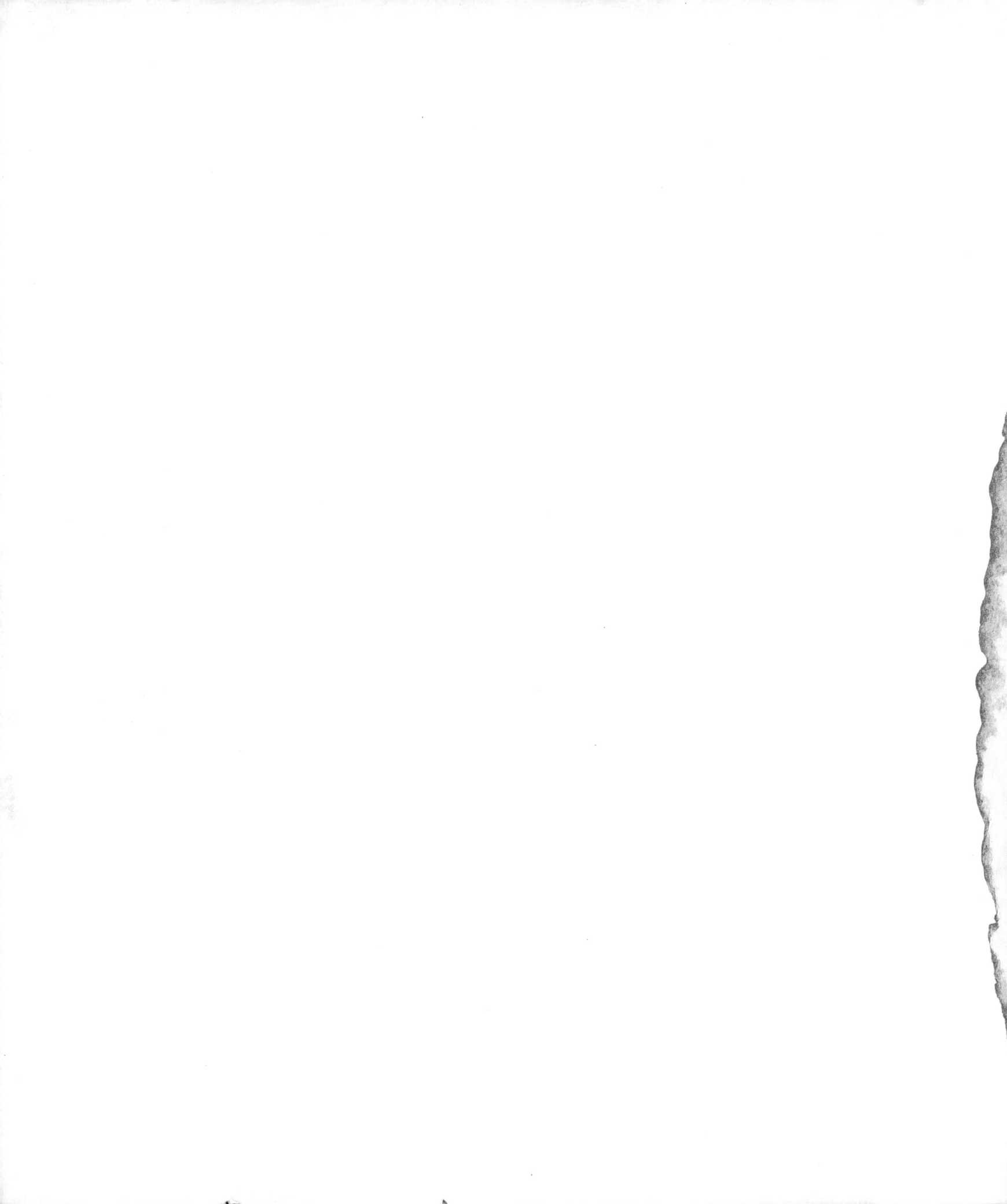

TEACHER EDITION with Solutions Key

Houghton
Mifflin
Harcourt

Geometry

TIMOTHY D. KANOLD

EDWARD B. BURGER

JULI K. DIXON

MATTHEW R. LARSON

STEVEN J. LEINWAND

Printed in the U.S.A.

ISBN 978-0-544-38582-5

4 5 6 7 8 9 10 0607 23 22 21 20 19 18 17 16 15

4500571052 ·   C D E F G

Authors

Timothy D. Kanold, Ph.D., is an award-winning international educator, author, and consultant. He is a former superintendent and director of mathematics and science at Adlai E. Stevenson High School District 125 in Lincolnshire, Illinois. He is a past president of the National Council of Supervisors of Mathematics (NCSM) and the Council for the Presidential Awardees of Mathematics (CPAM). He has served on several writing and leadership commissions for NCTM during the past decade. He presents motivational professional development seminars with a focus on developing professional learning communities (PLC's) to improve the teaching, assessing, and learning of students. He has recently authored nationally recognized articles, books, and textbooks for mathematics education and school leadership, including *What Every Principal Needs to Know about the Teaching and Learning of Mathematics.*

Edward B. Burger, Ph.D., is the President of Southwestern University, a former Francis Christopher Oakley Third Century Professor of Mathematics at Williams College, and a former vice provost at Baylor University. He has authored or coauthored more than sixty-five articles, books, and video series; delivered over five hundred addresses and workshops throughout the world; and made more than fifty radio and television appearances. He is a Fellow of the American Mathematical Society as well as having earned many national honors, including the Robert Foster Cherry Award for Great Teaching in 2010. In 2012, Microsoft Education named him a "Global Hero in Education."

Juli K. Dixon, Ph.D., is a Professor of Mathematics Education at the University of Central Florida. She has taught mathematics in urban schools at the elementary, middle, secondary, and post-secondary levels. She is an active researcher and speaker with numerous publications and conference presentations. Key areas of focus are deepening teachers' content knowledge and communicating and justifying mathematical ideas. She is a past chair of the NCTM Student Explorations in Mathematics Editorial Panel and member of the Board of Directors for the Association of Mathematics Teacher Educators.

Matthew R. Larson, Ph.D., is the K-12 mathematics curriculum specialist for the Lincoln Public Schools and served on the Board of Directors for the National Council of Teachers of Mathematics from 2010 to 2013. He is a past chair of NCTM's Research Committee and was a member of NCTM's Task Force on Linking Research and Practice. He is the author of several books on implementing the Common Core Standards for Mathematics. He has taught mathematics at the secondary and college levels and held an appointment as an honorary visiting associate professor at Teachers College, Columbia University.

Steven J. Leinwand is a Principal Research Analyst at the American Institutes for Research (AIR) in Washington, D.C., and has over 30 years in leadership positions in mathematics education. He is past president of the National Council of Supervisors of Mathematics and served on the NCTM Board of Directors. He is the author of numerous articles, books, and textbooks and has made countless presentations with topics including student achievement, reasoning, effective assessment, and successful implementation of standards.

Transformations and Congruence

MODULE 1

Tools of Geometry

COMMON CORE

MODULE 2

Transformations and Symmetry

COMMON CORE

© Houghton Mifflin Harcourt Publishing Company • Image Credits: (t) ©Jochen Tack/Imagebroker/Corbis; (b) ©Helen King/Corbis

MODULE 3

Congruent Figures

Kitchen

COMMON CORE

Lines, Angles, and Triangles

MODULE **4** — Lines and Angles

Real-World Video 161
Are You Ready? 162

MODULE **5** — Triangle Congruence Criteria

Real-World Video 217
Are You Ready? 218

MODULE 6

Applications of Triangle Congruence

Real-World Video 271
Are You Ready? 272

MODULE 7

Properties of Triangles

Real-World Video 311
Are You Ready? 312

MODULE 8

Special Segments in Triangles

© Houghton Mifflin Harcourt Publishing Company • Image Credit: ©AugustSnow/Alamy

UNIT 3

Quadrilaterals and Coordinate Proof

Volume 1

MODULE 9

Properties of Quadrilaterals

COMMON CORE

MODULE 10

Coordinate Proof Using Slope and Distance

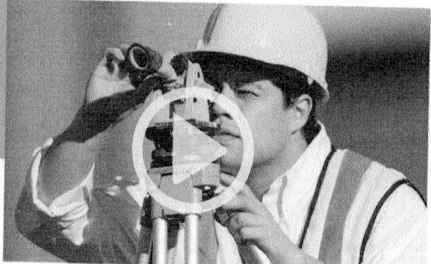

COMMON CORE

Similarity

MODULE 11 — Similarity and Transformations

COMMON CORE

MODULE 12 — Using Similar Triangles

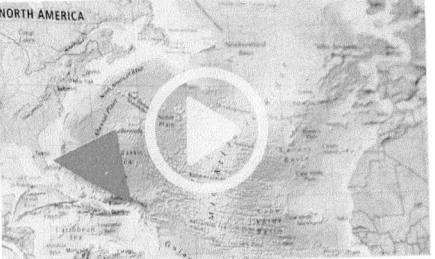

COMMON CORE

© Houghton Mifflin Harcourt Publishing Company • Image Credits: (t) ©Izzy Schwartz/Digital Vision/Getty Images; (b) ©Lightguard/iStockPhoto.com

UNIT 5

Trigonometry

Volume 2

MODULE 13

Trigonometry with Right Triangles

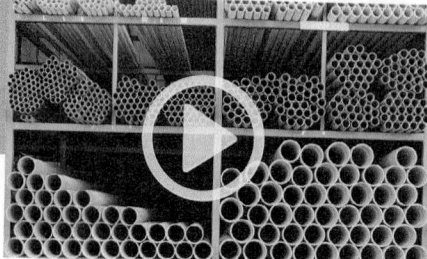

COMMON CORE

MODULE 14

Trigonometry with All Triangles

COMMON CORE

© Houghton Mifflin Harcourt Publishing Company • Image Credit: ©artzenter/Shutterstock; (b)©Carol Kohen/Cultura RM/Alamy

Properties of Circles

UNIT 6
COMMON CORE

Volume 2

MODULE 15 Angles and Segments in Circles

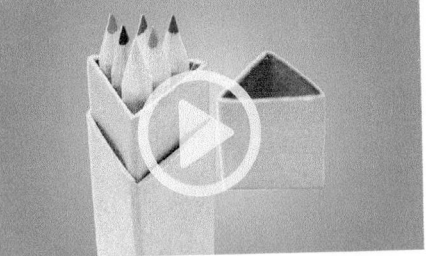

COMMON CORE

MODULE 16 Arc Length and Sector Area

COMMON CORE

Equations of Circles and Parabolas

COMMON
CORE

© Houghton Mifflin Harcourt Publishing Company • Image Credit: ©Adam Eggers/U.S. Coast Guard

Measurement and Modeling in Two and Three Dimensions

MODULE 18

Volume Formulas

MODULE 19

Visualizing Solids

MODULE 20

Modeling and Problem Solving

COMMON CORE

© Houghton Mifflin Harcourt Publishing Company • Image Credit: ©Doug Berry/iStockPhoto.com

Probability

 **MODULE 21**

Introduction to Probability

MODULE 22

Conditional Probability and Independence of Events

© Houghton Mifflin Harcourt Publishing Company • Image Credits: (t) ©Tetra Images/Alamy; (b) ©Sergey Nivens/Shutterstock

MODULE 23

Probability and Decision Making

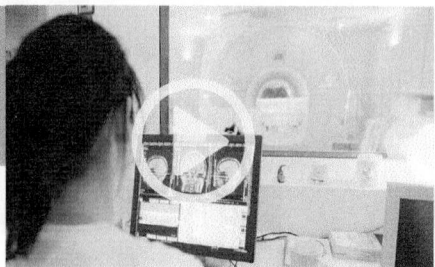

COMMON CORE

HMH Geometry
Online State Resources

Scan the QR code or visit:
my.hrw.com/nsmedia/osp/2015/ma/hs/te_1/tempaga
for correlations and other state-specific resources.

Common Core State Standards

HMH GEOMETRY

Standard	Descriptor	Citations
Geometry		
G-CO Congruence		
Experiment with transformations in the plane.		
G-CO.A.1	Know precise definitions of angle, circle, perpendicular line, parallel line, and line segment, based on the undefined notions of point, line, distance along a line, and distance around a circular arc.	**SE:** 5–18, 19–30, 63–72, 73–86
G-CO.A.2	Represent transformations in the plane using, e.g., transparencies and geometry software; describe transformations as functions that take points in the plane as inputs and give other points as outputs. Compare transformations that preserve distance and angle to those that do not (e.g., translation versus horizontal stretch).	**SE:** 31–44, 63–72, 73–86, 87–100, 115–126, 577–586, 601–610
G-CO.A.3	Given a rectangle, parallelogram, trapezoid, or regular polygon, describe the rotations and reflections that carry it onto itself.	**SE:** 101–108
G-CO.A.4	Develop definitions of rotations, reflections, and translations in terms of angles, circles, perpendicular lines, parallel lines, and line segments.	**SE:** 63–72, 73–86, 87–100
G-CO.A.5	Given a geometric figure and a rotation, reflection, or translation, draw the transformed figure using, e.g., graph paper, tracing paper, or geometry software. Specify a sequence of transformations that will carry a given figure onto another.	**SE:** 31–44, 63–72, 73–86, 87–100, 115–126, 127–138, 601–610
Understand congruence in terms of rigid motions.		
G-CO.B.6	Use geometric descriptions of rigid motions to transform figures and to predict the effect of a given rigid motion on a given figure; given two figures, use the definition of congruence in terms of rigid motions to decide if they are congruent.	**SE:** 63–72, 73–86, 87–100, 115–126, 127–138
G-CO.B.7	Use the definition of congruence in terms of rigid motions to show that two triangles are congruent if and only if corresponding pairs of sides and corresponding pairs of angles are congruent.	**SE:** 139–150, 219–230, 231–244, 245–254, 255–266
G-CO.B.8	Explain how the criteria for triangle congruence (ASA, SAS, and SSS) follow from the definition of congruence in terms of rigid motions.	**SE:** 231–244, 245–254, 255–266

★ Indicates a modeling standard linking mathematics to everyday life, work, and decision-making.
(+) Indicates additional mathematics to prepare students for advanced courses.

Scan the QR code or visit my.hrw.com/nsmedia/osp/2015/ma/hs/te_1/ tempaga for additional correlations and state specific resources.

Standard	Descriptor	Citations
Prove geometric theorems.		
G-CO.C.9	Prove theorems about lines and angles.	**SE:** 45–56, 163–174, 175–184, 185–194, 195–204, 371–380
G-CO.C.10	Prove theorems about triangles.	**SE:** 231–244, 245–254, 255–266, 313–326, 327–340, 341–352, 359–370, 371–380, 381–394, 395–404, 433–446, 521–536, 631–640
G-CO.C.11	Prove theorems about parallelograms.	**SE:** 419–432, 433–446, 447–458, 459–470, 537–548
Make geometric constructions.		
G-CO.D.12	Make formal geometric constructions with a variety of tools and methods (compass and straightedge, string, reflective devices, paper folding, dynamic geometric software, etc.).	**SE:** 5–18, 19–30, 73–86, 185–194, 195–204, 273–282, 341–352, 359–370, 371–380, 381–394, 395–404, 631–640, 641–652
G-CO.D.13	Construct an equilateral triangle, a square, and a regular hexagon inscribed in a circle.	**SE:** 273–282
G-SRT Similarity, Right Triangles, and Trigonometry		
Understand similarity in terms of similarity transformations.		
G-SRT.A.1	Verify experimentally the properties of dilations given by a center and a scale factor:	**SE:** 577–586
G-SRT.A.1a[1]	A dilation takes a line not passing through the center of the dilation to a parallel line, and leaves a line passing through the center unchanged.	**SE:** 577–586
G-SRT.A.1b[1]	The dilation of a line segment is longer or shorter in the ratio given by the scale factor.	**SE:** 577–586

[1] These standards are not included in the PARCC Model Content Framework for Geometry.

Common Core State Standards (continued)

Standard	Descriptor	Citations
G-SRT.A.2	Given two figures, use the definition of similarity in terms of similarity transformations to decide if they are similar; explain using similarity transformations the meaning of similarity for triangles as the equality of all corresponding pairs of angles and the proportionality of all corresponding pairs of sides.	**SE:** 587–600, 601–610
G-SRT.A.3	Use the properties of similarity transformations to establish the Angle-Angle (AA) criterion for two triangles to be similar.	**SE:** 611–622
Prove theorems involving similarity.		
G-SRT.B.4	Prove theorems about triangles.	**SE:** 631–640, 663–674
G-SRT.B.5	Use congruence and similarity criteria for triangles to solve problems and to prove relationships in geometric figures.	**SE:** 231–244, 245–254, 255–266, 273–282, 283–294, 295–304, 341–352, 419–432, 433–446, 447–458, 459–470, 471–486, 611–622, 631–640, 653–662, 663–674
Define trigonometric ratios and solve problems involving right triangles.		
G-SRT.C.6	Understand that by similarity, side ratios in right triangles are properties of the angles in the triangle, leading to definitions of trigonometric ratios for acute angles.	**SE:** 687–696, 697–708
G-SRT.C.7	Explain and use the relationship between the sine and cosine of complementary angles.	**SE:** 697–708
G-SRT.C.8	Use trigonometric ratios and the Pythagorean Theorem to solve right triangles in applied problems. ★	**SE:** 687–696, 697–708, 709–722, 723–736
Apply trigonometry to general triangles.		
G-SRT.D.9 [1]	(+) Derive the formula $A = \frac{1}{2} ab \sin(C)$ for the area of a triangle by drawing an auxiliary line from a vertex perpendicular to the opposite side.	**SE:** 723–736
G-SRT.D.10 [1]	(+) Prove the Laws of Sines and Cosines and use them to solve problems.	**SE:** 743–754, 755–766
G-SRT.D.11 [1]	(+) Understand and apply the Law of Sines and the Law of Cosines to find unknown measurements in right and non-right triangles (e.g., surveying problems, resultant forces).	**SE:** 743–754, 755–766

★ Indicates a modeling standard linking mathematics to everyday life, work, and decision-making.
(+) Indicates additional mathematics to prepare students for advanced courses.

Standard	Descriptor	Citations
G-C Circles		
Understand and apply theorems about circles.		
G-C.A.1	Prove that all circles are similar.	**SE:** 587–600, 863–872
G-C.A.2	Identify and describe relationships among inscribed angles, radii, and chords.	**SE:** 779–792, 805–814, 815–828, 829–842
G-C.A.3	Construct the inscribed and circumscribed circles of a triangle, and prove properties of angles for a quadrilateral inscribed in a circle.	**SE:** 359–370, 371–380, 793–804
G-C.A.4	(+) Construct a tangent line from a point outside a given circle to the circle.	**SE:** 805–814
Find arc lengths and areas of sectors of circles.		
G-C.B.5	Derive using similarity the fact that the length of the arc intercepted by an angle is proportional to the radius, and define the radian measure of the angle as the constant of proportionality; derive the formula for the area of a sector.	**SE:** 863–872, 873–882
G-GPE Expressing Geometric Properties with Equations		
Translate between the geometric description and the equation for a conic section.		
G-GPE.A.1	Derive the equation of a circle of given center and radius using the Pythagorean Theorem; complete the square to find the center and radius of a circle given by an equation.	**SE:** 889–900
G-GPE.A.2[1]	Derive the equation of a parabola given a focus and directrix.	**SE:** 901–912
Use coordinates to prove simple geometric theorems algebraically.		
G-GPE.B.4	Use coordinates to prove simple geometric theorems algebraically	**SE:** 5–18, 359–370, 381–394, 395–404, 495–508, 509–520, 521–536, 537–548, 889–901, 902–912
G-GPE.B.5	Prove the slope criteria for parallel and perpendicular lines and use them to solve geometric problems (e.g., find the equation of a line parallel or perpendicular to a given line that passes through a given point).	**SE:** 205–212, 359–370, 381–394, 395–404, 495–508, 509–520, 521–536, 537–548
G-GPE.B.6	Find the point on a directed line segment between two given points that partitions the segment in a given ratio.	**SE:** 641–652

[1] These standards are not included in the PARCC Model Content Framework for Geometry.

Common Core State Standards (continued)

Standard	Descriptor	Citations
G-GPE.B.7	Use coordinates to compute perimeters of polygons and areas of triangles and rectangles, e.g., using the distance formula. ★	**SE:** 521–536, 549–564, 723–736, 1037–1046
G-GMD Geometric Measurement and Dimension		
Explain volume formulas and use them to solve problems.		
G-GMD.A.1	Give an informal argument for the formulas for the circumference of a circle, area of a circle, volume of a cylinder, pyramid, and cone.	**SE:** 851–862, 863–872, 925–936, 937–948, 949–962
G-GMD.A.3	Use volume formulas for cylinders, pyramids, cones, and spheres to solve problems. ★	**SE:** 925–936, 937–948, 949–962, 963–974, 1037–1046
Visualize relationships between two-dimensional and three-dimensional objects.		
G-GMD.B.4	Identify the shapes of two-dimensional cross-sections of three-dimensional objects, and identify three-dimensional objects generated by rotations of two-dimensional objects.	**SE:** 981–990
G-MG Modeling with Geometry		
Apply geometric concepts in modeling situations.		
G-MG.A.1	Use geometric shapes, their measures, and their properties to describe objects (e.g., modeling a tree trunk or a human torso as a cylinder). ★	**SE:** 851–862, 863–872, 873–882, 925–936, 937–948, 949–962, 963–974, 991–1004, 1005–1018, 1019–1030, 1047–1056, 1057–1070
G-MG.A.2	Apply concepts of density based on area and volume in modeling situations (e.g., persons per square mile, BTUs per cubic foot). ★	**SE:** 925–936, 963–974, 1047–1056
G-MG.A.3	Apply geometric methods to solve design problems (e.g., designing an object or structure to satisfy physical constraints or minimize cost; working with typographic grid systems based on ratios). ★	**SE:** 73–86, 1057–1070
Statistics and Probability		
S-CP Conditional Probability and the Rules of Probability		
Understand independence and conditional probability and use them to interpret data.		
S-CP.A.1[1]	Describe events as subsets of a sample space (the set of outcomes) using characteristics (or categories) of the outcomes, or as unions, intersections, or complements of other events ("or," "and," "not"). ★	**SE:** 1083–1094

★ Indicates a modeling standard linking mathematics to everyday life, work, and decision-making.
(+) Indicates additional mathematics to prepare students for advanced courses.

Standard	Descriptor	Citations
S-CP.A.2[1]	Understand that two events A and B are independent if the probability of A and B occurring together is the product of their probabilities, and use this characterization to determine if they are independent. ★	**SE:** 1149–1164
S-CP.A.3[1]	Understand the conditional probability of A given B as $\frac{P(A \text{ and } B)}{P(B)}$, and interpret independence of A and B as saying that the conditional probability of A given B is the same as the probability of A, and the conditional probability of B given A is the same as the probability of B. ★	**SE:** 1137–1148, 1149–1164, 1165–1176
S-CP.A.4[1]	Construct and interpret two-way frequency tables of data when two categories are associated with each object being classified. Use the two-way table as a sample space to decide if events are independent and to approximate conditional probabilities. ★	**SE:** 1119–1130, 1137–1148, 1149–1164, 1165–1176, 1193–1204
S-CP.A.5[1]	Recognize and explain the concepts of conditional probability and independence in everyday language and everyday situations. ★	**SE:** 1137–1148, 1149–1164, 1165–1176, 1193–1204
Use the rules of probability to compute probabilities of compound events in a uniform probability model.		
S-CP.B.6[1]	Find the conditional probability of A given B as the fraction of B's outcomes that also belong to A, and interpret the answer in terms of the model. ★	**SE:** 1137–1148
S-CP.B.7[1]	Apply the Addition Rule, $P(A \text{ or } B) = P(A) + P(B) - P(A \text{ and } B)$, and interpret the answer in terms of the model. ★	**SE:** 1119–1130
S-CP.B.8[1]	(+) Apply the general Multiplication Rule in a uniform probability model, $P(A \text{ and } B) = P(A)P(B|A) = P(B)P(A|B)$, and interpret the answer in terms of the model. ★	**SE:** 1165–1176
S-CP.B.9[1]	(+) Use permutations and combinations to compute probabilities of compound events and solve problems. ★	**SE:** 1095–1106, 1107–1118

[1] These standards are not included in the PARCC Model Content Framework for Geometry.

Standard	Description	Citations
S-MD Using Probability to Make Decisions		
Use probability to evaluate outcomes of decisions.		
S-MD.B.6[1]	(+) Use probabilities to make fair decisions (e.g., drawing by lots, using a random number generator). ★	**SE:** 1183–1192
S-MD.B.7[1]	(+) Analyze decisions and strategies using probability concepts (e.g., product testing, medical testing, pulling a hockey goalie at the end of a game). ★	**SE:** 1193–1204

★ Indicates a modeling standard linking mathematics to everyday life, work, and decision-making.
(+) Indicates additional mathematics to prepare students for advanced courses.

STANDARDS FOR MATHEMATICAL PRACTICE

Standard	Description	Citations
MP.1	Make sense of problems and persevere in solving them.	*Integrated throughout the book. Examples:* **SE:** 58, 70, 86, 100, 110, 138, 369, 385–386, 445
MP.2	Reason abstractly and quantitatively.	*Integrated throughout the book. Examples:* **SE:** 27, 43, 45–56, 68, 77, 79–80, 142–143, 149–150
MP.3	Construct viable arguments and critique the reasoning of others.	*Integrated throughout the book. Examples:* **SE:** 17, 29, 45–56, 70, 77, 85, 137, 149, 183, 211
MP.4	Model with mathematics.	*Integrated throughout the book. Examples:* **SE:** 78–79, 83 86, 147–148, 158, 166, 212, 486
MP.5	Use appropriate tools strategically.	*Integrated throughout the book. Examples:* **SE:** 7–8, 11, 19, 23, 30, 63, 87–88, 94, 115, 273–274, 298, 419
MP.6	Attend to precision.	*Integrated throughout the book. Examples:* **SE:** 7, 21, 195, 231, 282, 567, 736, 1094
MP.7	Look for and make use of structure.	*Integrated throughout the book. Examples:* **SE:** 29, 33–34, 71, 99, 115, 137, 314–315, 324
MP.8	Look for and express regularity in repeated reasoning.	*Integrated throughout the book. Examples:* **SE:** 21, 31–32, 46, 50–51, 164–165, 232

[1] These standards are not included in the PARCC Model Content Framework for Geometry.

Common Core Cluster Progressions

HMH Geometry carefully develops the instructional progression of each cluster from the Common Core Standards. The table below shows where key topics from each cluster are taught in HMH Geometry.

HMH GEOMETRY

Common Core Clusters		Unit 1	Unit 2	Unit 3
G-CO.A	Experiment with transformations in the plane.	covered in full		
G-CO.B	Understand congruence in terms of rigid motions.	congruence and transformations	triangle congruence	
G-CO.C	Prove geometric theorems.		proofs of angle and triangle theorems	coordinate proofs
G-CO.D	Make geometric constructions.	segments and angles	parallel lines and polygons	
G-SRT.A	Understand similarity in terms of similarity transformations.			
G-SRT.B	Prove theorems involving similarity.		congruent triangles	
G-SRT.C	Define trigonometric ratios and solve problems involving right triangles.			
G-SRT.D	Apply trigonometry to general triangles.			
G-C.A	Understand and apply theorems about circles.		inscribed and circumscribed triangles and quadrilaterals	
G-C.B	Find arc lengths and areas of sectors of circles.			
G-GPE.A	Translate between the geometric description and the equation for a conic section.			

	Unit 4	Unit 5	Unit 6	Unit 7	Unit 8
	covered in full				
	similar triangles	right triangles			
		covered in full			
		covered in full			
	circles and similarity		angles in circles		
			covered in full		
			covered in full		

Common Core Cluster Progressions (continued)

HMH GEOMETRY

Common Core Clusters		Unit 1	Unit 2	Unit 3
G-GPE.B	Use coordinates to prove simple geometric theorems algebraically.		parallel and perpendicular lines	distance formula
G-GMD.A	Explain volume formulas and use them to solve problems.			
G-GMD.B	Visualize relationships between two-dimensional and three-dimensional objects.			
G-MG	Apply geometric concepts in modeling situations.			
S-CP.A	Understand independence and conditional probability and use them to interpret data.			
S-CP.B	Use the rules of probability to compute probabilities of compound events in a uniform probability model.			
S-MD.A	Calculate expected values and use them to solve problems.			
S-MD.B	Use probability to evaluate outcomes of decisions.			

	Unit 4	Unit 5	Unit 6	Unit 7	Unit 8
			circles and parabolas		
			circumference and area of a circle	volume formulas	
			arcs and sectors	solids	
			circles	volume and surface area	
					covered in full
					covered in full
					covered in full
					covered in full

Succeeding with HMH Geometry

HMH Geometry is built on the 5E instructional model--Engage, Explore, Explain, Elaborate, Evaluate--to develop strong conceptual understanding and mastery of key mathematics standards.

ENGAGE

Preview the Lesson Performance Task in the Interactive Student Edition.

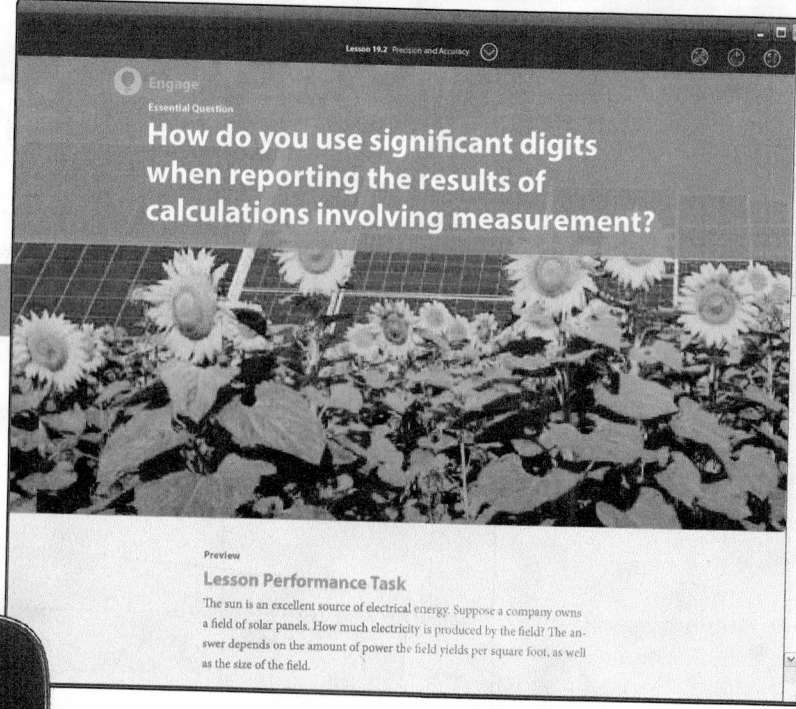

Lesson 19.2 Precision and Accuracy

Engage

Essential Question

How do you use significant digits when reporting the results of calculations involving measurement?

Preview

Lesson Performance Task

The sun is an excellent source of electrical energy. Suppose a company owns a field of solar panels. How much electricity is produced by the field? The answer depends on the amount of power the field yields per square foot, as well as the size of the field.

EXPLORE

Explore and interact with new concepts to develop a deeper understanding of mathematics in your book and the Interactive Student Edition.

Scan the QR code to access engaging videos, activities, and more in the Resource Locker for each lesson.

Lesson 19.2 Precision and Accuracy

Explore Concept 1

Comparing Precision of Measurements

Eric is a technician in a pharmaceutical lab. Every week, he needs to test the scales in the lab to make sure that they are. He uses a that is exactly 12.000 g and gets the following results:

Scale	Mass
Scale 1	12.03 g
Scale 2	12.029 g
Scale 3	11.98 g

Definition of Precision: The level of detail of a, determined by **the smallest** unit or fraction of a unit that can be reasonably measured.

Definition of Accuracy: The closeness of a given value to the actual measurement or value.

Which measuring tool is the most precise?

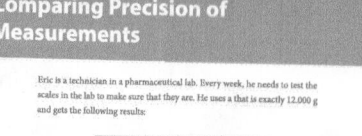

Which scale is the most accurate?

Scale 2

My answer

Reflect

Name _____ Class _____ Date _____

1.3 Reporting with Precision and Accuracy

Essential Question: How do you use significant digits when reporting the results of calculations involving measurement?

Explore Comparing Precision of Measurements.

Numbers are values without units. They can be used to compute or to describe measurements. Quantities are real-word values that represent specific amounts. For instance, 15 is a number, but 15 grams is a quantity.

Precision is the level of detail of a measurement, determined by the smallest unit or fraction of a unit that can be reasonably measured.

Accuracy is the closeness of a given measurement or value to the actual measurement or value. Suppose you know the actual measure of a quantity, and someone else measures it. You can find the accuracy of the measurement by finding the absolute value of the difference of the two.

Ⓐ Complete the table to choose the more precise measurement.

Measurement 1	Measurement 2	Smaller Unit	More Precise Measurement
4 g	4.3 g		
5.71 oz	5.7 oz		
4.2 m	422 cm		
7 ft 2 in.	7.2 in.		

Ⓑ Eric is a lab technician. Every week, he needs to test the scales in the lab to make sure that they are accurate. He uses a standard mass that is exactly 8.000 grams and gets the following results.

Scale	Mass
Scale 1	8.02 g
Scale 2	7.9 g
Scale 3	8.000 g

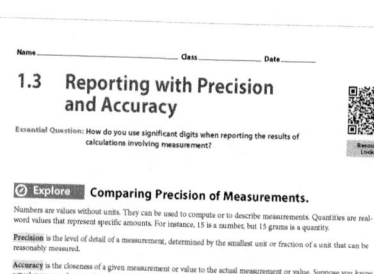

EXPLAIN

Learn concepts with step-by-step interactive examples. Every example is also supported by a Math On the Spot video tutorial.

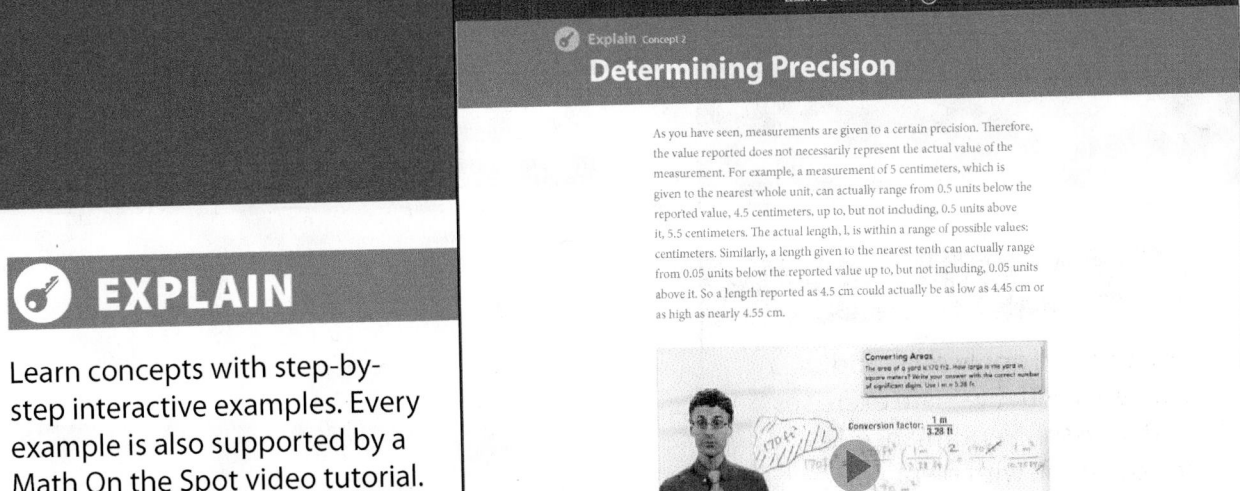

Explain Concept 2

Determining Precision

As you have seen, measurements are given to a certain precision. Therefore, the value reported does not necessarily represent the actual value of the measurement. For example, a measurement of 5 centimeters, which is given to the nearest whole unit, can actually range from 0.5 units below the reported value, 4.5 centimeters, up to, but not including, 0.5 units above it, 5.5 centimeters. The actual length, *l*, is within a range of possible values: centimeters. Similarly, a length given to the nearest tenth can actually range from 0.05 units below the reported value up to, but not including, 0.05 units above it. So a length reported as 4.5 cm could actually be as low as 4.45 cm or as high as nearly 4.55 cm.

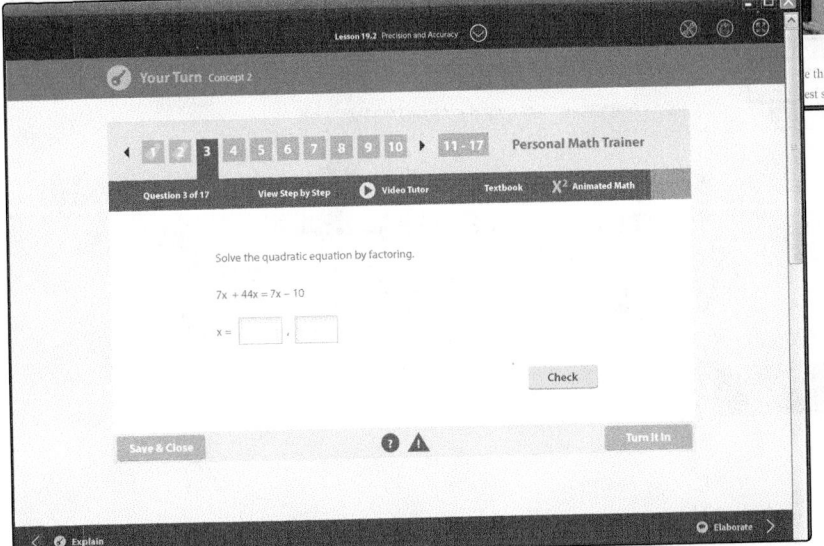

Your Turn Concept 2

Personal Math Trainer

Question 3 of 17 | View Step by Step | Video Tutor | Textbook | X² Animated Math

Solve the quadratic equation by factoring.

$7x + 44x = 7x - 10$

$x = \boxed{}, \boxed{}$

Check

Save & Close

Turn It In

Check your understanding of new concepts and skills with Your Turn exercises in your book or online with Personal Math Trainer.

Personal Math Trainer

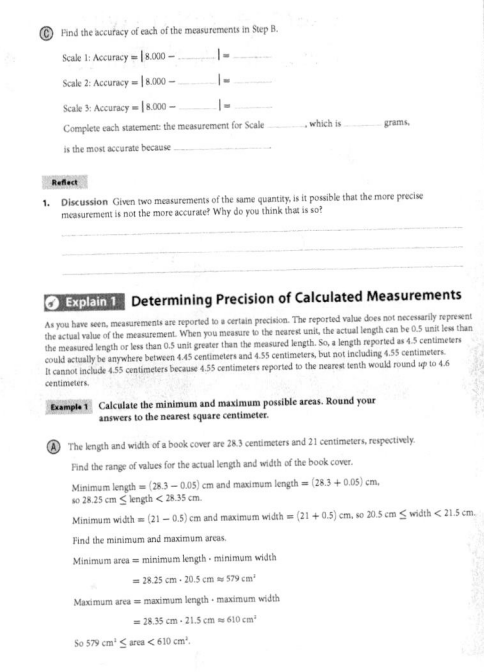

© Find the accuracy of each of the measurements in Step B.

Scale 1: Accuracy = |8.000 — ___ | = ___

Scale 2: Accuracy = |8.000 — ___ | = ___

Scale 3: Accuracy = |8.000 — ___ | = ___

Complete each statement: the measurement for Scale ___ , which is ___ grams, is the most accurate because ___

Reflect

1. **Discussion** Given two measurements of the same quantity, is it possible that the more precise measurement is not the more accurate? Why do you think that is so?

Explain 1 Determining Precision of Calculated Measurements

As you have seen, measurements are reported to a certain precision. The reported value does not necessarily represent the actual value of the measurement. When you measure to the nearest unit, the actual length can be 0.5 unit less than the measured length or less than 0.5 unit greater than the measured length. So, a length reported as 4.5 centimeters could actually be anywhere between 4.45 centimeters and 4.55 centimeters, but not including 4.55 centimeters. It cannot include 4.55 centimeters because 4.55 centimeters reported to the nearest tenth would round up to 4.6 centimeters.

Example 1 Calculate the minimum and maximum possible areas. Round your answers to the nearest square centimeter.

Ⓐ The length and width of a book cover are 28.3 centimeters and 21 centimeters, respectively.

Find the range of values for the actual length and width of the book cover.

Minimum length = $(28.3 - 0.05)$ cm and maximum length = $(28.3 + 0.05)$ cm, so $28.25 \le$ length < 28.35 cm.

Minimum width = $(21 - 0.5)$ cm and maximum width = $(21 + 0.5)$ cm, so 20.5 cm $\le$ width < 21.5 cm.

Find the minimum and maximum areas.

Minimum area = minimum length · minimum width

$= 28.25$ cm · 20.5 cm ≈ 579 cm²

Maximum area = maximum length · maximum width

$= 28.35$ cm · 21.5 cm ≈ 610 cm²

So 579 cm² $\le$ area < 610 cm².

Module 1 28 Lesson 3

ELABORATE

Show your understanding and reasoning with Reflect and Elaborate questions.

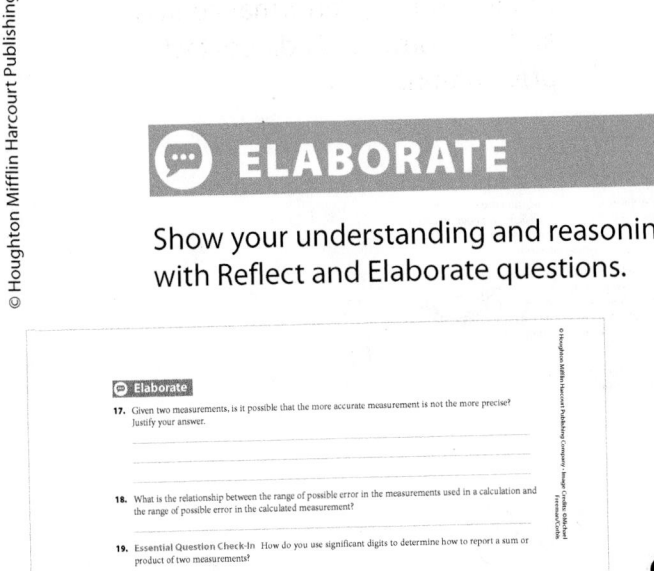

Elaborate

17. Given two measurements, is it possible that the more accurate measurement is not the more precise? Justify your answer.

18. What is the relationship between the range of possible error in the measurements used in a calculation and the range of possible error in the calculated measurement?

19. **Essential Question Check-In** How do you use significant digits to determine how to report a sum or product of two measurements?

Module 1 34 Lesson 3

Elaborate

Given two measurements, is it possible that the more precise measurement may not be the more accurate?

Formula | Send to Notebook

What is the relationship between the precision used in the length and width of the rectangle and the precision of the resulting area measurement?

Formula | Send to Notebook

How are the significant digits related to the calculations using measurements?

CC15

⭐ EVALUATE

Practice and apply skills and concepts with Evaluate exercises and a Lesson Performance Task in your book with plenty of workspace, or complete these exercises online with Personal Math Trainer.

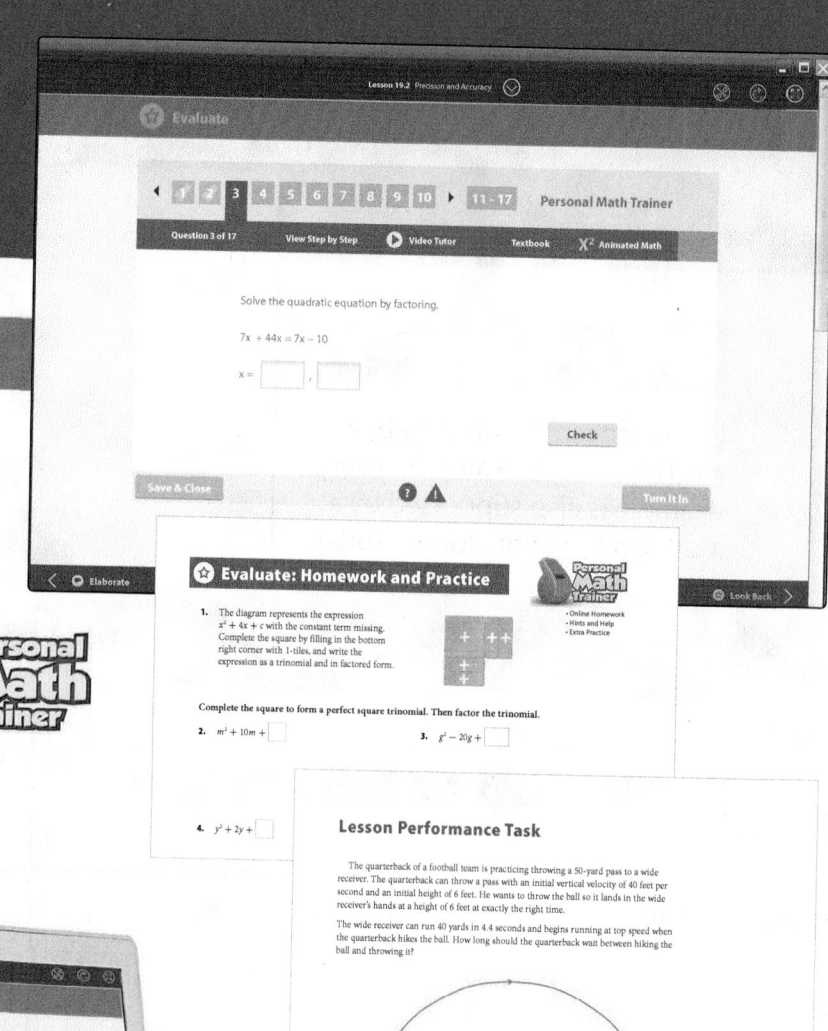

Evaluate

Question 3 of 17 | View Step by Step | ▶ Video Tutor | Textbook | X² Animated Math

Personal Math Trainer

Solve the quadratic equation by factoring.

$7x + 44x = 7x - 10$

$x =$ ☐ + ☐

Check

Save & Close | Turn It In

⭐ Evaluate: Homework and Practice

Personal Math Trainer
• Online Homework
• Hints and Help
• Extra Practice

1. The diagram represents the expression $x^2 + 4x + c$ with the constant term missing. Complete the square by filling in the bottom right corner with 1-tiles, and write the expression as a trinomial and in factored form.

Complete the square to form a perfect square trinomial. Then factor the trinomial.

2. $m^2 + 10m +$ ☐

3. $g^2 - 20g +$ ☐

4. $y^2 + 2y +$ ☐

Lesson Performance Task

The quarterback of a football team is practicing throwing a 50-yard pass to a wide receiver. The quarterback can throw a pass with an initial vertical velocity of 40 feet per second and an initial height of 6 feet. He wants to throw the ball so it lands in the wide receiver's hands at a height of 6 feet at exactly the right time.

The wide receiver can run 40 yards in 4.4 seconds and begins running at top speed when the quarterback hikes the ball. How long should the quarterback wait between hiking the ball and throwing it?

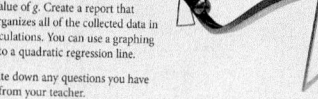

Journal

Discuss the solution method you used with some of your classmates. Did your thinking change? Summarize anything you learned or shared below.

Formula

Self-Evaluation

This lesson covered the concepts below.

• Using Ratios and Proportions to Solve Problems
• Using Scale Drawings and Models to Solve Problems
• Using Dimensional Analysis to Convert Measurements
• Using Dimensional Analysis to Convert and Compare Rates
• Graphing a Proportional Relationship

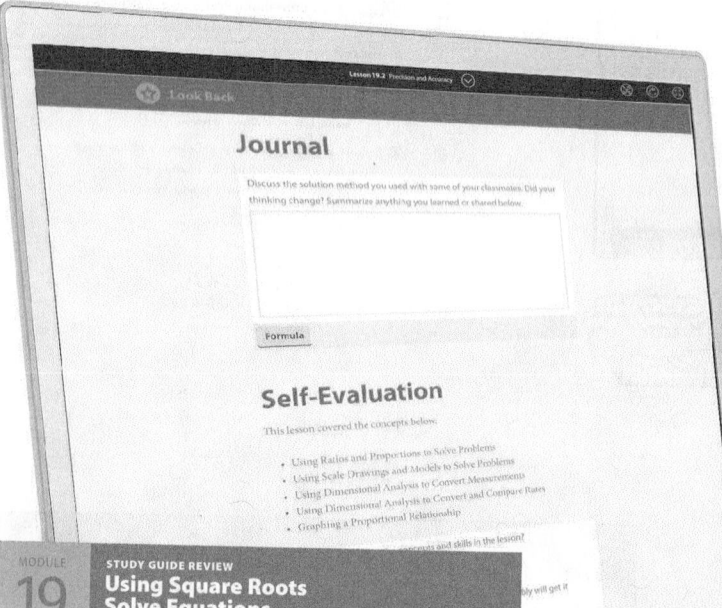

⭐ LOOK BACK

Review what you have learned and prepare for high-stakes tests with a variety of resources, including Study Guide Reviews, Performance Tasks, and Assessment Readiness test preparation.

MODULE 19
STUDY GUIDE REVIEW
Using Square Roots Solve Equations

Essential Question: How do you determine the best method for solving a quadratic equation or a system of equations?

Key Vocabulary
discriminant (discriminante)
end behavior (comportamiento extremo)
quadratic formula (fórmula cuadrática)

KEY EXAMPLE (Lesson 19.1)

Solve $(x - 3)^2 = 49$ using square roots.

$(x - 3)^2 = 49$

$x - 3 = \pm\sqrt{49}$ Take the square root of both sides.

$x - 3 = \pm 7$ Use ± to show both square roots.

$x = \pm 7 + 3$

$x = 7 + 3$ and $x = -7 + 3$

$x = 10$ $x = -4$ Simplify each equation.

The solutions are −4 and 10.

KEY EXAMPLE (Lesson 19.2)

Solve $x^2 - 6x - 12 = 0$ by completing the square.

$x^2 - 6x - 12 = 0$

$x^2 - 6x = 12$ Add 12 to both sides.

$x^2 - 6x + 9 = 12 + 9$ Complete the square.

$(x - 3)^2 = 21$ Factor left side.

$x - 3 = \pm\sqrt{21}$ Take square roots.

$x = 3 \pm \sqrt{21}$ Solve for x.

$x = 3 + \sqrt{21}$ or $x = 3 - \sqrt{21}$

KEY EXAMPLE (Lesson 19.3)

Solve $3x^2 - 5x - 4 = 0$ by using the quadratic formula.

$3x^2 - 5x - 4 = 0$

$a = 3, b = -5, c = -4$ Find a, b, c.

$x = \dfrac{-(-5) \pm \sqrt{(-5)^2 - 4(3)(-4)}}{2(3)}$ Use quadratic formula.

$= \dfrac{5 \pm \sqrt{25 - (-48)}}{6}$

MODULE PERFORMANCE TASK
Going Down?

Construct a ramp that is at least 4 feet long. The angle the ramp makes with the ground should be 30°. Working with a partner, release a ball from various points on the ramp. Measure the distance the ball rolls and the time (using a stopwatch) that it rolls. You should perform several trials for various distances.

The quadratic equation $d = \frac{1}{2}gt^2$ models the distance d (in feet) that the ball rolls in t seconds. Use your data and the equation to estimate the value of g. Create a report that explains your approach, organizes all of the collected data in tables, and shows your calculations. You can use a graphing calculator to fit your data to a quadratic regression line.

Use the space below to write down any questions you have or important information from your teacher.

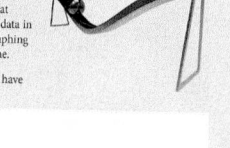

Module 19   3   Study Guide Review

Synergy Through Collaboration

Tim Kanold
Program Author

Great teaching materials do not provide great education in and of themselves. Educators who collaborate in Professional Learning Communities can have a profound impact on their students. As a mathematics teacher, your grade-level or course-based collaborative team is the engine that can drive your professional learning and the professional learning community (PLC) process.

You and your colleagues hold a critical key to helping *all* students successfully learn the Common Core Mathematics Standards in your school. Through your hard work and the work of your collaborative team, effective instruction, assessment, and intervention practices become more coherent and focused.

The National Board for Professional Teaching Standards states the following:

> Seeing themselves as partners with other teachers, [faculty members] are dedicated to improving the profession. They care about the quality of teaching in their schools, and, to this end, their collaboration with colleagues is continuous and explicit. They recognize that collaborating in a professional learning community contributes to their own professional growth, as well as to the growth of their peers, for the benefit of student learning. Teachers promote the ideal that working collaboratively increases knowledge, reflection, and quality of practice and benefits the instructional program. (*Mathematics Standards for Teachers of Students Ages 11–18+*, ©2010, p. 75)

As a highly accomplished mathematics teacher you understand the value in the practice of effective collaboration with your colleagues. Teacher collaboration is not the icing on top of the proverbial cake of your work. Instead, it is the egg in the batter, holding the cake together.

As your school becomes a learning institution for the adults, it also becomes a learning institution dedicated to preparing all students for the future. The process of your collaboration in a PLC culture capitalizes on the fact that you and your colleagues come together with diverse experiences and knowledge to create a whole that is larger than the sum of the parts. Teacher collaboration is the solution to your sustained professional learning—the ongoing and never-ending process of growth necessary to meet the classroom demands of the CCSS expectations and the unit-by-unit mathematics content described in our series.

Transformations and Congruence

CONTENTS

Unit Pacing Guide

45-Minute Classes

Module 1

DAY 1	DAY 2	DAY 3	DAY 4	DAY 5
Lesson 1.1	Lesson 1.2	Lesson 1.3	Lesson 1.4	Lesson 1.4

DAY 6
Module Review and Assessment Readiness

Module 2

DAY 1	DAY 2	DAY 3	DAY 4	DAY 5
Lesson 2.1	Lesson 2.2	Lesson 2.3	Lesson 2.3	Lesson 2.4

DAY 6
Module Review and Assessment Readiness

Module 3

DAY 1	DAY 2	DAY 3	DAY 4	DAY 5
Lesson 3.1	Lesson 3.2	Lesson 3.2	Lesson 3.3	Module Review and Assessment Readiness

DAY 6
Unit Review and Assessment Readiness

90-Minute Classes

Module 1

DAY 1	DAY 2	DAY 3
Lesson 1.1	Lesson 1.3	Lesson 1.4
Lesson 1.2	Lesson 1.4	Module Review and Assessment Readiness

Module 2

DAY 1	DAY 2	DAY 3
Lesson 2.1	Lesson 2.3	Lesson 2.4
Lesson 2.2		Module Review and Assessment Readiness

Module 3

DAY 1	DAY 2	DAY 3
Lesson 3.1	Lesson 3.2	Module Review and Assessment Readiness
Lesson 3.2	Lesson 3.3	Unit Review and Assessment Readiness

Program Resources

PLAN

HMH Teacher App

Access a full suite of teacher resources online and offline on a variety of devices. Plan present, and manage classes, assignments, and activities.

ePlanner
Easily plan your classes, create and view assignments, and access all program resources with your online, customizable planning tool.

Professional Development Videos

Authors Juli Dixon and Matt Larson model successful teaching practices and strategies in actual classroom settings.

QR Codes
Scan with your smart phone to jump directly from your print book to online videos and other resources.

Teacher's Edition

Support students with point-of-use Questioning Strategies, teaching tips, resources for differentiated instruction, additional activities, and more.

ENGAGE AND EXPLORE

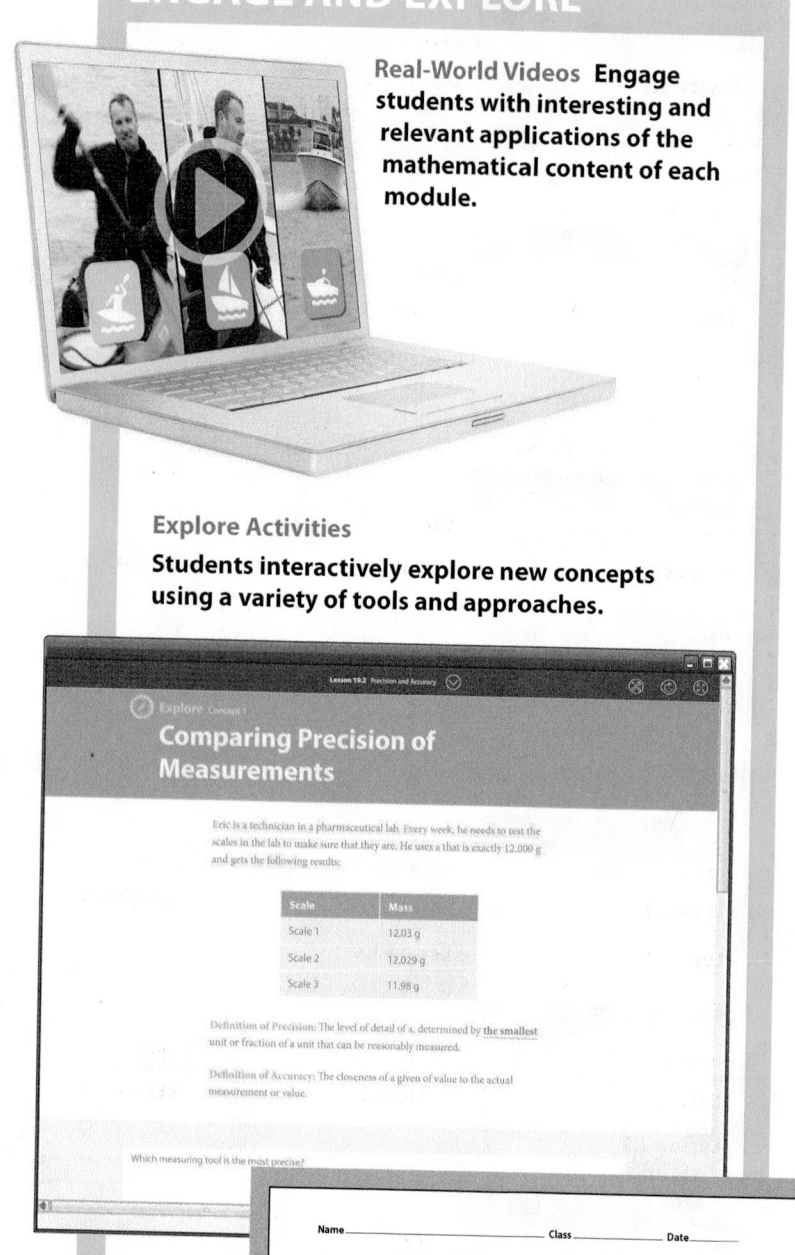

Real-World Videos
Engage students with interesting and relevant applications of the mathematical content of each module.

Explore Activities

Students interactively explore new concepts using a variety of tools and approaches.

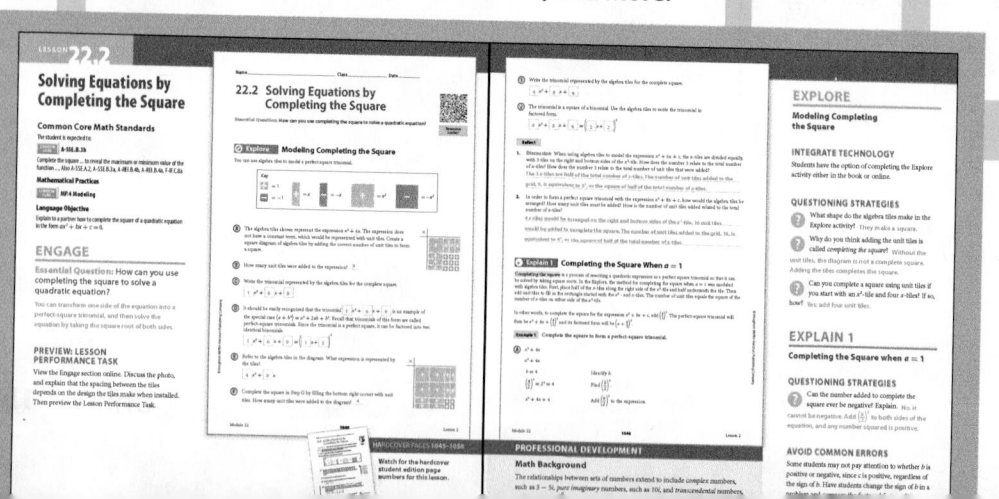

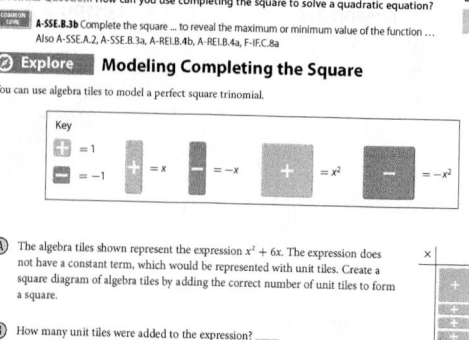

Name_____ Class_____ Date_____

22.2 Solving Equations by Completing the Square

Essential Question: How can you use completing the square to solve a quadratic equation?

COMMON CORE A-SSE.B.3b Complete the square ... to reveal the maximum or minimum value of the function ...
Also A-SSE.A.2, A-SSE.B.3a, A-REI.B.4b, A-REI.B.4a, F-IF.C.8a

Resource Locker

⊘ Explore — Modeling Completing the Square

You can use algebra tiles to model a perfect square trinomial.

(A) The algebra tiles shown represent the expression $x^2 + 6x$. The expression does not have a constant term, which would be represented with unit tiles. Create a square diagram of algebra tiles by adding the correct number of unit tiles to form a square.

(B) How many unit tiles were added to the expression? _____

(C) Write the trinomial represented by the algebra tiles for the complete square.

$\boxed{}x^2 + \boxed{}x + \boxed{}$

(D) It should be easily recognized that the trinomial $\boxed{}x^2 + \boxed{}x + \boxed{}$ is an example of the special case $(a + b)^2$

TEACH

Math On the Spot video tutorials, featuring program author Dr. Edward Burger, accompany every example in the textbook and give students step-by-step instructions and explanations of key math concepts.

Interactive Teacher Edition

Customize and present course materials with collaborative activities and integrated formative assessment.

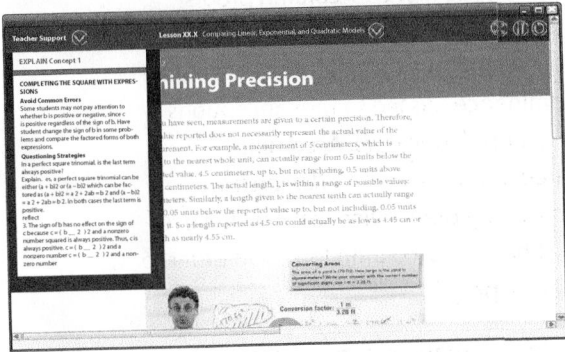

Differentiated Instruction Resources

Support all learners with Differentiated Instruction Resources, including

- **Leveled Practice and Problem Solving**
- **Reading Strategies**
- **Success for English Learners**
- **Challenge**

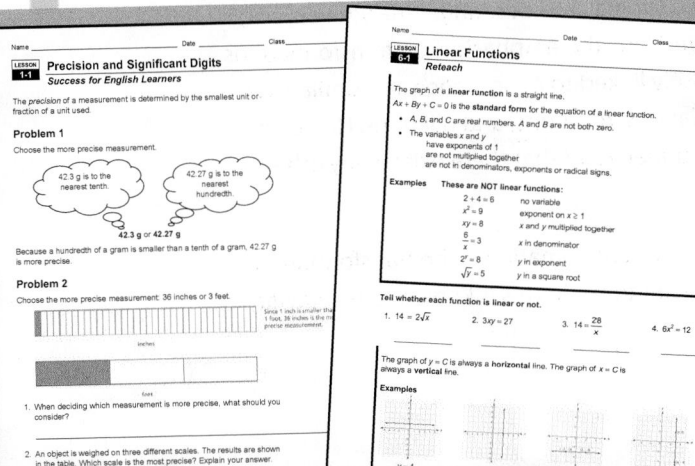

ASSESSMENT AND INTERVENTION

The Personal Math Trainer provides online practice, homework, assessments, and intervention. Monitor student progress through reports and alerts. Create and customize assignments aligned to specific lessons or Common Core standards.

- **Practice** – With dynamic items and assignments, students get unlimited practice on key concepts supported by guided examples, step-by-step solutions, and video tutorials.

- **Assessments** – Choose from course assignments or customize your own based on course content, Common Core standards, difficulty levels, and more.

- **Homework** – Students can complete online homework with a wide variety of problem types, including the ability to enter expressions, equations, and graphs. Let the system automatically grade homework, so you can focus where your students need help the most!

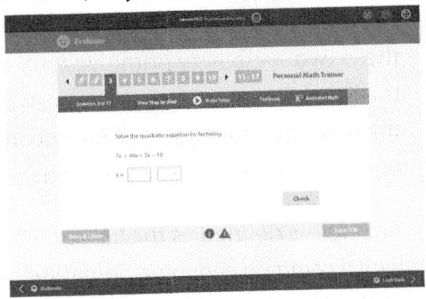

- **Intervention** – Let the Personal Math Trainer automatically prescribe a targeted, personalized intervention path for your students.

Focus on Higher Order Thinking

Raise the bar with homework and practice that incorporates higher-order thinking and mathematical practices in every lesson.

Assessment Readiness

Prepare students for success on high stakes tests for Geometry with practice at every module and unit

Assessment Resources

Tailor assessments and response to intervention to meet the needs of all your classes and students, including

- Leveled Module Quizzes
- Leveled Unit Tests
- Unit Performance Tasks
- Placement, Diagnostic, and Quarterly Benchmark Tests
- Tier 1, Tier 2, and Tier 3 Resources

Math Background

Tools of Geometry  G-CO.A.1
LESSONS 1.1 and 1.2

The geometry concepts that are presented here are largely based on ideas set forth more than 2000 years ago by the Greek mathematician Euclid. His series of books, *Elements* (circa 300 B.C.E.), is the first known work in which a logical, deductive system of reasoning is used as a means of unifying all mathematical knowledge.

Constructions with compass and straightedge date to antiquity. In fact, Euclid's first three postulates describe how these tools may be used. The straightedge is used to draw a line through two points or to extend an existing line segment. In contrast to a ruler, the unmarked straightedge is never used for measuring distance. Although a compass is often thought of as a tool for making circles, its primary use in constructions is marking equal distances. Using these two seemingly primitive tools and working within the limits described above, one can construct virtually all of the fundamental figures of Euclidean geometry, including equilateral triangles, squares, and regular pentagons.

An *angle* is defined as *the figure that is formed by two rays with a common endpoint*. Sometimes an angle is defined as *the figure formed by two noncollinear rays with a common endpoint*. This restriction eliminates straight angles and thus removes some of the ambiguity that can arise when straight angles are considered. (For example, either side of a straight angle could be considered the interior or exterior of the angle.)

On the other hand, angles with measures greater than or equal to 180° are essential in trigonometry and other areas of higher mathematics. For this reason, straight angles are discussed here. Students should be aware, however, that in work with proofs, the term *angle* generally refers to angles formed by noncollinear rays, unless otherwise stated.

Reasoning and Proof G-CO.C.9
LESSON 1.4

The essential doctrine of *Elements* is that when a certain set of fundamental ideas or understandings are assumed to be true, all other mathematical results can be logically derived and proved from these foundations.

There are many forms for proofs, such as two-column proofs, flowchart proofs, and paragraph proofs. However, the main purpose of any proof, regardless of its format, is to present a logically sound argument. To that end, it is essential to point out to students that finding a proof and communicating a proof are two entirely different things.

Students who see completed proofs should understand that these are models for how to present a finished logical argument; they are not models of the step-by-step thought process for finding a proof. The process of finding a proof is rarely a linear one. Instead, it is more often a matter of sorting through the pieces of a puzzle, looking for logical connections, stumbling into blind alleys, and returning to the starting point (sometimes more than once). Once this hit-and-miss process has been completed, the proof can be organized and communicated in any format.

It is interesting to note that the first two-column proofs began appearing in textbooks around 1900. Since then, such proofs have often occupied a central role in geometry courses, and their prominence has led to misconceptions about their role, even among educators. According to a study that appeared in the *Journal for Research in Mathematics Education*, many pre-service teachers believe that an argument must be in two-column format in order to constitute a mathematical proof.

Although the two-column format is practical because it reminds students that every statement must be supported with a reason, students should be reminded that the heart of any proof is the validity of the argument, not the format.

Transformations G-CO.A.4
LESSONS 2.1 to 2.3

A *transformation* is *a function that changes the position, size, or shape of a figure*. Here, the emphasis is on transformations that are most closely linked to congruence and similarity: reflections, translations, rotations, and dilations. However, it is important to understand that there exist many other transformations.

Perhaps the simplest transformation is the transformation that maps every point to itself. This is known as the *identity transformation*.

Another simple transformation is the one that maps every point to the origin.

An *isometry* is *a transformation that preserves distance*. This means that, under an isometry, the distance between any two points of the pre-image is the same as the distance between the corresponding points of the image. So, an isometry does not change the size or shape of a figure.

Isometries are also called *congruence mappings*. In fact, *congruence* may be defined in terms of isometries as follows: *Two figures are congruent if and only if there is an isometry that maps one figure to the other*. In the plane, there are four types of isometries: reflections, translations, rotations, and glide reflections.

The identity transformation, which maps every point to itself, may be considered a separate isometry or it may be considered a special case of a translation or rotation.

It is natural to ask whether there are other isometries. For example, it seems intuitively obvious that a composition of isometries (one isometry followed by another) is also an isometry. Therefore, it makes sense to ask whether the composition of a translation and a rotation is a new type of isometry or whether the resulting transformation is equivalent to one of the four basic isometries. The somewhat surprising answer is that every isometry is indeed a reflection, translation, rotation, or glide reflection.

As discussed above, every isometry is a reflection, translation, rotation, or glide reflection. Thus, the composition of any two of these isometries must be equivalent to one of the four basic isometries.

The following table summarizes the results of all possible compositions.

Composition of Isometries			
	Refl.	**Trans.**	**Rot.**	**Glide**
Refl.	Trans. or Rot.	Glide	Glide	Trans. or Rot.
Trans.	Glide	Trans.	Rot.	Refl. or Glide
Rot.	Glide	Rot.	Trans. or Rot.	Glide
Glide	Trans. or Rot.	Refl. or Glide	Glide	Trans. or Rot.

Symmetry  G-CO.A.3

LESSON 2.4

In general terms, an object, figure, or pattern has symmetry if a transformation can be performed on the object, figure, or pattern so that its image looks exactly like its preimage. If the relevant transformation is a reflection, the figure has line symmetry (or reflection symmetry). If the transformation is a rotation, the figure has rotational symmetry.

It is also possible for a figure to have translation symmetry or glide-reflection symmetry, but these terms apply only to patterns that continue indefinitely, such as frieze patterns and tessellations.

Congruence and Corresponding Parts G-CO.B.7

LESSONS 3.2 and 3.3

Two geometric figures are congruent if they are the same size and shape; in other words, if one of the figures can be moved so that it fits perfectly on top of the other figure.

This is the intuitive idea behind the more rigorous mathematical definition of *congruence*: *two figures are congruent if one can be transformed into the other by an isometry* (that is, by a combination of translations, reflections, and rotations).

For polygons, the definition of congruence can be stated in terms of corresponding sides and angles. In particular, *two triangles are congruent if and only if the sides and angles can be matched up so that the corresponding sides are congruent and the corresponding angles are congruent*.

This definition of triangle congruence means that six correspondences must be checked in order to conclude that two triangles are congruent (three pairs of corresponding sides and three pairs of corresponding angles).

Transformations and Congruence

MATH IN CAREERS
Unit Activity Preview

After completing this unit, students will complete a Math in Careers task by using given measurements in three dimensions to calculate distances. Critical skills include modeling real-world situations and using the distance formula.

For more information about careers in mathematics as well as various mathematics appreciation topics, visit The American Mathematical Society at http://www.ams.org.

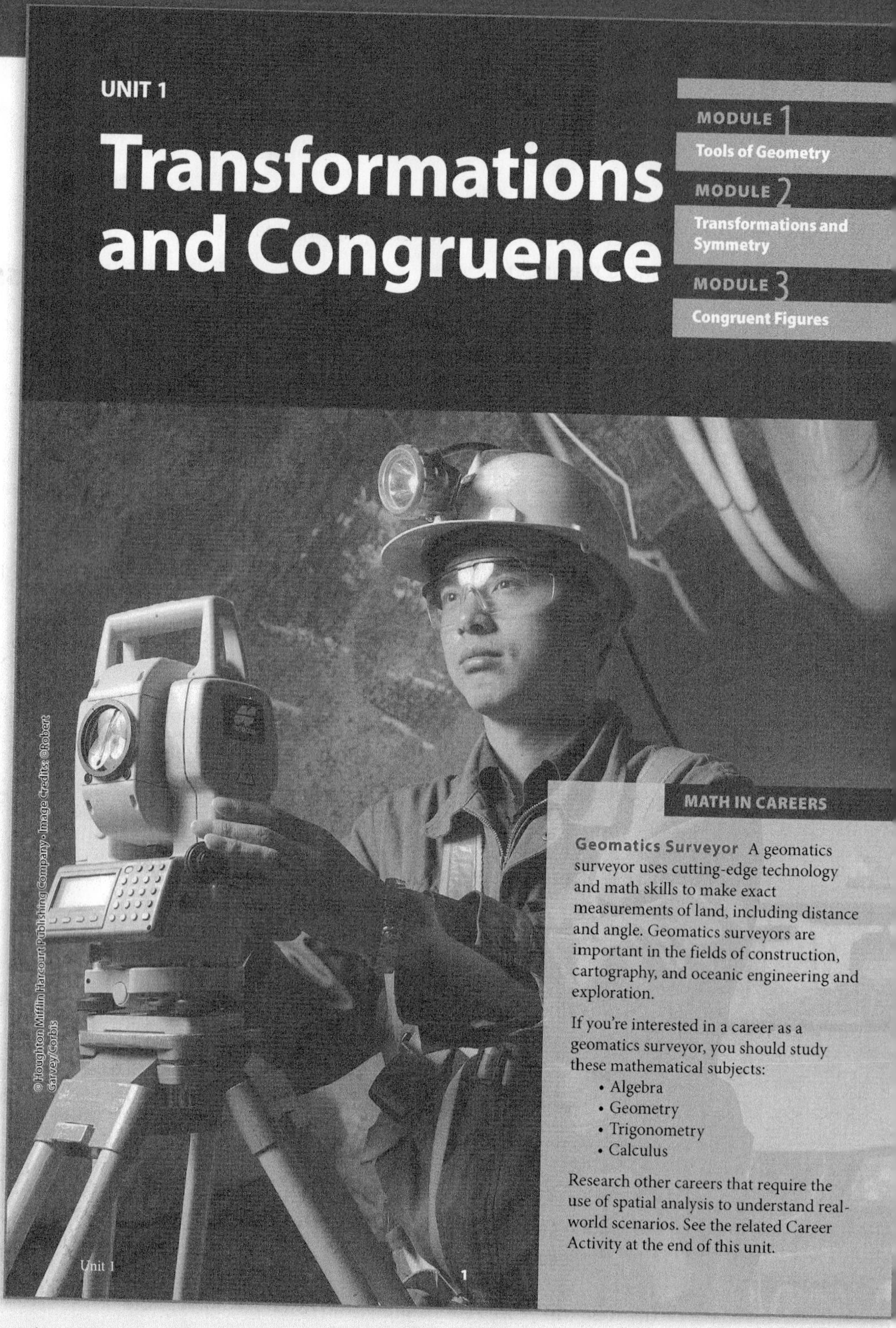

UNIT 1

Transformations and Congruence

MODULE 1
Tools of Geometry

MODULE 2
Transformations and Symmetry

MODULE 3
Congruent Figures

MATH IN CAREERS

Geomatics Surveyor A geomatics surveyor uses cutting-edge technology and math skills to make exact measurements of land, including distance and angle. Geomatics surveyors are important in the fields of construction, cartography, and oceanic engineering and exploration.

If you're interested in a career as a geomatics surveyor, you should study these mathematical subjects:
- Algebra
- Geometry
- Trigonometry
- Calculus

Research other careers that require the use of spatial analysis to understand real-world scenarios. See the related Career Activity at the end of this unit.

Unit 1   1

TRACKING YOUR LEARNING PROGRESSION

Before	In this Unit	After
Students understand: • order of operations • using variables and expressions to represent situations • locating points in a coordinate plane • solving equations	Students will learn about: • segments and angles • reasoning and proof • translations, reflections, and rotations • symmetry • corresponding parts of congruent figures	Students will study: • properties of intersecting lines, parallel lines, and perpendicular lines • special segments of triangles • congruent triangles • geometric constructions

Reading Start-Up

Visualize Vocabulary

Use the ✔ words to complete the chart. You may put more than one word in each box.

Angle	Description	Example	complementary angle	supplementary angle
acute	Angle whose measure is less than 90°	40°	50°	140°
obtuse	Angle whose measure is greater than 90°	110°	None	70°

Vocabulary

Review Words
✔ midpoint (*punto medio*)
✔ angle (*ángulo*)
✔ transformation (*transformación*)
✔ complementary angle (*ángulo complementario*)
✔ supplementary angle (*ángulo suplementario*)
✔ acute angle (*ángulo agudo*)
✔ obtuse angle (*ángulo obtuso*)

Preview Words
angle bisector (*bisectriz de un ángulo*)
vertex (*vértice*)
collinear (*colineales*)
postulate (*postulado*)

Understand Vocabulary

Complete the sentences using the preview words.

1. A(n) _angle bisector_ is a ray that divides an angle into two angles that both have the same measure.

2. The common endpoint of two rays that form an angle is the _vertex_ of the angle.

3. Points that lie on the same line are _collinear_.

Active Reading

Booklet Before beginning each module, create a booklet to help you organize what you learn. As you study each lesson, draw the different graphical concepts that you learn and write their definitions.

Reading Start Up

Have students complete the activities on this page by working alone or with others.

VISUALIZE VOCABULARY

The description and example chart graphic helps students review vocabulary associated with angles. If time allows, brainstorm definitions and examples of transformations that students recall.

UNDERSTAND VOCABULARY

Use the following explanations to help students learn the preview words.

A **postulate** is a statement that is accepted without proof. An **angle bisector** is a ray that divides an angle into two equal angles. The endpoint of the ray lies at the **vertex** of the angle. Every point on the ray is **collinear**.

ACTIVE READING

Students can use these reading and note-taking strategies to help them organize and understand the new concepts and vocabulary. Encourage students to speak up and ask for supplementary information to help them understand new vocabulary. Suggest that they include as much information as they need in their booklets to make included concepts clear.

ADDITIONAL RESOURCES

Differentiated Instruction

- Reading Strategies **EL**

Tools of Geometry

ESSENTIAL QUESTION:

Answer: Just about any real-world situation involving shapes or the location of objects in space can be represented using the tools of geometry.

PROFESSIONAL DEVELOPMENT VIDEO

Professional Development Video

Learn effective ways of integrating technology into your classroom to meet a variety of different needs.

Professional Development
my.hrw.com

Tools of Geometry

MODULE 1

Essential Question: How can you use the tools of geometry to solve real-world problems?

LESSON 1.1
Segment Length and Midpoints

LESSON 1.2
Angle Measures and Angle Bisectors

LESSON 1.3
Representing and Describing Transformations

LESSON 1.4
Reasoning and Proof

REAL WORLD VIDEO
Check out how the tools of geometry can be used to solve real-world problems, like planning a park fountain's location to be the same distance from the park's three entrances.

© Houghton Mifflin Harcourt Publishing Company • Image Credits: ©Jochen Tack/Imagebroker/Corbis

MODULE PERFORMANCE TASK PREVIEW

How Far Is It?

How does your cellphone know how far away the nearest restaurant is? In this module, you'll explore how apps and search engines use GPS coordinates to calculate distances. So enter your present location and let's find out!

Module 1   3

DIGITAL TEACHER EDITION

Access a full suite of teaching resources when and where you need them:

- Access content online or offline
- Customize lessons to share with your class
- Communicate with your students in real-time
- View student grades and data instantly to target your instruction where it is needed most

PERSONAL MATH TRAINER

Assessment and Intervention

Assign automatically graded homework, quizzes, tests, and intervention activities. Prepare your students with updated, Common Core-aligned practice tests.

Are (YOU) Ready?

Complete these exercises to review skills you will need for this module.

Algebraic Representations of Transformations

- Online Homework
- Hints and Help
- Extra Practice

Example 1 Shift $y = \sqrt{x}$ horizontally 2 units to the right.

$(0, 0)$ to $(2, 0)$ Write the starting point and its transformation.

$y - 0 = \sqrt{x - 2}$ Use the transformed point to write the equation.

$y = \sqrt{x - 2}$ Simplify.

Transform the equations.

1. Shift $y = 5x$ 3 units up.

$\underline{y = 5x + 3}$

2. Stretch $y = 5x$ vertically about the fixed x-axis by a factor of 2.

$\underline{y = 10x}$

3. Shift $y = 5\sqrt{x} + 3$ horizontally 2 units to the right and stretch by a factor of 3. (Stretch vertically about the fixed $y = 3$ line.)

$\underline{y = 15\sqrt{x - 2} + 3}$

Angle Relationships

Example 2 Find the angle complementary to the given angle, $75°$.

$x + 75° = 90°$ Write as an equation.

$x = 90° - 75°$ Solve for x.

$x = 15°$

Find the complementary angle.

4. $20°$ $\underline{\quad 70° \quad}$ **5.** $35°$ $\underline{\quad 55° \quad}$ **6.** $67°$ $\underline{\quad 23° \quad}$

Find the supplementary angle.

7. $80°$ $\underline{\quad 100° \quad}$ **8.** $65°$ $\underline{\quad 115° \quad}$ **9.** $34°$ $\underline{\quad 146° \quad}$

Distance and Midpoint Formulas

Example 3 Find the distance between $(2, 3)$ and $(5, 7)$.

$\sqrt{(5 - 2)^2 + (7 - 3)^2}$ Apply the distance formula.

$= \sqrt{9 + 16}$ Simplify each square.

$= 5$ Add and find the square root.

Find each distance and midpoint for the given points.

10. The points $(6, 14)$ and $(1, 2)$ Distance $\underline{\quad 13 \quad}$ Midpoint $\underline{\left(\frac{7}{2}, 8\right)}$

11. The points $(4, 6)$ and $(19, 14)$ Distance $\underline{\quad 17 \quad}$ Midpoint $\underline{\left(\frac{23}{2}, 10\right)}$

Are You Ready?

ASSESS READINESS

Use the assessment on this page to determine if students need strategic or intensive intervention for the module's prerequisite skills.

ASSESSMENT AND INTERVENTION

RtI Response to Intervention **TIER 1, TIER 2, TIER 3 SKILLS**

Personal Math Trainer will automatically create a standards-based, personalized intervention assignment for your students, targeting each student's individual needs!

ADDITIONAL RESOURCES

See the table below for a full list of intervention resources available for this module.

Response to Intervention Resources also includes:

- Tier 2 Skill Pre-Tests for each Module
- Tier 2 Skill Post-Tests for each skill

Response to Intervention			Differentiated Instruction
Tier 1 Lesson Intervention Worksheets	**Tier 2** Strategic Intervention Skills Intervention Worksheets	**Tier 3** Intensive Intervention Worksheets available online	
Reteach 1.1 Reteach 1.2 Reteach 1.3 Reteach 1.4	1 Algebraic Representations of Transformations 2 Angle Relationships 9 Distance and Midpoint Formulas	Building Block Skills 7, 10, 11, 15, 16, 27, 38, 45, 46, 51, 53, 55, 56, 66, 69, 70, 95, 98, 100, 102,	Challenge worksheets Extend the Math Lesson Activities in TE

Segment Length and Midpoints

Common Core Math Standards

The student is expected to:

COMMON CORE **G-CO.A.1**

Know precise definitions of ... line segment, based on the undefined notions of ... distance along a line, ... Also G-CO.D.12, G-GPE.B.4

Mathematical Practices

COMMON CORE **MP.5 Using Tools**

Language Objective

Work with a small group to match pictures to "geometry term cards."

ENGAGE

Essential Question: How do you draw a segment and measure its length?

Possible answer: You can use a compass and straightedge to draw a segment and use a ruler to measure it. Or, you can connect two points on a coordinate plane to form a segment and use the Distance Formula to find its length.

PREVIEW: LESSON PERFORMANCE TASK

View the Engage section online. Discuss the photo and the fact that the fence must be big enough to enclose the ride in all of its possible configurations. Then preview the Lesson Performance Task.

1.1 Segment Length and Midpoints

Essential Question: How do you draw a segment and measure its length?

Resource Locker

⊘ Explore **Exploring Basic Geometric Terms**

In geometry, some of the names of figures and other terms will already be familiar from everyday life. For example, a *ray* like a beam of light from a spotlight is both a familiar word and a geometric figure with a mathematical definition.

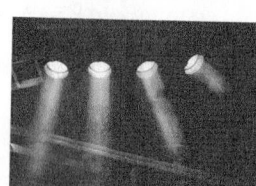

The most basic figures in geometry are *undefined terms*, which cannot be defined using other figures. The terms *point*, *line*, and *plane* are undefined terms. Although they do not have formal definitions, they can be described as shown in the table.

Undefined Terms

Term	Geometric Figure	Ways to Name the Figure
A **point** is a specific location. It has no dimension and is represented by a dot.	● *P*	point *P*
A **line** is a connected straight path. It has no thickness and it continues forever in both directions.	*A* *B* ℓ	line ℓ, line *AB*, line *BA*, $\overleftrightarrow{AB}$, or $\overleftrightarrow{BA}$
A **plane** is a flat surface. It has no thickness and it extends forever in all directions.	*X* *Z* ℛ *Y*	plane ℛ or plane *XYZ*

In geometry, the word *between* is another undefined term, but its meaning is understood from its use in everyday language. You can use undefined terms as building blocks to write definitions for defined terms, as shown in the table.

Defined Terms

Term	Geometric Figure	Ways to Name the Figure
A **line segment** (or *segment*) is a portion of a line consisting of two points (called **endpoints**) and all points between them.	*C* *D*	segment *CD*, segment *DC*, $\overline{CD}$, or $\overline{DC}$
A **ray** is a portion of a line that starts at a point (the *endpoint*) and continues forever in one direction.	*P* *Q*	ray *PQ* or $\overrightarrow{PQ}$

HARDCOVER PAGES 5–16

Turn to these pages to find this lesson in the hardcover student edition.

You can use points to sketch lines, segments, rays, and planes.

Ⓐ Draw two points J and K. Then draw a line through them. (Remember that a line shows arrows at both ends.)

Ⓑ Draw two points J and K again. This time, draw the line segment with endpoints J and K.

Ⓒ Draw a point K again and draw a ray from endpoint K. Plot a point J along the ray.

Ⓓ Draw three points J, K, and M so that they are not all on the same line. Then draw the plane that contains the three points. (You might also put a script letter such as B on your plane.)

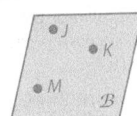

Ⓔ Give a name for each of the figures you drew. Then use a circle to choose whether the type of figure is an undefined term or a defined term.

Point	points J, K, and M	ⓤndefined term/defined term
Line	$\overleftrightarrow{JK}$ (or $\overleftrightarrow{KJ}$)	ⓤndefined term/defined term
Segment	$\overline{JK}$ or $\overline{KJ}$	undefined term/ⓓefined term
Ray	$\overrightarrow{KJ}$	undefined term/ⓓefined term
Plane	plane JKM (or plane B)	ⓤndefined term/defined term

Reflect

1. In Step C, would $\overrightarrow{JK}$ be the same ray as $\overrightarrow{KJ}$? Why or why not?
   No. The rays would have different endpoints and continue in opposite directions.

2. In Step D, when you name a plane using 3 letters, does the order of the letters matter?
   No. Using 3 letters, the plane in Step D can be named plane JKM, plane JMK, plane KJM,
   plane KMJ, plane MJK, or plane MKJ.

3. **Discussion** If $\overleftrightarrow{PQ}$ and $\overleftrightarrow{RS}$ are different names for the same line, what must be true about points P, Q, R, and S?
   The four points all lie on a common line.

EXPLORE

Exploring Basic Geometric Terms

INTEGRATE TECHNOLOGY

Geometry programs and other software contain tools to measure segment lengths and distances.

CONNECT VOCABULARY EL

Connect the words *collinear* and *coplanar* to the prefix *co-*. Let students know that *co-* usually means together or joint. For example, *coauthors* author a book together. *Collinear* means that points are on the same line, *coplanar* means "together on the same plane."

QUESTIONING STRATEGIES

? How are drawing and naming lines, rays, and line segments similar and how are they different? All of the figures can be named by two points. The line segment connects the two points, the ray extends beyond one of the named points with an arrow at the extended end, and the line extends beyond both named points, with arrows at each end.

? Does the order of the two points matter when naming a line segment, a ray, or a line? Explain. The order does not matter when naming a line or a line segment but it does matter when naming a ray. Each named ray has a different endpoint and continues forever in opposite directions.

PROFESSIONAL DEVELOPMENT

Math Background

Students have worked with geometric terms and figures since the elementary grades. This course revisits many ideas that may be familiar to students, but does so in a systematic way in order to build a deductive system. The Distance and Midpoint Formulas are key tools of coordinate geometry. Students will write coordinate proofs later in this course and they will find that these two formulas, along with facts about the slopes of parallel and perpendicular lines, are enough to prove a wide range of theorems.

EXPLAIN 1

Constructing a Copy of a Line Segment

CONNECT VOCABULARY **EL**

The definition of the distance used to measure the length of a line segment is called the *Ruler Postulate*.

QUESTIONING STRATEGIES

? Why is the first step in constructing a copy of a line segment to draw a line segment with an endpoint? It provides a place to set the compass point and draw the arc that shows the length of the copied segment.

AVOID COMMON ERRORS

Remind students to set the compass point on the endpoint of the line segment and to be careful not to change the distance setting before drawing the arc to copy a segment.

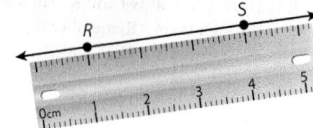

⊘ Explain 1   **Constructing a Copy of a Line Segment**

The distance along a line is undefined until a unit distance, such as 1 inch or 1 centimeter, is chosen. You can use a ruler to find the distance between two points on a line. The distance is the absolute value of the difference of the numbers on the ruler that correspond to the two points. This distance is the length of the segment determined by the points.

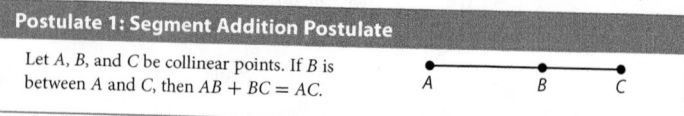

In the figure, the length of $\overline{RS}$, written RS (or SR), is the distance between R and S.

$$RS = |4 - 1| = |3| = 3 \text{ cm} \qquad \text{or} \qquad SR = |1 - 4| = |-3| = 3 \text{ cm}$$

Points that lie in the same plane are **coplanar**. Lines that lie in the same plane but do not intersect are **parallel**. Points that lie on the same line are **collinear**. The *Segment Addition Postulate* is a statement about collinear points. A **postulate** is a statement that is accepted as true without proof. Like undefined terms, postulates are building blocks of geometry.

Postulate 1: Segment Addition Postulate
Let A, B, and C be collinear points. If B is between A and C, then $AB + BC = AC$. 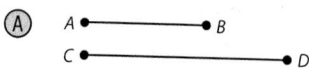

A *construction* is a geometric drawing that produces an accurate representation without using numbers or measures. One type of construction uses only a compass and straightedge. You can construct a line segment whose length is equal to that of a given segment using these tools along with the Segment Addition Postulate.

Example 1   Use a compass and straightedge to construct a segment whose length is $AB + CD$.

(A)   A •———————• B
      C •————————————• D

Step 1 Use the straightedge to draw a long line segment. Label an endpoint X. (See the art drawn in Step 4.)

Step 2 To copy segment AB, open the compass to the distance AB.

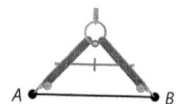

Step 3 Place the compass point on X, and draw an arc. Label the point Y where the arc and the segment intersect.

Step 4 To copy segment CD, open the compass to the distance CD. Place the compass point on Y, and draw an arc. Label the point Z where this second arc and the segment intersect.

$\overline{XZ}$ is the required segment.

COLLABORATIVE LEARNING

Peer-to-Peer Activity

Have students work in pairs and use a compass and straightedge to construct a fair ruler. Tell the students to draw a straight line, set the compass for the unit, and after marking an endpoint as 0, construct and label the ruler. Have students compare their rulers. Discuss which units are fair rulers and why they are, or are not. If time permits, discuss which rulers would be most appropriate to measure the lengths of different objects.

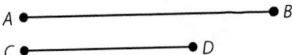

Step 1 Use the straightedge to draw a long line segment. Label an endpoint X.

Step 2 To copy segment AB, open the compass to the distance AB.

Step 3 Place the compass point on X, and draw an arc. Label the point Y where the arc and the segment intersect.

Step 4 To copy segment CD, open the compass to the distance CD. Place the compass point on Y, and draw an arc. Label the point Z where this second arc and the segment intersect.

$\overline{XZ}$ is the required segment.

Reflect

4. **Discussion** Look at the line and ruler above Example 1. Why does it not matter whether you find the distance from R to S or the distance from S to R?

The formula to find the distance between the two points involves taking the absolute

value of the difference between the two coordinates R and S, so the distance is always

positive; the order of the coordinates does not matter. From R to S or from S to R, the

coordinates are always 3 units apart.

5. In Part B, how can you check that the length of $\overline{YZ}$ is the same as the length of $\overline{CD}$?

Use a ruler to measure $\overline{YZ}$ and $\overline{CD}$ to see if the lengths are the same.

Your Turn

6. Use a ruler to draw a segment PQ that is 2 inches long. Then use your compass and straightedge to construct a segment MN with the same length as $\overline{PQ}$.

⦿ Explain 2   Using the Distance Formula on the Coordinate Plane

The Pythagorean Theorem states that $a^2 + b^2 = c^2$, where a and b are the lengths of the legs of a right triangle and c is the length of the hypotenuse. You can use the Distance Formula to apply the Pythagorean Theorem to find the distance between points on the coordinate plane.

© Houghton Mifflin Harcourt Publishing Company

DIFFERENTIATE INSTRUCTION

Communicating Math

Before introducing the Distance Formula, ask students to explain why $\sqrt{3^2 + 4^2} \neq 3 + 4$. You must first square each number and then take the square root of the sum. The answer is 5, not 7.

Visual Cues

Have students estimate the midpoint or distance of a line segment plotted in the coordinate plane. Then have them use a calculator and the appropriate formula to support their answers.

EXPLAIN 2

Using the Distance Formula on the Coordinate Plane

AVOID COMMON ERRORS

Students may confuse the coordinates when using the Distance Formula. Have them label the coordinates of any two points they are given as (x_1, y_1) and (x_2, y_2) before substituting the numbers into the Distance Formula.

QUESTIONING STRATEGIES

? How can you use the Pythagorean Theorem to find the distance between two points in the plane if you forget the Distance Formula? Use the endpoints to draw a right triangle with a vertical leg and a horizontal leg. The hypotenuse is the line connecting the points. Find the length of each leg and then use the Pythagorean Theorem to find the length of the hypotenuse.

© Houghton Mifflin Harcourt Publishing Company

The Distance Formula

The distance between two points (x_1, y_1) and (x_2, y_2) on the coordinate plane is $\sqrt{(x_2 - x_1)^2 + (y_2 - y_1)^2}$.

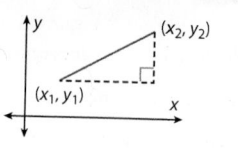

Example 2 Determine whether the given segments have the same length. Justify your answer.

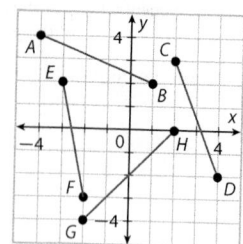

(A) $\overline{AB}$ and $\overline{CD}$

Write the coordinates of the endpoints. $A(-4, 4)$, $B(1, 2)$, $C(2, 3)$, $D(4, -2)$

Find the length of $\overline{AB}$. $AB = \sqrt{(1 - (-4))^2 + (2 - 4)^2}$

Simplify the expression. $= \sqrt{5^2 + (-2)^2} = \sqrt{29}$

Find the length of $\overline{CD}$. $CD = \sqrt{(4 - 2)^2 + (-2 - 3)^2}$

Simplify the expression. $= \sqrt{2^2 + (-5)^2} = \sqrt{29}$

So, $AB = CD = \sqrt{29}$. Therefore, $\overline{AB}$ and $\overline{CD}$ have the same length.

(B) $\overline{EF}$ and $\overline{GH}$

Write the coordinates of the endpoints. $E(-3, 2)$, $F\left(\boxed{-2}, \boxed{-3}\right)$, $G(-2, -4)$, $H\left(\boxed{2}, \boxed{0}\right)$

Find the length of $\overline{EF}$. $EF = \sqrt{\left(\boxed{-2} - (-3)\right)^2 + \left(\boxed{-3} - 2\right)^2}$

Simplify the expression. $= \sqrt{\left(\boxed{1}\right)^2 + \left(\boxed{-5}\right)^2} = \sqrt{\boxed{26}}$

Find the length of $\overline{GH}$. $GH = \sqrt{\left(\boxed{2} - (-2)\right)^2 + \left(\boxed{0} - (-4)\right)^2}$

Simplify the expression. $= \sqrt{\left(\boxed{4}\right)^2 + \left(\boxed{4}\right)^2} = \sqrt{\boxed{32}}$

So, $\underline{EF \neq GH}$. Therefore, $\underline{EF \text{ and } \overline{GH} \text{ do not have the same length}}$.

LANGUAGE SUPPORT **EL**

Connect Vocabulary

Have students look up the word *between* in the dictionary and compare that definition with the mathematical definition. Emphasize that the mathematical definition of *between* includes collinearity.

Reflect

7. Consider how the Distance Formula is related to the Pythagorean Theorem. To use the Distance Formula to find the distance from $U(-3, -1)$ to $V(3, 4)$, you write $UV = \sqrt{\left(3 - (-3)\right)^2 + \left(4 - (-1)\right)^2}$. Explain how $\left(3 - (-3)\right)$ in the Distance Formula is related to a in the Pythagorean Theorem and how $\left(4 - (-1)\right)$ in the Distance Formula is related to b in the Pythagorean Theorem.

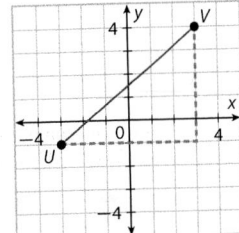

The Pythagorean Theorem states that $a^2 + b^2 = c^2$, where a and b are the lengths of the legs of a right triangle and c is the length of the hypotenuse. Applying this to the right triangle in the figure, $UV = c = \sqrt{a^2 + b^2}$, where a is the length of the horizontal leg of the triangle, or $\left(3 - (-3)\right)$, and b is the length of the vertical leg of the triangle, or $\left(4 - (-1)\right)$.

Your Turn

8. Determine whether $\overline{JK}$ and $\overline{LM}$ have the same length. Justify your answer.

$J(-4, 4)$, $K(-2, 1)$, $L(-1, -4)$, $M(2, -2)$

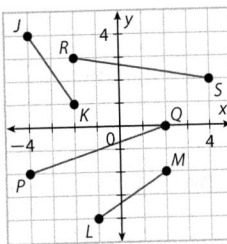

$JK = \sqrt{\left(-2 - (-4)\right)^2 + (1 - 4)^2} = \sqrt{13}$

$LM = \sqrt{\left(2 - (-1)\right)^2 + \left(-2 - (-4)\right)^2} = \sqrt{13}$

So, $JK = LM = \sqrt{13}$. Therefore, $\overline{JK}$ and $\overline{LM}$ have the same length.

⊘ Explain 3   Finding a Midpoint

The **midpoint** of a line segment is the point that divides the segment into two segments that have the same length. A line, ray, or other figure that passes through the midpoint of a segment is a **segment bisector**.

In the figure, the tick marks show that $PM = MQ$. Therefore, M is the midpoint of $\overline{PQ}$ and line ℓ bisects $\overline{PQ}$.

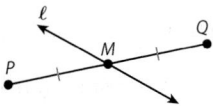

You can use paper folding as a method to construct a bisector of a given segment and locate the midpoint of the segment.

Finding a Midpoint

CONNECT VOCABULARY   EL

Explain that *bi-* is a prefix meaning *two* and *sect* means *to cut*, as into sections. A *segment bisector* divides the segment into two equal parts.

AVOID COMMON ERRORS

Some students may have difficulty aligning the points so that one is on top of the other. Have students enlarge and darken the endpoints so they are easier to locate. Students can fold either inward or outward as long as the points are put together.

QUESTIONING STRATEGIES

 When you use paper folding to bisect a line segment, why do you fold the paper so that the endpoints of the line segment are on top of each other? Placing one endpoint on top of the other creates a mirror image of the parts, with the crease corresponding to the midpoint and mirror line.

Example 3 Use paper folding to construct a bisector of each segment.

(A)

Step 1 Use a compass and straightedge to copy $\overline{AB}$ on a piece of paper.

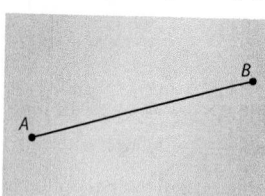

Step 2 Fold the paper so that point B is on top of point A.

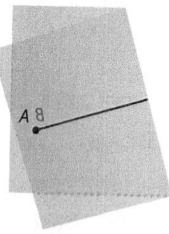

Step 3 Open the paper. Label the point where the crease intersects the segment as point M.

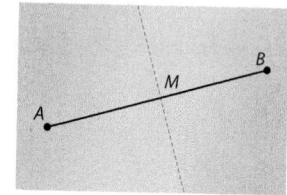

Point M is the midpoint of $\overline{AB}$ and the crease is a bisector of $\overline{AB}$.

(B) **Step 1** Use a compass and straightedge to copy $\overline{JK}$ on a piece of paper.

Step 2 Fold the paper so that point K is on top of point _____J_____.

Step 3 Open the paper. Label the point where the crease intersects the segment as point N.

Point N is the ___midpoint___ of $\overline{JK}$ and the crease is a ___bisector___ of $\overline{JK}$.

Step 4 Make a sketch of your paper folding construction or attach your folded piece of paper.

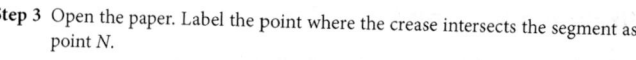

Reflect

9. Explain how you could use paper folding to divide a line segment into four segments of equal length.
   Use paper folding to construct the midpoint of the segment. Then use the same methods
   to construct the midpoint of each of the two new segments. The three midpoints divide
   the given segment into four segments of equal length.

© Houghton Mifflin Harcourt Publishing Company

10. Explain how to use a ruler to check your construction in Part B.
Measure each of the segments formed by the bisector. The two segments should each have

a length that is half as long as the given segment.

✏ Explain 4 Finding Midpoints on the Coordinate Plane

You can use the *Midpoint Formula* to find the midpoint of a segment on the coordinate plane.

The Midpoint Formula

The midpoint M of $\overline{AB}$ with endpoints $A(x_1, y_1)$ and $B(x_2, y_2)$ is given by $M\left(\dfrac{x_1 + x_2}{2}, \dfrac{y_1 + y_2}{2}\right)$.

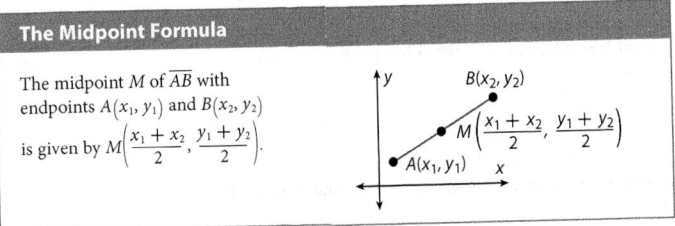

Example 4 Show that each statement is true.

Ⓐ If $\overline{PQ}$ has endpoints $P(-4, 1)$ and $Q(2, -3)$, then the midpoint M of $\overline{PQ}$ lies in Quadrant III.

Use the Midpoint Formula to find the midpoint of $\overline{PQ}$. $\qquad M\left(\dfrac{-4 + 2}{2}, \dfrac{1 + (-3)}{2}\right) = M(-1, -1)$

Substitute the coordinates, then simplify.

So M lies in Quadrant III, since the x- and y-coordinates are both negative.

Ⓑ If $\overline{RS}$ has endpoints $R(3, 5)$ and $S(-3, -1)$, then the midpoint M of $\overline{RS}$ lies on the y-axis.

Use the Midpoint Formula to find the midpoint of $\overline{RS}$. $\qquad M\left(\dfrac{3 + \boxed{-3}}{2}, \dfrac{5 + \boxed{-1}}{2}\right) = M\left(\boxed{0}, \boxed{2}\right)$

Substitute the coordinates, then simplify.

So M lies on the y-axis, since ___the x-coordinate is 0___.

Your Turn

Show that each statement is true.

11. If $\overline{AB}$ has endpoints $A(6, -3)$ and $B(-6, 3)$, then the midpoint M of $\overline{AB}$ is the origin.

$M\left(\dfrac{6 + (-6)}{2}, \dfrac{-3 + 3}{2}\right) = M(0, 0)$

So M is the origin, since the x- and y-coordinates are both 0.

12. If $\overline{JK}$ has endpoints $J(7, 0)$ and $K(-5, -4)$, then the midpoint M of $\overline{JK}$ lies in Quadrant IV.

$M\left(\dfrac{7 + (-5)}{2}, \dfrac{0 + (-4)}{2}\right) = M(1, -2)$

So M lies in Quadrant IV, since the x-coordinate is positive and the y-coordinate is negative.

© Houghton Mifflin Harcourt Publishing Company

EXPLAIN 4

Finding Midpoints on the Coordinate Plane

AVOID COMMON ERRORS

To avoid computation errors, caution students to pay attention to the signs of the endpoint coordinates when they are finding the midpoint. Students may benefit from plotting segments in the plane before using the formula to find the midpoint.

QUESTIONING STRATEGIES

❓ Does it matter which point is represented by (x_1, y_1)? Explain. No, the midpoint coordinates are the same due to the Commutative Property of Addition.

❓ How could you use the Distance Formula to check the location of a midpoint? Check that the distance from one endpoint to the midpoint equals the distance from the other endpoint to the midpoint.

ELABORATE

INTEGRATE MATHEMATICAL PRACTICES

Focus on Critical Thinking

MP.3 Discuss with students why they are applying the Ruler Postulate ("The distance between any two points is equal to the absolute value of the difference of their coordinates") when they find the length of a vertical or a horizontal segment on a coordinate plane.

AVOID COMMON ERRORS

Remind students that they can draw a quick sketch to help them recognize when a line is horizontal, vertical, or oblique to help them select the appropriate method to find the length of a line given its coordinates.

QUESTIONING STRATEGIES

? Can you use the Distance Formula to find the length of a vertical or horizontal line segment? Explain. **Yes, either the horizontal or vertical distance reduces to 0, so it is the same as finding the positive difference of using the other coordinate.**

SUMMARIZE THE LESSON

? If you know the endpoints of a line segment, how can you find the length of the line segment and its midpoint? **Use the Distance Formula to find the length of the segment and the Midpoint Formula to find the coordinates of its midpoint.**

---

13. Explain why the Distance Formula is not needed to find the distance between two points that lie on a horizontal or vertical line.
If two points lie on a horizontal or vertical line, they share a common x-coordinate or y-coordinate. To find the distance between the points, you just need to find the positive difference of the other coordinates.

14. When you use the Distance Formula, does the order in which you subtract the x- and y-coordinates matter? Explain.
No; $(x_1 - x_2)^2 = (x_2 - x_1)^2$ and $(y_1 - y_2)^2 = (y_2 - y_1)^2$.

15. When you use the Midpoint Formula, can you take either point as (x_1, y_1) or (x_2, y_2)? Why or why not?
Yes; $\dfrac{x_1 + x_2}{2} = \dfrac{x_2 + x_1}{2}$ and $\dfrac{y_1 + y_2}{2} = \dfrac{y_2 + y_1}{2}$.

16. Essential Question Check-In What is the difference between finding the length of a segment that is drawn on a sheet of blank paper and a segment that is drawn on a coordinate plane?
Possible answer: You use a ruler to find the length of a segment drawn on a sheet of blank paper and the Distance Formula to find the length of a segment on a coordinate plane.

☆ Evaluate: Homework and Practice

- Online Homework
- Hints and Help
- Extra Practice

Write the term that is suggested by each figure or description. Then state whether the term is an undefined term or a defined term.

1.

line segment; defined term

2.

point; undefined term

3.
$M \bullet \qquad \bullet L$

ray; defined term

4.

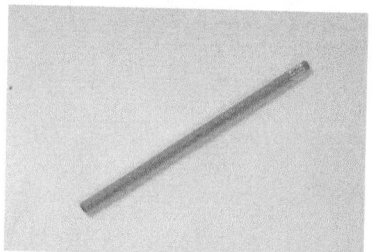

plane or line; undefined term

Use a compass and straightedge to construct a segment whose length is $AB + CD$.

5.
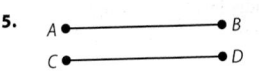

6.
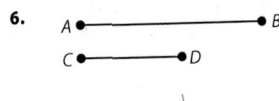

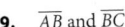

Copy each segment onto a sheet of paper. Then use paper folding to construct a bisector of the segment. Check students' constructions.

7.

8.
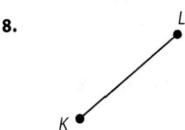

Determine whether the given segments have the same length. Justify your answer.

9. $\overline{AB}$ and $\overline{BC}$

$A(-4, 2), B(1, 4), C(2, -1)$

$AB = \sqrt{\left(1 - (-4)\right)^2 + (4 - 2)^2} = \sqrt{29}$

$BC = \sqrt{(2 - 1)^2 + \left(-1 - (4)\right)^2} = \sqrt{26}$

$AB \ne BC$, so $\overline{AB}$ and $\overline{BC}$ do not have the same length.

10. $\overline{EF}$ and $\overline{GH}$

$E(-4, -3), F(-1, 1), G(-2, -3), H(3, -3)$

$EF = \sqrt{\left(-1 - (-4)\right)^2 + \left(1 - (-3)\right)^2} = 5$

$GH = \sqrt{\left(3 - (-2)\right)^2 + \left(-3 - (-3)\right)^2} = 5$

$EF = GH = 5$, so $\overline{EF}$ and $\overline{GH}$ have the same length.

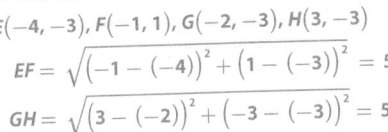

11. $\overline{AB}$ and $\overline{CD}$

$A(-4, 2), B(1, 4), C(2, -1), D(4, 4)$

$AB = \sqrt{\left(1 - (-4)\right)^2 + (4 - 2)^2} = \sqrt{29}$

$CD = \sqrt{(4 - 2)^2 + \left(4 - (-1)\right)^2} = \sqrt{29}$

So, $AB = CD = \sqrt{29}$. Therefore, $\overline{AB}$ and $\overline{CD}$ have the same length.

12. $\overline{BC}$ and $\overline{EF}$

$B(1, 4), C(2, -1), E(-4, -3), F(-1, 1)$

$BC = \sqrt{(2 - 1)^2 + \left(-1 - (-4)\right)^2} = \sqrt{26}$

$EF = \sqrt{\left(-1 - (-4)\right)^2 + \left(1 - (-3)\right)^2} = 5$

So, $BC \ne EF$. Therefore, $\overline{BC}$ and $\overline{EF}$ do not have the same length.

Show that each statement is true.

13. If $\overline{DE}$ has endpoints $D(-1, 6)$ and $E(3, -2)$, then the midpoint M of $\overline{DE}$ lies in Quadrant I.

$M\left(\dfrac{-1 + 3}{2}, \dfrac{6 + (-2)}{2}\right) = M(1, 2)$

So M lies in Quadrant I, since the x- and y-coordinates are both positive.

14. If $\overline{ST}$ has endpoints $S(-6, -1)$ and $T(0, 1)$, then the midpoint M of $\overline{ST}$ lies in on the x-axis.

$M\left(\dfrac{-6 + 0}{2}, \dfrac{-1 + 1}{2}\right) = M(-3, 0)$

So M lies on the x-axis, since the y-coordinate is 0.

Exercise	Depth of Knowledge (D.O.K.)	COMMON CORE Mathematical Practices
1–4	**1** Recall of Information	**MP.6** Precision
5–8	**2** Skills/Concepts	**MP.5** Using Tools
9–12	**2** Skills/Concepts	**MP.2** Reasoning
13–16	**2** Skills/Concepts	**MP.2** Reasoning
17–18	**1** Recall of Information	**MP.3** Logic
19–20	**2** Skills/Concepts	**MP.4** Modeling

EVALUATE

ASSIGNMENT GUIDE

Concepts and Skills	Practice
Explore Exploring Basic Geometric Terms	Exercises 1–4
Example 1 Constructing a Copy of a Line Segment	Exercises 5–6
Example 2 Using the Distance Formula on the Coordinate Plane	Exercises 9–12
Example 3 Finding a Midpoint	Exercises 7–8
Example 4 Finding Midpoints on the Coordinate Plane	Exercises 13–16

COMMUNICATING MATH

Students sometimes forget to place a symbol above letters used to name lines, segments, and rays. Remind them that two letters without a symbol represent a length.

INTEGRATE MATHEMATICAL PRACTICES
Focus on Communication

MP.3 As one student copies a line segment, have another student provide step-by-step instructions for how to copy the line segment. Repeat for finding the midpoint using paper folding. Then have students change roles.

Segment Length and Midpoints **14**

CONNECT VOCABULARY EL

Provide each small group with a deck of note cards with a highlighted term on each, such as *collinear, coplanar, line, segment, midpoint, coordinate plane*. Provide cards with pictures to illustrate each term. Have students shuffle and deal the cards. Students take turns putting down a card. If the picture or term matches a card another student is holding, that student picks it up and makes a pair. Students must agree on the pairings before play can resume.

AVOID COMMON ERRORS

Remind students of the techniques for accuracy in construction, including using a sharp pencil, lining up the compass tip and the pencil tip, and making sure the compass opening stays the same size.

Show that each statement is true.

15. If $\overline{JK}$ has endpoints $J(-2, 3)$ and $K(6, 5)$, and $\overline{LN}$ has endpoints $L(0, 7)$ and $N(4, 1)$, then $\overline{JK}$ and $\overline{LN}$ have the same midpoint.

$M_{\overline{JK}}\left(\frac{-2+6}{2}, \frac{3+5}{2}\right) = M_{\overline{JK}}(2, 4)$

$M_{\overline{LN}}\left(\frac{0+4}{2}, \frac{7+1}{2}\right) = M_{\overline{LN}}(2, 4)$

Both midpoints have the same coordinates, so the segments have the same midpoint.

16. If $\overline{GH}$ has endpoints $G(-8, 1)$ and $H(4, 5)$, then the midpoint M of $\overline{GH}$ lies on the line $y = -x + 1$.

$M\left(\frac{-8+4}{2}, \frac{1+5}{2}\right) = M(-2, 3)$

The midpoint lies on $y = -x + 1$ since its coordinates satisfy the equation: $3 = -(-2) + 1$.

Use the figure for Exercises 17 and 18.

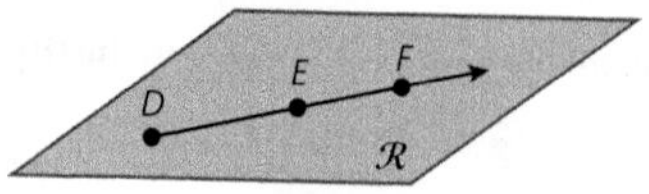

17. Name two different rays in the figure.

$\overrightarrow{DE}$ (or $\overrightarrow{DF}$) and $\overrightarrow{EF}$

18. Name three different segments in the figure.

$\overline{DE}$ (or $\overline{ED}$), $\overline{EF}$ (or $\overline{FE}$), and $\overline{DF}$ (or $\overline{FD}$)

Sketch each figure.

19. two rays that form a straight line and that intersect at point P

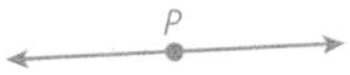

20. two line segments that both have a midpoint at point M

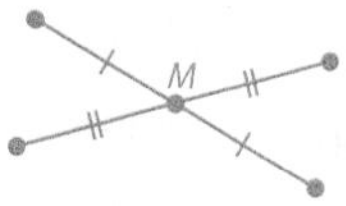

21. Draw and label a line segment, $\overline{JK}$, that is 3 inches long. Use a ruler to draw and label the midpoint M of the segment.

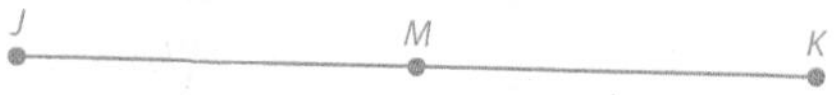

22. Draw the segment PQ with endpoints $P(-2, -1)$ and $Q(2, 4)$ on the coordinate plane. Then find the length and midpoint of $\overline{PQ}$.

$PQ = \sqrt{(2-(-2))^2 + (4-(-1))^2} = \sqrt{41}$

$M\left(\frac{-2+2}{2}, \frac{-1+4}{2}\right) = M(0, 1.5)$

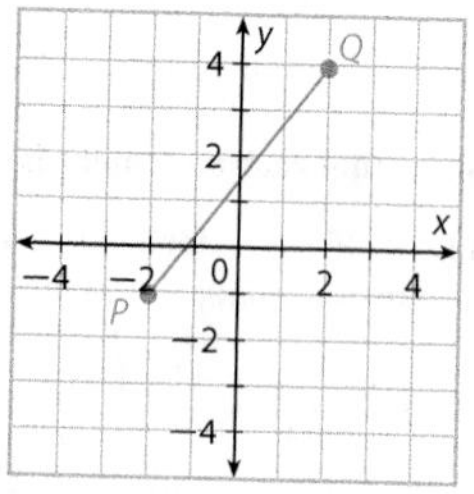

© Houghton Mifflin Harcourt Publishing Company

Exercise	Depth of Knowledge (D.O.K.)	COMMON CORE Mathematical Practices
21–22	1 Recall of Information	MP.4 Modeling
23–25	2 Skills/Concepts	MP.4 Modeling
26	3 Strategic Thinking	MP.3 Logic
27	2 Skills/Concepts	MP.2 Reasoning
28	3 Strategic Thinking H.O.T.	MP.5 Using Tools
29	3 Strategic Thinking H.O.T.	MP.2 Reasoning
30	3 Strategic Thinking H.O.T.	MP.6 Precision

23. Multi-Step The sign shows distances from a rest stop to the exits for different towns along a straight section of highway. The state department of transportation is planning to build a new exit to Freestone at the midpoint of the exits for Roseville and Edgewood. When the new exit is built, what will be the distance from the exit for Midtown to the exit for Freestone?

Midtown	17 mi
Roseville	35 mi
Edgewood	59 mi

The distance from the Roseville to Edgewood exits is $59 - 35 = 24$ mi, so the distance from the Roseville to Freestone exits will be $\frac{1}{2} \cdot 24 = 12$ mi. The distance from the Midtown to Roseville exits is $35 - 17 = 18$ mi, so the distance from the Midtown to Freestone exits will be $18 + 12 = 30$ mi.

24. On a town map, each unit of the coordinate plane represents 1 mile. Three branches of a bank are located at $A(-3, 1)$, $B(2, 3)$, and $C(4, -1)$. A bank employee drives from Branch A to Branch B and then drives halfway to Branch C before getting stuck in traffic. What is the minimum total distance the employee may have driven before getting stuck in traffic? Round to the nearest tenth of a mile.

The minimum total distance occurs when the employee drives along a straight line from A to B and from B to the midpoint of $\overline{BC}$.

The midpoint N of $\overline{BC}$ is $N(3, 1)$.

$AB = \sqrt{29}$, $BN = \sqrt{5}$, $AB + BN = \sqrt{29} + \sqrt{5} \approx 7.6$.

The minimum total distance the employee may have driven is 7.6 miles.

25. A city planner designs a park that is a quadrilateral with vertices at $J(-3, 1)$, $K(1, 3)$, $L(5, -1)$, and $M(-1, -3)$. There is an entrance to the park at the midpoint of each side of the park. A straight path connects each entrance to the entrance on the opposite side. Assuming each unit of the coordinate plane represents 10 meters, what is the total length of the paths to the nearest meter?

Midpoint P of $\overline{JK}$ is $P(-1, 2)$,
midpoint Q of $\overline{KL}$ is $Q(3, 1)$,
midpoint R of $\overline{LM}$ is $R(2, -2)$,
midpoint S of $\overline{MJ}$ is $S(-2, -1)$.

The paths are $\overline{PR}$ and $\overline{SQ}$.

$PR = \sqrt{25} = 5$
$SQ = \sqrt{29}$

The total length is $\sqrt{29} + 5 \approx 10.39$, which represents 103.9 meters.

The total length of the paths is approximately 104 meters.

26. Communicate Mathematical Ideas A video game designer places an anthill at the origin of a coordinate plane. A red ant leaves the anthill and moves along a straight line to $(1, 1)$, while a black ant leaves the anthill and moves along a straight line to $(-1, -1)$. Next, the red ant moves to $(2, 2)$, while the black ant moves to $(-2, -2)$. Then the red ant moves to $(3, 3)$, while the black ant moves to $(-3, -3)$, and so on. Explain why the red ant and the black ant are always the same distance from the anthill.

At any given moment, the red ant's coordinates may be written as (a, a) where $a > 0$. The red ant's distance from the anthill is $\sqrt{(a-0)^2 + (a-0)^2} = \sqrt{2a^2} = a\sqrt{2}$. The black ant's coordinates may be written as $(-a, -a)$ and the black ant's distance from the anthill is $\sqrt{(-a-0)^2 + (-a-0)^2} = \sqrt{2a^2} = a\sqrt{2}$. This shows both ants are always $a\sqrt{2}$ units from the anthill.

INTEGRATE MATHEMATICAL PRACTICES

Focus on Modeling

MP.4 When applying the Distance and Midpoint Formulas, students may benefit from using different colors to represent the coordinates and the operation symbols. This may help them distinguish the operation from the sign of the coordinate.

COGNITIVE STRATEGIES

Connect the Midpoint Formula to finding the average of two numbers. In the Midpoint Formula, the midpoint is the mean of the x-coordinates and the y-coordinates.

PEER-TO-PEER DISCUSSION

Ask students to discuss with a partner how to find the other endpoint of a line segment given one endpoint and the midpoint of the segment. Set the coordinates of the midpoint equal to the total of the missing endpoint and known endpoint coordinates divided by 2. Solve for the missing endpoint coordinates.

Have students compare the Distance and Midpoint Formulas. Ask them to draw an example of each on a grid.

27. Which of the following points are more than 5 units from the point $P(-2, -2)$? Select all that apply.

A. $A(1, 2)$ $AP = 5$, so AP is not greater than 5.

B. $B(3, -1)$ $BP \approx 5.1$, so BP is greater than 5.

C. $C(2, -4)$ $CP \approx 4.5$, so CP is not greater than 5.

D. $D(-6, -6)$ $DP \approx 5.7$, so DP is greater than 5.

E. $E(-5, 1)$ $EP \approx 4.2$, so EP is not greater than 5.
       Answer: B, D

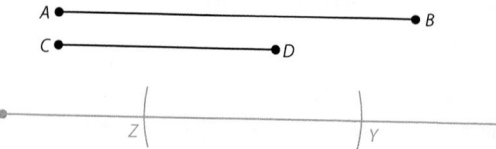

H.O.T. Focus on Higher Order Thinking

28. Analyze Relationships Use a compass and straightedge to construct a segment whose length is $AB - CD$. Use a ruler to check your construction.

$\overline{XZ}$ is the required segment.

29. Critical Thinking Point M is the midpoint of $\overline{AB}$. The coordinates of point A are $(-8, 3)$ and the coordinates of M are $(-2, 1)$. What are the coordinates of point B?

Let (x, y) be the coordinates of point B.

Solve for x: $-2 = \dfrac{-8 + x}{2}$, $4 = x$ Solve for y: $1 = \dfrac{3 + y}{2}$, $-1 = y$

The coordinates of point B are $(4, -1)$.

30. Make a Conjecture Use a compass and straightedge to copy $\overline{AB}$ so that one endpoint of the copy is at point X. Then repeat the process three more times, making three different copies of $\overline{AB}$ that have an endpoint at point X. Make a conjecture about the set of all possible copies of $\overline{AB}$ that have an endpoint at point X.

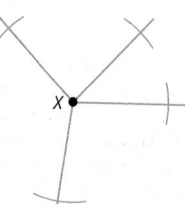

$A \bullet\!\!-\!\!-\!\!-\!\!\bullet B$

Constructions may vary. Possible answer: The set of all possible copies of $\overline{AB}$ that have an endpoint at point X form a circle and its interior. The center of the circle is X and the radius is AB.

Lesson Performance Task

A carnival ride consists of four circular cars—A, B, C, and D—each of which spins about a point at its center. The center points of cars A and B are attached by a straight beam, as are the center points of cars C and D. The two beams are attached at their midpoints by a rotating arm. The figure shows how the beams and arm can rotate.

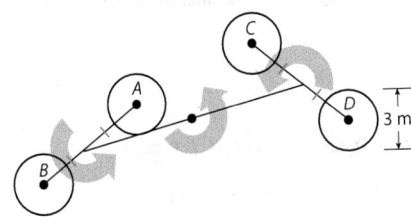

A plan for the ride uses a coordinate plane in which each unit represents one meter. In the plan, the center of car A is $(-6, -1)$, the center of car B is $(-2, -3)$, the center of car C is $(3, 4)$, and the center of car D is $(5, 0)$. Each car has a diameter of 3 meters.

The manager of the carnival wants to place a fence around the ride. Describe the shape and dimensions of a fence that will be appropriate to enclose the ride. Justify your answer.

Let P be the midpoint of $\overline{AB}$ and let Q be the midpoint of $\overline{CD}$.

The coordinates of P and Q are $P(-4, -2)$. and $Q(4, 2)$.

Find the length of the rotating arm PQ. $PQ = \sqrt{80}$

The maximum length of the ride occurs when the two beams lie along the rotating arm, as shown.

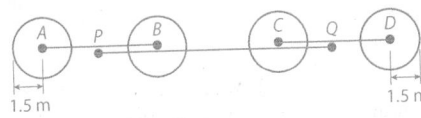

$AP = \sqrt{5}$ and $BP = \sqrt{5}$ since $AP = BP$.

$CQ = \sqrt{5}$ and $DQ = \sqrt{5}$ since $CQ = DQ$.

The total length L is $AP + PQ + QD$ plus half the diameter of a car on either end.

$L = 1.5 + \sqrt{5} + \sqrt{80} + \sqrt{5} + 1.5 \approx 16.4$ m.

Students' descriptions should allow extra space for clearance around the ride. Possibilities include a square fence that is about 18 meters long on each side or a circular fence about 18 meters in diameter.

Focus on Patterns

MP.8 Students can check that they have found the correct coordinates of P by seeing if the x-coordinate of P is midway between the x-coordinates of points A and B, and if the y-coordinate of P is midway between the y-coordinates of points A and B:

$$A(-6, -1)$$
$$P(-4, -2)$$
$$B(-2, -3)$$

They can use the same method to check the coordinates of Q:

$$C(3, 4)$$
$$Q(4, 2)$$
$$D(5, 0)$$

This process helps to make the calculation of midpoints more logical and less prone to error.

AVOID COMMON ERRORS

When finding PQ using the Distance Formula, students may calculate

$\sqrt{64 + 16}$ incorrectly:

$$\sqrt{64 + 16} = \sqrt{64} + \sqrt{16}$$
$$= 8 + 4$$
$$= 12$$

Stress that by the order of operations, sums and differences beneath a square root sign must be calculated first, before the square root is taken:

$$\sqrt{64 + 16} = \sqrt{64 + 16}$$
$$= \sqrt{80}$$

EXTENSION ACTIVITY

Have students graph two versions of the carnival ride on coordinate grids, using the given coordinates and scale. Ask them to show the ride in these configurations:

- when it is at its maximum horizontal length
- when it is at its maximum vertical height

When students have completed the two graphs, they should draw the fence that they described in the Lesson Performance Task and calculate its length.

Scoring Rubric

2 points: Student correctly solves the problem and explains his/her reasoning.

1 point: Student shows good understanding of the problem but does not fully solve or explain his/her reasoning.

0 points: Student does not demonstrate understanding of the problem.

Angle Measures and Angle Bisectors

Common Core Math Standards

The student is expected to:

COMMON CORE G-CO.A.1

Know precise definitions of angle ... based on the undefined notions of ... distance around a circular arc. Also G-CO.D.12

Mathematical Practices

COMMON CORE MP.5 Using Tools

Language Objective

Work with a partner to play "angle charades."

ENGAGE

Essential Question: How is measuring an angle similar to and different from measuring a line segment?

Possible answer: In both cases, the measure is undefined until a unit is chosen. Angles may be measured in degrees; there are 360° in a circle. The tool for measuring an angle in degrees is a protractor. Line segments are measured using linear units, such as centimeters or inches. The tool for measuring a line segment is a ruler.

PREVIEW: LESSON PERFORMANCE TASK

View the online Engage. Discuss the photo and the fact that 60° and 40° stands are available, but that a customer wants a 50° stand. Then preview the Lesson Performance Task.

Name_____ Class_____ Date_____

1.2 Angle Measures and Angle Bisectors

Essential Question: How is measuring an angle similar to and different from measuring a line segment?

Resource Locker

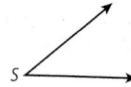 **Explore**   **Constructing a Copy of an Angle**

Start with a point X and use a compass and straightedge to construct a copy of $\angle S$.

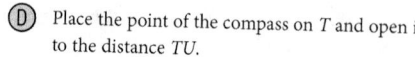

Ⓐ Use a straightedge to draw a ray with endpoint X.

Ⓑ Place the point of your compass on S and draw an arc that intersects both sides of the angle. Label the points of intersection T and U.

Ⓓ Place the point of the compass on T and open it to the distance TU.

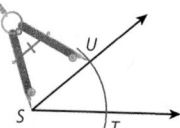

Ⓒ Without adjusting the compass, place the point of the compass on X and draw an arc that intersects the ray. Label the intersection Y.

Ⓔ Without adjusting the compass, place the point of the compass on Y and draw an arc. Label the intersection with the first arc Z.

Ⓕ Use a straightedge to draw $\overrightarrow{XZ}$. $\angle X$ is a copy of $\angle S$.

Reflect

1. If you could place the angle you constructed on top of $\angle S$ so that $\overrightarrow{XY}$ coincides with $\overrightarrow{ST}$, what would be true about $\overrightarrow{XZ}$? Explain.
    $\overrightarrow{XZ}$ would coincide with $\overrightarrow{SU}$. Since the angles are copies of each other, the rays in each angle form the same opening.

2. **Discussion** Is it possible to do the construction with a compass that is stuck open to a fixed distance? Why or why not?
    No; you could use the compass to make the required arcs in Steps B and C, but you would not be able to adjust the opening of the compass as required in Step D.

Module 1   **19**   Lesson 2

© Houghton Mifflin Harcourt Publishing Company

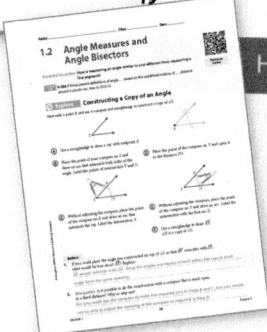

HARDCOVER PAGES 17–26

Turn to these pages to find this lesson in the hardcover student edition.

An **angle** is a figure formed by two rays with the same endpoint.
The common endpoint is the **vertex** of the angle.
The rays are the **sides** of the angle.

Example 1 Draw or name the given angle.

Ⓐ ∠PQR

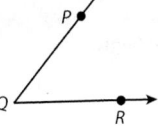

When an angle is named with three letters, the middle letter is the vertex. So, the vertex of angle ∠PQR is point Q.

The sides of the angle are two rays with common endpoint Q. So, the sides of the angle are $\overrightarrow{QP}$ and $\overrightarrow{QR}$.

Draw and label the angle as shown.

Ⓑ

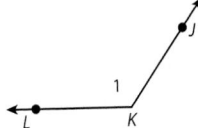

The vertex of the angle shown is point ⬚K⬚ . A name for the angle is ∠ ⬚K⬚ .

The vertex must be in the middle, so two more names for the angle are ∠ ⬚J⬚ ⬚K⬚ ⬚L⬚

and ∠ ⬚L⬚ ⬚K⬚ ⬚J⬚ .

The angle is numbered, so another name is ∠ ⬚1⬚ .

Reflect

3. Without seeing a figure, is it possible to give another name for ∠MKG?
   If so, what is it? If not, why not?
   Yes; ∠GKM

Your Turn

Use the figure for 4–5.

4. Name ∠2 in as many different ways as possible.
   ∠AEB, ∠BEA

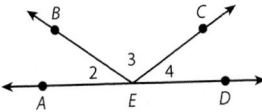

5. Use a compass and straightedge to copy ∠BEC.

EXPLORE

Constructing a Copy of an Angle

QUESTIONING STRATEGIES

? Do the rays of the angle you construct need to be the same length as the rays of the given angle? Why or why not? No; the measure of the angle is determined only by the size of the opening between the rays, not by the lengths of the rays.

? When you draw the initial arc that intersects the side of the angle to be copied, does it matter how wide you open the compass? Explain. No, as long as the arc intersects both sides of the angle, it doesn't matter.

INTEGRATE MATHEMATICAL PRACTICES
Focus on Modeling

MP.4 Have students practice constructing both acute and obtuse angles.

EXPLAIN 1

Naming Angles and Parts of an Angle

CONNECT VOCABULARY [EL]

Connect the word *degree* to the idea of measurement. A *degree* in science may be a measure of temperature in units known as Fahrenheit or Celsius. *Degree* in this context is the measure of an angle. Ask how many degrees are in a straight angle, a right angle, and so on.

PROFESSIONAL DEVELOPMENT

Math Background

Compass and straightedge constructions date to ancient Greece. In fact, one of the classic problems of ancient Greek mathematics was the trisection of an angle. That is, using a compass and straightedge, is it possible to construct an angle whose measure is one-third that of an arbitrary given angle? It was not until 1837 that this construction was proven to be impossible. On the other hand, it is a straightforward task to bisect any angle, and students learn this fundamental construction in this lesson.

QUESTIONING STRATEGIES

? When an angle is named using three letters, how can you identify the vertex of the angle? The vertex is the center letter of the angle name.

? An angle diagram may use letters or numbers to identify the angle. How are the diagrams different? Letters label individual points on the angle, while a number is inside the angle and names the entire angle.

EXPLAIN 2

Measuring Angles

AVOID COMMON ERRORS

Remind students to place the center mark of the protractor on the vertex and to align one side of the angle with the 0° mark. They may have to rotate the angle or the protractor for ease of alignment. On some protractors, the zero line is on the bottom edge, while on others, it is placed higher.

INTEGRATE MATHEMATICAL PRACTICES

Focus on Modeling

MP.4 Suggest that students use a straightedge, such as an index card, to extend the rays of an angle before they use a protractor to measure the angle. If the angle is smaller than the distance from the center mark to the edge of the protractor, this will make it easier to accurately measure the angle. Encourage students to estimate an angle measure before measuring to make sure the measurement is reasonable.

© Houghton Mifflin Harcourt Publishing Company

 Explain 2 Measuring Angles

The distance around a circular arc is undefined until a measurement unit is chosen. **Degrees** (°) are a common measurement unit for circular arcs. There are 360° in a circle, so an angle that measures 1° is $\frac{1}{360}$ of a circle. The measure of an angle is written $m\angle A$ or $m\angle PQR$.

You can classify angles by their measures.

Classifying Angles			
Acute Angle	**Right Angle**	**Obtuse Angle**	**Straight Angle**
$0° < m\angle A < 90°$	$m\angle A = 90°$	$90° < m\angle A < 180°$	$m\angle A = 180°$

Example 2 Use a protractor to draw an angle with the given measure.

(A) 53°

Step 1 Use a straightedge to draw a ray, $\overrightarrow{XY}$.

Step 2 Place your protractor on point X as shown. Locate the point along the edge of the protractor that corresponds to 53°. Make a mark at this location and label it point Z.

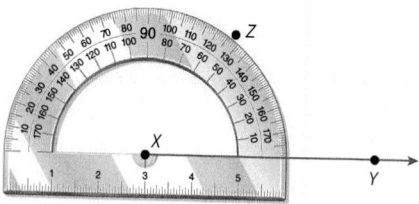

Step 3 Draw $\overrightarrow{XZ}$. $m\angle ZXY = 53°$.

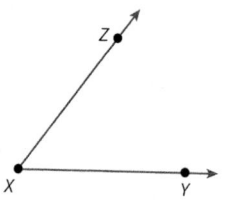

COLLABORATIVE LEARNING

Small Group Activity

Use pictures from magazines to find angles of different sizes. Ask students to identify the type of angle and estimate the measure. Then have students measure the angles with a protractor. If protractors are not available, they can use index cards or origami paper. The edges are already at a 90° angle, and anything greater would be an obtuse angle. A half-fold forms a 45° angle, a tri-fold approximately 30°, and so on. The pictures can be posted by classification and used for reference.

(B) 138°

Step 1 Use a straightedge to draw a ray, $\overrightarrow{AB}$.

Step 2 Place your protractor on point A so that $\overrightarrow{AB}$ is at zero.

Step 3 Locate the point along the edge of the protractor that corresponds to 138°. Make a mark at this location and label it point C.

Step 4 Draw $\overrightarrow{AC}$. m∠CAB = 138°.

Reflect

6. Explain how you can use a protractor to check that the angle you constructed in the Explore is a copy of the given angle.
   Measure the given angle and the constructed angle. They should have the same measure.

Your Turn

Each angle can be found in the rigid frame of the bicycle.
Use a protractor to find each measure.

7.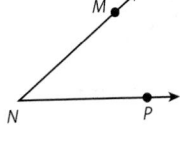

40°

8.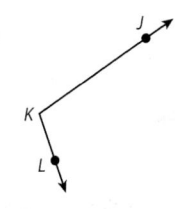

105°

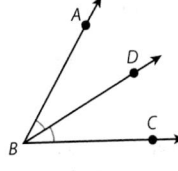

⚙ Explain 3   Constructing an Angle Bisector

An **angle bisector** is a ray that divides an angle into two angles that both have the same measure. In the figure, $\overrightarrow{BD}$ bisects ∠ABC, so m∠ABD = m∠CBD. The arcs in the figure show equal angle measures.

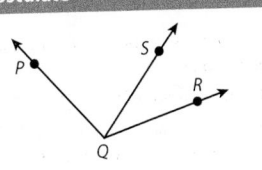

Postulate 2: Angle Addition Postulate
If S is in the interior of ∠PQR, then m∠PQR = m∠PQS + m∠SQR.

Module 1

22

Lesson 2

© Houghton Mifflin Harcourt Publishing Company • Image Credits: ©Gena73/ Shutterstock

---

QUESTIONING STRATEGIES

? If the vertex of an angle is placed on the center point of a protractor and both rays of the angle lie within the measures of the protractor, does one of the rays have to align with the 0° mark to find the measure of the angle? Explain. No, you can find the absolute value of the difference of the measures each ray intersects to find the measure of the angle. For example, if one ray aligns with 25° and the other with 67°, the angle measures 42°.

EXPLAIN 3

Constructing an Angle Bisector

CONNECT VOCABULARY **EL**

The postulates for angles are similar to the postulates for segments. The *Protractor Postulate* is similar to the Ruler Postulate. It says that the measure of an angle is the absolute value of the difference between the numbers matched on a protractor with the rays that form the sides of the angle.

DIFFERENTIATE INSTRUCTION

Manipulatives

Have students investigate how to find the bisector of an angle using a geometric reflecting tool. Have students draw an angle on a piece of paper. To use the tool, place it on the vertex of the angle so that one side is reflected onto the other side. Then draw the tool's line. Discuss how using the reflective device is similar to using paper folding to find the angle bisector.

Angle Measures and Angle Bisectors   **22**

AVOID COMMON ERRORS

Remind students not to change the compass setting when they draw the intersecting arcs from each side ray of an angle to create the angle bisector. In order to help students see why this is important, you many want to have them do a construction in which they change the compass setting between arcs. Students will see that the resulting ray does not bisect the angle.

QUESTIONING STRATEGIES

? If a ray divides an angle into two angles with equal measures, what must be true about the ray? Explain. **The ray is the angle bisector of the angle by the definition of an angle bisector.**

VISUAL CUES

Some students may have difficulty visualizing two angles that have the same measure, especially if the sides of the angles are shown with rays of different lengths. You may want to have students construct angle copies on tracing paper. Then they can place the copy on top of the original angle to check that the measures are the same.

© Houghton Mifflin Harcourt Publishing Company

Example 3 Use a compass and straightedge to construct the bisector of the given angle. Check that the measure of each of the new angles is one-half the measure of the given angle.

(A)

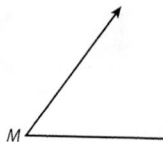

Step 1 Place the point of your compass on point M. Draw an arc that intersects both sides of the angle. Label the points of intersection P and Q.

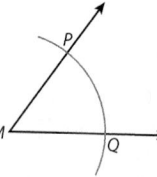

Step 2 Place the point of the compass on P and draw an arc in the interior of the angle.

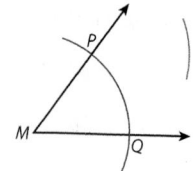

Step 3 Without adjusting the compass, place the point of the compass on Q and draw an arc that intersects the last arc you drew. Label the intersection of the arcs R.

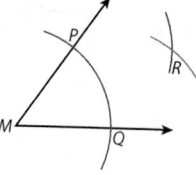

Step 4 Use a straightedge to draw $\overrightarrow{MR}$.

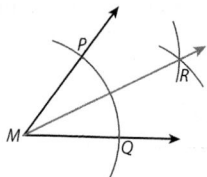

Step 5 Measure with a protractor to confirm that $m\angle PMR = m\angle QMR = \frac{1}{2}m\angle PMQ$.
$27° = 27° = \frac{1}{2}(54°)$ ✓

(B)

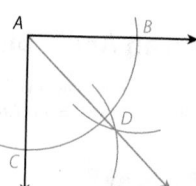

Step 1 Draw an arc centered at A that intersects both sides of the angle. Label the points of intersection B and C.

Step 2 Draw an arc centered at B in the interior of the angle.

Step 3 Without adjusting the compass, draw an arc centered at C that intersects the last arc you drew. Label the intersection of the arcs D.

Step 4 Draw $\overrightarrow{AD}$.

Step 5 Check that $m\angle BAD = m\angle CAD = \frac{1}{2}m\angle BAC$. **Yes;** $45° = 45° = \frac{1}{2}(90°)$

Module 1

23

Lesson 2

LANGUAGE SUPPORT **EL**

Connect Vocabulary

Remind students that the prefix *bi-* means "two" and that the root *sect* means "to cut." They can use these cues to help them remember that an angle bisector divides the angle into two equal parts.

9. **Discussion** Explain how you could use paper folding to construct the bisector of an angle.
   Fold the paper so that one side of the angle lies on top of the other. Unfold the paper.

   The crease is the angle bisector.

Use a compass and straightedge to construct the bisector of the given angle. Check that
the measure of each of the new angles is one-half the measure of the given angle.

10.

11.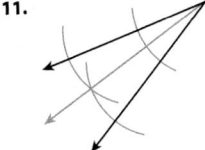

Elaborate

12. What is the relationship between a segment bisector and an angle bisector?
   A segment bisector divides a line segment into two segments that have the same length;

   an angle bisector divides an angle into two angles that have the same measure.

13. When you copy an angle, do the lengths of the segments you draw to represent the two rays affect whether
   the angles have the same measure? Explain.
   No; the measure of an angle depends only on the portion of a circle that the angle

   encompasses, not upon the apparent length of its sides.

14. **Essential Question Check-In** Many protractors have two sets of degree measures around the edge.
   When you measure an angle, how do you know which of the two measures to use?
   Answers may vary. Sample: First determine if the angle is acute or obtuse. If the angle

   is acute, use the measure between 0° and 90°. If the angle is obtuse, use the measure

   between 90° and 180°.

ELABORATE

INTEGRATE MATHEMATICAL PRACTICES
Focus on Math Connections

MP.1 Remind students to record angle measures using a protractor in degrees by using the degree symbol. Point out that not all angle measures are recorded in degrees. *Radians* are real number units of angle rotation. For example, π radians $= 180°$.

INTEGRATE TECHNOLOGY

Point out that a graphing calculator may need to be set to record angle measure in degrees, since either degree or radian measure can be selected. This feature is generally used for trigonometry calculations, however.

QUESTIONING STRATEGIES

What methods can you use to bisect an angle? Which method do you think is the most accurate? Explain. You can use a compass and straightedge, paper folding, or measurement with a protractor. Possible answer: You are more likely to draw the bisector accurately from the vertex by using a compass and straightedge because the method is exact.

SUMMARIZE THE LESSON

What is the Angle Addition Postulate and how does it relate to the bisector of an angle? If a ray from the vertex of an angle divides the angle into two parts, the sum of the measures of the parts is equal to the measure of the whole original angle. An angle bisector is a ray that divides an angle into two equal parts.

EVALUATE

ASSIGNMENT GUIDE

Concepts and Skills	Practice
Explore Constructing a Copy of an Angle	Exercises 1–3
Example 1 Naming Angles and Parts of an Angle	Exercises 4–7
Example 2 Measuring Angles	Exercises 8–11
Example 3 Constructing an Angle Bisector	Exercises 12–14

INTEGRATE MATHEMATICAL PRACTICES
Focus on Reasoning

MP.2 Discuss how the Protractor Postulate can be applied in addition to the Angle Addition Postulate to find the measure of angles outlined on top of a protractor.

KINESTHETIC EXPERIENCE

Have students work in pairs to write highlighted and prerequisite vocabulary from the lesson on index cards, such as *acute, obtuse,* and *straight angles; angle bisector,* and *ray.* Students talk about what each term means, then place the cards face down. One student draws a card and "acts out" the term on the card (for example, a right angle) using hands and arms. The other student guesses. Then they switch roles and the first student guesses while the second student acts out or draws the term.

⭐ Evaluate: Homework and Practice

- Online Homework
- Hints and Help
- Extra Practice

Use a compass and straightedge to construct a copy of each angle.

1. 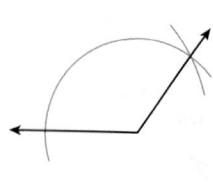   **2.**    **3.**

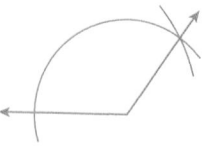      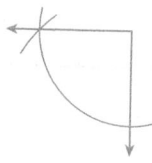

Draw an angle with the given name.

4. ∠JWT

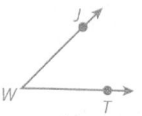

5. ∠NBQ

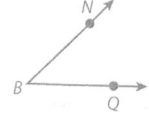

Name each angle in as many different ways as possible.

6.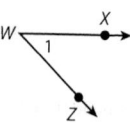

∠W, ∠ZWX, ∠XWZ, and ∠1

7.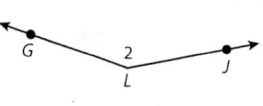

∠L, ∠GLJ, ∠JLG, and ∠2

Use a protractor to draw an angle with the given measure.

8. 19°

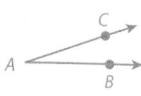

9. 100°

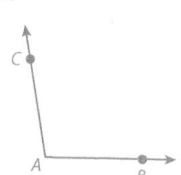

© Houghton Mifflin Harcourt Publishing Company

Exercise	Depth of Knowledge (D.O.K.)	COMMON CORE Mathematical Practices
1–3	**1** Recall of Information	**MP.5** Using Tools
4–7	**1** Recall of Information	**MP.6** Precision
8–14	**1** Recall of Information	**MP.5** Using Tools
15–16	**2** Skills/Concepts	**MP.2** Reasoning
17–19	**2** Skills/Concepts	**MP.5** Using Tools
20–21	**2** Skills/Concepts	**MP.4** Modeling
22	**2** Skills/Concepts	**MP.4** Modeling

Use a protractor to find the measure of each angle.

10.

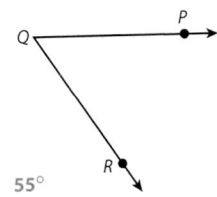

11.

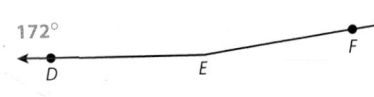

Use a compass and straightedge to construct the bisector of the given angle. Check that the measure of each of the new angles is one-half the measure of the given angle.

12.

13.

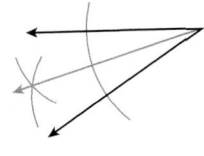

14.

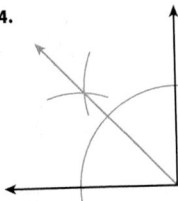

Use the Angle Addition Postulate to find the measure of each angle.

15. ∠BXC

$$m∠AXB + m∠BXC = m∠AXC$$
$$40° + m∠BXC = 70°$$
$$m∠BXC = 30°$$

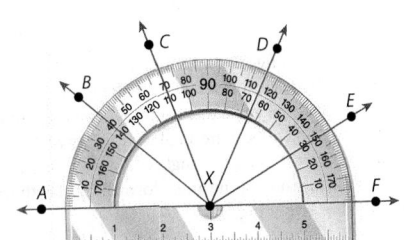

16. ∠BXE

$$m∠EXF + m∠BXE = m∠BXF$$
$$30° + m∠BXE = 140°$$
$$m∠BXE = 110°$$

Use a compass and straightedge to copy each angle onto a separate piece of paper. Then use paper folding to construct the angle bisector.

17.

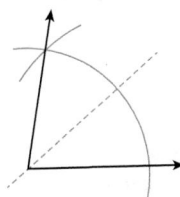

18.

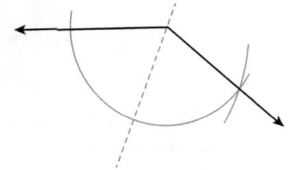

VISUAL CUES

Remind students to show all arcs and extend segments far enough when creating compass and straightedge constructions.

AVOID COMMON ERRORS

If students' compass settings are not tightly fixed, the compass setting may change without students' awareness. Stress to students that they must check compass tightness and keep the same fixed compass setting for accuracy.

Exercise	Depth of Knowledge (D.O.K.)	COMMON CORE Mathematical Practices
23	**2** Skills/Concepts	**MP.4** Modeling
24	**2** Skills/Concepts	**MP.6** Precision
25	**2** Skills/Concepts	**MP.2** Reasoning
26	**3** Strategic Thinking	**MP.2** Reasoning
27	**3** Strategic Thinking H.O.T.	**MP.3** Logic
28	**2** Skills/Concepts H.O.T.	**MP.5** Using Tools
29	**3** Strategic Thinking H.O.T.	**MP.5** Using Tools

Angle Measures and Angle Bisectors　**26**

COMMUNICATING MATH

Students will have to use algebra together with the Angle Addition Postulate to set up an equation to solve for the variable when one of the angles includes a variable. Point out that angles may not always have whole-number measures.

19. Use a compass and straightedge to construct an angle whose measure is $m\angle A + m\angle B$. Use a protractor to check your construction.

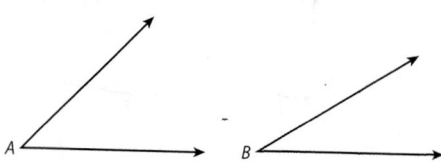

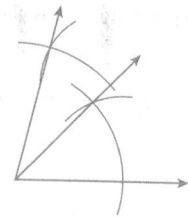

20. Find the value of x, given that $m\angle PQS = 112°$.

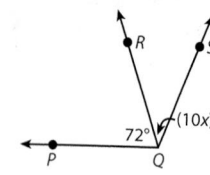

$$m\angle PQR + m\angle RQS = m\angle PQS$$
$$72 + 10x = 112$$
$$x = 4$$

21. Find the value of y, given that $m\angle KLM = 135°$.

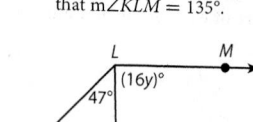

$$m\angle KLN + m\angle NLM = m\angle KLM$$
$$47 + 16y = 135$$
$$y = 5.5$$

22. Multi-Step The figure shows a map of five streets that meet at Concord Circle. The measure of the angle formed by Melville Road and Emerson Avenue is 118°. The measure of the angle formed by Emerson Avenue and Thoreau Street is 134°. Hawthorne Lane bisects the angle formed by Melville Road and Emerson Avenue. Dickinson Drive bisects the angle formed by Emerson Avenue and Thoreau Street. What is the measure of the angle formed by Hawthorne Lane and Dickinson Drive? Explain your reasoning.

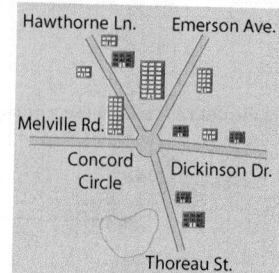

The measure of the angle formed by Melville and Emerson is 118°, so the measure of the angle formed by Hawthorne and Emerson is $\frac{1}{2}(118°) = 59°$. The measure of the angle formed by Emerson and Thoreau is 134°, so the measure of the angle formed by Emerson and Dickinson is $\frac{1}{2}(134°) = 67°$. By the Angle Addition Postulate, the measure of the angle formed by Hawthorne and Dickinson is $59° + 67° = 126°$.

23. **Represent Real-World Problems** A carpenter is building a rectangular bookcase with diagonal braces across the back, as shown. The carpenter knows that $\angle ADC$ is a right angle and that $m\angle BDC$ is $32°$ greater than $m\angle ADB$. Write and solve an equation to find $m\angle BDC$ and $m\angle ADB$.

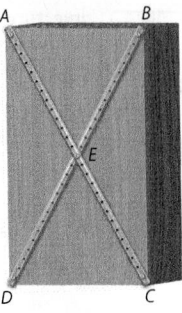

$$m\angle ADB + m\angle BDC = m\angle ADC$$
$$x + (x + 32) = 90$$
$$2x + 32 = 90$$
$$x = 29$$

So, $m\angle ADB = 29°$ and $m\angle BDC = 29 + 32 = 61°$

24. Describe the relationships among the four terms.

The definitions of the terms "angle bisector" and "angle" are each built upon the definitions of the term below it. The definition of the term "ray" is built upon the undefined term "line" below it.

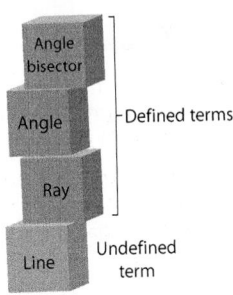

25. Determine whether each of the following pairs of angles have equal measures. Select the correct answer for each lettered part.

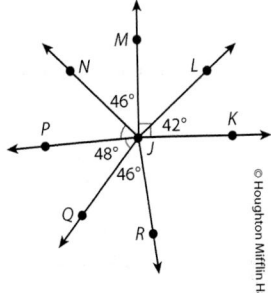

	Yes	No
A. $\angle KJL$ and $\angle LJM$	○ Yes	● No
B. $\angle MJP$ and $\angle PJR$	● Yes	○ No
C. $\angle LJP$ and $\angle NJR$	● Yes	○ No
D. $\angle MJK$ and $\angle PJR$	○ Yes	● No
E. $\angle KJR$ and $\angle MJP$	○ Yes	● No

a. no; $m\angle LJM = 90° - 42° = 48° \neq m\angle KJL$

b. yes; $m\angle NJP = 48°$ so $m\angle MJP = 46° + 48° = 94°$ and $m\angle PJR = 48° + 46° = 94°$

c. yes; $m\angle NJP = 48°$ and $m\angle LJM = 90° - 42° = 48°$, so $m\angle LJP = 48° + 46° + 48° = 142°$ and $m\angle NJR = 48° + 48° + 46° = 142°$

d. no; $m\angle MJK = 90°$, but $m\angle PJR = 48° + 46° = 94°$

e. no; $m\angle KJR = 360° - 90° - 46° - 48° - 48° - 46° = 82°$, but $m\angle MJP = 46° + 48° = 94°$

CRITICAL THINKING

Review why students can use the Angle Addition Postulate to find a missing angle measure if they know the measures of one angle and the total angle, in order to find the measure of the other angle, when an angle is divided into two angles that do not overlap.

MODELING

Students know the measure of a right angle. Discuss how to use the measure of a right angle to find the measure of a straight angle $(180°)$ and the total number of degrees in one full rotation $(360°)$.

PEER-TO-PEER DISCUSSION

Have students work with a partner to write a guide to copying and bisecting angles in the form of a comic strip. Encourage them to include enough information so that someone who has never done these constructions could follow the procedure.

Angle Measures and Angle Bisectors   **28**

26. **Make a Conjecture** A rhombus is a quadrilateral with four sides of equal length. Use a compass and straightedge to bisect one of the angles in each of the rhombuses shown. Then use your results to state a conjecture.

Constructions may vary. Sample:

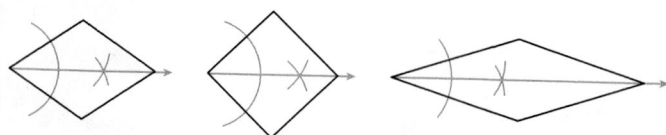

In a rhombus, the bisector of an angle also bisects the opposite angle.

H.O.T. Focus on Higher Order Thinking

27. **What If?** What happens if you perform the steps for constructing an angle bisector when the given angle is a straight angle? Does the construction still work? If so, explain why and show a sample construction. If not, explain why not.

Yes; the construction still works. In this case, the construction produces two right angles since each has half the measure of a straight angle (180°).

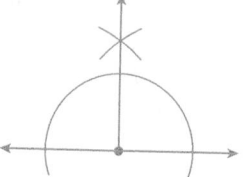

28. **Critical Thinking** Use a compass and straightedge to construct an angle whose measure is m∠A − m∠B. Use a protractor to check your construction.

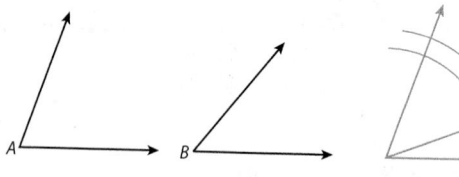
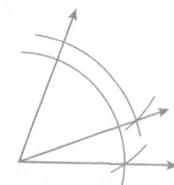

29. **Communicate Mathematical Ideas** Explain the steps for using a compass and straightedge to construct an angle with $\frac{1}{4}$ the measure of a given angle. Then draw an angle and show the construction.

Construct the bisector of the given angle. Then construct the bisector of one of the angles that was formed.

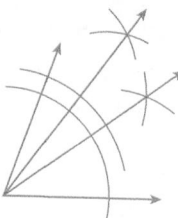

© Houghton Mifflin Harcourt Publishing Company

Module 1

29

Lesson 2

Lesson Performance Task

A store sells custom-made stands for tablet computers. When an order comes in, the customer specifies the angle at which the stand should hold the tablet. Then an employee bends a piece of aluminum to the correct angle to make the stand. The figure shows the templates that the employee uses to make a 60° stand and a 40° stand.

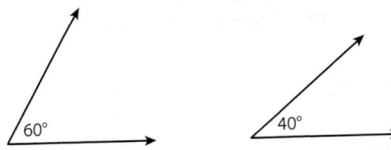

The store receives an order for a 50° stand. The employee does not have a template for a 50° stand and does not have a protractor. Can the employee use the existing templates and a compass and straightedge to make a template for a 50° stand? If so, explain how and show the steps the employee should use. If not, explain why not.

Yes; first construct the bisector of the template for the 60° stand to create two 30° angles. Then construct the bisector of the template for the 40° stand to create two 20° angles. Next, copy one of the 30° angles. Finally, copy one of the 20° angles so it shares a side with the 30° angle. The measure of the resulting angle is 20° + 30° = 50°.

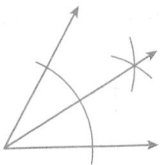  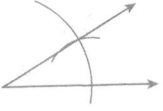 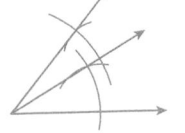

© Houghton Mifflin Harcourt Publishing Company

EXTENSION ACTIVITY

The Lesson Performance Task introduces the idea of combining simple constructions to produce more complex ones. Have students think about how they could use this idea to construct a 35° angle from a 30° angle and a 40° angle. Then have them make up problems that apply the idea. Each problem should give the measures of two or more angles and ask how an angle of specified measure could be constructed using the given ones. Students should provide answers for each of their problems.

QUESTIONING STRATEGIES

? You are given a 60° angle and an 80° angle. How could you use them to construct a 20° angle? Sample answer: Copy the 60° angle inside the 80° angle, with the two angles sharing a side. The angle adjacent to the 60° angle will measure 80° − 60° = 20°.

? You are given a 70° angle and a 60° angle. How could you use them to construct a 25° angle? Sample answer: Bisect the 70° angle to create two 35° angles. Copy a 35° angle inside the 60° angle, with the two angles sharing a side. The angle adjacent to the 35° angles will measure 60° − 35° = 25°.

? You are given a 50° angle and a 40° angle. How could you use them to construct a 5° angle? Sample answer: Copy the 40° angle inside the 50° angle, with the two angles sharing a side. The angle adjacent to the 40° angle will measure 50° − 40° = 10°. Then bisect the 10° angle to create two 5° angles.

AVOID COMMON ERRORS

Students may have difficulty completing the last step of the Lesson Performance Task, in which they must copy a 20° angle so that it shares the non-horizontal side of the 30° angle. This can happen when students are used to starting with horizontal lines in their constructions. Point out that there is nothing wrong with rotating their papers to start with a horizontal line.

Scoring Rubric
2 points: Student correctly solves the problem and explains his/her reasoning.
1 point: Student shows good understanding of the problem but does not fully solve or explain his/her reasoning.
0 points: Student does not demonstrate understanding of the problem.

Angle Measures and Angle Bisectors   **30**

Representing and Describing Transformations

Common Core Math Standards

The student is expected to:

 G-CO.A.2

Represent transformations in the plane ...; describe transformations as functions .... Compare transformations that preserve distance and angle to those that do not .... Also G-CO.B.5

Mathematical Practices

COMMON CORE **MP.6 Precision**

Language Objective

Students work together to give oral, verbal and pictorial clues and justify transformations drawn from clues.

ENGAGE

Essential Question: How can you describe transformations in the coordinate plane using algebraic representations and using words?

Possible answer: You can use coordinate notation to write rules that describe how preimage points are transformed to image points. You can describe transformations with words like *reflection, rotation, translation, stretch,* and *dilation.* You can say that a transformation is *rigid* (preserves length and angle measure) or *not rigid* (does not preserve length and angle measure.)

PREVIEW: LESSON PERFORMANCE TASK

View the online Engage. Discuss the photo and the fact that it has been stretched. Ask whether the angles in the photo match the real-life angles. Then preview the Lesson Performance Task.

Name _____ Class _____ Date _____

1.3 Representing and Describing Transformations

Essential Question: How can you describe transformations in the coordinate plane using algebraic representations and using words?

Resource Locker

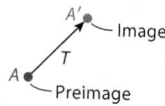 **Explore** Performing Transformations Using Coordinate Notation

A **transformation** is a function that changes the position, shape, and/or size of a figure. The inputs of the function are points in the plane; the outputs are other points in the plane. A figure that is used as the input of a transformation is the **preimage**. The output is the **image**. Translations, reflections, and rotations are three types of transformations. The decorative tiles shown illustrate all three types of transformations.

You can use *prime notation* to name the image of a point. In the diagram, the transformation T moves point A to point A' (read "A prime"). You can use function notation to write $T(A) = A'$. Note that a transformation is sometimes called a *mapping.* Transformation T maps A to A'.

A' ——— Image
    T
A ——— Preimage

Coordinate notation is one way to write a rule for a transformation on a coordinate plane. The notation uses an arrow to show how the transformation changes the coordinates of a general point, (x, y).

Find the unknown coordinates for each transformation and draw the image. Then complete the description of the transformation and compare the image to its preimage.

Ⓐ $(x, y) \rightarrow (x - 4, y - 3)$

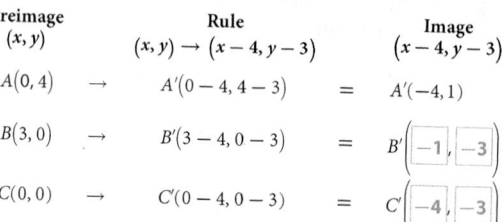
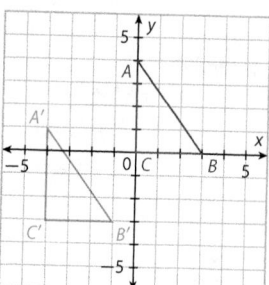

Preimage (x, y)		Rule $(x, y) \rightarrow (x - 4, y - 3)$		Image $(x - 4, y - 3)$
$A(0, 4)$	$\rightarrow$	$A'(0 - 4, 4 - 3)$	$=$	$A'(-4, 1)$
$B(3, 0)$	$\rightarrow$	$B'(3 - 4, 0 - 3)$	$=$	$B'(\boxed{-1}, \boxed{-3})$
$C(0, 0)$	$\rightarrow$	$C'(0 - 4, 0 - 3)$	$=$	$C'(\boxed{-4}, \boxed{-3})$

The transformation is a translation 4 units (left/right)

and 3 units (up/down).

A comparison of the image to its preimage shows that

Possible answer: the image is the same size and shape as the preimage

Module 1   31   Lesson 3

© Houghton Mifflin Harcourt Publishing Company · Image Credits: ©Antony McAulay/Shutterstock

---

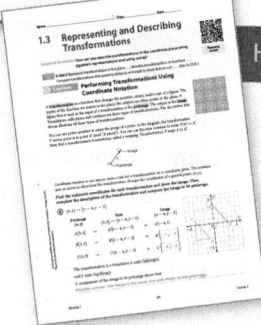

HARDCOVER PAGES 27–38

Turn to these pages to find this lesson in the hardcover student edition.

Ⓑ $(x, y) \rightarrow (-x, y)$

Preimage (x, y)	Rule $(x, y) \rightarrow (-x, y)$		Image $(-x, y)$
$R(-4, 3)$	$\rightarrow$	$R'(-(-4), 3)$	$= R'\boxed{4}, \boxed{3}$
$S(-1, 3)$	$\rightarrow$	$S'(-(-1), 3)$	$= S'\boxed{1}, \boxed{3}$
$T(-4, 1)$	$\rightarrow$	$T'(-(-4), 1)$	$= T'\boxed{4}, \boxed{1}$

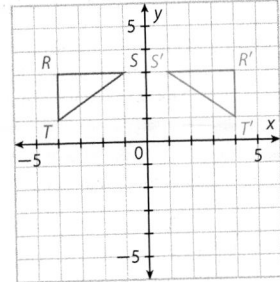

The transformation is a reflection across the (x-axis / ⓨ-axis).

A comparison of the image to its preimage shows that

Possible answer: the image is the same size and shape as the preimage, but it is flipped over

the y-axis
_____.

Ⓒ $(x, y) \rightarrow (2x, y)$

Preimage (x, y)	Rule $(x, y) \rightarrow (2x, y)$		Image $(2x, y)$
$J\boxed{-1}, \boxed{2}$	$\rightarrow$	$J'\boxed{2 \cdot -1}, \boxed{2}$	$= J'\boxed{-2}, \boxed{2}$
$K\boxed{2}, \boxed{2}$	$\rightarrow$	$K'\boxed{2 \cdot 2}, \boxed{2}$	$= K'\boxed{4}, \boxed{2}$
$L\boxed{2}, \boxed{-4}$	$\rightarrow$	$L'\boxed{2 \cdot 2}, \boxed{-4}$	$= L'\boxed{4}, \boxed{-4}$

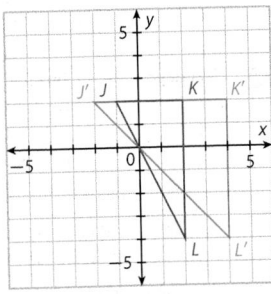

The transformation is a (ⓗorizontal / vertical) stretch by a

factor of ___2___.

A comparison of the image to its preimage shows that

Possible answer: the image and the preimage are both right triangles, but they do not

have the same size or shape
_____.

Reflect

1. **Discussion** How are the transformations in Steps A and B different from the transformation in Step C?
   The transformations in Steps A and B preserve the size and shape of the right triangle. The

   transformation in Step C changes the shape of the right triangle.

2. For each transformation, what rule could you use to map the image back to the preimage?
   A. $(x, y) \rightarrow (x + 4, y + 3)$; B. $(x, y) \rightarrow (-x, y)$; C. $(x, y) \rightarrow (0.5x, y)$

© Houghton Mifflin Harcourt Publishing Company

PROFESSIONAL DEVELOPMENT

 Integrate Mathematical Practices

This lesson provides an opportunity to address Mathematical Practice **MP.6**, which calls for students to "attend to precision." Students are already familiar with transformations in the plane and, in this lesson, students use graph paper to draw transformations. They use protractors, rulers, and coordinates to determine whether length and angle measure have been preserved. They also use concepts about functions to write the rules that express transformations algebraically.

EXPLORE

Performing Transformations Using Coordinate Notation

INTEGRATE TECHNOLOGY

You can use a spreadsheet to enter coordinates of vertices to create geometric figures and then transform the coordinates using a formula to create transformed figures.

INTEGRATE MATHEMATICAL PRACTICES
Focus on Communication

MP.3 Have students stand in front of a mirror. The student is the *preimage*. The *image* is the *reflection* of the student in the mirror. Ask students to use items on their desks to demonstrate a translation and a rotation. For each transformation, have them identify the preimage and the image.

QUESTIONING STRATEGIES

? How is the notation for an image related to the notation for its preimage? It is the same except that the notation for the image has a prime mark after each letter.

? How is the notation $T(A) = A'$ similar to the more familiar function notation $y = f(x)$? The object inside the parentheses is the input. The object on the other side of the equal sign is the output.

? How can you use the rule for transforming the coordinates of a general point of a figure to help you recognize if the transformation changes the size of the image? If a coordinate is changed by a multiplicative factor other than ±1, the image will change in size.

CONNECT VOCABULARY [EL]

Emphasize that the rule for the *transformation* shows how to change each *preimage* coordinate to its corresponding *image* coordinate.

Representing and Describing Transformations   **32**

EXPLAIN 1

Describing Rigid Motions Using Coordinate Notation

AVOID COMMON ERRORS

Sometimes students recognize that a rigid motion is a rotation, but do not correctly identify the angle of rotation. Review the angles by having students stand and physically turn to show various rotations, such as 90° clockwise or 180° counterclockwise.

QUESTIONING STRATEGIES

? To write a rule for a rigid motion transformation, does it matter which point on the figure you choose? Explain. No, the same rule is applied to each point to transform the figure.

? How does looking for a pattern in the coordinates from the preimage to the image help you identify the type of rigid motion? If the coordinates are changed by the same sum or difference, the rigid motion is a translation. If one coordinate stays the same and the other is the opposite of its original, the rigid motion is a reflection. If both coordinates change signs or if the x-and y-coordinates switch and one changes sign, the rigid motion is a rotation.

Explain 1 Describing Rigid Motions Using Coordinate Notation

Some transformations preserve length and angle measure, and some do not. A **rigid motion** (or *isometry*) is a transformation that changes the position of a figure without changing the size or shape of the figure. Translations, reflections, and rotations are rigid motions.

Properties of Rigid Motions	
• Rigid motions preserve distance.	• Rigid motions preserve collinearity.
• Rigid motions preserve angle measure.	• Rigid motions preserve parallelism.
• Rigid motions preserve betweenness.	

If a figure is determined by certain points, then its image after a rigid motion is determined by the images of those points. This is true because of the betweenness and collinearity properties of rigid motions. Rotations and translations also preserve *orientation*. This means that the order of the vertices of the preimage and image are the same, either clockwise or counterclockwise. Reflections do not preserve orientation.

Example 1 Use coordinate notation to write the rule that maps each preimage to its image. Then identify the transformation and confirm that it preserves length and angle measure.

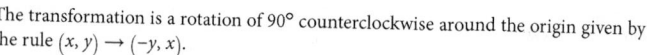

(A)

Preimage		Image
$A(1, 2)$	$\rightarrow$	$A'(-2, 1)$
$B(4, 2)$	$\rightarrow$	$B'(-2, 4)$
$C(3, -2)$	$\rightarrow$	$C'(2, 3)$

Look for a pattern in the coordinates.

The x-coordinate of each image point is the opposite of the y-coordinate of its preimage.

The y-coordinate of each image point equals the x-coordinate of its preimage.

The transformation is a rotation of 90° counterclockwise around the origin given by the rule $(x, y) \rightarrow (-y, x)$.

Find the length of each side of $\triangle ABC$ and $\triangle A'B'C'$. Use the Distance Formula as needed.

$AB = 3$ $A'B' = 3$

$BC = \sqrt{(3-4)^2 + (-2-2)^2}$ $B'C' = \sqrt{(2-(-2))^2 + (3-4)^2}$

$\quad = \sqrt{17}$ $\quad = \sqrt{17}$

$AC = \sqrt{(3-1)^2 + (-2-2)^2}$ $A'C' = \sqrt{(2-(-2))^2 + (3-1)^2}$

$\quad = \sqrt{20}$ $\quad = \sqrt{20}$

Since $AB = A'B'$, $BC = B'C'$, and $AC = A'C'$, the transformation preserves length.

Find the measure of each angle of $\triangle ABC$ and $\triangle A'B'C'$. Use a protractor.

$m\angle A = 63°$, $m\angle B = 76°$, $m\angle C = 41°$ $m\angle A' = 63°$, $m\angle B' = 76°$, $m\angle C' = 41°$

Since $m\angle A = m\angle A'$, $m\angle B = m\angle B'$, and $m\angle C = m\angle C'$, the transformation preserves angle measure.

COLLABORATIVE LEARNING ACTIVITY

Small Group Activity

Give each student three sheets of graph paper. Have each student draw a preimage and an image showing a translation on one sheet, a reflection on another, and a rotation on the third. Have them write the rule for each transformation on the back. Then, working in groups of three or four, have students analyze each other's graphs and determine the rule used to create each transformation.

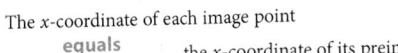

Ⓑ
Preimage		Image
$P(-3, -1)$	$\rightarrow$	$P'(-3, 1)$
$Q(3, -1)$	$\rightarrow$	$Q'(3, 1)$
$R(1, -4)$	$\rightarrow$	$R'(1, 4)$

Look for a pattern in the coordinates.

The x-coordinate of each image point ___**equals**___ the x-coordinate of its preimage.

The y-coordinate of each image point ___**is the opposite of**___ the y-coordinate of its preimage.

The transformation is a ___**reflection across the x-axis**___

given by the rule ___$(x, y) \rightarrow (x, -y)$___.

Find the length of each side of $\triangle PQR$ and $\triangle P'Q'R'$.

$PQ = \boxed{6}$

$QR = \sqrt{\left(1 - \boxed{3}\right)^2 + \left(-4 - \boxed{-1}\right)^2}$

$= \sqrt{\boxed{13}}$

$PR = \sqrt{\left(1 - \boxed{-3}\right)^2 + \left(-4 - \boxed{-1}\right)^2}$

$= \sqrt{\boxed{25}} = \boxed{5}$

$P'Q' = \boxed{6}$

$Q'R' = \sqrt{\left(1 - \boxed{3}\right)^2 + \left(4 - \boxed{1}\right)^2}$

$= \sqrt{\boxed{13}}$

$P'R' = \sqrt{\left(1 - \boxed{-3}\right)^2 + \left(4 - \boxed{1}\right)^2}$

$= \sqrt{\boxed{25}} = \boxed{5}$

Since ___$PQ = P'Q', QR = Q'R',$ and $PR = P'R'$___, the transformation preserves length.

Find the measure of each angle of $\triangle PQR$ and $\triangle P'Q'R'$. Use a protractor.

$m\angle P = \boxed{37°}$, $m\angle Q = \boxed{56°}$, $m\angle R = \boxed{87°}$ $m\angle P' = \boxed{37°}$, $m\angle Q' = \boxed{56°}$, $m\angle R' = \boxed{87°}$

Since ___$m\angle P = m\angle P', m\angle Q = m\angle Q',$ and $m\angle R = m\angle R'$___, the transformation preserves angle measure.

Reflect

3. How could you use a compass to test whether corresponding lengths in a preimage and image are the same?

___Place the point of the compass on one endpoint of the segment in the preimage and open it___

___to the length of the segment. Without adjusting the compass, move the point of the compass___

___to an endpoint of the corresponding segment in the image and make an arc. If the lengths___

___are the same, the arc will pass through the other endpoint of the segment in the image.___

4. Look back at the transformations in the Explore. Classify each transformation as a rigid motion or not a rigid motion.

___A. rigid motion; B. rigid motion; C. not a rigid motion___

INTEGRATE MATHEMATICAL PRACTICES

Focus on Modeling

MP.4 Some students have difficulty visualizing rotations. Have students copy the image on graph paper and then rotate the paper a given number of degrees. Tell them that the location and orientation of the figure on the graph after rotating the paper shows how the final image looks when the rotation rule is applied to the preimage.

DIFFERENTIATE INSTRUCTION

Multiple Representations

For each of the transformations, ask students to summarize all the possible ways to represent the transformation: graphically, using a rule, and using words. When students use words, encourage them to be as specific as possible, using the appropriate vocabulary from this lesson. Discuss the different advantages of each representation.

EXPLAIN 2

Describing Nonrigid Motions Using Coordinate Notation

CONNECT VOCABULARY **EL**

Note that the prefix *pre-* in *preimage* indicates "before," and that the preimage is before the *image* in a transformation.

INTEGRATE MATHEMATICAL PRACTICES

Focus on Modeling

MP.4 You may want to give students verbal descriptions of a variety of transformations. For example, the simplest transformation maps every point to itself. This is known as the *identity transformation*. Another transformation maps every point to the origin. Giving students examples of these "extreme" transformations will help them realize that not every transformation is a rigid motion.

© Houghton Mifflin Harcourt Publishing Company • Image Credits: ©Mary Hockenbery/Flickr/Getty Images

---

Your Turn

Use coordinate notation to write the rule that maps each preimage to its image. Then identify the transformation and confirm that it preserves length and angle measure.

5.

Preimage		Image
$D(-4, 4)$	$\rightarrow$	$D'(4, -4)$
$E(2, 4)$	$\rightarrow$	$E'(-2, -4)$
$F(-4, 1)$	$\rightarrow$	$F'(4, -1)$

Each coordinate maps to its opposite.

The transformation is a rotation of 180° around the origin given by the rule $(x, y) \rightarrow (-x, -y)$.

$DE = D'E' = 6$ $m\angle D = m\angle D' = 90°$

$EF = E'F' = \sqrt{45}$ $m\angle E = m\angle E' = 27°$

$DF = D'F' = 3$ $m\angle F = m\angle F' = 63°$

The transformation preserves length and angle measure.

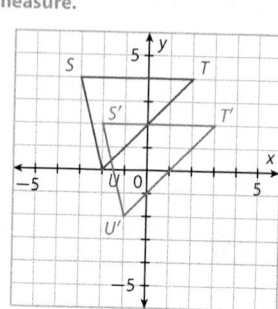

6.

Preimage		Image
$S(-3, 4)$	$\rightarrow$	$S'(-2, 2)$
$T(2, 4)$	$\rightarrow$	$T'(3, 2)$
$U(-2, 0)$	$\rightarrow$	$U'(-1, -2)$

x-coordinates: image is 1 more than preimage

y-coordinates: image is 2 less than preimage

The transformation is a translation given by the rule $(x, y) \rightarrow (x + 1, y - 2)$.

$ST = S'T' = 5$ $m\angle S = m\angle S' = 76°$

$TU = T'U' = \sqrt{32}$ $m\angle T = m\angle T' = 45°$

$SU = S'U' = \sqrt{17}$ $m\angle U = m\angle U' = 59°$

The transformation preserves length and angle measure.

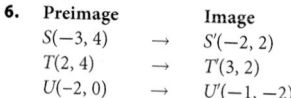 **Explain 2** **Describing Nonrigid Motions Using Coordinate Notation**

Transformations that stretch or compress figures are not rigid motions because they do not preserve distance.

The view in the fun house mirror is an example of a vertical stretch.

LANGUAGE SUPPORT **EL**

Connect Vocabulary

After reading the properties of rigid motions, discuss the meaning of "preserving" the characteristics of rigid motions. Have students explain in their own words what it means for each property to be preserved.

Example 2 Use coordinate notation to write the rule that maps each preimage to its image. Then confirm that the transformation is not a rigid motion.

(A) $\triangle JKL$ maps to triangle $\triangle J'K'L'$.

Preimage		Image
$J(4, 1)$	$\rightarrow$	$J'(4, 3)$
$K(-2, -1)$	$\rightarrow$	$K'(-2, -3)$
$L(0, -3)$	$\rightarrow$	$L'(0, -9)$

Look for a pattern in the coordinates.

The x-coordinate of each image point equals the x-coordinate of its preimage.
The y-coordinate of each image point is 3 times the y-coordinate of its preimage.
The transformation is given by the rule $(x, y) \rightarrow (x, 3y)$.

Compare the length of a segment of the preimage to the length of the corresponding segment of the image.

$$JK = \sqrt{(-2 - 4)^2 + (-1 - 1)^2} \qquad J'K' = \sqrt{(-2 - 4)^2 + (-3 - 3)^2}$$

$$= \sqrt{40} \qquad\qquad\qquad\qquad = \sqrt{72}$$

Since $JK \neq J'K'$, the transformation is not a rigid motion.

(B) $\triangle MNP$ maps to triangle $\triangle M'N'P'$.

Preimage		Image
$M(-2, 2)$	$\rightarrow$	$M'(-4, 1)$
$N(4, 0)$	$\rightarrow$	$N'(8, 0)$
$P(-2, -2)$	$\rightarrow$	$P'(-4, -1)$

The x-coordinate of each image point is __twice__ the x-coordinate of its preimage.

The y-coordinate of each image point is __half__ the y-coordinate of its preimage.

The transformation is given by the rule $(x, y) \rightarrow \left(2x, \frac{1}{2}y\right)$.

Compare the length of a segment of the preimage to the length of the corresponding segment of the image.

$$MN = \sqrt{(x_2 - x_1)^2 + (y_2 - y_1)^2} \qquad M'N' = \sqrt{(x_2 - x_1)^2 + (y_2 - y_1)^2}$$

$$= \sqrt{\left(4 - \boxed{-2}\right)^2 + \left(0 - \boxed{2}\right)^2} \qquad = \sqrt{\left(\boxed{8} - \boxed{-4}\right)^2 + \left(\boxed{0} - \boxed{1}\right)^2}$$

$$= \sqrt{\boxed{6}^2 + \boxed{-2}^2} \qquad\qquad = \sqrt{\boxed{12}^2 + \boxed{-1}^2}$$

$$= \sqrt{\boxed{40}} \qquad\qquad\qquad = \sqrt{\boxed{145}}$$

Since $\underline{MN \neq M'N'}$, the transformation is not a rigid motion.

© Houghton Mifflin Harcourt Publishing Company

QUESTIONING STRATEGIES

? How can you use an equation or write a ratio to find the multiplicative factor in a nonrigid motion? Possible answer: If the corresponding coordinates of the preimage and image are *a* and *b*, solve the equation $ax = b$ for x or use the ratio.

$\dfrac{b}{a}$ or $\dfrac{\text{image coordinate}}{\text{preimage coordinate}}$.

? How can you use the rule for a nonrigid motion to recognize if a figure is stretched or compressed? If the absolute value of the multiplicative factor is greater than 1, the figure is stretched. If it is less than 1, the figure is compressed.

? Can a nonrigid motion stretch a figure in one direction and compress it in another direction? Explain. No, because it preserves the shape of the figure.

ELABORATE

INTEGRATE MATHEMATICAL PRACTICES

Focus on Patterns

MP.8 Discuss with students why angle measure is preserved but length is not preserved in a nonrigid motion.

AVOID COMMON ERRORS

Make sure students understand that both coordinates are multiplied by the same factor to create a nonrigid motion transformation.

CRITICAL THINKING

Have students think about evaluating a classmate's work to check if the properties of a rigid motion transformation have been correctly verified. Discuss what students should look for as they assess the work. Repeat for the properties of a nonrigid motion transformation

SUMMARIZE THE LESSON

? How are transformations of nonrigid motions similar to and different from transformations of rigid motions? Rigid and nonrigid motions preserve betweenness and collinearity. Rigid motions preserve distance while nonrigid motions do not preserve distance.

Reflect

7. How could you confirm that a transformation is not a rigid motion by using a protractor?
   If any angle measure in the preimage is different from the corresponding angle measure in the image, then the transformation is not a rigid motion. Therefore, use the protractor to check corresponding angles. If all angle measures are preserved, then check lengths.

Your Turn

Use coordinate notation to write the rule that maps each preimage to its image. Then confirm that the transformation is not a rigid motion.

8. $\triangle ABC$ maps to triangle $\triangle A'B'C'$.

Preimage		Image
$A(2, 2)$	$\rightarrow$	$A'(3, 3)$
$B(4, 2)$	$\rightarrow$	$B'(6, 3)$
$C(2, -4)$	$\rightarrow$	$C'(3, -6)$

$(x, y) \rightarrow (1.5x, 1.5y)$

$\overline{AB}$ is horizontal and $AB = 2$.
$\overline{A'B'}$ is horizontal and $A'B' = 3$.
Since $AB \neq A'B'$, the transformation is not a rigid motion.

9. $\triangle RST$ maps to triangle $\triangle R'S'T'$.

Preimage		Image
$R(-2, 1)$	$\rightarrow$	$R'(-1, 3)$
$S(4, 2)$	$\rightarrow$	$S'(2, 6)$
$T(2, -2)$	$\rightarrow$	$T'(1, -6)$

$(x, y) \rightarrow \left(\frac{1}{2}x, 3y\right)$

$RS = \sqrt{(4 - (-2))^2 + (2 - 1)^2} = \sqrt{37}$
$R'S' = \sqrt{(2 - (-1))^2 + (6 - 3)^2} = \sqrt{18}$

Since $RS \neq R'S'$, the transformation is not a rigid motion.

💬 Elaborate

10. **Critical Thinking** To confirm that a transformation is not a rigid motion, do you have to check the length of every segment of the preimage and the length of every segment of the image? Why or why not?
    No; once you find a segment of the preimage whose length is not equal to the length of the corresponding segment of the image, you can stop checking lengths. You only need to find one pair whose lengths are not equal in order to confirm that the transformation is not a rigid motion.

11. **Make a Conjecture** A polygon is transformed by a rigid motion. How are the perimeters of the preimage polygon and the image polygon related? Explain.
    The perimeters are equal. Each side of the preimage polygon is transformed to a side of the image polygon with the same length. The sum of the side lengths of the preimage is equal to the sum of the side lengths of the image.

12. **Essential Question Check-In** How is coordinate notation for a transformation, such as $(x, y) \rightarrow (x + 1, y - 1)$, similar to and different from algebraic function notation, such as $f(x) = 2x + 1$?
    In both cases, the notation shows how an input is changed by the transformation or function. In coordinate notation, the input is a point of the coordinate plane. In algebraic function notation, the input is a real number.

Evaluate: Homework and Practice

• Online Homework
• Hints and Help
• Extra Practice

Draw the image of each figure under the given transformation.
Then describe the transformation in words.

1. $(x, y) \rightarrow (-x, -y)$

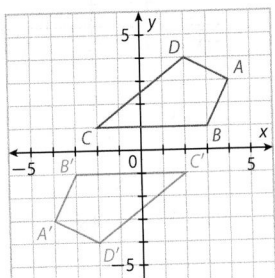

$A(4, 3) \rightarrow A'(-4, -3) = A'(-4, -3)$
$B(3, 1) \rightarrow B'(-3, -1) = B'(-3, -1)$
$C(-2, 1) \rightarrow C'(-(-2), -1) = C'(2, -1)$
$D(2, 4) \rightarrow D'(-2, -4) = D'(-2, -4)$

rotation of 180° around the origin

2. $(x, y) \rightarrow (x + 5, y)$

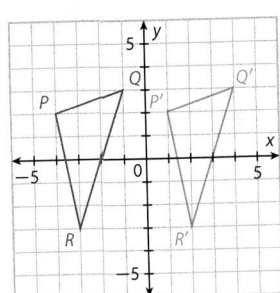

$P(-4, 2) \rightarrow P'(-4 + 5, 2) = P'(1, 2)$
$Q(-1, 3) \rightarrow Q'(-1 + 5, 3) = Q'(4, 3)$
$R(-3, -3) \rightarrow R'(-3 + 5, -3) = R'(2, -3)$

translation 5 units right

3. $(x, y) \rightarrow \left(x, \frac{1}{3}y\right)$

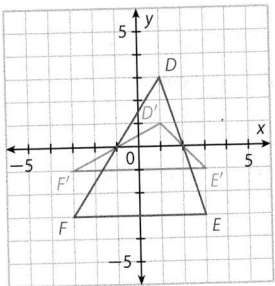

$D(1, 3) \rightarrow D'\left(1, \frac{1}{3} \cdot 3\right) = D'(1, 1)$
$E(3, -3) \rightarrow E'\left(3, \frac{1}{3} \cdot -3\right) = E'(3, -1)$
$F(-3, -3) \rightarrow F'\left(-3, \frac{1}{3} \cdot -3\right) = F'(-3, -1)$

vertical compression by a factor of $\frac{1}{3}$

4. $(x, y) \rightarrow (y, x)$

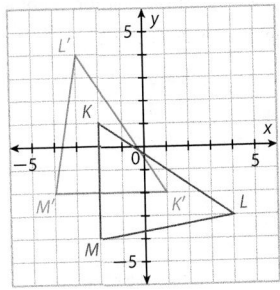

$K(-2, 1) \rightarrow K'(1, -2)$
$L(4, -3) \rightarrow L'(-3, 4)$
$M(-2, -4) \rightarrow M'(-4, -2)$

reflection across the line $y = x$

EVALUATE

ASSIGNMENT GUIDE

Concepts and Skills	Practice
Explore Performing Transformations Using Coordinate Notation	Exercises 1–4
Example 1 Describing Rigid Motions Using Coordinate Notation	Exercises 5–6
Example 2 Describing Nonrigid Motions Using Coordinate Notation	Exercises 7–9

INTEGRATE MATHEMATICAL PRACTICES
Focus on Modeling

MP.4 Encourage students to try to identify the transformation from its rule before drawing the image. Then have them draw the image to verify their predictions and highlight any misconceptions.

Exercise	Depth of Knowledge (D.O.K.)	COMMON CORE Mathematical Practices
1–4	**1** Recall of Information	**MP.4** Modeling
5–6	**1** Recall of Information	**MP.2** Reasoning
7–8	**2** Skills/Concepts	**MP.3** Logic
9	**2** Skills/Concepts	**MP.4** Modeling
10–11	**1** Recall of Information	**MP.4** Modeling
12	**2** Skills/Concepts	**MP.4** Modeling
13–14	**2** Skills/Concepts	**MP.4** Modeling

Representing and Describing Transformations **38**

GRAPHIC ORGANIZERS

Have students make a graphic organizer or table to compare properties of reflections, rotations, translations, and nonrigid motions.

AVOID COMMON ERRORS

Some students may draw an image and then incorrectly label the corresponding vertices of the image. Suggest that students label each vertex as they plot the point for the transformation.

Use coordinate notation to write the rule that maps each preimage to its image. Then identify the transformation and confirm that it preserves length and angle measure.

5.

Preimage		Image
$A(-4, 4)$	$\rightarrow$	$A'(4, 4)$
$B(-1, 2)$	$\rightarrow$	$B'(2, 1)$
$C(-4, 1)$	$\rightarrow$	$C'(1, 4)$

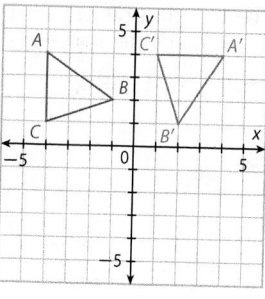

$(x, y) \rightarrow (y, -x)$; rotation of 90° clockwise around the origin

$AB = A'B' = \sqrt{13}$ $m\angle A = m\angle A' = 56°$

$BC = B'C' = \sqrt{10}$ $m\angle B = m\angle B' = 52°$

$AC = A'C' = 3$ $m\angle C = m\angle C' = 72°$

The transformation preserves length and angle measure.

6.

Preimage		Image
$J(0, 3)$	$\rightarrow$	$J'(-3, 0)$
$K(4, 3)$	$\rightarrow$	$K'(-3, -4)$
$L(2, 1)$	$\rightarrow$	$L'(-1, -2)$

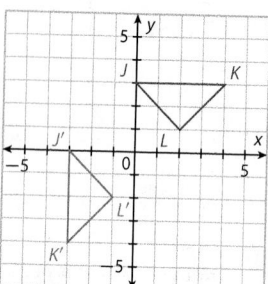

$(x, y) \rightarrow (-y, -x)$; reflection across the line $y = -x$

$JK = J'K' = 4$ $m\angle J = m\angle J' = 45°$

$KL = K'L' = \sqrt{8}$ $m\angle K = m\angle K' = 45°$

$JL = J'L' = \sqrt{8}$ $m\angle L = m\angle L' = 90°$

The transformation preserves length and angle measure.

Use coordinate notation to write the rule that maps each preimage to its image. Then confirm that the transformation is not a rigid motion.

7. $\triangle ABC$ maps to triangle $\triangle A'B'C'$.

Preimage		Image
$A(6, 6)$	$\rightarrow$	$A'(3, 3)$
$B(4, -2)$	$\rightarrow$	$B'(2, -1)$
$C(0, 0)$	$\rightarrow$	$C'(0, 0)$

$(x, y) \rightarrow \left(\frac{1}{2}x, \frac{1}{2}y\right)$

$AB = \sqrt{(4 - 6)^2 + (-2 - 6)^2}$

$\quad = \sqrt{68}$

$A'B' = \sqrt{(2 - 3)^2 + (-1 - 3)^2}$

$\quad = \sqrt{17}$

Since $AB \neq A'B'$, the transformation is not a rigid motion.

8. $\triangle FGH$ maps to triangle $\triangle F'G'H'$.

Preimage		Image
$F(-1, 1)$	$\rightarrow$	$F'(-2, 1)$
$G(1, -1)$	$\rightarrow$	$G'(2, -1)$
$H(-2, -2)$	$\rightarrow$	$H'(-4, -2)$

$(x, y) \rightarrow (2x, y)$

$FG = \sqrt{(1 - (-1))^2 + (-1 - 1)^2}$

$\quad = \sqrt{8}$

$F'G' = \sqrt{(2 - (-2))^2 + (-1 - 1)^2}$

$\quad = \sqrt{20}$

Since $FG \neq F'G'$, the transformation is not a rigid motion.

© Houghton Mifflin Harcourt Publishing Company

Module 1

39

Lesson 3

Exercise	Depth of Knowledge (D.O.K.)	COMMON CORE Mathematical Practices
15–16	**3** Strategic Thinking	**MP.3** Logic
17	**2** Skills/Concepts H.O.T.	**MP.3** Logic
18	**2** Skills/Concepts H.O.T.	**MP.6** Precision
19	**3** Strategic Thinking H.O.T.	**MP.2** Reasoning
20	**3** Strategic Thinking H.O.T.	**MP.6** Precision

39 Lesson 1.3

9. **Analyze Relationships** A mineralogist is studying a quartz crystal. She uses a computer program to draw a side view of the crystal, as shown. She decides to make the drawing 50% wider, but to keep the same height. Draw the transformed view of the crystal. Then write a rule for the transformation using coordinate notation. Check your rule using the original coordinates.

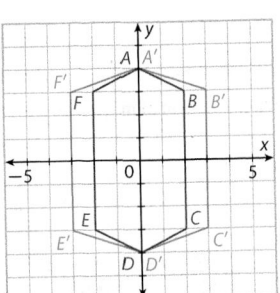

$(x, y) \rightarrow (1.5x, y)$

$A(0, 4) \quad \rightarrow A'(1.5 \cdot 0, 4) \quad = A'(0, 4)$

$B(2, 3) \quad \rightarrow B'(1.5 \cdot 2, 3) \quad = B'(3, 3)$

$C(2, -3) \rightarrow C'(1.5 \cdot 2, -3) \quad = C'(3, -3)$

$D(0, -4) \rightarrow D'(1.5 \cdot 0, -4) \quad = D'(0, -4)$

$E(-2, -3) \rightarrow E'(1.5 \cdot -2, -3) = E'(-3, -3)$

$F(-2, 3) \quad \rightarrow F'(1.5 \cdot -2, 3) \quad = F'(-3, 3)$

10. Use the points $A(2, 3)$ and $B(2, -3)$.

   a. Describe segment AB and find its length.

   Segment AB is a vertical segment that is 6 units long.

   b. Describe the image of segment AB under the transformation $(x, y) \rightarrow (x, 2y)$.

   $A(2, 3) \quad \rightarrow \quad A'(2, 2 \cdot 3) \quad = \quad A'(2, 6)$

   $B(2, -3) \quad \rightarrow \quad B'(2, 2 \cdot (-3)) \quad = \quad B'(2, -6)$

   The image of segment AB is a vertical segment that is 12 units long.

   c. Describe the image of segment AB under the transformation $(x, y) \rightarrow (x + 2, y)$.

   $A(2, 3) \quad \rightarrow \quad A'(2 + 2, 3) \quad = \quad A'(4, 3)$

   $B(2, -3) \quad \rightarrow \quad B'(2 + 2, -3) \quad = \quad B'(4, -3)$

   The image of segment AB is a vertical segment two units to the right of the original segment that is 6 units long.

   d. Compare the two transformations.

   Possible answer: $(x, y) \rightarrow (x + 2, y)$ is rigid, because it does not change the length of the segment. $(x, y) \rightarrow (x, 2y)$ is not rigid because it doubles the length of the segment. The segment remains vertical under both transformations.

CRITICAL THINKING

A reflection in the coordinate plane can be across either axis, any vertical or horizontal line, or any other line, such as $y = x$ or $y = -x$. Discuss with students how to identify the line of reflection for a reflection.

11. Use the points $H(-4, 1)$ and $K(4, 1)$.

    a. Describe segment HK and find its length.
    Segment HK is a horizontal segment that is 8 units long.

    b. Describe the image of segment HK under the transformation $(x, y) \rightarrow (-y, x)$.
    $H(-4, 1) \;\rightarrow\; H'(-1, -4)$

    $K(4, 1) \;\;\;\rightarrow\;\; K'(-1, 4)$
    The image of segment HK is a vertical segment that is 8 units long.

    c. Describe the image of segment HK under the transformation $(x, y) \rightarrow (2x, y)$.
    $H(-4, 1) \;\rightarrow\; H'(-8, 1)$

    $K(4, 1) \;\;\;\rightarrow\; K'(8, 1)$
    The image of segment HK is a horizontal segment that is 16 units long.

    d. Compare the two transformations.
    Possible answer: $(x, y) \rightarrow (-y, x)$ is rigid, because it does not change the length of the segment. $(x, y) \rightarrow (2x, y)$ is not rigid because it doubles the length of the segment. The transformation given by $(x, y) \rightarrow (-y, x)$ switches the segment from horizontal to vertical, while $(x, y) \rightarrow (2x, y)$ does not.

12. Make a Prediction A landscape architect designs a flower bed that is a quadrilateral, as shown in the figure. The plans call for a light to be placed at the midpoint of the longest side of the flower bed. The architect decides to change the location of the flower bed using the transformation $(x, y) \rightarrow (x, -y)$. Describe the location of the light in the transformed flower bed. Then make the required calculations to show that your prediction is correct.

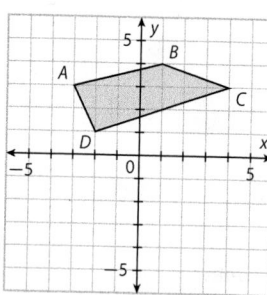

The longest side of $ABCD$ is $\overline{CD}$ and its midpoint is

$$M\left(\frac{4 + (-2)}{2}, \frac{3 + 1}{2}\right) = M(1, 2).$$

The coordinates of the transformed flower bed are:

$A(-3, 3) \;\rightarrow\; A'(-3, -3)$ $C(4, 3) \;\;\;\rightarrow\; C'(4, -3)$ $M(1, 2) \rightarrow M'(1, -2)$

$B(1, 4) \;\;\;\rightarrow\; B'(1, -4)$ $D(-2, 1) \;\rightarrow\; D'(-2, -1)$

The longest side of the transformed flower bed is $\overline{C'D'}$ and its midpoint is

$$M'\left(\frac{4 + (-2)}{2}, \frac{-3 + (-1)}{2}\right) = M'(1, -2).$$

This matches the coordinates of the image of M calculated above, so the prediction is correct.

13. Multiple Representations If a transformation moves points only up or down, how do the coordinates of the point change? What can you conclude about the coordinate notation for the transformation?

The x-coordinate does not change. The y-coordinate has a constant added to it (for a translation up) or subtracted from it (translation down). The coordinate notation has the form $(x, y) \rightarrow (x, y + b)$, where b is a real number, $b \neq 0$.

14. Match each transformation with the correct description.

A. $(x, y) \rightarrow (3x, y)$ __E__   dilation with scale factor 3

B. $(x, y) \rightarrow (x + 3, y)$ __D__   translation 3 units up

C. $(x, y) \rightarrow (x, 3y)$ __B__   translation 3 units right

D. $(x, y) \rightarrow (x, y + 3)$ __A__   horizontal stretch by a factor of 3

E. $(x, y) \rightarrow (3x, 3y)$ __C__   vertical stretch by a factor of 3

Draw the image of each figure under the given transformation. Then describe the transformation as a rigid motion or not a rigid motion. Justify your answer.

15. $(x, y) \rightarrow (2x + 4, y)$

$P(-2, 3) \rightarrow P'(2(-2) + 4, 3) = P'(0, 3)$
$Q(-1, -3) \rightarrow Q'(2(-1) + 4, -3) = Q'(2, -3)$
$R(-3, -3) \rightarrow R'(2(-3) + 4, -3) = R'(-2, -3)$
$QR = 2$
$Q'R' = 4$
Since $QR \neq Q'R'$, the transformation is not a rigid motion.

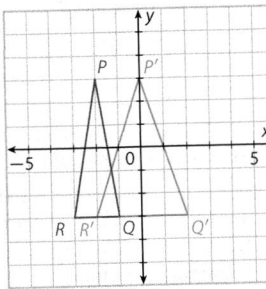

16. $(x, y) \rightarrow (0.5x, y - 4)$

$D(-4, 3) \rightarrow D'(0.5 \cdot -4, 3 - 4) = D'(-2, -1)$
$E(2, 3) \rightarrow E'(0.5 \cdot 2, 3 - 4) = E'(1, -1)$
$F(4, 1) \rightarrow F'(0.5 \cdot 4, 1 - 4) = F'(2, -3)$
$DE = 6$
$D'E' = 3$
Since $DE \neq D'E'$, the transformation is not a rigid motion.

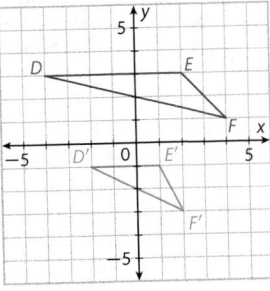

© Houghton Mifflin Harcourt Publishing Company

COMMUNICATING MATH

Have students work in pairs. One student draws a figure in a coordinate plane, and gives clues to the second student for drawing a second image. A sample clue: "Draw this preimage transformed into a mirror image, or reflection." The second student draws the image, and then explains the reason the image is a reflection. They switch roles; the second student draws a preimage, and asks the first student to draw a rotated image. The first student has to explain how the image drawn fulfills the clue.

MODELING

If the coordinates of a transformation have different multiplicative factors, the transformation is neither a rigid motion nor a nonrigid motion. Discuss why this is the case and how to use the multiplicative factor to recognize whether the transformation is a vertical or horizontal stretch or compression.

SMALL GROUP ACTIVITY

Is reflecting a figure across the x-axis and then across the y-axis the same as rotating it 180°? Have students work in small groups to explore the question both by drawing examples on the coordinate plane and by writing and analyzing the algebraic rules for the transformations. When they have had time to formulate an answer, have each group present their conclusion and the reasoning behind it.

JOURNAL

Have students explain and give an example on a coordinate plane of a reflection, a translation, a rotation, and a nonrigid motion transformation. Have them write the rules for their translations and nonrigid motion transformations.

17. Explain the Error A student claimed that the transformation $(x, y) \rightarrow (3x, y)$ is a rigid motion because the segment joining $(5, 0)$ to $(5, 2)$ is transformed to the segment joining $(15, 0)$ to $(15, 2)$, and both of these segments have the same length. Explain the student's error.

The transformation is a horizontal stretch by a factor of 3, so it preserves the length of vertical segments but not the length of horizontal or diagonal segments. In order to be a rigid motion, the transformation must preserve all lengths, so this transformation is not a rigid motion.

18. Critical Thinking Write a rule for a transformation that maps $\triangle STU$ to $\triangle S'T'U'$.

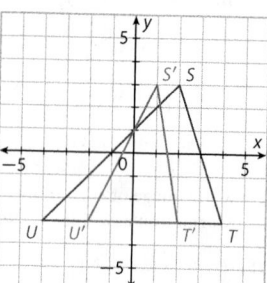

$S(2, 3) \quad \rightarrow \quad S'(1, 3)$

$T(4, -3) \quad \rightarrow \quad T'(2, -3)$

$U(-4, -3) \quad \rightarrow \quad U'(-2, -3)$

So, the transformation divides each

x-coordinate by 2 but leaves the y-coordinate unchanged.

The rule is $(x, y) \rightarrow \left(\frac{1}{2}x, y\right)$.

19. Justify Reasoning Consider the transformation given by the rule $(x, y) \rightarrow (0, 0)$. Describe the transformation in words. Then explain whether or not the transformation is a rigid motion and justify your reasoning.

The transformation maps all points to the origin, so the image of any figure under this transformation is a single point, $(0, 0)$. The transformation is not a rigid motion because all line segments are mapped to a point, so the length of the segment is not preserved.

20. Communicate Mathematical Ideas One of the properties of rigid motions states that rigid motions preserve parallelism. Explain what this means, and give an example using a specific figure and a specific rigid motion. Include a graph of the preimage and image.

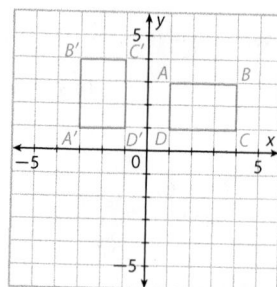

If two segments or lines are parallel in the preimage, then the corresponding lines or segments of the image are also parallel.

Possible example: In $ABCD$, $\overline{AB} \parallel \overline{CD}$. A rotation of 90° counterclockwise around the origin is a rigid motion, and after this transformation $\overline{A'B'} \parallel \overline{C'D'}$.

Lesson Performance Task

A Web designer has created the logo shown here for Matrix Engineers.

The logo is 100 pixels wide and 24 pixels high. Images placed in Web pages can be stretched horizontally and vertically by changing the dimensions in the code for the Web page.

The Web designer would like to change the dimensions of the logo so that lengths are increased or decreased but angle measures are preserved.

   a. Find three different possible sets of dimensions for the width and height so that lengths are changed but angle measures are preserved. The dimensions must be whole numbers of pixels. Justify your choices.

   b. Explain how the Web designer can use transformations to find additional possible dimensions for the logo.

   a. Possible dimensions: 150 pixels by 36 pixels, 200 pixels by 48 pixels, 250 pixels by 60 pixels

    A horizontal stretch changes lengths but does not preserve angle measures; a vertical stretch changes lengths but does not preserve angle measures. However, stretching both horizontally and vertically by the same scale factor (a dilation) changes lengths while preserving angle measures. The dimensions given represent dilations by a scale factor of 1.5, 2, and 2.5, respectively.

   b. In general, the required dimensions should be 100k pixels and 24k pixels, where k is any real number, $k > 0$, such that 100k and 24k are whole numbers. The Web designer should transform the logo using a dilation, $(x, y) \rightarrow (kx, ky)$, where $k > 0$ and such that 100k and 24k are whole numbers.

INTEGRATE TECHNOLOGY

Lengths and widths on a computer screen are measured in *pixels*. A *pixel* is the smallest visual element that a computer is capable of processing. Therefore, it is always a whole number. Typical dimensions for a smartphone portrait are 310 pixels by 352 pixels, and for a large computer screen 1024 pixels by 768 pixels.

INTEGRATE MATHEMATICAL PRACTICES
Focus on Modeling

MP.4 Ask students to visualize a rectangular piece of rubber that they are holding between their hands. In the middle is a large plus sign. Have them describe what happens to the plus sign in each of the following situations.

- They stretch the rubber horizontally by moving their hands farther apart. The horizontal bar of the plus sign increases in length. The vertical bar stays the same height.

- They stretch the rubber vertically by grabbing it at the top and bottom and moving their hands farther apart. The vertical bar of the plus sign increases in length. The horizontal bar stays the same width.

- Together with a friend, they stretch the rubber to an equal extent both vertically and horizontally. Both bars of the plus sign increase in length and the lengths increase proportionally. The result is that the plus sign gets larger but still looks like a plus sign.

EXTENSION ACTIVITY

Have students plot the points (5, 5), (8, 5), (8, 8), and (5, 8) on a coordinate grid. They should connect the points to form a square and draw the diagonals of the square. Ask them to experiment now by drawing on the same grid:

(a) rectangles with heights of 3 units, lengths other than 3 units, and diagonals; and

(b) rectangles with lengths of 3 units, heights other than 3 units, and diagonals.

The rectangles are the square stretched or compressed horizontally or vertically.

For each rectangle, students should compare the angles formed by the intersection of the diagonals with the angles at the intersection of the diagonals of the square.

Scoring Rubric
2 points: Student correctly solves the problem and explains his/her reasoning.
1 point: Student shows good understanding of the problem but does not fully solve or explain his/her reasoning.
0 points: Student does not demonstrate understanding of the problem.

Reasoning and Proof

Common Core Math Standards

The student is expected to:

 G-CO.C.9

Prove theorems about lines and angles. Also A-REI.A.1

Mathematical Practices

COMMON CORE **MP.8 Patterns**

Language Objective

Have students fill in a chart explaining the meaning of conditionals, counterexample and conditional.

ENGAGE

Essential Question: How do you go about proving a statement?

Possible answer: You can make a conjecture, or statement, that you believe is true. Then through inductive or deductive reasoning, you can prove the statement is true by showing specific cases are true or by using logical steps.

PREVIEW: LESSON PERFORMANCE TASK

View the online Engage. Discuss the photo. Discuss why the figure seems to be impossible. Then preview the Lesson Performance Task.

Name_____ Class_____ Date_____

1.4 Reasoning and Proof

Essential Question: How do you go about proving a statement?

Resource Locker

⊘ Explore Exploring Inductive and Deductive Reasoning

A **conjecture** is a statement that is believed to be true. You can use *inductive* or *deductive* reasoning to show, or *prove*, that a conjecture is true. **Inductive reasoning** is the process of reasoning that a rule or statement is true because specific cases are true. **Deductive reasoning** is the process of using logic to draw conclusions.

Complete the steps to make a conjecture about the sum of three consecutive counting numbers.

(A) Write a sum to represent the first three consecutive counting numbers, starting with 1.
$1 + 2 + 3$

(B) Is the sum divisible by 3?
Yes. $1 + 2 + 3 = 6$ and $6 \div 3 = 2$.

(C) Write the sum of the next three consecutive counting numbers, starting with 2.
$2 + 3 + 4$

(D) Is the sum divisible by 3?
Yes. $2 + 3 + 4 = 9$ and $9 \div 3 = 3$.

(E) Complete the conjecture:

The ____sum____ of three consecutive counting numbers is divisible by ____3____.

Recall that postulates are statements you accept are true. A **theorem** is a statement that you can prove is true using a series of logical steps. The steps of deductive reasoning involve using appropriate undefined words, defined words, mathematical relationships, postulates, or other previously-proven theorems to prove that the theorem is true.

Use deductive reasoning to prove that the sum of three consecutive counting numbers is divisible by 3.

(F) Let the three consecutive counting numbers be represented by n, $n + 1$, and $\boxed{n + 2}$.

(G) The sum of the three consecutive counting numbers can be written as $3n + \boxed{3}$.

© Houghton Mifflin Harcourt Publishing Company

Module 1   45   Lesson 4

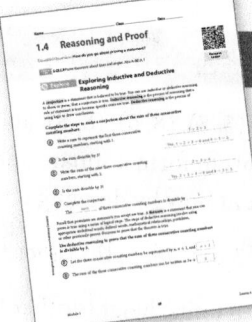

HARDCOVER PAGES 39–48

Turn to these pages to find this lesson in the hardcover student edition.

(H) The expression $3n + 3$ can be factored as $3\left(\boxed{n+1}\right)$.

(I) The expression $3(n + 1)$ is divisible by $\boxed{3}$ for all values of n.

(J) Recall the conjecture in Step E: The sum of three consecutive counting numbers is divisible by 3.

Look at the steps in your deductive reasoning. Is the conjecture true or false? __True__

Reflect

1. **Discussion** A **counterexample** is an example that shows a conjecture to be false. Do you think that counterexamples are used mainly in inductive reasoning or in deductive reasoning?
Possible answer: A counterexample would be used in inductive reasoning to show that at least one specific case makes the conjecture false.

2. Suppose you use deductive reasoning to show that an angle is not acute. Can you conclude that the angle is obtuse? Explain.
No; if the angle is not acute, I can conclude that it is right, obtuse, or straight.

⊘ Explain 1 Introducing Proofs

A **conditional statement** is a statement that can be written in the form "If p, then q" where p is the *hypothesis* and q is the *conclusion*. For example, in the conditional statement "If $3x - 5 = 13$, then $x = 6$," the hypothesis is "$3x - 5 = 13$" and the conclusion is "$x = 6$."

Most of the Properties of Equality can be written as conditional statements. You can use these properties to solve an equation like "$3x - 5 = 13$" to prove that "$x = 6$."

Properties of Equality	
Addition Property of Equality	If $a = b$, then $a + c = b + c$.
Subtraction Property of Equality	If $a = b$, then $a - c = b - c$.
Multiplication Property of Equality	If $a = b$, then $ac = bc$.
Division Property of Equality	If $a = b$ and $c \neq 0$, then $\frac{a}{c} = \frac{b}{c}$.
Reflexive Property of Equality	$a = a$
Symmetric Property of Equality	If $a = b$, then $b = a$.
Transitive Property of Equality	If $a = b$ and $b = c$, then $a = c$.
Substitution Property of Equality	If $a = b$, then b can be substituted for a in any expression.

PROFESSIONAL DEVELOPMENT

Integrate Mathematical Practices

This lesson provides an opportunity to address Mathematical Practice MP.3, which calls for students to "construct viable arguments." Students use deductive reasoning, and explain steps logically from definite premises to a definite general conclusion. They use inductive reasoning to make a conjecture about what is true in general by examining several cases, and they justify the falsehood of a conclusion by citing a counterexample.

EXPLORE

Exploring Inductive and Deductive Reasoning

QUESTIONING STRATEGIES

? When a detective solves a case, is the detective more likely to use inductive or deductive reasoning? Explain. deductive reasoning, because the solution is likely based on logical conclusions drawn from the evidence

? When might you want to make a conjecture about a set of numbers? If the numbers seem to form a pattern, you might want to make a conjecture based on the number pattern.

? Is one counterexample enough to prove that a conjecture is false? Explain. Yes, the conjecture must be true for every case. So, if even one counterexample exists, the conjecture is false.

INTEGRATE MATHEMATICAL PRACTICES
Focus on Reasoning

MP.2 Discuss why a conjecture is like a hypothesis in the scientific method. Elicit that a conjecture, like a hypothesis, is often based on inductive reasoning.

EXPLAIN 1

Introducing Proofs

AVOID COMMON ERRORS

Students may have difficulty identifying the correct property of equality to justify a step when solving an algebraic equation. Students may need to include steps where they show the property of equality to help them recognize how it is applied. For example, they may need to show the step where the value is added to both sides of the equation to apply the Addition Property of Equality.

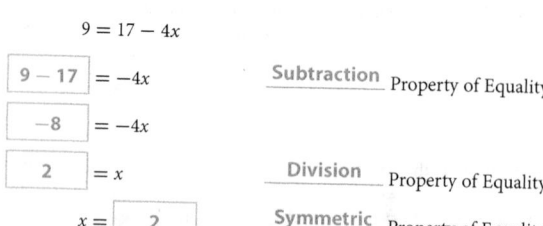

Will changing the order of the hypothesis and the conclusion in a true conditional statement change whether or not the statement is true? Explain. Yes, the statement may still be true but you would have to prove that it is.

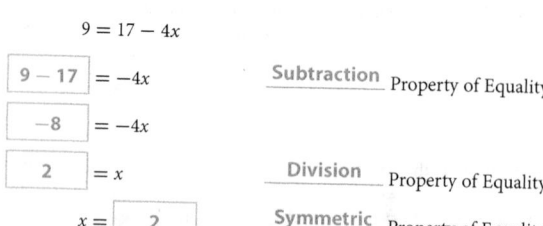

Do you always use deductive reasoning when you solve an equation algebraically? Explain. Yes, you should always be able to support each step in the solution using a property.

Example 1 Use deductive reasoning to solve the equation. Use the Properties of Equality to justify each step.

(A) $14 = 3x - 4$

$14 = 3x - 4$	
$18 = 3x$	Addition Property of Equality
$6 = x$	Division Property of Equality
$x = 6$	Symmetric Property of Equality

(B) $9 = 17 - 4x$

$9 = 17 - 4x$

$\boxed{9 - 17} = -4x$ — **Subtraction** Property of Equality

$\boxed{-8} = -4x$

$\boxed{2} = x$ — **Division** Property of Equality

$x = \boxed{2}$ — **Symmetric** Property of Equality

Your Turn

Write each statement as a conditional.

3. All zebras belong to the genus *Equus*.
   If an animal is a zebra, then it belongs to the genus *Equus*.

4. The bill will pass if it gets two-thirds of the vote in the Senate.
   If the bill gets two-thirds of the vote in the Senate, then it will pass.

5. Use deductive reasoning to solve the equation $3 - 4x = -5$.

$3 - 4x = -5$

$-4x = -8$ Subtraction Property of Equality

$x = 2$ Division Property of Equality

6. Identify the Property of Equality that is used in each statement.

If $x = 2$, then $2x = 4$.	Multiplication Property of Equality
$5 = 3a$; therefore, $3a = 5$.	Symmetric Property of Equality
If $T = 4$, then $5T + 7$ equals 27.	Substitution Property of Equality
If $9 = 4x$ and $4x = m$, then $9 = m$.	Transitive Property of Equality

COLLABORATIVE LEARNING

Small Group Activity

Have students work in small groups. The first student writes a number or draws a figure. The next student writes or draws a second item, beginning a pattern. Have them continue until each student has contributed to the pattern. Then ask the first student to describe a rule for the pattern. Have the groups repeat this activity until each student has gone first.

© Houghton Mifflin Harcourt Publishing Company · Image Credits: ©Digital Vision/Getty Images

⚙ Explain 2 Using Postulates about Segments and Angles

Recall that two angles whose measures add up to 180° are called *supplementary angles*. The following theorem shows one type of supplementary angle pair, called a *linear pair*. A **linear pair** is a pair of adjacent angles whose non-common sides are opposite rays. You will prove this theorem in an exercise in this lesson.

The Linear Pair Theorem

If two angles form a linear pair, then they are supplementary.

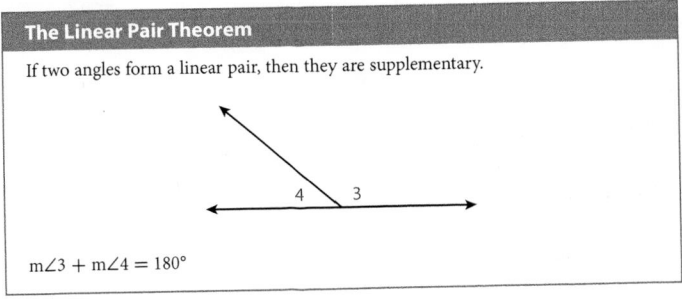

$m\angle 3 + m\angle 4 = 180°$

You can use the Linear Pair Theorem, as well as the Segment Addition Postulate and Angle Addition Postulate, to find missing values in expressions for segment lengths and angle measures.

Example 2 Use a postulate or theorem to find the value of x in each figure.

 Given: $RT = 5x - 12$

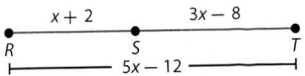

Use the Segment Addition Postulate.

$$RS + ST = RT$$

$$(x + 2) + (3x - 8) = 5x - 12$$

$$4x - 6 = 5x - 12$$

$$6 = x$$

$$x = 6$$

© Houghton Mifflin Harcourt Publishing Company

EXPLAIN 2

Using Postulates about Segments and Angles

INTEGRATE MATHEMATICAL PRACTICES
Focus on Modeling

MP.4 Have students identify the property of equality used as they complete each step to solve for the variable using the postulates about segments and angles.

QUESTIONING STRATEGIES

? How are the segment and angle addition postulates applied to solve for a variable? Set the sum of the non-overlapping segments or angles equal to the measure of the whole segment or angle.

AVOID COMMON ERRORS

When solving equations using the Segment or Angle Addition Postulates, students may forget to combine like terms or use inverse operations to solve. Review how to combine like terms and use inverse operations as needed.

DIFFERENTIATE INSTRUCTION

Kinesthetic Experience

Have students act out the Reflexive, Symmetric, and Transitive Properties. For the Reflexive Property, have students look in a mirror. For the Symmetric Property, have two students stand next to each other and then change places. For the Transitive Property, have one student give a second student a sheet of paper, and have the second student give the paper to a third. The result is the same as if the first student had given the paper directly to the third.

Ⓑ Given: m∠RST = $(15x - 10)°$

Use the [Angle Addition] Postulate.

m∠RST = m∠ [RSP] + m∠ [PST]

$(15x - 10)° = $ [$(x + 25)$]$° + $ [$5x + 10$]$°$

$15x - 10 = $ [$6x + 35$]

[9] $x = $ [45]

$x = $ [5]

Reflect

7. **Discussion** The Linear Pair Theorem uses the terms *opposite rays* as well as *adjacent angles*. Write a definition for each of these terms. Compare your definitions with your classmates.

Possible answers: Opposite rays are rays that share a common endpoint and form a line.

Adjacent angles are two angles in the same plane with a common vertex and a common

side, but no common interior points.

Your Turn

8. Two angles *LMN* and *NMP* form a linear pair. The measure of ∠LMN is twice the measure of ∠NMP. Find m∠LMN.

Use the Linear Pair Theorem. Substitute for m∠LMN.

m∠LMN + m∠NMP = 180°

(2 · m∠NMP) + m∠NMP = 180°

3 · m∠NMP = 180°

m∠NMP = 60°

m∠LMN = 2 · m∠NMP = 2 · 60° = 120°

© Houghton Mifflin Harcourt Publishing Company

LANGUAGE SUPPORT **EL**

Connect Vocabulary

For the properties of equality based on the operations, have students highlight the operation to connect to the corresponding property. For the *Reflexive, Symmetric,* and *Transitive Properties,* discuss what these words bring to mind. For example, *reflexive* might remind students of a *reflection* in a mirror. You see the same thing on both sides of a mirror, so, $a = a$.

⚙ Explain 3 Using Postulates about Lines and Planes

Postulates about points, lines, and planes help describe geometric figures.

Postulates about Points, Lines, and Planes

Through any two points, there is exactly one line.

Through any three noncollinear points, there is exactly one plane containing them.

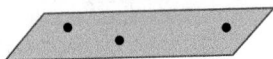

If two points lie in a plane, then the line containing those points lies in the plane.

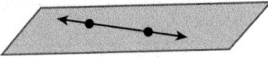

If two lines intersect, then they intersect in exactly one point.

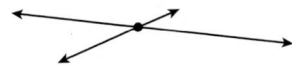

If two planes intersect, then they intersect in exactly one line.

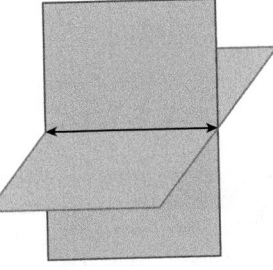

EXPLAIN 3

Using Postulates about Lines and Planes

COOPERATIVE LEARNING

To help students understand the rationale behind the postulates about points, lines, and planes, ask them to draw additional examples with the points and lines in different locations to demonstrate each postulate. Share the drawings with the class.

? Must any two planes intersect? Why or why not? Name planes in the classroom that support your answer. **No, if the planes are parallel they will never intersect. Possible example: opposite walls in the classroom**

? If a line lies in a plane, how many points of intersection do the line and the plane have? **an infinite number: every point that lies on the line**

VISUAL CUES

Students may have difficulty interpreting the diagrams showing intersecting planes. Make a slit in the side of one piece of paper and hold the paper in a horizontal plane. Slide a second sheet in a vertical plane perpendicular to the horizontal plane to provide students with a visual demonstration of two intersecting planes. Locate points and lines as needed.

Example 3 Use each figure to name the results described.

Ⓐ

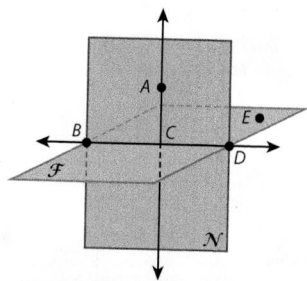

Description	Example from the figure
the line of intersection of two planes	Possible answer: The two planes intersect in line *BD*.
the point of intersection of two lines	The line through point *A* and the line through point *B* intersect at point *C*.
three coplanar points	Possible answer: The points *B*, *D*, and *E* are coplanar.
three collinear points	The points *B*, *C*, and *D* are collinear.

Ⓑ

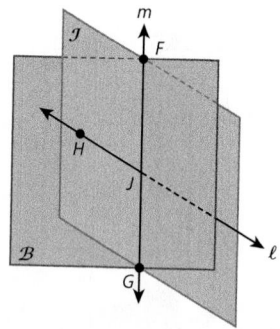

Description	Example from the figure
the line of intersection of two planes	Possible answer: The two planes intersect in line *JF*.
the point of intersection of two lines	The line through point *F* and the line through point *H* intersect at point *J*.
three coplanar points	Possible answer: The points *F*, *J*, and *H* are coplanar.
three collinear points	The points *F*, *J*, and *G* are collinear.

9. Find examples in your classroom that illustrate the postulates of lines, planes, and points.
   Possible answers: walls, floors, corners, desktops, blackboard

10. Draw a diagram of a plane with three collinear points and three points that are noncollinear.
    Possible answer: in the figure, *B*, *C*, and *A* are collinear; *D*, *C*, and *A* are noncollinear.

💬 Elaborate

11. What is the difference between a postulate and a definition? Give an example of each.
    Possible answers: A postulate is a statement that is self-evident or is generally accepted to

    be a true statement.

    A definition is a statement that explains the meaning of a word in terms of previously

    accepted words or statements.

    Possible examples:

    Postulate: $x = x$ is called the Reflexive Property of Equality.

    Definition: An *even number* is a number that is divisible by 2.

12. Give an example of a diagram illustrating the Segment Addition Postulate. Write the
    Segment Addition Postulate as a conditional statement.

    If *S* is between *R* and *T*, then $RS + ST = RT$.

13. Explain why photographers often use a tripod when taking pictures.
    Through any three noncollinear points,

    there is only one plane, so the feet of the

    tripod are all always flat against the plane

    of the ground, which steadies the camera.

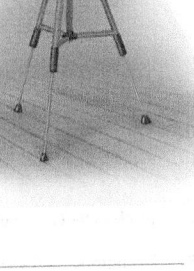

14. **Essential Question Check-In** What are some of the reasons you can
    give in proving a statement using deductive reasoning?
    You can use given facts, definitions, postulates or properties, and

    previously-proven theorems.

ELABORATE

INTEGRATE MATHEMATICAL PRACTICES
Focus on Reasoning

MP.2 Point out that students are starting to build a catalog of definitions, postulates, and theorems about geometric relationships that they will use throughout the course. Discuss why it is important to become familiar with using them as tools in deductive reasoning.

QUESTIONING STRATEGIES

? How can you use a Property of Equality to write the equation $4x = 8$ as a conditional statement? Using the Division Property of Equality, $x = 2$. The conditional statement is "If $4x = 8$, then $x = 2$."

CONNECT VOCABULARY **EL**

Connect conditionals in geometry to conditional statements in everyday life. For example: "If I walk in the rain without an umbrella, then I will get wet." Have students express their own conditional statements tied to reality so that they can see this connection.

SUMMARIZE THE LESSON

? How can you use deductive reasoning to establish a conclusion? Provide a logical sequence of statements supported by postulates and established theorems in which each statement logically follows from the preceding statement up to the conclusion.

EVALUATE

ASSIGNMENT GUIDE

Concepts and Skills	Practice
Explore Exploring Inductive and Deductive Reasoning	Exercises 1–12
Example 1 Introducing Proofs	Exercises 13–16
Example 2 Using Postulates about Segments and Angles	Exercises 17–20
Example 3 Using Postulates about Lines and Planes	Exercises 21–26

COMMUNICATING MATH

Have students compare counterexamples used to demonstrate conjectures that are not true.

GRAPHIC ORGANIZERS

Students work in pairs to complete a chart. The chart has three columns and each column is labeled with the highlighted vocabulary. Students must discuss in depth the meaning of each word, and take notes on their discussion. Then they write down their agreed-upon ideas under the word in each column.

⭐ Evaluate: Homework and Practice

• Online Homework
• Hints and Help
• Extra Practice

Explain why the given conclusion uses inductive reasoning.

1. Find the next term in the pattern: 3, 6, 9.
   The next term is 12 because the previous terms are multiples of 3.

   The conclusion is based on observing three numbers.

2. $3 + 5 = 8$ and $13 + 5 = 18$, therefore the sum of two odd numbers is an even number.

   The conclusion is based on two examples.

3. My neighbor has two cats and both cats have yellow eyes.
   Therefore when two cats live together, they will both have yellow eyes.

   The conclusion is based on two observations.

4. It always seems to rain the day after July 4th.

   The conclusion is based on a limited number of observations.

Give a counterexample for each conclusion.

5. If x is a prime number, then $x + 1$ is not a prime number.

   Counterexample: 2; if $x = 2$, then $x + 1 = 3$, which is a prime number.

6. The difference between two even numbers is positive.

   Counterexample: $6 - 10 = -4$, which is negative.

7. Points A, B, and C are noncollinear, so therefore they are noncoplanar.

   When I draw three points that are noncollinear, I can draw a single plane through all three points, so they are coplanar after all.

8. The square of a number is always greater than the number.

   The square of $\frac{1}{3}$ is $\frac{1}{9}$, which is less than $\frac{1}{3}$.

In Exercises 9–12 use deductive reasoning to write a conclusion.

9. If a number is divisible by 2, then it is even.
   The number 14 is divisible by 2.

   The number 14 is an even number.

Exercise	Depth of Knowledge (D.O.K.)	COMMON CORE Mathematical Practices
1–6	**1** Recall of Information	**MP.3** Logic
7–8	**2** Skills/Concepts	**MP.3** Logic
9–16	**1** Recall of Information	**MP.3** Logic
17–20	**2** Skills/Concepts	**MP.2** Reasoning
21–22	**1** Recall of Information	**MP.3** Logic
23–24	**2** Skills/Concepts	**MP.3** Logic
25	**3** Strategic Thinking	**MP.3** Logic

Use deductive reasoning to write a conclusion.

10. If two planes intersect, then they intersect in exactly one line. Planes ℜ and ℑ intersect.

    Planes ℜ and ℑ intersect in exactly one line.

11. Through any three noncollinear points, there is exactly one plane containing them. Points W, X, and Y are noncollinear.

    There is exactly one plane containing points W, X, and Y.

12. If the sum of the digits of an integer is divisible by 3, then the number is divisible by 3. The sum of the digits of 46,125 is 18, which is divisible by 3.

    The number 46,125 is divisible by 3.

Identify the hypothesis and conclusion of each statement.

13. If the ball is red, then it will bounce higher.
    Hypothesis: the ball is red   Conclusion: it will bounce higher

14. If a plane contains two lines, then they are coplanar.
    Hypothesis: a plane contains two lines   Conclusion: the lines are coplanar

15. If the light does not come on, then the circuit is broken.
    Hypothesis: the light does not come on   Conclusion: the circuit is broken

16. You must wear your jacket if it is cold outside.
    Hypothesis: it is cold outside   Conclusion: you must wear your jacket

Use a definition, postulate, or theorem to find the value of x in the figure described.

17. Point E is between points D and F. If $DE = x - 4$, $EF = 2x + 5$, and $DF = 4x - 8$, find x.

    Use the Segment Addition Postulate; $DE + EF = DF$; $(x - 4) + (2x + 5) = 4x - 8$; $3x + 1 = 4x - 8$; $9 = x$

18. Y is the midpoint of $\overline{XZ}$. If $XZ = 8x - 2$ and $YZ = 2x + 1$, find x.

    Because Y is the midpoint of $\overline{XZ}$, $XY = YZ$. Use this fact and the Segment Addition Postulate; $XY + YZ = XZ$; $(2x + 1) + (2x + 1) = 8x - 2$; $4x + 2 = 8x - 2$; $4 = 4x$; $1 = x$

19. $\overrightarrow{SV}$ is an angle bisector of $\angle RST$. If m$\angle RSV = (3x + 5)°$ and m$\angle RST = (8x - 14)°$, find x.

    Because $\overrightarrow{SV}$ is an angle bisector of $\angle RST$, m$\angle RSV =$ m$\angle VST$. Use this fact and the Angle Addition Postulate; m$\angle RSV +$ m$\angle VST =$ m$\angle RST$; $(3x + 5) + (3x + 5) = 8x - 14$; $6x + 10 = 8x - 14$; $24 = 2x$; $12 = x$

20. $\angle ABC$ and $\angle CBD$ are a linear pair. If m$\angle ABC =$ m$\angle CBD = 3x - 6$, find x.

    Use the Linear Pair Theorem.; m$\angle ABC +$ m$\angle CBD = 180°$; $(3x - 6)° + (3x - 6)° = 180°$; $6x - 12 = 180$; $6x = 192$; $x = 32$

Students may have difficulty identifying the hypothesis and the conclusion given a conditional statement when *then* is missing from the statement. Suggest that students first rewrite the statement in the "if, ... then" form before they identify the hypothesis and conclusion.

AVOID COMMON ERRORS

Remind students to combine like terms when they solve equations by applying the Segment and Angle Addition Postulates.

INTEGRATE MATHEMATICAL PRACTICES
Focus on Reasoning

MP.2 After students solve for the variable using the Segment and Angle Addition Postulates, have them use the value to find the actual lengths or angle measures represented by the expressions. They can also use this method to check their work.

Exercise	Depth of Knowledge (D.O.K.)	COMMON CORE Mathematical Practices
26	2 Skills/Concepts	**MP.3** Logic
27	3 Strategic Thinking H.O.T.	**MP.3** Logic
28	2 Skills/Concepts H.O.T.	**MP.6** Precision

Reasoning and Proof   **54**

PEER-TO-PEER DISCUSSION

Have students use a ruler to draw a line segment made from two non-overlapping segments. Have them label the lengths of one section and the total segment. Then have them exchange papers and explain how to use deductive reasoning to find the missing length.

JOURNAL

Have students write examples of the following: a conjecture, a counterexample to a conjecture, inductive reasoning, and deductive reasoning.

Use the figure for Exercises 21 and 22.

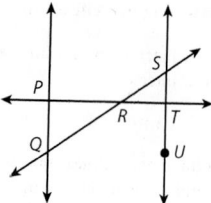

21. Name three collinear points.

Possible answer: *P, R,* and *T*

22. Name two linear pairs.

Possible answers: ∠PRQ and ∠QRT, ∠STR and ∠UTR

Explain the error in each statement.

23. Two planes can intersect in a single point.

When two planes cross, they intersect each other at an infinite number of points, i.e., in a line.

24. Three points have to be collinear.

The three points could be the vertices of a triangle.

25. A line is contained in exactly one plane

A line can be in more than one plane.

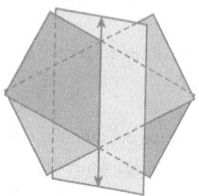

26. If $x^2 = 25$, then $x = 5$.

The value of x could also be -5.

H.O.T.   Focus on Higher Order Thinking

27. Analyze Relationships What is the greatest number of intersection points 4 coplanar lines can have? What is the greatest number of planes determined by 4 noncollinear points? Draw diagrams to illustrate your answers.

Four coplanar lines can intersect in up to 6 points.   Up to four planes can be determined by 4 noncollinear points.

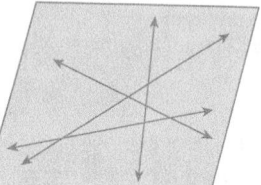

© Houghton Mifflin Harcourt Publishing Company

28. Justify Reasoning Prove the Linear Pair Theorem.
Given: ∠MJK and ∠MJL are a linear pair of angles.
Prove: ∠MJK and ∠MJL are supplementary.

Complete the proof by writing the missing reasons.
Choose from the following reasons.

Angle Addition Postulate   Definition of linear pair

Substitution Property of Equality   Given

Statements	Reasons
1. ∠MJK and ∠MJL are a linear pair.	1. **Given**
2. $\overrightarrow{JL}$ and $\overrightarrow{JK}$ are opposite rays.	2. **Definition of linear pair**
3. $\overrightarrow{JL}$ and $\overrightarrow{JK}$ form a straight line.	3. Definition of opposite rays
4. m∠LJK = 180°	4. Definition of straight angle
5. m∠MJK + m∠MJL = m∠LJK	5. **Angle Addition Postulate**
6. m∠MJK + m∠MJL = 180°	6. **Substitution Property of Equality**
7. ∠MJK and ∠MJL are supplementary.	7. Definition of supplementary angles

Lesson Performance Task

If two planes intersect, then they intersect in exactly one line.

Find a real-world example that illustrates the postulate above. Then formulate a conjecture by completing the following statement:

If three planes intersect, then _____.

Justify your conjecture with real-world examples or a drawing.

Possible example: a wall and the ceiling
Students may make any of the following conjectures:
If three planes intersect, then they intersect in a point.
If three planes intersect, then they intersect in a line.
If three planes intersect, then they intersect in either a point or a line.
Obviously the third conjecture is the most complete. Possible examples: two
walls and the ceiling intersect at a point; the pages of a book are planes that
intersect in a line, the spine of the book.

LANGUAGE SUPPORT **EL**

A *conjecture* is an opinion or proposition that is supported by evidence but has not been proven. It begins with an observation, such as: "I added twenty pairs of odd numbers, and the sums were all even." The conjecture based on this might be, "The sum of two odd numbers is always even." A conjecture doesn't have to be true. For example: "I saw eleven kids with apples at lunch today, and all the apples were red. Conjecture: All apples are red."

INTEGRATE MATHEMATICAL PRACTICES
Focus on Critical Thinking

MP.3 Ask students to state a possible conjecture for the statement, then support or refute it:

"I've seen thousands of creatures with wings and all of them could fly." Conjecture: If a creature has wings, then it can fly. Refute: Penguins and ostriches have wings but cannot fly.

"I've seen hundreds of bicycles and all of them had two wheels." Conjecture: If a vehicle is a bicycle, then it has two wheels. Support: The prefix *bi-* means two, and *cycle* refers to a wheel. So, the definition of *bicycle* includes the requirement that the vehicle have two wheels.

© Houghton Mifflin Harcourt Publishing Company

Module 1   56   Lesson 4

EXTENSION ACTIVITY

The "impossible" triangle in the photo in the online Engage activity is an example of an optical illusion. Have students research optical illusions and either sketch or print ones that especially intrigue them. For each illusion, students should describe what's intriguing about it, and then explain—if they can!—how the illusion is accomplished.

Scoring Rubric
2 points: Student correctly solves the problem and explains his/her reasoning.
1 point: Student shows good understanding of the problem but does not fully solve or explain his/her reasoning.
0 points: Student does not demonstrate understanding of the problem.

Reasoning and Proof   **56**

Study Guide Review

ASSESSMENT AND INTERVENTION

Assign or customize module reviews.

MODULE PERFORMANCE TASK

COMMON CORE

Mathematical Practices: MP.1, MP.2, MP.3, MP.4, MP.6
G-CO.A.1

SUPPORTING STUDENT REASONING

Students should begin this problem by focusing on what information they will need. Here are some issues they might bring up.

- **How to find their current GPS location:** The best way is to use a smartphone app or a map search engine.

- **A good representation of their GPS location:** A good representation is latitude and longitude given in decimal degrees, not in degrees, minutes, and seconds. The GPS coordinates are then expressed in (x, y) notation as the ordered pair (latitude, longitude).

- **What the decimal approximation using the distance formula represents, and what units are used:** distance measured in degrees

---

Essential Question: How can you use tools of geometry to solve real-world problems?

KEY EXAMPLE   (Lesson 1.1)

Find the midpoint of $(5, 6)$ and $(1, 3)$.

$\left(\dfrac{5+1}{2}, \dfrac{6+3}{2}\right)$ Apply the midpoint formula.

$= \left(\dfrac{6}{2}, \dfrac{9}{2}\right)$ Simplify the numerators.

$= \left(3, \dfrac{9}{2}\right)$ Simplify.

KEY EXAMPLE   (Lesson 1.2)

The ray $\overrightarrow{BD}$ is the angle bisector of $\angle ABC$ and $m\angle ABC = 40°$. Find $m\angle ABD$.

$\overrightarrow{BD}$ is the angle bisector of $\angle ABC$ so it divides the angle into two angles of equal measure.

Then $m\angle ABD + m\angle DBC = m\angle ABC$ and $m\angle ABD = m\angle DBC$.

So, $2 \cdot m\angle ABD = m\angle ABC$.

$m\angle ABD = 20°$ Substitute the angles and simplify.

KEY EXAMPLE   (Lesson 1.3)

Use the rule $(x, y) \rightarrow (x + 1, 2y)$ and the points of a triangle, $A(1, 2)$, $B(2, 4)$, and $C(2, 2)$ to draw the image. Determine whether this is a rigid motion.

$A'(1 + 1, 2(2))$, $B'(2 + 1, 2(4))$, $C'(2 + 1, 2(2))$ Use the transformation rule.

$A'(2, 4)$, $B'(3, 8)$, $C'(3, 4)$ Simplify.

$A'B' = \sqrt{(3-2)^2 + (8-4)^2}$ Use the distance formula to find the distance between A' and B'.

$= \sqrt{17} \approx 4.1$ Simplify.

$AB = \sqrt{(2-1)^2 + (4-2)^2}$ Use the distance formula to find the distance between A and B.

$= \sqrt{5} \approx 2.2$ Simplify.

The image is not a rigid motion because the side lengths are not equal.

Key Vocabulary

point *(punto)*
line *(línea)*
plane *(plano)*
line segment *(segmento de línea)*
endpoints *(punto final)*
ray *(rayo)*
coplanar *(coplanares)*
parallel *(paralelo)*
collinear *(colineales)*
postulate *(postulado)*
midpoint *(punto medio)*
segment bisector *(segmento bisectriz)*
angle *(ángulo)*
vertex *(vértice)*
side *(lado)*
degrees *(grados)*
angle bisector *(bisectriz de un ángulo)*
transformation *(transformación)*
preimage *(preimagen)*
image *(imagen)*
rigid motion *(movimiento rígido)*
conjecture *(conjetura)*
inductive reasoning *(razonamiento inductivo)*
deductive reasoning *(razonamiento deductivo)*
theorem *(teorema)*
counterexample *(contraejemplo)*
conditional statement *(sentencia condicional)*
linear pair *(par lineal)*

SCAFFOLDING SUPPORT

- Show students how to look up their current GPS location by using a computer search engine or a smartphone app, or give students their current location in decimal degrees.

- Students can use the conversion factor 1 degree = 69.2 miles to find distances. The Sample Solution on the next page mentions limitations associated with this value.

- Suggest that students make calculations to the nearest thousandth and round to the nearest hundredth.

- Distance calculations in this task are quite complex. You may wish to have students work on the task in pairs.

EXERCISES

Find the midpoint of the pairs of points. *(Lesson 1.1)*

1. $(4, 7)$ and $(2, 9)$ _____ $(3, 8)$

2. $(5, 5)$ and $(-1, 3)$ _____ $(2, 4)$

Find the measure of the angle formed by the angle bisector. *(Lesson 1.2)*

3. The ray $\overrightarrow{BD}$ is the angle bisector of $\angle ABC$ and $m\angle ABC = 110°$. Find $m\angle ABD$. _____ $55°$

Use the rule $(x, y) \rightarrow (3x, 2y)$ to find the image for the preimage defined by the points. Determine whether the transformation is a rigid motion. *(Lesson 1.3)*

4. $A(3, 5)$, $B(5, 3)$, $C(2, 2)$

The points of the image are _____ $A'(9, 10)$, $B'(15, 6)$, $C'(6, 4)$.

The image _____ is not _____ a rigid motion.

Determine whether the conjecture uses inductive or deductive reasoning. *(Lesson1.4)*

5. The child chose Rock in all four games of Rock-Paper-Scissors. The child always chooses Rock.

The conjecture uses inductive reasoning.

MODULE PERFORMANCE TASK

How Far Is It?

Many smartphone apps and online search engines will tell you the distances to nearby restaurants from your current location. How do they do that? Basically, they use latitude and longitude coordinates from GPS to calculate the distances. Let's explore how that works for some longer distances.

The table lists latitude and longitude for four state capitals. Use an app or search engine to find the latitude and longitude for your current location, and record them in the last line of the table.

- Which of the state capitals do you think is nearest to you? Which is farthest away? Use the distance formula to calculate your distance from each of the cities in degrees. Then convert each distance to miles.

- Use an app or search engine to find the distance between your location and each of the capital cities. How do these distances compare with the ones you calculated? How might you account for any differences?

City	Latitude	Longitude
Austin, TX	30.31° N	97.76° W
Columbus, OH	39.98° N	82.99° W
Nashville, TN	36.17° N	86.78 ° W
Sacramento, CA	38.57° N	121.5° W
Your Location		

DISCUSSION OPPORTUNITIES

- What are other ways to locate places on Earth?

- Why are some GPS coordinates expressed with negative numbers? A negative longitude represents a coordinate in the Western hemisphere (a positive longitude is in the Eastern hemisphere), while a negative latitude represents a coordinate in the Southern hemisphere (a positive latitude is in the Northern hemisphere).

SAMPLE SOLUTION

Current location: 33.57°N, 101.88°W

Distance, current location to Austin:

$$\sqrt{(33.57 - 30.31)^2 + (101.88 - 97.76)^2} =$$
$$\sqrt{(3.26)^2 + (4.12)^2} \approx \sqrt{27.602} \approx 5.25°$$

$5.25° \times 69.2$ miles $/° = 363.3$ miles

Distance, current location to Columbus:

$$\sqrt{(39.98 - 33.57)^2 + (101.88 - 82.99)^2} =$$
$$\sqrt{(6.41)^2 + (18.89)^2} \approx \sqrt{397.92} \approx 19.95°$$

$19.95° \times 69.2$ miles $/° = 1380.54$ miles

Distance, current location to Nashville:

$$\sqrt{(36.17 - 33.57)^2 + (101.88 - 86.78)^2} =$$
$$\sqrt{(2.6)^2 + (15.1)^2} \approx \sqrt{234.77} \approx 15.32°$$

$15.32° \times 69.2$ miles $/° = 1060.14$ miles

Distance, current location to Sacramento:

$$\sqrt{(38.57 - 33.57)^2 + (121.5 - 101.88)^2} =$$
$$\sqrt{(5)^2 + (19.62)^2} \approx \sqrt{409.94} \approx 20.25°$$

$20.25° \times 69.2$ miles $/° = 1401.3$ miles

Error, current location to Austin:
$363.3 - 333 = 30.3$ miles

Error, current location to Columbus:
$1380.54 - 1133 = 247.54$ miles

Error, current location to Nashville:
$1060.14 - 876 = 184.14$ miles

Error, current location to Sacramento:
$1401.3 - 1146 = 255.3$ miles

Possible error sources: Calculated distances are straight-line distances, which will be less than distances measured along the curved surface of the Earth; and although 1 degree of latitude measures 69.2 miles, degrees of longitude range from 69.2 miles at the Equator to 0 miles at the North Pole. Precise distance calculations would need to take this into account.

Assessment Rubric

2 points: Student correctly solves the problem and explains his/her reasoning.

1 point: Student shows good understanding of the problem but does not fully solve or explain.

0 points: Student does not demonstrate

Ready to Go On?

ASSESS MASTERY

Use the assessment on this page to determine if students have mastered the concepts and standards covered in this module.

ASSESSMENT AND INTERVENTION

Access Ready to Go On? assessment online, and receive instant scoring, feedback, and customized intervention or enrichment.

ADDITIONAL RESOURCES

Response to Intervention Resources

- Reteach Worksheets

Differentiated Instruction Resources

- Reading Strategies **EL**
- Success for English Learners **EL**
- Challenge Worksheets

Assessment Resources

- Leveled Module Quizzes

Ready to Go On?

1.1–1.4 Tools of Geometry

- Online Homework
- Hints and Help
- Extra Practice

Use a definition, postulate, or theorem to find the value desired.

1. Point M is the midpoint between points $A(-5, 4)$ and $B(-1, -6)$. Find the location of M. *(Lesson 1.1)*

Use the midpoint formula.

$$M\left(\frac{x_1 + x_2}{2}, \frac{y_1 + y_2}{2}\right) = M\left(\frac{-5 + (-1)}{2}, \frac{4 + (-6)}{2}\right) = M(-3, -1)$$

Given triangle EFG, graph its image $E'F'G'$ and confirm that the transformation preserves length and angle measure. *(Lesson 1.1)*

2. $(x, y) \rightarrow (x - 1, y + 5)$

$EF = E'F' = 6$, $FG = F'G' = 8$

$GE = \sqrt{(x_2 - x_1)^2 + (y_2 - y_1)^2}$

$\quad\ = \sqrt{(8 - 2)^2 + (-9 - (-1))^2}$

$\quad\ = 10$

$G'E' = \sqrt{(7 - 1)^2 + (-4 - 4)^2}$

$\quad\quad\ = 10$

$m\angle F = m\angle F' = 90°$, $m\angle E = m\angle E' = 53°$, and $m\angle G = m\angle G' = 37°$

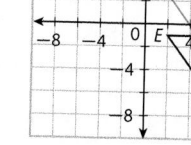

Find the measure of the angle formed by the angle bisector. *(Lesson 1.2)*

3. The ray $\overrightarrow{GJ}$ is the angle bisector of $\angle FGH$ and $m\angle FGH = 75°$. Find $m\angle FGJ$.
37.5°

4. The ray $\overrightarrow{XZ}$ is the angle bisector of $\angle WXY$ and $m\angle WXY = 155°$. Find $m\angle YXZ$.
77.5°

ESSENTIAL QUESTION

5. When is a protractor preferred to a ruler when finding a measurement?
Answers may vary. Sample: When finding the angle between two lines as opposed to finding the length of a line segment.

COMMON CORE Common Core Standards

Lesson	Items	Content Standards	Mathematical Practices
1.1	1	G-CO.A.1, G-GPE.B.4	MP.2
1.1, 1.3	2	G-CO.A.1, G-GPE.B.4	MP.7
1.2	3	G-CO.A.1	MP.2
1.2	4	G-CO.A.1	MP.2

MODULE 1
MIXED REVIEW

Assessment Readiness

1. For two angles, $\angle ABC$ and $\angle DBC$, m$\angle ABC = 30°$ and $\angle DBC$ is its complement. Ray $\overrightarrow{BE}$ is the angle bisector of $\angle ABD$. Consider each angle. Does the angle have a measure of 45°?

Select Yes or No for A–C.

A. $\angle DBC$ ○ Yes   ● No
B. $\angle ABE$ ● Yes   ○ No
C. $\angle DBE$ ● Yes   ○ No

2. The line $y = \sqrt{x}$ is transformed into $y = \sqrt{5x}$. Choose True or False for each statement.

A. A dilation can be used to obtain this transformation.   ● True   ○ False

B. A rotation can be used to obtain this transformation.   ○ True   ● False

C. A translation can be used to obtain this transformation.   ○ True   ● False

3. Triangle ABC is given by the points $A(1, 1)$, $B(3, 2)$, and $C(2, 3)$. Consider each rule of transformation. Does the rule result in an image with points $A'(2, 2)$, $B'(6, 3)$, and $C'(4, 4)$?

Select Yes or No for A–C.

A. $(x, y) \rightarrow (x, y + 1)$ ○ Yes   ● No
B. $(x, y) \rightarrow (2x, 2y)$ ○ Yes   ● No
C. $(x, y) \rightarrow (2x, y + 1)$ ● Yes   ○ No

4. Find the midpoint of (4, 5) and (–2, 12). Show your work.

$$\left(\frac{x_1 + x_2}{2}, \frac{y_1 + y_2}{2} \right) = \left(\frac{4 + (-2)}{2}, \frac{5 + 12}{2} \right)$$

$$= \left(\frac{2}{2}, \frac{17}{2} \right)$$

$$= \left(1, \frac{17}{2} \right)$$

MIXED REVIEW
Assessment Readiness

ASSESSMENT AND INTERVENTION

Assign ready-made or customized practice tests to prepare students for high-stakes tests.

ADDITIONAL RESOURCES

Assessment Resources

• Leveled Module Quizzes: Modified, B

AVOID COMMON ERRORS

Item 4 Some students may substitute into the midpoint formula incorrectly. They may use x and y from the first ordered pair in the first part of the formula, and use x and y from the second ordered pair for the second part. Encourage students to label their points to avoid confusion; for example:

(4, 2), (3, −1)

x_1, y_1 x_2, y_2

Common Core Standards

Lesson	Items	Content Standards	Mathematical Practices
1.2	1	G-CO.D.12	MP.2
1.3	2	G-CO.A.2	MP.7
1.3	3	G-CO.A.2	MP.8
1.1	4	G-GPE.B.4	MP.2

* Item integrates mixed review concepts from previous modules or a previous course.

Transformations and Symmetry

ESSENTIAL QUESTION:

Answer: Rigid transformations can represent situations in which objects slide, turn, or flip.

PROFESSIONAL DEVELOPMENT VIDEO

Professional Development Video

Author Juli Dixon models successful teaching practices in an actual high-school classroom.

Professional Development
my.hrw.com

Transformations and Symmetry

MODULE 2

★

Essential Question: How can you use transformations to solve real-world problems?

© Houghton Mifflin Harcourt Publishing Company • Image Credits: ©Helen King/Corbis

REAL WORLD VIDEO
Check out how transformations can be used to cut patterns out of fabric as efficiently as possible.

MODULE PERFORMANCE TASK PREVIEW

Animating Digital Images

In this module, you will use transformations to create a simple animation of a bird in flight. How do computer animators use translations, rotations, and reflections? Let's find out.

Module 2   61

DIGITAL TEACHER EDITION

Access a full suite of teaching resources when and where you need them:

- Access content online or offline
- Customize lessons to share with your class
- Communicate with your students in real-time
- View student grades and data instantly to target your instruction where it is needed most

PERSONAL MATH TRAINER

Assessment and Intervention

Assign automatically graded homework, quizzes, tests, and intervention activities. Prepare your students with updated, Common Core-aligned practice tests.

Are (YOU) Ready?

Complete these exercises to review the skills you will need for this module.

- Online Homework
- Hints and Help
- Extra Practice

Properties of Reflections

Example 1

A figure in the first quadrant is reflected over the *x*-axis. What quadrant is the image in?

The image is in the fourth quadrant. A figure drawn on tracing paper can be reflected across the *x*-axis by folding the paper along the axis.

Find the quadrant of each image.

1. The image from reflecting a figure in the first quadrant over the *y*-axis   The second quadrant

2. The image from reflecting a figure in the second quadrant over the *x*-axis   The third quadrant

Properties of Rotations

Example 2

A figure in the first quadrant is rotated 90° counterclockwise around the origin. What quadrant is the image in?

The image is in the second quadrant. In the second quadrant, each point of the figure forms a clockwise 90° angle around the origin with its corresponding point in the original figure.

Find the quadrant of each image.

3. The image from rotating a figure in the third quadrant 180° clockwise   The first quadrant

4. The image from rotating a figure in the first quadrant 360° clockwise   The first quadrant

Properties of Translations

Example 3

A figure in the first quadrant is translated up 3 units and to the right 1 unit. What quadrant is the image in?

The image is in the first quadrant. A translation only moves the image in a direction; the image is not reflected or rotated.

Answer each question.

5. A figure in the first quadrant is translated down and to the right. Is it known what quadrant the image is in?

   No

6. A figure is translated 3 units up and 2 units left. How large is the image in comparison to the figure?

   They are the same size.

© Houghton Mifflin Harcourt Publishing Company

Are You Ready?

ASSESS READINESS

Use the assessment on this page to determine if students need strategic or intensive intervention for the module's prerequisite skills.

ASSESSMENT AND INTERVENTION

RtI Response to Intervention   TIER 1, TIER 2, TIER 3 SKILLS

Personal Math Trainer will automatically create a standards-based, personalized intervention assignment for your students, targeting each student's individual needs!

ADDITIONAL RESOURCES

See the table below for a full list of intervention resources available for this module.

Response to Intervention Resources also includes:

- Tier 2 Skill Pre-Tests for each Module
- Tier 2 Skill Post-Tests for each skill

Response to Intervention			Differentiated Instruction
Tier 1	**Tier 2**	**Tier 3**	
Lesson Intervention Worksheets	Strategic Intervention Skills Intervention Worksheets	Intensive Intervention Worksheets available online	
Reteach 2.1 Reteach 2.2 Reteach 2.3 Reteach 2.4	17 Properties of Reflections 18 Properties of Rotations 19 Properties of Translations	Building Block Skills 46, 53, 56, 102, 103	Challenge worksheets Extend the Math Lesson Activities in TE

Translations

Common Core Math Standards

The student is expected to:

COMMON CORE **G-CO.A.4**

Develop definitions of ... translations in terms of ... parallel lines, and line segments. Also G-CO.A.1, G-CO.A.2, G-CO.A.5, G-CO.B.6

Mathematical Practices

COMMON CORE **MP.7 Using Structure**

Language Objective

Work with a partner to identify examples and non-examples of translations.

ENGAGE

Essential question: How do you draw the image of a figure under a translation?

Possible answer: You can use tracing paper to slide the figure parallel to a vector. On the coordinate plane, you can draw the image by using coordinate notation to calculate the coordinates of the images of the vertices.

PREVIEW: LESSON PERFORMANCE TASK

View the online Engage. Discuss the photo; ask students to describe repetitions they see in the pattern and tell whether they could create it by using copies of a smaller section. Then preview the Lesson Performance Task.

Name_____ Class_____ Date_____

2.1 Translations

Essential Question: How do you draw the image of a figure under a translation?

Resource Locker

⊘ Explore Exploring Translations

A translation slides all points of a figure the same distance in the same direction.

You can use tracing paper to model translating a triangle.

(A) First, draw a triangle on lined paper. Label the vertices A, B, and C. Then draw a line segment XY. An example of what your drawing may look like is shown.

(B) Use tracing paper to draw a copy of triangle ABC. Then copy $\overline{XY}$ so that the point X is on top of point A. Label the point made from Y as A'.

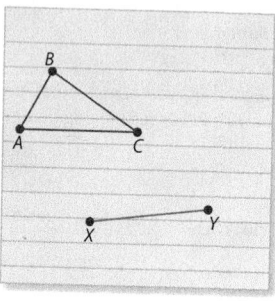

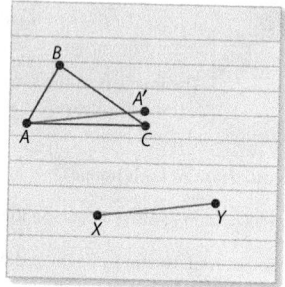

(C) Using the same piece of tracing paper, place A' on A and draw a copy of $\triangle ABC$. Label the corresponding vertices B' and C'. An example of what your drawing may look like is shown.

(D) Use a ruler to draw line segments from each vertex of the preimage to the corresponding vertex on the new image.

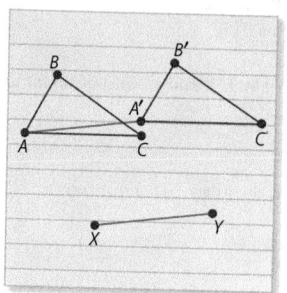

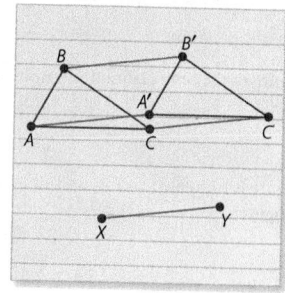

© Houghton Mifflin Harcourt Publishing Company

Module 2　　　　　　　　　　63　　　　　　　　　　Lesson 1

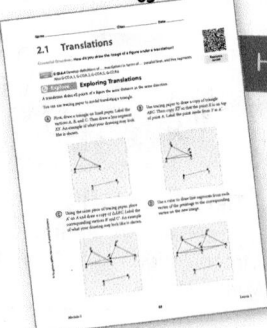

HARDCOVER PAGES 55–64

Turn to these pages to find this lesson in the hardcover student edition.

(E) Measure the distances *AA'*, *BB'*, *CC'*, and *XY*. Describe how *AA'*, *BB'*, and *CC'* compare to the length *XY*.

Possible answer: *BB'*, *AA'*, and *CC'* are each 2 inches. *XY* is also 2 inches. The segments are all the same length.

Reflect

1. Are *BB'*, *AA'*, and *CC'* parallel, perpendicular, or neither? Describe how you can check that your answer is reasonable.
   They are parallel. I can turn the tracing paper so that one of the lines is on one of the
   parallel rules of the lined paper. All of the segments line up with the lines on the paper.
   So, they are parallel.

2. How does the angle *BAC* relate to the angle *B'A'C*? Explain.
   Possible answer: The angles are congruent. Since translation is a rigid transformation, the
   side lengths and angle measures remain the same in the translated figure.

 Explain 1 **Translating Figures Using Vectors**

A **vector** is a quantity that has both direction and magnitude.
The **initial point** of a vector is the starting point.
The **terminal point** of a vector is the ending point. The vector
shown may be named $\overrightarrow{EF}$ or $\overrightarrow{v}$.

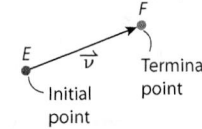

Translation

It is convenient to describe translations using vectors. A **translation** is a transformation along a vector such that the segment joining a point and its image has the same length as the vector and is parallel to the vector.

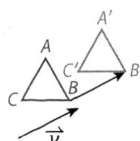

For example, *BB'* is a line segment that is the same length as and is parallel to vector $\overrightarrow{v}$.

You can use these facts about parallel lines to draw translations.

- Parallel lines are always the same distance apart and never intersect.
- Parallel lines have the same slope.

PROFESSIONAL DEVELOPMENT

COMMON CORE **Integrate Mathematical Practices**

This lesson provides an opportunity to address Mathematical Practice **MP.7**, which calls for students to "look for and make use of structure." Students are already familiar with translating a figure in the plane; in this lesson, they explore translations using tracing paper, and then describe translations using vectors, both in the plane and in the coordinate plane. Students use vector notation to describe the translation vector in component form, and then relate the vector to the associated algebraic rule used to transform the preimage figure in the coordinate plane.

Exploring Translations

INTEGRATE TECHNOLOGY

If you use software instead of tracing paper, begin by reviewing how to use geometry software to draw points and figures, to mark a vector, and to translate using a vector. Familiarity with those techniques will allow students to concentrate on the concepts they are exploring.

QUESTIONING STRATEGIES

? How does the given vector relate to the translation of the triangle? It gives both the distance and the direction between pairs of corresponding points from the preimage and the image.

EXPLAIN 1

Translating Figures Using Vectors

AVOID COMMON ERRORS

Some students may assume that they should slide the figure along the vector. Compare a vector to aspects of a map such as scale or location of north and south, since the vector gives information about the direction and distance of the move.

COOPERATIVE LEARNING

Have students pair up to check each other's drawings
of the vectors and translated figures. Remind students
to check the labels on their partners' drawings.

Example 1 Draw the image of △ABC after a translation along $\vec{v}$.

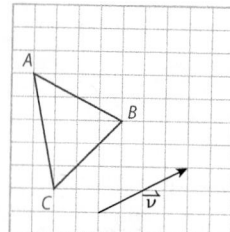

Draw a copy of $\vec{v}$ with its initial point at
vertex A of △ABC. The copy must be
the same length as $\vec{v}$, and it must be
parallel to $\vec{v}$. Repeat this process at
vertices B and C.

Draw segments to connect the
terminal points of the vectors.
Label the points A′, B′, and C′.
△A′B′C′ is the image of △ABC.

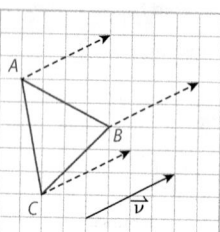

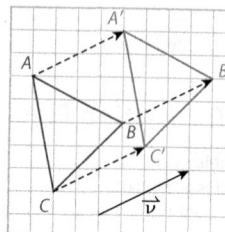

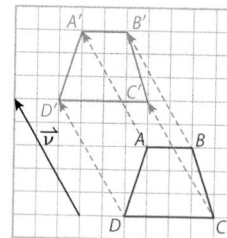

Draw a vector from the vertex A that is the same length as
and <u>parallel to</u> vector $\vec{v}$. The terminal point A′ will
be <u>5</u> units up and 3 units <u>left</u>.

Draw three more vectors that are parallel from <u>B</u>, <u>C</u>,
and <u>D</u> with terminal points B′, C′, and D′.

Draw segments connecting A′, B′, C′, and D′ to
form <u>quadrilateral A′B′C′D′</u>.

Reflect

3. How is drawing an image of quadrilateral ABCD like drawing an image of
    △ABC? How is it different?

    Possible answer: The steps to drawing an image of the quadrilateral are the same as

    drawing an image of the triangle. It is different because there is an extra vector when

    drawing the quadrilateral. Also, you must be careful to connect the vertices in the same

    order as the original shape.

© Houghton Mifflin Harcourt Publishing Company

COLLABORATIVE LEARNING

Peer-to-Peer Activity

Have students work in pairs. Instruct one student in each pair to give an example
of a translation that would move a given figure from Quadrant I to Quadrant III,
and write steps to show what was done. The partner then checks this work. Then
they switch roles and repeat, using a translation between two different quadrants.

4. Draw the image of △ABC after a translation along $\vec{v}$.

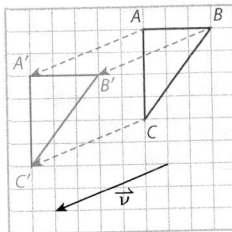

🔘 Explain 2   Drawing Translations on a Coordinate Plane

A vector can also be named using component form, $\langle a, b \rangle$, which specifies the horizontal change a and the vertical change b from the initial point to the terminal point. The component form for $\overrightarrow{PQ}$ is $\langle 5, 3 \rangle$.

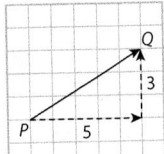

You can use the component form of the vector to draw coordinates for a new image on a coordinate plane. By using this vector to move a figure, you are moving the x-coordinate 5 units to the right. So, the new x-coordinate would be 5 greater than the x-coordinate in the preimage. Using this vector you are also moving the y-coordinate up 3 units. So, the new y-coordinate would be 3 greater than the y-coordinate in the preimage.

Rules for Translations on a Coordinate Plane	
Translation a units to the right	$\langle x, y \rangle \rightarrow \langle x + a, y \rangle$
Translation a units to the left	$\langle x, y \rangle \rightarrow \langle x - a, y \rangle$
Translation b units up	$\langle x, y \rangle \rightarrow \langle x, y + b \rangle$
Translation b units down	$\langle x, y \rangle \rightarrow \langle x, y - b \rangle$

So, when you move an image to the right a units and up b units, you use the rule $(x, y) \rightarrow (x + a, y + b)$ which is the same as moving the image along vector $\langle a, b \rangle$.

Example 2   Calculate the vertices of the image figure. Graph the preimage and the image.

Ⓐ Preimage coordinates: $(-2, 1), (-3, -2),$ and $(-1, -2)$. Vector: $\langle 4, 6 \rangle$

Predict which quadrant the new image will be drawn in: 1ˢᵗ quadrant.

Use a table to record the new coordinates. Use vector components to write the transformation rule.

Then use the preimage coordinates to draw the preimage, and use the image coordinates to draw the new image.

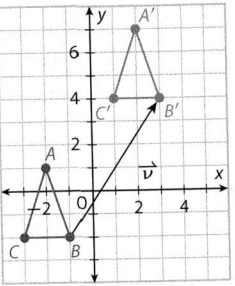

Preimage coordinates (x, y)	Image $(x + 4, y + 6)$
$(-2, 1)$	$(2, 7)$
$(-3, -2)$	$(1, 4)$
$(-1, -2)$	$(3, 4)$

DIFFERENTIATE INSTRUCTION

Critical Thinking

Remind students that they use the absolute value of the difference of coordinates when finding a vertical or horizontal distance. Ask, why don't we use the absolute value when finding the component form of a vector? Direction is an important part of a vector, whether positive or negative. Using the absolute value would make all components positive.

EXPLAIN 2

Drawing Translations on a Coordinate Plane

INTEGRATE MATHEMATICAL PRACTICES
Focus on Math Connections

MP.1 Relate the concept of slope, the ratio of the vertical change to the horizontal change between two points, to the component form of the vector.

QUESTIONING STRATEGIES

❓ What is the slope of the line that contains the vector $\langle a, b \rangle$? $\frac{b}{a}$

❓ Describe how two vectors could have the same slope but not be the same vector. They could have different magnitudes.

AVOID COMMON ERRORS

Some students may try to position the preimage at the beginning of the vector rather than the reverse. Help them position the vector at the vertices of the preimage.

AVOID COMMON ERRORS

Students sometimes confuse translation with transformation. Have them draw a Venn diagram to make clear that translation, or slide, is one kind of transformation.

CONNECT VOCABULARY 🔲EL

Relate the word *translation* in geometry to translating languages. For example, when we translate a sentence from English to Spanish, we want to keep the same meaning, from each word, for the translation to be accurate. When we translate an image, every point and line in that image is moved in the same direction and the same distance.

EXPLAIN 3

Specifying Translation Vectors

AVOID COMMON ERRORS

Some students may make an error when they subtract negative coordinates. Review the rules for subtracting integers, as needed.

QUESTIONING STRATEGIES

? In writing the component form of the vector, how would you indicate that there is no vertical change in the position of the figure? Use the number 0 to indicate no change.

INTEGRATE MATHEMATICAL PRACTICES
Cognitive Strategies

Discuss what happens when a point moves from one end of a vector to the other end, and how this relates to the translation of the vertices in the image figure.

INTEGRATE MATHEMATICAL PRACTICES
Multiple Representations

Ask students which method for specifying the translation of a figure they find most helpful in visualizing the image. Have them discuss the advantages of each kind of description.

© Houghton Mifflin Harcourt Publishing Company

B Preimage coordinates: $A(3, 0)$, $B(2, -2)$, and $C(4, -2)$. Vector $\langle -2, 3 \rangle$

Prediction: The image will be in Quadrant __1__.

Preimage coordinates (x, y)	Image $\left(x - \boxed{2}, y + \boxed{3}\right)$	
$(3, 0)$	$\boxed{1}$	$\boxed{3}$
$(2, -2)$	$\boxed{0}$	$\boxed{1}$
$(4, -2)$	$\boxed{2}$	$\boxed{1}$

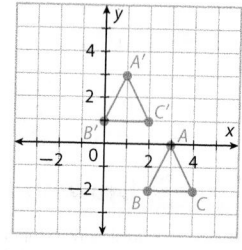

Your Turn

Draw the preimage and image of each triangle under a translation along $\langle -4, 1 \rangle$.

5. Triangle with coordinates: $A(2, 4)$, $B(1, 2)$, $C(4, 2)$.

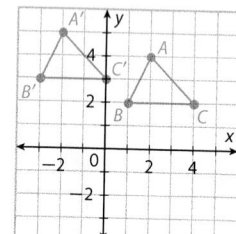

6. Triangle with coordinates: $P(2, -1)$, $Q(2, -3)$, $R(4, -3)$.

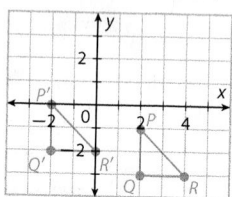

⚙ Explain 3 **Specifying Translation Vectors**

You may be asked to specify a translation that carries a given figure onto another figure. You can do this by drawing the translation vector and then writing it in component form.

Example 3 Specify the component form of the vector that maps $\triangle ABC$ to $\triangle A'B'C'$.

Ⓐ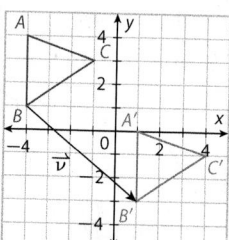

Determine the components of $\vec{v}$.

The horizontal change from the initial point $(-4, 1)$ to the terminal point $(1, -3)$ is $1 - (-4) = 5$.

The vertical change from the initial point $(-4, 1)$ to the terminal point $(1, -3)$ is $-3 - 1 = -4$

Write the vector in component form.

$$\vec{v} = \langle 5, -4 \rangle$$

Module 2

67

Lesson 1

LANGUAGE SUPPORT **EL**

Connect Vocabulary

Help students understand the difference between the *initial*, or beginning, point of a vector and the *terminal*, or ending, point. Discuss the effects of reversing the points. When talking about the *component form* of a vector, emphasize the importance of listing the horizontal (left and right) change first, and then the vertical (up and down) change. Point out how reversing the two numbers changes the definition of the vector and, therefore, the location of the image it defines.

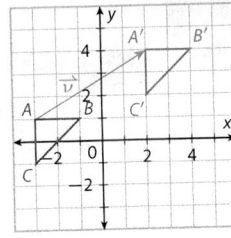

Ⓑ Draw the vector $\vec{v}$ from a vertex of △ABC to its image in △A'B'C'.

Determine the components of $\vec{v}$.

The horizontal change from the initial point $(-3, 1)$ to the terminal point $(2, 4)$ is $\underline{2} - \underline{-3} = \underline{5}$.

The vertical change from the initial point to the terminal point is $\underline{4} - \underline{1} = \underline{3}$

Write the vector in component form. $\vec{v} = \left\langle \boxed{5}, \boxed{3} \right\rangle$

Reflect

7. What is the component form of a vector that translates figures horizontally? Explain.
The vector has the form $\langle a, 0 \rangle$. There is no change in the vertical direction, so the value of

b is 0.

Your Turn

8. In Example 3A, suppose △A'B'C' is the preimage and △ABC is the image after translation. What is the component form of the translation vector in this case? How is this vector related to the vector you wrote in Example 3A?
$\langle -5, 4 \rangle$; the components are the opposites of the components of the vector in Example 3A.

💬 **Elaborate**

9. How are translations along the vectors $\langle a, -b \rangle$ and $\langle -a, b \rangle$ similar and how are they different?
They move the points the same distance, but in opposite directions.

10. A translation along the vector $\langle -2, 7 \rangle$ maps point P to point Q. The coordinates of point Q are $(4, -1)$. What are the coordinates of point P? Explain your reasoning.
$(6, -8)$; Solving equations $x - 2 = 4$ and $y + 7 = -1$ shows that $x = 6$ and $y = -8$.

11. A translation along the vector $\langle a, b \rangle$ maps points in Quadrant I to points in Quadrant III. What can you conclude about a and b? Justify your response.
Both a and b are negative. Points in Quadrant I have positive x- and y-coordinates and

points in Quadrant III have negative x- and y-coordinates. This means the horizontal and

vertical changes are both negative. So a is negative and b is negative.

12. **Essential Question Check-In** How does translating a figure using the formal definition of a translation compare to the previous method of translating a figure?
Possible answer: Rather than sliding a figure left or right and then up or down to translate

it, you slide it parallel to a given vector a distance equal to the length of the vector.

ELABORATE

QUESTIONING STRATEGIES

❓ What can you say about the length of the line segments drawn from each vertex to its image?
Each is equal to the magnitude of the vector used to draw the translation.

SUMMARIZE THE LESSON

❓ Give at least three different ways to describe a translation. Sample answer: A translation is
(1) a slide that moves the figure so many units horizontally and so many vertically;
(2) moving all points of the figure the same distance in the same direction;
(3) drawing an image by sliding a preimage parallel to a given vector a distance equal to the length of the vector;
(4) using a pair of coordinates to find the coordinates of the images of the vertices.

ASSIGNMENT GUIDE

Concepts and Skills	Practice
Explore Exploring Translations	Exercise 4
Example 1 Translating Figures Using Vectors	Exercises 3, 8—10
Example 2 Drawing Translations on a Coordinate Plane	Exercises 5–7
Example 3 Specifying Translation Vectors	Exercises 12–14

INTEGRATE MATHEMATICAL PRACTICES

Focus on Patterns

MP.8 Encourage students to predict, before constructing the translated image, where the image will lie, using the distance and direction given by the translation vector.

INTEGRATE MATHEMATICAL PRACTICES

Focus on Communication

MP.3 Provide students with graphic examples of translated images (preimage and image) and preimages that may have been transformed but are *not* translations. Have students sort the pictures into translations and non-translations, discuss why they are or are not translations, and write the justifications on note cards. Provide a list of key terms for students to use in their explanations.

✪ Evaluate: Homework and Practice

- Online Homework
- Hints and Help
- Extra Practice

Draw the image of △ABC after a translation along $\vec{v}$.

1.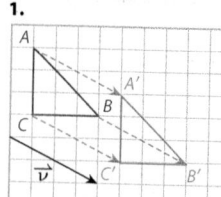

2.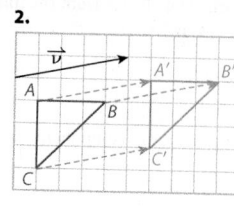

3.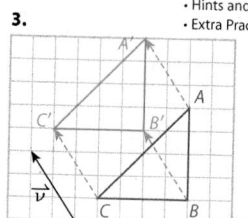

4. Line segment $\overline{XY}$ was used to draw a copy of △ABC. $\overline{XY}$ is 3.5 centimeters long. What is the length of $AA' + BB' + CC'$?
10.5 cm

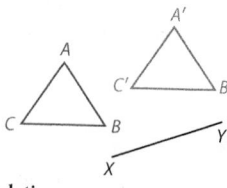

Draw the preimage and image of each triangle under the given translation.

5. Triangle: $A(-3, -1)$; $B(-2, 2)$; $C(0, -1)$; Vector: $\langle 3, 2 \rangle$

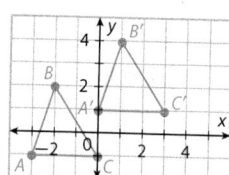

6. Triangle: $P(1, -3)$; $Q(3, -1)$; $R(4, -3)$; Vector: $\langle -1, 3 \rangle$

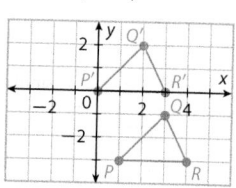

7. Triangle: $X(0, 3)$; $Y(-1, 1)$; $Z(-3, 4)$; Vector: $\langle 4, -2 \rangle$

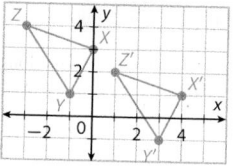

8. Find the coordinates of the image under the transformation $\langle 6, -11 \rangle$.

$(x, y) \rightarrow (x + 6, y - 11)$ $(2, -3) \rightarrow (8, -14)$

$(3, 1) \rightarrow (9, -10)$ $(4, -3) \rightarrow (10, -14)$

9. Name the vector. Write it in component form.

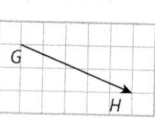

$\overrightarrow{GH}, \langle 5, -2 \rangle$

10. Match each set of coordinates for a preimage with the coordinates of its image after applying the vector $\langle 3, -8 \rangle$. Indicate a match by writing a letter for a preimage on the line in front of the corresponding image.

A. $(1, 1)$; $(10, 1)$; $(6, 5)$ ___C___ $(6, -10)$; $(6, -4)$; $(9, -3)$

B. $(0, 0)$; $(3, 8)$; $(4, 0)$; $(7, 8)$ ___D___ $(1, -6)$; $(5, -6)$; $(-1, -8)$; $(7, -8)$

C. $(3, -2)$; $(3, 4)$; $(6, 5)$ ___A___ $(4, -7)$; $(13, -7)$; $(9, -3)$

D. $(-2, 2)$; $(2, 2)$; $(-4, 0)$; $(4, 0)$ ___B___ $(3, -8)$; $(6, 0)$; $(7, -8)$; $(10, 0)$

© Houghton Mifflin Harcourt Publishing Company

Exercise	Depth of Knowledge (D.O.K.)	COMMON CORE Mathematical Practices
1–3	**2** Skills/Concepts	**MP.4** Modeling
4	**1** Recall of Information	**MP.2** Reasoning
5–7	**2** Skills/Concepts	**MP.4** Modeling
8	**1** Recall of Information	**MP.6** Precision
9	**1** Recall of Information	**MP.2** Reasoning
10	**2** Skills/Concepts	**MP.5** Using Tools

11. Persevere in Problem Solving Emma and Tony are playing a game. Each draws a triangle on a coordinate grid. For each turn, Emma chooses either the horizontal or vertical value for a vector in component form. Tony chooses the other value, alternating each turn. They each have to draw a new image of their triangle using the vector with the components they chose and using the image from the prior turn as the preimage. Whoever has drawn an image in each of the four quadrants first wins the game.

Emma's initial triangle has the coordinates $(-3, 0)$, $(-4, -2)$, $(-2, -2)$ and Tony's initial triangle has the coordinates $(2, 4)$, $(2, 2)$, $(4, 3)$. On the first turn the vector $\langle 6, -5 \rangle$ is used and on the second turn the vector $\langle -10, 8 \rangle$ is used. What quadrant does Emma need to translate her triangle to in order to win? What quadrant does Tony need to translate his triangle to in order to win?

Emma: Quadrant I; Tony: Quadrant III

Specify the component form of the vector that maps each figure to its image.

12.

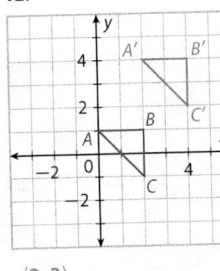

$\langle 2, 3 \rangle$

13.

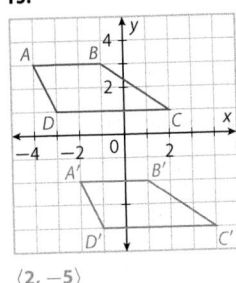

$\langle 2, -5 \rangle$

14.

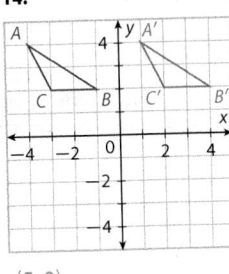

$\langle 5, 0 \rangle$

15. Explain the Error Andrew is using vector $\vec{v}$ to draw a copy of $\triangle ABC$. Explain his error.

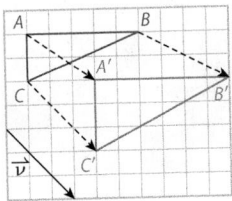

Possible answer: He drew vectors from A to A' and from B to B' that were not parallel to or the same length as $\vec{v}$. The correct vectors should each point 3 units right and 3 units down.

16. Explain the Error Marcus was asked to identify the vector that maps $\triangle DEF$ to $\triangle D'E'F'$. He drew a vector as shown and determined that the component form of the vector is $\langle 3, 1 \rangle$. Explain his error.

He should have drawn the vector from F to F' or from E to E'. The correct component form of the vector is $\langle 5, 1 \rangle$.

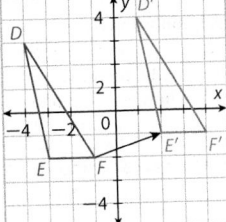

INTEGRATE MATHEMATICAL PRACTICES

Focus on Modeling

MP.4 Have students draw a vector on graph paper and then use it as the hypotenuse of a right triangle. Discuss how the legs of the triangle show the vertical and horizontal components.

AVOID COMMON ERRORS

When writing the component form of a given vector, some students may reverse the initial point and the terminal point. Suggest that they circle the arrow that shows the terminal point before writing the components.

Exercise	Depth of Knowledge (D.O.K.)	COMMON CORE Mathematical Practices
11	**3** Strategic Thinking	**MP.5** Using Tools
12–14	**2** Skills/Concepts	**MP.4** Modeling
15–16	**3** Strategic Thinking	**MP.3** Logic
17	**2** Skills/Concepts	**MP.3** Logic
18	**3** Strategic Thinking H.O.T.	**MP.3** Logic
19–20	**2** Skills/Concepts H.O.T.	**MP.3** Logic
21	**3** Strategic Thinking H.O.T.	**MP.3** Logic

Translations **70**

17. Algebra A cartographer is making a city map. Line m represents Murphy Street. The cartographer translates points on line m along the vector $\langle 2, -2 \rangle$ to draw Nolan Street. Draw the line for Nolan Street on the coordinate plane and write its equation. What is the image of the point $(0, 3)$ in this situation?

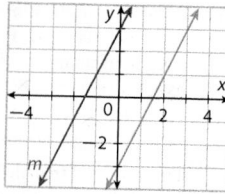

$y = 2x - 3;\ (2, 1)$

H.O.T. Focus on Higher Order Thinking

18. Represent Real-World Problems A builder is trying to level out some ground with a front-end loader. He picks up some excess dirt at (9, 16) and then maneuvers through the job site along the vectors $\langle -6, 0 \rangle$, $\langle 2, 5 \rangle$, $\langle 8, 10 \rangle$ to get to the spot to unload the dirt. Find the coordinates of the unloading point. Find a single vector from the loading point to the unloading point.

$(13, 31);\ \langle 4, 15 \rangle$

19. Look for a Pattern A checker player's piece begins at K and, through a series of moves, lands on L. What translation vector represents the path from K to L?

$\langle 4, -6 \rangle$

20. Represent Real-World Problems A group of hikers walks 2 miles east and then 1 mile north. After taking a break, they then hike 4 miles east to their final destination. What vector describes their hike from their starting position to their final destination? Let 1 unit represent 1 mile.

$\langle 6, 1 \rangle$

21. Communicate Mathematical Ideas In a quilt pattern, a polygon with vertices $(-4, -2)$, $(-3, -1)$, $(-2, -2)$, and $(-3, -3)$ is translated repeatedly along the vector $\langle 2, 2 \rangle$. What are the coordinates of the third polygon in the pattern? Explain how you solved the problem.

$(0, 2);\ (1, 3);\ (2, 2);\ (1, 1);$ Possible answer: I used a table to find the coordinates of the second polygon. Then I made a new table, using the coordinates from the second polygon to find the coordinates of the third polygon.

Lesson Performance Task

A contractor is designing a pattern for tiles in an entryway, using a sun design called Image A for the center of the space. The contractor wants to duplicate this design three times, labeled Image B, Image C, and Image D, above Image A so that they do not overlap. Identify the three vectors, labeled $\vec{m}$, $\vec{n}$, and $\vec{p}$ that could be used to draw the design, and write them in component form. Draw the images on grid paper using the vectors you wrote.

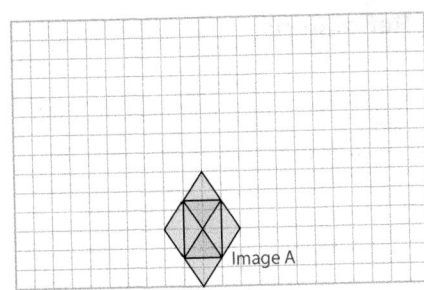

Image A

Drawings and vectors will vary. Possible drawing and vectors are shown.

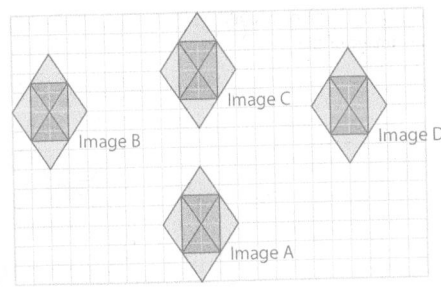

Image C
Image B
Image D
Image A

$\vec{m}$ moves Image A to Image B. $\vec{m} = \langle -8, 6 \rangle$

$\vec{n}$ moves Image A to Image C. $\vec{n} = \langle 0, 8 \rangle$

$\vec{p}$ moves Image A to Image D. $\vec{p} = \langle 8, 6 \rangle$

CONNECT VOCABULARY **EL**

Ask students to describe any similarities between the meaning of *translation* as it is used in this lesson and the word's meaning when it is used to describe the process of converting words from one language to another. **Sample answer: Each transforms something into something else. In this lesson, a translation transforms a point to a point in another position. A language translation transforms a word in one language into an equivalent word in another language.**

QUESTIONING STRATEGIES

? Suppose $\vec{m} = \langle 3, -5 \rangle$ translates $P(4, -2)$ to Q. How do you find the coordinates of Q? **Add 3 to 4 for the x-coordinate and add –5 to –2 for the y-coordinate.**

? What is a vector $\vec{n}$ that will translate Q to P? Why? **$\vec{n} = \langle -3, 5 \rangle$; each component is the opposite of the component in the translation vector.**

EXTENSION ACTIVITY

Provide students with grid paper. Have each student design and color a geometric shape. The design should be no larger than a 6 × 6 portion of the grid. The student should write three or more vectors indicating where additional designs like theirs are to be drawn, making sure that translated designs do not overlap the original or each other. Students then exchange grids with a partner and draw the translated designs indicated by their partner's vectors.

Scoring Rubric

2 points: Student correctly solves the problem and explains his/her reasoning.

1 point: Student shows good understanding of the problem but does not fully solve or explain his/her reasoning.

0 points: Student does not demonstrate understanding of the problem.

Translations **72**

Reflections

Common Core Math Standards

The student is expected to:

 G-CO.A.4

Develop definitions of ... reflections ... in terms of ... perpendicular lines .... Also G-CO.A.1, G-CO.A.2, G-CO.A.5, G-CO.B.6, G-CO.D.12, G-MG.A.3

Mathematical Practices

 MP.5 Using Tools

Language Objective

Work with a partner to discuss how to determine if a transformation is a reflection.

ENGAGE

Essential Question: How do you draw the image of a figure under a reflection?

Possible answer: To draw the image of a figure under a reflection across line ℓ, choose a vertex of the figure, vertex A. Draw a segment with an endpoint at vertex A so that the segment is perpendicular to line ℓ and is bisected by line ℓ. Label the other endpoint of the segment A'. Repeat the process with the other vertices of the figure. Connect the images of the vertices in the same order as the preimage to draw the image of the figure.

PREVIEW: LESSON PERFORMANCE TASK

View the online Engage. Discuss with students what a mirror does and how it reflects a person—the preimage. Ask students to describe similarities and differences between an object and the image of the object in a mirror. Then preview the Lesson Performance Task.

2.2 Reflections

Essential Question: How do you draw the image of a figure under a reflection?

⊘ Explore **Exploring Reflections**

Use tracing paper to explore reflections.

(A) Draw and label a line ℓ on tracing paper. Then draw and label a quadrilateral ABCD with vertex C on line ℓ.

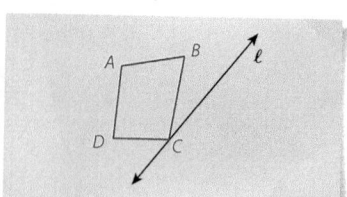

(B) Fold the tracing paper along line ℓ. Trace the quadrilateral. Then unfold the paper and draw the image of the quadrilateral. Label it A' B' C' D'.

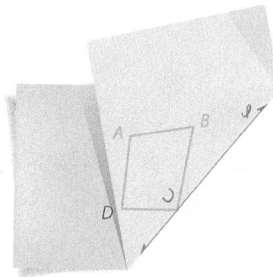

(C) Draw segments to connect each vertex of quadrilateral ABCD with its image. Use a protractor to measure the angle formed by each segment and line ℓ. What do you notice?

Each segment forms a right angle with line ℓ.

(D) Use a ruler to measure each segment and the two shorter segments formed by its intersection with line ℓ. What do you notice?

Line ℓ bisects each segment.

Reflect

1. In this activity, the fold line (line ℓ) is the line of reflection. What happens when a point is located on the line of reflection?

The image of the point is also on the line of reflection, in the same location as the preimage.

© Houghton Mifflin Harcourt Publishing Company

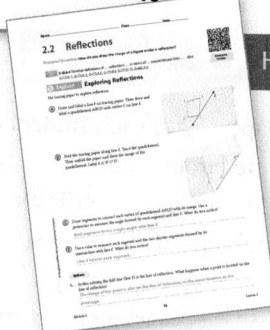

HARDCOVER PAGES 65–76

Turn to these pages to find this lesson in the hardcover student edition.

2. Discussion A student claims that a figure and its reflected image always lie on opposite sides of the line of reflection. Do you agree? Why or why not?

No; this is only true when the figure lies entirely on one side of the line of reflection.

The statement is not true when the line of reflection passes through one or more

points of the figure.

⊘ Explain 1 Reflecting Figures Using Graph Paper

Perpendicular lines are lines that intersect at right angles. In the figure, line ℓ is perpendicular to line m. The right angle mark in the figure indicates that the lines are perpendicular.

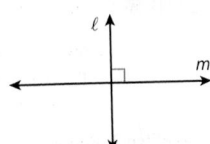

The **perpendicular bisector** of a line segment is a line perpendicular to the segment at the segment's midpoint. In the figure, line n is the perpendicular bisector of $\overline{AB}$.

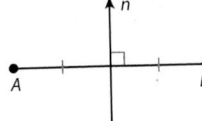

A **reflection** across line ℓ maps a point P to its image P'.

• If P is not on line ℓ, then line ℓ is the perpendicular bisector of $\overline{PP'}$.

• If P is on line ℓ, then $P = P'$.

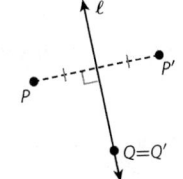

Example 1 Draw the image of $\triangle ABC$ after a reflection across line ℓ.

(A) **Step 1** Draw a segment with an endpoint at vertex A so that the segment is perpendicular to line ℓ and is bisected by line ℓ. Label the other endpoint of the segment A'.

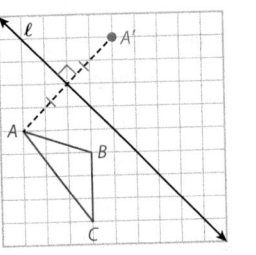

© Houghton Mifflin Harcourt Publishing Company

Exploring Reflections

INTEGRATE TECHNOLOGY

To carry out the Explore using geometry software, first have students construct a figure similar to the given preimage. Then have them construct a line and mark it as the line of reflection. Finally, have students select the preimage and choose how to reflect it.

QUESTIONING STRATEGIES

 What is the image of the line of reflection? **The line of reflection is its own image.**

EXPLAIN 1

Reflecting Figures Using Graph Paper

AVOID COMMON ERRORS

Some students might confuse the segments drawn to construct a reflection with the vectors used to draw translations. Point out that the vectors for translations all have equal magnitude, but the segments drawn to reflect a figure vary in length.

QUESTIONING STRATEGIES

For the term *perpendicular bisector*, describe the mark in the figure that results from *perpendicular*, and the marks that result from *bisector*.

PROFESSIONAL DEVELOPMENT

COMMON CORE Integrate Mathematical Practices

This lesson provides an opportunity to address Mathematical Practice **MP.5**, which calls for students to "use appropriate tools." Students are already familiar with reflecting a figure in the plane; in this lesson, students use the tools of tracing paper, ruler, and protractor to explore reflections. Students draw perpendicular bisectors on graph paper to draw reflected images and find midpoints to determine the line of reflection.

Step 2 Repeat Step 1 at vertices *B* and *C*.

Step 3 Connect points *A′*, *B′*, and *C′*.
△*A′B′C′* is the image of △*ABC*.

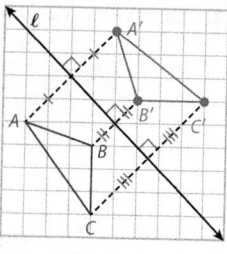

Ⓑ Draw the image of △*ABC* after a reflection across line ℓ.

Step 1 Draw a segment with an endpoint at vertex *A* so that the segment is perpendicular to line ℓ and is bisected by line ℓ. Label the other endpoint of the segment *A′*.

Step 2 Repeat Step 1 at vertex *B*.
Notice that *C* and *C′* are the same point because *C* is on the line of reflection.

Step 3 Connect points *A′*, *B′*, and *C′*. △*A′B′C′* is the image of △*ABC*.

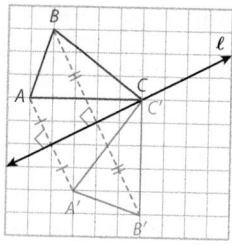

Reflect

3. How can you check that you drew the image of the triangle correctly?
Possible answer: Since a reflection is a rigid motion, it preserves length. Check that each side of △*ABC* has the same length as its image in △*A′B′C′*.

4. In Part A, how can you tell that $\overline{AA'}$ is perpendicular to line ℓ?
Possible answer: Line ℓ forms a diagonal through corners of grid squares. $\overline{AA'}$ forms a diagonal through corners of grid squares in the opposite direction.

Your Turn

Draw the image of △*ABC* after a reflection across line ℓ.

5.

6.

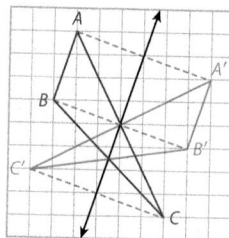

COLLABORATIVE LEARNING

Small Group Activity

Have students work in small groups to develop and write a list of what they would look for, or check, when they evaluate whether a classmate's paper shows a correctly drawn reflection.

Explain 2 Drawing Reflections on a Coordinate Plane

The table summarizes coordinate notation for reflections on a coordinate plane.

Rules for Reflections on a Coordinate Plane	
Reflection across the x-axis	$(x, y) \rightarrow (x, -y)$
Reflection across the y-axis	$(x, y) \rightarrow (-x, y)$
Reflection across the line $y = x$	$(x, y) \rightarrow (y, x)$
Reflection across the line $y = -x$	$(x, y) \rightarrow (-y, -x)$

Example 2 Reflect the figure with the given vertices across the given line.

(A) $M(1, 2), N(1, 4), P(3, 3)$; y-axis

Step 1 Find the coordinates of the vertices of the image.

$A(x, y) \rightarrow A'(-x, y)$.
$M(1, 2) \rightarrow M'(-1, 2)$
$N(1, 4) \rightarrow N'(-1, 4)$
$P(3, 3) \rightarrow P'(-3, 3)$

Step 2 Graph the preimage.

Step 3 Predict the quadrant in which the image will lie. Since $\triangle MNP$ lies in Quadrant I and the triangle is reflected across the y-axis, the image will lie in Quadrant II.

Graph the image.

(B) $D(2, 0), E(2, 2), F(5, 2), G(5, 1)$; $y = x$

Step 1 Find the coordinates of the vertices of the image.

$A(x, y) \rightarrow A'\left(\boxed{y}, \boxed{x}\right)$

$D(2, 0) \rightarrow D'\left(\boxed{0}, \boxed{2}\right)$

$E(2, 2) \rightarrow E'\left(\boxed{2}, \boxed{2}\right)$

$F(5, 2) \rightarrow F'\left(\boxed{2}, \boxed{5}\right)$

$G(5, 1) \rightarrow G'\left(\boxed{1}, \boxed{5}\right)$

Step 2 Graph the preimage.

Step 3 Since $DEFG$ lies in Quadrant I and the quadrilateral is reflected across the line $y = x$, the image will lie in Quadrant ____I____.

Graph the image.

© Houghton Mifflin Harcourt Publishing Company

EXPLAIN 2

Drawing Reflections on a Coordinate Plane

QUESTIONING STRATEGIES

? Describe in words what happens to the coordinates of a point when the point is reflected across the x-axis. The x-coordinate stays the same and the y-coordinate of the image is the opposite of the y-coordinate of the preimage.

? Does this mean that the y-coordinate of an image is always a negative number? Explain. No; it is always the opposite of the preimage, but the opposite of a negative number is a positive number.

INTEGRATE MATHEMATICAL PRACTICES
Focus on Communication

MP.3 Have students describe what is alike and what is different in the preimage and the image for a reflection.

COGNITIVE STRATEGIES

Have students determine if given preimages have been reflected onto an image. Explain that besides folding paper, or tracing and flipping the image, you can check the distance of each point from whichever axis the reflection occurs across (or whichever axis acts as the line of reflection). Encourage them to state whether or not the image is a reflection of the reimage across the x- or y-axis, and to check whether each point in the image and preimage is the same distance from the x- or y-axis.

DIFFERENTIATE INSTRUCTION

Visual Cues

To help students see how a reflection is different from the original image, use a mirror and have students draw an object such as someone facing the class with a pencil behind one ear. Then have the person turn so that the class sees the reflection in the mirror and have them sketch the reflection. Discuss how the two sketches differ.

EXPLAIN 3

Specifying Lines of Reflection

QUESTIONING STRATEGIES

(?) In order for a line to be a line of reflection, what two things must be true about the line and each segment connecting corresponding points of the preimage and image? The line must pass through the midpoint of each segment, and it must be perpendicular to each segment.

AVOID COMMON ERRORS

Some students may think that reflection over a line always puts the image in a different quadrant from the preimage. Help them draw examples of reflecting over a line that is *not* an axis to see why this is not always true.

Reflect

7. How would the image of △*MNP* be similar to and different from the one you drew in Part A if the triangle were reflected across the *x*-axis?
The image would have the same size and shape, but it would lie in Quadrant IV instead of Quadrant II.

8. A classmate claims that the rule $(x, y) \rightarrow (-x, y)$ for reflecting a figure across the *y*-axis only works if all the vertices are in the first quadrant because the values of *x* and *y* must be positive. Explain why this reasoning is not correct.
The rule says that the image of a point will have an *x*-coordinate that is the opposite of the value of the preimage. So, the point $(-1, 2)$ will have the image $(1, 2)$ when reflected across the *y*-axis.

Your Turn

Reflect the figure with the given vertices across the given line.

9. $S(3, 4), T(3, 1), U(-2, 1), V(-2, 4)$; *x*-axis

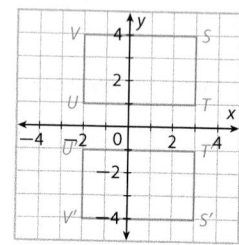

$(x, y) \rightarrow (x, -y)$
$S'(3, -4), T'(3, -1), U'(-2, -1), V'(-2, -4)$

10. $A(-4, -2), B(-1, -1), C(-1, -4)$; $y = -x$

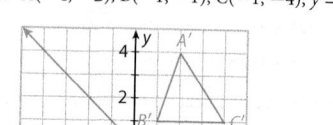

$(x, y) \rightarrow (-y, -x)$
$A'(2, 4), B'(1, 1), C'(4, 1)$

(◉) Explain 3 Specifying Lines of Reflection

Example 3 Given that △*A'B'C'* is the image of △*ABC* under a reflection, draw the line of reflection.

(A) Draw the segments $\overline{AA'}$, $\overline{BB'}$, and $\overline{CC'}$.

Find the midpoint of each segment.

The midpoint of $\overline{AA'}$ is $\left(\dfrac{-3 + 5}{2}, \dfrac{3 + (-1)}{2} \right) = (1, 1)$.

The midpoint of $\overline{BB'}$ is $\left(\dfrac{-2 + 2}{2}, \dfrac{0 + (-2)}{2} \right) = (0, -1)$.

The midpoint of $\overline{CC'}$ is $\left(\dfrac{-5 + 3}{2}, \dfrac{-1 + (-5)}{2} \right) = (-1, -3)$.

Plot the midpoints. Draw line ℓ through the midpoints.

Line ℓ is the line of reflection.

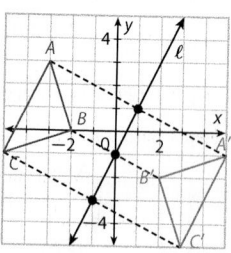

LANGUAGE SUPPORT **EL**

Connect Vocabulary

Students who are speakers of Spanish may benefit from learning that many polysyllabic English words that end in *–or* and *–al* are shared cognates with Spanish. Although pronounced differently, these words are written the same and are identical in meaning. Some examples are *vector, bisector, factor, divisor, numerator, denominator, initial, terminal, vertical, horizontal,* and *final.*

(B) Draw $\overline{AA'}$, $\overline{BB'}$, and $\overline{CC'}$. Find the midpoint of each segment.

The midpoint of $\overline{AA'}$ is $\left(\dfrac{-3 + -5}{2}, \dfrac{3 + -1}{2} \right) = \left(-4, 1 \right)$.

The midpoint of $\overline{BB'}$ is $\left(\dfrac{2 + -2}{2}, \dfrac{3 + -5}{2} \right) = \left(0, -1 \right)$.

The midpoint of $\overline{CC'}$ is $\left(\dfrac{5 + 3}{2}, \dfrac{-1 + -5}{2} \right) = \left(4, -3 \right)$.

Plot the midpoints. Draw line ℓ through the midpoints. Line ℓ is the line of reflection.

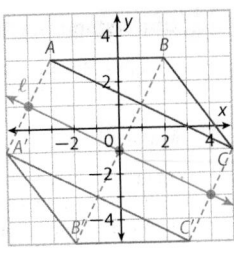

Reflect

11. How can you use a ruler and protractor to check that line ℓ is the line of reflection?
Use the ruler to check that line ℓ bisects $\overline{AA'}$, $\overline{BB'}$, and $\overline{CC'}$. Use the protractor to check that line ℓ is perpendicular to $\overline{AA'}$, $\overline{BB'}$, and $\overline{CC'}$.

Your Turn

Given that $\triangle A'B'C'$ is the image of $\triangle ABC$ under a reflection, draw the line of reflection.

12.

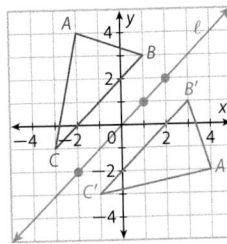

midpoints: $\overline{AA'}$: $\left(\dfrac{-2 + 4}{2}, \dfrac{4 + (-2)}{2} \right) = (1, 1)$;
$\overline{BB'}$: $\left(\dfrac{1 + 3}{2}, \dfrac{3 + 1}{2} \right) = (2, 2)$;
$\overline{CC'}$: $\left(\dfrac{-3 + (-1)}{2}, \dfrac{-1 + (-3)}{2} \right) = (-2, -2)$

13.

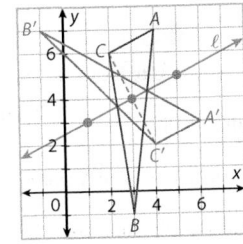

midpoints: $\overline{AA'}$: $\left(\dfrac{4 + 6}{2}, \dfrac{7 + 3}{2} \right) = (5, 5)$;
$\overline{BB'}$: $\left(\dfrac{3 + (-1)}{2}, \dfrac{-1 + 7}{2} \right) = (1, 3)$;
$\overline{CC'}$: $\left(\dfrac{2 + 4}{2}, \dfrac{6 + 2}{2} \right) = (3, 4)$

⊘ Explain 4   Applying Reflections

Example 4

The figure shows one hole of a miniature golf course. It is not possible to hit the ball in a straight line from the tee T to the hole H. At what point should a player aim in order to make a hole in one?

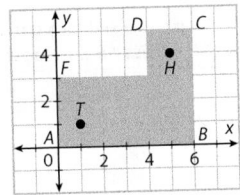

EXPLAIN 4

Applying Reflections

QUESTIONING STRATEGIES

? For reflected light, or for an object such as a ball bouncing off a wall, what does it mean to say "the angle of reflection equals the angle of incidence"? The angle that the object makes as it hits the reflecting surface is equal to the angle at which the object bounces off that surface.

PEER-TO-PEER DISCUSSION

Have students discuss and explain familiar events involving angles of reflection, such as playing golf, basketball, and soccer, or using light and mirrors.

⊞ Understand the Problem

The problem asks you to locate point X on the wall of the miniature golf hole so that the ball can travel in a straight line from T to X and from X to H.

⊞ Make a Plan

In order for the ball to travel directly from T to X to H, the angle of the ball's path as it hits the wall must equal the angle of the ball's path as it leaves the wall. In the figure, $m\angle 1$ must equal $m\angle 2$.

Let H' be the reflection of point H across $\overline{BC}$.

Reflections preserve angle measure, so $m\angle 2 = m\angle \boxed{3}$. Therefore, $m\angle 1$ is equal to $m\angle 2$ when $m\angle 1$ is equal to $m\angle 3$. This occurs when T, $\boxed{X}$, and H' are collinear.

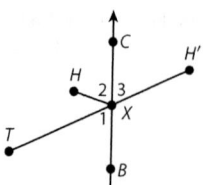

⊞ Solve

Reflect H across $\overline{BC}$ to locate H'.

The coordinates of H' are $\left(\boxed{7}, \boxed{4} \right)$.

Draw $\overline{TH'}$ and locate point X where $\overline{TH'}$ intersects $\overline{BC}$.

The coordinates of point X are $\left(\boxed{6}, \boxed{3.5} \right)$.

The player should aim at this point.

⊞ Look Back

To check that the answer is reasonable, plot point X using the coordinates you found. Then use a protractor to check that the angle of the ball's path as it hits the wall at point X is equal to the angle of the ball's path as it leaves the wall from point X.

Reflect

14. Is there another path the ball can take to hit a wall and then travel directly to the hole? Explain.

Yes; use a similar process to reflect H across $\overline{AB}$ and locate a point Y on $\overline{AB}$ so that the ball travels from T to Y to H.

15. Cara is playing pool. She wants to use the cue ball *C* to hit the ball at point *A* without hitting the ball at point *B*. To do so, she has to bounce the cue ball off the side rail and into the ball at point *A*. Find the coordinates of the exact point along the side rail that Cara should aim for.

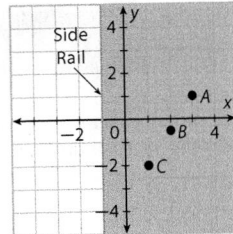

Reflect point *C* across the side rail to locate *C'*. The coordinates of *C'* are $(-3, -2)$. Locate point *X* where $\overline{AC'}$ intersects the side rail. The coordinates of point *X* are $(-1, -1)$. Cara should aim for the point $(-1, -1)$ along the side rail.

Elaborate

16. Do any points in the plane have themselves as images under a reflection? Explain.
Yes; every point on the line of reflection has itself as its image. This is how the reflection image is defined for points that lie on the line of reflection.

17. If you are given a figure and its image under a reflection, how can you use paper folding to find the line of reflection?
Fold the paper so that the figure coincides with its image. Then unfold the paper. The crease is the line of reflection.

18. **Essential Question Check-In** How do you draw the image of a figure under a reflection across the *x*-axis?
For each vertex of the figure, use the rule $(x, y) \rightarrow (x, -y)$ to find the coordinates of the image of the vertex. Plot the images of the vertices. Then connect these points to draw the image of the figure.

ELABORATE

QUESTIONING STRATEGIES

? Describe how you would draw the reflection of a figure drawn on graph paper across the line $y = -x$? Find the coordinates of each vertex of the preimage and change each using the rule. $(x,y) \rightarrow (-y,-x)$. Then join the new vertices to draw the image.

CONNECT VOCABULARY **EL**

Compare and contrast a translation and a reflection by having students write the words and then draw an example of each kind of transformation. Have them write some features of each underneath.

SUMMARIZE THE LESSON

? How can you check that a drawing of two figures represents a reflection? (1) The two figures must have the same size and shape. (2) There must be a line of reflection that is the perpendicular bisector of every segment joining the vertices of the preimage to the image (unless a vertex is on the line of reflection).

EVALUATE

ASSIGNMENT GUIDE

Concepts and Skills	Practice
Explore Exploring Reflections	Exercises 1–4
Example 1 Reflection Figures Using Graph Paper	Exercises 5–8
Example 2 Drawing Reflections on a Coordinate Plane	Exercises 9–12
Example 3 Specifying Lines of Reflection	Exercises 13–16
Example 4 Applying Reflections	Exercises 17–18

INTEGRATE MATHEMATICAL PRACTICES
Focus on Critical Thinking

MP.3 Discuss whether a preimage and its reflected image can have any points in common (can touch or overlap). Have students draw examples to explain their conclusions.

⭐ Evaluate: Homework and Practice

- Online Homework
- Hints and Help
- Extra Practice

Use tracing paper to copy each figure and line ℓ. Then fold the paper to draw and label the image of the figure after a reflection across line ℓ.

1.
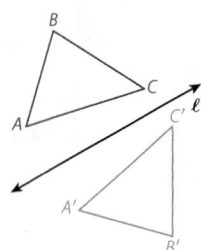

2.
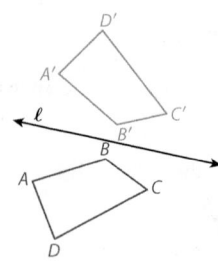

3.
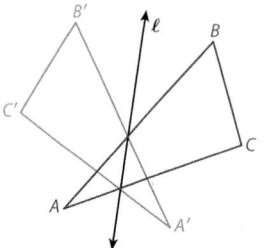

4.
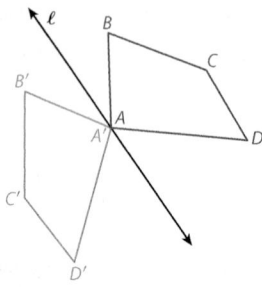

Draw the image of △ABC after a reflection across line ℓ.

5.
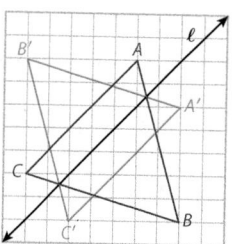

6.
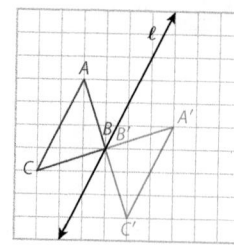

7.

8.
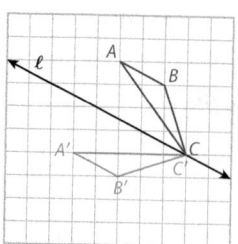

© Houghton Mifflin Harcourt Publishing Company

Exercise	Depth of Knowledge (D.O.K.)	COMMON CORE Mathematical Practices
1–4	**1** Recall of Information	**MP.5** Using Tools
5–8	**1** Recall of Information	**MP.6** Precision
9–12	**1** Recall of Information	**MP.4** Modeling
13–16	**2** Skills/Concepts	**MP.2** Reasoning
17–18	**2** Skills/Concepts	**MP.1** Problem Solving
19–20	**2** Skills/Concepts	**MP.4** Modeling
21	**2** Skills/Concepts	**MP.4** Modeling

Reflect the figure with the given vertices across the given line.

9. $P(-2, 3), Q(4, 3), R(-1, 0), S(-4, 1)$; x-axis

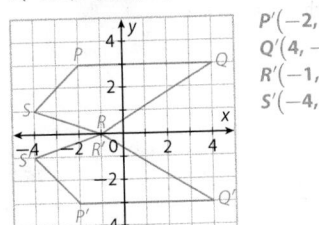

$P'(-2, -3),$
$Q'(4, -3),$
$R'(-1, 0),$
$S'(-4, -1)$

10. $A(-3, -3), B(1, 3), C(3, -1)$; y-axis

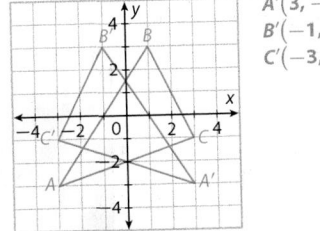

$A'(3, -3),$
$B'(-1, 3),$
$C'(-3, -1)$

11. $J(-1, 2), K(2, 4), L(4, -1); y = -x$

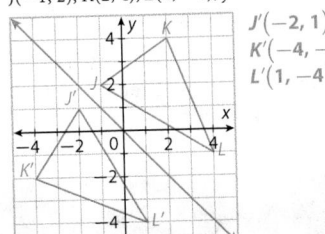

$J'(-2, 1),$
$K'(-4, -2),$
$L'(1, -4)$

12. $D(-1, 1), E(3, 2), F(4, -1), G(-1, -3); y = x$

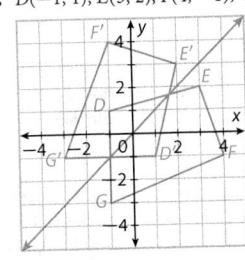

$D'(1, -1),$
$E'(2, 3),$
$F'(-1, 4),$
$G'(-3, -1)$

Given that $\triangle A'B'C'$ **is the image of** $\triangle ABC$ **under a reflection, draw the line of reflection.**

13.

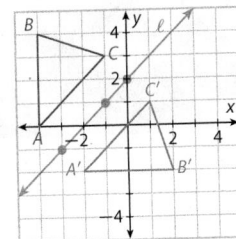

midpoint of $\overline{AA'}$ is $(-3, -1)$. midpoint of $\overline{BB'}$ is $(-1, 1)$. midpoint of $\overline{CC'}$ is $(0, 2)$.

14.

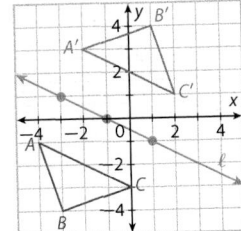

midpoint of $\overline{AA'}$ is $(-3, 1)$. midpoint of $\overline{BB'}$ is $(-1, 0)$. midpoint of $\overline{CC'}$ is $(1, -1)$.

15.

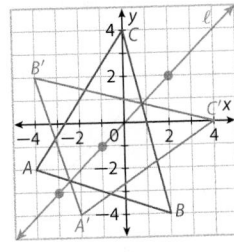

midpoint of $\overline{AA'}$ is $(-3, -3)$. midpoint of $\overline{BB'}$ is $(-1, -1)$. midpoint of $\overline{CC'}$ is $(2, 2)$.

16.

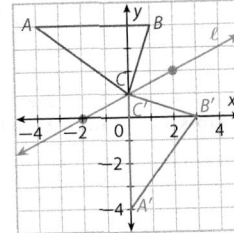

midpoint of $\overline{AA'}$ is $(-2, 0)$. midpoint of $\overline{BB'}$ is $(2, 2)$.

AVOID COMMON ERRORS

Some students may think that any line through the midpoint of a segment joining two vertices (such as $\overline{AA'}$) is the line of reflection. Have them draw a figure and its reflection as well as the segment joining two corresponding vertices. Then have them draw several different lines through the midpoint in order to identify as the line of reflection the only line that is perpendicular to the segment.

Exercise	Depth of Knowledge (D.O.K.)	COMMON CORE Mathematical Practices
22	**2** Skills/Concepts	**MP.3** Logic
23	**2** Skills/Concepts	**MP.6** Precision
24	**2** Skills/Concepts	**MP.2** Reasoning
25	**2** Skills/Concepts H.O.T.	**MP.6** Precision
26	**3** Strategic Thinking H.O.T.	**MP.4** Modeling
27	**2** Skills/Concepts H.O.T.	**MP.3** Logic
28	**3** Strategic Thinking H.O.T.	**MP.3** Logic

Focus on Math Connections

MP.1 Reflections, or flips, are one of the three rigid motions that students will study. Reflections may be considered the most basic of the three because the other two can be expressed in terms of reflections. In particular, every translation is a composition of reflections across parallel lines and every rotation is a composition of reflections across intersecting lines.

17. Jamar is playing a video game. The object of the game is to roll a marble into a target. In the figure, the shaded rectangular area represents the video screen and the striped rectangle is a barrier. Because of the barrier, it is not possible to roll the marble M directly into the target T. At what point should Jamar aim the marble so that it will bounce off a wall and roll into the target?

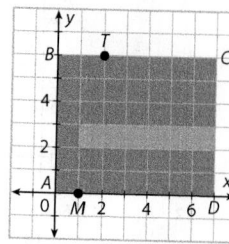

Reflect point M across the edge of the screen to locate M'. The coordinates of M' are $(-1, 0)$. Locate point X where $\overline{M'T}$ intersects the edge of the screen. The coordinates of point X are $(0, 2)$. Jamar should aim for the point $(0, 2)$ along the edge of the screen.

18. A trail designer is planning two trails that connect campsites A and B to a point on the river, line ℓ. She wants the total length of the trails to be as short as possible. At what point should the trails meet the river?

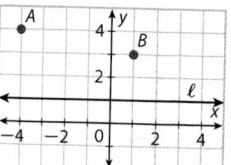

Reflect point B across the river to locate B'. The coordinates of B' are $(1, -1)$. Locate point X where $\overline{AB'}$ intersects the river. The coordinates of point X are $(-1, 1)$. The trail designer will have the trails meet the river at $(-1, 1)$.

Algebra In the figure, point K is the image of point J under a reflection across line ℓ. Find each of the following.

19. JM

Since line ℓ bisects $\overline{JK}$, $JM = MK$.

$2x + 4 = 4x - 6; 5 = x$

$JM = 2x + 4 = 2(5) + 4 = 14$

20. y

Since line ℓ is perpendicular to $\overline{JK}$, each angle formed by the intersection of line ℓ and $\overline{JK}$ measures $90°$.

$3y - 30 = 90; y = 40$

© Houghton Mifflin Harcourt Publishing Company · Image Credits: (b)©Comstock Images/Jupiterimages/Getty Images; (t)©Pavelk/Shutterstock

21. Make a Prediction Each time Jenny presses the tab key on her keyboard, the software reflects the logo she is designing across the x-axis. Jenny's cat steps on the keyboard and presses the tab key 25 times. In which quadrant does the logo end up? Explain.

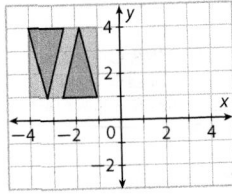 

When the tab key is pressed twice, the logo is reflected into Quadrant III and then reflected back to its original position in Quadrant II. So after the tab key is pressed 24 times, the logo is in its original position. When the tab key is pressed for the 25th time, the logo is reflected across the x-axis into Quadrant III.

22. Multi-Step Write the equation of the line of reflection.

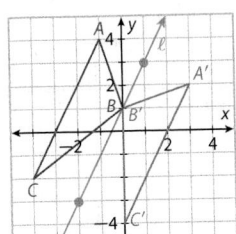

midpoint of $\overline{AA'} = \left(\dfrac{-1+3}{2}, \dfrac{4+2}{2}\right) = (1, 3)$

midpoint of $\overline{CC'} = \left(\dfrac{-4+0}{2}, \dfrac{-2+-4}{2}\right) = (-2, -3)$

$(-2, -3)$ and $(1, 3)$; $m = \dfrac{3-(-3)}{1-(-2)} = \dfrac{6}{3} = 2$

$y = 2x + b$; $3 = 2(1) + b$; $1 = b$; $y = 2x + 1$.

23. Communicate Mathematical Ideas
The figure shows rectangle *PQRS* and its image after a reflection across the y-axis. A student said that *PQRS* could also be mapped to its image using the translation $(x, y) \rightarrow (x + 6, y)$. Do you agree? Explain why or why not.

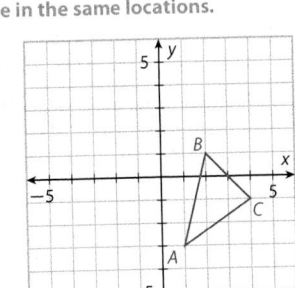

No; the translation would move rectangle *PQRS* into the same position as rectangle *P'Q'R'S'*, but the corresponding vertices would not be in the same locations.

24. Which of the following transformations map $\triangle ABC$ to a triangle that intersects the x-axis? Select all that apply.

(A.) $(x, y) \rightarrow (-x, y)$

(B.) $(x, y) \rightarrow (x, -y)$

C. $(x, y) \rightarrow (y, x)$

D. $(x, y) \rightarrow (-y, -x)$

(E.) $(x, y) \rightarrow (x, y + 1)$

A. $A'(-1, -3), B'(-2, 1), C'(-4, -1)$; $\overline{A'B'}$ intersects x-axis.

B. $A'(1, 3), B'(2, -1), C'(4, 1)$; $\overline{A'B'}$ intersects the x-axis.

C. $A'(-3, 1), B'(1, 2), C'(-1, 4)$; no side intersects the x-axis.

D. $A'(3, -1), B'(-1, -2), C'(1, -4)$; no side intersects the x-axis.

E. $A'(1, -2), B'(2, 2), C'(4, 0)$; $\overline{A'B'}$ intersects the x-axis.

© Houghton Mifflin Harcourt Publishing Company · Image Credits: ©Jim O Donnell/Alamy

JOURNAL

Have students list some everyday examples of reflections they have seen (such as reflections in water or in mirrors and windows) and then describe how a reflection is like the original object and how it is different.

25. Explain the Error $\triangle M'N'P'$ is the image of $\triangle MNP$. Casey draws $\overline{MM'}$, $\overline{NN'}$, and $\overline{PP'}$. Then she finds the midpoint of each segment and draws line ℓ through the midpoints. She claims that line ℓ is the line of reflection. Do you agree? Explain.

No; line ℓ is not perpendicular to $\overline{MM'}$, $\overline{NN'}$, and $\overline{PP'}$ so it cannot be the line of reflection. There is a translation required in addition to a reflection to map $\triangle MNP$ to $\triangle M'N'P'$.

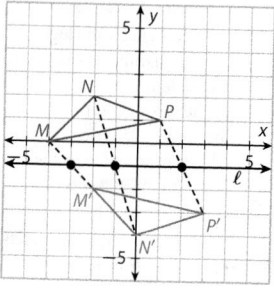

26. Draw Conclusions Plot the images of points D, E, F, and G after a reflection across the line $y = 2$. Then write an algebraic rule for the reflection.

The reflection maps points as follows:
$D(-3, 3) \rightarrow D'(-3, 1)$, $E(-1, 2) \rightarrow E'(-1, 2)$, $F(2, 0) \rightarrow F'(2, 4)$, $G(4, 4) \rightarrow G'(4, 0)$. The x-coordinate is unchanged and the y-coordinate is subtracted from 4. The rule is $(x, y) \rightarrow (x, 4 - y)$.

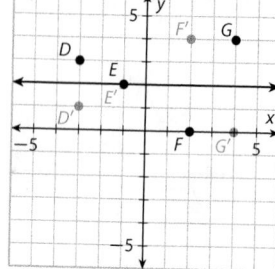

27. Critique Reasoning Mayumi wants to draw the line of reflection for the reflection that maps $\triangle ABC$ to $\triangle A'B'C'$. She claims that she just needs to draw the line through the points X and Y. Do you agree? Explain.

Yes; points X and Y are fixed under the reflection, so they must lie on the line of reflection. Since two points determine a line, the line of reflection is $\overleftrightarrow{XY}$.

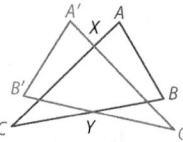

28. Justify Reasoning Point Q is the image of point P under a reflection across line ℓ. Point R lies on line ℓ. What type of triangle is $\triangle PQR$? Justify your answer.

Isosceles triangle; since a reflection is a rigid motion, it preserves distance. Since $\overline{RQ}$ is the image of $\overline{RP}$, $RQ = RP$. Therefore, the triangle has two sides with the same length, so it is isosceles.

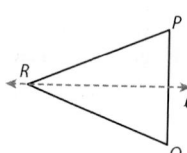

Lesson Performance Task

In order to see the entire length of your body in a mirror, do you need a mirror that is as tall as you are? If not, what is the length of the shortest mirror you can use, and how should you position it on a wall?

a. Let the *x*-axis represent the floor and let the *y*-axis represent the wall on which the mirror hangs. Suppose the bottom of your feet are at $F(3, 0)$, your eyes are at $E(3, 7)$, and the top of your head is at $H(3, 8)$. Plot these points and the points that represent their reflection images. (*Hint*: When you look in a mirror, your reflection appears to be as far behind the mirror as you are in front of it.) Draw the lines of sight from your eyes to the reflection of the top of your head and to the reflection of the bottom of your feet. Determine where these lines of sight intersect the mirror.

b. Experiment by changing your distance from the mirror, the height of your eyes, and/or the height of the top of your head. Use your results to determine the length of the shortest mirror you can use and where it should be positioned on the wall so that you can see the entire length of your body in the mirror.

a.

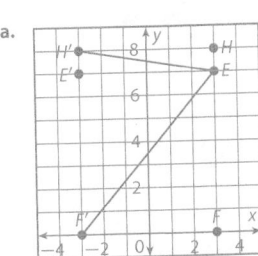

The lines of sight intersect the mirror at the midpoint of $\overline{EH'}$, which is $(0, 7.5)$, and at the midpoint of $\overline{EF'}$, which is $(0, 3.5)$.

b. No matter what values you use for your distance from the mirror, the height of your eyes, and/or the height of the top of your head, the length of the shortest mirror that shows the entire length of your body is one-half your height. For example, in the figure from Part a, the viewer's height is 8 units and the height of the shortest possible mirror is $7.5 - 3.5 = 4$ units. The top of the mirror should be placed halfway between the top of your head and eye level. The bottom of the mirror should be placed halfway between eye level and the bottom of your feet.

© Houghton Mifflin Harcourt Publishing Company · Image Credits: ©Eric Camden/Houghton Mifflin Harcourt

---

INTEGRATE MATHEMATICAL PRACTICES
Focus on Modeling

MP.4 Students may have difficulty understanding the graph they are asked to draw in (a). Each point on the left side of the mirror should be the same distance from the *y*-axis as the corresponding point is from the *x*-axis. Most important in terms of understanding the reflection is that only the portion of the mirror between $(0, 7.5)$ and $(0, 3.5)$ is involved in producing the reflection.

INTEGRATE MATHEMATICAL PRACTICES
Focus on Math Connections

MP.1 The branch of physics called *optics* is the study of the properties and behavior of light. One of the fundamental principles of the field is that when a beam of light strikes a reflective surface, the angle of incidence (the angle of the incoming beam) is congruent to the angle of reflection.

EXTENSION ACTIVITY

Students will need a protractor and a pocket mirror with a flat edge.

1. Draw a line segment $\overline{AB}$ on a piece of paper and line segment $\overline{CD}$ meeting $\overline{AB}$ at D, forming $\angle CDB$.

2. Place the mirror along $\overline{AB}$ so you can see $\overline{C'D}$, the reflection of $\overline{CD}$.

3. Observing $\overline{C'D}$ and placing a straightedge under the mirror, draw $\overline{DE}$, the extension of $\overline{C'D}$.

4. Measure $\angle CDB$ and $\angle EDA$. Suppose a light ray from C struck the mirror at D. Based on your results, at what angle do you think the ray would reflect off the mirror?   **an angle congruent to the angle at which the light ray struck the mirror**

Rotations

Common Core Math Standards

The student is expected to:

 G-CO.A.4

Develop definitions of rotations ... in terms of angles, circles, ... and line segments. Also G-CO.A.2, G-CO.A.5, G-CO.B.6

Mathematical Practices

COMMON CORE **MP.5 Using Tools**

Language Objective

Students work in small groups or pairs to identify and label the transformation shown on a coordinate plane and if a rotation, identify the point of rotation.

ENGAGE

Essential Question: How do you draw the image of a figure under a rotation?

Possible answer: To draw the image of a figure under a rotation of $m°$ around point P, choose a vertex of the figure, for example, vertex A. Draw $\overline{PA}$. Use a protractor to draw a ray that forms an angle of $m°$ with $\overline{PA}$. Use a ruler to mark point A' along the ray so that $PA' = PA$. Repeat the process with the other vertices of the figure. Connect the images of the vertices (A', B', etc.) to draw the image of the figure. If the figure is on a coordinate plane, use an algebraic rule to find the image of each vertex of the figure. Then connect the images of the vertices.

PREVIEW: LESSON PERFORMANCE TASK

View the online Engage. Discuss the motion of the minute hand of the clock with students. Then preview the Lesson Performance Task.

2.3 Rotations

Essential Question: How do you draw the image of a figure under a rotation?

Explore **Exploring Rotations**

You can use geometry software or an online tool to explore rotations.

(A) Draw a triangle and label the vertices A, B, and C. Then draw a point P. Mark P as a center. This will allow you to rotate figures around point P.

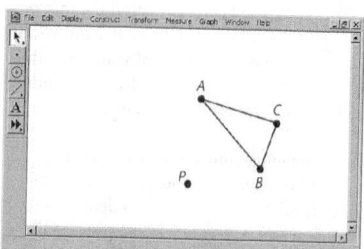

(B) Select $\triangle ABC$ and rotate it 90° around point P. Label the image of $\triangle ABC$ as $\triangle A'B'C'$. Change the shape, size, or location of $\triangle ABC$ and notice how $\triangle A'B'C'$ changes.

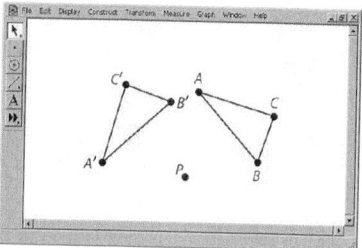

(C) Draw $\angle APA'$, $\angle BPB'$, and $\angle CPC'$. Measure these angles. What do you notice? Does this relationship remain true as you move point P? What happens if you change the size and shape of $\triangle ABC$?

The measure of each angle is 90°; this remains true regardless of the location of point P or the size and shape of $\triangle ABC$.

(D) Measure the distance from A to P and the distance from A' to P. What do you notice? Does this relationship remain true as you move point P? What happens if you change the size and shape of $\triangle ABC$?

$AP = AP'$; this remains true regardless of the location of point P or the size and shape of $\triangle ABC$.

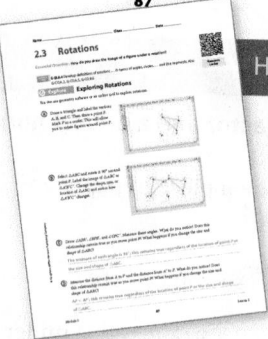

HARDCOVER PAGES 77–88

Turn to these pages to find this lesson in the hardcover student edition.

1. What can you conclude about the distance of a point and its image from the center of rotation?
   A point and its image are both the same distance from the center of rotation.

2. What are the advantages of using geometry software or an online tool rather than tracing paper or a protractor and ruler to investigate rotations?
   Sample answer: Software or an online tool makes it easy to observe the effect of changing the shape or location of the preimage or changing the location of the center of rotation.

✐ Explain 1   Rotating Figures Using a Ruler and Protractor

A **rotation** is a transformation around point P, the **center of rotation**, such that the following is true.

• Every point and its image are the same distance from P.

• All angles with vertex P formed by a point and its image have the same measure. This angle measure is the **angle of rotation**.

In the figure, the center of rotation is point P and the angle of rotation is 110°.

Example 1   Draw the image of the triangle after the given rotation.

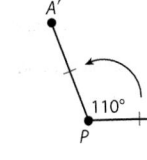

Ⓐ   Counterclockwise rotation of 150° around point P

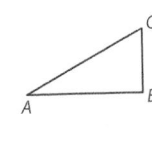

●
P

Step 1 Draw $\overline{PA}$. Then use a protractor to draw a ray that forms a 150° angle with $\overline{PA}$.

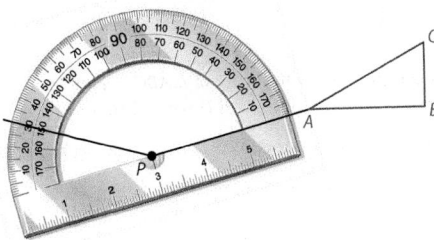

PROFESSIONAL DEVELOPMENT

 Learning Progressions

In this lesson, students extend the informal concept of a rotation as a "turn" to a more precise definition. Rotations are one of the three rigid motions that students study in this module (translations and reflections are the other two). Rotations are somewhat more difficult to draw than the other rigid motions and predicting the effect of a rotation may be more difficult for students than predicting the effect of a reflection or a translation. Geometry software is a useful tool for investigating rotations. Students will need a solid understanding of transformations, including rotations, when they combine transformations to solve real-world problems.

EXPLORE

Exploring Rotations

INTEGRATE TECHNOLOGY

If time permits, students can use the software to experiment with different angles of rotation. In particular, ask students to investigate a 360° angle of rotation. Students should discover that the image of a figure after a 360° rotation coincides exactly with the preimage. Point out that this means a 360° rotation is equivalent to a 0° rotation. Students may also explore angles of rotation greater than 360°. In this case, students should conclude that an equivalent rotation can be found by subtracting 360°(or multiples of 360°) from the angle of rotation.

QUESTIONING STRATEGIES

❓ In what direction does the software rotate figures? How could you use the software to produce a 90° clockwise rotation? Counterclockwise; enter 270° as the angle of rotation.

EXPLAIN 1

Rotating Figures Using a Ruler and Protractor

INTEGRATE MATHEMATICAL PRACTICES
Focus on Math Connections

MP.1 Encourage students to use their knowledge of right angles to visualize rotations. Remind students that a 90° rotation is a quarter turn; a 45° rotation is half that. For example, suggest students visualize what is approximately a triangle after a rotation of 40° around P.

QUESTIONING STRATEGIES

? How can you use tracing paper to check your construction? Trace the figure; place a pencil's point on P, and rotate the paper counterclockwise for the given angle of rotation. The traced version of the figure should lie on top of the rotated figure.

Step 2 Use a ruler to mark point A' along the ray so that $PA' = PA$.

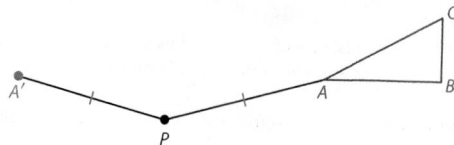

Step 3 Repeat Steps 1 and 2 for points B and C to locate points B' and C'. Connect points A', B', and C' to draw $\triangle A'B'C'$.

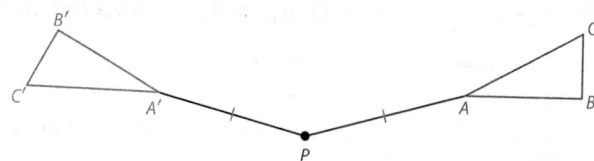

(B) Clockwise rotation of 75° around point Q

Step 1 Draw $\overline{QD}$. Use a protractor to draw a ray forming a clockwise 75° angle with $\overline{QD}$.

Step 2 Use a ruler to mark point D' along the ray so that $QD' = QD$.

Step 3 Repeat Steps1 and 2 for points E and F to locate points E' and F'. Connect points D', E', and F' to draw $\triangle D'E'F'$.

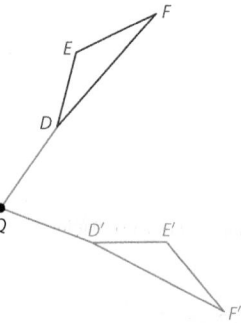

Reflect

3. How could you use tracing paper to draw the image of $\triangle ABC$ in Part A?
Put a piece of tracing paper on the page and trace $\triangle ABC$ and point P. Put the point of a pencil on point P and use a protractor to rotate the tracing paper counterclockwise 150°. Trace over $\triangle ABC$ in the new location, pressing firmly to make an impression on the page below.

COLLABORATIVE LEARNING

Small Group Activity

Have students work in small groups to write together a description of the similarities and differences they observe among the three transformations: translations, reflections, and rotations. Sample answer: All three transformations preserve the size and shape of the original figure. Each transformation uses a different geometric object (vector, line, or point) to perform the transformation. Translations always preserve the orientation of the original figure, while reflections and rotations may alter the orientation.

Draw the image of the triangle after the given rotation.

4. Counterclockwise rotation of 40° around point P **5.** Clockwise rotation of 125° around point Q

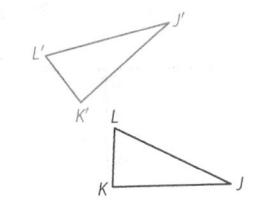

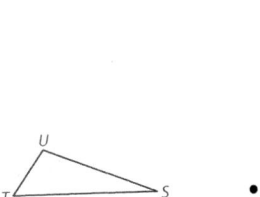

⊘ **Explain 2**   **Drawing Rotations on a Coordinate Plane**

You can rotate a figure by more than 180°. The diagram shows counterclockwise rotations of 120°, 240°, and 300°. Note that a rotation of 360° brings a figure back to its starting location.

When no direction is specified, you can assume that a rotation is counterclockwise. Also, a counterclockwise rotation of $x°$ is the same as a clockwise rotation of $(360 - x)°$.

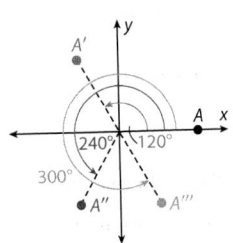

The table summarizes rules for rotations on a coordinate plane.

Rules for Rotations Around the Origin on a Coordinate Plane	
90° rotation counterclockwise	$(x, y) \rightarrow (-y, x)$
180° rotation	$(x, y) \rightarrow (-x, -y)$
270° rotation counterclockwise	$(x, y) \rightarrow (y, -x)$
360° rotation	$(x, y) \rightarrow (x, y)$

Example 2   Draw the image of the figure under the given rotation.

(A)   Quadrilateral $ABCD$; 270°

The rotation image of (x, y) is $(y, -x)$.

Find the coordinates of the vertices of the image.

$A(0, 2) \rightarrow A'(2, 0)$

$B(1, 4) \rightarrow B'(4, -1)$

$C(4, 2) \rightarrow C'(2, -4)$

$D(3, 1) \rightarrow D'(1, -3)$

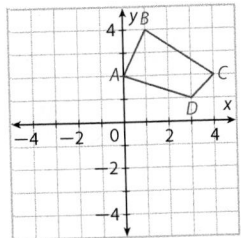

EXPLAIN 2

Drawing Rotations on a Coordinate Plane

QUESTIONING STRATEGIES

? How can you predict the quadrant in which the image of the quadrilateral will lie? Every 90° of rotation moves the preimage around the origin by one quadrant, so a 270° rotation moves the preimage from Quadrant I to Quadrant IV.

? How can you use the rule for rotation to show that the origin is fixed under the rotation? The rule is $(x, y) \rightarrow (y, -x)$, so $(0, 0) \rightarrow (0, 0)$, which shows that the origin is fixed.

AVOID COMMON ERRORS

Some students may confuse the direction of a rotation (clockwise or counterclockwise). Remind students that the direction is assumed to be counterclockwise unless otherwise stated. Associate this default direction with the way the quadrants are numbered.

COMMUNICATING MATH

Students analyze pictures of preimages and images, and discuss what kind of transformation is shown. The group must agree before labeling each picture. If a transformation is identified as a rotation, the group must determine the point of rotation. Each picture should be labeled, and this sentence completed: "This shows a (translation/reflection/rotation) because ———". Provide key terms to help students complete the statement.

Predict the quadrant in which the image will lie. Since quadrilateral $ABCD$ lies in Quadrant I and the quadrilateral is rotated counterclockwise by 270°, the image will lie in Quadrant IV.

Plot A', B', C', and D' to graph the image.

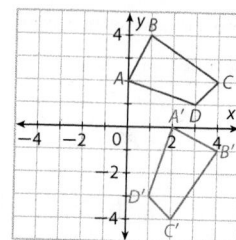

(B) $\triangle KLM$; 180°

The rotation image of (x, y) is $\left(\boxed{-x}, \boxed{-y}\right)$.

Find the coordinates of the vertices of the image.

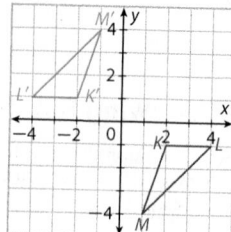

$K(2, -1) \rightarrow K'\left(\boxed{-2}, \boxed{1}\right)$

$L(4, -1) \rightarrow L'\left(\boxed{-4}, \boxed{1}\right)$

$M(1, -4) \rightarrow M'\left(\boxed{-1}, \boxed{4}\right)$

Predict the quadrant in which the image will lie. Since $\triangle KLM$ lies in Quadrant $\underline{IV}$ and the triangle is rotated by 180°, the image will lie in Quadrant $\underline{II}$.

Plot K', L', and M' to graph the image.

Reflect

6. **Discussion** Suppose you rotate quadrilateral $ABCD$ in Part A by 810°. In which quadrant will the image lie? Explain.

   Quadrant II; the quadrilateral $ABCD$ is in Quadrant 1. Every rotation of 360° brings the quadrilateral back to Quadrant I, and since 810° = 360° + 360° + 90°, the 810° rotation is equivalent to a 90° rotation. This maps the quadrilateral to Quadrant II.

© Houghton Mifflin Harcourt Publishing Company

LANGUAGE SUPPORT ᴇʟ

The words *rotation* and *transformation* (as well as *function* and *notation*) are all cognates with Spanish. They contain the same Latin root and have similar spellings and identical meanings. Point out that all these words in English end with *–tion*, and in Spanish they all end with *–ción*. This is a word pattern that may be useful to students who speak English and Spanish.

Your Turn

Draw the image of the figure under the given rotation.

7. △*PQR*; 90°

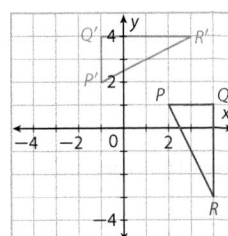

8. Quadrilateral *DEFG*; 270°

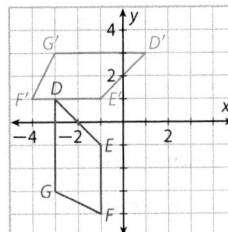

 Explain 3 **Specifying Rotation Angles**

Example 3 Find the angle of rotation and direction of rotation in the given figure. Point *P* is the center of rotation.

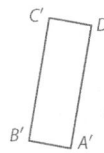 Ⓐ

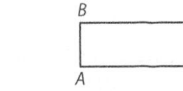

Draw segments from the center of rotation to a vertex and to the image of the vertex.

Measure the angle formed by the segments. The angle measure is 80°.

Compare the locations of the preimage and image to find the direction of the rotation.

The rotation is 80° counterclockwise.

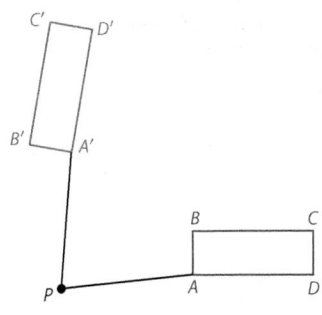

EXPLAIN 3

Specifying Rotation Angles

QUESTIONING STRATEGIES

❓ When a drawing of a rotation shows two figures, how can you tell which is the preimage and which is the image? The vertices of the image will have prime marks, for example, *A*'.

AVOID COMMON ERRORS

Some students may have difficulty identifying the direction of the rotation. Suggest that they visualize *P* as the center of a clock, with the minute hand pointing to a vertex on the preimage. As the minute hand moves to point at the corresponding vertex, which way is it moving (going the shortest way)?

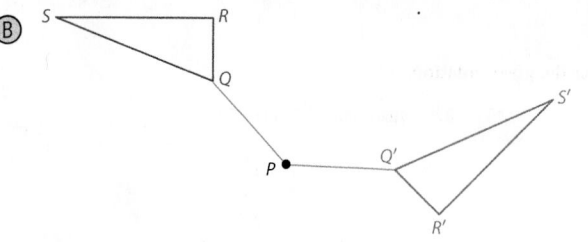

Ⓑ

Draw segments from the center of rotation to a vertex and to the image of the vertex.

Measure the angle formed by the segments.

The angle measure is ⟦ 135 ⟧°.

The rotation is ⟦ 135 ⟧° (clockwise/counterclockwise).

9. **Discussion** Does it matter which points you choose when you draw segments from the center of rotation to points of the preimage and image? Explain.
    No, as long as the points are corresponding points (i.e., a point and its image), the angle of
    rotation will be the same.

10. In Part A, is a different angle of rotation and direction possible? Explain.
    Yes; a rotation of 80° counterclockwise is equivalent to a rotation of 280° clockwise.

Your Turn

Find the angle of rotation and direction of rotation in the given figure. Point _P_ is the center of rotation.

11.

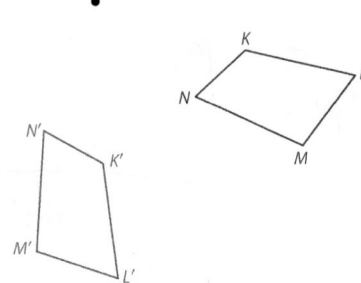

The transformation is a 70° clockwise rotation.

12. If you are given a figure, a center of rotation, and an angle of rotation, what steps can you use to draw the image of the figure under the rotation?

Sample answer: Draw a segment from the center of rotation, P, to one vertex of the

figure, A. Use a protractor to draw a ray that forms an angle with $\overline{PA}$ that is equal to the

angle of rotation. Use a ruler to mark a point along the ray so that $PA' = PA$. Repeat the

process with the other vertices of the figure. Connect the images of the vertices to draw

the image of the figure.

13. Suppose you are given $\triangle DEF$, $\triangle D'E'F'$, and point P. What are two different ways to prove that a rotation around point P cannot be used to map $\triangle DEF$ to $\triangle D'E'F'$?

(1) Show that $PD \neq PD'$, $PE \neq PE'$, or $PF \neq PF'$. (2) Show that $m\angle DPD' \neq m\angle EPE'$,

$m\angle EPE' \neq m\angle FPF'$, or $m\angle DPD' \neq m\angle FPF'$.

14. Essential Question Check-In How do you draw the image of a figure under a counterclockwise rotation of 90° around the origin?

For each vertex of the figure, use the rule $(x, y) \rightarrow (-y, x)$ to find the coordinates of the

image of the vertex. Plot the images of the vertices, then connect these points to draw the

image of the figure.

☆ Evaluate: Homework and Practice

• Online Homework
• Hints and Help
• Extra Practice

1. Alberto uses geometry software to draw $\triangle STU$ and point P, as shown. He marks P as a center and uses the software to rotate $\triangle STU$ 115° around point P. He labels the image of $\triangle STU$ as $\triangle S'T'U'$.

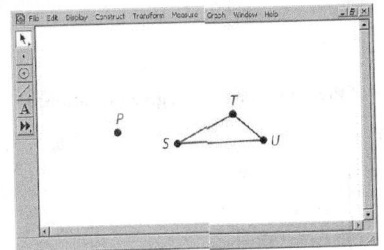

Which three angles must have the same measure? What is the measure of these angles?

$\angle SPS'$, $\angle TPT'$, and $\angle UPU'$; all three angles measure $115°$ since this is the amount by which the triangle was rotated around the point.

Exercise	Depth of Knowledge (D.O.K.)	COMMON CORE Mathematical Practices
1–4	**1** Recall of Information	**MP.5** Using Tools
5–8	**1** Recall of Information	**MP.4** Modeling
9–10	**1** Recall of Information	**MP.5** Using Tools
11–13	**2** Skills/Concepts	**MP.2** Reasoning
14	**2** Skills/Concepts	**MP.3** Logic
15	**2** Skills/Concepts	**MP.2** Reasoning

ELABORATE

QUESTIONING STRATEGIES

? Given a line segment $\overline{WP}$, describe how you would draw $\overline{WP}$ under a rotation of 120° around P. Draw a ray from P that forms a 120° angle with the segment. Mark point W' along this ray such that $WP = W'P$.

SUMMARIZE THE LESSON

? How do you draw the image of a figure under a clockwise rotation of 90° around the origin? For each vertex of the figure, use the rule $(x, y) \rightarrow (y, -x)$ to find the coordinates of the image of the vertex. Plot the images of the vertices; then connect these points to draw the image of the figure.

EVALUATE

ASSIGNMENT GUIDE

Concepts and Skills	Practice
Explore Exploring Rotations	Exercise 1
Example 1 Rotating Figures Using a Ruler and Protractor	Exercises 2–4
Example 2 Drawing Rotations on a Coordinate Plane	Exercises 5–8
Example 3 Specifying Rotation Angles	Exercises 9–10

INTEGRATE MATHEMATICAL PRACTICES

Focus on Communication

MP.3 Remind students that in mapping a figure onto itself, the center of rotation is inside the figure. If students are confused, show a square rotating around a point at its center and a square rotating around a point outside the square. Help students verbalize the difference.

CONNECT VOCABULARY EL

Have students complete a chart like the following vocabulary chart, filling in the blank areas with pictures and words to describe the transformation.

Transformations		
Translation	**Reflection**	**Rotation**
Define or describe:	Define or describe:	Define or describe:
Draw an example:	Draw an example:	Draw an example:

Draw the image of the triangle after the given rotation.

2. Counterclockwise rotation of 30° around point P

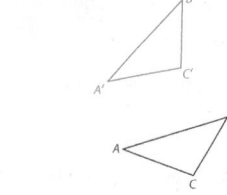

3. Clockwise rotation of 55° around point J

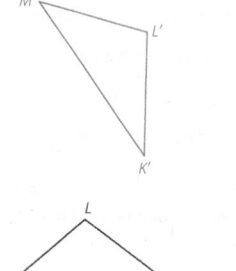

4. Counterclockwise rotation of 90° around point P

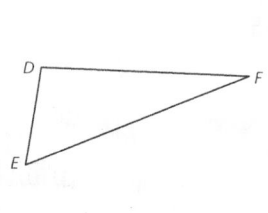

Draw the image of the figure under the given rotation.

5. $\triangle ABC$; 270°

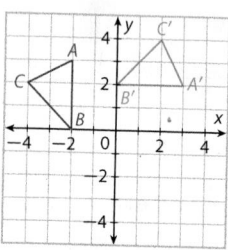

6. $\triangle RST$; 90°

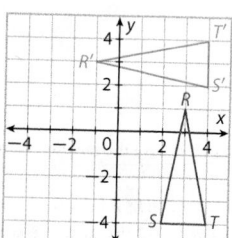

© Houghton Mifflin Harcourt Publishing Company

Exercise	Depth of Knowledge (D.O.K.)	COMMON CORE Mathematical Practices	
16	**2** Skills/Concepts	**MP.2** Reasoning	
17–20	**2** Skills/Concepts	**MP.4** Modeling	
21	**2** Skills/Concepts	**MP.2** Reasoning	
22	**3** Strategic Thinking H.O.T.	**MP.5** Using Tools	
23–24	**3** Strategic Thinking H.O.T.	**MP.3** Logic	
25	**3** Strategic Thinking H.O.T.	**MP.1** Problem Solving	

7. Quadrilateral *EFGH*; 180°

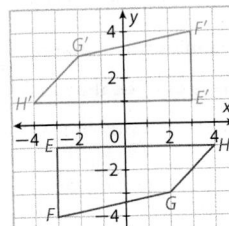

8. Quadrilateral *PQRS*; 270°

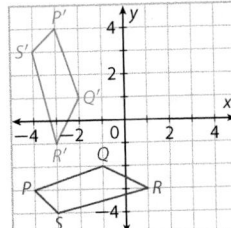

Find the angle of rotation and direction of rotation in the given figure. Point *P* is the center of rotation.

9.

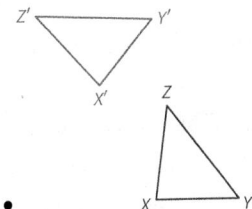

The rotation is 50° counterclockwise.

10.

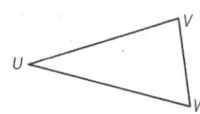

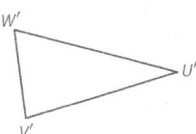

The rotation is 180°.

Write an algebraic rule for the rotation shown. Then describe the transformation in words.

11.

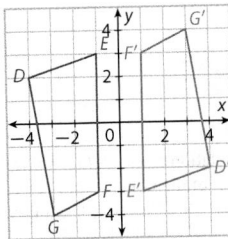

$D(-4, 2) \rightarrow D'(4, -2)$, $E(-1, 3) \rightarrow E'(1, -3)$, $F(-1, -3) \rightarrow F'(1, 3)$, $G(-3, -4) \rightarrow G'(3, 4)$ so the image of (x, y) is $(-x, -y)$. The rule is $(x, y) \rightarrow (-x, -y)$ and the transformation is a rotation of 180°.

12.

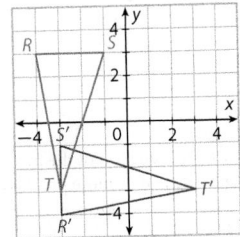

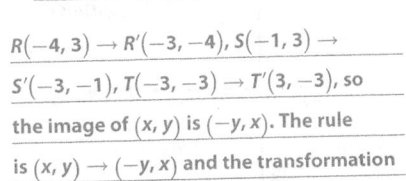

$R(-4, 3) \rightarrow R'(-3, -4)$, $S(-1, 3) \rightarrow$ $S'(-3, -1)$, $T(-3, -3) \rightarrow T'(3, -3)$, so the image of (x, y) is $(-y, x)$. The rule is $(x, y) \rightarrow (-y, x)$ and the transformation is a counterclockwise rotation of 90°.

Lesson 3

© Houghton Mifflin Harcourt Publishing Company

Some students may rotate a figure around its center or around one of its vertices, not around point *P*. Reread the instructions together. Ask students to explain the differences between rotating a figure around an exterior point, around a point on the figure, and around an interior point.

INTEGRATE MATHEMATICAL PRACTICES

Focus on Math Connections

MP.1 Discuss the fact that every rotation can be expressed as a composition of reflections across intersecting lines.

---

13. Vanessa used geometry software to apply a transformation to △ABC, as shown. According to the software, m∠APA′ = m∠BPB′ = m∠CPC′. Vanessa said this means the transformation must be a rotation. Do you agree? Explain.

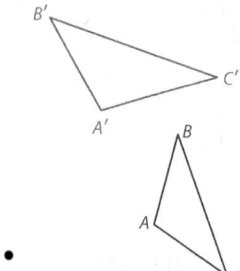

No; according to the definition of a rotation, every point and its image must be the same distance from P, and that is not the case in the given figure.

14. Make a Prediction In which quadrant will the image of △FGH lie after a counterclockwise rotation of 1980°? Explain how you made your prediction.

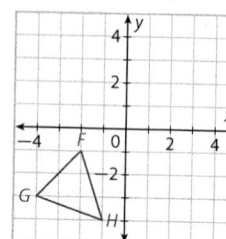

Quadrant I; a rotation of 360° brings the figure back to its original location, so you can subtract multiples of 360° from the angle of rotation. 360° × 5 = 1800° and 1980° − 1800° = 180°, so the rotation is equivalent to a rotation of 180°, which maps △FGH to Quadrant I.

15. Critical Thinking The figure shows the image of △MNP after a counterclockwise rotation of 270°. Draw and label △MNP.

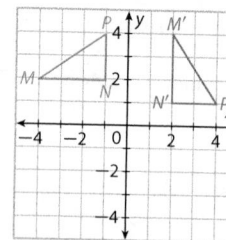

The rule for the rotation is $(x, y) \rightarrow (y, -x)$.

M′ has coordinates $(2, 4)$, so the coordinates of M are $(-4, 2)$.

N′ has coordinates $(2, 1)$, so the coordinates of N are $(-1, 2)$.

P′ has coordinates $(4, 1)$, so the coordinates of P are $(-1, 4)$.

16. Multi-Step Write the equation of the image of line ℓ after a clockwise rotation of 90°. (*Hint*: To find the image of line ℓ, choose two or more points on the line and find the images of the points.)

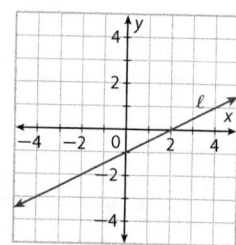

Line ℓ passes through A(2, 0) and B(0, −1). The rule for a clockwise rotation of 90° is $(x, y) \rightarrow (y, -x)$, so $A(2, 0) \rightarrow A′(0, -2)$ and $B(0, -1) \rightarrow B′(-1, 0)$. The line through A′ and B′ has slope $\frac{0 - (-2)}{-1 - 0} = -2$ and y-intercept −2, so the equation of the line is $y = -2x - 2$.

DIFFERENTIATE INSTRUCTION

Modeling

To reinforce the meaning of *rotation*, show some examples of rotations that might be familiar to students—for example, the turn of a steering wheel or Earth's orbit around the sun. Ask students to give other examples of turns or rotations in the real world, such as the motion of a DVD in a player, or of a doorknob. Discuss what all of the motions have in common. Help students see that all involve moving points around a fixed point.

© Houghton Mifflin Harcourt Publishing Company

17. A Ferris wheel has 20 cars that are equally spaced around the circumference of the wheel. The wheel rotates so that the car at the bottom of the ride is replaced by the next car. By how many degrees does the wheel rotate?

18°; there are 360° in a complete rotation

and there are 20 equally-spaced cars, so the

amount of rotation is 360° ÷ 20 = 18°.

18. The Skylon Tower, in Niagara Falls, Canada, has a revolving restaurant 775 feet above the falls. The restaurant makes a complete revolution once every hour. While a visitor was at the tower, the restaurant rotated through 135°. How long was the visitor at the tower?
Set up a proportion.

$$\frac{x}{60} = \frac{135}{360}$$

$$x = 22.5$$

The visitor was at the tower for 22.5 minutes.

19. Amani plans to use drawing software to make the design shown here. She starts by drawing Triangle 1. Explain how she can finish the design using rotations.
Possible answer: Starting with triangle 1, rotate clockwise 60° around

the vertex at the center of the hexagon. Repeat the process using each

successive image as a preimage.

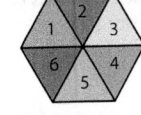

20. An animator is drawing a scene in which a ladybug moves around three mushrooms. The figure shows the starting position of the ladybug. The animator rotates the ladybug 180° around mushroom A, then 180° around mushroom B, and finally 180° around mushroom C. What are the final coordinates of the ladybug?

$(2, -4)$; the 180° rotation around A moves the ladybug from

$(-4, 2)$ to $(0, 2)$; the 180° rotation around B moves the ladybug

from $(0, 2)$ to $(4, 0)$; the 180° rotation around C moves the

ladybug from $(4, 0)$ to $(2, -4)$.

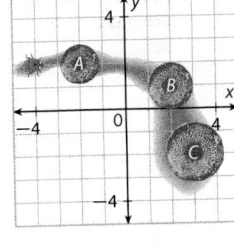

21. Determine whether each statement about the rotation $(x, y) \rightarrow (y, -x)$ is true or false. Select the correct answer for each lettered part.

a. Every point in Quadrant I is mapped to a point in Quadrant II.   ○ True   ● False

b. Points on the x-axis are mapped to points on the y-axis.   ● True   ○ False

c. The origin is a fixed point under the rotation.   ● True   ○ False

d. The rotation has the same effect as a 90° clockwise rotation.   ● True   ○ False

e. The angle of rotation is 180°.   ○ True   ● False

f. A point on the line $y = x$ is mapped to another point on the line $y = x$.   ○ True   ● False

JOURNAL

Have students list some everyday examples of rotations and how they are used, and then describe how a rotation is like the original object and how it is different.

22. **Communicate Mathematical Ideas** Suppose you are given a figure and a center of rotation P. Describe two different ways you can use a ruler and protractor to draw the image of the figure after a 210° counterclockwise rotation around P.

    Possible answer: (1) Use the ruler and protractor to draw a 150° clockwise rotation of the figure. (2) First draw a 180° rotation of the figure. Then draw a 30° counterclockwise rotation of the image.

23. **Explain the Error** Kevin drew the image of $\triangle ABC$ after a rotation of 85° around point P. Explain how you can tell from the figure that he made an error. Describe the error.

    Possible answer: $\triangle A'B'C'$ should be rotated so that B' is at the top of the figure. After correctly locating the image of point A, Kevin translated the figure rather than rotating it.

    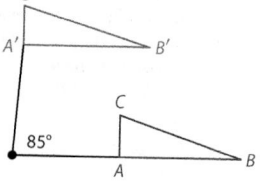

24. **Critique Reasoning** Isabella said that all points turn around the center of rotation by the same angle, so all points move the same distance under a rotation. Do you agree with Isabella's statement? Explain.

    No; although all points rotate through the same angle, points closer to the center of rotation move a shorter distance than points father from the center of rotation.

25. **Look for a Pattern** Isaiah uses software to draw $\triangle DEF$ as shown. Each time he presses the left arrow key, the software rotates the figure on the screen 90° counterclockwise. Explain how Isaiah can determine which quadrant the triangle will lie in if he presses the left arrow key n times.

    Sample answer: Make a table that shows the quadrant the triangle will lie in for various values of n.

    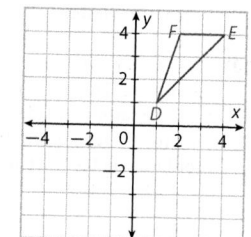

n	1	2	3	4	5	6	7	8
Quadrant	II	III	IV	I	II	III	IV	I

    The remainder after dividing n by 4 defines a pattern for the table.

    A remainder of 0 → QI   A remainder of 2 → QIII

    A remainder of 1 → QII   A remainder of 3 → QIV

Lesson Performance Task

A tourist in London looks up at the clock in Big Ben tower and finds that it is exactly 8:00. When she looks up at the clock later, it is exactly 8:10.

a. Through what angle of rotation did the minute hand turn? Through what angle of rotation did the hour hand turn?

b. Make a table that shows different amounts of time, from 5 minutes to 60 minutes, in 5-minute increments. For each number of minutes, provide the angle of rotation for the minute hand of a clock and the angle of rotation for the hour hand of a clock.

a. A complete rotation around the face of the clock is 360°. The face of the clock is divided into 12 equal parts, each representing 5-minute intervals. So the angle of rotation of the minute hand is $360° \div 12 = 30°$ for every 5 minutes. During an interval of 10 minutes, the angle of rotation of the minute hand is 60°.

In one hour, the hour hand moves from one number on the face of the clock to the next, which is an angle of rotation of 30°. Since an hour is 60 minutes, a 10-minute interval represents $\frac{1}{6}$ of this angle of rotation, or 5°.

b. As above, the angle of rotation of the minute hand is 30° for every 5 minutes. The angle of rotation of the hour hand is 5° for every 10 minutes, or 2.5° for every 5 minutes. Use these values to complete the table below.

Amount of Time (min)	Angle of Rotation, Minute Hand	Angle of Rotation, Hour Hand
5	30°	2.5°
10	60°	5.0°
15	90°	7.5°
20	120°	10.0°
25	150°	12.5°
30	180°	15.0°
35	210°	17.5°
40	240°	20.0°
45	270°	22.5°
50	300°	25.0°
55	330°	27.5°
60	360°	30.0°

EXTENSION ACTIVITY

Big Ben isn't the biggest clock in the world. Have students conduct research to find five clocks bigger than Big Ben. Ask them to present their findings as five congruent circles drawn to scale, with labels detailing the sizes of the clocks, and giving interesting facts about each. Students should include information about the angles formed on each clock as the time changes.

Have students consider how often during a 12-hour period the hour and minute hands of each clock are at a 180° degree angle to each other. They can then calculate or estimate one or more times that this would occur, other than at 6 o'clock.

INTEGRATE MATHEMATICAL PRACTICES
Focus on Reasoning

MP.2 Ask students to look at the table they made for the angles of rotation of the hour hand and minute hand of Big Ben. Ask: "How, if at all, would the table change if you made a similar table for a small pocket watch?" Explain your reasoning. The table would not change. A complete rotation around the face of any clock or any circle, no matter how big or how small, equals 360°. The values in the table are based on that fact, not on the size of the circle.

QUESTIONING STRATEGIES

Have students refer to their angles of rotation tables.

? When the amount of time doubles, how are the angles of rotation affected? They double.

? When the amount of time increases by 15 minutes, how are the angles of rotation affected? The angle of rotation of the minute hand increases by 90°. The angle of rotation of the hour hand increases by 7.5°.

? If you know the angle of rotation of the minute hand, how can you find the angle of rotation of the hour hand? Divide the angle of rotation of the minute hand by 12.

Scoring Rubric

2 points: Student correctly solves the problem and explains his/her reasoning.

1 point: Student shows good understanding of the problem but does not fully solve or explain his/her reasoning.

0 points: Student does not demonstrate understanding of the problem.

Rotations   **100**

Investigating Symmetry

Common Core Math Standards

The student is expected to:

 G-CO.A.3

Given a rectangle, parallelogram, trapezoid, or regular polygon, describe the rotations and reflections that carry it onto itself.

Mathematical Practices

 MP.7 Using Structure

Language Objective

Have students work with a partner to give clues about a figure, and identify whether figures have line symmetry, rotational symmetry, or both and draw the line(s) of symmetry.

ENGAGE

Essential Question: How do you determine whether a figure has line symmetry or rotational symmetry?

Possible answer: To identify line symmetry, look for a line of reflection, which is a line that divides the figure into mirror-image halves. To identify rotational symmetry, think of the figure rotating around its center. The figure has rotational symmetry if a rotation of at most 180° produces the original figure.

PREVIEW: LESSON PERFORMANCE TASK

View the online Engage. Discuss the photo of the flower with students. Consider whether you could turn the flower and have it still appear the same. Then preview the Lesson Performance Task.

2.4 Investigating Symmetry

Essential Question: How do you determine whether a figure has line symmetry or rotational symmetry?

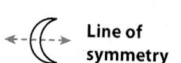
Resource Locker

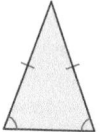 Explore 1 Identifying Line Symmetry

A figure has **symmetry** if a rigid motion exists that maps the figure onto itself. A figure has **line symmetry** (or *reflectional symmetry*) if a reflection maps the figure onto itself. Each of these lines of reflection is called a **line of symmetry**.

 Line of symmetry

You can use paper folding to determine whether a figure has line symmetry.

(A) Trace the figure on a piece of tracing paper.

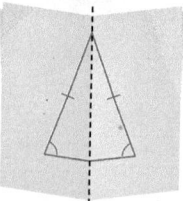

(B) If the figure can be folded along a straight line so that one half of the figure exactly matches the other half, the figure has line symmetry. The crease is the line of symmetry. Place your shape against the original figure to check that each crease is a line of symmetry.

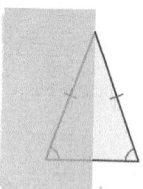

(C) Sketch any lines of symmetry on the figure.

The figure has _____one_____ line of symmetry.

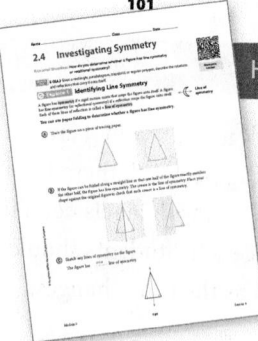

HARDCOVER PAGES 89–96

Turn to these pages to find this lesson in the hardcover student edition.

(D) Draw the lines of symmetry, if any, on each figure and tell the total number of lines of symmetry each figure has.

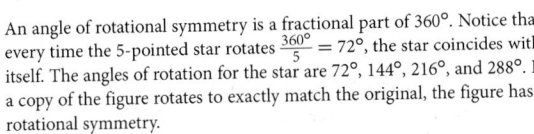

Figure			
How many lines of symmetry?	two	zero	one

Reflect

1. What do you have to know about any segments and angles in a figure to decide whether the figure has line symmetry?
   Pairs of segments in the figure must have the same length and pairs of angles must have the same measure, so that one half of the figure will coincide with the other half when the figure is folded across a line of symmetry.

2. What figure has an infinite number of lines of symmetry? A circle

3. **Discussion** A figure undergoes a rigid motion, such as a rotation. If the figure has line symmetry, does the image of the figure have line symmetry as well? Give an example.
   Yes. The line of symmetry also undergoes the rigid motion. For example, if the L-shape in Step D is rotated into a V-shape, the line of symmetry is rotated the same way.

Explore 2 Identifying Rotational Symmetry

A figure has **rotational symmetry** if a rotation maps the figure onto itself. The **angle of rotational symmetry**, which is greater than 0° but less than or equal to 180°, is the smallest angle of rotation that maps a figure onto itself.

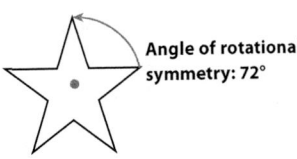

Angle of rotational symmetry: 72°

An angle of rotational symmetry is a fractional part of 360°. Notice that every time the 5-pointed star rotates $\frac{360°}{5} = 72°$, the star coincides with itself. The angles of rotation for the star are 72°, 144°, 216°, and 288°. If a copy of the figure rotates to exactly match the original, the figure has rotational symmetry.

(A) Trace the figure onto tracing paper. Hold the center of the traced figure against the original figure with your pencil. Rotate the traced figure counterclockwise until it coincides again with the original figure beneath.

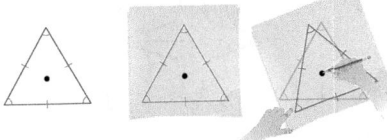

By how many degrees did you rotate the figure? 120°

What are all the angles of rotation? 120°, 240°

102

© Houghton Mifflin Harcourt Publishing Company

PROFESSIONAL DEVELOPMENT

COMMON CORE Math Background

A wallpaper pattern is a planar repeating pattern. Mathematicians classify wallpaper patterns based on the symmetries they exhibit, for example, only translation symmetry; translation and reflection symmetry; or all these plus rotational symmetry. Every wallpaper pattern can be classified by identifying its symmetries. Surprisingly, there are precisely 17 different classifications. That is, any repeating pattern that covers a plane can be reduced to one of 17 basic types. This unusual mathematical fact has had far-reaching applications in a number of fields, including chemistry and crystallography.

EXPLORE 1

Identifying Line Symmetry

INTEGRATE TECHNOLOGY

Have students use geometry software or cut out figures to examine the symmetry of regular polygons. Then have them use inductive reasoning to make conjectures about the number of lines of symmetry a regular n-gon has. n lines of symmetry

QUESTIONING STRATEGIES

? What are the three rigid motions explained in this module? What does a rigid motion transformation preserve? translation, reflection, rotation; shape and size

EXPLORE 2

Identifying Rotational Symmetry

INTEGRATE TECHNOLOGY

Ask students to discuss the pros and cons of using geometry software to investigate properties of rotations and symmetry. Be sure students recognize that such software has the advantage of making it easy to change parameters (such as the angle of rotation) so that they can observe the effects of the changes.

QUESTIONING STRATEGIES

? When you are testing a figure to see if it has rotational symmetry, where is P, the center of rotation? at the center of the figure

Describing Symmetries

INTEGRATE TECHNOLOGY

Human faces appear to have symmetry, but most people's faces aren't perfectly symmetric. Photocopy a picture of a face onto two transparencies and cut each one down the center of the face. Flip the pieces of one transparency over and put the two left sides together and the two right sides together to create two different faces with perfect symmetry. Discuss with students how to tell if a figure has symmetry.

QUESTIONING STRATEGIES

? How can you find the center point of a regular polygon? The center is the point that is equidistant from each vertex or corner.

AVOID COMMON ERRORS

Some students may think that any diagonal of a figure is a line of symmetry. Have them draw a rectangle that is not a square and one of the diagonals. Folding along this diagonal demonstrates that it is not a line of symmetry.

B Determine whether each figure has rotational symmetry. If so, identify all the angles of rotation less than 360°.

Figure	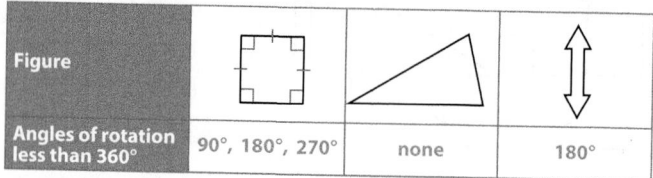		
Angles of rotation less than 360°	90°, 180°, 270°	none	180°

Reflect

4. What figure is mapped onto itself by a rotation of any angle? A circle

5. **Discussion** A figure is formed by line *l* and line *m*, which intersect at an angle of 60°. Does the figure have an angle of rotational symmetry of 60°? If not, what is the angle of rotational symmetry? No, the angle of rotational symmetry for the figure is 180°. A rotation of 60° about the intersection will only map one of the lines onto the other line.

🕐 Explain 1 Describing Symmetries

A figure may have line symmetry, rotational symmetry, both types of symmetry, or no symmetry.

Example 1 Describe the symmetry of each figure. Draw the lines of symmetry, name the angles of rotation, or both if the figure has both.

(A)

Step 1 Begin by finding the line symmetry of the figure. Look for matching halves of the figure. For example, you could fold the left half over the right half, and fold the top half over the bottom half. Draw one line of symmetry for each fold. Notice that the lines intersect at the center of the figure.

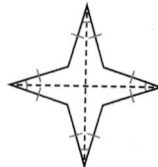

COLLABORATIVE LEARNING

Small Group Activity

Have students identify common shapes that do *not* have line symmetry, for example, the capital letters F, G, and J. Have students name a letter of the alphabet with each type of symmetry:

• one line of symmetry (horizontal) B C D E
• one line of symmetry (vertical) A M T U V W Y
• two lines of symmetry H I O X
• rotational symmetry but not line symmetry N S Z
• no symmetry F G J K L P Q R

Step 2 Now look for other lines of symmetry. The two diagonals also describe matching halves. The figure has a total of 4 lines of symmetry.

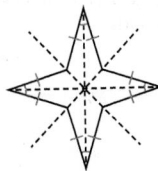

Step 3 Next, look for rotational symmetry. Think of the figure rotated about its center until it matches its original position. The angle of rotational symmetry of this figure is $\frac{1}{4}$ of 360°, or 90°.

The other angles of rotation for the figure are the multiples of 90° that are less than 360°. So the angles of rotation are 90°, 180°, and 270°.

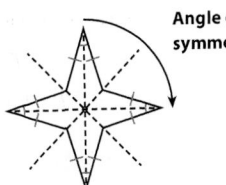

Angle of rotational symmetry: 90°

Number of lines of symmetry: 4   Angles of rotation: 90°, 180°, 270° _____

 B

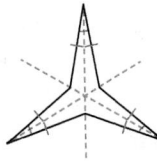

Step 1 Look for lines of symmetry. One line divides the figure into left and right halves. Draw this line on the figure. Then draw similar lines that begin at the other vertices of the figure.

Step 2 Now look for rotational symmetry. Think of the figure rotating about its center until it matches the original figure. It rotates around the circle by a

fraction of ____$\frac{1}{3}$____. Multiply by 360° to find the angle of rotation,

which is ____120°____. Find multiples of this angle to find other angles

of rotation.

Number of lines of symmetry: ____3____   Angles of rotation: ____120°, 240°____

© Houghton Mifflin Harcourt Publishing Company

CONNECT VOCABULARY EL

Connect the idea of a *reflection* to a figure with *line symmetry*. If you identify the line of symmetry on the figure, and superimpose that line on the *x*- or *y*-axis on a coordinate plane, then the line of symmetry becomes the line of reflection, and you can see the image and preimage on either side.

LANGUAGE SUPPORT EL

Connect Vocabulary

In English and in Spanish, we usually add –s or –es to the end of a noun to form the plural, for example, *triangles, points, figures*. In English, some nouns are irregular and don't follow that convention. The plural form of the noun *vertex* is *vertices*. Notice that the *x* becomes a *c* and then –es is added to form this plural. In Spanish, the same thing happens with words that end in *z*. The *z* becomes a *c* and then –es is added to form the plural.

ELABORATE

INTEGRATE MATHEMATICAL PRACTICES
Focus on Communication

MP.3 The number of angles of rotation less than 360° is called the *order* of the rotational symmetry, so a square is of order 3 and an equilateral triangle is of order 2. A five-pointed star is of order 4.

INTEGRATE MATHEMATICAL PRACTICES
Focus on Reasoning

MP.2 Give students pictures of figures or objects that have line symmetry, rotational symmetry, both, or neither. Students get two sets of each figure. One set of pictures is placed face up between the pair of students and one set is face down. The first student draws a card, such as the picture of a square, and gives oral clues such as, "This figure has both rotational symmetry and line symmetry. Its angle of rotation is 90 degrees; it has 4 sides and 4 angles; and has 4 lines of symmetry." The second student picks the picture that matches the clues. They switch roles and repeat the process.

SUMMARIZE THE LESSON

? How do you determine whether a figure has line symmetry or rotational symmetry? A figure has line symmetry if the figure can be reflected across a line so that the image coincides with the preimage. A figure has rotational symmetry if the figure can be rotated about a point by an angle greater than 0° and less than or equal to 180° so that the image coincides with the preimage.

Describe the type of symmetry for each figure. Draw the lines of symmetry, name the angles of rotation, or both if the figure has both.

6. Figure *ABCD*

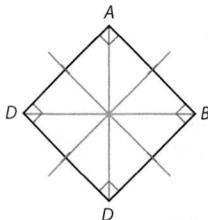

Types of symmetry: ___line, rotational___

Number of lines of symmetry: ___4___

Angles of rotation: ___90°, 180°, 270°___

7. Figure *EFGHI*

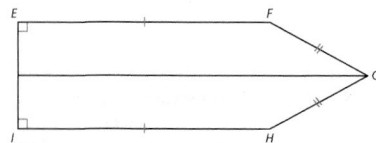

Types of symmetry: ___line___

Number of lines of symmetry: ___1___

Angles of rotation: ___none___

8. Figure *KLNPR*

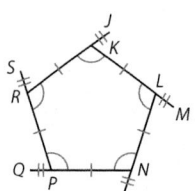

Types of symmetry: ___rotational___

Number of lines of symmetry: ___0___

Angles of rotation: ___72°, 144°, 216° and 288°___

9. Figure *TUVW*

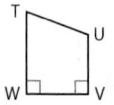

Types of symmetry: ___none___

Number of lines of symmetry: ___0___

Angles of rotation: ___none___

💬 Elaborate

10. How are the two types of symmetry alike? How are they different?
Both types of symmetry show how a figure can be mapped onto itself by a rigid motion. In line symmetry, the figure is mapped onto itself by reflection, and in rotational symmetry, the mapping is by rotation.

11. Essential Question Check-In How do you determine whether a figure has line symmetry or rotational symmetry?
Possible answer: To identify line symmetry, look for a line of reflection that divides the figure into mirror-image halves. To identify rotational symmetry, think of the figure rotating around its center. The figure has rotational symmetry if a rotation of at most 180° produces the original figure.

© Houghton Mifflin Harcourt Publishing Company

DIFFERENTIATE INSTRUCTION

Modeling

Bring in books or suggest websites that show examples of mandalas. Have students find and describe examples of rotational symmetry in each. Have them create an original mandala.

- Online Homework
- Hints and Help
- Extra Practice

Draw all the lines of symmetry for the figure, and give the number of lines of symmetry. If the figure has no line symmetry, write zero.

1.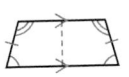

Lines of symmetry: ___1___

2.

Lines of symmetry: ___8___

3.

Lines of symmetry: ___1___

For the figures that have rotational symmetry, list the angles of rotation less than 360°. For figures without rotational symmetry, write "no rotational symmetry."

4.

Angles of rotation: no rotational symmetry

5.

Angles of rotation: 45°, 90°, 135°, 180°, 225°, 270°, 315°

6.

Angles of rotation: no rotational symmetry

In the tile design shown, identify whether the pattern has line symmetry, rotational symmetry, both line and rotational symmetry, or no symmetry.

7.

rotational symmetry

8.

both line and rotational symmetry

For figure *ABCDEF* shown here, identify the image after each transformation described. For example, a reflection across $\overline{AD}$ has an image of figure *AFEDCB*. In the figure, all the sides are the same length and all the angles are the same measure.

9. Reflection across $\overline{CF}$

Figure ___EDCBAF___

10. rotation of 240° clockwise, or 120° counterclockwise

Figure ___CDEFAB___

11. reflection across the line that connects the midpoint of $\overline{BC}$ and the midpoint of $\overline{EF}$

Figure ___DCBAFE___

Exercise	Depth of Knowledge (D.O.K.)	COMMON CORE Mathematical Practices
1	**1** Recall of Information	**MP.4** Modeling
2	**2** Skills/Concepts	**MP.4** Modeling
3–4	**1** Recall of Information	**MP.4** Modeling
5	**2** Skills/Concepts	**MP.4** Modeling
6	**1** Recall of Information	**MP.4** Modeling
7–8	**2** Skills/Concepts	**MP.4** Modeling

EVALUATE

ASSIGNMENT GUIDE

Concepts and Skills	Practice
Explore 1 Identifying Line Symmetry	Exercises 1–3
Explore 2 Identifying Rotational Symmetry	Exercises 4–6
Example 1 Describing Symmetries	Exercises 7–16

INTEGRATE MATHEMATICAL PRACTICES

Focus on Math Connections

MP.1 It is also possible to define a symmetry based on translations. A pattern has translation symmetry if it can be translated along a vector so that the image coincides with the preimage. Tiled floors may be examples of this.

AVOID COMMON ERRORS

Some students may stop when they have found one line of symmetry or one angle of rotation. Remind them to reread the directions to see if they are asked to find *all* lines of symmetry or *all* angles of rotation.

JOURNAL

Have students create four different, simple logos. For the first logo, there should be no rotations that map the logo onto itself. For the second, a rotation of 180° should map the logo onto itself; for the third, 120°; and for the fourth, 90°.

In the space provided, sketch an example of a figure with the given characteristics.   Possible answers are shown.

12. no line symmetry; angle of rotational symmetry: 180°

13. one line of symmetry; no rotational symmetry

14. Describe the line and rotational symmetry in this figure.

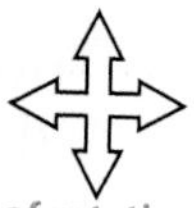

four lines of symmetry; angle of rotational symmetry: 90°

H.O.T. Focus on Higher Order Thinking

15. Communicate Mathematical Ideas How is a rectangle similar to an ellipse? Use concepts of symmetry in your answer.

Both have two perpendicular lines of symmetry, and both have 180° rotational symmetry.

16. Explain the Error A student was asked to draw all of the lines of symmetry on each figure shown. Identify the student's work as correct or incorrect. If incorrect, explain why.

a.

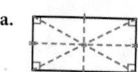

Incorrect; the two diagonals are not lines of symmetry.

b.

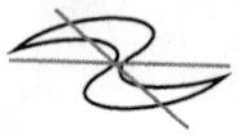

Incorrect; the figure has no lines of symmetry.

c.

Incorrect; the figure has three more lines of symmetry, each connecting the remaining pairs of opposite vertices.

Exercise	Depth of Knowledge (D.O.K.)	COMMON CORE Mathematical Practices
9–11	**2** Skills/Concepts	**MP.2** Reasoning
12–13	**2** Skills/Concepts	**MP.4** Modeling
14	**3** Strategic Thinking H.O.T.	**MP.4** Modeling
15	**2** Skills/Concepts H.O.T.	**MP.6** Precision
16	**3** Strategic/Thinking H.O.T.	**MP.5** Using Tools

Lesson Performance Task

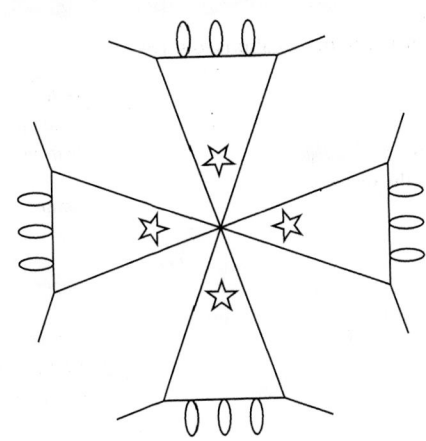

Use symmetry to design a work of art. Begin by drawing one simple geometric figure, such as a triangle, square, or rectangle, on a piece of construction paper. Then add other lines or two-dimensional shapes to the figure. Next, make identical copies of the figure, and then arrange them in a symmetric pattern.

Evaluate the symmetry of the work of art you created. Rotate it to identify an angle of rotational symmetry. Compare the line symmetry of the original figure with the line symmetry of the finished work.

Answers will vary. Students' responses should identify all lines of symmetry (horizontal, vertical, and diagonal) as well as all angles of rotational symmetry (90°, 180°, and 270°).

AVOID COMMON ERRORS

In evaluating rectangular shapes for symmetries, students sometimes identify the diagonals as lines of symmetry. Unless a rectangle is a square, its diagonals are not lines of symmetry.

INTEGRATE MATHEMATICAL PRACTICES
Focus on Critical Thinking

MP.3 Students should recognize that while single elements of their designs might exhibit symmetries, those symmetries might not extend to the entire design.

For example, in a design composed of a square and four isosceles triangles, each of those shapes contains lines of symmetry. None of those lines, however, is a line of symmetry for the entire design.

EXTENSION ACTIVITY

The flags of many nations have rotational symmetry or line symmetry. The flags of a few nations, such as Jamaica, have both. Research the flags of the nations of the world to find examples of symmetry. If you wish, disregard color and concentrate only on the designs of the flags. Draw or print out examples of designs you find especially interesting or attractive.

Scoring Rubric
2 points: Student correctly solves the problem and explains his/her reasoning.
1 point: Student shows good understanding of the problem but does not fully solve or explain his/her reasoning.
0 points: Student does not demonstrate understanding of the problem.

Investigating Symmetry   **108**

Study Guide Review

ASSESSMENT AND INTERVENTION

Assign or customize module reviews.

MODULE PERFORMANCE TASK

COMMON CORE

Mathematical Practices: MP.1, MP.4, MP.8
G-CO.A.2, G-CO.A.5, G-CO.B.6, G-MG.A.1

SUPPORTING STUDENT REASONING

Students should begin this problem by focusing on the transformations needed to simulate movement in the coordinate plane. Here are some issues they might bring up.

- **What movements the bird made:** Sample answer: translations up, rotations of 90° clockwise, translations down and to the right, translations to the right

- **How to represent the movements with coordinates:** Make a table showing the coordinates after every transformation.

- **If some images include more than one transformation:** Yes, some images can be a composition of a rotation and a translation, as is done with the second and third sets of coordinates in the sample answer.

- **How to perform the series of transformations:** Sample answer: draw the new position of the figure, give its coordinates, and then describe the composition of transformations needed to find the image figure.

Essential Question: How can you use transformations to solve real-world problems?

KEY EXAMPLE   (Lesson 2.1)

Translate the square $ABCD$ along the vector $\langle 2, 1 \rangle$.

$A(1, 2), B(3, 2), C(1, 4), D(3, 4)$.

$(x, y) \rightarrow (x + a, y + b)$ Write the rule for translation along the vector $\langle a, b \rangle$.

$A(1, 2) \rightarrow A'(1 + 2, 2 + 1)$ Apply the rule to each point.

$B(3, 2) \rightarrow B'(3 + 2, 2 + 1)$

$C(1, 4) \rightarrow C'(1 + 2, 4 + 1)$

$D(3, 4) \rightarrow D'(3 + 2, 4 + 1)$

$A'(3, 3), B'(5, 3),$ Now simplify.

$C'(3, 5), D'(5, 5)$

KEY EXAMPLE   (Lesson 2.2)

Determine the vertices of the image of $\triangle ABC$.

$A(2, 3), B(3, 4),$ and $C(3, 1)$ reflected across the line $y = x$.

$(x, y) \rightarrow (y, x)$ Write the rule for reflection across the line $y = x$.

$A(2, 3), A'(3, 2)$ Apply the rule to each point.

$B(3, 4), B'(4, 3)$

$C(3, 1), C'(1, 3)$

KEY EXAMPLE   (Lesson 2.3)

Determine the vertices of the image of $\triangle DFE$.

$D(1, 2), F(2, 2),$ and $E(2, 0)$, rotated 270° counterclockwise about the origin.

$(x, y) \rightarrow (y, -x)$ Write the rule for a rotation 270° counterclockwise.

$D(1, 2), \rightarrow D'(2, -1)$ Apply the rule to each point.

$F(2, 2), \rightarrow F'(2, -2)$

$E(2, 0), \rightarrow E'(0, -2)$

Key Vocabulary

vector *(vector)*
initial point *(punto inicial)*
terminal point *(punto terminal)*
translation *(translación)*
perpendicular lines *(líneas perpendiculares)*
perpendicular bisector *(mediatriz)*
reflection *(reflexión)*
rotation *(rotación)*
center of rotation *(centro de rotación)*
angle of rotation *(ángulo de rotación)*
symmetry *(simetría)*
line symmetry *(simetría de línea)*
line of symmetry *(línea de simetría)*
rotational symmetry *(simetría rotacional)*
angle of rotational symmetry *(ángulo de simetría rotacional)*

SCAFFOLDING SUPPORT

- Students may find it useful to cut out a set of triangles congruent to the given triangle and place them on the graph to plan the flight of the bird. Students can use the triangles as patterns to trace the successive positions of the bird.

- Explain that it is fine if the triangles overlap from one triangle to the next.

- Encourage students to be creative in their flight plans. The general outline is "exit the perch, swoop down and right, then off to the right," but students can add interesting movements to the basic plan if they wish.

EXERCISES

Translate each figure along each vector. *(Lesson 2.1)*

1. The line segment determined by $A(4, 7)$ and $B(2, 9)$ along $\langle 0, -2 \rangle$.
The endpoints of the image are _____ $A'(4, 5), B'(2, 7)$ _____.

2. The triangle determined by $A(-3, 2)$, $B(4, 4)$, and $C(1, 1)$ along $\langle -1, -3 \rangle$.
The vertices of the image are _____ $A'(-4, -1), B'(3, 1), C'(0, -2)$ _____.

Determine the vertices of each image. *(Lesson 2.2)*

3. The image of the rectangle $ABCD$ reflected across the line $y = -x$.
$A(-3, 2), B(3, 2), C(-3, -3), D(3, -3)$
The vertices of the image are _____ $A'(-2, 3), B'(-2, -3), C'(3, 3), D'(3, -3)$ _____.

4. The image of the polygon $ABCDE$ reflected across the x-axis.
$A(-1, -1), B(0, 1), C(4, 2), D(6, 0), E(3, -3)$
The vertices of the image are _____ $A'(-1, 1), B'(0, -1), C'(4, -2), D'(6, 0), E'(3, 3)$ _____.

Determine the vertices of the image. *(Lesson 2.3)*

5. The figure defined by $A(3, 5)$, $B(5, 3)$, $C(2, 2)$ rotated 180° counterclockwise about the origin.
The points of the image are _____ $A'(-3, -5), B'(-5, -3), C'(-2, -2)$ _____.

MODULE PERFORMANCE TASK

Animating Digital Images

A computer animator is designing an animation in which a bird flies off its perch, swoops down and to the right, and then flies off the right side of the screen. The graph shows the designer's preliminary sketch, using a triangle to represent the bird in its initial position (top) and one intermediate position.

Plan a series of rotations and translations to animate the flight of the bird. Sketch each rotation and translation on a graph and label the coordinates of the triangle's vertices at each position. If you wish, you can test out how well your animation works by making a flipbook of your graphs.

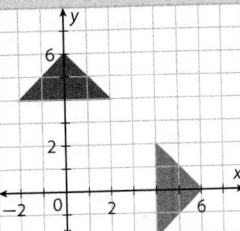

DISCUSSION OPPORTUNITIES

- Can the transformations be done in the same way but explained differently? How can you verify this?

- Why did you need to represent the triangle's movement as a series of individual transformations, instead of a single composition of transformations?

One transformation would not work for animation, because intermediate positions need to be shown.

SAMPLE SOLUTION

1. translation $(x, y) \rightarrow (x, y + 2)$:

   $(0, 6), (-2, 4), (2, 4)$ to $(0, 8), (-2, 6), (2, 6)$

2. 90° clockwise rotation about $(0, 6)$:

   $(0, 8), (-2, 6), (2, 6)$ to $(2, 6), (0, 8), (0, 4)$

3. translation $(x, y) \rightarrow (x + 4, y)$:

   $(2, 6), (0, 8), (0, 4)$ to $(6, 6), (4, 8), (4, 4)$

4. translation $(x, y) \rightarrow (x, y - 6)$:

   $(6, 6), (4, 8), (4, 4)$ to $(6, 0), (4, 2), (4, -2)$

Assessment Rubric

2 points: Student correctly solves the problem and explains his/her reasoning.

1 point: Student shows good understanding of the problem but does not fully solve or explain.

0 points: Student does not demonstrate understanding of the problem.

Ready to Go On?

ASSESS MASTERY

Use the assessment on this page to determine if students have mastered the concepts and standards covered in this module.

ASSESSMENT AND INTERVENTION

Access Ready to Go On? assessment online, and receive instant scoring, feedback, and customized intervention or enrichment.

ADDITIONAL RESOURCES

Response to Intervention Resources

- Reteach Worksheets

Differentiated Instruction Resources

- Reading Strategies **EL**
- Success for English Learners **EL**
- Challenge Worksheets

Assessment Resources

- Leveled Module Quizzes

(Ready) to Go On?

Transformations and Symmetry

- Online Homework
- Hints and Help
- Extra Practice

1. Line segment $\overline{YZ}$ was used to translate $ABCDE$. $\overline{YZ}$ is 6.2 inches long. What is the length of $AA' + BB' + CC' + DD' + EE'$?

31 inches

Given figure *FGHI* and its image *F′G′H′I′*, answer the following.

2a. Write an algebraic rule for the rotation shown and then describe the rotation in words.

$F(-10, 6) \rightarrow F'(10, -6)$, $G(-6, 9) \rightarrow G'(6, -9)$, $H(-3, 5) \rightarrow H'(3, -5)$, $I(-7, 2) \rightarrow I'(7, -2)$, The rule is $(x, y) \rightarrow (-x, -y)$, and the transformation is a rotation of $180°$.

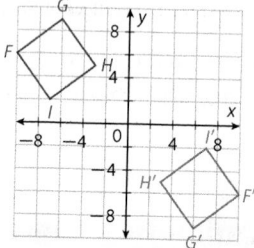

2b. Tell whether the figure *FGHI* has line symmetry, rotational symmetry, both types of symmetry, or no symmetry. If the figure has line symmetry, record the number. If the figure has rotational symmetry, list the angles of rotation that are less than 360°.

Types of symmetry	Number of lines of symmetry	Angles of rotation
line, rotational	4	90°, 180°, 270°

3. Given triangle ABC with $A(-2, 4)$, $B(-2, 1)$, and $C(-4, 0)$, and its image $A'B'C'$ with $A'(2, 0)$, $B'(-1, 0)$, and $C'(-2, -2)$, find the line of reflection.

$y = x + 2$

Essential Question

4. In which situations are translations useful for transformations? Reflections? Rotations?

Answers may vary. Sample: Translations are useful when shifting the points of an image along the same direction and length, reflections are useful when mirroring an image across a line, and rotations are useful when shifting an image around a fixed point.

Common Core Standards

Lesson	Items	Content Standards	Mathematical Practices
2.1	1	G-CO.A.4	MP.4
2.3, 2.4	2	G-CO.A.4, G-CO.A.2, G-CO.A.5, G-CO.A.6	MP.7
2.2	3	G-CO.A.4, G-CO.A.5, G-CO.A.6	MP.4

Assessment Readiness

1. Triangle *ABC* is given by the points $A(-1, 5)$, $B(0, 3)$, and $C(2, 4)$. It is reflected over the line $y = -2x - 2$. Does the image contain each of the points?

   Select Yes or No for A–C.

   A. $A'(-5, 3)$ ● Yes   ○ No

   B. $B'(-4, 6)$ ○ Yes   ● No

   C. $C'(-6, 0)$ ● Yes   ○ No

2. A triangle, $\triangle ABC$, is rotated 90° counterclockwise, reflected across the *x*-axis, and then reflected across the *y*-axis. Choose True or False for each statement.

   A. Rotating $\triangle ABC$ 180° clockwise is an equivalent transformation.   ○ True   ● False

   B. Rotating $\triangle ABC$ 270° counterclockwise is an equivalent transformation.   ● True   ○ False

   C. Reflecting $\triangle ABC$ across the *y*-axis is an equivalent transformation.   ○ True   ● False

3. Choose True or False for each statement about equilateral triangles.

   A. An equilateral triangle has 3 equal angle measures.   ● True   ○ False

   B. An equilateral triangle has 3 equal side measures.   ● True   ○ False

   C. An equilateral triangle has 3 lines of symmetry.   ● True   ○ False

4. A line segment with points $P(1, 2)$ and $Q(4, 3)$ is reflected across the line $y = x$. What are the new coordinates of the points of the line segment?

   $P'(2, 1)$, $Q'(3, 4)$

5. Draw on the figure all lines of symmetry and explain why those lines are the lines of symmetry. Give all angles of rotational symmetry less than 360°.

   Answers may vary. Sample: Because when the figure is folded along the lines, one half coincides with the other. The angles of rotational symmetry are 72°, 144°, 216°, and 288°.

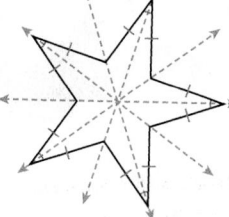

MIXED REVIEW
Assessment Readiness

ASSESSMENT AND INTERVENTION

Assign ready-made or customized practice tests to prepare students for high-stakes tests.

ADDITIONAL RESOURCES

Assessment Resources

- Leveled Module Quizzes: Modified, B

AVOID COMMON ERRORS

Item 4   Some students will follow the rule for reflecting over the *x*- or *y*-axis when trying to reflect over the line $y = x$. Remind students that they can graph the points and the line $y = x$ on graph paper, and then fold the paper along the line of symmetry to see where the points will land.

MODULE 2

COMMON CORE | Common Core Standards

Lesson	Items	Content Standards	Mathematical Practices
2.2	1	G-CO.A.3	MP.5
2.2, 2.3, 1.3	2*	G-CO.B.6	MP.5
2.4, 1.2	3*	G-CO.A.5, G-CO.A.1	MP.5
2.2	4	G-CO.B.6	MP.7
2.4	5	G-CO.A.5	MP.6

* Item integrates mixed review concepts from previous modules or a previous course.

Congruent Figures

ESSENTIAL QUESTION:

Answer: The principles of congruency can be used to establish whether two objects in the real world are the same shape or not.

PROFESSIONAL DEVELOPMENT VIDEO

Professional Development Video

 Author Juli Dixon models successful teaching practices in an actual high-school classroom.

Professional Development
my.hrw.com

Congruent Figures

MODULE 3

Essential Question: How can you use congruency to solve real-world problems?

LESSON 3.1
Sequences of Transformations

LESSON 3.2
Proving Figures Are Congruent Using Rigid Motions

LESSON 3.3
Corresponding Parts of Congruent Figures Are Congruent

© Houghton Mifflin Harcourt Publishing Company • Image Credits: (t) ©Scott E. Feuer/Shutterstock; (b) ©HildaBright/Shutterstock

REAL WORLD VIDEO
Check out how landscape architects use transformations of geometric shapes to design green space for parks and homes.

MODULE PERFORMANCE TASK PREVIEW

Jigsaw Puzzle

In this module, you will use congruency and a series of transformations to solve a portion of a jigsaw puzzle. What is some of the basic geometry behind a jigsaw puzzle? Let's get started on finding out how all the pieces fit together!

Module 3   113

DIGITAL TEACHER EDITION

Access a full suite of teaching resources when and where you need them:

- Access content online or offline
- Customize lessons to share with your class
- Communicate with your students in real-time
- View student grades and data instantly to target your instruction where it is needed most

PERSONAL MATH TRAINER
Assessment and Intervention

Assign automatically graded homework, quizzes, tests, and intervention activities. Prepare your students with updated, Common Core-aligned practice tests.

Are YOU Ready?

Complete these exercises to review skills you will need for this module.

• Online Homework
• Hints and Help
• Extra Practice

Properties of Reflections

Example 1

Find the points that define the reflection of the figure given by $A(1, 1)$, $B(2, 3)$, and $C(3, 1)$ across the y-axis.

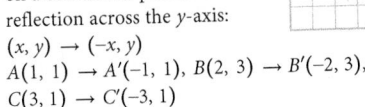

Use the rules for reflections on a coordinate plane. For a reflection across the y-axis:

$(x, y) \rightarrow (-x, y)$
$A(1, 1) \rightarrow A'(-1, 1)$, $B(2, 3) \rightarrow B'(-2, 3)$,
$C(3, 1) \rightarrow C'(-3, 1)$

Find the vertices of the reflected figure.

1. $\triangle ABC$ reflected across the x-axis $A'(1, -1)$, $B'(2, -3)$, $C'(3, -1)$

2. $\triangle ABC$ reflected across $y = x$ $A'(1, 1)$, $B'(3, 2)$, $C'(1, 3)$

Properties of Rotations

Example 2

Find the vertices of $\triangle ABC$ rotated 90° counterclockwise around the origin.

$(x, y) \rightarrow (-y, x)$ Write the rule for rotation.

$A(1, 1) \rightarrow A'(-1, 1)$, $B(2, 3) \rightarrow B'(-3, 2)$,

$C(3, 1) \rightarrow C'(-1, 3)$ Apply the rule.

Find the vertices of the rotated figure.

3. $\triangle ABC$ rotated 180° around the origin $A'(-1, -1)$, $B'(-2, -3)$, $C'(-3, -1)$

Properties of Translations

Example 3

Calculate the vertices of the image of $\triangle ABC$ translated using the rule $(x, y) \rightarrow (x + 2, y + 1)$.

$A(1, 1) \rightarrow A'(3, 2)$, $B(2, 3) \rightarrow B'(4, 4)$,

$C(3, 1) \rightarrow C'(5, 2)$ Apply the rule.

Calculate the vertices of the image.

4. $\triangle ABC$ translated using the rule $(x, y) \rightarrow (x - 2, y + 2)$ $A'(-1, 3)$, $B'(0, 5)$, $C'(1, 3)$

Are You Ready?

ASSESS READINESS

Use the assessment on this page to determine if students need strategic or intensive intervention for the module's prerequisite skills.

ASSESSMENT AND INTERVENTION

TIER 1, TIER 2, TIER 3 SKILLS

Personal Math Trainer will automatically create a standards-based, personalized intervention assignment for your students, targeting each student's individual needs!

ADDITIONAL RESOURCES

See the table below for a full list of intervention resources available for this module.

Response to Intervention Resources also includes:

- Tier 2 Skill Pre-Tests for each Module
- Tier 2 Skill Post-Tests for each skill

Response to Intervention			Differentiated Instruction
Tier 1 Lesson Intervention Worksheets	**Tier 2** Strategic Intervention Skills Intervention Worksheets	**Tier 3** Intensive Intervention Worksheets available online	
Reteach 3.1 Reteach 3.2 Reteach 3.3	7 Congruent Figures 17 Properties of Reflections 18 Properties of Rotations 19 Properties of Translations	Building Block Skills 8, 16, 46, 48, 53, 56, 74, 98, 102, 103	Challenge worksheets Extend the Math Lesson Activities in TE

Sequences of Transformations

Common Core Math Standards

The student is expected to:

 G-CO.A.5

... Specify a sequence of transformations that will carry a given figure onto another. Also G-CO.A.2, G-CO.B.6

Mathematical Practices

 MP.5 Using Tools

Language Objective

Explain to a partner why a transformation or sequence of transformations is rigid or nonrigid.

ENGAGE

Essential Question: What happens when you apply more than one transformation to a figure?

Possible answer: The transformations occur sequentially, and order matters. The result may be the same as a single transformation.

PREVIEW: LESSON PERFORMANCE TASK

View the Engage section online. Discuss the photo and ask students to describe the snowflake in general terms, such as "It has six arms that look alike." Then preview the Lesson Performance Task.

Name_____ Class_____ Date_____

3.1 Sequences of Transformations

Essential Question: What happens when you apply more than one transformation to a figure?

Resource Locker

◉ Explore Combining Rotations or Reflections

A transformation is a function that takes points on the plane and maps them to other points on the plane. Transformations can be applied one after the other in a sequence where you use the image of the first transformation as the preimage for the next transformation.

Find the image for each sequence of transformations.

Ⓐ Using geometry software, draw a triangle and label the vertices A, B, and C. Then draw a point outside the triangle and label it P.

Rotate $\triangle ABC$ 30° around point P and label the image as $\triangle A'B'C'$. Then rotate $\triangle A'B'C'$ 45° around point P and label the image as $\triangle A''B''C''$. Sketch your result.

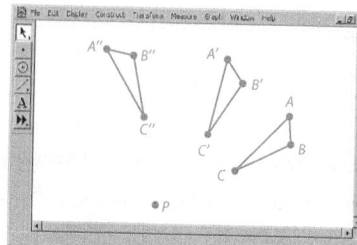

Ⓑ Make a conjecture regarding a single rotation that will map $\triangle ABC$ to $\triangle A''B''C''$. Check your conjecture, and describe what you did.

A rotation of 75° $\left(\text{because } 30 + 45 = 75\right)$ should map $\triangle ABC$ to $\triangle A''B''C''$. By using the software to rotate $\triangle ABC$ 75°, I can see that this image coincides with $\triangle A''B''C''$.

Ⓒ Using geometry software, draw a triangle and label the vertices D, E, and F. Then draw two intersecting lines and label them j and k.

Reflect $\triangle DEF$ across line j and label the image as $\triangle D'E'F'$. Then reflect $\triangle D'E'F'$ across line k and label the image as $\triangle D''E''F''$. Sketch your result.

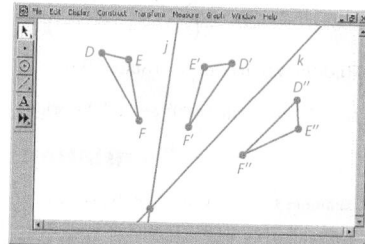

Ⓓ Consider the relationship between $\triangle DEF$ and $\triangle D''E''F''$. Describe the single transformation that maps $\triangle DEF$ to $\triangle D''E''F''$. How can you check that you are correct?

A rotation with center at the intersection of j and k maps $\triangle DEF$ to $\triangle D''E''F''$. Rotating $\triangle DEF$ around the intersection of j and k by the angle made between the lines rotates it about halfway to $\triangle D''E''F''$, so rotate it by twice that angle to see $\triangle DEF$ mapped to $\triangle D''E''F''$.

© Houghton Mifflin Harcourt Publishing Company

HARDCOVER PAGES 103–112

Turn to these pages to find this lesson in the hardcover student edition.

1. Repeat Step A using other angle measures. Make a conjecture about what single transformation will describe a sequence of two rotations about the same center.
   If a figure is rotated and then the image is rotated about the same center, a single rotation

   by the sum of the angles of rotation will have the same result.

2. Make a conjecture about what single transformation will describe a sequence of three rotations about the same center.
   A sequence of three rotations about the same center can be described by a single rotation

   by the sum of the angles of rotation.

3. **Discussion** Repeat Step C, but make lines *j* and *k* parallel instead of intersecting. Make a conjecture about what single transformation will now map △*DEF* to △*D″E″F″*. Check your conjecture and describe what you did.
   △*D″E″F″* looks like a translation of △*DEF*. I marked a vector from *D* to *D″* and

   translated △*DEF* by it . The image coincides with △*D″E″F″*, so two reflections in ‖ lines

   result in a translation.

🔑 Explain 1 Combining Rigid Transformations

In the Explore, you saw that sometimes you can use a single transformation to describe the result of applying a sequence of two transformations. Now you will apply sequences of rigid transformations that cannot be described by a single transformation.

Example 1 Draw the image of △*ABC* after the given combination of transformations.

Ⓐ Reflection over line *ℓ* then translation along $\vec{v}$

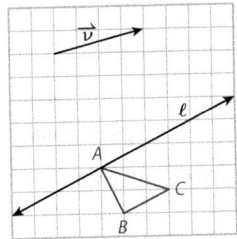

Step 1 Draw the image of △*ABC* after a reflection across line *ℓ*. Label the image △*A′B′C′*.

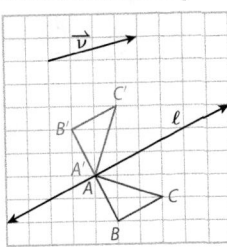

Step 2 Translate △*A′B′C′* along $\vec{v}$. Label this image △*A″B″C″*.

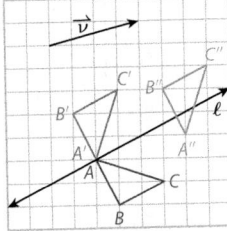

EXPLORE

Combining Reflections

INTEGRATE TECHNOLOGY

Students have the option of completing the combining reflections activity either in the book or online.

QUESTIONING STRATEGIES

? How can you use geometry software to check your transformations? For reflections in parallel lines, use the measuring features to see if all points move the same distance in the same direction. For reflections in intersecting lines, rotate the preimage figure to see if the images are the same size and shape.

EXPLAIN 1

Combining Rigid Transformations

AVOID COMMON ERRORS

Some students may transform the original figure twice instead of transforming the first image to get the second, and the second to get the third. Note that when performing two transformations with $A \rightarrow A'$ as the first transformation, A is the preimage and A' is the image. In the second transformation $A' \rightarrow A''$, A' is the preimage and A'' is the image.

PROFESSIONAL DEVELOPMENT

Math Background

Students have worked with individual transformations and should now be able to identify and describe translations, reflections, and rotations. In this lesson, they combine two or more of these transformations and may include sequences of nonrigid transformations. They must be able to visualize and predict the outcome of performing more than one transformation, as well as consider other transformations that produce the same final image. Throughout the lesson they must recall the properties of each transformation and the methods for drawing them.

After a rigid motion, an image has the same shape and size as the preimage. If you perform a sequence of rigid motions, will the final image have the same shape and size as the original? **Yes; each rigid motion preserves size and shape, so a sequence of rigid motions will also preserve size and shape.**

(B) 180° rotation around point P, then translation along $\vec{v}$, then reflection across line ℓ

Apply the rotation. Label the image $\triangle A'B'C'$.

Apply the translation to $\triangle A'B'C'$. Label the image $\triangle A''B''C''$.

Apply the reflection to $\triangle A''B''C''$. Label the image $\triangle A'''B'''C'''$.

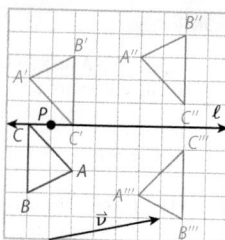

Reflect

4. Are the images you drew for each example the same size and shape as the given preimage? In what ways do rigid transformations change the preimage?

Yes. Rigid transformations move the figure in the plane and may change the orientation, but they do not change the size or shape.

5. Does the order in which you apply the transformations make a difference? Test your conjecture by performing the transformations in Part B in a different order.

Possible answer: Yes, if I reflect first, then rotate, and then translate, the final image is above line ℓ instead of below it.

6. For Part B, describe a sequence of transformations that will take $\triangle A''B''C''$ back to the preimage.

Possible answer: In this case, reversing the order of the transformations will take the final image back to the preimage.

Your Turn

Draw the image of the triangle after the given combination of transformations.

7. Reflection across ℓ then 90° rotation around point P

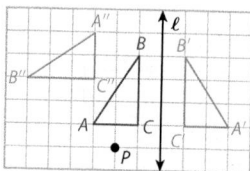

8. Translation along $\vec{v}$ then 180° rotation around point P then translation along $\vec{u}$

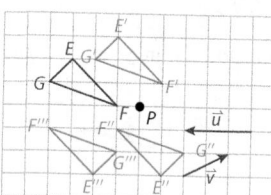

COLLABORATIVE LEARNING

Small Group Activity

Geometry software allows students to focus on their predictions rather than on drawing multiple transformations. Give students the coordinates of a figure and a series of transformations. Instruct them to plot the points on graph paper and to sketch a prediction of the final image. Then have them use geometry software to perform the transformations and check the results against their predictions. After students have done this for several figures, ask them to brainstorm ways to make their predictions more accurate.

🎯 Explain 2   Combining Nonrigid Transformations

Example 2   Draw the image of the figure in the plane after the given combination of transformations.

(A) $(x, y) \rightarrow \left(\frac{3}{2}x, \frac{3}{2}y\right) \rightarrow (-x, y) \rightarrow (x + 1, y - 2)$

1. The first transformation is a dilation by a factor of $\frac{3}{2}$. Apply the dilation. Label the image $A'B'C'D'$.

2. Apply the reflection of $A'B'C'D'$ across the y-axis. Label this image $A''B''C''D''$.

3. Apply the translation of $A''B''C''D''$. Label this image $A'''B'''C'''D'''$.

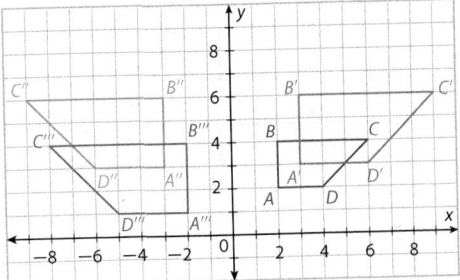

(B) $(x, y) \rightarrow (3x, y) \rightarrow \left(\frac{1}{2}x, -\frac{1}{2}y\right)$

1. The first transformation is a [horizontal]/vertical stretch by a factor of ___3___. Apply the stretch. Label the image ___$\triangle A'B'C'$___.

2. The second transformation is a dilation by a factor of ___$\frac{1}{2}$___ combined with a reflection. Apply the transformation to ___$\triangle A'B'C'$___. Label the image ___$\triangle A''B''C''$___.

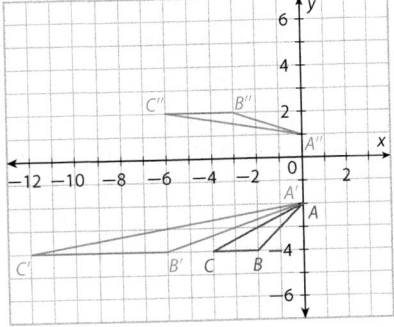

Reflect

9. If you dilated a figure by a factor of 2, what transformation could you use to return the figure back to its preimage? If you dilated a figure by a factor of 2 and then translated it right 2 units, write a sequence of transformations to return the figure back to its preimage.
   Dilate the figure by a factor of $\frac{1}{2}$. Possible answer: You could dilate the figure by a factor
   of $\frac{1}{2}$ then translate the figure left 2 units.

10. A student is asked to reflect a figure across the y-axis and then vertically stretch the figure by a factor of 2. Describe the effect on the coordinates. Then write one transformation using coordinate notation that combines these two transformations into one.
    The x-coordinates change to their opposites. The y-coordinates are multiplied by a factor
    of 2. $(x, y) \rightarrow (-x, 2y)$

DIFFERENTIATE INSTRUCTION

Multiple Representations

Have students graph any three points on a coordinate plane and connect them to form a triangle. Ask students to perform two transformations on this triangle. Then instruct them to use the algebra rules to perform the same transformations. Students should compare the coordinates they found algebraically with those they found with the physical transformation. Then have them study the preimage and the final image to decide whether they could have used one transformation to obtain the same result. If so, ask them to use the algebraic rules to show that the single transformation is equivalent to the two original transformations.

EXPLAIN 2

Combining Nonrigid Transformations

INTEGRATE MATHEMATICAL PRACTICES
Focus on Math Connections

MP.1 Relate *nonrigid transformation* to *rigid transformation* by comparing the size and shape of the original and image figures. Point out that a dilation preserves the shape but not the size of a figure, while a horizontal or vertical stretch does not preserve either the size or the shape of a figure.

QUESTIONING STRATEGIES

? How would you describe the image of a figure after a sequence of nonrigid transformations? **Either the size or the shape of the original figure changed, although it is possible that a subsequent transformation results in a figure of the original size and shape.**

? If you perform a sequence of nonrigid motions on a polygon, will the type of polygon change? Explain. **No. The polygon will have the same number of vertices, so it will be the same general polygon. If the original figure is regular, the nonrigid motions may give an image of a non-regular polygon. The image of a square may be a parallelogram, for example.**

CONNECT VOCABULARY 🔲 EL

The word *rigid* derives from *rigidus*, the Latin word for *stiff*. Help students understand how *nonrigid transformation* is used to represent a type of transformation that gives an image that is a different size and/or shape of a preimage figure. Point out that the transformation can be in the plane or in the coordinate plane, and that a nonrigid transformation can be included in any sequence of combined transformations.

EXPLAIN 3

Predicting the Effect of Transformations

INTEGRATE MATHEMATICAL PRACTICES
Focus on Patterns
MP.8 Encourage students to predict the effect of transformations and then actually perform the transformations described in the example to verify their predictions. Have students repeat the same sequence of transformations using a different figure as the original figure. Ask whether the sequence of transformations affects the new figure in the same way.

QUESTIONING STRATEGIES

? Why is it important to carefully label the vertices after each transformation? Labeling the vertices will help distinguish the types of rigid and nonrigid transformations used in the sequence of transformations. Mislabeling a transformation in the sequence will likely result in an incorrect final image.

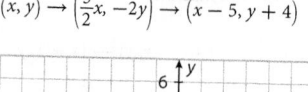

Your Turn

Draw the image of the figure in the plane after the given combination of transformations.

11. $(x, y) \rightarrow (x - 1, y - 1) \rightarrow (3x, y) \rightarrow (-x, -y)$ **12.** $(x, y) \rightarrow \left(\frac{3}{2}x, -2y\right) \rightarrow (x - 5, y + 4)$

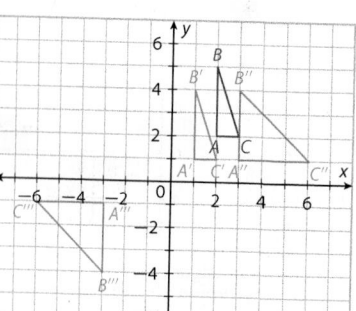
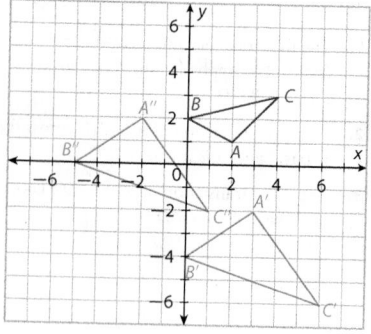

🔵 **Explain 3** **Predicting the Effect of Transformations**

Example 3 Predict the result of applying the sequence of transformations to the given figure.

Ⓐ △*LMN* is translated along the vector $\langle -2, 3 \rangle$, reflected across the *y*-axis, and then reflected across the *x*-axis.

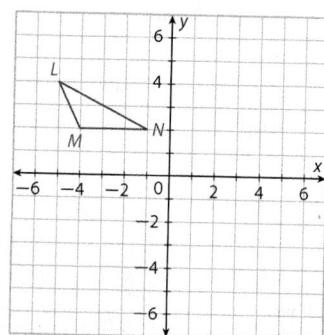

Predict the effect of the first transformation: A translation along the vector $\langle -2, 3 \rangle$ will move the figure left 2 units and up 3 units. Since the given triangle is in Quadrant II, the translation will move it further from the *x*- and *y*-axes. It will remain in Quadrant II.

Predict the effect of the second transformation: Since the triangle is in Quadrant II, a reflection across the *y*-axis will change the orientation and move the triangle into Quadrant I.

Predict the effect of the third transformation: A reflection across the *x*-axis will again change the orientation and move the triangle into Quadrant IV. The two reflections are the equivalent of rotating the figure 180° about the origin.

The final result will be a triangle the same shape and size as △*LMN* in Quadrant IV. It has been rotated 180° about the origin and is farther from the axes than the preimage.

LANGUAGE SUPPORT 🔲 EL

Communicate Math

Have students work in pairs. Have the first student show the partner a graph of a preimage and transformed image and ask whether it is an example of a rigid or nonrigid transformation. The second student should describe the transformation and tell whether it is rigid or nonrigid, and why. The first student writes the explanation under the images. Students change roles and repeat the sequence with another set of images.

Ⓑ Square *HIJK* is rotated 90° clockwise about the origin and then dilated by a factor of 2, which maps $(x, y) \rightarrow (2x, 2y)$.

Predict the effect of the first transformation: __A 90° clockwise__ rotation will map it to Quadrant IV. Due to its symmetry, it will appear to have been translated, but will be closer to the *x*-axis than it is to the *y*-axis.

Predict the effect of the second transformation: __A dilation__ by a factor of 2 will double the side lengths of the square. It will also be further from the origin than the preimage.

The final result will be __a square in Quadrant 4 with side lengths twice as long as the__ side lengths of the original. The image is further from the origin than the preimage.

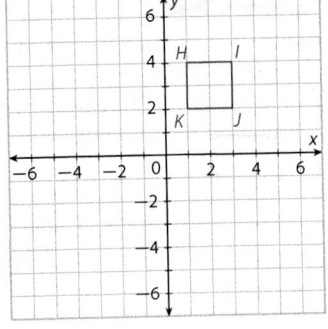

Your Turn

Predict the result of applying the sequence of transformations to the given figure.

13. Rectangle *GHJK* is reflected across the *y*-axis and translated along the vector $\langle 5, 4 \rangle$.

The reflection across the *y*-axis will move the rectangle from the right of the *y*-axis to the left of it. Due to the symmetry of the rectangle, it will appear to have been translated left 6 units. Then, translating along the vector $\langle 5, 4 \rangle$ will move the rectangle right 5 units and up 4 units. This will bring the rectangle fully into Quadrant I. The final result will be a rectangle that is the same shape and size as the preimage that has moved to sit on the *x*-axis in Quadrant I, closer to the *y*-axis than the preimage.

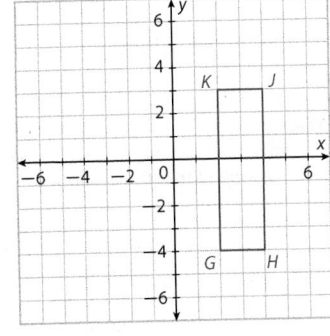

14. △*TUV* is horizontally stretched by a factor of $\frac{3}{2}$, which maps $(x, y) \rightarrow \left(\frac{3}{2}x, y\right)$, and then translated along the vector $\langle 2, 1 \rangle$.

A horizontal stretch will pull points *U* and *T* away from the *y*-axis, making the triangle longer in the left-to-right direction. The translation along the vector $\langle 2, 1 \rangle$ will move the stretched triangle 2 units right and 1 unit up, which will move the triangle closer to the origin with one vertex on the *x*-axis and another across the *y*-axis. The final image will not be the same shape or size as the preimage.

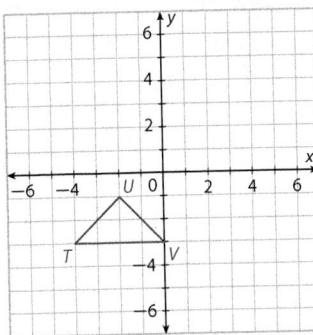

ELABORATE

INTEGRATE MATHEMATICAL PRACTICES

Focus on Patterns

MP.8 Discuss with students how to record and use algebraic patterns to represent a series of rigid and nonrigid motions in the coordinate plane. For example, a reflection in the x-axis is represented by $(x, y) \rightarrow (x, -y)$, while a reflection in the y-axis is represented by $(x, y) \rightarrow (-x, y)$. So, a reflection in the x-axis followed by a reflection in the y-axis is represented by $(x, y) \rightarrow (-x, -y)$.

QUESTIONING STRATEGIES

? Is a transformation from a sequence of rigid motions always rigid? Yes. Each rigid motion preserves the size and shape of a figure, so the final image must have the same size and shape as the original figure.

? What types of sequences of transformations can be undone? A sequence of transformations using the same rigid motion can sometimes be undone by reversing the order of the sequence. It is possible that a sequence using different rigid motions or nonrigid motions cannot be undone directly, but students may be able to write a series of related transformations to undo the transformations.

SUMMARIZE THE LESSON

? What features can you describe when predicting the result of more than one transformation? Sample answer: You can predict which quadrant(s) the final image will be in, how far and in what direction it will be from the origin or from the original figure, its orientation, and whether the size or shape of the figure has changed.

💬 Elaborate

15. Discussion How many different sequences of rigid transformations do you think you can find to take a preimage back onto itself? Explain your reasoning.

An infinite number. With rotations you just need to go 360° and you will be back where you started, and you can do that as many times as you want. You can always reflect back over a line. You can always go back left just as far as you went right, or up as many times as you went down in a translation, so you can take a preimage back onto itself in many ways. You can add extra transformations to find additional sequences.

16. Is there a sequence of a rotation and a dilation that will result in an image that is the same size and position as the preimage? Explain your reasoning.

Yes, a rotation of 360° and a dilation of 1 will work.

17. Essential Question Check-In In a sequence of transformations, the order of the transformations can affect the final image. Describe a sequence of transformations where the order does not matter. Describe a sequence of transformations where the order does matter.

Possible answer: A sequence of any number of rotations about the same point can be added together to make one rotation, even if they are a combination of clockwise and counterclockwise rotations. Any sequence of translations can also be done in any order. When a sequence includes a mix of different types of transformations, the order usually affects the final image, for example a rotation of 90° around a vertex followed by a dilation by a factor of 4 will have a different final image than the same figure dilated by a factor of 4 followed by a rotation of 90°.

✪ Evaluate: Homework and Practice

• Online Homework
• Hints and Help
• Extra Practice

Draw and label the final image of △ABC after the given sequence of transformations.

1. Reflect △ABC over the y-axis and then translate by ⟨2, −3⟩.

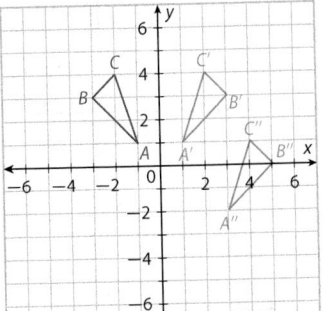

2. Rotate △ABC 90 degrees clockwise about the origin and then reflect over the x-axis.

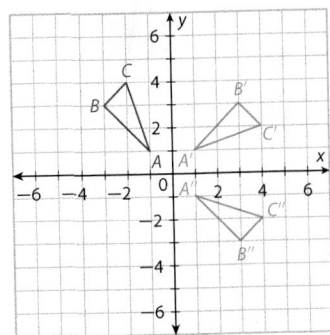

3. Translate △ABC by ⟨4, 4⟩, rotate 90 degrees counterclockwise around A, and reflect over the y-axis.

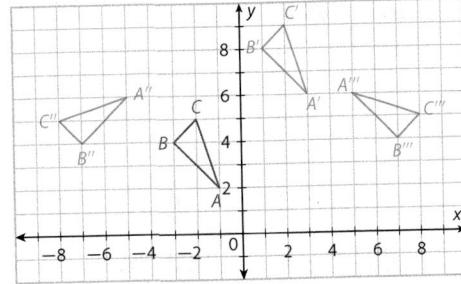

4. Reflect △ABC over the x-axis, translate by ⟨−3, −1⟩, and rotate 180 degrees around the origin.

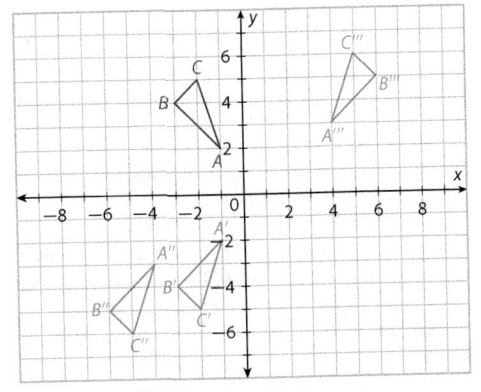

EVALUATE

ASSIGNMENT GUIDE

Concepts and Skills	Practice
Explore Combining Rotations or Reflections	
Example 1 Combining Rigid Transformations	Exercises 1–4
Example 2 Combining Nonrigid Transformations	Exercises 5–6
Example 3 Predicting the Effect of Transformations	Exercises 7–12

INTEGRATE MATHEMATICAL PRACTICES
Focus on Technology

MP.5 Students can use geometry software to do a sequence of transformations or to check a sequence of transformations. Remind students to use the measuring features to verify that a sequence of rigid motions preserves the size and shape of a figure.

Exercise	Depth of Knowledge (D.O.K.)	COMMON CORE Mathematical Practices
1–8	**2** Skills/Concepts	**MP.6** Precision
9–13	**2** Skills/Concepts	**MP.2** Reasoning
14	**1** Recall of Information	**MP.2** Reasoning
15–18	**2** Skills/Concepts	**MP.2** Reasoning
19	**2** Skills/Concepts	**MP.2** Reasoning

GRAPHIC ORGANIZERS

Suggest that students use a graphic organizer to keep track of the types of transformations and their properties in a sequence of transformations. This can help them remember to use the last image figure as they proceed with the sequence of transformations. For example:

Transformation 1	
Property 1	Property 2

↓

Transformation 2	
Property 1	Property 2

↓

Transformation 3	
Property 1	Property 2

AVOID COMMON ERRORS

Some students may perform a combination of transformations in the wrong order. Emphasize the importance of doing the transformations in the correct order by asking them to rotate a triangle 90° in the plane and then reflect it in the *x*-axis. They will get a different result if the order is reversed.

SMALL GROUP ACTIVITY

Have students work in small groups to make a poster showing how to find a sequence of transformations in the coordinate plane using both rigid and nonrigid motions. Give each group a different sequence to transform. Then have each group present its poster to the rest of the class, explaining each step.

123 Lesson 3.1

Draw and label the final image of △*ABC* after the given sequence of transformations.

5. $(x, y) \rightarrow \left(x, \frac{1}{3}y\right) \rightarrow (-2x, -2y)$

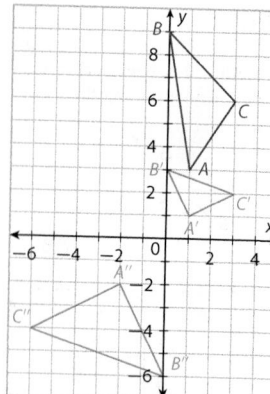

6. $(x, y) \rightarrow \left(-\frac{3}{2}x, \frac{2}{3}y\right) \rightarrow (x + 6, y - 4) \rightarrow \left(\frac{2}{3}x, -\right.$

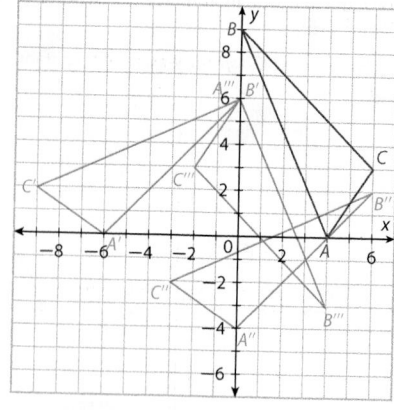

Predict the result of applying the sequence of transformations to the given figure.

7. △*ABC* is translated along the vector $\langle -3, -1 \rangle$, reflected across the *x*-axis, and then reflected across the *y*-axis.

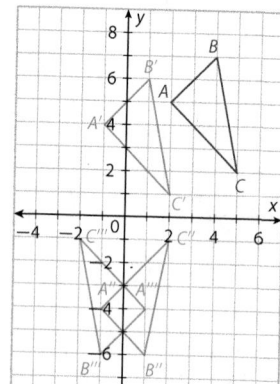

Possible answer: The translation moves the figure down one unit and left three units, mapping *A′* to the left of the *y*-axis and *C′* closer to the origin. The reflection first will map *A″B″C″* below the *x*-axis and change the orientation. The second reflection will map the figure mostly into Quadrant III, with *A‴* in Quadrant IV, and again change the orientation. The final image is the same size, shape, and orientation as the preimage.

Module 3

123

8. △*ABC* is translated along the vector $\langle -1, -3 \rangle$, rotated 180° about the origin, and then dilated by a factor of 2.

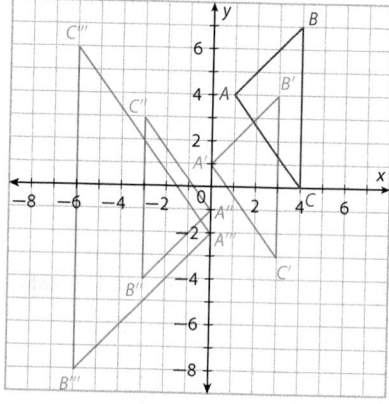

Possible answer: The translation moves the figure down and to the left without changing the shape or orientation. The rotation about the origin moves the figure from Quadrants I and IV to Quadrants II and III without changing the orientation. The dilation doubles the side lengths. The final image is the same shape as the preimage but larger. It has the same orientation.

Lesson 1

Exercise	Depth of Knowledge (D.O.K.)	COMMON CORE Mathematical Practices
20	**3** Strategic Thinking	**MP.6** Precision
21–23	**2** Skills/Concepts	**MP.2** Reasoning

In Exercises 9–12, use the diagram. Fill in the blank with the letter of the correct image described.

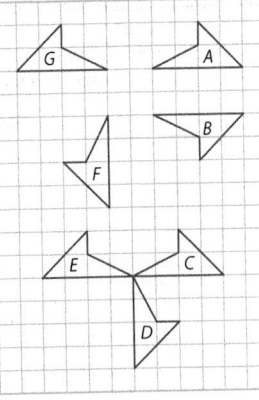

9. __B__ is the result of the sequence: *G* reflected over a vertical line and then a horizontal line.

10. __E__ is the result of the sequence: *D* rotated 90° clockwise around one of its vertices and then reflected over a horizontal line.

11. __F__ is the result of the sequence: *E* translated and then rotated 90° counterclockwise.

12. __A__ is the result of the sequence: *D* rotated 90° counterclockwise and then translated.

Choose the correct word to complete a true statement.

13. A combination of two rigid transformations on a preimage will always/sometimes/never produce the same image when taken in a different order.

14. A double rotation can always/sometimes/never be written as a single rotation.

15. A sequence of a translation and a reflection always/sometimes/never has a point that does not change position.

16. A sequence of a reflection across the *x*-axis and then a reflection across the *y*-axis always/sometimes/never results in a 180° rotation of the preimage.

17. A sequence of rigid transformations will always/sometimes/never result in an image that is the same size and orientation as the preimage.

18. A sequence of a rotation and a dilation will always/sometimes/never result in an image that is the same size and orientation as the preimage.

19. △*QRS* is the image of △*LMN* under a sequence of transformations. Can each of the following sequences be used to create the image, △*QRS*, from the preimage, △*LMN*? Select yes or no.

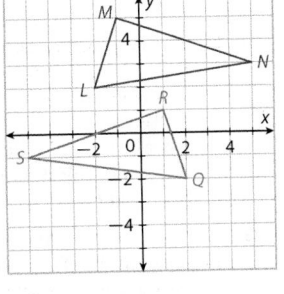

   a. Reflect across the *y*-axis and then translate along the vector ⟨0, −4⟩. ● Yes ○ No

   b. Translate along the vector ⟨0, −4⟩ and then reflect across the *y*-axis. ● Yes ○ No

   c. Rotate 90° clockwise about the origin, reflect across the *x*-axis, and then rotate 90° counterclockwise about the origin. ○ Yes ● No

   d. Rotate 180° about the origin, reflect across the *x*-axis, and then translate along the vector ⟨0, −4⟩. ● Yes ○ No

MP.4 When writing the algebraic rules for the rigid motions and other transformations, review the quadrants and coordinates. Students should remember that a rotation through a positive angle is in the counterclockwise direction, and a rotation through a negative angle is in the clockwise direction.

MP.1 Have students use the algebraic representation of a dilation in the coordinate plane as $(x, y) \rightarrow (kx, ky)$, where k is the scale factor. Ask students how they would represent the dilation that would "undo" this dilation. $(x, y) \rightarrow \left(\frac{1}{k}x, \frac{1}{k}y \right)$

PEER-TO-PEER DISCUSSION

Ask students to discuss with a partner how to predict the final image for a combination of rigid transformations and nonrigid transformations. Then ask students to make a conjecture about the result of dilating a triangle whose vertices have coordinates $(1, 1)$, $(1, 4)$, $(5, 1)$ with a scale factor of 2, followed by a reflection in the x-axis. The image has vertices $(2, -2)$, $(2, -8)$, $(10, -2)$.

JOURNAL

Have students compare and contrast the methods they have learned for combining rigid transformations and nonrigid transformations in the coordinate plane.

20. A teacher gave students this puzzle: "I had a triangle with vertex A at $(1, 4)$ and vertex B at $(3, 2)$. After two rigid transformations, I had the image shown. Describe and show a sequence of transformations that will give this image from the preimage."

Possible answer: Translate by the vector $\langle 2,1 \rangle$ then reflect over the line $x = 5$.

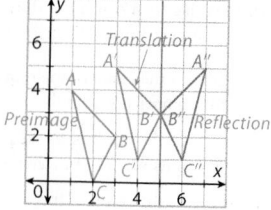

H.O.T. Focus on Higher Order Thinking

21. **Analyze Relationships** What two transformations would you apply to $\triangle ABC$ to get $\triangle DEF$? How could you express these transformations with a single mapping rule in the form of $(x, y) \rightarrow (?, ?)$?

Possible answer: Reflect $\triangle ABC$ across the y-axis and then translate it down 7 units. A single mapping rule would be $(x, y) \rightarrow (-x, y - 7)$.

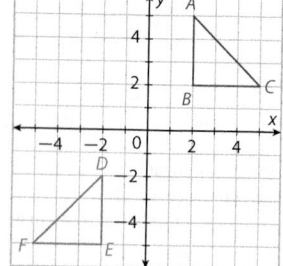

22. **Multi-Step** Muralists will often make a scale drawing of an art piece before creating the large finished version. A muralist has sketched an art piece on a sheet of paper that is 3 feet by 4 feet.

a. If the final mural will be 39 feet by 52 feet, what is the scale factor for this dilation?

Scale factor: 13

b. The owner of the wall has decided to only give permission to paint on the lower half of the wall. Can the muralist simply use the transformation $(x, y) \rightarrow \left(x, \frac{1}{2}y\right)$ in addition to the scale factor to alter the sketch for use in the allowed space? Explain.

Only if the artist wants the final version of the mural to be distorted. This mapping will shrink the height of the mural in half, but by keeping the original width, the shapes will change.

23. **Communicate Mathematical Ideas** As a graded class activity, your teacher asks your class to reflect a triangle across the y-axis and then across the x-axis. Your classmate gets upset because he reversed the order of these reflections and thinks he will have to start over. What can you say to your classmate to help him?

The order of these two reflections does not matter. The resulting image is the same for a reflection in the y-axis followed by a reflection in the x-axis as for a reflection in the x-axis followed by a reflection in the y-axis.

© Houghton Mifflin Harcourt Publishing Company • Image Credits: ©AJP/Shutterstock

Lesson Performance Task

The photograph shows an actual snowflake. Draw a detailed sketch of the "arm" of the snowflake located at the top left of the photo (10:00 on a clock face). Describe in as much detail as you can any translations, reflections, or rotations that you see.

Then describe how the entire snowflake is constructed, based on what you found in the design of one arm.

Check students' drawings.

In their descriptions, students should refer to specific features of their drawings. The line dividing the 10:00 arm in half is a line of reflection, with the portion of the flake on each side being (nearly) a reflection of the other side. There's a small imperfection in this description, with the large "ear" in the middle of the right side not quite having a mirror image where it should be. However, its almost-image on the other side can be created by reflecting the ear across the line of symmetry and then translating it slightly downward.

The entire flake can be created by rotating the arm through 60°, 120°, 180°, 240°, and 300°. For several of the new arms, the "ear" mentioned above appears in a slightly dilated form, or it appears several times as translations of one another.

EXTENSION ACTIVITY

Have students research the claim that "all snowflakes are different." Depending upon students' interests, the claim may lead them to investigate how and where snowflakes form, how they change as they fall through the atmosphere, why they have a hexagonal structure, and the effects that temperature and humidity have upon their structure.

INTEGRATE MATHEMATICAL PRACTICES
Focus on Modeling

MP.4 A visual pattern can be described as a form or shape that repeats. Ask students to describe the snowflake in terms of patterns. Sample answer: Each half of any one of the arms can be taken as a pattern that repeats approximately twelve times in the snowflake design, twice on each arm.

INTEGRATE MATHEMATICAL PRACTICES
Focus on Communication

MP.3 Ask students to write, say, or show sequences of rotations, reflections, and translations, using their hands. For example:

Reflection — both hands facing outward, thumbs nearly together.
Translation — one hand facing forward and one backward in the same orientation.
Rotation — one hand pointing left (thumb up) and one hand pointing right (thumb down), fingers facing each other.

CRITICAL THINKING

Ask students whether a snowflake is a two-dimensional object. Have them consider the effects of the third dimension on lines of symmetry, and how the snowflake appears from a side view rather than a top view.

Scoring Rubric
2 points: Student correctly solves the problem and explains his/her reasoning.
1 point: Student shows good understanding of the problem but does not fully solve or explain his/her reasoning.
0 points: Student does not demonstrate understanding of the problem.

Sequences of Transformations   **126**

Proving Figures are Congruent Using Rigid Motions

Common Core Math Standards

The student is expected to:

 G-CO.B.6

... given two figures, use the definition of congruence in terms of rigid motions to decide if they are congruent. Also G-CO.A.5

Mathematical Practices

 MP.3 Logic

Language Objective

Have students work in pairs to label congruent and noncongruent figures.

ENGAGE

Essential Question: How can you determine whether two figures are congruent?

Possible answer: If one figure can be obtained from the other by a sequence of rigid motions, then they are congruent.

PREVIEW: LESSON PERFORMANCE TASK

View the Engage section online. Discuss the photo and ask students to describe the pattern or patterns in the tile design. Then preview the Lesson Performance Task.

Name_____ Class_____ Date_____

3.2 Proving Figures are Congruent Using Rigid Motions

Essential Question: How can you determine whether two figures are congruent?

Resource Locker

⊘ Explore   Confirming Congruence

Two plane figures are congruent if and only if one can be obtained from the other by a sequence of rigid motions (that is, by a sequence of reflections, translations, and/or rotations).

A landscape architect uses a grid to design the landscape around a mall. Use tracing paper to confirm that the landscape elements are congruent.

(A) Trace planter *ABCD*. Describe a transformation you can use to move the tracing paper so that planter *ABCD* is mapped onto planter *EFGH*. What does this confirm about the planters?

You can map *ABCD* to *EFGH* with a translation right 4 units and

down 4 units. The planters are congruent because there is a rigid

transformation that maps one to the other.

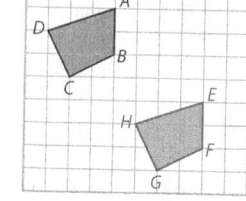

(B) Trace pools *JKLM* and *NPQR*. Fold the paper so that pool *JKLM* is mapped onto pool *NPQR*. Describe the transformation. What does this confirm about the pools?

You can map *JKLM* to *NPQR* with a reflection over the fold line.

The pools are congruent because there is a rigid transformation

that maps one to the other.

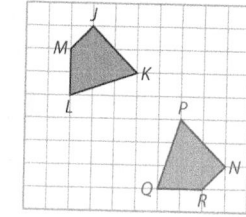

(C) Determine whether the lawns are congruent. Is there a rigid transformation that maps $\triangle LMN$ to $\triangle DEF$? What does this confirm about the lawns?

There is no sequence of rigid transformations that maps $\triangle DEF$

to $\triangle LMN$. The lawns are not congruent.

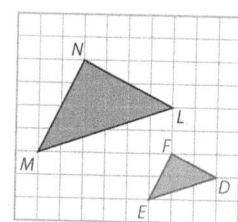

Reflect

1. How do the sizes of the pairs of figures help determine if they are congruent?
If the figures are not the same size, there is no rigid motion that can map one of them onto

the other. The transformation would need to include a dilation, which is not a rigid motion.

©Houghton Mifflin Harcourt Publishing Company

3.2 Proving Figures are Congruent Using Rigid Motions

HARDCOVER PAGES 113–122

Turn to these pages to find this lesson in the hardcover student edition.

🎤 Explain 1   Determining if Figures are Congruent

Example 1   Use the definition of congruence to decide whether the two figures are congruent. Explain your answer.

Ⓐ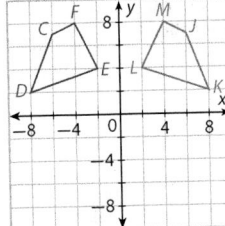

The two figures appear to be the same size and shape, so look for a rigid transformation that will map one to the other.

You can map *CDEF* onto *JKLM* by reflecting *CDEF* over the *y*-axis. This reflection is a rigid motion that maps *CDEF* to *JKLM*, so the two figures are congruent.

The coordinate notation for the reflection is $(x, y) \rightarrow (-x, y)$.

Ⓑ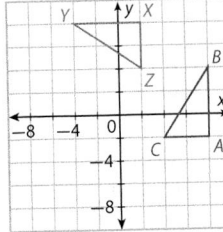

The two figures appear to be the ⟨same⟩/different.

You can map $\triangle ABC$ to $\triangle XYZ$ by ___a counter-clockwise rotation of 90° around the origin___

This ⟨is⟩/is not a rigid motion that maps $\triangle ABC$ to $\triangle XYZ$, so the two figures ⟨are⟩/are not congruent.

The coordinate notation for the rotation is $(x, y) \rightarrow (-y, x)$.

Your Turn

Use the definition of congruence to decide whether the two figures are congruent. Explain your answer.

2.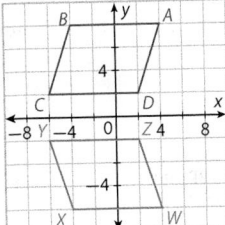

You can map *ABCD* to *WXYZ* with a reflection across the *x*-axis, so the figures are congruent. The coordinate notation for the reflection is $(x, y) \rightarrow (x, -y)$.

3.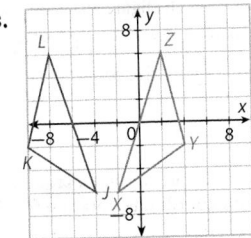

You can map $\triangle JKL$ to $\triangle XYZ$ with a reflection across the *y*-axis, followed by a horizontal translation, so the figures are congruent. The coordinate notation for the reflection is $(x, y) \rightarrow (-x, y)$ and for the translation is $(x, y) \rightarrow (x - 6, y)$.

PROFESSIONAL DEVELOPMENT

 Learning Progressions

In this lesson students learn that two figures are congruent if and only if there is a sequence of rigid motions that maps one figure to the other. That means if they can find the sequence of rigid motions that maps one figure to the other, then they can confirm that the preimage and image figures are congruent. It also means, if the figures are known to be congruent, that there is a sequence of rigid motions that maps one figure to the other. In upcoming lessons, students will use this transformations-based definition to develop congruence criteria for triangles.

EXPLORE

Confirming Congruence

INTEGRATE TECHNOLOGY

Students have the option of confirming congruence using the rigid motion activity either in the book or online.

QUESTIONING STRATEGIES

? Do the figures appear to be congruent? Why or why not? yes, because they have the same size and shape

? Can either figure be considered to be the preimage? Why or why not? Yes, if *ABCD* is congruent to *EFGH*, then the reverse is true.

EXPLAIN 1

Determining if Figures are Congruent

CONNECT VOCABULARY **EL**

Define *congruence*. Ask students to give examples of congruent figures in the classroom. Students might mention floor tiles with the same size and shape, or desktops that are rectangles of the same size and shape. Tell students that "the same size and shape" is an informal way of deciding whether two figures may be congruent, but a formal definition of congruence is based on rigid motions.

QUESTIONING STRATEGIES

? How can a rigid motion be used to determine if two figures are congruent? Each rigid motion preserves size and shape, so if a sequence of rigid motions can be found to map one figure to the other, then the preimage and image figure are congruent.

EXPLAIN 2

Finding a Sequence of Rigid Motions

INTEGRATE MATHEMATICAL PRACTICES

Focus on Math Connections

MP.1 Relate congruence to rigid motion by comparing the size and shape of the preimage and image. Point out that the sequence of rigid motions that maps one figure to another may not be unique. Encourage students to look for alternate sequences that work.

QUESTIONING STRATEGIES

? For each pair of figures, how do you know that a sequence of rigid motions that maps one figure to the other must exist? If the figures are known to be congruent—by the definition of congruent, there is a sequence of rigid motions that maps one to the other.

? What would the notation $(x, y) \rightarrow (-x, y + 2)$ mean? The transformation reflects each x-coordinate across the x-axis and raises the figure by 2 units.

AVOID COMMON ERRORS

Some students may think that if two figures are congruent, then there is one rigid motion that can map one figure to the other. Explain that it may take a sequence of rigid motions to map a figure to a congruent figure. Ask students to find examples of when this may be true.

CONNECT VOCABULARY **EL**

Help students understand how *congruence* is related to rigid motions by pointing out how a single rigid motion can produce a congruent figure. Therefore, a sequence of rigid motions must also produce a congruent figure. Point out that this is true both in a plane and on a coordinate plane.

Explain 2 · Finding a Sequence of Rigid Motions

The definition of congruence tells you that when two figures are known to be congruent, there must be some sequence of rigid motions that maps one to the other.

Example 2 The figures shown are congruent. Find a sequence of rigid motions that maps one figure to the other. Give coordinate notation for the transformations you use.

(A) $\triangle ABC \cong \triangle PQR$

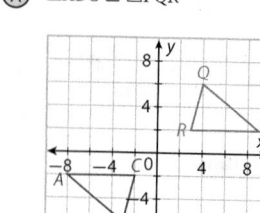

Map $\triangle ABC$ to $\triangle PQR$ with a rotation of 180° around the origin, followed by a horizontal translation.

Rotation: $(x, y) \rightarrow (-x, -y)$

Translation: $(x, y) \rightarrow (x + 1, y)$

(B) $ABCD \cong JKLM$

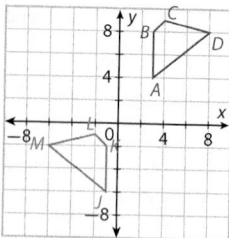

Map $ABCD$ to $JKLM$ with a

___reflection across the y-axis___

followed by a ___translation___.

___Reflection___ : $(x, y) \rightarrow$ ___$(-x, y)$___

___Translation___ : $(x, y) \rightarrow$ ___$(x + 2, y - 10)$___

Reflect

4. How is the orientation of the figure affected by a sequence of transformations?
If the transformations include a reflection, then the orientation will change. A translation or rotation will preserve the original orientation.

Your Turn

The figures shown are congruent. Find a sequence of rigid motions that maps one figure to the other. Give coordinate notation for the transformations you use.

5. $JKLM \cong WXYZ$

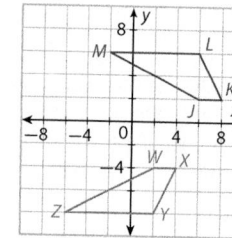

Reflect $JKLM$ across the x-axis: $(x, y) \rightarrow (x, -y)$. Then translate the image: $(x, y) \rightarrow (x - 4, y - 2)$.

6. $ABCDE \cong PQRST$

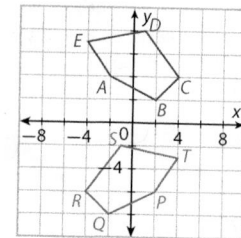

Reflect $ABCDE$ across the y-axis: $(x, y) \rightarrow (-x, y)$. Then translate the image: $(x, y) \rightarrow (x, y - 10)$.

Module 3

129

Lesson 2

COLLABORATIVE LEARNING

Small Group Activity

Give students the coordinates of a pair of congruent figures in the coordinate plane. Have each student describe a sequence of rigid motions that will map one figure to the other. Instruct them to switch papers and use another student's sequence of rigid motions to confirm that the given figures are congruent. Have them use geometry software to do the rigid motions and check the results against their own sequences.

Explain 3 **Investigating Congruent Segments and Angles**

Congruence can refer to parts of figures as well as whole figures. Two angles are congruent if and only if one can be obtained from the other by rigid motions (that is, by a sequence of reflections, translations, and/or rotations.) The same conditions are required for two segments to be congruent to each other.

Example 3 Determine which angles or segments are congruent. Describe transformations that can be used to verify congruence.

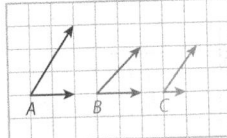

∠A and ∠C are congruent. The transformation is a translation. There is no transformation that maps ∠B to either of the other angles.

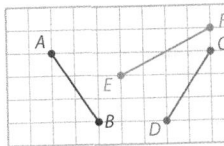

$\overline{AB}$ and $\overline{CD}$ are congruent. A sequence of transformations is a __reflection__ and a translation.

There is no transformation that maps $\overline{EF}$ to either of the other segments.

Your Turn

7. Determine which segments and which angles are congruent. Describe transformations that can be used to show the congruence.

∠B and ∠C are congruent. $\overline{EF}$ and $\overline{GH}$ are congruent. In both cases, a sequence of transformations is a reflection and a translation.

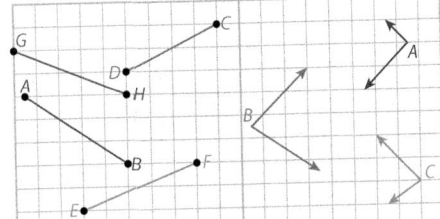

Elaborate

8. Can you say two angles are congruent if they have the same measure but the segments that identify the rays that form the angle are different lengths?
Yes, the definition of congruence for angles requires only that the angle between the rays be the same. The lengths of the segments does not matter.

9. **Discussion** Can figures have congruent angles but not be congruent figures?
Yes, two figures can have congruent angles but not be congruent figures. They could appear to be different sized versions of the same figure.

10. **Essential Question Check-In** Can you use transformations to prove that two figures are not congruent?
Maybe. If a dilation with scale factor ≠ 1 maps one figure onto the other, then the figures cannot not be mapped using only rigid motions, so they cannot be congruent.

Module 3   130   Lesson 2

DIFFERENTIATE INSTRUCTION

Visual Cues

Draw two congruent triangles and label the vertices. Highlight one side of one triangle blue. Have students name the corresponding side of the other triangle and highlight that side blue as well. Repeat with the other two pairs of corresponding sides using green and purple. Then shade one of the angles red. Have students name the corresponding angle of the other triangle and shade that red as well. Repeat with the other two pairs of corresponding angles using yellow and orange.

EXPLAIN 3

Investigating Congruent Segments and Angles

QUESTIONING STRATEGIES

? How does the congruence of angles and segments relate to the congruence of two figures? Why? Since rigid motions preserve angle measure and distance, verifying that corresponding angles and corresponding segments have the same measure determines whether two figures are congruent.

AVOID COMMON ERRORS

Students may believe that two angles cannot be congruent if the rays forming the angles have different lengths. Remind students that rays continue forever in one direction, so the length representing a ray in a diagram is arbitrary. Draw two congruent angles, one with longer rays. Discuss why the angles are congruent even though one appears to be larger.

ELABORATE

QUESTIONING STRATEGIES

? Can you say two angles are congruent if they have the same measure but the segments that identify the rays that form the angle are different lengths? Explain. Yes. The angle measures determine if the two angles are congruent, not the rays or parts of the rays that make up their sides.

? Can you say two segments are congruent if their orientation is different? Explain. Yes. The orientation of the segments does not affect their lengths, and therefore does not affect their congruence.

SUMMARIZE THE LESSON

? How are congruent figures related to transformations? Two figures are congruent if one can be mapped to the other by a rigid transformation (rotation, reflection, or translation) or by a sequence of rigid transformations.

Proving Figures are Congruent Using Rigid Motions **130**

EVALUATE

ASSIGNMENT GUIDE

Concepts and Skills	Practice
Explore Confirming Congruence	
Example 1 Determining if Figures are Congruent	Exercises 1–5, 14–15, 17
Example 2 Finding a Sequence of Rigid Motions	Exercises 6–9, 16, 18–21, 24, 26–31
Example 3 Investigating Congruent Segments and Angles	Exercises 10–13, 23, 25

INTEGRATE MATHEMATICAL PRACTICES

Focus on Technology

MP.5 Students can verify that two figures are congruent by using geometry software to do a sequence of rigid motions. Remind students to use the measuring features to show that angle measures and segment lengths are preserved.

☆ Evaluate: Homework and Practice

• Online Homework
• Hints and Help
• Extra Practice

Use the definition of congruence to decide whether the two figures are congruent. Explain your answer. Give coordinate notation for the transformations you use.

1.

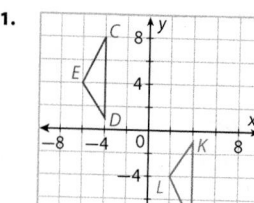

You can map △CDE to △JKL by reflecting △CDE over the x-axis, followed by a horizontal translation. So, the two figures are congruent. reflection: $(x, y) \rightarrow (x, -y)$; translation: $(x, y) \rightarrow (x + 8, y)$.

2.

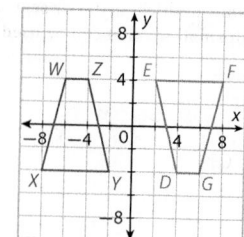

You can map WXYZ to DEFG with a reflection across the x-axis, followed by a horizontal translation. So, the two figures are congruent. reflection: $(x, y) \rightarrow (x, -y)$; translation: $(x, y) \rightarrow (x + 10, y)$.

3.

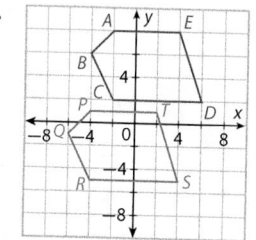

You can map ABCDE to PQRST with a translation. So, the figures are congruent. translation: $(x, y) \rightarrow (x - 2, y - 7)$.

4.

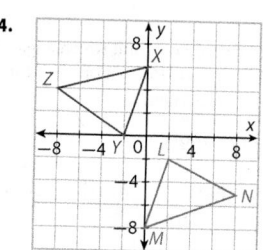

There is no sequence of rigid transformations that will map one figure onto the other, so they are not congruent.

5.

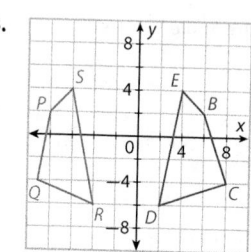

There is no sequence of rigid transformations that will map one figure onto the other, so they are not congruent.

Exercise	Depth of Knowledge (D.O.K.)	COMMON CORE Mathematical Practices	
1–5	**1** Recall of Information	**MP.5** Using Tools	
6–9	**1** Recall of Information	**MP.4** Modeling	
10–23	**1** Recall of Information	**MP.5** Using Tools	
24–29	**2** Skills/Concepts	**MP.5** Using Tools	

The figures shown are congruent. Find a sequence of rigid motions that maps one figure to the other. Give coordinate notation for the transformations you use.

6. $RSTU \cong WXYZ$

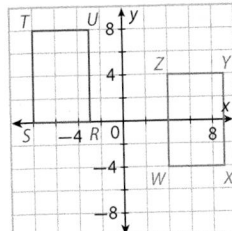

Map *RSTU* to *WXYZ* with a reflection across the *y*-axis, followed by a translation. reflection: $(x, y) \rightarrow (-x, y)$; translation: $(x, y) \rightarrow (x + 1, y - 4)$

7. $\triangle ABC \cong \triangle DEF$

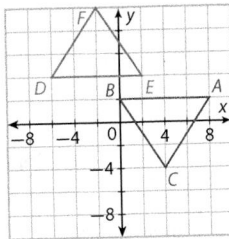

Map $\triangle ABC$ to $\triangle DEF$ with a rotation of 180° around the origin, followed by a translation. rotation: $(x, y) \rightarrow (-x, -y)$; translation: $(x, y) \rightarrow (x + 2, y + 6)$

8. $DEFGH \cong PQRST$

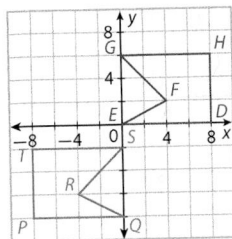

Map *DEFGH* to *PQRST* with a reflection across the *y*-axis, followed by a vertical translation. reflection: $(x, y) \rightarrow (-x, y)$; translation: $(x, y) \rightarrow (x, y - 8)$

9. $\triangle CDE \cong \triangle WXY$

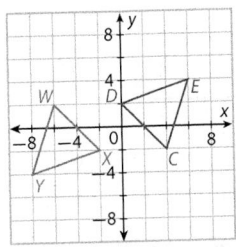

Map $\triangle CDE$ to $\triangle WXY$ with a rotation of 180° around the origin, followed by a horizontal translation. rotation: $(x, y) \rightarrow (-x, -y)$; translation: $(x, y) \rightarrow (x - 2, y)$

Determine which of the angles are congruent. Which transformations can be used to verify the congruence?

10.

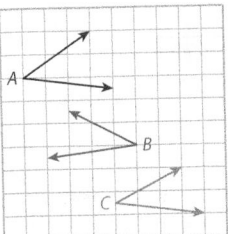

None of the angles are congruent. There is no transformation that maps one of the angles to another.

11.

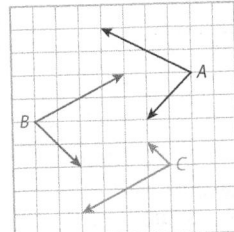

$\angle A$, $\angle B$ and $\angle C$ are all congruent. The sequence of transformations is a reflection and a translation.

INTEGRATE MATHEMATICAL PRACTICES

Focus on Modeling

MP.4 Suggest that students use tracing paper to investigate which corresponding segments for two figures are congruent and which pairs of corresponding angles are congruent. Have them fold the tracing paper to see if the figures are coincident and, if they are, then write a sequence of rigid motions that can map one figure to the other. Have them also use the tracing paper to draw the figure and its congruent image on graph paper and then give the algebraic rules that map one figure to the other.

Exercise	Depth of Knowledge (D.O.K.)	COMMON CORE Mathematical Practices
30–33	3 Strategic Thinking	**MP.2** Reasoning
34–35	3 Strategic Thinking H.O.T.	**MP.2** Reasoning
36	3 Strategic Thinking H.O.T.	**MP.4** Modeling

Focus on Math Connections

MP.1 When examining congruent figures on graph paper, students can see how each vertex is mapped to its corresponding vertex by circling corresponding vertices in the same color, using a different color for each pair of corresponding vertices. Students can also highlight pairs of corresponding sides in the same color, using a different color for each pair.

Determine which of the segments are congruent. Which transformations can be used to verify the congruence?

12.

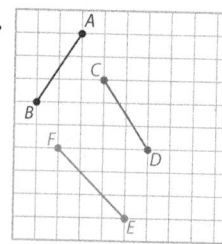

$\overline{AB}$ and $\overline{CD}$ are congruent; reflection, then translation. There is no transformation that maps $\overline{EF}$ to either of the other segments.

13.

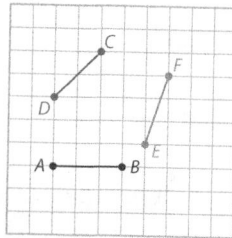

None of the segments are congruent. There is no rigid transformation that maps one of them to another.

Use the definition of congruence to decide whether the two figures are congruent. Explain your answer. Give coordinate notation for the transformations you use.

14.

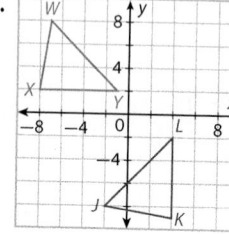

Yes. Map $\triangle JKL$ to $\triangle WXY$ with a clockwise rotation of $90°$ around the origin, followed by a translation. rotation: $(x, y) \rightarrow (y, -x)$ translation: $(x, y) \rightarrow (x + 1, y + 6)$.

15.

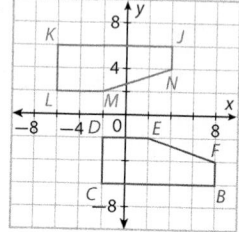

Yes. Map $BCDEF$ to $JKLMN$ with a reflection across the x-axis, followed by a horizontal translation. reflection: $(x, y) \rightarrow (x, -y)$ translation: $(x, y) \rightarrow (x - 4, y)$.

16.

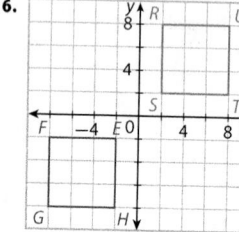

Yes. Map $EFGH$ to $RSTU$ with a counter-clockwise rotation of $90°$ around the origin, followed by a vertical translation. rotation: $(x, y) \rightarrow (-y, x)$ translation: $(x, y) \rightarrow (x, y + 10)$.

17.

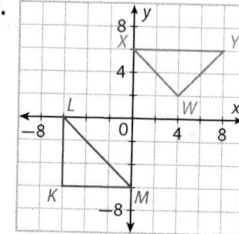

No, the figures are not congruent. There are no transformations to map $\triangle KLM$ to $\triangle WXY$.

The figures shown are congruent. Find a sequence of transformations for the indicated mapping. Give coordinate notation for the transformations you use.

18. Map *PQRST* to *DEFGH*.

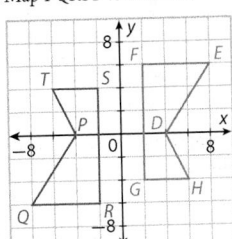

Map *PQRST* to *DEFGH* with a rotation of 180° around the origin. The coordinate notation for the rotation is $(x, y) \rightarrow (-x, -y)$.

19. Map *WXYZ* to *JKLM*.

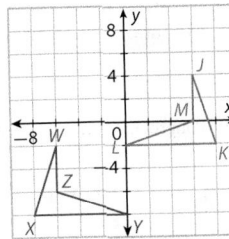

Map *WXYZ* to *JKLM* with a reflection across the y-axis, followed by a vertical translation. reflection: $(x, y) \rightarrow (-x, y)$; translation: $(x, y) \rightarrow (x, y + 6)$.

20. Map *PQRSTU* to *ABCDEF*.

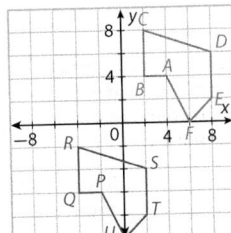

Map *PQRSTU* to *ABCDEF* with a combined translation. The coordinate notation for the translation is $(x, y) \rightarrow (x + 6, y + 10)$.

21. Map △*DEF* to △*KLM*.

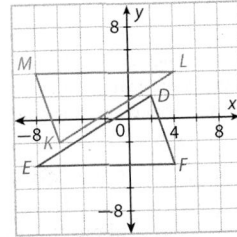

Map △*DEF* to △*KLM* with a rotation of 180° about the origin, followed by a horizontal translation. Rotation: $(x, y) \rightarrow (-x, -y)$; translation: $(x, y) \rightarrow (x - 4, y)$.

22. Determine whether each pair of angles is congruent or not congruent. Select the correct answer for each lettered part.

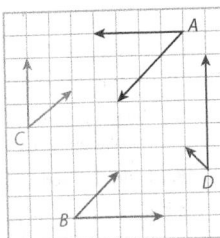

a. ∠A and ∠B   ● Congruent   ○ Not congruent

b. ∠A and ∠C   ○ Congruent   ● Not congruent

c. ∠B and ∠C   ○ Congruent   ● Not congruent

d. ∠B and ∠D   ● Congruent   ○ Not congruent

e. ∠C and ∠D   ○ Congruent   ● Not congruent

© Houghton Mifflin Harcourt Publishing Company

AVOID COMMON ERRORS

Students may make an error when using computations to determine if a transformed figure is congruent or not congruent. Emphasize that a resulting figure with the sides crossing each other is an indication of an error, not necessarily a noncongruent figure.

COLLABORATIVE LEARNING

Give each student a sheet of graph paper. On the top half, have students draw $\triangle ABC$. Then ask them to perform a sequence of two or three rigid motions to draw $\triangle A'B'C'$. They may use each transformation only once. On the bottom half, have them write the sequence of rigid motions using precise mathematical language or symbols, then cut the paper in half. Collect the half sheets, making one pile of drawings and one pile of descriptions. Randomly pass out the papers so that each student receives one from each pile. Students should try to match each drawing with its corresponding rigid motions.

23. If *ABCD* and *WXYZ* are congruent, then *ABCD* can be mapped to *WXYZ* using a rotation and a translation. Determine whether the statement is true or false. Then explain your reasoning.

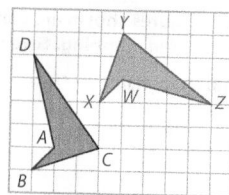

   False. The figures do not have the same orientation, so the sequence of transformations must include a reflection.

24. Which segments are congruent? Which are not congruent? Explain.

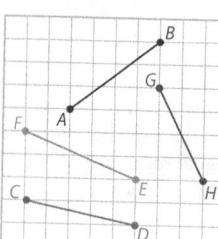

   None are congruent. No rigid motions map one segment onto another.

25. Which angles are congruent? Which are not congruent? Explain.

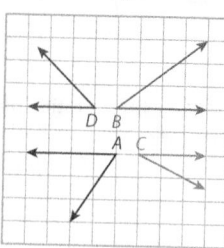

   None are congruent. No rigid motions map one angle onto another.

26. The figures shown are congruent. Find a sequence of transformations that will map *CDEFG* to *QRSTU*. Give coordinate notation for the transformations you use.

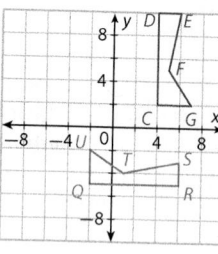

   Rotate *CDEFG* 90° clockwise about the origin: $(x, y) \rightarrow (y, -x)$. **Then reflect across the x-axis:** $(x, y) \rightarrow (x, -y)$. **Then translate:** $(x, y) \rightarrow (x - 4, y - 9)$.

27. The figures shown are congruent. Find a sequence of transformations that will map $\triangle LMN$ to $\triangle XYZ$. Give coordinate notation for the transformations you use.

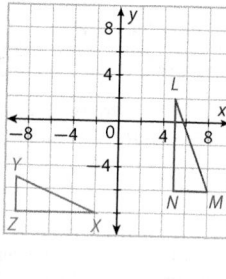

   Rotate $\triangle LMN$ 90° counter clockwise about the origin: $(x, y) \rightarrow (-y, x)$. **Reflect across the y-axis:** $(x, y) \rightarrow (-x, y)$. **Translate:** $(x, y) \rightarrow (x - 3, y - 13)$.

28. Which sequence of transformations does not map a figure onto a congruent figure? Explain.

   A. Rotation of 180° about the origin, reflection across the x-axis, horizontal translation $(x, y) \rightarrow (x + 4, y)$

   B. Reflection across the y-axis, combined translation $(x, y) \rightarrow (x - 5, y + 2)$

   C. Rotation of 180° about the origin, reflection across the y-axis, dilation $(x, y) \rightarrow (2x, 2y)$ **A dilation is not a rigid transformation.**

   D. Counterclockwise rotation of 90° about the origin, reflection across the y-axis, combined translation $(x, y) \rightarrow (x - 11, y - 12)$

29. The figures shown are congruent. Find a sequence of transformations that will map *DEFGH* to *VWXYZ*. Give coordinate notation for the transformations you use.

Map *DEFGH* to *VWXYZ* with a clockwise rotation of 90° around the origin, followed by a reflection across the y-axis, followed by a combined translation. rotation: $(x, y) \rightarrow (y, -x)$; reflection: $(x, y) \rightarrow (-x, y)$; translation: $(x, y) \rightarrow (x + 2, y - 9)$.

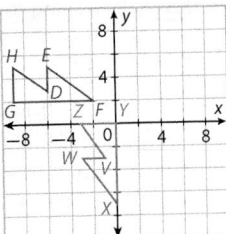

30. How can you prove that two arrows in the recycling symbol are congruent to each other?

The arrows can each be mapped to each other by a rotation, which is a rigid transformation.

31. The city of St. Louis was settled by the French in the mid 1700s and joined the United States in 1803 as part of the Louisiana Purchase. The city flag reflects its French history by featuring the fleur-de-lis. How can you prove that the left and right petals are congruent to each other?

The petals can be mapped onto each other by a reflection, which is a rigid transformation.

32. **Draw Conclusions** Two students are trying to show that the two figures are congruent. The first student decides to map *CDEFG* to *PQRST* using a rotation of 180° around the origin, followed by the translation $(x, y) \rightarrow (x, y + 6)$. The second student believes the correct transformations are a reflection across the y-axis, followed by the vertical translation $(x, y) \rightarrow (x, y - 2)$. Are both students correct, is only one student correct, or is neither student correct?

Only the first student is correct. The two figures have the same orientation, so a sequence of transformations including a single reflection will change the orientation of the result.

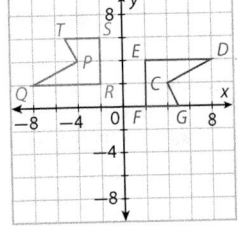

INTEGRATE MATHEMATICAL PRACTICES

Focus on Communication

MP.3 Be sure that students' answers are as detailed and precise as possible. When stating that two figures in the coordinate plane are congruent, students should describe the specific rigid motion(s) that map one figure to the other. For instance, "a reflection across the x-axis" or "the reflection $(x, y) \rightarrow (x, -y)$" are detailed descriptions of a rigid motion in the coordinate plane, while "reflection" is not.

PEER-TO-PEER DISCUSSION

Have students discuss with a partner how to predict the sequence of rigid motions that may map a figure to a congruent figure. Then have them predict and test whether reversing the order of the sequence of rigid motions will produce the preimage figure.

CONNECT VOCABULARY EL

Have students relate the word *congruent* to the terms *equal* and *equivalent*. If a figure is congruent to another it is equal in shape <u>and</u> size. Show students similar figures that are equal in shape but not size, and discuss why they are not congruent.

JOURNAL

Have students write a journal entry in which they summarize what they know so far about congruence. Prompt students to include examples and non-examples of congruent figures and the methods of obtaining them and determining them.

---

33. **Justify Reasoning** Two students are trying to show that the two figures are congruent. The first student decides to map *DEFG* to *RSTU* using a rotation of 180° about the origin, followed by the vertical translation $(x, y) \rightarrow (x, y + 4)$. The second student uses a reflection across the *x*-axis, followed by the vertical translation $(x, y) \rightarrow (x, y + 4)$, followed by a reflection across the *y*-axis. Are both students correct, is only one student correct, or is neither student correct?

    Both students are correct. Either of the sequences of transformation will map *DEFG* to *RSTU*. Recall that a rotation of 180° around the origin is the same as a reflection across both axes.

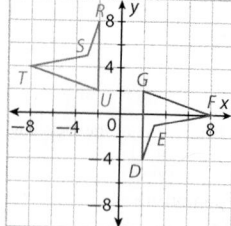

H.O.T. Focus on Higher Order Thinking

34. **Look for a Pattern** Assume the pattern of congruent squares shown in the figure continues forever.

    Write rules for rigid motions that map square 0 onto square 1, square 0 onto square 2, and square 0 onto square 3.

    $(x, y) \rightarrow (x + 2, y - 2)$
    $(x, y) \rightarrow (x + 4, y - 4)$
    $(x, y) \rightarrow (x + 6, y - 6)$

    Write a rule for a rigid motion that maps square 0 onto square *n*.

    $(x, y) \rightarrow (x + 2n, y - 2n)$

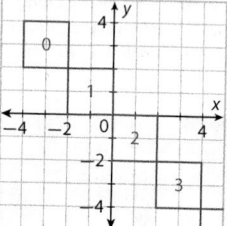

35. **Analyze Relationships** Suppose you know that $\triangle ABC$ is congruent to $\triangle DEF$ and that $\triangle DEF$ is congruent to $\triangle GHJ$. Can you conclude that $\triangle ABC$ is congruent to $\triangle GHJ$? Explain.

    Yes; by the definition of congruence, there is a sequence of rigid motions that maps $\triangle ABC$ onto $\triangle DEF$ and another that maps $\triangle DEF$ onto $\triangle GHJ$. The first sequence followed by the second sequence maps $\triangle ABC$ onto $\triangle GHJ$, so the triangles are congruent.

36. **Communicate Mathematical Ideas** Ella plotted the points $A(0, 0)$, $B(4, 0)$, and $C(0, 4)$. Then she drew $\overline{AB}$ and $\overline{AC}$. Give two different arguments to explain why the segments are congruent.

    Both segments are 4 units long. Because the segments are the same length, they are congruent. A rotation of 90° maps $\overline{AB}$ onto $\overline{AC}$. Because there is a rigid motion that maps one segment onto the other, the segments are congruent.

Lesson Performance Task

The illustration shows how nine congruent shapes can be fitted together to form a larger shape. Each of the shapes can be formed from Shape #1 through a combination of translations, reflections, and/or rotations.

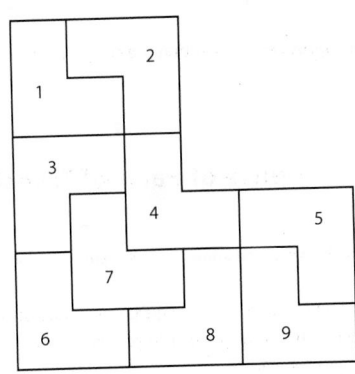

Describe how each of Shapes 2–9 can be formed from Shape #1 through a combination of translations, reflections, and/or rotations. Then design a figure like this one, using at least eight congruent shapes. Number the shapes. Then describe how each of them can be formed from Shape #1 through a combination of translations, reflections, and/or rotations.

Shape #2: Rotate Shape #1 180°.

Shape #3: Reflect Shape #1 vertically.

Shape #4: Translate Shape #1 down and right.

Shape #5: Rotate Shape #1 180° and then translate it down and right.

Shape #6: Translate Shape #1 down.

Shape #7: Translate Shape #1 down and right.

Shape #8: Translate Shape #1 down and then reflect it horizontally.

Shape #9: Translate Shape #1 down and right.

Answers will vary. Check students' answers.

EXTENSION ACTIVITY

The broken lines on the figure show how it can be divided into three congruent isosceles right triangles. Have students copy the figure and determine how it can be divided into eight congruent trapezoids.

INTEGRATE MATHEMATICAL PRACTICES
Focus on Modeling

MP.4 Ask students to show how each of the nine pieces in the Lesson Performance Task can be divided into two congruent shapes so that the entire shape can be constructed from 18 congruent shapes. The shapes are trapezoids that form an L when placed together.

INTEGRATE MATHEMATICAL PRACTICES
Focus on Critical Thinking

MP.3 An object viewed through certain types of lenses will appear to be flipped upside-down. Ask why the letters in the word STAR are flipped when seen through such a lens but the word CODE is not. The letters C, O, D, and E are symmetric with respect to a line drawn horizontally through their centers, while the letters S, T, A, and R are not. The result is that CODE is indeed "flipped" by the lens, and the image through the lens appears exactly as it did before. The same is not true of the letters of STAR.

Scoring Rubric

2 points: Student correctly solves the problem and explains his/her reasoning.

1 point: Student shows good understanding of the problem but does not fully solve or explain his/her reasoning.

0 points: Student does not demonstrate understanding of the problem.

Proving Figures are Congruent Using Rigid Motions   **138**

Corresponding Parts of Congruent Figures Are Congruent

Common Core Math Standards

The student is expected to:

 G-CO.B.7

Use the definition of congruence in terms of rigid motions to show that two triangles are congruent if and only if corresponding pairs of sides and corresponding pairs of angles are congruent.

Mathematical Practices

COMMON CORE **MP.2 Reasoning**

Language Objective

Have students fill in sentence stems to explain why figures are congruent or noncongruent.

ENGAGE

Essential Question: What can you conclude about two figures that are congruent?

The corresponding parts are congruent, and relationships within the figures, such as relative distances between vertices, are equal.

PREVIEW: LESSON PERFORMANCE TASK

View the online Engage. Discuss the photo and ask students to identify congruent shapes in the design. Then preview the Lesson Performance Task.

Name _____ Class _____ Date _____

3.3 Corresponding Parts of Congruent Figures Are Congruent

Essential Question: What can you conclude about two figures that are congruent?

Explore **Exploring Congruence of Parts of Transformed Figures**

You will investigate some conclusions you can make when you know that two figures are congruent.

(A) Fold a sheet of paper in half. Use a straightedge to draw a triangle on the folded sheet. Then cut out the triangle, cutting through both layers of paper to produce two congruent triangles. Label them △ABC and △DEF, as shown.

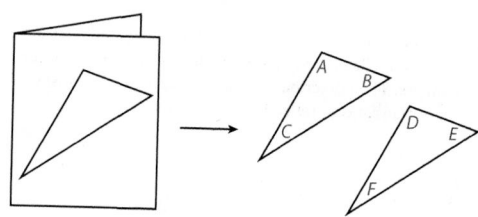

(B) Place the triangles next to each other on a desktop. Since the triangles are congruent, there must be a sequence of rigid motions that maps △ABC to △DEF. Describe the sequence of rigid motions.

A translation (perhaps followed by a rotation) maps △ABC to △DEF.

(C) The same sequence of rigid motions that maps △ABC to △DEF maps parts of △ABC to parts of △DEF. Complete the following.

$\overline{AB} \rightarrow \boxed{DE}$ $\overline{BC} \rightarrow \boxed{EF}$ $\overline{AC} \rightarrow \boxed{DF}$

$A \rightarrow \boxed{D}$ $B \rightarrow \boxed{E}$ $C \rightarrow \boxed{F}$

(D) What does Step C tell you about the corresponding parts of the two triangles? Why?

The corresponding parts are congruent because there is a sequence of rigid motions that

maps each side or angle of △ABC to the corresponding side or angle of △DEF.

© Houghton Mifflin Harcourt Publishing Company

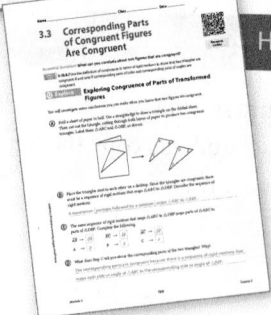

HARDCOVER PAGES 123–132

Turn to these pages to find this lesson in the hardcover student edition.

1. If you know that $\triangle ABC \cong \triangle DEF$, what six congruence statements about
segments and angles can you write? Why?
$\overline{AB} \cong \overline{DE}, \overline{BC} \cong \overline{EF}, \overline{AC} \cong \overline{DF}, \angle A \cong \angle D, \angle B \cong \angle E, \angle C \cong \angle F.$ The rigid motions that map
$\triangle ABC$ to $\triangle DEF$ also map the sides and angles of $\triangle ABC$ to the corresponding sides and
angles of $\triangle DEF$, which establishes congruence.

2. Do your findings in this Explore apply to figures
other than triangles? For instance, if you know that
quadrilaterals *JKLM* and *PQRS* are congruent, can
you make any conclusions about corresponding
parts? Why or why not?

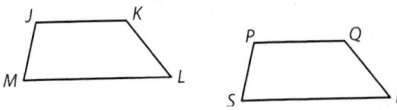

Yes; since quadrilateral *JKLM* is congruent to quadrilateral *PQRS*, there is a sequence of
rigid motions that maps *JKLM* to *PQRS*. This same sequence of rigid motions maps sides
and angles of *JKLM* to the corresponding sides and angles of *PQRS*.

✏ Explain 1   Corresponding Parts of Congruent Figures Are Congruent

The following true statement summarizes what you discovered in the Explore.

> **Corresponding Parts of Congruent Figures Are Congruent**
>
> If two figures are congruent, then corresponding sides are congruent and
> corresponding angles are congruent.

Example 1 $\triangle ABC \cong \triangle DEF.$ Find the given side length or angle measure.

 DE

    Step 1 Find the side that corresponds to $\overline{DE}$.

       Since $\triangle ABC \cong \triangle DEF$, $\overline{AB} \cong \overline{DE}$.

    Step 2 Find the unknown length.

       $DE = AB$, and $AB = 2.6$ cm,
so $DE = 2.6$ cm.

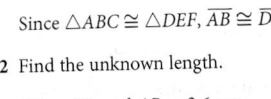

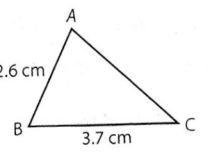

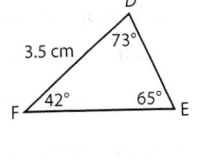

Ⓑ $m\angle B$

    Step 1 Find the angle that corresponds to $\angle B$.

       Since $\triangle ABC \cong \triangle DEF$, $\angle B \cong \angle \boxed{E}$.

    Step 2 Find the unknown angle measure.

       $m\angle B = m\angle \boxed{E}$, and $m\angle \boxed{E} = \boxed{65}°$, so $m\angle B = \boxed{65}°$.

© Houghton Mifflin Harcourt Publishing Company

Exploring Congruence of Parts of Transformed Figures

QUESTIONING STRATEGIES

❓ When you are given two congruent
triangles, how many pairs of corresponding
parts—angles and sides—are there? 6; 3 angles and
3 sides

EXPLAIN 1

Corresponding Parts of Congruent Figures Are Congruent

INTEGRATE MATHEMATICAL PRACTICES
Focus on Communication

MP.3 Have a student read the statement about
Corresponding Parts of Congruent Figures. Discuss
the meaning of the statement for general figures and
then in terms of two triangles. Emphasize that
the statement is a *biconditional*, an if-and-only-if
statement that is true when read as an if-then
statement in either direction.

PROFESSIONAL DEVELOPMENT

COMMON CORE   Math Background

In this lesson, students learn that if two figures (including triangles) are
congruent, then corresponding pairs of sides and corresponding pairs of angles of
the figures are congruent. This follows readily from the rigid-motion definition of
congruence and from the statement that Corresponding Parts of Congruent
Figures Are Congruent. This statement is a biconditional, a statement that is true
in either direction. That is, if corresponding pairs of sides and corresponding pairs
of angles in two figures are congruent, then the figures are congruent.

? How do you determine which sides of two congruent figures correspond? Use the order of letters in the congruence statement. The first letters correspond, the last letters correspond, and the other letters correspond in the same order.

VISUAL CUES

Have each student make a poster illustrating the concept of congruent figures. The illustrations should be labeled to show which pairs of corresponding parts are congruent. Have them show both examples and non-examples of congruent figures in the poster.

EXPLAIN 2

Applying the Properties of Congruence

INTEGRATE MATHEMATICAL PRACTICES

Focus on Modeling

MP.4 Suggest that students list all the congruencies that relate the parts of the figures and mark the figures to show them. Once they have clearly represented the corresponding parts, they can more easily answer the questions.

QUESTIONING STRATEGIES

? How could you use transformations to decide whether two figures are congruent? You could use transformations to create all pairs of corresponding parts congruent. Then the statement applies because if corresponding parts of congruent figures are congruent, then the figures are congruent.

Reflect

3. **Discussion** The triangles shown in the figure are congruent. Can you conclude that $\overline{JK} \cong \overline{QR}$? Explain.

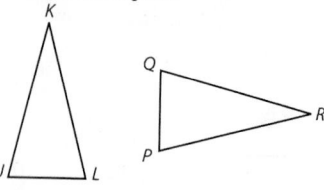

No; the segments appear to be congruent, but the correspondence between the triangles is not given, so you cannot assume $\overline{JK}$ and $\overline{QR}$ are corresponding parts.

Your Turn

$\triangle STU \cong \triangle VWX$. Find the given side length or angle measure.

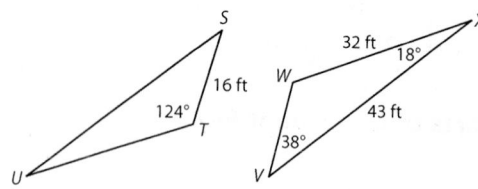

4. *SU*

Since $\triangle STU \cong \triangle VWX$, $\overline{SU} \cong \overline{VX}$.

$SU = VX = $ **43 ft.**

5. $m\angle S$

Since $\triangle STU \cong \triangle VWX$, $\angle S \cong \angle V$.

$m\angle S = m\angle V = $ **38°.**

⊘ Explain 2 **Applying the Properties of Congruence**

Rigid motions preserve length and angle measure. This means that congruent segments have the same length, so $\overline{UV} \cong \overline{XY}$ implies $UV = XY$ and vice versa. In the same way, congruent angles have the same measure, so $\angle J \cong \angle K$ implies $m\angle J = m\angle K$ and vice versa.

Properties of Congruence	
Reflexive Property of Congruence	$\overline{AB} \cong \overline{AB}$
Symmetric Property of Congruence	If $\overline{AB} \cong \overline{CD}$, then $\overline{CD} \cong \overline{AD}$.
Transitive Property of Congruence	If $\overline{AB} \cong \overline{CD}$ and $\overline{CD} \cong \overline{EF}$, then $\overline{AB} \cong \overline{EF}$.

Example 2 $\triangle ABC \cong \triangle DEF$. Find the given side length or angle measure.

(A) *AB*

Since $\triangle ABC \cong \triangle DEF$, $\overline{AB} \cong \overline{DE}$.
Therefore, $AB = DE$.

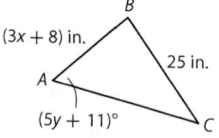 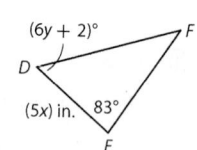

Write an equation. $3x + 8 = 5x$

Subtract $3x$ from each side. $8 = 2x$

Divide each side by 2. $4 = x$

So, $AB = 3x + 8 = 3(4) + 8 = 12 + 8 = 20$ in.

COLLABORATIVE LEARNING

Small Group Activity

Have each student draw a pair of congruent figures on paper. Instruct them to switch papers and to write a congruence statement for the pair of figures. Then have them switch papers several more times within groups, write new congruence statements that fit the pair of figures, and list the congruent pairs of corresponding parts of the figures.

Ⓑ m∠D

Since △ABC ≅ △DEF, ∠ $\boxed{A}$ ≅ ∠D. Therefore, m∠ $\boxed{A}$ = m∠D.

Write an equation. $5y + \boxed{11} = \boxed{6y} + 2$

Subtract 5y from each side. $11 = \boxed{y} + 2$

Subtract 2 from each side. $\boxed{9} = \boxed{y}$

So, m∠D = $(6y + 2)° = \left(6 \cdot \boxed{9} + 2\right)° = \boxed{56}°$.

Your Turn

Quadrilateral GHJK ≅ quadrilateral LMNP. Find the given side length or
angle measure.

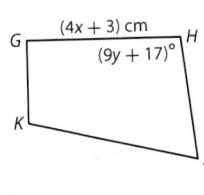
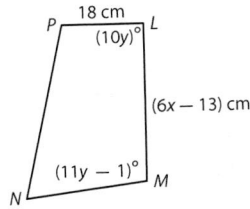

6. LM
Since GHJK ≅ LMNP, $\overline{GH} ≅ \overline{LM}$.
Therefore, GH = LM.
4x + 3 = 6x − 13 → 8 = x
LM = 6x − 13 = 6(8) − 13 = 35 cm

7. m∠H
Since quadrilateral GHJK ≅ quadrilateral
LMNP, ∠H ≅ ∠M. Therefore, m∠H = m∠M.
9y + 17 = 11y − 1 → 9 = y
m∠H = (9y + 17)° = (9 · 9 + 17)° = 98°

 **Explain 3** **Using Congruent Corresponding Parts in a Proof**

Example 3   Write each proof.

Ⓐ   Given: △ABD ≅ △ACD

    Prove: D is the midpoint of $\overline{BC}$.

Statements	Reasons
1. △ABD ≅ △ACD	1. Given
2. $\overline{BD} ≅ \overline{CD}$	2. Corresponding parts of congruent figures are congruent.
3. D is the midpoint of $\overline{BC}$.	3. Definition of midpoint.

© Houghton Mifflin Harcourt Publishing Company

DIFFERENTIATE INSTRUCTION

Technology

Have students use geometry software to create designs using congruent triangles.
They should arrange multiple congruent triangles using different colors, positions,
and orientations. Ask them to make three separate designs: one using congruent
equilateral triangles, one using congruent isosceles triangles, and one using
congruent scalene triangles.

AVOID COMMON ERRORS

Students may correctly solve for a variable but then
incorrectly give the value of the variable as a side
length or angle measure. Remind them to examine
the diagram carefully; sometimes a side length or
angle measure is described by an expression
containing a variable, not by the variable alone.

EXPLAIN 3

Using Congruent Corresponding Parts in a Proof

INTEGRATE MATHEMATICAL PRACTICES
Focus on Technology

MP.5 Encourage students to use geometry software
to reflect the triangle with the given conditions and
then to verify that corresponding congruent parts
have equal measure.

CONNECT VOCABULARY **EL**

In this lesson, students learn the *Corresponding Parts
of Congruent Figures Are Congruent*. Although
acronyms (such as CPCTC) may be helpful to some
students when referring to statements, postulates, or
theorems, such devices may be a bit more difficult for
English Learners at the Emerging level. Consider
making a poster or having students create or copy a
list of theorems, along with their meanings, for them
to refer to in this module. Students may want to come
up with a mnemonic for the CPCTC itself, such as
Cooks Pick Carrots Too Carefully.

? Why do pairs of corresponding congruent parts have equal measure? Since rigid motions preserve angle measure and length, and since there is a sequence of rigid motions that maps a figure to a congruent figure, pairs of corresponding parts must have equal measure.

ELABORATE

INTEGRATE MATHEMATICAL PRACTICES
Focus on Modeling

MP.4 When examining congruent figures, students can see how each vertex is mapped to its corresponding vertex by designating corresponding vertices in the same color and using a different color for each pair of corresponding vertices. Students can also highlight pairs of corresponding sides in the same color, using a different color for each pair.

QUESTIONING STRATEGIES

? Can you say two figures are congruent if their corresponding angles have the same measure? Explain. No. You must also determine that the corresponding sides have the same measure.

? Can you say that a pair of corresponding sides of two congruent figures has equal measure? Yes. If the figures are congruent, then each pair of corresponding sides is congruent and therefore has equal measure.

SUMMARIZE THE LESSON

? Suppose you know that $\triangle CBA \cong \triangle EFG$. What are six congruency statements? $\angle C \cong \angle E$, $\angle B \cong \angle F$, $\angle A \cong \angle G$, $\overline{CB} \cong \overline{EF}$, $\overline{CA} \cong \overline{EG}$, $\overline{BA} \cong \overline{FG}$

Ⓑ Given: Quadrilateral $JKLM \cong$ quadrilateral $NPQR$; $\angle J \cong \angle K$
Prove: $\angle J \cong \angle P$

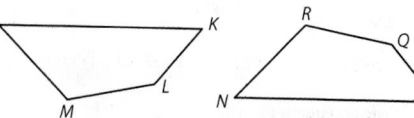

Statements	Reasons
1. Quadrilateral $JKLM \cong$ quadrilateral $NPQR$	1. Given
2. $\angle J \cong \angle K$	2. Given
3. $\angle K \cong \angle P$	3. Corresponding parts of congruent figures are congruent.
4. $\angle J \cong \angle P$	4. Transitive Property of Congruence

Your Turn

Write each proof.

8. Given: $\triangle SVT \cong \triangle SWT$
    Prove: $\overline{ST}$ bisects $\angle VSW$.

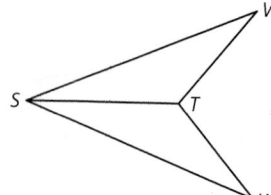

Statements	Reasons
1. $\triangle SVT \cong \triangle SWT$	1. Given
2. $\angle VST \cong \angle WST$	2. Corresponding parts of congruent figures are congruent.
3. $\overline{ST}$ bisects $\angle VSW$.	3. Definition of angle bisector.

9. Given: Quadrilateral $ABCD \cong$ quadrilateral $EFGH$;
    $\overline{AD} \cong \overline{CD}$
    Prove: $\overline{AD} \cong \overline{GH}$

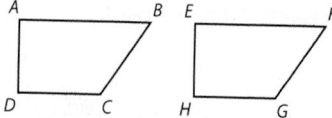

Statements	Reasons
1. Quadrilateral $ABCD \cong$ quadrilateral $EFGH$	1. Given
2. $\overline{AD} \cong \overline{CD}$	2. Given
3. $\overline{CD} \cong \overline{GH}$	3. Corresponding parts of congruent figures are congruent.
4. $\overline{AD} \cong \overline{GH}$	4. Transitive Property of Congruence

LANGUAGE SUPPORT 🄴🄻

Connect Vocabulary

Have students work in pairs. Provide each student with a protractor and ruler, and ask them to explain why two figures are congruent or noncongruent. Provide students with sentence stems to help them describe the attributes of the figures. For example: "The two (triangles/quadrilaterals/figures) are or are not congruent because their corresponding angles have/don't have equal measures. Angles ____ and ____ are corresponding, and measure _____ degrees. Corresponding sides have equal/not equal lengths." Students work together to complete the sentences.

Elaborate

10. A student claims that any two congruent triangles must have the same perimeter. Do you agree? Explain.

Yes; since the corresponding sides of congruent triangles are congruent, the sum of the lengths of the sides (perimeter) must be the same for both triangles.

11. If $\triangle PQR$ is a right triangle and $\triangle PQR \cong \triangle XYZ$, does $\triangle XYZ$ have to be a right triangle? Why or why not?

Yes; since $\triangle PQR$ is a right triangle, one of its angles is a right angle. Since corresponding parts of congruent figures are congruent, one of the angles of $\triangle XYZ$ must also be a right angle, which means $\triangle XYZ$ is a right triangle.

12. Essential Question Check-In Suppose you know that pentagon $ABCDE$ is congruent to pentagon $FGHJK$. How many additional congruence statements can you write using corresponding parts of the pentagons? Explain.

There are five statements using the congruent corresponding sides and five statements using the congruent corresponding angles.

⭐ Evaluate: Homework and Practice

- Online Homework
- Hints and Help
- Extra Practice

1. Danielle finds that she can use a translation and a reflection to make quadrilateral $ABCD$ fit perfectly on top of quadrilateral $WXYZ$. What congruence statements can Danielle write using the sides and angles of the quadrilaterals? Why?

The same sequence of rigid motions that maps $ABCD$ to $WXYZ$ also maps sides and angles of $ABCD$ to corresponding sides and angles of $WXYZ$. Therefore, those sides and angles are congruent: $\overline{AB} \cong \overline{WX}$, $\overline{BC} \cong \overline{XY}$, $\overline{CD} \cong \overline{YZ}$, $\overline{AD} \cong \overline{WZ}$, $\angle A \cong \angle W$, $\angle B \cong \angle X$, $\angle C \cong \angle Y$, $\angle D \cong \angle Z$.

$\triangle DEF \cong \triangle GHJ$. **Find the given side length or angle measure.**

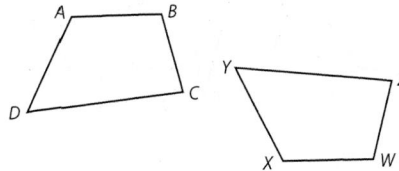

2. JH

Since $\triangle DEF \cong \triangle GHJ$, $\overline{FE} \cong \overline{JH}$.

$FE = JH = 31$ ft, so $JH = 31$ ft.

3. $m\angle D$

Since $\triangle DEF \cong \triangle GHJ$, $\angle D \cong \angle G$.

$m\angle D = m\angle G = 43°$

© Houghton Mifflin Harcourt Publishing Company

ASSIGNMENT GUIDE

Concepts and Skills	Practice
Explore Exploring Congruence of Parts of Transformed Figures	Exercises 1
Example 1 Corresponding Parts of Congruent Figures are Congruent	Exercises 2–5, 10–13
Example 2 Applying the Properties of Congruence	Exercises 6–9
Example 3 Using Congruent Corresponding Parts in a Proof	Exercises 14–16

INTEGRATE MATHEMATICAL PRACTICES

Focus on Math Connections

MP.1 Have students consider whether two quadrilaterals, both with side lengths of 1 foot on each side, are congruent. Students should recognize that the description is that of a rhombus. Demonstrate that a box with an open top and bottom lying on its side is not rigid, and although the side lengths stay the same when one side is pushed, the angles change. Thus it is possible for the two figures described to have different angle measures and not be congruent.

Exercise	Depth of Knowledge (D.O.K.)	COMMON CORE Mathematical Practices
1	**1** Recall of Information	**MP.6** Precision
2–5	**1** Recall of Information	**MP.2** Reasoning
6–9	**1** Recall of Information	**MP.4** Modeling
14–16	**2** Skills/Concepts	**MP.3** Logic
10–13, 17–18	**2** Skills/Concepts	**MP.2** Reasoning
19–22	**2** Skills/Concepts	**MP.4** Modeling

Focus on Communication

MP.3 Have students compare their congruence statements for a given diagram, and ask them to write other correct congruence statements for the same diagram. Then have them write a congruence statement that is not correct for the diagram and explain why it is not correct.

$KLMN \cong PQRS$. Find the given side length or angle measure.

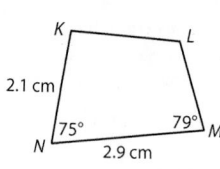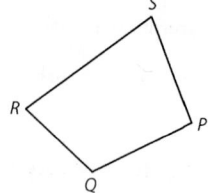

4. $m\angle R$ $\angle M \cong \angle R$.
$m\angle M = m\angle R = 79°$.

5. PS $\overline{KN} \cong \overline{PS}$. $KN = PS =$
2.1 cm

$\triangle ABC \cong \triangle TUV$. Find the given side length or angle measure.

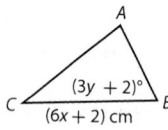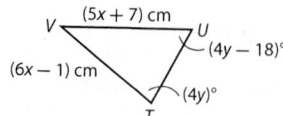

6. BC $\overline{BC} \cong \overline{UV}$. So, $BC = UV$.
$6x + 2 = 5x + 7 \rightarrow x = 5$
So, $BC = 6x + 2 = 6(5) + 2 =$
$30 + 2 = 32$ cm.

7. $m\angle U$ $\angle B \cong \angle U$. So, $m\angle B = m\angle U$.
$3y + 2 = 4y - 18 \rightarrow 20 = y$
So, $m\angle U = (4y - 18)° =$
$(4 \cdot 20 - 18)° = 62°$.

$DEFG \cong KLMN$. Find the given side length or angle measure.

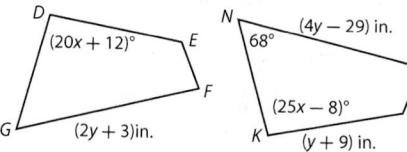

8. FG $\overline{FG} \cong \overline{MN}$. So, $FG = MN$.
$2y + 3 = 4y - 29 \rightarrow 16 = y$
So, $FG = 2y + 3 = 2(16) + 3 =$
$32 + 3 = 35$ in.

9. $m\angle D$ $\angle D \cong \angle K$. So, $m\angle D = m\angle K$.
$20x + 12 = 25x - 8 \rightarrow 4 = x$
So, $m\angle D = (20x + 12)° =$
$(20 \cdot 4 + 12)° = 92°$.

$\triangle GHJ \cong \triangle PQR$ and $\triangle PQR \cong \triangle STU$. Complete the following using a side or angle of $\triangle STU$. Justify your answers.

10. $\overline{GH} \cong$ $\underline{\overline{ST}}$

$\triangle GHJ \cong \triangle STU$ by the Transitive Prop. of Cong., and corr. parts of $\cong$ fig. $\cong$.

11. $\angle J \cong$ $\underline{\angle U}$

$\triangle GHJ \cong \triangle STU$ by the Transitive Prop. of Cong., and corr. parts of $\cong$ fig. $\cong$.

12. $GJ =$ $\underline{SU}$

$\triangle GHJ \cong \triangle STU$ by the Transitive Prop. of Cong., and corr. parts of $\cong$ fig. $\cong$.

Congruent segments have the same length.

13. $m\angle G =$ $\underline{m\angle S}$

$\triangle GHJ \cong \triangle STU$ by the Transitive Prop. of Cong., and corr. parts of $\cong$ fig. $\cong$. Cong. angles have the same measure.

Exercise	Depth of Knowledge (D.O.K.)	COMMON CORE Mathematical Practices	
23	**2** Skills/Concepts		**MP.2** Reasoning
24–25	**3** Strategic Thinking	H.O.T.	**MP.3** Logic
26	**3** Strategic Thinking	H.O.T.	**MP.6** Precision
27	**3** Strategic Thinking	H.O.T.	**MP.3** Logic

Write each proof.

14. Given: Quadrilateral $PQTU \cong$ quadrilateral $QRST$
Prove: $\overline{QT}$ bisects $\overline{PR}$.

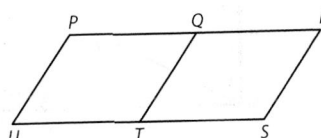

Statements	Reasons
1. Quadrilateral $PQTU \cong$ quadrilateral $QRST$	1. Given
2. $\overline{PQ} \cong \overline{QR}$	2. Corr. parts of $\cong$ fig. are $\cong$
3. Q is the midpoint of $\overline{PR}$.	3. Definition of midpoint
4. $\overline{QT}$ bisects $\overline{PR}$.	4. Definition of segment bisector

15. Given: $\triangle ABC \cong \triangle ADC$
Prove: $\overline{AC}$ bisects $\angle BAD$ and $\overline{AC}$ bisects $\angle BCD$.

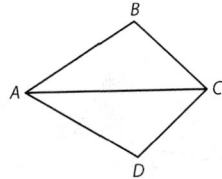

Statements	Reasons
1. $\triangle ABC \cong \triangle DEF$	1. Given
2. $\angle BAC \cong \angle DAC$	2. Corr. parts of $\cong$ fig. are $\cong$
3. $\angle BCA \cong \angle DCA$	3. Corr. parts of $\cong$ fig. are $\cong$
4. $\overline{AC}$ bisects $\angle BAD$ and $\overline{AC}$ bisects $\angle BCD$.	4. Definition of angle bisector

16. Given: Pentagon $ABCDE \cong$ pentagon $FGHJK$; $\angle D \cong \angle E$
Prove: $\angle D \cong \angle K$

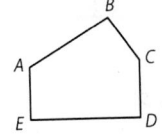 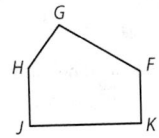

Statements	Reasons
1. Pentagon $ABCDE \cong$ pentagon $FGHJK$	1. Given
2. $\angle D \cong \angle E$	2. Given
3. $\angle E \cong \angle K$	3. Corr. parts of $\cong$ fig. are $\cong$
4. $\angle D \cong \angle K$	4. Transitive Property of Congruence

Students may find the value of a variable or the value of an algebraic expression as the solution to a problem when they are in fact only part of the way through the solving process. Remind students to always go back to the initial question to make sure the answer is the solution to the problem.

Students may write incorrect congruence statements. Make sure they understand that the order of the vertices in a congruence statement is not random. They should know that they can identify corresponding angles by choosing pairs of letters in corresponding positions in a congruence statement. For example, in $\triangle JZQ \cong \triangle MDH$, the letters J and M both appear in the first position in the names of their respective triangles. This means $\angle J \cong \angle M$. In a similar way, pairs of letters that are in corresponding positions yield pairs of corresponding sides.

$\triangle ABC \cong \triangle DEF$. Find the given side length or angle measure.

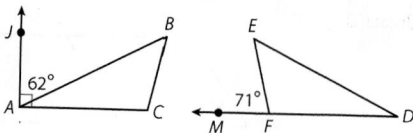

17. $m\angle D$ $m\angle JAB + m\angle BAC = 90°$, so $62° + m\angle BAC = 90°$ and $m\angle BAC = 28°$.
Since $\triangle ABC \cong \triangle DEF$, $\angle BAC \cong \angle D$. $m\angle BAC = m\angle D$, and $m\angle BAC = 28°$, so $m\angle D = 28°$.

18. $m\angle C$ $m\angle EFM + m\angle EFD = 180°$, so $71° + m\angle EFD = 180°$ and $m\angle EFD = 109°$.
Since $\triangle ABC \cong \triangle DEF$, $\angle C \cong \angle EFD$. $m\angle C = m\angle EFD$, and $m\angle EFD = 109°$, so $m\angle C = 109°$.

19. The figure shows the dimensions of two city parks, where $\triangle RST \cong \triangle XYZ$ and $\overline{YX} \cong \overline{YZ}$. A city employee wants to order new fences to surround both parks. What is the total length of the fences required to surround the parks?

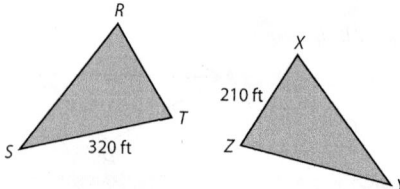

Since $\triangle RST \cong \triangle XYZ$, $\overline{ST} \cong \overline{YZ}$, so $ST = YZ = 320$ ft. Since $\overline{YX} \cong \overline{YZ}$, $YX = YZ = 320$ ft.
Since the triangles are congruent, they have the same perimeter, which is $210 + 320 + 320 = 850$ ft. The total length of the fences is $850 + 850 = 1700$ ft.

20. A tower crane is used to lift steel, concrete, and building materials at construction sites. The figure shows part of the horizontal beam of a tower crane, in which $\triangle ABG \cong \triangle BCH \cong \triangle HGB$

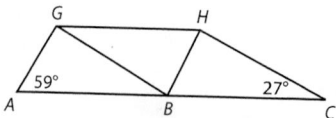

a. Is it possible to determine $m\angle GBH$? If so, how? If not, why not?
Yes; since corr. parts are $\cong$, $m\angle ABG = 27°$ and $m\angle HBC = 59°$, so
$m\angle GBH = 180° - 59° - 27° = 94°$.

b. A member of the construction crew claims that $\overline{AC}$ is twice as long as $\overline{AB}$. Do you agree? Explain.
Yes; since corr. parts are $\cong$, $\overline{AB} \cong \overline{BC}$ and so B is the midpoint of $\overline{AC}$.
This means AC is twice AB.

21. Multi-Step A company installs triangular pools at hotels. All of the pools are congruent and $\triangle JKL \cong \triangle MNP$ in the figure. What is the perimeter of each pool?

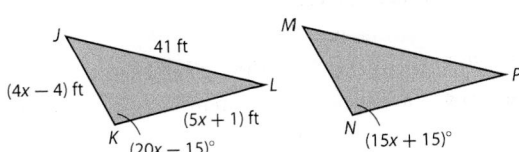

Since corresponding parts are congruent, $\angle K \cong \angle N$ and so $m\angle K = m\angle N$.

$20x - 15 = 15x + 15 \rightarrow x = 6$; $JK = 4(6) - 4 = 20$ ft, $KL = 5(6) + 1 = 31$ ft

The perimeter of $\triangle JKL$ is $20 + 31 + 41 = 92$ ft. The perimeter of $\triangle MNP$ is also 92 ft.

22. Kendall and Ava lay out the course shown below for their radio-controlled trucks. In the figure, $\triangle ABD \cong \triangle CBD$. The trucks travel at a constant speed of 15 feet per second. How long does it take a truck to travel on the course from A to B to C to D? Round to the nearest tenth of a second.

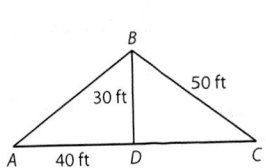

Since $\triangle ABD \cong \triangle CBD$, $\overline{AB} \cong \overline{CB}$, so $AB = 50$ ft. Also, $\overline{AD} \cong \overline{CD}$, so $CD = 40$ ft.

$AB + BC + CD = 50 + 50 + 40 = 140$ ft; distance = rate × time, so $140 = 15t \rightarrow t \approx 9.3$ s.

23. $\triangle MNP \cong \triangle QRS$. Determine whether each statement about the triangles is true or false. Select the correct answer for each lettered part.

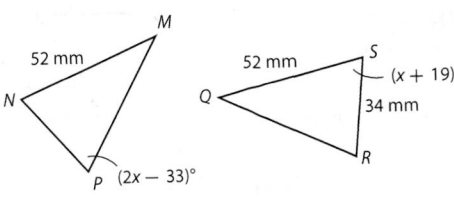

a. Since $\triangle MNP \cong \triangle QRS$, $\overline{MN} \cong \overline{QR}$, so $QR = 52$ mm. $\triangle QRS$ has two sides with the same length, so it is isosceles.

b. Since $\triangle MNP \cong \triangle QRS$, $\overline{MP} \cong \overline{QS}$, so $MP = 52$ mm. Therefore, $MP = MN$.

c. Since $\triangle MNP \cong \triangle QRS$, $\angle P \cong \angle S$, so $2x - 33 = x + 19$. Solving the equation shows that $x = 52$ and $m\angle P = (2x - 33)° = (2 \cdot 52 - 33)° = 71°$.

d. Since $\triangle MNP \cong \triangle QRS$, $\overline{MP} \cong \overline{QR}$, so $QR = 52$ mm. The perimeter of $\triangle QRS$ is $52 + 52 + 34 = 138$ mm.

e. Since $\triangle MNP \cong \triangle QRS$, $\angle M \cong \angle Q$ since corresponding parts of congruent figures are congruent.

a. $\triangle QRS$ is isosceles.   ● True   ○ False

b. $\overline{MP}$ is longer than $\overline{MN}$.   ○ True   ● False

c. $m\angle P = 52°$ ○ True   ● False

d. The perimeter of $\triangle QRS$ is 120 mm.   ○ True   ● False

e. $\angle M \cong \angle Q$ ● True   ○ False

INTEGRATE MATHEMATICAL PRACTICES

Focus on Reasoning

MP.2 When students solve algebraic equations to find the measures of congruent corresponding parts of figures, caution them to first verify that the correspondences are correct. Suggest that students start by listing the pairs of corresponding parts.

PEER-TO-PEER DISCUSSION

Ask students to discuss with a partner how to determine whether two figures are congruent. Have students give each other a pair of figures, look for the congruent corresponding parts, and then write a congruence statement for the figures. Repeat the exercise for other pairs of figures.

JOURNAL

Have students write a journal entry in which they discuss the statement that Corresponding Parts of Congruent Figures Are Congruent in their own words. Encourage them to include one or more labeled figures as part of the journal entry.

24. **Justify Reasoning** Given that $\triangle ABC \cong \triangle DEF$, $AB = 2.7$ ft, and $AC = 3.4$ ft, is it possible to determine the length of $\overline{EF}$? If so, find the length and justify your steps. If not, explain why not.

    No; the side of $\triangle ABC$ that corresponds to $\overline{EF}$ is $\overline{BC}$. The length of this side

    is not known and cannot be determined from the given information.

25. **Explain the Error** A student was told that $\triangle GHJ \cong \triangle RST$ and was asked to find GH. The student's work is shown below. Explain the error and find the correct answer.

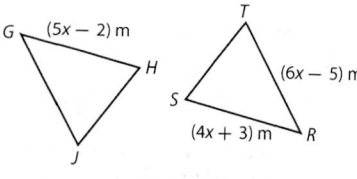

Student's Work
$5x - 2 = 6x - 5$
$-2 = x - 5$
$3 = x$
$GH = 5x - 2 = 5(3) - 2 = 13$ m

    The student incorrectly identified corresponding sides. Since $\triangle GHJ \cong \triangle RST$, $\overline{GH} \cong \overline{RS}$.

    $5x - 2 = 4x + 3 \rightarrow x = 5$; $GH = 5(5) - 2 = 23$ m.

26. **Critical Thinking** In $\triangle ABC$, $m\angle A = 55°$, $m\angle B = 50°$, and $m\angle C = 75°$. In $\triangle DEF$, $m\angle E = 50°$, and $m\angle F = 65°$. Is it possible for the triangles to be congruent? Explain.

    No; if the triangles were congruent, then corresponding angles would be congruent. Since $m\angle F = 65°$, there is no angle of $\triangle ABC$ that could be the corresponding angle to $\angle F$, so the triangles cannot be congruent.

27. **Analyze Relationships** $\triangle PQR \cong \triangle SQR$ and $\overline{RS} \cong \overline{RT}$. A student said that point R appears to be the midpoint of $\overline{PT}$. Is it possible to prove this? If so, write the proof. If not, explain why not. Yes;

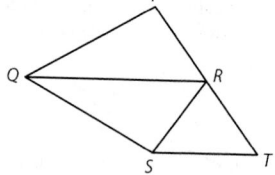

Statements	Reasons
1. $\triangle PQR \cong \triangle SQR$	1. Given
2. $\overline{RP} \cong \overline{RS}$	2. Corr parts of $\cong$ figs. are $\cong$
3. $\overline{RS} \cong \overline{RT}$	3. Given
4. $\overline{RP} \cong \overline{RT}$	4. Transitive Property
5. R is the midpoint of $\overline{PT}$	5. Definition of midpoint

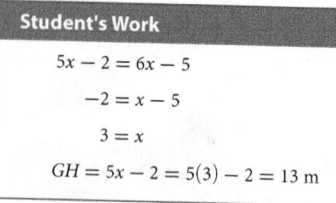

© Houghton Mifflin Harcourt Publishing Company

Lesson Performance Task

The illustration shows a "Yankee Puzzle" quilt.

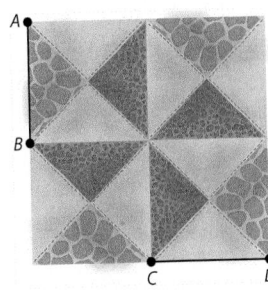

a. Use the idea of congruent shapes to describe the design of the quilt.

   The design is created from 16 congruent triangles. Each quarter of the design consists of 4 of the triangles joined to form a square.

b. Explain how the triangle with base $\overline{AB}$ can be transformed to the position of the triangle with base $\overline{CD}$.

   There are many ways to transform the triangle with base $\overline{AB}$ to the position of the triangle with base $\overline{CD}$. One way is to translate it to the position of the triangle directly beneath it, then, rotate it 90° counterclockwise about C, then translate to the right.

c. Explain how you know that $CD = AB$.

   $CD = AB$ because corresponding parts of congruent figures are congruent.

EXTENSION ACTIVITY

Challenge students to draw and color a design for a quilt that meets the following requirements:

- The design should be square.
- The design should consist of triangles and/or quadrilaterals only.
- The design should have 90-degree rotational symmetry.

INTEGRATE MATHEMATICAL PRACTICES
Focus on Patterns

MP.8 Sketch and number the eight inner triangles of the Yankee Puzzle quilt on the board.

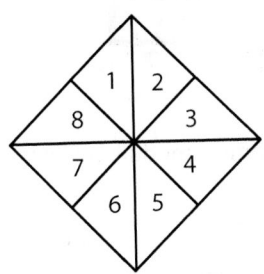

? Given Triangle 1, how could you find the locations of the other seven triangles using transformations? **Sample answer: Rotate Triangle 1 90°, 180°, and 270° clockwise around the center point to locate triangles 3, 5, and 7. Reflect Triangle 1 across the vertical center line to locate Triangle 2. Then rotate Triangle 2 90°, 180°, and 270° clockwise around the center point to locate triangles 4, 6, and 8.**

INTEGRATE MATHEMATICAL PRACTICES
Focus on Communication

MP.3 Describe how, starting with a square, you could draw the pattern of a Yankee Puzzle quilt. **Sample answer: Draw the diagonals of the square. Find the midpoints of the four sides. Connect the midpoint of each side with the midpoint of the side adjacent to it and the midpoint of the side opposite it.**

Scoring Rubric
2 points: Student correctly solves the problem and explains his/her reasoning.
1 point: Student shows good understanding of the problem but does not fully solve or explain his/her reasoning.
0 points: Student does not demonstrate understanding of the problem.

Study Guide Review

ASSESSMENT AND INTERVENTION

Assign or customize module reviews.

MODULE PERFORMANCE TASK

COMMON CORE

Mathematical Practices: MP.1, MP.3, MP.4, MP.6
G-CO.A.5, G-CO.B.6

SUPPORTING STUDENT REASONING

Students should begin this problem by focusing on the transformations needed to move one figure to a congruent figure in the plane. Here are some issues they might bring up.

- **How to identify an open space on the puzzle that is congruent to one of the available puzzle pieces:** The open space on the puzzle has at least two sides that can be matched to the available puzzle pieces.

- **The rotation(s) needed to position the available puzzle piece:** The center of the rotation will be close to the center of the available puzzle piece.

- **The translation(s) needed to move the available puzzle piece into position**: If the rotation to a vertical position is done first, then the translations will be vertical and horizontal.

- **If there are pieces that will not fit anywhere into the pieces already assembled:** Yes, the piece at the upper right appears not to fit anywhere.

Essential Question: How can you use congruency to solve real-world problems?

KEY EXAMPLE (Lesson 3.1)

Write the vertices of the image of the figure given by $A(2, 1)$, $B(3, 3)$, $C(2, 4)$ after the transformations.

$$(x, y) \rightarrow (x + 1, y + 2) \rightarrow (3x, y)$$

$A(2, 1) \rightarrow A'(3, 3)$

$B(3, 3) \rightarrow B'(4, 5)$ Apply the transformations in order to each point. Apply the first transformation.

$C(2, 4) \rightarrow C'(3, 6)$

$A'(3, 3) \rightarrow A''(9, 3)$

$B'(4, 5) \rightarrow B''(12, 5)$ Apply the second transformation.

$C'(3, 6) \rightarrow C''(9, 6)$

The image of the transformed figure is determined by the points $A''(9, 3)$, $B''(12, 5)$, $C''(9, 6)$.

KEY EXAMPLE (Lesson 3.2)

Determine whether a triangle $\triangle ABC$ is congruent to its image after the transformations $(x, y) \rightarrow (x + 1, y + 2) \rightarrow (2x, y)$.

The transformation $(x, y) \rightarrow (x + 1, y + 2)$ is a translation, which is a rigid motion, so after this transformation the image is congruent. The transformation $(x, y) \rightarrow (2x, y)$ is a dilation, which is not a rigid motion, so the image from this transformation is not congruent.

After the transformations, the image is not congruent to $\triangle ABC$ because one of the transformations is not a rigid motion.

KEY EXAMPLE (Lesson 3.3)

Find the angle in $\triangle DFE$ congruent to $\angle A$ and the side congruent to $\overline{BC}$ when $\triangle ABC \cong \triangle DFE$.

Since $\triangle ABC \cong \triangle DFE$, and corresponding parts of congruent figures are congruent, $\angle A \cong \angle D$ and $\overline{BC} \cong \overline{FE}$.

SCAFFOLDING SUPPORT

- Show students how to use a protractor to approximate the angle of rotation of a puzzle piece. Remind students to specify whether the rotation is clockwise or counterclockwise.

- Suggest that students draw a rough sketch of the pieces that have not yet been fitted into the puzzle and number them. Have them also draw a rough sketch of the edge of the puzzle showing the empty spaces and letter the spaces. Then students can begin their descriptions with phrases such as "To move piece 2 into slot E...".

EXERCISES

Write the vertices of the image of the figure after the transformations. *(Lesson 3.1)*

1. The figure given by $A(1, -2)$, $B(2, 5)$, $C(-3, 7)$, and the transformations
   $(x, y) \rightarrow (x, y-1) \rightarrow (-y, 2x)$ ___A' (3, 2), B' (−4, 4), C' (−6, −6)___

Find the rigid motions to transform one figure into its congruent figure. *(Lesson 3.2)*

2. In the figure, $\triangle ABC \cong \triangle DEF$.

   The rigid motions to transform from $\triangle ABC$ to $\triangle DEF$ are
   ___$(x, y) \rightarrow (-y, x) \rightarrow (x-2, y+2)$___ .

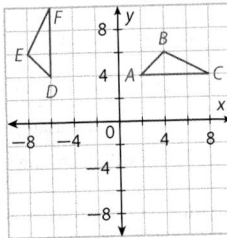

Find the congruent parts. *(Lesson 3.3)*

3. Given $\triangle ABC \cong \triangle DEF$, $\angle A \cong$ ___∠D___ .

4. Given $\triangle ABC \cong \triangle DEF$, $\overline{CA} \cong$ ___$\overline{FD}$___ .

MODULE PERFORMANCE TASK

Jigsaw Puzzle

A popular pastime, jigsaw puzzles are analogous to the series of transformations that can be performed to move one figure onto another congruent figure.

In the photo, identify at least three pieces that would likely fit into one of the empty spaces in the puzzle. Describe the rotations and translations necessary to move the piece to its correct position in the puzzle.

DISCUSSION OPPORTUNITIES

- Can any available piece be moved into position using a single transformation?
- The available pieces look very similar. How will you determine whether you chose the correct piece to transform to the congruent piece?

SAMPLE SOLUTION

I made a sketch of the pieces that had not yet been fitted into the puzzle and numbered them from 1 to 5. I also made a sketch of the empty spaces at the edge of the puzzle and lettered them A to F. Here are the moves I used to transfer the three pieces into the puzzle:

To move Piece 4 into Space C, rotate the piece approximately 75 degrees clockwise, then move it vertically upward and horizontally to the left.

To move Piece 1 into Space D, rotate the piece approximately 150 degrees counterclockwise, then move it vertically downward and horizontally to the left.

To move Piece 2 into Space A, rotate the piece approximately 100 degrees counterclockwise, then move it vertically upward and horizontally to the left.

Assessment Rubric

2 points: Student correctly solves the problem and explains his/her reasoning.

1 point: Student shows good understanding of the problem but does not fully solve or explain.

0 points: Student does not demonstrate understanding of the problem.

Ready to Go On?

ASSESS MASTERY

Use the assessment on this page to determine if students have mastered the concepts and standards covered in this module.

ASSESSMENT AND INTERVENTION

Access Ready to Go On? assessment online, and receive instant scoring, feedback, and customized intervention or enrichment.

ADDITIONAL RESOURCES

Response to Intervention Resources

- Reteach Worksheets

Differentiated Instruction Resources

- Reading Strategies **EL**
- Success for English Learners **EL**
- Challenge Worksheets

Assessment Resources

- Leveled Module Quizzes

(Ready) to Go On?

3.1–3.3 Congruent Figures

- Online Homework
- Hints and Help
- Extra Practice

Predict the results of the transformations. *(Lesson 3.1)*

1. Triangle △ABC is in the first quadrant and translated along ⟨2, 1⟩ and reflected across the x-axis.

Which quadrant will the triangle be in after the first transformation? ___The first quadrant___

Which quadrant will the triangle be in after the second transformation? ___The fourth quadrant___

Determine whether the triangles are congruent using rigid motions. *(Lesson 3.2)*

2. Using the graph with △ABC, △DEF, and △PQR:

  A. Determine whether △ABC is congruent to △DEF.

    △ABC is not congruent to △DEF.

  B. Determine whether △DEF is congruent to △PQR.

    △DEF is congruent to △PQR.

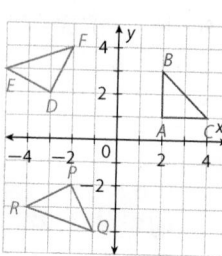

Find the congruent parts of the triangles. *(Lesson 3.3)*

3. List all of the pairs of congruent sides for two congruent triangles △ABC and △DEF.

$\overline{AB} \cong \overline{DE}$, $\overline{BC} \cong \overline{EF}$, $\overline{CA} \cong \overline{FD}$

ESSENTIAL QUESTION

4. How can you determine whether a figure is congruent to another figure?

Answers may vary. Sample: You can figure out whether a figure is congruent to another by determining whether a sequence of rigid motions will transform one figure into the other.

COMMON CORE	**Common Core Standards**		

Lesson	Items	Content Standards	Mathematical Practices
3.1	1	G-CO.A.5	MP.4
3.1, 3.2	2	G-CO.B.7	MP.7
3.3	3	G-CO.B.7	MP.4

Assessment Readiness

1. A line segment with points $R(3, 5)$ and $S(5, 5)$ is reflected across the line $y = -x$ and translated 2 units down. Determine whether each choice is a coordinate of the image of the line segment. Select Yes or No for A–C.

   A. $R'(-5, -3)$ ○ Yes   ● No

   B. $R'(-5, -5)$ ● Yes   ○ No

   C. $S'(-5, -7)$ ● Yes   ○ No

2. The polygon $ABCD$ is congruent to $PQRS$. The measure of angle B is equal to 65°. Choose True or False for each statement.

   A. The supplement of angle Q measures 115°.   ● True   ○ False

   B. Angle Q measures 115°.   ○ True   ● False

   C. The supplement of angle B measures 115°.   ● True   ○ False

3. Triangle LMN is a right triangle. The measure of angle L is equal to 35°. Triangle LMN is congruent to $\triangle PRQ$ with right angle R. Choose True or False for each statement.

   A. The measure of angle Q is 55°.   ● True   ○ False

   B. The measure of angle R is 90°.   ● True   ○ False

   C. The measure of angle P is 35°.   ● True   ○ False

4. The two triangles, $\triangle ABC$ and $\triangle DEF$, are congruent. Which side is congruent to $\overline{CA}$? Which side is congruent to $\overline{BA}$?

   $\overline{FD}; \overline{ED}$

MIXED REVIEW
Assessment Readiness

ASSESSMENT AND INTERVENTION

Personal Math Trainer

Assign ready-made or customized practice tests to prepare students for high-stakes tests.

ADDITIONAL RESOURCES

Assessment Resources

- Leveled Module Quizzes: Modified, B

AVOID COMMON ERRORS

Item 1 Some students will stop too soon when faced with a problem with multiple steps. Encourage students to number each step, and then make sure they have completed each one before choosing a final answer to the problem.

COMMON CORE | Common Core Standards

Lesson	Items	Content Standards	Mathematical Practices
3.1, 2.1, 2.2	1*	G-CO.A.5	MP.5
3.3, 1.2	2*	G-CO.A.1, G-CO.B.6	MP.2
3.3	3	G-CO.B.6	MP.2
3.3	4	G-CO.B.6	MP.7

* Item integrates mixed review concepts from previous modules or a previous course.

MIXED REVIEW
Assessment Readiness

ASSESSMENT AND INTERVENTION

Assign ready-made or customized practice tests to prepare students for high-stakes tests.

ADDITIONAL RESOURCES

Assessment Resources

- Leveled Unit Tests: Modified, A, B, C
- Performance Assessment

AVOID COMMON ERRORS

Item 7 Some students will attempt this problem without plotting the transformations. Encourage students to use a sheet of graph paper and test each transformation.

UNIT 1 MIXED REVIEW
Assessment Readiness

- Online Homework
- Hints and Help
- Extra Practice

1. Consider each expression. if $x = -2$, is the value of the expression a positive number? Select Yes or No.
   A. $-2(x - 2)^2$ — ○ Yes ● No
   B. $-3x(5 - 4x)$ — ● Yes ○ No
   C. $x^3 + 6x$ — ○ Yes ● No

2. A bedroom is shaped like a rectangular prism. The floor has a length of 4.57 meters and a width of 4.04 meters. The height of the room is 2.3 meters. Choose True or False for each statement.
   A. The perimeter of the floor with the correct number of significant digits is 17.22 meters. — ● True ○ False
   B. The area of the floor with the correct number of significant digits is 18.46 square meters. — ○ True ● False
   C. The volume of the room with the correct number of significant digits is 42 cubic meters. — ● True ○ False

3. Does the ray BD bisect $\angle ABC$?
   Select Yes or No for each pair of angles.
   A. $m\angle ABC = 60°$, $m\angle ABD = 30°$ — ● Yes ○ No
   B. $m\angle ABC = 96°$, $m\angle ABD = 47°$ — ○ Yes ● No
   C. $m\angle ABC = 124°$, $m\angle ABD = 62°$ — ● Yes ○ No

4. Is the point C the midpoint of the line $\overline{AB}$?
   Select Yes or No for each statement.
   A. $A(1, 2)$, $B(3, 4)$, and $C(2, 3)$ — ● Yes ○ No
   B. $A(-1, 2)$, $B(3, -1)$, and $C(1, 0)$ — ○ Yes ● No
   C. $A(-3, 0)$, $B(-1, 5)$, and $C(-2, 2)$ — ○ Yes ● No

5. Is $\overline{RS}$ a translation of $\overline{DF}$?
   Select Yes or No for each statement.
   A. $R(2, 2)$, $S(5, 2)$, and $D(3, 3)$, $F(5, 3)$ — ○ Yes ● No
   B. $R(-1, 3)$, $S(2, -2)$, and $D(-4, 2)$, $F(-1, -3)$ — ● Yes ○ No
   C. $R(5, -3)$, $S(2, 2)$, and $D(1, -4)$, $F(-1, -3)$ — ○ Yes ● No

---

COMMON CORE Common Core Standards

Items	Content Standards	Mathematical Practices
1	A-REI.B.3	MP.2
2	G-GMD.B.4	MP.6
3	G-CO.D.12	MP.6
4	G-CO.A.1	MP.6
5	N-CN.B.6	MP.5

* Item integrates mixed review concepts from previous modules or a previous course.

6. Does the shape have rotational symmetry?
   Select Yes or No for each statement.
   A. A square   ● Yes   ○ No
   B. A trapezoid   ○ Yes   ● No
   C. A right triangle   ○ Yes   ● No

7. Determine whether each image of △ABC, with A(1, 3), B(2, 3), C(4, 5), can be formed with only the given transformation. Select True or False for each statement.
   A. A′(2, 4), B′(3, 4), C′(5, 6) is formed by translation.   ● True   ○ False
   B. A′(−1, 3), B′(−2, 3), C′(−4, 5) is formed by rotation.   ○ True   ● False
   C. A′(1, −5), B′(2, −3), C′(4, −1) is formed by reflection.   ○ True   ● False

8. For △DEF, with D(2, 2), E(3, 5), F(4, 3), and △D′E′F′, with D′(4, 2), E′(3, 5), F′(2, 3), determine whether the image can be formed with the sequence of transformations. Select True or False for each statement.
   A. The image is formed by a reflection followed by a translation.   ● True   ○ False
   B. The image is formed by a rotation followed by a reflection.   ● True   ○ False
   C. The image is formed by two consecutive reflections.   ● True   ○ False

9. Use the figure to answer the questions below.
   A. What is a specific series of rigid transformations that maps △ABC to △DEF?

   Answers may vary. Sample: Reflect across the x-axis and translate to the right 5 units and up 1 unit.

   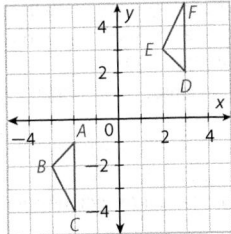

   B. List all congruent pairs of angles and sides for the two figures.

   $\overline{AB} \cong \overline{DE}, \overline{BC} \cong \overline{EF}, \overline{CA} \cong \overline{FD}$

   $\angle A \cong \angle D, \angle B \cong \angle E, \angle C \cong \angle F$

PERFORMANCE TASKS

There are three different levels of performance tasks:

  * **Novice:** These are short word problems that require students to apply the math they have learned in straightforward, real-world situations.

  ** **Apprentice:** These are more involved problems that guide students step-by-step through more complex tasks. These exercises include more complicated reasoning, writing, and open ended elements.

  ***Expert:** These are open-ended, nonroutine problems that, instead of stepping the students through, ask them to choose their own methods for solving and justify their answers and reasoning.

COMMON CORE **Common Core Standards**

Items	Content Standards	Mathematical Practices
6	G-CO.A.2	MP.5
7	G-CO.A.3	MP.5
8	G-CO.A.5	MP.5
9	G-CO.A.5, G-CO.A.6	MP.2, MP.7

* Item integrates mixed review concepts from previous modules or a previous course.

SCORING GUIDES

Item 10 (2 points) Award the student 1 point for a correct explanation of how to find the square, and 1 point for the correct vertices $(-2, 5)$, $(1, 2)$, $(-2, -1)$, and $(-5, 2)$.

Item 11 (6 points)

2 points for naming correct transformation type

4 points for full description

Item 12 (6 points)

A. 1 point for correct answer about straight lines
   1 point for correct answer about nonintersecting lines

B. 1 point for correct answer about straight lines
   1 point for correct answer about nonintersecting lines

C. 2 points for correct answer

Performance Tasks

★**10.** A student has drawn a figure of a square $PQRS$ with points $P(-5, 5)$, $Q(1, 5)$, $R(1, -1)$, and $S(-5, -1)$. For the next assignment, the teacher wants students to inscribe another square, but with sides of length $\sqrt{18}$, in the square. How would a student find the correct square? What are the vertices of the inscribed square?

Note that the square's side lengths are 6. All sides must be the same length, so the midpoints of each square side should be found. Confirm that using the midpoints of the square as the vertices for the inscribed square gives a square with side length $\sqrt{18}$. The vertices are $(-2, 5)$, $(1, 2)$, $(-2, -1)$, and $(-5, 2)$.

★★**11.** A square table is set with four identical place settings, one on each side of the table. Each setting consists of a plate and spoon. Choose one as the original place setting. What transformation describes the location of each of the other three? Express your answer in terms of degrees, lines of reflection, or directions from the original place setting.

Possible answer: They are rotations of the first place setting with the center of rotation in the center of the table. The second setting is a rotation of 90 degrees, the third is 180 degrees, and the fourth is 270 degrees.

★★★**12.** In spherical geometry, the plane is replaced by the surface of a sphere. In this context, straight lines are defined as great circles, which are circles that have the same center as the sphere. They are the largest possible circles on the surface of the sphere.

A. On a globe, lines of longitude run north and south. In spherical geometry, are lines of longitude straight lines? Are any lines of longitude parallel (nonintersecting)?

B. Lines of latitude run east and west. In spherical geometry, are lines of latitude straight lines? Are any lines of latitude parallel (nonintersecting)?

C. In general, in how many places does a pair of straight lines intersect in spherical geometry?

A. Lines of longitude are straight lines, and no lines of longitude are nonintersecting.

B. Most lines of latitude are not straight lines, but the equator is straight. All lines of latitude are nonintersecting.

C. All straight lines in spherical geometry intersect in exactly two places.

Geomatics Surveyor A geomatics surveyor is surveying a piece of land of length 400 feet and width 300 feet. Standing at one corner, he finds that the elevation of the opposite corner is 50 feet greater than his elevation. Find the distance between the surveyor and the middlemost point of the piece of land (ignoring elevation), the elevation of the middlemost point in comparison to his location (assuming that the elevation increases at a constant rate), and distance between the surveyor and the middlemost point of the piece of land considering its elevation.

The distance, ignoring elevation, is found with the distance

formula. $\sqrt{\left(\frac{300}{2}\right)^2 + \left(\frac{400}{2}\right)^2} = 250$ feet

The elevation of the middlemost point is found by dividing the

elevation of the opposite corner by 2.

$\frac{50}{2} = 25$ feet

The final distance is found using the distance

formula. $\sqrt{(250)^2 + (25)^2} \approx 251.25$ feet

© Houghton Mifflin Harcourt Publishing Company

MATH IN CAREERS

Geomatics Surveyor In this Unit Performance Task, students can see how a geomatics surveyor uses mathematics on the job.

For more information about careers in mathematics as well as various mathematics appreciation topics, visit the American Mathematical Society http://www.ams.org

SCORING GUIDES

Task (6 points)

2 points for the correct distance ignoring elevation

2 points for finding elevation

2 points for correct distance including elevation

UNIT 2

Lines, Angles, and Triangles

CONTENTS

Unit Pacing Guide

45-Minute Classes

Module 4

DAY 1	DAY 2	DAY 3	DAY 4	DAY 5
Lesson 4.1	Lesson 4.2	Lesson 4.3	Lesson 4.3	Lesson 4.4

DAY 6	DAY 7	DAY 8		
Lesson 4.5	Lesson 4.5	Module Review and Assessment Readiness		

Module 5

DAY 1	DAY 2	DAY 3	DAY 4	DAY 5
Lesson 5.1	Lesson 5.2	Lesson 5.3	Lesson 5.4	Module Review and Assessment Readiness

Module 6

DAY 1	DAY 2	DAY 3	DAY 4
Lesson 6.1	Lesson 6.2	Lesson 6.3	Module Review and Assessment Readiness

Module 7

DAY 1	DAY 2	DAY 3	DAY 4	DAY 5
Lesson 7.1	Lesson 7.2	Lesson 7.3	Lesson 7.3	Module Review and Assessment Readiness

Module 8

DAY 1	DAY 2	DAY 3	DAY 4	DAY 5
Lesson 8.1	Lesson 8.2	Lesson 8.2	Lesson 8.3	Lesson 8.3

DAY 6	DAY 7	DAY 8		
Lesson 8.4	Module Review and Assessment Readiness	Unit Review and Assessment Readiness		

90-Minute Classes

Module 4

DAY 1	DAY 2	DAY 3	DAY 4
Lesson 4.1 Lesson 4.2	Lesson 4.3	Lesson 4.4 Lesson 4.5	Lesson 4.5 Module Review and Assessment Readiness

Module 5

DAY 1	DAY 2	DAY 3
Lesson 5.1	Lesson 5.2 Lesson 5.3	Lesson 5.4 Module Review and Assessment Readiness

Module 6 / Module 7

DAY 1	DAY 2	DAY 1	DAY 2	DAY 3
Lesson 6.1 Lesson 6.2	Lesson 6.3 Module Review and Assessment Readiness	Lesson 7.1 Lesson 7.2	Lesson 7.2 Lesson 7.3	Lesson 7.3 Module Review and Assessment Readiness

Module 8

DAY 1	DAY 2	DAY 3	DAY 4
Lesson 8.1	Lesson 8.2 Lesson 8.3	Lesson 8.3 Lesson 8.4	Module and Unit Review and Assessment Readiness

Program Resources

PLAN

HMH Teacher App

Access a full suite of teacher resources online and offline on a variety of devices. Plan present, and manage classes, assignments, and activities.

ePlanner
Easily plan your classes, create and view assignments, and access all program resources with your online, customizable planning tool.

Professional Development Videos

Authors Juli Dixon and Matt Larson model successful teaching practices and strategies in actual classroom settings.

QR Codes
Scan with your smart phone to jump directly from your print book to online videos and other resources.

Teacher's Edition

Support students with point-of-use Questioning Strategies, teaching tips, resources for differentiated instruction, additional activities, and more.

ENGAGE AND EXPLORE

Real-World Videos
Engage students with interesting and relevant applications of the mathematical content of each module.

Explore Activities

Students interactively explore new concepts using a variety of tools and approaches.

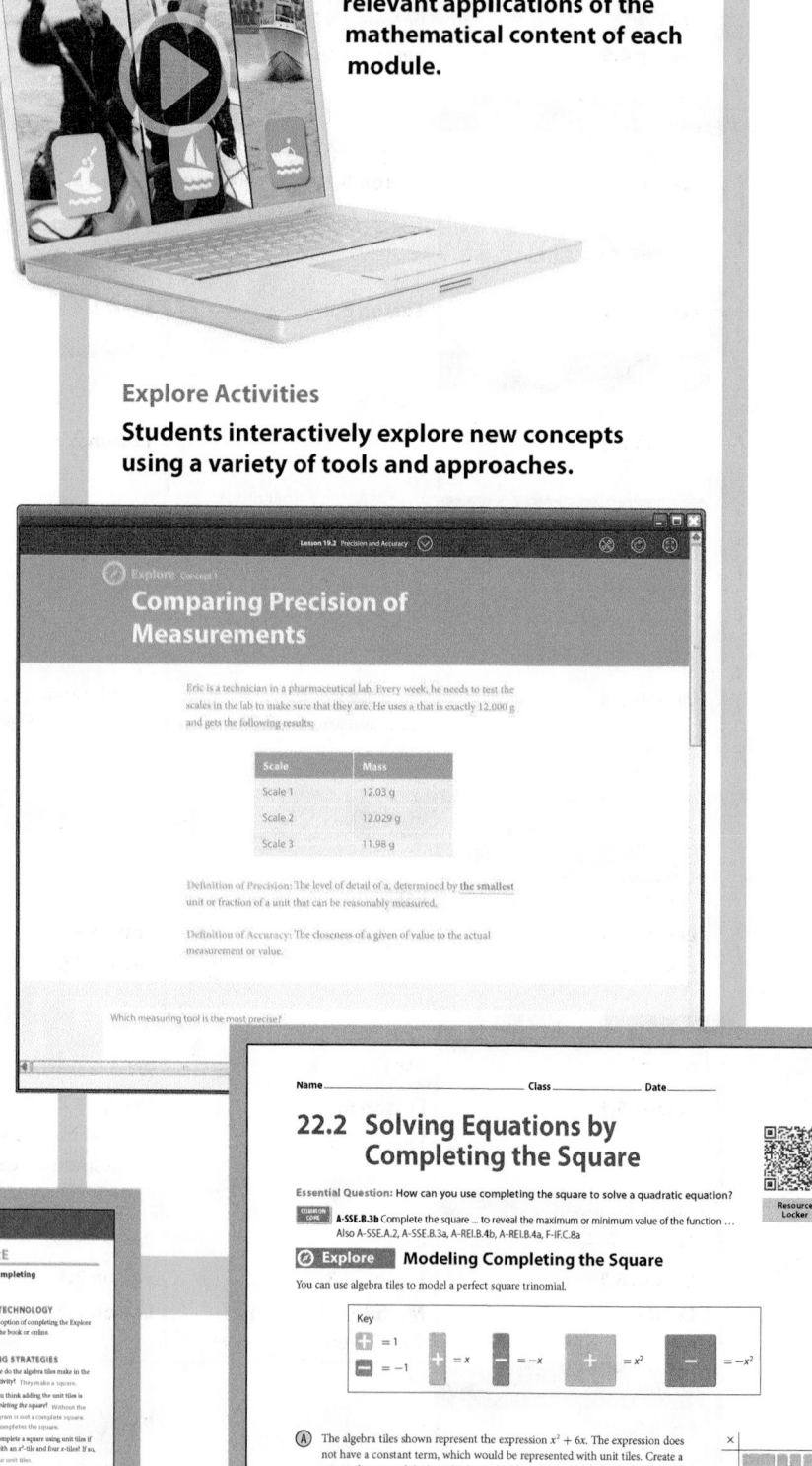

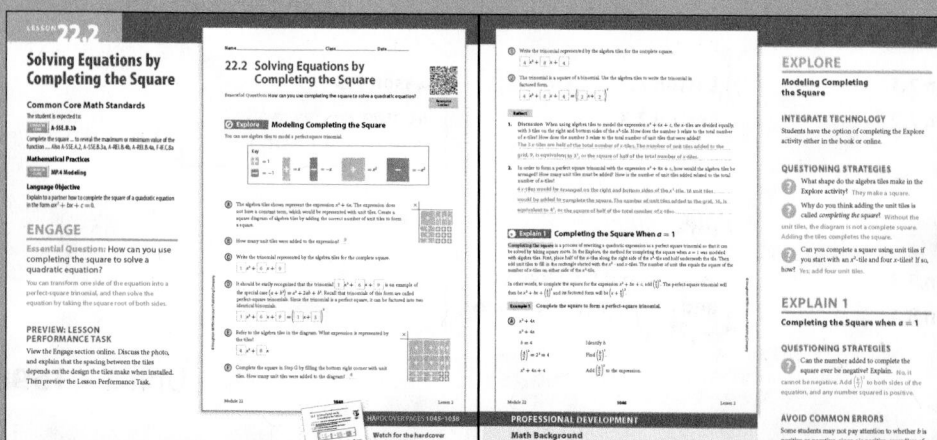

TEACH

Math On the Spot video tutorials, featuring program author Dr. Edward Burger, accompany every example in the textbook and give students step-by-step instructions and explanations of key math concepts.

Interactive Teacher Edition

Customize and present course materials with collaborative activities and integrated formative assessment.

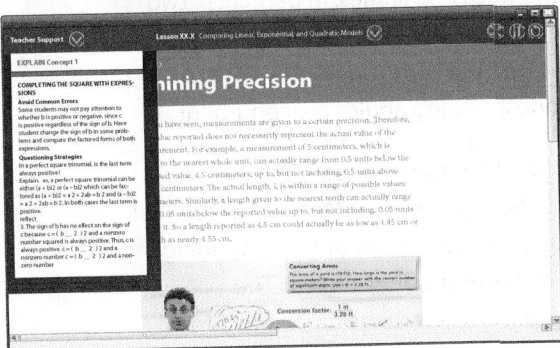

Differentiated Instruction Resources

Support all learners with Differentiated Instruction Resources, including

- **Leveled Practice and Problem Solving**
- **Reading Strategies**
- **Success for English Learners**
- **Challenge**

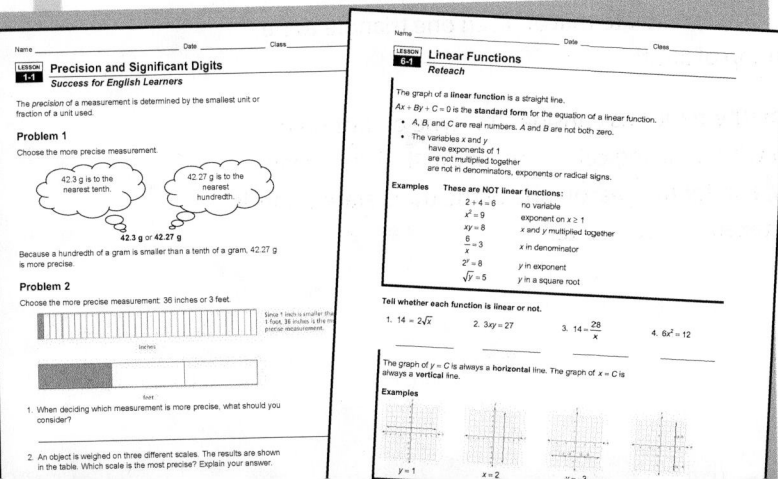

ASSESSMENT AND INTERVENTION

The **Personal Math Trainer** provides online practice, homework, assessments, and intervention. Monitor student progress through reports and alerts. Create and customize assignments aligned to specific lessons or Common Core standards.

- **Practice** – With dynamic items and assignments, students get unlimited practice on key concepts supported by guided examples, step-by-step solutions, and video tutorials.
- **Assessments** – Choose from course assignments or customize your own based on course content, Common Core standards, difficulty levels, and more.
- **Homework** – Students can complete online homework with a wide variety of problem types, including the ability to enter expressions, equations, and graphs. Let the system automatically grade homework, so you can focus where your students need help the most!

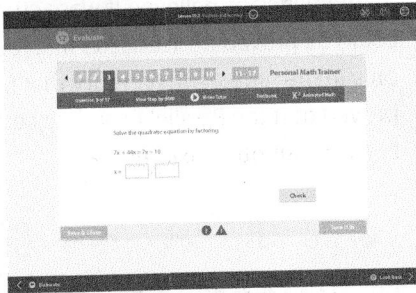

- **Intervention** – Let the Personal Math Trainer automatically prescribe a targeted, personalized intervention path for your students.

Focus on Higher Order Thinking

Raise the bar with homework and practice that incorporates higher-order thinking and mathematical practices in every lesson.

Assessment Readiness

Prepare students for success on high stakes tests for Geometry with practice at every module and unit

Assessment Resources

Tailor assessments and response to intervention to meet the needs of all your classes and students, including

- Leveled Module Quizzes
- Leveled Unit Tests
- Unit Performance Tasks
- Placement, Diagnostic, and Quarterly Benchmark Tests
- Tier 1, Tier 2, and Tier 3 Resources

Math Background

Parallel Lines G-CO.C.9

LESSONS 4.2 and 4.3

The Parallel Postulate was the fifth postulate proposed in Euclid's *Elements*. Euclid worded the postulate as follows: *If a straight line falling on two straight lines makes the interior angles on the same side less than two right angles, then the straight lines, if extended indefinitely, meet on the side on which the angles lie.*

Today, the postulate is usually presented in a logically equivalent form that is sometimes known as Playfair's Axiom: *Through a point P not on line ℓ, there is exactly one line parallel to ℓ.*

The Parallel Postulate has played an important role in the history of mathematics, initially because many mathematicians believed it was actually a theorem that could be proved from Euclid's first four postulates. It was only in the nineteenth century that Eugenio Beltrami proved that the Parallel Postulate could not be proven from Euclid's four other axioms.

Perpendicular Lines G-CO.C.9

LESSONS 4.4 and 4.5

Thus far, the concept of distance has been defined only for two points. However, it is possible to extend the notion of distance to other situations. For example, the distance from a point P to a line $ℓ$ is defined as the length of the perpendicular segment from P to $ℓ$.

As shown in the following figure, this perpendicular segment is the shortest segment from the point to the line.

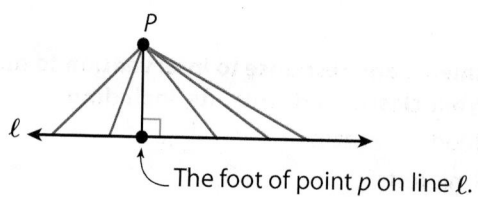

The foot of point *p* on line *ℓ*.

The point at which the perpendicular segment through P intersects line $ℓ$ is sometimes called the *foot* of the point on the line.

Congruent Triangles G-CO.B.7

LESSONS 5.1 to 5.4

Two geometric figures are congruent if they are the same size and shape; in other words, if one of the figures can be moved so that it fits perfectly on top of the other figure.

This is the intuitive idea behind the more rigorous mathematical definition of *congruence: two figures are congruent if one can be transformed into the other by an isometry* (that is, by a combination of translations, reflections, and rotations).

For polygons, the definition of congruence can be stated in terms of corresponding sides and angles. In particular, two triangles are congruent if and only if the sides and angles can be matched up so that the corresponding sides are congruent and the corresponding angles are congruent.

This definition of triangle congruence means that six correspondences must be checked in order to conclude that two triangles are congruent (three pairs of corresponding sides and three pairs of corresponding angles). The congruence theorems provide shortcuts for proving triangles congruent.

Strictly speaking, only one of SSS, SAS, or ASA needs to be taken as a postulate. In other words, any one of these may be assumed to be true, and the other two may then be proved as theorems.

Euclid actually proved all three results (SSS, SAS, and ASA) as theorems. However, he did so through the use of a "superposition" postulate that allowed one triangle to be placed on top of another.

Modern mathematicians consider this type of motion to be invalid within the logical system of classical Euclidean geometry, and for this reason one of the three statements is generally taken as a postulate.

Properties of Triangles G-CO.C.10

LESSONS 7.1 to 7.3

The Triangle Inequality is the mathematical statement of a well-known fact: the shortest path between two points is a straight line. In the case of a triangle with vertices A, B, and C, the straight path from A to B is shorter than the path that includes a detour to point C. In other words, $AB < AC + BC$.

One can use the Triangle Inequality to find other useful results. For example, the length of any side of a triangle is less than half the perimeter of the triangle. Another result is that the sum of the lengths of the diagonals of any quadrilateral is less than the perimeter of the quadrilateral. Specifically, in quadrilateral $ABCD$, four applications of the Triangle Inequality yield the four inequalities shown below.

$$AC < AB + BC$$
$$AC < AD + CD$$
$$BD < AD + AB$$
$$BD < CD + BC$$

Adding the four inequalities above gives

$2(AC + BD) < 2AB + 2BC + 2CD + 2AD$, and dividing both sides of this inequality by 2 proves the result.

Special Segments in Triangles G-CO.C.10

LESSONS 8.1 to 8.3

The medians of a triangle are concurrent at a point called the *centroid* of the triangle. The centroid has important physical properties. For a triangle of uniform thickness and density, the centroid is the point at which the triangle will balance.

In this sense, the centroid can be considered the "average" of all the points in the triangle. The triangle will also balance along any line that passes through the centroid. In particular, this means that a median of a triangle divides the triangle into two smaller triangles with equal areas. For example, in the figure below, area $(\triangle ABX) = $ area $(\triangle ACX)$.

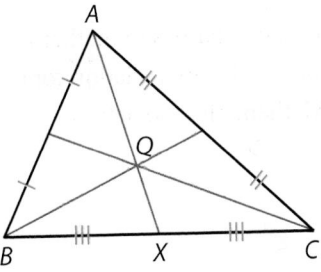

This is easy to see because the two smaller triangles have equal bases and heights.

Midsegments of Triangles G-CO.C.10

LESSON 8.4

A *midsegment of a triangle* is *a segment that joins the midpoints of two sides of the triangle*. Together, the three midsegments of a triangle form the midsegment triangle, which is $\triangle XYZ$ in the figure.

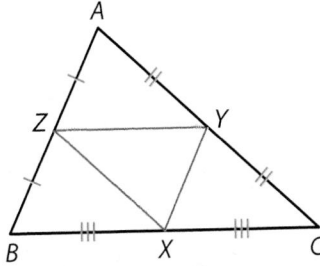

By the Triangle Midsegment Theorem,
$XY = \frac{1}{2} AB$, $ZY = \frac{1}{2} BC$, and $XZ = \frac{1}{2} AC$.
It follows by SSS Congruence that the four small triangles formed by the midsegments are congruent.

Since the four triangles together form $\triangle ABC$, each small triangle has one-fourth the area of $\triangle ABC$.

Lines, Angles, and Triangles

MATH IN CAREERS

Unit Activity Preview

After completing this unit, students will complete a Math in Careers task by applying triangle congruence theorems to the real world. Critical skills include modeling real-world situations.

For more information about careers in mathematics as well as various mathematics appreciation topics, visit The American Mathematical Society at http://www.ams.org.

UNIT 2

Lines, Angles, and Triangles

MODULE 4
Lines and Angles

MODULE 5
Triangle Congruence Criteria

MODULE 6
Applications of Triangle Congruence

MODULE 7
Properties of Triangles

MODULE 8
Special Segments in Triangles

MATH IN CAREERS

Architect An architect is responsible for designing spaces where people work and live. In addition to a keen eye for detail and strong artistic skills, architects use mathematics to create spaces that are both functional and aesthetically pleasing.

If you're interested in a career as an architect, you should study these mathematical subjects:
- Algebra
- Geometry
- Trigonometry

Research other careers that require the use of spatial analysis to understand real-world scenarios. See the related Career Activity at the end of this unit.

Unit 2   159

TRACKING YOUR LEARNING PROGRESSION

Before	In this Unit	After
Students understand: • using the distance formula on a coordinate plane • constructing an angle bisector • postulates about segments, angle, lines, and planes • rigid and non-rigid motions • congruence of corresponding parts	Students will learn about: • parallel lines, transversals, and angle relationships • perpendicular lines and bisectors • slopes and equations of parallel and perpendicular lines • congruence of triangles • geometric constructions • special triangles and triangle inequalities • special segments of triangles	Students will study: • properties of intersecting lines, parallel lines, and perpendicular lines in figures • properties of quadrilateral figures: parallelograms, rectangles, rhombuses, squares, kites, and trapezoids • perimeter and area on the coordinate plane

Reading Start-Up

Visualize Vocabulary

Use the ✔ words to complete the case diagram. Write the review words in the bubbles and draw a picture to illustrate each case.

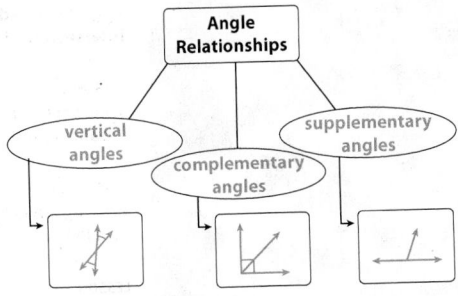

Understand Vocabulary

Complete the sentences using the preview words.

1. A(n) __equilateral triangle__ has three sides with the same length.

2. A circle is __inscribed__ in a polygon if each side of the polygon is tangent to the circle.

3. The __hypotenuse__ of a right triangle is the longest side of the triangle.

Active Reading

Key-Term Fold While reading each module, create a Key-Term Fold to help you organize vocabulary words. Write vocabulary terms on one side and definitions on the other side. Place a special emphasis on learning and speaking the English word while discussing the unit.

© Houghton Mifflin Harcourt Publishing Company

Vocabulary

Review Words

✔ adjacent angles (*ángulos adyacentes*)
✔ parallel lines (*líneas paralelas*)
✔ congruence (*congruencia*)
✔ vertical angles (*ángulos verticales*)
✔ complementary angles (*ángulos complementarios*)
✔ supplementary angles (*ángulos suplementarios*)
✔ transversal (*transversal*)

Preview Words

indirect proof (*demostración indirecta*)
hypotenuse (*hipotenusa*)
legs (*catetos*)
interior angle (*ángulo interior*)
exterior angle (*ángulo exterior*)
isosceles triangle (*triángulo isósceles*)
equilateral triangle (*triángulo equilátero*)
circumscribe (*circunscrito*)
inscribed (*apuntado*)

Reading Start Up

Have students complete the activities on this page by working alone or with others.

VISUALIZE VOCABULARY

The case diagram graphic helps students review vocabulary associated with angles. If time allows, review relationships among angles created by parallel lines and a transversal.

UNDERSTAND VOCABULARY

Use the following explanations to help students learn the preview words.

A triangle with three sides that are the same length is **equilateral**. A triangle with two sides that are the same length is **isosceles**. A triangle with a right angle is a **right triangle**. The sides of a right triangle that form the right angle are the **legs**. The side opposite the right angle is the **hypotenuse**. An **interior angle** of a triangle is formed by two sides of the triangle with a common vertex. An **exterior angle** is formed by one side of the triangle and an extension of an adjacent side.

ACTIVE READING

Students can use these reading and note-taking strategies to help them organize and understand the new concepts and vocabulary. Encourage students to ask questions to create definitions that are clear, correct, and helpful. Remind them to include diagrams to support their definitions. It may be beneficial to have students share information to help clarify definitions of any terms that seem confusing.

ADDITIONAL RESOURCES

Differentiated Instruction

• Reading Strategies **EL**

Lines and Angles

ESSENTIAL QUESTION:

Answer: The characteristics of parallel and perpendicular lines can help you to analyze real-world objects such as street intersections.

PROFESSIONAL DEVELOPMENT VIDEO

Professional Development Video

Learn effective ways of integrating technology into your classroom to meet a variety of different needs.

Professional
Development
my.hrw.com

Lines and Angles

MODULE 4

Essential Question: How can you use parallel and perpendicular lines to solve real-world problems?

LESSON 4.1
Angles Formed by Intersecting Lines

LESSON 4.2
Transversals and Parallel Lines

LESSON 4.3
Proving Lines Are Parallel

LESSON 4.4
Perpendicular Lines

LESSON 4.5
Equations of Parallel and Perpendicular Lines

REAL WORLD VIDEO
Check out how properties of parallel and perpendicular lines and angles can be used to create real-world illusions in a mystery spot building.

© Houghton Mifflin Harcourt Publishing Company • Image Credits: ©Alexander Demianchuk/Reuters/Corbis

MODULE PERFORMANCE TASK PREVIEW

Mystery Spot Building

In this module, you will use properties of parallel lines and angles to analyze the strange happenings in a mystery spot building. With a little bit of geometry, you'll be able to figure out whether mystery spot buildings are "on the up-and-up!"

Module 4   161

DIGITAL TEACHER EDITION

Access a full suite of teaching resources when and where you need them:

- Access content online or offline
- Customize lessons to share with your class
- Communicate with your students in real-time
- View student grades and data instantly to target your instruction where it is needed most

PERSONAL MATH TRAINER

Assessment and Intervention

Assign automatically graded homework, quizzes, tests, and intervention activities. Prepare your students with updated, Common Core-aligned practice tests.

Are(YOU)Ready?

Complete these exercises to review skills you will need for this module.

Angle Relationships

- Online Homework
- Hints and Help
- Extra Practice

Example 1

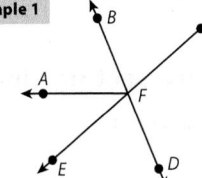

The measure of $\angle AFB$ is 70° and the measure of $\angle AFE$ is 40°. Find the measure of angle $\angle BFE$.

$m\angle BFE = m\angle AFB + m\angle AFE$ Angle Addition Postulate

$m\angle BFE = 70° + 40°$ Substitute.

$m\angle BFE = 110°$ Solve for $m\angle BFE$.

Find the measure of the angle in the image from the example.

1. The measure of $\angle BFE$ is 110°. Find $m\angle EFD$.
   $m\angle EFD = $ _____ 70°

2. The measure of $\angle BFE$ is 110°. Find $m\angle BFC$.
   $m\angle BFC = $ _____ 70°

Parallel Lines Cut by a Transversal

Example 2   The measure of $\angle 7$ is 110°. Find $m\angle 3$.
Assume $p \parallel q$.

$m\angle 3 = m\angle 7$ Corresponding Angles Theorem

$m\angle 3 = 110°$ Substitute.

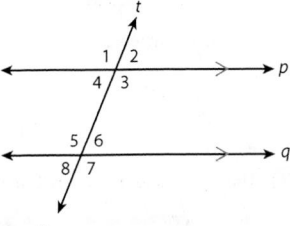

Find the measure of the angle in the image from the example. Assume $p \parallel q$.

3. The measure of $\angle 3$ is 110°. Find $m\angle 1$. $m\angle 1 = $ _____ 110°

4. The measure of $\angle 3$ is 110°. Find $m\angle 6$. $m\angle 6 = $ _____ 70°

Writing Equations of Parallel, Perpendicular, Vertical, and Horizontal Lines

Example 3   Find the line parallel to $y = 2x + 7$ that passes through the point $(3, 6)$.

$(y - y_1) = m(x - x_1)$ Use point-slope form.

$(y - 6) = 2(x - 3)$ Substitute for m, x_1, y_1. Parallel lines have the same slope, so $m = 2$.

$y - 6 = 2x - 6$ Simplify.

$y = 2x$ Solve for y.

Find the equation of the line described.

5. Perpendicular to $y = 3x + 5$; passing through the point $(-6, -4)$ $y = -\frac{1}{3}x - 6$

6. Parallel to the x-axis; passing through the point $(4, 1)$ $y = 1$

Are You Ready?

ASSESS READINESS

Use the assessment on this page to determine if students need strategic or intensive intervention for the module's prerequisite skills.

ASSESSMENT AND INTERVENTION

Rtl   Response to Intervention   **TIER 1, TIER 2, TIER 3 SKILLS**

Personal Math Trainer will automatically create a standards-based, personalized intervention assignment for your students, targeting each student's individual needs!

ADDITIONAL RESOURCES

See the table below for a full list of intervention resources available for this module.

Response to Intervention Resources also includes:

- Tier 2 Skill Pre-Tests for each Module
- Tier 2 Skill Post-Tests for each skill

Response to Intervention			Differentiated Instruction
Tier 1	**Tier 2**	**Tier 3**	
Lesson Intervention Worksheets	Strategic Intervention Skills Intervention Worksheets	Intensive Intervention Worksheets available online	
Reteach 4.1 Reteach 4.2 Reteach 4.3 Reteach 4.4 Reteach 4.5	2 Angle Relationships 12 Parallel Lines Cut by a Transversal 17 Properties of Reflections 28 Writing Equations...	Building Block Skills 7, 15, 16, 22, 23, 42, 46, 53, 56, 66, 71, 87, 95, 98, 102, 103	Challenge worksheets Extend the Math Lesson Activities in TE

Angles Formed by Intersecting Lines

Common Core Math Standards

The student is expected to:

COMMON CORE **G-CO.C.9**

Prove theorems about lines and angles.

Mathematical Practices

COMMON CORE **MP.3 Logic**

Language Objective

Explain to a partner the differences among complementary angles, supplementary angles, linear pairs, and vertical angles.

ENGAGE

Essential Question: How can you find the measures of angles formed by intersecting lines?

Possible answer: Identify any angles with known angle measures. Look for pairs of vertical angles and linear pairs of angles. Find angles that are complementary (if any) and supplementary. Use these relationships between pairs of angles together with the known angle measures to find the missing measures.

PREVIEW: LESSON PERFORMANCE TASK

View the Engage section online. Discuss the photo, making sure students understand that a multiplying effect is created by the long handle and the short "jaws." Then preview the Lesson Performance Task.

Name _____ Class _____ Date _____

4.1 Angles Formed by Intersecting Lines

Essential Question: How can you find the measures of angles formed by intersecting lines?

Resource Locker

⊘ Explore 1 Exploring Angle Pairs Formed by Intersecting Lines

When two lines intersect, like the blades of a pair of scissors, a number of angle pairs are formed. You can find relationships between the measures of the angles in each pair.

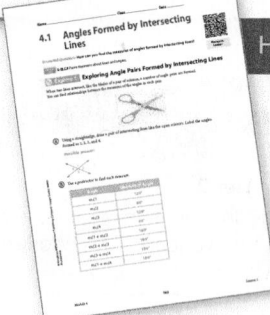

(A) Using a straightedge, draw a pair of intersecting lines like the open scissors. Label the angles formed as 1, 2, 3, and 4.

Possible answer:

(B) Use a protractor to find each measure.

Angle	Measure of Angle
m∠1	120°
m∠2	60°
m∠3	120°
m∠4	60°
m∠1 + m∠2	180°
m∠2 + m∠3	180°
m∠3 + m∠4	180°
m∠1 + m∠4	180°

HARDCOVER PAGES 145–152

Turn to these pages to find this lesson in the hardcover student edition.

You have been measuring *vertical angles* and *linear pairs* of angles. When two lines intersect, the angles that are opposite each other are **vertical angles**. Recall that a *linear pair* is a pair of adjacent angles whose non-common sides are opposite rays. So, when two lines intersect, the angles that are on the same side of a line form a linear pair.

Reflect

1. Name a pair of vertical angles and a linear pair of angles in your diagram in Step A.
   Possible answers: vertical angles: ∠1 and ∠3 or ∠2 and ∠4 ; linear pairs:

   ∠1 and ∠2, ∠2 and ∠3, ∠3 and ∠4, or ∠1 and ∠4

2. Make a conjecture about the measures of a pair of vertical angles.
   Vertical angles have the same measure and so are congruent.

3. Use the Linear Pair Theorem to tell what you know about the measures of angles that form a linear pair.
   The angles in a linear pair are supplementary, so the measures of the angles add

   up to 180°.

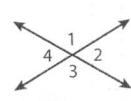 **Explore 2** **Proving the Vertical Angles Theorem**

The conjecture from the Explore about vertical angles can be proven so it can be stated as a theorem.

The Vertical Angles Theorem
If two angles are vertical angles, then the angles are congruent.
∠1 ≅ ∠3 and ∠2 ≅ ∠4

You have written proofs in two-column and paragraph proof formats. Another type of proof is called a *flow proof*. A **flow proof** uses boxes and arrows to show the structure of the proof. The steps in a flow proof move from left to right or from top to bottom, shown by the arrows connecting each box. The justification for each step is written below the box. You can use a flow proof to prove the Vertical Angles Theorem.

Follow the steps to write a Plan for Proof and a flow proof to prove the Vertical Angles Theorem.

Given: ∠1 and ∠3 are vertical angles.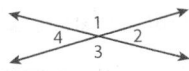

Prove: ∠1 ≅ ∠3

© Houghton Mifflin Harcourt Publishing Company

PROFESSIONAL DEVELOPMENT

 ## Math Background

Students will work with special angles. *Congruent angles* have the same measure. A pair of angles is *supplementary* if their sum is 180°. A pair of angles is *complementary* if their sum is 90°. *Adjacent angles* share one side without overlapping. *Vertical angles* are the non-adjacent angles formed by intersecting lines. They lie opposite each other at the point of intersection.

EXPLORE 1

Exploring Angle Pairs Formed by Intersecting Lines

INTEGRATE TECHNOLOGY

Students have the option of exploring the activity either in the book or online.

QUESTIONING STRATEGIES

? How would you describe a pair of supplementary angles in the drawing of intersecting lines? adjacent angles

? Which pair of angles, if any, are congruent in a drawing of two intersecting lines? Opposite angles are congruent.

EXPLORE 2

Proving the Vertical Angles Theorem

QUESTIONING STRATEGIES

? How do you identify vertical angles? They are opposite angles formed by intersecting lines.

AVOID COMMON ERRORS

A common error that students make in writing proofs is using the result they are trying to prove as an intermediate step in the proof. Remind students to be alert for this type of circular reasoning.

CURRICULUM INTEGRATION

The common error mentioned above is discussed in the study of logic; it is known as the logical fallacy of *begging the question*. This is not the same as the general use of the phrase to "beg the question," which often means "to raise another question."

(A) Complete the final steps of a Plan for Proof:

Because ∠1 and ∠2 are a linear pair and ∠2 and ∠3 are a linear pair, these pairs of angles are supplementary. This means that m∠1 + m∠2 = 180° and m∠2 + m∠3 = 180°. By the Transitive Property, m∠1 + m∠2 = m∠2 + m∠3. Next:

Subtract m∠2 from both sides to conclude that m∠1 = m∠3. So, ∠1 ≅ ∠3.

(B) Use the Plan for Proof to complete the flow proof. Begin with what you know is true from the Given or the diagram. Use arrows to show the path of the reasoning. Fill in the missing statement or reason in each step.

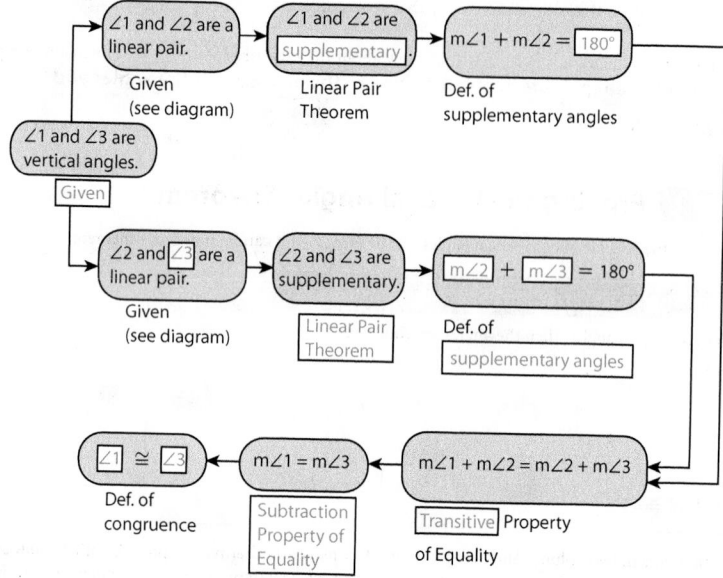

Reflect

4. **Discussion** Using the other pair of angles in the diagram, ∠2 and ∠4, would a proof that ∠2 ≅ ∠4 also show that the Vertical Angles Theorem is true? Explain why or why not.

   Yes, it does not matter which pair of vertical angles is used in the proof. Similar statements and reasons could be used for either pair of vertical angles.

5. Draw two intersecting lines to form vertical angles. Label your lines and tell which angles are congruent. Measure the angles to check that they are congruent.

   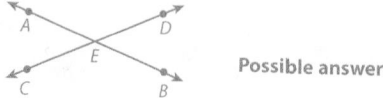

   Possible answer:

   By the Vertical Angles Theorem, ∠AEC ≅ ∠DEB and ∠AED ≅ ∠CEB. Checking by measuring, m∠AEC = m∠DEB = 45° and m∠AED = m∠CEB = 135°.

COLLABORATIVE LEARNING

Small Group Activity

Have students review the different angle pairs and lesson illustrations. Have each student draw one example of an angle pair, choosing from: a linear pair, supplementary angles, complementary angles, and vertical angles. Students then pass their drawings to others, who list all the information they know about that type of angle pair. Have them keep passing the drawings for other students to add more information until the drawing comes back to the student who drew it. Then have students identify and draw the angle that is a complement of an acute angle, a supplement of an obtuse angle, and the supplement of a right angle. acute, acute, right

You can use the Vertical Angles Theorem to find missing angle measures in situations involving intersecting lines.

Example 1 Cross braces help keep the deck posts straight. Find the measure of each angle.

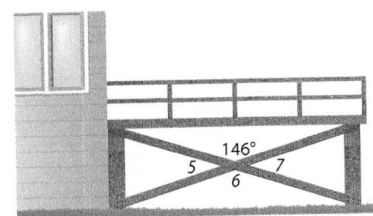

Ⓐ ∠6

Because vertical angles are congruent, m∠6 = 146°.

Ⓑ ∠5 and ∠7

From Part A, m∠6 = 146°. Because ∠5 and ∠6 form a ___linear pair___ , they are

supplementary and m∠5 = 180° − 146° = $\boxed{34°}$. m∠ $\boxed{7}$ = $\boxed{34°}$ because ∠ $\boxed{7}$

also forms a linear pair with ∠6, or because it is a ___vertical angle___ with ∠5.

Your Turn

6. The measures of two vertical angles are 58° and $(3x + 4)$°. Find the value of x.

$58 = 3x + 4$

$54 = 3x$

$18 = x$

7. The measures of two vertical angles are given by the expressions $(x + 3)$° and $(2x − 7)$°. Find the value of x. What is the measure of each angle?

$x + 3 = 2x − 7$

$x + 10 = 2x$

$10 = x$

The measure of each angle is $(x + 3)° = (10 + 3)° = 13°$.

EXPLAIN 1

Using Vertical Angles

QUESTIONING STRATEGIES

? If two lines intersect to form four angles and one angle is an 80-degree angle, how do you know there is another 80-degree angle? The 80-degree angle forms a linear pair with two 100-degree angles, and they each form a linear pair with the remaining angle, so that angle must measure 80 degrees.

CONNECT VOCABULARY **EL**

Differentiate the word *vertical*, meaning *up and down*, and the idea of vertical angles, which share a vertex but don't need to be in an up-and-down position. They are vertical in respect to one another.

DIFFERENTIATE INSTRUCTION

Graphic Organizers

Have students create a graphic organizer with a central oval titled *Pairs of Angles* with leader lines to boxes for *Adjacent angles, Linear pairs, Vertical angles, Supplementary angles,* and *Complementary angles.* Ask students to draw and label an example of each pair of angles and to write a definition of each type of angle pair.

EXPLAIN 2

Using Supplementary and Complementary Angles

INTEGRATE MATHEMATICAL PRACTICES
Focus on Critical Thinking

MP.3 Ask students what the maximum size of a supplementary angle might be. Encourage students to state that the angle measure is close to, but not exactly, 180°. Have them try to describe two lines that intersect to form these angles.

QUESTIONING STRATEGIES

? What fact do you use to find the angle measures in a linear pair? The angles in a linear pair are supplementary.

? What fact do you use to find the angle measures in a pair of complementary angles? Two angles are complementary if the sum of their measures is 90°.

? How does an angle complementary to an angle *A* compare with an angle supplementary to *A*? It measures 90° less.

INTEGRATE MATHEMATICAL PRACTICES
Focus on Reasoning

MP.2 Encourage students to write an equation to solve for the measure of an angle in an angle-pair relationship.Students will write an equation to represent the angle-pair relationship and substitute the information that they are given to solve for the unknown.

CONNECT VOCABULARY EL

To help students remember the definitions of *complementary* and *supplementary*, explain that the letter *c* for *complementary* comes before *s* for *supplementary,* just as 90° comes before 180°.

🌀 **Explain 2**   **Using Supplementary and Complementary Angles**

Recall what you know about complementary and supplementary angles. **Complementary angles** are two angles whose measures have a sum of 90°. **Supplementary angles** are two angles whose measures have a sum of 180°. You have seen that two angles that form a linear pair are supplementary.

Example 2   Use the diagram below to find the missing angle measures. Explain your reasoning.

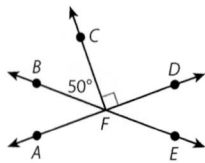

(A) Find the measures of ∠AFC and ∠AFB.

∠AFC and ∠CFD are a linear pair formed by an intersecting line and ray, $\overleftrightarrow{AD}$ and $\overrightarrow{FC}$, so they are supplementary and the sum of their measures is 180°. By the diagram, m∠CFD = 90°, so m∠AFC = 180° − 90° = 90° and ∠AFC is also a right angle.

Because together they form the right angle ∠AFC, ∠AFB and ∠BFC are complementary and the sum of their measures is 90°. So, m∠AFB = 90° − m∠BFC = 90° − 50° = 40°.

(B) Find the measures of ∠DFE and ∠AFE.

∠BFA and ∠DFE are formed by two ___intersecting lines___ and are opposite each other, so the angles are ___vertical___ angles. So, the angles are congruent. From Part A m∠AFB = 40°, so m∠DFE = ⟨40°⟩ also.

Because ∠BFA and ∠AFE form a linear pair, the angles are ___supplementary___ and the sum of their measures is ⟨180°⟩. So, m∠AFE = ⟨180°⟩ − m∠BFA = ⟨180°⟩ − ⟨40°⟩ = ⟨140°⟩.

Reflect

8. In Part A, what do you notice about right angles ∠AFC and ∠CFD? Make a conjecture about right angles.
Possible answer: Both angles have measure 90°. Conjecture: All right angles are
congruent.

LANGUAGE SUPPORT EL

Visual Cues

Have students work in pairs to fill out an organizer like the following, starting with prior knowledge:

Angle(s)	Definition	Picture
Right		
Obtuse		
Acute		
Complementary		
Supplementary		

You can represent the measures of an angle and its complement as $x°$ and $(90 − x)°$. Similarly, you can represent the measures of an angle and its supplement as $x°$ and $(180 − x)°$. Use these expressions to find the measures of the angles described.

9. The measure of an angle is equal to the measure of its complement.

$$x = 90 − x$$
$$2x = 90$$
$$x = 45; \text{ so, } 90 − x = 45$$

The measure of the angle is 45°
the measure of its complement is 45°.

10. The measure of an angle is twice the measure of its supplement.

$$x = 2(180 − x)$$
$$x = 360 − 2x$$
$$3x = 360$$
$$x = 120; \text{ so, } 180 − x = 60$$

The measure of the angle is 120°
the measure of its supplement is 60°.

💬 Elaborate

11. Describe how proving a theorem is different than solving a problem and describe how they are the same.
Possible answer: **A theorem is a general statement and can be used to justify steps in solving**

problems, which are specific cases of algebraic and geometric relationships. Both proofs and

problem solving use a logical sequence of steps to justify a conclusion or to find a solution.

12. Discussion The proof of the Vertical Angles Theorem in the lesson includes a Plan for Proof. How are a Plan for Proof and the proof itself the same and how are they different?
Possible answer: **A plan for a proof is less formal than a proof. Both start from the given**

information and reach the final conclusion, but a formal proof presents every logical step

in detail, while a plan describes only the key logical steps.

13. Draw two intersecting lines. Label points on the lines and tell what angles you know are congruent and which are supplementary.

Possible answer:

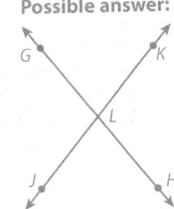

Vertical angles are congruent: $\angle GLK \cong \angle JLH$ and $\angle GLJ \cong \angle KLH$

Angles in a linear pair are supplementary: $\angle GLJ$ and $\angle GLK$; $\angle GLJ$ and $\angle JLH$; $\angle JLH$ and

$\angle HLK$; and $\angle HLK$ and $\angle GLK$

14. Essential Question Check-In If you know that the measure of one angle in a linear pair is 75°, how can you find the measure of the other angle?
The angles in a linear pair are supplementary, so subtract the known measure from 180°:

180 − 75 = 105, so the measure of the other angle is 105°.

ELABORATE

INTEGRATE MATHEMATICAL PRACTICES
Focus on Technology

MP.5 You may want to have students explore the theorems in this lesson using geometry software. For example, have students construct a linear pair of angles, determine the measure of each angle, and use the software's *calculate* tool to find the sum of the measures. Students can change the size of the angles and see that the measures change while their sum remains constant.

QUESTIONING STRATEGIES

? How many vertical angle pairs are formed where three lines intersect at a point? Explain. **6; if the small angles are numberered consecutively 1–6, the vertical angles are 1 and 4, 2 and 5, 3 and 6, and the adjacent angle pairs 1–2 and 4–5, 2–3 and 5–6, 3–4, and 6–1.**

SUMMARIZE THE LESSON

? Have students make a graphic organizer to show how some of the properties, postulates, and theorems in this lesson build upon one another. A sample is shown below.

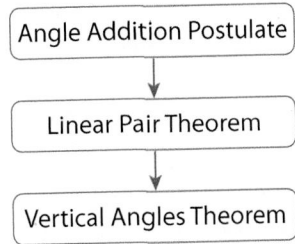

EVALUATE

ASSIGNMENT GUIDE

Concepts and Skills	Practice
Explore Exploring Angle Pairs Formed by Intersecting Lines	Exercise 1
Example 1 Using Vertical Angles	Exercises 2–11
Example 2 Using Supplementary and Complementary Angles	Exercises 12–14

CONNECT VOCABULARY EL

Suggest still another way for students to remember which sum is 90 and which is 180: *complementary* and *corner* both start with the letter *c*, and corners are often right angles. *Supplementary* and *straight* both start with the letter *s*, and a straight line is a 180° angle.

⭐ Evaluate: Homework and Practice

• Online Homework
• Hints and Help
• Extra Practice

Use this diagram and information for Exercises 1–4.

Given: m∠AFB = m∠EFD = 50°

Points B, F, D and points E, F, C are collinear.

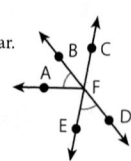

1. Determine whether each pair of angles is a pair of vertical angles, a linear pair of angles, or neither. Select the correct answer for each lettered part.

		Vertical	Linear Pair	Neither
A.	∠BFC and ∠DFE	⬤ Vertical	◯ Linear Pair	◯ Neither
B.	∠BFA and ∠DFE	◯ Vertical	◯ Linear Pair	⬤ Neither
C.	∠BFC and ∠CFD	◯ Vertical	⬤ Linear Pair	◯ Neither
D.	∠AFE and ∠AFC	◯ Vertical	⬤ Linear Pair	◯ Neither
E.	∠BFE and ∠CFD	⬤ Vertical	◯ Linear Pair	◯ Neither
F.	∠AFE and ∠BFC	◯ Vertical	◯ Linear Pair	⬤ Neither

2. Find m∠AFE.

m∠AFB + m∠AFE + m∠EFD = 180°
50° + m∠AFE + 50° = 180°
m∠AFE = 80°

3. Find m∠DFC.

m∠EFB = m∠AFB + m∠AFE = 80° + 50° = 130°
m∠DFC = m∠EFB, so m∠DFC = 130°

4. Find m∠BFC.

m∠BFC = m∠EFD = 50°

5. Represent Real-World Problems A sprinkler swings back and forth between A and B in such a way that ∠1 ≅ ∠2, ∠1 and ∠3 are complementary, and ∠2 and ∠4 are complementary. If m∠1 = 47.5°, find m∠2, m∠3, and m∠4.

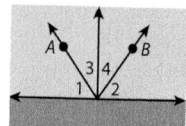

∠1 ≅ ∠2, so m∠2 = 47.5°

∠1 and ∠3 are complementary, so m∠3 = 90 − 47.5 = 42.5°

∠2 and ∠4 are complementary, so m∠4 = 90 − 47.5 = 42.5°

Exercise	Depth of Knowledge (D.O.K.)	COMMON CORE Mathematical Practices
1	**1** Recall of Information	**MP.4** Modeling
2–4	**1** Recall of Information	**MP.2** Reasoning
5–7	**2** Skills/Concepts	**MP.2** Reasoning
8–11	**1** Recall of Information	**MP.3** Logic
12–14	**2** Skills/Concepts	**MP.3** Logic
15	**2** Skills/Concepts	**MP.4** Modeling

Determine whether each statement is true or false. If false, explain why.

6. If an angle is acute, then the measure of its complement must be greater than the measure of its supplement.

False. The measure of an acute angle is less than 90°, so the measure of its complement will be less than 90° and the measure of its supplement will be greater than 90°. So, the measure of the supplement will be greater than the measure of the complement.

7. A pair of vertical angles may also form a linear pair.

False. Vertical angles do not share a common side.

8. If two angles are supplementary and congruent, the measure of each angle is 90°.

True

9. If a ray divides an angle into two complementary angles, then the original angle is a right angle.

True

You can represent the measures of an angle and its complement as $x°$ and $(90 − x)°$. Similarly, you can represent the measures of an angle and its supplement as $x°$ and $(180 − x)°$. Use these expressions to find the measures of the angles described.

10. The measure of an angle is three times the measure of its supplement.

$$x = 3(180 − x)$$
$$x = 540 − 3x$$
$$4x = 540$$
$$x = 135; \text{ so, } 180 − x = 45$$

The measure of the angle is 135° and the measure of its supplement is 45°.

11. The measure of the supplement of an angle is three times the measure of its complement.

$$180 − x = 3(90 − x)$$
$$180 − x = 270 − 3x$$
$$2x = 90$$
$$x = 45; \text{ so, } 90 − x = 45 \text{ and } 180 − x = 135$$

The measure of the angle is 45°, the measure of its complement is 45°, and the measure of its supplement is 135°.

12. The measure of an angle increased by 20° is equal to the measure of its complement.

$$x + 20 = 90 − x$$
$$2x = 70$$
$$x = 35; \text{ so, } 90 − x = 55$$

The measure of the angle is 35°, the measure of its complement is 55°.

© Houghton Mifflin Harcourt Publishing Company

INTEGRATE MATHEMATICAL PRACTICES

Focus on Communication

MP.3 As students answer the questions using the angle names in a pair of angles, encourage them to trace each angle along its letters and say the angle's name aloud as they write it. This will help students get used to naming an angle with three letters.

AVOID COMMON ERRORS

Some students may have difficulty organizing the reasons or steps for a proof. You may wish to have students write the given reasons or steps on sticky notes. Then they can rearrange the sticky notes as needed to write the proof in the correct order.

Exercise	Depth of Knowledge (D.O.K.)	COMMON CORE	Mathematical Practices
16–17	**3** Strategic Thinking H.O.T.		**MP.2** Reasoning
18–20	**3** Strategic Thinking H.O.T.		**MP.3** Logic

Angles Formed by Intersecting Lines **170**

INTEGRATE MATHEMATICAL PRACTICES

Focus on Modeling

MP.4 Remind students that the shape of the letter *X* suggests the idea of vertical angles.

INTEGRATE MATHEMATICAL PRACTICES

Focus on Math Connections

MP.1 Remind students of the definitions of vertical, complementary, supplementary, and linear pairs. Have students use mental math to find complements and supplements of angles before using variables or expressions.

Write a plan for a proof for each theorem.

13. If two angles are congruent, then their complements are congruent.

Given: $\angle ABC \cong \angle DEF$

Prove: The complement of $\angle ABC \cong$ the complement of $\angle DEF$.

Plan for Proof:

If $\angle ABC \cong \angle DEF$, then $m\angle ABC = m\angle DEF$.

The measure of the complement of $\angle ABC = 90° - m\angle ABC$.

The measure of the complement of $\angle DEF = 90° - m\angle DEF$.

Since $m\angle ABC = m\angle DEF$, the measure of the complement of $\angle DEF = 90° - m\angle ABC$.

Therefore, the measure of the complement of $\angle ABC =$ the measure of the complements of $\angle DEF$.

The measures of the complements of the angles are equal, so the complements of the angles are congruent.

14. If two angles are congruent, then their supplements are congruent.

Given: $\angle ABC \cong \angle DEF$

Prove: The supplement of $\angle ABC \cong$ the supplement of $\angle DEF$.

Plan for Proof:

If $\angle ABC \cong \angle DEF$, then $m\angle ABC = m\angle DEF$.

The measure of the supplement of $\angle ABC = 180° - m\angle ABC$.

The measure of the supplement of $\angle DEF = 180° - m\angle DEF$.

Since $m\angle ABC = m\angle DEF$, the measure of the supplement of $\angle DEF = 180° - m\angle ABC$.

Therefore, the measure of the supplement of $\angle ABC =$ the measure of the supplement of $\angle DEF$.

The measures of the supplements of the angles are equal, so the supplements of the angles are congruent.

15. Justify Reasoning Complete the two-column proof for the theorem "If two angles are congruent, then their supplements are congruent."

Statements	Reasons
1. $\angle ABC \cong \angle DEF$	1. Given
2. The measure of the supplement of $\angle ABC = 180° - m\angle ABC$.	2. Definition of the _____supplement_____ of an angle
3. The measure of the supplement of $\angle DEF = 180° - m\angle DEF$.	3. _Definition of the supplement of an angle_
4. _$m\angle ABC = m\angle DEF$_	4. If two angles are congruent, their measures are equal.
5. The measure of the supplement of $\angle DEF = 180° - m\angle ABC$.	5. Substitution Property of _Equality_
6. The measure of the supplement of $\angle ABC$ = the measure of the supplement of $\angle DEF$.	6. _Substitution Property of Equality_
7. The supplement of $\angle ABC \cong$ the supplement of _$\angle DEF$_.	7. If the measures of the supplements of two angles are equal, then supplements of the angles are congruent.

16. Probability The probability P of choosing an object at random from a group of objects is found by the fraction $P(\text{event}) = \dfrac{\text{Number of favorable outcomes}}{\text{Total number of outcomes}}$. Suppose the angle measures 30°, 60°, 120°, and 150° are written on slips of paper. You choose two slips of paper at random.

a. What is the probability that the measures you choose are complementary?

$$P(\text{complementary}) = \frac{1 \text{ possible pair } (30°, 60°)}{6 \text{ angle pairs total}} = \frac{1}{6}$$

b. What is the probability that the measures you choose are supplementary?

$$P(\text{supplementary}) = \frac{2 \text{ possible pairs } (30°, 150° \text{ and } 60°, 120°)}{6 \text{ angle pairs total}} = \frac{2}{6} = \frac{1}{3}$$

INTEGRATE MATHEMATICAL PRACTICES
Focus on Critical Thinking

MP.3 If students have difficulty supplying the missing reasons in a proof, give them the reasons in random order and ask them to write the correct reason in the appropriate line of the proof. This type of scaffolding can be helpful for English language learners until they become more comfortable with the vocabulary of deductive reasoning.

© Houghton Mifflin Harcourt Publishing Company

PEER-TO-PEER DISCUSSION

Ask students to discuss with a partner the names and diagrams for various pairs of angles introduced in this lesson. Ask them to write and solve a word problem using complementary or supplementary angles on index cards, then switch cards with their partners to solve the problem.

JOURNAL

Have students write about each angle-pair relationship discussed in this lesson (supplementary angles, complementary angles, and vertical angles). Students should include definitions and drawings to support their descriptions.

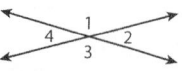

17. Communicate Mathematical Ideas Write a proof of the Vertical Angles Theorem in paragraph proof form.

Given: ∠2 and ∠4 are vertical angles.

Prove: ∠2 ≅ ∠4

In the diagram of intersecting lines, ∠2 and ∠4 are vertical angles. Also, ∠2 and ∠3 are a linear pair and ∠3 and ∠4 are a linear pair. By the Linear Pair Theorem, ∠2 and ∠3 are supplementary and ∠3 and ∠4 are supplementary. Then m∠2 + m∠3 = 180° and m∠3 + m∠4 = 180° by the definition of supplementary angles. By the Transitive Property of Equality, m∠2 + m∠3 = m∠3 + m∠4. Using the Subtraction Property of Equality, m∠2 = m∠4. So, ∠2 ≅ ∠4 by the definition of congruence.

18. Analyze Relationships If one angle of a linear pair is acute, then the other angle must be obtuse. Explain why.

The sum of the measures of the two angles of a linear pair must be 180°. If the measure of one angle is less than 90°, then the measure of the other angle must be greater than 90°.

19. Critique Reasoning Your friend says that there is an angle whose measure is the same as the measure of the sum of its supplement and its complement. Is your friend correct? What is the measure of the angle? Explain your friend's reasoning.

Yes; 90°: the measure of its complement is 0°, and the measure of its supplement is 90°, so 0° + 90° = 90°.

20. Critical Thinking Two statements in a proof are:

$$m\angle A = m\angle B$$

$$m\angle B = m\angle C$$

What reason could you give for the statement m∠A = m∠C? Explain your reasoning.

You could use either the Transitive Property of Equality, since both statements have m∠B in common; or you could use the Substitution Property of Equality by substituting m∠C for m∠B in the first statement.

Lesson Performance Task

The image shows the angles formed by a pair of scissors. When the scissors are closed, $m\angle 1 = 0°$. As the scissors are opened, the measures of all four angles change in relation to each other. Describe how the measures change as $m\angle 1$ increases from 0° to 180°.

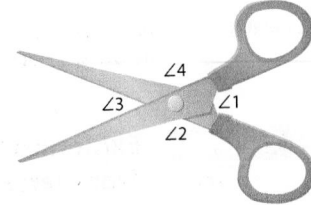

When $m\angle 1 = 0°$, $m\angle 3 = 0°$, and the measures of both $\angle 2$ and $\angle 4$ equal 180°. As $m\angle 1$ increases, the measure of $\angle 3$ increases as well, so that $m\angle 3$ always equals $m\angle 1$. At the same time, the measures of $\angle 2$ and $\angle 4$ decrease steadily, both angles being congruent to each other and supplementary to $\angle 1$. When $m\angle 1 = 90°$, the measures of the other three angles are also 90°. When $m\angle 1 > 90°$, the measures of $\angle 2$ and $\angle 4$ are less than 90° and continually decrease, reaching 0° when $m\angle 1 = 180°$.

© Houghton Mifflin Harcourt Publishing Company

CONNECT VOCABULARY EL

A *supplement* is something that *completes* something else, as a vitamin supplement may complete a person's daily vitamin requirement. The supplement of an angle completes a linear pair, with measures that complete a sum of 180°. A *complement* similarly brings something to completion, like a new coach who proves to be a perfect complement to the team. The complement of an angle brings a right angle to completion.

AVOID COMMON ERRORS

Students may have difficulty with the concept that as angle measures increase from 0° to 180°, their supplements change from obtuse to right to acute angles. Stress that supplementary angles have measures whose sum is 180°, and that one angle in a pair of supplementary angles that are not right angles will always be obtuse and one will be acute, and that supplements of right angles are right angles.

EXTENSION ACTIVITY

A lever is a simple machine that enables the user to lift or move an object using less force than the weight of the object. A teeter-totter is an example of a "class 1" lever, which has a fulcrum between the object being moved and the applied force. Have students research "double class 1 levers," of which pliers and scissors are examples. Students should explain how this type of lever differs from single class 1 levers, and describe how double class 1 levers create a mechanical advantage that allows users to produce forces greater than they apply.

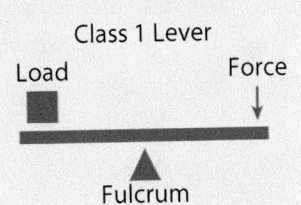

Scoring Rubric

2 points: Student correctly solves the problem and explains his/her reasoning.

1 point: Student shows good understanding of the problem but does not fully solve or explain his/her reasoning.

0 points: Student does not demonstrate understanding of the problem.

Angles Formed by Intersecting Lines   **174**

Transversals and Parallel Lines

Common Core Math Standards

The student is expected to:

COMMON CORE G-CO.C.9

Prove theorems about lines and angles.

Mathematical Practices

COMMON CORE MP.3 Logic

Language Objective

Explain to a partner how to identify the angles formed by two parallel lines cut by a transversal.

ENGAGE

Essential Question: How can you prove and use theorems about angles formed by transversals that intersect parallel lines?

Possible answer: Start by establishing a postulate about certain pairs of angles, such as same-side interior angles. The postulate allows you to prove a theorem about other pairs of angles, such as alternate interior angles. You can then use the postulate and the theorem to prove other theorems about other pairs of angles, such as corresponding angles.

PREVIEW: LESSON PERFORMANCE TASK

View the Engage section online. Discuss the photo. Ask students to describe ways that a real-world example of parallel lines and a transversal like this example differ from parallel lines and a transversal that might appear in a geometry book. Then preview the Lesson Performance Task.

Name_____ Class_____ Date_____

4.2 Transversals and Parallel Lines

Essential Question: How can you prove and use theorems about angles formed by transversals that intersect parallel lines?

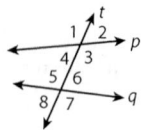
Resource Locker

⊚ Explore   Exploring Parallel Lines and Transversals

A **transversal** is a line that intersects two coplanar lines at two different points. In the figure, line *t* is a transversal. The table summarizes the names of angle pairs formed by a transversal.

Angle Pair	Example
Corresponding angles lie on the same side of the transversal and on the same sides of the intersected lines.	∠1 and ∠5
Same-side interior angles lie on the same side of the transversal and between the intersected lines.	∠3 and ∠6
Alternate interior angles are nonadjacent angles that lie on opposite sides of the transversal between the intersected lines.	∠3 and ∠5
Alternate exterior angles lie on opposite sides of the transversal and outside the intersected lines.	∠1 and ∠7

Recall that parallel lines lie in the same plane and never intersect. In the figure, line ℓ is parallel to line *m*, written $\ell \| m$. The arrows on the lines also indicate that they are parallel.

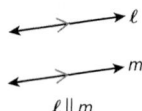

$\ell \| m$

© Houghton Mifflin Harcourt Publishing Company · Image Credits: ©Ruud Morijn Photographer/Shutterstock

Module 4   175   Lesson 2

HARDCOVER PAGES 153–160

Turn to these pages to find this lesson in the hardcover student edition.

When parallel lines are cut by a transversal, the angle pairs formed are either congruent or supplementary. The following postulate is the starting point for proving theorems about parallel lines that are intersected by a transversal.

Same-Side Interior Angles Postulate

If two parallel lines are cut by a transversal, then the pairs of same-side interior angles are supplementary.

Follow the steps to illustrate the postulate and use it to find angle measures.

Ⓐ Draw two parallel lines and a transversal, and number the angles formed from 1 to 8.

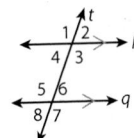

Ⓑ Identify the pairs of same-side interior angles.

∠4 and ∠5; ∠3 and ∠6

Ⓒ What does the postulate tell you about these same-side interior angle pairs?

Given $p \parallel q$, then ∠4 and ∠5 are supplementary and ∠3 and ∠6 are supplementary.

Ⓓ If m∠4 = 70°, what is m∠5? Explain.

m∠5 = 110°; ∠4 and ∠5 are supplementary, so m∠4 + m∠5 = 180°. Therefore

70° + m∠5 = 180°, so m∠5 = 110°.

Reflect

1. Explain how you can find m∠3 in the diagram if $p \parallel q$ and m∠6 = 61°.
    ∠3 and ∠6 are supplementary, so m∠3 + m∠6 = 180°. Therefore m∠3 + 61° = 180°, so

    m∠3 = 119°.

2. **What If?** If $m \parallel n$, how many pairs of same-side interior angles are shown in the figure? What are the pairs?
    Two pairs; ∠3 and ∠5, ∠4 and ∠6

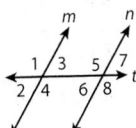

Exploring Parallel Lines and Transversals

INTEGRATE TECHNOLOGY

The properties of parallel lines and transversals can be explored using geometry software. Students can display lines and angle measures on screen, rotate a line so it is parallel to another, and observe the relationships between angles.

QUESTIONING STRATEGIES

? When two lines are cut by a transversal, how many pairs of corresponding angles are formed? How many pairs of same-side angles? 4; 2

? What does the Same-Side Interior Angles Postulate tell you about the measure of a pair of same-side interior angles? The sum of their measures is 180°.

PROFESSIONAL DEVELOPMENT

COMMON CORE Math Background

When two parallel lines are cut by a transversal, alternate interior angles have the same measure, corresponding angles have the same measure, and same-side interior angles are supplementary. One of these three facts must be taken as a postulate and then the other two may be proved. In the work text, the statement about same-side interior angles is taken as the postulate. This is closely related to one of the postulates stated in Euclid's *Elements*: "If a straight line falling on two straight lines makes the interior angles on the same side less than two right angles, the two straight lines, if produced indefinitely, meet on that side on which are the angles less than the two right angles."

Transversals and Parallel lines **176**

EXPLAIN 1

Proving that Alternate Interior Angles are Congruent

CONNECT VOCABULARY EL

Have students experience the idea of what the term *alternate* means by shading in alternating figures in a series of figures.

QUESTIONING STRATEGIES

? Do you have to write a separate proof for every pair of alternate interior angles in the figure? Why or why not? No, you can write the proof for any pair of alternate interior angles. The same reasoning applies to all the pairs.

⚙ Explain 1 **Proving that Alternate Interior Angles are Congruent**

Other pairs of angles formed by parallel lines cut by a transversal are alternate interior angles.

Alternate Interior Angles Theorem
If two parallel lines are cut by a transversal, then the pairs of alternate interior angles have the same measure.

To prove something to be true, you use definitions, properties, postulates, and theorems that you already know.

Example 1 Prove the Alternate Interior Angles Theorem.

Given: $p \parallel q$

Prove: $m\angle 3 = m\angle 5$

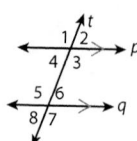

Complete the proof by writing the missing reasons. Choose from the following reasons. You may use a reason more than once.

- Same-Side Interior Angles Postulate
- Given
- Definition of supplementary angles
- Subtraction Property of Equality
- Substitution Property of Equality
- Linear Pair Theorem

Statements	Reasons
1. $p \parallel q$	1. Given
2. $\angle 3$ and $\angle 6$ are supplementary.	2. Same-Side Interior Angles Postulate
3. $m\angle 3 + m\angle 6 = 180°$	3. Definition of supplementary angles
4. $\angle 5$ and $\angle 6$ are a linear pair.	4. Given
5. $\angle 5$ and $\angle 6$ are supplementary.	5. Linear Pair Theorem
6. $m\angle 5 + m\angle 6 = 180°$	6. Definition of supplementary angles
7. $m\angle 3 + m\angle 6 = m\angle 5 + m\angle 6$	7. Substitution Property of Equality
8. $m\angle 3 = m\angle 5$	8. Subtraction Property of Equality

Reflect

3. In the figure, explain why $\angle 1$, $\angle 3$, $\angle 5$, and $\angle 7$ all have the same measure.
   $m\angle 1 = m\angle 3$ and $m\angle 5 = m\angle 7$ (Vertical Angles Theorem), $m\angle 3 = m\angle 5$ (Alternate Interior Angles Theorem), so $m\angle 1 = m\angle 3 = m\angle 5 = m\angle 7$ (Transitive Property of Equality).

COLLABORATIVE LEARNING

Peer-to-Peer Activity

Have students use lined paper or geometry software to draw two parallel lines and a transversal that is not perpendicular to the lines. Instruct the student's partner to shade or mark the acute angles with one color and the obtuse angles with another color. Let students use a protractor or geometry software to see that all the angles with the same color are congruent, and that pairs of angles with different colors are supplementary.

4. Suppose m∠4 = 57° in the figure shown. Describe two different ways to determine m∠6.
By the Alternate Interior Angles Theorem, m∠6 = 57°. Also ∠4 and ∠5 are supplementary,
so m∠5 = 123°. Since ∠5 and ∠6 are supplementary, m∠6 = 57°.

⊘ Explain 2 **Proving that Corresponding Angles are Congruent**

Two parallel lines cut by a transversal also form angle pairs called corresponding angles.

Corresponding Angles Theorem
If two parallel lines are cut by a transversal, then the pairs of corresponding angles have the same measure.

Example 2 Complete a proof in paragraph form for the Corresponding Angles Theorem.

Given: $p \| q$

Prove: m∠4 = m∠8

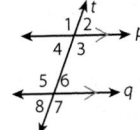

By the given statement, $p \| q$. ∠4 and ∠6 form a pair of ___alternate interior angles___

So, using the Alternate Interior Angles Theorem, ___m∠4 = m∠6___.

∠6 and ∠8 form a pair of vertical angles. So, using the Vertical Angles Theorem,

___m∠6 = m∠8___. Using the ___Substitution Property of Equality___

in m∠4 = m∠6, substitute ___m∠4___ for m∠6. The result is ___m∠4 = m∠8___.

Reflect

5. Use the diagram in Example 2 to explain how you can prove the Corresponding Angles Theorem using the Same-Side Interior Angles Postulate and a linear pair of angles.
By the Same-Side Interior Angles Theorem, m∠4 + m∠5 = 180°. As a linear pair,

m∠4 + m∠1 = 180°. Therefore m∠4 + m∠1 = m∠4 + m∠5, so m∠1 = m∠5.

6. Suppose m∠4 = 36°. Find m∠5. Explain.
m∠5 = 144°; Since ∠1 and ∠4 form a linear pair, they are supplementary. So,

m∠1 = 144°. Using the Corresponding Angles Theorem, you know that m∠1 = m∠5.

So, m∠5 = 144°.

© Houghton Mifflin Harcourt Publishing Company

DIFFERENTIATE INSTRUCTION

Kinesthetic Experience

Have students draw a pair of parallel lines and a transversal on translucent paper squares. Tear the paper between the parallel lines, and overlay the two parts to show that the angles are congruent.

EXPLAIN 2

Proving that Corresponding Angles are Congruent

INTEGRATE MATHEMATICAL PRACTICES

Focus on Reasoning

MP.2 Explaining and justifying arguments is at the heart of this proof-based lesson. You may wish to have students pair up with a "proof buddy." Students can exchange their work with this partner and check that the partner's logical arguments make sense.

QUESTIONING STRATEGIES

? What can you use as reasons in a proof? given information, properties, postulates, and previously-proven theorems

? How can you check that the first and last statements in a two-column proof are correct? The first statement should match the "Given" and the last statement should match the "Prove."

INTEGRATE MATHEMATICAL PRACTICES

Focus on Modeling

MP.4 Draw parallel lines and a transversal on a transparency. Trace an acute and an obtuse angle formed by the lines onto another transparency, and use them to find congruent angles.

AVOID COMMON ERRORS

Some students may have difficulty identifying the correct angles for two parallel lines cut by a transversal because they are unfamiliar with the angles. Have these students use highlighters to color-code the different angle pairs. For example, students can use a yellow highlighter to highlight the term *corresponding angles* and then use the same highlighter to mark the corresponding angles.

EXPLAIN 3

Using Parallel Lines to Find Angle Pair Relationships

INTEGRATE MATHEMATICAL PRACTICES

Focus on Modeling

MP.4 Have students look through magazines to find pictures with parallel lines and transversals, such as bridges, fences, furniture, etc. Use markers or colored tape to mark the lines, and then identify angles that appear to be congruent and angles that appear to be supplementary.

QUESTIONING STRATEGIES

? How can you check that the postulates and theorems about parallel lines apply to real-world situations? Sample answer: Measure some angle pair relationships with lines that appear parallel, and verify that the postulates and theorems apply.

ELABORATE

AVOID COMMON ERRORS

Students may incorrectly apply the postulates and theorems presented in this lesson when lines cut by a transversal are not parallel. Remind them that the postulates and theorems are only true for parallel lines.

QUESTIONING STRATEGIES

? Postulates may be used to prove theorems; which postulate was used to prove the two theorems in this lesson? Same-Side Interior Angles Postulate

---

⚙ Explain 3 **Using Parallel Lines to Find Angle Pair Relationships**

You can apply the theorems and postulates about parallel lines cut by a transversal to solve problems.

> **Example 3** Find each value. Explain how to find the values using postulates, theorems, and algebraic reasoning.

(A) In the diagram, roads a and b are parallel. Explain how to find the measure of $\angle VTU$.

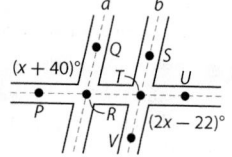

It is given that $m\angle PRQ = (x + 40)°$ and $m\angle VTU = (2x - 22)°$. $m\angle PRQ = m\angle RTS$ by the Corresponding Angles Theorem and $m\angle RTS = m\angle VTU$ by the Vertical Angles Theorem. So, $m\angle PRQ = m\angle VTU$, and $x + 40 = 2x - 22$. Solving for x, $x + 62 = 2x$, and $x = 62$. Substitute the value of x to find $m\angle VTU$: $m\angle VTU = (2(62) - 22)° = 102°$.

(B) In the diagram, roads a and b are parallel. Explain how to find the measure of $m\angle WUV$.

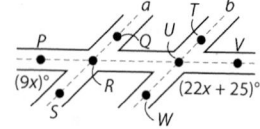

It is given that $m\angle PRS = (9x)°$ and $m\angle WUV = (22x + 25)°$.

$m\angle PRS = m\angle RUW$ by the ___Corresponding Angles Theorem___.

$\angle RUW$ and ___$\angle WUV$___ are supplementary angles.

So, $m\angle RUW + m\angle WUV = $ ___$180°$___. Solving for x, $31x + 25 = 180$,

and ___$x = 5$___. Substitute the value of x to find ___$m\angle WUV$___;

$m\angle WUV = (22(5) + 25)° $ ___$= 135°$___.

Your Turn

7. In the diagram of a gate, the horizontal bars are parallel and the vertical bars are parallel. Find x and y. Name the postulates and/or theorems that you used to find the values.

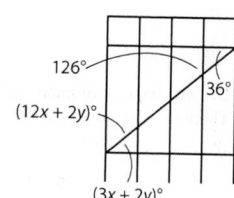

$x = 10, y = 3; (12x + 2y)° = 126°$ by the Corresponding Angles Theorem and $(3x + 2y)° = 36°$ by the Alternate Interior Angles Theorem. Solving the equations simultaneously results in $x = 10$ and $y = 3$.

© Houghton Mifflin Harcourt Publishing Company

LANGUAGE SUPPORT 🔲EL

Visual Cues

Have students work in pairs to add the following angle definitions and pictures to an organizer like the one below:

Angle(s)	Definition	Picture
Alternate interior angles		
Corresponding angles		
Same-side interior angles		

💬 Elaborate

8. How is the Same-Side Interior Angles Postulate different from the two theorems in the lesson (Alternate Interior Angles Theorem and Corresponding Angles Theorem)?

The postulate shows that pairs of angles are supplementary, while the theorems show that pairs of angles have the same measure.

9. Discussion Look at the figure below. If you know that *p* and *q* are parallel, and are given one angle measure, can you find all the other angle measures? Explain.

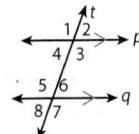

Yes; Possible explanation: Consider angles 1–4. If you knew one angle you can use the fact that angles that are linear pairs are supplementary and the Vertical Angles Theorem. You could use either the Alternate Interior Angles Theorem or the Corresponding Angles Theorem to find one of the angle measures for angles 5–8. Then you can use the Linear Pair Theorem and the Vertical Angles Theorem to find all of those angle measures.

10. Essential Question Check-In Why is it important to establish the Same-Side Interior Angles Postulate before proving the other theorems?

You need to use the Same-Side Interior Angles Postulate to prove the Alternate Interior Angles Theorem, and to prove the Corresponding Angles Theorem you need to use either the Same-Side Interior Angles Postulate or the Alternate Interior Angles Theorem.

☆ Evaluate: Homework and Practice

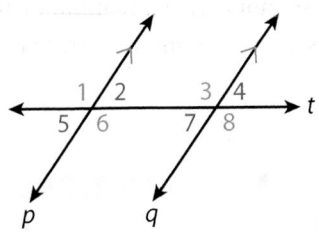

- Online Homework
- Hints and Help
- Extra Practice

1. In the figure below, *m*∥*n*. Match the angle pairs with the correct label for the pairs. Indicate a match by writing the letter for the angle pairs on the line in front of the corresponding labels.

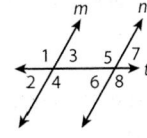

A. ∠4 and ∠6   ___C___ Corresponding Angles

B. ∠5 and ∠8   ___A___ Same-Side Interior Angles

C. ∠2 and ∠6   ___D___ Alternate Interior Angles

D. ∠4 and ∠5   ___B___ Vertical Angles

Exercise	Depth of Knowledge (D.O.K.)	COMMON CORE Mathematical Practices	
1	**1** Recall of Information	**MP.2**	Reasoning
2	**1** Recall of Information	**MP.3**	Logic
3	**1** Recall of Information	**MP.2**	Reasoning
4–14	**2** Skills/Concepts	**MP.2**	Reasoning
15	**3** Strategic Thinking	**MP.4**	Modeling
16	**2** Skills/Concepts	**MP.4**	Modeling
17	**2** Skills/Concepts	**MP.3**	Logic

SUMMARIZE THE LESSON

Have students use the diagram to identify the following:

Parallel lines *p* and *q*

Transversal *t*

Congruent angles: Corresponding ∠1 ≅ ∠3; ∠2 ≅ ∠4; ∠5 ≅ ∠7; ∠6 ≅ ∠8

Alternate interior ∠2 ≅ ∠7; ∠3 ≅ ∠6

Supplementary angles: Same-side interior ∠2 and ∠3; ∠6 and ∠7

EVALUATE

ASSIGNMENT GUIDE

Concepts and Skills	Practice
Explore Exploring Parallel Lines and Transversals	Exercises 1–4
Example 1 Proving that Alternate Interior Angles are Congruent	Exercises 5–14
Example 2 Proving that Corresponding Angles are Congruent	Exercises 5–14
Example 3 Using Parallel Lines to Find Angle Pair Relationships	Exercises 15–18

Students may incorrectly apply the postulates and theorems presented in this lesson when lines cut by a transversal are not parallel. Remind them that the postulates and theorems are only true for parallel lines.

INTEGRATE MATHEMATICAL PRACTICES

Focus on Modeling

MP.4 Some students may have difficulty identifying the correct angles for two parallel lines cut by a transversal because some combinations of angles can be visually distracting. Suggest that these students re-draw or trace the diagram for each exercise, labeling only the angles necessary for the exercise.

---

2. Complete the definition: A ___transversal___ is a line that intersects two coplanar lines at two different points.

Use the figure to find angle measures. In the figure, $p \parallel q$.

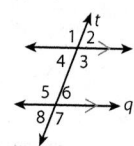

3. Suppose $m\angle 4 = 82°$. Find $m\angle 5$.
$m\angle 5 = 98°$, by the Same-Side Interior Angles Postulate.

4. Suppose $m\angle 3 = 105°$. Find $m\angle 6$.
$m\angle 6 = 75°$, by the Same-Side Interior Angles Postulate.

5. Suppose $m\angle 3 = 122°$. Find $m\angle 5$.
$m\angle 5 = 122°$, by the Alternate Interior Angles Theorem.

6. Suppose $m\angle 4 = 76°$. Find $m\angle 6$.
$m\angle 6 = 76°$, by the Alternate Interior Angles Theorem.

7. Suppose $m\angle 5 = 109°$. Find $m\angle 1$.
$m\angle 1 = 109°$, by the Corresponding Angles Theorem.

8. Suppose $m\angle 6 = 74°$. Find $m\angle 2$.
$m\angle 2 = 74°$, by the Corresponding Angles Theorem.

Use the figure to find angle measures. In the figure, $m \parallel n$ and $x \parallel y$.

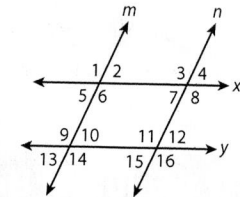

9. Suppose $m\angle 5 = 69°$. Find $m\angle 10$.
$m\angle 10 = 69°$, by the Alternate Interior Angles Theorem.

10. Suppose $m\angle 9 = 115°$. Find $m\angle 6$.
$m\angle 6 = 115°$, by the Alternate Interior Angles Theorem.

11. Suppose $m\angle 12 = 118°$. Find $m\angle 7$.
$m\angle 7 = 118°$, by the Alternate Interior Angles Theorem.

12. Suppose $m\angle 4 = 72°$. Find $m\angle 11$.
$m\angle 11 = 108°$, by the Corresponding Angles Theorem and Linear Pair Theorem.

13. Suppose $m\angle 4 = 114°$. Find $m\angle 14$.
$m\angle 14 = 66°$, by the Corresponding Angles Theorem, Linear Pair Theorem, and Corresponding Angles Theorem.

14. Suppose $m\angle 5 = 86°$. Find $m\angle 12$.
$m\angle 12 = 86°$, by the Alternate Interior Angles Theorem and Corresponding Angles Theorem.

Exercise	Depth of Knowledge (D.O.K.)	COMMON CORE Mathematical Practices
18–21	**3** Strategic Thinking	**MP.3** Logic
22–23	**3** Strategic Thinking H.O.T.	**MP.3** Logic

15. Ocean waves move in parallel lines toward the shore. The figure shows the path that a windsurfer takes across several waves. For this exercise, think of the windsurfer's wake as a line. If $m\angle 1 = (2x + 2y)°$ and $m\angle 2 = (2x + y)°$, find x and y. Explain your reasoning.

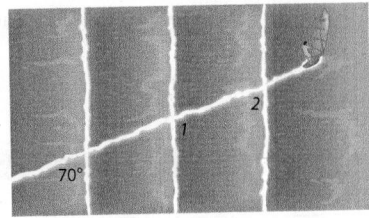

$x = 15$ and $y = 40$; $m\angle 2 = 70°$ by the Corresponding Angles Theorem and $m\angle 1 + m\angle 2 = 180°$ by the Same-Side Interior Angles Postulate. So, $m\angle 1 = 180° - 70° = 110°$. $m\angle 2 = (2x + y)°$ and $m\angle 2 = 70°$, so $(2x + y) = 70°$ by the Substitution Property of Equality and $2x = 70 - y$. $m\angle 1 = (2x + 2y)°$, so $m\angle 1 = (70 - y + 2y)° = (70 + y)°$, so $(70 + y)° = 110°$ and $y = 40$ by the Substitution Property of Equality.

Since $2x + y = 70$ and $y = 40$, $2x = 30$ and $x = 15$.

In the diagram of movie theater seats, the incline of the floor, f, is parallel to the seats, s.

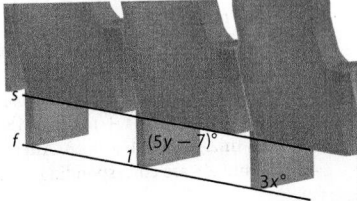

16. If $m\angle 1 = 60°$, what is x?

$x = 40$; by the Corr. $\angle$s Thm. and the Lin. Pair Thm., $3x° + m\angle 1 = 180°$, so $3x + 60 = 180$, and $x = 40$.

17. If $m\angle 1 = 68°$, what is y?

$y = 15$; by the Alt. Int. $\angle$s Thm., $m\angle 1 = (5y - 7)°$, so $68 = 5y - 7$, and $y = 15$.

18. Complete a proof in paragraph form for the Alternate Interior Angles Theorem.

Given: $p \parallel q$

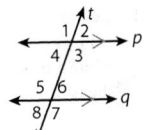

Prove: $m\angle 3 = m\angle 5$

It is given that $p \parallel q$, so using the Same-Side Interior Angles Postulate, $\angle 3$ and $\angle 6$ are ___supplementary___. So, the sum of their measures is ___180°___ and $m\angle 3 + m\angle 6 = 180°$.

You can see from the diagram that $\angle 5$ and $\angle 6$ form a line, so they are a ___linear pair___, which makes them ___supplementary___. Then $m\angle 5 + m\angle 6 = 180°$. Using the Substitution Property of Equality, you can substitute ___180°___ in $m\angle 3 + m\angle 6 = 180°$ with $m\angle 5 + m\angle 6$. This results in $m\angle 3 + m\angle 6 = m\angle 5 + m\angle 6$. Using the Subtraction Property of Equality, you can subtract ___$m\angle 6$___ from both sides. So, ___$m\angle 3 = m\angle 5$___.

Ask students to discuss with a partner the parallel line diagrams for various pairs of angles introduced in this lesson. Ask them to write and solve a word problem about parallel lines and their associated angles on index cards, and switch with their partners to solve the problem.

INTEGRATE MATHEMATICAL PRACTICES
Focus on Math Connections

MP.1 Remind students about how to use the Same-Side Interior Angles Postulate and the theorems about parallel lines to write equations that will help them find angle measures related to parallel lines.

JOURNAL

Have students list examples in the real world where they have seen parallel lines cut by a transversal. Ask them to name the pairs of angles that are congruent.

19. Write a proof in two-column form for the Corresponding Angles Theorem.

Given: $p \parallel q$

Prove: $m\angle 1 = m\angle 5$

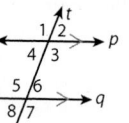

Statements	Reasons
1. $p \parallel q$	1. Given
2. $m\angle 3 = m\angle 5$	2. Alternate Interior Angles Theorem
3. $m\angle 1 = m\angle 3$	3. Vertical Angles Theorem
4. $m\angle 1 = m\angle 5$	4. Substitution Property of Equality

20. Explain the Error Angelina wrote a proof in paragraph form to prove that the measures of corresponding angles are congruent. Identify her error, and describe how to fix the error.

Angelina's proof:

I am given that $p \parallel q$. $\angle 1$ and $\angle 4$ are supplementary angles because they form a linear pair, so $m\angle 1 + m\angle 4 = 180°$. $\angle 4$ and $\angle 8$ are also supplementary because of the Same-Side Interior Angles Postulate, so $m\angle 4 + m\angle 8 = 180°$. You can substitute $m\angle 4 + m\angle 8$ for 180° in the first equation above. The result is $m\angle 1 + m\angle 4 = m\angle 4 + m\angle 8$. After subtracting $m\angle 4$ from each side, I see that $\angle 1$ and $\angle 8$ are corresponding angles and $m\angle 1 = m\angle 8$.

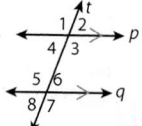

$\angle 4$ and $\angle 8$ are not same-side interior angles. $\angle 4$ and $\angle 5$ are same-side interior angles. So, in the paragraph proof, replace $\angle 8$ with $\angle 5$ to see that $m\angle 1 = m\angle 5$.

21. Counterexample Ellen thinks that when two lines that are not parallel are cut by a transversal, the measures of the alternate interior angles are the same. Write a proof to show that she is correct or use a counterexample to show that she is incorrect.

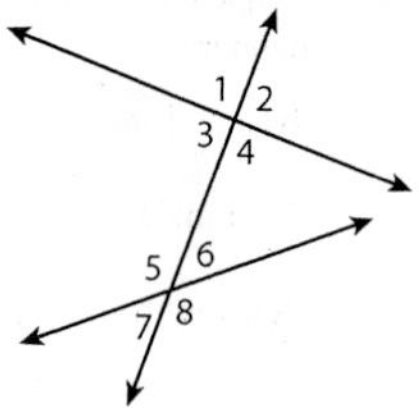

A possible diagram is shown, with two nonparallel lines cut by a transversal. I can measure the angles in my drawing with a protractor as a counterexample. $\angle 4$ and $\angle 5$ are alternate interior angles, but $m\angle 4 = 90°$ and $m\angle 5 = 130°$, so the measures are not the same when the lines are not parallel.

Analyzing Mathematical Relationships Use the diagram of a staircase railing for Exercises 22 and 23. $\overline{AG} \parallel \overline{CJ}$ and $\overline{AD} \parallel \overline{FJ}$. Choose the best answer.

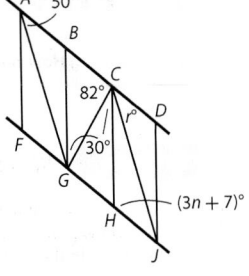

22. Which is a true statement about the measure of $\angle DCJ$?

    A. It is 30°, by the Alternate Interior Angles Theorem.

    B. It is 30°, by the Corresponding Angles Theorem.

    C. It is 50°, by the Alternate Interior Angles Theorem.

    (D.) It is 50°, by the Corresponding Angles Theorem.

23. Which is a true statement about the value of n?

    A. It is 25, by the Alternate Interior Angles Theorem.

    B. It is 25, by the Same-Side Interior Angles Postulate.

    (C.) It is 35, by Alternate Interior Angles Theorem.

    D. It is 35, by the Corresponding Angles Theorem.

Lesson Performance Task

Washington Street is parallel to Lincoln Street. The Apex Company's headquarters is located between the streets. From headquarters, a straight road leads to Washington Street, intersecting it at a 51° angle. Another straight road leads to Lincoln Street, intersecting it at a 37° angle.

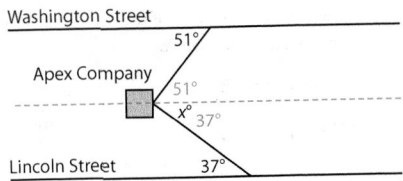

    a. Find x. Explain your method.

    b. Suppose that another straight road leads from the opposite side of headquarters to Washington Street, intersecting it at a $y°$ angle, and another straight road leads from headquarters to Lincoln Street, intersecting it at a $z°$ angle. Find the measure of the angle w formed by the two roads. Explain how you found w.

    a. Draw a line parallel to the two streets and passing through the vertex of the angle with measure $x°$. Because alternate interior angles formed by parallel lines and a transversal are congruent, the angle measuring $x°$ is divided into a 51° angle and a 37° angle, so $x = 51 + 37 = 88$.

    b. Use the method from part a. The top part of the unknown angle measures $y°$ and the bottom part measures $z°$. So, $w = y + z$.

INTEGRATE MATHEMATICAL PRACTICES
Focus on Critical Thinking

MP.3 Students may not have encountered geometry problems that can be solved by drawing a line or some other element on a given figure. Students may object that a problem of this kind isn't "fair." Point out that many problems omit information. To solve a problem, you use problem-solving skills, working your way logically from the statement of the problem to its solution. This problem introduces a new approach students can add to their arsenal of problem-solving skills.

INTEGRATE MATHEMATICAL PRACTICES
Focus on Modeling

MP.4 If students have difficulty drawing the figure for part b of the Lesson Performance Task, show them this figure:

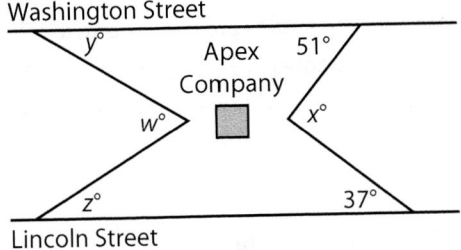

Scoring Rubric

2 points: Student correctly solves the problem and explains his/her reasoning.

1 point: Student shows good understanding of the problem but does not fully solve or explain his/her reasoning.

0 points: Student does not demonstrate understanding of the problem.

EXTENSION ACTIVITY

The easiest way to solve the problems in the Lesson Performance Task is to draw a line parallel to Washington and Lincoln streets through the angle with its vertex at the Apex Company. But what if there are two such possible lines, or even more?

Have students research and report on "Playfair's Axiom," which states that, in a plane, no more than one line can be drawn through a given point that is parallel to a given line. Students should be able to grasp this concept intuitively, as a second line through a point would form a nonzero angle with the parallel line and thus could not also be parallel.

Proving Lines are Parallel

Common Core Math Standards

The student is expected to:

 G-CO.C.9

Prove theorems about lines and angles. Also G-CO.D.12

Mathematical Practices

 MP.3 Logic

Language Objective

Explain to a partner whether the angles formed by two lines cut by a transversal determine parallel lines.

ENGAGE

Essential Question: How can you prove that two lines are parallel?

Possible answer: Look at the angles formed when a transversal crosses the two lines. If a pair of alternate interior angles are congruent, a pair of corresponding angles are congruent, or a pair of same-side interior angles are supplementary, then the lines are parallel.

PREVIEW: LESSON PERFORMANCE TASK

View the Engage section online. Discuss the photo. Ask students to speculate on advantages a system of parallel east-west and north-south streets at Giza might have had over another system. Then preview the Lesson Performance Task.

4.3 Proving Lines are Parallel

Essential Question: How can you prove that two lines are parallel?

Explore **Writing Converses of Parallel Line Theorems**

You form the **converse** of and if-then statement "if *p*, then *q*" by swapping *p* and *q*.
The converses of the postulate and theorems you have learned about lines cut by a transversal are true statements. In the Explore, you will write specific cases of each of these converses.

The diagram shows two lines cut by a transversal *t*. Use the diagram and the given statements in Steps A–D. You will complete the statements based on your work in Steps A–D.

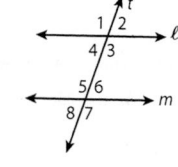

Statements	
lines ℓ and m are parallel	∠4 ≅ ∠ 6
∠6 and ∠ 3 are supplementary	∠ 3 ≅ ∠7

(A) Use two of the given statements together to complete a statement about the diagram using the Same-Side Interior Angles Postulate.

By the postulate: If ___lines ℓ and m are parallel___, then ∠6 and ∠ 3 are supplementary.

(B) Now write the converse of the Same-Side Interior Angles Postulate using the diagram and your statement in Step A.

By its converse: If ___∠6 and ∠3 are supplementary___,

then ___lines ℓ and m are parallel___.

(C) Repeat to illustrate the Alternate Interior Angles Theorem and its converse using the diagram and the given statements.

By the theorem: If ___lines ℓ and m are parallel___, then ∠4 ≅ ∠ 6 .

By its converse: If ___∠4 ≅ ∠6___

then ___lines ℓ and m are parallel___.

(D) Use the diagram and the given statements to illustrate the Corresponding Angles Theorem and its converse.

By the theorem: If ___lines ℓ and m are parallel___, then ∠ 3 ≅ ∠7.

By its converse: ___if ∠3 ≅ ∠7, then lines ℓ and m are parallel___

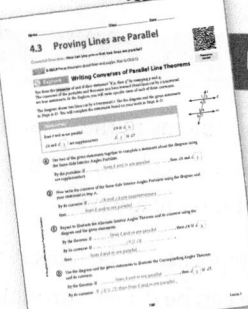

HARDCOVER PAGES 161–168

Turn to these pages to find this lesson in the hardcover student edition.

Reflect

1. How do you form the converse of a statement?
   Possible answer: Reverse the hypothesis and conclusion; for a statement "if p, then q", the

   converse is "if q, then p."

2. What kind of angles are $\angle 4$ and $\angle 6$ in Step C? What does the converse you wrote in Step C mean?
   Possible answer: alternate interior angles; if the two alternate interior angles $\angle 4$ and $\angle 6$

   are congruent, then the lines ℓ and m are parallel.

⚙ Explain 1   Proving that Two Lines are Parallel

The converses from the Explore can be stated formally as a postulate and two theorems. (You will prove the converses of the theorems in the exercises.)

> **Converse of the Same-Side Interior Angles Postulate**
>
> If two lines are cut by a transversal so that a pair of same-side interior angles are supplementary, then the lines are parallel.

> **Converse of the Alternate Interior Angles Theorem**
>
> If two lines are cut by a transversal so that any pair of alternate interior angles are congruent, then the lines are parallel.

> **Converse of the Corresponding Angles Theorem**
>
> If two lines are cut by a transversal so that any pair of corresponding angles are congruent, then the lines are parallel.

You can use these converses to decide whether two lines are parallel.

Example 1   A mosaic designer is using quadrilateral-shaped colored tiles to make an ornamental design. Each tile is congruent to the one shown here.

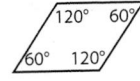

The designer uses the colored tiles to create the pattern shown here.

(A) Use the values of the marked angles to show that the two lines ℓ_1 and ℓ_2 are parallel.

Measure of $\angle 1$: 120°   Measure of $\angle 2$: 60°

Relationship between the two angles: They are supplementary.

Conclusion: $\ell_1 \parallel \ell_2$ by the Converse of the Same-Side Interior Angles Postulate.

PROFESSIONAL DEVELOPMENT

 Learning Progressions

Previously, students learned the Same-Side Interior Angles Postulate, the Alternate Interior Angles Theorem, and the Corresponding Angles Theorem. They now prove that the converses of the theorems are true given that the Converse of the Same-Side Interior Angles Postulate is also true. Presenting the converses of these statements reinforces the relationship between parallel lines cut by a transversal and the angles these lines form. Parallel lines are important to architecture, construction, and other disciplines. All students should develop fluency with parallel lines and the associated angles as they continue their study of the applications of geometry.

EXPLORE

Writing Converses of Parallel Line Theorems

INTEGRATE TECHNOLOGY

Students have the option of exploring the converses of parallel lines theorem activity either in the book or online.

INTEGRATE MATHEMATICAL PRACTICES
Focus on Math Connections

MP.1 Before introducing the converses of the Same-Side Interior Angles Postulate, the Alternate Interior Angles Theorem, and the Corresponding Angles Theorem, you may want to spend a few minutes talking about statements and their converses. Have students give the converse for statements based on everyday situations such as, "If you live in Cleveland, then you live in Ohio." Forming the converses of such statements can help students see that the converse of a true statement may or may not be true.

EXPLAIN 1

Proving that Two Lines are Parallel

QUESTIONING STRATEGIES

❓ How can you determine that a statement is the converse of a theorem?   The hypothesis and conclusion of the theorem are switched.

CONNECT VOCABULARY **EL**

Have students explore lines of latitude, often called *parallels,* on a map or globe. They might measure the distance between different parallels at several locations. The actual distance between successive degrees of latitude is about 69 miles.

AVOID COMMON ERRORS

As you work through the examples, watch for students who use a postulate or theorem for justification when its converse should be used. To help them choose the correct conditional, point out that any given information corresponds to the hypothesis in a conditional statement.

Ⓑ Now look at this situation. Use the values of the marked angles to show that the two lines are parallel.

Measure of ∠1: _____120°_____   Measure of ∠2: _____120°_____

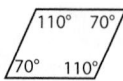

Relationship between the two

angles: __They are congruent corresponding angles.__

Conclusion:

__ℓ₁ ∥ ℓ₂ by the Converse of the Corresponding Angles Theorem.__

Reflect

3. **What If?** Suppose the designer had been working with this basic shape instead. Do you think the conclusions in Parts A and B would have been different? Why or why not?

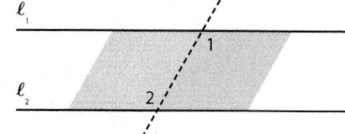

__No, because the tile pattern formed still has congruent corresponding angle and__

__supplementary angle pairs that can be used to produce parallel lines.__

Your Turn

Explain why the lines are parallel given the angles shown. Assume that all tile patterns use this basic shape.

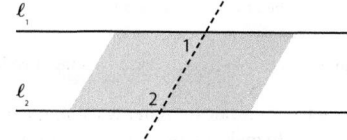

4.

m∠1 = 120° and m∠2 = 120°

They are congruent alternate interior angles. The lines are parallel because of the Converse of the Alternate Interior Angles Theorem.

5.

m ∠1 = 120° and m∠2 = 60°

The angles are supplementary. The lines are parallel because of the Converse of the Same-Side Interior Angles Postulate.

COLLABORATIVE LEARNING

Whole Class Activity

Have groups of students create posters to demonstrate how the Corresponding Angles Theorem and its converse are related and how the Alternate Interior Angles Theorem and its converse are related. Ask them to display their results as a graphic organizer that shows the answers to two questions for each theorem and converse: "How are the theorem and its converse the same?" and "How are the theorem and its converse different?"

⊘ Explain 2 Constructing Parallel Lines

The Parallel Postulate guarantees that for any line ℓ, you can always construct a parallel line through a point that is not on ℓ.

The Parallel Postulate

Through a point *P* not on line ℓ, there is exactly one line parallel to ℓ.

Example 2 Use a compass and straightedge to construct parallel lines.

Ⓐ Construct a line *m* through a point *P* not on a line ℓ so that *m* is parallel to ℓ.

Step 1 Draw a line ℓ and a point *P* not on ℓ.

P ●

ℓ ◄─────────────────────►

Step 2 Choose two points on ℓ and label them *Q* and *R*. Use a straightedge to draw $\overleftrightarrow{PQ}$.

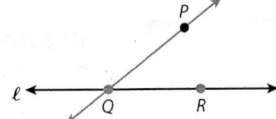

Step 3 Use a compass to copy ∠PQR at point *P*, as shown, to construct line *m*.

line *m* ∥ line ℓ

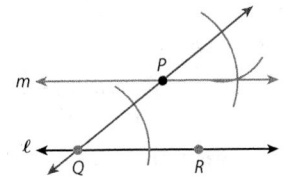

Ⓑ In the space provided, follow the steps to construct a line *r* through a point *G* not on a line *s* so that *r* is parallel to *s*.

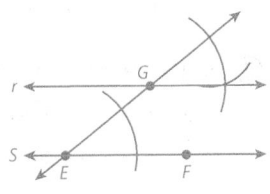

Step 1 Draw a line *s* and a point *G* not on *s*.

Step 2 Choose two points on *s* and label them *E* and *F*. Use a straightedge to draw $\overleftrightarrow{GE}$.

Step 3 Use a compass to copy ∠GEF at point *G*. Label the side of the angle as line *r*.
line *r* ∥ line *s*

© Houghton Mifflin Harcourt Publishing Company

DIFFERENTIATE INSTRUCTION

Manipulatives

Have students tape two pieces of uncooked spaghetti together to form four angles, then measure one angle. Have them place another piece of spaghetti so that the corresponding angle is congruent to the measured angle. Repeat with different angle pairs. Ask the students to discuss how they can justify whether they created pairs of parallel lines.

EXPLAIN 2

Constructing Parallel Lines

INTEGRATE MATHEMATICAL PRACTICES
Focus on Critical Thinking

MP.3 Make sure students understand that the construction is based on congruent corresponding angles. Have students develop a similar construction for parallel lines that is based on congruent alternate interior angles.

QUESTIONING STRATEGIES

? How is the Parallel Postulate used in the parallel lines construction? The Parallel Postulate guarantees that, for any line, you can always construct a parallel line through a point that is not on the line.

? Why must the constructed lines be parallel? Congruent corresponding angles were constructed, so the Converse of the Corresponding Angles Theorem applies.

INTEGRATE MATHEMATICAL PRACTICES
Focus on Modeling

MP.4 Ask students to compare constructions using a reflective device, tracing paper, compass and straightedge, and geometry software. Discuss the advantages of each. Have students consider not only how easy each is to use, but also how accurate, and how well each one helps them understand the geometric relationships being studied.

EXPLAIN 3

Using Angle Pair Relationships to Verify Lines are Parallel

CONNECT VOCABULARY EL

Point out to students that the word *converse* comes from the Latin *conversus*, which means *to turn around*. Connect *converse* to the word *conversation*, meaning *to have a back-and-forth discussion*.

QUESTIONING STRATEGIES

? What are some congruent angle pairs that can be used to prove two lines parallel? corresponding angles or alternate interior angles

? What are some angle pairs that must be supplementary to prove two lines parallel? same-side interior angles

INTEGRATE MATHEMATICAL PRACTICES

Focus on Technology

MP.5 Encourage students to use the geometry software to create congruent pairs of corresponding angles or alternate interior angles. Then have them use the congruent pairs to draw parallel lines. Discuss how congruence of corresponding angles may translate to lines being parallel.

Reflect

6. Discussion Explain how you know that the construction in Part A or Part B produces a line passing through the given point that is parallel to the given line.

In each case, the construction creates two congruent corresponding angles. In Part A, for example, lines ℓ and m are cut by a transversal and a pair of corresponding angles are congruent, so the lines are parallel (Converse of the Corresponding Angles Theorem).

Your Turn

7. Construct a line *m* through *P* parallel to line *ℓ*.

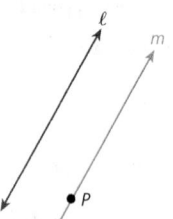

Check students' constructions.

⊘ Explain 3 Using Angle Pair Relationships to Verify Lines are Parallel

When two lines are cut by a transversal, you can use relationships of pairs of angles to decide if the lines are parallel.

Example 3 Use the given angle relationships to decide whether the lines are parallel. Explain your reasoning.

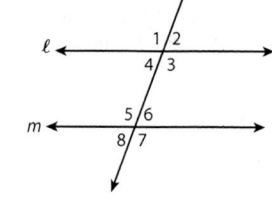

Ⓐ ∠3 ≅ ∠5

    Step 1 Identify the relationship between the two angles.
        ∠3 and ∠5 are congruent alternate interior angles.

    Step 2 Are the lines parallel? Explain.
        Yes, the lines are parallel by the Converse of the Alternate Interior Angles Theorem.

Ⓑ m∠4 = $(x + 20)°$, m∠8 = $(2x + 5)°$, and $x = 15$.

    Step 1 Identify the relationship between the two angles.

      m∠4 = $(x + 20)°$ m∠8 = $(2x + 5)°$

           = $\left(\boxed{15} + 20\right)° = \boxed{35°}$ = $\left(2 \cdot \boxed{15} + 5\right)° = \boxed{35°}$

    So, $\underline{∠4}$ and $\underline{∠8}$ are $\underline{\text{congruent corresponding}}$ angles.

    Step 2 Are the lines parallel? Explain.

    Yes, the lines are parallel by the Converse of the Corresponding Angles Theorem.

LANGUAGE SUPPORT EL

Connect Vocabulary

Help students understand how the term *converse* is used to write the Converse of the Same-Side Interior Angle Postulate, the Converse of the Corresponding Angles Theorem, and the Converse of the Alternate Interior Angles Theorem by first having them explain how to write the converses of simple, non-mathematical statements. Then have them explain how to write the converses of these mathematical statements.

Your Turn

Identify the type of angle pair described in the given condition. How do you know that lines ℓ and m are parallel?

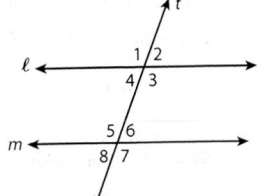

8. $m\angle 3 + m\angle 6 = 180°$
   same side interior angles; by the Converse of the Same Side
   Interior Angles Postulate

9. $\angle 2 \cong \angle 6$
   corresponding angles; by the Converse of the Corresponding
   Angles Theorem

💬 Elaborate

10. How are the converses in this lesson different from the postulate/theorems in the previous lesson?
    In the previous lesson, we knew lines were parallel and things about angles; here, we
    know things about angle pairs, and lines are parallel.

11. **What If?** Suppose two lines are cut by a transversal such that alternate interior angles are both congruent and supplementary. Describe the lines.
    The lines are parallel and all the angles are 90°. The transversal is perpendicular to the
    lines.

12. **Essential Question Check-In** Name two ways to test if a pair of lines is parallel, using the interior angles formed by a transversal crossing the two lines.
    Possible answer: Use given information or measure pairs of angles to decide if alternate
    interior angles are congruent or if same-side interior angles are supplementary.

☆ Evaluate: Homework and Practice

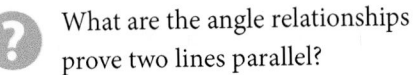

- Online Homework
- Hints and Help
- Extra Practice

The diagram shows two lines cut by a transversal *t*. Use the diagram and the given statements in Exercises 1–3 on the facing page.

Statements
lines ℓ and m are parallel
$m\angle\boxed{6} + m\angle 3 = 180°$
$\angle 1 \cong \angle\boxed{5}$
$\angle\boxed{4} \cong \angle 6$

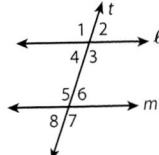

© Houghton Mifflin Harcourt Publishing Company

Exercise	Depth of Knowledge (D.O.K.)	COMMON CORE Mathematical Practices
1–3	1 Recall of Information	**MP.3** Logic
4–7	2 Skills/Concepts	**MP.3** Logic
8–11	2 Skills/Concepts	**MP.6** Precision
12	2 Skills/Concepts	**MP.4** Modeling
13	2 Skills/Concepts	**MP.5** Using Tools
14	1 Recall of Information	**MP.3** Logic
15–16	3 Strategic Thinking H.O.T.	**MP.3** Logic

ELABORATE

AVOID COMMON ERRORS

A common error when working with converses of the parallel lines postulate or theorems is to assume that the lines are already parallel. Emphasize the need to establish that there are congruent angle pairs (corresponding or alternate interior) or same-side interior angles supplementary before a statement about parallelism can be made.

QUESTIONING STRATEGIES

? How are the converses in this lesson different from the postulate/theorems in the previous lesson? There, we knew the lines were parallel and we were proving things about the angles; here, we know things about the angle pairs, and are proving the lines are parallel.

SUMMARIZE THE LESSON

? What are the angle relationships that would prove two lines parallel?

a pair of congruent corresponding angles; a pair of congruent alternate interior angles; a pair of same-side interior angles that are supplementary

EVALUATE

ASSIGNMENT GUIDE

Concepts and Skills	Practice
Explore Writing Converses of Parallel Line Theorems	Exercises 1–3
Example 1 Proving that Two Lines are Parallel	Exercises 4–8
Example 2 Constructing Parallel Lines	Exercises 13–14
Example 3 Using Angle Pair Relationships to Verify Lines are Parallel	Exercises 9–12

Proving Lines are Parallel   **190**

AVOID COMMON ERRORS

Students may incorrectly apply the converses presented in this lesson because they assume that lines are parallel and then "prove" that they are. Remind them that the converses of postulates and theorems have different given conditions than those of the original theorems.

1. Use two of the given statements together to complete statements about the diagram to illustrate the Corresponding Angles Theorem. Then write its converse.

   By the theorem: If _____lines ℓ and m are parallel_____, then ∠1 ≅ ∠ 5 .

   By its converse: _____If ∠1 ≅ ∠5, then lines ℓ and m are parallel._____

2. Use two of the given statements together to complete statements about the diagram to illustrate the Same-Side Interior Angles Postulate. Then write its converse.

   By the postulate: If _____lines ℓ and m are parallel_____, then m∠ 6 + m∠3 = 180°.

   By its converse: _____If m∠6 + m∠3 = 180°, then lines ℓ and m are parallel._____

3. Use two of the given statements together to complete statements about the diagram to illustrate the Alternate Interior Angles Theorem. Then write its converse.

   By the theorem: If _____lines ℓ and m are parallel_____, then ∠ 4 ≅ ∠6.

   By its converse: _____If ∠4 ≅ ∠6, then lines ℓ and m are parallel._____

4. **Matching** Match the angle pair relationship on the left with the name of a postulate or theorem that you could use to prove that lines ℓ and m in the diagram are parallel.

   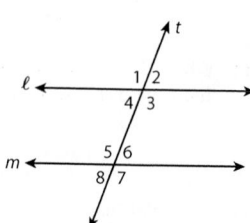

   A. ∠2 ≅ ∠6

   B. ∠3 ≅ ∠5

   C. ∠4 and ∠5 are supplementary.

   D. ∠4 ≅ ∠8

   E. m∠3 + m∠6 = 180°

   F. ∠4 ≅ ∠6

   __A, D__ Converse of the Corresponding Angles Theorem

   __C, E__ Converse of the Same-Side Interior Angles Postulate

   __B, F__ Converse of the Alternate Interior Angles Theorem

Use the diagram for Exercises 5–8.

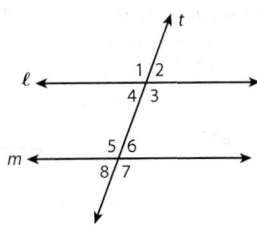

5. What must be true about $\angle 7$ and $\angle 3$ for the lines to be parallel? Name the postulate or theorem.

   $\angle 7 \cong \angle 3$; Converse of the Corresponding Angles Theorem

6. What must be true about $\angle 6$ and $\angle 3$ for the lines to be parallel? Name the postulate or theorem.

   $m\angle 6 + m\angle 3 = 180°$; Converse of the Same-Side Interior Angles Postulate

7. Suppose $m\angle 4 = (3x + 5)°$ and $m\angle 5 = (x + 95)°$, where $x = 20$. Are the lines parallel? Explain.

   $m\angle 4 = 65°$ and $m\angle 5 = 115°$, so $m\angle 4 + m\angle 5 = 180°$. Yes, the lines are parallel by the Converse of the Same-Side Interior Angles Postulate.

8. Suppose $m\angle 3 = (4x + 12)°$ and $m\angle 7 = (80 - x)°$, where $x = 15$. Are the lines parallel? Explain.

   $m\angle 3 = 72°$ and $m\angle 7 = 65°$, so $m\angle 3 \neq m\angle 7$. No, the lines are not parallel because a pair of corresponding angles are not congruent.

Use a converse to answer each question.

9. What value of x makes the horizontal parts of the letter Z parallel?

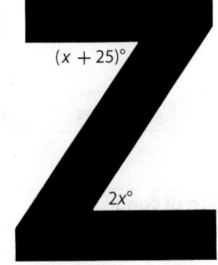

   When $x = 25$, $x + 25 = 2x = 50$; the alternate interior angles are congruent and the horizontal parts of the letter Z are parallel.

10. What value of x makes the vertical parts of the letter N parallel?

   When $x = 3$, $2x + 9 = 5x = 15$; the alternate interior angles are congruent and the vertical parts of the letter N are parallel.

Focus on Math Connections

MP.1 Remind students how to use the converse of the Same-Side Interior Angles Postulate and the converses of theorems about parallel lines to write equations that will help them find angle measures related to parallel lines.

INTEGRATE MATHEMATICAL PRACTICES

Focus on Critical Thinking

MP.3 You may want to have students write a plan for their proof of the theorems in the exercises. Start by assembling the given information that is part of the theorem's hypothesis, the *if* part. For example, before students work on the proof of the Converse of the Corresponding Angles Theorem, have them read the theorem and look for key words or phrases. In this case, students should identify *corresponding angles* as important given information in the theorem. Then ask students to identify the *then* part, which is to conclude that lines are parallel. For many students, a brief preliminary activity of this type can provide a running start for their work on the proof itself.

INTEGRATE MATHEMATICAL PRACTICES

Focus on Critical Thinking

MP.3 Ask students to discuss in groups how the proof of the Converse of the Alternate Interior Angles Theorem would change if the Converse of Same-Side Interior Angles Postulate were a theorem and the Converse of the Corresponding Angles Theorem were a postulate. Ask them to show a plan for the proof and a diagram illustrating the given information.

Ask students to sketch two parallel lines *m* and *n* and a transversal *p* and then label the angles formed with the numbers 1 through 8. Have them explain three ways of proving lines *m* and *n* are parallel.

JOURNAL

Have students explain how to construct parallel lines using one of the postulates or theorems in the lesson.

11. **Engineering** An overpass intersects two lanes of a highway. What must the value of *x* be to ensure the two lanes are parallel?

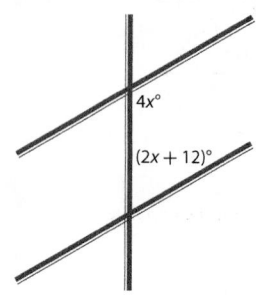

When $x = 28$, $2x + 12 = 68$ and $4x = 132$; the same-side interior angles are supplementary and the lanes are parallel.

12. A trellis consists of overlapping wooden slats. What must the value of *x* be in order for the two slats to be parallel?

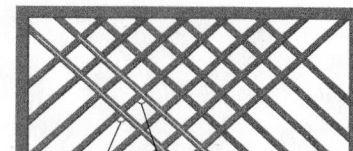

When $x = 6$, $3x + 24 = 42$ and $7x = 42$; the corresponding angles are congruent and the slats are parallel.

13. Construct a line parallel to ℓ that passes through *P*.

Check students' constructions.

14. **Communicate Mathematical Ideas** In Exercise 13, how many parallel lines can you draw through *P* that are parallel to ℓ? Explain.

One; by the Parallel Postulate, there is only one line through a point not on a given line that is parallel to the given line.

> **H.O.T.** Focus on Higher Order Thinking

15. **Justify Reasoning** Write a two-column proof of the Converse of the Alternate Interior Angles Theorem.

Given: lines ℓ and *m* are cut by a transversal *t*; $\angle 1 \cong \angle 2$

Prove: ℓ ∥ *m*

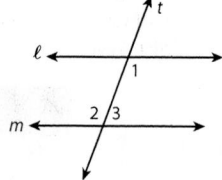

Statements	Reasons
1. lines ℓ and *m* are cut by a transversal; $\angle 1 \cong \angle 2$	1. Given
2. $m\angle 1 = m\angle 2$	2. Definition of congruence
3. $\angle 2$ and $\angle 3$ are supplementary.	3. Linear Pair Theorem
4. $m\angle 2 + m\angle 3 = 180°$	4. Definition of supplementary angles
5. $m\angle 1 + m\angle 3 = 180°$	5. Substitution Property of Equality
6. $\angle 1$ and $\angle 3$ are supplementary.	6. Definition of supplementary angles
7. ℓ ∥ *m*	7. Converse of Same-Side Interior Angles Postulate

© Houghton Mifflin Harcourt Publishing Company

16. Justify Reasoning Write a two-column proof of the Converse of the Corresponding Angles Theorem.

Given: lines ℓ and m are cut by a transversal t; $\angle 1 \cong \angle 2$
Prove: $\ell \parallel m$

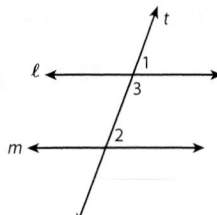

Statements	Reasons
1. lines ℓ and m are cut by a transversal; $\angle 1 \cong \angle 2$	1. Given
2. $m\angle 1 = m\angle 2$	2. Definition of congruence
3. $\angle 1$ and $\angle 3$ are supplementary.	3. Linear Pair Theorem
4. $m\angle 1 + m\angle 3 = 180°$	4. Definition of supplementary angles
5. $m\angle 2 + m\angle 3 = 180°$	5. Substitution Property of Equality
6. $\angle 2$ and $\angle 3$ are supplementary.	6. Definition of supplementary angles
7. $\ell \parallel m$	7. Converse of Same-Side Interior Angles Postulate

Lesson Performance Task

A simplified street map of a section of Harlem in New York City is shown at right. Draw a sketch of the rectangle bounded by West 110th Street and West 121st Street in one direction and Eighth Avenue and Lenox Avenue in the other. Include all the streets and avenues that run between sides of the rectangle. Show St. Nicholas Avenue as a diagonal of the rectangle.

Now imagine that you have been given the job of laying out these streets and avenues on a bare plot of land. Explain in detail how you would do it.

Students should use the fact that St. Nicholas Ave. is a transversal of both the parallel streets and the parallel avenues. One approach is to lay out the outside rectangle with right angles at the corners and St. Nicholas Ave. connecting opposite corners. Then measure the angles where St. Nicholas meets the corners and duplicate them as either alternate interior angles or corresponding angles to draw the streets and avenues between the boundaries.

© Houghton Mifflin Harcourt Publishing Company

Draw attention to the fact that St. Nicholas Avenue is a transversal of both the parallel streets and the parallel avenues.

QUESTIONING STRATEGIES

Sketch the map shown below on the board. Ask questions such as the following. (Answers shown are sample answers.)

? Name a pair of vertical angles. $\angle AMO$ and $\angle MOP$

? Name an angle congruent to $\angle LPQ$. $\angle OPC$

? Name an angle that corresponds to $\angle JRS$. $\angle KQR$

? Name an angle that is supplementary to $\angle OPL$. $\angle LPQ$

? Name a pair of same-side interior angles. $\angle CPQ$ and $\angle DQP$

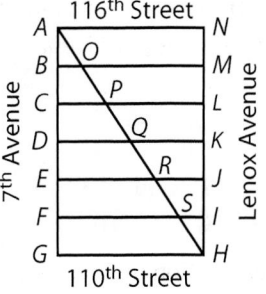

EXTENSION ACTIVITY

The grid on which New York City's street-and-avenue system is based was designed in 1811. The streets from 110th to 121st are 60 feet wide, except for 116th Street, which is 100 feet wide. The distance between each pair of streets is 200 feet. 8th Avenue, 7th Avenue, and Lenox Avenue are each 100 feet wide. The distance between each pair of avenues is 922 feet.

- Find the length and width of the rectangle bounded by 8th Avenue, 110th Street, Lenox Avenue, and 121st Street.

- Find the area of the rectangle in square feet and square miles.

dimensions: 2144 ft by 2960 ft; area: 6,346,240 ft²; 0.23 mi²

Scoring Rubric
2 points: Student correctly solves the problem and explains his/her reasoning.
1 point: Student shows good understanding of the problem but does not fully solve or explain his/her reasoning.
0 points: Student does not demonstrate understanding of the problem.

Proving Lines are Parallel   **194**

Perpendicular Lines

Common Core Math Standards

The student is expected to:

COMMON CORE G-CO.C.9

Prove theorems about lines and angles. Also G-CO.D.12

Mathematical Practices

COMMON CORE MP.5 Using Tools

Language Objective

Explain to a partner why a pair of lines is or is not perpendicular.

ENGAGE

Essential Question: What are the key ideas about perpendicular bisectors of a segment?

Possible answer: If you know that a line is the perpendicular bisector of a segment, then any point on the line is equidistant from the endpoints of the segment. If you know that a point on a line is equidistant from the endpoints of a segment, then the line must be the perpendicular bisector of the segment.

PREVIEW: LESSON PERFORMANCE TASK

View the Engage section online. Discuss the photo. Ask students how they would balance the competing factors that a power company might face in deciding where to build a wind farm. Then preview the Lesson Performance Task.

Name_____ Class_____ Date_____

4.4 Perpendicular Lines

Essential Question: What are the key ideas about perpendicular bisectors of a segment?

Resource Locker

🧭 Explore   Constructing Perpendicular Bisectors and Perpendicular Lines

You can construct geometric figures without using measurement tools like a ruler or a protractor. By using geometric relationships and a compass and a straightedge, you can construct geometric figures with greater precision than figures drawn with standard measurement tools.

A————————B

In Steps A–C, construct the perpendicular bisector of $\overline{AB}$.

(A) Place the point of the compass at point A. Using a compass setting that is greater than half the length of $\overline{AB}$, draw an arc.

(B) Without adjusting the compass, place the point of the compass at point B and draw an arc intersecting the first arc in two places. Label the points of intersection C and D.

(C) Use a straightedge to draw $\overleftrightarrow{CD}$, which is the perpendicular bisector of $\overline{AB}$.

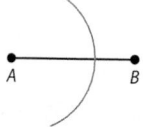
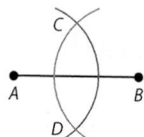
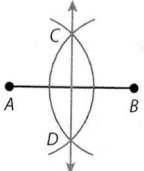

In Steps D–E, construct a line perpendicular to a line ℓ that passes through some point P that is not on ℓ.

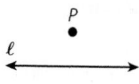

(D) Place the point of the compass at P. Draw an arc that intersects line ℓ at two points, A and B.

(E) Use the methods in Steps A–C to construct the perpendicular bisector of $\overline{AB}$.

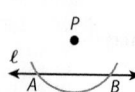
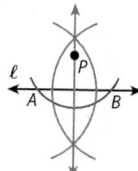

Because it is the perpendicular bisector of $\overline{AB}$, then the constructed line through P is perpendicular to line ℓ.

© Houghton Mifflin Harcourt Publishing Company

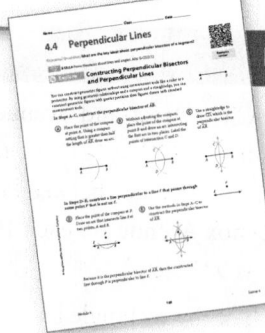

HARDCOVER PAGES 169–178

Turn to these pages to find this lesson in the hardcover student edition.

1. In Step A of the first construction, why do you open the compass to a setting that is greater than half the length of $\overline{AB}$?
This ensures that the two arcs will intersect at two points.

2. What If? Suppose Q is a point *on* line ℓ. Is the construction of a line perpendicular to ℓ through Q any different than constructing a perpendicular line through a point P *not* on the line, as in Steps D and E?
Constructing the points A and B on line ℓ is different in the two constructions. For a
point Q on line ℓ, you place the compass point at Q and draw arcs on either side of Q. The
intersection points will be points A and B. Then, you can follow the same methods as in
Steps A–C in the Explore.

Explain 1 · Proving the Perpendicular Bisector Theorem Using Reflections

You can use reflections and their properties to prove a theorem about perpendicular bisectors. These theorems will be useful in proofs later on.

Perpendicular Bisector Theorem

If a point is on the perpendicular bisector of a segment, then it is equidistant from the endpoints of the segment.

Example 1 Prove the Perpendicular Bisector Theorem.

Given: P is on the perpendicular bisector m of $\overline{AB}$.

Prove: $PA = PB$

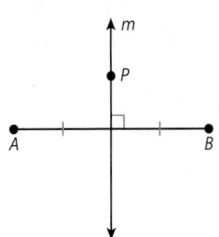

Consider the reflection across ___line m___. Then the reflection of point P across line m is also ___P___ because point P lies on ___line m___, which is the line of reflection.

Also, the reflection of ___point A___ across line m is B by the definition of ___reflection___.

Therefore, $PA = PB$ because ___reflection___ preserves distance.

Reflect

3. Discussion What conclusion can you make about $\triangle KLJ$ in the diagram using the Perpendicular Bisector Theorem?

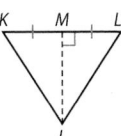

$JK = JL$ because point J lies on the perpendicular bisector of $\overline{KL}$.

Module 4   196   Lesson 4

PROFESSIONAL DEVELOPMENT

 Integrate Mathematical Practices

This lesson provides an opportunity to address Mathematical Practice **MP.5**, which calls for students to "use appropriate tools." They begin the lesson by constructing the perpendicular bisector of a segment; they may also use paper-folding or reflective devices to construct the perpendicular bisector. Students also construct the perpendicular to a line through a point not on the line. For each construction, they must be able to use the tools in a variety of ways in order to obtain accurate results and to understand the underlying mathematical relationships.

EXPLORE

Constructing Perpendicular Bisectors and Perpendicular Lines

INTEGRATE TECHNOLOGY

Students have the option of exploring the perpendicular bisector activity either in the book or online.

QUESTIONING STRATEGIES

Why do you have to use a compass setting greater than half the length of the segment when you construct the perpendicular bisector of the segment? This ensures that the two arcs will intersect.

INTEGRATE MATHEMATICAL PRACTICES
Focus on Critical Thinking

MP.3 Have students think about the steps used with each construction. Ask them to reflect on how they remember how to do each. In small groups, have students discuss strategies for remembering the steps. Then share each group's best strategies with the class.

EXPLAIN 1

Proving the Perpendicular Bisector Theorem Using Reflections

QUESTIONING STRATEGIES

Suppose you construct the perpendicular bisector of a segment and then choose any point on the perpendicular bisector. If you measure the distance from the point to each endpoint of the segment, what do you expect to find? The distances from the point to each endpoint of the segment are equal.

Perpendicular Lines   196

When finding the distance from a point on one side of a perpendicular bisector to its reflected point, students may give the distance to the bisector as the solution. Remind students to re-read the question to verify that they have answered it by using given information, such as congruence markings.

EXPLAIN 2

Proving the Converse of the Perpendicular Bisector Theorem

INTEGRATE MATHEMATICAL PRACTICES

Focus on Communication

MP.3 Make sure students understand that the proof of the Converse of the Perpendicular Bisector Theorem is based on the method of indirect proof. To write an indirect proof:

1. Identify the conjecture to be proven.

2. Assume the opposite of the conclusion is true.

3. Use direct reasoning to show the assumption leads to a contradiction.

4. Conclude that since the assumption is false, the original conjecture must be true.

QUESTIONING STRATEGIES

? How can you tell that an indirect proof is used? In the first step, you assume that what you are trying to prove is false.

? Near the end of an indirect proof, a step contradicts a known true statement. What does this mean in terms of the proof? The original assumption is false, so what you are trying to prove must be true.

197 Lesson 4.4

Your Turn

Use the diagram shown. $\overline{BD}$ is the perpendicular bisector of $\overline{AC}$.

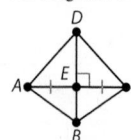

4. Suppose $ED = 16$ cm and $DA = 20$ cm. Find DC.
Because $\overline{BD}$ is the perpendicular bisector of $\overline{AC}$, then $DA = DC$ and $DC = 20$ cm.

5. Suppose $EC = 15$ cm and $BA = 25$ cm. Find BC.
Because $\overline{BD}$ is the perpendicular bisector of $\overline{AC}$, then $BA = BC$ and $BC = 25$ cm.

Explain 2 Proving the Converse of the Perpendicular Bisector Theorem

The converse of the Perpendicular Bisector Theorem is also true. In order to prove the converse, you will use an *indirect proof* and the *Pythagorean Theorem*.

In an **indirect proof**, you assume that the statement you are trying to prove is false. Then you use logic to lead to a contradiction of given information, a definition, a postulate, or a previously proven theorem. You can then conclude that the assumption was false and the original statement is true.

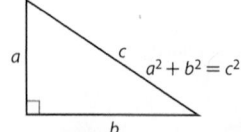

Recall that the Pythagorean Theorem states that for a right triangle with legs of length a and b and a hypotenuse of length c, $a^2 + b^2 = c^2$.

Converse of the Perpendicular Bisector Theorem

If a point is equidistant from the endpoints of a segment, then it lies on the perpendicular bisector of the segment.

Example 2 Prove the Converse of the Perpendicular Bisector Theorem

Given: $PA = PB$

Prove: P is on the perpendicular bisector m of $\overline{AB}$.

Step A: Assume what you are trying to prove is false.

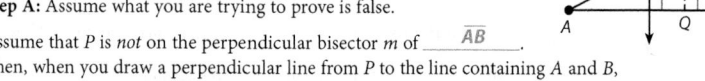

Assume that P is *not* on the perpendicular bisector m of ___$\overline{AB}$___.
Then, when you draw a perpendicular line from P to the line containing A and B,

it intersects $\overline{AB}$ at point Q, which is not the ___midpoint___ of $\overline{AB}$.

Step B: Complete the following to show that this assumption leads to a contradiction.

$\overline{PQ}$ forms two right triangles, $\triangle AQP$ and ___$\triangle BQP$___.

So, $AQ^2 + QP^2 = PA^2$ and $BQ^2 + QP^2 = \boxed{PB^2}$ by the ___Pythagorean___ Theorem.

Subtract these equations:

$AQ^2 + QP^2 = PA^2$

$\underline{BQ^2 + QP^2 = PB^2}$

$AQ^2 - BQ^2 = PA^2 - PB^2$

However, $PA^2 - PB^2 = 0$ because ___$PA = PB$___.

Therefore, $AQ^2 - BQ^2 = 0$. This means that $AQ^2 = BQ^2$ and $AQ = BQ$. This contradicts the fact that Q is not the midpoint of $\overline{AB}$. Thus, the initial assumption must be incorrect, and P must lie on the ___perpendicular bisector___ of $\overline{AB}$.

© Houghton Mifflin Harcourt Publishing Company

COLLABORATIVE LEARNING

Whole Class Activity

Have groups of students create posters to describe how to do an indirect proof. Then demonstrate the method for the Converse of the Perpendicular Bisector Theorem. Ask them to display their results as a graphic organizer that shows the steps for the proof.

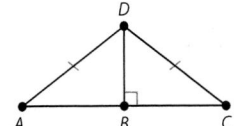

6. In the proof, once you know $AQ^2 = BQ^2$, why can you conclude that $AQ = BQ$?
Take the square root of both sides. Since distances are nonnegative, $AQ = BQ$.

Your Turn

7. $\overline{AD}$ is 10 inches long. $\overline{BD}$ is 6 inches long. Find the length of $\overline{AC}$.

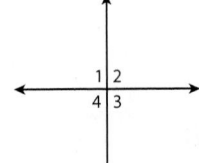

Since D is equidistant from A and C and $\overline{DB}$ is perpendicular to $\overline{AC}$ by the diagram, then $\overline{DB}$ must be the perpendicular bisector of $\overline{AC}$ and $AC = 2 \cdot BC$. $BC^2 + 6^2 = 10^2$, so $BC = 8$ in. and $AC = 16$ in.

⊘ Explain 3 Proving Theorems about Right Angles

The symbol $\perp$ means that two figures are perpendicular. For example, $\ell \perp m$ or $\overleftrightarrow{XY} \perp \overline{AB}$.

Example 3 Prove each theorem about right angles.

(A) If two lines intersect to form one right angle, then they are perpendicular and they intersect to form four right angles.

Given: $m\angle 1 = 90°$ **Prove:** $m\angle 2 = 90°$, $m\angle 3 = 90°$, $m\angle 4 = 90°$

Statement	Reason
1. $m\angle 1 = 90°$	1. Given
2. $\angle 1$ and $\angle 2$ are a linear pair.	2. Given
3. $\angle 1$ and $\angle 2$ are supplementary.	3. Linear Pair Theorem
4. $m\angle 1 + m\angle 2 = 180°$	4. Definition of supplementary angles
5. $90° + m\angle 2 = 180°$	5. Substitution Property of Equality
6. $m\angle 2 = 90°$	6. Subtraction Property of Equality
7. $m\angle 2 = m\angle 4$	7. Vertical Angles Theorem
8. $m\angle 4 = 90°$	8. Substitution Property of Equality
9. $m\angle 1 = m\angle 3$	9. Vertical Angles Theorem
10. $m\angle 3 = 90°$	10. Substitution Property of Equality

(B) If two intersecting lines form a linear pair of angles with equal measures, then the lines are perpendicular.

Given: $m\angle 1 = m\angle 2$ **Prove:** $\ell \perp m$

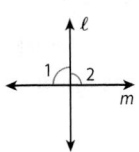

By the diagram, $\angle 1$ and $\angle 2$ form a linear pair so $\angle 1$ and $\angle 2$ are supplementary by the _Linear Pair Theorem_. By the definition of supplementary angles, $m\angle 1 + m\angle 2 = $ _180°_. It is also given that ___$m\angle 1 = m\angle 2$___, so $m\angle 1 + m\angle 1 = 180°$ by the _Substitution Property of Equality_. Adding gives $2 \cdot m\angle 1 = 180°$, and $m\angle 1 = 90°$ by the Division Property of Equality. Therefore, $\angle 1$ is a right angle and $\ell \perp m$ by the _definition of perpendicular lines_.

COMMUNICATING MATH

Help students understand the Converse of the Perpendicular Bisector Theorem by having them make a poster showing the theorem and its converse. Then have them explain what is given as the hypothesis of the theorem and of its converse, and what they have to prove for the theorem and its converse.

EXPLAIN 3

Proving Theorems About Right Angles

QUESTIONING STRATEGIES

? If a linear pair of angles has equal measure, why are the angles right angles? Since a linear pair of angles is supplementary, their sum must be 180°. So each angle must be half of 180°, or 90°.

INTEGRATE MATHEMATICAL PRACTICES
Focus on Technology

MP.5 Encourage students to use the geometry software to create linear pairs of angles and then measure them. Then have them construct perpendicular lines and measure each of the angles to verify that they are right angles.

DIFFERENTIATE INSTRUCTION

Visual Cues

Use colors to identify the steps in an indirect proof. Write each of the steps in a different color. Then place colored boxes around the parts of the proof that correspond to each step. For example, write the step "Assume the opposite of the conclusion is true" in blue and put a blue box around the assumption made in the indirect proof.

ELABORATE

QUESTIONING STRATEGIES

? How is constructing a perpendicular bisector related to constructing a segment bisector? The construction of a perpendicular bisector starts with a segment.

? How is constructing a perpendicular bisector related to constructing a perpendicular to a point on a line? The construction of a perpendicular to a point on a line starts with marking equal distances from the point along the line. This creates a segment with the point as the midpoint of the segment.

SUMMARIZE THE LESSON

If you are given a line and a point *P*, how do you construct a line that is perpendicular to the given line using a compass and straightedge? Sample answer: Use a compass to locate two points *A* and *B* on the line that are the same distance from point *P*. Then construct the perpendicular bisector of $\overline{AB}$.

© Houghton Mifflin Harcourt Publishing Company

Reflect

8. State the converse of the theorem in Part B. Is the converse true?
   If two intersecting lines are perpendicular, then they form a linear pair of angles with equal measures; yes.

Your Turn

9. Given: $b \parallel d$, $c \parallel e$, $m\angle 1 = 50°$, and $m\angle 5 = 90°$. Use the diagram to find $m\angle 4$.

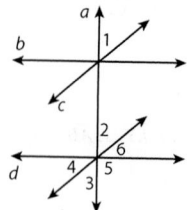

m∠4 = 40°; by corresponding angles because $c \parallel e$, $m\angle 1 = m\angle 2$, and by vertical angles, $m\angle 2 = m\angle 3$, so $m\angle 3 = 50°$; because $m\angle 5 = 90°$, then $a \perp d$ and $m\angle 3 + m\angle 4 = 90$, so $m\angle 4 = 40°$.

💬 Elaborate

10. **Discussion** Explain how the converse of the Perpendicular Bisector Theorem justifies the compass-and-straightedge construction of the perpendicular bisector of a segment.

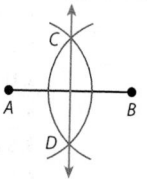

The construction involves making two arcs that intersect in two points. Each of these two intersection points is equidistant from the endpoints of the segment, because the arcs are the same radius. So, both of the intersection points are on the perpendicular bisector of the segment.

11. **Essential Question Check-In** How can you construct perpendicular lines and prove theorems about perpendicular bisectors?
    Constructing a line perpendicular to a given line involves using a compass to locate two points that are not on the given line but are equidistant from two points on the given line. You can prove the Perpendicular Bisector Theorem using a reflection and its properties, and you can prove the Converse of the Perpendicular Bisector Theorem using an indirect argument involving the Pythagorean Theorem.

LANGUAGE SUPPORT **EL**

Visual Cues

Have students work in pairs. Give students pictures of intersecting, parallel, skew, and perpendicular lines. Instruct one student in each pair to explain why a pair of lines is or is not perpendicular, and prove it to the partner. Have the student who is not explaining write notes about the proof explanation. Then have students switch roles.

✪ Evaluate: Homework and Practice

- Online Homework
- Hints and Help
- Extra Practice

1. How can you construct a line perpendicular to line ℓ that passes through point *P* using paper folding?

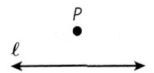

Fold line ℓ onto itself so that the crease passes through point *P*.

The crease is the required perpendicular line.

2. **Check for Reasonableness** How can you use a ruler and a protractor to check the construction in Elaborate Exercise 10?

Use the ruler to check that $\overleftrightarrow{CD}$ bisects $\overline{AB}$.

Use the protractor to check that $\overline{AB}$ and $\overleftrightarrow{CD}$ are perpendicular.

3. Describe the point on the perpendicular bisector of a segment that is closest to the endpoints of the segment.

The midpoint of the segment is the point on the perpendicular bisector that is closest to the endpoints of the segment.

4. **Represent Real-World Problems** A field of soybeans is watered by a rotating irrigation system. The watering arm, $\overline{CD}$, rotates around its center point. To show the area of the crop of soybeans that will be watered, construct a circle with diameter *CD*.

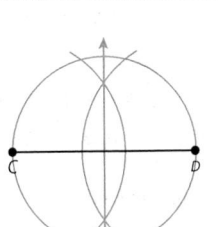

Use the diagram to find the lengths. $\overline{BP}$ is the perpendicular bisector of $\overline{AC}$. $\overline{CQ}$ is the perpendicular bisector of $\overline{BD}$. $AB = BC = CD$.

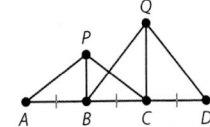

5. Suppose $AP = 5$ cm. What is the length of $\overline{PC}$?

By the Perpendicular Bisector Theorem, $PC = 5$ cm.

6. Suppose $AP = 5$ cm and $BQ = 8$ cm. What is the length of $\overline{QD}$?

By the Perpendicular Bisector Theorem, $QD = 8$ cm.

© Houghton Mifflin Harcourt Publishing Company • Image Credits: ©sima/Shutterstock

Exercise	Depth of Knowledge (D.O.K.)		COMMON CORE Mathematical Practices	
1	**1** Recall of Information		**MP.5** Using Tools	
2–4	**2** Skills/Concepts		**MP.5** Using Tools	
5–13	**2** Skills/Concepts		**MP.6** Precision	
14	**3** Strategic Thinking		**MP.6** Precision	
15–16	**2** Skills/Concepts		**MP.6** Precision	
17	**3** Strategic Thinking	H.O.T.	**MP.2** Reasoning	
18	**3** Strategic Thinking	H.O.T.	**MP.3** Logic	
19	**3** Strategic Thinking	H.O.T.	**MP.2** Reasoning	

EVALUATE

ASSIGNMENT GUIDE

Concepts and Skills	Practice
Explore Constructing Perpendicular Bisectors and Perpendicular Lines	Exercises 1–4
Example 1 Proving the Perpendicular Bisector Theorem	Exercises 5–8, 15–16
Example 2 Proving the Converse of the Perpendicular Bisector Theorem	Exercises 9–11, 14
Example 3 Proving Theorems about Right Angles	Exercises 12–13, 15–16

AVOID COMMON ERRORS

A common error when working with perpendicular lines is to assume that lines are perpendicular if they look perpendicular. Emphasize the need to establish that there are right angles before saying that lines are perpendicular.

Focus on Critical Thinking

MP.3 Ask students to compare constructions using a reflective device, tracing paper, compass and straightedge, and geometry software. Discuss the advantages of each. Have students consider not only how easy each is to use, but also how accurate, and how well each tool helps them understand the geometric relationships being studied.

INTEGRATE MATHEMATICAL PRACTICES

Focus on Technology

MP.5 Ask each student to draw a simple sketch that involves perpendicular lines and right angles. Have students exchange sketches and attempt to reproduce the one they receive using geometry software.

7. Suppose $AC = 12$ cm and $QD = 10$ cm. What is the length of $\overline{QC}$?

$QC = 8$ cm; $AC = 12$ cm so $BC = \frac{1}{2} \cdot$
$AC = 6$ cm and $CD = 6$ cm. By the
Pythagorean Theorem, $QD^2 = QC^2 + CD^2$,
so $10^2 = QC^2 + 6^2$ and $QC = 8$ cm.

8. Suppose $PB = 3$ cm and $AD = 12$ cm. What is the length of $\overline{PC}$?

$PC = 5$ cm; $AD = 12$ cm, so $AB = BC = CD = 4$ cm
By the Pythagorean Theorem, $PC^2 = PB^2 + BC^2$,
so $PC^2 = 3^2 + 4^2$ and $PC = 5$ cm.

Given: $PA = PC$ and $BA = BC$. Use the diagram to find the lengths or angle measures described.

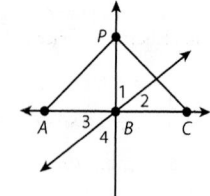

9. Suppose $m\angle 2 = 38°$. Find $m\angle 1$.

$m\angle 1 = 52°$; because $PA = PC$ and $BA = BC$, then $\overleftrightarrow{PB}$ is
the perpendicular bisector of $\overline{AC}$, and $m\angle PBC = 90°$.
Then $m\angle 1 = 90° - 38° = 52°$.

10. Suppose $PA = 10$ cm and $PB = 6$ cm. What is the length of $\overline{AC}$?

$AC = 16$ cm; because $PA = PC$ and $BA = BC$,
then $\overleftrightarrow{PB}$ is the perpendicular bisector of $\overline{AC}$ and
$\triangle PBA$ is a right triangle. By the Pythagorean
Theorem, $PA^2 = PB^2 + BA^2$, so $10^2 = 6^2 + BA^2$
and $BA = 8$ cm. Then $AC = 2 \cdot BA = 16$ cm.

11. Find $m\angle 3 + m\angle 4$.

$m\angle 3 + m\angle 4 = 90°$; because P and B are
equidistant from the endpoints, then $\overleftrightarrow{PB}$
is the perpendicular bisector of $\overline{AC}$.
So, $\overleftrightarrow{PB} \perp \overleftrightarrow{AC}$ and the lines meet at right
angles, and $m\angle 3 + m\angle 4 = 90°$.

Given: $m \parallel n$, $x \parallel y$, and $y \perp m$. Use the diagram to find the angle measures.

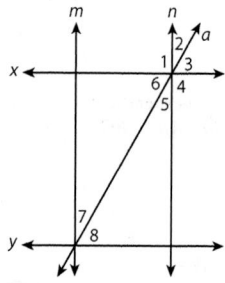

12. Suppose $m\angle 7 = 30°$. Find $m\angle 3$.

$y \perp m$, so $m\angle 7 + m\angle 8 = 90°$ and $m\angle 8 = 60°$.
Using alternate interior angles, because $x \parallel y$,
then $m\angle 8 = m\angle 6$, so $m\angle 6 = 60°$. $\angle 6$ and $\angle 3$
are vertical angles, so $m\angle 3 = 60°$.

13. Suppose $m\angle 1 = 90°$. What is $m\angle 2 + m\angle 3 + m\angle 5 + m\angle 6$?

Because $m\angle 1 = 90°$, then $x \perp n$ and the
lines intersect at four right angles. So,
$m\angle 2 + m\angle 3 + m\angle 5 + m\angle 6 = 180°$.

Use this diagram of trusses for a railroad bridge in Exercise 14.

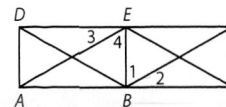

14. Suppose $\overline{BE}$ is the perpendicular bisector of $\overline{DF}$. Which of the following statements do you know are true? Select all that apply. Explain your reasoning.

A. $BD = BF$

B. $m\angle 1 + m\angle 2 = 90°$

C. E is the midpoint of $\overline{DF}$.   A, C, and D; the given information that $\overline{BE}$ is the perpendicular bisector

D. $m\angle 3 + m\angle 4 = 90°$ of $\overline{DF}$ means that both points E and B are equidistant from D and F so

E. $\overline{DA} \perp \overline{AC}$ answer choices A and C are true. Then, $\overline{EB} \perp \overline{DF}$ and $m\angle 3 + m\angle 4 = 90°$,

so answer choice D is known to be true. The given information does not tell anything

about $\overline{DA}$ or $\overline{AC}$, though, so answer choices B and E may or may not be true.

15. Algebra Two lines intersect to form a linear pair with equal measures. One angle has the measure $2x°$ and the other angle has the measure $(20y - 10)°$. Find the values of x and y. Explain your reasoning.

$x = 45$, $y = 5$; the linear pair formed has equal measures, so the lines are

perpendicular and then $2x° = 90°$, so $x = 45$, and $(20y - 10)° = 90°$, so $y = 5$.

16. Algebra Two lines intersect to form a linear pair of congruent angles. The measure of one angle is $(8x + 10)°$ and the measure of the other angle is $\left(\frac{15y}{2}\right)°$. Find the values of x and y. Explain your reasoning.

$x = 10$, $y = 12$; the linear pair formed are congruent angles, so the lines are

perpendicular and then $(8x + 10)° = 90°$, so $x = 10$, and $\left(\frac{15y}{2}\right)° = 90°$, so $y = 12$.

H.O.T. Focus on Higher Order Thinking

17. Communicate Mathematical Ideas The valve pistons on a trumpet are all perpendicular to the lead pipe. Explain why the valve pistons must be parallel to each other.

The valve pistons are lines that are perpendicular to the same line (the lead pipe), so they form right angles with the same line. By the converse of the corresponding angles theorem, all the congruent right angles mean the valve pistons are parallel to each other.

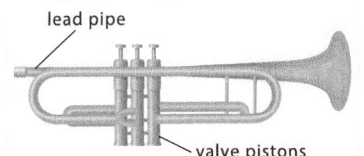

lead pipe

valve pistons

INTEGRATE MATHEMATICAL PRACTICES

Focus on Math Connections

MP.1 Remind students about how to use the Perpendicular Bisector Theorem and its converse to write equations that will help them find angle measures related to perpendicular lines.

INTEGRATE MATHEMATICAL PRACTICES

Focus on Modeling

MP.4 Have students explain how they can use a protractor or reflective device to check the accuracy of their constructions.

Have students work in groups of three or four. Ask them to choose one student to give directions. Instruct the other students to each draw a line and a point that is not on the line. The first student will then give a set of directions, step by step, for constructing a perpendicular to a line through a point that is either on the line or not on the line. The other students will not know which construction it is until they have followed the directions. Once the student has successfully guided the other students through the construction process, have another student take the lead and describe the construction to the others.

JOURNAL

Have students draw and mark a set of figures to illustrate the Perpendicular Bisector Theorem and its converse. Have students provide explanatory captions for the figures.

18. **Justify Reasoning** Prove the theorem: In a plane, if a transversal is perpendicular to one of two parallel lines, then it is perpendicular to the other.

Given: $\overline{RS} \perp \overline{CD}$ and $\overline{AB} \parallel \overline{CD}$ Prove: $\overline{RS} \perp \overline{AB}$

Statements	Reasons
1. $\overline{AB} \parallel \overline{CD}$	1. Given
2. m∠RTD = m∠RVB	2. Corresponding Angles Theorem
3. $\overline{RS} \perp \overline{CD}$	3. Given
4. m∠RTD = 90°	4. Definition of perpendicular lines
5. m∠RVB = 90°	5. Substitution Property of Equality
6. $\overline{RS} \perp \overline{AB}$	6. Definition of perpendicular lines

19. **Analyze Mathematical Relationships** Complete the indirect proof to show that two supplementary angles cannot both be obtuse angles.

Given: ∠1 and ∠2 are supplementary.

Prove: ∠1 and ∠2 cannot both be obtuse.

Assume that two supplementary angles *can* both be obtuse angles. So, assume that ∠1 and ∠2 ___are both obtuse___ . Then m∠1 > 90° and m∠2 > ⟨90°⟩ by ___the definition of obtuse angles___ . Adding the two inequalities, m∠1 + m∠2 > ⟨180°⟩. However, by the definition of supplementary angles, ___m∠1 + m∠2 = 180°___ . So m∠1 + m∠2 > 180° contradicts the given information.

This means the assumption is ___false___ , and therefore ___∠1 and ∠2 cannot both be obtuse___ .

© Houghton Mifflin Harcourt Publishing Company

Lesson Performance Task

A utility company wants to build a wind farm to provide electricity to the towns of Acton, Baxter, and Coleville. Because of concerns about noise from the turbines, the residents of all three towns do not want the wind farm built close to where they live. The company comes to an agreement with the residents to build the wind farm at a location that is equally distant from all three towns.

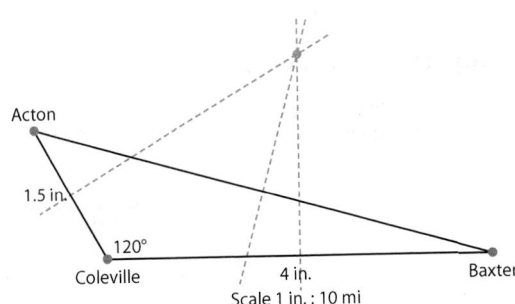

a. Use the drawing to draw a diagram of the locations of the towns using a scale of 1 in. : 10 mi. Draw the 4-inch and 1.5-inch lines with a 120° angle between them. Write the actual distances between the towns on your diagram.

b. Estimate where you think the wind farm will be located.

c. Use what you have learned in this lesson to find the exact location of the wind farm. What is the approximate distance from the wind farm to each of the three towns?

a. Distances: Acton–Baxter, about 49 miles; Baxter–Coleville, 40 miles; Acton–Coleville, 15 miles

b. Student answers will vary.

c. Students should construct perpendicular bisectors of the three lines of the triangle. The point of intersection of the bisectors is the point that is equidistant from the three vertices of the triangle. Any two of the bisectors is sufficient to locate the point, but a third one is useful for spotting possible errors in the drawing of the first two bisectors.

AVOID COMMON ERRORS

Students can use proportions to find the actual distances between towns, but they may set them up incorrectly. To find the distance between Acton and Coleville, they can write and solve this proportion:

$\dfrac{1 \text{ in.}}{10 \text{ mi}} = \dfrac{1.5 \text{ in.}}{x \text{ mi}}$. The correct pattern is

$\dfrac{\text{map distance}}{\text{actual distance}} = \dfrac{\text{map distance}}{\text{actual distance}}$.

INTEGRATE MATHEMATICAL PRACTICES
Focus on Critical Thinking

MP.3 Marcus said that it isn't necessary to draw three perpendicular bisectors to find the location of the wind farm. Two is sufficient, he said. Was he right? Explain. Yes; sample answer: Any two of the perpendicular bisectors will intersect at a point. That point must be the location of the wind farm because the two lines can intersect in only one point. The third perpendicular bisector provides a useful check on the accuracy of the constructions of the first two perpendicular bisectors.

EXTENSION ACTIVITY

Pose this challenge to students: Three other towns have signed up to obtain electricity from the wind farm. All are the same distance from the farm as Acton, Baxter, and Coleville. On your drawing, show three points that could be the locations of the towns. Explain how you found the points and how you know they meet the conditions of the problem.

Students should draw a circle with its center at the wind farm and passing through Acton, Baxter, and Coleville. They can choose any three points on the circle as the locations of the three new towns. Those points must be the same distance from the farm as Acton, Baxter, and Coleville because all radii of a circle are equal in length.

Scoring Rubric

2 points: Student correctly solves the problem and explains his/her reasoning.

1 point: Student shows good understanding of the problem but does not fully solve or explain his/her reasoning.

0 points: Student does not demonstrate understanding of the problem.

Equations of Parallel and Perpendicular Lines

Common Core Math Standards

The student is expected to:

 G-GPE.B.5

... find the equation of a line parallel or perpendicular to a given line that passes through a given point ....

Mathematical Practices

 MP.2 Reasoning

Language Objective

Explain to a partner how to use the slope of a line to find the equation of a parallel or perpendicular line.

ENGAGE

Essential Question: How can you find the equation of a line that is parallel or perpendicular to a given line?

Possible answer: The slopes of parallel lines are equal. Substitute the known slope and the coordinates of a point on the other line into the point-slope form to find the equation of the parallel line. The product of the slopes of perpendicular lines is −1. Substitute the opposite reciprocal of the known slope and the coordinates of a point on the other line into the point-slope form to find the equation of the perpendicular line.

PREVIEW: LESSON PERFORMANCE TASK

View the Engage section online. Discuss the photo. Explain that *GPS* stands for Global Positioning System, a system of 24 orbiting satellites that enables a person to pinpoint his or her precise location on Earth's surface. Then preview the Lesson Performance Task.

Name_____ Class_____ Date_____

4.5 Equations of Parallel and Perpendicular Lines

Essential Question: How can you find the equation of a line that is parallel or perpendicular to a given line?

Resource Locker

⊘ Explore　Exploring Slopes of Lines

Recall that the *slope* of a straight line in a coordinate plane is the ratio of the *rise* to the *run*. In the figure, the slope of $\overline{AB}$ is $\frac{\text{rise}}{\text{run}} = \frac{4}{8} = \frac{1}{2}$.

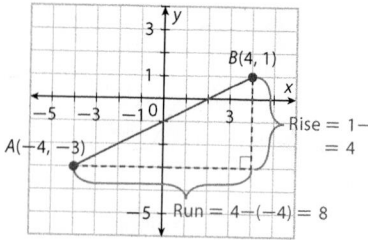

(A) Graph the equations $y = 2(x + 1)$ and $y = 2x - 3$.

(B) What do you notice about the graphs of the two lines? About the slopes of the lines?

The lines are parallel. The slopes are equal.

The graphs of $x + 3y = 22$ and $y = 3x - 14$ are shown.

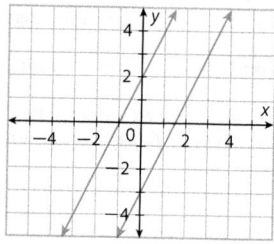

(C) Use a protractor. What is the measure of the angle formed by the intersection of the lines. What does that tell you about the lines?

90°; the lines are perpendicular.

(D) What are the slopes of the two lines? How are they related?

$-\frac{1}{3}$ and 3; the slopes are opposite reciprocals.

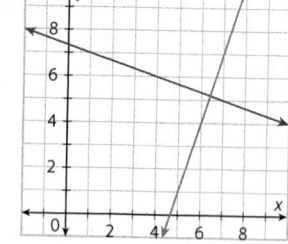

(E) Complete the statements: If two nonvertical lines

are ___parallel___, then they have equal slopes. If two nonvertical lines are perpendicular,

then the product of their slopes is ___−1___.

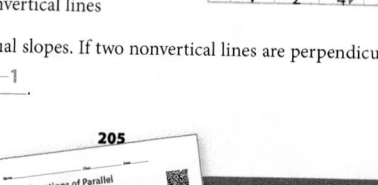

HARDCOVER PAGES 179–184

Turn to these pages to find this lesson in the hardcover student edition.

© Houghton Mifflin Harcourt Publishing Company

1. Your friend says that if two lines have opposite slopes, they are perpendicular.
   He uses the slopes 1 and −1 as examples. Do you agree with your friend? Explain.
   No; although lines with slopes of 1 and −1 are perpendicular, it's because the product
   of the slopes is −1. Slopes of 2 and −2 are opposites, but the corresponding lines are not
   perpendicular.

2. The frets on a guitar are all perpendicular to one of the strings. Explain why the
   frets must be parallel to each other.
   The frets are lines that are perpendicular to the same line (the string), so the frets must
   be parallel to each other.

⊘ Explain 1 Writing Equations of Parallel Lines

You can use slope relationships to write an equation of a line parallel to a given line.

Example 1 Write the equation of each line in slope-intercept form.

Ⓐ The line parallel to $y = 5x + 1$ that passes through $(-1, 2)$

Parallel lines have equal slopes. So the slope of the required line is 5.

Use point-slope form.	$y - y_1 = m(x - x_1)$
Substitute for m, x_1, y_1.	$y - 2 = 5(x - (-1))$
Simplify.	$y - 2 = 5x + 5$
Solve for y.	$y = 5x + 7$

The equation of the line is $y = 5x + 7$.

Ⓑ The line parallel to $y = -3x + 4$ that passes through $(9, -6)$

Parallel lines have $\boxed{\text{equal}}$ slopes. So the slope of the required line is $\boxed{-3}$.

Use point-slope form.	$y - y_1 = m(x - x_1)$
Substitute for m, x_1, y_1.	$y - \boxed{-6} = \boxed{-3}\left(x - \boxed{9}\right)$
Simplify.	$y + 6 = \boxed{-3}x + \boxed{27}$
Solve for y.	$y = \boxed{-3}x + \boxed{21}$

The equation of the line is $\boxed{y = -3x + 21}$.

© Houghton Mifflin Harcourt Publishing Company

PROFESSIONAL DEVELOPMENT

Math Background

In this lesson, students use the slope criterion for parallel lines and the slope
criterion for perpendicular lines to solve problems. Note that the slope criteria
given here assume that the lines are neither vertical nor horizontal. If the lines are
vertical, the criteria for parallel and perpendicular lines do not apply, since slope is
not defined for vertical lines. If the lines are horizontal, both lines have a slope of
zero, and the criterion for parallel lines is trivial.

EXPLORE

Exploring Slopes of Lines

INTEGRATE TECHNOLOGY

Students have used geometry software to construct
perpendicular lines and calculate their slopes. They
can use the calculation feature to find the product of
slopes of perpendicular lines is always −1.

QUESTIONING STRATEGIES

❓ What appears to be true about the slopes of
non-vertical parallel lines? They are equal.

❓ What appears to be true about the slopes of
two non-vertical perpendicular lines? The
slopes are opposite reciprocals.

INTEGRATE MATHEMATICAL
PRACTICES
Focus on Critical Thinking

MP.3 You may want to discuss the biconditional
nature of the slope criteria. Because they are *if and
only if* statements, the criteria can be used in either
direction. That is, if you know that two lines are
parallel (perpendicular), you can conclude that they
have the same (opposite reciprocal) slope. Conversely,
if you know that two lines have the same (opposite
reciprocal) slope, you can conclude that they are
parallel (perpendicular).

EXPLAIN 1

Writing Equations of Parallel Lines

QUESTIONING STRATEGIES

❓ How do you know if an equation is written in
slope-intercept form? It is of the form
$y = mx + b$, with m the slope and b the y-intercept.

❓ How can you use graphing to check your
answer? Graph the given line and your
answer line. They should be parallel.

AVOID COMMON ERRORS

Remind students that the *x*-coefficient gives the slope of a line only when the equation of the line is written in slope-intercept form. For example, some students might say that the slope of the line represented by the equation $y - 2x = 4$ is -2. However, the equation is not in slope-intercept form. Rewriting the equation in this form gives $y = 2x + 4$, which shows that the correct slope is 2.

EXPLAIN 2

Writing Equations of Perpendicular Lines

INTEGRATE MATHEMATICAL PRACTICES
Focus on Technology

MP.5 Students can use their graphing calculators to check that two equations represent perpendicular lines. However, students should be aware that perpendicular lines may or may not appear to be perpendicular on a graphing calculator, depending upon the viewing window that is used. To ensure that perpendicular lines appear to be perpendicular, students should go to the ZOOM menu and choose 5:ZSquare.

QUESTIONING STRATEGIES

? The given line has a positive slope. What does this tell you about the required perpendicular line? Why? It must have a negative slope because the product of the slopes is -1.

? How can you check your answers? Check that the product of the slopes is -1.

Reflect

3. What is the equation of the line through a given point and parallel to the *x*-axis? Why?
   The equation is $y = y_1$, where y_1 is the *y*-coordinate of the given point. This is because the *x*-axis is a horizontal line with equation $y = 0$.

Your Turn

Write the equation of each line in slope-intercept form.

4. The line parallel to $y = -x$ that passes through $(5, 2.5)$

$$y - 2.5 = -1(x - 5)$$
$$y - 2.5 = -x + 5$$
$$y = -x + 7.5$$

5. The line parallel to $y = \frac{3}{2}x + 4$ that passes through $(-4, 0)$

$$y - (0) = \frac{3}{2}(x - (-4))$$
$$y = \frac{3}{2}x + 6$$

⊘ Explain 2   Writing Equations of Perpendicular Lines

You can use slope relationships to write an equation of a line perpendicular to a given line.

Example 2   Write the equation of each line in slope-intercept form.

(A) The line perpendicular to $y = 4x - 2$ that passes through $(3, -1)$

Perpendicular lines have slopes that are opposite reciprocals, which means that the product of the slopes will be -1. So the slope of the required line is $-\frac{1}{4}$.

$y - y_1 = m(x - x_1)$	Use point-slope form.
$y - (-1) = -\frac{1}{4}(x - 3)$	Substitute for m, x_1, y_1.
$y + 1 = -\frac{1}{4}x + \frac{3}{4}$	Simplify.
$y = -\frac{1}{4}x - \frac{1}{4}$	Solve for y.

The equation of the line is $y = -\frac{1}{4}x - \frac{1}{4}$.

(B) The line perpendicular to $y = -\frac{2}{5}x + 12$ that passes through $(-6, -8)$

The product of the slopes of perpendicular lines is $\boxed{-1}$. So the slope of the required line is $\boxed{\frac{5}{2}}$.

$y - y_1 = m(x - x_1)$	Use point-slope form.
$y - \boxed{-8} = \boxed{\frac{5}{2}}\left(x - \boxed{-6}\right)$	Substitute for m, x_1, y_1.
$y + 8 = \boxed{\frac{5}{2}}x + \boxed{15}$	Simplify.
$y = \boxed{\frac{5}{2}}x + \boxed{7}$	Solve for y.

The equation of the line is y $\boxed{y = \frac{5}{2}x + 7}$.

© Houghton Mifflin Harcourt Publishing Company

COLLABORATIVE LEARNING

Whole Class Activity

Have groups of students create posters to describe the slope criteria. Then remind students about the biconditional nature of the criteria and ask them if the criteria are true in two directions. Ask them to display the criteria as graphic organizers. Sample organizers:

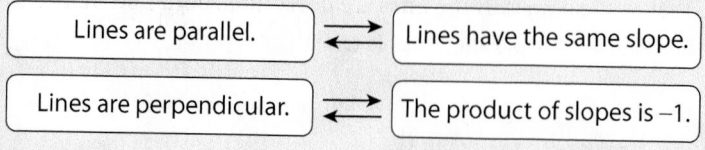

Reflect

6. A carpenter's square forms a right angle. A carpenter places the square so that one side is parallel to an edge of a board, and then draws a line along the other side of the square. Then he slides the square to the right and draws a second line. Why must the two lines be parallel?

   Both lines are perpendicular to the edge of the

   board. If two coplanar lines are perpendicular to

   the same line, then the two lines are parallel to each

   other, so the lines must be parallel to each other.

Your Turn

Write the equation of each line in slope-intercept form.

7. The line perpendicular to $y = \frac{3}{2}x + 2$ that passes through $(3, -1)$

   $$y - (-1) = -\frac{2}{3}(x - 3)$$
   $$y = -\frac{2}{3}x + 1$$

8. The line perpendicular to $y = -4x$ that passes through $(0, 0)$

   $$y - 0 = \frac{1}{4}(x - 0)$$
   $$y = \frac{1}{4}x$$

💬 **Elaborate**

9. **Discussion** Would it make sense to find the equation of a line parallel to a given line, and through a point on the given line? Explain.
   No; if the point is on the line, the line can't be parallel to the line, because it either

   intersects it or it is the same line.

10. Would it make sense to find the equation of a line perpendicular to a given line, and through a point on the given line? Explain.
    Yes; the line will be perpendicular to the given line at the point.

11. **Essential Question Check-In** How are the slopes of parallel lines and perpendicular lines related? Assume the lines are not vertical.
    Parallel lines have the same slope; perpendicular lines have slopes whose product is -1.

© Houghton Mifflin Harcourt Publishing Company • Image Credits: ©Zoran Zeremski/Shutterstock

ELABORATE

QUESTIONING STRATEGIES

? What is the equation of the line through a given point and parallel to the x-axis? Why? The equation is $y = b$, where b is the y-coordinate of the point.

? Can either of the lines referred to in the slope criterion for perpendicular lines be vertical? Why or why not? No; the slope criterion specifies that neither line is vertical. However, since the lines are perpendicular, if one line were horizontal, the other would be vertical.

SUMMARIZE THE LESSON

? Given the equation of a line and a point not on the line, how do you find the equation of a line parallel and perpendicular to the given line? Sample answer: Parallel: Use the slope-intercept form of a line, $y = mx + b$, and replace m with the slope from the given line. Use the given point and the slope to solve for b and then rewrite the equation using the same slope m and the new y-intercept b.

Perpendicular: Do the same steps as for parallel except replace m with the opposite reciprocal of m.

DIFFERENTIATE INSTRUCTION

Communicating Math

Group students in pairs and give each pair a sheet of graph paper with a non-vertical, non-horizontal line drawn on it. Have students draw axes and find the equation of the line. Then have each student plot a point that is not on the line, and find the equation of the line that is parallel, and the equation of the line that is perpendicular to the original line and that passes through the partner's point. When they are done, they should compare the slopes of their lines to show that the two new lines are parallel (or perpendicular) to each other.

EVALUATE

ASSIGNMENT GUIDE

Concept & Skills	Practice
Explore Exploring Slopes of Lines	Exercises 1–4
Example 1 Writing Equations of Parallel Lines	Exercises 5–7, 11–12, 14–15
Example 2 Writing Equations of Perpendicular Lines	Exercises 8–10, 13, 16–19

AVOID COMMON ERRORS

A common error students make when finding slopes of perpendicular lines is using the same sign for both slopes. One slope must be the opposite reciprocal of the other, not just the reciprocal of the other, so that the product is −1, not 1.

⭐ Evaluate: Homework and Practice

• Online Homework
• Hints and Help
• Extra Practice

Use the graph for Exercises 1–4.

1. A line with a positive slope is parallel to one of the lines shown. What is its slope?

$$\frac{6-2}{5-0} = \frac{4}{5}$$

2. A line with a negative slope is perpendicular to one of the lines shown. What is its slope?

$$-\frac{5}{4}$$

3. A line with a positive slope is perpendicular to one of the lines shown. What is its slope?

   The line will be perpendicular to the line with

   slope $\frac{5-1}{1-2} = -4$. So the slope is $\frac{1}{4}$.

4. A line with a negative slope is parallel to one of the lines shown. What is its slope?

   The line will be parallel to the line with

   slope $\frac{5-1}{1-2} = -4$. So the slope is -4.

Find the equation of the line that is parallel to the given line and passes through the given point.

5. $y = -3x + 1$; $(9, 0)$

   $y - 0 = -3\,(x - 9)$

   $y = -3x + 27$

6. $y = 0.6x - 3$; $(-2, 2)$

   $y - 2 = 0.6\,\big(x - (-2)\big)$

   $y = 0.6x + 3.2$

7. $y = 5(x + 1)$; $\left(\frac{1}{2}, -\frac{1}{2}\right)$

   $y = 5x + 5$

   $y - \left(-\frac{1}{2}\right) = 5\left(x - \frac{1}{2}\right)$

   $y = 5x - 3$

Find the equation of the line that is perpendicular to the given line and passes through the given point.

8. $y = 10x$; $(1, -3)$

   $y - (-3) = -0.10(x - 1)$

   $y = -0.1x - 2.9$

9. $y = -\frac{1}{3}x - 5$; $(12, 0)$

   $y = 3(x - 12)$

   $y = 3x - 36$

10. $y = \frac{5x + 1}{3}$; $(1, 1)$

   $3y = 5x + 1$

   $y = \frac{5}{3}x + \frac{1}{3}$

   $y - 1 = -\frac{3}{5}(x - 1)$

   $y = \frac{-3x + 8}{5}$

Exercise	Depth of Knowledge (D.O.K.)	COMMON CORE Mathematical Practices
1–4	**1** Recall of Information	**MP.6** Precision
5–10	**1** Recall of Information	**MP.2** Reasoning
11	**2** Skills/Concepts	**MP.2** Reasoning
12–15	**2** Skills/Concepts	**MP.4** Modeling
16	**2** Skills/Concepts	**MP.4** Modeling
17–19	**2** Skills/Concepts	**MP.2** Reasoning

11. Determine whether the lines are parallel. Use slope to explain your answer.

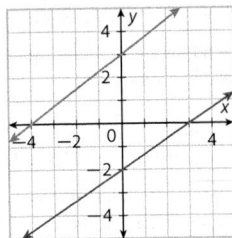

The top line passes through $(-4, 0)$ and $(0, 3)$, so its slope is $\frac{3}{4}$. The bottom line passes through $(0, -2)$ and $(3, 0)$, so its slope is $\frac{2}{3}$. The lines do not have the same slope, so they are not parallel.

The endpoints of a side of rectangle $ABCD$ in the coordinate plane are at $A(1, 5)$ and $B(3, 1)$. Find the equation of the line that contains the given segment.

12. $\overline{AB}$

The slope of the required line is -2.
$y - 1 = -2(x - 3); y - 1 = -2x + 6;$
$y = -2x + 7$

13. $\overline{BC}$

$\overline{BC} \perp \overline{AB}$, so the slope of the required line is $\frac{1}{2}$. $y - 1 = \frac{1}{2}(x - 3); y - 1 = \frac{1}{2}x - \frac{3}{2};$
$y = \frac{1}{2}x - \frac{1}{2}$

14. $\overline{AD}$

$\overline{AD} \parallel \overline{BC}$, so the slope of the required line is $\frac{1}{2}$.
$y - 5 = \frac{1}{2}(x - 1); y = \frac{1}{2}x + \frac{9}{2}$

15. $\overline{CD}$ if point C is at $(7, 3)$

$\overline{CD} \parallel \overline{AB}$, so the slope of the required line is -2. $y - 3 = -2(x - 7); y = -2x + 17$

16. A well is to be dug at the location shown in the diagram. Use the diagram for parts (a–c).

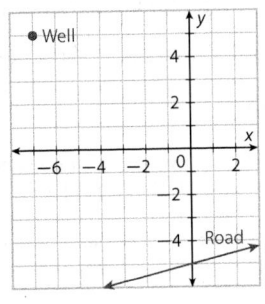

a. Find the equation that represents the road.

The slope is
$\frac{-6 - (-5)}{-4 - 0} = \frac{1}{4}$ and the
y-intercept is -5.

$y = \frac{1}{4}x - 5$

b. A path is to be made from the road to the well. Describe how this should be done to minimize the length of the path.

The line containing the path should be perpendicular to the road.

c. Find the equation of the line that contains the path.

$y - (-7) = -4(x - 5); y = -4x - 23$

© Houghton Mifflin Harcourt Publishing Company • Image Credits: ©Gary S. Chapman/Photographer's Choice RF/Getty Images

Exercise	Depth of Knowledge (D.O.K.)	COMMON CORE Mathematical Practices
20	**3** Strategic Thinking **H.O.T.**	**MP.2** Reasoning
21	**2** Skills/Concepts **H.O.T.**	**MP.3** Logic
22	**3** Strategic Thinking **H.O.T.**	**MP.2** Reasoning

INTEGRATE MATHEMATICAL PRACTICES
Focus on Critical Thinking

MP.3 Ask students to think about how they can use slope to solve geometry problems. Remind them that since parallel lines have the same slope, they can analyze lines containing sides of polygons, for example, to see whether the sides are parallel. They can also use slope to write the equation of a line that is parallel or perpendicular to a given line. Point out that since perpendicular lines have opposite reciprocal slopes, they can analyze the lines containing the sides of polygons, for example, to see if the polygon contains any right angles.

INTEGRATE MATHEMATICAL PRACTICES
Focus on Technology

MP.5 Ask each student to use geometry software to draw a simple sketch that involves perpendicular lines and right angles. Have students exchange sketches, measure the slopes of the lines, and find the product of the slopes. Have them do another sketch that involves parallel lines. Have students exchange sketches and measure the slopes of the lines.

INTEGRATE MATHEMATICAL PRACTICES
Focus on Math Connections

MP.1 Instruct students to write two equations in the form $y = mx + b$, one with a positive value of m and one with a negative value of m. Have them graph each line on a coordinate plane and then plot a point that is not on either line. For each of the original lines, instruct students to explain how to find the equation of a parallel line through the point and the perpendicular line through the point.

COOPERATIVE LEARNING

Have students work in groups of three or four. Ask them to choose one student to give directions. Instruct the other students to each draw a line and a point that is not on the line. The first student will then give a set of directions, step by step, for finding the equation of a parallel or of a perpendicular to the line through the point. The other students will not know which type of line it is until they have followed the directions. Once the student has successfully guided the other students through the process to find the equation of the line, have another student take the lead and describe the process to the others.

JOURNAL

Have students write and solve a problem involving finding the equation of a line that is parallel to a given line. Remind students to show all the steps of the solution and to explain how they can check the answer.

---

17. Use the graph for parts (a–c),

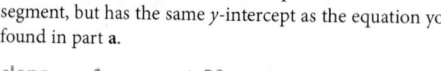

a. Find the equation of the perpendicular bisector of the segment. Explain your method.

$m = \dfrac{150 - 60}{30 - 120} = -1$; slope $M = \left(\dfrac{30 + 120}{2}, \dfrac{150 + 60}{2}\right) = (75, 105)$; midpoint equation; $y - 105 = 1(x - 75)$ or $y = x + 30$

b. Find the equation of the line that is parallel to the segment, but has the same y-intercept as the equation you found in part **a**.

slope $= -1$: $y = -x + 30$

c. What is the relationship between the two lines you found in parts (a) and (b)?

They are perpendicular.

18. Line m is perpendicular to $x - 3y = -1$ and passes through $(1, 5)$. What is the slope of line m?

A. -3 **B.** $\dfrac{1}{3}$ **C.** 3 **D.** 5

A; the slope of the given line is $\frac{1}{3}$ and its opposite reciprocal is -3.

19. Determine whether each pair of lines are parallel, perpendicular, or neither. Select the correct answer for each lettered part.

a. $x - 2y = 12$; $y = x + 5$ ○ Parallel ○ Perpendicular ● Neither

b. $\dfrac{1}{5}x + y = 8$; $y = 5x$ ○ Parallel ● Perpendicular ○ Neither

c. $3x - 2y = 12$; $3y = -2x + 5$ ○ Parallel ● Perpendicular ○ Neither

d. $y = 3x - 1$; $15x - 5y = 10$ ● Parallel ○ Perpendicular ○ Neither

e. $7y = 4x + 1$; $14x + 8y = 10$ ○ Parallel ● Perpendicular ○ Neither

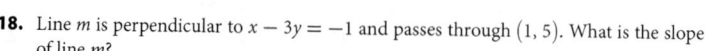

H.O.T. Focus on Higher Order Thinking

20. Communicate Mathematical Ideas Two lines in the coordinate plane have opposite slopes, are parallel, and the sum of their y-intercepts is 10. If one of the lines passes through $(5, 4)$, what are the equations of the lines?

$y = 4$ and $y = 6$; parallel lines have equal slopes if the slopes are opposites, they must be zero; a line with slope 0 through $(5, 4)$ has equation $y = 4$.

21. Explain the Error Alan says that two lines in the coordinate plane are perpendicular if and only if the slopes of the lines are m and $\frac{1}{m}$. Identify and correct two errors in Alan's statement.

He should have said "two nonvertical lines" because vertical lines have undefined slope. He should have had a negative sign on one of his expressions for slope because the slopes of nonvertical perpendicular lines have a product of -1.

22. Analyze Relationships Two perpendicular lines have opposite y-intercepts. The equation of one of these lines is $y = mx + b$. Express the x-coordinate of the intersection point of the lines in terms of m and b.

If one equation is $y = mx + b$, then the other is $y = -\dfrac{1}{m}x - b$. $mx + b = -\dfrac{1}{m}x - b$.

$mx + \dfrac{1}{m}x = -2b$; $x(m^2 + 1) = -2mb$; $x = \dfrac{-2mb}{m^2 + 1}$

Lesson Performance Task

Surveyors typically use a unit of measure called a rod, which equals $16\frac{1}{2}$ feet. (A rod may seem like an odd unit, but it's very useful for measuring sections of land, because an acre equals exactly 160 square rods.) A surveyor was called upon to find the distance between a new interpretive center at a park and the park entrance. The surveyor plotted the points shown on a coordinate grid of the park in units of 1 rod. The line between the Interpretive Center and Park Headquarters forms a right angle with the line connecting the Park Headquarters and Park Entrance.

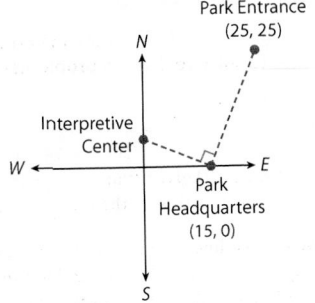

What is the distance, in feet, between the Interpretive Center and the park entrance? Explain the process you used to find the answer.

About 518 feet; one method is shown.

Find the slope of the line between Park Headquarters (PH) and the park entrance (PE):

$m = \dfrac{25 - 0}{25 - 15} = \dfrac{25}{10} = \dfrac{5}{2}$

Since the line connecting the Interpretive Center (IC) and Park Headquarters (PH) forms a right angle with the line connecting PH and PE, its slope must be the opposite reciprocal, $-\frac{2}{5}$.

Use the slope and the coordinates of PH (15, 0) to find the coordinates of IC:

$m = \dfrac{0 - y}{15 - x}$

$-\dfrac{2}{5} = \dfrac{-y}{15 - 0} = \dfrac{-y}{15}$

$-2 = \dfrac{-y}{3}$

$-6 = -y$

$y = 6$

So the coordinates of IC are (0, 6).

Use the distance formula to find the distance in rods between IC and PE:

$d = \sqrt{(25 - 0)^2 + (25 - 6)^2} \approx 31.4$

So the distance in feet equals 31.4 × 16.5, or approximately 518 feet.

© Houghton Mifflin Harcourt Publishing Company

The Lesson Performance Task mentions that an acre equals 160 square rods. Have students show that that is true, using the fact that 1 square mile equals 640 acres.

Possible explanation: 1 mi = 5280 ft so 1 mi^2 = 5280 × 5280 = 27,878,400 ft^2

1 acre = 27,878,400 ft^2 ÷ 640 = 43,560 ft^2

1 rod = 16.5 ft, so 1 rod^2 = 16.5 × 16.5 = 272.25 ft^2

1 acre = (43,560 ÷ 272.25) = 160 rod^2

AVOID COMMON ERRORS

In calculating the distance between the park entrance and the Interpretive Center, students may apply the Distance Formula incorrectly as:

$d = \sqrt{(25 - 0)^2 + (25 - 6)^2}$

$= \sqrt{25^2 + 19^2}$

$= \sqrt{25^2} + \sqrt{19^2}$

$= 25 + 19$

$= 44$

Remind students to find the sum beneath the radical sign first before finding the square root:

$d = \sqrt{(25 - 0)^2 + (25 - 6)^2}$

$= \sqrt{25^2 + 19^2}$

$= \sqrt{625 + 361}$

$= \sqrt{986}$

INTEGRATE MATHEMATICAL PRACTICES
Focus on Critical Thinking

MP.3 The distance between Park Headquarters and the Interpretive Center is approximately 267 feet. Explain how you could find the distance from the park entrance to Park Headquarters without using the Distance Formula. You know the distance from the Interpretive Center to Park Headquarters (267 feet) and the distance from the Interpretive Center to the park entrance (518 feet), the lengths of two sides of a right triangle. You can use the Pythagorean Theorem to find the length of the third side joining the park entrance and Park Headquarters.

Scoring Rubric
2 points: Student correctly solves the problem and explains his/her reasoning.
1 point: Student shows good understanding of the problem but does not fully solve or explain his/her reasoning.
0 points: Student does not demonstrate understanding of the problem.

Study Guide Review

ASSESSMENT AND INTERVENTION

Assign or customize module reviews.

MODULE PERFORMANCE TASK

COMMON CORE

Mathematical Practices: MP.1, MP.2, MP.3, MP.7
G-CO.C.9

SUPPORTING STUDENT REASONING

Students should begin this problem by focusing on how the table and chandelier will look in the room, both from the inside and the outside. Here are some issues they might bring up.

- **If you extended the tabletop, at what angle would it intersect the walls?** 90°

- **If you extended the tabletop, would it intersect the ground?** yes **Which pair of congruent corresponding angles would be formed?** the angle formed by the floor and the ground, and the angle formed by the tabletop and the ground

- **What is the angle made by the floor with the horizontal?** 25°

- **What type of angle pairs are the angle formed by the floor and the horizontal and the angle formed by the board and the floor?** alternate interior angles

---

Lines and Angles

Essential Question: How can you use parallel and perpendicular lines to solve real-world problems?

KEY EXAMPLE   *(Lesson 4.1)*

Find $m\angle ABD$ given that $m\angle CBE = 40°$ and the angles are formed by the intersection of the lines $\overleftrightarrow{AC}$ and $\overleftrightarrow{DE}$.

When two lines intersect, they form two pairs of vertical angles at their intersection. Note that $\angle ABD$ and $\angle CBE$ are vertical angles and $\angle DBC$ and $\angle ABE$ are vertical angles.

$\angle ABD \cong \angle CBE$	Vertical Angles Theorem
$m\angle ABD = m\angle CBE = 40°$	Definition of congruence of angles

KEY EXAMPLE   *(Lesson 4.2)*

Find $m\angle APD$ given that $\overleftrightarrow{AB}$ intersects the parallel lines $\overleftrightarrow{DE}$ and $\overleftrightarrow{FG}$ at the points P and Q, respectively, and $m\angle AQF = 70°$.

When a transversal intersects two parallel lines, it forms a series of angle pairs. Note that $\angle APD$ and $\angle AQF$ are a pair of corresponding angles.

$m\angle APD = m\angle AQF$	Corresponding Angles Theorem
$m\angle APD = 70°$	Substitute the known angle measure.

KEY EXAMPLE   *(Lesson 4.3)*

Determine whether the lines $\overleftrightarrow{DE}$ and $\overleftrightarrow{FG}$ are parallel given that $\overleftrightarrow{AB}$ intersects them at the points P and Q, respectively, $m\angle APE = 60°$, and $m\angle BQF = 60°$.

Lines $\overleftrightarrow{AB}$ and $\overleftrightarrow{DE}$ intersect, so they create two pairs of vertical angles. The angle which is the opposite of $\angle APE$ is $\angle DPB$, so they are called vertical angles.

$\angle APE \cong \angle DPB$	Vertical Angles Theorem
$m\angle APE = m\angle DPB$	Definition of congruence
$m\angle DPB = 60°$	Substitute the known angle measure.
$m\angle BQF = m\angle DPB = 60°$	
$\angle BQF \cong \angle DPB$	Definition of congruence

Thus, the lines $\overleftrightarrow{DE}$ and $\overleftrightarrow{FG}$ are parallel by the converse of the Corresponding Angles Theorem because their corresponding angles are congruent.

© Houghton Mifflin Harcourt Publishing Company

Key Vocabulary

vertical angles
(ángulos verticales)
complementary angles
(ángulos complementarios)
supplementary angles
(ángulos suplementarios)
transversal *(transversal)*
indirect proof *(prueba indirecta)*

SCAFFOLDING SUPPORT

- To better visualize relationships between the room and items inside it, suggest that students model the situation using a sheet of paper and a sticky note. Using the sheet of paper to represent the real world, students can draw a horizontal line on the paper to represent level ground. They can then attach the sticky note at a 25° angle to the paper, with one corner of the note touching the line.

- Point out that objects in the room that are affected by gravity, for example, a hanging object or a person standing in the room, must be oriented perpendicular to real-world horizontal. If students use the model described above, real-world horizontal is the line drawn on the paper.

EXERCISES

Find the angle measure.

1. $m\angle ABD$ given that $m\angle CBD = 40°$ and the angles are formed by the intersection of the lines $\overleftrightarrow{AC}$ and $\overleftrightarrow{DE}$. *(Lesson 4.1)*

    140°

2. $m\angle BPE$ given that $\overleftrightarrow{AB}$ intersects the parallel lines $\overleftrightarrow{DE}$ and $\overleftrightarrow{FG}$ at the points P and Q, respectively, and $m\angle AQF = 45°$. *(Lesson 4.2)*

    45°

Determine whether the lines are parallel. *(Lesson 4.3)*

3. $\overleftrightarrow{DE}$ and $\overleftrightarrow{FG}$, given that $\overleftrightarrow{AB}$ intersects them at the points P and Q, respectively, $m\angle APD = 60°$, and $m\angle BQG = 120°$.

    The lines are not parallel.

Find the distance and angle formed from the perpendicular bisector. *(Lesson 4.4)*

4. Find the distance of point D from B given that D is the point at the perpendicular bisector of the line segment $\overline{AB}$, $\overline{DE}$ intersects $\overline{AB}$, and $AD = 3$. Find $m\angle ADE$.

    $m\angle ADE = 90°$, $BD = 3$

Find the equation of the line. *(Lesson 4.5)*

5. Perpendicular to $y = \frac{2}{3}x + 2$ and passes through the point $(3, 4)$. $y = -\frac{3}{2}x + \frac{17}{2}$

MODULE PERFORMANCE TASK

Mystery Spot Geometry

Inside mystery spot buildings, some odd things can appear to occur. Water can appear to flow uphill, and people can look as if they are standing at impossible angles. That is because there is no view of the outside, so the room appears to be normal.

The illustration shows a mystery spot building constructed so that the floor is at a 25° angle with the ground.

- A table is placed in the room with its legs perpendicular to the floor and the tabletop perpendicular to the legs. Sketch or describe the relationship of the tabletop to the floor, walls, and ceiling of the room. What would happen if a ball were placed on the table?
- A chandelier hangs from the ceiling of the room. How does it appear to someone inside? How does it appear to someone standing outside of the room?

View from outside   View from inside

© Houghton Mifflin Harcourt Publishing Company

Use your own paper to complete the task. Use sketches, words, or geometry to explain how you reached your conclusions.

SAMPLE SOLUTION

- The tabletop is parallel to the floor and ceiling of the room and perpendicular to the walls. To an observer outside the room, the tabletop would appear to slope at a 25° angle. If a ball were placed on the tabletop, the ball would roll along a path slanted at a 25° angle to the horizontal until it fell off the table. When it fell, it would fall on a vertical path relative to true (outside) horizontal.

- To an outside observer, a chandelier inside the room would appear to hang perpendicular to true horizontal. To an inside observer, the chandelier would appear to hang at a 25° angle to the ceiling of the room.

DISCUSSION OPPORTUNITIES

- If a ball appears to roll up a ramp on the floor of the room, what can you say about the angle that the ramp makes with the floor?

    The angle is less than 25°.

- How can the chandelier help you determine whether you are viewing the room from the inside or from the outside? If you are viewing from the outside, a line containing the chandelier will be perpendicular to the true horizontal.

Assessment Rubric

2 points: Student correctly solves the problem and explains his/her reasoning.

1 point: Student shows good understanding of the problem but does not fully solve or explain.

0 points: Student does not demonstrate understanding of the problem.

Study Guide Review   **214**

Ready to Go On?

ASSESS MASTERY

Use the assessment on this page to determine if students have mastered the concepts and standards covered in this module.

ASSESSMENT AND INTERVENTION

Access Ready to Go On? assessment online, and receive instant scoring, feedback, and customized intervention or enrichment.

ADDITIONAL RESOURCES

Response to Intervention Resources

- Reteach Worksheets

Differentiated Instruction Resources

- Reading Strategies **EL**
- Success for English Learners **EL**
- Challenge Worksheets

Assessment Resources

- Leveled Module Quizzes

Module 4

(Ready) to Go On?

4.1–4.5 Lines and Angles

- Online Homework
- Hints and Help
- Extra Practice

Find the measure of each angle. Assume lines $\overleftrightarrow{GB}$ and $\overleftrightarrow{FC}$ are parallel. *(Lessons 4.1, 4.2)*

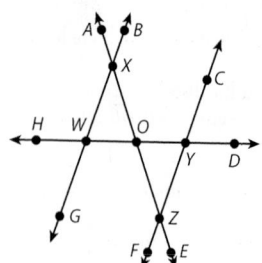

1. The measure of $\angle WOX$ is 70°. Find m$\angle YOZ$.

   70°

2. The measure of $\angle AXB$ is 40°. Find m$\angle FZE$.

   40°

3. The measure of $\angle XWO$ is 70°. Find m$\angle OYC$.

   110°

4. The measure of $\angle BXO$ is 110°. Find m$\angle OZF$.

   110°

Use the diagram to find lengths. $\overline{PB}$ is the perpendicular bisector of $\overline{AC}$. $\overline{QC}$ is the perpendicular bisector of $\overline{BD}$. $AB = BC = CD$. *(Lessons 4.3, 4.4)*

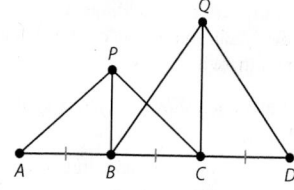

5. Given $BD = 24$ and $PC = 13$, find PB.

   $PB = 5$

6. Given $QB = 23$ and $BC = 12$, find QD.

   $QD = 23$

Find the equation of each line. *(Lessons 4.5)*

7. The line parallel to $y = -\frac{3}{7}x + 5$ and passing through the point $(-7, -1)$

   $y = -\frac{3}{7}x - 4$

8. The line perpendicular to $y = \frac{1}{5}x + 3$ and passing through the point $(2, 7)$

   $y = -5x + 17$

9. The perpendicular bisector to the line segment with endpoints $(-3, 8)$ and $(9, 4)$

   $y = 3x - 3$

ESSENTIAL QUESTION

10. Say you want to create a ladder. Which lines should be parallel or perpendicular to each other?

    Answers may vary. Sample: The sides, or rails, of a ladder are both parallel, as are the foot holds, or rungs. The rungs on a ladder are perpendicular to the rails.

© Houghton Mifflin Harcourt Publishing Company

Module 4   215   Study Guide Review

COMMON CORE | **Common Core Standards**

Lesson	Items	Content Standards	Mathematical Practices
4.1, 4.2	1	G-CO.C.9	MP.7
4.1, 4.2	2	G-CO.C.9	MP.7
4.1, 4.2	3	G-CO.C.9	MP.7
4.1, 4.2	4	G-CO.C.9	MP.7
4.1, 4.3	5	G-CO.C.9	MP.7
4.1, 4.3	6	G-CO.C.9	MP.7
4.5	7–9	G-GPE.B.5	MP.2

Assessment Readiness

1. Consider each equation. Is it the equation of a line that is parallel or perpendicular to $y = 3x + 2$?
   Select Yes or No for A–C.

   A. $y = -\frac{1}{3}x - 8$ ● Yes   ○ No

   B. $y = 3x - 10$ ● Yes   ○ No

   C. $y = 2x + 4$ ○ Yes   ● No

2. Consider the following statements about $\triangle ABC$. Choose True or False for each statement.

A. $AC = BC$	● True	○ False
B. $CD = BC$	○ True	● False
C. $AD = BD$	● True	○ False

   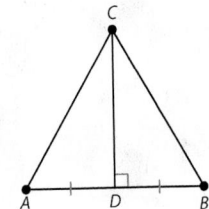

3. The measure of angle 3 is 130° and the measure of angle 4 is 50°. State two different relationships that can be used to prove m∠1 = 130°.

   Possible Answer: ∠1 and ∠4 are supplementary

   angles, ∠1 and ∠3 are vertical angles.

   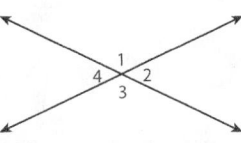

4. m∠1 = 110° and m∠6 = 70°. Use angle relationships to show that lines m and n are parallel.

   Answers may vary. Sample: Since ∠1 and ∠2 are a linear pair, they are supplementary. So, m∠2 = 70°. Then, m∠2 = m∠6. By the definition of congruence, corresponding angles ∠2 and ∠6 are congruent. So, line $m \parallel$ line n by the Converse of the Corresponding Angles Theorem.

   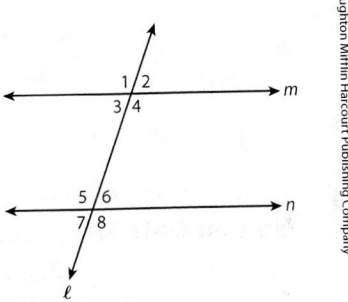

MIXED REVIEW
Assessment Readiness

ASSESSMENT AND INTERVENTION

Assign ready-made or customized practice tests to prepare students for high-stakes tests.

ADDITIONAL RESOURCES

Assessment Resources

- Leveled Module Quizzes: Modified, B

AVOID COMMON ERRORS

Item 1 The word *or* in this problem may be overlooked by some students. They will focus on either parallel or perpendicular but won't look for both. Encourage students to highlight, underline, or circle keywords like *or*.

 Common Core Standards

Lesson	Items	Content Standards	Mathematical Practices
4.5	1	**G-GPE.B.5**	**MP.6**
4.4, 1.1	2*	**G-CO.C.9**	**MP.6**
4.1	3	**G-CO.C.9**	**MP.6**
4.3, 1.4	4*	**G-CO.C.9**	**MP.3**

* Item integrates mixed review concepts from previous modules or a previous course.

Triangle Congruence Criteria

ESSENTIAL QUESTION:

Answer: You can use the principles of triangle congruence to analyze architectural and engineering features, such as trusses.

PROFESSIONAL DEVELOPMENT VIDEO

Professional Development Video

Author Juli Dixon models successful teaching practices in an actual high-school classroom.

Professional Development
my.hrw.com

Triangle Congruence Criteria

MODULE
5

Essential Question: How can you use triangle congruence to solve real-world problems?

LESSON 5.1
Exploring What Makes Triangles Congruent

LESSON 5.2
ASA Triangle Congruence

LESSON 5.3
SAS Triangle Congruence

LESSON 5.4
SSS Triangle Congruence

REAL WORLD VIDEO
Take a look at some of the geometry involved in the engineering marvels of the Golden Gate Bridge in San Francisco.

© Houghton Mifflin Harcourt Publishing Company • Image Credits: ©Corbis

MODULE PERFORMANCE TASK PREVIEW

Golden Gate Triangles

In this module, you will explore congruent triangles in the trusses of the lower deck of the Golden Gate Bridge. How can you use congruency to help figure out how far apart the two towers of the bridge are? Let's find out.

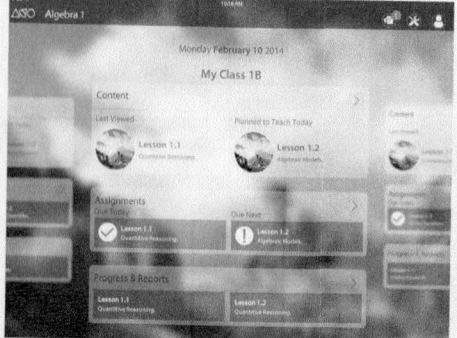

DIGITAL TEACHER EDITION

Access a full suite of teaching resources when and where you need them:

- Access content online or offline
- Customize lessons to share with your class
- Communicate with your students in real-time
- View student grades and data instantly to target your instruction where it is needed most

PERSONAL MATH TRAINER
Assessment and Intervention

Assign automatically graded homework, quizzes, tests, and intervention activities. Prepare your students with updated, Common Core-aligned practice tests.

Are (YOU) Ready?

Complete these exercises to review the skills you will need for this module.

- Online Homework
- Hints and Help
- Extra Practice

Angle Relationships

Example 1   Line segments AB and DC are parallel. Find the measure of angle ∠CDE.

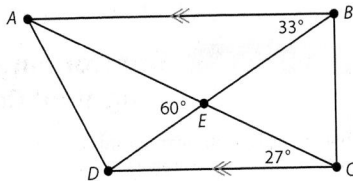

$m\angle CDE = m\angle ABE$ Equate alternate interior angles.

$m\angle CDE = 33°$ Substitute.

Find each angle in the image from the example.

1. m∠BEC

_____60°_____

2. m∠BAE

_____27°_____

Congruent Figures

Example 2   Find the length DF. Assume △DEF ≅ △GHJ.

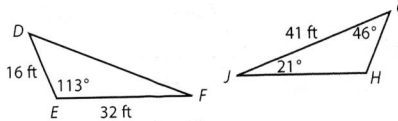

Since △DEF ≅ △GHJ, the sides $\overline{DF}$ and $\overline{GJ}$ are congruent, or $\overline{DF} \cong \overline{GJ}$. Thus, DF = GJ. Since GJ = 41 ft, length DF must also be 41 ft.

Use the figure from the example to find the given side length or angle measure. Assume △DEF ≅ △GHJ.

3. Find m∠GHJ.

_____m∠GHJ = 113°_____

4. Find the length GH.

_____GH = 16 ft_____

5. Find m∠FDE.

_____m∠FDE = 46°_____

6. Find the length HJ.

_____HJ = 32 ft_____

Are You Ready?

ASSESS READINESS

Use the assessment on this page to determine if students need strategic or intensive intervention for the module's prerequisite skills.

ASSESSMENT AND INTERVENTION

RtI Response to Intervention   **TIER 1, TIER 2, TIER 3 SKILLS**

Personal Math Trainer will automatically create a standards-based, personalized intervention assignment for your students, targeting each student's individual needs!

ADDITIONAL RESOURCES

See the table below for a full list of intervention resources available for this module.

Response to Intervention Resources also includes:

- Tier 2 Skill Pre-Tests for each Module
- Tier 2 Skill Post-Tests for each skill

Response to Intervention			Differentiated Instruction
Tier 1 Lesson Intervention Worksheets	**Tier 2** Strategic Intervention Skills Intervention Worksheets	**Tier 3** Intensive Intervention Worksheets available online	
Reteach 5.1 Reteach 5.2 Reteach 5.3 Reteach 5.4	7 Congruent Figures 12 Parallel Lines ... 17 Properties of Reflections 18 Properties of Rotations 19 Properties of Translations	Building Block Skills 8, 16, 46, 48, 53, 56, 71, 74, 98, 102, 103	Challenge worksheets Extend the Math Lesson Activities in TE

Exploring What Makes Triangles Congruent

Common Core Math Standards

The student is expected to:

 G-CO.B.7

Use the definition of congruence in terms of rigid motions to show that two triangles are congruent if and only if corresponding pairs of sides and corresponding pairs of angles are congruent.

Mathematical Practices

 MP.2 Reasoning

Language Objective

Have students explain to a partner why a pair of triangles is congruent or noncongruent.

ENGAGE

Essential Question: How can you show that two triangles are congruent?

Show that their corresponding sides and corresponding angles are congruent.

PREVIEW: LESSON PERFORMANCE TASK

View the Engage section online. Explain that *pollination* is the process in which bees collect pollen from flowers and deposit it on other flowers. Then preview the Lesson Performance Task.

Name _____ Class _____ Date _____

5.1 Exploring What Makes Triangles Congruent

Essential Question: How can you show that two triangles are congruent?

Resource Locker

Explore **Transforming Triangles with Congruent Corresponding Parts**

You can apply what you've learned about corresponding parts of congruent figures to write the following true statement about triangles.

If two triangles are congruent, then the corresponding parts of the triangles are congruent.

The statement is sometimes referred to as *CPCTC*. The converse of CPCTC can be stated as follows.

If all corresponding parts of two triangles are congruent, then the triangles are congruent.

Use a straightedge and tracing paper to explore this converse statement.

Ⓐ Trace the angles and segments shown to draw △*ABC*. Repeat the process to draw △*DEF* on a separate piece of tracing paper. Label the triangles.

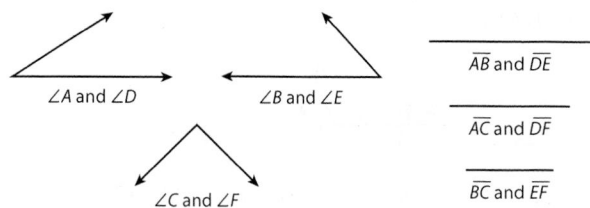

Ⓑ What must you do to show that the triangles are congruent?

Find a sequence of rigid motions that maps one triangle onto the other.

Ⓒ Flip the piece of tracing paper with △*ABC* and arrange the two triangles on a desk as shown in the figure. Then move the tracing paper with △*ABC* so that point *A* maps to point *D*. Name the rigid motion that you used.

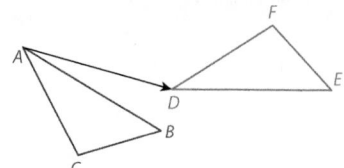

translation

© Houghton Mifflin Harcourt Publishing Company

Module 5 **219** Lesson 1

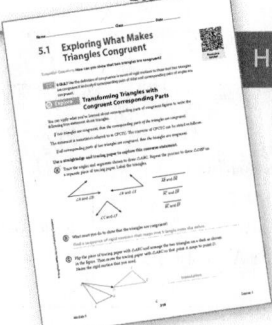

HARDCOVER PAGES 191–200

Turn to these pages to find this lesson in the hardcover student edition.

Ⓓ Name a rigid motion you can use to map point *B* to point *E*. How can you be sure the image of *B* is *E*?

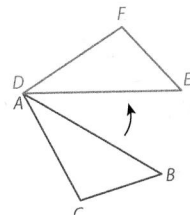

Counterclockwise rotation about point *D* by m ∠*BDE*; $\overline{AB} \cong \overline{DE}$, so the image of point *B*

must be point *E*.

Ⓔ Name a rigid motion you can use to map point *C* to point *F*.

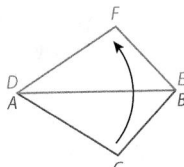

reflection across $\overleftrightarrow{DE}$

Ⓕ To show that the image of point *C* is point *F*, complete the following.

∠*A* is reflected across $\overleftrightarrow{DE}$, so the measure of the angle is preserved. Since ∠*A* ≅ ∠*D*, you

can conclude that the image of $\overrightarrow{AC}$ lies on ___$\overrightarrow{DF}$___. It is given that $\overline{AC} \cong$ ___$\overline{DF}$___, so the

image of point *C* must be ___point *F*___.

Ⓖ What sequence of rigid motions maps △*ABC* onto △*DEF*?

a translation followed by a rotation followed by a reflection

Reflect

1. **Discussion** Is there another sequence of rigid motions that maps △*ABC* onto △*DEF*?
    Explain.
    Yes; possible answer: you can first rotate △*ABC* so that $\overleftrightarrow{AB}$ ∥ $\overleftrightarrow{DE}$, then use a translation to

    map *A* to *D* followed by a reflection across $\overleftrightarrow{DE}$ to map △*ABC* onto △*DEF*.

2. **Discussion** Is the converse of CPCTC always true when you apply it to triangles?
    Explain why or why not based on the results of the Explore.
    Possible answer: Yes. If you draw two triangles that have congruent corresponding parts,

    you will always be able to find a series of rigid motions that maps one onto the other.

    So, the two triangles will always be congruent.

EXPLORE

Transforming Triangles with Congruent Corresponding Parts

INTEGRATE TECHNOLOGY

Have students use geometry software to create designs using congruent triangles. They should arrange multiple congruent triangles using different colors, positions, and orientations. Ask them to make three separate designs, one using congruent equilateral triangles, one using congruent isosceles triangles, and one using congruent scalene triangles.

QUESTIONING STRATEGIES

? When you translate a triangle so that one vertex maps to a new location, what happens to the other vertices and sides of the triangle? How does the triangle change? They are translated the same direction and the same distance. The triangle will have the same shape and size, but it will be in a different position.

PROFESSIONAL DEVELOPMENT

Learning Progressions

In this lesson, students apply the rigid-motion definition of congruence specifically to triangles. Some key understandings for students are as follows:

• If two triangles are congruent, then all pairs of corresponding sides and all pairs of corresponding angles are congruent.

• If all pairs of corresponding sides and all pairs of corresponding angles of two triangles are congruent, then the triangles are congruent.

Students will explore ways to prove that triangles are congruent and use information gained from congruent triangles to solve problems.

Exploring What Makes Triangles Congruent   **220**

EXPLAIN 1

Deciding if Triangles are Congruent by Comparing Corresponding Parts

INTEGRATE MATHEMATICAL PRACTICES

Focus on Communication

MP.3 Make sure students pay attention to the order of the vertices when writing a congruence statement. The order of the vertices communicates which pairs of angles and sides are congruent. Have students write several correct congruence statements for the diagram. Then have them write an incorrect congruence statement and explain why it is not correct.

QUESTIONING STRATEGIES

? How can you find the measure of a missing angle in a triangle with two given angle measures? You know that the sum of the measures of the angles of a triangle is always 180°, and you know the other two angle measures in the triangle. You can use this information to write and solve an equation.

LANGUAGE SUPPORT **EL**

Have students work in pairs to complete sentence stems explaining why a pair of triangles is congruent or not. For example: "This pair of triangles is congruent because _____." Possible answers: The corresponding angles have equal measures and the corresponding sides have equal lengths; when I trace one I can fit it exactly over the other.

A **biconditional** is a statement that can be written in the form "*p* if and only if *q*." You can combine what you learned in the Explore with the fact that corresponding parts of congruent triangles are congruent to write the following true biconditional.

Two triangles are congruent if and only if corresponding pairs of sides and corresponding pairs of angles are congruent.

To decide whether two triangles are congruent, you can compare the corresponding parts. If they are congruent, the triangles are congruent. If any of the corresponding parts are not congruent, then the triangles are not congruent.

Example 1 Determine whether the given triangles are congruent. Explain.

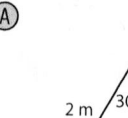 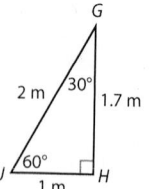 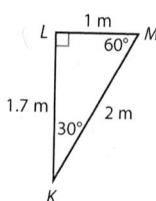

Compare corresponding sides to decide if they are congruent.

$GH = KL = 1.7$ m, $HJ = LM = 1$ m, and $GJ = KM = 2$ m.

So, $\overline{GH} \cong \overline{KL}$, $\overline{HJ} \cong \overline{LM}$, and $\overline{GJ} \cong \overline{KM}$.

Compare corresponding angles to decide if they are congruent.

$m\angle G = m\angle K = 30°$, $m\angle H = m\angle L = 90°$, and $m\angle J = m\angle M = 60°$.

So, $\angle G \cong \angle K$, $\angle H \cong \angle L$, and $\angle J \cong \angle M$.

$\triangle GHJ \cong \triangle KLM$ because all pairs of corresponding parts are congruent.

 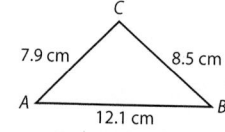 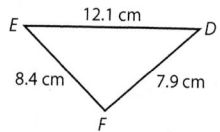

Compare corresponding sides to decide if they are congruent.

$AB = \boxed{DE} = \boxed{12.1}$ cm, so $\overline{AB} \cong \boxed{DE}$. $AC = \boxed{DF} = \boxed{7.9}$ cm, so $\overline{AC} \cong \boxed{DF}$.

However, $BC \neq \boxed{EF}$, so $\overline{BC}$ is not congruent to $\boxed{EF}$.

The triangles are not congruent because <u>there is a pair of corresponding sides that are not congruent.</u>

COLLABORATIVE LEARNING

Peer-to-Peer Activity

Working in pairs, one student draws and labels the vertices of a parallelogram and a rectangle that is not a square; the other draws a square and a trapezoid with exactly one pair of parallel sides. They exchange drawings and try to divide each quadrilateral into two congruent triangles by drawing one diagonal. For each divided quadrilateral, they identify the triangles' corresponding sides and angles, write congruence statements, and review each other's work.

3. Critique Reasoning The **contrapositive** of a conditional statement "if *p*, then *q*" is the statement "If not *q*, then not *p*." The contrapositive of a true statement is always true. Janelle says that you can justify Part B using the contrapositive of CPCTC. Is this accurate? Explain your reasoning.

Yes; the contrapositive of a true statement is true, so the contrapositive of CPCTC is true:

if the corresponding parts of two figures are not congruent, then the figures are not

congruent. In Part B, the fact that at least one pair of corresponding parts is not congruent

means that the triangles are not congruent.

Your Turn

Determine whether the given triangles are congruent. Explain your reasoning.

4.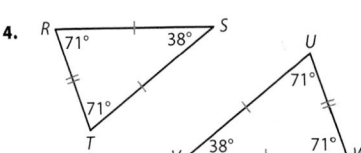

$\overline{RS} \cong \overline{UV}$, $\overline{ST} \cong \overline{VW}$, and $\overline{RT} \cong \overline{UW}$. $m\angle R = m\angle U = 71°$, $m\angle S = m\angle V = 38°$, and $m\angle T = m\angle W = 71°$, so $\angle R \cong \angle U$, $\angle S \cong \angle V$ and $\angle T \cong \angle W$. $\triangle RST \cong \triangle UVW$, because all six pairs of corresponding parts are congruent.

5.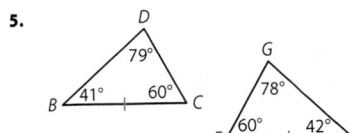

$\angle C \cong \angle F$, but $m\angle B \neq m\angle E$ and $m\angle D \neq m\angle G$, so $\angle B$ is not congruent to $\angle E$ and $\angle D$ is not congruent to $\angle G$. The triangles are not congruent because some pairs of the corresponding angles are not congruent.

⊘ Explain 2 **Applying Properties of Congruent Triangles**

Triangles are part of many interesting designs. You can ensure that triangles are congruent by making corresponding sides congruent and corresponding angles congruent. To do this, you may have to use the Triangle Sum Theorem, which states that the sum of the measures of the angles of a triangle is 180°. You will explore this theorem in more detail later in this course.

© Houghton Mifflin Harcourt Publishing Company • Image Credits: ©Michael Zegers/Westend61/Corbis

EXPLAIN 2

Applying Properties of Congruent Triangles

AVOID COMMON ERRORS

Students may correctly solve for a variable but then incorrectly give the value of the variable as a side length or angle measure. Remind them to examine the diagram carefully; sometimes a side length or angle measure is described by an expression containing a variable, not just the variable itself.

QUESTIONING STRATEGIES

? What must be true of the angle measures for the triangles to be congruent? The measures of corresponding angles must be equal.

CONNECT VOCABULARY **EL**

Have students review the prefixes *bi-*, *tri-*, *quad-*, and *pent-* to relate them to the number of sides and angles in a geometric figure.

DIFFERENTIATE INSTRUCTION

Critical Thinking

Ask students to use a ruler and protractor to draw and label two isosceles triangles $\triangle QRS$ and $\triangle UVW$: $m\angle R = m\angle V = 40°$, $m\angle Q = m\angle S = m\angle U = m\angle W = 70°$, $\overline{QS} \cong \overline{UW}$, and $\overline{RQ} \cong \overline{RS} \cong \overline{VU} \cong \overline{VW}$. Then ask them to write a congruence statement for the triangles. It is likely that not all students will write the same congruence statement. Discuss why both $\triangle QRS \cong \triangle UVW$ and $\triangle QRS \cong \triangle WVU$ are correct even though the first maps point *S* onto point *W* and the second maps point *S* onto point *U*.

Example 2 Find the value of the variable that results in congruent triangles.

 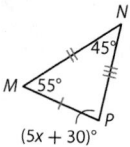

Step 1 Identify corresponding angles.

$\angle M$ corresponds to $\angle J$, because they have the same measure and they are formed by congruent corresponding sides. Similarly, $\angle N$ corresponds to $\angle K$. So, $\angle P$ corresponds to $\angle L$.

Step 2 Find $m\angle L$.

Triangle Sum Theorem	$m\angle J + m\angle K + m\angle L = 180°$
Substitute.	$55° + 45° + m\angle L = 180°$
Simplify.	$100° + m\angle L = 180°$
Subtract 100° from each side.	$m\angle L = 80°$

Step 3 Write an equation to find the value of x.

Set corresponding measures equal.	$m\angle P = m\angle L$
Substitute.	$5x + 30 = 80$
Subtract 30 from each side.	$5x = 50$
Divide each side by 5.	$x = 10$

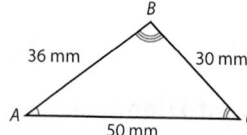 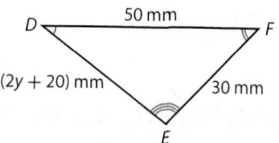

Step 1 Identify corresponding sides, beginning with side $\overline{DE}$.

$\angle A \cong \angle$ [D] , $\angle B \cong \angle$ [E] , and , $\angle C \cong \angle$ [F] , so $\overline{DE}$ corresponds to [AB] .

Step 2 Write an equation to find the value of y.

Set corresponding measures equal.	$DE =$ [36] mm
Substitute.	$2y + 20 =$ [36]
Subtract 20 from each side.	$2y =$ [16]
Divide each side by 2.	$y =$ [8]

LANGUAGE SUPPORT [EL]

Connect Context

Many English words have multiple meanings. In this lesson, the word *converse* means *opposite*. The word is pronounced with the stress on the first syllable: "CON-verse." English Learners may know the word as a verb, pronounced "con-VERSE," meaning *to have a conversation*. Words in English typically do not have accent marks, so words that serve as both nouns and verbs can be difficult to distinguish. Remind students that when *converse* is preceded by the word *to*, it is a verb. When preceded by the word *the*, it is a noun or adjective.

6. The measures of two angles of △QRS are 18° and 84°. The measures of two angles of △TUV are 18° and 76°. Is it possible for the triangles to be congruent? Explain.
   No; by the Triangle Sum Theorem, the measures of the angles of △QRS are 18°, 84°, and
   78°, and the measures of the angles of △TUV are 18°, 76°, and 86°. Since two pairs of
   corresponding angles are not congruent, the triangles cannot be congruent.

Find the value of the variable that results in congruent triangles.

7.

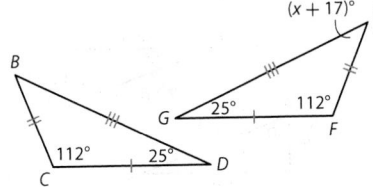

∠E corresponds to ∠B.

$m\angle B + 112° + 25° = 180°$

$m\angle B = 43°$

$m\angle E = 43°$, so $x + 17 = 43$, or $x = 26$

8.

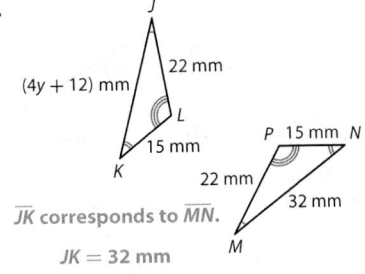

$\overline{JK}$ corresponds to $\overline{MN}$.

$JK = 32$ mm

$4y + 12 = 32$, so $4y = 20$, or $y = 5$

Elaborate

9. All three angles of △ABC measure 60° and all three sides are 4 inches long. All three angles of △PQR measure 60° and all three sides are 4 inches long. Can you conclude that the triangles are congruent? Why or why not?
   Yes; no matter how you set up the correspondence, corresponding angles will be
   congruent and corresponding sides will be congruent. By the converse of CPCTC,
   △ABC ≅ △PQR.

10. Use the concept of rigid motion to explain why two triangles cannot be congruent if any pair of corresponding parts is not congruent.
    Possible answer: For figures to be congruent there must exist a sequence of rigid motions
    that maps one to the other. If a pair of corresponding parts is not congruent, no rigid
    motion maps one to the other because distance, or angle measure, will not be preserved.

11. **Essential Question Check-In** △PQR and △STU have six pairs of congruent corresponding parts and △PQR can be mapped onto △STU by a translation followed by a rotation. How are the triangles related? Explain your reasoning.
    The triangles are congruent by the converse of CPCTC and because a sequence of rigid
    motions maps one triangle onto the other.

ELABORATE

INTEGRATE MATHEMATICAL PRACTICES

Focus on Math Connections

MP.1 Have students explain how they could use transformations to decide whether the triangles are congruent.

SUMMARIZE THE LESSON

? Suppose that △BUD ≅ △RIN. Write six congruency statements. ∠B ≅ ∠R, ∠U ≅ ∠I, ∠D ≅ ∠N, $\overline{BU} \cong \overline{RI}$, $\overline{UD} \cong \overline{IN}$, $\overline{DB} \cong \overline{NR}$

EVALUATE

ASSIGNMENT GUIDE

Concepts and Skills	Practice
Explore Transforming Triangles with Congruent Corresponding Parts	Exercise 1
Example 1 Deciding if Triangles are Congruent	Exercises 2–5
Example 2 Applying the Properties of Congruent Triangles	Exercises 6–9

INTEGRATE MATHEMATICAL PRACTICES

Focus on Modeling

MP.4 Suggest that students list the six congruencies that relate the parts of the triangles and mark the triangles to show them. Once they have clearly represented the corresponding parts, they can more easily answer the questions.

⭐ Evaluate: Homework and Practice

- Online Homework
- Hints and Help
- Extra Practice

1. Describe a sequence of rigid motions that maps △MNP onto △MQR to show that △MNP ≅ △MQR.

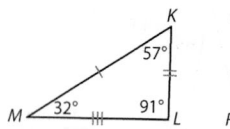

Possible answer: counterclockwise rotation about point M by m∠QMN followed by a reflection across $\overrightarrow{MQ}$

Determine whether the given triangles are congruent. Explain your reasoning.

2.

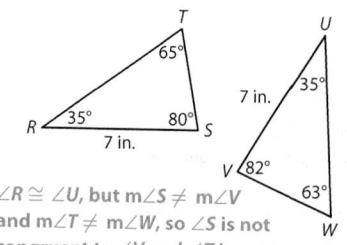

$\overline{KL} \cong \overline{QR}$, $\overline{LM} \cong \overline{RS}$, $\overline{KM} \cong \overline{QS}$, $\angle K \cong \angle Q$, $\angle L \cong \angle R$, and $\angle M \cong \angle S$; So, △KLM ≅ △QRS because all six pairs of corresponding parts are congruent.

3.

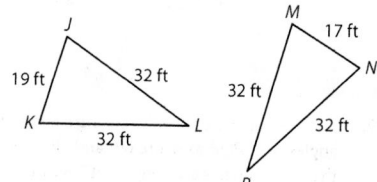

$\overline{AB} \cong \overline{DE}$, $\overline{BC} \cong \overline{EF}$, $\overline{AC} \cong \overline{DF}$, $\angle A \cong \angle D$, $\angle B \cong \angle E$, and $\angle C \cong \angle F$; So, △ABC ≅ △DEF because all six pairs of corresponding parts are congruent.

4.

$\angle R \cong \angle U$, but m∠S ≠ m∠V and m∠T ≠ m∠W, so ∠S is not congruent to ∠V and ∠T is not congruent to ∠W. Not congruent; there aren't six pairs of congruent corresponding parts.

5.

$\overline{KL} \cong \overline{NP}$ and $\overline{JL} \cong \overline{MP}$. However, since JK ≠ MN, JK is not congruent to $\overline{MN}$. Not congruent; there aren't six pairs of congruent corresponding parts.

Find the value of the variable that results in congruent triangles.

6.

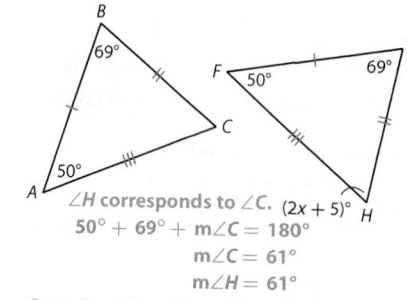

∠H corresponds to ∠C.
$50° + 69° + m∠C = 180°$
$m∠C = 61°$
$m∠H = 61°$
$2x + 5 = 61$, so $2x = 56$, and $x = 28$

7.

$\overline{RS}$ corresponds to $\overline{MN}$.
$RS = 1.8$ cm.
$3z - 3 = 1.8$, so $3z = 4.8$, and $z = 1.6$

Exercise	Depth of Knowledge (D.O.K.)	COMMON CORE Mathematical Practices
1	**1** Recall Information	**MP.6** Precision
2–5	**1** Recall Information	**MP.2** Reasoning
6–9	**1** Recall Information	**MP.4** Modeling
10–21	**2** Skills/Concept	**MP.2** Reasoning
22	**3** Strategic Thinking H.O.T.	**MP.3** Logic
23	**3** Strategic Thinkings H.O.T.	**MP.3** Logic
24	**3** Strategic Thinking H.O.T.	**MP.3** Logic

© Houghton Mifflin Harcourt Publishing Company

8.

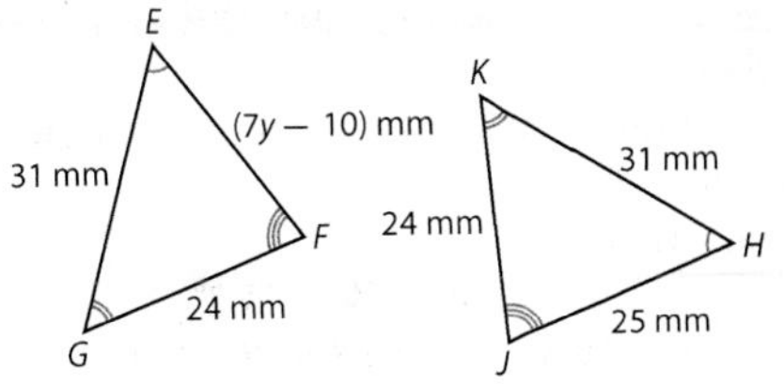

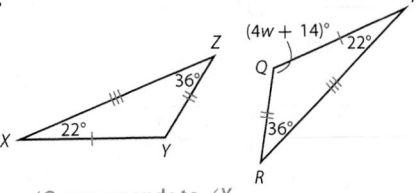

$\overline{EF}$ corresponds to $\overline{HJ}$.

$EF = 25$ mm

$7y - 10 = 25$, so $7y = 35$, and $y = 5$

9.

$\angle Q$ corresponds to $\angle Y$.

$22° + m\angle Y + 36° = 180°$

$m\angle Y = 122°$

$m\angle Q = 122°$

$4w + 14 = 122$, so $4w = 108$, and $w = 27$

Determine whether the given triangles are congruent. Explain.

10.

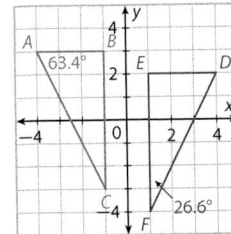

Since $\overline{AB}$ is horizontal and $\overline{BC}$ is vertical, $\angle B$ is a right angle, so $m\angle B = 90°$.

Since $\overline{DE}$ is horizontal and $\overline{EF}$ is vertical, $\angle E$ is a right angle, so $m\angle E = 90°$.

By the Triangle Sum Theorem, $63.4° + 90° + m\angle C = 180°$, so $m\angle C = 26.6°$.

Also, $m\angle D + 90° + 26.6° + 180°$, so $m\angle D = 63.4°$.

Therefore, $\angle A \cong \angle D$, $\angle B \cong \angle E$, and $\angle C \cong \angle F$.

$\overline{AB}$ is horizontal and its length is 3 units. $\overline{BC}$ is vertical and its length is 6 units.

$\overline{DE}$ is horizontal and its length is 3 units. $\overline{EF}$ is vertical and its length is 6 units.

By the Distance Formula, $AC = \sqrt{\left(-1-(-4)\right)^2 + (-3-3)^2} = \sqrt{45}$.

Also, $DF = \sqrt{(1-4)^2 + (-4-2)^2} = \sqrt{45}$.

Therefore, $\overline{AB} \cong \overline{DE}$, $\overline{BC} \cong \overline{EF}$, and $\overline{AC} \cong \overline{DF}$, so the triangles have six pairs of congruent corresponding parts, and are congruent by the converse of CPCTC.

11.

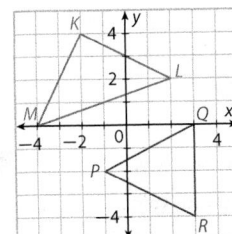

$KL = \sqrt{\left(2-(-2)\right)^2 + (2-4)^2} = \sqrt{20}$

$LM = \sqrt{(-4-2)^2 + (0-2)^2} = \sqrt{40}$

$KM = \sqrt{\left(-4-(-2)\right)^2 + (0-4)^2} = \sqrt{20}$

$PQ = \sqrt{\left(3-(-1)\right)^2 + \left(0-(-2)\right)^2} = \sqrt{20}$

$PR = \sqrt{\left(3-(-1)\right)^2 + \left(-4-(-2)\right)^2} = \sqrt{20}$

$\overline{QR}$ is vertical and its length is 4 units.

Therefore, $\overline{KL} \cong \overline{PQ}$ and $\overline{KM} \cong \overline{PR}$, but $LM \neq QR$, so $\overline{LM}$ is not congruent to $\overline{QR}$.

So, the triangles are not congruent.

Students may write congruence statements incorrectly. Make sure they understand that the order of the vertices in a congruence statement is not random. Students should know that they can identify corresponding angles by choosing pairs of letters in corresponding positions in a congruence statement.

Have each student design a poster to illustrate the concept of congruent triangles. The illustrations should show both an example and a nonexample.

12.

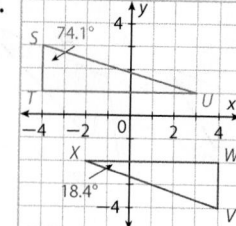

Since $\overline{ST}$ is vertical and $\overline{TU}$ is horizontal, $\angle T$ is a right angle, so m$\angle T = 90°$.

Since $\overline{VW}$ is vertical and $\overline{WX}$ is horizontal, $\angle W$ is a right angle, so m$\angle W = 90°$.

By the Triangle Sum Theorem,
$74.1° + 90° + m\angle U = 180°$, so m$\angle U = 15.9°$.

Also, m$\angle V + 90° + 18.4° = 180°$, so m$\angle V = 71.6°$.

Therefore, $\angle T \cong \angle W$, but $\angle S$ is not congruent to $\angle V$ or $\angle X$. So, the triangles are not congruent.

13.

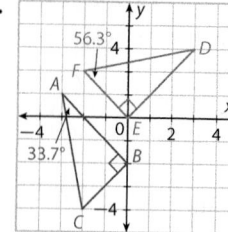

$\angle B$ is a right angle, so m$\angle B = 90°$.

$\angle E$ is a right angle, so m$\angle E = 90°$.

By the Triangle Sum Theorem,

$33.7° + 90° + m\angle C = 180°$, so m$\angle C = 56.3°$.

Also, m$\angle D + 90° + 56.3° = 180°$, so m$\angle D = 33.7°$.

Therefore, $\angle A \cong \angle D$, $\angle B \cong \angle E$, and $\angle C \cong \angle F$.

$$AB = \sqrt{\left(0-(-3)\right)^2 + (-2-1)^2} = \sqrt{18} \qquad DE = \sqrt{(0-3)^2 + (0-3)^2} = \sqrt{18}$$

$$BC = \sqrt{(-2-0)^2 + \left(-4-(-2)\right)^2} = \sqrt{8} \qquad EF = \sqrt{(-2-0)^2 + (2-0)^2} = \sqrt{8}$$

$$AC = \sqrt{\left(-2-(-3)\right)^2 + (-4-1)^2} = \sqrt{26} \qquad DF = \sqrt{(-2-3)^2 + (2-3)^2} = \sqrt{26}$$

Therefore $\overline{AB} \cong \overline{DE}$, $\overline{BC} \cong \overline{EF}$, and $\overline{AC} \cong \overline{DF}$, so the triangles have six pairs of congruent corresponding parts, and are congruent by the converse of CPCTC.

14. $\triangle FGH$ represents an artist's initial work on a design for a new postage stamp. What must be the values of x, y, and z in order for the artist's stamp to be congruent to $\triangle ABC$?

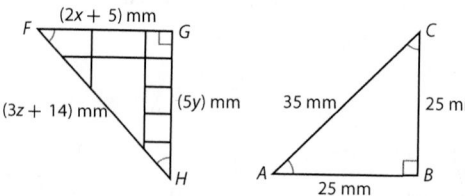

$\angle F$ corresponds to $\angle A$, $\angle G$ corresponds to $\angle B$, and $\angle H$ corresponds to $\angle C$.

$\overline{FG}$ corresponds to $\overline{AB}$. $\overline{GH}$ corresponds to $\overline{BC}$. $\overline{FH}$ corresponds to $\overline{AC}$.

$FG = 25$ mm $GH = 25$ mm $FH = 35$ mm

$2x + 5 = 25$ $5y = 25$ $3z + 14 = 35$

$x = 10$ $y = 5$ $z = 7$

© Houghton Mifflin Harcourt Publishing Company • Image Credits: ©Leonard de Selva/Corbis

15. Multi-Step Find the values of the variables that result in congruent triangles.

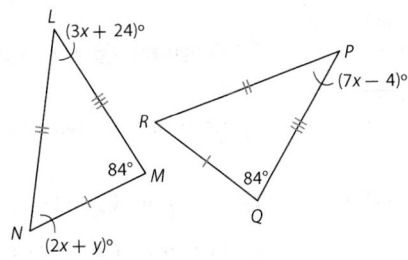

$\angle L$ corresponds to $\angle P$.

$m \angle L = m \angle P$

$3x + 24 = 7x - 4$

$3x + 28 = 7x$

$7 = x$

$m\angle L = (3x + 24)° = (3 \cdot 7 + 24)° = 45°$

$45° + 84° + m\angle N = 180°$

$m\angle N = 51°$

$2x + y = 51$

$2(7) + y = 51$, So $y = 37$.

Determine whether each statement is always, sometimes, or never true. Explain your reasoning.

16. If $\triangle ABC$ has angles that measure $10°$ and $40°$, and $\triangle DEF$ has angles that measure $40°$ and $120°$, then $\triangle ABC \cong \triangle DEF$.

Never true; by the Triangle Sum Theorem, the third angle of $\triangle ABC$ measures $130°$ and the third angle of $\triangle DEF$ measures $20°$. Since corresponding angles are not congruent, the triangles cannot be congruent.

17. Two triangles with different perimeters are congruent.

Never true; if the corresponding sides of two triangles are congruent, then the perimeters are equal. Therefore, if the perimeters are not equal, at least one pair of corresponding sides is not congruent, so the triangles are not congruent.

18. If $\triangle JKL \cong \triangle MNP$, then $m\angle L = m\angle N$.

Sometimes true; $\angle L$ corresponds to $\angle P$, so by CPCTC, $\angle L \cong \angle P$. If $\angle P \cong \angle N$, then $\angle L \cong \angle N$ by transitivity, and $m\angle L = m\angle N$.

19. Two triangles that each contain a right angle are congruent.

Sometimes true; the right angles in the triangles are congruent corresponding angles. Other corresponding angles may or may not be congruent, and corresponding sides may or may not be congruent.

20. Tenaya designed the earrings shown. She wants to be sure they are congruent. She knows that the three pairs of corresponding angles are congruent. What additional measurements should she make? Explain.

Corresponding sides must also be congruent. So, AB must equal DE, BC must equal EF, and AC must equal DF. She should check that $AC = 35$ mm, $BC = 12$ mm, and $DE = 37$ mm.

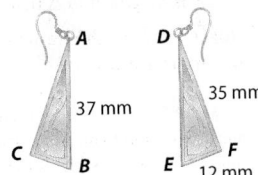

Have students write a journal entry in which they explain in their own words what CPCTC means. Encourage them to include one or more labeled figures as part of the journal entry.

21. Determine whether △*JKL* and △*PQR* are congruent or not congruent based on the given information. Select the correct answer for each lettered part.

a. m∠*J* = m∠*K* = m∠*L* = 60°, m∠*P* = m∠*Q* = m∠*R* = 60°,
   JK = *KL* = *JL* = 1.2 cm, *PQ* = *QR* = *PR* = 1.5 cm
   ○ Congruent ● Not congruent

b. m∠*J* = 48°, m∠*K* = 93°, m∠*P* = 48°, m∠*R* = 39°,
   $\overline{JK} \cong \overline{PQ}$, $\overline{KL} \cong \overline{QR}$, $\overline{JL} \cong \overline{PR}$
   ● Congruent ○ Not congruent

c. ∠*J* ≅ ∠*P*, ∠*K* ≅ ∠*Q*, ∠*L* ≅ ∠*R*,
   JK = *PQ* = 22 in., *KL* = *QR* = 34 in., *JL* = *PR* = 28 in.
   ● Congruent ○ Not congruent

d. m∠*J* = 51°, m∠*K* = 77°, m∠*P* = 51°, m∠*R* = 53°
   ○ Congruent ● Not congruent

e. m∠*J* = 45°, m∠*K* = 80°, m∠*Q* = 80°, m∠*R* = 55°,
   JK = *PQ* = 1.5 mm, *KL* = *QR* = 1.3 mm, *JL* = *PR* = 1.8 mm
   ● Congruent ○ Not congruent

a. **Not congruent; corresponding sides are not congruent.**
b. **Congruent; by the Triangle Sum Theorem, m∠*L* = 39°and m∠*Q* = 93°.**
c. **Congruent; there are six pairs of congruent corresponding parts.**
d. **Not congruent; by the Triangle Sum Theorem, m∠*L* = 52° and m∠*Q* = 76°.**
e. **Congruent; by the Triangle Sum Theorem, m∠*L* = 55° and m∠*P* = 45°.**

H.O.T. Focus on Higher Order Thinking

22. **Counterexamples** Isaiah says it is not necessary to check all six pairs of congruent corresponding parts to decide whether two triangles are congruent. He says that it is enough to check that the corresponding angles are congruent. Sketch a counterexample. Explain your counterexample.

Possible sketch:

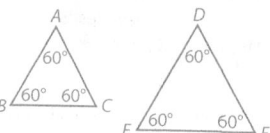

△*ABC* and △*DEF* have three pairs of congruent corresponding angles, but the triangles are not congruent because corresponding sides are not the same length.

23. **Critique Reasoning** Kelly was asked to determine whether △*KLN* is congruent to △*MNL*. She noted that $\overline{KL} \cong \overline{MN}$, $\overline{KN} \cong \overline{ML}$, and that the three pairs of corresponding angles are congruent. She said that this is only five pairs of congruent corresponding parts, so it is not possible to conclude that △*KLN* is congruent to △*MNL*. Do you agree? Explain.

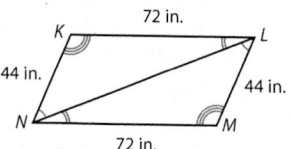

No; $\overline{LN} \cong \overline{LN}$ by the Reflexive Property of Congruence, so there are actually six pairs of congruent corresponding parts. Therefore, the triangles are congruent.

24. **Analyze Relationships** David uses software to draw two triangles. He finds that he can use a rotation and a reflection to map one triangle onto the other, and he finds that the image of vertex *D* is vertex *L*, the image of vertex *V* is vertex *C*, and the image of vertex *W* is vertex *Y*. In how many different ways can David write a congruence statement for the triangles? Explain.

12 ways; △*DVW* ≅ △*LCY*, △*DWV* ≅ △*LYC*, △*VDW* ≅ △*CLY*, △*VWD* ≅ △*CYL*, △*WDV* ≅ △*YLC*, or △*WVD* ≅ △*YCL*, and 6 more with the order of the triangles reversed.

Lesson Performance Task

For Kenny's science project, he is studying whether honeybees favor one color of eight-petal flowers over other colors. For his display, he is making eight-petal flowers from paper in various colors. For each flower, he'll cut out eight triangles like the one in the figure.

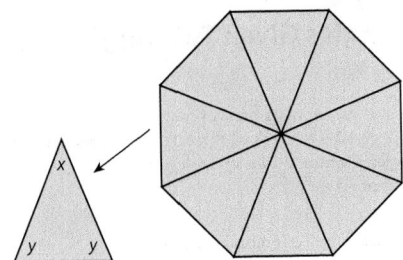

a. Find x, the measure in degrees of the top angle of each triangle. Explain how you found x.

b. Find y, the measure in degrees of the two base angles of each triangle. Explain how you found y.

c. Explain how Kenny could confirm that one of his triangles is congruent to the other seven.

a. To find x, use the fact that the sum of the measures of the eight angles at the center of the flower is 360°.

$x = 360° \div 8 = 45°$.

b. To find y, use the fact that the sum of the measures of the interior angles of a triangle is 180°.

$y = \dfrac{180° - 45°}{2} = \dfrac{135°}{2} = 67.5°$

c. Kenny could confirm that one of his triangles is congruent to the other seven by physically matching each of the seven to the first one to show that the three pairs of angles and the three pairs of sides are congruent. Or he could reason that one of the triangles can be mapped to each of the seven others through a series of 45° rotations.

INTEGRATE MATHEMATICAL PRACTICES
Focus on Modeling

MP.4 Have students describe, in as much detail as possible, the numerical and geometric features of the 8-sided polygon in the Lesson Performance Task diagram. Sample answer: The figure is a regular octagon. Drawing the four diagonals divides it into 8 isosceles triangles, each with base angles measuring 67.5° and apex angle measuring 45°. The 8 sides of the octagon are congruent.

INTEGRATE MATHEMATICAL PRACTICES
Focus on Reasoning

MP.2 A regular polygon is divided into congruent isosceles triangles. One of the base angles of each isosceles triangle measures 84°. How many sides does the polygon have? Explain how you found the answer. Sample answer: Since each triangle is isosceles, both base angles measure 84°. That leaves $180° - (84° + 84°) = 180° - 168° = 12°$ for the remaining angle, the angle at the center of the polygon. The sum of the angles at the center of the polygon is 360°, so the polygon must have $360° \div 12° = 30$ sides.

EXTENSION ACTIVITY

Extend the Lesson Performance Task by completing the table shown for regular polygons with the given numbers of sides. Describe any patterns you observe. Possible patterns: As the number of sides increases, the value of y increases, the value of x decreases, and the ratio $\dfrac{x}{y}$ decreases; the sum $x + y + y$ always equals 180°.

Number of Sides	x	y	y
9	40	70	70
10	36	72	72
12	30	75	75
15	24	78	78
18	20	80	80
20	18	81	81

Scoring Rubric

2 points: Student correctly solves the problem and explains his/her reasoning.

1 point: Student shows good understanding of the problem but does not fully solve or explain his/her reasoning.

0 points: Student does not demonstrate understanding of the problem.

Exploring What Makes Triangles Congruent   **230**

ASA Triangle Congruence

Common Core Math Standards

The student is expected to:

 G-CO.B.8

Explain how the criteria for triangle congruence (ASA . . .) follow from the definition of congruence in terms of rigid motions. Also G-CO.B.7, G-CO.C.10, G-SRT.B.5

Mathematical Practices

 MP.4 Modeling

Language Objective

Have students work in pairs to label and color code congruent angles and a side in pairs of triangles.

ENGAGE

Essential Question: What does the ASA Triangle Congruence Theorem tell you about triangles?

If two angles and the included side of one triangle are congruent to two angles and the included side of another triangle, the triangles are congruent.

PREVIEW: LESSON PERFORMANCE TASK

View the Engage section online. Explain that the flags of many countries incorporate geometric objects such as triangles. Then preview the Lesson Performance Task.

5.2 ASA Triangle Congruence

Essential Question: What does the ASA Triangle Congruence Theorem tell you about triangles?

Resource Locker

⊘ Explore 1 Drawing Triangles Given Two Angles and a Side

You have seen that two triangles are congruent if they have six pairs of congruent corresponding parts. However, it is not always possible to check all three pairs of corresponding sides and all three pairs of corresponding angles. Fortunately, there are shortcuts for determining whether two triangles are congruent.

(A) Draw a segment that is 4 inches long. Label the endpoints A and B.

(B) Use a protractor to draw a 30° angle so that one side is $\overline{AB}$ and its vertex is point A.

(C) Use a protractor to draw a 40° angle so that one side is $\overline{AB}$ and its vertex is point B. Label the point where the sides of the angles intersect as point C.

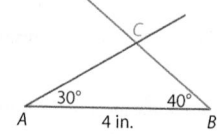

(D) Put your triangle and a classmate's triangle beside each other. Is there a sequence of rigid motions that maps one to the other? What does this tell you about the triangles?
Yes; the triangles are congruent.

Reflect

1. In a polygon, the side that connects two consecutive angles is the *included side* of those two angles. Describe the triangle you drew using the term *included side*. Be as precise as possible.
It is a triangle with a 30° angle, a 40° angle, and an included side that is 4 inches long.

2. **Discussion** Based on your results, how can you decide whether two triangles are congruent without checking that all six pairs of corresponding sides and corresponding angles are congruent?
Possible answer: If two angles and the included side of one triangle are congruent to two angles and the included side of another triangle, then the triangles are congruent.

© Houghton Mifflin Harcourt Publishing Company

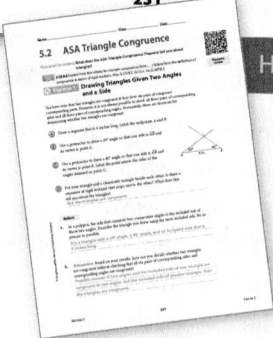

HARDCOVER PAGES 201–210

Turn to these pages to find this lesson in the hardcover student edition.

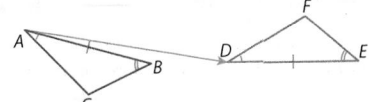

Explore 2 **Justifying ASA Triangle Congruence**

Explain the results of Explore 1 using transformations.

(A) Use tracing paper to make two copies of the triangle from Explore 1 as shown. Identify the corresponding parts you know to be congruent and mark these congruent parts on the figure.

$\angle A \cong$ ___ $\angle D$
$\angle B \cong$ ___ $\angle E$
$\overline{AB} \cong$ ___ $\overline{DE}$

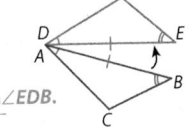

(B) What can you do to show that these triangles are congruent?
Find a sequence of rigid motions that maps one triangle onto the other triangle.

(C) Translate △ABC so that point A maps to point D. What translation vector did you use?
the vector with initial point A and terminal point D ($\vec{AD}$)

(D) Use a rotation to map point B to point E. What is the center of the rotation? What is the angle of the rotation?
The center of the rotation is point D (or A); the angle of the rotation is m∠EDB.

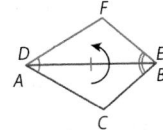

(E) How do you know the image of point B is point E?
It is given that $\overline{AB} \approx \overline{DE}$, so the image of point B must be point E.

(F) What rigid motion do you think will map point C to point F?
reflection across $\overleftrightarrow{DE}$

(G) To show that the image of point C is point F, notice that ∠A is reflected across $\overleftrightarrow{DE}$, so the measure of the angle is preserved. Since ∠A ≅ ∠D you can conclude that the image of $\overline{AC}$ lies on ___ $\vec{DF}$. In particular, the image of point C must lie on ___ $\vec{DF}$. By similar reasoning, the image of $\overline{BC}$ lies on ___ $\vec{EF}$ and the image of point C must lie on ___ $\vec{EF}$. The only point that lies on both $\vec{DF}$ and $\vec{EF}$ is ___ **point F**.

(H) Describe the sequence of rigid motions used to map △ABC to △DEF.
a translation followed by a rotation followed by a reflection

Reflect

3. **Discussion** Arturo said the argument in the activity works for any triangles with two pairs of congruent corresponding angles, and it is not necessary for the included sides to be congruent. Do you agree? Explain.
No; the included sides must be congruent to conclude that the image of

point B is point E after a rotation around point D.

Drawing Triangles Given Two Angles and a Side

INTEGRATE TECHNOLOGY

Have students explore the Angle-Side-Angle theorem using geometry software.

QUESTIONING STRATEGIES

? How can you check whether the triangles you draw are congruent to the triangles your classmates draw? Place one student's page on top of the other student's page and check to see if the triangles can be made to coincide exactly.

EXPLORE 2

Justifying ASA Triangle Congruence

INTEGRATE MATHEMATICAL PRACTICES
Focus on Reasoning

MP.2 Have students respond to this prompt in their math journals.

"If I know that two pairs of corresponding angles and the included sides of two triangles are congruent, I know _____. I know this because _____."

QUESTIONING STRATEGIES

? What is the benefit of using the Angle-Side-Angle Theorem instead of CPCTC? You need to find only three pairs of congruent corresponding parts with ASA, as opposed to six pairs with CPCTC.

PROFESSIONAL DEVELOPMENT

Math Background

Students know that when triangles are congruent, all pairs of corresponding sides and corresponding angles are congruent. As an extension of that, students to begin to develop converses of the Corresponding Parts of Congruent Triangles Theorem in which they do not need to know that all six pairs of corresponding parts are congruent in order to prove that triangles are congruent. In this lesson, they explore the Angle-Side-Angle (ASA) Theorem. They find that if they can prove that two angles and the included side of one triangle are congruent to two angles and the included side of another triangle, the triangles are congruent.

EXPLAIN 1

Deciding Whether Triangles Are Congruent Using ASA Triangle Congruence

CONNECT VOCABULARY **EL**

Remind students that *the ASA Triangle Congruence Theorem* is a shortened form of its full name, *the Angle-Side-Angle Triangle Congruence Theorem*. When you write *ASA*, it is helpful to read it aloud as *Angle-Side-Angle* and have students do the same to reinforce what it means.

QUESTIONING STRATEGIES

? Why do you need to find the measure of the missing angle to use the ASA Triangle Congruence Theorem? The two sides that you know are congruent need to be the included sides, so you need to know the measures of the angles at their endpoints.

LANGUAGE SUPPORT **EL**

Give each pair pictures of congruent and non-congruent triangles, highlighters, protractors, and rulers. Instruct them to prove which pairs are congruent by using Angle-Side-Angle to prove it. Have students highlight the angles and the side they used to show congruence, and write notes explaining why the triangles are congruent.

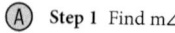

Explain 1 **Deciding Whether Triangles Are Congruent Using ASA Triangle Congruence**

You can state your findings about triangle congruence as a theorem. This theorem can help you decide whether two triangles are congruent.

> **ASA Triangle Congruence Theorem**
>
> If two angles and the included side of one triangle are congruent to two angles and the included side of another triangle, then the triangles are congruent.

Example 1 Determine whether the triangles are congruent. Explain your reasoning.

(A) **Step 1** Find m∠D.

$$m\angle D + m\angle E + m\angle F = 180°$$
$$m\angle D + 74° + 61° = 180°$$
$$m\angle D + 135° = 180°$$
$$m\angle D = 45°$$

Step 2 Compare the angle measures and side lengths.

m∠A = m∠D = 45°, AC = DF = 2.3 cm, and m∠C = m∠F = 61°

So, ∠A ≅ ∠D, $\overline{AC} \cong \overline{DF}$, and ∠C ≅ ∠F.

∠A and ∠C include side $\overline{AC}$, and ∠D and ∠F include side $\overline{DF}$.

So, △ABC ≅ △DEF by the ASA Triangle Congruence Theorem.

(B) **Step 1** Find m∠P.

$$m\angle M + m\angle N + m\angle P = 180°$$
$$\boxed{31}° + \boxed{38}° + m\angle P = 180°$$
$$\boxed{69}° + m\angle P = 180°$$
$$m\angle P = \boxed{111}°$$

Step 2 Compare the angle measures and side lengths.

None of the angles in △MNP has a measure of $\boxed{110°}$. Therefore, there ~~is~~/is not a sequence of rigid motions that maps △MNP onto △JKL, and △MNP ~~is~~/(is not) congruent to △JKL.

Reflect

4. In Part B, do you need to find m∠K? Why or why not?
No; you only need to know that △JKL has an angle (∠L) that is not congruent to any angle of △MNP. At that point, you can conclude that the triangles are not congruent.

© Houghton Mifflin Harcourt Publishing Company

COLLABORATIVE LEARNING

Small Group Activity

Have students experiment with congruent triangles and triangles that are not congruent but do have some congruent parts. Instruct them to draw a pair of congruent triangles and a pair of non-congruent triangles that meet the following criteria:

- at least two pairs of congruent sides
- at least one pair each of congruent sides and congruent angles
- all three pairs of congruent angles
- at least two pairs of congruent sides and one pair of congruent angles

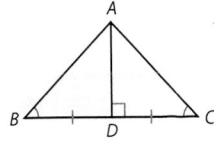

Your Turn

Determine whether the triangles are congruent. Explain your reasoning.

5.

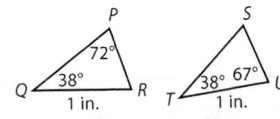

$\angle B \cong \angle C$, $\overline{BD} \cong \overline{CD}$, and $\angle ADB \cong$
$\angle ADC$ since both are right angles.
$\angle B$ and $\angle ADB$ include side $\overline{BD}$ and
$\angle ADC$ and $\angle C$ include side $\overline{DC}$. So,
$\triangle ADB \cong \triangle ADC$ by the ASA Triangle
Congruence Theorem.

6.

$72° + 38° + m\angle R = 180°$

$m\angle R = 70°$

None of the angles in $\triangle PQR$ has a
measure of 67°. So, $\triangle PQR$ is not
congruent to $\triangle STU$.

Explain 2 **Proving Triangles Are Congruent Using ASA Triangle Congruence**

The ASA Triangle Congruence Theorem may be used as a reason in a proof.

Example 2 Write each proof.

(A) Given: $\angle MQP \cong \angle NPQ$, $\angle MPQ \cong \angle NQP$

Prove: $\triangle MQP \cong \triangle NPQ$

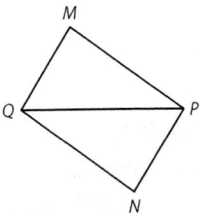

Statements	Reasons
1. $\angle MQP \cong \angle NPQ$	1. Given
2. $\angle MPQ \cong \angle NQP$	2. Given
3. $\overline{QP} \cong \overline{QP}$	3. Reflexive Property of Congruence
4. $\triangle MQP \cong \triangle NPQ$	4. ASA Triangle Congruence Theorem

---

EXPLAIN 2

Proving Triangles Are Congruent Using ASA Triangle Congruence

AVOID COMMON ERRORS

Some students may forget to include in their proofs the information that is given in the diagram. Remind them to start the proof by listing the given information.

QUESTIONING STRATEGIES

How do you know when you have enough information to complete the proof? To complete the proof, you need to show that two angles and the included side of one triangle are congruent to the corresponding angles and side of the other triangle.

CONNECT VOCABULARY EL

Have students review the different units used to measure triangles to show congruence. Length is measured in linear units such as cm, mm, or inches, while angles are measured in degrees.

DIFFERENTIATE INSTRUCTION

Modeling

Instruct students to draw and label three triangles according to the following specifications.

- There is just enough information to prove that they are congruent using the ASA Triangle CongruenceTheorem.

- There is enough information to prove that they are not congruent.

- There is some of the information required to prove that they are congruent, but not enough.

ASA Triangle Congruence   **234**

Ⓑ Given: ∠A ≅ ∠C, E is the midpoint of $\overline{AC}$.

Prove: △AEB ≅ △CED

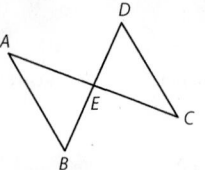

Statements	Reasons
1. ∠A ≅ ∠C	1. Given
2. E is the midpoint of $\overline{AC}$.	2. Given
3. $\overline{AE}$ ≅ $\overline{CE}$	3. Definition of midpoint
4. ∠AEB ≅ ∠CED	4. Vertical angles are congruent.
5. △AEB ≅ △CED	5. ASA Triangle Congruence Theorem

Reflect

7. In Part B, suppose the length of $\overline{AB}$ is 8.2 centimeters. Can you determine the length of any other segments in the figure? Explain.

Yes; CD = 8.2 cm because $\overline{AB}$ ≅ $\overline{CD}$ by CPCTC.

Your Turn

Write each proof.

8. Given: ∠JLM ≅ ∠KML, ∠JML ≅ ∠KLM

Prove: △JML ≅ △KLM

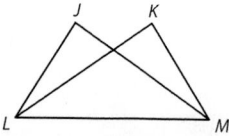

Statements	Reasons
1. ∠JLM ≅ ∠KML	1. Given
2. ∠JML ≅ ∠KLM	2. Given
3. $\overline{LM}$ ≅ $\overline{LM}$	3. Reflexive Property of Congruence
4. △JML ≅ △KLM	4. ASA Triangle Congruence Theorem

LANGUAGE SUPPORT 🔲EL

Vocabulary Development

Make sure students understand the meaning of *included side*. Sketch △BER, △MAT, and △SQU on the board. Use color to highlight $\overline{SQ}$ and define what it means for it to be included between ∠S and ∠Q. Ask questions such as "What side is included between ∠E and ∠R?" and "Between which two angles is $\overline{MT}$?" Continue to drill students until they can recognize and name included sides fluently.

9. Given: ∠S and ∠U are right angles, $\overline{RV}$ bisects $\overline{SU}$.

Prove: △RST ≅ △VUT

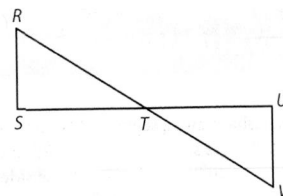

Statements	Reasons
1. ∠S and ∠U are right angles.	1. Given
2. ∠S ≅ ∠U	2. All right angles are congruent.
3. $\overline{RV}$ bisects $\overline{SU}$.	3. Given
4. $\overline{ST} \cong \overline{UT}$	4. Definition of bisector
5. ∠RTS ≅ ∠VTU	5. Vertical angles are congruent.
6. △RST ≅ △VUT	6. ASA Triangle Congruence Theorem

💬 Elaborate

10. Discussion Suppose you and a classmate both draw triangles with a 30° angle, a 70° angle, and a side that is 3 inches long. How will they compare? Explain your reasoning.

The triangles will be congruent by the ASA Triangle Congruence Theorem if the 3 inch side is the included side. Otherwise, the triangles will have the same shape but not necessarily the same size.

11. Discussion How can a diagram show you that corresponding parts of two triangles are congruent without providing specific angle measures or side lengths?

Possible answer: Vertical angles are congruent. Overlapping sides are congruent. Right angles are congruent. Angles or sides marked with congruence symbols are congruent.

12. Essential Question Check-In What must be true in order for you to use the ASA Triangle Congruence Theorem to prove that triangles are congruent?

Two angles and the included side of one triangle must be congruent to two angles and the included side of another triangle.

ELABORATE

VISUAL CUES

Use colored pencils to label congruent sides using ticks and congruent angles using arcs to help students better visualize the angles and sides that are congruent

SUMMARIZE THE LESSON

? Why would you use the ASA Triangle Congruence Theorem? What do you need to know to use it? You would use the ASA Triangle Congruence Theorem to prove that two triangles are congruent by using only three pairs of congruent parts. You need to know that two pairs of corresponding angles are congruent and the included sides between those angles are also congruent.

EVALUATE

ASSIGNMENT GUIDE

Concepts and Skills	Practice
Explore Drawing Triangles Given Two Angles and a Side	Exercise 1
Explore Justifying ASA Triangle Congruence	Exercise 2
Example 1 Deciding Whether Triangles Are Congruent Using ASA Triangle Congruence	Exercises 3–6
Example 2 Proving Triangles Are Congruent Using ASA Triangle Congruence	Exercises 7–9

QUESTIONING STRATEGIES

? You can take any quadrilateral and draw a segment between two opposite vertices to form two triangles. How do you know these two triangles will contain at least one pair of congruent sides? The diagonal is a side of both triangles and it is congruent to itself.

⭐ Evaluate: Homework and Practice

• Online Homework
• Hints and Help
• Extra Practice

1. Natasha draws a segment $\overline{PQ}$ that is 6 centimeters long. She uses a protractor to draw a 60° angle so that one side is $\overrightarrow{PQ}$ and its vertex is point P. Then she uses a protractor to draw an 35° angle so that one side is $\overrightarrow{PQ}$ and its vertex is point Q.

   a. Draw a triangle following the instructions that Natasha used. Label the vertices and the known side and angle measures.

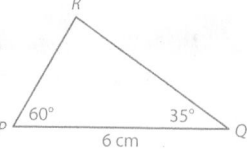

   b. Will there be a sequence of rigid motions that will map your triangle onto Natasha's triangle? Explain.

   Yes; the triangles are congruent by ASA. Therefore, there is a sequence of rigid motions that will map my triangle onto Natasha's triangle.

2. Tomas drew two triangles, as shown, so that $\angle B \cong \angle E$, $\overline{BC} \cong \overline{EC}$, and $\angle ACB \cong \angle DCE$. Describe a sequence of one or more rigid motions Tomas can use to show that $\triangle ABC \cong \triangle DEC$.

   He should use a counterclockwise rotation about point C with an angle of rotation of m$\angle BCE$.

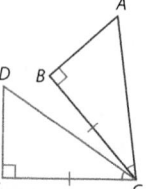

Determine whether the triangles are congruent. Explain your reasoning.

3.

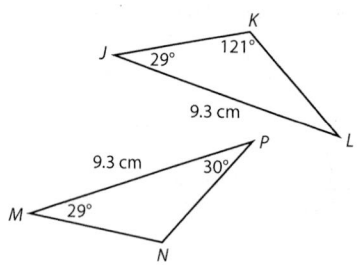

$29° + 121° + m\angle L = 180°$

$m\angle L = 30°$

$m\angle J = m\angle M$, $JL = MP$, and $m\angle L = m\angle P$. So $\angle J \cong \angle M$, $\overline{JL} \cong \overline{MP}$, and $\angle L \cong \angle P$. $\angle J$ and $\angle L$ include side $\overline{JL}$, and $\angle M$ and $\angle P$ include side $\overline{MP}$. Therefore, $\triangle JKL \cong \triangle MNP$ by ASA.

4.

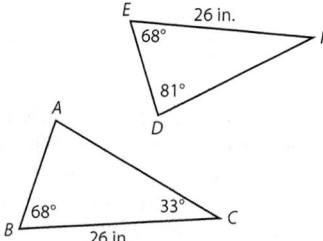

$81° + 68° + m\angle F = 180°$

$m\angle F = 31°$

None of the angles in $\triangle DEF$ has a measure of 33°. So, $\triangle DEF$ is not congruent to $\triangle ABC$.

© Houghton Mifflin Harcourt Publishing Company

Module 5   237   Lesson 2

Exercise	Depth of Knowledge (D.O.K.)	COMMON CORE Mathematical Practices	
1–2	**1** Recall of Information	**MP.3** Logic	
3–6	**1** Recall of Information	**MP.2** Reasoning	
7–9	**2** Skills/Concepts	**MP.3** Logic	
10–20	**2** Skills/Concepts	**MP.4** Modeling	
21	**3** Strategic Thinking H.O.T.	**MP.4** Modeling	
22	**3** Strategic Thinking H.O.T.	**MP.2** Reasoning	
23	**3** Strategic Thinking H.O.T.	**MP.2** Reasoning	

Determine whether the triangles are congruent. Explain your reasoning.

5.

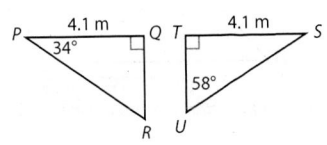

$m\angle S + 90° + 58° = 180°$

$m\angle S = 32°$

None of the angles in $\triangle STU$ has a measure of 34°. So, $\triangle STU$ is not congruent to $\triangle PQR$.

6.

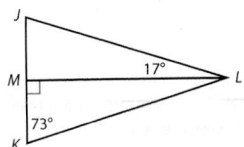

$m\angle LMK + m\angle K + m\angle MLK = 180°$

$163° + m\angle MLK = 180°$, so $m\angle MLK = 17°$

$m\angle JML = m\angle KML$, so $\angle JML \cong \angle KML$; $\overline{ML} \cong \overline{ML}$ by the Reflexive Property of Congruence; $m\angle MLJ = m\angle MLK$, so $\angle MLJ \cong \angle MLK$. $\angle JML$ and $\angle MLJ$ include side $\overline{ML}$, and $\angle KML$ and $\angle MLK$ include side $\overline{ML}$. Therefore $\triangle JML \cong \triangle KML$ by the ASA Triangle Congruence Theorem.

Write each proof.

7. **Given:** $\overline{AB}$ bisects $\angle CAD$ and $\angle CBD$.

Prove: $\triangle CAB \cong \triangle DAB$

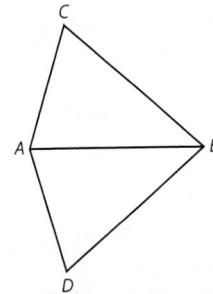

Statements	Reasons
1. $\overline{AB}$ bisects $\angle CAD$ and $\angle CBD$.	1. Given
2. $\angle CAB \cong \angle DAB$	2. Definition of bisector
3. $\angle CBA \cong \angle DBA$	3. Definition of bisector
4. $\overline{AB} \cong \overline{AB}$	4. Reflexive Property of Congruence
5. $\triangle CAB \cong \triangle DAB$	5. ASA Triangle Congruence Theorem

COGNITIVE STRATEGIES

Draw and label $\triangle OXF$. Have students name a side that is included between $\angle O$ and $\angle F$ and a side that is not. Then have them share the strategy they use to distinguish between the two.

8. Given: $\overline{AB}$ is parallel to $\overline{CD}$, $\angle ACB \cong \angle CAD$.

Prove: $\triangle ABC \cong \triangle CDA$

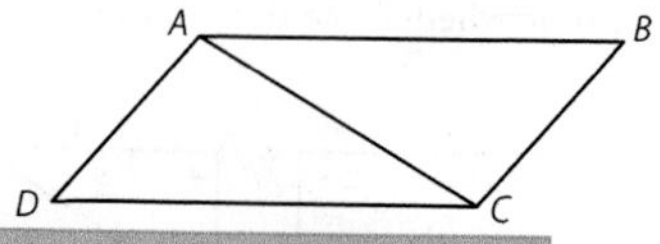

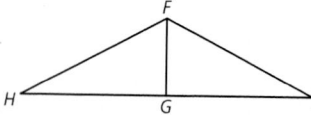

Statements	Reasons
1. $\overline{AB}$ is parallel to $\overline{CD}$.	1. Given
2. $\angle BAC \cong \angle DCA$	2. Alternate Interior Angles Theorem
3. $\overline{AC} \cong \overline{AC}$	3. Reflexive Property of Congruence
4. $\angle ACB \cong \angle CAD$	4. Given
5. $\triangle ABC \cong \triangle CDA$	5. ASA Triangle Congruence Theorem

9. Given: $\angle H \cong \angle J$, G is the midpoint of $\overline{HJ}$, $\overline{FG}$ is perpendicular to $\overline{HJ}$.

Prove: $\triangle FGH \cong \triangle FGJ$

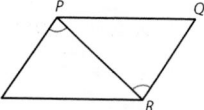

Statements	Reasons
1. $\angle H \cong \angle J$	1. Given
2. G is the midpoint of $\overline{HJ}$.	2. Given
3. $\overline{HG} \cong \overline{JG}$	3. Definition of midpoint
4. $\overline{FG}$ is perpendicular to $\overline{HJ}$.	4. Given
5. $\angle FGH$ and $\angle FGJ$ are right angles.	5. Definition of perpendicular
6. $\angle FGH \cong \angle FGJ$	6. All right angles are congruent.
7. $\triangle FGH \cong \triangle FGJ$	7. ASA Triangle Congruence Theorem

10. The figure shows quadrilateral $PQRS$. What additional information do you need in order to conclude that $\triangle SPR \cong \triangle QRP$ by the ASA Triangle Congruence Theorem? Explain.

$\angle SRP \cong \angle QPR$; you need to have two pairs of congruent corresponding angles with $\overline{PR}$ as the included side.

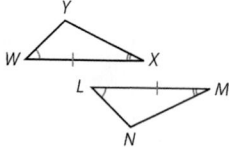

11. **Communicate Mathematical Ideas** In the figure, $\overline{WX}$ is parallel to $\overline{LM}$.

a. Describe a sequence of two rigid motions that maps $\triangle LMN$ to $\triangle WXY$.

Translate $\overline{LM}$ to $\overline{WX}$, then reflect $\triangle LMN$ across $\overleftrightarrow{WX}$.

b. How can you be sure that point N maps to point Y?

Since $\angle L \cong \angle W$ and $\angle M \cong \angle X$, the images of $\overline{LN}$ and $\overline{MN}$ lie on $\overrightarrow{WY}$ and $\overrightarrow{XY}$, respectively. The image of N must lie on both rays, so the image is the intersection point Y.

Use a compass and straightedge and the ASA Triangle Congruence Theorem to construct a triangle that is congruent to △ABC.

12.

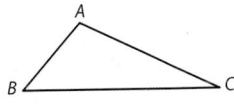

13.

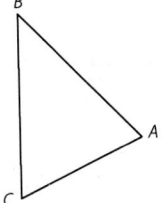

14. Multi-Step For what values of the variables is △QPR congruent to △SPR? In this case, what is m∠Q?

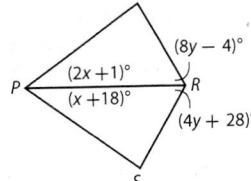

If ∠QPR ≅ ∠SPR,
then m∠QPR = m∠SPR.
$$2x + 1 = x + 18$$
$$2x = x + 17$$
$$x = 17$$

If ∠QRP ≅ ∠SRP,
then m∠QRP = m∠SRP.
$$8y - 4 = 4y + 28$$
$$4y = 32$$
$$y = 8$$

m∠QPR = $(2x + 1)° = (2 \cdot 17 + 1)° = 35°$ and
m∠QRP = $(8y - 4)° = (8 \cdot 8 - 4)° = 60°$
$$35° + m∠Q + 60° = 180°$$
$$m∠Q = 85°$$

Write each proof.

15. Given: $\angle A \cong \angle E$, C is the midpoint of $\overline{AE}$.

Prove: $\overline{AB} \cong \overline{ED}$

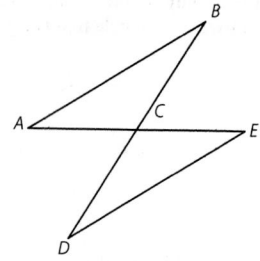

Statements	Reasons
1. $\angle A \cong \angle E$	1. Given
2. C is the midpoint of $\overline{AE}$.	2. Given
3. $\overline{AC} \cong \overline{EC}$	3. Definition of midpoint
4. $\angle ACB \cong \angle ECD$	4. Vertical angles are congruent.
5. $\triangle ACB \cong \triangle ECD$	5. ASA Triangle Congruence Theorem
6. $\overline{AB} \cong \overline{ED}$	6. CPCTC

16. The figure shows $\triangle GHJ$ and $\triangle PQR$ on a coordinate plane.

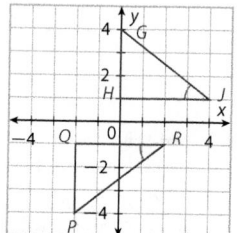

a. Explain why the triangles are congruent using the ASA Triangle Congruence Theorem.

$\angle J \cong \angle R$, $\angle H \cong \angle Q$ (both are right angles), and $\overline{HJ} \cong \overline{QR}$ (both are 4 units long). Two pairs of angles and their included sides are congruent, so the triangles are congruent by the ASA Triangle Congruence Theorem.

b. Explain why the triangles are congruent using rigid motions.

Possible answer: You can map $\triangle GHJ$ onto $\triangle PQR$ by a translation two units left followed by a reflection across the x-axis. By the definition of congruence in terms of rigid motions, the triangles must be congruent.

© Houghton Mifflin Harcourt Publishing Company

17. Justify Reasoning A factory makes triangular traffic signs. Each sign is an equilateral triangle with three 60° angles. Explain why two signs that each have a side 36 inches long must be congruent.

In each sign, the side that is 36 in. long is the included side between two 60° angles. Therefore, by the ASA Triangle Congruence Theorem, the signs are congruent.

18. Represent Real-World Problems Rob is making the kite shown in the figure.

a. Can Rob conclude that $\triangle ABD \cong \triangle ACD$? Why or why not?

Yes; $\angle BAD \cong \angle CAD$, $\overline{AD} \cong \overline{AD}$, and $\angle BDA \cong \angle CDA$, so $\triangle ABD \cong \triangle ACD$ by the ASA Triangle Congruence Theorem.

b. Rob says that $AB = AC$ and $BD = CD$. Do you agree? Explain.

Yes; by CPCTC, $\overline{AB} \cong \overline{AC}$ and $\overline{BD} \cong \overline{CD}$. Congruent segments have equal measures.

c. Given that $BD = x + 15$ cm and $AB = x$ cm, write an expression for the distance around the kite in centimeters.

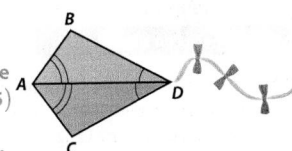

The distance around the kite is $AB + BD + CD + AC$. Since $AB = AC$ and $BD = CD$, $AB + BD + CD + AC = x + (x + 15) + (x + 15) + x$.

Combining like terms shows that this expression is equal to $4x + 30$.

19. In order to find the distance across a canyon, Mariela sites a tree across the canyon (point A) and locates points on her side of the canyon as shown. Explain how she can use this information to find the distance AB across the canyon.

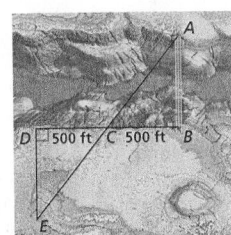

$\angle B$ and $\angle D$ are both right angles, so $\angle B \cong \angle D$; $CB = CD$, so $\overline{CB} \cong \overline{CD}$; $\angle ACB$ and $\angle ECD$ are vertical angles, so $\angle ACB \cong \angle ECD$. Therefore, $\triangle ACB \cong \triangle ECD$ by the ASA Triangle Congruence Theorem. Since corresponding parts of congruent triangles are congruent, $\overline{AB} \cong \overline{ED}$, so $AB = ED$. Mariela can find the distance AB across the canyon by measuring the distance ED.

AVOID COMMON ERRORS

Some students may not be able to answer a question because they do not notice all of the information given by the diagram. Remind them that a little square by an angle means it is a right angle.

Have students explain why identifying two pairs of congruent angles with their included sides congruent is enough to prove that two triangles are congruent.

20. Determine whether each of the following provides enough information to prove that $\triangle SQP \cong \triangle SQR$. Select the correct answer for each lettered part.

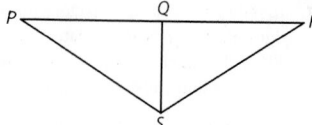

a. Q is the midpoint of $\overline{PR}$. ○ Yes ● No

b. $\angle P \cong \angle R$ ○ Yes ● No

c. $\angle SQP$ is a right angle, $\angle PSQ \cong \angle RSQ$ ● Yes ○ No

d. $\angle SQP$ is a right angle, $m\angle P = 32°$, $m\angle RSQ = 58°$. ● Yes ○ No

e. $\angle P \cong \angle R$, $\angle PSQ \cong \angle RSQ$ ● Yes ○ No

a. **No; there is no information about angle measures**

b. **No; only one pair of angles is known.**

c. **Yes; $\angle SQP \cong \angle SQR$; $\overline{QS} \cong \overline{QS}$; $\angle PSQ \cong \angle RSQ$. Therefore, $\triangle SQP \cong \triangle SQR$ by the ASA Triangle Congruence Theorem.**

d. **Yes; $\angle SQP \cong \angle SQR$; $\overline{QS} \cong \overline{QS}$ by the Triangle Sum Theorem, $m\angle PSQ = 58°$, so $\angle RSQ \cong \angle PSQ$. Therefore, $\triangle SQP \cong \triangle SQR$ by ASA.**

e. **Yes; $\angle P \cong \angle R$ and $\angle PSQ \cong \angle RSQ$, so by Triangle Sum, $\angle SQP \cong \angle SQR$. Since $\overline{QS} \cong \overline{QS}$, $\triangle SQP \cong \triangle SQR$ by the ASA Triangle Congruence Theorem.**

H.O.T. Focus on Higher Order Thinking

21. **Counterexamples** Jasmine said that the ASA Triangle Congruence Theorem works for quadrilaterals. That is, if two angles and the included side of one quadrilateral are congruent to two angles and the included side of another quadrilateral, then the quadrilaterals are congruent. Sketch and mark a figure of two quadrilaterals as a counterexample to show that Jasmine is incorrect.
Possible sketch:

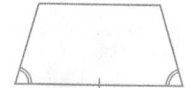 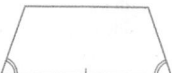

22. **Critique Reasoning** $\triangle ABC$ and $\triangle DEF$ are both right triangles and both triangles contain a 30° angle. Both triangles have a side that is 9.5 mm long. Yoshio claims that he can use the ASA Triangle Congruence Theorem to show that the triangles are congruent. Do you agree? Explain.

No; the triangles are congruent only if the sides that are 9.5 mm long are corresponding sides.

23. Draw Conclusions Do you think there is an ASAS Congruence Theorem for quadrilaterals? Suppose two quadrilaterals have a pair of congruent consecutive angles with a pair of congruent included sides and an additional pair of congruent corresponding sides. Must the quadrilaterals be congruent? Justify your response.

No; the quadrilaterals in the figure meet the conditions of the proposed ASAS Congruence Theorem, but they are not congruent. Therefore, the quadrilaterals serve as a counterexample to show that there is no such theorem.

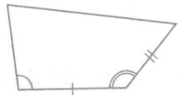 

Lesson Performance Task

The flag of the Congo Republic consists of green and red right triangles separated by a yellow parallelogram. Construct an argument to prove that $\triangle BAF \cong \triangle EDC$.

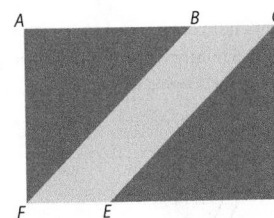

$\angle ABF \cong \angle ACE$ because they are corresponding angles on one side of transversal $\overline{AC}$ intersecting parallel lines $\overline{BF}$ and $\overline{CE}$.

$\angle ACE \cong \angle CED$ because they are alternate interior angles with transversal $\overline{EC}$ intersecting parallel lines $\overline{AC}$ and $\overline{FD}$.

$\angle ABF \cong \angle CED$ because both angles are congruent to $\angle ACE$.

$\angle A \cong \angle D$ because both are right angles.

$m\angle A + m\angle ABF + m\angle AFB = 180°$ because the sum of the measures of the angles of a triangle is 180°. For the same reason, $m\angle D + m\angle CED + m\angle DCE = 180°$

So, $m\angle A + m\angle ABF + m\angle AFB = m\angle D + m\angle CED + m\angle DCE$

$m\angle AFB = m\angle DCE$ because $\angle A \cong \angle D$ and $\angle ABF \cong \angle CED$.

Imaging connecting points B and E to form a diagonal of the parallelogram. Notice that this transversal forms the congruent corresponding angle pairs $\angle CBE \cong \angle FEB$ and $\angle FBE \cong \angle CEB$. Since $\overline{BE} \approx \overline{BE}$ by the reflexive property, $\triangle FBE \cong \triangle CEB$ by the ASA Triangle Congruence Theorem, and $\overline{BF} \cong \overline{EC}$ by CPCTC.

Since $\angle ABF \cong \angle CED$, $m\angle AFB = m\angle DCE$, and $\overline{BF} \cong \overline{EC}$, $\triangle BAF \cong \triangle EDC$ by the ASA Triangle Congruence Theorem.

© Houghton Mifflin Harcourt Publishing Company

MP.2 Using the flag of the Republic of the Congo, a student proved these three congruencies:

(a) $\angle A \cong \angle D$

(b) $\angle ABF \cong \angle DEC$

(c) $\angle AFB \cong \angle DCE$

The student then argued that $\triangle BAF \cong \triangle EDC$ because the three angles of one triangle are congruent to the three angles of the other triangle. Draw a sketch to show that the student's argument is not valid. Sample sketch: two equilateral triangles of different sizes. Three angles of one triangle are congruent to three angles of the other triangle, but the triangles are clearly not congruent.

INTEGRATE MATHEMATICAL PRACTICES
Focus on Communication

MP.3 Using the flag of the Republic of the Congo, a student argued that $\angle ABF \cong \angle BFE$ because the angles are alternate interior angles, with transversal $\overline{BF}$ intersecting parallel lines $\overline{AC}$ and $\overline{FD}$. Was the student correct? Explain. Sample answer: Yes; $\overline{AC}$ and $\overline{FD}$ are parallel because they are opposite sides of a rectangle.

EXTENSION ACTIVITY

Have students research national flags. Ask each student to choose a flag with a geometrical pattern containing at least two triangles. The student should sketch the flag, give sufficient information about the angles and lines of the flag to prove that two triangles are congruent, and write a proof showing that the triangles are congruent. Among national flags students might consider for this project are those of Antigua and Barbuda, Eritrea, Guyana, Namibia, and Trinidad and Tobago.

Scoring Rubric
2 points: Student correctly solves the problem and explains his/her reasoning.
1 point: Student shows good understanding of the problem but does not fully solve or explain his/her reasoning.
0 points: Student does not demonstrate understanding of the problem.

SAS Triangle Congruence

Common Core Math Standards

The student is expected to:

  G-CO.B.8

Explain how the criteria for triangle congruence (. . . SAS . . .) follow from the definition of congruence in terms of rigid motions. Also G-CO.B.7, G-CO.C.10, G-SRT.B.5

Mathematical Practices

  MP.3 Logic

Language Objective

Have students work in pairs to find an example in the lesson and write out a step-by-step explanation of how the SAS Triangle Congruence Theorem works.

ENGAGE

Essential Question: What does the SAS Triangle Congruence Theorem tell you about triangles?

If two sides and the included angle of one triangle are congruent to two sides and the included angle of another triangle, the triangles are congruent.

PREVIEW: LESSON PERFORMANCE TASK

View the Engage section online. Explain that triangle congruence is important in the design of structures like pyramids. Then preview the Lesson Performance Task.

245 Lesson 5.3

Name_____ Class_____ Date_____

5.3 SAS Triangle Congruence

Essential Question: What does the SAS Triangle Congruence Theorem tell you about triangles?

Resource Locker

⊘ Explore 1 Drawing Triangles Given Two Sides and an Angle

You know that when all corresponding parts of two triangles are congruent, then the triangles are congruent. Sometimes you can determine that triangles are congruent based on less information.

For this activity, cut two thin strips of paper, one 3 in. long and the other 2.5 in. long.

Ⓐ On a sheet of paper use a straightedge to draw a horizontal line. Arrange the 3 in. strip to form a 45° angle, as shown. Next, arrange the 2.5 in. strip to complete the triangle. How many different triangles can you form? Support your answer with a diagram.

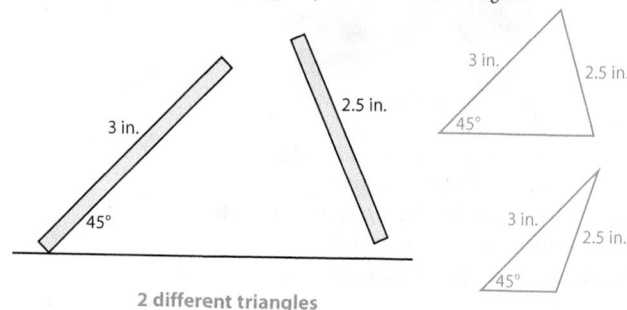

2 different triangles

Ⓑ Now arrange the two strips of paper to form a 45° angle so that the angle is *included* between the two consecutive sides, as shown. With this arrangement, can you construct more than one triangle? Why or why not?

No, only one triangle is possible.

Having the angle included between the

sides fixes the position of the sides.

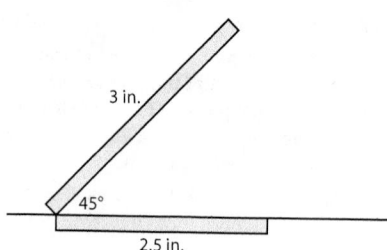

© Houghton Mifflin Harcourt Publishing Company

Module 5   **245**   Lesson 3

---

1. **Discussion** If two triangles have two pairs of congruent corresponding sides and one pair of congruent corresponding angles, under what conditions can you conclude that the triangles must be congruent? Explain.

   The triangles must be congruent if the congruent corresponding angles are the angles included between the congruent corresponding sides.

⊘ Explore 2 Justifying SAS Triangle Congruence

You can explain the results of Explore 1 using transformations.

Ⓐ Construct △DEF by copying ∠A, side $\overline{AB}$, and side $\overline{AC}$. Let point D correspond to point A, point E correspond to point B, and point F correspond to point C, and place point E on the segment shown.

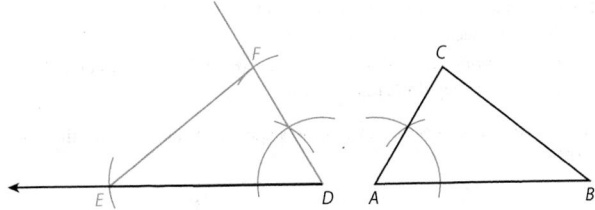

Ⓑ The diagram illustrates one step in a sequence of rigid motions that will map △DEF onto △ABC. Describe a complete sequence of rigid motions that will map △DEF onto △ABC.

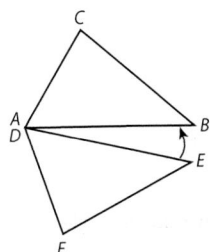

   Possible answer: Translate △DEF so that point D maps to point A. Then rotate △DEF 180° counterclockwise about point A. Point E will map to point B because DE = AB. Then reflect △DEF across $\overline{AB}$. Point F will map to point C because ∠A ≅ ∠D and DF = AC.

Ⓒ What can you conclude about the relationship between △ABC and △DEF? Explain your reasoning.

   △ABC ≅ △DEF because there is a sequence of rigid motions that maps one onto the other.

2. Is it possible to map △DEF onto △ABC using a single rigid motion? If so, describe the rigid motion.
   Yes; possible answer: reflect △DEF across a vertical line halfway between points A and D.

© Houghton Mifflin Harcourt Publishing Company

PROFESSIONAL DEVELOPMENT

 Integrate Mathematical Practices

This lesson provides an opportunity to address Mathematical Practice **MP.3**, which calls for students to "construct viable arguments and critique the reasoning of others." As students explore congruent triangles, ask them to share their observations and conclusions with the class. As they share their findings, ask if anyone got different results. Discuss the differences. Promoting this type of dialogue in the classroom is an essential aspect of the standard.

EXPLORE 1

Drawing Triangles Given Two Sides and an Angle

INTEGRATE TECHNOLOGY

Have students use geometry software to explore included angles.

QUESTIONING STRATEGIES

? If I hold up a compass and increase the angle, what happens to the distance between the tips? If I decrease the angle, what happens to the distance between the tips? If I keep the angle the same, what happens to the distance between the tips? The angle increases; it decreases; it stays the same.

EXPLORE 2

Justifying SAS Triangle Congruence

INTEGRATE MATHEMATICAL PRACTICES
Focus on Critical Thinking

MP.3 Each time the students perform a transformation, have them note the effect of the transformation on the angles and sides. They should notice that they are transformed in the same way and that their measures stay the same.

QUESTIONING STRATEGIES

? Does it matter on which side of the angle you place each segment? No; they will make the same triangle, with the only difference being a reflection.

EXPLAIN 1

Deciding Whether Triangles Are Congruent Using SAS Triangle Congruence

QUESTIONING STRATEGIES

? How do you know that two sides of a triangle are congruent? Two sides are congruent if they have the same length.

INTEGRATE MATHEMATICAL PRACTICES
Focus on Critical Thinking

MP.3 Remind students that they know how to find the measure of an angle of a triangle when they know the measures of the other two angles. This makes it possible to apply the ASA Triangle Congruence Theorem to many sets of triangles. Tell them to suppose that they know the lengths of two sides of a triangle. Is it possible to use that information to find the length of the third side? It is possible only if the triangle is a right triangle; then the length of the third side can be found using the Pythagorean Theorem.

⦿ Explain 1   **Deciding Whether Triangles are Congruent Using SAS Triangle Congruence**

What you explored in the previous two activities can be summarized in a theorem. You can use this theorem and the definition of congruence in terms of rigid motions to determine whether two triangles are congruent.

SAS Triangle Congruence Theorem
If two sides and the included angle of one triangle are congruent to two sides and the included angle of another triangle, then the triangles are congruent.

Example 1   Determine whether the triangles are congruent. Explain your reasoning.

Ⓐ   Look for congruent corresponding parts.

* Sides $\overline{DE}$ and $\overline{DF}$ do not correspond to side $\overline{BC}$, because they are not 15 cm long.
* $\overline{DE}$ corresponds to $\overline{AB}$, because $DE = AB = 20$ cm.
* $\overline{DF}$ corresponds to $\overline{AC}$, because $DF = AC = 19$ cm.
* $\angle A$ and $\angle D$ are corresponding angles because they are included between pairs of corresponding sides, but they don't have the same measure.

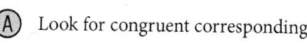

The triangles are not congruent, because there is no sequence of rigid motions that maps $\triangle ABC$ onto $\triangle DEF$.

Ⓑ

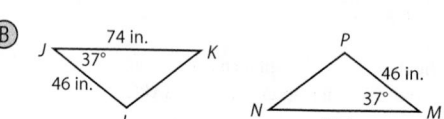

Look for congruent corresponding parts.

* $\overline{JL}$ corresponds to ___$\overline{MP}$___, because $JL = $ ___MP___ = ___46___ in.
* ___$\overline{JK}$___ corresponds to MN, because ___JK___ $= MN = 74$ in.
* ___$\angle J$___ corresponds to ___$\angle M$___, because m$\angle J$ = m$\angle M$ = ___37°___.

Two sides and the included angle of $\triangle JKL$ are congruent to two sides and the included angle of ___$\triangle MNP$___. $\triangle JKL \cong$ ___$\triangle MNP$___ by the ___SAS Triangle Congruence Theorem___.

COLLABORATIVE LEARNING

Small Group Activity

Instruct students to illustrate the difference between the ASA and SAS Triangle Congruence Theorems. They may make a poster, write an essay, create a model, or use another technique to convey the information. Have students share their work in small groups. Then have each group choose one project to present to the class.

3. Determine whether the triangles are congruent. Explain your reasoning.
$\overline{DE} \cong \overline{GH}$, $\overline{DF} \cong \overline{GJ}$, and $\angle D \cong \angle G$, and $\angle D$ and
$\angle G$ are included by congruent corresponding sides.
$\triangle EDF \cong \triangle HGJ$ by the SAS Triangle Congruence
Theorem.

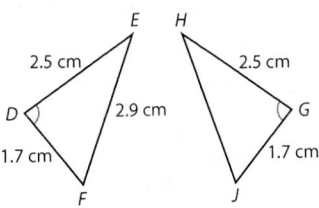

Explain 2 Proving Triangles Are Congruent Using SAS Triangle Congruence

Theorems about congruent triangles can be used to show that triangles in real-world objects are congruent.

Example 2 Write each proof.

Ⓐ Write a proof to show that the two halves of a triangular window are congruent if the vertical post is the perpendicular bisector of the base.

Given: $\overline{BD}$ is the perpendicular bisector of $\overline{AC}$.
Prove: $\triangle BDA \cong \triangle BDC$

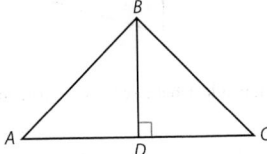

It is given that $\overline{BD}$ is the perpendicular bisector of $\overline{AC}$. By the definition of a perpendicular bisector, $AD = CD$, which means $\overline{AD} \cong \overline{CD}$, and $\overline{BD} \perp \overline{AC}$, which means $\angle BDA$ and $\angle BDC$ are congruent right angles. In addition, $\overline{BD} \cong \overline{BD}$ by the reflexive property of congruence. So two sides and the included angle of $\triangle BDA$ are congruent to two sides and the included angle of $\triangle BDC$. The triangles are congruent by the SAS Triangle Congruence Theorem.

Ⓑ Given: $\overline{CD}$ bisects $\overline{AE}$ and $\overline{AE}$ bisects $\overline{CD}$
Prove: $\triangle ABC \cong \triangle EBD$

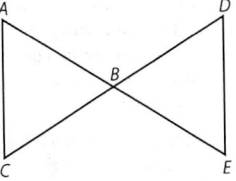

It is given that $\overline{CD}$ bisects $\overline{AE}$ and $\overline{AE}$ bisects $\overline{CD}$. So by the definition

of a bisector, $AB = EB$ and $\underline{\quad CB = DB \quad}$, which makes $\overline{AB} \cong \overline{EB}$

and $\underline{\quad \overline{CB} \cong \overline{DB} \quad}$. $\angle ABC \cong \underline{\quad \angle EBD \quad}$ because they are

$\underline{\quad \text{vertical angles} \quad}$. So two sides and the $\underline{\quad \text{included} \quad}$ angle of $\triangle ABC$

are congruent to two sides and the $\underline{\quad \text{included} \quad}$ angle of $\triangle EBD$. The

triangles are congruent by the $\underline{\quad \text{SAS Triangle Congruence Theorem} \quad}$.

EXPLAIN 2

Proving Triangles Are Congruent Using SAS Triangle Congruence

AVOID COMMON ERRORS

Remind students that they should not assume information from a figure unless it is marked or stated in the given information.

QUESTIONING STRATEGIES

? To use SAS, is it essential that the congruent angles be included between the pairs of congruent sides? Yes, because it is possible for an acute triangle and an obtuse triangle to have two pairs of corresponding congruent sides and a pair of corresponding congruent *nonincluded* angles. There is no Side-Side-Angle (SSA) Theorem.

DIFFERENTIATE INSTRUCTION

Kinesthetic Experience

Have students place two pencils on their desks so that the points intersect and the pencils model an angle. Have students measure the distance between the erasers. Have the students rotate one pencil to change the angle. Have them measure the distance between the erasers again. After they have experimented with different angles, discuss whether or not it is possible to change the distance between the erasers without changing the angle.

ELABORATE

QUESTIONING STRATEGIES

? The solution to an exercise is $\triangle JKL \cong \triangle MNP$. Suppose that Bud concludes that $\triangle JLK \cong \triangle MPN$ and Kim concludes that $\triangle KJL \cong \triangle MPN$. Can both students be correct? Explain. Bud's answer is correct because the order of the vertices lines up congruent angles. Kim's is not because the order of the vertices does not line up congruent angles.

SUMMARIZE THE LESSON

? Why would you use the SAS Triangle Congruence Theorem? What do you need to know to use it? You would use the SAS Triangle Congruence Theorem to prove that two triangles are congruent by using only three pairs of congruent parts. You need to know that two pairs of corresponding sides are congruent and the angles included between those sides are also congruent.

Your Turn

4. Given: $\overline{AB} \cong \overline{AD}$ and $\angle 1 \cong \angle 2$

   Prove: $\triangle BAC \cong \triangle DAC$

   Possible answer: You are given that $\overline{AB} \cong \overline{AD}$ and $\angle 1 \cong \angle 2$. You also know that $\overline{AC} \cong \overline{AC}$ by the reflexive property. Two sides and the included angle of $\triangle BAC$ are congruent to two sides and the included angle of $\triangle DAC$. The triangles are congruent by the SAS Triangle Congruence Theorem

   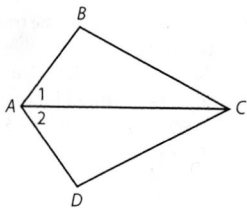

💬 Elaborate

5. Explain why the corresponding angles must be *included* angles in order to use the SAS Triangle Congruence Theorem.
   Possible answer: If the corresponding angles are not included angles, then there is more than one possible angle between the congruent corresponding sides.

6. Jeffrey draws $\triangle PQR$ and $\triangle TUV$. He uses a translation to map point P to point T and point R to point V as shown. What should be his next step in showing the triangles are congruent? Why?
   Reflect $\triangle PQR$ across $\overleftrightarrow{TV}$; this will map point Q to point U and show that there is a sequence of rigid motions that maps $\triangle PQR$ to $\triangle TUV$.

   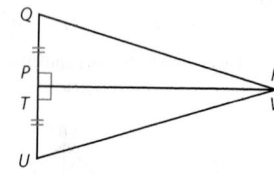

7. **Essential Question Check-In** If two triangles share a common side, what else must be true for the SAS Triangle Congruence Theorem to apply?
   A second side and an included angle must be congruent.

⭐ Evaluate: Homework and Practice

- Online Homework
- Hints and Help
- Extra Practice

1. Sarah performs rigid motions mapping point A to point D and point B to point E, as shown. Does she have enough information to confirm that the triangles are congruent? Explain your reasoning.

   No; she can map $\overrightarrow{AC}$ to $\overrightarrow{DF}$ by a reflection across $\overleftrightarrow{DE}$, but C will map to F only if $AC = DF$.

   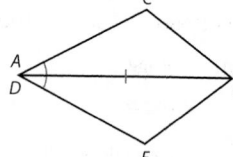

©Houghton Mifflin Harcourt Publishing Company

LANGUAGE SUPPORT 🔲EL

Connect Vocabulary

Open and shut a door and talk about the function of a hinge. Compare the concept of an included angle to a hinge. Draw a triangle on the board, labeling the vertices. Have students identify the angle that is included between each pair of sides.

Determine whether the triangles are congruent. Explain your reasoning.

2.

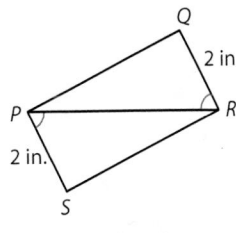

$\overline{PS} \cong \overline{RQ}$, $\overline{PR} \cong \overline{PR}$, $\angle SPR \cong \angle QRP$, and $\angle SPR$ and $\angle QRP$ are included by congruent corresponding sides.
$\triangle SPR \cong \triangle QRP$ by SAS.

3.

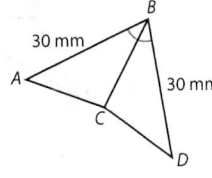

$\overline{AB} \cong \overline{DB}$, $\overline{BC} \cong \overline{BC}$, and $\angle ABC \cong \angle DBC$, and $\angle ABC$ and $\angle DBC$ are included by congruent corresponding sides.
$\triangle ABC \cong \triangle DBC$ by SAS.

4.

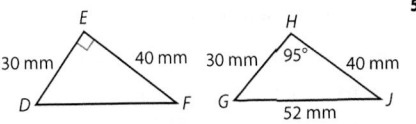

$\overline{DE} \cong \overline{GH}$ and $\overline{EF} \cong \overline{HJ}$, but included angles $\angle E$ and $\angle H$ are not congruent. The triangles are not congruent, because there is no sequence of rigid motions that maps $\triangle DEF$ onto $\triangle GHJ$.

5.

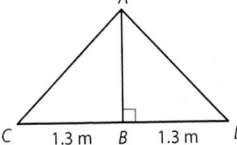

$\overline{AB} \cong \overline{AB}$, $\overline{CB} \cong \overline{DB}$, $\angle ABC \cong \angle ABD$ and $\angle ABC$ and $\angle ABD$ are included by congruent corresponding sides.
$\triangle ABC \cong \triangle ABD$ by SAS.

Find the value of the variable that results in congruent triangles. Explain.

6.

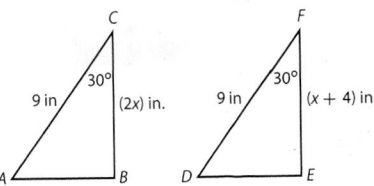

$2x = x + 4$; $x = 4$; $\triangle ABC \cong \triangle DEF$ by SAS when x is 4.

7.

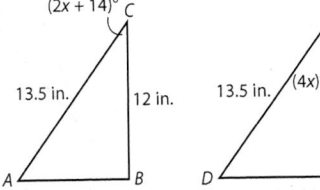

$2x + 14 = 4x$; $x = 7$; $\triangle ABC \cong \triangle DEF$ by SAS when x is 7.

© Houghton Mifflin Harcourt Publishing Company

ASSIGNMENT GUIDE

Concepts and Skills	Practice
Explore 2 Justifying SAS Triangle Congruence	Exercises 1–6
Example 1 Deciding Whether Triangles Are Congruent Using SAS Triangle Congruence	Exercises 7–11
Example 2 Proving Triangles Are Congruent Using SAS Triangle Congruence	Exercises 12–20

INTEGRATE MATHEMATICAL PRACTICES
Focus on Communication

MP.3 Write ASA and SAS on the board. Ask students to do each of the following in their Math Journals:

- Tell what each stands for in terms of triangle congruence.
- Draw and label a diagram illustrating each.
- Tell how the two theorems are the same.
- Tell how the two theorems are different.

Exercise	Depth of Knowledge (D.O.K.)	COMMON CORE Mathematical Practices
1–6	**2** Skills/Concepts	**MP.3** Logic
8	**2** Skills/Concepts	**MP.1** Problem Solving
9–10	**2** Skills/Concepts	**MP.4** Modeling
11–12	**2** Skills/Concepts	**MP.3** Logic
13	**3** Strategic Thinking H.O.T.	**MP.4** Modeling
14	**3** Strategic Thinking H.O.T.	**MP.2** Reasoning
15	**3** Strategic Thinking H.O.T.	**MP.6** Precision

SAS Triangle Congruence   **250**

CRITICAL THINKING

Draw non-collinear points *M*, *O*, and *U* on the board, connecting them to form an obtuse angle with vertex *O*. Ask students to visualize a translation, a rotation, and a reflection of the figure shown. In each case, have them describe the effect on the segment that connects point *M* with point *U*.

Sample response: The segment connecting points *M* and *U* will follow the same movements as the rest of the figure. Its length will remain the same no matter what rigid-motion transformation is used.

8. Given that polygon *ABCDEF* is a regular hexagon, prove that $\overline{AC} \cong \overline{AE}$.

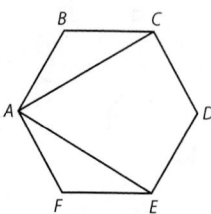

Statements	Reasons
1. *ABCDEF* is a regular hexagon.	1. Given
2. *AB = AF* and *BC = FE*	2. Definition of regular polygon
3. $\overline{AB} \cong \overline{AF}$ and $\overline{BC} \cong \overline{FE}$	3. Definition of congruence in terms of rigid motion
4. *m∠B = m∠F*	4. Definition of regular polygon
5. *∠B ≅ ∠F*	5. Definition of congruence in terms of rigid motion
6. △*ABC* ≅ △*AFE*	6. SAS Triangle Congruence Theorem
7. $\overline{AC} \cong \overline{AE}$	7. CPCTC

9. A product designer is designing an easel with extra braces as shown in the diagram. Prove that if $\overline{BD} \cong \overline{FD}$ and $\overline{CD} \cong \overline{ED}$, then the braces $\overline{BE}$ and $\overline{FC}$ are also congruent.

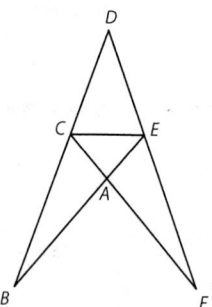

You are given that $\overline{BD} \cong \overline{FD}$ and $\overline{CD} \cong \overline{ED}$. You also know that ∠*D* ≅ ∠*D* by the reflexive property. Two sides and the included angle of △*BDE* are congruent to two sides and the included angle of △*FDC*. The triangles are congruent by the SAS Triangle Congruence Theorem. So, by CPCTC, the braces $\overline{BE}$ and $\overline{FC}$ and are also congruent.

© Houghton Mifflin Harcourt Publishing Company · Image Credits: ©Andreyuu/iStockPhoto.com

10. An artist is framing a large picture and wants to put metal poles across the back to strengthen the frame as shown in the diagram. If the metal poles are both the same length and they bisect each other, prove that $\overline{AB} \cong \overline{CD}$ and $\overline{AD} \cong \overline{CB}$.

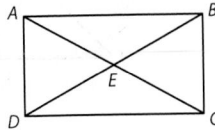

Because $\overline{BD}$ and $\overline{AC}$ bisect each other, $AE = CE$ and $BE = DE$, so $\overline{AE} \cong \overline{CE}$ and $\overline{BE} \cong \overline{DE}$ by the definition of congruence. By the Vertical Angle Theorem, you also know that $\angle AEB \cong \angle CED$. Two sides and the included angle of $\triangle AEB$ are congruent to two sides and the included angle of $\triangle CED$. The triangles are congruent by the SAS Triangle Congruence Theorem. By CPCTC, $\overline{AB} \cong \overline{CD}$. You can use similar reasoning to show that $\overline{AD} \cong \overline{CB}$

11. The figure shows a side panel of a skateboard ramp. Kalim wants to confirm that the right triangles in the panel are congruent.

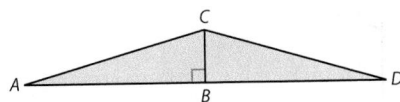

a. What measurements should Kalim take if he wants to confirm that the triangles are congruent by SAS? Explain.

Measure $\overline{AB}$ and $\overline{DB}$; so he can confirm that two pairs of sides and their included angles are congruent. $\left(\overline{AB} \cong \overline{DB}, \overline{CB} \cong \overline{CB}, \text{ and } \angle ABC \cong \angle DBC\right)$

b. What measurements should Kalim take if he wants to confirm that the triangles are congruent by ASA? Explain.

Measure $\angle ACB$ and $\angle DCB$; so he can confirm that two pairs of angles and their included sides are congruent. $\left(\angle ACB \cong \angle DCB, \angle ABC \cong \angle DBC, \text{ and } \overline{CB} \cong \overline{CB}\right)$

AVOID COMMON ERRORS

Students may choose the wrong angle when SAS is used to prove triangles congruent. Explain that the angle must be formed by the sides. The included angle is named by the letter the segments share.

JOURNAL

Have students describe how they can use color coding to help them recognize the SAS theorem. Have them support their descriptions with colored sketches.

12. Which of the following are reasons that justify why the triangles are congruent? Select all that apply.

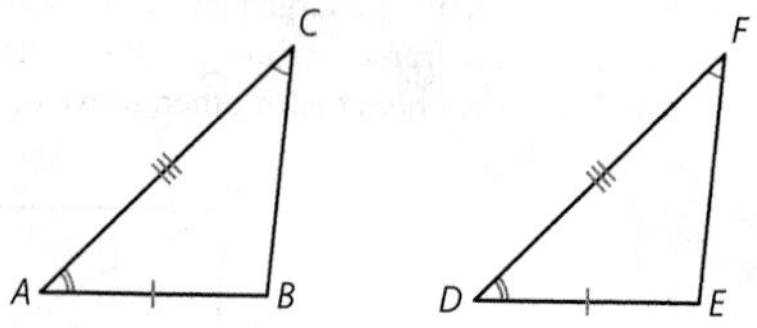

A. SSA Triangle Congruence Theorem

(B.) SAS Triangle Congruence Theorem

(C.) ASA Triangle Congruence Theorem

D. Converse of CPCTC

E. CPCTC

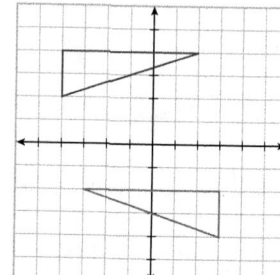

A. SSA is not a valid congruence theorem.

D. You do not know that all of the corresponding parts are congruent.

E. CPCTC is a property of congruent triangles, not a justification for congruence.

H.O.T. Focus on Higher Order Thinking

13. **Multi-Step** Refer to the following diagram to answer each question.

a. Use a triangle congruence theorem to explain why these triangles are congruent.

Each triangle has side lengths of 2 and 6 and an included right angle. By SAS they are congruent.

b. Describe a sequence of rigid motions to map the top triangle onto the bottom triangle to confirm that they are congruent.

Possible answer: Reflect the triangle across the *y*-axis. Next translate it 1 unit to the left. Then translate it 6 units down.

14. Explain the Error Mark says that the diagram confirms that a given angle and two given side lengths determine a unique triangle even if the angle is not an included angle. Explain Mark's error.

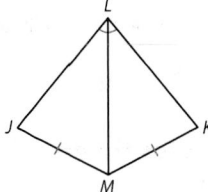

Possible answer: A circle with its center at *M* and radius *MJ* = *MK* will intersect $\overline{JL}$ and $\overline{KL}$ at two other points closer to *L*. The triangles formed by each of these two points and the points *L* and *M* will be different than the original triangles, even though they are formed by the same given angle and two given side lengths.

15. Justify Reasoning The opposite sides of a rectangle are congruent. Can you conclude that a diagonal of a rectangle divides the rectangle into two congruent triangles? Justify your response.

Yes; since the opposite sides of a rectangle are congruent and the included angles between the sides are right angles, the two triangles are congruent by the SAS Theorem.

Lesson Performance Task

The diagram of the Great Pyramid at Giza gives the approximate lengths of edge $\overline{AB}$ and slant height $\overline{AC}$. The slant height is the perpendicular bisector of $\overline{BD}$. Find the perimeter of $\triangle ABD$. Explain how you found the answer.

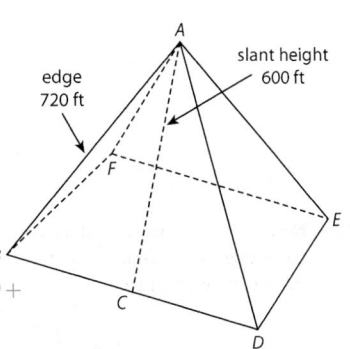

edge 720 ft

slant height 600 ft

Because $\overline{AC}$ is the perpendicular bisector of $\overline{BD}$, *BC* = *CD* and m∠*BCA* = m∠*DCA* = 90°. Also, *AC* = *AC* so △*BCA* ≅ △*DCA* by the SAS Triangle Congruence Theorem. Therefore, *AD* = 720 ft by CPCTC. To find *BC*, use the Pythagorean Theorem:
$(BC)^2 = 720^2 - 600^2 = 158,400$; $BC = \sqrt{158,400} \approx 398$;
CD = *BC*, so *CD* = 398 perimeter of △*ABD* = *AB* + *BC* + *CD* + *AD* ≈ 720 + 398 + 398 + 720 = 2,236 ft.

EXTENSION ACTIVITY

Some authorities claim that there is a relationship between the dimensions of the Great Pyramid at Giza and π, the ratio of the circumference of a circle to the radius. Have students research this claim and offer evidence as to its truth or falsity.

The claim is that the ratio of the perimeter of the base of the Great Pyramid to its height equals 2π. Some sources give 923 m as the perimeter of the base and 146.3 m as the height. $\frac{923}{146.3} \approx 6.309$; $2\pi \approx 6.283$

MP.2 Ask students to identify the single congruence they would need to establish, in addition to the given information, to enable them to prove $\triangle BCA \cong \triangle DCA$ by the ASA Triangle Congruence Theorem. ∠*BAC* ≅ ∠*DAC*

INTEGRATE MATHEMATICAL PRACTICES

Focus on Math Connections

MP.1 The base of the Great Pyramid is square. What is the area of the base in acres? $\left(1 \text{ acre} = 43,560 \text{ ft}^2\right)$ about 14.5 acres

Scoring Rubric

2 points: Student correctly solves the problem and explains his/her reasoning.

1 point: Student shows good understanding of the problem but does not fully solve or explain his/her reasoning.

0 points: Student does not demonstrate understanding of the problem.

SSS Triangle Congruence

Common Core Math Standards

The student is expected to:

COMMON CORE **G-CO.B.8**

Explain how the criteria for triangle congruence (... SSS) follow from the definition of congruence in terms of rigid motions. Also G-CO.B.7, G-CO.C.10, G-SRT.B.5

Mathematical Practices

COMMON CORE **MP.7 Using Structure**

Language Objective

Have small groups of students complete a triangle congruence chart.

ENGAGE

Essential Question: What does the SSS Triangle Congruence Theorem tell you about triangles?

If three sides of one triangle are congruent to three sides of another triangle, you can conclude that the triangles are congruent.

PREVIEW: LESSON PERFORMANCE TASK

View the Engage section online. Point out that the "structural beams" mentioned in the Preview refer to the steel sides of the triangles. Then preview the Lesson Performance Task.

Name_____ Class_____ Date_____

5.4 SSS Triangle Congruence

Essential Question: What does the SSS Triangle Congruence Theorem tell you about triangles?

Resource Locker

⊘ Explore **Constructing Triangles Given Three Side Lengths**

Two triangles are congruent if and only if a rigid motion transformation maps one triangle onto the other triangle. Many theorems can also be used to identify congruent triangles.

Follow these steps to construct a triangle with sides of length 5 in., 4 in., and 3 in. Use a ruler, compass, and either tracing paper or a transparency.

(A) Use a ruler to draw a line segment of length 5 inches. Label the endpoints A and B.

(B) Open a compass to 4 inches. Place the point of the compass on A, and draw an arc as shown.

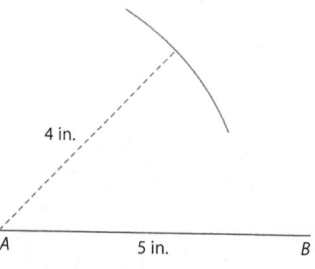

(C) Now open the compass to 3 inches. Place the point of the compass on B, and draw a second arc.

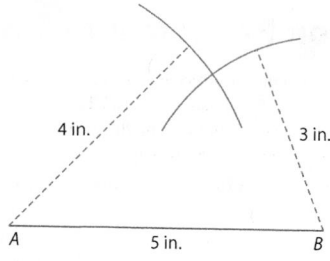

(D) Next, find the intersection of the two arcs. Label the intersection C. Draw $\overline{AC}$ and $\overline{BC}$. Label the side lengths on the figure.

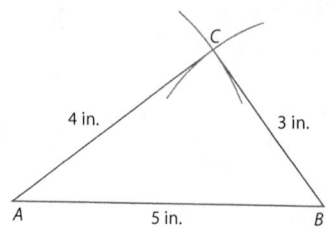

(E) Repeat steps A through D to draw $\triangle DEF$ on a separate piece of tracing paper. The triangle should have sides with the same lengths as $\triangle CAB$. Start with a segment that is 4 in. long. Label the endpoints D and E as shown.

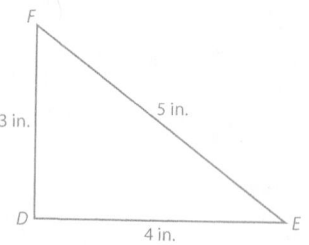

© Houghton Mifflin Harcourt Publishing Company

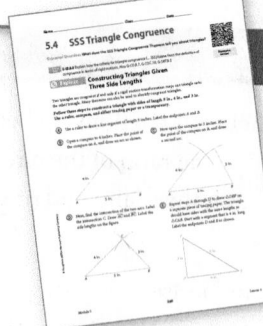

HARDCOVER PAGES 221–230

Turn to these pages to find this lesson in the hardcover student edition.

(F) Compare △CAB and △DEF. Are they congruent? How do you know?

Yes. Triangle *CAB* can be mapped to △DEF by a translation that maps

point *B* to point *F*, and then a rotation about point *F*.

Reflect

1. **Discussion** When you construct △CAB, how do you know that the intersection of the two arcs is a distance of 4 inches from *A* and 3 inches from *B*?
   The arcs are sections of circles sets of points, respectively, 3 inches and 4 inches from *A*. The other circle

   is the set of points that is 3 inches away from *B*. The intersection has the properties of both circles.

2. Compare your triangles to those made by other students. Are they all congruent? Explain.
   Yes, because there is a sequence of rigid motions that maps any one of the

   triangles onto any of the others.

✏ Explain 1   Justifying SSS Triangle Congruence

You can use rigid motions and the converse of the Perpendicular Bisector Theorem to justify this theorem.

SSS Triangle Congruence Theorem
If three sides of one triangle are congruent to three sides of another triangle, then the triangles are congruent.

Example 1   In the triangles shown, let $\overline{AB} \cong \overline{DE}$, $\overline{AC} \cong \overline{DF}$, and $\overline{BC} \cong \overline{EF}$. Use rigid motions to show that $\triangle ABC \cong \triangle DEF$.

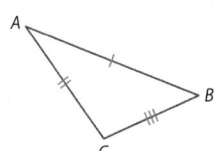 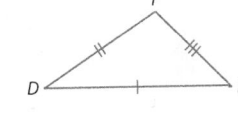

© Houghton Mifflin Harcourt Publishing Company

PROFESSIONAL DEVELOPMENT

Math Background

The Side-Side-Side Triangle Congruence Theorem is often presented as the first of the Triangle Congruence Theorems because it is easy to demonstrate concretely. In this course, it is the third theorem presented because the justification requires students to apply the Perpendicular Bisector Theorem. Reinforce this justification throughout the lesson.

EXPLORE

Constructing Triangles Given Three Side Lengths

INTEGRATE TECHNOLOGY

Students may use geometry software to explore the concept of constructing a triangle with given side lengths.

INTEGRATE MATHEMATICAL PRACTICES
Focus on Modeling

MP.4 Give each student a piece of dry spaghetti. They should measure and break the spaghetti so that they have three pieces that are the same length as the sides of the triangle in the exercise. Instruct them to make a triangle with these pieces on top of the triangle they drew. Have them compare the triangles and explain why they are congruent. Then ask them to consider whether it is possible to create a triangle from the spaghetti pieces that is not congruent to the triangle they drew in the exercise.

EXPLAIN 1

Justifying SSS Triangle Congruence

INTEGRATE MATHEMATICAL PRACTICES
Focus on Communication

MP.3 Some justifications in this exercise may be difficult for some students to understand. Have students model each step with the triangles they have drawn on tracing paper. Encourage students to restate the steps in their own words. Students should fully understand each step before moving on to the next one.

QUESTIONING STRATEGIES

(?) Draw two segments that share an endpoint. How many different segments could be drawn to turn this figure into a triangle? There is only one segment.

SSS Triangle Congruence   **256**

(A) Transform △ABC by a translation along $\overrightarrow{AD}$ followed by a rotation about point D, so that $\overline{AB}$ and $\overline{DE}$ coincide. The segments coincide because they are the same length.

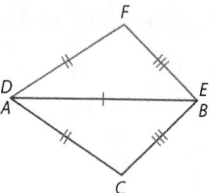

Does a reflection across $\overline{AB}$ map point C to point F? To show this, notice that $DC = DF$, which means that point D is equidistant from point C and point F.

Therefore, point D lies on the perpendicular bisector of $\overline{CF}$ by the converse of the perpendicular bisector theorem. Because $EC = EF$, point E also lies on the perpendicular bisector of $\overline{CF}$.

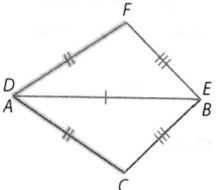

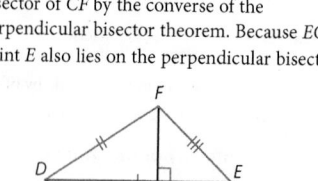

Since point D and point E both lie on the perpendicular bisector of $\overline{CF}$ and there is a unique line through any two points, $\overrightarrow{DE}$ is the perpendicular bisector of $\overline{CF}$. By the definition of reflection, the image of point C must be point F. Therefore, △ABC is mapped onto △DEF by a translation, followed by a rotation, followed by a reflection, and the two triangles are congruent.

(B) Show that △ABC ≅ △PQR.

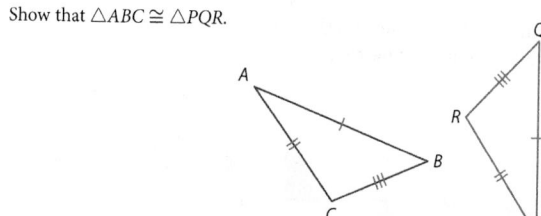

Triangle ABC is transformed by a sequence of rigid motions to form the figure shown below. Identify the sequence of rigid motions. (You will complete the proof on the following page.)

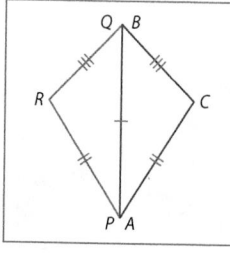

1. **Translation along $\overrightarrow{AP}$**

2. **Rotation about P so that $\overline{PQ}$ and $\overline{AB}$ coincide.**

3. **Reflection across $\overline{PQ}$.**

COLLABORATIVE LEARNING

Peer-to-Peer Activity

Give each student five index cards. Students should prepare a card that shows two labeled triangles for each of the following situations:

• The triangles can be proved congruent by SSS.
• The triangles can be proved congruent by SAS.
• The triangles can be proved congruent by ASA.
• The triangles can be proved noncongruent.
• There is not enough information to determine congruence.

Collect and shuffle them. Divide students into pairs and give each pair ten cards. Have them sort their cards into the above categories.

Complete the explanation by filling in the blanks with the name of a point, line segment, or geometric theorem.

Because $\overline{QR} \cong$ __QC__, point Q is equidistant from __R (or C)__ and __C (or R)__. Therefore,

by the converse of the __Perpendicular Bisector__ Theorem, point Q lies on the

__perpendicular bisector__ of $\overline{RC}$. Similarly, $\overline{PR} \cong$ __PC__. So point __P__ lies on

the perpendicular bisector of __RC__. Because two points determine a line, the line $\overleftrightarrow{PQ}$ is

the __perpendicular bisector of $\overline{RC}$__.

By the definition of reflection, the image of point C must be point __R__. Therefore,

$\triangle ABC \cong \triangle PQR$ because $\triangle ABC$ is mapped to __$\triangle PQR$__ by a translation, a rotation,

and a __reflection__.

Reflect

3. Can you conclude that two triangles are congruent if two pairs of corresponding sides are congruent? Explain your reasoning and include an example.

No; you need a third piece of information to ensure a rigid motion maps

one triangle to the other, such as congruent included angles or another

pair of congruent sides.

Your Turn

4. Use rigid motions and the converse of the perpendicular bisector theorem to explain why $\triangle ABC \cong \triangle ADC$.

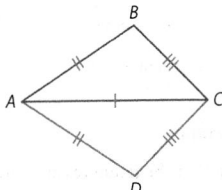

$\overline{AB} \cong \overline{AD}$ and $\overline{CB} \cong \overline{CD}$, so A is equidistant from B and D, and C is equidistant from B and D. By the converse of the Perpendicular Bisector Theorem, $\overleftrightarrow{AC}$ is the perpendicular bisector of $\overline{BD}$. By the definition of a reflection, point D is the image of point B reflected across $\overline{AC}$. The reflection also maps $\overline{AC}$ onto $\overline{AC}$, so $\triangle ABC \cong \triangle ADC$.

DIFFERENTIATE INSTRUCTION

Manipulatives

Have students create a triangle and a quadrilateral using strips of construction paper or tagboard and brass fasteners. Then have students attempt to change the angles in each without bending the strips of paper. Students should notice that the triangle always remains the same but that they can create many different quadrilaterals. Discuss how this activity illustrates the Side-Side-Side Triangle Congruence Theorem.

EXPLAIN 2

Proving Triangles Are Congruent Using SSS Triangle Congruence

INTEGRATE MATHEMATICAL PRACTICES
Focus on Math Connections

MP.1 Although the example emphasizes the SSS Triangle Congruence Theorem, it is important for students to keep in mind that the triangles are congruent because one can be mapped onto the other by one or more rigid motions. Maintain this connection by asking which segments of one triangle map onto certain segments of another triangle.

QUESTIONING STRATEGIES

? When do you use the SSS Triangle Congruence Theorem instead of the ASA or SAS Triangle Congruence Theorems to determine whether two triangles are congruent? When you know three pairs of corresponding congruent sides and no pairs of corresponding congruent angles, you cannot use a theorem that involves an angle.

LANGUAGE SUPPORT [EL]

Have students work in small groups. Have them complete a chart like the following, highlighting the sides and angles that are congruent in each pair of triangles.

Triangle Congruence Theorems		
Theorem	Definition	Picture

Explain 2 **Proving Triangles Are Congruent Using SSS Triangle Congruence**

You can apply the SSS Triangle Congruence Theorem to confirm that triangles are congruent. Remember, if any one pair of corresponding parts of two triangles is not congruent, then the triangles are not congruent.

Example 2 Prove that the triangles are congruent or explain why they are not congruent.

(A) $AB = DE = 1.7$ m, so $\overline{AB} \cong \overline{DE}$.

$BC = EF = 2.4$ m, so $\overline{BC} \cong \overline{EF}$.

$AC = DF = 2.3$ m, so $\overline{AC} \cong \overline{DF}$.

The three sides of $\triangle ABC$ are congruent to the three sides of $\triangle DEF$.

$\triangle ABC \cong \triangle DEF$ by the SSS Triangle Congruence Theorem.

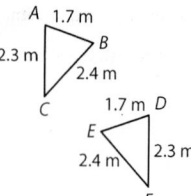

(B) $DE = \underline{FG} = 20$ cm, so $\underline{\overline{DE} \cong \overline{FG}}$.

$DH = \underline{FH} = 12$ cm, so $\underline{\overline{DH} \cong \overline{FH}}$.

$EH = \underline{GH} = 24$ cm, so $\underline{\overline{EH} \cong \overline{GH}}$.

The three sides of $\triangle DEH$ are congruent to the three sides of $\underline{\triangle FGH}$, so the two triangles are congruent by $\underline{\text{the SSS Triangle Congruence Theorem}}$.

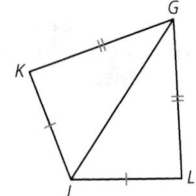

Your Turn

Prove that the triangles are congruent or explain why they are not congruent.

5.

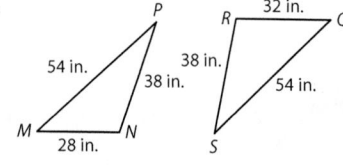

The corresponding sides $\overline{MN}$ and $\overline{QR}$ are not congruent. Therefore, the triangles are not congruent.

6.

It is given that $\overline{GK} \cong \overline{GL}$ and $\overline{JK} \cong \overline{JL}$, and $\overline{GJ} \cong \overline{GJ}$ by the Reflexive Property.

LANGUAGE SUPPORT [EL]

Connect Context

The phrase *Given Three Side Lengths* in the title of the Explore section may confuse some English Learners. Explain that it indicates that you will be constructing triangles when you are given the lengths of the sides. Remind students that in math, they are often given partial information to help solve a problem, and that the information is called a *given*.

Explain 3 — Applying Triangle Congruence

You can use the SSS Triangle Congruence Theorem and other triangle congruence theorems to solve many real-world problems that involve congruent triangles.

Example 3 Find the value of x for which you can show the triangles are congruent.

(A) Lexi bought matching triangular pendants for herself and her mom in the shapes shown. For what value of x can you use a triangle congruence theorem to show that the pendants are congruent? Which triangle congruence theorem can you use? Explain.

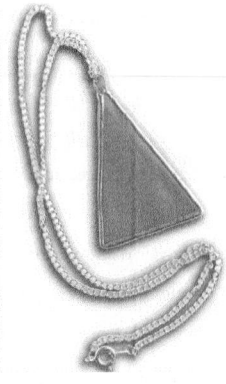

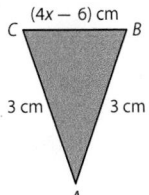 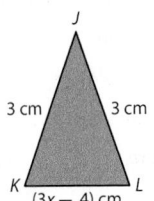

$\overline{AB} \cong \overline{JK}$ and $\overline{AC} \cong \overline{JL}$, because they have the same measure. So, if $\overline{BC} \cong \overline{KL}$, then $\triangle ABC \cong \triangle JKL$ by the SSS Triangle Congruence Theorem. Write an equation setting the lengths equal and solve for x. $4x - 6 = 3x - 4$; $x = 2$

(B) Adeline made a design using triangular tiles as shown. For what value of x can you use a triangle congruence theorem to show that the tiles are congruent? Which triangle congruence theorem can you use? Explain.

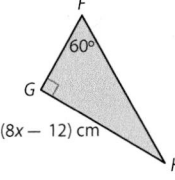 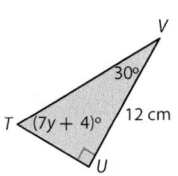

Notice that $\overline{PQ} \cong \overline{MN}$ and $\underline{\overline{PR}} \cong \overline{MO}$, because they have the same measure.

If $\overline{NO} \cong \overline{QR}$, then $\triangle MNO \cong \underline{\triangle PQR}$ by the $\underline{SSS}$ Triangle Congruence Theorem.

Write an equation setting the lengths equal and solve for x.

$3x - 11 = 4$, $3x = 15$, $x = 5$

Your Turn

7. Craig made a mobile using geometric shapes including triangles shaped as shown. For what value of x and y can you use a triangle congruence theorem to show that the triangles are congruent? Which triangle congruence theorem can you use? Explain.

$m\angle H = 30°$ by the Triangle Sum Theorem, so $\angle H \cong \angle V$. $\angle G \cong \angle U$, they are right angles. If $\overline{GH} \cong \overline{UV}$, then $\triangle FGH \cong \triangle TUV$ by the ASA. $x = 3$; $y = 8$

EXPLAIN 3

Applying Triangle Congruence

AVOID COMMON ERRORS

Because students are concentrating on sides when using the SSS Triangle Congruence Theorem, they may not write corresponding angles in the correct order in the congruence statement. Discuss methods they can use to make sure they get the order right.

QUESTIONING STRATEGIES

? How do you know whether angles in one triangle are congruent to the angles in the other triangle? You know the triangles are congruent by SSS, so you know that corresponding angles are also congruent because of CPCTC.

CONNECT VOCABULARY **EL**

Have students collaboratively write a definition for a triangle, providing supports. For example: "A triangle is a _____, It has _____ sides. It has 3 _____. A right triangle has a _____."

ELABORATE

QUESTIONING STRATEGIES

? Two triangles appear to be congruent. You know that three pairs of corresponding parts are congruent, but you have no information about the other corresponding parts. How can you determine whether the triangles really are congruent? Sample answer: If the congruent parts are two pairs of corresponding angles and the included side, or two pairs of corresponding sides and the included angle, you can use the ASA or SAS Triangle Congruence Theorem. If the congruent parts are three pairs of corresponding sides, you can use the SSS Triangle Congruence Theorem. Otherwise, check whether there is a sequence of rigid motions that map one triangle onto the other.

SUMMARIZE THE LESSON

? When do you use the SSS Triangle Congruence Theorem? What information do you need in order to use this theorem? You use the SSS Triangle Congruence Theorem to prove that two triangles are congruent by using three pairs of congruent sides. You need to know that all three pairs of corresponding sides are congruent to use it.

💬 Elaborate

8. An isosceles triangle has two sides of equal length. If we ask everyone in class to construct an isosceles triangle that has one side of length 8 cm and another side of length 12 cm, how many sets of congruent triangles might the class make?

   The class could make at most 2 sets of congruent triangles. One set would have sides of length 8 cm, 8 cm, and 12 cm. The second set would have sides of length 12 cm, 12 cm, and 8 cm.

9. **Essential Question Check-In** How do you explain the SSS Triangle Congruence Theorem?

   Possible answer: Two triangles are congruent if a series of rigid motion transformations maps one triangle onto the other. For two triangles that have pairs of congruent sides, begin by translating and then rotating one triangle so that it shares one side with the other triangle. Then apply the converse of the Perpendicular Bisector Theorem to show that a reflection completes the mapping.

⭐ Evaluate: Homework and Practice

- Online Homework
- Hints and Help
- Extra Practice

Use a compass and a straightedge to complete the drawing of △DEF so that it is congruent to △ABC.

1.
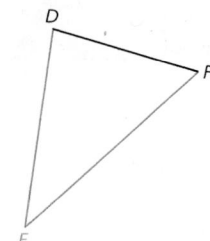

On a separate piece of paper, use a compass and a ruler to construct two congruent triangles with the given side lengths. Label the lengths of the sides.

2. 3 in., 3.5 in., 4 in.

3. 3 cm, 11 cm, 12 cm

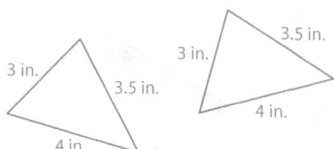

Identify a sequence of rigid motions that maps one side of △ABC onto one side of △DEF.

4.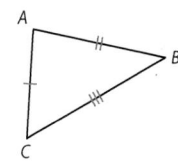

Possible answer: A translation along $\vec{CF}$, and then a clockwise rotation about F so that $\overline{CB}$ coincides with $\overline{FE}$.

5.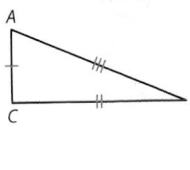

Possible answer: A translation along $\vec{AD}$, and then a counterclockwise rotation about D so that $\overline{AB}$ coincides with $\overline{DE}$.

6.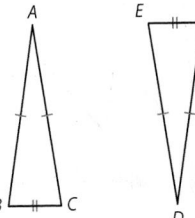

Possible answer: A translation along $\vec{AD}$, and then a clockwise rotation about D so that $\overline{AB}$ coincides with $\overline{DE}$.

7.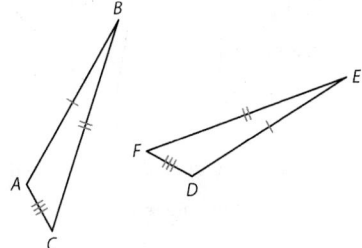

Possible answer: A translation along $\vec{CF}$, and then a counterclockwise rotation about F so that $\overline{CA}$ coincides with $\overline{FD}$.

In each figure, identify the perpendicular bisector and the line segment it bisects, and explain how to use the information to show that the two triangles are congruent.

8.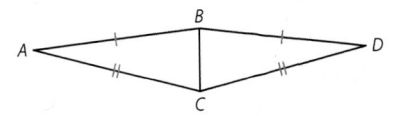

$\overleftrightarrow{BC}$ is the perpendicular bisector of $\overline{AD}$. This shows that A maps to D by a reflection across $\overleftrightarrow{BC}$.

9.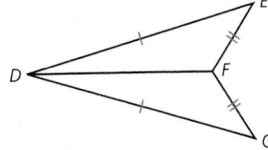

$\overleftrightarrow{DF}$ is the perpendicular bisector of $\overline{EG}$. This shows that E maps to G by a reflection across $\overleftrightarrow{DF}$.

© Houghton Mifflin Harcourt Publishing Company

EVALUATE

ASSIGNMENT GUIDE

Concepts and Skills	Practice
Explore Constructing Triangles Given Side Lengths	Exercises 1–3
Example 1 Justifying SSS Triangle Congruence	Exercises 4–9
Example 2 Proving Triangles Are Congruent Using SSS Triangle Congruence	Exercises 10–13
Example 3 Applying Triangle Congruence	Exercises 14–20

AVOID COMMON ERRORS

Some students may have trouble applying SSS to adjacent triangles. Adjacent triangles share a side, so you can apply the Reflexive Property to get a pair of congruent sides.

Exercise	Depth of Knowledge (D.O.K.)	COMMON CORE Mathematical Practices
1–3	**2** Skills/Concepts	**MP.4** Modeling
4–9	**2** Skills/Concepts	**MP.1** Problem Solving
10–13	**2** Skills/Concepts	**MP.2** Reasoning
14–20	**3** Strategic Thinking	**MP.1** Problem Solving
21–27	**2** Skills/Concepts	**MP.3** Logic

SSS Triangle Congruence   **262**

Introduce the word *criterion* and its plural, *criteria*. Ask students if they can define *criterion* and give an example of its use. For instance, you might discuss a college's criteria for accepting students (a completed application, a minimum grade-point average, a minimum SAT score, and so on). Tell students that they have developed three criteria for determining whether two triangles are congruent, the ASA, SAS, and SSS Triangle Congruence Theorems. Discuss how they can determine whether two given triangles meet any of these criteria.

Prove that the triangles are congruent or explain why this is not possible.

10.
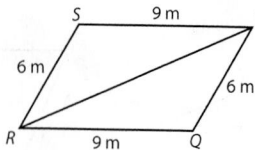

11.
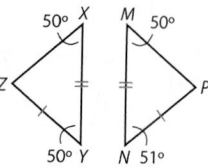

Congruent, by SSS congruence; $\overline{RS} \cong \overline{TQ}$ because they have the same measure, $\overline{RT} \cong \overline{RT}$ by the reflexive property, and $\overline{ST} \cong \overline{QR}$ because they have the same measure.

Not congruent, because only one triangle has an interior angle of 51° so there is no rigid motion that will map one to the other.

12.
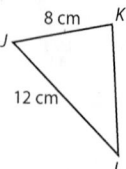

13.
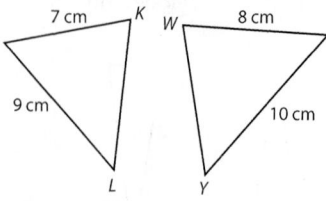

Possibly congruent, depending on the lengths of the unlabeled sides.

Not congruent. The diagrams show a total of 4 different side lengths, but two congruent triangles have only 3 different side lengths.

14. Carol bought two chairs with triangular backs. For what value of *x* can you use a triangle congruence theorem to show that the triangles are congruent? Which triangle congruence theorem can you use? Explain.

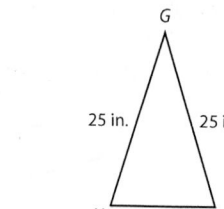
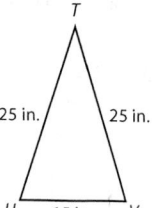

$X = 4$; $\overline{GH} \cong \overline{TU}$ and $\overline{GI} \cong \overline{TV}$, because they have the same measure.

So, if $\overline{HI} \cong \overline{UV}$, then $\triangle GHI \cong \triangle TUV$ by the SSS Triangle Congruence Theorem.

15. For what values of *x* and *y* can you use a triangle congruence theorem to show that the triangles are congruent? Which triangle congruence theorem can you use? Explain.

$x = 4$, $y = 4$; $\angle A \cong \angle E$,

$\angle C \cong \angle G$, and $\overline{AC} \cong \overline{EG}$, ASA

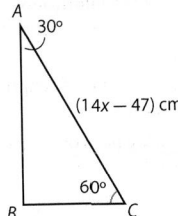 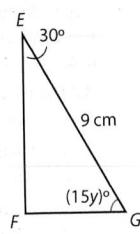

Find all possible solutions for *x* such that △ABC is congruent to △DEF. One or more of the problems may have no solution.

16. △ABC: sides of length 6, 8, and *x*.
△DEF: sides of length 6, 9, and $x - 1$.

$x = 9$

17. △ABC: sides of length 3, $x + 1$, and 14.
△DEF: sides of length 13, $x - 9$, and $2x - 6$

no solution

18. △ABC: sides of length 17, 17, and $2x + 1$.
△DEF: sides of length 17, 17, and $3x - 9$

$x = 10$

19. △ABC: sides of length 19, 25, and $5x - 2$.
△DEF: sides of length 25, 28, and $4 - y$

$x = 6$, $y = -15$

20. △ABC: sides of length 8, $x - y$, and $x + y$
△DEF: sides of length 8, 15, and 17

$x = 16$, $y = 1$; $x = 16$, $y = -1$

21. △ABC: sides of length 9, *x*, and $2x - y$
△DEF: sides of length 8, 9, and $2y - x$

Possible solution: $x = 8$, $y = 8$

22. These statements are part of an explanation for the SSS Triangle Congruence Theorem. Write the numbers 1 to 6 to place these strategies in a logical order. The statements refer to triangles *ABC* and *DEF* shown here.

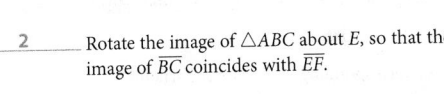 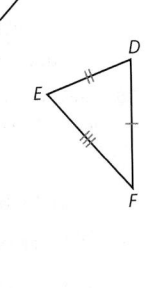

___2___ Rotate the image of △ABC about *E*, so that the image of $\overline{BC}$ coincides with $\overline{EF}$.

___5___ Apply the definition of reflection to show *D* is the reflection of *A* across $\overrightarrow{EF}$.

___6___ Conclude that △ABC ≅ △DEF because a sequence of rigid motions maps one triangle onto the other.

___1___ Translate △ABC along $\overrightarrow{BE}$.

___4___ Define $\overrightarrow{EF}$ as the perpendicular bisector of the line connecting *D* and the image of *A*.

___3___ Identify *E*, and then *F*, as equidistant from *D* and the image of *A*.

Students may find it useful to use geometry software to model exercises they are struggling with.

23. Determine whether the given information is sufficient to guarantee that two triangles are congruent. Select the correct answer for each lettered part.

A. The triangles have three pairs of congruent corresponding angles.

○ sufficient   ● not sufficient

B. The triangles have three pairs of congruent corresponding sides.

● sufficient   ○ not sufficient

C. The triangles have two pairs of congruent corresponding sides and one pair of congruent corresponding angles.

○ sufficient   ● not sufficient

D. The triangles have two pairs of congruent corresponding angles and one pair of congruent corresponding sides.

● sufficient   ○ not sufficient

E. Two angles and the included side of one triangle are congruent to two angles and the included side of the other triangle.

● sufficient   ○ not sufficient

F. Two sides and the included angle of one triangle are congruent to two sides and the included angle of the other triangle.

● sufficient   ○ not sufficient

A. the triangles have the same shape but not necessarily the same size.

B. SSS Triangle Congruence Theorem

C. These conditions do not produce a unique triangle.

D. The Triangle Sum Theorem will show that the third pair of angles is congruent, so the triangles are congruent by the ASA Triangle Congruence Theorem.

E. ASA Triangle Congruence Theorem

F. SAS Triangle Congruence Theorem

24. Make a Conjecture Does a version of SSS congruence apply to quadrilaterals? Provide an example to support your answer.

No; Possible example: a variety of non-congruent rhombuses, including a square, may have 4 sides of the same length.

25. Are two triangles congruent if all pairs of corresponding angles are congruent? Support your answer with an example.

No; At least one pair of sides must be congruent. For example, two triangles that have three 60 degree angles may not have at least one pair of congruent corresponding sides, such as a triangle with side lengths of 4 inches and another triangle with side lengths of 8 inches.

26. Explain the Error Ava wants to know the distance JK across a pond. She locates points as shown. She says that the distance across the pond must be 160 ft by the SSS Triangle Congruence Theorem. Explain her error.

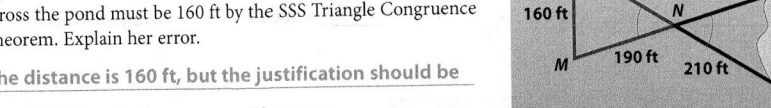

The distance is 160 ft, but the justification should be

the SAS Triangle Congruence Theorem.

27. Analyze Relationships Write a proof.

Given: $\angle BFC \cong \angle ECF$, $\angle BCF \cong \angle EFC$

$\overline{AB} \cong \overline{DE}$, $\overline{AF} \cong \overline{DC}$

Prove: $\triangle ABF \cong \triangle DEC$

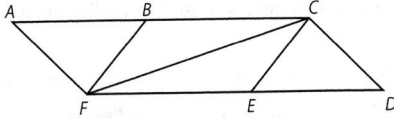

Statements	Reasons
1. $\angle BFC \cong \angle ECF$, $\angle BCF \cong \angle EFC$	1. Given
2. $\overline{FC} \cong \overline{FC}$	2. Reflexive Property of Congruence
3. $\triangle BFC \cong \triangle ECF$	3. ASA Triangle Congruence Theorem
4. $\overline{FB} \cong \overline{CE}$	4. CPCTC
5. $\overline{AB} \cong \overline{DE}$, $\overline{AF} \cong \overline{DC}$	5. Given
6. $\triangle ABF \cong \triangle DEC$	6. SSS Triangle Congruence Theorem

Lesson Performance Task

Mike and Michelle each hope to get a contract with the city to build benches for commuters to sit on while waiting for buses. The benches must be stable so that they don't collapse, and they must be attractive. Their designs are shown. Judge the two benches on stability and attractiveness. Explain your reasoning.

Mike   Michelle

Answers will vary. While Mike's bench will probably be chosen as the more attractive, students should note that Michelle's is more stable. There are many quadrilaterals with the same side lengths as Mike's bench. But, by the SSS Congruence Theorem, the triangles in Michelle's design cannot change shape.

© Houghton Mifflin Harcourt Publishing Company

EXTENSION ACTIVITY

Have students construct models of Mike and Michelle's benches from sturdy pieces of cardboard or photo-print paper cut into long, narrow strips and attached at the corners with brads. Students can explore further by making other polygons, checking their stability, and explaining why, for example, there is no SSSSS Pentagon Congruence Theorem. A 5-sided polygon is not stable. This means that there are many different shapes that can be constructed from the same 5 sides of a pentagon.

INTEGRATE MATHEMATICAL PRACTICES

Focus on Reasoning

MP.2 Ask students to consider the changes in Mike's bench if it were to transform from the original shape to complete collapse. Which properties of the bench would change and how would they change? Which properties would not change? Sample answer: Change: During collapse, the area inside the parallelogram would decrease continually; the measures of the angles would change, with the measures of one pair of opposite angles increasing continually and the measures of the other pair decreasing continually.

Not change: The lengths of the sides and the perimeter of the parallelogram would not change.

AVOID COMMON ERRORS

Students may argue that Mike's bench may be solidly constructed with screws, nails, and glue, so that it would not collapse. Stress that the bench is a real-world object introduced here to model an abstract geometrical principle, and that it is not a perfect model. The important conclusion to draw is the one relating to quadrilaterals, not to benches.

Scoring Rubric

2 points: Student correctly solves the problem and explains his/her reasoning.

1 point: Student shows good understanding of the problem but does not fully solve or explain his/her reasoning.

0 points: Student does not demonstrate understanding of the problem.

SSS Triangle Congruence   **266**

Study Guide Review

ASSESSMENT AND INTERVENTION

Assign or customize module reviews.

MODULE PERFORMANCE TASK

COMMON CORE

Mathematical Practices: MP.1, MP.2, MP.3, MP.4, MP.6
G-SRT.B.5, G-MG.A.1

SUPPORTING STUDENT REASONING

Students should begin this problem by focusing on the information they will need. Here are some issues they might bring up.

- **Whether the triangles are congruent:** Students can use the photo and measuring tools to conclude the triangles are congruent by the SSS Congruence Criteria.

- **How to find the length of one base of a triangle:** Students can estimate the length of the base as about 3 car lengths, or 50 ft.

- **How to determine the number of triangles in the trusses that fit between two towers:** Students can divide the distance between the towers (4200 ft) by 50 (the base) to get 84 triangles that are "vertical" and then another 84 triangles that are "inverted" to get a total of 168 triangles.

Essential Question: How can you use triangle congruence criteria to solve real-world problems?

KEY EXAMPLE   *(Lesson 5.1)*

Triangle $\triangle ABC$ is congruent to $\triangle DEF$. Given that $AB = 7$ and $DE = 5y - 3$, find y.

$\overline{AB} \cong \overline{DE}$	Corresponding parts of congruent triangles are congruent.
$AB = DE$	Definition of congruent sides
$5y - 3 = 7$	Write the equation.
$5y = 10$	Add 3 to each side.
$y = 2$	Divide each side by 5.

KEY EXAMPLE   *(Lesson 5.2)*

Given: $\overline{AB} \cong \overline{BC} \cong \overline{CD} \cong \overline{DA}$

$m\angle DAB = m\angle ABC = m\angle BCD$
$= m\angle ADC = 90°$

$\angle EDC \cong \angle ECD$

Prove: E is the midpoint of $\overline{AB}$.

$m\angle DAB = m\angle ABC$	Given.
$\angle DAB \cong \angle ABC$	Definition of congruent angles.
$\angle EDC \cong \angle ECD$	Given
$m\angle ADC = m\angle BCD$	Given
$m\angle ADC - m\angle EDC = m\angle BCD - m\angle ECD$	Subtraction property of equality.
$\angle ADE \cong \angle BCE$	
$\overline{AD} \cong \overline{BC}$	Given.
$\triangle ADE \cong \triangle BCE$	ASA Triangle Congruence Theorem.
$AE = EB$	CPCT

Therefore, E is the midpoint of $\overline{AB}$ by the definition of midpoint.

KEY EXAMPLE   *(Lesson 5.3)*

Determine whether the triangles are congruent. Explain your reasoning.

It is given that $\overline{AB} \cong \overline{AD}$ and $\angle BAC \cong \angle DAC$. By the reflexive property of congruence, $\overline{AC} \cong \overline{AC}$. Since two sides and an included angle of each triangle are congruent, $\triangle BAC \cong \triangle DAC$ by the SAS Triangle Congruence Theorem.

SCAFFOLDING SUPPORT

- To gain a sense of the scale of the photo, suggest that students place a piece of paper below one of the cars, mark its length on the paper, and then compare the length with the dimensions of a triangle beneath the roadway. Since the base of each triangle measures about 3 car lengths and an average car measures about 16 feet in length, students may wish to use the convenient conversion factor "triangle base = 50 feet" in their calculations.

- Use the following reference for other information about the bridge. http://goldengatebridge.org/research/school.php

EXERCISES

Solve for y given each set of constraints. *(Lesson 5.1)*

1. Given $\triangle PQR \cong \triangle DEF$, $PQ = 15$, $QR = 10$, $RP = 8$, and $EF = 6y + 4$. <u>   1   </u>

2. Given $\triangle PQR \cong \triangle ABC$, $m\angle P = 60°$, $m\angle Q = 40°$, and $m\angle C = (7y + 10)°$. <u>   10   </u>

Determine whether the triangles are congruent. Explain your reasoning. *(Lesson 5.3)*

The measure of angle QRS cannot be 35 degrees, so the triangles are not congruent.

3.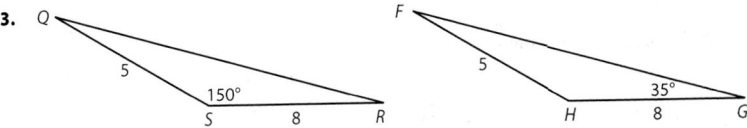

4. Barbara and Sherwin want to use the SSS Triangle Congruence Theorem to see if their triangular slices of watermelon are congruent. They each measure two sides of their slices. Barbara measures sides of lengths 7 inches and 6 inches, while Sherwin measures sides of lengths 8 inches and 5 inches. Do they need to measure the third sides of their slices to determine whether they are congruent? If so, what must the side lengths be for the slices to be congruent? Explain. *(Lesson 5.4)*

No; there is no way for the triangles to have 3 congruent sides.

MODULE PERFORMANCE TASK

Golden Gate Triangles

The Golden Gate Bridge in San Francisco is famous worldwide. The suspension bridge spans the Golden Gate strait with suspension cables attached to two towers that are 4200 feet apart. The bridge also uses trusses, support structures formed by triangles, to help support the weight of the towers and the rest of the bridge.

Use visual evidence from the photo to estimate how many isosceles triangles can be found between the two towers.

Use your own paper to complete the task. Be sure to write down all your data and assumptions. Then use graphs, numbers, words, or algebra to explain how you reached your conclusion.

DISCUSSION OPPORTUNITIES

- Would it be reasonable to assume that all triangles used to construct the trusses for the bridge are congruent?

- Is the distance between two towers of the bridge enough information to find the entire length of the bridge? If not, what additional information is needed?

SAMPLE SOLUTION

It appears that there are three types of triangles supporting the roadway. There are isosceles triangles with their vertices at the top and inverted versions of the isosceles triangles with their vertices at the bottom. I estimated that the corresponding sides of these triangles are congruent, so the equilateral triangles are all congruent by the SSS Congruence Theorem.

There are also two right triangles in each isosceles triangle, formed by an altitude constructed from the vertex angle to the base. The right triangles, too, are congruent by SSS.

By comparing the sides of the triangles with the lengths of the cars on the bridge, I estimated that the bases of the isosceles triangles are about 50 feet long. That means that there are about $4200 \div 50 = 84$ inverted triangles between the towers. There are an equal number of isosceles triangles with their bases at the bottom, for a total of about 168 isosceles triangles. Since each isosceles triangle contains two right triangles, the total number of right triangles is about $2 \times 168 = 336$ right triangles.

Assessment Rubric

2 points: Student correctly solves the problem and explains his/her reasoning.

1 point: Student shows good understanding of the problem but does not fully solve or explain.

0 points: Student does not demonstrate understanding of the problem.

Ready to Go On?

ASSESS MASTERY

Use the assessment on this page to determine if students have mastered the concepts and standards covered in this module.

ASSESSMENT AND INTERVENTION

Access Ready to Go On? assessment online, and receive instant scoring, feedback, and customized intervention or enrichment.

ADDITIONAL RESOURCES

Response to Intervention Resources

- Reteach Worksheets

Differentiated Instruction Resources

- Reading Strategies **EL**
- Success for English Learners **EL**
- Challenge Worksheets

Assessment Resources

- Leveled Module Quizzes

5.1–5.4 Triangle Congruence Criteria

- Online Homework
- Hints and Help
- Extra Practice

1. $\triangle ABC \cong \triangle EDF$. Determine the value of x. *(Lesson 5.1)*

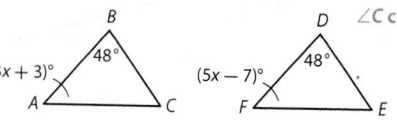

$\angle C$ corresponds to $\angle F$, so $m\angle C = m\angle F = (5x - 7)$

$m\angle A + m\angle B + m\angle C = 180°$

$(3x + 3) + 48 + (5x - 7) = 180$

$8x + 44 = 180$

$8x = 136$

$x = 17$

2. Plot point F so that $\triangle ABC \cong \triangle FGH$. Identify a sequence of rigid motions that maps $\triangle ABC$ onto $\triangle FGH$ and use a theorem to explain why the triangles are congruent. *(Lessons 5.3, 5.4)*

Point *F* is plotted at $(5, 2)$. Rigid motions answers may vary. Sample: Translate $\triangle ABC$ so that point *B* maps to point *G* and C maps to $(-2, 0)$. Then reflect across the *y*-axis. By the Distance Formula, side lengths are as follows:

$AB = \sqrt{(-4-1)^2 + (-1-(-2))^2} = \sqrt{(-5)^2 + 1^2} = \sqrt{26}$,

$FG = \sqrt{(5-0)^2 + (2-1)^2} = \sqrt{5^2 + 1^2} = \sqrt{26}$,

$BC = \sqrt{(1-(-1))^2 + (-2-(-3))^2} = \sqrt{2^2 + 1^2} = \sqrt{5}$,

$GH = \sqrt{(2-0)^2 + (0-1)^2} = \sqrt{2^2 + 1^2} = \sqrt{5}$,

$HF = \sqrt{(2-5)^2 + (0-2)^2} = \sqrt{(-3)^2 + (-2)^2} = \sqrt{13}$,

$CA = \sqrt{(-1-(-4))^2 + (-3-(-1))^2} = \sqrt{3^2 + (-2)^2} = \sqrt{13}$

$\overline{AB} \cong \overline{FG}, \overline{BC} \cong \overline{GH}$, and $\overline{CA} \cong \overline{HF}$.

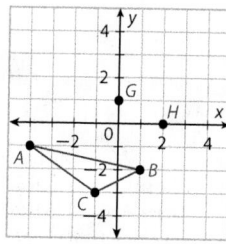

By the SSS Triangle Congruence Theorem, $\triangle ABC \cong \triangle FGH$.

ESSENTIAL QUESTION

3. How can you tell that triangles are congruent without knowing the lengths of all sides and the measures of all angles?

Answers may vary. Sample: The ASA Congruence Theorem, SAS Congruence Theorem, and SSS Congruence Theorems can all be used.

COMMON CORE **Common Core Standards**

Lesson	Items	Content Standards	Mathematical Practices
5.1	1	G-CO.B.7	MP.1
5.1, 5.4	2	G-CO.B.7, G-CO.B.8	MP.6

MODULE 5
MIXED REVIEW

Assessment Readiness

1. Two triangles, △ABC and △XYZ, are congruent. The measure of angle C, m∠C, is equal to 81°. The measure of angle X, m∠X, is equal to 56°.

   Select Yes or No for A–C.

   A. Does m∠A = 99°? ○ Yes ● No

   B. Does m∠B = 43°? ● Yes ○ No

   C. Are ∠A and ∠Z congruent? ○ Yes ● No

2. Look at the triangles to the right. Choose True or False for each of the statements about them.

   A. A value of x = 16 results in congruent triangles. ○ True ● False

   B. A value of x = 27 results in congruent triangles. ● True ○ False

   C. A value of x = 31 does not result in congruent triangles. ● True ○ False

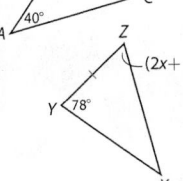

3. Write the equation of one line that is perpendicular to and one line that is parallel to y = 7x + 9.

   Possible Answers: perpendicular: $y = -\frac{1}{7}x - 2$; parallel: $y = 7x - 11$

4. In the figure, segment $\overline{AB}$ is parallel to $\overline{CD}$, $\overline{XY}$ is the perpendicular bisector of $\overline{AB}$, E is the midpoint of $\overline{XY}$. Prove that △AEB ≅ △DEC.

   Answers may vary. Sample:

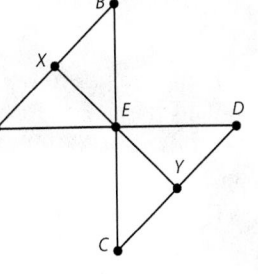

$\overline{XY} \perp \overline{AB}$	Definition of perpendicular bisector
$\overline{XY} \perp \overline{CD}$	In a plane, if a transversal is perpendicular to one of two parallel lines, then it is perpendicular to the other.
∠AXE and ∠DYE are right angles.	Definition of perpendicular lines
∠AXE ≅ ∠DYE	Right angles are congruent.
$\overline{XE} \cong \overline{YE}$	Definition of midpoint
∠AEX ≅ ∠DEY	Vertical Angles Theorem
△AXE ≅ △DYE	ASA Triangle Congruence Theorem
$\overline{AE} \cong \overline{DE}$	CPCTC
∠A ≅ ∠D	Alternate Interior Angles Theorem
∠AEB ≅ ∠DEC	Vertical Angles Theorem
△AEB ≅ △DEC	ASA Triangle Congruence Theorem

© Houghton Mifflin Harcourt Publishing Company

MIXED REVIEW

Assessment Readiness

ASSESSMENT AND INTERVENTION

Assign ready-made or customized practice tests to prepare students for high-stakes tests.

ADDITIONAL RESOURCES

Assessment Resources

• Leveled Module Quizzes: Modified, B

AVOID COMMON ERRORS

Item 2 Some students may be confused by the presence of both the variable *x* and the point label *X* in the same diagram. Remind them that capitalized and lowercase letters have different meanings in mathematical contexts.

Common Core Standards

Lesson	Items	Content Standards	Mathematical Practices
5.1	1	G-SRT.B.5	MP.2
5.1	2	G-CO.B.7	MP.2
4.5	3*	G-GPE.B.5	MP.8
5.2, 1.1	4*	G-CO.C.10	MP.3

* Item integrates mixed review concepts from previous modules or a previous course.

Applications of Triangle Congruence

ESSENTIAL QUESTION:

Answer: Triangle congruence is involved in the analysis and construction of structures such as geodesic domes.

PROFESSIONAL DEVELOPMENT VIDEO

Professional Development Video

Author Juli Dixon models successful teaching practices in an actual high-school classroom.

Professional Development
my.hrw.com

MODULE 6

Applications of Triangle Congruence

Essential Question: How can you use applications of triangle congruence to solve real-world problems?

LESSON 6.1
Justifying Constructions

LESSON 6.2
AAS Triangle Congruence

LESSON 6.3
HL Triangle Congruence

© Houghton Mifflin Harcourt Publishing Company • Image Credit: ©Gunter Marx/Gunter Marx Photography/Corbis

REAL WORLD VIDEO
A geodesic dome encloses the greatest volume of space for a given surface area. Check out how applications of triangles are involved in the design of geodesic domes.

MODULE PERFORMANCE TASK PREVIEW

Geodesic Domes

In this module, you will use a three-dimensional shape called an icosahedron to explore the geometry of a geodesic dome. Let's dive in and find out what triangles have to do with icosahedrons and geodesic domes.

Module 6   271

DIGITAL TEACHER EDITION

Access a full suite of teaching resources when and where you need them:

- Access content online or offline
- Customize lessons to share with your class
- Communicate with your students in real-time
- View student grades and data instantly to target your instruction where it is needed most

PERSONAL MATH TRAINER

Assessment and Intervention

Assign automatically graded homework, quizzes, tests, and intervention activities. Prepare your students with updated, Common Core-aligned practice tests.

Are (YOU) Ready?

Complete these exercises to review the skills you will need for this chapter.

Distance Formulas

Example 1 Find the distance between $(1, -6)$ and $(-1, -2)$.

$$\sqrt{(-1-1)^2 + (-2-(-6))^2}$$ Apply the distance formula.

$$= \sqrt{4 + 16}$$ Simplify each square.

$$= \sqrt{20}$$ Simplify.

Find the distance between the given points.

1. The points $(-1, 2)$ and $(2, -2)$ ___5___

2. The points $(-5, 21)$ and $(0, 19)$ ___$\sqrt{29}$___

Congruent Figures

Example 2 Determine whether the triangles are congruent. Explain your reasoning.

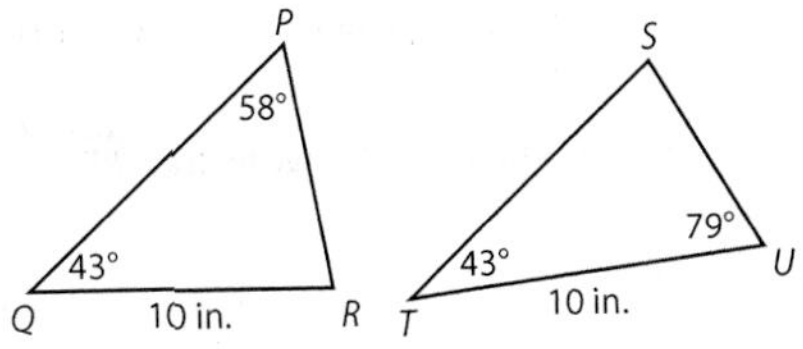

Step 1: Find $m\angle R$.

$$m\angle R + m\angle P + m\angle Q = 180°$$

$$m\angle R + 58° + 43° = 180°$$

$$m\angle R = 79°$$

So, $\triangle QPR \cong \triangle TSU$ by the ASA Triangle Congruence Theorem.

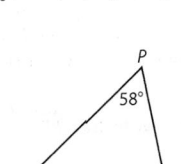
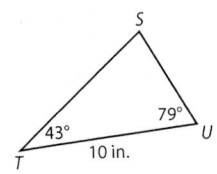

3. Determine whether the triangles are congruent. Explain your reasoning.

   ___$\triangle EHD \cong \triangle GHF$ by the SSS Triangle Congruence Theorem.___

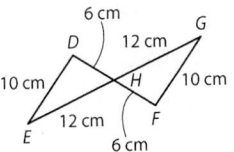

Angle Theorems for Triangles

Example 3 Given $a = 7$ cm and $b = 5$ cm, find the missing length.

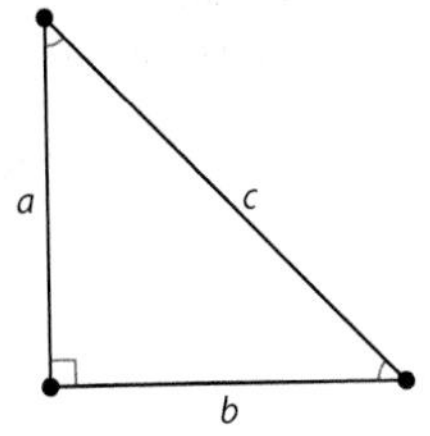

$$a^2 + b^2 = c^2$$ Pythagorean Theorem

$$(7)^2 + (5)^2 = c^2$$ Substitute $a = 7$ and $b = 5$.

$$c = \sqrt{49 + 25}$$ Solve for c.

$$c = \sqrt{74}\text{ cm}$$ Simplify.

Use the given values to find the missing lengths in the figure from the example.

4. $c = 13$ cm and $b = 5$ cm

   $a = $ ___12 cm___

5. $c = 7$ cm and $a = 6$ cm

   $b = $ ___$\sqrt{13}$ cm___

Are You Ready?

ASSESS READINESS

Use the assessment on this page to determine if students need strategic or intensive intervention for the module's prerequisite skills.

ASSESSMENT AND INTERVENTION

RtI Response to Intervention **TIER 1, TIER 2, TIER 3 SKILLS**

Personal Math Trainer will automatically create a standards-based, personalized intervention assignment for your students, targeting each student's individual needs!

ADDITIONAL RESOURCES

See the table below for a full list of intervention resources available for this module.

Response to Intervention Resources also includes:

- Tier 2 Skill Pre-Tests for each Module
- Tier 2 Skill Post-Tests for each skill

Response to Intervention			Differentiated Instruction
Tier 1 Lesson Intervention Worksheets	**Tier 2** Strategic Intervention Skills Intervention Worksheets	**Tier 3** Intensive Intervention Worksheets available online	
Reteach 6.1 Reteach 6.2 Reteach 6.3	3 Angle Theorems for Triangles 7 Congruent Figures 12 Parallel Lines Cut by a Transversal	Building Block Skills 8, 16, 48, 71, 74, 98, 103, 104	Challenge worksheets Extend the Math Lesson Activities in TE

Justifying Constructions

Common Core Math Standards

The student is expected to:

COMMON CORE G-CO.D.12

Make formal geometric constructions with a variety of tools and methods (compass and straightedge, string, reflective devices, paper folding, dynamic geometric software, etc.). Also G-CO.D.13, G-SRT.B.5

Mathematical Practices

COMMON CORE MP.3 Logic

Language Objective

Explain in your own words how to construct a copy of an angle.

ENGAGE

Essential Question: How can you be sure that the result of a construction is valid?

You can use geometric properties to prove that the drawn figure must have the properties of the expected shape.

PREVIEW: LESSON PERFORMANCE TASK

View the Engage section online. Make sure students understand the meaning of *tolerance* in the context of manufacturing. Then preview the Lesson Performance Task.

Name _____ Class _____ Date _____

6.1 Justifying Constructions

Essential Question: How can you be sure that the result of a construction is valid?

Resource Locker

⊘ Explore 1 Using a Reflective Device to Construct a Perpendicular Line

You have constructed a line perpendicular to a given line through a point not on the line using a compass and straightedge. You can also use a reflective device to construct perpendicular lines.

Ⓐ **Step 1** Place the reflective device along line ℓ. Look through the device to locate the image of point P on the opposite side of line ℓ. Draw the image of point P and label it P′.

Step 2 Use a straightedge to draw $\overleftrightarrow{PP'}$.

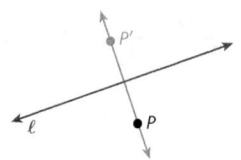

Explain why $\overleftrightarrow{PP'}$ is perpendicular to line ℓ.

By the definition of reflection, line ℓ is the perpendicular bisector of $\overleftrightarrow{PP'}$.

Ⓑ Place the reflective device so that it passes through point Q and is approximately perpendicular to line m. Adjust the angle of the device until the image of line m coincides with line m. Draw a line along the reflective device and label it line n. Explain why line n is perpendicular to line m.

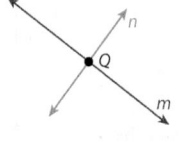
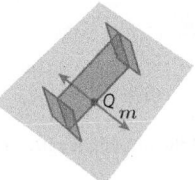

The reflective device is positioned so that for any point A on line m, the image, A′, is also on line m. Since line n is the line of reflection, it must be perpendicular to the line through A and A′, which is line m.

© Houghton Mifflin Harcourt Publishing Company

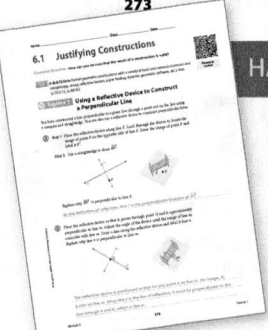

HARDCOVER PAGES 237–244

Turn to these pages to find this lesson in the hardcover student edition.

1. How can you check that the lines you drew are perpendicular to lines ℓ and m?
   Use a protractor to measure the angle formed by $\overrightarrow{PP'}$ and line ℓ, and the angle formed by
   line n and line m. In both cases, the angle should measure 90°.

2. Use the reflective device to draw two points on line ℓ that are reflections of each other. Label the
   points X and X'. What is true about PX and PX'? Why? Use a ruler to check your prediction.
   $PX = PX'$. $\overrightarrow{PP'}$ is the perpendicular bisector of $\overline{XX'}$, and any point on the perpendicular
   bisector of a segment is equidistant from the endpoints of the segment.

3. Describe how to construct a perpendicular bisector of a line segment using paper folding.
   Use a rigid motion to explain why the result is a perpendicular bisector.
   Fold the paper so that one endpoint of the line is mapped to the other endpoint. The fold
   is a reflection, and the crease is the line of reflection. By the definition of reflection, the
   crease is the perpendicular bisector of the segment that connects a point and its image.

⊘ Explore 2   Justifying the Copy of an Angle Construction

You have seen how to construct a copy of an angle, but how do you know that the copy must be
congruent to the original? Recall that to construct a copy of an angle A, you use these steps.

Step 1 Draw a ray with endpoint D.

Step 2 Draw an arc that intersects both rays of $\angle A$. Label the intersections B and C.

Step 3 Draw the same arc on the ray. Label the point of intersection E.

Step 4 Set the compass to the length BC.

Step 5 Place the compass at E and draw a new arc. Label the intersection of the new arc F.
Draw $\overrightarrow{DF}$. $\angle D$ is congruent to $\angle A$.

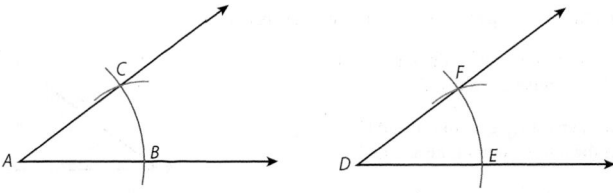

Ⓐ Sketch and name the two triangles that are created when you construct a copy of an angle.

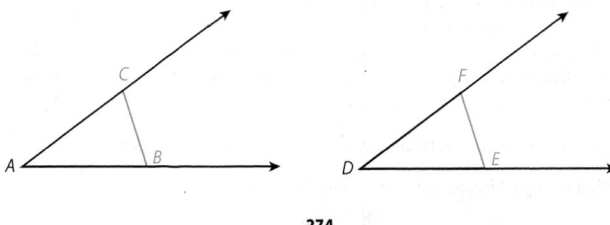

EXPLORE 1

Using a Reflective Device to Construct a Perpendicular Line

INTEGRATE TECHNOLOGY

Students may use geometry software to model the construction of a perpendicular to a given line.

QUESTIONING STRATEGIES

❓ What angle measure could you use to describe a straight line? What angle measures does the construction of a perpendicular line produce? Describe the relationship between the angle measure of the straight line and the angles created by the perpendicular line. 180°; 90°; the perpendicular divides the 180° angle into two equal halves of 90° each.

EXPLORE 2

Justifying the Copy of an Angle Construction

INTEGRATE TECHNOLOGY

Students may use geometry software to model the construction of an angle congruent to a given angle.

Math Background

Compass and straightedge constructions date to ancient Greece. In fact, one of the classic problems of ancient Greek mathematics was the trisection of the angle. That is, using a compass and straightedge, is it possible to construct an angle whose measure is one-third that of an arbitrary given angle? It was not until 1837 that this construction was proven to be impossible. On the other hand, it is a straightforward task to bisect any angle, and students prove the validity of this fundamental construction in this lesson.

? How do you know that the sides of the triangles are congruent? **They were constructed using the same compass setting.**

EXPLAIN 1

Proving the Angle Bisector and Perpendicular Bisector Constructions

AVOID COMMON ERRORS

Some students may use the angles resulting from the bisected angle to prove the triangles are congruent by SAS. Remind these students that they are trying to prove the congruence of those two angles, so they cannot be used in the justification.

QUESTIONING STRATEGIES

? What role does the angle bisector play in proving the two triangles are congruent? **The angle bisector forms a side that is common to both triangles, so it is congruent to itself.**

COMMUNICATE MATH ᴇʟ

Have students work in pairs to write the steps for constructing an angle bisector. The first student does the construction and explains the steps. The second student writes down the steps. The students switch roles and repeat the procedure with parallel line construction.

Ⓑ What segments do you know are congruent? Explain how you know.

$\overline{AB} \cong \overline{DE}$ because the arcs that created these segments have the same radius.

$\overline{BC} \cong \overline{EF}$ because the arcs that created these segments have the same radius.

$\overline{AC} \cong \overline{DF}$ because the arcs that created these segments have the same radius.

Ⓒ Are the triangles congruent? How do you know?

Yes. They are congruent by the SSS Triangle Congruence Theorem.

Reflect

4. **Discussion** Suppose you used a larger compass setting to create $\overline{AB}$ than another student when copying the same angle. Will your copied angles be congruent?
Yes. Even though our triangles *ABC* and *DEF* will not be congruent, our angles *A* and *D* will

be congruent because of the transitive property of congruence.

5. Does the justification above for constructing a copy of an angle work for obtuse angles?
Yes. The construction method is the same, and it will still result in two triangles with three

pairs of congruent corresponding sides. So the two triangles are congruent, and the copy

of the angle will be congruent to the original.

⊘ Explain 1 **Proving the Angle Bisector and Perpendicular Bisector Constructions**

You have constructed angle bisectors and perpendicular bisectors. You now have the tools you need to prove that these compass and straightedge constructions result in the intended figures.

Example 1 Prove two bisector constructions.

Ⓐ You have used the following steps to construct an angle bisector.

Step 1 Draw an arc intersecting the sides of the angle. Label the intersections *B* and *C*.

Step 2 Draw intersecting arcs from *B* and *C*. Label the intersection of the arcs as *D*.

Step 3 Use a straightedge to draw $\overline{AD}$.

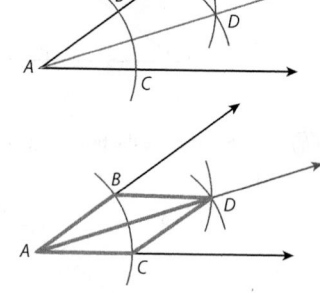

Prove that the construction results in the angle bisector.

The construction results in the triangles *ABD* and *ACD*. Because the same compass setting was used to create them, $\overline{AB} \cong \overline{AC}$ and $\overline{BD} \cong \overline{CD}$. The segment $\overline{AD}$ is congruent to itself by the Reflexive Property of Congruence. So, by the SSS Triangle Congruence Theorem, $\triangle ABD \cong \triangle ACD$.

Corresponding parts of congruent figures are congruent, so $\angle BAD \cong \angle DAC$.

By the definition of angle bisector, $\overrightarrow{AD}$ is the angle bisector of $\angle A$.

COLLABORATIVE LEARNING

Peer-to-Peer Activity

Have students work in pairs and give them the following prompt: "You know how to draw a perpendicular bisector, copy a segment, and copy an angle. How can you use a sequence of these constructions to construct a square?" **Sample answer: You can draw a segment and construct its perpendicular bisector to get a right angle. Copy one of the halves of the original segment on the perpendicular bisector so that you now have two sides of the square. Then copy the right angle and a side length two more times until you have four right angles and four congruent sides.**

(B) You have used the following steps to construct a perpendicular bisector.

Step 1 Draw an arc centered at A.

Step 2 Draw an arc with the same diameter centered at B. Label the intersections C and D.

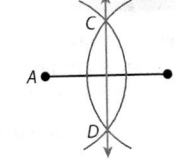

Step 3 Draw $\overline{CD}$.

Prove that the construction results in the perpendicular bisector.

The point C is equidistant from the endpoints of $\overline{AB}$, so by the __Converse of the Perpendicular__

__Bisector__ Theorem, it lies on the __perpendicular bisector__ of $\overline{AB}$. The point D is also equidistant

from the endpoints of $\overline{AB}$, so it also lies on the __perpendicular bisector__ of $\overline{AB}$. Two points

determine a line, so __$\overleftrightarrow{CD}$ is the perpendicular bisector of $\overline{AB}$__.

Reflect

6. In Part B, what can you conclude about the measures of the angles made by the intersection of $\overline{AB}$ and $\overleftrightarrow{CD}$?
   __The four angles are congruent 90° angles.__

7. **Discussion** A classmate claims that in the construction shown in Part B, $\overline{AB}$ is the perpendicular bisector of $\overline{CD}$. Is this true? Justify your answer.
   __The claim is true for the same reason that $\overleftrightarrow{CD}$ is the perpendicular bisector of $\overline{AB}$.__

Your Turn

8. The construction in Part B is also used to construct the midpoint R of $\overline{MN}$. How is the proof of this construction different from the proof of the perpendicular bisector construction in Part B?
   __You need to add an extra step to say that because $\overleftrightarrow{PQ}$ is the__

   __perpedicular bisector of $\overline{MN}$, the point of intersection will be the__

   __midpoint of $\overline{MN}$ by the definition of midpoint.__

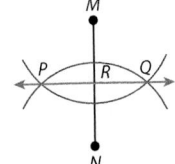

9. How could you combine the constructions in Example 1 to construct a 45° angle?
   __First construct a perpendicular bisector of a segment. This creates 90° angles. Choose one__

   __of the angles to bisect. This will construct two 45° angles.__

© Houghton Mifflin Harcourt Publishing Company

DIFFERENTIATE INSTRUCTION

Critical Thinking

Have students use a protractor to draw a 60° angle. Then challenge them to use compass and straightedge constructions to create angles with the following measures:

30°	120°	90°
15°	45°	105°

After they complete as many as they can, have them use a protractor to check for accuracy.

AVOID COMMON ERRORS

When proving that a construction resulted in a perpendicular bisector, some students may use the Perpendicular Bisector Theorem. Make sure they understand why it is the Converse of the Perpendicular Bisector Theorem that is used.

ELABORATE

CONNECT VOCABULARY EL

Point out to students that the word *converse* comes from the Latin *converses*, which means *to turn around.*

SUMMARIZE THE LESSON

? Why is it important to justify and prove constructions? The construction itself is just a concrete example. Proving the construction ensures that it works for every possible example.

© Houghton Mifflin Harcourt Publishing Company

💬 **Elaborate**

10. Describe how you can construct a line that is parallel to a given line using the construction of a perpendicular to a line.

Construct a perpendicular to the given line. Then construct a perpendicular to the perpendicular. This line is parallel to the given line.

11. Use a straightedge and a piece of string to construct an equilateral triangle that has *AB* as one of its sides. Then explain how you know your construction works. (*Hint*: Consider an arc centered at *A* with radius *AB* and an arc centered at *B* with radius *AB*.)

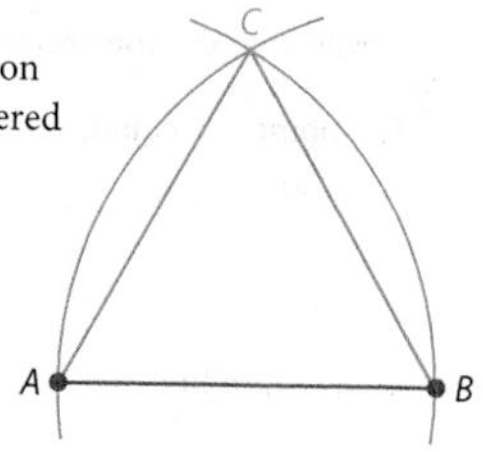

$\overline{AC} \cong \overline{AB}$ since $\overline{AC}$ and $\overline{AB}$ are radii of the same circle.

$\overline{BC} \cong \overline{AB}$, since $\overline{BC}$ and $\overline{AB}$ are radii of the same circle.

So, the three sides of the triangle all have the same length.

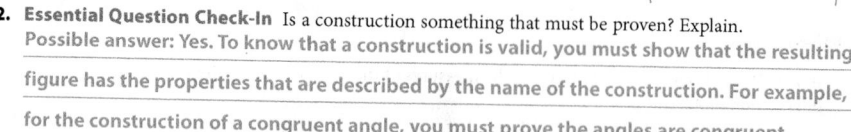

12. **Essential Question Check-In** Is a construction something that must be proven? Explain.

Possible answer: Yes. To know that a construction is valid, you must show that the resulting figure has the properties that are described by the name of the construction. For example, for the construction of a congruent angle, you must prove the angles are congruent.

⭐ **Evaluate: Homework and Practice**

Personal **Math Trainer**
• Online Homework
• Hints and Help
• Extra Practice

1. Julia is given a line ℓ and a point *P* not on line ℓ. She is asked to use a reflective device to construct a line through *P* that is perpendicular to line ℓ. She places the device as shown in the figure. What should she do next to draw the required line?

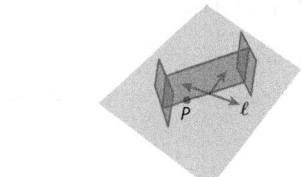

She should adjust the angle of the reflective device until the image of line ℓ coincides with line ℓ. Then she should draw a line along the edge of the reflective device. This is the required line.

2. Describe how to construct a copy of a segment. Explain how you know that the segments are congruent.

Draw a segment longer than the segment to be copied. Set the compass opening to the length of the given segment. Using that compass setting, draw an arc centered at one endpoint of the segment you drew. Mark the intersection to label the copied segment. The segments are congruent because the compass ensures the two segments have the same length.

LANGUAGE SUPPORT EL

Connect Vocabulary

Analyze the parts of the word *bisect* or *bisector* with students. They previously identified the prefix *bi-* as meaning *two.* The root *sect* comes from the word *secare,* which means *to cut.* So, to *bisect* means *to cut into two equal parts.*

Complete the proof of the construction of a segment bisector.

3. **Given:** the construction of the segment bisector of $\overline{AB}$

Prove: $\overleftrightarrow{CD}$ bisects $\overline{AB}$

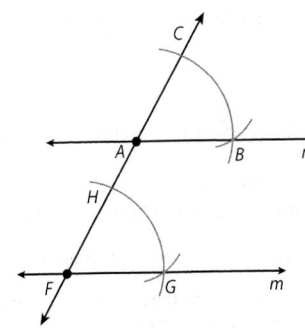

Statements	Reasons
1. $AC = \underline{BC}$ and $AD = \underline{BD}$.	1. Same compass setting used
2. C is on the perpendicular bisector of $\overline{AB}$.	2. Converse of the Perpendicular Bisector Theorem
3. D is on the perpendicular bisector of $\overline{AB}$.	3. Converse of the Perpendicular Bisector Theorem
4. $\overleftrightarrow{CD}$ is the perpendicular bisector of $\overline{AB}$.	4. Through any two points, there is exactly one line.
5. $\overleftrightarrow{CD}$ bisects AB.	5. Definition of perpendicular bisector

4. Complete the proof of the construction of a congruent angle.

Given: the construction of $\angle CAB$ given $\angle HFG$

Prove: $\angle CAB \cong \angle HFG$

Statements	Reasons
1. $FG = FH = \underline{AB} = AC$	1. same compass setting
2. $GH = CB$	2. Same compass setting used
3. $\triangle FGH \cong \triangle ABC$	3. SSS Triangle Congruence Theorem
4. $\angle CAB \cong \angle HFG$	4. CPCTC

ASSIGNMENT GUIDE

Concepts and Skills	Practice
Explore 1 Using a Reflective Device to Construct a Perpendicular Line	Exercise 1
Explore 2 Justifying the Copy of an Angle Construction	Exercises 2–15
Example 1 Proving the Angle Bisector and Perpendicular Bisector Constructions	Exercises 16–18

Exercise	Depth of Knowledge (D.O.K.)	COMMON CORE Mathematical Practices
1	**2** Skills/Concepts	**MP.5** Using Tools
2–18	**2** Skills/Concepts	**MP.6** Precision
19	**3** Strategic Thinking H.O.T.	**MP.1** Problem Solving
20	**3** Strategic Thinking H.O.T.	**MP.6** Precision

Justifying Constructions   **278**

Focus on Communication

MP.3 Model precise mathematical vocabulary when discussing the constructions in the exercises. Using terms such as *intersect*, *arc*, and *congruent*, and naming figures by their correct geometric names help accustom students to communicate using mathematical language.

To construct a line through the given point P, parallel to line ℓ, you use the following steps.

Step 1 Choose a point Q on line ℓ and draw $\overline{QP}$.

Step 2 Construct an angle congruent to $\angle$l at P.

Step 3 Construct the line through the given point, parallel to the line shown.

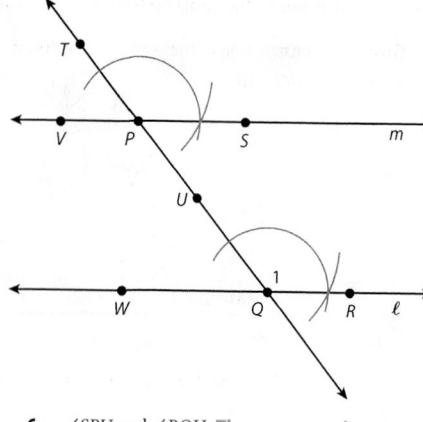

Describe the relationship between the given angles or segments. Justify your answer.

5. $\angle TPS$ and $\angle UQR$ They are congruent; these are the original angle and the angle that was copied.

6. $\angle SPU$ and $\angle RQU$ They are supplementary; same-side interior angles of parallel lines are supplementary.

7. $\angle VPU$ and $\angle UQR$ They are congruent; alternate interior angles of parallel lines are congruent.

8. $\angle TPS$ and $\angle WQU$ They are supplementary; $\angle WQU$ and $\angle UQR$ form a linear pair and are supplementary, and $\angle TPS \cong \angle UQR$, so $\angle TPS$ and $\angle WQU$ are supplementary.

9. $\overline{QU}$ and $\overline{PS}$ They are congruent; radii of congruent circles are congruent.

10. $\overline{QU}$ and $\overline{PT}$ They are congruent; radii of congruent circles are congruent.

11. To construct a line through the given point P, parallel to line ℓ, you use the following steps.

    Step 1 Draw line m through P and intersecting line ℓ.

    Step 2 Construct an angle congruent to $\angle$l at P.

    Step 3 Construct the line through the given point, parallel to the line shown.

    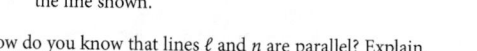

    How do you know that lines ℓ and n are parallel? Explain.

    Line m is a transversal of lines ℓ and n. Angles 1 and 2 are congruent corresponding angles, because angle 2 is a constructed copy of angle 1. By the Converse of the Corresponding Angles Postulate, $\ell \parallel n$.

12. Construct an angle whose measure is $\frac{1}{4}$ the measure of $\angle Z$. Justify the construction.

    Bisect $\angle Z$ and then bisect one of the smaller angles.
    $$\frac{1}{2} \cdot \left(\frac{1}{2} \cdot m\angle Z\right) = \frac{1}{4} \cdot m\angle Z.$$

    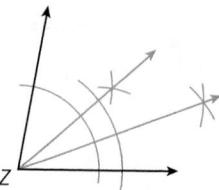

In Exercises 13 and 14, use the diagram shown. The diagram shows the result of constructing a copy of an angle adjacent to one of the rays of the original angle. Assume the pattern continues.

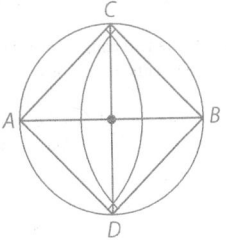

13. If it takes 10 more copies of the angle for the last angle to overlap the first ray (the horizontal ray), what is the measure of each angle?

There will be total of 12 copies of the angle.

The sum of the measures will be 360°.

$\frac{360}{12} = 30$; The measure of each angle is 30°.

14. If it takes 8 more copies of the angle for the last angle to overlap the first ray (the horizontal ray), what is the measure of each angle?

There will be total of 10 copies of the angle.

The sum of the measures will be 360°.

$\frac{360}{10} = 30$; The measure of each angle is 36°.

15. Sonia draws a segment on a piece of paper. She wants to find three points that are equidistant from the endpoints of the segment. Explain how she can use paper folding to help her locate the three points.

Fold the paper so that the segment's endpoints coincide. The fold line is the segment's perpendicular bisector, so any three points on the fold line will be equidistant from the endpoints.

In Exercises 16–18, a polygon is inscribed in a circle if all of the polygon's vertices lie on the circle.

16. Follow the given steps to construct a square inscribed in a circle.

Use your compass to draw a circle. Mark the center.

Draw a diameter, $\overline{AB}$, using a straightedge.

Construct the perpendicular bisector of $\overline{AB}$. Label the points where the perpendicular bisector intersects the circle as C and D.

Use the straightedge to draw $\overline{AC}$, $\overline{CB}$, $\overline{BD}$, and $\overline{DA}$.

17. Suppose you are given a piece of tracing paper with a circle on it and you do not have a compass. How can you use paper folding to inscribe a square in the circle?

Fold the circle so that one half coincides with the other. The crease is a diameter. Then fold the diameter onto itself to make another crease that is the perpendicular bisector of the diameter. The two creases determine the four vertices of the square on the circle.

Have students think about the steps used with each construction. Ask them to reflect on how they remember how to do each one. In small groups, have students discuss strategies for remembering the steps. Then share each group's best strategies with the class.

Some students may use a ruler or protractor to make measurements during their constructions. Reinforce that measuring tools should be used only *after* a construction to verify the results. Measurements should not be made *during* a construction.

JOURNAL

Have students explain the importance of proving constructions.

18. Follow the given steps to construct a regular hexagon inscribed in a circle.

Tie a pencil to one end of the string.

Mark a point O on your paper. Place the string on point O and hold it down with your finger. Pull the string taut and draw a circle. Mark and label a point A.

Hold the point on the string that you placed on point O, and move it to point A. Pull the string taut and draw an arc that intersects the circle. Label the point as B.

Hold the point on the string that you placed on point A, and move it to point B. Draw an arc to locate point C on the circle. Repeat to locate points D, E, and F. Use your straightedge to draw ABCDEF.

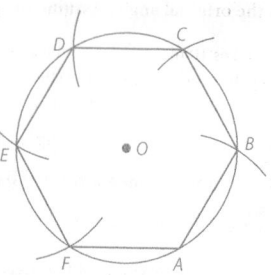

H.O.T. Focus on Higher Order Thinking

19. Your teacher constructed the figure shown. It shows the construction of line PT through point P and parallel to line AB.

   a. Compass settings of length AB and AP were used in the construction. Complete the statements:

   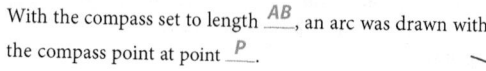

   With the compass set to length AP, an arc was drawn with the compass point at point __B__.

   With the compass set to length __AB__, an arc was drawn with the compass point at point __P__.

   The two arcs intersect at point __T__.

   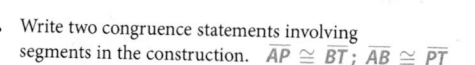

   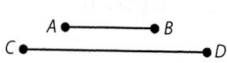

   b. Write two congruence statements involving segments in the construction. $\overline{AP} \cong \overline{BT}$; $\overline{AB} \cong \overline{PT}$

   c. Write a proof that the construction is true. That is, given the construction, prove $\overline{PT} \| \overline{AB}$. (*Hint*: Draw segments to create two congruent triangles.)

   Draw $\overline{PB}$. $\overline{PB} \cong \overline{PB}$ by the Reflexive Property of Congruence. $\triangle PAB \cong \triangle BTP$ by SSS, and therefore $\angle ABP \cong \angle TPB$ by CPCTC. So by the Converse of the Alternate Interior Angles Theorem, $\overline{PT} \| \overline{AB}$.

20. Use the segments shown. Construct and label a segment, $\overline{XY}$, whose length is the average of the lengths of $\overline{AB}$ and $\overline{CD}$. Justify the method you used.

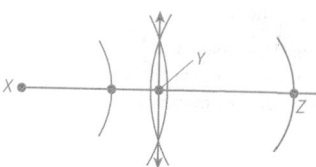

The length of $\overline{XZ}$ is $AB + CD$. The perpendicular bisector of $\overline{XZ}$ passes through its midpoint, Y. The length of $\overline{XY}$ is $\frac{AB + CD}{2}$, which is the average of the given lengths.

Lesson Performance Task

A plastic "mold" for copying a 30° angle is shown here.

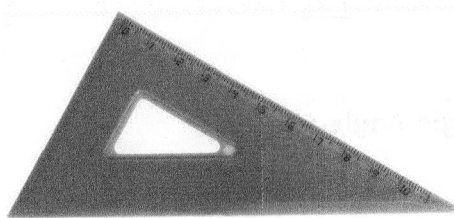

a. If you drew a 30°–60°–90° triangle using the mold, how would you know that your triangle and the mold were congruent?

b. Explain how you know that any angle you would draw using the lower right corner of the mold would measure 30°.

c. Explain the meaning of "tolerance" in the context of drawing an angle using the mold.

a. The SSS Congruence Theorem

b. CPCTC

c. Because your pencil would be "outside" the 30°–60°–90° triangle, your triangle would be slightly larger than the 30°–60°–90° triangle. The tolerance would be the difference in the sizes of the two triangles.

© Houghton Mifflin Harcourt Publishing Company • Image Credits: ©mihalec/Shutterstock

INTEGRATE MATHEMATICAL PRACTICES
Focus on Reasoning

MP.2 An art supply manufacturer produces 30°-60°-90° plastic triangles like the one in the Lesson Performance Task. The most popular such triangle has sides measuring 9.3 cm, 16.1 cm, and 18.6 cm. with allowable tolerances of ±1%. What is the difference between the maximum and minimum allowable perimeters of the triangle? maximum perimeter: 44.44 cm; minimum perimeter: 43.56 cm; difference: 0.88 cm

EXTENSION ACTIVITY

Have students research tolerances typically found in the manufacture of familiar products such as batteries or eyeglasses. Among topics they may choose to investigate are effects on the product when tolerances are not met; reasons a company may choose to employ tolerances that are greater than the most precise; and changes in tolerances made as a product becomes more and more technically precise over the years. (An Internet search for "tolerance chart" will get students off to a good start.)

Scoring Rubric
2 points: Student correctly solves the problem and explains his/her reasoning.
1 point: Student shows good understanding of the problem but does not fully solve or explain his/her reasoning.
0 points: Student does not demonstrate understanding of the problem.

Justifying Constructions   **282**

AAS Triangle Congruence

Common Core Math Standards

The student is expected to:

 G-SRT.B.5

Use congruence ... criteria for triangles to solve problems and to prove relationships in geometric figures.

Mathematical Practices

 MP.3 Logic

Language Objective

Explain in your own words the difference between the AAS and ASA congruence theorems.

ENGAGE

Essential Question: What does the AAS Triangle Congruence Theorem tell you about two triangles?

If two angles and a non-included side of one triangle are congruent to the corresponding angles and side of another triangle, the triangles are congruent.

PREVIEW: LESSON PERFORMANCE TASK

View the Engage section online. Discuss the figure, making sure students understand why a triangle with the given side lengths cannot be drawn. Then preview the Lesson Performance Task.

6.2 AAS Triangle Congruence

Essential Question: What does the AAS Triangle Congruence Theorem tell you about two triangles?

Resource Locker

⊘ Explore   Exploring Angle-Angle-Side Congruence

If two angles and a non-included side of one triangle are congruent to the corresponding angles and side of another triangle, are the triangles congruent?

In this activity you'll be copying a side and two angles from a triangle.

(A) Use a compass and straightedge to copy segment *AC*. Label it as segment *EF*.

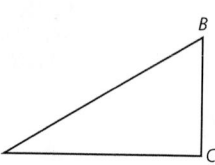

(B) Copy ∠A using $\overline{EF}$ as a side of the angle.

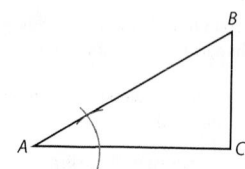

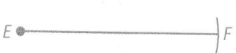

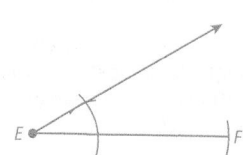

(C) On a separate transparent sheet or a sheet of tracing paper, copy ∠B. Label its vertex *G*. Make the rays defining ∠G longer than their corresponding sides on △*ABC*.

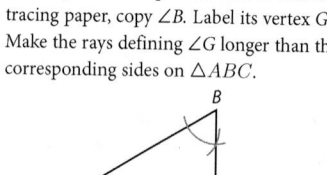

(D) Now overlay the ray from ∠E with the ray from ∠G to form a triangle. Make sure that side $\overline{EF}$ maintains the length you defined for it.

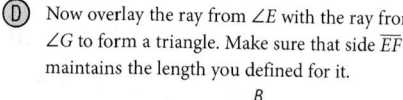

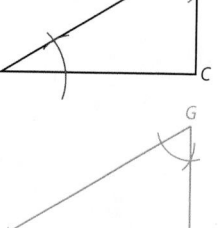

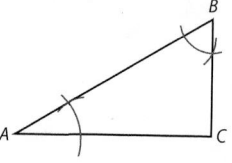

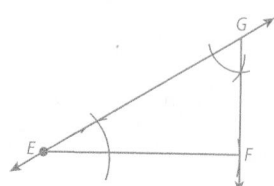

© Houghton Mifflin Harcourt Publishing Company

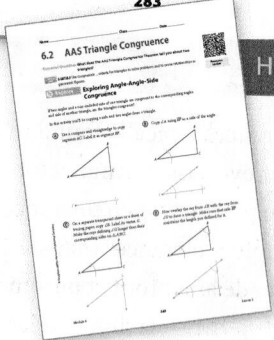

HARDCOVER PAGES 245–254

Turn to these pages to find this lesson in the hardcover student edition.

(E) How many triangles can you construct?

Only one triangle is possible.

(F) Copy all of △EFG to the transparency. Then overlay it on △ABC. Are the triangles congruent? How do you know?

Yes; possible answer: All sides are

congruent, so they are congruent by SSS.

Reflect

1. Suppose you had started this activity by copying segment BC and then angles A and C. Would your results have been the same? Why or why not?

Yes; no specific side lengths and angle measures were involved.

2. Compare your results to those of your classmates. Does this procedure work with any triangle?

Yes. All triangles with congruent angles and a congruent non-included side are congruent.

⊘ Explain 1   Justifying Angle-Angle-Side Congruence

The following theorem summarizes the previous activity.

> **Angle-Angle-Side (AAS) Congruence Theorem**
>
> If two angles and a non-included side of one triangle are congruent to the corresponding angles and non-included side of another triangle, then the triangles are congruent.

Prove the AAS Congruence Theorem.

Given: $\angle A \cong \angle D$, $\angle C \cong \angle F$, $\overline{BC} \cong \overline{EF}$

Prove: $\triangle ABC \cong \triangle DEF$

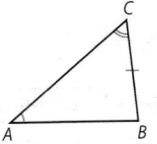 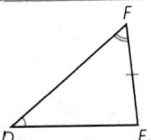

Statements	Reasons
1. $\angle A \cong \angle D$, $\angle C \cong \angle$ F , $\overline{BC} \cong \overline{EF}$	1. Given
2. $m\angle A + m\angle B + m\angle C = 180°$	2. Triangle Sum Theorem
3. $m\angle B = 180° - m\angle A - m\angle$ C	3. Subtraction Property of Equality
4. $m\angle$ D $+ m\angle E + m\angle F = 180°$	4. Triangle Sum Theorem
5. $m\angle E = 180° - m\angle D - m\angle$ F	5. Subtraction Property of Equality
6. $m\angle A = m\angle D$, $m\angle C = m\angle F$	6. Definition of congruent angles
7. $m\angle E = 180° - m\angle A - m\angle C$	7. Substitution
8. $m\angle$ E $\cong m\angle B$	8. Transitive Property of Equality
9. $\angle B \cong m\angle E$	9. Definition of congruent angles
10. $\triangle ABC \cong \triangle DEF$	10. ASA Triangle Congruence Theorem

PROFESSIONAL DEVELOPMENT

 Integrate Mathematical Practices

This lesson provides an opportunity to address Mathematical Practice **MP.3**, which calls for students to "construct viable arguments and critique the reasoning of others." Students learn to justify the Angle-Angle-Side Congruence Theorem by using a paragraph proof. Mathematical proofs must use precise language to ensure their validity. As students continue to explore congruent triangles, ask them to justify their conclusions and communicate them with the class. Promoting this type of dialogue in the classroom is an essential aspect of the standard.

EXPLORE

Exploring Angle-Angle-Side Congruence

INTEGRATE TECHNOLOGY

Students can use geometry software to explore how much they know about a triangle when given two angle measures and the length of a nonincluded side.

QUESTIONING STRATEGIES

? If you know the measures of two angles in a triangle, and the length of a side that is not included, does this describe a unique triangle? What is the relationship between the information necessary to describe a unique triangle and the information necessary to prove two triangles congruent? Yes; the same sides and angles that must be known to be congruent to prove two triangles congruent must be given to describe a unique triangle (two angles and the included side, two sides and the included angle, etc.).

EXPLAIN 1

Justifying Angle-Angle-Side Congruence

QUESTIONING STRATEGIES

? If you know the measures of two angles of a triangle, what theorem gives you a way to determine the measure of the third angle? Third Angles Theorem

AVOID COMMON ERRORS

After finding the measure of the third angle, some students may want to say the triangles are congruent by AAA. Remind them that there is no AAA congruence theorem because having three pairs of congruent angles does not ensure two triangles have the same size.

EXPLAIN 2

Using Angle-Angle-Side Congruence

QUESTIONING STRATEGIES

? How does the AAS Congruence Theorem differ from the ASA Congruence Theorem? While both the ASA and AAS Congruence Theorems require you to know that two pairs of corresponding angles are congruent between two triangles, the ASA Congruence Theorem requires you to also know that a pair of corresponding included sides are congruent. The AAS Congruence Theorem requires you to know also that a pair of corresponding non-included sides are congruent.

? If AAS is used as the method of proof, can the triangles also be proved congruent using ASA? Yes; you can use the Third Angles Theorem to show the third pair of angles is congruent, and then you can use ASA.

Reflect

3. **Discussion** The Third Angles Theorem says "If two angles of one triangle are congruent to two angles of another triangle, then the third pair of angles are congruent." How could using this theorem simplify the proof of the AAS Congruence Theorem?

   Steps 2–8 could be simplified to one step, $\angle B \cong \angle E$, making the whole proof only three steps.

4. Could the AAS Congruence Theorem be used in the proof? Explain.

   No, that is the theorem being proved, so it cannot be used until it has been proven.

⚡ Explain 2 **Using Angle-Angle-Side Congruence**

Example 2 Use the AAS Theorem to prove the given triangles are congruent.

(A) Given: $\overline{AC} \cong \overline{EC}$ and $m \parallel n$

   Prove: $\triangle ABC \cong \triangle EDC$

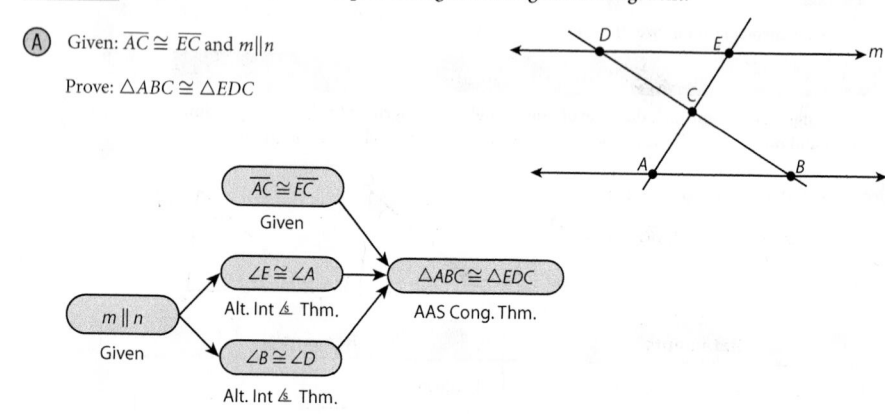

(B) Given: $\overline{CB} \parallel \overline{ED}$, $\overline{AB} \parallel \overline{CD}$, and $\overline{CB} \cong \overline{ED}$.

   Prove: $\triangle ABC \cong \triangle CDE$

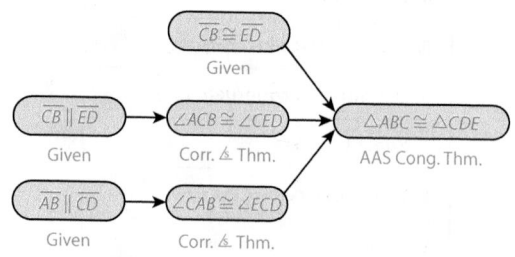

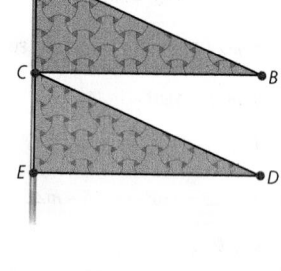

© Houghton Mifflin Harcourt Publishing Company

COLLABORATIVE LEARNING

Small Group Activity

Students may benefit from exploring conditions that do not guarantee congruent triangles. Have students work in small groups and use a protractor to draw triangles with angles that measure 35°, 50°, and 95°. Then then compare their triangles within each group. Students will see that all the triangles have the same shape, but not necessarily the same size. Since the triangles are not all congruent, the activity shows that there is no AAA Congruence Criteria.

5. Given: $\angle ABC \cong \angle DEF$, $\overline{BC} \parallel \overline{EF}$, $\overline{AC} \cong \overline{DF}$. Use the AAS Theorem to prove the triangles are congruent.

Write a paragraph proof.

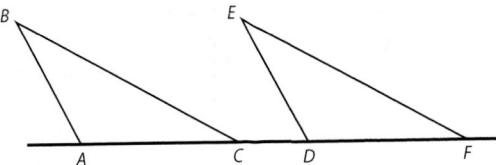

Because $\overline{BC}$ is parallel to $\overline{EF}$, this means that $\angle ACB$ is congruent to $\angle DFE$, using the Corresponding Angles Theorem. Since $\angle ABC$ is congruent to $\angle DEF$ and $\overline{AC}$ is congruent to $\overline{DF}$, then one pair of corresponding angles and two pairs of non-included corresponding sides are congruent. This means that $\triangle ABC$ is congruent to $\triangle DEF$ using the AAS Triangle Congruence Theorem.

⚡ Explain 3 Applying Angle-Angle-Side Congruence

Example 3 The triangular regions represent plots of land. Use the AAS Theorem to explain why the same amount of fencing will surround either plot.

(A) Given: $\angle A \cong \angle D$

It is given that $\angle A \cong \angle D$. Also, $\angle B \cong \angle E$ because both are right angles. Compare AC and DF using the Distance Formula.

$$AC = \sqrt{(x_2 - x_1)^2 + (y_2 - y_1)^2}$$
$$= \sqrt{(-1-(-4))^2 + (4-0)^2}$$
$$= \sqrt{3^2 + 4^2}$$
$$= \sqrt{25}$$
$$= 5$$

$$DF = \sqrt{(x_2 - x_1)^2 + (y_2 - y_1)^2}$$
$$= \sqrt{(4-0)^2 + (1-4)^2}$$
$$= \sqrt{4^2 + (-3)^2}$$
$$= \sqrt{25}$$
$$= 5$$

Because two pairs of angles and a pair of non-included sides are congruent, $\triangle ABC \cong \triangle DEF$ by AAS. Therefore the triangles have the same perimeter and the same amount of fencing is needed.

EXPLAIN 3

Applying Angle-Angle-Side Congruence

AVOID COMMON ERRORS

The real-world situation may distract some students. Make sure they are certain what they are solving for before they begin.

DIFFERENTIATE INSTRUCTION

Auditory Cues

As students work through the lesson, have them identify orally whether the triangles are congruent by ASA, AAS, SAS, or SSS. Then have them work with a partner to identify the congruent parts and to determine if the congruent pairs of angles or sides are corresponding parts.

When is the distance formula useful for proving two triangles to be congruent? How would you use it? It is useful when the triangles are on a coordinate grid and their side lengths are not given; you would use it to find the lengths of corresponding sides and determine whether or not the sides are congruent.

Ⓑ Given: $\angle P \cong \angle Z$, $\angle Q \cong \angle X$

It is given that $\angle P \cong \angle Z$ and $\angle Q \cong \angle X$.

Compare YZ and $\underline{OP}$ using the distance formula.

$$YZ = \sqrt{(x_2 - x_1)^2 + (y_2 - y_1)^2}$$

$$= \sqrt{\left((-1) - \boxed{-5}\right)^2 + \left((-2) - \boxed{-4}\right)^2}$$

$$= \sqrt{\boxed{4}^2 + \boxed{2}^2}$$

$$= \sqrt{\boxed{16} + \boxed{4}}$$

$$= \sqrt{\boxed{20}}$$

$$\underline{OP} = \sqrt{(x_2 - x_1)^2 + (y_2 - y_1)^2}$$

$$= \sqrt{\left(\boxed{2} - 0\right)^2 + \left(\boxed{-4} - 0\right)^2}$$

$$= \sqrt{\boxed{2}^2 + \boxed{-4}^2}$$

$$= \sqrt{\boxed{4} + \boxed{16}}$$

$$= \sqrt{\boxed{20}}$$

Because two pairs of angles and a pair of non-included sides are congruent,

$\triangle XYZ \cong \triangle \boxed{QOP}$ by AAS. Therefore the triangles have the same perimeter and the same amount of fencing is needed.

Reflect

6. Explain how you could have avoided using the distance formula in Example 2B.
    I could have used $\overline{XY}$ and $\overline{QO}$ as corresponding sides. By counting
    gridlines, it is easy to see that $XY = QO = 7$. These are also not the
    included sides between the angles, so AAS applies.

© Houghton Mifflin Harcourt Publishing Company

LANGUAGE SUPPORT EL

Communicate Math

Divide students into pairs. Give each pair pictures of congruent and non-congruent triangles, highlighters, protractors, and rulers. Instruct them to prove which pairs are congruent by angle-angle-side. Have students highlight the angles and the side they used to show congruence, and write notes explaining why the triangles are congruent.

Refer to the diagram to answer the questions.

Given: $\angle A \cong \angle D$ and $\angle B \cong \angle E$

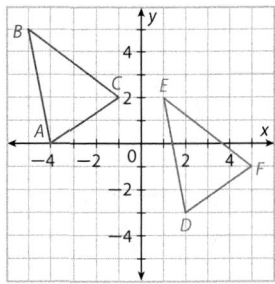

7. Show that the two triangles are congruent using the AAS Theorem. Use the distance formula to compare BC and EF.

It is given that $\angle A \cong \angle D$ and $\angle B \cong \angle E$.

$BC = \sqrt{\left(-5-(-1)\right)^2 + (5-2)^2}$ $\qquad EF = \sqrt{(1-5)^2 + \left(2-(-1)\right)^2}$

$\quad = \sqrt{16+9}$ $\qquad\qquad\qquad = \sqrt{16+9}$

$\quad = 5$ $\qquad\qquad\qquad\qquad = 5$

Sides BC and EF are equal. Therefore, because two angles and a non-included side are congruent, $\triangle ABC \cong \triangle DEF$ by the AAS Theorem.

8. Show that the two triangles are congruent using the AAS Theorem. Use the distance formula to compare AC and DF.

It is given that $\angle A \cong \angle D$ and $\angle B \cong \angle E$.

$AC = \sqrt{\left(-4-(-1)\right)^2 + (0-2)^2}$ $\qquad DF = \sqrt{(2-5)^2 + \left(-3-(-1)\right)^2}$

$\quad = \sqrt{9+4}$ $\qquad\qquad\qquad\quad = \sqrt{9+4}$

$\quad = \sqrt{13}$ $\qquad\qquad\qquad\quad = \sqrt{13}$

Sides AC and DF are equal. Therefore, because two angles and a non-included side are congruent, $\triangle ABC \cong \triangle DEF$ by the AAS Theorem.

CONNECT VOCABULARY **EL**

Students can create a chart, or add to a chart, proving triangle congruence, defining angle/angle/side, and showing a picture that demonstrates this condition.

ELABORATE

INTEGRATE MATHEMATICAL PRACTICES

Focus on Modeling

MP.4 Students may benefit from seeing the proof of the AAS Congruence Criterion presented as a flowchart proof.

SUMMARIZE THE LESSON

? When do you use the AAS Triangle Congruence Theorem? What information do you need in order to use this theorem? You use the AAS Triangle Congruence Theorem to prove that two triangles are congruent by using three pairs of congruent corresponding parts. You need to know that two pairs of corresponding angles and one pair of corresponding non-included sides are congruent in order to use it.

9. Two isosceles triangles share a side. With which diagram can the AAS Theorem be used to show the triangles are congruent? Explain.

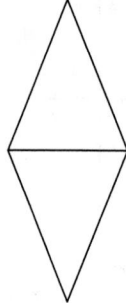 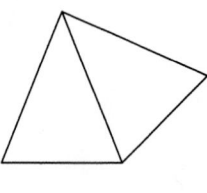

The one on the right. The shared side is the non-included side.

10. What must be true of the right triangles in the roof truss to use the AAS Congruence Theorem to prove the two triangles are congruent? Explain.

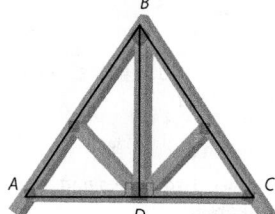

Because ∠BDA and ∠BDC are right angles, ∠BDA ≅ ∠BDC. Since $\overline{BD}$ is a shared side for both triangles, it must be the non-included side. So to use the AAS Theorem, ∠BAD must be congruent to ∠BCD. This gives two angles and a non-included side.

11. **Essential Question Check-In** You know that a pair of triangles has two pairs of congruent corresponding angles. What other information do you need to show that the triangles are congruent?

You need a pair of congruent sides that are either both included or both not included.

© Houghton Mifflin Harcourt Publishing Company

⭐ Evaluate: Homework and Practice

Decide whether you have enough information to determine that the triangles are congruent. If they are congruent, explain why.

- Online Homework
- Hints and Help
- Extra Practice

1.

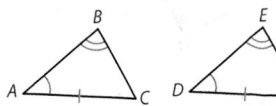

Congruent, by AAS Congruence

2.

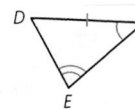

Congruent, by AAS Congruence

3.

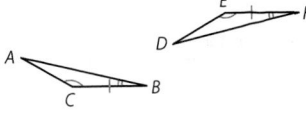

Congruent, by ASA Congruence

4.

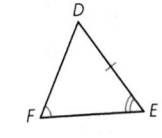

Cannot be determined.

5.

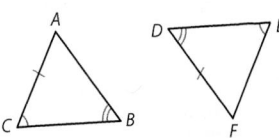

Cannot be determined.

6.

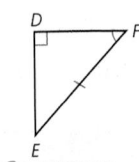

Congruent, AAS Congruence

Each diagram shows two triangles with two congruent angles or sides. Identify one additional pair of corresponding angles or sides such that, if the pair were congruent, the two triangles could be proved congruent by AAS.

7.

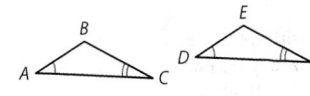

$\overline{AB} \cong \overline{DE}$, or $\overline{BC} \cong \overline{EF}$

8.

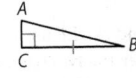

$\angle A \cong \angle E$

9.

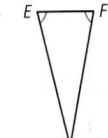

$\overline{AB} \cong \overline{DE}$, $\overline{AB} \cong \overline{DF}$, $\overline{AC} \cong \overline{DE}$, or $\overline{AC} \cong \overline{DF}$

10.

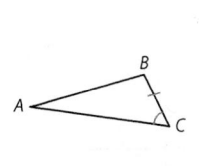

$\angle A \cong \angle E$

11.

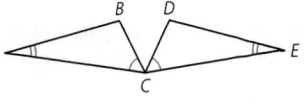

$\overline{AB} \cong \overline{DE}$, or $\overline{BC} \cong \overline{DC}$

12.

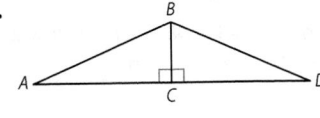

$\angle A \cong \angle D$

© Houghton Mifflin Harcourt Publishing Company

Exercise	Depth of Knowledge (D.O.K.)	COMMON CORE Mathematical Practices
1–12	**1** Recall of information	**MP.6** Precision
13–21	**2** Skills/Concepts	**MP.4** Modeling
22	**3** Strategic Thinking H.O.T.	**MP.2** Reasoning
23	**3** Strategic Thinking H.O.T.	**MP.2** Reasoning
24	**3** Strategic Thinking H.O.T.	**MP.2** Reasoning

EVALUATE

ASSIGNMENT GUIDE

Concepts and Skills	Practice
Explore Exploring Angle-Angle-Side Congruence	Exercises 1–12
Example 1 Justifying Angle-Angle-Side Congruence	Exercises 13–14
Example 2 Using Angle-Angle-Side Congruence	Exercises 13–14
Example 3 Applying Angle-Angle-Side Congruence	Exercises 15–21

QUESTIONING STRATEGIES

? If you know the measures of two angles of a triangle, how can you find the measure of the third angle? Find the difference between 180° and the sum of the two known angle measures.

Have students each make a poster on which they describe and illustrate the AAS theorem. The illustrations should show both an example and a nonexample.

13. Complete the proof.

Given: $\angle B \cong \angle D$, $\overleftrightarrow{AC}$ bisects $\angle BCD$.

Prove: $\triangle ABC \cong \triangle ADC$

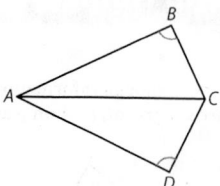

Statements	Reasons
1. $\overline{AC} \cong \overline{AC}$	1. **Reflexive Property of Congruence**
2. $\overleftrightarrow{AC}$ bisects $\angle BCD$.	2. Given
3. $\angle ACB \cong \angle ACD$	3. Definition of angle bisector
4. $\angle B \cong \angle D$	4. Given
5. $\triangle ABC \cong \triangle ADC$	5. **AAS Triangle Congruence Theorem**

14. Write a two-column proof or a paragraph proof.

Given: $\overline{AB} \| \overline{DE}$, $\overline{CB} \cong \overline{CD}$.

Prove: $\triangle ABC \cong \triangle EDC$

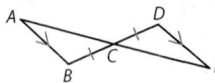

Statements	Reasons
1. $\overline{AB} \| \overline{DE}$, $\overline{CB} \cong \overline{CD}$	1. **Given**
2. $\angle A \cong \angle E$, $\angle B \cong \angle D$	2. **Alternate Interior Angles Theorem**
3. $\triangle ABC \cong \triangle EDC$	3. **AAS Triangle Congruence Theorem**

Each diagram shows $\triangle ABC$ and $\triangle DEF$ on the coordinate plane, with $\angle A \cong \angle E$, and $\angle C \cong \angle F$. Identify whether the two triangles are congruent. If they are not congruent, explain how you know. If they are congruent, find the length of each side of each triangle.

15.

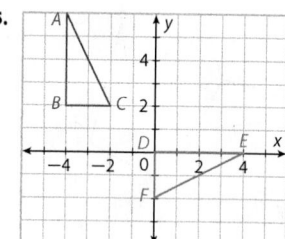

Congruent; $AB = DE = 4$; $BC = DF = 2$; $AC = EF = 4.47$

16.

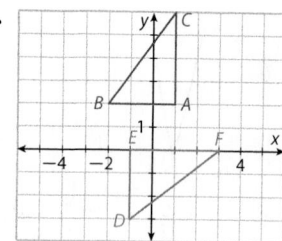

Congruent. $AB = ED = 3$, $AC = EF = 4$, $BC = DF = 5$

© Houghton Mifflin Harcourt Publishing Company

Exercise	Depth of Knowledge (D.O.K.)	COMMON CORE Mathematical Practices	
25	**3** Strategic Thinking H.O.T.	**MP.3**	Logic
26	**3** Strategic Thinking H.O.T.	**MP.3**	Logic
27	**3** Strategic Thinking H.O.T.	**MP.4**	Modeling

17.

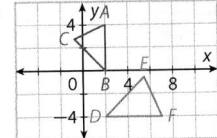

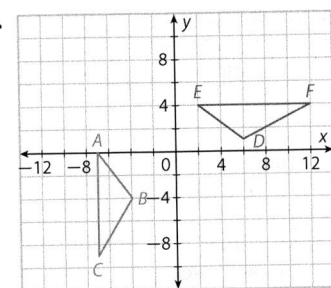

Not congruent. Segments $\overline{AB}$ and $\overline{DF}$ are corresponding, but they have different lengths $(AB = 4, DF = 5)$.

18.

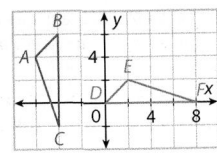

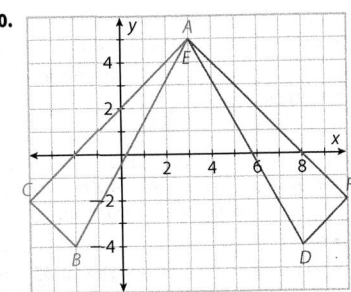

Congruent; $AB = DE = 2.8$; $BC = DF = 8$; $AC = EF = 6.3$

19.

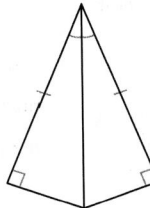

Not congruent. Segments $\overline{AC}$ and $\overline{EF}$ are corresponding, but they have different lengths $(AC = 9, EF = 10)$.

20.

Congruent. $AB = DE = 10.29$, $AC = EF = 9.9$, $BC = DF = 2.8$

21. Which theorem or postulate can be used to prove that the triangles are congruent? Select all that apply.

(**A.**) ASA   (**B.**) SAS   **C.** SSS   (**D.**) AAS

H.O.T. Focus on Higher Order Thinking

22. Analyze Relationships $\triangle XYZ$ and $\triangle KLM$ have two congruent angles: $\angle X \cong \angle K$ and $\angle Y \cong \angle L$. Can it be concluded that $\angle Z \cong \angle M$? Can it be concluded that the triangles are congruent? Explain.

It can be concluded that $\angle Z \cong \angle M$, because the sum of the three angles of a triangle equals $180°$. While the two triangles are similar, it cannot be concluded that the triangles are congruent without identifying at least one congruent side.

23. Communicate Mathematical Ideas $\triangle GHJ$ and $\triangle PQR$ have two congruent angles: $\angle G \cong \angle P$ and $\angle H \cong \angle Q$. If $\overline{HJ}$ is congruent to one of the sides of $\triangle PQR$, are the two triangles congruent? Explain.

They are not necessarily congruent. Only if $\overline{HJ}$ is congruent to the corresponding side, which is $\overline{QR}$, will the triangles be congruent.

Some students may think that two pairs of congruent angles and any pair of non-included sides is enough to use AAS. They need to be sure the non-included sides are corresponding sides, otherwise they may be looking at triangles that are not congruent.

Have students write a journal entry in which they explain and illustrate the AAS Theorem.

24. **Make a Conjecture** Combine the theorems of ASA Congruence and AAS Congruence into a single statement that describes a condition for congruency between triangles.

If two triangles have two congruent angles and one corresponding congruent side, then the two triangles are congruent.

25. **Justify Reasoning** Triangles *ABC* and *DEF* are constructed with the following angles: $m\angle A = 35°$, $m\angle B = 45°$, $m\angle D = 65°$, $m\angle E = 45°$. Also, $AC = DF = 12$ units. Are the two triangles congruent? Explain.

The two triangles cannot be congruent. Because the sum of the three angles of a triangle equals 180°, it can be calculated that $m\angle C = 100°$ and that $m\angle F = 70°$. The triangles do not have matching angles, so they are not congruent.

26. **Justify Reasoning** Triangles *ABC* and *DEF* are constructed with the following angles: $m\angle A = 65°$, $m\angle B = 60°$, $m\angle D = 65°$, $m\angle F = 55°$. Also, $AB = DE = 7$ units. Are the two triangles congruent? Explain.

The two triangles are congruent by either AAS or ASA Congruence. The triangles each have angles of 65°, 60°, and 55°, and each has a side of length 7 that is opposite the angle of 55°.

27. **Algebra** A bicycle frame includes $\triangle VSU$ and $\triangle VTU$, which lie in intersecting planes. From the given angle measures, can you conclude that $\triangle VSU \cong \triangle VTU$? Explain.

$$m\angle VUS = (7y - 2)°$$
$$m\angle USV = 5\tfrac{2}{3}y°$$
$$m\angle SVU = (3y - 6)°$$

$$m\angle VUT = \left(5\tfrac{1}{2}x - \tfrac{1}{2}\right)°$$
$$m\angle UTV = (4x + 8)°$$
$$m\angle TVU = 2x°$$

Yes, the sum of the $\angle$ measures in each triangle must be 180°, which makes it possible to solve for *x* and *y*. The value of *x* is 15, and the value of *y* is 12. Each triangle has angles measuring 82°, 68°, and 30°. $\overline{VU} \cong \overline{VU}$ by the Reflexive Property of Congruence. So $\triangle VSU \cong \triangle VTU$ by ASA or AAS.

Lesson Performance Task

A mapmaker has successfully mapped Carlisle Street and River Avenue, as shown in the diagram. The last step is to map Beacon Street correctly. To save time, the mapmaker intends to measure just one more angle or side of the triangle.

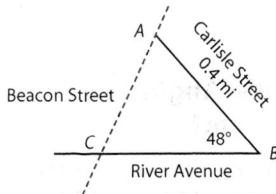

a. Which angle(s) or side(s) could the mapmaker measure to be sure that only one triangle is possible? For each angle or side that you name, justify your answer.

b. Suppose that instead of measuring the length of Carlisle Street, the mapmaker measured ∠A and ∠C along with ∠B. Would the measures of the three angles alone assure a unique triangle? Explain.

a. ∠C, by the AAS Triangle Congruence Theorem; ∠A, by the ASA Triangle Congruence Theorem; $\overline{BC}$, by the SAS Triangle Congruence Theorem

b. No; there is no AAA Triangle Congruence Theorem. There are many similar triangles with the same angle measures.

Module 6   294   Lesson 2

© Houghton Mifflin Harcourt Publishing Company

INTEGRATE MATHEMATICAL PRACTICES
Focus on Critical Thinking

MP.3 Draw attention to the figure in the Lesson Performance Task. State that m∠CAB = 85°. Ask students to imagine that the 48° angle where Carlisle Street and River Avenue intersect increases in size until Carlisle Street and Beacon Street no longer intersect. Ask: "What is the smallest measure of ∠B for which this would be possible? Explain your reasoning." 133°; Sample answer: The smallest measure of ∠B for which this would be possible would be when the streets became parallel. ∠B and ∠ACB would be supplementary interior angles on the same side of the River Avenue transversal: m∠ACB = 180° − (48° + 85°) = 47°. So, m∠B = 180° − 47° = 133°.

INTEGRATE MATHEMATICAL PRACTICES
Focus on Modeling

MP.4 Ask students to explain how they could use equilateral triangles to show that AAA Congruence does not hold. Sample answer: All equilateral triangles from small ones on a company's logo to large "Yield" traffic signs share three pairs of congruent (60°) angles. Yet the triangles are clearly not congruent.

Scoring Rubric

2 points: Student correctly solves the problem and explains his/her reasoning.

1 point: Student shows good understanding of the problem but does not fully solve or explain his/her reasoning.

0 points: Student does not demonstrate understanding of the problem.

EXTENSION ACTIVITY

A surveyor has a contract to lay out the boundaries of a triangular park. Here are the instructions given to the surveyor. (All of the streets are straight.)

- The vertex of one angle of the park will be the 30° angle where Charles Street and Barton Street intersect.
- One side of the park will start at the Charles-Barton vertex and extend 100 yards along Charles Street.
- The side of the park opposite the 30° angle will connect Barton Street and Charles Street and measure 60 yards.

What problem did the surveyor run into? Explain and draw a diagram.

There are two possible triangles that meet the given conditions.

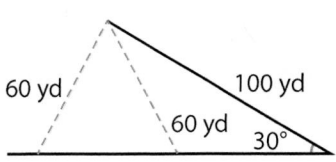

AAS Triangle Congruence   **294**

HL Triangle Congruence

Common Core Math Standards

The student is expected to:

 G-SRT.B.5

Use congruence ... criteria for triangles to solve problems and to prove relationships in geometric figures.

Mathematical Practices

 MP.7 Using Structure

Language Objective

Explain the HL Congruence Theorem in your own words.

ENGAGE

Essential Question: What does the HL Triangle Congruence Theorem tell you about two triangles?

If a leg and the hypotenuse of one right triangle are congruent to the corresponding leg and hypotenuse another right triangle, the triangles are congruent.

PREVIEW: LESSON PERFORMANCE TASK

View the Engage section online. Discuss the photo, asking students to describe the shape of the kite in terms of angles, triangles, and any other geometrical terms that seem relevant. Then preview the Lesson Performance Task.

6.3   HL Triangle Congruence

Essential Question: What does the HL Triangle Congruence Theorem tell you about two triangles?

Resource Locker

⊘ Explore   Is There a Side-Side-Angle Congruence Theorem?

You have already seen several theorems for proving that triangles are congruent. In this Explore, you will investigate whether there is a SSA Triangle Congruence Theorem.

Follow these steps to draw △ABC such that m∠A = 30°, AB = 6 cm, and BC = 4 cm. The goal is to determine whether two side lengths and the measure of a non-included angle (SSA) determine a unique triangle.

(A) Use a protractor to draw a large 30° angle on a separate sheet of paper. Label it ∠A.

(B) Use a ruler to locate point B on one ray of ∠A so that AB = 6 cm.

(C) Now draw $\overline{BC}$ so that BC = 4 cm. To do this, open a compass to a distance of 4 cm. Place the point of the compass on point B and draw an arc. Plot point C where the arc intersects the side of ∠A. Draw $\overline{BC}$ to complete △ABC.

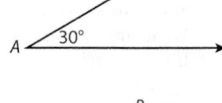

(D) What do you notice? Is it possible to draw only one △ABC with the given side length? Explain.
If extended, the arc would intersect $\overrightarrow{AC}$ in two places. So, it is possible to draw two different triangles with side length BC.

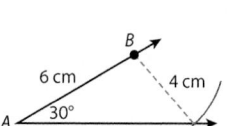

Reflect

1. Do you think that SSA is sufficient to prove congruence? Why or why not?
   No. SSA is not sufficient to determine congruence because a given set of values does not necessarily describe a unique triangle. It is possible to draw two different triangles that have two congruent sides and a congruent non-included angle.

2. **Discussion** Your friend said that there is a special case where SSA can be used to prove congruence. Namely, when the non-included angle was a right angle. Is your friend right? Explain.
   Yes; if the congruent non-included angle were a right angle, then SSA would work. Given a right angle, one set of congruent sides would be legs and the other set the hypotenuses. Given a leg and the hypotenuse of a right triangle, the Pythagorean theorem guarantees a unique triangle.

HARDCOVER PAGES 255–262

Turn to these pages to find this lesson in the hardcover student edition.

Explain 1 Justifying the Hypotenuse-Leg Congruence Theorem

In a right triangle, the side opposite the right angle is the **hypotenuse**.
The two sides that form the sides of the right angle are the **legs**.

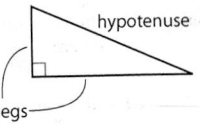

You have learned four ways to prove that triangles are congruent.

- Angle-Side-Angle (ASA) Congruence Theorem
- Side-Angle-Side (SAS) Congruence Theorem
- Side-Side-Side (SSS) Congruence Theorem
- Angle-Angle-Side (AAS) Congruence Theorem

The Hypotenuse-Leg (HL) Triangle Congruence Theorem is a special case that
allows you to show that two right triangles are congruent.

Hypotenuse-Leg (HL) Triangle Congruence Theorem
If the hypotenuse and a leg of a right triangle are congruent to the hypotenuse and a leg of another right triangle, then the triangles are congruent.

Example 1 Prove the HL Triangle Congruence Theorem.

Given: △ABC and △DEF are right triangles;
∠C and ∠F are right angles.

$\overline{AB} \cong \overline{DE}$ and $\overline{BC} \cong \overline{EF}$

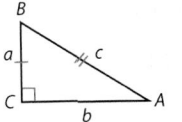
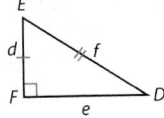

Prove: △ABC ≅ △DEF

By the Pythagorean Theorem, $a^2 + b^2 = c^2$ and $\boxed{d}^2 + \boxed{e}^2 = f^2$. It is given that

$\overline{AB} \cong \overline{DE}$, so $AB = DE$ and $c = f$. Therefore, $c^2 = f^2$ and $a^2 + b^2 = \boxed{d}^2 + \boxed{e}^2$. It is given that

$\overline{BC} \cong \overline{EF}$, so $BC = EF$ and $a = d$. Substituting a for d in the above equation, $a^2 + b^2 = \boxed{a}^2 + \boxed{e}^2$.

Subtracting a^2 from each side shows that $b^2 = \boxed{e}^2$, and taking the square root of each side, $b = \boxed{e}$.

This shows that $\overline{AC} \cong \boxed{\overline{DF}}$.

Therefore, △ABC ≅ △DEF by ___the SSS Triangle Congruence Theorem___

Your Turn

3. Determine whether there is enough information to prove that
    triangles △VWX and △YXW are congruent. Explain.
    **Yes. △VWX and △YXW are right triangles
    that share hypotenuse $\overline{WX}$. $\overline{WX} \cong \overline{WX}$ by the
    Reflexive Property of Congruence. It is given
    that $\overline{WV} \cong \overline{XY}$, therefore △VWX ≅ △YXW by
    the HL Triangle Congruence Theorem.**

© Houghton Mifflin Harcourt Publishing Company

EXPLORE

Is there a Side-Side-Angle Congruence Theorem?

INTEGRATE TECHNOLOGY

Students can use geometry software to explore what
you can do with two sides and a non-included angle.

QUESTIONING STRATEGIES

 Could you use SAS on the triangles we are
discussing here? Explain. No; SAS requires
the angle to be included between the two pairs of
congruent sides.

EXPLAIN 1

Justifying the Hypotenuse-Leg Congruence Theorem

AVOID COMMON ERRORS

Students may use *hypotenuse* to describe the longest
side of any triangle. Remind them that the term is
used only with right triangles.

QUESTIONING STRATEGIES

With what kind of triangles can you use the
Pythagorean Theorem? right triangles only

PROFESSIONAL DEVELOPMENT

Integrate Mathematical Practices

This lesson provides an opportunity to address Mathematical Practice **MP.7**,
which calls for students to "look for and make use of structure." Students look at
pairs of triangles that have two congruent sides and congruent non-included
angles. They analyze these relationships to determine that this information is
sufficient only to prove right triangles congruent.

EXPLAIN 2

Applying the Hypotenuse-Leg Congruence Theorem

QUESTIONING STRATEGIES

Are all right angles congruent? Explain. **Yes; a right angle is an angle that measures 90°, so all right angles have the same measure. This means that all right angles are congruent.**

AVOID COMMON ERRORS

Students may assume that the hypotenuses of two given right triangles are congruent. Remind them not to assume anything is true, and to use only the information that is given.

CONNECT VOCABULARY **EL**

Have students label the parts of a right triangle, identifying the hypotenuse, the legs, and the right angle, and then measure and write the measures of the other two angles.

⚙ Explain 2   Applying the HL Triangle Congruence Theorem

Example 2 Use the HL Congruence Theorem to prove that the triangles are congruent.

Ⓐ Given: ∠P and ∠R are right angles. $\overline{PS} \cong \overline{RQ}$
   Prove: △PQS ≅ △RSQ

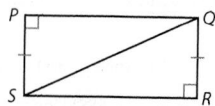

Statements	Reasons
1. ∠P and ∠R are right angles.	1. Given
2. $\overline{PS} \cong \overline{RQ}$	2. Given
3. $\overline{SQ} \cong \overline{SQ}$	3. Reflexive Property of Congruence
4. △PQS ≅ △RSQ	4. HL Triangle Congruence Theorem

Ⓑ Given: ∠J and ∠L are right angles. K is the midpoint of $\overline{JL}$ and $\overline{MN}$.
   Prove: △JKN ≅ △LKM

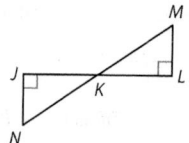

Statements	Reasons
1. ∠J and ∠L are right angles.	1. Given
2. K is the midpoint of $\overline{JL}$ and $\overline{MN}$.	2. Given
3. $\overline{JK} \cong \overline{LK}$ and $\overline{MK} \cong \overline{NK}$	3. Definition of midpoint
4. △JKN ≅ △LKM	4. HL Triangle Congruence Theorem

Reflect

4. Is it possible to write the proof in Part B without using the HL Triangle Congruence Theorem? Explain.
   Yes, you can use the SAS Triangle Congruence Theorem (∠J ≅ ∠L, $\overline{JK} \cong \overline{LK}$, and vertical angles JKN and LKM are congruent) or the SAS Triangle Congruence Theorem ($\overline{JK} \cong \overline{LK}$ and $\overline{MK} \cong \overline{NK}$, and vertical angles JKN and LKM are congruent).

Your Turn

Use the HL Congruence Theorem to prove that the triangles are congruent.

5. Given: ∠CAB and ∠DBA are right angles. $\overline{AD} \cong \overline{BC}$
   Prove: △ABC ≅ △BAD
   It is given that and ∠CAB and ∠DBA are right angles and $\overline{AD} \cong \overline{BC}$. $\overline{AB} \cong \overline{AB}$ by the Reflexive Property of Congruence. Then △ABC ≅ △BAD by the HL Triangle Congruence Theorem.

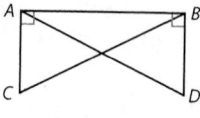

© Houghton Mifflin Harcourt Publishing Company

COLLABORATIVE LEARNING

Small Group Activity

Have students work in small groups to illustrate the differences between the HL and SAS Triangle Congruence Theorems. They may convey the information in any way, including making a poster, writing an essay, or creating a model. Have each group present their project to the class.

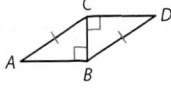

😀 Elaborate

6. You draw a right triangle with a hypotenuse that is 5 inches long. A friend also draws a right triangle with a hypotenuse that is 5 inches long. Can you conclude that the triangles are congruent using the HL Congruence Theorem? If not, what else would you need to know in order to conclude that the triangles are congruent?

No; you cannot apply the HL Triangle Congruence Theorem if you only know the

hypotenuses are congruent. You also need to know that a leg in one triangle is congruent

to a leg in the other triangle.

7. Essential Question Check-In How is the HL Triangle Congruence Theorem similar to and different from the ASA, SAS, SSS, and AAS Triangle Congruence Theorems?

Possible answer: The HL Triangle Congruence Theorem is similar to the other theorems

because it provides criteria you can use to prove that two triangles are congruent. It is

different from the other theorems because it only applies to right triangles.

⭐ Evaluate: Homework and Practice

• Online Homework
• Hints and Help
• Extra Practice

1. Tyrell used geometry software to construct $\angle ABC$ so that $m\angle ABC = 20°$. Then he dragged point A so that $AB = 6$ cm. He used the software's compass tool to construct a circle centered at point A with radius 3 cm. Based on this construction, is there a unique $\triangle ABC$ with $m\angle ABC = 20°$, $AB = 6$ cm, and $AC = 3$ cm? Explain.

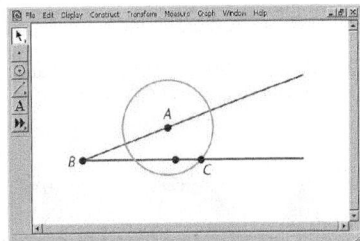

No. The circle intersects $\overrightarrow{BC}$ at two different points. Either of those intersection points can be vertex C of the triangle, so there is a not a unique triangle with these side and angle measures.

Determine whether enough information is given to prove that the triangles are congruent. Explain your answer.

2. $\triangle ABC$ and $\triangle DCB$

Yes. $\triangle ABC$ and $\triangle DCB$ are right triangles that share leg $\overline{BC}$. $\overline{BC} \cong \overline{BC}$ by the Reflexive Property of Congruence. It is given that $\overline{AC} \cong \overline{BD}$, therefore $\triangle ABC \cong \triangle DCB$ by the HL Triangle Congruence Theorem.

3. $\triangle PQR$ and $\triangle STU$

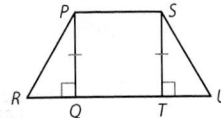

No. The triangles are right triangles and a pair of legs are congruent ($\overline{PQ} \cong \overline{ST}$), but it is not known whether the hypotenuses are congruent.

© Houghton Mifflin Harcourt Publishing Company

ELABORATE

QUESTIONING STRATEGIES

❓ Will a right angle ever be the included angle between the hypotenuse and a leg? No; the right angle is always opposite the hypotenuse, so it will always be non-included.

SUMMARIZE THE LESSON

❓ How is the HL Congruence Theorem different from the other congruence theorems we have studied? It can be used only with right triangles; it uses a non-included angle with two sides.

EVALUATE

ASSIGNMENT GUIDE

Concepts and Skills	Practice
Explore Is there a Side-Side-Angle Congruence Theorem?	Exercise 1
Example 1 Justifying the Hypotenuse-Leg Congruence Theorem	Exercises 2–5
Example 2 Applying the Hypotenuse-Leg Congruence Theorem	Exercises 6–9

Exercise	Depth of Knowledge (D.O.K.)	COMMON CORE Mathematical Practices
1	2 Skills/Concepts	MP.5 Using Tools
2–5	1 Recall information	MP.2 Reasoning
6–9	2 Skills/Concepts	MP.3 Logic
10–13	2 Skills/Concepts	MP.4 Modeling
14–20	2 Skills/Concepts	MP.4 Modeling
21	3 Strategic Thinking H.O.T.	MP.2 Reasoning

? What type of triangle must be given to use HL as a method of proof? It must be a right triangle.

4. △GKJ and △JHG

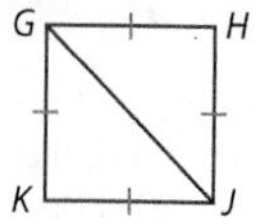

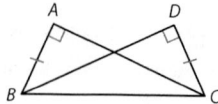

Yes. You cannot use the HL Triangle Congruence Theorem since it is not known whether the triangles are right triangles, but you can use the SSS Triangle Congruence Theorem.

5. △EFG and △SQR

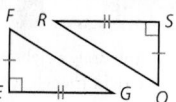

Yes. You can use the Pythagorean Theorem to show that $\overline{FG} \cong \overline{QR}$ and then use the HL Triangle Congruence Theorem, or you can use the SAS Triangle Congruence Theorem with the given information.

Write a two-column proof, using the HL Congruence Theorem, to prove that the triangles are congruent.

6. Given: ∠A and ∠B are right angles. $\overline{AB} \cong \overline{DC}$
Prove: △ABC ≅ △DCB

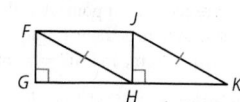

Statements	Reasons
1. ∠A and ∠B are right angles.	1. Given
2. $\overline{AB} \cong \overline{DC}$	2. Given
3. $\overline{BC} \cong \overline{BC}$	3. Reflexive Property of Congruence
4. △ABC ≅ △DCB	4. HL Triangle Congruence Theorem

7. Given: ∠FGH and ∠JHK are right angles. H is the midpoint of $\overline{GK}$. $\overline{FH} \cong \overline{JK}$
Prove: △FGH ≅ △JHK

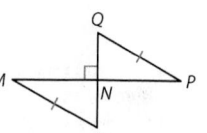

Statements	Reasons
1. ∠FGH and ∠JHK are right angles.	1. Given
2. H is the midpoint of $\overline{GK}$.	2. Given
3. $\overline{GH} \cong \overline{HK}$	3. Definition of midpoint
4. $\overline{FH} \cong \overline{JK}$	4. Given
5. △FGH ≅ △JHK	5. HL Triangle Congruence Theorem

8. Given: $\overline{MP}$ is perpendicular to $\overline{QR}$. N is the midpoint of $\overline{MP}$. $\overline{QP} \cong \overline{RM}$
Prove: △MNR ≅ △PNQ

$\overline{MP} \perp \overline{QR}$ so ∠QNP and ∠MNR are right angles (definition of perpendicular). N is the midpoint of $\overline{MP}$, so $\overline{MN} \cong \overline{PN}$ (definition of midpoint). Then, since it is given that $\overline{QP} \cong \overline{RM}$, △MNR ≅ △PNQ by the HL Triangle Congruence Theorem.

© Houghton Mifflin Harcourt Publishing Company

Exercise	Depth of Knowledge (D.O.K.)	COMMON CORE Mathematical Practices
22	3 Strategic Thinking H.O.T.	MP.2 Reasoning
23	3 Strategic Thinking H.O.T.	MP.2 Reasoning

9. Given: $\angle ADC$ and $\angle BDC$ are right angles. $\overline{AC} \cong \overline{BC}$
   Prove: $\overline{AD} \cong \overline{BD}$

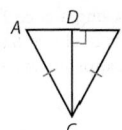

Statements	Reasons
1. $\angle ADC$ and $\angle BDC$ are right angles.	1. Given
2. $\overline{AC} \cong \overline{BC}$	2. Given
3. $\overline{DC} \cong \overline{DC}$	3. Reflexive Property of Congruence
4. $\triangle ADC \cong \triangle BDC$	4. HL Triangle Congruence Theorem
5. $\overline{AD} \cong \overline{BD}$	5. Corresponding parts of congruent triangles are congruent.

Algebra What value of x will make the given triangles congruent? Explain.

10. $\triangle JKL$ and $\triangle JKM$

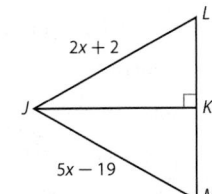

$\overline{JK} \cong \overline{JK}$ by the Reflexive Property of
Congruence. If $\overline{JL} \cong \overline{JM}$, then $\triangle JKL \cong \triangle JKM$
by the HL Triangle Congruence Theorem.
If $JL = JM$, then $2x + 2 = 5x - 19$,
so $x = 7$.

11. $\triangle ABC$ and $\triangle ABD$

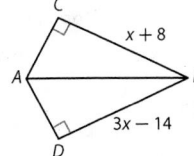

$\overline{AB} \cong \overline{AB}$ by the Reflexive Property of
Congruence. If $\overline{BC} \cong \overline{BD}$, then $\triangle ABC \cong \triangle ABD$
by the HL Triangle Congruence Theorem.
If $BC = BD$, then $x + 8 = 3x - 14$,
so $x = 11$.

12. $\triangle STV$ and $\triangle UVT$

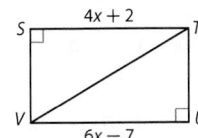

$\overline{TV} \cong \overline{TV}$ by the Reflexive Property of
Congruence. If $\overline{ST} \cong \overline{UV}$, then $\triangle STV \cong \triangle UVT$
by the HL Triangle Congruence Theorem.
If $ST = UV$, then $4x + 2 = 6x - 7$, so $x = 4.5$.

13. $\triangle MPQ$ and $\triangle PMN$

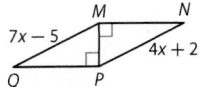

$\overline{MP} \cong \overline{MP}$ by the Reflexive Property of
Congruence. If $\overline{MQ} \cong \overline{PN}$, then $\triangle MPQ \cong \triangle PMN$
by the HL Triangle Congruence Theorem.
If $MQ = PN$, then $7x - 5 = 4x + 25$, so $x = 10$.

© Houghton Mifflin Harcourt Publishing Company

Use colored pencils to trace over congruent legs and
hypotenuses in different colors to help students better
visualize the sides that are congruent.

Algebra Use the HL Triangle Congruence Theorem to show that $\triangle ABC \cong \triangle DEF$. (*Hint:* Use the Distance Formula to show that appropriate sides are congruent. Use the slope formula to show that appropriate angles are right angles.)

14.

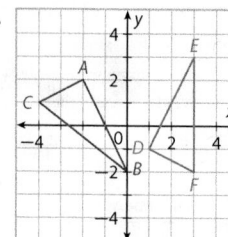

By the Distance Formula,

$$AB = \sqrt{\left(0 - (-2)\right)^2 + (-2 - 2)^2} = \sqrt{20},$$

$$DE = \sqrt{(3 - 1)^2 + \left(3 - (-1)\right)^2} = \sqrt{20},$$

$$BC = \sqrt{(4 - 0)^2 + \left(1 - (-2)\right)^2} = 5,$$

and $EF = 5$ by counting units along the vertical segment.

Therefore, $\overline{AB} \cong \overline{DE}$ and $\overline{BC} \cong \overline{EF}$. By the Slope Formula,

slope of $\overline{AB} = \dfrac{-2 - 2}{0 - (-2)} = -2$, slope of $\overline{AC} = \dfrac{1 - 2}{-4 - (-2)} = \dfrac{1}{2}$,

slope of $\overline{DE} = \dfrac{3 - (-1)}{3 - 1} = 2$, and slope of $\overline{DF} = \dfrac{-2 - (-1)}{3 - 1} = -\dfrac{1}{2}$.

Since $\left(\text{slope of } \overline{AB}\right) \cdot \left(\text{slope of } \overline{AC}\right) = -1$, $\overline{AB} \perp \overline{AC}$ and $\angle A$ is a right angle.

Since $\left(\text{slope of } \overline{DE}\right) \cdot \left(\text{slope of } \overline{DF}\right) = -1$, $\overline{DE} \perp \overline{DF}$ and $\angle D$ is a right angle.

So, $\triangle ABC \cong \triangle DEF$ by the HL Triangle Congruence Theorem.

15.

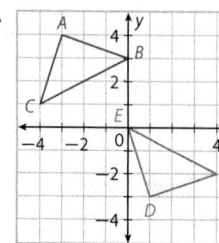

By the Distance Formula,

$$AB = \sqrt{\left(0 - (-3)\right)^2 + (3 - 4)^2} = \sqrt{10},$$

$$DE = \sqrt{(1 - 0)^2 + (-3 - 0)^2} = \sqrt{10},$$

$$BC = \sqrt{(-4 - 0)^2 + (1 - 3)^2} = \sqrt{20},$$

and $EF = \sqrt{(4 - 0)^2 + (-2 - 0)^2} = \sqrt{20}.$

Therefore, $\overline{AB} \cong \overline{DE}$ and $\overline{BC} \cong \overline{EF}$. By the Slope Formula,

slope of $\overline{AB} = \dfrac{3 - 4}{0 - (-3)} = -\dfrac{1}{3}$, slope of $\overline{AC} = \dfrac{1 - 4}{-4 - (-3)} = 3$,

slope of $\overline{DE} = \dfrac{0 - (-3)}{0 - 1} = -3$, slope of $\overline{DF} = \dfrac{-2 - (-3)}{4 - 1} = \dfrac{1}{3}$.

Since $\left(\text{slope of } \overline{AB}\right) \cdot \left(\text{slope of } \overline{AC}\right) = -1$, $\overline{AB} \perp \overline{AC}$ and $\angle A$ is a right angle.

Since $\left(\text{slope of } \overline{DE}\right) \cdot \left(\text{slope of } \overline{DF}\right) = -1$, $\overline{DE} \perp \overline{DF}$ and $\angle D$ is a right angle.

So, $\triangle ABC \cong \triangle DEF$ by the HL Triangle Congruence Theorem.

16. Communicate Mathematical Ideas A vertical tower is supported by two guy wires, as shown. The guy wires are both 58 feet long. Is it possible to determine the distance from the bottom of guy wire $\overline{AB}$ to the bottom of the tower? If so, find the distance. If not, explain why not.

Yes. It is given that $\overline{AB} \cong \overline{AC}$, and $\overline{AD} \cong \overline{AD}$ by the Reflexive Property of Congruence. Since the tower is vertical, $\angle ADB$ and $\angle ADC$ are right angles, so $\triangle ADB \cong \triangle ADC$ by the HL Triangle Congruence Theorem. Therefore, $\overline{BD} \cong \overline{CD}$ since corresponding parts of congruent triangles are congruent. This means $BD = CD = 34$ ft.

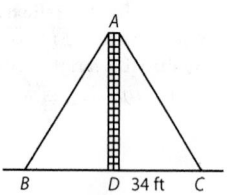

17. A carpenter built a truss, as shown, to support the roof of a doghouse.

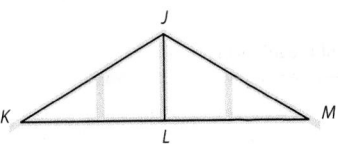

a. The carpenter knows that $\overline{KJ} \cong \overline{MJ}$. Can the carpenter conclude that $\triangle KJL \cong \triangle MJL$? Why or why not?

No; there is not enough information to use any of the triangle congruence theorems.

b. **What If?** Suppose the carpenter also knows that $\angle JLK$ is a right angle. Can the carpenter now conclude that $\triangle KJL \cong \triangle MJL$? Explain.

Yes; $\triangle KJL \cong \triangle MJL$ by the HL Triangle Congruence Theorem since $\overline{KJ} \cong \overline{MJ}$ and $\overline{JL} \cong \overline{JL}$.

18. **Counterexamples** Denise said that if two right triangles share a common hypotenuse, then the triangles must be congruent. Sketch a figure that serves as a counterexample to show that Denise's statement is not true.

Sample figure:

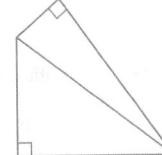

19. **Multi-Step** The front of a tent is covered by a triangular flap of material. The figure represents the front of the tent, with $\overline{PS} \perp \overline{QR}$ and $\overline{PQ} \cong \overline{PR}$. Jonah needs to determine the perimeter of $\triangle PQR$ so that he can replace the zipper on the tent. Find the perimeter. Explain your steps.

Since $\overline{PQ} \cong \overline{PR}$ and $\overline{PS} \cong \overline{PS}$, $\triangle PSQ \cong \triangle PSR$ by the HL Triangle Congruence Theorem. Therefore, $\overline{QS} \cong \overline{RS}$ since corresponding parts of congruent triangles are congruent. By the Pythagorean Theorem, $QS^2 + 4^2 = 5^2$, so $QS^2 = 9$, and $QS = 3$ ft. The perimeter of $\triangle PQR$ is 16 ft.

© Houghton Mifflin Harcourt Publishing Company • Image Credits: (t) ©Jacek Tarczyski/Panther Media/age fotostock

Have students describe how proving two triangles congruent by HL is different from using the SAS method.

20. A student is asked to write a two-column proof for the following.

Given: $\angle ABC$ and $\angle DCB$ are right angles. $\overline{AC} \cong \overline{BD}$

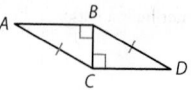

Prove: $\overline{AB} \cong \overline{DC}$

Assuming the student writes the proof correctly, which of the following will appear as a statement or reason in the proof? Select all that apply.

A. ASA Triangle Congruence Theorem   **D.** Reflexive Property of Congruence

B. $\overline{BC} \cong \overline{BC}$ **E.** CPCTC

C. $\angle A \cong \angle D$ **F.** HL Triangle Congruence Theorem

Statements	Reasons
1. $\angle ABC$ and $\angle DCB$ are right angles.	1. Given
2. $\overline{AC} \cong \overline{BD}$	2. Given
3. $\overline{BC} \cong \overline{BC}$	3. Reflexive Property of Congruence
4. $\triangle ABC \cong \triangle DCB$	4. HL Triangle Congruence Theorem
5. $\overline{AB} \cong \overline{DC}$	5. CPCTC

Answer: B, D, E, F

H.O.T. Focus on Higher Order Thinking

21. Analyze Relationships Is it possible for a right triangle with a leg that is 10 inches long and a hypotenuse that is 26 inches long to be congruent to a right triangle with a leg that is 24 inches long and a hypotenuse that is 26 inches long? Explain.

Yes. Let the remaining leg of the first triangle have a length of x inches. Then by the Pythagorean Theorem, $x^2 + 10^2 = 26^2$. So, $x^2 = 576$, and $x = 24$. Therefore, the hypotenuse and a leg of the first right triangle are congruent to the hypotenuse and a leg of the second right triangle, so the triangles are congruent by the HL Triangle Congruence Theorem.

22. Communicate Mathematical Ideas In the figure, $\overline{JK} \cong \overline{LM}, \overline{JM} \cong \overline{LK}$, and $\angle J$ and $\angle L$ are right angles. Describe how you could use three different congruence theorems to prove that $\triangle JKM \cong \triangle LMK$.

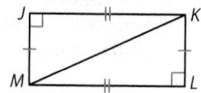

Sample answer: (1) Since $\angle J$ and $\angle L$ are right angles, $\overline{JM} \cong \overline{LK}$, and $\overline{MK} \cong \overline{MK}$, $\triangle JKM \cong \triangle LMK$ by the HL Triangle Congruence Theorem.

(2) Since $\angle J$ and $\angle L$ are right angles, $\angle J \cong \angle L$. Also, $\overline{JK} \cong \overline{LM}$ and $\overline{JM} \cong \overline{LK}$, so $\triangle JKM \cong \triangle LMK$ by the SAS Triangle Congruence Theorem.

(3) By the Reflexive Property of Congruence, $\overline{MK} \cong \overline{MK}$. Also, $\overline{JK} \cong \overline{LM}$ and $\overline{JM} \cong \overline{LK}$, so $\triangle JKM \cong \triangle LMK$ by the SSS Triangle Congruence Theorem.

23. Justify Reasoning Do you think there is an LL Triangle Congruence Theorem? That is, if the legs of one right triangle are congruent to the legs of another right triangle, are the triangles necessarily congruent? If so, write a proof of the theorem. If not, provide a counterexample.

There is an LL Triangle Congruence Theorem.

Given: $\triangle ABC$ $\triangle DEF$ are right triangles;
$\angle A$ and $\angle D$ are right angles.
$\overline{AB} \cong \overline{DE}$ and $\overline{AC} \cong \overline{DF}$

Prove: $\triangle ABC \cong \triangle DEF$

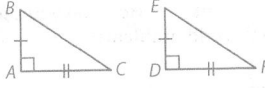

Statements	Reasons
1. $\angle A$ and $\angle D$ are right angles.	1. Given
2. $\angle A \cong \angle D$	2. All right angles are congruent.
3. $\overline{AB} \cong \overline{DE}$	3. Given
4. $\overline{AC} \cong \overline{DF}$	4. Given
5. $\triangle ABC \cong \triangle DEF$	5. SAS Triangle Congruence Theorem

Lesson Performance Task

The figure shows kite *ABCD*.

a. What would you need to know about the relationship between $\overline{AC}$ and $\overline{DB}$ in order to prove that $\triangle ADE \cong \triangle ABE$ and $\triangle CDE \cong \triangle CBE$ by the HL Triangle Congruence Theorem?

b. Can you prove that $\triangle ADC$ and $\triangle ABC$ are congruent using the HL Triangle Congruence Theorem? Explain why or why not.

c. How can you prove that the two triangles named in Part b are in fact congruent, even without the additional piece of information?

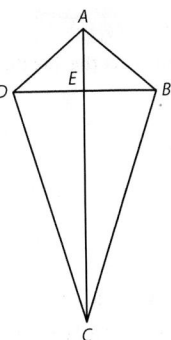

a. $\overline{AC}$ is the perpendicular bisector of $\overline{DB}$

b. You cannot prove that $\triangle ADC$ and $\triangle ABC$ are congruent using the HL Triangle Congruence Theorem because you do not know that $\angle ADC$ and $\angle ABC$ are right angles.

c. The SSS Triangle Congruence Theorem $\left(\overline{AD} \cong \overline{AB}, \overline{CD} \cong \overline{CB}, \overline{AC} \cong \overline{AC}\right)$

© Houghton Mifflin Harcourt Publishing Company

MP.3 To prove that two triangles are congruent by SSS, you must meet three conditions, showing that the three sides of one triangle are congruent respectively to the three sides of the other triangle. Renaldo said that, in fact, for all five methods of proving triangles congruent, it is necessary to meet three conditions. Do you agree or disagree? Explain. Agree. Sample answer: For ASA, SAS, SSS, and AAS, the three letters specify that three pairs of angles, sides, or combinations of the two must be shown congruent. HL appears at first to require that only two conditions be met. But in addition to showing that the hypotenuses and one pair of legs are congruent, the theorem requires that a third condition must be met: You must show that the triangles are right triangles.

INTEGRATE MATHEMATICAL PRACTICES
Focus on Communication

MP.3 Explain that figure *ABCD* in the Lesson Performance Task not only looks like a kite, it's known geometrically as a *kite*. Ask students to study the kite's features and then write a concise, precise definition of a geometrical kite. Students will study kites in Module 9. Their definitions will vary but should address the fact that a kite is a quadrilateral with two pairs of adjacent congruent sides, and that the pairs have different lengths.

EXTENSION ACTIVITY

Students have studied five congruence theorems: ASA, SAS, SSS, AAS, and HL. Have students draw five diagrams, each as simple or as complicated as they wish, with each diagram showing at minimum a pair of triangles, and each illustrating one of the five congruence theorems. For each diagram, students should write what is given, what is to be proved, and which congruence theorem is illustrated, then add a formal or informal proof.

Scoring Rubric
2 points: Student correctly solves the problem and explains his/her reasoning.
1 point: Student shows good understanding of the problem but does not fully solve or explain his/her reasoning.
0 points: Student does not demonstrate understanding of the problem.

HL Triangle Congruence   **304**

Study Guide Review

ASSESSMENT AND INTERVENTION

Assign or customize module reviews.

Applications of Triangle Congruence

MODUL **6**

Essential Question: How can you use triangle congruence to solve real-world problems?

Key Vocabulary
hypotenuse *(hipotenusa)*
legs *(catetos)*

KEY EXAMPLE   Lesson 6.1

Construct the bisector of the angle shown.

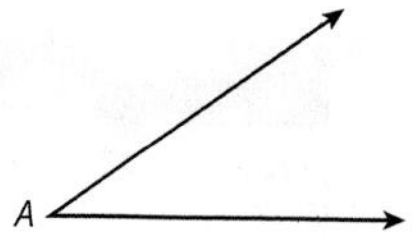

Place the point of the compass at A and draw an arc intersecting the sides of the angle. Label its points of intersection as B and C.

Use the same compass setting to draw intersecting arcs from B and C. Label the intersection of the arcs as point D.

Use a straight edge to draw $\overrightarrow{AD}$.

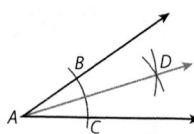

KEY EXAMPLE   (Lesson 6.2)

Construct the line through the given point, parallel to the line shown.

Use a straightedge to draw $\overrightarrow{AC}$.

Copy $\angle CAB$. Start by constructing a pair of arcs.

Then construct the pair of arc intersections.

Draw line ℓ through C and the arc intersection. This line is parallel to m.

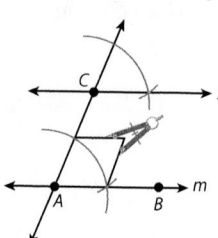

The triangular regions represent plots of land. Use the AAS Theorem to explain why the same amount of fencing will surround either plot.

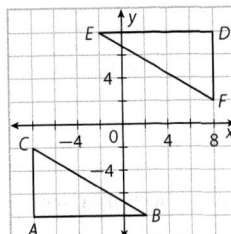

Given: $\angle B \cong \angle E$

$\angle A \cong \angle D$ Both right angles

Compare AC and DF using the Distance Formula.

$$AC = \sqrt{(x_2 - x_1)^2 + (y_2 - y_1)^2} \qquad DF = \sqrt{(x_2 - x_1)^2 + (y_2 - y_1)^2}$$

$$= \sqrt{(-8 - (-8))^2 + (-2 - (-8))^2} \qquad = \sqrt{(8 - 8)^2 + (2 - 8)^2}$$

$$= \sqrt{0 + 36} \qquad\qquad\qquad\qquad = \sqrt{0 + 36}$$

$$= 6 \qquad\qquad\qquad\qquad\qquad = 6$$

Because two angles and a nonincluded side are congruent, $\triangle ABC \cong \triangle DEF$ by AAS. Therefore the triangles have the same perimeter by CPCTC and the same amount of fencing is needed.

Write the given proof.

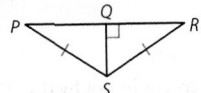

Given: $\overline{PS} \cong \overline{RS}$

Prove: $\triangle PQS \cong \triangle RSQ$

Statements	Reasons
1. $\angle PQS$ and $\angle RQS$ are right angles.	1. Given
2. $\overline{PS} \cong \overline{SR}$	2. Given
3. $\overline{SQ} \cong \overline{SQ}$	3. Reflexive Property of Congruence
4. $\triangle PQS \cong \triangle RQS$	4. HL Triangle Congruence Theorem

MODULE PERFORMANCE TASK

Mathematical Practices: MP.1, MP.2, MP.4, MP.7, MP.8
G-SRT.B.5, G-MG.A.1

SUPPORTING STUDENT REASONING

Students should begin this problem by focusing on the triangles that make up the icosahedron. Here are some issues they might bring up.

- **If all of the triangular faces are congruent:** The best way to find out is to prove that the triangles are congruent by the ASA Congruence Criteria.

- **What the area is of each triangle:** Use a triangle area formula to find the area of each triangle.

- **How the surface area is found:** Students should understand that the surface area is the sum of the areas of all 20 equilateral triangles. The formula can be derived by multiplying the area formula of one equilateral triangle by 20,

  or $SA = 20\left(\dfrac{\sqrt{3}}{4}s^2\right) = 5\sqrt{3}s^2$.

EXERCISES

Refer to the diagram, which shows isosceles triangle *ABC* to find the measure of the angle. $\overline{AD}$ and $\overline{CD}$ are angle bisectors. *(Lesson 6.1)*

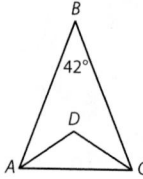

1. m∠*BAC* __69°__

2. m∠*ADC* __111°__

Identify the sides or angles that need to be congruent in order to make the given triangles congruent by AAS. *(Lesson 6.2)*

3.

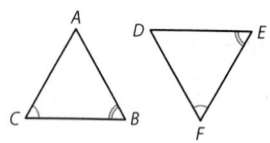

$\overline{AB} \cong \overline{DE}$ or $\overline{AC} \cong \overline{DF}$

4.

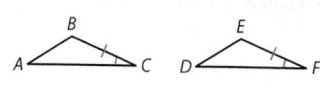

$\angle BAC \cong \angle EDF$

Determine whether the two triangles are congruent or not by the HL Theorem. Show all work. *(Lesson 6.3)*

5.

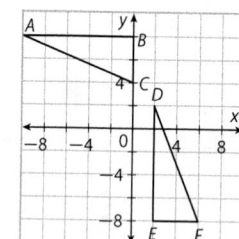

$AC = \sqrt{AB^2 + CB^2}$

$\quad = \sqrt{5^2 + 2^2}$

$\quad = \sqrt{29}$

$DF = \sqrt{DE^2 + EF^2}$

$\quad = \sqrt{5^2 + 2^2}$

$\quad = \sqrt{29}$

So, $\overline{AC} \cong \overline{DF}$. Also $CB = EF = 2$, so $\overline{CB} \cong \overline{EF}$.

Therefore $\triangle ABC \cong \triangle DEF$ by the HL Congruence Theorem.

SCAFFOLDING SUPPORT

- Use the figure to help students find the area of each triangle in the dome. An altitude is drawn from one vertex. By the Pythagorean Theorem,

  $4^2 + h^2 = 8^2$

  $16 + h^2 = 64$

  $h^2 = 48$

  $h = \sqrt{48}$

  $h = 4\sqrt{3}$

So, the area of each triangle equals $\frac{1}{2}bh = \frac{1}{2}(8)(4\sqrt{3}) = 16\sqrt{3}$ in².

MODULE PERFORMANCE TASK
Geodesic Dome Design

A geodesic dome is derived from a 20-sided structure called an icosahedron, made up of equilateral triangles. The illustration shows an icosahedron with the length of one side of a triangle labeled.

Are all of the triangles that make up the icosahedron congruent? How can you find the total surface area of the icosahedron?

Use the space below to complete the task. Be sure to write down all your data and assumptions. Then use graphs, numbers, words, or algebra to explain how you reached your conclusion.

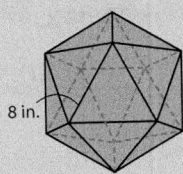

8 in.

SAMPLE SOLUTION

The dome has 20 equilateral triangles for faces. Since all the angles measure 60° and each triangle shares a side with each adjacent triangle, the triangles are all congruent by the ASA Congruence Theorem.

The area of each of the 20 congruent triangles that make up the dome is $16\sqrt{3}$ in². [See "Scaffolding Support" for the derivation of this area.] So, the total surface area is $20(16\sqrt{3}) = 320\sqrt{3}$

$$\approx 320(1.732)$$

$$\approx 554.26 \text{ in}^2.$$

DISCUSSION OPPORTUNITIES

- Would it be reasonable to assume that knowing the length of one side of a regular icosahedron is enough to find the surface area?

- Is there a formula for the surface area of a non-regular icosahedron?

Assessment Rubric

2 points: Student correctly solves the problem and explains his/her reasoning.

1 point: Student shows good understanding of the problem but does not fully solve or explain.

0 points: Student does not demonstrate understanding of the problem.

Ready to Go On?

ASSESS MASTERY

Use the assessment on this page to determine if students have mastered the concepts and standards covered in this module.

ASSESSMENT AND INTERVENTION

Access Ready to Go On? assessment online, and receive instant scoring, feedback, and customized intervention or enrichment.

ADDITIONAL RESOURCES

Response to Intervention Resources

- Reteach Worksheets

Differentiated Instruction Resources

- Reading Strategies **EL**
- Success for English Learners **EL**
- Challenge Worksheets

Assessment Resources

- Leveled Module Quizzes

- Online Homework
- Hints and Help
- Extra Practice

Given the figure below, answer the following.

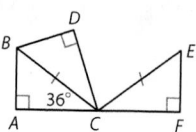

1. Given: $\angle A \cong \angle D$, $\overrightarrow{BC}$ bisects $\angle ACD$. Prove: $\triangle ABC \cong \triangle DBC$ *(Lessons 6.1, 6.3)*

Answers may vary. Sample:

1. $\overline{BC} \cong \overline{BC}$	Reflexive property of congruence
2. $\overline{BC}$ bisects $\angle ACD$.	Given
3. $\angle ACB \cong \angle DCB$	Definition of angle bisector
4. $\angle A \cong \angle D$	Given
5. $\triangle ABC \cong \triangle DBC$	AAS Congruence Theorem

2. Given: $\angle A$ and $\angle F$ are right angles, C is the midpoint of $\overline{AF}$, $\overline{BC} \cong \overline{EC}$. Prove: $\triangle ABC \cong \triangle FEC$ *(Lesson 6.3)*

Answers may vary. Sample:

1. $\angle A$ and $\angle F$ are right angles.	Given
2. C is the midpoint of $\overline{AF}$.	Given
3. $\overline{AC} \cong \overline{FC}$	Definition of midpoint
4. $\overline{BC} \cong \overline{EC}$	Given
5. $\triangle ABC \cong \triangle FEC$	HL Triangle Congruence Theorem

3. Given: $\overrightarrow{BC}$ bisects $\angle ACD$ and m$\angle ACB$ is 36°. Find m$\angle BCD$. *(Lesson 6.1)*

m$\angle BCD = 36°$

ESSENTIAL QUESTION

4. When given two sides and an angle of two triangles are equal, when can it be proven and when can't it be proven that the two triangles are congruent?

Answers may vary. Sample: If the two triangles are right triangles, then HL will prove they are congruent. Also, if the angle is included in the sides, then SAS will prove the triangles are congruent. But, if the angle is not included in the sides, then it cannot be proven that the triangles are congruent.

COMMON CORE Common Core Standards

Lesson	Items	Content Standards	Mathematical Practices
6.2	1	G-SRT.B.5	MP.3
6.3	2	G-SRT.B.5	MP.3
6.1	3	G-CO.D.12	MP.2

MODULE 6
MIXED REVIEW

Assessment Readiness

1. Which of these are theorems that can be used to prove two triangles are congruent?
   Select Yes or No for A–C.
   A. SSA   ○ Yes   ● No
   B. AAS   ● Yes   ○ No
   C. SAS   ● Yes   ○ No

2. Line D bisects $\angle ABC$, $m\angle ABD = 4x$, and $m\angle DBC = x + 36$. Choose True or False for each statement.
   A. $m\angle ABC = 48°$ ○ True   ● False
   B. $m\angle ABC = 96°$ ● True   ○ False
   C. $m\angle DBC = 48°$ ● True   ○ False

3. Given $\triangle GHI$ and $\triangle JKL$, $GI = 5$, $HI = 4$, $JK = 4$, and $JL = 5$, what else do you need to know to prove the two triangles are congruent using HL?

   Possible Answer: You need to know that angles *H* and *K* are right angles

   because HL only works with right triangles.

4. Given: $\overline{AB} \cong \overline{BC}$, $\overline{BD}$ is the perpendicular bisector of $\overline{AC}$
   Prove: $\triangle ABD \cong \triangle CBD$

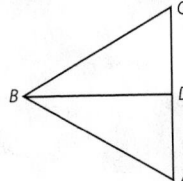

Answers may vary. Sample:

$\overline{AB} \cong \overline{BC}$	Given
$\overline{BD}$ is the perpendicular bisector of $\overline{AC}$.	Given
$\overline{BD} \cong \overline{BD}$	Reflexive property of congruence
$\angle BDA$ and $\angle BDC$ are right angles.	Definition of perpendicular bisector
$\triangle ABD \cong \triangle CBD$	HL triangle congruence theorem

---

MIXED REVIEW
Assessment Readiness

ASSESSMENT AND INTERVENTION

Assign ready-made or customized practice tests to prepare students for high-stakes tests.

ADDITIONAL RESOURCES

Assessment Resources

- Leveled Module Quizzes: Modified, B

AVOID COMMON ERRORS

Item 2 Some students will have a hard time visualizing the problem. Encourage students to draw a picture to match the verbal description. It will help them see the relationships between the angles.

COMMON CORE **Common Core Standards**

Lesson	Items	Content Standards	Mathematical Practices
6.2, 5.3	1*	G-SRT.B.5	MP.6
1.2	2*	G-CO.D.12	MP.2
6.3	3	G-SRT.B.5	MP.6
6.3	4	G-SRT.B.5	MP.3

* Item integrates mixed review concepts from previous modules or a previous course.

Properties of Triangles

ESSENTIAL QUESTION:

Answer: The properties of triangles can be used to solve problems wherever triangles appear in the real world, such as in the shape of a building or a park.

PROFESSIONAL DEVELOPMENT VIDEO

Professional Development Video

Learn effective ways of integrating technology into your classroom to meet a variety of different needs.

Professional Development
my.hrw.com

MODULE 7

Properties of Triangles

Essential Question: How can you use properties of triangles to solve real-world problems?

LESSON 7.1
Interior and Exterior Angles

LESSON 7.2
Isosceles and Equilateral Triangles

LESSON 7.3
Triangle Inequalities

UNITED STATES

FEDERAL TRADE COMMISSION BUILDING

© Houghton Mifflin Harcourt Publishing Company • Image Credits: ©Gary Cameron/Reuters/Corbis

REAL WORLD VIDEO
Check out some of the famous buildings and landmarks in the Federal Triangle area of Washington, DC.

MODULE PERFORMANCE TASK PREVIEW

The Federal Triangle

Is the Federal Triangle really a triangle? In this module, you will use a map of the Federal Triangle to explore the geometric properties of the entire area. Time to "capitalize" on your geometry knowledge!

DIGITAL TEACHER EDITION

Access a full suite of teaching resources when and where you need them:

- Access content online or offline
- Customize lessons to share with your class
- Communicate with your students in real-time
- View student grades and data instantly to target your instruction where it is needed most

PERSONAL MATH TRAINER

Assessment and Intervention

Assign automatically graded homework, quizzes, tests, and intervention activities. Prepare your students with updated, Common Core-aligned practice tests.

Are YOU Ready?

Complete these exercises to review the skills you will need for this module.

- Online Homework
- Hints and Help
- Extra Practice

Solving Inequalities

Example 1   What values of x make both inequalities true?

$x + 7 > 2$	$3 + x < 9$	Write the inequalities
$x > 2 - 7$	$x < 9 - 3$	Solve for x.
$x > -5$	$x < 6$	Simplify.
	$-5 < x < 6$	Combine solved inequalities.

The solutions to the system are all values greater than −5 and less than 6.

What values of the variable make both inequalities true?

1. $\dfrac{d + 176}{3} < 116$

    $248 + d > 368$

       $\underline{120 < d < 172}$

2. $n + 14 > 16$

    $2(n + 68) < 148$

       $\underline{2 < n < 6}$

Angle Relationships

Example 2   Find the measure of $\angle x$.

$m\angle x + 72° = 180°$	Definition of supplementary angles
$m\angle x = 180° - 72°$	Solve for $m\angle x$.
$m\angle x = 108°$	Simplify.

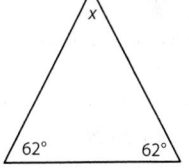

Find the measure of each angle in the image from the example.

3. $m\angle y = \underline{\quad 71° \quad}$

4. $m\angle z = \underline{\quad 37° \quad}$

Angle Theorems for Triangles

Example 3   Find the missing angle.

$62° + 62° + m\angle x = 180°$	Triangle Sum Theorem
$m\angle x = 180° - 62° - 62°$	Solve for $m\angle x$.
$m\angle x = 56°$	Simplify.

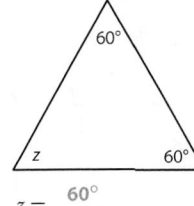

Find the missing angle measures in the given triangles.

5.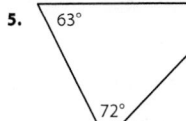

$y = \underline{\quad 45° \quad}$

6.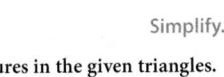

$z = \underline{\quad 60° \quad}$

© Houghton Mifflin Harcourt Publishing Company

Are You Ready?

ASSESS READINESS

Use the assessment on this page to determine if students need strategic or intensive intervention for the module's prerequisite skills.

ASSESSMENT AND INTERVENTION

RtI Response to Intervention   **TIER 1, TIER 2, TIER 3 SKILLS**

Personal Math Trainer will automatically create a standards-based, personalized intervention assignment for your students, targeting each student's individual needs!

ADDITIONAL RESOURCES

See the table below for a full list of intervention resources available for this module.

Response to Intervention Resources also includes:

- Tier 2 Skill Pre-Tests for each Module
- Tier 2 Skill Post-Tests for each skill

Response to Intervention			Differentiated Instruction
Tier 1 Lesson Intervention Worksheets	**Tier 2** Strategic Intervention Skills Intervention Worksheets	**Tier 3** Intensive Intervention Worksheets available online	
Reteach 7.1 Reteach 7.2 Reteach 7.3	2 Angle Relationships 3 Angle Theorems for Triangles 9 Distance and Midpoint Formula	Building Block Skills 7, 8, 10, 11, 15, 16, 27, 38, 45, 48, 53, 56, 66, 69, 70, 74, 95, 98, 100, 102, 104	Challenge worksheets Extend the Math Lesson Activities in TE

Interior and Exterior Angles

Common Core Math Standards

The student is expected to:

COMMON CORE G-CO.C.10

Prove theorems about triangles.

Mathematical Practices

COMMON CORE MP.8 Patterns

Language Objective

Work in small groups to play angle jeopardy.

ENGAGE

Essential Question: What can you say about the interior and exterior angles of a triangle and other polygons?

The sum of the interior angle measures of a triangle is 180°. You can find the sum of the interior angle measures of any *n*-gon, where *n* represents the number of sides of the polygon, by multiplying $(n - 2)180°$. In a polygon, an exterior angle forms a linear pair with its adjacent interior angle, so the sum of their measures is 180°. In a triangle, the measure of an exterior angle is equal to the sum of the measures of its two remote interior angles.

PREVIEW: LESSON PERFORMANCE TASK

View the Engage section online. Discuss the photo, asking students to recall and describe the designs of game boards of their favorite games. Then preview the Lesson Performance Task.

Name_____ Class_____ Date_____

7.1 Interior and Exterior Angles

Essential Question: What can you say about the interior and exterior angles of a triangle and other polygons?

Resource Locker

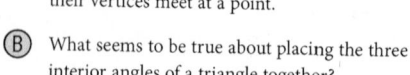 **Explore 1** **Exploring Interior Angles in Triangles**

You can find a relationship between the measures of the three angles of a triangle. An **interior angle** is an angle formed by two sides of a polygon with a common vertex. So, a triangle has three interior angles.

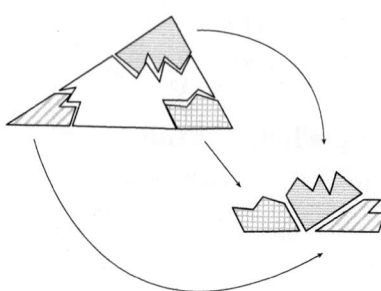

interior angles

(A) Use a straightedge to draw a large triangle on a sheet of paper and cut it out. Tear off the three corners and rearrange the angles so their sides are adjacent and their vertices meet at a point.

(B) What seems to be true about placing the three interior angles of a triangle together?

They form a straight angle.

(C) Make a conjecture about the sum of the measures of the interior angles of a triangle.

The sum of the measures of the interior

angles of a triangle is 180°.

The conjecture about the sum of the interior angles of a triangle can be proven so it can be stated as a theorem. In the proof, you will add an *auxiliary line* to the triangle figure. An **auxiliary line** is a line that is added to a figure to aid in a proof.

The Triangle Sum Theorem

The sum of the angle measures of a triangle is 180°.

(D) Fill in the blanks to complete the proof of the Triangle Sum Theorem.

Given: △ABC

Prove: $m\angle 1 + m\angle 2 + m\angle 3 = 180°$

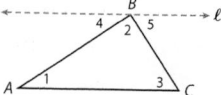

Statements	Reasons
1. Draw line ℓ through point *B* parallel to $\overline{AC}$.	1. Parallel Postulate
2. $m\angle 1 = m\angle$ __4__ and $m\angle 3 = m\angle$ __5__	2. Alternate Interior Angles Theorem
3. $m\angle 4 + m\angle 2 + m\angle 5 = 180°$	3. Angle Addition Postulate and definition of straight angle
4. $m\angle$ __1__ $+ m\angle 2 + m\angle$ __3__ $= 180°$	4. Substitution Property of Equality

Module 7

313

Lesson 1

© Houghton Mifflin Harcourt Publishing Company

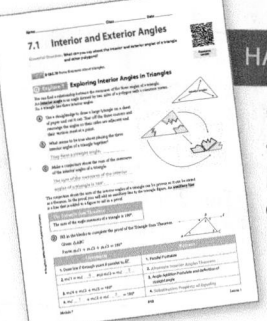

HARDCOVER PAGES 271–282

Turn to these pages to find this lesson in the hardcover student edition.

1. Explain how the Parallel Postulate allows you to add the auxiliary line into the triangle figure.
Since there is only one line parallel to a given line that passes through a given point, I can

draw that line into the triangle and know it is the only one possible.

2. What does the Triangle Sum Theorem indicate about the angles of a triangle that has
three angles of equal measure? How do you know?
$\frac{180}{3} = 60$, so each angle of the triangle must have a measure of 60°.

⊘ Explore 2 Exploring Interior Angles in Polygons

To determine the sum of the interior angles for any polygon, you can use what you know
about the Triangle Sum Theorem by considering how many triangles there are in other
polygons. For example, by drawing the diagonal from a vertex of a quadrilateral, you can
form two triangles. Since each triangle has an angle sum of 180°, the quadrilateral must
have an angle sum of 180° + 180° = 360°.

quadrilateral

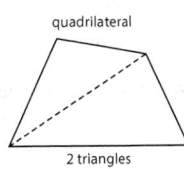

2 triangles

Ⓐ Draw the diagonals from any one vertex for each polygon. Then state the
number of triangles that are formed. The first two have already been completed.

triangle

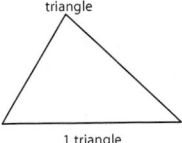

1 triangle

quadrilateral

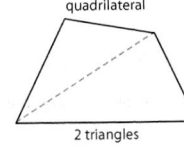

2 triangles

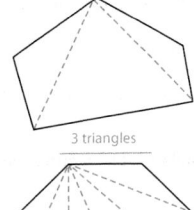

3 triangles

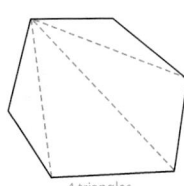

4 triangles

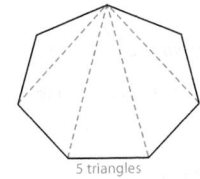

5 triangles

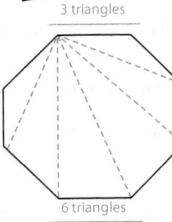

6 triangles

Ⓑ For each polygon, identify the number of sides and triangles, and determine the angle sums.
Then complete the chart. The first two have already been done for you.

Polygon	Number of Sides	Number of Triangles	Sum of Interior Angle Measures
Triangle	3	1	(1)180° = 180°
Quadrilateral	4	2	(2)180° = 360°
Pentagon	5	3	(_3_)180° = _540°_
Hexagon	6	4	(_4_)180° = _720°_
Decagon	10	8	(_8_)180° = _1440°_

EXPLORE 1

Exploring Interior Angles in Triangles

INTEGRATE TECHNOLOGY

Students have the option of completing the interior
angles in triangles activity either in the book or
online.

QUESTIONING STRATEGIES

? What can you say about angles that come
together to form a straight line? Why? The
sum of the angle measures must be 180° by the
definition of a straight angle and the Angle Addition
Postulate.

? Is it possible for a triangle to have two obtuse
angles? Why or why not? No; the sum of
these angles would be greater than 180°.

EXPLORE 2

Exploring Interior Angles in Polygons

AVOID COMMON ERRORS

When attempting to determine the sum of the
interior angles of a polygon, some students may
divide the figure into too many triangles. For
example, a student may draw both diagonals of a
quadrilateral and conclude that the sum of the
interior angles of a polygon is 720°. Point out that
four of the angles of the triangles are not part of an
interior angle of the quadrilateral, and demonstrate
the correct division.

PROFESSIONAL DEVELOPMENT

 Integrate Mathematical Practices

This lesson provides an opportunity to address Mathematical Practice **MP.8**,
which calls for students to "look for and identify patterns." Throughout the lesson,
students use hands-on investigations or geometry to predict patterns and
relationships for the interior and exterior angles of a triangle or polygon. They
prove the Triangle Sum Theorem, the Polygon Angle Sum Theorem, and the
Exterior Angle Theorem. The hands-on investigations give students a chance to
use inductive reasoning to make a conjecture. This is followed by a proof in which
students use deductive reasoning to justify their conjectures.

EXPLAIN 1

Using Interior Angles

INTEGRATE MATHEMATICAL PRACTICES

Focus on Math Connections

MP.1 You may want to review with students how to evaluate algebraic expressions and how to use inverse operations to solve equations.

Ⓒ Do you notice a pattern between the number of sides and the number of triangles? If n represents the number of sides for any polygon, how can you represent the number of triangles? $\underline{n-2}$

Ⓓ Make a conjecture for a rule that would give the sum of the interior angles for any n-gon.

Sum of interior angle measures = $\underline{(n-2)180°}$

Reflect

3. In a regular hexagon, how could you use the sum of the interior angles to determine the measure of each interior angle?

Since the polygon is regular, you can divide the sum by 6 to determine each interior angle

measure.

4. How might you determine the number of sides for a polygon whose interior angle sum is 3240°?

Write and solve an equation for n, where $(n-2)180° = 3240°$.

⊘ Explain 1 **Using Interior Angles**

You can use the angle sum to determine the unknown measure of an angle of a polygon when you know the measures of the other angles.

Polygon Angle Sum Theorem
The sum of the measures of the interior angles of a convex polygon with n sides is $(n-2)180°$.

Example 1 Determine the unknown angle measures.

Ⓐ For the nonagon shown, find the unknown angle measure $x°$.

First, use the Polygon Angle Sum Theorem to find the sum of the interior angles:

$n = 9$

$(n-2)180° = (9-2)180° = (7)180° = 1260°$

Then solve for the unknown angle measure, $x°$:

$125 + 130 + 172 + 98 + 200 + 102 + 140 + 135 + x = 1260$

$x = 158$

The unknown angle measure is 158°.

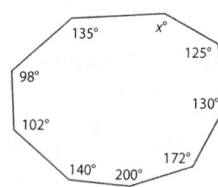

© Houghton Mifflin Harcourt Publishing Company

COLLABORATIVE LEARNING

Small Group Activity

Geometry software allows students to explore the theorems in this lesson. For the Triangle Sum Theorem and the Exterior Angle Theorem, students should construct a triangle, measure the three angles, and use the Calculate tool (in the Measure menu) to find the sum of the interior angle measures and also to find the sum of the exterior angles. As students drag the vertices of the triangle to change its shape, the individual angle measures will change, but the sum of the measures will remain 180° for the interior angles and 360° for the exterior angles.

Ⓑ Determine the unknown interior angle measure of a convex octagon in which the measures of the seven other angles have a sum of 940°.

$n = \boxed{8}$

$\text{Sum} = \left(\boxed{8} - 2\right)180° = \left(\boxed{6}\right)180° = \boxed{1080°}$

$\boxed{940} + x = \boxed{1080}$

$x = \boxed{140}$

The unknown angle measure is $\underline{140°}$.

Reflect

5. How might you use the Polygon Angle Sum Theorem to write a rule for determining the measure of each interior angle of any regular convex polygon with n sides?

You can divide the angle sum by n. $\dfrac{(n-2)180°}{n}$ gives the measure of an interior angle for any regular polygon.

Your Turn

6. Determine the unknown angle measures in this pentagon.

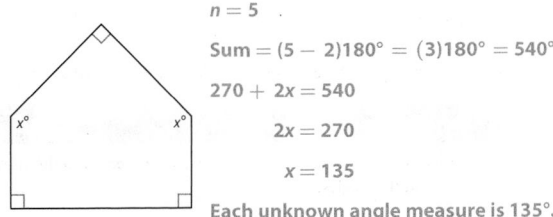

$n = 5$

$\text{Sum} = (5 - 2)180° = (3)180° = 540°$

$270 + 2x = 540$

$2x = 270$

$x = 135$

Each unknown angle measure is 135°.

7. Determine the measure of the fourth interior angle of a quadrilateral if you know the other three measures are 89°, 80°, and 104°.

$n = 4$

$\text{Sum} = (4 - 2)180° = 2(180°) = 360°$

$89 + 80 + 104 + x = 360$

$x = 87$

The unknown angle measure is 87°.

8. Determine the unknown angle measures in a hexagon whose six angles measure 69°, 108°, 135°, 204°, $b°$, and $2b°$.

$n = 6$

$\text{Sum} = (6 - 2)180° = (4)180° = 720°$

$b + 2b + 69 + 108 + 135 + 204 = 720$

$3b + 516 = 720$

$3b = 204$

$b = 68$

$2b = 136$

The two unknown angle measures are 68° and 136°.

QUESTIONING STRATEGIES

❓ How do you use the sum of the interior angle measures of a polygon to find the measure of an unknown interior angle? Use the Polygon Sum Theorem to find the total measure of the interior angles, then solve an algebraic equation to find the unknown angle.

DIFFERENTIATE INSTRUCTION

Manipulatives

Have students fold and crease the four corners of a sheet of paper. Next, ask them to open the folds to reveal a creased polygon shape. Have students classify the polygon (octagon). Ask them to find the sum of the interior and exterior angle measures (1080°; 360°). Then have students measure the interior and exterior angles to verify their sums.

EXPLAIN 2

Proving the Exterior Angle Theorem

QUESTIONING STRATEGIES

? How does finding the measure of an exterior angle differ from finding the measure of an interior angle? The measure of an exterior angle is the supplement of its adjacent interior angle because the angles form linear pairs with the interior angles. The measure of an interior angle is not found by using linear pairs.

? Why is the Exterior Angle Theorem sometimes called a corollary of the Triangle Sum Theorem? because the Exterior Angle Theorem follows from the Triangle Sum Theorem

Lesson 7.1

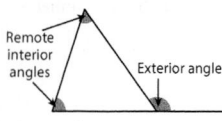

⌀ Explain 2 **Proving the Exterior Angle Theorem**

An **exterior angle** is an angle formed by one side of a polygon and the extension of an adjacent side. Exterior angles form linear pairs with the interior angles.

A **remote interior angle** is an interior angle that is not adjacent to the exterior angle.

Example 2 Follow the steps to investigate the relationship between each exterior angle of a triangle and its remote interior angles.

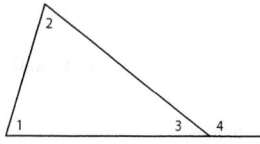

Step 1 Use a straightedge to draw a triangle with angles 1, 2, and 3. Line up your straightedge along the side opposite angle 2. Extend the side from the vertex at angle 3. You have just constructed an exterior angle. The exterior angle is drawn *supplementary* to its adjacent interior angle.

Step 2 You know the sum of the measures of the interior angles of a triangle.

$m\angle 1 + m\angle 2 + m\angle 3 = \boxed{180}°$

Since an exterior angle is supplementary to its adjacent interior angle, you also know:

$m\angle 3 + m\angle 4 = \boxed{180}°$

Make a conjecture: What can you say about the measure of the exterior angle and the measures of its remote interior angles?

Conjecture: The measure of the exterior angle is the same as the sum of the measures of its two remote interior angles.

The conjecture you made in Step 2 can be formally stated as a theorem.

Exterior Angle Theorem
The measure of an exterior angle of a triangle is equal to the sum of the measures of its remote interior angles.

Step 3 Complete the proof of the Exterior Angle Theorem.

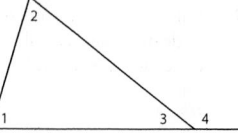

∠4 is an exterior angle. It forms a linear pair with interior angle ∠3. Its remote interior angles are ∠1 and ∠2.

By the ___Triangle Sum Theorem___, $m\angle 1 + m\angle 2 + m\angle 3 = 180°$.

Also, $m\angle 3 + m\angle 4 = \underline{180°}$ because they are supplementary and make a straight angle.

By the Substitution Property of Equality, then, $m\angle 1 + m\angle 2 + m\angle 3 = m\angle \underline{3} + m\angle \underline{4}$.

Subtracting $m\angle 3$ from each side of this equation leaves $\underline{m\angle 1 + m\angle 2 = m\angle 4}$.

This means that the measure of an exterior angle of a triangle is equal to the sum of the measures of the remote interior angles.

© Houghton Mifflin Harcourt Publishing Company

LANAGUAGE SUPPORT **EL**

Communicate Math

Have students write clues about interior and exterior angles in polygons, for example: "The sum of the interior angles of this three-sided polygon is 180 degrees" or "The sum of the exterior angles of this three-sided polygon is 360 degrees." Have each student write two clue cards about different polygons. They then read their clues to the rest of the group, and the group must decide which polygon fits the clue.

9. **Discussion** Determine the measure of each exterior angle. Add them together. What can you say about their sum? Explain.

The exterior angles will measure 140°, 120°, and 100°.

Their sum is 360°. Each exterior angle is equal to the sum

of the measures of the two remote interior angles, and

the sum of all 3 exterior angles includes each interior

angle twice.

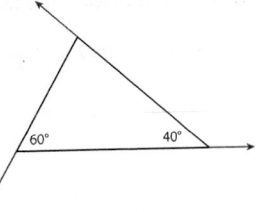

10. According to the definition of an exterior angle, one of the sides of the triangle must be extended in order to see it. How many ways can this be done for any vertex? How many exterior angles is it possible to draw for a triangle? for a hexagon?

Two exterior angles can be drawn from any vertex by extending either side, so a triangle

can have 6 exterior angles. You could draw 12 different exterior angles for a hexagon.

Explain 3   Using Exterior Angles

You can apply the Exterior Angle Theorem to solve problems with unknown angle measures by writing and solving equations.

Example 3 Determine the measure of the specified angle.

(A) Find m∠B.

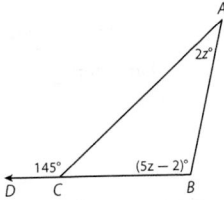

Write and solve an equation relating the exterior and remote interior angles.

$145 = 2z + 5z - 2$

$145 = 7z - 2$

$z = 21$

Now use this value for the unknown to evaluate the expression for the required angle.

$m\angle B = (5z - 2)° = (5(21) - 2)°$

$= (105 - 2)°$

$= 103°$

(B) Find m∠PRS.

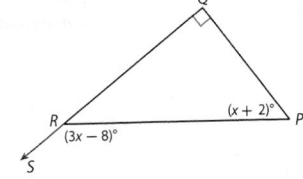

Write an equation relating the exterior and remote interior angles.

$3x - 8 = (x + 2) + 90$

Solve for the unknown.

$3x - 8 = x + 92$

$2x = 100$

$x = 50$

Use the value for the unknown to evaluate the expression for the required angle.

$m\angle PRS = (3x - 8)° = (3(50) - 8)° = 142°$

AVOID COMMON ERRORS

Some students may confuse the theorems in this lesson and incorrectly assume that the sum of the interior angles of a polygon is 360°. Remind students of the Triangle Sum Theorem. Have them draw an equilateral triangle and show that its interior angle measures add to 180° and its exterior angle measures add to 360°.

EXPLAIN 3

Using Exterior Angles

INTEGRATE MATHEMATICAL PRACTICES
Focus on Patterns

MP.8 Encourage students to make a table listing the sums of the exterior angles of regular triangles, quadrilaterals, pentagons, and hexagons. Ask them what they notice about the sum of the exterior angles. (The sum is always 360°.) Ask them to find the pattern in the measure of each individual exterior angle for these regular polygons. (They each have the same measure.)

CONNECT VOCABULARY EL

Help students understand the meanings of *interior*, *exterior*, and *remote* by writing the definitions on note cards. An *interior* angle is *inside* the figure, an *exterior* angle is *outside* the figure, and a *remote interior angle* is *interior and away* from the exterior angle. Relate the idea of a remote interior angle to a television remote control that sends a signal across the room and away from you.

QUESTIONING STRATEGIES

? What kind of angle is formed by extending one of the sides of a triangle? What is its relationship to the adjacent interior angle? an exterior angle; the angles are supplementary.

ELABORATE

QUESTIONING STRATEGIES

? How do you use the sum of the interior angle measures of a regular polygon to find the measure of each interior angle? Divide the sum of the interior angles by the number of sides.

? What happens to the measure of each exterior angle as the number of sides of a regular polygon increases? Why? The measures get smaller and smaller because the sum must remain 360°.

SUMMARIZE THE LESSON

Have students fill out a chart to summarize the theorems in this lesson. Sample:

Triangle Sum Theorem
$m\angle 1 + m\angle 2 + m\angle 3 = 180°$

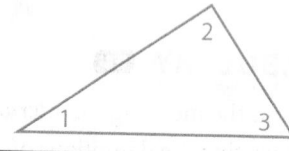

Polygon Sum Theorem
$(n-2)\,180° = (6-2)\,180° = 720°$

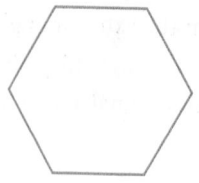

Exterior Angle Theorem
$m\angle 4 = m\angle 1 + m\angle 2$

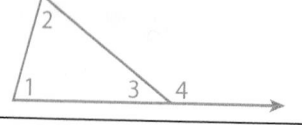

Determine the measure of the specified angle.

11. Determine $m\angle N$ in $\triangle MNP$.

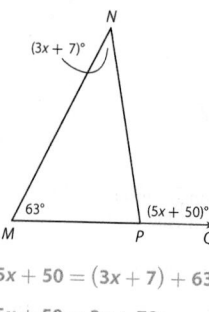

$5x + 50 = (3x + 7) + 63$

$5x + 50 = 3x + 70$

$2x = 20$

$x = 10$

$m\angle N = (3x + 7)° = \big(3(10) + 7\big)° = 37°$

12. If the exterior angle drawn measures 150°, and the measure of $\angle D$ is twice that of $\angle E$, find the measure of the two remote interior angles.

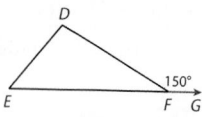

$x + 2x = 150$

$3x = 150$

$x = 50$

$m\angle E = x° = 50°$

$m\angle D = 2x° = 100°$

💬 Elaborate

13. In your own words, state the Polygon Angle Sum Theorem. How does it help you find unknown angle measures in polygons?
Possible answer: The sum of the measures of the interior angles of a convex polygon equals $180(n-2)°$. You can use it to find an unknown measure of an interior angle of a polygon when you know the measures of the other angles.

14. When will an exterior angle be acute? Can a triangle have more than one acute exterior angle? Describe the triangle that tests this.
An exterior angle will be acute when paired with an obtuse adjacent interior angle; therefore, the triangle must be obtuse. Since a triangle must have two or three acute interior angles, at least two exterior angles must be obtuse.

15. Essential Question Check-In Summarize the rules you have discovered about the interior and exterior angles of triangles and polygons.
The sum of the measures of the interior angles of a triangle is 180°. The sum of the measures of the interior angles for any polygon can be found by the rule $(n-2)180°$, where n represents the number of sides of the polygon. The measure of an exterior angle of a triangle is equal to the sum of the measures of the two remote interior angles.

⭐ Evaluate: Homework and Practice

• Online Homework
• Hints and Help
• Extra Practice

1. Consider the Triangle Sum Theorem in relation to a right triangle. What conjecture can you make about the two acute angles of a right triangle? Explain your reasoning.

They must be complementary. One angle of the right triangle measures 90°. So the sum of the remaining two angles is 180° − 90° = 90°.

2. Complete a flow proof for the Triangle Sum Theorem.

Given △ABC

Prove m∠1 + m∠2 + m∠3 = 180°

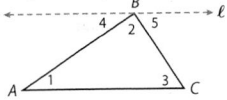

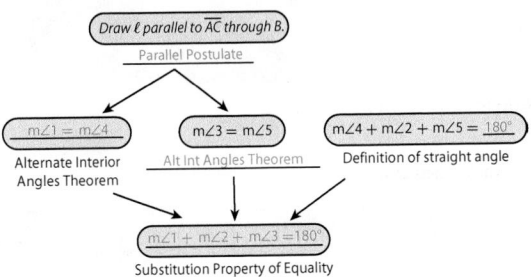

3. Given a polygon with 13 sides, find the sum of the measures of its interior angles.

$(n-2)180° = (13-2)180° = (11)180° = 1980°$

A polygon with 13 sides has an interior angle measure sum of 1980°.

4. A polygon has an interior angle sum of 3060°. How many sides must the polygon have?

$3060 = (n-2)180$

$19 = n$

The polygon must have 19 sides.

5. Two of the angles in a triangle measure 50° and 27°. Find the measure of the third angle.

$50 + 27 + x = 180$

$x = 103$

The measure of the third angle is 103°.

Solve for the unknown angle measures of the polygon.

6. A pentagon has angle measures of 100°, 105°, 110° and 115°. Find the fifth angle measure.

$(5-2)180° = (3)180° = 540°$

$540 = 100 + 105 + 110 + 115 + x$

$110 = x$

The measure of the fifth angle is 110°.

7. The measures of 13 angles of a 14-gon add up to 2014°. Find the fourteenth angle measure?

$(14-2)180° = (12)180° = 2160°$

$2014 + x = 2160$

$x = 146$

The measure of the 14th angle is 146°.

Module 7   320   Lesson 1

© Houghton Mifflin Harcourt Publishing Company

Exercise	Depth of Knowledge (D.O.K.)	COMMON CORE Mathematical Practices	
1–2	2 Skills/Concepts	MP.2	Reasoning
3–5	2 Skills/Concepts	MP.6	Precision
6–9	2 Skills/Concepts	MP.5	Using Tools
10–26	2 Skills/Concepts	MP.4	Modeling
27	3 Strategic Thinking H.O.T.	MP.3	Logic
28	3 Strategic Thinking H.O.T.	MP.6	Precision
29	3 Strategic Thinking H.O.T.	MP.2	Reasoning

EVALUATE

ASSIGNMENT GUIDE

Concepts and Skills	Practice
Explore 1 Exploring Interior Angles in Triangles	Exercises 1–2
Explore 2 Exploring Interior Angles in Polygons	Exercises 3–5
Example 1 Using Interior Angles	Exercises 6–9
Example 2 Proving the Exterior Angle Theorem	Exercises 10
Example 3 Using Exterior Angles	Exercises 11–14

INTEGRATE MATHEMATICAL PRACTICES

Focus on Technology

MP.5 Students can use a spreadsheet as a reference to find the sum of the interior angles of a convex polygon with n sides for $n = 3$ to 30 (or higher). They could also use the spreadsheet to give the measure of each interior and exterior angle of a regular polygon with n sides.

Interior and Exterior Angles   **320**

8. Determine the unknown angle measures for the quadrilateral in the diagram.

$(4 - 2)180° = (2)180° = 360°$

$x + 2x + 3x + 4x = 360$

$x = 36$

$2x = 72$

$3x = 108$

$4x = 144$

The measures of the interior angles of the quadrilateral are 36°, 72°, 108°, and 144°.

9. The cross-section of a beehive reveals it is made of regular hexagons. What is the measure of each angle in the regular hexagon?

$(n - 2)180° = (6 - 2)180° = (4)180° = 720°$

$6x = 720$

$x = 120$

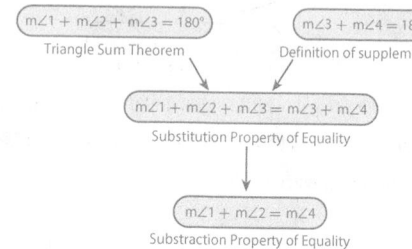

Each angle of a regular hexagon measures 120°.

10. Create a flow proof for the Exterior Angle Theorem.

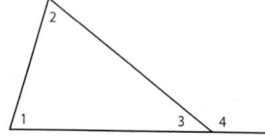

| m∠1 + m∠2 + m∠3 = 180° |
Triangle Sum Theorem

| m∠3 + m∠4 = 180° |
Definition of supplementary

| m∠1 + m∠2 + m∠3 = m∠3 + m∠4 |
Substitution Property of Equality

| m∠1 + m∠2 = m∠4 |
Substraction Property of Equality

Find the value of the variable to find the unknown angle measure(s).

11. Find w to find the measure of the exterior angle.

$w = 68 + 68$

$w = 136$

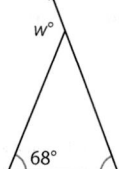

12. Find x to find the measure of the remote interior angle.

$x + 46 = 134$

$x = 88$

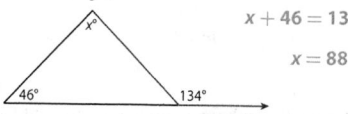

© Houghton Mifflin Harcourt Publishing Company · Image Credits: ©StudioSmart/Shutterstock

13. Find m∠H.

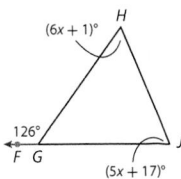

$(6x - 1) + (5x + 17) = 126$

$x = 10$

$m\angle H = (6x - 1)° = (6(10) - 1)° = 59°$

14. Determine the measure of the indicated exterior angle in the diagram.

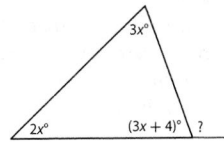

$180 - (3x + 4) = 2x + 3x$

$22 = x$

$180 - (3(22) + 4) = 180 - (66 + 4) = 180 - 70 = 110$

The measure of the indicated exterior angle is 110°.

15. Match each angle with its corresponding measure, given $m\angle 1 = 130°$ and $m\angle 7 = 70°$. Indicate a match by writing the letter for the angle on the line in front of the corresponding angle measure.

A. m∠2

B. m∠3

C. m∠4

D. m∠5

E. m∠6

____A____ 50°

____B____ 60°

____D____ 70°

____E____ 110°

____C____ 120°

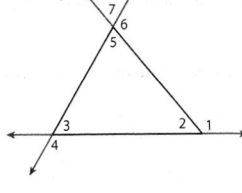

16. The map of France commonly used in the 1600s was significantly revised as a result of a triangulation survey. The diagram shows part of the survey map. Use the diagram to find the measure of ∠KMJ .

$m\angle KMN + m\angle MNK + m\angle NKM = 180°$

$88° + 48° + m\angle NKM = 180°$

$136° + m\angle NKM = 180°$

$m\angle NKM = 44°$

$\angle KMJ \cong \angle NKM$, so $m\angle KMJ = m\angle NKM = 44°$.

17. An artistic quilt is being designed using computer software. The designer wants to use regular octagons in her design. What interior angle measures should she set in the computer software to create a regular octagon?

$(n - 2)180° = (8 - 2)180° = (6)180° = 1080°$

$\dfrac{1080°}{8} = 135°$

The designer should set the interior angles of the regular octagon at 135°.

INTEGRATE MATHEMATICAL PRACTICES

Focus on Communication

MP.3 Discuss each of the following questions about triangles as a class. Have students explain how the Triangle Sum Theorem justifies their responses.

1. A triangle can have only one obtuse angle or only one right angle.

2. The acute angles of a right triangle are complementary.

18. A ladder propped up against a house makes a 20° angle with the wall. What would be the ladder's angle measure with the ground facing away from the house?

The house is perpendicular to the ground, so the other remote interior angle is 90°. 20 + 90 = 110, so the measure of the indicated exterior angle is 110°.

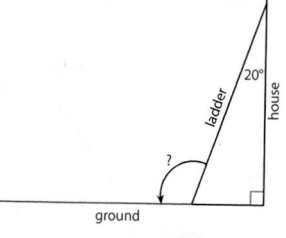

19. Photography The aperture of a camera is made by overlapping blades that form a regular decagon.

a. What is the sum of the measures of the interior angles of the decagon?

$(10 - 2)180° = (8)180° = 1440°$

b. What would be the measure of each interior angle? each exterior angle?

$1440° \div 10 = 144°; 180° - 144° = 36°$

c. Find the sum of all ten exterior angles.

$36°(10) = 360°$

20. Determine the measure of ∠UXW in the diagram.

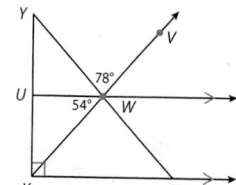

$m\angle WUX = 90°$

$180° = 54° + 90° + m\angle UXW$

$m\angle UXW = 36°$

21. Determine the measures of angles x, y, and z.

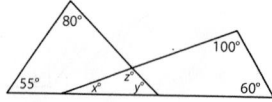

$x = 180 - (100 + 60) = 20°$

$y = 180 - (80 + 55) = 45°$

$z = 180 - (20 + 45) = 115°$

22. Given the diagram in which $\overrightarrow{BD}$ bisects $\angle ABC$ and $\overrightarrow{CD}$ bisects $\angle ACB$, what is m$\angle BDC$?

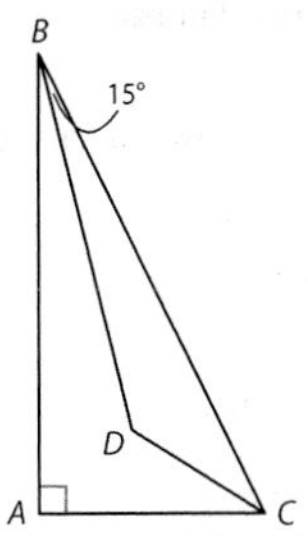

$$m\angle ABC = 2(m\angle DBC) = 2(15°) = 30°$$

$$30° + m\angle ACB + 90° = 180°, \text{ so } m\angle ACB = 60°.$$

Then, $m\angle DCB = \frac{1}{2}(m\angle ACB) = \frac{1}{2}(60°) = 30°.$

$$15° + m\angle BDC + 30° = 180°, \text{ so } m\angle BDC = 135°.$$

23. What If? Suppose you continue the congruent angle construction shown here. What polygon will you construct? Explain.

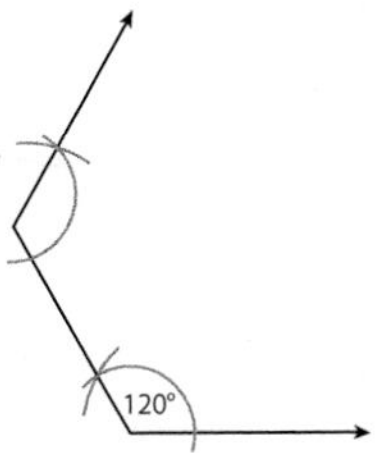

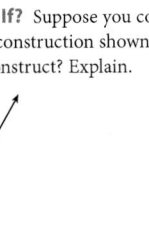

A regular hexagon; if the construction continues and the sides are kept congruent, the polygon will include six 120° angles and six congruent sides, so it is a regular hexagon.

24. Algebra Draw a triangle ABC and label the measures of its angles $a°$, $b°$, and $c°$. Draw ray BD that bisects the exterior angle at vertex B. Write an expression for the measure of angle CBD.

Possible answer:

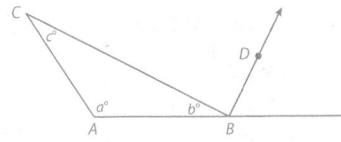

$$m\angle CBD = \left(\frac{a+c}{2}\right)°$$

25. Look for a Pattern Find patterns within this table of data and extend the patterns to complete the remainder of the table. What conjecture can you make about polygon exterior angles from Column 5?

Column 1 Number of Sides	Column 2 Sum of the Measures of the Interior Angles	Column 3 Average Measure of an Interior Angle	Column 4 Average Measure of an Exterior Angle	Column 5 Sum of the Measures of the Exterior Angles
3	180°	60°	120°	120°(3) = 360°
4	360°	90°	90°	90°(4) = 360°
5	540°	108°	72°	72°(5) = 360°
6	720°	120°	60°	60°(6) = 360°

Conjecture: It appears from the table that the sum of the measures of the exterior angles of any polygon is always 360°.

AVOID COMMON ERRORS

Some students may multiply the number of sides of a polygon by 180 to find the sum of the interior angles of the polygon. Remind them that the sum is based on the number of triangles. Since the sum of the angles of a triangle (3 sides) is 180°, to find the sum of the interior angles, they must subtract 2 from the number of sides before multiplying by 180.

Have students review the Polygon Angle Sum Theorem and the Polygon Exterior Angle Theorem, and then draw a pentagon and show how to find its interior angle sum measures and its exterior angle sum measures. 540°, 360°

26. Explain the Error Find and explain what this student did incorrectly when solving the following problem.

What type of polygon would have an interior angle sum of 1260°?

$$1260 = (n - 2)180$$
$$7 = n - 2$$
$$5 = n$$

The polygon is a pentagon.

The error is that the student subtracted 2 from both sides instead of adding 2. The value of n should be 9, and the polygon is a nonagon.

H.O.T. Focus on Higher Order Thinking

27. Communicate Mathematical Ideas Explain why if two angles of one triangle are congruent to two angles of another triangle, then the third pair of angles are also congruent.

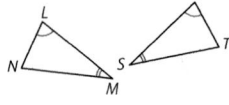

Given: $\angle L \cong \angle R$, $\angle M \cong \angle S$

Prove: $\angle N \cong \angle T$

By the Triangle Sum Theorem, $m\angle L + m\angle M + m\angle N = 180°$ and $m\angle R + m\angle S + m\angle T = 180°$. Since each set of angle measures total 180°, they are equal using the substitution property of equality. So, $m\angle L + m\angle M + m\angle N = m\angle R + m\angle S + m\angle T$. Since $\angle L \cong \angle R$ and $\angle M \cong \angle S$, then $m\angle L = m\angle R$ and $m\angle M = m\angle S$ by the definition of congruence. Subtracting equals from both sides gives $m\angle N = m\angle T$. Then $\angle N \cong \angle T$ by the definition of congruence.

28. Analyze Relationships Consider a right triangle. How would you describe the measures of its exterior angles? Explain.

An exterior angle will be right when paired with a right adjacent interior angle. There can be only one right angle in a triangle. Since a triangle must have two or three acute interior angles, the other two exterior angles must be obtuse.

29. Look for a Pattern In investigating different polygons, diagonals were drawn from a vertex to break the polygon into triangles. Recall that the number of triangles is always two less than the number of sides. But diagonals can be drawn from all vertices. Make a table where you compare the number of sides of a polygon with how many diagonals can be drawn (from all the vertices). Can you find a pattern in this table?

Number of Sides, n	3	4	5	6	7	8
Number of Diagonals, d	0	2	5	9	14	20

The number of diagonals increases by 2, then 3, 4, 5, etc. A formula relating n and d is $d = \dfrac{n(n-3)}{2}$.

Lesson Performance Task

You've been asked to design the board for a new game called Pentagons. The board consists of a repeating pattern of regular pentagons, a portion of which is shown in the illustration. When you write the specifications for the company that will make the board, you include the measurements of ∠BAD, ∠ABC, ∠BCD and ∠ADC. Find the measures of those angles and explain how you found them.

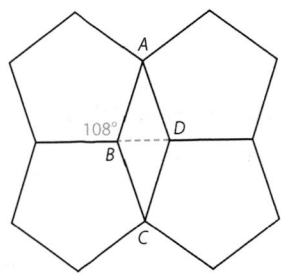

$m\angle BAD = m\angle BCD = 36°$

$m\angle ABC = m\angle ADC = 144°$

To find the measure of each interior angle of one of the pentagons, divide it into three triangles. This gives the sum of the measures of the five angles of the pentagon, $3 \times 180° = 540°$. Each angle measures $540° \div 5 = 108°$.

Draw $\overline{BD}$.

$m\angle ABD = 180° - 108° = 72°$.

$m\angle ABC = m\angle ADC = 2 \times 72° = 144°$

$m\angle BAD = m\angle BCD = 180° - (72° + 72°) = 180° - 144° = 36°$

EXTENSION ACTIVITY

Have students design and draw game boards consisting of congruent quadrilaterals, congruent pentagons, and/or congruent hexagons. Each design should show at least two different classes of polygons (for example, quadrilaterals and hexagons) and a total of at least six polygons. Students should write the measure of each angle directly on the figures, and write elsewhere an explanation of how, without protractors, they found each measure.

INTEGRATE MATHEMATICAL PRACTICES
Focus on Communication

MP.3 Direct students' attention to quadrilateral *ABCD*. Ask:

- Without knowing anything about the angles of *ABCD*, how could you identify the type of quadrilateral that it is? What type is it? The sides of *ABCD* are sides of congruent regular pentagons, so they are congruent. A quadrilateral with four congruent sides is a rhombus.

- What does the type of quadrilateral that *ABCD* is tell you about the angles of the figure? The opposite angles are congruent. The adjacent angles are supplementary.

INTEGRATE MATHEMATICAL PRACTICES
Focus on Critical Thinking

MP.3 The perimeter of each pentagon in the diagram is 16 cm. What is the perimeter of quadrilateral *ABCD*? Explain. 12.8 cm; length of each side of each pentagon = 16 cm ÷ 5 = 3.2 cm; perimeter of *ABCD* = 4 x 3.2 = 12.8 cm

Scoring Rubric
2 points: Student correctly solves the problem and explains his/her reasoning.
1 point: Student shows good understanding of the problem but does not fully solve or explain.
0 points: Student does not demonstrate understanding of the problem.

Interior and Exterior Angles   **326**

Isosceles and Equilateral Triangles

Common Core Math Standards

The student is expected to:

COMMON CORE **G-CO.C.10**

Prove theorems about triangles.

Mathematical Practices

COMMON CORE **MP.3 Logic**

Language Objective

Explain to a partner what you can deduce about a triangle if it has two sides with the same length.

ENGAGE

Essential Question: What are the special relationships among angles and sides in isosceles and equilateral triangles?

In an isosceles triangle, the angles opposite the congruent sides are congruent. In an equilateral triangle, all the sides and angles are congruent, and the measure of each angle is 60°.

PREVIEW: LESSON PERFORMANCE TASK

View the Engage section online. Discuss the photo, explaining that the instrument is a sextant and that long ago it was used to measure the elevation of the sun and stars, allowing one's position on Earth's surface to be calculated. Then preview the Lesson Performance Task.

Name _____ Class _____ Date _____

7.2 Isosceles and Equilateral Triangles

Essential Question: What are the special relationships among angles and sides in isosceles and equilateral triangles?

⊘ Explore   Investigating Isosceles Triangles

An **isosceles triangle** is a triangle with at least two congruent sides.

The congruent sides are called the **legs** of the triangle.

The angle formed by the legs is the **vertex angle**.

The side opposite the vertex angle is the **base**.

The angles that have the base as a side are the **base angles**.

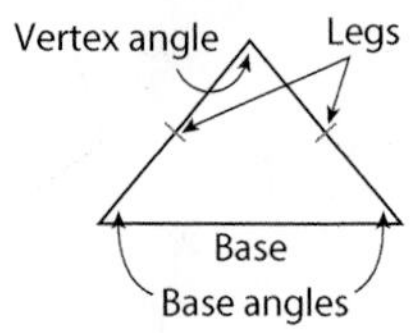

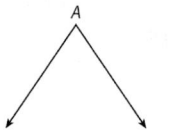

In this activity, you will construct isosceles triangles and investigate other potential characteristics/properties of these special triangles.

(A) Do your work in the space provided. Use a straightedge to draw an angle. Label your angle ∠A, as shown in the figure.

A

Check students' construtions.

(B) Using a compass, place the point on the vertex and draw an arc that intersects the sides of the angle. Label the points B and C.

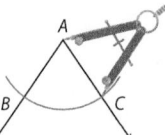

Module 7   **327**   Lesson 2

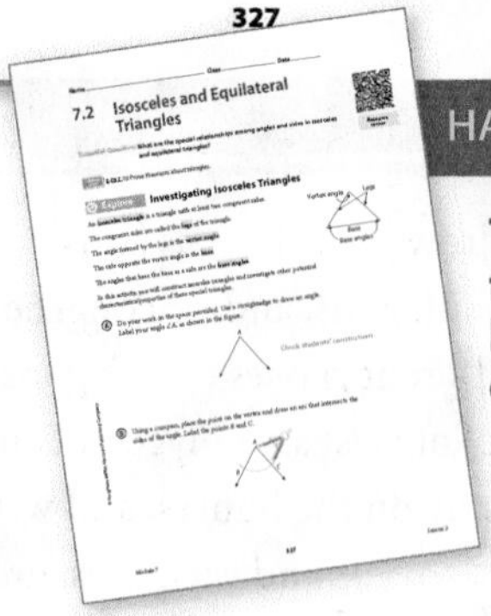

HARDCOVER PAGES 283–292

Turn to these pages to find this lesson in the hardcover student edition.

Ⓒ Use the straightedge to draw line segment $\overline{BC}$.

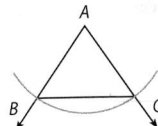

Ⓓ Use a protractor to measure each angle. Record the measures in the table under the column for Triangle 1.

	Triangle 1	Triangle 2	Triangle 3	Triangle 4
m∠A				
m∠B				
m∠C				

Possible answer for Triangle 1: m∠A = 70°; m∠B = ∠55°; m∠C = 55°.

Ⓔ Repeat steps A–D at least two more times and record the results in the table. Make sure ∠A is a different size each time.

Reflect

1. How do you know the triangles you constructed are isosceles triangles?
   The compass marks equal lengths on both sides of ∠A; therefore, $\overline{AB} \cong \overline{AC}$.

2. **Make a Conjecture** Looking at your results, what conjecture can be made about the base angles, ∠B and ∠C?
   The base angles are congruent.

⚙ **Explain 1** **Proving the Isosceles Triangle Theorem and Its Converse**

In the Explore, you made a conjecture that the base angles of an isosceles triangle are congruent. This conjecture can be proven so it can be stated as a theorem.

Isosceles Triangle Theorem
If two sides of a triangle are congruent, then the two angles opposite the sides are congruent.

This theorem is sometimes called the Base Angles Theorem and can also be stated as "Base angles of an isosceles triangle are congruent."

© Houghton Mifflin Harcourt Publishing Company

Investigating Isosceles Triangles

INTEGRATE TECHNOLOGY

Students have the option of completing the isosceles triangle activity either in the book or online.

QUESTIONING STRATEGIES

❓ What must be true about the triangles you construct in order for them to be isosceles triangles? They must have two congruent sides.

❓ How could you draw isosceles triangles without using a compass? Possible answer: Draw ∠A and plot point B on one side of ∠A. Then use a ruler to measure $\overline{AB}$ and plot point C on the other side of ∠A so that AC = AB.

EXPLAIN 1

Proving the Isosceles Triangle Theorem and Its Converse

CONNECT VOCABULARY 🔲EL

Ask a volunteer to define *isosceles triangle* and have students give real-world examples of them. If possible, show the class a baseball pennant or other flag in the shape of an isosceles triangle. Tell students they will be proving theorems about isosceles triangles and investigating their properties in this lesson.

PROFESSIONAL DEVELOPMENT

 Learning Progressions

In this lesson, students add to their prior knowledge of isosceles and equilateral triangles by investigating the Isosceles Triangle Theorem from both an inductive and deductive perspective. The opening activity leads students to make a conjecture about the measures of the base angles of an isosceles triangle. Students prove their conjecture and its converse later in the lesson. They also prove the Equilateral Triangle Theorem and its converse, and use the properties of both types of triangles to find the unknown measure of angles and sides in a triangle. All students should develop fluency with various types of triangles as they continue their study of geometry.

 What can you say about an isosceles triangle, △ABC, with base angles ∠B and ∠C, if you know that m∠A = 100°? Explain. **By the Isosceles Triangle Theorem, ∠B ≅ ∠C, and m∠B + m∠C = 80° by the Triangle Sum Theorem, so m∠B = m∠C = 40°.**

 What can you say about the angles of an isosceles right triangle? **The angles of the triangle measure 90°, 45°, and 45°.**

Example 1 Prove the Isosceles Triangle Theorem and its converse.

Step 1 Complete the proof of the Isosceles Triangle Theorem.

Given: $\overline{AB} \cong \overline{AC}$

Prove: ∠B ≅ ∠C

Statements	Reasons
1. $\overline{BA} \cong \overline{CA}$	1. Given
2. ∠A ≅ ∠A	2. **Reflexive Property of Congruence**
3. $\overline{CA} \cong \overline{BA}$	3. Symmetric Property of Equality
4. △BAC ≅ △CAB	4. **SAS Triangle Congruence Theorem**
5. ∠B ≅ ∠C	5. CPCTC

Step 2 Complete the statement of the Converse of the Isosceles Triangle Theorem.

If two ___angles___ of a ___triangle___ are congruent, then the two ___sides___ opposite those ___angles___ are ___congruent___.

Step 3 Complete the proof of the Converse of the Isosceles Triangle Theorem.

Given: ∠B ≅ ∠C

Prove: $\overline{AB} \cong \overline{AC}$

Statements	Reasons
1. ∠ABC ≅ ∠ACB	1. Given
2. $\overline{BC} \cong \overline{CB}$	2. Reflexive Property of Congruence
3. ∠ACB ≅ ∠ABC	3. Symmetric Property of Equality
4. △ABC ≅ △ACB	4. **ASA Triangle Congruence Theorem**
5. $\overline{AB} \cong \overline{AC}$	5. CPCTC

Reflect

3. **Discussion** In the proofs of the Isosceles Triangle Theorem and its converse, how might it help to sketch a reflection of the given triangle next to the original triangle, so that vertex B is on the right?

Possible answer: Sketching a copy of the triangle makes it easier to see the two pairs of congruent corresponding sides and the two pairs of congruent corresponding angles.

Module 7

329

Lesson 2

COLLABORATIVE LEARNING

Small Group Activity

Geometry software allows students to explore the theorems in this lesson. For the Isosceles Triangle Theorem (or the Equilateral Triangle Theorem), students should construct an isosceles (or equilateral) triangle and measure the angles. As students drag the vertices of the triangle to change its size or shape, the individual base angle measures will change (for isosceles only), but the relationship between the lengths of the sides and the measures of the angles will remain the same.

⊘ Explain 2 Proving the Equilateral Triangle Theorem and Its Converse

An **equilateral triangle** is a triangle with three congruent sides.

An **equiangular triangle** is a triangle with three congruent angles.

> **Equilateral Triangle Theorem**
>
> If a triangle is equilateral, then it is equiangular.

Example 2 Prove the Equilateral Triangle Theorem and its converse.

Step 1 Complete the proof of the Equilateral Triangle Theorem.

Given: $\overline{AB} \cong \overline{AC} \cong \overline{BC}$

Prove: $\angle A \cong \angle B \cong \angle C$

Given that $\overline{AB} \cong \overline{AC}$ we know that $\angle B \cong \angle$ __C__ by the

__Isosceles Triangle Theorem__

It is also known that $\angle A \cong \angle B$ by the Isosceles Triangle Theorem, since __$\overline{AC} \cong \overline{BC}$__ .

Therefore, $\angle A \cong \angle C$ by __substitution__ .

Finally, $\angle A \cong \angle B \cong \angle C$ by the __Transitive__ Property of Congruence.

The converse of the Equilateral Triangle Theorem is also true.

> **Converse of the Equilateral Triangle Theorem**
>
> If a triangle is equiangular, then it is equilateral.

Step 2 Complete the proof of the Converse of the Equilateral Triangle Theorem.

Given: $\angle A \cong \angle B \cong \angle C$

Prove: $\overline{AB} \cong \overline{AC} \cong \overline{BC}$

Because $\angle B \cong \angle C$, $\overline{AB} \cong$ __$\overline{AC}$__ by the

__Converse of the Isosceles Triangle Theorem__

$\overline{AC} \cong \overline{BC}$ by the Converse of the Isosceles Triangle Theorem because

__$\angle A$__ $\cong \angle B$.

Thus, by the Transitive Property of Congruence, __$\overline{AB} \cong \overline{BC}$__ , and therefore, $\overline{AB} \cong \overline{AC} \cong \overline{BC}$.

Reflect

4. To prove the Equilateral Triangle Theorem, you applied the theorems of isosceles triangles. What can be concluded about the relationship between equilateral triangles and isosceles triangles?

   Possible answer: Equilateral/equiangular triangles are a special type of isosceles triangles.

EXPLAIN 2

Proving the Equilateral Triangle Theorem and Its Converse

COLLABORATIVE LEARNING

The converse of this theorem is proved interactively using a paragraph proof. Have small groups of students discuss the proof and highlight the important statements (steps) and reasons for the statements. Ask them how they would present the same proof using the two-column method.

QUESTIONING STRATEGIES

? What is the connection between equilateral triangles and equiangular triangles? If a triangle is equilateral, then it is also equiangular. If a triangle is equiangular, then it is also equilateral.

AVOID COMMON ERRORS

Some students may confuse the theorems in this lesson because they are so similar. Have students draw and label diagrams to illustrate the theorems and then add visual cues, if needed, to help them remember how the theorems are applied.

DIFFERENTIATE INSTRUCTION

Visual Cues

Visually represent the Equilateral Triangle Theorem and its converse:

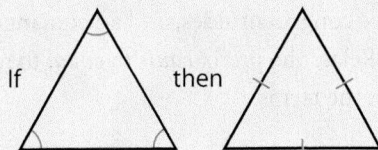

Equilateral Triangle Theorem: If [triangle] then [triangle]   Converse: If [triangle] then [triangle]

Isosceles and Equilateral Triangles   **330**

EXPLAIN 3

Using Properties of Isosceles and Equilateral Triangles

INTEGRATE MATHEMATICAL PRACTICES

Focus on Math Connections

MP.1 Encourage students to discuss how the Triangle Sum Theorem and the theorems in this lesson help them solve for the unknown angles and sides of an isosceles or equilateral triangle. Have them share their ideas about the best method to use to solve for the unknown quantities in each problem.

QUESTIONING STRATEGIES

? If the triangle is equiangular, how do you find the measure of one of its angles? Divide the sum of the interior angles by the number of interior angles: $180° \div 3 = 60°$.

⚡ Explain 3 **Using Properties of Isosceles and Equilateral Triangles**

You can use the properties of isosceles and equilateral triangles to solve problems involving these theorems.

Example 3 Find the indicated measure.

(A) Katie is stitching the center inlay onto a banner that she created to represent her new tutorial service. It is an equilateral triangle with the following dimensions in centimeters. What is the length of each side of the triangle?

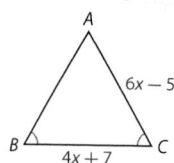

To find the length of each side of the triangle, first find the value of x.

$\overline{AC} \cong \overline{BC}$	Converse of the Equilateral Triangle Theorem
$AC = BC$	Definition of congruence
$6x - 5 = 4x + 7$	Substitution Property of Equality
$x = 6$	Solve for x.

Substitute 6 for x into either $6x - 5$ or $4x + 7$.

$$6(6) - 5 = 36 - 5 = 31 \quad \text{or} \quad 4(6) + 7 = 24 + 7 = 31$$

So, the length of each side of the triangle is 31 cm.

(B) $m\angle T$

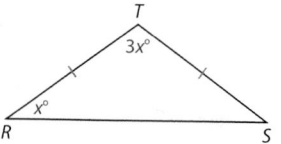

To find the measure of the vertex angle of the triangle, first find the value of __x__.

$m\angle R = m\angle S = x°$	[Isosceles Triangle] Theorem
$m\angle R + m\angle S + \boxed{m\angle T} = 180°$	Triangle Sum Theorem
$x + x + 3x = 180$	Substitution Property of Equality
$\boxed{5x} = 180$	Addition Property of Equality
$x = \boxed{36}$	[Division] Property of Equality

So, $m\angle T = 3x° = 3\left(\boxed{36}\right)° = \boxed{108}°$.

© Houghton Mifflin Harcourt Publishing Company · Image Credits: ©Nelvin C. Cepeda/ZUMA Press/Corbis

---

LANGUAGE SUPPORT 🔵EL

Connect Vocabulary

Help students understand the meanings of *isosceles*, *equilateral*, and *equiangular* by having them make a poster showing each type of triangle along with its definition. An isosceles triangle has two congruent sides, an equilateral triangle has three congruent sides, and an equiangular triangle has three congruent angles. Relate the prefix *equi-* to *equal* to help students make connections between the terms.

Your Turn

5. Find $m\angle P$.

$(3x + 3)^\circ$ Q

P

$(5x - 2)^\circ$

R

$m\angle P = m\angle Q = (3x + 3)^\circ$

$2(3x + 3) + (5x - 2) = 180$

$x = 16$

$m\angle P = (3x + 3)^\circ = (3(16) + 3)^\circ = 51^\circ$

6. Katie's tutorial service is going so well that she is having shirts made with the equilateral triangle emblem. She has given the t-shirt company these dimensions. What is the length of each side of the triangle in centimeters?

A

$\frac{3}{10}y + 9$ $\frac{4}{5}y - 1$

B   C

$\overline{AB} \cong \overline{AC}$ $\Rightarrow$ $AB = AC$

$\frac{3}{10}y + 9 = \frac{4}{5}y - 1$ $\Rightarrow$ $20 = y$

Therefore, $\frac{3}{10}y + 9 = \frac{3}{10}(20) + 9 = 6 + 9 = 15$

The length of each side is 15 cm.

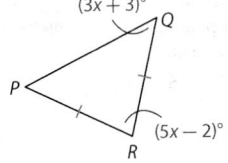 **Elaborate**

7. Discussion Consider the vertex and base angles of an isosceles triangle. Can they be right angles? Can they be obtuse? Explain.

The vertex angle of an isosceles triangle can be acute, right, or obtuse as long as its

measure is less than 180°. The base angles of an isosceles triangle can only be acute,

meaning they have a measurement less than 90°. because otherwise they would cause the

sum of the base angles to be $\geq$ 180° before adding in the third angle, which contradicts

the Triangle Sum Theorem.

8. Essential Question Check-In Discuss how the sides of an isosceles triangle relate to its angles.

The legs of an isosceles triangle are opposite from the base angles and because the base

angles are congruent, the legs are also congruent because of the Converse of the Isosceles

Triangle Theorem.

ELABORATE

QUESTIONING STRATEGIES

? How do you use the Isosceles Triangle Theorem to find the measures of the base angles of an isosceles triangle, given a known value for the measure of the vertex angle? Subtract the measure of the vertex angle from 180°, and then divide the answer by 2 to find the measure of each base angle.

? How do you use the Equilateral Triangle Theorem to find the measures of the angles of an equilateral triangle? The theorem says that the triangle is equiangular, so each angle must measure 60°.

SUMMARIZE THE LESSON

Have students fill out charts for the two theorems and their converses. Sample:

Isosceles Triangle		
	If	Then
Theorem	2 sides congruent	2 angles congruent
Converse	2 angles congruent	2 sides congruent

Equilateral Triangle		
	If	Then
Theorem	3 sides congruent	3 angles congruent
Converse	3 angles congruent	3 sides congruent

EVALUATE

ASSIGNMENT GUIDE

Concepts and Skills	Practice
Explore Investigating Isosceles Triangles	Exercise 1
Example 1 Proving the Isosceles Triangle Theorem and Its Converse	Exercise 2
Example 2 Proving the Equilateral Triangle Theorem and Its Converse	Exercise 3
Example 3 Using Properties of Isosceles and Equilateral Triangles	Exercises 4–13

INTEGRATE MATHEMATICAL PRACTICES

Focus on Reasoning

MP.2 Have students analyze the following statement: "If a triangle is equilateral, then the triangle is isosceles." Is the statement true? (yes) Is the converse of the statement true? (no) Have them use the properties of isosceles and equilateral triangles to justify their answers.

⭐ Evaluate: Homework and Practice

• Online Homework
• Hints and Help
• Extra Practice

1. Use a straightedge. Draw a line. Draw an acute angle with vertex A along the line. Then use a compass to copy the angle. Place the compass point at another point B along the line and draw the copied angle so that the angle faces the original angle. Label the intersection of the angle sides as point C. Look at the triangle you have formed. What is true about the two base angles of $\triangle ABC$? What do you know about $\overline{CA}$ and $\overline{CB}$? What kind of triangle did you form? Explain your reasoning.

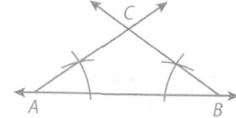

$\angle CAB \cong \angle CBA$, so opposite sides $\overline{CA}$ and $\overline{CB}$ are congruent. Therefore, it is an isosceles triangle.

2. Prove the Isosceles Triangle Theorem as a paragraph proof.

   Given: $\overline{AB} \cong \overline{AC}$

   Prove: $\angle B \cong \angle C$

   Proof: It is given that $\overline{AB} \cong \overline{AC}$. By the Reflexive Property of Congruence, $\angle A \cong \angle A$. Given that $\overline{BA} \cong \overline{CA}$, then $\triangle ABC \cong \triangle ACB$ by the SAS Triangle Congruence Theorem. Therefore, $\angle B \cong \angle C$ because corresponding parts of congruent triangles are congruent.

3. Complete the flow proof of the Equilateral Triangle Theorem.

   Given: $\overline{AB} \cong \overline{AC} \cong \overline{BC}$

   Prove: $\angle A \cong \angle B \cong \angle C$

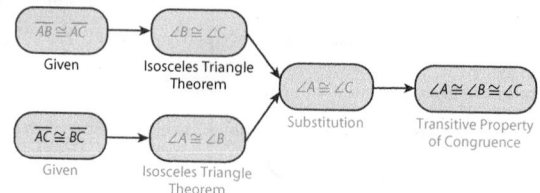

© Houghton Mifflin Harcourt Publishing Company

Exercise	Depth of Knowledge (D.O.K.)	COMMON CORE Mathematical Practices
1	**2** Skills/Concepts	**MP.6** Precision
2–3	**2** Skills/Concepts	**MP.4** Modeling
4–11	**2** Skills/Concepts	**MP.2** Reasoning
12–20	**2** Skills/Concepts	**MP.4** Modeling
21	**3** Strategic Thinking H.O.T.	**MP.3** Logic
22	**3** Strategic Thinking H.O.T.	**MP.5** Using Tools
23	**3** Strategic Thinking H.O.T.	**MP.5** Using Tools

Find the measure of the indicated angle.

4. $m\angle A$

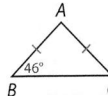

$m\angle B = m\angle C = 46°$

$m\angle A = 180° - m\angle B - m\angle C$

$m\angle A = (180 - 46 - 46)°$

$m\angle A = 88°$

5. $m\angle R$

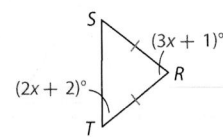

$m\angle S = m\angle T = (2x + 2)°$

$m\angle S + m\angle T + m\angle R = 180°$

$2m\angle T + m\angle R = 180°$

$2(2x + 2) + (3x + 1) = 180$

$4x + 4 + 3x + 1 = 180$

$7x + 5 = 180$

$7x = 175$

$x = 25$

$m\angle R = (3x + 1)° = (3(25) + 1)° = (75 + 1)° = 76°$

6. $m\angle O$

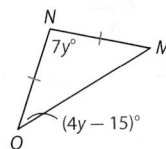

$m\angle O = m\angle M = (4y - 15)°$

$m\angle O + m\angle M + m\angle N = 180°$

$2m\angle O + m\angle N = 180°$

$2(4y - 15) + 7y = 180$

$8y - 30 + 7y = 180$

$15y - 30 = 180$

$y = 14$

$m\angle O = (4y - 15)° = (4(14) - 15)° = (56 - 15)° = 41°$

7. $m\angle E$

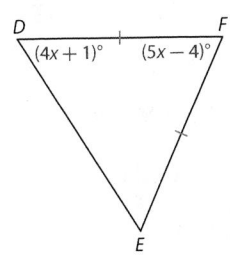

$m\angle D = m\angle E = (4x + 1)°$

$m\angle D + m\angle E + m\angle F = 180°$

$2m\angle E + m\angle F = 180°$

$2(4x + 1) + (5x - 4) = 180$

$8x + 2 + 5x - 4 = 180$

$13x - 2 = 180$

$13x = 182$

$x = 14$

$m\angle E = (4x + 1)° = (4(14) + 1)° = (56 + 1)° = 57°$

INTEGRATE MATHEMATICAL PRACTICES

Focus on Communication

MP.3 Discuss each of the following questions about triangles as a class. Have students explain how the theorems in this lesson justify their responses.

1. Each acute angle of an obtuse isosceles triangle must be less than 45°.
2. Each angle of an equilateral triangle must be 60°.
3. Each acute angle of an isosceles right triangle must be 45°.

Isosceles and Equilateral Triangles   **334**

AVOID COMMON ERRORS

In this lesson, students prove the Isosceles Triangle Theorem by using the SAS Congruence Criterion. Having seen this congruence criterion, students may assume another congruence criterion can be used to prove the theorem. Encourage students to try other methods of proof, but be sure students understand that some conditions may not apply to isosceles triangles.

Find the length of the indicated side.

8. $\overline{DE}$

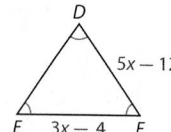

$\overline{DF} \cong \overline{EF}$, so $DF = EF$.

$3x - 4 = 5x - 12$

$-4 = 2x - 12$

$8 = 2x$

$4 = x$

$DE = DF = EF$

$DE = 3x - 4 = 3(4) - 4 = 12 - 4 = 8$

$DE = 8$

9. $\overline{KL}$

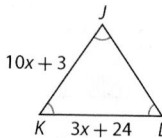

$\overline{JK} \cong \overline{KL}$, so $JK = KL$

$10x + 3 = 3x + 24$

$7x + 3 = 24$

$7x = 21$

$x = 3$

$KL = 3x + 24 = 3(3) + 24 = 33$

$KL = 33$

10. $\overline{AB}$

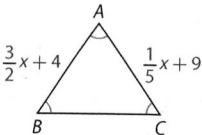

$\overline{AB} \cong \overline{AC}$, so $AB = AC$.

$\frac{3}{2}x + 4 = \frac{1}{5}x + 9$

$\frac{13}{10}x + 4 = 9$

$\frac{13}{10}x = 5$

$x = \frac{50}{13}$

$AB = \frac{3}{2}\left(\frac{50}{13}\right) + 4$

$= \frac{75}{13} + \frac{52}{13}$

$= \frac{127}{13}$

$AB = \frac{127}{13}$

11. $\overline{BC}$

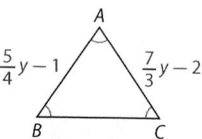

$\overline{AB} \cong \overline{BC} \cong \overline{AC}$, so $AB = BC = AC$.

$\frac{5}{4}y - 1 = \frac{7}{3}y - 2$

$\frac{15}{12}y - 1 = \frac{28}{12}y - 2$

$-\frac{13}{12}y = -1$

$y = \frac{12}{13}$

$BC = \frac{5}{4}\left(\frac{12}{13}\right) - 1$

$BC = \frac{60}{52} - \frac{52}{52}$

$BC = \frac{2}{13}$

12. Given △JKL with m∠J = 63° and m∠L = 54°, is the triangle an acute, isosceles, obtuse, or right triangle?

By the Triangle Sum Theorem, m∠K = 63°, so the triangle is an acute isosceles triangle because all angle measures are less than 90°.

13. Find *x*. Explain your reasoning. The horizontal lines are parallel.

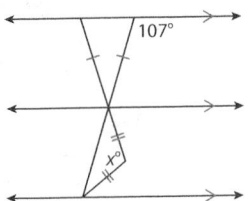

By the def. supp. ∠, the base angles of the top triangle have a measure of 73°. Therefore, the measure of the vertex angle is 34° by the Triangle Sum Theorem. The base angles of the bottom isosceles triangle will also measure 34° by the Vertical Angles Theorem. Thus, x° will equal 112° by the Triangle Sum Theorem.

14. Summarize Complete the diagram to show the cause and effect of the theorems covered in the lesson. Explain why the arrows show the direction going both ways.

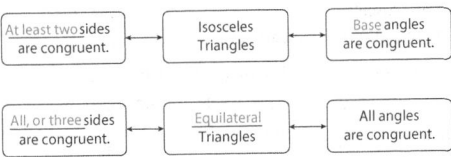

Possible explanation: The arrows go both ways because each theorem and its converse are both true.

15. A plane is flying parallel to the ground along $\overrightarrow{AC}$. When the plane is at *A*, an air-traffic controller in tower *T* measures the angle to the plane as 40°. After the plane has traveled 2.4 miles to *B*, the angle to the plane is 80°. How can you find *BT*?

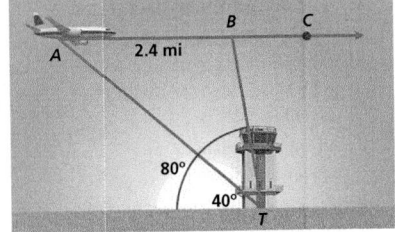

By the Angle Addition Postulate, m∠ATB = 80° − 40° = 40°.

m∠BAT = 40° by Alt. Int. ∠ Thm.

∠ATB ≅ ∠BAT by the definition of congruence and $\overline{BA} ≅ \overline{BT}$ by the Converse of the Isosceles Triangle Theorem.

Then BA = BT = 2.4 mi.

PEER-TO-PEER DISCUSSION

Have students work in pairs to create a poster that shows examples of how to find the unknown sides or angles of an isosceles and an equilateral triangle, when given the measure of one angle or an algebraic expression.

16. John is building a doghouse. He decides to use the roof truss design shown. If $m\angle DBF = 35°$, what is the measure of the vertex angle of the isosceles triangle?

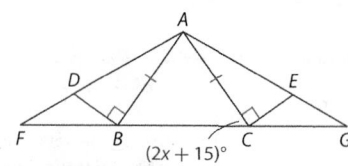

By the Isosceles Triangle Theorem,
$\angle ACB \cong \angle ABC$, so $m\angle ABC = (2x + 15)°$.
$m\angle DBF + m\angle ABD + m\angle ABC = 180°$
$$35 + 90 + (2x + 15) = 180$$
$$2x + 140 = 180$$
$$2x = 40$$
$$x = 20$$

$m\angle ABC = (2(20) + 15)° = 55°$
$m\angle BAC = 180° - m\angle ABC - m\angle ACB$
$$= 180° - 2(55°)$$
$$= 180° - 110°$$
$$= 70°$$
The measure of the vertex angle is 70°.

17. The measure of the vertex angle of an isosceles triangle is 12 more than 5 times the measure of a base angle. Determine the sum of the measures of the base angles.

$2(\text{measure of base angle}) + (\text{measure of vertex angle}) = 180°$
$$2(x) + (5x + 12) = 180 \;\Rightarrow\; x = 24$$
The sum of the measures of the base angles is $24° + 24° = 48°$.

18. Justify Reasoning Determine whether each of the following statements is true or false. Select the correct answer for each lettered part. Explain your reasoning.

a. All isosceles triangles have at least two acute angles.   ● True ○ False

b. If the perimeter of an equilateral triangle is P, then the length of each of its sides is $\frac{P}{3}$.   ● True ○ False

c. All isosceles triangles are equilateral triangles.   ○ True ● False

d. If you know the length of one of the legs of an isosceles triangle, you can determine its perimeter.   ○ True ● False

e. The exterior angle of an equilateral triangle is obtuse.   ● True ○ False

a. **At least the base angles have to be acute.**

b. **Because all three sides are equal, dividing P by 3 gives the length of each side.**

c. **An isosceles triangle requires only a minimum of two sides being congruent, not all three.**

d. **You need to know the length of one leg and the base to determine perimeter.**

e. **The exterior angle of a triangle is equal to the sum of its remote interior angles. The exterior angle measures $60° + 60° = 120°$, which is obtuse.**

19. Critical Thinking Prove $\angle B \cong \angle C$, given point M is the midpoint of $\overline{BC}$.

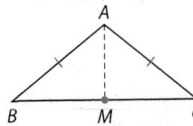

Statements	Reasons
1. M is the midpoint of $\overline{BC}$.	1. Given
2. $\overline{BM} \cong \overline{CM}$	2. Definition of midpoint
3. $\overline{AB} \cong \overline{AC}$	3. Given
4. $\overline{AM} \cong \overline{AM}$	4. Reflexive Property of Congruence
5. $\triangle AMB \cong \triangle AMC$	5. SSS Triangle Congruence Theorem
6. $\angle B \cong \angle C$	6. CPCTC

20. Given that $\triangle ABC$ is an isosceles triangle and $\overline{AD}$ and $\overline{CD}$ are angle bisectors, what is $m\angle ADC$?

$m\angle BAC = m\angle BCA = 70°$, so $m\angle DAC = m\angle DCA = 35°$. Then, $m\angle ADC = 180° - (35° + 35°) = 110°$.

H.O.T. Focus on Higher Order Thinking

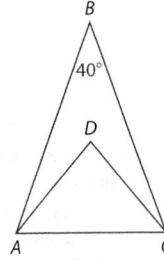

21. Analyze Relationships Isosceles right triangle ABC has a right angle at B and $\overline{AB} \cong \overline{CB}$. $\overline{BD}$ bisects angle B, and point D is on $\overline{AC}$. If $\overline{BD} \perp \overline{AC}$, describe triangles ABD and CBD. Explain. HINT: Draw a diagram.

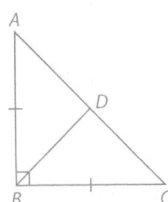

The triangles are congruent isosceles triangles; the bisected right angle results in two 45° angles, and the perpendicular segments result in two right angles, so angles A and C must also measure 45°. Since $\overline{BD} \cong \overline{BD}$ by the Reflexive Property, triangles ABD and CBD are congruent by ASA.

INTEGRATE MATHEMATICAL PRACTICES

Focus on Math Connections

MP.1 Remind students that an isosceles triangle has at least two congruent sides, and its properties can be used to prove that it also has at least two congruent angles.

Compare the hypothesis and the conclusion of the Isosceles Triangle Theorem with its converse. Support your comparison with a sketch.

Communicate Mathematical Ideas Follow the method to construct a triangle. Then use what you know about the radius of a circle to explain the congruence of the sides.

22. Construct an isosceles triangle. Explain how you know that two sides are congruent.
- Use a compass to draw a circle. Mark two different points on the circle.
- Use a straightedge to draw a line segment from the center of the circle to each of the two points on the circle (radii).
- Draw a line segment (chord) between the two points on the circle.

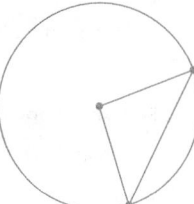

I know two sides are congruent because the two line segments I drew from the center each represent the radius of the circle and so are the equal-length sides of an isosceles triangle.

23. Construct an equilateral triangle. Explain how you know the three sides are congruent.
- Use a compass to draw a circle.
- Draw another circle of the same size that goes through the center of the first circle. (Both should have the same radius length.)
- Mark one point where the circles intersect.
- Use a straightedge to draw line segments connecting both centers to each other and to the intersection point.

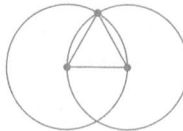

I know the three sides are congruent because the three line segments drawn are radii, which have the same length in both circles, since the circles are the same size. Therefore, all of the line segments are congruent and form the three sides of an equilateral triangle.

Lesson Performance Task

The control tower at airport A is in contact with an airplane flying at point P, when it is 5 miles from the airport, and 30 seconds later when it is at point Q, 4 miles from the airport. The diagram shows the angles the plane makes with the ground at both times. If the plane flies parallel to the ground from P to Q at constant speed, how fast is it traveling?

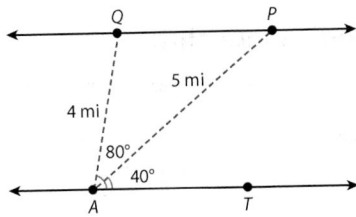

$m\angle QAP = 80° - 40° = 40°$

$\overline{QP}$ and $\overline{AT}$ are parallel, so $m\angle QPA = m\angle PAT = 40°$ because the angles form alternate interior angles.

By the converse of the Isosceles Triangle Theorem, $\triangle QAP$ is isosceles because $m\angle QPA = m\angle QAP = 40°$.

In isosceles $\triangle QAP$, $QP = QA = 4$ miles.

It took the plane 30 seconds to travel 4 miles, so it was traveling $4 \times 2 = 8$ miles per minute, or $8 \times 60 = 480$ miles per hour.

EXTENSION ACTIVITY

Have students research a technique used by marine navigators called a *doubled angle fix* or *doubled angle on the bow*. The problem in the Lesson Performance Task is based on this method. Students should describe how a marine navigator could use the method to find the distance of an object on shore, and how an isosceles triangle would be used in the calculation.

AVOID COMMON ERRORS

When students have determined that the plane has traveled 4 miles in 30 seconds, they may convert units incorrectly to find the plane's speed in miles per hour. The correct conversion is:

$$\frac{4 \text{ mi}}{30 \text{ sec}} \cdot \frac{60 \text{ sec}}{1 \text{ min}} \cdot \frac{60 \text{ min}}{1 \text{ hr}} = \frac{14{,}400 \text{ mi}}{30 \text{ hr}} = \frac{480 \text{ mi}}{1 \text{ hr}}$$

INTEGRATE MATHEMATICAL PRACTICES

Focus on Reasoning

MP.2 Have students refer to the diagram in the Lesson Performance Task, changing the angles measuring 40° and 80° to angles measuring $a°$ and $(2a)°$. Ask them to justify the conclusion that no matter how high the plane is, the distance it will travel from P to Q will equal the distance from Q to A. Sample answer: $m\angle QAP = (2a)° - a° = a°$. $m\angle QPA = m\angle PAT = a°$ because the angles are congruent alternate interior angles for parallel lines $\overleftrightarrow{QP}$ and $\overleftrightarrow{AT}$. $\triangle QAP$ is isosceles by the converse of the Isosceles Triangle Theorem. Therefore, $PQ = QA$.

Scoring Rubric

2 points: Student correctly solves the problem and explains his/her reasoning.

1 point: Student shows good understanding of the problem but does not fully solve or explain.

0 points: Student does not demonstrate understanding of the problem.

Isosceles and Equilateral Triangles   **340**

Triangle Inequalities

Common Core Math Standards

The student is expected to:

 COMMON CORE G-SRT.B.5

Use congruence ... criteria for triangles to solve problems and to prove relationships in geometric figures. Also G-CO.C.10, G-CO.D.12

Mathematical Practices

 COMMON CORE MP.5 Using Tools

Language Objective

Explain to a partner how to show the three inequalities generated for a triangle with side lengths a, b, and c.

ENGAGE

Essential Question: How can you use inequalities to describe the relationships among side lengths and angle measures in a triangle?

The sum of any two side lengths of a triangle will be greater than the length of the third side. If the sides of a triangle are not congruent, then the largest angle will be opposite the longest side and the smallest angle will be opposite the shortest side.

PREVIEW: LESSON PERFORMANCE TASK

View the Engage section online. Discuss the photo, making sure that students understand the objective of an orienteering competition and the tools used by competing teams. Then preview the Lesson Performance Task.

Name_____ Class_____ Date_____

7.3   Triangle Inequalities

Essential Question: How can you use inequalities to describe the relationships among side lengths and angle measures in a triangle?

Resource Locker

⊘ Explore   Exploring Triangle Inequalities

A triangle can have sides of different lengths, but are there limits to the lengths of any of the sides?

Ⓐ Consider a △ABC where you know two side lengths, AB = 4 inches and BC = 2 inches. On a separate piece of paper, draw $\overline{AB}$ so that it is 4 inches long.

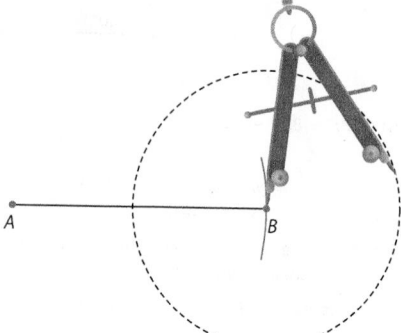

Ⓑ To determine all possible locations for C with $\overline{BC}$ = 2 inches, set your compass to 2 inches. Draw a circle with center at B.

Ⓒ Choose and label a final vertex point C so it is located on the circle. Using a straightedge, draw the segments to form a triangle.

Are there any places on the circle where point C cannot lie? Explain.

<u>Point C cannot lie on the two points of the</u>
<u>circle that intersect $\overrightarrow{AB}$ because then the</u>
<u>sides will overlap to form a straight line.</u>

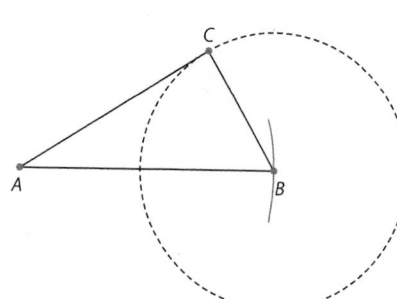

Ⓓ Measure and record the lengths of the three sides of your triangle.
Possible answer: AB = 4 in., BC = 2 in., AC = 3.2 in.

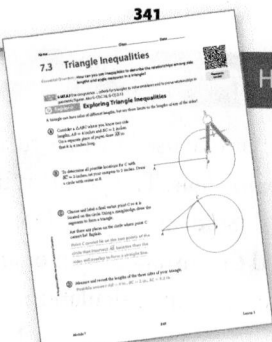

HARDCOVER PAGES 293–302

Turn to these pages to find this lesson in the hardcover student edition.

Ⓔ The figures below show two other examples of △ABC that could have been formed. What are the values that $\overline{AC}$ approaches when point C approaches $\overline{AB}$?

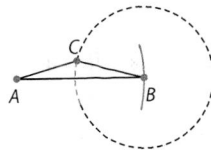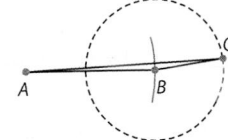

AC approaches 2 inches or 6 inches.

Reflect

1. Use the side lengths from your table to make the following comparisons. What do you notice?

$AB + BC$? AC $BC + AC$? AB $AC + AB$? BC

The sum of any of the two sides is greater than the third side.

2. Measure the angles of some triangles with a protractor. Where is the smallest angle in relation to the shortest side? Where is the largest angle in relation to the longest side?
The smallest angle is opposite the shortest side; the largest angle is opposite the longest

side.

3. **Discussion** How does your answer to the previous question relate to isosceles triangles or equilateral triangles?
When angles in a triangle have the same measure, the sides opposite those angles also

have the same measure.

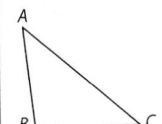 **Explain 1** **Using the Triangle Inequality Theorem**

The Explore shows that the sum of the lengths of any two sides of a triangle is greater than the length of the third side. This can be summarized in the following theorem.

Triangle Inequality Theorem
The sum of any two side lengths of a triangle is greater than the third side length.

$AB + BC > AC$

$BC + AC > AB$

$AC + AB > BC$

To be able to form a triangle, each of the three inequalities must be true. So, given three side lengths, you can test to determine if they can be used as segments to form a triangle. To show that three lengths cannot be the side lengths of a triangle, you only need to show that one of the three triangle inequalities is false.

Module 7   342   Lesson 3

 © Houghton Mifflin Harcourt Publishing Company

PROFESSIONAL DEVELOPMENT

COMMON CORE **Learning Progressions**

In this lesson, students add to their knowledge of triangles by using a variety of tools to verify the Triangle Inequality Theorem. Students also explore how to order the side lengths given the angle measures of the triangle and how to predict the possible lengths of the third side of a triangle, given the lengths of two of the sides. Triangles have important uses in everyday life and in future mathematics study, including trigonometry. All students should develop fluency with the properties of triangles as they continue their study of geometry.

EXPLORE

Exploring Triangle Inequalities

INTEGRATE TECHNOLOGY

Students have the option of completing the triangle inequality activity either in the book or online.

QUESTIONING STRATEGIES

❓ How do you decide if three lengths can be the side lengths of a triangle? Check the sum of each pair of two sides. The sum must be greater than the third side.

EXPLAIN 1

Using the Triangle Inequality Theorem

AVOID COMMON ERRORS

Some students may have difficulty understanding why all three inequalities must be checked for the Triangle Inequality Theorem. One example may be side lengths of 5 cm, 5 cm, and 10 cm. Straws with these lengths look like they will make a triangle, but they do not. Have them do several examples with different side lengths to test the theorem.

QUESTIONING STRATEGIES

❓ For side lengths a, b, and c of a triangle, how many inequalities must be true? Write them. $3; a < b + c, b < a + c, c < a + b$

Example 1 Use the Triangle Inequality Theorem to tell whether a triangle can have sides with the given lengths. Explain.

(A) 4, 8, 10

$$\overset{?}{4 + 8 > 10} \qquad\qquad \overset{?}{4 + 10 > 8} \qquad\qquad \overset{?}{8 + 10 > 4}$$
$$12 > 10 \checkmark \qquad\qquad 14 > 8 \checkmark \qquad\qquad 18 > 4 \checkmark$$

Conclusion: The sum of each pair of side lengths is greater than the third length. So, a triangle can have side lengths of 4, 8, and 10.

(B) 7, 9, 18

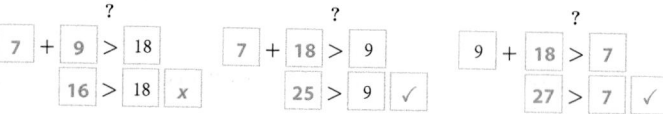

$$\boxed{7} + \boxed{9} \overset{?}{>} \boxed{18} \qquad \boxed{7} + \boxed{18} \overset{?}{>} \boxed{9} \qquad \boxed{9} + \boxed{18} \overset{?}{>} \boxed{7}$$

$$\boxed{16} > \boxed{18} \;\; x \qquad\qquad \boxed{25} > \boxed{9} \;\; \checkmark \qquad\qquad \boxed{27} > \boxed{7} \;\; \checkmark$$

Conclusion:

Not all three inequalities are true. So, a triangle cannot have these three side lengths.

Reflect

4. Can an isosceles triangle have these side lengths? Explain. 5, 5, 10
No; These numbers do not result in three true inequalities.

$5 + 5 \not> 10$, so no triangle can be drawn with these side lengths.

5. How do you know that the Triangle Inequality Theorem applies to all equilateral triangles?
Since all sides are congruent, the sum of any two side lengths will be greater than the third side.

Your Turn

Determine if a triangle can be formed with the given side lengths. Explain your reasoning.

6. 12 units, 4 units, 17 units
No; $12 + 4 \not> 17$

7. 24 cm, 8 cm, 30 cm
Yes; $24 + 8 > 30$, $8 + 30 > 24$, and $24 + 30 > 8$

© Houghton Mifflin Harcourt Publishing Company

COLLABORATIVE LEARNING

Small Group Activity

Give all students in groups pieces of raw spaghetti. Have each student break three pieces of spaghetti in different lengths and measure the length of each piece. Then have a group member write the three inequalities for those lengths. Have another group member analyze the inequalities and conjecture if the three lengths will form a triangle. Ask the fourth student to position the pieces to show a triangle or to show no triangle. Switch roles and repeat the activity.

Explain 2   Finding Possible Side Lengths in a Triangle

From the Explore, you have seen that if given two side lengths for a triangle, there are an infinite number of side lengths available for the third side. But the third side is also restricted to values determined by the Triangle Inequality Theorem.

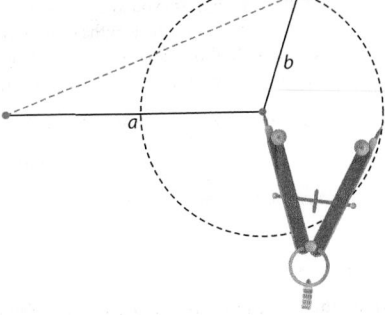

Example 2   Find the range of values for x using the Triangle Inequality Theorem.

Ⓐ   Find possible values for the length of the third side using the Triangle Inequality Theorem.

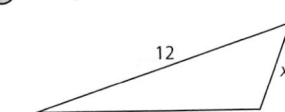

$$x + 10 > 12 \qquad\qquad x + 12 > 10 \qquad\qquad 10 + 12 > x$$
$$x > 2 \qquad\qquad\qquad x > -2 \qquad\qquad\quad 22 > x$$

$$2 < x < 22$$

Ignore the inequality with a negative value, since a triangle cannot have a negative side length. Combine the other two inequalities to find the possible values for x.

Ⓑ

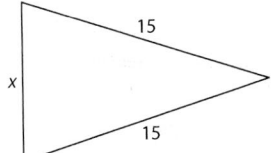

$$\boxed{x} + \boxed{15} > \boxed{15} \qquad \boxed{x} + \boxed{15} > \boxed{15} \qquad \boxed{15} + \boxed{15} > \boxed{x}$$
$$\boxed{x} > \boxed{0} \qquad\qquad \boxed{x} > \boxed{0} \qquad\qquad \boxed{30} > \boxed{x}$$

$$\boxed{0} < x < \boxed{30}$$

Module 7   **344**   Lesson 3

Finding Possible Side Lengths in a Triangle

CONNECT VOCABULARY   EL

Relate the *range of values* for a third side length of a triangle given two side lengths by stating that the third side length must be greater than the difference of the other two side lengths and also less than the sum of the other two side lengths.

© Houghton Mifflin Harcourt Publishing Company

DIFFERENTIATE INSTRUCTION

Manipulatives

Give students a number of straws and ask them to cut them into various lengths. Then have them measure each length. Ask them to make a table listing the measures of all possible combinations of the three lengths. Then have them manipulate the straws to see if they can form a triangle. Highlight sets of three measurements that do not form a triangle.

Triangle Inequalities   **344**

? How do find the range for the length of the third side of a triangle? **The range is $r < x < s$, where r is the difference of the two given side lengths and s is the sum of the two given side lengths.**

? How do you interpret the compound inequality $a < x < b$ as individual inequalities? **$a < x$ and $x < b$**

EXPLAIN 3

Ordering a Triangle's Angle Measures Given Its Side Lengths

INTEGRATE MATHEMATICAL PRACTICES

Focus on Technology

MP.5 Have students use geometry software to create a scalene triangle. Ask them to use the measuring features to measure the side lengths. Then have them measure each angle and verify that the largest angle is opposite the longest side length and that the smallest angle is opposite the shortest side length. Ask them to drag the vertices to vary the side lengths and then observe that the angle measures are ordered in the same way as in the original triangle.

Reflect

8. **Discussion** Suppose you know that the length of the base of an isosceles triangle is 10, but you do not know the lengths of its legs. How could you use the Triangle Inequality Theorem to find the range of possible lengths for each leg? Explain.

Possible answer: If x represents the length of one leg, then by the Triangle Inequality Theorem, solve for $x + x > 10$ and $x + 10 > x$. The solution of the first inequality is $x > 5$. The solution of the second inequality is $10 > 0$, which is always true. So the range of possible lengths for each leg is $x > 5$.

Your Turn

Find the range of values for x using the Triangle Inequality Theorem.

9.

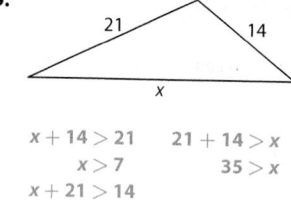

$$x + 14 > 21 \qquad 21 + 14 > x$$
$$x > 7 \qquad\qquad 35 > x$$
$$x + 21 > 14$$
$$x > -7 \qquad 7 < x < 35$$

10.

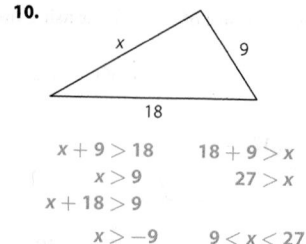

$$x + 9 > 18 \qquad 18 + 9 > x$$
$$x > 9 \qquad\qquad 27 > x$$
$$x + 18 > 9$$
$$x > -9 \qquad 9 < x < 27$$

⊘ Explain 3 **Ordering a Triangle's Angle Measures Given Its Side Lengths**

From the Explore Step D, you can see that changing the length of $\overline{AC}$ also changes the measure of $\angle B$ in a predictable way.

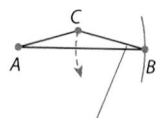

As side AC gets shorter, $m\angle B$ approaches $0°$

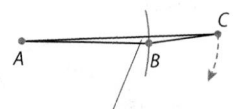

As side AC gets longer, $m\angle B$ approaches $180°$

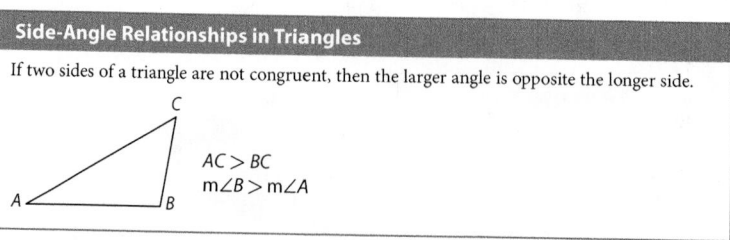

Side-Angle Relationships in Triangles

If two sides of a triangle are not congruent, then the larger angle is opposite the longer side.

$$AC > BC$$
$$m\angle B > m\angle A$$

LANGUAGE SUPPORT **EL**

Visual Cues

Help students understand how to apply the inequality relationships in this lesson by suggesting they list all the angles and sides before doing an example or exercise. Then, they can list the angles in increasing order and write the side lengths opposite those angles in the same order.

Example 3   For each triangle, order its angle measures from least to greatest.

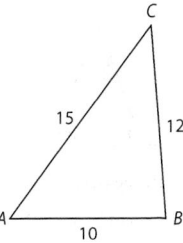   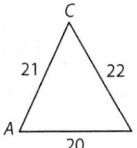

Longest side length: *AC*

Greatest angle measure: m∠*B*

Shortest side length: *AB*

Least angle measure: m∠*C*

Order of angle measures from least to greatest:
m∠*C*, m∠*A*, m∠*B*

Longest side length: __BC__

Greatest angle measure: __m∠A__

Shortest side length: __AB__

Least angle measure: __m∠C__

Order of angle measures from
least to greatest: __m∠C, m∠B, m∠A__

Your Turn

For each triangle, order its angle measures from least to greatest.

11.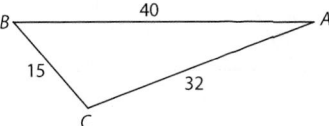

Longest side length: *AB*
Shortest side length: *CB*
m∠*A*, m∠*B*, m∠*C*

12.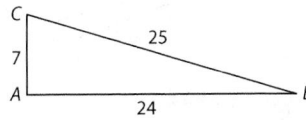

Longest side length: *BC*
Shortest side length: *AC*
m∠*B*, m∠*C*, m∠*A*

⊙ Explain 4   **Ordering a Triangle's Side Lengths Given Its Angle Measures**

From the Explore Step D, you can see that changing the the measure of ∠*B* also changes length of $\overline{AC}$ in a predictable way.

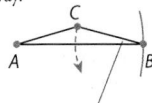   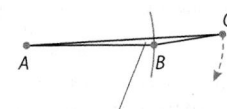

As m∠*B* approaches 0°, side *AC* gets shorter   As m∠*B* approaches 180°, side *AC* gets longer

Angle-Side Relationships in Triangles
If two angles of a triangle are not congruent, then the longer side is opposite the larger angle.

QUESTIONING STRATEGIES

?   How do you know the greatest angle is opposite the longest side in a triangle?   If one side of a triangle is longer than another, then the angle opposite the longer side is larger than the angle opposite the shorter side.

EXPLAIN 4

Ordering a Triangle's Side Lengths Given Its Angle Measures

AVOID COMMON ERRORS

Some students may think that they can use angle measures to compare the side lengths of different triangles. Explain that angle measures can be used to order the side lengths only within a single triangle. Give an example of why this must be the case, such as a very small triangle with an obtuse angle and a very large equilateral triangle. The obtuse angle is greater than the 60° angle of the equilateral triangle, but its opposite side may be shorter.

QUESTIONING STRATEGIES

?   How do you order the side lengths of a triangle given the angle measures?
Explain.   The side lengths will be in the same order as the measure of the angles opposite the side lengths. For example, the greatest side length is opposite the greatest angle measure. Use the rule that if one angle of a triangle is larger than another, then the side opposite the larger angle is longer than the side opposite the smaller angle.

ELABORATE

AVOID COMMON ERRORS

Some students may list angle measures in order and side lengths in order, but not make the connection that the largest side length must be opposite the largest angle measure. Suggest that they list the angles with the corresponding opposite side before they order their measures.

QUESTIONING STRATEGIES

? Can a triangle have side lengths of 7 cm, 12 cm, and 20 cm? Explain. No; the Triangle Inequality Theorem states that the sum of each pair of lengths must be greater than the third length in order for 3 lengths to be side lengths of a triangle. Since $7 + 12 \not> 20$, these lengths cannot be lengths of sides of a triangle.

? A triangle has angle measures of 30°, 60°, and 90°. Which angle is opposite the longest side of the triangle? Explain. The 90° angle, because the side lengths of a triangle are ordered in the same way as the angle measures.

SUMMARIZE THE LESSON

? How do you know if three segment lengths can be the side lengths of a triangle? Test the sum of each two pairs of segment lengths. By the Triangle Inequality Theorem, if the sum of each pair of segment lengths is greater than the third length, then the segments can be the side lengths of a triangle.

Example 4 For each triangle, order the side lengths from least to greatest.

 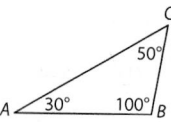 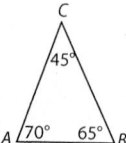

(A)

Greatest angle measure: m∠B

Longest side length: AC

Least angle measure: m∠A

Shortest side length: BC

Order of side lengths from least to greatest: BC, AB, AC

(B)

Greatest angle measure: ___m∠A___

Longest side length: ___BC___

Least angle measure: ___m∠C___

Shortest side length: ___AB___

Order of side lengths from least to great: ___AB, AC, BC___

Your Turn

For each triangle, order the side lengths from least to greatest.

13.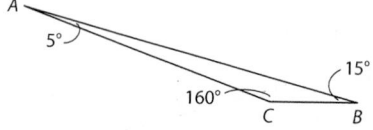

Greatest angle measure: m∠C

Least angle measure: m∠A

CB, AC, AB

14.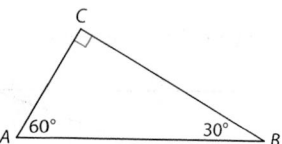

Greatest angle measure: m∠C

Least angle measure: m∠B

AC, BC, AB

💬 Elaborate

15. When two sides of a triangle are congruent, what can you conclude about the angles opposite those sides?
They are also congruent.

16. What can you conclude about the side opposite the obtuse angle in an obtuse triangle?
It is the longest side of the triangle.

17. **Essential Question Check-In** Suppose you are given three values that could represent the side lengths of a triangle. How can you use one inequality to determine if the triangle exists?
If the sum of the two least values is greater than the remaining value, the triangle exists.
Otherwise it does not exist.

Evaluate: Homework and Practice

• Online Homework
• Hints and Help
• Extra Practice

Use a compass and straightedge to decide whether each set of lengths can form a triangle.

1. 7 cm, 9 cm, 18 cm

No; if the base is 18 cm compass arcs of lengths 7 cm and 9 cm from each end of the base do not intersect.

2. 2 in., 4 in., 5 in.

Yes; if the base is 5 in. compass arcs of lengths 2 in. and 4 in. from each end of the base have two intersections, each forming a triangle.

3. 1 in., 2 in., 10 in.

No; if the base is 10 in. compass arcs of lengths 1 in. and 2 in. from each end of the base do not intersect.

4. 9 cm, 10 cm, 11 cm

Yes; if the base is 11 cm compass arcs of lengths 9 cm and 10 cm from each end of the base have two intersections, each forming a triangle.

Determine whether a triangle can be formed with the given side lengths.

5. 10 ft, 3 ft, 15 ft   No; $10 + 3 \not> 15$

6. 12 in., 4 in., 15 in. Yes; $12 + 4 > 15$, $4 + 15 > 12$, and $12 + 15 > 4$

7. 9 in., 12 in., and 18 in.   Yes

8. 29 m, 59 m, and 89 m   No; $29 + 59 \not> 89$

Find the range of possible values for x using the Triangle Inequality Theorem.

9.

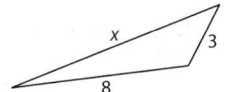

$5 < x < 11$

$3 + 8 > x$ $3 + x > 8$ $8 + x > 3$

$11 > x$ $x > 5$ $x > -5$

10.

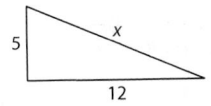

$7 < x < 19$

$5 + 12 > x$ $5 + x > 12$ $12 + x > 5$

$19 > x$ $x > 7$ $x > -7$

11. A triangle with side lengths 22.3, 27.6, and x $5.3 < x < 49.9$

$22.3 + 27.6 > x$ $22.3 + x > 27.6$ $27.6 + x > 22.3$

$49.9 > x$ $x > 5.3$ $x > -5.3$

12. **Analyze Relationships** Suppose a triangle has side lengths AB, BC, and x, where $AB = 2 \cdot BC$. Find the possible range for x in terms of BC. $BC < x < 3 \cdot BC$

$AB + BC > x$ $BC + x > AB$ $x + AB > BC$

$2 \cdot BC + BC > x$ $BC + x > 2 \cdot BC$ $x + 2 \cdot BC > BC$

$3 \cdot BC > x$ $x > BC$ $x > -BC$

© Houghton Mifflin Harcourt Publishing Company

ASSIGNMENT GUIDE

Concepts and Skills	Practice
Explore Exploring Triangle Inequalities	Exercises 1–4
Example 1 Using the Triangle Inequality Theorem	Exercises 5–8
Example 2 Finding Possible Side Lengths in a Triangle	Exercises 9–12
Example 3 Ordering a Triangle's Angle Measures Given Its Side Lengths	Exercises 13–15
Example 4 Ordering a Triangle's Side Lengths Given Its Angle Measures	Exercises 16–19

INTEGRATE MATHEMATICAL PRACTICES

Focus on Technology

MP.5 Students can check their solutions for correctness by using geometry software to create triangles with the same side lengths or angle measures. When checking solutions, remind students the order of the side lengths gives the order of the opposite angle measures.

Exercise	Depth of Knowledge (D.O.K.)	COMMON CORE Mathematical Practices
1–19	**2** Skills/Concepts	**MP.4** Modeling
20–27	**2** Skills/Concepts	**MP.4** Modeling
28	**3** Strategic Thinking H.O.T.	**MP.4** Modeling
29	**3** Strategic Thinking H.O.T.	**MP.3** Logic
30	**3** Strategic Thinking H.O.T.	**MP.3** Logic

Triangle Inequalities   **348**

13.

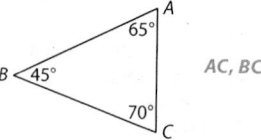

$m\angle A, m\angle B, m\angle C$

14.

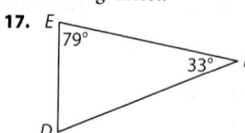

$m\angle E, m\angle F, m\angle D$

15. Analyze Relationships Suppose a triangle has side lengths PQ, QR, and PR, where $PR = 2PQ = 3QR$. Write the angle measures in order from least to greatest.

$$PR = 2PQ \qquad PR = 3QR \qquad \tfrac{1}{3}PR < \tfrac{1}{2}PR < PR$$

$$\tfrac{1}{2}PR = PQ \qquad \tfrac{1}{3}PR = QR \qquad QR < PQ < PR$$

So $m\angle P < m\angle R < m\angle Q$; Order from least to greatest: $m\angle P, m\angle R, m\angle Q$

For each triangle, write the side lengths in order from least to greatest.

16.

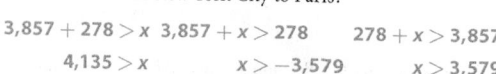

AC, BC, AB

17.

$m\angle D = 68°$

DE, EF, DF

18. In $\triangle JKL$, $m\angle J = 53°$, $m\angle K = 68°$, and $m\angle L = 59°$. KL, JK, JL

19. In $\triangle PQR$, $m\angle P = 102°$ and $m\angle Q = 25°$. $m\angle R = 53°$ PR, PQ, QR

20. Represent Real-World Problems Rhonda is traveling from New York City to Paris and is trying to decide whether to fly via Frankfurt or to get a more expensive direct flight. Given that it is 3,857 miles from New York City to Frankfurt and another 278 miles from Frankfurt to Paris, what is the range of possible values for the direct distance from New York City to Paris?

$3,857 + 278 > x \quad 3,857 + x > 278 \qquad 278 + x > 3,857$

$\qquad 4,135 > x \qquad\qquad x > -3,579 \qquad\qquad x > 3,579$

$3,579 < x < 4,135$

The direct distance is between 3,579 miles and 4,135 miles.

©Houghton Mifflin Harcourt Publishing Company · Image Credits: ©Carlos Davila/Photographer's Choice RF/Getty Images

---

VISUAL CUES EL

Suggest that students label a side and its corresponding opposite angle in one color and then do the same with other side-angle combinations in different colors. This visual cue can help them to remember the order of the measures of the sides or angles.

AVOID COMMON ERRORS

If students have trouble with compound inequalities, have them write the inequalities separately and then use a number line to help them combine the inequalities into one.

COLLABORATIVE LEARNING

Have students work in small groups to make a poster showing a triangle, the side-angle relationships, and the triangle inequality relationship they learned in this lesson. Give each group a different triangle to draw. Then have each group present its poster to the rest of the class, explaining each relationship they listed.

21. Represent Real-World Problems A large ship is sailing between three small islands. To do so, the ship must sail between two pairs of islands, avoiding sailing between a third pair. The safest route is to avoid the closest pair of islands. Which is the safest route for the ship?

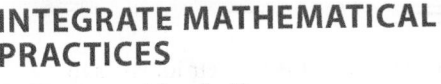

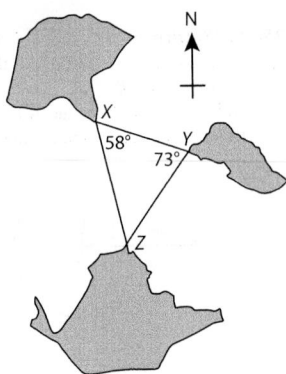

$58° + 73° + m\angle Z = 180°; m\angle Z = 49°$

$m\angle Z < m\angle X < m\angle Y$, so $XY < YZ < XZ$. Therefore, the safest route is to avoid sailing between the islands at X and Y.

22. Represent Real-World Problems A hole on a golf course is a dogleg, meaning that it bends in the middle. A golfer will usually start by driving for the bend in the dogleg (from A to B), and then using a second shot to get the ball to the green (from B to C). Sandy believes she may be able to drive the ball far enough to reach the green in one shot, avoiding the bend (from A direct to C). Sandy knows she can accurately drive a distance of 250 yd. Should she attempt to drive for the green on her first shot? Explain. **Yes;**

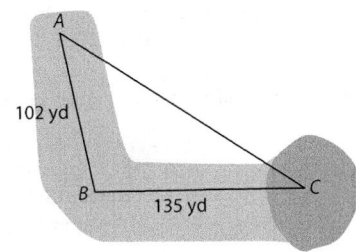

$102 + 135 > AC$	$102 + AC > 135$	$135 + AC > 102$
$237 > AC$	$AC > 33$	$AC > -33$

$33 < AC < 237$

Since AC is less than 250 yd, Sandy has a good chance of reaching the green in one shot.

23. Represent Real-World Problems Three cell phone towers form a triangle, $\triangle PQR$. The measure of $\angle Q$ is 10° less than the measure of $\angle P$. The measure of $\angle R$ is 5° greater than the measure of $\angle Q$. Which two towers are closest together?

$m\angle Q = m\angle P - 10°$ and

$m\angle R = m\angle Q + 5° = (m\angle P - 10°) + 5° = m\angle P - 5°$

So, $m\angle Q < m\angle R < m\angle P$, and therefore $PR < PQ < QR$. The towers at Q and R are closest together.

24. Algebra In $\triangle PQR$, $PQ = 3x + 1$, $QR = 2x - 2$, and $PR = x + 7$. Determine the range of possible values of x. **First, each side length must be positive.**

$3x + 1 > 0$	$2x - 2 > 0$	$x + 7 > 0$
$x > -\dfrac{1}{3}$	$x > 1$	$x > -7$
$(3x + 1) + (2x - 2) > x + 7$	$(3x + 1) + (x + 7) > 2x - 2$	$(2x - 2) + (x + 7) > (3x + 1)$
$x > 2$	$x > -5$	$4 > 0$

Since the last inequality is always true, $x > 2$.

INTEGRATE MATHEMATICAL PRACTICES

Focus on Modeling

MP.4 When writing side measures or side-angle measure relationships for a triangle, students should remember that there is a range of possible side lengths for making a triangle, and that the side lengths and angle measures must be in the same order.

AVOID COMMON ERRORS

Some students may think that all three inequalities associated with the Triangle Inequality Theorem must be false. Point out that you need to show only that one of the three triangle inequalities is false to state that the three lengths are not side lengths of a triangle.

Have students use diagrams in their journals to illustrate the angle-side relationships in triangles.

25. In any triangle ABC, suppose you know the lengths of $\overline{AB}$ and $\overline{BC}$, and suppose that $AB > BC$. If x is the length of the third side, $\overline{AC}$, use the Triangle Inequality Theorem to prove that $AB - BC < x < AB + BC$. That is, x must be between the difference and the sum of the other two side lengths. Explain why this result makes sense in terms of the constructions shown in the figure.

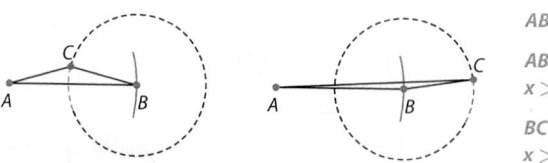

$$AB + BC > x$$
$$AB + x > BC$$
$$x > BC - AB$$

$$BC + x > AB$$
$$x > AB - BC$$

Since $AB > BC$, $BC - AB < 0$, so the second inequality is not relevant. Combining the first and last inequalities gives $AB - BC < x < AB + BC$.

The constructions show that AC approaches but is always greater than $AB - BC$, and that AC approaches but is always less than $AB + BC$.

26. Given the information in the diagram, prove that $m\angle DEA < m\angle ABC$.

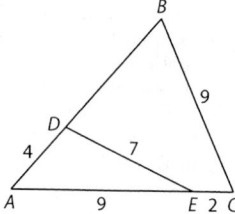

In , $\triangle ADE$, $DA < DE$, so $m\angle DEA < m\angle DAE = m\angle BAC$. In $\triangle ABC$, $AC = 9 + 2 = 11$ (Segment Addition Postulate), so $BC < AC$, and therefore $m\angle BAC < m\angle ABC$. Therefore, $m\angle DEA < m\angle ABC$ (Transitive Property Of Inequality).

27. An isosceles triangle has legs with length 11 units. Which of the following could be the perimeter of the triangle? Choose all that apply. Explain your reasoning.

a. 22 units **B, C, D**

b. 24 units   If x represents the length of the third side of the triangle, then by the Triangle Inequality Theorem, solve for $11 + x > 11$ and $11 + 11 > x$. The solution of the first inequality is $x > 0$, which is always true. The solution of the second inequality

c. 34 units

d. 43 units   is $22 > x$. So the range of possible lengths for the third side is $0 < x < 22$. Use both limits to solve for perimeter. $11 + 11 + 0 = 22$ and $11 + 11 + 22 = 44$. So, the

e. 44 units   perimeter for all possible triangles must be greater than 22 units and less than 44 units. So choices A and E are not possible.

H.O.T. Focus on Higher Order Thinking

28. Communicate Mathematical Ideas Given the information in the diagram, prove that $PQ < PS$.

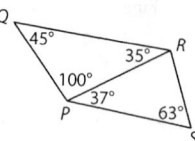

In, $\triangle PQR$, $m\angle PRQ < m\angle Q$, so $PQ < PR$. In $\triangle PRS$, $m\angle PRS = 180° - 37° - 63° = 80°$, so $m\angle S < m\angle PRS$, and therefore $PR < PS$. Therefore, $PQ < PS$ (Transitive Property of Inequality).

29. Justify Reasoning In obtuse $\triangle ABC$, $m\angle A < m\angle B$. The auxiliary line segment $\overline{CD}$ perpendicular to $\overrightarrow{AB}$ (extended beyond B) creates right triangles ADC and BDC. Describe how you could use the Pythagorean Theorem to prove that $BC < AC$.

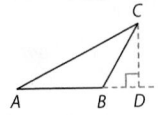

Write two equations, $AD^2 + CD^2 = AC^2$ and $BD^2 + CD^2 = BC^2$. Equating expressions for CD^2, $AC^2 - AD^2 = BC^2 - BD^2$ and therefore $AC^2 - BC^2 = AD^2 - BD^2$. Since the right side is positive, so is the left side, which leads to $BC < AC$.

30. Make a Conjecture In acute $\triangle DEF$, $m\angle D < m\angle E$. The auxiliary line segment $\overline{FG}$ creates $\triangle EFG$, where $EF = FG$. What would you need to prove about the points D, G, and E to prove that $\angle DGF$ is obtuse, and therefore that $EF < DF$? Explain.

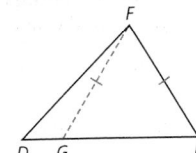

You would need to show that G lies on $\overline{DE}$, i.e. between D and E. In that case, since $\angle DGF$ and $\angle EGF$ are supplementary and $\angle EGF$ is acute, then $\angle DGF$ is obtuse. So $\angle DGF$ is the largest angle in $\triangle DGF$ and $FG < DF$. Since $EF = FG$, then by substitution, $EF < DF$.

Lesson Performance Task

As captain of your orienteering team, it's your job to map out the shortest distance from point A to point H on the map. Justify each of your decisions.

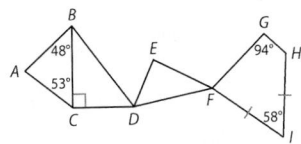

The shortest route is A-C-D-F-G-H.

In $\triangle ABC$ the smallest angle measures $48°$, so the shortest side is $\overline{AC}$.

In $\triangle BCD$ the route from C to D is shorter than the route from C to B to D, because $\overline{BD}$ is the longest side of the triangle.

In $\triangle DEF$ the route from D to F is shorter than the route from D to E to F by the Triangle Inequality Theorem.

In quadrilateral $FGHI$, draw $\overline{FH}$. Since $FI = HI$, $\triangle FIH$ is isosceles, with base angles each measuring $61°$. So, $\overline{FH}$ is the shortest side of $\triangle FIH$. $\overline{FH}$ is opposite the largest angle in $\triangle FGH$, so $\overline{FH}$ is the longest side in triangle in $\triangle FGH$ by the Triangle Inequality Theorem. So, $FI > FH > FG$ and $IH > FH > GH$. So, the path from F to G to H is shorter than the path from F to I to H.

EXTENSION ACTIVITY

Have students design orienteering courses like the one in the Lesson Performance Task. Courses should consist of at least four stages. At each stage of a course, angle measures or other information should be given that will allow an orienteer to apply the Triangle Inequality Theorem, angle-side relationships, and/or side-angle relationships, in order to gauge the shortest route to follow. Students may wish to work in teams of two or three and tackle routes other students have designed.

AVOID COMMON ERRORS

Students may attempt to apply the methods discussed in this lesson to figures other than triangles, an approach that is likely to lead to false conclusions. The solution, when confronted with a figure like quadrilateral $FGHI$ in the Lesson Performance Task, is to draw one or more diagonals, dividing the figure into triangles whose inequalities can then be analyzed.

INTEGRATE MATHEMATICAL PRACTICES
Focus on Critical Thinking

MP.3 Define the side *opposite* an angle in a pentagon as the side that neither forms the angle nor is adjacent to a side that forms the angle.

Ask students to draw and label a pentagon in which, unlike a triangle, the side opposite the largest angle is the *shortest* side of the pentagon. Sample figure:

Scoring Rubric
2 points: Student correctly solves the problem and explains his/her reasoning.
1 point: Student shows good understanding of the problem but does not fully solve or explain.
0 points: Student does not demonstrate understanding of the problem.

Study Guide Review

ASSESSMENT AND INTERVENTION

Assign or customize module reviews.

MODULE PERFORMANCE TASK

COMMON CORE

Mathematical Practices: MP.1, MP.3, MP.4, MP.6
G-MG.A.1

SUPPORTING STUDENT REASONING

Students should begin this problem by analyzing the shape of the Federal Triangle. Here are some issues they might bring up.

- **If any part of the Federal Triangle is a triangle:** Students can research this. Since the Federal Triangle extends, on the east, past 6th Street, a large section of it is a triangle.

- **The number of sides for the outline of the Federal Triangle:** The illustration shows a polygon, so students can count the number of sides.

- **The angle measure at each vertex of the polygon:** One approach is to find angle measures at each vertex of the polygon and then add them if necessary.

- **How to find the area of the Federal Triangle:** Students can break it up in a variety of ways. Using the streets as edges of the polygons may be convenient.

Properties of Triangles

Essential Question: How can you use the properties of triangles to solve real-world problems?

KEY EXAMPLE   (Lesson 7.1)

Determine the measure of the fifth interior angle of a pentagon if you know the other four measures are 100°, 50°, 158°, and 147°.

$\text{Sum} = (5 - 2)180° = 540°$ Apply the Polygon Angle Sum Theorem.

$100 + 50 + 158 + 147 + x = 540$ Set the sum of the angle measures equal to 540.

$455 + x = 540$

$x = 85$ Solve for x.

KEY EXAMPLE   (Lesson 7.2)

Given an isosceles triangle $\triangle ABC$ with $\overline{AB} \cong \overline{AC}$, $AB = 4x + 3$, and $AC = 8x - 13$, find AB.

$\overline{AB} \cong \overline{AC}$ Given

$4x + 3 = 8x - 13$ Substitution

$x = 4$ Solve for x.

$AB = 4(4) + 3$ Substitute the value of x into AB.

$AB = 19$ Simplify.

KEY EXAMPLE   (Lesson 7.3)

Given a triangle with sides 7, 12, and x, find the range of values for x.

According to the Triangle Inequality Theorem, the sum of any two side lengths of a triangle is greater than the third side length

$7 + 12 > x$	$7 + x > 12$	$x + 12 > 7$	Apply the Triangle Inequality Theorem.
$19 > x$	$x > 5$	$x > -5$	Simplify.
$5 < x < 19$			Combine the inequalities together.

Key Vocabulary

interior angle *(ángulo interior)*
auxiliary line *(línea auxiliar)*
exterior angle *(ángulo exterior)*
remote interior angle *(ángulo interior remoto)*
isosceles triangle *(triángulo isósceles)*
legs *(catetos)*
vertex angle *(ángulo del vértice)*
base *(base)*
base angles *(ángulos de la base)*
equilateral triangle *(triángulo equilátero)*
equiangular triangle *(triángulo equiangular)*

SCAFFOLDING SUPPORT

- In the actual Federal Triangle, there are some small curves and other departures from straight lines that result in a figure that is not exactly a polygon. Encourage students to disregard these departures and use the polygonal figure on the page as their pattern.

- Students can use a search engine to find a map of the "Triangle" and the map scale. You may wish to review writing and solving proportions, which students will need to do to convert map dimensions to actual dimensions.

- Many estimates will go into each student's solution, so reassure students that there may be wide variations in their answers. You can use the answers in the Sample Solution as good approximations of answers.

EXERCISES

Find how many sides a polygon has with the given interior angle sum. *(Lesson 7.1)*

1. 2700° _____17_____

2. 1800° _____12_____

Find the sum of interior angles a polygon has with the given number of sides.
(Lesson 7.1)

3. 3 _____180°_____

4. 19 _____3060°_____

Given an isosceles triangle $\triangle DEF$ with $\overline{DE} \cong \overline{DF}$, $DE = 26$, and $m\angle F = 45°$, find the desired measurements. *(Lesson 7.2)*

5. DF _____26_____

6. $m\angle D$ _____90°_____

Determine whether a triangle can have sides with the given lengths. *(Lesson 7.3)*

7. 5 mi, 19 mi, 15 mi _____Yes_____

8. 4 ft, 3 ft, 10 ft _____No_____

Find the range of the unknown side of a triangle with the given sides. *(Lesson 7.3)*

9. 5 mi, 19 mi, x mi _____$14 < x < 24$_____

10. 4 ft, 3 ft, x ft _____$1 < x < 7$_____

MODULE PERFORMANCE TASK

What's Up in the Federal Triangle?

The diagram shows a schematic of the Federal Triangle, an area located in Washington, DC. The area is bounded by Constitution Avenue on the south and Pennsylvania Avenue on the north and extends from 12ᵗʰ Street on the west to just past 6ᵗʰ Street on the east.

Is the shape of the Federal Triangle a triangle? How many sides does the Federal Triangle have? What is the actual shape of the Federal Triangle? What is the sum of the internal angles of the Federal Triangle? What portion of the area is actually a triangle?

Do some research and find the lengths of each side. Find the perimeter and area of the Federal Triangle. Find the area of the portion of the Federal Triangle that is a triangle.

Federal Triangle

DISCUSSION OPPORTUNITIES

- Would it be reasonable to assume that adding the areas of the footprints of all the buildings will give the total area of the Federal Triangle?

- Are there other ways to find the area of the polygon that is the Federal Triangle?

SAMPLE SOLUTION

The Federal Triangle has four sides, so it is a quadrilateral, not a triangle. Since the western end of Pennsylvania Avenue, one side of the quadrilateral, is parallel to Constitution Avenue, the Federal "Triangle" is actually a trapezoid. That means that the sum of its interior angles is 360°. I drew a map of the trapezoid to scale and found that the angle at the intersection of Constitution Avenue and Pennsylvania Avenue measures about 20°. That means that the angle where Pennsylvania Avenue "bends" is about 180° − 20° = 160°.

Using my map and scale I found these dimensions:

Pennsylvania Avenue, left end: 1150 ft

Pennsylvania Avenue, right end: 3450 ft

Constitution Avenue: 3900 ft

15ᵗʰ Street: 1250 ft

perimeter: 9750 ft

area (triangular portion): 1,718,750 ft²

area (rectangular portion): 1,437,500 ft²

total area: 3,156,250 ft²

portion of total area that is a triangle: about 54%

Assessment Rubric

2 points: Student correctly solves the problem and explains his/her reasoning.

1 point: Student shows good understanding of the problem but does not fully solve or explain.

0 points: Student does not demonstrate understanding of the problem.

Ready to Go On?

ASSESS MASTERY

Use the assessment on this page to determine if students have mastered the concepts and standards covered in this module.

ASSESSMENT AND INTERVENTION

Access Ready to Go On? assessment online, and receive instant scoring, feedback, and customized intervention or enrichment.

ADDITIONAL RESOURCES

Response to Intervention Resources

- Reteach Worksheets

Differentiated Instruction Resources

- Reading Strategies **EL**
- Success for English Learners **EL**
- Challenge Worksheets

Assessment Resources

- Leveled Module Quizzes

(Ready) to Go On?

7.1–7.3 Properties of Triangles

- Online Homework
- Hints and Help
- Extra Practice

Determine whether a triangle can be formed with the given side lengths. If the side lengths can form a triangle, determine if they will form an isosceles triangle, equilateral triangle, or neither. *(Lesson 7.1)*

1. 3 mi, 8 mi, 3 mi

No, $3 + 3 < 8$

2. 7 cm, 7cm, 7cm

Yes, equilateral

3. 4 ft, 4 ft, 2 ft

Yes, isosceles

4. 20 m, 30 m, 10 m

No, $10 + 20 = 30$

5. 3 m, 4 m, 5 m

Yes, neither isosceles nor equilateral

6. 26 yd, 26 yd, 26 yd

Yes, equilateral

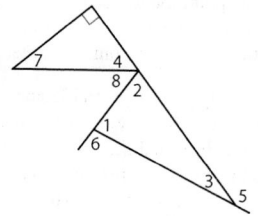

Use the figure to answer the following. *(Lesson 7.2)*

7. Given m∠2 = 76°, m∠1 = 3 · m∠3, and ∠4 ≅ ∠8, find m∠1, m∠3, m∠4, m∠5, m∠6, m∠7, and m∠8.

m∠1 = 78°, m∠3 = 26°, m∠4 = 52°, m∠5 = 154°, m∠6 = 102°, m∠7 = 38°, m∠8 = 52°

ESSENTIAL QUESTION

8. Is it possible for one angle of a triangle to be 180°? If so, demonstrate with an example. If not, explain why not.

Answers may vary. Sample: It is not possible. The three angles of a triangle add up to 180°, and if one angle were 180°, then the other two angles would be 0°, and a triangle cannot have angles of 0°.

©Houghton Mifflin Harcourt Publishing Company

COMMON CORE Common Core Standards

Lesson	Items	Content Standards	Mathematical Practices
7.3	1	G-CO.C.10	MP.7
7.2	2	G-CO.C.10	MP.7
7.2	3	G-CO.C.10	MP.7
7.3	4	G-CO.C.10	MP.7
7.2	5	G-CO.C.10	MP.7
7.2	6	G-CO.C.10	MP.7
7.1	7	G-CO.C.10	MP.7

MODULE 7
MIXED REVIEW

Assessment Readiness

1. Two angles in a triangle have measurements of 34° and 84°.
   Select Yes or No for A–C.
   - **A.** Does the third angle measure 62°?   ● Yes   ○ No
   - **B.** Could a triangle congruent to this one contain an angle of 75°?   ○ Yes   ● No
   - **C.** Is this triangle congruent to a right triangle?   ○ Yes   ● No

2. Consider the following statements about a seven-sided polygon. Choose True or False for each statement.
   - **A.** Each interior angle measures 135°.   ○ True   ● False
   - **B.** The sum of the measures of the interior angles is 1260°.   ○ True   ● False
   - **C.** The sum of the measures of the interior angles is 900°.   ● True   ○ False

3. $\triangle ABC$ is an equilateral triangle, $AB = 4x + 45$, and $BC = 6x - 3$. Choose True or False for each statement.
   - **A.** $x = 24$ ● True   ○ False
   - **B.** The length of one side of the triangle is 141 units.   ● True   ○ False
   - **C.** The distance from one vertex of the triangle to the midpoint of an adjacent side is 12 units.   ○ True   ● False

4. Given a triangle with a side of length 6 and another side of length 13, find the range of possible values for the third side, x.

   $7 < x < 19$

5. Given $\triangle DEF$, with $DE = 3EF$ and $DF = 4DE$, explain how to write the sides and angles in order of least to greatest.

   Answers may vary. Sample: $DE = 3EF$, so $\frac{1}{3}DE = EF$. $DF = 4DE$, so the order of sides in terms of DE is $\frac{1}{3}DE < DE < 4DE$, or $EF < DE < DF$. The order of sides from least to greatest is EF, DE, and DF. Since the longer side corresponds to the larger angle, $\angle D < \angle F < \angle E$.

© Houghton Mifflin Harcourt Publishing Company

Module 7 356 Study Guide Review

Assessment Readiness

ASSESSMENT AND INTERVENTION

Assign ready-made or customized practice tests to prepare students for high-stakes tests.

ADDITIONAL RESOURCES

Assessment Resources
- Leveled Module Quizzes: Modified, B

AVOID COMMON ERRORS

Item 2 Some students will divide by n when using the Interior Angle Sum theorem. Remind students to double-check what they are looking for. Students should only divide the sum by n when trying to find the measure of one angle in a regular polygon.

Common Core Standards

Lesson	Items	Content Standards	Mathematical Practices
7.1, 5.1	1*	G-CO.C.10	MP.2
7.1	2	G-CO.C.10	MP.2
7.2, 1.1	3*	G-MG.A.3	MP.2
7.3	4	G-MG.A.3	MP.6
7.3	5	G-MG.A.3	MP.6

* Item integrates mixed review concepts from previous modules or a previous course.

Study Guide Review **356**

Special Segments in Triangles

ESSENTIAL QUESTION:

Answer: Special segments can be used to find many characteristics of real-world triangles, such as their areas or centers of mass.

PROFESSIONAL DEVELOPMENT VIDEO

Professional Development Video

STEM Consultant Michael DiSpezio offers engaging suggestions and activities for integrating science, technology, and engineering into the math classroom.

Professional Development

my.hrw.com

MODULE **8**

Special Segments in Triangles

Essential Question: How can you use special segments in triangles to solve real-world problems?

LESSON 8.1
Perpendicular Bisectors of Triangles

LESSON 8.2
Angle Bisectors of Triangles

LESSON 8.3
Medians and Altitudes of Triangles

LESSON 8.4
Midsegments of Triangles

REAL WORLD VIDEO
Check out how the properties of triangles can be used by architects and urban planners to solve problems involving the positioning of landmarks.

MODULE PERFORMANCE TASK PREVIEW

Where Is the Heart of the Texas Triangle?

The Texas Triangle is a region with the cities of Dallas, Houston, and San Antonio as the vertices of the triangle. In this module, you will use theorems about triangles to explore the geometry of the region and locate its center. Are even triangles bigger in Texas?

© Houghton Mifflin Harcourt Publishing Company • Image Credits: ©AugustSnow/Alamy

---

DIGITAL TEACHER EDITION

Access a full suite of teaching resources when and where you need them:

- Access content online or offline
- Customize lessons to share with your class
- Communicate with your students in real-time
- View student grades and data instantly to target your instruction where it is needed most

PERSONAL MATH TRAINER
Assessment and Intervention

Assign automatically graded homework, quizzes, tests, and intervention activities. Prepare your students with updated, Common Core-aligned practice tests.

Are YOU Ready?

Complete these exercises to review the skills you will need for this module.

- Online Homework
- Hints and Help
- Extra Practice

Distance and Midpoint Formulas

Example 1 Find the midpoint between $(7, 1)$ and $(-4, 8)$.

$\left(\dfrac{x_1 + x_2}{2}, \dfrac{y_1 + y_2}{2}\right)$ Midpoint Formula

$\left(\dfrac{7 - 4}{2}, \dfrac{1 + 8}{2}\right)$ Substitute.

$\left(\dfrac{3}{2}, \dfrac{9}{2}\right)$ Simplify.

Find each midpoint for the given points.

1. $(2, 3)$ and $(14, 9)$ _____ $(8, 6)$

2. $(-4, 7)$ and $(-1, -11)$ _____ $\left(-\dfrac{5}{2}, -2\right)$

Angle Theorems for Triangles

Example 2 Given that $m\angle a = 72°$ and $m\angle c = 48°$, find the missing angle.

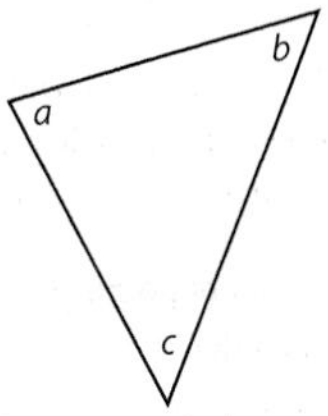

$m\angle a + m\angle b + m\angle c = 180°$ Triangle Sum Theorem

$72° + m\angle b + 48° = 180°$ Substitute.

$m\angle b + 120° = 180°$ Simplify.

$m\angle b = 60°$ Solve for $m\angle b$.

Find the missing angle in the figure from the example for the given values.

3. $m\angle b = 66°$ and $m\angle c = 75°$

$m\angle a = 39°$

4. $m\angle a = 103°$ and $m\angle c = 49°$

$m\angle b = 28°$

Geometric Drawings

Example 3 Use a compass and straightedge to construct the bisector of the given angle.

Angle with Bisector

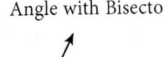
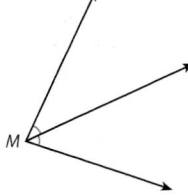

Use a compass and straightedge to construct the bisector of the given angle.

5.

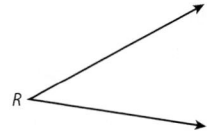

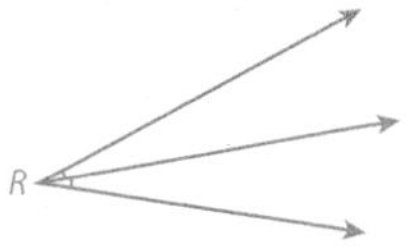

Check students' constructions.

© Houghton Mifflin Harcourt Publishing Company

Are You Ready?

ASSESS READINESS

Use the assessment on this page to determine if students need strategic or intensive intervention for the module's prerequisite skills.

ASSESSMENT AND INTERVENTION

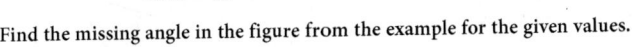

RtI Response to Intervention **TIER 1, TIER 2, TIER 3 SKILLS**

Personal Math Trainer will automatically create a standards-based, personalized intervention assignment for your students, targeting each student's individual needs!

ADDITIONAL RESOURCES

See the table below for a full list of intervention resources available for this module.

Response to Intervention Resources also includes:

- Tier 2 Skill Pre-Tests for each Module
- Tier 2 Skill Post-Tests for each skill

Response to Intervention			Differentiated Instruction
Tier 1 Lesson Intervention Worksheets	**Tier 2** Strategic Intervention Skills Intervention Worksheets	**Tier 3** Intensive Intervention Worksheets available online	
Reteach 8.1 Reteach 8.2 Reteach 8.3 Reteach 8.4	3 Angle Theorems for Triangles 9 Distance and Midpoint Formula 10 Geometric Drawings	Building Block Skills 8, 10, 11, 27, 38, 45, 48, 69, 70, 74, 98, 99, 100, 104	Challenge worksheets Extend the Math Lesson Activities in TE·

Perpendicular Bisectors of Triangles

Common Core Math Standards

The student is expected to:

 **G-C.A.3**

Construct the . . . circumscribed circles of a triangle . . . . Also G-CO.C.10, G-CO.D.12, G-GPE.B.4, G-GPE.B.5

Mathematical Practices

 MP.6 Precision

Language Objective

Work in small groups to match terms to picture cards.

ENGAGE

Essential Question: How can you use perpendicular bisectors to find the point that is equidistant from all the vertices of a triangle?

Graph or find the equations for at least two of the three perpendicular bisectors of the sides of the triangle. The circumcenter, which is the point that is equidistant from the vertices, will be located at the intersection of any of the two perpendicular bisectors.

PREVIEW: LESSON PERFORMANCE TASK

View the Engage section online. Discuss the photo, asking students to explain the meanings of the words *botany, geology,* and *ecology.* Then preview the Lesson Performance Task.

Name_____ Class_____ Date_____

8.1 Perpendicular Bisectors of Triangles

Essential Question: How can you use perpendicular bisectors to find the point that is equidistant from all the vertices of a triangle?

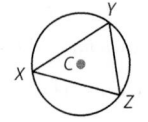

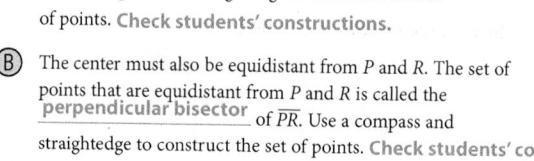 **Explore** **Constructing a Circumscribed Circle**

A circle that contains all the vertices of a polygon is **circumscribed** about the polygon. In the figure, circle C is circumscribed about $\triangle XYZ$, and circle C is called the **circumcircle** of $\triangle XYZ$. The center of the circumcircle is called the **circumcenter** of the triangle.

In the following activity, you will construct the circumcircle of $\triangle PQR$. Copy the triangle onto a separate piece of paper.

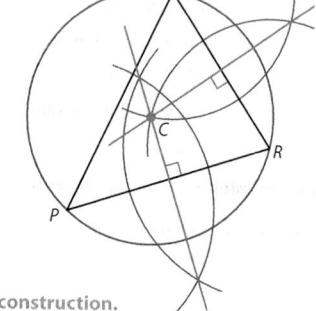

(A) The circumcircle will pass through P, Q, and R. So, the center of the circle must be equidistant from all three points. In particular, the center must be equidistant from Q and R.

The set of points that are equidistant from Q and R is called the ___perpendicular bisector___ of $\overline{QR}$.

Use a compass and straightedge to construct the set of points. **Check students' constructions.**

(B) The center must also be equidistant from P and R. The set of points that are equidistant from P and R is called the ___perpendicular bisector___ of $\overline{PR}$. Use a compass and straightedge to construct the set of points. **Check students' construction.**

(C) The center must lie at the intersection of the two sets of points you constructed. Label the point C. Then place the point of your compass at C and open it to distance CP. Draw the circumcircle. **Check students' drawings.**

Module 8   **359**   Lesson 1

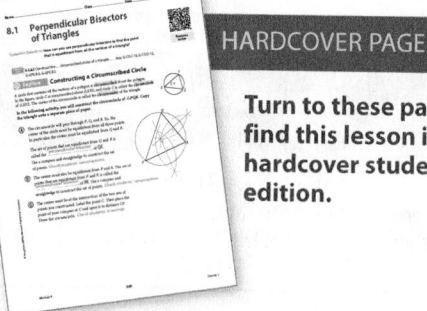

HARDCOVER PAGES 309–316

Turn to these pages to find this lesson in the hardcover student edition.

1. **Make a Prediction** Suppose you started by constructing the set of points equidistant from P and Q and then constructed the set of points equidistant from Q and R. Would you have found the same center? Check by doing this construction.
   Yes; because P, Q, and R are all on the circumcircle you constructed in the activity, C is the
   same distance from all three points, so it is on all three perpendicular bisectors. Check
   students' constructions.

2. Can you locate the circumcenter of a triangle without using a compass and straightedge? Explain.
   Yes; you can use paper folding to construct the perpendicular bisectors of the sides. Fold
   each side of the triangle over on itself so the endpoints meet. Their intersection is the
   circumcenter of the triangle.

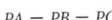 **Explain 1** **Proving the Concurrency of a Triangle's Perpendicular Bisectors**

Three or more lines are **concurrent** if they intersect at the same point. The point of intersection is called the **point of concurrency**. You saw in the Explore that the three perpendicular bisectors of a triangle are concurrent. Now you will prove that the point of concurrency is the circumcenter of the triangle. That is, the point of concurrency is equidistant from the vertices of the triangle.

Circumcenter Theorem

The perpendicular bisectors of the sides of a triangle intersect at a point that is equidistant from the vertices of the triangle.

$$PA = PB = PC$$

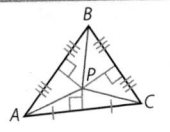

Example 1 Prove the Circumcenter Theorem.

Given: Lines ℓ, m, and n are the perpendicular bisectors of $\overline{AB}$, $\overline{BC}$, and $\overline{AC}$, respectively. P is the intersection of ℓ, m, and n.

Prove: $PA = PB = PC$

P is the intersection of ℓ, m, and n. Since P lies on the <u>perpendicular bisector</u> of $\overline{AB}$, $PA = PB$ by the <u>Perpendicular Bisector</u> Theorem. Similarly, P lies on the <u>perpendicular bisector</u> of $\overline{BC}$, so <u>PB</u> $= PC$. Therefore, $PA = $ <u>PB</u> $= $ <u>PC</u> by the <u>Transitive</u> Property of Equality.

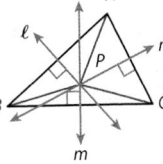

PROFESSIONAL DEVELOPMENT

 Math Background

By constructing the perpendicular bisectors of the sides of many different triangles, students can convince themselves that the following statement is likely to be true: The perpendicular bisectors of the sides of any triangle intersect in a point (are *concurrent*). The inductive approach described above may be convincing, but it does not constitute a proof. To prove the theorem, it is necessary to show that the point of intersection of two of the perpendicular bisectors lies on the third.

EXPLORE

Constructing a Circumscribed Circle

INTEGRATE TECHNOLOGY

Students have the option of doing the circumscribed circle activity either in the book or online.

QUESTIONING STRATEGIES

? What is true of the intersection of perpendicular bisectors of the sides of a triangle? The intersection is a point that is equidistant from the vertices of a triangle.

EXPLAIN 1

Proving the Concurrency of a Triangle's Perpendicular Bisectors

INTEGRATE MATHEMATICS PRACTICES
Focus on Math Connections

MP.1 Understanding the proof of the concurrency of a triangle's perpendicular bisectors depends on students understanding that all of the points on the perpendicular bisector of a segment are equidistant from the endpoints of the segment. This is the Perpendicular Bisector Theorem and its converse from Module 4. You may want to review these theorems with students.

QUESTIONING STRATEGIES

? What do you have to do to construct the circumcircle of a triangle? Find a point that is equidistant from the vertices of the triangle. This point is the center of the required circle, and its radius is equal to the distance from the point to any vertex.

? In the proof of the Circumcenter Theorem, why do you show that the point of concurrency lies on the perpendicular bisector of each side of the triangle? If the point of concurrency is on the perpendicular bisector of each side of the triangle, then it is equidistant from each vertex of the triangle. This makes the distances from each vertex possible radii of the same circle.

EXPLAIN 2

Using Properties of Perpendicular Bisectors

INTEGRATE MATHEMATICAL PRACTICES
Focus on Modeling

MP.4 Have students copy a larger version of the triangle in the example, and construct the circumcenter of the triangle by paper folding. Discuss the point of concurrency and the Circumcenter Theorem, and how the perpendicular bisectors each divide sides of a triangle at midpoints. Remind students of how they constructed perpendicular bisectors in Module 4.

Reflect

3. **Discussion** How might you determine whether the circumcenter of a triangle is always inside the triangle? Make a plan and then determine whether the circumcenter is always inside the triangle.
You could draw different triangles and construct their circumcenters using either a compass and straightedge or paper folding. The circumcenter of an acute triangle is inside the triangle. The circumcenter of an obtuse triangle is outside the triangle. The circumcenter of a right triangle is on the triangle.

⊘ Explain 2 **Using Properties of Perpendicular Bisectors**

You can use the Circumcenter Theorem to find segment lengths in a triangle.

Example 2 $\overline{KZ}$, $\overline{LZ}$, and $\overline{MZ}$ are the perpendicular bisectors of $\triangle GHJ$. Use the given information to find the length of each segment. Note that the figure is not drawn to scale.

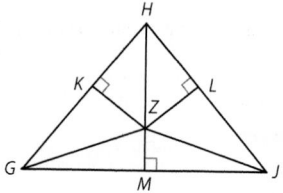

(A) Given: $ZM = 7$, $ZJ = 25$, $HK = 20$

Find: ZH and HG

Z is the circumcenter of $\triangle GHJ$, so $ZG = ZH = ZJ$.

$ZJ = 25$, so $ZH = 25$.

K is the midpoint of $\overline{GH}$, so $HG = 2 \cdot KH = 2 \cdot 20 = 40$.

(B) Given: $ZH = 85$, $MZ = 13$, $HG = 136$

Find: KG and ZJ

K is the $\underline{\text{midpoint}}$ of $\overline{HG}$, so $KG = \boxed{\frac{1}{2}} HG = \boxed{\frac{1}{2}} \cdot \boxed{136} = \boxed{68}$.

Z is the $\underline{\text{circumcenter}}$ of $\triangle GHJ$, so $ZG = \underline{ZH} = \underline{ZJ}$.

$ZH = \underline{85}$, so $ZJ = \underline{85}$.

COLLABORATIVE LEARNING

Whole Class Activity

Give students a triangular region in the plane and a triangle drawn on the coordinate plane. Have students construct the perpendicular bisectors of the triangle in the plane and identify the circumcenter of the triangle. Ask a volunteer to explain how it was identified. Then ask students to locate the circumcenter for the triangle drawn on the coordinate plane. They should give the equations of the perpendicular bisectors of the triangle's sides and the coordinates of their intersection point. Ask a volunteer to explain the process, then compare the two methods as a class.

4. In △*ABC*, ∠*ACB* is a right angle and *D* is the circumcenter of the triangle. If *CD* = 6.5, what is *AB*? Explain your reasoning.

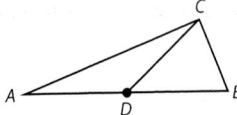

13; *D* is the circumcenter of the triangle, so *DA = DB = DC*.

Then *AB = AD + DB = CD + CD* = 2(6.5) = 13.

$\overline{KZ}$, $\overline{LZ}$, and $\overline{MZ}$ are the perpendicular bisectors of △*GHJ*. Copy the sketch and label the given information. Use that information to find the length of each segment. Note that the figure is not drawn to scale.

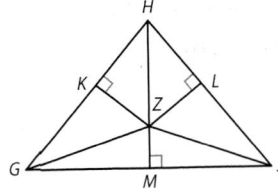

5. Given: *ZG* = 65, *HL* = 63, *ZL* = 16
Find: *HJ* and *ZJ*

Z is the circumcenter of △*GHJ*, so *ZG = ZH = ZJ*.

ZG = 65, so *ZJ* = 65.

L is the midpoint of $\overline{HJ}$, so *HJ* = 2 · *HL* = 2 · 63 = 126.

6. Given: *ZM* = 25, *ZH* = 65, *GJ* = 120
Find: *GM* and *ZG*

M is the midpoint of $\overline{GJ}$, so *GM* = $\frac{1}{2}$ *GJ* = $\frac{1}{2}$· 120 = 60.

Z is the circumcenter of △*GHJ*, so *ZG = ZH = ZJ*.

ZH = 65, so *ZG* = 65.

QUESTIONING STRATEGIES

? **How does a perpendicular bisector divide a triangle?** The perpendicular bisector of a triangle divides it at the midpoint of the side of the triangle.

? **What is true of the circumcenter of a triangle?** The point is equidistant from the three triangle vertices.

? **What is the advantage in exploring circumcenters with geometry software rather than by drawing triangles and perpendicular bisectors with a compass and straightedge?** The software makes it easy to change the size and shape of the triangle to see how the circumcenter changes.

DIFFERENTIATE INSTRUCTION

Multiple Representations

Have students find the circumcenter of a triangle by paper folding. Then compare this to how to find the circumcenter of a triangle in the coordinate plane, which may involve finding the intersection of the equations of lines. Finally, have students use geometry software to construct a triangle and the perpendicular bisectors of the sides. Have them drag a vertex of the triangle to change its shape and note that the perpendicular bisectors are still concurrent.

EXPLAIN 3

Finding a Circumcenter on a Coordinate Plane

INTEGRATE TECHNOLOGY

Some properties of a circumcenter on a coordinate plane that students can verify using a geometry program are that the circumcenter is the middle point of the circumscribed circle; the circumcenter is exactly the same distance from each vertex; the circumcenter may be located outside of the triangle or it may be located on the triangle. You might also ask students to use the geometry software to find the equations of the perpendicular bisectors of the sides, and the intersection point of the perpendicular bisectors.

QUESTIONING STRATEGIES

? How do you find the circumcenter of a triangle when given the coordinates of the three vertices? You graph the triangle, find the equations of the perpendicular bisectors of two sides of the triangle, then find the intersection point of the two equations.

⊘ Explain 3 **Finding a Circumcenter on a Coordinate Plane**

Given the vertices of a triangle, you can graph the triangle and use the graph to find the circumcenter of the triangle.

Example 3 Graph the triangle with the given vertices and find the circumcenter of the triangle.

(A) $R(-6, 0)$, $S(0, 4)$, $O(0, 0)$

Step 1: Graph the triangle.

Step 2: Find equations for two perpendicular bisectors.

Side $\overline{RO}$ is on the x-axis, so its perpendicular bisector is vertical: the line $x = -3$.

Side $\overline{SO}$ is on the y-axis, so its perpendicular bisector is horizontal: the line $y = 2$.

Step 3: Find the intersection of the perpendicular bisectors.

The lines $x = -3$ and $y = 2$ intersect at $(-3, 2)$.

$(-3, 2)$ is the circumcenter of $\triangle ROS$.

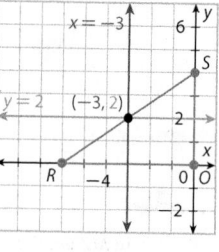

(B) $A(-1, 5)$, $B(5, 5)$, $C(5, -1)$

Step 1 Graph the triangle.

Step 2 Find equations for two perpendicular bisectors.

Side $\overline{AB}$ is <u>horizontal</u>, so its perpendicular bisector is vertical.

The perpendicular bisector of $\overline{AB}$ is the line <u>$x = 2$</u>.

Side $\overline{BC}$ is <u>vertical</u>, so the perpendicular bisector of $\overline{BC}$ is the horizontal line <u>$y = 2$</u>.

Step 3 Find the intersection of the perpendicular bisectors.

The lines <u>$x = 2$</u> and <u>$y = 2$</u> intersect at <u>$(2, 2)$</u>.

<u>$(2, 2)$</u> is the circumcenter of $\triangle ABC$.

LANGUAGE SUPPORT **EL**

Connect Vocabulary

To help students remember the meanings of *circumcenter* and *circumscribed*, remind them that the prefix *circum-* means *around*. Point out that *circum-* and *circle* begin with the same four letters: *circ*.

7. Draw Conclusions Could a vertex of a triangle also be its circumcenter?
If so, provide an example. If not, explain why not.

No; possible answer: if the vertex were the circumcenter, the distance from all of the

vertices to the circumcenter would have to be 0. The vertices cannot all be the same point.

Your Turn

Graph the triangle with the given vertices and find the circumcenter of the triangle.

8. $Q(-4, 0), R(0, 0), S(0, 6)$

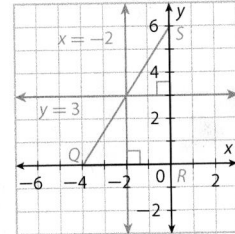

The circumcenter of $\triangle QRS$ is $(-2, 3)$

9. $K(1, 1), L(1, 7), M(6, 1)$

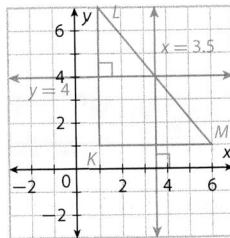

The circumcenter of $\triangle KLM$ is $(3.5, 4)$.
Check students' graphs.

Elaborate

10. A company that makes and sells bicycles has its largest stores in three cities. The company wants to build a new factory that is equidistant from each of the stores. Given a map, how could you identify the location for the new factory?

Draw the segments connecting the three cities and construct the perpendicular bisectors

of two of the segments. The intersection of the perpendicular bisectors is equidistant from

the three cities.

11. A sculptor builds a mobile in which a triangle rotates around its circumcenter. Each vertex traces the shape of a circle as it rotates. What circle does it trace? Explain.

The circumcircle of the triangle. Each vertex is on the circumcircle. As the mobile rotates,

each vertex moves to other points on the circumcircle.

AVOID COMMON ERRORS

Students may be confused when asked to calculate the radius of the circumcircle. The radius is the same as the distance from the circumcenter to any vertex. In the coordinate plane, they can use the distance formula to find the radius.

ELABORATE

QUESTIONING STRATEGIES

? Why is the point where the perpendicular bisectors intersect the middle point of the circumscribed circle? The point is the center of the circumscribed circle, so it is the middle point of the circumscribed circle.

? Why isn't the circumcenter always inside the perimeter of the triangle? The lines representing the perpendicular bisectors of the triangle give the circumcenter, and these lines may intersect outside or on the triangle.

? How many perpendicular bisectors do you need to construct to find the circumcenter of a triangle? Explain. Two; since all three perpendicular bisectors intersect in the same point, you need only two lines to determine the point.

SUMMARIZE THE LESSON

? What feature can you use to describe the circumcenter of a triangle? **Sample answer:** The circumcenter is the point that is equidistant from each of the vertices of the triangle.

EVALUATE

ASSIGNMENT GUIDE

Concepts and Skills	Practice
Explore Constructing a Circumscribed Circle	Exercises 1–4
Example 1 Proving the Concurrency of a Triangle's Perpendicular Bisectors	Exercises 9–10
Example 2 Using Properties of Perpendicular Bisectors	Exercises 5–8
Example 3 Finding a Circumcenter on a Coordinate Plane	Exercises 11–13

12. **What If?** Suppose you are given the vertices of a triangle PQR. You plot the points in a coordinate plane and notice that $\overline{PQ}$ is horizontal but neither of the other sides is vertical. How can you identify the circumcenter of the triangle? Justify your reasoning.

Choose one of the other sides. Use the opposite of the reciprocal of its slope and the coordinates of its midpoint to write an equation of its perpendicular bisector in point-slope form. The perpendicular bisector of a segment passes through its midpoint, and its slope is the opposite of the reciprocal of the slope of the segment.

13. **Essential Question Check-In** How is the point that is equidistant from the three vertices of a triangle related to the circumcircle of the triangle?

The point is the center of the circumcircle, or the circumcenter of the triangle.

☆ **Evalute: Homework and Practice**

- Online Homework
- Hints and Help
- Extra Practice

Construct the circumcircle of each triangle. Label the circumcenter P.

1.

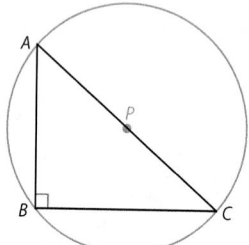

Check students' constructions.

2.

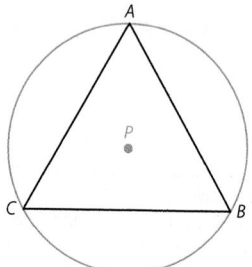

Check students' constructions.

3.

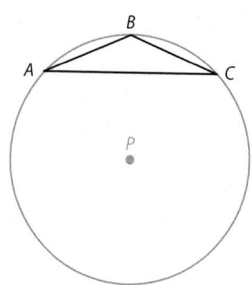

Check students' constructions.

4.

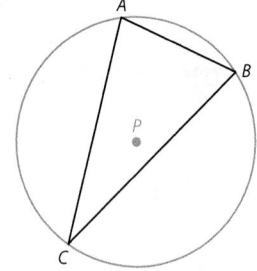

Check students' constructions.

© Houghton Mifflin Harcourt Publishing Company

Exercise	Depth of Knowledge (D.O.K.)	COMMON CORE Mathematical Practices
1–4	**1** Recall of information	**MP.4** Modeling
5–13	**2** Skills/Concepts	**MP.2** Reasoning
14	**3** Strategic Thinking H.O.T.	**MP.3** Logic
15	**3** Strategic Thinking H.O.T.	**MP.3** Logic
16	**3** Strategic Thinking H.O.T.	**MP.6** Precision

Complete the proof of the Circumcenter Theorem.

Use the diagram for Exercise 5–8. $\overline{ZD}$, $\overline{ZE}$, and $\overline{ZF}$ are the perpendicular bisectors of $\triangle ABC$. Use the given information to find the length of each segment. Note that the figure is not drawn to scale.

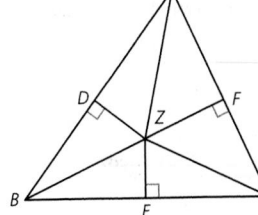

5. Given: $DZ = 40$, $ZA = 85$, $FC = 77$

Find: ZC and AC

Z is the circumcenter of $\triangle ABC$, so $ZA = ZB = ZC$.

$ZA = 85$, so $ZC = 85$.

F is the midpoint of $\overline{AC}$, so $AC = 2 \cdot FC = 2 \cdot 77 = 154$.

6. Given: $FZ = 36$, $ZA = 85$, $AB = 150$

Find: AD and ZB

D is the midpoint of $\overline{AB}$, so $AD = \frac{1}{2}AB = \frac{1}{2} \cdot 150 = 75$.

Z is the circumcenter of $\triangle ABC$, so $ZA = ZB = ZC$.

$ZA = 85$, so $ZB = 85$.

7. Given: $AZ = 85$, $ZE = 51$

Find: BC

(*Hint*: Use the Pythagorean Theorem.)

Z is the circumcenter of $\triangle ABC$, so $ZA = ZB = ZC$.

$AZ = 85$, so $ZC = 85$.

By the Pythagorean Theorem, $EC^2 = ZC^2 - ZE^2 = 85^2 - 51^2 = 4624$.

Then $EC = \sqrt{4624} = 68$. So, $BC = 2 \cdot 68 = 136$.

8. Analyze Relationships How can you write an algebraic expression for the radius of the circumcircle of $\triangle ABC$ in Exercises 5–7? Explain.

ZA, ZB, or ZC; the radius of the circumcircle is the distance from Z to a vertex of the triangle.

© Houghton Mifflin Harcourt Publishing Company

INTEGRATE MATHEMATICAL PRACTICES

Focus on Reasoning

MP.2 Encourage students to try different types of triangles when testing the validity of statements in the exercises.

When learning to find the circumcenter, students may use only an equilateral triangle. Encourage them to use other types of triangles to discover the various positions of the points of concurrency.

Complete the proof of the Circumcenter Theorem.

9. **Given:** Lines ℓ, m, and n are the perpendicular bisectors of $\overline{AB}$, $\overline{BC}$, and $\overline{AC}$, respectively. P is the intersection of ℓ, m, and n.

   Prove: $PA = PB = PC$

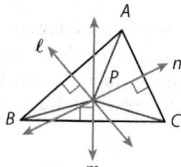

Statements	Reasons
1. Lines ℓ, m, and n are the perpendicular bisectors of $\overline{AB}$, $\overline{BC}$, and $\overline{AC}$.	1. **Given**
2. P is the intersection of ℓ, m, and n.	2. **Given**
3. $PA = \underline{PB}$	3. P lies on the perpendicular bisector of $\overline{AB}$.
4. $\underline{PB} = PC$	4. P lies on the perpendicular bisector of $\overline{BC}$.
5. $PA = \underline{PB} = \underline{PC}$	5. **Transitive Property of Equality**

10. $\overline{PK}$, $\overline{PL}$, and $\overline{PM}$ are the perpendicular bisectors of sides $\overline{AB}$, $\overline{BC}$, and $\overline{AC}$. Tell whether the given statement is justified by the figure. Select the correct answer for each lettered part.

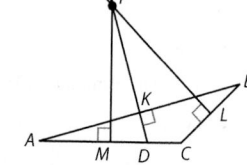

   a. $AK = KB$ ● Justified   ○ Not Justified

   b. $PA = PB$ ● Justified   ○ Not Justified

   c. $PM = PL$ ○ Justified   ● Not Justified

   d. $BL = \frac{1}{2}BC$ ● Justified   ○ Not Justified

   e. $PK = KD$ ○ Justified   ● Not Justified

   a. Justified; $\overline{PK}$ bisects $\overline{AB}$, so $AK = KB$

   b. Justified; P is the circumcenter of the triangle, so $PA = PB$.

   c. Not justified

   d. Justified; $\overline{PL}$ bisects $\overline{BC}$,

   e. Not justified

Graph the triangle with the given vertices and find the circumcenter of the triangle.

11. $D(-5, 0), E(0, 0), F(0, 7)$

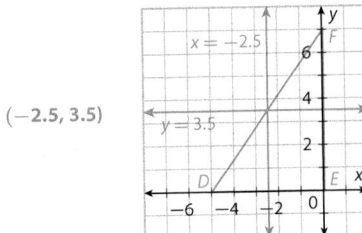

$(-2.5, 3.5)$

12. $Q(3, 4), R(7, 4), S(3, -2)$

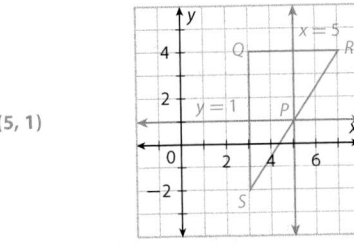

$(5, 1)$

13. Represent Real-World Problems For the next Fourth of July, the towns of Ashton, Bradford, and Clearview will launch a fireworks display from a boat in the lake. Draw a sketch to show where the boat should be positioned so that it is the same distance from all three towns. Justify your sketch.

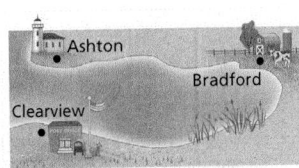

Let the three towns be vertices of a triangle. By the Circumcenter Theorem, the circumcenter of the triangle is equidistant from the vertices. Trace the outline of the lake. Draw the triangle formed by the towns. To find the circumcenter, find the perpendicular bisectors of each side. The position of the boat is the circumcenter, F.

H.O.T. Focus on Higher Order Thinking

14. Analyze Relationships Explain how can you draw a triangle JKL whose circumcircle has a radius of 8 centimeters.

Use a compass to draw circle C with a radius of 8 centimeters. Choose any three distinct points J, K, and L on the circle and draw segments to form a triangle. C is the circumcircle of △JKL, and its radius is 8 centimeters.

MP.1 When students are given the coordinates of the vertices of a triangle, encourage them to graph the triangle first and then find the midpoints of the sides. Then have them find the equation of each perpendicular bisector the opposite reciprocal of the slope of a side of the triangle and the midpoint of that side. Remind them that they need to find the equations of only two perpendicular bisectors of the triangle. They should find the point where the perpendicular bisectors intersect using a system of equations or other algebraic method.

PEER-TO-PEER DISCUSSION

Ask students to discuss with a partner how to locate the circumcenter of a triangle drawn in the coordinate plane. One student can draw a triangle in the coordinate plane and challenge the partner to find the coordinates of the circumcenter. Then switch roles. Have them use the Circumcenter Theorem to verify that the point where the perpendicular bisectors intersect is the circumcenter of the triangle. Have them draw additional examples of triangles to justify their reasoning.

JOURNAL

Have students describe how they remember that the circumcenter is the intersection of the perpendicular bisectors of the sides of the triangle.

15. **Persevere in Problem Solving** $\overline{ZD}$, $\overline{ZE}$ and $\overline{ZF}$ are the perpendicular bisectors of $\triangle ABC$, which is not drawn to scale.

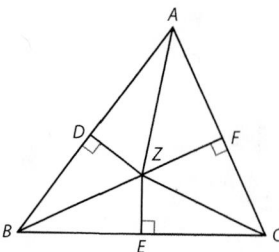

a. Suppose that $ZB = 145$, $ZD = 100$, and $ZF = 17$. How can you find AB and AC?

To find AB, note that $\overline{DB}$ is a leg of right triangle $\triangle ZBD$ and $\overline{ZB}$ is the hypotenuse. Use the Pythagorean Theorem to find DB and multiply by 2 because D is the midpoint of $\overline{AB}$. To find AC, use the same method, noting first that $ZC = ZB$ because C is the circumcenter of $\triangle ABC$. Also, $\overline{ZF}$ is a leg of right triangle $\triangle ZCF$ and $\overline{ZC}$ is the hypotenuse.

b. Find AB and AC.

$AB = 2BD$, $BD^2 = ZB^2 - ZD^2 = 11{,}025$; $BD = \sqrt{11{,}025} = 105$, so $AB = 210$.

$AC = 2FC$, $FC^2 = ZC^2 - ZF^2 = 20{,}736$; $FC = \sqrt{20{,}736} = 144$, so $AC = 288$.

c. Can you find BC? If so, explain how and find BC. If not, explain why not.

No; the only information given about isosceles $\triangle ZBC$ is the length of two sides, which is insufficient for finding BC.

16. **Multiple Representations** Given the vertices $A(-2, -2)$, $B(4, 0)$, and $C(4, 4)$ of a triangle, the graph shows how you can use a graph and construction to locate the circumcenter P of the triangle. You can draw the perpendicular bisector of $\overline{CB}$ and construct the perpendicular bisector of $\overline{AB}$. Consider how you could identify P algebraically.

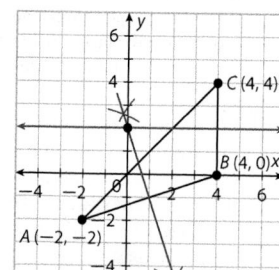

a. The perpendicular bisector of $\overline{AB}$ passes through its midpoint. Use the Midpoint Formula to find the midpoint of $\overline{AB}$.

$$M = \left(\frac{x_1 + x_2}{2}, \frac{y_1 + y_2}{2} \right) = \left(\frac{-2 + 4}{2}, \frac{-2 + 0}{2} \right) = (1, -1)$$

b. What is the slope m of the perpendicular bisector of $\overline{AB}$? Explain how you found it.

$m = -3$; m is the opposite of the reciprocal of the slope of $\overline{AB}$, $\dfrac{y_2 - y_1}{x_2 - x_1} = \dfrac{0 - (-2)}{4 - (-2)} = \dfrac{1}{3}$.

c. Write an equation of the perpendicular bisector of $\overline{AB}$ and explain how you can use it find P.

Use the point-slope form of a linear equation: $y - y_1 = m(x - x_1)$; $y - (-1) = -3(x - 1)$;

$y + 1 = -3x + 3$; $y = -3x + 2$. Find the intersection of that line and the perpendicular bisector of $\overline{CB}$, $y = 2$. The lines intersect at $(0, 2)$, the circumcenter P of the triangle.

Lesson Performance Task

A landscape architect wants to plant a circle of flowers around a triangular garden. She has sketched the triangle on a coordinate grid with vertices at $A(0, 0)$, $B(8, 12)$, and $C(18, 0)$.

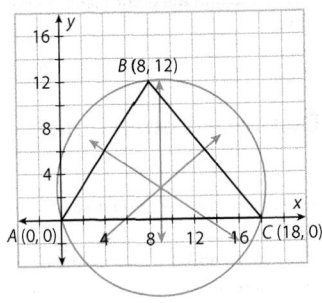

Explain how the architect can find the center of the circle that will circumscribe triangle ABC. Then find the radius of the circumscribed circle.

Answers will vary. Students can sketch the perpendicular bisectors to find the circumcenter of the triangle and estimate its coordinates to be approximately $(9, 2.5)$.

The radius of the circle can be found using the Pythagorean Theorem with the triangle formed by $A(0, 0)$, the midpoint of $\overline{AC}$ $(9, 0)$, and the circumcenter $(9, 2.5)$.

$r^2 = 9^2 + (2.5)^2$

$r^2 = 81 + 6.25$

$r = \sqrt{87.25} \approx 9.3$

The radius of the circle is approximately 9.3 feet.

(Note: the actual y-coordinate of the circumcenter is $\frac{8}{3} = 2.6667$. This will change the final result to approximately 9.4 feet.)

EXTENSION ACTIVITY

Review dilations. Have students chose a scale factor, and then use it to dilate the triangle in the Performance Task on the same coordinate grid. Ask students to find the circumcenter of the new triangle.

- What do you notice about the circumcenter of the new triangle?
  Sample answer: It is the same point as the circumcenter of the original.

- Make a conjecture as to why that might be the case.
  Sample answer: Dilating a figure changes its size but not its shape. The relative location of a triangle's circumcenter must depend on its shape and not its size.

MP.2 The landscape architect in the Lesson Performance Task could have sketched the triangle anywhere on the coordinate plane. What advantage did she gain by drawing the triangle with one side on the x-axis and one vertex at the origin? Sample answer: Doing so gave her a midpoint of one side of the triangle with one coordinate of zero (9, 0) and a vertex with two coordinates of zeros (0, 0). The zeros greatly simplify the calculation of the length of the radius when it comes time to apply the Pythagorean Theorem.

INTEGRATE MATHEMATICAL PRACTICES

Focus on Critical Thinking

MP.3 Explain how the landscape architect can find the area of the circle of flowers that lies outside the triangular garden. She can subtract the area of the triangle from the area of the circle.

Scoring Rubric

2 points: Student correctly solves the problem and explains his/her reasoning.

1 point: Student shows good understanding of the problem but does not fully solve or explain his/her reasoning.

0 points: Student does not demonstrate understanding of the problem.

Perpendicular Bisectors of Triangles   **370**

Angle Bisectors of Triangles

Common Core Math Standards

The student is expected to:

 G-C.A.3

Construct the inscribed ... circles of a triangle .... Also G-CO.C.9, G-CO.C.10, G-CO.D.12

Mathematical Practices

 MP.3 Logic

Language Objective

Students work in pairs to complete a compare/contrast chart for circumscribed and inscribed circles.

ENGAGE

Essential Question: How can you use angle bisectors to find the point that is equidistant from all the sides of a triangle?

Bisect any two of the angles of a triangle; the point of intersection of the angle bisectors is equidistant from the sides of the triangle.

PREVIEW: LESSON PERFORMANCE TASK

View the Engage section online. Discuss the photo, asking students to explain how central pivot irrigation works. Then preview the Lesson Performance Task.

Name_____ Class_____ Date_____

8.2 Angle Bisectors of Triangles

Essential Question: How can you use angle bisectors to find the point that is equidistant from all the sides of a triangle?

Resource Locker

🧭 Explore   Investigating Distance from a Point to a Line

Use a ruler, a protractor, and a piece of tracing paper to investigate points on the bisector of an angle.

Ⓐ Use the ruler to draw a large angle on tracing paper. Label it $\angle ABC$. Fold the paper so that $\overrightarrow{BC}$ coincides with $\overrightarrow{BA}$. Open the paper. The crease is the bisector of $\angle ABC$. Plot a point P on the bisector.

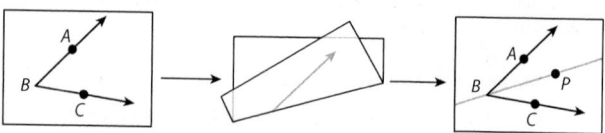

Ⓑ Use the ruler to draw several different segments from point P to $\overrightarrow{BA}$. Measure the lengths of the segments. Then measure the angle each segment makes with $\overrightarrow{BA}$. What do you notice about the shortest segment you can draw from point P to $\overrightarrow{BA}$?

The segment is most nearly perpendicular to $\overrightarrow{BA}$.

Ⓒ Draw the shortest segment you can from point P to $\overrightarrow{BC}$. Measure its length. How does its length compare with the length of the shortest segment you drew from point P to $\overrightarrow{BA}$?

The lengths should be approximately equal.

Reflect

1. Suppose you choose a point Q on the bisector of $\angle XYZ$ and you draw the perpendicular segment from Q to $\overrightarrow{YX}$ and the perpendicular segment from Q to $\overrightarrow{YZ}$. What do you think will be true about these segments?
They will be the same length.

2. **Discussion** What do you think is the best way to measure the distance from a point to a line? Why?
Measure the distance from the point to the line along the perpendicular segment from the point to the line. Among all the segments from the point to the line, this segment is shortest.

© Houghton Mifflin Harcourt Publishing Company

Module 8   371   Lesson 2

HARDCOVER PAGES 317–326

Turn to these pages to find this lesson in the hardcover student edition.

✪ Explain 1 Applying the Angle Bisector Theorem and Its Converse

The **distance from a point to a line** is the length of the perpendicular segment from the point to the line. You will prove the following theorems about angle bisectors and the sides of the angle they bisect in Exercises 16 and 17.

Angle Bisector Theorem

If a point is on the bisector an of angle, then it is equidistant from the sides of the angle.

$\angle APC \cong \angle BPC$, so $AC = BC$.

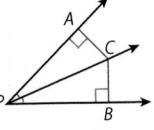

Converse of the Angle Bisector Theorem

If a point in the interior of an angle is equidistant from the sides of the angle, then it is on the bisector of the angle.

$AC = BC$, so $\angle APC \cong \angle BPC$

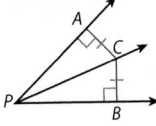

Example 1 Find each measure.

Ⓐ *LM*

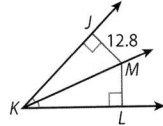

$\overrightarrow{KM}$ is the bisector of $\angle JKL$, so $LM = JM = 12.8$.

Ⓑ $m\angle ABD$, given that $m\angle ABC = 112°$

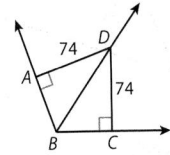

Since $AD = DC$, $\overline{AD} \perp \overrightarrow{BA}$, and $\overline{DC} \perp \overrightarrow{BC}$, you know that $\overrightarrow{BD}$ bisects $\angle ABC$ by the __Converse of the Angle Bisector__ Theorem.

So, $m\angle ABD = \frac{1}{2}m\angle$ __ABC__ = $\boxed{56}$ °.

Reflect

3. In the Converse of the Angle Bisector Theorem, why is it important to say that the point must be in the *interior* of the angle?

    If a point lies in the exterior of the angle, it is not necessarily possible to draw

    perpendicular segments to each ray. The distance to each ray is not necessarily defined.

© Houghton Mifflin Harcourt Publishing Company

PROFESSIONAL DEVELOPMENT

🔷 COMMON CORE Learning Progressions

In this lesson, students add to their prior knowledge of constructing geometrical figures by investigating the angle bisectors of a triangle. The opening activity leads students to make a conjecture that the distance from a point to a line is the perpendicular distance. This fact helps students understand that the perpendicular distances from the intersection point of the angle bisectors of a triangle serve as radii of the incircle of a triangle. By constructing the angle bisectors of the angles of many different triangles, students can convince themselves that the angle bisectors of any triangle intersect in a point (are concurrent). This point is called the *incenter* of the triangle.

EXPLORE

Investigating Distance from a Point to a Line

INTEGRATE TECHNOLOGY

Students have the option of doing the distance from a point to a line activity either in the book or online.

QUESTIONING STRATEGIES

❓ You can draw many segments from a point to a line. Which segment is the distance from a point to the line? the segment that is perpendicular to the line

---

EXPLAIN 1

Applying the Angle Bisector Theorem and Its Converse

INTEGRATE MATHEMATICAL PRACTICES
Focus on Math Connections

MP.1 The Converse of the Angle Bisector Theorem does not apply if the point is in the exterior of the angle. An angle bisector must be in the interior of the angle it bisects. Therefore, a point equidistant from the sides must also be in the angle's interior in order to be on the bisector.

QUESTIONING STRATEGIES

❓ How do you know which theorem to use in the example? If a point is given on the angle bisector, use the Angle Bisector Theorem to state that the point is equidistant from the sides of the angle. If it is given that the point is equidistant from the sides of the angle, use the Converse of the Angle Bisector Theorem to state that the point must be on the angle bisector.

Angle Bisectors of Triangles   **372**

? How many angle bisectors does a triangle have? 3

? What is true about the points on the bisector of an angle? The points are all equidistant from the sides of the angle.

EXPLAIN 2

Constructing an Inscribed Circle

INTEGRATE MATHEMATICAL PRACTICES
Focus on Modeling

MP.4 Have students copy a larger version of the triangle in the example, and construct the incenter of the triangle by paper folding. To construct an angle bisector, have them fold one side of an angle of the triangle onto the other side of the angle. Discuss the point of concurrency and Angle Bisector Theorem. Remind students of the properties of angle bisectors.

INTEGRATE MATHEMATICAL PRACTICES
Focus on Technology

MP.5 Have students use geometry software to draw a triangle and then construct the bisector of each angle. Have them mark the point of concurrency of the bisectors. Then have them measure the distances from the point to each side of the triangle and confirm that they are equal. Have them finish by constructing a circle with the point of concurrency as center and the distance to the side of the triangle as radius.

QUESTIONING STRATEGIES

? How do you use the angle bisectors to find the incenter? The incenter is the point of concurrency of the angle bisectors.

? What is true of the incenter of a triangle? The point is equidistant from the sides of the triangle.

373 Lesson 8.2

Your Turn

Find each measure.

4. QS

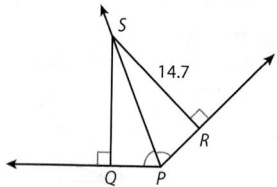

$\overrightarrow{PS}$ is the bisector of ∠QPR. By the Angle Bisector Theorem, QS = RS = 14.7.

5. m∠LJM, given that m∠KJM = 29°

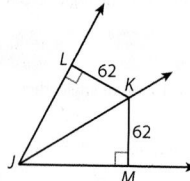

KL = KM, $\overline{KL} \perp \overrightarrow{JL}$, and $\overline{KM} \perp \overrightarrow{JM}$, so $\overrightarrow{JK}$ bisects ∠LJM by the Converse of the Angle Bisector Theorem. Then m∠LJM = 2m∠KJM = 58°.

⊘ Explain 2 **Constructing an Inscribed Circle**

A circle is **inscribed** in a polygon if each side of the polygon is tangent to the circle. In the figure, circle C is inscribed in quadrilateral WXYZ and this circle is called the **incircle (inscribed circle)** of the quadrilateral.

In order to construct the incircle of a triangle, you need to find the center of the circle. This point is called the **incenter** of the triangle.

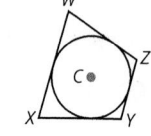

Example 2 Use a compass and straightedge to construct the inscribed circle of △PQR.

Step 1 The center of the inscribed circle must be equidistant from $\overline{PQ}$ and $\overline{PR}$. What is the set of points equidistant from $\overline{PQ}$ and $\overline{PR}$? the bisector of ∠P
Construct this set of points.

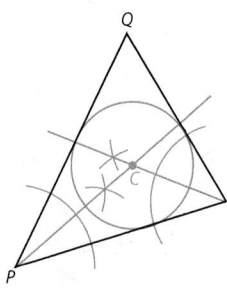

Step 2 The center must also be equidistant from $\overline{PR}$ and $\overline{QR}$. What is the set of points equidistant from $\overline{PR}$ and $\overline{QR}$? the bisector of ∠R Construct this set of points.

Step 3 The center must lie at the intersection of the two sets of points you constructed. Label this point C.

Step 4 Place the point of your compass at C and open the compass until the pencil just touches a side of △PQR. Then draw the inscribed circle.

Reflect

6. Suppose you started by constructing the set of points equidistant from $\overline{PR}$ and $\overline{QR}$, and then constructed the set of points equidistant from $\overline{QR}$ and $\overline{QP}$. Would you have found the same center point? Check by doing this construction.
Yes, all three angle bisectors intersect at the same point.

Module 8   **373**   Lesson 2

© Houghton Mifflin Harcourt Publishing Company

COLLABORATIVE LEARNING

Whole Class Activity

Give groups of students different triangular regions in the plane. Have each group construct the angle bisectors of their triangle and identify the incenter of the triangle. Ask a volunteer from each group to display their triangle and explain to the class how they found the incenter.

As you have seen, the angle bisectors of a triangle are concurrent. The point of concurrency is the incenter of the triangle.

Incenter Theorem

The angle bisectors of a triangle intersect at a point that is equidistant from the sides of the triangle.

$PX = PY = PZ$

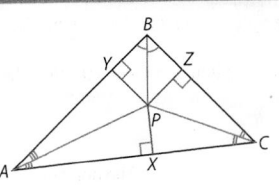

Example 3 $\overline{JV}$ and $\overline{KV}$ are angle bisectors of $\triangle JKL$. Find each measure.

Ⓐ the distance from V to $\overline{KL}$

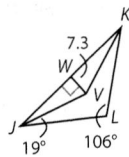

V is the incenter of $\triangle JKL$. By the Incenter Theorem, V is equidistant from the sides of $\triangle JKL$. The distance from V to $\overline{JK}$ is 7.3. So the distance from V to $\overline{KL}$ is also 7.3.

Ⓑ m∠VKL

$\overline{JV}$ is the bisector of ∠ $\boxed{KJL}$. $m\angle KJL = 2\left(\boxed{19°}\right) = \boxed{38°}$

Triangle Sum Theorem $\boxed{38°} + \boxed{106°} + m\angle JKL = 180°$

Subtract $\boxed{144°}$ from each side. $m\angle JKL = \boxed{36°}$

$\overline{KV}$ is the bisector of ∠JKL. $m\angle VKL = \frac{1}{2}\left(\boxed{36°}\right) = \boxed{18°}$

Reflect

7. In Part A, is there another distance you can determine? Explain.
   Yes the incenter is equidistant from all three sides, so the distance from V to $\overline{JL}$ is 7.3.

Your Turn

$\overline{QX}$ and $\overline{RX}$ are angle bisectors of $\triangle PQR$. Find each measure.

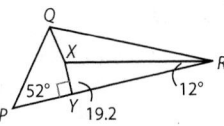

8. the distance from X to $\overline{PQ}$
   X is the incenter of $\triangle PQR$. By the Incenter Theorem, X is equidistant from the sides of $\triangle PQR$. So the distance $= XY = 19.2$.

9. m∠PQX
   $\overline{RX}$ is the bisector of ∠QRP, so m∠QRP = 2m∠XRP = 24°.
   By the Triangle Sum Theorem, 52° + 24° + m∠PQR = 180°, and m∠PQR = 104°.
   $\overline{QX}$ is the bisector of ∠PQR, so m∠PQX = $\frac{1}{2}$ m∠PQR = 52°.

© Houghton Mifflin Harcourt Publishing Company

DIFFERENTIATE INSTRUCTION

Multiple Representations

Have students use geometry software to construct a triangle and its angle bisectors. Have students drag a vertex to verify that the angle bisectors are still concurrent. Finally, have students construct the inscribed circle and verify that the incenter is the same distance from each side of the triangle.

EXPLAIN 3

Using Properties of Angle Bisectors

INTEGRATE TECHNOLOGY

Some properties of the incenter on a coordinate plane that students can verify using a geometry program are: the incenter is the middle point of the inscribed circle; the incenter is exactly the same distance from each side of the triangle; the incenter is always located in the interior of the triangle. You can also ask students to use geometry software to find the angle bisectors of the sides, and the intersection point of the angle bisectors.

QUESTIONING STRATEGIES

? How do you use the angle bisectors of a triangle to find the indicated measures in a triangle? You find the incenter from the intersection of the angle bisectors, then use the fact that the incenter is equidistant from the sides of the triangle to solve for various measures in the triangle.

AVOID COMMON ERRORS

Students may be confused when asked to calculate the radius of the incircle. The radius is the same as the distance from the incenter to any side. In the coordinate plane, they can use the distance formula to find the radius.

ELABORATE

QUESTIONING STRATEGIES

? How does the incenter of a triangle compare with the circumcenter of the circumscribed circle of the triangle? The incenter is the center of the inscribed circle, while the circumcenter is the center of the circumscribed circle.

? When are the incenter and the circumcenter of a triangle concurrent? when the triangle is equilateral

? How many angle bisectors do you need to construct to find the incenter of a triangle? Explain. Two; since all three angle bisectors intersect in the same point, you need only two lines to determine the point.

SUMMARIZE THE LESSON

? How do you construct the incenter of a triangle? Sample answer: Construct the angle bisectors of the circle and find their intersection point.

Elaborate

10. P and Q are the circumcenter and incenter of $\triangle RST$, but not necessarily in that order. Which point is the circumcenter? Which point is the incenter? Explain how you can tell without constructing any bisectors.

Q is the circumcenter and P is the incenter. The incenter is always inside the triangle, therefore P must be the incenter.

11. Complete the table by filling in the blanks to make each statement true.

	Circumcenter	Incenter
Definition	The point of concurrency of the <u>perpendicular bisectors</u>	The point of concurrency of the <u>angle bisectors</u>
Distance	Equidistant from the <u>vertices of the triangle</u>	Equidistant from the <u>sides of the triangle</u>
Location (Inside, Outside, On)	Can be <u>inside, outside, or on</u> the triangle	Always <u>inside</u> the triangle

12. Essential Question Check-In How do you know that the intersection of the bisectors of the angles of a triangle is equidistant from the sides of the triangle?

The points on the bisector of an angle are equidistant from the sides of the angle. So the intersection of the three angle bisectors is equidistant from the three sides of the triangle.

⭐ Evaluate: Homework and Practice

- Online Homework
- Hints and Help
- Extra Practice

1. Use a compass and straightedge to investigate points on the bisector of an angle. On a separate piece of paper, draw a large angle A.

  a. Construct the bisector of $\angle A$.

  b. Choose a point on the angle bisector you constructed. Label it P. Construct a perpendicular through P to each side of $\angle A$.

  c. Explain how to use a compass to show that P is equidistant from the sides of $\angle A$.
    Use the compass to measure both perpendicular segments from P to the sides of $\angle A$.

Find each measure.

2. VP

$\overrightarrow{SP}$ is the bisector of $\angle VSW$. By the Angle Bisector Theorem, $VP =$ $WP = 4.9$.

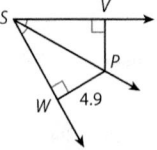

3. $m\angle LKM$, given that $m\angle JKL = 63°$

$JM = LM$, $\overline{LM} \perp \overrightarrow{KL}$, and $\overline{JM} \perp \overrightarrow{KJ}$, so $\overrightarrow{KM}$ bisects $\angle JKL$ (Converse of the Angle Bisector Theorem). Then $m\angle LKM = 0.5 m\angle JKL = 31.5°$.

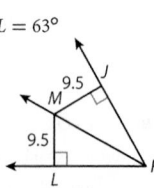

LANGUAGE SUPPORT **EL**

Connect Vocabulary

To help students remember the meanings of the words *incenter, incircle,* and *inscribed,* remind them that the prefix *in-* means *inside or within.* Have students make a poster showing examples and diagrams of the use of *incenter, inscribed,* and *incircle.*

4. AD

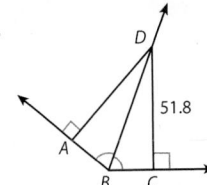

$\overrightarrow{BD}$ is the bisector of ∠ABC. By the Angle Bisector Theorem, AD = CD = 51.8.

5. m∠HFJ, given that m∠GFJ = 45°

HG = JG, $\overline{HG} \perp \overline{FH}$, and $\overline{JG} \perp \overline{FJ}$, $\overrightarrow{FG}$ bisects ∠HFJ (Converse of the Angle Bisector Theorem). Then m∠HFJ = 2m∠GFJ = 90°.

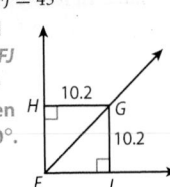

Construct an inscribed circle for each triangle.

6.

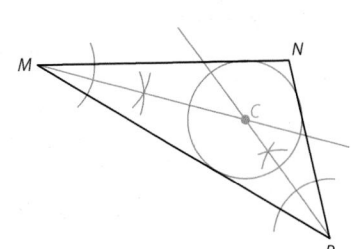

7.

$\overline{CF}$ and $\overline{EF}$ are angle bisectors of △CDE. Find each measure.

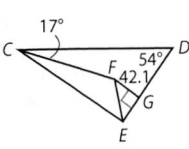

8. the distance from F to $\overline{CD}$

F is the incenter of △CDE. By the Incenter Theorem, F is equidistant from the sides of △CDE. So the distance = FG = 42.1.

9. m∠FED

$\overline{CF}$ bisects ∠DCE, so m∠DCE = 2m∠DCF = 34°. By the Triangle Sum Theorem, 34° + 54° + m∠DEC = 180°, and m∠DEC = 92°.

So, m∠FED = 0.5m∠DEC = 46°.

$\overline{TJ}$ and $\overline{SJ}$ are angle bisectors of △RST. Find each measure.

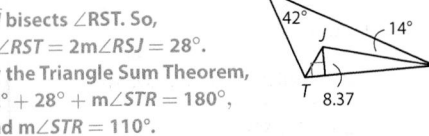

10. the distance from J to $\overline{RS}$

J is the incenter of △RST. By the Incenter Theorem, J is equidistant from the sides of △RST. So the distance = 8.37.

11. m∠RTJ

$\overline{SJ}$ bisects ∠RST. So, m∠RST = 2m∠RSJ = 28°. By the Triangle Sum Theorem, 42° + 28° + m∠STR = 180°, and m∠STR = 110°.

So, m∠RTJ = 0.5m∠STR = 55°.

EVALUATE

Personal Math Trainer

ASSIGNMENT GUIDE

Concepts and Skills	Practice
Explore Investigating Distance from a Point to a Line	Exercise 1
Example 1 Applying the Angle Bisector Theorem and Its Converse	Exercises 2–5
Example 2 Constructing an Inscribed Circle	Exercises 6–7
Example 3 Using Properties of Angle Bisectors	Exercises 8–11

INTEGRATE MATHEMATICAL PRACTICES

Focus on Modeling

MP.4 Some students may benefit from a hands-on approach to finding the incenter. Have students copy a larger version of the triangle in an exercise onto a sheet of paper and then cut it out. Students can then fold the angles of the triangle along the sides (a reflection) to get the angle bisectors. The three creases represent the angle bisectors of the triangle, and students should find that the creases intersect at a common point.

Exercise	Depth of Knowledge (D.O.K.)	COMMON CORE Mathematical Practices	
1	**2** Skills/Concepts	**MP.5** Using Tools	
2–5	**1** Recall	**MP.2** Reasoning	
6–7	**1** Recall	**MP.5** Using Tools	
8–11	**1** Recall	**MP.2** Reasoning	
12–21	**1** Recall	**MP.5** Using Tools	
22	**3** Strategic Thinking	H.O.T.	**MP.3** Logic

Angle Bisectors of Triangles   **376**

Find each measure.

12. *BC*

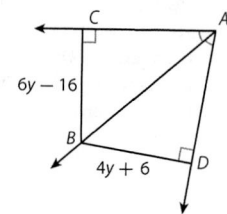

$\overrightarrow{AB}$ is the bisector of $\angle CAD$. By the Angle Bisector Theorem, $BC = BD$, so $6y - 16 = 4y + 6$, and $y = 11$. $BC = 6y - 16 = 50$

13. *VY*

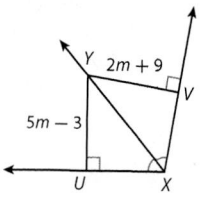

$\overrightarrow{XY}$ is the bisector of $\angle UXV$. By the Angle Bisector Theorem, $VY = UY$, so $2m + 9 = 5m - 3$ and $m = 4$. $VY = 2m + 9 = 17$

14. $m\angle JKL$

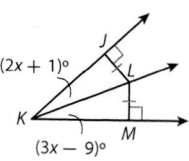

$JL = ML$, $\overline{JL} \perp \overrightarrow{KJ}$, and $\overline{ML} \perp \overrightarrow{KM}$, so $\overrightarrow{KL}$ bisects $\angle JKM$ (Converse of the Angle Bisector Theorem). $m\angle JKL = m\angle MKL$, so $2x + 1 = 3x - 9$ and $x = 10$. $m\angle JKL = (2x + 1)° = 21°$

15. $m\angle GDF$

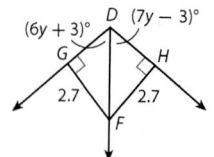

$FG = FH$, $\overline{FG} \perp \overrightarrow{DG}$, and $\overline{FH} \perp \overrightarrow{DH}$, so $\overrightarrow{DF}$ bisects $\angle GDH$ (Converse of the Angle Bisector Theorem). $m\angle GDF = m\angle HDF$, so $6y + 3 = 7y - 3$ and $y = 6$. $m\angle GDF = (6y + 3)° = 39°$

16. Complete the following proof of the Angle Bisector Theorem.

Given: $\overrightarrow{PS}$ bisects $\angle QPR$.
$\overline{SQ} \perp \overrightarrow{PQ}$, $\overline{SR} \perp \overrightarrow{PR}$

Prove: $SQ = SR$

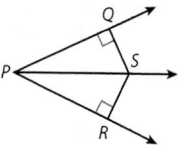

Statements	Reasons
1. $\overrightarrow{PS}$ bisects $\angle QPR$. $\overline{SQ} \perp \overrightarrow{PQ}, \overline{SR} \perp \overrightarrow{PR}$	1. Given
2. $\angle QPS \cong \angle RPS$	2. Definition of angle bisector
3. $\angle SQP$ and $\angle SRP$ are right angles.	3. Definition of perpendicular
4. $\angle SQP \cong \angle SRP$	4. All right angles are congruent.
5. $\overline{PS} \cong \overline{PS}$	5. Reflexive Property of Congruence
6. $\triangle PQS \cong \triangle PRS$	6. AAS Triangle Congruence Theorem
7. $\overline{SQ} \cong \overline{SR}$	7. Corresponding parts of congruent triangles are congruent.
8. $SQ = SR$	8. Congruent segments have the same length.

Exercise	Depth of Knowledge (D.O.K.)	COMMON CORE Mathematical Practices
23	3 Strategic Thinking H.O.T.	MP.2 Reasoning

17. Complete the following proof of the Converse of the Angle Bisector Theorem.

Given: $\overrightarrow{VX} \perp \overrightarrow{YX}$, $\overrightarrow{VZ} \perp \overrightarrow{YZ}$, $VX = VZ$.

Prove: $\overrightarrow{YV}$ bisects $\angle XYZ$.

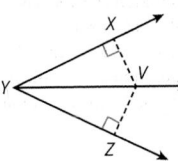

Statements	Reasons
1. $\overrightarrow{VX} \perp \overrightarrow{YX}$, $\overrightarrow{VZ} \perp \overrightarrow{YZ}$, $VX = VZ$	1. **Given**
2. $\angle VXY$ and $\angle VZY$ are right angles.	2. **Definition of perpendicular**
3. $\overline{YV} \cong \overline{YV}$	3. **Reflexive Property of Congruence**
4. $\triangle YXV \cong \triangle YZV$	4. **HL Triangle Congruence Theorem**
5. $\angle XYV \cong \angle ZYV$	5. **Corresponding parts of congruent triangles are congruent.**
6. $\overrightarrow{YV}$ **bisects** $\angle XYZ$.	6. **Definition of angle bisector**

18. Complete the following proof of the Incenter Theorem.

Given: $\overrightarrow{AP}, \overrightarrow{BP},$ and $\overrightarrow{CP}$ bisect $\angle A, \angle B$ and $\angle C$, respectively. $\overline{PX} \perp \overline{AC}, \overline{PY} \perp \overline{AB}, \overline{PZ} \perp \overline{BC}$

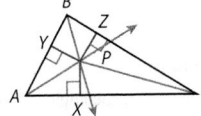

Prove: $PX = PY = PZ$

Let P be the incenter of $\triangle ABC$. Since P lies on the bisector of $\angle A$, $PX = PY$ by the __Angle Bisector__ Theorem. Similarly, P also __lies on the bisector of $\angle B$__, so $PY = PZ$. Therefore, $PX = PY = PZ$, by the __Transitive Property of Equality__.

19. A city plans to build a firefighter's monument in a triangular park between three streets. Draw a sketch on the figure to show where the city should place the monument so that it is the same distance from all three streets. Justify your sketch.

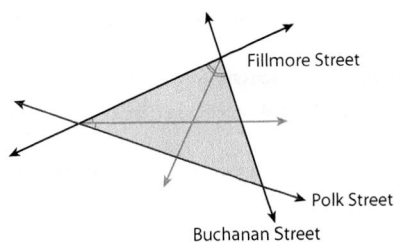

Fillmore Street

Polk Street

Buchanan Street

Draw the bisectors of two angles of the triangular park. The monument should be at the intersection of the bisectors. This point is the incenter of the triangle. By the Incenter Theorem, it is equidistant from the sides of the triangle.

Focus on Math Connections

MP.1 When students are given a triangle in the plane, encourage them to use a protractor to help locate the angle bisectors. Remind them that they need to find only two angle bisectors of the triangle to locate the incenter.

Have students write the Angle Bisector Theorem and its converse in their own words and explain how they are used to find the incircle of a triangle.

20. A school plans to place a flagpole on the lawn so that it is equidistant from Mercer Street and Houston Street. They also want the flagpole to be equidistant from a water fountain at W and a bench at B. Find the point F where the school should place the flagpole. Mark the point on the figure and explain your answer.

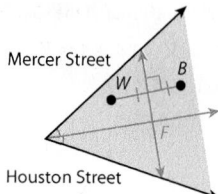

Mercer Street

Houston Street

A point that is equidistant from Mercer Street and Houston street must lie on the bisector of the angle formed by the streets. A point that is equidistant from the water fountain and the bench, must lie on the perpendicular bisector of the segment connecting those points. Therefore, the flagpole should be located at the intersection of the bisector of the angle formed by the streets and the perpendicular bisector of the segment determined by the water fountain and the bench.

21. P is the incenter of $\triangle ABC$. Determine whether each statement is true or false. Select the correct answer for each lettered part.

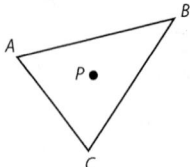

a. Point P must lie on the perpendicular bisector of $\overline{BC}$.   ○ True   ● False

b. Point P must lie on the angle bisector of $\angle C$.   ● True   ○ False

c. If AP is 23 mm long, then CP must be 23 mm long.   ○ True   ● False

d. If the distance from point P to $\overline{AB}$ is x, then the distance from point P to $\overline{BC}$ must be x.   ● True   ○ False

e. The perpendicular segment from point P to $\overline{AC}$ is longer than the perpendicular segment from point P to $\overline{BC}$.   ○ True   ● False

a. *P* is the incenter of the triangle *P* does not necessarily lie on any of the perpendicular bisectors of the sides.

b. *P* is the intersection of the angle bisectors, so point *P* must lie on the angle bisector of $\angle C$.

c. *P* is equidistant from the sides of the triangle, not necessarily from the vertices.

d. *P* is equidistant from the sides of the triangle. The distance from *P* to $\overline{AB}$ must equal the distance from *P* to $\overline{BC}$.

e. *P* is is equidistant from the sides of the triangle. The perpendicular segments from *P* to $\overline{AC}$ and from *P* to $\overline{BC}$ must be the same length.

H.O.T. Focus on Higher Order Thinking

22. **What If?** In the Explore, you constructed the angle bisector of acute $\angle ABC$ and found that if a point is on the bisector, then it is equidistant from the sides of the angle. Would you get the same results if $\angle ABC$ were a straight angle? Explain.

Yes. In this case, the angle bisector is a line through point B that is perpendicular to the straight angle. For any point P on the bisector, the shortest distance to the sides of $\angle ABC$ is the distance along the perpendicular to point B, or PB.

23. **Explain the Error** A student was asked to draw the incircle for $\triangle PQR$. He constructed angle bisectors as shown. Then he drew a circle through points J, K, and L. Describe the student's error.

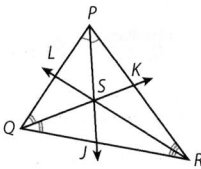

The circle will not necessarily pass through the points where the angle bisectors intersect the sides of the triangle. Instead, the student should have used S as the center of the circle and made a circle that just touches the three sides of the triangle.

Lesson Performance Task

Teresa has just purchased a farm with a field shaped like a right triangle. The triangle has the measurements shown in the diagram. Teresa plans to install central pivot irrigation in the field. In this type of irrigation, a circular region of land is irrigated by a long arm of sprinklers—the radius of the circle—that rotates around a central pivot point like the hands of a clock, dispensing water as it moves.

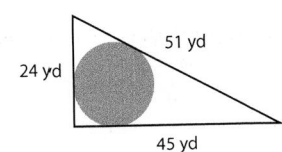

51 yd
24 yd
45 yd

a. Describe how she can find where to locate the pivot.

b. Find the area of the irrigation circle. To find the radius, r, of a circle inscribed in a triangle with sides of length a, b, and c, you can use the formula $r = \frac{\sqrt{k(k-a)(k-b)(k-c)}}{k}$, where $k = \frac{1}{2}(a+b+c)$.

c. About how much of the field will *not* be irrigated?

a. She can bisect each of the three angles of the triangle. The point of intersection of the three angle bisectors is the center of the circle.

b. $a = 24$ yd, $b = 45$ yd, $c = 51$ yd, so $k = \frac{1}{2}(24 + 45 + 51) = 60$. Then

$r = \frac{\sqrt{(60)(60-24)(60-45)(60-51)}}{60} = 9$, and area $= \pi r^2 \approx 3.14(9)^2 \approx 254$

c. Area of triangle $= \frac{1}{2}(45)(24) = 540$ yd², so area NOT irrigated $\approx 540 - 254 = 286$ yd².

INTEGRATE MATHEMATICAL PRACTICES

Focus on Math Connections

MP.1 The formula given in Part (b) of the Lesson Performance Task is derived from Heron's Formula, named after the ancient Greek mathematician Heron of Alexandria. The formula finds T, the area of a triangle, given a, b, and c, the lengths of the sides:

$T = \sqrt{s(s-a)(s-b)(s-c)}$, where s is the *semi-perimeter* (half the perimeter) of the triangle:

$s = \frac{a+b+c}{2}$

INTEGRATE MATHEMATICAL PRACTICES

Focus on Critical Thinking

MP.3 Tell students that by constructing the angle bisectors of the angles of an equilateral triangle, they have found the incenter of the triangle. Ask them to explain how they can now find the circumcenter of the triangle without carrying out any further constructions. They have already found the circumcenter, because the circumcenter and incenter of an equilateral triangle are the same point.

EXTENSION ACTIVITY

A farmer intends to install central pivot irrigation in a square field measuring 400 feet on a side. The farmer is considering three possible systems: using 1, 4, or 16 circles.

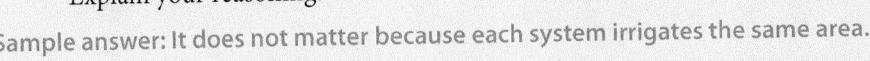

- Calculate and compare the total areas that will be irrigated by each system. Use 3.14 for π.

All three systems irrigate 125,600 ft².

- Which system do you think the farmer should choose? Explain your reasoning.

Sample answer: It does not matter because each system irrigates the same area.

Scoring Rubric
2 points: Student correctly solves the problem and explains his/her reasoning.
1 point: Student shows good understanding of the problem but does not fully solve or explain.
0 points: Student does not demonstrate understanding of the problem.

Angle Bisectors of Triangles   **380**

Medians and Altitudes of Triangles

Common Core Math Standards

The student is expected to:

 G-CO.C.10

Prove theorems about triangles. Also G-CO.D.12, G-GPE.B.4, G-GPE.B.5

Mathematical Practices

 MP.5 Using Tools

Language Objective

With a partner, label the orthocenter, medians, and altitudes of triangles drawn on coordinate planes.

ENGAGE

Essential Question: How can you find the balancing point, or center of gravity, of a triangle?

Graph or find the equations for at least two of the three medians of the triangle; the centroid, which is the balancing point of the triangle, will be located at their intersection.

PREVIEW: LESSON PERFORMANCE TASK

View the Engage section online. Discuss the photo, making certain that students understand that the spinning plates are balancing on their centers of gravity. Then preview the Lesson Performance Task.

Name _____ Class _____ Date _____

8.3 Medians and Altitudes of Triangles

Essential Question: How can you find the balance point or *center of gravity* of a triangle?

⊙ Explore Finding the Balance Point of a Triangle

If a triangle were cut out of a sheet of wood or paper, the triangle could be balanced around exactly one point inside the triangle.

A **median** of a triangle is a segment whose endpoints are a vertex of a triangle and the midpoint of the opposite side.

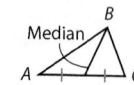

Every triangle has three distinct medians. You can use construction tools to show that the intersection of the three medians is the balance point of the triangle.

(A) Draw a large triangle on a sheet of construction paper. Label the vertices *A*, *B*, and *C*.

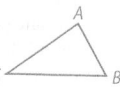

(B) Find the midpoint of the side opposite *A*, which is $\overline{BC}$. You may use a compass to find points equidistant to *B* and *C* and then draw the perpendicular bisector. Or you can use paper folding or a ruler. Write the label *X* for the midpoint.

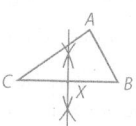

(C) Draw a segment to connect *A* and *X*. The segment is one of the three medians of the triangle.

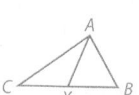

(D) Repeat Steps B and C, this time to draw the other two medians of the triangle. Write the label *Y* for the midpoint of the side opposite point *B*, and the label *Z* for the midpoint of the side opposite point *C*. Write the label *P* for the intersection of the three medians.

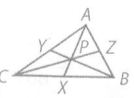

© Houghton Mifflin Harcourt Publishing Company

8.3 Medians and Altitudes of Triangles

HARDCOVER PAGES 327–338

Turn to these pages to find this lesson in the hardcover student edition.

Ⓔ Use a ruler to measure the lengths of each median and the subsegments defined by P in your triangle. Record your measurements in the table.

Median $\overline{AX}$:	AX = ____	AP = ____	PX = ____
Median $\overline{BY}$:	BY = ____	BP = ____	PY = ____
Median $\overline{CZ}$:	CZ = ____	CP = ____	PZ = ____

Answers will vary. For each median, the longer length should be twice the shorter length.

Ⓕ What pattern do you observe in the measurements?

Answers will vary. Possible answer: For each median, the longer subsegment has twice the

length of the shorter subsegment.

Ⓖ Let AX be the length of any median of a triangle from a vertex A, and let P be the intersection of the three medians. Write an equation to describe the relationship between AP and PX.

$AP = 2PX$, or $PX = \frac{1}{2}AP$

Ⓗ Let AX be the length of any median of a triangle from a vertex A, and let P be the intersection of the three medians. Write an equation to show the relationship between AX and AP.

$AP = \frac{2}{3}AX$, or $\frac{3}{2}AP = AX$

Ⓘ Cut out the triangle, and then punch a very small hole through P. Stick a pencil point through the hole, and then try to spin the triangle around the pencil point. How easily does it spin? Repeat this step with another point in the triangle, and compare the results.

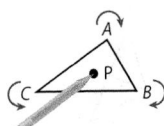

The triangle spins more easily around point P than around any other point of

the triangle.

INTEGRATE TECHNOLOGY

Students have the option of doing the balance point activity either in the book or online.

QUESTIONING STRATEGIES

 Is it possible for the medians of a triangle to intersect on the triangle? Why or why not? No; if the medians were to intersect on a side of the triangle, the median drawn from an adjacent vertex would have to lie coincident with that side. Since the median connects a vertex to the midpoint of the opposite side, that would mean the midpoint of the opposite side lies on the adjacent side that contains the median and the point of intersection, which is impossible.

PROFESSIONAL DEVELOPMENT

COMMON CORE Integrate Mathematical Practices

This lesson provides an opportunity to address Mathematical Practice **MP.5**, which calls for students to "use appropriate tools." Throughout the lesson, students use paper and pencil, protractors and rulers, and algebraic rules to predict and draw the indicated segments related to triangles. They must be able to use the tools in a variety of ways to explore concepts, do measurements of segments and subsegments related to triangles, and to solve problems that involve segments of triangles.

Medians and Altitudes of Triangles   **382**

EXPLAIN 1

Using the Centroid Theorem

INTEGRATE MATHEMATICAL PRACTICES

Focus on Math Connections

MP.1 Define the median of a triangle and point out that every triangle has three medians, which intersect at the centroid. Explain that the centroid is also called the *center of gravity* and that the Centroid Theorem can be used to find segment lengths in triangles.

1. Why is "balance point" a descriptive name for point P, the intersection of the three medians?

   The triangle can be balanced at this point. If the triangle is suspended or held up at this point, it does not list to one side.

2. **Discussion** By definition, median $\overline{AX}$ intersects $\triangle ABC$ at points A and X. Could it intersect the triangle at a third point? Explain why or why not.

   No. The median intersects $\overline{AB}$ and $\overline{AC}$ at point A, and it intersects $\overline{BC}$ at point X, the midpoint. If the median intersected the triangle at a third point, then the median would be coincident with one of the three sides of the triangle.

⊘ Explain 1   Using the Centroid Theorem

The intersection of the three medians of a triangle is the *centroid* of the triangle. The centroid is always inside the triangle and divides each median by the same ratio.

Centroid Theorem

The centroid theorem states that the **centroid** of a triangle is located $\frac{2}{3}$ of the distance from each vertex to the midpoint of the opposite side.

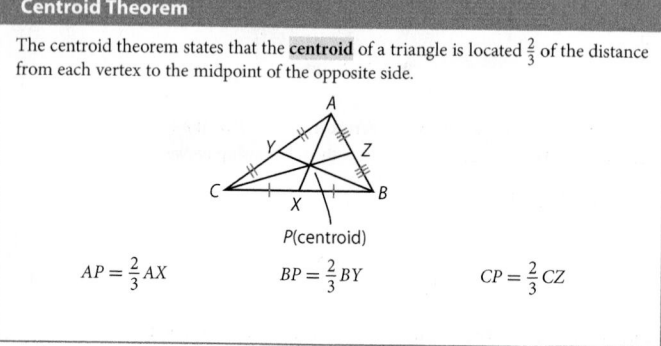

$$AP = \frac{2}{3}AX \qquad BP = \frac{2}{3}BY \qquad CP = \frac{2}{3}CZ$$

Example 1   Use the Centroid Theorem to find the length.

$AF = 9$, and $CE = 7.2$

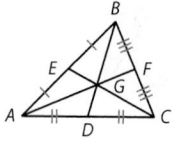

 AG

Centroid Theorem	$AG = \frac{2}{3}AF$
Substitute 9 for AF.	$AG = \frac{2}{3}(9)$
Simplify.	$AG = 6$

COLLABORATIVE LEARNING

Small Group Activity

Give each group of students a triangular region cut out of heavy construction paper and a triangle drawn on the coordinate plane. Have half of the group find the center of gravity of the triangular region by balancing it on the end of a pencil, and then explain to the other group members what they found. Have the other half find the intersection of the medians of the triangle on the coordinate plane, and explain what they found and how they found it.

(B) GE

Centroid Theorem	$CG = \dfrac{2}{3}\;\underline{CE}$
Substitute for the given value.	$CG = \dfrac{2}{3}\;\underline{(7.2)}$
Simplify.	$CG = \underline{4.8}$
Segment Addition Postulate	$CG + \underline{GE} = CE$
Subtraction Property of Equality	$GE = CE - \underline{CG}$
Substitute for the value of CG.	$GE = 7.2 - \underline{4.8}$
Simplify.	$GE = \underline{2.4}$

? The centroid divided each median into two segment lengths. What is their ratio? **2:1**

? How does the length from a vertex to P, the intersection of the medians, compare to the distance from the vertex to the midpoint of the opposite side? **The length from a vertex to P is $\frac{2}{3}$ the distance from the vertex to the midpoint of the opposite side.**

Reflect

3. To find the centroid of a triangle, how many medians of the triangle must you construct?
You need to construct two medians. The centroid will be located at their intersection.

4. Compare the lengths of $\overline{CG}$ and $\overline{GE}$ in Part B. What do you notice?
$CG = 4.8$ and $GE = 2.4$, so their ratio is 2:1.

5. **Make a Conjecture** The three medians of $\triangle FGH$ divide the triangle into six smaller triangles. Is it possible for the six smaller triangles to be congruent to one another? If yes, under what conditions?
Yes, when $\triangle FGH$ is an equilateral triangle. All three medians will be congruent with each other, as will matching sets of segments among the six smaller triangles.

Your Turn

6. Vertex L is 8 units from the centroid of $\triangle LMN$. Find the length of the median that has one endpoint at L.

$$\frac{2}{3}(x) = 8$$

$$\frac{3}{2} \cdot \frac{2}{3}(x) = 8 \cdot \frac{3}{2}$$

$$x = 12$$

The length of the median is 12 units.

7. Let P be the centroid of $\triangle STU$, and let $\overline{SW}$ be a median of $\triangle STU$. If $SW = 18$, find SP and PW.

$$\frac{2}{3}(SW) = SP \qquad \frac{1}{3}(SW) = PW$$

$$\frac{2}{3}(18) = SP \qquad \frac{1}{3}(18) = PW$$

$$12 = SP \qquad 6 = PW$$

$$SP = 12;\ PW = 6$$

8. In $\triangle ABC$, the median $\overline{AD}$ is perpendicular to $\overline{BC}$. If $AD = 21$ feet, describe the position of the centroid of the triangle.
The centroid is located 7 feet above the ground along AD, or 14 feet below point A.

Let F be the centroid.

$$\frac{2}{3}(AD) = AF \qquad \frac{1}{3}(AD) = FD$$

$$\frac{2}{3}(21) = AF \qquad \frac{1}{3}(21) = FD$$

$$14 = AF \qquad 7 = FD$$

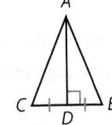

DIFFERENTIATE INSTRUCTION

Modeling

Have groups of students divide up and draw different types of triangles, including right, acute, obtuse, scalene, isosceles, and equilateral. Ask them to use construction methods or technology to find the orthocenter of each type of triangle. Then have them discuss the location of the orthocenter in relation to the triangle (inside, outside, or on the triangle) within the group and then with the whole class.

Ask students to make conjectures about the relationship between the orthocenter and a specific type of triangle.

EXPLAIN 2

Finding the Intersection of Medians of a Triangle

INTEGRATE MATHEMATICAL PRACTICES

Focus on Math Connections

MP.1 Point out that the problem solving model is in four parts:

(1) Understanding the problem so that the important given information is highlighted and the focus is on the desired answer;

(2) Making a plan for how to solve the problem;

(3) Solving the problem; and

(4) Checking the answer by looking back at the problem statement.

✪ Explain 2 **Finding the Intersection of Medians of a Triangle**

When a triangle is plotted on the coordinate plane, the medians can be graphed and the location of the centroid can be identified.

Example 2 Find the coordinates of the centroid of the triangle shown on the coordinate plane.

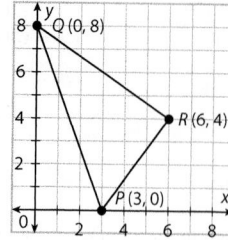

🧩 Analyze Information

What does the problem ask you to find? the centroid of the triangle

What information does the graph provide that will help you find the answer?
the coordinates of the three vertices of the triangle

🧩 Formulate a Plan

The centroid is the ___intersection___ of the medians of the triangle. Begin by calculating the ___midpoint___ of one side of the triangle. Then draw a line to connect that point to a ___vertex___. You need to draw only ___two___ medians to find the centroid.

🧩 Solve

Find and plot midpoints.
Let M be the midpoint of $\overline{QR}$.

$$M = \left(\frac{0+6}{2}, \frac{8+4}{2}\right) = \underline{(3, 6)}$$

Let N be the midpoint of $\overline{QP}$.

$$N = \left(\frac{0+3}{2}, \frac{8+0}{2}\right) = \underline{(1.5, 4)}$$

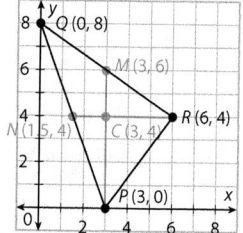

Draw the medians and identify equations.
Draw a segment to connect M and ___P___.
The segment is a median and is described by the equation ___$x = 3$___.
Draw a segment to connect N and ___R___.
The segment is also a median and is described by the equation ___$y = 4$___.

Find the centroid.
Identify the intersection of the two medians, which is (___3, 4___). Label it C.

LANGUAGE SUPPORT 🇪🇱

Connect Vocabulary

The prefix *ortho-* means *perpendicular or straight*. To help students remember this, explain that an orthodontist straightens teeth with braces. The altitude of a triangle is straight (vertical) in relation to the side to which it is perpendicular.

© Houghton Mifflin Harcourt Publishing Company

The answer seems reasonable because it is positioned in the middle of the triangle. To check it, find the midpoint of $\overline{RP}$, which is ___(4.5, 2)___ . Label the midpoint L, and draw the third median, which is ___QL___ . The slope of the third median is

$\frac{2-8}{4.5-0} = -\frac{4}{3}$, and the equation that describes it is $y = -\frac{4}{3}x + \underline{\ 8\ }$. It intersects the

other two medians at (___3, 4___), which confirms C as the centroid.

You can also apply the Centroid Theorem to check your answer.

$RC = \frac{2}{3}RN$

$RN = \underline{\ 4.5\ }$

$RC = \underline{\ 3\ }$

Substitute values into the first equation:

$3 = \frac{2}{3}\,(4.5)$

The equality is true, which confirms the answer.

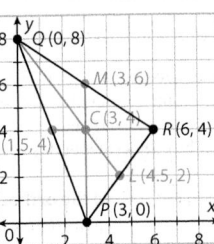

Find the centroid of the triangles with the given vertices. Show your work and check your answer.

9. $P(-1, 7),\ Q(9, 5),\ R(4, 3)$

Let M be the midpoint of $\overline{QR}$.

$M = \left(\frac{9+4}{2}, \frac{5+3}{2}\right) = (6.5, 4)$

Let N be the midpoint of $\overline{QP}$.

$N = \left(\frac{-1+9}{2}, \frac{7+5}{2}\right) = (4, 6)$

$\overline{MP}: y = -\frac{2}{5}x + \frac{33}{5};\ \overline{NR}: x = 4$

Check: Let L be the midpoint of $\overline{PR}$.

$L = \left(\frac{-1+4}{2}, \frac{7+3}{2}\right) = (1.5, 5)$

Equation of $\overline{QL}$ is $y = 5$, which intersects $x = 4$ at $S(4, 5)$.

$y = -\frac{2}{5}\,(4) + \frac{33}{5}$

$y = -\frac{8}{5} + \frac{33}{5}$

$y = 5$

The coordinates of the centroid are $S(4, 5)$.

10. $A(-6, 0),\ B(0, 12),\ C(6, 0)$

Let D be the midpoint of $\overline{AB}$.

$D = \left(\frac{-6+0}{2}, \frac{0+12}{2}\right) = (-3, 6)$

Let F be the midpoint of $\overline{BC}$.

$F = \left(\frac{0+6}{2}, \frac{12+0}{2}\right) = (3, 6)$

$\overline{DC}: y = -\frac{2}{3}x + 4;\ \overline{FA}: y = \frac{2}{3}x + 4$

Check: Let G be the midpoint of $\overline{AC}$.

$G = \left(\frac{-6+6}{2}, \frac{0+0}{2}\right) = (0, 0)$

Equation of $\overline{BG}$ is $x = 0$, which intersects $y = 4$ at $S(0, 4)$.

$-\frac{2}{3}x + 4 = \frac{2}{3}x + 4$

$x = 0$

$y = \frac{2}{3}(0) + 4$

$y = 4$

The coordinates of the centroid are $S(0, 4)$.

QUESTIONING STRATEGIES

? How do you find the point at which a triangular region will balance? **Find the intersection point of the medians.**

? How does finding the point of intersection of the medians help solve a real-world problem? **Finding this point will help decide how to balance a triangular structure.**

? What is the advantage in exploring medians with geometry software rather than by drawing triangles and medians with a ruler? **The software makes it easy to change the triangle's size and shape to see if the relationship among the medians still holds.**

AVOID COMMON ERRORS

When using the Centroid Theorem, students may identify the wrong part of the median as $\frac{2}{3}$ of the total length. Remind them that the centroid is closer to each side than to the opposite vertex. Watch for correct notation when students describe the length of the segments. This indicates an understanding of how the theorem is applied.

EXPLAIN 3

Finding the Orthocenter of a Triangle

INTEGRATE MATHEMATICAL PRACTICES

Focus on Math Connections

MP.1 Point out that an *altitude* is a line segment from the vertex of a triangle perpendicular to the opposite side of the triangle. Make the distinction between the altitudes of the triangle and the perpendicular lines from the vertex of a triangle to the lines containing the opposite sides of the triangle. The *orthocenter* is located at the intersection of the perpendicular lines containing the opposite sides of the triangle. These lines may intersect outside the triangle.

✏ Explain 3 **Finding the Orthocenter of a Triangle**

Like the centroid, the *orthocenter* is a point that characterizes a triangle. This point involves the *altitudes* of the triangle rather than the medians.

An **altitude** of a triangle is a perpendicular segment from a vertex to the line containing the opposite side. Every triangle has three altitudes. An altitude can be inside, outside, or on the triangle.

In the diagram of △*ABC*, the three altitudes are $\overline{AX}$, $\overline{BZ}$, and $\overline{CY}$. Notice that two of the altitudes are outside the triangle.

The length of an altitude is often called the height of a triangle.

The **orthocenter** of a triangle is the intersection (or point of concurrency) of the lines that contain the altitudes. Like the altitudes themselves, the orthocenter may be inside, outside, or on the triangle. Notice that the lines containing the altitudes are concurrent at *P*. The orthocenter of this triangle is *P*.

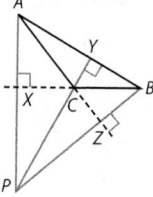

Example 3 Find the orthocenter of the triangle by graphing the perpendicular lines to the sides of the triangle.

(A) **Step 1** Draw the triangle. Choose one vertex and then find and graph the equation of the line containing the altitude from that vertex.

Triangle with vertices $O(0, 0)$, $P(2, 6)$, and $Q(8, 0)$

Choose *P*. The side opposite *P* is $\overline{OQ}$, which is horizontal, so the altitude is vertical. The altitude is a segment of the line $x = 2$.

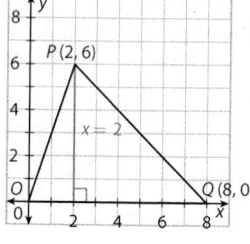

Step 2 Repeat Step 1 with a second vertex.

Choose *O*, the origin. The altitude that contains *O* is perpendicular to $\overline{PQ}$. Calculate the slope of $\overline{PQ}$ as $\frac{y_2 - y_1}{x_2 - x_1} = \frac{6 - 0}{2 - 8} = -1$.

Since the slope of the altitude is the opposite reciprocal of the slope of $\overline{PQ}$, the slope of the altitude is 1. The altitude is a segment of the line that passes through the origin and has a slope of 1. The equation of the line is $y = x$.

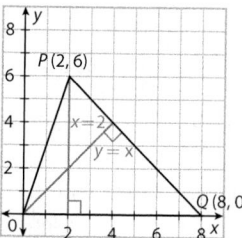

Step 3 Find the intersection of the two lines.

The orthocenter is the intersection of the two lines that contain the altitudes. The lines $x = 2$ and $y = x$ intersect at $(2, 2)$, which is the orthocenter.

© Houghton Mifflin Harcourt Publishing Company

Ⓑ

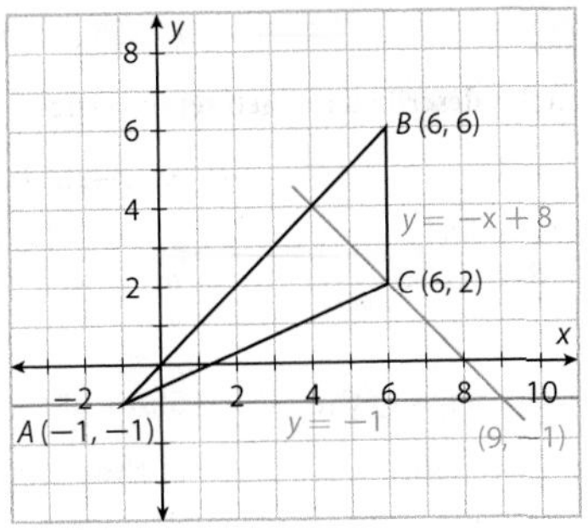

Step 1 Find the altitude that contains vertex A.

Because $\overline{BC}$ is vertical, the altitude through A is a __horizontal__ segment. The equation of the line that contains the segment is $y = \underline{-1}$. Draw this line.

Step 2 Find the altitude that contains vertex C.

First, calculate the slope of $\overline{AB}$. The slope is $\dfrac{6-(-1)}{6-(-1)}$, which equals $\underline{1}$.

The slope of the altitude to $\overline{AB}$ is the __opposite reciprocal__ of 1, which is -1.

Use the point-slope form to find the equation of the line that has a slope of -1 and passes through $\underline{C}$:

$y - \underline{2} = -1(x - \underline{6})$, which simplifies to $y = -x + 8$.

Draw this line.

Step 3 Find the intersection of the two lines.

$y = -1$

$y = -x + 8$

Substitute for y:

$\underline{-1} = -x + 8$

$x = \underline{9}$

The orthocenter is at $(\underline{9, -1})$.

Reflect

11. Could the orthocenter of a triangle be concurrent with one of its vertices?
If yes, provide an example. If not, explain why not.
Yes. The orthocenter of a right triangle is the vertex where the right angle forms.

12. An altitude is defined to be a perpendicular segment from a vertex to the line containing the opposite side. Why are the words "the line containing" important in this definition?
An altitude may lie outside the triangle. It will intersect an extension of the opposite side, but not the side itself.

© Houghton Mifflin Harcourt Publishing Company

QUESTIONING STRATEGIES

❓ Why isn't the orthocenter always inside the perimeter of the triangle? The orthocenter is located at the intersection of the perpendicular lines from the vertices of the triangle to the lines containing the opposite sides of the triangle. This point may be on the triangle (right triangle) or outside the triangle (obtuse triangle).

❓ Which point allows a triangular region to balance, the centroid or the orthocenter? centroid

Medians and Altitudes of Triangles   **388**

ELABORATE

QUESTIONING STRATEGIES

? Do the centroid and orthocenter ever coincide? Explain. Yes, in an equilateral triangle, these points are the same.

? Can the orthocenter ever be a vertex of a triangle? Explain. Yes, in a right triangle, the orthocenter is the point where the two legs intersect.

? Can the orthocenter ever be a balancing point of a triangle? Explain. Yes, but only in equilateral triangles.

? Why must the balancing point of the medians be inside the triangle? All three medians are inside the triangle, so their intersection point must also be inside the triangle.

SUMMARIZE THE LESSON

? Have students fill out a vocabulary chart to summarize what they know about the centroid and the orthocenter. Sample:

Centroid	
Definition	The point of intersection of the three medians of a triangle
Diagram	Diagrams will vary.
Attributes	Always a point inside the triangle; balancing point of a triangular surface

Orthocenter	
Definition	The point of intersection of the lines containing the altitudes of the vertices of a triangle
Diagram	Diagrams will vary.
Attributes	Can be outside, inside, or on the triangle

Your Turn

Find the orthocenter for the triangles described by each set of vertices.

13. $Q(4, -3)$, $R(8, 5)$, $S(8, -8)$

Since $\overline{RS}$ is vertical, the altitude line through Q is horizontal, so the equation is $y = -3$.

Slope of $\overline{QR}$ is $\frac{5+3}{8-4} = 2$, so the slope of the altitude line through S is $-\frac{1}{2}$. In point-slope form, the equation is $y + 8 = -\frac{1}{2}(x - 8)$.

$y = -3$, so $-3 + 8 = -\frac{1}{2}(x - 8)$

$$5 = -\frac{1}{2}(x - 8)$$

$$-10 = x - 8$$

$$x = -2$$

The coordinates of the orthocenter are $(-2, -3)$.

14. $K(2, -2)$, $L(4, 6)$, $M(8, -2)$

Since $\overline{KM}$ is horizontal, the altitude line through L is vertical, so the equation is $x = 4$.

Slope of $\overline{LM}$ is $\frac{-2-6}{8-4} = -2$, so the slope of the altitude line through K is $\frac{1}{2}$.

In point-slope form, the equation is $y + 2 = \frac{1}{2}(x - 2)$.

$x = 4$, so $y + 2 = \frac{1}{2}(4 - 2)$

$$y + 2 = 2 - 1$$

$$y = -1$$

The coordinates of the orthocenter are $(4, -1)$.

💬 Elaborate

15. Could the centroid of a triangle be coincident with the orthocenter? If so, give an example.
Yes. An equilateral triangle has its centroid and orthocenter at the same point.

16. Describe or sketch an example in which the orthocenter P of $\triangle ABC$ is far away from the triangle. That is, PA, PB, and PC are each greater than the length of any side of the triangle.
An example is an obtuse triangle with one angle slightly less than 180°. For example, the triangle with vertices $A(-100, 0)$, $B(0, 1)$, and $C(100, 0)$ has an orthocenter at $(0, 10^4)$.

17. A sculptor is assembling triangle-shaped pieces into a mobile. Describe circumstances when the sculptor would need to identify the centroid and orthocenter of each triangle.
Possible answer: Identifying the centroid of the triangle would allow the sculptor to dangle the triangle at the end of a bar or wire, and the triangle would be balanced there. Identifying the orthocenter would allow the triangle to be attached to a single point by three bars or straight wires, each perpendicular to one side of the triangle.

18. **Essential Question Check-In** How can you find the centroid, or balance point, of a triangle?
Graph or find the equations for at least two of the three medians of the triangle. The centroid will be located at their intersection.

⭐ Evaluate: Homework and Practice

• Online Homework
• Hints and Help
• Extra Practice

Use a compass and a straightedge to draw the medians and identify the centroid of the triangle. Label the centroid P.

1.

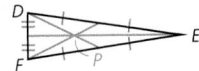

2.

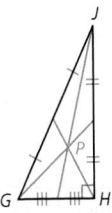

3. **Critique Reasoning** Paul draws △ABC and the medians from vertices A and B. He finds that the medians intersect at a point, and he labels this point X. Paul claims that point X lies outside △ABC. Do you think this is possible? Explain.

No; no matter how you change the shape of △ABC, the point at which the medians intersect is always in the interior of the triangle.

4. For △ABC and its medians, match the segment on the left with its length.

A. AM   C   1.5

B. AP   F   2

C. PM   I   2.5

D. BK   B   3

E. BP   E   4

F. PK   A   4.5

G. CL   H   5

H. CP   D   6

I. PL   G   7.5

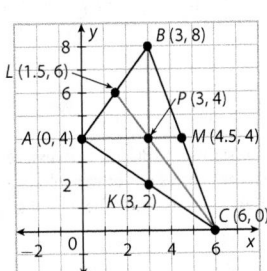

EVALUATE

ASSIGNMENT GUIDE

Concepts and Skills	Practice
Explore Finding the Balance Point of a Triangle	Exercises 1–4
Example 1 Using the Centroid Theorem	Exercises 5–11
Example 2 Finding the Intersection of Medians of a Triangle	Exercises 12–18
Example 3 Finding the Orthocenter of a Triangle	Exercises 19–25

Exercise	Depth of Knowledge (D.O.K.)	COMMON CORE Mathematical Practices
1–4	**1** Recall of information	**MP.4** Modeling
5–22	**2** Skills/Concepts	**MP.5** Using Tools
23–25	**2** Skills/Concepts	**MP.1** Problem Solving
26	**3** Strategic Thinking H.O.T.	**MP.3** Logic
27	**3** Strategic Thinking H.O.T.	**MP.2** Reasoning
28	**3** Strategic Thinking H.O.T.	**MP.3** Logic
29	**3** Strategic Thinking H.O.T.	**MP.3** Logic

Medians and Altitudes of Triangles   **390**

INTEGRATE MATHEMATICAL PRACTICES

Focus on Critical Thinking

MP.3 Remind students that by the Centroid Theorem, the centroid is located $\frac{2}{3}$ of the distance from each vertex to the midpoint of the opposite side. In the coordinate plane, to find the point that is $\frac{2}{3}$ of the distance from $(2, 7)$ to $(5, -11)$, for example, find the difference between the x-coordinates (3) and the y-coordinates (-18). Multiply each difference by $\frac{2}{3}$ and add this to the coordinates of the first point. $\frac{2}{3}(3) = 2$, and $\frac{2}{3}(-18) = -12$. Since $2 + 2 = 4$ and $7 + (-12) = (-5)$, the point is $(4, -5)$.

The diagram shows $\triangle FGH$, its medians, centroid P, and the lengths of some of the subsegments. Apply the Centroid Theorem to find other lengths.

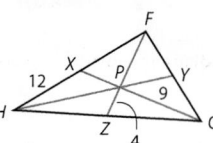

5. FH
$2(XH) = FH; 24 = FH$

6. PF
$PF = 2(PZ); PF = 8$

7. GX
$GX = GP + \frac{1}{2}(GP);$
$GX = 13.5$

The diagram shows $\triangle XYZ$, which has side lengths of 8 inches, 12 inches, and 15 inches. The diagram also shows the medians, centroid P, and the lengths of some of the subsegments. Apply the Centroid Theorem to find other lengths.

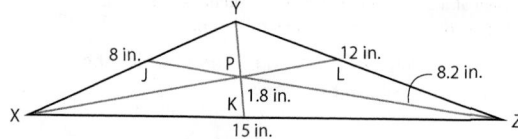

8. LY
$LY = \frac{1}{2}ZY; LY = 6$
6 in.

9. KY
$KY = 3(KP); KY = 5.4$
5.4 in.

10. ZJ
$ZJ = ZP + \frac{1}{2}(ZP);$
$ZJ = 12.3$
12.3 in.

11. The diagram shows $\triangle ABC$, its medians, centroid P, and the lengths of some of the subsegments as expressions of variables x and y. Apply the Centroid Theorem to solve for the variables and to find other lengths.

a. x
b. y
c. BP
d. BD
e. CP
f. PE

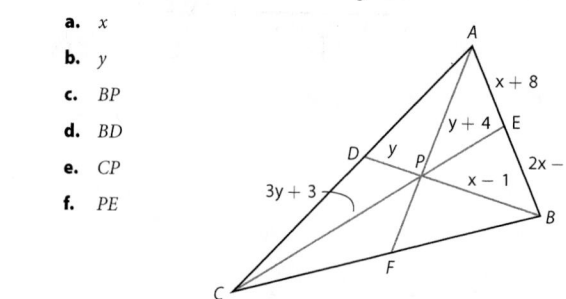
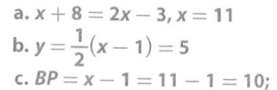

a. $x + 8 = 2x - 3, x = 11$
b. $y = \frac{1}{2}(x - 1) = 5$
c. $BP = x - 1 = 11 - 1 = 10;$

d. $BD = PD + BP, BD = 15$
e. $CP = 3y + 3 = 18$
f. $PE = \frac{1}{2}(CP) PE = 9$

© Houghton Mifflin Harcourt Publishing Company

12. Draw the medians from A to $\overline{BC}$ and from C to $\overline{AB}$.

Midpoint of $\overline{AB}$: $= \left(\dfrac{-2+4}{2}, \dfrac{2+4}{2}\right) = (1,3)$

Midpoint of $\overline{BC}$: $N = \left(\dfrac{1+4}{2}, \dfrac{0+4}{2}\right) = (2.5, 2)$

The centroid is $(1, 2)$. The third median
will also pass through $(1, 2)$.

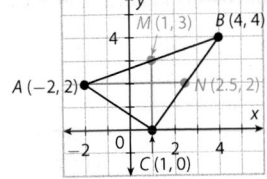

The vertices of a triangle are $A(-2, 3)$, $B(5, 10)$, and $C(12, -4)$.
Find the coordinates or equations for each feature of the triangle.

13. the coordinates of the midpoint of $\overline{AC}$

$\left(\dfrac{-2+12}{2}, \dfrac{3-4}{2}\right) = (5, -0.5)$

14. the coordinates of the midpoint of $\overline{BC}$

$\left(\dfrac{5+12}{2}, \dfrac{10-4}{2}\right) = (8.5, 3)$

15. the equation of the line that contains the median
through point B

$x = 5$

16. the equation of the line that contains the median
through point A

$y = 3$

17. the coordinates of the intersection of the two medians

$(5, 3)$

18. the coordinates of the center of balance of the triangle

$(5, 3)$

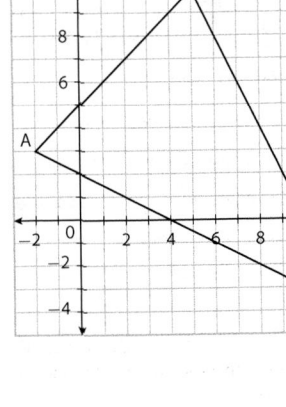

For each triangle, draw the three altitudes and find the orthocenter. Label it P.

19.

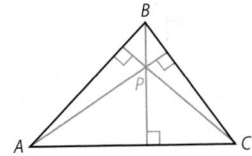

20.

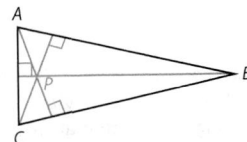

21.

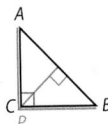

22.

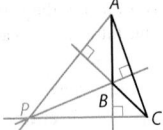

© Houghton Mifflin Harcourt Publishing Company

INTEGRATE MATHEMATICAL PRACTICES

Focus on Math Connections

MP.1 Remind students that the lines containing the three altitudes of a triangle intersect at the orthocenter of the triangle. Point out that two of the altitudes of a right triangle are its legs.

AVOID COMMON ERRORS

Some students may confuse the ratios of part to part and part to whole when working with segments along the medians of a triangle. Suggest that these students write the ratios of the parts using segment notation before substituting in the lengths of the segments.

Medians and Altitudes of Triangles   **392**

PEER-TO-PEER DISCUSSION

Ask students to discuss with a partner how to locate the centroid of a triangle drawn in the coordinate plane. Have them use the Centroid Theorem to verify that the centroid is located at $\frac{2}{3}$ of the distance from the vertex of a triangle to the midpoint of the opposite side. Have them draw additional examples to justify their reasoning.

JOURNAL

Have students write a journal entry in which they describe the Centroid Theorem in their own words. Remind students to include a labeled figure with their descriptions.

Find the orthocenter of each triangle with the given vertices.

23. $A(2, 2)$, $B(2, 10)$, $C(4, 2)$

Since $\overline{AB}$ is vertical, the altitude is horizontal, so the equation of the line containing the altitude through C is $y = 2$. Find the equation of the line containing the altitude from B to $\overline{AC}$. $\overline{AC}$ is horizontal and the altitude is vertical, so the equation is $x = 2$. Since $y = 2$ and $x = 2$, the coordinates of the orthocenter are $(2, 2)$.

24. $A(2, 5)$, $B(10, -3)$, $C(4, 5)$

Since $\overline{AC}$ is horizontal, the altitude is vertical, so the equation of the line containing the altitude through B is $x = 10$. Find the equation of the line containing the altitude from A to $\overline{BC}$. The slope of $\overline{BC}$ is $\frac{5+3}{4-10} = -\frac{4}{3}$. So, the equation is $y - 5 = \frac{3}{4}(x - 2)$. Since $x = 10$, $y - 5 = \frac{3}{4}(10 - 2)$. So, $y = 11$. The coordinates of the orthocenter are $(10, 11)$.

25. $A(9, 3)$, $B(9, -1)$, $C(6, 0)$

Since $\overline{AB}$ is vertical, the altitude is horizontal, so the equation of the line containing the altitude through C is $y = 0$. Find the equation of the line containing the altitude from A to $\overline{BC}$. The slope of $\overline{BC}$ is $\frac{0+1}{6-9} = -\frac{1}{3}$. So, the equation is $y - 3 = 3(x - 9)$. Since $y = 0$, $0 - 3 = 3(x - 9$ So, $x = 8$. The coordinates of the orthocenter are $(8, 0)$.

> **H.O.T. Focus on Higher Order Thinking**

26. Draw Conclusions Triangles ABC, DBE, and FBG are all symmetric about the y–axis. Show that each triangle has the same centroid. What are the coordinates of the centroid?

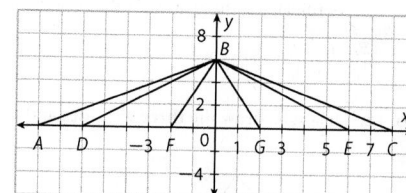

In each triangle, the side opposite point B has a midpoint at the origin. This means that each triangle has $\overline{BO}$ as a median. As explained by the centroid theorem, the centroid is located $\frac{2}{3}$ along $\overline{BO}$, which is at $(0, 2)$.

27. Analyze Relationships Triangle ABC is plotted on the coordinate plane. $\overline{AB}$ is horizontal, meaning it is parallel to the x-axis. $\overline{BC}$ is vertical, meaning it is parallel to the y-axis. Based on this information, can you determine the location of the orthocenter? Explain.

Yes. The orthocenter is B. The orthocenter is the intersection of the three altitudes of the triangle, but identifying only two altitudes is necessary to locate the intersection. $\overline{AB} \perp \overline{BC}$, so each segment is an altitude of the triangle. They intersect at B.

28. What if? The equilateral triangle shown here has its orthocenter and centroid on the y-axis. Suppose the triangle is stretched by moving A up the y-axis, while keeping B and C stationary. Describe and compare the changes to the centroid and the orthocenter of the triangle.
The centroid moves up the y-axis and the orthocenter moves down the y-axis. The centroid is above the orthocenter, and the distance between them increases as the triangle is stretched.

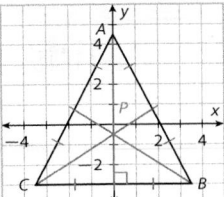

29. What If? The diagram shows right triangle ABC on the coordinate plane, and it shows the three medians and centroid P. How does the position of the centroid change when the triangle is stretched by moving B to the right along the x-axis, and keeping A and C stationary? How does the orthocenter change?

As the triangle is stretched to the right, the centroid moves to the right along a horizontal line. The orthocenter remains at C, the origin.

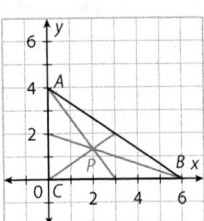

Lesson Performance Task

A bicycle frame consists of two adjacent triangles. The diagram shows some of the dimensions of the two triangles that make up the frame.

Answer these questions about the bicycle frame ABCD. Justify each of your answers.

a. Find the measures of all the angles in the frame.

b. Copy the figure on a piece of paper. Then find the center of gravity of each triangle.

c. Estimate the center of gravity of the entire frame and show it on your diagram.

d. Explain how you could modify the frame to lower its center of gravity and improve stability.

a. m∠A = m∠ADB = m∠ABD = 60°; m∠CBD + m∠CDB = 74°; m∠C = 32°.

b. Students should find the intersection of the medians of each triangle.

c. Possible answer: Find the midpoint of the line segment joining the centroids.

d. Possible answer: Make ∠CBD smaller so that $\overline{BC}$ angles downward.

© Houghton Mifflin Harcourt Publishing Company

INTEGRATE MATHEMATICAL PRACTICES
Focus on Reasoning

MP.2 With the intent of saving money, the president of a bicycle manufacturing company ordered the design department to eliminate the seat-to-pedal bar ($\overline{BD}$ in the diagram) in all new bicycle designs. Was that a good idea? Explain. No.
Sample answer: The design shown consists of two triangles, each of which, by the SSS Triangle Congruence Theorem, is stable. Eliminating the seat-to-pedal bar would leave quadrilateral ABCD, which is not stable (a heavy rider could cause the frame to collapse).

INTEGRATE MATHEMATICAL PRACTICES
Focus on Critical Thinking

MP.3 An artist carved a piece of very rough rock into a triangle. The artist then located the point where the three medians of the triangle intersected and attempted to balance the triangle on that point. The rock did not balance. It did balance, however, on a nearby point that the artist found by trial and error. Explain why the centroid might not have been the balance point of the rock triangle. Then complete this sentence: The centroid is the balance point of a triangle, as long as _____. Sample answers: The rock may not have had the same density at all points. Sentence completion: The centroid is the balance point of a triangle, as long as the triangle is of uniform density throughout.

EXTENSION ACTIVITY

Give students large pieces of light cardboard such as cereal-box cardboard, or photo-print paper. Each student should use a straightedge to draw a large scalene triangle on the cardboard, then cut out the triangle. Now challenge students to find the centroids of their triangles without using rulers or other measuring instruments. (The key is to fold adjacent vertices together to find the midpoint of each side.) Having found the midpoints, students can draw the medians and mark the centroid at their point of intersection. Finally, have students attempt to balance their triangles on the points of pens or sharpened pencils.

Scoring Rubric
2 points: Student correctly solves the problem and explains his/her reasoning.
1 point: Student shows good understanding of the problem but does not fully solve or explain.
0 points: Student does not demonstrate understanding of the problem.

Medians and Altitudes of Triangles   **394**

Midsegments of Triangles

Common Core Math Standards

The student is expected to:

COMMON CORE **G-CO.C.10**

Prove theorems about triangles. Also G-CO.D.12, G-GPE.B.4, G-GPE.B.5

Mathematical Practices

COMMON CORE **MP.2 Reasoning**

Language Objective

Explain to a partner why a drawn segment in a triangle is or is not a midsegment.

ENGAGE

Essential Question: How are the segments that join the midpoints of a triangle's sides related to the triangle's sides?

Each midsegment is half the length of the side to which it is parallel; the sum of the lengths of the midsegments is half the perimeter of the triangle.

PREVIEW: LESSON PERFORMANCE TASK

View the Engage section online. Discuss the photo, drawing attention to the horizontal crossbeams that extend between the slanting beams and stabilize them. Then preview the Lesson Performance Task.

Name_____ Class_____ Date_____

8.4   Midsegments of Triangles

Essential Question: How are the segments that join the midpoints of a triangle's sides related to the triangle's sides?

Resource Locker

⊘ Explore   **Investigating Midsegments of a Triangle**

The **midsegment** of a triangle is a line segment that connects the midpoints of two sides of the triangle. Every triangle has three midsegments. Midsegments are often used to add rigidity to structures. In the support for the garden swing shown, the crossbar $\overline{DE}$ is a midsegment of $\triangle ABC$

You can use a compass and straightedge to construct the midsegments of a triangle.

(A) Sketch a scalene triangle and label the vertices A, B, and C.

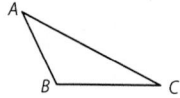

(B) Use a compass to find the midpoint of $\overline{AB}$. Label the midpoint D.

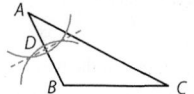

(C) Use a compass to find the midpoint of $\overline{AC}$. Label the midpoint E.

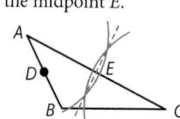

(D) Use a straightedge to draw $\overline{DE}$. $\overline{DE}$ is one of the midsegments of the triangle.

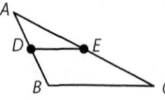

(E) Repeat the process to find the other two midsegments of $\triangle ABC$. You may want to label the midpoint of $\overline{BC}$ as F.

Module 8   **395**   Lesson 4

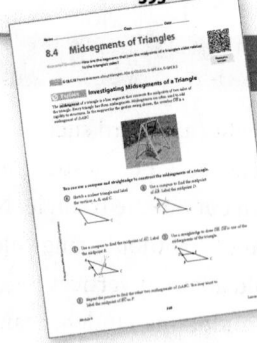

HARDCOVER PAGES 339–346

Turn to these pages to find this lesson in the hardcover student edition.

© Houghton Mifflin Harcourt Publishing Company

1. Use a ruler to compare the length of $\overline{DE}$ to the length of $\overline{BC}$. What does this tell you about $\overline{DE}$ and $\overline{BC}$?
   The length of $\overline{DE}$ is half the length of $\overline{BC}$.

2. Use a protractor to compare m∠ADE and m∠ABC. What does this tell you about $\overline{DE}$ and $\overline{BC}$? Explain.
   m∠ADE = m∠ABC, so $\overline{DE} \parallel \overline{BC}$ since corresponding angles are congruent.

3. Compare your results with your class. Then state a conjecture about a midsegment of a triangle.
   A midsegment of a triangle is parallel to the third side of the triangle and is half as long as the third side.

⚙ Explain 1 Describing Midsegments on a Coordinate Grid

You can confirm your conjecture about midsegments using the formulas for the midpoint, slope, and distance.

Example 1 Show that the given midsegment of the triangle is parallel to the third side of the triangle and is half as long as the third side.

(A) The vertices of $\triangle GHI$ are $G(-7, -1)$, $H(-5, 5)$, and $I(1, 3)$. J is the midpoint of $\overline{GH}$, and K is the midpoint of $\overline{IH}$. Show that $\overline{JK} \parallel \overline{GI}$ and $JK = \frac{1}{2}GI$. Sketch $\overline{JK}$.

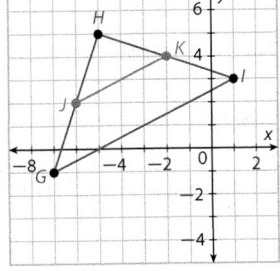

Step 1 Use the midpoint formula, $\left(\dfrac{x_1 + x_2}{2}, \dfrac{y_1 + y_2}{2}\right)$, to find the coordinates of J and K.

The midpoint of $\overline{GH}$ is $\left(\dfrac{-7 - 5}{2}, \dfrac{-1 + 5}{2}\right) = (-6, 2)$. Graph and label this point J.

The midpoint of $\overline{IH}$ is $\left(\dfrac{-5 + 1}{2}, \dfrac{5 + 3}{2}\right) = (-2, 4)$. Graph and label this point K. Use a straightedge to draw $\overline{JK}$.

Step 2 Use $\left(\dfrac{y_2 - y_1}{x_2 - x_1}\right)$ to compare the slopes of $\overline{JK}$ and $\overline{GI}$.

Slope of $\overline{JK} = \dfrac{4 - 2}{-2 - (-6)} = \dfrac{1}{2}$ Slope of $\overline{GI} = \dfrac{3 - (-1)}{1 - (-7)} = \dfrac{1}{2}$

Since the slopes are the same, $\overline{JK} \parallel \overline{GI}$.

Step 3 Use $\sqrt{(x_2 - x_1)^2 + (y_2 - y_1)^2}$ to compare the lengths of $\overline{JK}$ and $\overline{GI}$.

$JK = \sqrt{(-2 - (-6))^2 + (4 - 2)^2} = \sqrt{20} = 2\sqrt{5}$

$GI = \sqrt{(1 - (-7))^2 + (3 - (-1))^2} = \sqrt{80} = 4\sqrt{5}$

Since $2\sqrt{5} = \frac{1}{2}(4\sqrt{5})$, $JK = \frac{1}{2}GI$.

PROFESSIONAL DEVELOPMENT

COMMON CORE Math Background

A *midsegment* of a triangle is a segment that joins the midpoints of two sides of the triangle. Together, the three midsegments of a triangle form the sides of the *midsegment triangle*. Using the Triangle Midsegment Theorem and the SSS Triangle Congruence Theorem, it can be proven that the four small triangles formed by the midsegments are congruent. Since the four triangles together form the original triangle, each small triangle has one-fourth of its area.

EXPLORE

Investigating Midsegments of a Triangle

INTEGRATE TECHNOLOGY

Students have the option of completing the midsegments activity either in the book or online.

QUESTIONING STRATEGIES

? How are the length of the midsegment and the third side of the triangle related? The midsegment is one-half the length of the third side.

EXPLAIN 1

Describing Midsegments on a Coordinate Grid

INTEGRATE MATHEMATICAL PRACTICES

Focus on Math Connections

MP.1 Remind students that two lines with equal slopes are parallel and that the slope of a segment is the difference of its y-coordinates divided by the difference of its x-coordinates. Also remind them to subtract the coordinates in the same order.

© Houghton Mifflin Harcourt Publishing Company

? To which side of the triangle does the midsegment appear to be parallel? **the side that does not contain the endpoints of the midsegment**

? How do you find the midsegments of a triangle in the coordinate plane? **Use the Midpoint Formula to find the coordinates of the midpoint of two sides of the triangle. Plot the midpoints and connect them to form a midsegment.**

? What are some ways you can show that two line segments are parallel when using the Triangle Midsegment Theorem in a coordinate plane? **Sample answer: Show that the lines have the same slope.**

B The vertices of $\triangle LMN$ are $L(2, 7)$, $M(10, 9)$, and $N(8, 1)$. P is the midpoint of $\overline{LM}$, and Q is the midpoint of $\overline{MN}$.

Show that $\overline{PQ} \parallel \overline{LN}$ and $PQ = \frac{1}{2}LN$. Sketch $\overline{PQ}$.

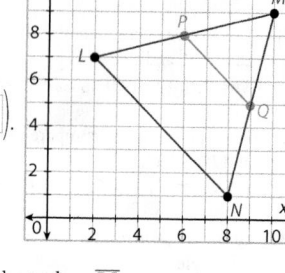

Step 1 The midpoint of $\overline{LM} = \left(\dfrac{2 + \boxed{10}}{2}, \dfrac{7 + \boxed{9}}{2} \right) = \left(\boxed{6}, \boxed{8} \right)$. Graph and label this point P.

The midpoint of $\overline{NM} = \left(\dfrac{\boxed{8} + \boxed{10}}{2}, \dfrac{\boxed{1} + \boxed{9}}{2} \right)$

$= \left(\boxed{9}, \boxed{5} \right)$. Graph and label this point Q. Use a straightedge to draw $\overline{PQ}$.

Step 2 Slope of $\overline{PQ} = \dfrac{5 - 8}{9 - 6} = \boxed{-1}$ Slope of $\overline{LN} = \dfrac{1 - 7}{8 - 2} = \boxed{-1}$

Since the slopes are the same, $\overline{PQ}$ and $\overline{LN}$ are **parallel**.

Step 3 $PQ = \sqrt{\left(\boxed{9} - 6 \right)^2 + (5 - 8)^2} = \sqrt{\boxed{9} + 9} = \sqrt{18} = 3\sqrt{2}$

$LN = \sqrt{\left(\boxed{8} - \boxed{2} \right)^2 + \left(\boxed{1} - \boxed{7} \right)^2} = \sqrt{\boxed{36} + \boxed{36}} = \sqrt{\boxed{72}} = 6\sqrt{2}$

Since $\boxed{3}\sqrt{\boxed{2}} = \frac{1}{2}\left(\boxed{6}\sqrt{\boxed{2}} \right)$, $\boxed{PQ} = \frac{1}{2}\boxed{LN}$.

The length of $\overline{PQ}$ is **half** the length of $\overline{LN}$.

Your Turn

4. The vertices of $\triangle XYZ$ are $X(3, 7)$, $Y(9, 11)$, and $Z(7, 1)$. U is the midpoint of $\overline{XY}$, and W is the midpoint of $\overline{XZ}$. Show that $\overline{UW} \parallel \overline{YZ}$ and $UW = \frac{1}{2}YZ$. Sketch $\triangle XYZ$ and $\overline{UW}$.

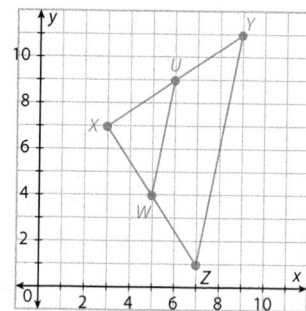

$U = \left(\dfrac{3 + 9}{2}, \dfrac{7 + 11}{2} \right) = (6, 9);$

$W = \left(\dfrac{3 + 7}{2}, \dfrac{7 + 1}{2} \right)$

$= (5, 4);$

slope of $\overline{UW} = \dfrac{4 - 9}{5 - 6} = 5;$ slope of $\overline{YZ} = \dfrac{1 - 11}{7 - 9} = 5;$

Since the slopes are the same, $\overline{UW} \parallel \overline{YZ}$.

$UW = \sqrt{(5 - 6)^2 + (4 - 9)^2} = \sqrt{26};$

$YZ = \sqrt{(7 - 9)^2 + (1 - 11)^2} = 2\sqrt{26};$

So $UW = \frac{1}{2}YZ$.

COLLABORATIVE LEARNING

Small Group Activity

Have one student in each group use geometry software to construct the midsegment of a triangle. Ask another student in the group to measure the midsegment and the sides of the triangle and make a conjecture about the relationship of the two measures. Ask a third student to measure the angles to make a conjecture about midsegment and the third side of the triangle. Have the fourth student drag the vertices of the triangle to verify the conjectures made by the other students: the midsegments are half the measure of the third side and are parallel to the third side.

Using the Triangle Midsegment Theorem

The relationship you have been exploring is true for the three midsegments of every triangle.

> **Triangle Midsegment Theorem**
>
> The segment joining the midpoints of two sides of a triangle is parallel to the third side, and its length is half the length of that side.

You explored this theorem in Example 1 and will be proving it later in this course.

Example 2 Use triangle *RST*.

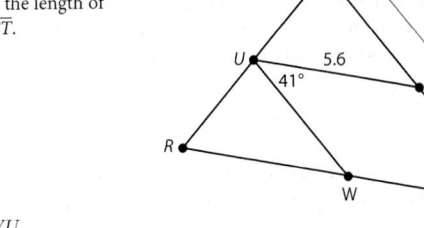

(A) Find *UW*.

By the Triangle Midsegment Theorem, the length of midsegment $\overline{UW}$ is half the length of $\overline{ST}$.

$UW = \frac{1}{2}ST$

$UW = \frac{1}{2}(10.2)$

$UW = 5.1$

(B) Complete the reasoning to find m ∠*SVU*.

△Midsegment Thm.	$\overline{UW}\|\overline{ST}$
Alt. Int. Angles Thm.	m ∠*SVU* = m ∠*VUW*
Substitute $\underline{41°}$ for $\underline{m∠VUW}$	m ∠*SVU* = $\boxed{41°}$

Reflect

5. How do you know to which side of a triangle a midsegment is parallel?
   Since a midsegment connects the midpoints of two sides, it is parallel to the third side.

Your Turn

6. Find *JL*, *PM*, and m ∠*MLK*.
   $JL = 2\,(PN) = 2(39) = 78; PM = \frac{1}{2}KL = \frac{1}{2}(95) = 47.5;$
   m ∠*MLK* = m ∠*JMP* = 105°

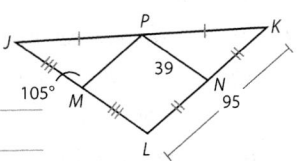

Elaborate

7. **Discussion** Explain why $\overline{XY}$ is NOT a midsegment of the triangle.
   The endpoints of $\overline{XY}$ are not midpoints of the sides of
   the triangle.

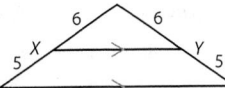

EXPLAIN 2

Using the Triangle Midsegment Theorem

INTEGRATE MATHEMATICAL PRACTICES
Focus on Math Connections

MP.1 Point out that if the midsegments of a triangle are found, then the Triangle Midsegment Theorem can be used to state that the midsegment is half the length of the third side and is parallel to the third side. Explain that the theorem gives a way to indirectly find the side lengths of a triangle, and that it gives similar triangles, which will be studied in Unit 4.

QUESTIONING STRATEGIES

? In the example, how do you know that you can use the Triangle Midsegment Theorem? The midsegment of a triangle was found, so the Triangle Midsegment Theorem applies.

AVOID COMMON ERRORS

Sometimes students write the incorrect algebraic expressions to indirectly find the lengths of segments in triangles when using the Triangle Midsegment Theorem. Have these students use the theorem to write the relationships among the segments before they substitute algebraic expressions for the segments. The correct expressions should give the correct equations to solve for the lengths.

DIFFERENTIATE INSTRUCTION

Modeling

Have students cut a large scalene triangle from heavy paper. Have them construct the midpoints of two sides and connect them, forming a *midsegment*. Then have them cut along this segment to form a triangle and a trapezoid. Have them rotate the small triangle and place it next to the trapezoid to form a parallelogram. Ask students to make conjectures about the relationship between the midsegment and the base of the triangle.

ELABORATE

QUESTIONING STRATEGIES

? How could you use a property of midsegments to find a measurement for something that is difficult to measure directly? Sample answer: If you cannot measure directly across something like a pond, you can construct a triangle around it so that the distance you want to measure is a midsegment of the triangle. Then you can measure the third side of the triangle and divide it by 2 to find the measure you are looking for.

SUMMARIZE THE LESSON

? Have students fill out a chart to summarize what they know about triangle midsegments. Sample:

Triangle Midsegment	
Definition	A line segment that connects the midpoints of two sides of the triangle
Properties	Half the length of the third side; parallel to the third side
Example	Answers will vary.
Non-example	Answers will vary.

---

8. **Essential Question Check–In** Explain how the perimeter of △DEF compares to that of △ABC.

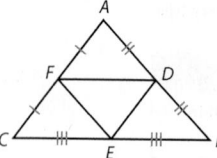

The perimeter of △DEF = $\frac{1}{2}$ (perimeter of △ABC).

⭐ Evaluate: Homework and Practice

• Online Homework
• Hints and Help
• Extra Practice

1. Use a compass and a ruler or geometry software to construct an obtuse triangle. Label the vertices. Choose two sides and construct the midpoint of each side; then label and draw the midsegment. Describe the relationship between the length of the midsegment and the length of the third side.

   Drawings will vary. Students should conclude that the midsegment is half the length of the third side.

2. The vertices of △WXY are $W(-4, 1)$, $X(0, -5)$, and $Y(4, -1)$. A is the midpoint of $\overline{WY}$, and B is the midpoint of $\overline{XY}$. Show that $\overline{AB} \parallel \overline{WX}$ and $AB = \frac{1}{2}WX$.

   The coordinates of A and B are $(0, 0)$ and $(2, -3)$. The slope of $\overline{AB}$ and $\overline{WX}$ is $-\frac{3}{2}$, so the lines are parallel. The length of $\overline{AB}$ is $\sqrt{13}$ and the length of $\overline{WX}$ is $2\sqrt{13}$, so $AB = \frac{1}{2}WX$.

3. The vertices of △FGH are $F(-1, 1)$, $G(-5, 4)$, and $H(-5, -2)$. X is the midpoint of $\overline{FG}$, and Y is the midpoint of $\overline{FH}$. Show that $\overline{XY} \parallel \overline{GH}$ and $XY = \frac{1}{2}GH$.

   The coordinates of X and Y are $\left(-3, \frac{5}{2}\right)$ and $\left(-3, -\frac{1}{2}\right)$. The slope of $\overline{XY}$ and $\overline{GH}$ is undefined, so the lines are parallel. The length of $\overline{XY}$ is 3 and the length of $\overline{GH}$ is 6, so $XY = \frac{1}{2}GH$.

4. One of the vertices of △PQR is $P(3, -2)$. The midpoint of $\overline{PQ}$ is $M(4, 0)$. The midpoint of $\overline{QR}$ is $N(7, 1)$. Show that $\overline{MN} \parallel \overline{PR}$ and $MN = \frac{1}{2}PR$.

   $\frac{3+x}{2} = 4$, So $x = 5$; $\frac{-2+y}{2} = 0$, So $y = 2$.

   The coordinates of Q are $(5, 2)$.

   $\frac{5+x}{2} = 7$, So $x = 9$; $\frac{2+y}{2} = 1$, So $y = 0$.

   The coordinates of R are $(9, 0)$.

   The slope of $\overline{MN}$ and $\overline{PR}$ is $\frac{1}{3}$, so the lines are parallel. The length of $\overline{MN}$ is $\sqrt{10}$ and the length of $\overline{PR}$ is $2\sqrt{10}$, so $MN = \frac{1}{2}PR$.

LANGUAGE SUPPORT 🔲EL

Communicate Math

Divide students into pairs. Provide each pair with pictures of triangles with segments joining two sides. Have one student explain why a drawing does or does not show a midsegment. Encourage the use of the words *parallel* and *midpoint*. Have students measure the distance between the segment and the base at different intervals to see if the segment and the base are parallel, and to measure the sides joined by the segment, to see if the segment's endpoints are the midpoints of the sides. Students switch roles and repeat the process.

5. One of the vertices of $\triangle ABC$ is $A(0, 0)$. The midpoint of $\overline{AC}$ is $J\left(\frac{3}{2}, 2\right)$. The midpoint of $\overline{BC}$ is $K(4, 2)$. Show that $\overline{JK} \parallel \overline{BA}$ and $JK = \frac{1}{2} BA$.

$\dfrac{0 + x}{2} = \dfrac{3}{2}$ $\quad$ $\dfrac{0 + y}{2} = 2$ $\qquad$ So, the coordinates of C are $(3, 4)$.

$\quad x = 3 \qquad y = 4$

Use the midpoint formula to find the coordinates of $B\,(x, y)$.

$\dfrac{3 + x}{2} = 4$ $\qquad$ $\dfrac{4 + y}{2} = 2$

$3 + x = 8 \qquad 4 + y = 4$

$\quad x = 5 \qquad\qquad y = 0$

So, the coordinates of B are $(5, 0)$.

The slope of $\overline{JK}$ and $\overline{BA}$ is 0, so the lines are parallel. The length of $\overline{JK}$ is $\dfrac{5}{2}$ and the length of $\overline{BA}$ is 5, so $JK = \frac{1}{2} BA$.

Find each measure.

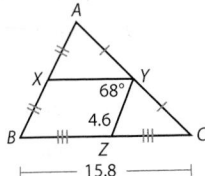

6. XY
$XY = \dfrac{1}{2} BC = \dfrac{1}{2}(15.8) = 7.9$

7. BZ
$BZ = \dfrac{1}{2} BC = \dfrac{1}{2}(15.8) = 7.9$

8. AX
Since $AX = \dfrac{1}{2} AB$, find AB first.

$AB = 2(YZ) = 2(4.6) = 9.2$

$AX = \dfrac{1}{2} AB = \dfrac{1}{2}(9.2) = 4.6$

9. $m\angle YZC$
$\angle YZC$ and $\angle XYZ$ are alternate interior angles, so they are congruent.

$m\angle YZC = 68°$

10. $m\angle BXY$
$m\angle BXY + m\angle ZYX = 180°$ (same-side interior angles)

$\quad m\angle BXY + 68° = 180°$

$\qquad m\angle BXY = 112°$

© Houghton Mifflin Harcourt Publishing Company

EVALUATE

ASSIGNMENT GUIDE

Concepts and Skills	Practice
Explore Investigating Midsegments of a Triangle	Exercises 1–3
Example 1 Describing Midsegments on a Coordinate Grid	Exercises 4–5
Example 2 Using the Triangle Midsegment Theorem	Exercises 6–15

INTEGRATE MATHEMATICAL PRACTICES

Focus on Math Connections

MP.1 Remind students of the key concepts they need to do the exercises. Define *midsegment*. Make a sketch on the board showing students how to draw a midsegment, and point out that every triangle has three midsegments. Add that, in this lesson, students will primarily work with one midsegment at a time.

Exercise	Depth of Knowledge (D.O.K.)	COMMON CORE	Mathematical Practices
1–15	**2** Skills/Concepts		**MP.6** Precision
16–21	**2** Skills/Concepts		**MP.2** Reasoning
22	**3** Strategic Thinking	H.O.T.	**MP.4** Modeling
23	**3** Strategic Thinking	H.O.T.	**MP.6** Precision
24	**3** Strategic Thinking	H.O.T.	**MP.4** Modeling

INTEGRATE MATHEMATICAL PRACTICES

Focus on Communication

MP.3 Discuss each of the following statements as a class. Have students explain how the Triangle Midsegment Theorem justifies their responses.

1. A triangle has three midsegments.

2. The midsegments form a triangle with a perimeter equal to one-half the perimeter of the original triangle.

3. The midsegments form a triangle with area equal to one-fourth the area of the original triangle.

Algebra Find the value of n in each triangle.

11.

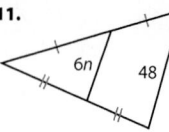

$$6n = \frac{1}{2}(48)$$
$$6n = 24$$
$$n = 4$$

12.

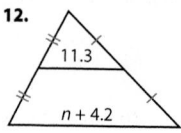

$$2(11.3) = n + 4.2$$
$$22.6 = n + 4.2$$
$$18.4 = n$$

13.

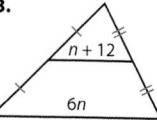

$$6n = 2(n + 12)$$
$$6n = 2n + 24$$
$$4n = 24$$
$$n = 6$$

14.

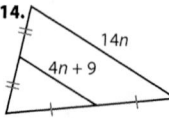

$$14n = 2(4n + 9)$$
$$14n = 8n + 18$$
$$6n = 18$$
$$n = 3$$

15. Line segment XY is a midsegment of $\triangle MNP$. Determine whether each of the following statements is true or false. Select the correct answer for each lettered part.

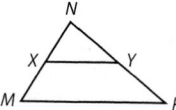

a. $MP = 2XY$ ● True   ○ False

b. $MP = \frac{1}{2}XY$ ○ True   ● False

c. $MX = XN$ ● True   ○ False

d. $MX = \frac{1}{2}NX$ ○ True   ● False

e. $NX = YN$ ○ True   ● False

f. $XY = \frac{1}{2}MP$ ● True   ○ False

16. What do you know about two of the midsegments in an isosceles triangle? Explain.

Two of the midsegments will be congruent because their lengths are $\frac{1}{2}$ the length of congruent sides.

17. Suppose you know that the midsegments of a triangle are all 2 units long. What kind of triangle is it?

an equilateral triangle with sides 4 units long

18. In $\triangle ABC$, $m\angle A = 80°$, $m\angle B = 60°$, $m\angle C = 40°$. The midpoints of $\overline{AB}$, $\overline{BC}$, and $\overline{AC}$ are D, E, and F, respectively. Which midsegment will be the longest? Explain how you know.

$\overline{BC}$ **is the longest side because it is opposite the largest angle, so midsegment $\overline{DF}$ will be**

the longest.

19. Draw Conclusions Carl's Construction is building a pavilion with an A-frame roof at the local park. Carl has constructed two triangular frames for the front and back of the roof, similar to $\triangle ABC$ in the diagram. The base of each frame, represented by $\overline{AC}$, is 36 feet long. He needs to insert a crossbar connecting the midpoints of $\overline{AB}$ and $\overline{BC}$, for each frame. He has 32 feet of timber left after constructing the front and back triangles. Is this enough to construct the crossbar for both the front and back frame? Explain.

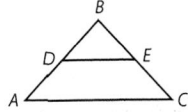

No. If $\overline{AC}$ is 36 feet long, $\overline{DE}$ is 18 feet long. Because he needs to insert two crossbars, he

needs 2 × 18, or 36, feet of timber. He needs 4 more feet.

20. Critique Reasoning Line segment AB is a midsegment in $\triangle PQR$. Kayla calculated the length of $\overline{AB}$. Her work is shown below. Is her answer correct? If not, explain her error.

$2(QR) = AB$
$2(25) = AB$
$50 = AB$.

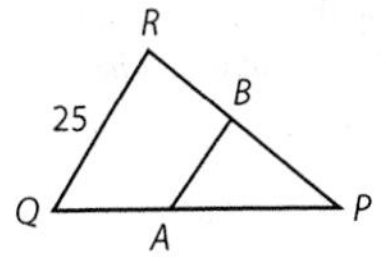

No, it is not correct. The equation should have $\frac{1}{2}QR$ on the left instead of $2(QR)$.

21. Using words or diagrams, tell how to construct a midsegment using only a straightedge and a compass.

Possible answer: First construct a triangle with a straightedge. Next use the compass to find the midpoint of two sides of the triangle. Finally, connect the two midpoints to create a midsegment parallel to the third side.

© Houghton Mifflin Harcourt Publishing Company · Image Credits: ©Polianskyi Igor/Shutterstock

Ask students to discuss with a partner how to locate the midsegments of a triangle drawn in the coordinate plane. Have them use the slope formula or distance formula and the Triangle Midsegment Theorem to verify that the midsegments are equal to one-half the third side and are parallel to the third side. Have them draw examples to justify their reasoning.

AVOID COMMON ERRORS

When using triangles in the coordinate plane, some students may assume that the Triangle Midsegment Theorem applies only to acute, scalene triangles. Have students work in groups to draw other types of triangles in the coordinate plane and use algebraic expressions to write the triangle relationships that apply to these triangles.

JOURNAL

Have students explain how to find the length of a midsegment when given the length of the parallel side.

22. Multi–Step A city park will be shaped like a right triangle, and there will be two pathways for pedestrians, shown by $\overline{VT}$ and $\overline{VW}$ in the diagram. The park planner only wrote two lengths on his sketch as shown. Based on the diagram, what will be the lengths of the two pathways?

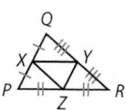

$$VW = \frac{1}{2}(XZ) = \frac{1}{2}(24) = 12$$

$$24^2 + (YZ)^2 = 30^2 \text{ (Pyth. Thm.)}$$

$$VT = \frac{1}{2}(YZ) = \frac{1}{2}(18) = 9$$

$$576 + (YZ)^2 = 900$$

$$VW = 12 \text{ yd}; VT = 9 \text{ yd}$$

$$(YZ)^2 = 324$$

$$YZ = 18$$

23. Communicate Mathematical Ideas $\triangle XYZ$ is the midsegment of $\triangle PQR$. Write a congruence statement involving all four of the smaller triangles. What is the relationship between the area of $\triangle XYZ$ and $\triangle PQR$?

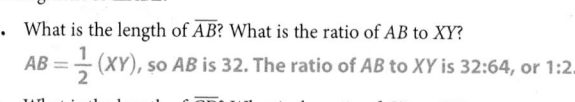

$$\triangle QXY \cong \triangle XPZ \cong \triangle YZR \cong \triangle ZYX;$$

area of $\triangle XYZ = \frac{1}{4}$ area of $\triangle PQR$

24. Copy the diagram shown. $\overline{AB}$ is a midsegment of $\triangle XYZ$. $\overline{CD}$ is a midsegment of $\triangle ABZ$.

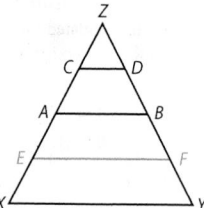

a. What is the length of $\overline{AB}$? What is the ratio of AB to XY?

$$AB = \frac{1}{2}(XY), \text{ so } AB \text{ is 32. The ratio of } AB \text{ to } XY \text{ is 32:64, or 1:2.}$$

b. What is the length of $\overline{CD}$? What is the ratio of CD to XY?

$$CD = \frac{1}{2}(AB), \text{ so } CD \text{ is 16. The ratio of } CD \text{ to } XY \text{ is 16:64, or 1:4.}$$

c. Draw $\overline{EF}$ such that points E and F are $\frac{3}{4}$ the distance from point Z to points X and Y. What is the ratio of EF to XY? What is the length of $\overline{EF}$?

$$EF = \frac{3}{4}(XY) = \frac{3}{4}(64) = 48$$

The length of $\overline{EF}$ is 48, so the ratio of EF to XY is 48:64, or 3:4.

d. Make a conjecture about the length of non-midsegments when compared to the length of the third side.

The length of the non-midsegment compared to the length of the third side is the same as the ratio of the distance of the segment from the vertex opposite the third side compared to the whole triangle.

Lesson Performance Task

The figure shows part of a common roof design using very strong and stable triangular *trusses*. Points B, C, D, F, G, and I are midpoints of $\overline{AC}$, $\overline{AE}$, $\overline{CE}$, $\overline{GE}$, $\overline{HE}$ and $\overline{AH}$ respectively. What is the total length of all the stabilizing bars inside $\triangle AEH$? Explain how you found the answer.

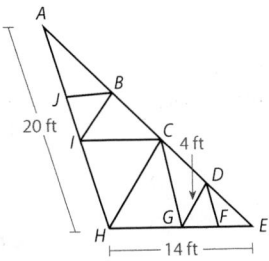

By the Midsegment Theorem, $IC = 7$ ft and $CG = 10$ ft because they are, respectively, half of HE and AH. $CH = 8$ ft because it is twice DG. $DF = 5$ ft, $JB = 3.5$ ft, and $IB = 4$ ft because they are, respectively, half of CG, IC, and HC.

Total length: $JB + IB + IC + CH + CG + DG + DF = 3.5 + 4 + 7 + 8 + 10 + 4 + 5 = 41.5$ ft

© Houghton Mifflin Harcourt Publishing Company

AVOID COMMON ERRORS

Students may mistakenly assume that because B, C, and D divide $\overline{AE}$ into four congruent segments, G and F must divide $\overline{HE}$ into three congruent segments, and that J and I divide $\overline{AH}$ into three congruent segments. Point out that because G is the midpoint of $\overline{HE}$, GF and FE are each only half of HG. Similarly, because I is the midpoint of $\overline{AH}$, AJ and JI are each only half of IH.

INTEGRATE MATHEMATICAL PRACTICES
Focus on Critical Thinking

MP.3 On the roof truss diagrammed below, D, E, and F are the midpoints of, respectively, $\overline{AC}$, $\overline{AB}$, and $\overline{CB}$.

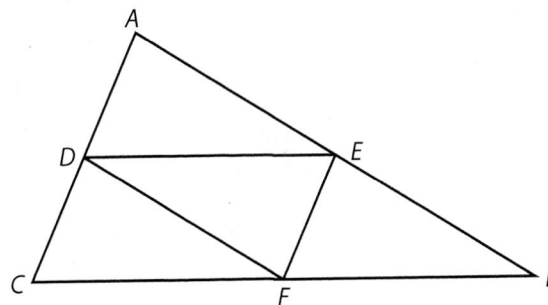

Compare the perimeter and area of $\triangle ABC$ with those of $\triangle DEF$. Explain how you found your answers.

Students can use the Midsegment Theorem and the facts that $\overline{DE}$, $\overline{EF}$, and $\overline{DF}$ are parallel to and half the length of, respectively, $\overline{CB}$, $\overline{AC}$, and $\overline{AB}$ to establish that (1) the perimeter of $\triangle DEF$ is half that of $\triangle ABC$, and (2) the four small triangles in the diagram are congruent, which means that the area of $\triangle DEF$ is one-fourth that of $\triangle ABC$.

EXTENSION ACTIVITY

Have students research tri-bearing roof trusses. Among topics they can report on:

- the definition of tri-bearing roof truss;
- the design of such a truss, together with a drawing and typical measurements;
- the meaning of the term *tri-bearing*;
- a description of the relationship between tri-bearing roof trusses and the Midsegment Theorem.

Scoring Rubric

2 points: Student correctly solves the problem and explains his/her reasoning.

1 point: Student shows good understanding of the problem but does not fully solve or explain.

0 points: Student does not demonstrate understanding of the problem.

Study Guide Review

ASSESSMENT AND INTERVENTION

Assign or customize module reviews.

Special Segments in Triangles

MODULE **8**

Essential Question: How can you use special segments in triangles to solve real-world problems?

KEY EXAMPLE *(Lesson 8.1)*

Find the coordinates of the circumcenter of the triangle.

Coordinates: $A(-2, -2)$, $B(2, 3)$, $C(2, -2)$

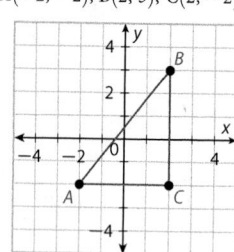

$M_{\overline{AC}} = \left(\dfrac{-2 + 2}{2}, \dfrac{-2 + (-2)}{2} \right) = (0, -2)$ Midpoint of $\overline{AC}$

$\overline{AC}$ is horizontal, so the line perpendicular to it is vertical and passes through the midpoint. The equation is $x = 0$.

Find the equation of the line perpendicular to $\overline{AC}$.

$M_{\overline{BC}} = \left(\dfrac{2 + 2}{2}, \dfrac{3 + (-2)}{2} \right) = \left(2, \dfrac{1}{2} \right)$ Midpoint of $\overline{BC}$

$\overline{BC}$ is vertical, so the line perpendicular to it is horizontal and passes through the midpoint. The equation is $y = \dfrac{1}{2}$.

Find the equation of the line perpendicular to $\overline{BC}$.

The coordinates of the circumcenter are $\left(0, \dfrac{1}{2} \right)$.

KEY EXAMPLE *(Lesson 8.2)*

$\overline{AP}$ and $\overline{CP}$ are angle bisectors of $\triangle ABC$, where P is the incenter of the triangle. The measure of $\angle BAC$ is 56°. The measure of $\angle BCA$ is 42°.

Find the measures of $\angle PAC$ and $\angle PCB$.

Since $\overline{AP}$ is an angle bisector of $\angle BAC$, the measures of $\angle PAC$ and $\angle PAB$ are equal. Since the measure of $\angle BAC$ is 56°, the measure of $\angle PAC$ is 28°.

Since $\overline{CP}$ is an angle bisector of $\angle BCA$, the measures of $\angle PCB$ and $\angle PCA$ are equal. Since the measure of $\angle BCA$ is 42°, the measure of $\angle PCB$ is 21°.

Key Vocabulary

altitude of a triangle
  (altura de un triángulo)
centroid of a triangle
  (centroide de un triángulo)
circumcenter of a triangle
  (circuncentro de un triángulo)
circumscribed circle
  (círculo circunscrito)
concurrent *(concurrente)*
distance from a point to a line
  (distancia desde un punto hasta una línea)
equidistant *(equidistante)*
incenter of a triangle
  (incentro de un triángulo)
inscribed circle
  (círculo inscrito)
median of a triangle
  (mediana de un triángulo)
midsegment of a triangle
  (segmento medio de un triángulo)
orthocenter of a triangle
  (ortocentro de un triángulo)
point of concurrency
  (punto de concurrencia)

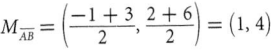

KEY EXAMPLE   *(Lesson 8.3)*

Find the coordinates of the centroid of the triangle.

Coordinates: $A(-1, 2)$, $B(3, 6)$, $C(4, 2)$

Centroid:

$M_{\overline{AB}} = \left(\dfrac{-1+3}{2}, \dfrac{2+6}{2}\right) = (1, 4)$ Midpoint of $\overline{AB}$

$m_{\overline{MC}} = \dfrac{2-4}{4-1} = -\dfrac{2}{3}$ Slope of line passing through midpoint and C

$y - 4 = -\dfrac{2}{3}(x - 1)$

$y = -\dfrac{2}{3}x + \dfrac{14}{3}$ Find the equation of the median from C to $\overline{AB}$.

$M_{\overline{AC}} = \left(\dfrac{-1+4}{2}, \dfrac{2+2}{2}\right) = \left(\dfrac{3}{2}, 2\right)$ Midpoint of $\overline{AC}$

$m_{\overline{MB}} = \dfrac{6-2}{3-\dfrac{3}{2}} = \dfrac{8}{3}$ Slope of line passing through midpoint and B

$y - 6 = \dfrac{8}{3}(x - 3)$

$y = \dfrac{8}{3}x - 2$ Find the equation of the median $\overline{AC}$.

$-\dfrac{2}{3}x + \dfrac{14}{3} = \dfrac{8}{3}x - 2$ Set the equations equal to each other to find the intersection.

$x = 2$

$y = \dfrac{8}{3}(2) - 2 = \dfrac{10}{3}$

The coordinates of the centroid are $\left(2, \dfrac{10}{3}\right)$.

KEY EXAMPLE   *(Lesson 8.4)*

$\overline{DE}$ **is a midsegment of** $\triangle ABC$**, and it is parallel to** $\overline{AC}$**. If the length of** $\overline{BD}$ **is 5 and the length of** $\overline{EC}$ **is 3, find the lengths of** $\overline{DA}$ **and** $\overline{BE}$**.**

$\overline{DE}$ is a midsegment of $\triangle ABC$, so $\overline{BD}$ is half of $\overline{BA}$. $\overline{DA}$ is the other half of $\overline{BA}$. So, $DA = BD = 5$.

$\overline{DE}$ is a midsegment of $\triangle ABC$, so $\overline{EC}$ is half of $\overline{BC}$. $\overline{BE}$ is the other half of $\overline{BC}$. So, $EC = BE = 3$.

MODULE PERFORMANCE TASK

Mathematical Practices: MP.1, MP.2, MP.3, MP.4, MP.6
G-GPE.B.4, G-GPE.B.5

SUPPORTING STUDENT REASONING

Students should begin this problem by focusing on what information they will need. Here are some issues they might bring up.

- **How to find the midpoints of the Texas Triangle region bounded by Dallas, Houston, and San Antonio:** Students should use the coordinates of the triangle to find the midpoints.

- **Which center of a triangle would be the best to use:** Students should use the coordinates of the midpoints and vertices to locate the centroid, circumcenter, and orthocenter of the given triangle. Then they should analyze their positions in relation to Bryan, TX.

- **If the distance to Bryan is the only important consideration in choosing a center:** Students can argue for the circumcenter, since it is approximately equal driving distance to the triangle vertices, or for the centroid, since it seems to be closest to the physical center of the triangle.

Find the coordinates of the points. *(Lesson 8.1)*

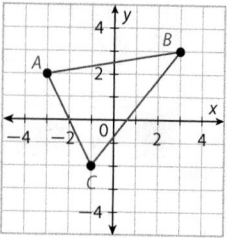

1. Circumcenter $\left(\dfrac{3}{13}, \dfrac{29}{26}\right)$

$\overline{AP}$, $\overline{BP}$, and $\overline{CP}$ are angle bisectors of $\triangle ABC$, where P is the incenter of the triangle. The measure of $\angle BAC$ is 24°. The measure of $\angle BCA$ is 91°. Find the measures of the angles. *(Lesson 8.2)*

2. $\angle BAP$ 12°   3. $\angle ABP$ 32.5°   4. $\angle BCP$ 45.5°

Find the coordinates of the points. *(Lesson 8.3)*

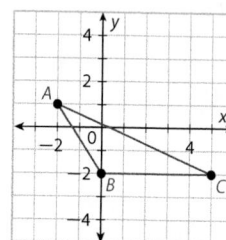

5. Centroid $(1, -1)$

6. Orthocenter $\left(-2, -\dfrac{20}{3}\right)$

$\overline{DE}$, $\overline{DF}$, and $\overline{EF}$ are midsegments of $\triangle ABC$. Find the lengths of the segments. *(Lesson 8.4)*

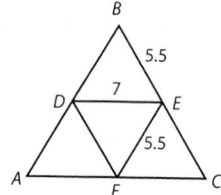

7. $\overline{BD}$ 5.5

8. $\overline{EC}$ 5.5

9. $\overline{AF}$ 7

SCAFFOLDING SUPPORT

- Remind students that the circumcenter of a triangle is the point of intersection of the perpendicular bisectors of the three sides; the orthocenter is the point of intersection of the altitudes to each of the three sides; and the centroid is the point of intersection of the medians.

- Students can approximate the three centers using compass and straightedge. If they choose this method, you may wish to review the various constructions they use.

- If students choose to solve the problem using algebra, they may need to be reminded that the slope of a line perpendicular to a given line is the negative reciprocal of the slope of the given line.

MODULE PERFORMANCE TASK
What's the Center of the Triangle?

The Texas Triangle Park in Bryan, Texas bills itself as being at the center of the Texas Triangle region. That is the region with the cities of Dallas, Houston, and San Antonio at the vertices of the triangle. The diagram shows a simple representation of the region with San Antonio located at the origin. The point B also gives you coordinates for the location of Bryan. So just how close is Bryan to the center of this triangle?

Before you tackle this problem, decide what you think is the best measure of the triangle's center in this context—the centroid, circumcenter, or orthocenter? Be prepared to support your decision.

Start by listing in the space below the information you will need to solve the problem. Then use your own paper to complete the task. Be sure to write down all your data and assumptions. Then use graphs, numbers, words, or algebra to explain how you reached your conclusion.

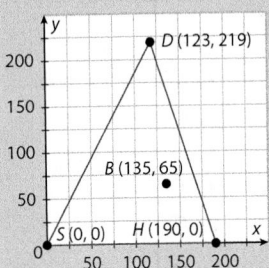

SAMPLE SOLUTION

Start by finding the equation of each side of the triangle, using the fact that you know two points on each side.

To find the perpendicular bisectors of the three sides of the triangle, find the midpoints of the three sides: (95, 0), (156.5, 109.5), (61.5, 109.5). Then, for each midpoint, find the equation of the line that passes through that point and has a slope that is the negative reciprocal of the slope of that side of the triangle. When you know the three equations, solve the system given by one pair of them. The solution is the circumcenter of the triangle, (95, 90.7).

To find the altitudes, find the equation of each line that passes through a vertex of the triangle and is perpendicular to the opposite side. The slope of each such line is the negative reciprocal of the slope of the side to which the altitude is being drawn. When you know the three equations, solve the system given by one pair of them. The solution is the orthocenter of the triangle, (123, 37.6).

To find the centroid, find the equation of each line that joins a vertex and the midpoint of the opposite side. When you know the three equations, solve the system given by one pair of them. The solution is the centroid of the triangle, (104.3, 73).

Use the Distance Formula to find the distance of each center from Bryan. Of the three centers, the orthocenter is closest to Bryan, 29.9 miles distant.

DISCUSSION OPPORTUNITIES
- Are there any other ways to describe what a "center" for this region might be? (for example, population)
- Why is knowing the distance from Bryan to the chosen center of the Texas Triangle region helpful?

Assessment Rubric

2 points: Student correctly solves the problem and explains his/her reasoning.

1 point: Student shows good understanding of the problem but does not fully solve or explain.

0 points: Student does not demonstrate understanding of the problem.

Ready to Go On?

ASSESS MASTERY

Use the assessment on this page to determine if students have mastered the concepts and standards covered in this module.

ASSESSMENT AND INTERVENTION

Access Ready to Go On? assessment online, and receive instant scoring, feedback, and customized intervention or enrichment.

ADDITIONAL RESOURCES

Response to Intervention Resources

- Reteach Worksheets

Differentiated Instruction Resources

- Reading Strategies **EL**
- Success for English Learners **EL**
- Challenge Worksheets

Assessment Resources

- Leveled Module Quizzes

409 Module 8

(Ready) to Go On?

Special Segments in Triangles

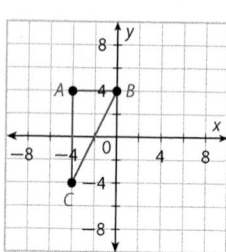

Segments $\overline{DE}$, $\overline{EF}$, and $\overline{DF}$ are midsegments of $\triangle ABC$
Find the lengths of the indicated segments.

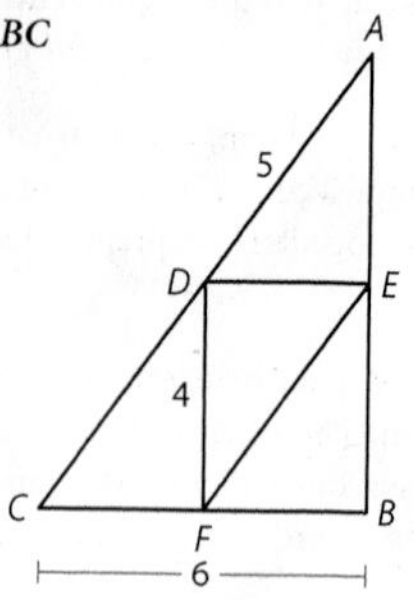

1. $\overline{AC}$ __10__
2. $\overline{CF}$ __3__
3. $\overline{DE}$ __3__
4. $\overline{AE}$ __4__
5. $\overline{AB}$ __8__
6. $\overline{EF}$ __5__

Locate centroids, circumcenters, and incenters.

7. Find the points of concurrency of $\triangle ABC$.

   a. Determine the coordinates of the centroid of $\triangle ABC$.

   $$\left(-\frac{8}{3}, \frac{4}{3}\right)$$

   b. Determine the coordinates of the circumcenter of $\triangle ABC$.

   $$(-2, 0)$$

   c. In what quadrant or on what axis does the incenter of $\triangle ABC$ lie?

   Quadrant II

ESSENTIAL QUESTION

8. Describe a triangle for which the centroid, circumcenter, incenter, and orthocenter are the same point. What features of this triangle cause these points to be concurrent and why?

   An equilateral/equiangular triangle; since the triangle's sides are congruent, all medians, perpendicular bisectors, angle bisectors, and altitudes are segments that connect a vertex to the midpoint of the opposite side. So, they all intersect at the same point.

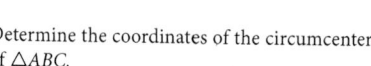

COMMON CORE Common Core Standards

Lesson	Items	Content Standards	Mathematical Practices
8.4	1	G-CO.C.10	MP.7
8.4	2	G-CO.C.10	MP.7
8.4	3	G-CO.C.10	MP.7
8.4	4	G-CO.C.10	MP.7
8.4	5	G-CO.C.10	MP.7
8.4	6	G-CO.C.10	MP.7
8.1	7	G-CO.C.10, G-CO.D.12, G-GPE.B.4	MP.7

MODULE 8
MIXED REVIEW

Assessment Readiness

1. Given △ABC and altitude $\overline{AH}$, decide whether each statement is necessarily true about △AHC. Select Yes or No for A–C.

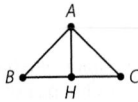

   A. $\overline{AH} < \overline{HC}$ ○ Yes   ● No
   B. $\overline{AH} < \overline{AC}$ ● Yes   ○ No
   C. △AHC ≅ △AHB   ○ Yes   ● No

2. $\overline{YZ}$ is the image of $\overline{YX}$ after a reflection across line M. Choose True or False for each statement.

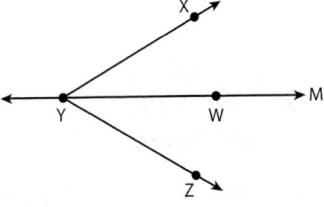

   A. M is the angle bisector of ∠XYZ.   ● Yes   ○ No
   B. ∠XYZ is acute.   ○ Yes   ● No
   C. M is horizontal.   ○ Yes   ● No

3. Given △ABC is equilateral, what can be determined about its centroid and circumcenter?

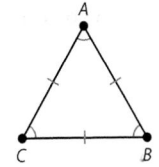

   They are at the same point inside of the triangle.

4. $\overline{DE}$, $\overline{EF}$, and $\overline{DF}$ are the midsegments of △ABC. How does the perimeter of △DEF compare to the perimeter of △ABC? Explain.

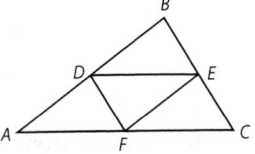

   Using the Triangle Midsegment Theorem, $\overline{DE}$,

   $\overline{EF}$, $\overline{DF}$ are half the distance of their parallel

   counterpart, therefore, the perimeter of △DEF is

   half the perimeter of △ABC.

© Houghton Mifflin Harcourt Publishing Company

MIXED REVIEW
Assessment Readiness

ASSESSMENT AND INTERVENTION

Assign ready-made or customized practice tests to prepare students for high-stakes tests.

ADDITIONAL RESOURCES

Assessment Resources

- Leveled Module Quizzes: Modified, B

AVOID COMMON ERRORS

Item 4   Some students will not remember that the midsegments are exactly half the length of the corresponding side. Remind students that they can use the edge of a piece of paper to compare lengths. Line up the paper with the larger segment, and then mark its length on the paper. Then, see how many times the midsegment fits inside the marks.

COMMON CORE	**Common Core Standards**

Lesson	Items	Content Standards	Mathematical Practices
8.3, 7.3	1*	G-CO.C.10	MP.7
2.2	2*	G-CO.C.9	MP.8
8.4	3	G-MG.A.3	MP.6
8.4	4	G-CO.C.10	MP.5

* Item integrates mixed review concepts from previous modules or a previous course.

MIXED REVIEW
Assessment Readiness

ASSESSMENT AND INTERVENTION

Assign ready-made or customized practice tests to prepare students for high-stakes tests.

ADDITIONAL RESOURCES

Assessment Resources

- Leveled Unit Tests: Modified, A, B, C
- Performance Assessment

AVOID COMMON ERRORS

Item 1   Some students may have difficulty isolating the correct angles when there are several lines and rays involved. Encourage students to lightly trace the angles they are considering.

- Online Homework
- Hints and Help
- Extra Practice

1. Determine whether each pair of angles is a pair of vertical angles, a linear pair of angles, or neither.
   Select the correct answer for each lettered part.

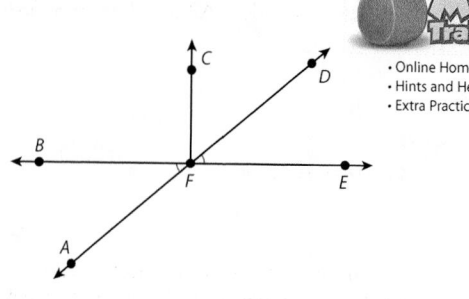

A. ∠AFC and ∠CFD — ○ Vertical ● Linear Pair ○ Neither
B. ∠AFB and ∠CFD — ○ Vertical ○ Linear Pair ● Neither
C. ∠BFD and ∠AFE — ● Vertical ○ Linear Pair ○ Neither

2. Does each transformation map a triangle in Quadrant II to Quadrant I?
   Select Yes or No for A–C.
   A. A rotation of 270° — ● Yes ○ No
   B. A translation along the vector $(-2, -2)$ — ○ Yes ● No
   C. A reflection across the y-axis — ● Yes ○ No

3. △ABC ≅ △DEF.
   Select Yes or No for each statement.

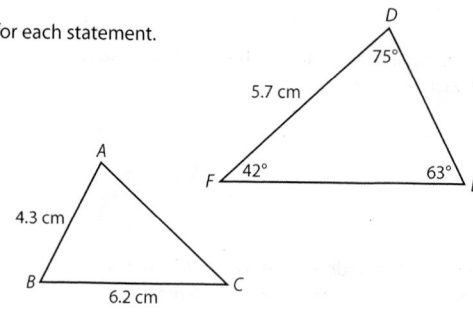

A. $AC = 5.7$ cm — ○ Yes ● No
B. m∠BAC = 75°, m∠ABC = 63°, and $DE = 4.3$ cm — ● Yes ○ No
C. m∠ACB = 42°, m∠ABC = 63°, and $FE = 8.2$ cm — ○ Yes ● No

© Houghton Mifflin Harcourt Publishing Company

COMMON CORE ## Common Core Standards

Items	Content Standards	Mathematical Practices
1	G-CO.C.9	MP.2, MP.7
2	G-CO.A.2	MP.1
3	G-CO.B.7	MP.2, MP.7
4	G-CO.A.4	MP.1
5*	G-CO.C.10	MP.6

* Item integrates mixed review concepts from previous modules or a previous course.

4. Triangle △ABC is in the second quadrant and translated along (−3, 2) and reflected across the y-axis. Determine if the translation will be in the given quadrant. Select Yes or No for each statement.

A. In the first quadrant after the first transformation   ○ Yes   ● No

B. In the second quadrant after the first transformation   ● Yes   ○ No

C. In the third quadrant after the second transformation   ○ Yes   ● No

5. Given △ABC where A(2, 3), B(5, 8), C(8, 3), $\overline{RS}$ is the midsegment parallel to $\overline{AC}$, $\overline{ST}$ is the midsegment parallel to $\overline{AB}$, and $\overline{RT}$ is the midsegment parallel to $\overline{BC}$, determine if the statements are true or false. Select True or False for each statement.

A. $\overline{ST} = 4$ ○ True   ● False
B. $\overline{RT} = 5$ ○ True   ● False
C. $\overline{RS} = 3$ ● True   ○ False

6. Find each angle measure.

$m\angle X = 112°$
$m\angle Z = 52°$
$m\angle Y = 60°$

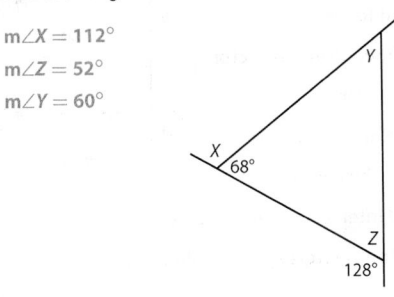

7. Write a proof in two-column form for the Corresponding Angles Theorem.

Given: ℓ ∥ m

Prove: m∠3 = m∠7

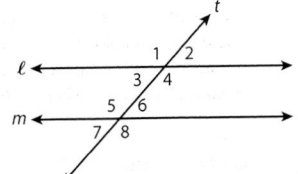

Statements	Reasons
1. ℓ ∥ m	1. Given
2. m∠3 = m∠6	2. Alternate Interior Angles Theorem
3. m∠6 = m∠7	3. Vertical Angles Theorem
4. m∠3 = m∠7	4. Substitution Property of Equality

© Houghton Mifflin Harcourt Publishing Company

PERFORMANCE TASKS

There are three different levels of performance tasks:

 * **Novice:** These are short word problems that require students to apply the math they have learned in straightforward, real-world situations.

 ** **Apprentice:** These are more involved problems that guide students step-by-step through more complex tasks. These exercises include more complicated reasoning, writing, and open ended elements.

 ***Expert:** These are open-ended, nonroutine problems that, instead of stepping the students through, ask them to choose their own methods for solving and justify their answers and reasoning.

COMMON CORE **Common Core Standards**

Items	Content Standards	Mathematical Practices
6*	G-CO.C.10	MP.6
7	G-CO.B.8, G-CO.C.10	MP.3, MP.8

* Item integrates mixed review concepts from previous modules or a previous course.

Item 8 (2 points)   Award the student 1 point for finding a good estimate of *AB*, about 4.34 miles, and 1 point for finding the difference between the routes, about 1.56 miles.

Item 9 (6 points)

2 points for drawing the correct lines

3 points for explaining the solution steps

1 point for giving the correct point

Item 10 (6 points)

2 points for giving the correct amount of wood

3 points for a reasonable explanation

1 point for drawing the image

Performance Tasks

★ **8.** An employee is walking home from work and wants to take the long way to get more exercise. The diagram represents the two different routes, where *A* is the employee's work and *B* is the employee's home. Which route is longer and by how much? Show your work.

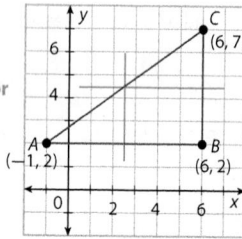

First, find the length of $\overline{AB}$.

$$(3.8)^2 + (2.1)^2 = AB^2$$

$$18.85 = AB^2$$

$$4.34 \approx AB$$

Since $3.8 + 2.1$ is greater than 4.34, going the 3.8 miles and then turning to go 2.1 miles is longer than taking path $\overline{AB}$ by about 1.56 miles.

★★ **9.** A student was given the following triangle and asked to find the circumcenter. Find the point and explain the steps for finding it.

Possible answer: Find the perpendicular bisector of side *AB* by first finding the midpoint using the midpoint formula. The midpoint of this side is $(2.5, 2)$. Draw the perpendicular bisector of this side, which is parallel to the *y*-axis. Next, find the perpendicular bisector of side *BC*. The midpoint is at $(6, 4.5)$. Draw the perpendicular bisector of this side, which is parallel to the *x*-axis. The circumcenter is the point of intersection of these two perpendicular bisectors, which is $(2.5, 4.5)$. This point is also the midpoint of the hypotenuse.

★★★ **10.** While constructing a roof, a construction company built a triangle frame with a base 25 feet long. A cross bar needs to be inserted that connects the midpoints of both sides of the frame. Draw an image to represent the situation and then describe how much wood is needed for the crossbar. Assume the triangle is isosceles. Explain your answer.

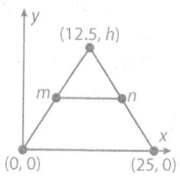

Let the height be *h*. The apex of the triangle is at $\left(\dfrac{25}{2}, h\right) = (12.5, h)$.

$$m\left(\frac{0 + 12.5}{2}, \frac{0 + h}{2}\right) = \left(6.25, \frac{h}{2}\right)$$

$$n\left(\frac{12.5 + 25}{2}, \frac{0 + h}{2}\right) = \left(18.75, \frac{h}{2}\right)$$

$$d = \sqrt{(x_2 - x_1)^2 + (y_2 - y_1)^2} = \sqrt{(18.75 - 6.25)^2 + \left(\frac{h}{2} - \frac{h}{2}\right)^2} = 12.5$$

The length of wood needed for the crossbar is 12.5 feet.

© Houghton Mifflin Harcourt Publishing Company

Architect An architect is writing the blueprints for a large triangular building to go in the middle of a city. The building needs to be congruent to a building that is already made, but the blueprints for the previous building were lost. What information will need to be known about each triangular face of the building in order to make sure all faces are congruent, knowing the building does not have any right triangles? Explain each possibility using known triangle congruence theorems and postulates.

AAS could be used where only two angles and a nonincluded side are known.

SAS could be used where only two sides and the included angle are known.

SSS could be used where all three sides are known.

ASA could be used where only two angles and the included side are known.

MATH IN CAREERS

Architect In this Unit Performance Task, students can see how an architect uses mathematics on the job.

For more information about careers in mathematics as well as various mathematics appreciation topics, visit the American Mathematical Society http://www.ams.org

SCORING GUIDES

Task (6 points)

6 points for naming all four congruence possibilities and giving explanations

Quadrilaterals and Coordinate Proof

CONTENTS

Unit Pacing Guide

45-Minute Classes

Module 9

DAY 1	DAY 2	DAY 3	DAY 4	DAY 5
Lesson 9.1	Lesson 9.2	Lesson 9.3	Lesson 9.3	Lesson 9.4

DAY 6	DAY 7	DAY 8		
Lesson 9.5	Lesson 9.5	Module Review and Assessment Readiness		

Module 10

DAY 1	DAY 2	DAY 3	DAY 4	DAY 5
Lesson 10.1	Lesson 10.1	Lesson 10.2	Lesson 10.2	Lesson 10.3

DAY 6	DAY 7	DAY 8	DAY 9	DAY 10
Lesson 10.4	Lesson 10.5	Lesson 10.5	Module Review and Assessment Readiness	Unit Review and Assessment Readiness

90-Minute Classes

Module 9

DAY 1	DAY 2	DAY 3	DAY 4
Lesson 9.1 Lesson 9.2	Lesson 9.3	Lesson 9.4 Lesson 9.5	Lesson 9.5 Module Review and Assessment Readiness

Module 10

DAY 1	DAY 2	DAY 3	DAY 4	DAY 5
Lesson 10.1	Lesson 10.2	Lesson 10.3 Lesson 10.4	Lesson 10.5	Module Review and Assessment Readiness Unit Review and Assessment Readiness

Program Resources

PLAN

HMH Teacher App

Access a full suite of teacher resources online and offline on a variety of devices. Plan present, and manage classes, assignments, and activities.

ePlanner
Easily plan your classes, create and view assignments, and access all program resources with your online, customizable planning tool.

Professional Development Videos

Authors Juli Dixon and Matt Larson model successful teaching practices and strategies in actual classroom settings.

QR Codes
Scan with your smart phone to jump directly from your print book to online videos and other resources.

Teacher's Edition

Support students with point-of-use Questioning Strategies, teaching tips, resources for differentiated instruction, additional activities, and more.

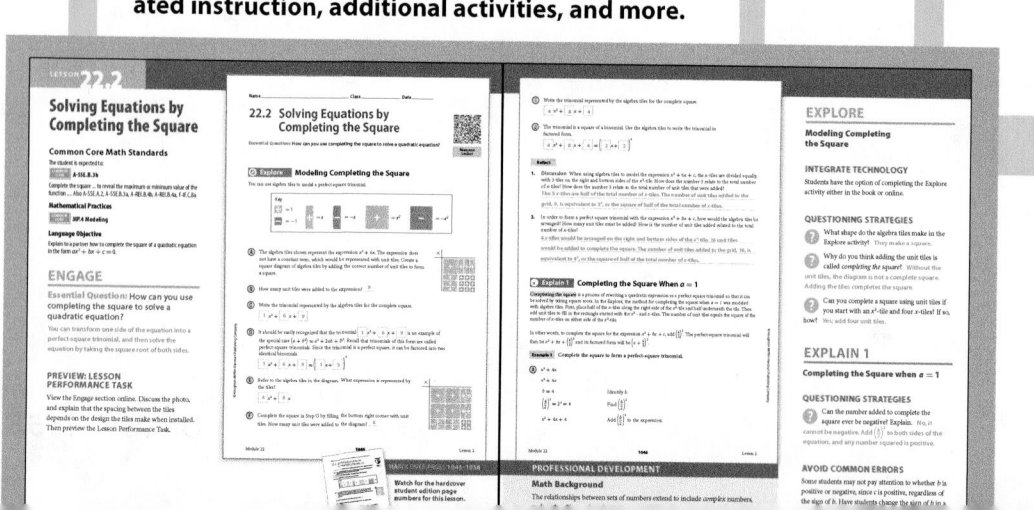

ENGAGE AND EXPLORE

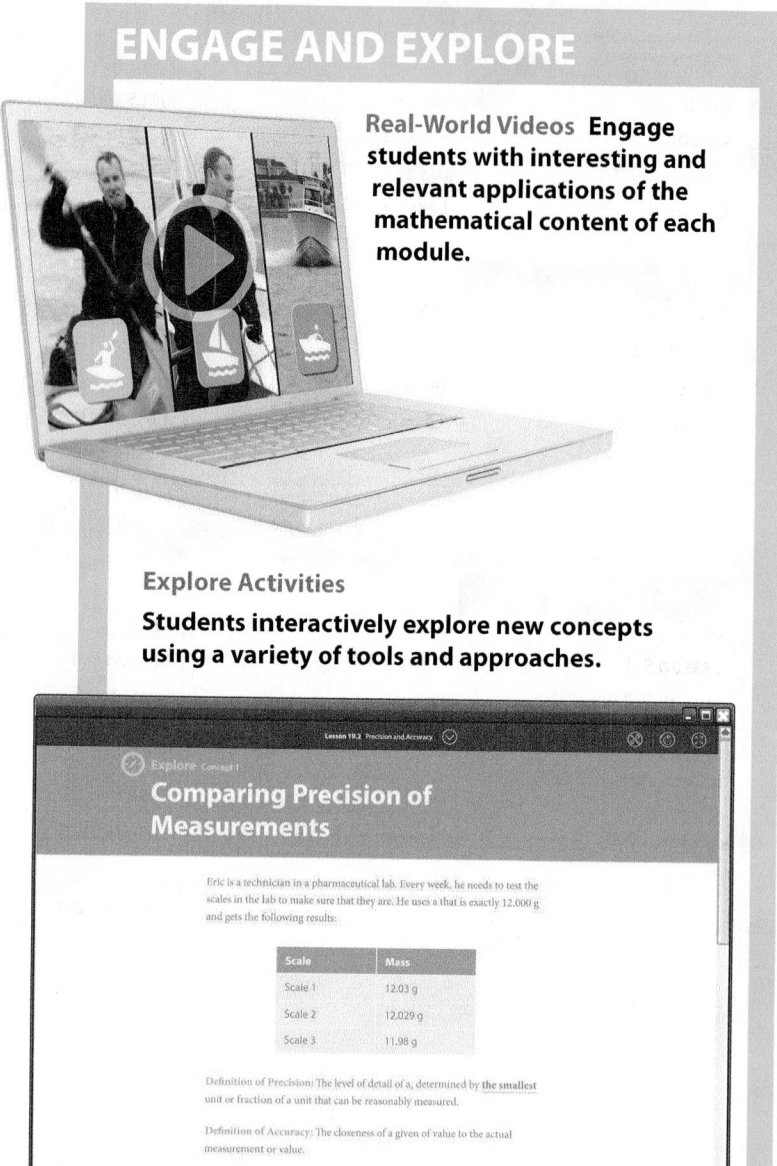

Real-World Videos Engage students with interesting and relevant applications of the mathematical content of each module.

Explore Activities

Students interactively explore new concepts using a variety of tools and approaches.

Comparing Precision of Measurements

Eric is a technician in a pharmaceutical lab. Every week, he needs to test the scales in the lab to make sure that they are. He uses a that is exactly 12.000 g and gets the following results:

Scale	Mass
Scale 1	12.03 g
Scale 2	12.029 g
Scale 3	11.98 g

Definition of Precision: The level of detail of a, determined by the smallest unit or fraction of a unit that can be reasonably measured.

Definition of Accuracy: The closeness of a given of value to the actual measurement or value.

Which measuring tool is the most precise?

Name _____ Class _____ Date _____

22.2 Solving Equations by Completing the Square

Resource Locker

Essential Question: How can you use completing the square to solve a quadratic equation?

A-SSE.B.3b Complete the square ... to reveal the maximum or minimum value of the function ... Also A-SSE.A.2, A-SSE.B.3a, A-REI.B.4b, A-REI.B.4a, F-IF.C.8a

Explore Modeling Completing the Square

You can use algebra tiles to model a perfect square trinomial.

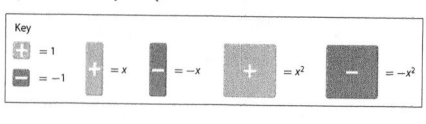

Key

(A) The algebra tiles shown represent the expression $x^2 + 6x$. The expression does not have a constant term, which would be represented with unit tiles. Create a square diagram of algebra tiles by adding the correct number of unit tiles to form a square.

(B) How many unit tiles were added to the expression? _____

(C) Write the trinomial represented by the algebra tiles for the complete square.

$$\boxed{\ }x^2 + \boxed{\ }x + \boxed{\ }$$

(D) It should be easily recognized that the trinomial $\boxed{\ }x^2 + \boxed{\ }x + \boxed{\ }$ is an example of

TEACH

Math On the Spot video tutorials, featuring program author Dr. Edward Burger, accompany every example in the textbook and give students step-by-step instructions and explanations of key math concepts.

Interactive Teacher Edition

Customize and present course materials with collaborative activities and integrated formative assessment.

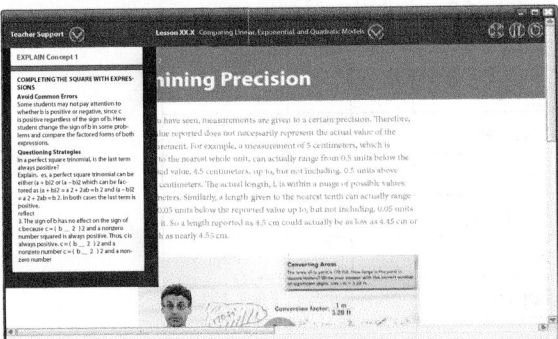

Differentiated Instruction Resources

Support all learners with Differentiated Instruction Resources, including

- **Leveled Practice and Problem Solving**
- **Reading Strategies**
- **Success for English Learners**
- **Challenge**

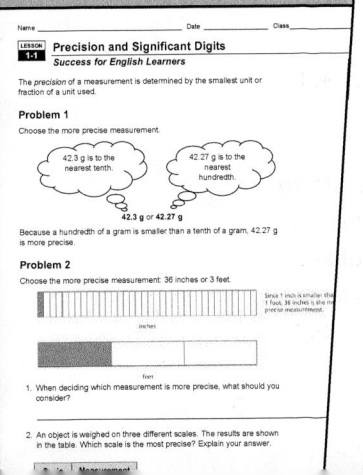

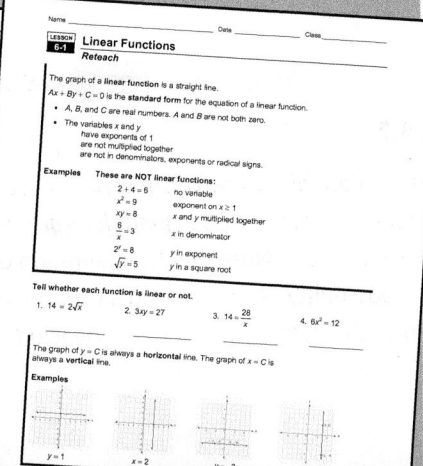

ASSESSMENT AND INTERVENTION

The **Personal Math Trainer** provides online practice, homework, assessments, and intervention. Monitor student progress through reports and alerts. Create and customize assignments aligned to specific lessons or Common Core standards.

- **Practice** – With dynamic items and assignments, students get unlimited practice on key concepts supported by guided examples, step-by-step solutions, and video tutorials.

- **Assessments** – Choose from course assignments or customize your own based on course content, Common Core standards, difficulty levels, and more.

- **Homework** – Students can complete online homework with a wide variety of problem types, including the ability to enter expressions, equations, and graphs. Let the system automatically grade homework, so you can focus where your students need help the most!

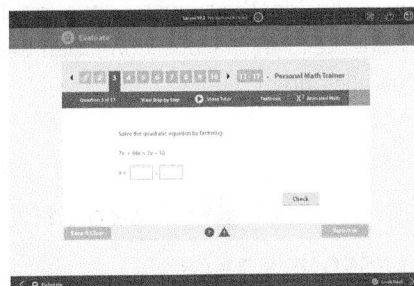

- **Intervention** – Let the Personal Math Trainer automatically prescribe a targeted, personalized intervention path for your students.

Focus on Higher Order Thinking

Raise the bar with homework and practice that incorporates higher-order thinking and mathematical practices in every lesson.

Assessment Readiness

Prepare students for success on high stakes tests for Geometry with practice at every module and unit

COMMON CORE

Assessment Resources

Tailor assessments and response to intervention to meet the needs of all your classes and students, including

- Leveled Module Quizzes
- Leveled Unit Tests
- Unit Performance Tasks
- Placement, Diagnostic, and Quarterly Benchmark Tests
- Tier 1, Tier 2, and Tier 3 Resources

Math Background

Parallelograms COMMON CORE G-CO.C.11

LESSONS 9.1 to 9.5

A *parallelogram* is *a quadrilateral whose opposite sides are parallel*. Like every polygon, parallelograms are named by listing consecutive vertices. Because of this convention, the pairs of parallel sides can be identified from the parallelogram's name.

For example, $\square$ *JKLM* has sides $\overline{JK}$, $\overline{KL}$, $\overline{LM}$, and $\overline{MJ}$ with $\overline{JK} \parallel \overline{LM}$ and $\overline{KL} \parallel \overline{MJ}$. This relationship is easily verified by sketching a parallelogram with consecutive vertices *J*, *K*, *L*, and *M*.

It is worth emphasizing to students the form of the theorems. Some may have the form "If a quadrilateral is a parallelogram, then [property]." In contrast, others may consider the converse situation. Those theorems have the form, "If [condition], then the quadrilateral is a parallelogram."

Rectangles, Rhombuses, and Squares COMMON CORE G-CO.C.11

LESSONS 9.3 and 9.4

Three special quadrilaterals are discussed: the rectangle, the rhombus, and the square. Each is defined to be a quadrilateral with specific properties.

- Rectangle: a quadrilateral with four congruent (right) angles
- Rhombus: a quadrilateral with four congruent sides
- Square: a quadrilateral with four congruent (right) angles and four congruent sides

The first order of business is to demonstrate that each of these special quadrilaterals is a parallelogram. In general, the proofs are straightforward, because the properties that define the special quadrilaterals readily fit one or more of the conditions for parallelograms.

Once you know that the special quadrilaterals are parallelograms, you can conclude that the special quadrilaterals inherit all of the properties of parallelograms.

This is a good application of the Law of Detachment (if $p \rightarrow q$ is true and p is true, then q is true).

For example, if a quadrilateral is a parallelogram, then its opposite sides are congruent. A rectangle is a parallelogram. Therefore, the opposite sides of a rectangle are congruent.

The special quadrilaterals have additional properties beyond those of parallelograms. Students can discover these properties by using inductive reasoning and can then prove the properties through coordinate or synthetic proofs. Such proofs can be instructive because they often draw upon triangle congruence theorems.

It is also useful to step back and consider the relationships among the special quadrilaterals and their properties. To that end, students might organize their findings in a Venn diagram or in a flowchart.

The following table of properties also illustrates the connections among the quadrilaterals.

Properties of Quadrilaterals				
Property	$\square$	$\square$	$\diamond$	$\square$
Opposite sides congruent	·	·	·	·
Opposite angles congruent	·	·	·	·
Consecutive angles supp.	·	·	·	·
Diagonals bisect each other	·	·	·	·
Diagonals congruent		·		·
Diagonals perpendicular			·	·
Diags. bisect opp. angles			·	·

The first four rows show that any property of a parallelogram is a property of all special quadrilaterals. The table also shows that any property that is true for parallelograms, rectangles, or rhombuses is true for squares.

This makes sense because a square is also a parallelogram, rectangle, and rhombus; a property of any of these quadrilaterals thus applies to squares.

Kites and Trapezoids COMMON CORE G-SRT.B.5

LESSON 9.5

A *kite* is *a quadrilateral with two distinct pairs of congruent consecutive sides*. A *trapezoid* is *a quadrilateral with at least one pair of parallel sides*. Note that the definition of kite *excludes* the possibility of considering a rhombus to be a kite, whereas the definition of trapezoid *includes* the possibility of considering a parallelogram to be a trapezoid. Consequently, the definition of kite is called an exclusive definition while the definition of trapezoid is called an inclusive definition.

Decisions about whether to make definitions be exclusive or inclusive are somewhat arbitrary. For example, a trapezoid can be defined as a quadrilateral with exactly one pair of parallel sides, in which case parallelograms are not considered to be trapezoids.

Variations of definitions do not change the facts of mathematics, but they do change the way facts are expressed. The decision to use an inclusive definition of trapezoid means that all parallelograms share the properties of trapezoids. If the exclusive definition of trapezoid is used instead, properties established for trapezoids would need to be re-established for parallelograms.

Coordinate Proof COMMON CORE G-GPE.B.4

LESSONS 10.1 to 10.5

Coordinate geometry, also known as *analytic geometry,* is *the branch of mathematics that merges geometry and algebra.* The French mathematician René Descartes is credited with introducing the key principles of coordinate geometry in his 1637 work, *Discourse on Method.* In honor of Descartes, coordinate geometry is also called *Cartesian geometry.*

The coordinate plane is the tool that links algebra and geometry. For example, through the use of the coordinate plane, *a straight line* is not only *a straight path that has no thickness and extends forever* but also *the graph of a linear equation.* These two definitions have far-reaching ramifications.

In synthetic geometry (the deductive approach studied by Euclid and others), two lines are perpendicular if and only if they intersect to form right angles. A coordinate geometry perspective provides a powerful test of perpendicularity: *two lines are perpendicular if and only if the product of their slopes is −1.*

The familiar Cartesian coordinate system uniquely names a point in the plane using two numbers, called *the coordinates of the point.* The coordinates are defined with respect to two perpendicular axes that intersect at a point called *the origin.*

It is worth noting that the standard Cartesian coordinate system is just one of many possible coordinate systems.

Polar coordinates provide another familiar example of a coordinate system. In addition, it is sometimes useful to name points using an oblique coordinate system in which the axes are not perpendicular to each other. In the oblique system shown here, the axes intersect at an angle of $\alpha°$. (When $\alpha = 90$, the system is an ordinary Cartesian system.) The point P has coordinates $(5, 3)$.

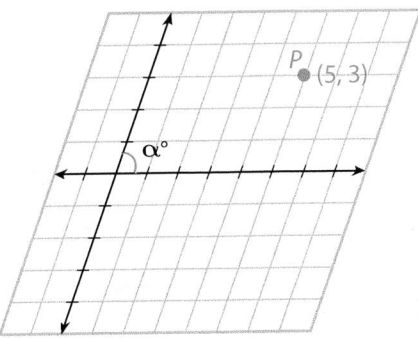

Although the idea of the distance between two points is intuitively familiar, it is instructive to look at the concept of distance from a purely mathematical point of view.

Mathematicians define *a distance function* (called a *metric*) as *a function that assigns a real number to any two points A and B in a plane such that:*

$d(A, B) = d(B, A)$

$d(A, B) \geq 0$, with $d(A, B) = 0$ only if $A = B$

$d(A, B) \leq d(A, C) + d(C, B)$ for any point C

Our standard notion of the distance between two points, based on the Distance Formula, satisfies all three of the above properties. The last property is known as the *Triangle Inequality* when C is not collinear with A and B and the symbol can be changed to a less-than symbol.

Quadrilaterals and Coordinate Proof

MATH IN CAREERS
Unit Activity Preview

After completing this unit, students will complete a Math in Careers task by finding the line that completes a square. Critical skills include interpreting figures on the coordinate plane and finding slope and distance.

For more information about careers in mathematics as well as various mathematics appreciation topics, visit The American Mathematical Society at http://www.ams.org.

UNIT 3

Quadrilaterals and Coordinate Proof

MODULE 9
Properties of Quadrilaterals

MODULE 10
Coordinate Proof Using Slope and Distance

MATH IN CAREERS

Urban Planners Urban planners design the way a city looks and functions. Urban planners use math to determine the size and placement of crucial elements in cities, based on factors such as population, industry, and transportation.

If you're interested in a career as an urban planner, you should study these mathematical subjects:
- Algebra
- Geometry
- Calculus
- Statistics
- Linear Algebra

Research other careers that require the use of spatial analysis and statistics to understand real-world scenarios. See the related Career Activity at the end of this unit.

TRACKING YOUR LEARNING PROGRESSION

Before	In this Unit	After
Students understand: • parallel and perpendicular lines in a plane • altitudes, medians, and midsegments in a triangle • isosceles and equilateral triangles • centroid and orthocenter of triangles	Students will learn about: • properties of parallelograms, rectangles, rhombuses, and squares • theorems about parallelograms • properties of kites and trapezoids • coordinate proofs with slopes and lines that are parallel and perpendicular • the distance and midpoint formulas • perimeter and area on the coordinate plane • finding areas of composite figures	Students will study: • similarity • corresponding parts of similar figures • geometric means • proving the Pythagorean Theorem with similar triangles

Reading Start-Up

Visualize Vocabulary

Use the review words to complete the chart.

distance formula	A formula that finds the distance between two points, written as $(x_2 - x_1)^2 + (y_2 - y_1)^2 = d^2$.
parallel	Two lines that lie in the same plane and never intersect.
midpoint formula	A formula that finds the midpoint of a line segment, written as $M = \left(\dfrac{x_1 + x_2}{2}, \dfrac{y_1 + y_2}{2}\right)$.
slope	A ratio that is used to determine how steep a line is.
opposite angles	When two lines intersect, four angles result. This refers to either pair of angles that are not adjacent to each other.

Understand Vocabulary

To become familiar with some of the vocabulary terms in the unit, consider the following. You may refer to the module, the glossary, or a dictionary.

1. A __rhombus__ is a quadrilateral with four congruent sides.
2. A __composite figure__ is made up of simple shapes, such as triangles and quadrilaterals.
3. A __parallelogram__ is any quadrilateral whose opposite sides are parallel.

Active Reading

Before beginning the unit, create a booklet to help you organize what you learn. Write a main topic from each module on each page of the booklet. Write details of each main topic on the appropriate page to create an outline of the module. The ability to reword and retell the details of a module will help in understanding complex materials.

Reading Start Up

Have students complete the activities on this page by working alone or with others.

VISUALIZE VOCABULARY

The definition chart graphic helps students review vocabulary associated with lines in the coordinate plane. If time allows, provide the endpoints of a line and review how to use the distance and midpoint formulas.

UNDERSTAND VOCABULARY

Use the following explanations to help students learn the preview words.

A **quadrilateral** is a four-sided polygon. A quadrilateral with two pairs of parallel sides is a **parallelogram**. A parallelogram with four sides that have the same length is a **rhombus.** A figure made of triangles, quadrilaterals, and other simple shapes is a **composite figure**. You can use a **coordinate proof** to prove relationships pertaining to figures in the coordinate plane.

ACTIVE READING

Students can use these reading and note-taking strategies to help them organize and understand the new concepts and vocabulary. Encourage students to write explanations in their own words. Remind them to question vocabulary or sentence structures that they have difficulty interpreting.

ADDITIONAL RESOURCES

Differentiated Instruction

- Reading Strategies **EL**

Vocabulary

Review Words

✔ distance formula *(fórmula de la distancia)*
✔ midpoint formula *(fórmula de punto medio)*
✔ opposite angles *(ángulos opuestos)*
✔ parallel *(paralelo)*
✔ slope *(pendiente)*

Preview Words

composite figure *(figura compuesta)*
coordinate proof *(demostración coordenado)*
parallelogram *(paralelogramo)*
quadrilateral *(cuadrilátero)*
rhombus *(rombo)*

MODULE **9**

Properties of Quadrilaterals

ESSENTIAL QUESTION:

Answer: Wherever quadrilaterals are found in the real world, such as in buildings, billboards, or paving stones, their properties can be used to answer questions about them.

PROFESSIONAL DEVELOPMENT VIDEO

Professional Development Video

Author Juli Dixon models successful teaching practices in an actual high-school classroom.

Professional Development
my.hrw.com

MODULE **9**

Properties of Quadrilaterals

Essential Question: How can you use properties of quadrilaterals to solve real-world problems?

© Houghton Mifflin Harcourt Publishing Company · Image Credits: ©Raimund Koch/Corbis

REAL WORLD VIDEO
Check out how architects use properties of quadrilaterals to design unusual buildings, such as the National Gallery of Art in Washington, D.C., or the Seattle Central Library.

MODULE PERFORMANCE TASK PREVIEW

How Big Is That Face?

In this module, you will use the geometry of trapezoids and other quadrilaterals to solve a problem related to the external dimensions of the Seattle Central Library. Let's get started and explore this interesting "slant" on architecture!

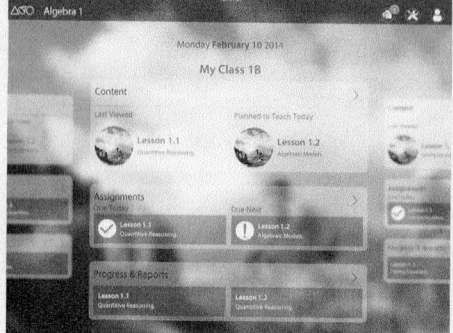

DIGITAL TEACHER EDITION

Access a full suite of teaching resources when and where you need them:

- Access content online or offline
- Customize lessons to share with your class
- Communicate with your students in real-time
- View student grades and data instantly to target your instruction where it is needed most

PERSONAL MATH TRAINER

Assessment and Intervention

Assign automatically graded homework, quizzes, tests, and intervention activities. Prepare your students with updated, Common Core-aligned practice tests.

Are (YOU) Ready?

Complete these exercises to review the skills you will need for this module.

Congruent Figures

Example 1

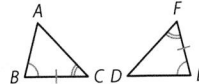

Determine if the pairs of figures are congruent and state the appropriate congruence theorem if applicable.

△ABC is congruent to △DEF via the ASA Congruence Theorem.

- Online Homework
- Hints and Help
- Extra Practice

1. Determine if the figures are congruent and state the appropriate congruence theorem if applicable.

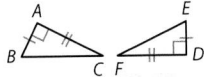

<u>   Yes, SAS   </u>   <u>   No   </u>

Example 2

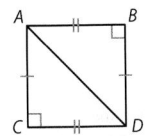

Determine whether the figure contains a pair of congruent triangles and state the appropriate congruence theorem if applicable.

Since $\overline{AD}$ is congruent to $\overline{DA}$ via the Reflexive Property of Congruence, △ABD is congruent to △DCA because of the SSS Congruence Theorem.

2. Determine whether the figure contains a pair of congruent triangles and state the appropriate congruence theorem if applicable.

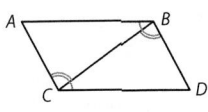 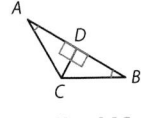

<u>   Yes, ASA   </u>   <u>   Yes, AAS   </u>

Parallelograms

Example 3

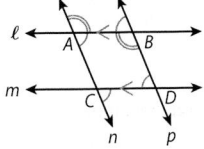

Determine if the figure is a parallelogram.

It is given that lines ℓ and m are parallel. Lines n and p are also parallel because of the Converse of the Corresponding Angles Theorem. Therefore, ABCD is a parallelogram.

3. Determine if the figure is a parallelogram.

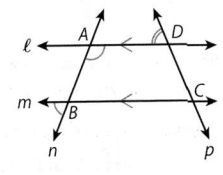

<u>   No   </u>   <u>   Yes   </u>

© Houghton Mifflin Harcourt Publishing Company

Are You Ready?

ASSESS READINESS

Use the assessment on this page to determine if students need strategic or intensive intervention for the module's prerequisite skills.

ASSESSMENT AND INTERVENTION

RtI Response to Intervention **TIER 1, TIER 2, TIER 3 SKILLS**

Personal Math Trainer will automatically create a standards-based, personalized intervention assignment for your students, targeting each student's individual needs!

ADDITIONAL RESOURCES

See the table below for a full list of intervention resources available for this module.

Response to Intervention Resources also includes:

- Tier 2 Skill Pre-Tests for each Module
- Tier 2 Skill Post-Tests for each skill

Response to Intervention			Differentiated Instruction
Tier 1 Lesson Intervention Worksheets	**Tier 2** Strategic Intervention Skills Intervention Worksheets	**Tier 3** Intensive Intervention Worksheets available online	
Reteach 9.1 Reteach 9.2 Reteach 9.3 Reteach 9.4 Reteach 9.5	7 Congruent Figures 13 Parallelograms	Building Block Skills 8, 16, 48, 49, 74, 98, 103	Challenge worksheets Extend the Math Lesson Activities in TE

Properties of Parallelograms

Common Core Math Standards

The student is expected to:

 G-CO.C.11

Prove theorems about parallelograms. Also G-SRT.B.5

Mathematical Practices

 MP.3 Logic

Language Objective

Explain to a partner why pictures of quadrilaterals are or are not parallelograms.

ENGAGE

Essential Question: What can you conclude about the sides, angles, and diagonals of a parallelogram?

Opposite sides are congruent, opposite angles are congruent, consecutive angles are supplementary, and diagonals bisect each other.

PREVIEW: LESSON PERFORMANCE TASK

View the Engage section online. Discuss the photo, asking students to identify the geometric figures formed by a scissor lift. Then preview the Lesson Performance Task.

Name _____ Class _____ Date _____

9.1 Properties of Parallelograms

Essential Question: What can you conclude about the sides, angles, and diagonals of a parallelogram?

Resource Locker

⊘ Explore Investigating Parallelograms

A **quadrilateral** is a polygon with four sides. A **parallelogram** is a quadrilateral that has two pairs of parallel sides. You can use geometry software to investigate properties of parallelograms.

(A) Draw a straight line. Then plot a point that is not on the line. Construct a line through the point that is parallel to the line. This gives you a pair of parallel lines.

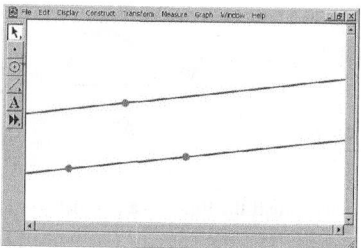

(B) Repeat Step A to construct a second pair of parallel lines that intersect those from Step A.

(C) The intersections of the parallel lines create a parallelogram. Plot points at these intersections. Label the points A, B, C, and D.

Identify the *opposite sides* and *opposite angles* of the parallelogram.

Opposite sides: Side $\overline{AB}$ is opposite side $\overline{DC}$. Side $\overline{AD}$ is opposite side $\overline{BC}$.

Opposite angles: $\angle A$ is opposite $\angle C$. $\angle B$ is opposite $\angle D$.

© Houghton Mifflin Harcourt Publishing Company

Module 9 · 419 · Lesson 1

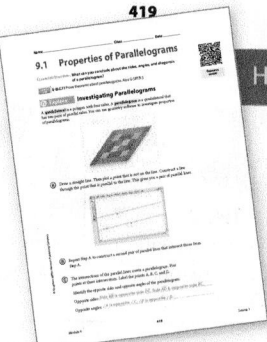

HARDCOVER PAGES 361–370

Turn to these pages to find this lesson in the hardcover student edition.

Ⓓ Measure each angle of the parallelogram.

Measure the length of each side of the parallelogram. You can do this by measuring the distance between consecutive vertices.

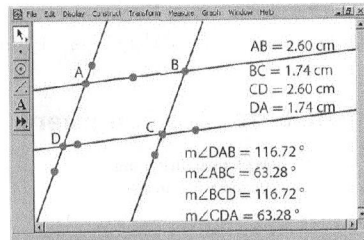

Ⓔ Then drag the points and lines in your construction to change the shape of the parallelogram. As you do so, look for relationships in the measurements. Make a conjecture about the sides and angles of a parallelogram.

Conjecture: **Opposite sides of a parallelogram are congruent. Opposite angles of a parallelogram are congruent.**

Ⓕ A segment that connects two nonconsecutive vertices of a polygon is a **diagonal**. Construct diagonals $\overline{AC}$ and $\overline{BD}$. Plot a point at the intersection of the diagonals and label it E.

Ⓖ Measure the length of $\overline{AE}$, $\overline{BE}$, $\overline{CE}$, and $\overline{DE}$.

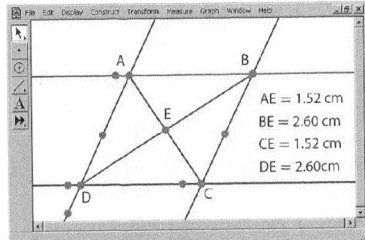

Ⓗ Drag the points and lines in your construction to change the shape of the parallelogram. As you do so, look for relationships in the measurements in Step G. Make a conjecture about the diagonals of a parallelogram.

Conjecture: **The diagonals of a parallelogram bisect each other.**

Reflect

1. *Consecutive angles* are the angles at consecutive vertices, such as $\angle A$ and $\angle B$, or $\angle A$ and $\angle D$. Use your construction to make a conjecture about consecutive angles of a parallelogram.
Conjecture: **Consecutive angles of a parallelogram are supplementary.**

© Houghton Mifflin Harcourt Publishing Company

EXPLORE

Investigating Parallelograms

INTEGRATE TECHNOLOGY

Students have the option of doing the parallelogram activity either in the book or online.

QUESTIONING STRATEGIES

❓ As you drag points, does the quadrilateral remain a parallelogram? Yes, the lines that form opposite sides remain parallel.

❓ What do you notice about consecutive angles in the parallelogram? Why does this make sense? Consecutive angles are supplementary. This makes sense because opposite sides are parallel, so consecutive angles are same-side interior angles. By the Same-Side Interior Angles Postulate, these angles are supplementary.

PROFESSIONAL DEVELOPMENT

Math Background

In this lesson, students extend their earlier work with triangle congruence criteria and triangle properties to prove facts about parallelograms. A *parallelogram* is a quadrilateral whose opposite sides are parallel. Like every polygon, parallelograms are named by listing consecutive vertices. Because of this convention, the pairs of parallel sides can be identified from the parallelogram's name. For example, ▱*JKLM* has sides $\overline{JK}$, $\overline{KL}$, $\overline{LM}$, and $\overline{MJ}$ with $\overline{JK} \parallel \overline{LM}$ and $\overline{KL} \parallel \overline{MJ}$. This relationship is easily verified by sketching a parallelogram with consecutive vertices *J*, *K*, *L*, and *M*.

EXPLAIN 1

Proving Opposite Sides Are Congruent

INTEGRATE MATHEMATICAL PRACTICES

Focus on Math Connections

MP.1 The proof that the opposite sides of a parallelogram are congruent depends on students understanding that the opposite sides of a quadrilateral do not share a vertex (that is, they do not intersect). Consecutive sides of a quadrilateral do share a vertex (that is, they intersect). You may want to help students draw and label a quadrilateral for reference.

QUESTIONING STRATEGIES

? Why do you think the proof is based on drawing a diagonal of the parallelogram?

Drawing the diagonal creates two triangles, which lets you use triangle congruence criteria and the fact that corresponding parts of congruent triangles are congruent.

---

2. **Critique Reasoning** A student claims that the perimeter of △AEB in the construction is always equal to the perimeter of △CED. Without doing any further measurements in your construction, explain whether or not you agree with the student's statement.

Agree; $AE = CE$, $BE = DE$, and $BA = DC$, since the diagonals of the parallelogram bisect each other and the opposite sides are congruent. So $AE + EB + BA = CE + ED + DC$.

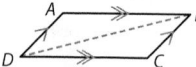 **Explain 1** **Proving Opposite Sides Are Congruent**

The conjecture you made in the Explore about opposite sides of a parallelogram can be stated as a theorem. The proof involves drawing an *auxiliary line* in the figure.

Theorem
If a quadrilateral is a parallelogram, then its opposite sides are congruent.

Example 1 Prove that the opposite sides of a parallelogram are congruent.

Given: $ABCD$ is a parallelogram.

Prove: $\overline{AB} \cong \overline{CD}$ and $\overline{AD} \cong \overline{CB}$

Statements	Reasons
1. $ABCD$ is a parallelogram.	1. Given
2. Draw $\overline{DB}$.	2. Through any two points, there is exactly one line.
3. $\overline{AB} \parallel \overline{DC}$, $\overline{AD} \parallel \overline{BC}$	3. Definition of parallelogram
4. $\angle ADB \cong \angle CBD$ $\angle ABD \cong \angle CDB$	4. Alternate Interior Angles Theorem
5. $\overline{DB} \cong \overline{DB}$	5. Reflexive Property of Congruence
6. △$ABD \cong$ △CDB	6. ASA Triangle Congruence Theorem
7. $\overline{AB} \cong \overline{CD}$ and $\overline{AD} \cong \overline{CB}$	7. CPCTC

Reflect

3. Explain how you can use the rotational symmetry of a parallelogram to give an argument that supports the above theorem.

Under a 180° rotation around the center, each side is mapped to its opposite side.

Since rotations preserve distance, this shows that opposite sides are congruent.

© Houghton Mifflin Harcourt Publishing Company

COLLABORATIVE LEARNING

Small Group Activity

Using geometry software, have one student construct a parallelogram. Ask a second student to measure both the opposite angles and the opposite sides of the parallelogram to verify the corresponding theorems in this lesson. Ask a third student to add the diagonals to the parallelogram and use the measuring features to verify that the diagonals of a parallelogram bisect each other. Ask a fourth student to verify that the consecutive angles of a parallelogram are supplementary by verifying this property. As students change the parallelogram, opposite sides and angles remain congruent.

Explain 2 Proving Opposite Angles Are Congruent

The conjecture from the Explore about opposite angles of a parallelogram can also be proven and stated as a theorem.

Theorem

If a quadrilateral is a parallelogram, then its opposite angles are congruent.

Example 2 Prove that the opposite angles of a parallelogram are congruent.

Given: ABCD is a parallelogram.

Prove: ∠A ≅ ∠C (A similar proof shows that ∠B ≅ ∠D.)

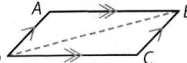

Statements	Reasons
1. ABCD is a parallelogram.	1. **Given**
2. Draw $\overline{DB}$.	2. **Through any two points, there is exactly one line.**
3. $\overline{AB} \| \overline{DC}$, $\overline{AD} \| \overline{BC}$	3. **Definition of parallelogram**
4. ∠ADB ≅ ∠CBD, ∠ABD ≅ ∠CDB	4. Alternate Interior Angles Theorem
5. $\overline{DB} \cong \overline{DB}$	5. Reflexive Property of Congruence
6. △ABD ≅ △CDB	6. ASA Triangle Congruence Theorem
7. ∠A ≅ ∠C	7. CPCTC

Reflect

4. Explain how the proof would change in order to prove ∠B ≅ ∠D.
   In the second step, draw the diagonal $\overline{AC}$. The remaining steps are all
   similar to those in the above proof.

5. In Reflect 1, you noticed that the consecutive angles of a parallelogram are supplementary. This can be stated as the theorem, *If a quadrilateral is a parallelogram, then its consecutive angles are supplementary.*

   Explain why this theorem is true.
   Each pair of consecutive angles of a parallelogram are same-side interior

   angles for a pair of parallel lines (the opposite sides of the parallelogram),

   so the angles are supplementary by the Same-Side Interior Angles Postulate.

Explain 3 Proving Diagonals Bisect Each Other

The conjecture from the Explore about diagonals of a parallelogram can also be proven and stated as a theorem. One proof is shown on the facing page.

Theorem

If a quadrilateral is a parallelogram, then its diagonals bisect each other.

© Houghton Mifflin Harcourt Publishing Company

DIFFERENTIATE INSTRUCTION

Modeling

Give each group a different model parallelogram made with straws. Ask each student in the group to use measuring tools to investigate the opposite angles and the opposite sides of their parallelogram and then record the results in a table. Since a parallelogram is not a rigid figure, ask students to change the angle measures of their parallelogram, redo the measurements and record their results in the table. After several parallelograms are explored, have the group make a conjecture about the opposite angles and opposite sides of a parallelogram, and then present their data and conjecture to the class.

EXPLAIN 2

Proving Opposite Angles Are Congruent

CONNECT VOCABULARY **EL**

The proof that the opposite angles of a parallelogram are congruent depends on students understanding the difference between *opposite* angles and *consecutive* angles. The opposite angles of a quadrilateral do not share a side, while the consecutive angles of a quadrilateral do share a side. You may want to help students draw and label a parallelogram for reference.

QUESTIONING STRATEGIES

? How are the opposite angles of a parallelogram related? They are congruent.

? How is the proof of this theorem similar to the proof that the opposite sides of a parallelogram are congruent? They both start with drawing a diagonal and then using a triangle congruence criterion and the fact that corresponding parts of congruent traingles are congruent.

EXPLAIN 3

Proving Diagonals Bisect Each Other

INTEGRATE MATHEMATICAL PRACTICES

Focus on Reasoning

MP.2 As students work on the proof in this lesson, ask them to think about how the format of the proof makes it easier to understand the underlying structure of the argument. Students should recognize that a flow proof shows how one statement connects to the next, which may not be as apparent in a two-column format. A two-column format, on the other hand, may make the justification for each step clearer than a flow proof.

QUESTIONING STRATEGIES

? Why do you think this theorem was introduced after the theorems about the sides and angles of a parallelogram? The proof of this theorem depends upon the fact that opposite sides of a parallelogram are congruent.

AVOID COMMON ERRORS

Students may be confused when asked to label the congruent parts of the parallelogram in this proof. Have students use one color pencil to mark the pairs of congruent sides, a second color pencil to mark the pairs of congruent angles on the parallelogram, and a third and fourth color pencil to mark the congruent segments on the diagonals of the parallelogram.

Example 3 Complete the flow proof that the diagonals of a parallelogram bisect each other.

Given: *ABCD* is a parallelogram.

Prove: $\overline{AE} \cong \overline{CE}$ and $\overline{BE} \cong \overline{DE}$

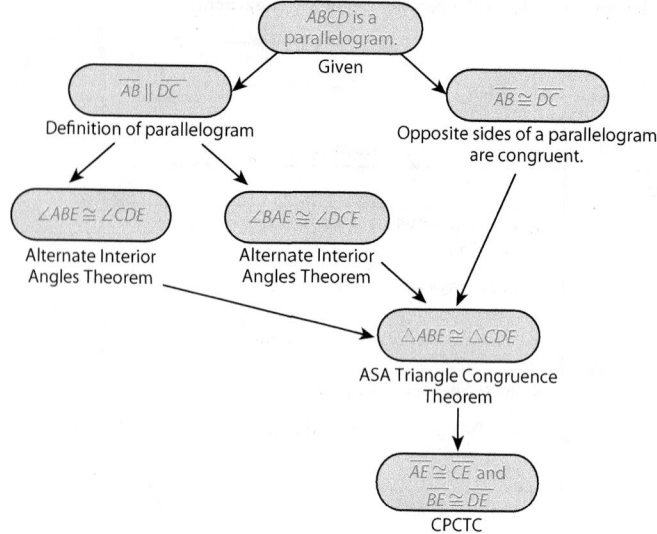

ABCD is a parallelogram.
Given

$\overline{AB} \parallel \overline{DC}$
Definition of parallelogram

$\overline{AB} \cong \overline{DC}$
Opposite sides of a parallelogram are congruent.

$\angle ABE \cong \angle CDE$
Alternate Interior Angles Theorem

$\angle BAE \cong \angle DCE$
Alternate Interior Angles Theorem

$\triangle ABE \cong \triangle CDE$
ASA Triangle Congruence Theorem

$\overline{AE} \cong \overline{CE}$ and $\overline{BE} \cong \overline{DE}$
CPCTC

Reflect

6. **Discussion** Is it possible to prove the theorem using a different triangle congruence theorem? Explain.

Yes; $\angle AEB \cong \angle CED$ because they are vertical angles. Together with

$\angle ABE \cong \angle CDE$ and $\overline{AB} \cong \overline{CD}$, you can prove the theorem using the

AAS Triangle Congruence Theorem.

© Houghton Mifflin Harcourt Publishing Company

LANGUAGE SUPPORT EL

Communicate Math

Provide each pair of students with pictures of different quadrilaterals, including rectangles, squares, and other parallelograms, and rulers and protractors. The first student chooses a picture, measures angles and side lengths, and tells the second student why this picture is or is not a parallelogram. The second student writes notes about the picture as the first student explains. Students switch roles and repeat the process.

Explain 4 **Using Properties of Parallelograms**

You can use the properties of parallelograms to find unknown lengths or angle measures in a figure.

 Example 4 ABCD is a parallelogram. Find each measure.

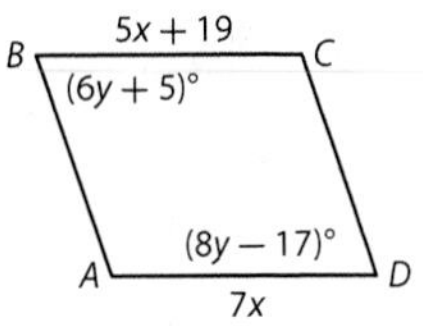

(A) *AD*

Use the fact that opposite sides of a parallelogram are congruent, so $\overline{AD} \cong \overline{CB}$ and therefore $AD = CB$.

Write an equation. $\qquad 7x = 5x + 19$

Solve for *x*. $\qquad x = 9.5$

$AD = 7x = 7(9.5) = 66.5$

(B) m∠B

Use the fact that opposite angles of a parallelogram are congruent,

so $\angle B \cong \angle \boxed{D}$ and therefore m∠B = m∠ $\boxed{D}$.

Write an equation. $\qquad 6y + 5 = \dfrac{8y - 17}{}$

Solve for *y*. $\qquad \dfrac{11}{} = y$

$m\angle B = (6y + 5)^\circ = \left(6\boxed{11} + 5\right)^\circ = \boxed{71}^\circ$

Reflect

7. Suppose you wanted to find the measures of the other angles of parallelogram *ABCD*. Explain your steps.
   Possible answer (using congruent opposite angles; can also be done using
   supplementary consecutive angles): Since the sum of the measures of a
   quadrilateral is 360°, m∠A + 71° + m∠C + 71° = 360°. Since opposite angles of
   a parallelogram are congruent, ∠A ≅ ∠C, so m∠A + 71° + m∠A + 71° = 360°.
   Solving shows that m∠A = 109°. Therefore, m∠A = m∠C = 109°.

© Houghton Mifflin Harcourt Publishing Company

EXPLAIN 4

Using Properties of Parallelograms

AVOID COMMON ERRORS

As students prepare to solve these types of problems, they may get confused about which segments or angles correspond. Ask them to mark the congruent parts carefully and then think about which property applies to the information that is marked.

QUESTIONING STRATEGIES

? How are the opposite sides of a parallelogram related? How are the diagonals of a parallelogram related? The opposite sides are congruent and the diagonals bisect each other.

Properties of Parallelograms **424**

ELABORATE

QUESTIONING STRATEGIES

? What do we have to know first to apply any of these theorems? **The quadrilateral is a parallelogram.**

SUMMARIZE THE LESSON

? Have students make a graphic organizer to summarize what they know about the sides, angles, and diagonals of a parallelogram.

Sample:

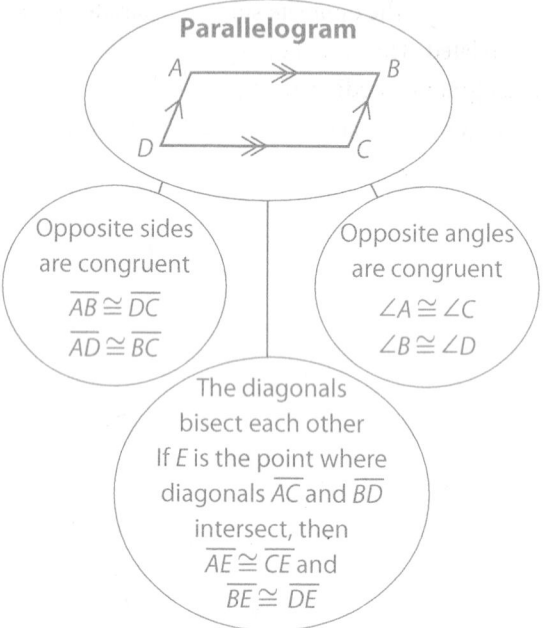

© Houghton Mifflin Harcourt Publishing Company

PQRS is a parallelogram. Find each measure.

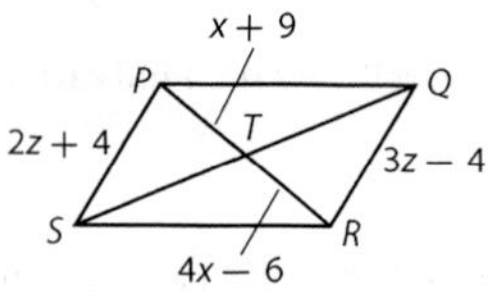

8. *QR*

$\overline{PS} \cong \overline{QR}$, so $PS = QR$

$2z + 4 = 3z - 4$

$8 = z$

$QR = 3z - 4 = 3(8) - 4 = 20$

9. *PR*

$\overline{PT} \cong \overline{RT}$, so $PT = RT$

$x + 9 = 4x - 6$

$5 = x$

$PT = x + 9 = 5 + 9 = 14$

$PR = 2PT$, so $PR = 2(14) = 28$

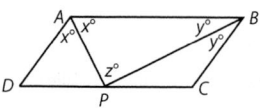

10. What do you need to know first in order to apply any of the theorems of this lesson? **You must know that the given quadrilateral is a parallelogram.**

11. In parallelogram *ABCD*, point *P* lies on $\overline{DC}$, as shown in the figure. Explain why it must be the case that $DC = 2AD$. Use what you know about base angles of an isosceles triangle.

$\angle DAP \cong \angle BAP$ since $\overline{AP}$ is an angle bisector. Also, $\angle DPA \cong \angle BAP$ by the Alternate Interior Angles Theorem. Therefore, $\angle DAP \cong \angle DPA$. This means $\triangle DAP$ is isosceles, with $\overline{AD} \cong \overline{DP}$. Similarly, $\overline{BC} \cong \overline{PC}$. Also, $\overline{BC} \cong \overline{AD}$ as opposite sides of a parallelogram. So, $DC = DP + PC = AD + BC = AD + AD = 2AD$.

12. **Essential Question Check-In** *JKLM* is a parallelogram. Name all of the congruent segments and angles in the figure.

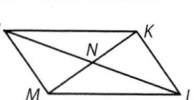

$\overline{JK} \cong \overline{LM}$, $\overline{JM} \cong \overline{LK}$, $\overline{JN} \cong \overline{LN}$, $\overline{MN} \cong \overline{KN}$, $\angle KJM \cong \angle MLK$, $\angle JKL \cong \angle LMJ$

★ Evaluate: Homework and Practice

1. Pablo traced along both edges of a ruler to draw two pairs of parallel lines, as shown. Explain the next steps he could take in order to make a conjecture about the diagonals of a parallelogram.

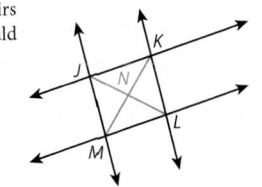

Possible answer: He can use the ruler to draw $\overline{JL}$ and $\overline{KM}$, label their intersection as point N, and use the ruler to find that $JN = LN$ and $KN = MN$. His conjecture would be that the diagonals of a parallelogram bisect each other.

2. Sabina has tiles in the shape of a parallelogram. She labels the angles of each tile as $\angle A$, $\angle B$, $\angle C$, and $\angle D$. Then she arranges the tiles to make the pattern shown here and uses the pattern to make a conjecture about opposite angles of a parallelogram. What conjecture does she make? How does the pattern help her make the conjecture?

Possible conjecture: Opposite angles of a parallelogram are congruent. In the pattern, vertical angles $\angle A$ and $\angle C$, are congruent, as are vertical angles and $\angle B$ and $\angle D$.

3. Complete the flow proof that the opposite sides of a parallelogram are congruent. Given: $ABCD$ is a parallelogram. Prove: $\overline{AB} \cong \overline{CD}$ and $\overline{AD} \cong \overline{CB}$

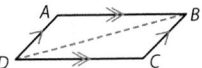

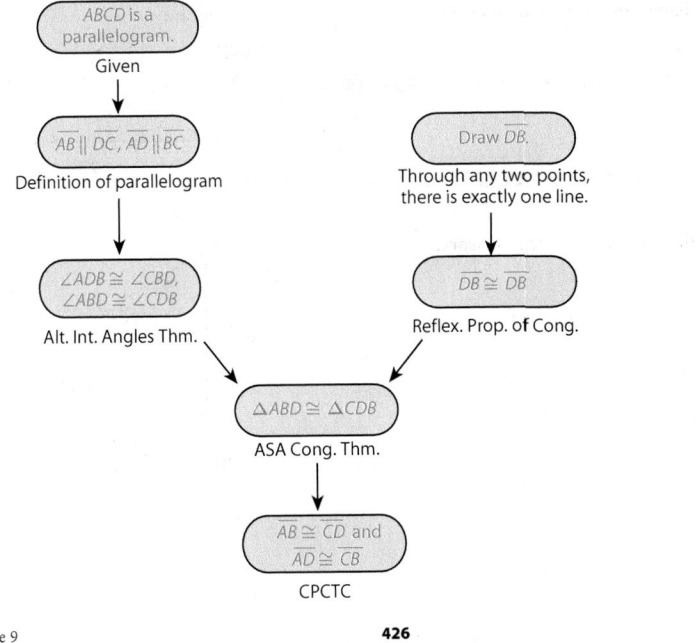

Exercise	Depth of Knowledge (D.O.K.)	COMMON CORE Mathematical Practices
1–2	**2** Skills/Concepts	**MP.5** Using Tools
3–5	**2** Skills/Concepts	**MP.3** Logic
6–9	**2** Skills/Concepts	**MP.4** Modeling
10–13	**2** Skills/Concepts	**MP.4** Modeling
14–16	**2** Skills/Concepts	**MP.3** Logic
17–24	**2** Skills/Concepts	**MP.2** Reasoning
25	**3** Strategic Thinking H.O.T.	**MP.4** Modeling

EVALUATE

ASSIGNMENT GUIDE

Concepts and Skills	Practice
Explore Investigating Parallelograms	Exercises 1–2
Example 1 Proving Opposite Sides Are Congruent	Exercise 3
Example 2 Proving Opposite Angles Are Congruent	Exercise 4
Example 3 Proving Diagonals Bisect Each Other	Exercise 5
Example 4 Using Properties of Parallelograms	Exercises 6–13

INTEGRATE MATHEMATICAL PRACTICES

Focus on Modeling

MP.4 Some students may benefit from a hands-on approach for finding the properties of parallelograms. Have students copy a larger version of the parallelogram in an exercise onto a sheet of paper and then cut it out. Make sure the diagonals are drawn in. Have them use a ruler to find the segment lengths of the diagonals and verify that the diagonals bisect each other. Students can then cut the parallelogram along one diagonal and place the opposite sides on top of each other to confirm that they are coincident, and therefore congruent.

Properties of Parallelograms   **426**

Focus on Modeling

MP.4 Encourage students to copy the parallelograms in the exercises onto their papers and use colored pencils to keep track of the congruent angles and segments.

---

4. Write the proof that the opposite angles of a parallelogram are congruent as a paragraph proof.

Given: *ABCD* is a parallelogram.

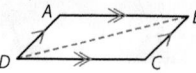

Prove: $\angle A \cong \angle C$ (A similar proof shows that $\angle B \cong \angle D$.)

Possible answer: It is given that *ABCD* is a parallelogram, so $\overline{AB} \| \overline{DC}$ and $\overline{AD} \| \overline{BC}$ by the def. of a parallelogram. By the Alt. Int. Angles Thm., $\angle ADB \cong \angle CBD$ and $\angle ABD \cong \angle CDB$. Since two points determine a line, you can draw $\overline{DB}$. $\overline{DB} \cong \overline{DB}$ by the Reflex. Prop. of Cong. You can conclude that $\triangle ABD \cong \triangle CDB$ by the ASA Cong. Thm., and so, $\angle A \cong \angle C$ by CPCTC.

5. Write the proof that the diagonals of a parallelogram bisect each other as a two-column proof.

Given: *ABCD* is a parallelogram.

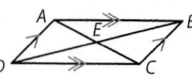

Prove: $\overline{AE} \cong \overline{CE}$ and $\overline{BE} \cong \overline{DE}$

Statements	Reasons
1. *ABCD* is a parallelogram.	1. Given
2. $\overline{AB} \| \overline{DC}$	2. Definition of parallelogram
3. $\angle ABE \cong \angle CDE$, $\angle BAE \cong \angle DCE$	3. Alt. Int. Angles Thm.
4. $\overline{AB} \cong \overline{DC}$	4. Opposite sides of a parallelogram are congruent.
5. $\triangle ABE \cong \triangle CDE$	5. ASA Triangle Cong. Thm.
6. $\overline{AE} \cong \overline{CE}$ and $\overline{BE} \cong \overline{DE}$	6. CPCTC

EFGH is a parallelogram. Find each measure.

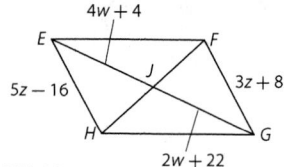

6. *FG*

$\overline{HE} \cong \overline{FG}$; $5z - 16 = 3z + 8$; $z = 12$; *FG* = 44

7. *EG*

$\overline{EJ} \cong \overline{GJ}$; $4w + 4 = 2w + 22$; $w = 9$; *EJ* = 40; *EG* = 2*EJ*, 80

ABCD is a parallelogram. Find each measure.

8. m$\angle B$

$\angle B \cong \angle D$; $9x - 5 = 10x - 19$; $14 = x$; m$\angle B$ = 121°

9. *AD*

$\overline{AD} \cong \overline{CB}$; $3y - 1 = y + 15$; $y = 8$; *AD* = 23

Exercise	Depth of Knowledge (D.O.K.)	COMMON CORE	Mathematical Practices
26	**3** Strategic Thinking H.O.T.		**MP.3** Logic
27	**3** Strategic Thinking H.O.T.		**MP.2** Reasoning

A staircase handrail is made from congruent parallelograms. In ▱*PQRS*, *PQ* = 17.5, *ST* = 18, and m∠*QRS* = 110°. Find each measure. Explain.

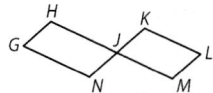

10. *RS*

Opp. sides of *PRQS* are congruent, so *RS* = *PQ* = 17.5.

11. *QT*

The diag. of *PRQS* bisect each other, so *QT* = *ST* = 18.

12. m∠*PQR*

Consec. angles of *PRQS* are supplementary, so m∠*PQR* = 70°.

13. m∠*SPQ*

Opp. angles of *PRQS* are congruent, so m∠*SPQ* = m∠*QRS* = 110°.

Write each proof as a two-column proof.

14. Given: *GHJN* and *JKLM* are parallelograms.
Prove: ∠*G* ≅ ∠*L*

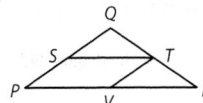

Statements	Reasons
1. *GHJN* and *JKLM* are parallelograms.	1. Given
2. ∠*G* ≅ ∠*HJN*, ∠*KJM* ≅ ∠*L*	2. Opp. angles of a ▱ are congruent.
3. ∠*HJN* ≅ ∠*KJM*	3. Vertical angles are congruent.
4. ∠*G* ≅ ∠*L*	4. Transitive Property of Congruence

15. Given: *PSTV* is a parallelogram. $\overline{PQ} \cong \overline{RQ}$
Prove: ∠*STV* ≅ ∠*R*

Statements	Reasons
1. *PSTV* is a parallelogram.	1. Given
2. ∠*STV* ≅ ∠*P*	2. Opp. angles of a ▱ are congruent.
3. $\overline{PQ} \cong \overline{RQ}$	3. Given
4. △*PQR* is isosceles.	4. Definition of isosceles triangle
5. ∠*P* ≅ ∠*R*	5. Isosceles Triangle Theorem
6. ∠*STV* ≅ ∠*R*	6. Transitive Property of Congruence

© Houghton Mifflin Harcourt Publishing Company • Image Credits: ©Byjeng/Shutterstock

Focus on Reasoning

MP.2 When working with proofs related to properties of parallelograms, encourage students to focus on the accuracy of the hypothesis and conclusion of each statement. In this lesson, the hypothesis of each proof includes a statement that a quadrilateral is a parallelogram. The conclusion of the proof will be a property of the parallelogram.

Advise students to pay close attention to the markings on a diagram, especially when writing a proof. Explain that a quadrilateral with only one set of parallel lines is not a parallelogram.

16. Given: *ABCD* and *AFGH* are parallelograms.
Prove: ∠*C* ≅ ∠*G*

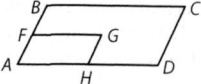

Statements	Reasons
1. *ABCD* and *AFGH* are parallelograms.	1. Given
2. ∠*C* ≅ ∠*A*, ∠*A* ≅ ∠*G*	2. Opposite angles of a parallelogram are congruent.
3. ∠*C* ≅ ∠*G*	3. Trans. Prop. of Cong.

Justify Reasoning Determine whether each statement is always, sometimes, or never true. Explain your reasoning.

17. If quadrilateral *RSTU* is a parallelogram, then $\overline{RS} \cong \overline{ST}$.

Sometimes; opposite sides of a parallelogram are congruent, but consecutive sides, such as $\overline{RS}$ and $\overline{ST}$, may or may not be congruent.

18. If a parallelogram has a 30° angle, then it also has a 150° angle.

Always; consecutive angles of a parallelogram are supplementary, so the angle that is a consecutive angle to the 30° angle must measure 150°.

19. If quadrilateral *GHJK* is a parallelogram, then $\overline{GH}$ is congruent to $\overline{JK}$.

Always; opposite sides of a parallelogram are congruent.

20. In parallelogram *ABCD*, ∠*A* is acute and ∠*C* is obtuse.

Never; opposite angles of a parallelogram are congruent; ∠*A* and ∠*C* are opposite angles, so they must have the same measure.

21. In parallelogram *MNPQ*, the diagonals $\overline{MP}$ and $\overline{NQ}$ meet at *R* with *MR* = 7 cm and *RP* = 5 cm.

Never; diagonals of a parallelogram bisect each other.

22. Communicate Mathematical Ideas Explain how you can use the rotational symmetry of a parallelogram to give an argument that supports the fact that opposite angles of a parallelogram are congruent.

Under a 180° rotation around the center of the parallelogram, each angle is mapped to its opposite angle. Since rotations preserve angle measure, this shows that opposite angles are congruent.

23. To repair a large truck or bus, a mechanic might use a parallelogram lift. The figure shows a side view of the lift. *FGKL*, *GHJK*, and *FHJL* are parallelograms.

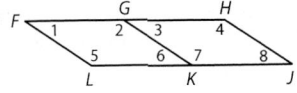

a. Which angles are congruent to ∠1? Explain.

∠3, ∠6, ∠8; ∠3 ≅ ∠1 since $\overline{FL} \parallel \overline{GK}$ and ∠3 and ∠1 are corresponding angles; ∠6 ≅ ∠1 since opposite angles of a parallelogram are congruent; ∠8 ≅ ∠1 since opposite angles of a parallelogram are congruent.

b. What is the relationship between ∠1 and each of the remaining labeled angles? Explain.

∠1 is supplementary to ∠2, ∠4, ∠5, and ∠7; ∠1 is supplementary to ∠2, ∠4, and ∠5 since consecutive angles of a parallelogram are supplementary. Because opposite angles of a parallelogram are congruent, ∠7 ≅ ∠4. So if ∠1 is supplementary to ∠4, then ∠1 is also supplementary to ∠7.

24. Justify Reasoning *ABCD* is a parallelogram. Determine whether each statement must be true. Select the correct answer for each lettered part. Explain your reasoning.

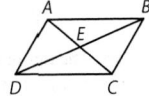

A. The perimeter of *ABCD* is 2*AB* + 2*BC*.   ● Yes ○ No

B. $DE = \frac{1}{2}DB$ ● Yes ○ No

C. $\overline{BC} \cong \overline{DC}$ ○ Yes ● No

D. ∠*DAC* ≅ ∠*BCA*   ● Yes ○ No

E. △*AED* ≅ △*CEB*   ● Yes ○ No

F. ∠*DAC* ≅ ∠*BAC*   ○ Yes ● No

a. Yes; opposite sides of a parallelogram are congruent so *AB* = *DC* and *AD* = *BC*. The perimeter of *ABCD* is *AB* + *BC* + *DC* + *AD* = *AB* + *BC* + *AB* + *BC* = 2*AB* + 2*BC*.

b. Yes; the diag. of a parallelogram bisect each other, so *DE* = *EB* and *DE* = $\frac{1}{2}$*DB*.

c. No; opp. sides are cong., but consecutive sides may or may not be cong.

d. Yes; $\overline{AD} \parallel \overline{BC}$, so ∠*DAC* ≅ ∠*BCA* because they are alternate interior angles.

e. Yes; the diag. of a parallelogram bisect each other, so $\overline{AE} \cong \overline{CE}$ and $\overline{DE} \cong \overline{BE}$; ∠*AED* ≅ ∠*CEB* because they are vert. angles; △*AED* ≅ △*CEB* by the SAS Cong. Thm.

f. No; the diag. of a parallelogram bisect each other, but they may or may not bisect opp. angles of the parallelogram.

PEER-TO-PEER DISCUSSION

Ask students to discuss with a partner how to create a graphic organizer that will display all the properties of parallelograms that they have learned in the lesson. Then have them create the graphic organizer, making sure they include the following properties:

- Opposite sides are parallel.
- Opposite sides are congruent.
- Opposite angles are congruent.
- Consecutive angles are supplementary.
- Diagonals bisect each other.

JOURNAL

Have students summarize the relationships they discovered about parallelograms.

25. Represent Real-World Problems A store sells tiles in the shape of a parallelogram. The perimeter of each tile is 29 inches. One side of each tile is 2.5 inches longer than another side. What are the side lengths of the tile? Explain your steps.

Possible answer: Represent the side lengths as x and $(x + 2.5)$. Since opposite sides of a parallelogram are congruent, the perimeter can be written as $x + (x + 2.5) + x + (x + 2.5)$, or $4x + 5$. Write an equation to solve for x.

$4x + 5 = 29$

So, $x = 6$, and $(x + 2.5) = 8.5$.

So, the side lengths of the tile are 6 inches and 8.5 inches.

26. Critique Reasoning A student claims that there is an SSSS congruence criterion for parallelograms. That is, if all four sides of one parallelogram are congruent to the four sides of another parallelogram, then the parallelograms are congruent. Do you agree? If so, explain why. If not, give a counterexample. Hint: Draw a picture.

No; two parallelograms may have four congruent sides, but their four angles do not also have to be congruent. The figures show a counterexample.

27. Analyze Relationships The figure shows two congruent parallelograms. How are x and y related? Write an equation that expresses the relationship. Explain your reasoning.

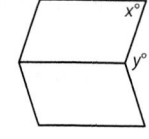

$y = 2x$; Possible explanation: Since opposite sides of a parallelogram are parallel, if the common side of the parallelograms is extended, the angles formed by the extended side each measure $x°$ because alternate interior angles are congruent.

Lesson Performance Task

The principle that allows a scissor lift to raise the platform on top of it to a considerable height can be illustrated with four freezer pop sticks attached at the corners.

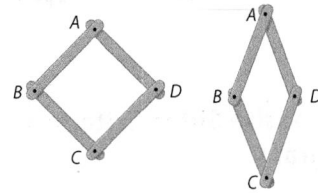

Answer these questions about what happens to parallelogram *ABCD* when you change its shape as in the illustration.

   a. Is it still a parallelogram? Explain.

   b. Is its area the same? Explain.

   c. Compare the lengths of the diagonals in the two figures as you change them.

   d. Describe a process that might be used to raise the platform on a scissor lift.

a. Yes. Its opposite sides are still parallel and congruent.

b. No. As you move points *B* and *D* closer to each other, the area decreases.

c. Horizontal diagonal $\overline{BD}$ decreases in length. Vertical diagonal $\overline{AC}$ increases in length.

d. Possible answer: Apply an inward horizontal force from both sides on the bottom parallelogram.

INTEGRATE MATHEMATICAL PRACTICES
Focus on Math Connections

MP.1 An inventor considered building a scissor lift from triangles rather than parallelograms. The inventor believed that simpler and cheaper 3-sided shapes would appeal to budget-minded customers. What advice would you give to the inventor and why? Sample answer: Triangles are rigid, meaning their shapes can't change. A triangular scissor lift wouldn't work because the triangular sections could not be made to expand or contract.

INTEGRATE MATHEMATICAL PRACTICES
Focus on Critical Thinking

MP.3 One angle of a parallelogram is a right angle. Describe the other angles. Explain your reasoning. The other angles are also right angles; Sample answer: Since the opposite angles of a parallelogram are congruent, the angle opposite the right angle must also be a right angle. Since consecutive angles of a parallelogram are supplementary, the measures of the two remaining angles must each be $180° - 90° = 90°$. So, both are also right angles.

EXTENSION ACTIVITY

Supply students with sheets of light cardboard or photo-print paper, and some brads. Instruct students to cut out twelve 5-inch-by-0.5-inch strips and to attach the ends with brads in such a way as to make a model of a 3-parallelogram scissor lift. Have students demonstrate the operation of the lift, describing how the elements of the parallelogram (angle measures, side length, shape, area) change as the lift increases and decreases in total height.

Scoring Rubric

2 points: Student correctly solves the problem and explains his/her reasoning.

1 point: Student shows good understanding of the problem but does not fully solve or explain.

0 points: Student does not demonstrate understanding of the problem.

Properties of Parallelograms   **432**

Conditions for Parallelograms

Common Core Math Standards

The student is expected to:

COMMON CORE **G-CO.C.11**

Prove theorems about parallelograms. Also G-CO.C.10, G-SRT.B.5

Mathematical Practices

COMMON CORE **MP.2 Reasoning**

Language Objective

Explain to a partner how to identify the opposite sides, opposite angles, and consecutive angles and sides of a quadrilateral.

ENGAGE

Essential Question: What criteria can you use to prove that a quadrilateral is a parallelogram?

Opposite sides are congruent; opposite sides are parallel; opposite angles are congruent; one angle is supplementary to both its consecutive angles; a pair of opposite sides are congruent and parallel; diagonals bisect one another.

PREVIEW: LESSON PERFORMANCE TASK

View the Engage section online. Discuss the photo. Be sure students understand that the stars in a constellation are at various distances from Earth, and that the shape the constellation appears to take is purely a line-of-sight effect. Then preview the Lesson Performance Task.

Name_____ Class_____ Date_____

9.2 Conditions for Parallelograms

Essential Question: What criteria can you use to prove that a quadrilateral is a parallelogram?

Resource Locker

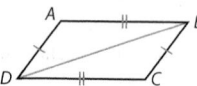 **Explore** **Proving the Opposite Sides Criterion for a Parallelogram**

You can prove that a quadrilateral is a parallelogram by using the definition of a parallelogram. That is, you can show that both pairs of opposite sides are parallel. However, there are other conditions that also guarantee that a quadrilateral is a parallelogram.

Theorem
If both pairs of opposite sides of a quadrilateral are congruent, then the quadrilateral is a parallelogram.

Complete the proof of the theorem.

Given: $\overline{AB} \cong \overline{CD}$ and $\overline{AD} \cong \overline{CB}$

Prove: *ABCD* is a parallelogram.

(A) Draw diagonal $\overline{DB}$.

Why is it helpful to draw this diagonal?

Drawing the auxiliary line, diagonal $\overline{DB}$, creates two triangles to use in the proof.

_____

(B) Use triangle congruence theorems and corresponding parts to complete the proof that the opposite sides are parallel so the quadrilateral is a parallelogram.

Statements	Reasons
1. Draw $\overline{DB}$.	1. Through any two points, there is exactly one line.
2. $\overline{DB} \cong \overline{DB}$	2. Reflexive Property of Congruence
3. $\overline{AB} \cong \overline{CD}$; $\overline{AD} \cong \overline{CB}$	3. Given
4. $\triangle ABD \cong \triangle CDB$	4. SSS Triangle Congruence Theorem
5. $\angle ABD \cong \angle CDB$; $\angle ADB \cong \angle CBD$	5. CPCTC
6. $\overline{AB} \parallel \overline{DC}$; $\overline{AD} \parallel \overline{BC}$	6. Converse of the Alternate Interior Angles Theorem
7. *ABCD* is a parallelogram.	7. Definition of parallelogram

© Houghton Mifflin Harcourt Publishing Company

Module 9 **433** Lesson 2

HARDCOVER PAGES 371–382

Turn to these pages to find this lesson in the hardcover student edition.

It is possible to combine the theorem from the Explore and the definition of a parallelogram to state the following condition for proving a quadrilateral is a parallelogram. You will prove this in the exercises.

Theorem

If one pair of opposite sides of a quadrilateral are parallel and congruent, then the quadrilateral is a parallelogram.

Reflect

1. **Discussion** A quadrilateral has two sides that are 3 cm long and two sides that are 5 cm long. A student states that the quadrilateral must be a parallelogram. Do you agree? Explain.

   Disagree; you can only conclude that the quadrilateral is a parallelogram if you know that

   the congruent sides are opposite each other.

⊘ Explain 1   Proving the Opposite Angles Criterion for a Parallelogram

You can use relationships between angles to prove that a quadrilateral is a parallelogram.

Theorem

If both pairs of opposite angles of a quadrilateral are congruent, then the quadrilateral is a parallelogram.

Example 1 Prove that a quadrilateral is a parallelogram if its opposite angles are congruent.

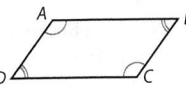

Given: $\angle A \cong \angle C$ and $\angle B \cong \angle D$ Prove: $ABCD$ is a parallelogram.

$m\angle A + m\angle B + m\angle C + m\angle D = 360°$ by ___the Polygon Angle Sum Theorem___.

From the given information, $m\angle A = m\angle$ **C** and $m\angle B = m\angle$ **D** . By substitution,

$m\angle A + m\angle D + m\angle A + m\angle D = 360°$ or $2m\angle$ **A** $+ 2m\angle$ **D** $= 360°$. Dividing

both sides by 2 gives ___$m\angle A + m\angle D = 180°$___. Therefore, $\angle A$ and $\angle D$ are

supplementary and so $\overline{AB} \parallel \overline{DC}$ by the ___Converse of the Same-Side Interior Angles Postulate.___

A similar argument shows that $\overline{AD} \parallel \overline{BC}$, so $ABCD$ is a parallelogram

by ___the definition of parallelogram___.

Reflect

2. What property or theorem justifies dividing both sides of the equation by 2 in the above proof?
   Division Property of Equality

PROFESSIONAL DEVELOPMENT

 ### Math Background

In this lesson, students extend their earlier work with the properties of parallelograms to establish sufficient conditions for concluding that a quadrilateral is a parallelogram. A quadrilateral is a parallelogram if its opposite sides are parallel, if its opposite sides are congruent, if its opposite angles are congruent, if its diagonals bisect each other, or if one pair of opposite sides is congruent and parallel. It is worth emphasizing that the statements to prove in the previous lesson all have the form "If a quadrilateral is a parallelogram, then [property]." In contrast, the statements to prove in this lesson all have the form, "If [condition], then the quadrilateral is a parallelogram."

EXPLORE

Proving the Opposite Sides Criterion for a Parallelogram

INTEGRATE TECHNOLOGY

Students have the option of doing the proof activity either in the book or online.

QUESTIONING STRATEGIES

? What is a sufficient condition to prove that a quadrilateral is a parallelogram? Either both pairs of opposite sides are parallel, or both pairs of opposite sides are congruent.

EXPLAIN 1

Proving the Opposite Angles Criterion for a Parallelogram

INTEGRATE MATHEMATICS PRACTICES
Focus on Math Connections

MP.1 The proof of this criterion depends on students understanding the hypothesis and conclusion of the statement. Both pairs of opposite angles are given to be congruent, and that is part of the hypothesis. Having these angles congruent leads to both pairs of opposite sides of the quadrilateral being parallel, which satisfies the definition of a parallelogram. Stating that the quadrilateral is a parallelogram is the conclusion.

QUESTIONING STRATEGIES

? Suppose only one pair of opposite angles of a quadrilateral are congruent. Can you still conclude that the quadrilateral is a parallelogram? Explain. No; in this case, the quadrilateral could be a kite.

Conditions for Parallelograms   **434**

EXPLAIN 2

Proving the Bisecting Diagonals Criterion for a Parallelogram

INTEGRATE MATHEMATICAL PRACTICES

Focus on Reasoning

MP.2 Students should read this criterion carefully and pay attention to the sufficient conditions given and to how the criterion is proved. The proof depends on students using the SAS Congruence Criterion, the Vertical Angles Theorem, and the Opposite Sides Criterion. Pairs of triangles formed by the diagonals are congruent, and this makes the opposite sides of the quadrilateral congruent, so that the Opposite Sides Criterion (for a parallelogram) applies.

QUESTIONING STRATEGIES

? How does the proof of this criterion use the Opposite Sides Criterion? The proof uses the SAS triangle congruence criteria and the fact that corresponding parts of congruent triangles are congruent to show that the opposite sides of a quadrilateral are congruent. Then the Opposite Sides Criterion is applied to state that the quadrilateral must be a parallelogram.

? In the proof of the Opposite Sides Criterion, which theorem justifies that both pairs of opposite sides are parallel? Once the alternate interior angles are stated to be congruent, the Converse of the Alternate Interior Angles Theorem states that the lines are parallel.

Explain 2 **Proving the Bisecting Diagonals Criterion for a Parallelogram**

You can use information about the diagonals in a given figure to show that the figure is a parallelogram.

Theorem
If the diagonals of a quadrilateral bisect each other, then the quadrilateral is a parallelogram.

Example 2 Prove that a quadrilateral whose diagonals bisect each other is a parallelogram.

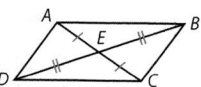

Given: $\overline{AE} \cong \overline{CE}$ and $\overline{DE} \cong \overline{BE}$

Prove: ABCD is a parallelogram.

Statements	Reasons
1. $\overline{AE} \cong \overline{CE}, \overline{DE} \cong \overline{BE}$	1. Given
2. $\angle AEB \cong \angle CED, \angle AED \cong \angle CEB$	2. Vertical angles are congruent.
3. $\triangle AEB \cong \triangle CED, \triangle AED \cong \triangle CEB$	3. SAS Triangle Congruence Theorem
4. $\overline{AB} \cong \overline{CD}, \overline{AD} \cong \overline{CB}$	4. CPCTC
5. ABCD is a parallelogram.	5. If both pairs of opposite sides of a quadrilateral are congruent, then it is a parallelogram.

Reflect

3. **Critique Reasoning** A student claimed that you can also write the proof using the SSS Triangle Congruence Theorem since $\overline{AB} \cong \overline{CD}$ and $\overline{AD} \cong \overline{CB}$. Do you agree? Justify your response.
No; in order to use the fact that opposite sides are congruent, you must first know that the quadrilateral is a parallelogram.

Explain 3 **Using a Parallelogram to Prove the Concurrency of the Medians of a Triangle**

Sometimes properties of one type of geometric figure can be used to recognize properties of another geometric figure. Recall that you explored triangles and found that the medians of a triangle are concurrent at a point that is $\frac{2}{3}$ of the distance from each vertex to the midpoint of the opposite side. You can prove this theorem using one of the conditions for a parallelogram from this lesson.

Example 3 Complete the proof of the Concurrency of Medians of a Triangle Theorem.

Given: $\triangle ABC$

Prove: The medians of $\triangle ABC$ are concurrent at a point that is $\frac{2}{3}$ of the distance from each vertex to the midpoint of the opposite side.

COLLABORATIVE LEARNING

Peer-to-Peer Activity

Divide students into pairs. Have one student draw different quadrilaterals (kites, rhombuses, rectangles, etc.). Have the other student determine whether the quadrilateral meets any of the criteria for a parallelogram, and list them. After a while, have the students switch roles.

© Houghton Mifflin Harcourt Publishing Company

Let $\triangle ABC$ be a triangle such that M is the midpoint of $\overline{AB}$ and N is the midpoint of $\overline{BC}$. Label the point where the two medians intersect as P. Draw $\overline{MN}$.

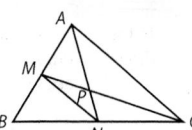

$\overline{MN}$ is a midsegment of $\triangle ABC$ because it connects the midpoints of two sides of the triangle.

$\overline{MN}$ is parallel to __AC__ and $MN = \underline{\frac{1}{2}AC}$ by the Triangle Midsegment Theorem.

Let Q be the midpoint of $\overline{PA}$ and let R be the midpoint of $\overline{PC}$. Draw $\overline{QR}$.

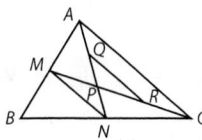

$\overline{QR}$ is a midsegment of $\triangle APC$ because it connects the midpoints of two sides of the triangle.

$\overline{QR}$ is parallel to __AC__ and $QR = \underline{\frac{1}{2}AC}$ by the Triangle Midsegment Theorem.

So, you can conclude that $MN = \underline{QR}$ by substitution and that $\overline{MN} \parallel \overline{QR}$ because __both segments are parallel to the same segment__.

Now draw $\overline{MQ}$ and $\overline{NR}$ and consider quadrilateral $MQRN$.

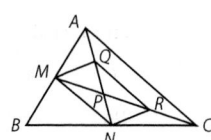

Quadrilateral $MQRN$ is a parallelogram because __a pair of opposite sides are congruent and parallel__.

Since the diagonals of a parallelogram bisect each other, then $QP = \underline{NP}$.

Also, $AQ = QP$ since __Q is the midpoint of $\overline{PA}$__.

Therefore, $AQ = QP = \underline{NP}$. This shows that point P is located on $\overline{AN}$ at a point that is $\frac{2}{3}$ of the distance from A to N.

By similar reasoning, the diagonals of a parallelogram bisect each other, so $RP = \underline{MP}$.

Also, $CR = RP$ since __R is the midpoint of $\overline{PC}$__.

Therefore, $CR = RP = \underline{MP}$. This shows that point P is located on $\overline{CM}$ at a point that is $\frac{2}{3}$ of the distance from C to M.

You can repeat the proof using any two medians of $\triangle ABC$. The same reasoning shows that the medians from vertices B and C intersect at a point that is also $\frac{2}{3}$ of the distance from C to M, so this point must also be point P. This shows that the three medians intersect at a unique point P and that the point is $\frac{2}{3}$ of the distance from each vertex to the midpoint of the opposite side.

© Houghton Mifflin Harcourt Publishing Company

EXPLAIN 3

Using a Parallelogram to Prove the Concurrency of the Medians of a Triangle

QUESTIONING STRATEGIES

? How is the Triangle Midsegment Theorem used in proving the concurrency of the medians in a triangle? The Triangle Midsegment Theorem is used to show that the opposite sides of a quadrilateral are parallel. This creates a parallelogram within the triangle. Then, since the diagonals of a parallelogram bisect each other, the parallelogram in turn is used to prove the concurrency of the medians in the triangle.

AVOID COMMON ERRORS

Students may be confused when asked to locate the midsegments in a triangle that already has the medians labeled for this proof. Have students use one color pencil to mark the medians, a second color pencil to mark the midsegments, and a third color pencil to mark the congruent segments on the diagonals of the parallelogram.

DIFFERENTIATE INSTRUCTION

Kinesthetic Experience

Have students use raw spaghetti to demonstrate the theorems in the lesson. For example, ask them to try to form a parallelogram with opposite sides that are congruent but not parallel, or vice versa. This emphasizes that, in the statement that a quadrilateral with a pair of opposite sides parallel and congruent leads to a parallelogram, the same pair of opposite sides must be congruent *and* parallel.

EXPLAIN 4

Verifying Figures Are Parallelograms

QUESTIONING STRATEGIES

? How is the Opposite Sides Criterion used to show that the given quadrilateral is a parallelogram? Algebra is used to show that the opposite sides are congruent after the given values are substituted into the expression. The figure meets the criterion and must be a parallelogram.

AVOID COMMON ERRORS

Some students may not know which criterion to use when proving that a quadrilateral is a parallelogram. Explain that they should study the given information carefully to determine which condition is best to apply. For example, if they are given congruent angles, then they should look only at the two criteria that deal with angles: both pairs of opposite angles are congruent, or one angle is supplementary to both of its consecutive angles.

Reflect

4. In the proof, how do you know that point P is located on $\overline{AN}$ at a point that is $\frac{2}{3}$ of the distance from A to N?
Possible answer: Since $AQ = QP = PN$, $\overline{AN}$ is divided into three segments of equal length $(AQ = QP = PN)$. So, points P and Q divide $\overline{AN}$ into thirds. Therefore, since $AP = AQ + QP = \frac{1}{3}AN + \frac{1}{3}AN = \frac{2}{3}AN$, then point P is $\frac{2}{3}$ of the distance from A to N.

Explain 4 **Verifying Figures Are Parallelograms**

You can use information about sides, angles, and diagonals in a given figure to show that the figure is a parallelogram.

Example 4 Show that each quadrilateral is a parallelogram for the given values of the variables.

(A) $x = 7$ and $y = 4$

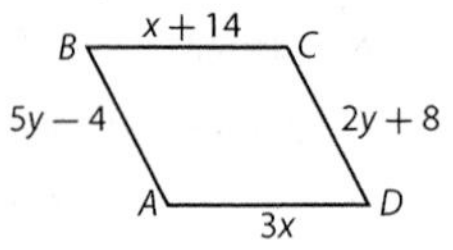

Step 1 Find BC and DA.

$BC = x + 14 = 7 + 14 = 21$

$DA = 3x = 3(7) = 21$

Step 2 Find AB and CD.

$AB = 5y - 4 = 5(4) - 4 = 16$

$CD = 2y + 8 = 2(4) + 8 = 16$

So, $BC = DA$ and $AB = CD$. $ABCD$ is a parallelogram since both pairs of opposite sides are congruent.

(B) $z = 11$ and $w = 4.5$

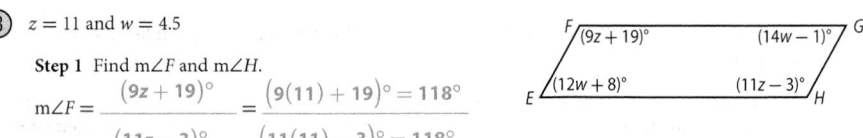

Step 1 Find $m\angle F$ and $m\angle H$.

$m\angle F = \dfrac{(9z + 19)^\circ}{} = \dfrac{(9(11) + 19)^\circ = 118^\circ}{}$

$m\angle H = \dfrac{(11z - 3)^\circ}{} = \dfrac{(11(11) - 3)^\circ = 118^\circ}{}$

Step 2 Find $m\angle E$ and $m\angle G$.

$m\angle E = \dfrac{(12w + 8)^\circ}{} = \dfrac{(12(4.5) + 8)^\circ = 62^\circ}{}$

$m\angle G = \dfrac{(14w - 1)^\circ}{} = \dfrac{(14(4.5) - 1)^\circ = 62^\circ}{}$

So, $m\angle F = m\angle \boxed{H}$ and $m\angle E = m\angle \boxed{G}$. $EFGH$ is a parallelogram since both pairs of opposite angles are congruent.

Reflect

5. What conclusions can you make about $\overline{FG}$ and $\overline{EH}$ in Part B? Explain.
$\overline{FG}$ is parallel and congruent to $\overline{EH}$; $EFGH$ is a parallelogram and opposite sides of a parallelogram are parallel and congruent.

LANGUAGE SUPPORT **EL**

Connect Vocabulary

Encourage students to pay close attention to the key words in each theorem, such as *opposite, parallel,* and *congruent.* Have them write each of the theorems on note cards, illustrate the theorems, and highlight these key words.

Your Turn

Show that each quadrilateral is a parallelogram for the given values of the variables.

6. $a = 2.4$ and $b = 9$

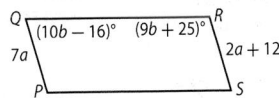

$PQ = 7a = 7(2.4) = 16.8$

$RS = 2a + 12 = 2(2.4) + 12 = 16.8$

$m\angle Q = (10b - 16)^\circ = (10(9) - 16)^\circ = 74^\circ$

$m\angle R = (9b + 25)^\circ = (9(9) + 25)^\circ = 106^\circ$

So, $PQ = RS$. Also, $\overline{PQ} \parallel \overline{RS}$ since same-side

interior angles are supplementary.

$PQRS$ is a parallelogram since a pair of

opposite sides are parallel and congruent.

7. $x = 6$ and $y = 3.5$

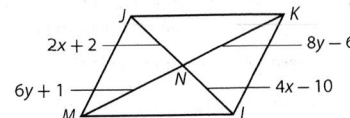

$JN = 2x + 2 = 2(6) + 2 = 14$

$LN = 4x - 10 = 4(6) - 10 = 14$

$KN = 8y - 6 = 8(3.5) - 6 = 22$

$MN = 6y + 1 = 6(3.5) + 1 = 22$

So $JN = LN$ and $KN = MN$. $JKLM$ is a

parallelogram since the diagonals

bisect each other.

💬 Elaborate

8. How are the theorems in this lesson different from the theorems in the previous lesson, Properties of Parallelograms?

In the previous lesson, you begin with a quadrilateral that is known to be a parallelogram

and each theorem states a property of the parallelogram. In this lesson, you begin with a

quadrilateral and each theorem states conditions that guarantee that the quadrilateral is

a parallelogram.

9. Why is the proof of the Concurrency of the Medians of a Triangle Theorem in this lesson and not in the earlier module when the theorem was first introduced?

The proof involves creating a quadrilateral that needs to be shown is a parallelogram.

This could not be done before this lesson.

10. Essential Question Check-In Describe three different ways to show that quadrilateral $ABCD$ is a parallelogram.

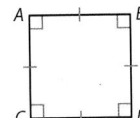

Possible answer: Since right angles are congruent, opposite angles of $ABCD$ are congruent.

Therefore, $ABCD$ is a parallelogram. Opposite sides of $ABCD$ are congruent, so $ABCD$ is a

parallelogram. $\angle A$ is supplementary to $\angle D$, so $\overline{AB} \parallel \overline{CD}$. Therefore, $ABCD$ is a parallelogram

since a pair of opposite sides are congruent and parallel.

ELABORATE

QUESTIONING STRATEGIES

? How do the theorems in this lesson differ from the ones in the previous lesson? They are converses. Here we know the properties, and are proving the quadrilateral is a parallelogram; previously, we knew the figure was a parallelogram and we were proving properties.

SUMMARIZE THE LESSON

? Two opposite angles in a quadrilateral each measure 103°. Can you conclude that this quadrilateral is a parallelogram? Explain why or draw a counterexample. No, we can't, because only one pair of opposite angles is congruent. Possible counterexample:

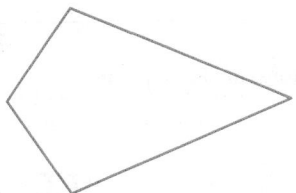

EVALUATE

ASSIGNMENT GUIDE

Concepts and Skills	Practice
Explore Proving the Opposite Sides Criterion for a Parallelogram	Exercise 1
Example 1 Proving the Opposite Angles Criterion for a Parallelogram	Exercise 2
Example 2 Proving the Bisecting Diagonals Criterion for a Parallelogram	Exercise 3
Example 3 Using a Parallelogram to Prove the Concurrency of the Medians of a Triangle	Exercise 4
Example 4 Verifying Figures are Parallelograms	Exercises 5–12

INTEGRATE MATHEMATICAL PRACTICES

Focus on Modeling

MP.4 Some students may benefit from a hands-on approach for exploring which quadrilaterals are parallelograms. Have students copy a larger version of the quadrilateral in an exercise onto a sheet of paper and then cut it out. Have them use a ruler to verify that the opposite sides are congruent, or a protractor to verify that the opposite angles are congruent, so that the criteria for the quadrilateral to be a parallelogram are satisfied.

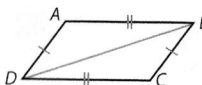
1. You have seen a proof that if both pairs of opposite sides of a quadrilateral are congruent, then the quadrilateral is a parallelogram. Write the proof as a flow proof.

Given: $\overline{AB} \cong \overline{CD}$ and $\overline{AD} \cong \overline{CB}$

Prove: $ABCD$ is a parallelogram.

Possible answer:

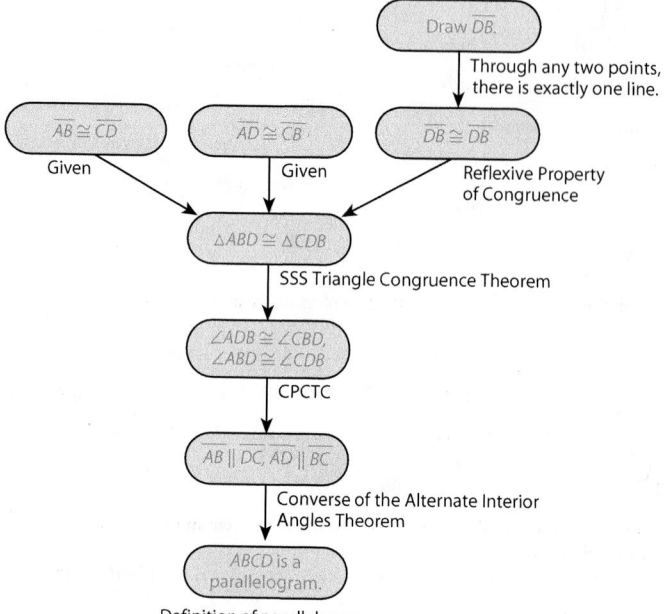

© Houghton Mifflin Harcourt Publishing Company

Exercise	Depth of Knowledge (D.O.K.)	COMMON CORE Mathematical Practices
1–4	**2** Skills/Concepts	**MP.3** Logic
5–12	**1** Recall	**MP.5** Using Tools
13–18	**2** Skills/Concepts	**MP.2** Reasoning
19	**3** Strategic Thinking H.O.T.	**MP.3** Logic
20	**3** Strategic Thinking H.O.T.	**MP.4** Modeling
21	**3** Strategic Thinking H.O.T.	**MP.2** Reasoning

2. You have seen a proof that if both pairs of opposite angles of a quadrilateral are congruent, then the quadrilateral is a parallelogram. Write the proof as a two-column proof.

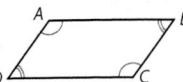

Given: $\angle A \cong \angle C$ and $\angle B \cong \angle D$

Prove: $ABCD$ is a parallelogram.

Statements	Reasons
1. $\angle A \cong \angle C$ and $\angle B \cong \angle D$	1. Given
2. $m\angle A + m\angle B + m\angle C + m\angle D = 360°$	2. Polygon Angle Sum Theorem
3. $m\angle A + m\angle B + m\angle A + m\angle B = 360°$; $m\angle A + m\angle D + m\angle A + m\angle D = 360°$	3. Substitution Property of Equality
4. $2m\angle A + 2m\angle B = 360°$; $2m\angle A + 2m\angle D = 360°$	4. Distributive Property
5. $m\angle A + m\angle B = 180°$; $m\angle A + m\angle D = 180°$	5. Division Property of Equality
6. $\angle A$ and $\angle B$ are supplementary; $\angle A$ and $\angle D$ are supplementary.	6. Definition of supplementary angles
7. $\overline{AD} \parallel \overline{BC}$ and $\overline{AB} \parallel \overline{DC}$	7. Converse of the Same-Side Interior Angles Postulate
8. $ABCD$ is a parallelogram.	8. Definition of parallelogram

3. You have seen a proof that if the diagonals of a quadrilateral bisect each other, then the quadrilateral is a parallelogram. Write the proof as a paragraph proof.

Given: $\overline{AE} \cong \overline{CE}$ and $\overline{DE} \cong \overline{BE}$

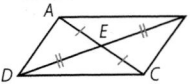

Prove: $ABCD$ is a parallelogram.

Possible answer: It is given that $\overline{AE} \cong \overline{CE}$ and $\overline{DE} \cong \overline{BE}$. Since vertical angles are congruent, $\angle AEB \cong \angle CED$ and $\angle AED \cong \angle CEB$. Therefore, $\triangle AEB \cong \triangle CED$ and $\triangle AED \cong \triangle CEB$ by the SAS Triangle Congruence Theorem. Since corresponding parts of congruent triangles are congruent, $\overline{AB} \cong \overline{CD}$ and $\overline{AD} \cong \overline{CB}$. So, $ABCD$ is a parallelogram because if both pairs of opposite sides of a quadrilateral are congruent, then the quadrilateral is a parallelogram.

4. Complete the following proof of the Triangle Midsegment Theorem.

Given: D is the midpoint of $\overline{AC}$, and E is the midpoint of $\overline{BC}$.

Prove: $\overline{DE} \parallel \overline{AB}$, $DE = \frac{1}{2}AB$

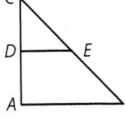

Extend $\overline{DE}$ to form $\overline{DF}$ such that $\overline{DE} \cong \overline{FE}$. Then draw $\overline{BF}$, as shown.

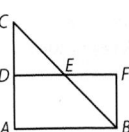

MP.2 Point out that only one criterion of the six listed below needs to be met to show that a quadrilateral is a parallelogram:

Both pairs of opposite sides are parallel.

One pair of opposite sides is parallel and congruent.

Both pairs of opposite sides are congruent.

Both pairs of opposite angles are congruent.

One angle is supplementary to both of its consecutive angles.

The diagonals bisect each other.

It is given that E is the midpoint of $\overline{CB}$, so $\overline{CE} \cong$ $\underline{\overline{BE}}$.

By the Vertical Angles Theorem, $\angle CED \cong$ $\underline{\angle BEF}$.

So, $\triangle CED \cong$ $\underline{\triangle BEF}$ by $\underline{\text{the SAS Triangle Congruence Theorem}}$

Since corresponding parts of congruent triangles are congruent, $\overline{CD} \cong$ $\underline{\overline{BF}}$.

D is the midpoint of $\overline{AC}$, so $\overline{CD} \cong$ $\underline{\overline{AD}}$.

By the Transitive Property of Congruence, $\overline{AD} \cong$ $\underline{\overline{BF}}$.

Also, since corresponding parts of congruent triangles are congruent, $\angle CDE \cong$ $\underline{\angle BFE}$

So, $\overline{AC} \parallel \overline{FB}$ by $\underline{\text{Converse of the Alternate Interior Angles Theorem}}$

This shows that $DFBA$ is a parallelogram because $\underline{\text{a pair of opposite sides}}$ $\underline{\text{are congruent and parallel}}$

By the definition of parallelogram, $\overline{DE}$ is parallel to $\underline{\overline{AB}}$.

Since opposite sides of a parallelogram are congruent, $AB = \underline{FD}$.

$\overline{DE} \cong \overline{FE}$, so $DE = \frac{1}{2}\boxed{DF}$ and by substitution, $DE = \frac{1}{2}\boxed{AB}$.

Show that each quadrilateral is a parallelogram for the given values of the variables.

5. $x = 4$ and $y = 9$

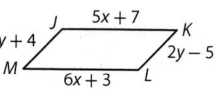

$JK = 5x + 7 = 5(4) + 7 = 27$
$LM = 6x + 3 = 6(4) + 3 = 27$
$KL = 2y - 5 = 2(9) - 5 = 13$
$MJ = y + 4 = 9 + 4 = 13$
So, $JK = LM$ and $KL = MJ$. $JKLM$ is a parallelogram.

6. $u = 8$ and $v = 3.5$

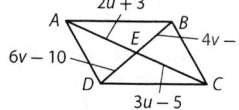

$AE = 2u + 3 = 2(8) + 3 = 19$
$CE = 3u - 5 = 3(8) - 5 = 19$
$BE = 4v - 3 = 4(3.5) - 3 = 11$
$DE = 6v - 10 = 6(3.5) - 10 = 11$
So $AE = CE$ and $BE = DE$. $ABCD$ is a parallelogram.

Determine if each quadrilateral must be a parallelogram. Justify your answer.

7.

No. One pair of opposite sides are parallel. A different pair of opposite sides are congruent.

8.

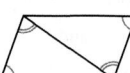

Yes. the third pair of angles in the triangles are congruent. So, both pairs of opposite angles are congruent.

9.

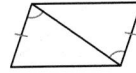

Yes. A pair of alternate interior angles are congruent, so a pair of opposite sides are parallel. The same pair of opposite sides are congruent by SAS and CPCTC.

10.

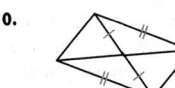

No. One pair of opposite sides are congruent and one diagonal is bisected by the other.

11.

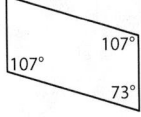

Yes. The 73° angle is supplementary to both of the 107° angles. This shows that both pairs of opposite sides are parallel by the Converse of the Same-Side Interior Angles Postulate.

12.

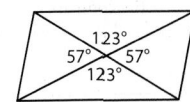

No. You are only given the measures of the four angles formed by the intersecting diagonals of the quadrilateral.

13. Communicate Mathematical Ideas Kalil wants to write the proof that the medians of a triangle are concurrent at a point that is $\frac{2}{3}$ of the distance from each vertex to the midpoint of the opposite side. He starts by drawing $\triangle PQR$ and two medians, $\overline{PK}$ and $\overline{QL}$. He labels the point of intersection as point J, as shown. What segment should Kalil draw next? What conclusions can he make about this segment? Explain.

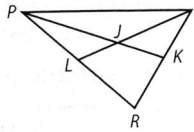

He should draw $\overline{KL}$. $\overline{KL}$ is a midsegment of $\triangle PQR$ because it connects the midpoints of two sides of the triangle. $\overline{KL}$ is parallel to $\overline{PQ}$ and $KL = \frac{1}{2} PQ$ by the Triangle Midsegment Theorem.

14. Critical Thinking Jasmina said that you can draw a parallelogram using the following steps.

1. Draw a point P.

2. Use a ruler to draw a segment that is 1 inch long with its midpoint at P.

3. Use the ruler to draw a segment that is 2 inches long with its midpoint at P.

4. Use the ruler to connect the endpoints of the segments to form a parallelogram.

Does Jasmina's method always work? Is there ever a time when it would not produce a parallelogram? Explain.

The method always works as long as the second segment does not overlap the first segment. The two segments are diagonals. Since the diagonals bisect each other, the quadrilateral is a parallelogram.

PEER-TO-PEER DISCUSSION

Ask students to discuss with a partner how to create a graphic organizer that will display all the criteria they have learned that make a quadrilateral a parallelogram. Then have them create the graphic organizer and make sure they include the following criteria:

- Opposite sides parallel
- Opposite sides congruent
- Opposite angles congruent
- Consecutive angles supplementary
- Diagonals bisecting each other
- One pair of sides congruent and parallel

15. Critique Reasoning Matthew said that there is another condition for parallelograms. He said that if a quadrilateral has two congruent diagonals, then the quadrilateral is a parallelogram. Do you agree? If so, explain why. If not, give a counterexample to show why the condition does not work.

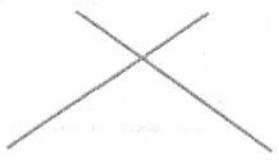

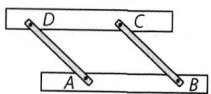

No. The figure shows a counterexample. The diagonals are congruent, but the quadrilateral does not have two pairs of parallel opposite sides, so it is not a parallelogram.

16. A parallel rule can be used to plot a course on a navigation chart. The tool is made of two rulers connected at hinges to two congruent crossbars, $\overline{AD}$ and $\overline{BC}$. You place the edge of one ruler on your desired course and then move the second ruler over the compass rose on the chart to read the bearing for your course. If $\overline{AD} \parallel \overline{BC}$, why is $\overline{AB}$ always parallel to $\overline{CD}$?

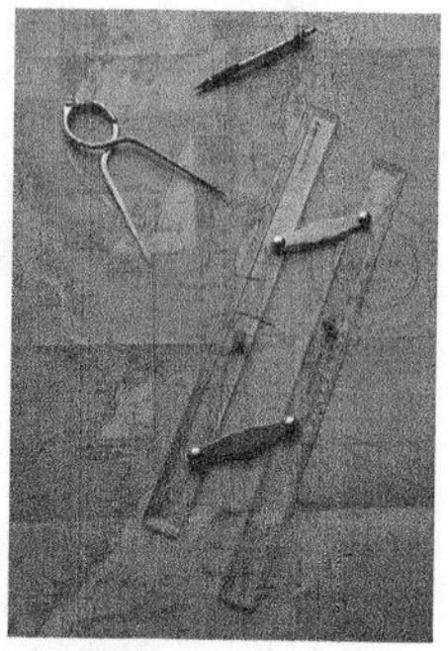

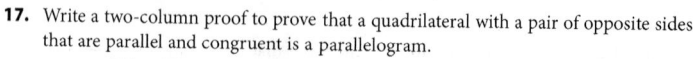

Possible answer: $\overline{AD}$ and $\overline{BC}$ are opposite sides of a quadrilateral. It is given that $\overline{AD} \parallel \overline{BC}$ and $\overline{AD} \cong \overline{BC}$. Therefore, $ABCD$ is a parallelogram. So, $\overline{AB}$ is always parallel to $\overline{CD}$.

17. Write a two-column proof to prove that a quadrilateral with a pair of opposite sides that are parallel and congruent is a parallelogram.

Given: $\overline{AB} \cong \overline{CD}$ and $\overline{AB} \parallel \overline{CD}$

Prove: $ABCD$ is a parallelogram. (*Hint*: Draw $\overline{DB}$.)

Statements	Reasons
1. Draw $\overline{DB}$	1. 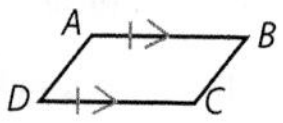 Through any two points, there is exactly one line.
2. $\overline{AB} \cong \overline{CD}$	2. Given
3. $\overline{AB} \parallel \overline{CD}$	3. Given
4. $\angle ABD \cong \angle CDB$	4. Alternate Interior Angles Theorem
5. $\overline{DB} \cong \overline{DB}$	5. Reflexive Property of Congruence
6. $\triangle ABD \cong \triangle CDB$	6. SAS Triangle Congruence Theorem
7. $\overline{AD} \cong \overline{CB}$	7. CPCTC
8. $ABCD$ is a parallelogram.	8. If both pairs of opposite sides of a quadrilateral are congruent, then the quadrilateral is a parallelogram.

18. Does each set of given information guarantee that quadrilateral *JKLM* is a parallelogram? Select the correct answer for each lettered part.

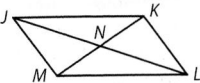

A. $JN = 25$ cm, $JL = 50$ cm, $KN = 13$ cm, $KM = 26$ cm   ⬤ Yes   ◯ No

B. $\angle MJL \cong \angle KLJ$, $\overline{JM} \cong \overline{LK}$ ⬤ Yes   ◯ No

C. $\overline{JM} \cong \overline{JK}$, $\overline{KL} \cong \overline{LM}$ ◯ Yes   ⬤ No

D. $\angle MJL \cong \angle MLJ$, $\angle KJL \cong \angle KLJ$ ◯ Yes   ⬤ No

E. $\triangle JKN \cong \triangle LMN$ ⬤ Yes   ◯ No

a. Yes; The diagonals of the quadrilateral bisect each other, so *JKLM* is a parallelogram.

b. Yes; A pair of opposite sides are both parallel and congruent, so *JKLM* is a parallelogram.

c. No; none of the conditions for a parallelogram are met.

d. No; none of the conditions for a parallelogram are met.

e. Yes; A pair of opposite sides are both parallel and congruent, so *JKLM* is a parallelogram.

H.O.T. Focus on Higher Order Thinking

19. Explain the Error A student wrote the two-column proof below. Explain the student's error and explain how to write the proof correctly.

Given: $\angle 1 \cong \angle 2$, *E* is the midpoint of $\overline{AC}$.

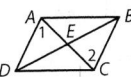

Prove: *ABCD* is a parallelogram.

Statements	Reasons
1. $\angle 1 \cong \angle 2$	1. Given
2. *E* is the midpoint of $\overline{AC}$.	2. Given
3. $\overline{AE} \cong \overline{CE}$	3. Definition of midpoint
4. $\angle AED \cong \angle CEB$	4. Vertical angles are congruent.
5. $\triangle AED \cong \triangle CEB$	5. ASA Triangle Congruence Theorem
6. $\overline{AD} \cong \overline{CB}$	6. Corresponding parts of congruent triangles are congruent
7. *ABCD* is a parallelogram.	7. If a pair of opposite sides of a quadrillateral are congruent, then the quadrillateral is a parallelogram.

Possible answer: The student used an invalid reason in Step 7. The student should also show that $\overline{AD} \parallel \overline{CB}$. This is true because $\angle 1 \cong \angle 2$ and these are alternate interior angles. Then the student can conclude that *ABCD* is a parallelogram because a pair of opposite sides are both parallel and congruent.

INTEGRATE MATHEMATICAL PRACTICES

Focus on Critical Thinking

MP.3 At this point, students may be thinking of the theorems from Lesson 9–1 and Lesson 9–2 as "if and only if statements" (biconditionals) about the relationship between quadrilaterals and parallelograms. Many of the theorems can be combined to be biconditionals, but make sure students can still focus on which phrase is the hypothesis and which phrase is the conclusion when they apply the theorems. For the exercises in this lesson, the hypothesis includes a statement that a quadrilateral has certain given attributes. The conclusion of the statement is that the quadrilateral is a parallelogram.

JOURNAL

Have students describe how to use the measures of the sides of a quadrilateral to determine whether it is a parallelogram.

---

20. Persevere in Problem Solving The plan for a city park shows that the park is a quadrilateral with straight paths along the diagonals. For what values of the variables is the park a parallelogram? In this case, what are the lengths of the paths?

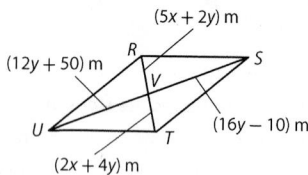

If the diagonals bisect each other, then *RSTU* will be a parallelogram, so assume $RV = TV$ and $SV = UV$.

$$16y - 10 = 12y + 50$$
$$4y - 10 = 50$$
$$4y = 60$$
$$y = 15$$
$$5x + 2y = 2x + 4y$$
$$5x + 2(15) = 2x + 4(15)$$
$$5x + 30 = 2x + 60$$
$$3x + 30 = 60$$
$$3x = 30$$
$$x = 10$$

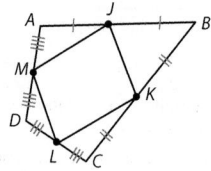

$UV = 12y + 50 = 12(15) + 50 = 230$ m

$US = 2UV = 2(230) = 460$ m

$RV = 5x + 2y = 5(10) + 2(15) = 80$ m

$RT = 2RV = 2(80) = 160$ m

The lengths of the paths are 230 m and 160 m.

21. Analyze Relationships When you connect the midpoints of the consecutive sides of any quadrilateral, the resulting quadrilateral is a parallelogram. Use the figure below to explain why this is true. (*Hint:* Draw a diagonal of *ABCD*.)

Possible answer: When you draw $\overline{AC}$, you form $\triangle DAC$ and $\triangle BAC$. $\overline{LM}$ is a midsegment of $\triangle DAC$, so $\overline{LM} \parallel \overline{AC}$ and $LM = \frac{1}{2}AC$. $\overline{JK}$ is a midsegment of $\triangle BAC$, so $\overline{JK} \parallel \overline{AC}$ and $JK = \frac{1}{2}AC$. This shows that $\overline{LM} \parallel \overline{JK}$ and $LM = JK$, so $\overline{LM} \cong \overline{JK}$. A pair of opposite sides of *JKLM* are both parallel and congruent, so *JKLM* is a parallelogram.

Module 9

445

Lesson 2

© Houghton Mifflin Harcourt Publishing Company • Image Credits: ©Beth Reitmeyer/Houghton Mifflin Harcourt

445 Lesson 9.2

Lesson Performance Task

In this lesson you've learned three theorems for confirming that a figure is a parallelogram.

- If both pairs of opposite sides of a quadrilateral are congruent, then the quadrilateral is a parallelogram.
- If both pairs of opposite angles of a quadrilateral are congruent, then the quadrilateral is a parallelogram.
- If the diagonals of a quadrilateral bisect each other, then the quadrilateral is a parallelogram.

For each of the following situations, choose one of the three theorems and use it in your explanation. You should choose a different theorem for each explanation.

a. You're an amateur astronomer, and one night you see what appears to be a parallelogram in the constellation of Lyra. Explain how you could verify that the figure is a parallelogram.

b. You have a frame shop and you want to make an interesting frame for an advertisement for your store. You decide that you'd like the frame to be a parallelogram but not a rectangle. Explain how you could construct the frame.

c. You're using a toolbox with cantilever shelves like the one shown here. Explain how you can confirm that the brackets that attach the shelves to the box form a parallelogram ABCD.

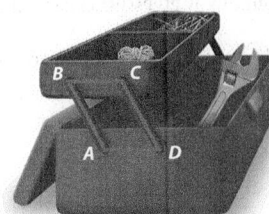

a. **Possible answer:** You could take a photograph of the figure and with a protractor measure to see if the opposite angles are congruent. (If both pairs of opposite angles of a quadrilateral are congruent, then the quadrilateral is a parallelogram.)

b. **Possible answer:** Choose two lengths of framing materials of one length and two of another. (If both pairs of opposite sides of a quadrilateral are congruent, then the quadrilateral is a parallelogram.) As long as the angles of the frame are not right angles, the frame is not a rectangle.

c. **Possible answer:** Attach diagonal braces to opposite corners and check to see if they bisect each other. (If the diagonals of a quadrilateral bisect each other, then the quadrilateral is a parallelogram.)

CONNECT VOCABULARY EL

- What is the *converse* of a statement? The converse is the statement that results from interchanging the hypothesis and conclusion of the given statement.

- What is the converse of this statement: "If a quadrilateral is a parallelogram, then both pairs of opposite sides are congruent"? If both pairs of opposite sides of a quadrilateral are congruent, then the quadrilateral is a parallelogram.

INTEGRATE MATHEMATICAL PRACTICES
Focus on Critical Thinking

MP.3 Give an example of a theorem involving quadrilaterals that is true but whose converse is false. Explain why the converse is false. Sample answer: Theorem: If a figure is a square, then it has four sides. Converse: If a figure has four sides, then it is a square. The converse is false because there are many four-sided figures that are not squares, including trapezoids and rhombuses that contain no right angles.

EXTENSION ACTIVITY

The night sky is divided into 88 constellations, groups of stars that appear to form figures or shapes. Many of the constellations are wholly or partially geometrical in design. Have students research the constellations, looking for triangles and quadrilaterals in the shapes. Students may wish to start with the parallelogram in Lyra, shown in the photo in the Lesson Performance Task Preview. Students may draw or print the shapes they find, and add to them interesting information about the shapes, such as the names of the stars that form them, the distances of the stars, and traditional stories told about the constellations in which the shapes appear.

Scoring Rubric
2 points: Student correctly solves the problem and explains his/her reasoning.
1 point: Student shows good understanding of the problem but does not fully solve or explain.
0 points: Student does not demonstrate understanding of the problem.

Properties of Rectangles, Rhombuses, and Squares

Common Core Math Standards

The student is expected to:

 G-CO.C.11

Prove theorems about parallelograms. Also G-SRT.B.5

Mathematical Practices

 MP.6 Precision

Language Objective

Explain to a partner how to classify different types of quadrilaterals as rectangles, rhombuses, or squares.

ENGAGE

Essential Question: What are the properties of rectangles, rhombuses, and squares?

A rectangle is a parallelogram with congruent diagonals; a rhombus is a parallelogram with perpendicular diagonals, each of which bisects a pair of opposite angles; a square is both a rectangle and a rhombus and has the properties of each.

PREVIEW: LESSON PERFORMANCE TASK

View the Engage section online. Discuss the photo, drawing attention to the geometrical shapes that form the design of the flag. Then preview the Lesson Performance Task.

Name_____ Class_____ Date_____

9.3 Properties of Rectangles, Rhombuses, and Squares

Essential Question: What are the properties of rectangles, rhombuses, and squares?

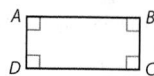 **Explore** **Exploring Sides, Angles, and Diagonals of a Rectangle**

A **rectangle** is a quadrilateral with four right angles. The figure shows rectangle *ABCD*.

Investigate properties of rectangles.

Ⓐ Use a tile or pattern block and the following method to draw three different rectangles on a separate sheet of paper.

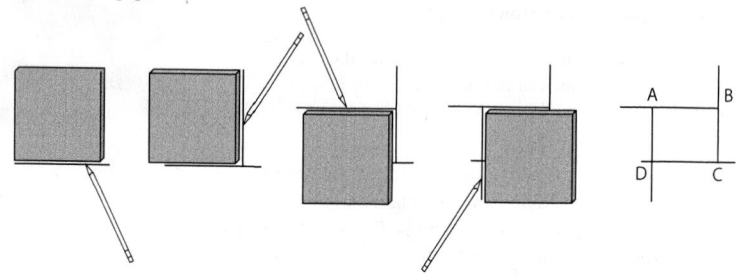

Ⓑ Use a ruler to measure the sides and diagonals of each rectangle. Keep track of the measurements and compare your results to other students.

Reflect

1. Why does this method produce a rectangle? What must you assume about the tile?
   You must assume that the corners of the tile are right angles. Therefore, each stage of the drawing produces a line that meets the previous line at a right angle. The completed quadrilateral has four right angles, so it is a rectangle.

2. **Discussion** Is every rectangle also a parallelogram? Make a conjecture based upon your measurements and explain your thinking.
   Yes; in every case, opposite sides are congruent. All rectangles are parallelograms because a quadrilateral in which both pairs of opposite sides are congruent is a parallelogram.

3. Use your measurements to make two conjectures about the diagonals of a rectangle.
   Conjecture: The diagonals of a rectangle are congruent.
   Conjecture: The diagonals of a rectangle bisect each other.

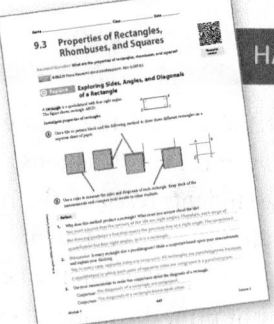

HARDCOVER PAGES 383–392

Turn to these pages to find this lesson in the hardcover student edition.

You can use the definition of a rectangle to prove the following theorems.

Properties of Rectangles

If a quadrilateral is a rectangle, then it is a parallelogram.
If a parallelogram is a rectangle, then its diagonals are congruent.

Example 1 Use a rectangle to prove the Properties of Rectangles Theorems.

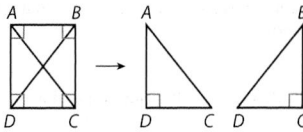

Given: ABCD is a rectangle.

Prove: ABCD is a parallelogram; $\overline{AC} \cong \overline{BD}$.

Ⓐ

Statements	Reasons
1. ABCD is a rectangle.	1. Given
2. ∠A and ∠C are right angles.	2. Definition of rectangle
3. ∠A ≅ ∠C	3. All right angles are congruent.
4. ∠B and ∠D are right angles.	4. Definition of rectangle
5. ∠B ≅ ∠D	5. All right angles are congruent.
6. ABCD is a parallelogram.	6. If both pairs of opposite angles of a quadrilateral are congruent, then the quadrilateral is a parallelogram.
7. $\overline{AD} \cong \overline{CB}$	7. If a quadrilateral is a parallelogram, then its opposite sides are congruent.
8. $\overline{DC} \cong \overline{DC}$	8. Reflexive Property of Congruence
9. ∠D and ∠C are right angles.	9. Definition of rectangle
10. ∠D ≅ ∠C	10. All right angles are congruent.
11. △ADC ≅ △BCD	11. SAS Triangle Congruence Theorem
12. $\overline{AC} \cong \overline{BD}$	12. CPCTC

Reflect

4. Discussion A student says you can also prove the diagonals are congruent in Example 1 by using the SSS Triangle Congruence Theorem to show that △ADC ≅ △BCD. Do you agree? Explain.
No; in order to use the SSS Triangle Congruence Theorem, you would have to know that
$\overline{AC} \cong \overline{BD}$, which is what you are trying to prove.

Your Turn

Find each measure.

5. AD = 7.5 cm and DC = 10 cm. Find DB.
By the Pythagorean Theorem, $AC^2 = 7.5^2 + 10^2$, so AC = 12.5 cm.
Diagonals of a rectangle are congruent, so DB = AC = 12.5 cm.

6. AB = 17 cm and BC = 12.75 cm. Find DB.
Opposite sides of the rectangle are congruent, so DC = AB = 17 cm.
By the Pythagorean Theorem, $DB^2 = 17^2 + 12.75^2$, so DB = 21.25 cm.

PROFESSIONAL DEVELOPMENT

 Learning Progressions

In this lesson, students extend their earlier work with parallelograms to explore the properties of three special quadrilaterals: the *rectangle*, a quadrilateral with four congruent (right) angles; the *rhombus*, a quadrilateral with four congruent sides; and the *square*, a quadrilateral with four congruent (right) angles and four congruent sides. The proofs demonstrate that each of these quadrilaterals is a parallelogram; as such, they inherit all of the properties of parallelograms. Proving these theorems is an application of the Law of Detachment (if $p \rightarrow q$ is true and p is true, then q is true), which students will use as they further their study of mathematics.

EXPLORE

Exploring Sides, Angles, and Diagonals of a Rectangle

INTEGRATE TECHNOLOGY

Students have the option of doing the rectangle activity either in the book or online.

QUESTIONING STRATEGIES

❓ Is a rectangle a parallelogram? How do you know? Yes; since the opposite sides are congruent, the Opposite Sides Criterion applies.

EXPLAIN 1

Proving Diagonals of a Rectangle Are Congruent

QUESTIONING STRATEGIES

❓ What two things do you have to prove in order to prove the theorem? Prove the figure is a parallelogram and then prove triangles that contain the diagonals of the rectangle are congruent.

❓ Does it matter which pair of triangles you prove congruent for this proof? Explain. Yes; you need to choose a pair of triangles that contain the diagonals of the rectangle as sides.

AVOID COMMON ERRORS

Students may try to prove that a rectangle is a parallelogram by stating that the opposite sides are congruent and using the Opposite Sides Criterion for a parallelogram. However, the given information states only that the figure is a rectangle (that is, it has four right angles). The fact that a rectangle has opposite sides that are congruent is a consequence of the fact that a rectangle is a parallelogram. In order to avoid circular reasoning, congruent opposite sides cannot be used as part of this proof.

EXPLAIN 2

Proving Diagonals of a Rhombus Are Perpendicular

QUESTIONING STRATEGIES

? Why do the diagonals of a rhombus bisect each other? Because a rhombus is a parallelogram, the diagonals bisect each other.

? To prove the diagonals of a rhombus are perpendicular, do you need to show that each of the four angles formed by the intersecting diagonals is a right angle? Why or why not? No; you need to show only that one angle is a right angle. If one angle is a right angle, it's easy to see that the others must also be right angles by the Vertical Angles Theorem and the Linear Pair Theorem.

CONNECT VOCABULARY EL

Have students complete a quadrilateral chart, with pictures and explanations for each type of quadrilateral they have encountered in this unit (rhombus, square, rectangle, other parallelograms, and so on).

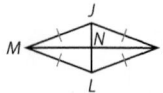

⊘ Explain 2 **Proving Diagonals of a Rhombus are Perpendicular**

A **rhombus** is a quadrilateral with four congruent sides. The figure shows rhombus *JKLM*.

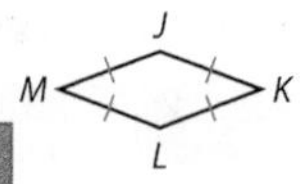

Properties of Rhombuses
If a quadrilateral is a rhombus, then it is a parallelogram. If a parallelogram is a rhombus, then its diagonals are perpendicular. If a parallelogram is a rhombus, then each diagonal bisects a pair of opposite angles.

Example 2 Prove that the diagonals of a rhombus are perpendicular.

Given: *JKLM* is a rhombus.

Prove: $\overline{JL} \perp \overline{MK}$

Since *JKLM* is a rhombus, $\overline{JM} \cong$ <u>$\overline{JK}$</u> . Because *JKLM* is also a parallelogram, $\overline{MN} \cong \overline{KN}$ because <u>diagonals of a parallelogram bisect each other</u>. By the Reflexive Property of Congruence, $\overline{JN} \cong \overline{JN}$, so $\triangle JNM \cong \triangle JNK$ by the <u>SSS Triangle Congruence Theorem</u>. So, <u>$\angle JNM \cong \angle JNK$</u> by CPCTC. By the Linear Pair Theorem, $\angle JNM$ and $\angle JNK$ are supplementary. This means that $m\angle JNM + m\angle JNK =$ <u>180°</u>. Since the angles are congruent, $m\angle JNM = m\angle JNK$ so by <u>substitution</u>, $m\angle JNM + m\angle JNK = 180°$ or $2m\angle JNK = 180°$. Therefore, $m\angle JNK =$ <u>90°</u> and <u>$\overline{JL}$</u> $\perp \overline{MK}$.

Reflect

7. What can you say about the image of *J* in the proof after a reflection across $\overline{MK}$? Why?
   That its image is *L* because $\overline{MK}$ is the perpendicular bisector of $\overline{JL}$.

8. What property about the diagonals of a rhombus is the same as a property of all parallelograms? What special property do the diagonals of a rhombus have?
   The diagonals of rhombuses bisect each other, which is a property of all parallelograms.

   The diagonals of rhombuses are perpendicular, which is a property unique to rhombuses.

Your Turn

9. Prove that if a parallelogram is a rhombus, then each diagonal bisects a pair of opposite angles.
   Given: *JKLM* is a rhombus.
   Prove: $\overline{MK}$ bisects $\angle JML$ and $\angle JKL$; $\overline{JL}$ bisects $\angle MJK$ and $\angle MLK$.

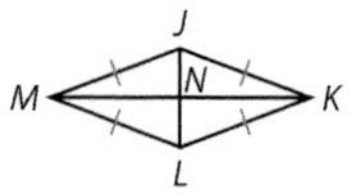

   Since *JKLM* is a rhombus, $\overline{JM} \cong \overline{LM}$ and $\overline{JK} \cong \overline{LK}$. $\overline{MK} \cong \overline{MK}$ by the Reflexive Property of Congruence. So, $\triangle MJK \cong \triangle MLK$ by the SSS Triangle Congruence Theorem. Therefore, $\angle JMK \cong \angle LMK$ and $\angle JKM \cong \angle LKM$ by CPCTC, so $\overline{MK}$ bisects $\angle JML$ and $\angle JKL$. A similar argument shows that $\overline{JL}$ bisects $\angle MJK$ and $\angle MLK$.

COLLABORATIVE LEARNING

Whole Class Activity

As a class, come up with a list of the properties common to some of the quadrilaterals studied in the lesson, such as "Opposite sides congruent" and "Diagonals perpendicular." Use the list to construct a table summarizing which quadrilateral (parallelogram, rectangle, rhombus, square) has each property. Save the table as a class review resource.

Explain 3   Using Properties of Rhombuses to Find Measures

Example 3   Use rhombus *VWXY* to find each measure.

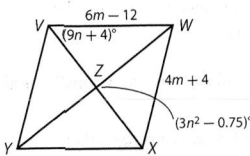

(A) Find *XY*.

All sides of a rhombus are congruent, so $\overline{VW} \cong \overline{WX}$ and $VW = WX$.

Substitute values for *VW* and *WX*. $6m - 12 = 4m + 4$

Solve for *m*. $m = 8$

Sustitute the value of *m* to find *VW*. $VW = 6(8) - 12 = 36$

Because all sides of the rhombus are congruent, then $\overline{VW} \cong \overline{XY}$, and $XY = 36$.

(B) Find $\angle YVW$.

The diagonals of a rhombus are __perpendicular__, so $\angle WZX$ is a right angle and

$m\angle WZX = \boxed{90°}$.

Since $m\angle WZX = (3n^2 - 0.75)°$, then $\underline{(3n^2 - 0.75°) = 90°}$.

Solve for *n*. $3n^2 - 0.75 = 90$

$n = \boxed{5.5}$

Substitute the value of *n* to find $m\angle WVZ$.

$m\angle WVZ = \boxed{53.5°}$

Since $\overline{VX}$ bisects $\angle YVW$, then $\underline{\angle YVZ \cong \angle WVZ}$

Substitute 53.5° for $m\angle WVZ$. $m\angle YVW = 2(53.5°) = 107°$

Your Turn

Use the rhombus *VWXY* from Example 3 to find each measure.

10. Find $m\angle VYX$.

From Part B, $m\angle YVW = 107°$
$107° + m\angle VYX = 180°$
$m\angle VYX = 73°$

11. Find $m\angle XYZ$.

$m\angle XYZ = \frac{1}{2}(m\angle VYX)$
$m\angle XYZ = \frac{1}{2}(73°)$
$m\angle XYZ = 36.5°$

EXPLAIN 3

Using Properties of Rhombuses to Find Measures

QUESTIONING STRATEGIES

 What type of angles do the diagonals of a rhombus form? **right angles**

AVOID COMMON ERRORS

Students may be confused when asked to solve equations to find segments of special quadrilaterals. Remind students that the sides and angles marked in the figure are not necessarily the ones asked for in the problem. Have students, when they read a problem, copy the figure and circle the length or measure they are asked to find.

DIFFERENTIATE INSTRUCTION

Modeling

Divide students into groups. Have each group cut out models of a rectangle, a rhombus, and a square from construction paper. Then have students use a protractor and a ruler to verify the properties of rectangles and rhombuses from the theorems in this lesson.

EXPLAIN 4

Investigating the Properties of a Square

QUESTIONING STRATEGIES

? Why is a square also a rhombus? A square is a quadrilateral with 4 congruent sides, so a square is a rhombus.

AVOID COMMON ERRORS

When working with shapes they are familiar with, like squares, some students have trouble distinguishing between properties that belong to the shape by definition and properties that must be proven. When discussing these definitions, point out which properties are included and which are not.

ELABORATE

QUESTIONING STRATEGIES

? How do the definitions of the special quadrilaterals in this lesson differ from the theorems in this lesson? The definitions only identify the figures as quadrilaterals. Proving the properties as theorems shows they are also parallelograms.

SUMMARIZE THE LESSON

? Have students make a graphic organizer or chart to summarize properties of rectangles and rhombuses. Sample:

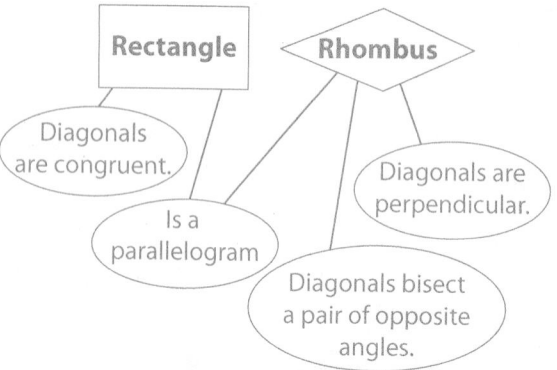

A **square** is a quadrilateral with four sides congruent and four right angles.

Example 4 Explain why each conditional statement is true.

(A) If a quadrilateral is a square, then it is a parallelogram.

By definition, a square is a quadrilateral with four congruent sides. Any quadrilateral with both pairs of opposite sides congruent is a parallelogram, so a square is a parallelogram.

(B) If a quadrilateral is a square, then it is a rectangle.

By definition, a square is a quadrilateral with four ___right angles___.

By definition, a rectangle is also a quadrilateral with four ___right angles___. Therefore, a square is a rectangle.

Your Turn

12. Explain why this conditional statement is true: If a quadrilateral is a square, then it is a rhombus.

By definition, a rhombus is a quadrilateral with four congruent sides. Since a square is also a quadrilateral that has four congruent sides, then a square is a rhombus.

13. Look at Part A. Use a different way to explain why this conditional statement is true: If a quadrilateral is a square, then it is a parallelogram.

Possible answer: All four angles of a square are right angles. All right angles are congruent. Any quadrilateral with both pairs of opposite angles congruent is a parallelogram, so a square is a parallelogram.

Elaborate

14. Discussion The Venn diagram shows how quadrilaterals, parallelograms, rectangles, rhombuses, and squares are related to each other. From this lesson, what do you notice about the definitions and theorems regarding these figures?

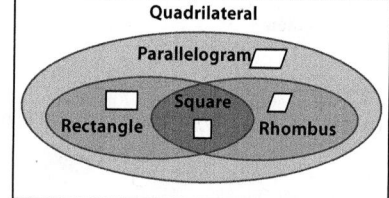

A rectangle, a rhombus, and a square are all

defined as quadrilaterals, but they can only be shown to be parallelograms by theorems

that prove their properties.

15. Essential Question Check-In What are the properties of rectangles and rhombuses? How does a square relate to rectangles and rhombuses?

A rectangle is a parallelogram with four right angles and congruent diagonals. A rhombus

is a parallelogram with four congruent sides, diagonals that are perpendicular, and each of

its diagonals bisects a pair of opposite angles. A square is both a rectangle and a rhombus,

so it has the properties of both.

LANGUAGE SUPPORT [EL]

Connect Vocabulary

Students may have difficulty distinguishing the special quadrilaterals in this lesson. Have them write the definitions on a poster, and look through magazines or books to find pictures of rectangles, rhombuses, and squares that they can add to the poster. Have them group the pictures based on the type of figure, show the pictures to the class, and then describe the identifying characteristics of each type of figure.

⭐ Evaluate: Homework and Practice

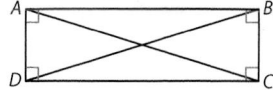

• Online Homework
• Hints and Help
• Extra Practice

1. Complete the paragraph proof of the Properties of Rectangles Theorems.
Given: *ABCD* is a rectangle.
Prove: *ABCD* is a parallelogram; $\overline{AC} \cong \overline{BD}$.

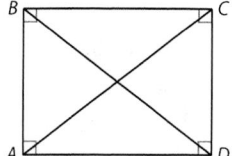

Proof that *ABCD* is a ___parallelogram___: Since *ABCD* is a rectangle, ∠*A* and ∠*C* are right angles. So ∠*A* ≅ ∠*C* because ___all right angles are congruent___.

By similar reasoning, ∠*B* ≅ ∠*D*. Therefore, *ABCD* is a parallelogram because **it is a quadrilateral that has congruent opposite angles.**

Proof that the diagonals are congruent: Since *ABCD* is a parallelogram, $\overline{AD} \cong \overline{BC}$ because ___opposite sides of a parallelogram are congruent___.

Also, $\overline{DC} \cong \overline{DC}$ by the Reflexive Property of Congruence. By the definition of a rectangle, ∠*D* and ∠*C* are right angles, and so $\dfrac{\angle D \cong \angle C}{}$ because all right angles are ___congruent___. Therefore, △*ADC* ≅ △*BCD* by the **SAS Triangle Congruence Theorem** and $\boxed{AC} \cong \boxed{BD}$ by CPCTC.

Find the lengths using rectangle *ABCD*.

2. *AB* = 21; *AD* = 28. What is the value of *AC* + *BD*?

$BD^2 = 21^2 + 28^2$, so *BD* = 35. Then, *AC* = 35, so *AC* + *BD* = 70.

3. *BC* = 40; *CD* = 30. What is the value of *BC* − *AC*?

The diagonals of the rectangle are congruent, so *BD* = *AC*.
Then, *BD* − *AC* = 0.

4. An artist connects stained glass pieces with lead strips. In this rectangular window, the strips are cut so that *FH* = 34 in. Find *JG*. Explain.

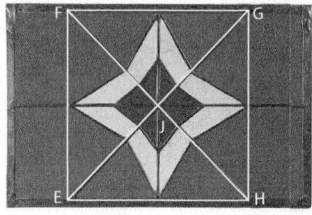

$\overline{EG} \cong \overline{FH}$ because the diagonals of a rectangle are congruent. Since *FH* measures 34 inches, *EG* also measures 34 inches. Since diagonals of a parallelogram bisect each other, $JG = \frac{1}{2}EG$. So, $JG = \frac{1}{2}(34) = 17$ in.

© Houghton Mifflin Harcourt Publishing Company • Image Credits: Courtesy of Wimberley Stain Glass/Houghton Mifflin Harcourt Photo by Pet

---

EVALUATE

ASSIGNMENT GUIDE

Concepts and Skills	Practice
Explore Exploring Properties of Rectangles	Exercise 1
Example 1 Proving Diagonals of a Rectangle Are Congruent	Exercises 2–6
Example 2 Proving Diagonals of a Rhombus Are Perpendicular	Exercise 8
Example 3 Using Properties of Rhombuses to Find Measures	Exercises 9–12
Example 4 Investigating the Properties of a Square	Exercise 19

INTEGRATE MATHEMATICAL PRACTICES

Focus on Modeling

MP.4 Some students may benefit from a hands-on approach for exploring special quadrilaterals. Have students make a physical model of a parallelogram with paper strips and brads. Ask them to adjust the model until it is a rectangle, as shown in an exercise, and then measure its diagonals. Then have them adjust the model to form a rhombus and measure the angles made by the intersecting diagonals.

Exercise	Depth of Knowledge (D.O.K.)	COMMON CORE Mathematical Practices
1–3	**2** Skills/Concepts	**MP.2** Reasoning
4–6	**2** Skills/Concepts	**MP.4** Modeling
7–19	**2** Skills/Concepts	**MP.2** Reasoning
20	**3** Strategic Thinking H.O.T.	**MP.3** Logic
21	**3** Strategic Thinking H.O.T.	**MP.3** Logic

INTEGRATE MATHEMATICAL PRACTICES

Focus on Math Connections

MP.1 You may want to review the properties of parallelograms before assigning the exercises. Then summarize the properties of rectangles and rhombuses and point out that these figures are also parallelograms. Explain that a square has all the properties of a parallelogram, a rectangle, and a rhombus.

The rectangular gate has diagonal braces. Find each length.

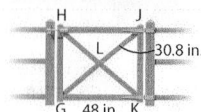

5. Find HJ.

$\overline{HJ} \cong \overline{KG}$

$HJ = KG$

$\quad = 48$ in.

6. Find HK.

$HK = JG$

$\quad = 2(JL)$

$\quad = 2(30.8 \text{ in.})$

$\quad = 61.6$ in.

7. Find the measure of each numbered angle in the rectangle.

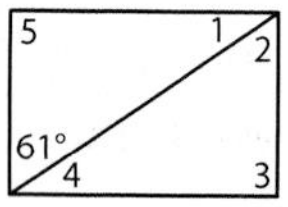

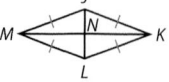

$\angle 3$ and $\angle 5$ are right angles, so they each measure $90°$.

$\angle 2 \cong$ to the give angle, so m$\angle 2 = 61°$.

m$\angle 1 = 90° - 61° = 29°$; $\angle 4 \cong \angle 1$, so m$\angle 4 = $ m$\angle 1 = 29°$.

So, m$\angle 1 = 29°$, m$\angle 2 = 61°$, m$\angle 3 = 90°$, m$\angle 4 = 29°$, and m$\angle 5 = 90°$.

8. Complete the two-column proof that the diagonals of a rhombus are perpendicular.

Given: $JKLM$ is a rhombus.

Prove: $\overline{JL} \perp \overline{MK}$

Statements	Reasons
1. $\overline{JM} \cong \overline{JK}$	1. Definition of rhombus
2. $\overline{MN} \cong \overline{KN}$	2. Diagonals of a parallelogram bisect each other.
3. $\overline{JN} \cong \overline{JN}$	3. Reflexive Property of Congruence
4. $\triangle JNM \cong \triangle JNK$	4. SSS Triangle Congruence Theorem
5. $\angle JNM \cong \angle JNK$	5. CPCTC
6. $\angle JNM$ and $\angle JNK$ are supplementary.	6. Linear Pair Theorem
7. m$\angle JNM +$ m$\angle JNK = 180°$	7. Definition of supplementary
8. $\angle JNM = \angle JNK$	8. Definition of congruence
9. $\boxed{\text{m}\angle JNK} + \angle JNK = 180°$	9. Substitution Property of Equality
10. 2m$\angle JNK = 180°$	10. Addition
11. m$\angle JNK = 90°$	11. Division Property of Equality
12. $\overline{JL} \perp \overline{MK}$	12. Definition of perpendicular lines

Exercise	Depth of Knowledge (D.O.K.)	COMMON CORE Mathematical Practices
22	**3** Strategic Thinking **H.O.T.**	**MP.3** Logic
23	**3** Strategic Thinking **H.O.T.**	**MP.3** Logic

ABCD is a rhombus. Find each measure.

9. Find AB.

Possible answer:

$4x + 15 = 7x + 2$

$13 = 3x$

$4\frac{1}{3} = x$

$\overline{AB} \cong \overline{CD}$, so $AB = CD = 7x + 2 = 7\left(4\frac{1}{3}\right) + 2 = 32\frac{1}{3}$

10. Find m∠ABC.

Possible answer:

$\overline{AC} \perp \overline{BD}$, so m∠AFB = 90°; $12y = 90$, so $y = 7.5$.

$m\angle ABC = 180° - 2(4y - 1)°$

$\qquad = 180° - 2(4 \cdot 7.5 - 1)° = 122°$

Find the measure of each numbered angle in the rhombus.

11.

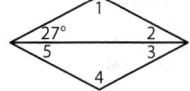

∠2 ≅ ∠3 ≅ ∠5 ≅ to the given angle,
so they each measure 27°.

$m\angle 1 + m\angle 2 + 27° = 180°$

$m\angle 1 + 27° + 27° = 180°$

$\qquad m\angle 1 = 126°$

∠4 ≅ ∠1, so m∠4 = 126°

So, m∠1 = 126°, m∠2 = 27°, m∠3 = 27°,
m∠4 = 126°, and m∠5 = 27°.

12.

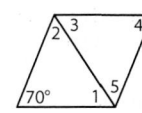

∠4 ≅ to the given angle, so m∠4 = 70°.

∠1 ≅ ∠2 ≅ ∠3 ≅ ∠5

$m\angle 1 + m\angle 2 + 70° = 180°$

$m\angle 1 + m\angle 1 + 70° = 180°$

$\qquad m\angle 1 = 55°$

So, m∠1 = 55°, m∠2 = 55°, m∠3 = 55°,
m∠4 = 70° and m∠5 = 55°.

13. Select the word that best describes when each of the following statements are true.
Select the correct answer for each lettered part.

A. A rectangle is a parallelogram.   ● always   ○ sometimes   ○ never

B. A parallelogram is a rhombus.   ○ always   ● sometimes   ○ never

C. A square is a rhombus.   ● always   ○ sometimes   ○ never

D. A rhombus is a square.   ○ always   ● sometimes   ○ never

E. A rhombus is a rectangle.   ○ always   ● sometimes   ○ never

AVOID COMMON ERRORS

Students might expect to use only the current lesson's properties and theorems when writing proofs. Point out that proofs often build on previous knowledge and thus use concepts learned in earlier lessons.v

Properties of Rectangles, Rhombuses, and Squares   **454**

14. Use properties of special parallelograms to complete the proof.

Given: *EFGH* is a rectangle. *J* is the midpoint of $\overline{EH}$.

Prove: $\triangle FJG$ is isosceles.

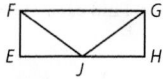

Statements	Reasons
1. *EFGH* is a rectangle. *J* is the midpoint of $\overline{EH}$.	1. Given
2. $\angle E$ and $\angle H$ are right angles.	2. Definition of rectangle
3. $\angle E \cong \angle H$	3. **All right angles are congruent.**
4. *EFGH* is a parallelogram.	4. **A rectangle is a parallelogram.**
5. $\overline{EF} \cong \overline{GH}$	5. **In a parallelogram, opposite sides are congruent.**
6. $\overline{EJ} \cong \overline{HJ}$	6. **Definition of midpoint**
7. $\triangle FJE \cong \triangle GJH$	7. **SAS Triangle Congruence Theorem**
8. $\overline{FJ} \cong \overline{GJ}$	8. **CPCTC**
9. $\triangle FJE$ is isosceles.	9. **Definition of isosceles triangle**

15. Explain the Error Find and explain the error in this paragraph proof. Then describe a way to correct the proof.

Given: *JKLM* is a rhombus.

Prove: *JKLM* is a parallelogram.

Proof: It is given that *JLKM* is a rhombus. So, by the definition of a rhombus, $\overline{JK} \cong \overline{LM}$, and $\overline{KL} \cong \overline{MJ}$. If a quadrilateral is a parallelogram, then its opposite sides are congruent. So *JKLM* is a parallelogram.

You cannot use a theorem that assumes the quadrilateral is a parallelogram to justify the final statement because you do not know that *JKLM* is a parallelogram. That is what you are trying to prove. Instead, use the converse, which states that if both pairs of opposite sides of a quadrilateral are congruent, then the quadrilateral is a parallelogram. So therefore, *JKLM* is a parallelogram.

© Houghton Mifflin Harcourt Publishing Company

The opening of a soccer goal is shaped like a rectangle.

16. Draw a rectangle to represent a soccer goal. Label the rectangle $ABCD$ to show that the distance between the goalposts, $\overline{BC}$, is three times the distance from the top of the goalpost to the ground. If the perimeter of $ABCD$ is 64 feet, what is the length of $\overline{BC}$?

Possible drawing:

Perimeter $= AB + BC + CD + DA$

$$64 = x + 3x + x + 3x$$
$$64 = 8x$$
$$8 = x$$
$$BC = 3x = 3(8) = 24 \text{ feet}$$

17. In your rectangle from Evaluate 16, suppose the distance from B to D is $(y + 10)$ feet, and the distance from A to C is $(2y - 5.3)$ feet. What is the approximate length of $\overline{AC}$?

The diagonals of a rectangle are congruent, so $\overline{AC} \cong \overline{BD}$.

$$AC = BD$$
$$2y - 5.3 = y + 10$$
$$y = 15.3$$
$$\text{So, } AC = 2(15.3) - 5.3 = 30.6 - 5.3 = 25.3 \text{ feet.}$$

18. $PQRS$ is a rhombus, with $PQ = (7b - 5)$ meters and $QR = (2b - 0.5)$ meters. If S is the midpoint of $\overline{RT}$, what is the length of $\overline{RT}$?

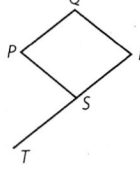

Possible answer:

By the midpoint, $\overline{TS} \cong \overline{RS}$.

By the definition of a rhombus, $\overline{PQ} \cong \overline{QR} \cong \overline{RS} \cong \overline{SP}$.

$$PQ = QR$$
$$7b - 5 = 2b - 0.5$$
$$b = 0.9$$
$$RT = TS + RS = 2(RS) = 2(QR)$$
$$= 2(2b - 0.5) = 2(2(0.9) - 0.5) = 2(1.8 - 0.5) = 2(1.3) = 2.6$$

So, the length of $\overline{RT}$ is 2.6 meters.

© Houghton Mifflin Harcourt Publishing Company • Image Credits: ©belterz/iStockPhoto.com

---

Ask students to work with a partner to write conditional statements in the form "If a quadrilateral is a [figure], then it is a [figure]." An example would be "If a quadrilateral is a rectangle, then it is a parallelogram." Also have them write conditional statements in the form "If a parallelogram is a [figure], then it is a [figure]," for example, "If a parallelogram is a square, then it is a rhombus." Have them write as many of these statements as possible and then compare their statements with other student pairs.

Have students describe the properties of a rectangle and a rhombus, then have them draw and label examples of each type of figure.

19. **Communicate Mathematical Ideas** List the properties that a square "inherits" because it is each of the following quadrilaterals.

   a. a parallelogram

   - Both pairs of opposite sides are parallel.
   - Both pairs of opposite sides are congruent.
   - Both pairs of opposite angles are congruent.
   - One angle is supplementary to both of its consecutive angles.
   - The diagonals bisect each other.

   b. a rectangle

   - The diagonals are congruent.

   c. a rhombus

   - The diagonals are perpendicular.
   - Each diagonal bisects a pair of opposite angles.

   H.O.T. Focus on Higher Order Thinking

   Justify Reasoning For the given figure, describe any rotations or reflections that would carry the figure onto itself. Explain.

20. A rhombus that is not a square

   180° rotation around its center; reflectional symmetry across a line that contains opposite vertices (two lines)

21. A rectangle that is not a square

   180° rotation around its center; reflectional symmetry across a line that contains the midpoints of opposite sides (two lines)

22. A square

   90° rotation around its center; reflectional symmetry across a line that contains opposite vertices (two lines), or a line that contains the midpoints of opposite sides (two lines)

23. **Analyze Relationships** Look at your answers for Exercises 20–22. How does your answer to Exercise 22 relate to your answers to Exercises 20 and 21? Explain.

   A square has the reflectional properties of both a rhombus that is not a square and a rectangle that is not a square. Because squares have all angles congruent and all sides congruent, as opposed to only all sides congruent (rhombuses) or only all angles congruent (rectangles), a square has 90° rotational symmetry.

© Houghton Mifflin Harcourt Publishing Company

Lesson Performance Task

The portion of the Arkansas state flag that is not red is a rhombus. On one flag, the diagonals of the rhombus measure 24 inches and 36 inches. Find the area of the rhombus. Justify your reasoning.

432 in.²

Possible answer: Draw the diagonals of the rhombus. Since they are perpendicular, the four triangles into which you have divided the rhombus are right triangles. The area of each is $\frac{1}{2}bh = \frac{1}{2}(18)(12) = 108$ in². There are four such triangles with a total area of $4 \cdot 108 = 432$ in².

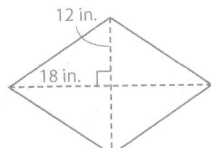

INTEGRATE MATHEMATICAL PRACTICES
Focus on Patterns

MP.8 Have students look at the rhombus on the Arkansas flag with diagonals measuring 24 inches and 36 inches. Pose these questions:

- Suppose you cut the rhombus along its diagonals to make four shapes, and then rearranged the shapes to form another type of quadrilateral that you studied in this lesson. Name the quadrilateral and its dimensions. a rectangle measuring 18 in. × 24 in. or 12 in. × 36 in.

- Find the area of the new quadrilateral. Then propose a method for finding the area of a rhombus if you know the lengths of its diagonals. Divide the product of the diagonals by 2.

INTEGRATE MATHEMATICAL PRACTICES
Focus on Modeling

MP.4 What is the relationship between the combined areas of the four red triangles on an Arkansas flag, and the area of the rest of the flag? Answer without referring to the actual dimensions of the flag. They are equal. Sample answer: The four red triangles can be rearranged to form the rhombus that makes up the rest of the flag. So, the two are equal in area.

EXTENSION ACTIVITY

The design of the Arkansas flag is composed of a number of geometrical shapes. Ask students to write and solve at least four problems involving the names, perimeters, areas, and/or other information relating to the shapes on the flag. Students should continue to use 24 inches and 36 inches as the lengths of the diagonals of the larger rhombus.

Scoring Rubric

2 points: Student correctly solves the problem and explains his/her reasoning.

1 point: Student shows good understanding of the problem but does not fully solve or explain.

0 points: Student does not demonstrate understanding of the problem.

Properties of Rectangles, Rhombuses, and Squares   **458**

Conditions for Rectangles, Rhombuses, and Squares

Common Core Math Standards

The student is expected to:

 G-CO.C.11

Prove theorems about parallelograms. Also G-SRT.B.5

Mathematical Practices

 MP.7 Using Structure

Language Objective

Explain to a partner how to distinguish between a condition for a quadrilateral to be a rectangle, rhombus, or square, and a property of a rectangle, rhombus, or square.

ENGAGE

Essential Question: How can you use given conditions to show that a quadrilateral is a rectangle, rhombus, or square?

You can use the converses of the theorems in the previous lesson to prove that a quadrilateral is a rectangle, rhombus, or square.

PREVIEW: LESSON PERFORMANCE TASK

View the Engage section online. Discuss the photo. Ask students to name some other animals that are related to tigers, and to explain how they are related. Then preview the Lesson Performance Task.

9.4 Conditions for Rectangles, Rhombuses, and Squares

Essential Question: How can you use given conditions to show that a quadrilateral is a rectangle, a rhombus, or a square?

Resource Locker

Explore **Properties of Rectangles, Rhombuses, and Squares**

In this lesson we will start with given properties and use them to prove which special parallelogram it could be.

Ⓐ Start by drawing two line segments of the same length that bisect each other but are not perpendicular. They will form an X shape, as shown.

Ⓑ Connect the ends of the line segments to form a quadrilateral.

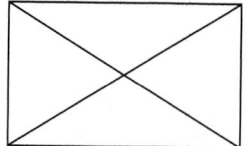

Ⓒ Measure each of the four angles of the quadrilateral, and use those measurements to name the shape.

The measure of each angle is 90°. The quadrilateral is a rectangle.

© Houghton Mifflin Harcourt Publishing Company • Image Credits: ©Aninka/iStockPhoto.com

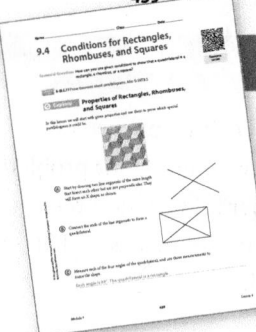

HARDCOVER PAGES 393–402

Turn to these pages to find this lesson in the hardcover student edition.

(D) Now, draw two line segments that are perpendicular and bisect each other but that are not the same length.

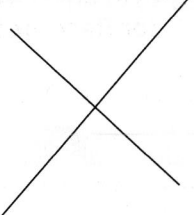

(E) Connect the ends of the line segments to form a quadrilateral.

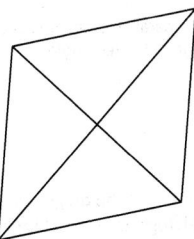

(F) Measure each side length of the quadrilateral. Then use those measurements to name the shape.

The side lengths are all equal. The quadrilateral is a rhombus.

Reflect

1. **Discussion** How are the diagonals of your rectangle in Step B different from the diagonals of your rhombus in Step E?

The diagonals of the rectangle have the same lengths, but are not perpendicular bisectors of each other. The diagonals of the rhombus are perpendicular bisectors of each other, but do not necessarily have the same lengths.

2. Draw a line segment. At each endpoint draw line segments so that four congruent angles are formed as shown. Then extend the segments so that they intersect to form a quadrilateral. Measure the sides. What do you notice? What kind of quadrilateral is it? How does the line segment relate to the angles drawn on either end of it?

The side lengths are equal. The quadrilateral is a rhombus. The line segment bisects both angles.

© Houghton Mifflin Harcourt Publishing Company

EXPLORE

Properties of Rectangles, Rhombuses, and Squares

INTEGRATE TECHNOLOGY

Students have the option of doing the special parallelograms activity either in the book or online.

QUESTIONING STRATEGIES

? If you draw a quadrilateral with congruent diagonals, what shape is the quadrilateral? rectangle

? If you draw two congruent segments that are perpendicular bisectors of one another and then connect the ends to form a quadrilateral, which shape is the quadrilateral? rhombus

PROFESSIONAL DEVELOPMENT

Integrate Mathematical Practices

This lesson provides an opportunity to address Mathematical Practice **MP.7**, which calls for students to "look for and make use of structure." Students are already familiar with the properties of rectangles, rhombuses, and squares, but in this lesson they must analyze the conditions that would be sufficient to make a parallelogram a more special figure. Each theorem in the lesson presents a single condition that leads to a broader conclusion that a figure is a special quadrilateral. For example, it is sufficient for one angle of a parallelogram to be a right angle to conclude that the parallelogram has four right angles (it is a rectangle).

EXPLAIN 1

Proving that Congruent Diagonals Is a Condition for Rectangles

INTEGRATE MATHEMATICAL PRACTICES

Focus on Math Communication

MP.3 Point out to students that in the previous lesson they were introduced to the properties of rectangles, rhombuses, and squares. Explain that in this lesson, they will be given a quadrilateral and will learn what conditions can be used to classify it as a rectangle, rhombus, or square. You may want to call on students to read each theorem aloud. Then ask them to explain the theorem in their own words. Challenge students to come up with unique ways to explain the theorems.

QUESTIONING STRATEGIES

? How does knowing that the diagonals of a parallelogram are congruent allow you to prove that the parallelogram is a rectangle? If the diagonals of a parallelogram are congruent, then they form congruent triangles. That makes the corresponding angles of the congruent triangles congruent. Since the largest angles are also supplementary, each must be a right angle. A quadrilateral with four right angles is a rectangle.

AVOID COMMON ERRORS

Some students may have trouble identifying a piece of additional information that is sufficient to make a conclusion valid. Suggest that once they have an answer, they write a complete statement of the given information, sketch the figure, mark it with this information, and then re-check their work.

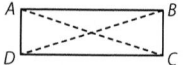

Explain 1   Proving that Congruent Diagonals Is a Condition for Rectangles

When you are given a parallelogram with certain properties, you can use the properties to determine whether the parallelogram is a rectangle.

Theorems: Conditions for Rectangles	
If one angle of a parallelogram is a right angle, then the parallelogram is a rectangle.	*(figure: parallelogram ABCD with right angle at A)*
If the diagonals of a parallelogram are congruent, then the parallelogram is a rectangle.	*(figure: parallelogram ABCD with diagonals)* $\overline{AC} \cong \overline{BD}$

Example 1   Prove that if the diagonals of a parallelogram are congruent, then the parallelogram is a rectangle.

Given: *ABCD* is a parallelogram; $\overline{AC} \cong \overline{BD}$.

Prove: *ABCD* is a rectangle.

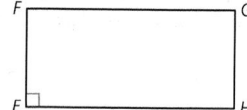

Because ___opposite sides of a parallelogram are congruent___, $\overline{AB} \cong \overline{CD}$.

It is given that $\overline{AC} \cong \overline{BD}$, and ___$\overline{AD} \cong \overline{AD}$___ by the Reflexive Property of Congruence.

So, ___$\triangle ABD \cong \triangle DCA$___ by the SSS Triangle Congruence Theorem,

and ___$\angle BAD \cong \angle CDA$___ by CPCTC. But these angles are ___supplementary___

since $\overline{AB} \| \boxed{DC}$. Therefore, $m\angle BAD + m\angle CDA = \boxed{180°}$. So

$m\angle BAD + \boxed{m\angle BAD} = \boxed{180°}$ by substitution, $2 \cdot m\angle BAD = 180°$,

and $m\angle BAD = 90°$. A similar argument shows that the other angles

of *ABCD* are also ___right___ angles, so *ABCD* is a ___rectangle___.

Reflect

3. **Discussion** Explain why this is a true condition for rectangles: *If one angle of a parallelogram is a right angle, then the parallelogram is a rectangle.*

(figure: rectangle FGHE with right angle at E)

Suppose ∠E is a right angle. Opposite angles in a parallelogram are congruent, so ∠G is also a right angle. Consecutive angles in a parallelogram are supplementary. When one of two supplementary angles is a right angle, then both are right angles. So ∠F and ∠H are also right angles. Since all four angles are right angles, the parallelogram is a rectangle.

COLLABORATIVE LEARNING

Small Group Activity

Ask students to work in small groups to classify the figure. Have each student write a conjecture about one of the *most* special figures possible: parallelogram, rectangle, rhombus, or square. Ask them to justify their conjectures to group members using the theorems they have learned in this lesson. Then have a student volunteer present the group's results to the class.

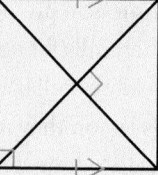

Use the given information to determine whether the quadrilateral is necessarily a rectangle. Explain your reasoning.

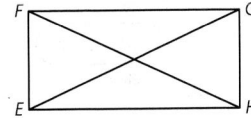

4. Given: $\overline{EF} \cong \overline{GF}$, $\overline{FG} \cong \overline{HE}$, $\overline{FH} \cong \overline{GE}$

    Yes; the figure is a parallelogram because of congruent opposite sides, and it is a rectangle because it is a parallelogram with congruent diagonals.

5. Given: m∠FEG = 45°, m∠GEH = 50°

    No; by the Angle Addition Postulate, m∠FEH = 45° + 50° = 95°, so ∠FEH is not a right angle and EFGH is not a rectangle.

⊘ Explain 2 Proving Conditions for Rhombuses

You can also use given properties of a parallelogram to determine whether the parallelogram is a rhombus.

Theorems: Conditions for Rhombuses	
If one pair of consecutive sides of a parallelogram are congruent, then the parallelogram is a rhombus.	
If the diagonals of a parallelogram are perpendicular, then the parallelogram is a rhombus.	
If one diagonal of a parallelogram bisects a pair of opposite angles, then the parallelogram is a rhombus.	

You will prove one of the theorems about rhombuses in Example 2 and the other theorems in Your Turn Exercise 6 and Evaluate Exercise 22.

© Houghton Mifflin Harcourt Publishing Company

EXPLAIN 2

Proving Conditions for Rhombuses

QUESTIONING STRATEGIES

? How can you use the diagonals of a parallelogram to classify a figure as a rhombus? You can show the diagonals are perpendicular, then apply the theorem that if a parallelogram has perpendicular diagonals, it is a rhombus.

DIFFERENTIATE INSTRUCTION

Communicating Math

Have a student say aloud four words, one of which does not fit with the other three. Have another student identify which word does not belong and explain to the class why. For example, the first student might say, "rhombus, rectangle, square, equilateral triangle." A possible response is that the rectangle does not belong because it does not necessarily have all sides congruent.

INTEGRATE MATHEMATICAL PRACTICES

Focus on Communication

MP.3 When students make statements about what conditions prove that a parallelogram is a rhombus or any other special quadrilateral, encourage them to write a complete statement of the given information and then compare the form and content with the theorems or other statements in the lesson.

Example 2 Complete the flow proof that if one diagonal of a parallelogram bisects a pair of opposite angles, then the parallelogram is a rhombus.

Given: *ABCD* is a parallelogram; ∠*BCA* ≅ ∠*DCA*; ∠*BAC* ≅ ∠*DAC*

Prove: *ABCD* is a rhombus.

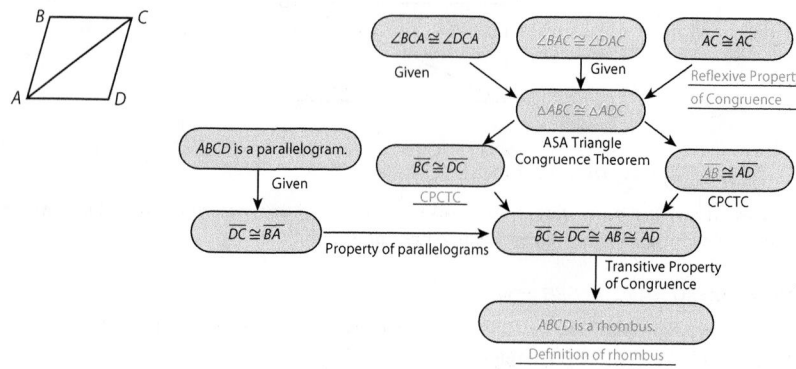

Your Turn

6. Prove that If one pair of consecutive sides of a parallelogram are congruent, then it is a rhombus.

   Given: *JKLM* is a parallelogram. $\overline{JK} \cong \overline{KL}$

   Prove: *JKLM* is a rhombus.

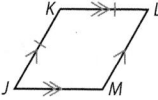

It is given that $\overline{JK} \cong \overline{KL}$. Because opposite sides of a parallelogram are congruent, $\overline{KL} \cong \overline{MJ}$ and $\overline{JK} \cong \overline{LM}$. By substituting the sides $\overline{JK}$ for $\overline{KL}$ and visa versa, $\overline{JK} \cong \overline{MJ}$ and $\overline{KL} \cong \overline{LM}$. So, $\overline{JK} \cong \overline{KL} \cong \overline{LM} \cong \overline{MJ}$, making *JKLM* a rhombus.

© Houghton Mifflin Harcourt Publishing Company

Module 9

463

Lesson 4

LANGUAGE SUPPORT EL

Connect Vocabulary

Students may have difficulty distinguishing the conditions for rectangles, rhombuses, and squares. Have them write the conditions on note cards and then list all the special quadrilaterals that can be further classified if those conditions are met. Have them group the note cards based on the type of figure.

463 Lesson 9.4

In Example 3, you will decide whether you are given enough information to conclude that a figure is a particular type of special parallelogram.

| Example 3 | Determine if the conclusion is valid. If not, tell what additional information is needed to make it valid. |

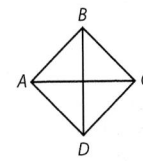

(A) Given: $\overline{AB} \cong \overline{CD}$; $\overline{BC} \cong \overline{DA}$; $\overline{AD} \perp \overline{DC}$; $\overline{AC} \perp \overline{BD}$

Conclusion: *ABCD* is a square.

To prove that a given quadrilateral is a square, it is sufficient to show that the figure is both a rectangle and a rhombus.

Step 1: Determine if *ABCD* is a parallelogram.

$\overline{AB} \cong \overline{CD}$ and $\overline{BC} \cong \overline{DA}$ are given. Since a quadrilateral with opposite sides congruent is a parallelogram, we know that *ABCD* is a parallelogram.

Step 2: Determine if *ABCD* is a rectangle.

Since $\overline{AD} \perp \overline{DC}$, by definition of perpendicular lines, $\angle ADC$ is a right angle. A parallelogram with one right angle is a rectangle, so *ABCD* is a rectangle.

Step 3: Determine if *ABCD* is a rhombus.

$\overline{AC} \perp \overline{BD}$. A parallelogram with perpendicular diagonals is a rhombus. So *ABCD* is a rhombus.

Step 4: Determine if *ABCD* is a square.

Since *ABCD* is a rectangle and a rhombus, it has four right angles and four congruent sides. So *ABCD* is a square by definition.

So, the conclusion is valid.

(B) Given: $\overline{AB} \cong \overline{BC}$

Conclusion: *ABCD* is a rhombus.

The conclusion is not valid. It is true that if two consecutive sides of a <u>parallelogram</u> are congruent, then the <u>parallelogram</u> is a <u>rhombus</u>. To apply this theorem, however, you need to know that *ABCD* is a <u>parallelogram</u>. The given information is not sufficient to conclude that the figure is a parallelogram.

EXPLAIN 3

Applying Conditions for Special Parallelograms

INTEGRATE MATHEMATICAL PRACTICES
Focus on Critical Thinking

MP.3 Some math textbooks define a rectangle as a parallelogram with one right angle. Point out to students that this definition is equivalent to "a quadrilateral with four right angles," because if one angle of a parallelogram is a right angle, the other three angles must also be right (opposite angles are equal; consecutive angles are supplementary).

QUESTIONING STRATEGIES

? How do you determine what additional information is needed to make a conclusion valid? Sample answer: Make sure all parts of the hypothesis of the statement are given or established as true. Then, the conclusion is valid (by the law of detachment).

? Can there be more than one way to demonstrate that a conclusion is valid? Explain. Sample answer: Yes; for example, you can also prove that a given quadrilateral is a rectangle, rhombus, or square by using the definitions of the special quadrilaterals.

ELABORATE

QUESTIONING STRATEGIES

? How are these theorems different from those in the previous lesson? They are converses; here we know the property and are trying to prove the parallelogram type.

? What is sufficient to prove that a quadrilateral is a square? Prove that it is both a rectangle and a rhombus.

SUMMARIZE THE LESSON

? Have students fill in the blanks in the table below to summarize the conditions that lead to special parallelograms.

If a parallelogram has _____	... then the parallelogram is a _____.
one right angle	rectangle
congruent diagonals	rectangle
one pair of consecutive sides congruent	rhombus
perpendicular diagonals	rhombus
one diagonal that bisects a pair of opposite angles	rhombus

---

7. Draw a figure that shows why this statement is not necessarily true: If one angle of a quadrilateral is a right angle, then the quadrilateral is a rectangle.

Possible answer:

Your Turn

Determine if the conclusion is valid. If not, tell what additional information is needed to make it valid.

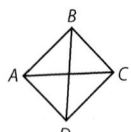

8. Given: ∠ABC is a right angle.
Conclusion: ABCD is a rectangle.

The conclusion is not valid. You must also first be given that ABCD is a parallelogram.

💬 **Elaborate**

9. Look at the theorem boxes in Example 1 and Example 2. How do the diagrams help you remember the conditions for proving a quadrilateral is a special parallelogram?
Possible answer: The diagrams give a quick picture of the conditions stated in the theorems. The congruence marks, parallel marks, and right angles show at a glance what must be known about a figure to say it is a rectangle or a rhombus.

10. EFGH is a parallelogram. In EFGH, $\overline{EG} \cong \overline{FH}$. Which conclusion is incorrect?
A. EFGH is a rectangle.

B. EFGH is a square.

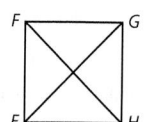

Conclusion B is incorrect. The diagonals of EFGH are congruent, so the parallelogram is a rectangle. However, we are given no information about how the sides are related, so we cannot conclude that it is a square.

11. **Essential Question Check-In** How are theorems about conditions for parallelograms different from the theorems regarding parallelograms used in the previous lesson?
The theorems in this lesson are the converses of the theorems in the previous lesson. In this lesson, information known about the sides, angles, or diagonals of a figure is used to prove whether the figure is a parallelogram, rectangle, rhombus, or square.

⭐ Evaluate: Homework and Practice

• Online Homework
• Hints and Help
• Extra Practice

1. Suppose Anna draws two line segments, $\overline{AB}$ and $\overline{CD}$ that intersect at point E. She draws them in such a way that $\overline{AB} \cong \overline{CD}$, $\overline{AB} \perp \overline{CD}$, and $\angle CAD$ is a right angle. What is the best name to describe $ACBD$? Explain.

   Square; because the diagonals are congruent, it is a rectangle and because

   the diagonals are perpendicular, it is a rhombus. A figure that is both a

   rectangle and a rhombus must be a square.

2. Write a two-column proof that if the diagonals of a parallelogram are congruent, then the parallelogram is a rectangle.

   Given: $EFGH$ is a parallelogram; $\overline{EG} \cong \overline{HF}$.

   Prove: $EFGH$ is a rectangle.

   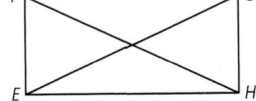

Statements	Reasons
1. $EFGH$ is a parallelogram; $\overline{EG} \cong \overline{HF}$.	1. Given
2. $\overline{EF} \cong \overline{GH}$	2. If a quadrilateral is a parallelogram, then its opposite sides are congruent.
3. $\overline{EH} \cong \overline{EH}$	3. Reflexive Property of Congruence
4. $\triangle EFH \cong \triangle HGE$	4. SSS Triangle Congruence Theorem
5. $\angle FEH \cong \angle GHE$	5. CPCTC
6. $\angle FEH$ and $\angle GHE$ are supplementary.	6. Consecutive angles of a parallelogram are supplementary.
7. $m\angle FEH = 90°$	7. Congruent supplementary angles are right angles.
8. $EFGH$ is a rectangle.	8. Definition of rectangle

Determine whether each quadrilateral must be a rectangle. Explain.

3.

   Given: $BD = AC$

   No information is known about its sides or

   angles, so it may not be a parallelogram. So,

   it cannot be determined if it is a rectangle.

4.

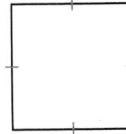

   No information about the angles is

   known, so it cannot be determined if it

   is a rectangle.

EVALUATE

ASSIGNMENT GUIDE

Concepts and Skills	Practice
Explore Properties of Rectangles, Rhombuses, and Squares	Exercise 1
Example 1 Proving that Congruent Diagonals Is a Condition for Rectangles	Exercises 2–4
Example 2 Proving Conditions for Rhombuses	Exercises 5–7
Example 3 Applying Conditions for Special Parallelograms	Exercises 8–16

INTEGRATE MATHEMATICAL PRACTICES

Focus on Communication

MP.3 Some students may not realize how important each word is in a definition or theorem. To explain one of the theorems in this lesson, ask students to focus on exactly what they know about a given parallelogram (or quadrilateral) in order to make a conclusion about how to further classify the parallelogram. Tell them to make sure that the statement they are trying to prove contains no more and no less information than is needed to proceed deductively to the conclusion.

Exercise	Depth of Knowledge (D.O.K.)	COMMON CORE Mathematical Practices
1–10	**2** Skills/Concepts	**MP.2** Reasoning
11–16	**2** Skills/Concepts	**MP.5** Using Tools
17–18	**2** Skills/Concepts	**MP.4** Modeling
19	**2** Skills/Concepts	**MP.2** Reasoning
20	**3** Strategic Thinking H.O.T.	**MP.2** Reasoning
21	**3** Strategic Thinking H.O.T.	**MP.3** Logic
22	**3** Strategic Thinking H.O.T.	**MP.3** Logic

INTEGRATE MATHEMATICAL PRACTICES

Focus on Math Connections

MP.1 Before doing the exercises, you may want to review the conditions for rectangles, rhombuses, and squares. In particular, if a parallelogram

- has one right angle, it is a rectangle.
- has congruent diagonals, it is a rectangle.
- has congruent consecutive sides, it is a rhombus.
- has perpendicular diagonals, it is a rhombus.
- is a rectangle and a rhombus, it is a square.

Each quadrilateral is a parallelogram. Determine whether each parallelogram is a rhombus or not.

5.

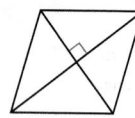

Rhombus; a parallelogram with perpendicular diagonals is a rhombus.

6.

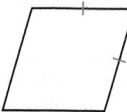

Rhombus; a parallelogram with a pair of consecutive sides congruent is a rhombus.

Give one characteristic about each figure that would make the conclusion valid.

7. Conclusion: *JKLM* is a rhombus.

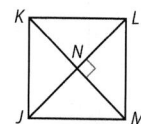

You need to know that *JKLM* is a parallelogram.

8. Conclusion: *PQRS* is a square.

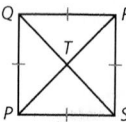

Possible answer: You need to know that ∠*QPS* is a right angle.

Determine if the conclusion is valid. If not, tell what additional information is needed to make it valid.

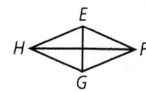

9. Given: $\overline{EG}$ and $\overline{FH}$ bisect each other. $\overline{EG} \perp \overline{FH}$

Conclusion: *EFGH* is a rhombus.

The conclusion is valid.

10. $\overline{FH}$ bisects ∠*EFG* and ∠*EHG*.

Conclusion: *EFGH* is a rhombus.

The conclusion is not valid. You need to know that *EFGH* is a parallelogram.

Find the value of *x* that makes each parallelogram the given type.

11. square

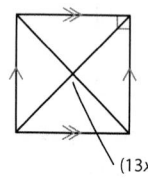

$(13x + 5.5)°$

$x = 6.5$

12. rhombus

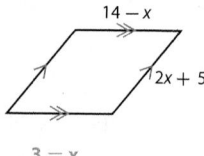

$14 - x$

$2x + 5$

$3 = x$

© Houghton Mifflin Harcourt Publishing Company

In Exercises 13–16, Determine which quadrilaterals match the figure: parallelogram, rhombus, rectangle, or square? List all that apply.

13. Given: $\overline{WY} \cong \overline{XZ}$, $\overline{WY} \perp \overline{XZ}$, $\overline{XY} \cong \overline{ZW}$

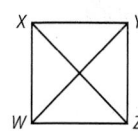

parallelogram, rhombus, rectangle, square

14. Given: $\overline{XY} \cong \overline{ZW}$, $\overline{WY} \cong \overline{ZX}$

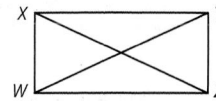

parallelogram, rectangle

15. Given: $\overline{XY} \cong \overline{ZW}$, $\angle XWY \cong \angle YWZ$, $\angle XYW \cong \angle ZYW$

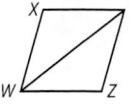

parallelogram, rhombus

16. Given: $m\angle WXY = 130°$, $m\angle XWZ = 50°$, $m\angle WZY = 130°$

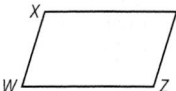

parallelogram

17. Represent Real-World Problems A framer uses a clamp to hold together pieces of a picture frame. The pieces are cut so that $\overline{PQ} \cong \overline{RS}$ and $\overline{QR} \cong \overline{SP}$. The clamp is adjusted so that PZ, QZ, RZ, and SZ are all equal lengths. Why must the frame be a rectangle?

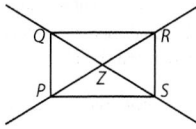

Since both pairs of opposite sides are congruent, *PQRS* is a parallelogram. Since *PZ*, *QZ*, *RZ*, and *SZ* are all equal lengths, *PZ* + *RZ* = *QZ* + *SZ*. So $\overline{QS} \cong \overline{PR}$. Since the diagonals are congruent, *PQRS* is a rectangle.

18. Represent Real-World Problems A city garden club is planting a square garden. They drive pegs into the ground at each corner and tie strings between each pair. The pegs are spaced so that $\overline{WX} \cong \overline{XY} \cong \overline{YZ} \cong \overline{ZW}$. How can the garden club use the diagonal strings to verify that the garden is a square?

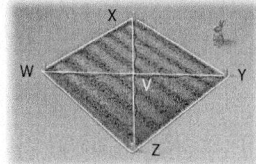

The club members can measure the lengths of the diagonals to see if they are equal.

19. A quadrilateral is formed by connecting the midpoints of a rectangle. Which of the following could be the resulting figure? Select all that apply.

- ● parallelogram
- ○ rectangle
- ● rhombus
- ○ square

AVOID COMMON ERRORS

Students may be confused about how to use the theorems in this lesson. Explain how some of the theorems in the lesson can be used as alternate definitions. For example, some people define a rectangle as a parallelogram with one right angle. In this case, the remaining properties and the definition as a quadrilateral with four right angles follow.

Ask students to work with a partner to make a physical model of a parallelogram with paper strips and brads. Ask them to manipulate the side lengths and angle measures in the parallelogram to discover the conditions necessary for a rectangle, rhombus, or square. Have students take turns making conjectures about how to get these special figures from a parallelogram.

JOURNAL

Have students explain the relationships between parallelograms, rectangles, rhombuses, and squares.

---

20. Critical Thinking The diagonals of a quadrilateral are perpendicular bisectors of each other. What is the best name for this quadrilateral? Explain your answer.

Rhombus; Since the diagonals bisect each other, the quadrilateral is a parallelogram. Since the diagonals are perpendicular, the parallelogram is a rhombus.

21. Draw Conclusions Think about the relationships between angles and sides in this triangular prism to decide if the given face is a rectangle.

Given: $\overline{AC} \cong \overline{DF}$, $\overline{AB} \cong \overline{DE}$, $\overline{AB} \perp \overline{BC}$, $\overline{DE} \perp \overline{EF}$, $\overline{BE} \perp \overline{EF}$, $\overline{BC} \parallel \overline{EF}$

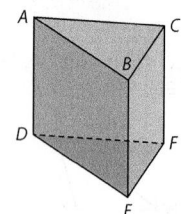

Prove: $EBCF$ is a rectangle.

It is given that $\overline{AC} \cong \overline{DF}$ and $\overline{AB} \cong \overline{DE}$. Since $\overline{AB} \perp \overline{BC}$, $\angle ABC$ is a right angle. And since $\overline{DE} \perp \overline{EF}$, $\angle DEF$ is a right angle. By the Hypotenuse-Leg (HL) Triangle Congruence Theorem, $\triangle ABC \cong \triangle DEF$. By CPCTC, $\overline{BC} \cong \overline{EF}$. Since the opposite sides of $EBCF$ are parallel and congruent, it is a parallelogram. Since $\overline{BE} \perp \overline{EF}$, then $\angle BEF$ is a right angle, which makes $EBCF$ a rectangle.

22. Justify Reasoning Use one of the other rhombus theorems to prove that if the diagonals of a parallelogram are perpendicular, then the parallelogram is a rhombus.

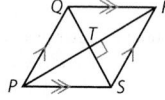

Given: $PQRS$ is a parallelogram. $\overline{PR} \perp \overline{QS}$

Prove: $PQRS$ is a rhombus.

Statements	Reasons
1. $PQRS$ is a parallelogram.	1. Given
2. $\overline{PT} \cong \overline{RT}$	2. Diagonals of a parallelogram bisect each other.
3. $\overline{QT} \cong \overline{QT}$	3. Reflexive Property of Congruence
4. $\overline{PR} \perp \overline{QS}$	4. Given
5. $\angle QTP$ and $\angle QTR$ are right angles.	5. Definition of perpendicular lines
6. $\angle QTP \cong \angle QTR$	6. Right angles are congruent.
7. $\triangle QTP \cong \triangle QTR$	7. SAS Congruence Criterion
8. $\overline{QP} \cong \overline{QR}$	8. CPCTC
9. $PQRS$ is a rhombus.	9. If one pair of consecutive sides of a parallelogram are congruent, then it is a rhombus.

Lesson Performance Task

The diagram shows the organizational ladder of groups to which tigers belong.

a. Use the terms below to create a similar ladder in which each term is a subset of the term above it.

Parallelogram Geometric figures Squares
Quadrilaterals Figures Rhombuses

b. Decide which of the following statements is true. Then write three more statements like it, using terms from the list in part (a).

If a figure is a rhombus, then it is a parallelogram.

If a figure is a parallelogram, then it is a rhombus.

c. Explain how you can use the ladder you created above to write if-then statements involving the terms on the list.

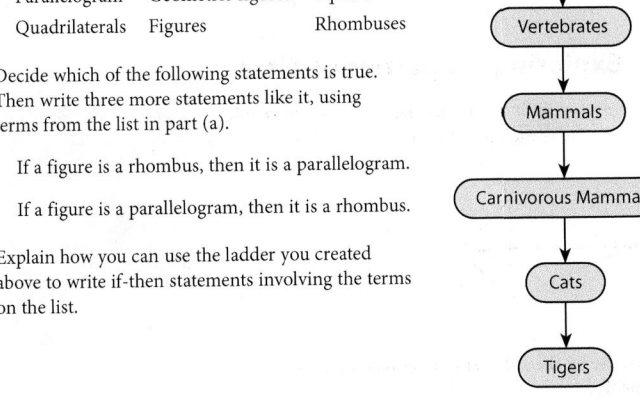

a.

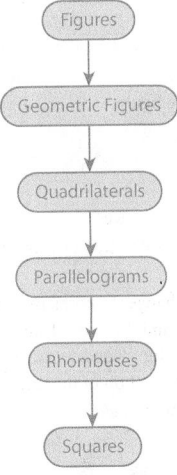

b. The true statement is "If a figure is a rhombus, then it is a parallelogram." Other statements will vary.

c. The term following "If" must be below the term following "then."

EXTENSION ACTIVITY

Have students draw the *Animals* ladder and the *Figures* ladder, using large boxes for each step. In each box, have them write information about the subject of the box, beginning by referring to the subject of the box above. For example, in the *Tigers* box they would begin, "A tiger is a cat that ...." In the *Parallelogram* box they would begin, "A parallelogram is a quadrilateral that ...." Students will likely need to research information for the *Animals* ladder. Encourage them to write precise, concise information, describing the main properties that distinguish the subject of the box and not digressing to discuss other interesting but irrelevant details.

INTEGRATE MATHEMATICAL PRACTICES
Focus on Modeling

MP.4 Have students redraw the Figures ladder, adding a box for each of these categories: Hexagons, Regular Hexagons, Pentagons, Regular Pentagons, and Rectangles.

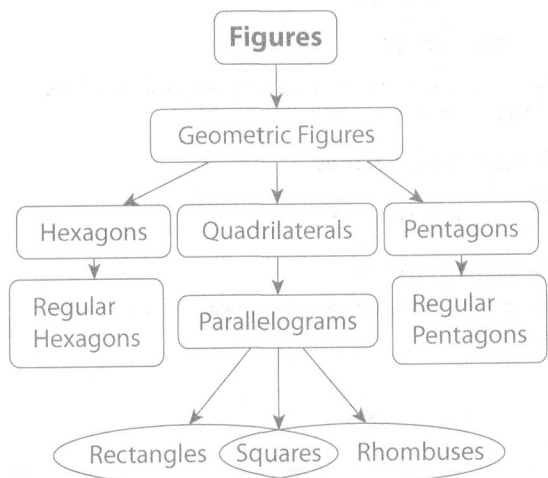

INTEGRATE MATHEMATICAL PRACTICES
Focus on Math Connections

MP.1 • Define the term *square* using the word *regular*.

A square is a regular rectangle.

• Define the term *rhombus* using the word *regular*.

A rhombus is a regular parallelogram.

Scoring Rubric

2 points: Student correctly solves the problem and explains his/her reasoning.

1 point: Student shows good understanding of the problem but does not fully solve or explain.

0 points: Student does not demonstrate understanding of the problem.

Properties and Conditions for Kites and Trapezoids

Common Core Math Standards

The student is expected to:

 G-SRT.B.5

Use congruence ... criteria for triangles to solve problems and to prove relationships in geometric figures.

Mathematical Practices

 MP.6 Precision

Language Objective

Explain to a partner how to describe the properties of kites and trapezoids.

ENGAGE

Essential Question: What are the properties of kites and trapezoids?

The diagonals of a kite are perpendicular; the diagonals of an isosceles trapezoid are congruent; a kite has exactly one pair of congruent opposite angles; an isosceles trapezoid has two pairs of congruent base angles.

PREVIEW: LESSON PERFORMANCE TASK

View the Engage section online. Discuss the photo. Ask students to describe the spider web and in particular its geometrical properties. Then preview the Lesson Performance Task.

9.5 Properties and Conditions for Kites and Trapezoids

Essential Question: What are the properties of kites and trapezoids?

Resource Locker

⊘ Explore Exploring Properties of Kites

A **kite** is a quadrilateral with two distinct pairs of congruent consecutive sides. In the figure, $\overline{PQ} \cong \overline{PS}$, and $\overline{QR} \cong \overline{SR}$, but $\overline{QR} \not\cong \overline{QP}$.

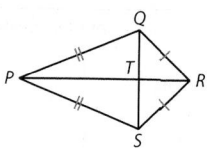

Measure the angles made by the sides and diagonals of a kite, noticing any relationships.

Ⓐ Use a protractor to measure $\angle PTQ$ and $\angle QTR$ in the figure. What do your results tell you about the kite's diagonals, $\overline{PR}$ and $\overline{QS}$?

$m\angle PTQ = 90°$, $m\angle QTR = 90°$; the diagonals $\overline{PR}$ and $\overline{QS}$ are perpendicular.

Ⓑ Use a protractor to measure $\angle PQR$ and $\angle PSR$ in the figure. How are these opposite angles related?

$\angle PQR \cong \angle PSR$

Ⓒ Measure $\angle QPS$ and $\angle QRS$ in the figure. What do you notice?

$\angle QPS \not\cong \angle QRS$, so only one pair of opposite angles in the kite are congruent.

Ⓓ Use a compass to construct your own kite figure on a separate sheet of paper. Begin by choosing a point B. Then use your compass to choose points A and C so that $AB = BC$.

Ⓔ Now change the compass length and draw arcs from both points A and C. Label the intersection of the arcs as point D.

Ⓕ Finally, draw the sides and diagonals of the kite.

Mark the intersection of the diagonals as point E.

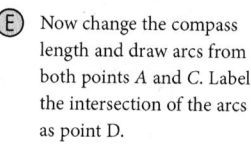

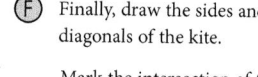

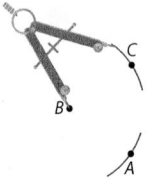

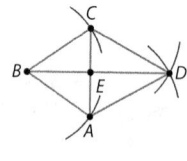

© Houghton Mifflin Harcourt Publishing Company · Image Credits: ©Larry Mulvehill/Corbis

Turn to these pages to find this lesson in the hardcover student edition.

HARDCOVER PAGES 403–416

Ⓖ Measure the angles of the kite *ABCD* you constructed in Steps D–F
and the measure of the angles formed by the diagonals. Are your
results the same as for the kite *PQRS* you used in Steps A–C?

Yes, for kite *ABCD*, m∠AEB = 90° and m∠CEB = 90°, so, again, the diagonals of the kite

are perpendicular. Also, for the constructed kite, ∠ABC ≇ ∠ADC, but ∠BAD ≅ ∠BCD, so,

again, one pair of opposite angles are congruent but the other pair are not.

Reflect

1. In the kite *ABCD* you constructed in Steps D–F, look at ∠CDE and ∠ADE. What do
   you notice? Is this true for ∠CBE and ∠ABE as well? How can you state this in terms
   of diagonal $\overline{AC}$ and the pair of non-congruent opposite angles ∠CBA and ∠CDA?

   ∠CDE ≅ ∠ADE; yes, ∠CBE ≅ ∠ABE; so, diagonal $\overline{BD}$ bisects the pair of non-

   congruent opposite angles ∠CBA and ∠CDA.

2. In the kite *ABCD* you constructed in Steps D–F, look at $\overline{EC}$ and $\overline{EA}$. What do you
   notice? Is this true for $\overline{EB}$ and $\overline{ED}$ as well? Which diagonal is a perpendicular
   bisector?

   $\overline{EC}$ ≅ $\overline{EA}$; no, $\overline{EB}$ ≇ $\overline{ED}$; so, diagonal $\overline{BD}$ is the perpendicular bisector of

   diagonal $\overline{AC}$, but not vice versa.

⊘ Explain 1   Using Relationships in Kites

The results of the Explore can be stated as theorems.

> **Four Kite Theorems**
>
> If a quadrilateral is a kite, then its diagonals are perpendicular.
>
> If a quadrilateral is a kite, then exactly one pair of opposite angles are congruent.
>
> If a quadrilateral is a kite, then one of the diagonals bisects the pair of
> non-congruent angles.
>
> If a quadrilateral is a kite, then exactly one diagonal bisects the other.
>
>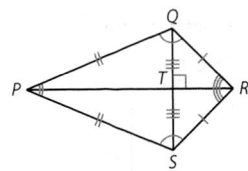

You can use the properties of kites to find unknown angle measures.

PROFESSIONAL DEVELOPMENT

 Math Background

A *kite* is a quadrilateral with two distinct pairs of congruent consecutive sides.
A *trapezoid* is a quadrilateral with at least one pair of parallel sides. These
definitions may not be the same as definitions in other textbooks. Such decisions
about definitions are somewhat arbitrary. Variations of definitions do not change
the facts of mathematics, but they do change the way the facts are expressed. The
decision to use an inclusive definition for trapezoid means that all parallelograms
share the properties of trapezoids. The decision to use an exclusive definition for
kite means that other quadrilaterals do not necessarily share the properties of kites.

EXPLORE

Exploring Properties of Kites

INTEGRATE TECHNOLOGY

Students have the option of doing the kite activity
either in the book or online.

QUESTIONING STRATEGIES

? What kind of triangles do the diagonals of a
kite form? Are any of these triangles
congruent? Explain. Right triangles; yes; there are
two pairs of congruent triangles by the HL Triangle
Congruence Theorem.

EXPLAIN 1

Using Relationships in Kites

INTEGRATE MATHEMATICAL PRACTICES
Focus on Math Communication

MP.3 Point out to students that in the previous
lesson they were introduced to the properties of
rectangles, rhombuses, and squares. Explain that in
this lesson, they will be given a quadrilateral and will
learn what conditions can be used to classify it as a
kite or a trapezoid. You may want to call on students
to read each theorem aloud. Then ask them to
explain the theorem in their own words. Challenge
students to come up with unique ways to explain the
theorems.

INTEGRATE TECHNOLOGY

Have students use geometry software to draw the
figures in some of the examples. This will allow them
to check their answers.

Properties and Conditions for Kites and Trapezoids   **472**

QUESTIONING STRATEGIES

? How do you use the properties of a kite to find the measure of its angles? Since the diagonals of a kite are perpendicular, they form right angles. That makes the acute angles of the right triangles complementary.

EXPLAIN 2

Proving that Base Angles of Isosceles Trapezoids Are Congruent

INTEGRATE MATHEMATICAL PRACTICES

Focus on Communication

MP.3 You may want to review the Parallel Postulate and the Corresponding Angles Theorem before you present a plan for the proof. The Parallel Postulate guarantees that there is a unique line through one vertex of the trapezoid that is parallel to one leg of the trapezoid. The segment determined by this line creates a parallelogram, which in turn creates an isosceles triangle (with congruent base angles). The Corresponding Angles Theorem applies to the figure because the lines are parallel, and the transitive property will give congruent base angles.

Example 1 In kite $ABCD$, $m\angle BAE = 32°$ and $m\angle BCE = 62°$. Find each measure.

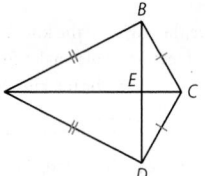

(A) $m\angle CBE$

Use angle relationships in $\triangle BCE$.

Use the property that the diagonals of a kite are perpendicular, so $m\angle BEC = 90°$.

$\triangle BCE$ is a right triangle.

Therefore, its acute angles are complementary.

$m\angle BCE + m\angle CBE = 90°$

Substitute 62° for $m\angle BCE$, then solve for $m\angle CBE$.

$62° + m\angle CBE = 90°$

$m\angle CBE = 28°$

(B) $m\angle ABE$

$\triangle ABE$ is also a right triangle.

Therefore, its acute angles are complementary.

$m\angle ABE + m\angle \boxed{BAE} = \boxed{90}°$

Substitute 32° for $m\angle \boxed{BAE}$, then solve for $m\angle ABE$.

$m\angle ABE + \boxed{32}° = \boxed{90}°$

$m\angle ABE = \boxed{58}°$

Reflect

3. From Part A and Part B, what strategy could you use to determine $m\angle ADC$?

One pair of opposite angles in $ABCD$ is congruent, so $m\angle ADC = m\angle ABC$. Also, $m\angle ABC$ is the sum of $m\angle ABE$ and $m\angle CBE$.

Your Turn

4. Determine $m\angle ADC$ in kite $ABCD$.

$\angle ADC \cong \angle ABC$, since exactly one pair of opposite angles are congruent.

$m\angle ADC = m\angle ABC = m\angle ABE + m\angle CBE = 58° + 28° = 86°$

⊘ Explain 2 **Proving that Base Angles of Isosceles Trapezoids Are Congruent**

A **trapezoid** is a quadrilateral with at least one pair of parallel sides. The pair of parallel sides of the trapezoid (or either pair of parallel sides if the trapezoid is a parallelogram) are called the *bases* of the trapezoid. The other two sides are called the *legs* of the trapezoid.

A trapezoid has two pairs of *base angles*: each pair consists of the two angles adjacent to one of the bases. An **isosceles trapezoid** is one in which the legs are congruent but not parallel.

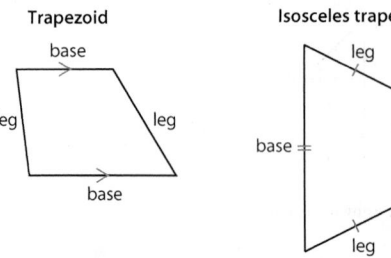

COLLABORATIVE LEARNING

Peer-to-Peer Activity

Ask students to work with a partner to make a physical model of a kite and of a trapezoid with paper strips and brads. Have one student make a conjecture about how to find the other three angle measures for the kite, and ask the other student to make a conjecture about how to find the other three angle measures for the trapezoid. Ask them to confirm each other's conjecture by measuring the angles.

Three Isosceles Trapezoid Theorems

If a quadrilateral is an isosceles trapezoid, then each pair of base angles are congruent.

If a trapezoid has one pair of congruent base angles, then the trapezoid is isosceles.

A trapezoid is isosceles if and only if its diagonals are congruent.

You can use auxiliary segments to prove these theorems.

Example 2   Complete the flow proof of the first Isosceles Trapezoid Theorem.

Given: $ABCD$ is an isosceles trapezoid
with $\overline{BC} \parallel \overline{AD}$, $\overline{AB} \cong \overline{DC}$.

Prove: $\angle A \cong \angle D$

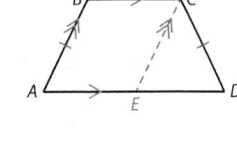

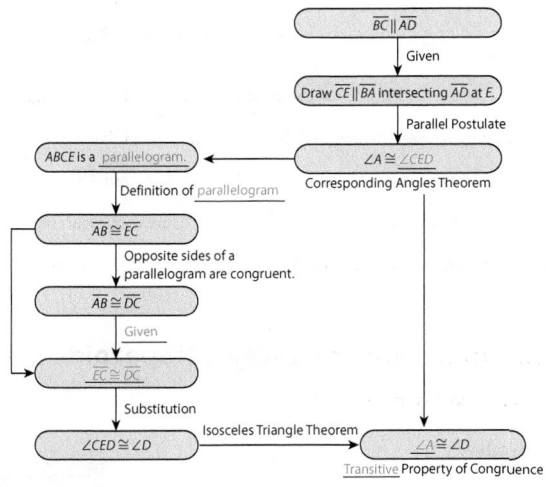

BC ∥ AD
↓ Given
Draw $\overline{CE} \parallel \overline{BA}$ intersecting $\overline{AD}$ at E.
↓ Parallel Postulate
$\angle A \cong \underline{\angle CED}$
Corresponding Angles Theorem

$ABCE$ is a parallelogram.
↓ Definition of parallelogram

$\overline{AB} \cong \overline{EC}$
↓ Opposite sides of a parallelogram are congruent.

$\overline{AB} \cong \overline{DC}$
↓ Given

$\overline{EC} \cong \overline{DC}$
↓ Substitution

$\angle CED \cong \angle D$ — Isosceles Triangle Theorem → $\underline{\angle A} \cong \angle D$
   Transitive Property of Congruence

Reflect

5. Explain how the auxiliary segment was useful in the proof.
Introducing the auxiliary segment breaks the trapezoid into familiar figures, a

parallelogram and an isosceles triangle. Then the properties of the simpler figures could

be used to prove the theorem about the more complex figure.

? How is the isosceles triangle in this proof used to show that the base angles of the isosceles trapezoid are congruent? Sample answer: The congruent sides of the isosceles triangle are used to show that its base angles are congruent. Then the proof establishes that the base angles of the isosceles trapezoid are congruent by the transitive property.

DIFFERENTIATE INSTRUCTION

Multiple Representations

Have students make a table of the properties of kites and trapezoids. Have them list the properties of each in their own words and draw a diagram to represent each. Then have students compare different types of quadrilaterals. For example, ask: "How are kites and squares alike?" Sample answer: Both are quadrilaterals, and both have perpendicular diagonals.

Properties and Conditions for Kites and Trapezoids   **474**

EXPLAIN 3

Using Theorems about Isosceles Trapezoids

INTEGRATE MATHEMATICAL PRACTICES
Focus on Critical Thinking

MP.3 Some math textbooks define a trapezoid as a quadrilateral with exactly one pair of parallel sides. Remind students that this definition is not used here. Parallelograms are a subset of trapezoids because a trapezoid has *at least* one pair of parallel sides, as they are defined here. Students need to consider this as they are using the theorems about isosceles trapezoids to find segment lengths for trapezoids.

QUESTIONING STRATEGIES

? If you are trying to find the length of one part of a diagonal of an isosceles trapezoid, what information do you need? You need to know that the diagonals of an isosceles trapezoid are congruent.

? Can the bases of a trapezoid be congruent? Explain. Yes, if the trapezoid is also a parallelogram.

---

6. The flow proof in Example 2 only shows that one pair of base angles is congruent. Write a plan for proof for using parallel lines to show that the other pair of base angles (∠B and ∠C) are also congruent.

   Plan for Proof: In the isosceles trapezoid, the bases are parallel, so ∠B is supplementary to ∠A and ∠C is supplementary to ∠D by the Same–Side Interior Angles Postulate. From Example 2, ∠A ≅ ∠D. So ∠B ≅ ∠C because angles supplementary to ≅ angles are ≅

7. Complete the proof of the second Isosceles Trapezoid Theorem: If a trapezoid has one pair of base angles congruent, then the trapezoid is isosceles.

   Given: ABCD is a trapezoid with $\overline{BC} \parallel \overline{AD}$, ∠A ≅ ∠D.
   Prove: ABCD is an isosceles trapezoid.

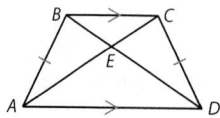

   It is given that $\overline{BC} \parallel \overline{AD}$. By the Parallel Postulate , $\overline{CE}$ can be drawn parallel to $\overline{BA}$ so that $\overline{CE}$ intersects $\overline{AD}$ at E. By the Corresponding Angles Theorem, ∠A ≅ ∠CED . It is given that ∠A ≅ ∠D , so by substitution, ∠CED ≅ ∠D . By the Converse of the Isosceles Triangle Theorem, $\overline{CE}$ ≅ $\overline{CD}$. By definition, ABCE is a parallelogram. In a parallelogram, opposite sides are congruent, so $\overline{AB}$ ≅ $\overline{CE}$. By the Transitive Property. of Congruence, $\overline{AB}$ ≅ $\overline{CD}$. Therefore, by definition, ABCD is an isosceles trapezoid .

⊘ Explain 3 Using Theorems about Isosceles Trapezoids

You can use properties of isosceles trapezoids to find unknown values.

Example 3 Find each measure or value.

(A) A railroad bridge has side sections that show isosceles trapezoids. The figure ABCD represents one of these sections. AC = 13.2 m and BE = 8.4 m. Find DE.

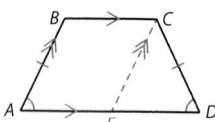

Use the property that the diagonals are congruent.	$\overline{AC} \cong \overline{BD}$
Use the definition of congruent segments.	$AC = BD$
Substitute 13.2 for AC.	$13.2 = BD$
Use the Segment Addition Postulate.	$BE + DE = BD$
Substitute 8.4 for BE and 13.2 for BD.	$8.4 + DE = 13.2$
Subtract 8.4 from both sides.	$DE = 4.8$

LANGUAGE SUPPORT 🔲

Connect Vocabulary

Have students draw a kite and an isosceles trapezoid on poster board and label the diagrams accordingly. For kites, include that their diagonals are perpendicular and that they have one pair of congruent opposite angles. For isosceles trapezoids, include that each pair of base angles is congruent and that the diagonals are congruent.

(B) Find the value of x so that trapezoid $EFGH$ is isosceles.

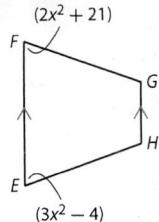
$(2x^2 + 21)$

$(3x^2 - 4)$

For $EFGH$ to be isosceles, each pair of base angles are congruent.

In particular, the pair at E and __F__ are congruent. $\angle E \cong \angle$ __F__

Use the definition of congruent angles. $m\angle E = m\angle$ __F__.

Substitute __$3x^2 - 4$__ for $m\angle E$ and __$2x^2 + 21$__ for $m\angle$ __F__. $3x^2 - 4 = 2x^2 + 21$

Substract __$2x^2$__ from both sides and add __4__ to both sides. $x^2 =$ __25__

Take the square root of both sides. $x =$ __5__ or $x =$ __-5__

Your Turn

8. In isosceles trapezoid $PQRS$, use the Same-Side Interior Angles Postulate to find $m\angle R$.

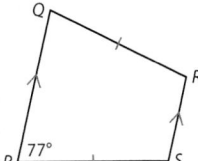
$77°$

Since $PQRS$ is isosceles, each pair of base angles must be congruent.

$\angle P \cong \angle Q$; $m\angle P = m\angle Q$; $77° = m\angle Q$

Using the Same-Side Interior Angles Postulate,

$m\angle Q + m\angle R = 180°$; $77° + m\angle R = 180°$

$m\angle R = 103°$

9. $JL = 3y + 6$ and $KM = 22 - y$. Determine the value of y so that trapezoid $JKLM$ is isosceles.

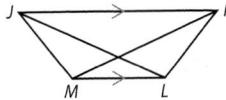

For $JKLM$ to be isosceles, its diagonals must be congruent.

$\overline{JL} \cong \overline{KM}$

$JL = KM$

$3y + 6 = 22 - y$

$4y = 16$

$y = 4$

Explain 4   Using the Trapezoid Midsegment Theorem

The **midsegment of a trapezoid** is the segment whose endpoints are the midpoints of the legs.

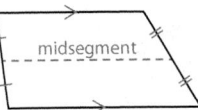
midsegment

EXPLAIN 4

Using the Trapezoid Midsegment Theorem

QUESTIONING STRATEGIES

? In the formula for the length of the midsegment, how do you know which segment lengths to substitute where? Sample answer: The midsegment length will be the length inside the trapezoid connecting the midpoints of the legs; the base lengths will be the lengths of the parallel sides.

AVOID COMMON ERRORS

Students may have trouble keeping track of given information, especially when algebraic expressions are involved. Encourage students to color code measures on each diagram. This may help students identify the information needed for their calculations.

Trapezoid Midsegment Theorem

The midsegment of a trapezoid is parallel to each base, and its length is one half the sum of the lengths of the bases.

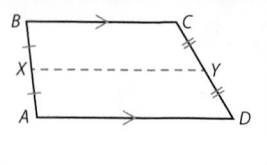

$\overline{XY} \parallel \overline{BC}, \overline{XY} \parallel \overline{AD}$

$XY = \frac{1}{2}(BC + AD)$

You can use the Trapezoid Midsegment Theorem to find the length of the midsegment or a base of a trapezoid.

Example 4 Find each length.

(A) In trapezoid *EFGH*, find *XY*.

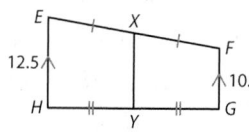

Use the second part of the Trapezoid Midsegment Theorem. $XY = \frac{1}{2}(EH + FG)$

Substitute 12.5 for *EH* and 10.3 for *FG*. $= \frac{1}{2}(12.5 + 10.3)$

Simplify. $= 11.4$

(B) In trapezoid *JKLM*, find *JM*.

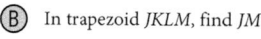

Use the second part of the Trapezoid Midsegment Theorem. $PQ = \frac{1}{2}(\underline{KL} + JM)$

Substitute __9.8__ for *PQ* and __8.3__ for __KL__. $\underline{9.8} = \frac{1}{2}(\underline{8.3} + JM)$

Multiply both sides by 2. $\underline{19.6} = \underline{8.3} + JM$

Subtract __8.3__ from both sides. $\underline{11.3} = JM$

Your Turn

10. In trapezoid *PQRS*, $PQ = 2RS$. Find *XY*.

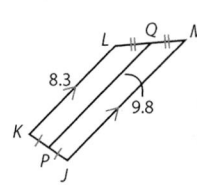

$$PQ = 2RS$$
$$16.8 = 2RS$$
$$8.4 = RS$$
$$XY = \frac{1}{2}(PQ + RS)$$
$$= \frac{1}{2}(16.8 + 8.4)$$
$$= 12.6$$

© Houghton Mifflin Harcourt Publishing Company

11. Use the information in the graphic organizer to complete the Venn diagram.

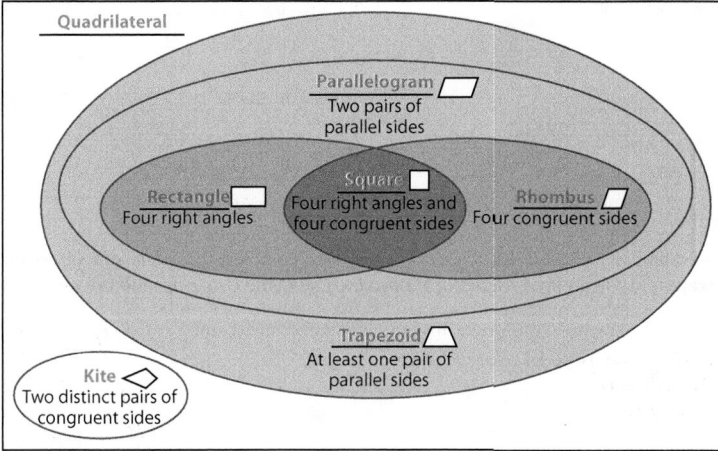

Rectangle
Four right angles

Rhombus
Four congruent sides

Parallelogram
Two pairs of
parallel sides

Quadrilateral

Trapezoid
At least one pair of
parallel sides

Square
Four right angles and
four congruent sides

Kite
Two distinct pairs of
congruent sides

What can you conclude about all parallelograms? <u>Possible answer: All</u>
<u>parallelograms are quadrilaterals and all parallelograms are also trapezoids.</u>

12. Discussion The Isosceles Trapezoid Theorem about congruent diagonals is in the form
of a biconditional statement. Is it possible to state the two isosceles trapezoid theorems
about base angles as a biconditional statement? Explain.
<u>No; the hypotheses and conclusions are not reverses. One has "isosceles trapezoid" as a</u>
<u>hypothesis and "each pair of base angles are ≅" as a conclusion; the other has "a trapezoid</u>
<u>and one pair of ≅ base angles" as a hypothesis and "isosceles trapezoid" as a conclusion.</u>

13. Essential Question Check-In Do kites and trapezoids have properties that are related
to their diagonals? Explain.
<u>Yes; the diagonals of a kite are perpendicular, while the diagonals of an</u>
<u>isosceles trapezoid are congruent.</u>

© Houghton Mifflin Harcourt Publishing Company

ELABORATE

QUESTIONING STRATEGIES

❓ Why can't theorems about the base angles of
an isosceles trapezoid be written as
biconditionals while theorems about the diagonals
can? Sample answer: One starts with an isosceles
trapezoid and results in finding two pairs of base
angles congruent; the other starts with a trapezoid
and one pair of congruent base angles and reasons
the trapezoid is isosceles. So, the hypothesis and
conclusion of the two theorems are not the reverse
of each other.

SUMMARIZE THE LESSON

❓ Have students list the properties of kites and
trapezoids and the difference between a
trapezoid and an isosceles trapezoid. Sample
answer: The diagonals of a kite are perpendicular;
the diagonals of an isosceles trapezoid are
congruent; a kite has exactly one pair of congruent
opposite angles; an isosceles trapezoid has two
pairs of congruent base angles. An isosceles
trapezoid has legs that are congruent but not
parallel.

EVALUATE

ASSIGNMENT GUIDE

Concepts and Skills	Practice
Explore Exploring Properties of Kites	Exercises 16–18
Example 1 Using Relationships in Kites	Exercises 1–4
Example 2 Proving that Base Angles of Isosceles Trapezoids Are Congruent	Exercises 5–6
Example 3 Using Theorems about Isosceles Trapezoids	Exercises 7–10
Example 4 Using the Trapezoid Midsegment Theorem	Exercises 11–14

INTEGRATE MATHEMATICAL PRACTICES

Focus on Communication

MP.3 For some exercises, some students may not realize how to begin solving the problem. Point out that they must first determine if the figure is a kite, a trapezoid, or an isosceles trapezoid. Then suggest that they redraw each figure, marking known properties for that type of quadrilateral.

479 Lesson 9.5

⭐ Evaluate: Homework and Practice

In kite $ABCD$, m$\angle BAE = 28°$ and m$\angle BCE = 57°$. Find each measure.

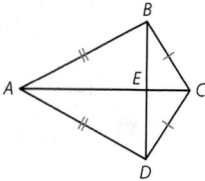

1. m$\angle ABE$

m$\angle ABE$ + m$\angle BAE = 90°$

m$\angle ABE + 28° = 90°$

m$\angle ABE = 62°$

2. m$\angle CBE$

m$\angle BCE$ + m$\angle CBE = 90°$

$57°$ + m$\angle CBE = 90°$

m$\angle CBE = 33°$

3. m$\angle ABC$

m$\angle ABC$ = m$\angle ABE$ + m$\angle CBE$

$= 62° + 33°$

$= 95°$

4. m$\angle ADC$

$\angle ADC \cong \angle ABC$

m$\angle ADC$ = m$\angle ABC$

m$\angle ADC = 95°$

Using the first and second Isosceles Trapezoid Theorems, complete the proofs of each part of the third Isosceles Trapezoid Theorem: *A trapezoid is isosceles if and only if its diagonals are congruent.*

5. Prove part 1: If a trapezoid is isosceles, then its diagonals are congruent.

Given: $ABCD$ is an isosceles trapezoid with $\overline{BC} \parallel \overline{AD}$, $\overline{AB} \cong \overline{DC}$.

Prove: $\overline{AC} \cong \overline{DB}$

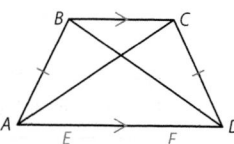

It is given that $\overline{AB} \cong \overline{DC}$. By the first Trapezoid Theorem, $\angle BAD \cong$ ___$\angle CDA$___, and by the Reflexive Property of Congruence, ___$AD \cong AD$___. By the SAS Triangle Congruence Theorem, $\triangle ABD \cong \triangle DCA$, and by ___CPCTC___, $\overline{AC} \cong \overline{DB}$.

Exercise	Depth of Knowledge (D.O.K.)	COMMON CORE Mathematical Practices
1–4	**1** Recall of information	**MP.4** Modeling
5–6	**2** Skills/Concepts	**MP.3** Logic
7–19	**2** Skills/Concepts	**MP.4** Modeling
20–21	**2** Skills/Concepts	**MP.4** Modeling
22–24	**2** Skills/Concepts	**MP.2** Reasoning
25	**3** Strategic Thinking H.O.T.	**MP.3** Logic
26	**3** Strategic Thinking H.O.T.	**MP.3** Logic

6. Prove part 2: If the diagonals of a trapezoid are congruent, then the trapezoid is isosceles.

Given: $ABCD$ is a trapezoid with $\overline{BC} \parallel \overline{AD}$ and diagonals $\overline{AC} \cong \overline{DB}$.

Prove: $ABCD$ is an isosceles trapezoid.

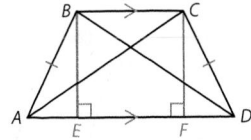

Statements	Reasons
1. Draw $\overline{BE} \perp \overline{AD}$ and $\overline{CF} \perp \overline{AD}$.	1. There is only one line through a given point perpendicular to a given line, so each auxiliary line can be drawn.
2. $\overline{BE} \parallel \overline{CF}$	2. Two lines perpendicular to the same line are parallel.
3. $\overline{BC} \parallel \overline{AD}$	3. Given
4. $BCFE$ is a parallelogram.	4. **Definition of parallelogram** *(Steps 2, 3)*
5. $\overline{BE} \cong \overline{CF}$	5. If a quadrilateral is a parallelogram, then its opposite sides are congruent.
6. $\overline{AC} \cong \overline{DB}$	6. **Given**
7. $\angle BED$ and $\angle CFA$ are right angles.	7. Definition of perpendicular lines
8. $\triangle BED \cong \triangle CFA$	8. HL Triangle Congruence Theorem *(Steps 5–7)*
9. $\angle BDE \cong \angle CAF$	9. **CPCTC**
10. $\angle CBD \cong \angle BDE$, $\angle BCA \cong \angle CAF$	10. Alternate Interior Angles Theorem
11. $\angle CBD \cong \angle BCA$	11. Transitive Property of Congruence *(Steps 9, 10)*
12. $\overline{AC} \cong \overline{DB}$	12. Given
13. $\overline{BC} \cong \overline{BC}$	13. **Reflexive Property of Congruence**
14. $\triangle ABC \cong \triangle DCB$	14. **SAS Triangle Congruence Theorem** *(Steps 12, 13)*
15. $\angle BAC \cong \angle CDB$	15. CPCTC
16. $\angle BAD \cong \angle CDA$	16. Angle Addition Postulate
17. $ABCD$ is isosceles.	17. If a trapezoid has one pair of base angles congruent, then the trapezoid is isosceles.

INTEGRATE MATHEMATICAL PRACTICES

Focus on Patterns

MP.8 Encourage students to develop their own work patterns when they analyze the many types of quadrilaterals in the exercises, especially when algebraic expressions are involved. For example, they may want to color code the measures on each diagram to help them identify the information needed for their calculations.

Properties and Conditions for Kites and Trapezoids   **480**

Use the isosceles trapezoid to find each measure or value.

7. $LJ = 19.3$ and $KN = 8.1$. Determine MN.

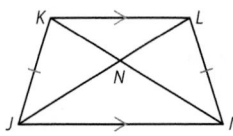

$\overline{LJ} \cong \overline{KM}$; $LJ = KM$; $19.3 = KM$;

$KN + MN = KM$; $8.1 + MN = 19.3$; $MN = 11.2$

8. Find the positive value of x so that trapezoid $PQRS$ is isosceles.

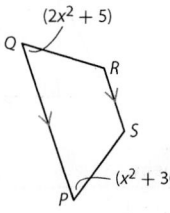

$(2x^2 + 5)$

$(x^2 + 30)$

$\angle Q \cong \angle P$

$m\angle Q = m\angle P$

$2x^2 + 5 = x^2 + 30$

$x^2 = 25$

$x = 5$

9. In isosceles trapezoid $EFGH$, use the Same-Side Interior Angles Postulate to determine $m\angle E$.

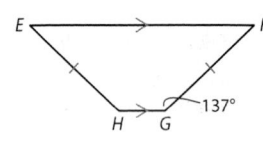

137°

$\angle G \cong \angle H$; $m\angle G = m\angle H$; $137° = m\angle H$

$m\angle E + m\angle H = 180°$; $m\angle E + 137° = 180°$;

$m\angle E = 43°$

10. $AC = 3y + 12$ and $BD = 27 - 2y$. Determine the value of y so that trapezoid $ABCD$ is isosceles.

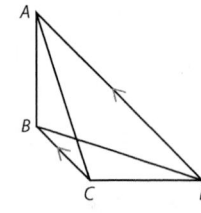

$\overline{AC} \cong \overline{BD}$

$AC = BD$

$3y + 12 = 27 - 2y$

$5y = 15$

$y = 3$

Find the unknown segment lengths in each trapezoid.

11. In trapezoid $ABCD$, find XY.

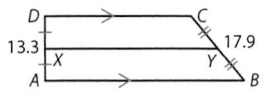

D C

13.3 17.9

X Y

A B

$XY = \frac{1}{2}(AD + BC)$; $= \frac{1}{2}(13.3 + 17.9)$; $= 15.6$

12. In trapezoid $EFGH$, find FG.

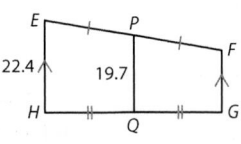

22.4 19.7

$PQ = \frac{1}{2}(EH + FG)$

$19.7 = \frac{1}{2}(22.4 + FG)$

$39.4 = 22.4 + FG$

$17.0 = FG$

13. In trapezoid $PQRS$, $PQ = 4RS$. Determine XY.

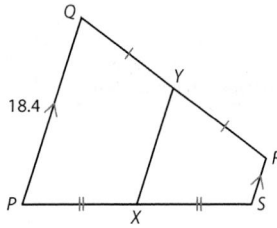

18.4

$PQ = 4RS$; $18.4 = 4RS$; $4.6 = RS$; $XY = \frac{1}{2}(PQ + RS)$; $= \frac{1}{2}(18.4 + 4.6)$; $= 11.5$

14. In trapezoid $JKLM$, $PQ = 2JK$. Determine LM.

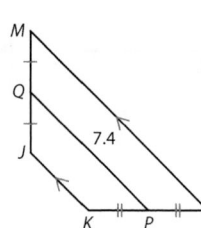

7.4

$PQ = 2JK$

$7.4 = 2JK$

$3.7 = JK$

$PQ = \frac{1}{2}(JK + LM)$

$7.4 = \frac{1}{2}(3.7 + LM)$

$14.8 = 3.7 + LM$

$11.1 = LM$

15. Determine whether each of the following describes a kite or a trapezoid. Select the correct answer for each lettered part.

A. Has two distinct pairs of congruent consecutive sides   ● kite   ○ trapezoid

B. Has diagonals that are perpendicular   ● kite   ○ trapezoid

C. Has at least one pair of parallel sides   ○ kite   ● trapezoid

D. Has exactly one pair of opposite angles that are congruent   ● kite   ○ trapezoid

E. Has two pairs of base angles   ○ kite   ● trapezoid

16. Multi-Step Complete the proof of each of the four Kite Theorems. The proof of each of the four theorems relies on the same initial reasoning, so they are presented here in a single two-column proof.

Given: $ABCD$ is a kite, with $\overline{AB} \cong \overline{AD}$ and $\overline{CB} \cong \overline{CD}$.

Prove: (i) $\overline{AC} \perp \overline{BD}$;
(ii) $\angle ABC \cong \angle ADC$;
(iii) $\overline{AC}$ bisects $\angle BAD$ and $\angle BCD$;
(iv) $\overline{AC}$ bisects $\overline{BD}$.

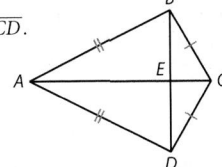

Statements	Reasons
1. $\overline{AB} \cong \overline{AD}$, $\overline{CB} \cong \overline{CD}$	1. Given
2. $\overline{AC} \cong \overline{AC}$	2. Reflexive Property of Congruence
3. $\triangle ABC \cong \triangle ADC$	3. **SSS Triangle Congruence Theorem** *(Steps 1, 2)*
4. $\angle BAE \cong \underline{\angle DAE}$	4. CPCTC
5. $\overline{AE} \cong \overline{AE}$	5. Reflexive Property of Congruence
6. $\underline{\triangle ABE} \cong \triangle ADE$	6. SAS Triangle Congruence Theorem *(Steps 1, 4, 5)*
7. $\angle AEB \cong \angle AED$	7. **CPCTC**
8. $\overline{AC} \perp \overline{BD}$	8. If two lines intersect to form a linear pair of congruent angles, then the lines are perpendicular.
9. $\angle ABC \cong \underline{\angle ADC}$	9. **CPCTC** *(Step 3)*
10. $\angle BAC \cong \underline{\angle DAC}$ and $\underline{\angle BCA} \cong \angle DCA$	10. **CPCTC** *(Step 3)*
11. $\overline{AC}$ bisects $\angle BAD$ and $\angle BCD$.	11. Definition of **angle bisector**
12. $\underline{\overline{BE}} \cong \underline{\overline{DE}}$	12. CPCTC *(Step 6)*
13. $\overline{AC}$ bisects $\overline{BD}$.	13. **Definition of segment bisector**

AVOID COMMON ERRORS

Some students may have trouble understanding how a trapezoid is isosceles if and only if its diagonals are congruent. Ask them to break up this biconditional statement into two statements to prove. They should see that if the diagonals are congruent, they can use triangle criteria to show congruent triangles and then use corresponding parts of congruent figures to show the trapezoid is isosceles. Conversely, they can start with an isosceles trapezoid to show triangles are congruent and then use corresponding parts of congruent figures to show the diagonals are congruent.

17. Given: *JKLN* is a parallelogram. *JKMN* is an isosceles trapezoid.

Prove: △*KLM* is an isosceles triangle.

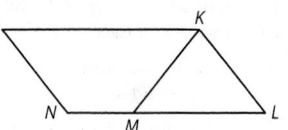

1. *JKLN* is a parallelogram. (Given); 2. $\overline{KL} \cong \overline{NJ}$
(Opposite sides of a parallelogram are congruent.);
3. *JKMN* is an isosceles trapezoid. (Given); 4. $\overline{NJ} \cong \overline{MK}$ (Definition of isosceles trapezoid);
5. $\overline{KL} \cong \overline{KM}$ (Transitive Property of Congruence); 6. △*KLM* is an isosceles triangle. (Definition of isosceles triangle)

Algebra Find the length of the midsegment of each trapezoid.

18.

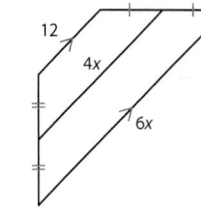

$4x = \frac{1}{2}(12 + 6x)$
$8x = 12 + 6x$
$x = 6$, so $4x = 4(6) = 24$

19.

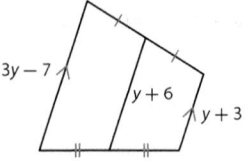

$y + 6 = \frac{1}{2}\big((y + 3) + (3y - 7)\big)$
$2(y + 6) = (y + 3) + (3y - 7)$
$2y + 12 = 4y - 4$
$8 = y$, so $y + 6 = 8 + 6 = 14$

20. Represent Real-World Problems A set of shelves fits an attic room with one sloping wall. The left edges of the shelves line up vertically, and the right edges line up along the sloping wall. The shortest shelf is 32 in. long, and the longest is 40 in. long. Given that the three shelves are equally spaced vertically, what total length of shelving is needed?

The shelves form a trapezoid and the middle shelf forms its midsegment.
Middle shelf: $\frac{1}{2}$(32 in. + 40 in.) = 36 in. Total: 32 + 36 + 40 = 108 in.

21. Represent Real-World Problems A common early stage in making an origami model is known as the kite. The figure shows a paper model at this stage unfolded.

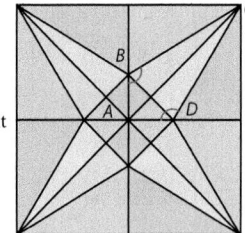

The folds create four geometric kites. Also, the 16 right triangles adjacent to the corners of the paper are all congruent, as are the 8 right triangles adjacent to the center of the paper. Find the measures of all four angles of the kite labeled *ABCD* (the point A is the center point of the diagram). Use the facts that ∠*B* ≅ ∠*D* and that the interior angle sum of a quadrilateral is 360°.

The 8 congruent central triangles are isosceles right triangles; so, m∠*A* = 2(45)° = 90°. The four angles at each corner of the paper are congruent, so m∠*BCA* = m∠*DCA* = $\frac{1}{4}$(90°) = 22.5° and m∠*C* = 22.5° + 22.5° = 45°.
Since ∠*B* ≅ ∠*D*, m∠*B* = m∠*D* = *x*°; then:
90 + *x* + 45 + *x* = 360°, 135 + 2*x* = 360, and *x* = 112.5.
So m∠*B* = m∠*D* = 112.5°.

22. Analyze Relationships The window frame is a regular octagon. It is made from eight pieces of wood shaped like congruent isosceles trapezoids. What are $m\angle A$, $m\angle B$, $m\angle C$, and $m\angle D$ in trapezoid $ABCD$?

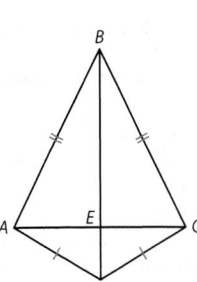

Extend $\overline{BA}$ and $\overline{CD}$ to their intersection E. Since
$m\angle E = \frac{1}{8}(360°) = 45°$, and since $\angle B \cong \angle C$,

$m\angle B + m\angle C + m\angle E = 180°$

$2m\angle B + 45° = 180°$

$2m\angle B = 135°$

$m\angle B = 67.5°$

$m\angle C = 67.5°$

By the Same-Side Int. $\angle$s Post., $m\angle A + m\angle B = 180°$,
so $m\angle A = 180° - 67.5° = 112.5°$.
Since $\angle A \cong \angle D$, $m\angle D = 112.5°$.

23. Explain the Error In kite $ABCD$, $m\angle BAE = 66°$ and $m\angle ADE = 59°$. Terrence is trying to find $m\angle ABC$. He knows that $\overline{BD}$ bisects $\overline{AC}$, and that therefore $\triangle AED \cong \triangle CED$. He reasons that $\angle ADE \cong \angle CDE$, so that $m\angle ADC = 2(59°) = 118°$, and that $\angle ABC \cong \angle ADC$ because they are opposite angles in the kite, so that $m\angle ABC = 118°$. Explain Terrence's error and describe how to find $m\angle ABC$.

Terrence mistakenly reasoned that $\angle ABC \cong \angle ADC$; only one pair of opposite angles in a kite are congruent, and they are adjacent to the bisected diagonal, not the bisecting diagonal. To find $m\angle ABC$: Since $\angle BAE$ and $\angle ABE$ are complementary, $m\angle ABE$ can be found by $90° - 66° = 24°$. Then, since $\triangle AEB \cong \triangle CEB$ so that $\angle ABE \cong \angle CBE$, $m\angle ABC$ is twice $m\angle ABE$, or $2(24°) = 48°$.

24. Complete the table to classify all quadrilateral types by the rotational symmetries and line symmetries they must have. Identify any patterns that you see and explain what these patterns indicate.

Quadrilateral	Angle of Rotational Symmetry	Number of Line Symmetries
kite	none	1
non-isosceles trapezoid	none	0
isosceles trapezoid	none	1
parallelogram	180°	0
rectangle	180°	2
rhombus	180°	2
square	90°	4

The quadrilaterals with rotational symmetry are parallelograms and special cases of parallelograms; the more restricted cases of quadrilaterals tend to have more line symmetries, up to the square with 4; there are two pairs of quadrilateral types with the same symmetries, kites and isosceles trapezoids, and rectangles and rhombuses.

JOURNAL

Have students draw an isosceles trapezoid. Have them label the angle measures in terms of x and write a justification for each measure.

---

25. Communicate Mathematical Ideas Describe the properties that rhombuses and kites have in common, and the properties that are different.

Rhombuses and kites both have pairs of congruent consecutive sides, but in a rhombus, this is because all four sides are congruent. In a kite, two distinct pairs of consecutive sides are congruent. The diagonals of both types of quadrilaterals are perpendicular. In a kite, exactly one diagonal is bisected by the other, while in a rhombus, each diagonal bisects the other. Finally, in a kite, exactly one pair of opposite angles are congruent, while both pairs of opposite angles of a rhombus are congruent.

26. Analyze Relationships In kite $ABCD$, triangles ABD and CBD can be rotated and translated, identifying $\overline{AD}$ with $\overline{CD}$ and joining the remaining pair of vertices, as shown in the figure. Why is this process guaranteed to produce an isosceles trapezoid?

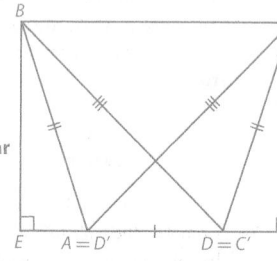

Next, suggest a process guaranteed to produce a kite from an isosceles trapezoid, using figures to illustrate your process.

Sample answer for the case of producing an isosceles trapezoid from a kite where the congruent angles are obtuse: By the definition of a kite and the Reflexive Property of Congruence, $\overline{BA} \cong \overline{BC}$, $\overline{AD} \cong \overline{CD}$, $\overline{BA} \not\cong \overline{AD}$, and $\overline{BD} \cong \overline{BD}$. Rotate and translate the triangles BAD and BCD so that sides $\overline{AD}$ and $\overline{CD}$ coincide, to produce the quadrilateral $BB'DA$ shown. Draw $\overline{BE}$ and $\overline{B'F}$ perpendicular to the line containing $\overline{AD}$ at points E and F. $\overline{BE}$ and $\overline{B'F}$ are parallel because they are perpendicular to the same line. $\triangle BAD \cong \triangle B'C'D'$ by SSS, so $\angle BAD \cong \angle B'C'D'$ because corresponding parts of congruent figures are congruent. Then $\angle BAE \cong \angle B'C'F$ because supplements of congruent angles are congruent. $\angle BEA \cong \angle B'FC'$ because they are both right angles. Also, $\overline{BA} \cong \overline{B'C'}$ (from the kite), so $\triangle BAE \cong \triangle B'C'F$ by AAS. So, $\overline{BE} \cong \overline{B'F}$ because corresponding parts of congruent figures are congruent. Quadrilateral $BB'FE$ is a parallelogram, because one pair of opposite sides are parallel and congruent. By the definition of a parallelogram, $\overleftrightarrow{BB'}$ and $\overleftrightarrow{EF}$ (which includes $\overline{AD}$ (or $\overline{C'D'}$)) are parallel, so $BB'DA$ is a trapezoid because it has a pair of parallel sides. Consider the lines BA and $B'C'$ cut by transversal $\overleftrightarrow{EF}$. Then $\angle BAE$ and $\angle B'C'D'$ are corresponding angles. Because $\angle BAD$ is obtuse, its supplement, $\angle BAE$, is acute. But $\angle B'C'D'$ is obtuse, which means that $\angle BAE$ and $\angle B'C'D'$ cannot be congruent. Thus, $\overline{BA}$ is not parallel to $\overline{B'C'}$ and $BB'DA$ is not a parallelogram. A trapezoid that is not a parallelogram but has congruent legs is isosceles, so $BB'DA$ is an isosceles trapezoid.

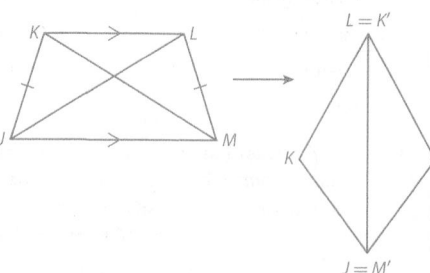

Sample answer: $JKLM$ is an isosceles trapezoid, with $\overline{JK} \cong \overline{ML}$ but $\overline{JK} \not\cong \overline{KL}$ or $\overline{JM}$. Rotate and translate triangles JKL and MLK so that sides $\overline{JL}$ and $\overline{M'K'}$ coincide. This can be done because the diagonals of an isosceles trapezoid are congruent. The resulting figure has two distinct pairs of congruent sides, $\overline{JK} \cong \overline{M'L'}$ (given) and $\overline{KL} \cong \overline{L'K'}$ (Reflexive Property of Congruence), so the figure is a kite.

© Houghton Mifflin Harcourt Publishing Company

Lesson Performance Task

This model of a spider web is made using only isosceles triangles and isosceles trapezoids.

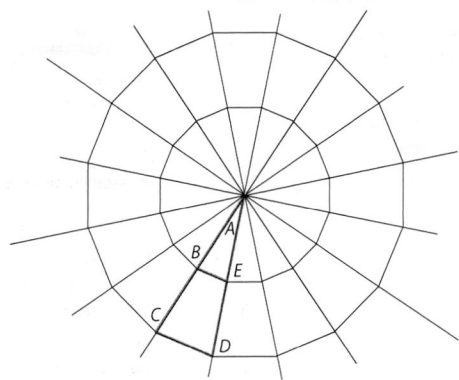

a. All of the figures surrounding the center of the web are congruent to figure *ABCDE*. Find m∠*A*. Explain how you found your answer.

b. Find m∠*ABE* and m∠*AEB*.

c. Find m∠*CBE* and m∠*DEB*.

d. Find m∠*C* and m∠*D*.

a. 22.5°; 16 triangles congruent to △*ABE* surround the center of the web, making up a total of 360°. 360° ÷ 16 = 22.5°

b. m∠*A* = 22.5° and △*ABE* is an isosceles triangle. So,
∠*ABE* ≅ ∠*AEB* and m∠*ABE* = m∠*AEB*
180° = m∠*ABE* + m∠*AEB* + 22.5°
180° = m∠*ABE* + m∠*ABE* + 22.5°
157.5° = 2 · m∠*ABE*
78.75° = m∠*ABE*
Thus, each angle measures 78.75°.

c. Because the angles form a linear pair, then m∠*ABE* + m∠*CBE* = 180°.
So 78.75° + m∠*CBE* = 180° and m∠*CBE* = 101.25°.
In an isosceles trapezoid, base angles are congruent, so m∠*DBE* = 101.25°.

d. In isosceles trapezoid *CBED*, $\overline{BE}\overline{PCD}$. Then corresponding angles are congruent and ∠*ABE* ≅ ∠*C* and ∠*AEB* ≅ ∠*D*. So m∠*C* = m∠*D* = 78.75°.

© Houghton Mifflin Harcourt Publishing Company

INTEGRATE MATHEMATICAL PRACTICES
Focus on Math Connections

MP.1 In the model of the spider web, $CD = 6$ cm and $BE = 3$ cm. Without referring to the circumference of either the outer or the inner circle, explain how you know that the radius of the inner circle is half the radius of the outer circle. By the converse of the Triangle Midsegment Theorem, *B* is the midpoint of $\overline{AC}$. So, $\overline{AB}$, a radius of the inner circle, has half the measure of $\overline{AC}$, a radius of the outer circle.

INTEGRATE MATHEMATICAL PRACTICES
Focus on Math Connections

MP.1 Explain how you know that $\overline{BE}$ is parallel to $\overline{CD}$. Sample answer: m∠*ABE* = 78.75° = m∠*C*, so ∠*ABE* ≅ ∠*C*. So, $\overline{BE} \parallel \overline{CD}$ because corresponding angles ∠*ABE* and ∠*C* are congruent.

EXTENSION ACTIVITY

The Lesson Performance Task deals with triangles and trapezoids in spider webs. Have students research other examples that illustrate quadrilaterals in the animal world, the plant world, or both. For each example students find, they should make a sketch, identify the quadrilateral, and provide additional information they feel is relevant, particularly as it relates to geometry.

Scoring Rubric
2 points: Student correctly solves the problem and explains his/her reasoning.
1 point: Student shows good understanding of the problem but does not fully solve or explain his/her reasoning.
0 points: Student does not demonstrate understanding of the problem.

ASSESSMENT AND INTERVENTION

Assign or customize module reviews.

Essential Question: How can you use properties of quadrilaterals to solve real-world problems?

KEY EXAMPLE (Lesson 9.1)

Given: *ABCD* and *EDGF* are parallelograms.

Prove: $\angle A \cong \angle G$

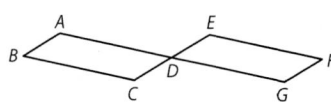

Statements	Reasons
ABCD and *EDGF* are parallelograms.	Given
$\angle A \cong \angle C$	Opposite angles of a parallelogram are congruent.
$\overline{BC} \parallel \overline{AG}$	Definition of a parallelogram
$\angle C \cong \angle CDG$	Alt. interior angles theorem
$\angle CDG \cong \angle ADE$	Vertical angles theorem
$\overline{CE} \parallel \overline{FG}$	Definition of a parallelogram
$\angle ADE \cong \angle G$	Corres. angles theorem
$\angle A \cong \angle G$	Transitive property of congruence

KEY EXAMPLE (Lesson 9.2)

Find the angle and side lengths when *t* is 19 to see if the figure is a parallelogram.

$2t + 13$

$(3t - 15)°$ $3t - 6$

$(7t + 5)°$

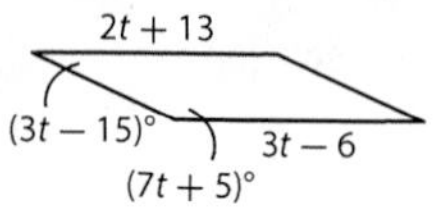

$2(19) + 13 = 51$

$3(19) - 6 = 51$

$3(19) - 15 = 42$

$7(19) + 5 = 138$

The top side is equivalent to the bottom. Also, the top side is parallel to the bottom because the same-side interior angles are supplementary. Therefore, this figure is a parallelogram because a pair of opposite sides are parallel and congruent.

Key Vocabulary

diagonal *(diagonal)*
isosceles trapezoid *(trapecio isósceles)*
kite *(el deltoide)*
midsegment of a trapezoid *(segmento medio de un trapecio)*
parallelogram *(paralelogramo)*
quadrilateral *(cuadrilátero)*
rectangle *(rectángulo)*
rhombus *(rombo)*
square *(cuadrado)*
trapezoid *(trapecio)*

© Houghton Mifflin Harcourt Publishing Company

Prove that $\triangle ABE \cong \triangle ADE$ given that $ABCD$ is a rhombus.

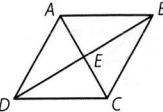

$\overline{AE} \cong \overline{AE}$ by the Reflexive Property.

Since $ABCD$ is a rhombus, $\overline{AB} \cong \overline{AD}$. Since a rhombus is also a parallelogram, $\overline{BE} \cong \overline{DE}$. Therefore, $\triangle ABE \cong \triangle ADE$ via the SSS Congruence Theorem.

Determine which quadrilaterals match the figure: parallelogram, rhombus, rectangle, or square.

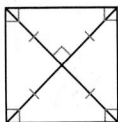

Since the figure has four 90° angles and a perpendicular bisector, then the figure is a square. Since the figure is a square, then it is also a rectangle, rhombus, and parallelogram.

Prove that $\triangle ADC \cong \triangle BCD$ given that $ABCD$ is an isosceles trapezoid.

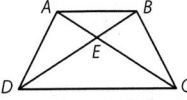

Statements	Reasons
$\overline{AD} \cong \overline{BC}$	Definition of an isosceles trapezoid
$\overline{AC} \cong \overline{BD}$	Diagonals of an isosceles trapezoid are congruent
$\overline{DC} \cong \overline{CD}$	Reflexive Property of Congruence
$\triangle ADC \cong \triangle BCD$	SSS Congruence Theorem

MODULE PERFORMANCE TASK

Mathematical Practices: MP.1, MP.2, MP.4, MP.6
G-MG.A.1

SUPPORTING STUDENT REASONING

Students should begin this problem by focusing on what information they will need. Here are some issues they might bring up.

- **Which figures are used for the facade:** Students can determine this from the given dimensions. The façade consists of one triangle with side lengths 18, 76, and 69, one rectangle with side lengths 179 and 44, another rectangle with side lengths 18 and 144, one trapezoid with bases 144 and 179 and height to be measured, and one quadrilateral with side lengths 179, 50, 182, and 39.

- **Which dimensions are needed to find the area of each figure:** Students can use construction tools to find the altitudes and other dimensions needed to calculate area. Students can also use the tools to break a figure into triangles so that the triangle formula will apply.

EXERCISES

EFGH is a parallelogram. Find the given side length. *(Lesson 9.1)*

1. EF $\qquad$ $y = 7, EF = 35$

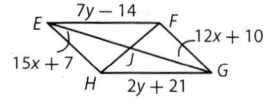

2. EG $\qquad$ $x = 1, EG = 44$

Determine if each quadrilateral is a parallelogram. Justify your answer. *(Lesson 9.2)*

3.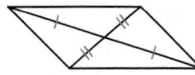

Yes, diagonals bisect each other

4.

Yes, opposite sides congruen

Find the measures of the numbered angles in each rhombus. *(Lesson 9.3)*

5.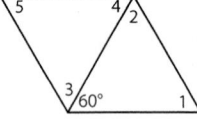

$\angle 1 = \angle 2 = \angle 3 = \angle 4 = \angle 5 = 60°$

6.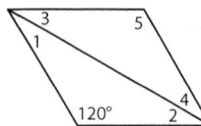

$\angle 1 = \angle 2 = \angle 3 = \angle 4 = 30°, \angle 5 = 120°$

Find the value of *x* that makes each parallelogram the given type. *(Lesson 9.4)*

7. Rectangle

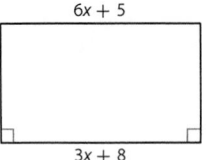

$x = 1$

8. Square

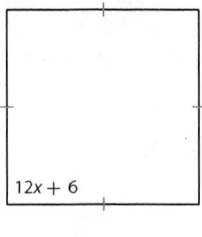

$x = 7$

9. A farm, in the shape of an isosceles trapezoid, is putting up fences on its diagonals. If one fence has sixteen 9-foot segments, how many 8-foot segments will the other fence have? *(Lesson 9.5)* 18

© Houghton Mifflin Harcourt Publishing Company

SCAFFOLDING SUPPORT

- Of the five figures that make up the façade, two are rectangles. Their areas can be found using the formula for the area of a rectangle.

- Finding the areas of the other three figures will require students to draw auxiliary lines to create figures whose areas *can* be found using formulas.

  1. For the triangle, students can draw an altitude from one vertex to the opposite side, measure its length, then find its actual length by writing and solving a proportion involving a different side.

  2. For each of the two remaining quadrilaterals, students can draw diagonals to divide the figure into triangles, then use the above method to find the areas of the triangles.

MODULE PERFORMANCE TASK

How Big Is That Face?

This strange image is the flattened east façade of the central library in Seattle, WA, designed by architect Rem Koolhaas. The faces of this unusual and striking building take the form of triangles, trapezoids, and other quadrilaterals.

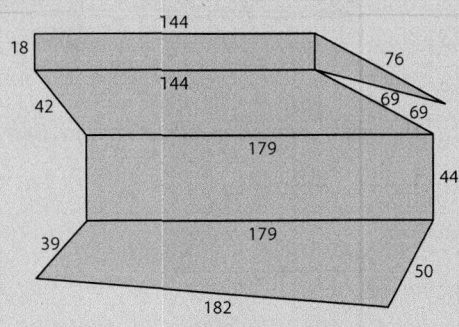

The diagram shows the dimensions of the faces labeled in feet. What is the total surface area of the east façade?

Use the space below to write down any questions you have and describe how you would find the area. Then use your own paper to complete the task. Be sure to write down all your data and assumptions. Then use numbers, words, or algebra to explain how you reached your conclusion.

SAMPLE SOLUTION

Use $A = bh$ to find the area of each rectangle.

area (top rectangle) = $144 \times 18 = 2592$ ft^2

area (bottom rectangle) = $179 \times 44 = 7876$ ft^2

Triangle: Draw an altitude to its 18-foot base and use proportions to find its length, about 62 feet. Use $A = \frac{1}{2}bh$ to find the area of the triangle.

area (triangle): $0.5(62)(18) = 558$ ft^2

Trapezoid: Draw an altitude to either of its bases and use proportions to find its length, about 30 feet. Use $A = \frac{1}{2}h(b_1 + b_2)$ to find the area of the trapezoid.

$0.5(30)(144 + 179) = 4845$ ft^2

Bottom quadrilateral: Divide the quadrilateral into two triangles; draw and measure the altitudes, about 28 feet and 40 feet.

$0.5(28)(182) + 0.5(40)(179) = 6128$ ft^2

Total area: $2592 + 7876 + 558 + 4845 + 6128 = 21,999$, or about 22,000 ft^2.

DISCUSSION OPPORTUNITIES

- Are there any other ways to find the area of the façade?
- How might the architect have shown each part of the façade in the blueprints?

Assessment Rubric

2 points: Student correctly solves the problem and explains his/her reasoning.

1 point: Student shows good understanding of the problem but does not fully solve or explain.

0 points: Student does not demonstrate understanding of the problem.

Ready to Go On?

ASSESS MASTERY

Use the assessment on this page to determine if students have mastered the concepts and standards covered in this module.

ASSESSMENT AND INTERVENTION

Access Ready to Go On? assessment online, and receive instant scoring, feedback, and customized intervention or enrichment.

ADDITIONAL RESOURCES

Response to Intervention Resources

- Reteach Worksheets

Differentiated Instruction Resources

- Reading Strategies **EL**
- Success for English Learners **EL**
- Challenge Worksheets

Assessment Resources

- Leveled Module Quizzes

491   Module 9

9.1–9.5 Properties of Quadrilaterals

- Online Homework
- Hints and Help
- Extra Practice

Find angle measure *x* on each given figure. *(Lessons 9.2, 9.4, 9.5)*

1.

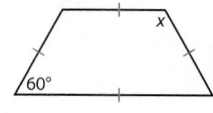

120°

2.

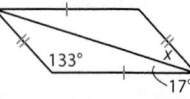

30°

3.

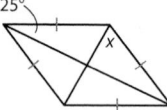

65°

4.

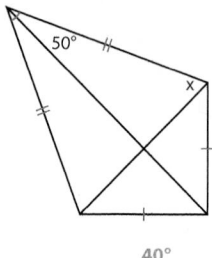

40°

5. Determine whether the trapezoids are congruent. *(Lesson 9.5)*

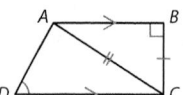 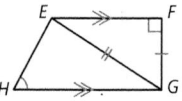

Yes, the trapezoids are congruent.
△*ABC* ≅ △*EFG* by the HL Triangle Congruence Theorem. Then $\overline{AB} \cong \overline{EF}$ and ∠*CAB* ≅ ∠*GEF* by CPCTC. Using the pairs of parallel lines, ∠*CAB* ≅ ∠*ACD* and ∠*GEF* ≅ ∠*EGH* by the Alternate Interior Angles Theorem. By transitivity, ∠*ACD* ≅ ∠*EGH*. Then △*ADC* ≅ △*EHG* by the AAS Triangle Congruence Theorem. The triangle congruences show that there exist sequences of rigid motions that map *A* to *E*, *B* to *F*, *C* to *G*, and *D* to *H*, so the trapezoids are congruent.

ESSENTIAL QUESTION

6. Name a time when it would be useful to know when a shape is a rectangle or a trapezoid.
It would be helpful to know that the shape is a rectangle if you needed to know whether its angles are right angles and whether any of the sides are congruent.
It would be helpful to know that the shape is a trapezoid if you needed to know whether at least one pair of sides are parallel, but you didn't need to know any information about its side lengths or angle measures.

COMMON CORE **Common Core Standards**

Lesson	Items	Content Standards	Mathematical Practices
9.5	1	**G-SRT.B.5**	**MP.7**
9.2	2	**G-CO.C.11, G-SRT.B.5**	**MP.7**
9.4	3	**G-CO.C.11, G-SRT.B.5**	**MP.7**
9.5	4	**G-SRT.B.5**	**MP.7**
9.5	5	**G-CO.C.11, G-SRT.B.5**	**MP.7**

Assessment Readiness

1. Consider each of the following quadrilaterals. Decide whether each is also necessarily a parallelogram. Select Yes or No for A–C.

    A. Trapezoid   ○ Yes   ● No
    B. Rhombus   ● Yes   ○ No
    C. Square   ● Yes   ○ No

2. Which conclusions are valid given that *ABCD* is a parallelogram? Choose True or False for each statement.

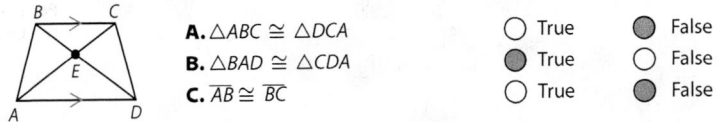

    A. $\angle A \cong \angle C$ ● True   ○ False
    B. $\angle A$ and $\angle B$ are complimentary.   ○ True   ● False
    C. $\overline{AD} \parallel \overline{BC}$ ● True   ○ False

3. *ABCD* is a trapezoid with $\overline{BC} \parallel \overline{AD}$ and $\angle BAD \cong \angle CDA$. Which of the following statements are valid conclusions? Choose True or False for each statement.

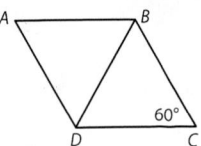

    A. $\triangle ABC \cong \triangle DCA$ ○ True   ● False
    B. $\triangle BAD \cong \triangle CDA$ ● True   ○ False
    C. $\overline{AB} \cong \overline{BC}$ ○ True   ● False

4. Given that *ABCD* is a rhombus, prove that $\triangle ABD \cong \triangle CDB$ and that both triangles are equilateral.

    The rhombus is a parallelogram, so consecutive angles are supplementary and $m\angle ABC = m\angle CDA = 180° - 60° = 120°$. The diagonals of a rhombus bisect the opposite angles, so $m\angle ABD = m\angle CBD = \frac{1}{2}(120°) = 60°$.
    Similarly, $m\angle ADB = m\angle CDB = \frac{1}{2}(120°) = 60°$. $\angle A$ is opposite $\angle C$ in the rhombus, so $m\angle A = m\angle C = 60°$. Both of the triangles are equiangular so both triangles are equilateral.

MIXED REVIEW
Assessment Readiness

ASSESSMENT AND INTERVENTION

Assign ready-made or customized practice tests to prepare students for high-stakes tests.

ADDITIONAL RESOURCES

Assessment Resources

• Leveled Module Quizzes: Modified, B

AVOID COMMON ERRORS

Item 3 Some students will attempt to apply the properties of a rectangle or parallelogram to the trapezoid. Encourage students to make a quick summary of the properties of the quadrilateral they are dealing with.

Common Core Standards

Lesson	Items	Content Standards	Mathematical Practices
9.2	1	G-CO.C.11	MP.8
9.1	2	G-CO.C.11	MP.5
9.5, 5.3	3*	G-SRT.B.5	MP.8
9.3, 7.2	4*	G-CO.C.11	MP.3

* Item integrates mixed review concepts from previous modules or a previous course.

Coordinate Proof Using Slope and Distance

ESSENTIAL QUESTION:

Answer: The use of coordinates can make it easier to represent the orientations, locations, and dimensions of objects in space, helping to solve any number of real-world problems.

PROFESSIONAL DEVELOPMENT VIDEO

Professional Development Video

Author Juli Dixon models successful teaching practices in an actual high-school classroom.

Professional Development
my.hrw.com

MODULE **10**

Coordinate Proof Using Slope and Distance

Essential Question: How can you use coordinate proofs using slope and distance to solve real-world problems?

© Houghton Mifflin Harcourt Publishing Company • Image Credits:
©Sportstock/iStockPhoto.com

REAL WORLD VIDEO
Check out how workers use surveying tools and coordinate geometry to measure real-world distances and areas for the construction of roads and bridges.

MODULE PERFORMANCE TASK PREVIEW

How Do You Calculate the Containment of a Fire?

In this module, you will use concepts of perimeter and area to determine the percentage containment of a wildfire. To successfully complete this task, you'll need to master the skills of finding area and perimeter on the coordinate plane. So put on your safety gear and let's get started!

Module 10　　493

DIGITAL TEACHER EDITION

Access a full suite of teaching resources when and where you need them:

- Access content online or offline
- Customize lessons to share with your class
- Communicate with your students in real-time
- View student grades and data instantly to target your instruction where it is needed most

PERSONAL MATH TRAINER
Assessment and Intervention

Assign automatically graded homework, quizzes, tests, and intervention activities. Prepare your students with updated, Common Core-aligned practice tests.

Are (YOU) Ready?

Complete these exercises to review the skills you will need for this module.

Area of Composite Figures

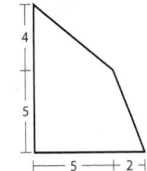 **Example 1**

Find the area of the given figure.

Think of the shape as a square and two triangles. The square has sides of length 5 and an area of 25. The top triangle has a height of 4 and a base of 5, so its area is 10. The triangle on the right has a base of 2 and a height of 5, so its area will be 5. Altogether, the area will be 40.

Find the area of the given figure to the nearest hundredth as needed. Use 3.14 for π.

1.

86

2.

132.52

Distance and Midpoint Formula

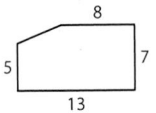 **Example 2** $(3, 3)$ $(5, 6)$

Find the distance and midpoint for each set of ordered pairs.

$\sqrt{(5-3)^2 + (6-3)^2} = d$ Set up points in the distance formula.

$d = \sqrt{13}$ Simplify.

$M = \left(\dfrac{3+5}{2}, \dfrac{3+6}{2}\right)$ Set up points in the midpoint formula.

$M = (4, 4.5)$ Simplify.

Find the distance and midpoint for each set of ordered pairs, rounded to the nearest hundredth as needed.

3. $(0, 9)$ $(2, 5)$
4.47; (1,7)

4. $(2, 7)$ $(4, 9)$
2.83; (3,8)

5. $(1, 8)$ $(3, 8)$
2; (2,8)

Writing Equations of Parallel, Perpendicular, Vertical, and Horizontal Lines

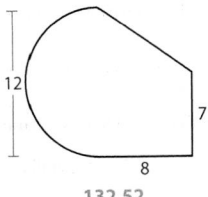 **Example 3**   Using the given xy-graph, find the equation of line C in slope-intercept form. The equation for this line is $y = 2$.

Using the given xy—graph, find the equation of the given line in slope-intercept form.

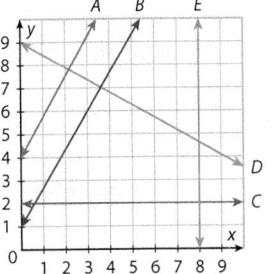

6. E $x = 8$

7. B $y = \frac{5}{3}x + 1$

8. A $y = \frac{5}{3}x + 4$

9. D $y = -\frac{5}{9}x + 9$

Are You Ready?

ASSESS READINESS

Use the assessment on this page to determine if students need strategic or intensive intervention for the module's prerequisite skills.

ASSESSMENT AND INTERVENTION

RtI Response to Intervention **TIER 1, TIER 2, TIER 3 SKILLS**

Personal Math Trainer will automatically create a standards-based, personalized intervention assignment for your students, targeting each student's individual needs!

ADDITIONAL RESOURCES

See the table below for a full list of intervention resources available for this module.

Response to Intervention Resources also includes:

- Tier 2 Skill Pre-Tests for each Module
- Tier 2 Skill Post-Tests for each skill

Response to Intervention			Differentiated Instruction
Tier 1 Lesson Intervention Worksheets	**Tier 2** Strategic Intervention Skills Intervention Worksheets	**Tier 3** Intensive Intervention Worksheets available online	
Reteach 10.1 Reteach 10.2 Reteach 10.3 Reteach 10.4 Reteach 10.5	5 Area of Composite Figures 9 Distance and Midpoint Formula 21 Rate of Change... 26 Using Slope... 28 Writing Equations...	Building Block Skills 9, 10, 11, 22, 23, 27, 35, 38, 42, 45, 69, 70, 73, 87, 98, 100, 112	Challenge worksheets Extend the Math Lesson Activities in TE

Slope and Parallel Lines

Common Core Math Standards

The student is expected to:

COMMON CORE G-GPE.B.5

Prove the slope criteria for parallel ... lines and use them to solve geometric problems .... Also G-GPE.B.4

Mathematical Practices

COMMON CORE MP.7 Using Structure

Language Objective

Explain to a partner how to use slopes to find missing vertices and classify quadrilaterals.

ENGAGE

Essential Question: How can you use slope to solve problems involving parallel lines?

Because parallel lines have equal slopes, you can determine whether two lines are parallel by finding their slopes. You can also find a line parallel to a given line by finding a line with the same slope as the given line.

PREVIEW: LESSON PERFORMANCE TASK

View the Engage section online. Discuss the photo, being sure students understand the reason that archeological digs are laid out on a coordinate grid. Then preview the Lesson Performance Task.

Name_____ Class_____ Date_____

10.1 Slope and Parallel Lines

Essential Question: How can you use slope to solve problems involving parallel lines?

Resource Locker

⊘ Explore   Proving the Slope Criteria for Parallel Lines

The following theorem states an important connection between slope and parallel lines.

> **Theorem: Slope Criteria for Parallel Lines**
> Two nonvertical lines are parallel if and only if they have the same slope.

Follow these steps to prove the slope criteria for parallel lines.

(A) First prove that if two lines are parallel, then they have the same slope.

Suppose lines m and n are parallel lines that are neither vertical nor horizontal.

Let A and B be two points on line m, as shown. You can draw a horizontal line through A and a vertical line through B to create the "slope triangle," $\triangle ABC$.

You can extend $\overline{AC}$ to intersect line n at point D and then extend it to point F so that $AC = DF$. Finally, you can draw a vertical line through F intersecting line n at point E.

Mark the figure to show parallel lines, right angles, and congruent segments.

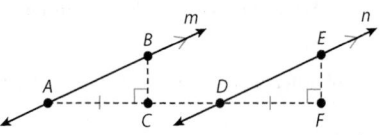

(B) When parallel lines are cut by a transversal, corresponding angles are congruent, so

$\angle BAC \cong \underline{\angle EDF}$.

$\triangle BAC \cong \underline{\triangle EDF}$ by the ___ASA___ Triangle Congruence Theorem.

By CPCTC, $\overline{BC} \cong \underline{EF}$ and $BC = \underline{EF}$.

The slope of line $m = \dfrac{BC}{AC}$, and the slope of line $n = \dfrac{EF}{DF}$.

The slopes of the lines are equal because the numerators of the fractions are equal and the denominators of the fractions are equal (Division Property of Equality).

Module 10   **495**   Lesson 1

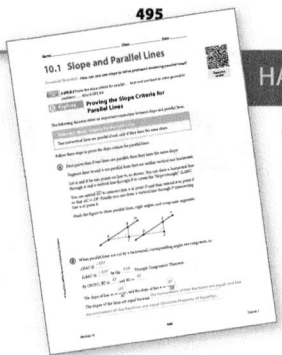

HARDCOVER PAGES 425–434

Turn to these pages to find this lesson in the hardcover student edition.

Ⓒ Now prove that if two lines have the same slope, then they are parallel.

Suppose lines m and n are two lines with the same nonzero slope. You can set up a figure in the same way as before.

Let A and B be two points on line m, as shown. You can draw a horizontal line through A and a vertical line through B to create the "slope triangle," $\triangle ABC$.

You can extend $\overline{AC}$ to intersect line n at point D and then extend it to point F so that $AC = DF$. Finally, you can draw a vertical line through F intersecting line n at point E.

Mark the figure to show right angles and congruent segments.

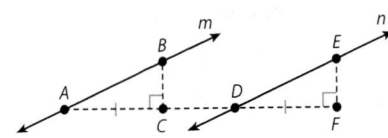

Ⓓ Since line m and line n have the same slope, $\dfrac{BC}{AC} = \dfrac{EF}{DF}$.

But $DF = AC$, so by substitution, $\dfrac{BC}{AC} = \dfrac{EF}{AC}$.

Multiplying both sides by AC shows that $BC = EF$.

Now you can conclude that $\triangle BAC \cong \triangle EDF$ by the SAS Triangle Congruence Theorem.

By CPCTC, $\angle BAC \cong \angle EDF$.

Line m and line n are two lines that are cut by a transversal so that a pair of corresponding angles are congruent.

You can conclude that line m is parallel to line n.

Reflect

1. Explain why the slope criteria can be applied to horizontal lines.
   If two parallel lines are horizontal, then both lines have a slope of 0. If two lines both have a slope of 0, then both lines are horizontal, so they are parallel.

2. Explain why the slope criteria cannot be applied to vertical lines even though all vertical lines are parallel.
   The slope of a vertical line is undefined. So, you can't say that two vertical lines have the same slope.

EXPLORE

Proving the Slope Criteria for Parallel Lines

INTEGRATE TECHNOLOGY

Students have the option of completing the Explore activity either in the book or online.

INTEGRATE MATHEMATICAL PRACTICES

Focus on Reasoning

MP.2 Discuss the phrase *if and only if*. Note that a statement containing *if and only if* is true only when both the conditional statement (if p, then q) and its converse (if q, then p) are true.

PROFESSIONAL DEVELOPMENT

Learning Progressions

In this lesson, students prove that two nonvertical lines have the same slope if and only if they are parallel. Students are expected to move from defining slope as the rate of change between two points on a line to using slope to write equations for parallel lines, and then to using parallelism and coordinates to prove simple geometric theorems algebraically. Rather than focusing on a few topics, students in high school focus on a few seed ideas about slope as a ratio and rate of change. These concepts lead to a variety of Mathematical Practices necessary for college readiness.

EXPLAIN 1

Using Slopes to Classify Quadrilaterals by Sides

AVOID COMMON ERRORS

Many times students substitute coordinates into the slope formula incorrectly. It may be helpful for students to write the slope formula on an index card with the numerator in one color (such as red) and the denominator in a second color (such as blue). Then, before substituting coordinates into the formula, have students circle or write the x–coordinates in blue and circle or write the y–coordinates in red. If students make errors finding differences between coordinates, review integer subtraction.

© Houghton Mifflin Harcourt Publishing Company · Image Credits: ©BuildPix/Construction Photography/Alamy

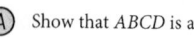 **Explain 1** **Using Slopes to Classify Quadrilaterals by Sides**

You can use the slope criteria for parallel lines to analyze figures in the coordinate plane.

Example 1 Show that each figure is the given type of quadrilateral.

(A) Show that $ABCD$ is a trapezoid.

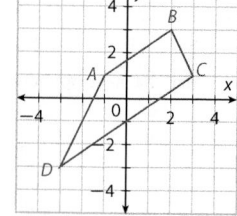

Step 1 Find the coordinates of the vertices of quadrilateral $ABCD$.

$A(-1, 1), B(2, 3), C(3, 1), D(-3, -3)$

Step 2 Use the slope formula to find the slope of $\overline{AB}$ and the slope of $\overline{DC}$.

slope of $\overline{AB} = \dfrac{y_2 - y_1}{x_2 - x_1} = \dfrac{3 - 1}{2 - (-1)} = \dfrac{2}{3}$

slope of $\overline{DC} = \dfrac{y_2 - y_1}{x_2 - x_1} = \dfrac{1 - (-3)}{3 - (-3)} = \dfrac{4}{6} = \dfrac{2}{3}$

Step 3 Compare the slopes.

Since the slopes are the same, $\overline{AB}$ is parallel to $\overline{DC}$.

Quadrilateral $ABCD$ is a trapezoid because it is a quadrilateral with at least one pair of parallel sides.

(B) Show that $PQRS$ is a parallelogram.

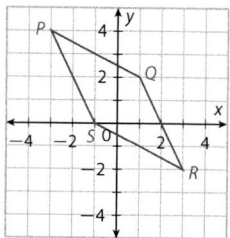

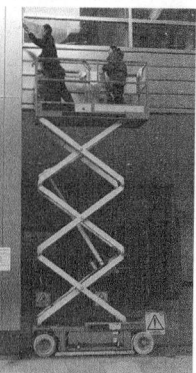

Step 1 Find the coordinates of the vertices of quadrilateral $PQRS$.

$P(-3, 4), Q(1, 2), R\left(\boxed{3}, \boxed{-2}\right), S\left(\boxed{-1}, \boxed{0}\right)$

Step 2 Use the slope formula to find the slope of each side.

$\overline{PQ}: \dfrac{y_2 - y_1}{x_2 - x_1} = \dfrac{2 - 4}{1 - (-3)} = \dfrac{-2}{4} = -\dfrac{1}{2}$

$\overline{QR}: \dfrac{y_2 - y_1}{x_2 - x_1} = \dfrac{\boxed{-2} - 2}{\boxed{3} - 1} = \dfrac{\boxed{-4}}{\boxed{2}} = \boxed{-2}$

$\overline{RS}: \dfrac{y_2 - y_1}{x_2 - x_1} = \dfrac{\boxed{0} - \boxed{-2}}{\boxed{-1} - \boxed{3}} = \dfrac{\boxed{2}}{\boxed{-4}} = -\dfrac{1}{2}$

$\overline{SP}: \dfrac{y_2 - y_1}{x_2 - x_1} = \dfrac{4 - \boxed{0}}{-3 - \boxed{-1}} = \dfrac{\boxed{4}}{\boxed{-2}} = \boxed{-2}$

COLLABORATIVE LEARNING

Peer-to-Peer Activity

Group students in pairs and give each pair a sheet of graph paper with a non-vertical, non-horizontal line drawn on it. Have students draw axes and find the equation of the line. Then have each student plot a point that is not on the line. They should then each find the equation of the line that is parallel to the original line and that passes through their partner's point. When they are done, have them compare the slopes of their lines to show that the two new lines are parallel to each other.

Step 3 Compare the slopes.

Since the slope of $\overline{PQ}$ is the same as the slope of $\underline{\quad RS \quad}$, $\overline{PQ}$ is parallel to $\underline{\quad RS \quad}$.

Since the slope of $\overline{QR}$ is the same as the slope of $\underline{\quad SP \quad}$, $\overline{QR}$ is parallel to $\underline{\quad SP \quad}$.

Quadrilateral $PQRS$ is a parallelogram because $\underline{\text{both pairs of opposite sides are parallel}}$.

Reflect

3. **What If?** Suppose you know that the lengths of $\overline{PQ}$ and $\overline{QR}$ in the figure in Example 1B are each $\sqrt{20}$. What type of parallelogram is quadrilateral $PQRS$? Explain.
   $PQRS$ is a rhombus; Since $\overline{PQ} \cong \overline{QR}$ and opposite sides of a parallelogram are congruent,

   you can conclude that all four sides are congruent. A quadrilateral with four congruent

   sides is a rhombus.

Your Turn

Show that each figure is the given type of quadrilateral.

4. Show that $JKLM$ is a trapezoid.

   $J(-2, 3), K(4, 1), L(-1, 0), M(-4, 1)$

   slope of $\overline{JK} = \dfrac{1-3}{4-(-2)} = \dfrac{-2}{6} = -\dfrac{1}{3}$

   slope of $\overline{LM} = \dfrac{1-0}{-4-(-1)} = \dfrac{1}{-3} = -\dfrac{1}{3}$

   slopes are the same, so $\overline{JK}$ is parallel to $\overline{LM}$

   Quadrilateral $JKLM$ is a trapezoid because it is a

   quadrilateral with at least one pair of parallel sides.

   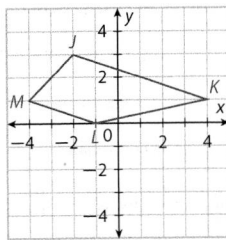

5. Show that $ABCD$ is a parallelogram.

   $A(-3, -2), B(1, 4), C(2, 2), D(-2, -4)$

   slope of $\overline{AB} = \dfrac{4-(-2)}{1-(-3)} = \dfrac{3}{2}$; slope of $\overline{BC} = \dfrac{2-4}{2-1} = -2$

   slope of $\overline{CD} = \dfrac{-4-2}{-2-2} = \dfrac{3}{2}$; slope of $\overline{DA} = \dfrac{-4-(-2)}{-2-(-3)} = -2$

   Quadrilateral $ABCD$ is a parallelogram because both pairs of

   opposite sides are parallel.

   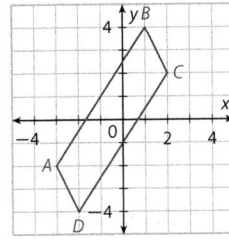

? What must you show to prove that a quadrilateral is a trapezoid? How do you prove it? At least one pair of opposite sides must be parallel; find the slopes of all sides and check whether there are two opposite sides with equal slopes.

DIFFERENTIATE INSTRUCTION

Critical Thinking

To explore translations of parallel lines in the coordinate plane, ask students to draw a pair of parallel lines in the coordinate plane and sketch a slope triangle on each. Challenge them to translate one of the lines in such a way that the image is not parallel to the original lines, and to write the algebraic rule for the translation. Students should eventually determine that there is no such translation. Discuss how translations of the slope triangles explain why the lines will always remain parallel after any translation.

EXPLAIN 2

Using Slopes to Find Missing Vertices

AVOID COMMON ERRORS

Students may put the missing vertex in the wrong place since there is more than one possibility of making a parallelogram. Remind them that the name of the figure gives the order of the vertices.

QUESTIONING STRATEGIES

? How are the slopes of the sides of a parallelogram related? Opposite sides of parallelograms are parallel, so their slopes are equal.

CONNECT VOCABULARY **EL**

Have students review the meanings of the terms *vertices*, *quadrilaterals* and *parallel lines* by describing the meanings using drawings, objects, or their arms and hands.

⊘ Explain 2 Using Slopes to Find Missing Vertices

Example 2 Find the coordinates of the missing vertex in each parallelogram.

(A) $\square ABCD$ with vertices $A(1, -2)$, $B(-2, 3)$, and $D(5, -1)$

Step 1 Graph the given points.

Step 2 Find the slope of $\overline{AB}$ by counting units from A to B.

The rise from -2 to 3 is 5. The run from 1 to -2 is -3.

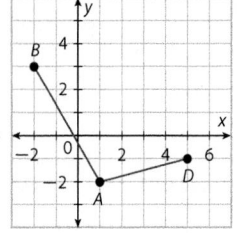

Step 3 Start at D and count the same number of units.

A rise of 5 from -1 is 4. A run of -3 from 5 is 2.

Label $(2, 4)$ as vertex C.

Step 4 Use the slope formula to verify that $\overline{BC} \parallel \overline{AD}$.

$$\text{slope of } \overline{BC} = \frac{4-3}{2-(-2)} = \frac{1}{4}$$

$$\text{slope of } \overline{AD} = \frac{-1-(-2)}{5-1} = \frac{1}{4}$$

The coordinates of vertex C are $(2, 4)$.

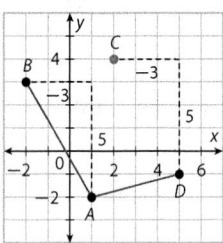

(B) $\square PQRS$ with vertices $P(-3, 0)$, $Q(-2, 4)$, and $R(2, 2)$

Step 1 Graph the given points.

Step 2 Find the slope of $\overline{PQ}$ by counting units from Q to P.

The rise from 4 to 0 is $\boxed{-4}$.   The run from -2 to -3 is $\boxed{-1}$.

Step 3 Start at R and count the same number of units.

A rise of $\boxed{-4}$ from 2 is $\boxed{-2}$.   A run of $\boxed{-1}$ from 2 is $\boxed{1}$.

Label $\left(\boxed{1}, \boxed{-2}\right)$ as vertex S.

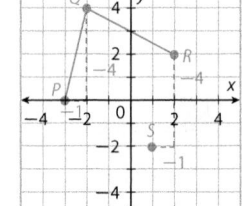

Step 4 Use the slope formula to verify that $\overline{QR} \parallel \overline{PS}$.

$$\text{slope of } \overline{QR} = \frac{\boxed{2}-\boxed{4}}{\boxed{2}-\boxed{-2}} = -\frac{\boxed{1}}{\boxed{2}}$$ $$\text{slope of } \overline{PS} = \frac{\boxed{-2}-\boxed{0}}{\boxed{1}-\boxed{-3}} = -\frac{\boxed{1}}{\boxed{2}}$$

The coordinates of vertex S are $\left(\boxed{1}, \boxed{-2}\right)$.

LANGUAGE SUPPORT **EL**

Communicate Math

Have students work in pairs. The first student explains the steps for using slopes to find missing vertices, while the second student asks clarifying questions and writes down the steps. Students switch roles and repeat the procedure, this time explaining how to use slopes to classify quadrilaterals.

Reflect

6. Discussion In Part A, you used the slope formula to verify that $\overline{BC} \parallel \overline{AD}$. Describe another way you can check that you found the correct coordinates of vertex C.

Possible answer: You could use the slope formula to verify that $\overline{AB} \parallel \overline{CD}$. The slope of

$\overline{AB}$ is $-\frac{5}{3}$ and the slope of $\overline{CD}$ is $-\frac{5}{3}$, so the sides are parallel.

Your Turn

Find the coordinates of the missing vertex in each parallelogram.

7. $\square JKLM$ with vertices $J(-3, -2)$, $K(0, 1)$, and $M(1, -3)$

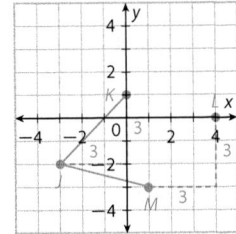

From J to K, rise = 3; run = 3; L is at $(4, 0)$.

Check: slope of $\overline{KL} = \frac{0-1}{4-0} = -\frac{1}{4}$;

slope of $\overline{JM} = \frac{-3-(-2)}{1-(-3)} = -\frac{1}{4}$

8. $\square DEFG$ with vertices $E(-2, 2)$, $F(4, 1)$, and $G(3, -2)$

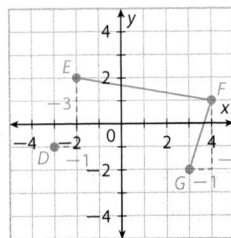

From F to G, rise = -3; run = -1; D is at $(-3, -1)$.

Check: slope of $\overline{EF} = \frac{1-2}{4-(-2)} = -\frac{1}{6}$;

slope of $\overline{DG} = \frac{-2-(-1)}{3-(-3)} = -\frac{1}{6}$

💬 Elaborate

9. Suppose you are given the coordinates of the vertices of a quadrilateral. Do you always need to find the slopes of all four sides of the quadrilateral in order to determine whether the quadrilateral is a trapezoid? Explain.

No; you only need to find one pair of opposite parallel sides to conclude that the

quadrilateral is a trapezoid. Once you have found that pair, you can stop finding slopes.

10. A student was asked to determine whether quadrilateral $ABCD$ with vertices $A(0, 0)$, $B(2, 0)$, $C(5, 7)$, and $D(0, 2)$ was a parallelogram. Without plotting points, the student looked at the coordinates of the vertices and quickly determined that quadrilateral $ABCD$ could not be a parallelogram. How do you think the student solved the problem?

Possible answer: $\overline{AD}$ is horizontal, so in order for $ABCD$ to be a parallelogram, the slope of

the opposite side, $\overline{BC}$, would have to be 0. However, the slope of $\overline{BC}$ is $\frac{7-0}{5-2} = \frac{7}{3} \neq 0$.

11. Essential Question Check-In What steps can you use to determine whether two given lines on a coordinate plane are parallel?

Possible answer: Find two points on each line and determine the slope of each line. If the

slopes are equal, then the lines are parallel.

QUESTIONING STRATEGIES

? When an equation is written in slope-intercept form, what is the easiest way to find its slope? Just read the equation: m, the coefficient of x, is the slope.

SUMMARIZE THE LESSON

? How can you use slope to solve geometry problems? Parallel lines have the same slope, so you can analyze lines containing sides of polygons to see whether the sides are parallel. You can also use slope to write the equation of a line that is parallel to a given line.

EVALUATE

ASSIGNMENT GUIDE

Concepts and Skills	Practice
Explore Proving the Slope Criteria for Parallel Lines	Exercise 1
Example 1 Using Slopes to Classify Quadrilaterals by Sides	Exercises 2–3
Example 2 Using Slopes to Find Missing Vertices	Exercises 4–5

⭐ Evaluate: Homework and Practice

• Online Homework
• Hints and Help
• Extra Practice

1. Jodie draws parallel lines p and q. She sets up a figure as shown to prove that the lines must have the same slope. First she proves that $\triangle JKL \cong \triangle RST$ by the ASA Triangle Congruence Theorem. What should she do to complete the proof?

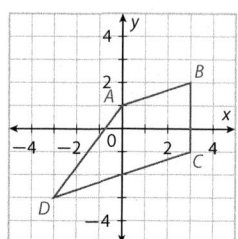

She should use the fact that corresponding parts of congruent triangles are congruent to show that $KL = ST$, which will allow her to conclude that $\frac{KL}{JL} = \frac{ST}{RT}$.

Show that each figure is the given type of quadrilateral.

2. Show that $ABCD$ is a trapezoid.

   $A(0, 1), B(3, 2), C(3, -1), D(-3, -3)$

   slope of $\overline{AB} = \frac{1}{3}$; slope of $\overline{CD} = \frac{1}{3}$

   Quadrilateral $ABCD$ is a trapezoid because it is a quadrilateral with at least one pair of parallel sides.

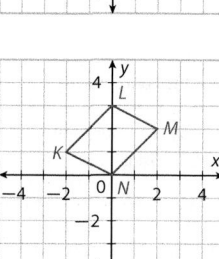

3. Show that $KLMN$ is a parallelogram.

   $K(-2, 1), L(0, 3), M(2, 2), N(0, 0)$

   slope of $\overline{KL} = 1$;

   slope of $\overline{LM} = -\frac{1}{2}$;

   slope of $\overline{MN} = 1$;

   slope of $\overline{NK} = -\frac{1}{2}$

   Quadrilateral $KLMN$ is a parallelogram because both pairs of opposite sides are parallel.

Exercise	Depth of Knowledge (D.O.K.)	COMMON CORE Mathematical Practices	
1	**2** Skills/Concepts	**MP.3** Logic	
2–7	**1** Recall of information	**MP.6** Precision	
8–16	**2** Skills/Concepts	**MP.2** Reasoning	
17–19	**2** Skills/Concepts	**MP.5** Using Tools	
20–24	**2** Skills/Concepts	**MP.1** Problem Solving	
25	**3** Strategic Thinking H.O.T.	**MP.3** Logic	

Find the coordinates of the missing vertex in each parallelogram. Use slopes to check your answer.

4. $\square ABCD$ with vertices $A(3, -3)$, $B(-1, -2)$, and $D(5, -1)$

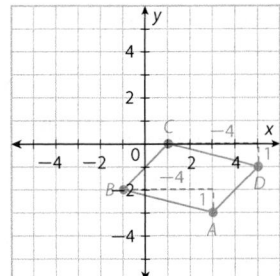

from A to B

rise: $-2 - (-3) = 1$

run: $-1 - 3 = -4$

C is at $(1, 0)$.

Check: slope of $\overline{BC} = \frac{0 - (-2)}{1 - (-1)} = \frac{2}{2} = 1$;

slope of $\overline{AD} = \frac{-1 - (-3)}{5 - 3} = \frac{2}{2} = 1$

5. $\square STUV$ with vertices $S(-3, -1)$, $T(-1, 1)$ and $V(0, 0)$

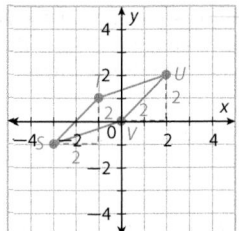

from S to T

rise: $1 - (-1) = 2$

run: $-1 - (-3) = 2$

U is at $(2, 2)$.

Check: slope of $\overline{TU} = \frac{2 - 1}{2 - (-1)} = \frac{1}{3}$;

slope of $\overline{SV} = \frac{0 - (-1)}{0 - (-3)} = \frac{1}{3}$

6. Show that quadrilateral $ABCD$ is *not* a trapezoid.

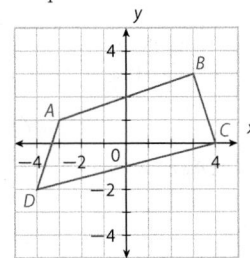

$A(-3, 1)$, $B(3, 3)$, $C(4, 0)$, $D(-4, -2)$

slope of $\overline{AB} = \frac{3 - 1}{3 - (-3)} = \frac{2}{6} = \frac{1}{3}$;

slope of $\overline{BC} = \frac{0 - 3}{4 - 3} = \frac{-3}{1} = -3$

slope of $\overline{CD} = \frac{-2 - 0}{-4 - 4} = \frac{-2}{-8} = \frac{1}{4}$;

slope of $\overline{DA} = \frac{1 - (-2)}{-3 - (-4)} = \frac{3}{1} = 3$

No two sides of $ABCD$ have the same slope, so no two sides of $ABCD$ are parallel. Therefore, $ABCD$ is not a trapezoid.

7. Show that quadrilateral $FGHJ$ is a trapezoid, but is not a parallelogram.

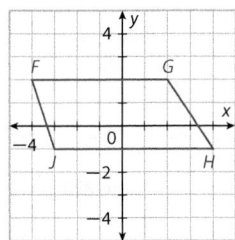

$F(-4, 2)$, $G(2, 2)$, $H(4, -1)$, $J(-3, -1)$

$\overline{FG}$ is horizontal, so the slope of $\overline{FG}$ is 0.

slope of $\overline{GH} = \frac{-1 - 2}{4 - 2} = \frac{-3}{2} = -\frac{3}{2}$

$\overline{HJ}$ is horizontal, so the slope of $\overline{HJ}$ is 0.

slope of $\overline{JF} = \frac{2 - (-1)}{-4 - (-3)} = \frac{3}{-1} = -3$

slope of $\overline{FG} = \overline{HJ}$, so $\overline{FG}$ is parallel to $\overline{HJ}$.

slope of $\overline{GH} \neq \overline{JF}$, so $\overline{GH}$ is not parallel to $\overline{JF}$.

The quadrilateral has only one pair of parallel sides, so it is a trapezoid but not a parallelogram.

© Houghton Mifflin Harcourt Publishing Company

KINESTHETIC EXPERIENCE

Give students a sheet of one-inch-ruled graph paper, two drinking straws, four toothpicks, and some glue. Have them glue the straws to the paper to model parallel lines and then glue the toothpicks to show congruent slope triangles. Then ask them to explain why the slope triangles show that the lines are parallel. Have them do this by using labels and symbols on the graph paper and/or by writing a short paragraph.

Exercise	Depth of Knowledge (D.O.K.)	COMMON CORE	Mathematical Practices
26	**3** Strategic Thinking H.O.T.		**MP.4** Modeling
27	**3** Strategic Thinking H.O.T.		**MP.3** Logic

Determine whether each statement is always, sometimes, or never true. Explain your reasoning.

8. If quadrilateral $ABCD$ is a trapezoid and the slope of $\overline{AB}$ is 3, then the slope of $\overline{CD}$ is 3.

   Sometimes; a trapezoid is a quadrilateral with at least one pair of parallel sides. $\overline{AB}$ and $\overline{CD}$ are opposite sides, but they are not necessarily the parallel sides, so their slopes may or may not be equal.

9. A parallelogram has vertices at $(0, 0)$, $(2, 0)$, $(0, 2)$, and at a point on the line $y = x$.

   Sometimes; when the fourth vertex is a point on the line $y = x$, the quadrilateral is not a parallelogram, except when the fourth vertex is $(2, 2)$. In this case, the quadrilateral is a parallelogram since one pair of sides are horizontal and one pair of sides are vertical.

10. If the slope of $\overline{PQ}$ is $\frac{1}{3}$ and the slope of $\overline{RS}$ is $-\frac{1}{3}$, the quadrilateral $PQRS$ is a parallelogram.

    Never; a parallelogram is a quadrilateral with two pairs of parallel sides, but if the slopes of the opposite sides $\overline{PQ}$ and $\overline{RS}$ are not equal, then these sides are not parallel.

11. If line m is parallel to line n and the slope of line m is greater than 1, then the slope of line n is greater than 1.

    Always; if line m is parallel to line n, then the lines have the same slope. Therefore, if the slope of line m is greater than 1, the slope of line n is also greater than 1.

12. If trapezoid $JKLM$ has vertices $J(-4, 1)$, $K(-3, 3)$, and $L(-1, 4)$, then the coordinates of vertex M are $(2, 4)$.

    Sometimes; a quadrilateral with vertices with the given coordinates is a trapezoid because the slope of $\overline{KL} = \frac{4 - 3}{-1 - (-3)} = \frac{1}{2}$ and the slope of $\overline{MJ} = \frac{1 - 4}{-4 - 2} = \frac{-3}{-6} = \frac{1}{2}$, so a pair of sides are parallel. However, there are other possible coordinates for vertex M that also result in a pair of parallel opposite sides, such as $(-2, 2)$, $(0, 3)$, or $(4, 5)$.

© Houghton Mifflin Harcourt Publishing Company

Explain whether the quadrilateral determined by the intersections of the given lines is a trapezoid, a parallelogram, both, or neither.

13.

Line	Equation
Line ℓ	$y = 2x + 3$
Line m	$2y = -x + 6$
Line n	$y = x - 3$
Line p	$x + y = -3$

Neither; Line ℓ: $m = 2$

Line m: $y = -\frac{1}{2}x + 3$; $m = -\frac{1}{2}$

Line n: $m = 1$

Line p: $y = -x - 3$; $m = -1$

14.

Line	Equation
Line ℓ	$y = x + 3$
Line m	$y - x = 0$
Line n	$x + 2y = 6$
Line p	$y = -0.5x - 3$

Both; Line ℓ: $m = 1$

Line m: $m = 1$

Line n: $y = -0.5x + 3$; $m = -0.5$

Line p: $m = -0.5$

15.

Line	Equation
Line ℓ	$2y = x + 4$
Line m	$y + 5 = 2x$
Line n	$-2x + y = 2$
Line p	$x + 2y = -6$

Trapezoid; Line ℓ: $y = \frac{1}{2}x + 2$; $m = \frac{1}{2}$

Line m: $m = 2$

Line n: $m = 2$

Line p: $y = -\frac{1}{2}x - 3$; $m = -\frac{1}{2}$

16.

Line	Equation
Line ℓ	$3x + y = 4$
Line m	$y + 3 = 0$
Line n	$y = 3x + 5$
Line p	$y = 3$

Trapezoid; Line ℓ: $y = -3x + 4$; $m = -3$

Line m: $m = 0$

Line n: $m = 3$

Line p: $m = 0$

Algebra Find the value of each variable in the parallelogram.

17.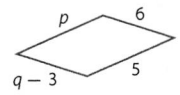

$p = 5$
$q - 3 = 6$
$q = 9$

18.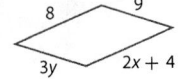

$2x + 4 = 8$
$x = 2$
$3y = 9$
$y = 3$

19.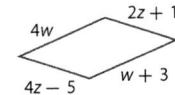

$4w = w + 3$
$w = 1$
$4z - 5 = 2z + 1$
$z = 3$

Some students may find an incorrect slope because their equations are not in the correct form. Remind students that they must write the equation of a line in slope-intercept form before identifying the coefficient of x as the slope.

20. Use the slope-intercept form of a linear equation to prove that if two lines are parallel, then they have the same slope. (*Hint:* Use an indirect proof. Assume the lines have different slopes, m_1 and m_2. Write the equations of the lines and show that there must be a point of intersection.)

Assume the lines have different slopes, m_1 and m_2. Then the equations of the lines are $y = m_1x + b_1$ and $y = m_2x + b_2$. By substitution, $m_1x + b_1 = m_2x + b_2$, and solving for x shows that $x = \frac{b_2 - b_1}{m_1 - m_2}$, so the lines intersect at this x-value, but this is a contradiction since the lines are parallel. So, $m_1 = m_2$.

21. Critique Reasoning Mayumi was asked to determine whether quadrilateral $RSTU$ is a trapezoid given the vertices $R(-2, 3)$, $S(1, 4)$, $T(1, -4)$, and $U(-2, 1)$. She noticed that the slopes of $\overline{RU}$ and $\overline{ST}$ are undefined, so she concluded that the quadrilateral could not be a trapezoid. Do you agree? Explain.

No; since the slopes of $\overline{RU}$ and $\overline{ST}$ are undefined, these two segments are vertical. Since all vertical lines are parallel, this means a pair of sides of the quadrilateral are parallel, and therefore the quadrilateral is a trapezoid.

22. Kaitlyn is planning the diagonal spaces for the parking lot at a mall. Each space is a parallelogram. Kaitlyn has already planned the spaces shown in the figure and wants to continue the pattern to draw the next space to the right. What are the endpoints of the next line segment she should draw? Explain your reasoning.

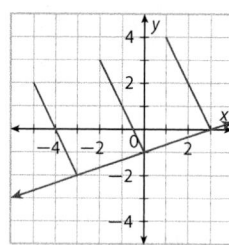

The line passes through points $(0, -1)$ to $(3, 0)$ and has slope, $m = \frac{0 - (-1)}{3 - 0} = \frac{1}{3}$.

Start at each endpoint of the segment for the rightmost parking space and use the slope to count units. Starting at $(1, 4)$, a rise of 1 and a run of 3 results in the point $(4, 5)$. Starting at $(3, 0)$, a rise of 1 and a run of 3 results in the point $(6, 1)$. Kaitlyn should use the points $(4, 5)$ and $(6, 1)$ as endpoints of the next line segment.

23. Multi-Step Two carpenters are using a coordinate plane to design a tabletop in the shape of a trapezoid. They have already drawn the two sides of the tabletop shown in the figure. They want side $\overline{AD}$ to lie on the line $x = -2$. What is the equation of the line on which side $\overline{CD}$ will lie? Explain your reasoning.

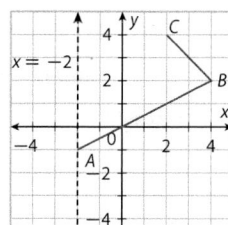 

Since side $\overline{AD}$ will not be parallel to side $\overline{BC}$, the remaining two sides must be parallel in order for $ABCD$ to be a trapezoid. The slope of $\overline{AB} = \frac{2-(-1)}{4-(-2)} = \frac{3}{6} = \frac{1}{2}$.

Therefore, the slope of $\overline{CD}$ must also be $\frac{1}{2}$. The line on which $\overline{CD}$ lies has slope $\frac{1}{2}$ and passes through the point $C(2, 4)$. The slope-intercept form of the equation is $y = mx + b$ or $y = \frac{1}{2}x + b$. Substituting the coordinates of C gives $4 = \frac{1}{2}(2) + b$, so $4 = 1 + b$ and $b = 3$. The equation of the line is $y = \frac{1}{2}x + 3$.

24. Quadrilateral $PQRS$ has vertices $P(-3, 2)$, $Q(-1, 4)$, and $R(5, 0)$. For each of the given coordinates of vertex S, determine whether the quadrilateral is a parallelogram, a trapezoid that is not a parallelogram, or neither. Select the correct answer for each lettered part.

a. $S(0, 0)$ ○ Parallelogram   ● Trapezoid but not parallelogram   ○ Neither

b. $S(3, -2)$ ● Parallelogram   ○ Trapezoid but not parallelogram   ○ Neither

c. $S(2, -1)$ ○ Parallelogram   ○ Trapezoid but not parallelogram   ● Neither

d. $S(6, -4)$ ○ Parallelogram   ● Trapezoid but not parallelogram   ○ Neither

e. $S(5, -3)$ ○ Parallelogram   ○ Trapezoid but not parallelogram   ● Neither

a. the slope of $\overline{PQ} = 1$, the slope of $\overline{QR} = -\frac{2}{3}$, the slope of $\overline{RS} = \frac{0-0}{0-5} = 0$, and the slope of $\overline{SP} = -\frac{2}{3}$.

b. the slope of $\overline{PQ} = 1$, the slope of $\overline{QR} = -\frac{2}{3}$, the slope of $\overline{RS} = 1$, and the slope of $\overline{SP} = -\frac{2}{3}$.

c. the slope of $\overline{PQ} = 1$, the slope of $\overline{QR} = -\frac{2}{3}$, the slope of $\overline{RS} = \frac{1}{3}$, and the slope of $\overline{SP} = -\frac{3}{5}$.

d. the slope of $\overline{PQ} = 1$, the slope of $\overline{QR} = -\frac{2}{3}$, the slope of $\overline{RS} = -4$, and the slope of $\overline{SP} = -\frac{2}{3}$.

e. the slope of $\overline{PQ} = 1$, the slope of $\overline{QR} = -\frac{2}{3}$, the slope of $\overline{RS}$ is undefined, and the slope of $\overline{SP} = -\frac{5}{8}$.

Have students explain how to show that a quadrilateral is a parallelogram.

25. Explain the Error Tariq was given the points $P(0, 3)$, $Q(3, -3)$, $R(0, -4)$, and $S(-2, -1)$ and was asked to decide whether quadrilateral $PQRS$ is a trapezoid. Explain his error.

slope of $\overline{SP} = \dfrac{3 - (-1)}{0 - (-2)} = \dfrac{4}{2} = 2$

slope of $\overline{QP} = \dfrac{3 - (-3)}{3 - 0} = \dfrac{6}{3} = 2$

The slope of $\overline{QP}$ should be $\dfrac{3 - (-3)}{0 - 3} = -2$. The slope of $\overline{QR} = \dfrac{1}{3}$ and the slope of $\overline{RS} = -\dfrac{3}{2}$. No sides of $PQRS$ are parallel, so $PQRS$ is not a trapezoid.

Since at least two sides are parallel, the quadrilateral is a trapezoid.

26. Analyze Relationships Four members of a marching band are arranged to form the vertices of a parallelogram. The coordinates of three band members are $M(-3, 1)$, $G(1, 3)$, and $Q(2, -1)$. Find all possible coordinates for the fourth band member.

Find the slope of $\overline{MG}$ by counting units from M to G.

The rise is 2. The run is 4.

Start at Q and count the same number of units.

A rise of 2 from -1 is 1. A run of 4 from 2 is 6. In this case, the fourth band member is at $(6, 1)$. Find the slope of $\overline{GQ}$ by counting units from G to Q. The rise from 3 to -1 is -4. The run from 1 to 2 is 1. Start at M and count the same number of units. A rise of -4 from 1 is -3. A run of 1 from -3 is -2. In this case, the fourth band member is at $(-2, -3)$. Find the slope of $\overline{QM}$ by counting units from Q to M. The rise from -1 to 1 is 2. The run from 2 to -3 is -5. Start at G and count the same number of units. A rise of 2 from 3 is 5. A run of -5 from 1 is -4. In this case, the fourth band member is at $(-4, 5)$. The possible coordinates for the fourth band member are $(6, 1)$, $(-2, -3)$, and $(-4, 5)$.

27. Make a Conjecture Plot any four points on the coordinate plane and connect them to form a quadrilateral. Find the midpoint of each side of the quadrilateral and connect consecutive midpoints to form a new quadrilateral. What type of quadrilateral is formed? Repeat the process by starting with a different set of four points. Do you get the same result? State a conjecture about your findings.

Possible answer: Plot the points $A(-4, 2)$, $B(2, 4)$, $C(4, 0)$, $D(0, -2)$.

midpoint of $\overline{AB} = M(-1, 3)$; midpoint of $\overline{BC} = N(3, 2)$; midpoint of $\overline{CD} = P(2, -1)$; midpoint of $\overline{DA} = Q(-2, 0)$; slope of $\overline{MN} = -\dfrac{1}{4}$; slope of $\overline{NP} = 3$; slope of $\overline{PQ} = -\dfrac{1}{4}$; slope of $\overline{QM} = 3$.

Since opposite sides are parallel, $MNPQ$ is a parallelogram. This is true when starting with any set of four points. Conjecture: The quadrilateral formed by connecting the midpoints of consecutive sides of a quadrilateral is a parallelogram.

© Houghton Mifflin Harcourt Publishing Company · Image Credits: ©Kelly-Mooney Photography/Corbis

Lesson Performance Task

Suppose archeologists uncover an ancient city with the foundations of 16 houses. The locations of the houses are as follows:

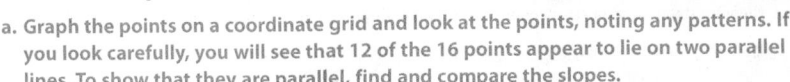

$(2, 2)$ $(-5, 6)$ $(3, -6)$ $(-1, 0)$ $(5, -8)$ $(3, 5)$ $(-3, 3)$ $(0, 5)$

$(-8, 1)$ $(4, -1)$ $(1, -3)$ $(-4, -3)$ $(8, -7)$ $(-5, -4)$ $(-2, 8)$ $(6, -4)$

a. How could you show that the streets are parallel? Explain.

b. Are the streets parallel?

a. Graph the points on a coordinate grid and look at the points, noting any patterns. If you look carefully, you will see that 12 of the 16 points appear to lie on two parallel lines. To show that they are parallel, find and compare the slopes.

b. Yes; the lines each have a slope of $-\frac{3}{2}$.

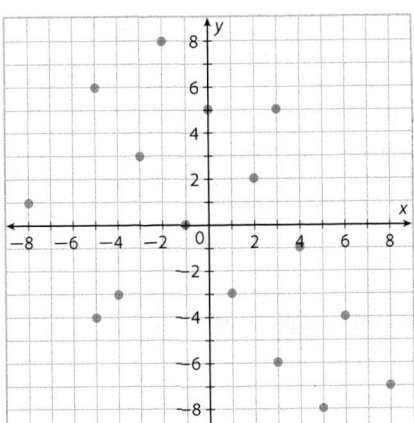

© Houghton Mifflin Harcourt Publishing Company • Image Credits: ©Dmitry Vasilyev/AP Images

---

INTEGRATE MATHEMATICAL PRACTICES
Focus on Patterns

MP.8 The points $(-5, 6)$, $(-3, 3)$, $(-1, 0)$, $(1, -3)$, and $(3, -6)$ all mark the locations of houses in the excavated city described in the Lesson Performance Task. Without calculating slopes or the equation of the line, how can you tell that all the points lie on the same line? Starting at x–coordinate -5 for the point $(-5, 6)$, the x–coordinate of each succeeding point, as listed, decreases by 2. Starting at y–coordinate 6 for the point $(-5, 6)$, the y-coordinate of each succeeding point, as listed, decreases by 3.

INTEGRATE MATHEMATICAL PRACTICES
Focus on Critical Thinking

MP.3 Find the coordinates of all points that form a parallelogram with the points $A(3, 2)$, $B(7, 3)$, and $C(5, 6)$. $(1, 5)$, $(9, 7)$, and $(5, -1)$

EXTENSION ACTIVITY

Have students draw 5×5 grids and number the squares from $(0, 0)$ to $(4, 4)$. Next, have them decide secretly on something that has been buried for centuries (such as a house) and sketch its outlines on the grid. Have them then make a list of things archeologists might find that would help to identify what has been buried, and note the locations of each. Students exchange lists with a partner, write the listed items in the correct places on their own coordinate grids, and use the clues to try to identify what is buried.

Scoring Rubric
2 points: Student correctly solves the problem and explains his/her reasoning.
1 point: Student shows good understanding of the problem but does not fully solve or explain.
0 points: Student does not demonstrate understanding of the problem.

Slope and Parallel Lines   **508**

Slope and Perpendicular Lines

Common Core Math Standards

The student is expected to:

 G-GPE.B.5

Prove the slope criteria for ... perpendicular lines and use them to solve geometric problems .... Also G-GPE.B.4

Mathematical Practices

 MP.7 Using Structure

Language Objective

Work in small groups to draft an explanation for students beginning to study geometry of how you can use slope to solve problems involving perpendicular lines.

ENGAGE

Essential Question: How can you use slope to solve problems involving perpendicular lines?

Slopes of perpendicular lines have a product of −1. Multiply the slopes of two lines; if the product is −1, the lines form a right angle. You can also use this information to write equations of perpendicular lines. If a given line has a slope of m, you know that the slope of a line perpendicular to it is $-\frac{1}{m}$.

PREVIEW: LESSON PERFORMANCE TASK

View the Engage section online. Discuss the photo. Point out that the Global Positioning System began operating in 1995; before GPS, determining one's position in remote places on Earth's surface was more difficult than it is now. Then preview the Lesson Performance Task.

10.2 Slope and Perpendicular Lines

Essential Question: How can you use slope to solve problems involving perpendicular lines?

Resource Locker

⊘ Explore   Proving the Slope Criteria for Perpendicular Lines

The following theorem states an important connection between slope and perpendicular lines.

> **Theorem: Slope Criteria for Perpendicular Lines**
>
> Two nonvertical lines are perpendicular if and only if the product of their slopes is −1.

Follow these steps to prove the slope criteria for perpendicular lines.

(A) First prove that if two lines are perpendicular, then the product of their slopes is −1.

Suppose lines m and n are perpendicular lines that intersect at point P, and that neither line is vertical. Assume the slope of line m is positive. (You can write a similar proof if the slope of line m is negative.)

Copy the figure on a separate piece of paper. Mark your figure to show the perpendicular lines.

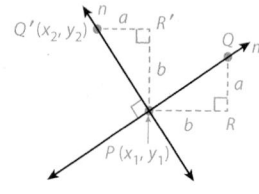

(B) Let Q be a point on line m, and draw a right triangle, $\triangle PQR$, as shown. Which line is this a "slope triangle" for?

_____line m_____

Mark the figure to show the perpendicular segments.

(C) Assume that a and b are both positive. The slope of line m is $\dfrac{a}{b}$.

(D) Rotate $\triangle PQR$ 90° around point P. The image is $\triangle PQ'R'$, as shown.

Which line is $\triangle PQ'R'$ a slope triangle for? _____line n_____

Let the coordinates of P be (x_1, y_1) and let the coordinates of Q' be (x_2, y_2).

Then the slope of line n is $\dfrac{y_2 - y_1}{x_2 - x_1} = \dfrac{b}{-a} = -\dfrac{b}{a}$.

(E) Now find the product of the slopes.

(slope of line m) · (slope of line n) = $\dfrac{a}{b} \cdot \left(-\dfrac{b}{a}\right) = \boxed{-1}$

Module 10   **509**   Lesson 2

HARDCOVER PAGES 435–444

Turn to these pages to find this lesson in the hardcover student edition.

(F) Now prove that if the product of the slopes of two lines is -1, then the lines are perpendicular.

Let the slope of line m be $\frac{a}{b}$, where a and b are both positive. Let line n have slope z.

It is given that $z \cdot \frac{a}{b} = -1$. Solving for z gives the slope of line n.

$$z = -\boxed{\dfrac{b}{a}}$$

(G) Assume the lines intersect at P. Since the slope of m is positive and the slope of n is negative, you can set up slope triangles.

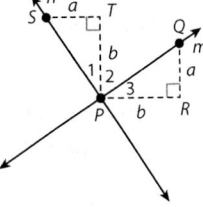

Based on the figure, $\overline{ST} \cong \underline{\overline{QR}}$ and $\overline{PT} \cong \underline{\overline{PR}}$.

Also, $\angle T \cong \underline{\angle R}$ because all right angles are congruent.

Therefore, $\underline{\triangle STP} \cong \underline{\triangle QRP}$ by the SAS Triangle Congruence Theorem.

(H) By CPCTC, $\angle 1 \cong \underline{\angle 3}$.

Since $\overline{TP}$ is vertical and $\overline{PR}$ is horizontal, $\angle TPR$ is a right angle.

So $\angle 2$ and $\underline{\angle 3}$ are complementary angles. You can conclude by substitution that

$\angle 2$ and $\underline{\angle 1}$ are complementary angles.

By the Angle Addition Postulate, $m\angle 1 + m\angle 2 = m\angle SPQ$, so $\angle SPQ$ must

measure $\underline{90°}$, and therefore line m is perpendicular to line n.

Reflect

1. In Step D, when you calculate the slope of line n, why is $x_2 - x_1$ negative?
   Point Q' lies to the left of point P, so $x_2 < x_1$ and $x_2 - x_1 < 0$.

2. The second half of the proof begins in Step F by assuming that line m has a positive slope. If the product of the slopes of two lines is -1, how do you know that one of the lines must have a positive slope?
   If both slopes were negative, the product of the slopes would be positive, so one of the slopes must be negative and one must be positive.

3. Does this theorem apply when one of the lines is horizontal? Explain.
   No; in this case, the other line is vertical and has undefined slope, so you cannot find the product of the slopes.

© Houghton Mifflin Harcourt Publishing Company

Proving the Slope Criteria for Perpendicular Lines

INTEGRATE TECHNOLOGY

Students have the option of doing the Explore activity either in the book or online.

INTEGRATE MATHEMATICAL PRACTICES

Focus on Reasoning

MP.2 Ask students to consider this statement:

If two lines are perpendicular, one must have a positive slope and the other a negative slope.

Have them decide if it is sometimes true, never true, or always true. Have students explain the reasoning behind their decisions. It is always true when neither line is vertical; the product of perpendicular slopes is negative, and for the product of two numbers to be negative, the numbers must have opposite signs.

PROFESSIONAL DEVELOPMENT

 Learning Progressions

In this lesson, students prove that two non-vertical lines are perpendicular if and only if the product of their slopes is -1. Students are expected to move from using slope to write equations for parallel lines to using slope to write equations for perpendicular lines. They then use perpendicular lines and coordinates to prove simple geometric theorems algebraically.

EXPLAIN 1

Using Slopes to Classify Figures by Right Angles

AVOID COMMON ERRORS

When looking for slopes that are opposite reciprocals, remind students to make sure that the slopes are in simplest form. Otherwise, they may incorrectly identify perpendicular lines as non-perpendicular.

© Houghton Mifflin Harcourt Publishing Company

🎯 Explain 1 **Using Slopes to Classify Figures by Right Angles**

You can use the slope criteria for perpendicular lines to analyze figures in the coordinate plane.

Example 1 Show that each figure is the given type of quadrilateral.

(A) Show that $ABCD$ is a rectangle.

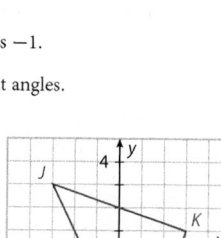

Step 1 Find the coordinates of the vertices of quadrilateral $ABCD$.

$A(-3, -1)$, $B(3, 2)$, $C(4, 0)$, $D(-2, -3)$

Step 2 Use the slope formula to find the slope of each side.

$\overline{AB}: \dfrac{2-(-1)}{3-(-3)} = \dfrac{1}{2}$ $\overline{BC}: \dfrac{0-2}{4-3} = -2$

$\overline{CD}: \dfrac{-3-0}{-2-4} = \dfrac{1}{2}$ $\overline{DA}: \dfrac{-1-(-3)}{-3-(-2)} = -2$

Step 3 Compare the slopes.

$\left(\text{slope of } \overline{AB}\right) \cdot \left(\text{slope of } \overline{BC}\right) = \dfrac{1}{2} \cdot (-2) = -1$

$\left(\text{slope of } \overline{BC}\right) \cdot \left(\text{slope of } \overline{CD}\right) = -2 \cdot \dfrac{1}{2} = -1$

$\left(\text{slope of } \overline{CD}\right) \cdot \left(\text{slope of } \overline{DA}\right) = \dfrac{1}{2} \cdot (-2) = -1$

$\left(\text{slope of } \overline{DA}\right) \cdot \left(\text{slope of } \overline{AB}\right) = -2 \cdot \dfrac{1}{2} = -1$

Consecutive sides are perpendicular since the product of the slopes is -1.

Quadrilateral $ABCD$ is a rectangle because it is a quadrilateral with four right angles.

(B) Show that $JKLM$ is a trapezoid with two right angles.

Step 1 Find the coordinates of the vertices of quadrilateral $JKLM$.

$J(-3, 3)$, $K(3, 1)$, $L\left(\boxed{2}, \boxed{-2}\right)$, $M\left(\boxed{-1}, \boxed{-1}\right)$

Step 2 Use the slope formula to find the slope of each side.

$\overline{JK}: \dfrac{1-3}{3-(-3)} = \dfrac{-2}{6} = -\dfrac{1}{3}$

$\overline{KL}: \dfrac{\boxed{-2} - \boxed{1}}{\boxed{2} - \boxed{-3}} = \dfrac{\boxed{-3}}{\boxed{-1}} = \boxed{3}$

$\overline{LM}: \dfrac{\boxed{-1} - \boxed{-2}}{\boxed{-1} - \boxed{2}} = \dfrac{\boxed{1}}{\boxed{-3}} = -\dfrac{\boxed{1}}{\boxed{3}}$

$\overline{MJ}: \dfrac{3 - \boxed{-1}}{-3 - \boxed{-1}} = \dfrac{\boxed{4}}{\boxed{-2}} = \boxed{-2}$

COLLABORATIVE LEARNING

Whole Class Activity

Instruct students to write equations of two lines in which the product of the slopes is -1. Have them graph each equation on a separate sheet of graph paper. Collect and shuffle the papers. Give each student two pages at random. Have students circulate through the room trying to match the graph of each line with the graph showing a line that is perpendicular to it. When students find a pair of perpendicular lines, have them tape the pair together on a wall.

Step 3 Compare the slopes.

Since the slope of $\overline{JK}$ is the same as the slope of $\underline{\quad LM \quad}$, $\overline{JK}$ is parallel to $\underline{\quad LM \quad}$.

Since the $\left(\text{slope of } \overline{JK}\right) \cdot \left(\text{slope of } \overline{KL}\right) = -\dfrac{1}{3} \cdot \boxed{3} = \boxed{-1}$ and

$\left(\text{slope of } \overline{KL}\right).\left(\text{slope of } \overline{LM}\right) = \boxed{3} \cdot \left(-\dfrac{\boxed{1}}{\boxed{3}}\right) = \boxed{-1}, \overline{JK} \perp \underline{\quad KL \quad}$

and $\overline{KL} \perp \underline{\quad LM \quad}$.

Quadrilateral *JKLM* is a trapezoid with two right angles because $\underline{\text{a pair of opposite sides are}}$ parallel and two pairs of consecutive sides are perpendicular.

Reflect

4. In Part B, is quadrilateral *JKLM* a parallelogram? Why or why not?
   No; a parallelogram has two pairs of opposite sides that are parallel. Quadrilateral *JKLM* has only one pair of opposite sides that are parallel.

Your Turn

Show that each figure is the given type of quadrilateral.

5. Show that *DEFG* is a rectangle.

   $D(-2, 3), E(4, -1), F(2, -4), G(-4, 0)$

   slope of $\overline{DE} = \dfrac{-1 - 3}{4 - (-2)} = -\dfrac{2}{3};$

   slope of $\overline{EF} = \dfrac{-4 - (-1)}{2 - 4} = \dfrac{3}{2};$

   slope of $\overline{FG} = \dfrac{0 - (-4)}{-4 - 2} = -\dfrac{2}{3};$

   slope of $\overline{GD} = \dfrac{3 - 0}{(-2) - (-4)} = \dfrac{3}{2}$

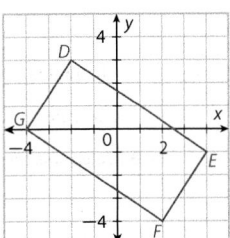

   $\left(\text{slope of } \overline{DE}\right) \cdot \left(\text{slope of } \overline{EF}\right) = -1; \left(\text{slope of } \overline{EF}\right) . \left(\text{slope of } \overline{FG}\right) = -1;$
   $\left(\text{slope of } \overline{FG}\right) \cdot \left(\text{slope of } \overline{GD}\right) = -1; \left(\text{slope of } \overline{GD}\right) . \left(\text{slope of } \overline{DE}\right) = -1$

   Consecutive sides are perpendicular since the product of the slopes is −1.
   Quadrilateral *DEFG* is a rectangle because it is a quadrilateral with four right angles.

QUESTIONING STRATEGIES

? What must you show to prove that a quadrilateral is a parallelogram by definition? You must show that both pairs of opposite sides are parallel.

DIFFERENTIATE INSTRUCTION

Modeling

Instruct students to write a pair of numbers $\dfrac{a}{b}$ and $-\dfrac{b}{a}$ with a product of −1. Ask them to plot a point anywhere on a sheet of graph paper. Have them plot, in red, a second point that is *a* vertical units and *b* horizontal units from the point. Have them draw a line through the two points and label it with the slope. Have them repeat the process, but marking, in blue, a new point as −*b* vertical units and *a* horizontal units from the original point. Instruct them to write a sentence or two at the bottom of the page explaining what the diagram illustrates.

EXPLAIN 2

Using Slopes and Systems of Equations to Classify Figures

AVOID COMMON ERRORS

Given an equation, some students may assume that the coefficient of x is always the slope. Remind students that they can only conclude that the coefficient of x is the slope if the equation is in slope-intercept form.

 Explain 2 **Using Slopes and Systems of Equations to Classify Figures**

You can use slope to help you analyze a system of equations.

Example 2 A city block is a quadrilateral bounded by four streets shown in the table. Classify the quadrilateral bounded by the streets.

Ⓐ

Street	Equation
Pine Street	$-x + 2y = 4$
Elm Road	$2x + y = 7$
Chestnut Street	$2y = x - 6$
Cedar Road	$y + 8 = -2x$

Step 1 Write each equation in slope-intercept form, $y = mx + b$.

Pine Street equation: $y = \frac{1}{2}x + 2$ Elm Road equation: $y = -2x + 7$

Chestnut Street equation: $y = \frac{1}{2}x - 3$ Cedar Road equation: $y = -2x - 8$

Step 2 Use the equations to determine the slope of each street.

Pine Street: $y = \frac{1}{2}x + 2$, so the slope is $\frac{1}{2}$.

Elm Road: $y = -2x + 7$, so the slope is -2.

Chestnut Street: $y = \frac{1}{2}x - 3$, so the slope is $\frac{1}{2}$.

Cedar Road: $y = -2x - 8$, so the slope is -2.

Step 3 Determine the type of quadrilateral bounded by the streets.

The product of the slopes of consecutive sides is -1.

So, the quadrilateral is a rectangle since it has four right angles.

Step 4 Check by graphing the equations.

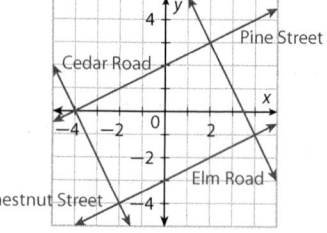

LANGUAGE SUPPORT **EL**

Connect Vocabulary

Have students show they understand the meaning of *perpendicular* lines by pointing out places in the classroom with perpendicular lines. Some examples include the intersection of two walls and the ceiling, the edges of desks, and the sides of textbooks.

Ⓑ

Street	Equation
Clay Avenue	$3y - 9 = x$
Fresno Road	$2x + y = 3$
Ward Street	$3y = x - 5$
Oakland Lane	$y + 4 = -2x$

Step 1 Write each equation in slope-intercept form, $y = mx + b$.

Clay Avenue equation: $y = \dfrac{1}{3}x + \boxed{3}$

Fresno Road equation: $y = \underline{-2x + 3}$

Ward Street equation: $y = \dfrac{1}{3}x - \dfrac{5}{3}$

Oakland Lane equation: $y = \underline{-2x - 4}$

Step 2 Use the equations to determine the slope of each street.

Clay Avenue: $\underline{y = \frac{1}{3}x + 3}$, so the slope is $\underline{\frac{1}{3}}$.

Fresno Road $\underline{y = -2x + 3}$, so the slope is $\underline{-2}$.

Ward Street $\underline{y = \frac{1}{3}x + -\frac{5}{3}}$, so the slope is $\underline{\frac{1}{3}}$.

Oakland Lane: $\underline{y = -2x - 4}$, so the slope is $\underline{-2}$.

Step 3 Determine the type of quadrilateral bounded by the streets.

The slopes of opposite sides of the quadrilateral are __equal__.

So, the quadrilateral is __a parallelogram__ since __both pairs of opposite sides are parallel.__

Step 4 Check by graphing the equations.

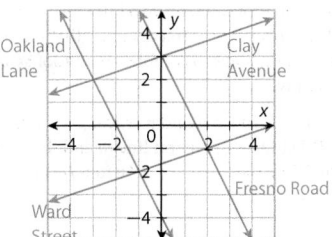

Reflect

6. **Discussion** Is it possible for four streets to form a rectangle if each of the four streets has a positive slope? Explain.

No; the product of the slopes of consecutive sides of the quadrilateral must be −1 in order

for the quadrilateral to be a rectangle. One pair of opposite sides must have positive

slopes, and the other pair must have negative slopes.

QUESTIONING STRATEGIES

? How could you determine that a set of four equations written in slope-intercept form will not produce a rectangle? If there are not two positive and two negative slopes, it is impossible to form four right angles, and the lines will not form a rectangle.

ELABORATE

INTEGRATE MATHEMATICAL PRACTICES
Focus on Technology

MP.5 Students can use graphing calculators to check that two equations represent perpendicular lines. However, students should be aware that perpendicular lines may or may not appear to be perpendicular on a graphing calculator, depending upon the viewing window that is used. To ensure that perpendicular lines appear as perpendicular, students should go to the ZOOM menu and choose 5:ZSquare.

SUMMARIZE THE LESSON

? How can you classify a quadrilateral by finding the slopes of its sides? After you find the slope of each side, compare the slopes. When the slopes are equal, the sides are parallel; identify parallelograms and trapezoids by the number of pairs of parallel sides. When the slopes have a product of −1, the sides are perpendicular; use this to identify rectangles.

Your Turn

7. A farmers market is set up as a quadrilateral bounded by four streets shown in the table. Classify the quadrilateral bounded by the streets.

Taft Road: $y = \frac{2}{3}x + \frac{13}{3}; m = \frac{2}{3}$

Harding Lane: $y = -3x - 3; m = -3$

Wilson Avenue: $y = \frac{2}{3}x + \frac{2}{3}; m = \frac{2}{3}$

Hoover Street: $y = -3x - 14; m = -3$

Street	Equation
Taft Road	$-2x + 3y = 13$
Harding Lane	$\frac{1}{3}y = -x - 1$
Wilson Avenue	$3y = 2x + 2$
Hoover Street	$3x + y = -14$

The slopes of opposite sides are equal. So, the quadrilateral is a parallelogram since both pairs of opposite sides are parallel.

💬 Elaborate

8. Suppose line ℓ has slope $\frac{a}{b}$ where $a \neq 0$ and $b \neq 0$, and suppose lines m and n are both perpendicular to line ℓ. Explain how you can use the slope criteria to show that line m must be parallel to line n.
   Since line m is perpendicular to line ℓ, the product of the slopes of these lines is −1, so line m has slope $-\frac{b}{a}$. Similarly, line n has slope $-\frac{b}{a}$. Then lines m and n are parallel.

9. **Essential Question Check-In** What steps can you use to determine whether two given lines on a coordinate plane are perpendicular?
   Find two points on each line and determine the slope of each line. If the product of the slopes is −1, or if one of the lines is vertical and one is horizontal, then the lines are perpendicular.

⭐ Evaluate: Homework and Practice

- Online Homework
- Hints and Help
- Extra Practice

1. In the Explore, you proved that if two lines are perpendicular, then the product of their slopes is −1. You assumed that the slope of line m was positive. Follow these steps to complete the proof assuming that the slope of line m is negative.

   a. Suppose lines m and n are nonvertical perpendicular lines that intersect at point P. Let Q be a point on line m and draw a slope triangle, $\triangle PQR$, as shown. Write the slope of line m in terms of a and b, where a and b are both positive. $-\frac{a}{b}$

   b. Rotate $\triangle PQR$ 90° around point P. The image is $\triangle PQ'R'$, as shown in the figure. Using $\triangle PQ'R'$, write the slope of line n in terms of a and b. $\frac{b}{a}$

   c. Explain how to complete the proof.
   The product of the slopes of the lines is $-\frac{a}{b} \cdot \frac{b}{a} = -1$.

Show that each figure is the given type of quadrilateral.

2. Show that *QRST* is a rectangle.

$Q(-4, 2)$, $R(-2, 3)$, $S(1, -3)$, $T(-1, -4)$: slope of $\overline{QR} =$
slope of $\overline{ST} = \frac{1}{2}$; slope of $\overline{TQ} =$ slope of $\overline{RS} = -2$;
$\left(\text{slope of } \overline{QR}\right) \cdot \left(\text{slope of } \overline{RS}\right) = \left(\text{slope of } \overline{RS}\right) \cdot \left(\text{slope of } \overline{ST}\right) = -1$
$\left(\text{slope of } \overline{ST}\right) \cdot \left(\text{slope of } \overline{TQ}\right) = \left(\text{slope of } \overline{TQ}\right) \cdot \left(\text{slope of } \overline{QR}\right) = -1$
consecutive sides are perpendicular since the product of
the slopes is -1.
QRST is a rectangle because it is a quadrilateral with four right angles.

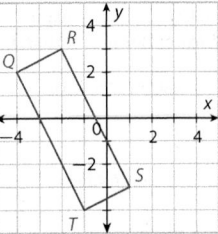

3. Show that *KLMN* is a trapezoid with two right angles.

$K(-2, 3)$, $L(4, -1)$, $M(2, -4)$, $N(-1, -2)$: slope of
$\overline{KL} =$ slope of $\overline{MN} = -\frac{2}{3}$; slope of $\overline{LM} = \frac{3}{2}$; slope of $\overline{NK} = -5$;
Slope of $\overline{KL} =$ slope of $\overline{MN}$, so $\overline{KL}$ is parallel to $\overline{MN}$.
Since $\left(\text{slope of } \overline{KL}\right) \cdot \left(\text{slope of } \overline{LM}\right) = -\frac{2}{3} \cdot \frac{3}{2} = -1$ and
$\left(\text{slope of } \overline{LM}\right) \cdot \left(\text{slope of } \overline{MN}\right) = \frac{3}{2} \cdot \left(-\frac{2}{3}\right) = -1$, $\overline{KL} \perp \overline{LM}$
and $\overline{LM} \perp \overline{MN}$.
KLMN is a trapezoid with two right angles because a pair of
opposite sides are parallel and two pairs of consecutive sides are perpendicular.

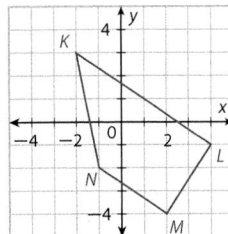

The boundary of a farm consists of four straight roads. Classify the
quadrilateral bounded by the roads in each table.

4.

Road	Equation
Lewiston Road	$y - 8 = 2x$
Johnson Road	$2y = -x + 1$
Chavez Road	$-2x + y = -2$
Brannon Road	$x + 2y = -4$

Lewiston Road: $y = 2x + 8$, $m = 2$; Johnson Road:
$y = -\frac{1}{2}x + \frac{1}{2}$, $m = -\frac{1}{2}$; Chavez Road: $y = 2x - 2$, $m = 2$;
Brannon Road: $y = -\frac{1}{2}x - 2$, $m = -\frac{1}{2}$; The product of the
slopes of consecutive sides of the quadrilateral is -1. So,
the quadrilateral is a rectangle since it has four right angles.

5.

Road	Equation
Larson Road	$y + 1 = 2x$
Cortez Road	$2x + y = 3$
Madison Road	$2x = y + 5$
Jackson Road	$2x + y = -5$

Larson Road: $y = 2x - 1$; $m = 2$;
Cortez Road: $y = -2x + 3$; $m = -2$;
Madison Road: $y = 2x - 5$; $m = 2$;
Jackson Road: $y = -2x - 5$; $m = -2$; The
slopes of opposite sides are equal. So, the
quadrilateral is a parallelogram since both
pairs of opposite sides are parallel.

© Houghton Mifflin Harcourt Publishing Company • Image Credits: ©Frans Lemmens/Corbis

ASSIGNMENT GUIDE

Concept and Skills	Practice
Explore Proving the Slope Criteria for Perpendicular Lines	Exercise 1
Example 1 Using Slopes to Classify Figures by Right Angles	Exercises 2–3
Example 2 Using Slopes and Systems of Equations to Classify Figures	Exercises 4–5

QUESTIONING STRATEGIES

What kinds of quadrilaterals are formed by
intersecting perpendicular lines? rectangles,
including squares

Exercise	Depth of Knowledge (D.O.K.)	COMMON CORE Mathematical Practices
1	**2** Skills/Concepts	**MP.3** Logic
2–3	**1** Recall	**MP.2** Reasoning
4–5	**1** Recall	**MP.4** Modeling
6–18	**2** Skills/Concepts	**MP.2** Reasoning
19	**2** Skills/Concepts	**MP.4** Modeling
20	**2** Skills/Concepts	**MP.4** Modeling
21	**3** Strategic Thinking **H.O.T.**	**MP.2** Reasoning

Slope and Perpendicular Lines   **516**

Multi-Step Determine whether the quadrilateral with the given vertices is a parallelogram. If so, determine whether it is a rhombus, a rectangle, or neither. Justify your conclusions. (*Hint*: Recall that a parallelogram with perpendicular diagonals is a rhombus.)

6. Quadrilateral $ABCD$ with $A(-3, 0)$, $B(1, 2)$, $C(2, 0)$, and $D(-2, -2)$

slope of $\overline{AB} = \dfrac{2-0}{1-(-3)} = \dfrac{1}{2}$; slope of $\overline{BC} = \dfrac{0-2}{2-1} = -2$;

slope of $\overline{CD} = \dfrac{-2-0}{-2-2} = \dfrac{1}{2}$; slope of $\overline{DA} = \dfrac{0-(-2)}{-3-(-2)} = -2$;

Opposite sides have the same slope, so opposite sides are parallel, and $ABCD$ is a parallelogram. The product of the slopes of consecutive sides is -1, so consecutive sides are perpendicular. Therefore, $ABCD$ is a rectangle. slope of $\overline{AC} = \dfrac{0-0}{2-(-3)} = 0$;

slope of $\overline{BD} = \dfrac{-2-2}{-2-1} = \dfrac{4}{3}$ The product of the slopes of the diagonals is not -1, so the diagonals are not perpendicular. Therefore, $ABCD$ is not a rhombus. So, $ABCD$ is a parallelogram and a rectangle, but not a rhombus.

7. Quadrilateral $KLMN$ with $K(-4, 2)$, $L(-1, 4)$, $M(3, 3)$, and $N(-3, -1)$

slope of $\overline{KL} = \dfrac{4-2}{-1-(-4)} = \dfrac{2}{3}$; slope of $\overline{LM} = \dfrac{3-4}{3-(-1)} = -\dfrac{1}{4}$;

slope of $\overline{MN} = \dfrac{2}{3}$; slope of $\overline{NK} = \dfrac{2-(-1)}{-4-(-3)} = -3$; A pair of opposite sides do not have the same slope, so these sides are not parallel. Therefore, $KLMN$ is not a parallelogram.

8. Quadrilateral $FGHJ$ with $F(-2, 3)$, $G(1, 2)$, $H(2, -1)$, and $J(-1, 0)$

slope of $\overline{FG} = \dfrac{2-3}{1-(-2)} = -\dfrac{1}{3}$; slope of $\overline{GH} = \dfrac{-1-2}{2-1} = -3$;

slope of $\overline{HJ} = \dfrac{0-(-1)}{-1-2} = -\dfrac{1}{3}$; slope of $\overline{JF} = \dfrac{3-0}{-2-(-1)} = -3$; Opposite sides have the same slope, so opposite sides are parallel, and $FGHJ$ is a parallelogram. The product of the slopes of consecutive sides is not -1, so consecutive sides are not perpendicular. Therefore, $FGHJ$ is not a rectangle. slope of $\overline{FH} = \dfrac{-1-3}{2-(-2)} = -1$; and slope of $\overline{GJ} = \dfrac{0-2}{-1-1} = 1$; The product of the slopes of the diagonals is -1, so the diagonals are perpendicular. Therefore, $FGHJ$ is a rhombus. So, $FGHJ$ is a parallelogram and a rhombus, but not a rectangle.

Exercise	Depth of Knowledge (D.O.K.)	COMMON CORE	Mathematical Practices
22	**3** Strategic Thinking H.O.T.		**MP.3** Logic

Determine whether each statement is always, sometimes, or never true. Explain.

9. If quadrilateral $ABCD$ is a rectangle and the slope of $\overline{AB}$ is positive, then the slope of $\overline{BC}$ is negative.

Always; consecutive sides of a rectangle are perpendicular, so the product of the slopes of consecutive sides is -1. If one side of a rectangle has a positive slope, then a consecutive side must have a negative slope.

10. If line m is perpendicular to line n, then the slope of line n is 0.

Sometimes; if line m is vertical, then line n is horizontal and has a slope of 0.

11. If quadrilateral $JKLM$ is a rhombus and one diagonal has a slope of 3, then the other diagonal has a slope of $\frac{1}{3}$.

Never; the diagonals of a rhombus are perpendicular, so the product of the slopes of the diagonals is -1 and $3 \cdot \frac{1}{3} \neq -1$.

12. If k is a real number, then the line $y = x + k$ is perpendicular to the line $y = -x + k$.

Always; for any value of k, the slope of the line $y = x + k$ is 1 and the slope of the line $y = -x + k$ is -1. Since the product of the slopes is -1, the lines are perpendicular.

13. The slopes of two consecutive sides of a rectangle are $\frac{2}{3}$ and $\frac{3}{2}$.

Never; consecutive sides of a rectangle are perpendicular, so the product of the slopes of consecutive sides is -1, and $\frac{2}{3} \cdot \frac{3}{2} \neq -1$.

Algebra The perimeter of $\square PQRS$ is 84. Find the length of each side of $\square PQRS$ under the given conditions.

14. $PQ = QR$

If $PQ = QR$, then all sides of the parallelogram are equal. The length of each side is $\frac{84}{4} = 21$. So $PQ = QR = RS = SP = 21$.

15. $QR = 3(RS)$

Let $QR = SP = x$ and $PQ = RS = y$. Then $2x + 2y = 84$. Since $QR = 3(RS)$, $x = 3y$ and $8y = 84$. Then $y = 10.5$ and $x = 31.5$. So $PQ = RS = 10.5$ and $QR = SP = 31.5$.

16. $RS = SP - 7$

Let $QR = SP = x$ and $PQ = RS = y$. Then $2x + 2y = 84$. Since $y = x - 7$, $2x + 2(x - 7) = 84$, and $x = 24.5$. Then $PQ = RS = 17.5$ and $QR = SP = 24.5$.

17. $SP = RS^2$

Let $QR = SP = x$ and $PQ = RS = y$. Then $2x + 2y = 84$. Since $x = y^2$, $2y^2 + 2y = 84$, and $(y + 7)(y - 6) = 0$. Since y must be positive, $y = 6$ and $x = 36$. So $PQ = RS = 6$ and $QR = SP = 36$.

KINESTHETIC EXPERIENCE

Give each student a geoboard and rubber bands. Instruct students to create a rectangle with sides that are <u>not</u> parallel to the edges of the board. Have them envision slope triangles to find the slope of each side and confirm that the quadrilateral is a rectangle.

18. **Multiple Representations** Line m has the equation $2x + 3y = 6$, line n passes through the points in the table, and line p has the graph shown in the figure. Which of these lines, if any, are perpendicular? Explain.

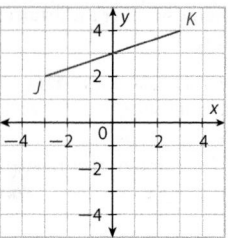

Line *n*	
x	**y**
4	5
6	8
8	11

Line m may be written as $y = -\frac{2}{3}x + 2$, so m is $-\frac{2}{3}$.

Line n, use points $(4, 5)$ and $(6, 8)$; $m = \frac{8-5}{6-4} = \frac{3}{2}$

Line p, use points $(3, 4)$ and $(-3, 2)$; $m = \frac{2-4}{-3-3} = \frac{-2}{-6} = \frac{1}{3}$

The product of the slopes of lines m and n is $-\frac{2}{3} \cdot \frac{3}{2} = -1$, so lines m and n are perpendicular.

19. Three subway lines run along straight tracks in the city. The equation for each subway line is given. City planners want to add a fourth subway line and want the tracks for the four lines to form a rectangle. What is a possible equation for the fourth subway line? Justify your answer.

Subway Line	Equation
B	$-2x + y = 4$
N	$2y = -x + 8$
S	$y + 11 = 2x$

Write each equation in slope-intercept form to find the slope of the line. B line: $y = 2x + 4$; $m = 2$; N line: $y = -\frac{1}{2}x + 4$; $m = -\frac{1}{2}$; S line: $y = 2x - 11$; $m = 2$; for the lines to form a rectangle, the fourth line must be parallel to the N line, so the slope of the fourth line must be $-\frac{1}{2}$. A possible equation is $y = -\frac{1}{2}x - 2$, since the slope of this line is $-\frac{1}{2}$.

20. Quadrilateral $JKLM$ is a rectangle. One side of the rectangle is shown in the figure. Which of the following are possible coordinates for vertices L and M? Select all that apply.

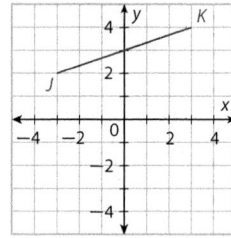

A. $L(4, 1)$ and $M(-2, -1)$ Answer: A, D

B. $L(5, -2)$ and $M(-1, -3)$ B. $\overline{KL}$ and $\overline{MJ}$ are not parallel.

C. $\overline{MJ}$ and $\overline{JK}$ are not perpendicular.

C. $L(4, 7)$ and $M(-2, 5)$ E. $\overline{JK}$ and $\overline{LM}$ are not parallel.

D. $L(5, -2)$ and $M(-1, -4)$

E. $L(3, 0)$ and $M(-3, 0)$

21. Analyze Relationships Quadrilateral *ABCD* is a rectangle. The coordinates of vertices *A* and *B* are *A*(−2, 2) and *B*(2, 0). Vertex *C* lies on the *y*-axis. What are the coordinates of vertices *C* and *D*? Explain.

slope of $\overline{AB} = -\dfrac{1}{2}$. Since consecutive sides of a rectangle are perpendicular, the slope of

$\overline{BC}$ must be 2. Since *C* lies on the *y*-axis, let its coordinates be (0, *y*). Then, slope of $\overline{BC} = \dfrac{y}{-2}$

and *y* = −4, so the coordinates of *C* are (0, −4). To find the coordinates of *D*, use the fact

that when moving from *B* to *A* and the run is −4 and the rise is 2. So moving from *C* to *D*,

the run and rise must be the same. From 0, a run of −4 is −4. From −4, a rise of 2 is −2.

The coordinates of *D* are $\left(-4, -2\right)$.

22. Counterexamples A student said that any three noncollinear points can be three of the vertices of a rectangle because it is always possible to choose a fourth vertex that completes the rectangle. Give a counterexample to show that the student's statement is false and explain the counterexample.

Possible answer: Let *P*, *Q*, and *R* have coordinates *P*(−3, 1), *Q*(3, 4), and *R*(6, 3). Then the

slope of $\overline{PQ} = \dfrac{4-1}{3-(-3)} = \dfrac{1}{2}$ and slope of $\overline{QR} = \dfrac{3-4}{6-3} = -\dfrac{1}{3}$. $\overline{PQ}$ and $\overline{QR}$ are neither

parallel nor perpendicular, because their slopes are not equal nor is their product −1, So

they cannot be sides of a rectangle.

Lesson Performance Task

Each unit on the grid represents 1 mile. A ship is in distress at the point shown. The navigator knows that the shortest distance from a point to a line is on a perpendicular to the line. So, the navigator directs the captain to head the ship on a perpendicular course toward the shoreline.

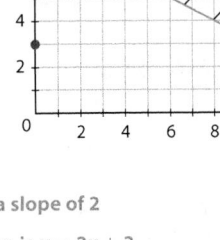

If the ship succeeds in staying on course, where will it hit land? Explain your method.

The ship will hit land at the point (2, 7). To solve, first find the

equation of the shoreline. The slope is $-\dfrac{1}{2}$ and the *y*-intercept is 8,

so the equation is $y = -\dfrac{1}{2}x + 8$. The line the captain will follow has a slope of 2

(the opposite reciprocal of $-\dfrac{1}{2}$) and a *y*-intercept of 3, so the equation is $y = 2x + 3$.

To find the point where the ship makes land, solve the system of equations

$\begin{cases} y = -\dfrac{1}{2}x + 8 \\ y = 2x + 3 \end{cases}$. The solution is (2, 7).

© Houghton Mifflin Harcourt Publishing Company

AVOID COMMON ERRORS

Students may have forgotten methods of solving systems of equations, leading them to err in solving the system that arises in the Lesson Performance Task:

$$\begin{cases} y = -\dfrac{1}{2}x + 8 \\ y = 2x + 3 \end{cases}$$

Point out that this system can be solved without system-of-equation methods by noting that the expressions on the right sides of the equations both equal *y*, so they must equal each other. This allows the system to be transformed at once into an equation in one variable:

$$-\dfrac{1}{2}x + 8 = 2x + 3$$

QUESTIONING STRATEGIES

? A line has a slope of *m*. A second line is perpendicular to the first. What is its slope? $-\dfrac{1}{m}$

? A third line is perpendicular to the second. What is its slope? Prove your answer algebraically. *m*; let *n* represent the slope of the third line:

$$n\left(-\dfrac{1}{m}\right) = -1$$
$$n = \dfrac{-1}{-\dfrac{1}{m}}$$
$$= -1\left(-\dfrac{m}{1}\right)$$
$$= m$$

EXTENSION ACTIVITY

How does a sailboat move forward when the wind direction is perpendicular to the centerline of the boat? By adopting a maneuver called *reaching*. Not only does reaching allow the sailboat to move forward, it can help the sailboat achieve its maximum possible speed. Have students research reaching and other sailboat maneuvers such as running and close hauling, describing the maneuvers and explaining how they utilize the wind to effect forward motion.

Scoring Rubric
2 points: Student correctly solves the problem and explains his/her reasoning.
1 point: Student shows good understanding of the problem but does not fully solve or explain.
0 points: Student does not demonstrate understanding of the problem.

Slope and Perpendicular Lines   **520**

Coordinate Proof Using Distance with Segments and Triangles

Common Core Math Standards

The student is expected to:

 G-GPE.B.4

Use coordinates to prove simple geometric theorems. Also G-CO.C.10, G-GPE.B.5, G-GPE.B.7

Mathematical Practices

 MP.6 Precision

Language Objective

Describe to a partner how to prove the Concurrency of Medians Theorem.

ENGAGE

Essential Question: How do you write a coordinate proof?

To write a coordinate proof, use variables to assign general coordinates to a figure and then use the distance formula, the midpoint formula, and/or other algebraic facts to construct a logical argument.

PREVIEW: LESSON PERFORMANCE TASK

View the Engage section online. Discuss the photo. Be sure students understand that each contestant competes in all three triathlon events, as opposed to teams of three competing in the events. Then preview the Lesson Performance Task.

10.3 Coordinate Proof Using Distance with Segments and Triangles

Essential Question: How do you write a coordinate proof?

⊘ Explore   **Deriving the Distance Formula and the Midpoint Formula**

Complete the following steps to derive the Distance Formula and the Midpoint Formula.

Ⓐ To derive the Distance Formula, start with points J and K as shown in the figure.

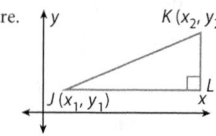

   Given: $J(x_1, y_1)$ and $K(x_2, y_2)$ with $x_1 \neq x_2$ and $y_1 \neq y_2$

   Prove: $JK = \sqrt{(x_2 - x_1)^2 + (y_2 - y_1)^2}$

   Locate point L so that $\overline{JK}$ is the hypotenuse of right triangle JKL. What are the coordinates of L?

   (x_2, y_1)

Ⓑ Find JL and LK.

   $JL = x_2 - x_1, LK = y_2 - y_1$

Ⓒ By the Pythagorean Theorem, $JK^2 = JL^2 + LK^2$. Use this to find JK. Explain your steps.

   $JK^2 = (x_2 - x_1)^2 + (y_2 - y_1)^2$ **by substitution.**

   Taking the square root of both sides shows that $JK = \sqrt{(x_2 - x_1)^2 + (y_2 - y_1)^2}$.

Ⓓ To derive the Midpoint Formula, start with points A and B as shown in the figure.

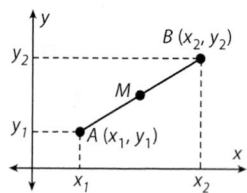

   Given: $A(x_1, y_1)$ and $B(x_2, y_2)$

   Prove: The midpoint of $\overline{AB}$ is $M\left(\dfrac{x_1 + x_2}{2}, \dfrac{y_1 + y_2}{2}\right)$.

   What is the horizontal distance from point A to point B? What is the vertical distance from point A to point B?

   horizontal distance: $x_2 - x_1$; **vertical distance:** $y_2 - y_1$

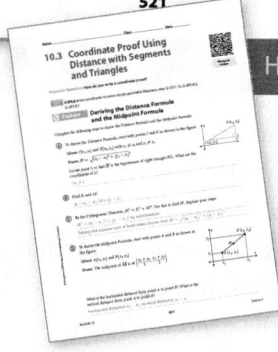

HARDCOVER PAGES 445–456

Turn to these pages to find this lesson in the hardcover student edition.

© Houghton Mifflin Harcourt Publishing Company

(E) The horizontal and vertical distances from A to M must be half these distances.

What is the horizontal distance from point A to point M? $\dfrac{x_2 - x_1}{2}$

What is the vertical distance from point A to point M? $\dfrac{y_2 - y_1}{2}$

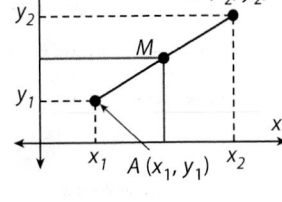

(F) To find the coordinates of point M, add the distances from Step E to the x- and y-coordinates of point A and simplify.

x-coordinate of point M: $x_1 + \dfrac{x_2 - x_1}{2} = \dfrac{2x_1}{2} + \dfrac{x_2 - x_1}{2} = \dfrac{2x_1 + x_2 - x_1}{2} = \dfrac{x_1 + x_2}{2}$

y-coordinate of point M: $y_1 + \dfrac{y_2 - y_1}{2} = \dfrac{2y_1}{2} + \dfrac{y_2 - y_1}{2} = \dfrac{2y_1 + y_2 - y_1}{2} = \dfrac{y_1 + y_2}{2}$

Reflect

1. In the proof of the Distance Formula, why do you assume that $x_1 \neq x_2$ and $y_1 \neq y_2$?
   If $x_1 = x_2$ or $y_1 = y_2$, the segment is vertical or horizontal and it is not possible to form a
   right triangle as in the figure.

2. Does the Distance Formula still apply if $x_1 = x_2$ or $y_1 = y_2$? Explain.
   Yes; if $x_1 = x_2$, the formula simplifies to $JK = |y_2 - y_1|$, and if $y_1 = y_2$, the formula simplifies
   to $JK = |x_2 - x_1|$.

3. Does the Midpoint Formula still apply if $x_1 = x_2$ or $y_1 = y_2$? Explain.
   Yes; if $x_1 = x_2$, the formula simplifies to $M\left(x_1, \dfrac{y_1 + y_2}{2}\right)$, and if $y_1 = y_2$, the formula simplifies
   to $M\left(\dfrac{x_1 + x_2}{2}, y_1\right)$.

EXPLORE

Deriving the Distance Formula and the Midpoint Formula

INTEGRATE TECHNOLOGY

Students have the option of completing the Explore activity either in the book or online.

QUESTIONING STRATEGIES

 Why do we need the small *1* and *2* (subscripts) next to the x and y? The subscripts help us know which point the coordinates come from. We choose one point to be *Point 1 (P_1)* and one point to be *Point 2 (P_2)*, and then write the subscripts *1* and *2* to show which point each pair of coordinates belongs to.

PROFESSIONAL DEVELOPMENT

COMMON CORE Math Background

The distance formula is a direct consequence of the Pythagorean Theorem. Note that the distance formula reduces to a simpler version in the case of points that lie on a horizontal or vertical line. For example, if two points lie on a vertical line, then they have the same x-coordinates and the distance between the points is
$\sqrt{(x_2 - x_1)^2 + (y_2 - y_1)^2} = \sqrt{(y_2 - y_1)^2} = |y_2 - y_1|$. Similarly, the distance between two points on a horizontal line is $|x_2 - x_1|$. The distance and midpoint formulas, along with facts about the slopes of parallel and perpendicular lines, are key tools of coordinate geometry.

Coordinate Proof Using Distance with Segments and Triangles **522**

EXPLAIN 1

Positioning a Triangle on the Coordinate Plane

AVOID COMMON ERRORS

Students may automatically try to use both axes to position a triangle. Make sure they understand you can position a triangle on both axes only if it is a right triangle.

 Explain 1 Positioning a Triangle on the Coordinate Plane

A **coordinate proof** is a style of proof that uses coordinate geometry and algebra. The first step of a coordinate proof is to position the given figure in the plane. You can use any position, but some strategies can make the steps of the proof simpler.

Strategies for Positioning Figures in the Coordinate Plane
• Use the origin as a vertex, keeping the figure in Quadrant I.
• Center the figure at the origin.
• Center a side of the figure at the origin.
• Use one or both axes as sides of the figure.

Example 1 Write each coordinate proof.

(A) **Given:** $\angle B$ is a right angle in $\triangle ABC$. D is the midpoint of $\overline{AC}$.

Prove: The area of $\triangle DBC$ is one half the area of $\triangle ABC$.

Step 1 Assign coordinates to each vertex. Since you will use the Midpoint Formula to find the coordinates of D, use multiples of 2 for the leg lengths.

The coordinates of A are $(0, 2j)$.

The coordinates of B are $(0, 0)$.

The coordinates of C are $(2n, 0)$.

Step 2 Position the figure on the coordinate plane.

Step 3 Write a coordinate proof.

$\triangle ABC$ is a right triangle with height $2j$ and base $2n$.

$$\text{area of } \triangle ABC = \tfrac{1}{2}bh$$
$$= \tfrac{1}{2}(2n)(2j)$$
$$= 2nj \text{ square units}$$

By the Midpoint Formula, the coordinates of $D = \left(\dfrac{0 + 2n}{2}, \dfrac{2j + 0}{2}\right) = (n, j)$.

The height of $\triangle DBC$ is j units, and the base is $2n$ units.

$$\text{area of } \triangle DBC = \tfrac{1}{2}bh$$
$$= \tfrac{1}{2}(2n)(j)$$
$$= nj \text{ square units}$$

Since $nj = \tfrac{1}{2}(2nj)$, the area of $\triangle DBC$ is one half the area of $\triangle ABC$.

COLLABORATIVE LEARNING

Whole Class Activity

Divide the class into two groups. Have one group complete a proof that a triangle with coordinates $(0, 4)$, $(0, 0)$, and $(3, 0)$ is a right triangle. Have the second group use the coordinates $(0, a)$, $(0, 0)$, and $(b, 0)$ and then verify that the triangle is a right triangle. Compare and contrast the two methods of proof. Emphasize that when you use variables, you prove that the statement is true for all right triangles, not just for a specific triangle.

(B) **Given:** $\angle B$ is a right angle in $\triangle ABC$. D is the midpoint of $\overline{AC}$.

Prove: The area of $\triangle ADB$ is one half the area of $\triangle ABC$.

Assign coordinates and position the figure as in Example 1A.

$\triangle ABC$ is a right triangle with height $\boxed{2j}$ and base $\boxed{2n}$.

area of $\triangle ABC = \frac{1}{2}bh$

$\qquad = \frac{1}{2} \boxed{2n} \cdot \boxed{2j}$

$\qquad = \boxed{2nj}$ square units

By the Midpoint Formula, the coordinates of $D = \left(\dfrac{0 + \boxed{2n}}{2}, \dfrac{\boxed{2j} + 0}{2}\right) = \left(\boxed{n}, \boxed{j}\right)$.

The height of $\triangle ADB$ is $\boxed{n}$ units, and the base is $\boxed{2j}$ units.

area of $\triangle ADB = \frac{1}{2}bh = \frac{1}{2} \boxed{2j} \cdot \boxed{n} = \boxed{jn}$ square units

Since $\underline{jn = \frac{1}{2}(2\,nj)}$, the area of $\triangle ADB$ is one half the area of $\triangle ABC$.

Reflect

4. Why is it possible to position $\triangle ABC$ so that two of its sides lie on the axes of the coordinate plane?

It is given that $\triangle ABC$ has a right angle at $\angle B$. The axes of the coordinate plane intersect at a right angle, so if vertex B is at the origin, then two sides of the triangle will lie on the axes.

Your Turn

Position the given triangle on the coordinate plane. Then show that the result about areas from Example 1 holds for the triangle.

5. A right triangle, $\triangle ABC$, with legs of length 2 units and 4 units

Possible answer: Let the coordinates of the vertices be $A(0, 4)$, $B(0, 0)$, and $C(2, 0)$.

The height of $\triangle ABC$ is 4 units, and the base is 2 units. area of $\triangle ABC = \frac{1}{2}(2)(4) = 4$ units^2

The coordinates of D, the midpoint of $\overline{AC}$, are $\left(\dfrac{0+2}{2}, \dfrac{4+0}{2}\right) = (1, 2)$.

The height of $\triangle DBC$ is 2 units, and the base is 2 units. area of $\triangle DBC = \frac{1}{2}(2)(2) = 2$ units^2

Since $2 = \frac{1}{2}(4)$, the area of $\triangle DBC$ is one half the area of $\triangle ABC$.

DIFFERENTIATE INSTRUCTION

Multiple Representations

Have students plot and connect two points on a coordinate plane. Ask them to find the midpoint of the segment and the equation of a line passing through the midpoint that is perpendicular to the segment. Then have them use a compass and straightedge to construct the perpendicular bisector of the segment. Have students compare the midpoints and the equations of the lines to show that the algebraic method and the construction yield the same results.

QUESTIONING STRATEGIES

? Why is it helpful to position a triangle on an axis? If a side is on an axis, one of the coordinates for every point on that side is zero. This makes calculations much easier.

Proving the Triangle Midsegment Theorem

CONNECT VOCABULARY EL

Review the term *midsegment*. Make a sketch on the board showing how to draw a midsegment, and remind students that every triangle has three midsegments. Explain that in this lesson, students will primarily work with one midsegment at a time.

QUESTIONING STRATEGIES

? What are some ways you can prove that two line segments are parallel? Which of these methods may work best in a coordinate proof? Sample answer: Show corresponding angles have the same measure, or show the lines have the same slope. In a coordinate proof, it may be easiest to show that the lines have the same slope.

---

6. A right triangle, $\triangle ABC$, with both legs of length 8 units
   Possible answer: Let the coordinates of the vertices be $A(0, 8)$, $B(0, 0)$, and $C(8, 0)$.

   The height of $\triangle ABC$ is 8 units, and the base is 8 units. area of $\triangle ABC = \frac{1}{2}(8)(8) = 32$ units²

   The coordinates of D, the midpoint of $\overline{AC}$, are $\left(\frac{0+8}{2}, \frac{8+0}{2}\right) = (4, 4)$.

   The height of $\triangle DBC$ is 4 units, and the base is 8 units. area of $\triangle DBC = \frac{1}{2}(8)(4) = 16$ units²

   Since $16 = \frac{1}{2}(32)$, the area of $\triangle DBC$ is one half the area of $\triangle ABC$.

⊘ Explain 2 Proving the Triangle Midsegment Theorem

In Module 8, you learned that the Triangle Midsegment Theorem states that a midsegment of a triangle is parallel to the third side of the triangle and is half as long as the third side. You can now use a coordinate proof to show that the theorem is true.

Example 2 Prove the Triangle Midsegment Theorem.

Given: $\overline{XY}$ is a midsegment of $\triangle PQR$.

Prove: $\overline{XY} \parallel \overline{PQ}$ and $XY = \frac{1}{2}PQ$

Place $\triangle PQR$ so that one vertex is at the origin. For convenience, assign vertex P the coordinates $(2a, 2b)$ and assign vertex Q the vertices $(2c, 2d)$.

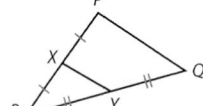

Use the Midpoint Formula to find the coordinates of X and Y.

The coordinates of X are $X\left(\frac{0 + 2a}{2}, \frac{0 + 2b}{2}\right) = X(a,b)$.

The coordinates of Y are $Y\left(\frac{0}{2} + \boxed{2c}, \frac{0}{2} + \boxed{2d}\right) = Y\left(\boxed{c}, \boxed{d}\right)$.

Find the slope of $\overline{PQ}$ and $\overline{XY}$.

slope of $\overline{PQ} = \frac{y_2 - y_1}{x_2 - x_1} = \frac{2d - 2b}{2c - 2a} = \frac{\boxed{d} - \boxed{b}}{\boxed{c} - \boxed{a}}$; slope of $\overline{XY} = \frac{y_2 - y_1}{x_2 - x_1} = \frac{\boxed{d} - \boxed{b}}{\boxed{c} - \boxed{a}}$

Therefore, $\overline{PQ} \parallel \overline{XY}$ since the slopes are the same .

Use the Distance Formula to find PQ and XY.

$PQ = \sqrt{(x_2 - x_1)^2 + (y_2 - y_1)^2}$
$= \sqrt{(2c - 2a)^2 + (2d - 2b)^2}$

$= \sqrt{\boxed{4} \cdot (c - a)^2 + \boxed{4} \cdot (d - b)^2}$
$= \sqrt{\boxed{4} \cdot (c - a)^2 + (d - b)^2}$

$= \sqrt{\boxed{4}} \cdot \sqrt{(c - a)^2 + (d - b)^2}$
$= \boxed{2}\sqrt{(c - a)^2 + (d - b)^2}$

$XY = \sqrt{(x_2 - x_1)^2 + (y_2 - y_1)^2}$
$= \sqrt{\left(\boxed{c} - \boxed{a}\right)^2 + \left(\boxed{d} - \boxed{b}\right)^2}$

This shows that $XY = \dfrac{1}{\boxed{2}}PQ$.

© Houghton Mifflin Harcourt Publishing Company

LANGUAGE SUPPORT EL

Connect Vocabulary

Remind students that one way to figure out the meaning of new words they encounter is to determine whether they are compound words. Compound words are words made up of two smaller words that maintain their original meanings. For example, a *midpoint* is a *point* that is *midway* on the line. Two other compound words that appear in this lesson are *endpoint* and *midsegment*. Help students figure out their meanings by highlighting the words that make up each compound word.

7. **Discussion** Why is it more convenient to assign vertex P the coordinates $(2a, 2b)$ and vertex Q the coordinates $(2c, 2d)$ rather than using the coordinates (a, b) and (c, d)?

The proof requires finding the coordinates of the midpoints of $\overline{RP}$ and $\overline{RQ}$. Assigning

coordinates that are multiples of 2 eliminates the need for fractions in the coordinates of

the midpoints.

Explain 3 Proving the Concurrency of Medians Theorem

You used the Concurrency of Medians Theorem in Module 8 and proved it in Module 9. Now you will prove the theorem again, this time using coordinate methods.

Example 3 Prove the Concurrency of Medians Theorem.

Given: $\triangle PQR$ with medians $\overline{PL}$, $\overline{QM}$, and $\overline{RN}$

Prove: $\overline{PL}$, $\overline{QM}$, and $\overline{RN}$ are concurrent.

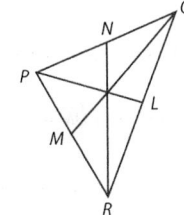

Place $\triangle PQR$ so that vertex R is at the origin. Also, place the triangle so that point N lies on the y-axis. For convenience, assign point N the vertices $(0, 6a)$. (The factor of 6 will result in easier calculations later.)

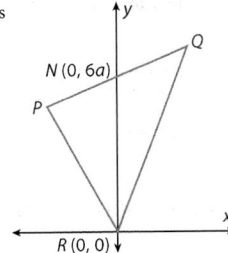

Since N is the midpoint of $\overline{PQ}$, assign coordinates to P and Q as follows.

The horizontal distance from N to P must be the same as the horizontal distance from N to Q. Let this distance be $2b$.

Then the x-coordinate of point P is $-2b$ and the x-coordinate of point Q is ___2b___.

The vertical distance from N to P must be the same as the vertical distance from N to Q. Let this distance be $2c$.

Then the y-coordinate of point P is $6a - 2c$ and the y-coordinate of point Q is ___$6a + 2c$___.

Complete the figure by writing the coordinates of points P and Q.

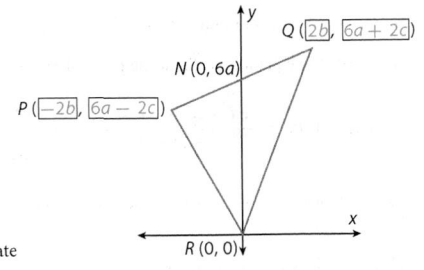

© Houghton Mifflin Harcourt Publishing Company

EXPLAIN 3

Proving the Concurrency of Medians Theorem

AVOID COMMON ERRORS

Students may get lost in the algebra that is required to complete the proof and lose track of the overall structure of the proof. To help students stay on track, you may want to have them write the main steps of the proof and then check off the steps as they complete them:

1. Assign coordinates to the vertices.

2. Find the coordinates of the midpoint of each side.

3. Write equations for the lines containing the medians.

4. Find the point of intersection of two of the lines.

5. Show that the point of intersection lies on the third line.

In the proof of the Concurrency of Medians Theorem, why do you write equations for the lines containing the medians? This allows you to determine the point of intersection of two of the lines. Then you can show that this intersection point lies on the third line.

Now use the Midpoint Formula to find the coordinates of L and M.

The midpoint of $\overline{RQ}$ is $L\left(\dfrac{0 + 2b}{2}, \dfrac{0 + 6a + 2c}{2}\right) = L\left(\boxed{b}, \boxed{3a+c}\right)$.

The midpoint of $\overline{RP}$ is $M\left(\dfrac{0 + -2b}{2}, \dfrac{0 + 6a - 2c}{2}\right) = M\left(\boxed{-b}, \boxed{3a-c}\right)$.

Complete the figure by writing the coordinates of points L and M.

To complete the proof, write the equation of $\overleftrightarrow{QM}$ and use the equation to find the coordinates of point C, which is the intersection of the medians $\overline{QM}$ and $\overline{RN}$. Then show that point C lies on $\overleftrightarrow{PL}$.

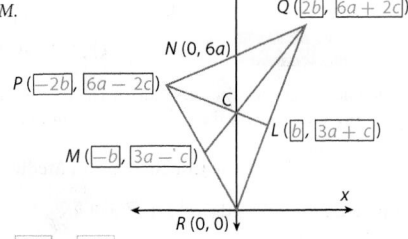

$Q\,(\boxed{2b}, \boxed{6a+2c})$

$N\,(0, 6a)$

$P\,(\boxed{-2b}, \boxed{6a-2c})$

C

$L\,(\boxed{b}, \boxed{3a+c})$

$M\,(\boxed{-b}, \boxed{3a-c})$

$R\,(0, 0)$

Write the equation of $\overleftrightarrow{QM}$ using point-slope form.

The slope of $\overleftrightarrow{QM}$ is $\dfrac{(6a + 2c) - (3a - c)}{2b - (-b)} = \dfrac{3\boxed{a} + 3\boxed{c}}{3\boxed{b}} = \dfrac{\boxed{a} + \boxed{c}}{\boxed{b}}$.

Use the coordinates of point Q for the point on $\overleftrightarrow{QM}$.

Therefore, the equation of $\overleftrightarrow{QM}$ is $y - \boxed{6a+2c} = \dfrac{\boxed{a} + \boxed{c}}{\boxed{b}} \cdot \left(x - \boxed{2b}\right)$.

Since point C lies on the y-axis, the x-coordinate of point C is 0. To find the y-coordinate of C, substitute $x = 0$ in the equation of $\overleftrightarrow{QM}$ and solve for y.

Substitute $x = 0$. $y - \boxed{6a+2c} = \dfrac{\boxed{a} + \boxed{c}}{\boxed{b}} \cdot \left(0 - \boxed{2b}\right)$

Simplify the right side of the equation. $y - \boxed{6a+2c} = -2\boxed{a+c}$

Distributive property $y - \boxed{6a+2c} = -2\boxed{a} - 2\boxed{c}$

Add $6a + 2c$ to each side and simplify. $y = \boxed{4a}$

So, the coordinates of point C are $C\left(\boxed{0}, \boxed{4a}\right)$.

Now write the equation of $\overleftrightarrow{PL}$ using point-slope form.

The slope of $\overleftrightarrow{PL}$ is $\dfrac{(6a - 2c) - (3a + c)}{-2b - b} = \dfrac{3\boxed{a} - 3\boxed{c}}{-3\boxed{b}} = \dfrac{\boxed{a} - \boxed{c}}{-\boxed{b}}$.

Use the coordinates of point P for the point on $\overleftrightarrow{PL}$.

Therefore, the equation of $\overleftrightarrow{PL}$ is $y - \boxed{6a-2c} = \dfrac{\boxed{a} - \boxed{c}}{-\boxed{b}} \cdot \left(x + \boxed{2b}\right)$.

Finally, show that point C lies on $\overleftrightarrow{PL}$. To do so, show that when $x = 0$ in the equation for $\overleftrightarrow{PL}$, $y = 4a$.

Substitute $x = 0$.
$$y - \boxed{6a - 2c} = \frac{\boxed{a} - \boxed{c}}{-\boxed{b}} \cdot \left(0 + \boxed{2b}\right)$$

Simplify right side of equation.
$$y - \boxed{6a - 2c} = -2\boxed{a} + 2\boxed{c}$$

Add $6a - 2c$ to each side and simplify.
$$y = \boxed{4a}$$

Reflect

8. A student claims that the averages of the x-coordinates and of the y-coordinates of the vertices of the triangle are x- and y-coordinates of the point of concurrency, C. Does the coordinate proof of the Concurrency of Medians Theorem support the claim? Explain.
Yes. The x-coordinates of the vertices of the triangle are $-2b$, 0, and $2b$. The average of these coordinates is 0. The y-coordinates of the vertices of the triangle are $6a - 2c$, 0, and $6a + 2c$. The average of these coordinates is $4a$. These averages match the coordinates of point C, $(0, 4a)$.

⊘ Explain 4   Using Triangles on the Coordinate Plane

Example 4   Write each proof.

(A) **Given:** $A(2, 3)$, $B(5, -1)$, $C(1, 0)$, $D(-4, -1)$, $E(0, 2)$, $F(-1, -2)$

Prove: $\angle ABC \cong \angle DEF$

Step 1 Plot the points on a coordinate plane.

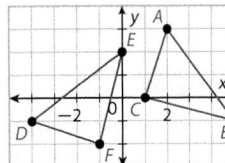

Step 2 Use the Distance Formula to find the length of each side of each triangle.

$$AB = \sqrt{(5 - 2)^2 + (-1 - 3)^2} = \sqrt{25} = 5; \quad BC = \sqrt{(1 - 5)^2 + 0 - (-1)^2} = \sqrt{17};$$

$$AC = \sqrt{(1 - 2)^2 + (0 - 3)^2} = \sqrt{10}; \quad DE = \sqrt{(0 - (-4))^2 + (2 - (-1))^2} = \sqrt{25} = 5;$$

$$EF = \sqrt{(-1 - 0)^2 + (-2 - 2)^2} = \sqrt{1 + 16} = \sqrt{17}; \quad DF = \sqrt{(-1 - (-4))^2 + (-2 - (-1))^2}$$

$$= \sqrt{9 + 1} = \sqrt{10}$$

So, $\overline{AB} \cong \overline{DE}$, $\overline{BC} \cong \overline{EF}$, and $\overline{AC} \cong \overline{DF}$. Therefore, $\triangle ABC \cong \triangle DEF$ by the SSS Triangle Congruence Theorem and $\angle ABC \cong \angle DEF$ by CPCTC.

© Houghton Mifflin Harcourt Publishing Company

Using Triangles on the Coordinate Plane

VISUAL CUES

Sometimes students confuse the distance formula and the midpoint formula because the distance formula involves finding the differences of two x- and two y-coordinates and the midpoint formula involves finding their sum. Ask students to write and label the two formulas on a sheet of construction paper. Then have them use color or another technique to emphasize that the distance formula uses the difference of coordinates and the midpoint formula uses sums.

Ⓑ **Given:** $J(-4, 1)$, $K(0, 5)$, $L(3, 1)$, $M(-1, -3)$, R is the midpoint of $\overline{JK}$, S is the midpoint of $\overline{LM}$.

Prove: $\angle JSK \cong \angle LRM$

Step 1 Plot the points on a coordinate plane.

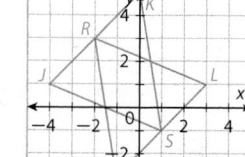

Step 2 Use the Midpoint Formula to find the coordinates of R and S.

$$R\left(\frac{\boxed{-4} + \boxed{0}}{2}, \frac{\boxed{1} + \boxed{5}}{2}\right) = R\left(\boxed{-2}, \boxed{3}\right)$$

$$S\left(\frac{\boxed{3} + \boxed{-1}}{2}, \frac{\boxed{1} + \boxed{-3}}{2}\right) = S\left(\boxed{1}, \boxed{-1}\right)$$

Step 3 Use the Distance Formula to find the length of each side of each triangle.

$$JK = \sqrt{\left(0 - (-4)\right)^2 + (5 - 1)^2} = \sqrt{16 + 16} = \sqrt{32}$$

$$KS = \sqrt{\left(\boxed{1} - 0\right)^2 + \left(\boxed{-1} - 5\right)^2} = \sqrt{\boxed{1} + \boxed{36}} = \sqrt{\boxed{37}}$$

$$JS = \sqrt{\left(\boxed{1} - (-4)\right)^2 + \left(\boxed{-1} - 1\right)^2} = \sqrt{\boxed{25} + \boxed{4}} = \sqrt{\boxed{29}}$$

$$LM = \sqrt{(-1 - 3)^2 + (-3 - 1)^2} = \sqrt{16 + 16} = \sqrt{32}$$

$$MR = \sqrt{\left(\boxed{-2} - (-1)\right)^2 + \left(\boxed{3} - (-3)\right)^2} = \sqrt{\boxed{1} + \boxed{36}} = \sqrt{\boxed{37}}$$

$$LR = \sqrt{\left(\boxed{-2} - 3\right)^2 + \left(\boxed{3} - 1\right)^2} = \sqrt{\boxed{25} + \boxed{4}} = \sqrt{\boxed{29}}$$

So, $\overline{JK} \cong \boxed{\overline{LM}}$, $\overline{KS} \cong \boxed{\overline{MR}}$, and $\overline{JS} \cong \boxed{\overline{LR}}$. Therefore, $\triangle JKS \cong \boxed{\triangle LMR}$ by the SSS Triangle Congruence Theorem and $\angle JSK \cong \angle LRM$ since __corresponding parts of congruent triangles are congruent__.

Reflect

9. In Part B, what other pairs of angles can you prove to be congruent? Why?
   $\angle JKS \cong \angle LMR$ and $\angle KJS \cong \angle MLR$ because these are corresponding parts of congruent triangles.

Your Turn

Write each proof.

10. Given: $A(-4, -2), B(-3, 2), C(-1, 3), D(-5, 0), E(-1, -1), F(0, -3)$
Prove: $\angle BCA \cong \angle EFD$

By the Distance Formula, $AB = \sqrt{17}, BC = \sqrt{5}, AC = \sqrt{34}, DE = \sqrt{17}, EF = \sqrt{5},$

$DF = \sqrt{34}$. So, $\overline{AB} \cong \overline{DE}, \overline{BC} \cong \overline{EF}$, and $\overline{AC} \cong \overline{DF}$. Therefore, $\triangle ABC \cong \triangle DEF$ by the

SSS Triangle Congruence Theorem and $\angle BCA \cong \angle EFD$ since corresponding parts of

congruent triangles are congruent.

11. Given: $P(-3, 5), Q(-1, -1), R(4, 5), S(2, -1)$, M is the midpoint of $\overline{PQ}$, N is the midpoint of $\overline{RS}$.
Prove: $\angle PQN \cong \angle RSM$

By the Midpoint Formula, the coordinates of M are $M\left(\frac{-3+(-1)}{2}, \frac{5+(-1)}{2}\right) = M(-2, 2)$ and

the coordinates of N are $N\left(\frac{4+2}{2}, \frac{5+(-1)}{2}\right) = N(3, 2)$.

By the Distance Formula, $PQ = \sqrt{40}, QN = 5, PN = \sqrt{45}, RS = \sqrt{40}, SM = 5, RM = \sqrt{45}$.

So, $\overline{PQ} \cong \overline{RS}, \overline{QN} \cong \overline{SM}$, and $\overline{PN} \cong \overline{RM}$. Therefore, $\triangle PQN \cong \triangle RSM$ by the SSS Triangle

Congruence Theorem and $\angle PQN \cong \angle RSM$ since corresponding parts of congruent triangles

are congruent.

Elaborate

12. When you write a coordinate proof, why might you assign $2p$ as a coordinate rather than p?
If the proof includes finding the midpoint of a segment, assigning the coordinate $2p$ might

make it possible to avoid fractions in the coordinates of the midpoint.

13. Essential Question Check-In What makes a coordinate proof different from the other types of proofs you have written so far?
A coordinate proof depends upon assigning coordinates to a figure and using coordinate

geometry and algebra to draw conclusions. Coordinate proofs often involve the Distance

Formula, the Midpoint Formula, and/or the Slope Formula.

ELABORATE

QUESTIONING STRATEGIES

Is it possible for the medians of a triangle to intersect at a point on the triangle? No; no matter the size or shape of the triangle, the medians always intersect in the interior of the triangle.

SUMMARIZE THE LESSON

Why are the distance formula and the midpoint formula important in using the triangle theorems in this lesson? The Midsegment Theorem and the Concurrency of Medians Theorem both use the lengths and midpoints of sides of triangles.

Coordinate Proof Using Distance with Segments and Triangles **530**

EVALUATE

ASSIGNMENT GUIDE

Concept and Skills	Practice
Explore Deriving the Distance Formula and the Midpoint Formula	Exercise 1
Example 1 Positioning a Triangle on the Coordinate Plane	Exercises 2–5
Example 2 Proving the Triangle Midsegment Theorem	Exercise 6
Example 3 Proving the Concurrency of Medians Theorem	Exercise 7
Example 4 Using Triangles on the Coordinate Plane	Exercises 8–11

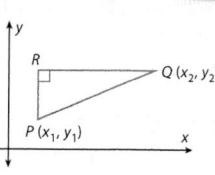 **Evaluate: Homework and Practice**

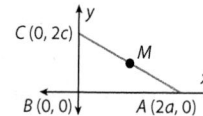

- Online Homework
- Hints and Help
- Extra Practice

1. Explain how to derive the Distance Formula using $\triangle PQR$.

   The coordinates of point R are $R(x_1, y_2)$.

   $PR = y_2 - y_1$ and $RQ = x_2 - x_1$

   $\triangle PQR$ is a right triangle with hypotenuse

   $\overline{PQ}$, $PQ^2 = RQ^2 + PR^2$

   By substitution, $PQ^2 = (x_2 - x_1)^2 + (y_2 - y_1)^2 = \sqrt{(x_2 - x_1)^2 + (y_2 - y_1)^2}$.

Write each coordinate proof.

2. **Given:** $\angle B$ is a right angle in $\triangle ABC$. M is the midpoint of $\overline{AC}$.

   Prove: M is equidistant from all three vertices of $\triangle ABC$.

   Use the coordinates that have been assigned in the figure.

   By the Midpoint Formula, the coordinates of M are $M\left(\dfrac{2a+0}{2}, \dfrac{0+2c}{2}\right) = M(a, c)$.

   Use the Distance Formula to find MA, MB, and MC.

   $MA = \sqrt{(2a - a)^2 + (0 - c)^2} = \sqrt{a^2 + c^2}$; $MB = \sqrt{(0 - a)^2 + (0 - c)^2} = \sqrt{a^2 + c^2}$

   $MC = \sqrt{(0 - a)^2 + (2c - c)^2} = \sqrt{a^2 + c^2}$

   Since $MA = MB = MC$, point M is equidistant from all three vertices of $\triangle ABC$.

3. **Given:** $\triangle ABC$ is isosceles. X is the midpoint of $\overline{AB}$, Y is the midpoint of $\overline{AC}$, Z is the midpoint of $\overline{BC}$.

   Prove: $\triangle XYZ$ is isosceles.

   Use the coordinates that have been assigned in the figure.

   By the Midpoint Formula, the coordinates of X, Y, and Z are as follows.

   $X\left(\dfrac{2a+0}{2}, \dfrac{2b+0}{2}\right) = X(a, b)$, $Y\left(\dfrac{2a+4a}{2}, \dfrac{2b+0}{2}\right) = Y(3a, b)$, $Z\left(\dfrac{0+4a}{2}, \dfrac{0+0}{2}\right) = Z(2a, 0)$

   By the Distance Formula, $XZ = \sqrt{(2a - a^2) + (0 - b^2)} = \sqrt{a^2 + b^2}$ and

   $YZ = \sqrt{(2a - 3a)^2 + (0 - b)^2} = \sqrt{a^2 + b^2}$.

   Since $XZ = YZ$, $\overline{XZ} \cong \overline{YZ}$ and $\triangle XYZ$ is isosceles.

Exercise	Depth of Knowledge (D.O.K.)	COMMON CORE Mathematical Practices
1–19	**2** Skills/Concepts	**MP.3** Logic
20	**2** Skills/Concepts	**MP.4** Modeling
21	**3** Strategic Thinking H.O.T.	**MP.2** Reasoning

4. Given: $\angle R$ is a right angle in $\triangle PQR$. A is the midpoint of $\overline{PR}$. B is the midpoint of $\overline{QR}$.

Prove: $\overline{AB}$ is parallel to $\overline{PQ}$.

Assign coordinates as shown in the figure.

By the Midpoint Formula, the coordinates of A and B are as follows.

$$A\left(\frac{0+2a}{2}, \frac{0+0}{2}\right) = A(a, 0), \quad B\left(\frac{0+0}{2}, \frac{0+2b}{2}\right) = B(0, b)$$

By the Slope Formula, the slope of $\overline{AB} = \frac{b-0}{0-a} = -\frac{b}{a}$ and the slope of $\overline{PQ} = \frac{2b-0}{0-2a} = -\frac{b}{a}$.

Since the slopes are the same, $\overline{AB}$ is parallel to $\overline{PQ}$.

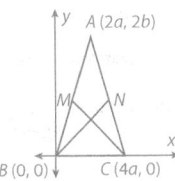

5. Given: $\triangle ABC$ is isosceles. M is the midpoint of $\overline{AB}$. N is the midpoint of $\overline{AC}$. $\overline{AB} \cong \overline{AC}$

Prove: $\overline{MC} \cong \overline{NB}$

Assign coordinates as shown in the figure.

By the Midpoint Formula, the coordinates of M and N are as follows.

$$M\left(\frac{0+2a}{2}, \frac{0+2b}{2}\right) = M(a, b); \quad N\left(\frac{2a+4a}{2}, \frac{2b+0}{2}\right) = N(3a, b)$$

By the Distance Formula, $MC = \sqrt{(4a-a)^2 + (0-b)^2} = \sqrt{9a^2 + b^2}$ and

$NB = \sqrt{(0-3a)^2 + (0-b)^2} = \sqrt{9a^2 + b^2}$, so $MC = NB$ and $\overline{MC} \cong \overline{NB}$.

6. Prove the Triangle Midsegment Theorem using the figure shown here.

Given: $\overline{DE}$ is a midsegment of $\triangle ABC$.

Prove: $\overline{DE} \parallel \overline{BC}$ and $DE = \frac{1}{2}BC$

By the Midpoint Formula, the coordinates of D and E are as follows.

$$D\left(\frac{2q+0}{2}, \frac{2r+0}{2}\right) = D(q, r); \quad E\left(\frac{2q+2p}{2}, \frac{2r+0}{2}\right) = E(q+p, r)$$

By the Slope Formula, the slope of $\overline{DE} = \frac{r-r}{q+p-q} = 0$ and the slope of $\overline{BC} = \frac{0-0}{2p-0} = 0$.

Since the slopes are the same, $\overline{DE} \parallel \overline{BC}$.

By the Distance Formula, $DE = \sqrt{(q+p-q)^2 + (r-r)^2} = \sqrt{p^2} = p$ and

$BC = \sqrt{(2p-0)^2 + (0-0)^2} = \sqrt{4p^2} = 2p$, so $DE = \frac{1}{2}BC$.

7. Critique Reasoning A student proves the Concurrency of Medians Theorem by first assigning coordinates to the vertices of $\triangle PQR$ as $P(0, 0)$, $Q(2a, 0)$, and $R(2a, 2c)$. The student says that this choice of coordinates makes the algebra in the proof a bit easier. Do you agree with the student's choice of coordinates? Explain.

No; these coordinates result in a triangle that is a right triangle, so the proof would not hold for triangles in general.

© Houghton Mifflin Harcourt Publishing Company

COGNITIVE STRATEGIES

Present the following statement:

Finding the midpoint of a segment is the same as averaging the x-coordinates and averaging the y-coordinates.

Is this a true statement? (yes) Suggest that the statement is a way to remember how to find the midpoint of a segment.

Write each proof.

8. **Given:** $J(-2, 2)$, $K(0, 1)$, $L(-3, -1)$, $P(4, -2)$, $Q(3, -4)$, $R(1, -1)$

   Prove: $\angle JKL \cong \angle PQR$

   $JK = \sqrt{5}$, $KL = \sqrt{13}$, $JL = \sqrt{10}$, $PQ = \sqrt{5}$, $QR = \sqrt{13}$, $PR = \sqrt{10}$.

   So, $\overline{JK} \cong \overline{PQ}$, $\overline{KL} \cong \overline{QR}$, and $\overline{JL} \cong \overline{PR}$. Therefore, $\triangle JKL \cong \triangle PQR$ by the

   SSS Triangle Congruence Theorem and $\angle JKL \cong \angle PQR$ since corresponding

   parts of congruent triangles are congruent.

9. **Given:** $D(-3, 2)$, $E(3, 3)$, $F(1, 1)$, $S(9, -2)$, $T(3, -1)$, $U(5, -3)$

   Prove: $\angle FDE \cong \angle UST$

   $DE = \sqrt{37}$, $EF = \sqrt{8}$, $DF = \sqrt{17}$, $ST = \sqrt{37}$, $TU = \sqrt{8}$, $SU = \sqrt{17}$.

   So, $\overline{DE} \cong \overline{ST}$, $\overline{EF} \cong \overline{TU}$, and $\overline{DF} \cong \overline{SU}$. Therefore, $\triangle DEF \cong \triangle STU$ by the

   SSS Triangle Congruence Theorem and $\angle FDE \cong \angle UST$ since corresponding

   parts of congruent triangles are congruent.

10. **Given:** $A(-2, 2)$, $B(4, 4)$, $M(-2, -1)$, $N(4, -3)$, X is the midpoint of $\overline{AB}$, Y is the midpoint of $\overline{MN}$.

    Prove: $\angle ABY \cong \angle MNX$

    The coordinates of X are $X\left(\dfrac{-2+4}{2}, \dfrac{2+4}{2}\right) = X(1, 3)$ and the coordinates of Y are $Y\left(\dfrac{-2+4}{2}, \dfrac{-1+(-3)}{2}\right) = Y(1, -2)$.

    $AB = \sqrt{40}$, $BY = \sqrt{45}$, $AY = 5$, $MN = \sqrt{40}$, $NX = \sqrt{45}$, $MX = 5$.

    So, $\overline{AB} \cong \overline{MN}$, $\overline{BY} \cong \overline{NX}$, and $\overline{AY} \cong \overline{MX}$. Therefore, $\triangle ABY \cong \triangle MNX$ by the

    SSS Triangle Congruence Theorem and $\angle ABY \cong \angle MNX$ since corresponding

    parts of congruent triangles are congruent.

11. **Given:** $J(-1, 4)$, $K(3, 0)$, $P(3, -6)$, $Q(-1, -2)$, U is the midpoint of $\overline{JK}$, V is the midpoint of $\overline{PQ}$.

    Prove: $\angle KVJ \cong \angle QUP$

    The coordinates of U are $U\left(\dfrac{-1+3}{2}, \dfrac{4+0}{2}\right) = U(1, 2)$ and the coordinates of V are $V\left(\dfrac{3+(-1)}{2}, \dfrac{-6+(-2)}{2}\right) = V(1, -4)$.

    $JK = \sqrt{32}$, $KV = \sqrt{20}$, $JV = \sqrt{68}$, $PQ = \sqrt{32}$, $QU = \sqrt{20}$, $PU = \sqrt{68}$.

    So, $\overline{JK} \cong \overline{PQ}$, $\overline{KV} \cong \overline{QU}$, and $\overline{JV} \cong \overline{PU}$. Therefore, $\triangle JKV \cong \triangle PQU$ by the

    SSS Triangle Congruence Theorem and $\angle KVJ \cong \angle QUP$ since corresponding

    parts of congruent triangles are congruent.

Prove or disprove each statement.

12. The triangle with vertices $R(-2, -2)$, $S(1, 4)$, and $T(4, -5)$ is an equilateral triangle.

$RS = \sqrt{45}$, $ST = \sqrt{90}$, and $RT = \sqrt{45}$. Since the three sides do not have the

same length, the triangle is not equilateral.

13. The triangle with vertices $J(-2, 2)$, $K(2, 3)$, and $L(-1, -2)$ is an isosceles triangle.

$JK = \sqrt{17}$, $KL = \sqrt{34}$, and $JL = \sqrt{17}$.

Since $\overline{JK}$ and $\overline{JL}$ have the same length, $\overline{JK} \cong \overline{JL}$, and therefore the triangle is isosceles.

14. The triangle with vertices $A(-1, 3)$, $B(2, 1)$, and $C(0, -2)$ is a scalene triangle.

$AB = \sqrt{13}$, $BC = \sqrt{13}$, and $AC = \sqrt{26}$.

Since $\overline{AB}$ and $\overline{BC}$ have the same length, $\overline{AB} \cong \overline{BC}$, and therefore the triangle is not a

scalene triangle.

15. Two container ships depart from a port at $P(20, 10)$. The first ship travels to a location at $A(-30, 50)$, and the second ship travels to a location at $B(70, -30)$. Each unit represents one nautical mile. Find the distance between the ships to the nearest nautical mile. Verify that the port is the midpoint between the two ships.

The distance between the ships is

$AB = \sqrt{16400} \approx 128$ nautical miles.

$AP = \sqrt{4100} \approx 64$ nautical miles and

$BP = \sqrt{4100} \approx 64$ nautical miles. Since $AP = BP = \frac{1}{2}AB$,

P is the midpoint of $\overline{AB}$.

16. The support structure for a hammock includes a triangle whose vertices have coordinates $G(-1, 3)$, $H(-3, -2)$, and $J(1, -2)$.

a. Classify the triangle and justify your answer.

$GH = \sqrt{29}$, $HJ = 4$, and $GJ = \sqrt{29}$.

Since two sides of the triangle have the same length, the triangle is isosceles.

b. **Algebra** Each unit of the coordinate plane represents one foot. To the nearest tenth of a foot, how much metal is needed to make one of the triangular parts for the support structure?

The perimeter of $\triangle GHJ$ is $GH + HJ + GJ = \sqrt{29} + 4 + \sqrt{29} \approx 14.8$

so approximately 14.8 feet of metal are needed for the triangular part.

Coordinate Proof Using Distance with Segments and Triangles   **534**

Have students describe strategies for positioning a triangle on a coordinate plane.

17. **Communicate Mathematical Ideas** Explain how the perimeter of $\triangle JKL$ compares to the perimeter of $\triangle MNP$.

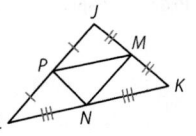

$\overline{PM}$, $\overline{MN}$, and $\overline{NP}$ are midsegments of $\triangle JKL$. By the Triangle Midsegment Theorem, $PM = \frac{1}{2}LK$, $MN = \frac{1}{2}JL$, and $NP = \frac{1}{2}KJ$. $PM + MN + NP = \frac{1}{2}(LK + JL + KJ)$, so the perimeter of $\triangle JKL$ is twice the perimeter of $\triangle MNP$.

18. The coordinates of the vertices of $\triangle LMN$ are shown in the figure. Determine whether each statement is true or false. Select the correct answer for each lettered part.

   a. $\triangle LMN$ is isosceles. **True** ○ False

   b. One side of $\triangle LMN$ has a length of $2c$ units. ○ True **False**

   c. If P is the midpoint of $\overline{LN}$, then $\overline{OP}$ is parallel to $\overline{LM}$. **True** ○ False

   d. The area of $\triangle LMN$ is $4cd$ square units. ○ True **False**

   e. The midpoint of $\overline{MN}$ is the origin. **True** ○ False

   a. **True; By the Distance Formula**, $LM = \sqrt{(-2c - 0)^2 + (0 - d)^2} = \sqrt{4c^2 + d^2}$, $MN = \sqrt{(2c - (-2c))^2 + (0 - 0)^2} = \sqrt{16c^2} = 4c$, and $LN = \sqrt{(2c - 0)^2 + (0 - d)^2} = \sqrt{4c^2 + d^2}$. Since two sides have the same length, $\triangle LMN$ is isosceles.

   b. **False; By the Distance Formula**, $LM = \sqrt{(-2c - 0)^2 + (0 - d)^2} = \sqrt{4c^2 + d^2}$, $MN = \sqrt{(2c - (-2c))^2 + (0 - 0)^2} = \sqrt{16c^2} = 4c$, and $LN = \sqrt{(-2c - 0)^2 + (0 - d)^2} = \sqrt{4c^2 + d^2}$. There is no side with a length of $2c$ units.

   c. **True.** By the Midpoint Formula, the coordinates of P are $P\left(\frac{0 + 2c}{2}, \frac{0 + d}{2}\right) = P\left(c, \frac{d}{2}\right)$. By the Slope Formula, the slope of $\overline{OP} = \frac{\frac{d}{2} - 0}{c - 0} = \frac{d}{2c}$ and the slope of $\overline{LM} = \frac{0 - d}{-2c - 0} = \frac{d}{2c}$. Since the slopes are the same, $\overline{OP}$ is parallel to $\overline{LM}$.

   d. **False; The base** of $\triangle LMN$ is $4c$ units and the height is d units. The area of $\triangle LMN$ is $\frac{1}{2}bh = \frac{1}{2} \cdot 4c \cdot d = 2cd$.

   e. **True.** By the Midpoint Formula, the midpoint of $\overline{MN}$ has coordinates $\left(\frac{-2c + 2c}{2}, \frac{0 + 0}{2}\right) = (0, 0)$, which is the origin.

H.O.T. Focus on Higher Order Thinking

19. **Explain the Error** A student assigns coordinates to a right triangle as shown in the figure. Then he uses the Distance Formula to show that $PQ = a$ and $RQ = a$. Since $PQ = RQ$, the student says he has proved that every right triangle is isosceles. Explain the error in the student's proof.

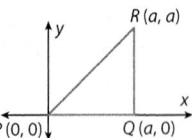

   The proof is incorrect because the assigned coordinates do not result in a general right triangle. For a general right triangle, the coordinates of R should be (a, b).

20. A carpenter wants to make a triangular bracket to hold up a bookshelf. The plan for the bracket shows that the vertices of the triangle are $R(-2, 2)$, $S(1, 4)$, and $T(1, -2)$. Can the carpenter conclude that the bracket is a right triangle? Explain.

No. The slope of $\overline{RS} = \frac{4-2}{1-(-2)} = \frac{2}{3}$, the slope of $\overline{ST} = \frac{-2-4}{1-1}$, which is

undefined, and the slope of $\overline{RT} = \frac{-2-2}{1-(-2)} = -\frac{4}{3}$. There are no two sides for

which the product of the slopes is -1, so no two sides are perpendicular.

This means the triangle is not a right triangle.

21. Analyze Relationships The vertices chosen to represent an isosceles right triangle for a coordinate proof are at $(-2s, 2s)$, $(0, 2s)$, and $(0, 0)$. What other coordinates could be used so that the coordinate proof would be easier to complete? Explain.

Possible answer: A right triangle with the same side lengths can be placed so that the

coordinates are $(0, 0)$, $(0, 2s)$ and $(4s, 0)$. This results in an easier coordinate proof

since there are no negative coordinates and more of the coordinates are 0. If the

proof does not involve midpoints, an even easier choice is $(0, 0)$, $(0, s)$, and $(2s, 0)$.

Lesson Performance Task

A triathlon course was mapped on a coordinate grid marked in 1-kilometer units. The starting point was $(0, 0)$. The triathlon was broken into three stages:

- Stage 1: Contestants swim from $(0, 0)$ to $(0.6, 0.8)$.
- Stage 2: Contestants bicycle from the previous stopping point to $(30.6, 16.8)$.
- Stage 3: Contestants run from the previous stopping point to $(25.6, 28.8)$.

The winner averaged 4 kilometers per hour for Stage 1, 50 kilometers per hour for Stage 2, and 13 kilometers per hour for Stage 3. What was the winner's time for the entire race? (Assume that no time elapsed between stages.) Explain how you found the answer.

Using the Distance Formula, Stage 1 was 1 kilometer in length. At a rate of

4 kilometers per hour, the winner needed 0.25 hour to complete the stage.

Stage 2 ran from $(0.6, 0.8)$ to $(30.6, 16.8)$. Using the Distance Formula, Stage 2

was 34 kilometers in length. At a rate of 50 kilometers per hour, the winner

needed $\frac{34}{50} = 0.68$ hour to complete the stage. Stage 3 ran from $(30.6, 16.8)$ to

$(25.6, 28.8)$. Using the Distance Formula, Stage 3 was 13 kilometers in length.

At a rate of 13 kilometers per hour, the winner needed 1 hour to complete the

stage. Total time: $0.25 + 0.68 + 1 = 1.93$ hours.

CONNECT VOCABULARY **EL**

The word *triathlon* is derived from the Greek word *tri*, which means three, and *athlon*, which means contest.

AVOID COMMON ERRORS

To solve each of the three parts of the Lesson Performance Task, students use the distance formula to find a distance. They are then given the rate of speed for that stage of the triathlon and must calculate the length of time the contestant needed to complete that stage. To help students avoid errors in calculating the time, urge them to start with the basic relationship between distance, rate, and time: $d = rt$. So, for 34-kilometer Stage 2, completed at a rate of 50 kilometers per hour:

$$d = rt$$

$$34 = 50t$$

$$\frac{34}{50} = t$$

$$0.68 = t$$

EXTENSION ACTIVITY

Explain how a 3–4–5 triangle can be used to find the lengths of the legs of any right triangle with a hypotenuse that is divisible by 5. For example, if the hypotenuse measures 30, which equals 6×5, the legs must measure $6 \times 3 = 18$ and $6 \times 4 = 24$. Have students draw a triathlon course on a coordinate grid. The 1.5-kilometer swim begins at $(0, 0)$. The 40-kilometer bike ride starts where the swim ends. The 10-kilometer run begins where the bike ride ends. The length of each section is divisible by 5, so students can use that distance as the hypotenuse, calculate the lengths of the legs of right triangles, and draw them to find where each event ends. Possible answer: $(1.2, 0.9)$, $(33.2, 24.9)$, and $(41.2, 30.9)$

Scoring Rubric

2 points: Student correctly solves the problem and explains his/her reasoning.

1 point: Student shows good understanding of the problem but does not fully solve or explain.

0 points: Student does not demonstrate understanding of the problem.

Coordinate Proof Using Distance with Quadrilaterals

Common Core Math Standards

The student is expected to:

 G-CO.C.11

Prove theorems about parallelograms. Also G-GPE.B.4, G-GPE.B.5

Mathematical Practices

MP.6 Precision

Language Objective

Explain in your own words how to prove that a quadrilateral on a coordinate plane is a rectangle.

ENGAGE

Essential Question: How can you use slope and the distance formula in coordinate proofs?

You can use the slope to show that opposite sides of a quadrilateral have the same slope and are parallel. You can also use slope to show that adjacent sides of a quadrilateral are perpendicular if the product of their slopes is −1. You can use the distance formula to find the lengths of diagonals and sides of quadrilaterals to show congruence.

PREVIEW: LESSON PERFORMANCE TASK

View the Engage section online. Discuss the photo. Connect the photo to the Lesson Performance Task by mentioning that the task will show how "orderly" congruent line segments can be found inside a figure composed of "disorderly" line segments of different lengths. Then preview the Lesson Performance Task.

Name_____ Class_____ Date_____

10.4 Coordinate Proof Using Distance with Quadrilaterals

Essential Question: How can you use slope and the distance formula in coordinate proofs?

Resource Locker

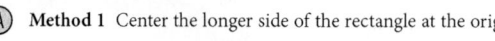 **Positioning a Quadrilateral on the Coordinate Plane**

You have used coordinate geometry to find the midpoint of a line segment and to find the distance between two points. Coordinate geometry can also be used to prove conjectures.

Remember that in Lesson 10.3 you learned several strategies that make using a coordinate proof simpler. They are:

- Use the origin as a vertex, keeping the figure in Quadrant I.
- Center the figure at the origin.
- Center a side of the figure at the origin.
- Use one or both axes as sides of the figure.

Position a rectangle with a length of 8 units and a width of 3 units in the coordinate plane as described.

(A) **Method 1** Center the longer side of the rectangle at the origin.

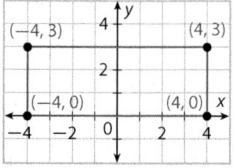

(B) **Method 2** Use the origin as a vertex of the rectangle.
Depending on what you are using the figure to prove, one method may be better than the other. For example, if you need to find the midpoint of the longer side, use the first method.

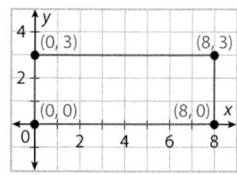

A coordinate proof can also be used to prove that a certain relationship is always true. You can prove that a statement is true for all right triangles without knowing the side lengths. To do this, assign variables as the coordinates of the vertices.

Position a square, with side lengths 2a, on a coordinate plane and give the coordinates of each vertex.

(C) Sketch the square. Label the side lengths.

Possible answer: Position the square so that one side is on the x-axis and another side is on the y-axis.

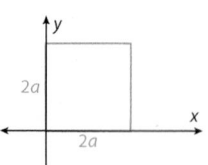

Module 10 | 537 | Lesson 4

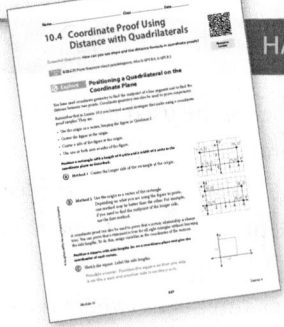

HARDCOVER PAGES 457–464

Turn to these pages to find this lesson in the hardcover student edition.

© Houghton Mifflin Harcourt Publishing Company

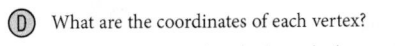

Ⓓ What are the coordinates of each vertex?

The vertices are $(0, 0)$, $(0, 2a)$, $(2a, 2a)$, and $(2a, 0)$.

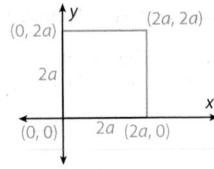

Reflect

1. **Discussion** Describe another way you could have positioned the square and give the coordinates of its vertices.
   Possible answer: You could have positioned the square so that $(0, 0)$ was the midpoint of
   one side. Then the coordinates of its vertices would be $(-a, 0)$, $(-a, a)$, (a, a), and $(a, 0)$.

2. When writing a coordinate proof why are variables used instead of numbers as coordinates for the vertices of a figure?
   Possible answer: By using variables, your results are not limited to specific numbers.

🕐 Explain 1 Proving Properties of a Parallelogram

You have already used the Distance Formula and the Midpoint Formula in coordinate proofs. As you will see, slope is useful in coordinate proofs whenever you need to show that lines are parallel or perpendicular.

Example 1 Prove or disprove that the quadrilateral determined by the points $A(4, 4)$, $B(3, 1)$, $C(-2, -1)$, and $D(-1, 2)$ is a parallelogram.

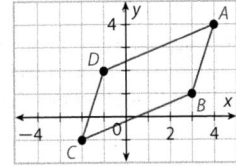

Ⓐ Use slopes to write the coordinate proof.

To determine whether $ABCD$ is a parallelogram, find the slope of each side of the quadrilateral.

Slope of $\overline{AB} = \frac{y_2 - y_1}{x_2 - x_1} = \frac{1 - 4}{3 - 4} = \frac{-3}{-1} = 3$; Slope of $\overline{BC} = \frac{y_2 - y_1}{x_2 - x_1} = \frac{-1 - 1}{-2 - 3} = \frac{-2}{-5} = \frac{2}{5}$;

Slope of $\overline{CD} = \frac{y_2 - y_1}{x_2 - x_1} = \frac{2 - (-1)}{-1 - (-2)} = \frac{3}{1} = 3$; Slope of $\overline{DA} = \frac{y_2 - y_1}{x_2 - x_1} = \frac{4 - 2}{4 - (-1)} = \frac{2}{5}$

Compare slopes. The slopes of opposite sides are equal. This means opposite sides are parallel. So, quadrilateral $ABCD$ is a parallelogram.

© Houghton Mifflin Harcourt Publishing Company

EXPLORE

Positioning a Quadrilateral on the Coordinate Plane

INTEGRATE TECHNOLOGY

Students have the option of completing the Explore activity either in the book or online.

QUESTIONING STRATEGIES

? Are rectangles the only quadrilaterals that you can position with a side on each of the axes?

No, you can position any quadrilateral that contains at least one right angle so that two of its sides are on an axis.

EXPLAIN 1

Proving Properties of a Parallelogram

AVOID COMMON ERRORS

Advise students to pay close attention to the markings on a diagram, especially when writing a proof. Some quadrilaterals have only one set of parallel lines; these are not parallelograms.

PROFESSIONAL DEVELOPMENT

Math Background

Analytic geometry is the study of geometry using a coordinate system. Although certain aspects of the subject date to ancient times, the French mathematician René Descartes (1596–1650) is traditionally considered the father of analytic geometry. The strength of analytic geometry lies in its use of tools from algebra to solve geometry problems. In particular, this lesson shows how it is possible to use a Cartesian coordinate system to classify quadrilaterals.

How could you use triangles in trying to prove properties of quadrilaterals? You can divide a quadrilateral into triangles and then use triangle congruence to show that angles, sides, or diagonals of a quadrilateral are congruent.

Ⓑ Use the Distance Formula to write the coordinate proof.

To determine whether $ABCD$ is a parallelogram, find the length of each side of the quadrilateral. Remember that the Distance Formula is length $= \sqrt{(x_2-x_1)^2+(y_2-y_1)^2}$.

$$AB = \sqrt{\left(\boxed{3} - 4\right)^2 + (1 - 4)^2}$$
$$= \sqrt{(-1)^2 + \boxed{-3}^2}$$
$$= \sqrt{\boxed{10}}$$

$$BC = \sqrt{\left(-2 - \boxed{3}\right)^2 + \left(\boxed{-1} - 1\right)^2}$$
$$= \sqrt{(-5)^2 + \boxed{-2}^2}$$
$$= \sqrt{\boxed{29}}$$

$$CD = \sqrt{\left(-1 - \boxed{-2}\right)^2 + \left(\boxed{2} - (-1)\right)^2}$$
$$= \sqrt{(1)^2 + \boxed{3}^2}$$
$$= \sqrt{\boxed{10}}$$

$$DA = \sqrt{\left(4 - \boxed{-1}\right)^2 + \left(4 - \boxed{2}\right)^2}$$
$$= \sqrt{\boxed{5}^2 + \boxed{2}^2}$$
$$= \sqrt{\boxed{29}}$$

Compare the side lengths. The lengths of the opposite sides are _equal_. By the _Opposites Sides Criterion for a Parallelogram_, we can conclude that $ABCD$ is a _parallelogram_.

Reflect

3. Suppose you want to prove that a general parallelogram $WXYZ$ has diagonals that bisect each other. Why is it convenient to use general vertex coefficients, such as $2a$ and $2b$?

   To prove that the diagonals bisect each other, you can show that the diagonals share the same midpoint. Because the midpoint formula involves dividing by 2, if the vertices have a coefficient of 2, then the result will be a whole number.

Your Turn

Write a coordinate proof given quadrilateral $ABCD$ with vertices $A(3, 2)$, $B(8, 2)$, $C(5, 0)$, and $D(0, 0)$.

4. Prove that $ABCD$ is a parallelogram.

   Possible answer: $AB = \sqrt{(8-3)^2 + (2-2)^2} = 5$; $DC = \sqrt{(5-0)^2 + (0-0)^2} = 5$
   $AD = \sqrt{(3-0)^2 + (2-0)^2} = \sqrt{13}$; $BC = \sqrt{(8-5)^2 + (2-0)^2} = \sqrt{13}$

   Since the opposite sides have the same lengths, $ABCD$ is a parallelogram.

5. Prove that the diagonals of $ABCD$ bisect each other.

   Show that the diagonals share the same midpoint.

   Midpoint of $\overline{DB}$: $\left(\dfrac{0+8}{2}, \dfrac{0+2}{2}\right) = (4, 1)$. **Midpoint of $\overline{AC}$:** $\left(\dfrac{3+5}{2}, \dfrac{2+0}{2}\right) = (4, 1)$.

   Since the diagonals share a midpoint, they bisect each other.

COLLABORATIVE LEARNING

Small Group Activity

Divide students into groups. Have each student draw a rectangle, a rhombus, and a square on a coordinate plane. Then have students trade drawings and use coordinate proofs to verify the properties of rectangles and rhombuses from the theorems they have learned.

Proving Conditions for Special Parallelograms

Example 2 Prove or disprove each statement about the quadrilateral determined
by the points $Q(2, -3)$, $R(-4, 0)$, $S(-2, 4)$, and $T(4, 1)$.

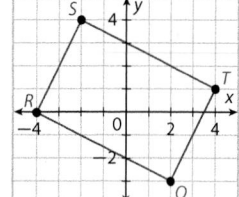

Ⓐ The diagonals of $QRST$ are congruent.

The length of $\overline{SQ} = \sqrt{\left(2 - (-2)\right)^2 + (-3 - 4)^2} = \sqrt{65}$.

The length of $\overline{RT} = \sqrt{(-4 - 4)^2 + (0 - 1)^2} = \sqrt{65}$.

So, the diagonals of $QRST$ are congruent.

Ⓑ $QRST$ is a rectangle.

Find the slope of each side of the quadrilateral.

Slope of $\overline{QR} = \dfrac{y_2 - y_1}{x_2 - x_1} = \dfrac{0 - (-3)}{-4 - 2} = \dfrac{3}{-6} = -\dfrac{1}{2}$; Slope of $\overline{RS} = \dfrac{y_2 - y_1}{x_2 - x_1} = \dfrac{\boxed{4} - \boxed{0}}{\boxed{-2} - \boxed{-4}} = \dfrac{\boxed{4}}{\boxed{2}} = \boxed{2}$;

Slope of $\overline{ST} = \dfrac{y_2 - y_1}{x_2 - x_1} = \dfrac{\boxed{1} - \boxed{4}}{\boxed{4} - \boxed{-2}} = \dfrac{\boxed{-3}}{\boxed{6}} = \boxed{-\dfrac{1}{2}}$;

Slope of $\overline{TQ} = \dfrac{y_2 - y_1}{x_2 - x_1} = \dfrac{\boxed{-3} - \boxed{1}}{\boxed{2} - \boxed{4}} = \dfrac{\boxed{-4}}{\boxed{-2}} = \boxed{2}$

Find the products of the slopes of adjacent sides.

$\left(\text{slope of } \overline{QR}\right)\left(\text{slope of } \overline{RS}\right) = \boxed{-\dfrac{1}{2}} \cdot \boxed{2} = \boxed{-1}$; $\left(\text{slope of } \overline{RS}\right)\left(\text{slope of } \overline{ST}\right) = \boxed{2} \cdot \boxed{-\dfrac{1}{2}} = \boxed{-1}$;

$\left(\text{slope of } \overline{ST}\right)\left(\text{slope of } \overline{TQ}\right) = \boxed{-\dfrac{1}{2}} \cdot \boxed{2} = \boxed{-1}$; $\left(\text{slope of } \overline{TQ}\right)\left(\text{slope of } \overline{QR}\right) = \boxed{2} \cdot \boxed{-\dfrac{1}{2}} = \boxed{-1}$

You can conclude that adjacent sides are __perpendicular__ . So, quadrilateral $QRST$ is a __rectangle__ .

Reflect

6. Explain how to prove that $QRST$ is not a square.
   Use the Distance Formula to compare adjacent sides; because the sides are not all

   congruent, $QRST$ is not a square.

© Houghton Mifflin Harcourt Publishing Company

EXPLAIN 2

Proving Conditions for Special Parallelograms

INTEGRATE MATHEMATICAL PRACTICES
Focus on Communication

MP.3 Look through magazines or books to find pictures of rectangles, rhombuses, and squares. Group the pictures based on the type of figure. Then show the pictures to the class and ask students to describe the identifying characteristics of each type of figure.

QUESTIONING STRATEGIES

❓ What must you show to prove that a quadrilateral is a rectangle? How can you show this? Show that the quadrilateral has four right angles (that is, that adjacent sides are perpendicular); show that the product of the slopes of adjacent sides is −1.

DIFFERENTIATE INSTRUCTION

Visual Cues

Have students draw a rectangle, a square, and a non-rectangular parallelogram. Then have them use colored pencils to mark the diagonals as bisected, congruent, and/or perpendicular.

EXPLAIN 3

Identifying Figures on the Coordinate Plane

VISUAL CUES

Students often confuse the relationships between diagonals of different types of special parallelograms. Have them review how diagonals can be used to classify rectangles, rhombuses, and squares.

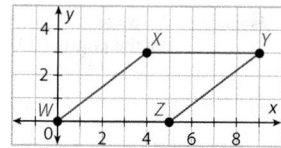

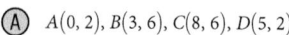

Your Turn

Prove or disprove each statement about quadrilateral WXYZ determined by the points $W(0, 0)$, $X(4, 3)$, $Y(9, 3)$, and $Z(5, 0)$.

7. WXYZ is a rhombus.

$$WX = \sqrt{(4-0)^2 + (3-0)^2} = \sqrt{25} = 5$$
$$XY = \sqrt{(9-4)^2 + (3-3)^2} = \sqrt{25} = 5$$
$$YZ = \sqrt{(5-9)^2 + (0-3)^2} = \sqrt{25} = 5$$
$$ZW = \sqrt{(0-5)^2 + (0-0)^2} = \sqrt{25} = 5$$

Since all four sides have the same length, WXYZ is a rhombus.

8. The diagonals of WXYZ are perpendicular.

Slope of $\overline{WY} = \dfrac{3-0}{9-0} = \dfrac{1}{3}$

Slope of $\overline{XZ} = \dfrac{0-3}{5-4} = \dfrac{-3}{1}$

$\left(\text{Slope of } \overline{WY}\right)\left(\text{Slope of } \overline{XZ}\right) = \dfrac{1}{3} \cdot \dfrac{-3}{1} = -1$

So, $\overline{WY}$ is perpendicular to $\overline{XZ}$.

⚙ Explain 3 Identifying Figures on the Coordinate Plane

Example 3 Use the diagonals to determine whether a parallelogram with the given vertices is a rectangle, rhombus, or square. Give all the names that apply.

Ⓐ $A(0, 2)$, $B(3, 6)$, $C(8, 6)$, $D(5, 2)$

Step 1 Graph ABCD.

Step 2 Determine if ABCD is a rectangle.

$$AC = \sqrt{(8-0)^2 + (6-2)^2} = \sqrt{80} = 4\sqrt{5}$$
$$BD = \sqrt{(5-3)^2 + (2-6)^2} = \sqrt{20} = 2\sqrt{5}$$

Since $4\sqrt{5} \neq 2\sqrt{5}$, ABCD is not a rectangle. Thus, ABCD is not a square.

Step 3 Determine if ABCD is a rhombus.

Slope of $\overline{AC} = \dfrac{6-2}{8-0} = \dfrac{1}{2}$

Slope of $\overline{BD} = \dfrac{2-6}{5-3} = -2$

Since $\left(\dfrac{1}{2}\right)(-2) = -1$, $\overline{AC} \perp \overline{BD}$. ABCD is a rhombus.

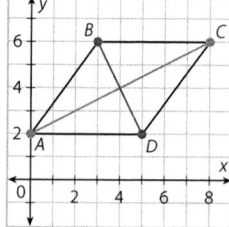

© Houghton Mifflin Harcourt Publishing Company

LANGUAGE SUPPORT EL

Connect Vocabulary

Students have been working on the coordinate plane in both algebra and geometry. Make sure they understand what is meant by *plane figures* and by a *coordinate plane*, and how these meanings of *plane* are different from everyday English uses of the word (such as the noun *plane* meaning *airplane*, or the verb *plane*, meaning *to level or smooth a wood surface*).

(B) $E(-4, -1)$, $F(-3, 2)$, $G(3, 0)$, $H(2, -3)$

Step 1 Graph *EFGH*.

Step 2 Determine if *EFGH* is a rectangle.

$$EG = \sqrt{\left(3 - \boxed{-4}\right)^2 + \left(0 - \boxed{-1}\right)^2} = \sqrt{\boxed{50}} = \boxed{5\sqrt{2}}$$

$$FH = \sqrt{\left(\boxed{2} - (-3)\right)^2 + \left(\boxed{-3} - 2\right)^2} = \sqrt{\boxed{50}} = 5\sqrt{\boxed{2}}$$

Since $\boxed{5\sqrt{2}} = 5\sqrt{\boxed{2}}$, the diagonals are ___congruent___. *EFGH* ___is___ a rectangle.

Step 3 Determine if *EFGH* is a rhombus.

Slope of $\overline{EG} = \dfrac{0 - (-1)}{3 - (-4)} = \dfrac{1}{7}$; Slope of $\overline{FH} = \dfrac{-3 - 2}{2 - (-3)} = \dfrac{-5}{5} = -1$

Since $\left(\dfrac{1}{7}\right)(-1) \neq -1$, $\overline{EG}$ is ___not perpendicular___ to $\overline{FH}$. So, *EFGH* is not a rhombus and cannot be a ___square___.

Your Turn

Use the diagonals to determine whether a parallelogram with the given vertices is a rectangle, rhombus, or square. Give all the names that apply.

9. $K(-5, -1)$, $L(-2, 4)$, $M(3, 1)$, $N(0, -4)$

$LN = \sqrt{\left(0 - (-2)\right)^2 + (-4 - 4)^2} = 2\sqrt{17}$

$KM = \sqrt{\left(3 - (-5)\right)^2 + \left(1 - (-1)\right)^2} = 2\sqrt{17}$

Since $2\sqrt{17} = 2\sqrt{17}$, the diagonals are congruent; *KLMN* is a rectangle.

Slope of $\overline{LN} = \dfrac{-4 - 4}{0 - (-2)} = \dfrac{-4}{1}$

Slope of $\overline{KM} = \dfrac{1 - (-1)}{3 - (-5)} = \dfrac{1}{4}$

Since $\left(\dfrac{-4}{1}\right)\left(\dfrac{1}{4}\right) = -1$, the diagonals are perpendicular; *KLMN* is a rhombus.

Since *KLMN* is both a rectangle and a rhombus, it is also a square.

10. $P(-4, 6)$, $Q(2, 5)$, $R(3, -1)$, $S(-3, 0)$

$PR = \sqrt{\left(3 - (-4)\right)^2 + (-1 - 6)^2} = 7\sqrt{2}$

$QS = \sqrt{(-3 - 2)^2 + (0 - 5)^2} = 5\sqrt{2}$

Since $7\sqrt{2} \neq 5\sqrt{2}$, the diagonals are not congruent. So *PQRS* is not a rectangle, and thus not a square.

Slope of $\overline{PR} = \dfrac{-1 - 6}{3 - (-4)} = -1$

Slope of $\overline{QS} = \dfrac{0 - 5}{-3 - 2} = 1$

Since $(-1)(1) = -1$, the diagonals are perpendicular, so *PQRS* is a rhombus.

💬 **Elaborate**

11. How can you use slopes to show that two line segments are parallel? Perpendicular?
___Parallel lines have the same slopes. Perpendicular lines have slopes that are opposite inverses, so when you multiply them, the product will be −1.___

12. When you use the distance formula, you find the square root of a value. When finding the square root of a value, you must consider both the positive and negative outcomes. Explain why the negative outcome is not used in the coordinate proofs in the lesson.
___Length is always a positive number, so the negative result of evaluating the square root does not apply to the situation.___

QUESTIONING STRATEGIES

? How are the slopes of the sides of rectangles related? **Opposite sides have equal slopes, adjacent sides have slopes with a product of −1.**

ELABORATE

QUESTIONING STRATEGIES

? Can you place a rhombus on a coordinate plane so that one side is on the *x*-axis and one side is on the *y*-axis? **only if the rhombus is a square**

SUMMARIZE THE LESSON

? How can you use slope in coordinate proofs involving quadrilaterals? **You can use slope to show that opposite sides of a quadrilateral have the same slope, and are therefore parallel. You can also use slope to show that the product of the slopes of any pair of adjacent sides of a quadrilateral is −1, and the sides are therefore perpendicular.**

ASSIGNMENT GUIDE

Concepts and Skills	Practice
Explore Positioning a Quadrilateral on the Coordinate Plane	Exercises 1–2
Example 1 Proving Properties of a Parallelogram	Exercises 3–6
Example 2 Proving Conditions for Special Parallelograms	Exercises 7–10
Example 3 Identifying Figures on the Coordinate Plane	Exercises 11–16

© Houghton Mifflin Harcourt Publishing Company

13. Essential Question Check-In How can you use slope in coordinate proofs?

You can use slope to show that opposite sides of a quadrilateral have the same slope.

This shows that the opposite sides are parallel, so the quadrilateral is a parallelogram.

You can also use slope to show that the product of the slopes of any pair of adjacent

sides of a quadrilateral is −1. This shows that the adjacent sides are perpendicular, so the

quadrilateral is a rectangle.

⭐ Evaluate: Homework and Practice

• Online Homework
• Hints and Help
• Extra Practice

1. Suppose you have a right triangle. If you want to write a proof about the midpoints of the legs of the triangle, which placement of the triangle would be most helpful? Explain.

A. Use the origin as a vertex, keeping the figure in Quadrant I with vertices $(0, 2b)$, $(2a, 0)$, and $(0, 0)$.

B. Center the triangle at the origin.

C. Use the origin as a vertex, keeping the figure in Quadrant I with vertices $(0, b)$, $(a, 0)$, and $(0, 0)$.

D. Center one leg of the triangle on the y-axis with vertices $(0, a)$, $(0, -a)$, and $(b, -a)$.

E. Use the x-axis as one leg of the triangle with vertices $(a, 0)$, (a, b), and $(a + c, 0)$.

A; Use the origin as a vertex, keeping the figure in Quadrant I with vertices $(0, 2b)$, $(2a, 0)$, and $(0, 0)$. Positioning the triangle in Quadrant I will mean that all the vertices are positive. Also, if you need to find the midpoints of the sides, using a coefficient of 2 for the vertices will mean that the coordinates of the midpoint will be whole numbers.

2. Describe the position of a general isosceles trapezoid $WXYZ$ determined by the points $W(0, 0)$, $X(a, 0)$, $Y(a - c, b)$, and $Z(c, b)$. Then sketch the trapezoid.

The origin is a vertex, and the x-axis contains one side of the trapezoid.

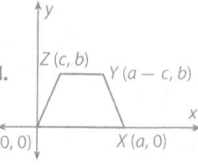

Write a coordinate proof for the quadrilateral determined by the points $A(2, 4)$, $B(4, -1)$, $C(-1, -3)$, and $D(-3, 2)$.

3. Prove that $ABCD$ is a parallelogram.

Slope of $\overline{AB} = \frac{-5}{2}$; Slope of $\overline{BC} = \frac{2}{5}$;

Slope of $\overline{DC} = \frac{-5}{2}$; Slope of $\overline{DA} = \frac{2}{5}$

The slopes of opposite sides are equal.

This means that opposite sides are

parallel, so $ABCD$ is a parallelogram.

4. Prove that $ABCD$ is a rectangle.

Since we already proved that $ABCD$ is a

parallelogram, if the diagonals are

congruent then $ABCD$ is a rectangle.

$AC = \sqrt{58}$; $DB = \sqrt{58}$

The diagonals are congruent, so $ABCD$

is a rectangle.

Exercise	Depth of Knowledge (D.O.K.)	COMMON CORE Mathematical Practices	
1–10	**2** Skills/Concepts	**MP.3** Logic	
11–16	**3** Strategic Thinking	**MP.2** Reasoning	
17–21	**2** Skills/Concepts	**MP.4** Modeling	
22	**2** Skills/Concepts	**MP.1** Problem Solving	
23	**3** Strategic Thinking	H.O.T.	**MP.2** Reasoning
24	**3** Strategic Thinking	H.O.T.	**MP.2** Reasoning
25	**3** Strategic Thinking	H.O.T.	**MP.2** Reasoning
26	**3** Strategic Thinking	H.O.T.	**MP.2** Reasoning

5. Prove that *ABCD* is a rhombus.

In Evaluate3 we proved that *ABCD* is a parallelogram.

Slope of $\overline{AC} = \frac{7}{3}$; Slope of $\overline{DB} = \frac{-3}{7}$

Since $\left(\frac{7}{3}\right)\left(\frac{-3}{7}\right) = -1$, the diagonals are perpendicular. So, *ABCD* is a rhombus.

6. Prove that *ABCD* is a square.

Since *ABCD* is both a rectangle and rhombus, it is also a square.

Prove or disprove each statement about the quadrilateral determined by the points *W* (−2, 5), *X* (5, 5), *Y* (5, 0), **and** *Z* (−2, 0).

7. Prove that the diagonals are congruent.

$WY = \sqrt{(-2-5)^2 + (5-0)^2} = \sqrt{74}$

$XZ = \sqrt{(-2-5)^2 + (0-5)^2} = \sqrt{74}$

So the diagonals are congruent.

8. Prove that the diagonals are perpendicular.

Slope of $\overline{WY} = \frac{-5}{7}$; Slope of $\overline{XZ} = \frac{5}{7}$

When you multiply the slopes, the product is not −1: $\left(\frac{-5}{7}\right)\left(\frac{5}{7}\right) = \frac{-25}{49}$. So the diagonals are not perpendicular.

9. Prove that the diagonals bisect each other.

midpoint of $\overline{WY} = \left(\frac{-2+5}{2}, \frac{5+0}{2}\right) = \left(\frac{3}{2}, \frac{5}{2}\right)$

midpoint of $\overline{XZ} = \left(\frac{5+(-2)}{2}, \frac{5+0}{2}\right) = \left(\frac{3}{2}, \frac{5}{2}\right)$

Since they share a midpoint, the diagonals bisect each other.

10. Prove that *WXYZ* is a square.

Since the diagonals bisect each other, *WXYZ* is a parallelogram. Since the diagonals are congruent, *WXYZ* is a rectangle. Since the diagonals are not perpendicular, it is not a rhombus. So, it is not a square.

Algebra Use the diagonals to determine whether a parallelogram with the given vertices is a rectangle, rhombus, or square. Give all the names that apply.

11. *A*(−10, 4), *B*(−2, 10), *C*(4, 2), *D*(−4, −4)

Slope of $\overline{BD} = 7$; Slope of $\overline{AC} = \frac{-1}{7}$

Since $(7)\left(\frac{-1}{7}\right) = -1$, the diagonals are perpendicular. *ABCD* is a rhombus.

$BD = AC = \sqrt{200}$

Since the lengths of the diagonals are equal. *ABCD* is a rectangle. Since *ABCD* is both a rhombus and a rectangle, it is also a square.

12. *J*(−9, −7), *K*(−4, −2), *L*(3, −3), *M*(−2, −8)

Slope of $\overline{JL} = \frac{1}{3}$; Slope of $\overline{KM} = -3$

Since $\left(\frac{1}{3}\right)(-3) = -1$, the diagonals are perpendicular. *JKLM* is a rhombus.

$JL = \sqrt{160}$; $KM = \sqrt{40}$

Since the diagonals are not congruent, *JKLM* is not a rectangle. So *JKLM* is not a square either.

© Houghton Mifflin Harcourt Publishing Company

VISUAL CUES

Some students may have difficulty using the formula to calculate slopes. You might suggest that these students try a more visual approach. Have them place the figure on a coordinate plane, then determine the rise and run visually.

How do you find the lengths of the diagonals of a quadrilateral in the coordinate plane? Use the distance formula to find the distance between the coordinates of the endpoints of each diagonal.

Analyze Relationships The coordinates of three vertices of parallelogram *ABCD* are given. Find the coordinates of the fourth point so that the given type of figure is formed.

13. $A(4, -2)$, $B(-5, -2)$, $D(4, 4)$, rectangle

Slope of $\overline{AB} = \dfrac{0}{-9} = 0$

Slope of $\overline{AD} = \dfrac{6}{0}$ so the slope is undefined.

$\overline{AD}$ is a vertical line.

For *ABCD* to be a rectangle, $\overline{BC}$ must be parallel to $\overline{AD}$. Thus, the slope of $\overline{BC}$ must be undefined. So, $\overline{BC}$ must be a vertical line and *C* must be $(-5, 4)$.

14. $A(-5, 5)$, $B(0, 0)$, $C(7, 1)$, rhombus

For *ABCD* to be a rhombus, opposite sides should be parallel and all four sides should be congruent.

Slope from *B* to *A*:

rise $= 5 - 0 = 5$

run $= -5 - 0 = -5$

Use the same slope from *C* to *D*: Start at $(7, 1)$ and move 5 units to the left and 5 units up. *D* is at $(2, 6)$.

Slope of $\overline{AB} = -1$; Slope of $\overline{BC} = \dfrac{1}{7}$;

Slope of $\overline{CD} = \dfrac{6-1}{2-7} = \dfrac{5}{-5} = -1$; Slope of

$\overline{DA} = \dfrac{5-6}{-5-2} = \dfrac{-1}{-7} = \dfrac{1}{7}$

Opposite sides are parallel.

Check: $AB = BC = CD = AD = 5\sqrt{2}$

ABCD is a rhombus.

15. $A(0, 2)$, $B(4, -2)$, $C(0, -6)$, square

Show that the product of the slopes of adjacent sides is -1 and that all four sides are congruent.

Slope from *B* to *A*:

rise $= 2 - (-2) = 4$

run $= 0 - 4 = -4$

Use the same slope from *C* to *D*: Start at $(0, -6)$ and move 4 units to the left and 4 units up. *D* is at $(-4, -2)$.

Slope of $\overline{AB} = -1$; Slope of $\overline{BC} = 1$;

Slope of $\overline{CD} = -1$; Slope of $\overline{DA} = 1$

Adjacent sides are perpendicular.

Check: $AB = BC = CD = AD = 4\sqrt{2}$

ABCD is a square.

16. $A(2, 1)$, $B(-1, 5)$, $C(-5, 2)$, square

Show that the product of the slopes of adjacent sides is -1 and that all four sides are congruent.

Slope from *B* to *A*:

rise $= 1 - 5 = -4$

run $= 2 - (-1) = 3$

Use the same slope from *C* to *D*:

Start at $(-5, 2)$ and move down 4 units and 3 units to the right. *D* is at $(-2, -2)$.

Slope of $\overline{AB} = -\dfrac{4}{3}$; Slope of $\overline{BC} = \dfrac{3}{4}$;

Slope of $\overline{CD} = -\dfrac{4}{3}$; Slope of $\overline{DA} = \dfrac{3}{4}$

Adjacent sides are perpendicular.

Check: $AB = BC = CD = AD = 5$

ABCD is a square.

Paul designed a doghouse to fit against the side of his house. His plan consisted of a right triangle on top of a rectangle. Use the drawing for Exercises 17–18.

17. Find *BD*, *CE*, and *BE*.

$BD = BC + CD = AE + CD = 28 + 10 = 38$ in.

$DE = \sqrt{CD^2 + CE^2}$; $CE^2 = DE^2 - CD^2$; $CE = \sqrt{26^2 - 10^2} = \sqrt{576} = 24$ in.

$BE^2 = BC^2 + EC^2$; $BE = \sqrt{BC^2 + EC^2} = \sqrt{28^2 + 24^2} = \sqrt{1360} \approx 36.88$ in.

18. Before building the doghouse, Paul sketched his plan on a coordinate plane. He placed *A* at the origin and $\overline{AB}$ on the x-axis. Find the coordinates of *B*, *C*, *D*, and *E*, assuming that each unit of the coordinate plane represents one inch.

$B = (24, 0)$; $C = (24, 28)$; $D = (24, 38)$; $E = (0, 28)$

19. Critical Thinking On the National Mall in Washington, D.C., a reflecting pool lies between the Lincoln Memorial and the World War II Memorial. The pool has two 2300-foot-long sides and two 150-foot-long sides. Tell what additional information you need to know in order to determine whether the reflecting pool is a rectangle. (*Hint*: Remember that you have to show it is a parallelogram first.)

Possible answer: To know that the reflecting pool is a parallelogram, the congruent sides must be opposite each other. If this is true, then knowing that one angle in the pool is a right angle or that the diagonals are congruent proves that the pool is a rectangle.

Algebra Write a coordinate proof.

20. The Bushmen in South Africa use the Global Positioning System to transmit data about endangered animals to conservationists. The Bushmen have sighted animals at the following coordinates: $(-25, 31.5)$, $(-23.2, 31.4)$, and $(-24, 31.1)$. Prove that the distance between two of these locations is approximately twice the distance between two other locations.

$$\sqrt{\left(-23.2 - (-25)\right)^2 + (31.4 - 31.5)^2} \approx 1.8 \text{ units}$$

$$\sqrt{\left(-24 - (-23.2)\right)^2 + (31.1 - 31.4)^2} \approx 0.9 \text{ units}$$

$$\sqrt{\left(-24 - (-25)\right)^2 + (31.1 - 31.5)^2} \approx 1.1 \text{ units}$$

1.8 is twice 0.9. The distance between 2 of the locations is approx. twice the distance between another 2 locations.

21. Two cruise ships leave a port located at $P(10, 50)$. One ship sails to an island located at $A(-40, -10)$, and the other sails to an island located at $B(60, 110)$. Suppose that each unit represents one nautical mile. Find the midpoint of the line segment connecting the two cruise ships. Verify that the port and the two cruise ships are in a line.

Midpoint of $\overline{AB} = \left(\dfrac{-40 + 60}{2}, \dfrac{-10 + 110}{2}\right) = (10, 50)$

Since P is the midpoint of $\overline{AB}$ it lies on $\overline{AB}$. Therefore, points A, B, and P are collinear and the port and the two cruise ships are in a line.

AVOID COMMON ERRORS

Students may unintentionally make an exercise harder than it needs to be by positioning a figure over positive and negative quadrants. Advise them to keep their figures in one quadrant if possible, preferably Quadrant I.

Coordinate Proof Using Distance with Quadrilaterals   **546**

Have students write a journal entry in which they give the coordinates of four points and then prove or disprove that the quadrilateral determined by the points is a parallelogram or rectangle.

22. A parallelogram has vertices at $(0, 0)$, $(5, 6)$, and $(10, 0)$. Which could be the fourth vertex of the parallelogram? Choose all that apply.

A. $(5, -6)$ **A, B, D, E; these coordinates result in a parallelogram because opposite sides have equal slopes.**

B. $(15, 6)$

C. $(0, -6)$

D. $(10, 6)$

E. $(-5, 6)$

H.O.T. Focus on Higher Order Thinking

23. Draw Conclusions The diagonals of a parallelogram intersect at $(-2, 1.5)$. Two vertices are located at $(-7, 2)$ and $(2, 6.5)$. Find the coordinates of the other two vertices.

Let A be at $(-7, 2)$, B at $(2, 6.5)$, C at (x, y), D at (a, b), and E at $(-2, 1.5)$

Midpoint of $\overline{AC} = \left(\dfrac{-7+x}{2}, \dfrac{2+y}{2}\right) = (-2, 1.5)$, so $\dfrac{-7+x}{2} = -2$ and $\dfrac{2+y}{2} = 1.5$.

$x = 3$ and $y = 1$, so point C is at (3.1).

Midpoint of $\overline{BD} = \left(\dfrac{2+a}{2}, \dfrac{6.5+b}{2}\right) = (-2, 1.5)$, so $\dfrac{2+a}{2} = -2$ and $\dfrac{6.5+b}{2} = 1.5$.

$a = -6$ and $b = -3.5$, so point D is at $(-6, -3.5)$

24. Analyze Relationships Consider points $L(3, -4)$, $M(1, -2)$, and $N(5, 2)$.

a. Find coordinates for point P so that the quadrilateral determined by points L, M, N, and P is a parallelogram. Is there more than one possibility? Explain.

The coordinates of P may be $(7, 0)$, $(3, 4)$, or $(-1, -8)$. These coordinates result in a parallelogram because opposite sides have equal slopes.

b. Are any of the parallelograms a rectangle? Why?

When the coordinates of P are $(7, 0)$, the quadrilateral is a rectangle because the product of the slopes of adjacent sides is -1.

25. Critical Thinking Rhombus $OPQR$ has vertices $O(0, 0)$, $P(a, b)$, $Q(a + b, a + b)$, and $R(b, a)$. Prove the diagonals of the rhombus are perpendicular.

Slope of $\overline{OQ} = \dfrac{(a+b)-0}{(a+b)-0} = \dfrac{a+b}{a+b} = 1$; Slope of $\overline{PR} = \dfrac{a-b}{b-a} = \dfrac{a-b}{-1(a-b)} = -1$

Because the product of the slopes is -1, the diagonals are perpendicular.

26. Multi-Step Use coordinates to verify the Trapezoid Midsegment Theorem which states "The midsegment of a trapezoid is parallel to each base, and its length is one half the sum of the lengths of the bases."

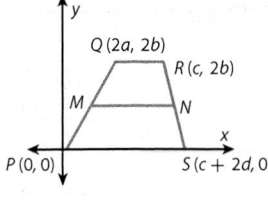

a. M is the midpoint of $\overline{QP}$. What are its coordinates?

$$\left(\frac{2a+0}{2}, \frac{2b+0}{2}\right) = (a, b)$$

b. N is the midpoint of $\overline{RS}$. What are its coordinates?

$$\left(\frac{c+c+2d}{2}, \frac{2b}{2}\right) = \left(\frac{2(c+d)}{2}, \frac{2b}{2}\right) = (c+d, b)$$

c. Find the slopes of $\overline{QR}$, $\overline{PS}$, $\overline{MN}$. What can you conclude?

Slope of $\overline{QR} = \dfrac{2b - 2b}{c - 2a} = \dfrac{0}{c - 2a} = 0$; Slope of $\overline{PS} = \dfrac{0 - 0}{c + 2d - 0} = \dfrac{0}{c + 2d} = 0$;

Slope of $\overline{MN} = \dfrac{b - b}{c + d - a} = \dfrac{0}{c + d - a} = 0$

All three line segments are parallel, and are horizontal lines.

d. Find $\overline{QR}$, $\overline{PS}$, $\overline{MN}$. Show that $MN = \frac{1}{2}(PS + QR)$.

$$QR = \sqrt{(c - 2a)^2 + (2b - 2b)^2} = \sqrt{(c - 2a)^2} = c - 2a$$

$$PS = \sqrt{(c + 2d - 0)^2 + (0 - 0)^2} = \sqrt{(c + 2d)^2} = c + 2d$$

$$MN = \sqrt{(c + d - a)^2 + (b - b)^2} = \sqrt{(c + d - a)^2} = c + d - a$$

$$\tfrac{1}{2}(PS + QR) = \tfrac{1}{2}(c + 2d + c - 2a) = \tfrac{1}{2}(2c + 2d - 2a) = \tfrac{1}{2}\big(2(c + d - a)\big) = c + d - a = MN$$

Lesson Performance Task

According to the new mayor, the shape of City Park is downright ugly. While the parks in all of the other towns in the vicinity have nice, regular polygonal shapes, City Park is the shape of an irregular quadrilateral. On a coordinate map of the park, the four corners are located at $(-3, 4)$, $(5, 2)$, $(1, -2)$, and $(-5, -4)$. The mayor's chief assistant knows a little mathematics and proposes that a special "inner park" be created by joining the midpoints of the sides of City Park. The assistant claims that the boundaries of the inner park will create a nice, regular polygonal shape, just like the parks in all the other towns. The mayor thinks the idea is ridiculous, saying, "You can't create order out of chaos."

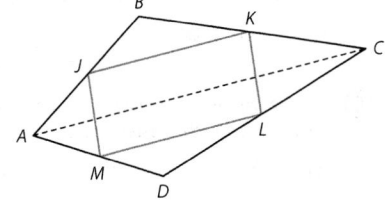

1. Who was right? Explain your reasoning in detail.

2. Irregular quadrilateral ABCD is shown here. Points J, K, L, and M are midpoints.

   a. What must you show to prove that quadrilateral JKLM is a parallelogram?

   b. How can you show this?

   c. If the adjacent sides of JKLM are perpendicular, what type of figure does that make JKLM?

1. The assistant was right. The coordinates of the inner park are $(1, 3)$, $(3, 0)$, $(-2, -3)$, and $(-4, 0)$. The slopes of opposite sides are equal. One pair of sides has a slope of $\frac{3}{5}$. The other pair of sides has a slope of $-\frac{3}{2}$. This means that inner park is a parallelogram.

2. a. Show that both pairs of opposite sides are parallel.
  b. Show that slopes of both pairs of opposite sides are equal.
  c. If adjacent sides are perpendicular, then quadrilateral JKLM would be a rectangle.

© Houghton Mifflin Harcourt Publishing Company

AVOID COMMON ERRORS

The Distance Formula contains the terms $(x_2 - x_1)$ and $(y_2 - y_1)$ The Midpoint Formula contains the terms $(x_1 + x_2)$ and $(y_1 + y_2)$. Because the terms are so similar, they are easily confused, particularly when students are just beginning to use the formulas. Caution students to be sure they're using the Midpoint Formula correctly when they find the coordinates of the midpoints of the quadrilateral in the Lesson Performance Task.

INTEGRATE MATHEMATICAL PRACTICES
Focus on Reasoning

MP.2 In the Lesson Performance Task, quadrilateral JKLM is shown to be a parallelogram by showing that its opposite sides $\overline{JK}$ and $\overline{LM}$ are both congruent and parallel. Explain how you could prove that JKLM is a parallelogram by showing that both pairs of opposite sides are congruent. Sample answer: $\overline{JK} \cong \overline{LM}$ as shown in the Lesson Performance Task. Draw auxiliary line segment $\overline{BD}$. By the Midline Theorem, both $\overline{JM}$ and $\overline{KL}$ are half the length of $\overline{BD}$. Therefore, $\overline{JM} \cong \overline{KL}$. Since $\overline{JK} \cong \overline{LM}$ and $\overline{JM} \cong \overline{KL}$, JKLM is a parallelogram.

EXTENSION ACTIVITY

In the Lesson Performance Activity, students use the Midline Theorem to prove that the figure formed by joining the midpoints of a quadrilateral–*any* quadrilateral–is a parallelogram. Even after this is proven, the conclusion remains one of the most amazing in all of plane geometry. (It holds even for concave quadrilaterals and quadrilaterals with intersecting sides.) Have students draw a collection of quadrilaterals of widely varying shapes and side lengths. Urge them to draw the most irregular-looking quadrilaterals they can think of. For each, students should measure the sides to find the midpoints and then join them to create a quadrilateral. They can then measure the angles or side lengths of the new quadrilateral to show that it is a parallelogram.

Scoring Rubric
2 points: Student correctly solves the problem and explains his/her reasoning.
1 point: Student shows good understanding of the problem but does not fully solve or explain.
0 points: Student does not demonstrate understanding of the problem.

Perimeter and Area on the Coordinate Plane

Common Core Math Standards

The student is expected to:

 G-GPE.B.7

Use coordinates to compute perimeters of polygons and areas of triangles and rectangles, e.g., using the distance formula.

Mathematical Practices

 MP.1 Problem Solving

Language Objective

Work in small groups to develop a series of written steps to explain how to calculate perimeter and area in the coordinate plane.

ENGAGE

Essential Question: How do you find the perimeter and area of polygons in the coordinate plane?

To find the perimeter, use the distance formula to find the length of each side and then add the side lengths. To find the area, divide the polygon into rectangles and/or triangles, then add the areas of the rectangles and triangles.

PREVIEW: LESSON PERFORMANCE TASK

View the Engage section online. Discuss the photo. Ask students to explain what is odd or does not make sense about the object in the photo. Then preview the Lesson Performance Task.

10.5 Perimeter and Area on the Coordinate Plane

Essential Question: How do you find the perimeter and area of polygons in the coordinate plane?

Resource Locker

 Explore **Finding Perimeters of Figures on the Coordinate Plane**

Recall that the perimeter of a polygon is the sum of the lengths of the polygon's sides. You can use the Distance Formula to find perimeters of polygons in a coordinate plane.

Follow these steps to find the perimeter of a pentagon with vertices $A(-1, 4)$, $B(4, 4)$, $C(3, -2)$, $D(-1, -4)$, and $E(-4, 1)$. Round to the nearest tenth.

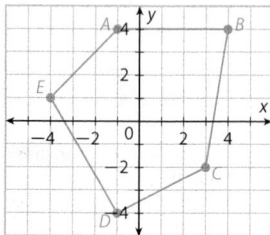

(A) Plot the points. Then use a straightedge to draw the pentagon that is determined by the points.

(B) Are there any sides for which you do not need to use the Distance Formula? Explain, and give their length(s). Yes; $\overline{AB}$, because it is horizontal; $AB = 5$

(C) Use the Distance Formula to find the remaining side lengths. Round your answers to the nearest tenth.

$BC = \sqrt{37} \approx 6.1;$ $\quad CD = \sqrt{20} \approx 4.5;$ $\quad DE = \sqrt{34} \approx 5.8;$ $\quad AE = \sqrt{18} \approx 4.2$

(D) Find the sum of the side lengths.

$AB + BC + CD + DE + AE = 5 + 6.1 + 4.5 + 5.8 + 4.2 = 25.6$; So, the perimeter is 25.6 units.

Reflect

1. Explain how you can find the perimeter of a rectangle to check that your answer is reasonable.
   The perimeter of pentagon *ABCDE* is approximately equal to the perimeter of the rectangle with vertices $(-1, 4)$, $(4, 4)$, $(-1, -4)$, and $(4, -4)$. This rectangle has a perimeter of 26 units, so the answer is reasonable.

© Houghton Mifflin Harcourt Publishing Company

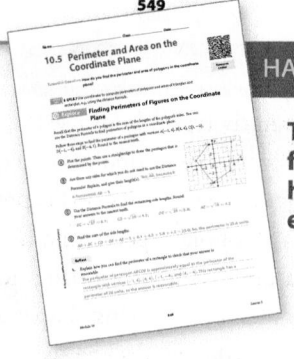

HARDCOVER PAGES 465–476

Turn to these pages to find this lesson in the hardcover student edition.

Explain 1   Finding Areas of Figures on the Coordinate Plane

You can use area formulas together with the Distance Formula to determine areas of figures such as triangles, rectangles and parallelograms.

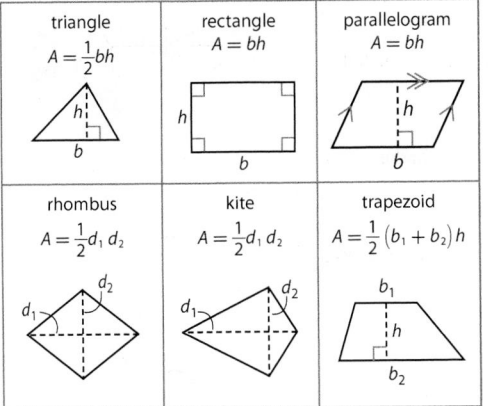

triangle	rectangle	parallelogram
$A = \frac{1}{2}bh$	$A = bh$	$A = bh$

rhombus	kite	trapezoid
$A = \frac{1}{2}d_1 d_2$	$A = \frac{1}{2}d_1 d_2$	$A = \frac{1}{2}(b_1 + b_2)h$

Example 1   Find the area of each figure.

 Step 1   Find the coordinates of the vertices of $\triangle ABC$.

$A(-4, -2), B(-2, 2), C(5, 1)$

Step 2   Choose a base for which you can easily find the height of the triangle.

Use $\overline{AC}$ as the base. A segment from the opposite vertex, B, to point $D(-1, -1)$ appears to be perpendicular to the base $\overline{AC}$. Use slopes to check.

slope of $\overline{AC} = \dfrac{1 - (-2)}{5 - (-4)} = \dfrac{1}{3}$; slope of $\overline{BD} = \dfrac{-1 - 2}{-1 - (-2)} = -3$

The product of the slopes is $\dfrac{1}{3} \cdot (-3) = -1$. $\overline{BD}$ is perpendicular to $\overline{AC}$, so $\overline{BD}$ is the height for the base $\overline{AC}$.

Find the length of the base and the height.

$AC = \sqrt{\left(5 - (-4)\right)^2 + \left(1 - (-2)\right)^2} = \sqrt{90} = 3\sqrt{10}$; $BD = \sqrt{\left(-1 - (-2)\right)^2 + (-1 - 2)^2} = \sqrt{10}$

Step 3   Determine the area of $\triangle ABC$.

$\text{Area} = \dfrac{1}{2}bh = \dfrac{1}{2}(AC)(BD) = \dfrac{1}{2} \cdot \left(3\sqrt{10}\right)\left(\sqrt{10}\right) = \dfrac{1}{2} \cdot 30 = 15$ square units

---

PROFESSIONAL DEVELOPMENT

Learning Progressions

In this lesson, students find the perimeter and area of polygons in the coordinate plane. Methods include:

- using the distance formula to find the length of each side
- using slopes of perpendicular lines to determine when a side of a triangle or quadrilateral may be used as the height
- using a system of equations and the distance formula to find the height of a nonright triangle

---

EXPLORE

Finding Perimeters of Figures on the Coordinate Plane

INTEGRATE TECHNOLOGY

Students have the option of doing the Explore activity either in the book or online.

QUESTIONING STRATEGIES

?   What do you need to know to find the perimeter of a polygon? If you don't remember the distance formula, how can you find the lengths of the sides? The lengths of the sides; you could use the Pythagorean Theorem after finding the vertical and horizontal distances between each two vertices. It is essentially the same as using the distance formula.

EXPLAIN 1

Finding Areas of Figures on the Coordinate Plane

AVOID COMMON ERRORS

Students may find the wrong sum for radical expressions because they are not using the correct rules. Remind students that they cannot add radical expressions with unlike radicands.

Can you use the formula $A = bh$ to find the areas of all quadrilaterals? Explain. **No, it is the area formula only for parallelograms, rectangles, rhombuses, and squares.**

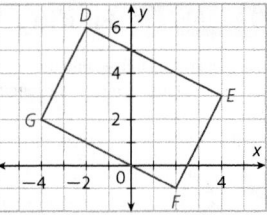

Ⓑ **Step 1** Find the coordinates of the vertices of *DEFG*.

$D(-2, 6)$, $E(4, 3)$, $F(2, -1)$, $G(-4, 2)$

Step 2 *DEFG* appears to be a rectangle. Use slopes to check that adjacent sides are perpendicular.

slope of $\overline{DE}$: $\dfrac{\boxed{3} - \boxed{6}}{4 - (-2)} = \dfrac{\boxed{-3}}{6} = -\dfrac{1}{2}$; slope of $\overline{EF}$: $\dfrac{\boxed{-1} - 3}{2 - \boxed{4}} = \dfrac{\boxed{-4}}{\boxed{-2}} = \boxed{2}$

slope of $\overline{FG}$: $\dfrac{2 - \boxed{-1}}{-4 - \boxed{2}} = \dfrac{\boxed{3}}{\boxed{-6}} = -\dfrac{1}{2}$; slope of $\overline{DG}$: $\dfrac{2 - \boxed{6}}{-4 - \boxed{-2}} = \dfrac{\boxed{-4}}{\boxed{-2}} = \boxed{2}$

so *DEFG* is a $\underline{\text{rectangle}}$.

Step 3 Find the area of *DEFG*.

$b = FG = \sqrt{\left(2 - \boxed{-4}\right)^2 + \left(\boxed{-1} - 2\right)^2} = \sqrt{\boxed{45}} = \boxed{3}\sqrt{\boxed{5}}$

$h = GD = \sqrt{\left(\boxed{-2} - (-4)\right)^2 + \left(6 - \boxed{2}\right)^2} = \sqrt{\boxed{20}} = \boxed{2}\sqrt{\boxed{5}}$

Area of *DEFG*: $A = bh = \left(\boxed{3}\sqrt{\boxed{5}}\right)\left(\boxed{2}\sqrt{\boxed{5}}\right) = \boxed{30}$ square units

Reflect

2. In Part A, is it possible to use another side of $\triangle ABC$ as the base? If so, what length represents the height of the triangle?
   Yes; you can use any side as the base. If you use $\overline{AB}$ as the base, then the height is the length of the perpendicular line segment from vertex *C* to $\overleftrightarrow{AB}$; if you use $\overline{BC}$ as the base, then the height is the length of the perpendicular line segment from vertex *A* to $\overleftrightarrow{BC}$.

3. **Discussion** In Part B, why was it necessary to find the slopes of the sides?
   Possible answer: To use one side as the base and another as the height, you must be sure that the two sides are perpendicular by confirming that the product of their slopes is −1.

© Houghton Mifflin Harcourt Publishing Company

COLLABORATIVE LEARNING

Small Group Activity

Divide students into groups. Have each group member find the area of one simple shape in a composite figure. Then have each group work together to add or subtract the areas.

Your Turn

4. Find the area of quadrilateral *JKLM* with vertices $J(-4, -2)$, $K(2, 1)$, $L(3, 4)$, $M(-3, 1)$.

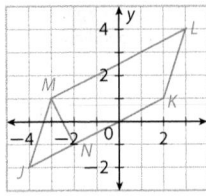

JKLM appears to be a parallelogram. Use slopes to show that opposite sides are parallel:

slope of $\overline{JK}$: $\frac{1-(-2)}{2-(-4)} = \frac{1}{2}$; slope of $\overline{KL}$: $\frac{4-1}{3-2} = 3$; slope of $\overline{LM}$: $\frac{1-4}{-3-3} = \frac{1}{2}$; slope of $\overline{JM}$: $\frac{1-(-2)}{-3-(-4)} = 3$

The slopes of opposite sides are equal, so *DEFG* is a parallelogram.

Use $\overline{JK}$ as the base and draw height $\overline{MN}$; Coordinates of *N*: $(-2, -1)$

slope of $\overline{MN}$: $\frac{-1-1}{-2-(-3)} = \frac{-2}{1} = -2$; so $\overline{MN} \perp \overline{JK}$

$b = JK = \sqrt{\left(2-(-4)\right)^2 + \left(1-(-2)\right)^2} = \sqrt{45} = 3\sqrt{5}$; $h = MN = \sqrt{\left(-2-(-3)\right)^2 + (-1-1)^2} = \sqrt{5}$

Area of *JKLM*: $A = bh = \left(3\sqrt{5}\right)\left(\sqrt{5}\right) = 15$ square units

---

⊘ **Explain 2** **Finding Areas of Composite Figures**

A **composite figure** is made up of simple shapes, such as triangles, rectangles, and parallelograms. To find the area of a composite figure, find the areas of the simple shapes and then use the Area Addition Postulate. You can use the Area Addition Postulate to find the area of a composite figure.

Area Addition Postulate

The area of a region is equal to the sum of the areas of its nonoverlapping parts.

Example 2 Find the area of each figure.

Ⓐ Possible solution: *ABCDE* can be divided up into a rectangle and two triangles, each with horizontal bases.

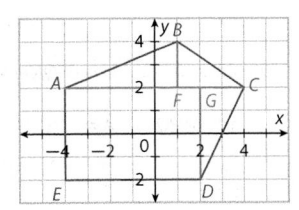

area of rectangle *AGDE*: $A = bh = (DE)(AE) = (6)(4) = 24$

area of $\triangle ABC$: $A = \frac{1}{2}bh = \frac{1}{2}(AC)(BF) = \frac{1}{2}(8)(2) = 8$

area of $\triangle CDG$: $A = \frac{1}{2}bh = \frac{1}{2}(CG)(DG) = \frac{1}{2}(2)(4) = 4$

area of *ABCDE*: $A = 24 + 8 + 4 = 36$ square units

EXPLAIN 2

Finding Areas of Composite Figures

AVOID COMMON ERRORS

Students may divide composite figures into shapes for which they are unable to find the area. Remind them that some figures can be divided in more than one way. If they are having difficulty, encourage them to divide the figures in a different way.

DIFFERENTIATE INSTRUCTION

Multiple Representations

Point out to students that there are two formulas for finding the area of a rhombus: $A = bh$ and $\frac{d_1 \cdot d_2}{2}$, where d_1 and d_2 are the lengths of the two diagonals of the rhombus. Have students draw a rhombus on a coordinate plane. Instruct them to orient the rhombus so that none of the sides is parallel to an axis. Have them then find the coordinates of the vertices, and use the two formulas in conjunction with the slope and distance formulas, to show that both formulas yield the same result.

? How do you know when to add and when to subtract areas? If you can divide the figure into simple shapes with areas you can easily find, you should add. Otherwise, you should try subtraction.

Ⓑ *PQRST* can be divided into a parallelogram and a triangle.

△*PQT* appears to be a right triangle. Check that $\overline{PT}$ and $\boxed{\overline{QT}}$ are perpendicular:

slope of $\overline{PT}$: $\dfrac{1 - \boxed{4}}{-3 - \boxed{-4}} = \dfrac{\boxed{-3}}{1} = \boxed{-3}$

slope of $\boxed{\overline{QT}}$: $\dfrac{\boxed{1} - 3}{-3 - \boxed{3}} = \dfrac{\boxed{-2}}{\boxed{-6}} = \boxed{\dfrac{1}{3}}$

△*PQT* is a right triangle with base $\overline{PT}$ and height $\boxed{\overline{QT}}$.

$PT = \sqrt{\left(-3 - \boxed{-4}\right)^2 + \left(1 - \boxed{4}\right)^2} = \sqrt{\boxed{10}}$

$\boxed{QT} = \sqrt{\left(-3 - \boxed{3}\right)^2 + \left(1 - \boxed{3}\right)^2} = \sqrt{\boxed{40}} = 2\sqrt{\boxed{10}}$

area of △*PQT*: $A = \dfrac{1}{2}bh = \dfrac{1}{2}\left(\sqrt{\boxed{10}}\right)\left(2\sqrt{\boxed{10}}\right) = \boxed{10}$

$\overline{QR} \parallel \overline{TS}$ since both sides are vertical.

slope of $\boxed{\overline{RS}} = \dfrac{\boxed{-1} - 1}{-3 - \boxed{3}} = \dfrac{\boxed{-2}}{\boxed{-6}} = \boxed{\dfrac{1}{3}}$, so $\overline{QT} \parallel \boxed{\overline{RS}}$. Therefore, *QRST* is a parallelogram.

$\overline{RT}$ is an ___diagonal___ of △*QRST* and is horizontal. Because $\overline{RT} \perp \overline{RQ}$, △*QRT* is a right triangle with base $\boxed{\overline{RT}}$ and height $\boxed{\overline{QR}}$. Therefore, the area of △*QRST* = 2 · (area of △*QRT*).

$RT = \boxed{6}$, $QR = \boxed{2}$, so the area of △*QRT* = $\dfrac{1}{2}\left(\boxed{6}\right)\left(\boxed{2}\right) = 6$.

△*QRST* = 2 · (area of *QRT*) = 2 · $\boxed{6}$ = 12

area of *PQRST*: $A = \boxed{10} + \boxed{12} = \boxed{22}$ square units

Reflect

5. **Discussion** How could you use subtraction to find the area of a figure on the coordinate plane? **For some figures, drawing a rectangle around the figure creates triangles around the figure, and its area can be found by subtracting the areas of the triangles from the area of the rectangle.**

LANGUAGE SUPPORT EL

Connect Vocabulary

To help them remember what a *composite figure* is, ask students to think of the word *compose*, which means *to form by putting together*. A composite figure is formed by putting together simple shapes.

6. Find the area of the polygon by addition.

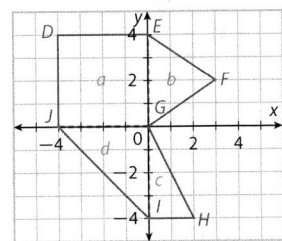

7. Find the area of polygon by subtraction.

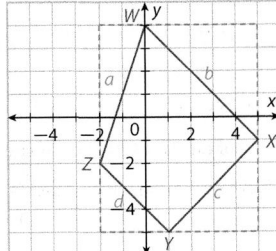

a: $A = 4^2 = 16 \text{ units}^2$;

b: $A = \frac{1}{2}(4)(3) = 6 \text{ units}^2$

c: $A = \frac{1}{2}(2)(4) = 4 \text{ units}^2$;

d: $A = \frac{1}{2}(4)(4) = 8 \text{ units}^2$

Area of the polygon = 34 units².

area of large rectangle:

$A = (7)(9) = 63 \text{ units}^2$

a: $A = \frac{1}{2}(2)(6) = 6 \text{ units}^2$;

b: $A = \frac{1}{2}(5)(5) = 12.5 \text{ units}^2$

c: $A = \frac{1}{2}(4)(4) = 8 \text{ units}^2$;

d: $A = \frac{1}{2}(3)(3) = 4.5 \text{ units}^2$

Area of the polygon = 63 − 31

= 32 units².

🔎 Explain 3 Using Perimeter and Area in Problem Solving

You can use perimeter and area techniques to solve problems.

Example 3 Miguel is planning and costing an ornamental garden in the a shape of an irregular octagon. Each unit on the coordinate grid represents one yard. He wants to lay the whole garden with turf, which costs $3.25 per square yard, and surround it with a border of decorative stones, which cost $7.95 per yard. What is the total cost of the turf and stones?

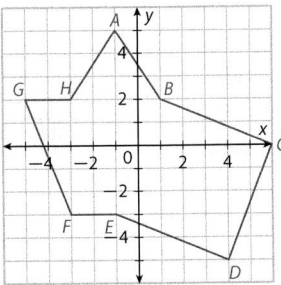

© Houghton Mifflin Harcourt Publishing Company • Image Credits: ©Alena Brozova/Shutterstock

EXPLAIN 3

Using Perimeter and Area in Problem Solving

AVOID COMMON ERRORS

Students may come to a conclusion that is not reasonable. Remind them that when they work on real-world problems, they should always check their answers for reasonableness in the context of the given situation.

Analyze Information

Identify the important information.

- The vertices are $A\left(\boxed{-1}, 5\right)$, $B\left(1, \boxed{2}\right)$, $C\left(6, \boxed{0}\right)$, $D\left(4, \boxed{-5}\right)$, $E(-1, -3)$, $F\left(\boxed{-3}, -3\right)$, $G\left(-5, \boxed{2}\right)$, and $H\left(\boxed{-3}, 2\right)$.
- The cost of turf is $\$\ \boxed{3.25}$ per square yard.
- The cost of the ornamental stones is $\$\ \boxed{7.95}$ per yard.

Formulate a Plan

- Divide the garden up into <u>smaller figures</u>.
- Add up the <u>areas</u> of the smaller figures.
- Find the cost of turf by <u>multiplying</u> the total area by the cost per square yard.
- Find the perimeter of the garden by adding the <u>lengths</u> of the sides.
- Find the cost of the border by <u>multiplying</u> the perimeter by the cost per yard.
- Find total cost by adding the <u>cost for the turf</u> and <u>cost for the border</u>.

Solve

Divide the garden into smaller figures.

The garden can be divided into square $BCDE$, kite $ABEH$, and parallelogram $EFGH$.

Find the area of each smaller figure.

area of $BCDE$:

slope of $\overline{BC}$: $\dfrac{\boxed{0} - 2}{6 - \boxed{1}} = -\boxed{\dfrac{2}{5}}$

slope of $\boxed{\overline{CD}}$: $\dfrac{\boxed{-5} - 0}{4 - \boxed{6}} = \boxed{\dfrac{5}{2}}$

Also, $BC = \sqrt{\left(\boxed{6} - 1\right)^2 + \left(0 - \boxed{2}\right)^2} = \sqrt{\boxed{29}}$ and

$CD = \sqrt{\left(4 - \boxed{6}\right)^2 + \left(\boxed{-5} - 0\right)^2} = \sqrt{\boxed{29}}$.

So $BCDE$ is a square, with area $A = s^2 = \left(\sqrt{\boxed{29}}\ \text{yd}\right)^2 = \boxed{29}\ \text{yd}^2$.

© Houghton Mifflin Harcourt Publishing Company

area of kite *ABEH*:

$$HA = \sqrt{\left(-1 - \boxed{-3}\right)^2 + \left(\boxed{5} - 2\right)^2} = \sqrt{4 + \boxed{9}} = \sqrt{\boxed{13}} \approx \boxed{3.6};$$

$$AB = \sqrt{\left(\boxed{1} - (-1)\right)^2 + \left(2 - \boxed{5}\right)^2} = \sqrt{\boxed{4} + 9} = \sqrt{\boxed{13}} \approx \boxed{3.6};$$

$$HE = \sqrt{\left(-1 - \boxed{-3}\right)^2 + \left(\boxed{-3} - 2\right)^2} = \sqrt{\boxed{4} + 25} = \sqrt{\boxed{29}} \approx \boxed{5.4};$$

$$BE = \sqrt{\left(\boxed{-1} - 1\right)^2 + \left(-3 - \boxed{2}\right)^2} = \sqrt{4 + \boxed{25}} = \sqrt{\boxed{29}} \approx 5.4$$

So, $\boxed{HA} \cong \boxed{AB}$ and $\boxed{HE} \cong \boxed{BE}$. Therefore *ABEH* is a kite.

$$b = d_1 = 8, h = d_2 = 4$$

$$A = \tfrac{1}{2}d_1 d_2 = \tfrac{1}{2}\left(\boxed{8}\right)\left(\boxed{4}\right) = \boxed{16} \text{ yd}^2$$

area of parallelogram *EFGH*:

$\boxed{EF}$ and $\overline{GH}$ are both horizontal, so are parallel;

slope of $\overline{EH}$: $\dfrac{2 - \boxed{-3}}{-3 - \boxed{-1}} = \dfrac{\boxed{5}}{\boxed{-2}} = -\tfrac{5}{2}$; slope of $\boxed{FG}$: $\dfrac{2 - \boxed{-3}}{-5 - \boxed{-3}} = \dfrac{\boxed{5}}{\boxed{-2}} = -\tfrac{5}{2}$

So *EFGH* is a parallelogram, with base $\boxed{EF} = \boxed{2}$ and height. $FH = \boxed{5}$.

area of *EFGH*: $A = bh = \left(\boxed{2}\ yd\right)\left(\boxed{5}\ yd\right) = \boxed{10} \text{ yd}^2$

Find the total area of the garden and the cost of turf.

area of garden: $A = \boxed{29} \text{ yd}^2 + \boxed{16} \text{ yd}^2 + \boxed{10} \text{ yd}^2 = \boxed{55} \text{ yd}^2$

cost of turf: $\left(\boxed{55}\ \text{yd}^2\right)\left(\$\ \boxed{3.25}\ /\text{yd}^2\right) = \$\ \boxed{178.75}$

Find the perimeter of the garden.

$EF = 2$ yd, $GH = 2$ yd

From area calculations, $BC = CD = DE = \sqrt{\boxed{29}} \approx \boxed{5.4}$ yd, and $AB = AH = \boxed{3.6}$ yd

$$FG = \sqrt{\left(\boxed{-5} - \boxed{-3}\right)^2 + \left(\boxed{2} - (-3)\right)^2} = \sqrt{\boxed{29}},$$

perimeter of garden $= GH + HA + AB + BC + CD + DE + EF + FG$

$$= \boxed{2} + \boxed{3.6} + \boxed{3.6} + \boxed{5.4} + \boxed{5.4} + \boxed{5.4} + \boxed{2} + \boxed{5.4} = \boxed{32.8} \text{ yd}$$

Find the cost of the stones for the border.

cost of stones: $\left(\boxed{32.8}\ \text{yd}\right)\left(\$\boxed{7.95}\ \text{per yd}\right) = \$\ \boxed{260.76}$

Find the total cost.

total cost: $\$\ \boxed{178.75} + \$\ \boxed{260.76} = \$\ \boxed{439.51}$

© Houghton Mifflin Harcourt Publishing Company

QUESTIONING STRATEGIES

? What do you need to do before you find the perimeter or area of any figure on the coordinate plane? Use the distance formula to find at least some of the side lengths.

The area can be checked by subtraction:

area of large rectangle $= (11)(10) = 110$ square units

area $= (11)\boxed{10} - \boxed{2}(3) - \frac{1}{2}(2)\boxed{3} - \frac{1}{2}\boxed{2}\boxed{3}$

$\quad - (5)\boxed{3} - \frac{1}{2}\boxed{5}(2) - \frac{1}{2}\boxed{2}(5)$

$\quad - \frac{1}{2}\boxed{5}\boxed{2} - \boxed{4}\boxed{2} - \frac{1}{2}\boxed{2}\boxed{5}$

$\quad = \boxed{110} - \boxed{6} - \boxed{3} - \boxed{3} - \boxed{15} - \boxed{5} - \boxed{5} - \boxed{5} - \boxed{8} - \boxed{5} = \boxed{55}$

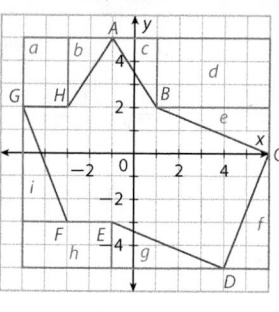

The perimeter is approximately the perimeter of the polygon shown:

The perimeter of the polygon shown is $\boxed{36}$,

so the answer is reasonable.

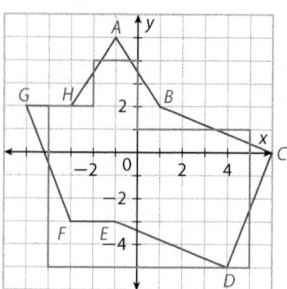

Your Turn

8. A designer is making a medallion in the shape of the letter "L." Each unit on the coordinate grid represents an eighth of an inch, and the medallion is to be cut from a 1-in. square of metal. How much metal is wasted to make each medallion? Write your answer as a decimal.

Divide the medallion into two parallelograms by drawing $\overline{RV}$. Find the area of each parallelogram, and sum them.

$\overline{PQ}$ and $\overline{UV}$ are both horizontal, so they are parallel;

slope of $\overline{PU}$: $\frac{-4-4}{-2-0} = \frac{-8}{-2} = 4$;

slope of $\overline{QV}$: $\frac{-4-4}{0-2} = \frac{-8}{-2} = 4$

So $PQVU$ is a parallelogram with base $UV = 2$ units and height $PV = 8$ units.

area of $PQVU$: $A = (2)(8) = 16$ units²

$\overline{RS}$ and $\overline{VT}$ are both horizontal, so are parallel;

slope of $\overline{RV}$: $\frac{-4+2}{0-0.5} = \frac{-2}{-0.5} = 4$;

slope of $\overline{ST}$: $\frac{-4+2}{4-4.5} = \frac{-2}{-0.5} = 4$

So $RSTV$ is a parallelogram, with base $VT = 4$ units and height 2 units.

area of $RSTV$: $A = (4)(2) = 8$ units²

area of medallion: 16 units² + 8 units² = 24 units²

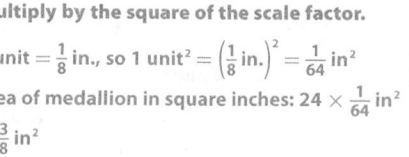

Multiply by the square of the scale factor.

1 unit $= \frac{1}{8}$ in., so 1 unit² $= \left(\frac{1}{8}\text{ in.}\right)^2 = \frac{1}{64}$ in²

area of medallion in square inches: $24 \times \frac{1}{64}$ in²

$= \frac{3}{8}$ in²

Subtract this from 1 in² to find the wastage.

area of wastage: 1 in² $- \frac{3}{8}$ in² $= \frac{5}{8}$ in² $= 0.625$ in²

© Houghton Mifflin Harcourt Publishing Company

Elaborate

9. Create a flowchart for the process of finding the area of the polygon *ABCDEFG*. Your flowchart should show when, and why, the Slope and Distance Formulas are used.

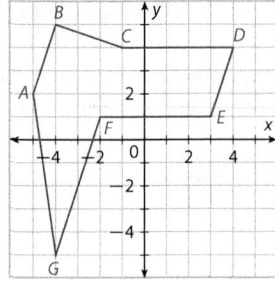

Possible answer:

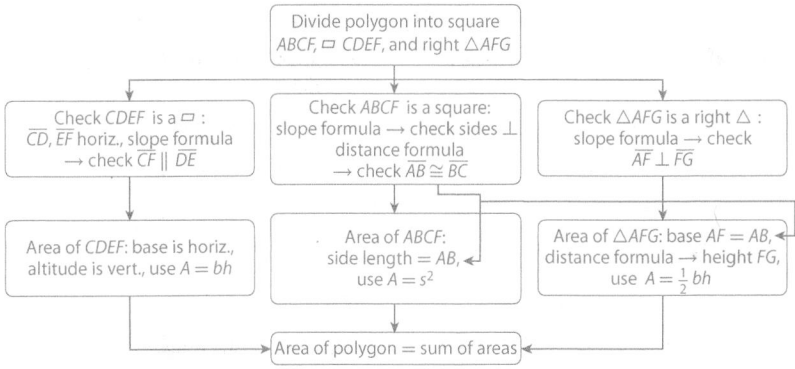

Divide polygon into square *ABCF*, ▱ *CDEF*, and right △*AFG*

Check *CDEF* is a ▱ :
$\overline{CD}$, $\overline{EF}$ horiz., slope formula → check $\overline{CF} \parallel \overline{DE}$

Check *ABCF* is a square:
slope formula → check sides ⊥ distance formula → check $\overline{AB} \cong \overline{BC}$

Check △*AFG* is a right △ :
slope formula → check $\overline{AF} \perp \overline{FG}$

Area of *CDEF*: base is horiz., altitude is vert., use $A = bh$

Area of *ABCF*: side length = *AB*, use $A = s^2$

Area of △*AFG*: base *AF* = *AB*, distance formula → height *FG*, use $A = \frac{1}{2}bh$

Area of polygon = sum of areas

10. **Discussion** If two polygons have approximately the same area, do they have approximately the same perimeter? Draw a picture to justify your answer.
   Not necessarily. You can increase the perimeter of a polygon by any amount, by making its sides "crinkly," without significantly changing the area:

11. **Essential Question Check-In** What formulas might you need to solve problems involving the perimeter and area of triangles and quadrilaterals in the coordinate plane?
   Besides the formulas for perimeter and area, you may need the Distance Formula to find lengths of sides and heights. You might also need to use the Slope Formula to see if two sides are perpendicular or to find the slope of the height segment if the sides are not perpendicular.

ELABORATE

INTEGRATE MATHEMATICAL PRACTICES
Focus on Technology

MP.5 Different calculators have different methods for finding the square root of a number. Have students work with a variety of calculators and figure out how to use the square root feature on each. Remind them that they can check the square root by squaring the result to see if it is the original number.

SUMMARIZE THE LESSON

? How can you use the formulas for perimeter and area in conjunction with the distance formula to solve problems about triangles and quadrilaterals in the coordinate plane? Use the distance formula to find the lengths of sides and heights, and then substitute those values into the formulas for perimeter and area.

EVALUATE

ASSIGNMENT GUIDE

Concepts and Skills	Practice
Explore Finding Perimeters of Figures on the Coordinate Plane	Exercises 1–4
Example 1 Finding Areas of Figures on the Coordinate Plane	Exercises 5–8
Example 2 Finding Areas of Composite Figures	Exercises 9–12
Example 3 Using Perimeter and Area in Problem Solving	Exercises 13–14

QUESTIONING STRATEGIES

? What must you do before you use two sides of a triangle for the height and base to find the area? You must verify that the two sides are perpendicular. Otherwise, you must choose a convenient height and base.

Evaluate: Homework and Practice

- Online Homework
- Hints and Help
- Extra Practice

Find the perimeter of the figure with the given vertices. Round to the nearest tenth.

1. $D(0, 1)$, $E(5, 4)$, and $F(2, 6)$

$DE = \sqrt{34} \approx 5.8$ units,

$EF = \sqrt{13} \approx 3.6$ units,

$FD = \sqrt{29} \approx 5.4$ units

$P = 5.8 + 3.6 + 5.4 = 14.8$ units

2. $P(2, 5)$, $Q(-3, 0)$, $R(2, -5)$, and $S(6, 0)$

$PQ = \sqrt{50} \approx 7.1$ units,

$QR = \sqrt{50} \approx 7.1$ units,

$RS = \sqrt{41} \approx 6.4$ units,

$SP = \sqrt{41} \approx 6.4$ units

$P = 7.1 + 7.1 + 6.4 + 6.4 = 27$ units

3. $M(-3, 4)$, $N(1, 4)$, $P(4, 2)$, $Q(4, -1)$, and $R(2, 2)$

$MN = \sqrt{16} = 4$ units,

$NP = \sqrt{13} \approx 3.6$ units,

$PQ = \sqrt{9} = 3$ units,

$QR = \sqrt{13} \approx 3.6$ units,

$RM = \sqrt{29} \approx 5.4$ units

$P = 4 + 3.6 + 3 + 3.6 + 5.4 = 19.6$ units

4. $A(-5, 1)$, $B(0, 3)$, $C(5, 1)$, $D(4, -2)$, $E(0, -4)$, and $F(-2, -4)$

$AB = \sqrt{29} \approx 5.4$ units,

$BC = \sqrt{29} \approx 5.4$ units,

$CD = \sqrt{10} \approx 3.2$ units,

$DE = \sqrt{20} \approx 4.5$ units,

$EF = \sqrt{4} = 2$ units,

$FA = \sqrt{34} \approx 5.8$ units,

$P = 5.4 + 5.4 + 3.2 + 4.5 + 2 + 5.8 = 26.3$ units

Find the area of each figure.

5.

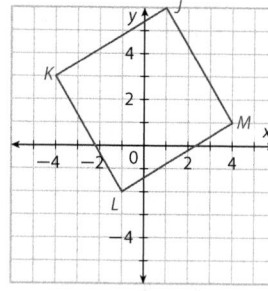

slope of $\overline{JK} = \frac{3}{5}$; slope of $\overline{KL} = -\frac{5}{3}$; slope of $\overline{LM} = \frac{3}{5}$; slope of $\overline{JM} = -\frac{5}{3}$

$JK = \sqrt{34}$; $KL = \sqrt{34}$

Adjacent sides are perpendicular and congruent, so JKLM is a square.

area of JKLM: $A = s^2 = \left(\sqrt{34}\right)^2 = 34$ units²

6.

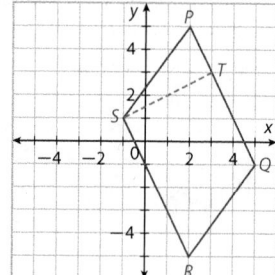

slope of $\overline{PQ} = -2$; slope of $\overline{QR} = \frac{4}{3}$; slope of $\overline{RS} = -2$; slope of $\overline{PS} = \frac{4}{3}$; Opposite sides have the same slope, so PQRS is a parallelogram. $\overline{ST}$ appears to be an altitude of $\square PQRS$. slope of $\overline{ST} = \frac{1}{2}$; so $\overline{ST} \perp \overline{PQ}$

$b = PQ = \sqrt{45} = 3\sqrt{5}$; $h = ST = \sqrt{20} = 2\sqrt{5}$

area of PQRS:

$A = bh = \left(3\sqrt{5}\right)\left(2\sqrt{5}\right) = 30$ units²

© Houghton Mifflin Harcourt Publishing Company

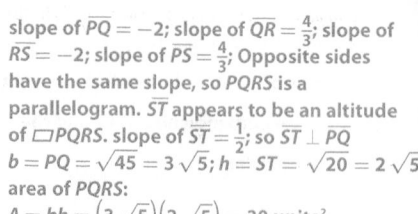

Exercise	Depth of Knowledge (D.O.K.)	COMMON CORE Mathematical Practices
1–12	**2** Skills/Concepts	**MP.2** Reasoning
13–15	**2** Skills/Concepts	**MP.4** Modeling
16–17	**2** Skills/Concepts	**MP.4** Modeling
18–19	**2** Skills/Concepts H.O.T.	**MP.4** Modeling
20	**3** Strategic Thinking H.O.T.	**MP.3** Logic

Find the area of each figure by addition.

7.

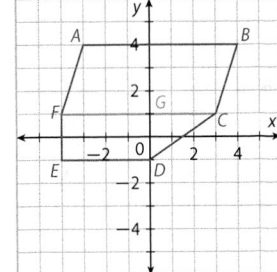

Divide the polygon into ▱ABCF, rectangle DEFG, and right △CDG.

area of ▱ABCF: $A = (7)(3) = 21$

area of DEFG: $A = (4)(2) = 8$

area of △CDG: $A = \frac{1}{2}(3)(2) = 3$

area of ABCDEF: $A = 21 + 8 + 3 = 32$ units²

8.

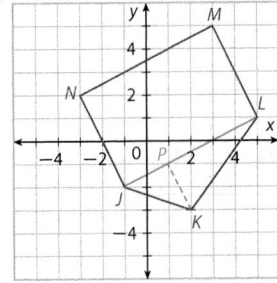

Divide the polygon into △JKL, and quadrilateral JLMN.

slope of $\overline{JL} = \frac{1}{2}$; slope of $\overline{LM} = -2$; slope of $\overline{MN} = \frac{1}{2}$;

slope of $\overline{JN} = -2$

Adjacent sides are perpendicular, so JLMN is a rectangle.

$b = JL = \sqrt{45} = 3\sqrt{5}; h = LM = \sqrt{20} = 2\sqrt{5}$

area of JLMN: $A = (3\sqrt{5})(2\sqrt{5}) = 30$

Use $\overline{JL}$ as the base and $\overline{KP}$ as the height of △JKL.

slope of $\overline{KP} = -2$; so $\overline{KP} \perp \overline{JL}$

$b = JL = 3\sqrt{5}; h = KP = \sqrt{5}$

area of △JKL: $A = \frac{1}{2}(3\sqrt{5})(\sqrt{5}) = 7.5$

area of JKLMN: $A = 30 + 7.5 = 37.5$ units²

Find the area of each figure by subtraction.

9.

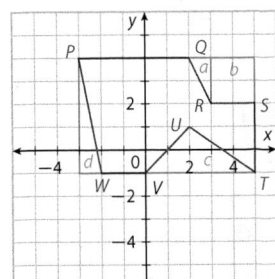

area of large rectangle: $A = (8)(5) = 40$

a. $A = \frac{1}{2}(1)(2) = 1$ b. $A = (2)^2 = 4$

c. $A = \frac{1}{2}(5)(2) = 5$ d. $A = \frac{1}{2}(1)(5) = 2.5$

area of PQRSTUVW: $A = 40 - 1 - 4 - 5 - 2.5 = 27.5$ units²

10.

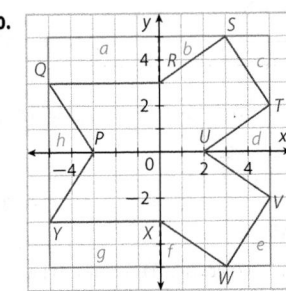

area of large rectangle: $A = (10)(10) = 100$ unit²

a. $A = (5)(2) = 10$ units²   b. $A = \frac{1}{2}(3)(2) = 3$ units²

c. $A = \frac{1}{2}(3)(2) = 3$ units²   d. $A = \frac{1}{2}(4)(3) = 6$ units²

e. $A = \frac{1}{2}(3)(2) = 3$ units²   f. $A = \frac{1}{2}(3)(2) = 3$ units²

g. $A = (5)(2) = 10$ units²   h. $A = \frac{1}{2}(6)(2) = 6$ units²

area of polygon:

$A = 100 - 10 - 3 - 3 - 6 - 3 - 3 - 10 - 6 = 56$ units²

MODELING

Give each student a sheet of graph paper. Ask students to draw the x- and y-axes and a triangle or quadrilateral in which none of the sides are congruent or parallel to one of the axes. Have them visually estimate the perimeter and area of their figures by counting units and squares. Then have them find the coordinates of the vertices and find the exact perimeter and area of their figures. Ask them to compare the results.

11. Fencing costs $1.45 per yard, and each unit on the grid represents 50 yd. How much will it cost to fence the plot of land represented by the polygon *ABCDEF*?

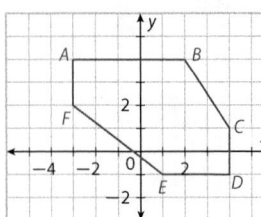

$AB = 5$, $CD = 2$, $DE = 3$, $AF = 2$

$BC = \sqrt{13}$, $EF = \sqrt{25} = 5$

perimeter of $ABCDEF = 17 + \sqrt{13} \approx 20.61$

length of fencing: 20.61×50 yd $= 1{,}030.5$ yd

cost of fencing: $1{,}030.5$ yd $\times \$1.45$/yd $= \$1{,}494.23$

12. A machine component has a geometric shaped plate, represented on the coordinate grid. Each unit on the grid represents 1 cm. Each plate is punched from an 8-cm square of alloy. The cost of the alloy is $0.43/cm², but $0.28/cm² can be recovered on wasted scraps of alloy. What is the net cost of alloy for each component?

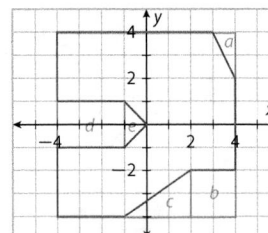

Area of alloy used: $A = (8 \text{ cm})^2 = 64 \text{ cm}^2$

Cost of alloy used: $64 \text{ cm}^2 \times \$0.43/\text{cm}^2 = \$27.52$

Area of wasted scraps:

a: $A = 1$ b: $A = 4$ c: $A = 3$

d: $A = 6$ e: $A = 1$

$A = 1 + 4 + 3 + 6 + 1 = 15 \text{ cm}^2$

Savings from wasted scraps: $15 \times \$0.28 = \$4.20$

Net cost of component: $\$27.52 - \$4.20 = \$23.32$

13. $\triangle ABC$ with vertices $A(1, 1)$ and $B(3, 5)$ has an area of 10 units². What is the location of the third vertex? Select all that apply. **B, C, and D**

A. $C(-5, 5)$ $b = 8, h = 4; A = \frac{1}{2}bh = \frac{1}{2}(8)(4) = 16$ units²

B. $C(3, -5)$ $b = 10, h = 2; A = \frac{1}{2}bh = \frac{1}{2}(10)(2) = 10$ units²

C. $C(-2, 5)$ $b = 5, h = 4; A = \frac{1}{2}bh = \frac{1}{2}(5)(4) = 10$ units²

D. $C(6, 1)$ $b = 5, h = 4; A = \frac{1}{2}bh = \frac{1}{2}(5)(4) = 10$ units²

E. $C(3, -3)$ $b = 8, h = 2; A = \frac{1}{2}bh = \frac{1}{2}(8)(2) = 8$ units²

14. Pentagon *ABCDE* shows the path of an obstacle course, where each unit of the coordinate plane represents 10 meters. Find the length of the course to the nearest meter.

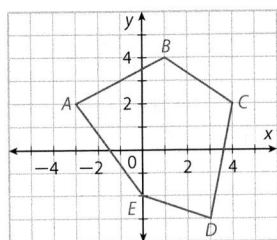

$A(-3, 2), B(1, 4), C(4, 2), D(3, -3), E(0, -2)$

$AB = \sqrt{20} \approx 4.5; BC = \sqrt{13} \approx 3.6; CD = \sqrt{26} \approx 5.1; DE = \sqrt{10} \approx 3.2; EA = \sqrt{25} = 5$

$P = 4.5 + 3.6 + 5.1 + 3.2 + 5 = 21.4;$ course $= 21.4$ units $\times 10$ meter/unit $= 214$ meters

Algebra Graph each set of lines to form a triangle. Find the area and perimeter.

15. $y = 2, x = 5,$ and $y = x$

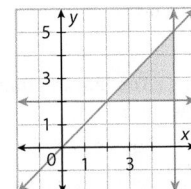

$b = 3, h = 3,$ 3rd side $= \sqrt{18} = 3\sqrt{2}$

$P = 3 + 3 + 3\sqrt{2} \approx 10.2$ units

$A = \frac{1}{2}(3)(3) = 4.5$ units^2

16. $y = -5, x = 2,$ and $y = -2x + 7$

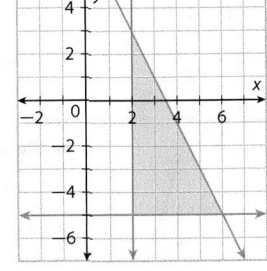

$b = 4, h = 8,$ 3rd side $= \sqrt{80} = 4\sqrt{5}$

$P \approx 20.9$ units; $A = 16$ units^2

17. Prove that quadrilateral *JKLM* with vertices $J(1, 5), K(4, 2), L(1, -4),$ and $M(-2, 2)$ is a kite, and find its area.

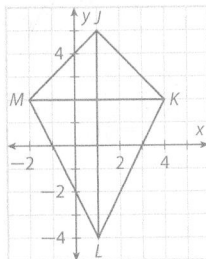

$JK = \sqrt{18} = 3\sqrt{2}; KL = \sqrt{45} = 3\sqrt{5};$

$LM = \sqrt{45} = 3\sqrt{5}; JM = \sqrt{18} = 3\sqrt{2}$

So $\overline{JK} \cong \overline{JM} \not\cong \overline{KL} \cong \overline{LM}$, and therefore *JKLM* is a kite.

$b = d_1 = 9, h = d_2 = 6$

$A = \frac{1}{2}d_1d_2 = \frac{1}{2}(9)(6) = 27$ units^2

AVOID COMMON ERRORS

Remind students to divide composite figures into shapes that are not overlapping. Otherwise, some of the area will be counted twice and the answer will not be correct.

JOURNAL

Have students write a journal entry in which they draw a polygon on a coordinate plane and then explain the steps for finding the polygon's perimeter and area.

18. **Explain the Error** Wendell is trying to prove that $ABCD$ is a rhombus and to find its area. Identify and correct his error. (*Hint:* A rhombus is a quadrilateral with four congruent sides.)

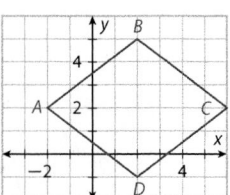

$$AB = \sqrt{\left(2 - (-2)\right)^2 + \left(5 - 2\right)^2} = \sqrt{25} = 5,$$

$$BC = \sqrt{\left(6 - 2\right)^2 + \left(2 - 5\right)^2} = \sqrt{25} = 5$$

$$CD = \sqrt{\left(2 - 6\right)^2 + \left(-1 - 2\right)^2} = \sqrt{25} = 5,$$

$$AD = \sqrt{\left(2 - (-2)\right)^2 + \left(-1 - (2)\right)^2} = \sqrt{25} = 5$$

So $\overline{AB} \cong \overline{BC} \cong \overline{CD} \cong \overline{AD}$, and therefore $ABCD$ is a rhombus.

area of $ABCD$: $b = AB = 5$ and $h = BC = 5$, so $A = bh = (5)(5) = 25$

Wendell's area calculation is incorrect because $\overline{BC}$ is not an altitude of $ABCD$. Instead, divide $ABCD$ into triangles ABC and ADC. For both these triangles, $b = AC = 8$ and $h = 3$.

area of $\triangle ABC$ and $\triangle ADC$: $A = \frac{1}{2}(8)(3) = 12$; area of $ABCD$: $A = 2(12) = 24$

19. **Communicate Mathematical Ideas** Using the figure, prove that the area of a kite is half the product of its diagonals. (Do not make numerical calculations.)

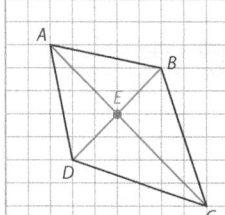

Since $ABCD$ is a kite, $\overline{AD} \cong \overline{AB}$ and $\overline{CD} \cong \overline{CB}$ The kite can then be divided into two triangles with the same base.

Therefore, $\overline{AE}$ is an altitude for $\triangle ABD$ with base $\overline{BD}$, and $\overline{CE}$ is an altitude for $\triangle CBD$ with base $\overline{BD}$.

area of $\triangle ABD$: $A = \frac{1}{2}(BD)(AE)$; area of $\triangle CBD$: $A = \frac{1}{2}(BD)(CE)$

area of $ABCD$: $A = \frac{1}{2}(BD)(AE) + \frac{1}{2}(BD)(CE) = \frac{1}{2}(BD)(AE + CE)$
$$= \frac{1}{2}(BD)(AC)$$

20. **Justify Reasoning** Use the Trapezoid Midsegment Theorem to show that the area of a trapezoid is the product of its midsegment and its height.

area of left triangle: $\frac{1}{2}xh$; area of rectangle: $b_2 h$;

area of right triangle: $\frac{1}{2}yh$

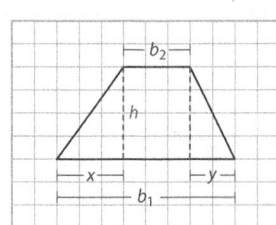

area of trapezoid: $A = \frac{1}{2}xh + b_2 h + \frac{1}{2}yh = \frac{1}{2}\left(x + 2b_2 + y\right)h$.

However, $b_1 = x + b_2 + y$, so area of trapezoid is

$A = \frac{1}{2}\left(x + b_2 + y + b_2\right)h = \frac{1}{2}(b_1 + b_2)h$

By Trapezoid Midsegment Theorem, length of midsegment

is $m = \frac{1}{2}(b_1 + b_2)$, so $A = \frac{1}{2}(b_1 + b_2)h = mh$.

Lesson Performance Task

The coordinate plane shows the floor plan of two rooms in Fritz's house. Because he enjoys paradoxes, Fritz has decided to entertain his friends with one by drawing lines on the floor of his tiled kitchen, on the left, and his tiled recreation room, on the right. The four sections in the kitchen are congruent to the four sections in the recreation room. Each square on the floor plan measures 1 yard on a side.

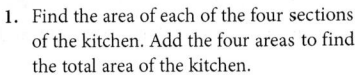

1. Find the area of each of the four sections of the kitchen. Add the four areas to find the total area of the kitchen.

2. Find the area of the kitchen by finding the product of the length and the width.

3. Find the area of the recreation room by finding the product of the length and the width.

4. Describe the paradox.

5. Explain the paradox.

1. Section 1 and Section 2 have areas of 20 yd². Section 3 and Section 4 have areas of 12 yd². The area of the kitchen is 20 + 20 + 12 + 12 = 64 yd².

2. Area of kitchen = 8 × 8 = 64 yd²

3. Area of recreation room = 5 × 13 = 65 yd²

4. It appears that the four pieces have different total areas when they are rearranged. That doesn't make sense. The sum of the four areas should be the same no matter how the pieces are arranged.

5. The paradox is easiest to explain by analyzing the slope of the long diagonal of the recreation room. The top third of the diagonal is the right edge of Section 1. Its slope is $\frac{5}{2}$. The middle third of the diagonal divides Section 3 and Section 4. Its slope is 3. The bottom third of the diagonal is the left edge of Section 2. Its slope is $\frac{5}{2}$. The diagonal is not a line segment at all but rather three separate segments, two with slopes of $\frac{5}{2}$ and one with a slope of 3. The four sections don't quite fit together. Here's a more accurate picture of the recreation room: The thin section in the middle is the location of the extra area, the difference between 65 yd² and 64 yd².

EXTENSION ACTIVITY

Have students research geometrical area paradoxes. There are many, including the "64 = 65 Paradox," the "Rectangle Paradox," and the "Business Card Paradox." Students should choose paradoxes that intrigue them. Ask students to create a presentation that displays the paradox, gives viewers an opportunity to study the paradox and try to explain it, and then reveals the reasons behind it.

INTEGRATE MATHEMATICAL PRACTICES
Focus on Modeling

MP.4 If students are still puzzled after the reasons behind the kitchen-rec-room paradox are revealed, encourage them to carefully draw the four kitchen sections on grid paper, cut them out, and reassemble them in the shape of the recreation room. They will see that, when reassembled, the pieces along the diagonal don't quite fit together. The small discrepancy accounts for the missing 1 square yard of space.

INTEGRATE MATHEMATICAL PRACTICES
Focus on Critical Thinking

MP.3 Give students a chance to practice their algebra by explaining this paradox:

Assume that $a = b$. Then:

(1)	$a^2 = ab$	Multiply by a.
(2)	$a^2 - b^2 = ab - b^2$	Subtract b^2.
(3)	$(a + b)(a - b) = b(a - b)$	Factor.
(4)	$a + b = b$	Divide by $(a - b)$.
(5)	$b + b = b$	Substitute b for a.
(6)	$2b = b$	Simplify.
(7)	$2 = 1$	Divide by b.

The explanation is that there's a mistake in Step 4: Since $a = b$, $a - b = 0$. So, Step 4 involves division by zero, which is not permitted.

Scoring Rubric

2 points: Student correctly solves the problem and explains his/her reasoning.

1 point: Student shows good understanding of the problem but does not fully solve or explain.

0 points: Student does not demonstrate understanding of the problem.

Study Guide Review

ASSESSMENT AND INTERVENTION

Assign or customize module reviews.

MODULE PERFORMANCE TASK

COMMON CORE

Mathematical Practices: MP.1, MP.2, MP.4, MP.6
G-GPE.B.7

SUPPORTING STUDENT REASONING

Students should begin this problem by focusing on what information they will need. Here are some issues they might bring up.

- **How to find the perimeter of a polygon in the plane:** Students can identify the coordinates of each side of the polygon and then use the distance formula to find the length of each side.

- **If the area of the fire affects how much of the fire is contained:** Students should understand that the area of the fire may make the perimeter larger, but it is the perimeter that is used to calculate fire containment.

- **How to find the area of a polygon in the coordinate plane:** Students can experiment with ways to find the area, or you can offer suggestions.

Coordinate Proof Using Slope and Distance

Essential Question: How can you use coordinate proofs using slope and distance to solve real-world problems?

Key Vocabulary
coordinate proof
  (prueba coordenada)
composite figure
  (figura compuesta)

KEY EXAMPLE (Lesson 10.1)

Show that the figure given by the points $A(2, 4)$, $B(3, 2)$, $C(2, 1)$, and $D(0, 5)$ is a trapezoid.

Determine whether the slopes of $\overline{AB}$ and $\overline{CD}$ are equal to determine whether they are parallel, and whether the figure is a trapezoid.

slope of $\overline{AB} = \dfrac{4-2}{2-3} = \dfrac{2}{-1} = -2$

slope of $\overline{CD} = \dfrac{5-1}{0-2} = \dfrac{4}{-2} = -2$

Thus, the figure $ABCD$ is a trapezoid.

KEY EXAMPLE (Lesson 10.2)

Show that $\triangle ABC$ with points $A(-2, 1)$, $B(-3, 3)$, and $C(2, 3)$ is a right triangle.

A right triangle should have a pair of sides that are perpendicular.

slope of $\overline{AB} = \dfrac{1-3}{-2-(-3)} = \dfrac{-2}{1} = -2$

slope of $\overline{BC} = \dfrac{3-3}{-3-2} = \dfrac{0}{-5} = 0$

slope of $\overline{CA} = \dfrac{3-1}{2-(-2)} = \dfrac{2}{4} = \dfrac{1}{2}$

One pair of slopes has a product of -1, so the triangle is a right triangle.

KEY EXAMPLE (Lesson 10.3)

Prove the triangles $\triangle ABC$ and $\triangle DCB$ are congruent given $A(1, 1)$, $B(3, 1)$, $C(1, 4)$, and $D(3, 4)$.

Note that the triangles share a side. Find the length of each other side.

$AC = \sqrt{(1-1)^2 + (4-1)^2} = \sqrt{0+9} = 3$

$AB = \sqrt{(3-1)^2 + (1-1)^2} = \sqrt{4+0} = 2$

$DC = \sqrt{(3-1)^2 + (4-4)^2} = \sqrt{4+0} = 2$

$DB = \sqrt{(3-3)^2 + (4-1)^2} = \sqrt{0+9} = 3$

$AC = DB$, so $\overline{AC} \cong \overline{DB}$, and $AB = DC$, so $\overline{AB} \cong \overline{DC}$. Additionally, CB is congruent to itself by the Reflexive Property.

The triangles have three congruent sides, so are congruent by SSS.

SCAFFOLDING SUPPORT

- Discuss with students methods they can use to find the area that has been burned. No single formula applies since the area is an irregular polygon. However, students can break the area into smaller triangles whose areas they can find using the formula for the area of a triangle. Ask students to identify ways that the burned region can be divided into triangles.

- As an alternative, students can calculate the area of the burn by counting squares and half-squares. Some estimation will be required.

- Students can find the length of the diagonal portion of the fire line by applying either the Distance Formula or the Pythagorean Formula (from which the Distance Formula is derived).

EXERCISES

Determine whether the statement is True or False. *(Lesson 10.1)*

1. The figure given by the points $A(0, -1)$, $B(3, -2)$, $C(5, -4)$, and $D(-1, -2)$ is a trapezoid. **True**

2. The figure given by the points $A(0, 3)$, $B(5, 3)$, and $C(2, 0)$ is a right triangle. **False**

Prove or disprove the statement.

3. $\triangle ABC$ and $\triangle DEF$ are congruent, given $A(-4, 4)$, $B(-2, 5)$, $C(-3, 1)$, $D(-2, -1)$, $E(-1, -3)$, and $F(-5, -2)$. *(Lesson 10.2)*

$AB = \sqrt{(-4-(-2))^2 + (4-5)^2} = \sqrt{4+1} = \sqrt{5}$,

$AC = \sqrt{(-4-(-3))^2 + (4-1)^2} = \sqrt{1+9} = \sqrt{10}$,

$BC = \sqrt{(-2-(-3))^2 + (5-1)^2} = \sqrt{1+16} = \sqrt{17}$,

$DE = \sqrt{(-2-(-1))^2 + (-1-(-3))^2} = \sqrt{1+4} = \sqrt{5}$,

$DF = \sqrt{(-2-(-5))^2 + (-1-(-2))^2} = \sqrt{9+1} = \sqrt{10}$,

$EF = \sqrt{(-1-(-5))^2 + (-3-(-2))^2} = \sqrt{16+1} = \sqrt{17}$,

The triangles are congruent by SSS.

Find the area of the polygon. *(Lesson 10.3)*

4. *ABCDE* defined by the points $A(-3, 4)$, $B(-1, 4)$, $C(1, 1)$, $D(-1, 1)$, and $E(-4, -1)$ $6 + 2\sqrt{13}$

MODULE PERFORMANCE TASK

How Do You Calculate the Containment of a Fire?

Most news stories about large wildfires report some level of "containment" reached by firefighters. To prevent a blaze from spreading, firefighters dig a "fire line" around its perimeter. For example, if 3 miles of fire line have been dug around a fire that is 10 miles in perimeter, then the fire is said to be 30 percent contained.

The image shows a forest fire, the forest is shown by the shaded square while the fire is shown by the irregular pentagon. The darker lines show where fire lines have been dug. What is the percentage containment of the fire as well as the total area that has been burned?

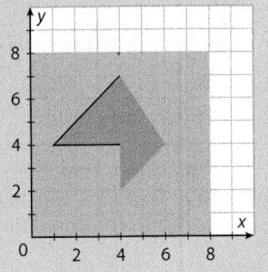

Use your own paper to complete the task. Be sure to write down all your data and assumptions. Then use graphs, numbers, words, or algebra to explain how you reached your conclusions.

© Houghton Mifflin Harcourt Publishing Company

SAMPLE SOLUTION

The burned area has a perimeter consisting of 5 line segments. First, find the lengths of the segments, beginning with the horizontal section of the fire line and moving clockwise:

- 3 units horizontally;

- Find the distance between $(1, 4)$ and $(4, 7)$:

$$\sqrt{(4-1)^2 + (7-4)^2} = \sqrt{3^2 + 3^2} = \sqrt{18} = 3\sqrt{2}$$

- Find the distance between $(4, 7)$ and $(6, 4)$:

$$\sqrt{(4-6)^2 + (7-4)^2} = \sqrt{(-2)^2 + 3^2} = \sqrt{13}$$

Find the distance between $(6, 4)$ and $(4, 2)$:

$$\sqrt{(6-4)^2 + (4-2)^2} = \sqrt{2^2 + 2^2} = \sqrt{8} = 2\sqrt{2}$$

- 2 units vertically

Total:

$3 + 3\sqrt{2} + \sqrt{13} + 2\sqrt{2} + 2 = 5 + 5\sqrt{2} + \sqrt{13}$ units; assuming 1 unit equals 1 mile, the perimeter is $5 + 5\sqrt{2} + \sqrt{13}$ miles.

Percent containment

$$= \frac{\text{dark lines}}{\text{perimeter}} = \frac{3 + 3\sqrt{2}}{5 + 5\sqrt{2} + \sqrt{13}} \times 100\%$$

$$\approx 46.2\%$$

Area of burn:

- triangle with base 3, height 3:
  area $= 0.5(3)(3) = 4.5$ square miles

- triangle with base 5, height 2:
  area $= 0.5(5)(2) = 5$ square miles

Total: $4.5 + 5 = 9.5$ square miles

DISCUSSION OPPORTUNITIES

- Can the perimeter of the fire be found by enclosing the fire region in a rectangle and then subtracting segments? Why or why not?

- Are there suppositions that need to be made so that the estimate of the level of fire containment is realistic?

Assessment Rubric

2 points: Student correctly solves the problem and explains his/her reasoning.

1 point: Student shows good understanding of the problem but does not fully solve or explain.

0 points: Student does not demonstrate understanding of the problem.

Ready to Go On?

ASSESS MASTERY

Use the assessment on this page to determine if students have mastered the concepts and standards covered in this module.

ASSESSMENT AND INTERVENTION

Access Ready to Go On? assessment online, and receive instant scoring, feedback, and customized intervention or enrichment.

ADDITIONAL RESOURCES

Response to Intervention Resources

- Reteach Worksheets

Differentiated Instruction Resources

- Reading Strategies **EL**
- Success for English Learners **EL**
- Challenge Worksheets

Assessment Resources

- Leveled Module Quizzes

(Ready) to Go On?

10.1–10.5 Coordinate Proof Using Slope and Distance

- Online Homework
- Hints and Help
- Extra Practice

Determine and prove what shaped is formed for the given coordinates for *ABCD*, and then find the perimeter and area as an exact value and rounded to the nearest tenth. *(Lessons 10.1, 10.2)*

1. $A(-10, 6)$, $B(-7, 2)$, $C(1, 8)$, $D(-6, 9)$

Trapezoid; The slope of AB is $-\frac{4}{3}$, the slope of BC is $\frac{3}{4}$, the slope of CD is $-\frac{1}{7}$, and the slope of AD is $\frac{3}{4}$. There is one pair of parallel sides, so the figure is a trapezoid. Perimeter is

$5 + 5 + 10 + 5\sqrt{2} = 27.1$; area is $\frac{3}{2} \times 5^2 = 37.5$ units^2.

2. $A(10, -6)$, $B(6, -9)$, $C(3, -5)$, $D(7, -2)$

A square, $AB = \sqrt{(6-10)^2 + (-9-(-6))^2} = \sqrt{25} = 5$

$BC = \sqrt{(6-3)^2 + (-9-(-5))^2} = \sqrt{25} = 5$

$CD = \sqrt{(7-3)^2 + (-2-(-5))^2} = \sqrt{25} = 5$

$AD = \sqrt{(7-10)^2 + (-2-(-6))^2} = \sqrt{25} = 5$ so the shape is a rhombus. The slope of AB is $\frac{-6-(-9)}{10-6} = \frac{3}{4}$, the slope of BC is $\frac{-9-(-5)}{6-3} = -\frac{4}{3}$, the slope of CD is $\frac{-2-(-5)}{7-3} = \frac{3}{4}$, and the slope of AD is $\frac{-6-(-2)}{10-7} = -\frac{4}{3}$; thus, adjacent sides are perpendicular, so $ABCD$ is a rectangle. If a figure is a rhombus and a rectangle, then it must be a square. Perimeter is

$5 + 5 + 5 + 5 = 20$; area is $5^2 = 25$ units^2.

ESSENTIAL QUESTION

3. When is a quadrilateral both a trapezoid and a parallelogram? Is a quadrilateral ever a parallelogram but not a trapezoid?

Answers may vary. Sample: When there are two pairs of parallel lines, which are two pairs of lines with the same slopes. No, since a parallelogram is a quadrilateral with two pairs of parallel lines and a trapezoid is a quadrilateral with at least one pair of parallel lines, a quadrilateral can never be a parallelogram but not a trapezoid.

© Houghton Mifflin Harcourt Publishing Company

COMMON CORE Common Core Standards

Lesson	Items	Content Standards	Mathematical Practices
10.1, 10.5	1	G-GPE.B.5, G-GPE.B.4, G-GPE.B.7	MP.4
10.3, 10.4, 10.5	2	G-GPE.B.5, G-GPE.B.4, G-GPE.B.7, G-CO.C.11	MP.4

MODULE 10
MIXED REVIEW

Assessment Readiness

1. Does the name correctly describe the shape given by the points $A(2, 2)$, $B(3, 4)$, $C(6, 4)$, and $D(5, 2)$?

   A. Rectangle   ○ Yes   ● No

   B. Parallelogram   ● Yes   ○ No

   C. Square   ○ Yes   ● No

2. Triangle ABC is given by the points $A(3, 2)$, $B(4, 4)$, and $C(5, 1)$. Choose True or False for each statement.

   A. The perimeter of $\triangle ABC$ is 9.9 units.   ○ True   ● False

   B. $\triangle ABC$ is an equilateral triangle.   ○ True   ● False

   C. The perimeter of $\triangle ABC$ is 7.6 units.   ● True   ○ False

3. Triangle DEF is given by the points $D(1, 1)$, $E(3, 8)$, and $F(8, 0)$. Choose True or False for each statement.

   A. The area of $\triangle DEF$ is 25.5 square units.   ● True   ○ False

   B. $\triangle DEF$ is a scalene triangle.   ● True   ○ False

   C. The area of $\triangle DEF$ is 30 square units.   ○ True   ● False

4. What type of triangle is given by the points $D(1, 1)$, $E(3, 8)$, and $F(5, 1)$? Explain how you could find the perimeter of the triangle.

   Possible Answer: isosceles triangle; You find the length of each side by finding the distance between each pair of points, then you find the perimeter of the triangle by adding the lengths of the sides.

5. For the polygon shown, specify how to find its area using triangles, parallelograms, and rectangles.

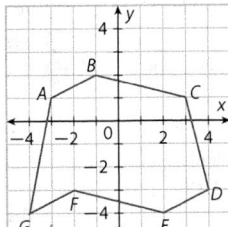

   Answers may vary. Sample: Draw segments $\overline{BF}$ and $\overline{CE}$ and then find the area of the two parallelograms and triangle. Then add them together.

MIXED REVIEW
Assessment Readiness

ASSESSMENT AND INTERVENTION

Assign ready-made or customized practice tests to prepare students for high-stakes tests.

ADDITIONAL RESOURCES

Assessment Resources

- Leveled Module Quizzes: Modified, B

AVOID COMMON ERRORS

Item 4 Some students will use the distance formula three times, which takes significant time and is not necessary. Point out that a sketch of the points will show the triangle's type and that the problem only asks for the method for finding the perimeter, not for the actual value of the perimeter.

COMMON CORE
Common Core Standards

Lesson	Items	Content Standards	Mathematical Practices
10.4, 9.2	1*	G-GPE.B.4	MP.5
10.5	2	G-GPE.B.7	MP.5
10.5	3	G-GPE.B.7	MP.1
10.3, 7.2	4*	G-GPE.B.4	MP.5
10.5	5	G-GPE.B.7	MP.6

* Item integrates mixed review concepts from previous modules or a previous course.

MIXED REVIEW
Assessment Readiness

ASSESSMENT AND INTERVENTION

Assign ready-made or customized practice tests to prepare students for high-stakes tests.

ADDITIONAL RESOURCES

Assessment Resources

- Leveled Unit Tests: Modified, A, B, C
- Performance Assessment

AVOID COMMON ERRORS

Item 3   Some students may substitute points into the slope formula incorrectly. Encourage students to label points to avoid confusion; for example:

$(-6, 2) , (4, 6)$

x_1, y_1 , x_2, y_2

- Online Homework
- Hints and Help
- Extra Practice

1. Using known properties, determine if the statements are true or not. Select True or False for each statement.

   A. If one pair of consecutive sides of a parallelogram is congruent, then the parallelogram is a rectangle. ○ True ● False

   B. If one pair of consecutive sides of a rhombus is perpendicular then the rhombus is a square. ● True ○ False

   C. If a quadrilateral has four right angles then it is a square. ○ True ● False

2. Given the line $y = -\frac{2}{5}x + 3$, determine if the given line is parallel, perpendicular, or neither. Select the correct answer for each lettered part.

   A. $y = \frac{2}{5}x + 7$ ○ Parallel ○ Perpendicular ● Neither

   B. $5y + 2x = -10$ ● Parallel ○ Perpendicular ○ Neither

   C. $-5x + 2y = 4$ ○ Parallel ● Perpendicular ○ Neither

3. Is $\overline{AB}$ parallel to $\overline{CD}$?

   Select Yes or No for each statement.

   A. $A(-5, 12), B(7, 18), C(0, -4),$ and $D(-8, 0)$ ○ Yes ● No

   B. $A(-6, 2), B(4, 6), C(7, -4),$ and $D(-3, -8)$ ● Yes ○ No

   C. $A(-6, 2), B(4, 6), C(7, -4),$ and $D(-4, -8)$ ○ Yes ● No

4. Is $\overline{RS}$ perpendicular to $\overline{DF}$?

   Select Yes or No for each statement.

   A. $R(6, -2)\ S(-1, 8)$ and $D(-1, 11)\ F(11, 4)$ ○ Yes ● No

   B. $R(1, 3)\ S(4, 7)$ and $D(3, 9)\ F(15, 0)$ ● Yes ○ No

   C. $R(-5, -5)\ S(0, 2)$ and $D(8, 3)\ F(1, 8)$ ● Yes ○ No

5. Use the distance formula to determine if $\angle ABC \cong \angle DEF$.

   Select Yes or No for each statement.

   A. $A(-5, -7), B(0, 0), C(4, -7), D(-6, -6),$ $E(-1, 1), F(5, -8)$ ○ Yes ● No

   B. $A(-3, 1), B(1, 1), C(-4, -8), D(1, 1),$ $E(-3, 1), F(4, 8)$ ○ Yes ● No

   C. $A(-8, 8), B(-4, 6), C(-10, 2), D(4, -4),$ $E(8, -2), F(2, 2)$ ● Yes ○ No

569

Common Core Standards

Items	Content Standards	Mathematical Practices
1	**G-CO.C.11**	**MP.2, MP.7**
2	**G-GPE.B.5**	**MP.2, MP.7**
3*	**G-GPE.B.5**	**MP.5**
4*	**G-GPE.B.5**	**MP.5**
5*	**N-CN.B.6**	**MP.2, MP.7**

* Item integrates mixed review concepts from previous modules or a previous course.

6. Is Point M the midpoint of $\overline{AB}$? Select Yes or No for each statement.

Select True or False for each statement.

A. $A(1, 2)$, $B(3,4)$, $M(2, 3)$ ● Yes   ○ No

B. $A(0, 8)$, $B(10,-1)$, $M(5, 3.5)$ ● Yes   ○ No

C. $A(-7, -5)$, $B(6, 4)$, $M(-1, -1)$ ○ Yes   ● No

D. $A(4, -2)$, $B(6, -8)$, $M(5, -5)$ ● Yes   ○ No

7. Determine whether the statement about $QRST$ is true or false using the given image.

Select True or False for each statement.

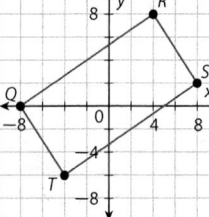

A. The diagonals of $QRST$ are congruent.   ● True   ○ False

B. $QRST$ is a square.   ○ True   ● False

C. $QRST$ is a rectangle.   ● True   ○ False

D. The diagonals of $QRST$ are perpendicular.   ○ True   ● False

8. In trapezoid $JKLM$, determine LM.

$$PQ = \frac{1}{2}(JK + LM)$$

$$11.4 = \frac{1}{2}(10.7 + LM)$$

$$11.4 = 5.35 + \frac{1}{2}LM$$

$$6.05 = \frac{1}{2}LM$$

$$12.1 = LM$$

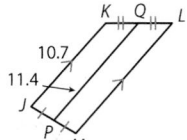

9. The midpoints of an irregular quadrilateral $ABCD$ are connected to form another quadrilateral inside $ABCD$. Explain why the quadrilateral is a parallelogram.

Draw a diagonal of $ABCD$. Because of the midsegment theorem, the diagonal is parallel to two opposite sides of the new quadrilateral. Each of these two sides is also half the length of the diagonal, so they are congruent. If opposite sides of a quadrilateral are both parallel and congruent, then the quadrilateral is a parallelogram.

PERFORMANCE TASKS

There are three different levels of performance tasks:

*Novice: These are short word problems that require students to apply the math they have learned in straightforward, real-world situations.

****Apprentice:** These are more involved problems that guide students step-by-step through more complex tasks. These exercises include more complicated reasoning, writing, and open ended elements.

*****Expert:** These are open-ended, nonroutine problems that, instead of stepping the students through, ask them to choose their own methods for solving and justify their answers and reasoning.

Common Core Standards

Items	Content Standards	Mathematical Practices
6	N-CN.B.6	MP.2, MP.7
7	G-CO.C.11	MP.3, MP.8
8	G-CO.C.11	MP.2
9	G-CO.C.11	MP.6

* Item integrates mixed review concepts from previous modules or a previous course.

SCORING GUIDES

Item 10 (2 points) Award the student 2 points for correctly identifying the shape as a rhombus and justifying answer.

Item 11 (6 points)

2 points for correctly finding the area of the given figure

2 points for correctly finding the area of the new logo

2 points for showing work

Item 12 (6 points)

2 points for correctly finding the perimeter of the kite

2 points for correctly finding the perimeter of the whole figure

2 points for correct explanations

Performance Tasks

★**10.** Streets of a city can be represented by the equations in the given table. Use the equations to find the type of quadrilateral that the streets form. Justify your answer.

Street	Equation
Pine Street	$3x - y = -4$
Danis Road	$3y - x = 4$
Granite Park	$3y = x + 12$
Jason Drive	$y = 3x - 4$

Granite Park and Danis Road both have equal slopes of $\frac{1}{3}$, so these roads are parallel. Pine Street and Jason Drive both have equal slopes of 3, so these roads are parallel. The roads form a parallelogram, and because each side is the same length, the streets form a rhombus.

★★**11.** The composite figure shown below represents the design for a new logo. Determine the area of a logo that has twice the area of the image provided. Allow 1 unit to represent two inches. Show your work.

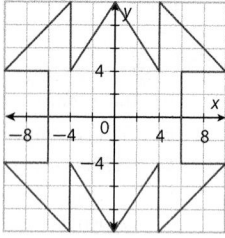

Possible answer: Divide the figure into triangles and a rectangle.

Four triangles have an area equal to $A = \frac{1}{2}(3)(3) = 4.5$ squares.

The two central triangles have an area equal to $A = \frac{1}{2}(4)(3) = 6$ squares. The rectangle has an area equal to 24 squares. The total area of the figure is $4(4.5) + 2(6) + 24 = 54$ squares. Since each square on the coordinate grid is equal to $(2)(2) = 4$ in², the area of the design is $4(54) = 216$ in². Twice this area is $(2)(216) = 432$ in².

★★★**12.** Each square section in an iron railing contains four small kites. The figure shows the dimensions of one kite. What length of iron is needed to outline one small kite? How much iron is needed to outline one complete section, including the square? Explain how each answer was found.

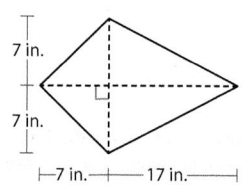 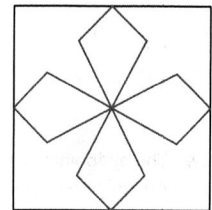

The kite can be thought of as a composite of four right triangles.

The smaller triangles have legs equal to 7 in. and hypotenuse of $c = \sqrt{7^2 + 7^2} = 7\sqrt{2}$ in. The two larger triangles have legs of 7 in. and 17 in., and a hypotenuse of $c = \sqrt{7^2 + 17^2} = \sqrt{338} = 13\sqrt{2}$ in. The length of iron needed to outline one small kite is $2(7\sqrt{2}) + 2(13\sqrt{2}) = 40\sqrt{2}$ in. The square has a side length equal to twice the longer length of one kite, which is $(2)(7 + 17) = 48$ in. The perimeter of the square is $(4)(48) = 192$ in. So the total length of iron is $4(40\sqrt{2}) + 192 = 192 + 160\sqrt{2} \approx 418.3$ in.

© Houghton Mifflin Harcourt Publishing Company

Urban planners A city planner is working to add a new street for the purpose of easing traffic congestion. The current streets can be represented by the image given. Where could the planner add the new street so that the streets form a square? Give the equation and add the line to the drawing.

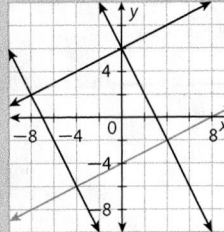

$$y = \frac{1}{2}x - 4$$

MATH IN CAREERS

Urban Planner In this Unit Performance Task, students can see how an urban planner uses mathematics on the job.

For more information about careers in mathematics as well as various mathematics appreciation topics, visit the American Mathematical Society http://www.ams.org

SCORING GUIDES

Task (6 points)

2 points for correctly finding the slope of the line

2 points for correctly finding the equation of the line

2 points for correctly adding the line to the drawing

Similarity

CONTENTS

Unit Pacing Guide

45-Minute Classes

Module 11

DAY 1	DAY 2	DAY 3	DAY 4	DAY 5
Lesson 11.1	Lesson 11.1	Lesson 11.2	Lesson 11.2	Lesson 11.3

DAY 6	DAY 7	DAY 8		
Lesson 11.3	Lesson 11.4	Module Review and Assessment Readiness		

Module 12

DAY 1	DAY 2	DAY 3	DAY 4	DAY 5
Lesson 12.1	Lesson 12.2	Lesson 12.2	Lesson 12.3	Lesson 12.3

DAY 6	DAY 7	DAY 8		
Lesson 12.4	Module Review and Assessment Readiness	Unit Review and Assessment Readiness		

90-Minute Classes

Module 11

DAY 1	DAY 2	DAY 3	DAY 4
Lesson 11.1	Lesson 11.2	Lesson 11.3	Lesson 11.4
			Module Review and Assessment Readiness

Module 12

DAY 1	DAY 2	DAY 3	DAY 4
Lesson 12.1	Lesson 12.2	Lesson 12.3	Module Review and Assessment Readiness
Lesson 12.2	Lesson 12.3	Lesson 12.4	Unit Review and Assessment Readiness

Program Resources

PLAN

HMH Teacher App

Access a full suite of teacher resources online and offline on a variety of devices. Plan present, and manage classes, assignments, and activities.

ePlanner **Easily plan your classes, create and view assignments, and access all program resources with your online, customizable planning tool.**

Professional Development Videos

Authors Juli Dixon and Matt Larson model successful teaching practices and strategies in actual classroom settings.

QR Codes **Scan with your smart phone to jump directly from your print book to online videos and other resources.**

Teacher's Edition

Support students with point-of-use Questioning Strategies, teaching tips, resources for differentiated instruction, additional activities, and more.

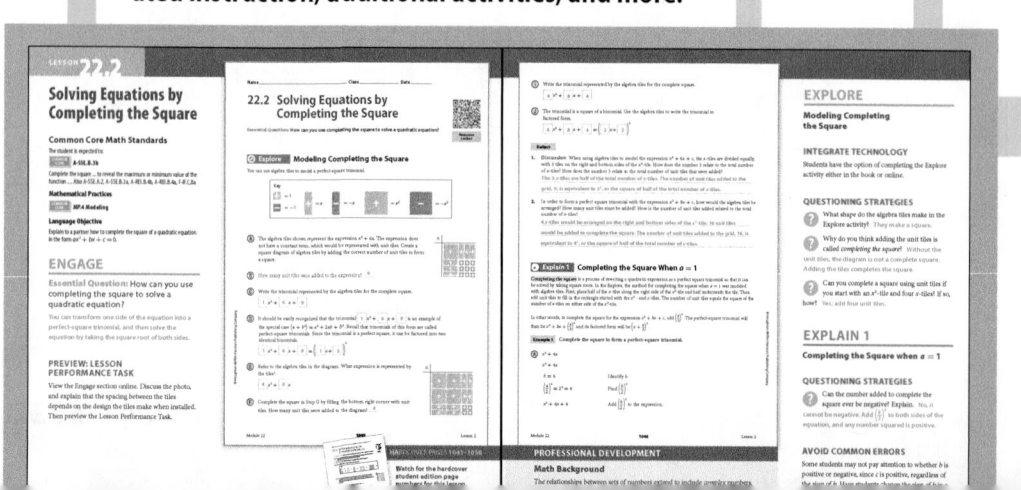

ENGAGE AND EXPLORE

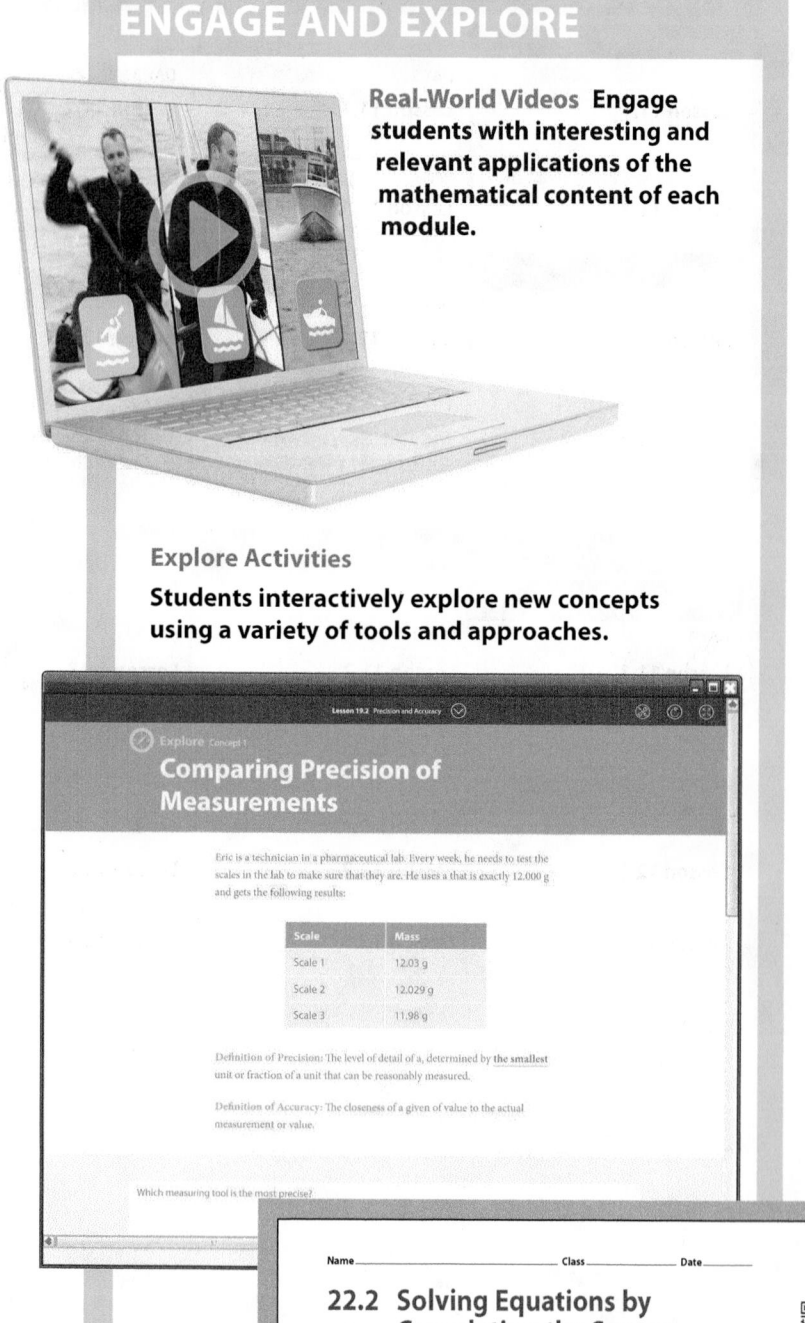

Real-World Videos **Engage students with interesting and relevant applications of the mathematical content of each module.**

Explore Activities

Students interactively explore new concepts using a variety of tools and approaches.

Lesson 19.2 Precision and Accuracy

Explore Concept 1

Comparing Precision of Measurements

Eric is a technician in a pharmaceutical lab. Every week, he needs to test the scales in the lab to make sure that they are. He uses a that is exactly 12.000 g and gets the following results:

Scale	Mass
Scale 1	12.03 g
Scale 2	12.029 g
Scale 3	11.98 g

Definition of Precision: The level of detail of a, determined by **the smallest** unit or fraction of a unit that can be reasonably measured.

Definition of Accuracy: The closeness of a given value to the actual measurement or value.

Which measuring tool is the most precise?

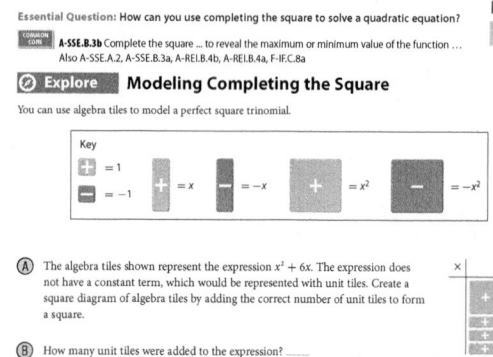

Name_____ Class_____ Date_____

22.2 Solving Equations by Completing the Square

Essential Question: How can you use completing the square to solve a quadratic equation?

A-SSE.B.3b Complete the square ... to reveal the maximum or minimum value of the function ... Also A-SSE.A.2, A-SSE.B.3a, A-REI.B.4b, A-REI.B.4a, F-IF.C.8a

Explore   Modeling Completing the Square

You can use algebra tiles to model a perfect square trinomial.

Key

$+$ = 1 $+$ = x $-$ = −x $+$ = x^2 $-$ = $-x^2$

$-$ = −1

(A) The algebra tiles shown represent the expression $x^2 + 6x$. The expression does not have a constant term, which would be represented with unit tiles. Create a square diagram of algebra tiles by adding the correct number of unit tiles to form a square.

(B) How many unit tiles were added to the expression? _____

(C) Write the trinomial represented by the algebra tiles for the complete square.

☐ $x^2 +$ ☐ $x +$ ☐

(D) It should be easily recognized that the trinomial ☐ $x^2 +$ ☐ $x +$ ☐ is an example of

TEACH

Math On the Spot video tutorials, featuring program author Dr. Edward Burger, accompany every example in the textbook and give students step-by-step instructions and explanations of key math concepts.

Interactive Teacher Edition

Customize and present course materials with collaborative activities and integrated formative assessment.

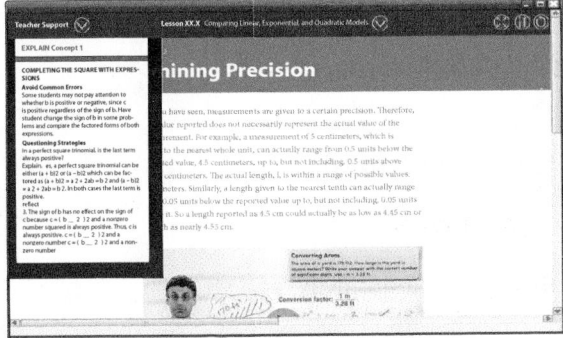

Differentiated Instruction Resources

Support all learners with Differentiated Instruction Resources, including

- **Leveled Practice and Problem Solving**
- **Reading Strategies**
- **Success for English Learners**
- **Challenge**

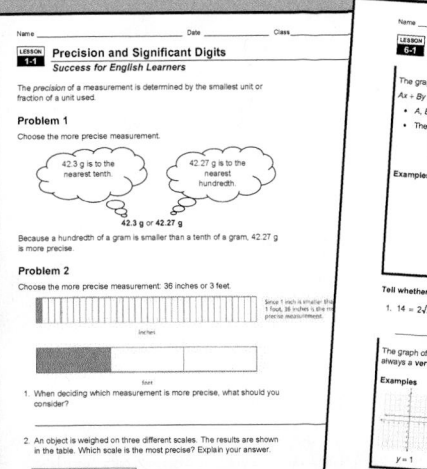
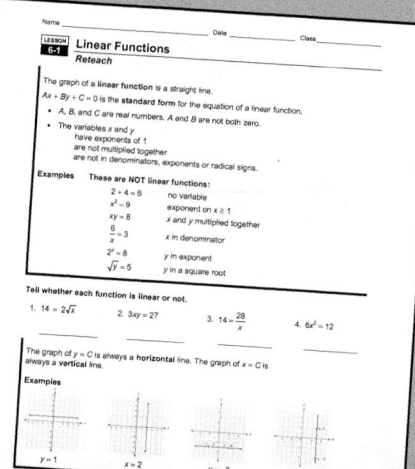

ASSESSMENT AND INTERVENTION

The **Personal Math Trainer** provides online practice, homework, assessments, and intervention. Monitor student progress through reports and alerts. **Create and customize assignments aligned to specific lessons or Common Core standards.**

- **Practice** – With dynamic items and assignments, students get unlimited practice on key concepts supported by guided examples, step-by-step solutions, and video tutorials.

- **Assessments** – Choose from course assignments or customize your own based on course content, Common Core standards, difficulty levels, and more.

- **Homework** – Students can complete online homework with a wide variety of problem types, including the ability to enter expressions, equations, and graphs. Let the system automatically grade homework, so you can focus where your students need help the most!

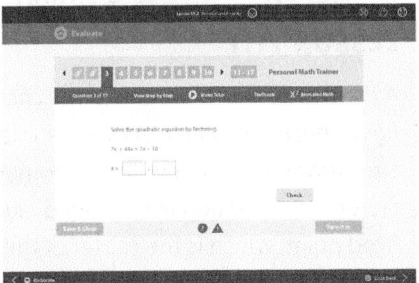

- **Intervention** – Let the Personal Math Trainer automatically prescribe a targeted, personalized intervention path for your students.

Focus on Higher Order Thinking

Raise the bar with homework and practice that incorporates higher-order thinking and mathematical practices in every lesson.

Assessment Readiness

Prepare students for success on high stakes tests for Geometry with practice at every module and unit

Assessment Resources

Tailor assessments and response to intervention to meet the needs of all your classes and students, including

- Leveled Module Quizzes
- Leveled Unit Tests
- Unit Performance Tasks
- Placement, Diagnostic, and Quarterly Benchmark Tests
- Tier 1, Tier 2, and Tier 3 Resources

Math Background

Transformations G-SRT.A.2

LESSONS 11.1 and 11.2

A *transformation* is *a function that changes the position, size, or shape of a figure*. In this course, the emphasis is on transformations that are most closely linked to congruence and similarity: reflections, translations, rotations, and dilations.

However, it is important to understand that there exist many other transformations. Perhaps the simplest transformation is the transformation that maps every point to itself. This is known as *the identity transformation*. Another simple transformation is the one that maps every point to the origin.

Dilations G-SRT.A.1

LESSON 11.1

A *dilation* is *a transformation that changes the size of a figure, but not its shape*. As such, a dilation is an example of a transformation that is not an isometry (unless the scale factor of the dilation is 1). Every dilation has exactly one fixed point, which is the center of the dilation.

Although dilations do not preserve distance, they do preserve other properties of a figure. For example, dilations preserve angle measure. In other words, under a dilation, an angle in the preimage is congruent to the corresponding angle in the image.

Dilations also preserve parallel lines. That is, two lines that are parallel in the preimage are mapped to two parallel lines in the image.

If two figures are congruent, then there is an isometry that maps one figure onto the other. If two figures are similar, one may be mapped onto the other through a combination of a dilation and an isometry.

A dilation with a scale factor greater than 1 is an enlargement. A dilation with a scale factor greater than 0 but less than 1 is a reduction.

It is also possible to extend the definition of a dilation to allow a scale factor of 0 (in this case, the entire preimage is collapsed to a single point, the center of dilation) and negative scale factors.

A dilation with a scale factor of $-k$, where $k > 0$, is equivalent to the dilation with scale factor k followed by a rotation of 180° about the center of dilation.

Similarity G-SRT.A.2

LESSONS 11.2 to 11.4

Recall that two figures can be defined as congruent if there is a sequence of isometries—reflections, translations, and/or rotations—that maps one figure onto the other. Likewise, *similarity* may be defined in terms of transformations. In particular, *two figures are similar if one may be obtained from the other through a combination of a dilation and one or more isometries*. Dilations transform figures by enlarging or reducing them.

Finally, it is worth noting that similarity is an equivalence relation; that is, similarity is reflexive, symmetric, and transitive.

For figures F_1, F_2, and F_3, $F_1 \sim F_1$ (reflexivity);

if $F_1 \sim F_2$, then $F_2 \sim F_1$ (symmetry); and

if $F_1 \sim F_2$ and $F_2 \sim F_3$, then $F_1 \sim F_3$ (transitivity).

Triangle Proportionality G-SRT.B.4

LESSON 12.1

The Triangle Proportionality Theorem states that if a line is parallel to a side of a triangle and intersects the other two sides, then it divides those sides proportionally. In the figure, $\overleftrightarrow{EF} \parallel \overline{BC}$. Therefore, $\frac{AE}{EB} = \frac{AF}{FC}$.

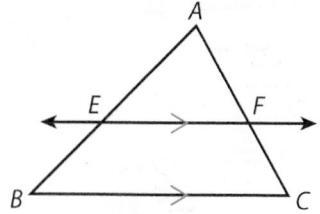

The proof, which uses similarity and facts about proportions, runs as follows. Because they are corresponding angles, $\angle AEF \cong \angle ABC$. Since $\angle A \cong \angle A$, $\triangle AEF \sim \triangle ABC$ by AA Similarity.

Thus, $\frac{AE}{AB} = \frac{AF}{AC}$, so the reciprocals are also equal, $\frac{AB}{AE} = \frac{AC}{AF}$.

By the Segment Addition Postulate, $AB = AE + EB$ and $AC = AF + FC$. By substitution, $\frac{AE + EB}{AE} = \frac{AF + AC}{AF}$ or $1 + \frac{EB}{AE} = 1 + \frac{FC}{AF}$. Therefore, $\frac{EB}{AE} = \frac{FC}{AF}$, which is equivalent to the required proportion.

Proportional Relationships

 **G-SRT.B.5**

LESSONS 12.2 and 12.3

A *proportion* is *an equation that states that two ratios are equal.* Students should realize that the steps for solving a proportion such as $\frac{x}{3} = \frac{5}{8}$ are the same as those for solving any other type of equation; that is, the equation must be transformed into simpler equivalent equations with the goal of isolating the variable on one side of the equation. A possible first step in solving $\frac{x}{3} = \frac{5}{8}$ is to clear the fractions by multiplying both sides of the equation by $3 \cdot 8$ or 24. This results in the equivalent equation $8x = 15$, which may be solved by dividing both sides by 8.

Students may already be familiar with the shortcut that results from performing the initial multiplication on a general proportion—the Cross Product Property. This property states that if $\frac{a}{b} = \frac{c}{d}$, where $b \neq 0$ and $d \neq 0$, then $ad = bc$.

To see why the Cross Product Property is true, begin by multiplying both sides of the proportion $\frac{a}{b} = \frac{c}{d}$ by bd.

$$\frac{a}{b} = \frac{c}{d},$$

$(bd)\frac{a}{b} = (bd)\frac{c}{d},$ *Multiplication Property of Equality*

$\frac{bda}{b} = \frac{bdc}{d}$ *Multiply.*

$da = bc$ *Simplify.*

$ad = bc$ *Commutative Property of Mult.*

Similarity in Right Triangles

 G-SRT.B.4

LESSON 12.4

In 1816, the French mathematician August Leopold Crelle stated, "It is indeed wonderful that so simple a figure as the triangle is so inexhaustible in properties." It is possible to develop and prove theorems that are increasingly elegant and unexpected, for example, the rather surprising fact that the three altitudes of any triangle are concurrent.

This lesson contains the following important theorems:

- The altitude to the hypotenuse of a right triangle forms two triangles that are similar to each other and to the original triangle.
- The length of the altitude to the hypotenuse of a right triangle is the geometric mean of the lengths of the two segments of the hypotenuse.
- The length of a leg of a right triangle is the geometric mean of the lengths of the hypotenuse and segment of the hypotenuse adjacent to that leg.
- The Pythagorean Theorem

The Pythagorean Theorem, one of the best-known relationships in mathematics, can be traced back almost as far as recorded history itself. Most of the early appearances of the theorem occur in the form of Pythagorean triples (sets of three nonzero whole numbers a, b, and c such that $a^2 + b^2 = c^2$). One example is the clay tablet known as Plimpton 322, which was written in Babylonia around 1800 B.C.E.; it contains 15 rows of numbers based on Pythagorean triples.

Such archaeological findings show that the relationship was known long before the time of the Greek mathematician Pythagoras (c. 582 B.C.E.–507 B.C.E.); it is because of the work of later Greek and Roman historians that the theorem has come to bear Pythagoras's name.

Regardless of its beginnings, the theorem has continued to inspire both professional and amateur mathematicians because of its elegance and adaptability to diverse methods of proof.

In fact, The Pythagorean Proposition by Elisha Scott Loomis presents more than 350 different proofs of the Pythagorean Theorem!

Similarity

MATH IN CAREERS
Unit Activity Preview

After completing this unit, students will complete a Math in Careers task by using similarity to make a calculation for a special effects engineer. Critical skills include modeling real-world situations and using similar figures to find missing measurements.

For more information about careers in mathematics as well as various mathematics appreciation topics, visit The American Mathematical Society at http://www.ams.org.

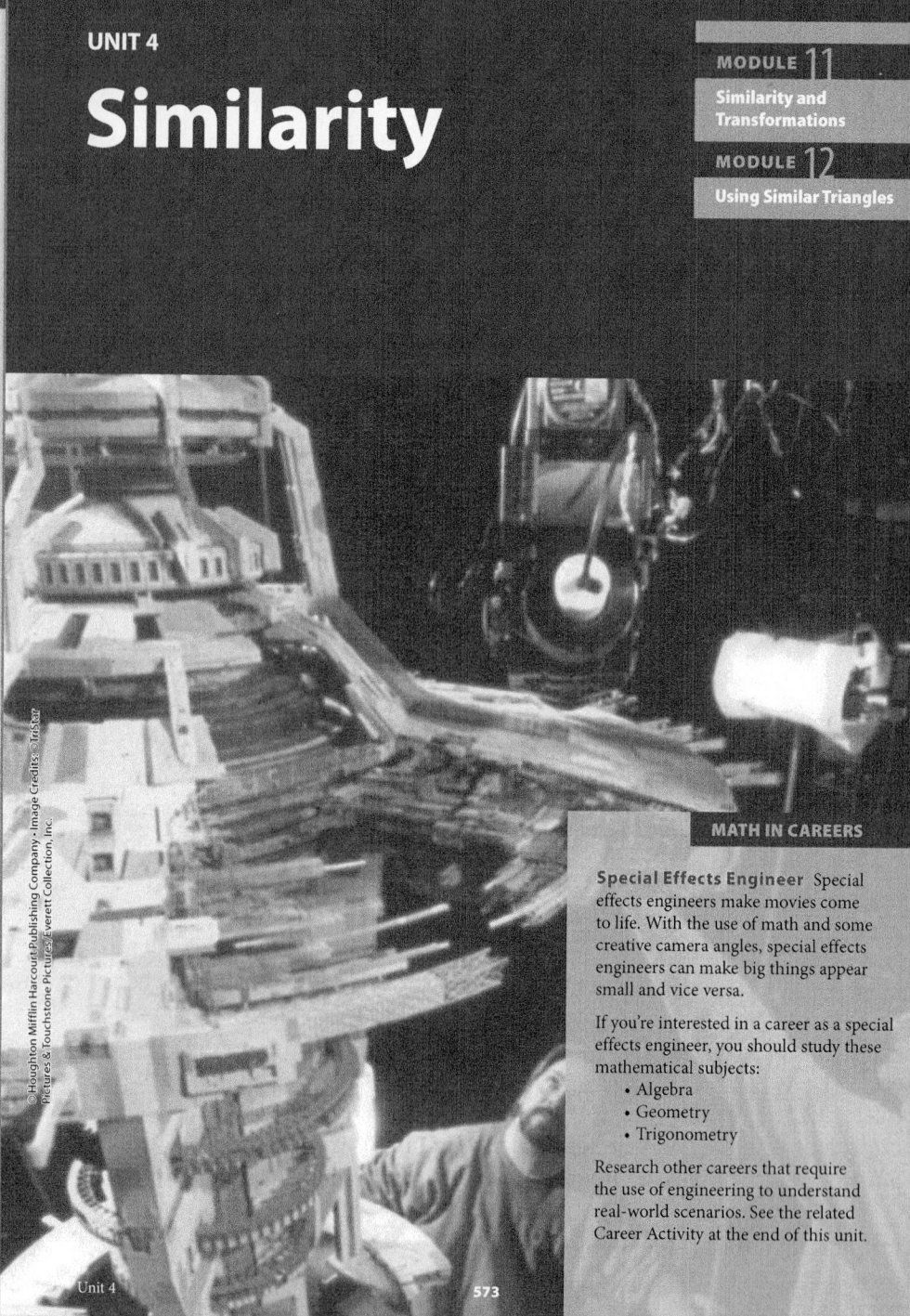

Similarity

MODULE **11**
Similarity and Transformations

MODULE **12**
Using Similar Triangles

MATH IN CAREERS

Special Effects Engineer Special effects engineers make movies come to life. With the use of math and some creative camera angles, special effects engineers can make big things appear small and vice versa.

If you're interested in a career as a special effects engineer, you should study these mathematical subjects:
- Algebra
- Geometry
- Trigonometry

Research other careers that require the use of engineering to understand real-world scenarios. See the related Career Activity at the end of this unit.

Unit 4   573

TRACKING YOUR LEARNING PROGRESSION

Before	In this Unit	After
Students understand: • relationships among angles, sides, and diagonals in a parallelogram • proving that a quadrilateral is a parallelogram • conditions for special quadrilaterals • using slope with lines and quadrilaterals • finding perimeters and areas	Students will learn about: • similarity and dilations • similarity of circles • corresponding parts of similar figures • proving triangles similar • the triangle proportionality theorem • dividing segments in a given ratio • geometric means theorems • proving the Pythagorean Theorem	Students will study: • trigonometric ratios in right triangles • using a tangent to find a side length • inverse trigonometric ratios • special right triangles • Pythagorean triples • finding an angle measure using a tangent

Reading Start-Up

Visualize Vocabulary

Use the ✔ words to complete the main idea web. Write the review words in the squares and include definitions.

Translation

A translation slides all points of a figure the same distance in the same direction.

Images formed by rigid transformations are congruent to their preimages.

Reflection

A reflection across a line maps each point to its image such that the line forms the perpendicular bisector of the point and its image. if the point is on the line, then the image is as well.

Rotation

A rotation moves each point about a center such that the distance from the center doesn't change and all angles formed by a point and its image have the same measure.

Understand Vocabulary

Complete the sentences using the preview words.

1. The image formed by a(n) ___similarity transformation/dilation___ has the same shape as its pre-image.

2. The ___scale factor___ indicates the ratio of the lengths of corresponding sides of two similar figures.

3. In the proportion $\frac{a}{x} = \frac{x}{b}$, x is called the ___geometric mean___.

Active Reading

Double-Door Fold Create a Double-Door Fold prior to starting the unit. Write characteristics of congruency under one flap. Fill out the other flap with corresponding characteristics of similarity so that the two topics can be compared more easily.

Unit 4   574

© Houghton Mifflin Harcourt Publishing Company

Reading Start Up

Have students complete the activities on this page by working alone or with others.

VISUALIZE VOCABULARY

The word web graphic helps students review vocabulary associated with transformations. If time allows, brainstorm other connections among the review words.

UNDERSTAND VOCABULARY

Use the following explanations to help students learn the preview words.

A **dilation** or **similarity transformation** is a transformation that changes the size of a figure but not its shape. The image of a dilation is a figure **similar** to the preimage. The **center of dilation** is the intersection of the lines that connect each point of the image with the corresponding point of the preimage. **Indirect measurement** is a method of measurement that uses similar figures. The multiplier used on each dimension to change one figure into a similar figure is the **scale factor**.

ACTIVE READING

Students can use these reading and note-taking strategies to help them organize and understand the new concepts and vocabulary. Encourage students to ask questions about any references to new vocabulary and associated concepts that seem unclear. Emphasize the importance of understanding precise mathematical language to accurately work through problems.

ADDITIONAL RESOURCES

Differentiated Instruction

- Reading Strategies

Similarity and Transformations

MODULE 11

Similarity and Transformations

ESSENTIAL QUESTION:

Answer: Similarity and transformations are useful tools in any real-world things that have the same shape but different sizes.

PROFESSIONAL DEVELOPMENT VIDEO

Professional Development Video

Author Juli Dixon models successful teaching practices in an actual high-school classroom.

Professional Development
my.hrw.com

Essential Question: How can you use similarity and transformations to solve real-world problems?

REAL WORLD VIDEO
Check out how properties of similarity and transformations can be used to create scale models of large, real-world structures like monuments.

MODULE PERFORMANCE TASK PREVIEW

Modeling the Washington Monument

In this module, you will be challenged to create a plan for a scale model of the Washington Monument. How can you use similarity and dilations to help you produce an accurate model? Let's find out.

© Houghton Mifflin Harcourt Publishing Company • Image Credits: ©Izzy Schwartz/Digital Vision/Getty Images

Module 11   575

DIGITAL TEACHER EDITION

Access a full suite of teaching resources when and where you need them:

- Access content online or offline
- Customize lessons to share with your class
- Communicate with your students in real-time
- View student grades and data instantly to target your instruction where it is needed most

PERSONAL MATH TRAINER

Assessment and Intervention

Assign automatically graded homework, quizzes, tests, and intervention activities. Prepare your students with updated, Common Core-aligned practice tests.

Are (YOU) Ready?

Complete these exercises to review skills you will need for this module.

- Online Homework
- Hints and Help
- Extra Practice

Properties of Dilations

Example 1 Stretch $\triangle ABC$ with points $A(1, 2)$, $B(3, 2)$, and $C(3, -1)$ horizontally and vertically by a factor of 4.

$(x, y) \rightarrow (4x, 4y)$ Write the transformation rule.

$A'(4, 8)$, $B'(12, 8)$, $C'(12, -4)$ Use the transformation to write each transformed point.

Describe the transformation.

1. Stretch $\triangle DEF$ with points $D(-2, 1)$, $E(-1, -1)$, and $F(-2, -2)$ horizontally and vertically by a factor of -3.

$$D'(6, -3),\ E'(3, 3),\ F'(6, 6)$$

2. Is the stretch a rigid motion?

No

3. Is it true that $\triangle DEF \cong \triangle D'E'F'$?

No

Similar Figures

Example 2 Transform $\triangle ABC$ with points $A(3, 4)$, $B(-1, 6)$, and $C(0, 1)$ by shifting it 2 units to the right and 1 unit up.

$(x, y) \rightarrow (x + 2, y + 1)$ Write the transformation rule.

$A'(5, 5)$, $B'(1, 7)$, $C'(2, 2)$ Write each transformed point.

Describe the transformation shown in the graph.

4. Write the rule used to transform $\triangle ABC$.
$$(x, y) \rightarrow \left(\frac{x}{2} + 1,\ \frac{y}{2} - 4\right)$$

5. Describe in words the transformation shown in the figure.
Answers may vary. Sample: Compress $\triangle ABC$ vertically and horizontally by a factor of 2, and then shift it to the right 1 unit and down 4 units.

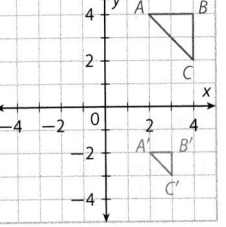

Are You Ready?

ASSESS READINESS

Use the assessment on this page to determine if students need strategic or intensive intervention for the module's prerequisite skills.

ASSESSMENT AND INTERVENTION

RtI Response to Intervention **TIER 1, TIER 2, TIER 3 SKILLS**

Personal Math Trainer will automatically create a standards-based, personalized intervention assignment for your students, targeting each student's individual needs!

ADDITIONAL RESOURCES

See the table below for a full list of intervention resources available for this module.

Response to Intervention Resources also includes:

- Tier 2 Skill Pre-Tests for each Module
- Tier 2 Skill Post-Tests for each skill

Response to Intervention			Differentiated Instruction
Tier 1 Lesson Intervention Worksheets	**Tier 2** Strategic Intervention Skills Intervention Worksheets	**Tier 3** Intensive Intervention Worksheets available online	
Reteach 11.1 Reteach 11.2 Reteach 11.3 Reteach 11.4	10 Geometric Drawings 16 Properties of Dilations 23 Similar Figures	Building Block Skills 36, 50, 80, 86, 95, 99, 103, 104, 112	Challenge worksheets Extend the Math Lesson Activities in TE

Dilations

Common Core Math Standards

The student is expected to:

COMMON CORE G-SRT.A.1a, G-SRT.A.1.b

Verify experimentally the properties of dilations given by a center and a scale factor .... Also G-CO.A.2

Mathematical Practices

COMMON CORE MP.5 Using Tools

Language Objective

Work with a partner to identify the center of dilation and scale factor in a dilation.

ENGAGE

Essential Question: How does a dilation transform a figure?

A dilation changes the size of a figure without changing its shape, so the image is similar to the pre-image but not congruent.

PREVIEW: LESSON PERFORMANCE TASK

View the Engage section online. Discuss the photo. Ask students to describe the relationship between the forms created by the hands and the shapes that appear on the wall. Then preview the Lesson Performance Task.

Name_____ Class_____ Date_____

11.1 Dilations

Essential Question: How does a dilation transform a figure?

Resource Locker

⊘ Explore 1 Investigating Properties of Dilations

A **dilation** is a transformation that can change the size of a polygon but leaves the shape unchanged. A dilation has a *center of dilation* and a *scale factor* which together determine the position and size of the image of a figure after the dilation.

Use $\triangle ABC$ and its image $\triangle A'B'C'$ after a dilation to answer the following questions.

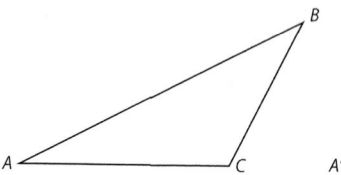
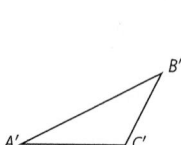

(A) Use a ruler to measure the following lengths. Measure to the nearest tenth of a centimeter.

$AB = \boxed{6.0}$ cm $A'B' = \boxed{3.0}$ cm

$AC = \boxed{4.0}$ cm $A'C' = \boxed{2.0}$ cm

$BC = \boxed{3.0}$ cm $B'C' = \boxed{1.5}$ cm

(B) Use a protractor to measure the corresponding angles.

$m\angle A = \boxed{22°}$ $m\angle A' = \boxed{22°}$

$m\angle B = \boxed{33°}$ $m\angle B' = \boxed{33°}$

$m\angle C = \boxed{125°}$ $m\angle C' = \boxed{125°}$

(C) Complete the following ratios

$\dfrac{A'B'}{AB} = \dfrac{\boxed{3.0}}{\boxed{6.0}} = \boxed{\dfrac{1}{2}}$ $\dfrac{A'C'}{AC} = \dfrac{\boxed{2.0}}{\boxed{4.0}} = \boxed{\dfrac{1}{2}}$ $\dfrac{B'C'}{BC} = \dfrac{\boxed{1.5}}{\boxed{3.0}} = \boxed{\dfrac{1}{2}}$

Reflect

1. What do you notice about the corresponding sides of the figures? What do you notice about the corresponding angles?

    The ratios of the lengths of corresponding sides are equal. Corresponding angles are

    congruent because the measures of the corresponding angles are the same.

2. **Discussion** What similarities are there between reflections, translations, rotations, and dilations? What is the difference?

    Reflections, translations, rotations, and dilations all preserve angle measure. Reflections,

    translations, and rotations all preserve distance but dilations do not preserve distance.

© Houghton Mifflin Harcourt Publishing Company

HARDCOVER PAGES 489–498

Turn to these pages to find this lesson in the hardcover student edition.

⊘ Explore 2 Dilating a Line Segment

The dilation of a line segment (the pre-image) is a line segment whose length is the product of the scale factor and the length of the pre-image.

Use the following steps to apply a dilation by a factor of 3, with center at the point O, to $\overleftrightarrow{AC}$.

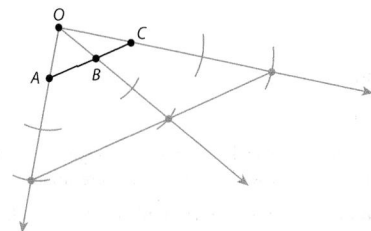

Ⓐ To locate the point A', draw a ray from O through A. Place A' on this ray so that the distance from O to A' is three times the distance from O to A.

Ⓑ To locate point B', draw a ray from O through B. Place B' on this ray so that the distance from O to B' is three times the distance from O to B.

Ⓒ To locate point C', draw a ray from O through C. Place C' on this ray so that the distance from O to C' is three times the distance from O to C.

Ⓓ Draw a line through A', B', and C'.

Ⓔ Measure $\overline{AB}$, $\overline{AC}$, and $\overline{BC}$. Measure $\overline{A'B'}$, $\overline{A'C'}$, and $\overline{B'C'}$. Make a conjecture about the lengths of segments that have been dilated.

The length of a segment that has been dilated is the original length times the scale factor.

Reflect

3. Make a conjecture about the length of the image of a 4 cm segment after a dilation with scale factor k. Can the image ever be shorter than the preimage?
The image will be 4k cm long. Yes, if k is between 0 and 1, the image will be shorter than the preimage.

4. What can you say about the image of a segment under a dilation? Does your answer depend upon the location of the segment? Explain
The image of segment m is parallel to m. The only exception is when line m passes through the center of dilation. In that case, the dilation lies along line m.

© Houghton Mifflin Harcourt Publishing Company

PROFESSIONAL DEVELOPMENT

 Math Background

Dilations are one of the major transformations that students study. Unlike earlier transformations (reflections, translations, and rotations), dilations are not rigid motions. That is, they do not preserve both the shape and the size of a figure. However, dilations do preserve the shape of a figure. Thus, every dilation is either an enlargement or a reduction. The image that results from a dilation is generally not congruent to the pre-image, so a dilation is not an isometry. An exception is a dilation with a scale factor of –1, which is equivalent to a 180° rotation about the center of dilation.

EXPLORE 1

Investigating Properties of Dilations

INTEGRATE TECHNOLOGY

Students have the option of doing the dilation activity either in the book or online.

QUESTIONING STRATEGIES

? Do dilations appear to preserve angle measure? yes

? Do dilations appear to preserve distance? no

? What happens when you dilate with a scale factor of 1? The image and pre-image coincide.

EXPLORE 2

Dilating a Line Segment

INTEGRATE MATHEMATICAL PRACTICES
Focus on Modeling

MP.4 Use an overhead projector to project a shape onto the board and then trace the shape. Move the projector closer and trace the shape again to demonstrate a reduction. Move it farther away and trace it again to demonstrate an enlargement.

QUESTIONING STRATEGIES

? Is it ever possible for the image of a point to coincide exactly with the pre-image?
Explain. yes; when the scale factor is 1

Dilations   **578**

EXPLAIN 1

Applying Properties of Dilations

INTEGRATE MATHEMATICAL PRACTICES

Focus on Math Connections

MP.1 Have students review the characteristics of dilated figures. Help them see that a dilation is a transformation that changes the size of a figure but not the shape.

🔘 **Explain 1**   **Applying Properties of Dilations**

The **center of dilation** is the fixed point about which all other points are transformed by a dilation. The ratio of the lengths of corresponding sides in the image and the preimage is called the **scale factor**.

Properties of Dilations
• Dilations preserve angle measure.
• Dilations preserve betweenness.
• Dilations preserve collinearity.
• Dilations preserve orientation.
• Dilations map a line segment (the pre-image) to another line segment whose length is the product of the scale factor and the length of the pre-image.
• Dilations map a line not passing through the center of dilation to a parallel line and leave a line passing through the center unchanged.

Example 1   Determine if the transformation on the coordinate plane is a dilation. If it is, give the scale factor.

Ⓐ   Preserves angle measure: yes

Preserves betweenness: yes

Preserves collinearity: yes

Preserves orientation: no

Ratio of corresponding sides: 1 : 1

Is this transformation a dilation? No, it does not preserve orientation.

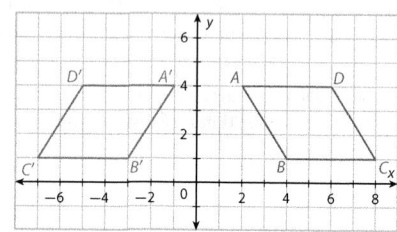

Ⓑ   Preserves angle measure (Y/N) _____ yes

Preserves betweenness (Y/N) _____ yes

Preserves collinearity (Y/N) _____ yes

Preserves orientation (Y/N) _____ yes

Scale Factor _____ 2

Is this transformation a dilation? _____ Yes

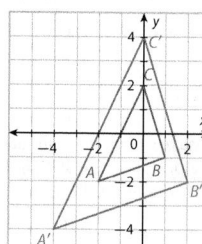

COLLABORATIVE LEARNING

Peer-to-Peer Activity

Divide students into pairs. Have one student draw a pre-image and an image, and then have the other determine whether the image is a dilation and explain why or why not. If it is a dilation, they should find the scale factor. Then have students switch roles.

Your Turn

Determine if the transformations are dilations.

5.

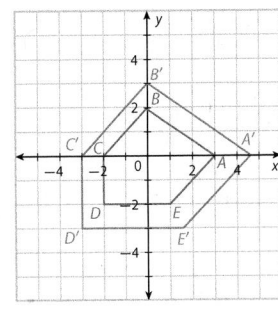

The transformation preserves angle measures, betweenness, collinearity, and orientation but not distance. The ratios of corresponding lengths are all the same. Therefore, it is a dilation. The scale factor is $\frac{3}{2}$.

6.

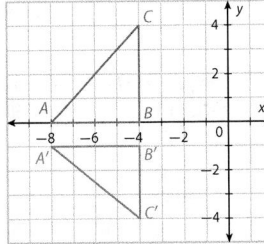

The transformation preserves betweenness and collinearity. It does not preserve angle measure, ratio of corresponding side lengths, or orientation. This is not a dilation.

🧨 **Explain 2** **Determining the Center and Scale of a Dilation**

When you have a figure and its image after dilation, you can find the center of dilation by drawing lines that connect corresponding vertices. These lines will intersect at the center of dilation.

Example 2 Determine the center of dilation and the scale factor of the dilation of the triangles.

Ⓐ Draw $\overleftrightarrow{AA'}$, $\overleftrightarrow{BB'}$, and $\overleftrightarrow{CC'}$. The point where the lines cross is the center of dilation. Label the intersection O. Measure to find the scale factor.

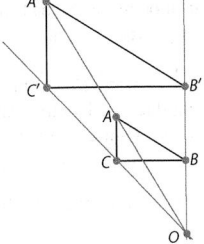

$OA = 25$ mm	$OB = 13$ mm	$OC = 19$ mm
$OA' = 50$ mm	$OB' = 26$ mm	$OC' = 38$ mm

The scale factor is 2 to 1.

© Houghton Mifflin Harcourt Publishing Company

DIFFERENTIATE INSTRUCTION

Critical Thinking

Students may wonder how to construct the dilation image of a figure when the scale factor is not a whole number. While it is not possible to use a compass and straightedge to construct the image for every scale factor, it is possible for certain scale factors, using a combination of the construction for copying a segment, the construction of a segment bisector, and the construction for dividing a segment into a given ratio. You may want to challenge students to use some combination of these constructions to draw the image of a triangle after a dilation with center of dilation O and scale factor 1.75.

QUESTIONING STRATEGIES

❓ If a transformation preserves angle measure, betweenness, and collinearity, is the transformation a dilation? Explain. Not necessarily; rigid transformations such as translations also preserve these things.

AVOID COMMON ERRORS

Some students may think that any larger or smaller figure is a dilation. Use examples to show that the shape and angles of the pre-image and image must be the same, and the lengths of the corresponding sides proportional.

EXPLAIN 2

Determining the Center and Scale of a Dilation

INTEGRATE MATHEMATICAL PRACTICES
Focus on Critical Thinking

MP.3 Discuss the reason that dilation does not affect a line through the center of dilation, but does affect a line not through the center. Remind students that the image of a point on a line through the center of dilation will remain on the line, and move only along it.

How can you use the given scale factor to predict whether the image is an enlargement? A scale factor >1 produces an enlargement.

ELABORATE

QUESTIONING STRATEGIES

? How can a dilation produce an image in which the pre-image and the image are two different congruent figures? The image under a dilation with a scale factor of –1 is congruent to the pre-image and is rotated 180°.

SUMMARIZE THE LESSON

? How can you determine whether the image of a figure is the result of a dilation? How might you determine the scale factor? If the lengths of the sides of the image are proportional to the lengths of the sides of the pre-image, and the corresponding angles are congruent, the image is the result of a dilation. If the figures are on a coordinate grid, you could divide the distance between the coordinates of the points of the image by the distance between the coordinates of the corresponding points of the pre-image to find the scale factor.

Ⓑ Draw $\overleftrightarrow{AA'}$, $\overleftrightarrow{BB'}$, and $\overleftrightarrow{CC'}$. Measure from each point to the intersection O to the nearest millimeter.

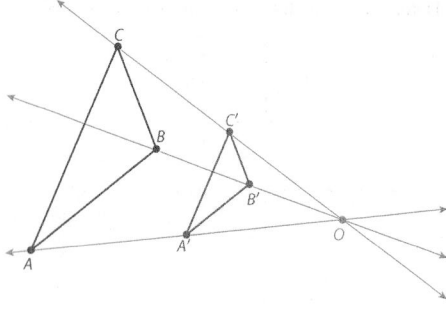

$OA = \underline{60\ mm}$

$OA' = \underline{30\ mm}$

$OB = \underline{38\ mm}$

$OB' = \underline{19\ mm}$

$OC = \underline{52\ mm}$

$OC' = \underline{26\ mm}$

The scale factor is $\underline{1\ to\ 2}$.

Reflect

7. For the dilation in Your Turn 5, what is the center of dilation? Explain how you can tell without drawing lines.

   The origin; several of the points and their images lie on axes, which intersect at the origin. For the points that are not on axes, you can use slopes to check that the lines connecting the point and image go through the origin.

Your Turn

8. Determine the center of dilation and the scale factor of the dilation.

   Measurements may vary but scale factor should not.

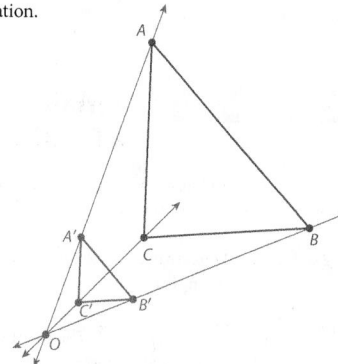

$OA' = \underline{18\ mm}$ cm, $OA = \underline{54\ mm}$

The scale factor of the dilation is $\underline{1\ to\ 3}$.

💬 **Elaborate**

9. How is the length of the image of a line segment under a dilation related to the length of its preimage?

   The ratio of the length of the image to the length of the preimage is the scale factor.

10. **Discussion** What is the result of dilating a figure using a scale factor of 1? For this dilation, does the center of dilation affect the position of the image relative to the preimage? Explain.

    A dilation by a scale factor of 1 will leave the figure unchanged. It will remain in the same position no matter what point is used as the center of dilation.

© Houghton Mifflin Harcourt Publishing Company

LANGUAGE SUPPORT 🇪🇱

Connect Vocabulary

Relate the word *dilation* to its meaning of becoming larger or smaller by using the example of the human eye. Pupils dilate in response to changes in light; in darkness, they get larger to let in more light, and in bright light, pupils get smaller to reduce the light entering the eye. Explain to students that when people talk about pupils *dilating*, they are using the mathematical term correctly.

11. **Essential Question Check-In** In general how does a dilation transform a figure?
A dilation changes the size of a figure without changing the shape. Dilations preserve

angle measures and orientation, but not length.

⭐ Evaluate: Homework and Practice

• Online Homework
• Hints and Help
• Extra Practice

1. Consider the definition of a dilation. A dilation is a transformation that can change the size of a polygon but leaves the shape unchanged. In a dilation, how are the ratios of the measures of the corresponding sides related?

The ratios of the lengths of the corresponding sides are equal.

Tell whether one figure appears to be a dilation of the other figure Explain.

2.

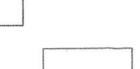

It appears to be a dilation that preserves angle measure, betweenness, collinearity and orientation. Also, the ratios of the lengths of corresponding sides appears to be equal.

3.

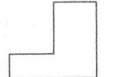

No, this is not a dilation, since the ratios of the lengths of corresponding sides are not equal. Some sides are about the same length and others are not.

4. Is the scale factor of the dilation of $\triangle ABC$ equal to $\frac{1}{2}$? Explain.

No, the scale factor is 2. The center of dilation is at $(0, 0)$. The measure from the center of dilation to A' is twice the measure from the center of dilation to A. The image is larger than the pre-image so the scale factor must be greater than 1.

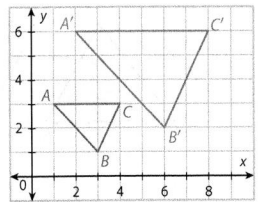

5. Square A is a dilation of square B.
What is the scale factor?

a. $\frac{1}{7}$ The answer is (c). The ratio is $\frac{35}{28} = \frac{5}{4}$

b. $\frac{4}{5}$

c. $\frac{5}{4}$

d. 7

e. $\frac{25}{16}$

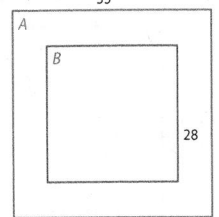

EVALUATE

ASSIGNMENT GUIDE

Concepts and Skills	Practice
Explore 1 Investigating Properties of Dilations	Exercises 1–5
Explore 2 Dilating a Line Segment	Exercises 6–11
Example 1 Applying Properties of Dilations	Exercises 12–13
Example 2 Determining the Center and Scale of a Dilation	Exercises 14–15

INTEGRATE MATHEMATICAL PRACTICES

Focus on Math Connections

MP.1 If two figures are congruent, is there a dilation that maps one onto the other? Why or why not? Yes; if figures are congruent, then there is a sequence of rigid motions that maps one to the other. Corresponding side lengths are equal (so the ratios of the side lengths is 1:1) and corresponding angles have equal measure, so the transformation is a dilation with scale factor 1.

Exercise	Depth of Knowledge (D.O.K.)	COMMON CORE Mathematical Practices	
1–5	**2** Skills/Concepts	**MP.2** Reasoning	
6–15	**2** Skills/Concepts	**MP.5** Using Tools	
16–17	**2** Skills/Concepts	**MP.3** Logic	
18	**2** Skills/Concepts	**MP.4** Modeling	
19	**3** Strategic Thinking	H.O.T.	**MP.1** Problem Solving
20	**3** Strategic Thinking	H.O.T.	**MP.1** Problem Solving

AVOID COMMON ERRORS

Some students may have trouble determining scale factors. In particular, they may have difficulty distinguishing a dilation with a scale factor of k from a dilation with a scale factor of $\frac{1}{k}$. Remind students that they should always compare the image to the pre-image. Also, remind students that if the image is an enlargement of the pre-image, then the scale factor must be greater than 1.

6. Apply a dilation to $\overline{AC}$ with a scale factor of 2 and center at the point O.

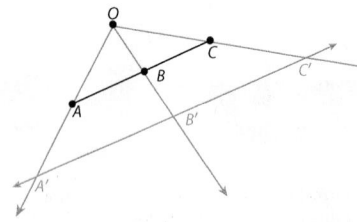

7. Apply a dilation to $\overline{AC}$ with a scale factor of $\frac{1}{3}$ and center at the point O.

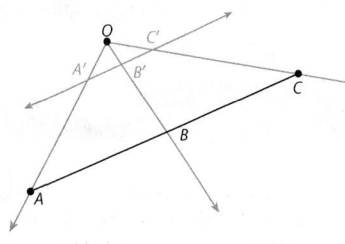

8. What happens when a triangle is dilated using one of the vertices as the center of dilation?

The sides of the triangles adjacent to the center of dilation will be collinear. The third sides of the preimage and image will be parallel. The vertex used as the center of dilation will be in the same location in both triangles.

9. Draw an image of $WXYZ$. The center of the dilation is O, and the scale factor is 2.

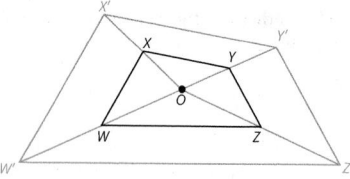

10. Draw an image of $\triangle ABC$. The center of dilation is C, and the scale factor is 1.5.

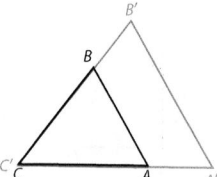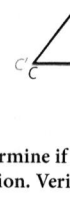

11. Compare dilations to rigid motions. How are they the same? How are they different?

Rigid motions preserve distance, angle measure, betweenness, and collinearity. Dilations preserve all of these except distance. The dilation of a line segment (preimage) is another line segment whose length is the product of the scale factor and the length of the preimage.

Determine if the transformation of figure A to figure B on the coordinate plane is a dilation. Verify ratios of corresponding side lengths for a dilation.

12.

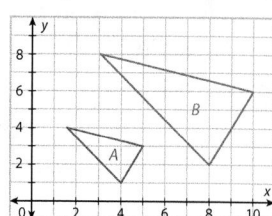

It is a dilation. The ratio for corresponding side lengths is $\frac{2}{1}$.

13.

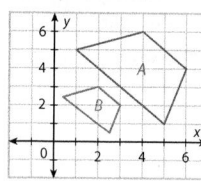

It is a dilation. The ratio for corresponding side lengths is $\frac{1}{2}$.

Determine the center of dilation and the scale factor of the dilation.

14.

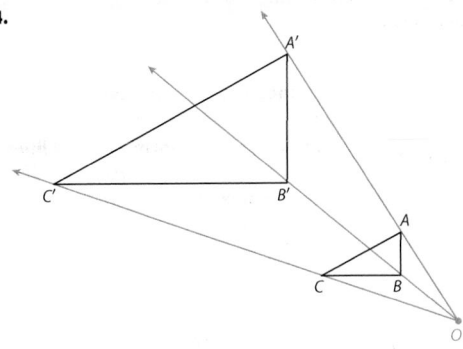

The scale factor is ___3 to 1___.

15.

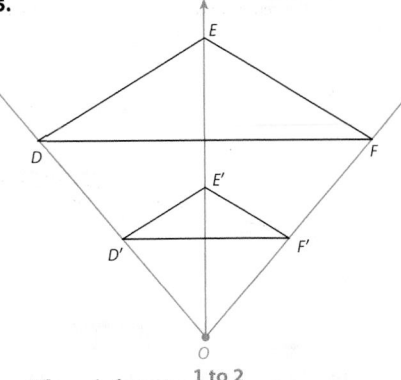

The scale factor is ___1 to 2___.

16. You work at a photography store. A customer has a picture that is 4.5 inches tall. The customer wants a reduced copy of the picture to fit a space of 1.8 inches tall on a postcard. What scale factor should you use to reduce the picture to the correct size?

$$\frac{1.8 \text{ in}}{4.5 \text{ in}} = \frac{2}{5}$$

A scale factor of $\frac{2}{5}$ should be used.

17. Computer Graphics An artist uses a computer program to enlarge a design, as shown. What is the scale factor of the dilation?

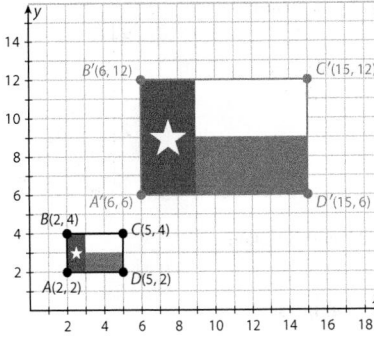

The length of the pre-image is $|5 - 2| = 3$ units.

The length of the image is $|15 - 6| = 9$ units.

The height of the pre-image is $|4 - 2| = 2$ units.

The height of the image is $|12 - 6| = 6$ units.

The ratio of the heights is $\frac{9}{3} = \frac{3}{1}$. The ratio of the

lengths is $\frac{6}{2} = \frac{3}{1}$. The scale factor is 3 to 1.

Have students write an explanation of how, given a triangle and its image under a dilation, you could use a ruler to find the scale factor of the dilation.

18. Explain the Error What mistakes did the student make when trying to determine the center of dilation? Determine the center of dilation.

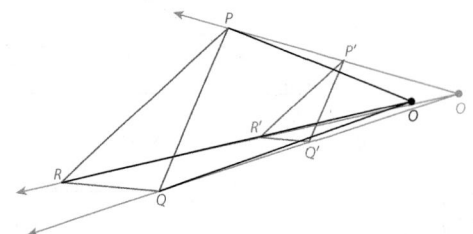

The lines were constructed incorrectly. $\overrightarrow{PO}$ should go through the points P and P′ to form $\overleftrightarrow{PP'}$. The lines must go through the vertex and the corresponding vertex to meet at the center of dilation O.

H.O.T. Focus on Higher Order Thinking

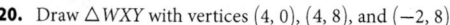

19. Draw △*DEF* with vertices D $(3, 1)$ E $(3, 5)$ F $(0, 5)$.

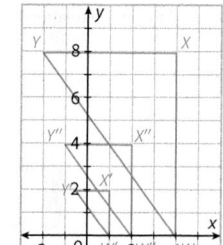

  a. Determine the perimeter and the area of △*DEF*.

  Perimeter is 12 units, Area is 6 square units

  b. Draw an image of △*DEF* after a dilation having a scale factor of 3, with the center of dilation at the origin $(0, 0)$. Determine the perimeter and area of the image.

  Perimeter is 36 units, Area is 54 square units

  c. How is the scale factor related to the ratios $\frac{\text{perimeter } \triangle D'E'F'}{\text{perimeter } \triangle DEF}$ and $\frac{\text{area } \triangle D'E'F'}{\text{area } \triangle DEF}$?

  $\frac{\text{perimeter } \triangle D'E'F'}{\text{perimeter } \triangle DEF} = \frac{36}{12} = \frac{3}{1} =$ **scale factor;** $\frac{\text{area } \triangle D'E'F'}{\text{area } \triangle DEF} = \frac{54}{6} = \frac{9}{1} =$ **scale factor squared**

20. Draw △*WXY* with vertices $(4, 0)$, $(4, 8)$, and $(-2, 8)$.

  a. Dilate △*WXY* using a factor of $\frac{1}{4}$ and the origin as the center. Then dilate its image using a scale factor of 2 and the origin as the center. Draw the final image.

  b. Use the scale factors given in part (a) to determine the scale factor you could use to dilate △*WXY* with the origin as the center to the final image in one step.

  Multiply the scale factors: $\frac{1}{4} \times 2 = \frac{1}{2} =$ the scale factor you multiply the pre-image by to draw the final image in one step.

  c. Do you get the same final image if you switch the order of the dilations in part (a)? Explain your reasoning.

  Yes. If you multiply $2 \times \frac{1}{4} = \frac{1}{2}$ it will give you the same scale factor because multiplication is commutative.

Lesson Performance Task

You've hung a sheet on a wall and lit a candle. Now you move your hands into position between the candle and the sheet and, to the great amusement of your audience, create an image of an animal on the sheet.

Compare and contrast what you're doing with what happens when you draw a dilation of a triangle on a coordinate plane. Point out ways that dilations and hand puppets are alike and ways they are different. Discuss measures that are preserved in hand-puppet projections and those that are not. Some terms you might like to discuss:

- pre-image
- image
- center of dilation
- scale factor
- transformation
- input
- output

Points that students may make:
- A coordinate-plane dilation takes place in two dimensions, a shadow puppet in three dimensions.
- When a shadow puppet is projected on a surface, angle measures are preserved. Lengths are not preserved. The depth of the hands is not preserved but is transformed into a two-dimensional image.
- The pre-image is the hands. The image is the shadow. The center of dilation is the light source.
- The scale factor for a shadow puppet projection is the ratio of a given measurement on the wall to the corresponding hand measurement in a plane parallel to the wall.

© Houghton Mifflin Harcourt Publishing Company • Image Credits: ©Digital Vision/Getty Images

EXTENSION ACTIVITY

Teams of three or four will need a flashlight, an index card, and a way of supporting the card at a fixed distance from the wall and parallel to it (one team member can hold the card, keeping it as parallel as possible). One student holds the flashlight, another measures the flashlight's distance from the rectangle, and a third measures the dimensions of the projected rectangle. Teams should take measurements with the flashlight at various distances from the rectangle. They can then study their data and hypothesize about the relationship between an object's dimensions and the dimensions of its image when it is projected on a wall.

INTEGRATE MATHEMATICAL PRACTICES
Focus on Patterns

MP.8 A rectangle measuring 3 inches by 6 inches is projected on a wall. The image of the rectangle on the wall has an area of 200 square inches. What are the dimensions of the wall rectangle? Explain. 10 in. x 20 in. ; sample answer: Since the length of the smaller rectangle is twice its width, the length of the larger rectangle must also be twice its width. The problem becomes one of finding two numbers in the ratio 2:1 with a product of 200. The solutions 10 in. and 20 in. can be found using the guess-and-check problem solving strategy.

INTEGRATE MATHEMATICAL PRACTICES
Focus on Math Connections

MP.1 A small rectangle is suspended halfway between a flashlight and a wall. It is parallel to the wall. Viewed from the side, what figure and special segment does this situation resemble? How could you use your knowledge of the segment to find unknown dimensions? Sample answer: The light from the flashlight, a side of the rectangle, and a side of the shadow form a triangle with a midsegment drawn. By the Midsegment Theorem, the side of the rectangle has half the length of the side of the shadow.

Scoring Rubric
2 points: Student correctly solves the problem and explains his/her reasoning.
1 point: Student shows good understanding of the problem but does not fully solve or explain his/her reasoning.
0 points: Student does not demonstrate understanding of the problem.

Dilations   586

Proving Figures are Similar Using Transformations

Common Core Math Standards

The student is expected to:

 G-SRT.A.2

Given two figures, use the definition of similarity in terms of similarity transformations to decide if they are similar . . . . Also G-C.A.1

Mathematical Practices

 MP.6 Precision

Language Objective

Work with a partner to list the essential components needed to prove a figure is similar to another.

ENGAGE

Essential Question: How can similarity transformations be used to show two figures are similar?

If a sequence of similarity transformations can be shown to map one figure to another, the figures are similar.

PREVIEW: LESSON PERFORMANCE TASK

View the Engage section online. Discuss the photo. Ask students to identify the game that's being played and the game board on which it is being played. Then preview the Lesson Performance Task.

11.2 Proving Figures are Similar Using Transformations

Essential Question: How can similarity transformations be used to show two figures are similar?

⊘ Explore   Confirming Similarity

A **similarity transformation** is a transformation in which an image has the same shape as its pre-image. Similarity transformations include reflections, translations, rotations, and dilations. Two plane figures are **similar** if and only if one figure can be mapped to the other through one or more similarity transformations.

A grid shows a map of the city park. Use tracing paper to confirm that the park elements are similar.

Ⓐ Trace patio *EFHG*. Turn the paper so that patio *EFHG* is mapped onto patio *LMON*. Describe the transformation. What does this confirm about the patios?

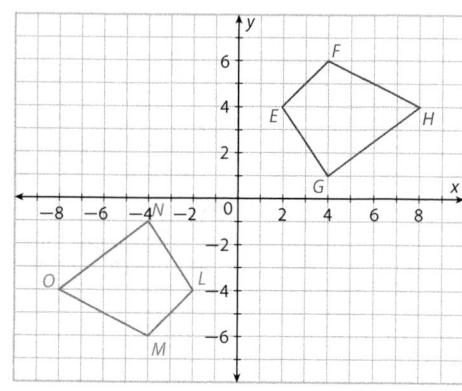

A rotation of 180° around the origin; The fountains are similar.

Ⓑ Trace statues *ABCDEF* and *JKLMNO*. Fold the paper so that statue *ABCDEF* is mapped onto statue *JKLMNO*. Describe the transformation. What does this confirm about the statues?

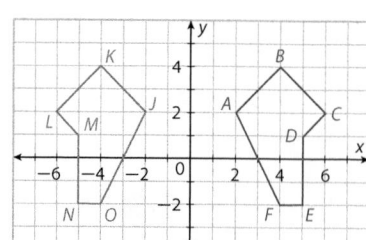

A reflection across the *y*-axis; The figures are similar.

© Houghton Mifflin Harcourt Publishing Company

HARDCOVER PAGES 499–510

Turn to these pages to find this lesson in the hardcover student edition.

© Describe the transformation you can use to map vertices of garden *RST* to corresponding vertices of garden *DEF*. What does this confirm about the gardens?

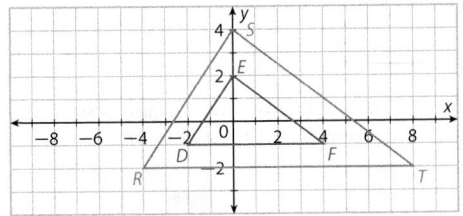

A dilation with scale factor $\frac{1}{2}$; The gardens are similar.

1. Look back at all the steps. Were any of the images congruent to the pre-images? If so, what types of similarity transformations were performed with these figures? What does this tell you about the relationship between similar and congruent figures?

    The two figures in Steps A and B are congruent to each other. The types of transformations that were performed with these figures were rotations and reflections, which are rigid motions. So congruent figures are also similar figures.

2. If two figures are similar, can you conclude that corresponding angles are congruent? Why or why not?

    Yes, the corresponding angles are congruent because rigid motions and dilations preserve angle measures.

⊘ Explain 1   Determining If Figures are Similar

You can represent dilations using the coordinate notation $(x, y) \rightarrow (kx, ky)$, where k is the scale factor and the center of dilation is the origin. If $0 < k < 1$, the dilation is a reduction. If $k > 1$, the dilation is an enlargement.

Example 1   Determine whether the two figures are similar using similarity transformations. Explain.

Ⓐ $\triangle RST$ and $\triangle XYZ$

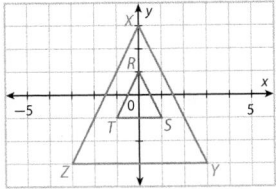

To map $\triangle RST$ onto $\triangle XYZ$, there must be some factor k that dilates $\triangle RST$.

Pre-image	Image
$R(0, 1)$	$X(0, 3)$
$S(1, -1)$	$Y(3, -3)$
$T(-1, -1)$	$Z(-3, -3)$

© Houghton Mifflin Harcourt Publishing Company

PROFESSIONAL DEVELOPMENT

 Math Background

Two conditions must be met in order to state that two polygons are similar. Two polygons are similar if and only if their corresponding angles are congruent and their corresponding sides are proportional. Similarity is an equivalence relation; that is, similarity is reflexive, symmetric, and transitive. For figures *A*, *B*, and *C*, $A \sim A$ (reflexivity); if $A \sim B$, then $B \sim A$ (symmetry); and if $A \sim B$ and $B \sim C$, then $A \sim C$ (transitivity).

EXPLORE

Confirming Similarity

INTEGRATE TECHNOLOGY

Students have the option of doing the transformation activity either in the book or online.

QUESTIONING STRATEGIES

? What kind of transformations result in similar figures? similarity transformations.

? Of these transformations, what kind give congruent figures? Which transformation could result in figures that are similar but not congruent? rigid motions; dilation

EXPLAIN 1

Determining If Figures Are Similar

QUESTIONING STRATEGIES

? Are dilations the only transformations that result in an image that is similar to the pre-image? Explain. No, rigid motions like translations result in figures that are congruent, and therefore similar.

INTEGRATE MATHEMATICAL PRACTICES

Focus on Math Connections

MP.1 Have students discuss the various approaches to defining similarity, including the intuitive approach (same shape, may be different size); meeting the conditions of congruent angles and proportional sides; and the transformational approach–if one can be obtained from the other by similarity transformations.

You can see that each coordinate of the pre-image is multiplied by 3 to get the image, so this is a dilation with scale factor 3. Therefore, $\triangle RST$ can be mapped onto $\triangle XYZ$ by a dilation with center at the origin, which is represented by the coordinate notation $(x, y) \rightarrow (3x, 3y)$. A dilation is a similarity transformation, so $\triangle RST$ is similar to $\triangle XYZ$.

Ⓑ *PQRS* and *WXYZ*

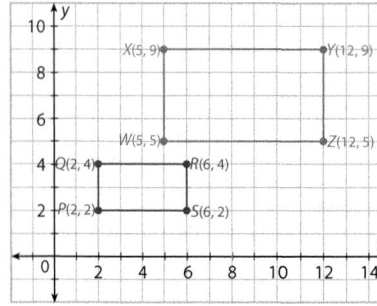

To map *PQRS* onto *WXYZ*, there must be some factor k that enlarges *PQRS*.

Pre-image	Image
$P(2, 2)$	$W(5, 5)$
$Q(2, 4)$	$X(5, 9)$
$R(6, 4)$	$Y(12, 9)$
$S(6, 2)$	$Z(12, 5)$

Find each distance: $PQ = 2$, $QR = \boxed{4}$, $WX = \boxed{4}$, and $\dfrac{XY}{} = 7$

If $kPQ = WX$, then $k = 2$. However. $2QR = \cancel{=} XY$.

No value of k can be determined that will map *PQRS* to *WXYZ*.

So, the figures are/(are not) similar.

Your Turn

Determine whether the two figures are similar using similarity transformations. Explain.

3.   *LMNO* and *GHJK*

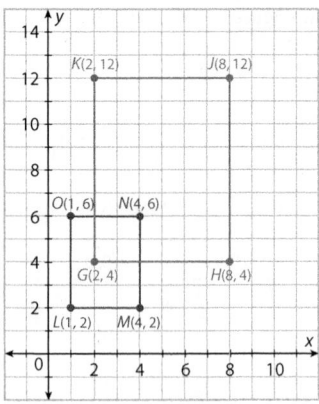

Yes, you can use a dilation with scale factor 2 and center at the origin to map *LMNO* onto *GHJK*. The figures are similar because a dilation is a similarity transformation.

COLLABORATIVE LEARNING

Small Group Activity

Have students work in small groups to design a logo for an imaginary company; the logo should repeat a single design as several similar figures. Have them write a description accompanying the logo that describes the transformations they used.

4. △JKL and △MNP

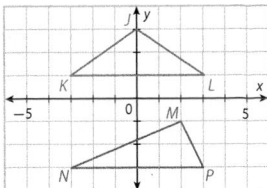

No, the angles are different. △JKL and △MNP are not similar figures.

5. CDEF and TUVF

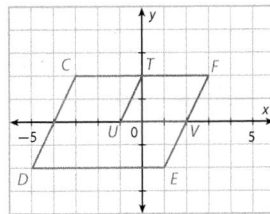

Yes, there is a dilation centered at point F with a scale factor of 2. CDEF is similar to TUVF.

⚙ **Explain 2** Finding a Sequence of Similarity Transformations

In order for two figures to be similar, there has to be some sequence of similarity transformations that maps one figure to the other. Sometimes there will be a single similarity transformation in the sequence. Sometimes you must identify more than one transformation to describe a mapping.

Example 2 Find a sequence of similarity transformations that maps the first figure to the second figure. Write the coordinate notation for each transformation.

Ⓐ ABDC to EFHG

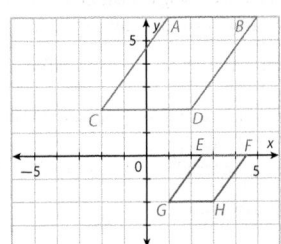

Since EFHG is smaller than ABDC, the scale factor k of the dilation must be between 0 and 1. The length of $\overline{AB}$ is 4 and the length of $\overline{EF}$ is 2; therefore, the scale factor is $\frac{1}{2}$. Write the new coordinates after the dilation:

Original Coordinates	$A(1,6)$	$B(5,6)$	$C(-2,2)$	$D(2,2)$
Coordinates after dilation $k=\frac{1}{2}$	$A'\left(\frac{1}{2},3\right)$	$B'\left(\frac{5}{2},3\right)$	$C'(-1,1)$	$D'(1,1)$

A translation right 2 units and down 3 units completes the mapping.

Coordinates after dilation	$A'\left(\frac{1}{2},3\right)$	$B'\left(\frac{5}{2},3\right)$	$C'(-1,1)$	$D'(1,1)$
Coordinates after translation $(x+2,\,y-3)$	$E\left(\frac{5}{2},0\right)$	$F\left(\frac{9}{2},0\right)$	$G(1,-2)$	$H(3,-2)$

The coordinates after translation are the same as the coordinates of EFGH, so you can map ABDC to EFHG by the dilation $(x,y) \rightarrow \left(\frac{1}{2}x, \frac{1}{2}y\right)$ followed by a translation $(x,y) \rightarrow (x+2, y-3)$.

Module 11   590   Lesson 2

Finding a Sequence of Similarity Transformations

INTEGRATE MATHEMATICAL PRACTICES
Focus on Math Connections

MP.1 Help students see that scale factors are the same as similarity ratios.

DIFFERENTIATE INSTRUCTION

Modeling

To help students understand the concepts in this lesson, have them draw figures and their transformed images on a coordinate plane. Then have them cut out the figures and see when they can be made to coincide, and when they cannot.

? How do you use the scale factor of a dilation to find the coordinates of points on the image of a figure? Multiply the coordinates of points on the pre-image by the scale factor.

AVOID COMMON ERRORS

Students may think that all rectangles are similar. Challenge them to draw two rectangles that do not have proportional sides.

Ⓑ △JKL to △PQR

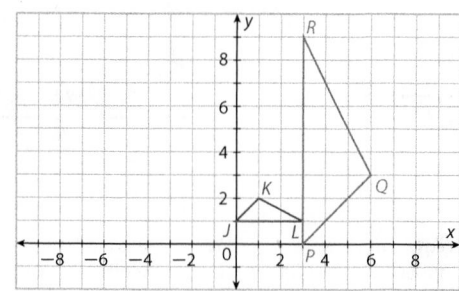

You can map △JKL to △PQR with a reflection across the x-axis followed by a ___dilation___ followed by a

90 ° counterclockwise rotation about the origin.

Reflection: $(x, y) \rightarrow (x, -y)$ ___Dilation___ : $(x, y) \rightarrow (\,3x, 3y\,)$ 90 ° counterclockwise rotation: $(x, y) \rightarrow (\,-y, x\,)$

Reflect

6. Using the figure in Example 3A, describe a single dilation that maps *ABDC* to *EFHG*.
   By connecting the corresponding vertices, you can identify $(4, -6)$ as the center of dilation
   for a dilation with scale factor $\frac{1}{2}$ that maps *ABDC* to *EFHG*.

7. Using the figure in Example 3B, describe a different sequence of transformations that will map
   △JKL to △PQR.
   Reflect △JKL across the y-axis. Then dilate with center at the origin and scale factor 3. Then
   rotate 90° clockwise around the origin.

Your Turn

For each pair of similar figures, find a sequence of similarity transformations that maps one figure to the other. Use coordinate notation to describe the transformations.

8. *PQRS* to *TUVW*

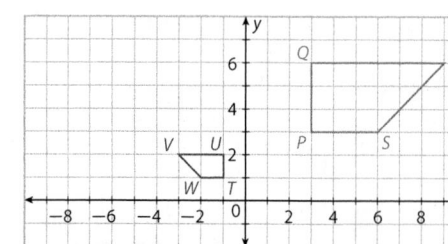

You can map *PQRS* to *TUVW* by a reflection followed by a dilation.

Reflection: $(x, y) \rightarrow (-x, y)$
Followed by...
Dilation: $(x, y) \rightarrow \left(\frac{1}{3}x, \frac{1}{3}y\right)$

LANGUAGE SUPPORT ⬛EL

Connect Vocabulary

Make sure students are not confused by the meanings of *similarity* in everyday English and in math. In everyday life, things may be called *similar* based only on how they appear. But, in math, we must look at the scale factors in corresponding sides and the angle measures in two similar figures before we call the figures *similar*.

9. △ABC to △DEF

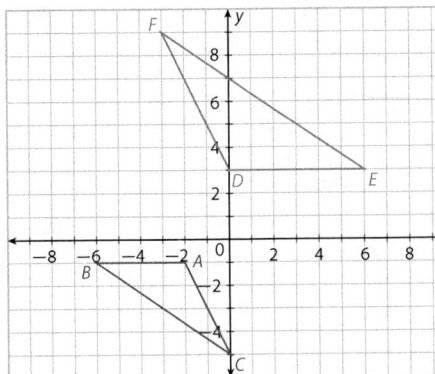

You can map △ABC to △DEF by a rotation about the origin 180° followed by a dilation followed by a translation.

Rotation: $(x, y) \rightarrow (-x, -y)$

Followed by...

Dilation: $(x, y) \rightarrow \left(\frac{3}{2}x, \frac{3}{2}y\right)$

Followed by...

Translation: $(x, y) \, (x - 3, y + 1.5)$

10. Describe a sequence of similarity transformations that maps *JKLMN* to *VWXYZ*.

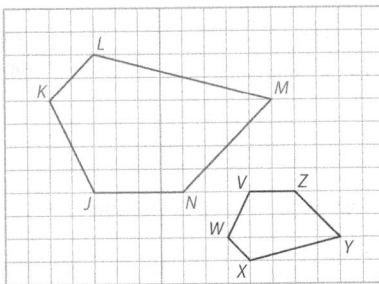

Translate *JKLMN* right 7 units so that *J* maps to *V*.

Reflect *JKLMN* across $\overleftrightarrow{JN}$.

Dilate *JKLMN* with center *J* and scale factor $\frac{1}{2}$.

🌀 Explain 3   Proving All Circles Are Similar

You can use the definition of similarity to prove theorems about figures.

Circle Similarity Theorem
All circles are similar.

Example 3   Prove the Circle Similarity Theorem.

Given: Circle *C* with center *C* and radius *r*.
        Circle *D* with center *D* and radius *s*.

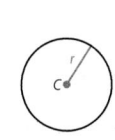 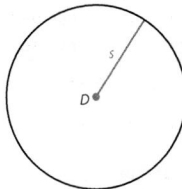

Prove: Circle *C* is similar to circle *D*.

To prove similarity, you must show that there is a sequence of similarity transformations that maps circle *C* to circle *D*.

EXPLAIN 3

Proving All Circles Are Similar

INTEGRATE MATHEMATICAL PRACTICES
Focus on Critical Thinking

MP.3 Help students realize that every dilation has an inverse, and the scale factors are reciprocals.

QUESTIONING STRATEGIES

❓ How can you perform the dilation in the proof that two circles are similar without knowing the lengths of their radii? Using the ratio of the lengths of the radii as the scale factor ensures that the dilation will map the circles onto one another. This is true of all circles of any size, so you do not need to know specific lengths.

ELABORATE

QUESTIONING STRATEGIES

? What scale factor is needed to dilate a circle with radius 2 to get a circle with radius 3? $\frac{3}{2}$

SUMMARIZE THE LESSON

? How do you use transformations to determine whether two polygons are similar? Determine whether one figure can be mapped to the other by a similarity transformation.

Ⓐ Start by transforming circle C with a ___translation___ along the vector $\vec{CD}$.

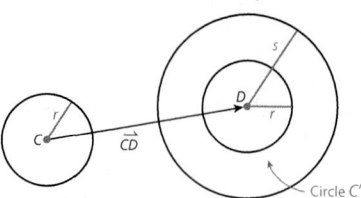

Circle C'

Through this ___translation___, the image of point C is ___point D___.

Let the image of circle C be circle C'. The center of circle C' coincides with point ___D___.

Ⓑ Transform circle C' with the dilation with center of dilation ___D___ and scale factor $\frac{s}{r}$.

Circle C' is made up of all the points at distance ___r___ from point ___D___.

After the dilation, the image of circle C' will consist of all the points at distance $\frac{s}{r} \times r = s$ from point D.

These are the same points that form circle ___D___. Therefore, the ___translation___ followed by the dilation maps circle C to circle ___D___. Because ___translations___ and dilations are ___similarity transformations___, you can conclude that circle C is ___similar___ to circle ___D___.

Reflect

11. Can you show that circle C and circle D are similar through another sequence of similarity transformations? Explain.

Yes, can reflect circle C across the perpendicular bisector of $\overline{CD}$, mapping point C to point D.

Then, follow the same steps for dilation.

12. Discussion Is it possible that circle C and circle D are congruent? If so, does the proof of the similarity of the circles still work? Explain.

Yes, if the ratio of each circle is the same positive value. The proof still works, because the

ratio of s to r is 1, so the dilation does not affect the size of the circle.

💬 Elaborate

13. Translations, reflections, and rotations are rigid motions. What unique characteristic keeps dilations from being considered a rigid motion?

Unlike the other transformations, dilations don't preserve distance, meaning the length

of the sides will not stay the same between the pre-image and its image. The lengths of

corresponding sides will be proportional according to the scale factor used.

14. Essential Question Check-In Two squares in the coordinate plane have horizontal and vertical sides. Explain how they are similar using similarity transformations.

Possible answer: translate the bottom left vertex of one square to the other square. Then

dilate the first square by the ratio of the side lengths.

© Houghton Mifflin Harcourt Publishing Company

• Online Homework
• Hints and Help
• Extra Practice

In Exercises 1–4, determine if the two figures are similar using similarity transformations. Explain.

1. *EFGH* and *ABCD*

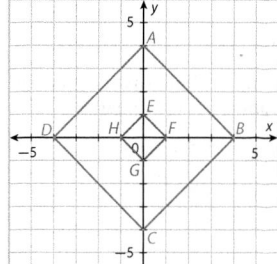

Looking at the two figures, you can see that *EFGH* has to be enlarged by some factor k to be mapped to *ABCD*.

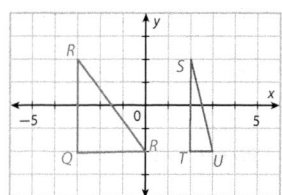

Pre-Image	Image
$E(0, 1)$	$A(0, 4)$
$F(1, 0)$	$B(4, 0)$
$G(0, -1)$	$C(0, -4)$
$H(-1, 0)$	$D(-4, 0)$

From the table, you can determine that $k = 4$. Therefore, *EFGH* can be mapped onto *ABCD* with a dilation of 4 with center at the origin, which is represented by the coordinate notation $(x, y) \rightarrow (4x, 4y)$.

2. $\triangle PQR$ and $\triangle STU$

The ratios of the lengths of corresponding sides are not equal. Therefore, there is no similarity transformation that maps $\triangle PQR$ onto $\triangle STU$, and $\triangle PQR$ is not similar to $\triangle STU$.

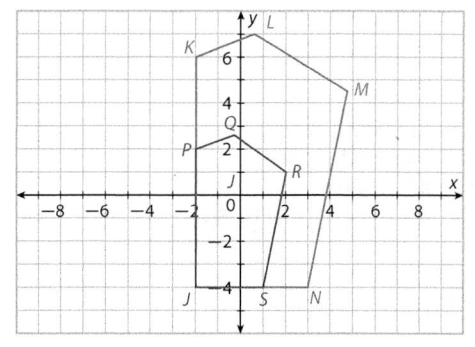

3. *JKLMN* and *JPQRS*

In order to map *JKLMN* to *JPQRS*, there must be a scale factor k that reduces *JKLMN*. In this situation, the center of the dilation is not the origin but point *J*. The scale factor is $\frac{3}{5}$ for the dilation. Since dilations are similarity transformations, *JKLMN* is similar to *JPQRS*.

EVALUATE

ASSIGNMENT GUIDE

Concepts and Skills	Practice
Explore Confirming Similarity	Exercises 11–12
Example 1 Determining If Figures Are Similar	Exercises 1–4
Example 2 Finding a Sequence of Similarity Transformations	Exercises 5–10
Example 3 Proving All Circles Are Similar	Lesson Performance Task

Exercise	Depth of Knowledge (D.O.K.)	COMMON CORE Mathematical Practices
1–4	**1** Recall of Information	**MP.1** Problem Solving
5–10	**2** Skills/Concepts	**MP.4** Modeling
11–13	**2** Skills/Concepts	**MP.3** Logic
14–17	**2** Skills/Concepts	**MP.4** Modeling
18–19	**2** Skills/Concepts	**MP.2** Reasoning
20	**3** Strategic Thinking H.O.T.	**MP.2** Reasoning

AVOID COMMON ERRORS

Some students may confuse *congruence* and *similarity*. Have them draw two similar triangles that are not congruent, and two similar triangles that are congruent, and label each set of figures with the appropriate term. Then have them repeat with pairs of circles, to make clear that all circles are similar, but all circles are not congruent.

4. △*UVW* and △*GHI*

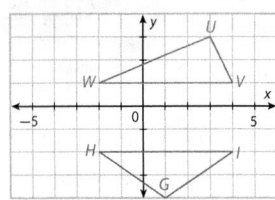

No, the angles are different. Similarity transformations preserve angle measures in similar figures, so △*UVW* and △*GHI* are not similar figures.

For the pair of similar figures in each of Exercises 5–10, find a sequence of similarity transformations that maps one figure to the other. Provide the coordinate notation for each transformation.

5. Map △*ABC* to △*PQR*.

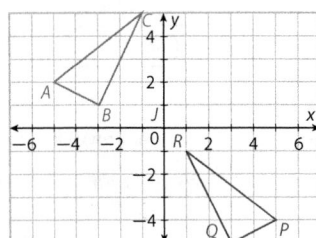

You can map △*ABC* to △*PQR* by a reflection followed by a translation.

Reflection: $(x, y) \rightarrow (-x, y)$

Translation: $(x, y) \rightarrow (x, y-6)$

6. Map *ABCD* to *EFGH*.

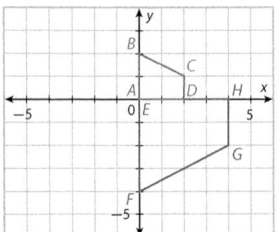

You can map *ABCD* to *EFGH* by a reflection followed by a dilation.

Reflection: $(x, y) \rightarrow (x, -y)$

Dilation: $(x, y) \rightarrow (2x, 2y)$

7. Map △*CED* to △*CBA*.

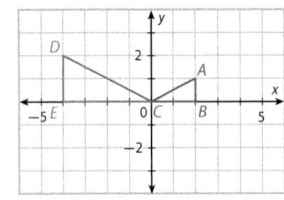

You can map △*CED* to △*CBA* by a reflection followed by a dilation.

Reflection: $(x, y) \rightarrow (-x, y)$

Dilation: $(x, y) \rightarrow \left(\frac{1}{2}x, \frac{1}{2}y\right)$

8. Map *ABCDE* to *JKLMN*.

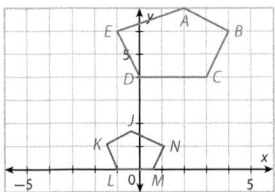

You can map *ABCDE* to *JKLMN* by a reflection followed by a dilation centered at the origin followed by a translation.

Reflection: $(x, y) \rightarrow (-x, y)$

Dilation: $(x, y) \rightarrow \left(\frac{1}{2}x, \frac{1}{2}y\right)$

Translation: $(x, y) \rightarrow \left(x + \frac{1}{2}, y - 2\right)$

Exercise	Depth of Knowledge (D.O.K.)	COMMON CORE Mathematical Practices
21	**3** Strategic Thinking H.O.T.	**MP.3** Logic
22	**3** Strategic Thinking H.O.T.	**MP.3** Logic
23	**3** Strategic Thinking H.O.T.	**MP.3** Logic

9. Map *ABCD* to *JKLM*.

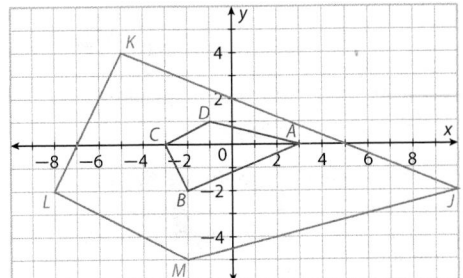

You can map *ABCD* to *JKLM* by a reflection followed by a dilation centered at the origin followed by a translation.

Reflection: $(x, y) \rightarrow (x, -y)$

Dilation: $(x, y) \rightarrow (3x, 3y)$

Translation: $(x, y) \rightarrow (x + 1, y - 2)$

10. Map $\triangle JKL$ to $\triangle PQR$

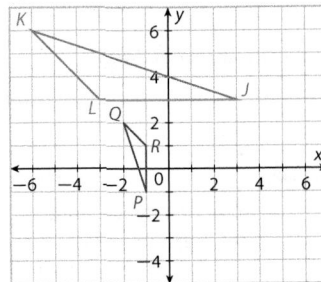

You can map $\triangle JKL$ to $\triangle PQR$ by a reflection followed by a dilation followed by a 90° clockwise rotation about the origin.

Reflection: $(x, y) \rightarrow (x, -y)$

Dilation: $(x, y) \rightarrow \left(\frac{1}{3}x, \frac{1}{3}y\right)$

Rotation: $(x, y) \rightarrow (y, -x)$

Complete the proof.

11. Given: Square *ABCD* with side length *x*.
Square *EFGH* with side length *y*.

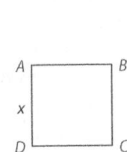 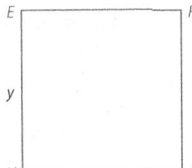

Prove: Square *ABCD* is similar to square *EFGH*.

Step A: Dilate *ABCD* with center of dilation *A* and scale factor $\frac{y}{x}$, producing square *A'B'C'D'*. Square *ABCD* has four sides of length *x*. Square *A'B'C'D'* will have four sides of length $\frac{y}{x}(x) = y$. These are the same side lengths as *EFGH*. The angles are all 90° in each square, so *A'B'C'D'* is congruent to *EFGH*.

Step B: Translate *A'B'C'D'* with a translation along the vector $\overrightarrow{A'E}$, producing *A''B''C''D''*. Through this translation, *A''* is mapped to *E*. It may be true that *B''* is mapped to *F*, *C''* is mapped to *G*, and *D''* is mapped to *H*. If not, rotate *A''B''C''D''* about *E* so that *B'''* is mapped to *F*. Then, *C'''* lands on *G* and *D'''* lands on *H*.

Proving Figures are Similar Using Transformations   **596**

Multiple Representations

Ask students to rewrite dilation rules that use fractions without using fractions. For example: $(x, y) \rightarrow \left(\frac{3}{4}x, \frac{3}{4}y\right)$. $(x, y) \rightarrow (0.75x, 0.75y)$

12. Given: Equilateral $\triangle JKL$ with side length j.
Equilateral $\triangle PQR$ with side length p

Prove: $\triangle JKL$ is similar to $\triangle PQR$.

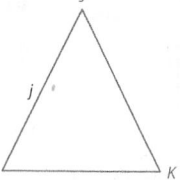
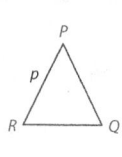

Step A: Dilate $\triangle JKL$ with center of dilation J and scale factor $\frac{p}{j}$, producing $\triangle J'K'L'$.
$\triangle JKL$ has three sides of length j. After the dilation $\triangle J'K'L'$ will have three sides of length $\frac{p}{j}(j) = p$. These are the same side lengths as $\triangle PQR$. By SSS Triangle Congruence, $\triangle J'K'L'$ is congruent to $\triangle PQR$.

Step B: Translate $\triangle J'K'L'$ along the vector $\overrightarrow{J'P}$, producing $\triangle J''K''L''$. Through this translation, J'' is mapped to P. It may be true that K'' and L'' are mapped to Q and R. If not, rotate $\triangle J''K''L''$ about P so that K''' is mapped to Q. Then, L''' is mapped to R.

13. Given: $\triangle ABC$ with $AB = c$, $BC = a$, $AC = b$
$\triangle XYZ$ with $YZ = x$, $XY = \frac{cx}{a}$, $XZ = \frac{bx}{a}$

Prove: $\triangle ABC$ is similar to $\triangle XYZ$.

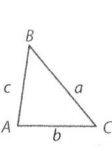
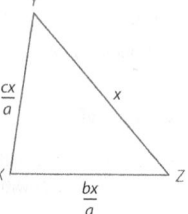

Step A: Dilate $\triangle ABC$ with center of dilation B and scale factor $k = \frac{x}{a}$, producing $\triangle A'B'C'$. After the dilation $\triangle A'B'C'$ will have sides of length $B'C' = ka = \frac{x}{a}(a) = x$, $A'C' = kb = \frac{x}{a}(b) = \frac{bx}{a}$, and $A'B' = kc = \frac{x}{a}(c) = \frac{cx}{a}$. These are the same side lengths of $\triangle XYZ$. By SSS Triangle Congruence, $\triangle A'B'C'$ is congruent to $\triangle XYZ$.

Step B: Translate $\triangle A'B'C'$ along the vector $\overrightarrow{B'Y}$, producing $\triangle A''B''C''$. Through this translation, B'' is mapped to Y. It may be true that A'' and C'' are mapped to X and Z. If not, rotate $\triangle A''B''C''$ about Y so that A'' is mapped to X. Then, C'' is mapped to Z.

14. The dimensions of a standard tennis court are 36 feet × 78 feet with a net that is 3 feet high in the center. The court is modified for players aged 10 and under such that the dimensions are 27 feet × 60 feet, and the same net is used. Use similarity to determine if the modified court is similar to the standard court.

Dilation factor for the width is $\frac{4}{3}$ and dilation factor for the length is $\frac{13}{10}$. Therefore the courts are not similar because the dilation factor is not constant between the width and length.

15. **Represent Real-World Problems** A scuba flag is used to indicate there is a diver below. In North America, scuba flags are red with a white stripe from the upper left corner to the lower right corner. Justify the triangles formed on the scuba flag are similar triangles.

Since the base and the height of the triangles are equal, no dilation has occurred.
The triangles are 180° reflections of each other. The triangles are similar to each other.

16. The most common picture size is 4 inches ×6 inches. Other common pictures sizes
(in inches) are 5 × 7, 8 × 10, 9 × 12, 11 × 14, 14 × 18, and 16 × 20.

a. Are any of these picture sizes similar? Explain using similarity transformations.

In order for any of the pictures to be similar, there needs to be a scale factor *k* which maps one picture to another. The ratio of the sides of each picture are 2:3, 5:7, 4:5, 3:4, 11:14, 7:9, and 4:5, respectively. Therefore, the only picture sizes that are similar are the 8" × 10" and 16" × 20", with a scale factor of *k* = 2.

b. What does your conclusion indicate about resizing pictures?
When resizing pictures one of two things will occur: the picture will be distorted or part of the picture will need to be cropped out.

17. Nicole wants to know the height of the snow sculpture but it is too tall to measure. Nicole measured the shadow of the snow sculpture's highest point to be 10 feet long. At the same time of day Nicole's shadow was 40 inches long. If Nicole is 5 feet tall, what is the height of the snow sculpture?

Since the shadows were measured at the same time of day the angle measures are equal and the triangles are similar.
Therefore a proportion can be used to determine the height.

10 ft. = 120 inches   Let *h* represent the height of the snow sculpture.

5 ft. = 60 inches $\dfrac{h}{120} = \dfrac{60}{40}$; *h* = 180 in., or 15 ft

18. Which of the following is a dilation?

A. $(x, y) \rightarrow (x, 3y)$

B. $(x, y) \rightarrow (3x, -y)$

C. $(x, y) \rightarrow (3x, 3y)$

D. $(x, y) \rightarrow (x, y - 3)$

E. $(x, y) \rightarrow (x - 3, y - 3)$

19. What is not preserved under dilation? Select all that apply.

A. Angle measure

B. Betweenness

C. Collinearity

D. Distance

E. Proportionality

JOURNAL

Have students define *similarity* in their own words, and then justify the definition using properties of similar figures.

---

20. Analyze Relationships Consider the transformations below.

    I. Translation   **II.** Reflection   **III.** Rotation   **IV.** Dilation

  a. Which transformations preserve distance?
    I, II, III

  b. Which transformations preserve angle measure?
    I, II, III, IV

  c. Use your knowledge of rigid transformations to compare and contrast congruency and similarity.

    Rigid transformations preserve angle measure and distance. Therefore, rigid transformations (translations, reflections, rotations) guarantee congruency. Similarity transformations (dilations) only preserve angle measures.

Justify Reasoning For Exercises 21–23, use the figure shown. Determine whether the given assumptions are enough to prove that the two triangles are similar. Write the correct correspondence of the vertices. If the two triangles must be similar, describe a sequence of similarity transformations that maps one triangle to the other. If the triangles are not necessarily similar, explain why.

21. The lengths AX, BX, CX, and DX satisfy the equation $\frac{AX}{BX} = \frac{DX}{CX}$.

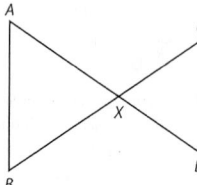

  Step A: Rearrange $\frac{AX}{BX} = \frac{DX}{CX}$ into $\frac{AX}{DX} = \frac{BX}{CX}$. Let $k = \frac{AX}{DX}$.

  Step B: Rotate $\triangle DXC$ 180° around point X so that $\angle DXC$ coincides with $\angle AXB$.

  Step C: Dilate $\angle DXC$ by a factor of k about the center X. This dilation moves the point D to A, since $k(DX) = AX$, and moves C to B, since $k(CX) = BX$. Since the dilation is through point X and dilations take line segments to line segments, $\triangle DXC$ is mapped to $\triangle AXB$. So $\triangle DXC$ is similar to $\triangle AXB$.

22. Lines AB and CD are parallel.

  Step A: Rotate $\triangle DXC$ so that $\triangle DXC$ coincides with $\triangle AXB$. Then the image $\overline{C'D'}$ is parallel to the pre-image of $\overline{CD}$. So the new side $\overline{C'D'}$ is still parallel to side $\overline{AB}$.

  Step B: Dilate $\triangle D'X'C'$ with center at point X. This moves vertex C' to point B and $\overline{C'D'}$ to a line through B parallel to $\overleftrightarrow{CD}$. Since $\overleftrightarrow{AB}$ is parallel to $\overleftrightarrow{C'D'}$, the dilation moves $\overleftrightarrow{C'D'}$ to $\overleftrightarrow{AB}$. Since D' moves to a point on $\overleftrightarrow{XA}$ and on $\overleftrightarrow{AB}$, D' must move to A. Therefore, the rotation and dilation map $\triangle DXC$ to $\triangle AXB$. So $\triangle DXC$ is similar to $\triangle AXB$.

23. $\angle XAB$ is congruent to $\angle XCD$.

  Step A: Draw the bisector of $\angle AXC$.

  Step B: Reflect $\triangle CXD$ across the angle bisector. This maps $\overline{XC}$ onto $\overline{XA}$. Since reflections preserve angles, it also maps $\overline{XD}$ to $\overline{XB}$. Since $\triangle XCD \cong \triangle XAB$, the image of $\overline{CD}$ is parallel to $\overline{AB}$.

  Step C: Dilate $\triangle XCD$ about point X. This moves the new point C to A. Since $\overleftrightarrow{AB}$ is parallel to $\overleftrightarrow{CD}$, the new $\overleftrightarrow{CD}$ moves to $\overleftrightarrow{AB}$. Therefore, the new point D is mapped to B and $\triangle XCD$ is mapped to $\triangle XAB$. So $\triangle XCD$ is similar to $\triangle XAB$.

Lesson Performance Task

Answer the following questions about the dartboard pictured here.

1. Are the circles similar? Explain, using the concept of a dilation in your explanation.

2. You throw a dart and it sticks in a random location on the board. What is the probability that it sticks in Circle A? Circle B? Circle C? Circle D? Explain how you found your answers.

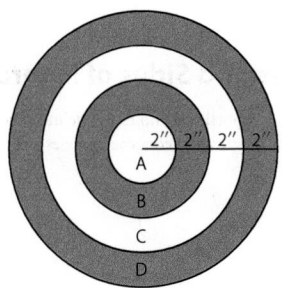

1. Yes. Each circle can be regarded as a pre-image that can be transformed through a dilation with its center at the center of the dartboard into any of the other circles.

2. Area Circle A $= \pi r^2 = \pi(2)^2 = 4\pi$

   Area Circle B $= \pi r^2 = \pi(4)^2 = 16\pi$

   Area Circle C $= \pi r^2 = \pi(6)^2 = 36\pi$

   Area Circle D $= \pi r^2 = \pi(8)^2 = 64\pi$

   Area Ring B $=$ Area Circle B $-$ Area Circle A $= 16\pi - 4\pi = 12\pi$

   Area Ring C $=$ Area Circle C $-$ Area Circle B $= 36\pi - 16\pi = 20\pi$

   Area Ring D $=$ Area Circle D $-$ Area Circle C $= 64\pi - 36\pi = 28\pi$

   Area of dartboard $=$ Area Circle D $= 64\pi$

   $P(A) = \dfrac{\text{area Circle A}}{\text{area of dartboard}} = \dfrac{4\pi}{64\pi} = \dfrac{1}{16}$

   $P(B) = \dfrac{\text{area Ring B}}{\text{area of dartboard}} = \dfrac{12\pi}{64\pi} = \dfrac{3}{16}$

   $P(C) = \dfrac{\text{area Ring C}}{\text{area of dartboard}} = \dfrac{20\pi}{64\pi} = \dfrac{5}{16}$

   $P(D) = \dfrac{\text{area Ring D}}{\text{area of dartboard}} = \dfrac{28\pi}{64\pi} = \dfrac{7}{16}$

AVOID COMMON ERRORS

Students may correctly calculate the areas of circles A, B, C, and D, but may forget that in order to calculate the required probabilities, they need to find the areas of *rings*. So, for example, Area Ring C = Area Circle C − Area Circle B.

INTEGRATE MATHEMATICAL PRACTICES

Focus on Patterns

MP.8 Study the pattern in the probabilities you obtained as answers in the Lesson Performance Task. Then, predict the probabilities of landing darts in each ring if a fifth ring of radius 10 inches were added outside the 8-inch circle. $\dfrac{1}{25}, \dfrac{3}{25}, \dfrac{5}{25}, \dfrac{7}{25}, \dfrac{9}{25}$

EXTENSION ACTIVITY

Have students design dartboards in basic shapes different from the circular board (for example, squares or equilateral triangles) but with the same basic properties: each should have four sections, and the sections should differ in dimensions from adjacent sections by the same amount. Have students answer the same questions about their designs that they answered about the circular dartboard. For squares and equilateral triangles, they should obtain the same results: the figures are similar and the probabilities of landing a dart in each are (smallest to largest) $\dfrac{1}{16}, \dfrac{3}{16}, \dfrac{5}{16}$, and $\dfrac{7}{16}$.

Scoring Rubric

2 points: Student correctly solves the problem and explains his/her reasoning.

1 point: Student shows good understanding of the problem but does not fully solve or explain his/her reasoning.

0 points: Student does not demonstrate understanding of the problem.

Proving Figures are Similar Using Transformations   **600**

Corresponding Parts of Similar Figures

Common Core Math Standards

The student is expected to:

 G-SRT.A.2

... explain using similarity transformations the meaning of similarity for triangles .... Also G-CO.A.2, G-CO.A.5

Mathematical Practices

 MP.4 Modeling

Language Objective

Play "similar or not" with a partner given pairs of figures on coordinate planes.

ENGAGE

Essential Question: If two figures are similar, what can you determine about measures of corresponding angles and lengths?

Similar figures have corresponding angles that are congruent and have corresponding sides that are proportional.

PREVIEW: LESSON PERFORMANCE TASK

View the Engage section online. Discuss the floor plan and ask students to explain the relationship of the floor plan to the house. Then preview the Lesson Performance Task.

11.3 Corresponding Parts of Similar Figures

Essential Question: If you know two figures are similar, what can you determine about measures of corresponding angles and lengths?

Resource Locker

⊙ Explore   Connecting Angles and Sides of Figures

You know that if figures are similar, the side lengths are proportional and the angle measures are equal. If you have two figures with proportional side lengths and congruent angles, can you conclude that they are similar?

Ⓐ Consider the graph of *ABCD* and *KLMN*.

Are corresponding angles congruent? (Yes)/No

Measure the angles.

$m\angle A = \underline{\quad 90° \quad}$ $\qquad$ $m\angle K = \underline{\quad 90° \quad}$

$m\angle B = \underline{\quad 63.4° \quad}$ $\qquad$ $m\angle L = \underline{\quad 63.4° \quad}$

$m\angle C = \underline{\quad 116.6° \quad}$ $\qquad$ $m\angle M = \underline{\quad 116.6° \quad}$

$m\angle D = \underline{\quad 90° \quad}$ $\qquad$ $m\angle N = \underline{\quad 90° \quad}$

Accept reasonable measures; opposite angles should be supplementary

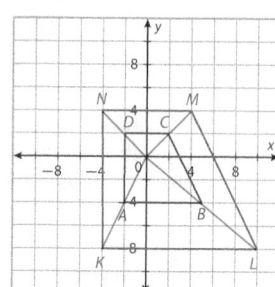

Ⓑ Are the ratios of corresponding side lengths equal? (Yes)/No

$\dfrac{AB}{KL} = \dfrac{1}{2}$ $\qquad$ $\dfrac{BC}{LM} = \dfrac{1}{2}$ $\qquad$ $\dfrac{CD}{MN} = \dfrac{1}{2}$ $\qquad$ $\dfrac{AD}{KN} = \dfrac{1}{2}$

Ⓒ Are the figures similar? Describe how you know using similarity transformations.

Yes, there is a dilation centered at the origin that you can find by connecting the corresponding vertices.

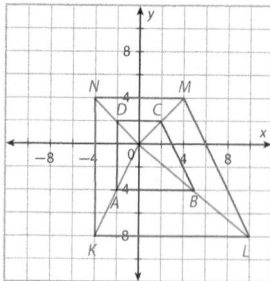

© Houghton Mifflin Harcourt Publishing Company

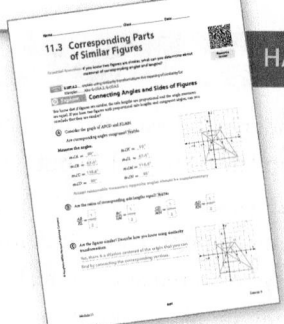

HARDCOVER PAGES 511–518

Turn to these pages to find this lesson in the hardcover student edition.

(D) Consider the graph of *ABCD* and *EFGH*.

Are corresponding angles congruent? (Yes)/No Explain.

The figures are both rectangles, so the measure of each

angle is 90°.

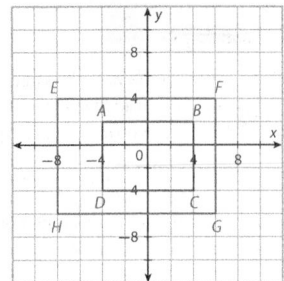

(E) Are the ratios of corresponding side lengths equal? Yes/(No)

$$\frac{AB}{EF} = \boxed{\frac{4}{7}} \qquad \frac{BC}{FG} = \boxed{\frac{3}{5}} \qquad \frac{CD}{GH} = \boxed{\frac{4}{7}} \qquad \frac{AD}{EH} = \boxed{\frac{3}{5}}$$

(F) Are the figures similar? Describe how you know using similarity transformations.

No. If you translate *ABCD* so that *A* maps to *E*, and dilate *A′B′C′D′* by the ratio $\frac{EF}{AD}$, *D′* will

map to *H* but *B′* and *C′* will not map to *F* and *G*.

(G) Consider the graph of *PQRS* and *WXYZ*.

Are corresponding angles congruent? Yes/(No)

Measure the angles.

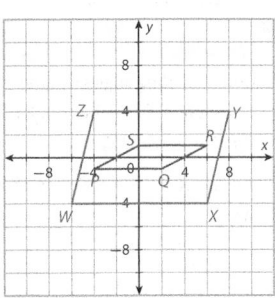

m∠P = 26.6°   m∠W = 76°

m∠Q = 153.4°   m∠X = 104°

m∠R = 26.6°   m∠Y = 76°

m∠S = 153.4°   m∠Z = 104°

Accept reasonable measures; opposite angles should be supplementary

(H) Are the ratios of corresponding side lengths equal? Yes/(No)

$$\frac{PQ}{WX} = \boxed{\frac{1}{2}} \qquad \frac{QR}{XY} = \boxed{\frac{\sqrt{5}}{\sqrt{17}}} \qquad \frac{RS}{YZ} = \boxed{\frac{1}{2}} \qquad \frac{PS}{WZ} = \boxed{\frac{\sqrt{5}}{\sqrt{17}}}$$

(I) Are the figures similar? Describe how you know using similarity transformations.

No. Dilations map line segments to parallel line segments, so there is no dilation that will

map $\overline{SP}$ to $\overline{ZW}$. The other similarity transformations are all rigid motions, which preserve

length and angle, so no sequence of similarity transformations will map *PQRS* to *WXYZ*.

EXPLORE

Connecting Angles and Sides of Figures

INTEGRATE TECHNOLOGY

Students have the option of doing the angle measure activity either in the book or online.

QUESTIONING STRATEGIES

? Given a figure that appears to be a dilation of another, how could you check whether a center of dilation exists? Draw lines through corresponding vertices of the figures. If they intersect at a point, it is the center of dilation. If they do not intersect at the point, no center of dilation exists.

PROFESSIONAL DEVELOPMENT

Math Background

Students use similarity to solve a variety of real-world problems. The general process is this: First, show that two figures are similar; then, use the fact that corresponding sides are proportional to find an unknown side length.

EXPLAIN 1

Justifying Properties of Similar Figures Using Transformations

INTEGRATE MATHEMATICAL PRACTICES
Focus on Modeling

MP.4 Use drawings to discuss how similar triangles can be used to find the heights of buildings or trees that are difficult to measure directly. The objects' shadows, measured at the same time of day, are proportional to the heights of the objects.

QUESTIONING STRATEGIES

? How do you know when two rectangles are similar? They are similar if corresponding sides are proportional.

Reflect

1. If two figures have the same number of sides and the corresponding angles are congruent, does this mean that a pair of corresponding sides are either congruent or proportional?
No, congruence of corresponding angles does not mean there is any relationship between a pair of corresponding sides. For example, consider a square and a rectangle.

2. If two figures have a center of dilation, is a corresponding pair of sides necessarily proportional?
Yes. If two figures have a center of dilation, the figures are similar and any pair of corresponding sides is proportional.

3. If two figures have a correspondence of proportional sides, do the figures necessarily have a center of dilation?
No. It's possible to establish a correspondence of proportional sides between two figures that are not similar (for example, if they don't have a center of dilation).

⌀ Explain 1 Justifying Properties of Similar Figures Using Transformations

Two figures that can be mapped to each other by similarity transformations (dilations and rigid motions) are similar. Similar figures have certain properties.

Properties of Similar Figures
Corresponding angles of similar figures are congruent. Corresponding sides of similar figures are proportional. If $\triangle ABC \sim \triangle XYZ$, then $\angle A \cong \angle X \quad \angle B \cong \angle Y \quad \angle C \cong \angle Z$ $\dfrac{AB}{XY} = \dfrac{BC}{YZ} = \dfrac{AC}{XZ}$

To show that two figures with all pairs of corresponding sides having equal ratio k and all pairs of corresponding angles congruent are similar, you can use similarity transformations.

Dilate one figure using k. The dilated figure is congruent to the second figure by the definition of congruence. So, there is a sequence of rigid motions (which are also similarity transformations) that maps one to the other.

Example 1 Identify properties of similar figures.

(A) Figure *EFGH* maps to figure *RSTU* by a similarity transformation. Write a proportion that contains *EF* and *RU*. List any angles that must be congruent to $\angle G$ or congruent to $\angle U$.

$\dfrac{EF}{RS} = \dfrac{EH}{RU}$ $\angle T$ is congruent to $\angle G$, and $\angle H$ is congruent to $\angle U$.

(B) Figure *JKLMN* maps to figure *TUVWX* by a similarity transformation. Write a proportion that contains *TX* and *LM*. List any angles that must be congruent to $\angle V$ or congruent to $\angle K$.

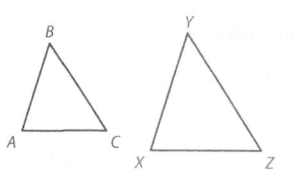

$\dfrac{\boxed{JN}}{TX} = \dfrac{LM}{\boxed{VW}}$ $\angle \underline{\ L\ }$ is congruent to $\angle V$, and $\angle \underline{\ U\ }$ is congruent to $\angle K$.

COLLABORATIVE LEARNING

Whole Class Activity

Have students bring in magazines and newspapers, and challenge them to find sets of similar figures. Discuss the use of similar figures in art and design, and the visual effects that such designs create.

© Houghton Mifflin Harcourt Publishing Company

Reflect

4. If you know two figures are similar, what angle or side measurements must you know to find the dilation used in the transformations mapping one figure to another?
You must know measurements of one pair of corresponding sides to find the scale factor.

Your Turn

5. Triangles $\triangle PQR$ and $\triangle LMN$ are similar. If $QR = 6$ and $MN = 9$, what similarity transformation (in coordinate notation) maps $\triangle PQR$ to $\triangle LMN$?
The ratio $\frac{MN}{QR} = 1.5$, therefore the similarity transformation is $(x, y) \rightarrow (1.5x, 1.5y)$.

6. **Error Analysis** Triangles $\triangle DEF$ and $\triangle UVW$ are similar. $\frac{DE}{UV} = \frac{VW}{EF}$ Is the statement true?
No. The proportion must compare corresponding sides. One possibility is $\frac{DE}{UV} = \frac{EF}{VW}$.

⚙ Explain 2 Applying Properties of Similar Figures

The properties of similar figures can be used to find the measures of corresponding parts.

Example 2 Given that the figures are similar, find the values of x and y.

Ⓐ

Find the value of x.

$\angle C \cong \angle R$, so m$\angle C =$ m$\angle R$

$4x + 27 = 95$

$4x = 68$

$x = 17$

Find the value of y.

$\frac{AB}{PS} = \frac{AD}{PQ}$

$\frac{4y}{10} = \frac{3y - 5}{5}$

$\frac{4y}{10} \cdot 10 = \frac{3y - 5}{5} \cdot 10$

$4y = 6y - 10$

$y = 5$

Ⓑ

Find the value of x.

m$\angle LMN =$ m$\angle XYZ$

$5(x - 5) = 4x$

$5x - 25 = 4x$

$x = 25$

Find the value of y.

$\frac{JK}{VW} = \frac{MN}{YZ}$

$\frac{2x - 8}{4} = \frac{1.5}{1}$

$2x - 8 = 1.5(4)$

$2x - 8 = 6$

$2x = 14$

$x = 7$

© Houghton Mifflin Harcourt Publishing Company

EXPLAIN 2

Applying Properties of Similar Figures

QUESTIONING STRATEGIES

? How can you use similar figures to solve problems? Use the fact that corresponding sides are proportional to find an unknown side length.

AVOID COMMON ERRORS

Students may sometimes write proportions that fail to use corresponding sides. While there are multiple ways to write a correct proportion, encourage students to use a pattern that they can remember. For example, so that the numerators always give side lengths from one triangle and the denominators always give side lengths from the other triangle.

COMMUNICATE MATH EL

Give student pairs different pictures of two figures drawn on coordinate planes. The first student decides whether a pair of figures is similar or not, and states three reasons why. The other student must agree or provide an alternative explanation. Students switch roles and repeat the process with another pair of figures.

DIFFERENTIATE INSTRUCTION

Modeling

Have students work with pattern blocks to explore the concept of similarity. Students can work in pairs, with one student creating a block design and the other creating a figure that is similar, but not congruent, to the first one. For more sets of pattern blocks, search for websites that feature "virtual pattern blocks." These sites allow students to select, combine, and rearrange blocks on a computer screen.

ELABORATE

QUESTIONING STRATEGIES

? Is an image always similar to its pre-image? Explain. No; for example, stretching and shrinking a figure disproportionally can produce an image that is not similar.

? Can two congruent angles have sides that are of different lengths? Explain. Yes, the measure of the angle refers to the amount of opening between the two sides; the length of the sides of the angle does not affect its size.

SUMMARIZE THE LESSON

? When two figures are given as similar, what can you conclude about their sides and angles? In similar figures, the corresponding sides are proportional and the corresponding angles are congruent.

---

7. **Discussion** What are some things you need to be careful about when solving problems involving finding the values of variables in similar figures?
Possible Answer: When finding side lengths, you need to be sure to set up the proportion correctly, and you need to remember that the side lengths are proportional rather than equal. Once you have the algebraic equation set up, you need to be careful not to make errors in the calculations.

Your Turn

Use the diagram, in which $\triangle ABE \sim \triangle ACD$.

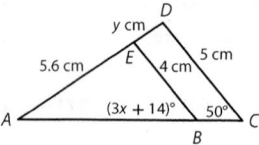

8. Find the value of x.

$$m\angle C = m\angle ABE$$
$$50 = 3x + 14$$
$$36 = 3x$$
$$12 = x$$

9. Find the value of y.

$$\frac{AD}{AE} = \frac{CD}{BE}$$
$$\frac{5.6 + y}{5.6} = \frac{5}{4}$$
$$5.6 + y = \frac{5}{4} \cdot 5.6$$
$$y = 1.4$$

💬 Elaborate

10. Consider two similar triangles $\triangle ABC$ and $\triangle A'B'C'$. If both $m\angle A' = m\angle C$ and $m\angle B' = m\angle A$, what can you conclude about triangle $\triangle ABC$? Explain your reasoning.
Since the two triangles are similar, we know $m\angle A' = m\angle A$ and $m\angle B' = m\angle B$.

Along with the given information, this tells us $m\angle A = m\angle C$ and $m\angle B = m\angle A$.

Therefore, $\triangle ABC$ is equilateral.

11. Rectangle $JKLM$ maps to rectangle $RSTU$ by the transformation $(x, y) \rightarrow (4x, 4y)$. If the perimeter of $RSTU$ is x, what is the perimeter of $JKLM$ in terms of x?
The ratio of corresponding sides is 1:4, and therefore the ratio of the perimeters is 1:4.

The perimeter of $JKLM$ is $\frac{x}{4}$.

12. **Essential Question Check-In** If two figures are similar, what can we conclude about their corresponding parts?
Similar figures have corresponding angles that are congruent and have corresponding sides that are proportional.

LANGUAGE SUPPORT **EL**

Connect Vocabulary

Students may be very familiar with the connotation of the word *translation* as it refers to interpretation between languages. In fact, this use of the word comes from its mathematically rigorous sense: translating between languages "moves" the meaning from one to another, just as translating a figure moves it from one place to another. Make the connection that mathematical translation does not change the essence of the original figure, much as a linguistic translation does not significantly alter the original meaning of the message as it enters another language.

In the figures, are corresponding angles congruent? Are corresponding sides proportional? Are the figures similar? Describe how you know using similarity transformations.

1.

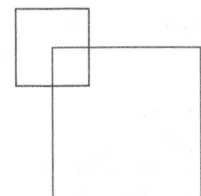

Yes; yes; yes. Translate the smaller square down and right so its upper left vertex coincides with that of the larger square. Then dilate with a scale factor of 2 about this vertex.

2.

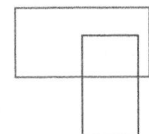

Yes; no; no. Rotate the smaller square 90° around its upper right corner, then translate it down and left until the lower left vertices coincide. If you dilate it with a scale factor of 3 to 2.5, the short edges will be congruent but the long edges will not be.

3.

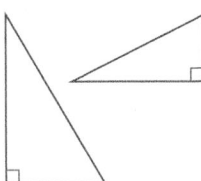

No; no; no. You can rotate and translate the triangle on the right so the right angles coincide, but no similarity transformation will make the acute angles congruent.

4.

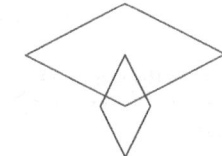

Yes; yes; yes. Rotate the smaller figure 90°, then translate it so that two corresponding vertices coincide. Then dilate the smaller figure the centers by a factor of 2 about that vertex.

5. Figure $ABCD$ is similar to figure $MNKL$. Write a proportion that contains BC and KL.

$$\frac{BC}{NK} = \frac{CD}{KL}$$

6. $\triangle DEF$ is similar to $\triangle STU$. Write a proportion that contains ST and SU.

$$\frac{ST}{DE} = \frac{SU}{DF}$$

7. $\triangle XYZ$ is similar to $\triangle XVW$. Write the congruence statements that must be true.

$\angle X \cong \angle X$, $\angle Y \cong \angle V$, and $\angle Z \cong \angle W$.

8. $\triangle MNP$ is similar to $\triangle HJK$, and both triangles are isosceles. If $m\angle P > 90°$, name all angles that are congruent to $\angle H$.

If $m\angle P > 90°$, then $\angle M \cong \angle N$. So, $\angle M$, $\angle J$ and $\angle N$ are all $\cong$ to $\angle H$.

9. $CDEF$ maps to $JKLM$ with the transformations $(x, y) \rightarrow (5x, 5y) \rightarrow (x - 4, y - 4)$. What is the value of $\frac{EF}{LM}$? $\frac{1}{5}$

10. $\triangle PQR$ maps to $\triangle VWX$ with the transformation $(x, y) \rightarrow (x + 3, y - 1) \rightarrow (2x, 2y)$. If $WX = 12$, what does QR equal? $QR = \frac{1}{2}(12) = 6$

Exercise	Depth of Knowledge (D.O.K.)	COMMON CORE Mathematical Practices	
1–4	**2** Skills/Concepts	**MP.3** Logic	
5–17	**2** Skills/Concepts	**MP.5** Using Tools	
18–20	**2** Skills/Concepts	**MP.2** Reasoning	
21–22	**2** Skills/Concepts	**MP.4** Modeling	
23–24	**2** Skills/Concepts	**MP.4** Modeling	
25	**3** Strategic Thinking	H.O.T.	**MP.3** Logic
26	**3** Strategic Thinking	H.O.T.	**MP.3** Logic
27	**3** Strategic Thinking	H.O.T.	**MP.3** Logic

EVALUATE

ASSIGNMENT GUIDE

Concepts and Skills	Practice
Explore Connecting Angles and Sides of Figures	Exercises 1–4
Example 1 Justifying Properties of Similar Figures Using Transformations	Exercises 9–12
Example 2 Applying Properties of Similar Figures	Exercises 5–8

INTEGRATE MATHEMATICAL PRACTICES

Focus on Modeling

MP.4 Compare the symbols for equality, similarity, and congruence. Point out that combining the equality and similarity symbols gives the symbol for congruence. Connect the composition of the symbol to its meaning: congruence combines equality and similarity, because congruent figures have the same size and shape.

When solving a proportion about a scale model, some students may make mistakes because they failed to read the units carefully. Remind them that the lengths of corresponding sides do not necessarily appear in the same units, and they may need to convert one or more of the measures.

11. $\triangle QRS$ maps to $\triangle XYZ$ with the transformation $(x, y) \rightarrow (6x, 6y)$. If $QS = 7$, what is the length of XZ?

$XZ = 42$

12. **Algebra** Two similar figures are similar based on the transformation $(x, y) \rightarrow (12x, 3a^2y)$. What is/are the value(s) of a?

If the figures are similar, then $12 = 3a^2$, and $a = 2$ or $a = -2$.

13. **Algebra** $\triangle PQR$ is similar to $\triangle XYZ$. If $PQ = n + 2$, $QR = n - 2$, and $XY = n^2 - 4$, what is the value of YZ, in terms of n?

Since $n^2 - 4 = (n + 2)(n - 2)$, the ratio of a pair corresponding sides is $(n - 2):1$. Then the value of YZ is $(n - 2)(n - 2) = n^2 - 4n + 4$.

14. Which transformations will not produce similar figures? Select all that apply and explain your choices.

A. $(x, y) \rightarrow (x - 4, y) \rightarrow (-x, -y) \rightarrow (8x, 8y)$

B. $(x, y) \rightarrow (x + 1, y + 1) \rightarrow (3x, 2y) \rightarrow (-x, -y)$

C. $(x, y) \rightarrow (5x, 5y) \rightarrow (x, -y) \rightarrow (x + 3, y - 3)$

D. $(x, y) \rightarrow (x, 2y) \rightarrow (x + 6, y - 2) \rightarrow (2x, y)$

E. $(x, y) \rightarrow (x, 3y) \rightarrow (2x, y) \rightarrow (x - 3, y - 2)$

Choices B and E will not produce similar figures, because each sequence contains transformations that are not dilations or rigid motions, and are not balanced elsewhere in the sequence. Choice D contains two transformations that are not dilations or rigid motions, but together create a dilation.

15. The figures in the picture are similar to each other. Find the value of x.

The longer bases of the trapezoids are 6 units and 3 units, so the scale factor is 2:1. Set up the equation $x + 1 = 2(x - 3)$ and solve to get $x = 7$.

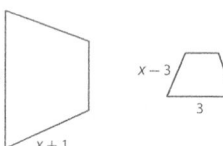

16. In the diagram, $\triangle NPQ \sim \triangle NLM$ and $PL = 5$.

a. Find the value of x.

$3x + 18 = 60$

$3x = 42$

$x = 14$

b. Find the lengths NP and NL.

$$\frac{NL}{NM} = \frac{NP}{NQ}$$

$$\frac{5 - y}{4} = \frac{y}{3.2}$$

$$3.2(5 - y) = 4y$$

$$16 = 7.2y$$

$$\frac{20}{9} = y$$

So $NP = \frac{20}{9}$ and $NL = \frac{25}{9}$.

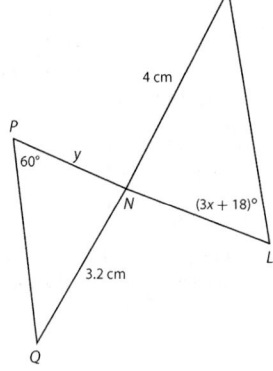

© Houghton Mifflin Harcourt Publishing Company

17. △CDE maps to △STU with the transformations

$(x, y) \rightarrow (x - 2, y - 2) \rightarrow (3x, 3y) \rightarrow (x, -y)$.

If $CD = a + 1$, $DE = 2a - 1$, $ST = 2b + 3$, and $TU = b + 6$, find the values of a and b.

Lengths of sides of △STU are 3 times the lengths of corresponding sides of △CDE. This produces the equations $3(a + 1) = 2b + 3$ and $3(2a - 1) = b + 6$. Solve this system of equations to get $a = 2$ and $b = 3$.

18. If a sequence of transformations contains the transformation (ax, by), with $a \neq b$, could the pre-image and image represent congruent figures? Could they represent similar, non-congruent figures? Justify your answers with examples.

Yes; if $ab = \pm 1$, then the pre-image and image are congruent (and therefore also similar). The pre-image and image could represent similar, non-congruent figures if the sequence of transformations also contains (bx, ay). The transformation (ax, by) followed by (bx, ay) is equivalent to the dilation (abx, aby).

19. Is any pair of equilateral triangles similar to each other? Why or why not?

Yes, the triangles will be similar. All the angles of each triangle are equal to 60°, and therefore corresponding angles are congruent. The sides of each triangle are congruent, and therefore the ratio of corresponding sides is constant.

20. Figure CDEF is similar to figure KLMN. Which statements are false? Select all that apply and explain why.

A. $\dfrac{CD}{KL} = \dfrac{EF}{MN}$ **B.** $\dfrac{CF}{KN} = \dfrac{EF}{MN}$ **C.** $\dfrac{DE}{LM} = \dfrac{CF}{KN}$ **D.** $\dfrac{LM}{DE} = \dfrac{KL}{CD}$ **E.** $\dfrac{LM}{DE} = \dfrac{KN}{CD}$

Choice E is false. The proportion doesn't match corresponding sides with each other.

Consider this model of a train locomotive when answering the next two questions.

21. If the model is 18 inches long and the actual locomotive is 72 feet long, what is the similarity transformation to map from the model to the actual locomotive? Express the answer using the notation $x \rightarrow ax$, where x is a measurement on the model and ax is the corresponding measurement on the actual locomotive.

The length of the model is 1.5 feet and so the similarity transformation is $x \rightarrow 48x$.

22. If the diameter of the front wheels on the locomotive is 4 feet, what is the diameter of the front wheels on the model? Express the answer in inches.

The diameter of the front wheels on the model is 1 inch.

Have students write a journal entry in which they make up their own problems using an unknown length that must be found using similar triangles. Remind students to include the solutions to their problems.

Use the following graph to answer the next two problems.

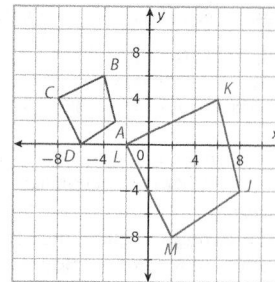

23. Specify a sequence of two transformations that will map *ABCD* onto *JKLM*.

Possible answer: $(x, y) \rightarrow (2x, 2y) \rightarrow (x + 14, y - 8)$ **or** $(x, y) \rightarrow (x + 7, y - 4) \rightarrow (2x, 2y)$

24. Find the value of $\frac{AC + BD}{JL + KM}$.

The two figures are similar, so all corresponding sides/diagonals have the same ratio. $\frac{AC}{JL}$
$= \frac{1}{2}$ and $\frac{BD}{KM} = \frac{1}{2}$, and so $\frac{AC + BD}{JL + KM} = \frac{1}{2}$.

H.O.T. Focus on Higher Order Thinking

25. Counterexamples Consider the statement "All rectangles are similar." Is this statement true or false? If true, explain why. If false, provide a counterexample.

The statement is false. For example, a rectangle measuring 5 units by 2 units is not similar to a rectangle measuring 4 units by 3 units.

26. Justify Reasoning If *ABCD* is similar to *KLMN* and *MNKL*, what special type of quadrilateral is *KLMN*? Justify your reasoning.

Looking at the corresponding angles, $\angle A \cong \angle K$ and $\angle A \cong \angle M$, which means $\angle K \cong \angle M$ by the Transitive Property of Congruence. Also, $\angle B \cong \angle L$ and $\angle B \cong \angle N$, which means $\angle L \cong \angle N$ by the Transitive Property of Congruence. If both pairs of opposite angles of a quadrilateral are congruent, then the quadrilateral is a parallelogram. Therefore, *KLMN* is a parallelogram. It could also be a rhombus, rectangle, or square, but more information would be needed to justify that conclusion.

27. Critique Reasoning Consider the statement "If $\triangle PQR$ is similar to $\triangle QPR$, then $\triangle PQR$ is similar to $\triangle RPQ$." Explain whether or not this statement is true.

The statement is false. If $\triangle PQR$ is similar to $\triangle QPR$, then $\angle P \cong \angle Q$ and the triangle is isosceles. This does not prove any correspondence between $\angle P$ and $\angle R$, or between $\angle Q$ and $\angle R$. For $\triangle PQR$ to be similar to $\triangle RPQ$, the triangle would have to be equilateral.

Lesson Performance Task

You've hired an architect to design your dream house and now the house has been built. Before moving in, you've decided to wander through the house with a tape measure to see how well the builders have followed the architect's floor plan. Describe in as much detail as you can how you could accomplish your goal. Then discuss how you can decide whether the room shapes and other features of the house are similar to the corresponding shapes on the floor plan.

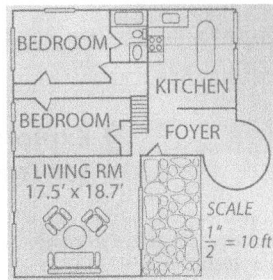

Among things students should discuss:
- the scale of the floor plan and how they could use it to check the dimensions of the rooms;
- a method they could use to check whether the shapes of the rooms and other features on the floor plan could be mapped to the corresponding shapes in the house by a series of transformations, including dilations;
- the measurements that should be preserved in the transformation from floor plan to house (e.g. angles) and those that would not be (e.g. lengths).

EXTENSION ACTIVITY

Supply yardsticks or meter sticks to students and have them make a floor plan of the classroom. Students should concentrate on features of the room that are permanent, such as dimensions and shape, omitting those that are not—desks and tables, for example. You may wish to specify the approximate size of the floor plan (for example, an 8.5 in. × 11 in. sheet of paper), thereby forcing students to calculate an appropriate scale. Students may exchange floor plans with a partner and check the partner's scale, shapes, and calculations.

INTEGRATE MATHEMATICAL PRACTICES
Focus on Critical Thinking

MP.3 Rectangle 1 is a units in length and b units in width. Rectangle 2 is obtained by multiplying the sides of Rectangle 1 by 10.

- Is Rectangle 2 similar to Rectangle 1? Explain. Yes; multiplying the sides by the same scale factor changes the size of the figure but not the shape, so the rectangles are similar.

- How does the area of Rectangle 2 compare to that of Rectangle 1? Explain. The area of Rectangle 1 is ab, and the area of Rectangle 2 is $100ab$, so the area of Rectangle 2 is 100 times as great as the area of Rectangle 1.

INTEGRATE MATHEMATICAL PRACTICES
Focus on Reasoning

MP.2 Three streets meet to form an equilateral triangle 100 yards on each side. In a photo of the triangle taken directly overhead, each side measures 4 inches. How are the actual triangle of streets and the triangle in the photo alike? How are they different? Explain. Their sizes are different but their shapes are the same; the sides of the triangle in the photograph are shorter than the actual triangle, but because they are both equilateral triangles, their sides are proportional and each has three 60° angles.

Scoring Rubric
2 points: Student correctly solves the problem and explains his/her reasoning.
1 point: Student shows good understanding of the problem but does not fully solve or explain his/her reasoning.
0 points: Student does not demonstrate understanding of the problem.

Corresponding Parts of Similar Figures   **610**

AA Similarity of Triangles

Common Core Math Standards

The student is expected to:

COMMON CORE **G-SRT.A.3**

Use the properties of similarity transformations to establish the AA criterion for two triangles to be similar. Also G-SRT.B.5

Mathematical Practices

COMMON CORE **MP.5 Using Tools**

Language Objective

Explain to a partner how to use the Angle-Angle criterion to show similarity in triangles.

ENGAGE

Essential Question: How can you show that two triangles are similar?

We can use the AA, SSS, or SAS similarity criteria to prove that triangles are similar.

PREVIEW: LESSON PERFORMANCE TASK

View the Engage section online. Discuss the illustration and ask students to speculate on what it depicts. Then preview the Lesson Performance Task.

Name _____ Class _____ Date _____

11.4 AA Similarity of Triangles

Essential Question: How can you show that two triangles are similar?

⊘ Explore **Exploring Angle-Angle Similarity for Triangles**

Two triangles are similar when their corresponding sides are proportional and their corresponding angles are congruent. There are several shortcuts for proving triangles are similar.

(A) Draw a triangle and label it △ABC. Elsewhere on your page, draw a segment longer than $\overline{AB}$ and label the endpoints D and E.

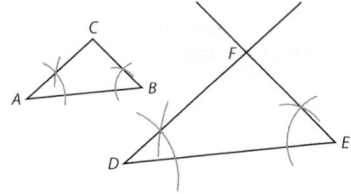

(B) Copy ∠CAB and ∠ABC to points D and E, respectively. Extend the rays of your copied angles, if necessary, and label their intersection point F. You have constructed △DEF.

(C) You constructed angles D and E to be congruent to angles A and B, respectively. Therefore, angles C and F must also be __congruent__ because of the __Third Angle__ Theorem.

(D) Check the proportionality of the corresponding sides. **Possible answer (ratios should be equal):**

$$\frac{AB}{DE} = \frac{4}{10} = 0.4 \qquad \frac{AC}{DF} = \frac{3}{7.5} = 0.4 \qquad \frac{BC}{EF} = \frac{2}{5} = 0.4$$

Since the ratios are __equal,__ the sides of the triangles are __proportional__.

Reflect

1. **Discussion** Compare your results with your classmates. What conjecture can you make about two triangles that have two corresponding congruent angles?
   If two triangles have two corresponding congruent angles, the triangles must be similar.

© Houghton Mifflin Harcourt Publishing Company

HARDCOVER PAGES 519–528

Turn to these pages to find this lesson in the hardcover student edition.

ⓘ Explain 1 Proving Angle-Angle Triangle Similarity

The Explore suggests the following theorem for determining whether two triangles are similar.

Angle-Angle (AA) Triangle Similarity Theorem
If two angles of one triangle are congruent to two angles of another triangle, then the two triangles are similar.

Example 1 Prove the Angle-Angle Triangle Similarity Theorem.

Given: $\angle A \cong \angle X$ and $\angle B \cong \angle Y$

Prove: $\triangle ABC \sim \triangle XYZ$

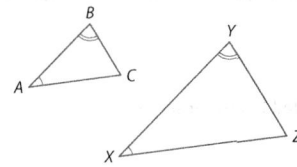

① Apply a dilation to $\triangle ABC$ with scale factor $k = \dfrac{XY}{AB}$. Let the image of $\triangle ABC$ be $\triangle A'B'C$.

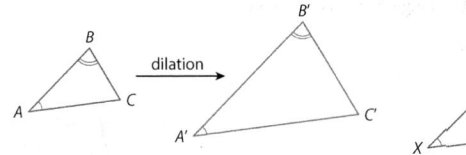

$\triangle A'B'C$ is similar to $\triangle ABC$, and $\angle A' \cong$ ___$\angle A$___ and $\angle B' \cong$ ___$\angle B$___

because ___corresponding angles of similar triangles are congruent___.

Also, $A'B' = k \cdot AB = \dfrac{XY}{AB} \cdot AB = XY$ _____.

② It is given that $\angle A \cong \angle X$ and $\angle B \cong \angle Y$

By the Transitive Property of Congruence, $\angle A' \cong$ ___$\angle X$___ and $\angle B' \cong$ ___$\angle Y$___.

So, $\triangle A'B'C' \cong \triangle XYZ$ by ___the ASA Triangle Congruence Theorem___.

This means there is a sequence of rigid motions that maps $\triangle A'B'C'$ to $\triangle YYZ$.

The dilation followed by this sequence of rigid motions shows that there is a sequence of similarity transformations that maps $\triangle ABC$ to $\triangle XYZ$. Therefore, $\triangle ABC \sim \triangle XYZ$.

Reflect

2. **Discussion** Compare and contrast the AA Similarity Theorem with the ASA Congruence Theorem.

   ___Both theorems require that two pairs of angles be congruent, but for congruence you also___
   ___need to know that the included sides are congruent, so that the figures are the same size.___
   ___The AA Similarity Theorem shows only that the two triangles are the same shape.___

PROFESSIONAL DEVELOPMENT

🔵 Learning Progression

Students have already proved triangles congruent using SAS, SSS, and ASA. The same kind of reasoning is used here to explore AA similarity, and to use this similarity to solve problems.

Exploring Angle-Angle Similarity for Triangles

INTEGRATE TECHNOLOGY

Students have the option of doing the similar triangles activity either in the book or online.

QUESTIONING STRATEGIES

? What does Angle-Angle similarity claim about triangles? According to the Angle-Angle similarity criterion, triangles with two pairs of congruent angles are similar.

EXPLAIN 1

Proving Angle-Angle Triangle Similarity

INTEGRATE MATHEMATICAL PRACTICES
Focus on Math Connections

MP.1 Compare proving two triangles similar with proving two triangles congruent.

QUESTIONING STRATEGIES

? How do you use AA similarity to show two triangles are similar? Show that two angles of one triangle are congruent to two angles of the other triangle. This lets you conclude that the two triangles are similar.

EXPLAIN 2

Applying Angle-Angle Similarity

INTEGRATE MATHEMATICAL PRACTICES

Focus on Communication

MP.3 Remind students that, in triangle similarity, they should identify sides that are *proportional*, rather than congruent.

---

3. In $\triangle JKL$, $m\angle J = 40°$ and $m\angle K = 55°$. In $\triangle MNP$, $m\angle M = 40°$ and $m\angle P = 85°$. A student concludes that the triangles are not similar. Do you agree or disagree? Why?

Disagree; by the Triangle Sum Theorem, $m\angle N = 55°$, so the triangles are similar by the

AA Similarity Theorem.

 Explain 2 **Applying Angle-Angle Similarity**

Architects and contractors use the properties of similar figures to find any unknown dimensions, like the proper height of a triangular roof. They can use a bevel angle tool to check that the angles of construction are congruent to the angles in their plans.

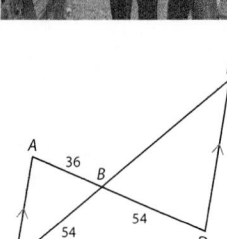

Example 2 Find the indicated length, if possible.

(A) *BE*

First, determine whether $\triangle ABC \sim \triangle DBE$.

By the Alternate Interior Angles Theorem, $\angle A \cong \angle D$ and $\angle C \cong \angle E$, so $\triangle ABC \sim \triangle DBE$ by the AA Triangle Similarity Theorem.

Find *BE* by solving a proportion.

$$\frac{BD}{BA} = \frac{BE}{BC}$$

$$\frac{54}{36} = \frac{BE}{54}$$

$$\frac{54}{36} \cdot 54 = \frac{BE}{54} \cdot 54$$

$$BE = 81$$

(B) *RT*

Check whether $\triangle RSV \sim \triangle RTU$:

It is given in the diagram that $\angle \boxed{RSV} \cong \angle \boxed{T}$. $\angle R$ is shared by both triangles,

so $\angle R \cong \angle R$ by the ____Reflexive____ Property of Congruence.

So, by the ____AA Triangle Similarity Theorem____, $\triangle RST \sim \triangle RTU$.

Find *RT* by solving a proportion.

$$\frac{RT}{RS} = \frac{TU}{SV}$$

$$\frac{RT}{\boxed{10}} = \frac{\boxed{12}}{\boxed{8}}$$

$$RT = \boxed{15}$$

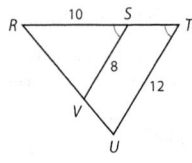

COLLABORATIVE LEARNING

Small Group Activity

Have students work in small groups and draw diagrams to illustrate each of these statements: all squares are similar; all rectangles are not similar; if two polygons are congruent, they are also similar; all right triangles are not similar.

4. In Example 2A, is there another way you can set up the proportion to solve for *BE*?

Yes; $\dfrac{BA}{BC} = \dfrac{BD}{BE}$ would also give the correct result for *BE*.

5. **Discussion** When asked to solve for *y*, a student sets up the proportion as shown. Explain why the proportion is wrong. How should you adjust the proportion so that it will give the correct result?

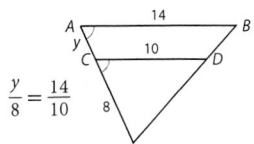

$\dfrac{y}{8} = \dfrac{14}{10}$

The variable *y* does not refer to the side of a triangle but just a segment of a side.

$\dfrac{y+8}{8} = \dfrac{14}{10}$ would be a correct way to solve for *y*.

6. A builder was given a design plan for a triangular roof as shown. Explain how he knows that $\triangle AED \sim \triangle ACB$. Then find *AB*.

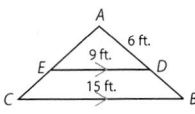

By the Corresponding Angles Theorem, $\angle AED \cong \angle C$ and $\angle ADE \cong \angle B$ (or $\angle A \cong \angle A$ by the Reflexive Property of Congruence), so $\triangle AED \sim \triangle ACB$ by the AA Triangle Similarity Theorem.

$$\dfrac{6}{9} = \dfrac{AB}{15} \rightarrow AB = 10 \text{ feet}$$

7. Find *PQ*, if possible.

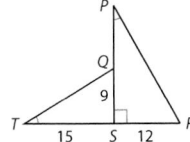

$\angle TSQ$ is a right angle because $\overline{PS}$ and $\overline{TR}$ are perpendicular. So $\triangle PRS \sim \triangle TQS$ by the AA Triangle Similarity Theorem. Let $x = PQ$.

$$\dfrac{x+9}{15} = \dfrac{12}{9} \rightarrow x = 11$$

So, $PQ = 11$.

⊘ Explain 3 Applying SSS and SAS Triangle Similarity

In addition to Angle-Angle Triangle Similarity, there are two additional shortcuts for proving two triangles are similar.

Side-Side-Side (SSS) Triangle Similarity Theorem

If the three sides of one triangle are proportional to the corresponding sides of another triangle, then the triangles are similar.

Side-Angle-Side (SAS) Triangle Similarity Theorem

If two sides of one triangle are proportional to the corresponding sides of another triangle and their included angles are congruent, then the triangles are similar.

? How can you use the AA similarity postulate to find unknown dimensions? You can use AA similarity to establish that two triangles with two congruent pairs of angles are similar, and then write a proportion to find unknown lengths of sides.

AVOID COMMON ERRORS

Some students may use an incorrect sequence of points when writing a similarity statement. Compare the process to writing a congruence statement and remind them to list corresponding vertices in the same order.

DIFFERENTIATE INSTRUCTION

Cognitive Strategies

Have students write their own AAA Similarity Theorems. Then ask them to explain why this theorem is not necessary. An AAA Similarity Theorem is not required because of this theorem: Given two triangles, if two pairs of corresponding angles are congruent, then the remaining pair of corresponding angles must also be congruent.

EXPLAIN 3

Applying SSS and SAS for Triangle Similarity

INTEGRATE MATHEMATICAL PRACTICES

Focus on Math Connections

MP.1 Remind students that similarity statements indicate corresponding parts in the same way congruence statements do.

(A)

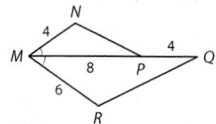

You are given two pairs of corresponding side lengths and one pair of congruent corresponding angles, so try using SAS.

Check that the ratios of corresponding sides are equal.

$$\frac{MN}{MR} = \frac{4}{6} = \frac{2}{3} \qquad \frac{MP}{MQ} = \frac{8}{8+4} = \frac{8}{12} = \frac{2}{3}$$

Check that the included angles are congruent: $\angle NMP \cong \angle QMR$ is given in the diagram.

Therefore $\triangle NMP \sim \triangle RMQ$ by the SAS Triangle Similarity Theorem.

(B)

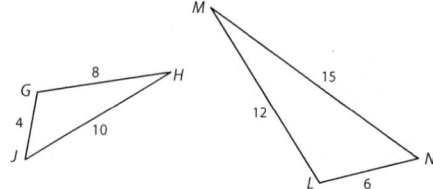

You are given ___three___ pairs of corresponding side lengths and ___zero___ congruent corresponding angles, so try using ___the SSS Triangle Similarity Theorem___.

Check that the ratios of corresponding sides are equal.

$$\frac{LM}{GH} = \boxed{\frac{12}{8}} = \boxed{\frac{3}{2}} \qquad \frac{MN}{HJ} = \boxed{\frac{15}{10}} = \boxed{\frac{3}{2}} \qquad \frac{GJ}{LN} = \boxed{\frac{6}{4}} = \boxed{\frac{3}{2}}$$

Therefore $\triangle$ $\boxed{GHJ}$ $\sim\triangle$ $\boxed{LMN}$ by ___the SSS Triangle Similarity Theorem___.

Since you are given all three pairs of sides, you don't need to check for congruent angles.

Reflect

8. Are all isosceles right triangles similar? Explain why or why not.
Let the legs of one isoc. triangle be *x* and the legs of another be *y*. Then the ratios of the sides would be $\frac{x}{y}$ and $\frac{x}{y}$. The included angle in each triangle is the right angle, so two isosceles right triangles are similar by SAS Similarity.

9. Why isn't Angle-Side-Angle (ASA) used to prove two triangles similar?
ASA implies two pairs of angles are congruent, which is sufficient to show the triangles similar, so checking the included sides is unnecessary.

LANGUAGE SUPPORT EL

Connect Vocabulary

Relate the idea of *proof* to justifying ideas in math. You use established rules and conventions to draw some conclusions. In real life, *proof* means *showing something by gathering evidence by established rules and conventions.*

Your Turn

If possible, determine whether the given triangles are similar. **Justify your answer.**

10.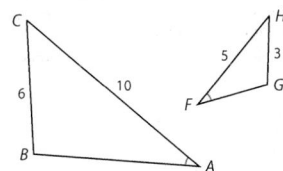

The two triangles cannot be proven similar. Although the two given sides are in proportion, there is not a pair of included congruent angles.

11.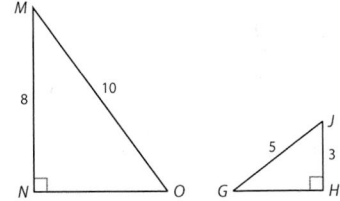

By the Pythagorean Theorem, $NO = 6$ and $GH = 4$, so $\frac{HJ}{NO} = \frac{GH}{MN} = \frac{GJ}{MO} = \frac{1}{2}$. $\triangle MNO \sim \triangle GHI$ by the SSS Triangle Similarity Theorem.

💬 **Elaborate**

12. Is triangle similarity transitive? If you know $\triangle ABC \sim \triangle DEF$ and $\triangle DEF \sim \triangle GHJ$, is $\triangle ABC \sim \triangle GHJ$? Explain.

Yes. If the first two triangles have three pairs of congruent angles and the second two triangles do as well, then the first and third triangles will also have those three pairs of congruent angles.

13. The AA Similarity Theorem applies to triangles. Is there an AAA Similarity Theorem for quadrilaterals? Use your geometry software to test your conjecture or create a counterexample.

No; a square and a rectangle each have three pairs of right angles, but they won't be similar because the sides aren't proportional.

14. Essential Question Check-In How can you prove triangles are similar?

Triangles are similar when their corresponding angles are congruent and their corresponding sides are in proportion, but it is sufficient to use AA Similarity (show two pairs of congruent angles), SSS Similarity (show three pairs of sides in proportion), or SAS Similarity (show two pairs of sides are in proportion and their included angles are congruent).

QUESTIONING STRATEGIES

❓ Why are ASA and AAS not similarity theorems? Both of these contain two pairs of corresponding congruent angles, so ASA and AAS triangles are already similar by the AA similarity theorem.

AVOID COMMON ERRORS

Some students may have difficulty identifying corresponding sides in similar triangles because of the orientation of the figures. Show these students how they can copy one of the triangles onto a piece of paper, then cut it out and rotate it, so that the two triangles have the same orientation.

ELABORATE

QUESTIONING STRATEGIES

❓ Two isosceles triangles have congruent vertex angles. Explain why the two triangles must be similar. Let the measure of the vertex angles be $x°$. Then, by the Isosceles Triangle Theorem, the base angle in each of the triangles must measure half of $(180 - x)°$. So, the triangles are similar by AA similarity.

SUMMARIZE THE LESSON

Which theorems allow you to conclude that triangles are similar without using transformations to map one to the other? What do you need to know before you can apply them? The AA similarity Theorem, the SSS similarity Theorem, and the SAS similarity Theorem; you need to know than the triangles have two pairs of congruent angles, or that all three pairs of sides are proportional, or that two pairs of sides are proportional and the included angles are congruent.

EVALUATE

ASSIGNMENT GUIDE

Concepts and Skills	Practice
Explore Exploring Angle-Angle Similarity in Triangles	Exercises 1–2
Example 1 Proving Angle-Angle Triangle Similarity	Exercises 3–6
Example 2 Applying Angle-Angle Similarity	Exercises 7–10
Example 3 Applying SSS and SAS for Triangle Similarity	Exercises 11–14

Show that the triangles are similar by measuring the lengths of their sides and comparing the ratios of the corresponding sides.

1.

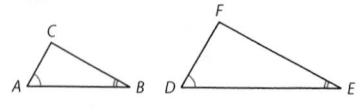

$$\frac{DE}{AB} = \frac{4.5}{3} = \frac{3}{2} \text{ or } 1.5$$

$$\frac{DF}{AC} = \frac{2.1}{1.4} = \frac{3}{2} \text{ or } 1.5$$

$$\frac{EF}{BC} = \frac{3.9}{2.6} = \frac{3}{2} \text{ or } 1.5$$

2.

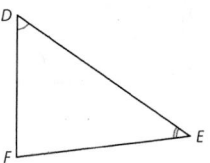

$$\frac{AB}{DE} = \frac{3}{6} = \frac{1}{2}$$

$$\frac{AC}{DF} = \frac{2}{4} = \frac{1}{2}$$

$$\frac{BC}{EF} = \frac{2.5}{5} = \frac{1}{2}$$

Determine whether the two triangles are similar. If they are similar, write the similarity statement.

3.

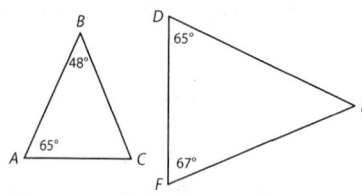

By the Triangle Angle Sum Theorem, $m\angle C = 67°$. So $\angle A \cong \angle D$ and $\angle C \cong \angle F$.
By the AA Triangle Similarity Theorem, $\triangle ABC \sim \triangle DEF$.

4.

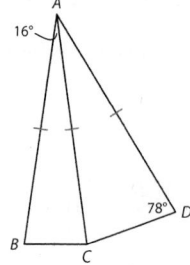

$\triangle ABC$ and $\triangle ACD$ are isosceles triangles, so $\angle B \cong \angle ACB$ and $\angle D \cong \angle ACD$. $16° + 2 \cdot m\angle B = 180°$, so $m\angle B = 82°$. However, $m\angle D = m\angle ACD = 78°$. None of the angles in $\triangle ABC$ is congruent to $\angle D$, so the triangles are not similar.

© Houghton Mifflin Harcourt Publishing Company

Exercise	Depth of Knowledge (D.O.K.)	COMMON CORE Mathematical Practices	
1–2	**2** Skills/Concepts	**MP.5** Using Tools	
3–17	**2** Skills/Concepts	**MP.2** Reasoning	
18	**2** Skills/Concepts	**MP.4** Modeling	
19	**3** Strategic Thinking H.O.T.	**MP.3** Logic	

Determine whether the two triangles are similar. If they are similar, write the similarity statement.

5.

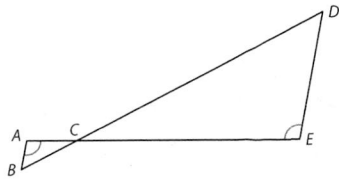

∠A ≅ ∠E, and ∠ACB ≅ ∠ECD by the Vertical Angles Theorem. Therefore △ABC ∼ △EDC by the AA Triangle Similarity Theorem.

6.

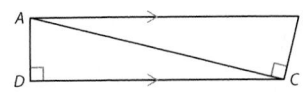

∠D ≅ ∠BCA, and ∠BAC ≅ ∠DCA by the Alternate Interior Angles Theorem. Therefore △ADC ∼ △BCA by the AA Triangle Similarity.

Explain how you know whether the triangles are similar. If possible, find the indicated length.

7. *AC*

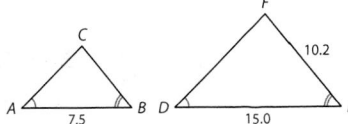

The triangles are similar by the AA Triangle Similarity Theorem. It is not possible to find the indicated length because, the length of the corresponding side, *DF*, is not known.

8. *AD*

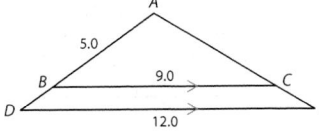

The triangles are similar by AA Similarity.

$\frac{AD}{12} = \frac{5}{9} \rightarrow AD = 6.7$

9. *QR*

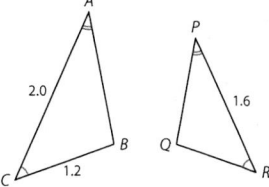

The triangles are similar by AA Similarity.

$\frac{QR}{1.6} = \frac{1.2}{2} \rightarrow QR = 0.96$

10. Find *BD*.

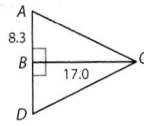

Not possible. Only one congruent angle is identified between △ABC and △DBC, so similarity cannot be established.

Exercise	Depth of Knowledge (D.O.K.)	COMMON CORE Mathematical Practices
20	**3** Strategic Thinking H.O.T.	**MP.2** Reasoning
21–22	**3** Strategic Thinking H.O.T.	**MP.3** Logic

AVOID COMMON ERRORS

Because they need to know only that two angles of two triangles are congruent in order to prove similarity, students might think they need to know only three angles of two quadrilaterals to do the same, and so on for any *n*-gon. Use counter examples to show that this is incorrect. Stress that triangles are a special case because they are rigid structures.

Focus on Patterns

MP.8 When using the SSS and SAS Similarity Theorems, some students have difficulty matching up the corresponding sides. Tell these students to match up the smallest side to the smallest side, the longest side to the longest side, and match the sides that are neither longest nor shortest.

Show whether or not each pair of triangles are similar, if possible. Justify your answer, and write a similarity statement when the triangles are similar.

11.

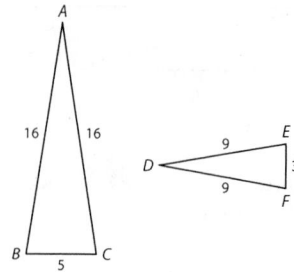

$\frac{AB}{DE} = \frac{AC}{DF} = \frac{16}{9}$; $\frac{BC}{EF} = \frac{5}{3}$. The ratios are not equal, so the two triangles are not similar.

12.

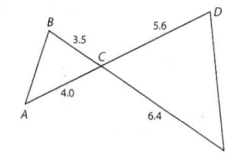

$\angle ACB \cong \angle ECD$ by the Vertical Angle Theorem. $\frac{BC}{DC} = \frac{3.5}{5.6} = 0.625$; $\frac{AC}{EC} = (4.0/6.4) = 0.625$. Therefore $\triangle ABC \sim \triangle EDC$ by SAS Similarity.

13.

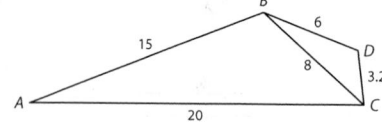

$\frac{BC}{DC} = \frac{8}{3.2} = 2.5$; $\frac{AB}{BD} = \frac{15}{6} = 2.5$; $\frac{AC}{BC} = \frac{20}{8} = 2.5$. Therefore $\triangle ABC \sim \triangle BDC$ by SSS Similarity.

14.

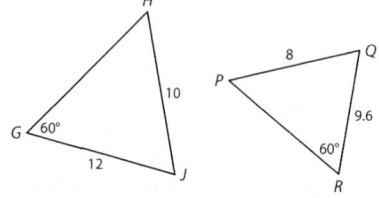

The triangles cannot be proven similar using the given information, because the congruent angle is not an included angle.

15. Explain the Error A student analyzes the two triangles shown below. Explain the error that the student makes.

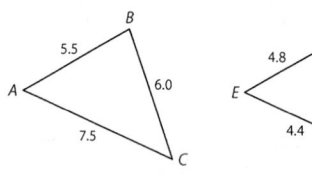

$\frac{AB}{EF} = \frac{5.5}{4.8} = 1.15$, and $\frac{BC}{DF} = \frac{6}{6} = 1$

Because the two ratios are not equal, the two triangles are not similar.

The student did not compare corresponding sides of the two triangles. $\overline{AB}$ is the shortest side of $\triangle ABC$, so its corresponding side is $\overline{DE}$ the shortest side of $\triangle DEF$. The ratios $\frac{AB}{DE}$, $\frac{BC}{EF}$ and $\frac{AC}{DF}$ are equal, so the triangles are similar by SSS Similarity.

16. Algebra Find all possible values of x for which these two triangles are similar.

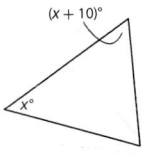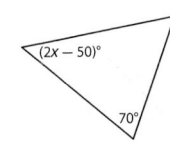

The possible values of x are the solutions of $x = 70$, $x = 2x - 50$, $x + 10 = 70$, $x + 10 = 2x - 50$, $x + x + 10 + 70 = 180$, and $x + x + 10 + 2x - 50 = 180$. These result in 50, 55, 60, or 70, of which only 50 results in similar triangles. So $x = 50°$ is the only possible value.

17. Multi-Step Identify two similar triangles in the figure, and explain why they are similar. Then find AB.

$\angle A \cong \angle A$, and $\angle ABD \cong \angle C$, so $\triangle ABD \sim \triangle ACB$ by the AA Triangle Similarity Theorem. $\dfrac{AB}{AC} = \dfrac{AD}{AB} \rightarrow \dfrac{AB}{16} = \dfrac{4}{AB} \rightarrow AB = 8$

18. The picture shows a person taking a pinhole photograph of himself. Light entering the opening reflects his image on the wall, forming similar triangles. What is the height of the image to the nearest inch?

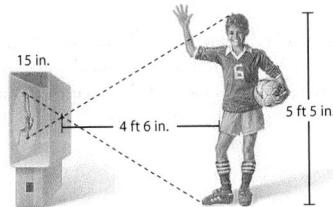

$\dfrac{h}{15} = \dfrac{5'5''}{4'6''} = \dfrac{65}{54} \rightarrow h = 18$ inches

19. Analyze Relationships Prove the SAS Triangle Similarity Theorem.

Given: $\dfrac{XY}{AB} = \dfrac{XZ}{AC}$ and $\angle A \cong \angle X$

Prove: $\triangle ABC \sim \triangle XYZ$

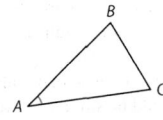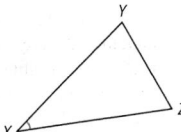

Apply a dilation to $\triangle ABC$ with scale factor $k = \dfrac{XY}{AB}$ and let the image of $\triangle ABC$ be $\triangle A'B'C'$.

Then $\angle A' \cong \angle A$. It is given that $\angle A \cong \angle X$, so by transitivity $\angle A' \cong \angle X$.

Also $A'B' = k \cdot AB = \dfrac{XY}{AB} \cdot AB = XY$ and $A'C' = k \cdot AC = \dfrac{XY}{AB} \cdot AC = \dfrac{XZ}{AC} \cdot AC = XZ$. Therefore, $\triangle A'B'C' \cong \triangle XYZ$ by SAS Congruence. So a sequence of rigid motions maps $\triangle A'B'C'$ to $\triangle XYZ$.

The dilation followed by this sequence of rigid motions shows that there is a sequence of similarity transformations that maps $\triangle ABC$ to $\triangle XYZ$. So $\triangle ABC \sim \triangle XYZ$.

Have students write a journal entry to explain what a scale on a map means, how it is used, and how it is related to the concept of similarity.

20. Analyze Relationships Prove the SSS Triangle Similarity Theorem.

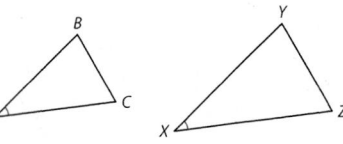

Given: $\dfrac{XY}{AB} = \dfrac{XZ}{AC} = \dfrac{YZ}{BC}$

Prove: $\triangle ABC \sim \triangle XYZ$

(Hint: The main steps of the proof are similar to those of the proof of the AA Triangle Similarity Theorem.)

Apply a dilation to $\triangle ABC$ with scale factor $k = \dfrac{XY}{AB}$ and let the image of

$\triangle ABC$ be $\triangle A'B'C'$. Then:

$A'B' = k \cdot AB = \dfrac{XY}{AB} \cdot AB = XY$

$A'C' = k \cdot AC = \dfrac{XY}{AB} \cdot AC = \dfrac{XZ}{AC} \cdot AC = XZ$

$B'C' = k \cdot BC = \dfrac{XY}{AB} \cdot BC = \dfrac{YZ}{BC} \cdot BC = YZ$. Therefore, $\triangle A'B'C \cong \triangle XYZ$ by the

SSS Congruence Theorem. This means there is a sequence of similarity

transformations that maps $\triangle ABC$ to $\triangle XYZ$. So $\triangle ABC \sim \triangle XYZ$.

21. Communicate Mathematical Ideas A student is asked to find point X on $\overleftrightarrow{BC}$ such that $\triangle ABC \sim \triangle XBA$ and XB is as small as possible. The student does so by constructing a perpendicular line to $\overleftrightarrow{AC}$ at point A, and then labeling X as the intersection of the perpendicular line with $\overleftrightarrow{BC}$. Explain why this procedure generates the similar triangle that the student was requested to construct.

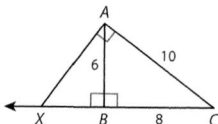

Possible Answer: For XB to be as small as possible, it should correspond to the shortest side of $\triangle ABC$, which is $\overline{AB}$. Thus, X corresponds to A.

22. Make a Conjecture Builders and architects use scale models to help them design and build new buildings. An architecture student builds a model of an office building in which the height of the model is $\dfrac{1}{400}$ of the height of the actual building, while the width and length of the model are each $\dfrac{1}{200}$ of the corresponding dimensions of the actual building. The model includes several triangles. Describe how a triangle in this model could be similar to the corresponding triangle in the actual building, then describe how a triangle in this model might not be similar to the corresponding triangle in the actual building. Use a similarity theorem to support each answer.

A triangle that lies entirely in a plane parallel to the ground will have side lengths that are

each $\dfrac{1}{200}$ of the side lengths of the corresponding triangle in the actual building. So the two

triangles are similar by the SSS Triangle Similarity Theorem. A triangle that has vertices at

several heights will not have side lengths that form a constant ratio with the side lengths of

the corresponding triangle in the actual building, and so would not be similar.

Lesson Performance Task

The figure shows a camera obscura and the object being "photographed." Answer the following questions about the figure:

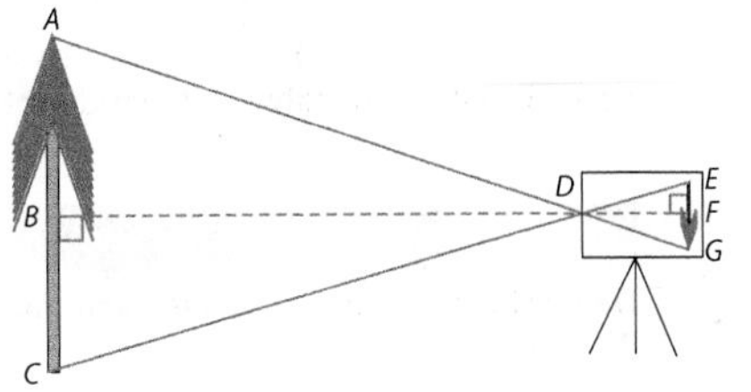

1. Explain how the image of the object would be affected if the camera were moved closer to the object. How would that limit the height of objects that could be photographed?

2. How do you know that $\triangle ADC$ is similar to $\triangle GDE$?

3. Write a proportion you could use to find the height of the pine tree.

4. $DF = 12$ in., $EG = 8$ in., $BD = 96$ ft. How tall is the pine tree?

1. **As the object gets closer the vertical angle at D will get larger, and since $\triangle ADC$ remains similar to $\triangle GDE$, the height of the image on the back surface will increase. So the camera must be placed far enough from the object that the image is no taller than the height of the back surface, or else the object will not be able to be photographed.**

2. **Possible answer: $\angle A \cong \angle G$ because the angles are alternate interior angles for parallel lines $\overline{AC}$ and $\overline{EG}$. $\angle ADC \cong \angle GDE$ because vertical angles are congruent. So, $\triangle ADC \sim \triangle GDE$ by the AA Similarity Theorem.**

3. $\dfrac{AC}{BD} = \dfrac{EG}{DF}$

4. $\dfrac{AC}{96} = \dfrac{8}{12} \Rightarrow AC = 64$ ft

EXTENSION ACTIVITY

Have students research methods of making simple models of a *camera obscura*. For some models, no more than a cereal box or shoe box, tape, scissors, and a pin are required. A more elaborate model can be made by blocking a window of the classroom and projecting an outside scene onto a sheet in the classroom. Either method will give reasonable results when students compare the dimensions and angles of the external object with those of the projected image.

CONNECT VOCABULARY EL

The name *camera obscura* comes from the Latin words *camera*, meaning room, and *obscura*, meaning dark. The plural of Latin words ending in the letter *a* is formed by changing *a* to *ae*. So, more than one of these instruments would be referred to as *camerae obscurae*.

INTEGRATE MATHEMATICAL PRACTICES

Focus on Patterns

MP.8 A camera obscura is square. This means that in the figure in the Lesson Performance Task, $DF = EG$. Suppose you want to photograph an object that is *n* feet from the front of the camera. What is the maximum height of such an object if you want to photograph its entire height? Explain your reasoning. **The maximum height is *n* feet.**
Sample answer: Because $DF = EG$, and, $\dfrac{AC}{BD} = \dfrac{EG}{DF}$, $AC = BD = 1$.

Scoring Rubric
2 points: Student correctly solves the problem and explains his/her reasoning.
1 point: 1 point: Student shows good understanding of the problem but does not fully solve or explain his/her reasoning.
0 points: Student does not demonstrate understanding of the problem.

AA Similarity of Triangles   **622**

Study Guide Review

ASSESSMENT AND INTERVENTION

Assign or customize module reviews.

Similarity and Transformations

Essential Question: How can you use similarity and transformations to solve real-world problems?

KEY EXAMPLE (Lesson 11.1)

Determine the center of dilation and the scale factor of the dilation.

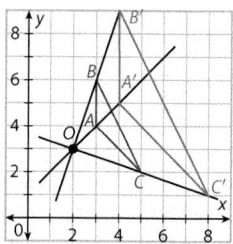

Draw a line through A and A'. Draw a line through B and B'. Draw a line through C and C'.

The three lines intersect at point $O(2, 3)$.

Find the distance from point O to points A and A'.

$$d_A = \sqrt{(2-3)^2 + (3-4)^2} = \sqrt{2} \qquad \text{Find the distance to point } A.$$

$$d_{A'} = \sqrt{(2-4)^2 + (3-5)^2} = 2\sqrt{2} \qquad \text{Find the distance to point } A'.$$

The distance from point O to point A' is twice the distance from point O to point A. The scale factor of dilation is 2 to 1.

KEY EXAMPLE (Lesson 11.3)

$\triangle ABCD$ maps to $\triangle EFGH$ by a similarity transformation. Write a proportion that contains $\overline{BC}$ and $\overline{EH}$. Then list any angles that are congruent to $\angle D$ or $\angle E$.

Corresponding sides of similar figures are proportional.

$\overline{BC} \cong \overline{FG}$ and $\overline{EH} \cong \overline{AD}$, so $\dfrac{BC}{FG} = \dfrac{AD}{EH}$.

Corresponding angles of similar figures are congruent.

$\angle D \cong \angle H$ and $\angle E \cong \angle A$.

Key Vocabulary

center of dilation *(centro de dilatación)*

dilation *(dilatación)*

scale factor *(factor de escala)*

Side-Side-Side Similarity *(Similitud Lado -Lado -Lado)*

Side-Angle-Side Similarity *(Similitud Lado-Ángulo-Lado)*

similar *(semejantes)*

similarity transformation *(transformación de semejanza)*

© Houghton Mifflin Harcourt Publishing Company

Determine whether $\triangle ABC$ and $\triangle DEF$ are similar. If so, justify by SSS Similarity or SAS Similarity.

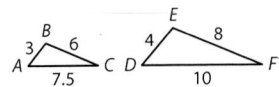

Check that the ratios of the lengths of corresponding sides are equal.

$$\frac{3}{4}$$

$$\frac{6}{8} = \frac{3}{4}$$

$$\frac{7.5}{10} = \frac{3}{4}$$

Since all the ratios of the lengths of corresponding sides are equal, the triangles are similar by SSS Similarity.

EXERCISES

Determine the following for the dilation. *(Lesson 11.1)*

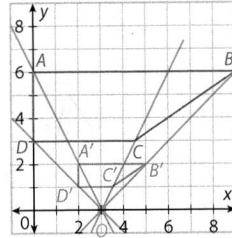

1. center ____(3, 0)____

2. scale factor ____1 to 3____

MODULE
PERFORMANCE TASK

Mathematical Practices: MP.1, MP.2, MP.4, MP.6
G-MG.A.1, G-MG.A.3

SUPPORTING STUDENT REASONING

Students should begin this problem by focusing on what information they will need. Here are some issues they might bring up.

- **What should be the maximum height of the model:** Students can either work backwards from the desired height or find a percent of the actual height and use it to determine the scale.

- **Which dimensions are not needed for a scale model:** Students can decide which dimensions might not be needed, such as the height at which the stone color changes.

- **How to determine the dimensions of the model:** Students should use proportions to convert the actual dimensions to the scaled dimensions. Students may first want to convert the actual dimensions to decimals.

- **What materials should be used:** Students can research the appropriate materials to use or you can make suggestions.

Determine whether the two figures are similar using similarity transformations. *(Lesson 11.2)*

3. $\triangle ABC$ to $\triangle DEF$ _____similar_____

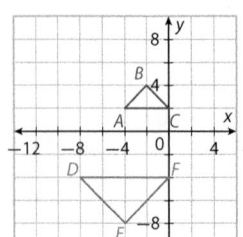

4. $\triangle ABCD$ to $\triangle EFGH$ ___not similar___

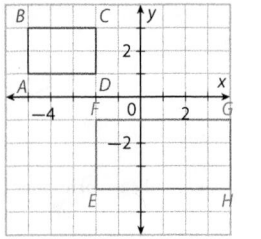

$\triangle ABC$ maps to $\triangle DEF$ by a similarity transformation. *(Lesson 11.3)*

5. Write a proportion that contains $\overline{AB}$ and $\overline{EF}$. $\dfrac{AB}{DE} = \dfrac{BC}{EF}$

6. Write a proportion that contains $\overline{BC}$ and $\overline{DF}$. $\dfrac{BC}{EF} = \dfrac{AC}{DF}$

7. List any angles that are congruent to $\angle A$ or $\angle E$. $\angle A \cong \angle D;\ \angle E \cong \angle B$

Determine whether $\triangle ABC$ and $\triangle DEF$ are similar. If so, justify by *SSS* or *SAS*. *(Lesson 11.4)*

8. _____not similar_____

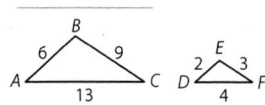

9. _____SAS_____

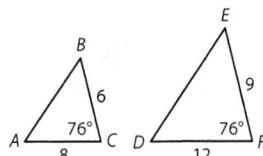

SCAFFOLDING SUPPORT

- Students should recognize that they will need to convert units of the given measurements so that all units are the same. Possible units are feet, inches, meters, or centimeters.

- If students choose to solve the problem by first deciding on a scale factor, they will need to make sure the scale factor they use results in a model which will fit inside a classroom.

MODULE PERFORMANCE TASK

Designing a Model of the Washington Monument

Your challenge is to design a scale model of the Washington Monument that would be small enough to fit inside your classroom. Here are some key dimensions of the Washington Monument for you to consider in determining the scale factor for your model. (Note that the color of the stone changes part way up the monument because of a halt in construction between 1854 and 1877.)

Key Dimension	Measurement
Total height	555 ft 5 in.
Height to top of trapezoidal side	500 ft
Width at base	55 ft 1 in.
Width at top of trapezoidal side	34 ft 5 in.
Height at which stone color changes	151 ft

What scale factor will you use for your model? What are the key dimensions of your model?

Begin by making some notes in the space below about your strategy for designing the model. Then use your own paper to complete the task. Present your plan using diagrams, words, and/or numbers.

© Houghton Mifflin Harcourt Publishing Company · Image Credits: ©Izzy Schwartz/Digital Vision/Getty Images

Module 11　　　626　　　Study Guide Review

SAMPLE SOLUTION

Use the scale 1 in. = 10 ft.

First, convert units so that all measurements are in feet, by multiplying inches by the ratio $\frac{1 \text{ ft}}{12 \text{ in.}}$ and adding that to the number of feet. The results are:

Total height: 555.42 ft

Width at base: 55.08 ft

Width at top of trapezoidal side: 34.42 ft

To find the model's dimensions, solve the proportion:

$$\frac{1 \text{ in.}}{10 \text{ ft}} = \frac{\text{model height}}{\text{actual height}}$$

Using the proportion, check the total height of the model to see if it will fit inside the classroom.

$$\frac{1 \text{ in.}}{10 \text{ ft}} = \frac{x}{555.42 \text{ ft}} \rightarrow x \approx 55.5 \text{ in.}$$

This is $55.54\left(\frac{1 \text{ ft}}{12 \text{ in.}}\right) \approx 4.6$ ft tall, so the scale factor is reasonable.

The remaining dimensions are as follows.

Height to top of trapezoidal side: 50 in.

Width at base: 5.5 in.

Width at top of trapezoidal side: 3.4 in.

Height at which stone color changes: 15.1 in.

DISCUSSION OPPORTUNITIES

- If students choose to work backwards from a desired height of exactly six feet, how will this change the calculations and scale factor used?

- What are some advantages to choosing a scale that makes the model no more than a foot tall? Sample answer: The amount of material needed to construct the model will be much less, which in turn will lower both the cost and the weight and make the model more portable.

Assessment Rubric

2 points: Student correctly solves the problem and explains his/her reasoning.

1 point: Student shows good understanding of the problem but does not fully solve or explain.

0 points: Student does not demonstrate understanding of the problem.

Ready to Go On?

ASSESS MASTERY

Use the assessment on this page to determine if students have mastered the concepts and standards covered in this module.

ASSESSMENT AND INTERVENTION

Access Ready to Go On? assessment online, and receive instant scoring, feedback, and customized intervention or enrichment.

ADDITIONAL RESOURCES

Response to Intervention Resources

- Reteach Worksheets

Differentiated Instruction Resources

- Reading Strategies **EL**
- Success for English Learners **EL**
- Challenge Worksheets

Assessment Resources

- Leveled Module Quizzes

627 Module 11

(Ready) to Go On?

11.1–11.4 Similarity and Transformations

 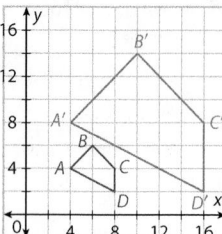

- Online Homework
- Hints and Help
- Extra Practice

Answer each problem about the image. *(Lesson 11.1)*

1. Are the two shapes similar? ____Yes____

2. Find the scale factor k. ____3____

3. Find the center of dilation. ____(4, 2)____

4. Compare k to the ratio $\dfrac{\text{area } \triangle A'D'C'}{\text{area } \triangle ADC}$.

   The ratio equals 9, which is the square of the scale factor.

Determine which of the following transformations are dilations. *(Lesson 11.1)*

5. $(x, y) \rightarrow (4x, 4y)$

   ____Dilation____

6. $(x, y) \rightarrow (-x, 3y)$

   ____Not a dilation____

7. $(x, y) \rightarrow (x - 2, y - 2)$

   ____Not a dilation____

8. $(x, y) \rightarrow \left(\frac{1}{3}x, \frac{1}{3}y\right)$

   ____Dilation____

Find the missing length. *(Lesson 11.3)*

9. $\triangle XYZ$ maps to $\triangle MNO$ with the transformation $(x, y) \rightarrow (7x, 7y)$. If $XY = 3$, what is the length of MN?

   ____21____

Find the appropriate statements about the triangles. *(Lesson 11.4)*

10. $\triangle ABC$ is similar to $\triangle RTS$. Write a proportion that contains AC and RT. Also write the angle congruence statements that must be true.

    $\dfrac{AC}{RS} = \dfrac{AB}{RT}$, $\angle A \cong \angle R$, $\angle B \cong \angle T$, $\angle C \cong \angle S$

ESSENTIAL QUESTION

11. How can you determine whether a shape is similar to another shape?

    Answers may vary. Sample: Two shapes are similar only if one shape can be mapped to the other through similarity transformations. These transformations are the rigid motions, meaning reflections, translations, and rotations, as well as dilations.

© Houghton Mifflin Harcourt Publishing Company

COMMON CORE	**Common Core Standards**		

Lesson	*Items*	**Content Standards**	**Mathematical Practices**
11.2	1	**G-SRT.A.2, G-SRT.A.1b, G-CO.A.2**	**MP.7**
11.1	2–4	**G-SRT.A.1b**	**MP.7**
11.2	5–8	**G-SRT.A.1b, G-CO.A.2**	**MP.2**
11.2	9	**G-SRT.A.1b, G-CO.A.2**	**MP.4**
11.3	10	**G-SRT.A.2**	**MP.4**

Assessment Readiness

1. Consider each transformation. Does the transformation preserve distance? Select Yes or No for A–C.

A.	Dilations	⚪ Yes	🔘 No
B.	Reflections	🔘 Yes	⚪ No
C.	Rotations	🔘 Yes	⚪ No

2. $\triangle MNO$ maps to $\triangle RST$ with the transformation $(x, y) \rightarrow \left(\frac{1}{3}x, \frac{1}{3}y\right)$. Choose True or False for each statement.

A.	If $RT = 3$, $MO = 9$.	🔘 True	⚪ False
B.	If $RT = 12$, $MO = 4$.	⚪ True	🔘 False
C.	If $RT = 9$, $MO = 27$.	🔘 True	⚪ False

3. Determine if the following pair of triangles are similar. If so, explain how. Note that $\overline{AC} \parallel \overline{BD}$.

   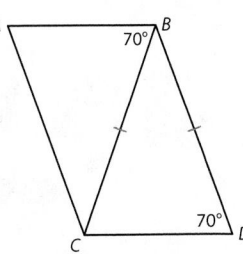

   Possible Answer: $\angle ACB$ and $\angle CBD$ are congruent because they are alternate interior angles. $\angle ABC$ and $\angle CDB$ are congruent because it is given they have the same measure. So the two triangles are similar by Angle–Angle Similarity.

4. If $\triangle ABC$ is similar to $\triangle XYZ$ and $\triangle YZX$, what special type of triangle is $\triangle ABC$? Justify your reasoning.

   Answers may vary. Sample: Examine the corresponding angles. Since $\triangle ABC$ is similar to $\triangle XYZ$, this means $\angle A \cong \angle X$. Likewise, since $\triangle ABC$ is similar to $\triangle YZX$, this means $\angle A \cong \angle Y$. Thus, by the Transitive Property of Congruence, it can be said that $\angle X \cong \angle Y$. Also, $\angle B \cong \angle Y$ and $\angle B \cong \angle Z$, which means $\angle Y \cong \angle Z$ by the Transitive Property of Congruence. Putting these facts together, it can be shown that $\angle X \cong \angle Y \cong \angle Z$. Therefore, $\triangle XYZ$, $\triangle YZX$, and by similarity, $\triangle ABC$ are all equilateral triangles.

Assessment Readiness

ASSESSMENT AND INTERVENTION

Assign ready-made or customized practice tests to prepare students for high-stakes tests.

ADDITIONAL RESOURCES

Assessment Resources

- Leveled Module Quizzes: Modified, B

AVOID COMMON ERRORS

Item 2 Some students have trouble following a dilation rule backward. Remind students that if moving from the image to the original figure, multiply by the reciprocal of the original dilation.

COMMON CORE Common Core Standards

Lesson	Items	Content Standards	Mathematical Practices
11.1, 1.3	1*	**G-SRT.A.2**	**MP.7**
11.3	2	**G-SRT.A.1**	**MP.7**
11.4	3	**G-SRT.A.3**	**MP.7**
11.3, 7.2	4*	**G-SRT.A.2**	**MP.3**

* Item integrates mixed review concepts from previous modules or a previous course.

Using Similar Triangles

ESSENTIAL QUESTION:

Answer: For one example, similar triangles can be used to find the height of a tall object by measuring its shadow.

PROFESSIONAL DEVELOPMENT VIDEO

Professional Development Video

Author Juli Dixon models successful teaching practices in an actual high-school classroom.

Professional Development
my.hrw.com

Using Similar Triangles

MODULE 12

Essential Question: How can you use similar triangles to solve real-world problems?

© Houghton Mifflin Harcourt Publishing Company • Image Credits: ©Lightguard/iStockPhoto.com

REAL WORLD VIDEO
Check out how properties of similar triangles can be used to determine real-world areas of geographic regions like the Bermuda Triangle.

MODULE PERFORMANCE TASK PREVIEW

How Large Is the Bermuda Triangle?

In this module, you will be asked to determine the area of the Bermuda Triangle from a map. How can indirect measurement and the properties of similar triangles help you find the answer? Let's get started on solving this "mystery" of the Bermuda Triangle!

Module 12   **629**

DIGITAL TEACHER EDITION

Access a full suite of teaching resources when and where you need them:

- Access content online or offline
- Customize lessons to share with your class
- Communicate with your students in real-time
- View student grades and data instantly to target your instruction where it is needed most

PERSONAL MATH TRAINER

Assessment and Intervention

Assign automatically graded homework, quizzes, tests, and intervention activities. Prepare your students with updated, Common Core-aligned practice tests.

Are YOU Ready?

Complete these exercises to review skills you will need for this module.

Scale Factor and Scale Drawings

Example 1
Determine the length of the side $\overline{A'B'}$ given $AB = 4$, $BC = 3$, and $B'C' = 6$.

The image of $\triangle ABC$ is created as a result of a scale drawing, so the transformation is a dilation.

$2BC = B'C'$, so $2AB = A'B'$.

$A'B' = 2(4) = 8$

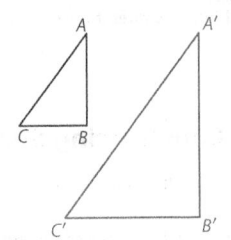

- Online Homework
- Hints and Help
- Extra Practice

Give the side length in $\triangle RST$.

1. ST, given $RT = 5$, $R'T' = 15$, and $S'T' = 18$ _____ 6

Similar Figures

Example 2
The figures $PQRS$ and $KLMN$ are similar. Determine the angle in figure $KLMN$ that is congruent to $\angle Q$ and find its measure if $m\angle Q = 45°$.

$\angle Q \cong \angle L$ Corresponding angles of similar figures are congruent.

$m\angle Q = m\angle L = 45°$ Definition of congruency of angle.

Give each angle measure.

2. $m\angle A$, given $\triangle ABC \cong \triangle DEF$ and $m\angle D = 67°$ _____ 67°

3. $m\angle E$, given $\triangle PQR \cong \triangle DEF$, $m\angle R = 13°$, and $m\angle D = 67°$ _____ 100°

The Pythagorean Theorem

Example 3
A right triangle $\triangle ABC$ has side lengths $AB = 3$ and $BC = 4$. Find the length of the hypotenuse $\overline{AC}$.

$\triangle ABC$ is a right triangle, so the Pythagorean Theorem can be used.

$AC = \sqrt{(AB)^2 + (BC)^2}$ Write the Pythagorean Theorem.

$AC = \sqrt{3^2 + 4^2} = \sqrt{9 + 16}$ Substitute and simplify.

$AC = 5$ Simplify.

Find the side length for each right triangle.

4. DE, given $DF = 5$, $EF = 12$, and $\overline{DE}$ is the hypotenuse _____ 13

5. BC, given $AB = 15$, $AC = 17$, and $\overline{AC}$ is the hypotenuse _____ 8

© Houghton Mifflin Harcourt Publishing Company

Are You Ready?

ASSESS READINESS

Use the assessment on this page to determine if students need strategic or intensive intervention for the module's prerequisite skills.

ASSESSMENT AND INTERVENTION

RtI Response to Intervention **TIER 1, TIER 2, TIER 3 SKILLS**

Personal Math Trainer will automatically create a standards-based, personalized intervention assignment for your students, targeting each student's individual needs!

ADDITIONAL RESOURCES

See the table below for a full list of intervention resources available for this module.

Response to Intervention Resources also includes:

- Tier 2 Skill Pre-Tests for each Module
- Tier 2 Skill Post-Tests for each skill

Response to Intervention			Differentiated Instruction
Tier 1 Lesson Intervention Worksheets	**Tier 2** Strategic Intervention Skills Intervention Worksheets	**Tier 3** Intensive Intervention Worksheets available online	
Reteach 12.1 Reteach 12.2 Reteach 12.3 Reteach 12.4	22 Scale Factor and Scale Drawings 23 Similar Figures 25 The Pythagorean Theorem 29 Proportional Relationships	Building Block Skills 36, 38, 46, 48, 50, 63, 80, 82, 86, 90, 95, 100	Challenge worksheets Extend the Math Lesson Activities in TE

Triangle Proportionality Theorem

Common Core Math Standards

The student is expected to:

 G-SRT.B.4

Prove theorems about triangles. Also G-CO.C.10, G-CO.D.12, G-SRT.B.5

Mathematical Practices

 MP.5 Using Tools

Language Objective

Work with a partner to describe the triangle proportionality theorem and its converse.

ENGAGE

Essential Question: When a line parallel to one side of a triangle intersects the other two sides, how does it divide those sides?

The line cuts two sides of the triangle into segments, and the ratios between the two segments of each side are equal.

PREVIEW: LESSON PERFORMANCE TASK

View the Engage section online. Discuss the photograph and ask students to identify the geometrical shapes seen in the sail. Then preview the Lesson Performance Task.

Name_____ Class_____ Date_____

12.1 Triangle Proportionality Theorem

Essential Question: When a line parallel to one side of a triangle intersects the other two sides, how does it divide those sides?

Resource Locker

⊘ Explore **Constructing Similar Triangles**

In the following activity you will see one way to construct a triangle similar to a given triangle.

(A) Do your work for Steps A–C in the space provided. Draw a triangle. Label it *ABC* as shown.

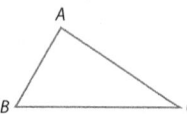

Check students' constructions.

(B) Select a point on $\overline{AB}$. Label it *E*.

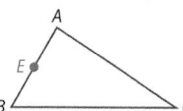

(C) Construct an angle with vertex *E* that is congruent to ∠*B*. Label the point where the side of the angle you constructed intersects $\overline{AC}$ as *F*.

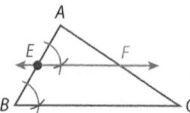

(D) Why are $\overleftrightarrow{EF}$ and $\overline{BC}$ parallel?

Coplanar lines $\overleftrightarrow{EF}$ and $\overleftrightarrow{BC}$ are cut by transversal $\overrightarrow{AB}$ so that ∠*AEF* ≅ ∠*B*. By the Converse of the Corresponding Angles Theorem, $\overleftrightarrow{EF} \parallel \overline{BC}$.

(E) Use a ruler to measure $\overline{AE}$, $\overline{EB}$, $\overline{AF}$, and $\overline{FC}$. Then compare the ratios $\frac{AE}{EB}$ and $\frac{AF}{FC}$.

Measurements will vary, but, if the constructions are accurate, the ratios should be approximately equal.

Module 12   631   Lesson 1

© Houghton Mifflin Harcourt Publishing Company

HARDCOVER PAGES 537–546

Turn to these pages to find this lesson in the hardcover student edition.

1. **Discussion** How can you show that $\triangle AEF \sim \triangle ABC$? Explain.
   You can show that there are three pairs of congruent angles. $\angle A \cong \angle A$ (Reflexive Property of Equality) and $\angle AEF \cong \angle B$ (by construction). Also, because $\overleftrightarrow{EF} \parallel BC$, $\angle AFE \cong \angle C$. Then you can use the AA Similarity Criterion because you can show that there are two pairs of congruent angles.

2. What do you know about the ratios $\frac{AE}{AB}$ and $\frac{AF}{AC}$? Explain.
   Because $\triangle ABC \sim \triangle AEF$ and corresponding sides of similar triangles are proportional, $\frac{AE}{AB} = \frac{AF}{AC}$.

3. **Make a Conjecture** Use your answer to Step E to make a conjecture about the line segments produced when a line parallel to one side of a triangle intersects the other two sides.
   The parallel line divides the other two sides so the lengths of the segments are proportional.

⊘ Explain 1   Proving the Triangle Proportionality Theorem

As you saw in the Explore, when a line parallel to one side of a triangle intersects the other two sides of the triangle, the lengths of the segments are proportional.

Triangle Proportionality Theorem		
Theorem	**Hypothesis**	**Conclusion**
If a line parallel to a side of a triangle intersects the other two sides, then it divides those sides proportionally.	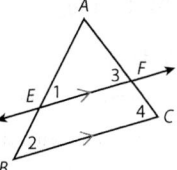 $\overrightarrow{EF} \parallel \overline{BC}$	$\dfrac{AE}{EB} = \dfrac{AF}{FC}$

Example 1   Prove the Triangle Proportionality Theorem

(A)   Given: $\overleftrightarrow{EF} \parallel \overline{BC}$

Prove: $\dfrac{AE}{EB} = \dfrac{AF}{FC}$

Step 1 Show that $\triangle AEF \sim \triangle ABC$.

Because $\overleftrightarrow{EF} \parallel \overline{BC}$, you can conclude that $\angle 1 \cong \angle 2$ and

$\angle 3 \cong \angle 4$ by the ___Corresponding Angles___ Theorem.

So, $\triangle AEF \sim \triangle ABC$ by the ___AA Similarity Criterion___.

PROFESSIONAL DEVELOPMENT

COMMON CORE Math Background

The Triangle Proportionality Theorem and its converse may be stated as a single biconditional: a line that intersects two sides of a triangle is parallel to the third side of the triangle if and only if it divides the intersected sides proportionally.

EXPLORE

Constructing Similar Triangles

INTEGRATE TECHNOLOGY

Students have the option of doing the Explore activity either in the book or online.

QUESTIONING STRATEGIES

? How do you use the AA Similarity Criterion to show two triangles are similar? Show that two angles of one triangle are congruent to two angles of the other triangle. This lets you conclude that the two triangles are similar.

EXPLAIN 1

Proving the Triangle Proportionality Theorem

INTEGRATE MATHEMATICAL PRACTICES
Focus on Reasoning

MP.2 Review with students which geometric statements can be used to provide justification for each step of a proof.

QUESTIONING STRATEGIES

? Is it always true that the fraction $\dfrac{x + y}{z}$ can be written as $\dfrac{x}{z} + \dfrac{y}{z}$? Yes, provided that $z \neq 0$.

? How do you take the reciprocal of both sides of an equation such as $x = y$? The reciprocal of an expression is 1 divided by the expression. One way is to multiply both sides by $\dfrac{1}{xy}$ $(xy \neq 0)$.

EXPLAIN 2

Applying the Triangle Proportionality Theorem

INTEGRATE MATHEMATICAL PRACTICES
Focus on Communication

MP.3 Some students may misunderstand the Triangle Proportionality Theorem to mean that a line parallel to one side of a triangle divides the other two sides into congruent segments rather than proportional ones. Show these students that congruent segments result only in the special case of the line intersecting the two sides at their midpoints.

Step 2 Use the fact that corresponding sides of similar triangles are proportional to prove that $\frac{AE}{EB} = \frac{AF}{FC}$.

$\frac{AB}{AE} =$	$\frac{AC}{AF}$	Corresponding sides are proportional.
$\frac{AE + EB}{AE} =$	$\frac{AF + FC}{AF}$	Segment Addition Postulate
$1 + \frac{EB}{AB} =$	$1 + \frac{FC}{AF}$	Use the property that $\frac{a+b}{c} = \frac{a}{c} + \frac{b}{c}$.
$\frac{EB}{AE} =$	$\frac{FC}{AF}$	Subtract 1 from both sides.
$\frac{AE}{EB} =$	$\frac{AF}{FC}$	Take the reciprocal of both sides.

Reflect

4. Explain how you conclude that $\triangle AEF \sim \triangle ABC$ without using $\angle 3$ and $\angle 4$.
$\angle A \cong \angle A$ **by the Reflexive Property of Congruence, and $\angle 1 \cong \angle 2$ since they are corresponding angles; $\triangle AEF \sim \triangle ABC$ by the AA Similarity Criterion.**

⊘ Explain 2 Applying the Triangle Proportionality Theorem

Example 2 Find the length of each segment.

(A) $\overline{CY}$

It is given that $\overline{XY} \parallel \overline{BC}$ so $\frac{AX}{XB} = \frac{AY}{YC}$ by the Triangle Proportionality Theorem.

Substitute 9 for AX, 4 for XB, and 10 for AY.

Then solve for CY.

$$\frac{9}{4} = \frac{10}{CY}$$

Take the reciprocal of both sides.

$$\frac{4}{9} = \frac{CY}{10}$$

Next, multiply both sides by 10.

$$10\left(\frac{4}{9}\right) = \left(\frac{CY}{10}\right)10 \quad \rightarrow \quad \frac{40}{9} = CY, \text{ or } 4\frac{4}{9} = CY$$

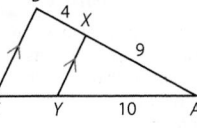

(B) Find PN.

It is given that $\overline{PQ} \parallel \overline{LM}$, so $\frac{NQ}{QM} = \frac{\boxed{NP}}{\boxed{PL}}$ by the Triangle Proportionality Theorem.

Substitute $\underline{5}$ for NQ, $\underline{2}$ for QM, and 3 for $\underline{PL}$.

$$\frac{5}{2} = \frac{NP}{3}$$

Multiply both sides by $\underline{3}$: $\boxed{3}\left(\frac{5}{2}\right) = \boxed{3}\left(\frac{NP}{3}\right) \rightarrow$  $\frac{15}{2} \text{ or } 7\frac{1}{2} = NP$

COLLABORATIVE LEARNING

Small Group Activity

Give small groups of students each a sheet with three parallel lines cut by a transversal. Have students measure the segments of the transversal and verify the ratio formed. Then have them draw another transversal across the parallel lines and measure the resulting segments. Have students try to form a conjecture based on their results.

Your Turn

Find the length of each segment.

5. $\overline{DG}$

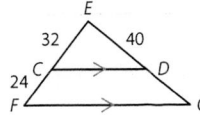

$\dfrac{EC}{CF} = \dfrac{ED}{DG}$; $\dfrac{32}{24} = \dfrac{40}{DG}$; $\dfrac{24}{32} = \dfrac{DG}{40}$;

$40\left(\dfrac{24}{32}\right) = DG$; $DG = \dfrac{960}{32} = 30$

6. $\overline{RN}$

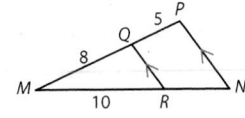

$\dfrac{MR}{RN} = \dfrac{MQ}{QP}$; $\dfrac{10}{RN} = \dfrac{8}{5}$; $\dfrac{RN}{10} = \dfrac{5}{8}$; $RN = \left(\dfrac{5}{8}\right)10$

$RN = \dfrac{50}{8} = \dfrac{25}{4}$ or $6\dfrac{1}{4}$

⚙ Explain 3 ### Proving the Converse of the Triangle Proportionality Theorem

The converse of the Triangle Proportionality Theorem is also true.

Converse of the Triangle Proportionality Theorem		
Theorem	**Hypothesis**	**Conclusion**
If a line divides two sides of a triangle proportionally, then it is parallel to the third side.	$\dfrac{AE}{EB} = \dfrac{AF}{FC}$	$\overleftrightarrow{EF} \parallel \overline{BC}$

Example 3 Prove the Converse of the Triangle Proportionality Theorem

Ⓐ Given: $\dfrac{AE}{EB} = \dfrac{AF}{FC}$

Prove: $\overleftrightarrow{EF} \parallel \overline{BC}$

Step 1 Show that $\triangle AEF \sim \triangle ABC$.

It is given that $\dfrac{AE}{EB} = \dfrac{AF}{FC}$, and taking the reciprocal

of both sides shows that $\underline{\dfrac{EB}{AE} = \dfrac{FC}{AF}}$. Now add 1 to

both sides by adding $\dfrac{AE}{AE}$ to the left side and $\dfrac{AF}{AF}$ to the right side.

This gives $\underline{\dfrac{AE}{AE} + \dfrac{EB}{AE} = \dfrac{AF}{AF} + \dfrac{FC}{AF}}$.

Adding and using the Segment Addition Postulate gives $\underline{\dfrac{AB}{AE} = \dfrac{AC}{AF}}$.

Since $\angle A \cong \angle A$, $\triangle AEF \sim \triangle ABC$ by the __SAS Similarity__ Criterion.

Step 2 Use corresponding angles of similar triangles to show that $\overleftrightarrow{EF} \parallel \overline{BC}$.

$\angle AEF \cong \angle$ __ABC__ and are corresponding angles.

So, $\overleftrightarrow{EF} \parallel \overline{BC}$ by the __Converse of the Corresponding Angles__ Theorem.

© Houghton Mifflin Harcourt Publishing Company

DIFFERENTIATE INSTRUCTION

Modeling

Use transparencies to explain the Triangle Proportionality Theorem. Put the parallel line on a separate transparency from the diagram of the triangle. Slide the line up and down relative to the triangle to show that regardless of the line's position, the sides will be divided proportionally.

QUESTIONING STRATEGIES

? How can you use the Triangle Proportionality Theorem to find unknown dimensions? If a line cutting two sides of a triangle is parallel to the third, you know that it cuts the two sides proportionally. Knowing this allows you to set up and solve a proportion for the missing side length.

AVOID COMMON ERRORS

Some students may write proportions that do not compare corresponding parts of the figure. Have them use different colors to show the proportional parts.

EXPLAIN 3

Proving the Converse of the Triangle Proportionality Theorem

INTEGRATE MATHEMATICAL PRACTICES

Focus on Math Connections

MP.1 Remind students that the converse of a theorem switches the condition and the conclusion. Review converses from previous lessons, such as converses of triangle congruence theorems, and discuss why they are useful.

QUESTIONING STRATEGIES

? What are the main steps of the proof? First, show that the two triangles are similar by SAS. Then, use congruent corresponding angles to show that the lines are parallel.

? How is this proof similar to that of the Triangle Proportionality Theorem? Both proofs use properties of fractions and the Segment Addition Postulate to work with proportions. Both proofs also use the fact that you can take the reciprocal of both sides of a proportion.

EXPLAIN 4

Applying the Converse of the Triangle Proportionality Theorem

INTEGRATE MATHEMATICAL PRACTICES
Focus on Critical Thinking

MP.3 Have students discuss the special case in which the parallel line intersects the two sides at their midpoints.

QUESTIONING STRATEGIES

? How is using the Converse of the Triangle Proportionality Theorem different from using the theorem itself? You use the TPT when you are given that a line cutting two sides of a triangle is parallel to the third side, and want to prove that it cuts the sides proportionally. You use the converse when you are given that the line cuts two sides proportionally, and want to prove that it is parallel to the third side.

Reflect

7. **Critique Reasoning** A student states that $\overline{UV}$ must be parallel to $\overline{ST}$. Do you agree? Why or why not?

Yes; because $RU = US$ and $RV = VS$, $\frac{RU}{US} = \frac{RV}{VT} = 1$.

So $\overline{UV} \parallel \overline{ST}$ by the Converse of the Triangle Proportionality Theorem.

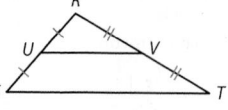

⊘ Explain 4 **Applying the Converse of the Triangle Proportionality Theorem**

You can use the Converse of the Triangle Proportionality Theorem to verify that a line is parallel to a side of a triangle.

Example 4 Verify that the line segments are parallel.

Ⓐ $\overline{MN}$ and $\overline{KL}$

$\frac{JM}{MK} = \frac{42}{21} = 2$ $\frac{JN}{NL} = \frac{30}{15} = 2$

Since $\frac{JM}{MK} = \frac{JN}{NL}$, $\overline{MN} \parallel \overline{KL}$ by the Converse of the Triangle Proportionality Theorem.

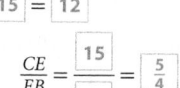

Ⓑ $\overline{DE}$ and $\overline{AB}$ (Given that $AC = 36$ cm, and $BC = 27$ cm)

$AD = AC - DC = 36 - 20 = 16$

$BE = BC - \boxed{EC} = 27 - \boxed{15} = \boxed{12}$

$\frac{CD}{DA} = \frac{\boxed{20}}{\boxed{16}} = \frac{\boxed{5}}{\boxed{4}}$ $\frac{CE}{EB} = \frac{\boxed{15}}{\boxed{12}} = \frac{5}{4}$

Since $\frac{CD}{DA} = \frac{CE}{EB}$, $\overline{DE} \parallel \overline{AB}$ by the ___Converse of the Triangle Proportionality___ Theorem.

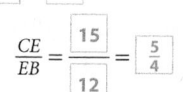

Reflect

8. **Communicate Mathematical Ideas** In $\triangle ABC$, in the example, what is the value of $\frac{AB}{DE}$? Explain how you know.

$\frac{AB}{DE} = \frac{AC}{DC} = \frac{9}{5}$; Possible answer: because $\overline{DE} \parallel \overline{AB}$, corresponding angles A and CDE are congruent, as are corresponding angles B and CED. So, $\triangle ABC \sim \triangle DEC$ and $\frac{AB}{DE} = \frac{AC}{DC} = \frac{BC}{EC}$.

Your Turn

9. Verify that $\overline{TU}$ and $\overline{RS}$ are parallel.

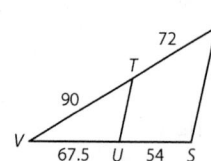

$\frac{VT}{TR} = \frac{90}{72} = \frac{5}{4}$, $\frac{VU}{US} = \frac{67.5}{54} = \frac{135}{108} = \frac{5}{4}$

$\frac{VT}{TR} = \frac{VU}{US}$, so $\overline{RS} \parallel \overline{TU}$.

LANGUAGE SUPPORT 🔲

Connect Vocabulary

Some students may have difficulty identifying a *transversal*. Remind them that the prefix *trans-* means *across*, as in *transportation*, *transfer*, and *transatlantic*. *Transverse* means *situated or lying across*. Therefore, the *transversal* is the line that lies across other lines.

ELABORATE

Elaborate

10. In $\triangle ABC$, $\overline{XY} \| \overline{BC}$. Use what you know about similarity and proportionality to identify as many different proportions as possible.

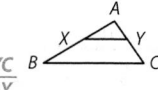

Possible answers: $\dfrac{AX}{AB} = \dfrac{AY}{AC}$; $\dfrac{AB}{AX} = \dfrac{AC}{AY}$; $\dfrac{AX}{XB} = \dfrac{AY}{YC}$; $\dfrac{XB}{AX} = \dfrac{YC}{AY}$

11. Discussion What theorems, properties, or strategies are common to the proof of the Triangle Proportionality Theorem and the proof of Converse of the Triangle Proportionality Theorem?

Possible answers: Segment Addition Postulate; properties of fractions;

taking reciprocals of both sides of a proportion, and use of Similarity Criteria

(AA for the Triangle Proportionality Theorem and SAS for its converse)

12. Essential Question Check-In Suppose a line parallel to side $\overline{BC}$ of $\triangle ABC$ intersects sides $\overline{AB}$ and $\overline{AC}$ at points X and Y, respectively, and $\frac{AX}{XB} = 1$. What do you know about X and Y? Explain.

X and Y are the midpoints of sides $\overline{AB}$ and $\overline{AC}$. If $\frac{AX}{XB} = 1$, then $\frac{AY}{YC} = 1$.

Then $AX = XB$, so X is the midpoint of $\overline{AB}$. Similarly, Y is the midpoint

of $\overline{AC}$.

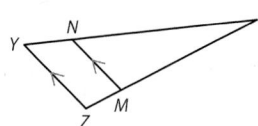

⭐ Evaluate: Homework and Practice

- Online Homework
- Hints and Help
- Extra Practice

1. Copy the triangle ABC that you drew for the Explore activity. Construct a line $\overleftrightarrow{FG}$ parallel to $\overline{AB}$ using the same method you used in the Explore activity.

Check students' constructions.

2. $\overline{ZY} \| \overleftrightarrow{MN}$. Write a paragraph proof to show that $\frac{XM}{MZ} = \frac{XN}{NY}$.

Since $\overline{ZY} \| \overleftrightarrow{MN}$, $\angle XNM \cong \angle XYZ$ and $\angle XMN \cong \angle XZY$ by the Corresponding Angles Theorem.

So $\triangle XYZ \sim \triangle XNM$ by the AA Similarity Criterion. Since

corresponding sides of similar triangles are proportional, $\frac{XZ}{XM} = \frac{XY}{XN}$. Use the Segment Addition Postulate to rewrite XZ as $XM + MZ$, and rewrite XY as $XN + NY$. So $\frac{XM + MZ}{XM}$ $= \frac{XN + NY}{XN}$. This can be rewritten as $\frac{XM}{XM} + \frac{MZ}{XM} = \frac{XN}{XN} + \frac{NY}{XN}$. Since any number divided by itself is 1, you can rewrite the expression as $1 + \frac{MZ}{XM} = 1 + \frac{NY}{XN}$. Subtracting 1 from both sides, $\frac{MZ}{XM}$ $= \frac{NY}{XN}$. Taking the reciprocals of both sides, $\frac{XM}{MZ} = \frac{XN}{NY}$.

© Houghton Mifflin Harcourt Publishing Company

QUESTIONING STRATEGIES

? What is the difference between triangles having congruent sides and triangles having proportional sides? Congruent sides have equal measures, but proportional sides have equal ratios to one another.

SUMMARIZE THE LESSON

? When does a line cut two sides of a triangle proportionally? What does it mean for the sides to be cut proportionally? When it is parallel to the third side; the ratios of the corresponding parts are equal.

EVALUATE

ASSIGNMENT GUIDE

Concepts and Skills	Practice
Explore Constructing Similar Triangles	Exercise 1
Example 1 Proving the Triangle Proportionality Theorem	Exercise 2
Example 2 Applying the Triangle Proportionality Theorem	Exercises 3–5
Example 3 Proving the Converse of the Triangle Proportionality Theorem	Exercise 13
Example 4 Applying the Converse of the Triangle Proportionality Theorem	Exercises 6–9

Find the length of each segment.

3. $\overline{KL}$

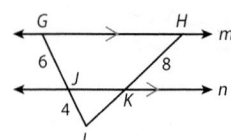

$$\frac{4}{6} = \frac{KL}{8}; \quad KL = \left(\frac{4}{6}\right)8 = 5\frac{1}{3}$$

4. $\overline{XZ}$

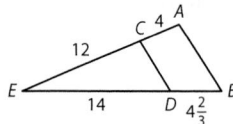

$$XY = 12; \frac{XY}{YU} = \frac{XZ}{ZV};$$

$$\frac{12}{18} = \frac{XZ}{30}; XZ = \left(\frac{12}{18}\right)30 = 20$$

5. $\overline{VM}$

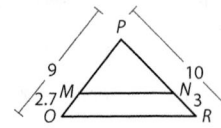

$$\frac{VN}{NT} = \frac{VM}{MU}; \frac{35}{14} = \frac{VM}{8};$$

$$VM = \left(\frac{35}{14}\right)8 = 20$$

Verify that the given segments are parallel.

6. $\overline{AB}$ and $\overline{CD}$

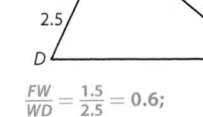

$$\frac{ED}{DB} = \frac{14}{4\frac{2}{3}} = 14 \cdot \frac{3}{14} = 3$$

$$\frac{EC}{CA} = \frac{12}{4} = 3$$

So, $\frac{ED}{DB} = \frac{EC}{CA}$. So, $\overline{AB} \parallel \overline{CD}$.

7. $\overline{MN}$ and $\overline{QR}$

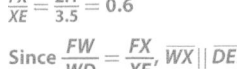

$$PM = 9 - 2.7 = 6.3$$

$$PN = 10 - 3 = 7$$

$$\frac{PM}{MQ} = \frac{6.3}{2.7} = \frac{7}{3} = \frac{PN}{NR}$$

So, $\overline{MN} \parallel \overline{QR}$.

8. $\overline{WX}$ and $\overline{DE}$

$$\frac{FW}{WD} = \frac{1.5}{2.5} = 0.6;$$

$$\frac{FX}{XE} = \frac{2.1}{3.5} = 0.6$$

Since $\frac{FW}{WD} = \frac{FX}{XE}$, $\overline{WX} \parallel \overline{DE}$.

9. Use the Converse of the Triangle Proportionality Theorem to identify parallel lines in the figure.

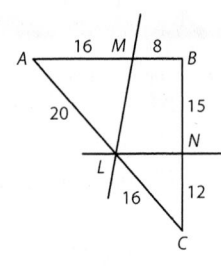

$$\frac{CN}{NB} = \frac{12}{15} = \frac{4}{5}; \frac{CL}{LA} = \frac{16}{20} = \frac{4}{5}; \frac{AL}{LC} = \frac{20}{16} = \frac{5}{4}; \frac{AM}{MB} = \frac{16}{8} = 2$$

So, $\frac{CN}{NB} = \frac{CL}{LA}$ and $\overline{LN} \parallel \overline{AB}$.

So, $\frac{AL}{LC} \neq \frac{AM}{MB}$ and $\overline{LM}$ is not parallel to $\overline{BC}$.

10. On the map, 1st Street and 2nd Street are parallel. What is the distance from City Hall to 2nd Street along Cedar Road?

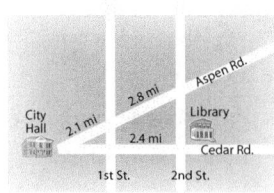

Let x be the distance in miles from City Hall to 1st Street.

$$\frac{x}{2.4} = \frac{2.1}{2.8} \qquad x = \left(\frac{2.1}{2.8}\right)2.4 = 1.8$$

$$1.8 + 2.4 = 4.2 \text{ miles}$$

The distance is 4.2 miles.

© Houghton Mifflin Harcourt Publishing Company

Exercise	Depth of Knowledge (D.O.K.)	COMMON CORE Mathematical Practices
1–9	**2** Skills/Concepts	**MP.4** Modeling
10–12	**2** Skills/Concepts	**MP.4** Modeling
13–15	**2** Skills/Concepts	**MP.2** Reasoning
16	**3** Strategic Thinking H.O.T.	**MP.2** Reasoning
17	**3** Strategic Thinking H.O.T.	**MP.3** Logic
18	**3** Strategic Thinking H.O.T.	**MP.1** Problem Solving

11. On the map, 5th Avenue, 6th Avenue, and 7th Avenue are parallel. What is the length of Main Street between 5th Avenue and 6th Avenue?

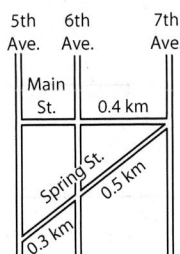

Let m be the length in kilometers of Main Street between 5th Avenue and 6th Ave.

$$\frac{0.4}{m} = \frac{0.5}{0.3} \quad \frac{m}{0.4} = \frac{0.3}{0.5} \quad m = \left(\frac{0.3}{0.5}\right)0.4 = 0.24$$

The length is 0.24 kilometer.

12. Multi-Step The storage unit has horizontal siding that is parallel to the base.

a. Find LM.

$$\frac{GL}{LM} = \frac{GH}{HJ}; \frac{11.3}{LM} = \frac{10.4}{2.6}; \frac{LM}{11.3} = \frac{2.6}{10.4}; LM = 11.3\left(\frac{2.6}{10.4}\right) = 2.825 \text{ ft}$$

b. Find GM.

$$GM = GL + LM = 11.3 + 2.825 = 14.125$$

c. Find MN to the nearest tenth of a foot.

$$\frac{GM}{MN} = \frac{GJ}{JK}; \frac{14.125}{MN} = \frac{13}{2.2}; \frac{MN}{14.125} = \frac{2.2}{13}; MN = 14.125\left(\frac{2.2}{13}\right) \approx 2.4\text{ft}$$

d. Make a Conjecture Write the ratios $\frac{LM}{MN}$ and $\frac{HJ}{JK}$ as decimals to the nearest hundredth and compare them. Make a conjecture about the relationship between parallel lines $\overleftrightarrow{LD}$, $\overleftrightarrow{ME}$, and $\overleftrightarrow{NF}$ and transversals $\overleftrightarrow{GN}$ and $\overleftrightarrow{GK}$.

$\frac{LM}{MN} \approx 1.18$ and $\frac{HJ}{JK} = 1.18$.

The parallel lines divide the transversals proportionally.

13. A corollary to the Converse of the Triangle Proportionality Theorem states that if three or more parallel lines intersect two transversals, then they divide the transversals proportionally. Complete the proof of the corollary.

Given: Parallel lines $\overleftrightarrow{AB} \parallel \overleftrightarrow{CD}$, $\overleftrightarrow{CD} \parallel \overleftrightarrow{EF}$
Prove: $\frac{AC}{CE} = \frac{BX}{XE}$, $\frac{BX}{XE} = \frac{BD}{DF}$, $\frac{AC}{CE} = \frac{BD}{DF}$

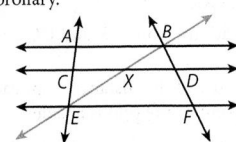

Statements	Reasons
1. $\overleftrightarrow{AB} \parallel \overleftrightarrow{CD}$, $\overleftrightarrow{CD} \parallel \overleftrightarrow{AF}$	1. Given
2. Draw $\overleftrightarrow{EB}$ intersecting $\overleftrightarrow{CD}$ at X.	2. Two points determine a line.
3. $\frac{AC}{CE} = \frac{BX}{XE}$	3. Triangle Proportionality Theorem
4. $\frac{BX}{XE} = \frac{BD}{DF}$	4. Triangle Proportionality Theorem
5. $\frac{AC}{CE} = \frac{BD}{DF}$	5. Transitive Property of Equality

---

AVOID COMMON ERRORS

In exercises that give a length with an algebraic expression, a common error is to give the value of the variable as the answer. Remind students they need to use the value of the variable to evaluate the expressions and find the segment lengths.

INTEGRATE MATHEMATICAL PRACTICES
Focus on Modeling

MP.4 For problems with two triangles, encourage students to draw (or color) the two triangles separately to identify corresponding parts.

JOURNAL

Have students write a journal entry in which they explain in their own words the Triangle Proportionality Theorem and its converse. Ask students to include figures with their explanations.

14. Suppose that $LM = 24$. Use the Triangle Proportionality Theorem to find PM.

$\frac{PM}{LP} = \frac{15}{10}$, $\frac{PM}{24 - PM} = \frac{3}{2}$

$PM = \frac{3}{2}(24 - PM)$; $PM = 36 - \frac{3}{2}PM$; $PM + \frac{3}{2}PM = 36$

$= \frac{5}{2}PM = 36$; $PM = \frac{72}{5}$

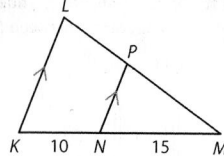

15. Which of the given measures allow you to conclude that $\overline{UV} \parallel \overline{ST}$? Select all that apply.

A. $SR = 12$, $TR = 9$ $\qquad \frac{20}{12} = \frac{5}{3}$, $\frac{20}{12} \neq \frac{16}{9}$

B. $SR = 16$, $TR = 20$ $\qquad \frac{20}{16} = \frac{5}{4}$, $\frac{16}{20} = \frac{4}{5}$, $\frac{20}{16} \neq \frac{16}{20}$

C. $SR = 35$, $TR = 28$ $\qquad \frac{20}{35} = \frac{4}{7}$, $\frac{16}{28} = \frac{4}{7}$, $\frac{20}{35} = \frac{16}{28}$

D. $SR = 50$, $TR = 48$ $\qquad \frac{20}{50} = \frac{2}{5}$, $\frac{16}{48} = \frac{1}{3}$, $\frac{20}{50} \neq \frac{16}{48}$

E. $SR = 25$, $TR = 20$ $\qquad \frac{20}{25} = \frac{4}{5}$, $\frac{16}{20} = \frac{4}{5}$, $\frac{20}{25} = \frac{16}{20}$

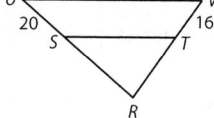

Answer: Only C and E allow you to conclude that $\overline{UV} \parallel \overline{ST}$.

H.O.T. Focus on Higher Order Thinking

16. Algebra For what value of x is $\overline{GF} \parallel \overline{HJ}$?

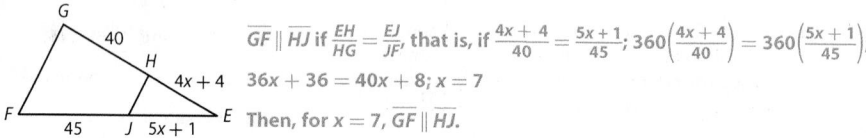

$\overline{GF} \parallel \overline{HJ}$ if $\frac{EH}{HG} = \frac{EJ}{JF}$, that is, if $\frac{4x + 4}{40} = \frac{5x + 1}{45}$; $360\left(\frac{4x + 4}{40}\right) = 360\left(\frac{5x + 1}{45}\right)$;

$36x + 36 = 40x + 8$; $x = 7$

Then, for $x = 7$, $\overline{GF} \parallel \overline{HJ}$.

17. Communicate Mathematical Ideas John used $\triangle ABC$ to write a proof of the Centroid Theorem. He began by drawing medians $\overline{AK}$ and $\overline{CL}$, intersecting at Z. Next he drew midsegments $\overline{LM}$ and $\overline{NP}$, both parallel to median $\overline{AK}$.

Given: $\triangle ABC$ with medians $\overline{AK}$ and $\overline{CL}$, and midsegments $\overline{LM}$ and $\overline{NP}$

Prove: Z is located $\frac{2}{3}$ of the distance from each vertex of $\triangle ABC$ to the midpoint of the opposite side.

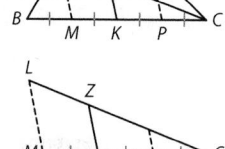

a. Complete each statement to justify the first part of John's proof.

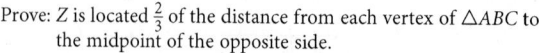

By the definition of __midsegment__, $MK = \frac{1}{2}BK$. By the definition of __median__, $BK = KC$. So, by __substitution__, $MK = \frac{1}{2}KC$, or $\frac{KC}{MK} = 2$.

Consider $\triangle LMC$. $\overline{LM} \parallel \overline{AK}$ (and therefore $\overline{LM} \parallel \overline{ZK}$), so $\frac{ZC}{LZ} = \frac{KC}{MK}$ by the __Triangle Proportionality__ Theorem, and $ZC = 2LZ$. Because

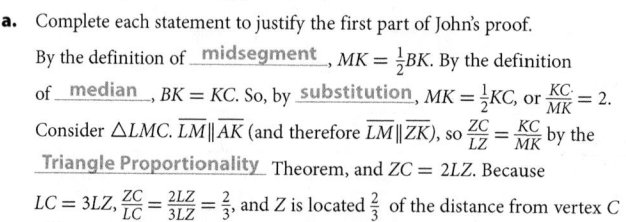

$LC = 3LZ$, $\frac{ZC}{LC} = \frac{2LZ}{3LZ} = \frac{2}{3}$, and Z is located $\frac{2}{3}$ of the distance from vertex C of $\triangle ABC$ to the midpoint of the opposite side.

b. Explain how John can complete his proof.

He can repeat the same process twice to show that Z is also located $\frac{2}{3}$ of the distance from vertices A and B of $\triangle ABC$ to the midpoints of their opposite sides.

18. Persevere in Problem Solving Given $\triangle ABC$ with $FC = 5$, you want to find BF. First, find the value that y must have for the Triangle Proportionality Theorem to apply. Then describe more than one way to find BF, and find BF.

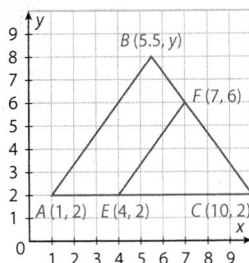

For the triangle Proportionality Theorem to apply, y must be such that $\overline{AB}$ and $\overline{EF}$ are parallel.

Slope of $\overline{EF} = \frac{6-2}{7-4} = \frac{4}{3}$, and slope of $\overline{AB} = \frac{y-2}{5.5-1} = \frac{y-2}{4.5}$.

Let $\frac{y-2}{4.5} = \frac{4}{3}$ and solve for y: $y - 2 = 4.5\left(\frac{4}{3}\right) = 6$; $y = 8$.

To find BF, you can use the Distance Formula or the Triangle Proportionality Theorem: $AE = 3$, $EC = 6$, $FC = 5$; $\frac{BF}{FC} = \frac{AE}{EC}$;

$\frac{BF}{5} = \frac{3}{6}$; $BF = 5\left(\frac{3}{6}\right) = 2.5$

Lesson Performance Task

Shown here is a triangular striped sail, together with some of its dimensions. In the diagram, segments BJ, CI, and DH are all parallel to segment EG. Find each of the following:

1. AJ

2. CD

3. HG

4. GF

5. the perimeter of $\triangle AEF$

6. the area of $\triangle AEF$

7. the number of sails you could make for $10,000 if the sail material costs $30 per square yard

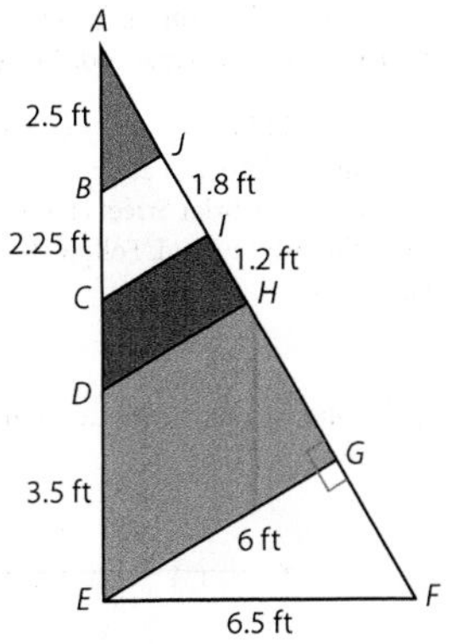

(Diagram labels: A; 2.5 ft; J; B; 1.8 ft; I; 2.25 ft; 1.2 ft; C; H; D; G; 3.5 ft; 6 ft; E; F; 6.5 ft)

1. Use triangles ABJ and ACI.
$$\frac{2.5}{2.25} = \frac{AJ}{1.8}$$
$$2.25(AJ) = 4.5$$
$$AJ = 2$$

2. Use triangles ACI and ADH.
$$\frac{2.5 + 2.25}{CD} = \frac{2 + 1.8}{1.2}$$
$$3.8(CD) = 5.7$$
$$CD = 1.5$$

3. Use triangles ADH and AEG.
$$\frac{2.5 + 2.25 + 1.5}{3.5} = \frac{2 + 1.8 + 1.2}{HG}$$
$$6.25(HG) = 17.5$$
$$HG = 2.8$$

4. $6^2 + (GF)^2 = (6.5)^2$
$36 + (GF)^2 = 42.25$
$(GF)^2 = 6.25$
$GF = 2.5$

5. Perimeter $= 2.5 + 2.25 +$
$1.5 + 3.5 + 6.5 +$
$2.5 + 2.8 + 1.2 +$
$1.8 + 2 = 26.55$

6. Use $\overline{AF}$ as the base of the triangle. Then the height is EG.
Area $= \frac{1}{2} \cdot$ base $\cdot$ height
$= \frac{1}{2}(10.3)(6)$
$= 30.9$

7. $\frac{30.9 \text{ ft}^2}{9 \frac{\text{ft}^2}{\text{yd}^2}} \approx 3.43 \text{ yd}^2$
$3.43 \text{ yd}^2 \cdot \frac{\$30}{\text{yd}^2} = \$103 \text{ per sail}$
$\frac{\$10,000 \text{ total}}{\$103 \text{ per sail}} \approx 97.1$; at most
97 sails

AVOID COMMON ERRORS

When students attempt to find the area of $\triangle AEF$, they may mistake the triangle for a right triangle with right angle $\angle AEF$, then use $A = \frac{1}{2}bh$ to find the area. This gives an incorrect area of 31.6875 ft^2, slightly greater than the actual area, which can be found by adding the areas of two different right triangles, $\triangle AGE$ and $\triangle EGF$.

INTEGRATE MATHEMATICAL PRACTICES

Focus on Reasoning

MP.2 A theorem for rectangles similar to the Triangle Proportionality Theorem might go like this: If a line segment parallel to one side of a rectangle intersects the two sides that are perpendicular to the segment, then the segment divides the perpendicular sides proportionally. Is the theorem true? Give an example to support your answer. Yes; possible answer: In rectangle $ABCD$, segment $\overline{EF}$ is drawn parallel to $\overline{AB}$, intersecting $\overline{AD}$ and $\overline{BC}$. $AF = 3$ and $FD = 5$. Since $AB = FE$, $ABEF$ is a rectangle, so $BE = 3$. Since $FE = DC$, $FECD$ is a rectangle, so $EC = 5$. So, $\frac{AF}{FD} = \frac{BE}{EC} = \frac{3}{5}$ and the segment divides the perpendicular sides proportionally.

EXTENSION ACTIVITY

Refer students to the sail in the Lesson Performance Task. Then give these directions:

1. Use your knowledge of similar triangles to find the lengths of $\overline{BJ}$, $\overline{CI}$, and $\overline{DH}$. 1.5 ft; 2.85 ft; 3.75 ft

2. Find the perimeters of $\triangle ABJ$, $\triangle ACI$, $\triangle ADH$, and $\triangle AEG$. 6 ft; 11.4 ft; 15 ft; 23.55

3. Are the perimeters of the triangles in the same ratio as the side lengths? Explain. The perimeters are in the same ratio as the side lengths. Students should give sample results such as $\frac{AC}{AB} = 1.9 = \frac{\text{perimeter of } \triangle ACI}{\text{perimeter of } \triangle ABJ}$.

Scoring Rubric
2 points: Student correctly solves the problem and explains his/her reasoning.
1 point: Student shows good understanding of the problem but does not fully solve or explain his/her reasoning.
0 points: Student does not demonstrate understanding of the problem.

Triangle Proportionality Theorem   **640**

Subdividing a Segment in a Given Ratio

Common Core Math Standards

The student is expected to:

 G-GPE.B.6

Find the point on a directed line segment between two given points that partitions the segment in a given ratio. Also G-CO.D.12

Mathematical Practices

MP.5 Using Tools

Language Objective

Work in groups to find ratios of subdivided segments.

ENGAGE

Essential Question: How do you find the point on a directed line segment that partitions the given segment in a given ratio?

If the segment lies on a number line, subtract the coordinates to find the distance between the endpoints. Then multiply the length by the ratio to find the coordinate of the point that divides the segment in that ratio. If there are no coordinates, use a compass and straightedge to divide the given segment into equal parts, and identify the point that divides the segment in the given ratio.

PREVIEW: LESSON PERFORMANCE TASK

View the Engage section online. Discuss the photograph and point out that the Golden Ratio is found throughout nature—even, some say, in the ratio of the length of a person's forearm to the length of the person's hand. Then preview the Lesson Performance Task.

Name_____ Class_____ Date_____

12.2 Subdividing a Segment in a Given Ratio

Essential Question: How do you find the point on a directed line segment that partitions the given segment in a given ratio?

Explore **Partitioning a Segment in a One-Dimensional Coordinate System**

It takes just one number to specify an exact location on a number line. For this reason, a number line is sometimes called a one-dimensional coordinate system. The mile markers on a straight stretch of a highway turn that part of the highway into a one-dimensional coordinate system.

On a straight highway, the exit for Arthur Avenue is at mile marker 14. The exit for Collingwood Road is at mile marker 44. The state highway administration plans to put an exit for Briar Street at a point that is $\frac{2}{3}$ of the distance from Arthur Avenue to Collingwood Road. Follow these steps to determine where the new exit should be placed.

(A) Mark Arthur Avenue (point A) and Collingwood Road (point C) on the number line.

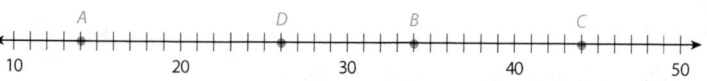

(B) What is the distance from Arthur Avenue to Collingwood Road? Explain.

30 miles; find the absolute value of the difference of the coordinates: $|44 - 14| = 30$.

(C) How far will the Briar Street exit be from Arthur Avenue? Explain.

20 miles; $\frac{2}{3} \cdot$ 30 miles = 20 miles

(D) What is the mile marker number for the Briar Street exit? Why?

mile marker 34; $14 + 20 = 34$

(E) Plot and label the Briar Street exit (point B) on the number line.

Check students' number lines.

Module 12 **641** Lesson 2

12.2 Subdividing a Segment in a Given Ratio

HARDCOVER PAGES 547–554

Turn to these pages to find this lesson in the hardcover student edition.

(F) The highway administration also plans to put an exit for Dakota Lane at a point that divides the highway from Arthur Avenue to Collingwood Road in a ratio of 2 to 3. What is the mile marker number for Dakota Lane? Why? (*Hint*: Let the distance from Arthur Avenue to Dakota Lane be 2x and let the distance from Dakota Lane to Collingwood Road be 3x.)

mile marker 26; since the distance from Arthur Avenue to Collingwood Road is 30 miles,

$2x + 3x = 30, 5x = 30$, and $x = 6$. Therefore, the distance from Arthur Avenue to Dakota

Lane is $2x = 12$ miles.

(G) Plot and label the Dakota Lane exit (point *D*) on the number line.

Check students' number lines.

Reflect

1. How can you tell that the location at which you plotted point *B* is reasonable?
   Point *B* appears to be about $\frac{2}{3}$ of the way (or about 67% of the way) from point *A* to

   point *C*.

2. Would your answer in Step F be different if the exit for Dakota Lane divided the highway from Arthur Avenue to Collingwood Road in a ratio of 3 to 2? Explain.
   Yes; in this case, the exit would be closer to Collingwood Avenue. It would be at mile

   marker 32.

⊙ Explain 1   Partitioning a Segment in a Two-Dimensional Coordinate System

A *directed line segment* is a segment between two points *A* and *B* with a specified direction, from *A* to *B* or from *B* to *A*. To partition a directed line segment is to divide it into two segments with a given ratio.

Example 1   Find the coordinates of the point *P* that divides the directed line segment from *A* to *B* in the given ratio.

(A) $A(-8, -7)$, $B(8, 5)$; 3 to 1

   Step 1   Write a ratio that expresses the distance of point *P* along the segment from *A* to *B*.

   Point *P* is $\frac{3}{3+1} = \frac{3}{4}$ of the distance from *A* to *B*.

   Step 2   Find the run and the rise of the directed line segment.

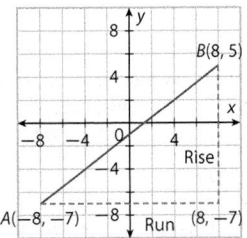

   run $= 8 - (-8) = 16$

   rise $= 5 - (-7) = 12$

Partitioning a Segment in a One-Dimensional Coordinate System

INTEGRATE TECHNOLOGY

Show how to use geometry software to partition a segment.

QUESTIONING STRATEGIES

What does it mean to say that point *P* divides $\overline{AB}$ in the ratio 3 to 1? Point *P* divides the segment into two segments, and the length of one is three times the length of the other.

EXPLAIN 1

Partitioning a Segment in a Two-Dimensional Coordinate System

INTEGRATE MATHEMATICAL PRACTICES
Focus on Patterns

MP.8 Have students draw a segment and find the midpoint to divide it into two segments with a ratio of 1 to 1. Then have them find the midpoint of one of those segments to divide the segment with a ratio of 3 to 1. Ask students what other ratios they could divide the segments into by using midpoints.

© Houghton Mifflin Harcourt Publishing Company

PROFESSIONAL DEVELOPMENT

 Learning Progressions

Students have previously studied slope and learned to find the slope of a line. They also used slope to write the equation of a line, either in slope-intercept form $(y = mx + b)$ or in point-slope form $(y - y_1 = m(x - x_1))$. Here students use the definition of *slope* (*the ratio of the rise to the run*) to help them find a point that divides a given line segment in a given ratio.

QUESTIONING STRATEGIES

? How can you predict whether the point to divide a line in a given ratio will be closer to one end or the other? **If the ratio is less than one-half, the point will be closer to the first endpoint, and if it is greater than one-half, the point will be closer to the second endpoint.**

? Can a proportion compare measurements that have different units? Explain. **Yes; if the numerators are both in one unit and the denominators in another, or if one fraction is in one unit and the other fraction is in another**

Step 3 Point P is $\frac{3}{4}$ of the distance from point A to point B, so find $\frac{3}{4}$ of both the rise and the run.

$\frac{3}{4}$ of run $= \frac{3}{4}(16) = 12$ $\qquad$ $\frac{3}{4}$ of rise $= \frac{3}{4}(12) = 9$

Step 4 To find the coordinates of point P, add the values from Step 3 to the coordinates of point A.

x-coordinate of point $P = -8 + 12 = 4$

y-coordinate of point $P = -7 + 9 = 2$

The coordinates of point P are $(4, 2)$.

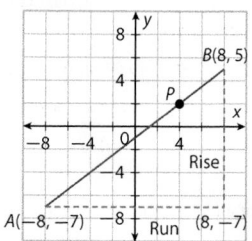

B $A(-4, 4)$, $B(2, 1)$; 1 to 2

Step 1 Write a ratio that expresses the distance of point P along the segment from A to B.

Point P is $\dfrac{\boxed{1}}{\boxed{1} + \boxed{2}} = \dfrac{\boxed{1}}{\boxed{3}}$ of the distance from A to B.

Step 2 Graph the directed line segment. Find the rise and the run of the directed line segment.

run $= 2 - (-4) = 6$

rise $= \boxed{1} - \boxed{4} = \boxed{-3}$

Step 3 Point P is $\dfrac{\boxed{1}}{\boxed{3}}$ of the distance from point A to point B.

$\dfrac{\boxed{1}}{\boxed{3}}$ of run $= \dfrac{\boxed{1}}{\boxed{3}}(6) = \boxed{2}$ $\qquad$ $\dfrac{\boxed{1}}{\boxed{3}}$ of run $= \dfrac{\boxed{1}}{\boxed{3}}\left(\boxed{-3}\right) = \boxed{-1}$

Step 4 To find the coordinates of point P, add the values from Step 3 to the coordinates of point A.

x-coordinate of point $P = -4 + \boxed{2} = \boxed{-2}$ $\qquad$ y-coordinate of point $P = 4 + \boxed{-1} = \boxed{3}$

The coordinates of point P are $\left(\boxed{-2}, \boxed{3}\right)$. Plot point P on the above graph.

Reflect

3. In Part A, show how you can use the Distance Formula to check that point P partitions the directed line segment in the correct ratio.

$AP = \sqrt{\left(4 - (-8)\right)^2 + \left(2 - (-7)\right)^2} = \sqrt{225} = 15; PB = \sqrt{(8-4)^2 + (5-2)^2} = \sqrt{25} = 5.$

The ratio of AP to BP is 15 to 5 or 3 to 1, which is the correct ratio.

4. **Discussion** What can you conclude about a point that partitions a segment in the ratio 1 to 1? How can you find the coordinates of such a point?
The point is the midpoint of the segment. Use the Midpoint Formula.

© Houghton Mifflin Harcourt Publishing Company

COLLABORATIVE LEARNING

Peer-to-Peer Activity

Have students work in pairs to draw and label a line, a line segment, and a directed line segment. Have them discuss their similarities and differences.

Find the coordinates of the point P that divides the directed line segment from A to B in the given ratio.

5. $A(-6, 5), B(2, -3)$; 5 to 3

Point P is $\dfrac{5}{5+3} = \dfrac{5}{8}$ of the distance from A to B.

$\text{run} = 2 - (-6) = 8$; $\text{rise} = -3 - 5 = -8$

$\dfrac{5}{8}$ of run $= 5$; $\dfrac{5}{8}$ of rise $= -5$

x-coordinate of point $P = -6 + 5 = -1$;

y-coordinate of point $P = 5 + (-5) = 0$

The coordinates of point P are $(-1, 0)$.

6. $A(4, 2), B(-6, -13)$; 3 to 2

Point P is $\dfrac{3}{3+2} = \dfrac{3}{5}$ of the distance from A to B.

$\text{run} = -6 - 4 = -10$; $\text{rise} = -13 - 2 = -15$

$\dfrac{3}{5}$ of run $= -6$; $\dfrac{3}{5}$ of rise $= -9$

x-coordinate of point $P = 4 - 6 = -2$;

y-coordinate of point $P = 2 + (-9) = -7$

The coordinates of point P are $(-2, -7)$.

⟡ Explain 2   Constructing a Partition of a Segment

Example 2   Given the directed line segment from A to B, construct the point P that divides the segment in the given ratio from A to B.

(A)   2 to 1

Step 1 Use a straightedge to draw $\overrightarrow{AC}$. The exact measure of the angle is not important, but the construction is easiest for angles from about 30° to 60°.

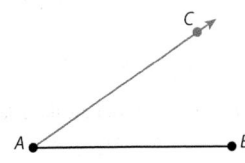

Step 2 Place the compass point on A and draw an arc through $\overrightarrow{AC}$. Label the intersection D. Using the same compass setting, draw an arc centered on D and label the intersection E. Using the same compass setting, draw an arc centered on E and label the intersection F.

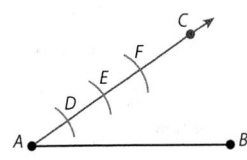

Step 3 Use the straightedge to connect points B and F. Construct an angle congruent to $\angle AFB$ with D as its vertex. Construct an angle congruent to $\angle AFB$ with E as its vertex.

Step 4 The construction partitions $\overline{AB}$ into 3 equal parts. Label point P at the point that divides the segment in the ratio 2 to 1 from A to B.

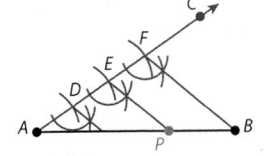

EXPLAIN 2

Constructing a Partition of a Segment

QUESTIONING STRATEGIES

? Can you partition a line (as opposed to a line segment)? Explain. No; because a line continues infinitely in both directions, it cannot be divided into segments with a definite ratio.

DIFFERENTIATE INSTRUCTION

Multiple Representations

Discuss whether it matters if the segment with endpoints C and D is named as $\overline{DC}$ or as $\overline{CD}$. Both are correct. The order does not matter as long as C and D are endpoints. If the segment is a *directed* line segment, the order does matter.

645 Lesson 12.2

AVOID COMMON ERRORS

Remind students to pay attention to the order of the letters in the problem in order to ensure they find the correct point for the given direction.

Ⓑ 1 to 3

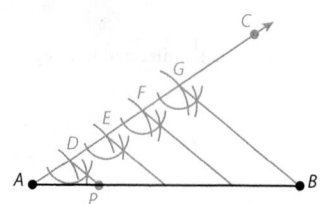

Step 1 Use a straightedge to draw $\overrightarrow{AC}$.

Step 2 Place the compass point on A and draw an arc through $\overrightarrow{AC}$. Label the intersection D. Using the same compass setting, draw an arc centered on D and label the intersection E. Using the same compass setting, draw an arc centered on E and label the intersection F. Using the same compass setting, draw an arc centered on F and label the intersection G.

Step 3 Use the straightedge to connect points B and G. Construct angles congruent to ∠AGB with D, E, and F as the vertices.

Step 4 The construction partitions $\overline{AB}$ into [4] equal parts. Label point P at the point that divides the segment in the ratio [1] to [3] from A to B.

Reflect

7. In Part A, why is $\overline{EP}$ is parallel to $\overline{FB}$?
   ∠AEP was constructed to be congruent to ∠AFB. These are congruent corresponding angles, so $\overline{EP} \parallel \overline{FB}$.

8. How can you use the Triangle Proportionality Theorem to explain why this construction method works?
   The construction ensures that the segments of the ray you constructed are congruent.
   Also, the segments that are drawn in Step 3 are all parallel. By the Triangle Proportionality
   Theorem, you can conclude that the segments along $\overline{AB}$ are congruent to each other.

Your Turn

Given the directed line segment from A to B, construct the point P that divides the segment in the given ratio from A to B.

9. 1 to 2

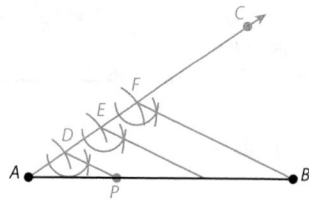

10. 3 to 2

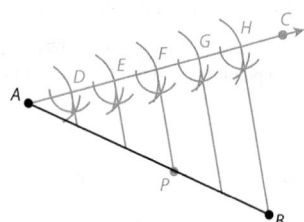

© Houghton Mifflin Harcourt Publishing Company

LANGUAGE SUPPORT 🄴🄻

Connect Vocabulary

Help students develop an understanding of the meaning of *dimension* by considering *one-dimensional* figures, such as a line, whose only dimension is length, and *two-dimensional* figures, such as a square. The two dimensions of a square are length and width.

11. How is a one-dimensional coordinate system similar to a two-dimensional coordinate system? How is it different?

    In both types of coordinate systems, numbers are used to specify the locations of points.

    In a one-dimensional coordinate system, a single number is used to specify the location of

    a point on a line. In a two-dimensional coordinate system, two numbers are used to specify

    the location of a point on a plane.

12. Is finding a point that is $\frac{4}{5}$ of the distance from point A to point B the same as finding a point that divides $\overline{AB}$ in the ratio 4 to 5? Explain.

    No; the point that is $\frac{4}{5}$ of the distance from point A to point B is 80% of the distance from

    point A to point B; the point that divides $\overline{AB}$ in the ratio 4 to 5 is $\frac{4}{9}$ or approximately 44% of

    the distance from point A to point B.

13. **Essential Question Check-In** What are some different ways to divide a segment in the ratio 2 to 1?

    If the segment lies on a number line, subtract the coordinates to find the distance between

    the endpoints. Then find the point that is $\frac{2}{3}$ of the distance from one endpoint to the other.

    If the segment is on a coordinate plane, use the run and the rise to find the point that is

    $\frac{2}{3}$ of the distance from one endpoint to the other. If there are no coordinates, use a

    compass and straightedge to divide the given segment into 3 equal parts. Then identify

    the point that divides the segment in the ratio 2 to 1.

⭐ Evaluate: Homework and Practice

A choreographer uses a number line to position dancers for a ballet. Dancers A and B have coordinates 5 and 23, respectively. In Exercises 1–4, find the coordinate for each of the following dancers based on the given locations.

1. Dancer C stands at a point that is $\frac{5}{6}$ of the distance from Dancer A to Dancer B.

   $AB = |23 - 5| = 18$

   $\frac{5}{6} \cdot 18 = 15$

   Dancer C is 15 units from Dancer A, so the coordinate for Dancer C is $5 + 15 = 20$.

2. Dancer D stands at a point that is $\frac{1}{3}$ of the distance from Dancer A to Dancer B.

   $AB = |23 - 5| = 18$

   $\frac{1}{3} \cdot 18 = 6$

   Dancer D is 6 units from Dancer A, so the coordinate for Dancer D is $5 + 6 = 11$.

ELABORATE

QUESTIONING STRATEGIES

❓ Can a proportion compare measurements that have different units? Explain. Yes, but each ratio must compare measurements with the same unit; for example, you can write a proportion with a ratio of feet to feet equal to a ratio of meters to meters.

SUMMARIZE THE LESSON

❓ How can you divide a directed line segment in a given ratio? Directed line segments are always read in the order in which the points are given. A segment partition divides the segment from a given point A to another point B in a ratio of $a : b$. In a coordinate plane, the rise and run can be used to find the point dividing the segment in the ratio $a : b$. Segment partitions can also be constructed using a compass and straightedge.

EVALUATE

Personal Math Trainer

ASSIGNMENT GUIDE

Concepts and Skills	Practice
Explore Partitioning a Segment in a One-Dimensional Coordinate System	Exercises 1–4
Example 1 Partitioning a Segment in a Two-Dimensional Coordinate System	Exercises 5–8
Example 2 Constructing a Partition of a Segment	Exercises 9–12

INTEGRATE MATHEMATICAL PRACTICES

Focus on Modeling

MP.4 Discuss the importance of careful constructions and labels in the portioning of segments.

---

3. Dancer E stands at a point that divides the line segment from Dancer A to Dancer B in a ratio of 2 to 1.

   $AB = |23 - 5| = 18$

   Let the distance from Dancer A to Dancer E be $2x$ and let the distance from Dancer E to Dancer B be x. Then $2x + x = 18$, $3x = 18$, and $x = 6$. So the distance from Dancer A to Dancer E is $2x = 2(6) = 12$.

   The coordinate for Dancer E is $5 + 12 = 17$.

4. Dancer F stands at a point that divides the line segment from Dancer A to Dancer B in a ratio of 1 to 5.

   $AB = |23 - 5| = 18$

   Let the distance from Dancer A to Dancer F be x and let the distance from Dancer F to Dancer B be $5x$. Then $x + 5x = 18$, $6x = 18$, and $x = 3$. So the distance from Dancer A to Dancer F is $x = 3$.

   The coordinate for Dancer F is $5 + 3 = 8$.

Find the coordinates of the point P that divides the directed line segment from A to B in the given ratio.

5. $A(-3, -2)$, $B(12, 3)$; 3 to 2

   P is $\frac{3}{3+2} = \frac{3}{5}$ of the distance from A to B.

   run $= 12 - (-3) = 15$; rise $= 3 - (-2) = 5$

   $\frac{3}{5}$ of run $= \frac{3}{5}(15) = 9$; $\frac{3}{5}$ of rise $= \frac{3}{5}(5) = 3$

   x-coordinate of point $P = -3 + 9 = 6$;

   y-coordinate of point $P = -2 + 3 = 1$

   The coordinates of point P are $(6, 1)$.

6. $A(-1, 5)$, $B(7, -3)$; 7 to 1

   P is $\frac{7}{7+1} = \frac{7}{8}$ of the distance from A to B.

   run $= 7 - (-1) = 8$; rise $= -3 - 5 = -8$

   $\frac{7}{8}$ of run $= \frac{7}{8}(8) = 7$; $\frac{7}{8}$ of rise $= \frac{7}{8}(-8) = -7$

   x-coordinate of point $P = -1 + 7 = 6$;

   y-coordinate of point $P = 5 + (-7) = -2$

   The coordinates of point P are $(6, -2)$.

7. $A(-1, 4)$, $(B-9, 0)$; 1 to 3

   P is $\frac{1}{1+3} = \frac{1}{4}$ of the distance from A to B.

   run $= -9 - (-1) = -8$; rise $= 0 - 4 = -4$

   $\frac{1}{4}$ of run $= \frac{1}{4}(-8) = -2$; $\frac{1}{4}$ of rise $= \frac{1}{4}(-4) = -1$

   x-coordinate of point $P = -1 + (-2) = -3$;

   y-coordinate of point $P = 4 + (-1) = 3$

   The coordinates of point P are $(-3, 3)$.

8. $A(7, -3)$, $B(-7, 4)$; 3 to 4

   P is $\frac{3}{3+4} = \frac{3}{7}$ of the distance from A to B.

   run $= -7 - 7 = -14$; rise $= 4 - (-3) = 7$

   $\frac{3}{7}$ of run $= \frac{3}{7}(-14) = -6$; $\frac{3}{7}$ of rise $= \frac{3}{7}(7) = 3$

   x-coordinate of point $P = 7 + (-6) = 1$;

   y-coordinate of point $P = -3 + 3 = 0$

   The coordinates of point P are $(1, 0)$.

Given the directed line segment from A to B, construct the point P that divides the segment in the given ratio from A to B.

9. 3 to 1

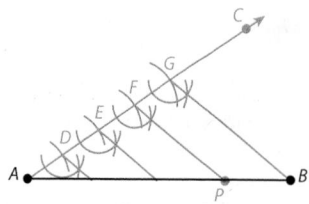

10. 2 to 3

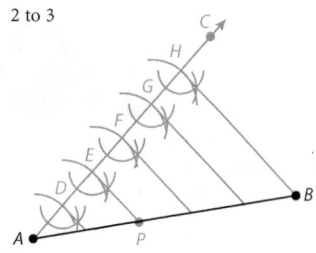

Exercise	Depth of Knowledge (D.O.K.)	COMMON CORE Mathematical Practices
1–4	**2** Skills/Concepts	**MP.4** Modeling
5–8	**2** Skills/Concepts	**MP.2** Reasoning
9–12	**2** Skills/Concepts	**MP.5** Using Tools
13–16	**2** Skills/Concepts	**MP.4** Modeling
17–20	**2** Skills/Concepts	**MP.4** Modeling
21	**2** Skills/Concepts	**MP.2** Reasoning
22	**3** Strategic Thinking **H.O.T.**	**MP.3** Logic
23	**3** Strategic Thinking **H.O.T.**	**MP.3** Logic

Given the directed line segment from A to B, construct the point P that divides the segment in the given ratio from A to B.

11. 1 to 4

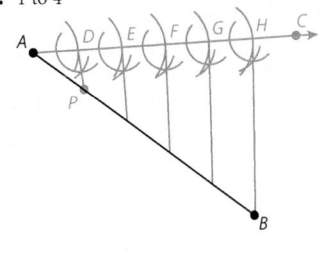

12. 4 to 1

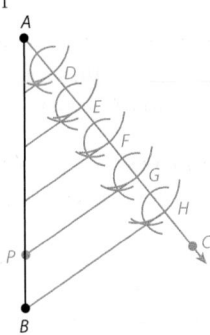

Find the coordinate of the point P that divides each directed line segment in the given ratio.

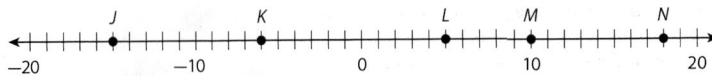

13. from J to M; 1 to 9

$JM = \left| 10 - (-15) \right| = 25$

Let $JP = x$ and let $PM = 9x$.

Then $x + 9x = 25$, $10x = 25$, and $x = 2.5$.

The coordinate of point P is $-15 + 2.5 = -12.5$

14. from K to L; 1 to 1

$KL = \left| 5 - (-6) \right| = 11$

Let $KP = x$ and let $PL = x$.

Then $x + x = 11$, $2x = 11$, and $x = 5.5$.

The coordinate of point P is $-6 + 5.5 = -0.5$

15. from N to K; 3 to 5

$NK = \left| -6 - 18 \right| = 24$

Let $NP = 3x$ and let $PK = 5x$.

Then $3x + 5x = 24$, $8x = 24$, and $x = 3$.

So $NP = 3(3) = 9$.

The coordinate of point P is $18 - 9 = 9$.

16. from K to J; 7 to 11

$KJ = \left| -15 - (-6) \right| = 9$

Let $KP = 7x$ and let $PJ = 11x$.

Then $7x + 11x = 9$, $18x = 9$, $x = 0.5$.

So $KP = 7(0.5) = 3.5$.

The coordinate of point P is $-6 - 3.5 = -9.5$.

17. Communicate Mathematical Ideas Leon constructed a point P that divides the directed segment from A to B in the ratio 2 to 1. Chelsea constructed a point Q that divides the directed segment from B to A in the ratio 1 to 2. How are points P and Q related? Explain.

Points P and Q are the same point. Sample explanation: Point P is $\frac{2}{3}$ of the distance from A to B. Point Q is $\frac{1}{3}$ of the distance from B to A. This means the points lie at the same location along the line segment.

AVOID COMMON ERRORS

Some students may confuse various ratios. Remind them that the similarity ratio refers only to the ratio of the lengths of the sides. It is equal to the perimeter ratio and the square root of the area ratio.

Exercise	Depth of Knowledge (D.O.K.)	COMMON CORE Mathematical Practices
24	**3** Strategic Thinking H.O.T.	**MP.2** Reasoning
25	**3** Strategic Thinking H.O.T.	**MP.2** Reasoning

18. City planners use a number line to place landmarks along a new street. Each unit of the number line represents 100 feet. A fountain F is located at coordinate -3 and a plaza P is located at coordinate 21. The city planners place two benches along the street at points that divide the segment from F to P in the ratios 1 to 2 and 3 to 1. What is the distance between the benches?

$FP = \left| 21 - (-3) \right| = 24$; Then $x + 2x = 24$, $3x = 24$, and $x = 8$.

Let the distance from F to the first bench be x and let the distance from the first bench to P be $2x$.

The coordinate for the first bench is $-3 + 8 = 5$.

Let the distance from F to the second bench be $3x$ and let the distance from the second bench to P be x.

Then $3x + x = 24$, $4x = 24$, $x = 6$. So the distance from F to the second bench is $3x = 3(6) = 18$ units.

The coordinate for the second bench is $-3 + 18 = 15$.

The distance between the benches is $15 - 5 = 10$ units or 1000 feet.

19. The course for a marathon includes a straight segment from city hall to the main library. The planning committee wants to put water stations along this part of the course so that the stations divide the segment into three equal parts. Find the coordinates of the points at the which the water stations should be placed.

From C to M, run $= 3 - (-3) = 6$; rise $= 3 - (-2) = 5$

Let the water stations be at points P and Q. Point P is $\frac{1}{3}$ of the distance from C to M.

$\frac{1}{3}$ of run $= \frac{1}{3}(6) = 2$; $\frac{1}{3}$ of rise $= \frac{1}{3}(5) = 1\frac{2}{3}$

x-coordinate of $P = -3 + 2 = -1$; y-coordinate of $P = -2 + 1\frac{2}{3} = -\frac{1}{3}$

The coordinates of point P are $\left(-1, -\frac{1}{3} \right)$.

Point Q is $\frac{2}{3}$ of the distance from C to M.

$\frac{2}{3}$ of run $= \frac{2}{3}(6) = 4$; $\frac{2}{3}$ of rise $= \frac{2}{3}(5) = 3\frac{1}{3}$

x-coordinate of $Q = -3 + 4 = 1$; y-coordinate of $Q = -2 + 3\frac{1}{3} = 1\frac{1}{3}$

The coordinates of point Q are $\left(1, 1\frac{1}{3} \right)$.

The water stations should be placed at $\left(-1, -\frac{1}{3} \right)$ and $\left(1, 1\frac{1}{3} \right)$.

© Houghton Mifflin Harcourt Publishing Company • Image Credits: ©sportgraphic/Fotolia

20. **Multi-Step** Carlos is driving on a straight section of highway from Ashford to Lincoln. Ashford is at mile marker 433 and Lincoln is at mile marker 553. A rest stop is located along the highway $\frac{2}{3}$ of the distance from Ashford to Lincoln. Assuming Carlos drives at a constant rate of 60 miles per hour, how long will it take him to drive from Ashford to the rest stop?

The distance from Ashford to Lincoln is $|553 - 433| = 120$ miles.

$\frac{2}{3} \cdot 120 = 80$, so Carlos must drive 80 miles from Ashford to the rest stop.

$d = rt$, where d is the distance, r is the rate, and t is the time, so $80 = 60t$, and $t = 1\frac{1}{3}$.

So it will take $1\frac{1}{3}$ hours (1 hour and 20 minutes) to drive from Ashford to the rest stop.

21. The directed segment from J to K is shown in the figure.

Points divide the segment from J to K in the each of the following ratios. Which points have integer coordinates? Select all that apply

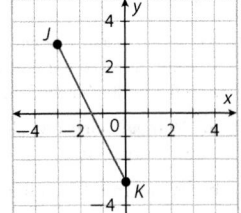

A. 1 to 1

(B.) 2 to 1

C. 2 to 3

D. 1 to 3

(E.) 1 to 2

From J to K, run $= 0 - (-3) = 3$; rise $= -3 - 3 = -6$

A. The point is $\frac{1}{1+1} = \frac{1}{2}$ of the distance from J to K. $\frac{1}{2}$ of run $= \frac{1}{2}(3) = 1\frac{1}{2}$; $\frac{1}{2}$
of rise $= \frac{1}{2}(-6) = -3$. x-coordinate of the point is $-3 + 1\frac{1}{2} = -1\frac{1}{2}$; y-coordinate of the
point is $3 + (-3) = 0$. The point does not have integer coordinates.

B. The point is $\frac{2}{2+1} = \frac{2}{3}$ of the distance from J to K. $\frac{2}{3}$ of run $= \frac{2}{3}(3) = 2$; $\frac{2}{3}$
of rise $= \frac{2}{3}(-6) = -4$. x-coordinate of the point is $-3 + 2 = -1$; y-coordinate of the
point is $3 + (-4) = -1$. The point has integer coordinates.

C. The point is $\frac{2}{2+3} = \frac{2}{5}$ of the distance from J to K. $\frac{2}{5}$ of run $= \frac{2}{5}(3) = 1\frac{1}{5}$; $\frac{2}{5}$
of rise $= \frac{2}{5}(-6) = -2\frac{2}{5}$. x-coordinate of the point is $-3 + 1\frac{1}{5} = -1\frac{4}{5}$; y-coordinate of the
point is $3 + \left(-2\frac{2}{5}\right) = \frac{3}{5}$. The point does not have integer coordinates.

D. The point is $\frac{1}{1+3} = \frac{1}{4}$ of the distance from J to K. $\frac{1}{4}$ of run $= \frac{1}{4}(3) = \frac{3}{4}$; $\frac{1}{4}$
of rise $= \frac{1}{4}(-6) = -1\frac{1}{2}$. x-coordinate of the point is $-3 + \frac{3}{4} = -2\frac{1}{4}$; y-coordinate of the
point is $3 + \left(-1\frac{1}{2}\right) = 1\frac{1}{2}$. The point does not have integer coordinates.

E. The point is $\frac{1}{1+2} = \frac{1}{3}$ of the distance from J to K. $\frac{1}{3}$ of run $= \frac{1}{3}(3) = 1$; $\frac{1}{3}$
of rise $= \frac{1}{3}(-6) = -2$. x-coordinate of the point is $-3 + 1 = -2$; y-coordinate of the
point is $3 + (-2) = 1$. The point has integer coordinates.

AVOID COMMON ERRORS

Students may forget to use the correct direction to partition line segments. Remind students to double-check direction in order to choose the correct partition point.

JOURNAL

Have students summarize the process for finding the point on a directed line segment that partitions the segment in a given ratio.

22. Critique Reasoning Jeffrey was given a directed line segment and was asked to use a compass and straightedge to construct the point that divides the segment in the ratio 4 to 2. He said he would have to draw a ray and then construct 6 congruent segments along the ray. Tamara said it is not necessary to construct 6 congruent segments along the ray. Do you agree? If so, explain Tamara's shortcut. If not, explain why not.

Yes; the ratio 4 to 2 is equivalent to the ratio 2 to 1. To construct a point that divides a segment in the ratio 2 to 1, it is only necessary to construct 3 congruent segments along the ray.

23. Explain the Error Point A has coordinate -9 and point B has coordinate 9. A student was asked to find the coordinate of the point P that is $\frac{2}{3}$ of the distance from A to B. The student said the coordinate of point P is -3.

a. Without doing any calculations, how can you tell that the student made an error?

Point P must be closer to point B than to point A, so the coordinate of point P should be positive.

b. What error do you think the student made?

Sample answer: The student found the coordinate of the point that is $\frac{2}{3}$ of the distance from B to A.

24. Analyze Relationships Point P divides the directed segment from A to B in the ratio 3 to 2. The coordinates of point A are $(-4, -2)$ and the coordinates of point P are $(2, 1)$. Find the coordinates of point B.

Point P is $\frac{3}{3+2} = \frac{3}{5}$ of the distance from A to B.

The run from A to P is $2 - (-4) = 6$. Let the run from A to B be x. Then $6 = \frac{3}{5}x$ and $x = 10$.

The rise from A to P is $1 - (-2) = 3$. Let the rise from A to B be y. Then $3 = \frac{3}{5}y$ and $y = 5$.

x-coordinate of point $B = -4 + 10 = 6$; y-coordinate of point $B = -2 + 5 = 3$

The coordinates of point B are $(6, 3)$

25. Critical Thinking $\overline{RS}$ passes through $R(-3, 1)$ and $S(4, 3)$. Find a point P on $\overline{RS}$ such that the ratio of RP to SP is 5 to 4. Is there more than one possibility? Explain.

If point P is on $\overline{RS}$, then point P is $\frac{5}{5+4} = \frac{5}{9}$ of the distance from R to S.

$\text{run} = 4 - (-3) = 7$; $\text{rise} = 3 - 1 = 2$

$\frac{5}{9}$ of run $= \frac{5}{9}(7) = 3\frac{8}{9}$; $\frac{5}{9}$ of rise $= \frac{5}{9}(2) = 1\frac{1}{9}$

x-coordinate of point $P = -3 + 3\frac{8}{9} = \frac{8}{9}$; y-coordinate of point $P = 1 + 1\frac{1}{9} = 2\frac{1}{9}$

In this case, the coordinates of point P are $\left(\frac{8}{9}, 2\frac{1}{9}\right)$.

There is also a point P, not on $\overline{RS}$, that lies beyond point S. Let P have coordinates (x, y).

Then $\frac{\text{rise of } \overline{RP}}{\text{rise of } \overline{SP}} = \frac{5}{4}$ so $\frac{x - (-3)}{x - 4} = \frac{5}{4}$, $4(x + 3) = 5(x - 4)$, $4x + 12 = 5x - 20$, $12 = x - 20$, and $x = 32$.

Also, $\frac{\text{rise of } \overline{RP}}{\text{rise of } \overline{SP}} = \frac{5}{4}$, so $\frac{y - 1}{y - 3} = \frac{5}{4}$, $4(y - 1) = 5(y - 3)$, $4y - 4 = 5y - 15$, $-4 = y - 15$, and $y = 11$.

In this case, the coordinates of point P are $(32, 11)$.

Lesson Performance Task

In this lesson you will subdivide line segments in given ratios. The diagram shows a line segment divided into two parts in such a way that the longer part divided by the shorter part equals the entire length divided by the longer part:

$$\frac{a}{b} = \frac{a+b}{a}$$

Each of these ratios is called the Golden Ratio. To find the point on a line segment that divides the segment this way, study this figure:

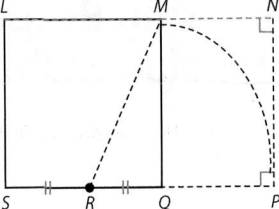

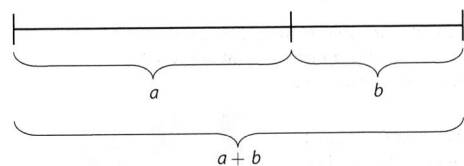

In the figure, $LMQS$ is a square. $\frac{LN}{LM}$ equals the Golden Ratio (the entire segment length divided by the longer part).

1. Describe how, starting with line segment $\overline{LM}$, you can find the location of point N.

2. Letting LM equal 1, find $\frac{LN}{LM} = \frac{LN}{1} = LN$, the Golden Ratio. Describe your method.

1. Using $\overline{LM}$ as one side, construct square $LMQS$. Construct R, the midpoint of $\overline{SQ}$. Place the compass point on R and use $\overline{RM}$ as a radius to construct an arc intersecting line SQ. Mark point P where $\overline{RM}$ intersects SQ. Construct a perpendicular through P intersecting line RM. Mark point N where the perpendicular intersects LM.

2. RM equals the length of the hypotenuse of a right triangle with sides 1 and 0.5. By the Pythagorean Theorem, $RM \approx 1.118$. So, $RP \approx 1.118$. $SR = 0.5$, so $SP \approx 1.118 + 0.5 \approx 1.618$. $LN = SP$, so LN, the Golden Ratio, equals approximately 1.618.

© Houghton Mifflin Harcourt Publishing Company

INTEGRATE MATHEMATICAL PRACTICES

Focus on Modeling

MP.4 The opening of the Lesson Performance Task states that for the divided line segment $a + b$, "the longer part divided by the shorter part equals the entire length divided by the longer part." So, $\frac{a}{b} = \frac{a+b}{a}$. Use that same relationship to complete this equation relating to line segment $\overline{LN}$: $\frac{LM}{MN} = ?. \frac{LN}{LM}$

INTEGRATE MATHEMATICAL PRACTICES

Focus on Math Connections

MP.1 The Lesson Performance Task shows a line segment divided into two parts a and b such that $\frac{a}{b} = \frac{a+b}{a}$. If $b = 1$, then $\frac{a}{1} = \frac{a+1}{a}$. Solve the equation for a. Compare your results with your results in the Lesson Performance Task and make a conjecture about the value of a.

$a = \frac{1 + \sqrt{5}}{2} \approx 1.618$; a appears to equal the Golden Ratio.

EXTENSION ACTIVITY

The first two numbers in the Fibonacci sequence of natural numbers are 1 and 1. To find each new term in the sequence, add the two previous terms. So, the first few terms are 1, 1, 2, 3, 5, and 8. Have students use calculators to write the ratios of each of the first ten numbers in the sequence to the previous number, rounding to the nearest ten-thousandth. Here are the first four ratios: $\frac{1}{1} = 1; \frac{2}{1} = 2; \frac{3}{2} = 1.5; \frac{5}{3} \approx 1.333$. After students complete their calculations, have them compare their results with their results in the Lesson Performance Task, and then make a conjecture about the ratios they calculated. The ratios get closer and closer to the Golden Ratio the farther the sequence of ratios continues.

Scoring Rubric

2 points: Student correctly solves the problem and explains his/her reasoning.

1 point: Student shows good understanding of the problem but does not fully solve or explain his/her reasoning.

0 points: Student does not demonstrate understanding of the problem.

Subdividing a Segment in a Given Ratio   **652**

Using Proportional Relationships

Common Core Math Standards

The student is expected to:

 G-SRT.B.5

Use congruence and similarity criteria for triangles to solve problems and to prove relationships in geometric figures.

Mathematical Practices

COMMON CORE **MP.5 Using Tools**

Language Objective

Explain the difference between direct and indirect measurement to a partner.

ENGAGE

Essential Question: How can you use similar triangles to solve problems?

You can use similar triangles to measure things indirectly, using the fact that similar triangles have side lengths that are proportional.

PREVIEW: LESSON PERFORMANCE TASK

View the Engage section online. Discuss the photograph and ask if students can cite evidence that suggests the Earth is round. Then preview the Lesson Performance Task.

12.3 Using Proportional Relationships

Essential Question: How can you use similar triangles to solve problems?

Resource Locker

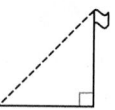 **Explore** **Exploring Indirect Measurement**

In this Explore, you will consider how to find heights, lengths, or distances that are too great to be measured directly, that is, with measuring tools like rulers. **Indirect measurement** involves using the properties of similar triangles to measure such heights or distances.

(A) During the day sunlight creates shadows, as shown in the figure below. The dashed segment represents the ray of sunlight. What kind of triangle is formed by the flagpole, its shadow, and the ray of sunlight?

A right triangle

(B) Suppose the sun is shining, and you are standing near a flagpole, but out of its shadow. You will cast a shadow as well. You can assume that the rays of the sun are parallel. What do you know about the two triangles formed? Explain your reasoning.

 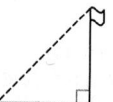

The triangles are similar. The rays of the sun are parallel and the line representing the

ground is a transversal. So the acute angles formed by the bases and hypotenuses of the

right triangles are congruent, as are the right angles. So the triangles are similar by the AA

Similarity Criterion.

(C) In the diagram, what heights or lengths do you already know?

You probably know your own height.

(D) What heights or lengths can be measured directly?

Your height (if necessary) and the lengths of your shadow and the shadow of the flagpole.

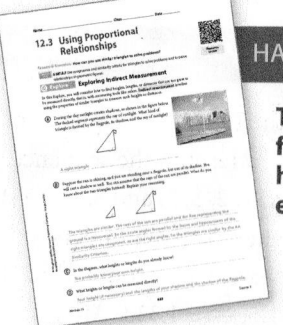

HARDCOVER PAGES 555–562

Turn to these pages to find this lesson in the hardcover student edition.

1. How could you use similar triangles to measure the height of the flagpole indirectly?
   Have someone measure the length of your shadow and the shadow of the flagpole. Write

   and solve a proportion in which the unknown is the height of the flagpole. Use the fact

   that corresponding sides of similar triangles are proportional.

✏ Explain 1 Finding an Unknown Height

Example 1 Find the indicated dimension using the measurements shown in the figure
and the properties of similar triangles.

(A) In order to find the height of a palm tree, you measure
the tree's shadow and, at the same time of day, you
measure the shadow cast by a meter stick that you hold at
a right angle to the ground. Find the height h of the tree.

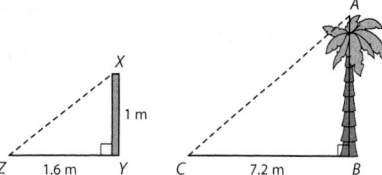

Because $\overline{ZX} \parallel \overline{CA}$, $\angle Z \cong \angle C$. All right angles are
congruent, so $\angle Y \cong \angle B$. So $\triangle XYZ \cong \triangle ABC$.

Set up proportion. $\dfrac{AB}{XY} = \dfrac{BC}{YZ}$

Substitute. $\dfrac{h}{7.2} = \dfrac{1}{1.6}$

Multiply each side by 7.2. $h = 7.2\left(\dfrac{1}{1.6}\right)$

Simplify. $h = 4.5$

The tree is 4.5 meters high.

(B) Sid is 72 inches tall. To measure a flagpole, Sid stands near the flag. Sid's
friend Miranda measures the lengths of Sid's shadow and the flagpole's
shadow. Find the height h of the flagpole.

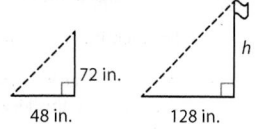

The triangles are similar by the AA Similarity Criterion.

Set up proportion. $\dfrac{\text{flagpole's height}}{\text{person's height}} = \dfrac{\text{flagpole's shadow}}{\text{person's shadow}}$

Substitute. $\dfrac{h}{72} = \dfrac{\boxed{128}}{48}$

Multiply each side by 72. $h = 72\left(\dfrac{\boxed{128}}{48}\right)$

Simplify. $x = \boxed{192}$

The flagpole is $\underline{\text{192 inches}}$ tall.

EXPLORE

Exploring Indirect Measurement

INTEGRATE TECHNOLOGY

After you have the known measurements, use
geometry software to calculate the missing
measurements.

QUESTIONING STRATEGIES

❓ What assumptions are made, in this kind of
indirect measurement, about the rays of the
Sun and the time of day when the shadows are
measured? The Sun's rays are parallel and the
measurements of the shadows are made at the
same time of day.

EXPLAIN 1

Finding an Unknown Height

INTEGRATE MATHEMATICAL PRACTICES
Focus on Math Connections

MP.1 Have students compare the process of using
similar triangles to the process of using congruent
triangles.

PROFESSIONAL DEVELOPMENT

🔷 Learning Progressions

Students have already used congruence to solve real-world problems. For example,
to find the distance across a pond, students showed that two triangles were
congruent and then used CPCTC to find an unknown side length that
corresponded to the distance across the pond. This lesson presents similar
problems (problems in which unknown lengths must be determined), but now
students will use similarity and the proportionality of corresponding sides to find
the unknown length.

? Which line in the figure is the transversal that is cutting two parallel lines? the ground

EXPLAIN 2

Finding an Unknown Distance

INTEGRATE MATHEMATICAL PRACTICES

Focus on Communication

MP.3 Have students name the corresponding parts before they begin to solve for any lengths.

QUESTIONING STRATEGIES

? How could you predict if an unknown length is longer or shorter than the corresponding given length? If the triangle with the unknown length looks smaller than the triangle with the given length, you can predict that the unknown length will be smaller. If the triangle with the unknown length looks greater than the triangle with the given length, you can predict that the unknown length will be greater.

Reflect

2. In the tree example, how can you check that your answer is reasonable?
The length of the meter stick's shadow is a little more than 1.5 times the length of the meter stick. So the length of the tree's shadow, should be a little more than 1.5 times the height of the tree. Since $1.5(4.5) = 6.75$, an answer of 4.5 is reasonable

Your Turn

3. Liam is 6 feet tall. To find the height of a tree, he measures his shadow and the tree's shadow. The measurements of the two shadows are shown. Find the height h of the tree.

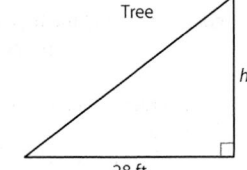

The triangles are similar by the AA Similarity Criterion.

$$\frac{\text{tree's height}}{\text{Liam's height}} = \frac{\text{tree's shadow}}{\text{Liam's shadow}}$$

$$\frac{h}{6} = \frac{28}{8} \qquad h = 6\left(\frac{28}{8}\right)$$

$$h = \frac{168}{8} \qquad h = 21$$

The tree is 21 feet tall.

Explain 2   Finding an Unknown Distance

In real-world situations, you may not be able to measure an object directly because there is a physical barrier separating you from the object. You can use similar triangles in these situations as well.

Example 2 Explain how to use the information in the figure to find the indicated distance.

Ⓐ A hiker wants to find the distance d across a canyon. She locates points as described.

1. She identifies a landmark at X. She places a marker (Y) directly across the canyon from X.

2. At Y, she turns 90° away from X and walks 400 feet in a straight line. She places a marker (Z) at this location.

3. She continues walking another 600 feet, and places a marker (W) at this location.

4. She turns 90° away from the canyon and walks until the marker Z aligns with X. She places a marker (V) at this location and measures $\overline{WV}$.

$\angle VWZ \cong \angle XYZ$ (All right angles are congruent) and $\angle VZW \cong \angle XZY$ (Vertical angles are congruent). So, $\triangle VWZ \sim \triangle XYZ$ by the AA Similarity Criterion.

$\frac{XY}{VW} = \frac{YZ}{WZ}$, So $\frac{d}{327} = \frac{400}{600}$, or $\frac{d}{327} = \frac{2}{3}$

Then $d = 327\left(\frac{2}{3}\right) = 218$.

The distance across the canyon is 218 feet.

COLLABORATIVE LEARNING

Small Group Activity

Have students work in a small group to estimate the length of something in the school building that would be difficult to measure. Examples include the height of a stairwell or a flagpole. Then have the group write an explanation of how to measure the structure, including diagrams.

Ⓑ To find the distance d across the gorge, a student identifies points as shown in the figure. Find d.

$\triangle JKL \sim \triangle NML$ by the AA Triangle Similarity Theorem.

$\dfrac{JK}{NM} = \dfrac{KL}{\boxed{ML}}$

$\dfrac{d}{35} = \dfrac{24}{\boxed{42}}$

$d = \boxed{35} \cdot \dfrac{\boxed{24}}{42} = \boxed{35} \cdot \dfrac{\boxed{4}}{7}$

$d = \dfrac{\boxed{140}}{7}$

$d = \boxed{20}$

The distance across the gorge is ___20 meters___.

Reflect

4. In the example, why is $\angle JLK \cong \angle NLM$?
   $\angle JLK \cong \angle NLM$ are vertical angles and vertical angles are congruent.

Your Turn

5. To find the distance d across a stream, Levi located points as shown in the figure. Use the given information to find d.

$\triangle ABC \sim \triangle DEC$ by the AA Triangle Similarity Theorem.

$\dfrac{AB}{DE} = \dfrac{BC}{EC}; \dfrac{d}{12} = \dfrac{12}{6}; d = 12\left(\dfrac{12}{6}\right) = 24$

$d = 24$ meters

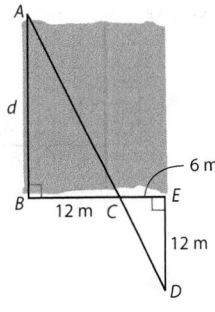

💬 Elaborate

6. **Discussion** Suppose you want to help a friend prepare for solving indirect measurement problems. What topics would you suggest that your friend review?
   Possible answers: The triangle similarity criteria, theorems about congruent angles (such as the Vertical Angles Theorem), writing and solving proportions, and properties of similar triangles, including the relationships between corresponding angles and between corresponding sides.

7. **Essential Question Check-In** You are given a figure including triangles that represent a real-world situation. What is the first step you should take to find an unknown measurement?
   You must first be sure that the triangles are similar.

AVOID COMMON ERRORS

Remind students to pay attention to the units in their final answers, and to make sure that the lengths they find for real-world problems are reasonable ones.

ELABORATE

QUESTIONING STRATEGIES

❓ What is the difference between direct and indirect measurement? If you can use a measurement tool like a ruler to measure a dimension, the measurement is direct. If you use the measurement tool to measure a corresponding dimension and relate it to the desired dimension using a proportion, the measurement is indirect.

SUMMARIZE THE LESSON

❓ How can you use indirect measurement and similar triangles to solve problems? You can show that two triangles are similar using the AA or SAS Similarity Criterion. Then, you can use the fact that corresponding sides are proportional to find an unknown side length.

DIFFERENTIATE INSTRUCTION

Modeling

If possible, encourage students to go outdoors to construct and solve indirect measurement problems with shadows. Find a distance that may be difficult to measure directly with a measuring tape and use similar triangles to find the distance. Direct students to draw a diagram of the problem, make measurements, write distance measurements on the diagram, and use these measurements and the appropriate steps to find the distance.

Using Proportional Relationships   **656**

EVALUATE

ASSIGNMENT GUIDE

Concepts and Skills	Practice
Explore Exploring Indirect Measurement	Exercise 1
Example 1 Finding an Unknown Height	Exercises 2–5
Example 2 Finding an Unknown Distance	Exercises 6–9

INTEGRATE MATHEMATICAL PRACTICES

Focus on Modeling

MP.4 Discuss how you could use a yardstick or a ruler to take an indirect measurement of objects in the classroom that are difficult to measure directly, such as a chalkboard or a door.

• Online Homework
• Hints and Help
• Extra Practice

1. Finding distances using similar triangles is called ___Indirect measurement___

Use similar triangles △ABC and △XYZ to find the missing height h.

2.

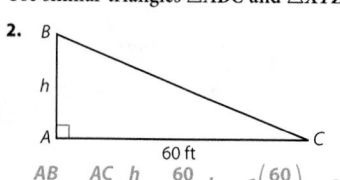

$$\frac{AB}{XY} = \frac{AC}{XZ}; \frac{h}{6} = \frac{60}{15}; h = 6\left(\frac{60}{15}\right) = 24 \text{ ft}$$

3.

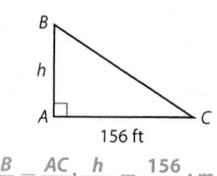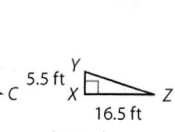

$$\frac{AB}{XY} = \frac{AC}{XZ}; \frac{h}{5.5} = \frac{156}{16.5}; m = \left(\frac{156}{16.5}\right)5.5 = 52 \text{ ft}$$

4.

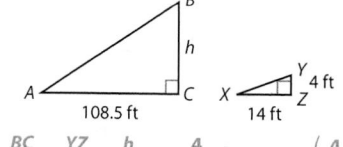

$$\frac{BC}{AC} = \frac{YZ}{XZ}; \frac{h}{108.5} = \frac{4}{14}; h = 108.5\left(\frac{4}{14}\right) = 31$$
$$h = 31 \text{ feet}$$

5.

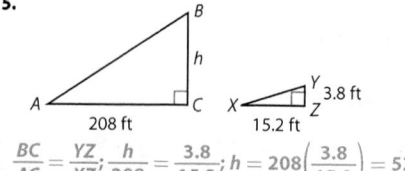

$$\frac{BC}{AC} = \frac{YZ}{XZ}; \frac{h}{208} = \frac{3.8}{15.2}; h = 208\left(\frac{3.8}{15.2}\right) = 52$$
$$h = 52 \text{ feet}$$

Use similar triangles △EFG and △IHG to find the missing distance d.

6.

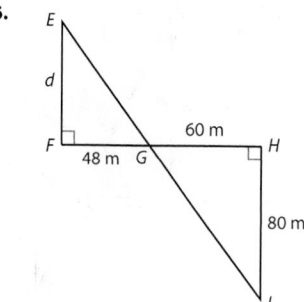

$$\frac{EF}{IH} = \frac{FG}{HG}; \frac{d}{80} = \frac{48}{60};$$
$$d = 80\left(\frac{48}{60}\right) = 64$$
$$d = 64 \text{ meters}$$

7.

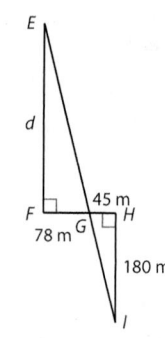

$$\frac{EF}{IH} = \frac{FG}{HG}; \frac{d}{180} = \frac{78}{45};$$
$$EF = 180\left(\frac{78}{45}\right) = 312$$
$$d = 312 \text{ meters}$$

8.

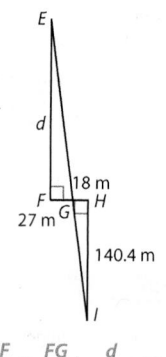

$$\frac{EF}{IH} = \frac{FG}{HG}; \frac{d}{140.4} = \frac{27}{18};$$
$$EF = 140.4\left(\frac{27}{18}\right) = 210.6$$
$$d = 210.6 \text{ meters}$$

9.

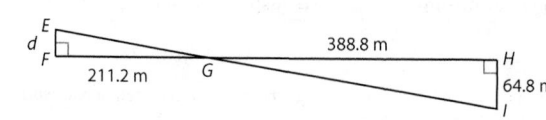

$$\frac{EF}{FG} = \frac{IH}{HG}; \frac{d}{211.2} = \frac{64.8}{388.8}; d = 211.2\left(\frac{64.8}{388.8}\right) = 35.2; d = 35.2 \text{ meters}$$

Exercise	Depth of Knowledge (D.O.K.)	COMMON CORE Mathematical Practices
1–5	**1** Recall of Information	**MP.4** Modeling
6–9	**2** Skills/Concepts	**MP.2** Reasoning
10–16	**2** Skills/Concepts	**MP.4** Modeling
17–19	**2** Skills/Concepts	**MP.2** Reasoning
20	**3** Strategic Thinking H.O.T.	**MP.3** Logic
21	**3** Strategic Thinking H.O.T.	**MP.2** Reasoning

10. To find the height h of a dinosaur in a museum, Amir placed a mirror on the ground 40 feet from its base. Then he stepped back 4 feet so that he could see the top of the dinosaur in the mirror. Amir's eyes were approximately 5 feet 6 inches above the ground. What is the height of the dinosaur?

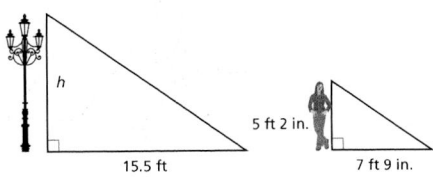

5 ft 6 in.

4 ft — 40 ft

The two triangles are similar by the AA Similarity Criterion. All the dimensions have to be in the same units, so write 5 feet 6 inches as 5.5 feet.

$\dfrac{h}{5.5} = \dfrac{40}{4}$; $h = 5.5\left(\dfrac{40}{4}\right) = 55$; The dinosaur is 55 feet tall.

11. Jenny is 5 feet 2 inches tall. To find the height h of a light pole, she measured her shadow and the pole's shadow. What is the height of the pole?

h

5 ft 2 in.

15.5 ft   7 ft 9 in.

The two triangles are similar by the AA

Similarity Criterion. All the dimensions

have to be in the same units, so write 5 feet 2 as $5\frac{2}{12} = 5\frac{1}{6}$ feet. Write 7 feet 9 inches as

$7\frac{9}{12} = 7\frac{3}{4}$ feet. To avoid mixing decimals and fractions, write 15.5 feet as $15\frac{1}{2}$ feet.

$\dfrac{h}{15\frac{1}{2}} = \dfrac{5\frac{1}{6}}{7\frac{3}{4}} = \dfrac{31}{2}\left(\dfrac{31}{6} \div \dfrac{31}{4}\right) = \dfrac{31}{2}\left(\dfrac{31}{6}\right)\left(\dfrac{4}{31}\right) = \dfrac{31}{2}\left(\dfrac{4}{6}\right) = \dfrac{62}{6} = 10\frac{1}{3}$

The light pole is $10\frac{1}{3}$ feet, or 10 feet 4 inches tall.

12. A student wanted to find the height h of a statue of a pineapple in Nambour, Australia. She measured the pineapple's shadow and her own shadow. The student's height is 5 feet 4 inches. What is the height of the pineapple?

$\triangle ABC \sim \triangle DEF$ by the AA Similarity Criterion.

$AC = 5$ ft 4 in. $= 64$ in.

$BC = 2$ ft $= 24$ in.

$EF = 8$ ft 9 in. $= 105$ in.

$\dfrac{AC}{DF} = \dfrac{BC}{EF}$; $\dfrac{64}{h} = \dfrac{24}{105}$; $\dfrac{h}{64} = \dfrac{105}{24}$; $h = 64\left(\dfrac{105}{24}\right) = 280$

The height h of the pineapple is 280 inches or 23 feet 4 inches.

D

h

A

B $\angle 1$ $\angle 2$
2 ft C E 8 ft 9 in. F

13. To find the height h of a flagpole, Casey measured her own shadow and the flagpole's shadow. Given that Casey's height is 5 feet 4 inches, what is the height of the flagpole?

The triangles are similar by the AA Similarity Criterion.

Casey's height: 5 ft 4 in. $= 64$ in.; Casey's shadow: 3 ft $= 36$ in.

flagpole's shadow: 14 ft 3 in. $= 171$ in.

$\dfrac{\text{flagpole's height}}{\text{Casey's height}} = \dfrac{\text{flagpole's shadow}}{\text{Casey's shadow}}$; $\dfrac{h}{64} = \dfrac{171}{36}$; $h = 64\left(\dfrac{171}{36}\right) = 304$

The height h of the flagpole is 304 inches or 25 feet 4 inches.

5 ft 4 in.

3 ft   14 ft 3 in.

h

AVOID COMMON ERRORS

Some students may not think they can find the similarity ratio of two figures without knowing the lengths of the sides. Remind them that the perimeters have the same similarity ratio as the corresponding sides, and the areas have the same ratio as the squares of the corresponding sides.

A city is planning an outdoor concert for an Independence Day celebration. To hold speakers and lights, a crew of technicians sets up a scaffold with two platforms by the stage. The first platform is 8 feet 2 inches off the ground. The second platform is 7 feet 6 inches above the first platform. The shadow of the first platform stretches 6 feet 3 inches across the ground.

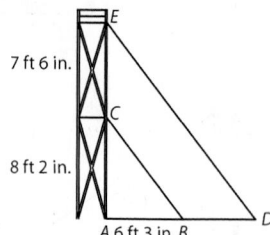

14. Explain why $\triangle ABC$ is similar to $\triangle ADE$. (*Hint*: rays of light are parallel.)

Possible answer: Because rays of light are parallel and $\overrightarrow{AD}$ is a transversal, $\angle ABC$ and $\angle ADE$ are corresponding angles, so they are congruent. $\angle A$ is common to both triangles. So $\triangle ABC \sim \triangle ADE$ by the AA Similarity Theorem.

15. Find the length of the shadow of the second platform in feet and inches to the nearest inch.

First, convert all lengths to inches:

$AC = 8 \text{ ft } 2 \text{ in.} = 98 \text{ in.}$

$CE = 7 \text{ ft } 6 \text{ in.} = 90 \text{ in.}$

$AB = 6 \text{ ft } 3 \text{ in.} = 75 \text{ in.}$

$AE = AC + CE = 98 + 90 = 188$

$\dfrac{AE}{AC} = \dfrac{AD}{AB}; \dfrac{188}{98} = \dfrac{AD}{75}; AD = 75\left(\dfrac{188}{98}\right) = 144$

The shadow of the second platform is represented by $\overline{BD}$.

$BD = AD - AB = 144 - 75 = 69$

So the shadow of the second platform is 69 inches or 5 feet 9 inches.

16. A technician is 5 feet 8 inches tall. The technician is standing on top of the second platform. Find the length s of the shadow that is cast by the scaffold and the technician to the nearest inch.

Height of technician: 5 ft 8 in. = 68 in.

Height of scaffold with technician: $188 + 68 = 256$ in.

$\dfrac{256}{98} = \dfrac{s}{75}; s = 75\left(\dfrac{256}{98}\right) = 196$

The shadow cast by the scaffold and the technician is 196 inches or 16 feet 4 inches.

17. To find the distance *XY* across a lake, you locate points as shown in the figure. Explain how to use this information to find *XY*.

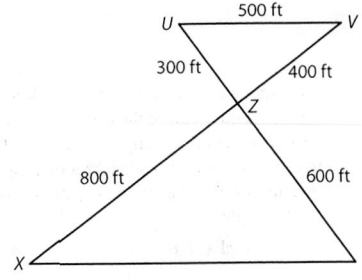

$\triangle XYZ \sim \triangle VUZ$ by the SAS Similarity Criterion,

so $\dfrac{XY}{VU} = \dfrac{XZ}{VZ}$. Then $\dfrac{XY}{500} = \dfrac{800}{400}$, so $XY = 1{,}000$ ft.

18. In order to find the height of a cliff, you stand at the bottom of the cliff, walk 60 feet from the base, and place a mirror on the ground. Then you face the cliff and step back 5 feet so that can see the top of the cliff in the mirror. Assuming your eyes are 6 feet above the ground, explain how to use this information to find the height of the cliff. (The angles marked congruent are congruent because of the nature of the reflection of light in a mirror.)

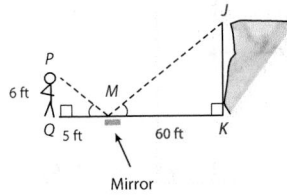

$\triangle JKM \sim \triangle PQM$ by the AA Similarity Criterion, so $\dfrac{JK}{PQ} = \dfrac{MK}{MQ}$. Then $\dfrac{JK}{6} = \dfrac{60}{5}$, so $JK = 72$, and the height of the cliff is 72 feet.

19. To find the height of a tree, Adrian measures the tree's shadow and then his shadow. Which proportion could Adrian use to find the height of the tree? Select all that apply.

(A.) $\dfrac{AC}{DF} = \dfrac{BC}{EF}$

(B.) $\dfrac{DF}{AC} = \dfrac{EF}{BC}$

C. $\dfrac{AB}{DF} = \dfrac{BC}{EF}$

D. $\dfrac{DF}{BC} = \dfrac{EF}{AC}$

(E.) $\dfrac{BC}{EF} = \dfrac{AC}{DF}$

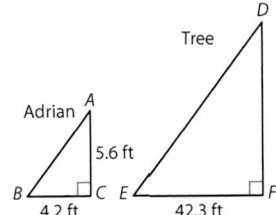

A. $\overline{AC}$ and $\overline{DF}$ are corresponding sides, as are $\overline{BC}$ and $\overline{EF}$.

B. $\overline{DF}$ and $\overline{AC}$ are corresponding sides, as are $\overline{EF}$ and $\overline{BC}$.

C. $\overline{AB}$ and $\overline{DF}$ are not corresponding sides.

D. $\overline{DF}$ and $\overline{BC}$ are not corresponding sides, nor are $\overline{EF}$ and $\overline{AC}$.

E. $\overline{BC}$ and $\overline{EF}$ are corresponding sides, as are $\overline{AC}$ and $\overline{DF}$.

JOURNAL

Have students make up their own problem in which an unknown length must be found using similar triangles. Remind students to include the solutions to their problems.

20. Critique Reasoning Jesse and Kyle are hiking. Jesse is carrying a walking stick. They spot a tall tree and use the walking stick as a vertical marker to create similar triangles and measure the tree indirectly. Later in the day they come upon a rock formation. They measure the rock formation's shadow and again want to use similar triangles to measure its height indirectly. Kyle wants to use the shadow length they measured earlier for the stick. Jesse says they should measure it again. Who do you think is right?

Jesse is right. The length of a shadow is dependent not only on the height of an object, but on the position of the sun in the sky. To create similar triangles, the shadows of the two objects must be measured at the same time of day.

21. Error Analysis Andy wants to find the distance d across a river. He located points as shown in the figure and then used similar triangles to find that $d = 220.5$ feet. How can you tell without calculating that he must be wrong? Tell what you think he did wrong and correct his error.

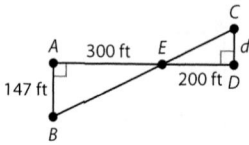

$\overline{AB}$ is the shortest side of right $\triangle ABE$, so corresponding side $\overline{DC}$ of $\triangle DCE$ must be shorter than $\overline{DE}$, that is, $DE < 200$. The triangles are similar, but Andy must have used the wrong proportion. The correct proportion is $\frac{d}{147} = \frac{200}{300}$, so $d = 147\left(\frac{200}{300}\right) = 98$. The distance across the river is 98 ft.

Lesson Performance Task

Around 240 B.C., the Greek astronomer Eratosthenes was residing in Alexandria, Egypt. He believed that the Earth was spherical and conceived of an experiment to measure its circumference. At noon in the town of Syene, the sun was directly overhead. A stick stuck vertically in the ground cast no shadow. At the same moment in Alexandria, 490 miles from Syene, a vertical stick cast a shadow that veered 7.2° from the vertical.

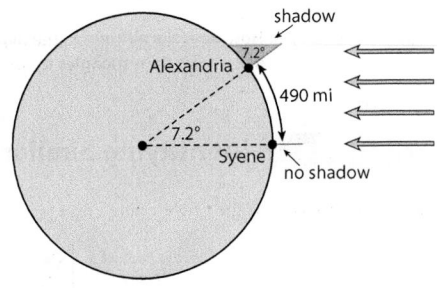

1. Refer to the diagram. Explain why Eratosthenes reasoned that the angle at the center of the Earth that intercepted a 490-mile arc measured 7.2 degrees.

2. Calculate the circumference of the Earth using Eratosthenes's figures. Explain how you got your answer.

3. Calculate the radius of the Earth using Eratosthenes's figures.

4. The accepted circumference of the Earth today is 24,901 miles. Calculate the percent error in Eratosthenes's calculations.

1. The line from the center of the Earth to Syene and the line from the top of the Alexandria stick to the north end of the Alexandria shadow are parallel. By the Alternate Interior Angles Theorem, the angle at the center of the Earth is congruent to the 7.2° angle at Alexandria.

2. In a complete rotation of 360° at the Earth's center, each 7.2° angle will intercept a 490-mile arc. There are $\frac{360}{7.2} = 50$ such 490-mile arcs in the entire circumference. So, by Eratosthenes' figures, the circumference of the Earth measures $50 \times 490 = 24,500$ miles.

3.
$$C = 2\pi r$$
$$24,500 \approx 2(3.14)r$$
$$\frac{24,500}{2(3.14)} \approx r$$
$$3901.3 \approx r$$

The radius of the Earth is about 3901.3 miles

4. $24,901 - 24,500 = 401$ miles; $\frac{401}{24,901} \approx 1.6\%$

© Houghton Mifflin Harcourt Publishing Company

Percent error compares the error in a measurement to the *correct* measurement. So, to find the percent error in Eratosthenes' calculations, students should compare the 401-mile error to the correct circumference, not to the incorrect circumference. The correct ratio is $\frac{401}{24,901}$, not $\frac{401}{24,500}$.

INTEGRATE MATHEMATICAL PRACTICES
Focus on Math Connections

MP.1 The ancient Greeks used several different units of length. One was the *stadion* (plural, *stadia*), which, by one modern estimate, equaled 185.4 meters. How far was Alexandria from Syene, in stadia? (1 mi ≈ 1609 meters) about 4252 stadia

---

EXTENSION ACTIVITY

Give these directions to students:

1. Choose one of the planets of the Solar System other than Earth and conduct research to find its radius or diameter.

2. Calculate the circumference of the planet (use 3.14 for π).

3. Suppose that you placed two sticks in the ground 490 miles apart on your planet. At the moment the Sun was directly over one of the sticks, what angle from the vertical would the shadow of the second stick cast? Explain.

Example: Mars: diameter 4200 mi; circumference: 13,888 mi;

$$\frac{490}{13,888} = \frac{x}{360°}; x = 12.7°$$

Scoring Rubric
2 points: Student correctly solves the problem and explains his/her reasoning.
1 point: Student shows good understanding of the problem but does not fully solve or explain his/her reasoning.
0 points: Student does not demonstrate understanding of the problem.

Using Proportional Relationships **662**

Similarity in Right Triangles

Common Core Math Standards

The student is expected to:

 G-SRT.B.4

Prove theorems about triangles. Also G-SRT.B.5

Mathematical Practices

 MP.8 Patterns

Language Objective

Explain to a partner how to use the Angle/Angle criterion to show similarity in triangles.

ENGAGE

Essential Question: How does the altitude to the hypotenuse of a right triangle help you use similar right triangles to solve problems?

The altitude to the hypotenuse of a right triangle divides the triangle into two smaller triangles that are similar to each other and to the original triangle. You can use the geometric means theorems to find missing measurements using indirect measurement.

PREVIEW: LESSON PERFORMANCE TASK

View the Engage section online. Discuss the photograph, asking students if they can describe what is happening and where. Then preview the Lesson Performance Task.

Name_____ Class_____ Date_____

12.4 Similarity in Right Triangles

Essential Question: How does the altitude to the hypotenuse of a right triangle help you use similar right triangles to solve problems?

Resource Locker

⊘ Explore Identifying Similarity in Right Triangles

Ⓐ Make two copies of the right triangle on a piece of paper and cut them out.

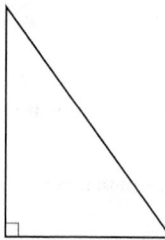

Ⓑ Choose one of the triangles. Fold the paper to find the altitude to the hypotenuse.

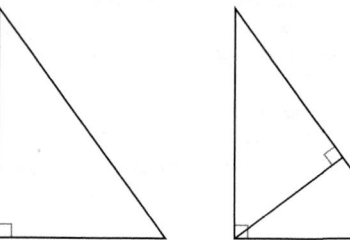

Ⓒ Cut the second triangle along the altitude. Label the triangles as shown.

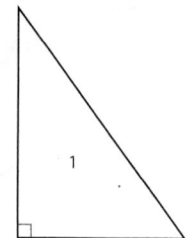
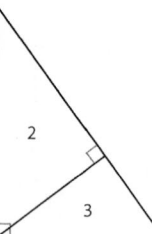

© Houghton Mifflin Harcourt Publishing Company

Module 12   663   Lesson 4

HARDCOVER PAGES 563–572

Turn to these pages to find this lesson in the hardcover student edition.

Ⓓ Place triangle 2 on top of triangle 1. What do you notice about the angles?

The corresponding angles are congruent.

Ⓔ What is true of triangles 1 and 2? How do you know?

They are congruent by the AA Similarity Criterion.

Ⓕ Repeat Steps 1 and 2 for triangles 1 and 3. Does the same relationship hold true for triangles 1 and 3?

Yes; the corresponding angles are congruent, and the triangles are similar by the AA Similarity Criterion.

Reflect

1. How are the hypotenuses of the triangles 2 and 3 related to triangle 1?
The hypotenuses of the smaller triangles are the legs of the original triangle.

2. What is the relationship between triangles 2 and 3? Explain.
They are similar because triangle similarity is transitive.

3. When you draw the altitude to the hypotenuse of a right triangle, what kinds of figures are produced?
Two triangles that are similar to the original triangle and to each other.

4. Suppose you draw △ABC such that ∠B is a right angle and the altitude to the hypotenuse intersects hypotenuse $\overline{AC}$ at point P. Match each triangle to a similar triangle. Explain your reasoning.

A. △ABC   B   △PAB

B. △PBC   C   △CAB

C. △BAP   A   △BPC

A. Angles B and P are corresponding right angles. Angle C corresponds to itself.

B. ∠BPC corresponds to ∠APB and ∠BCP corresponds to ∠ABP.

C. Angles B and P are corresponding right angles. Angle A corresponds to itself.

© Houghton Mifflin Harcourt Publishing Company

Identifying Similarity in Right Triangles

INTEGRATE TECHNOLOGY

Use geometry software to explore drawing a right angle and an altitude to the hypotenuse.

QUESTIONING STRATEGIES

 What kind of angle is formed by the altitude to the hypotenuse? The altitude to the hypotenuse forms a right angle with the hypotenuse.

 What does it mean when you say that two triangles are similar? The triangles have the same shape; that is, corresponding angles are congruent and corresponding sides are proportional.

PROFESSIONAL DEVELOPMENT

COMMON CORE Math Background

In mathematics, the word *mean* describes a relationship between numbers. The *arithmetic mean* of two numbers is the average of the numbers. This is different from the *geometric mean*, which, for positive numbers, is the positive square root of their product. The geometric mean of a and b is the positive number x such that $x = \sqrt{ab}$. In later math courses, students may also study *harmonic means*.

Finding Geometric Means of Pairs of Numbers

Focus on Reasoning

MP.2 Point out that only a positive number can represent the length of a segment in a triangle.

QUESTIONING STRATEGIES

? In a proportion involving a and b, where is the geometric mean between the two numbers? The geometric mean is the denominator of one fraction and the numerator of the other.

⌀ Explain 1 **Finding Geometric Means of Pairs of Numbers**

Consider the proportion $\frac{a}{x} = \frac{x}{b}$ where two of the numbers in the proportion are the same. The number x is the *geometric mean* of a and b. The **geometric mean** of two positive numbers is the positive square root of their product. So the geometric mean of a and b is the positive number x such that $x = \sqrt{ab}$ or $x^2 = ab$.

Example 1 Find the geometric mean x of the numbers.

Ⓐ 4 and 25

Write proportion.	$\frac{4}{x} = \frac{x}{25}$
Multiply both sides by the product of the denominators.	$25x \cdot \frac{4}{x} = 25x \cdot \frac{x}{25}$
Multiply.	$\frac{100x}{x} = \frac{25x^2}{25}$
Simplify.	$100 = x^2$
Take the square root of both sides.	$\sqrt{100} = \sqrt{x^2}$
Simplify.	$10 = x$

Ⓑ 9 and 20

Write proportion.	$\frac{\boxed{9}}{x} = \frac{x}{20}$
Multiply both sides by the product of the denominators.	$20x \cdot \frac{\boxed{9}}{x} = 20x \cdot \frac{x}{20}$
Multiply.	$\frac{\boxed{180}x}{x} = \frac{20x^2}{20}$
Simplify.	$\boxed{180} = x^2$
Take the square root of both sides.	$\sqrt{\boxed{180}} = \sqrt{x^2}$
Simplify.	$\boxed{6}\sqrt{\boxed{5}} = x$

Reflect

5. How can you show that if positive numbers a and b are such that $\frac{a}{x} = \frac{x}{b}$, then $x = \sqrt{ab}$? **Multiply both sides of the proportion by xb, then take the square root of both sides:**

$xb\left(\frac{a}{x}\right) = xb\left(\frac{x}{b}\right); ab = x^2; \sqrt{ab} = \sqrt{x^2}; \sqrt{ab} = x.$

Your Turn

Find the geometric mean of the numbers. If necessary, give the answer in simplest radical form.

6. 6 and 24

$\sqrt{6 \cdot 24} = \sqrt{144} = 12$

7. 5 and 12

$\sqrt{60} = \sqrt{4 \cdot 15} = 2\sqrt{15}$

© Houghton Mifflin Harcourt Publishing Company

COLLABORATIVE LEARNING

Small Group Activity

Have small groups of students work together to research and present to the class other proofs of the Pythagorean Theorem.

Explain 2   Proving the Geometric Means Theorems

In the Explore activity, you discovered a theorem about right triangles and similarity.

The altitude to the hypotenuse of a right triangle forms two triangles that are similar to each other and to the original triangle.

That theorem leads to two additional theorems about right triangles. Both of the theorems involve geometric means.

Geometric Means Theorems		
Theorem	**Example**	**Diagram**
The length of the altitude to the hypotenuse of a right triangle is the geometric mean of the lengths of the segments of the hypotenuse.	$h^2 = xy$ or $h = \sqrt{xy}$	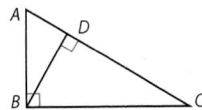
The length of a leg of a right triangle is the geometric mean of the lengths of the hypotenuse and the segment of the hypotenuse adjacent to that leg.	$a^2 = xc$ or $a = \sqrt{xc}$ $b^2 = yc$ or $b = \sqrt{yc}$	

Example 2   Prove the first Geometric Means Theorem.

Given: Right triangle ABC with altitude $\overline{BD}$

Prove: $\dfrac{CD}{BD} = \dfrac{BD}{AD}$

Statements	Reasons
1. $\triangle ABC$ with altitude $\overline{BD}$	1. Given
2. $\triangle CBD \sim \triangle BAD$	2. The altitude to the hypotenuse of a right triangle forms two triangles that are similar to the original triangle and to each other.
3. $\dfrac{CD}{BD} = \dfrac{BD}{AD}$	3. Corresponding sides of similar triangles are proportional.

Reflect

8.   **Discussion**   How can you prove the second Geometric Means Theorem?
Use the triangle shown in the Example. Show that $\triangle ABC \sim \triangle ADB$ because the altitude

to the hypotenuse of a right triangle forms two triangles that are similar to the original

triangle and to each other. Then show that $\dfrac{AD}{AB} = \dfrac{AB}{AC}$ because corresponding sides of similar

triangles are proportional. Then prove that $\dfrac{DC}{BC} = \dfrac{BC}{AC}$ in the same way.

EXPLAIN 2

Proving the Geometric Means Theorems

INTEGRATE MATHEMATICAL PRACTICES

Focus on Communication

MP.3 Make sure that students can identify the right angle and the hypotenuse, as well as the altitude to the hypotenuse.

QUESTIONING STRATEGIES

? What is the relationship between the altitude of a hypotenuse and the segments on the hypotenuse? It is the geometric mean of the lengths of the segments.

? How could you express this relationship as a proportion? The ratio of one segment to the altitude is equal to the ratio of the altitude to the other segment.

DIFFERENTIATE INSTRUCTION

Modeling

Have students cut a 15–20–25-unit right triangle out of a sheet of graph paper. Ask them to draw the altitude to the hypotenuse, forming a 12–16–20-unit right triangle and a 9–12–15-unit right triangle. Then have students use the side lengths in these triangles to verify the relationships in this lesson.

EXPLAIN 3

Using the Geometric Means Theorems

QUESTIONING STRATEGIES

 If you know the lengths of the segments that the altitude divides the hypotenuse into, how can you find the length of the altitude? You can write a proportion with the lengths of the segments and length of the hypotenuse and solve for the unknown.

AVOID COMMON ERRORS

Some students may find it puzzling that a leg in one triangle can become the hypotenuse in a related triangle. Have them use colored pencils to distinguish the various triangles, marking the hypotenuse in each with a double or darker line.

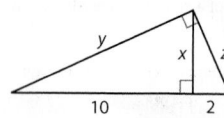

You can use the Geometric Means Theorems to find unknown segment lengths in a right triangle.

Example 3 Find the indicated value.

(A) x

Write proportion.	$\frac{2}{x} = \frac{x}{10}$
Multiply both sides by the product of the denominators.	$10x \cdot \frac{2}{x} = 10x \cdot \frac{x}{10}$
Multiply.	$\frac{20x}{x} = \frac{10x^2}{10}$
Simplify.	$20 = x^2$
Take the square root of both sides.	$\sqrt{20} = \sqrt{x^2}$
Simplify.	$2\sqrt{5} = x$

(B) y

Write proportion.	$\frac{10}{y} = \frac{y}{12}$
Multiply both sides by the product of the denominators.	$12y\,\frac{10}{y} = 12y\,\frac{y}{12}$
Multiply.	$\frac{120y}{y} = \frac{12y^2}{12}$
Simplify.	$\boxed{120} = \boxed{y^2}$
Take the square root of both sides.	$\sqrt{\boxed{120}} = \sqrt{\boxed{y^2}}$
Simplify.	$\boxed{2\sqrt{30}} = y$

Reflect

9. **Discussion** How can you check your answers?
   Possible answer: Use the Pythagorean Theorem.

Your Turn

10. Find x.

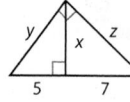

$\frac{5}{x} = \frac{x}{7}$; $7x\left(\frac{5}{x}\right) = 7x\left(\frac{x}{7}\right)$; $35 = x^2$; $\sqrt{35} = x$

Module 12   **667**   Lesson 4

© Houghton Mifflin Harcourt Publishing Company

LANGUAGE SUPPORT **EL**

Connect Vocabulary

Differentiate the *geometric mean* from previous uses of *mean* such as the *arithmetic mean*, in which we add a set of numbers and divide by the number of values. The *geometric mean* is *the nth root of the product of* n *numbers*. That means, we multiply the set of numbers, then take the *n*th root, where *n* is the number of values that were multiplied.

Explain 4 · Proving the Pythagorean Theorem using Similarity

You have used the Pythagorean Theorem in earlier courses as well as in this one. There are many, many proofs of the Pythagorean Theorem. You will prove it now using similar right triangles.

> ### The Pythagorean Theorem
> In a right triangle, the square of the sum of the lengths of the legs is equal to the square of the length of the hypotenuse.

Example 4 Complete the proof of the Pythagorean Theorem.

Given: Right $\triangle ABC$

Prove: $a^2 + b^2 = c^2$

Part 1

Draw the altitude to the hypotenuse.
Label the point of intersection X.

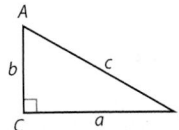

$\angle BXC \cong \angle BCA$ because __all right angles are congruent__.

$\angle B \cong \angle B$ by __the Reflexive Property of Congruence__.

So, $\triangle BXC \sim \triangle BCA$ by __the AA Similarity Criterion__.

$\angle AXC \cong \angle ACB$ because __all right angles are congruent__.

$\angle A \cong \angle A$ by __the Reflexive Property of Congruence__.

So, $\triangle AXC \sim \triangle ACB$ by __the AA Similarity Criterion__.

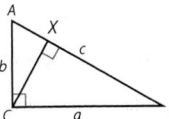

Part 2

Let the lengths of the segments of the hypotenuse be d and e, as shown in the figure.

Use the fact that corresponding sides of similar triangles are proportional to write two proportions.

Proportion 1: $\triangle BXC \sim \triangle BCA$, so $\dfrac{a}{c} = \dfrac{\boxed{e}}{a}$.

Proportion 2: $\triangle AXC \sim \triangle ACB$, so $\dfrac{b}{c} = \dfrac{\boxed{d}}{b}$.

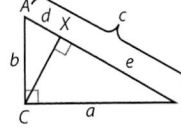

© Houghton Mifflin Harcourt Publishing Company

EXPLAIN 4

Proving the Pythagorean Theorem using Similarity

INTEGRATE MATHEMATICAL PRACTICES
Focus on Math Connections

MP.1 The Pythagorean Theorem was known in many ancient civilizations, including those of Egypt, India, and China. The oldest known axiomatic proof of the theorem, however, dates to Euclid's *Elements* (circa 300 BCE). Since then, hundreds of proofs have been given, including proofs that rely on area, proofs that use calculus, and the proof that is given in this lesson, which is based on similar triangles.

QUESTIONING STRATEGIES

To which triangles does the Pythagorean Theorem apply? Why is it useful? To right triangles only; it allows you to relate the lengths of the sides of right triangles.

Part 3

Now perform some algebra to complete the proof as follows.

Multiply both sides of Proportion1 by ac. Write the resulting equation. $a^2 = ce$

Multiply both sides of Proportion12 by bc. Write the resulting equation. $b^2 = cd$

Adding the two resulting equations give this: $a^2 + b^2 = ce + cd$

Factor the right side of the equation: $a^2 + b^2 = c(e + d)$

Finally, use the fact that $e + d =$ c by the Segment Addition Postulate to rewrite the equation as $a^2 + b^2 = c^2$.

Reflect

11. **Error Analysis** A student used the figure in Part 2 of the example, and wrote the following incorrect proof of the Pythagorean Theorem. Critique the student's proof. $\triangle BXC \sim \triangle BCA$ and $\triangle BCA \sim \triangle CXA$, so $\triangle BXC \sim \triangle CXA$ by transitivity of similarity. Let $CX = f$. Since corresponding sides of similar triangles are proportional, $\frac{e}{f} = \frac{f}{d}$ and $f^2 = ed$. Because $\triangle BXC \sim \triangle CXA$ and they are right triangles, $a^2 = e^2 + f^2$ and $b^2 = f^2 + d^2$.

Add the equations.	$a^2 + b^2 = e^2 + 2f^2 + d^2$
Substitute.	$= e^2 + 2ed + d^2$
Factor.	$= (e + d)^2$
Segment Addition Postulate	$= c^2$

The proof is incorrect because the student assumes the result that is to be proved. The student assumes that the Pythagorean Theorem is true in order to write that $a^2 = e^2 + f^2$ and $b^2 = f^2 + d^2$.

12. How would you explain to a friend how to find the geometric mean of two numbers?
Possible answers: Write a proportion and multiply both sides by the product of the

denominators, then simplify and take the square root of both sides; multiply the two

numbers and then take the square root.

13. $\triangle XYZ$ is an isosceles right triangle and the right angle is $\angle Y$. Suppose the altitude to hypotenuse $\overline{XZ}$ intersects $\overline{XZ}$ at point P. Describe the relationships among triangles $\triangle XYZ$, $\triangle YPZ$ and $\triangle XPY$.
Possible answer: All three triangles are similar. In addition, $\triangle YPZ \cong \triangle XPY$.

14. Can two different pairs of numbers have the same geometric mean? If so, give an example. If not, explain why not.
Yes; possible answer: the geometric mean of 4 and 16 is 8, and the geometric mean of

2 and 32 is also 8.

15. Essential Question Check-In How is the altitude to the hypotenuse of a right triangle related to the segments of the hypotenuse it creates?
The length of the altitude is the geometric mean of the lengths of the segments of the

hypotenuse.

ELABORATE

QUESTIONING STRATEGIES

? What is the relationship between the original triangle and the two smaller triangles formed by the altitude to the hypotenuse? All three triangles are similar to one another.

? How can you identify the hypotenuse in a right triangle? It is opposite the right angle, and it is the longest side.

SUMMARIZE THE LESSON

? How are geometric means related to the Pythagorean Theorem? Geometric means can be used to prove the Pythagorean Theorem.

EVALUATE

ASSIGNMENT GUIDE

Concepts and Skills	Practice
Explore Identifying Similarity in Right Triangles	Exercises 1–3
Example 1 Finding Geometric Means of Pairs of Numbers	Exercises 4–9
Example 2 Proving the Geometric Means Theorems	Exercises 13–18
Example 3 Using the Geometric Means Theorems	Exercises 10–12
Example 4 Proving the Pythagorean Theorem using Similarity	Exercise 22

INTEGRATE MATHEMATICAL PRACTICES

Focus on Modeling

MP.4 Have students draw and label a right triangle with the altitude drawn to the hypotenuse. Have them identify three similar triangles. Ask them to write three different proportions involving a geometric mean.

• Online Homework
• Hints and Help
• Extra Practice

⭐ Evaluate: Homework and Practice

Write a similarity statement comparing the three triangles to each diagram.

1.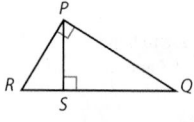

$\triangle PQR \sim \triangle SPR \sim \triangle SQP$

2.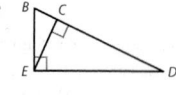

$\triangle BDE \sim \triangle EDC \sim \triangle BEC$

3.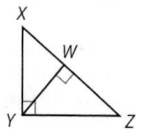

$\triangle XYZ \sim \triangle XWY \sim \triangle YWZ$

Find the geometric mean x of each pair of numbers. If necessary, give the answer in simplest radical form.

4. 5 and 20

$\dfrac{5}{x} = \dfrac{x}{20}; x^2 = 100; x = 10$

5. 3 and 12

$\dfrac{3}{x} = \dfrac{x}{12}; x^2 = 36; x = 6$

6. 8 and 13

$\dfrac{8}{x} = \dfrac{x}{13}; x^2 = 104; x = 2\sqrt{26}$

7. 3.5 and 20

$\dfrac{3.5}{x} = \dfrac{x}{20}; x^2 = 70; x = \sqrt{70}$

8. 1.5 and 84

$\dfrac{1.5}{x} = \dfrac{x}{84}; x^2 = 126; x = 3\sqrt{14}$

9. $\dfrac{2}{3}$ and $\dfrac{27}{40}$

$\dfrac{\frac{2}{3}}{x} = \dfrac{x}{\frac{27}{40}}; x^2 = \dfrac{9}{20}; x = \dfrac{3\sqrt{5}}{10}$

Find x, y, and z.

10.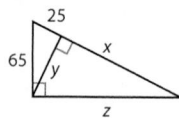

$y = \sqrt{65^2 - 25^2} = \sqrt{3600} = 60$

$\dfrac{25}{y} = \dfrac{y}{x}; \dfrac{25}{60} = \dfrac{60}{x}; 25x = 3600; x = 144$

$\dfrac{25 + x}{z} = \dfrac{z}{x}; \dfrac{169}{z} = \dfrac{z}{144}; z^2 = 24{,}366;$
$z = \sqrt{24{,}336} = 156$

11.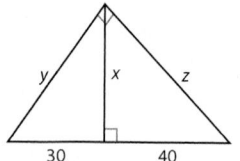

$\dfrac{30}{x} = \dfrac{x}{40}; x^2 = 1200; x = 20\sqrt{3}$

$\dfrac{70}{y} = \dfrac{y}{30}; y^2 = 2100; y = 10\sqrt{21}$

$\dfrac{70}{z} = \dfrac{z}{40}; z^2 = 2800; z = 20\sqrt{7}$

Exercise	Depth of Knowledge (D.O.K.)	COMMON CORE Mathematical Practices
1–9	**2** Skills/Concepts	**MP.2** Reasoning
10–12	**2** Skills/Concepts	**MP.4** Modeling
13–18	**2** Skills/Concepts	**MP.1** Problem Solving
19–22	**2** Skills/Concepts	**MP.5** Using Tools
23	**3** Strategic Thinking H.O.T.	**MP.1** Problem Solving
24	**3** Strategic Thinking H.O.T.	**MP.3** Logic

12.

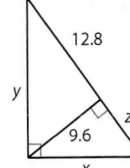

12.8
y
9.6
z
x

$$y^2 = (12.8)^2 + (9.6)^2 = 256; y = \sqrt{256} = 16$$

$$\frac{12.8}{9.6} = \frac{9.6}{z}; 12.8z = 92.16; z = 7.2$$

$$\frac{12.8 + 7.2}{x} = \frac{x}{7.2}; x^2 = 144; x = 12$$

Use the diagram to complete each equation.

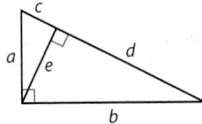

c
a
e
d
b

13. $\dfrac{c}{e} = \dfrac{\boxed{e}}{d}$

14. $\dfrac{c}{a} = \dfrac{a}{\boxed{c+d}}$

15. $\dfrac{c+d}{b} = \dfrac{b}{\boxed{d}}$

16. $\dfrac{d}{\boxed{e}} = \dfrac{e}{c}$

17. $c(c+d) = \boxed{a}^2$

18. $\boxed{e}^2 = cd$

Find the length of the altitude to the hypotenuse under the given conditions.

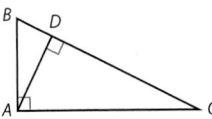

B
D
A
C

19. $BC = 5$
$AC = 4$

$AB = 3; \dfrac{AD}{3} = \dfrac{4}{5};$
$AD = 2.4$

20. $BC = 17$
$AC = 15$

$AB = 8; \dfrac{AD}{8} = \dfrac{15}{17};$
$AD \approx \dfrac{120}{17} \approx 7.06$

21. $BC = 13$
$AC = 12$

$AB = 5; \dfrac{AD}{5} = \dfrac{12}{13};$
$AD = \dfrac{60}{13} \approx 4.62$

AVOID COMMON ERRORS

Some students may have difficulty visualizing the corresponding angles in the overlapping triangles. Suggest that they redraw the diagram to separate the three triangles.

Ask students to demonstrate, with examples and reasons, that the geometric mean of two positive numbers is always smaller than their arithmetic mean.

22. **Communicate Mathematical Ideas** The area of a rectangle with a length of ℓ and a width of w has the same area as a square. Show that the side length of the square is the geometric mean of the length and width of the rectangle.

Area of the square $= s^2 =$ Area of rectangle $= \ell w; s^2 = \ell w; s = \sqrt{\ell w}$

H.O.T. Focus on Higher Order Thinking

23. **Algebra** An 8-inch-long altitude of a right triangle divides the hypotenuse into two segments. One segment is 4 times as long as the other. What are the lengths of the segments of the hypotenuse?

x in. = shorter segment; $4x$ in. = longer segment; The length of the hypotenuse is the geometric mean of these lengths, so $\frac{x}{8} = \frac{8}{4x}$. Then $4x^2 = 64$, $x^2 = 16$, and $x = 4$.

The segments of the hypotenuse measure 4 inches and 16 inches.

24. **Error Analysis** Cecile and Amelia both found a value for EF in $\triangle DEF$. Both students work are shown. Which student's solution is correct? What mistake did the other student make?

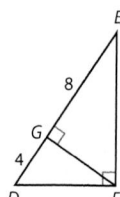

Cecile: $\frac{12}{EF} = \frac{EF}{8}$

So $EF^2 = 12(8) = 96$.

Then $EF = \sqrt{96} = 4\sqrt{6}$.

Amelia: $\frac{8}{EF} = \frac{EF}{4}$

So $EF^2 = 8(4) = 32$.

Then $EF = \sqrt{32} = 4\sqrt{2}$.

Cecile's solution is correct. Amelia wrote the wrong proportion.

Lesson Performance Task

In the example at the beginning of the lesson, a $100 investment grew for one year at the rate of 50%, to $150, then fell for one year at the rate of 50%, to $75. The arithmetic mean of +50% and −50%, which is 0%, was not a good predictor of the change, for it predicted the investment would still be worth $100 after two years, not $75.

1. Find the geometric mean of $1 + 50\%$ and $1 - 50\%$. (Each 1 represents the fact that at the beginning of each year, an investment is worth 100% of itself.) Round to the nearest thousandth.

2. It is the geometric mean, not the arithmetic mean, that tells you what the interest rate would have had to have been over an entire investment period to achieve the end result. You can use your answer to Exercise 1 to check this claim. Find the value of a $100 investment after it increased or decreased at the rate you found in Exercise 1 for two years. Show your work.

3. Copy the right triangle shown here. Write the terms "Year 1 Rate", "Year 2 Rate", and "Average Rate" to show geometrically how the three investment rates relate to each other.

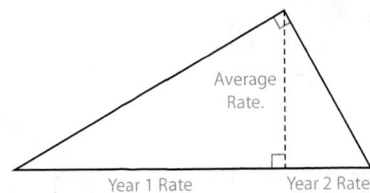

Average Rate.

Year 1 Rate   Year 2 Rate

4. The geometric mean of n numbers is the nth root of the product of the numbers. Find what the interest rate would have had to have been over 4 years to achieve the result of a $100 investment that grew 20% in Year 1 and 30% in Year 2, then lost 20% in Year 3 and 30% in Year 4. Show your work. Round your answer to the nearest tenth of a percent.

1. $\sqrt{(1 + .5)(1 - .5)} = \sqrt{(1.5)(.5)}$

   $= \sqrt{.75}$

   $= .866$

2. After 1 year: $100 \times 0.866 = 86.6$

   After 2 years: $86.6 \times 0.866 = 74.9956$, or $75

3. See diagram.

4. $\sqrt[4]{(1.2)(1.3)(0.8)(0.7)} = \sqrt[4]{0.8736}$

   ≈ 0.967

   Since 1 represents 0% change, 0.967 represents $(1 - 0.967) = 0.033$,

   or a 3.3% average loss per year.

EXTENSION ACTIVITY

The Pythagorean Theorem is only one of many contributions the Greek mathematician and philosopher Pythagoras made to mathematics. He was the first to identify three means for weighting numbers: the arithmetic mean (or average), the geometric mean, and the harmonic mean. Have students research and explain the harmonic mean. Then they should show how to find all three Pythagorean means for the numbers 4 and 9. arithmetic: 6.5; geometric: 6; harmonic: $\frac{72}{13} \approx 5.54$

INTEGRATE MATHEMATICAL PRACTICES

MP.8 Focus on Patterns

- Find the geometric mean of 1, 1, 2, 4, and 4. 2

- Write an expression representing the geometric mean of the numbers a, b, c, d, and e. $\sqrt[5]{a \cdot b \cdot c \cdot d \cdot e}$ or $\sqrt[5]{abcde}$

AVOID COMMON ERRORS

In Question 4 of the Lesson Performance Task, some students may calculate the geometric mean and then assume that it represents the interest rate they are looking for. Remind students that a geometric mean of 1 represents 0% change, and they must subtract the mean they found from 1 to find the average percent change per year.

Scoring Rubric

2 points: Student correctly solves the problem and explains his/her reasoning.

1 point: Student shows good understanding of the problem but does not fully solve or explain his/her reasoning.

0 points: Student does not demonstrate understanding of the problem.

Similarity in Right Triangles   **674**

Study Guide Review

ASSESSMENT AND INTERVENTION

Personal Math Trainer

Assign or customize module reviews.

MODULE PERFORMANCE TASK

COMMON CORE

Mathematical Practices: MP.1, MP.2, MP.4, MP.6
G-SRT.B.5, G-MG.A.1

SUPPORTING STUDENT REASONING

Students should begin this problem by focusing on what information they will need. Here are some issues they might bring up.

- **The GPS coordinates of the vertices of the Bermuda Triangle:** Students can research these. The GPS coordinates for Miami are (25.789106, –80.226529), for San Juan are (18.4663188, –66.1057427), and for Hamilton are (32.294887, –64.781380).

- **The best way to work with the GPS coordinates:** Students may want to express the coordinates as (latitude, longitude) so they can use the distance formula to find the lengths of the sides of the triangle (see Module 1 Performance Task). This gives the following coordinates: Miami: (–80.226529, 25.789106); San Juan: (–66.1057427, 18.4663188); Hamilton: (–64.781380, 32.294887)

- **How to find the area from the lengths of the sides:** Students can experiment with ways to find the area or you can make a suggestion.

Using Similar Triangles

Essential Question: How can you use similar triangles to solve real-world problems?

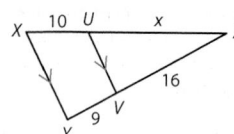

Key Vocabulary
indirect measurement
  (medición indirecta)
geometric mean *(media geométrica)*

KEY EXAMPLE (Lesson 12.1)

Find the missing length x.

$\dfrac{ZU}{UX} = \dfrac{ZV}{VY}$ Write a proportion.

$\dfrac{x}{10} = \dfrac{16}{9}$ Substitute.

$x = \left(\dfrac{16}{9}\right)(10)$ Multiply both sides by 10.

$x \approx 17.8$ Simplify.

KEY EXAMPLE (Lesson 12.2)

Given the directed line segment from A to B, construct the point P that divides the segment in the ratio 2 to 3 from A to B.

Use a straightedge to draw $\overrightarrow{AC}$.

Place a compass on point A and draw an arc through $\overrightarrow{AC}$. Label the intersection D. Continue this for intersections D through H.

Use a straightedge to connect points B and H.

Construct angles congruent to $\angle AHB$ with points D through G.

$\overline{AB}$ is partitioned into five equal parts. Label point P at the point that divides the segment in the ratio 2 to 3 from A to B.

KEY EXAMPLE (Lesson 12.3)

A 5.8-foot-tall man is standing next to a basketball hoop that casts an 11.2-foot shadow. The man's shadow is 6.5 feet long. How tall is the basketball hoop?

Let x be the height of the basketball hoop.

$\dfrac{x}{11.2} = \dfrac{5.8}{6.5}$ Write a proportion.

$x = \left(\dfrac{5.8}{6.5}\right)(11.2)$ Multiply both sides by 11.2.

$x \approx 10$

SCAFFOLDING SUPPORT

- For this region of the globe, assume that each unit of latitude or longitude is equal to 100 km.

- One way to find the area is to enclose the triangle shown in the figure in a rectangle then find the area of the rectangle, and subtract the areas in the rectangle that are outside of the triangle.

- Students can also use the area formula for a triangle with side lengths a, b and c given by $A = \sqrt{s(s-a)(s-b)(s-c)}$, where $s = \dfrac{a+b+c}{2}$.

EXERCISES

Find the missing lengths. *(Lesson 12.1)*

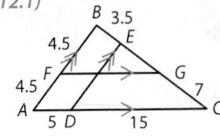

1. $BG = \underline{\quad 7 \quad}$

2. $CE = \underline{\quad 10\frac{1}{2} \quad}$

Given the directed line segment from A to B, construct the point P that divides the segment in the ratio 3 to 1 from A to B. *(Lesson 12.2)*

3.

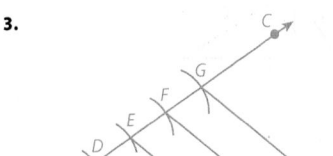

Find the unknown length. *(Lesson 12.3)*

4. A 5.9-foot-tall-man stands near a 12-foot statue. The man places a mirror on the ground a certain distance from the base of the statue, and then stands another 7 feet from the mirror to see the top of the statue in it. How far is the mirror from the base of the statue?

$\underline{\quad 14.2 \text{ feet} \quad}$

5. A 45-foot flagpole casts a 22-foot shadow. At the same time of day, a woman casts a 2.7-foot shadow. How tall is the woman?

$\underline{\quad 5.5 \text{ feet} \quad}$

Find the lengths. *(Lesson 12.4)*

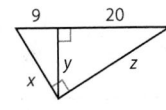

6. $x = \underline{\quad 16.2 \quad}$

7. $y = \underline{\quad 13.4 \quad}$

8. $z = \underline{\quad 24.1 \quad}$

MODULE PERFORMANCE TASK

How Large Is the Bermuda Triangle?

The boundaries of the Bermuda Triangle are not well defined, but the region is often represented as a triangle with vertices at Miami, Florida; San Juan, Puerto Rico; and Hamilton, Bermuda. The distance between Miami and San Juan is about 1,034 miles. What is the approximate area of this region? One tool that you may find helpful in solving this problem is the similar triangle shown here with angle measures labeled.

Use your own paper to complete the task. Be sure to record all your data and assumptions. Then use graphs, diagrams, words, or numbers to explain how you reached your conclusion.

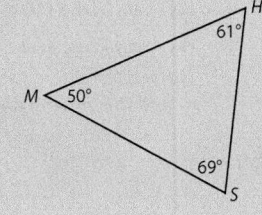

DISCUSSION OPPORTUNITIES

- If students choose to add a height of the triangle to the drawing they are provided, and then use the familiar area of a triangle formula, how does this affect the accuracy of their calculations?

- How does the fact that the Bermuda Triangle is not actually a triangle in the plane, but a triangle on a sphere, affect the accuracy of the calculations? Is the actual area more or less than the one calculated?

SAMPLE SOLUTION

Methodology:

Find the GPS coordinates of the three locations and write them as $(x, y) = (\text{latitude}, \text{longitude})$. Then use the distance formula, $d = \sqrt{(x_2 - x_1)^2 + (y_2 - y_1)^2}$, to find the lengths of the three sides, a, b, and c, of the triangle. To find the distances, multiply the results by 100 km. Finally, use the area formula for a triangle,

$A = \sqrt{s(s-a)(s-b)(s-c)}$ where $s = \dfrac{a+b+c}{2}$,

to determine the area.

Coordinates:

Miami: $(-80.226529, 25.789106)$;

San Juan: $(-66.1057427, 18.4663188)$;

Hamilton: $(-64.781380, 32.294887)$

Using the distance formula and multiplying the results by 100 km gives the following distances.

Miami to San Juan: 1590 km

San Juan to Hamilton: 1389 km

Hamilton to Miami: 1676 km

Calculate s, $s - a$, $s - b$, and $s - c$.

$s = \dfrac{1590 + 1389 + 1676}{2} = 2327.5$

$s - a = 2327.5 - 1590 = 737.5$

$s - b = 2327.5 - 1389 = 938.5$

$s - c = 2327.5 - 1676 = 651.5$

Find the area:

$A = \sqrt{s(s-a)(s-b)(s-c)}$

$= \sqrt{2327.5(737.5)(938.5)(651.5)}$

$\approx 1,024,472 \text{ km}^2$

Ready to Go On?

ASSESS MASTERY

Use the assessment on this page to determine if students have mastered the concepts and standards covered in this module.

ASSESSMENT AND INTERVENTION

Access Ready to Go On? assessment online, and receive instant scoring, feedback, and customized intervention or enrichment.

ADDITIONAL RESOURCES

Response to Intervention Resources

- Reteach Worksheets

Differentiated Instruction Resources

- Reading Strategies **EL**
- Success for English Learners **EL**
- Challenge Worksheets

Assessment Resources

- Leveled Module Quizzes

(Ready) to Go On?

12.1–12.4 Using Similar Triangles

- Online Homework
- Hints and Help
- Extra Practice

Find the missing lengths. *(Lesson 12.1)*

1.

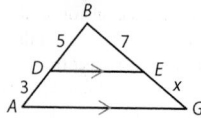

$x = 4.2$

2.

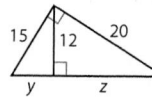

$z = 16 ; y = 9$

Given the directed line segment from *A* to *B*, construct the point *P* that divides the segment in the given ratio from *A* to *B*. *(Lesson 12.2)*

3. 3 to 4

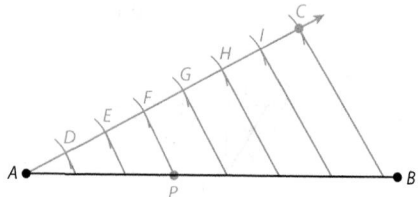

Find the missing height. *(Lesson 12.3)*

4. The height of a street light is 25 feet. It casts a 12-foot shadow. At the same time, a man standing next to the street light casts a 3-foot shadow. How tall is the man?

6.25 feet

ESSENTIAL QUESTION

5. How can you use similar triangles to find the missing parts of a triangle?

You can use proportions or corresponding parts of a triangle to find the missing parts of a triangle that is similar to another.

© Houghton Mifflin Harcourt Publishing Company

Module 12   677   Study Guide Review

COMMON CORE **Common Core Standards**

Lesson	Items	Content Standards	Mathematical Practices
12.1, 12.3	1	G-SRT.B.4, G-SRT.B.5, G-CO.C.10	MP.7
12.1, 12.3, 12.4	2	G-SRT.B.4, G-SRT.B.5, G-CO.C.10	MP.7
12.2	3	G-CO.D.12, G-GPE.B.6	MP.5
12.1, 12.3, 12.4	4	G-SRT.B.4, G-SRT.B.5, G-CO.C.10	MP.4

MODULE 12
MIXED REVIEW

Assessment Readiness

SELECTED RESPONSE

1. $\triangle XYZ$ is given by the points $X(-1, -1)$, $Y(3, 5)$, and $Z(5, 1)$. Consider each of the points below. Is each point a vertex of the image under the transformation

$$(x, y) \rightarrow (x + 3, y - 2) \rightarrow \left(\tfrac{1}{2}x, y\right) \rightarrow (y, -x)?$$

Select Yes or No for A–C.

A. $X'''(-3, -1)$ ● Yes   ○ No
B. $Y'''(3, -3)$ ● Yes   ○ No
C. $Z'''(-1, -4)$ ● Yes   ○ No

2. Which of the following statements are true about the triangle at the right? Choose True or False for each statement.

A. The value of x is 15. ○ True   ● False
B. The value of y is 12. ○ True   ● False
C. The value of y is 16. ○ True   ● False

3. $\triangle ABC$ is given by the points $A(-1, 2)$, $B(2, 5)$, and $C(4, -1)$. What is the point $\left(\tfrac{1}{2}, \tfrac{5}{2}\right)$? Explain what this means.

Possible Answer: The orthocenter; When the altitude is drawn from each of the three vertices of the triangle, the point they intersect at is $\left(\tfrac{1}{2}, \tfrac{5}{2}\right)$.

4. Given the directed segment from A to B, construct the point P that divides the segment in the ratio 1 to 5 from A to B. Explain your process and how it relates to similar triangles.

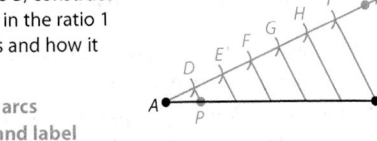

Draw $\overrightarrow{AC}$. Use a compass to draw 6 arcs (equidistant spacing) through $\overrightarrow{AC}$ and label each intersection D through I. Connect the points B and I. Construct angles congruent to $\angle AIB$ for the remaining intersections. $\overline{AB}$ is partitioned into 6 equal parts. Label the point P that divides the segment in the ratio 1 to 5 from A to B. Each triangle created is a similar triangle to $\triangle AIB$.

MIXED REVIEW
Assessment Readiness

ASSESSMENT AND INTERVENTION

Personal Math Trainer

Assign ready-made or customized practice tests to prepare students for high-stakes tests.

ADDITIONAL RESOURCES

Assessment Resources

• Leveled Module Quizzes: Modified, B

AVOID COMMON ERRORS

Item 1   Some students will stop working on this problem too early, not completing all three transformations. Encourage students to double-check the problem to make sure they have completely finished before making their answer choices.

COMMON CORE **Common Core Standards**

Lesson	Items	Content Standards	Mathematical Practices
3.1	1*	G-SRT.B.5, G-CO.A.5	MP.6
12.4	2	G-SRT.C.8	MP.6
8.3	3*	G-CO.D.12, G-CO.C.10, G-GPE.B.5	MP.6
12.2	4	G-GPE.B.6, G-CO.D.12	MP.5

* Item integrates mixed review concepts from previous modules or a previous course.

ASSESSMENT AND INTERVENTION

Assign ready-made or customized practice tests to prepare students for high-stakes tests.

ADDITIONAL RESOURCES

Assessment Resources

- Leveled Unit Tests: Modified, A, B, C
- Performance Assessment

UNIT 4 MIXED REVIEW
Assessment Readiness

- Online Homework
- Hints and Help
- Extra Practice

1. Determine whether the statements are true.
   Select True or False for each statement.
   - **A.** Dilations preserve angle measure. ● True ○ False
   - **B.** Dilations preserve distance. ○ True ● False
   - **C.** Dilations preserve collinearity. ● True ○ False
   - **D.** Dilations preserve orientation. ● True ○ False

2. Was the given transformation used to map $ABCD$ to $QRST$?
   Select Yes or No for each statement.
   - **A.** Reflection across the y-axis ○ Yes ● No
   - **B.** Reflection across the x-axis ● Yes ○ No
   - **C.** Dilation ● Yes ○ No
   - **D.** Translation ● Yes ○ No

3. The vertices of quadrilateral $JKLM$ are $J(-2, 0)$, $K(-1, 2)$, $L(1, 3)$, and $M(0, 1)$. Can you use slopes and/or the distance formula to prove each statement?
   Select Yes or No for A–C.
   - **A.** Quadrilateral $JKLM$ is a parallelogram. ● Yes ○ No
   - **B.** Quadrilateral $JKLM$ is a rhombus. ● Yes ○ No
   - **C.** Quadrilateral $JKLM$ is a rectangle. ○ Yes ● No

4. Will the transformation produce similar figures?
   Select Yes or No for each statement.
   - **A.** $(x, y) \rightarrow (x - 5, y + 5) \rightarrow (-x, -y) \rightarrow (3x, 3y)$ ● Yes ○ No
   - **B.** $(x, y) \rightarrow (3x, y + 5) \rightarrow (x, 3y) \rightarrow (x - 1, y - 1)$ ● Yes ○ No
   - **C.** $(x, y) \rightarrow (x, y + 5) \rightarrow (2x, y) \rightarrow (x + 5, y)$ ○ Yes ● No

5. Is ABC similar to DEF? Select Yes or No for each statement.
   - **A.** $A(-1, -3)$, $B(1, 3)$, $C(3, -5)$
     $D(2, -6)$, $E(3, 0)$, $F(6, -8)$ ○ Yes ● No
   - **B.** $A(-1, -3)$, $B(1, 3)$, $C(3, -5)$
     $D(-5, -1)$, $E(-4, 2)$, $F(-3, -2)$ ● Yes ○ No
   - **C.** $A(-1, -3)$, $B(1, 3)$, $C(3, -5)$
     $D(-2, -2)$, $E(2, 4)$, $F(2, -4)$ ○ Yes ● No

Common Core Standards

Items	Content Standards	Mathematical Practices
1	G-SRT.A.1	MP.2, MP.7
2*	G-SRT.A.1	MP.2, MP.7
3	G-SRT.B.5	MP.5
4*	G-SRT.A.2, G-CO.A.2	MP.2, MP.7
5	G-SRT.A.2, G-CO.A.2	MP.2, MP.7

* Item integrates mixed review concepts from previous modules or a previous course.

6. Are the triangles similar? Select Yes or No for each pair of figures.

A. ● Yes ○ No

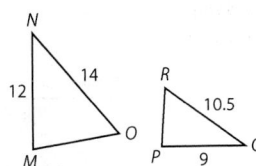

B. ● Yes ○ No

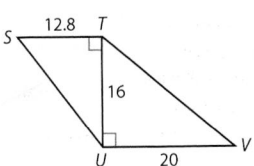

C. ○ Yes ● No

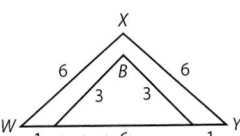

7. Find the missing side lengths PQ, PR, and TU.

Using AA Similarity, the triangles are similar.

$\dfrac{PQ}{50} = \dfrac{45}{30}$ $(PQ)^2 + (QR)^2 = (PR)^2$

$PQ = \dfrac{45}{30} \cdot 50$ $(75)^2 + (50)^2 = (PR)^2$

$PQ = 75$ $25\sqrt{13} = PR$

$(ST)^2 + (SU)^2 = (TU)^2$

$(45)^2 + (30)^2 = (TU)^2$

$5\sqrt{117} = TU$

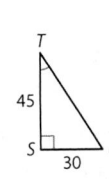

AVOID COMMON ERRORS

Item 6   Some students will have trouble deciding which sides correspond on the triangles, especially when the triangles have different orientations. Remind students that the smallest side on one shape will always correspond to the smallest side on the other shape. The same goes for the largest side.

PERFORMANCE TASKS

There are three different levels of performance tasks:

*Novice: These are short word problems that require students to apply the math they have learned in straightforward, real-world situations.

**Apprentice: These are more involved problems that guide students step-by-step through more complex tasks. These exercises include more complicated reasoning, writing, and open ended elements.

***Expert: These are open-ended, nonroutine problems that, instead of stepping the students through, ask them to choose their own methods for solving and justify their answers and reasoning.

COMMON CORE **Common Core Standards**

Items	Content Standards	Mathematical Practices
6	G-SRT.B.4, G-SRT.B.5	MP.5
7	G-SRT.A.3, G-SRT.B.5	MP.6

* Item integrates mixed review concepts from previous modules or a previous course.

SCORING GUIDES

Item 8 (2 points) Award the student 1 point for the correct distance of 4.5 miles, and 1 point for correctly naming the Triangle Proportionality Theorem.

Item 9 (6 points)

1 point for finding each coordinate point, 3 in all

1 point for correctly graphing each coordinate point, 3 in all

Item 10 (6 points)

2 points for finding AB

1 point for recognizing similar triangles

2 points for the correct distance

1 point for explaining the ball will hit the table

Performance Tasks

★ **8.** The map shows that A Street and B Street are parallel. Find the distance on 6th Ave between A Street and the library. Explain any theorems that come into play here.

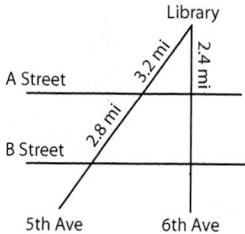

$$\frac{x}{2.4} = \frac{2.8}{3.2}$$
$$x = 2.1$$

Distance: $2.1 + 2.4 = 4.5$; 4.5 miles

The Triangle Proportionality Theorem

★★ **9.** A city has a walkway between the middle school and the library that can be represented in the image given. The city decides it wants to place three trash cans, equally spaced along the walkway, to help reduce any littering. Find the coordinates of the points at which the trash cans should be placed, and then plot them on the graph.

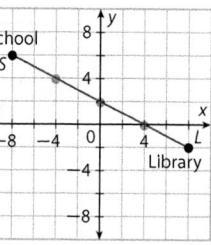

Subdivide the line segment SL into four equal parts. The horizontal distance from point S to point L is 16, and one-fourth of this is 4. So each trash can should be placed at horizontal intervals of 4 units. The vertical distance from point S to point L is 8, and one-fourth of this is 2, so each trash can should be placed at vertical intervals of 2 units. The coordinates are $(-4, 4)$, $(0, 2)$, and $(4, 0)$.

★★★**10.** A person playing table tennis can be represented by the image shown, where A is the point where the person hits the ball with the paddle, at a vertical distance of 152.25 cm from the floor. The height of the table is 76 cm and the net is 15.25 cm tall. Determine the path of the ball.

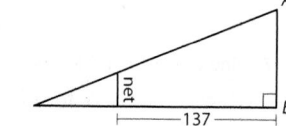

The distance from A to B is $152.25 - 76 = 76.25$ cm. Let the distance from the net to the point where the ball impacts the table be x; then the distance from B to the impact point is $137 + x$. The two triangles in the figure are similar, so use ratios to find x:

$$\frac{15.25}{x} = \frac{76.25}{137 + x}$$
$$15.25(137 + x) = 76.25x$$
$$2089.25 + 15.25x = 76.25x$$
$$2089.25 = 61x$$
$$34.25 = x$$

The ball hits the table a distance of 34.25 cm from the net. The distance the ball travels is the hypotenuse of the triangle with legs 76.25 cm and $(137 + 34.25)$ cm, which is $\sqrt{(76.25)^2 + (171.25)^2} \approx 187.5$ cm.

Special Effects Engineers A special effects engineer is helping create a movie and needs to add a shadow to a tall totem pole that is next to a 6-foot-tall man. The totem pole is 48 feet tall and is next to the man, who has a shadow that is 2.5 feet long. Create an image with the given information and then use the image to find the length of the shadow that the engineer needs to create for the totem pole.

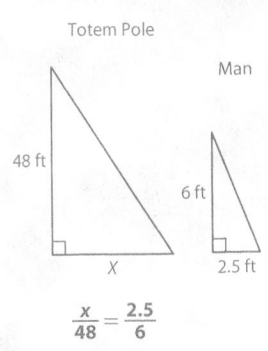

Totem Pole

48 ft

Man

6 ft

X

2.5 ft

$$\frac{x}{48} = \frac{2.5}{6}$$

$$x = 20$$

MATH IN CAREERS

Special Effects Engineer In this Unit Performance Task, students can see how a special effects engineer uses mathematics on the job.

For more information about careers in mathematics as well as various mathematics appreciation topics, visit the American Mathematical Society http://www.ams.org

SCORING GUIDES

Task (6 points)

3 points for creating a diagram that represents the situation, with distances labeled

3 points for correctly setting up the proportion and solving

UNIT 5

Trigonometry

CONTENTS

Unit Pacing Guide

45-Minute Classes

Module 13

DAY 1	DAY 2	DAY 3	DAY 4	DAY 5
Lesson 13.1	Lesson 13.2	Lesson 13.2	Lesson 13.3	Lesson 13.3

DAY 6	DAY 7	DAY 8		
Lesson 13.4	Lesson 13.4	Module Review and Assessment Readiness		

Module 14

DAY 1	DAY 2	DAY 3	DAY 4	DAY 5
Lesson 14.1	Lesson 14.1	Lesson 14.2	Lesson 14.2	Module Review and Assessment Readiness

DAY 6				
Unit Review and Assessment Readiness				

90-Minute Classes

Module 13

DAY 1	DAY 2	DAY 3	DAY 4
Lesson 13.1	Lesson 13.2	Lesson 13.3	Lesson 13.4
Lesson 13.2	Lesson 13.3	Lesson 13.4	Module Review and Assessment Readiness

Module 14

DAY 1	DAY 2	DAY 3
Lesson 14.1	Lesson 14.2	Module Review and Assessment Readiness
		Unit Review and Assessment Readiness

Program Resources

PLAN

HMH Teacher App

Access a full suite of teacher resources online and offline on a variety of devices. Plan present, and manage classes, assignments, and activities.

ePlanner
Easily plan your classes, create and view assignments, and access all program resources with your online, customizable planning tool.

Professional Development Videos

Authors Juli Dixon and Matt Larson model successful teaching practices and strategies in actual classroom settings.

QR Codes
Scan with your smart phone to jump directly from your print book to online videos and other resources.

Teacher's Edition

Support students with point-of-use Questioning Strategies, teaching tips, resources for differentiated instruction, additional activities, and more.

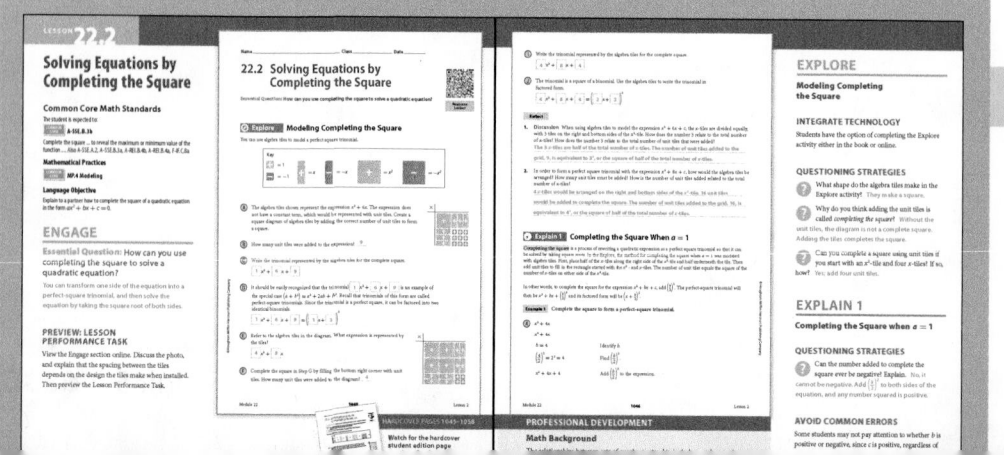

ENGAGE AND EXPLORE

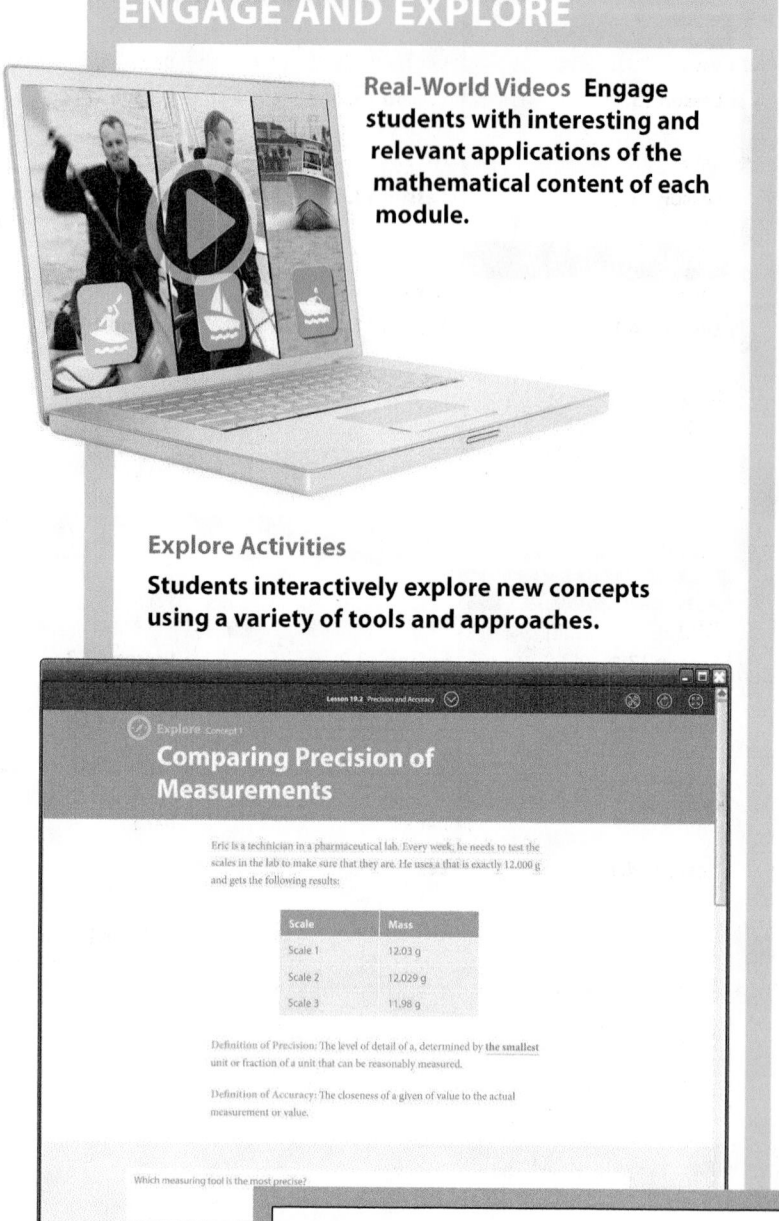

Real-World Videos
Engage students with interesting and relevant applications of the mathematical content of each module.

Explore Activities

Students interactively explore new concepts using a variety of tools and approaches.

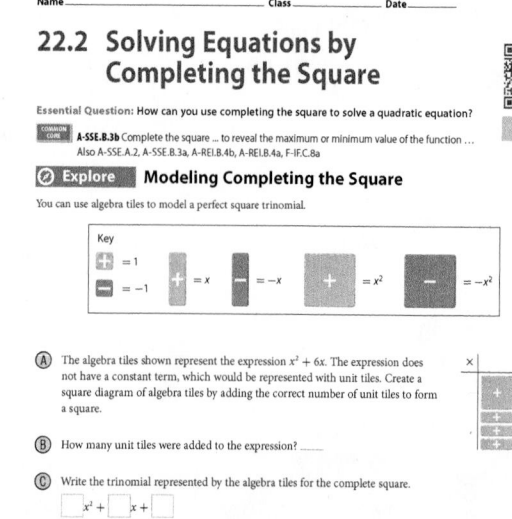

TEACH

Math On the Spot video tutorials, featuring program author Dr. Edward Burger, accompany every example in the textbook and give students step-by-step instructions and explanations of key math concepts.

Interactive Teacher Edition

Customize and present course materials with collaborative activities and integrated formative assessment.

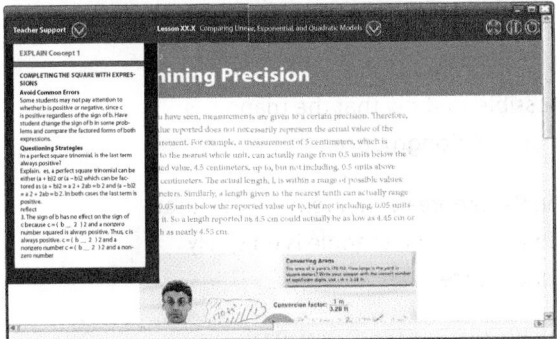

Differentiated Instruction Resources

Support all learners with Differentiated Instruction Resources, including

- **Leveled Practice and Problem Solving**
- **Reading Strategies**
- **Success for English Learners**
- **Challenge**

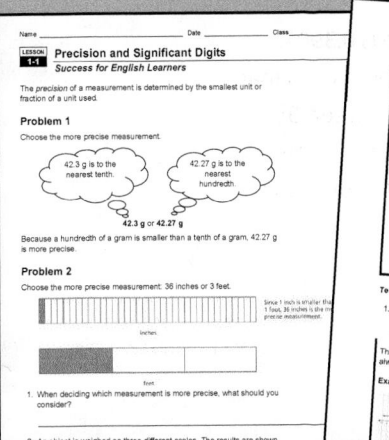
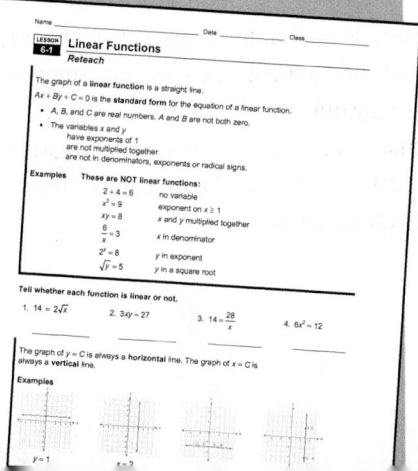

ASSESSMENT AND INTERVENTION

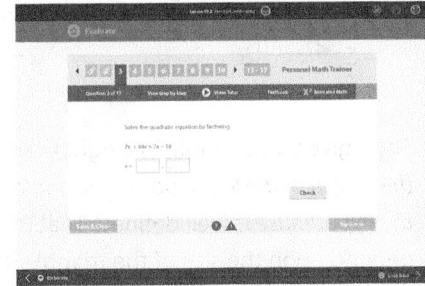

The **Personal Math Trainer** provides online practice, homework, assessments, and intervention. Monitor student progress through reports and alerts. Create and customize assignments aligned to specific lessons or Common Core standards.

- **Practice** – With dynamic items and assignments, students get unlimited practice on key concepts supported by guided examples, step-by-step solutions, and video tutorials.

- **Assessments** – Choose from course assignments or customize your own based on course content, Common Core standards, difficulty levels, and more.

- **Homework** – Students can complete online homework with a wide variety of problem types, including the ability to enter expressions, equations, and graphs. Let the system automatically grade homework, so you can focus where your students need help the most!

- **Intervention** – Let the Personal Math Trainer automatically prescribe a targeted, personalized intervention path for your students.

Focus on Higher Order Thinking

Raise the bar with homework and practice that incorporates higher-order thinking and mathematical practices in every lesson.

Assessment Readiness

Prepare students for success on high stakes tests for Geometry with practice at every module and unit

Assessment Resources

Tailor assessments and response to intervention to meet the needs of all your classes and students, including

- Leveled Module Quizzes
- Leveled Unit Tests
- Unit Performance Tasks
- Placement, Diagnostic, and Quarterly Benchmark Tests
- Tier 1, Tier 2, and Tier 3 Resources

Math Background

Trigonometry G-SRT.C.6

LESSONS 13.1 and 13.2

Trigonometry comes from the Greek words *trigonon* (triangle) and *metron* (measure). As a branch of mathematics, trigonometry dates to ancient times. Its first recorded use is attributed to the Greek astronomer Hipparchus (c. 190 B.C.E. – 120 B.C.E.), who prepared a table of values for the sine function.

The foundation of trigonometry is the observation that all right triangles with a given acute angle are similar by the AA Similarity Theorem. For the triangles shown below, this means that the ratios $\frac{AB}{AC}$, $\frac{JK}{JL}$, and $\frac{PQ}{PR}$ are all equal.

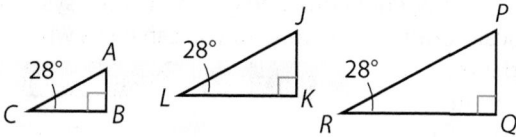

Thus, given a 28° angle in a right triangle, *the ratio of the length of the leg opposite the angle to the length of the hypotenuse* is well defined. That is, the ratio does not depend upon the size of the triangle. This ratio is defined to be the *sine* of 28°, written sin 28°.

Students sometimes regard trigonometric ratios as random numbers that are mysteriously assigned to angle measures. They should recognize that they can estimate trigonometric ratios by using basic drawing tools or geometry software.

For example, it may be worthwhile to have students use a protractor to draw right triangles with 28° angles as shown above and then use a ruler to measure the side lengths. Calculating the ratios $\frac{AB}{AC}$, $\frac{JK}{JL}$, and $\frac{PQ}{PR}$ shows that the three ratios are all equal to approximately 0.47, which is the value of sin 28°. This is the same value that can be found in a trigonometric table or by using a calculator.

Other trigonometric ratios are defined by considering the ratios of other combinations of side lengths.

The *cosine* of an angle is *the ratio of the length of the leg adjacent to the angle to the length of the hypotenuse.*

The *tangent* of an angle *is the ratio of the length of the leg opposite the angle to the length of the leg adjacent to the angle.*

Again, students should understand that these ratios can be approximated by drawing a right triangle that contains the given angle, measuring the side lengths, and calculating the desired ratio.

Solving Right Triangles G-SRT.C.8

LESSON 13.4

Solving a right triangle is the process of using given measures in the triangle to find unknown side lengths or angle measures. Note that a right triangle is uniquely determined given either of the following sets of information.

- The measure of an acute angle and the length of any side
- The length of any two sides

In the first case, it is possible to show that the triangle is uniquely determined by ASA Congruence.

In the second case, the Pythagorean Theorem may be used to find the third side length and the triangle is uniquely determined by SSS Congruence.

In either case, it is possible to use trigonometry to determine all of the unknown side lengths and angle measures.

In order to solve a right triangle, it is sometimes necessary to know the measure of an angle given the value of the angle's sine, cosine, or tangent. This is possible because, for angle measures between 0° and 90°, the trigonometric ratios are one-to-one functions.

For example, given that the cosine of an angle is 0.3907, the fact that the cosine is a one-to-one function means that there is exactly one angle whose measure is between 0° and 90° that has this cosine. This angle measure is written as $\cos^{-1}(0.3907)$, and a calculator can be used to determine that the angle measures 67°.

When introducing the notation for inverse trigonometric functions, students must understand the meaning of the superscript notation $^{-1}$.

In the context of functions, $f^{-1}(x)$ represents the inverse of the function $f(x)$, rather than a reciprocal.

The Law of Sines may be used to solve any triangle given either of the following.

- Two angle measures and any side length
- Two side lengths and a non-included angle measure

Note that, in the second case, two side lengths and a non-included angle measure are known (SSA), and that this is generally not enough information to uniquely determine a triangle. (Thus, there is no SSA Congruence Theorem.)

The ambiguity arises when you are given an acute angle measure and the side opposite the known angle is shorter than the other side. As the figures show, this situation may result in no triangle or two triangles.

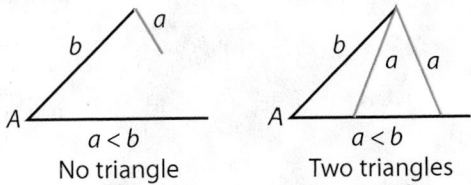

Similarly, when the given angle is right or obtuse, there will be no triangle if the side opposite the given angle is shorter than the other side.

All of the situations described here are known as *the ambiguous case of the Law of Sines*.

The Law of Cosines may be used to solve a triangle given either of the following.

- Two side lengths and the included angle measure
- Three side lengths

The Law of Cosines may be considered to be a generalization of the Pythagorean Theorem.

For the following triangle, the Law of Cosines states that $c^2 = a^2 + b^2 - 2ab \cos C$.

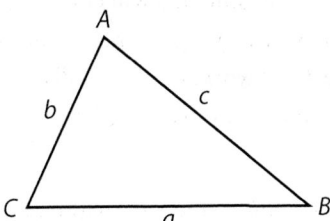

In the case that $\angle C$ is a right angle, $\cos C = \cos 90° = 0$, and the Law of Cosines reduces to $c^2 = a^2 + b^2 - 2ab(0)$ or $c^2 = a^2 + b^2$, which is the Pythagorean Theorem.

Trigonometry

MATH IN CAREERS
Unit Activity Preview

After completing this unit, students will complete a Math in Careers task by using trigonometric ratios in the context of a detective's work. Critical skills include using trigonometric ratios to find an unknown angle.

For more information about careers in mathematics as well as various mathematics appreciation topics, visit The American Mathematical Society at http://www.ams.org.

UNIT 5

Trigonometry

MODULE 13
Trigonometry with Right Triangles

MODULE 14
Trigonometry with All Triangles

MATH IN CAREERS

Detective A detective uses clues to determine the time and place that an event has occurred. With the use of logic and math skills, a detective can pinpoint the time of day shown in a photograph, based on the position of shadows in the image.

If you're interested in a career as a detective, you should study these mathematical subjects:
- Algebra
- Geometry
- Trigonometry
- Calculus

Research other careers that require the use of forensics to understand real-world scenarios. See the related Career Activity at the end of this unit.

Unit 5   683

TRACKING YOUR LEARNING PROGRESSION

Before	In this Unit	After
Students understand: • dilations and similarity • indirect measurement • the relationship of the altitude to the hypotenuse of a right triangle to other parts of the triangle • the Pythagorean Theorem	Students will learn about: • ratios in right triangles • using tangents • using sine and cosine • special right triangles • Pythagorean triples • solving right triangles • inverse trigonometric ratios	Students will study: • central and inscribed angles; chords, secants, tangent lines, and arcs • inscribed quadrilaterals and circumscribed angles • angles formed by intersecting lines of a circle • formulas for circumference and area of a circle, area of a sector, and the equation of a circle • arc lengths, concentric circles, radian measure

Reading Start-Up

Visualize Vocabulary

Use the review words to complete the chart.

Term	Description
right triangle	A triangle with a right angle
right angle	An angle whose measure is 90°
hypotenuse	The longest side of a right triangle
legs	The shorter sides of a right triangle
complementary angles	Angles whose measures sum to 90°
supplementary angles	Angles whose measures sum to 180°
ratio	A representation of the relative sizes of two or more values

Understand Vocabulary

Complete the sentences using the preview words.

1. In a right triangle, the side __adjacent__ to an acute angle is the leg that forms one side of the angle.

2. Sine, cosine, and tangent are examples of __trigonometric ratios__.

3. A set of positive integers a, b, and c that satisfy the equation $a^2 + b^2 = c^2$ is called a(n) __Pythagorean triple__.

Active Reading

Booklet Create a booklet at the start of the unit. During discussions of the material in class, write vocabulary that you know toward the front, vocabulary that you recognize but are unsure of toward the middle, and vocabulary that you do not know toward the back. Use the booklet as a tool for studying the vocabulary.

© Houghton Mifflin Harcourt Publishing Company

Reading Start Up

Have students complete the activities on this page by working alone or with others.

VISUALIZE VOCABULARY

The definition chart helps students review vocabulary associated with trigonometry. If time allows, ask students to draw diagrams to illustrate the terms.

UNDERSTAND VOCABULARY

Use the following explanations to help students learn the preview words.

A **Pythagorean triple** is a set of three nonzero whole numbers that satisfy the Pythagorean Theorem. A **trigonometric ratio** is a ratio of two sides of a right triangle. In a right triangle, the **sine** is the ratio of the length of the leg **opposite** one of the acute angles to the hypotenuse, the **cosine** is the ratio of the leg **adjacent** to the acute angle to the hypotenuse, and the **tangent** is the ratio of the leg opposite the acute angle to the adjacent leg.

ACTIVE READING

Students can use these reading and note-taking strategies to help them organize and understand the new concepts and vocabulary. Encourage students to look for the vocabulary in familiar applications and situations and to ask for clarification whenever needed.

ADDITIONAL RESOURCES

Differentiated Instruction

- Reading Strategies

Trigonometry with Right Triangles

ESSENTIAL QUESTION:

Answer: Trigonometric ratios allow you to find the side length of a right triangle given an angle measure, or vice versa. This can be useful whenever a triangular shape appears in the real world, such as in a metal bracket or a sculpture.

PROFESSIONAL DEVELOPMENT VIDEO

Professional Development Video

STEM Consultant Michael DiSpezio offers engaging suggestions and activities for integrating science, technology, and engineering into the math classroom.

Professional Development
my.hrw.com

MODULE 13

Trigonometry with Right Triangles

Essential Question: How can you use trigonometry with right triangles to solve real-world problems?

REAL WORLD VIDEO
Check out how right triangle trigonometry is used in real-world warehouses to minimize the space needed for items being shipped or stored.

© Houghton Mifflin Harcourt Publishing Company • Image Credits: ©artzenter/Shutterstock

MODULE PERFORMANCE TASK PREVIEW

How Much Shorter Are Staggered Pipe Stacks?

In this module, you will investigate how much space can be saved by stacking pipes in a staggered pattern rather than directly on top of each other. How can trigonometry help you find the answer to this problem? Get prepared to discover the "staggering" results!

Module 13   **685**

DIGITAL TEACHER EDITION

Access a full suite of teaching resources when and where you need them:

- Access content online or offline
- Customize lessons to share with your class
- Communicate with your students in real-time
- View student grades and data instantly to target your instruction where it is needed most

PERSONAL MATH TRAINER

Assessment and Intervention

Assign automatically graded homework, quizzes, tests, and intervention activities. Prepare your students with updated, Common Core-aligned practice tests.

Are (YOU) Ready?

Complete these exercises to review skills you will need for this module.

Angle Relationships

- Online Homework
- Hints and Help
- Extra Practice

Example 1 Find the angle complementary to the given angle. 75°

$x + 75° = 90°$ Write as an equation.

$x = 90° - 75°$ Solve for x.

$x = 15°$

Find the complementary angle.

1. 20° _____ 70°
2. 35° _____ 55°
3. 67° _____ 23°

Find the supplementary angle.

4. 80° _____ 100°
5. 65° _____ 115°
6. 34° _____ 146°

Find the remaining angle or angles for △ABC.

7. $m\angle A = 50°, m\angle B = 40°$ _____ $m\angle C = 90°$

8. $m\angle A = 60°, m\angle C = 20°$ _____ $m\angle B = 100°$

9. $m\angle B = 70°$ and $\angle A \cong \angle C$ _____ $m\angle A = 55°, m\angle C = 55°$

10. $\angle A \cong \angle B \cong \angle C$ _____ $m\angle A = 60°, m\angle B = 60°, m\angle C = 60°$

11. $m\angle B = 30°$ and $m\angle A = \frac{1}{2}m\angle C$ _____ $m\angle A = 50°, m\angle C = 100°$

12. △ABC is similar to △DEF and $m\angle D = 70°$ and $m\angle F = 50°$ _____ $m\angle A = 70°, m\angle B = 60°, m\angle C = 50°$

13. △ABC is similar to △PQR and $m\angle R = 50°$ and $\angle P \cong \angle Q$ _____ $m\angle A = 65°, m\angle B = 65°, m\angle C = 50°$

14. $m\angle A = 45°$ and $m\angle B = m\angle C$ _____ $m\angle B = 67.5°, m\angle C = 67.5°$

15. $m\angle B = 105°$ and $m\angle A = 2 \cdot m\angle C$ _____ $m\angle A = 50°, m\angle C = 25°$

16. $m\angle A = 5°$ and $m\angle B = 9 \cdot m\angle C$ _____ $m\angle B = 157.5°, m\angle C = 17.5°$

Are You Ready?

ASSESS READINESS

Use the assessment on this page to determine if students need strategic or intensive intervention for the module's prerequisite skills.

ASSESSMENT AND INTERVENTION

RtI Response to Intervention **TIER 1, TIER 2, TIER 3 SKILLS**

Personal Math Trainer will automatically create a standards-based, personalized intervention assignment for your students, targeting each student's individual needs!

ADDITIONAL RESOURCES

See the table below for a full list of intervention resources available for this module.

Response to Intervention Resources also includes:

- Tier 2 Skill Pre-Tests for each Module
- Tier 2 Skill Post-Tests for each skill

Response to Intervention			Differentiated Instruction
Tier 1 Lesson Intervention Worksheets	**Tier 2** Strategic Intervention Skills Intervention Worksheets	**Tier 3** Intensive Intervention Worksheets available online	
Reteach 13.1 Reteach 13.2 Reteach 13.3 Reteach 13.4	2 Angle Relationships 25 The Pythagorean Theorem 29 Proportional Relationships	Building Block Skills 7, 15, 16, 38, 46, 53, 56, 63, 66, 82, 90, 95, 98, 100, 102	Challenge worksheets Extend the Math Lesson Activities in TE

Tangent Ratio

Common Core Math Standards

The student is expected to:

 G-SRT.C.6

Understand that by similarity, side ratios in right triangles are properties of the angles in the triangle, leading to definitions of trigonometric ratios for acute angles. Also G-SRT.C.8

Mathematical Practices

COMMON CORE **MP.4 Modeling**

Language Objective

Explain to a partner how to find the tangent of an angle given a diagram of a right triangle with given angle measure and leg lengths.

ENGAGE

Essential Question: How do you find the tangent ratio for an acute angle?

For an acute angle in a right triangle, the tangent ratio is the ratio of the length of the opposite leg to the length of the adjacent leg.

PREVIEW: LESSON PERFORMANCE TASK

View the Engage section online. Discuss the photograph, asking students to describe the forces that might create the shape of a sand dune. Then preview the Lesson Performance Task.

Name_____ Class_____ Date_____

13.1 Tangent Ratio

Essential Question: How do you find the tangent ratio for an acute angle?

Resource Locker

⊘ Explore   Investigating a Ratio in a Right Triangle

In a given a right triangle, $\triangle ABC$, with a right angle at vertex C, there are three sides. The side adjacent to $\angle A$ is the leg that forms one side of $\angle A$. The side opposite $\angle A$ is the leg that does not form a side of $\angle A$. The side that connects the adjacent and opposite legs is the hypotenuse.

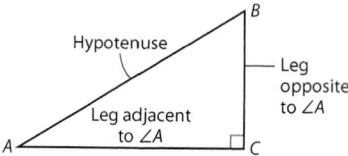

(A) In $\triangle DEF$, label the legs opposite and adjacent to $\angle D$. Then measure the lengths of the legs in centimeters and record their values in the rectangles provided.

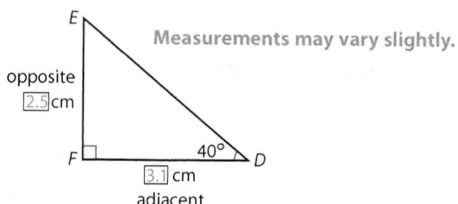

Measurements may vary slightly.

(B) What is the ratio of the opposite leg length to the adjacent leg length, rounded to the nearest hundredth?

$\dfrac{EF}{DF} \approx$ 0.81   Ratios may vary slightly depending on measurements.

(C) Using a protractor and ruler, draw right triangle $\triangle JKL$ with a right angle at vertex L and $\angle J = 40°$ so that $\triangle JKL \sim \triangle DEF$. Label the opposite and adjacent legs to $\angle J$ and include their measurements.

Drawings will vary but should be similar to the triangle in Step A. For all

triangles, it is true that opposite length < adjacent length.

(D) What is the ratio of the opposite leg length to the adjacent leg length, rounded to the nearest hundredth?

$\dfrac{KL}{JL} \approx$ 0.81

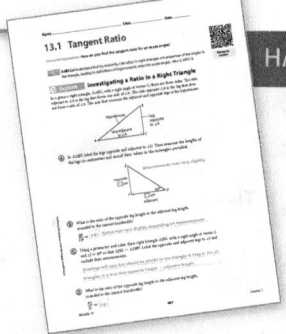

HARDCOVER PAGES 585–592

Turn to these pages to find this lesson in the hardcover student edition.

1. **Discussion** Compare your work with that of other students. Do all the triangles have the same angles? Do they all have the same side lengths? Do they all have the same leg ratios? Summarize your findings.

   The triangles are all similar, so they have angles that have the same

   measure but not the same side lengths. Yet, for a given angle, the ratio of

   the length of the opposite leg to the length of the adjacent leg is constant.

2. If you repeated Steps A–D with a right triangle having a 30° angle, how would your results be similar? How would they be different?

   The triangles would all be similar, with the ratio of the length of the leg

   opposite the 30° angle to the length of the leg adjacent to the 30° angle

   constant, but the actual value of the ratio would be different from 0.81.

⊘ Explain 1 Finding the Tangent of an Angle

The ratio you calculated in the Explore section is called the *tangent* of an angle. The **tangent** of acute angle A, written $\tan \angle A$, is defined as follows:

$$\tan A = \frac{\text{length of leg opposite } \angle A}{\text{length of leg adjacent to } \angle A}$$

You can use what you know about similarity to show why the tangent of an angle is constant. By the AA Similarity Theorem, given $\angle D \cong \angle J$ and also $\angle F \cong \angle L$, then $\triangle DEF \sim \triangle JKL$. This means the lengths of the sides of $\triangle JKL$ are each the same multiple, k, of the lengths of the corresponding sides of $\triangle DEF$. Substituting into the tangent equation shows that the ratio of the length of the opposite leg to the length of the adjacent leg is always the same value for a given acute angle.

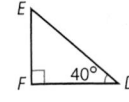

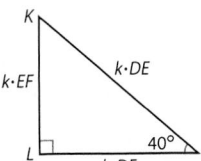

tangent defined for specified angle $\triangle DEF$ $\triangle JKL$

$$\tan 40° = \frac{\text{leg opposite } \angle 40°}{\text{leg adjacent to } \angle 40°} = \frac{EF}{DF} = \frac{KL}{JL} = \frac{k \cdot EF}{k \cdot DF} = \frac{EF}{DF}$$

Example 1 Find the tangent of each specified angle. Write each ratio as a fraction and as a decimal rounded to the nearest hundredth.

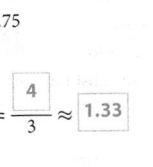

Ⓐ $\angle A$

$\tan A = \dfrac{\text{length of leg opposite } \angle A}{\text{length of leg adjacent to } \angle A} = \dfrac{18}{24} = \dfrac{3}{4} = 0.75$

Ⓑ $\angle B$

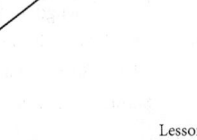

$\tan B = \dfrac{\text{length of leg } \boxed{\text{opposite}} \; \angle B}{\text{length of leg } \boxed{\text{adjacent}} \; \text{to } \angle B} = \dfrac{\boxed{24}}{\boxed{18}} = \dfrac{4}{3} \approx \boxed{1.33}$

© Houghton Mifflin Harcourt Publishing Company

PROFESSIONAL DEVELOPMENT

Learning Progressions

Students work with three trigonometric ratios in this course: tangent, sine, and cosine. The tangent is treated separately for two reasons. First, working with a single ratio gives students a chance to focus on the conceptual underpinnings of trigonometry. That is, right triangles with a given acute angle, $\angle A$, are all similar, so the ratio of the length of the leg opposite $\angle A$ to the length of the leg adjacent to $\angle A$ is constant for all such triangles. Second, students sometimes have difficulty deciding which trigonometric ratio to use when solving a problem. By working with tangents first, students can instead focus on the general process for solving a problem using trigonometry.

EXPLORE

Investigating a Ratio in a Right Triangle

INTEGRATE TECHNOLOGY

Students have the option of doing the Explore activity either in the book or online.

CONNECT VOCABULARY 🔲EL

Draw and label a variety of right triangles with different orientations. For each of the triangles, have students name the *hypotenuse*, the leg *adjacent* to a given angle, and the *leg opposite* the angle.

QUESTIONING STRATEGIES

? The ratio of the length of the opposite leg to the adjacent leg of an angle of a right triangle is constant for any right triangle with the same angle measures. What does this imply about right triangles with that given angle measure? Explain. The triangles must be similar because the angle measures are constant and the ratios of the sides are proportional.

AVOID COMMON ERRORS

If students use calculators to compute the tangent ratio of an angle, remind them to check that their calculators are in degree mode. Otherwise, they will not find the correct value.

EXPLAIN 1

Finding the Tangent of an Angle

CONNECT VOCABULARY 🔲EL

The abbreviation *tan* is read *tangent*. For example, $\tan 30°$ is read as *tangent of 30 degrees*.

QUESTIONING STRATEGIES

? If you know the tangent ratio for an acute angle of a right triangle, and the length of one of the legs, can you reconstruct the triangle? Explain. **Yes; you can use the ratio to find the length of the other leg, and then use the Pythagorean Theorem to find the length of the hypotenuse.**

? You can use a table of values to find the tangent of a given acute angle. How do you think the tables were compiled? **by constructing right triangles with the given angle measure and its complement, measuring the opposite and adjacent side lengths, and then computing the tangent ratio**

EXPLAIN 2

Finding a Side Length using Tangent

QUESTIONING STRATEGIES

? Why is it important to draw and label a diagram when solving a real-world problem about relationships in a right triangle? **The diagram makes it possible to identify values and relationships that you can use to solve the problem.**

? What if you want to find the tangent of the other acute angle in the triangle? How would you find the angle? When might this be necessary? **The measure of the angle is the complement of the given angle. You might want to do this if the missing side is in the denominator of the tangent ratio.**

Reflect

3. What is the relationship between the ratios for tan A and tan B? Do you believe this relationship will be true for acute angles in other right triangles? Explain. **The ratios are reciprocals of each other. This will always be true because the opposite side of one acute angle is the adjacent side of the other acute angle, and vice versa.**

4. Why does it not make sense to ask for the value of tan L? **The tangent ratio is defined only for the acute angles of a right triangle, not for the right angle.**

Your Turn

Find the tangent of each specified angle. Write each ratio as a fraction and as a decimal rounded to the nearest hundredth.

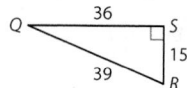

5. $\angle Q$ 6. $\angle R$

$$\tan \angle Q = \frac{15}{36} = \frac{5}{12} \approx 0.42 \qquad \tan \angle R = \frac{36}{15} = \frac{12}{5} = 2.4$$

⚡ Explain 2 Finding a Side Length using Tangent

When you know the length of a leg of a right triangle and the measure of one of the acute angles, you can use the tangent to find the length of the other leg. This is especially useful in real-world problems.

Example 2 Apply the tangent ratio to find unknown lengths.

(A) In order to meet safety guidelines, a roof contractor determines that she must place the base of her ladder 6 feet away from the house, making an angle of 76° with the ground. To the nearest tenth of a foot, how far above the ground is the eave of the roof?

Step 1 Write a tangent ratio that involves the unknown length.

$$\tan A = \frac{\text{length of leg opposite } \angle A}{\text{length of leg adjacent to } \angle A} = \frac{BC}{BA}$$

Step 2 Identify the given values and substitute into the tangent equation.

Given: $BA = 6$ ft and $m\angle A = 76°$

Substitute: $\tan 76° = \dfrac{BC}{6}$

© Houghton Mifflin Harcourt Publishing Company

COLLABORATIVE LEARNING

Peer-to-Peer Activity

Provide pairs of students with graph paper and ask each student to draw two different right triangles, with unit side lengths for the legs. Have them use a protractor to estimate one of the acute angles in one triangle, then have pairs work together to find the tangent. Then, have them choose an acute angle in the remaining triangle and find the inverse tangent of the angle. For additional work, have students exchange triangles with other pairs.

Step 3 Solve for the unknown leg length. Be sure the calculator is in degree mode and do not round until the final step of the solution.

Multiply each side by 6.	$6 \cdot \tan 76° = \dfrac{6}{1} \cdot \dfrac{BC}{6}$
Use a calculator to find $\tan 76°$.	$6 \cdot \tan 76° = BC$
Substitute this value in for $\tan 76°$.	$6(4.010780934) = BC$
Multiply. Round to the nearest tenth.	$24.1 \approx BC$

So, the eave of the roof is about 24.1 feet above the ground.

(B) For right triangle $\triangle STU$, what is the length of the leg adjacent to $\angle S$?

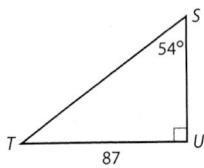

Step 1 Write a tangent ratio that involves the unknown length.

$$\tan S = \frac{\text{length of leg} \quad \boxed{\text{opposite}} \quad \angle S}{\text{length of leg} \quad \boxed{\text{adjacent}} \quad \text{to } \angle S} = \frac{\boxed{TU}}{\boxed{SU}}$$

Step 2 Identify the given values and substitute into the tangent equation.

Given: $TU = \boxed{87}$ and $m\angle S = \boxed{54}°$

Substitute: $\tan \boxed{54}° = \dfrac{87}{SU}$

Step 3 Solve for the unknown leg length.

Multiply both sides by SU, then divide both sides by $54°$. $SU \approx \dfrac{\boxed{87}}{\tan \boxed{54}°}$

Use a calculator to find $54°$ and substitute. $SU \approx \dfrac{\boxed{87}}{\boxed{1.37638192}}$

Divide. Round to the nearest tenth. $SU \approx \boxed{63.2}$

Your Turn

7. A ladder needs to reach the second story window, which is 10 feet above the ground, and make an angle with the ground of 70°. How far out from the building does the base of the ladder need to be positioned?

3.6 ft; $\tan 70° = \dfrac{10}{x}$, so $x = \dfrac{10}{\tan 70°} \approx \dfrac{10}{2.747477419} \approx 3.6$

⚙ **Explain 3**   **Finding an Angle Measure using Tangent**

In the previous section you used a given angle measure and leg measure with the tangent ratio to solve for an unknown leg. What if you are given the leg measures and want to find the measures of the acute angles? If you know the tan A, read as "tangent of $\angle A$," then you can use the **tan⁻¹ A**, read as "**inverse tangent of $\angle A$**," to find $m\angle A$. So, given an acute angle $\angle A$, if $\tan A = x$, then $\tan^{-1} x = m\angle A$.

AVOID COMMON ERRORS

When solving an equation of the form $\tan 35° = \dfrac{x}{12}$, students may forget to multiply by 12 to solve for x after they find $\tan 35°$. These students may benefit from rewriting the equation as $12 \cdot \tan 35° = x$ before evaluating $\tan 35°$.

EXPLAIN 3

Finding an Angle Measure using Tangent

QUESTIONING STRATEGIES

? In the equation $y = \tan^{-1}x$, explain what x and y represent. In the equation, x represents the tangent of the angle with measure $y°$.

? If $\tan x = 1$, what is the measure of angle x? Explain. The measure of angle x must be 45° because the legs of the triangle must be the same length to make the tangent ratio 1.

? How could you evaluate the inverse tangent of an angle without using a calculator's inverse tangent key or a table of values? Use the measurements of the tangent ratio as the legs to draw the corresponding right triangle. Then use a protractor to measure the angle formed by the hypotenuse and the adjacent side to estimate the angle measure.

DIFFERENTIATE INSTRUCTION

Kinesthetic Experience

To help students identify the opposite and adjacent legs, model a right triangle on the floor with masking tape. Have a student stand at one acute angle and walk to the leg next to, or touching, that angle. That is the adjacent leg. Then have the student walk from the acute angle to the leg opposite, or across from, the angle. This is the opposite leg.

INTEGRATE MATHEMATICAL PRACTICES

Focus on Critical Thinking

MP.3 Discuss why students will get more accurate results if they evaluate an expression like $\tan^{-1}\left(\frac{1}{3}\right)$ rather than finding a decimal approximation for the fraction $\frac{1}{3}$, rounding, and evaluating $\tan^{-1}(0.33)$.

ELABORATE

INTEGRATE TECHNOLOGY

Have students graph $y = \tan x$ on their graphing calculators on the interval $[0, 90°]$. Discuss how to interpret the graph, especially as x nears $90°$.

AVOID COMMON ERRORS

Some students may have the misconception that the opposite leg is always a vertical side of the triangle and the adjacent leg is always a horizontal side of the triangle. Remind students that the opposite and adjacent sides are determined by the location of the associated angle, not by the orientation of the triangle.

QUESTIONING STRATEGIES

How are tangent and inverse tangent related? The tangent of an acute angle of a right triangle is the ratio of the lengths of the opposite side to the adjacent side of the right triangle. The inverse tangent is the angle with that tangent ratio.

SUMMARIZE THE LESSON

How do you find the tangent ratio for an acute angle of a right triangle? Find the ratio of the length of the leg opposite the angle to the length of the leg adjacent to the angle.

Example 3 Find the measure of the indicated angle. Round to the nearest degree.

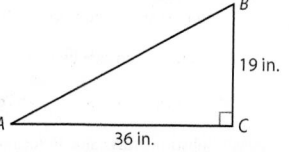

(A) What is $m\angle A$?

Step 1 Write the tangent ratio for $\angle A$ using the known values.	Step 2 Write the inverse tangent equation.	Step 3 Evaluate using a calculator and round as indicated.
$\tan A = \frac{19}{36}$	$\tan^{-1}\frac{19}{36} = m\angle A$	$m\angle A \approx 27.82409638 \approx 28°$

(B) What is $m\angle B$?

Step 1 Write the tangent ratio for $\angle B$ using the known values.	Step 2 Write the inverse tangent equation.	Step 3 Evaluate using a calculator and round as indicated.
$\tan B = \dfrac{\boxed{36}}{\boxed{19}}$	$\tan^{-1}\dfrac{\boxed{36}}{\boxed{19}} = m\angle B$	$m\angle B \approx \boxed{62.17590362}° \approx \boxed{62}°$

Your Turn

8. Find $m\angle J$.

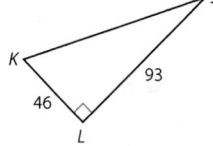

$26°, m\angle J = \tan^{-1}\frac{46}{93} \approx 26.31808814$

💬 **Elaborate**

9. Explain how to identify the opposite and adjacent legs of a given acute angle.
   The opposite leg does not form a side of the given angle. The adjacent leg forms a side of the given angle and is not the hypotenuse.

10. **Discussion** How does $\tan A$ change as $m\angle A$ increases? Explain the basis for the identified relationship.
   Tan A increases as $m\angle A$ increases. As $m\angle A$ increases, the length of the leg adjacent to $\angle A$ remains the same and the length of the leg opposite $\angle A$ increases. Since the length of the opposite leg is the numerator of the tangent ratio, and the denominator of that ratio does not change, the ratio increases.

LANGUAGE SUPPORT EL

Connect Vocabulary

Have students look up the word *inverse* in the dictionary. A definition may include *reversed in position*. Discuss how this corresponds to the relationship between the inverse tangent and the tangent of an angle.

11. Essential Question Check-In Compare and contrast the use of the tangent and inverse tangent ratios for solving problems.

The tangent and inverse tangent both apply only to acute angles in right triangles. When the leg lengths are known, the tangent can be used to solve for the constant ratio. Whereas, the inverse tangent can be used to solve for the associated acute angle. When the measures of one leg and one angle are known, the tangent can be used to solve for the unknown leg whereas the inverse tangent is not applicable.

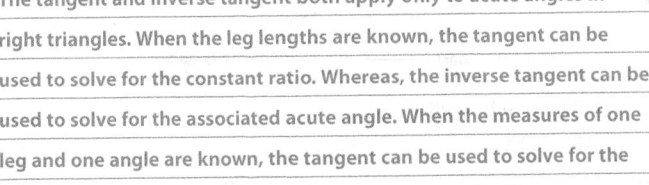

☆ Evaluate: Homework and Practice

1. In each triangle, measure the length of the adjacent side and the opposite side of the 22° angle. Then calculate and compare the ratios.

$\frac{\text{Opposite}}{\text{Adjacent}} = 0.40$; $\frac{\text{Opposite}}{\text{Adjacent}} = 0.40$; the ratios are the same.

In each right triangle, find the tangent of each angle that is not the right angle.

2.

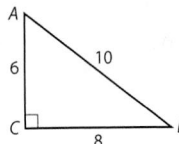

$\tan \angle A = \frac{8}{6}$ $\tan \angle B = \frac{6}{8}$

$\tan \angle A = 1.33$ $\tan \angle B = 0.75$

3.

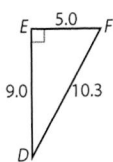

$\tan \angle D = \frac{5}{9}$ $\tan \angle F = \frac{9}{5}$

$\tan \angle D = 0.56$ $\tan \angle F = 1.8$

4.

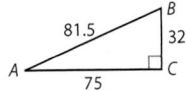

$\tan \angle A = \frac{32}{75}$ $\tan \angle B = \frac{75}{32}$

$\tan \angle A = 0.43$ $\tan \angle B = 2.34$

5.

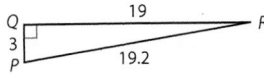

$\tan \angle P = \frac{19}{3}$ $\tan \angle R = \frac{3}{19}$

$\tan \angle P = 6.33$ $\tan \angle R = 0.16$

© Houghton Mifflin Harcourt Publishing Company

Exercise	Depth of Knowledge (D.O.K.)	COMMON CORE Mathematical Practices
1–5	**1** Recall of Information	**MP.6** Precision
6–17	**2** Skills/Concepts	**MP.5** Using Tools
18–22	**2** Skills/Concepts	**MP.2** Reasoning
23–24	**2** Skills/Concepts	**MP.4** Modeling
25–26	**2** Skills/Concepts H.O.T.	**1.A** Everyday life

EVALUATE

ASSIGNMENT GUIDE

Concepts and Skills	Practice
Explore Investigating a Ratio in a Right Triangle	Exercise 1
Example 1 Finding the Tangent of an Angle	Exercises 2–8
Example 2 Finding a Side Length using Tangent	Exercises 9–14, 18–19
Example 3 Finding an Angle Measure using Tangent	Exercises 15–17, 20–21

COMMUNICATING MATH

Point out that the hypotenuse of a right triangle will never be the opposite or the adjacent side for the tangent ratio. Discuss why this must be so.

INTEGRATE MATHEMATICAL PRACTICES
Focus on Modeling

MP.4 Discuss rounding errors that occur when finding the tangent and inverse tangent of an angle. Have students find the tangent of an angle on their calculators. Then have them use the value to find the inverse tangent for that tangent. Compare results. Repeat with several exercises. Have students also start with the inverse tangent.

AVOID COMMON ERRORS

Students may confuse the opposite and the adjacent sides of a given angle in a right triangle. Suggest that students use one color to highlight the opposite side and another color to highlight the adjacent side of a given acute angle. Emphasize that the adjacent side forms the given angle's ray that is not the hypotenuse of the triangle.

Let $\triangle ABC$ be a right triangle, with $m\angle C = 90°$. Given the tangent of one of the complementary angles of the triangle, find the tangent of the other angle.

6. $\tan \angle A = 1.25$
   $\tan \angle B = \frac{1}{1.25}$
   $\tan \angle B = 0.80$

7. $\tan \angle B = 0.50$
   $\tan \angle A = \frac{1}{0.50}$
   $\tan \angle A = 2.0$

8. $\tan \angle B = 1.0$
   $\tan \angle A = \frac{1}{1.0}$
   $\tan \angle A = 1.0$

Use the tangent to find the unknown side length.

9. Find QR.

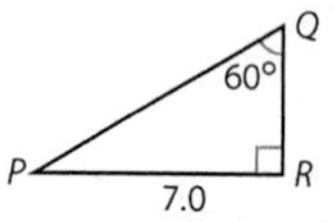

$\tan 60° = \frac{7.0}{QR}$

$QR = \frac{7.0}{\tan 60°}$

$QR = 4.0$

10. Find AC.

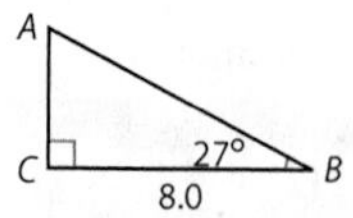

$\tan 27° = \frac{AC}{8.0}$

$AC = \tan 27°(8.0)$

$AC = 4.1$

11. Find PQ.

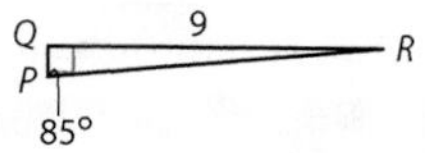

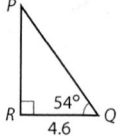

$\tan 85° = \frac{9}{PQ}$

$PQ = \frac{9}{\tan 85°}$

$PQ = 0.79$

12. Find DE.

$\tan 21° = \frac{13}{DE}$

$DE = \frac{13}{\tan 21°}$

$DE = 33.9$

13. Find AB.

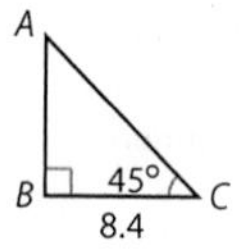

$\tan 45° = \frac{AB}{8.4}$

$AB = \tan 45°(8.4)$

$AB = 8.4$

14. Find PR.

$\tan 54° = \frac{PR}{4.6}$

$PR = \tan 54°(4.6)$

$PR = 6.3$

Find the measure of the angle specified for each triangle. Use the inverse tangent (tan⁻¹) function of your calculator. Round your answer to the nearest degree.

15. Find ∠A.

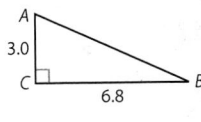

$$\tan^{-1}\frac{6.8}{3.0} = m\angle A$$

$$m\angle A = 66°$$

16. Find ∠R.

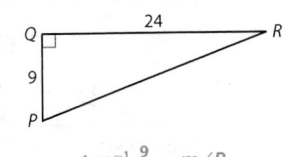

$$\tan^{-1}\frac{9}{24} = m\angle R$$

$$m\angle R = 21°$$

17. Find ∠B.

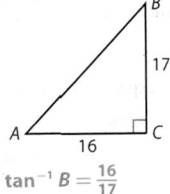

$$\tan^{-1}B = \frac{16}{17}$$

$$m\angle B = 43°$$

Write an equation using either tan or tan⁻¹ to express the measure of the angle or side. Then solve the equation.

18. Find BC.

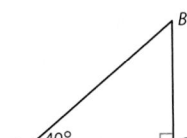

$$BC = 10 \tan 40° = 8.4$$

19. Find PQ.

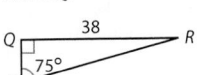

$$PQ = \frac{38}{\tan 75°} = 10.2$$

20. Find ∠A and ∠C.

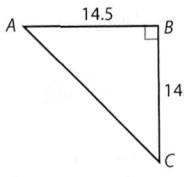

$$m\angle A = m\angle C = \tan^{-1}A\left(\frac{14.5}{14.5}\right) = 45°$$

21. Multi-Step Find the measure of angle D. Show your work.

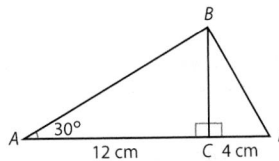

$$\tan 30° = \frac{BC}{12}; \quad BC = 12 \tan 30°$$

$$m\angle D = \tan^{-1}\left(\frac{BC}{CD}\right) = \tan^{-1}\left(\frac{12 \tan 30°}{4}\right) = 60°$$

MANIPULATIVES

For right triangles with unit side lengths for the legs, when they are finding the inverse tangent, students may benefit from drawing the right triangle on graph paper and then using a protractor to estimate the acute angle measure. They can also do this to check their work.

AVOID COMMON ERRORS

Call attention to the notation used to represent the inverse tangent: $\tan^{-1}x$. The expression $\tan^{-1}x$ is a short way to indicate "the angle whose tangent ratio is x." Be sure students understand that the raised −1 is *not* an exponent and that $\tan^{-1}x$ does not mean $\frac{1}{\tan x}$. Emphasize that when students find the inverse tangent, the result will be an angle with a degree measure.

Have students summarize what they know about the tangent ratio. Remind them to include at least one figure and at least one example in their descriptions.

22. Engineering A client wants to build a ramp that carries people to a height of 1.4 meters, as shown in the diagram. What additional information is necessary to identify the measure of angle a, the angle the ramp forms with the horizontal? After the additional measurement is made, describe how to find the measure of the angle. **Possible answer: Measure the distance x of the ramp across**

the horizontal. Then find $\tan^{-1}\left(\frac{1.4}{x}\right)$, which equals the measure of angle a.

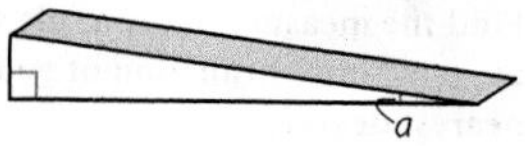

23. Explain the Error A student uses the triangle shown to calculate a. Find and explain the student's error.

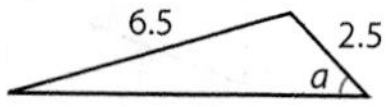

$a = \tan^{-1}\left(\frac{6.5}{2.5}\right) = \tan^{-1}(2.6)$ **The student's calculations are correct only if the triangle is a right triangle.**

$a = 69.0°$

24. When $m\angle A + m\angle B = 90°$, what relationship is formed by $\tan \angle A$ and $\tan \angle B$? Select all that apply.

A. $\tan\angle A = \dfrac{1}{\tan B}$ **C.** $(\tan\angle A)(\tan\angle B) = 1$

B. $\tan\angle A + \tan\angle B = 1$ **D.** $(\tan\angle A)(\tan\angle B) = -1$

A, C; Tan A and tan B are reciprocals of each other so they have a product of 1.

H.O.T. Focus on Higher Order Thinking

25. Analyze Relationships To travel from Pottstown to Cogsville, a man drives his car 83 miles due east on one road, and then 15 miles due north on another road. Describe the path that a bird could fly in a straight line from Pottstown to Cogsville. What angle does the line make with the two roads that the man used?

The bird's path is the hypotenuse of the right triangle formed by the path of the man. The bird's path forms an angle of 10.2° with the first road and an angle of 79.8° with the second road.

26. Critical Thinking A right triangle has only one 90° angle. Both of its other angles have measures greater than 0° and less than 90°. Why is it useful to define the tangent of 90° to equal 1, and the tangent of 0° to equal 0?

Answers will vary. Possible answer: Consider a right triangle in which the complementary angles are very close to 0° and 90°. Let the length of the hypotenuse be 1. The tangent of the small angle is very close to $\frac{0}{1}$. The tangent of the larger angle will be very close to $\frac{1}{1}$.

Lesson Performance Task

When they form conical piles, granular materials such as salt, gravel, and sand settle at different "angles of repose," depending on the shapes of the grains. One particular 13-foot tall cone of dry sand has a base diameter of 38.6 feet.

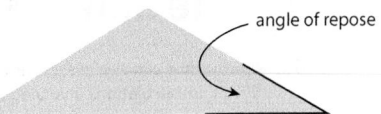

angle of repose

1. To the nearest tenth of a degree, what is the angle of repose of this type of dry sand?

2. A different conical pile of the same type of sand is 10 feet tall. What is the diameter of the cone's base?

3. Henley Landscaping Supply sells a type of sand with a 30° angle of repose for $32 per cubic yard. Find the cost of an 11-foot-tall cone of this type of sand. Show your work.

1. $\tan(x) = \dfrac{13}{\left(\frac{38.6}{2}\right)}$

   $\tan(x) = \dfrac{13}{19.3}$

   $x = \tan^{-1}\left(\dfrac{13}{19.3}\right)$

   $x = 34°$

2. $\tan(34) = \dfrac{10}{\left(\frac{x}{2}\right)}$

   $\tan(34) = \dfrac{20}{x}$

   $x = 29.7$

3. Let r = radius of cone. Then:

   $\tan 30° = \dfrac{11}{r}$

   $0.5774 = \dfrac{11}{r}$

   $r \approx 19.1$ ft

   Volume of cone:

   $V = \dfrac{1}{3}Bh$

   $= \dfrac{1}{3}\pi r^2 h$

   $= \dfrac{1}{3}(3.14)(19.1)^2(11)$

   $= 4200.2$ ft^3

   1 yd^3 = 27 ft^3 so 4200.2 ft^3 = 4200.2 ÷ 27 ≈ 155.6 yd^3

   At $32 per yd^3, 155.6 yd^3 will cost 155.6 × 32 = $4979.20.

EXTENSION ACTIVITY

Have students research the angle of repose of at least four granular substances. For each one they should draw an equilateral triangle showing a cross-section of a pile of the substance labeled with a base diameter of 20 feet, base angles measuring the angle of repose, and the correct height to the nearest tenth.

AVOID COMMON ERRORS

When using the tangent function to find the angle of repose of a conical pile, students may mistakenly use the diameter of the base of the pile as the side adjacent to the angle of repose. The triangle they should use has the *radius* of the base as the side adjacent to the angle of repose and the height of the pile as the side opposite.

INTEGRATE MATHEMATICAL PRACTICES

Focus on Math Connections

MP.1 Are values of the tangent function proportional? If they are, the tangent of 40°, for example, should be double the tangent of 20°. Use tangent tables or a calculator to investigate the question. Give examples to support your conclusion. Not proportional; example: tan 20° ≈ 0.36, but tan 40° ≈ 0.84 ≠ 2tan 20°

Scoring Rubric

2 points: Student correctly solves the problem and explains his/her reasoning.

1 point: Student shows good understanding of the problem but does not fully solve or explain his/her reasoning.

0 points: Student does not demonstrate understanding of the problem.

Tangent Ratio　**696**

Sine and Cosine Ratios

Common Core Math Standards

The student is expected to:

 G-SRT.C.6

Understand that by similarity, side ratios in right triangles are properties of the angles in the triangle, leading to definitions of trigonometric ratios for acute angles. Also G-SRT.C.7, G-SRT.C.8

Mathematical Practices

 MP.4 Modeling

Language Objective

Explain to a partner how to find the sine and cosine of an angle given a diagram of a right triangle with given angle measure and opposite or adjacent leg and hypotenuse lengths.

ENGAGE

Essential Question: How can you use the sine and cosine ratios, and their inverses, in calculations involving right triangles?

Given the measure of one acute angle and the length of the hypotenuse, you can use the sine and cosine ratios to find the lengths of each leg. Given the length of the hypotenuse and the length of a leg, you can use their inverses to find the measure of each acute angle.

PREVIEW: LESSON PERFORMANCE TASK

View the Engage section online. Discuss the photograph, asking students to speculate on what the person in the photo might be doing. Then preview the Lesson Performance Task.

Name_____ Class_____ Date_____

13.2 Sine and Cosine Ratios

Essential Question: How can you use the sine and cosine ratios, and their inverses, in calculations involving right triangles?

Resource Locker

🧭 Explore   Investigating Ratios in a Right Triangle

You can use geometry software or an online tool to explore ratios of side lengths in right triangles.

(A) Construct three points A, B, and C.
Construct rays $\vec{AB}$ and $\vec{AC}$. Move C so that $\angle A$ is acute.

(B) Construct point D on $\overline{AC}$. Construct a line through D perpendicular to $\overline{AB}$. Construct point E as the intersection of the perpendicular line and $\overline{AB}$.

(C) Measure $\angle A$. Measure the side lengths DE, AE, and AD of $\triangle ADE$.

(D) Calculate the ratios $\frac{DE}{AD}$ and $\frac{AE}{AD}$.

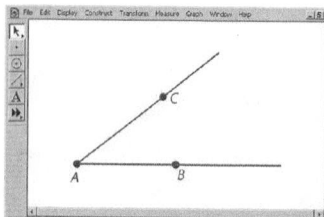

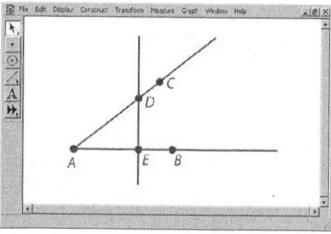

Reflect

1. Drag D along $\vec{AC}$. What happens to m$\angle A$ as D moves along $\vec{AC}$? What postulate or theorem guarantees that the different triangles formed are similar to each other?
   m$\angle A$ does not change; AA Similarity Theorem, given also that $\angle AED$ remains a right angle.

2. As you move D along $\vec{AC}$, what happens to the values of the ratios $\frac{DE}{AD}$ and $\frac{AE}{AD}$?
   Use the properties of similar triangles to explain this result.
   The ratios do not change; Given similar triangles $\triangle ADE$, and $\triangle AD'E'$,
   $\frac{AD}{AD'} = \frac{DE}{D'E'} \rightarrow \frac{D'E'}{AD'} = \frac{DE}{AD}$ and $\frac{AD}{AD'} = \frac{AE}{AE'} \rightarrow \frac{AE'}{AD'} = \frac{AE}{AD}$.

3. Move C. What happens to m$\angle A$? With a new value of m$\angle A$, note the values of the two ratios. What happens to the ratios if you drag D along $\vec{AC}$?
   m$\angle A$ changes in value; the new values of the ratios do not change as D is dragged along $\vec{AC}$.

© Houghton Mifflin Harcourt Publishing Company

Module 13   **697**   Lesson 2

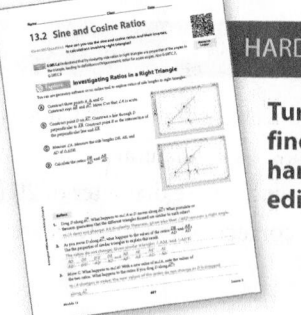

HARDCOVER PAGES 593–602

Turn to these pages to find this lesson in the hardcover student edition.

Trigonometric Ratios

A **trigonometric ratio** is a ratio of two sides of a right triangle. You have already seen one trigonometric ratio, the tangent. There are two additional trigonometric ratios, the sine and the cosine, that involve the hypotenuse of a right triangle.

The **sine** of $\angle A$, written $\sin A$, is defined as follows:

$$\sin A = \frac{\text{length of leg opposite } \angle A}{\text{length of hypotenuse}} = \frac{BC}{AB}$$

The **cosine** of $\angle A$, written $\cos A$, is defined as follows:

$$\cos A = \frac{\text{length of leg adjacent to } \angle A}{\text{length of hypotenuse}} = \frac{AC}{AB}$$

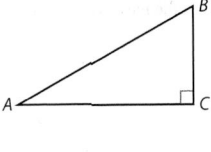

You can use these definitions to calculate trigonometric ratios.

Example 1 Write sine and cosine of each angle as a fraction and as a decimal rounded to the nearest thousandth.

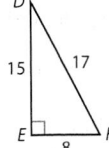

(A) $\angle D$

$$\sin D = \frac{\text{length of leg opposite } \angle D}{\text{length of hypotenuse}} = \frac{EF}{DF} = \frac{8}{17} \approx 0.471$$

$$\cos D = \frac{\text{length of leg adjacent to } \angle D}{\text{length of hypotenuse}} = \frac{DE}{DF} = \frac{15}{17} \approx 0.882$$

(B) $\angle F$

$$\sin F = \frac{\text{length of leg opposite to } \angle F}{\text{length of hypotenuse}} = \frac{DE}{DF} = \frac{15}{17} \approx \boxed{0.882}$$

$$\cos F = \frac{\text{length of leg adjacent to } \angle F}{\text{length of hypotenuse}} = \frac{8}{17} \approx \boxed{0.471}$$

Reflect

4. What do you notice about the sines and cosines you found? Do you think this relationship will be true for any pair of acute angles in a right triangle? Explain.
   $\sin D = \cos F$ and $\cos D = \sin F$; this relationship always holds because the leg opposite one acute angle is adjacent to the other one.

5. In a right triangle $\triangle PQR$ with $PR = 5$, $QR = 3$, and $m\angle Q = 90°$, what are the values of $\sin P$ and $\cos P$?

   $\sin P = \boxed{\dfrac{3}{5}}$

   $\cos P = \boxed{\dfrac{4}{5}}$

PROFESSIONAL DEVELOPMENT

Math Background

Trigonometry is the branch of mathematics concerned with angle relationships in triangles. The ancient Egyptians used trigonometry to reset land boundaries after the Nile River flooded each year. The Babylonians used trigonometry to measure distances to nearby stars. Trigonometry is used in modern engineering, cartography, medical imaging, and many other fields.

EXPLORE

Investigating Ratios in a Right Triangle

INTEGRATE TECHNOLOGY

Students have the option of doing the Explore activity either in the book or online.

INTEGRATE MATHEMATICAL PRACTICES
Focus on Critical Thinking

MP.3 Have students examine what happens to the ratio of the opposite side length to the hypotenuse length as the acute angle gets closer to 90°. Repeat for the ratio of the adjacent side length to the hypotenuse length as the acute angle gets closer to 0°.

QUESTIONING STRATEGIES

? If the measure of the acute angle of the right triangle does not change but the side lengths of the triangle change, how do the ratios change? Explain. The values of the numerator and the denominators will change but the ratios are equal to the original ratios of opposite length to hypotenuse and adjacent length to hypotenuse because the triangles are similar.

EXPLAIN 1

Finding the Sine and Cosine of an Angle

AVOID COMMON ERRORS

Students often use the wrong ratio for sine or cosine. Help students review these relationships by using flashcards, mnemonics, or other memory aids. Encourage students to research mnemonics or produce their own.

? If you know only the sine for an acute angle of a right triangle, how could you find the cosine? The sine gives the ratio of the opposite side to the hypotenuse, so you can construct a right triangle with a hypotenuse and a leg that match the ratio. Then you can use the Pythagorean Theorem to find the length of the other leg, and use it to write the cosine ratio.

? Do you think it is possible for the value of a sine or cosine to be greater than 1? Why or why not? It is not possible; because the hypotenuse is the longest side of a right triangle, any ratio that has the length of the hypotenuse as the denominator will be less than 1.

EXPLAIN 2

Using Complementary Angles

QUESTIONING STRATEGIES

? Why do the sine and cosine have a complementary angle relationship? The ratios are for a right triangle. Since one angle must be a right angle, the other two angles must be complementary because the sum of the measures of the angles of a triangle is 180°.

? How can you write equivalent expressions for $\sin x°$ using cosine and $\cos y°$ using sine? Explain. Use the complement to write $\sin x° = \cos\left(90° - x°\right)$ and $\cos y° = \sin\left(90° - y°\right)$.

? How can the relationship between the sine and cosine of complementary angles help you solve equations involving sines and cosines? Apply the fact that the total measure of the angles is 90° to set up an equation to solve for unknown values.

699 Lesson 13.2

⚙ Explain 2 **Using Complementary Angles**

The acute angles of a right triangle are complementary. Their trigonometric ratios are related to each other as shown in the following relationship.

> **Trigonometric Ratios of Complementary Angles**
>
> If $\angle A$ and $\angle B$ are the acute angles in a right triangle, then $\sin A = \cos B$ and $\cos A = \sin B$.
>
> Therefore, if θ ("theta") is the measure of an acute angle, then $\sin \theta = \cos\left(90° - \theta\right)$ and $\cos \theta = \sin\left(90° - \theta\right)$.
>
>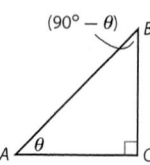

You can use these relationships to write equivalent expressions.

Example 2 Write each trigonometric expression.

Ⓐ Given that $\sin 38° \approx 0.616$, write the cosine of a complementary angle in terms of the sine of 38°. Then find the cosine of the complementary angle.

Use an expression relating trigonometric ratios of complementary angles.

$$\sin \theta = \cos(90° - \theta)$$

Substitute 38 into both sides. $\qquad \sin 38° = \cos(90° - 38°)$

Simplify. $\qquad \sin 38° = \cos 52°$

Substitute for $\sin 38°$. $\qquad 0.616 \approx \cos 52°$

So, the cosine of the complementary angle is about 0.616.

Ⓑ Given that $\cos 60° = 0.5$, write the sine of a complementary angle in terms of the cosine of 60°. Then find the sine of the complementary angle.

Use an expression relating trigonometric ratios of complementary angles.

$$\cos \theta = \sin(90° - \theta)$$

Substitute $\boxed{60}$ into both sides. $\qquad \cos \boxed{60}° = \sin\left(90° - \boxed{60}°\right)$

Simplify the right side. $\qquad \cos \boxed{60}° = \sin \boxed{30}°$

Substitute for the cosine of $\boxed{60}°$. $\qquad \boxed{0.5} = \sin \boxed{30}°$

So, the sine of the complementary angle is 0.5.

COLLABORATIVE LEARNING

Small Group Activity

Have students work in small groups to investigate the relationship between the size of an angle and its sine, using geometry software or graph paper, rulers, and protractors. They should draw several triangles with unit side lengths and an angle that increases. Those using graph paper will need to measure with protractor and ruler. Have them determine how the sine changes as the angle size increases; then repeat for cosine. Have students share their results and how they drew their conclusions.

Reflect

6. What can you conclude about the sine and cosine of 45°? Explain.
   $\sin 45° = \cos 45°$; 45° is complementary to itself.

7. **Discussion** Is it possible for the sine or cosine of an acute angle to equal 1? Explain.
   No; the hypotenuse of a right triangle is always longer than its legs, so the side ratios
   defining sine and cosine must always be less than 1.

Your Turn

Write each trigonometric expression.

8. Given that $\cos 73° \approx 0.292$, write the sine of a complementary angle.
   $\theta = 73°$, so $90 - \theta = 17°$.

   $\sin 17° \approx 0.292$

9. Given that $\sin 45° \approx 0.707$, write the cosine of a complementary angle.
   $\theta = 45°$, so $90 - \theta = 45°$.

   $\cos 45° \approx 0.707$

⏺ Explain 3   Finding Side Lengths using Sine and Cosine

You can use sine and cosine to solve real-world problems.

Example 3   A 12-ft ramp is installed alongside some steps to provide wheelchair access to a library. The ramp makes an angle of 11° with the ground. Find each dimension, to the nearest tenth of a foot.

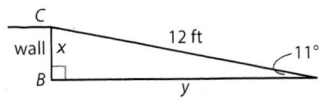

Ⓐ Find the height x of the wall.

Use the definition of sine. $\sin A = \dfrac{\text{length of leg opposite } \angle A}{\text{length of hypotenuse}} = \dfrac{AB}{AC}$

Substitute 11° for A, x for BC, and 12 for AC. $\sin 11° = \dfrac{x}{12}$

Multiply both sides by 12. $12\sin 11° = x$

Use a calculator to evaluate the expression. $x \approx 2.3$

So, the height of the wall is about 2.3 feet.

© Houghton Mifflin Harcourt Publishing Company

DIFFERENTIATE INSTRUCTION

Critical Thinking

Discuss how to use the trigonometric ratios to prove that $\tan x = \dfrac{\sin x}{\cos x}$. Ask students if they find this surprising and why or why not.

COLLABORATIVE LEARNING

Have students construct right triangles with unit side lengths on graph paper, then use a protractor to measure each of the acute angles to the nearest degree. Have students verify the complementary relationship between the sine and cosine for their triangles for each of the acute angles, and then share their results with the class.

EXPLAIN 3

Finding Side Lengths using Sine and Cosine

INTEGRATE TECHNOLOGY

It may be helpful to review with students how to evaluate expressions of the form $a\sin(x°)$ and $b\cos(y°)$, with given values for a, b, x, and y, using their calculators.

QUESTIONING STRATEGIES

? Why is a trigonometric ratio useful in solving a real-world problem involving right triangles? Sample answer: It makes it possible to use known lengths and angle measures to find unknown lengths that might be difficult to measure.

? If you use a trigonometric ratio, such as sine or cosine, to find the length of one of the legs of a right triangle, do you have to use a trigonometric ratio to find the length of the other leg as well? Explain. No, you could also use the Pythagorean Theorem to find the other leg since you will know the lengths of the hypotenuse and one leg.

Finding Angle Measures using Sine and Cosine

QUESTIONING STRATEGIES

? In the equation $y = \sin^{-1} x$, explain what x and y represent. In the equation, x represents the sine of the angle with measure $y°$.

Ⓑ Find the distance y that the ramp extends in front of the wall.

Use the definition of cosine.

$$\cos A = \frac{\text{length of leg adjacent to } \angle A}{\text{length of hypotenuse}} = \frac{AB}{AC}$$

Substitute $\boxed{11}°$ for A, y for AB, and $\boxed{12}$ for AC.

$$\cos \boxed{11}° = \frac{y}{\boxed{12}}$$

Multiply both sides by $\boxed{12}$.

$$\boxed{12} \cos \boxed{11}° = y$$

Use a calculator to evaluate the expression.

$$y \approx \boxed{11.8}$$

So, the ramp extends in front of the wall about $\boxed{11.8}$ feet.

Reflect

10. Could you find the height of the wall using the cosine? Explain.
Since $\angle A$ and $\angle B$ are complementary, $m\angle C = 79°$. Then $\cos 79° = \frac{x}{12}$ and

$x = 12\cos 79° \approx 2.3$ ft.

Your Turn

11. Suppose a new regulation states that the maximum angle of a ramp for wheelchairs is 8°. At least how long must the new ramp be? Round to the nearest tenth of a foot.

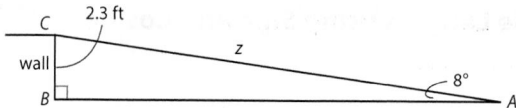

The ramp must be at least long enough to create an 8° angle at $\angle A$.

$$\sin A = \frac{BC}{AC} \Rightarrow \sin 8° \approx \frac{2.3}{z}$$

$$z \approx 16.5$$

The ramp must be at least 16.5 ft long.

⊘ Explain 4 **Finding Angle Measures using Sine and Cosine**

In the triangle, $\sin A = \frac{5}{10} = \frac{1}{2}$. However, you already know that $\sin 30° = \frac{1}{2}$. So you can conclude that $m\angle A = 30°$,

and write $\sin^{-1}\left(\frac{1}{2}\right) = 30°$.

Extending this idea, the **inverse trigonometric ratios** for sine and cosine are defined as follows:

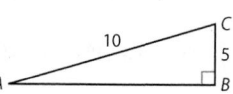

Given an acute angle, $\angle A$,

- if $\sin A = x$, then $\sin^{-1} x = m\angle A$, read as "inverse sine of x"
- if $\cos A = x$, then $\cos^{-1} x = m\angle A$, read as "inverse cosine of x"

You can use a calculator to evaluate inverse trigonometric expressions.

LANGUAGE SUPPORT **EL**

Connect Vocabulary

Distinguishing between *sine* and *cosine* may be challenging for some students. Explain that the prefix *co-* can mean *together*, as it does in the word *cooperate*. Point out that the cosine ratio for an acute angle of a triangle involves the adjacent leg. Tell students to remember this by thinking of the adjacent leg as "coming together" with the hypotenuse from the angle.

Example 4 Find the acute angle measures in △PQR, to the nearest degree.

(A) Write a trigonometric ratio for ∠R.

Since the lengths of the hypotenuse and the opposite leg are given,

use the sine ratio.

$\sin R = \dfrac{PQ}{PR}$

Substitute 7 for PQ and 13 for PR.

$\sin R = \dfrac{7}{13}$

(B) Write and evaluate an inverse trigonometric ratio to find m∠R and m∠P.

Start with the trigonometric ratio for ∠R.

$\sin R = \boxed{\dfrac{7}{13}}$

Use the definition of the inverse sine ratio.

$m\angle R = \sin^{-1} \boxed{\dfrac{7}{13}}$

Use a calculator to evaluate the inverse sine ratio.

$m\angle R = \boxed{33}\,^{\circ}$

Write a cosine ratio for ∠P.

$\cos P = \dfrac{PQ}{PR}$

Substitute $\boxed{7}$ for PQ and $\boxed{13}$ for PR.

$\cos P = \boxed{\dfrac{7}{13}}$

Use the definition of the inverse cosine ratio.

$m\angle P = \cos^{-1} \boxed{\dfrac{7}{13}}$

Use a calculator to evaluate the inverse cosine ratio.

$m\angle P = \boxed{57}\,^{\circ}$

Reflect

12. How else could you have determined m∠P?

∠P and ∠R are complementary. Therefore, m∠P = 90° − m∠R ≈ 90° − 33° = 57°.

Your Turn

Find the acute angle measures in △XYZ, to the nearest degree.

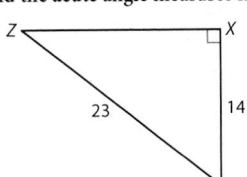

13. m∠Y $\cos Y = \dfrac{XY}{YZ} = \dfrac{14}{23}$

$m\angle Y = \cos^{-1}\left(\dfrac{14}{23}\right) \approx 53°$

14. m∠Z   m∠Z = 90° − m∠Y ≈ 90° − 53° = 37°

Elaborate

15. How are the sine and cosine ratios for an acute angle of a right triangle defined?

$\sin A = \dfrac{\text{opposite}}{\text{hypotenuse}} = \dfrac{BC}{AB}$ and $\cos A = \dfrac{\text{adjacent}}{\text{hypotenuse}} = \dfrac{AC}{AB}$

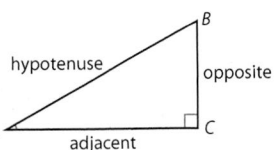

QUESTIONING STRATEGIES

? How could you evaluate the inverse sine or cosine of an angle without using the calculator's inverse trigonometric keys or a table of values? Use the measurements of the sine or cosine ratio in the Pythagorean Theorem to find the length of the missing leg. Then draw a right triangle with the side lengths and use a protractor to measure the angle formed by the hypotenuse and the opposite side or the adjacent side to estimate the angle measure.

AVOID COMMON ERRORS

Remind students about the notation used to represent the inverse sine and cosine: $\sin^{-1} x$ and $\cos^{-1} x$. As with the inverse tangent, the −1 is not an exponent. Rather, it denotes the inverse trigonometric ratio whose value is an angle with a degree measure.

ELABORATE

INTEGRATE TECHNOLOGY

Have students graph $y = \sin x$ and $y = \cos x$ on their graphing calculators on the interval [0°, 90°]. Discuss similarities and differences.

QUESTIONING STRATEGIES

? How are cosine and the inverse cosine related? The cosine of an acute angle of a right triangle is the ratio of the lengths of the adjacent side to the hypotenuse of the right triangle. The inverse cosine is the angle with that cosine ratio.

SUMMARIZE THE LESSON

? How do you decide which trigonometric ratio to use to find a missing side length or angle measure in a right triangle? Use sine or inverse sine for opposite side and hypotenuse relationships and cosine or inverse cosine for adjacent side and hypotenuse relationships.

---

16. How are the inverse sine and cosine ratios for an acute angle of a right triangle defined?
Because the sine ratio for a given acute angle is always the same, the measure of that angle

can be defined as an inverse sine ratio:

$$\sin A = \frac{BC}{AB} \rightarrow m\angle A = \sin^{-1}\left(\frac{BC}{AB}\right) \text{ or } \sin A = x \rightarrow m\angle A = \sin^{-1} x$$

Similarly,

$$\cos A = \frac{AC}{AB} \rightarrow m\angle A = \cos^{-1}\left(\frac{AC}{AB}\right) \text{ or } \cos A = y \rightarrow m\angle A = \cos^{-1} y$$

17. Essential Question Check-In How do you find an unknown angle measure in a right triangle?
First, use two known side lengths to form a ratio. Then use the appropriate inverse

trigonometric ratio to find the angle measure.

☆ Evaluate: Homework and Practice

- Online Homework
- Hints and Help
- Extra Practice

Write each trigonometric expression. Round trigonometric ratios to the nearest thousandth.

1. Given that sin 60° ≈ 0.866, write the cosine of a complementary angle.

$$\sin 60° = \cos(90° - 60°)$$
$$0.866 \approx \cos 30°$$

2. Given that cos 26° ≈ 0.899, write the sine of a complementary angle.

$$\cos 26° = \sin(90° - 26°)$$
$$0.899 \approx \sin 64°$$

Write each trigonometric ratio as a fraction and as a decimal, rounded (if necessary) to the nearest thousandth.

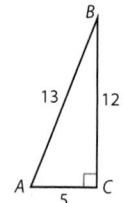

3. sin A $\sin A = \dfrac{\text{opposite}}{\text{hypotenuse}} = \dfrac{BC}{AB} = \dfrac{12}{13} \approx 0.923$

4. cos A $\cos A = \dfrac{\text{adjacent}}{\text{hypotenuse}} = \dfrac{AC}{AB} = \dfrac{5}{13} \approx 0.385$

5. cos B $\cos B = \dfrac{\text{adjacent}}{\text{hypotenuse}} = \dfrac{BC}{AB} = \dfrac{12}{13} \approx 0.923$

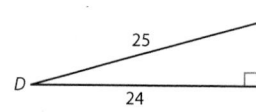

6. sin D $\cos A = \dfrac{\text{opposite}}{\text{hypotenuse}} = \dfrac{EF}{DF} = \dfrac{7}{25} = 0.28$

7. cos F $\cos F = \dfrac{\text{adjacent}}{\text{hypotenuse}} = \dfrac{EF}{DF} = \dfrac{7}{25} = 0.28$

8. sin F $\sin F = \dfrac{\text{opposite}}{\text{hypotenuse}} = \dfrac{24}{25} = 0.96$

Find the unknown length x in each right triangle, to the nearest tenth.

9.

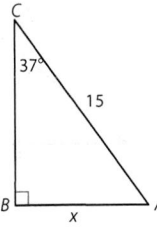

$$\sin C = \frac{AB}{AC}$$

$$\sin 37° = \frac{x}{15} \Rightarrow 9.0 \approx x$$

10.

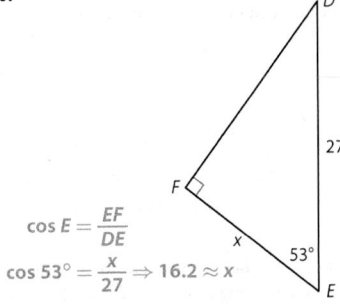

$$\cos E = \frac{EF}{DE}$$

$$\cos 53° = \frac{x}{27} \Rightarrow 16.2 \approx x$$

11.

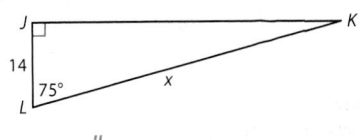

$$\cos L = \frac{JL}{KL}$$

$$\cos 75° = \frac{14}{x} \Rightarrow \approx 54.1$$

12.

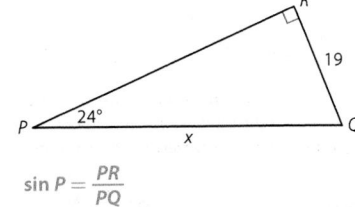

$$\sin P = \frac{PR}{PQ}$$

$$\sin 24° = \frac{19}{x} \Rightarrow \approx 46.7$$

Find each acute angle measure, to the nearest degree.

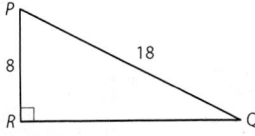

13. $m\angle P$

$$\cos P = \frac{PR}{PQ} = \frac{8}{18}$$

$$m\angle P = \cos^{-1}\left(\frac{8}{18}\right) \approx 64°$$

14. $m\angle Q$

$$m\angle Q = 90° - m\angle P \approx 90° - 64° = 26°$$

15. $m\angle U$

$$\sin U = \frac{VW}{UW} = \frac{11}{15}$$

$$m\angle U = \sin^{-1}\left(\frac{11}{15}\right) \approx 47°$$

16. $m\angle W$

$$m\angle W = 90° - m\angle U \approx 90° - 47° = 43°$$

© Houghton Mifflin Harcourt Publishing Company

EVALUATE

ASSIGNMENT GUIDE

Concepts and Skills	Practice
Explore Investigating Ratios in a Right Triangle	Exercise 17
Example 1 Finding the Sine and Cosine of an Angle	Exercises 3–8
Example 2 Using Complementary Angles	Exercises 1–2
Example 3 Finding Side Lengths using Sine and Cosine	Exercises 9–12
Example 4 Finding Angle Measures using Sine and Cosine	Exercises 13–16

AVOID COMMON ERRORS

Remind students that their calculators must be set on degrees, not radians, to get the correct values for the trigonometric ratios.

Communicating Math

Discuss the importance of being able to draw and interpret right triangle diagrams to use trigonometric ratios to solve real-world problems.

Exercise	Depth of Knowledge (D.O.K.)	COMMON CORE	Mathematical Practices
1–16	**1** Recall of Information		**MP.4** Modeling
17–24	**2** Skills/Concepts		**MP.4** Modeling
25	**3** Strategic Thinking H.O.T.		**MP.3** Logic
26	**3** Strategic Thinking H.O.T.		**MP.2** Reasoning
27	**3** Strategic Thinking H.O.T.		**MP.3** Logic

Sine and Cosine Ratios　**704**

Students may have difficulty solving equations such as $\sin x = \frac{a}{c}$ when the variable is in the denominator. Review with students how to use inverse operations to write an equivalent equation with the variable in the numerator, such as $c = \frac{a}{\sin x}$.

INTEGRATE TECHNOLOGY

In addition to calculators, students can use geometry software and spreadsheets to evaluate trigonometric ratios.

---

17. Use the property that corresponding sides of similar triangles are proportional to explain why the trigonometric ratio sin A is the same when calculated in △ADE as in △ABC.

$\angle A \cong \angle A$ and $\angle ABC \cong \angle ADE$, since both are right angles.

By AA ∼, △ABC∼△ADE, so corresponding sides are proportional:

$$\frac{AC}{AE} = \frac{BC}{DE} \Rightarrow AC = \frac{(BC)(AE)}{DE} \Rightarrow \frac{AC}{BC} = \frac{AE}{DE}$$

These ratios determine sin A, and since they are equal, sin A is the same when calculated in either right triangle.

18. Technology The specifications for a laptop computer describe its screen as measuring 15.6 in. However, this is actually the length of a diagonal of the rectangular screen, as represented in the figure. How wide is the screen horizontally, to the nearest tenth of an inch?

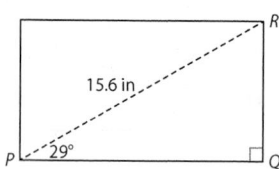

$$\cos P = \frac{PQ}{PR} \Rightarrow \cos 29° = \frac{PQ}{15.6} \Rightarrow 13.6 \text{ in.} = PQ$$

19. Building Sharla's bedroom is directly under the roof of her house. Given the dimensions shown, how high is the ceiling at its highest point, to the nearest tenth of a foot?

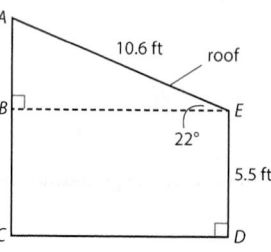

$$\sin(m\angle AEB) = \frac{AB}{AE} \Rightarrow \sin 22° = \frac{AB}{10.6} \Rightarrow AB \approx 4.0$$

Maximum height: $AC = AB + BC \approx 4.0 + 5.5 = 9.5$ ft

20. Zoology You can sometimes see an eagle gliding with its wings flexed in a characteristic double-vee shape. Each wing can be modeled as two right triangles as shown in the figure. Find the measure of the angle in the middle of the wing, $\angle DHG$ to the nearest degree.

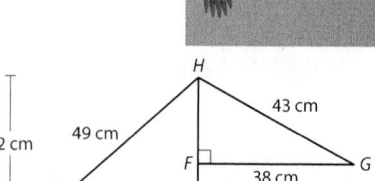

$$\cos(m\angle DHE) = \frac{EH}{DH} = \frac{32}{49}$$

$$m\angle DHE = \cos^{-1}\left(\frac{32}{49}\right) \approx 49.2°$$

$$\sin(m\angle FHG) = \frac{FG}{GH} = \frac{38}{43}$$

$$m\angle FHG = \sin^{-1}\left(\frac{38}{43}\right) \approx 62.1°$$

$$m\angle DHG = m\angle DHE + m\angle FHG \approx$$

$$49.2 + 62.1 = 111.3°$$

21. Algebra Find a pair of acute angles that satisfy the equation $\sin(3x + 9) = \cos(x + 5)$. Check that your answers make sense.

The expressions must be the measures of two complementary angles:

$(3x + 9) + (x + 5) = 90 \Rightarrow x = 19$

$(3x + 9)° = (3(19) + 9)° = 66°$ and $(x + 5)° = ((19) + 5)° = 24°$

Check: $66° + 24° = 90°$

22. Multi-Step Reginald is planning to fence his back yard. Every side of the yard except for the side along the house is to be fenced, and fencing costs \$3.50/yd. How much will the fencing cost?

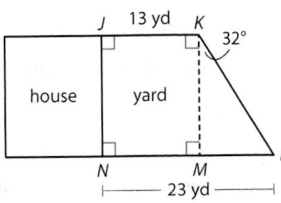

$\sin(m\angle LKM) = \dfrac{LM}{LK} \Rightarrow \sin 32° = \dfrac{(23 - 13)}{LK} \Rightarrow LK \approx 18.9$

distance to fence: $JK + KL + LN \approx 13 + 18.9 + 23 = 54.9$ yd

cost of fencing: about $54.9(3.50) = \$192.15$

23. Architecture The sides of One World Trade Center in New York City form eight isosceles triangles, four of which are 200 ft long at their base BC. The length AC of each sloping side is approximately 1185 ft.

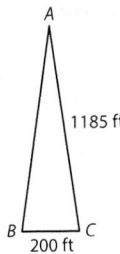

Find the measure of the apex angle BAC of each isosceles triangle, to the nearest tenth of a degree. (*Hint:* Use the midpoint D of $\overline{BC}$ to create two right triangles.)

In $\triangle ABD$, $AB = 1185$ ft and $BD = \dfrac{1}{2}(200 \text{ ft}) = 100$ ft. Therefore,

$\sin(m\angle BAD) = \dfrac{BD}{AB} = \dfrac{100}{1185} \Rightarrow m\angle BAD = \sin^{-1}\left(\dfrac{100}{1185}\right)$

So $m\angle BAC = 2m\angle BAD = 2\sin^{-1}\left(\dfrac{100}{1185}\right) \approx 9.7°$.

Discuss how students can use the facts that $\sin 0° = 0$ and the sine increases as the angle increases (between 0° and 90°), and $\cos 0° = 1$ and the cosine decreases as the angle increases (between 0° and 90°), as a quick check when they evaluate sine and cosine trigonometric ratios.

PEER-TO-PEER DISCUSSION

Have students investigate the following identities by evaluating them for different angles:
$\sin^{-1}(\sin x) = x$ and $\cos^{-1}(\cos x) = x$.

JOURNAL

Have students describe how they remember the difference between the sine and cosine ratios, and the relationship between the ratios. Remind them to include at least one figure and at least one example in their descriptions.

24. Explain the Error Melissa has calculated the length of $\overline{XZ}$ in $\triangle XYZ$. Explain why Melissa's answer must be incorrect, and identify and correct her error.

Melissa's solution:

$\cos X = \dfrac{XZ}{XY}$

$XZ = \dfrac{XY}{\cos X}$

$XZ = 27 \cos 42° \approx 20.1$

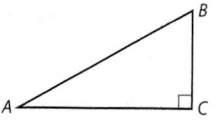

20.1 < 27, but the hypotenuse should be the longest side. Her definition of cosine was inverted.

$\cos X = \dfrac{XY}{XZ} \Rightarrow XZ = \dfrac{27}{\cos 42°} \approx 36.3$

25. Communicate Mathematical Ideas Explain why the sine and cosine of an acute angle are always between 0 and 1.

$0 < BC < AB \Rightarrow \dfrac{0}{AB} < \dfrac{BC}{AB} < \dfrac{AB}{AB} \Rightarrow 0 < \sin A < 1$

The same argument shows that $0 < \cos A < 1$.

26. Look for a Pattern In $\triangle ABC$, the hypotenuse $\overline{AB}$ has a length of 1. Use the Pythagorean Theorem to explore the relationship between the squares of the sine and cosine of $\angle A$, written $\sin^2 A$ and $\cos^2 A$. Could you derive this relationship using a right triangle without any lengths specified? Explain.

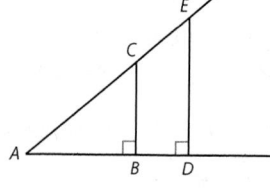

$\sin A = \dfrac{BC}{AB} = \dfrac{BC}{1} = BC$ and $\cos A = \dfrac{AC}{AB} = \dfrac{AC}{1} = AC$

By the Pythagorean Theorem, $AC^2 + BC^2 = AB^2$

$(\sin A)^2 + (\cos A)^2 = 1^2$

$\sin^2 A + \cos^2 A = 1$

Yes: $\sin^2 A + \cos^2 A = \left(\dfrac{BC}{AB}\right)^2 + \left(\dfrac{AC}{AB}\right)^2 = \dfrac{BC^2 + AC^2}{AB^2} = \dfrac{AB^2}{AB^2} = 1$

27. Justify Reasoning Use the Triangle Proportionality Theorem to explain why the trigonometric ratio $\cos A$ is the same when calculated in $\triangle ADE$ as in $\triangle ABC$.

Two segments $\perp$ to the same line are $\parallel$ to each other,

so $\overline{BC} \parallel \overline{DE}$. By the Triangle Proportionality Theorem, $\overline{BC}$

divides sides $\overline{AD}$ and $\overline{AE}$ of $\triangle ADE$ proportionally:

$\dfrac{BD}{AB} = \dfrac{CE}{AC} \Rightarrow 1 + \dfrac{BD}{AB} = 1 + \dfrac{CE}{AC} \Rightarrow \dfrac{AB + BD}{AB} = \dfrac{AC + CE}{AC} \Rightarrow \dfrac{AD}{AB} = \dfrac{AE}{AC} \Rightarrow \dfrac{AD}{AE} = \dfrac{AB}{AC}$

These ratios determine $\cos A$, and since they are equal, $\cos A$ is the same when

calculated in either triangle.

Lesson Performance Task

As light passes from a vacuum into another medium, it is *refracted*—that is, its direction changes. The ratio of the sine of the angle of the incoming *incident* ray, I, to the sine of the angle of the outgoing *refracted* ray, r, is called the *index of refraction*:

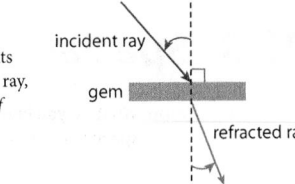

incident ray

gem

refracted ray

$n = \frac{\sin I}{\sin r}$. where n is the index of refraction.

This relationship is important in many fields, including gemology, the study of precious stones. A gemologist can place an unidentified gem into an instrument called a refractometer, direct an incident ray of light at a particular angle into the stone, measure the angle of the refracted ray, and calculate the index of refraction. Because the indices of refraction of thousands of gems are known, the gemologist can then identify the gem.

Gem	Index of Refraction
Hematite	2.94
Diamond	2.42
Zircon	1.95
Azurite	1.85
Sapphire	1.77
Tourmaline	1.62
Serpentine	1.56
Coral	1.49
Opal	1.39

1. Identify the gem, given these angles obtained from a refractometer:

   a. $I = 71°$, $r = 29°$

   b. $I = 51°$, $r = 34°$

   c. $I = 45°$, $r = 17°$

2. A thin slice of sapphire is placed in a refractometer. The angle of the incident ray is $56°$. Find the angle of the refracted ray to the nearest degree.

3. An incident ray of light struck a slice of serpentine. The resulting angle of refraction measured $21°$. Find the angle of incidence to the nearest degree.

4. Describe the error(s) in a student's solution and explain why they were error(s):

$$n = \frac{\sin I}{\sin r}$$
$$= \frac{\sin 51°}{\sin 34°}$$
$$= \frac{51°}{34°}$$
$$= 1.5 \rightarrow coral$$

1. a. $\frac{\sin(71°)}{\sin(29°)} = 1.95$ zircon

   b. $\frac{\sin(51°)}{\sin(34°)} = 1.39$ opal

   c. $\frac{\sin(45°)}{\sin(17°)} = 2.42$ diamond

2. $1.77 = \frac{\sin(56°)}{\sin(x°)}$

   $\sin(x°) = \frac{\sin(56°)}{1.77}$

   $x = \sin^{-1}\left(\frac{\sin(56°)}{1.77}\right) = 28°$

3. $1.56 = \frac{\sin(x°)}{\sin(21°)}$

   $x = \sin^{-1}\left(1.56 \cdot \sin(21°)\right) = 34°$

4. Possible answer: The student divided out the word "sin" from the numerator and the denominator in Step 2. This was incorrect because "sin 51°" and "sin 34°" are indivisible units, with each representing a single real number.

Module 13   708   Lesson 2

© Houghton Mifflin Harcourt Publishing Company

Sine and Cosine Ratios   708

AVOID COMMON ERRORS

Question 4 in the Lesson Performance Task identifies an error commonly made by students in working with the trigonometric functions. Here is a similar error:

$$\frac{\sin 50°}{\sin 10°} = \sin\frac{50°}{10°} = \sin 5° \approx 0.0872$$

Explain to students that the function and the angle cannot be separated. The correct solution is:

$$\frac{\sin 50°}{\sin 10°} \approx \frac{0.7660}{0.1736} \approx 4.41$$

INTEGRATE MATHEMATICAL PRACTICES

Focus on Reasoning

MP.2 Using a refractometer, a gemologist found that the index of refraction of a substance was 2.0. Using the same angle of incidence, the gemologist found that the angle of the refracted ray for a second substance was greater than the angle of the refracted ray for the first substance. Was the index of refraction of the second substance greater or less than 2.0? Explain. Sample answer: Let i = angle of incidence, r_1 = refraction angle 1, and r_2 = refraction angle 2. Then, $2 = \frac{\sin i}{\sin r_1}$. Since the sine function increases as an angle increases from 0° to 90°, $\sin r_2 > \sin r_1$ and $\frac{\sin i}{\sin r_2} < \frac{\sin i}{\sin r_1} = 2$. So, $\frac{\sin i}{\sin r_2}$, the index of refraction of the second substance, was less than 2.

EXTENSION ACTIVITY

Physicists define the index of refraction of a material in terms of the speed of light. Research the formula used by physicists that relates the index of refraction of a substance, n, the speed of light in a vacuum, c, and the speed of light through the substance, v. $n = \frac{c}{v}$

The speed of light in azurite is approximately 100,693 miles per second. Use that fact and the table in the Lesson Performance Task to find the speed of light in a vacuum. Express your answer in miles per second and miles per hour.
186,282 mi/sec; 670,615,200 mi/hr

The Sun is about 93 million miles from Earth. How long does it take light from the Sun to reach Earth? about 8.3 min

Scoring Rubric
2 points: Student correctly solves the problem and explains his/her reasoning.
1 point: Student shows good understanding of the problem but does not fully solve or explain his/her reasoning.
0 points: Student does not demonstrate understanding of the problem.

Special Right Triangles

Common Core Math Standards

The student is expected to:

 G-SRT.C.8

Use trigonometric ratios and the Pythagorean Theorem to solve right triangles in applied problems.

Mathematical Practices

MP.2 Reasoning

Language Objective

Explain to a partner how to find the sine, cosine, and tangent of a $30° — 60° — 90°$ triangle or a $45° — 45° — 90°$ triangle.

ENGAGE

Essential Question: What do you know about the side lengths and the trigonometric ratios in special right triangles?

The side lengths of a $45° — 45° — 90°$ triangle are always in the ratio $1 : 1 : \sqrt{2}$. The trigonometric ratios associated with this triangle are $\sin 45° = \frac{\sqrt{2}}{2}$ and $\tan 45° = 1$. The side lengths of a $30° — 60° — 90°$ triangle are always in the ratio $1 : \sqrt{3} : 2$. The trigonometric ratios associated with this triangle are

$\sin 45° = \cos 60° = \frac{1}{2}$,

$\sin 60° = \cos 30° = \frac{\sqrt{3}}{2}$, $\tan 30° = \frac{\sqrt{3}}{3}$,

and $\tan 60° = \sqrt{3}$.

PREVIEW: LESSON PERFORMANCE TASK

View the Engage section online. Discuss the photograph, asking students to speculate on whether the Lesson Performance Task will involve the dog or the flying disc, and why. Then preview the Lesson Performance Task.

13.3 Special Right Triangles

Essential Question: What do you know about the side lengths and the trigonometric ratios in special right triangles?

Resource Locker

⊘ Explore 1 Investigating an Isosceles Right Triangle

Discover relationships that always apply in an isosceles right triangle.

Ⓐ The figure shows an isosceles right triangle. Identify the base angles, and use the fact that they are complementary to write an equation relating their measures.

$\angle A, \angle B; m\angle A + m\angle B = 90°$

Ⓑ Use the Isosceles Triangle Theorem to write a different equation relating the base angle measures.

$m\angle A = m\angle B$

Ⓒ What must the measures of the base angles be? Why?

$m\angle A = m\angle B = 45°$; using substitution, $2m\angle A = 90°$, so $m\angle A = 45°$.

Ⓓ Use the Pythagorean Theorem to find the length of the hypotenuse in terms of the length of each leg, x.

$AB^2 = x^2 + x^2 \qquad AB^2 = 2x^2 \qquad AB = x\sqrt{2}$

Reflect

1. Is it true that if you know one side length of an isosceles right triangle, then you know all the side lengths? Explain.

   Yes; If you know either leg length x, then the other leg length is also equal to x, and the length of the hypotenuse is this value multiplied by $\sqrt{2}$. If you know the hypotenuse length, then each leg length is this value divided by $\sqrt{2}$.

2. **What if?** Suppose you draw the perpendicular from C to $\overline{AB}$. Explain how to find the length of $\overline{CD}$.

   Since $\triangle ABC$ is isosceles, $m\angle A = 45°$, and since $\triangle ADC$ is a right triangle, $m\angle ACD = 90° - m\angle A = 45°$. Therefore $\triangle ADC$ is an isosceles right triangle, so $CD = \frac{1}{\sqrt{2}}$ or $\frac{\sqrt{2}}{2}$.

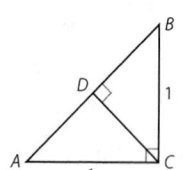

© Houghton Mifflin Harcourt Publishing Company

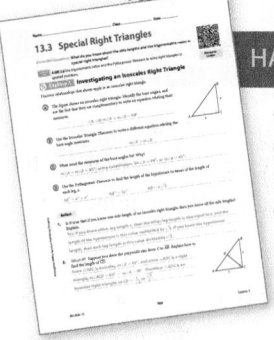

HARDCOVER PAGES 603–612

Turn to these pages to find this lesson in the hardcover student edition.

⚡ Explore 2   Investigating Another Special Right Triangle

Discover relationships that always apply in a right triangle formed as half of an equilateral triangle.

Ⓐ △ABD is an equilateral triangle and $\overline{BC}$ is a perpendicular from B to $\overline{AD}$. Determine all three angle measures in △ABC.

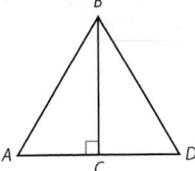

m∠C = 90°; each angle in an equilateral triangle measures 60°,

so m∠A = 60°, and therefore m∠ABC = 90° − m∠A = 30°.

Ⓑ Explain why △ABC ≅ △DBC.

∠A ≅ ∠D (Equilateral Triangle Theorem), ∠ACB ≅ ∠DCB (all right angles are congruent),

and $\overline{BC}$ ≅ $\overline{BC}$ (Reflexive Property of Congruence), so △ABC ≅ △DBC by AAS Congruence.

Or, $\overline{AB}$ ≅ $\overline{DB}$ (△ABD equilateral), $\overline{BC}$ ≅ $\overline{BC}$ (Reflexive Property of Congruence), and since

△ABC and △DBC are right triangles, △ABC ≅ △DBC by HL Congruence.

Ⓒ Let the length of $\overline{AC}$ be x. What is the length of $\overline{AB}$, and why?

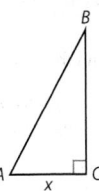

From Step B, △ABC ≅ △DBC, so $\overline{AC}$ ≅ $\overline{DC}$ (CPCTC) and therefore

CD = AC = x. In △ABD, AD = AC + DC = x + x = 2x (Seg. Add. Post.);

since $\overline{AB}$ ≅ $\overline{AD}$ (△ABD equilateral), AB = AD = 2x.

Ⓓ Using the Pythagorean Theorem, find the length of $\overline{BC}$.

$(2x)^2 = x^2 + BC^2$ $3x^2 = BC^2$ $x\sqrt{3} = BC$

Reflect

3. What is the numerical ratio of the side lengths in a right triangle with acute angles that measure 30° and 60°? Explain.

The right triangle is similar to △ABC (AA Similarity), so its side lengths are in the ratio

$x : x\sqrt{3} : 2x$, or $1 : \sqrt{3} : 2$.

4. Explain the Error A student has drawn a right triangle with a 60° angle and a hypotenuse of 6. He has labeled the other side lengths as shown. Explain how you can tell at a glance that he has made an error and how to correct it.

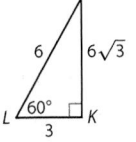

Since $6\sqrt{3} > 6$, leg $\overline{JK}$ is longer than the hypotenuse, which is

impossible. The side lengths must be in the ratio $1 : \sqrt{3} : 2$.

For this to be true, the length of $\overline{JK}$ should be $3\sqrt{3}$.

© Houghton Mifflin Harcourt Publishing Company

EXPLORE 1

Investigating an Isosceles Right Triangle

INTEGRATE TECHNOLOGY

Students have the option of doing the Explore activity either in the book or online.

QUESTIONING STRATEGIES

? How can you use the relationship between the angle measure and the length of the sides to help you reconstruct the simplest form of an isosceles right triangle? The legs are opposite the 45° angles and measure 1 unit while the hypotenuse is opposite the right angle and measures $\sqrt{2}$ units.

EXPLORE 2

Investigating Another Special Right Triangle

QUESTIONING STRATEGIES

? How can you use the relationship between the angle measure and the length of the side opposite the angle to help you reconstruct the simplest form of a 30° −60° −90° triangle? The shortest side is opposite the 30° angle and the longest side is the hypotenuse. So label the side opposite the 30° angle 1 unit, the side opposite the 60° angle $\sqrt{3}$ units, and the hypotenuse 2 units.

PROFESSIONAL DEVELOPMENT

Integrate Mathematical Practices

This lesson provides an opportunity to address Mathematical Practice **MP.2**, which calls for students to "reason abstractly and quantitatively." Students investigate the relationships among the side lengths and angles of the special right triangles, and use them to find the trigonometric ratios and angle measures associated with these relationships. This recognition can often provide a quicker solution to a problem involving a special triangle.

AVOID COMMON ERRORS

Students may confuse the side lengths when labeling the sides of a standard $30° - 60° - 90°$ triangle. Review with students why $\sqrt{3} > 1$ and why this side length or its multiple must be opposite the 60° angle.

EXPLAIN 1

Applying Relationships in Special Right Triangles

QUESTIONING STRATEGIES

? If you know the exact value of the length of one side of a special right triangle, can you always find the exact value of the remaining sides? Explain. Yes, because of the special side-length relationships that exist in the special right triangles.

INTEGRATE MATHEMATICAL PRACTICES

Focus on Math Connections

MP.1 Work with students to find the lengths of the legs of an isosceles right triangle with a hypotenuse of one unit. The lengths are $\frac{1}{\sqrt{2}}$. Review how to write the length without the radical in the denominator $\left(\frac{1}{\sqrt{2}} \cdot \frac{\sqrt{2}}{\sqrt{2}} = \frac{\sqrt{2}}{2}\right)$. Remind students this is called rationalizing the denominator.

Applying Relationships in Special Right Triangles

The right triangles you explored are sometimes called $45°-45°-90°$ and $30°-60°-90°$ triangles. In a $45°-45°-90°$ triangle, the hypotenuse is $\sqrt{2}$ times as long as each leg. In a $30°-60°-90°$ triangle, the hypotenuse is twice as long as the shorter leg and the longer leg is $\sqrt{3}$ times as long as the shorter leg. You can use these relationships to find side lengths in these special types of right triangles.

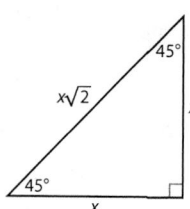 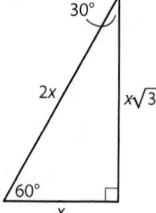

Example 1 Find the unknown side lengths in each right triangle.

Ⓐ Find the unknown side lengths in $\triangle ABC$.

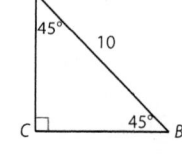

The hypotenuse is $\sqrt{2}$ times as long as each leg.

Substitute 10 for AB.

Multiply by $\sqrt{2}$.

Divide by 2.

$$AB = AC\sqrt{2} = BC\sqrt{2}$$
$$10 = AC\sqrt{2} = BC\sqrt{2}$$
$$10\sqrt{2} = 2AC = 2BC$$
$$5\sqrt{2} = AC = BC$$

Ⓑ In right $\triangle DEF$, m$\angle D = 30°$ and m$\angle E = 60°$. The shorter leg measures $5\sqrt{3}$. Find the remaining side lengths.

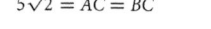

The hypotenuse is twice as long as the shorter leg. $DE = 2 \boxed{EF}$

Substitute $\boxed{5\sqrt{3}}$ for $\boxed{EF}$. $DE = 2 \boxed{5\sqrt{3}}$

Simplify. $DE = \boxed{10\sqrt{3}}$

The longer leg is $\sqrt{3}$ times as long as the shorter leg. $\boxed{DF} = \boxed{EF}\sqrt{3}$

Substitute $\boxed{5\sqrt{3}}$ for $\boxed{EF}$. $\boxed{DF} = \boxed{5\sqrt{3}}\sqrt{3}$

Simplify. $\boxed{DF} = \boxed{15}$

© Houghton Mifflin Harcourt Publishing Company

COLLABORATIVE LEARNING

Small Group Activity

Have students work in small groups to draw and label right triangles with the following properties:

- isosceles right triangles with legs whose lengths are whole numbers greater than 1
- isosceles right triangles with a hypotenuse whose length is a whole number greater than 1
- $30° - 60° - 90°$ triangles with a shortest leg whose length is a whole number greater than 1
- $30° - 60° - 90°$ triangles with a hypotenuse whose length is a whole number greater than 2

Find the unknown side lengths in each right triangle.

5.
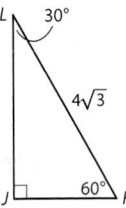

$$KL = 2JK \qquad JL = JK\sqrt{3}$$
$$4\sqrt{3} = 2JK \qquad JL = (2\sqrt{3})\sqrt{3}$$
$$2\sqrt{3} = JK \qquad JL = 6$$

6.
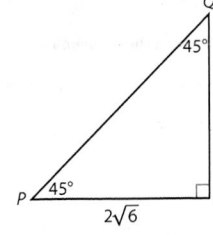

$$\overline{PR} \cong \overline{QR}, \text{ so } QR = PR = 2\sqrt{6}$$
$$PQ = PR\sqrt{2}$$
$$= (2\sqrt{6})\sqrt{2} = 4\sqrt{3}$$

⚙ Explain 2 Trigonometric Ratios of Special Right Triangles

You can use the relationships you found in special right triangles to find trigonometric ratios for the angles 45°, 30°, and 60°.

Example 2 For each triangle, find the unknown side lengths and trigonometric ratios for the angles.

(A) A 45°—45°—90° triangle with a leg length of 1

Step 1

Since the lengths of the sides opposite the 45° angles are congruent, they are both 1. The length of the hypotenuse is $\sqrt{2}$ times as long as each leg, so it is $1(\sqrt{2})$, or $\sqrt{2}$.

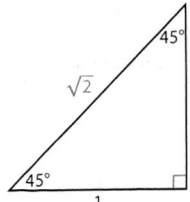

Step 2

Use the triangle to find the trigonometric ratios for 45°. Write each ratio as a simplified fraction.

Angle	Sine = $\dfrac{\text{opp}}{\text{hyp}}$	Cosine = $\dfrac{\text{adj}}{\text{hyp}}$	Tangent = $\dfrac{\text{opp}}{\text{adj}}$
45°	$\dfrac{\sqrt{2}}{2}$	$\dfrac{\sqrt{2}}{2}$	1

DIFFERENTIATE INSTRUCTION

Kinesthetic Experience

Kinesthetic learners may benefit from verifying the relationships of an isosceles right triangle through a simple paper-folding activity. Have students take a square piece of paper and fold it in half diagonally. This creates an isosceles right triangle. Then ask students to measure one leg of the triangle to the nearest millimeter, and apply their understanding of the relationships among the legs and the hypotenuse to predict the length of the hypotenuse. Finally, have students measure the length of the hypotenuse to check their predictions.

EXPLAIN 2

Trigonometric Ratios of Special Right Triangles

QUESTIONING STRATEGIES

? If a trigonometric ratio includes $\sqrt{2}$ in the ratio, which special right triangle does it likely refer to? Explain. an isosceles right triangle because that is the length of the hypotenuse

? If a trigonometric ratio includes $\sqrt{3}$ in the ratio, which special right triangle does it likely refer to? Explain. a 30°—60°—90° triangle because that is the length of the side opposite the 60° angle

? If you know the exact value of a trigonometric ratio for a special right triangle, can you find the measure of the angle that corresponds to the ratio? Explain. Yes. Draw the corresponding special right triangle and then find the angle that corresponds to the trigonometric ratio.

INTEGRATE MATHEMATICAL PRACTICES
Focus on Math Connections

MP.1 Point out to students that the side lengths and the trigonometric ratios for the special right triangles are usually left in exact answer form. This means they are often expressed as ratios in simplest form, with rationalized denominators, when applicable.

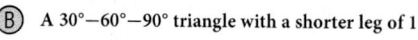 **B** A 30°—60°—90° triangle with a shorter leg of 1

Step 1

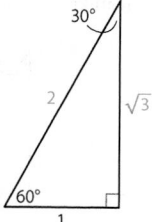

The hypotenuse is ___twice___ as long as the ___shorter___ leg,

so the length of the hypotenuse is ___2___.

The longer leg is ___$\sqrt{3}$___ times as long as the ___shorter___ leg,

so the length of the longer leg is ___$\sqrt{3}$___.

Step 2

Use the triangle to complete the table. Write each ratio as a simplified fraction.

Angle	Sine $= \dfrac{\text{opp}}{\text{hyp}}$	Cosine $= \dfrac{\text{adj}}{\text{hyp}}$	Tangent $= \dfrac{\text{opp}}{\text{adj}}$
30°	$\dfrac{1}{2}$	$\dfrac{\sqrt{3}}{2}$	$\dfrac{\sqrt{3}}{3}$
60°	$\dfrac{\sqrt{3}}{2}$	$\dfrac{1}{2}$	$\sqrt{3}$

Reflect

7. Write any patterns or relationships you see in the tables in Part A and Part B as equations. Why do these patterns or relationships make sense?

   $\sin 30° = \cos 60° = \frac{1}{2}$; $\sin 45° = \cos 45° = \frac{\sqrt{2}}{2}$; $\sin 60° = \cos 30° = \frac{\sqrt{3}}{2}$; the sine of an angle equals the cosine of its complement.

8. For which acute angle measure θ, is $\tan\theta$ less than 1? equal to 1? greater than 1?

   $\tan\theta < 1$ for $\theta < 45°$; $\tan\theta = 1$ for $\theta = 45°$; $\tan\theta > 1$ for $\theta > 45°$.

Your Turn

Find the unknown side lengths and trigonometric ratios for the 45° angles.

9.

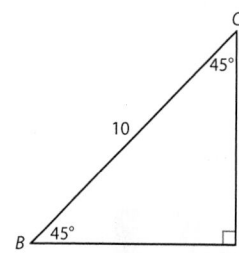

$AB = \dfrac{CB}{\sqrt{2}}, AB = \dfrac{10}{\sqrt{2}} = 5\sqrt{2};$

$AC = AB, AC = 5\sqrt{2}$

$\sin 45° = \cos 45° = \dfrac{5\sqrt{2}}{10} = \dfrac{\sqrt{2}}{2}$

$\tan 45° = 1$

LANGUAGE SUPPORT **EL**

Connect Vocabulary

Point out that what makes *special* right triangles special are the unique relationships among the sides. It may be easier for students to focus on the special triangles by referring to them by their angle measures. Instead of discussing an *isosceles right triangle*, refer to the triangle as a *45° —45° —90° triangle*.

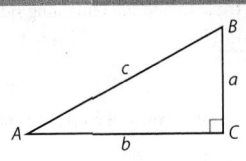 **Explain 3** **Investigating Pythagorean Triples**

Pythagorean Triples

A **Pythagorean triple** is a set of positive integers a, b, and c that satisfy the equation $a^2 + b^2 = c^2$. This means that a, b, and c are the legs and hypotenuse of a right triangle. Right triangles that have non-integer sides will not form Pythagorean triples.

Examples of Pythagorean triples include 3, 4, and 5; 5, 12, and 13; 7, 24, and 25; and 8, 15, and 17.

Example 3 Use Pythagorean triples to find side lengths in right triangles.

(A) Verify that the side lengths 3, 4, and 5; 5, 12, and 13; 7, 24, and 25; and 8, 15, and 17 are Pythagorean triples.

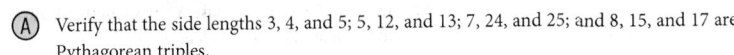
$3^2 + 4^2 = 9 + 16 = 25 = 5^2 \checkmark$ $\qquad$ $5^2 + 12^2 = 25 + 144 = 169 = 13^2 \checkmark$

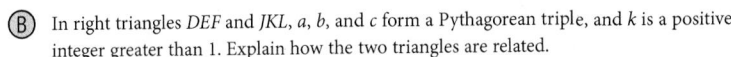
$7^2 + 24^2 = 49 + 576 = 625 = 25^2 \checkmark$ $\qquad$ $8^2 + 15^2 = 64 + 225 = 289 = 17^2 \checkmark$

The numbers in Step A are not the only Pythagorean triples. In the following steps you will discover that multiples of known Pythagorean triples are also Pythagorean triples.

(B) In right triangles DEF and JKL, a, b, and c form a Pythagorean triple, and k is a positive integer greater than 1. Explain how the two triangles are related.

$\triangle DEF$ is similar to $\underline{\triangle JKL}$ by the $\underline{\text{Side-Side-Side (SSS) Triangle Similarity Theorem}}$ because the corresponding sides are proportional. Complete the ratios to verify Side-Side-Side (SSS) Triangle Similarity.

$a : \underline{b} : c = \underline{ka} : \underline{kb} : \underline{kc}$

(C) You can use the Pythagorean Theorem to compare the lengths of the sides of $\triangle JKL$. What must be true of the set of numbers ka, kb, and kc?

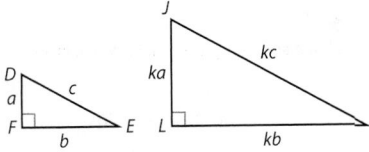
$(ka^2) + (kb^2) = \underline{k^2a^2} + k^2b^2$

$= k^2 \underline{(a^2 + b^2)}$

$= k^2(c^2) = \underline{(kc)^2}$

The set of numbers ka, kb, and kc form a $\underline{\text{Pythagorean triple}}$.

© Houghton Mifflin Harcourt Publishing Company

EXPLAIN 3

Investigating Pythagorean Triples

QUESTIONING STRATEGIES

? How can understanding the relationship between a Pythagorean triple and its multiples help you find the missing side in a right triangle? If you can identify the triple and the multiple, you can multiply the missing triple length by the multiple to find the missing side length without having to use the Pythagorean Theorem.

INTEGRATE MATHEMATICAL PRACTICES
Focus on Patterns

MP.8 Have students create a list of Pythagorean triples. Students do not need to memorize every triple on the list, but they can use it as a reference to help them recognize the triples and to look for multiples. Students may want to include side columns with multiples to help them recognize the patterns between the original triple and its multiples.

ELABORATE

AVOID COMMON ERRORS

Students may confuse Pythagorean triples. Emphasize that students can always use the Pythagorean Theorem to verify that a triple or a multiple of a triple is correct.

SUMMARIZE THE LESSON

? What can you say about the side lengths and the trigonometric ratios associated with special right triangles? The sides of an isosceles right triangle are in the ratio $1:1:\sqrt{2}$. The sides of a $30°-60°-90°$ triangle are in the ratio $1:\sqrt{3}:2$. You can find the related trigonometric ratios by drawing the triangles and finding the sine, cosine, and tangent of the corresponding 30°, 45°, and 60° angles from the triangles.

Reflect

10. Suppose you are given a right triangle with two side lengths. What would have to be true for you to use a Pythagorean triple to find the remaining side length?

   The given side lengths would have to be two numbers in a Pythagorean triple. Also, if the legs are given, the side lengths would have to be the smaller two numbers in the triple, whereas if one leg and the hypotenuse are given, the side lengths would have to include the largest number in the triple.

Your Turn

Use Pythagorean triples to find the unknown side length.

11.

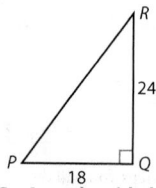

   $18:24 = 3:4$, so the side lengths are multiples of the Pythagorean triple 3, 4, 5.
   $3:4:5 = 6(3):6(4):6(5) = 18:24:30$, so $PR = 30$.

12. In $\triangle XYZ$, the hypotenuse $\overline{XY}$ has length 68, and the shorter leg $\overline{XZ}$ has length 32.

   $32:68 = 8:17$, so the side lengths are multiples of 8, 15, and 17.
   $8:15:17 = 4(8):4(15):4(17) = 32:60:6$
   so $YZ = 60$.

⬤ Elaborate

13. Describe the type of problems involving special right triangles you can solve.

   Once you identify the side (longer leg, shorter leg, hypotenuse) that is given, you can find the lengths of the other two sides by applying relationships such as the length of the hypotenuse in a 30°-60°-90° triangle being twice as long as the length of the shorter leg.

14. How can you use Pythagorean triples to solve right triangles?

   Suppose two side lengths of a right triangle are given and correspond to two numbers in a Pythagorean triple. If one of the given sides is the hypotenuse and one of the lengths is the largest number of the triple, then the unknown length is the remaining number in the triple. Likewise, if neither given side is the hypotenuse and the lengths are the smaller two numbers of the triple, the unknown side length must be the largest number of the triple.

15. **Discussion** How many Pythagorean triples are there?

   Infinitely many; for example, since 3, 4, and 5 is a Pythagorean triple, so are $2(3) = 6$, $2(4) = 8$, and $2(5) = 10$; 9, 12, and 15; 12, 16, and 20; and so on.

16. **Essential Question Check-In** What is the ratio of the length of the hypotenuse to the length of the shorter leg in any 30°-60°-90° triangle?

   The ratio is 2 to 1.

★ Evaluate: Homework and Practice

• Online Homework
• Hints and Help
• Extra Practice

For each triangle, state whether the side lengths shown are possible.
Explain why or why not.

1.

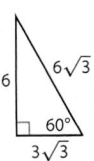

No; $3\sqrt{3} : 6 : 6\sqrt{3} = 1 : \dfrac{6}{3\sqrt{3}} : \dfrac{6\sqrt{3}}{3\sqrt{3}} =$
$1 : \dfrac{2\sqrt{3}}{3} : 2 \neq 1 : \sqrt{3} : 2$

2.

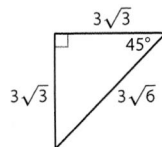

Yes; $3\sqrt{3} : 3\sqrt{3} : 3\sqrt{6} =$
$1 : 1 : \dfrac{3\sqrt{6}}{3\sqrt{3}} = 1 : 1 : \sqrt{2}$

3.

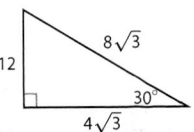

Yes; $4\sqrt{3} : 12 : 8\sqrt{3} = 1 : \dfrac{12}{4\sqrt{3}} : \dfrac{8\sqrt{3}}{4\sqrt{3}} =$
$1 : \sqrt{3} : 2$

4.

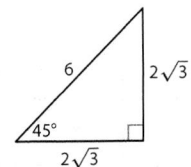

No; $2\sqrt{3} : 2\sqrt{3} : 6 = 1 : 1 : \dfrac{6}{2\sqrt{3}} \neq$
$1 : 1 : \sqrt{2}$

Find the unknown side lengths in each right triangle.

5.

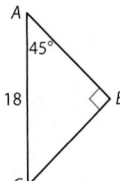

$AC = AB\sqrt{2} = BC\sqrt{2}$
$18 = AB\sqrt{2} = BC\sqrt{2}$
$18\sqrt{2} = 2AB = 2BC$
$9\sqrt{2} = AB = BC$

6.

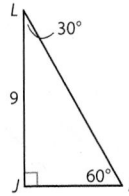

$JL = JK\sqrt{3} \quad KL = 2JK$
$9 = JK\sqrt{3} \quad KL = 2(3\sqrt{3})$
$9\sqrt{3} = 3JK \quad KL = 6\sqrt{3}$
$3\sqrt{3} = JK$

© Houghton Mifflin Harcourt Publishing Company

EVALUATE

ASSIGNMENT GUIDE

Concepts and Skills	Practice
Explore 1 Investigating an Isosceles Right Triangle	Exercises 2, 4
Explore 2 Investigating Another Special Right Triangle	Exercises 1, 3
Example 1 Applying Relationships in Special Right Triangles	Exercises 5–8
Example 2 Trigonometric Ratios of Special Right Triangles	Exercises 9–12
Example 3 Investigating Pythagorean Triples	Exercises 13–16

INTEGRATE TECHNOLOGY

Although students should write answers in exact form for special right triangles, they can use a calculator to check that their answers make sense.

Exercise	Depth of Knowledge (D.O.K.)	COMMON CORE Mathematical Practices
1–21	**2** Skills/Concepts	**MP.4** Modeling
22	**2** Skills/Concepts	**MP.4** Modeling
23–24	**2** Strategic Thinking	**MP.4** Modeling
25	**3** Strategic Thinking H.O.T.	**MP.3** Logic
26	**3** Strategic Thinking H.O.T.	**MP.3** Logic

AVOID COMMON ERRORS

Students working with special right triangles can mislabel diagrams when the side lengths differ from the standard reference triangles. Remind students they can refer to those triangles, but that they must identify the appropriate relationship for each triangle based on its corresponding problem statement.

MANIPULATIVES

Have students construct several triangles with legs whose measures are the legs of Pythagorean triples using centimeter graph paper. Then have them use a ruler to verify that the length of the hypotenuse corresponds to the length of the hypotenuse in the corresponding Pythagorean triple.

7. Right triangle UVW has acute angles U measuring 30° and W measuring 60°. Hypotenuse $\overline{UW}$ measures 12. (You may want to draw the triangle in your answer.)

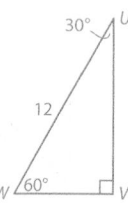

$UW = 2VW$ $UV = VW\sqrt{3}$

$12 = 2VW$ $UV = 6\sqrt{3}$

$6 = VW$

8. Right triangle PQR has acute angles P and Q measuring 45°. Leg $\overline{PR}$ measures $5\sqrt{10}$. (You may want to draw the triangle in your answer.)

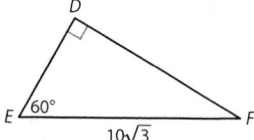

$PQ = PR\sqrt{2}$

$= \left(5\sqrt{10}\right)\sqrt{2}$

$= 5\sqrt{20}$

$= 10\sqrt{5}$

Use trigonometric ratios to solve each right triangle.

9.

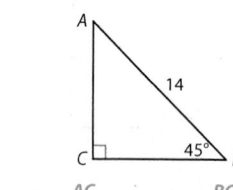

$\sin 45° = \dfrac{AC}{AB}$ $\cos 45° = \dfrac{BC}{AB}$

$\dfrac{\sqrt{2}}{2} = \dfrac{AC}{14}$ $\dfrac{\sqrt{2}}{2} = \dfrac{BC}{14}$

$7\sqrt{2} = AC$ $7\sqrt{2} = BC$

10.

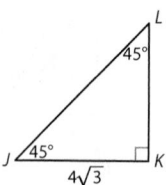

$\sin 60° = \dfrac{DF}{EF}$ $\cos 60° = \dfrac{DE}{EF}$

$\dfrac{\sqrt{3}}{2} = \dfrac{DF}{10\sqrt{3}}$ $\dfrac{1}{2} = \dfrac{DE}{10\sqrt{3}}$

$15 = DF$ $5\sqrt{3} = DE$

11. Right $\triangle KLM$ with m$\angle J = 45°$, leg $JK = 4\sqrt{3}$

$\sin 45° = \dfrac{JK}{JL}$ $\tan 45° = \dfrac{KL}{JK}$

$\dfrac{\sqrt{2}}{2} = \dfrac{4\sqrt{3}}{JL}$ $1 = \dfrac{KL}{4\sqrt{3}}$

$JL = \left(4\sqrt{3}\right)\sqrt{2} = 4\sqrt{6}$ $KL = 4\sqrt{3}$

12. Right $\triangle PQR$ with m$\angle Q = 30°$, leg $QR = 15$

$\tan 30° = \dfrac{PR}{QR}$ $\sin 30° = \dfrac{PR}{PQ}$

$\dfrac{\sqrt{3}}{3} = \dfrac{PR}{15}$ $\dfrac{1}{2} = \dfrac{5\sqrt{3}}{PQ}$

$5\sqrt{3} = PR$ $PQ = 2\left(5\sqrt{3}\right) = 10\sqrt{3}$

© Houghton Mifflin Harcourt Publishing Company

For each right triangle, find the unknown side length using a Pythagorean triple. If it is not possible, state why.

13.

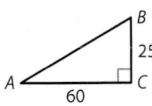

25:60 = 5:12, so the side lengths are multiples of 5, 12, and 13.

$5:12:13 = 5(5):5(12):5(13) = 25:60:65$, so $AB = 65$.

14.

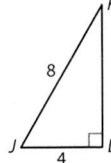

Not possible: $8^2 - 4^2 = 64 - 16 = 48$; 48 is not a perfect square.

15. In right $\triangle PQR$, the legs have lengths $PQ = 9$ and $QR = 21$.

Not possible: $9^2 + 21^2 = 81 + 441 = 522$; 522 is not a perfect square.

16. In right $\triangle XYZ$, the hypotenuse $\overline{XY}$ has length 35, and the shorter leg $\overline{YZ}$ has length 21.

$21:35 = 3:5$, so the side lengths are multiples of 3, 4, and 5.

$3:4:5 = 7(3):7(4):7(5) = 21:28:35$, so $XZ = 28$.

17. Solve for x.

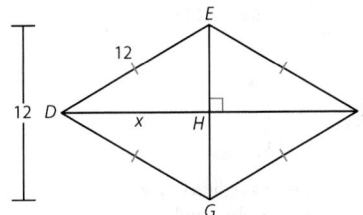

DEFG is a rhombus, so its diagonals bisect each other, and $EH = HG$. Since $EH + HG = EG = 12$ (Seg. Add. Post.), $2EH = 12$, and therefore $EH = 6$. By the Pythagorean Thm.,

$x^2 + 6^2 = 12^2$

$x^2 + 36 = 144$

$x^2 = 108$

$x = \sqrt{108} = 6\sqrt{3}$

18. Represent Real-World Problems A baseball "diamond" actually forms a square, each side measuring 30 yards. How far, to the nearest yard, must the third baseman throw the ball to reach first base?

The line from first base to third base forms the diagonal of the square, so with home plate they form a 45°-45°-90° triangle with legs of length 30 yd. Therefore, the third baseman must throw the ball $30\sqrt{2}$ yd ≈ 42 yd.

COGNITIVE STRATEGIES

Discuss the importance of being able to draw and interpret right triangle diagrams to use trigonometric ratios to solve real-world problems.

19. In a right triangle, the longer leg is exactly $\sqrt{3}$ times the length of the shorter leg. Use the inverse tangent trigonometric ratio to prove that the acute angles of the triangle measure 30° and 60°.

Given: $BC = AC\sqrt{3}$. Since $\tan A = \dfrac{BC}{AC}$, use an inverse tangent ratio:

$$\tan A = \frac{BC}{AC} = \frac{AC\sqrt{3}}{AC} = \sqrt{3}$$

$$m\angle A = \tan^{-1}\sqrt{3} = 60°$$

$\angle A$ and $\angle B$ are complementary, so $m\angle B = 90° - m\angle A = 90° - 60° = 30°$.

Algebra Find the value of x in each right triangle.

20.

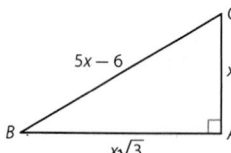

Since the longer leg is $\sqrt{3}$ times the length of the shorter leg, $\triangle ABC$ is a 30°-60°-90° triangle. Therefore,

$$BC = 2AC$$
$$5x - 6 = 2x$$
$$3x = 6$$
$$x = 2$$

21.

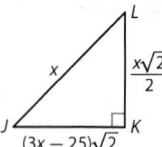

Since the hypotenuse is $\sqrt{2}$ times the length of one of the legs, $\triangle JKL$ is a 45°-45°-90° triangle. Therefore,

$$JK = KL$$
$$\frac{x\sqrt{2}}{2} = (3x - 25)\sqrt{2}$$
$$x = 2(3x - 25)$$
$$x = 6x - 50$$
$$50 = 5x$$
$$10 = x$$

22. Explain the Error Charlene is trying to find the unknown sides of a right triangle with a 30° acute angle, whose hypotenuse measures $12\sqrt{2}$. Identify, explain, and correct Charlene's error.

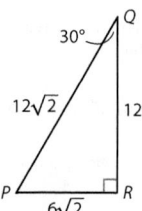

Charlene appears to have used the ratio $1 : \sqrt{2} : 2$, whereas the correct ratio for a 30°-60°-90° triangle is $1 : \sqrt{3} : 2$. $PR = 6\sqrt{2}$ is correct, but $QR = PR\sqrt{3} = \left(6\sqrt{2}\right)\sqrt{3} = 6\sqrt{6}$.

23. Represent Real-World Problems Honeycomb blinds form a string of almost-regular hexagons when viewed end-on. Approximately how much material, to the nearest ten square centimeters, is needed for each 3.2-cm deep cell of a honeycomb blind that is 125 cm wide? (*Hint: Draw a picture.* A regular hexagon can be divided into 6 equilateral triangles.)

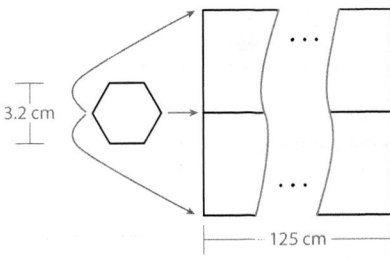

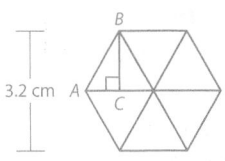

$\triangle ABC$ is a $30°$–$60°$–$90°$ triangle, and $BC = \dfrac{1}{2}$ (3.2 cm) = 1.6 cm. Therefore,

$$\cos 30° = \frac{BC}{AB}$$

$$\frac{\sqrt{3}}{2} = \frac{1.6 \text{ cm}}{AB}$$

$$AB = 3.2\sqrt{3} \approx 5.542 \text{ cm}$$

The amount of material needed is the perimeter of the hexagon × the width of the blind:

$$6(AB) \times \text{width} = 6(5.542) \times 125 \approx 4{,}160 \text{ cm}^2$$

24. Which of these pairs of numbers are two out of three integer-valued side lengths of a right triangle? (*Hint:* for positive integers a, b, c, and k, ka, kb, and kc are side lengths of a right triangle if and only if a, b, and c are side lengths of a right triangle.)

A. 15, 18	○ True	● False
B. 15, 30	○ True	● False
C. 15, 51	○ True	● False
D. 16, 20	● True	○ False
E. 16, 24	○ True	● False

A. False; $15 = 3(5)$ and $18 = 3(6)$; $5^2 + 6^2 = 25 + 36 = 61$ and $6^2 - 5^2 = 36 - 25 = 11$, and neither are perfect squares.

B. False; $15 = 15(1)$ and $30 = 15(2)$; $1^2 + 2^2 = 5$ and $2^2 - 1^2 = 3$, and neither are perfect squares.

C. False; $15 = 3(5)$ and $51 = 3(17)$; $17^2 + 5^2 = 314$ and $17^2 - 5^2 = 264$, and neither are perfect squares.

D. True; $16 = 4(4)$ and $20 = 4(5)$; 3, 4, 5 is a Pythagorean triple.

E. False; $16 = 8(2)$ and $24 = 8(3)$; $2^2 + 3^2 = 13$ and $3^2 - 2^2 = 5$, and neither are perfect squares.

PEER-TO-PEER DISCUSSION

Have students use the special right triangles to make up several inverse trigonometric problems to evaluate, such as $\sin^{-1}\frac{1}{2}$. Have them exchange and solve problems with another pair of students. Have students use a calculator to check their work.

JOURNAL

Have students summarize what they know about special right triangles. Remind them to include a chart that summarizes trigonometric ratios for relevant angles and diagrams that support the ratios.

H.O.T. Focus on Higher Order Thinking

25. **Communicate Mathematical Ideas** Is it possible for the three side lengths of a right triangle to be odd integers? Explain.

   No; if the two shorter side lengths are odd, then their squares are odd, because the square of an odd number is always odd. But the sum of their squares is even, because the sum of two odd numbers is always even. Therefore the sum of the squares of the two shorter side lengths cannot itself be the square of an odd number.

26. **Make a Conjecture** Use spreadsheet software to investigate this question: are there sets of positive integers a, b, and c such that $a^3 + b^3 = c^3$? You may choose to begin with these formulas:

	A	B	C	D
1	1	=A1+1	=A1^3+B1^3	=C1^(1/3)
2	=A1	=B1+1	=A2^3+B2^3	=C2^(1/3)

   Actually there are no sets of positive integers a, b, and c such that $a^3 + b^3 = c^3$, but this is very hard indeed to prove. Students should be able to extend the spreadsheet example as follows, testing triples with different smallest numbers by changing the value in cell A1; for example:

	A	B	C	D
1	5	6	341	6.986368
2	5	7	468	7.763936
3	5	8	637	8.604252
4	5	9	854	9.487518
5	5	10	1125	10.40042
6	5	11	1456	11.3341
7	5	12	1853	12.28264
8	5	13	2322	13.24201
9	5	14	2869	14.20944
10	5	15	3500	15.18294

Lesson Performance Task

Kate and her dog are longtime flying disc players. Kate has decided to start a small business making circles of soft material that dogs can catch without injuring their teeth. Since she also likes math, she's decided to see whether she can apply Pythagorean principles to her designs. She used the Pythagorean triple 3-4-5 for the dimensions of her first three designs.

| $r = 3$ in. | $r = 4$ in. | $r = 5$ in. |
| small | medium | large |

1. Is it true that the (small area) + (medium area) = (large area)? Explain.

2. If the circles had radii based on the Pythagorean triple 5—12—13, would the above equation be true? Explain.

3. Three of Kate's circles have radii of a, b, and c, where a, b, and c form a Pythagorean triple $(a^2 + b^2 = c^2)$. Show that the sum of the areas of the small and medium circles equals the area of the large circle.

4. Kate has decided to go into the beach ball business. Sticking to her Pythagorean principles, she starts with three spherical beach balls--a small ball with radius 3 in., a medium ball with radius 4 in., and a large ball with radius 5 in. Is it true that (small volume) + (medium volume) = (large volume)? Show your work.

5. Explain the discrepancy between your results in Exercises 3 and 4.

1. yes; small area + medium area = 9 in² + 16 in² = 25 in² = large area
2. yes; small area + medium area = 25 in² + 144 in² = 169 in² = large area
3. small area + medium area = $a^2 + b^2 = (a^2 + b^2) = c^2$ = large area
4. no; small volume + medium volume = 36 in² + $85\frac{1}{3}$ in² = $121\frac{1}{3}$ in² $\neq 166\frac{2}{3}$ in² (large area)
5. Possible answer: Numbers are squared in both the Pythagorean Theorem and the formula for the area of a circle. In the formula for the volume of a sphere, numbers are cubed. There is no theorem analogous to the Pythagorean Theorem for cubes of numbers.

AVOID COMMON ERRORS

When students check three measurements to see if they could represent the sides of a right triangle, they may add the two smaller measurements *before* squaring them to see if the result is the square of the third measurement. Caution students to square each smaller measurement first, before finding their sum.

INTEGRATE MATHEMATICAL PRACTICES
Focus on Critical Thinking

MP.3 If you look at a list of Pythagorean Triples, you'll notice that at least one of the numbers forming the triple is even. Must this be true for all Pythagorean Triples? Explain. Yes; sample answer: The square of an odd number is always odd. The sum of two odd numbers is always even. So, if a and b are both odd, $a^2 + b^2$ must be even, which means that c must also be even.

EXTENSION ACTIVITY

Choose two whole numbers m and n, such that $m < n$. Make a table like the following for at least 10 pairs of values of m and n:

m	n	$n^2 - m^2$	$2mn$	$n^2 + m^2$	Pythagorean Triple?
1	2	3	4	5	yes

Describe your results, and use algebra to explain them. m and n always generate a Pythagorean Triple.

$$(n^2 - m^2)^2 + (2mn)^2 = n^4 - 2n^2m^2 + m^4 + 4m^2n^2$$
$$= n^4 + 2n^2m^2 + m^4$$
$$= (n^2 + m^2)^2$$

Scoring Rubric
2 points: Student correctly solves the problem and explains his/her reasoning.
1 point: Student shows good understanding of the problem but does not fully solve or explain his/her reasoning.
0 points: Student does not demonstrate understanding of the problem.

Special Right Triangles   **722**

Problem Solving with Trigonometry

Common Core Math Standards

The student is expected to:

 G-SRT.C.8

Use trigonometric ratios and the Pythagorean Theorem to solve right triangles in applied problems. Also G-SRT.D.9(+), G-GPE.B.7

Mathematical Practices

 MP.2 Reasoning

Language Objective

Explain to a partner how to solve a right triangle, and how to solve a right triangle in the coordinate plane.

ENGAGE

Essential Question: How can you solve a right triangle?

You can use trigonometric ratios to find side lengths, or their inverses to find angle measures; you can use the Pythagorean Theorem to find the third side length; you can use the fact that the acute angles are complementary; if the triangle is in the coordinate plane, you can use the distance formula to find side lengths.

PREVIEW: LESSON PERFORMANCE TASK

View the Engage section online. Discuss the photograph. Ask students if they know why water is sometimes referred to as H_2O. Then preview the Lesson Performance Task.

13.4 Problem Solving with Trigonometry

Essential Question: How can you solve a right triangle?

⊘ Explore　Deriving an Area Formula

You can use trigonometry to find the area of a triangle without knowing its height.

Ⓐ　Suppose you draw an altitude $\overline{AD}$ to side $\overline{BC}$ of $\triangle ABC$. Then write an equation using a trigonometric ratio in terms of $\angle C$, the height h of $\triangle ABC$, and the length of one of its sides.

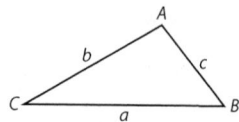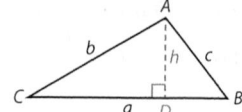

$\sin C = \dfrac{AD}{AC} = \dfrac{h}{b}$

Ⓑ　Solve your equation from Step A for h.

$b \sin C = h$

Ⓒ　Complete this formula for the area of $\triangle ABC$ in terms of h and another of its side lengths:　Area $= \dfrac{1}{2} \boxed{ah}$

Ⓓ　Substitute your expression for h from Step B into your formula from Step C.

$\dfrac{1}{2} ab \sin C$

Reflect

1.　Does the area formula you found work if $\angle C$ is a right angle? Explain.
Yes; in this case, $\sin C = \sin 90° = 1$, so the formula becomes Area $= \frac{1}{2}ab$, and this is correct since a and b are now the base and height of $\triangle ABC$.

© Houghton Mifflin Harcourt Publishing Company

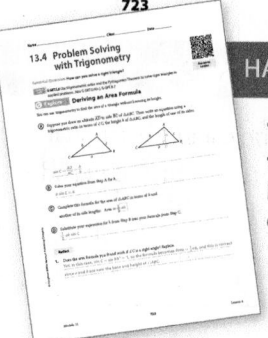

HARDCOVER PAGES 613–622

Turn to these pages to find this lesson in the hardcover student edition.

2. Suppose you used a trigonometric ratio in terms of $\angle B$, h, and a different side length. How would this change your findings? What does this tell you about the choice of sides and included angle?

Step C would be the same, but the other steps would change:

$$\sin B = \frac{AD}{AB} = \frac{h}{c}$$

$$c \sin B = h$$

$$\text{Area} = \frac{1}{2} ac \sin B$$

You can choose different sides and included angle and derive a slightly different

formula for the area, but in the same form.

⚬ Explain 1 Using the Area Formula

Area Formula for a Triangle in Terms of its Side Lengths

The area of $\triangle ABC$ with sides a, b, and c can be found using the lengths of two of its sides and the sine of the included angle: Area $= \frac{1}{2} bc \sin A$, Area $= \frac{1}{2} ac \sin B$, or Area $= \frac{1}{2} ab \sin C$.

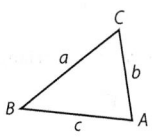

You can use any form of the area formula to find the area of a triangle, given two side lengths and the measure of the included angle.

Example 1 Find the area of each triangle to the nearest tenth.

 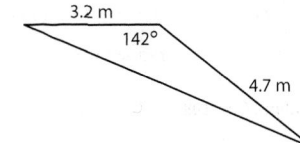

Let the known side lengths be a and b. $a = 3.2$ m and $b = 4.7$ m

Let the known angle be $\angle C$.   m $\angle C = 142°$

Substitute in the formula Area $= \frac{1}{2} ab \sin C$.   Area $= \frac{1}{2}(3.2)(4.7)\sin 142°$

Evaluate, rounding to the nearest tenth.   Area ≈ 4.6 m²

© Houghton Mifflin Harcourt Publishing Company

PROFESSIONAL DEVELOPMENT

 Integrate Mathematical Practices

This lesson provides an opportunity to address Mathematical Practice **MP.2**, which calls for students to "reason abstractly and quantitatively." Students derive the formula for the area of a triangle by recognizing the relationships that occur within the triangle when the altitude is constructed. They apply this formula to a variety of triangles. As students solve a right triangle, they must identify relationships that can be used to find missing measures, and they can often choose which of the three inverse trigonometric ratios to apply.

Deriving an Area Formula

INTEGRATE TECHNOLOGY

Students have the option of doing the Explore activity either in the book or online.

INTEGRATE TECHNOLOGY

Students are familiar with the trigonometric ratios from 0° to 90°. Ask them to graph $y = \sin x$ from 0° to 180° using their graphing calculators to see that the ratios are defined for angles greater (and less) than 90°.

QUESTIONING STRATEGIES

? Trigonometric ratios are defined using right triangles. Why does the area formula work for all types of triangles when it uses the sine ratio? The formula works because when the altitude, or height, is drawn to apply the usual formula for the area of a triangle, a right triangle is created.

? If you know the area of a triangle and the lengths of two sides, how can you find the measure of the included angle? Find the inverse sine of twice the area divided by the product of the two sides.

EXPLAIN 1

Using the Area Formula

AVOID COMMON ERRORS

Students may have difficulty substituting values into the sine area formula from a diagram. Emphasize that the two sides are both adjacent to the angle. Or, the angle is the included angle formed by the sides of the triangle.

? Why is the sine area formula useful when there is already a formula for the area of a triangle? It provides another method to find the area of a triangle without having to construct the height.

? Why does the angle have to be the included angle to use the sine area formula? The formula is derived by constructing a right triangle so that the height is opposite the angle and the hypotenuse is adjacent to the angle to make it possible to apply the sine ratio.

CONNECT VOCABULARY EL

Remind students that another word for the *altitude* of a triangle is its *height*.

INTEGRATE MATHEMATICAL PRACTICES

Focus on Modeling

MP.4 Discuss why students need remember only one version of the sine area formula to apply the formula to find the area of any triangle.

B In △DEF, DE = 9 in., DF = 13 in., and m∠D = 57°.

Sketch △DEF and check that ∠D is the included angle.

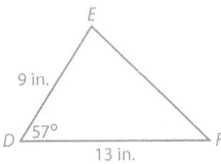

Write the area formula in terms of △DEF.	Area = $\frac{1}{2}$ (DE)(**DF**) sin **D**
Substitute in the area formula.	Area = $\frac{1}{2}$ (**9**)(**13**) sin **57** °
Evaluate, rounding to the nearest tenth.	Area ≈ **49.1** in.²

Your Turn

Find the area of each triangle to the nearest tenth.

3.

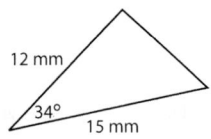

Let the known side lengths be *a* and *b*.	*a* = **12 mm** and *b* = **15 mm**
Let the known angle be ∠C.	m ∠C = **34°**
Substitute in the formula Area = $\frac{1}{2}$ *ab* sin C.	Area = $\frac{1}{2}$ (12)(15) sin 34°
Evaluate, rounding to the nearest tenth.	Area ≈ **50.3 mm²**

4. In △PQR, PQ = 3 cm, QR = 6 cm, and m∠Q = 108°.

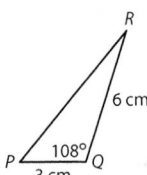

Area = $\frac{1}{2}$ (PQ)(QR) sin Q

= $\frac{1}{2}$ (3)(6) sin 108°

≈ 8.6 cm²

© Houghton Mifflin Harcourt Publishing Company

COLLABORATIVE LEARNING

Small Group Activity

Have students verify that they can use different trigonometric ratios and different inverse trigonometric ratios to solve a right triangle. Have students work together to solve a right triangle. Then have each student verify the measures using different trigonometric and inverse trigonometric ratios.

⏺ Explain 2   Solving a Right Triangle

Solving a right triangle means finding the lengths of all its sides and the measures of all its angles. To solve a right triangle you need to know two side lengths or one side length and an acute angle measure. Based on the given information, choose among trigonometric ratios, inverse trigonometric ratios, and the Pythagorean Theorem to help you solve the right triangle.

A shelf extends perpendicularly 7 in. from a wall. You want to place a 9-in. brace under the shelf, as shown. To the nearest tenth of an inch, how far below the shelf will the brace be attached to the wall? To the nearest degree, what angle will the brace make with the shelf and with the wall?

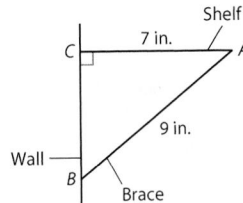

(A)   Find *BC*.

Use the Pythagorean Theorem to find the length of the third side.	$AC^2 + BC^2 = AB^2$
Substitute 7 for *AC* and 9 for *AB*.	$7^2 + BC^2 = 9^2$
Find the squares.	$49 + BC^2 = 81$
Subtract 49 from both sides.	$BC^2 = 32$
Find the square root and root.	$BC \approx 5.7$

(B)   Find m∠*A* and m∠*B*.

Use an inverse trigonometric ratio to find m∠*A*. You know the lengths of the adjacent side and the hypotenuse, so use the cosine ratio.

Write a cosine ratio for ∠*A*.	$\cos A = \boxed{\dfrac{7}{9}}$
Write an inverse cosine ratio.	$m\angle A = \cos^{-1}\left(\boxed{\dfrac{7}{9}}\right)$
Evaluate the inverse cosine ratio and round.	$m\angle A \approx \boxed{39}°$
∠ $\boxed{A}$ and ∠*B* are complementary.	$m\angle \boxed{A} + m\angle B = 90°$
Substitute $\boxed{39}°$ for m∠ $\boxed{A}$.	$\boxed{39}° + m\angle B \approx 90°$
Subtract $\boxed{39}°$ from both sides.	$m\angle B \approx \boxed{51}°$

Reflect

5.   Is it possible to find m∠*B* before you find m∠*A*? Explain.
   Yes; use an inverse sine ratio; $\sin B = \dfrac{7}{9}$, so $m\angle B = \sin^{-1}\left(\dfrac{7}{9}\right) \approx 51°$.

EXPLAIN 2

Solving a Right Triangle

QUESTIONING STRATEGIES

❓ **What information do you need to solve a right triangle? Explain.** You need the lengths of two sides or the length of one side and one acute angle measure. With this information you can find the remaining angle measures and side lengths.

AVOID COMMON ERRORS

Be sure students remember how to interpret the notation that represents an inverse function. Remind them that the −1 in an expression such as $\tan^{-1}\left(\dfrac{a}{b}\right)$ represents the angle whose tangent is $\dfrac{a}{b}$. It does *not* represent the reciprocal $\dfrac{1}{\tan\left(\dfrac{a}{b}\right)}$. It should generally be clear from the context whether the −1 is an inverse function or a negative exponent.

DIFFERENTIATE INSTRUCTION

Modeling

Have students draw an acute triangle with two adjacent sides that have whole number measures. Ask them to use a protractor to measure the included angle. Then have them find the area of the triangle using the sine area formula. Repeat with an obtuse triangle.

Auditory Cues

Students can use the mnemonic *soh-cah-toa* to remember that
$$\sin A = \frac{\text{opposite leg}}{\text{hypotenuse}}, \cos A = \frac{\text{adjacent leg}}{\text{hypotenuse}}, \text{ and } \tan A = \frac{\text{opposite leg}}{\text{adjacent leg}}.$$

EXPLAIN 3

Solving a Right Triangle in the Coordinate Plane

INTEGRATE MATHEMATICAL PRACTICES
Focus on Modeling

MP.4 Discuss how to identify the legs and the hypotenuse of a right triangle in the coordinate plane if the legs of the right triangle are not formed by horizontal and vertical line segments. Use the distance formula to find the length of each side. The longest side is the hypotenuse.

QUESTIONING STRATEGIES

? How is solving a right triangle in the coordinate plane different from solving a labeled right triangle? Neither side lengths nor an angle measure are given in the coordinate plane. You must use the distance formula to find side lengths and then use the inverses of trigonometric ratios to find the angles.

Your Turn

A building casts a 33-m shadow when the Sun is at an angle of 27° to the vertical. How tall is the building, to the nearest meter? How far is it from the top of the building to the tip of the shadow? What angle does a ray from the Sun along the edge of the shadow make with the ground?

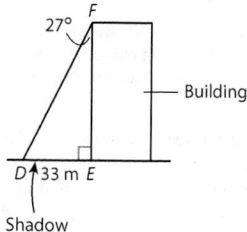

Building

D 33 m E

Shadow

6. Use a trigonometric ratio to find the distance EF.

$$\tan F = \frac{DE}{EF}$$

$$\tan 27° = \frac{33}{EF}$$

$$EF = \frac{33}{\tan 27°} \approx 65 \text{ m}$$

7. Use another trigonometric ratio to find the distance DF.

$$\sin F = \frac{DE}{DF}$$

$$\sin 27° = \frac{33}{DF}$$

$$DF = \frac{33}{\sin 27°} \approx 73 \text{ m}$$

8. Use the fact that acute angles of a right triangle are complementary to find $m\angle D$.

$$m\angle D + m\angle F = 90°$$

$$m\angle D + 27° = 90°$$

$$m\angle D = 63°$$

Explain 3 Solving a Right Triangle in the Coordinate Plane

You can use the distance formula as well as trigonometric tools to solve right triangles in the coordinate plane.

Example 3 Solve each triangle.

(A) Triangle ABC has vertices $A(-3, 3)$, $B(-3, -1)$, and $C(4, -1)$. Find the side lengths to the nearest hundredth and the angle measures to the nearest degree.

Plot points A, B, and C, and draw $\triangle ABC$.

Find the side lengths: $AB = 4$, $BC = 7$

Use the distance formula to find the length of $\overline{AC}$.

$$AC = \sqrt{\left(4 - (-3)\right)^2 + (-1 - 3)^2} = \sqrt{65} \approx 8.06$$

Find the angle measures: $\overline{AB} \perp \overline{BC}$, so $m\angle B = 90°$.

Use an inverse tangent ratio to find

$$m\angle C = \tan^{-1}\left(\frac{AB}{BC}\right) = \tan^{-1}\left(\frac{4}{7}\right) \approx 30°.$$

$\angle A$ and $\angle C$ are complementary, so $m\angle A \approx 90° - 30° = 60°$.

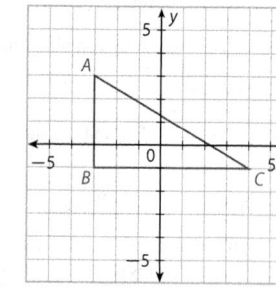

© Houghton Mifflin Harcourt Publishing Company

Module 13 **727** Lesson 4

LANGUAGE SUPPORT EL

Connect Vocabulary

Discuss the meaning of *solve* in the phrase *solve a right triangle*. Compare solving a triangle to solving an equation. To use the non-mathematical meaning of *solve*, compare solving a triangle to solving a mystery. A detective uses clues to find missing information. Similarly, to solve a right triangle means to use given information and tools such as the trigonometric ratios to find all the missing side lengths and angle measures.

727 Lesson 13.4

Ⓑ Triangle DEF has vertices $D(-4, 3)$, $E(3, 4)$, and $F(0, 0)$. Find the side lengths to the nearest hundredth and the angle measures to the nearest degree.

Plot points D, E, and F, and draw $\triangle DEF$.

$\angle F$ appears to be a right angle. To check, find the slope

of $\overline{DF}$: $\dfrac{\boxed{0} - 3}{0 - \boxed{-4}} = \dfrac{\boxed{-3}}{\boxed{4}} = \boxed{-\dfrac{3}{4}}$;

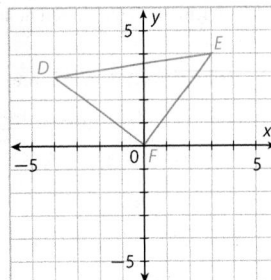

slope of $\boxed{EF}$: $\dfrac{\boxed{0} - \boxed{4}}{\boxed{0} - 3} = \dfrac{\boxed{-4}}{\boxed{-3}} = \dfrac{\boxed{4}}{\boxed{3}}$;

so m$\angle F = \boxed{90}$ °.

Find the side lengths using the distance formula:

$DE = \sqrt{\left(3 - \boxed{-4}\right)^2 + \left(\boxed{4} - 3\right)^2} = \sqrt{\boxed{50}} = \boxed{5}\sqrt{\boxed{2}} \approx \boxed{7.07}$,

$DF = \sqrt{\left(\boxed{0} - \boxed{-4}\right)^2 + \left(\boxed{0} - 3\right)^2} = \sqrt{\boxed{25}} = \boxed{5}$,

$\boxed{EF} = \sqrt{\left(\boxed{0} - \boxed{3}\right)^2 + \left(\boxed{0} - 4\right)^2} = \sqrt{\boxed{25}} = \boxed{5}$

Use an inverse sine ratio to find m$\angle D$.

$m\angle D = \sin^{-1}\left(\dfrac{\boxed{EF}}{\boxed{DE}}\right) = \sin^{-1}\left(\dfrac{\boxed{5}}{\boxed{5\sqrt{2}}}\right) = \boxed{45}$ °

$\angle D$ and $\angle\ \boxed{E}$ are complementary, so m$\angle\ \boxed{E} = 90° - \boxed{45}° = \boxed{45}°$.

Reflect

9. How does the given information determine which inverse trigonometric ratio you should use to determine an acute angle measure?

   It doesn't – you can use any inverse trigonometric ratio, as long as you use the correct

   two side lengths. However, if two sides are vertical and horizontal, it makes sense to use

   inverse tangent.

Problem Solving with Trigonometry   **728**

ELABORATE

INTEGRATE MATHEMATICAL PRACTICES
Focus on Modeling

MP.4 Some students may find it difficult to choose a trigonometric or inverse trigonometric ratio to solve a right triangle. Discuss with the class how students choose a particular relationship. For example, some students may prefer to always use the inverse tangent ratio if the lengths of both legs are known to find an acute angle measure.

AVOID COMMON ERRORS

Students may miss parts when solving a right triangle. Remind students that three side lengths and three angle measures are needed. Encourage students to always draw a diagram and to label it whenever they determine a measure.

SUMMARIZE THE LESSON

How do you solve a right triangle? Use the Pythagorean Theorem, trigonometric ratios, inverse trigonometric ratios, and complementary angle relationships to find missing side lengths and angle measures in a right triangle.

Your Turn

10. Triangle *JKL* has vertices $J(3, 5)$, $K(-3, 2)$, and $L(5, 1)$. Find the side lengths to the nearest hundredth and the angle measures to the nearest degree.

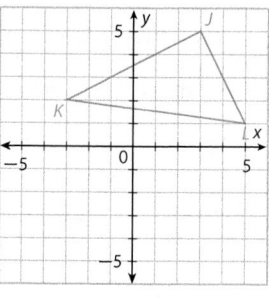

Plot points *J*, *K*, and *L*, and draw $\triangle JKL$.

Find the side lengths using the distance formula:

$JK = \sqrt{(-3-3)^2 + (2-5)^2} = \sqrt{45} = 3\sqrt{5} \approx 6.71$,

$JL = \sqrt{(5-3)^2 + (1-5)^2} = \sqrt{20} = 2\sqrt{5} \approx 4.47$,

$KL = \sqrt{(5-(-3))^2 + (1-2)^2} = \sqrt{65} \approx 8.06$

$\angle J$ appears to be a right angle. To check, find the slope of $\overline{JK}$.

Slope of $\overline{JK}$: $\dfrac{2-5}{-3-3} = \dfrac{-3}{-6} = \dfrac{1}{2}$; slope of $\overline{JL}$: $\dfrac{1-5}{5-3} = \dfrac{-4}{2} = -2$; so m$\angle J = 90°$.

Use an inverse cosine ratio to find m$\angle K = \cos^{-1}\left(\dfrac{JK}{KL}\right) = \cos^{-1}\left(\dfrac{\sqrt{45}}{\sqrt{65}}\right) \approx 34°$.

$\angle K$ and $\angle L$ are complementary, so m$\angle L \approx 90° - 34° = 66°$.

💬 Elaborate

11. Would you use the area formula you determined in this lesson for a right triangle? Explain.

Possible answer: No. You could use this formula, but since in a right triangle, the lengths of the legs are the base and height, it is simpler to use the formula $A = \dfrac{1}{2}bh$.

12. **Discussion** How does the process of solving a right triangle change when its vertices are located in the coordinate plane?

Generally, you need to find all the side lengths and all the angles, checking that one is a right angle. The distance formula is generally used to find side lengths rather than trigonometric ratios or the Pythagorean Theorem (although the distance formula depends on the Pythagorean Theorem). The acute angles are found in the same way in both cases.

13. **Essential Question Check-In** How do you find the unknown angle measures in a right triangle?

You first use two known side lengths to form a ratio and then use the appropriate inverse trigonometric ratio to find one angle measure. Then subtract that measure from 90° to find the measure of the other acute angle.

• Online Homework
• Hints and Help
• Extra Practice

Find the area of each triangle to the nearest tenth.

1.

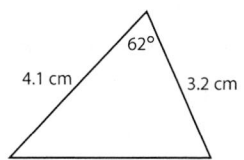

62°

4.1 cm   3.2 cm

$a = 4.1$ cm, $b = 3.2$ cm, and m$\angle C = 62°$;

Area $= \frac{1}{2}ab \sin C = \frac{1}{2}(4.1)(3.2)\sin 62° \approx 5.8$ cm²

2. In $\triangle PQR$, $PR = 23$ mm, $QR = 39$ mm, and m$\angle R = 163°$.

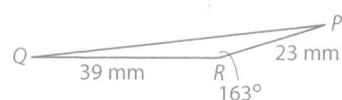

Area $= \frac{1}{2}(PR)(QR)\sin R = \frac{1}{2}(23)(39)\sin 163° \approx 131.1$ mm².

Solve each right triangle. Round lengths to the nearest tenth and angles to the nearest degree.

3.

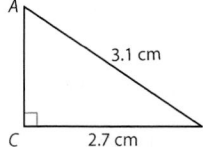

3.1 cm

2.7 cm

$AC^2 + BC^2 = AB^2$

$AC^2 + (2.7)^2 = (3.1)^2$

$AC^2 = 2.32$

$AC = \sqrt{2.32} \approx 1.5$ cm

m$\angle A = \sin^{-1}\left(\frac{BC}{AB}\right) = \sin^{-1}\left(\frac{2.7}{3.1}\right) \approx 61°$

$\angle A$ and $\angle B$ are complementary, so m$\angle B \approx 90° - 61° = 29°$.

4.

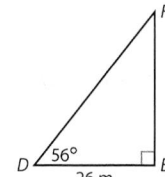

56°
26 m

$\angle D$ and $\angle F$ are complementary, so m$\angle F = 90° - 56° = 34°$.

$\tan D = \frac{EF}{DE}$ $\cos D = \frac{DE}{DF}$

$\tan 56° = \frac{EF}{26}$ $\cos 56° = \frac{26}{DF}$

$26\tan 56° = EF$ $DF = \frac{26}{\cos 56°} \approx 46.5$ m

38.5 m $\approx EF$

5. Right $\triangle PQR$ with $\overline{PQ} \perp \overline{PR}$, $QR = 47$ mm, and m$\angle Q = 52°$

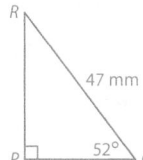

47 mm

52°

$\angle Q$ and $\angle R$ are complementary, so m$\angle R = 90° - 52° = 38°$.

$\sin Q = \frac{PR}{QR}$ $\cos Q = \frac{PQ}{QR}$

$\sin 52° = \frac{PR}{47}$ $\cos 52° = \frac{PQ}{47}$

$47 \sin 52° = PR$ $47 \cos 52° = PQ$

37.0 mm $\approx PR$ 28.9 mm $\approx PQ$

Exercise	Depth of Knowledge (D.O.K.)	COMMON CORE Mathematical Practices	
1–8	**1** Recall of Information	**MP.4** Modeling	
9–15	**2** Skills/Concepts	**MP.4** Modeling	
16	**3** Strategic Thinking	**MP.3** Logic	
17	**3** Strategic Thinking H.O.T.	**MP.2** Reasoning	
18	**3** Strategic Thinking H.O.T.	**MP.4** Modeling	
19	**3** Strategic Thinking H.O.T.	**MP.3** Logic	

EVALUATE

ASSIGNMENT GUIDE

Concepts and Skills	Practice
Explore Deriving an Area Formula	Exercise 16
Example 1 Using the Area Formula	Exercises 1–2
Example 2 Solving a Right Triangle	Exercises 3–5
Example 3 Solving a Right Triangle in the Coordinate Plane	Exercises 6–8

AVOID COMMON ERRORS

Students may forget to include units when solving area problems. Remind students that the units are an important part of the answer.

COMMUNICATING MATH

Encourage students solving right triangles to communicate their understanding of the relationships between the trigonometric ratios and their inverses.

Problem Solving with Trigonometry   **730**

AVOID COMMON ERRORS

Students may have difficulty solving right triangles. They may find it easier when they first identify whether they are looking for a ratio or an angle measure. If they are looking for a ratio, they should use sin, cos, or tan. If they are looking for an angle measure, they should use $\sin^{-1}$, $\cos^{-1}$, or $\tan^{-1}$.

INTEGRATE MATHEMATICAL PRACTICES

Focus on Modeling

MP.4 For greater accuracy, remind students to use given measurements instead of calculated values in the later steps of solving a right triangle.

Solve each triangle. Find the side lengths to the nearest hundredth and the angle measures to the nearest degree.

6. Triangle ABC with vertices $A(-4, 4)$, $B(3, 4)$, and $C(3, -2)$

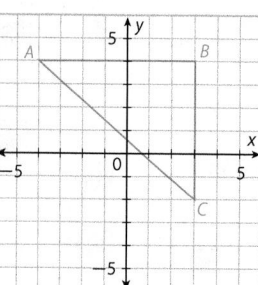

Plot points A, B, and C, and draw $\triangle ABC$.

$\overline{AB} \perp \overline{BC}$, so $m\angle B = 90°$

$AB = 7$, $BC = 6$, $AC = \sqrt{\left(3 - (-4)\right)^2 + (-2 - 4)^2} = \sqrt{85} \approx 9.$

$m\angle A = \tan^{-1}\left(\dfrac{BC}{AB}\right) = \tan^{-1}\left(\dfrac{6}{7}\right) \approx 41°$

$\angle A$ and $\angle C$ are complementary, so $m\angle C \approx 90° - 41° = 49°.$

7. Triangle JKL with vertices $J(-3, 1)$, $K(-1, 4)$, and $L(6, -5)$

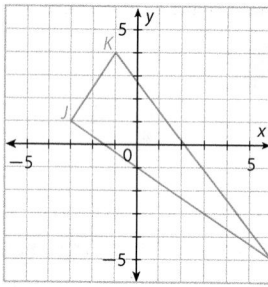

Plot points J, K, and L, and draw $\triangle JKL$.

$\angle J$ appears to be a right angle. To check,

slope of $\overline{JK}$: $\dfrac{4 - 1}{-1 - (-3)} = \dfrac{3}{2}$;

slope of $\overline{JL}$: $\dfrac{-5 - 1}{6 - (-3)} = \dfrac{-6}{9} = -\dfrac{2}{3}$; so $m\angle J = 90°$.

$JK = \sqrt{\left(-1 - (-3)\right)^2 + (4 - 1)^2} = \sqrt{13} \approx 3.6,$

$JL = \sqrt{\left(6 - (-3)\right)^2 + (-5 - 1)^2} = \sqrt{117} \approx 10.8,$

$KL = \sqrt{\left(6 - (-1)\right)^2 + \left(5 - (-4)\right)^2} = \sqrt{130} \approx 11.4$

$m\angle L = \sin^{-1}\left(\dfrac{JK}{KL}\right) = \sin^{-1}\left(\dfrac{\sqrt{13}}{\sqrt{130}}\right) \approx 18°$

$\angle K$ and $\angle L$ are complementary, so $m\angle K \approx 90° - 18° = 72°$.

8. Triangle PQR with vertices $P(5, 5)$, $Q(-5, 3)$, and $R(-4, -2)$

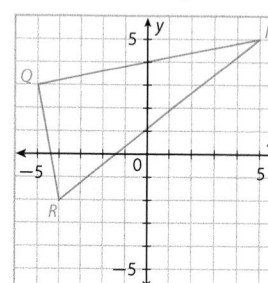

Plot points P, Q, and R, and draw $\triangle PQR$.

$\angle Q$ appears to be a right angle. To check,

slope of $\overline{PQ}$: $\dfrac{3 - 5}{-5 - 5} = \dfrac{-2}{-10} = \dfrac{1}{5}$;

slope of $\overline{QR}$: $\dfrac{-2 - 3}{-4 - (-5)} = \dfrac{-5}{1} = -5$; so $m\angle Q = 90°$.

$PQ = \sqrt{(-5 - 5)^2 + (3 - 5)^2} = \sqrt{104} = 2\sqrt{26} \approx 10.2,$

$QR = \sqrt{\left(-4 - (-5)\right)^2 + (-2 - 3)^2} = \sqrt{26} \approx 5.1,$

$PR = \sqrt{(-4 - 5)^2 + (-2 - 5)^2} = \sqrt{130} \approx 11.4$

$m\angle P = \tan^{-1}\left(\dfrac{QR}{PQ}\right) = \tan^{-1}\left(\dfrac{1}{2}\right) \approx 27°$

$\angle P$ and $\angle R$ are complementary, so $m\angle R \approx 90° - 27° = 63°.$

9. **Surveying** A plot of land is in the shape of a triangle, as shown. Find the area of the plot, to the nearest hundred square yards.

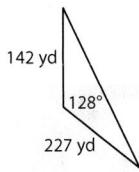

142 yd

128°

227 yd

$$\text{Area} = \frac{1}{2}ab \sin C$$

$$= \frac{1}{2}(142)(227) \sin 128° \approx 12{,}700 \text{ yd}^2$$

10. **History** A drawbridge at the entrance to an ancient castle is raised and lowered by a pair of chains. The figure represents the drawbridge when flat. Find the height of the suspension point of the chain, to the nearest tenth of a meter, and the measures of the acute angles the chain makes with the wall and the drawbridge, to the nearest degree.

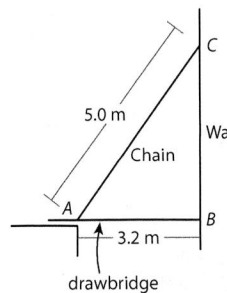

C

5.0 m

Chain

Wall

A

3.2 m

B

drawbridge

height of wall: $AB^2 + BC^2 = AC^2$

$$(3.2)^2 + BC^2 = (5.0)^2$$

$$10.24 + BC^2 = 25$$

$$BC^2 = 14.76$$

$$BC \approx 3.8 \text{ m}$$

$$m\angle A = \cos^{-1}\left(\frac{AB}{AC}\right) = \cos^{-1}\left(\frac{3.2}{5.0}\right) \approx 50°$$

$\angle A$ and $\angle C$ are complementary, so $m\angle C \approx 90° - 50° = 40°$.

11. **Building** For safety, the angle a wheelchair ramp makes with the horizontal should be no more than 3.5°. What is the maximum height of a ramp of length 30 ft? What distance along the ground would this ramp cover? Round to the nearest tenth of a foot.

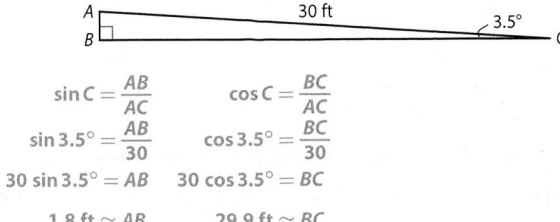

A

30 ft

3.5°

B

C

$$\sin C = \frac{AB}{AC} \qquad \cos C = \frac{BC}{AC}$$

$$\sin 3.5° = \frac{AB}{30} \qquad \cos 3.5° = \frac{BC}{30}$$

$$30 \sin 3.5° = AB \qquad 30 \cos 3.5° = BC$$

$$1.8 \text{ ft} \approx AB \qquad 29.9 \text{ ft} \approx BC$$

COLLABORATIVE LEARNING

Have students construct a right triangle and measure the lengths of two sides. Ask them to find the length of the third side and the acute angle measures without using the Pythagorean Theorem or a protractor. Have students construct a second right triangle and measure one acute angle and a side. Have them find the other acute angle measure and the lengths of the other two sides. Finally, have students exchange triangles and check each other's work.

COMMUNICATE MATH EL

Have students explain to each other when they would use the Pythagorean Theorem, the sin, cos, or tan ratios, and the $\sin^{-1}$, $\cos^{-1}$, or $\tan^{-1}$ ratios to solve a right triangle.

12. Multi-Step The figure shows an origami crane as well as a stage of its construction. The area of each wing is shown by the shaded part of the figure, which is symmetric about its vertical center line. Use the information in the figure to find the total wing area of the crane, to the nearest tenth of a square inch.

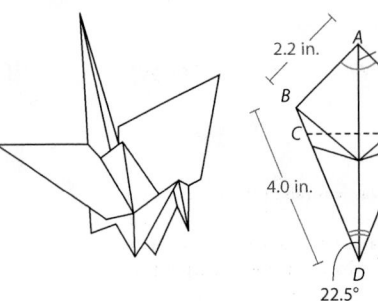

Area of each wing = Area of △ABF + Area of △DBF − Area of △DCE

Area of △ABF $= \frac{1}{2}(2.2)(2.2)\sin 45°; \approx 1.711$ **in.**^{2}

Area of △DBF $= \frac{1}{2}(4.0)(4.0)\sin 22.5°; \approx 3.061$ **in.**^{2}

Area of △DCE $= \frac{1}{2}(3.7 \text{ in.})(3.7 \text{ in.})\sin 22.5°; \approx 2.619$ **in.**^{2}

Area of each wing: 1.711 in.^{2} **+ 3.061 in.**^{2} **− 2.619 in.**^{2} **= 2.153 in.**^{2}

Area of both wings: 2(2.153) in.^{2} **≈ 4.3 in.**^{2}

13. Right triangle △XYZ has vertices $X(1, 4)$ and $Y(2, -3)$. The vertex Z has positive integer coordinates, and $XZ = 5$. Find the coordinates of Z and solve △XYZ; give exact answers.

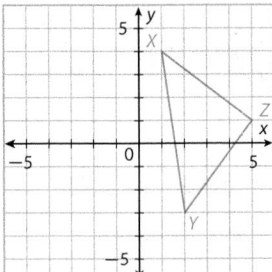

Based on 3–4–5 right triangles as well as horizontal and vertical displacements of 5, possible coordinates for Z are $(1, 9)$, $(4, 8)$, $(5, 7)$, $(6, 4)$, and $(5, 1)$. $Z(5, 1)$ is the only possibility that appears to create a right triangle.

To check, slope of $\overline{XZ}$: $\frac{1-4}{5-1} = \frac{-3}{4} = -\frac{3}{4}$; slope of $\overline{YZ}$: $\frac{1-(-3)}{5-2} = \frac{4}{3}$; so m∠Z = 90°.

$XY = \sqrt{(2-1)^2 + (-3-4)^2} = \sqrt{50} = 5\sqrt{2}$, $XZ = \sqrt{(5-1)^2 + (1-4)^2} = \sqrt{25} = 5$,

$YZ = \sqrt{(5-2)^2 + (1-(-3))^2} = \sqrt{25} = 5$

Since $\overline{XZ} \cong \overline{YZ}$, △XYZ is a 45°−45°−90° triangle. Therefore, m∠X = m∠Y = 45°.

Module 13 · 733 · Lesson 4

14. Critique Reasoning Shania and Pedro are discussing whether it is always possible to solve a right triangle, given enough information, without using the Pythagorean Theorem. Pedro says that it is always possible, but Shania thinks that when two side lengths and no angle measures are given, the Pythagorean Theorem is needed. Who is correct, and why?

Pedro; Possible answer: When one side and one acute angle are given, trigonometric ratios can be used to find the other sides, and complementary angles give the other acute angle. When two sides are given, an inverse trigonometric ratio can be used to find one acute angle, and this angle together with a given side can be used with a different trigonometric ratio to find the other side. The other acute angle is complementary as before.

15. Design The logo shown is symmetrical about one of its diagonals. Find the angle measures in $\triangle CAE$, to the nearest degree. (*Hint:* First find an angle in $\triangle ABC$, $\triangle CDE$ or $\triangle AEF$.) Then, find the area of $\triangle CAE$, without first finding the areas of the other triangles.

$m\angle BAC = \tan^{-1}\left(\frac{BC}{AB}\right) = \tan^{-1}\left(\frac{3}{6}\right) \approx 26.565°$

$\angle BAC \cong \angle EAF$, so $m\angle EAF = m\angle BAC \approx 26.565°$

$m\angle BAC + m\angle CAE + m\angle EAF = 90°$

$26.565° + m\angle CAE + 26.565° \approx 90°$

$m\angle CAE \approx 90° - 2(26.565°)$

$\approx 36.87° \approx 37°$

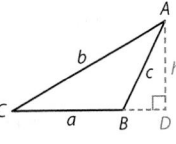

6 mm

A   B

3 mm

C

3 mm

F   E   D

$\angle AEC \cong \angle ACE$, so $m\angle AEC = m\angle ACE$ $AC^2 = AB^2 + BC^2$

$m\angle AEC + m\angle ACE + m\angle CAE = 180°$ $AC^2 = 6^2 + 3^2 = 45$

$2(m\angle AEC) + 36.87° \approx 180°$ $AC = \sqrt{45} = 3\sqrt{5}$

$m\angle AEC \approx 71.5°$ Area $= \frac{1}{2}(AC)(AE)\sin(\angle CAE)$

$m\angle ACE \approx 71.5°$ $\approx \frac{1}{2}\left(3\sqrt{5}\right)\left(3\sqrt{5}\right)\sin(36.87°) \approx 13.5$ mm²

16. Use the area formula for obtuse $\angle B$ in the diagram to show that if an acute angle and an obtuse angle are supplementary, then their sines are equal.

Area formula: Area $= \frac{1}{2}ac \sin B$

But $\triangle ABC$ has base a and height $h = c\sin(\angle ABD)$,

so Area $= \frac{1}{2}(a)\left(c\sin(\angle ABD)\right)$.

Equating these two expressions for the area, $\sin B = \sin \angle ABD$

But since, for any obtuse $\angle B$, $\angle B$ and $\angle ABD$ are supplementary in this construction, this proves the result.

JOURNAL

Have students create an example that shows how to solve a right triangle. Students should specify the known side or angle measures and explain how to find the unknown side lengths and angle measures.

17. Communicate Mathematical Ideas The HL Congruence Theorem states that for right triangles ABC and DEF such that $\angle A$ and $\angle D$ are right angles, $\overline{BC} \cong \overline{EF}$, and $\overline{AB} \cong \overline{DE}$, $\triangle ABC \cong \triangle DEF$.

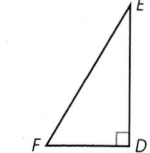

Explain, without formal proof, how solving a right triangle with given leg lengths, or with a given side length and acute angle measure, shows that right triangles with both legs congruent, or with corresponding sides and angles congruent, must be congruent.

Suppose $\overline{AB} \cong \overline{DE}$ and $\overline{AC} \cong \overline{DF}$. Solving either of these right triangles determines the length of the hypotenuse in the same way, e.g., using the Pythagorean Theorem, so $BC = EF$ and therefore, by SSS $\cong$, $\triangle ABC \cong \triangle DEF$.

Suppose $\angle B \cong \angle E$. The given corresponding side lengths allow the unknown sides to be calculated in the same way using trigonometric ratios, so that all corresponding side lengths are equal and therefore all corresponding sides are congruent. Again, by SSS $\cong$, $\triangle ABC \cong \triangle DEF$.

18. Persevere in Problem Solving Find the perimeter and area of $\triangle ABC$, as exact numbers. Then, find the measures of all the angles to the nearest degree.

$BC = 6$, $AB = \sqrt{\left(3 - (-2)\right)^2 + (3 - 2)^2} = \sqrt{26}$,

$AC = \sqrt{\left(3 - (-2)\right)^2 + \left(-3 - (-2)\right)^2} = \sqrt{50} = 5\sqrt{2}$

perimeter: $BC + AB + AC = 6 + \sqrt{26} + 5\sqrt{2}$

With base $b = BC = 6$, height $h = 5$,

so area $= \frac{1}{2}bh = \frac{1}{2}(6)(5) = 15$.

$$\text{Area} = \frac{1}{2}ab \sin C \qquad\qquad 15 = \frac{1}{2}\left(5\sqrt{2}\right)\left(\sqrt{26}\right)\sin A$$

$$15 = \frac{1}{2}(6)\left(5\sqrt{2}\right)\sin C \qquad\qquad \frac{3\sqrt{13}}{13} = \sin A$$

$$\frac{\sqrt{2}}{2} = \sin C \qquad\qquad \sin^{-1}\left(\frac{3\sqrt{13}}{13}\right) = m\angle A$$

$$45° = m\angle C \qquad\qquad 56° \approx m\angle A$$

Angle sum of a triangle: $56° + m\angle B + 45° \approx 180°$; $m\angle B \approx 79°$

19. Analyze Relationships Find the area of the triangle using two different formulas, and deduce an expression for $\sin 2\theta$.

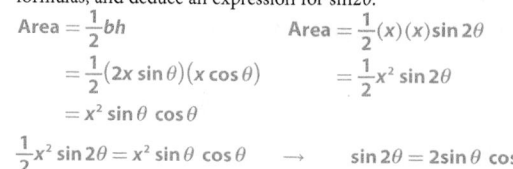 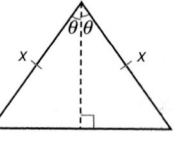

$$\text{Area} = \frac{1}{2}bh \qquad\qquad \text{Area} = \frac{1}{2}(x)(x)\sin 2\theta$$

$$= \frac{1}{2}(2x \sin \theta)(x \cos \theta) \qquad\qquad = \frac{1}{2}x^2 \sin 2\theta$$

$$= x^2 \sin \theta \, \cos \theta$$

$$\frac{1}{2}x^2 \sin 2\theta = x^2 \sin \theta \, \cos \theta \quad \longrightarrow \quad \sin 2\theta = 2\sin \theta \, \cos \theta$$

Lesson Performance Task

Every molecule of water contains two atoms of hydrogen and one atom of oxygen. The drawing shows how the atoms are arranged in a molecule of water, along with the incredibly precise dimensions of the molecule that physicists have been able to determine. (1 pm = 1 picometer = 10^{-12}m)

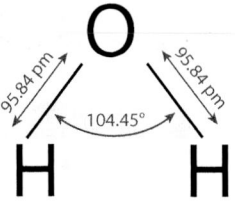

1. Draw and label a triangle with the dimensions shown.

2. Find the area of the triangle in square centimeters. Show your work.

3. Find the distance between the hydrogen atoms in centimeters. Explain your method.

1.

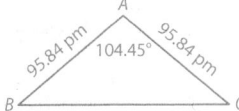

2. $AB = AC = 95.84 \text{ pm} = 95.84 \times 10^{-12} \text{ m} = 95.84 \times 10^{-10} \text{ cm} = 9.584 \times 10^{-9} \text{ cm}$

$\text{area} = \frac{1}{2} AB(AC) \, \sin A = \frac{1}{2}(9.584 \times 10^{-9} \text{ cm})(9.584 \times 10^{-9} \text{ cm}) \sin 104.45°$

$\quad = \frac{1}{2}(9.584 \times 10^{-9} \text{ cm})(9.584 \times 10^{-9} \text{ cm})(0.9684)$

$\quad \approx 44.48 \times 10^{-18} \text{ cm}^2$

$\quad \approx 4.45 \times 10^{-17} \text{ cm}^2$

3. Possible answer: Label the midpoint of $\overline{BC}$ point D. Draw $\overline{AD}$. $\overline{AD}$ bisects $\angle A$, forming two 52.225° angles.

In right triangle ABD,

$\sin 52.225 = \dfrac{BD}{AB}$

$\quad 0.79 \approx \dfrac{BD}{95.84}$

$\quad 75.71 \approx BD$

$BC = 2 \times 75.71 = 151.42 \text{ pm} = 151.42 \times 10^{-12} \text{ m} = 151.42 \times 10^{-10} \text{ cm} = 1.51 \times 10^{-8} \text{cm}$

EXTENSION ACTIVITY

This Lesson Performance Task will give students a glimpse into the complex field of molecular geometry. While most of the subject lies beyond the range of high-school geometry students, there are many questions students can research and report on at a basic level. Among them:

- What is molecular geometry?
- How was the molecular structure of water discovered?
- What determines the angles between the atoms in a molecule?
- What holds a molecule together?

CONNECT VOCABULARY EL

Students are probably familiar with the metric prefixes *deci-*, *centi-*, and *milli-*, but may not know the next three smaller prefixes. They are:

$micro\text{-} = 10^{-6} = 0.000\,001$

$nano\text{-} = 10^{-9} = 0.000\,000\,001$

$pico\text{-} = 10^{-12} = 0.000\,000\,000\,001$

AVOID COMMON ERRORS

The conversion from 95.84 picometers to centimeters may be difficult for students. Here are the steps and reasons:

$95.84 \text{ pm} = 95.84 \times 10^{-12} \text{ m}$

$\qquad\qquad (\textit{Definition of pm})$

$\qquad = 95.84 \times 10^{-10} \text{ cm}$

$\qquad\qquad (\textit{Multiply by } 10^2 \textit{ cm} = 1 \textit{ m.})$

$\qquad = 9.584 \times 10^{-9} \text{ cm}$

$\qquad\qquad (\textit{Divide 95.84 by 10 and multiply } 10^{-10} \textit{ by 10})$

Scoring Rubric

2 points: Student correctly solves the problem and explains his/her reasoning.

1 point: Student shows good understanding of the problem but does not fully solve or explain his/her reasoning.

0 points: Student does not demonstrate understanding of the problem.

Problem Solving with Trigonometry　**736**

Study Guide Review

ASSESSMENT AND INTERVENTION

Personal **Math** Trainer

Assign or customize module reviews.

MODULE PERFORMANCE TASK

COMMON CORE

Mathematical Practices: MP.1, MP.2, MP.3, MP.4, MP.7
G-SRT.C.8, G-MG.A.1

SUPPORTING STUDENT REASONING

Students should begin this problem by focusing on what information they will need. Here are some issues they might bring up.

- **How to find the total height of layers of staggered pipes:** Students need to realize that the centers of three staggered pipes form an equilateral triangle. The height can be found in multiple ways, including the Pythagorean Theorem or trigonometry, or you can provide an algorithm to find the height.

- **How to find the height of _n_ layers of staggered pipes:** Students need to generalize the relationship from the height of 10 layers of staggered pipes to _n_ layers.

- **If the thickness of the pipes matters:** Students can brainstorm possibilities for both a stack and a staggered stack of pipes. The thickness adds to the height of the stack, but will add less to the height of the staggered stack.

Trigonometry with Right Triangles

Essential Question: How can you use trigonometry with right triangles to solve real-world problems?

Key Vocabulary
adjacent _(adyacente)_
opposite _(opuesto)_
tangent _(tangente)_
$tan^{-1} A$ _($tan^{-1} A$)_
inverse tangent of $\angle A$
   (tangente inversa de $\angle A$)
trigonometric ratio
   (proporción trigonométrica)
sine _(seno)_
cosine _(coseno)_
inverse trigonometric ratios
   (proporción inversa trigonométrica)
Pythagorean triple
   (terna pitagórica)

KEY EXAMPLE _(Lesson 13.1)_

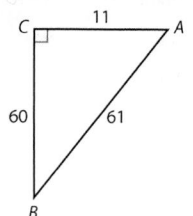

Find the tangent of angle A.

$$\tan A = \frac{\text{length of leg opposite } \angle A}{\text{length of leg adjacent to } \angle A}$$ Definition of tangent

$$\tan A = \frac{60}{11} \approx 5.45$$ Substitute and simplify

KEY EXAMPLE _(Lesson 13.2)_

Find the sine and cosine of angle A.

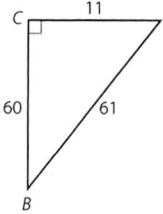

$$\sin A = \frac{\text{length of leg opposite } \angle A}{\text{length of hypotenuse}}$$ Definition of sine

$$\sin A = \frac{60}{61} \approx .98$$ Simplify.

$$\cos A = \frac{\text{length of leg adjacent to } \angle A}{\text{length of hypotenuse}}$$ Definition of cosine

$$\cos A = \frac{11}{61} \approx .18$$ Simplify.

KEY EXAMPLE _(Lesson 13.3)_

Given an isosceles right triangle _DEF_ with m$\angle F$ = 90° and _DE_ = 7, find the length of the other two sides.

$$DE = DF\sqrt{2}$$ Apply the relationship of 45°-45°-90° triangles.

$$7 = DF\sqrt{2}$$ Substitute.

$$\frac{7}{\sqrt{2}} = DF$$ Simplify.

$$DF = EF = \frac{7}{\sqrt{2}} = \frac{7\sqrt{2}}{2}$$ Apply properties of isosceles triangles.

SCAFFOLDING SUPPORT

- Suggest that students use the strategy of solving a simpler problem to help them find the height of stacked pipes. Have them first find the height of two layers, then find the height as another layer is added until they recognize a pattern.

- One way to determine the height for two layers is to look at three pipes that form an equilateral triangle, and determine the total height using the students' knowledge of triangles. They can continue this process, adding more layers to form larger triangles.

EXERCISES

Given a right triangle $\triangle XYZ$ where $\angle Z$ is a right angle, $XY = 53$, $YZ = 28$, and $XZ = 45$, find the following rounded to the nearest hundredth. *(Lessons 13.1, 13.2)*

1. $\sin X$ __0.53__
2. $\cos X$ __0.85__
3. $\tan X$ __0.62__

Find the lengths of the other two sides of the following triangle. Find exact answers in order of least to greatest. *(Lesson 13.3)*

4. 30°-60°-90° triangle with a hypotenuse of length 14   __$7, 7\sqrt{3}$__

Find the area of the following triangle, rounded to the nearest tenth. *(Lesson 13.4)*

5. triangle $\triangle ABC$, where m$\angle C = 127°$, $AC = 5$, and $BC = 9$ __18.0__

MODULE PERFORMANCE TASK

How Much Shorter Are Staggered Pipe Stacks?

How much space can be saved by stacking pipe in a staggered pattern? The illustration shows you the difference between layers of pipe stacked directly on top of each other (left) and in a staggered pattern (right). Suppose you have pipes that are 2 inches in diameter. How much shorter will a staggered stack of 10 layers be than a non-staggered stack with the same number of layers? In general, how much shorter are n layers of staggered pipe?

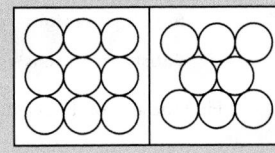

Start by listing in the space below how you plan to tackle the problem. Then use your own paper to complete the task. Be sure to write down all your data and assumptions. Then use numbers, graphs, diagrams, or algebraic equations to explain how you reached your conclusion.

DISCUSSION OPPORTUNITIES

- What assumptions are made when finding the height of a stack of pipes?
- What could be sources of error in finding the height of a staggered stack of pipes?

SAMPLE SOLUTION

Methodology:

The centers of three staggered pipes form an equilateral triangle. Find an expression for the height of this triangle, which is two layers. Next, add another layer to form an equilateral triangle using 6 pipes. Find an expression for the height of this triangle, which is three layers. Continue the process until a clear pattern emerges, then generalize to n layers.

The height of an equilateral triangle formed by the centers of three pipes can be found using the Pythagorean Theorem, $a^2 + b^2 = c^2$, where $a = 1$ in., $c = 2$ in.

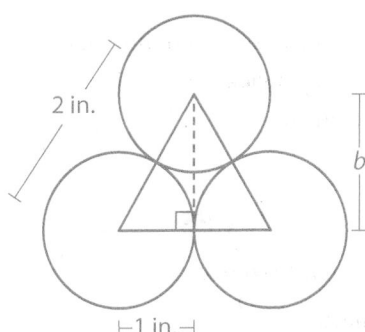

The total height of the three pipes is the height of the triangle plus two times the radius of the pipes.

$$h_{2\,layers} = 2 + \sqrt{3}$$

Continuing the calculations, we get:

$$h_{3\,layers} = 2 + 2\sqrt{3}$$

$$h_{4\,layers} = 2 + 3\sqrt{3}$$

Or, generalizing,

$$h_{n\,layers} = 2 + (n-1)\sqrt{3}$$

So the difference in the heights of 10 layers staggered versus non-staggered is

$$10(2) - \left[2 + (10-1)\sqrt{3}\right] \approx 2.41 \text{ in.}$$

Assessment Rubric

2 points: Student correctly solves the problem and explains his/her reasoning.

1 point: Student shows good understanding of the problem but does not fully solve or explain.

0 points: Student does not demonstrate understanding of the problem.

Study Guide Review   **738**

Ready to Go On?

ASSESS MASTERY

Use the assessment on this page to determine if students have mastered the concepts and standards covered in this module.

ASSESSMENT AND INTERVENTION

Access Ready to Go On? assessment online, and receive instant scoring, feedback, and customized intervention or enrichment.

ADDITIONAL RESOURCES

Response to Intervention Resources

- Reteach Worksheets

Differentiated Instruction Resources

- Reading Strategies **EL**
- Success for English Learners **EL**
- Challenge Worksheets

Assessment Resources

- Leveled Module Quizzes

13.1–13.4 Trigonometry with Right Triangles

- Online Homework
- Hints and Help
- Extra Practice

Solve the problem. *(Lesson 13.1)*

1. A painter is placing a ladder to reach the third story window, which is 20 feet above the ground and makes an angle with the ground of 70°. How far out from the building does the base of the ladder need to be positioned?

$$\tan 70° = \frac{20}{x}, \text{ so } x = \frac{20}{\tan 70°} \approx \frac{20}{2.747477419} \approx 7.3 \text{ feet}$$

2. Given the value of $\cos 30° = \frac{\sqrt{3}}{2}$, write the sine of a complementary angle. Use an expression relating trigonometric ratios of complementary angles. *(Lesson 13.2)*

	$\cos\theta = \sin(90° - \theta)$
Substitute 30 into both sides.	$\cos 30° = \sin(90° - 30°)$
Simplify the right side.	$\cos 30° = \sin 60°$
Substitute for $\cos 30°$.	$\frac{\sqrt{3}}{2} = \sin 60°$

Find the area of the regular polygon. *(Lesson 13.3)*

3. What is the area of a regular hexagon with a distance from its center to a vertex of 1 cm? (Hint: A regular hexagon can be divided into six equilateral triangles.)

Each of the six equilateral triangles has sides of length 1.

You can split each of these triangles into two congruent 30°-60°-90° triangles. These make twelve 30°-60°-90° triangles. Each of these triangles has a base of $\frac{1}{2}$ and a height of $\frac{\sqrt{3}}{2}$. The area of each of these 30°-60°-90° triangles is $\frac{1}{2}bh = \frac{1}{2} \cdot \frac{1}{2} \cdot \frac{\sqrt{3}}{2} = \frac{\sqrt{3}}{8}$. The area of the hexagon is twelve times that, or $\frac{12\sqrt{3}}{8} = \frac{3\sqrt{3}}{2}$.

ESSENTIAL QUESTION

4. How would you go about finding the area of a regular pentagon given the distance from its center to the vertices?

Answers may vary. Sample: You can determine the area of a regular pentagon by splitting it into 5 congruent triangles (each including a 360/5 = 72 degree angle). Find the angles of the triangles and use trigonometric ratios to find their height and base. With this information we can find the area of one triangle and multiply by 5 to get the area of the pentagon.

COMMON CORE Common Core Standards

Lesson	Items	Content Standards	Mathematical Practices
13.1, 13.4	1	**G-SRT.C.6, G-SRT.C.8**	**MP.2**
13.2	2	**G-SRT.C.7**	**MP.6**
13.3	3	**G-SRT.C.8**	**MP.6**

Assessment Readiness

1. Julia is standing 2 feet away from a lamppost. She casts a shadow of 5 feet and the light makes a 20° angle relative to the ground from the top of her shadow. Consider each expression. Does the expression give you the height of the lamppost?

   Select Yes or No for A–C.

   A. $7 \sin 20°$ ○ Yes   ● No

   B. $7 \tan 20°$ ● Yes   ○ No

   C. $7 \tan 70°$ ○ Yes   ● No

2. A right triangle has two sides with lengths 10 and 10. Choose True or False for each statement.

   A. The triangle has two angles that measure 45° each.   ● True   ○ False

   B. The triangle is equilateral.   ○ True   ● False

   C. The length of the third side is $10\sqrt{2}$.   ● True   ○ False

3. The measure of angle 1 is 125° and the measure of angle 2 is 55°. State two different relationships that can be used to prove $m\angle 3 = 125°$.

   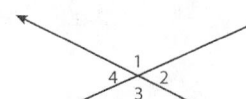

   Possible Answer: $\angle 2$ and $\angle 3$ are supplementary

   angles, $\angle 1$ and $\angle 3$ are vertical angles.

4. For the rhombus, specify how to find its area using the four congruent right triangles with variable angle θ.

   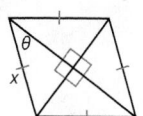

   Answers may vary. Sample: Find the base and height of each

   right triangle using trigonometric ratios of θ. Multiply by 4 to

   get the area of the rhombus, as all the triangles are congruent.

   $A_r = 4 \cdot \frac{1}{2}bh = 2x^2 \cos\theta \sin\theta$, where x is the side length of the

   rhombus.

MIXED REVIEW
Assessment Readiness

ASSESSMENT AND INTERVENTION

Assign ready-made or customized practice tests to prepare students for high-stakes tests.

ADDITIONAL RESOURCES

Assessment Resources

- Leveled Module Quizzes: Modified, B

AVOID COMMON ERRORS

Item 1 Some students will have a hard time visualizing the problem. Encourage students to draw and label a quick sketch to help them see which trigonometric function best fits the situation.

COMMON CORE — Common Core Standards

Lesson	Items	Content Standards	Mathematical Practices
13.1	1	**G-SRT.C.8**	**MP.4**
13.3, 7.2	2*	**G-SRT.C.8**	**MP.2**
4.1	3*	**G-CO.C.9**	**MP.6**
13.2	4	**G-SRT.C.8**	**MP.5**

* Item integrates mixed review concepts from previous modules or a previous course.

Trigonometry with All Triangles

ESSENTIAL QUESTION:

Answer: Understanding triangle trigonometry can help you solve real-world real estate problems when direct measurement of a property is impossible.

PROFESSIONAL DEVELOPMENT VIDEO

Professional Development Video

Author Juli Dixon models successful teaching practices in an actual high-school classroom.

Professional
Development
my.hrw.com

MODULE **14**

Trigonometry with All Triangles

Essential Question: How can you use triangle trigonometry to solve real-world problems?

LESSON 14.1
Law of Sines

LESSON 14.2
Law of Cosines

© Houghton Mifflin Harcourt Publishing Company • Image Credits: ©Carol Kohen/Cultura RM/Alamy

REAL WORLD VIDEO
Air traffic controllers must understand trigonometry and other mathematics to make rapid judgments about the positions of aircraft and the distances between them.

MODULE PERFORMANCE TASK PREVIEW

Controlling the Air

You've probably seen photos of air traffic controllers studying green-tinted screens covered with blinking blips. Their job is to analyze the positions of every plane in the airspace near the airport and see to it that the planes land safely. In this module, you'll learn to solve triangles of the type air traffic controllers encounter. Then you'll apply what you've learned to find the distance between two planes approaching an airport.

Module 14   741

DIGITAL TEACHER EDITION

Access a full suite of teaching resources when and where you need them:

- Access content online or offline
- Customize lessons to share with your class
- Communicate with your students in real-time
- View student grades and data instantly to target your instruction where it is needed most

PERSONAL MATH TRAINER

Assessment and Intervention

Assign automatically graded homework, quizzes, tests, and intervention activities. Prepare your students with updated, Common Core-aligned practice tests.

Are (YOU) Ready?

Complete these exercises to review skills you will need for this module.

- Online Homework
- Hints and Help
- Extra Practice

Similar Triangles

Example 1

In $\triangle PRK$, $PK = 34$, $RK = 50$, and $m\angle K = 74°$. Why is this triangle similar to $\triangle ABC$? What is the similarity statement?

$PK = 34 = 2AB$ (Side),

$m\angle K = 74° = m\angle A$ (Angle), and $RK = 50 = 2AC$ (Side). So, $\triangle ABC \sim \triangle KPR$ by $SAS\triangle\sim$.

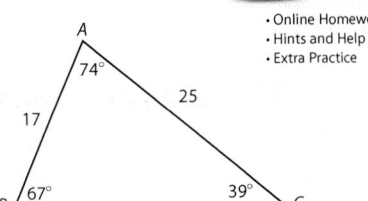

Complete each similarity statement and name the theorem that supports it.

1. Given: In $\triangle MNT$, $MN = 8.5$, $TM = 13$, and $TN = 12.5$.

$\triangle ABC \sim \triangle NMT$ by $SSS\triangle\sim$

2. Given: In $\triangle ZQE$, $m\angle E = 67°$, $ZQ = 4$, and $m\angle Q = 39°$.

$\triangle ABC \sim \triangle ZEQ$ by $AA\triangle\sim$

Proportional Relationships

Example 2

Given: $\triangle PQR \sim \triangle NCL$, $PQ = 15$, $QR = 12$, $PR = 18$, and $CL = 15$.

What is NL?

$\dfrac{CL}{QR} = \dfrac{NL}{PR}$ Write a proportion.

$\dfrac{15}{12} = \dfrac{NL}{18}$ Substitute.

$NL = 22.5$ Solve.

Solve, given that $\triangle RST \sim \triangle FGH$, $RT = 9$, $ST = 6$, $FG = 7.5$, and $FH = 13.5$.

3. Find RS.

    5

4. Find GH.

    9

Multi-Step Equations

Example 3

Solve $4x + 15 = 1$ for x.

$4x + 15 - 15 = 1 - 15$ Subtract 15 from both sides.

$4x = -14$ Combine like terms.

$x = -3.5$ Divide.

Solve each equation.

5. $2r - 5 = -9$

    -2

6. $\dfrac{4m - 5}{3} = -7$

    -4

7. $9.9 - 4.2k = 3k - 0.9$

    1.5

Are You Ready?

ASSESS READINESS

Use the assessment on this page to determine if students need strategic or intensive intervention for the module's prerequisite skills.

ASSESSMENT AND INTERVENTION

RtI Response to Intervention TIER 1, TIER 2, TIER 3 SKILLS

Personal Math Trainer will automatically create a standards-based, personalized intervention assignment for your students, targeting each student's individual needs!

ADDITIONAL RESOURCES

See the table below for a full list of intervention resources available for this module.

Response to Intervention Resources also includes:

- Tier 2 Skill Pre-Tests for each Module
- Tier 2 Skill Post-Tests for each skill

Response to Intervention			Differentiated Instruction
Tier 1	**Tier 2**	**Tier 3**	
Lesson Intervention Worksheets	Strategic Intervention Skills Intervention Worksheets	Intensive Intervention Worksheets available online	
Reteach 14.1 Reteach 14.2	23 Similar Figures 29 Proportional Relationships 30 Multi-Step Equations	Building Block Skills 36, 50, 59, 63, 80, 82, 86, 90, 95, 98	Challenge worksheets Extend the Math Lesson Activities in TE

Law of Sines

Common Core Math Standards

The student is expected to:

 G-SRT.D.10$(+)$

Prove the Laws of Sines and Cosines and use them to solve problems. Also G-SRT.D.11$(+)$

Mathematical Practices

COMMON CORE **MP.3 Logic**

Language Objective

Explain to a partner how to find the unknown measures of a triangle using the Law of Sines.

ENGAGE

Essential Question: How can you use trigonometric ratios to find side lengths and angle measures of non-right triangles?

The Law of Sines allows you to find unknown side lengths and angle measures for any given triangle, as long as you know its AAS, ASA, or SSA information.

PREVIEW: LESSON PERFORMANCE TASK

View the Engage section online. Discuss the photo and how to use trigonometry to find the measures of a triangular park. Then preview the Lesson Performance Task.

Name_____ Class_____ Date_____

14.1 Law of Sines

Essential Question: How can you use trigonometric ratios to find side lengths and angle measures of non-right triangles?

⊘ Explore Use an Area Formula to Derive the Law of Sines

Recall that the area of a triangle can be found using the sine of one of the angles.

Area $= \frac{1}{2}b \cdot c \cdot \sin(A)$

You can write variations of this formula using different angles and sides from the same triangle.

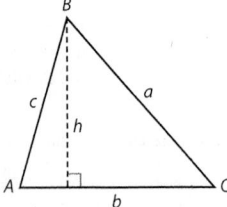

Ⓐ Rewrite the area formula using side length a as the base of the triangle and $\angle C$.

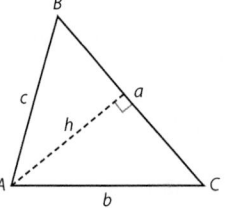

Area $= \frac{1}{2}a \cdot b \cdot \sin(C)$

Ⓑ Rewrite the area formula using side length c as the base of the triangle and $\angle B$.

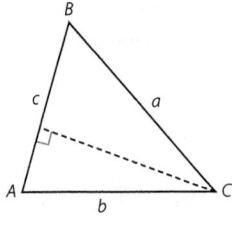

Area $= \frac{1}{2}c \cdot a \cdot \sin(B)$

Ⓒ What do all three formulas have in common?

They measure the same area.

Ⓓ Why is this statement true?

$\frac{1}{2}b \cdot c \cdot \sin(A) = \frac{1}{2}a \cdot b \cdot \sin(C) = \frac{1}{2}c \cdot a \cdot \sin(B)$

All three areas are the same.

Ⓔ Multiply each area by the expression $\frac{2}{abc}$. Write an equivalent statement.

$\frac{\sin(A)}{a} = \frac{\sin(B)}{b} = \frac{\sin(C)}{c}$

© Houghton Mifflin Harcourt Publishing Company

Module 14 **743** Lesson 1

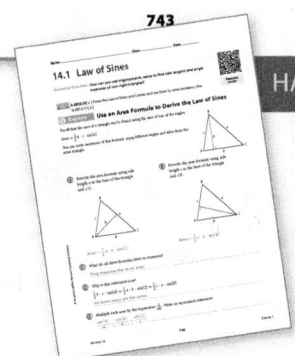

HARDCOVER PAGES 629–638

Turn to these pages to find this lesson in the hardcover student edition.

1. In the case of a right triangle, where C is the right angle, what happens to the area formula?
   Since $\sin(90°) = 1$, the area formula becomes the familiar Area $= \frac{1}{2}ab$.

2. **Discussion** In all three cases of the area formula you explored, what is the relationship between the angle and the two side lengths in the area formula?
   It is the included angle.

Explain 1   Applying the Law of Sines

The results of the Explore activity are summarized in the Law of Sines.

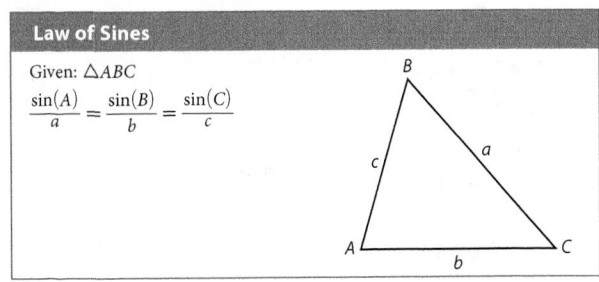

Law of Sines

Given: △ABC

$$\frac{\sin(A)}{a} = \frac{\sin(B)}{b} = \frac{\sin(C)}{c}$$

The Law of Sines allows you to find the unknown measures for a given triangle, as long as you know either of the following:

1. Two angle measures and any side length—angle-angle-side (AAS) or angle-side-angle (ASA) information

2. Two side lengths and the measure of an angle that is not between them—side-side-angle (SSA) information

Example 1   Find all the unknown measures using the given triangle. Round to the nearest tenth.

(A)   **Step 1**   Find the third angle measure.

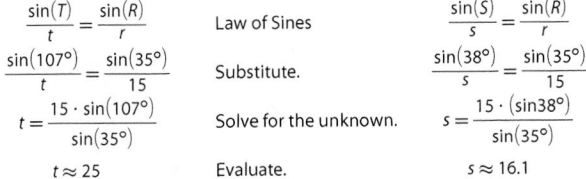

$m\angle R + m\angle S + m\angle T = 180°$ Triangle Sum Theorem

$35° + 38° + m\angle T = 180°$ Substitute the known angle measures.

$m\angle T = 107°$ Solve for the measure of $\angle T$.

Step 2   Find the unknown side lengths. Set up proportions using the Law of Sines and solve for the unknown.

$\dfrac{\sin(T)}{t} = \dfrac{\sin(R)}{r}$	Law of Sines	$\dfrac{\sin(S)}{s} = \dfrac{\sin(R)}{r}$
$\dfrac{\sin(107°)}{t} = \dfrac{\sin(35°)}{15}$	Substitute.	$\dfrac{\sin(38°)}{s} = \dfrac{\sin(35°)}{15}$
$t = \dfrac{15 \cdot \sin(107°)}{\sin(35°)}$	Solve for the unknown.	$s = \dfrac{15 \cdot (\sin 38°)}{\sin(35°)}$
$t \approx 25$	Evaluate.	$s \approx 16.1$

PROFESSIONAL DEVELOPMENT

Learning Progressions

In geometry, students learn to *solve a triangle*. This phrase refers to the process of using given measures to find the unknown angle measures or side lengths of the triangle. For general triangles, additional relationships are needed. The Law of Sines may be used to find the unknown measures of a triangle given either of the following: two angle measures and any side length (AAS or ASA); or two side lengths and a non-included angle measure (SSA). Note that, in the case of SSA, two side lengths and a non-included angle measure are known, and solving the triangle may result in no triangle or two triangles.

EXPLORE

Use an Area Formula to Derive the Law of Sines

INTEGRATE TECHNOLOGY

Students have the option of doing the Explore activity either in the book or online.

QUESTIONING STRATEGIES

?   When is it necessary to use the formula $A = \frac{1}{2}b \cdot c \cdot \sin(A)$ to find the area of a triangle?   When the triangle is not a right triangle, because you cannot use the length of a side as the height in the formula $A = \frac{1}{2}bh$.

EXPLAIN 1

Applying the Law of Sines

INTEGRATE MATHEMATICAL PRACTICES
Focus on Math Connections

MP.1   Remind students that the Triangle Sum Theorem states that the sum of the measures of the angles of a triangle is $180°$.

QUESTIONING STRATEGIES

?   How can you use the Triangle Sum Theorem to find the measure of the third angle of the triangle?   The Triangle Sum Theorem justifies subtracting the sum of the two known angles from $180°$ to get the measure of the third angle.

?   Once you have substituted measurements into the Law of Sines, how do you solve for an unknown side length?   Use the sines of the known angles and the properties of proportions to solve for the unknown side.

AVOID COMMON ERRORS

Some students may want to use ratios in the Law of Sines that include calculated side lengths (or angles) from applying the Law of Sines to other parts of the triangle. Point out that no calculated lengths should be used when other side lengths of the triangle are known exactly. This provides greater accuracy (because a calculated value of a side length is an approximation) and helps avoid additional errors (in case the student calculated a side length incorrectly).

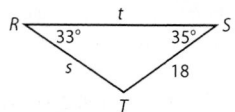

Ⓑ Step 1 Find the third angle measure.

$$m\angle R + m\angle S + m\angle T = 180°$$ Triangle Sum Theorem

$$\boxed{33}° + \boxed{35}° + m\angle T = 180°$$ Substitute the known angle measures.

$$m\angle T = \boxed{112}°$$ Solve for the measure of $\angle T$.

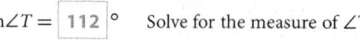

Step 2 Find the unknown side lengths. Set up proportions using the Law of Sines and solve for the unknown.

$$\frac{\sin(T)}{t} = \frac{\sin(R)}{r}$$ Law of Sines $$\frac{\sin(S)}{s} = \frac{\sin(R)}{r}$$

$$\frac{\sin\left(\boxed{112}°\right)}{t} = \frac{\sin\left(\boxed{33}°\right)}{\boxed{18}}$$ Substitute. $$\frac{\sin\left(\boxed{35}°\right)}{s} = \frac{\sin\left(\boxed{33}°\right)}{\boxed{18}}$$

$$t = \frac{\boxed{18} \cdot \sin\left(\boxed{112}°\right)}{\sin\left(\boxed{33}°\right)}$$ Solve for the unknown. $$s = \frac{\boxed{18} \cdot \sin\left(\boxed{35}°\right)}{\sin\left(\boxed{33}°\right)}$$

$$t \approx \boxed{30.6}$$ Evaluate. $$s \approx \boxed{19.0}$$

Reflect

3. Suppose that you are given $m\angle A$. To find c, what other measures do you need to know?

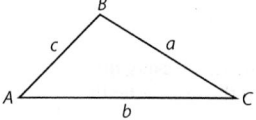

$m\angle C$ and a

COLLABORATIVE LEARNING

Small Group Activity

To help students understand how to use the Law of Sines in the SSA case, have one student create a diagram of a triangle for which two sides and a non-included angle are given. The given angle should be either right or obtuse angle A, or an acute angle A. Then ask another student to identify the number of triangles that can be found. Have a third student find the unknown side and angle measures using the Law of Sines. Finally, ask a fourth student to check the calculations and share the results with the group.

Find all the unknown measures using the given triangle. Round to the nearest tenth.

4.

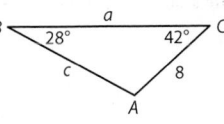

5.

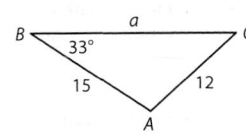

$m\angle A = 180° - 28° - 42° = 110°$

$$\frac{\sin(110°)}{a} = \frac{\sin(28°)}{8}$$

$$a \approx \frac{8 \cdot \sin(110°)}{\sin(28°)}$$

$$\approx 16.0$$

$$\frac{\sin(28°)}{8} = \frac{\sin(42°)}{c}$$

$$c = \frac{8 \cdot \sin(42°)}{\sin(28°)}$$

$$\approx 11.4$$

$$\frac{\sin(33°)}{12} = \frac{\sin(C)}{15}$$

$$\sin(C) = \frac{15 \cdot \sin(33°)}{12}$$

$$m\angle C \approx 42.9°$$

$m\angle A = 180° - 33° - 42.9° = 104.1°$

$$\frac{\sin(33°)}{12} = \frac{\sin(104.1°)}{a}$$

$$a = \frac{12 \cdot \sin(104.1°)}{\sin(33°)}$$

$$\approx 21.4$$

⚙ Explain 2   Evaluating Triangles When SSA is Known Information

When you use the Law of Sines to solve a triangle for which you know side-side-angle (SSA) information, zero, one, or two triangles may be possible. For this reason, SSA is called the ambiguous case.

Ambiguous Case

Given a, b, and $m\angle A$.

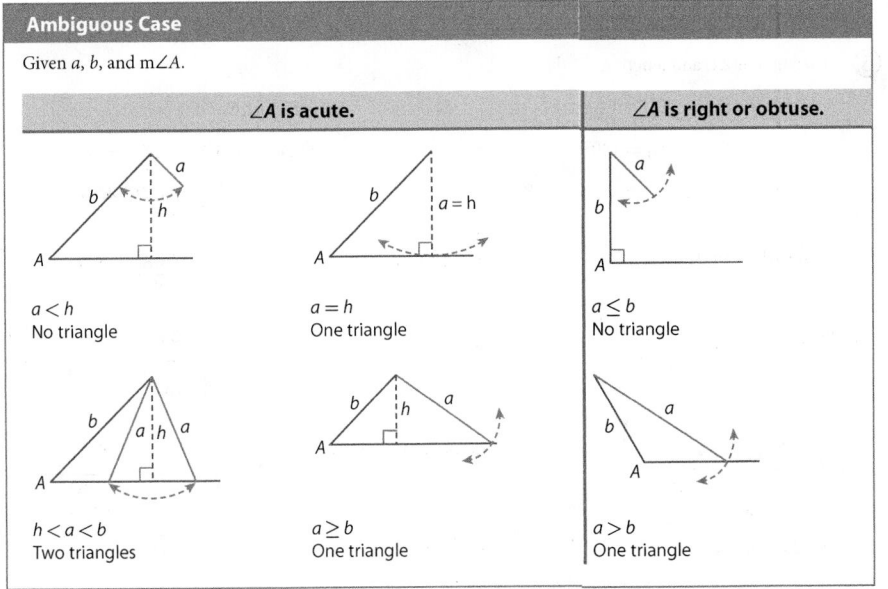

∠A is acute.		∠A is right or obtuse.

$a < h$
No triangle

$a = h$
One triangle

$a \leq b$
No triangle

$h < a < b$
Two triangles

$a \geq b$
One triangle

$a > b$
One triangle

EXPLAIN 2

Evaluating Triangles When SSA is Known Information

QUESTIONING STRATEGIES

? When two triangles are possible, how do you find the two possible values for the unknown angle measures of the triangle? Find one acute angle and subtract it from 180° to get the other angle. Then use the Triangle Sum Theorem to find the corresponding third-angle measures (and side lengths) for each case.

AVOID COMMON ERRORS

Some students may not understand why, when SSA is known information, one, two, or zero triangles may be possible. Remind students that there is no SSA Triangle Congruence Theorem because two sides and a non-included angle do not define a unique triangle.

DIFFERENTIATE INSTRUCTION

Visual Cues

Help students set up equations correctly when they use the Law of Sines by suggesting that they use highlighters to mark each side with the corresponding angle opposite that side in the same color. Tell students that an angle and the side opposite that angle are called a *side-angle pair,* and that using this strategy helps avoid using the ratio of the sine of an angle and the length of a side that is *not* opposite that angle.

Law of Sines   **746**

Example 2 **Design** Each triangular wing of a model airplane has one side that joins the wing to the airplane. The other sides have lengths $b = 18$ in. and $a = 15$ in. The side with length b meets the airplane at an angle A with a measure of $30°$, and meets the side with length a at point C. Find each measure.

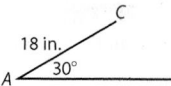

(A) Find $m\angle B$.

Step 1 Determine the number of possible triangles. Find h.

$\sin(30°) = \dfrac{h}{18}$, so $h = 18 \cdot \sin(30°) = 9$

Because $h < a < b$, two triangles are possible.

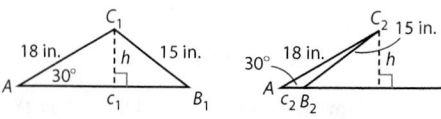

Step 2 Determine $m\angle B_1$ and $m\angle B_2$.

$\dfrac{\sin(A)}{a} = \dfrac{\sin(B)}{b}$ Law of Sines

$\dfrac{\sin(30°)}{15} = \dfrac{\sin(B)}{18}$ Substitute.

$\sin(B) = \dfrac{18 \cdot \sin(30°)}{15}$ Solve for $\sin(B)$.

Let $\angle B_1$ be the acute angle with the given sine, and let $\angle B_2$ be the obtuse angle. Use the inverse sine function on your calculator to determine the measures of the angles.

$m\angle B_1 = \sin^{-1}\left(\dfrac{18 \cdot \sin(30°)}{15}\right) \approx 36.9°$ and $m\angle B_2 = 180° - 36.9° = 143.1°$

(B) Determine $m\angle C$ and length c.

Solve for $m\angle C_1$.

$\boxed{36.9}° + 30° + m\angle C_1 = 180°$

$m\angle C_1 = \boxed{113.1}°$

$\dfrac{\sin(A)}{a} = \dfrac{\sin(C_1)}{c_1}$ Law of Sines

$\dfrac{\sin\left(\boxed{30}°\right)}{\boxed{15}} = \dfrac{\sin\left(\boxed{113.1}°\right)}{c_1}$ Substitute.

$c_1 = \dfrac{\boxed{15} \cdot \sin\left(\boxed{113.1}°\right)}{\sin\left(\boxed{30}°\right)}$ Solve for the unknown.

$c_1 \approx \boxed{27.6}$ in.   Evaluate.

Solve for $m\angle C_2$.

$\boxed{143.1}° + 30° + m\angle C_2 = 180°$

$m\angle C_2 = \boxed{6.9}°$

$\dfrac{\sin(A)}{a} = \dfrac{\sin(C_2)}{c_2}$

$\dfrac{\sin\left(\boxed{30}°\right)}{\boxed{15}} = \dfrac{\sin\left(\boxed{6.9}°\right)}{c_2}$

$c_2 = \dfrac{\boxed{15} \cdot \sin\left(\boxed{6.9}°\right)}{\sin\left(\boxed{30}°\right)}$

$c_2 \approx \boxed{3.6}$ in.

LANGUAGE SUPPORT EL

Connect Vocabulary

Students may have difficulty distinguishing the ASA, AAS, or SSA cases for the Law of Sines. Have them write several examples of each of these types of triangles on note cards, list the side and angle measures that are known, and then show the steps for finding the unknown measures of the triangle. Have them share their examples with other students.

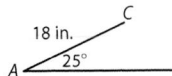
Your Turn

In Exercises 6 and 7, suppose that for the model airplane in the Example, $a = 21$ in., $b = 18$ in., and $m\angle A = 25°$.

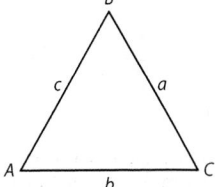

18 in.   C
A ⟍25°

6. How many triangles are possible with this configuration? Explain.
   Only one triangle; $\angle A$ is acute and $a > b$.

7. Find the unknown measurements. Round to the nearest tenth.

$$\frac{\sin(25°)}{21} = \frac{\sin(B)}{18}$$

$$\sin(B) = \frac{18 \cdot \sin(25°)}{21}$$

$$m\angle B \approx 21.2°$$

$$m\angle C = 180° - 25° - 21.2° = 133.8°$$

$$\frac{\sin(133.8°)}{c} = \frac{\sin(25°)}{21}$$

$$c = \frac{21 \cdot \sin(133.8°)}{\sin(25°)}$$

$$\approx 35.9 \text{ in.}$$

💬 **Elaborate**

8. If the base angles of a triangle are congruent, use the Law of Sines to show the triangle is isosceles.

$$\angle A \cong \angle C$$

$$\frac{\sin(A)}{a} = \frac{\sin(C)}{c}$$

$$\frac{1}{a} = \frac{1}{c}$$

$$a = c$$

9. Show that when $h = a$, $\angle C$ is a right angle.

$$\frac{1}{2}a \cdot b \cdot \sin(C) = \frac{1}{2}b \cdot h$$

Since $h = a$, $\sin(C) = 1$, so $m\angle C = 90°$.

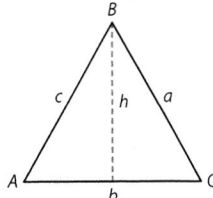

ELABORATE

QUESTIONING STRATEGIES

? How do you determine the number of triangles possible when using the Law of Sines for the SSA case, with h equal to the height opposite angle A, and $h = b \sin A$? If angle A is right or obtuse, and $a \leq b$, then there is no triangle. If angle A is right or obtuse, and $a > b$, then there is one triangle. If angle A is acute, and $h > a$, then there is no triangle. If angle A is acute, and $h = a$ or $a \geq b$, then there is one triangle. If $h < a < b$, then there are two triangles.

SUMMARIZE THE LESSON

Have students make a graphic organizer showing the possibilities for the ambiguous case. The organizer should show the conditions for which the ambiguous case results in zero, one, or two triangles. Sample:

SSA: Given a, b, and $m\angle A$			
Angle A	0 Triangles	1 Triangle	2 Triangles
Right or Obtuse	$a \leq b$	$a > b$	n/a
Acute	$a < h$	$a = h;$ $a \geq b$	$h < a < b$

EVALUATE

ASSIGNMENT GUIDE

Concepts and Skills	Practice
Explore Use an Area Formula to Derive the Law of Sines	Exercises 1–6
Example 1 Applying the Law of Sines	Exercises 7–14, 19–22
Example 2 Evaluating Triangles When SSA is Known Information	Exercises 15–18

INTEGRATE MATHEMATICAL PRACTICES

Focus on Math Connections

MP.1 Remind students that the SSA case is different from the AAS and ASA cases because the SSA combination (two sides and a non-included angle) does not always determine exactly one triangle.

---

10. Essential Question Check-In Given the measures of △ABC, describe a method for finding any of the altitudes of the triangle.

The solution for any of the altitudes should be of the following form:

$$\frac{\sin \theta}{h} = \frac{\sin(90°)}{c}$$

$$h = c \cdot \sin \theta$$

☆ Evaluate: Homework and Practice

• Online Homework
• Hints and Help
• Extra Practice

Find the area of each triangle. Round to the nearest tenth.

1.

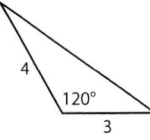

$$\text{Area} = \frac{1}{2}4 \cdot 3 \cdot \sin(120°)$$
$$\approx 5.2$$

2.

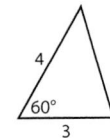

$$\text{Area} = \frac{1}{2}4 \cdot 3 \cdot \sin(60°)$$
$$\approx 5.2$$

3.

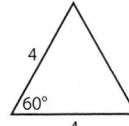

$$\text{Area} = \frac{1}{2}4 \cdot 4 \cdot \sin(60°)$$
$$\approx 6.9$$

4.

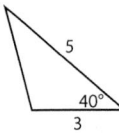

$$\text{Area} = \frac{1}{2}3 \cdot 5 \cdot \sin(40°)$$
$$\approx 4.8$$

5.

$$\text{Area} = \frac{1}{2}7 \cdot 7 \cdot \sin(130°)$$
$$\approx 18.8$$

6.

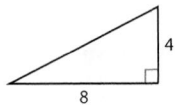

$$\text{Area} = \frac{1}{2}4 \cdot 8 \cdot \sin(90°)$$
$$= 16$$

7. What is the area of an isosceles triangle with congruent side lengths x and included angle θ?

$$\frac{x^2}{2}\sin(\theta)$$

8. What is the area of an equilateral triangle of side length x?

$$\frac{\sqrt{3} \cdot x^2}{4}$$

Exercise	Depth of Knowledge (D.O.K.)	COMMON CORE Mathematical Practices
1–6	**1** Recall of information	**MP.2** Reasoning
7–8	**2** Skills/Concepts	**MP.7** Using Structure
9–14	**2** Skills/Concepts	**MP.1** Problem Solving
15–22	**2** Skills/Concepts	**MP.4** Modeling
23	**3** Strategic Thinking H.O.T.	**MP.2** Reasoning
24	**3** Strategic Thinking H.O.T.	**MP.2** Reasoning

Find all the unknown measurements using the Law of Sines.

9.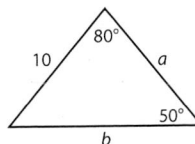

$m\angle A = 180° - 80° - 50°$

$= 50°$

Since this is an isosceles

triangle, $a = 10$.

$\dfrac{\sin(80°)}{b} = \dfrac{\sin(50°)}{10}$

$b = \dfrac{10 \cdot \sin(80°)}{\sin(50°)}$

≈ 12.9

10.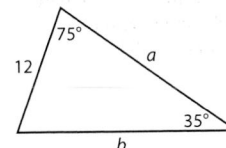

$m\angle A = 180° - 75° - 35°$

$= 70°$

$\dfrac{\sin(75°)}{b} = \dfrac{\sin(35°)}{12}$

$b = \dfrac{12 \cdot \sin(75°)}{\sin(35°)}$

≈ 20.2

$\dfrac{\sin(35°)}{12} = \dfrac{\sin(70°)}{a}$

$a = \dfrac{12 \cdot \sin(70°)}{\sin(35°)}$

≈ 19.7

11.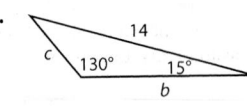

$m\angle B = 180° - 130° - 15°$

$= 35°$

$\dfrac{\sin(35°)}{b} = \dfrac{\sin(130°)}{14}$

$b = \dfrac{14 \cdot \sin(35°)}{\sin(130°)}$

≈ 10.5

$\dfrac{\sin(15°)}{c} = \dfrac{\sin(130°)}{14}$

$c = \dfrac{14 \cdot \sin(15°)}{\sin(130°)}$

≈ 4.7

12.

$m\angle C = 180° - 80° - 40°$

$= 60°$

$\dfrac{\sin(60°)}{7} = \dfrac{\sin(40°)}{a}$

$a = \dfrac{7 \cdot \sin(40°)}{\sin(60°)}$

≈ 5.2

$\dfrac{\sin(80°)}{b} = \dfrac{\sin(60°)}{7}$

$c = \dfrac{7 \cdot \sin(80°)}{\sin(60°)}$

≈ 8.0

13.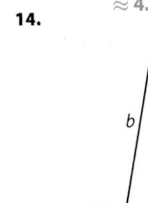

$m\angle C = 180° - 150° - 20°$

$= 10°$

$\dfrac{\sin(10°)}{18} = \dfrac{\sin(150°)}{a}$

$a = \dfrac{18 \cdot \sin(150°)}{\sin(10°)}$

≈ 51.8

$\dfrac{\sin(10°)}{18} = \dfrac{\sin(20°)}{b}$

$b = \dfrac{18 \cdot \sin(20°)}{\sin(10°)}$

≈ 35.5

14.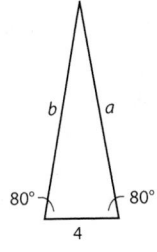

$m\angle C = 180° - 80° - 80° = 20°$

$\dfrac{\sin(20°)}{4} = \dfrac{\sin(80°)}{a}$

$a = \dfrac{4 \cdot \sin(80°)}{\sin(20°)}$

≈ 11.5

Since this is an isosceles triangle, the measure for a is also the measure for b.

INTEGRATE MATHEMATICAL PRACTICES

Focus on Patterns

MP.8 Remind students that they can organize their work to find the unknown measures of a triangle by using the following steps.

1. Determine the number of possible triangles by using the values of a, b, and $\angle A$.

2. If there is one triangle, use the Law of Sines to solve for the unknowns.

3. If there are two triangles, use the Law of Sines to find the two possible measures for the second angle. Then use the two possible angle measures to find the unknowns for each of the two possible triangles.

Exercise	Depth of Knowledge (D.O.K.)	COMMON CORE Mathematical Practices
25	**3** Strategic Thinking H.O.T.	**MP.2** Reasoning
26	**3** Strategic Thinking H.O.T.	**MP.2** Reasoning

AVOID COMMON ERRORS

Students may make errors finding the unknown measures for triangles that are not shown in a diagram. Suggest that students begin by sketching a triangle that is approximately to scale for the given measurements. Students should carefully label their sketches and double-check the labels before beginning to calculate the unknowns.

Design A model airplane designer wants to design wings of the given dimensions. Determine the number of different triangles that can be formed. Then find all the unknown measurements. Round values to the nearest tenth.

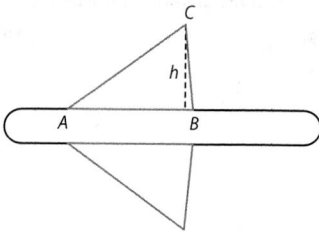

15. $a = 7$ m, $b = 9$ m, $m\angle A = 55°$

Find h.

$$\sin(55°) = \frac{h}{9}$$

$$h \approx 7.4 \text{ m}$$

Since $a < h$, no triangles are possible.

16. $a = 12$ m, $b = 4$ m, $m\angle A = 120°$

Since $\angle A$ is obtuse and $a > b$, one triangle is possible.

$$\frac{\sin(120°)}{12} = \frac{\sin(B)}{4}$$

$$m\angle B \approx 16.8°$$

$$m\angle C = 180° - 120° - 16.8° = 43.2°$$

$$\frac{\sin(120°)}{12} = \frac{\sin(43.2°)}{c}$$

$$c \approx 9.5 \text{ m}$$

17. $a = 9$ m, $b = 10$ m, $m\angle A = 35°$

Find h.

$$\sin(35°) = \frac{h}{10}$$

$$h \approx 5.7$$

Since $h < a < b$, there are two triangles.

First triangle measurements.

$$\frac{\sin(35°)}{9} = \frac{\sin(B)}{10}$$

$$m\angle B \approx 39.6°$$

$$m\angle C = 180° - 35° - 39.6° = 105.4°$$

$$\frac{\sin(35°)}{9} = \frac{\sin(105.4°)}{c}$$

$$c \approx 15.1 \text{ m}$$

Second triangle measurements.

$$m\angle B \approx 180° - 39.6° = 140.4°$$

$$m\angle C = 180° - 35° - 140.4° = 4.6°$$

$$\frac{\sin(35°)}{9} = \frac{\sin(4.6°)}{c}$$

$$c \approx 1.3 \text{ m}$$

18. $a = 7$ m, $b = 5$ m, $m\angle A = 45°$

Since $\angle A$ is acute and $a > b$, there is one triangle.

$$\frac{\sin(45°)}{7} = \frac{\sin(B)}{5}$$

$$m\angle B \approx 30.3°$$

$$m\angle C = 180° - 45° - 30.3° = 104.7°$$

$$\frac{\sin(45°)}{7} = \frac{\sin(104.7°)}{c}$$

$$c \approx 9.6 \text{ m}$$

19. Space Travel Two radio towers that are 50 miles apart track a satellite in orbit. The first tower's signal makes a 76° angle between the ground and satellite. The second tower forms an 80.5° angle.

a. How far is the satellite from each tower?

$$m\angle C = 23.5°$$

$$\frac{\sin(23.5°)}{50} = \frac{\sin(76°)}{a}$$

$$a \approx 121.7 \text{ mi}$$

$$\frac{\sin(23.5°)}{50} = \frac{\sin(80.5°)}{b}$$

$$b \approx 123.7 \text{ mi}$$

Satellite C

76°   80.5°

Tower A   Tower B

b. How could you determine how far above Earth the satellite is? What is the satellite's altitude?

Possible answer: Calculate the area using the sine formula. Use the value of the area to solve for h using the other form of the area formula.

$$\frac{1}{2} b \cdot c \cdot \sin(A) = \frac{1}{2} c \cdot h$$

$$b \cdot \sin(A) = h$$

$$123.7 \cdot \sin(76°) = h$$

$$h \approx 120 \text{ mi}$$

20. Biology The dorsal fin of a shark forms an obtuse triangle with these measurements. Find the missing measurements and determine if another triangle can be formed.

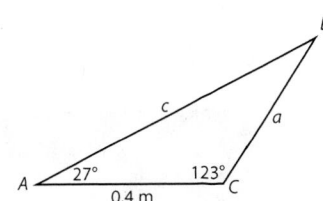

B

c

a

A   27°   123°
      0.4 m   C

$$m\angle B = 30°$$

$$\frac{\sin(27°)}{a} = \frac{\sin(30°)}{0.4}$$

$$a \approx 0.36 \text{ m; Since } h < a < b, \text{ another triangle is possible.}$$

21. Navigation As a ship approaches the dock, it forms a 70° angle between the dock and lighthouse. At the lighthouse, an 80° angle is formed between the dock and the ship. How far is the ship from the dock?

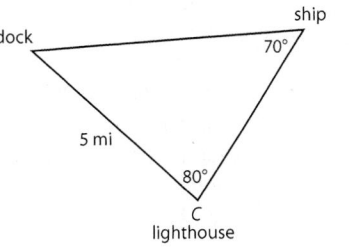

dock   ship
                70°

5 mi

            80°
            C
        lighthouse

$$\frac{\sin(70°)}{5} = \frac{\sin(80°)}{c}$$

$$c \approx 5.2 \text{ mi}$$

© Houghton Mifflin Harcourt Publishing Company • Image Credits: ©Matt9122/ Shutterstock

INTEGRATE MATHEMATICAL PRACTICES

Focus on Critical Thinking

MP.3 If students have difficulty with an exercise, point out that they will need to know at least two of the side lengths of the triangle to apply the SSA cases to find the unknown angle measures of the triangle, and to find the length of the third side using the Law of Sines. Also point out that they will need to know two of the angle measures to apply the AAS or the ASA cases to find the unknown measures of a triangle with only one known side length.

AVOID COMMON ERRORS

Some students may not be able to determine how many triangles can be found using given measurements for the sides and angles. Stress the importance of first determining the number of possible triangles by using the values of a, b, and $\angle A$. If only one side value (side a) and two angles are given, then only one triangle is possible.

PEER-TO-PEER DISCUSSION

Ask students to work in pairs. Have each student draw a triangle and use a ruler and protractor to label it with AAS or ASA information. Have students exchange drawings with their partners. Ask students to use the Law of Sines to solve each other's triangles and explain their reasoning. Students can check their work by direct measurement of the unlabeled sides and angles.

JOURNAL

Have students explain how to solve a triangle when given angle-side-angle (ASA) information.

---

22. For the given triangle, match each altitude with its equivalent expression.

A. h_1 $\underline{c \cdot \sin(A)}$ $a \cdot \sin(B)$

B. h_2 $\underline{b \cdot \sin(C)}$ $c \cdot \sin(A)$

C. h_3 $\underline{a \cdot \sin(B)}$ $b \cdot \sin(C)$

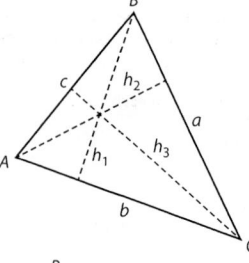

H.O.T. Focus on Higher Order Thinking

Use the diagram, in which $\triangle ABC \approx \triangle DEF$.

23. To find the missing measurements for either triangle using the Law of Sines, what must you do first?

Transfer corresponding angle measures from each triangle to the other.

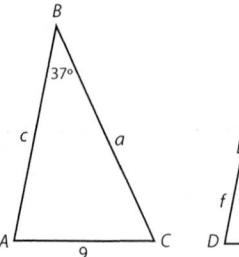

24. Find the missing measurements for $\triangle ABC$.

$$\frac{\sin(37°)}{9} = \frac{\sin(65°)}{c}$$

$$c \approx 13.5$$

$$m\angle A = 78°$$

$$\frac{\sin(37°)}{9} = \frac{\sin(78°)}{a}$$

$$a \approx 14.6$$

25. Find the missing measurements for $\triangle DEF$.

$$\frac{\sin(78°)}{6} = \frac{\sin(65°)}{f}$$

$$f \approx 5.6$$

$$\frac{\sin(78°)}{6} = \frac{\sin(37°)}{e}$$

$$e \approx 3.7$$

26. Surveying Two surveyors are at the same altitude and are 10 miles apart on opposite sides of a mountain. They each measure the angle relative to the ground and the top of the mountain. Use the given diagram to indirectly measure the height of the mountain.

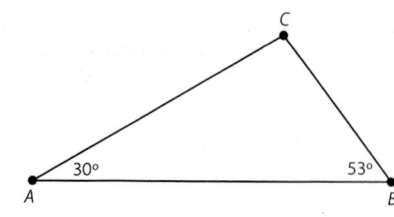

1. Find one of the sides.

$$m\angle C = 97°$$

$$\frac{\sin(97°)}{10} = \frac{\sin(53°)}{b}$$

$$b \approx 8 \text{ mi}$$

2. Find the area of the triangle using the formula that includes sine.

$$\text{Area} = \frac{1}{2}8 \cdot 10 \cdot \sin(30°)$$

$$= 20 \text{ sq. mi}$$

3. Solve for the height using the other area formula.

$$\frac{1}{2} \cdot 10 \cdot h = 20$$

$$h = 4 \text{ mi}$$

Module 14   **753**   Lesson 1

Lesson Performance Task

In the middle of town, State and Elm streets meet at an angle of 40°. A triangular pocket park between the streets stretches 100 yards along State Street and 53.2 yards along Elm Street.

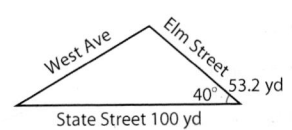

a. Find the area of the pocket park using the given dimensions.

$A = \frac{1}{2}(100)(53.2)\sin(40°) \approx 1709.8 \text{ yd}^2$

b. If the total distance around the pocket park is 221.6 yards, find ∠S, the angle that West Avenue makes with State Street, to the nearest degree.

Find the length of the park along West Avenue.

$221.6 - (100 + 53.2) = 68.4 \text{ yards}$

Use the Law of Sines.

$\dfrac{\sin S}{53.2} = \dfrac{\sin(40°)}{68.4}$

So, m∠S = 30°.

c. Suppose West Avenue makes angles of 55° with State Street and 80° with Elm Street. The distance from State to Elm along West Avenue is 40 yards. Find the distance from West Avenue to Elm Street along State Street.

Determine the measure of the third angle of the triangular area.

$180° - 55° - 80° = 45°$

By the law of sines the distance from West Avenue to Elm Street is $\dfrac{40\sin(80°)}{\sin(45°)} \approx 55.7 \text{ yards.}$

EXTENSION ACTIVITY

Prove the Law of Sines for a triangle with one obtuse angle, such as the one shown.

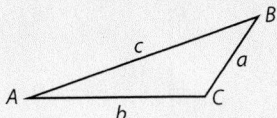

Possible answer: Draw a perpendicular from B to the extension of AC at point D, and let $BD = h$.

$\sin A = \frac{h}{c}$ and $\sin BCD = \frac{h}{a}$. Since ∠BCD and ∠C are supplements, $\sin C = \frac{h}{a}$.

Solving for h gives $\dfrac{a}{\sin A} = \dfrac{c}{\sin C}$. Draw another perpendicular from ∠C and repeat the process to find $\dfrac{a}{\sin A} = \dfrac{b}{\sin B} = \dfrac{c}{\sin C}$.

Scoring Rubric

2 points: Student correctly solves the problem and explains his/her reasoning.

1 point: Student shows good understanding of the problem but does not fully solve or explain his/her reasoning.

0 points: Student does not demonstrate understanding of the problem.

QUESTIONING STRATEGIES

? How can you use the Law of Sines to solve a triangle given two angles and the side length between the two given angles? Use the Triangle Sum Theorem to find the third angle, then apply the Law of Sines.

AVOID COMMON ERRORS

Students may be tempted to round intermediate answers when applying the Law of Sines, which can result in an incorrect final answer. Encourage students to perform the full calculation with their calculators, using parentheses if needed, to avoid rounding errors.

Law of Cosines

Common Core Math Standards

The student is expected to:

 G-SRT.D.10(+)

Prove the Laws of Sines and Cosines and use them to solve problems. Also G-SRT.D.11(+)

Mathematical Practices

 MP.3 Logic

Language Objective

Explain to a partner how to find the unknown measures of a triangle using the Law of Cosines.

ENGAGE

Essential Question: How can you use the Law of Cosines to find measures of any triangle?

You can use the Law of Cosines to solve triangles for which SAS or SSS information is given.

PREVIEW: LESSON PERFORMANCE TASK

View the Engage section online. Discuss the photo and how to use the Law of Cosines to find the width of a pond. Then preview the Lesson Performance Task.

14.2 Law of Cosines

Essential Question: How can you use the Law of Cosines to find measures of any triangle?

Resource Locker

⊘ Explore Deriving the Law of Cosines

You learned to solve triangle problems by using the Law of Sines. However, the Law of Sines cannot be used to solve triangles for which side-angle-side (SAS) or side-side-side (SSS) information is given. Instead, you must use the Law of Cosines.

To derive the Law of Cosines, draw $\triangle ABC$ with altitude $\overline{BD}$. If x represents the length of $\overline{AD}$, the length of $\overline{DC}$ is $b - x$.

(A) Use the Pythagorean Theorem to write a relationship for the side lengths of $\triangle BCD$ and for the side lengths of $\triangle ABD$.

$$a^2 = (b - x)^2 + h^2 \qquad\qquad c^2 = x^2 + h^2$$
$$= b^2 - 2bx + x^2 + h^2$$

(B) Notice that c^2 is equal to a sum of terms in the equation for a^2. Substitute c^2 for those terms.

$$a^2 = b^2 - 2bx + c^2$$

(C) In $\triangle ABD$, $\cos A = \frac{x}{c}$. Solve for x. Then substitute into the equation you wrote for a^2.

$$\cos A = \frac{x}{c}, \text{ or } x = \underline{\quad c\cos A \quad}.$$
$$a^2 = b^2 - \underline{\quad -2b(c\cos A) \quad} + c^2$$

Reflect

1. The equation you wrote in Step D is the Law of Cosines, which is usually written as $a^2 = b^2 + c^2 - 2bc\cos A$. Write formulas using $\cos B$ or $\cos C$ to describe the same relationships in this triangle.

$$b^2 = a^2 + c^2 - 2ac\cos B$$
$$c^2 = a^2 + b^2 - 2ab\cos C$$

© Houghton Mifflin Harcourt Publishing Company

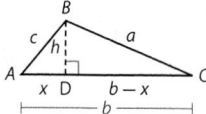

HARDCOVER PAGES 639–646

Turn to these pages to find this lesson in the hardcover student edition.

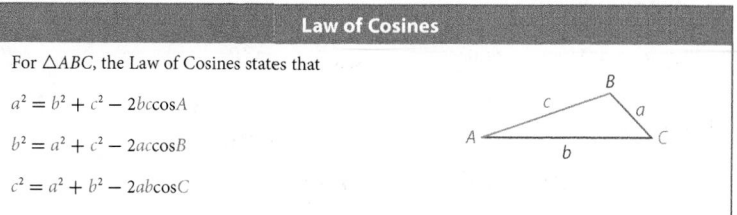

Explain 1   Using the Law of Cosines

To find the missing side length of a right triangle, you can use the Pythagorean Theorem. To find a missing side length of a general triangle, you can use the Law of Cosines.

Law of Cosines
For $\triangle ABC$, the Law of Cosines states that

$$a^2 = b^2 + c^2 - 2bc\cos A$$

$$b^2 = a^2 + c^2 - 2ac\cos B$$

$$c^2 = a^2 + b^2 - 2ab\cos C$$

Example 1   Solve $\triangle ABC$. Round to the nearest tenth.

(A)   **Step 1** Find the length of the third side.

$b^2 = a^2 + c^2 - 2ac\cos B$	Law of Cosines
$b^2 = 7^2 + 5^2 - 2(7)(5)\cos 100°$	Substitute.
$b^2 \approx 86.2$	Evaluate.
$b \approx 9.3$	Solve for a positive value of b.

Step 2 Find an angle measure.

$\dfrac{\sin A}{a} = \dfrac{\sin B}{b}$	Law of Sines
$\dfrac{\sin A}{7} = \dfrac{\sin 100°}{9.3}$	Substitute.
$\sin A = \dfrac{7\sin 100°}{9.3}$	Solve for $\sin A$.
$m\angle A = \sin^{-1}\left(\dfrac{7\sin 100°}{9.3}\right) \approx 47.8°$	Solve for $m\angle A$.

Step 3 Find the third angle measure.

$$47.8° + 100° + m\angle C = 180°$$
$$m\angle C = 32.2°$$

(B)   **Step 1** Find the measure of the largest angle, $\angle C$.

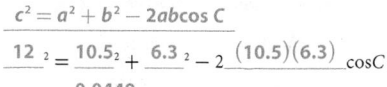

$c^2 = a^2 + b^2 - 2ab\cos C$	Law of Cosines
$12^2 = 10.5^2 + 6.3^2 - 2\,(10.5)(6.3)\cos C$	Substitute.
$\cos C \approx 0.0449$	Solve for $\cos C$.
$m\angle C \approx \cos^{-1}(0.0449) \approx 87.4°$	Solve for $m\angle C$.

EXPLORE

Deriving the Law of Cosines

INTEGRATE TECHNOLOGY

Students have the option of doing the Explore activity either in the book or online.

QUESTIONING STRATEGIES

? What is the difference between the application of the formula $b^2 = a^2 + c^2 - 2ac\cos B$ and the application of the Pythagorean Theorem? The Pythagorean Theorem applies only to right triangles, but the formula $b^2 = a^2 + c^2 - 2ac\cos B$ applies to any triangle.

EXPLAIN 1

Using the Law of Cosines

INTEGRATE MATHEMATICAL PRACTICES
Focus on Reasoning

MP.2 Point out that while there are three forms of the Law of Cosines, only one is necessary if the measurements of the triangle are relabeled to reflect which form of the law is being used.

QUESTIONING STRATEGIES

? How can you check that the measurements you found for the unknown sides or angles are correct? Substitute the values into the Law of Cosines or Law of Sines and show that both sides of the equation are equal.

? When do you use the Law of Sines along with the Law of Cosines to find the unknown measures for a triangle? You use the Law of Sines when you need to find an unknown measurement for which the Law of Cosines does not apply.

PROFESSIONAL DEVELOPMENT

Math Background

The Law of Cosines has a long history. In more recent times, the relationship has played a central role in surveying, navigation, and other fields that depend on the principle of triangulation. The Law of Cosines may be used to solve a triangle given either of the following:

- two side lengths and the included angle measure (SAS)
- three side lengths (SSS)

Note that the Law of Cosines, which states that $a^2 = b^2 + c^2 - 2bc\cos A$, may be viewed as a generalization of the Pythagorean Theorem. When A is a right angle, $\cos A = 0$, and the Law of Cosines reduces to $a^2 = b^2 + c^2$.

Law of Cosines   **756**

AVOID COMMON ERRORS

Some students may want to use calculated side lengths or angle measures when applying the Law of Cosines to other parts of a triangle. Point out that no calculated measures should be used when other side lengths or angles of the triangle are known exactly. This provides greater accuracy (because a calculated value of a side length is an approximation) and helps avoid additional errors (in case the student made errors in the calculations).

Step 2 Find another angle measure.

$b^2 = a^2 + c^2 - 2ac \cos B$ <u>Law of Cosines</u>

$\underline{6.3}^2 = \underline{10.5}^2 + \underline{12}^2 - 2(\underline{\,10.5\,})(\underline{\,12\,})\cos B$ Substitute.

$\cos B \approx \underline{\,0.8514\,}$ Solve for $\underline{\cos B}$.

$m\angle B \approx \cos^{-1}(\underline{\,0.8514\,}) \approx \underline{\,31.6°\,}$ Solve for $\underline{m\angle B}$.

Step 3 Find the third angle measure.

$m\angle A + \underline{\,31.6°\,} + \underline{\,87.4°\,} = 180°$ <u>Triangle Sum Theorem</u>

$m\angle A = \underline{\,61.0°\,}$ Solve for $m\angle A$.

> **Reflect**

2. Suppose a student used the Law of Sines to solve this triangle. Determine whether the measurements are correct. Explain.

Use the Law of Cosines to check.

$a^2 = b^2 + c^2 - 2bc \cos A$ $b^2 = a^2 + c^2 - 2ac \cos B$

$10^2 = 9^2 + 6^2 - 2(9)(6) \cos 80.9°$ $9^2 = 10^2 + 6^2 - 2(10)(6) \cos 62.7°$

$100 = 100$ $81 = 81$

$c^2 = a^2 + b^2 - 2ab \cos C$

$6^2 = 10^2 + 9^2 - 2(10)(9) \cos 36.4°$

$36 = 36$

The student's measurements are correct; substituting the measurements into the Law of Cosines equations produced true statements.

> **Your Turn**

Solve △ABC. Round to the nearest tenth.

3. $b = 23, c = 18, m\angle A = 173°$

Find length of a.

$a^2 = b^2 + c^2 - 2bc \cos A$

$a^2 = 23^2 + 18^2 - 2(23)(18) \cos 173°$

$a^2 \approx 1{,}674.8$

$a \approx 40.9$

Find an angle measure.

$b^2 = a^2 + c^2 - 2ac \cos B$

$23^2 = 40.9^2 + 18^2 - 2(40.9)(18)\cos B$

$\cos B \approx 0.9968$

$m\angle B \approx \cos^{-1}(0.9968) \approx 4.5°$

Find the other angle measure.

$173° + 4.5° + m\angle C = 180°$

$m\angle C = 2.5°$

4. $a = 35, b = 42, c = 50.3$

Find an angle measure.

$a^2 = b^2 + c^2 - 2bc \cos A$

$35^2 = 42^2 + 50.3^2 - 2(42)(50.3) \cos A$

$\cos A \approx 0.726$

$m\angle A \approx \cos^{-1}(0.726) \approx 43.4°$

Find another angle measure.

$b^2 = a^2 + c^2 - 2ac \cos B$

$42^2 = 35^2 + 50.3^2 - 2(35)(50.3)\cos B$

$\cos B \approx 0.565$

$m\angle B \approx \cos^{-1}(0.565) \approx 55.6°$

Find the last angle measure.

$43.4° + 55.6° + m\angle C = 180°$

$m\angle C = 81.0°$

COLLABORATIVE LEARNING

Small Group Activity

To help students understand how to use the Law of Cosines in the SAS or SSS cases, have one student create a diagram of a triangle for which either case applies. Then have the student pass the triangle to another student, who identifies which form of the law should be used. Ask another student to find the unknown side or angle measures using the Law of Cosines and the Law of Sines, if necessary. Have a fourth student check the calculations and share the results with the group.

⊘ Explain 2   **Problem Solving Using the Law of Cosines**

You now know many triangle relationships that you can use to solve real-world problems.

Example 2

A coast guard patrol boat and a fishing boat leave a dock at the same time at the courses shown. The patrol boat travels at a speed of 12 nautical miles per hour (12 knots), and the fishing boat travels at a speed of 5 knots. After 3 hours, the fishing boat sends a distress signal picked up by the patrol boat. If the fishing boat does not drift, how long will it take the patrol boat to reach it at a speed of 12 knots?

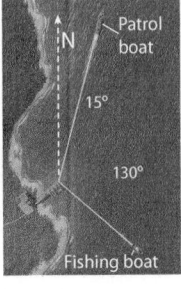

Step 1 Understand the Problem

The answer will be the number of hours that the patrol boat needs to reach the fishing boat.

List the important information:

- The patrol boat's speed is 12 knots. Its direction is 15° east of north.
- The fishing boat's speed is 5 knots. Its direction is 130° east of north.
- The boats travel for 3 hours before the distress call is given.

Step 2 Make a Plan

Determine the angle between the boats' courses and the distance that each boat travels in 3 hours. Use this information to draw and label a diagram.

Then use the Law of Cosines to find the distance d between the boats at the time of the distress call. Finally, determine how long it will take the patrol boat to travel this distance.

Step 3 Draw and Label a Diagram

- The angle between the boats' courses is $130° - 15° = 115°$. In 3 hours, the patrol boat travels $3(12) = 36$ nautical miles and the fishing boat travels $3(5) = 15$ nautical miles.
- Find the distance d between the boats.

$d^2 = p^2 + f^2 - 2pf\cos D$	Law of Cosines
$d^2 = 15^2 + 36^2 - 2(15)(36)\cos 115°$	Substitute.
$d^2 \approx 1,977.4$	Evaluate.
$d \approx 44.5$	Solve for the positive value of d.

- Determine the number of hours.
  The patrol boat must travel about 44.5 nautical miles to reach the fishing boat. At a speed of 12 nautical miles per hour, it will take the patrol boat $\frac{44.5}{12} \approx 3.7$ hours to reach the fishing boat.

Step 4 Look Back

To reach the fishing boat, the patrol boat will have to travel a greater distance than it did during the first 3 hours of its trip. Therefore, it makes sense that it will take the patrol boat longer than 3 hours to reach the fishing boat. An answer of 3.7 hours seems reasonable.

EXPLAIN 2

Problem Solving Using the Law of Cosines

INTEGRATE MATHEMATICAL PRACTICES
Focus on Reasoning

MP.2 Explain to students that the Law of Cosines can be used to find the unknown measures of triangles that cannot be found by using the Law of Sines alone. Stress that when students use the Law of Cosines to find angle measures, they should find the measure of the triangle's largest angle first, if it is not already known. By doing so, they will not need to worry about the ambiguous case if they use the Law of Sines to find another angle measure.

AVOID COMMON ERRORS

When using the Law of Cosines to determine a side length of a triangle, some students may solve for the square of the side length and then forget to take the positive square root of each side of the equation. Remind students that one way to check that they have correctly solved for the side length is to substitute its value into the original equation to see whether it makes the equation true.

QUESTIONING STRATEGIES

? How can you use the Law of Cosines to find the distance between two vertices of a real-world triangle? The distance is the length of a side of the triangle, so the Law of Cosines will apply if the angle opposite the distance and the other two side lengths are known.

DIFFERENTIATE INSTRUCTION

Cognitive Strategies

Have students make note cards for each of the following cases: AAS, ASA, SAS, SSS, and SSA. For each case, have students list the steps they would use to solve a triangle if given this information. In the SSS case, for example, students might write the following:

1. Use the Law of Cosines twice to find the measures of the two largest angles.

2. Use the Triangle Sum Theorem to find the measure of the third angle.

AVOID COMMON ERRORS

Some students may want to use a negative value for a, b, or c when using the Law of Cosines for a real-world triangle because of the squares in the formulas. Point out that no lengths can be negative.

ELABORATE

QUESTIONING STRATEGIES

? What information do you need to find the unknown measures of a triangle using the Law of Cosines? You need to know one angle measure and two side lengths—side-angle-side (SAS), or three side lengths—side-side-side (SSS).

SUMMARIZE THE LESSON

? Which law would you use to find the unknown measures in each triangle described below, Law of Sines or Law of Cosines? Justify your answer.

- $a = 14$, $b = 8$, $c = 9$

Law of Cosines; SSS is given.

- $a = 26$, $m\angle A = 46°$, $m\angle B = 80°$

Law of Sines; AAS is given.

- $b = 4$, $m\angle A = 27°$, $m\angle C = 100°$

Law of Sines; ASA is given.

- $a = 12$, $b = 15$, $m\angle C = 45°$

Law of Cosines; SAS is given.

5. If Lucas hikes at an average of 2.5 miles per hour, how long will it take him to travel from the cave to the waterfall? Round to the nearest tenth of an hour.

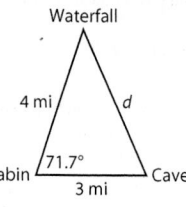

Use the Law of Cosines to find the distance between the cave and the waterfall.

$d^2 = 4^2 + 3^2 - 2(4)(3)\cos 71.7°$

$d^2 \approx 17.46$

$d \approx 4.18$

If Lucas is walking 4.18 miles at a rate of 2.5 miles per hour, it will take him $\frac{4.18}{2.5} \approx 1.7$ **hours.**

6. A pilot is flying from Houston to Oklahoma City. To avoid a thunderstorm, the pilot flies 28° off of the direct route for a distance of 175 miles. He then makes a turn and flies straight on to Oklahoma City. To the nearest mile, how much farther than the direct route was the route taken by the pilot?

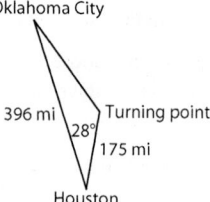

Find the distance from the turning point to Oklahoma City, d, using the Law of Cosines.

$d^2 = 396^2 + 175^2 - 2(396)(175)\cos 28°$

$d^2 \approx 65,064.46$

$d \approx 255$

The route taken by the pilot was $255 + 175 = 430$ miles, which is 34 miles greater than the direct route.

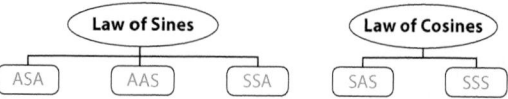 **Elaborate**

7. Explain why you cannot solve a triangle if you are given only angle-angle-angle information. All triangles that are similar to each other have the same angle measures. Therefore, you

must know the length of at least one side of a triangle in order to solve it.

8. When using the Law of Cosines, $a^2 = b^2 + c^2 - 2bc\cos A$, you can take the square root of both sides to find the value of a. Explain why the negative square root is not used when considering the answer. The Law of Cosines is used to find distance, and distance is not a negative.

9. **Essential Question Check-In** Copy and complete the graphic organizer. List the types of triangles that can be solved by using each law. Consider the following types of triangles: ASA, AAS, SAS, SSA, and SSS.

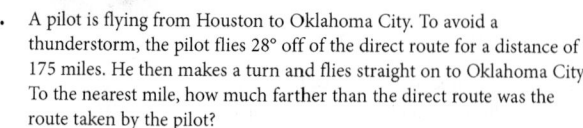

LANGUAGE SUPPORT EL

Connect Vocabulary

Students may have difficulty distinguishing the Law of Cosines from the Law of Sines. Have them create a poster displaying different triangles whose unknown measures can be found with one law, the other law, or both laws. Have them share their posters with other students and then display the posters for the class.

Evaluate: Homework and Practice

• Online Homework
• Hints and Help
• Extra Practice

Draw and label the diagram you would use to derive the given form of the Law of Cosines.

1. $b^2 = a^2 + c^2 - 2ac\cos B$

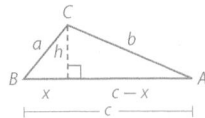

2. $c^2 = a^2 + b^2 - 2ab\cos C$

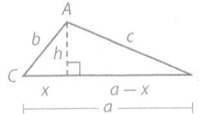

3. What information do you need to be able to use the Law of Cosines to solve a triangle?

You need two side lengths and the angle measure for the unknown side, or you need all three side lengths.

Solve each triangle. Round to the nearest tenth.

4.

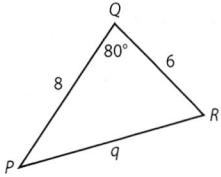

$q^2 = 8^2 + 6^2 - 2(8)(6)\cos(80°)$

$q^2 \approx 83.33$

$q \approx 9.1$

$6^2 = 8^2 + 9.1^2 - 2(8)(9.1)\cos P$

$\cos P \approx 0.76$

$m\angle P \approx \cos^{-1}(0.76) \approx 40.5°$

$8^2 = 6^2 + 9.1^2 - 2(6)(9.1)\cos R$

$\cos R \approx 0.50$

$m\angle R = 60°$

5.

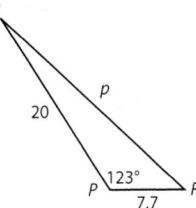

$p^2 = 20^2 + 7.7^2 - 2(20)(7.7)\cos 123°$

$p^2 \approx 627.04$

$p \approx 25.0$

$20^2 = 25^2 + 7.7^2 - 2(25)(7.7)\cos R$

$\cos R \approx 0.74$

$m\angle R \approx \cos^{-1}(0.74) \approx 42.3°$

$7.7^2 = 20^2 + 25^2 - 2(20)(25)\cos Q$

$\cos Q \approx 0.97$

$m\angle Q \approx \cos^{-1}(0.97) \approx 15.0°$

EVALUATE

ASSIGNMENT GUIDE

Concepts and Skills	Practice
Explore Deriving the Law of Cosines	Exercises 1–3
Example 1 Using the Law of Cosines	Exercises 4–15
Example 2 Problem Solving Using the Law of Cosines	Exercises 16–17

INTEGRATE MATHEMATICAL PRACTICES
Focus on Math Connections

MP.1 Remind students that the SSA case is different from the SAS case because the SSA combination (two sides and a non-included angle) does not always determine exactly one triangle and is solved using the Law of Sines, while the SAS case determines exactly one triangle and is solved using the Law of Cosines.

Exercise	Depth of Knowledge (D.O.K.)	COMMON CORE Mathematical Practices
1–2	2 Skills/Concepts	**MP.3** Logic
3	2 Skills/Concepts	**MP.5** Using Tools
4–15	2 Skills/Concepts	**MP.2** Reasoning
16–17	2 Skills/Concepts	**MP.1** Problem Solving
18	3 Strategic Thinking	**MP.8** Patterns
19	2 Skills/Concepts	**MP.2** Reasoning
20	3 Strategic Thinking	**MP.3** Logic

AVOID COMMON ERRORS

Students might make errors finding the unknown measures for triangles that are not shown in a diagram. Suggest that students begin by sketching a triangle that is approximately to scale for the given measurements. Ask students to carefully label their sketches and double-check the labels before beginning to calculate the unknowns. A carefully labeled sketch should also help students choose the version of the Law of Cosines that is appropriate.

6.

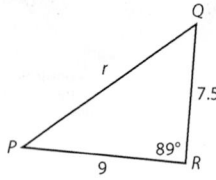

$$r^2 = 7.5^2 + 9^2 - 2(7.5)(9)\cos 89°$$
$$r^2 \approx 134.90$$
$$r \approx 11.6$$
$$9^2 = 11.6^2 + 7.5^2 - 2(11.6)(7.5)\cos Q$$
$$\cos Q \approx 0.63$$
$$m\angle Q \approx \cos^{-1}(0.63) \approx 50.9°$$
$$7.5^2 = 11.6^2 + 9^2 - 2(11.6)(9)\cos P$$
$$\cos P \approx 0.76$$
$$m\angle P \approx \cos^{-1}(0.76) \approx 40.3°$$

7.

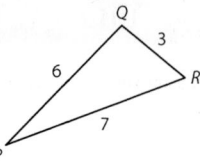

$$3^2 = 6^2 + 7^2 - 2(6)(7)\cos P$$
$$\cos P \approx 0.90$$
$$m\angle P \approx \cos^{-1}(0.90) \approx 25.2°$$
$$6^2 = 3^2 + 7^2 - 2(3)(7)\cos R$$
$$\cos R \approx 0.52$$
$$m\angle R \approx \cos^{-1}(0.52) \approx 58.4°$$
$$25.2° + 58.4° + m\angle Q = 180°$$
$$m\angle Q \approx 96.4°$$

8.

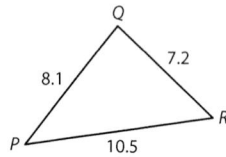

$$10.5^2 = 8.1^2 + 7.2^2 - 2(8.1)(7.2)\cos Q$$
$$\cos Q \approx 0.06$$
$$m\angle Q \approx \cos^{-1}(0.06) \approx 86.5°$$
$$7.2^2 = 8.1^2 + 10.5^2 - 2(8.1)(10.5)\cos P$$
$$\cos P \approx 0.73$$
$$m\angle P \approx \cos^{-1}(0.73) \approx 43.2°$$
$$86.5° + 43.2° + m\angle R = 180°$$
$$m\angle R = 50.3°$$

9.

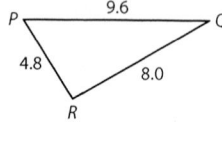

$$9.6^2 = 8^2 + 4.8^2 - 2(8)(4.8)\cos R$$
$$\cos R \approx -0.07$$
$$m\angle R \approx \cos^{-1}(-0.07) \approx 93.8°$$
$$4.8^2 = 9.6^2 + 8^2 - 2(9.6)(8)\cos Q$$
$$\cos Q \approx 0.87$$
$$m\angle Q \approx \cos^{-1}(0.87) \approx 29.9°$$
$$93.8° + 29.9° + m\angle P = 180°$$
$$m\angle P = 56.3°$$

Solve △ABC. Round to the nearest tenth.

10. $m\angle A = 120°, b = 16, c = 20$

$$a^2 = 16^2 + 20^2 - 2(16)(20)\cos 120°$$
$$a^2 \approx 976$$
$$a \approx 31.2$$
$$16^2 = 31.2^2 + 20^2 - 2(31.2)(20)\cos B$$
$$\cos B \approx 0.90$$
$$m\angle B \approx \cos^{-1}(0.90) \approx 25.8°$$
$$120° + 25.8° + m\angle C = 180°$$
$$m\angle C = 34.2°$$

11. $m\angle B = 78°, a = 6, c = 4$

$$b^2 = 6^2 + 4^2 - 2(6)(4)\cos 78°$$
$$b^2 \approx 42.0$$
$$b \approx 6.5$$
$$6^2 = 6.5^2 + 4^2 - 2(6.5)(4)\cos A$$
$$\cos A \approx 0.43$$
$$m\angle A \approx \cos^{-1}(0.43) \approx 64.7°$$
$$78° + 64.7° + m\angle C = 180°$$
$$m\angle C = 37.3°$$

© Houghton Mifflin Harcourt Publishing Company

Exercise	Depth of Knowledge (D.O.K.)	COMMON CORE Mathematical Practices
21	**2** Skills/Concepts	**MP.1** Problem solving
22	**3** Strategic Thinking H.O.T.	**MP.1** Problem solving
23	**3** Strategic Thinking H.O.T.	**MP.2** Reasoning
24	**3** Strategic Thinking H.O.T.	**MP.2** Reasoning
25	**3** Strategic Thinking H.O.T.	**MP.3** Logic

12. $m\angle C = 96°$, $a = 13$, $b = 9$

$c^2 = 13^2 + 9^2 - 2(13)(9)\cos 96°$

$c^2 \approx 274.46$

$c \approx 16.6$

$13^2 = 9^2 + 16.6^2 - 2(9)(16.6)\cos A$

$\cos A \approx 0.63$

$m\angle A \approx \cos^{-1}(0.63) \approx 51.1°$

$51.1° + m\angle B + 96° = 180°$

$m\angle B = 32.9°$

13. $a = 14$, $b = 9$, $c = 10$

$14^2 = 9^2 + 10^2 - 2(9)(10)\cos A$

$\cos A \approx -0.08$

$m\angle A \approx \cos^{-1}(-0.08) \approx 94.6°$

$9^2 = 10^2 + 14^2 - 2(10)(14)\cos B$

$\cos B \approx 0.77$

$m\angle B \approx \cos^{-1}(0.77) \approx 39.8°$

$94.7° + 39.8° + m\angle C = 180°$

$m\angle C = 45.5°$

14. $a = 5$, $b = 8$, $c = 6$

$5^2 = 8^2 + 6^2 - 2(8)(6)\cos A$

$\cos A \approx 0.78$

$m\angle A \approx \cos^{-1}(0.78) \approx 38.7°$

$8^2 = 5^2 + 6^2 - 2(5)(6)\cos B$

$\cos B \approx -0.05$

$m\angle B = \cos^{-1}(-0.05) \approx 92.9°$

$38.7° + 92.9° \; m\angle C = 180°$

$m\angle C = 48.4°$

15. $a = 30$, $b = 26$, $c = 35$

$30^2 = 26^2 + 35^2 - 2(26)(35)\cos A$

$\cos A = 0.55$

$m\angle A = \cos^{-1}(0.55) \approx 56.6°$

$26^2 = 30^2 + 35^2 - 2(30)(35)\cos B$

$\cos B = 0.69$

$m\angle B = \cos^{-1}(0.69) \approx 46.4°$

$56.6° + 46.4° + m\angle C = 180°$

$m\angle C = 77°$

16. A triangular hiking trail is being planned. At an average walking speed of 2 m/s, how many minutes will it take a hiker to make a complete circuit around the trail? Round to the nearest minute.

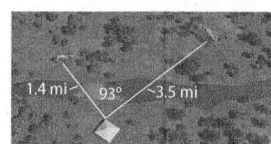

Find length of third side.

$s^2 = 410^2 + 200^2 - 2(410)(200)\cos 100°$

$s^2 \approx 236{,}578.3$

$s \approx 486.4$

The entire circuit is $486.4 + 410 + 200 = 1{,}096.4$ meters. Walking at an average speed of 2 m/s, the hike would take $\frac{1{,}096.4}{2} \approx 548$ seconds, or $\frac{548}{60} \approx 9$ minutes, to walk the circuit.

17. An ecologist is studying a pair of zebras fitted with radio-transmitter collars. One zebra is 1.4 miles from the ecologist, and the other is 3.5 miles from the ecologist. To the nearest tenth of a mile, how far apart are the two zebras?

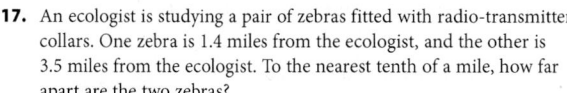

$d^2 = 1.4^2 + 3.5^2 - 2(1.4)(3.5)\cos 93°$

$d^2 \approx 14.72$

$d \approx 3.8$

3.8 miles

INTEGRATE MATHEMATICAL PRACTICES

Focus on Technology

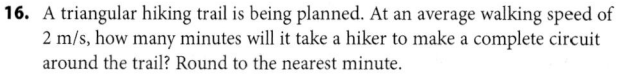 **MP.5** Remind students that they can use a graphing calculator (in degree mode) to check their work with the Law of Cosines. For the SSS case, students should input the side lengths **A**, **B**, and **C**, with **C** the side opposite the unknown angle to be determined. Then the calculator will output the measure of angle **C** using the expression $\cos^{-1}\left(\dfrac{(C^2 - A^2 - B^2)}{(-2AB)}\right)$.

For the SAS case, students should input the side lengths **A** and **B**, and the measure of angle **C**, with **c** being the unknown side length opposite the known angle. Then the calculator will output the measure of side **c** using the expression $\sqrt{(A^2 + B^2 - 2AB\cos(C))}$.

AVOID COMMON ERRORS

When using the Law of Cosines to determine a side length of a triangle, caution students to take the positive square root of each side of the equation during the solving process. Remind students that one way to check that they have correctly solved for the side length is to substitute its value into the original equation to see whether the value makes the equation true.

18. **Critical Thinking** Find the length of $\overline{AE}$.

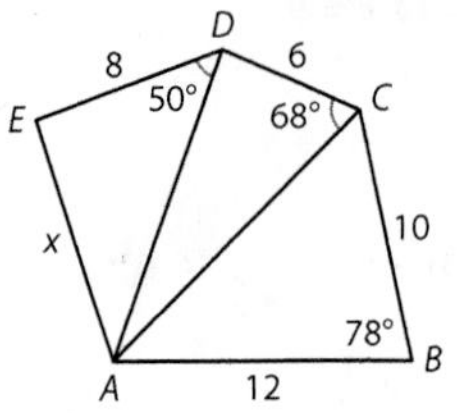

$AC^2 = 10^2 + 12^2 - 2(10)(12)\cos 78°$

$AC^2 \approx 194.1$

$AC \approx 13.9$

$AD^2 = 13.9^2 + 6^2 - 2(13.9)(6)\cos 68°$

$AD^2 \approx 166.7$

$AD \approx 12.9$

$AE^2 = 12.9^2 + 8^2 - 2(12.9)(8)\cos 50°$

$AE^2 \approx 97.7$

$AE \approx 9.9$

19. Which is the approximate measure of $\angle K$ in the triangle shown?

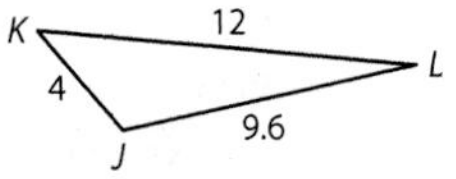

A. $-30°$ D. $45°$

B. $-45°$ E. $54°$

C. $30°$ F. $60°$

$9.6^2 = 4^2 + 12^2 - 2(4)(12)\cos K$

$\cos K \approx 0.71$

$m\angle K \approx \cos^{-1}(0.71) \approx 45°$

D. $45°$

20. **Critical Thinking** Use the Law of Cosines to explain why $c^2 = a^2 + b^2$ for $\triangle ABC$, where $\angle C$ is a right angle.

Possible answer: If $\angle C$ is a right angle, then its measure is 90°.

$c^2 = a^2 + b^2 - 2ab\cos C$

$c^2 = a^2 + b^2 - 2ab\cos 90°$

$c^2 = a^2 + b^2 - 2ab(0)$

$c^2 = a^2 + b^2$

21. A graphic artist is asked to draw a triangular logo with sides measuring 15 cm, 18 cm, and 20 cm. If she draws the triangle correctly, what will be the measures of its angles to the nearest degree?

$15^2 = 18^2 + 20^2 - 2(18)(20)\cos A$ $18^2 = 15^2 + 20^2 - 2(15)(20)\cos B$

$\cos A \approx 0.69$ $\cos B \approx 0.5$

$m\angle A \approx \cos^{-1}(0.69) \approx 46°$ $m\angle B \approx \cos^{-1}(0.5) \approx 60°$

$20^2 = 15^2 + 18^2 - 2(15)(18)\cos C$

$\cos C \approx 0.28$

$m\angle C \approx \cos^{-1}(0.28) \approx 74°$

© Houghton Mifflin Harcourt Publishing Company

22. Represent Real-World Problem Two performers hang by their knees from trapezes, as shown.

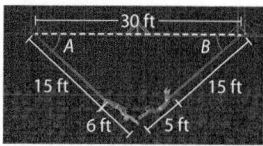

a. To the nearest degree, what acute angles A and B must the ropes of each trapeze make with the horizontal if the performer on the left is to grab the wrists of the performer on the right and pull her away from her trapeze?

b. Later, the performer on the left grabs the trapeze of the performer on the right and lets go of his trapeze. To the nearest degree, what angles A and B must the ropes of each trapeze make with the horizontal for this trick to work?

a. The left side of the triangle is 21 feet long, and the right side of the triangle is 20 feet long.

$$20 = 21^2 + 30^2 - 2(21)(30)\cos A$$

$\cos A \approx 0.75$

$m\angle A \approx 41°$

$$21^2 = 20^2 + 30^2 - 2(20)(30)\cos B$$

$\cos B \approx 0.72$

$m\angle B \approx 44°$

b. The left side is 21 feet long, and the right side length does not include the length of the person, so it is only 15 feet long.

$$15^2 = 21^2 + 30^2 - 2(21)(30)\cos A \qquad 21^2 = 15^2 + 30^2 - 2(15)(30)\cos B$$

$\cos A \approx 0.89 \qquad\qquad\qquad \cos B \approx 0.76$

$m\angle A \approx 28° \qquad\qquad\qquad m\angle B \approx 41°$

23. Barrington Crater in Arizona was produced by the impact of a meteorite. Based on the measurements shown, what is the diameter d of Barrington Crater to the nearest tenth of a kilometer?

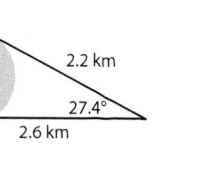

$$d^2 = 2.6^2 + 2.2^2 - 2(2.6)(2.2)\cos 27.4°$$

$d^2 \approx 1.44$

$d \approx 1.2$

1.2 km

© Houghton Mifflin Harcourt Publishing Company • Image Credits: ©Francois Gohier/Science Source

INTEGRATE MATHEMATICAL PRACTICES

Focus on Critical Thinking

MP.3 If students have difficulty with an exercise, point out that they will need to know two side lengths and the included angle measure of the triangle to apply the SAS case to find the third side length (opposite the known angle measure of the triangle). From there, they may want to use the Law of Sines to find the other unknown angle measures. For the SSS case, they will need to know all three side lengths to find the angle measures. The Law of Cosines can then be used to find all of the unknown angle measures.

PEER-TO-PEER DISCUSSION

Ask students to work in pairs. Have each student draw a triangle and use a ruler and protractor to label it with SAS or SSS information. Then have partners use the Law of Cosines to solve each other's triangles and explain their reasoning. Students can check their work by direct measurement of the unlabeled sides and angles.

JOURNAL

Have students explain how the Law of Cosines enables them to solve a triangle when given SAS information.

24. **Analyze Relationships** What are the angle measures of an isosceles triangle whose base is half as long as its congruent legs? Round to the nearest tenth.

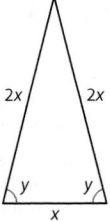

$$(2x)^2 = x^2 + (2x)^2 - 2(x)(2x)\cos y$$

$$4x^2 = x^2 + 4x^2 - 4x^2 \cos y$$

$$4x^2 = 5x^2 - 4x^2 \cos y$$

$$-x^2 = -4x^2 \cos y$$

$$\frac{1}{4} = \cos y$$

$$m\angle y = \cos^{-1}\left(\frac{1}{4}\right) \approx 75.5°$$

75.5°, 75.5°, 29°

25. **Explain the Error** Abby uses the Law of Cosines to find $m\angle A$ when $a = 2$, $b = 3$, $c = 5$. The answer she gets is $0°$. Did she make an error? Explain.

$$2^2 = 3^2 + 5^2 - 2(3)(5)\cos A$$

$$\cos A = 1$$

$$m\angle A \approx \cos^{-1}(1) = 0°$$

Abby did not make an error. The three lengths cannot form a triangle because $a + b = c$.

© Houghton Mifflin Harcourt Publishing Company

Lesson Performance Task

Standing on a small bluff overlooking a local pond, Clay wants to calculate the width of the pond.

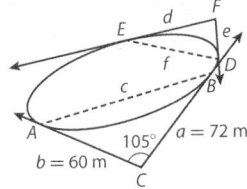

a. From point C, Clay walks the distances CA and CB. Then he measures the angle between these line segments. What is the distance to the nearest meter from A to B?

$c^2 = 72^2 + 60^2 - 2(72)(60)\cos105° \approx 11{,}020$

$c \approx 105$ m

b. From another point F, Clay measures 20 meters to D and 50 meters to E. Reece says that last summer this area dried out so much that he could walk the 49 meters from D to E. What is the measure of $\angle F$?

$m\angle F = \cos^{-1}\left(\dfrac{(50^2 + 20^2 - 49^2)}{2(50)(20)}\right) \approx 75.6°$

c. Reece tells Clay that when the area defined by $\triangle DEF$ dries out, it becomes covered with native grasses and plants. What is the area of this section?

$A = \frac{1}{2}(20)(20)\sin75.6° \approx 484.3$ m^2

© Houghton Mifflin Harcourt Publishing Company • Image Credits: ©Dieter Heinemann/Westend61 GmbH/Alamy

---

QUESTIONING STRATEGIES

What three triangle measures cannot be used to solve the triangle using either the Law of Sines or Law of Cosines, and why? AAA; at least one side must be known to use the Law of Sines, and at least two sides must be known to use the Law of Cosines.

AVOID COMMON ERRORS

Students might confuse which angle measure to use when applying the Law of Cosines. That angle is always the one opposite the unknown side.

EXTENSION ACTIVITY

Prove the Law of Cosines for a triangle with one obtuse angle, such as the one shown. Possible answer: Draw a perpendicular from B to the extension of AC at point D, and let $BD = h$ and

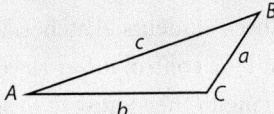

$CD = x$. $\cos BCD = \dfrac{x}{a}$ and since $m\angle BCD = 180° - m\angle C$, $\cos BCD = -\cos C$ and $x = -a\cos C$. Applying the Pythagorean Theorem to both right triangles gives $x^2 + h^2 = a^2$ and $(x + b)^2 + h^2 = c^2$. Substitute and simplify to find $c^2 = a^2 + b^2 - 2ab \cos C$; repeat to find the other two formulas.

Scoring Rubric

2 points: Student correctly solves the problem and explains his/her reasoning.

1 point: Student shows good understanding of the problem but does not fully solve or explain his/her reasoning.

0 points: Student does not demonstrate understanding of the problem.

Law of Cosines   **766**

Study Guide Review

ASSESSMENT AND INTERVENTION

Assign or customize module reviews.

MODULE PERFORMANCE TASK

COMMON CORE

Mathematical Practices: MP.1, MP.4, MP.5, MP.6
G-SRT.D.10, G-SRT.D.11

SUPPORTING STUDENT REASONING

Students should begin this problem by focusing on the information they will need. Here are some questions they might ask.

- **How can I understand the relationships among the angles and distances that are given?** Draw and label a sketch. Make a list of what you know and what you want to know. Then use your knowledge of trigonometry to write an equation you can solve to find what you want to know.

- **How can I sketch an angle whose measure is given as "45° east of north?"** Draw a point to represent the control tower, the vertex of the angle. From it, draw a vertical line to represent north. From the same point, draw a second line angling to the right (east) of the first line and forming a 35° angle with it.

Essential Question: How can you use triangle trigonometry to solve real-world problems?

Key Vocabulary
cosine *(coseno)*
sine *(seno)*
trigonometric ratio
(razón trigonométrica)

KEY EXAMPLE (Lesson 14.1)

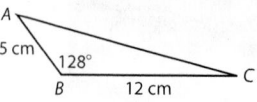

Find the area of the triangle. Round to the nearest tenth.

$$\text{area} = \frac{1}{2}\,ac\,\sin B \qquad \text{Write the area formula.}$$

$$= \frac{1}{2}\,(5)(12)\,\sin 128° \qquad \text{Substitute the known values.}$$

$$\approx 23.6 \qquad \text{Use a calculator to evaluate the expression.}$$

The area of the triangle is about 23.6 cm².

KEY EXAMPLE (Lesson 14.1)

Solve the triangle. Round to the nearest tenth.

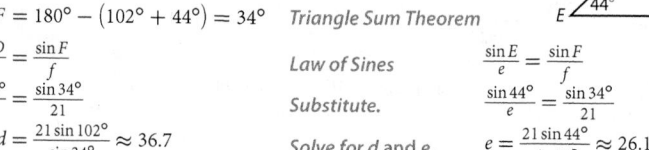

$m\angle F = 180° - (102° + 44°) = 34°$ *Triangle Sum Theorem*

$\dfrac{\sin D}{d} = \dfrac{\sin F}{f}$ *Law of Sines*

$\dfrac{\sin 102°}{d} = \dfrac{\sin 34°}{21}$ *Substitute.*

$d = \dfrac{21\sin 102°}{\sin 34°} \approx 36.7$ *Solve for d and e.*

$\dfrac{\sin E}{e} = \dfrac{\sin F}{f}$

$\dfrac{\sin 44°}{e} = \dfrac{\sin 34°}{21}$

$e = \dfrac{21\sin 44°}{\sin 34°} \approx 26.1$

KEY EXAMPLE (Lesson 14.2)

Find *a*. Round to the nearest tenth.

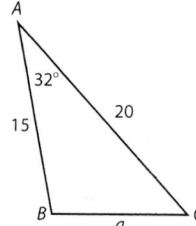

$a^2 = b^2 + c^2 - 2bc\cos A$ *Law of Cosines*

$a^2 = 20^2 + 15^2 - 2(20)(15)\cos 32°$ *Substitute.*

$a^2 \approx 116.2$ *Use a calculator to simplify.*

$a \approx 10.8$ *Solve for the positive value of a.*

SCAFFOLDING SUPPORT

- Check students' sketches, which should include a triangle with the two planes and the control tower as vertices. Ask students to identify the parts of the triangles they know (two sides and the included angle), the part they want to find (the third side), and the law they can use to relate all of these (the Law of Cosines).

EXERCISES

Find the area of each triangle. Round to the nearest tenth. *(Lesson 14.1)*

1.

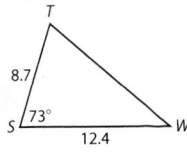

area = 51.6 units²

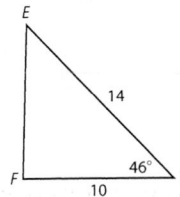

area = 50.4 units²

Solve each triangle. Round to the nearest tenth. *(Lesson 14.1)*

2.

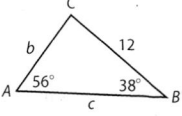

$m\angle C = 86°$; $b = 8.9$; $c = 14.4$

3.

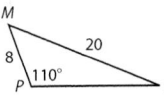

$m\angle M = 47.9°$; $m\angle N = 22.1°$; $m = 15.8$

Solve each triangle. Round to the nearest tenth. *(Lesson 14.2)*

4.

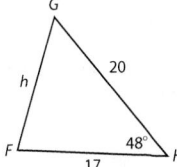

$h = 15.3$; $m\angle F = 76.3°$; $m\angle G = 55.7°$

5.

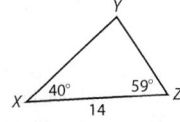

$x = 9.1$; $z = 12.1$; $m\angle Y = 81°$

MODULE PERFORMANCE TASK

Controlling the Air

It's a busy day in the airspace above Metropolitan Airport and the traffic controllers in the tower below have their hands full. Right now there's a passenger jet that's located at a bearing of 45° east of north and 22 miles from the airport. A private plane is located 34° east of north and 14 miles from the airport. The planes are at the same altitude. How far apart are they?

Start by listing in the space below the information you will need to solve the problem. Then use your own paper to work on the task. Then use numbers, words, or algebra to explain how you reached your conclusion.

© Houghton Mifflin Harcourt Publishing Company

SAMPLE SOLUTION

If *A* is the private plane, *B* is the passenger jet, and *C* is the control tower, the diagram shows their relative locations as described in the problem.

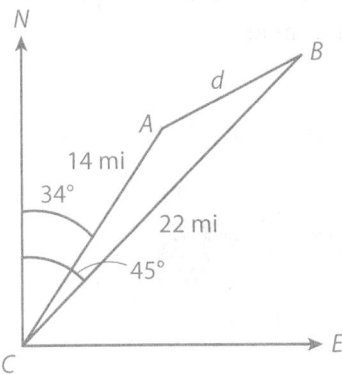

$$m\angle ABC = 45° - 34° = 11°$$

By the Law of Cosines:

$$d^2 = 14^2 + 22^2 - 2(14)(22)\cos 11°$$

$$\approx 196 + 484 - 616(0.9816)$$

$$\approx 680 - 604.7$$

$$= 75.3$$

$$d = \sqrt{75.3}$$

$$\approx 8.7$$

The planes are about 8.7 miles apart.

DISCUSSION OPPORTUNITIES

- Are the planes in any danger of colliding? Sample answer: If they are traveling in opposite directions there is no danger of a collision. If they are traveling toward each other or on paths that are destined to intersect, they are in danger and should change course immediately.

- How many minutes would it take a plane traveling 400 miles per hour to travel 8.7 miles? about 1.3 min

- What other factors besides a plane's speed, altitude, and direction might affect the plane's flight path? Possible answers: wind speed, wind direction, rain, lightning

Assessment Rubric

2 points: Student correctly solves the problem and explains his/her reasoning.

1 point: Student shows good understanding of the problem but does not fully solve or explain his/her reasoning.

0 points: Student does not demonstrate understanding of the problem.

Ready to Go On?

ASSESS MASTERY

Use the assessment on this page to determine if students have mastered the concepts and standards covered in this module.

ASSESSMENT AND INTERVENTION

Access Ready to Go On? assessment online, and receive instant scoring, feedback, and customized intervention or enrichment.

ADDITIONAL RESOURCES

Response to Intervention Resources

- Reteach Worksheets

Differentiated Instruction Resources

- Reading Strategies **EL**
- Success for English Learners **EL**
- Challenge Worksheets

Assessment Resources

- Leveled Module Quizzes

14.1–14.2 Trigonometry with All Triangles

- Online Homework
- Hints and Help
- Extra Practice

Solve. Round answers to the nearest tenth. *(Lesson 14.1)*

1. The sides of a triangle measure 31 inches, 23 inches, and 17 inches. What is the area of the triangle?

192.2 in²

2. The sides of a triangle measure 11 centimeters, 13 centimeters, and 15 centimeters. What are the measures of the angles of the triangles?

45.6°; 57.6°; 76.9°

3. A triangle has two sides measuring 10 inches and 16 inches. The angle opposite the 16-inch side measures 70.3°. Solve the triangle.

36.0°; 73.7°; 16.3 in.

4. One of the base angles of an isosceles triangle measures 72°. The base of the triangle measures 11 centimeters. What is the perimeter of the triangle?

46.6 centimeters

5. Tony is standing at sea level. From his location, the angle of elevation of the top of Blue Mountain is 23°. Staying at sea level, he walks 200 yards toward the mountain. The angle of elevation of the top is now 27°. Find the height of Blue Mountain.

508.6 yards

ESSENTIAL QUESTION

6. How can you use trigonometric ratios to find a side length in a non-right triangle?

Sample answer: If you know another side length and the measures of the angles opposite that side and opposite the unknown side, apply the Law of Sines. If you know the angle opposite the unknown side and the lengths of the other two sides of the triangle, apply the Law of Cosines.

© Houghton Mifflin Harcourt Publishing Company

COMMON CORE	**Common Core Standards**

Lesson	Items	Content Standards	Mathematical Practices
14.1	1	**G-SRT.D.9, G-SRT.D.11**	**MP.4**
14.1	2	**G-SRT.D.11**	**MP.4**
14.2	3	**G-SRT.D.11**	**MP.4**
14.2	4	**G-SRT.D.11**	**MP.4**
14.1	5	**G-SRT.D.11**	**MP.4**

Assessment Readiness

1. You know the two legs of a right triangle. You also know the measure of one of the acute angles of the triangle. Could you use the given law or theorem to find the length of the hypotenuse? Select Yes or No for A–C.

   A. Law of Sines   ● Yes   ○ No

   B. Law of Cosines   ● Yes   ○ No

   C. Pythagorean Theorem   ● Yes   ○ No

2. Consider each statement about finding the measurements of triangles. Choose True or False for each statement.

   A. If you know the measures of the three angles of a triangle, you can find the lengths of the sides.   ○ True   ● False

   B. If you know the lengths of the three sides of a triangle, you can find the measures of the angles.   ● True   ○ False

   C. If you know the measures of the two sides of a triangle and the measure of an angle not included between the two sides, you can solve the triangle.   ● True   ○ False

3. In the figure, O is the center of the circle and G and H are points on the circle. What is the circumference of the circle? Round your answer to the nearest tenth. Explain how you found the answer.

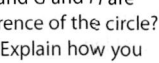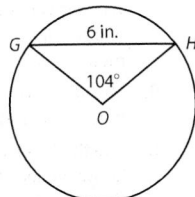

   23.9 inches; sample answer: The radii $\overline{GO}$ and $\overline{HO}$ are

   congruent, so $m\angle G = m\angle H = \frac{1}{2}(180° - 104°) = 38°$.

   By the Law of Sines, $\frac{6}{\sin 104°} = \frac{GO}{\sin 38°}$, so $GO = 3.8$ inches.

   Circumference $= 2\pi r \approx 2(3.14)(3.8) \approx 23.9$ inches.

4. In solving triangle ABC, Dawn found that the cosine of $\angle B$ and the sine of $\angle A$ were both negative. What conclusions can she draw about her solution? Why?

   Sample answer: $\angle B$ is obtuse because any angle with a negative cosine must

   be obtuse. No interior angle of a triangle can have a negative sine, however, so

   she must have made an error in her calculations involving $\angle A$.

MIXED REVIEW
Assessment Readiness

ASSESSMENT AND INTERVENTION

Assign ready-made or customized practice tests to prepare students for high-stakes tests.

ADDITIONAL RESOURCES

Assessment Resources

- Leveled Module Quizzes: Modified, B

AVOID COMMON ERRORS

Item 4   Some students will not know where to begin with this problem. Encourage them to calculate the cosines and sines of a few possible angles of a triangle, and see which come out negative.

COMMON CORE Common Core Standards

Lesson	Items	Content Standards	Mathematical Practices
14.1, 14.2	1*	G-SRT.D.10	MP.2
14.1, 14.2	2	G-SRT.D.10	MP.2
14.1	3*	G-SRT.D.10	MP.6
14.1, 14.2	4	G-SRT.D.10	MP.2

* Item integrates mixed review concepts from previous modules or a previous course.

MIXED REVIEW

Assessment Readiness

ASSESSMENT AND INTERVENTION

Assign ready-made or customized practice tests to prepare students for high-stakes tests.

ADDITIONAL RESOURCES

Assessment Resources

- Leveled Unit Tests: Modified, A, B, C

- Performance Assessment

AVOID COMMON ERRORS

Item 2 Some students will forget which sides correspond with which trigonometric functions. One way to help students remember is the phrase "soh cah toa," which allows them to relate the trigonometric function (for example: *soh* stands for $\sin = \dfrac{\text{opposite}}{\text{hypotenuse}}$) with the sides.

© Houghton Mifflin Harcourt Publishing Company

UNIT 5 MIXED REVIEW

Assessment Readiness

- Online Homework
- Hints and Help
- Extra Practice

1. Given $\triangle JKL$ where $\angle K$ is a right angle, determine which measurements will produce $m\angle J$ to be greater than 45°.
   Select Yes or No for each pair of sides.
   - **A.** $KL = 27$, $JK = 23$ ● Yes ○ No
   - **B.** $KL = 15$, $JK = 32$ ○ Yes ● No
   - **C.** $KL = 10$, $JK = 10$ ○ Yes ● No

2. Using the image provided, which of the following equations could be used to find x?
   Select Yes or No for each equation.
   - **A.** $\sin 40 = \dfrac{x}{13}$ ● Yes ○ No
   - **B.** $\tan 40 = \dfrac{x}{7}$ ● Yes ○ No
   - **C.** $\cos 40 = \dfrac{13}{x}$ ○ Yes ● No

   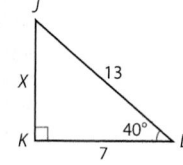

3. Which of the following statements are true?
   Select True or False for each statement.
   - **A.** When given an angle and the opposite leg, you should use cosine to find the measure of the adjacent leg.   ○ True ● False
   - **B.** The values of sine and cosine are always between 0 and 1.   ● True ○ False
   - **C.** Use the inverse sine ratio when you know the length of the leg opposite the required angle and the length of the hypotenuse.   ● True ○ False

4. The following points are graphed on the coordinate plane: $A(-3, 5)$, $B(4, 1)$, and $C(-1, 1)$. Does the given point make $ABCD$ a trapezoid?
   Select Yes or No for ordered pairs A—C.
   - **A.** $D(-2, 3)$ ○ Yes ● No
   - **B.** $D(3, 3)$ ● Yes ○ No
   - **C.** $D(-3, 6)$ ○ Yes ● No

COMMON CORE ## Common Core Standards

Items	Content Standards	Mathematical Practices
1	**G-SRT.C.6**	**MP.5**
2	**G-SRT.C.8**	**MP.5**
3	**G-SRT.C.7**	**MP.6**
4*	**G-GPE.B.4**	**MP.5**
5	**G-SRT.C.6**	**MP.2, MP.7**

* Item integrates mixed review concepts from previous modules or a previous course.

5. Which of the relationships are true?

Select True or False for each statement.

A. $\sin 90° = \cos 90° = \frac{1}{2}$ ○ True ● False

B. $\sin 45° = \cos 45° = \frac{\sqrt{2}}{2}$ ● True ○ False

C. $\sin 60° = \cos 30° = \frac{\sqrt{3}}{2}$ ● True ○ False

D. $\tan \theta < 1$ for $\theta \leq 45°$ ○ True ● False

6. Is the triangle a Pythagorean triple?

Select Yes or No for each set of numbers.

A. $3 - 4 - 5$ ● Yes ○ No

B. $11 - 12 - 13$ ○ Yes ● No

C. $9 - 24 - 25$ ○ Yes ● No

7. Is $\triangle DEF$ a right triangle?

Select True or False for each statement.

A. $D(0, 2), E(-2, 5), F(5, 5)$ ○ True ● False

B. $D(-1, 0), E(-1, -7), F(0, 3)$ ○ True ● False

C. $D(-8, 8), E(-10, -2), F(0, -4)$ ● True ○ False

8. The plans for a new house include a wall with two triangular windows, $\triangle ABC$ and $\triangle A'B'C'$. The vertices of $\triangle ABC$ are $A(-4, 1)$, $B(-1, 1)$, and $C(-1, 5)$. The vertices of $\triangle A'B'C'$ are $A'(-1, -5)$, $B'(-1, -2)$, and $C'(-5, -2)$. The architect wants to give a sequence of rigid motions that maps $\triangle ABC$ to $\triangle A'B'C'$. Provide verbal descriptions and algebraic rules for the appropriate sequence of rigid motions.

Sample answer: Rotate $\triangle ABC$ by $90°$ around the origin, and then

translate the image one unit down. The algebraic rules are

$(x,y) \rightarrow (-y, x)$ followed by $(x,y) \rightarrow (x, y-1)$.

9. Find the side lengths to the nearest hundredth and the angle measures to the nearest degree.

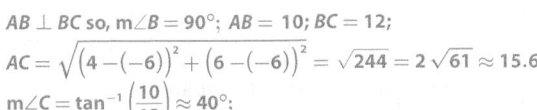

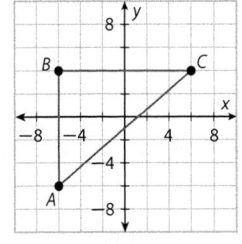

$AB \perp BC$ so, $m\angle B = 90°$; $AB = 10$; $BC = 12$;

$AC = \sqrt{\left(4 - (-6)\right)^2 + \left(6 - (-6)\right)^2} = \sqrt{244} = 2\sqrt{61} \approx 15.6$

$m\angle C = \tan^{-1}\left(\frac{10}{12}\right) \approx 40°$;

$m\angle A$ and $m\angle C$ are complementary so $m\angle A = 90° - 40° = 50°$.

PERFORMANCE TASKS

There are three different levels of performance tasks:

* **Novice:** These are short word problems that require students to apply the math they have learned in straightforward, real-world situations.

** **Apprentice:** These are more involved problems that guide students step-by-step through more complex tasks. These exercises include more complicated reasoning, writing, and open ended elements.

*****Expert:** These are open-ended, nonroutine problems that, instead of stepping the students through, ask them to choose their own methods for solving and justify their answers and reasoning.

COMMON CORE Common Core Standards

Items	Content Standards	Mathematical Practices
6	G-SRT.B.4	MP.2, MP.7
7	G-SRT.B.5	MP.5
8*	G-CO.A.5	MP.2, MP.7
9	G-CO.C.10	MP.1

* Item integrates mixed review concepts from previous modules or a previous course.

Item 10 (2 points) Award the student 1 point for correctly finding the maximum distance of 6.9 feet, and 1 point for the minimum distance of 3.2 feet.

Item 11 (6 points)

3 points for correct distance

3 points for showing work

Item 12 (6 points)

2 points for finding *PN* and *JK*

1 point for recognizing $\angle JKL$ and $\angle PMN$ are congruent

1 point for correct length of fence, rounding up to nearest yard

2 points for correct dollar amount

Performance Tasks

★**10.** A painter is using a ladder to help reach the top of a house. If the house is 12 feet tall and the angle of the ladder needs to be at an angle of at least 60° and no greater than 75° to be safe, how far away should the painter place the ladder from the house? Show your work.

$$\tan(60°) = \frac{12}{x} \qquad \tan(75°) = \frac{12}{x}$$

$$x = \frac{12}{\tan(60°)} \qquad x = \frac{12}{\tan(75°)}$$

$$x \approx 6.9 \qquad\qquad x \approx 3.2$$

The ladder needs to be between 3.2 and 6.9 feet away from the house.

★★**11.** Gerta and Jeremy are talking on their two-way hand-held radios, which have a range of 35 miles. Gerta is sitting in her car on the side of the road as Jeremy drives past. He continues along the straight road for 28 miles, and then makes a right turn onto a straight road, turning through an angle of 100°. How many miles can Jeremy drive along this second road until he is out of range of Gerta's radio? Show your work.

Use the law of cosines.

$$35^2 = 28^2 + x^2 - 2(28)(x)\cos 100°$$

$$441 \approx x^2 + 9.72x$$

$$x^2 + 9.72x - 441 \approx 0$$

$$x \approx \frac{-9.72 \pm \sqrt{(9.72)^2 - 4(-441)}}{2} \approx 16.7 \text{ miles}$$

★★★**12.** Sam is planning to fence his backyard. Every side of the yard except for the side along the house is to be fenced, and fencing costs $3/yd and can only be bought in whole yards. (Note that $m\angle NPM = 28°$, and the side of his yard opposite the house measures 35 yd.) How much will the fencing cost? Explain how you found your answer.

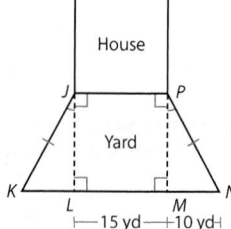

The distance from *K* to *L* is $35 - (15 + 10) = 10$ yd, so triangles *JKL* and *MNP* are congruent. The distance *JK* (and *PN*) is $\frac{10}{\sin 28°} \approx 21.3$ yd. So the total length of fencing needed is $(2)(21.3) + 35 = 77.6$ yd. Because the fencing can only be bought in whole yards, Sam will need to buy 78 yd. The cost is $(78 \text{ yd})(\$3/\text{yd}) = \$234$.

A detective knows what time of day it is based on the angle at which the sun is hitting a man. Suppose a detective is looking at a photograph of a 6-foot-tall man with a shadow that is 3.5 feet long. Find the angle at which the sun was hitting the ground.

$$\tan^{-1}\left(\frac{3.5}{6}\right) \approx 30.26°$$

The sun was hitting the ground at an angle of about 30°.

MATH IN CAREERS

Detective In this Unit Performance Task, students can see how a detective uses mathematics on the job.

For more information about careers in mathematics as well as various mathematics appreciation topics, visit the American Mathematical Society http://www.ams.org

SCORING GUIDES

Task (6 points)

3 points for correctly setting up a trigonometric equation to find an appropriate angle

3 points for finding the correct angle measure

© Houghton Mifflin Harcourt Publishing Company

Properties of Circles

CONTENTS

Unit Pacing Guide

45-Minute Classes

Module 15

DAY 1	DAY 2	DAY 3	DAY 4	DAY 5
Lesson 15.1	Lesson 15.1	Lesson 15.2	Lesson 15.3	Lesson 15.3

DAY 6	DAY 7	DAY 8		
Lesson 15.4	Lesson 15.5	Module Review and Assessment Readiness		

Module 16

DAY 1	DAY 2	DAY 3	DAY 4
Lesson 16.1	Lesson 16.2	Lesson 16.3	Module Review and Assessment Readiness

Module 17

DAY 1	DAY 2	DAY 3	DAY 4	DAY 5
Lesson 17.1	Lesson 17.1	Lesson 17.2	Lesson 17.2	Module Review and Assessment Readiness

DAY 6				
Unit Review and Assessment Readiness				

90-Minute Classes

Module 15

DAY 1	DAY 2	DAY 3	DAY 4
Lesson 15.1	Lesson 15.2	Lesson 15.3	Lesson 15.5
	Lesson 15.3	Lesson 15.4	Module Review and Assessment Readiness

Module 16

DAY 1	DAY 2
Lesson 16.1	Lesson 16.3
Lesson 16.2	Unit Review and Assessment Readiness

Module 17

DAY 1	DAY 2	DAY 3
Lesson 17.1	Lesson 17.2	Module Review and Assessment Readiness
		Unit Review and Assessment Readiness

Program Resources

PLAN

HMH Teacher App

Access a full suite of teacher resources online and offline on a variety of devices. Plan present, and manage classes, assignments, and activities.

ePlanner
Easily plan your classes, create and view assignments, and access all program resources with your online, customizable planning tool.

Professional Development Videos

Authors Juli Dixon and Matt Larson model successful teaching practices and strategies in actual classroom settings.

QR Codes
Scan with your smart phone to jump directly from your print book to online videos and other resources.

Teacher's Edition

Support students with point-of-use Questioning Strategies, teaching tips, resources for differentiated instruction, additional activities, and more.

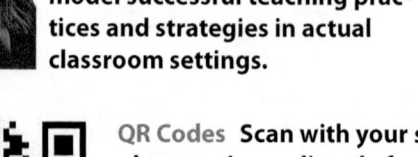

ENGAGE AND EXPLORE

Real-World Videos **Engage students with interesting and relevant applications of the mathematical content of each module.**

Explore Activities

Students interactively explore new concepts using a variety of tools and approaches.

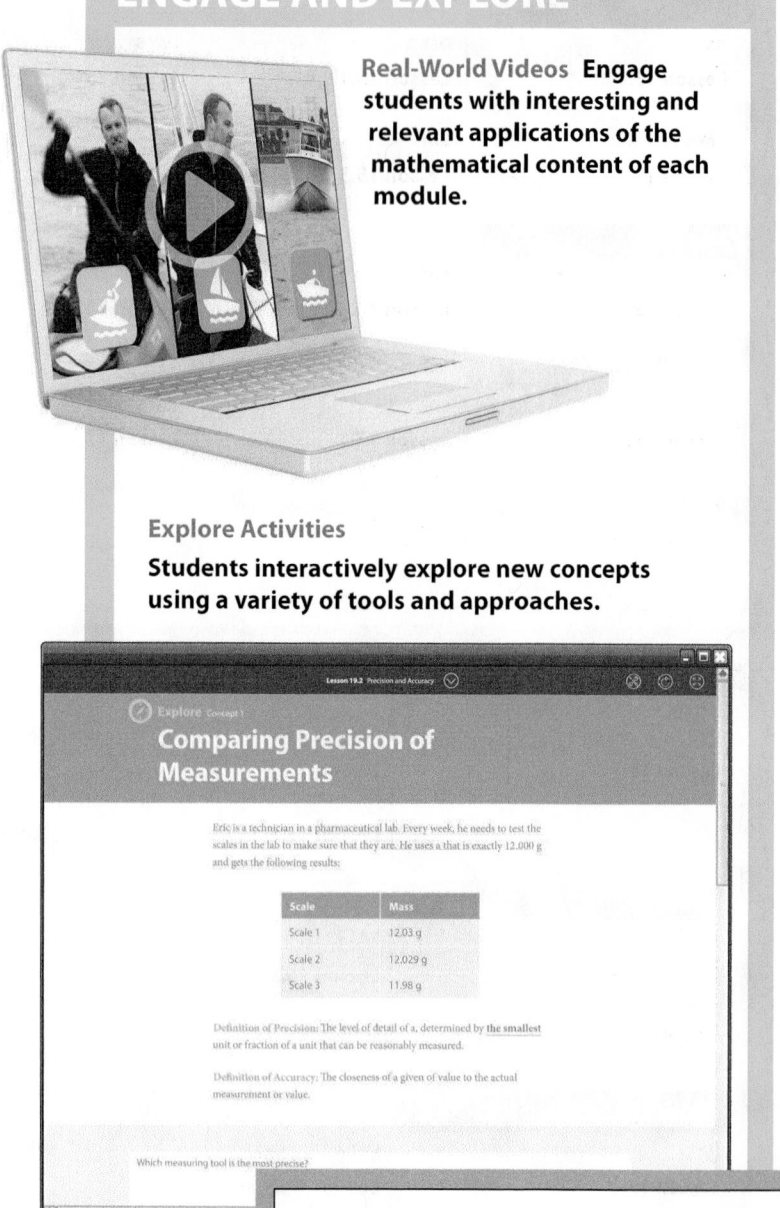

Lesson 19.2 Precision and Accuracy

Explore Concept 1
Comparing Precision of Measurements

Eric is a technician in a pharmaceutical lab. Every week, he needs to test the scales in the lab to make sure that they are. He uses a that is exactly 12.000 g and gets the following results:

Scale	Mass
Scale 1	12.03 g
Scale 2	12.029 g
Scale 3	11.98 g

Definition of Precision: The level of detail of a, determined by the smallest unit or fraction of a unit that can be reasonably measured.

Definition of Accuracy: The closeness of a given of value to the actual measurement or value.

Which measuring tool is the most precise?

Name _____ Class _____ Date _____

22.2 Solving Equations by Completing the Square

Essential Question: How can you use completing the square to solve a quadratic equation?

Resource Locker

Explore Modeling Completing the Square

You can use algebra tiles to model a perfect square trinomial.

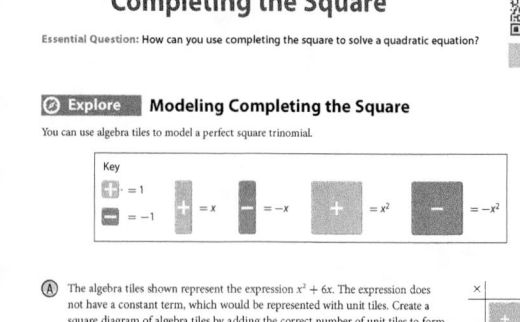

Key

(A) The algebra tiles shown represent the expression $x^2 + 6x$. The expression does not have a constant term, which would be represented with unit tiles. Create a square diagram of algebra tiles by adding the correct number of unit tiles to form a square.

(B) How many unit tiles were added to the expression? 9

(C) Write the trinomial represented by the algebra tiles for the complete square.

$1\ x^2 + 6\ x + 9$

(D) It should be easily recognized that the trinomial $1\ x^2 + 6\ x + 9$ is an example of

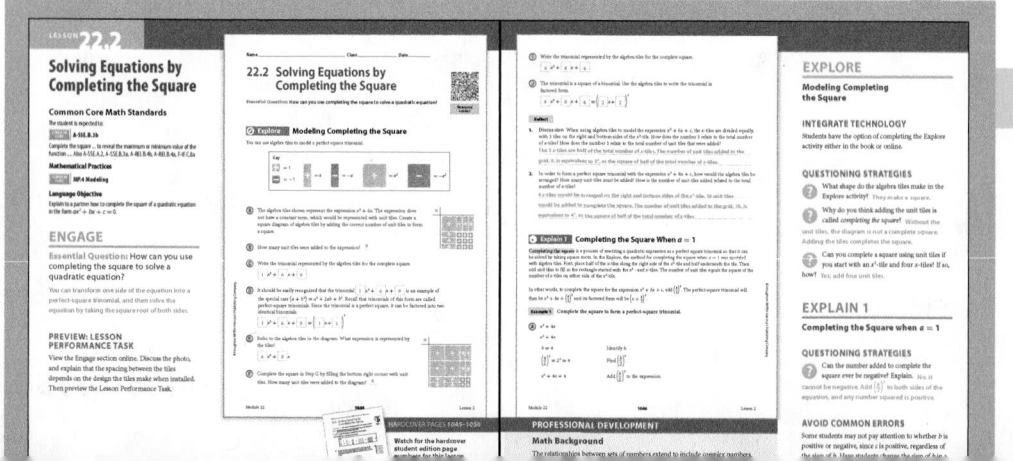

TEACH

Math On the Spot video tutorials, featuring program author Dr. Edward Burger, accompany every example in the textbook and give students step-by-step instructions and explanations of key math concepts.

Interactive Teacher Edition

Customize and present course materials with collaborative activities and integrated formative assessment.

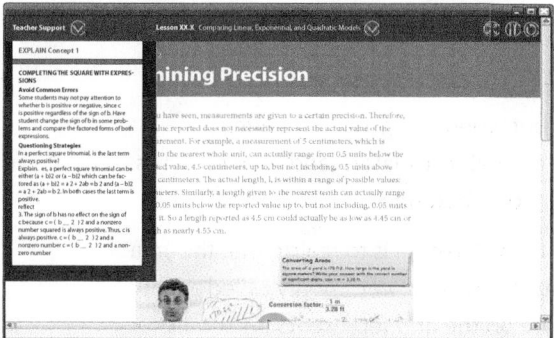

Differentiated Instruction Resources

Support all learners with Differentiated Instruction Resources, including

- **Leveled Practice and Problem Solving**
- **Reading Strategies**
- **Success for English Learners**
- **Challenge**

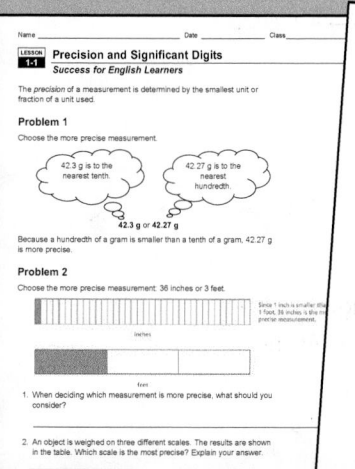

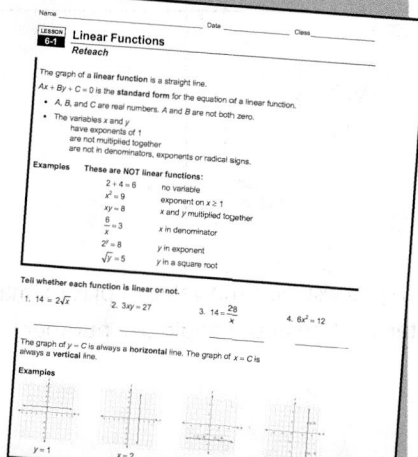

ASSESSMENT AND INTERVENTION

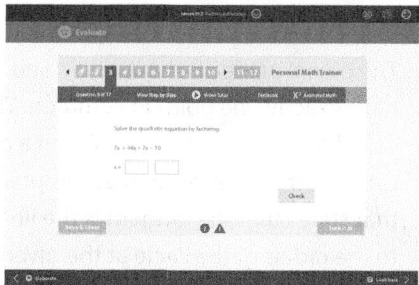

The **Personal Math Trainer** provides online practice, homework, assessments, and intervention. Monitor student progress through reports and alerts.

Create and customize assignments aligned to specific lessons or Common Core standards.

- **Practice** – With dynamic items and assignments, students get unlimited practice on key concepts supported by guided examples, step-by-step solutions, and video tutorials.

- **Assessments** – Choose from course assignments or customize your own based on course content, Common Core standards, difficulty levels, and more.

- **Homework** – Students can complete online homework with a wide variety of problem types, including the ability to enter expressions, equations, and graphs. Let the system automatically grade homework, so you can focus where your students need help the most!

- **Intervention** – Let the Personal Math Trainer automatically prescribe a targeted, personalized intervention path for your students.

Focus on Higher Order Thinking

Raise the bar with homework and practice that incorporates higher-order thinking and mathematical practices in every lesson.

Assessment Readiness

Prepare students for success on high stakes tests for Geometry with practice at every module and unit

Assessment Resources

Tailor assessments and response to intervention to meet the needs of all your classes and students, including

- Leveled Module Quizzes
- Leveled Unit Tests
- Unit Performance Tasks
- Placement, Diagnostic, and Quarterly Benchmark Tests
- Tier 1, Tier 2, and Tier 3 Resources

Math Background

Angles and Segments in Circles   COMMON CORE G-C.A.2

LESSONS 15.1 to 15.5

The Inscribed Angle Theorem states that the measure of an inscribed angle is half the measure of its intercepted arc. The theorem has several interesting corollaries, including the fact that an inscribed angle subtends a semicircle if and only if the angle is a right angle.

Most theorems related to circles that appear here were known to the mathematicians of antiquity. In fact, Euclid devoted Book III of his *Elements* to definitions and propositions about circles. One of the first definitions in *Elements* states that a straight line touches a circle if the line meets the circle but does not cut it. In modern terms, such a line is called a *tangent* to the circle, with the word *tangent* originating from the Latin *tangere*, which means *to touch*.

The essential idea is that a circle and a tangent to the circle have exactly one point in common. This common point is called *the point of tangency*. Given a point on a circle, you can construct the tangent at this point by the theorem that states that the tangent is the line that is perpendicular to the radius of the circle at the given point. This is the only tangent line by the contrapositive of the theorem that states that if a line is tangent to a circle, then it is perpendicular to the radius drawn to the point of tangency.

The theorems that are presented here are sometimes known as *power theorems*. In particular, the Chord-Chord Product Theorem, the Secant-Secant Product Theorem, and the Secant-Tangent Product Theorem may be stated in an all-inclusive general form called the Power of a Point Theorem.

The Power of a Point Theorem: Given a circle, a point P not on the circle, and two lines through P that intersect the circle at points A and B and at points C and D, respectively, $AP \cdot BP = CP \cdot DP$.

As shown in the figures, P may lie in the interior or exterior of the circle. In the case where a line through P is tangent to the circle, the two points of intersection coincide and the theorem reduces to the Secant-Tangent Product Theorem.

Circumference and Area of a Circle   COMMON CORE G-GMD.A.1

LESSON 16.1

The ratio of the circumference to the diameter of any circle is a constant. Ancient Egyptian, Babylonian, and Greek geometers all recognized that this constant ratio is a little greater than 3, with the Babylonians settling on the approximation $3\frac{1}{8}$, or 3.125. In 1706, the mathematician William Jones was the first to represent the constant by the Greek letter pi (π). Pi is an irrational number, which means that its decimal representation neither terminates nor repeats. The first 20 digits to the right of the decimal point are shown below.

3.14159265358979323846...

For most practical purposes, 3.14 is a satisfactory approximation of pi, but whenever possible, students should use the π key on their calculators, and then round as needed in the last step of the solution.

One way to visualize the value of pi is to realize that the area of a circle with a radius of one unit (commonly called a unit circle) is pi. Each square on the grid represents 0.1 square unit. You can count to find there are about 314 squares inside the circle.

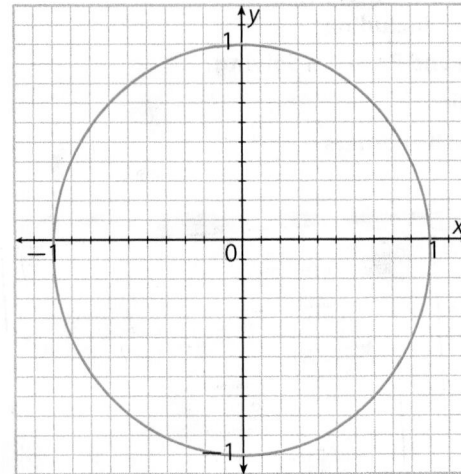

Another way to visualize the value of pi is to imagine a circle of diameter 1 sitting at the origin of a number line. As the circle rolls to the right, the point at the bottom of the circle that was originally touching the number line will next touch the number line again at π.

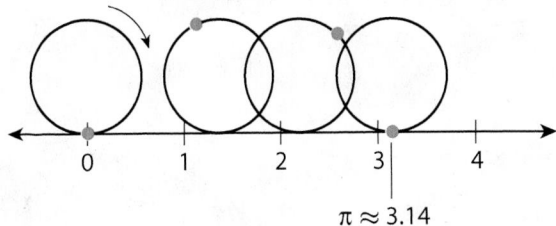

$\pi \approx 3.14$

Arc Length and Radian Measure COMMON CORE G-C.B.5

LESSON 16.1

In the most general terms, an *arc* is *any smooth curve that joins two points*. In the context of circles, an *arc* is *a continuous portion of a circle*. An arc of a circle is closely related to the central angle that is defined by the endpoints of the arc and the center of the circle. Students should be aware that most of the theorems about arcs have proofs that depend on working back and forth between properties of arcs and properties of angles.

The Arc Addition Postulate states that the measure of an arc formed by two adjacent arcs is the sum of the measures of the two adjacent arcs. This postulate is analogous to the Angle Addition Postulate. In fact, the Arc Addition Postulate can be stated as a theorem, with its proof drawing on the Angle Addition Postulate. However, a rigorous proof is somewhat tedious in that it requires several cases to account for various combinations of major arcs, minor arcs, and semicircles. For this reason, the principle is simply presented as a postulate in this text.

A *radian* is a unit of angle measure that may be defined as follows:

In a unit circle, a central angle that measures 1 radian intercepts an arc with a length of 1 unit. The circumference of the unit circle is 2π. Thus, 2π radians corresponds to 360°. This basic relationship, combined with proportional reasoning, is the key to converting between degrees and radians.

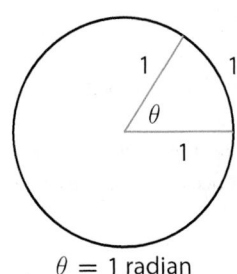

$\theta = 1$ radian

Students may wonder why radians are needed at all. They should be aware that radians give rise to more natural relationships than do degrees. For example, in a circle of radius r, the arc length s intercepted by a central angle θ is given by $s = r\theta$, but this simple formula holds only when θ is measured in radians. Students will see additional examples in calculus courses, where all angles are measured in radians.

Sector Area COMMON CORE G-C.B.5

LESSON 16.3

The underlying idea of this lesson is proportionality. Students should realize that they can use proportional reasoning to find areas of sectors and arc lengths. They can also use proportionality to derive the relevant formulas if they forget them. For example, to derive the formula for the area of a sector of a circle, set up a proportion as shown.

$$\frac{\text{Area of sector}}{\text{Area of circle}} = \frac{\text{Measure of central angle}}{360°}$$

$$\frac{A}{\pi r^2} = \frac{m°}{360°}$$

Solving the proportion for A gives $A = \pi r^2 \left(\frac{m°}{360°}\right)$. Similar reasoning yields the formula for the length of an arc.

Equation of a Circle COMMON CORE G-GPE.A.1

LESSON 17.1

The equation of a circle with center (h, k) and radius r is $(x - h)^2 + (y - k)^2 = r^2$. This equation follows immediately from the Distance Formula.

In addition, squaring and simplifying show that every circle is the graph of an equation of the form $x^2 + y^2 + Ax + By + C = 0$.

Given an equation in this form, the center and radius of the circle may be found by completing the square.

The equation of a circle easily generalizes to three dimensions to give the equation of a sphere. In particular, the equation of a sphere with center (h, j, k) and radius r is $(x - h)^2 + (y - j)^2 + (z - k)^2 = r^2$. This equation may be derived directly from the Distance Formula in three dimensions.

Properties of Circles

MATH IN CAREERS
Unit Activity Preview

After completing this unit, students will complete a Math in Careers task by using knowledge of the properties of circles in the context of an astronomical event. Critical skills include modeling real-world situations and applying theorems about tangents, secants, and arc measures in a circle.

For more information about careers in mathematics as well as various mathematics appreciation topics, visit The American Mathematical Society at http://www.ams.org.

UNIT 6

Properties of Circles

MODULE 15
Angles and Segments in Circles

MODULE 16
Arc Length and Sector Area

MODULE 17
Equations of Circles and Parabolas

MATH IN CAREERS

Astronomer An astronomer uses advanced technology and mathematics to study outer space. Astronomers apply mathematics to study the positions, movement, and energy of celestial objects.

If you're interested in a career as an astronomer, you should study these mathematical subjects:
- Algebra
- Geometry
- Trigonometry
- Calculus

Research other careers that require the use of physics to understand real-world scenarios. See the related Career Activity at the end of this unit.

Unit 6   **775**

TRACKING YOUR LEARNING PROGRESSION

Before	In this Unit	After
Students understand: • using tangent, sine, and cosine to find measures in right triangles • using Pythagorean triples to solve right triangles	Students will learn about: • central and inscribed angles • chords, secants, tangent lines, and arcs • segment lengths in circles • angles formed by intersecting lines of a circle • formulas for circumference and area of a circle • area of a sector • the equation of a circle	Students will study: • volumes of 3-D figures • cross sections of solids • surface area of 3-D figures • perimeter and area for composite figures • scale factor • calculating densities • modeling to meet constraints

Reading Start-Up

Visualize Vocabulary

Use the ✔ words to complete the sequence diagram.

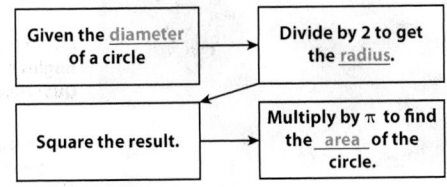

Given the <u>diameter</u> of a circle	Divide by 2 to get the <u>radius</u>.
Square the result.	Multiply by π to find the <u>area</u> of the circle.

Understand Vocabulary

Complete the sentences using the preview words.

1. An angle with a vertex on a circle formed by two rays that intersect other points on the circle is called a(n) _____<u>inscribed angle</u>_____.

2. A radius of a circle is perpendicular to a tangent line at _____<u>the point of tangency</u>_____.

3. A _____<u>chord</u>_____ of a circle is a line segment with both endpoints on the circle.

Active Reading

Four-Corner Fold Create a Four-Corner Fold with flaps for segments, angles, arcs, and sectors. Add relevant vocabulary terms while reading the modules. Emphasize using the written words when discussing these topics with teachers and classmates.

© Houghton Mifflin Harcourt Publishing Company

Vocabulary

Review Words

✔ area (*área*)
✔ circumference (*circunferencia*)
✔ diameter (*diámetro*)
✔ perpendicular (*perpendicular*)
✔ radius (*radio*)
✔ vertical angles (*ángulos verticales*)

Preview Words

adjacent arcs (*arcos adyacentes*)
arc (*arco*)
arc length (*longitud de arco*)
central angle (*ángulo central*)
chord (*acorde*)
circumscribed (*circunscrito*)
inscribed angle (*ángulo apuntado*)
point of tangency (*punto de tangencia*)
radian measure (*radianes*)
secant (*secante*)
sector (*sector*)
semicircle (*semicírculo*)
tangent (*tangente*)

Reading Start Up

Have students complete the activities on this page by working alone or with others.

VISUALIZE VOCABULARY

The sequence diagram helps students review vocabulary associated with circles. If time allows, review definitions and connections among the remaining terms.

UNDERSTAND VOCABULARY

Use the following explanations to help students learn the preview words.

An angle whose vertex is the center of a circle is a **central angle**. An angle whose vertex is on a circle and whose side contains chords of the circle is an **inscribed angle**. A **chord** is a segment with both endpoints on the circle. A **secant** is a line that intersects a circle at two points. A **tangent** is a line that intersects a circle at exactly one point. An **arc** is an unbroken part of a circle consisting of two points on the circle and all the points on the circle between them.

ACTIVE READING

Students can use these reading and note-taking strategies to help them organize and understand the new concepts and vocabulary. Encourage students to use the new vocabulary and to be as specific as possible to create four-corner folds that are illustrated, descriptive, and helpful.

ADDITIONAL RESOURCES

Differentiated Instruction

- Reading Strategies

MODULE 15

Angles and Segments in Circles

ESSENTIAL QUESTION:

Answer: Angles and segments in circles can be used to solve real-world problems wherever linear and circular shapes appear, such as in clockwork or machinery.

PROFESSIONAL DEVELOPMENT VIDEO

Professional Development Video

Learn effective ways of integrating technology into your classroom to meet a variety of different needs.

Professional
Development
my.hrw.com

MODULE
15

Angles and Segments in Circles

Essential Question: How can you use angles and segments in circles to solve real-world problems?

© Houghton Mifflin Harcourt Publishing Company • Image Credits: ©Dolas/ iStockPhoto.com

REAL WORLD VIDEO
Check out how package designers make use of the mathematics of angles and segments to design efficient and attractive packages and containers.

MODULE PERFORMANCE TASK PREVIEW

How Many Marbles Will Fit?

In this module, you will be challenged to determine the size of the largest marble that can fit into a triangular package. How can an understanding of segment and angle relationships in circles help you to solve this problem? Don't "lose your marbles" before you get a chance to find out!

Module 15   **777**

DIGITAL TEACHER EDITION

Access a full suite of teaching resources when and where you need them:

- Access content online or offline
- Customize lessons to share with your class
- Communicate with your students in real-time
- View student grades and data instantly to target your instruction where it is needed most

PERSONAL MATH TRAINER
Assessment and Intervention

Assign automatically graded homework, quizzes, tests, and intervention activities. Prepare your students with updated, Common Core-aligned practice tests.

Are(YOU)Ready?

Complete these exercises to review skills you will need for this module.

Angle Relationships

- Online Homework
- Hints and Help
- Extra Practice

Example 1   Find m∠ABD given that m∠CBE = 40° and the angles are formed by the intersection of the lines $\overleftrightarrow{AC}$ and $\overleftrightarrow{DE}$ at point m.

When two lines intersect, they form two pairs of vertical angles at their intersection. Note that ∠ABD and ∠CBE are vertical angles and ∠DBC and ∠ABE are vertical angles.

∠ABD ≅ ∠CBE   Theorem: Vertical Angles are Congruent

m∠ABD = m∠CBE = 40°   Definition of congruence of angles

Find the measure of the complementary or supplementary angle.

1. Complementary to 40°   50°
2. Complementary to 67°   23°
3. Supplementary to 80°   100°
4. Supplementary to 65°   115°

Use the image to find the angles or their measures assuming $\overleftrightarrow{CD}$ is parallel to $\overleftrightarrow{EF}$.

5. All angles congruent to ∠APD
   ∠AQF, ∠BQE, ∠BPC

6. m∠BPD when m∠BQE = 165°
   15°

7. m∠APG when m∠DPG = 55° and m∠BPC = 110°
   55°

8. All angles congruent to ∠GPC
   None

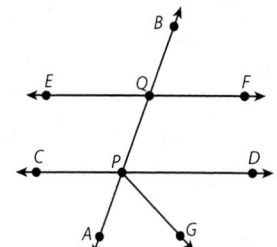

Determine whether the lines $\overleftrightarrow{CD}$ and $\overleftrightarrow{EF}$ in the image are parallel for the given angle measures.

9. m∠BPG = 135°, m∠GPC = 95°, and m∠BQF = 110°
   The lines are not parallel.

10. m∠BPD = 35°, m∠APG = 115°, and m∠EQA = 35°
    The lines are parallel.

Are You Ready?

ASSESS READINESS

Use the assessment on this page to determine if students need strategic or intensive intervention for the module's prerequisite skills.

ASSESSMENT AND INTERVENTION

TIER 1, TIER 2, TIER 3 SKILLS

Personal Math Trainer will automatically create a standards-based, personalized intervention assignment for your students, targeting each student's individual needs!

ADDITIONAL RESOURCES

See the table below for a full list of intervention resources available for this module.

Response to Intervention Resources also includes:

- Tier 2 Skill Pre-Tests for each Module
- Tier 2 Skill Post-Tests for each skill

Response to Intervention			Differentiated Instruction
Tier 1 Lesson Intervention Worksheets	**Tier 2** Strategic Intervention Skills Intervention Worksheets	**Tier 3** Intensive Intervention Worksheets available online	
Reteach 15.1 Reteach 15.2 Reteach 15.3 Reteach 15.4 Reteach 15.5	2 Angle Relationships 3 Angle Theorems for Triangles 13 Parallelograms	Building Block Skills 7, 8, 15, 16, 48, 49, 53, 56, 66, 74, 95, 98, 102, 104	Challenge worksheets Extend the Math Lesson Activities in TE

Central Angles and Inscribed Angles

Common Core Math Standards

The student is expected to:

 G-C.A.2

Identify and describe relationships among inscribed angles, radii, and chords.

Mathematical Practices

 MP.2 Reasoning

Language Objective

Work with a partner to compare and contrast central angles and inscribed angles.

ENGAGE

Essential Question: How can you determine the measures of central and inscribed angles of a circle?

The measure of an inscribed angle is half the measure of its intercepted arc. The measure of the arc is equal to the measure of its central angle (for minor arcs) or 360° minus the measure of its central angle (for major arcs).

PREVIEW: LESSON PERFORMANCE TASK

View the Engage section online. Discuss the photograph. Ask students to describe the apparent shape of the theater and to describe possible advantages and disadvantages of this shape compared with other designs. Then preview the Lesson Performance Task.

Name_____ Class_____ Date_____

15.1 Central Angles and Inscribed Angles

Essential Question: How can you determine the measures of central angles and inscribed angles of a circle?

Resource Locker

⊘ Explore Investigating Central Angles and Inscribed Angles

A **chord** is a segment whose endpoints lie on a circle.

A **central angle** is an angle less than 180° whose vertex lies at the center of a circle.

An **inscribed angle** is an angle whose vertex lies on a circle and whose sides contain chords of the circle.

The diagram shows two examples of an inscribed angle and the corresponding central angle.

Chords
$\overline{AB}$ and $\overline{BD}$
Central Angle
∠ACD
Inscribed Angle
∠ABD

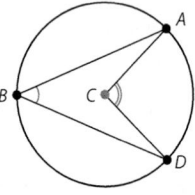

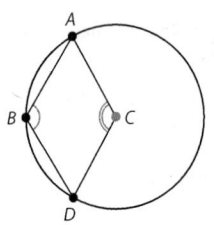

(A) Use a compass to draw a circle. Label the center C.

(B) Use a straightedge to draw an acute inscribed angle on your circle from Step A. Label the angle as ∠DEF.

Check students' drawings.

(C) Use a straightedge to draw the corresponding central angle, ∠DCF.

Check students' drawings.

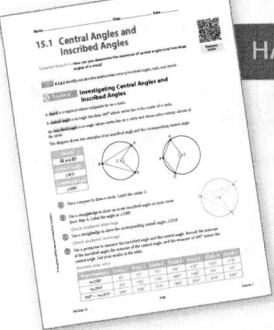

(D) Use a protractor to measure the inscribed angle and the central angle. Record the measure of the inscribed angle, the measure of the central angle, and the measure of 360° minus the central angle. List your results in the table.

Answers may vary.

Angle Measure	Circle C	Circle 2	Circle 3	Circle 4	Circle 5	Circle 6	Circle 7
m∠DEF	32°	51°	75°	90°	127°	155°	173°
m∠DCF	64°	102°	150°	180°	106°	50°	14°
360° − m∠DCF	296°	258°	210°	180°	254°	310°	346°

© Houghton Mifflin Harcourt Publishing Company

HARDCOVER PAGES 659–668

Turn to these pages to find this lesson in the hardcover student edition.

(E) Repeat Steps A-D six more times. Examine a variety of inscribed angles (two more acute, one right, and three obtuse). Record your results in the table in Step D.

Answers may vary. Possible answers are given.

1. Examine the values in the first and second rows of the table. Is there a mathematical relationship that exists for some or all of the values? Make a conjecture that summarizes your observation.
   For inscribed angles with measures less than or equal to 90°, the measure of the inscribed
   angle is equal to half the measure of the corresponding central angle.

2. Examine the values in the first and third rows of the table. Is there a mathematical relationship that exists for some or all of the values? Make a conjecture that summarizes your observation.
   For inscribed angles with measures greater than or equal to 90°, the measure of the
   inscribed angle is equal to half the difference between 360° and the measure of the
   corresponding central angle.

✏ Explain 1   Understanding Arcs and Arc Measure

An **arc** is a continuous portion of a circle consisting of two points (called the endpoints of the arc) and all the points on the circle between them.

Arc	Measure	Figure
A **minor arc** is an arc whose points are on or in the interior of a corresponding central angle.	The measure of a minor arc is equal to the measure of the central angle. $$m\widehat{AB} = m\angle ACB$$	
A **major arc** is an arc whose points are on or in the exterior of a corresponding central angle.	The measure of a major arc is equal to 360° minus the measure of the central angle. $$m\widehat{ADB} = 360° - m\angle ACB$$	
A **semicircle** is an arc whose endpoints are the endpoints of a diameter.	The measure of a semicircle is 180°.	

© Houghton Mifflin Harcourt Publishing Company

PROFESSIONAL DEVELOPMENT

Learning Progressions

In Unit 6, students investigate circles. This first lesson introduces key vocabulary that students should be able to recall to help them continue their exploration of the properties of circles. Students will discover important facts about relationships between central and inscribed angles and their arc lengths. Theorems in later lessons build upon these ideas. The connection between central angles and arcs is the foundation of students' continued work with circles, especially as they investigate angles in inscribed quadrilaterals, circumscribed angles, and other angle relationships in circles in the other lessons in this module.

EXPLORE

Investigating Central Angles and Inscribed Angles

INTEGRATE TECHNOLOGY

Students have the option of doing the Explore activity either in the book or online.

QUESTIONING STRATEGIES

? How can you tell whether an angle in a circle is a central angle or an inscribed angle? **A central angle has its vertex at the center and rays that are radii. An inscribed angle has its vertex on the circle and rays that are chords.**

? Is it possible for multiple inscribed angles to have the same associated central angle? Explain. **Yes; given two points on a circle, only one central angle can be drawn, but different inscribed angles can be drawn by placing the vertex point anywhere on the circle. Each of these inscribed angles has the same associated central angle.**

EXPLAIN 1

Understanding Arcs and Arc Measure

INTEGRATE MATHEMATICAL PRACTICES
Focus on Math Connections

MP.1 Arcs are measured in the same units as the angles that intercept them—degrees. Students may notice that an arc length is part of the circumference and can be measured using units of length. This relationship can be used to find arc length in standard units.

Adjacent arcs are arcs of the same circle that intersect in exactly one point. $\overset{\frown}{DE}$ and $\overset{\frown}{EF}$ are adjacent arcs.

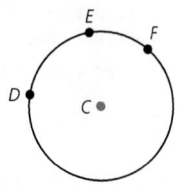

Arc Addition Postulate

The measure of an arc formed by two adjacent arcs is the sum of the measures of the two arcs.

$m\overset{\frown}{ADB} = m\overset{\frown}{AD} + m\overset{\frown}{DB}$

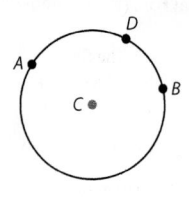

Example 1

(A) If $m\angle BCD = 18°$ and $m\overset{\frown}{EF} = 33°$, determine $m\overset{\frown}{ABD}$ using the appropriate theorems and postulates. $\overleftrightarrow{AF}$ and $\overleftrightarrow{BE}$ intersect at Point C.

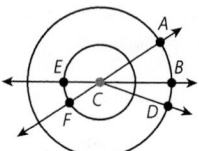

If $m\overset{\frown}{EF} = 33°$, then $m\angle ECF = 33°$. If $m\angle ECF = 33°$, then $m\angle ACB = 33°$ by the Vertical Angles Theorem. If $m\angle ACB = 33°$ and $m\angle BCD = 18°$, then $m\overset{\frown}{AB} = 33°$ and $m\overset{\frown}{BD} = 18°$. By the Arc Addition Postulate, $m\overset{\frown}{ABD} = m\overset{\frown}{AB} + m\overset{\frown}{BD}$, and so $m\overset{\frown}{ABD} = 51°$.

(B) If $m\overset{\frown}{JK} = 27°$, determine $m\overset{\frown}{NP}$ using the appropriate theorems and postulates. $\overleftrightarrow{MK}$ and $\overrightarrow{NJ}$ intersect at Point C.

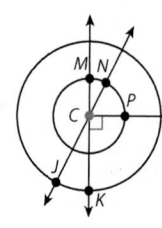

If $m\overset{\frown}{JK} = 27°$, then $m\angle JCK = 27°$. If $m\angle JCK = 27°$, then

$m\angle$ ⟦MCN⟧ $= 27°$ by the ⟦Vertical Angles Theorem⟧.

If $m\angle MCN = 27°$ and $m\angle MCP =$ ⟦90⟧°, then $m\overset{\frown}{MN} = 27°$

and $m\overset{\frown}{MNP} =$ ⟦90⟧°. By the ⟦Arc Addition Postulate⟧,

$m\overset{\frown}{MNP} = m\overset{\frown}{MN} + m\overset{\frown}{NP}$, and so $m\overset{\frown}{NP} = m$ ⟦MNP⟧ $- m\overset{\frown}{MN} =$ ⟦63⟧°

COLLABORATIVE LEARNING

Small Group Activity

Ask each group to choose an angle measure that is a fraction of the whole circle (for example, $\frac{1}{3}$ or $\frac{1}{8}$). Have students use a compass and a protractor to draw the circle with a central angle of the required number of degrees (for example, 120° or 45°). Then ask students to draw an inscribed angle with the same central angle. As students share their drawings, have them give the arc measure, the central angle measure, or the inscribed angle measure. Ask the class to find the other measures.

3. The minute hand of a clock sweeps out an arc as time moves forward. From 3:10 p.m. to 3:30 p.m., what is the measure of this arc? Explain your reasoning.

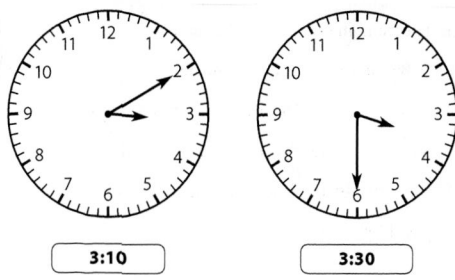

A complete rotation corresponds to 60 minutes, so 20 minutes is $\frac{1}{3}$ of a complete rotation.

Since $\frac{1}{3} \times 360° = 120°$, the measure of the arc is 120°.

4. If $m\widehat{EF} = 45°$ and $m\angle ACD = 56°$, determine $m\widehat{BD}$ using the appropriate theorems and postulates. $\overleftrightarrow{AE}$, $\overleftrightarrow{BF}$, and $\overleftrightarrow{DC}$ intersect at Point C.

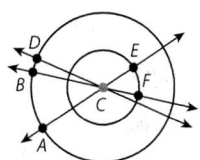

If $m\widehat{EF} = 45°$, then $m\angle ECF = 45°$. If $m\angle ECF = 45°$, then $m\angle ACB = 45°$ by the Vertical

Angles Theorem. If then $m\angle ACB = 45°$ and $m\angle ACD = 56°$, then $m\widehat{AB} = 45°$ and $m\widehat{ABD} =$

56°. By the Arc Addition Postulate, $m\widehat{ABD} = m\widehat{AB} + m\widehat{BD}$, and so $m\widehat{BD} = 11°$.

⊘ Explain 2 Using the Inscribed Angle Theorem

In the Explore you looked at the relationship between central angles and inscribed angles. Those results, combined with the definitions of arc measure, lead to the following theorem about inscribed angles and their *intercepted arcs*. An **intercepted arc** consists of endpoints that lie on the sides of an inscribed angle and all the points of the circle between them.

Inscribed Angle Theorem

The measure of an inscribed angle is equal to half the measure of its intercepted arc.

$$m\angle ADB = \frac{1}{2}m\widehat{AB}$$

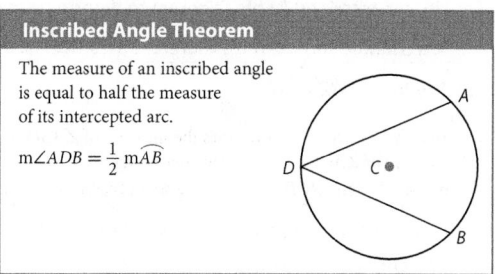

? How do you distinguish between the minor and major arc of a central angle? Why is this important? The minor arc has its points on the interior of the central angle while the major arc has its points on the exterior. The measures of the arcs are different, although both depend on the central angle.

EXPLAIN 2

Using the Inscribed Angle Theorem

QUESTIONING STRATEGIES

? What is the arc measure of any semicircle? Why? 180°; because a semicircle always has a central angle of 180°; the diameter intercepts half a circle and, by the Inscribed Angle Theorem, it is half the measure of a full circle, which has a measure of 360°.

DIFFERENTIATE INSTRUCTION

Cognitive Strategies

Draw a circle with diameter $\overline{AB}$ and radius $\overline{AC}$. Use colored pens to emphasize the minor and major arcs on the circle. Explain that a semicircle measures 180°. Since a minor arc is shorter than a semicircle, it must have a measure that is less than 180°. A major arc is longer than a semicircle, so it must have a measure that is more than 180°.

Example 2 Use the Inscribed Angle Theorem to find inscribed angle measures.

Ⓐ Determine $m\widehat{DE}$, $m\widehat{BD}$, $m\angle DAB$, and $m\angle ADE$ using the appropriate theorems and postulates.

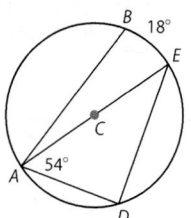

By the Inscribed Angle Theorem, $m\angle DAE = \frac{1}{2}m\widehat{DE}$, and so $m\widehat{DE} = 2 \times 54° = 108°$. By the Arc Addition Postulate, $m\widehat{BD} = m\widehat{BE} + m\widehat{ED} = 18° + 108° = 126°$. By the Inscribed Angle Theorem, $m\angle DAB = \frac{1}{2}m\widehat{BD} = \frac{1}{2} \times 126° = 63°$. Note that $\widehat{ABE}$ is a semicircle, and so $m\widehat{ABE} = 180°$. By the Inscribed Angle Theorem, $m\angle ADE = \frac{1}{2}m\widehat{ABE} = \frac{1}{2} \times 180° = 90°$.

Ⓑ Determine $m\widehat{WX}$, $m\widehat{XZ}$, $m\angle XWZ$, and $m\angle WXZ$ using the appropriate theorems and postulates.

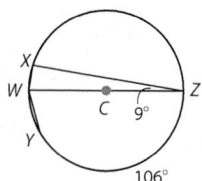

By the Inscribed Angle Theorem, $m\angle WZX = \boxed{\frac{1}{2}}\, m\widehat{WX}$, and so $m\widehat{WX} = 2 \times 9° = \boxed{18°}$. Note that $\widehat{WXZ}$ is a $\underline{\text{semicircle}}$ and, therefore, $m\widehat{WXZ} = 180°$. By the $\underline{\text{Arc Addition Postulate}}$, $m\widehat{WXZ} = m\widehat{WX} + m\widehat{XZ}$ and then $m\widehat{XZ} = 180° - 18° = \boxed{162°}$

By the $\underline{\text{Inscribed Angle Theorem}}$, $m\angle XWZ = \frac{1}{2}m\widehat{XZ} = \frac{1}{2} \times 162° = 81°$.

Note that $\boxed{\widehat{WYZ}}$ is a semicircle, and so $m\widehat{WYZ} = \boxed{180°}$. By the Inscribed Angle Theorem, $m\angle WXZ = \frac{1}{2}m\boxed{\widehat{WYZ}} = \frac{1}{2} \times \boxed{180°} = \boxed{90°}$.

Reflect

5. **Discussion** Explain an alternative method for determining $m\angle\widehat{XZ}$ in Example 2B.
   Use the Inscribed Angle Theorem to determine $m\angle WXZ = 90°$. The angle measures
   in a triangle sum to 180°, therefore $m\angle XWZ = 81°$ and by the Inscribed Angles
   Theorem, $m\widehat{XZ} = 162°$.

6. **Justify Reasoning** How does the measure of $\angle ABD$ compare to the measure of $\angle ACD$? Explain your reasoning.
   $m\angle ABD = m\angle ACD$; Each angle intercepts $\widehat{AD}$. Since the measure
   of each angle is equal to half the measure of $\widehat{AD}$, the measures
   of $\angle ABD$ and $\angle ACD$ are the same.

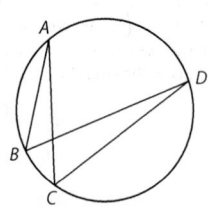

Module 15

783

Lesson 1

© Houghton Mifflin Harcourt Publishing Company

LANGUAGE SUPPORT EL

Communicate Math

Have students work with a partner to discuss the differences and similarities between inscribed and central angles in circles. Ask them to complete a compare and contrast table, such as this one. Sample:

Central Angle	Both	Inscribed Angle
Vertex point on the center of the circle	Intercept an arc	Vertex point on the circumference
Measure equal to intercepted arc measure	Measure related to intercepted arc measure	Measure equal to half intercepted arc measure

7. If m∠EDF = 15°, determine m∠ABE using the appropriate theorems and postulates.

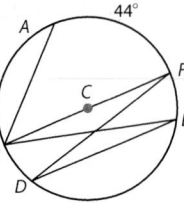

Since ∠EDF and ∠EBF intercept the same arc, they have the same

measure. By the Inscribed Angle Theorem,

$m\angle ABF = \frac{1}{2}m\widehat{AF} = \frac{1}{2} \times 44° = 22°$. By the Angle Addition

Postulate,

$m\angle ABE = m\angle ABF + m\angle EBF$. Therefore,

$m\angle ABE = 22° + 15° = 37°$.

⚙ Explain 3   Investigating Inscribed Angles on Diameters

You can examine angles that are inscribed in a semicircle. Example 3 Construct and analyze an angle inscribed in a semicircle.

Ⓐ Use a compass to draw a circle with center C. Use a straightedge to draw a diameter of the circle. Label the diameter $\overline{DF}$.

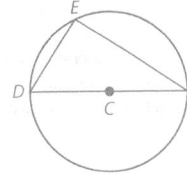

Ⓑ Use a straightedge to draw an inscribed angle ∠DEF on your circle from Step A whose sides contain the endpoints of the diameter.

Check students' drawings.

Ⓒ Use a protractor to determine the measure of ∠DEF (to the nearest degree). Record the results in the table.

Angle Measure	Circle C	Circle 2	Circle 3	Circle 4
m∠DEF	90°	90°	90°	90°

Ⓓ Repeat the process three more times. Make sure to vary the size of the circle, and the location of the vertex of the inscribed angle. Record the results in the table in Part C.

Ⓔ Examine the results, and make a conjecture about the measure of an angle inscribed in a semicircle.

The measure of an angle inscribed in a semicircle is 90°.

Ⓕ How can does the Inscribed Angle Theorem justify your conjecture?

The Inscribed Angle Theorem states that the measure of an inscribed angle is equal to

half the measure of its intercepted arc. The arc formed by a diameter is a semicircle with a

measure equal to 180°. Therefore, the measure of the inscribed angle is 90°.

EXPLAIN 3

Investigating Inscribed Angles on Diameters

INTEGRATE TECHNOLOGY

Have students use geometry software to draw a variety of different inscribed right angles to visually support the theorem.

QUESTIONING STRATEGIES

? How could you use the Angle Inscribed in a Semicircle Theorem to find the center of a circle? Sample answer: Inscribe a right angle in a circle, then draw a chord connecting its endpoints. By the Angle Inscribed in a Semicircle Theorem, the chord is a diameter, and the center is a point on it. Inscribe another right angle and connect its endpoints. The intersection of the two diameters is the center of the circle.

ELABORATE

AVOID COMMON ERRORS

Students may not be able to find all the required measures in a problem. Encourage students to do a *consistency check*. They should label a figure with all of the measures found and make sure that the sum of the angle measures of any triangle is 180°; that the sum of any arc measures that make up a full circle is 360°; that the measure of any arc subtended by a central angle is the measure of the central angle; and that the measure of any inscribed angle is half the measure of its intercepted arc.

SUMMARIZE THE LESSON

? What is the relationship between central angles and inscribed angles in a circle? The measure of an inscribed angle is half the measure of its intercepted arc. The measure of the arc is equal to the measure of its central angle (for minor arcs) or 360° minus the measure of its central angle (for major arcs).

> **Inscribed Angle of a Diameter Theorem**
>
> The endpoints of a diameter lie on an inscribed angle if and only if the inscribed angle is a right angle.
>
>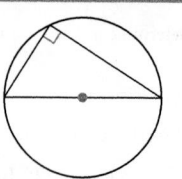

Reflect

8. A right angle is inscribed in a circle. If the endpoints of its intercepted arc are connected by a segment, must the segment pass through the center of the circle?

Yes, the endpoints of the intercepted arc lie on a diameter. And by definition, a diameter passes through the center of the circle.

● Elaborate

9. An equilateral triangle is inscribed in a circle. How does the relationship between the measures of the inscribed angles and intercepted arcs help determine the measure of each angle of the triangle?

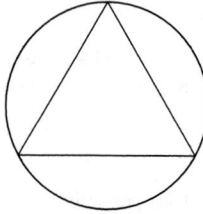

Together the three angles intercept the entire circle, which has a measure of 360°. Since the angles of an equilateral triangle are congruent, they each intercept an arc of 120°. The measure of an inscribed angle is equal to half the measure of its intercepted arc, so each angle of the triangle measures 60°.

10. Essential Question Check-In What is the relationship between inscribed angles and central angles in a circle?

If an inscribed angle is acute, its measure is equal to half the measure of its associated central angle. If an inscribed angle is obtuse, its measure is equal to half the difference between the measure of its associated central angle and 360°.

Identify the chord(s), inscribed angle(s), and central angle(s) in the figure. The center of the circles in Exercises 1, 2, and 4 is C.

1.

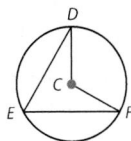

Chord(s): $\overline{DE}, \overline{EF}$

InscribedAngle(s): $\angle DEF$

Central Angle(s): $\angle DCF$

2.

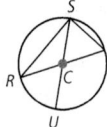

Chord(s): $\overline{SR}, \overline{SU}, \overline{ST}, \overline{RT}$

Inscribed Angle(s): $\angle RST, \angle SRT, \angle RTS, \angle RSU, \angle UST$

Central Angle(s): $\angle RCS, \angle SCT, \angle RCU, \angle UCT$

3.

Chord(s): $\overline{DF}, \overline{DG}, \overline{EF}, \overline{EG}$

Inscribed Angle(s):

$\angle DGE, \angle DFE, \angle FDG, \angle FEG$

Central Angle(s): none

4.

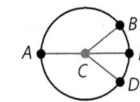

Chord(s): $\overline{AE}$

Inscribed Angle(s): none

Central Angle(s): $\angle ACB, \angle ACE, \angle ACD,$

$\angle BCE \ \angle DCE, \angle BCD$

In circle C, $m\widehat{DE} = 84°$. Find each measure.

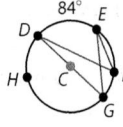

5. $m\angle DGE$

$\angle DGE$ is an inscribed angle, so $m\angle DGE$ is equal to half the measure of its intercepted arc, or $\frac{1}{2}(84)° = 42°$.

6. $m\angle EFD$

$\angle EFD$ is an inscribed angle, so $m\angle EFD$ is equal to half the measure of its intercepted arc, or $\frac{1}{2}(84)° = 42°$.

© Houghton Mifflin Harcourt Publishing Company

ASSIGNMENT GUIDE

Concepts and Skills	Practice
Explore Investigating Central Angles and Inscribed Angles	Exercises 1–4
Example 1 Understanding Arcs and Arc Measure	Exercises 5–8
Example 2 Using the Inscribed Angle Theorem	Exercises 9–11
Example 3 Investigating Inscribed Angles on Diameters	Exercises 12–14

INTEGRATE MATHEMATICAL PRACTICES
Focus on Modeling

MP.4 Students can redraw diagrams and use colored pencils to mark inscribed angles and their intercepted arcs.

Exercise	Depth of Knowledge (D.O.K.)	COMMON CORE Mathematical Practices	
1–4	**1** Recall of Information		**MP.6** Precision
5–17	**2** Skills/Concepts		**MP.2** Reasoning
18–20	**2** Skills/Concepts		**MP.4** Modeling
21–23	**2** Skills/Concepts		**MP.2** Reasoning
24	**3** Strategic Thinking	H.O.T.	**MP.3** Logic
25	**3** Strategic Thinking	H.O.T.	**MP.2** Reasoning
26	**3** Strategic Thinking	H.O.T.	**MP.3** Logic

AVOID COMMON ERRORS

Caution students to make sure they match the inscribed angle with its correct intercepted arc.

The center of the circle is A. Find each measure using the appropriate theorems and postulates.

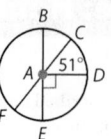

7. $\overarc{mCE}$

$\overarc{mCE} = \overarc{mCD} + \overarc{mDE}$ by the Arc Addition Postulate.
$\overarc{mCD} = 51°$ and $\overarc{mDE} = 90°$ because the measure of an arc is equal to the measure of its central angle. So, $\overarc{mCE} = 51° + 90° = 141°$ by substitution.

8. $\overarc{mDF}$ Since $\overline{CF}$ is a diameter, $\overarc{CDF} = \frac{1}{2}(360°) = 180°$. Since the measure of a minor arc is equal to the measure of its central angle, $\overarc{mCD} = 51°$. $\overarc{mCDF} = \overarc{mCD} + \overarc{mDF}$ by the Arc Addition Postulate. So, $\overarc{mDF} = 180° - 51° = 129°$ by substitution and subtraction.

9. $\overarc{mBEC}$ Since $\overline{BE}$ is a diameter, $\overarc{BFE} = \frac{1}{2}(360°) = 180°$. Since the measure of a minor arc is equal to the measure of its central angle, $\overarc{mDE} = 90°$ and $\overarc{mCD} = 51°$. $\overarc{mCE} = \overarc{mCD} + \overarc{mDE}$ by the Arc Addition Postulate. So, $\overarc{mCE} = 90° + 51° = 141°$ by substitution. $\overarc{mBEC} = \overarc{mBFE} + \overarc{mCE}$ by the Arc Addition Postulate. So, $\overarc{mBEC} = 180° + 141° = 321°$ by substitution.

Find each measure using the appropriate theorems and postulates. $\overarc{mAC} = 116°$

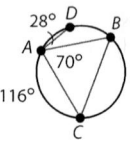

10. $\overarc{mBC}$

$m\angle CAB = 70°$, so $\overarc{mBC} = 140°$ by the Inscribed Angle Theorem.

11. $\overarc{mAD}$

$m\angle CAB = 70°$, so $\overarc{mBC} = 140°$ by the Inscribed Angle Theorem.
$\overarc{mAB} = 360° - (140° + 116°) = 104°$ by the Arc Addition Postulate and subtraction.
$m\angle DAB = 28°$, so $\overarc{mDB} = 2(28)° = 56°$ by the Inscribed Angle Theorem.
$\overarc{mAD} = 104° - 56° = 48°$ by the Arc Addition Postulate and subtraction.

The center of the circle is C. Find each measure using the appropriate theorems and postulates. $\overarc{mLM} = 70°$ and $\overarc{mNP} = 60°$.

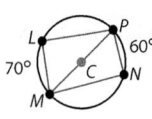

12. $m\angle MNP$

By the Inscribed Angle of a Diameter Theorem, since $\overline{MP}$ is a diameter, $m\angle MNP = 90°$.

13. $m\angle LMN$

By the Inscribed Angle Theorem, $m\angle PMN = \frac{1}{2}(60°) = 30°$ and $m\angle LPM = \frac{1}{2}(70°) = 35°$. By the Inscribed Angle of a Diameter Theorem, $m\angle MLP = 90°$. So, $m\angle LMP = 180° - (90° + 35°) = 55°$. By the Angle Addition Postulate, $m\angle LMN = 55° + 30° = 85°$.

© Houghton Mifflin Harcourt Publishing Company

The center of the circle is *O*. Find each arc or angle measure using the appropriate theorems and postulates.

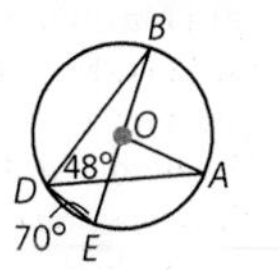

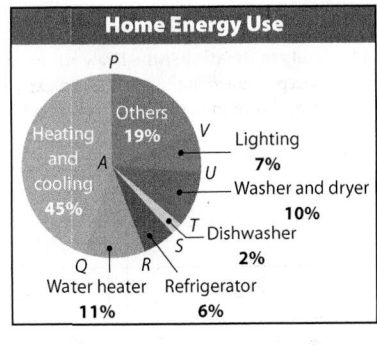

14. m∠*BDE*

Since $\overline{BE}$ is a diameter, by the Inscribed Angle of a Diameter Theorem, m∠*BDE* = 90°.

15. m$\widehat{ABD}$

By the Inscribed Angle Theorem, m$\widehat{DB}$ = 2(70°) = 140° and m$\widehat{AB}$ = 2(48°) = 96°. By the Arc Addition Postulate, m$\widehat{ABD}$ = 140° + 96° = 236°.

16. m$\widehat{ED}$

By the Inscribed Angle Theorem, m$\widehat{DB}$ = 2(70°) = 140° and m$\widehat{AB}$ = 2(48°) = 96°. m∠*AOB* = 96° because the measure of a minor arc is equal to its central angle. ∠*AOE* is the supplement of ∠*AOB*, so m∠*AOE* = 84°. Hence, m$\widehat{AE}$ = 84° because the measure of a minor arc is equal to the measure of its central angle. By the Arc Addition Postulate and subtraction, m$\widehat{ED}$ = 360° − (140° + 96° + 84°) = 40°.

17. m∠*DBE*

By the Inscribed Angle Theorem, m$\widehat{DB}$ = 2(70°) = 140° and m$\widehat{AB}$ = 2(48°) = 96°. m∠*AOB* = 96° because the measure of a minor arc is equal to the measure of its central angle. ∠*AOE* is the supplement of ∠*AOB*, so m∠*AOE* = 84°. Hence, m$\widehat{AE}$ = 84° because the measure of a minor arc is equal to the measure of its central angle. By the Arc Addition Postulate and subtraction, m$\widehat{ED}$ = 360° − (140° + 96° + 84°) = 40°. By the Inscribed Angle Theorem, m∠*DBE* = $\frac{1}{2}$(40°) = 20°.

Represent Real-World Problems The circle graph shows how a typical household spends money on energy. Use the graph to find the measure of each arc.

18. m$\widehat{PQ}$

m∠*PAQ* is 45% of 360°. 45% of 360° is 162°, so m∠*PAQ* = 162°. Since the measure of an arc is equal to the measure of its central angle, m$\widehat{PQ}$ = 162°.

19. m$\widehat{UPT}$

m∠*UAT* is 10% of 360° and 10% of 360° is 36°, so m∠*UT* = 36°. So m$\widehat{UT}$ and m∠*UPT* = 360° − 36° = 324°.

Home Energy Use

P — Others 19%
Heating and cooling 45% — A
V — Lighting 7%
U — Washer and dryer 10%
T — Dishwasher 2%
S
Q — Water heater 11%
R — Refrigerator 6%

AVOID COMMON ERRORS

Students may confuse central and inscribed angles and their special relationships with arc length. Suggest that students refer to or draw a simple diagram of a circle showing a central angle and a corresponding inscribed angle to help them recall the relationships.

Remind students that if the center point of a circle is not labeled, or if a segment is not given as a diameter of a circle, they cannot assume that a chord is a diameter.

20. **Communicate Mathematical Ideas** A carpenter's square is a tool that is used to draw right angles. Suppose you are building a toy car and you have four small circles of wood that will serve as the wheels. You need to drill a hole in the center of each wheel for the axle. Explain how you can use the carpenter's square to find the center of each wheel.

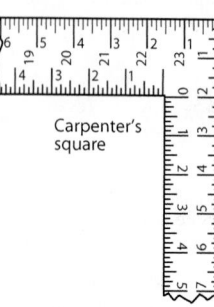

Carpenter's square

Use the carpenter's square to draw an inscribed right angle. The sides of the angle intersect the circle at the endpoints of a diameter. Draw the diameter. Then repeat the process to draw a different diameter. The point of intersection of the two diameters is the center of the circle.

21. Choose the expressions that are equivalent to m∠AOB. Select all that apply.

A. $\frac{1}{2}$m∠ACB

B. m∠ACB

C. 2m∠ACB

D. m$\widehat{AB}$

E. m∠DOE

F. m∠DFE

G. 2m∠DFE

H. m$\widehat{DE}$

C, D, E, G, H; m∠AOB = 2m∠ACB = m$\widehat{AB}$ = m∠DOE = 2m∠DFE = m$\widehat{DE}$

22. **Analyze Relationships** Draw arrows to connect the concepts shown in the boxes. Then explain how the terms shown in the concept map are related.

Possible Answer:

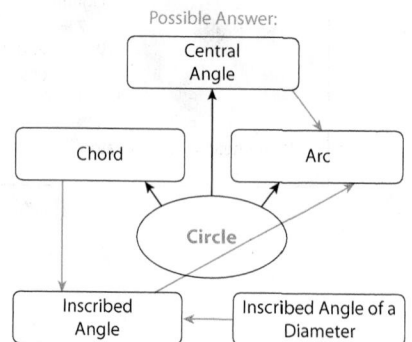

The term "inscribed angle" is connected to the term "chord," because an inscribed angle of a circle is defined to be an angle whose vertex is on the circle and whose sides contain chords of the circle. The term "arc" is connected to the term "central angle," because the measure of an arc is defined to be the measure of its central angle. The term "inscribed angle of a diameter" is connected to "inscribed angle" because an inscribed angle of a diameter is a particular kind of inscribed angle. The term "inscribed angle" is connected to the term "arc" because the measure of an inscribed angle is one-half the measure of the intercepted arc.

23. In circle E, the measures of $\angle DEC$, $\angle CEB$, and $\angle BEA$ are in the ratio 3:4:5. Find $m\overset{\frown}{AC}$.

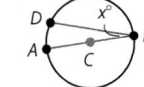

$m\overset{\frown}{AD} = \frac{1}{2}(360°) = 180°$ because $\overline{AD}$ is a diameter.

Solve $5x + 4x + 3x = 180$ to get $x = 15$. So, $m\angle BEA = 5x = 75°$,

$m\angle CEB = 4x = 60°$. Since the measure of a minor arc is equal

to the measure of its central angle, $m\overset{\frown}{AB} = 75°$ and $m\overset{\frown}{BC} = 60°$.

So $m\overset{\frown}{AC} = 75° + 60° = 135°$ by the Arc Addition Postulate.

H.O.T. **Focus on Higher Order Thinking**

24. Explain the Error The center of the circle is G. Below is a student's work to find the value of x. Explain the error and find the correct value of x.

$\overline{AD}$ is a diameter, so $m\overset{\frown}{ACD} = 180°$.

Since $m\overset{\frown}{ACD} = m\overset{\frown}{AB} + m\overset{\frown}{BC} + m\overset{\frown}{CD}$, $m\overset{\frown}{AB} + m\overset{\frown}{BC} + m\overset{\frown}{CD} = 180°$.

$5x + 90 + 15x = 180$

$20x = 90$

$x = 4.5$

The solution is incorrect because it assumes that $\angle BGC$ is a right angle. Because they are vertical angles, $\angle AGF \cong \angle CGD$. So, $m\overset{\frown}{AF} = m\overset{\frown}{CD}$. So $16x - 5 = 15x$ and $x = 5$.

25. Multi-Step An inscribed angle with a diameter as a side has measure $x°$. If the ratio of $m\overset{\frown}{AD}$ to $m\overset{\frown}{DB}$ is 1:4, what is $m\overset{\frown}{DB}$?

$m\overset{\frown}{AD} = 2x°$ by the Inscribed Angle Theorem. Since $\overline{AB}$ is a diameter of the circle, $m\overset{\frown}{ADB} = 180°$. Since the ratio of $m\overset{\frown}{AD}$ to $m\overset{\frown}{DB}$ is 1:4, $m\overset{\frown}{DB} = 8x°$. By the Arc Addition Postulate, $2x + 8x = 180$. So $10x = 180$ and $x = 18$. So $m\overset{\frown}{DB} = 8x° = 8(18°) = 144°$.

26. Justify Reasoning To prove the Inscribed Angle Theorem you need to prove three cases. In Case 1, the center of the circle is on a side of the inscribed angle. In Case 2, the center the circle is in the interior of the inscribed angle. In Case 3, the center the circle is in the exterior of the inscribed angle.

a. Fill in the blanks in the proof for Case 1 to show that $m\angle DAB = \frac{1}{2}m\overset{\frown}{DB}$.

Given: $\angle DAB$ is inscribed in circle C.

Prove: $m\angle DAB = \frac{1}{2}m\overset{\frown}{DB}$

Proof: Let $m\angle A = x°$. Draw $\overline{DC}$.

$\triangle ADC$ is $\underline{\text{isosceles}}$. So $m\angle A = m\angle \boxed{ADC}$ by the Isosceles Triangle Theorem.

Then $\boxed{m\angle DCB} = 2x°$ by the Exterior Angle Theorem. So, $m\overset{\frown}{DB} = \boxed{2x°}$ by the definition of the measure of an arc of a circle.

Since $m\overset{\frown}{DB} = \boxed{2x°}$ and $m\angle DAB = \boxed{x°}$, $m\angle DAB = \frac{1}{2}\overset{\frown}{DB}$.

VISUAL CUES

To help students remember the Inscribed Angle Theorem, encourage them to draw a circle similar to those they drew in the first Explore activity to discover the relationship between an inscribed angle and a central angle that intercept the same arc. The diagram will show that the inscribed angle is smaller; this should help them remember that its measure is half that of the central angle.

JOURNAL

Have students summarize the main vocabulary and theorems from this lesson. Encourage students to illustrate the vocabulary and theorems.

b. Draw and label a diagram for Case 2. Then use a paragraph proof to prove that the inscribed angle is one-half the intercepted arc.

Possible Answer:

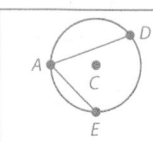

Given: $\angle DAE$ is inscribed in circle C.

Prove: $m\angle DAE = \frac{1}{2}m\widehat{DE}$

Proof:

Draw diameter $\overline{AB}$. Let $m\angle DAB = x°$ and $m\angle EAB = y°$. Draw $\overline{DC}$ and $\overline{EC}$.

$\triangle ADC$ and $\triangle AEC$ are isosceles. So, $m\angle DAB = m\angle ADC = x°$ and $m\angle EAB = m\angle AEC = y°$ by the Isosceles Triangle Theorem.

Then $m\angle DCB = 2x°$ and $m\angle ECB = 2y°$ by the Exterior Angle Theorem. So, $m\widehat{DB} = 2x°$, and $m\widehat{EB} = 2y°$ by the definition of the measure of an arc of a circle. $m\widehat{DE} = m\widehat{DB} + m\widehat{EB}$ by the Arc Addition Postulate, and $m\angle DAE = m\angle DAB + m\angle EAB$ by the Angle Addition Postulate.

Since $m\widehat{DE} = m\widehat{DB} + m\widehat{EB}$, $2x° + 2y° = 2(x + y)°$ and $m\angle DAE = (x + y)°$, this proves the theorem.

c. Draw and label a diagram for Case 3. Then use a paragraph proof to prove that the inscribed angle is one-half the intercepted arc.

Possible Answer:

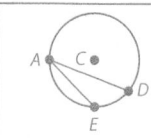

Given: $\angle DAE$ is inscribed in circle C.

Prove: $m\angle DAE = \frac{1}{2}m\widehat{DE}$

Proof:

Draw diameter $\overline{AB}$. Let $m\angle EAB = x°$ and $m\angle DAB = y°$. Draw $\overline{DC}$ and $\overline{EC}$.

$\triangle ADC$ and $\triangle AEC$ are isosceles. So, $m\angle DAB = m\angle ADC$ and $= y°$ and $m\angle EAB = m\angle AEC = x°$ by the Isosceles Triangle Theorem.

Then $m\angle DCB = 2y°$ and $m\angle ECB = 2x°$ by the Exterior Angle Theorem. So $m\widehat{DB} = 2y°$ and $m\widehat{EB} = 2x°$ by the definition of the measure of an arc of a circle. $m\widehat{DE} = m\widehat{EB} - m\widehat{DB}$ by the Arc Addition Postulate, and subtraction, and $m\angle EAD = m\angle EAB - m\angle DAB$ by the Angle Addition Postulate and subtraction.

Since $m\widehat{ED} = m\widehat{EB} - m\widehat{DB} = 2x° - 2y° = 2(x - y)°$ and $m\angle EAD = (x - y)°$, this proves the theorem.

Lesson Performance Task

Diana arrives late at the theater for a play. Her ticket entitles her to sit anywhere in Circle G. She had hoped to sit in Seat D, which she thought would give her the widest viewing angle of the stage. But Seat D is taken, as are all the other nearby seats in Circle G. The seating chart for the theater is shown.

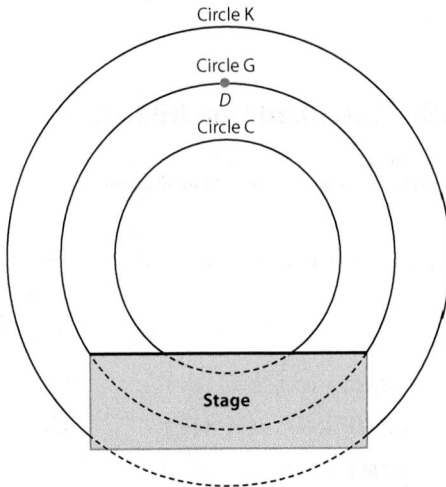

Identify two other spots where Diana can sit that will give her the same viewing angle she would have had in Seat D. Explain how you know how your points would provide the same viewing angle, and support your claim by showing the viewing angles on the drawing.
Students can choose any two points on Circle G. They should explain that all of the viewing angles on the circle are congruent because they are inscribed in the same circle and include the same intercepted arc. Drawings should show the inscribed angles. Two sample points, Y and Z, are shown.

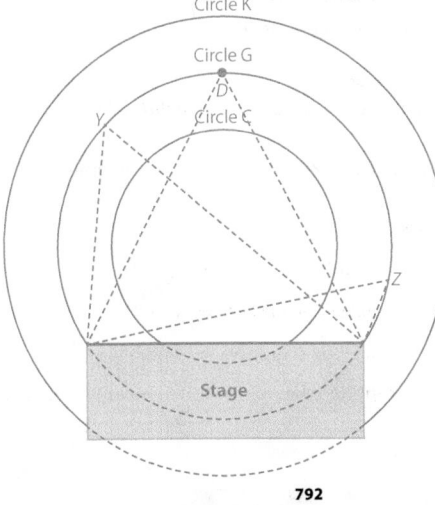

EXTENSION ACTIVITY

Theater designs have changed dramatically through the centuries, from L-shaped to semicircular to square to the complete circles of theater-in-the-round. Have students research the history of theater design and describe their findings in geometric terms. Reports may include drawings of important innovations in theater design, advantages and disadvantages of given designs, and descriptions of specific theaters.

INTEGRATE MATHEMATICAL PRACTICES
Focus on Reasoning

MP.2 If you were to move from point Y to point D to point Z, your viewing angle of the stage would remain constant. Describe how the angles your line of sight made with the two ends of the stage would change as you moved. The angle your line of sight made with the left end of the stage (closest to Y) would be at its greatest when you started, and the angle with the right end of the stage (closest to Z) would be at its least. As you moved, the first angle would continue to decrease in measure while the second angle would increase.

INTEGRATE MATHEMATICAL PRACTICES
Focus on Critical Thinking

MP.3 Look at the illustration of the theater in the Lesson Performance Task. Suppose you were seated at point E in Circle K, directly behind the person at point D in Circle G. Would your viewing angle of the stage be greater than or less than the viewing angle of the person at point D? Explain. Less than; if you drew lines from E to the endpoints of the stage, you would create an isosceles triangle with the two lines as sides and the stage as the base. Those base angles would be greater than the base angles of the isosceles triangle with point D at its vertex and the stage as its base. Since the base angles of the isosceles triangle with E as its vertex are greater than the base angles of the isosceles triangle with D as its vertex, and since the sum of the measures of the angles of both triangles is 180°, the measure of ∠E must be less than the measure of ∠D.

Scoring Rubric
2 points: Student correctly solves the problem and explains his/her reasoning.
1 point: Student shows good understanding of the problem but does not fully solve or explain his/her reasoning.
0 points: Student does not demonstrate understanding of the problem.

Central Angles and Inscribed Angles   **792**

Angles in Inscribed Quadrilaterals

Common Core Math Standards

The student is expected to:

 G-C.A.3

Construct the incribed and circumscribed circles of a triangle, and prove properties of angles for a quadrilateral inscribed in a circle. Also G-C.D.13

Mathematical Practices

 MP.4 Modeling

Language Objective

Work with a small group to decide whether statements about inscribed quadrilaterals are true or false.

ENGAGE

Essential Question: What can you conclude about the angles of a quadrilateral inscribed in a circle?

If a quadrilateral is inscribed in a circle, then its opposite angles are supplementary.

PREVIEW: LESSON PERFORMANCE TASK

View the Engage section online. Discuss the photograph. Point out the main features of the ballpark—the diamond, the outfield, the stands, and the foul territory. Then preview the Lesson Performance Task.

15.2 Angles in Inscribed Quadrilaterals

Essential Question: What can you conclude about the angles of a quadrilateral inscribed in a circle?

Resource Locker

⊘ Explore   Investigating Inscribed Quadrilaterals

There is a relationship among the angles of a quadrilateral that is inscribed in a circle. You can use a protractor and compass to explore the angle measures of a quadrilateral inscribed in a circle.

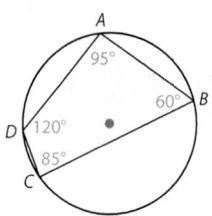

Ⓐ Measure the four angles of quadrilateral *ABCD* and record their values to the nearest degree on the diagram.

Ⓑ Find the sums of the indicated angles.

m∠*DAB* + m∠*ABC* = 155 °   m∠*ABC* + m∠*BCD* = 145 °

m∠*DAB* + m∠*BCD* = 180 °   m∠*ABC* + m∠*CDA* = 180 °

m∠*DAB* + m∠*CDA* = 215 °   m∠*BCD* + m∠*CDA* = 205 °

Ⓒ Use a compass to draw a circle with a diameter greater than the circle in Step A. Plot points *E*, *F*, *G*, and *H* consecutively around the circumference of the circle so that the center of the circle is not inside quadrilateral *EFGH*. Use a straightedge to connect each pair of consecutive points to draw quadrilateral *EFGH*.

Drawings will vary. Vertices should be on the circle and labeled *E*, *F*, *G*, *H* consecutively.

Ⓓ Measure the four angles of *EFGH* to the nearest degree and record their values on your diagram.

Measurements will vary but should be recorded to the nearest degree.

Ⓔ Find the sums of the indicated angles.

m∠*HEF* + m∠*EFG* = ____ °   m∠*EFG* + m∠*FGH* = ____ °

m∠*HEF* + m∠*FGH* = 180 °   m∠*EFG* + m∠*GHE* = 180 °

m∠*HEF* + m∠*GHE* = ____ °   m∠*FGH* + m∠*GHE* = ____ °

Answers will vary for all values except for pairs of opposite angles which sum to 180°.

© Houghton Mifflin Harcourt Publishing Company

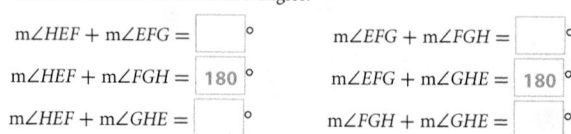

HARDCOVER PAGES 669–678

Turn to these pages to find this lesson in the hardcover student edition.

1. **Discussion** Compare your work with that of other students. What conclusions can you make about the angles of a quadrilateral inscribed in a circle?
   The opposite angles are supplementary. There appears to be no relationship between
   consecutive angles.

2. Based on your observations, does it matter if the center of the circle is inside or outside the inscribed quadrilateral for the relationship between the angles to hold? Explain.
   It does not matter if the center is inside or outside the quadrilateral. Opposite angles will
   always be supplementary for any inscribed quadrilateral.

⚙ Explain 1   Proving the Inscribed Quadrilateral Theorem

The result from the Explore can be formalized in the Inscribed Quadrilateral Theorem.

> **Inscribed Quadrilateral Theorem**
>
> If a quadrilateral is inscribed in a circle, then its opposite angles are supplementary.

Example 1 Prove the Inscribed Quadrilateral Theorem.

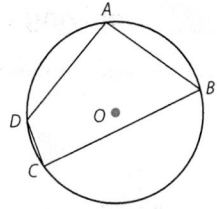

Given: Quadrilateral ABCD is inscribed in circle O.

Prove: $\angle A$ and $\angle C$ are supplementary.
$\angle B$ and $\angle D$ are supplementary.

Step 1 The union of $\overset{\frown}{BCD}$ and $\overset{\frown}{DAB}$ is circle O.

Therefore, $m\overset{\frown}{BCD} + m\overset{\frown}{DAB} = \boxed{360}$ °

Step 2 $\angle A$ is an inscribed angle and its intercepted arc is $\boxed{\overset{\frown}{BCD}}$.

$\angle\,\boxed{C}$ is an inscribed angle and its intercepted arc is $\overset{\frown}{DAB}$.

By the Inscribed Angle Theorem, $m\angle A = \dfrac{1}{\boxed{2}}\,m\,\boxed{\overset{\frown}{BCD}}$ and

$m\angle C = \dfrac{1}{\boxed{2}}\,m\,\boxed{\overset{\frown}{DAB}}$.

Step 3 So, $m\angle A + m\angle C = \boxed{\dfrac{1}{2}\,m\overset{\frown}{BCD} + \dfrac{1}{2}\,m\overset{\frown}{DAB}}$ Substitution Property of Equality

$= \boxed{\dfrac{1}{2}\left(m\overset{\frown}{BCD} + m\overset{\frown}{DAB}\right)}$ Distributive Property

$= \boxed{\dfrac{1}{2}\left(360°\right)}$ Substitution Property of Equality

$= \boxed{180°}$ Simplify.

So, $\angle A$ and $\angle C$ are supplementary, by the definition of supplementary. Similar reasoning shows that $\angle B$ and $\angle D$ are also supplementary.

PROFESSIONAL DEVELOPMENT

 Integrate Mathematical Practices

This lesson provides an opportunity to address Mathematical Practice **MP.4**, which calls for students to "model with mathematics." Students create and use representations to extend their understanding of the Inscribed Angle Theorem to prove the Inscribed Quadrilateral Theorem. They recognize that the theorem is bi-conditional and implies that an inscribed parallelogram must be a rectangle and an inscribed rhombus must be a square. They use these ideas to find missing angle measures in quadrilaterals inscribed in circles and to inscribe a square in a circle.

EXPLORE

Investigating Inscribed Quadrilaterals

INTEGRATE TECHNOLOGY

Students have the option of doing the Explore activity either in the book or online.

QUESTIONING STRATEGIES

(?) What can you say about two arcs that together form a complete circle? The sum of the measures of the arcs is 360°.

(?) Does the conjecture apply to all quadrilaterals inside a circle? Explain. No, the special relationship results from the quadrilateral having vertices that are inscribed angles on a circle.

EXPLAIN 1

Proving the Inscribed Quadrilateral Theorem

INTEGRATE MATHEMATICAL PRACTICES

Focus on Modeling

MP.4 Challenge students to inscribe different parallelograms in a circle. Discuss why each parallelogram must be either a rectangle or a square.

CONNECT VOCABULARY EL

Remind students that the words *if and only if* mean the statement is biconditional. For a statement to be biconditional, the theorem and its converse must both be proven.

QUESTIONING STRATEGIES

? What does it mean to say that two angles are supplementary? The sum of their angle measures is 180°.

? What if three vertices of a quadrilateral lie on a circle? Will the opposite angles necessarily be supplementary? Explain. No; since the vertices are not all inscribed angles, they will not necessarily intercept arcs that contain the whole circle.

EXPLAIN 2

Applying the Inscribed Quadrilateral Theorem

AVOID COMMON ERRORS

Students may set the opposite angles of a quadrilateral equal to each other or select consecutive angles as supplements. To help students identify the opposite angles as supplementary pairs, suggest that they use a color to mark one pair of opposite angles. Emphasize that this pair is supplementary and that the same is true for the uncolored pair.

The converse of the Inscribed Quadrilateral Theorem is also true. That is, if the opposite angles of a quadrilateral are supplementary, it can be inscribed in a circle. Taken together, these statements can be stated as the following biconditional statement. A quadrilateral can be inscribed in a circle *if and only if* its opposite angles are supplementary.

Reflect

3. What must be true about a parallelogram that is inscribed in a circle? Explain.
It must be a rectangle. Opposite angles of a parallelogram are congruent, but for a parallelogram to be inscribed in a circle, the opposite angles must also be supplementary. Only angles with measures of 90° meet both criteria and a parallelogram with four right angles is a rectangle.

4. Quadrilateral PQRS is inscribed in a circle and $m\angle P = 57°$. Is it possible to find the measure of some or all of the other angles? Explain.
You can only find that $m\angle R = 123°$ because $\angle P$ and $\angle R$ are opposite angles and thus supplementary. You know the other two angles are supplementary, but their measures are unknown without further information.

Explain 2 Applying the Inscribed Quadrilateral Theorem

Example 2 Find the angle measures of each inscribed quadrilateral.

(A) *PQRS*

Find the value of y.

$$m\angle P + m\angle R = 180° \qquad \text{PQRS is inscribed in a circle.}$$

$$(5y + 3) + (15y + 17) = 180 \qquad \text{Substitute.}$$

$$20y + 20 = 180 \qquad \text{Simplify.}$$

$$y = 8 \qquad \text{Solve for } y.$$

Find the measure of each angle.

$$m\angle P = 5(8) + 3 = 43° \qquad \text{Substitute the value of } y \text{ into each angle expression and evaluate.}$$

$$m\angle R = 15(8) + 17 = 137°$$

$$m\angle Q = 8^2 + 53 = 117°$$

$$m\angle S + m\angle Q = 180° \qquad \text{Definition of supplementary}$$

$$m\angle S + 117° = 180° \qquad \text{Substitute.}$$

$$m\angle S = 63° \qquad \text{Subtract 117 from both sides.}$$

So, $m\angle P = 43°$, $m\angle R = 137°$, $m\angle Q = 117°$, and $m\angle S = 63°$.

COLLABORATIVE LEARNING

Peer-to-Peer Activity

Ask each student to inscribe a quadrilateral in a circle using a compass and straightedge. Working in pairs, have each student select a different color, then choose one inscribed angle on the quadrilateral and outline the chords that create the inscribed angle in the color. Ask them to use the same color to outline the arc intercepted by the inscribed angle. Then have students exchange papers and use their colors to outline the chords that create the inscribed angle opposite the angle chosen by the partner. Again ask students to outline the arc intercepted by the inscribed angle. Discuss how the diagrams support the Inscribed Quadrilateral Theorem.

Ⓑ *JKLM*

Find the value of *x*.

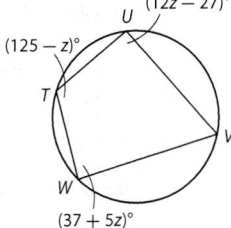

$$m\angle J + m\angle\boxed{L} = \boxed{180}^\circ$$ *JKLM* is inscribed in a circle.

$$\left(\boxed{39} + \boxed{7x}\right) + \left(\boxed{6x} - \boxed{15}\right) = \boxed{180}$$ Substitute.

$$\boxed{13}x + \boxed{24} = \boxed{180}$$ Simplify.

$$\boxed{13}x = \boxed{156}$$ Subtract 24 from both sides.

$$x = \boxed{12}$$ Divide both sides by 13.

Find the measure of each angle.

$$m\angle J = 39 + 7\left(\boxed{12}\right) = \boxed{123}^\circ$$ Substitute the value of *x* into each angle expression and evaluate.

$$m\angle L = 6\left(\boxed{12}\right) - 15 = \boxed{57}^\circ$$

$$m\angle K = \frac{20\left(\boxed{12}\right)}{3} = \boxed{80}^\circ$$

$$m\angle M + m\angle\boxed{K} = \boxed{180}^\circ$$ Definition of supplementary

$$m\angle M + \boxed{80}^\circ = \boxed{180}^\circ$$ Substitute.

$$m\angle M = \boxed{100}^\circ$$ Subtract 80 from both sides.

So, $m\angle J = \boxed{123}^\circ$, $m\angle L = \boxed{57}^\circ$, $m\angle K = \boxed{80}^\circ$, and $m\angle M = \boxed{100}^\circ$.

Your Turn

5. Find the measure of each angle of inscribed quadrilateral *TUVW*.

$$(12z - 27) + (37 + 5z) = 180;\ 17z + 10 = 180;\ z = 10$$

$$m\angle T = 125^\circ - 10^\circ = 115^\circ;$$

$$m\angle U = 12(10^\circ) - 27^\circ = 93^\circ;$$

$$m\angle V = 180^\circ - 115^\circ = 65^\circ;$$

$$m\angle W = 37^\circ + 5(10^\circ) = 87^\circ$$

QUESTIONING STRATEGIES

? Is it possible to draw any conclusions about the consecutive angles of an inscribed quadrilateral? Why or why not? No; you know only that the opposite angles are supplementary, unless one pair of opposite angles measures 90° each. Then, you know the other angles each measure 90°.

? When finding angle measurements for a quadrilateral, how can you check if the angle measurements are reasonable answers? Sample answer: Verify that opposite angles are supplementary and that the total angle measure of the quadrilateral is 360°.

DIFFERENTIATE INSTRUCTION

Critical Thinking

Ask students to determine whether the following method of inscribing a square in a circle is valid and explain why or why not.

First, draw two points on the circle so that they define an arc. Connect the two points to form a chord. Construct a second chord that is perpendicular to the first chord at one of its endpoints. Repeat the process until you have four chords that form a quadrilateral with four right angles.

Students should realize that the above construction does not ensure that the chords are congruent unless the original arc was exactly *one-quarter* of the circle.

Angles in Inscribed Quadrilaterals   **796**

EXPLAIN 3

Constructing an Inscribed Square

INTEGRATE MATHEMATICAL PRACTICES
Focus on Modeling

MP.4 Discuss how to use paper folding to construct the inscribed square. Fold the circle in half and then fold it in half again. Unfold it and use a straightedge to connect the points at which the folds intersect the circle.

QUESTIONING STRATEGIES

? What basic construction is used to inscribe a square in a circle? Why? The perpendicular bisector of a diameter construction; possible answer: The perpendicular bisector makes it possible to create 4 congruent isosceles right triangles. This means the sides of the square are congruent since each side is a congruent hypotenuse and each vertex angle is the sum of two 45° angles, or 90°.

? How could you use a protractor and ruler to check the construction? How could you use paper folding? Use a protractor to check that the angles are right angles and a ruler to make sure the sides have the same length.

© Houghton Mifflin Harcourt Publishing Company • Image Credits: ©Kevin Hsieh/Shutterstock

---

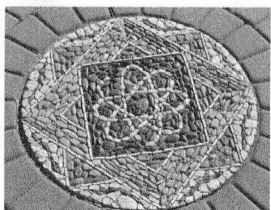

⊘ Explain 3 **Constructing an Inscribed Square**

Many designs are based on a square inscribed in a circle. Follow the steps to construct rectangle *ACBD* inscribed in a circle. Then show *ACBD* is a square.

Example 3 Construct an inscribed square.

Step 1 Use your compass to draw a circle. Mark the center, *O*. Draw diameter $\overline{AB}$ using a straightedge.

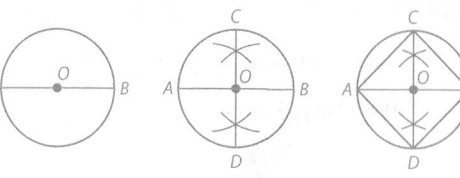

Step 2 Use your compass to construct the perpendicular bisector of $\overline{AB}$. Label the points where the bisector intersects the circle as *C* and *D*. **See Step 1 answer.**

Step 3 Use your straightedge to draw $\overline{AC}$, $\overline{CB}$, $\overline{BD}$, and $\overline{DA}$. **See Step 1 answer.**

Step 4 To show that *ACBD* is a square, you need to show that it has 4 ___congruent___ sides and 4 ___right___ angles.

Step 5 Complete the two-column proof to prove that *ACBD* has four congruent sides.

Statements	Reasons
$\overline{OA} \cong \boxed{OC} \cong \boxed{OB} \cong \boxed{OD}$	Radii of the circle *O*
$m\angle AOC = m\angle COB = m\angle \boxed{BOD} = m\angle \boxed{DOA} = \boxed{90}°$	$\overline{CD}$ is the perpendicular bisector of $\overline{AB}$.
$\triangle AOC \cong \triangle COB \cong \triangle BOD \cong \triangle DOA$	SAS
$\overline{AC} \cong \overline{CB} \cong \overline{BD} \cong \overline{DA}$	CPCTC

Use the diagram to complete the paragraph proof in Steps 6 and 7 that *ACBD* has four right angles.

Step 6 Since $\triangle AOC \cong \triangle COB$, then $\angle 1 \cong \angle \boxed{3}$ by CPCTC. By reasoning similar to that in the previous proof, it can be shown that $\triangle BOC \cong \triangle COB$. Therefore, by the Transitive Property of Congruence, $\triangle AOC \cong \triangle \boxed{BOC}$, and $\angle 1 \cong \angle 4$ by CPCTC. Also by the Transitive Property of Congruence, $\angle \boxed{3} \cong \angle 4$. Similar arguments show that $\angle 1 \cong \angle \boxed{2}$, $\angle 5 \cong \angle \boxed{6}$, and $\angle 7 \cong \angle \boxed{8}$.

LANGUAGE SUPPORT **EL**

Connect Vocabulary

Divide students into groups. Have each student write two or three clues about inscribed quadrilaterals on separate index cards, some true and some false. Then shuffle the cards and have students take turns drawing one and stating that it is *true* or *false*. If the group disagrees with the student, ask the student to justify his or her answer.

Step 7 The sum of all the angle measures in a triangle is $\underline{180}°$, so $m\angle 1 + m\angle 2 + m\angle \boxed{AOC} = 180°$.

Since $m\angle AOC = \boxed{90}°$, $m\angle 1 + m\angle 2 + 90° = 180°$. This means that $m\angle 1 + m\angle 2 = \boxed{90}°$.

Since $m\angle 1 = m\angle 2$, it can be concluded that $m\angle 1 = m\angle 2 = \boxed{45}°$. By similar reasoning, it is

shown that the measure of each of the congruent numbered angles is $\boxed{45}°$. Therefore, the measure

of each of the four angles of quadrilateral *ACBD* is the $\underline{sum}$ of the measures of two of the adjacent

numbered angles, which is $\underline{90}°$.

Reflect

6. How could reflections be used to construct an inscribed square?
<u>Reflect one half of the circle onto the other. The line of reflection is a diameter. Use a</u>

<u>different reflection to create a second diameter, making sure that the first diameter maps</u>

<u>onto itself. Connect the endpoints of the two diameters to create the square.</u>

Your Turn

7. Finish the quilt block pattern by inscribing a square in the circle. Shade in
your square.

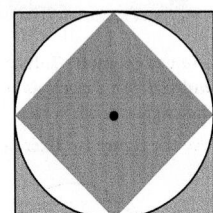

💬 Elaborate

8. Critique Reasoning Marcus said he thought some information was missing from one
of his homework problems because it was impossible to answer the question based on the given
information. The question and his work are shown. Critique Marcus's work and reasoning.

<u>Homework Problem</u>

Find the measures of the angles of
quadrialatral *ABCD*, which can be
inscribed in a circle.

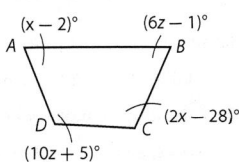

Marcus's Work
$x - 2 + 6z - 1 + 2x - 28 + 10z + 5 = 360$
$3x + 16z - 26 = 360$
$\boxed{3x} + \boxed{16z} = 386$
Cannot solve for two
different variables!

<u>Marcus correctly reasoned that the sum of the angle measures of a quadrilateral is equal</u>

<u>to 360° and that you cannot solve a single equation with two unknowns. However, he</u>

<u>failed to recognize that the Inscribed Quadrilateral Theorem must be used to solve the</u>

<u>problem. The problem states the quadrilateral can be inscribed in a circle, which means</u>

<u>that opposite angles are supplementary. He should have written two separate equations,</u>

<u>each with only one variable, $((x - 2) + (2x - 28) = 180$ and $(6z - 1) + (10z + 5) = 180)$</u>

<u>and used those equations to solve the problem.</u>

Module 15   **798**   Lesson 2

© Houghton Mifflin Harcourt Publishing Company

QUESTIONING STRATEGIES

? Does it matter whether the center of the circle
lies inside, outside, or on the quadrilateral to
apply the Inscribed Quadrilateral Theorem?
Explain. No, in all of these cases, the opposite
angles of the quadrilateral are supplementary.

SUMMARIZE THE LESSON

? What can you conclude about the angles of a
quadrilateral inscribed in a circle? Why? If a
quadrilateral is inscribed in a circle, then its
opposite angles are supplementary. The opposite
angles are inscribed angles, and the sum of their
intercepted arcs is 360°. So, the sum of the opposite
inscribed angles is 180°.

Angles in Inscribed Quadrilaterals   **798**

EVALUATE

ASSIGNMENT GUIDE

Concepts and Skills	Practice
Explore Investigating Inscribed Quadrilaterals	Exercises 1–3
Example 1 Proving the Inscribed Quadrilateral Theorem	Exercise 4
Example 2 Applying the Inscribed Quadrilateral Theorem	Exercises 5–13
Example 3 Constructing an Inscribed Square	Exercise 14

INTEGRATE MATHEMATICAL PRACTICES

Focus on Communication

MP.3 Students may feel overwhelmed with the variety of problems. Ask them to summarize what they remember about central and inscribed angle relationships, arc length, and the inscribed angles of a quadrilateral.

---

9. What must be true about a rhombus that is inscribed in a circle? Explain.
It is a square. A rhombus has opposite angles that are equal in measure. For a quadrilateral to be inscribed in a circle, the opposite angles must be supplementary. Therefore the rhombus must have four right angles. However, a rhombus with four right angles is a square.

10. **Essential Question Check-In** Can all types of quadrilaterals be inscribed in a circle? Explain.
No; The Inscribed Angle Theorem states that if a quadrilateral is inscribed in a circle, then its opposite angles are supplementary. Only rectangles (and thus squares) meet this criterion.

⭐ Evaluate: Homework and Practice

You use geometry software to inscribe quadrilaterals *ABCD* and *GHIJ* in a circle as shown in the figures. You then measure the angle at each vertex.

- Online Homework
- Hints and Help
- Extra Practice

Use the figure for Exercises 1–2.

Use the figure for Exercises 3–4.

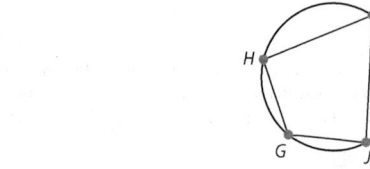

1. Suppose you drag the vertices of ∠A and ∠C to new positions on the circle and then measure ∠A and ∠C again. Does the relationship between ∠A and ∠C change? Explain.
   No. ∠A and ∠C are still supplementary. Opposite angles of an inscribed quadrilateral are always supplementary.

2. Suppose you know that m∠B is 74°. Is m∠D = 74°? Explain.
   No. ∠B and ∠D are supplementary, so m∠D = 180° − 74° = 106°.

3. Suppose m∠HIJ = 65° and that m∠H = m∠J. Can you find the measures of all the angles? Explain.
   Yes. ∠HIJ and ∠HGJ are supplementary, so m∠HGJ = 180° − 65° = 115°. Also, ∠H and ∠J are supplementary and have equal measures, so each angle must measure $\frac{1}{2}(180°) = 90°$.

4. **Justify Reasoning** You have found that m∠H = m∠J, but then you drag the vertex of ∠H so that m∠H changes. Is the statement m∠H = m∠J still true? Justify your reasoning.
   No. The opposite angles still have to be supplementary, which means that m∠H ≠ m∠J if m∠H changes. If m∠H becomes greater, then m∠J becomes less and vice versa.

Exercise	Depth of Knowledge (D.O.K.)	COMMON CORE Mathematical Practices
1–8	**2** Skills/Concepts	**MP.3** Logic
9–12	**2** Skills/Concepts	**MP.4** Modeling
13–16	**2** Skills/Concepts	**MP.2** Reasoning
17	**2** Skills/Concepts	**MP.4** Modeling
18	**2** Skills/Concepts	**MP.2** Reasoning
19	**3** Strategic Thinking H.O.T.	**MP.2** Reasoning

Use the figure for Exercices 5–6. Find each measure using the appropriate theorems and postulates.

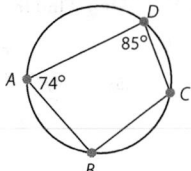

5. m∠B

By the Inscribed Quadrilateral Theorem, ∠B and ∠D are supplementary, so m∠B = 180° − 85° = 95°.

6. m$\widehat{DAB}$

By the Inscribed Quadrilateral Theorem, ∠A and ∠C are supplementary, so m∠C = 180° − 74° = 106°. By the Inscribed Angle Theorem, m$\widehat{DAB}$ = 2(106°) = 212°.

7. GHIJ is a quadrilateral. If m∠HIJ + m∠HGJ = 180° and m∠H + m∠J = 180°, could the points G, H, I, and J points of a circle? Explain.

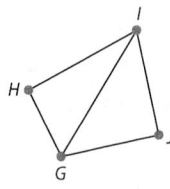

Yes. Since the opposite angles of quadrilateral GHIJ are supplementary, the quadrilateral can be inscribed in a circle.

8. LMNP is a quadrilateral inscribed in a circle. If m∠L = m∠N, is $\overline{MP}$ a diameter of the circle? Explain.

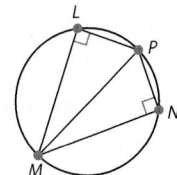

Yes. Since LMNP is a quadrilateral inscribed in a circle, the opposite angles of the quadrilateral are supplementary. Since m∠L = m∠N and m∠L + m∠N = 180°, they are congruent and supplementary angles, and must therefore be right angles. Since ∠L is a right angle, by the Inscribed Angle of a Diameter Theorem, $\overline{MP}$ must be a diameter of the circle.

9. Rafael was asked to construct a square inscribed in a circle. He drew a circle and a diameter of the circle. Describe how to complete his construction. Then, complete the construction.

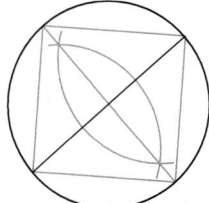

Construct the perpendicular bisector of the diameter. Connect the points where the perpendicular bisector and the diameter intersect the circle.

Exercise	Depth of Knowledge (D.O.K.)	COMMON CORE Mathematical Practices
20	**3** Strategic Thinking H.O.T.	**MP.6** Precision
21	**3** Strategic Thinking H.O.T.	**MP.4** Modeling

When finding angle measures with variables, students may solve for the variable and forget to use the value of the variable to find the actual angle measure. Remind students to look back at the problem to answer what is asked for. It may be the variable, a single angle measure, or several angle measures.

Multi-Step Find the angle measures of each inscribed quadrilateral.

10.

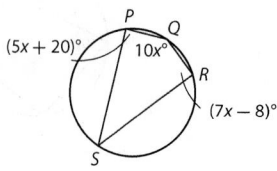

$(5x + 20) + (7x - 8) = 180$

$12x + 12 = 180$

$12x = 168$

$x = 14$

$m\angle P = 5(14) + 20 = 90°$

$m\angle Q = 10(14) = 140°$

$m\angle R = 7(14) - 8 = 90°$

Since $\angle S$ and $\angle Q$ are supplementary,

$m\angle S = 180° - 140° = 40°.$

11.

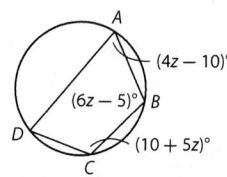

$(4z - 10) + (10 + 5z) = 180$

$9z = 180$

$z = 20$

$m\angle A = 4(20) - 10 = 70°$

$m\angle B = 6(20) - 5 = 115°$

$m\angle C = 10 + 5(20) = 110°$

Since $\angle B$ and $\angle D$ are supplementary,

$m\angle D = 180 - 115 = 65°.$

12.

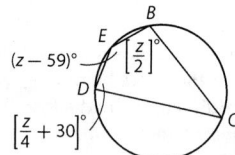

$\left(\dfrac{z}{4} + 30\right) + \dfrac{z}{2} = 180$

$\dfrac{3z}{4} = 150$

$z = 200$

$m\angle B = \dfrac{200}{2} = 100°$

$m\angle E = 200 - 59 = 141°$

$m\angle D = \dfrac{200}{4} + 30 = 80°$

Since $\angle E$ and $\angle C$ are supplementary,

$m\angle C = 180 - 141 = 39°.$

13.

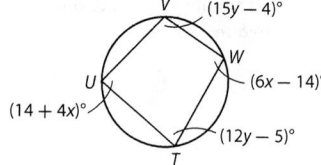

$(15y - 4) + (12y - 5) = 180$

$27y = 189$

$y = 7$

$m\angle V = 15(7) - 4 = 101°$

$m\angle T = 12(7) - 5 = 79°$

$(14 + 4x) + (6x - 14) = 180$

$10x = 180$

$x = 18$

$m\angle U = 14 + 4(18) = 86°$

$m\angle W = 6(18) - 14 = 94°.$

14. Critical Thinking Haruki is designing a fountain that consists of a square pool inscribed in a circular base represented by circle O. He wants to construct the square so that one of its vertices is point X. Construct the square and then explain your method.

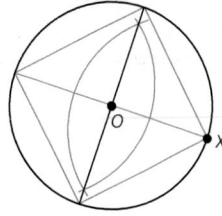

Draw a diameter with an endpoint at X. Then construct the perpendicular bisector of the diameter. Connect the points where the perpendicular bisector and the diameter intersect the circle.

For each quadrilateral, tell whether it can be inscribed in a circle. If so, describe a method for doing so using a compass and straightedge. If not, explain why not.

15. a parallelogram that is not a rectangle

A parallelogram that is not a rectangle cannot be inscribed in a circle because opposite angles are congruent. Since the opposite angles are not right angles, they cannot be supplementary.

16. a kite with two right angles

Can be inscribed in a circle. A kite has exactly one pair of opposite angles that are congruent. So the two right angles of the kite must be opposite angles. Draw the diagonal of the kite that connects the two noncongruent angles. This represents a diameter of the circle. Use the compass and straightedge to find the perpendicular bisector of the diagonal. The point of intersection is the center of the circle. Open the compass to the radius of the circle and draw the circle around the kite.

17. Represent Real-World Problems Lisa has not yet learned how to stop on ice skates, so she just skates straight across the circular rink until she reaches a wall. If she starts at P, turns $75°$ at Q, and turns $100°$ at R, find how many degrees she must turn at S to go back to her starting point.

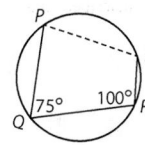

By the Inscribed Quadrilateral Theorem $m\angle S + m\angle Q = 180°$, so $m\angle S = 180° - 75° = 105°$.

18. In the diagram, C is the center of the circle and $\angle YXZ$ is inscribed in the circle. Classify each statement.

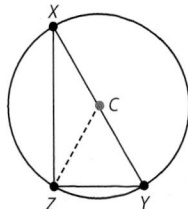

a. $\overline{CX} \cong \overline{CY}$		(True)/False/Cannot be determined
b. $\overline{CZ} \cong \overline{XY}$		True/(False)/Cannot be determined
c. $\triangle CXZ$ is isosceles.		(True)/False/Cannot be determined
d. $\triangle CYZ$ is equilateral.		True/False/(Cannot be determined)
e. $\overline{XY}$ is a diameter of circle C.		(True)/False/Cannot be determined

© Houghton Mifflin Harcourt Publishing Company

Students may not remember which angle pairs are supplementary in a quadrilateral. Emphasize that they must identify and match the opposite angles of a quadrilateral to apply the Inscribed Quadrilateral Theorem.

Have students find similarities and differences
between a right triangle inscribed in a circle, and a
square or a rectangle inscribed in a circle.

JOURNAL

Have students inscribe a quadrilateral in a circle. Ask
them to label the vertices of their quadrilaterals and
write equations that show the relationship between
the opposite angles of their quadrilaterals.

H.O.T. Focus on Higher Order Thinking

19. Multi-Step In the diagram, $m\overarc{JKL} = 198°$ and $m\overarc{KLM} = 216°$. Find the measures of
the angles of quadrilateral *JKLM*.

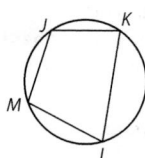

By the Inscribed Angle Theorem, $m\angle M = \frac{1}{2} m\overarc{JKL} = \frac{1}{2}(198°) = 99°$
and $m\angle J = \frac{1}{2} m\overarc{KLM} = \frac{1}{2}(216°) = 108°$. By the Inscribed Quadrilateral
Theorem $m\angle M + m\angle K = 180°$, so $m\angle K = 180° - 99° = 81°$, and
$m\angle J + m\angle L = 180°$, so $m\angle L = 180° - 108° = 72°$.

20. Critical Thinking Explain how you can construct a regular octagon inscribed in
a circle.

Start by constructing a square inscribed in a circle. Then construct the perpendicular
bisector of each side to locate four additional points around the circle. Form the octagon
by using a straightedge to connect consecutive points around the circle.

21. Represent Real-World Problems A patio tile design is constructed from a square
inscribed in a circle. The circle has radius $5\sqrt{2}$ feet.

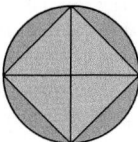

a. Find the area of the square.
Let *x* be the length of one side of the square in feet. Using the Pythagorean Theorem,

$$\left(5\sqrt{2}\right)^2 + \left(5\sqrt{2}\right)^2 = x^2$$
$$50 + 50 = x^2$$
$$100 = x^2$$
$$10 = x$$

So each side of the square is 10 feet. The area of the square is 10^2, or 100 square feet.

b. Find the area of the shaded region outside the square.
From part a, the area of the square is 100 square feet.

Find the area of the circle.

$$A = \pi r^2$$
$$= \pi\left(5\sqrt{2}\right)^2$$
$$= 50\pi$$

The area of the shaded region outside the circle is $(50\pi - 100)$ square feet.

Lesson Performance Task

Here are some facts about the baseball field shown here:

- *ABCD* is the baseball "diamond," a square measuring 90 feet on a side.
- Points *A, B, E, H* are collinear.
- The distance from third base (Point *B*) to the left field fence (Point *E*) equals the distance from first base (point *D*) to the right field fence (Point *G*).

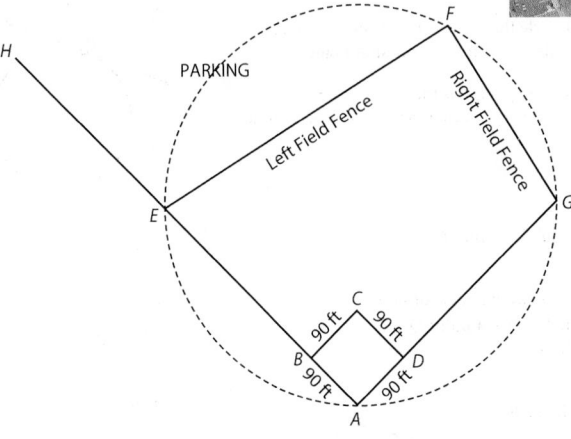

a. Is $\overset{\frown}{EA}$ congruent to $\overset{\frown}{AG}$? Explain why or why not.

b. Find m∠*F*. Explain your reasoning.

c. Identify an angle congruent to ∠*HEF*. Explain your reasoning.

a. Yes. *AB = AD* and *BE = DG*. *AE = AB + BE* and *AG = AD + DG*. Thus, *AE = AG*, which means $\overline{AE} \cong \overline{AG}$. Because in a circle congruent chords intersect congruent arcs, $\overset{\frown}{EA} \cong \overset{\frown}{AG}$.

b. m∠*F* = 90°. Possible answer: ∠*F* is supplementary to ∠*A* because the two are angles are opposite angles in an inscribed quadrilateral; m∠*A* = 90°; 180° − 90° = 90°

c. ∠*G* ≅ ∠*HEF*; Possible answer: ∠*HEF* and ∠*FEA* form a linear pair, so they are supplementary; ∠*FEA* and ∠*G* are opposite angles in an inscribed quadrilateral so they are supplementary; ∠*G* ≅ ∠*HEF* because both angles are supplementary to ∠*FEA*.

© Houghton Mifflin Harcourt Publishing Company • Image Credits: ©SuperStock/age fotostock

---

EXTENSION ACTIVITY

Ask students to research the dimensions and shapes of famous baseball parks. They should draw a diagram of a park, then show how to find its area. If the park is an irregular shape, students can divide it into component figures with areas they know how to find, and then add the areas.

Tangents and Circumscribed Angles

Common Core Math Standards

The student is expected to:

 G-C.A.2

Identify and describe relationships among inscribed angles, radii, and chords. Also G-C.A.4(+)

Mathematical Practices

MP.2 Reasoning

Language Objective

Work in pairs to identify tangents and points of tangency.

ENGAGE

Essential Question: What are the key theorems about tangents to a circle?

If a line is tangent to a circle, then it is perpendicular to the radius drawn to the point of tangency. Conversely, if a line is perpendicular to a radius at a point on the circle, then the line is tangent to the circle. Also, a circumscribed angle of a circle and its associated central angle are supplementary.

PREVIEW: LESSON PERFORMANCE TASK

View the Engage section online. Discuss the photograph. Ask students to describe some of the ways satellites benefit people on Earth. Then preview the Lesson Performance Task.

Name _____ Class _____ Date _____

15.3 Tangents and Circumscribed Angles

Essential Question: What are the key theorems about tangents to a circle?

Resource Locker

🧭 Explore Investigating the Tangent-Radius Theorem

A **tangent** is a line in the same plane as a circle that intersects the circle in exactly one point. The point where a tangent and a circle intersect is the **point of tangency**.

In the figure, the line is tangent to circle *C*, and point *P* is the point of tangency. You can use a compass and straightedge to construct a circle and a line tangent to it.

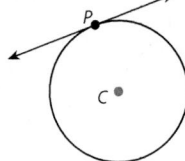

(A) Use a compass to draw a circle. Label the center *C*.

(B) Mark a point *P* on the circle. Using a straightedge, draw a tangent to the circle through point *P*. Mark a point *Q* at a different position on the tangent line.

(C) Use a straightedge to draw the radius $\overline{CP}$.

(D) Use a protractor to measure ∠*CPQ*. Record the result in the table. Repeat the process two more times. Make sure to vary the size of the circle and the location of the point of tangency.

	Circle 1	Circle 2	Circle 3
Measure of ∠CPQ	90°	90°	90°

Reflect

1. **Make a Conjecture** Examine the values in the table. Make a conjecture about the relationship between a tangent line and the radius to the point of tangency.
   A tangent line and the radius to the point of tangency are perpendicular to each other.

2. **Discussion** Describe any possible inaccuracies related to the tools you used in this Explore.
   It is difficult to accurately construct the tangent using just a straightedge and a point on the circle. This may cause the angle measurements to vary slightly from 90°.

© Houghton Mifflin Harcourt Publishing Company

Module 15 Lesson 3

HARDCOVER PAGES 679–686

Turn to these pages to find this lesson in the hardcover student edition.

⊘ Explain 1 Proving the Tangent-Radius Theorem

The Explore illustrates the Tangent-Radius Theorem.

> **Tangent-Radius Theorem**
>
> If a line is tangent to a circle, then it is perpendicular to a radius drawn to the point of tangency.

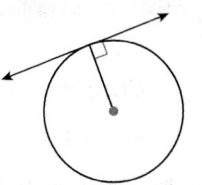

Example 1 Complete the proof of the Tangent–Radius Theorem.

Given: Line m is tangent to circle C at point P.

Prove: $\overline{CP} \perp m$

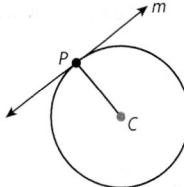

Ⓐ Use an indirect proof. Assume that $\overline{CP}$ is not perpendicular to line m. There must be a point Q on line m such that $\overline{CQ} \perp m$.

If $\overline{CQ} \perp m$, then $\triangle CQP$ is a __right__ triangle, and $CP > CQ$ because __$\overline{CP}$__ is the __hypotenuse__ of the right triangle.

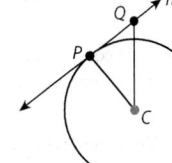

Ⓑ Since line m is a tangent line, it can intersect circle C at only point __P__, and all other points

of line m are in the __exterior__ of the circle.

Ⓒ This means point Q is in the __exterior__ of the circle. You can conclude that $CP < CQ$ because

__$\overline{CP}$__ is a __radius__ of circle C.

Ⓓ This contradicts the initial assumption that a point Q exists such that $\overline{CQ} \perp m$, because that meant that $CP > CQ$. Therefore, the assumption

is __false__ and __$\overline{CP}$__ must be perpendicular to line m.

> **Reflect**
>
> 3. Both lines in the figure are tangent to the circle, and $\overline{AB}$ is a diameter. What can you conclude about the tangent lines?
> Since the tangent lines are both perpendicular to $\overline{AB}$, they are
>
> parallel to each other.

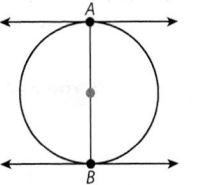

© Houghton Mifflin Harcourt Publishing Company

PROFESSIONAL DEVELOPMENT

🄲 Integrate Mathematical Practices

This lesson provides an opportunity to address Mathematical Practice **MP.2**, which calls for students to "reason abstractly and quantitatively." Students begin by making a conjecture about the relationship between a tangent line to a circle and the radius at the point of tangency, and then provide a proof. In addition to proving the Tangent-Radius Theorem and its converse, students construct a tangent to a circle from a given point outside the circle using the Converse of the Tangent-Radius Theorem. Finally, students prove the Circumscribed Angle Theorem, which depends upon the Tangent-Radius Theorem and the Quadrilateral Sum Theorem.

EXPLORE

Investigating the Tangent-Radius Theorem

INTEGRATE TECHNOLOGY

Students have the option of doing the Explore activity either in the book or online.

QUESTIONING STRATEGIES

? Do you think your observation about the perpendicular relationship between a tangent line and a radius to the point of tangency will prove to be biconditional? Explain. Yes; there is only one point of tangency for a given tangent, and only one radius can be drawn to that point, so it seems likely that the relationship will prove to be biconditional.

EXPLAIN 1

Proving the Tangent-Radius Theorem

AVOID COMMON ERRORS

Some students may assume a segment is tangent to a circle based only on its appearance. Reinforce the fact that a segment is tangent to a circle if and only if it intersects the circle at a point where it is perpendicular to the radius of the circle.

QUESTIONING STRATEGIES

? How does an indirect proof demonstrate that an assertion must be true? Sample answer: It shows that an absurdity results from the assumption that the assertion is not true. Therefore, the assertion must be true.

EXPLAIN 2

Constructing Tangents to a Circle

INTEGRATE TECHNOLOGY

You may wish to have students use geometry software to construct a tangent line from an exterior point, *P*. Once students have completed the construction, encourage them to move point *P* to see what elements of the construction change and what elements remain the same.

CONNECT VOCABULARY [EL]

Compare the definition of a *circumscribed angle* to the definition of an *inscribed angle*. Emphasize that the circumscribed angle is formed by two tangents. Review similarities and highlight the differences between the angles.

QUESTIONING STRATEGIES

? Why do you construct the midpoint of the line segment that connects the point to the center of the circle? The midpoint becomes the center of the circle that intersects the original circle at a right angle.

? How are the two tangent lines that are constructed through the point outside the circle related? Possible answer: They are mirror images of each other because of the way they are constructed using the midpoint of the line that connects the point outside the circle and the center of the circle.

The converse of the Tangent-Radius Theorem is also true. You will be asked to prove this theorem as an exercise.

> **Converse of the Tangent-Radius Theorem**
>
> If a line is perpendicular to a radius of a circle at a point on the circle, then it is tangent to the circle at that point on the circle.

⚙ Explain 2 Constructing Tangents to a Circle

From a point outside a circle, two tangent lines can be drawn to the circle.

Example 2   Use the steps to construct two tangent lines from a point outside a circle.

Ⓐ Use a compass to draw a circle. Label the center *C*.

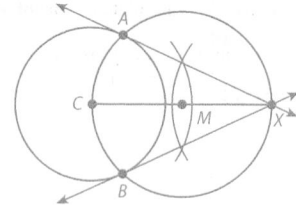

Ⓑ Mark a point *X* outside the circle and use a straightedge to draw $\overline{CX}$.

Ⓒ Use a compass and straightedge to construct the midpoint of $\overline{CX}$ and label the midpoint *M*.

Ⓓ Use a compass to construct a circle with center *M* and radius *CM*.

Ⓔ Label the points of intersection of circle *C* and circle *M* as *A* and *B*. Use a straightedge to draw $\overleftrightarrow{XA}$ and $\overleftrightarrow{XB}$. Both lines are tangent to circle *C*.

> **Reflect**
>
> **4.** How can you justify that $\overleftrightarrow{XA}$ (or $\overleftrightarrow{XB}$) is a tangent line? (Hint: Draw $\overline{CA}$ on the diagram.)
> The endpoints of diameter $\overline{CX}$ lie on the inscribed angle $\angle CAX$ of circle *M*. By the
> Angle Inscribed in a Semicircle Theorem, $\angle CAX$ is a right angle. By the Converse of the
> Tangent-Radius Theorem, $\overleftrightarrow{XA}$ is a tangent line to circle *C*. The same reasoning shows
> that $\overleftrightarrow{XB}$ is a tangent line.
>
> **5.** Draw $\overline{CA}$ and $\overline{CB}$ on the diagram. Consider quadrilateral *CAXB*. State any conclusions you can reach about the measures of the angles of *CAXB*.
> The sum of the measures of the angles is 360°. There are two right angles, $\angle CAX$ and $\angle CBX$.
> $\angle AXB$ and $\angle ACB$ are supplementary.

© Houghton Mifflin Harcourt Publishing Company

COLLABORATIVE LEARNING

Peer-to-Peer Activity

Ask students to use a compass to draw a circle. Then have them draw a point anywhere outside the circle and construct the tangents to the circle from the point. Have the students use a protractor to measure either the circumscribed angle or the associated central angle. Then have them exchange papers with a partner and apply the Circumscribed Angle Theorem to find the other related angle. Finally, have students check their work using a protractor and share their constructions with the class.

⚙ Explain 3 Proving the Circumscribed Angle Theorem

A **circumscribed angle** is an angle formed by two rays from a common endpoint that are tangent to a circle.

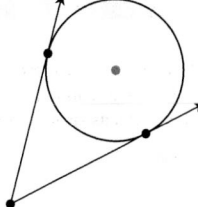

Circumscribed Angle Theorem
A circumscribed angle of a circle and its associated central angle are supplementary.

Example 3   Prove the Circumscribed Angle Theorem.

Given: $\angle AXB$ is a circumscribed angle of circle C.

Prove: $\angle AXB$ and $\angle ACB$ are supplementary.

Since $\angle AXB$ is a circumscribed angle of circle C, $\overline{XA}$ and $\overline{XB}$ are

<u>tangents</u> to the circle. Therefore, $\angle XAC$ and $\angle XBC$ are

<u>right angles</u> by the <u>Tangent-Radius Theorem</u>.

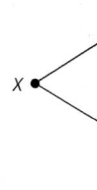

In quadrilateral $XACB$, the sum of the measures of its four angles is <u>360°</u>.

Since $m\angle XAC + m\angle XBC = \boxed{180°}$, this means $m\angle AXB + m\angle ACB = 360° - 180° = \boxed{180°}$.

So, $\angle AXB$ and $\angle ACB$ are supplementary by the <u>definition of supplementary angles</u>.

Reflect

6. Is it possible for quadrilateral $AXBC$ to be a parallelogram? If so, what type of parallelogram must it be? If not, why not?
    Yes. If $AXBC$ is a parallelogram, it must be a square.

💬 Elaborate

7. $\overrightarrow{KM}$ and $\overrightarrow{KN}$ are tangent to circle C. Explain how to show that $\overline{KM} \cong \overline{KN}$, using congruent triangles.
    Draw $\overline{KC}$. This creates two right triangles, $\triangle KCM$ and

    $\triangle KCN$. Since $\overline{CM} \cong \overline{CN}$ and $\overline{CK} \cong \overline{CK}$, the triangles are

    congruent by the Hypotenuse-Leg Theorem.

    It follows that $\overline{KM} \cong \overline{KN}$ by CPCTC.

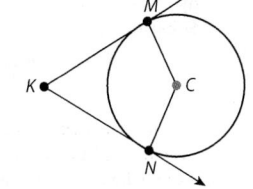

8. **Essential Question Check-In** What are the key theorems regarding tangent lines to a circle?
    If a line is tangent to a circle, it is perpendicular to the radius drawn to the point of

    tangency. Conversely, if a line is perpendicular to a radius of a circle at a point on the

    circle, it is tangent to the circle. Also, a circumscribed angle of a circle and its associated

    central angle are supplementary.

DIFFERENTIATE INSTRUCTION

Multiple Representations

Students may wonder whether there is a connection between the term *tangent* as it is defined in this lesson and the trigonometric ratio called the *tangent*. In a circle drawn on the coordinate plane with a radius of 1 and its center at the origin, the tangent of an angle with measure $m°$ is $\frac{y}{1}$ or y. This is the length of the line segment that is *tangent* to the circle and that has its endpoints on the sides of the angle.

EXPLAIN 3

Proving the Circumscribed Angle Theorem

INTEGRATE MATHEMATICAL PRACTICES
Focus on Reasoning

MP.2 Discuss similarities and differences between the Circumscribed Angle Theorem and the Inscribed Quadrilateral Theorem.

QUESTIONING STRATEGIES

❓ Why do you construct a quadrilateral to prove the Circumscribed Angle Theorem? to use the fact that the sum of the angle measures of a quadrilateral is 360° in conjunction with the total angle measures at the point of tangency

ELABORATE

INTEGRATE MATHEMATICAL PRACTICES
Focus on Reasoning

MP.2 Check that students understand how to use the Tangent-Radius Theorem and its converse. Discuss why it is necessary to verify that a line is perpendicular to a radius at a point on the circle to confirm that the line is a tangent to the circle.

SUMMARIZE THE LESSON

❓ What are the key theorems about tangent lines to a circle? If a line is tangent to a circle, then it is perpendicular to the radius drawn to the point of tangency. Conversely, if a line is perpendicular to a radius of a circle at a point on the circle, then the line is a tangent to the circle.

ASSIGNMENT GUIDE

Concepts and Skills	Practice
Explore Investigating the Tangent-Radius Theorem	Exercises 1–2
Example 1 Proving the Tangent-Radius Theorem	Exercises 3–4
Example 2 Constructing Tangents to a Circle	Exercises 5–8
Example 3 Proving the Circumscribed Angle Theorem	Exercises 9–12

GRAPHIC ORGANIZERS

Have students make a graphic organizer or illustrated guide that shows the steps for constructing a tangent line to a circle from a point outside the circle.

⭐ Evaluate: Homework and Practice

• Online Homework
• Hints and Help
• Extra Practice

Use the figure for Exercises 1–2. You use geometry software to construct a tangent to circle O at point X on the circle, as shown in the diagram.

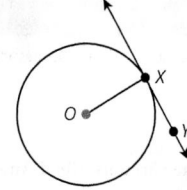

1. What do you expect to be the measure of $\angle OXY$? Explain.

> 90°; By the Tangent-Radius Theorem, $\overline{XC}$ and $\overline{XY}$ are perpendicular, so $m\angle OXY = 90°$.

2. Suppose you drag point X so that is in a different position on the circle. Does the measure of $\angle OXY$ change? Explain.

> No. The Tangent-Radius Theorem still holds so the measure of $\angle OXY$ stays the same.

3. **Make a Conjecture** You use geometry software to construct circle A, diameters $\overline{AB}$ and $\overline{AD}$, and lines m and n which are tangent to circle A at points D and B, respectively. Make a conjecture about the relationship of the two tangents. Explain your conjecture.

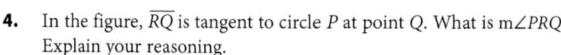

> The tangents are perpendicular. $\angle A$ is given to be a right angle. By the Tangent-Radius Theorem, $\overline{AD} \perp \overline{CD}$ and $\overline{AB} \perp \overline{CB}$, so both $\angle ADC$ and $\angle ABC$ are right angles. Since the sum of the angle measures of a quadrilateral is 360°, $\angle C$ must be a right angle. Thus, the tangents are perpendicular.

4. In the figure, $\overline{RQ}$ is tangent to circle P at point Q. What is $m\angle PRQ$? Explain your reasoning.

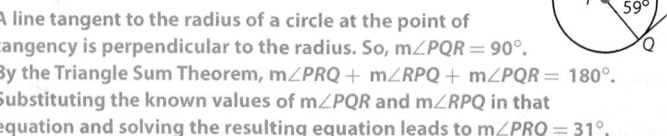

> A line tangent to the radius of a circle at the point of tangency is perpendicular to the radius. So, $m\angle PQR = 90°$. By the Triangle Sum Theorem, $m\angle PRQ + m\angle RPQ + m\angle PQR = 180°$. Substituting the known values of $m\angle PQR$ and $m\angle RPQ$ in that equation and solving the resulting equation leads to $m\angle PRQ = 31°$.

5. **Represent Real-World Problems** The International Space Station orbits Earth at an altitude of about 240 miles. In the diagram, the Space Station is at point E. The radius of Earth is approximately 3960 miles. To the nearest ten miles, what is EH, the distance from the space station to the horizon?

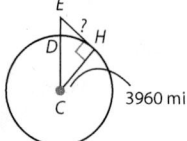

> $ED = 240$ mi; $EC = CD + ED = 3960$ mi $+ 240$ mi $= 4200$ mi. $EC^2 = EH^2 + CH^2$ by the Pythagorean Theorem; $4200^2 = EH^2 + 3960^2$. $1{,}958{,}400 = EH^2$, so EH is approximately 1400 mi.

Module 15   809   Lesson 3

Exercise	Depth of Knowledge (D.O.K.)	COMMON CORE Mathematical Practices
1–4	**2** Skills/Concepts	**MP.3** Logic
5	**2** Skills/Concepts	**MP.4** Modeling
6–10	**2** Skills/Concepts	**MP.4** Modeling
11–19	**2** Skills/Concepts	**MP.2** Reasoning
20	**3** Strategic Thinking H.O.T.	**MP.3** Logic
21	**3** Strategic Thinking H.O.T.	**MP.3** Logic

Multi-Step Find the length of each radius. Identify the point of tangency, and write the equation of the tangent line at that point.

6.

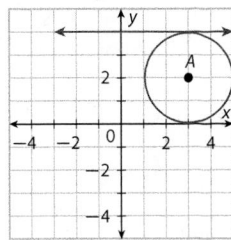

The radius of the circle is 2 units, and the point of tangency is $(3, 4)$. The equation of a horizontal line through $(3, 4)$ is $y = 4$.

7.

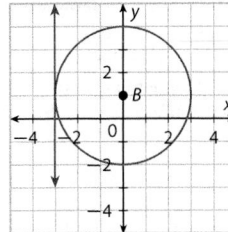

The radius of the circle is 3 units, and the point of tangency is $(-3, 1)$. The equation of a vertical line through $(-3, 1)$ is $x = -3$.

8. In the figure, $QS = 5$, $RT = 12$, and $\overleftrightarrow{RT}$ is tangent to radius $\overline{QR}$ with the point of tangency at R. Find QT.

$\overline{QR}$ is a radius, so $QR = QS = 5$. Since $\overleftrightarrow{RT}$ is a tangent to radius $\overline{QR}$ at the point of tangency R, $\overleftrightarrow{RT} \perp \overline{QR}$ and $\triangle RQT$ is a right triangle. By the Pythagorean Theorem,

$QT^2 = QR^2 + RT^2 = 5^2 + 12^2 = 25 + 144 = 169$. So $QT = 13$.

The segments in each figure are tangent to the circle at the points shown. Find each length.

9.

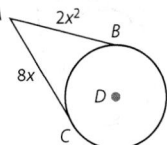

The tangents from point A are congruent.

Solve $2x^2 = 8x$ to get the value of x.

$2x^2 = 8x$, or $2x(x - 4) = 0$, and $x = 0$ or 4.

Choose $x = 4$. $AC = 2(4)^2 = 32$.

$AB = 8(4) = 32$.

10.

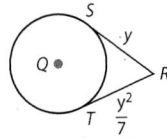

The tangents from point R are congruent.

Solve $y = \dfrac{y^2}{7}$ to get the value of y.

$y = \dfrac{y^2}{7}$, or $7y = y^2$, and $0 = y^2 - 7y = y(y - 7)$.

The solutions are $y = 0$ or 7.

Choose $y = 7$. $SR = 7$. $RT = \dfrac{y^2}{7} = \dfrac{49}{7} = 7$.

Focus on Communication

MP.3 Have students support their work by explaining how and why they applied a theorem to solve a problem or complete a diagram.

Exercise	Depth of Knowledge (D.O.K.)	COMMON CORE Mathematical Practices
22	**3** Strategic Thinking H.O.T.	**MP.3** Logic
23	**3** Strategic Thinking H.O.T.	**MP.5** Using Tools

11. Justify Reasoning Suppose you construct a figure with $\overline{PR}$ tangent to circle Q at R and $\overline{PS}$ tangent to circle Q at S. Make a conjecture about $\angle P$ and $\angle Q$. Justify your reasoning.

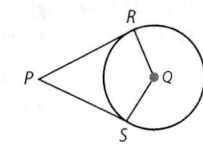

    $\angle P$ and $\angle Q$ are supplementary angles. The sum of the angle measures in quadrilateral $PRQS$ is 360°. Since a line tangent to a circle is $\perp$ to a radius, $\angle R$ and $\angle S$ are right angles. By substitution, $m\angle P + m\angle R + m\angle Q + m\angle S = m\angle P + 90° + m\angle Q + 90° = 360°$. So, $m\angle P + m\angle Q = 180°$. So $\angle P$ and $\angle Q$ are supplementary angles.

12. $\overline{PR}$ is tangent to circle Q at R and $\overline{PS}$ is tangent to circle Q at S. Find $m\angle Q$.

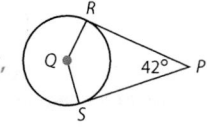

    Since $\overline{PR}$ is tangent to circle Q at R and $\overline{PS}$ is tangent to circle Q at S, $\angle P$ and $\angle Q$ are supplementary by the Circumscribed Angle Theorem. So, $m\angle Q = 180° - 42° = 138°$.

13. $\overline{PR}$ is tangent to circle Q at R and $\overline{PS}$ is tangent to circle Q at S. Find $m\angle P$.

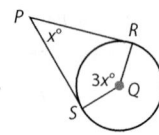

    Since $\overline{PR}$ is tangent to circle Q at R and $\overline{PS}$ is tangent to circle Q at S, $\angle P$ and $\angle Q$ are supplementary by the Circumscribed Angle Theorem. Solve for x. $x + 3x = 180$; $4x = 180$, $x = 45$. So, $m\angle P = 45°$.

$\overline{PA}$ is tangent to circle O at A and $\overline{PB}$ is tangent to circle O at B, and $m\angle P = 56°$. Use the figure to find each measure.

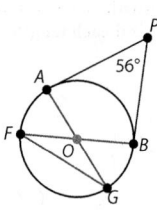

14. $m\angle AOB$

    Since $\overline{PA}$ is tangent to circle O at A and $\overline{PB}$ is tangent to circle O at B, $\angle P$ and $\angle AOB$ are supplementary by the Circumscribed Angle Theorem. So, $m\angle AOB = 180° - 56° = 124°$.

15. $m\angle OGF$

    Since $\overline{PA}$ is tangent to circle O at A and $\overline{PB}$ is tangent to circle O at B, $\angle P$ and $\angle AOB$ are supplementary by the Circumscribed Angle Theorem. So, $m\angle AOB = 180° - 56° = 124°$. Since $\angle AOB$ and $\angle FOG$ are vertical angles, $m\angle FOG = 124°$. $\triangle FOB$ is isosceles, so its base angles are congruent. So, $m\angle OGF = \dfrac{180 - 124}{2} = 28°$.

16. Which statements correctly relate ∠BDC and ∠BAC? Select all that apply.

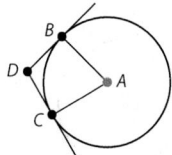

A. ∠BDC and ∠BAC are complementary.

B. ∠BDC and ∠BAC are supplementary.

C. ∠BDC and ∠BAC are congruent.

D. ∠BDC and ∠BAC are right angles.

E. The sum of the measures of ∠BDC and ∠BAC is 180°.

F. It is impossible to determine a relationship between ∠BDC and ∠BAC.

B and E; The Circumscribed Angle Theorem states that ∠BDC and ∠BAC are
supplementary and the measures of supplementary angles sum to 180°.

17. Critical Thinking Given a circle with diameter $\overline{BC}$, is it possible to construct
tangents to B and C from an external point X? If so, make a construction. If not,
explain why it is not possible.

It is not possible. If it were possible, △XBC would contain two right
angles, one each where the ends of the diameter intersect the tangents.
This contradicts the Triangle Sum Theorem.

$\overrightarrow{KJ}$ is tangent to circle C at J, $\overrightarrow{KL}$ is tangent to circle C at L,
and $m\overset{\frown}{ML} = 138°$.

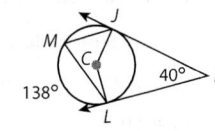

18. Find m∠M.

$\overrightarrow{KJ}$ *and* $\overrightarrow{KL}$ *are tangents to circle C, ∠K and ∠JCL are supplementary by the Circumscribed*
Angle Theorem.
So, m∠JCL = 180° − 40° = 140°. Since an arc is equal to its central angle, m$\overset{\frown}{JL}$ = 140°.
So, m∠M = 70° by the Inscribed Angle Theorem.

19. Find $m\overset{\frown}{MJ}$.

$\overrightarrow{KJ}$ *and* $\overrightarrow{KL}$ *are tangents to circle C, ∠K and ∠JCL are supplementary by the Circumscribed*
Angle Theorem. So, m∠JCL = 180° − 40° = 140°. Since an arc is equal to its central angle,
m$\overset{\frown}{JL}$ = 140°. So, m$\overset{\frown}{MJ}$ = 360° − (140° + 138°) = 82.

© Houghton Mifflin Harcourt Publishing Company

Students may confuse angle and arc length
relationships when they solve problems with missing
measures. Suggest that students identify one measure
at a time. Encourage them to look back and find the
appropriate theorem or definition to help them
identify a measure. As they become familiar with the
relationships, they will become easier to identify.
Emphasize that they should understand the reasoning
that supports a computed measure before they write
down a measure because it seems probable.

Have students explain why distance from the center of a circle is determined by a radius drawn perpendicularly to a tangent at the point of tangency. Have them support their explanations with sketches.

H.O.T. Focus on Higher Order Thinking

20. **Justify Reasoning** Prove the converse of the Tangent-Radius Theorem.
Given: Line m is in the plane of circle C, P is a point of circle C, and $\overline{CP} \perp m$
Prove: m is tangent to circle C at P.

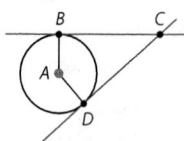

Let Q be any point on m other than P. Then $\triangle CPQ$ is a right triangle with hypotenuse $\overline{CQ}$. Therefore, $CQ > CP$ since the hypotenuse is the longest side of a right triangle. Since $\overline{CP}$ is a radius, point Q must be in the exterior of circle C. So, P is the only point of line m on circle C. Since line m intersects circle C at exactly one point, line m is tangent to the circle at P.

21. **Draw Conclusions** A grapic designer created a preliminary sketch for a company logo. In the figure, $\overleftrightarrow{BC}$ and $\overleftrightarrow{CD}$ are tangent to circle A and $BC > BA$. What type of quadrilateral is figure $ABCD$ that she created? Explain.

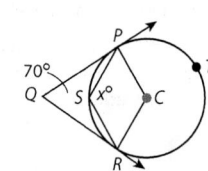

$ABCD$ is a kite; $\overline{AB} \cong \overline{AD}$ because they are radii. $\overline{CB} \cong \overline{CD}$ because they are tangents drawn to a circle from an external point. This shows $ABCD$ is a kite because it has two pairs of consecutive sides congruent, but opposite sides are not congruent.

22. **Explain the Error** In the given figure, $\overleftrightarrow{QP}$ and $\overleftrightarrow{QR}$ are tangents. A student was asked to find m$\angle PSR$. Critique the student's work and correct any errors.

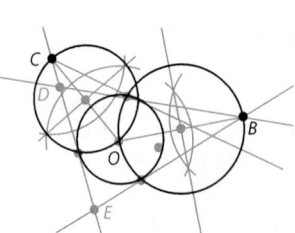

Since $\angle PQR$ is a circumscribed angle, $\angle PQR$ and $\angle PCR$ are supplementary. So m$\angle PCR = 110°$. Since $\angle PSR \cong \angle PQR$, m$\angle PCR = 110°$.

The student made an error in assuming $\angle PSR \cong \angle PCR$. The student should have realized that since m$\angle PCR = 110°$, m$\widehat{PR} = 110°$. The student should have subtracted $110°$ from $360°$ to conclude that m$\widehat{PTR} = 250°$. The student should then have concluded that m$\angle PSR = \frac{1}{2}(m\angle PTR) = \frac{1}{2}(250°) = 125°$ by the Inscribed Angle Theorem.

23. Given circle O and points B and C, construct a triangle that is circumscribed around the circle.

From point B, construct two tangents to circle O. From point C, construct two tangents to circle O. Label the point of intersection of the tangent from B and the tangent from C as point D. Triangle DEB is circumscribed about circle O.

Lesson Performance Task

A communications satellite is in a synchronous orbit 22,000 miles above Earth's surface. Points *B* and *D* in the figure are points of tangency of the satellite signal with the Earth. They represent the greatest distance from the satellite at which the signal can be received directly. Point *C* is the center of the Earth.

1. Find distance *AB*. Round to the nearest mile. Explain your reasoning.

2. m∠*BAC* = 9°. If the circumference of the circle represents the Earth's equator, what percent of the Earth's equator is within range of the satellite's signal? Explain your reasoning.

3. How much longer does it take a satellite signal to reach point *B* than it takes to reach point *E*? Use 186,000 mi/sec as the speed of a satellite signal. Round your answer to the nearest hundredth.

4. The satellite is in orbit above the Earth's equator. Along with the point directly below it on the Earth's surface, the satellite makes one complete revolution every 24 hours. How fast must it travel to complete a revolution in that time? You can use the formula *C* = 2π*r* to find the circumference of the orbit. Round your answer to the nearest whole number.

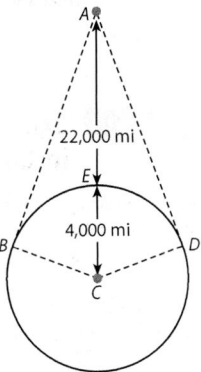

1. 25,690 miles; $\overline{AB}$ and $\overline{AD}$ are tangents to the circle at *B* and *D*. Triangle *ABC* is a right triangle with hypotenuse *AC* = 26,000 miles and leg *BC* = 4000 miles. By the Pythagorean Theorem, *AB* = 25,690 miles.

2. 45%; m∠*BCA* = m∠*DCA* = 180° − (90° + 9°) = 81°. So, central angle m∠*BCD* = 81° + 81° = 162°. So, m$\overset{\frown}{BED}$ = 162°. This is $\frac{162}{360}$ = 45% of the circumference of the circle.

3. About 0.02 sec; The signal must travel 25,690 − 22,000 = 3,690 miles farther to reach *B* than to reach *E*. At a speed of 186,000 miles per second, the extra distance will take $\frac{3690}{186,000}$ = 0.02 second.

4. About 6803 mi/h; circumference of orbit = 2π*r* ≈ 2(3.14)(26,000) = 163,280 mi;

   To travel this distance in 24 hours the satellite must travel $\frac{163,280}{24}$ ≈ 6803 miles per hour.

© Houghton Mifflin Harcourt Publishing Company

Module 15   **814**   Lesson 3

INTEGRATE MATHEMATICAL PRACTICES
Focus on Patterns

MP.8 A satellite is in Earth orbit at a lower altitude than a satellite in geosynchronous orbit. Is it visible within a greater or lesser range than the range of a geosynchronous satellite? Explain your answer by referring to the Lesson Performance Task diagram. A lesser range; Sample answer: Tangents drawn to the satellite will have points of tangency with the circle that are closer to point *E* than *B* or *D* are. Therefore, the length of the arc connecting them will be less than the length of $\overset{\frown}{BD}$.

INTEGRATE MATHEMATICAL PRACTICES
Focus on Critical Thinking

MP.3 As the Lesson Performance Task shows (Question 2), at an altitude of 22,000 miles, about 45% of Earth's equator is within range of a synchronous satellite's signal. At what altitude would a satellite have to be in order for 50% of Earth's equator to be within range of the satellite's signal? Explain. A satellite can never be within range of 50% of Earth's equator. If it were at such an altitude, $\overline{BD}$ in the figure would be a diameter of the circle, and triangles *ABC* and *ADC* would each contain two right angles, which is impossible.

EXTENSION ACTIVITY

The velocity, *v*, of an object orbiting the Earth, in meters per second, is given approximately by $v = \sqrt{\frac{(6.67 \times 10^{-11})m}{r}}$, where *m* is Earth's mass $(6 \times 10^{24} \text{ kg})$ and *r* is the object's distance from the center of the Earth (that is, its distance above Earth's surface plus Earth's radius of 6.4×10^6 m). Ask students to find the Moon's velocity in its orbit, in meters per second (using the formula) and miles per hour. They'll need to research the Moon's distance from Earth $(3.8 \times 10^8 \text{ m})$. They can extend this activity by finding the orbital velocities of other moons in our solar system. about 1018 m/sec

Scoring Rubric
2 points: Student correctly solves the problem and explains his/her reasoning.
1 point: Student shows good understanding of the problem but does not fully solve or explain his/her reasoning.
0 points: Student does not demonstrate understanding of the problem.

Tangents and Circumscribed Angles   **814**

Segment Relationships in Circles

Common Core Math Standards

The student is expected to:

 G-C.A.2

Identify and describe relationships among inscribed angles, radii, and chords.

Mathematical Practices

 MP.2 Reasoning

Language Objective

Explain to a partner how to interpret the Chord-Chord Product Theorem.

ENGAGE

Essential Question: What are the relationships between the segments in circles?

Chords intersecting in a circle form four segments. The product of the lengths of the segments of one chord equals the product of the lengths of the segments of the other chord. Secants to a circle form a secant segment and an external secant segment. For two secants from the same point, the product of the lengths of one secant segment and its external segment equals the product of the lengths of the other secant segment and its external segment. For a tangent and secant from the same point, the product of the lengths of the secant segment and its external segment equals the square of the length of the tangent segment.

PREVIEW: LESSON PERFORMANCE TASK

View the Engage section online. Discuss the photograph. Ask students if they can explain how a car converts gasoline to energy to propel the car. Then preview the Lesson Performance Task.

15.4 Segment Relationships in Circles

Essential Question: What are the relationships between the segments in circles?

Resource Locker

⊙ Explore   **Exploring Segment Length Relationships in Circles**

Any segment connecting two points on a circle is a chord. In some cases, two chords drawn inside the same circle will intersect, creating four segments. In the following activity, you will look for a pattern in how these segments are related and form a conjecture.

(A) Using geometry software or a compass and straightedge, construct circle A with two chords $\overline{CD}$ and $\overline{EF}$ that intersect inside the circle. Label the intersection point G.

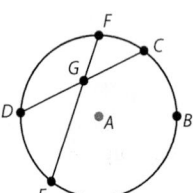

Circle 1

Students' circles may vary.

(B) Repeat your construction with two more circles. Vary the size of the circles and where you put the intersecting chords inside them.

Circle 2

Students' circles may vary.

Circle 3

Students' circles may vary.

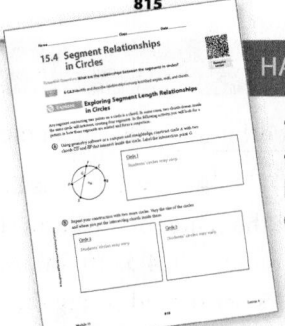

HARDCOVER PAGES 687–698

Turn to these pages to find this lesson in the hardcover student edition.

(C) Fill in the chart with the lengths of the segments measured to the nearest millimeter and calculate their products.

Students' results may vary. Possible results are shown.

	DG	GC	EG	GF	DG · GC	EG · GF
Circle 1	13.5	26.8	25.2	14.4	362	362
Circle 2	15.0	29.9	28.1	16.0	449	449
Circle 3	19.0	26.0	35.0	14.1	494	494

(D) Look for a pattern among the measurements and calculations of the segments. From the table, it appears that _DG · GC_ will always equal _EG · GF_.

Reflect

1. **Discussion** Compare your results with those of your classmates. What do you notice?
   Possible answer: Everyone answered Step D the same; the values of *DG · GC* and *EG · GF* were always the same.

2. What conjecture can you make about the products of the segments of two chords that intersect inside a circle?
   Conjecture: The products of the lengths of the segments of two chords that intersect inside a circle will be equal.

⟡ Explain 1   Applying the Chord-Chord Product Theorem

In the Explore, you discovered a pattern in the relationship between the parts of two chords that intersect inside a circle. In this Example, you will apply the following theorem to solve problems.

Chord-Chord Product Theorem

If two chords intersect inside a circle, then the products of the lengths of the segments of the chords are equal.

$AE \cdot EB = CE \cdot ED$

PROFESSIONAL DEVELOPMENT

Math Background

The theorems that are presented in this lesson are sometimes known as the *power theorems*. In particular, the Chord-Chord Product Theorem, the Secant-Secant Product Theorem, and the Secant-Tangent Product Theorem may be stated in an all-inclusive general form called the Power of a Point Theorem. This theorem states that, given a circle, a point *P* not on the circle, and two lines through *P* that intersect the circle at points *A* and *B* and at points *C* and *D*, respectively, $AP \times BP = CP \times DP$. *P* may lie in the interior of or exterior to the circle. If *P* is tangent to the circle, the two points of intersection coincide and the theorem reduces to the Secant-Tangent Product Theorem.

EXPLORE

Exploring Segment Length Relationships in Circles

INTEGRATE TECHNOLOGY

Students have the option of doing the Explore activity either in the book or online.

INTEGRATE MATHEMATICAL PRACTICES
Focus on Communication

MP.3 As students explore the segment length relationships, have them note whether they are constructing chords, secants, or tangents. Discuss with students the different ways they are relating the segment lengths to one another, based on whether the segments intersect inside or outside the circle.

QUESTIONING STRATEGIES

? How does drawing triangles to connect the endpoints help you recognize the relationship between the chords? Sample answer: It makes it possible to identify the congruent angles because the inscribed angles intercept the same arc. The triangles are similar, so the sides are proportional. Then the products of the lengths of the chord segments of each chord are equal.

EXPLAIN 1

Applying the Chord-Chord Product Theorem

AVOID COMMON ERRORS

Some students might multiply the wrong segments for the Chord-Chord Product Theorem. Have them use two colors to distinguish the chords. Emphasize that the segments lie on the same chord, or line segment.

QUESTIONING STRATEGIES

? Do intersecting chords have to be equal in length to use the Chord-Chord Product Theorem? Explain. No, the theorem applies to any two chords that intersect inside a circle.

? How can you check that the length of each chord is reasonable? Check that the segment that looks longer has the greater length. Then verify that the products of the chord segments are equal.

Example 1 Find the value of x and the length of each chord.

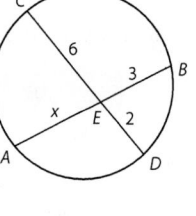

(A) Set up an equation according to the Chord-Chord Product Theorem and solve for x.

$$CE \cdot ED = AE \cdot EB$$
$$6(2) = 3(x)$$
$$12 = 3x$$
$$4 = x$$

Add the segment lengths to find the length of each chord.

$$CD = CE + ED = 6 + 2 = 8$$
$$AB = AE + EB = 4 + 3 = 7$$

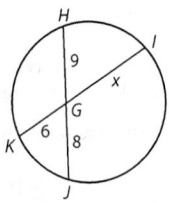

(B) Set up an equation according to the Chord-Chord Product Theorem and solve for x:

$$HG \cdot GJ = KG \cdot GI$$
$$\boxed{9}\left(\boxed{8}\right) = \boxed{6}\left(\boxed{x}\right)$$
$$\boxed{72} = 6x$$
$$\boxed{12} = x$$

Add the segment lengths together to find the lengths of each chord:

$$HJ = HG + GJ = \boxed{9} + 8 = \boxed{17}$$
$$KI = \boxed{KG} + GI = 6 + \boxed{12} = \boxed{18}$$

Your Turn

3. Given $AD = 12$. Find the value of x and the length of each chord.

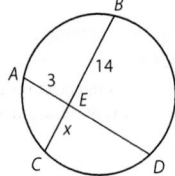

$$AE \cdot ED = CE \cdot CB$$
$$3(12 - 3) = 14(x)$$
$$27 = 14x$$
$$1.93 \approx x$$
$$CB \approx 15.93$$
$$AD = 12 \text{ (given)}$$

© Houghton Mifflin Harcourt Publishing Company

COLLABORATIVE LEARNING

Peer-to-Peer Activity

Ask pairs of students to work together to draw an example of one of the theorems in the lesson, assigning different theorems to various pairs. Then have the pairs exchange drawings and state the theorem that applies to the drawings. Ask each pair to verify their choice using the Chord-Chord, Secant-Secant, or Secant-Tangent Product Theorems.

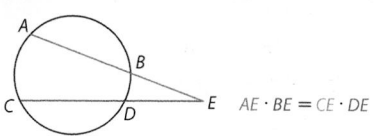 **Explain 2** **Proving the Secant-Secant Product Theorem**

A secant is any line that intersects a circle at exactly two points. A secant segment is part of a secant line with at least one point on the circle. A secant segment that lies in the exterior of the circle with one point on the circle is called an external secant segment. Secant segments drawn from the same point in the exterior of a circle maintain a certain relationship that can be stated as a theorem.

Secant-Secant Product Theorem

If two secants intersect in the exterior of a circle, then the product of the lengths of one secant segment and its external segment equals the product of the lengths of the other secant segment and its external segment.

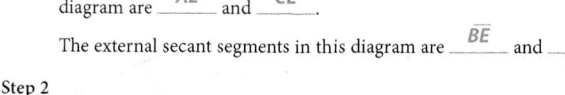

$AE \cdot BE = CE \cdot DE$

Example 2   Use similar triangles to prove the Secant-Secant Product Theorem.

Step 1 Identify the segments in the diagram. The whole secant segments in this

diagram are ___$\overline{AE}$___ and ___$\overline{CE}$___.

The external secant segments in this diagram are ___$\overline{BE}$___ and ___$\overline{DE}$___.

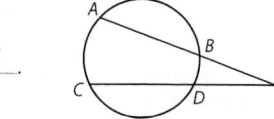

Step 2

Given the diagram as shown, prove that $AE \cdot BE = CE \cdot DE$.

Prove: $AE \cdot BE = CE \cdot DE$

Proof: Draw auxiliary line segments $\overline{AD}$ and $\overline{CB}$. $\angle EAD$ and $\angle ECB$ both

intercept ___$\overparen{BD}$___, so $\angle$ ☐EAD ≅ $\angle$ ☐ECB. $\angle E \cong \angle E$ by the

___Reflexive___ Property. Thus, $\triangle EAD \sim \triangle ECB$ by

the ___AA Triangle Similarity Theorem___. Therefore, corresponding sides

are proportional, so $\dfrac{AE}{\boxed{CE}} = \dfrac{\boxed{DE}}{BE}$. By the ___Multiplication___ Property of Equality,

$BE(CE) \cdot \frac{AE}{CE} = \frac{DE}{BE} \cdot BE(CE)$, and thus $AE \cdot BE = CE \cdot DE$.

Reflect

4. Rewrite the Secant-Secant Theorem in your own words. Use a diagram or shortcut
notation to help you remember what it means.
Possible answer: For two secant segments drawn to a circle from the same point, (whole)

(outside) of first segment equals (whole)(outside) of second segment.

5. **Discussion:** Suppose that two secants are drawn so that they intersect on the circle.
Can you determine anything about the lengths of the segments formed? Explain.
No; if the endpoints of the secants lie outside the circle, the lengths outside the circle can

be extended without changing the segments inside the circle. So no relationship exists

using the external segments and whole secant segments.

EXPLAIN 2

Proving the Secant-Secant Product Theorem

INTEGRATE MATHEMATICAL PRACTICES
Focus on Math Connections

MP.1 Discuss how the proof of the Secant-Secant Product Theorem is similar to and different than the Chord-Chord Product Theorem.

QUESTIONING STRATEGIES

? Must the two secant segments and the two external secant segments be equal in length to use the Secant-Secant Product Theorem? Explain. No, the theorem does not require the lengths of the secant segments to be equal.

? What provides the basis for the proof of the Secant-Secant Product Theorem? As with the Chord-Chord Product Theorem, the proof is based on similar triangles that are formed by the segments within the circle.

? Why does the Secant-Secant Product Theorem relate the products of the external secant segments and the whole secant segment? These are the parts that are proportional using the similar triangles constructed to derive the theorem.

DIFFERENTIATE INSTRUCTION

Visual Cues

As you discuss each theorem with the class, use colored chalk or markers to highlight the segments that are proportional to one another. Use the same colors to write the parts of the proportion so students can better see and understand the relationships. Encourage students to use colored pencils in their notes.

EXPLAIN 3

Applying the Secant-Secant Product Theorem

AVOID COMMON ERRORS

Some students may have difficulty setting up the segment length equation to apply the Secant-Secant Product Theorem. Encourage students to get in the habit of drawing and labeling the entire secant as well as the external secant segment to help them avoid errors in setting up the segment length equations.

QUESTIONING STRATEGIES

? How can you use the Secant-Secant Product Theorem to find the length of a secant, its secant segment, and its external secant segment, if their given measures contain a variable? Use the given information to set up an equation that shows the product of the lengths of one secant segment and its external segment equal to the product of the lengths of the other secant segment and its external segment. Solve the equation for the variable and then use the variable to find each unknown length.

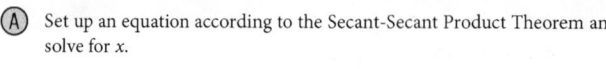

Explain 3 Applying the Secant-Secant Product Theorem

You can use the Secant-Secant Product Theorem to find unknown measures of secants and secant segments by setting up an equation.

Example 3 Find the value of x and the length of each secant segment.

(A) Set up an equation according to the Secant-Secant Product Theorem and solve for x.

$$AC \cdot AB = AE \cdot AD$$
$$(5 + x)(5) = (12)(6)$$
$$5x + 25 = 72$$
$$5x = 47$$
$$x = 9.4$$

Add the segments together to find the lengths of each secant segment.

$$AC = 5 + 9.4 = 14.4; \; AE = 6 + 6 = 12$$

(B) Set up an equation according to the Secant-Secant Product Theorem and solve for x.

$$UP \cdot TP = SP \cdot RP$$

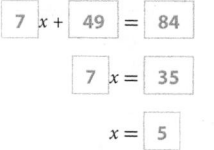

$$7x + \boxed{49} = \boxed{84}$$
$$7x = \boxed{35}$$
$$x = \boxed{5}$$

Add the segments together to find the lengths of each secant segment.

$$UP = 7 + \boxed{5} = \boxed{12}; \; SP = 8 + 6 = 14$$

Your Turn

Find the value of x and the length of each secant segment.

6.

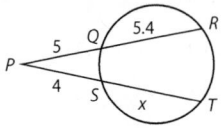

$$PT \cdot PS = PR \cdot PQ$$
$$(4 + x)(4) = (10.4)(5)$$
$$x = 9$$
$$PT = 13; PR = 10.4$$

7.

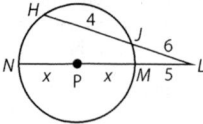

$$NL \cdot ML = HL \cdot JL$$
$$(5 + 2x)(5) = (10)(6)$$
$$x = 3.5$$
$$HL = 10; NL = 12$$

LANGUAGE SUPPORT EL

Connect Vocabulary

Explain to students that the name of each theorem depends on understanding the vocabulary associated with the special line of the circle. Present students with a variety of drawings that show *chords, secants,* and *tangents.* Have them identify each line segment by its name. This should help them associate the vocabulary with the theorem and its corresponding name. Students will still have to learn the special relationships that characterize each theorem but recognizing the specific name of each line segment should facilitate their understanding.

© Houghton Mifflin Harcourt Publishing Company

⊘ Explain 4   Applying the Secant-Tangent Product Theorem

A similar theorem applies when both a secant segment and tangent segment are drawn to a circle from the same exterior point. A **tangent segment** is a segment of a tangent line with exactly one endpoint on the circle.

Secant-Tangent Product Theorem	
If a secant and a tangent intersect in the exterior of a circle, then the product of the lengths of the secant segment and its external segment equals the length of the tangent segment squared.	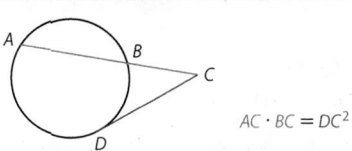 $AC \cdot BC = DC^2$

Example 4   Find the value of x.

(A)   Given the diameter of the Earth as 8,000 miles, a satellite's orbit is 6,400 miles above the Earth. Its range, shown by $\overline{SP}$, is a tangent segment.

Set up an equation according to the Secant-Tangent Product Theorem and solve for x:

$$SA \cdot SE = SP^2$$
$$(8000 + 6400)(6400) = x^2$$
$$(14400)(6400) = x^2$$
$$92,160,000 = x^2$$
$$\pm 9600 = x$$

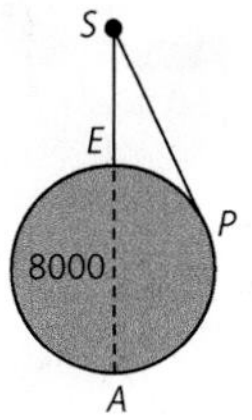

Since distance must be positive, the value of x must be 9600 miles.

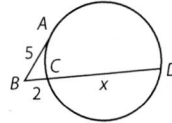

(B)   Set up an equation according to the Secant-Tangent Product Theorem and solve for x:

$$BD \cdot BC = BA^2$$
$$\left(\boxed{x + 2}\right)(2) = 5^2$$
$$\boxed{2}\,x + \boxed{4} = \boxed{25}$$
$$\boxed{2}\,x = \boxed{21}$$
$$x = \boxed{10.5}$$

EXPLAIN 4

Applying the Secant-Tangent Product Theorem

QUESTIONING STRATEGIES

❓ **How do you know when to use the Secant-Secant Product Theorem or the Secant-Tangent Product Theorem?** Use the Secant-Secant Product Theorem when the problem has information about the lengths of two secants, secant segments, or external secant segments; use the Secant-Tangent Product theorem when the problem involves a secant and a tangent or tangent segment.

❓ **Why does a secant segment lie inside a circle while a tangent segment lies outside the circle?** The definitions are different. A secant intersects a circle in two places. The segment that lies inside the circle is the *secant segment* and the segment that lies outside the circle from the point on the circumference to the point outside the circle is the *external secant segment*. A tangent passes through a circle in only one point. The segment from the point outside the circle to the point of tangency is the *tangent segment*.

Segment Relationships in Circles   **820**

INTEGRATE MATHEMATICAL PRACTICES

Focus on Math Connections

MP.1 Point out to students that, in the Secant-Tangent Product Theorem, the tangent is the mean proportional between the secant segment and its external segment.

© Houghton Mifflin Harcourt Publishing Company • Image Credits: ©Roy Toft/ National Geographic/Getty Images

8. Compare and contrast the Secant-Secant Product Theorem with the Secant-Tangent Product Theorem.

   Both theorems involve equations where two lengths are being multiplied together on

   each side of the equal sign. In the Secant-Tangent Product Theorem, since the tangent

   segment has only one length to consider, it is multiplied by itself.

Your Turn

Find the value of x.

9. On a bird-watching trip, you travel along a path tangent to a circular pond to a lookout station that faces a hawk's nest. Given the measurements in the diagram on your bird-watching map, how far is the nest from the lookout station?

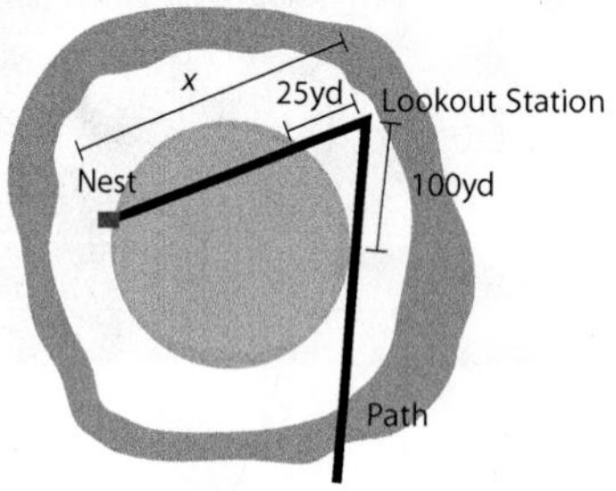

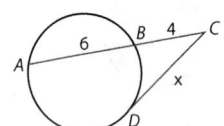

$(x)(25) = 100^2$

$25x = 10000$

$x = 400$

The nest is 400 yards from the lookout station.

10.

$AC \cdot BC = CD^2$

$(10)(4) = x^2$

$40 = x^2$

$\pm 2\sqrt{10} = x$

Since distance must be positive, the value of x must be $2\sqrt{10} \approx 6.32$.

11. How is solving for y in the following diagram different from Example 3?

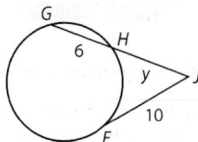

For the secant segment in this case, both the secant external segment and the whole

segment involve the number y, so the equation would be $GJ \cdot HJ = FJ^2$, or $(6 + y)y = 10^2$.

Then, when we multiply y by $(6 + y)$, it would result in a quadratic equation to solve.

12. A circle is constructed with two secant segments that intersect outside the circle. If both external secant segments are equal, is it reasonable to conclude that both secant segments are equal? Explain.
Yes. Suppose the length of the external part of each secant segment equals a and the

lengths of the whole secant segments are b and c. By the Secant-Secant Product Theorem,

$b(a) = c(a)$. Dividing both sides by a leaves $b = c$, which means that the two secant

segments must be equal.

13. Essential Question Check-In How are the theorems in this lesson related?
All three theorems involve segments drawn intersecting with a circle. They also involve

equations where you multiply two segment lengths on each side of an equal sign. The two

segments either intersect inside or outside the circle.

ELABORATE

AVOID COMMON ERRORS

Make sure students do not confuse secants and tangents. A *secant* intersects the circle in two points. The *tangent* intersects at exactly one point.

INTEGRATE MATHEMATICAL PRACTICES
Focus on Reasoning

MP.2 Discuss how the circle segment theorems in this lesson are similar and how they are different. Have students suggest ways to remember the specific equations that are the conclusions of each theorem.

SUMMARIZE THE LESSON

? What are some properties of chords, secants, and tangents to a circle? For chords, secants, and tangents to a circle, the products of pairs of lengths are equal by the Chord-Chord, Secant-Secant, and Secant Product Theorems.

EVALUATE

ASSIGNMENT GUIDE

Concepts and Skills	Practice
Explore Exploring Segment Length Relationships in Circles	Exercises 1–4
Example 1 Applying the Chord-Chord Product Theorem	Exercises 5–8
Example 2 Proving the Secant-Secant Product Theorem	Exercise 9
Example 3 Applying the Secant-Secant Product Theorem	Exercises 10–13
Example 4 Applying the Secant-Tangent Product Theorem	Exercises 14–18

GRAPHIC ORGANIZERS

Have students make a graphic organizer or illustrated guide that characterizes each of the segment length relationships covered in the lesson.

• Online Homework
• Hints and Help
• Extra Practice

Use the figure for Exercises 1–2.

Suppose you use geometry software to construct two chords $\overline{RS}$ and $\overline{TU}$ that intersect inside a circle at V.

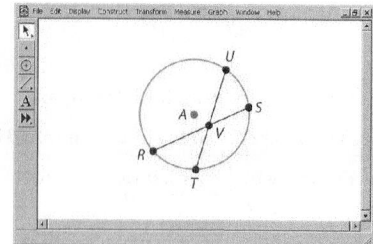

1. If you measured $\overline{RV}$, $\overline{VS}$, $\overline{TV}$, and $\overline{VU}$, what would be true about the relationship between their lengths?

The product of the lengths of the segments on one chord will equal the product of the lengths of the segments on the other chord: $RV \cdot VS = TV \cdot VU$.

2. Suppose you drag the points around the circle and examine the changes in the measurements. Would your answer to Exercise 1 change? Explain.

No. The product of the lengths of the segments on one chord will still equal the product of the lengths of the segments on the other chord.

Use the figure for Exercises 3–4.

Suppose you use geometry software to construct two secants $\overleftrightarrow{DC}$ and $\overrightarrow{BE}$ that intersect outside a circle at F.

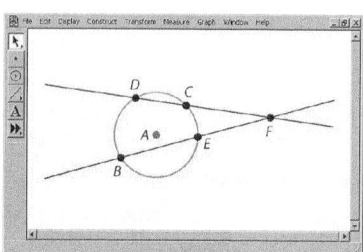

3. If you measured $\overline{DF}$, $\overline{CF}$, $\overline{BF}$, and $\overline{EF}$, what would be true about the relationship between their lengths?

$DF \cdot CF = BF \cdot EF$

4. Suppose you drag F and examine the changes in the measurements. Would your answer to Exercise 3 change? Explain.

No. $DF \cdot CF = BF \cdot EF$ would still be true.

Find the value of the variable and the length of each chord.

5.

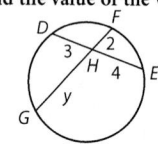

By the Chord-Chord Product Theorem,
$3 \cdot 4 = y \cdot 2$; $2y = 12$; $y = 6$. $DE = 7$; $FG = 8$.

6.

By the Chord-Chord Product Theorem, $6 \cdot 7 = x \cdot 10$;
$10x = 42$; $x = 4.2$ $JL = 14.2$; $MN = 13$.

© Houghton Mifflin Harcourt Publishing Company

Exercise	Depth of Knowledge (D.O.K.)	COMMON CORE Mathematical Practices
1–7	**2** Skills/Concepts	**MP.2** Reasoning
8–9	**3** Strategic Thinking	**MP.3** Logic
10–22	**2** Skills/Concepts	**MP.2** Reasoning
23	**3** Strategic Thinking H.O.T.	**MP.3** Logic
24	**3** Strategic Thinking H.O.T.	**MP.3** Logic
25	**3** Strategic Thinking H.O.T.	**MP.3** Logic
26	**3** Strategic Thinking H.O.T.	**MP.3** Logic

7. *M* is the midpoint of $\overline{PQ}$, The diameter of circle *O* is 13 in. and $RM = 4$ in.

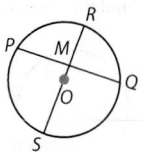

   a. Find *PM*.

   Since *M* is the midpoint of $\overline{PQ}$, let *x* be the length of $\overline{PM}$. Since the diameter is 13 in. and $RM = 4$ in., $MS = 9$ in. By the Chord-Chord Product Theorem, $4 \cdot 9 = x \cdot x$; $x^2 = 36$; $x = 6$; $PM = 6$ in.

   b. Find *PQ*.

   $PQ = 2(6) = 12$ in.

8. **Representing a Real-World Problem** A broken pottery shard found at archaeological dig has a curved edge. Find the diameter of the original plate. (Use the fact that the diameter $\overline{PR}$ is the perpendicular bisector of chord $\overline{AB}$.)

$\overline{PR}$ is the perpendicular bisector of $\overline{AB}$, so $AQ = QB = 5$.

$PQ \cdot QR = AQ \cdot QB$

   $3(x) = 5(5)$

     $x = \frac{25}{3}$

   $AB = 5 + 5 = 10$ in. $PR = 3 + \frac{25}{3} = \frac{34}{3} = 11\frac{1}{3}$ in.

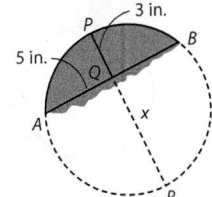

9. **Critique Reasoning** A student drew a circle and two secant segments. He concluded that if $\overline{PQ} \cong \overline{PS}$, then $\overline{QR} \cong \overline{ST}$. Do you agree with the student's conclusion? Why or why not?

I agree. Given: $\overline{PQ} \cong \overline{PS}$. Then $PQ = PS$. Since $PR \cdot PQ = PT \cdot PS$ by the Secant-Secant Product Theorem, $PR \cdot PQ = PT \cdot PS$, and so $PR = PT$. Since $PR = PQ + QR$ and $PT = PS + ST$, $PQ + QR = PS + ST$. Since $PQ = PS$, $QR = ST$. Therefore, $\overline{QR} \cong \overline{ST}$.

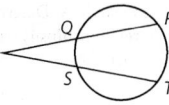

Find the value of the variable and the length of each secant segment.

10.

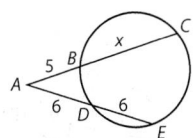

By the Secant-Secant Product Theorem, $(5 + x)5 = 12(6)$. $5x + 25 = 72$; $x = 9.4$; $AC = 14.4$; $AE = 12$

11.

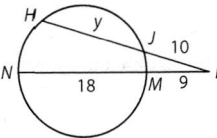

By the Secant-Secant Product Theorem, $(y + 10)10 = 27(9)$. $10y + 100 = 243$; $y = 14.3$; $HL = 24.3$; $NL = 27$

© Houghton Mifflin Harcourt Publishing Company · Image Credits: ©vonSteck/ iStockPhoto.com

INTEGRATE MATHEMATICAL PRACTICES

Focus on Communication

MP.3 Discuss how students recognized which theorem to apply to solve given problems about segment relationships in circles.

AVOID COMMON ERRORS

Students may confuse the products when they apply the segment length equations to solve problems. Have students first identify the segments in a problem. Then have them find the theorem that states how the products of the segments are related. Next, ask them to set up equations that apply the theorems. Finally, ask them to solve the equations. Point out that, to reach a correct solution, they must use only the appropriate products.

12. Find the value of x.

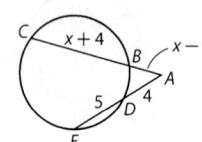

Since $\overleftrightarrow{AE}$ and $\overleftrightarrow{AC}$ are secants, $AC \cdot AB = AE \cdot AD$. Substituting the given values and solving for x: $(x - 2 + x + 4)(x - 2) = 9 \cdot 4$; $(2x + 2)(x - 2) = 36$; $2x^2 - 2x - 4 = 36$; $2x^2 - 2x - 40 = 0$; $2(x^2 - x - 20) = 0$; $2(x - 5)(x + 4) = 0$; $x = 5$ or $x = -4$. Rejecting the negative value of x, then $x = 5$.

Find the value of the variable.

13.

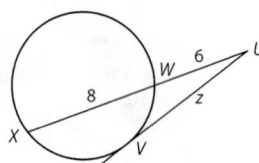

By the Secant-Tangent Product Theorem, $z^2 = 14(6) = 84; z = \sqrt{84} = 2\sqrt{21}$

14.

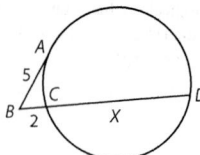

By the Secant-Tangent Product Theorem, $5^2 = (x + 2)2; 25 = 2x + 4; x = 10.5$

15.

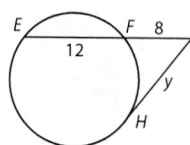

By the Secant-Tangent Product Theorem,

$y^2 = 20(8) = 160; y = \sqrt{160} = 4\sqrt{10}$

16. Tangent $\overleftrightarrow{PF}$ and secants $\overrightarrow{PD}$ and $\overleftrightarrow{PB}$ are drawn to circle A. Determine whether each of the following relationships is true or false. Select the correct answer for each lettered part.

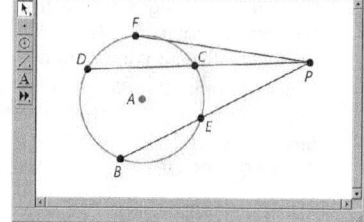

a. $PB \cdot EB = PD \cdot DC$ ○ True ● False
b. $PE \cdot EB = PC \cdot DC$ ○ True ● False
c. $PB \cdot PE = PF^2$ ● True ○ False
d. $PB \cdot DC = PD \cdot EB$ ○ True ● False
e. $PB \cdot PE = PD \cdot PC$ ● True ○ False
f. $PB \cdot PE = PF \cdot PC$ ○ True ● False

17. Which of these is closest to the length of tangent segment $\overline{PQ}$?

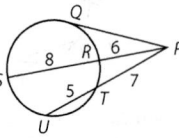

A. 6.9   B. 9.2
C. 9.9   D. 10.6

B; by the Secant-Tangent Product Theorem,

$PQ^2 = 14(6) = 84. PQ \approx 9.2$

18. Explain the Error Below is a student's work to find the value of x. Explain the error and find the correct value of x.

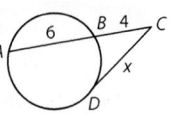

$AB \cdot BC = DC^2$

$6(4) = x^2$

$x^2 = 24$

$x = \pm\sqrt{24} = \pm 2\sqrt{6}$

The first step should be $AC \cdot BC = DC^2$.

$10(4) = x^2$

$x^2 = 40$

$x = \pm\sqrt{40} = \pm 2\sqrt{10}$

The value of x cannot be negative. Therefore $x = 2\sqrt{10}$.

19. Represent Real-World Problems Molokini is a small, crescent-shaped island $2\frac{1}{2}$ miles from the Maui, Hawaii, coast. It is all that remains of an extinct volcano. To approximate the diameter of the mouth of the volcano, a geologist used a diagram like the one shown. The geologist assumed that the mouth of the volcano was a circle. What was the approximate diameter of the volcano's mouth to the nearest ten feet?

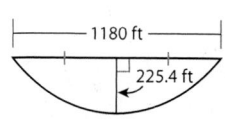

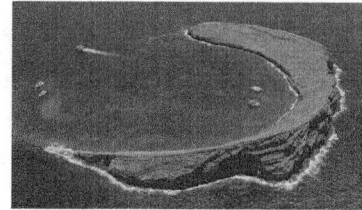

Let x be the diameter of the circle in feet. Since the vertical segment in the diagram is a perpendicular bisector of the horizontal segment, the vertical segment is part of a diameter of the circle. So the length of the part of that diameter (chord) above the vertical 225.4 ft segment is $x - 225.4$. Since $1180 \div 2 = 590$, the length of each half of the horizontal chord is 590 ft. By the Chord-Chord Product Theorem, $225.4(x - 225.4) = 590^2$. So $225.4x - 225.4^2 = 590^2$. So $x \approx 1770$. So the approximate diameter of the volcano's mouth was 1770 feet.

20. Multi-step Find the value of both variables in the figure.

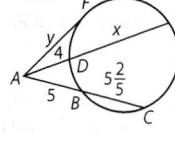

By the Secant-Secant Product Theorem,

$(4 + x)4 = \left(5 + 5\frac{2}{5}\right)5 = \left(10\frac{2}{5}\right)5 = 52; 16 + 4x = 52;$

$4x = 36; x = 9; \left(5 + 5\frac{2}{5}\right)5 = y^2; 52 = y^2; y = \sqrt{52} = 2\sqrt{13}.$

21. $\overline{KL}$ is a tangent segment of circle N and $\overline{KM}$ and $\overline{LM}$ are secants of the circle. Find the value of x.

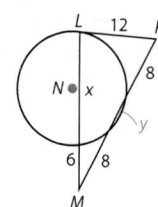

Let y be the length of the chord along $\overline{MK}$.

Then $(8 + y)8 = 12^2 = 144$ by the Secant-Tangent Product Theorem; $64 + 8y = 144; 8y = 80;$ so $y = 10$. $(6 + x)6 = (8 + 10)8$ by the Secant-Secant Product Theorem; $36 + 6x = 144; 6x = 108; x = 18$.

© Houghton Mifflin Harcourt Publishing Company · Image Credits: ©M Swiet Productions/Flickr/Getty Images

KINESTHETIC EXPERIENCE

Have students model each theorem using cut-out circles taped to their desks, lengths of different colored string for chords, secants, and tangents, and rulers to find and compare segment measures. Students may also benefit from using a compass to draw a circle and then using paper folding to create chords and secants, which they can measure to compare lengths.

JOURNAL

Have students describe and use colored pencils to make sketches that will help them remember when each theorem should be used.

22. **Justify Reasoning** Prove the Chord-Chord Product Theorem

    Given: Chords $\overline{AB}$ and $\overline{CD}$ intersect at point E.

    Prove: $AE \cdot EB = CE \cdot ED$ (*Hint*: Draw $\overline{AC}$ and $\overline{BD}$.)

    Since through any two points there exists exactly one line, then $\overline{AC}$

    and $\overline{BD}$ can be drawn. $\angle ACD \cong \angle DBA$ because they intercept the same

    arc. $\angle CEA \cong \angle DEB$ by the Vertical Angles Theorem. Therefore,

    $\triangle ECA \sim \triangle DEB$ by the AA Similarity Theorem. Corresponding sides

    are proportional, so $\frac{AE}{ED} = \frac{CE}{EB}$.

    $\frac{AE}{ED} \cdot (EB \cdot ED) = \frac{CE}{EB} \cdot (EB \cdot ED)$, or $AE \cdot EB = CE \cdot ED$.

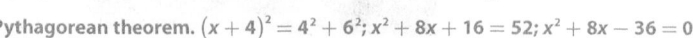

23. **Justify Reasoning** $\overline{PQ}$ is a tangent segment of a circle with radius 4 in. Q lies on the circle, and $PQ = 6$ in. Make a sketch and find the distance from P to the circle. Round to the nearest tenth of an inch. Explain your reasoning.

    Let x be the distance from P to the circle. Since the tangent segment

    is perpendicular to the radius $\overline{QA}$, $\triangle AQP$ is a right triangle. Use the

    Pythagorean theorem. $(x + 4)^2 = 4^2 + 6^2$; $x^2 + 8x + 16 = 52$; $x^2 + 8x - 36 = 0$;

    $x = \frac{-b \pm \sqrt{b^2 - 4ac}}{2a}$; $x = \frac{-8 \pm \sqrt{8^2 - 4(1)(-36)}}{2(1)}$; $x = \frac{-8 \pm \sqrt{208}}{2}$; $x = 3.2$ or -11.2.

    Choose the positive solution. So, the distance from P to the circle is about 3.2 in.

24. **Justify Reasoning** The circle in the diagram has radius c. Use this diagram and the Chord-Chord Product Theorem to prove the Pythagorean Theorem.

    If a diameter of a circle is perpendicular to a chord, then the diameter bisects the chord. So the dashed line segment also has length b. By the Chord-Chord Product Theorem, $(c + a)(c - a) = b \cdot b$. So $c^2 - a^2 = b^2$, or $a^2 + b^2 = c^2$.

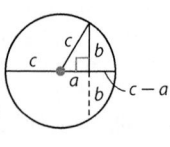

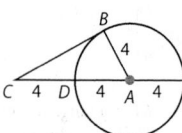

25. **Critical Thinking** The radius of circle A is 4. $CD = 4$, and $\overline{CB}$ is a tangent segment. Describe two different methods you can use to find BC.

    Method 1: By the Secant-Tangent Product Theorem, $BC^2 = 12 \cdot 4$ and so $BC = \sqrt{48} = 4\sqrt{3}$.

    Method 2: Because a line tangent to a circle is a line $\perp$ to the radius, $\angle ABC$ is a right angle. By the Pythagorean Theorem, $BC^2 + 4^2 = 8^2$. Thus $BC^2 = 64 - 16 = 48$ and $BC = \sqrt{48} = 4\sqrt{3}$.

Lesson Performance Task

The figure shows the basic design of a Wankel rotary engine. The triangle is equilateral, with sides measuring 10 inches. An arc on each side of the triangle has as its center the vertex on the opposite side of the triangle. In the figure, the arc *ADB* is an arc of a circle with its center at *C*.

a. Use the sketch of the engine. What is the measure of each arc along the side of the triangle?

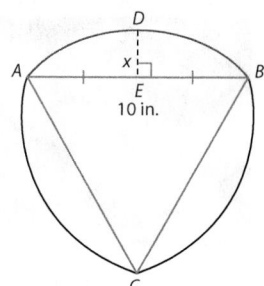

b. Use the relationships in an equilateral triangle to find the value of *x*. Explain.

c. Use the Chord-Chord Product Theorem to find the value of *x*. Explain.

a. 120°

b. *CE* is the length of the side of a 30°–60°–90° triangle opposite the 60° angle, so $CE = AE\sqrt{3} = 5\sqrt{3}$. $CD = CA = CB = 10$ in. So $x = CD - CE = \left(10 - 5\sqrt{3}\right)$ in.

c. By the Chord-Chord Product Theorem,

$$AE \times EB = DE \times (\text{diameter of circle} - x)$$

$$5 \times 5 = x(20 - x)$$

$$25 = 20x - x^2$$

$$0 = -x^2 + 20x - 25$$

$$x = \frac{-20 \pm \sqrt{20^2 - 4(-1)(-25)}}{2(-1)}$$

$$= \frac{-20 \pm \sqrt{300}}{-2}$$

$$= 10 - 5\sqrt{3}$$

© Houghton Mifflin Harcourt Publishing Company • Image Credits: ©dpa/dpa/Corbis

EXTENSION ACTIVITY

In a conventional car engine, pistons move up and down at a speed determined by the car's engine speed, which is measured in RPMs (revolutions per minute). Have students research to find the engine speed of a specific car. Then have them calculate the distance a piston would move in the engine of the car in one minute, assuming a typical distance of 6 inches per revolution. Finally, have them calculate the speed of the piston in miles per hour. **Sample answer:** For an engine speed of 6000 RPMs, a piston would move 3000 feet per minute, or about 34.1 miles per hour.

AVOID COMMON ERRORS

When students apply the Chord-Chord Product Theorem, they may mistakenly use 10 inches as the diameter of the circle that has $\overset{\frown}{ADB}$ as an arc. The diameter of the circle is 20 inches.

INTEGRATE MATHEMATICAL PRACTICES
Focus on Reasoning

MP.2 Rotary engines have many advantages over piston engines, but fuel efficiency is not one of them. Car A with a piston engine gets 24 miles per gallon. Car B with a rotary engine gets 20 miles per gallon. If gas costs $3.20 per gallon, how much farther can you drive on $400 worth of gas in Car A than you can in Car B?

Car A: $\dfrac{24\text{ mi}}{1\text{ gal}} \cdot \dfrac{1\text{ gal}}{\$3.20} \cdot \$400 = 3000\text{ mi}$;

Car B: $\dfrac{20\text{ mi}}{1\text{ gal}} \cdot \dfrac{1\text{ gal}}{\$3.20} \cdot \$400 = 2500\text{ mi}$;

$3000 - 2500 = 500\text{ mi}$

Scoring Rubric

2 points: Student correctly solves the problem and explains his/her reasoning.

1 point: Student shows good understanding of the problem but does not fully solve or explain his/her reasoning.

0 points: Student does not demonstrate understanding of the problem.

Angle Relationships in Circles

Common Core Math Standards

The student is expected to:

 G-C.A.2

Identify and describe relationships among inscribed angles, radii, and chords.

Mathematical Practices

COMMON CORE **MP.3 Logic**

Language Objective

Explain to a partner how to find the measure of an angle formed by intersecting chords if the measures of the intercepted arcs are known.

ENGAGE

Essential Question: What are the relationships between angles formed by lines that intersect a circle?

The measure of an angle whose vertex is on the circle is half the measure of its intercepted arc. The measure of an angle whose vertex is inside the circle is half the sum of its two intercepted arcs. The measure of an angle whose vertex is outside the circle is half the difference of its two intercepted arcs.

PREVIEW: LESSON PERFORMANCE TASK

View the Engage section online. Discuss the photograph. Ask students to describe some of the Moon's features that we can see from Earth. Then preview the Lesson Performance Task.

15.5 Angle Relationships in Circles

Essential Question: What are the relationships between angles formed by lines that intersect a circle?

Resource Locker

Explore   Exploring Angle Measures in Circles

The sundial is one of many instruments that use angles created in circles for practical applications, such as telling time.

In this lesson, you will observe the relationships between angles created by various line segments and their intercepted arcs.

(A) Using geometry software, construct a circle with two secants $\overleftrightarrow{CD}$ and $\overleftrightarrow{EF}$ that intersect inside the circle at G, as shown in the figure.

(B) Create two new points H and I that are on the circle as shown. These will be used to measure the arcs. Hide B if desired.

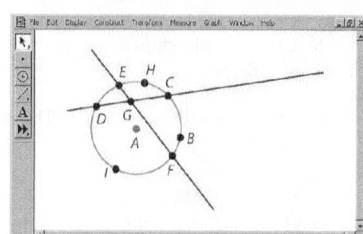

(C) Measure $\angle DGF$ formed by the secant lines, and measure $\overarc{CHE}$ and $\overarc{DIF}$. Record angle and arc measurements in the first column of the table.

m∠DGF	120°	75°	90°			
mCHE	80°	110°	63°			
mDIF	160°	40°	117°			
Sum of Arc Measures	240°	150°	180°			

Students' answers will vary. Possible answers are given.

(D) Drag F around the circle and record the changes in measures in the table in Part C. Try to create acute, right, and obtuse angles. Be sure to keep H between C and E and I between D and F for accurate arc measurement. Move them if necessary.

Students' answers will vary. Possible answers are given.

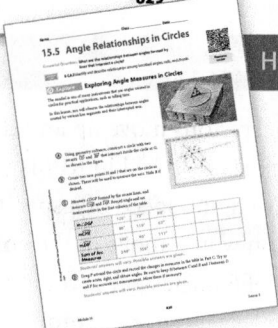

HARDCOVER PAGES 699–710

Turn to these pages to find this lesson in the hardcover student edition.

Reflect

1. Can you make a conjecture about the relationship between the angle measure and the two arc measures?

The angle measure is half the sum of the two arc measures.

2. Using the same circle you created in step A, drag points around the circle so that the intersection is outside the circle, as shown. Measure ∠FGC formed by the secant lines and measure $\overarc{CIF}$ and $\overarc{DHE}$. Drag points around the circle and observe the changes in measures. Record some measures in the table.

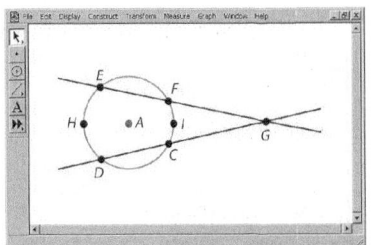

m∠FGC	120°	75°	90°
m$\overarc{CIF}$	65°	42°	110°
m$\overarc{DHE}$	305°	192°	290°
Difference of Arc Measures	240°	150°	180°

What is similar and different about the relationships between the angle measure and the arc measures when the secants intersect outside the circle?

Although finding the angle measure still involves taking half the measurement of the

intercepted arcs, you halve the *difference* of the arc measures instead of the sum of the

arc measures.

🔘 Explain 1   Proving the Intersecting Chords Angle Measure Theorem

In the Explore section, you discovered the effects that line segments, such as chords and secants, have on angle measures and their intercepted arcs. These relationships can be stated as theorems, with the first one about chords.

The Intersecting Chords Angle Measure Theorem

If two secants or chords intersect in the interior of a circle, then the measure of each angle formed is half the sum of the measures of its intercepted arcs.

Chords $\overline{AD}$ and $\overline{BC}$ intersect at E.

$m\angle 1 = \frac{1}{2}\left(m\overarc{AB} + m\overarc{CD}\right)$

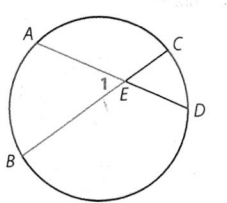

© Houghton Mifflin Harcourt Publishing Company

INTEGRATE TECHNOLOGY

Students have the option of doing the Explore activity either in the book or online.

QUESTIONING STRATEGIES

 The opposite arc lengths intercepted by the chords do not have the same measure but the angles formed do. Why? If the shared vertex of the angles is not on the center of the circle, the angles are not central angles and their measures are not the same as the measures of their intercepted arcs. The angles formed are vertical angles, and vertical angles have the same measure.

EXPLAIN 1

Proving the Intersecting Chords Angle Measure Theorem

INTEGRATE MATHEMATICAL PRACTICES
Focus on Critical Thinking

MP.3 Discuss other ways students could prove the Intersecting Chords Angle Measure Theorem.

PROFESSIONAL DEVELOPMENT

🔲 Integrate Mathematical Practices

This lesson provides an opportunity to address Mathematical Practice **MP.3**, which calls for students to "construct viable arguments." Students must recognize angle relationships that occur based on intersections of specific segment relationships in circles. They must justify their choices of theorems to use based on the segment relationships. Students then apply the theorem (or theorems) to find missing measures in circles.

? Why is the inscribed Angle Theorem used in the proof? **It provides a way to measure the inscribed angle with respect to the arc length.**

? If the chords intersect at the center of the circle, can you still apply the theorem? Explain. **Yes, the result will be the same, but it may be easier to use the fact that the angles will be central angles to find the measures.**

? Why does the theorem apply to both chords and secants? **The secants intersect inside the circle to form chords.**

Example 1 Prove the Intersecting Chords Angle Measure Theorem

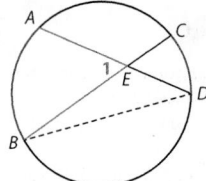

Given: $\overline{AD}$ and $\overline{BC}$ intersect at E.

Prove: $m\angle 1 = \frac{1}{2}\left(m\widehat{AB} + m\widehat{CD}\right)$

Statements	Reasons
1. $\overline{AD}$ and $\overline{BC}$ intersect at E.	1. Given
2. Draw $\overline{BD}$.	2. Through any two points, there is exactly one line.
3. $m\angle 1 = m\angle EDB + m\angle EBD$	3. Exterior Angle Theorem
4. $m\angle EDB = \frac{1}{2}m\widehat{AB}$, $m\angle EBD = \frac{1}{2}m\widehat{CD}$	4. Inscribed Angle Theorem
5. $m\angle 1 = \frac{1}{2}m\widehat{AB} + \frac{1}{2}m\boxed{\widehat{CD}}$	5. Substitution Property
6. $m\angle 1 = \frac{1}{2}\left(m\widehat{AB} + m\widehat{CD}\right)$	6. Distributive Property

Reflect

3. **Discussion** Explain how an auxiliary segment and the Exterior Angle Theorem are used in the proof of the Intersecting Chords Angle Measure Theorem.

∠1 is formed by two intersecting chords. An auxiliary line is drawn to create a triangle

using parts of the chords as the other two sides. Then, ∠1 is an exterior angle for the

triangle formed, and its measure is the sum of the measures of its remote interior angles.

Those interior angles intercept the same arcs as ∠1, so its measure can be found.

Your Turn

Find each unknown measure.

4. $m\angle MPK$

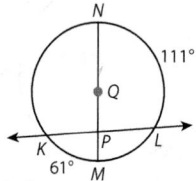

5. $m\widehat{PR}$

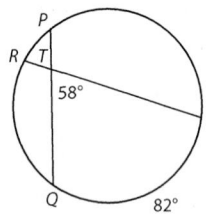

$m\angle MPK = \frac{1}{2}\left(m\widehat{MK} + m\widehat{LN}\right) = \frac{1}{2}\left(61° + 111°\right)$
$= \frac{1}{2}\left(172°\right) = 86°$

$m\angle QTS = \frac{1}{2}\left(m\widehat{QS} + m\widehat{PR}\right);\ 58° = \frac{1}{2}\left(82° + m\widehat{PR}\right);\ 116° = \left(82° + m\widehat{PR}\right);\ 116° - 82° = m\widehat{PR};\ 34° = m\widehat{PR}$

© Houghton Mifflin Harcourt Publishing Company

COLLABORATIVE LEARNING

Peer-to-Peer Activity

Have students work in pairs to draw figures similar to the ones given in each of the theorems in the lesson. Suggest they use different colored pencils to indicate the different angles formed. Have students exchange papers with another pair and measure each angle. Then have them identify each angle by the lines that form it.

Explain 2   Applying the Tangent-Secant Interior Angle Measure Theorem

The angle and arc formed by a tangent and secant intersecting *on* a circle also have a special relationship.

The Tangent-Secant Interior Angle Measure Theorem

If a tangent and a secant (or a chord) intersect on a circle at the point of tangency, then the measure of the angle formed is half the measure of its intercepted arc.

Tangent $\overrightarrow{BC}$ and secant $\overrightarrow{BA}$ intersect at B.

$$m\angle ABC = \tfrac{1}{2}\,m\widehat{AB}$$

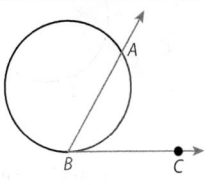

Example 2   Find each unknown measure.

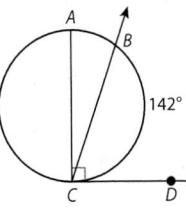

Ⓐ $m\angle BCD$

$$m\angle BCD = \tfrac{1}{2}m\widehat{BC}$$
$$= \tfrac{1}{2}(142°)$$
$$= 71°$$

Ⓑ $m\widehat{ABC}$

$$m\angle ACD = \tfrac{1}{2}\left(m\widehat{ABC}\right)$$
$$\boxed{90°} = \tfrac{1}{2}\left(m\widehat{ABC}\right)$$
$$\boxed{180°} = m\widehat{ABC}$$

Your Turn

Find the measure.

6. $m\widehat{PN}$

$$m\angle P = \tfrac{1}{2}\left(m\widehat{PN}\right)$$
$$61° = \tfrac{1}{2}\left(m\widehat{PN}\right)$$
$$122° = m\widehat{PN}$$

7. $m\angle MNP$

$$m\angle MNP = \tfrac{1}{2}m\widehat{NQP}$$
$$= \tfrac{1}{2}(238°)$$
$$= 119°$$

Explain 3   Applying the Tangent-Secant Exterior Angle Measure Theorem

You can use the *difference* in arc measures to find measures of angles formed by tangents and secants intersecting *outside* a circle.

EXPLAIN 2

Applying the Tangent-Secant Interior Angle Measure Theorem

INTEGRATE MATHEMATICAL PRACTICES
Focus on Communication

MP.3 Discuss how to find all the angle and arc measures from diagrams with tangent-chord and inscribed angles.

QUESTIONING STRATEGIES

? How are problems with tangent-secant angles similar to those with inscribed angles? The measure of the angle formed is half the measure of its intercepted arc, as with inscribed angles.

? How are tangent-secant angles different than inscribed angles? Each ray of an inscribed angle intersects the circle in two places. The tangent ray of the tangent-secant angle intersects the circle in only one point, at the vertex of the angle.

DIFFERENTIATE INSTRUCTION

Auditory Cues

Ask students to note the key words that will help them determine the method of solving a problem involving angle relationships in circles. Have one student recite each of the three relationships in this lesson. Then have the student's partner draw a diagram of what the first student has said. Each student should then measure the angles in the diagram as a check.

1. Vertex *on* a circle means you take half the *measure* of *one* arc.

2. Vertex *inside* a circle means you take half the *sum* of *two* arcs.

3. Vertex *outside* a circle means you take half the *difference* of *two* arcs.

EXPLAIN 3

Applying the Tangent-Secant Exterior Angle Measure Theorem

INTEGRATE MATHEMATICAL PRACTICES

Focus on Reasoning

MP.2 The theorem covers three types of exterior angles. Discuss why students need recall only one case to apply the theorem.

QUESTIONING STRATEGIES

? How is finding an angle measure that is exterior to a circle different from finding an angle measure in the interior of a circle? The measure of the angle formed in the exterior is half the difference of the measures of its intercepted arcs, while the measure of the angle formed in the interior is half the sum of the measures of its intercepted arcs.

The Tangent-Secant Exterior Angle Measure Theorem

If a tangent and a secant, two tangents, or two secants intersect in the exterior of a circle, then the measure of the angle formed is half the difference of the measures of its intercepted arcs.

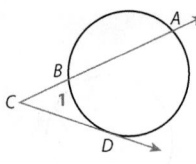 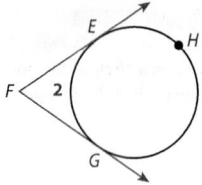 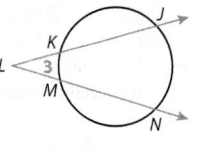

$$m\angle 1 = \frac{1}{2}\left(m\widehat{AD} - m\widehat{BD}\right) \qquad m\angle 2 = \frac{1}{2}\left(m\widehat{EHG} - m\widehat{EG}\right) \qquad m\angle 3 = \frac{1}{2}\left(m\widehat{JN} - m\widehat{KM}\right)$$

Example 3   Find the value of x.

 A

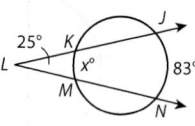

$$m\angle L = \frac{1}{2}\left(m\widehat{JN} - m\widehat{KM}\right)$$
$$25° = \frac{1}{2}\left(83° - x°\right)$$
$$50 = 83 - x$$
$$-33 = -x$$
$$33 = x$$

 B

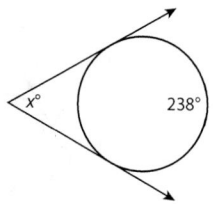

$$x° = \frac{1}{2}\left(238° - \left(360° - \boxed{238°}\right)\right)$$
$$x = \frac{1}{2}\left(238 - \boxed{122}\right)$$
$$x = \frac{1}{2}\left(\boxed{116}\right)$$
$$x = \boxed{58}$$

Your Turn

Find the value of x.

8.

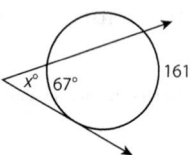

$$x° = \frac{1}{2}\left(161° - 67°\right)$$
$$x = \frac{1}{2}(94)$$
$$x = 47$$

LANGUAGE SUPPORT [EL]

Connect Vocabulary

Provide each student with two blank index cards or small squares of paper. Ask students to sketch an example of a tangent-secant interior angle on one card and an example of a tangent-secant exterior angle on the other card. Collect the cards, mix them up, and display them one by one, asking students to identify the type of angle shown.

9. The superior oblique and inferior oblique are two muscles that help control eye movement. They intersect behind the eye to create an angle, as shown. If $m\widehat{AEB} = 225°$, what is $m\angle ACB$?

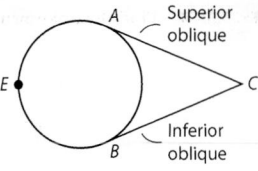

$$x° = \frac{1}{2}\left(225° - \left(360° - 225°\right)\right)$$

$$x = \frac{1}{2}(225 - 135)$$

$$x = \frac{1}{2}(90)$$

$$x = 45$$

So, the measure of the angle between the two muscles is 45°.

⊘ Explain 4 **Understanding Angle Relationships in Circles**

You can summarize angle relationships in circles by looking at where the vertex of the angle lies: on the circle, inside the circle, or outside the circle.

Angle Relationships in Circles		
Vertex of the Angle	**Measure of Angle**	**Diagrams**
On a circle	Half the measure of its intercepted arc	120° $m\angle 1 = 60°$ 200° $m\angle 2 = 100°$
Inside a circle	Half the sum of the measures of its intercepted arcs	44° 1 86° $m\angle 1 = \frac{1}{2}(44° + 86°)$ $= 65°$
Outside a circle	Half the difference of the measures of its intercepted arcs	1 78° 202° 2 45° 125° $m\angle 1 = \frac{1}{2}(202° - 78°)$ $= 62°$ $m\angle 2 = \frac{1}{2}(125° - 45°)$ $= 40°$

EXPLAIN 4

Understanding Angle Relationships in Circles

AVOID COMMON ERRORS

Before students can apply the results of a theorem about angle relationships in circles, they must be able to recognize the angle relationships. Discuss strategies students can use to help them identify the types of angle relationship. Next, have them look up the corresponding theorem and write the relationships using the names of the angles and arc lengths. Finally, have them substitute values and find the missing measure.

INTEGRATE MATHEMATICAL PRACTICES
Focus on Communication

MP.3 Ask students to support each step with a reason as they find missing angle and arc measures.

ELABORATE

AVOID COMMON ERRORS

Students may forget whether they need to find the sum or difference of the measures of the intercepted arcs. Draw several examples on the board, with lines intersecting inside the circle and outside the circle. Have students name the lines and say whether they would add or subtract arc measures to find the angle measure.

INTEGRATE MATHEMATICAL PRACTICES
Focus on Reasoning

MP.2 Discuss how the angle relationship theorems in this lesson are similar and how they are different. Have students suggest ways to remember the specific equations that are the conclusions of each theorem.

SUMMARIZE THE LESSON

? What are some angle relationships created by chords, secants, and tangents to a circle?
The measure of an angle formed by two chords that intersect inside a circle is one half the sum of the measures of the intercepted arcs. The measure of an angle formed outside a circle by tangents and/or secants is one half the difference of the measures of the intercepted arcs. If a chord and a tangent intersect on a circle, the measure of the angle formed is one half that of the intercepted arc.

835 Lesson 15.5

Example 4 Find the unknown arc measures.

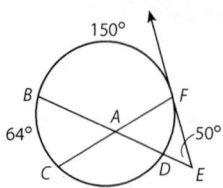

(A) Find m$\widehat{FD}$.

$$m\angle E = \frac{1}{2}\left(m\widehat{BF} - m\widehat{FD}\right)$$
$$50° = \frac{1}{2}\left(150° - m\widehat{FD}\right)$$
$$100° = \left(50° - m\widehat{FD}\right)$$
$$-50° = -m\widehat{FD}$$
$$50° = m\widehat{FD}$$

(B) Find m$\widehat{CD}$.

$$m\widehat{CD} = \boxed{360°} - \left(m\widehat{BC} + m\widehat{BF} + m\widehat{FD}\right)$$
$$= \boxed{360°} - \left(\boxed{64°} + \boxed{150°} + \boxed{50°}\right)$$
$$= \boxed{360°} - \boxed{264°}$$
$$= \boxed{96°}$$

Your Turn

10. Find m$\widehat{KN}$.

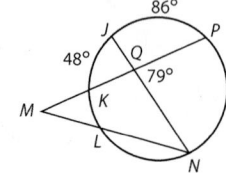

$$m\angle PQN = \frac{1}{2}\left(m\widehat{JK} + m\widehat{PN}\right)$$
$$79° = \frac{1}{2}\left(48° + m\widehat{PN}\right)$$
$$110° = m\widehat{PN}$$
$$m\widehat{KN} = 360° - \left(m\widehat{JK} + m\widehat{JP} + m\widehat{PN}\right)$$
$$= 360° - \left(48° + 86° + 110°\right)$$
$$= 116°$$

Elaborate

11. Complete the graphic organizer that shows the relationship between the angle measurement and the location of its vertex.

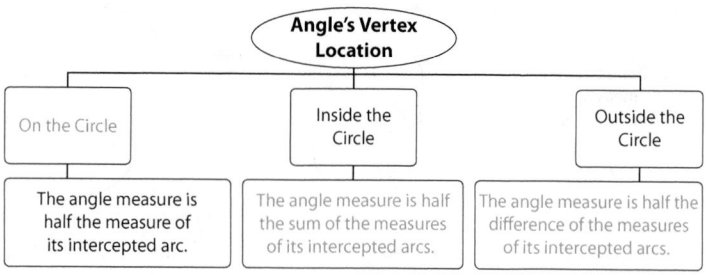

12. Essential Question Check-In What is similar about all the relationships between angle measures and their intercepted arcs?
The arc measurements have to be halved to obtain the angle measurement.

⭐ Evaluate: Homework and Practice

• Online Homework
• Hints and Help
• Extra Practice

Use the figure for Exercises 1–2.

Suppose you use geometry software to construct a secant $\overleftrightarrow{CE}$ and tangent $\overleftrightarrow{CD}$ that intersect on a circle at point C.

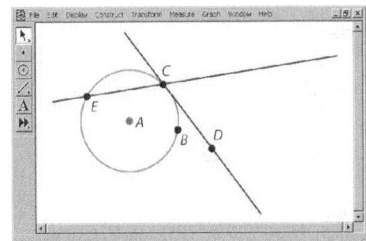

1. Suppose you measure $\angle DCE$ and you measure $\overset{\frown}{CBE}$. Then you drag the points around the circle and measure the angle and arc three more times. What would you expect to find each time? Which theorem from the lesson would you be demonstrating?

   The measure of the angle will be half the measure of its intercepted arc; the Tangent-Secant Interior Angle Theorem

2. When the measure of the intercepted arc is 180°, what is the measure of the angle? What does that tell you about the secant?

   When $m\overset{\frown}{CBE} = 180°$, then $m\angle DCE = \frac{1}{2}(180°) = 90°$; the secant (or chord) and the tangent are perpendicular at the point of tangency, so the secant must be a diameter of the circle.

Find each measure.

3. $m\angle QPR$

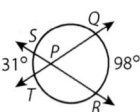

$m\angle QPR = \frac{1}{2}\left(m\overset{\frown}{QR} + m\overset{\frown}{ST}\right)$

$= \frac{1}{2}(98° + 31°) = 64.5°$

4. $m\angle ABC$

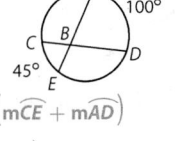

$m\angle CBE = \frac{1}{2}\left(m\overset{\frown}{CE} + m\overset{\frown}{AD}\right)$

$= \frac{1}{2}(45° + 100°) = 72.5;$

$m\angle ABC = 180° - 72.5° = 107.5°.$

5. $m\angle MKJ$

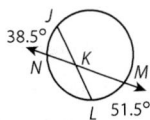

$m\angle JKN = \frac{1}{2}\left(m\overset{\frown}{JN} + m\overset{\frown}{ML}\right)$

$= \frac{1}{2}(38.5° + 51.5°) = 45°;$

$m\angle MKJ = 180° - 45° = 135°$

6. $m\angle NPK$

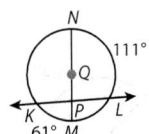

$m\angle KPM = \frac{1}{2}\left(m\overset{\frown}{KM} + m\overset{\frown}{NL}\right)$

$= \frac{1}{2}(61° + 111°) = 86°;$

$m\angle NPK = 180° - 86° = 94°$

Exercise	Depth of Knowledge (D.O.K.)	COMMON CORE Mathematical Practices	
1–6	**2** Skills/Concepts	**MP.2** Reasoning	
7–10	**2** Skills/Concepts	**MP.1** Problem Solving	
11–18	**2** Skills/Concepts	**MP.2** Reasoning	
19	**2** Skills/Concepts	**MP.4** Modeling	
20	**3** Strategic Thinking	**MP.2** Reasoning	
21	**3** Strategic Thinking	**MP.3** Logic	

EVALUATE

ASSIGNMENT GUIDE

Concept and Skills	Practice
Explore Exploring Angle Measures in Circles	Exercises 1–2
Example 1 Proving the Intersecting Chords Angle Measure Theorem	Exercises 3–6
Example 2 Applying the Tangent-Secant Interior Angle Measure Theorem	Exercises 7–10
Example 3 Applying the Tangent-Secant Exterior Angle Measure Theorem	Exercises 11–13
Example 4 Understanding Angle Relationships in Circles	Exercises 14–18

GRAPHIC ORGANIZERS

Have students make a graphic organizer that characterizes each of the angle relationships in circles covered in the lesson.

INTEGRATE MATHEMATICAL PRACTICES

Focus on Communication

MP.3 Discuss how students decided which theorem to apply in solving given problems involving angle relationships in circles.

Find each measure. Use the figure for Exercises 7–8.

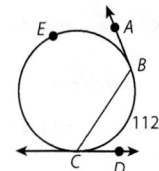

7. m∠BCD

$m\angle BCD = \frac{1}{2}\left(m\widehat{BC}\right) = \frac{1}{2}(112°) = 56°$

8. m∠ABC

$m\angle ABC = \frac{1}{2}m\widehat{BEC} = \frac{1}{2}(360° - 112°) = \frac{1}{2}(248°) = 124°$

Find each measure. Use the figure for Exercises 9–10.

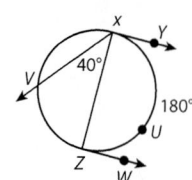

9. m∠XZW

By the Tangent-Secant Interior Angle Measure Theorem,

$m\angle XZW = \frac{1}{2}\left(m\widehat{XUZ}\right) = \frac{1}{2}(180)° = 90°$.

10. m∠YXZ

By the Tangent-Secant Interior Angle Measure Theorem, $m\angle YXZ = \frac{1}{2}\widehat{XUZ} = \frac{1}{2}(180°) = 90°$.

By the Inscribed Angle Theorem, $m\widehat{ZV} = 2(40°) = 80°$.

By the Angle Addition Postulate,

$m\angle YXV = m\angle YXZ + m\angle ZXV = 90° + 40° = 130°$.

Find the value of x.

11.

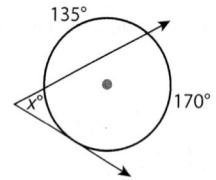

Find the missing arc measure.

$360° - (135° + 170°) = 55°$. By the Tangent-Secant Exterior Angle Measure Theorem,

$x° = \frac{1}{2}(170° - 55°) = 57.5°$.

12.

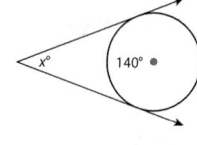

Find the missing arc measure.

$360° - 140° = 220°$. By the Tangent-Secant Exterior Angle Measure Theorem,

$x° = \frac{1}{2}(220° - 140°) = 40°$.

13.

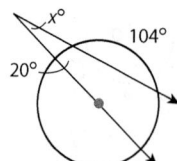

Find the missing arc measure of the other intercepted arc.

$180° - (20° + 104°) = 56$. By the Tangent-Secant Exterior Angle Measure Theorem, $x° = \frac{1}{2}(56° - 20°) = 18°$.

© Houghton Mifflin Harcourt Publishing Company

Exercise	Depth of Knowledge (D.O.K.)	COMMON CORE Mathematical Practices
22	**3** Strategic Thinking H.O.T.	**MP.3** Logic
23	**3** Strategic Thinking H.O.T.	**MP.3** Logic
24	**3** Strategic Thinking H.O.T.	**MP.3** Logic

14. Represent Real-World Problems Stonehenge is a circular arrangement of massive stones near Salisbury, England. A viewer at V observes the monument from a point where two of the stones A and B are aligned with stones at the endpoints of a diameter of the circular shape. Given that $\overset{\frown}{mAB} = 48°$, what is $m\angle AVB$?

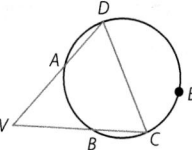

Since $\overline{CD}$ is a diameter, $\overset{\frown}{mCED} = 180°$. By the Tangent-Secant Exterior Angle Measure Theorem, $m\angle AVB = \frac{1}{2}(180° - 48°) = 66°$.

15. Multi-Step Find each measure.

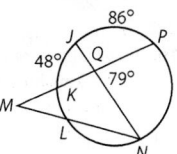

a. Find $\overset{\frown}{mPN}$.

$m\angle PQN = \frac{1}{2}\left(\overset{\frown}{mJK} + \overset{\frown}{mPN}\right)$; Let x be $\overset{\frown}{mPN}$. Then $79° = \frac{1}{2}(48° + x)$; $158° = 48° + x$; $x = 110°$. So, $\overset{\frown}{mPN} = 110°$.

b. Use your answer to part a to find $\overset{\frown}{mKN}$.

$m\angle KQN = 180° - 79° = 101°$; $m\angle KQN = \frac{1}{2}\left(\overset{\frown}{mJP} + \overset{\frown}{mKN}\right)$; Let x be $\overset{\frown}{mKN}$ in degrees. Then $101° = \frac{1}{2}(86° + x)$; $202° = 86° + x$; $x = 116°$. So, $\overset{\frown}{mKN} = 116°$.

16. Multi-Step Find each measure.

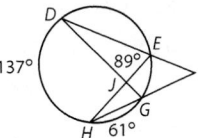

a. Find $\overset{\frown}{mDE}$.

$m\angle DJE = \frac{1}{2}\left(\overset{\frown}{mHG} + \overset{\frown}{mDE}\right)$. Let x be $\overset{\frown}{mDE}$; Then $89° = \frac{1}{2}(61° + x)$; $178° = 61° + x$; $x = 117°$. So, $\overset{\frown}{mDE} = 117°$.

b. Use your answer to part a to find $m\angle F$.

Find the missing arc measure.

$\overset{\frown}{mEG} = 360° - \left(117° + 137° + 61°\right) = 45°$. By the Tangent-Secant Exterior Angle Measure Theorem. $m\angle F = \frac{1}{2}\left(\overset{\frown}{mDH} - \overset{\frown}{mEG}\right) = \frac{1}{2}(137° - 45°) = 46°$.

© Houghton Mifflin Harcourt Publishing Company · ©Jason Hawkes/Corbis

VISUAL CUES

Remind students they can copy problems and use different colors to help them keep track of the measures they find as they solve for several missing measures in circle problems.

Some students may have difficulty with problems that have more than one angle relationship. To help students keep their information organized, suggest that they each write a brief plan before performing any calculations.

$\overrightarrow{MS} \parallel \overrightarrow{PQ}$ and $m\angle PNS = 50°$. Find each measure.

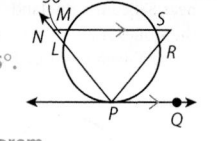

17. $m\widehat{PR}$

By the Inscribed Angle Theorem, $m\angle LPR = \frac{1}{2}(m\widehat{LR}) = \frac{1}{2}(170°) = 85°$.

So, the missing angle of the triangle is $180° - (50 + 85)° = 45°$.

Since $\overrightarrow{MS} \parallel \overrightarrow{PQ}$, $m\angle RPQ = 45°$ by the Alternate Interior Angles Theorem.

By the Inscribed Angle Theorem, $m\widehat{PR} = 2(45°) = 90°$.

18. $m\widehat{LP}$

Find the missing arc measure. $m\angle LPR = 360° - 170° = 190°$. By the Inscribed

Angle Theorem, $m\angle LPR = \frac{1}{2}(m\widehat{LR}) = \frac{1}{2}(170°) = 85°$. So, the missing angle of

the triangle is $180° - (50 + 85)° = 45°$. Since $\overrightarrow{MS} \parallel \overrightarrow{PQ}$, $m\angle RPQ = 45°$ by the

Alternate Interior Angles Theorem. By the Inscribed Angle Theorem,

$m\widehat{PR} = 2(45°) = 90°$. $m\widehat{LP} = m\widehat{LPR} - m\widehat{PR} = 190° - 90° = 100°$.

19. Represent Real-World Problems A satellite orbits Mars. When it reaches S it is about 12,000 km above the planet. What is $x°$, the measure of the arc that is visible to a camera in the satellite?

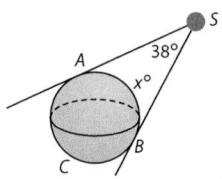

By the Tangent-Secant Exterior Angle Measure Theorem,

$m\angle S = \frac{1}{2}(m\angle ACB - m\widehat{AB}) = \frac{1}{2}((360° - x°) - x°)$;

$38° = \frac{1}{2}(360° - 2x°)$; $76° = 360° - 2x°$; $2x° = 284°$; $x° = 142°$.

So, $142°$ of arc is visible to a camera in the satellite.

20. Use the circle with center J. Match each angle or arc on the left with its measure on the right. Indicate a match by writing the letter for the angle or arc on the line in front of the corresponding measure.

A. $\angle BAE$ __D__   41°

B. $\angle ACD$ __E__   180°

C. $\widehat{AF}$ __B__   101°

D. $\angle AED$ __A__   90°

E. $\widehat{ADE}$ __C__   60°

21. Use the Plan for Proof to write a proof for one case of the Tangent-Secant Exterior Angle Measure Theorem.

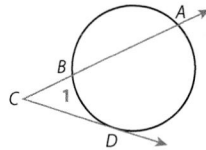

Given: Tangent $\overrightarrow{CD}$ and secant $\overrightarrow{CA}$

Prove: $m\angle ACD = \frac{1}{2}\left(m\overset{\frown}{AD} - m\overset{\frown}{BD}\right)$

Plan: Draw auxiliary line segment $\overline{BD}$. Use the Exterior Angle Theorem to show that $m\angle ACD = m\angle ABD - m\angle BDC$. Then use the Inscribed Angle Theorem and the Tangent-Secant Interior Angle Measure Theorem.

Since though any two points, there exists exactly one line, then $\overline{BD}$ can be drawn. By the Exterior Angle Theorem, $m\angle ABD = m\angle ACD + m\angle BDC$, so $m\angle ACD = m\angle ABD - m\angle BDC$. $m\angle ABD = \frac{1}{2}m\overset{\frown}{AD}$ by the Inscribed Angle Theorem, and $m\angle BCD = \frac{1}{2}m\overset{\frown}{BD}$ because the measure of an angle formed by a tangent and a secant intersecting on a circle at the point of tangency is half the measure of the intercepted arc. By subst., $m\angle ACD = \frac{1}{2}m\overset{\frown}{AD} - \frac{1}{2}m\overset{\frown}{BD}$. Thus by the Distributive Property, $m\angle ACD = \frac{1}{2}\left(m\overset{\frown}{AD} - m\overset{\frown}{BD}\right)$.

22. Justify Reasoning Write a proof that the figure shown is a square.

Given: $\overline{YZ}$ and $\overline{WZ}$ are tangent to circle X, $m\overset{\frown}{WY} = 90°$

Prove: $WXYZ$ is a square.

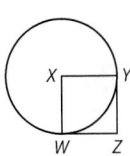

Since $m\overset{\frown}{WY} = 90°$, $m\angle YXW = 90°$ because it is a central angle. Because a line tangent to a circle is a line perpendicular to a radius at the point of tangency, $\angle XYZ$ and $\angle XWZ$ are right angles. The sum of the measures of the angles of a quadrilateral is $360°$, so $m\angle WZY = 90°$. Thus all 4 angles of $WXYZ$ are right, so $WXYZ$ is a rectangle. $\overline{XY} \cong \overline{XW}$ because they are radii. Because a parallelogram with one pair consecutive sides congruent is a rhombus, $WXYZ$ is a rhombus. Since $WXYZ$ is both a rectangle and a rhombus, it must also be a square.

COGNITIVE STRATEGIES

Have students make a study guide by folding a sheet of paper in fourths. Have them write *Angle Relationships in Circles* on one section of the guide. On the other sections, ask students to write the process for finding the measure of an angle whose vertex is on a circle, inside a circle, and outside a circle. Have them include a diagram of each, using colored pencils to draw the angles.

Ask students to explain in their own words the angle relationships in circles from the lesson. Encourage them to include diagrams and suggestions about how to remember each relationship.

23. Justify Reasoning Prove the Tangent-Secant Interior Angle Theorem.

Given: Tangent $\vec{BC}$ and secant $\vec{BA}$

Prove: $m\angle ABC = \frac{1}{2}m\widehat{AB}$

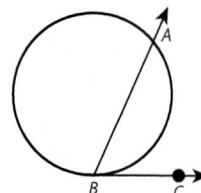

$\left(Hint:$ Consider two cases, one where $\overline{AB}$ is a diameter and one where $\overline{AB}$ is not a diameter.$\right)$

Case 1: Assume $\overline{AB}$ is a diameter of the circle. Then $m\widehat{AB} = 180°$, and $\angle ABC$ is a right angle, because a diameter is perpendicular to a tangent at the point of tangency. Thus $m\angle ABC = \frac{1}{2}m\widehat{AB}$.

Case 2: Assume $\overline{AB}$ is not a diameter of the circle. Let X be the center of the circle and draw radii $\overline{XA}$ and $\overline{XB}$. Since they are radii, $\overline{XA} \cong \overline{XB}$ so $\triangle AXB$ is isosceles. Thus $\angle XAB \cong \angle XBA$, and $2m\angle XBA + m\angle AXB = 180°$. This means that $m\angle XBA = 90° - \frac{1}{2}m\angle AXB$. Because a line tangent to a circle is perpendicular to the radius at the point of tangency, $\angle XBC$ is a right angle, so $m\angle XBA + m\angle ABC = 90°$ or $m\angle ABC = 90° - m\angle XBA$. By substitution, $m\angle ABC = 90° - \left(90° - \frac{1}{2}m\angle AXB\right)$. Simplifying gives $m\angle ABC = \frac{1}{2}m\angle AXB$. $m\angle AXB = m\widehat{AB}$ because $\angle AXB$ is a central angle. Thus $m\angle ABC = \frac{1}{2}m\widehat{AB}$.

24. Critical Thinking Suppose two secants intersect in the exterior of a circle as shown. Which is greater, $m\angle 1$ or $m\angle 2$? Justify your answer.

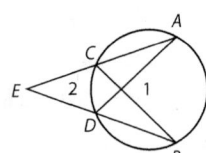

$m\angle 1 > m\angle 2$ because $m\angle 1 = \frac{1}{2}\left(m\widehat{AB} + m\widehat{CD}\right)$ and $m\angle 2 = \frac{1}{2}\left(m\widehat{AB} - m\widehat{CD}\right)$.

Since $m\widehat{CD} > 0$ the expression for $m\angle 1$ is greater.

© Houghton Mifflin Harcourt Publishing Company

Lesson Performance Task

The diameter of the Moon is about 2160 miles. From Earth, the portion of the Moon's surface that an observer can see is from a circumscribed angle of approximately 0.5°.

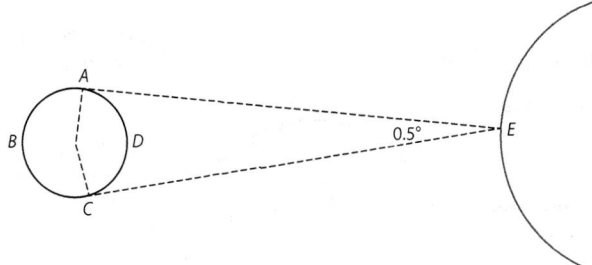

a. Find the measure of $\overset{\frown}{ADC}$. Explain how you found the measure.

b. What fraction of the circumference of the Moon is represented by $\overset{\frown}{ADC}$?

c. Find the length of $\overset{\frown}{ADC}$. You can use the formula $C = 2\pi r$ to find the circumference of the Moon.

a. Let $x = m\overset{\frown}{ADC}$. Then $m\overset{\frown}{ABC} = 360° - x$.

$$m\angle E = \tfrac{1}{2}\left(m\overset{\frown}{ABC} - m\overset{\frown}{ADC}\right)$$
$$0.5° = \tfrac{1}{2}\left([360° - x] - x\right)$$
$$= \tfrac{1}{2}(360° - 2x)$$
$$= 180° - x$$
$$x = 179.5°$$

So, $m\overset{\frown}{ADC} = 179.5°$.

b. $\dfrac{179.5}{360} \approx 49.9\%$

c. radius of the Moon ≈ 1080 miles

$$\text{length } \overset{\frown}{ADC} = 49.9\% \times \text{circumference}$$
$$= 0.499 \times 2\pi r$$
$$\approx 0.499(2)(3.14)(1080)$$
$$= 3384.4$$

The length of $\overset{\frown}{ADC}$ is about 3384.4 miles.

INTEGRATE MATHEMATICAL PRACTICES

Focus on Reasoning

MP.2 $\overline{AB}$ is a diameter of a circle. Tangents are drawn to points A and B. How can you use the Tangent-Tangent Exterior Angle Theorem to show that the tangents do not intersect? If the tangents intersect, the angle they form measures half the difference of the arcs they intercept. Since $\overline{AB}$ is a diameter, those intercepted arcs are congruent. Half their difference equals 0°. Since no angle measures 0°, the tangents cannot intersect.

INTEGRATE MATHEMATICAL PRACTICES

Focus on Critical Thinking

MP.3 Imagine points A and B are the farthest points with which a satellite above Earth at point S can directly communicate. Measured along the Earth's surface, A and B are 8000 miles apart. Find the measure of $\angle S$. Use 4000 miles for the radius of Earth.

$$\text{circumference} = 2\pi(4000) \approx 25{,}120$$
$$\frac{m\overset{\frown}{AB}}{360°} = \frac{4000}{25{,}120}$$
$$m\overset{\frown}{AB} \approx 57°$$
$$m\angle S = \frac{1}{2}\left[(360° - 57°) - 57°\right]$$
$$= 123°$$

EXTENSION ACTIVITY

When the Moon passes directly in front of the Sun, a total solar eclipse occurs. The discs of the Sun and Moon, as seen from Earth, are the same size. Students saw in the Lesson Performance Task that the Moon subtends an angle of about 0.5°, as seen from Earth. So does the Sun, even though it is 93 million miles away—nearly 400 times as far away as the Moon. Ask students to prove that at that distance and with a radius of 430,000 miles, the Sun also subtends a 0.5° angle. To do so, they can draw a right triangle with a point on the Earth at one vertex, the distance to the Sun as one leg of the right triangle, and the radius of the Sun as the other leg. The tangent ratio shows that half the angle as seen from Earth is about 0.25°. The full angle is thus 0.5°.

Scoring Rubric
2 points: Student correctly solves the problem and explains his/her reasoning.
1 point: Student shows good understanding of the problem but does not fully solve or explain his/her reasoning.
0 points: Student does not demonstrate understanding of the problem.

Angle Relationships in Circles   **842**

Study Guide Review

ASSESSMENT AND INTERVENTION

Assign or customize module reviews.

Angles and Segments in Circles

Essential Question: How can you use angles and segments in circles to solve real-world problems?

KEY EXAMPLE (Lesson 15.1)

Determine $m\widehat{DE}$, $m\widehat{BD}$, $m\widehat{DAB}$, and $m\angle ADE$.

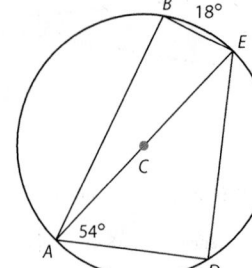

Since chord AE passes through the center of the circle at C, the chord AE is a diameter of the circle. $\widehat{ABE}$ is then a semicircle, and $m\widehat{ABE} = 180°$.

But $m\angle ADE = \frac{1}{2}m\widehat{ABE} = 90°$. $\triangle ADE$ is a right triangle with $m\angle AED = 36°$.

Also, $m\angle DAE = \frac{1}{2}m\widehat{DE}$, which implies that $m\widehat{DE} = 2m\angle DAE = 108°$. Since $m\widehat{BD} = m\widehat{BE} + m\widehat{DE}$, $m\widehat{BD} = 18° + 108° = 126°$. Finally, $m\angle DAB = \frac{1}{2}m\widehat{BD} = 63°$.

KEY EXAMPLE (Lesson 15.2)

Determine the angles J, K, L, and M in the given quadrilateral.

$(40 + 8x) + (5x - 16) = 180$.
$24 + 13x = 180$.
$13x = 156.\ x = 12$.

$m\angle J = 40 + 8x = 40 + 8(12)$
$\quad = 136°$

$m\angle L = 5x - 16 = 5(12) - 16$
$\quad = 60 - 16 = 44°$

$m\angle K = \dfrac{20(12)}{4} = 60°.\ m\angle M + m\angle K = 180°$.

$m\angle M = 180° - 60° = 120°$

Key Vocabulary

chord *(cuerda)*
central angle *(ángulo central)*
inscribed angle
(ángulo inscrito)
arc *(arco)*
minor arc *(arco menor)*
major arc *(arco principal)*
semicircle *(semicírculo)*
adjacent arcs
(arcos adyacentes)
Inscribed Angle Theorem
(teorema del ángulo inscrito)
Inscribed Quadrilateral
Theorem *(teorema del
ángulo inscrito)*
tangent *(tangent)*
point of tangency
(punto de tangencia)
Tangent-Radius Theorem
*(teorema de la tangente-
radio)*
Chord-Chord Product Theorem
*(teorema del producto de la
cuerda de la cuerda)*
secant *(secante)*
secant segment
(segmente secante)
external secant segment
(segmento externo secante)
Secant-Secant Theorem
*(Teorema de la secante-
secante)*
tangent segment
(segmento tangente)
Intersecting Chords Angle
Measure Theorem *(teorema
de medida de ángulo de
intersección acordes)*
Tangent-Secant Interior Angle
Measure Theorem *(teorema
de la medida de ángulo
interior tangente-secante)*
Tangent-Secant Exterior Angle
Measure Theorem *(teorema
de la medida de ángulo
exterior tangente-secante)*

Two tangent lines are drawn to a circle from point K intersecting the circle at points M and N. If $m\widehat{MPN} = 210°$, what is $m\angle MKN$?

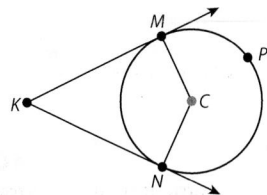

If $m\widehat{MPN} = 210°$, then $m\widehat{MN} = 360° - 210° = 150°$.

$m\angle MKN = \frac{1}{2}\left(m\widehat{MPN} - m\widehat{MN}\right)$

$m\angle MKN = \frac{1}{2}(210° - 150°) = \frac{1}{2}(60°) = 30°$

A tangent and a secant are drawn to a circle from the external point B. The point of tangency is at point A, and the secant intersects the circle at points C and D. Find x.

From the Secant-Tangent Product Theorem, we can say that $BD \cdot BC = AB^2$. So $(2 + x) \cdot 2 = 8^2$.

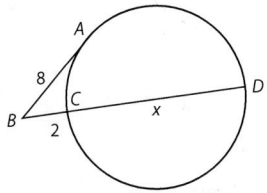

So $4 + 2x = 64$. $2x = 60$ and $x = 30$.

Two chords intersect the interior of a circle at point T. Find $m\widehat{PR}$.

By the Intersecting Chords Angle Measure Theorem we can say the following:

$m\angle QTS = \frac{1}{2}\left(m\widehat{QS} + m\widehat{PR}\right)$

$60° = \frac{1}{2}\left(80° + m\widehat{PR}\right)$

$120° = \left(80° + m\widehat{PR}\right)$

$120° - 80° = m\widehat{PR}$

$40° = m\widehat{PR}$

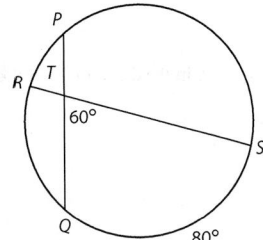

MODULE PERFORMANCE TASK

COMMON CORE

Mathematical Practices: MP.1, MP.2, MP.4, MP.6
G-C.A.2, G-C.A.3, G-SRT.C.8

SUPPORTING STUDENT REASONING

Students should begin this problem by focusing on what information they will need. Here are some issues they might bring up.

- **How a marble fits inside the package:** Students need to assume that a marble will be tangent to all sides of the package, so a cross section of the package will be a circle inscribed in an equilateral triangle.

- **How to find the diameter of a marble that is tangent to all sides of the package:** Students should work with the cross section of the marble (a circle) in the package and use special triangles or trigonometry to find the radius and diameter of the circle.

EXERCISES

Use the Inscribed Angle Theorem. *(Lesson 15.1)*

1. Find the measure of the intercepted arc for an inscribed angle of 50°.

100°

Use the Inscribed Quadrilateral Theorem. *(Lesson 15.2)*

2. If one angle of a quadrilateral inscribed in a circle is 50°, what is the measure of its opposite angle?

130°

Use the Circumscribed Angle Theorem. *(Lesson 15.3)*

3. Two tangents are drawn from an external point A to a circle. If one of the intercepted arcs on the circle is 120°, what must be the measure of the other intercepted arc?

240°

Use the Chord-Chord Product Theorem. *(Lesson 15.4)*

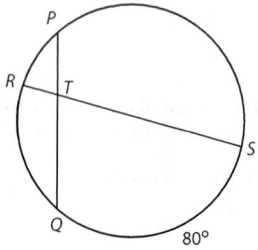

4. Given $RT = 2$, $TS = 6$, and $PT = 3$. Find TQ

4

Use the Tangent-Secant Exterior Angle Measure Theorem. *(Lesson 15.5)*

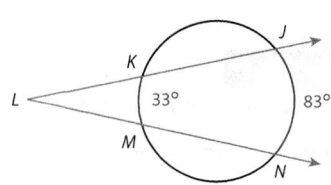

5. Find m∠L in the diagram given the m$\widehat{KM}$ and m$\widehat{JN}$.

25°

© Houghton Mifflin Harcourt Publishing Company

SCAFFOLDING SUPPORT

- Suggest that students draw a diagram to show the cross section of the marble as it relates to the triangular base of the package. This should help them see the relationship between the radius of the inscribed circle and the length of a side of the equilateral triangle. Students should think about a way to form a right triangle using the radius of the marble and one of the sides of the triangular base.

- To calculate the number of marbles, students can divide the length of the package by the diameter of one marble. Make sure students understand that only a whole number of marbles will fit in the package.

MODULE PERFORMANCE TASK

How Many Marbles Will Fit?

Consider a package of marbles in the shape of a triangular prism. The cross-section of the package is an equilateral triangle with a side length of 1.5 inches, and the length of the package is 10 inches. What is the diameter of the largest marble that will fit inside the package? How many such marbles can fit within the package?

Start by listing in the space below how you plan to tackle the problem. Then use your own paper to complete the task. Be sure to write down all your data and assumptions. Then use words, numbers, diagrams, or algebra to explain how you reached your conclusion.

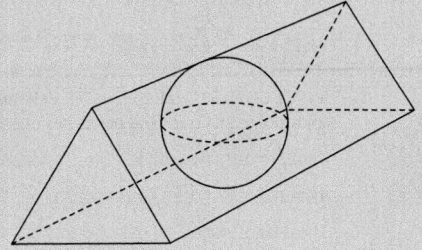

SAMPLE SOLUTION

A diagram of the cross section of the package with the largest marble inside is shown, with a right triangle formed by a perpendicular bisector of one of the sides and an angle bisector for one angle. The two intersect at the center of the circle.

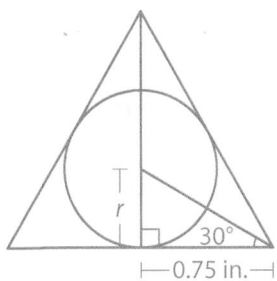

Using the trigonometry of right triangles:

$$\tan 30° = \frac{r}{0.75}$$

$$r = 0.75 \tan 30°$$

$$r \approx 0.43$$

The radius of the largest marble that can fit in the package is 0.43 inch, so the diameter is 0.86 inch.

Divide the length of the package by the diameter of the marble to find how many can fit in the package.

$$\frac{10}{0.86} \approx 11.6$$

Eleven marbles with a diameter of 0.86 inch can fit in the package.

DISCUSSION OPPORTUNITIES

- What assumptions are made when finding how many marbles will fit into the package? Sample: the marbles are packed tightly into the package and thus are tangent to the sides of the package.

- What are some sources of error in finding the diameter of the circle that is the cross section of the marble?

- Why might manufacturers want to leave space in a container when packaging items? Why might they not want to leave space?

Assessment Rubric

2 points: Student correctly solves the problem and explains his/her reasoning.

1 point: Student shows good understanding of the problem but does not fully solve or explain.

0 points: Student does not demonstrate understanding of the problem.

Ready to Go On?

ASSESS MASTERY

Use the assessment on this page to determine if students have mastered the concepts and standards covered in this module.

ASSESSMENT AND INTERVENTION

Access Ready to Go On? assessment online, and receive instant scoring, feedback, and customized intervention or enrichment.

ADDITIONAL RESOURCES

Response to Intervention Resources

- Reteach Worksheets

Differentiated Instruction Resources

- Reading Strategies **EL**
- Success for English Learners **EL**
- Challenge Worksheets

Assessment Resources

- Leveled Module Quizzes

15.1–15.5 Angles and Segments in Circles

- Online Homework
- Hints and Help
- Extra Practice

1. If $m\angle BCD = 20°$ and $m\widehat{EF} = 34°$, determine $m\widehat{ABD}$ using the appropriate theorems and postulates. (Lesson 15.1)

    If $m\widehat{EF} = 34°$, then $m\angle ECF = \underline{\ 34°\ }$. If $m\angle ECF = 34°$,

    then $m\angle ACB = \underline{\ 34°\ }$ by the $\underline{\text{vertical angles}}$

    Theorem. If $m\angle ACB = 34°$ and $m\angle BCD = 20°$, then

    $m\widehat{AB} = \underline{\ 34°\ }$ and $\underline{\ m\widehat{BD} = 20°\ }$. By the

    $\underline{\text{Arc Addition Postulate}}$, $m\widehat{ABD} = m\widehat{AB} + m\widehat{BD}$, and

    so $m\widehat{ABD} = \underline{\ 54°\ }$.

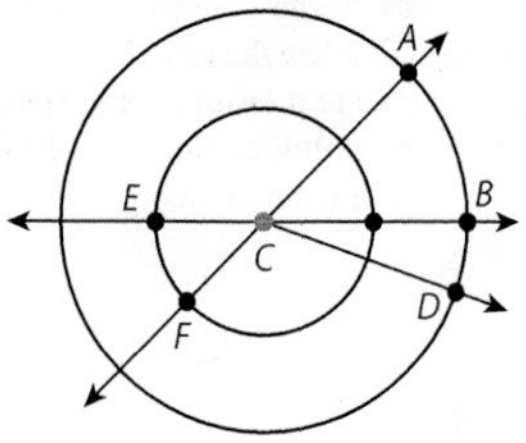

2. Find the measures of each angle in the inscribed quadrilateral. (Lesson 15.2)

    $m\angle P + m\angle R = 180°$

    $(5y + 4) + (15y + 16) = 180$

    $\qquad 20y + 20 = 180$

    $\qquad\qquad 20y = 160$

    $\qquad\qquad\quad y = 8$

    $m\angle P = 5(8) + 4 = 44°$

    $m\angle R = 15(8) + 16 = 136°$

    $m\angle Q = 8^2 + 53 = 117°$

    $m\angle S = 63°$

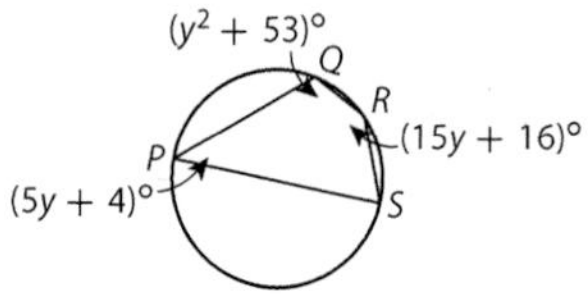

Fill in the proper conclusions based on known theorems and relationships. (Lesson 15.5)

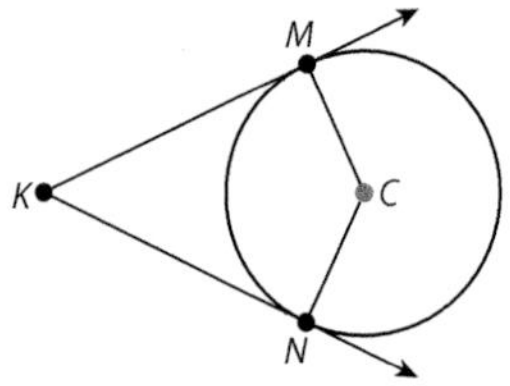

3. Using the given figure where $\overline{KM}$ and $\overline{KN}$ are tangent to the circle at M and N respectively, what can you say about the following?

    a. What angles are right angles? $\qquad \underline{\angle M, \angle N}$

    b. Suppose that $m\angle MKN = 80°$. What is $m\angle MCN$?

    $\qquad m\angle MCN + m\angle MKN = 180°$, so $m\angle MCN = 100°$

ESSENTIAL QUESTION

4. What are the major theorems that allow you to determine the relationships between angles formed by lines that intersect a circle?

    Answers may vary. There are many theorems that were developed in this module. Sample: You can determine the measure of an inscribed angle by $\frac{1}{2}$ the measure of its intercepted arc. You can use the Intersecting Chords Theorem to find missing lengths and angles.

COMMON CORE Common Core Standards

Lesson	Items	Content Standards	Mathematical Practices
15.3, 15.4, 15.5	1	G-C.B.5, G-C.A.2	MP.3
15.2	2	G-C.A.3	MP.7
15.3	3	G-C.A.2	MP.7

Assessment Readiness

SELECTED RESPONSE

1. An angle of 20° is inscribed in a circle. Could the given value be the measure of the arc intercepted by this angle?
   Select Yes or No for A–C.
   - **A.** 10°   ○ Yes   ● No
   - **B.** 20°   ○ Yes   ● No
   - **C.** 40°   ● Yes   ○ No

2. The points A, B, C, and D are taken in order on the circumference of a circle. Chords AC and BD intersect at point E. $m\widehat{AB} = 76°$ and $m\widehat{CD} = 80°$. Choose True or False for each statement.
   - **A.** $m\widehat{ABC} = 156°$ ○ True   ● False
   - **B.** $m\angle AEB = 78°$ ● True   ○ False
   - **C.** $m\angle AED = 72°$ ○ True   ● False

3. Line F bisects $\angle ABC$, $\angle ABF = 6x$, and $\angle FBC = 2x + 60$. Choose True or False for each statement.
   - **A.** $m\angle FBC = 45°$ ○ True   ● False
   - **B.** $m\angle ABC = 180°$ ● True   ○ False
   - **C.** $\angle ABF$ is a right angle.   ● True   ○ False

4. If two chords intersect inside a circle, then what do you know about the products of the lengths of the segments of the chords? How can you determine whether two circles are similar?

   Possible answer: The products of the lengths of the segments of the chords are always equal. All circles are similar.

5. $\triangle ABC$ is inscribed in a circle such that vertices A and B lie on a diameter of the circle. If the length of the diameter of the circle is 13 and the length of chord BC is 5, find side AC.

   $AC = 12$; solution requires knowledge of the Inscribed Angle Theorem and the Pythagorean Theorem. The student is expected to supply his or her own diagram.

MIXED REVIEW

Assessment Readiness

ASSESSMENT AND INTERVENTION

Assign ready-made or customized practice tests to prepare students for high-stakes tests.

ADDITIONAL RESOURCES

Assessment Resources

- Leveled Module Quizzes: Modified, B

AVOID COMMON ERRORS

Item 5   After placing two vertices of the triangle on the diameter of the circle, some students may automatically place the third vertex as far as possible from the first two, creating an isosceles triangle. Remind them to be careful to avoid making assumptions that are not supported by the problem.

Common Core Standards

Lesson	Items	Content Standards	Mathematical Practices
15.1	1	G-C.A.2	MP.5
15.5	2	G-C.A.2	MP.5
1.2	3*	G-CO.D.12	MP.2
15.4, 11.2	4*	G-C.A.2	MP.3
15.4	5	G-SRT.C.8	MP.5

* Item integrates mixed review concepts from previous modules or a previous course.

Arc Length and Sector Area

ESSENTIAL QUESTION:

Answer: Arc length and sector area are useful when you want to analyze a part of a circular shape, such as a slice of pizza.

PROFESSIONAL DEVELOPMENT VIDEO

Professional Development Video

Author Juli Dixon models successful teaching practices in an actual high-school classroom.

Professional
Development
my.hrw.com

MODULE **16**

Arc Length and Sector Area

Essential Question: How can the arc length and sector area of a circle be used to solve real-world problems?

© Houghton Mifflin Harcourt Publishing Company • Image Credits:
©primopiano/Shutterstock

REAL WORLD VIDEO
Check out how you can use sector areas to help you order wisely the next time you're buying pizza.

MODULE PERFORMANCE TASK PREVIEW

What's the Better Deal on Pizza?

In this module, you will use geometry to figure out which pizza order gets you more pizza for your money. How can calculating sector area help you to solve this problem? Let's find out.

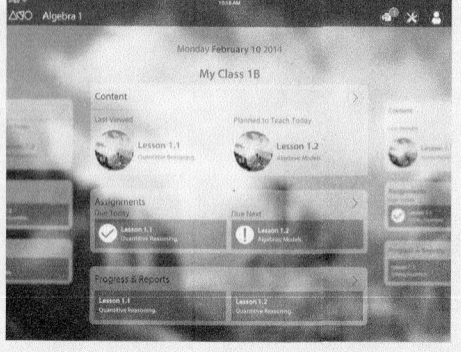

DIGITAL TEACHER EDITION

Access a full suite of teaching resources when and where you need them:

- Access content online or offline
- Customize lessons to share with your class
- Communicate with your students in real-time
- View student grades and data instantly to target your instruction where it is needed most

PERSONAL MATH TRAINER
Assessment and Intervention

Assign automatically graded homework, quizzes, tests, and intervention activities. Prepare your students with updated, Common Core-aligned practice tests.

Are (YOU) Ready?

Complete these exercises to review skills you will need for this module.

Area of a Circle

Example 1   Find the area of a circle with radius equal to 5.

$A = \pi r^2$ Write the equation for the area of a circle of radius r.

$A = \pi(5)^2$ Substitute the radius.

$A = 25\pi$ Simplify.

Find each area.

1. A circle with radius 3 9π
                                     2. A circle with radius 6 36π

3. A circle with radius 2π $4\pi^3$
                                     4. A circle with radius $\frac{5}{\pi}$ $\frac{25}{\pi}$

Circumference

Example 2   Find the circumference of a circle with radius equal to 6.

$C = 2\pi r$ Write the equation for the circumference of a circle with radius r.

$C = 2\pi(6)$ Substitute the radius.

$C = 12\pi$ Simplify.

Find each circumference.

5. A circle with radius 4   **6.** A circle with radius 3π

             8π $6\pi^2$

7. A circle with diameter 2   **8.** A circle with diameter $\frac{6}{\pi}$

             2π 6

Quadratic Functions

Example 3   Write x in terms of y. $10yx^2 = 60$

$10yx^2 = 60$ Write the equation.

$yx^2 = 6$ Divide both sides by 10.

$x^2 = \frac{6}{y}$ Divide both sides by y.

$x = \sqrt{\frac{6}{y}}, x = -\sqrt{\frac{6}{y}}$ Find the square root and its negative.

Solve each equation for x.

9. $4x^2 + 8x + 4 = 100$ **10.** $5y^2x^2 = 125$

     $x = 4, x = -6$ $x = \frac{5}{y}, x = -\frac{5}{y}$

Are You Ready?

ASSESS READINESS

Use the assessment on this page to determine if students need strategic or intensive intervention for the module's prerequisite skills.

ASSESSMENT AND INTERVENTION

RtI Response to Intervention TIER 1, TIER 2, TIER 3 SKILLS

Personal Math Trainer will automatically create a standards-based, personalized intervention assignment for your students, targeting each student's individual needs!

ADDITIONAL RESOURCES

See the table below for a full list of intervention resources available for this module.

Response to Intervention Resources also includes:

- Tier 2 Skill Pre-Tests for each Module
- Tier 2 Skill Post-Tests for each skill

Response to Intervention			Differentiated Instruction
Tier 1 Lesson Intervention Worksheets	**Tier 2** Strategic Intervention Skills Intervention Worksheets	**Tier 3** Intensive Intervention Worksheets available online	
Reteach 16.1 Reteach 16.2 Reteach 16.3	4 Area of a Circle 6 Circumference 20 Quadratic Functions	Building Block Skills 9, 14, 22, 23, 38, 53, 65, 100, 102	Challenge worksheets Extend the Math Lesson Activities in TE

Justifying Circumference and Area of a Circle

Common Core Math Standards

The student is expected to:

 **G-GMD.A.1**

Give an informal argument for the formulas for the circumference of a circle, area of a circle, volume of a cylinder, pyramid, and cone. Also G-MG.A.1

Mathematical Practices

 MP.8 Patterns

Language Objective

Explain to a partner how to justify the circumference and area formulas for a circle.

ENGAGE

Essential Question: How can you justify and use the formulas for the circumference and area of a circle?

To justify the formulas, inscribe a series of regular n-gons in a circle of radius r. Then write expressions to represent the perimeter and area of a circle, respectively. Then show that the expression for the perimeter gets closer to $C = 2\pi r$ as n gets larger and that the expression for area gets closer to $A = \pi r^2$ as n gets larger. To use the formulas, find the radius or diameter of a circle, substitute into the equation, and solve.

PREVIEW: LESSON PERFORMANCE TASK

View the Engage section online. Discuss the photograph. Ask students to speculate on the event that is taking place and to describe it. Then preview the Lesson Performance Task.

Name_____ Class_____ Date_____

16.1 Justifying Circumference and Area of a Circle

Essential Question: How can you justify and use the formulas for the circumference and area of a circle?

Resource Locker

⊘ Explore   Justifying the Circumference Formula

To find the circumference of a given circle, consider a regular polygon that is inscribed in the circle. As you increase the number of sides of the polygon, the perimeter of the polygon gets closer to the circumference of the circle.

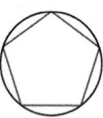  

Inscribed pentagon   Inscribed hexagon   Inscribed octagon

Let circle O be a circle with center O and radius r. Inscribe a regular n–gon in circle O and draw radii from O to the vertices of the n-gon.

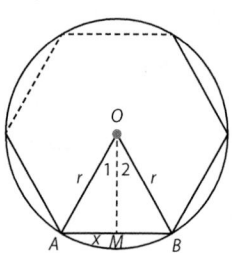

Let $\overline{AB}$ be one side of the n-gon. Draw $\overline{OM}$, the segment from O to the midpoint of $\overline{AB}$.

(A) Then $\triangle AOM \cong \triangle BOM$ by _____the SSS Congruence Criterion_____.

(B) So, $\angle 1 \cong \angle 2$ by ___CPCTC___.

(C) There are n triangles, all congruent to $\triangle AOB$, that surround point O and fill the n-gon.

Therefore, $m\angle AOB = \boxed{\dfrac{360°}{n}}$ and $m\angle 1 = \boxed{\dfrac{180°}{n}}$.

© Houghton Mifflin Harcourt Publishing Company

Module 16   **851**   Lesson 1

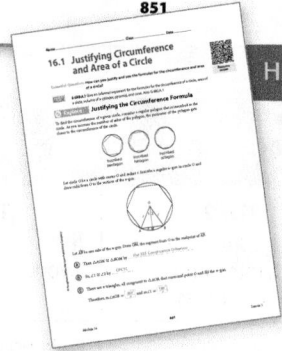

HARDCOVER PAGES 719–728

Turn to these pages to find this lesson in the hardcover student edition.

Ⓓ Since $\angle OMA \cong \angle OMB$ by CPCTC, and $\angle OMA$ and $\angle OMB$ form a linear pair, these angles are supplementary and must have measures of 90°. So $\triangle AOM$ and $\triangle BOM$ are right triangles.

In $\triangle AOM$, $\sin\angle 1 = \dfrac{\text{length of opposite leg}}{\text{length of hypotenuse}} = \dfrac{x}{r}$.

So, $x = r\sin\angle 1$ and substituting the expression for $m\angle 1$ from above gives

$x = r\sin \boxed{\dfrac{180°}{n}}$.

Ⓔ Now express the perimeter of the n-gon in terms of x.

The length of $\overline{AB}$ is $2x$, because $\underline{\text{since } M \text{ is the midpoint of } \overline{AB}}$.

This means the perimeter of the n-gon is $\underline{\ 2nx\ }$.

Substitute the expression for x in Step D.

The perimeter of the n-gon in terms of x is $\underline{\ 2nr\sin\left(\dfrac{180°}{n}\right)\ }$.

Ⓕ Your expression for the perimeter of the n-gon should include the factor $n\sin\left(\dfrac{180°}{n}\right)$. What happens to this factor as n gets larger?

Use your calculator to do the following.

- Enter the expression $x\sin\left(\dfrac{180}{x}\right)$ as Y_1.
- Go to the Table Setup menu and enter the values shown.
- View a table for the function.
- Use arrow keys to scroll down.

What happens to the value of $x\sin\left(\dfrac{180°}{x}\right)$ as x gets larger?

The value gets closer to π.

Ⓖ Look at the expression you wrote for the perimeter of the n-gon. What happens to the value of this expression, as n gets larger?

The expression gets closer to $2\pi r$.

Reflect

1. When n is very large, does the perimeter of the n-gon ever equal the circumference of the circle? Why or why not?
No; the perimeter of the n-gon gets very close to the circumference, but is always a bit less than the circumference.

2. How does the above argument justify the formula $C = 2\pi r$?
When n is very large, the regular n-gon is virtually indistinguishable from the circle and the expression for the n-gon's perimeter is virtually indistinguishable from $2\pi r$.

EXPLORE

Justifying the Circumference Formula

INTEGRATE TECHNOLOGY

Students have the option of doing the Explore activity either in the book or online.

QUESTIONING STRATEGIES

? How many sides does a regular n-gon have? How many angles does it have? *n sides and n angles*

? What is an expression for the perimeter of an n-gon in terms of the radius r of the circle that circumscribes the n-gon? *$2nr\sin\dfrac{180°}{n}$*

PROFESSIONAL DEVELOPMENT

 Learning Progressions

Students have already seen the formulas for the circumference and area of a circle in earlier grades. In this lesson, they will explore a justification of the formula for the circumference of a circle that is based on an informal limit argument, and then use the circumference formula to help them justify the area formula. These types of arguments are of central importance in calculus. Although the term *limit* is not used here, and there is no attempt to give a rigorous explanation of the concept, the underlying idea should be accessible to students at this level, and it offers a preview of the mathematical thinking that students will do in future courses.

EXPLAIN 1

Applying the Circumference Formula

INTEGRATE MATHEMATICS PRACTICES
Focus on Math Connections

MP.1 When students use the circumference formula for real-world applications, remind them that π is a mathematical constant that is approximately equal to 3.14159. Tell students that they will often use approximations for π, since π is an irrational number.

QUESTIONING STRATEGIES

? What units should you choose when using the circumference formula in a real-life application? How do you know? Sample answer: Use the same units of length that are given for the linear dimensions of the real-life circle, because the circumference is measured in units of length.

© Houghton Mifflin Harcourt Publishing Company · Image Credits: ©Nikada/ iStockPhoto.com

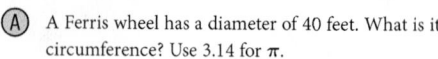

Explain 1 Applying the Circumference Formula

Example 1 Find the circumference indicated.

(A) A Ferris wheel has a diameter of 40 feet. What is its circumference? Use 3.14 for π.

Diameter $= 2r$

$40 = 2r$

$20 = r$

Use the formula $C = 2\pi r$ to find the circumference.

$C = 2\pi r$

$C = 2\pi(20)$

$C = 2(3.14)(20)$

$C \approx 125.6$

The circumference is about 125.6 feet.

(B) A pottery wheel has a diameter of 2 feet. What is its circumference? Use 3.14 for π.

The diameter is 2 feet, so the radius in inches is $r = \boxed{12}$.

$C = 2\pi r$

$C = \boxed{2} \cdot \boxed{3.14} \cdot \boxed{12}$

$C \approx \boxed{75.36}$ in.

Reflect

3. Discussion Suppose you double the radius of a circle. How does the circumference of this larger circle compare with the circumference of the smaller circle? Explain.

The circumference is also doubled. The new radius is 2r and the new circumference is

$2\pi(2r) = 2(2\pi r)$.

Your Turn

4. The circumference of a tree is 20 feet. What is its diameter? Round to the nearest tenth of a foot. Use 3.14 for π.

Since, $d = 2r$, $C = 2\pi r = \pi d$.

$C = \pi d$

$\frac{20}{\pi} = d$

$6.37 \approx d$

So, the diameter is about 6.4 feet.

5. The circumference of a circular fountain is 32 feet. What is its diameter? Round to the nearest tenth of a foot. Use 3.14 for π.

Since, $d = 2r$, $C = 2\pi r = \pi d$.

$C = \pi d$

$\frac{32}{\pi} = d$

$10.19 \approx d$

So, the diameter is about 10.2 feet.

COLLABORATIVE LEARNING

Small Group Activity

Geometry software allows students to explore how to approximate the circumference formula and the area formula. Have one student construct a regular polygon. Ask a second student to measure both the perimeter of the polygon and the area of the polygon. Continue to increase the sides of the polygon and repeat the activity until the perimeter and area approach a nearly constant value. Then use geometry software to circumscribe the final figure and measure its circumference and area. Ask students to compare these results to the nearly constant value for the polygons.

⚙ Explain 2 Justifying the Area Formula

To find the area of a given circle, consider a regular polygon that is inscribed in the circle. As you increase the number of sides of the polygon, the area of the polygon gets closer to the area of the circle.

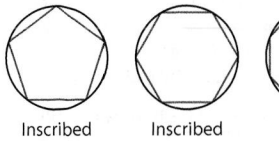

Inscribed pentagon   Inscribed hexagon   Inscribed octagon

Let circle O be a circle with center O and radius r. Inscribe a regular n-gon in circle O and draw radii from O to the vertices of the n-gon.

Let $\overline{AB}$ be one side of the n-gon. Draw $\overline{OM}$, the segment from O to the midpoint of $\overline{AB}$.

We know that $\overline{OM}$ is perpendicular to $\overline{AB}$ because triangle AOM is congruent to triangle BOM.

Let the length of $\overline{OM}$ be h.

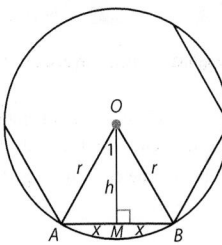

Example 2 Justify the formula for the area of a circle.

Ⓐ There are n triangles, all congruent to $\triangle AOB$, that surround point O and fill the n-gon.

Therefore, the measure of $\angle AOB$ is $\frac{360°}{n}$, and the measure of $\angle 1$ is $\frac{180°}{n}$.

We know that $x = r\sin\left(\frac{180°}{n}\right)$. Write a similar expression for h. $\underline{h = r\cos\left(\frac{180°}{n}\right)}$

Ⓑ The area of $\triangle AOB$ is $\frac{1}{2}(2x)(h) = xh = r\sin\left(\frac{180°}{n}\right)h$.

Substitute your value for h to get area $\triangle AOB = \underline{r^2\sin\left(\frac{180°}{n}\right)\cos\left(\frac{180°}{n}\right)}$.

Ⓒ There are n of these triangles, so the area of the n-gon is $\underline{nr^2\sin\left(\frac{180°}{n}\right)\cos\left(\frac{180°}{n}\right)}$.

Ⓓ Your expression for the area of the n-gon includes the factor $n\sin\left(\frac{180°}{n}\right)\cos\left(\frac{180°}{n}\right)$. What happens to this expression as n gets larger?

Use your graphing calculator to do the following.

- Enter the expression $x\sin\left(\frac{180°}{x}\right)\cos\left(\frac{180°}{x}\right)$ as Y_1.
- View a table for the function.
- Use arrow keys to scroll down.

What happens to the value of $x\sin\left(\frac{180°}{x}\right)\cos\left(\frac{180°}{x}\right)$ as x gets larger? **The value gets closer to π.**

Ⓔ Look at the expression you wrote for the area of the n-gon. What happens to the value of this expression as n gets larger? **The expression gets closer to πr^2.**

EXPLAIN 2

Justifying the Area Formula

INTEGRATE MATHEMATICAL PRACTICES
Focus on Critical Thinking

MP.3 Just as the circumference (perimeter) of a circle can be approximated by finding the perimeters of the inscribed regular polygons with n sides in terms of the radius of the circumscribed circle, so can the area of the circle be approximated by the areas of polygons with n sides in terms of the radius of the circumscribed circle. As the number of sides of the inscribed polygon increases, the perimeter of the polygon approaches a limit called the circumference of the circle, and the area of the polygon approaches a different limit called the area of the circle.

QUESTIONING STRATEGIES

❓ How is the area of a circle related to the circumference? Justify your reasoning.
$A = \frac{C^2}{4\pi}$; since $C = 2\pi r$, $r = \frac{C}{2\pi}$. Substitute for r in the area formula: $A = \pi r^2 = \pi\left(\frac{C}{2\pi}\right)^2 = \frac{C^2}{4\pi}$.

DIFFERENTIATE INSTRUCTION

Modeling

Give groups of students congruent circles. Ask each group to approximate the perimeter of their circle using different methods and then record the results in a table. Methods include: measuring with a ruler; using a string to encircle the circle, then stretching and measuring the string; or rolling the circle along the board and measuring the distance it travels. After several methods are explored, have each group make a conjecture about the perimeter of their circle, compare the conjecture to a calculation of the circumference using a formula, and then present their data and conjecture to the class.

EXPLAIN 3

Applying the Area Formula

INTEGRATE MATHEMATICAL PRACTICES
Focus on Patterns

MP.8 Students should be able to apply the area formula when given the radius or the diameter of a circle, just as they should be able to find the circumference of a circle given these values. Ask students to work with a partner to draw example circles and explain to each other how they would find the area of the circle if they are given either the radius or diameter.

QUESTIONING STRATEGIES

? How would you find the circumference of the circle if you are given the area? Sample answer: Solve for the radius using the area formula and then substitute the radius into the formula for circumference, $C = 2\pi r$, where C is the circumference and r is the radius.

AVOID COMMON ERRORS

Students may be confused about using π when asked to find the area of a circle. Point out that most applications of area specify whether they should find the approximate area, in which case an approximation for π is appropriate, or find the exact area, in which case the answer is given in terms of π. Remind students that they should wait until the end of the calculations before they round their answers.

Reflect

6. When n is very large, does the area of the n-gon ever equal the area of the circle? Why or why not?
No; the area of the n-gon is always less than the area of the circle.

7. How does the above argument justify the formula $A = \pi r^2$?
When n is very large, the regular n-gon is virtually indistinguishable from the circle and the expression for the n-gon's area is virtually indistinguishable from πr^2.

⊘ Explain 3 Applying the Area Formula

Example 3 Find the area indicated.

(A) A rectangular piece of cloth is 3 ft by 6 ft. What is the area of the largest circle that can be cut from the cloth? Round the nearest square inch.

The diameter of the largest circle is 3 feet, or 36 inches. The radius of the circle is 18 inches.

$A = \pi r^2$
$A = \pi(18)^2$
$A = 324\pi$
$A \approx 1{,}017.9 \text{ in}^2$

So, the area is about 1,018 square inches.

(B) A slice of a circular pizza measures 9 inches in length. What is the area of the entire pizza? Use 3.14 for π.

The 9-in. side of the pizza is also the length of the __radius__ of the circle. So, $r = \boxed{9}$.

$A = \pi r^2$
$A = \pi \boxed{9}^2$
$A = \boxed{81}\pi \approx \boxed{254.34}$

To the nearest square inch, the area of the pizza is ____$\boxed{255 \text{ in}^2}$____.

Reflect

8. Suppose the slice of pizza represents $\frac{1}{6}$ of the whole pizza. Does this affect your answer to Example 3B? What additional information can you determine with this fact?
No; the pizza is still assumed to be a circle with a radius of 9 in. The area of the slice of pizza is $\frac{1}{6}$ the area of the whole pizza, or about 42 square inches.

Your Turn

9. A circular swimming pool has a diameter of 18 feet. To the nearest square foot, what is the smallest amount of material needed to cover the surface of the pool? Use 3.14 for π.
$d = 18$ so $r = 9$; $A = \pi r^2 = (3.14)(9)^2 \approx 254.34$; 254 ft^2

© Houghton Mifflin Harcourt Publishing Company

LANGUAGE SUPPORT **EL**

Connect Vocabulary

To help students remember the formulas used to find the circumference and area of a circle and their associated vocabulary, have students draw example circles. Then have them use colored pencils to mark the radius of each in one color, the diameters in another color, and then list the formulas for area and circumference in different colors. Have them label the circles with the terms *radius*, *diameter*, *circumference*, *area*.

10. If the radius of a circle is doubled, is the area doubled? Explain.

No; if the radius is doubled, then the area is multiplied by 4. The area of the larger circle

is $\pi(2r)^2 = 4\pi r^2$.

11. **Essential Question Check-In** How do you justify and use the formula for the circumference of a circle?

To justify the formula, inscribe a series of regular n-gons in a circle of radius r. The

perimeter of each n-gon is $2nr \sin\left(\dfrac{180°}{n}\right)$. As n gets larger, the expression gets closer to

$2\pi r$. To use the formula $C = 2\pi r$, find the radius of the circle, and substitute this value for r.

Use a calculator to evaluate the expression.

⭐ Evaluate: Homework and Practice

- Online Homework
- Hints and Help
- Extra Practice

1. Which inscribed figure has a perimeter closer to the circumference of a circle, a regular polygon with 20 sides or a regular polygon with 40 sides? Explain.
A regular polygon with 40 sides because as the number of sides of a polygon increases, the perimeters of the polygons get closer to the circumference of the circle.

Find the circumference of each circle with the given radius or diameter. Round to the nearest tenth. Use 3.14 for π.

2. $r = 9$ cm
$C = 2\pi r = 2\pi(9) \approx 56.5$ cm

3. $r = 24$ in.
$C = 2\pi r = 2\pi(24) \approx 150.7$ cm

4. $d = 14.2$ mm
$C = \pi d = \pi(14.2) \approx 44.6$ mm

5. A basketball rim has a radius of 9 inches. Find the circumference of the rim. Round to the nearest tenth. Use 3.14 for π.
$C = 2\pi r$
$C = 2(3.14)(9)$
$C \approx 56.5$ in.

6. The diameter of a circular swimming pool is 12 feet. Find its circumference. Use 3.14 for π.
$C = \pi d$
$C = (3.14)(12)$
$C \approx 37.7$ ft

7. The diameter of the U.S. Capitol Building's dome is 96 feet at its widest point. Find its circumference. Use 3.14 for π.
$C = \pi d$
$C = (3.14)(96)$
$C \approx 301.4$ ft

Find the area of each circle with the given radius or diameter. Use 3.14 for π.

8. $r = 7$ yd
$A = \pi r^2 = (3.14)(7)^2 = 153.86$ yd²

9. $d = 5$ m
$A = \pi r^2 = (3.14)\left(\dfrac{5}{2}\right)^2 = 19.625$ m²

10. $d = 16$ ft
$A = \pi r^2 = (3.14)(8)^2 = 200.96$ ft²

11. A drum has a diameter of 10 inches. Find the area of the top of the drum. Use 3.14 for π.
$A = \pi r^2$
$= (3.14)(5)^2$
$= 78.5$ in²

Exercise	Depth of Knowledge (D.O.K.)	COMMON CORE Mathematical Practices	
1–10	**1** Recall of Information	**MP.5** Using Tools	
11–15	**2** Skills/Concepts	**MP.5** Using Tools	
16–22	**2** Skills/Concepts	**MP.4** Modeling	
23–28	**2** Skills/Concepts	**MP.2** Reasoning	
29	**3** Strategic Thinking H.O.T.	**MP.2** Reasoning	
30	**3** Strategic Thinking H.O.T.	**MP.2** Reasoning	

ELABORATE

QUESTIONING STRATEGIES

? How can you find the area of a circle when given its circumference? Solve the circumference formula for the radius and then substitute the radius into the area formula.

SUMMARIZE THE LESSON

? Suppose a regular polygon is inscribed in a circle with radius r. What formulas are used to find the area and circumference of the circle in terms of the radius, and the perimeter of the inscribed polygon in terms of the radius?
Circle: $C = 2\pi r$ and $A = \pi r^2$;
polygon perimeter $= 2nr \sin\dfrac{180°}{n}$, where n is the number of sides

EVALUATE

ASSIGNMENT GUIDE

Concept and Skills	Practice
Explore Justifying the Circumference Formula	Exercise 1
Example 1 Applying the Circumference Formula	Exercises 2–7
Example 2 Justifying the Area Formula	Exercise 32
Example 3 Applying the Area Formula	Exercises 8–15

AVOID COMMON ERRORS

When students are given the diameter of a circle in a figure, they may sometimes make the mistake of using the given diameter as r in the formulas $C = 2\pi r$ or $A = \pi r^2$. Remind students to pay close attention to whether they are given the radius or the diameter in a figure.

12. The circumference of a quarter is about 76 mm. What is the area? Round to the nearest tenth.

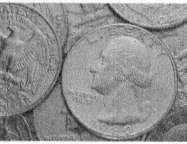

$C = 2\pi r$

$\frac{C}{2\pi} = r$

$\frac{76}{2\pi} = r$

$12.1 \approx r$

$A = \pi r^2$

$\approx \pi(12.1)^2$

$\approx 460.0 \text{ mm}^2$

Algebra **Find the area of the circle with the given circumference C. Use 3.14 for π.**

13. $C = 31.4$ ft

$C = 2\pi r$

$31.4 = 2\pi r$

$\frac{31.4}{2\pi} = r$

$5 = r$

$A = \pi(5)^2 \approx 78.5 \text{ ft}^2$

14. $C = 21.98$ ft

$C = 2\pi r$

$21.98 = 2\pi r$

$\frac{21.98}{2\pi} = r$

$3.5 = r$

$A = \pi(3.5)^2 \approx 38.5 \text{ ft}^2$

15. $C = 69.08$ ft

$C = 2\pi r$

$69.08 = 2\pi r$

$\frac{69.08}{2\pi} = r$

$11 = r$

$A = \pi(11)^2 \approx 379.9 \text{ ft}^2$

16. A Ferris wheel has a diameter of 56 ft. How far will a rider travel during a 4-minute ride if the wheel rotates once every 20 seconds? Use $\frac{22}{7}$ for π.

$C = \pi d$

$C = \left(\frac{22}{7}\right)(56)$

$C = 176$

4 min = 240 sec

$\frac{240}{20} = 12$, so the Ferris wheel rotates 12 times in 4 minutes

$176 \times 12 = 2{,}112$

rider will travel 2,112 ft on a 4-min ride.

17. A giant water lily pad is shaped like a circle with a diameter of up to 5 feet. Find the circumference and area of the pad. Round to the nearest tenth.

$C = \pi d = \pi(5) \approx 15.7$ ft.

$A = \pi r^2 = \pi(2.5)^2 \approx 19.6 \text{ ft}^2$

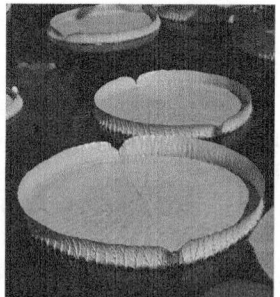

Exercise	Depth of Knowledge (D.O.K.)	COMMON CORE Mathematical Practices
31	**3** Strategic Thinking H.O.T.	**MP.2** Reasoning
32	**3** Strategic Thinking H.O.T.	**MP.2** Reasoning

18. A pizza parlor offers pizzas with diameters of 8 in., 10 in., and 12 in. Find the area of each size pizza. Round to the nearest tenth. If the pizzas cost $9, $12, and $18 respectively, which is the better buy?

$A = \pi r^2 = \pi(4)^2 \approx 50.3 \text{ in}^2$

$A = \pi r^2 = \pi(5)^2 \approx 78.5 \text{ in}^2$

$A = \pi r^2 = \pi(6)^2 \approx 113.1 \text{ in}^2$

The 8-in. pizza cost $\dfrac{\$9}{50.3} = \$0.179$ per in²; the 10-in. pizza cost $\dfrac{\$12}{78.5} = \$0.153$ per in²; the 12-in. pizza cost $\dfrac{\$18}{113.1} = \$0.159$ per in². So, the 10-inch pizza is the better buy.

19. Critical Thinking Which do you think would seat more people, a 4 ft by 6 ft rectangular table or a circular table with a diameter of 6 ft? How many people would you sit at each table? Explain your reasoning.

Possible answer: The circular table would fit at least as many people as the rectangular table. At the rectangular table, 2 people would fit at each of the 4 ft sides and 3 people would fit at each of the 6 ft sides, for a total of 10 people. Each person would have 2 ft of space. The circumference of the circular table is $C = \pi d = \pi(6) \approx 18.8$ ft. If 11 people sat at the circular table, each person would have $\dfrac{18.8}{11} \approx 1.7$ ft, or about 1 ft 8 in. of space.

20. You can estimate a tree's age in years by using the formula $a = \dfrac{r}{w}$, where r is the tree's radius without bark and w is the average thickness of the tree's rings. The circumference of a white oak tree is 100 inches. The bark is 0.5 in. thick, and the average thickness of a ring is 0.2 in. Estimate the tree's age and the area enclosed by the outer circumference of the widest ring.

If the circumference of the tree is 100 in., then the circumference of the widest ring is the circumference of the tree minus twice the thickness of the bark

$100 - 2(0.5) = 99$ in.

$C = 2\pi r$

$\dfrac{C}{2\pi} = r$

$\dfrac{99}{2\pi} = r$

$15.8 \approx r$

$a = \dfrac{r}{w} \approx \dfrac{15.8}{0.2} = 79$ years

$A = \pi r^2 \approx \pi(15.8)^2 \approx 784.3 \text{ in}^2$

© Houghton Mifflin Harcourt Publishing Company • Image Credits: ©aleximbro/iStockPhoto.com

INTEGRATE MATHEMATICAL PRACTICES

Focus on Modeling

MP.4 Some students may benefit from a hands-on approach for finding the area of a circle. Have students copy a circle with a small whole-number radius onto a sheet of graph paper and then cut it out. Have them count the whole-number squares and then cut out the pieces of the squares that are not whole. Ask them to rearrange the pieces like a puzzle to closely approximate more squares. Have them count these additional squares and add the number to their previous total. Have them compare their total to the area found by applying the formula.

To remember the first five digits of π, count the letters in each word of this statement: "Wow, I made a great discovery!"

21. **Multi-Step** A circular track for a model train has a diameter of 8.5 feet. The train moves around the track at a constant speed of 0.7 ft/s.

   a. To the nearest foot, how far does the train travel when it goes completely around the track 10 times?

   $C = \pi d$

   $= \pi(8.5)$

   ≈ 26.7

   $26.7(10) = 267$ ft

   b. To the nearest minute, how long does it take the train to go completely around the track 10 times?

   $\dfrac{267 \text{ ft}}{0.7 \text{ ft/s}} = 381.4$ s

   $\dfrac{381.4 \text{ s}}{60 \text{ s/min}} \approx 6$ min

22. The Parthenon is a Greek temple dating to about 445 BCE. The temple features 46 Doric columns, which are roughly cylindrical. The circumference of each column at the base is about 5.65 meters. What is the approximate diameter of each column? Round to the nearest tenth.

   $C = \pi d$

   $\dfrac{C}{\pi} = d$

   $\dfrac{5.65}{\pi} = d$

   $1.8 \approx d$

   $d \approx 1.8$ m

23. **Explain the Error** A circle has a diameter of 2π in. Which calculation of the area is incorrect? Explain.

   The calculation shown in A is incorrect because the diameter, instead of the radius, is used to find the area.

   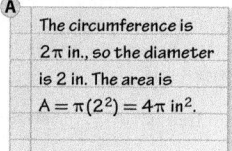

   A The circumference is 2π in., so the diameter is 2 in. The area is $A = \pi(2^2) = 4\pi$ in^2.

   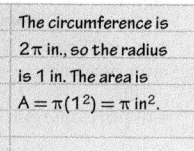

   B The circumference is 2π in., so the radius is 1 in. The area is $A = \pi(1^2) = \pi$ in^2.

24. **Write About It** The center of each circle in the figure lies on the number line. Describe the relationship between the circumference of the largest circle and the circumferences of the four smaller circles.

   The circumference of the largest circle is equal to the sum of the circumferences of the four smaller circles.

   $10\pi = 4\pi + \pi + 2\pi + 3\pi$

   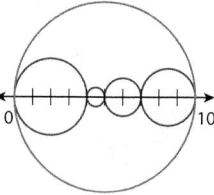

25. Find the diameter of a data storage disk with an area 113.1 cm^2.

   Since $A = \pi r^2$, $113.1 = \pi r^2$; $36.0 \approx r^2$ and r is about 6 cm. So, the diameter is about 12 cm.

© Houghton Mifflin Harcourt Publishing Company • Image Credits: ©Adam Crowley/Photodisc/Getty Images

26. Which of the following ratios can be derived from the formula for the circumference of a circle? Select all that apply.

A. $\dfrac{C}{d}$

B. $\dfrac{C}{2r}$

C. $\dfrac{C}{\pi}$

D. $\dfrac{C}{2\pi}$

E. $\dfrac{C}{2c}$

A, B, C, and D

Since $C = 2\pi r$ or $C = \pi d$, $\pi = \dfrac{C}{d}$, $\pi = \dfrac{C}{2r}$, $d = \dfrac{C}{\pi}$, and $r = \dfrac{C}{2\pi}$.

27. A meteorologist measured the eyes of hurricanes to be 15 to 20 miles in diameter during one season. What is the range of areas of the land underneath the eyes of the hurricanes?

15 mi diameter: $A = \pi r^2 = \left(\dfrac{15}{2}\right)^2 \approx 176.7 \text{ mi}^2$

20 mi diameter: $A = \pi r^2 = \pi(10)^2 \approx 314.2 \text{ mi}^2$

The range of areas is about 177 square miles to about 314 square miles.

28. A circle with a 6 in. diameter is stamped out of a rectangular piece of metal as shown. Find the area of the remaining piece of metal. Use 3.14 for π.

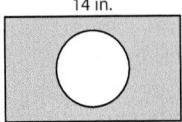

Area of metal $= (14)(8) - \pi(3)^2 = 112 - 28.26 = 83.74 \text{ in}^2$

H.O.T. Focus on Higher Order Thinking

29. Critique Reasoning A standard bicycle wheel has a diameter of 26 inches. A student claims that during a one-mile bike ride the wheel makes more than 1000 complete revolutions. Do you agree or disagree? Explain. (*Hint:* 1 mile = 5280 feet)

Disagree; the total distance is $5280 \cdot 12 = 63,360$ inches and the number of revolutions equals the total distance divided by the circumference, which is $\dfrac{63,360}{26\pi} \approx 775.7$ revolutions.

INTEGRATE MATHEMATICAL PRACTICES

Focus on Reasoning

MP.2 When working with area and circumference formulas, remind students that if they use 3.14 instead of the π button on a calculator, they are automatically giving an approximation to the circumference or area of the circle. Have small groups of students discuss when using the π key on a calculator is appropriate and when it is not necessary.

PEER-TO-PEER DISCUSSION

Ask students to discuss with a partner how to create a graphic organizer that will display all the circle formulas that they have learned in the lesson. Then have them create the graphic organizer and make sure they include the following:

- Circumference formulas
- Area formula
- Area formula in terms of circumference formulas
- Circumference formulas in terms of area formula

JOURNAL

Have students summarize the main steps in the argument that justifies the formula for the circumference of a circle and for the area of a circle. Remind students to include at least one figure in the journal entry.

---

30. **Algebra** A graphic artist created a company logo from two tangent circles whose diameters are in the ratio 3:2. What percent of the total logo is the area of the region outside of the smaller circle?

    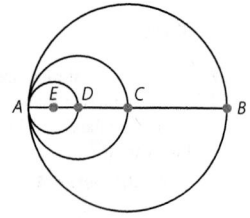

    The diameters are in the ratio 3:2, so the radii are also in the ratio 3:2.

    Let x be the common factor between the ratios. The area of the larger circle is $\pi(3x)^2 = 9x^2\pi$, and the area of the smaller circle is $\pi(2x)^2 = 4x^2\pi$.

    The area of the region outside the smaller circle is $9x^2\pi - 4x^2\pi = 5x^2\pi$.

    The percent of the total logo that is outside the smaller circle is $\frac{5x^2\pi}{9x^2\pi} = \frac{5}{9}$, or about 55.6%.

31. **Communicate Mathematical Ideas** In the figure, $\overline{AB}$ is a diameter of circle C, D is the midpoint of $\overline{AC}$, and E is the midpoint of $\overline{AD}$. How does the circumference of circle E compare to the circumference of circle C? Explain.

    The circumference of circle E is $\frac{1}{4}$ the circumference of circle C because the radius of circle E is $\frac{1}{4}$ the radius of circle C.

32. **Critical Thinking** Evelyn divides the circle and rearranges the pieces to make a shape that resembles a parallelogram.

    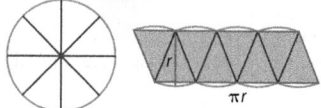

    She then divides the circle into more pieces and rearranges them into a shape that resembles a parallelogram. She thinks that the area of the new parallelogram will be closer to the area of a circle. Is she correct? Explain.

    Yes. Dividing the circle and rearranging it to make a shape that resembles a parallelogram gives a figure whose area is an estimate for the area of the circle. The more pieces you divide the circle into, the more accurate the estimate will be.

© Houghton Mifflin Harcourt Publishing Company

Lesson Performance Task

In the lesson, you saw that the more wedges into which you divide a circle, the more closely each wedge resembles a triangle, and the closer to the area of a circle the area of the reassembled wedges becomes. In the branch of mathematics called calculus, this process is called finding a *limit*. Even though you can't cut a circle into millions of tiny wedges to calculate the actual area of the circle, you can see what the area is going to be long before that, by spotting a pattern. You can apply this method in many ways, some of them unexpected.

Mac is a race walker. He is training for a race. He has decided that in the weeks leading up to the race, he'll work up to a level where he is walking 20 kilometers a day. His plan is to walk 10 kilometers the first day of training and increase the distance he walks each day until he reaches his goal.

1. Complete the table for Mac's first 6 days of training.

Day	Increase in distance walked from the day before (in kilometers)	Total distance walked that day (in kilometers)
1	10	10
2	5	$10 + 5 = \boxed{15}$
3	2.5	$\boxed{15} + 2.5 = \boxed{17.5}$
4	1.25	$17.5 + 1.25 = 18.75$
5	0.625	$18.75 + 0.625 = 19.375$
6	0.3125	$19.375 + 0.3125 = 19.6875$

2. Describe your results in relation to Mac's plan to reach a level where he walks 20 kilometers a day.

3. Suppose Mac continues his training plan. Will Mac ever reach his goal?

2. Possible answer: On the second day and beyond, Mac increases his distance by half of the increase from the day before. Mac's race walk distance on the sixth day is 19.6875 km. His added distances each day are getting very short and it seems unlikely that he'll ever reach 20 km.

3. Possible answer: I found his total after 10 days (about 19.98 km) and though it is very close to 20 km, it's still less than 20. No, it seems that Mac will approach his goal of 20 km but never quite reach it, no matter how many days he continues.

© Houghton Mifflin Harcourt Publishing Company

INTEGRATE MATHEMATICAL PRACTICES
Focus on Reasoning

MP.2 What reasons can you give to explain why the sum $10 + 5 + 2.5 + \ldots$ never seems to reach 20? Sample answer: Each new number that is added is only half of the last one, so the amount added gets smaller every time. Cumulatively, never is enough added to bring the total to 2×10 (the first number).

INTEGRATE MATHEMATICAL PRACTICES
Focus on Patterns

MP.8 Dexter drew some circles. In the first circle he inscribed an equilateral triangle, in the next a square, in the next a regular pentagon, in the next a regular hexagon, and so on. If he continued to the 100th polygon, what would it look like? Explain your reasoning. Sample answer: a circle; each succeeding figure that he drew had one additional side, each side of which would be slightly shorter than the sides of the previous figure. By the time he reached the 100th polygon, the sides would be extremely short, causing the figure to closely approximate the shape of the circle in which it was inscribed.

EXTENSION ACTIVITY

In the Lesson Performance Task, students saw that no matter how many terms in the given sequence were added, the sum never reached 20. For each sequence, ask students to hypothesize whether the sequence is bounded by an ultimate sum, as the 20 sequence was, then attempt to give a rule for deciding whether or not a sequence is bounded.

1. $1 + 2 + 3 + 4 + \ldots$ no

2. $81 + 27 + 9 + 3 + \ldots$ 122

3. $\frac{1}{2} + \frac{1}{4} + \frac{1}{8} + \frac{1}{16} + \ldots$ 1

4. $\frac{1}{3} + \frac{2}{3} + \frac{3}{3} + \frac{4}{3} + \ldots$ no

Sample answer: If each consecutive addend is equal to the previous multiplied by a factor less than 1, the sequence is bounded.

Scoring Rubric

2 points: Student correctly solves the problem and explains his/her reasoning.

1 point: Student shows good understanding of the problem but does not fully solve or explain his/her reasoning.

0 points: Student does not demonstrate understanding of the problem.

Arc Length and Radian Measure

Common Core Math Standards

The student is expected to:

 **G-C.A.1**

Prove that all circles are similar. Also G-C.B.5, G-GMD.A.1, G-MG.A.1

Mathematical Practices

 MP.4 Modeling

Language Objective

Explain to a partner how to convert the measure of an arc from degrees to radians.

ENGAGE

Essential Question: How do you find the length of an arc?

The arc length s of an arc with measure m° and radius r is given by the formula $\frac{m}{360} \cdot 2\pi$.

PREVIEW: LESSON PERFORMANCE TASK

View the Engage section online. Discuss the map. Ask students to speculate on problems that might arise for a mapmaker who set out to map a portion of the spherical Earth on a flat sheet of paper. Then preview the Lesson Performance Task.

Name _____ Class _____ Date _____

16.2 Arc Length and Radian Measure

Essential Question: How do you find the length of an arc?

Resource Locker

⊘ Explore Deriving the Formula for Arc Length

An **arc** is an unbroken part of a circle consisting of two points called the endpoints and all the points on the circle between them. **Arc length** is understood to be the distance along a circular arc measured in linear units (such as feet or centimeters). You can use proportional reasoning to find arc length.

Find the arc length of $\overset{\frown}{AB}$. Express your answer in terms of π and rounded to the nearest tenth.

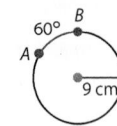

(A) First find the circumference of the circle.

$C = 2\pi r$ Substitute the radius, 9, for r.

$C = \boxed{18\pi}$

(B) The entire circle has 360°. Therefore, the arc's length is $\frac{60}{360}$ or $\frac{1}{6}$ of the circumference.

Fill in the blanks to find the arc length.

Arc length of $\overset{\frown}{AB} = \frac{1}{6} \cdot \underline{18\pi}$ Arc length is $\frac{1}{6}$ of the circumference.

$= \underline{3\pi}$ Multiply.

$\approx \underline{9.4}$ Use a calculator to evaluate. Then round.

So, the arc length of $\overset{\frown}{AB}$ is $\underline{3\pi \text{ cm}}$ or $\underline{9.4 \text{ cm}}$.

Reflect

1. How could you use the reasoning process you used above to find the length of an arc of the circle that measures $m°$?

The arc length is $\frac{m}{360}$ of the circumference, or $\frac{m}{360} \cdot 18\pi$. This can be written as $\frac{m}{20}\pi$.

© Houghton Mifflin Harcourt Publishing Company

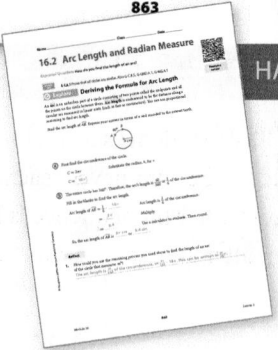

HARDCOVER PAGES 729–736

Turn to these pages to find this lesson in the hardcover student edition.

⚙ Explain 1   Applying the Formula for Arc Length

You were able to find an arc length using concepts of circumference. Using the same reasoning results in the formula for finding arc length.

Arc Length
The arc length, s, of an arc with measure $m°$ and radius r is given by the formula $s = \frac{m}{360} \cdot 2\pi r$.   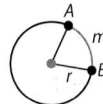

Example 1   Find the arc length.

Ⓐ On a clock face, the minute hand of a clock is 10 inches long. To the nearest tenth of an inch, how far does the tip of the minute hand travel as the time progresses from 12:00 to 12:15?

The minute hand moves 15 minutes.

$\frac{15 \text{ minutes}}{60 \text{ minutes}} = \frac{1}{4}$ so the central angle formed is $\frac{1}{4} \cdot 360° = 90°$.

$s = \frac{m}{360} \cdot 2\pi r$ Use the formula for arc length.

$ = \frac{90}{360} \cdot 2\pi(10)$ Substitute 10 for r and 90 for m.

$ = 5\pi$ Simplify.

$ \approx 15.7$ in.   Simplify.

Ⓑ The minute hand of a clock is 6 inches long. To the nearest tenth of an inch, how far does the tip of the minute hand travel as the time progresses from 12:00 to 12:30?

The minute hand moves 30 minutes.

$\frac{30 \text{ minutes}}{60 \text{ minutes}} = \boxed{\frac{1}{2}}$, so the central angle formed is $\frac{1}{2} \cdot \boxed{360°} = \boxed{180°}$.

$s = \frac{m}{360} \cdot \boxed{2\pi r}$ Use the formula for arc length.

$ = \frac{\boxed{180}}{360} \cdot 2\pi \left(\boxed{6} \right)$ Substitute $\underline{\ \ 6\ \ }$ for r and $\underline{\ \ 180\ \ }$ for m.

$ = \boxed{6\pi}$ Simplify.

$ \approx \boxed{18.8}$ in.   Simplify.

The length of the arc is $\boxed{18.8}$ inches.

Reflect

2. **Discussion** Why does the formula represent the length of an arc of a circle?
   Suppose a circle has a radius r. Find the length of an arc of the circle that measures $m°$.

   Since a circle is 360°, each arc is $\frac{m}{360}$ of the circumference of the circle. The circumference is

   $2\pi r$, so the arc length is $\frac{m}{360} \cdot 2\pi r$.

© Houghton Mifflin Harcourt Publishing Company • Image Credits: ©Multiart/iStockPhoto.com

PROFESSIONAL DEVELOPMENT

Math Background

This is the first of two lessons in which students apply proportional reasoning to circles. In this lesson, students find arc lengths by considering the fraction of a circle that a given arc represents. The formula for the arc length s of an arc with measure $m°$ and radius r is $s = \frac{m°}{360°} \cdot 2\pi r$. The length of the arc is proportional to the radius of the circle, with $\frac{m°}{360°} \cdot 2\pi$, the radian measure of its intercepted angle, the constant of proportionality. A similar process will be used in the following lesson to find the area of a sector.

EXPLORE

Deriving the Formula for Arc Length

INTEGRATE TECHNOLOGY

Students have the option of doing the Explore activity either in the book or online.

QUESTIONING STRATEGIES

❓ In a circle, how is an arc length related to the measure of the arc? The length of an arc is the circumference of the circle multiplied by the measure of the arc divided by 360.

❓ Why is the answer for arc length in units and not in square units? Sample answer: Arc length is a fraction of the circumference of a circle, which is given in units, not square units.

EXPLAIN 1

Applying the Formula for Arc Length

AVOID COMMON ERRORS

Students may confuse arc measure and arc length. Point out the difference between these measures. The notation for the measure of the arc is m $\overset{\frown}{AB}$, given in degrees, while the length of an arc is given in the same units as the circumference of the associated circle.

QUESTIONING STRATEGIES

❓ What units should you use when using the arc length formula in a real-life application? How do you know? Sample answer: Use the same units as given for the circumference, because arc length is a fraction of the circumference.

EXPLAIN 2

Investigating Arc Lengths in Concentric Circles

INTEGRATE MATHEMATICAL PRACTICES

Focus on Critical Thinking

MP.3 The length of an arc of a circle is proportional to the circumference of the circle (and therefore the radius) in terms of π. So, if the circle has a radius of 1, then the arc length for $\frac{1}{4}$ of the circle is $\frac{1}{4}(2\pi)$, or $\frac{\pi}{2}$ units. If a concentric circle has a radius of 2, then the arc length for $\frac{1}{4}$ of the circle is $\frac{1}{4}(2\pi)2$, or π units. In the next example, students will learn that radians may be used for the measure of an angle. This means that in terms of radians, the angle that corresponds to $\frac{1}{4}$ of a circle measures $\frac{\pi}{2}$ radians.

QUESTIONING STRATEGIES

? What is the general equation of a proportional relationship? $y = ax$

? What is the name for the constant a in the equation? the constant of proportionality

? What are some characteristics of the graph of this type of proportional relationship? Sample answer: The graph is a straight line that passes through the origin.

---

3. The minute hand of a clock is 8 inches long. To the nearest tenth of an inch, how far does the tip of the minute hand travel as the time progresses from 12:00 to 12:45?

$$\frac{45 \text{ minutes}}{60 \text{ minutes}} = \frac{3}{4}, \text{ so } \frac{3}{4} \cdot 360° = 270°$$

$$s = \frac{m}{360} \cdot 2\pi r$$

$$= \frac{270}{360} \cdot 2\pi(8) \approx 37.7 \text{ in.}$$

⏱ Explain 2 Investigating Arc Lengths in Concentric Circles

Consider a set of concentric circles with center O and radius 1, 2, and 3, and so on. The central angle shown in the figure is a right angle and it cuts off arcs that measure 90°.

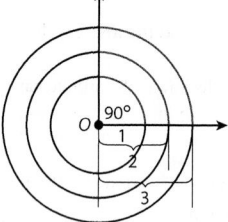

Example 2 Find and graph arc lengths for different radii.

(A) For each value of the radius r listed in the table below, find the corresponding arc length. Write the length in terms of π and rounded to the nearest hundredth.

For example, when $r = 1$, the arc length is $\frac{90}{360} \cdot 2\pi(1) = \frac{1}{2}\pi \approx 1.57$.

Radius r	1	2	3	4	5
Arc length s in terms of π	$\frac{1}{2}\pi$	π	$\frac{3}{2}\pi$	2π	$\frac{5}{2}\pi$
Arc length s to the nearest hundredth	1.57	3.14	4.71	6.28	7.85

(B) Plot the ordered pairs from your table on the coordinate plane.

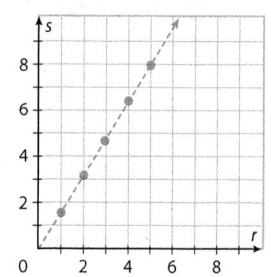

What do you notice about the points?

The points lie on a straight line through the origin.

What type of relationship is the relationship between arc length and radius?

proportional relationship (direct variation)

What is the constant of proportionality for this relationship?

$\frac{1}{2}\pi$

© Houghton Mifflin Harcourt Publishing Company

COLLABORATIVE LEARNING

Peer-Peer Activity

Students may gain a better understanding of how two arcs can have the same arc measure but different arc lengths by working with different circles. Working in pairs, have one student construct a circle with a diameter of 4 centimeters and another student construct a circle with a diameter of 6 centimeters. Have each draw a 60° angle with vertex at the center of the circle. Ask them to identify the measure of each arc (60°). Then, have them use a piece of string to measure the length of each arc. Have them discuss their results and make a conjecture about arc length.

Reflect

4. What happens to the arc length when you double the radius? How is this connected to the idea that all circles are similar?

   The arc length doubles. Since all circles are similar, the ratio of the radii (2:1) equals the

   ratio of the arc length (2:1).

Explain 3   Converting Radian Measure

As you discovered in Explain 2, when the central angle is fixed at $m°$, the length of the arc cut off by a central angle is proportional to (or varies directly with) the radius. In fact, you can see that the formula for arc length is a proportional relationship when m is fixed.

$$s = \underbrace{\frac{m}{360} \cdot 2\pi r}$$

constant of proportionality

The constant of proportionality for the proportional relationship is $\frac{m}{360} \cdot 2\pi$. This constant of proportionality is defined to be the **radian measure** of the angle.

Example 3   Convert each angle measure to radian measure.

(A)   180°

To convert to a radian measure, let $m = 180$ in the expression $\frac{m}{360} \cdot 2\pi$.

$180° = \frac{180}{360} \cdot 2\pi$ Substitute 180 for m.

$\quad = \pi$ radians   Simplify.

(B)   60°

To convert to a radian measure, let $m = 60$ in the expression $\frac{m}{360} \cdot 2\pi$.

$60° = \dfrac{\boxed{60}}{360} \cdot 2\pi$ Substitute $\boxed{60}$ for m.

$\quad = \boxed{\frac{\pi}{3}}$ radians   Simplify.

Reflect

5. Explain why the radian measure for an angle $m°$ is sometimes defined as the length of the arc cut off on a circle of radius 1 by a central angle of $m°$.

   By the arc length formula, the length of the arc cut off on a circle of radius 1 by a central

   angle of m° is $\frac{m}{360} \cdot 2\pi$, and this is the radian measure of the angle.

6. Explain how to find the degree measure of an angle whose radian measure is $\frac{\pi}{4}$.

   Solve $\frac{\pi}{4} = \frac{m}{360} \cdot 2\pi$. Dividing both sides by π and simplifying gives $\frac{1}{4} = \frac{m}{180}$ and

   multiplying both sides by 180 shows that $m = 45$, so the angle measures 45°.

EXPLAIN 3

Converting Radian Measure

INTEGRATE MATHEMATICAL PRACTICES
Focus on Patterns

MP.8 Have students use the formula for conversion from degrees to radians to make a table of fractions of a circle, including $\frac{1}{4}$, $\frac{1}{3}$, $\frac{1}{2}$, and $\frac{3}{4}$. Encourage them to discuss any pattern that they find.

QUESTIONING STRATEGIES

? How do you convert an angle's degree measure to radian measure? Substitute the angle's degree measure for m in the expression $\frac{m}{360} \cdot 2\pi$.

? You know that 360° is the degree measure that corresponds to a full circle. What radian measure corresponds to a full circle? 2π

? What degree measure and what radian measure correspond to a semicircle? 180°; π

DIFFERENTIATE INSTRUCTION

Cognitive Strategies

Some students may benefit from referring to a summary of how to convert between degrees and radians, and between radians and degrees. Ask them to use the patterns below.

Degrees to radians: Multiply the degree measure by $\frac{\pi}{180}$ and reduce the fraction, if necessary.

Radians to degrees: Multiply the radian measure by $\frac{180°}{\pi}$ and reduce the fraction, if necessary.

ELABORATE

QUESTIONING STRATEGIES

? What is the difference between arc length and arc measure? Arc length is measured in linear units, while arc measure is measured in degrees.

SUMMARIZE THE LESSON

? How do you use proportional reasoning to find the length of an arc? The length of an arc is the constant of proportionality times a variable. Using r as the independent variable, the constant of proportionality is $\frac{m°}{360°} \cdot 2\pi$, and the length s of the arc is $s = \frac{m°}{360°} \cdot 2\pi r$.

Your Turn

Convert each angle measure to radian measure.

7. 90°

$$90° = \frac{90}{360} \cdot 2\pi = \frac{\pi}{2} \text{ radians}$$

8. 45°

$$45° = \frac{45}{360} \cdot 2\pi = \frac{\pi}{4} \text{ radians}$$

💬 Elaborate

9. You know that 360° is the degree measure that corresponds to a full circle. What is the radian measure that corresponds to a full circle?

2π

10. Suppose you are given that the measure in radians of an arc of a circle with radius r is θ. How can you find the length of the arc in radians?

The radian measure of an angle of measure m° is $\left(\frac{m}{360}\right) \cdot 2\pi r$. Then you can substitute θ.

11. **Essential Question Check-In** What two pieces of information do you need to calculate arc length?

You need the measure of the arc and the radius.

⭐ Evaluate: Homework and Practice

• Online Homework
• Hints and Help
• Extra Practice

Use the formula, $s = \frac{m}{360} \cdot 2\pi r$, to answer the questions.

1. What part of the circle does the expression $2\pi r$ represent?

$2\pi r$ represents the circumference of the circle.

2. What part of the circle does $\frac{m}{360}$ represent?

$\frac{m}{360}$ represents the portion of the circumference of the circle that the arc spans.

3. What part of the circle does the expression $2r$ represent?

The expression $2r$ represents the diameter of the circle.

4. **Critical Thinking** Suppose an arc were intercepted by a central angle measuring 15°. The diameter of the circle is 9 cm. Can both of these values be substituted into the arc length formula? Explain.

Yes; The central angle of 15° intercepts an arc of the same measure, so substitute 15 for m. The diameter and not the radius, r, is given and the diameter is represented by $2r$, so substitute 9 for $2r$.

LANGUAGE SUPPORT 🔲 EL

Connect Vocabulary

To help students distinguish between the measure of an arc and the length of an arc, ask them to think of riding a bicycle on a circular track. A bicycle riding along the track will go farther if it travels $\frac{1}{3}$ of the track $(120°)$ than if it travels $\frac{1}{4}$ of the track $(90°)$. Since these distances are fractions of the length of the track, the degree measure is used to find the length the bicycle travels, but the length is not given in degrees.

Find the arc length of $\overparen{AB}$ to the nearest tenth.

5.

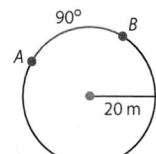

$s = \dfrac{m}{360} \cdot 2\pi r$

$= \dfrac{90}{360} \cdot 2\pi(20)$

$= 10\pi$

≈ 31.4

$s \approx 31.4$ m

6.

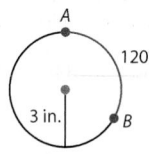

$s = \dfrac{m}{360} \cdot 2\pi r$

$= \dfrac{120}{360} \cdot 2\pi(3)$

$= 2\pi$

≈ 6.3

$s \approx 6.3$ in.

7.

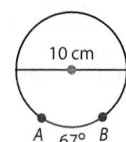

The diameter is 10 cm, so substitute 5 for r.

$s = \dfrac{m}{360} \cdot 2\pi r$

$= \dfrac{67}{360} \cdot 2\pi(5)$

$= \dfrac{67}{36}\pi$

≈ 5.8

$s \approx 5.8$ cm

8. The minute hand of a clock is 5 inches long. To the nearest tenth of an inch, how far does the tip of the minute hand travel as the time progresses from 12:00 to 12:25?

$\dfrac{25 \text{ minutes}}{60 \text{ minutes}} = \dfrac{5}{12}$, so $\dfrac{5}{12} \cdot 360° = 150°$

$s = \dfrac{m}{360} \cdot 2\pi r$

$= \dfrac{150}{360} \cdot 2\pi(5) \approx 13.1$ in.

9. The circles are concentric. Find the length of the intercepted arc in the larger circle.

$\dfrac{40}{10} = \dfrac{x}{8.7}$

$\dfrac{40(8.7)}{10} = x$

$34.8 = x$

Arc length = 34.8 m.

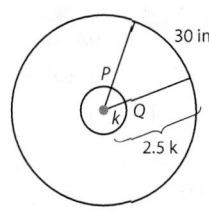

10. The circles are concentric. Find the length of $\overparen{PQ}$

$\dfrac{x}{30} = \dfrac{k}{2.5k}$

$\dfrac{x}{30} = \dfrac{1}{2.5}$

$\dfrac{30}{1} \cdot \dfrac{x}{30} = \dfrac{1}{2.5} \cdot \dfrac{30}{1}$

$x = \dfrac{30}{2.5}$

$x = 12$

The length of $\overparen{PQ}$ is 12 in.

ASSIGNMENT GUIDE

Concepts and Skills	Practice
Explore Deriving the Formula for Arc Length	Exercises 1–4
Example 1 Applying the Formula for Arc Length	Exercises 5–8
Example 2 Investigating Arc Lengths in Concentric Circles	Exercises 9–12
Example 3 Converting Radian Measure	Exercises 13–19

INTEGRATE MATHEMATICAL PRACTICES
Focus on Critical Thinking

MP.3 Explain to students that when they divide the measure of an arc by 360°, they are actually finding the percentage of the circumference of the circle covered by the arc. Show how an arc that measures 180° covers 0.5, or 50%, of the circumference of a circle.

Exercise	Depth of Knowledge (D.O.K.)	COMMON CORE Mathematical Practices
1–3	**1** Recall of Information	**MP.6** Precision
4	**3** Strategic Thinking	**MP.2** Reasoning
5–7	**1** Recall of Information	**MP.5** Using Tools
8	**2** Skills/Concepts	**MP.4** Modeling
9–21	**2** Skills/Concepts	**MP.5** Using Tools
22	**2** Skills/Concepts	**MP.4** Modeling
23	**3** Strategic Thinking	**MP.3** Logic

Arc Length and Radian Measure　**868**

Point out that the m in the formula for length of an arc represents the arc measure, not the central angle measure, although the two are related.

INTEGRATE TECHNOLOGY

Students may want to use graphing calculators to check their work when converting from degrees to radians. First, set the mode of the calculator to *radian*. Then enter the degree and choose "°" from the ANGLE menu. The calculator will display the degree as a radian measure.

11. Two arcs of concentric circles are intercepted by the same central angle. The resulting arc length of the arc of the larger circle is 16 m and the radius of the larger circle is 12 m. The radius of the smaller circle is 7.5 m. Find the length of the corresponding arc of the smaller circle.
Let m represent the length of the arc of the small circle.

$$\frac{m}{16} = \frac{7.5}{12}$$

$$\frac{16}{1} \cdot \frac{m}{16} = \frac{7.5}{12} \cdot \frac{16}{1}$$

$$m = \frac{7.5(16)}{12}$$

$$m = 10 \text{ m}$$

12. Two arcs of concentric circles are intercepted by the same central angle. The resulting arc length of the arc of the smaller circle is 36 ft and its radius is 30 ft. The radius of the larger circle is 45 ft. Find the length of the corresponding arc of the larger circle.
Let n represent the length of the arc of the large circle.

$$\frac{n}{36} = \frac{45}{30}$$

$$\frac{36}{1} \cdot \frac{n}{36} = \frac{45}{30} \cdot \frac{36}{1}$$

$$n = \frac{45(36)}{30}$$

$$n = 54 \text{ ft}$$

Convert each angle measure to radian measure.

13. 40°
Let $m = 40$ in the expression $\frac{m}{360} \cdot 2\pi$.

$$\frac{40}{360} \cdot 2\pi = \frac{1}{9} \cdot 2\pi = \frac{2}{9}\pi$$

14. 80°
Let $m = 80$ in the expression $\frac{m}{360} \cdot 2\pi$.

$$\frac{80}{360} \cdot 2\pi = \frac{2}{9} \cdot 2\pi = \frac{4\pi}{9}$$

15. 100°
Let $m = 100$ in the expression $\frac{m}{360} \cdot 2\pi$.

$$\frac{100}{360} \cdot 2\pi = \frac{5}{18} \cdot 2\pi = \frac{5\pi}{9}$$

16. 12°
Let $m = 12$ in the expression $\frac{m}{360} \cdot 2\pi$.

$$\frac{12}{360} \cdot 2\pi = \frac{1}{30} \cdot 2\pi = \frac{\pi}{15}$$

17. It is convenient to know the radian measure for benchmark angles such as 0°, 30°, 45°, and so on. Complete the table by finding the radian measure for each of the given benchmark angles.

Benchmark Angles									
Degree Measure	0°	30°	45°	60°	90°	120°	135°	150°	180°
Radian Measure	0	$\frac{\pi}{6}$	$\frac{\pi}{4}$	$\frac{\pi}{3}$	$\frac{\pi}{2}$	$\frac{2\pi}{3}$	$\frac{3\pi}{4}$	$\frac{5\pi}{6}$	π

For 0°: $\frac{0}{360} \cdot 2\pi = 0$; For 30°: $\frac{30}{360} \cdot 2\pi = \frac{1}{12} \cdot 2\pi = \frac{\pi}{6}$; For 45°: $\frac{45}{360} \cdot 2\pi = \frac{1}{8} \cdot 2\pi = \frac{\pi}{4}$;

For 60°: $\frac{60}{360} \cdot 2\pi = \frac{1}{6} \cdot 2\pi = \frac{\pi}{3}$; For 90°: $\frac{90}{360} \cdot 2\pi = \frac{1}{4} \cdot 2\pi = \frac{\pi}{2}$;

For 120°: $\frac{120}{360} \cdot 2\pi = \frac{1}{3} \cdot 2\pi = \frac{2\pi}{3}$; For 135°: $\frac{135}{360} \cdot 2\pi = \frac{3}{8} \cdot 2\pi = \frac{3\pi}{4}$;

For 150°: $\frac{150}{360} \cdot 2\pi = \frac{5}{12} \cdot 2\pi = \frac{5\pi}{6}$; For 180°: $\frac{180}{360} \cdot 2\pi = \frac{1}{2} \cdot 2\pi = \pi$

Exercise	Depth of Knowledge (D.O.K.)	COMMON CORE Mathematical Practices
24	**3** Strategic Thinking H.O.T.	**MP.3** Logic
25	**3** Strategic Thinking H.O.T.	**MP.4** Modeling
26	**3** Strategic Thinking H.O.T.	**MP.4** Modeling

Convert each radian measure to degree measure.

18. $\dfrac{5\pi}{8}$

$$\frac{5\pi}{8} = \frac{m}{360} \cdot 2\pi$$
$$\frac{1}{2\pi} \cdot \frac{5\pi}{8} = \frac{m}{360} \cdot 2\pi \cdot \frac{1}{2\pi}$$
$$\frac{5}{16} = \frac{m}{360}$$
$$\frac{360}{1} \cdot \frac{5}{16} = \frac{m}{360} \cdot \frac{360}{1}$$
$$112.5° = m$$

19. $\dfrac{8\pi}{9}$

$$\frac{8\pi}{9} = \frac{m}{360} \cdot 2\pi$$
$$\frac{1}{2\pi} \cdot \frac{8\pi}{9} = \frac{m}{360} \cdot 2\pi \cdot \frac{1}{2\pi}$$
$$\frac{4}{9} = \frac{m}{360}$$
$$\frac{360}{1} \cdot \frac{4}{9} = \frac{m}{360} \cdot \frac{360}{1}$$
$$160° = m$$

20. In the diagram, $\overline{WY}$, and $\overline{XZ}$ are diameters of $\odot T$, and $WY = XZ = 6$. If $m\widehat{XY} = 140°$, what is the length of $\widehat{YZ}$? Select all that apply.

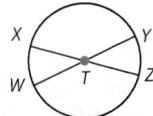

   (A.) $\dfrac{4\pi}{6}$

   B. $\dfrac{4\pi}{3}$

   (C.) $\dfrac{2}{3}\pi$

   D. 4π

   E. 6π

Since $\overline{WY}$ is a diameter, then $m\widehat{XYZ} = 180°$, so $m\widehat{YZ} = (180 - 140)° = 40°$.

$$s = \frac{m}{360} \cdot 2\pi r = \frac{40}{360} \cdot 2\pi(3) = \frac{2\pi}{3}$$
$$\frac{2\pi}{3} = \frac{2}{3}\pi \text{ and } \frac{2\pi}{3} = \frac{2\pi}{3} \cdot \frac{2}{2} = \frac{4\pi}{6}$$

21. Algebra The length of $\widehat{TS}$ is 12 in. Find the length of $\widehat{RS}$.

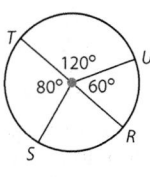

$360 - 80 - 120 - 60 = 100°$. So, the arc measure is $100°$.

Since $80°$ is $\dfrac{80}{360} = \dfrac{2}{9}$ of the circumference, the length of $\widehat{TS}$

is $\dfrac{2}{9}$ of the circumference. So, $\dfrac{2}{9}C = 12$, or $C = \dfrac{9}{2} \cdot 12 = 54$ in.

$$s = \frac{m}{360} \cdot 2\pi r = \frac{100}{360} \cdot 54 = 15$$

$\widehat{RS} = 15$ in.

22. Multi-Step The diagram shows the plan for a putting a decorative trim around a corner desk. The trim will be 4-inch high around the perimeter of the desk. The curve is one quarter of the circumference of a circle. Find the length of trim needed to the nearest half foot.

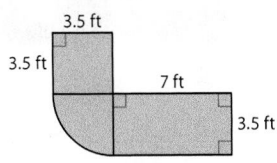

$$s = \frac{m}{360} \cdot 2\pi r = \frac{90}{360} \cdot 2\pi(3.5) = 1.75\pi \text{ ft}$$

$$1.75\pi + 4 \cdot 3.5 + 2 \cdot 7 = 1.75\pi + 28 \approx 33.5 \text{ ft}$$

INTEGRATE MATHEMATICAL PRACTICES

Focus on Math Connections

MP.1 Since radius, diameter, circumference, and arc length are linear dimensions, the effect is that arc length and the other dimensions are doubled if the linear dimension is doubled, and arc length and the other dimensions are tripled if the linear dimension is tripled.

Ask students to discuss with a partner how to find the length of an arc using the circumference formula. One student should draw a circle and give the radius. The other student should then identify various arc measures on the circle and give the lengths of the arcs. Have students switch roles and repeat the exercise.

JOURNAL

Have students summarize how to use proportional reasoning to find the length of an arc. Ask them to include a summary of radian measure, with at least one example of how to convert degree measure to radian measure.

23. **Explain the Error** A student was asked to find the arc length of $\overset{\frown}{PQ}$. The student's work is shown. Explain the student's error and give the correct arc length.

The student used the diameter instead of the radius in the circumference formula. The student should have substituted 8 for r or 16 for $2r$ and used 45 for m in the formula $s = \frac{m}{360} \cdot 2\pi r$ to get $s = \frac{45}{360} \cdot 16\pi = 2\pi$ m.

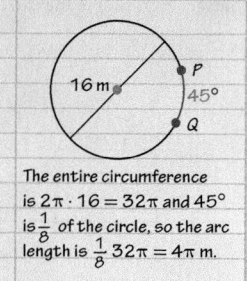

The entire circumference is $2\pi \cdot 16 = 32\pi$ and $45°$ is $\frac{1}{8}$ of the circle, so the arc length is $\frac{1}{8} 32\pi = 4\pi$ m.

H.O.T. Focus on Higher Order Thinking

24. **Critique Reasoning** A friend tells you two arcs from different circles have the same arc length if their central angles are equal. Is your friend correct? Explain your reasoning.

No; they have the same arc length only if the two circles are congruent circles.

25. **Multi-Step** A carpenter is making a tray to fit between two circular pillars in the shape of the shaded area as shown. She is using a jigsaw to cut along the edge of the tray. What is the length of the cut encompassing the tray? Round to the nearest half foot.

$$s = \frac{m}{360} \cdot 2\pi r$$
$$= \frac{90}{360} \cdot 2\pi(3)$$
$$= 1.5\pi$$

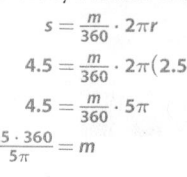

$$2 \cdot 1.5\pi + 2 \cdot 6 =$$
$$3\pi + 12 \approx 21.4 \text{ ft}$$

26. **Critical Thinking** The pedals of a penny-farthing Bicycle are directly connected to the front wheel.

   a. Suppose a penny-farthing bicycle has a front wheel with a diameter of 5 ft. To the nearest tenth of a foot, how far does the bike move when you turn the pedals through an angle of 90°?

$$s = \frac{m}{360} \cdot 2\pi r = \frac{90}{360} \cdot 2\pi(2.5) \approx 3.9 \text{ ft}$$

   b. Through what angle should you turn the pedals in order to move forward by a distance of 4.5 ft? Round to the nearest degree.

$$s = \frac{m}{360} \cdot 2\pi r$$
$$4.5 = \frac{m}{360} \cdot 2\pi(2.5)$$
$$4.5 = \frac{m}{360} \cdot 5\pi$$
$$\frac{4.5 \cdot 360}{5\pi} = m$$
$$103° \approx m$$

Lesson Performance Task

The latitude of a point is a measure of its position north or south on the Earth's surface. Latitudes North (N) are measured from 0° N at the equator to 90° N at the North Pole. Latitudes South (S) are measured from 0° S at the equator to 90° S at the South Pole.

The figure shows the latitudes of Washington, D.C. and Lima, Peru. The radius of the Earth is approximately 6,370 kilometers.

1. Find the angle at the Earth's center between radii drawn to Washington and Lima.

2. Find the distance between Washington and Lima. Show your work.

3. A point's longitude is a measure of its position east or west on the Earth's surface. In order for your calculation of the distance between Washington and Lima to be accurate, what must be true about the longitudes of the two cities?

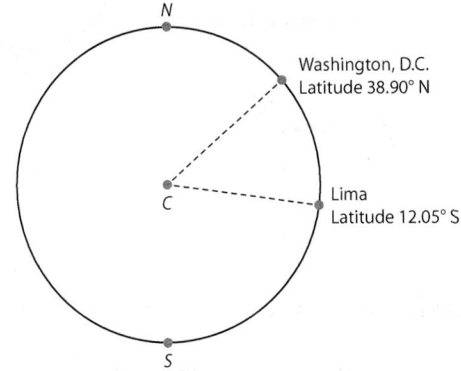

1. $38.90° + 12.05° = 50.95°$

2. circumference of Earth $= 2\pi r$

$$\approx 2(3.14)(6370)$$

$$\approx 40,003.6 \text{ kilometers}$$

$$\frac{50.95°}{360°} = \frac{\text{Washington-Lima distance}}{40,003.6}$$

Washington-Lima distance ≈ 5661.6 kilometers

3. The cities must be located on the same longitude. Distance calculations in this problem will turn out to be quite accurate, since Washington is located at 77.04° W longitude and Lima is at 77.05° W longitude.

AVOID COMMON ERRORS

In the Lesson Performance Task, latitudes are given in degrees but with the fractional portion of the latitude in decimal form rather than in minutes and seconds. This is common practice for latitudes and longitudes given on the Internet. Caution students to beware of this difference. Washington's latitude of 38.90°N, written as minutes and seconds, will be

$$38 \text{ degrees} + 0.9 \times \frac{60 \text{ minutes}}{1 \text{ degree}} = 38°54'.$$

INTEGRATE MATHEMATICAL PRACTICES
Focus on Critical Thinking

MP.3 How would your solution to the Lesson Performance Task change if Lima were located at latitude 12.05°N instead of 12.05°S? The answer to Question 1 would be $38.90° - 12.05° = 26.85°$. This value rather than 50.95° would be used in the proportion in Question 2 to find the distance between the two cities.

EXTENSION ACTIVITY

An ambitious mining engineer has decided to build a tunnel straight through the Earth from Washington, D.C. to Lima. Ask these questions:

1. How long will the tunnel be? Explain your method. Students can use the sine function in a right triangle with half a 50.95° angle opposite half the tunnel length. Total tunnel length: 5479 kilometers

2. How much time will a passenger save riding from Washington to Lima on a 200-kilometer-per-hour tunnel train compared to a train moving at the same speed above ground? difference in distance: $(5662 - 5479) = 183$ mi; $\frac{183 \text{ mi}}{200 \text{ mi}} \times 60 \text{ min} \approx 55 \text{ min}$

Scoring Rubric

2 points: Student correctly solves the problem and explains his/her reasoning.

1 point: Student shows good understanding of the problem but does not fully solve or explain his/her reasoning.

0 points: Student does not demonstrate understanding of the problem.

Arc Length and Radian Measure　**872**

Sector Area

Common Core Math Standards

The student is expected to:

 G-C.B.5

Derive ... the formula for the area of a sector. Also G-MG.A.1

Mathematical Practices

COMMON CORE **MP.7 Using Structure**

Language Objective

Explain to a partner how to find the area of a sector of a circle.

ENGAGE

Essential Question: How do you find the area of a sector of a circle?

The area A of a sector of a circle with a central angle of $m°$ and radius r is given by the formula.

$$A = \frac{m}{360} \cdot 2\pi r^2$$

PREVIEW: LESSON PERFORMANCE TASK

View the Engage section online. Discuss the map. Ask whether Earth is closer to the Sun in summer or in winter, and why students think so. Then preview the Lesson Performance Task.

Name _____ Class _____ Date _____

16.3 Sector Area

Essential Question: How do you find the area of a sector of a circle?

Resource Locker

⊘ Explore Derive the Formula for the Area of a Sector

A **sector** of a circle is a region bounded by two radii and their intercepted arc. A sector is named by the endpoints of the arc and the center of the circle. For example, the figure shows sector POQ.

In the same way that you used proportional reasoning to find the length of an arc, you can use proportional reasoning to find the area of a sector.

Find the area of sector AOB. Express your answer in terms of π and rounded to the nearest tenth.

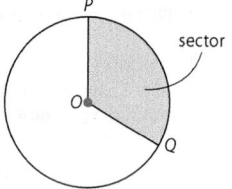

(A) First find the area of the circle.

$$A = \pi r^2 = \pi(\underline{15})^2$$
$$= \underline{225\pi}$$

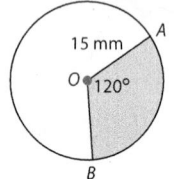

(B) The entire circle is 360°, but $\angle AOB$ measures 120°. Therefore, the sector's area is $\frac{120}{360}$ or $\frac{1}{3}$ of the circle's area.

Area of sector $AOB = \frac{1}{3} \cdot \underline{225\pi}$ The area is $\frac{1}{3}$ of the circle's area.

$\qquad\qquad\qquad = \underline{75\pi}$ Simplify.

$\qquad\qquad\qquad = \underline{235.6}$ Use a calculator to evaluate. Then round.

So, the area of sector AOB is $\underline{75\pi \text{ mm}^2}$ or $\underline{235.6 \text{ mm}^2}$.

Reflect

1. How could you use the above process to find the area of a sector of the circle whose central angle measures $m°$?

   The area of the sector is $\frac{m}{360}$ of the circle's area, or $\frac{m}{360} \cdot 225\pi$. This can be written as $\frac{5m}{8}\pi$.

2. **Make a Conjecture** What do you think is the formula for the area of a sector with a central angle of $m°$ and radius r?

   $$A = \frac{m}{360} \cdot \pi r^2$$

© Houghton Mifflin Harcourt Publishing Company

HARDCOVER PAGES 737–744

Turn to these pages to find this lesson in the hardcover student edition.

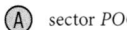 **Explain 1** **Using the Formula for the Area of a Sector**

Explain 1 Using the Formula for the Area of a Sector

The proportional reasoning process you used in the Explore can be generalized. Given a sector with a central angle of $m°$ and radius r, the area of the entire circle is πr^2 and the area of the sector is $\frac{m}{360}$ times the circle's area. This gives the following formula.

Area of a Sector
The area A of a sector with a central angle of $m°$ of a circle with radius r is given by $A = \frac{m}{360} \cdot \pi r^2$

Example 1 Find the area of each sector, as a multiple of π and to the nearest hundredth.

(A) sector POQ

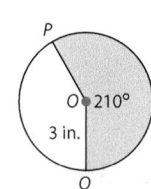

$A = \frac{m}{360} \cdot \pi r^2$

$= \frac{210}{360} \cdot \pi(3)^2$

$= \frac{7}{12} \cdot 9\pi$

$= \frac{21}{4}\pi$

$\approx 16.49 \text{ in}^2$

(B) sector HGJ

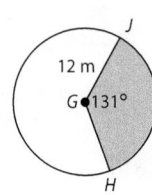

$A = \frac{m}{360} \cdot \pi r^2$

$= \frac{\boxed{131}}{360} \cdot \pi \left(\boxed{12}\right)^2$

$= \frac{\boxed{131}}{360} \cdot \boxed{144}\,\pi$

$= \boxed{52.4}\,\pi$

$\approx \boxed{164.62}\ \text{m}^2$

Reflect

3. **Discussion** Your friend said that the value of $m°$ in the formula for the area of a sector can never be larger than 360°. Do you agree or disagree? Explain your reasoning.
Agree; a complete revolution is 360°, so a sector which is a part of a circle will always have a central angle that is less than 360°.

PROFESSIONAL DEVELOPMENT

COMMON CORE Math Background

This is the second of two lessons in which students apply proportional reasoning to circles. In this lesson, students find the area of a sector of a circle using proportional reasoning. To derive the formula for the area of a sector of a circle, set up a proportion as shown.

$$\frac{\text{Area of sector}}{\text{Area of circle}} = \frac{\text{Measure of central angle}}{360°}$$

$$\frac{A}{\pi r^2} = \frac{m°}{360°}$$

$$A = \frac{m°}{360°} \cdot \pi r^2$$

EXPLORE

Derive the Formula for the Area of a Sector

INTEGRATE TECHNOLOGY

Students have the option of doing the Explore activity either in the book or online.

QUESTIONING STRATEGIES

? What are the appropriate units for the area of a sector? Why? Sample answer: The area of a sector is a fraction of the area of a circle, which is given in square units, so the appropriate units are square units.

EXPLAIN 1

Using the Formula for the Area of a Sector

CONNECT VOCABULARY EL

Compare the *sector* of a circle to a piece of pie. If a pie is sliced into 6 congruent wedges, then each wedge is a *sector* of the circular pie. The pie slice sector has radii for two sides and an arc of a circle for the third side.

QUESTIONING STRATEGIES

? How can you find the area of a sector by using the formula for the area of a circle? Find the fraction of the circle represented by the sector and then multiply the fraction by the expression representing the area of a circle.

EXPLAIN 2

Applying the Formula for the Area of a Sector

INTEGRATE MATHEMATICAL PRACTICES
Focus on Critical Thinking

MP.3 The area of a sector of a circle varies as the square of the radius of the circle because it is equal to a fraction of the area of the circle. The constant of proportionality is $\frac{m}{360} \cdot \pi$, where m is the measure of the central angle. So, if the circle has a radius of 1, the area of a sector representing $\frac{1}{4}$ of the circle is $\frac{1}{4} \cdot \pi$ or $\frac{\pi}{4}$ square units.

QUESTIONING STRATEGIES

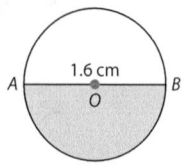

What units should you choose when using the sector formula in a real-life application? How do you know? Sample answer: Use the square of the unit given for the radius of the circle because sector area is a fraction of the area of the circle.

AVOID COMMON ERRORS

Some students may not realize that an answer that contains π is an appropriate answer, and may automatically give an approximate decimal answer. Explain that an answer containing π is an exact answer, and caution students to check whether a question asks for an approximate or exact answer.

Your Turn

Find the area of each sector, as a multiple of π and to the nearest hundredth.

4. sector AOB

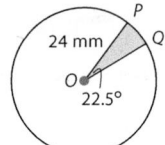

$\angle AOB$ is a straight angle, so $m° = 180°$, $r = 0.8$ cm

$A = \dfrac{m}{360} \cdot \pi r^2$

$= \dfrac{180}{360} \cdot \pi (0.8)^2$

$= \dfrac{1}{2} \cdot (0.64)\pi$

$= 0.32\pi$

≈ 1.01 cm²

5. sector POQ

$A = \dfrac{m}{360} \cdot \pi r^2$

$= \dfrac{22.5}{360} \cdot \pi (24)^2$

$= \dfrac{1}{16} \cdot 576\pi$

$= 36\pi$

≈ 113.10 mm²

⊘ Explain 2 Applying the Formula for the Area of a Sector

You can apply the formula for the area of a sector to real-world problems.

Example 2 Find the area described.

Ⓐ A beam from a lighthouse is visible for a distance of 3 mi. To the nearest square mile, what is the area covered by the beam as it sweeps in an arc of 150°?

$A = \dfrac{m}{360} \cdot \pi r^2$

$= \dfrac{150}{360} \cdot \pi (3)^2$

$= \dfrac{5}{12} \cdot 9\pi$

$= 3.75\pi \approx 12$ mi²

Ⓑ A circular plot with a 180 foot diameter is watered by a spray irrigation system. To the nearest square foot, what is the area that is watered as the sprinkler rotates through an angle of 50°?

$d = 180$ ft, so $r = \underline{90}$ ft

$A = \dfrac{m}{360} \cdot \pi r^2$

$= \dfrac{\boxed{50}}{\boxed{360}} \cdot \pi \left(\boxed{90}\right)^2$

$= \boxed{\dfrac{5}{36}} \cdot \boxed{8100}\ \pi$

$= \boxed{1125}\ \pi \approx \boxed{3534}$ ft²

© Houghton Mifflin Harcourt Publishing Company · Image Credits: ©Narvikk/ Vetta/Getty Images

---

COLLABORATIVE LEARNING

Small Group Activity

Students will have a better understanding of finding the area of sectors in a real-world situation if they choose circles to measure, either from the exercises or from the classroom. Have students discuss how to measure the appropriate parts of each type of circle and what tools to use for measuring. Have students take turns measuring, and record the measurements in a table. Students should then use the table values to find the area of the circle and sectors. Have them make a conjecture about how the area of a sector is related to finding the area of a circle, and invite them to share their work with the class.

6. To the nearest square foot, what is the area watered in Example 2B as the sprinkler rotates through a semicircle?

semicircle $= 180°$

$A = \frac{m}{360} \cdot \pi r^2 = \frac{180}{360} \cdot \pi (90)^2 = 4{,}050\pi \approx 12{,}723 \text{ mi}^2$

 **Elaborate**

7. **Discussion** When can you use proportional reasoning to find the area of a sector without knowing or finding its central angle? Explain your reasoning by giving an example.
Possible answer: If you are told that the size a sector is proportional to the size of a circle,
then the area of the sector will have the same proportion to the area of the circle. So, you
can simply multiply the area of the circle by the fraction.
For example, if you are told that a sector is $\frac{1}{4}$ the size of a circle with area 24 cm^2, then you
can find the area of the sector by multiplying 24 cm^2 by $\frac{1}{4}$.

8. **Essential Question Check-In** What information do you need to find the area of a sector?
You need the measure of the central angle and the radius.

⭐ Evaluate: Homework and Practice

- Online Homework
- Hints and Help
- Extra Practice

1. The region within a circle that is bounded by two radii and an arc is called a ___sector___.

2. Suppose you know the area and the measure of the central angle of a sector. Describe the process of finding the area of the sector.

Divide the measure of the central angle by 360 and multiply the result by the
area of the circle.

3. What is the formula for the area of a circle? Define all variables in the formula.

$A = \pi r^2$, where A represents the area and r represents the length of the radius.

4. If the angle of a sector measures 45°, what fraction of the circle is the sector?

$\frac{45}{360} = \frac{1}{8}$

© Houghton Mifflin Harcourt Publishing Company

Exercise	Depth of Knowledge (D.O.K.)	COMMON CORE Mathematical Practices
1–4	**1** Recall of Information	**MP.6** Precision
5–10	**1** Recall of Information	**MP.5** Using Tools
11–13	**2** Skills/Concepts	**MP.4** Modeling
14–17	**1** Recall of Information	**MP.5** Using Tools
18–22	**2** Skills/Concepts	**MP.4** Modeling
23–26	**2** Skills/Concepts	**MP.5** Using Tools

ELABORATE

QUESTIONING STRATEGIES

? How do you use percent to calculate the area of a sector from the area of a circle? You find what percent of the circle the area represents by dividing the measure of the central angle by 360, then you multiply the percent by the area of the circle.

SUMMARIZE THE LESSON

? What information do you need to find the area of a sector of a circle? How does the information allow you to find the area? You need to know the radius of the circle, r, and the measure of the central angle, m. These values allow you to find the portion of the circle that the sector represents. Then, multiply the portion by the total area, $A = \frac{m}{360} \cdot \pi r^2$.

EVALUATE

ASSIGNMENT GUIDE

Concepts and Skills	Practice
Explore Derive the Formula for the Area of a Sector	Exercises 1–4
Example 1 Using the Formula for the Area of a Sector	Exercises 5–10
Example 2 Applying the Formula for the Area of a Sector	Exercises 11–17

AVOID COMMON ERRORS

Some students may substitute the length of the diameter into the area formula instead of the length of the radius. Caution students to take careful note of what information they are given.

Find the area of sector *AOB*. Express your answer in terms of π and rounded to the nearest tenth.

5.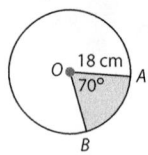

$$A = \frac{m}{360} \cdot \pi r^2$$
$$= \frac{70}{360} \cdot \pi (18)^2$$
$$= 63\pi$$
$$A = 63\pi \approx 197.7 \text{ cm}^2$$

6.

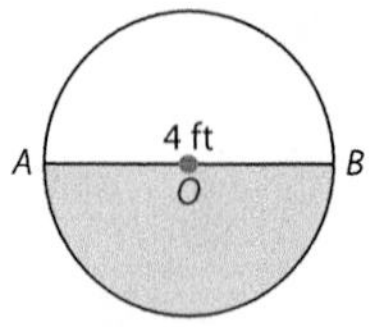

$$A = \frac{m}{360} \cdot \pi r^2$$
$$= \frac{180}{360} \cdot \pi (2)^2$$
$$= 2\pi$$
$$A = 2\pi \approx 6.3 \text{ ft}^2$$

7.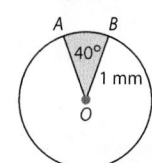

$$A = \frac{m}{360} \cdot \pi r^2$$
$$= \frac{40}{360} \cdot \pi (1)^2$$
$$= \frac{\pi}{9}$$
$$A = \frac{\pi}{9} \approx 0.3 \text{ mm}^2$$

8.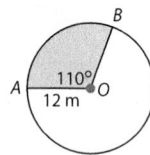

$$A = \frac{m}{360} \cdot \pi r^2$$
$$= \frac{110}{360} \cdot \pi (12)^2$$
$$= 44\pi$$
$$A = 44\pi \approx 138.2 \text{ m}^2$$

9.

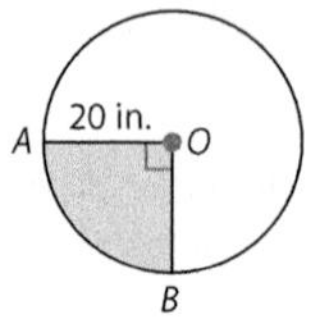

$$A = \frac{m}{360} \cdot \pi r^2$$
$$= \frac{90}{360} \cdot \pi (20)^2$$
$$= 100\pi$$
$$A = 100\pi \approx 314.2 \text{ in}^2$$

10.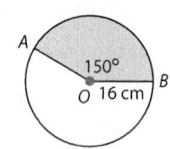

$$A = \frac{m}{360} \cdot \pi r^2$$
$$= \frac{150}{360} \cdot \pi (16)^2$$
$$= \frac{320}{3}\pi$$
$$A = \frac{320}{3}\pi \approx 335.1 \text{ cm}^2$$

11. A round pizza is cut into congruent sectors. If the angle measure of the pizza slice is 20°, how many pieces are in the whole pizza?

$$\frac{360}{20} = 18$$

18 pieces

12. The area of a piece of pie in the shape of a sector is 7.1 in². The angle of the sector is 40°.

a. What is the area of the entire pie?

The piece of pie is $\frac{40}{360} = \frac{1}{9}$ of the pie.

So, the area of the entire pie is $9 \cdot 7.1 = 63.9$ in².

b. What is the diameter of the pie?

$$A = \pi r^2$$
$$63.9 = \pi r^2$$
$$\frac{63.9}{\pi} = r^2$$
$$4.5 \approx r$$
$$d = 2r \approx 2(4.5) \approx 9 \text{ in.}$$

© Houghton Mifflin Harcourt Publishing Company

Exercise	Depth of Knowledge (D.O.K.)	COMMON CORE	Mathematical Practices
27	**3** Strategic Thinking	H.O.T.	**MP.3** Logic
28	**3** Strategic Thinking	H.O.T.	**MP.1** Problem Solving
29	**3** Strategic Thinking	H.O.T.	**MP.2** Reasoning
30	**3** Strategic Thinking	H.O.T.	**MP.3** Logic

13. A *lunette* is a semicircular window that is sometimes placed above a doorway or above a rectangular window. The diameter of the lunette is 40 inches. To the nearest square inch, what is the area of the lunette?

$r = \frac{40}{2} = 20$ in.

$A = \frac{m}{360} \cdot \pi r^2$

$ = \frac{180}{360} \cdot \pi (20)^2$

$ = 200\pi$

$ \approx 628.3$ in²

Find the area of each sector. Give your answer in terms of π and rounded to the nearest hundredth.

14. sector *PQR*

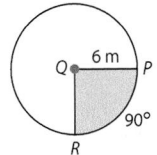

$A = \frac{m}{360} \cdot \pi r^2$

$ = \frac{90}{360} \cdot \pi (6)^2.$

$ = 9\pi$

$ \approx 28.7$ m²

15. sector *JKL*

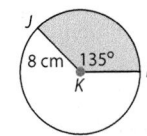

$A = \frac{m}{360} \cdot \pi r^2$

$ = \frac{135}{360} \cdot \pi (8)^2.$

$ = 24\pi$

$ \approx 75.40$ cm²

16. sector *ABC*

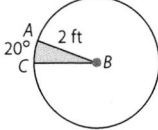

$A = \frac{m}{360} \cdot \pi r^2$

$ = \frac{20}{360} \cdot \pi (2)^2.$

$ = \frac{2}{9}\pi$

$ \approx 0.70$ ft²

17. sector *RST*

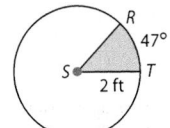

$A = \frac{m}{360} \cdot \pi r^2$

$ = \frac{47}{360} \cdot \pi (2)^2.$

$ = \frac{47}{90}\pi$

$ \approx 1.64$ ft²

18. The beam from a lighthouse is visible for a distance of 15 mi. To the nearest square mile, what is the area covered by the beam as it sweeps in an arc of 270°?

$A = \frac{270}{360} \cdot \pi (15)^2 = \frac{3}{4} \cdot (225)\pi \approx 530$ mi²

19. The radius of circle O is 6 mm. The area of sector AOB is $\frac{9}{2}\pi$ mm². Explain how to find m$\angle AOB$.

Let m$\angle AOB = x°$, then $\frac{x}{360} \cdot \pi (6)^2 = \frac{9}{2}\pi$. Solving for x shows that m$\angle AOB = 45°$.

© Houghton Mifflin Harcourt Publishing Company · Image Credits: ©Paul O'Connell/Shutterstock

INTEGRATE MATHEMATICAL PRACTICES

Focus on Reasoning

MP.2 Point out that the area of a sector of a circle varies as the square of the radius of the circle. Using r as the independent variable, the constant of variation is $\frac{m°}{360°} \cdot \pi$, and the area of the sector is $A = \frac{m°}{360°} \cdot \pi r^2$.

INTEGRATE MATHEMATICAL PRACTICES
Focus on Math Connections

MP.1 Since radius and diameter are linear dimensions and the area of a circle and sector increase by the square of the linear dimensions, the effect is that the area is multiplied by four if the linear dimension is doubled, and the area is multiplied by nine if the linear dimension is tripled.

INTEGRATE MATHEMATICAL PRACTICES
Focus on Reasoning

MP.2 Real-life circles such as pizzas or pies are often cut into congruent wedges (sectors). So, if a pie is cut into congruent wedges, each with an angle of 45°, there must be 8 wedges, because $\frac{360°}{45°} = 8$.

The Artisan Pizza Co sells take-out pizza in two shapes: an "individual" 6-in. square slice and a circular "party" wheel with an 18 in. diameter. The party wheel is cut into 8 slices/sectors for the customer. An individual slice of the party wheel costs $2.95 and the entire party wheel costs $15.95.

20. Which is larger, the square slice or one sector of the wheel?

Area of square slice $= (6 \text{ in.})^2 = 36 \text{ in}^2$

Area of a sector $= \frac{1}{8}\pi r^2 = \frac{1}{8}\pi(9 \text{ in.})^2 = \frac{1}{8}(81\pi \text{ in}^2) \approx 31.8 \text{ in}^2$

The square slice is larger.

21. Which option is the better value, buying by the slice or buying the entire wheel?

Cost of slice per square inch $= \frac{\$2.95}{36 \text{ in}^2} \approx \$0.08 \text{ per in}^2$

Cost of wheel per square inch $= \frac{\$15.95}{81\pi \text{ in}^2} \approx \$0.07 \text{ per in}^2$

Buying an entire wheel is the better value.

22. Greek mathematicians studied the *salinon*, a figure bounded by four semicircles. What is the area of this salinon to the nearest tenth of a square inch?

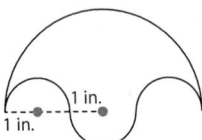

The salinon is one half circle with a 3-inch radius minus one half circle with a 1-inch radius.

$A = \frac{180}{360} \cdot \pi(3)^2 - \frac{180}{360} \cdot \pi(1)^2$

$= \frac{9}{2}\pi - \frac{1}{2}\pi$

$= 4\pi$

$\approx 12.6 \text{ in}^2$

23. Which of the following express the measure of the angle of a sector, *m*, as a ratio between the area of the sector and the radius of the circle? Select all that apply.

A. $\frac{360\pi}{Ar^2}$

B. $\frac{360\,A}{\pi r^2}$

C. $360r^2 \cdot \frac{A}{\pi}$

D. $\frac{A\pi r^2}{360}$

E. $\frac{Ar^2}{360\pi}$

F. $360A \cdot \frac{1}{\pi r^2}$

$A = \frac{m}{360} \cdot \pi r^2$

$\frac{A}{\pi r^2} = \frac{m}{360}$

$\frac{360\,A}{\pi r^2} = m$

$\frac{360\,A}{\pi r^2} = 360\,A \cdot \frac{1}{\pi r^2}$

B, F

© Houghton Mifflin Harcourt Publishing Company

24. Algebra The table shows how students get to school.

Methods	% of Students
Bus	65%
Walk	25%
Other	10%

a. Explain why a circle graph is appropriate for the data.

Each group is expressed as a percent and their sum is 100%. So, a full circle can represent the entire data.

b. Use a proportion to find the measure of the central angle for each sector. Then use a protractor and a compass to draw the circle graph.

$$\frac{65}{100} = \frac{a}{360°}; \quad \frac{25}{100} = \frac{a}{360°}; \quad \frac{10}{100} = \frac{a}{360°}$$

$$a = 234° \qquad a = 90° \qquad a = 36°$$

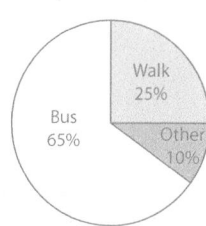

c. Find the area of each sector. Use a radius of 2 inches.

Bus: $A = \frac{65}{100} \cdot \pi(2)^2 = 2.6\pi \approx 8.2$ in^2

Walk: $A = \frac{25}{100} \cdot \pi(2)^2 = \pi \approx 3.1$ in^2

Other: $A = \frac{10}{100} \cdot \pi(2)^2 = 0.4\pi \approx 1.3$ in^2

Multi-Step A *segment of a circle* is a region bounded by an arc and its chord. Find the area of each segment to the nearest hundredth.

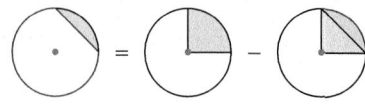

area of segment = area of sector − area of triangle

25.

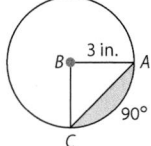

Sector *ABC*: $A = \frac{90}{360} \cdot \pi(3)^2 = 2.25\pi \approx 7.07$ in^2

Triangle *ABC*: $A = \frac{1}{2}(3)(3) = 4.5$ in^2

$7.07 - 4.5 = 2.57$ in^2.

26.

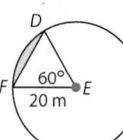

The base of triangle *DEF* is 20 m, and the height is $10\sqrt{3}$ m.

$A = \frac{1}{2}(20)(10\sqrt{3}) \approx 173.21$ m^2

$A = \frac{60}{360} \cdot \pi(20)^2 = 66\frac{2}{3}\pi \approx 209.44$ m^2

$209.44 - 173.21 = 36.23$ m^2

INTEGRATE MATHEMATICAL PRACTICES

Focus on Math Connections

MP.1 A *segment* of a circle is a region bounded by an arc and its chord. Point out that to find the area of the segment, you should subtract the area of the isosceles triangle from the area of the sector of the circle. Segment *RPQ* is shaded in the figure below. Tell students to name a segment with three letters. The first and third letters are the endpoints of the chord and the middle letter is the center of the circle.

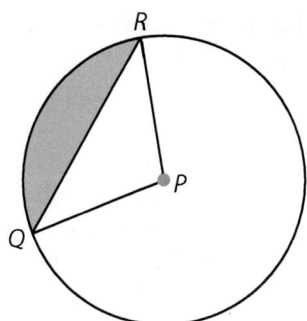

PEER-TO-PEER DISCUSSION

Ask students to discuss with a partner how to find the area of a sector of a circle using a formula. One student should draw a circle and give the radius. Then the other student should identify various central angle measures on the circle and give the area of the sectors. Have students switch roles and repeat the exercise.

JOURNAL

Have students describe the steps for finding the area of a sector. Have them include specific examples to illustrate the steps.

---

27. Critique Reasoning A student claims that when you double the radius of a sector while keeping the measure of the central angle constant, you double the area of the sector. Do you agree or disagree? Explain

Disagree; the original area is $\frac{m}{360} \cdot \pi r^2$ and the new area is $\frac{m}{360} \cdot \pi(2r)^2$ or $4 \cdot \frac{m}{360} \cdot \pi r^2$, so the area becomes 4 times greater.

28. Multi-Step The exclamation point (!) on a billboard consists of a circle sector and circle. The radius of the sector is 9 ft, and the radius of the circle is 1.5 ft. The angle of the sector is 24°. What is the total area of the exclamation point on the billboard? Round to the nearest tenth.

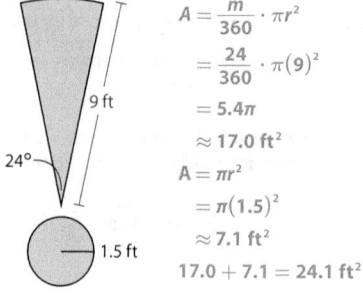

$$A = \frac{m}{360} \cdot \pi r^2$$
$$= \frac{24}{360} \cdot \pi(9)^2$$
$$= 5.4\pi$$
$$\approx 17.0 \text{ ft}^2$$
$$A = \pi r^2$$
$$= \pi(1.5)^2$$
$$\approx 7.1 \text{ ft}^2$$
$$17.0 + 7.1 = 24.1 \text{ ft}^2$$

29. Analyze Relationships Compare finding arc length to finding the area of a sector. Name any common and different processes.

Arc length requires using the circumference of the circle, whereas area requires the circle's area. In each, the central angle is used to find the fraction of the circumference or area of the circle.

30. Critique Reasoning Melody says that she needs only to know the length of an arc and radius of a circle to find the area of the corresponding sector. If arc length is L and sector area is A, then $A = \frac{2L}{r}$. Is she correct? Justify your answer.

She is correct that she only needs the arc length and radius to find the area, but her equation is incorrect.

$A = \frac{m}{360} \cdot \pi(r)^2$ and $L = \frac{m}{360} \cdot 2\pi r$, so $\frac{A}{L} = \frac{\frac{m}{360} \cdot \pi(r)^2}{\frac{m}{360} \cdot 2\pi r}$. Thus, $\frac{A}{L} = \frac{r}{2}$, and $A = \frac{rL}{2}$.

Lesson Performance Task

The planets orbit the Sun not in circles but in ellipses, which are "flattened" circles. The Earth's orbit, however, isn't flattened much. Its greatest distance from the Sun, 94.5 million miles, differs from its least distance, 91.4 million miles, by only about 3%.

To answer the following questions, make the following assumptions:

a. Summer includes all of the days from June 21 through September 21. During that time Earth travels in a circular orbit with a radius of 94.5 million miles. A year lasts 365 days.

b. Winter includes all of the days from December 21 through March 20. During that time Earth travels in a circular orbit with a radius of 91.4 million miles. The year you will consider lasts 365 days and is not a leap year.

Solve. Show your work. Use 3.14 for π.

1. Find the distances that the Earth travels in summer and in winter. Give your answers in millions of miles rounded to the nearest tenth.

2. Find the Earth's average rate of speed in summer and in winter. Give your answers in millions of miles per day rounded to the nearest hundredth.

3. Find the areas of the sectors that the Earth traverses in summer and in winter. Give your answers in millions of miles squared rounded to the nearest tenth.

1. number of days in summer = 10 (June) + 31 (July) + 31 (August) + 21(September) = 93
number of days in winter = 11 (December) + 31 (January) + 28 (February) + 20 (March) = 90

circumference of orbit (summer): $2\pi r =$ 2(3.14)(94.5) = 593.46 million miles

distance traveled in summer (93 of 365 days of year):
$\frac{93}{365} \times 593.46 = 151.2$ million miles

circumference of orbit (winter):
$2\pi r = 2(3.14)(91.4)$
$= 573.99$ million miles

distance traveled in winter (90 of 365 days of year):
$\frac{90}{365} \times 573.99 = 141.5$ million miles

2. average speed in summer:
$\frac{distance}{time} = \frac{151.2}{93}$
$= 1.63$ million miles/day

average speed in winter:
$\frac{distance}{time} = \frac{141.5}{90}$
$= 1.57$ million miles/day

3. area of orbit (summer):
$\pi r^2 = (3.14)(94.5)^2$
$= 28,040.99$ million miles squared

sector area in summer (93 of 365 days of year):
$\frac{93}{365} \times 28,040.99 = 7144.7$ million miles squared

area of orbit (winter):
$\pi r^2 = (3.14)(91.4)^2$
$= 26,231.43$ million miles squared

sector area in winter (90 of 365 days of year):
$\frac{90}{365} \times 26,231.43 = 6468.0$ million miles squared

© Houghton Mifflin Harcourt Publishing Company

EXTENSION ACTIVITY

Provide these statistics: Earth's average distance from the Sun is 93 million miles, and Mars's average distance from the Sun is 142 million miles. Ask, "During one-quarter of their orbits around the Sun, by how many square miles does the area of the sector that Mars traverses exceed the area of the sector that Earth traverses? Assume that both planets move in circular orbits." area of Earth's 90° sector ≈ 6.79 × 10¹⁵ square miles; area of Mars's 90° sector ≈ 1.58 × 10¹⁶ square miles; difference ≈ 9 × 10¹⁵ square miles

INTEGRATE MATHEMATICAL PRACTICES

Focus on Reasoning

MP.2 The Lesson Performance Task states that Earth's greatest distance from the Sun differs from its least distance by only about 3%. Show the calculations that give this result. greatest distance: 94.5 million miles; least distance: 91.4 million miles; difference: 3.1 million miles; $\frac{3.1}{91.4} \approx 3.4\%$

INTEGRATE MATHEMATICAL PRACTICES

Focus on Math Connections

MP.1 Mars takes 687 days to orbit the Sun at an average distance of 142 million miles. Earth takes 365 days to orbit the Sun at an average distance of 93 million miles. Which planet moves at the faster average rate of speed? Explain. (Assume that the planets move in circular orbits.) Earth moves faster. The circumference of Earth's orbit is 93 × 2π ≈ 584 million miles, and the circumference of Mars's orbit is 142 × 2π ≈ 892 million miles. Earth's average speed is $\frac{584}{365} \approx 1.6$ million miles per day, and Mars's average speed is $\frac{892}{687} \approx 1.3$ million miles per day.

Scoring Rubric
2 points: Student correctly solves the problem and explains his/her reasoning.
1 point: Student shows good understanding of the problem but does not fully solve or explain his/her reasoning.
0 points: Student does not demonstrate understanding of the problem.

Sector Area   **882**

Study Guide Review

ASSESSMENT AND INTERVENTION

Assign or customize module reviews.

MODULE PERFORMANCE TASK

Mathematical Practices: MP.1, MP.2, MP.3, MP.4, MP.6
G-C.B.5, G-MG.A.1

SUPPORTING STUDENT REASONING

Students should begin this problem by focusing on what information they will need. Here are some issues they might bring up.

- **What are ways to compare the pizzas:** Students can find the area of the slice of pizza and of the whole small pizza and then compare them.

- **What about the thicknesses of the pizzas:** For the purpose of this problem, students can assume that each type of pizza is the same thickness.

Essential Question: How can the arc length and sector area of a circle be used to solve a real-world problem? How are they related?

KEY EXAMPLE (Lesson 16.1)

The circumference of a tire is 90 inches. What is its radius? Round to the nearest inch.

$C = 2\pi r$	Write the circumference formula.
$90 = 2\pi r$	Substitute the circumference.
$\frac{90}{2\pi} = r$	Simplify.
$14 \text{ in} \approx r$	Substitute 3.14 for π to approximate the solution.

KEY EXAMPLE (Lesson 16.2)

Find the arc length of an arc that measures 150° in a circle with a radius of 8 meters. Give your answer in terms of π.

$A = \frac{m}{360} \cdot 2\pi r$	Write the arc length formula.
$A = \frac{150}{360} \cdot 2\pi 8$	Substitute the angle measure and radius.
$A = \frac{20}{3}\pi$	Simplify.

KEY EXAMPLE (Lesson 16.3)

A sandwich shop sells sandwiches on two types of bread: a 9-inch square flatbread and a round roll with a 4-inch radius. Which type of bread is larger?

$A = s^2$	Write the area of a square.
$A = (9\,\text{in})^2$	Substitute the side length of the flatbread.
$A = 81\,\text{in}^2$	Simplify.
$A = \pi r^2$	Write the area of a circle.
$A = \pi(4)^2\,\text{in}^2$	Substitute the radius of the roll.
$A = 16\pi\,\text{in}^2$	Simplify.
$A \approx 50.24\,\text{in}^2$	Substitute 3.14 for π to approximate the solution.

The flatbread is larger than the roll.

SCAFFOLDING SUPPORT

- Students should be able to devise a formula to find the area of one-eighth of a pizza.

- To calculate the price per square inch of pizza, divide the cost of the pizza by the number of square inches of pizza. Students should do this for the slice of pizza and for the personal-size pizza so that they can be compared.

EXERCISES

Find the radius of the circle with the given circumference. *(Lesson 16.1)*

1. $C = 15$ in

$r \approx 2.39$ in

2. $C = \pi$ cm

$r = 0.5$ cm

Find the arc length given the angle measure and radius of the circle. Give your answer in terms of π. *(Lesson 16.2)*

3. $m = 180°, r = 4$ inches

$A = 4\pi$ in

Apply the formula for the area of a sector to solve the real-world problem. *(Lesson 16.3)*

4. A paper airplane can be made out of two different pieces of paper: a circular piece 10 inches wide and a square piece 11 inches wide. Which piece of paper will provide the greater area for flight?

The square piece of paper will provide the greater area for flight.

MODULE PERFORMANCE TASK

What's the Better Deal on Pizza?

You are ordering pizza and you have two choices: a slice of pizza from a large pizza with a diameter of 22 inches or an entire personal-size pizza that has a diameter of 6 inches. The slice costs $4.95, and the smaller pizza costs $3.75. Assuming that the large pizza is cut into 8 slices, will you get more pizza for your money by buying one slice of the larger pizza or by buying the personal-size pizza?

Use your own paper to complete the task. Be sure to write down all of your assumptions and data. Then use words, diagrams, numbers, or geometry to explain how you came to your conclusion.

DISCUSSION OPPORTUNITIES

- What are reasons why you might choose to buy the personal-size pizza instead of a slice? Sample: The personal-size pizza costs less, or has more crust.

- What are some sources of error in finding the area of a sector of a circle?

SAMPLE SOLUTION

Method:

Determine the price per square inch for the personal-size pizza, by first calculating the area.

Find a formula for the area of one slice of the larger pizza, and use the formula to determine the cost per square inch for one slice.

Finally, compare the costs for the two choices.

Find the area of the personal-size pizza.

Use $r = d/2 = 3$ in.

$A = \pi r^2 = \pi(3 \text{ in.})^2 = 9\,\pi \text{ in.}^2 \approx 28.27 \text{ in.}^2$

The cost per square inch for the personal-size pizza is $\frac{\$3.75}{28.27 \text{ in.}^2} = \$0.13/\text{in.}^2$.

The area of one slice of the larger pizza is given by the formula $A = \frac{1}{8}(\pi r^2)$. The radius of the pizza is $22/2 = 11$ in.

$A = \frac{1}{8}\pi r^2 = \frac{1}{8}\pi(11 \text{ in.})^2 \approx 47.52 \text{ in.}^2$

The cost per square inch for the slice is $\frac{\$4.95}{47.52 \text{ in.}^2} = \$0.10/\text{in.}^2$

It is a better deal to buy the slice of the large pizza.

Assessment Rubric

2 points: Student correctly solves the problem and explains his/her reasoning.

1 point: Student shows good understanding of the problem but does not fully solve or explain.

0 points: Student does not demonstrate understanding of the problem.

Ready to Go On?

ASSESS MASTERY

Use the assessment on this page to determine if students have mastered the concepts and standards covered in this module.

ASSESSMENT AND INTERVENTION

Access Ready to Go On? assessment online, and receive instant scoring, feedback, and customized intervention or enrichment.

ADDITIONAL RESOURCES

Response to Intervention Resources

- Reteach Worksheets

Differentiated Instruction Resources

- Reading Strategies **EL**
- Success for English Learners **EL**
- Challenge Worksheets

Assessment Resources

- Leveled Module Quizzes

(Ready) to Go On?

16.1–16.3 Arc Length and Sector Area

- Online Homework
- Hints and Help
- Extra Practice

Apply the appropriate area formula. *(Lesson 16.1)*

1. At a campground, the area of a rectangular fire pit is 5 feet by 4 feet. What is the area of the largest circular fire than can be made in this fire pit? Round to the nearest square inch.

The diameter of the largest circle is 4 feet, or 48 inches.

$A = \pi r^2$

$A = \pi (24 \text{ in})^2$

$A = 576\pi \text{ in}^2 \approx 1808.6 \text{ in}^2$

The area is about 1809 square inches.

Find the arc length. Give your answer in terms of π and round to the nearest hundredth. *(Lesson 16.2)*

2. $\overset{\frown}{AB}$

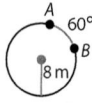

$\overset{\frown}{AB} = \frac{m}{360} \cdot 2\pi r$

$= \frac{60}{360} \cdot 2\pi 8\,m$

$= \frac{960}{360}\pi\,m = \frac{8}{3}\pi\,m$, or about 8.38 m

Apply the formula for the area of a sector to solve the real-world problem. *(Lesson 16.3)*

3. A Mexican restaurant sells quesadillas in two sizes: a "large" 10-inch round quesadilla and a "small" 6-inch round quesadilla. Which is larger, half of the 10-inch quesadilla or the entire 6-inch quesadilla?

Area of small quesadilla $= \pi r^2 = \pi (6 \text{ in})^2 = \pi 36 \text{ in}^2 \approx 113.10 \text{ in}^2$

Area of half of large quesadilla

$= \frac{1}{2}\pi r^2 = \frac{1}{2}\pi (10 \text{ in})^2 = \frac{1}{2}\pi 100 \text{ in}^2 = 50\pi \text{ in}^2 \approx 157.08 \text{ in}^2$

Half of the large quesadilla is larger than the small quesadilla.

ESSENTIAL QUESTION

4. What is the relationship between the arc length and sector area of a circle?

Answers may vary. Sample Answer: Start with a circle that has a central angle of measure $m°$. Consider the arc and sector the central angle subtends. The arc has length of $\frac{m}{360}$ times the circumference of the circle. The sector has an area of $\frac{m}{360}$ times the area of the circle. The ratio of arc length to circumference is the same as the ratio of sector area to circle area, the ratio of $\frac{m}{360}$. Once you know one, you can solve for the other. The area of the sector is $\frac{r}{2}$ times the length of the arc length, taking away the units.

© Houghton Mifflin Harcourt Publishing Company

COMMON CORE **Common Core Standards**

Lesson	Items	Content Standards	Mathematical Practices
16.1	1	**G-GMD.A.1, G-MG.A.1**	**MP.4**
16.2	2	**G-C.B.5**	**MP.7**
16.3	3	**G-C.B.5, G-MG.A.1**	**MP.4**

MODULE 16
MIXED REVIEW

Assessment Readiness

SELECTED RESPONSE

1. Consider each equation. Does it show a true relationship between degree measure and radian measure? Select Yes or No for A–C.

   A. $\frac{5\pi}{12}$ radians = 75°   ● Yes   ○ No

   B. $\frac{\pi}{2}$ radians = 180°   ○ Yes   ● No

   C. $\frac{\pi}{3}$ radians = 60°   ● Yes   ○ No

2. Consider a circle with a radius of 2 meters that has an arc angle of 90°. Choose True or False for each statement.

   A. The arc measure is 90°.   ● True   ○ False

   B. The circumference and the area of this circle, taking away the units, are equal.   ● True   ○ False

   C. The arc length is π meters.   ● True   ○ False

3. $\triangle ABC$ is an equilateral triangle, $AB = 3x + 27$, and $BC = 5x - 9$. Choose True or False for each statement.

   A. $x = 18$ ● True   ○ False

   B. The length of one side of the triangle is 162 units.   ○ True   ● False

   C. The perimeter of the triangle is 243 units.   ● True   ○ False

4. Write an equation that represents the circumference of a circle with a radius of 6 feet. What is the diameter of the circle?

   $y = 12\pi$; 12 feet

5. Given the sector area, how can the radius be determined? From the radius, how can the arc length be determined?

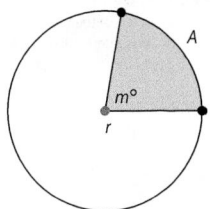

Answers may vary. Sample: Use $A = \frac{m\pi}{360} r^2$, and solve for the radius, r. Keep only the positive result since a negative radius is impossible. To find the arc length, multiply the radius by $\frac{m\pi}{180}$.

MIXED REVIEW
Assessment Readiness

ASSESSMENT AND INTERVENTION

Assign ready-made or customized practice tests to prepare students for high-stakes tests.

ADDITIONAL RESOURCES

Assessment Resources

- Leveled Module Quizzes: Modified, B

AVOID COMMON ERRORS

Item 3 Some students will have difficulty remembering how to solve an equation with the same variable on both sides of the equal sign. Remind students that they can also work backward when given a value for x in the answer choices.

COMMON CORE Common Core Standards

Lesson	Items	Content Standards	Mathematical Practices
16.2	1	G-C.B.5	MP.2
16.2, 14.1	2*	G-C.B.5	MP.2
7.2	3*	G-CO.D.13	MP.2
16.1	4	G-GMD.A.1	MP.2
16.3	5	G-C.B.5	MP.7

* Item integrates mixed review concepts from previous modules or a previous course.

Equations of Circles and Parabolas

ESSENTIAL QUESTION:

Answer: Parabolic equations help creators of fireworks displays synchronize the explosions accurately. Circle equations are used to measure how loud a sound is from the point of sound emission.

PROFESSIONAL DEVELOPMENT VIDEO

Professional Development Video

Author Juli Dixon models successful teaching practices in an actual high-school classroom.

Professional Development
my.hrw.com

MODULE **17**

Equations of Circles and Parabolas

Essential Question: How can you use equations of circles and parabolas to solve real-world problems?

LESSON 17.1
Equation of a Circle

LESSON 17.2
Equation of a Parabola

© Houghton Mifflin Harcourt Publishing Company • Image Credits: Adam Eggers/U.S. Coast Guard

REAL WORLD VIDEO
Check out some of the mathematics involved in the flight of rescue helicopters, such as this H-65 helicopter flown by the United States Coast Guard.

MODULE PERFORMANCE TASK PREVIEW

Rescue at Sea

One of the critical functions of the United States Coast Guard is carrying out search and rescue missions at sea. Teams of H-65 helicopters, each carrying two pilots, a flight mechanic, and a rescue swimmer, conduct coordinated sweeps over huge areas of ocean in search of the missing craft. The mathematics involved in executing such missions is complex, but you'll learn some of the basics in this module. Then you'll plan an ocean rescue of your own.

DIGITAL TEACHER EDITION

Access a full suite of teaching resources when and where you need them:

- Access content online or offline
- Customize lessons to share with your class
- Communicate with your students in real-time
- View student grades and data instantly to target your instruction where it is needed most

PERSONAL MATH TRAINER
Assessment and Intervention

Assign automatically graded homework, quizzes, tests, and intervention activities. Prepare your students with updated, Common Core-aligned practice tests.

Are **YOU** Ready?

Complete these exercises to review skills you will need for this module.

Circumference

Example 1

The center of a circle is $(-4, 1)$, and a point on the circle is $(1, -11)$. Find the circumference of the circle to the nearest tenth.

The circumference formula is $C = 2\pi r$.

$r = \sqrt{(-4-1)^2 + (1-(-11))^2} = 13$ Use the distance formula.

$C = 2\pi(13)$ Substitute.

$C = 26\pi$, or about 81.7.   Simplify.

The center and a point on a circle are given. Find the circumference to the nearest tenth.

1. center: $(5, -5)$
point on the circle: $(25, 10)$

157.1

2. center: $(-12, -20)$
point on the circle: $(3, -12)$

106.8

3. center: $(8, 8)$
point on the circle: $(-2, 1)$

76.7

Characteristics of Quadratic Functions

Example 2

The vertex of a quadratic function is at $(2, 5)$ and one of the x-intercepts is at $(-1, 0)$. Find the other x-intercept.

The missing x-intercept is of the form $(x, 0)$. The midpoint between the two x-intercepts lies on the axis of symmetry, which passes through the vertex of the parabola. The x-value of the vertex is 2, so the axis of symmetry is $x = 2$, and the midpoint between the intercepts is $(2, 0)$. Therefore, 2 is the mean of the x-values of the intercepts: $2 = \dfrac{x + (-1)}{2}$, so $x = 5$. The missing x-intercept is $(5, 0)$.

The vertex and one x-intercept are given. Find the other x-intercept.

4. $(-3, 4), (6, 0)$

$(-12, 0)$

5. $(8, 1), (7, 0)$

$(9, 0)$

6. $(-9-1), (-4, 0)$

$(-14, 0)$

© Houghton Mifflin Harcourt Publishing Company

Are You Ready?

ASSESS READINESS

Use the assessment on this page to determine if students need strategic or intensive intervention for the module's prerequisite skills.

ASSESSMENT AND INTERVENTION

RtI Response to Intervention **TIER 1, TIER 2, TIER 3 SKILLS**

Personal Math Trainer will automatically create a standards-based, personalized intervention assignment for your students, targeting each student's individual needs!

ADDITIONAL RESOURCES

See the table below for a full list of intervention resources available for this module.

Response to Intervention Resources also includes:

- Tier 2 Skill Pre-Tests for each Module
- Tier 2 Skill Post-Tests for each skill

Response to Intervention			Differentiated Instruction
Tier 1 Lesson Intervention Worksheets	**Tier 2** Strategic Intervention Skills Intervention Worksheets	**Tier 3** Intensive Intervention Worksheets available online	
Reteach 17.1 Reteach 17.2	6 Circumference 9 Distance and Midpoint Formula 31 Characteristics of Quadratic Functions 32 Solving Quadratic Functions Graphically	Building Block Skills 10, 11, 14, 27, 34, 38, 45, 65, 69, 70, 97, 98, 100, 102	Challenge worksheets Extend the Math Lesson Activities in TE

Personal Math Trainer

• Online Homework
• Hints and Help
• Extra Practice

Equation of a Circle

Common Core Math Standards

The student is expected to:

 G-GPE.A.1

Derive the equation of a circle of given center and radius using the Pythagorean Theorem; complete the square to find the center and radius of a circle given by an equation. Also G-GPE.B.4

Mathematical Practices

COMMON CORE **MP.6 Precision**

Language Objective

Explain to a partner how to find the equation of a circle given its radius and the coordinates of its center.

ENGAGE

Essential Question: How can you write the equation of a circle if you know its radius and the coordinates of its center?

The equation of a circle with center (h, k) and radius r is $(x - h)^2 + (y - k)^2 = r^2$.

PREVIEW: LESSON PERFORMANCE TASK

View the Engage section online. Discuss the map. Tell students that something is hidden in the tree and ask them to guess what it might be. Then preview the Lesson Performance Task.

17.1 Equation of a Circle

Essential Question: How can you write the equation of a circle if you know its radius and the coordinates of its center?

⊘ Explore **Deriving the Equation of a Circle**

You have already worked with circles in several earlier lessons. Now you will investigate circles in a coordinate plane and learn how to write an equation of a circle.

We can define a **circle** as the set of all points in the coordinate plane that are a fixed distance r from the center (h, k).

Consider the circle in a coordinate plane that has its center at $C(h, k)$ and that has radius r.

Ⓐ Let P be any point on the circle and let the coordinates of P be (x, y).

Create a right triangle by drawing a horizontal line through C and a vertical line through P, as shown.

What are the coordinates of point A? $\underline{A(x, k)}$ Explain how you found the coordinates of A.

A has the same x-coordinate as P and the same y-coordinate as C.

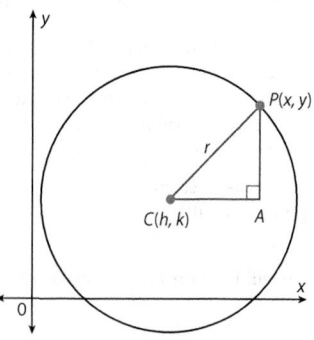

Ⓑ Use absolute value to write expressions for the lengths of the legs of $\triangle CAP$.

$CA = \underline{|x - h|}$; $PA = \underline{|y - k|}$

Ⓒ Use the Pythagorean Theorem to write a relationship among the side lengths of $\triangle CAP$.

$\underline{(x - h)^2} + \underline{(y - k)^2} = \underline{r^2}$

© Houghton Mifflin Harcourt Publishing Company

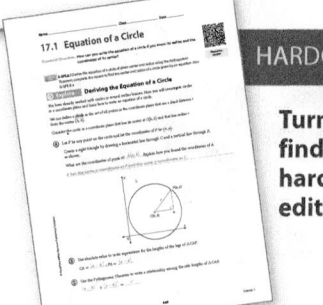

HARDCOVER PAGES 751–758

Turn to these pages to find this lesson in the hardcover student edition.

1. Compare your work with that of other students. Then, write an equation for the circle with center $C(h, k)$ and radius r.
$(x - h)^2 + (y - k)^2 = r^2$

2. Why do you need absolute values when you write expressions for the lengths of the legs in Step B, but not when you write the relationship among the side lengths in Step C?
In Step B, the absolute values ensure that the lengths are nonnegative.

In Step C, the lengths are squared, so the absolute values are no longer needed.

3. Suppose a circle has its center at the origin. What is the equation of the circle in this case?
$x^2 + y^2 = r^2$

⊘ Explain 1 Writing the Equation of a Circle

You can write the equation of a circle given its coordinates and radius.

> **Equation of a Circle**
>
> The equation of a circle with center (h, k) and radius r is $(x - h)^2 + (y - k)^2 = r^2$.

Example 1 Write the equation of the circle with the given center and radius.

(A) Center: $(-2, 5)$; radius: 3

$(x - h)^2 + (y - k)^2 = r^2$ Write the general equation of a circle.

$(x - (-2))^2 + (y - 5)^2 = 3^2$ Substitute -2 for h, 5 for k, and 3 for r.

$(x + 2)^2 + (y - 5)^2 = 9$ Simplify.

(B) Center: $(4, -1)$; radius: $\sqrt{5}$

$(x - h)^2 + (y - k)^2 = r^2$ Write the general equation of a circle.

$\left(x - \boxed{4}\right)^2 + \left(y - \boxed{-1}\right)^2 = \boxed{\sqrt{5}}^2$ Substitute $\boxed{4}$ for h, $\boxed{-1}$ for k, and $\boxed{\sqrt{5}}$ for r.

$\left(x \boxed{-4}\right)^2 + \left(y \boxed{+1}\right)^2 = \boxed{5}$ Simplify.

Reflect

4. Suppose the circle with equation $(x - 2)^2 + (y + 4)^2 = 7$ is translated by $(x, y) \rightarrow (x + 3, y - 1)$. What is the equation of the image of the circle? Explain.
The center of the circle, $(2, -4)$, is translated to $(2 + 3, -4 - 1) = (5, -5)$,

and the radius does not change. Therefore, the image of the circle has

equation $(x - 5)^2 + (y - (-5))^2 = 7$ or $(x - 5)^2 + (y + 5)^2 = 7$.

PROFESSIONAL DEVELOPMENT

 Integrate Mathematical Practices

This lesson provides an opportunity to address Mathematical Practice **MP.6**, which calls for students to "communicate with precision." In this lesson, students analyze the conditions that would be sufficient to write the equation of a circle in the coordinate plane. The equation of a circle with center (h, k) and radius r is $(x - h)^2 + (y - k)^2 = r^2$. This equation follows immediately from the Distance Formula. In addition, squaring and simplifying show that every circle is the graph of an equation of the form $x^2 + y^2 + Ax + By + C = 0$. Given an equation in this form, the center and radius of the circle may be found by completing the square.

EXPLORE

Deriving the Equation of a Circle

INTEGRATE TECHNOLOGY

Students have the option of doing the Explore activity either in the book or online.

QUESTIONING STRATEGIES

? How do you find the length of a horizontal segment in the coordinate plane? Take the absolute value of the difference of the x-coordinates.

? Why do you take the absolute value to find the length of segments in the coordinate plane? Distance cannot be negative.

EXPLAIN 1

Writing the Equation of a Circle

INTEGRATE MATHEMATICAL PRACTICES
Focus on Math Connections

MP.1 Point out that the values of h and k do not change the graph of a circle but they do translate the center of the circle. The value of r does change the graph of a circle because the size of the circle depends on its radius.

QUESTIONING STRATEGIES

? Can you write the equation of a circle from a given point if the point does not lie on the circle? Explain. No, you need the center of the circle and a point on the circle to determine the radius of the circle. The radius of the circle is needed to write the equation of the circle.

EXPLAIN 2

Finding the Center and Radius of a Circle

INTEGRATE MATHEMATICAL PRACTICES

Focus on Patterns

MP.8 Remind students of the definition of a circle. Be sure students know how to graph a circle. They should plot the center first and then count units up, down, right, and left from the center equal to the length of the radius. This plots four points that lie on the circle. Then, students can use a compass to help draw the rest of the circle.

Your Turn

Write the equation of the circle with the given center and radius.

5. Center: $(4, 3)$; radius: 4

$(x - 4)^2 + (y - 3)^2 = 16$

6. Center: $(-1, -1)$; radius: $\sqrt{3}$

$(x + 1)^2 + (y + 1)^2 = 3$

⊘ Explain 2   Finding the Center and Radius of a Circle

Sometimes you may find an equation of a circle in a different form. In that case, you may need to rewrite the equation to determine the circle's center and radius. You can use the process of completing the square to do so.

Example 2   Find the center and radius of the circle with the given equation. Then graph the circle.

(A) $x^2 - 4x + y^2 + 2y = 20$

Step 1 Complete the square twice to write the equation in the form $(x - h)^2 + (y - k)^2 = r^2$.

$x^2 - 4x + (\ )^2 + y^2 + 2y + (\ )^2 = 20 + (\ )^2$ Set up to complete the square.

$x^2 - 4x + \left(\dfrac{-4}{2}\right)^2 + y^2 + 2y + \left(\dfrac{2}{2}\right)^2 = 20 + \left(\dfrac{-4}{2}\right)^2 + \left(\dfrac{2}{2}\right)^2$ Add $\left(\dfrac{-4}{2}\right)^2$ and $\left(\dfrac{2}{2}\right)^2$ to both sides.

$x^2 - 4x + 4 + y^2 + 2y + 1 = 20 + 5$ Simplify.

$(x - 2)^2 + (y + 1)^2 = 25$ Factor.

Step 2 Identify h, k, and r to determine the center and radius.

$h = 2$ $k = -1$ $r = \sqrt{25} = 5$

So, the center is $(2, -1)$ and the radius is 5.

Step 3 Graph the circle.

- Locate the center of the circle.

- Place the point of your compass at the center

- Open the compass to the radius.

- Use the compass to draw the circle.

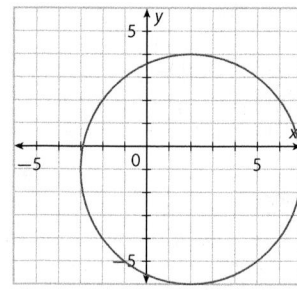

COLLABORATIVE LEARNING

Small Group Activity

To help students understand how to find the radius, center, and equation of a circle, give students graph paper and four circles cut out of transparent paper. The diameters of the circles should match the units of the grid and be whole numbers. Have students place their transparent circles on their grids, one in each of the four quadrants. Have each student find the radius, center, and equation for one of the circles. Have them conjecture how to find the equation of the circle and share their results with the group and with the class.

Ⓑ $x^2 + 6x + y^2 - 4y + 4 = 0$

Step 1 Complete the square twice to write the equation in the form $(x - h)^2 + (y - k)^2 = r^2$.

$$x^2 + 6x + \left(\boxed{\dfrac{6}{2}}\right)^2 + y^2 - 4y + \left(\boxed{\dfrac{-4}{2}}\right)^2 = -4 + \left(\boxed{\dfrac{6}{2}}\right)^2 + \left(\boxed{\dfrac{-4}{2}}\right)^2 \quad \text{Add } \left(\boxed{\dfrac{6}{2}}\right)^2 \text{ and } \left(\boxed{\dfrac{-4}{2}}\right)^2$$
to both sides.

Subtract 4 from both sides.

$$x^2 + 6x + \boxed{9} + y^2 - 4y + \boxed{4} = -4 + \boxed{13} \qquad \text{Simplify.}$$

$$\left(x \boxed{+3}\right)^2 + \left(y \boxed{-2}\right)^2 = \boxed{9} \qquad \text{Factor.}$$

Step 2 Identify h, k, and r to determine the center and radius.

$$h = \boxed{-3} \quad k = \boxed{2} \qquad r = \sqrt{\boxed{9}} = \boxed{3}$$

So, the center is $\left(\boxed{-3}, \boxed{2}\right)$ and the radius is $\boxed{3}$.

Step 3 Graph the circle.

- Locate the center of the circle.
- Place the point of your compass at the center
- Open the compass to the radius.
- Use the compass to draw the circle.

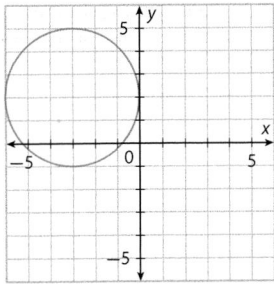

Reflect

7. How can you check your graph by testing specific points from the graph in the original equation? Give an example.

Check that points on the graph satisfy the equation. For Example 2A, $(5, 3)$ is on the graph and this point satisfies the equation: $5^2 - 4(5) + 3^2 + 2(3) = 20$.

Your Turn

8. Find the center and radius of the circle with the equation. $x^2 + 2x + y^2 - 8y + 13 = 0$. Then graph the circle.

$$x^2 + 2x + 1 + y^2 - 8y + 16 = -13 + 1 + 16$$

$$(x + 1)^2 + (y - 4)^2 = 2^2$$

Center: $(-1, 4)$, radius: 2

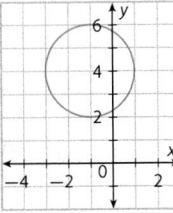

? What three values do you need to find the equation of a circle by completing the square? **the x- and y-coordinates of the center, and the length of the radius**

? How do you complete the square? **Add half the coefficient of the x-term squared and add half the coefficient of the y-term squared. Add the same quantities to the other side of the equation. Now, the equation will contain two perfect squares, one involving the variable x and one involving the variable y.**

AVOID COMMON ERRORS

Some students may say that the circle with equation $(x + 2)^2 + (y - 1)^2 = 9$ has center $(2, -1)$. It may help these students to rewrite the equation as $\left(x - (-2)\right)^2 + (y - 1)^2 = 9$ and compare this to the general equation, $(x - h)^2 + (y - k)^2 = r^2$, which has center (h, k). This may help them see that the correct center is $(-2, 1)$.

DIFFERENTIATE INSTRUCTION

Multiple Representations

Use geometry software to show students the relationship between the equation of a circle and its graph. By dragging the center of the circle to a different position, students can see how the equation changes as the position of the circle changes.

EXPLAIN 3

Writing a Coordinate Proof

INTEGRATE MATHEMATICAL PRACTICES
Focus on Critical Thinking

MP.3 Given the center of a circle and the radius, students can easily identify four points that lie on the circle. There are infinitely many points on the circle, however, and the coordinates of these points are solutions to the equation $r = \sqrt{(x-h)^2 + (y-k)^2}$, where r, h, and k are known values.

9. Find the center and radius of the circle with the equation $x^2 + y^2 + 4y = 5$. Then graph the circle.

$$x^2 + y^2 + 4y + 4 = 5 + 4$$

$$(x-0)^2 + (y+2)^2 = 3^2$$

Center $(0, -2)$, radius 3

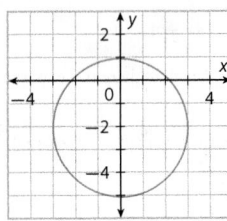

⊘ Explain 3 **Writing a Coordinate Proof**

You can use a coordinate proof to determine whether or not a given point lies on a given circle in the coordinate plane.

Example 3 **Prove or disprove that the given point lies on the given circle.**

(A) Point $(3, \sqrt{7})$ circle centered at the origin and containing the point $(-4, 0)$

Step 1 Plot a point at the origin and at $(-4, 0)$. Use these to help you draw the circle centered at the origin that contains $(-4, 0)$.

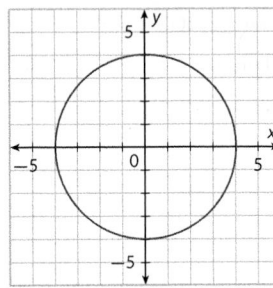

Step 2 Determine the radius: $r = 4$

Step 3 Use the radius and the coordinates of the center to write the equation of the circle.

$$(x-h)^2 + (y-k)^2 = r^2 \qquad \text{Write the equation of the circle.}$$

$$(x-0)^2 + (y-0)^2 = (4)^2 \qquad \text{Substitute 0 for } h, 0 \text{ for } k, \text{ and 4 for } r.$$

$$x^2 + y^2 = 16 \qquad \text{Simplify.}$$

Step 4 Substitute the x- and y-coordinates of the point $(3, \sqrt{7})$ in the equation of the circle to check whether they satisfy the equation of the circle.

$$(3)^2 + (\sqrt{7})^2 \stackrel{?}{=} 16 \qquad \text{Substitute 3 for } x \text{ and } \sqrt{7} \text{ for } y.$$

$$9 + 7 = 16 \qquad \text{Simplify.}$$

So, the point $(3, \sqrt{7})$ lies on the circle because the point's x- and y-coordinates satisfy the equation of the circle.

Ⓑ Point $\left(1, \sqrt{6}\right)$, circle with center $(-1, 0)$ and containing the point $(-1, 3)$

Step 1 Plot a point at $\left(\boxed{-1}, 0\right)$ and at $\left(-1, \boxed{3}\right)$. Draw the circle centered at $\left(\boxed{-1}, 0\right)$ that contains $\left(-1, \boxed{3}\right)$.

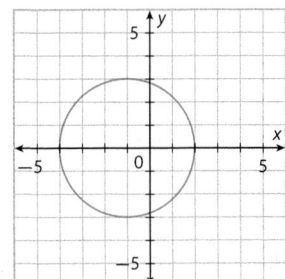

Step 2 Determine the radius: $r = \boxed{3}$

Step 3 Use the radius and the coordinates of the center to write the equation of the circle.

$(x - h)^2 + (y - k)^2 = r^2$ Write the equation of the circle.

$\left(x - \left(\boxed{-1}\right)\right)^2 + \left(y - \left(\boxed{0}\right)\right)^2 = \left(\boxed{3}\right)^2$ Substitute $\boxed{-1}$ for h, $\boxed{0}$ for k, and $\boxed{3}$ for r.

$\left(x \boxed{+1}\right)^2 + y^2 = \boxed{9}$ Simplify.

Step 4 Substitute the x- and y-coordinates of the point $\left(1, \sqrt{6}\right)$ in the equation of the circle to check whether they satisfy the equation of the circle.

$\left(\boxed{1+1}\right)^2 + \left(\boxed{\sqrt{6}}\right)^2 \overset{?}{=} \boxed{9}$ Substitute $\boxed{1}$ for x and $\boxed{\sqrt{6}}$ for y.

$\boxed{4} + \boxed{6} \neq \boxed{9}$ Simplify.

So the point $\left(1, \sqrt{6}\right)$ $\boxed{\text{does not lie}}$ on the circle because the x- and y-coordinates of the point $\boxed{\text{do not satisfy}}$ the equation of the circle.

Reflect

10. How do you know that the radius of the circle in Example 3A is 4?
The line segment joining the center, $(0, 0)$, to point $(-4, 0)$ is a radius of the circle, and
since it is horizontal, you can count squares to determine the radius.

11. Name another point with noninteger coordinates that lies on the circle in Example 3A. Explain.
Possible answer: $\left(3, -\sqrt{7}\right)$, because $3^2 + \left(-\sqrt{7}\right)^2 = 16$.

© Houghton Mifflin Harcourt Publishing Company

QUESTIONING STRATEGIES

? What steps can you use to write a coordinate proof that a point lies on a circle, given the center and radius of the circle? Sample answer: First, write the equation of the circle. Then, check to see whether the given point is a solution of the equation. If so, the point lies on the circle.

? How can you determine the radius of a circle? Sample answer: Count units on the coordinate grid, moving horizontally or vertically from the center to the circle.

ELABORATE

QUESTIONING STRATEGIES

? How do you write the equation of a circle given the center (h, k) and the radius r?
Substitute the radius, r, and the coordinates of the center (h, k) into the equation of a circle in the form $(x - h)^2 + (y - k)^2 = r^2$.

SUMMARIZE THE LESSON

? What do the different parts of an equation of a circle with the form $(x - h)^2 + (y - k)^2 = r^2$ represent? The variables x and y are the coordinates of points on the circle, and h and k give the coordinates of the center of the circle. The variable r represents the length of the radius.

Prove or disprove that the given point lies on the given circle.

12. Point $(\sqrt{18}, -4)$, circle centered at the origin and containing the point $(6, 0)$

$r = 6$

$(x - 0)^2 + (y - 0)^2 = (6)^2$

$x^2 + y^2 = 36$

$(\sqrt{18})^2 + (-4)^2 \stackrel{?}{=} 36$

$18 + 16 \neq 36$

So the point $(\sqrt{18}, -4)$ does not lie on the circle because the point's x- and y-coordinates do not satisfy the equation of the circle.

13. Point $(4, -4)$, circle with center $(1, 0)$ and containing the point $(1, 5)$

$r = 5$

$(x - 1)^2 + (y - 0)^2 = (5)^2$

$(x - 1)^2 + y^2 = 25$

$(4 - 1)^2 + (-4)^2 \stackrel{?}{=} 25$

$9 + 16 = 25$

So the point $(4, -4)$ lies on the circle because the point's x- and y-coordinates satisfy the equation of the circle.

💬 Elaborate

14. **Discussion** How is the distance formula related to the equation of a circle?
Possible answer: Given the points (x, y) and (h, k) and the distance formula. You get $d = \sqrt{(x - h)^2 + (y - k)^2}$. But if you square both sides, you get $d^2 = (x - h)^2 + (y - k)^2$, which is the same as the equation of a circle centered at the origin with radius d.

15. **Essential Question Check-In** What information do you need to know to write the equation of a circle?
You need the coordinates of the center and the radius.

© Houghton Mifflin Harcourt Publishing Company

LANGUAGE SUPPORT **EL**

Connect Vocabulary

Ask students to articulate the differences among a *chord*, a *radius*, and a *diameter*. Have students create drawings to support their explanations. Suggest that they keep the drawings to use as references.

☆ Evaluate: Homework and Practice

• Online Homework
• Hints and Help
• Extra Practice

1. Given the equation, $(x - h)^2 = (y - k)^2 = r^2$, what are the coordinates of the center?

(h, k)

Write the equation of the circle with the given center and radius.

2. center: $(0, 2)$; radius: 5

$x^2 + (y - 2)^2 = 25$

3. center: $(-1, 3)$; radius 8

$(x + 1)^2 + (y - 3)^2 = 64$

4. center: $(-4, -5)$; radius $\sqrt{2}$

$(x + 4)^2 + (y + 5)^2 = 2$

5. center: $(9, 0)$; radius $\sqrt{3}$

$(x - 9)^2 + y^2 = 3$

Find the center and radius of the circle with the given equation. Then graph the circle.

6. $x^2 + y^2 = 16$

center: $(0, 0)$; radius: 4

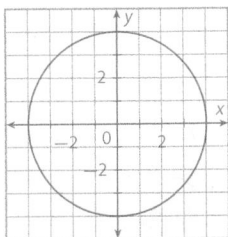

7. $x^2 - 6x + y^2 + 8y + 16 = 0$

center: $(3, -4)$; radius: 3

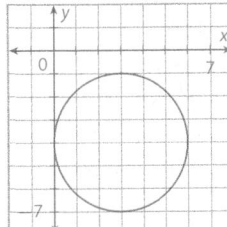

8. $x^2 - 2x + y^2 + 4y - 4 = 0$

center: $(1, -2)$; radius: 3

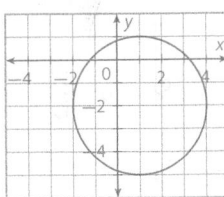

9. $x^2 - 6x + y^2 - 6y + 14 = 0$

center: $(3, 3)$; radius: 2

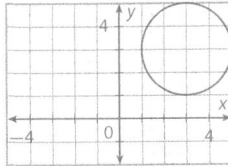

10. Prove or disprove that the point $(1, \sqrt{3})$ lies on the circle that is centered at the origin and contains the point $(0, 2)$.

The radius of the circle is 2, so its equation is $x^2 + y^2 = 4$. The point does lie on the circle, because its x- and y-coordinates satisfy the equation: $1^2 + (\sqrt{3})^2 = 1 + 3 = 4$.

EVALUATE

ASSIGNMENT GUIDE

Concepts and Skills	Practice
Explore Deriving the Equation of a Circle	Exercise 1
Example 1 Writing the Equation of a Circle	Exercises 2–5
Example 2 Finding the Center and Radius of a Circle	Exercises 6–9
Example 3 Writing a Coordinate Proof	Exercises 10–13

INTEGRATE TECHNOLOGY

Students can check circle graphs using a graphing calculator if they first write the equation in y-form. For example, to graph, $x^2 + y^2 = 9$, solve for y to get equations $y = \sqrt{9 - x^2}$ and $y = -\sqrt{9 - x^2}$, and then graph the equations. Point out to students that the graph of a circle on a graphing calculator will look like an ellipse if the window setting is not a square window.

Exercise	Depth of Knowledge (D.O.K.)	COMMON CORE Mathematical Practices
1–5	**1** Recall of Information	**MP.5** Using Tools
6–9	**2** Skills/Concepts	**MP.4** Modeling
10–13	**2** Skills/Concepts	**MP.3** Logic
14–23	**2** Skills/Concepts	**MP.2** Reasoning
24	**3** Strategic Thinking H.O.T.	**MP.4** Modeling
25	**3** Strategic Thinking H.O.T.	**MP.5** Using Tools
26	**3** Strategic Thinking H.O.T.	**MP.6** Precision

AVOID COMMON ERRORS

When students are writing the equation of a circle or when they are given the equation of a circle, they often write the incorrect signs for h and k. Point out that the standard equation of a circle includes subtraction, and that this may mean taking the opposite of the values of h and k.

INTEGRATE MATHEMATICAL PRACTICES

Focus on Math Connections

MP.1 Remind students that both h and k can be 0 in the equation of a circle, $(x - h)^2 + (y - k)^2 = r^2$. If their values are 0, then the equation can be written as $x^2 + y^2 = r^2$.

---

11. Prove or disprove that the point $\left(2, \sqrt{3}\right)$ lies on the circle that is centered at the origin and contains the point $(-3, 0)$.

The radius of the circle is 3, so its equation is $x^2 + y^2 = 9$. The point $\left(2, \sqrt{3}\right)$ does not lie on the circle because its x- and y-coordinates do not satisfy the equation:
$2^2 + \left(\sqrt{3}\right)^2 = 4 + 3 = 7 \neq 9$.

12. Prove or disprove that the circle with equation $x^2 - 4x + y^2 = -3$ intersects the y-axis.

Points on the y-axis have x-coordinate 0. Substituting $x = 0$ in the equation gives $y^2 = -3$. This equation has no real solutions, so there are no points of the form $(0, y)$ on the circle. Therefore, the circle does not intersect the y-axis.

13. Prove or disprove that the circle with equation $x^2 + y^2 - 10y = -16$ intersects the x-axis.

Points on the x-axis have y-coordinate 0. Substituting $y = 0$ in the equation gives $x^2 = 9$, so $x = \pm 3$. Therefore, the graph of the circle intersects the x-axis at both $(3, 0)$ and $(-3, 0)$.

14. The center of a circle is $(0, -8)$. The radius is 9. What is the equation of the circle? Select all that apply.

A. $x^2 + (y + 8)^2 = 3$ $(x - 0)^2 + \left(y - (-8)\right)^2 = 9^2$

B. $x^2 + (y + 8)^2 = 9$ $x^2 + (y + 8)^2 = 81$

C.) $x^2 + (y + 8)^2 = 81$ $x^2 + y^2 + 16y + 64 = 81$

D.) $x^2 + y^2 + 16y = 17$ $x^2 + y^2 + 16y = 17$

E. $x^2 + y^2 + 16y = -55$

Algebra Write the equation of each circle.

15.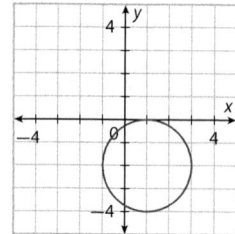

center: $(1, -2)$; radius: 2
$(x - 1)^2 + \left(y - (-2)\right)^2 = 2^2$
$(x - 1)^2 + (y + 2)^2 = 4$

16.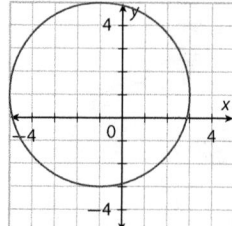

center: $(-1, 1)$; radius: 4
$\left(x - (-1)\right)^2 + (y - 1)^2 = 4^2$
$(x + 1)^2 + (y - 1)^2 = 16$

© Houghton Mifflin Harcourt Publishing Company

17. Prove or disprove that the circle with equation $x^2 + 4x + y^2 - 4y = 0$ contains the point $(0, 4)$.

The point does lie on the equation because its x- and y coordinates satisfy the equation: $0^2 + 4(0) + 4^2 - 4(4) = 0$.

18. The point $(2, n)$ lies on the circle whose equation is $(x - 3)^2 + (y + 2)^2 = 26$. Find the value of n.

$$(2 - 3)^2 + (n + 2)^2 = 26$$
$$(-1)^2 + (n + 2)^2 = 26$$
$$1 + (n + 2)^2 = 26$$
$$(n + 2)^2 = 25$$
$$n + 2 = \pm 5$$

$$n + 2 = 5 \qquad \text{or} \qquad n + 2 = -5$$
$$n = 3 \qquad\qquad\qquad n = -7$$

Determine whether each statement is true or false. If false, explain why.

19. The circle $x^2 + y^2 = 7$ has radius 7.

False; $r = \sqrt{7}$

20. The circle $(x - 2)^2 + (y + 3)^2 = 9$ passes through the point $(-1, -3)$.

True; $(-1 - 2)^2 + (-3 + 3)^2 = 9$

21. The center of the circle $(x - 6)^2 + (y + 4)^2 = 1$ lies in the second quadrant.

False; the center is $(6, -4)$, which is in the fourth quadrant

22. The circle $(x + 1)^2 + (y - 4)^2 = 4$ intersects the y-axis.

True; $\left(0, 4 \pm \sqrt{3}\right)$ lie on the y-axis and the circle

23. The equation of the circle centered at the origin with diameter 6 is $x^2 + y^2 = 36$.

False; the equation is $x^2 + y^2 = 3^2 = 9$

© Houghton Mifflin Harcourt Publishing Company

INTEGRATE MATHEMATICAL PRACTICES

Focus on Critical Thinking

MP.3 Point out that the area of a circle in the coordinate plane can be found by finding the radius of the circle with equation $(x - h)^2 + (y - k)^2 = r^2$, or $r = \sqrt{(x - h)^2 + (y - k)^2}$, and then solving for the area using the formula $A = \pi r^2$.

AVOID COMMON ERRORS

Some students may not be able to determine whether a point lies on a circle. Point out that if a point does lie on a circle, its x-and y-coordinates must satisfy the equation $(x - h)^2 + (y - k)^2 = r^2$, if the circle is translated in the coordinate plane, or they must satisfy the equation $x^2 + y^2 = r^2$, if the circle is centered at the origin.

PEER-TO-PEER DISCUSSION

Ask students to discuss with a partner how to write the equation of a circle in the coordinate plane. Have one student draw a circle on graph paper using a whole-number radius length. Ask the other student to identify the center of the circle, the length of the radius, and the equation of the circle. Then, have students switch roles and repeat the exercise several times.

JOURNAL

Have students explain how to write an equation for a circle with center $(2, 3)$ and radius 9, and to describe how they would graph the circle. Then have them graph the circle.

24. Multi-Step Carousels can be found in many different settings, from amusement parks to city plazas. Suppose that the center of a carousel is at the origin and that one of the animals on the circumference of the carousel has coordinates $(24, 32)$.

   a. If one unit of the coordinate plane equals 1 foot, what is the diameter of the carousel?

$$r = \sqrt{24^2 + 32^2} = 40$$

$$d = 2(40) = 80 \text{ units or } 80 \text{ ft}$$

   b. As the carousel turns, the animals follow a circular path. Write the equation of this circle.

$$x^2 + y^2 = 40^2$$

$$x^2 + y^2 = 1600$$

25. Critical Thinking The diameter of a circle has endpoints $(-6, 4)$ and $(0, 2)$.

   a. Write an equation for the circle in standard form.

$$d = \sqrt{(-6 - 0)^2 + (4 - 2)^2}$$

$$= \sqrt{36 + 4}$$

$$= 2\sqrt{10}$$

$$r = \frac{1}{2}d$$

$$= \frac{1}{2}(2\sqrt{10})$$

$$= \sqrt{10}$$

Center: $\left(\dfrac{-6 + 0}{2}, \dfrac{4 + 2}{2}\right) = (-3, 3)$

$$(x - h)^2 + (y - h)^2 = r^2$$

$$(x - (-3))^2 + (y - (3))^2 = (\sqrt{10})^2$$

$$(x + 3)^2 + (y - 3)^2 = 10$$

   b. Prove or disprove that the point $(0, 4)$ lies on the circle.

It does lie on the circle because $x = 0$ and $y = 4$ satisfies the equation $(x + 3)^2 + (y - 3)^2 = 10$: $(0 + 3)^2 + (4 - 3)^2 = 9 + 1 = 10$.

26. Communicate Mathematical Ideas Can a unique circle be constructed from three nonlinear points? Explain.

Yes; the three points form a triangle. The center of the circle is the intersection of the perpendicular bisectors of the sides of the triangle, which intersect in one point. This point is equidistant from the vertices of the triangle. The distance from the point to one of the vertices is the radius of the circle. The circle is circumscribed about the triangle.

Lesson Performance Task

Cell phone towers are expensive to build, so phone companies try to build as few towers as possible, while still ensuring that all of their customers are within range of a tower. The top figure represents the ranges of three towers that each serve customers within the shaded areas but leave customers outside the shaded areas. The bottom figure shows towers that are too close together. Customers between the towers are not left out, but many customers are served by two towers, a waste of the phone company's money.

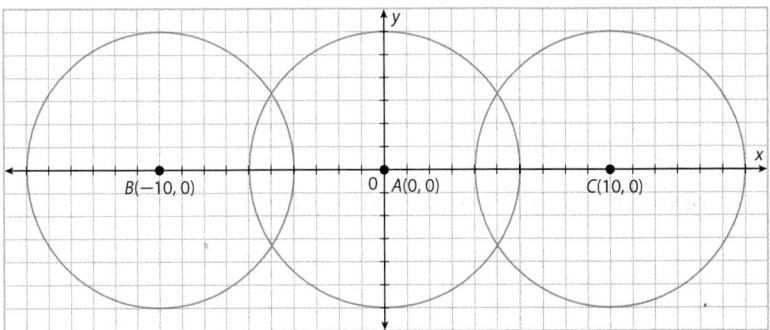

On a coordinate grid of three cell phone towers, each unit represents 1 mile. The graph of the range of Tower A has the equation $x^2 + y^2 = 36$. Tower B is 10 miles west of Tower A. Tower C is 10 miles east of Tower A.

1. Graph the ranges of the three towers. (All three have the same range.)

2. Write the equations of the ranges of Tower B and Tower C.

3. Estimate the area of the overlap between Tower A and Tower B.

4. A new tower with a range of 8 miles is being built 5 miles west and 11 miles north of Tower A. Write the equation of the range of the new tower.

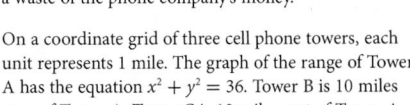
(graph with circles centered at B(−10, 0), A(0, 0), C(10, 0))

1. Check students' graphs.

2. Tower B: $(x + 10)^2 + y^2 = 36$

   Tower C: $(x - 10)^2 + y^2 = 36$

3. Estimates will vary; about 8 square miles

4. $(x + 5)^2 + (y - 11)^2 = 64$

© Houghton Mifflin Harcourt Publishing Company

AVOID COMMON ERRORS

Because the center of Circle B is at $(-10, 0)$, students may mistakenly write $(x - 10)^2$ as the first part of the equation of Circle B. Similarly, because the center of Circle C is at $(10, 0)$, they may mistakenly write $(x + 10)^2$ as the first part of the equation for Circle C. Stress that because the general equation of a circle with center at (a, b) is $(x - a)^2 + (y - b)^2 = r^2$, the $-a$ and $-b$ terms effectively change the signs of the coordinates of the center of the circle. The correct equation of Circle B is $(x + 10)^2 + y^2 = 36$ and the correct equation of Circle C is $(x - 10)^2 + y^2 = 36$.

INTEGRATE MATHEMATICAL PRACTICES
Focus on Math Connections

MP.1 Circle A in the Lesson Performance Task covers a portion of Dallas, a city with a population density of 3518 people per square mile. How many people live within the circle? Explain. About 397,675; the area of the circle is $\pi r^2 \approx 3.14(6)^2 \approx$ 113.04 mi². The total population is about 113.04 × 3518 ≈ 397,675 people.

EXTENSION ACTIVITY

In Question 3 of the Lesson Performance Task, students are asked to estimate the area of the overlapping sections of two circles. Explain to students that they can calculate the exact overlapping area using the formula

$A = 2r^2 \cos^{-1}\left(\frac{d}{2r}\right) - \frac{d}{2}\sqrt{4r^2 - d^2}$, where r is the radius of each circle and d is the distance between the centers of the circles. Have students calculate the overlapping area, explaining that $\cos^{-1}\left(\frac{d}{2r}\right)$ represents "the angle whose cosine equals $\frac{d}{2r}$" and that the angle should be expressed in radians. about 9.0 square miles

Scoring Rubric

2 points: Student correctly solves the problem and explains his/her reasoning.

1 point: Student shows good understanding of the problem but does not fully solve or explain his/her reasoning.

0 points: Student does not demonstrate understanding of the problem.

Equation of a Circle   **900**

Equation of a Parabola

Common Core Math Standards

The student is expected to:

 G-GPE.A.2

Derive the equation of a parabola given a focus and directrix.
Also G-GPE.B.4

Mathematical Practices

COMMON CORE **MP.3 Logic**

Language Objective

Explain to a partner how to find the equation of a parabola given its focus and directrix.

ENGAGE

Essential Question: How do you write the equation of a parabola that opens up or down given its focus and directrix?

If the parabola has vertex (0, 0), focus (0, p) and directrix $y = -p$, the equation of the parabola is $y = \frac{1}{4p}x^2$. If the parabola has vertex (h, k), the equation of the parabola is $(x - h)^2 = 4p(y - k)$, where $|p|$ is the distance from the vertex to the focus.

PREVIEW: LESSON PERFORMANCE TASK

View the Engage section online. Discuss the photo and how to use a parabolic function to design a half-pipe skateboard park. Then preview the Lesson Performance Task.

17.2 Equation of a Parabola

Essential Question: How do you write the equation of a parabola that opens up or down given its focus and directrix?

Resource Locker

Explore 1 Identify Points That Are Equidistant From a Point and a Line

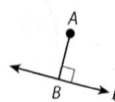

Remember that the distance from a point to a line is the length of the perpendicular segment from the point to the line. In the figure, the distance from point A to line ℓ is AB.

You will use the idea of the distance from a point to a line below.

You are given the point R and line ℓ as shown on the graph. Follow these instructions to plot a point.

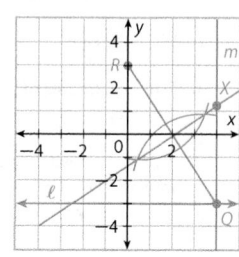

(A) Choose a point on line ℓ. Plot point Q at this location.

  Check students' work.

(B) Using a straightedge, draw a perpendicular to ℓ that passes through point Q. Label this line m.

  Check students' work.

Possible construction shown.

(C) Use the straightedge to draw $\overline{RQ}$. Then use a compass and straightedge to construct the perpendicular bisector of $\overline{RQ}$.

  Check students' work.

(D) Plot a point X where the perpendicular bisector intersects the line m.

  Check students' work.

(E) Write the approximate coordinates of point X.

  Possible answer: $\left(4, 1\frac{1}{3}\right)$

(F) Repeat Steps A–D to plot multiple points. You may want to work together with other students, plotting all of your points on each of your graphs.

  Check students' work.

© Houghton Mifflin Harcourt Publishing Company

HARDCOVER PAGES 759–766

Turn to these pages to find this lesson in the hardcover student edition.

The figure shows the construction of point Q, along with several other points constructed using the same method.

1. Explain why point X is equidistant from point R and line ℓ.

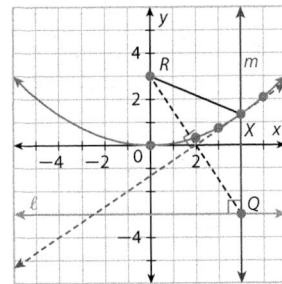

Since X is on the perpendicular bisector of $\overline{RQ}$, $XR = XQ$, and XQ is the distance from

point X to line ℓ.

2. What do you notice about the points you plotted?
The points lie along a curve in the approximate shape of a parabola.

⊘ Explore 2   Deriving the Equation of a Parabola

A **parabola** is the set of all points P in a plane that are equidistant from a given point, called the **focus**, and a given line, called the **directrix**. The **vertex** of a parabola is the midpoint of the segment, perpendicular to the directrix, that connects the focus and the directrix.

For the parabola shown, the vertex is at the origin.

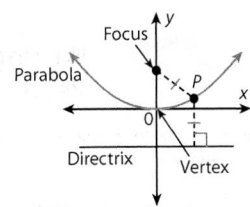

To derive the general equation of a parabola, you can use the definition of a parabola, the distance formula, and the idea that the distance from a point to a line is the length of the perpendicular segment from the point to the line.

Ⓐ Let the focus of the parabola be $F(0, p)$ and let the directrix be the line $y = -p$. Let P be a point on the parabola with coordinates (x, y).

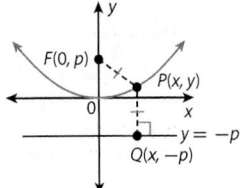

Ⓑ Let Q be the point of intersection of the perpendicular from P and the directrix. Then the coordinates of Q are _____$(x, -p)$_____.

PROFESSIONAL DEVELOPMENT

Learning Progressions

In geometry, a *locus* is a collection of points that share a property or satisfy a given condition. In previous lessons, students worked with circles. A circle may be defined as the locus of points in a plane that are a fixed distance from a given point. In this lesson, students explore parabolas. A parabola is the locus of points in a plane that are equidistant from a given point (the focus) and a given line (the directrix). Tell students that a parabola is a kind of *conic section*, which they will study in future math classes.

EXPLORE 1

Identify Points That Are Equidistant From a Point and a Line

INTEGRATE TECHNOLOGY

Students have the option of doing the Explore activity either in the book or online.

QUESTIONING STRATEGIES

? When identifying points that are equidistant from a point and a line, will everyone in the class identify the same point? Why or why not? No; there are infinitely many points that are equidistant from a point on a graph to a given line.

? What happens as you plot more and more points? The points begin to form a curve that has the shape of a parabola.

EXPLORE 2

Deriving the Equation of a Parabola

QUESTIONING STRATEGIES

? If Q is the point of intersection of the perpendicular from P, a point on the parabola, with the directrix, how do you find QP without using the distance formula? Because QP is the length of a vertical segment, you can find its length by subtracting the y-coordinates of Q and P and taking the absolute value of the result.

? How do you know the origin is a point on the parabola with focus $(0, p)$ and directrix $y = -p$? Its distance from the focus, $(0, p)$, is $|p|$, and its distance from the directrix, $y = -p$, is also $|p|$, so it is equidistant from the focus and the directrix.

Focus on Math Connections

MP.3 Review with students the connection between a parabola and quadratic functions. The equations $y = x^2$ and $y = -x^2$ represent both quadratic functions and parabolas. The equations $x = y^2$ and $x = -y^2$ represent parabolas only.

AVOID COMMON ERRORS

Some students may have difficulty deriving the equation of the parabola using the distance formula because of the algebraic steps. Remind them that a radical (square root) expression needs to be isolated on one side of the equation before solving the equation (by squaring both sides). Point out that students need to carefully find the squares of binomials to expand the squared terms.

EXPLAIN 1

Writing an Equation of a Parabola with Vertex at the Origin

INTEGRATE MATHEMATICAL PRACTICES

Focus on Math Connections

MP.1 Remind students that the equation of a parabola with vertex at $(0, 0)$ is $y = \frac{1}{4p}x^2$, where $(0, p)$ is the focus and $y = -p$ is the directrix. If $p > 0$, then the parabola opens upward. If $p < 0$, the parabola opens downward.

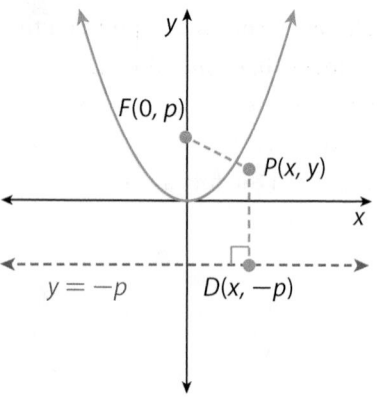

Ⓒ By the definition of a parabola, $FP = QP$.

By the distance formula, $FP = \sqrt{(x-0)^2 + (y-p)^2} = \sqrt{x^2 + (y-p)^2}$ and

$QP = \sqrt{(x-x)^2 + \left(y - (-p)\right)^2} = \sqrt{0 + (y+p)^2} = |y+p|$.

Set FP equal to QP.	$\sqrt{x^2 + (y-p)^2} = \|y+p\|$
Square both sides.	$x^2 + \underline{(y-p)^2} = \|y+p\|^2$
Expand the squared terms.	$x^2 + y^2 - \underline{2py} + p^2 = y^2 + \underline{2py} + p^2$
Subtract y^2 and p^2 from both sides.	$\underline{x^2 - 2py} = \underline{2py}$
Add $2py$ to both sides.	$x^2 = \underline{4py}$
Solve for y.	$\frac{1}{4p}x^2 = y$

Reflect

3. Explain how the value of p determines whether the parabola opens up or down.
   When p is positive, the focus is on the positive y-axis, and the directrix is a horizontal line below the x-axis, so the parabola opens up; when p is negative, the focus is on the negative y-axis, and the directrix is a horizontal line above the x-axis, so the parabola opens down.

4. Explain why the origin $(0, 0)$ is always a point on a parabola with focus $F(0, p)$ and directrix $y = -p$.
   The distance from $(0, 0)$ to $(0, p)$ is $|p|$, and the distance from $(0, 0)$ to the directrix is also $|p|$, so $(0, 0)$ is on the parabola by definition.

⊘ Explain 1   Writing an Equation of a Parabola with Vertex at the Origin

You can use the focus and directrix of a parabola to write an equation of the parabola with vertex at the origin.

Example 1   Write the equation of the parabola with the given focus and directrix. Then graph the parabola.

Ⓐ   focus: $(0, 5)$; directrix : $y = -5$

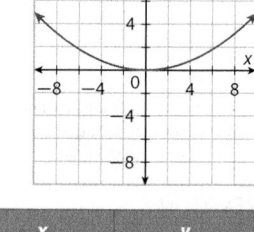

- The focus of the parabola is $(0, p)$, so $p = 5$.

  The general equation of a parabola is $y = \frac{1}{4p}x^2$.

  So, the equation of this parabola is $y = \frac{1}{4(5)}x^2$ or $y = \frac{1}{20}x^2$.

- To graph the parabola, complete the table of values. Then plot points and draw the curve.

x	y
−10	5
−5	1.25
0	0
5	1.25
10	5

COLLABORATIVE LEARNING

Small Group Activity

To help students understand how to write the equation of a parabola from a graph and with the vertex at the origin, give each group a different graph of a parabola. Have one student identify the focus and vertex, then give the value of p, where $(0, p)$ is the focus. Have another student identify the equation of the directrix and tell whether p is positive or negative. Ask a third student to find the equation of the parabola, and a fourth student to check the equation and share the results with the group.

(B) Write the equation of the parabola with focus $(0, -4)$ and directrix $y = 4$.

- The focus of the parabola is $(0, p)$, so $p = \underline{-4}$.

  The general equation of a parabola is $y = \frac{1}{4p}x^2$.

  So, the equation of this parabola is $\underline{y = -\frac{1}{16}x^2}$.

- To graph the parabola, complete the table of values. Then plot points and draw the curve.

x	y
−4	−1
−2	−0.25
0	0
2	−0.25
4	−1

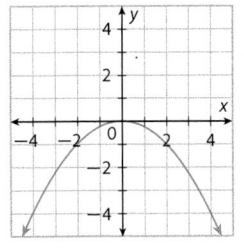

Reflect

5. Describe any symmetry in your graph from Example 1B. Why does this make sense based on the parabola's equation?

   The parabola has reflection symmetry, with the y-axis as the line of symmetry.

   This makes sense because every value of x and its opposite have the same value:

   $-\frac{1}{16}x^2 = -\frac{1}{16}(-x)^2$

Your Turn

Write the equation of the parabola with the given focus and directrix.
Then graph the parabola.

6. Parabola with focus $(0, -1)$ and directrix $y = 1$.

   The focus of the parabola is $(0, p)$, so $p = -1$.

   So, the equation of this parabola is $y = -\frac{1}{4}x^2$.

x	y
−4	−4
−2	−1
0	0
2	−1
2	−4

QUESTIONING STRATEGIES

? What does the value of p tell you about the parabola? If p is positive, the parabola opens upward. If p is negative, the parabola opens downward.

? What are the domain and range for the function described by a parabola that opens downward with its vertex at the origin? The domain is all real numbers; the range is all numbers less than or equal to zero.

DIFFERENTIATE INSTRUCTION

Critical Thinking

Help students learn how to analyze the graph of a parabola opening upward or downward to find its equation. The following steps may be useful.

1) Locate the vertex and name its coordinates (h, k).

2) Locate the focus along the line $x = h$. Then count the units from k to the focus. This is the value of $|p|$.

3) Substitute (h, k) and p into the equation $(x - h)^2 = 4p(y - k)$. If the parabola opens downward, use $-|p|$ for p. If the parabola opens upward, use $|p|$ for p.

Equation of a Parabola **904**

EXPLAIN 2

Writing the Equation of a Parabola with Vertex Not at the Origin

INTEGRATE MATHEMATICAL PRACTICES

Focus on Math Connections

MP.1 Remind students that the equation of a parabola with vertex (h, k) is $(x - h)^2 = 4p(y - k)$, where p is the distance from the vertex to the focus $(h, k + p)$, and $y = k - p$ is the equation of the directrix. If $p > 0$, then the parabola opens upward. If $p < 0$, the parabola opens downward.

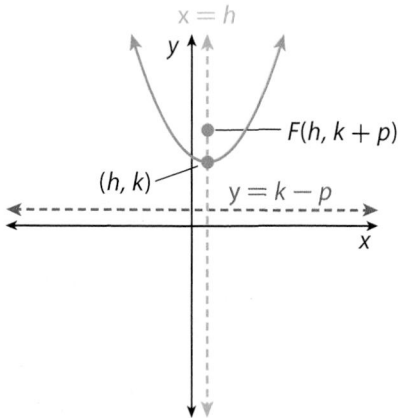

QUESTIONING STRATEGIES

What are the domain and range for the function described by a parabola that opens upward with vertex (h, k)? The domain is all real numbers; the range is all numbers greater than or equal to k.

The vertex of a parabola may not be at the origin. But given the focus and directrix of a parabola, you can find the coordinates of the vertex and write an equation of the parabola.

A parabola with vertex (h, k) that opens up or down has equation $(x - h)^2 = 4p(y - k)$ where $|p|$ is the distance from the vertex to the focus.

Example 2 Write the equation of the parabola with the given focus and directrix. Then graph the parabola.

(A) focus: $(3, 5)$, directrix: $y = -3$

* Draw the focus and the directrix on the graph.
* Draw a segment perpendicular to the directrix from the focus.
* Find the midpoint of the segment. The segment is 8 units long, so the vertex is 4 units below the focus. Then $p = 4$, and the coordinates of the vertex are $(3, 1)$.

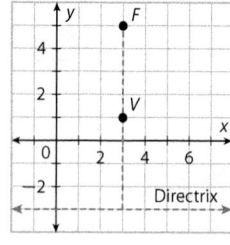

* Since the formula for a parabola is $(x - h)^2 = 4p(y - k)$, the equation of the parabola is $(x - 3)^2 = 16(y - 1)$.
* To graph the parabola, complete the table of values. Round to the nearest tenth if necessary. Then plot the points and draw the curve.

x	y
−1	2
1	1.3
2	1.1
3	1
4	1.1
6	1.6
7	2

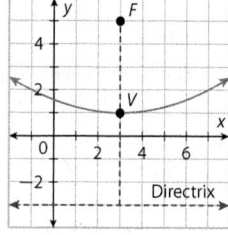

LANGUAGE SUPPORT EL

Connect Context

Help students to understand how the terms *focus* and *directrix* are used to find the equation of a parabola in the coordinate plane. Point out that both use the value of p, the distance from the vertex to the focus and to the directrix, and discuss how the terms are related in this context.

Ⓑ focus: $(-1, 4)$; directrix: $y = 6$

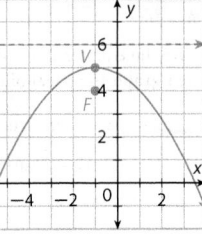

- Draw the focus and the directrix on the graph.

- Draw a segment perpendicular to the directrix through the focus.

- Find the midpoint of the segment. The segment is ___2___ units long,

  so the vertex is ___1___ units (above)/below the focus. The coordinates

  of the vertex are __(-1, 5)__. The parabola opens down

  so $p = $ ___-1___.

- Since the formula for a parabola is $(x - h)^2 = 4p(y - k)$, the equation of the parabola is

  $(x - \dfrac{(-1)}{\quad})^2 = \dfrac{-4}{\quad}(y - \dfrac{5}{\quad})$.

- To graph the parabola, complete the table of values. Round to the nearest tenth if necessary.
  Then plot the points and draw the curve.

x	y
−4	2.8
−3	4
−2	4.8
−1	5
0	4.8
1	4
2	2.8

Reflect

7. **Discussion** Without calculating, how can you determine by considering the focus and directrix of a parabola whether the parabola opens up or down?
Possible answers: All the points on a parabola are equidistant to the focus and the directrix.

Given a graph, you can observe whether the focus is above or below the directrix. Given the

coordinates (h, k) of the focus and the equation of the directrix, $y = n$, you can either draw

the focus and directrix and observe their positions, or you can compare the values k and n.

If $k > n$, the parabola opens up. If $k < n$, the parabola opens down.

© Houghton Mifflin Harcourt Publishing Company

ELABORATE

QUESTIONING STRATEGIES

? How do you write the equation of a parabola that is translated in the coordinate plane so that its vertex is (h, k)? Substitute $y - k$ for y and $x - h$ for x in $y = \frac{1}{4p}x^2$, the equation of the parabola when the vertex is $(0, 0)$, to get $(y - k) = \frac{1}{4p}(x - h)^2$. Then multiply both sides by $4p$ to get the general equation of a parabola, $(x - h)^2 = 4p(y - k)$.

SUMMARIZE THE LESSON

? Have students make chart organizers for the equations of a parabola when the vertex is $(0, 0)$ and when the vertex is (h, k). The charts should include the focus, directrix, and equation for each type of parabola. **Sample:**

Parabola with Vertex (0, 0)	
Focus	$(0, p)$
Directrix	$y = -p$
Equation	$y = \frac{1}{4p}x^2$

Parabola with Vertex (h, k)	
Focus	$(h, k + p)$
Directrix	$y = k - p$
Equation	$(x - h)^2 = 4p(y - k)$

Write the equation of the parabola with the given focus and directrix. Then graph the parabola.

8. focus: $(3, 2)$, directrix: $y = -4$

The segment from the focus to the directrix is 6 units long. The vertex is 3 units below the focus. Then $p = 3$ and $V = (3, -1)$; equation of parabola: $(x - 3)^2 = 12(y - (-1))$ or $(x - 3)^2 = 12(y + 1)$.

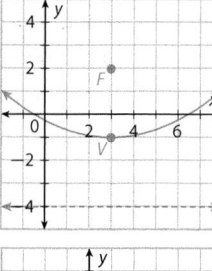

9. focus: $(2, 1)$, directrix: $y = 9$

The segment from the focus to the directrix is 8 units long. The vertex is 4 units above the focus. Then $p = -4$ and $V = (2, 5)$; equation of parabola: $(x - 2)^2 = -16(y - 5)$.

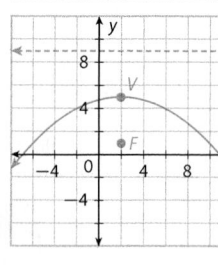

💬 Elaborate

10. What does the sign of p in the equation of a parabola tell you about the parabola?
When p is positive, the parabola opens up. When p is negative, the parabola opens down.

11. Explain how to choose appropriate x-values when completing a table of values given the equation of a parabola.
Possible answer: Choose pairs of x-values that are the same amount more and less than the x-coordinate of the focus so the parabola is centered east-west on the grid.

12. **Essential Question Check-In** How is an equation for the general parabola related to the equation for a parabola with a vertex of $(0, 0)$?
The general formula is $(x - h)^2 = 4p(y - k)$. If the vertex (h, k) is $(0, 0)$, the formula is $x^2 = 4py$, which can be written as $\frac{1}{4p}x^2 = y$.

Write the equation of the parabola with the given focus and directrix. Then graph the parabola.

1. focus: $(0, 2)$; directrix: $y = -2$

The focus of the parabola is $(0, 2)$, so $p = 2$;

equation of parabola: $y = \frac{1}{4(2)} x^2 = \frac{1}{8} x^2$.

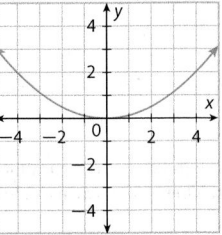

2. focus: $(0, -3)$; directrix: $y = 3$

The focus of the parabola is $(0, -3)$, so $p = -3$;

equation of parabola: $y = \frac{1}{4(-3)} x^2 = -\frac{1}{12} x^2$.

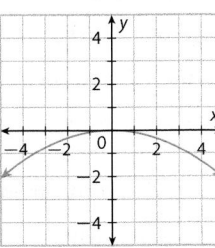

3. focus: $(0, -5)$; directrix: $y = 5$

The focus of the parabola is $(0, -5)$, so $p = -5$;

equation of parabola: $y = \frac{1}{4(-5)} x^2 = -\frac{1}{20} x^2$.

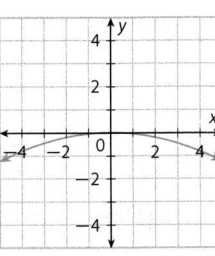

4. focus: $(0, 4)$; directrix: $y = -4$

The focus of the parabola is $(0, 4)$, so $p = 4$;

equation of parabola: $y = \frac{1}{4(4)} x^2 = \frac{1}{16} x^2$.

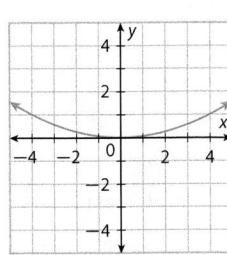

Find the directrix and focus of a parabola with the given equation.

5. $y = -\frac{1}{24} x^2$ $y = -\frac{1}{24} x^2 = \frac{1}{4(-6)} x^2$ so $p = -6$; focus: $(0, -6)$; directrix is $y = 6$.

EVALUATE

ASSIGNMENT GUIDE

Concepts and Skills	Practice
Explore 1 Identify Points That Are Equidistant from a Point and a Line	Exercise 18
Explore 2 Deriving the Equation of a Parabola	Exercise 17
Example 1 Writing an Equation of a Parabola with the Vertex at the Origin	Exercises 1-8
Example 2 Writing the Equation of a Parabola with Vertex Not at the Origin	Exercises 9–16

INTEGRATE MATHEMATICAL PRACTICES

Focus on Math Connections

MP.1 Remind students that in this lesson they are working only on parabolas that open upward or downward. Parabolas also open to the right or to the left; the equations then have the form $x = \frac{1}{4p} y^2$ or $(y - k)^2 = 4p(x - h)$.

Exercise	Depth of Knowledge (D.O.K.)	COMMON CORE Mathematical Practices
1–16	**2** Skills/Concepts	**MP.2** Reasoning
17	**2** Skills/Concepts	**MP.5** Using Tools
18	**2** Skills/Concepts	**MP.2** Reasoning
19–20	**3** Strategic Thinking	**MP.4** Modeling
21	**3** Strategic Thinking H.O.T.	**MP.7** Using Structure
22	**3** Strategic Thinking H.O.T.	**MP.7** Using Structure

AVOID COMMON ERRORS

Students might make errors finding the domain and range of a parabola. Help students see that a parabola that opens upward or downward always has a domain of all real numbers (unless it represents a real-world situation), and has a range that is greater than or equal to the y-coordinate of the vertex if the parabola opens upward, and a range that is less than or equal to the y-coordinate of the vertex if the parabola opens downward.

INTEGRATE MATHEMATICAL PRACTICES

Focus on Technology

MP.5 Encourage students to use their graphing calculators to help them understand the equations and graphs of parabolas. Remind them that they need to convert the equation of the parabola to "y-form" before graphing the equation.

© Houghton Mifflin Harcourt Publishing Company

6. $y = 2x^2$

   $y = 2x^2 = \dfrac{1}{4\left(\frac{1}{8}\right)} x^2$, so $p = \dfrac{1}{8}$; focus: $\left(0, \dfrac{1}{8}\right)$; directrix: $y = -\dfrac{1}{8}$.

7. $y = -\dfrac{1}{2} x^2$

   $y = -\dfrac{1}{2} x^2 = \dfrac{1}{4\left(-\frac{1}{2}\right)} x^2$, so $p = -\dfrac{1}{2}$; focus: $\left(0, -\dfrac{1}{2}\right)$; directrix is $y = \dfrac{1}{2}$.

8. $y = \dfrac{1}{40} x^2$

   $y = \dfrac{1}{40} x^2 = \dfrac{1}{4(10)} x^2$, so $p = 10$; focus: $(0, 10)$; directrix is $y = -10$.

Write the equation of the parabola with the given focus and directrix. Then graph the parabola.

9. focus: $(2, 3)$; directrix: $y = 7$

   The segment from the focus to the directrix is 4 units long.

   The vertex is 2 units above the focus. Then $p = -2$ and $V = (2, 5)$;

   equation of parabola: $(x - 2)^2 = -8(y - 5)$.

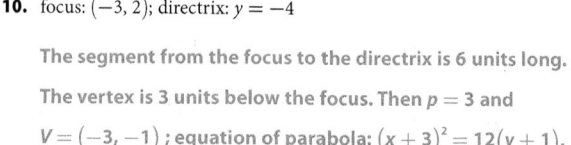

10. focus: $(-3, 2)$; directrix: $y = -4$

    The segment from the focus to the directrix is 6 units long.

    The vertex is 3 units below the focus. Then $p = 3$ and

    $V = (-3, -1)$; equation of parabola: $(x + 3)^2 = 12(y + 1)$.

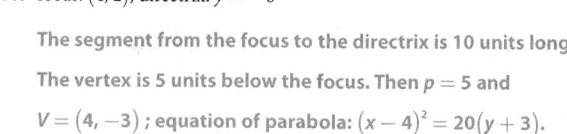

11. focus: $(4, 2)$; directrix: $y = -8$

    The segment from the focus to the directrix is 10 units long.

    The vertex is 5 units below the focus. Then $p = 5$ and

    $V = (4, -3)$; equation of parabola: $(x - 4)^2 = 20(y + 3)$.

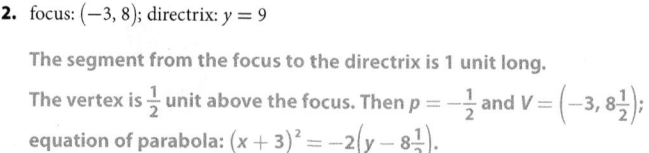

12. focus: $(-3, 8)$; directrix: $y = 9$

    The segment from the focus to the directrix is 1 unit long.

    The vertex is $\dfrac{1}{2}$ unit above the focus. Then $p = -\dfrac{1}{2}$ and $V = \left(-3, 8\dfrac{1}{2}\right)$;

    equation of parabola: $(x + 3)^2 = -2\left(y - 8\dfrac{1}{2}\right)$.

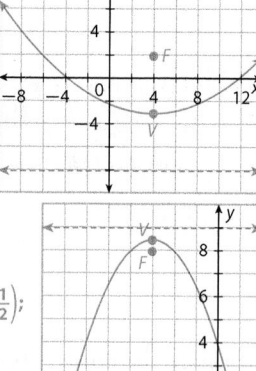

Exercise	Depth of Knowledge (D.O.K.)	COMMON CORE Mathematical Practices
23	**3** Strategic Thinking H.O.T.	**MP.4** Modeling

Find the focus and directrix of a parabola with the given equation.

13. $(x + 2)^2 = 16(y + 1)$

The value of p is $\frac{16}{4} = 4$, and the vertex is $(-2, -1)$. The parabola opens

up so the focus is 4 units above the vertex and the directrix is 4 units

below the vertex; focus is $(-2, 3)$ and directrix is $y = -5$.

14. $(x - 4)^2 = 40(y - 4)$

The value of p is $\frac{40}{4} = 10$, and the vertex is $(4, 4)$. The parabola opens

up so the focus is 10 units above the vertex and the directrix is 10 units

below the vertex; focus is $(4, 14)$ and directrix is $y = -6$.

15. $-(x + 5)^2 = y + 3.25$

The value of p is $\frac{-1}{4} = -0.25$, and the vertex is $(-5, -3.25)$. The parabola opens

down so the focus is 0.25 unit below the vertex and the directrix is 0.25 unit

above the vertex; focus is $(-5, -3.5)$ and directrix is $y = -3$.

16. $(x - 3)^2 = -24(y + 4)$

The value of p is $\frac{-24}{4} = -6$, and the vertex is $(3, -4)$. The parabola opens

down so the focus is 6 units below the vertex and the directrix is 6 units

above the vertex; focus is $(3, -10)$ and directrix is $y = 2$.

17. Make a Conjecture Complete the table by writing the equation of each parabola.
Then use a calculator to graph the equations in the same window to help you make
a conjecture: What happens to the graph of a parabola as the focus and directrix
move apart?

Focus	$(0, 1)$	$(0, 2)$	$(0, 3)$	$(0, 4)$
Directrix	$y = -1$	$y = -2$	$y = -3$	$y = -4$
Equation	$y = \frac{1}{4}x^2$	$y = \frac{1}{8}x^2$	$y = \frac{1}{12}x^2$	$y = \frac{1}{16}x^2$

As the focus and directrix move apart, the parabola is vertically compressed.

© Houghton Mifflin Harcourt Publishing Company

INTEGRATE MATHEMATICAL PRACTICES

Focus on Critical Thinking

MP.3 Point out that the algebraic properties of
parabolas include the equation of the parabola and all
of the key points related to finding the equation of
the parabola, including the vertex, focus, equation of
the directrix, and the domain and range of the graph.
On the other hand, the geometric properties of the
parabola include the nature of the graph of the
parabola, the direction in which it opens, and how to
construct the graph in the plane from the focus and
the directrix.

AVOID COMMON ERRORS

Some students may have trouble remembering where
the focus is in relation to the graph of a parabola.
Point out that the focus is always in the interior of the
parabola. So, if the parabola opens upward, the
distance from the vertex to the focus is positive and
$p > 0$. If $p < 0$, then the focus is p units down from
the vertex in its interior and the parabola opens
downward.

JOURNAL

Have students give an example of how to write the equation of a parabola that opens up or down given its focus and directrix. Ask students to include a graph with their explanation.

18. Find the length of the line segment that is parallel to the directrix of a parabola, that passes through the focus, and that has endpoints on the parabola. Explain your reasoning.

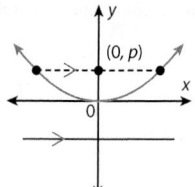

$|4p|$; the y-coordinate of each of the points is p. To find the x-coordinates, solve the equation $y = \frac{1}{4p}x^2$ for x; $x = \pm 2p$, so the endpoints are $(-2p, p)$ and $(2p, p)$.

19. **Represent Real-World Problems** The light from the lamp shown has parabolic cross sections. Write an equation for a cross section of the lamp if the bulb is 6 inches from the vertex and the vertex is placed at the origin. (Hint: The bulb of the lamp is the focus of the parabola.)

Possible answer: Suppose the lamp is pointing straight up.

The value of p is the distance from the focus to the vertex, or 6 inches. An equation of the parabola is $y = \frac{1}{24}x^2$.

20. At a bungee-jumping contest, Gavin makes a jump that can be modeled by the equation $(x - 6)^2 = 12(y - 4)$ with dimensions in feet.

   a. Which point on the path identifies the lowest point that Gavin reached? What are the coordinates of this point? How close to the ground was he?

   $(6, 4)$; for the given equation, $p = 3$, and the parabola opens up. The vertex represents the lowest point that Gavin reached. The coordinates of the vertex are $(h, k) = (6, 4)$, so Gavin's lowest point was 4 feet off the ground.

   b. **Analyze Relationships** Nicole makes a similar jump that can be modeled by the equation $(x - 2)^2 = 8(y - 8.5)$. How close to the ground did Nicole get? Did Nicole get closer to the ground than Gavin? If so, by how much?

   In the equation for Nicole's jump, $p = 2$ so the parabola opens up. The vertex has coordinates $(2, 8.5)$. This means that Nicole's lowest point was 8.5 feet off the ground, and Gavin got 4.5 feet closer to the ground than Nicole.

H.O.T. Focus on Higher Order Thinking

21. **Critical Thinking** Some parabolas open to the left or right rather than up or down. For such parabolas, if $p > 0$, the parabola opens to the right. If $p < 0$, the parabola opens to the left. What is the value of p for the parabola shown? Explain your reasoning.

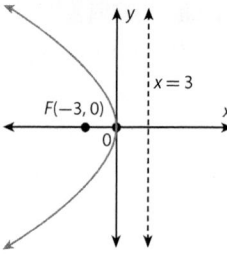

-3; Since the parabola opens to the left, $p < 0$. Because p is the distance between the focus and vertex, the value of p is -3.

22. Critical Thinking Which equation represents the parabola shown?

A. $(x - 2)^2 = -16(y - 2)$

B. $(y - 2)^2 = -16(x - 2)$

C. $(x - 2)^2 = 16(y - 2)$

D. $(y - 2)^2 = 16(x - 2)$

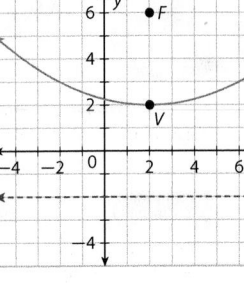

C; The vertex is $(2, 2)$, so $h = k = 2$. The distance between the focus F and the vertex V is 4, so $p = 4$. The parabola opens up, so its equation is $(x - 2)^2 = 16(y - 2)$.

23. Amber and James are lying on the ground, each tossing a ball into the air, and catching it. The paths of the balls can be represented by the following equations, with the x-values representing the horizontal distances traveled thrown and the y-values representing the heights of the balls, both measured in feet.

Amber: $-20(x - 15)^2 = y - 11.25$ James: $-24(x - 12)^2 = y - 6$

a. What are the bounds of the equations for the physical situation? Explain.

Since the ball can't be thrown below the ground or thrown a negative distance, both x and y must be positive. So, $x \geq 0$, $y \geq 0$.

b. Whose ball went higher? Which traveled the farthest horizontal distance? Justify your answers.

Amber's ball went higher; vertex for Amber: $(15, 11.25)$, vertex for James: $(12, 6)$; the y-coordinate represents the height of the ball. Since $11.25 > 6$, Amber's ball went higher. Amber's ball traveled the farthest horizontal distance. Amber's x-intercepts are $(14.25, 0)$ and $(15.75, 0)$. Her ball traveled 1.5 feet horizontally. James's x-intercepts are $(11.5, 0)$ and $(12.5, 0)$. His ball traveled 1 foot horizontally.

Lesson Performance Task

Suppose a park wants to build a new half-pipe structure for the skateboarders. To make sure all parts of the ramp are supported, the inside of the ramp needs to be equidistant from a focus point, which is at a height of 3 feet. Find the equation of the half-pipe and sketch it, along with the focus point and the directrix. Would the ramp get steeper or flatten out if the focus point height were at a height of 4 feet? Explain.

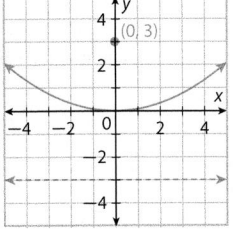

The focus point is $(0, 3)$ and the directrix is $y = -3$. The equation is $y = \frac{1}{12}x^2$. If the focus were at a height of 4 feet, the focus point would change to $(0, 4)$, which would make the equation $y = \frac{1}{16}x^2$.

This would cause the ramp to flatten out.

INTEGRATE MATHEMATICAL PRACTICES

Focus on Technology

MP.5 Students can use their graphing calculators to see how changing the coefficient of x^2 in the standard form of a parabola affects the graph.

AVOID COMMON ERRORS

Often students think that p is the reciprocal of the coefficient of x^2. Remind students to set the coefficient of x^2 equal to $\frac{1}{4p}$ when solving for p.

EXTENSION ACTIVITY

Suppose instead the park staff want to build a half-pipe with height equal to 4 feet and width equal to 12 feet. Have students find the equation for this half-pipe, the focus, and the directrix. Ask students to compare the ramp of this half-pipe to the original design. Equation: $y = \frac{1}{9}x^2$, focus: $(0, 2.25)$, directrix: $y = -2.25$; it is steeper.

Scoring Rubric

2 points: Student correctly solves the problem and explains his/her reasoning.

1 point: Student shows good understanding of the problem but does not fully solve or explain his/her reasoning.

0 points: Student does not demonstrate understanding of the problem.

Equation of a Parabola   **912**

Study Guide Review

ASSESSMENT AND INTERVENTION

Assign or customize module reviews.

MODULE PERFORMANCE TASK

COMMON
CORE

Mathematical Practices: MP.1, MP.3, MP.4, MP.5, MP.6
G-GPE.A.1

SUPPORTING STUDENT REASONING

Students should begin this problem by focusing on what information they will need. Here are some questions students might have:

- **What is the "range" of a helicopter?** The range is the greatest distance the helicopter can fly from its home base. A helicopter with a range of 290 nautical miles and a home base at SFO can search a circular region with its center at SFO and a radius of 290 nautical miles.

- **What is a nautical mile?** A nautical mile is a unit of distance used primarily by air and sea navigators, and should be distinguished from the more familiar mile, which is called a statute mile or land mile. One nautical mile is approximately equal to 1.15 statute miles.

Equations of Circles and Parabolas

MODULE
17

Essential Question: How can you use equations of circles and parabolas to solve real-world problems?

Key Vocabulary
circle *(círculo)*
parabola *(parábola)*
focus *(foco)*
directrix *(directriz)*

KEY EXAMPLE	(Lesson 17.1)

Find the center and radius of the circle with the equation $x^2 + 2x + y^2 - 6y = 6$.

$x^2 + 2x + (\ )^2 + y^2 - 6y + (\ )^2 = 6 + (\ )^2$ Set up to complete the square.

$x^2 + 2x + \left(\frac{2}{2}\right)^2 + y^2 - 6y + \left(\frac{-6}{2}\right)^2 = 6 + \left(\frac{2}{2}\right)^2 + \left(\frac{-6}{2}\right)^2$ Add $\left(\frac{2}{2}\right)^2$ and $\left(\frac{-6}{2}\right)^2$ to both sides.

$x^2 + 2x + 1 + y^2 - 6y + 9 = 6 + 10$ Simplify.

$(x + 1)^2 + (y - 3)^2 = 16$ Factor.

$h = -1, k = 3, r = \sqrt{16} = 4$ Identify h, k, and r to determine the center and radius.

The center is $(-1, 3)$ and the radius is 4.

KEY EXAMPLE	(Lesson 17.2)

Find the focus and directrix of the parabola with the equation $y = -\frac{1}{12}x^2$.

$h = 0, k = 0, p = -3$ Use the general equation $y - k = \frac{1}{4p}(x - h)^2$ to identify h, k, and p.

focus: $(0, -3)$ The vertex is at $(0, 0)$, so the focus is at $(0, p)$.

directrix: $y = 3$ The vertex is at $(0, 0)$, so the directrix is $y = -p$.

KEY EXAMPLE	(Lesson 17.2)

Find the equation of the parabola with focus $(1, 6)$ and directrix $y = 2$.

vertex: $(1, 4)$ The vertex is the midpoint of the line through the focus and perpendicular to the directrix.

$h = 1, k = 4, p = 2$ Identify h, k, and p.

$y - 4 = \frac{1}{8}(x - 1)^2$ Substitute h, k, and p in the general equation $y - k = \frac{1}{4p}(x - h)^2$

The equation of the parabola is $y - 4 = \frac{1}{8}(x - 1)^2$.

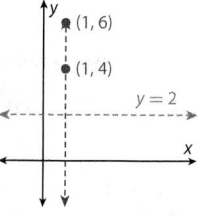

SCAFFOLDING SUPPORT

- Students will need to research the latitude-longitude coordinates of LAX and SFO. LAX is located at approximately 33.9° N, 118.4° W. SFO is located at approximately 37.8° N, 122.4° W.

- Students will also need to research methods for converting between nautical miles and degrees of latitude and longitude. One degree of longitude at the locations in this task is approximately equal to 50 nautical miles. One degree of latitude is equal to 60 nautical miles.

EXERCISES

Find the center and radius of the circle with the given equation. *(Lesson 17.1)*

1. $(x - 3)^2 + (y + 5)^2 = 49$

center: $(3, -5)$; radius: 7

2. $(x + 8.5)^2 + y^2 = 75$

center: $(-8.5, 0)$; radius: $5\sqrt{3}$

3. $x^2 + 6x + y^2 - 2y = 15$

center: $(-3, 1)$; radius: 5

4. $x^2 - 18x + y^2 - 18y + 53 = 0$

center: $(9, 9)$; radius: $\sqrt{109}$

Find the focus, vertex, and directrix of the parabola with the given equation. *(Lesson 17.2)*

5. $y = \frac{1}{32}x^2$

focus: $(0, 8)$; vertex $(0, 0)$;
directrix: $y = -8$

6. $y + 3 = -\frac{1}{2}(x + 5)^2$

focus: $(-5, -3.5)$; vertex $(-5, -3)$;
directrix: $y = -2.5$

Find the equation of the parabola with the given focus and directrix. *(Lesson 17.2)*

7. focus $(-2, 3)$; directrix $y = -5$

$y + 1 = \frac{1}{16}(x + 2)^2$

8. focus $(5, -4)$; directrix $y = 8$

$y - 2 = -\frac{1}{24}(x - 5)^2$

MODULE PERFORMANCE TASK

Rescue at Sea

Radio contact with a sailboat off the coast of California has been lost. The craft's last known position was 35.5° North, 123.7° West. The Coast Guard is mounting a search-and-rescue operation from either Los Angeles International Airport (LAX), located at 33.9° N, 118.4° W; San Francisco International Airport (SFO), located at 37.8° N, 122.4° W; or both. The Coast Guard will use H-65 helicopters with ranges of approximately 290 nautical miles.

Should helicopters be flown from LAX, SFO, or both?

Start by listing in the space below the information you will need to solve the problem. Then use your own paper to work on the task. Use numbers, words, or algebra to explain how you reached your conclusion.

DISCUSSION OPPORTUNITIES

- What is the significance of the statement that the sailboat's last *known* position was 35.5° North, 123.7° W? The sailboat may have drifted or been sailed a considerable distance from that position by the time the helicopters get there. Therefore, they may have to search a wide area around that location.

- Is a 1-degree-by-1-degree zone on a globe a square? Explain. No; using the rescue area as an example, 1 degree of longitude measures about 50 nautical miles, while 1 degree of latitude measures about 60 nautical miles.

SAMPLE SOLUTION

A helicopter based at LAX can search a circular region with a radius of 290 nautical miles. One degree of longitude in this region measures approximately 50 nautical miles, so the circular region that can be searched has a radius of about $290 \div 50 = 5.8$ degrees. That means that the equation of the circular region a helicopter based at LAX $(-118.4, 33.9)$ can cover is:

$$(x + 118.4)^2 + (y - 33.9)^2 = (5.8)^2$$

The equation of the circular region a helicopter based at SFO $(-122.4, 37.8)$ can cover is:

$$(x + 122.4)^2 + (y - 37.8)^2 - (5.8)^2$$

Graphically:

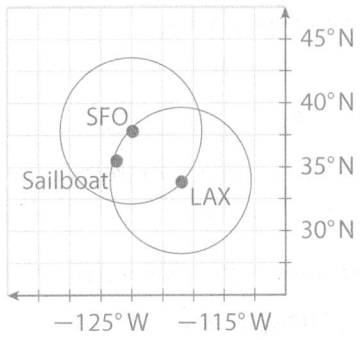

The last known location of the sailboat was at the extreme edge of an LAX-based helicopter's range. Given that the helicopter must also make allowances for returning to shore, LAX is not a good base for this mission. SFO-based helicopters, on the other hand, can easily reach the last known location and locations considerably beyond, and still have plenty of fuel to return to shore.

Assessment Rubric

2 points: Student correctly solves the problem and explains his/her reasoning.

1 point: Student shows good understanding of the problem but does not fully solve or explain his/her reasoning.

0 points: Student does not demonstrate understanding of the problem.

Ready to Go On?

ASSESS MASTERY

Use the assessment on this page to determine if students have mastered the concepts and standards covered in this module.

ASSESSMENT AND INTERVENTION

Access Ready to Go On? assessment online, and receive instant scoring, feedback, and customized intervention or enrichment.

ADDITIONAL RESOURCES

Response to Intervention Resources

- Reteach Worksheets

Differentiated Instruction Resources

- Reading Strategies **EL**
- Success for English Learners **EL**
- Challenge Worksheets

Assessment Resources

- Leveled Module Quizzes

915 Module 17

17.1–17.2 Equation of Circles and Parabolas

- Online Homework
- Hints and Help
- Extra Practice

Solve. Round answers to the nearest tenth. *(Lessons 17.1, 17.2)*

1. Find the center and radius of the circle $x^2 + 4x + y^2 - 2y - 4 = 0$.

center: $(-2, 1)$; radius: 3

2. Find the focus, vertex, and directrix of the parabola with the equation $y = (x - 8)^2 - 6$

focus: $(8, -5.75)$; vertex: $(8, -6)$; directrix: $y = -6.25$

3. A circle has its center at $(-2, 4)$ and a radius of $5\sqrt{2}$. Does the point $(3, -1)$ lie on the circle? Explain.

Yes; sample answer: The equation of the circle is $(x + 2)^2 + (y - 4)^2 = 50$. The point $(3, -1)$ satisfies the equation: $(3 + 2)^2 + (-1 - 4)^2 = 25 + 25 = 50$. So $(3, -1)$ is on the circle.

4. Does the graph of the parabola $y = -\frac{1}{100}x^2$ open upward or downward? Explain.

Downward; sample answer: The focus is $(0, -25)$. The directrix is $y = 25$. The directrix is above the focus, so the parabola opens downward.

5. A new cellular phone tower services all phones within a 17 mile radius. Doreen lives 15 miles east and 8 miles south of the tower. Is she within the area serviced by the tower? Explain. *(Lesson 17.2)*

Yes; sample answer: The range of the tower can be modeled by a circle with a radius of 17 and center at the origin. The equation of the circle is $x^2 + y^2 = 17^2 = 289$. Doreen lives at the point $(15, -8)$, which is on the circle: $15^2 + (-8)^2 = 225 + 64 = 289$.

ESSENTIAL QUESTION

6. What information about a circle and a parabola do you need in order to draw their graphs on the coordinate plane?

Sample answer: To draw a circle you need to know the radius r and the center (h, k). The equation of the circle is $(x - h)^2 + (y - k)^2 = r^2$. To draw a parabola you need to know the vertex (h, k) and p, which equals half the distance from the focus to the directrix. The equation of the parabola is $y - k = \frac{1}{4p}(x - h)^2$.

COMMON CORE ## Common Core Standards

Lesson	Items	Content Standards	Mathematical Practices
17.1	1	G-GPE.A.1, G-GPE.B.4	MP.2
17.2	2	G-GPE.A.2, G-GPE.B.4	MP.1
17.1	3	G-GPE.A.1, G-GPE.B.4	MP.6
17.2	4	G-GPE.A.2, G-GPE.B.4	MP.6
17.1	5	G-GPE.A.1	MP.6

MODULE 17
MIXED REVIEW

Assessment Readiness

1. The graph of the equation $x^2 + 6x + y^2 - 16y = -9$ is a circle. Choose True or False for each statement.
   - **A.** The center of the circle is $(3, -8)$.   ○ True ● False
   - **B.** The circle is tangent to the x-axis.   ● True ○ False
   - **C.** The circle has a radius of 64.   ○ True ● False

2. Consider the graph of the parabola $y = x^2 + 4$. Select Yes or No for A–C.
   - **A.** The vertex is $(0, 4)$ ● Yes ○ No
   - **B.** The parabola opens upward.   ● Yes ○ No
   - **C.** The directrix is $y = -4.25$.   ○ Yes ● No

3. An engineer drew the graph of a new tire on a coordinate plane. The equation of the tire was $x^2 + y^2 - 26y = 0$. How many feet will the tire roll in 100 complete revolutions? Explain.

   About 681 ft; sample answer: The graph of the equation of the tire is a circle with radius 13 inches. The circumference of the tire equals $2\pi r$ for $r = 13$ inches, or about 81.68 inches. In 100 revolutions, the tire will roll $100 \times 81.68 = 8168$ inches, or $8168 \div 12 \approx 681$ feet.

4. Find the points of intersection of the circle $x^2 + y^2 = 25$ and the parabola $y = x^2 - 5$. Explain how you found the points.

   Sample answer: Solving the equation of the circle for x^2 gives $x^2 = 25 - y^2$. Substitute this in the equation of the parabola: $y = 25 - y^2 - 5$. Rewrite and simplify this equation as the quadratic equation: $y^2 + y - 20 = 0$. Now factor and solve for y: $(y + 5)(y - 4) = 0$. The solution is $y = 4$ or $y = -5$. Substituting $y = 4$ in the equation $y = x^2 - 5$ gives $x = \pm 3$. So two points of intersection are $(3, 4)$ and $(-3, 4)$. Substituting $y = -5$ in the same equation gives $x = 0$. This gives one more point of intersection, $(0, -5)$. So the points of intersection are $(0, -5)$, $(3, 4)$, and $(-3, 4)$.

© Houghton Mifflin Harcourt Publishing Company

MIXED REVIEW
Assessment Readiness

ASSESSMENT AND INTERVENTION

Assign ready-made or customized practice tests to prepare students for high-stakes tests.

ADDITIONAL RESOURCES

Assessment Resources

- Leveled Module Quizzes: Modified, B

AVOID COMMON ERRORS

Item 4 Some students will attempt to graph these functions on the calculator but will only see one side of the circle. Remind the students that, when graphing a circle, both the negative and positive square roots need to be entered into the calculator as two different equations.

COMMON CORE **Common Core Standards**

Lesson	Items	Content Standards	Mathematical Practices
17.1	1	**G-GPE.A.1**	**MP.6**
17.2	2	**G-GPE.A.2**	**MP.6**
17.1, 16.1	3*	**G-GPE.A.1**	**MP.3**
17.1	4*	**G-GPE.A.1, G-GPE.A.2**	**MP.3**

* Item integrates mixed review concepts from previous modules or a previous course.

MIXED REVIEW
Assessment Readiness

ASSESSMENT AND INTERVENTION

Assign ready-made or customized practice tests to prepare students for high-stakes tests.

ADDITIONAL RESOURCES

Assessment Resources

- Leveled Unit Tests: Modified, A, B, C
- Performance Assessment

AVOID COMMON ERRORS

Item 2 Some students may be led astray by the information that *ABCD* is inscribed in a circle. Point out that sometimes information is given in a problem that is not needed when finding the solution.

UNIT 6 MIXED REVIEW
Assessment Readiness

- Online Homework
- Hints and Help
- Extra Practice

1. Determine whether each arc is a minor arc, a major arc, or a semicircle.
   Select the correct answer for each arc.
   A. $\overarc{AB}$ (Minor Arc)   Major Arc   Semicircle
   B. $\overarc{ABE}$ Minor Arc   Major Arc   (Semicircle)
   C. $\overarc{ADB}$ Minor Arc   (Major Arc)   Semicircle

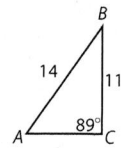

2. Quadrilateral *ABCD* is inscribed in a circle with angle measures $m\angle A = (11x - 8)°$, $m\angle B = (3x^2 + 1)°$, $m\angle C = (15x + 32)°$, and $m\angle D = (2x^2 - 1)°$. Are each of the following measures of the quadrilateral's angles?
   Select Yes or No for each statement.
   A. $m\angle A = 135°$ ○ Yes ● No
   B. $m\angle B = 109°$ ● Yes ○ No
   C. $m\angle C = 227°$ ○ Yes ● No
   D. $m\angle D = 71°$ ● Yes ○ No

3. $\triangle ABC$ and $\triangle DEF$ are congruent.
   Select True or False for each statement.

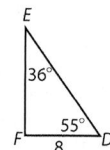

   A. $m\angle F = 91°$ ○ True ● False
   B. $m\angle A = 55°$ ● True ○ False
   C. $EF = 11$ ● True ○ False

4. Determine whether the vertex of $\angle 1$ is on the circle, inside the circle, or outside the circle given its measure and the measure of its intercepted arc(s).
   Select the correct answer for each set of angle measures.
   A. $m\angle 1 = 58°$, $m\overarc{2} = 85°$, $m\overarc{3} = 31°$ On circle   (Inside circle)   Outside circle
   B. $m\angle 1 = 52°$, $m\overarc{2} = 104°$ (On circle)   Inside circle   Outside circle
   C. $m\angle 1 = 27°$, $m\overarc{2} = 85°$, $m\overarc{3} = 31°$ On circle   Inside circle   (Outside circle)

© Houghton Mifflin Harcourt Publishing Company

COMMON CORE **Common Core Standards**

Items	Content Standards	Mathematical Practices
1	G-CO.A.1	MP.2, MP.7
2	G-C.A.2	MP.2, MP.7
3*	G-CO.B.7	MP.2, MP.7
4	G-C.A.2	MP.2, MP.7
5	G-C.A.4	MP.2, MP.7

* Item integrates mixed review concepts from previous modules or a previous course.

5. Are each of the following lengths of chords in the circle?

Select Yes or No for each statement.

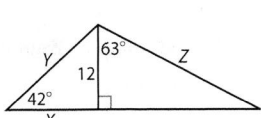

- **A.** $AC = 13.5$ ● Yes   ○ No
- **B.** $EF = 7.1$ ○ Yes   ● No
- **C.** $BF = 2.9$ ○ Yes   ● No

6. Are each of the following lengths of the segments in the triangle?

Select Yes or No for each statement.

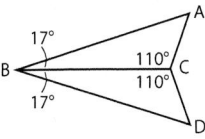

- **A.** $x = 13.3$ ● Yes   ○ No
- **B.** $y = 16.1$ ○ Yes   ● No
- **C.** $z = 13.5$ ○ Yes   ● No

7. Given that $\triangle ABC$ is a right triangle, determine if it is a special right triangle.

Select Yes or No for each statement.

- **A.** $AC = BC = 3\sqrt{2}$ and $AB = 6$ ● Yes   ○ No
- **B.** $AC = BC = 5\sqrt{2}$ and $AB = 10$ ● Yes   ○ No
- **C.** $m\angle A = 30°$ ● Yes   ○ No

8. Renee is designing a logo for an airline. She starts by making a figure with angle measures as shown. She measures $\overline{AB}$ and finds that the length of the segment is 5 inches. Can she determine the length of $\overline{DB}$ without measuring? If so, explain how. If not, explain why not.

Yes; $\triangle ABC \cong \triangle DBC$ by the ASA Triangle Congruence Theorem. $\overline{AB}$ and $\overline{DB}$ are corresponding parts, and corresponding parts of congruent triangles are congruent, so she can conclude that $DB = 5$ inches.

9. A car tire has a diameter of 21.3 inches. What is the circumference and the area of the tire?

$$C = 2\pi r \qquad\qquad A = \pi r^2$$
$$= 2\pi\left(\frac{21.3}{2}\right) \qquad = \pi\left(\frac{23.1}{2}\right)^2$$
$$= 21.3\pi \qquad\qquad = 133.4025\pi$$
$$\approx 66.9 \text{ in.} \qquad\qquad \approx 419.1 \text{ in}^2$$

PERFORMANCE TASKS

There are three different levels of performance tasks:

* **Novice:** These are short word problems that require students to apply the math they have learned in straightforward, real-world situations.

** **Apprentice:** These are more involved problems that guide students step-by-step through more complex tasks. These exercises include more complicated reasoning, writing, and open ended elements.

*****Expert:** These are open-ended, nonroutine problems that, instead of stepping the students through, ask them to choose their own methods for solving and justify their answers and reasoning.

COMMON CORE   Common Core Standards

Items	Content Standards	Mathematical Practices
6*	G-SRT.B.4	MP.2, MP.7
7*	G-SRT.C.8	MP.4
8	G-CO.B.7	MP.6
9	G-GMD.A.1	MP.1

* Item integrates mixed review concepts from previous modules or a previous course.

SCORING GUIDES

Item 10 (2 points)   Award the student 1 point for the correct angle of 62° for the left footpath, and 1 point for the angle of 118° for the right footpath.

Item 11 (6 points)

2 points for correct area

2 points for correct fraction

2 points for explanation

Item 12 (6 points)

2 points for correct paint cost

2 points for correct fencing cost

2 points for explanation

Performance Tasks

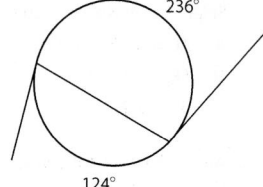

★**10.** A city planner is designing a bridge to cross a circular lake in the park. There will be two footpaths, both tangent to the lake, that connect to each side of the bridge. At what angles do the footpaths connect with the bridge?

$\frac{1}{2}(124°) = 62°$

The left footpath connects with the bridge at a 62° angle.

$\frac{1}{2}(236°) = 118°$

The right footpath connects with the bridge at a 118° angle.

★★**11.** Nestor cuts a cake with a 12-inch diameter. One of the pieces he cuts has a central angle of 24°. What is the area of the slice of cake? What fraction of the entire cake is this? Explain.

The total area of the cake is πr^2, and the area of the slice is $\frac{24°}{360°} \cdot \pi r^2 = \frac{12\pi}{5}$ in². Dividing this by the area of the entire cake is $36\pi = \frac{1}{15}$ of the cake.

★★★**12.** Jeanine's swimming pool has a diameter of 27 feet. Surrounding the pool is a deck that extends 5 feet from the edges of the pool. Jeanine wants to paint the deck and then put a fence around it. Paint costs $0.85 per square foot and fencing costs $8.25 per foot. How much will it cost Jeanine to paint the deck and add fencing? Explain how you found your answer.

The area of the deck is the combined area of the deck and pool, minus the area of the pool. The radius of the combined area is $\frac{27}{2} + 5 = 18.5$ ft, and the combined area is $\pi(18.5)^2 = 342.25\pi$. The area of the pool is $\pi(13.5)^2 = 182.25\pi$, so the area of the deck is $342.25\pi - 182.25\pi = 160\pi$ ft². The cost of the paint is $(160\pi \text{ ft}^2)(\$0.85/\text{ft}^2) = \$427.26$. The cost of adding fencing around the deck is the cost of the fencing per foot times the circumference of the deck, which is $\pi(27 + 5 + 5)\text{ft} \times (\$8.25/\text{ft}) = 37\pi(\$8.25) = \$958.98$. So, to paint the deck and add fencing would be $\$427.26 + \$958.98 = \$1386.24$.

© Houghton Mifflin Harcourt Publishing Company

Astronomer During a partial solar eclipse, the moon aligns with the sun and Earth such that it partially covers the sun from view on a circular area on Earth's surface with a radius of 130 kilometers (km). The lines tangent to both the moon and this area meet at a 144° angle. What is the measure and length of the arc on the area in which a person on Earth will be able to witness a partial eclipse?

Use the Tangent-Secant Exterior Angle Measure Theorem to find the measure of the arc.

$$144° = \frac{1}{2}\left(x - (360° - x)\right)$$

$$144° = \frac{1}{2}(2x - 360°)$$

$$144° = x - 180°$$

$$324° = x$$

$$360° - 324° = 36°$$

The measure of the arc is 36°.

Use the formula for arc length to find the length of the arc.

$$s = \frac{36°}{360°} \cdot 2\pi(130 \text{ km})$$

$$= 26\pi \text{ km}$$

$$\approx 81.7 \text{ km}$$

The length of the arc is approximately 81.7 kilometers.

© Houghton Mifflin Harcourt Publishing Company

MATH IN CAREERS

Astronomer In this Unit Performance Task, students can see how an astronomer uses mathematics on the job.

For more information about careers in mathematics as well as various mathematics appreciation topics, visit the American Mathematical Society http://www.ams.org

SCORING GUIDES

Task (6 points)

3 points for the correct measure of the arc

3 points for the correct arc length

Measurement and Modeling in Two and Three Dimensions

CONTENTS

Unit Pacing Guide

45-Minute Classes

Module 18

DAY 1	DAY 2	DAY 3	DAY 4	DAY 5
Lesson 18.1	Lesson 18.1	Lesson 18.2	Lesson 18.3	Lesson 18.4

DAY 6				
Module Review and Assessment Readiness				

Module 19

DAY 1	DAY 2	DAY 3	DAY 4	DAY 5
Lesson 19.1	Lesson 19.1	Lesson 19.2	Lesson 19.3	Lesson 19.4

DAY 6				
Module Review and Assessment Readiness				

Module 20

DAY 1	DAY 2	DAY 3	DAY 4	DAY 5
Lesson 20.1	Lesson 20.1	Lesson 20.2	Lesson 20.2	Lesson 20.3

DAY 6	DAY 7	DAY8		
20.3	Module Review and Assessment Readiness	Unit Review and Assessment Readiness		

90-Minute Classes

Module 18

DAY 1	DAY 2	DAY 3
Lesson 18.1	Lesson 18.2 Lesson 18.3	Lesson 18.4 Module Review and Assessment Readiness

Module 19

DAY 1	DAY 2	DAY 3
Lesson 19.1	Lesson 19.2 Lesson 19.3	Lesson 19.4 Module Review and Assessment Readiness

Module 20

DAY 1	DAY 2	DAY 3	DAY 4
Lesson 20.1	Lesson 20.2	Lesson 20.3	Module Review and Assessment Readiness Unit Review and Assessment Readiness

Program Resources

PLAN

HMH Teacher App

Access a full suite of teacher resources online and offline on a variety of devices. Plan present, and manage classes, assignments, and activities.

ePlanner
Easily plan your classes, create and view assignments, and access all program resources with your online, customizable planning tool.

Professional Development Videos

Authors Juli Dixon and Matt Larson model successful teaching practices and strategies in actual classroom settings.

QR Codes
Scan with your smart phone to jump directly from your print book to online videos and other resources.

Teacher's Edition

Support students with point-of-use Questioning Strategies, teaching tips, resources for differentiated instruction, additional activities, and more.

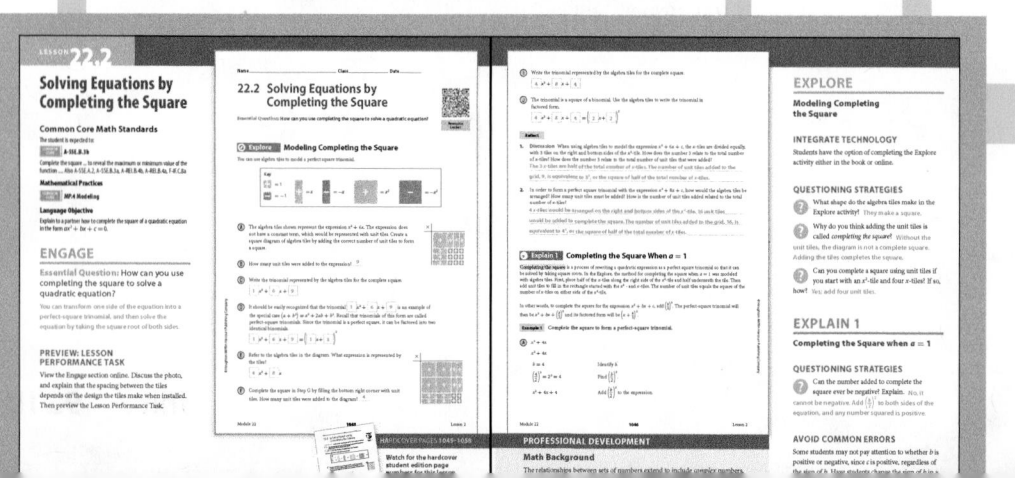

ENGAGE AND EXPLORE

Real-World Videos Engage students with interesting and relevant applications of the mathematical content of each module.

Explore Activities
Students interactively explore new concepts using a variety of tools and approaches.

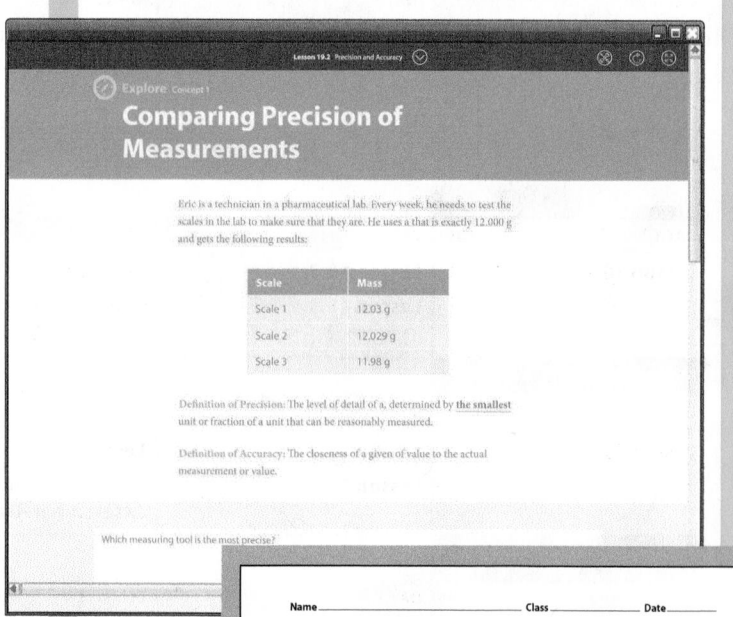

Comparing Precision of Measurements

Eric is a technician in a pharmaceutical lab. Every week, he needs to test the scales in the lab to make sure that they are. He uses a that is exactly 12.000 g and gets the following results:

Scale	Mass
Scale 1	12.03 g
Scale 2	12.029 g
Scale 3	11.98 g

Definition of Precision: The level of detail of a, determined by **the smallest** unit or fraction of a unit that can be reasonably measured.

Definition of Accuracy: The closeness of a given of value to the actual measurement or value.

Which measuring tool is the most precise?

Name _____ Class _____ Date _____

22.2 Solving Equations by Completing the Square

Essential Question: How can you use completing the square to solve a quadratic equation?

A-SSE.B.3b Complete the square ... to reveal the maximum or minimum value of the function ... Also A-SSE.A.2, A-SSE.B.3a, A-REI.B.4b, A-REI.B.4a, F-IF.C.8a

Resource Locker

Explore   Modeling Completing the Square

You can use algebra tiles to model a perfect square trinomial.

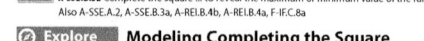

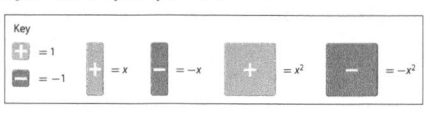

(A) The algebra tiles shown represent the expression $x^2 + 6x$. The expression does not have a constant term, which would be represented with unit tiles. Create a square diagram of algebra tiles by adding the correct number of unit tiles to form a square.

(B) How many unit tiles were added to the expression? _____

(C) Write the trinomial represented by the algebra tiles for the complete square.

$\boxed{} x^2 + \boxed{} x + \boxed{}$

(D) It should be easily recognized that the trinomial $\boxed{} x^2 + \boxed{} x + \boxed{}$ is an example of

TEACH

Math On the Spot video tutorials, featuring program author Dr. Edward Burger, accompany every example in the textbook and give students step-by-step instructions and explanations of key math concepts.

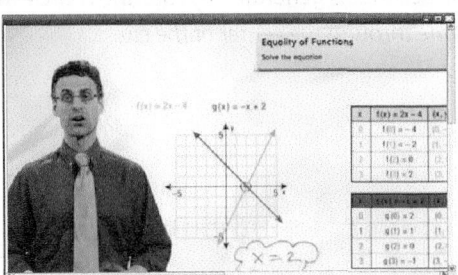

Interactive Teacher Edition

Customize and present course materials with collaborative activities and integrated formative assessment.

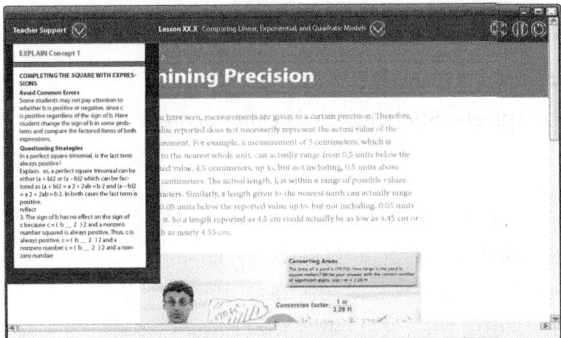

Differentiated Instruction Resources

Support all learners with Differentiated Instruction Resources, including

- **Leveled Practice and Problem Solving**
- **Reading Strategies**
- **Success for English Learners**
- **Challenge**

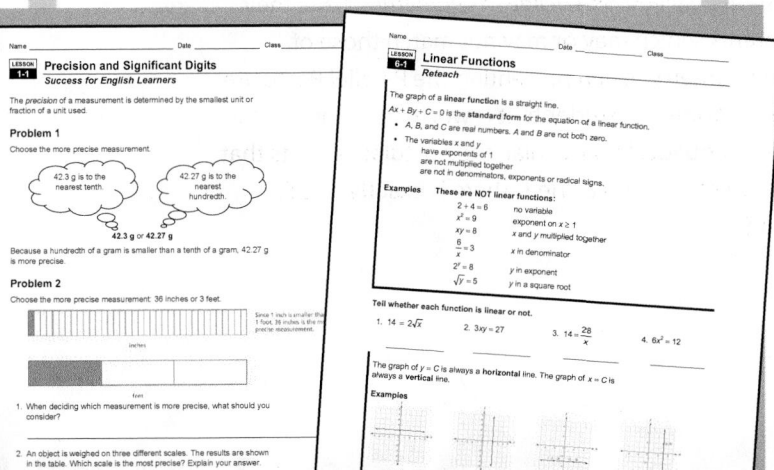

ASSESSMENT AND INTERVENTION

The **Personal Math Trainer** provides online practice, homework, assessments, and intervention. Monitor student progress through reports and alerts. **Create and customize assignments aligned to specific lessons or Common Core standards.**

- **Practice** – With dynamic items and assignments, students get unlimited practice on key concepts supported by guided examples, step-by-step solutions, and video tutorials.

- **Assessments** – Choose from course assignments or customize your own based on course content, Common Core standards, difficulty levels, and more.

- **Homework** – Students can complete online homework with a wide variety of problem types, including the ability to enter expressions, equations, and graphs. Let the system automatically grade homework, so you can focus where your students need help the most!

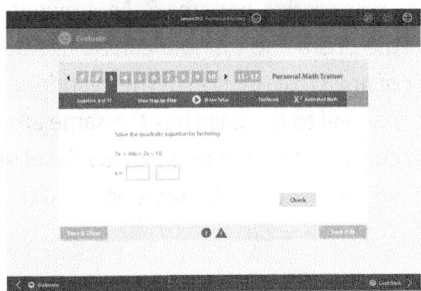

- **Intervention** – Let the Personal Math Trainer automatically prescribe a targeted, personalized intervention path for your students.

Focus on Higher Order Thinking

Raise the bar with homework and practice that incorporates higher-order thinking and mathematical practices in every lesson.

Assessment Readiness

Prepare students for success on high stakes tests for Geometry with practice at every module and unit

Assessment Resources

Tailor assessments and response to intervention to meet the needs of all your classes and students, including

- Leveled Module Quizzes
- Leveled Unit Tests
- Unit Performance Tasks
- Placement, Diagnostic, and Quarterly Benchmark Tests
- Tier 1, Tier 2, and Tier 3 Resources

Math Background

Volume G-GMD.A.2

LESSONS 18.1 to 18.4

The formula for the volume of a rectangular prism $(V = Bh)$ is the starting point for developing the volume formulas for other three-dimensional figures.

Another important ingredient in developing volume formulas is Cavalieri's Principle. This principle says that if two three-dimensional figures have the same height and the same cross-sectional area at every level, then they have the same volume.

To illustrate the use of Cavalieri's Principle, consider the following informal argument for the volume formula for a cylinder with height h and base area B. Construct a rectangular prism of height h so that each rectangular cross-section has area B. As shown in the following figure, the prism and cylinder can be positioned so that the area of any cross-section of the cylinder created by a plane parallel to the base has the same area as the corresponding cross-section of the prism. By Cavalieri's Principle, the volume of the cylinder is equal to that of the prism. That is, $V = Bh$.

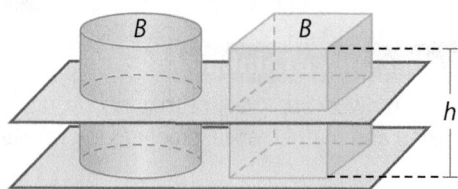

Note that the above argument works for all cylinders, oblique or right, and regardless of the shape of the base. In the case of a cylinder with a circular base, the volume formula may be written as $V = \pi r^2 h$.

For pyramids, cones, and spheres, the situation is somewhat more complex. Students can fill models of solids with sand or water to gain an intuitive sense of how the volumes of pyramids and cones are related to the volumes of prisms and cylinders, respectively. However, rigorous justifications of the volume formulas for pyramids, cones, and spheres all rely on clever applications of Cavalieri's Principle.

Geometry on a Sphere G-GMD.B.4

LESSON 19.4

A *sphere* is *the locus of points in space that are a fixed distance from a given point*. In three dimensions, a *sphere* may also be defined as *the surface that is generated by rotating a circle in space about any line through the center of the circle.*

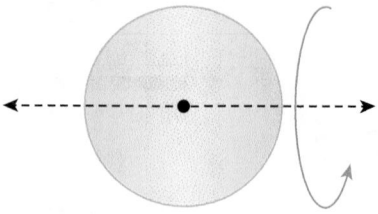

When a sphere and a plane intersect, their intersection is either a single point (when the plane is tangent to the sphere) or a circle. If the plane passes through the center of the sphere, the circle that is formed has the same radius and same center as the sphere. Such a circle is called a *great circle*.

Great circles are the largest circles that lie on a sphere. Great circles also have another important property: Given two points on a sphere, the shortest path on the sphere between the points lies along the great circle that passes through the points. For this reason, ships and airplanes generally follow routes that are arcs of great circles.

In the nineteenth century, mathematicians began to recognize that logically consistent mathematical systems could be developed without assuming the Parallel Postulate.

These systems, called *non-Euclidean geometries*, have their own theorems, which may or may not match those of Euclidean geometry. When presenting the Parallel Postulate (as Playfair's Axiom) to students, it is worth focusing on the postulate's language. In particular, the postulate asserts that through a point P not on a line ℓ, there is exactly one line parallel to ℓ.

In other words, a parallel line exists, and it is unique. Thus, non-Euclidean geometries are based on one of two assumptions: that there is no line through P parallel to ℓ (which gives rise to elliptic geometry) or that there are multiple lines through P parallel to ℓ (which gives rise to hyperbolic geometry).

In Euclidean geometry, a *line* is *a straight path that extends forever in two directions in a plane*. In spherical geometry, a *line* is *a great circle*. This is a circle that divides a sphere into equal halves.

Scale Factor G-MG.A.3

LESSON 20.1

When all dimensions of a figure are multiplied by a nonzero constant k, the perimeter or circumference changes by a factor of k and the area changes by a factor of k^2. This principle can be proved for various categories of figures by using established formulas.

Consider the case of a triangle, $\triangle ABC$, with sides of length a, b, and c. When all dimensions are multiplied by k $(k \neq 0)$, the resulting triangle has sides of length ka, kb, and kc. The perimeter of the new triangle is therefore $ka + kb + kc$ or $k(a + b + c)$, which is k times the perimeter of $\triangle ABC$.

The three-dimensional analogue of this principle says that, when all the dimensions of a three-dimensional figure are multiplied by a nonzero constant k, the surface area changes by a factor of k^2 and the volume changes by a factor of k^3.

Geometric Probability G-MG.A.2

LESSON 20.3

In general, the probability of an event is a ratio. Given a sample space in which every outcome is equally likely, the probability of an event is the ratio of the number of outcomes in the event to the number of outcomes in the sample space. In geometric probability, the probability of an event is based on a ratio of geometric measures, such as lengths or areas.

The history of geometric probability dates back at least as far as a famous problem that was first posed in 1777 by George Louis Leclerc, Comte de Buffon. At the time, a popular wagering game consisted of tossing a small coin onto a floor with square tiles.

Players bet on whether the coin would land entirely within a tile. Buffon recognized that the probability of the coin landing inside a tile depended upon the location of the coin's center within the tile. In particular, a coin of 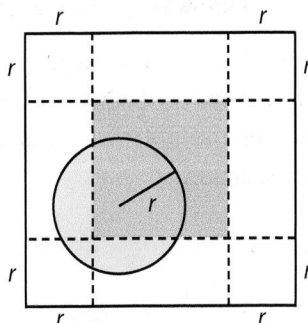 radius r will land entirely within a square tile if the coin's center falls within the smaller, shaded square shown in the figure. In this way, Buffon reduced the problem to one that could be solved by calculating some areas.

In a similar way, Buffon explored the probability that a needle tossed onto a surface that is marked with equidistant parallel lines will land across one of the lines. This is the well-known Buffon Needle Problem.

If the length of the needle is equal to the distance between the lines, it is possible to show that the probability P of the needle landing across a line is $\frac{2}{\pi}$, or about 0.64.

This result provides an interesting method for estimating the value of pi. Toss a needle several times onto a surface that satisfies the above conditions and record the number of times the needle hits a line. Let P be the ratio of hits to the total number of tosses. Then $\pi \approx \frac{2}{P}$. This approximation will become more accurate as the number of tosses increases.

Measurement and Modeling in Two and Three Dimensions

MATH IN CAREERS
Unit Activity Preview

After completing this unit, students will complete a Math in Careers task relating to a scale model of a sphere. Critical skills include finding a scale factor and applying knowledge of spherical geometry.

For more information about careers in mathematics as well as various mathematics appreciation topics, visit The American Mathematical Society at http://www.ams.org.

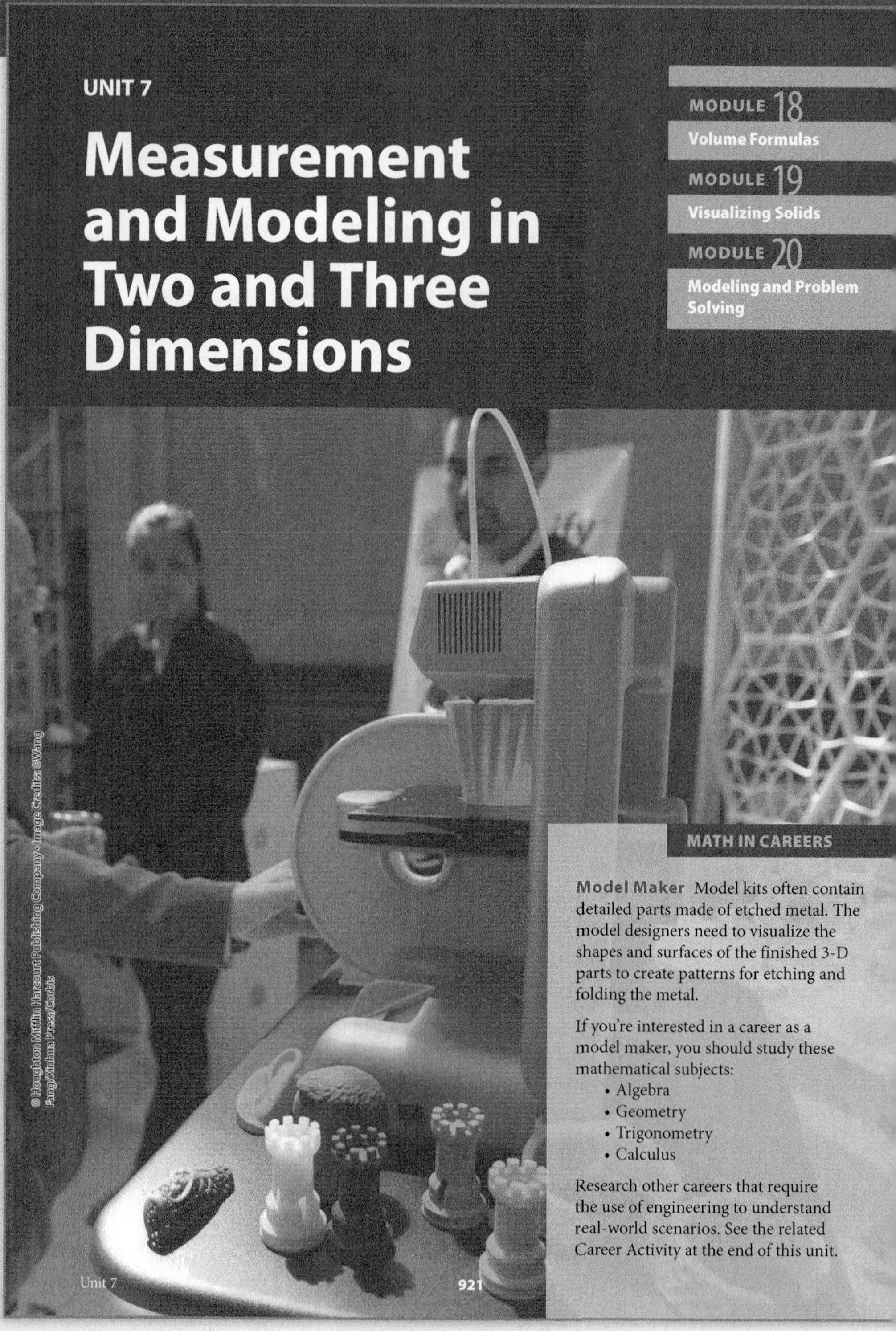

UNIT 7

Measurement and Modeling in Two and Three Dimensions

MODULE 18
Volume Formulas

MODULE 19
Visualizing Solids

MODULE 20
Modeling and Problem Solving

MATH IN CAREERS

Model Maker Model kits often contain detailed parts made of etched metal. The model designers need to visualize the shapes and surfaces of the finished 3-D parts to create patterns for etching and folding the metal.

If you're interested in a career as a model maker, you should study these mathematical subjects:
- Algebra
- Geometry
- Trigonometry
- Calculus

Research other careers that require the use of engineering to understand real-world scenarios. See the related Career Activity at the end of this unit.

Unit 7   921

TRACKING YOUR LEARNING PROGRESSION

Before	In this Unit	After
Students understand: • central and inscribed angles • chords, secants, tangent lines, and arcs • inscribed quadrilaterals • segment lengths in circles • formulas for circumference, area, and equation of a circle • arc lengths, concentric circles, radian measure • area of a sector	Students will learn about: • formulas for the volume of a prism, cylinder, pyramid, cone, and sphere • cross sections and solids of rotation • formulas for the surface area of a prism, cylinder, pyramid, cone, and sphere • scale factor • calculating densities • modeling to meet constraints	Students will study: • probability • permutations and combinations • conditional probability • independent and dependent events • making and analyzing decisions using probability

Reading Start-Up

Visualize Vocabulary

Use the ✔ words and draw examples to complete the chart.

Object	Example
cone	
cylinder	
pyramid	
sphere	

Vocabulary

Review Words
- ✔ area (*área*)
- ✔ composite figure (*figura compuesta*)
- ✔ cone (*cono*)
- ✔ cylinder (*cilindro*)
- ✔ pyramid (*pirámide*)
- ✔ sphere (*esfera*)
- ✔ volume (*volume*)

Preview Words
apothem (*apotema*)
cross section (*sección transversal*)
great circle (*gran círculo*)
net (*neto*)
oblique cylinder (*cilindro oblicuo*)
oblique prism (*prisma oblicuo*)
regular pyramid (*pirámide regular*)
right cone (*cono recto*)
right cylinder (*cilindro recto*)
right prism (*prisma recto*)
surface area (*área de la superficie*)

Understand Vocabulary

Complete the sentences using the preview words.

1. A(n) **cross section** is the region of a plane that intersects a solid figure.

2. A cross section of a sphere with the same radius as the sphere is called a **great circle**.

3. The **net** of a right prism is a two-dimensional image containing six rectangles.

Active Reading

Pyramid Create a Pyramid and organize the adjectives used to describe different objects—right, regular, oblique—on each of its faces. When listening to descriptions of objects, look for these words and associate them with the object that follows.

Reading Start Up

Have students complete the activities on this page by working alone or with others.

VISUALIZE VOCABULARY

The example chart helps students review vocabulary associated with three-dimensional figures. If time allows, discuss the characteristics that helped students identify each figure.

UNDERSTAND VOCABULARY

Use the following explanations to help students learn the preview words.

A **net** is a diagram of the faces of a three-dimensional figure arranged so that the diagram can be folded to form the figure. The total area of all faces and curved surfaces of a three-dimensional figure is its **surface area**. A **regular pyramid** has a base that is a regular polygon and lateral faces that are congruent isosceles triangles.

ACTIVE READING

Students can use these reading and note-taking strategies to help them organize and understand the new concepts and vocabulary. Encourage students to make connections among the figures and their properties by using descriptive vocabulary when constructing their vocabulary pyramids. Remind students to keep asking questions about any vocabulary that they find confusing or unclear.

ADDITIONAL RESOURCES

Differentiated Instruction

- Reading Strategies

ESSENTIAL QUESTION:

Answer: For one example, volume formulas are useful when you want to find how much liquid something can hold, such as a cup or a swimming pool.

PROFESSIONAL DEVELOPMENT VIDEO

Professional Development Video

Author Juli Dixon models successful teaching practices in an actual high-school classroom.

Professional Development
my.hrw.com

MODULE 18

Volume Formulas

Essential Question: How can you use volume formulas to solve real-world problems?

© Houghton Mifflin Harcourt Publishing Company · Image Credits ©Stringer/Reuters/Corbis

REAL WORLD VIDEO
Check out how volume formulas can be used to find the volumes of real-world objects, including sinkholes.

MODULE PERFORMANCE TASK PREVIEW

How Big Is That Sinkhole?

In 2010, a giant sinkhole opened up in a neighborhood in Guatemala and swallowed up the three-story building that stood above it. In this module, you will choose and apply an appropriate formula to determine the volume of this giant sinkhole.

Module 18   923

DIGITAL TEACHER EDITION

Access a full suite of teaching resources when and where you need them:

- Access content online or offline
- Customize lessons to share with your class
- Communicate with your students in real-time
- View student grades and data instantly to target your instruction where it is needed most

PERSONAL MATH TRAINER

Assessment and Intervention

Assign automatically graded homework, quizzes, tests, and intervention activities. Prepare your students with updated, Common Core-aligned practice tests.

Are YOU Ready?

Complete these exercises to review skills you will need for this module.

Area of a Circle

Example 1   Find the area of a circle with radius equal to 5.

$A = \pi r^2$ Write the equation for the area of a circle of radius r.

$A = \pi(5)^2$ Substitute the radius.

$A = 25\pi$ Simplify.

• Online Homework
• Hints and Help
• Extra Practice

Find each area.

1. A circle with radius 4 16π

2. A circle with radius 6 36π

3. A circle with radius 3π $9\pi^3$

4. A circle with radius $\frac{2}{\pi}$ $\frac{4}{\pi}$

Volume Properties

Example 2   Find the number of cubes that are 1 cm^3 in size that fit into a cube of size 1 m^3.

Notice that the base has a length and width of 1 m or 100 cm, so its area is 1 m^2 or 10,000 cm^2.

The 1 m^3 cube is 1 m or 100 cm high, so multiply the area of the base by the height to find the volume of 1,000,000 cm^3.

Find the volume.

5. The volume of a 1 km^3 body of water in m^3

1,000,000,000 m^3

6. The volume of a 1 ft^3 box in in.^{3}

1728 in^3

Volume of Rectangular Prisms

Example 3   Find the volume of a rectangular prism with height 4 cm, length 3 cm, and width 5 cm.

$V = Bh$ Write the equation for the volume of a rectangular prism.

$V = (3)(5)(4)$ The volume of a rectangular prism is the area of the base times the height.

$V = 60$ cm^3 Simplify.

Find each volume.

7. A rectangular prism with length 3 m, width 4 m, and height 7 m

84 m^3

8. A rectangular prism with length 2 cm, width 5 cm, and height 12 cm

120 cm^3

Are You Ready?

ASSESS READINESS

Use the assessment on this page to determine if students need strategic or intensive intervention for the module's prerequisite skills.

ASSESSMENT AND INTERVENTION

RtI Response to Intervention **TIER 1, TIER 2, TIER 3 SKILLS**

Personal Math Trainer will automatically create a standards-based, personalized intervention assignment for your students, targeting each student's individual needs!

ADDITIONAL RESOURCES

See the table below for a full list of intervention resources available for this module.

Response to Intervention Resources also includes:

- Tier 2 Skill Pre-Tests for each Module
- Tier 2 Skill Post-Tests for each skill

Response to Intervention			Differentiated Instruction
Tier 1	**Tier 2**	**Tier 3**	
Lesson Intervention Worksheets	Strategic Intervention Skills Intervention Worksheets	Intensive Intervention Worksheets available online	
Reteach 18.1 Reteach 18.2 Reteach 18.3 Reteach 18.4	24 Surface Area 27 Volume	Building Block Skills 9, 10, 11, 14, 30, 31, 77, 83, 101, 106	Challenge worksheets Extend the Math Lesson Activities in TE

Volume of Prisms and Cylinders

Common Core Math Standards

The student is expected to:

 G-GMD.A.1

Give an informal argument for the formulas for the circumference of a circle, area of a circle, volume of a cylinder, pyramid, and cone. Also G-GMD.A.2, G-GMD.A.3, G-MG.A.1, G-MG.A.2

Mathematical Practices

COMMON CORE **MP.4 Modeling**

Language Objective

Explain to a partner how to apply the formulas for the volume of a prism and a cylinder.

ENGAGE

Essential Question: How do the formulas for the volume of a prism and a cylinder relate to area formulas that you already know?

The formula for the volume of a prism involves the formula for the area of a rectangle, and the formula for the volume of a cylinder involves the formula for the area of a circle.

PREVIEW: LESSON PERFORMANCE TASK

View the Engage section online. Discuss the photograph. Ask students to suggest possible connections between the photo and the subject of this lesson, the volume of prisms and cylinders. Then preview the Lesson Performance Task.

Name_____ Class_____ Date_____

18.1 Volume of Prisms and Cylinders

Essential Question: How do the formulas for the volume of a prism and cylinder relate to area formulas that you already know?

Resource Locker

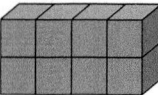 **Explore**   **Developing a Basic Volume Formula**

The volume of a three-dimensional figure is the number of nonoverlapping cubic units contained in the interior of the figure. This prism is made up of 8 cubes, each with a volume of 1 cubic centimeter, so it has a volume of 8 cubic centimeters. You can use this idea to develop volume formulas.

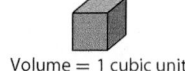
Volume = 1 cubic unit

In this activity you'll explore how to develop a volume formula for a right prism and a right cylinder.

A **right prism** has lateral edges that are perpendicular to the bases, with faces that are all rectangles.	A **right cylinder** has bases that are perpendicular to its center axis.
right prism	right cylinder

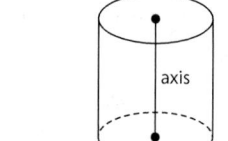

Ⓐ On a sheet of paper draw a quadrilateral shape. Make sure the sides aren't parallel. Assume the figure has an area of *B* square units.

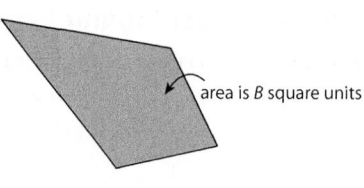
area is *B* square units

Ⓑ Use it as the base for a prism. Take a block of Styrofoam and cut to the shape of the base. Assume the prism has a height of 1 unit.

How would changing the area of the base change the volume of the prism?

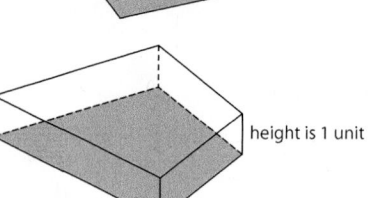
height is 1 unit

An increase in the area of the base would

increase the volume. A decrease in the area of

the base would decrease the volume.

© Houghton Mifflin Harcourt Publishing Company

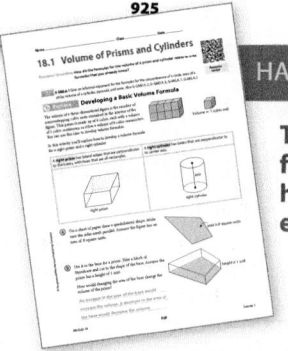

HARDCOVER PAGES 779–790

Turn to these pages to find this lesson in the hardcover student edition.

Ⓒ If the base has an area of *B* square units, how many cubic units does the prism contain?

B cubic units

Ⓓ Now use the base to build a prism with a height of *h* units.

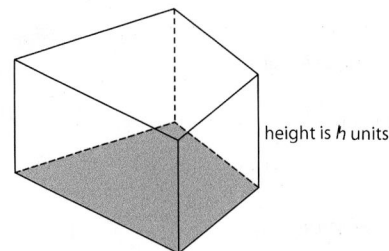

height is *h* units

How much greater is the volume of this prism compared to the one with a height of 1?

The volume of the prism is *B* · *h*, which is *h* times the volume of the original prism.

Reflect

1. Suppose the base of the prism was a rectangle of sides *l* and *w*. Write a formula for the volume of the prism using *l*, *w*, and *h*.
   $V = lwh$

2. A cylinder has a circular base. Use the results of the Explore to write a formula for the volume of a cylinder. Explain what you did.
   $V = \pi r^2 h$; I multiplied the area of a circle, πr^2, by the height of the cylinder.

🔍 **Explain 1** **Finding the Volume of a Prism**

The general formula for the volume of a prism is $V = B \cdot h$. With certain prisms the volume formula can include the formula for the area of the base.

Volume of a Prism	
The formula for the volume of a right rectangular prism with length ℓ, width *w*, and height *h* is $V = \ell wh$.	The formula for the volume of a cube with edge length *s* is $V = s^3$.
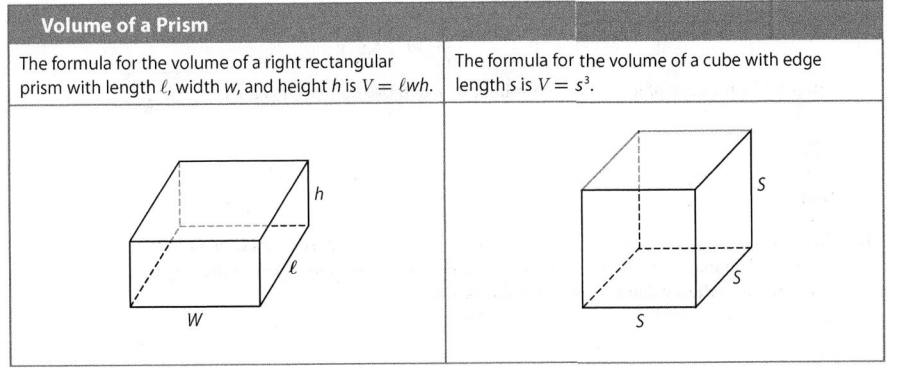	

© Houghton Mifflin Harcourt Publishing Company

PROFESSIONAL DEVELOPMENT

 Learning Progressions

Previously, students saw that the formula for the area of a rectangle is the starting point for developing the area formulas for other polygons. In much the same way, the formula for the volume of a rectangular prism $(V = Bh)$ is the starting point for developing the volume formulas for other three-dimensional figures. Another important idea in developing volume formulas is Cavalieri's Principle, which states that if two three-dimensional figures have the same height and the same cross-sectional area at every level, then they have the same volume. As students progress through more advanced courses, such as calculus, they will apply Cavalieri's Principle to more complex solid figures.

Developing a Basic Volume Formula

INTEGRATE TECHNOLOGY

Students have the option of doing the Explore activity either in the book or online.

QUESTIONING STRATEGIES

❓ How are the units used to measure volume related to the units used to measure length? The units used to measure volume are cubes of the units used to measure length.

❓ How can you estimate the volume of a cylinder whose radius and height are both 1 cm? $\pi r^2 h = \pi(1)^2 \cdot 1 \approx 3.14 \text{ cm}^3$

INTEGRATE MATHEMATICAL PRACTICES

Focus on Communication

MP.3 Begin by briefly reviewing the definitions of *prism* and *cylinder*. Be sure that students recognize the similarities in these three-dimensional figures and that they can identify the bases of a given prism or cylinder.

EXPLAIN 1

Finding the Volume of a Prism

AVOID COMMON ERRORS

Students may have difficulty finding the volume of a prism if they need to use conversion factors. Review how to use unit analysis and conversion factors to find volume.

Volume of Prisms and Cylinders   **926**

How would you find the volume of the contents of a right prism that is $\frac{3}{4}$ full? **Multiply the volume found by using the volume formula by $\frac{3}{4}$.**

Example 1 Use volume formulas to solve real world problems.

(A) A shark and ray tank at the aquarium has the dimensions shown. Estimate the volume of water in gallons. Use the conversion 1 gallon = 0.134 ft³.

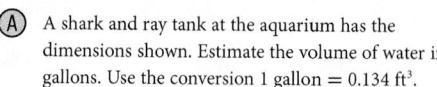

Step 1 Find the volume of the aquarium in cubic feet.

$$V = \ell wh = (120)(60)(8) = 57,600 \text{ ft}^3$$

Step 2 Use the conversion factor $\dfrac{1 \text{ gallon}}{0.134 \text{ ft}^3}$ to estimate the volume of the aquarium in gallons.

$$57,600 \text{ ft}^3 \cdot \frac{1 \text{ gallon}}{0.134 \text{ ft}^3} \approx 429,851 \text{ gallons} \qquad \frac{1 \text{ gallon}}{0.134 \text{ ft}^3} = 1$$

Step 3 Use the conversion factor $\dfrac{1 \text{ gallon}}{8.33 \text{ pounds}}$ to estimate the weight of the water.

$$429,851 \text{ gallons} \cdot \frac{8.33 \text{ pounds}}{1 \text{ gallon}} \approx 3,580,659 \text{ pounds} \qquad \frac{8.33 \text{ pounds}}{1 \text{ gallon}} = 1$$

The aquarium holds about 429,851 gallons. The water in the aquarium weighs about 3,580,659 pounds.

(B) **Chemistry** Ice takes up more volume than water. This cubic container is filled to the brim with ice. Estimate the volume of water once the ice melts.

Density of ice: 0.9167 g/cm³   Density of water: 1 g/cm³

Step 1 Find the volume of the cube of ice.

$$V = s^3 = \boxed{3}^3 = \boxed{27} \text{ cm}^3$$

Step 2 Convert the volume to mass using the conversion factor $\boxed{0.9167} \dfrac{\text{g}}{\text{cm}^3}$.

$$\boxed{27} \text{ cm}^3 \cdot \boxed{0.9167} \frac{\text{g}}{\text{cm}^3} \approx \boxed{24.8} \text{ g}$$

Step 3 Use the mass of ice to find the volume of water. Use the conversion factor $\boxed{1 \dfrac{\text{cm}^3}{\text{g}}}$.

$$24.8 \text{ g} \cdot \boxed{1 \frac{\text{cm}^3}{\text{g}}} \approx \boxed{24.8} \text{ cm}^3$$

Reflect

3. The general formula for the volume of a prism is $V = B \cdot h$. Suppose the base of a prism is a parallelogram of length l and altitude h. Use H as the variable to represent the height of the prism. Write a volume formula for this prism.

$$V = \ell \cdot h \cdot H$$

COLLABORATIVE LEARNING

Small Group Activity

Have students work in groups to make cylinders out of modeling clay. Then have them use string to slice the cylinders into eight congruent sectors and arrange the sectors to approximate a rectangular prism. Have them use this shape to explain the volume formula for a cylinder.

4. Find the volume of the figure.

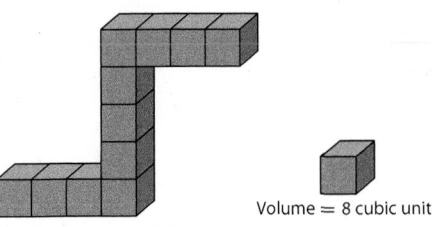

88 cubic units

Volume = 8 cubic units

5. Find the volume of the figure.

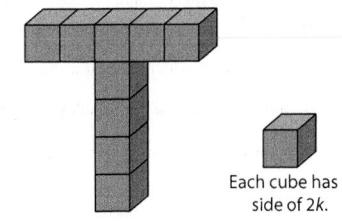

Each cube has a side of 2k.

72k³ cubic units

🔘 **Explain 2**   **Finding the Volume of a Cylinder**

You can also find the volume of prisms and cylinders whose edges are not perpendicular to the base.

Oblique Prism	Oblique Cylinder
An **oblique prism** is a prism that has at least one non-rectangular lateral face.	An **oblique cylinder** is a cylinder whose axis is not perpendicular to the bases.

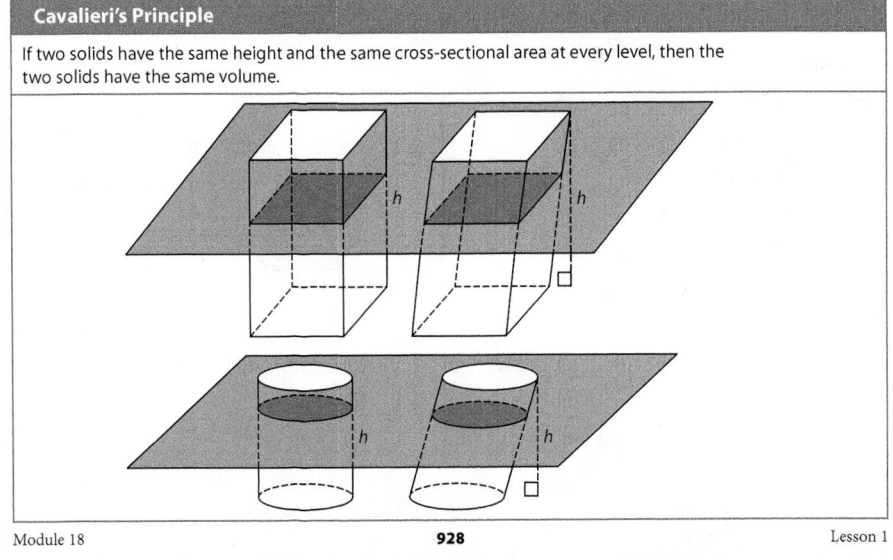

Cavalieri's Principle
If two solids have the same height and the same cross-sectional area at every level, then the two solids have the same volume.

EXPLAIN 2

Finding the Volume of a Cylinder

QUESTIONING STRATEGIES

? How is an oblique cylinder similar to a right cylinder? The bases are circles. The bases are connected by a curved lateral surface. The same volume formula works for both types of cylinders.

? How is an oblique cylinder different from a right cylinder? In an oblique cylinder, the axis is not perpendicular to the base.

DIFFERENTIATE INSTRUCTION

Kinesthetic Experience

Kinesthetic learners can use a stack of pennies to understand Cavalieri's Principle. Have students arrange the pennies to form a right cylinder and ask them to estimate the volume. Then have students push the stack to form an oblique cylinder. Students should see that the volume of the stack does not change, because the number and size of the pennies have not changed. This is supported by Cavalieri's Principle because the cross-sectional area at each level (that is, the area of the face of a penny) is unchanged when the stack is pushed to form the oblique cylinder.

AVOID COMMON ERRORS

Students may make careless errors if they do not read the problem carefully and use the given information correctly. For example, if the diameter of a cylinder is given, they must divide by 2 to find the radius before using the formula. Also, the base area may be given instead of the radius.

Example 2 To find the volume of an oblique cylinder or oblique prism, use Cavalieri's Principle to find the volume of a comparable right cylinder or prism.

(A) The height of this oblique cylinder is three times that of its radius. What is the volume of this cylinder? Round to the nearest tenth.

Use Cavalieri's Principle to find the volume of a comparable right cylinder.

Represent the height of the oblique cylinder: $h = 3r$

Use the area of the base to find r: $\pi r^2 = 81\pi$ cm², so $r = 9$.

Calculate the height: $h = 3r = 27$ cm

Calculate the volume: $V = Bh = (81\pi)27 \approx 6870.7$

The volume is about 6870.7 cubic centimeters.

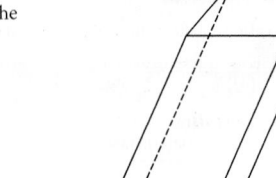

$B = 81\pi$ cm²

(B) The height of this oblique square-based prism is four times that of side length of the base. What is the volume of this prism? Round to the nearest tenth.

Calculate the height of the oblique prism:

$h = \underline{4}\ s$, where s is the length of the square base.

Use the area of the base to find s.

$s^2 = \boxed{75}$ cm²

$s = \sqrt{\boxed{75}}$ cm

Calculate the height.

$h = 4s = 4\boxed{\sqrt{75}}$ cm

Calculate the volume.

$V = Bh$

$= (75 \text{ cm}^2)\left(\boxed{4\sqrt{75}} \text{ cm}\right)$

$= \boxed{2598.1}$ cm³

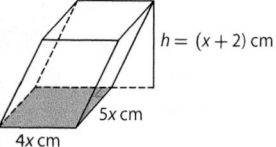

$B = 75$ cm²

Your Turn

Find the volume.

6.

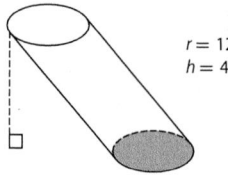

$r = 12$ in.
$h = 45$ in.

$V = \pi r^2 h = \pi(12 \text{ in.})^2(45 \text{ in.}) \approx 20{,}357.5 \text{ in.}^3$

7.

$h = (x + 2)$ cm

$5x$ cm

$4x$ cm

$V = (4x)(5x)(x + 2) = 20x^2(x + 2)$

Module 18   **929**   Lesson 1

LANGUAGE SUPPORT **EL**

Connect Vocabulary

To help students remember the vocabulary in the lesson, including *right prism*, *right cylinder*, *oblique prism*, and *oblique cylinder*, have students make a small poster showing examples of each solid figure. Then have them use colored pencils to mark the dimensions of the base of each in one color, the heights in another color, and then list the formulas for volume in different colors. Have them label the figures with the vocabulary words, and display the posters in the classroom. Invite students to present their posters to the class.

© Houghton Mifflin Harcourt Publishing Company

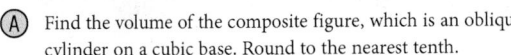
Explain 3 Finding the Volume of a Composite Figure

Recall that a composite figure is made up of simple shapes that combine to create a more complex shape. A composite three-dimensional figure is formed from prisms and cylinders. You can find the volume of each separate figure and then add the volumes together to find the volume of the composite figure.

Example 3 Find the volume of each composite figure.

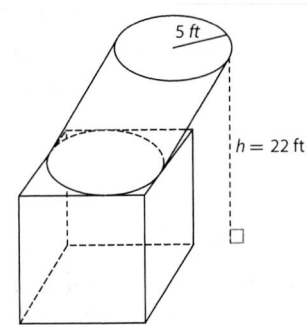

(A) Find the volume of the composite figure, which is an oblique cylinder on a cubic base. Round to the nearest tenth.

The base area of the cylinder is $B = \pi r^2 = \pi(5)^2 = 25\pi$ ft².

The cube has side lengths equal to the diameter of the cylinder's circular base: $s = 10$.

The height of the cylinder is $h = 22 - 10 = 12$ ft.

The volume of the cube is $V = s^3 = 10^3 = 1000$ ft³.

The volume of the cylinder is $V = Bh = (25\pi \text{ ft}^2)(12 \text{ ft}) \approx 942.5$ ft³.

The total volume of the composite figure is the sum of the individual volumes.

$V = 1000 \text{ ft}^3 + 942.5 \text{ ft}^3 = 1942.5 \text{ ft}^3$

(B) This periscope is made up of two congruent cylinders and two congruent triangular prisms, each of which is a cube cut in half along one of its diagonals. The height of each cylinder is 6 times the length of the radius. Use the measurements provided to estimate the volume of this composite figure. Round to the nearest tenth.

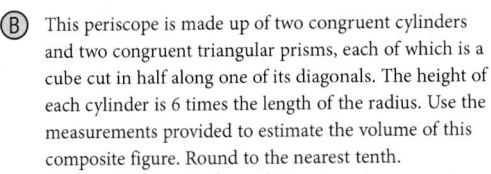

Use the area of the base to find the radius. $B = \pi r^2$

$\pi r^2 = \boxed{36} \pi$, so $r = \boxed{6}$ in.

Calculate the height of each cylinder:

$h = 6r = 6 \cdot \boxed{6} = \boxed{36}$ in.

The faces of the triangular prism that intersect the cylinders are congruent squares. The side length s of each square is the same as the diameter of the circle.

$s = d = 2 \cdot \boxed{6} = \boxed{12}$ in.

The two triangular prisms form a cube. What is the volume of this cube?

$V = s^3 = \boxed{12}^3 = \boxed{1728}$ in³

Find the volume of the two cylinders: $V = 2 \cdot 36\pi \cdot \boxed{6} = \boxed{432\pi}$ in³

The total volume of the composite figure is the sum of the individual volumes.

$V = \boxed{1728}$ in³ $+ \boxed{432\pi}$ in³ $\approx \boxed{3085.17}$ in³

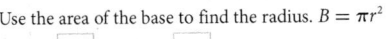

© Houghton Mifflin Harcourt Publishing Company

EXPLAIN 3

Finding the Volume of a Composite Figure

INTEGRATE MATHEMATICAL PRACTICES
Focus on Patterns

MP.8 Students should be able to recognize the solid figures that make up a composite figure. Ask them to make an organized list of all figures comprising the composite figures and then give the formulas for their volumes. Emphasize that while the volume of each cylinder or prism has the formula $V = Bh$, where B is the area of the base and h is the height, finding B changes from one solid figure to the next, depending on the figure. After organizing how to find the volume of the composite figure, have students substitute for the variables in each formula, find the volume of each solid, and then add the volumes to get the total.

QUESTIONING STRATEGIES

? How can you find the volume of a composite figure? You can divide a composite figure into component figures, use the volume formula for each component figure, then add the individual volumes.

ELABORATE

QUESTIONING STRATEGIES

? How do you find the volume of a prism or cylinder? **Multiply the area of the base of the figure by the height.**

SUMMARIZE THE LESSON

? How is the formula for the volume of a prism similar to the formula for the volume of a cylinder? How are the formulas different? **Both of the formulas may be written as $V = Bh$, where B is the area of the base and h is the height, but in the formula for the volume of a cylinder, B represents a circular area, while in the formula for the volume of a prism, B represents the area of a polygon.**

Reflect

8. A pipe consists of two concentric cylinders, with the inner cylinder hollowed out. Describe how you could calculate the volume of the solid pipe. Write a formula for the volume.

    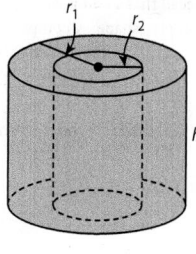

    Find the volume of the large cylinder and subtract the volume of the smaller cylinder. If r_1 is the radius of the larger cylinder and r_2 is the radius of the smaller cylinder and h is the common height, this is the volume of the solid pipe.

    $$V = \pi r_1^2 h - \pi r_2^2 h = \pi h\left(r_1^2 - r_2^2\right)$$

Your Turn

9. This robotic arm is made up of two cylinders with equal volume and two triangular prisms for a hand. The volume of each prism is $\frac{1}{2}r \times \frac{1}{3}r \times 2r$, where r is the radius of the cylinder's base. What fraction of the total volume does the hand take up?

    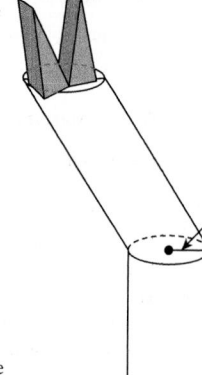

    $$V_{Hand} = 2\left(\frac{1}{3}r^3\right) = \frac{2}{3}r^3$$

    $$V_{Total} = 2\left(\pi r^2 \cdot h\right) + \frac{2}{3}r^3 = 2\pi r^2 h + \frac{2}{3}r^3 = 2r^2 \cdot \left(\pi h + \frac{1}{3}r\right)$$

    $$\frac{V_{Hand}}{V_{Total}} = \frac{\frac{2}{3}r^3}{2r^2\left(\pi h + \frac{1}{3}r\right)} = \frac{r}{3\left(\pi h + \frac{1}{3}r\right)} = \frac{r}{3\pi h + r}$$

💬 **Elaborate**

10. If an oblique cylinder and a right cylinder have the same height but not the same volume, what can you conclude about the cylinders?
    They have different radii.

11. A right square prism and a right cylinder have the same height and volume. What can you conclude about the radius of the cylinder and side lengths of the square base?
    Let V_1 be the volume of the prism.

    Let V_2 be the volume of the cylinder.

    $$V_1 = V_2$$
    $$s^2 \cdot h = \pi r^2 \cdot h$$
    $$s^2 = \pi r^2$$
    $$s = \sqrt{\pi} \cdot r$$

12. **Essential Question Check-In** How does the formula for the area of a circle relate to the formula for the volume of a cylinder?
    Sample answer: I can multiply the expression for the area of a circle by the height of the cylinder to get an expression for the volume of the cylinder.

Module 18   931   Lesson 1

• Online Homework
• Hints and Help
• Extra Practice

1. The volume of prisms and cylinders can be represented with Bh, where B represents the area of the base. Identify the type of figure shown and match the prism or cylinder with the appropriate volume formula.

A. $V = (\pi r^2)h$ **B.** $V = (\frac{1}{2}bh)h$ **C.** $V = \ell wh$

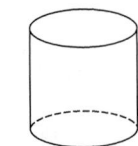

rectangular prism

C. $V = \ell wh$

cylinder

A. $V = (\pi r^2) \cdot h$

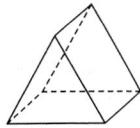

triangular prism

B. $V = (\frac{1}{2}bh) \cdot h$

Find the volume of each prism or cylinder. Round to the nearest hundredth.

2.

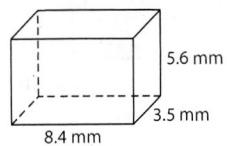

5.6 mm
3.5 mm
8.4 mm

$V = (8.4 \text{ mm})(3.5 \text{ mm})(5.6 \text{ mm})$

$= 164.64 \text{ mm}^3$

3.

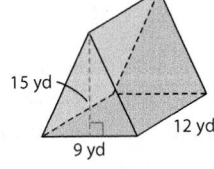

15 yd
12 yd
9 yd

$V = (\frac{1}{2} \cdot 9 \text{ yd} \cdot 15 \text{ yd})12 \text{ yd}$

$= (67.5 \text{ yd}^2)12 \text{ yd}$

$= 810 \text{ yd}^3$

4. The area of the hexagonal base is $(\frac{54}{\tan 30°})$ m². Its height is 8 m.

$V = Bh = (\frac{54}{\tan 30°}) \text{ m}^2 \cdot 8 \text{ m}$

$\approx 748.25 \text{ m}^3$

5. The area of the pentagonal base is $(\frac{125}{\tan 36°})$ m². Its height is 15 m.

$V = Bh = (\frac{125}{\tan 36°}) \text{ m}^2 \cdot 15 \text{ m}$

$\approx 2580.72 \text{ m}^3$

6.

6 cm
4 cm
9 cm

$V = 9 \text{ cm} \cdot 4 \text{ cm} \cdot 6 \text{ cm}$

$= 216 \text{ cm}^3$

7.

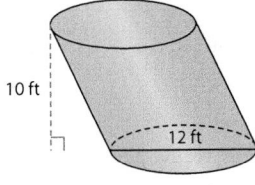

10 ft
12 ft

$V = \pi \cdot (6 \text{ ft})^2 \cdot 10 \text{ ft}$

$\approx 1130.97 \text{ ft}^3$

© Houghton Mifflin Harcourt Publishing Company

ASSIGNMENT GUIDE

Concepts and Skills	Practice
Explore Developing a Basic Volume Formula	Exercise 1
Example 1 Finding the Volume of a Prism	Exercises 2–6
Example 2 Finding the Volume of a Cylinder	Exercises 7–8
Example 3 Finding the Volume of a Composite Figure	Exercises 9–12

INTEGRATE MATHEMATICAL PRACTICES
Focus on Modeling

MP.4 Some students may benefit from a hands-on approach to finding the volume of a prism. Have students imagine an arrangement of 3 rows of 4 unit cubes each. The cubes form a 3 × 4 × 1 rectangular prism with a volume of 12 cubic units. To find the volume of a 3 × 4 × 2 prism, imagine another layer of cubes stacked on top of the first one.

Exercise	Depth of Knowledge (D.O.K.)	COMMON CORE Mathematical Practices	
1–12	**1** Recall of Information	**MP.5**	Using Tools
13–15	**2** Skills/Concepts	**MP.4**	Modeling
16	**2** Skills/Concepts	**MP.5**	Using Tools
17–18	**2** Skills/Concepts	**MP.1**	Problem Solving

AVOID COMMON ERRORS

When finding the volume of composite figures, some students may think they need to subtract the areas of the common surfaces that are shared by the touching cubes, as they would if they were finding the surface area of a composite figure. Using concrete models, show them that the volume of a composite figure made up of stacked blocks is the sum of the volumes of the individual blocks.

CONNECT VOCABULARY EL

To remember how the volume of a prism is connected to the volume of familiar figures like cubes and boxes, have students make a graphic organizer listing the volume formulas they know and adding the volume formulas from this module. Sample:

Shape	Volume	Volume
Cube	$V = s^3$	$V = Bh$
Box (prism)	$V = lwh$	$V = Bh$
Cylinder	$V = \pi r^2 h$	$V = Bh$

---

8. **Multi-Step** A vase in the shape of an oblique cylinder has the dimensions shown. What is the volume of the vase in liters? Round to the nearest thundredth. (*Hint:* Use the right triangle in the cylinder to find its height.)

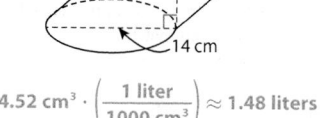

$$h^2 + 14^2 = 17^2 \qquad\qquad V = Bh$$
$$h^2 + 196 = 289 \qquad\qquad\quad = \pi r^2 h$$
$$h^2 = 93 \qquad\qquad\quad = \pi \cdot (7 \text{ cm})^2 \cdot \sqrt{93} \text{ cm}$$
$$h = \sqrt{93} \text{ cm} \qquad\qquad \approx 1484.52 \text{ cm}^3$$

$$1484.52 \text{ cm}^3 \cdot \left(\frac{1 \text{ liter}}{1000 \text{ cm}^3} \right) \approx 1.48 \text{ liters}$$

The volume is 1.5 liters.

Find the volume of each composite figure. Round to the nearest tenth.

9.

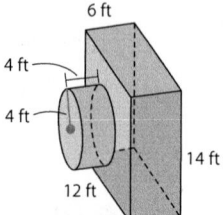

Cylinder	Prism
$V = \pi \cdot (4 \text{ ft})^2 \cdot 4 \text{ ft}$	$V = 12 \text{ ft} \cdot 6 \text{ ft} \cdot 14 \text{ ft}$
$\approx 201.06 \text{ ft}^3$	$\approx 1008 \text{ ft}^3$

$201.06 \text{ ft}^3 + 1008 \text{ ft}^3 = 1209.06 \text{ ft}^3$
$V \approx 1209.1 \text{ ft}^3$

10.

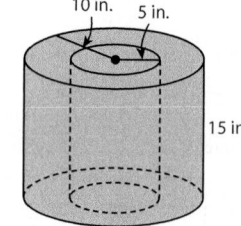

Large cylinder	Small cylinder
$V = \pi \cdot (10 \text{ in})^2 \cdot 15 \text{ in}$	$V = \pi \cdot (5 \text{ in})^2 \cdot 15 \text{ in}$
$\approx 4712.39 \text{ in}^3$	$\approx 1178.10 \text{ in}^3$

$V = 4712.39 \text{ in}^3 - 1178.10 \text{ in}^3 = 3534.29 \text{ in}^3$

11.

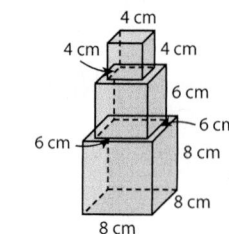

$V = (4 \text{ cm})^3$
$\quad = 64 \text{ cm}^3$
$V = (6 \text{ cm})^3$
$\quad = 216 \text{ cm}^3$
$V = (8 \text{ cm})^3$
$\quad = 512 \text{ cm}^3$
$64 \text{ cm}^3 + 216 \text{ cm}^3 + 512 \text{ cm}^3 = 792 \text{ cm}^3$

12. The two figures on each end combine to form a right cylinder.

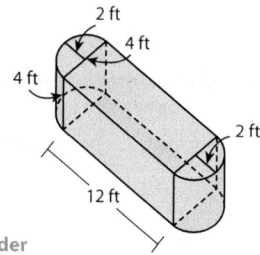

One whole cylinder
$V = \pi \cdot (2 \text{ ft})^2 \cdot 4 \text{ ft}$
$\quad \approx 50.27 \text{ ft}^3$

Prism
$V = (12 \text{ ft}) \cdot (4 \text{ ft}) \cdot (4 \text{ ft})$
$\quad = 192 \text{ ft}^3$

$50.27 \text{ ft}^3 + 192 \text{ ft}^3 = 242.27 \text{ ft}^3$

Exercise	Depth of Knowledge (D.O.K.)	COMMON CORE Mathematical Practices	
19	**3** Strategic Thinking **H.O.T.**	**MP.1**	Problem Solving
20	**3** Strategic Thinking **H.O.T.**	**MP.4**	Modeling
21	**3** Strategic Thinking **H.O.T.**	**MP.2**	Reasoning

13. Colin is buying dirt to fill a garden bed that is a 9 ft by 16 ft rectangle. If he wants to fill it to a depth of 4 in., how many cubic yards of dirt does he need? Round to the nearest cubic yard. If dirt costs \$25 per yd³, how much will the project cost?

$V = Bh = \ell wh = 9 \text{ ft} \cdot 16 \text{ ft} \cdot \left(\frac{4}{12} \text{ ft}\right) = 48 \text{ ft}^3;\ 48 \text{ ft}^3 \cdot \left(\frac{1 \text{ yd}}{3 \text{ ft}}\right) \cdot \left(\frac{1 \text{ yd}}{3 \text{ ft}}\right) \cdot \left(\frac{1 \text{ yd}}{3 \text{ ft}}\right) = 1.\overline{7} \approx 2 \text{ yd}^3;$

$2 \text{ yd}^3 \cdot \dfrac{\$25}{\text{yd}^3} = \$50;\ 2 \text{ yd}^3;\ \$50$

14. Persevere in Problem Solving A cylindrical juice container with a 3 in. diameter has a hole for a straw that is 1 in. from the side. Up to 5 in. of a straw can be inserted.

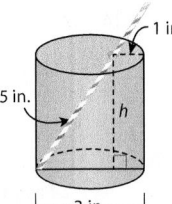

a. Find the height h of the container to the nearest tenth.

$a^2 + b^2 = c^2;\ h^2 + 2^2 = 5^2;\ h^2 + 4 = 25;\ h^2 = 21;\ h = \sqrt{21};\ h \approx 4.6 \text{ in.}$

b. Find the volume of the container to the nearest tenth.

$V = Bh = \pi r^2 h = \pi \cdot (1.5 \text{ in})^2 \cdot 4.6 \text{ in.} \approx 32.5 \text{ in}^3$

c. How many ounces of juice does the container hold? (*Hint*: 1 in³ ≈ 0.55 oz)

$32.5 \text{ in}^3 \cdot \dfrac{0.55 \text{ oz}}{1 \text{ in}^3} \approx 17.9 \text{ oz}$

15. Abigail has a cylindrical candle mold with the dimensions shown. If Abigail has a rectangular block of wax measuring 15 cm by 12 cm by 18 cm, about how many candles can she make after melting the block of wax? Round to the nearest tenth.

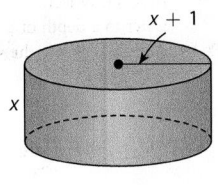

Wax	Mold
$V = Bh$	$V = Bh$
$= \ell wh$	$= \pi r^2 h$
$= 15 \text{ cm} \cdot 12 \text{ cm} \cdot 18 \text{ cm}$	$= \pi \cdot 3.4^2 \cdot 6$
$= 3240 \text{ cm}^3$	$\approx 218 \text{ cm}^3$

$3240 \text{ cm}^3 \div 218 \text{ cm}^3 \approx 14.9$

Because 0.9 of a candle would not make an entire candle, the answer rounds down to 14 candles.

16. Algebra Find the volume of the three-dimensional figure in terms of x.

$V = Bh$
$= \pi r^2 h$
$= \pi \cdot (x + 1)^2 \cdot x$
$= \pi \cdot (x^2 + 2x + 1) \cdot x$
$= \pi \cdot (x^3 + 2x^2 + x)$
$= \pi x^3 + 2\pi x^2 + \pi x$
$V = \pi x^3 + 2\pi x^2 + \pi x$

INTEGRATE MATHEMATICAL PRACTICES

Focus on Reasoning

MP.2 When working with the volume of a cylinder formulas, remind students that if they use 3.14 instead of the π key on a calculator, they are automatically giving an approximation to the volume of a cylinder. Have small groups of students discuss when using the π key on a calculator is appropriate and when it is not necessary.

INTEGRATE MATHEMATICAL PRACTICES

Focus on Math Connections

MP.1 If the corresponding linear dimensions of two similar solid figures have a scale factor of k, then their volumes are in the ratio of $1:k^3$. For example, if the dimensions of a cube with an edge length of 4 cm are doubled, then the volumes are in the ratio $1:2^3$, or 1:8. This means, the volume goes from $4^3 = 64 \text{ cm}^3$ to $8^3 = 512 \text{ cm}^3$.

PEER-TO-PEER DISCUSSION

Have students work in pairs. Each student should make up four application problems, two involving the volumes of prisms and two involving the volumes of cylinders. Then have them exchange problems with their partners, and solve the problems.

JOURNAL

Have students describe how to use the general volume formula $V = Bh$ to write a formula for the volume of a rectangular prism with base length ℓ and width w, and for a cylinder with radius r.

17. One cup is equal to 14.4375 in³. If a 1-cup measuring cylinder has a radius of 2 in., what is its height? If the radius is 1.5 in., what is its height? Round to the nearest tenth.

2 in. radius	1.5 in. radius
$V = Bh$	$V = Bh$
$V = \pi r^2 h$	$V = \pi r^2 h$
$14.4375 \text{ in}^3 = \pi 2^2 h$	$14.4375 \text{ in}^3 = \pi(1.5 \text{ in.})^2 h$
$\dfrac{14.4375 \text{ in}^3}{\pi(2 \text{ in.})^2} = h$	$\dfrac{14.4375 \text{ in}^3}{\pi(1.5 \text{ in.})^2} = h$
$1.1489 \text{ in.} \approx h$	$2.0425 \text{ in.} \approx h$
$h \approx 1.2 \text{ in.}$	$h \approx 2.0 \text{ in.}$

18. **Make a Prediction** A cake is a cylinder with a diameter of 10 in. and a height of 3 in. For a party, a coin has been mixed into the batter and baked inside the cake. The person who gets the piece with the coin wins a prize.

   a. Find the volume of the cake. Round to the nearest tenth.
   $V = \pi(5 \text{ in.})^2(3 \text{ in.}) \approx 235.6 \text{ in.}^3$

   b. Keka gets a piece of cake that is a right rectangular prism with a 3 in. by 1 in. base. What is the probability that the coin is in her piece? Round to the nearest hundredth.
   $V = (3 \text{ in.})(1 \text{ in.})(3 \text{ in.}) = 9 \text{ in.}^3$; Probability $= \dfrac{9 \text{ in}^3}{235.6 \text{ in}^3} \approx 0.04$

H.O.T. Focus on Higher Order Thinking

19. **Multi-Step** What is the volume of the three-dimensional object with the dimensions shown in the three views?
   Top prism: $V = 10 \text{ cm} \cdot 6 \text{ cm} \cdot 4 \text{ cm} = 240 \text{ cm}^3$

   Bottom prism: $V = 10 \cdot 10 \cdot 6 = 600 \text{ cm}^3$

   $V = 840 \text{ cm}^3$

   10 cm | 4 cm | 10 cm | 4 cm
   10 cm | Front | Top | 10 cm | Side

20. **Draw Conclusions** You can use *displacement* to find the volume of an irregular object, such as a stone. Suppose a 2 foot by 1 foot tank is filled with water to a depth of 8 in. A stone is placed in the tank so that it is completely covered, causing the water level to rise by 2 in. Find the volume of the stone.

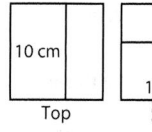

   Before the stone: $V = 2 \text{ ft} \cdot 1 \text{ ft} \cdot \dfrac{8}{12} \text{ ft} = \dfrac{4}{3} \text{ ft}^3$, or $V = 24 \text{ in.} \cdot 12 \text{ in.} \cdot 8 \text{ in.} = 2304 \text{ in}^3$

   After the stone: $V = 2 \text{ ft} \cdot 1 \text{ ft} \cdot \dfrac{10}{12} \text{ ft} = \dfrac{5}{3} \text{ ft}^3$, or $V = 24 \text{ in.} \cdot 12 \text{ in.} \cdot 10 \text{ in.} = 2880 \text{ in}^3$

   Volume of the stone $= \dfrac{5}{3} - \dfrac{4}{3} = \dfrac{1}{3} \text{ ft}^3$, or $2880 - 2304 = 576 \text{ in}^3$

21. Analyze Relationships One juice container is a rectangular prism with a height of 9 in. and a 3 in. by 3 in. square base. Another juice container is a cylinder with a radius of 1.75 in. and a height of 9 in. Describe the relationship between the two containers.

Prism	Cylinder
$V = Bh$	$V = Bh$
$= \ell wh$	$= \pi r^2 h$
$= 3 \text{ in.} \cdot 3 \text{ in.} \cdot 9 \text{ in.}$	$= \pi \cdot (1.75 \text{ in.})^2 \cdot 9 \text{ in.}$
$= 81 \text{ in}^3$	$\approx 86.6 \text{ in}^3$

The cylinder's volume is greater than the rectangular prism's volume by 5.6 in³.

Lesson Performance Task

A full roll of paper towels is a cylinder with a diameter of 6 inches and a hollow inner cylinder with a diameter of 2 inches.

1. Find the volume of the paper on the roll. Explain your method.

2. Each sheet of paper on the roll measures 11 inches by 11 inches by $\frac{1}{32}$ inch. Find the volume of one sheet. Explain how you found the volume.

3. How many sheets of paper are on the roll? Explain.

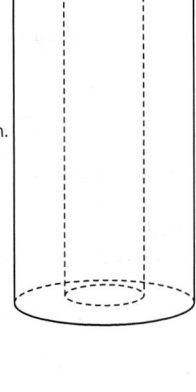
2 in.   2 in.   2 in.

11 in.

1. The volume of paper on the roll equals the volume of the larger 3-in. radius cylinder minus the volume of the smaller 1-in. radius cylinder.

   Volume of outer roll:
   $\pi r^2 h = 3.14(3)^2 11$
   $= 310.86 \text{ in}^3$

   Volume of inner roll:
   $\pi r^2 h = 3.14(1)^2 11$
   $= 34.54 \text{ in}^3$

   Volume of paper: $310.86 - 34.54 = 276.32 \text{ in}^3$

2. Each sheet is a rectangular prism measuring 11 in. by 11 in. by $\frac{1}{32}$ in.
   $V = 11 \times 11 \times \frac{1}{32}$
   $\approx 3.78 \text{ in}^3$

3. 73 sheets; The number of sheets is the total volume of paper divided by the volume of each sheet.
   $276.32 \div 3.78 \approx 73.1$

© Houghton Mifflin Harcourt Publishing Company

EXTENSION ACTIVITY

Students should work in teams of two or more. Each team should have a new roll of paper towels. Direct teams to find the volume of paper on the roll by subtracting the volume of the inside tube from the volume of the entire roll. Then, using the number of sheets in the roll, a figure that will be given on the outside of the package, they should determine the thickness of the paper. If teams work with different brands of towels, they can compare thicknesses, which affect the ability of a towel to absorb moisture.

INTEGRATE MATHEMATICAL PRACTICES
Focus on Math Connections

MP.1 Discuss with the class different methods of calculating the volume of paper towels in the Lesson Performance Task. The solution accompanying the task is to subtract the volume of a 1-inch-radius cylinder from the volume of a 3-inch-radius cylinder:

$$\pi(3^2)(11) - \pi(1^2)(11) = 3.14(9)(11) - 3.14(1)(11)$$

Ask students to suggest a shortcut for evaluating the expression on the right, one that reduces the number of products that must be found. The key is to factor the expression:

$$3.14(9)(11) - 3.14(1)(11) = (9 - 1)(3.14)(11)$$
$$= 8(3.14)(11)$$

INTEGRATE MATHEMATICAL PRACTICES
Focus on Critical Thinking

MP.3 Some students may be skeptical of the method used to calculate the number of paper towel sheets, because it may seem to erroneously convert a three-dimensional measurement—the volume of the paper towel roll—into a two-dimensional one—a flat sheet of 73 towel sections. Besides pointing out that the sheet of towel sections, while very thin, is in fact three-dimensional, mention that once the volume of the paper towel roll has been calculated, it can be used to find the parameters of any substance with that same volume, for example, the weight of water that would fill a container shaped like the paper towel roll.

Scoring Rubric
2 points: Student correctly solves the problem and explains his/her reasoning.
1 point: Student shows good understanding of the problem but does not fully solve or explain his/her reasoning.
0 points: Student does not demonstrate understanding of the problem.

Volume of Prisms and Cylinders   **936**

Volume of Pyramids

Common Core Math Standards

The student is expected to:

 G-GMD.A.1

Give an informal argument for the formulas for the circumference of a circle, area of a circle, volume of a cylinder, pyramid, and cone. Also G-GMD.A.2, G-GMD.A.3, G-MG.A.1

Mathematical Practices

COMMON CORE **MP.2 Reasoning**

Language Objective

Explain to a partner how to apply the formulas for the volume of a pyramid.

ENGAGE

Essential Question: How do you find the volume of a pyramid?

Find the area of the base and multiply it by one third times the height of the pyramid.

PREVIEW: LESSON PERFORMANCE TASK

View the Engage section online. Discuss the photograph. Ask students to explain why the long handle cannot simply be pulled directly through the rings and away from the puzzle. Then preview the Lesson Performance Task.

18.2 Volume of Pyramids

Essential Question: How do you find the volume of a pyramid?

Resource Locker

🧭 Explore   Developing a Volume Formula

As shown at the left below, $\overline{AB}$ has length b, and C is any point on line ℓ parallel to $\overline{AB}$. The distance between the line containing $\overline{AB}$ and line ℓ is h. No matter where C is located on line ℓ, the area of the resulting $\triangle ABC$ is always a constant equal to $\frac{1}{2}bh$. Similarly, given a polygon and a plane R that is parallel to the plane containing the polygon, suppose you choose a point on R and create a pyramid with the chosen point as the vertex and the polygon as the base. Both the base area and the height of the pyramid remain constant as you vary the location of the vertex on R, so it is reasonable to assume that the volume of the pyramid remains constant.

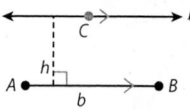
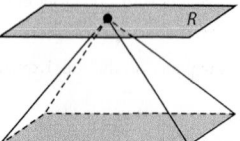

Postulate

Pyramids that have equal base areas and equal heights have equal volumes.

Consider a triangular pyramid with vertex A directly over vertex D of the base BCD. This triangular pyramid A-BCD can be thought of as part of a triangular prism with $\triangle EFA \cong \triangle BCD$. Let the area of the base be B and let $AD = h$.

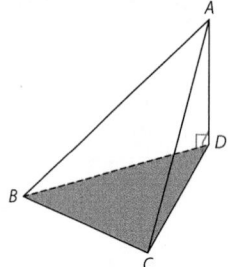
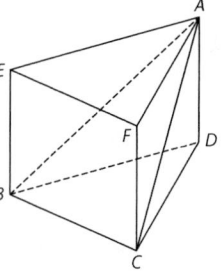

(A) What is the volume of the triangular prism?

$V = Bh$; the volume of the prism is the product of the base and height.

© Houghton Mifflin Harcourt Publishing Company

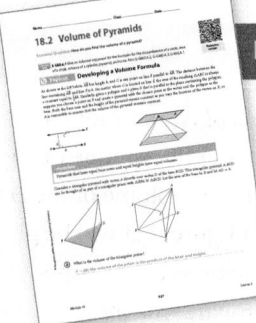

HARDCOVER PAGES 791–800

Turn to these pages to find this lesson in the hardcover student edition.

(B) Draw $\overline{EC}$ on one face of the triangular prism. Consider the three pyramids: *A-BCD*, *A-EBC*, and *A-CFE*. Explain why the sum of the volumes of these three pyramids is equal to the volume of the prism.

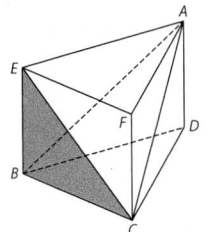 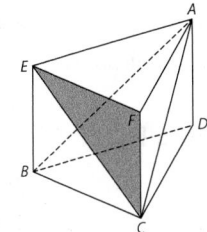 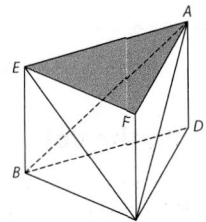 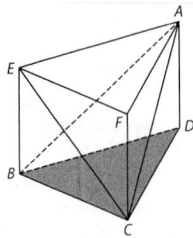

If you remove *A-BCD* from the prism, and then slice the remaining solid on the plane *AEC*, you get pyramids *A-EBC* and *A-CFE*. The three pyramids do not overlap and contain the entire prism, so the sum of their volumes is equal to the volume of the prism.

(C) $\overline{EC}$ is the diagonal of a rectangle, so $\triangle [EBC] \cong \triangle [CFE]$.
Explain why pyramids *A-EBC* and *A-CFE* have the same volume. Explain why pyramids *C-EFA* and *A-BCD* have the same volume.

In pyramids *A-EBC* and *A-CFE*, the bases *EBC* and *CFE* are congruent and the heights are equal, so by the preceding postulate, the volumes are equal. In the pyramids *C-EFA* and *A-BCD*, the bases *EFA* and *BCD* are congruent and the heights are equal, so by the preceding postulate, the volumes are equal.

(D) *A-CFE* and *C-EFA* are two names for the same pyramid, so you now have shown that the three pyramids that form the triangular prism all have equal volume. Compare the volume of the pyramid *A-BCD* and the volume of the triangular prism. Write the volume of pyramid *A-BCD* in terms of *B* and *h*.

The volume of pyramid *A-BCD* is one-third the volume of the triangular prism. The volume of the pyramid *A-BCD* is $\frac{1}{3} Bh$.

© Houghton Mifflin Harcourt Publishing Company

EXPLORE

Developing a Volume Formula

INTEGRATE TECHNOLOGY

Students have the option of doing the Explore activity either in the book or online.

QUESTIONING STRATEGIES

 What information do you need to find the volume of a pyramid? You need the base area of the pyramid and the height. The volume is $\frac{1}{3}$ the base area times the height.

What is the shape of the base of the pyramid affect the volume? The shape of the base affects how the area of the base is calculated, which in turn affects the volume.

INTEGRATE MATHEMATICAL PRACTICES
Focus on Communication

MP.3 Begin by briefly reviewing the definition of *pyramid* and the associated vocabulary (*lateral face, vertex, base*). You may also want to review how to sketch a pyramid. Suggest that students start by drawing a polygonal base and plotting a point for the vertex. Then, students can draw segments from the vertex to each vertex of the polygonal base. Remind students to use dashed lines for edges that are hidden when the pyramid is viewed from the front.

PROFESSIONAL DEVELOPMENT

Math Background

In this lesson, students develop and use a formula for the volume of a pyramid. They find that the volume of a pyramid is related to the volume of a prism by a factor of one third. That is, the volume of a pyramid is equal to one-third the volume of the associated prism, or one-third the area of the base of the pyramid times its height. Cavalieri's Principle also applies to pyramids, although the application is less straightforward than it is with prisms and cylinders, because the cross-sectional area of a pyramid is different at different points along its height.

EXPLAIN 1

Finding the Volume of a Pyramid

QUESTIONING STRATEGIES

? What must you know about a line before you can use it as a height in the formula for the volume of a pyramid? The line must be perpendicular to the base and contain the vertex.

Reflect

1. Explain how you know that the three pyramids that form the triangular prism all have the same volume.

   Pyramids *A-EBC* and *A-CFE* have the same volume and pyramids *C-EFA* and *A-BCD* have

   the same volume. Because *A-CFE* and *C-EFA* are two names for the same pyramid, by the

   Transitive Property of Equality, the three pyramids all have the same volume.

✏ Explain 1 Finding the Volume of a Pyramid

In the Explore, you showed that the volume of a "wedge pyramid" having its vertex directly over one of the vertices of the base is one-third the product of the base area and the height. Now consider a general pyramid. As shown in the figure, a pyramid can be partitioned into nonoverlapping wedge pyramids by drawing a perpendicular from the vertex to the base. The volume V of the given pyramid is the sum of the volumes of the wedge pyramids.

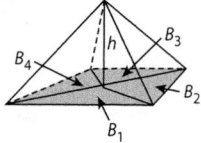

That is, $V = \frac{1}{3}B_1 h + \frac{1}{3}B_2 h + \frac{1}{3}B_3 h + \frac{1}{3}B_4 h.$

Using the distributive property, this may be rewritten as $V = \frac{1}{3}h(B_1 + B_2 + B_3 + B_4).$

Notice that $B_1 + B_2 + B_3 + B_4 = B$, where B is the base area of the given pyramid.

So, $V = \frac{1}{3}Bh.$

The above argument provides an informal justification for the following result.

Volume of a Pyramid

The volume V of a pyramid with base area B and height h is given by $V = \frac{1}{3}Bh.$

Example 1 Solve a volume problem.

(A) Ashton built a model square-pyramid with the dimensions shown. What is the volume of the pyramid?

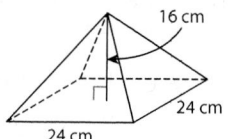

The pyramid is composed of wooden blocks that are in the shape of cubes. A block has the dimensions 4 cm by 4 by 4 cm. How many wooden blocks did Ashton use to build the pyramid?

- Find the volume of the pyramid.

  The area of the base B is the area of the square with sides of length 24 cm. So, $B = 576$ cm².

  The volume V of the pyramid is $\frac{1}{3}Bh = \frac{1}{3} \cdot 576 \cdot 16.$

  So $V = 3072$ cm³.

- Find the volume of an average block.

  The volume of a cube is given by the formula $V = s^3$. So the volume W of a wooden block is 64 cm³.

- Find the approximate number of stone blocks in the pyramid, divide V by W. So the number of blocks that Ashton used is 144.

COLLABORATIVE LEARNING

Small Group Activity

Have students make nets for a square-based pyramid and a square-based prism that has the same height as the pyramid. Then, have students cut out, fold, and tape the nets to form the three-dimensional figures. Students can model the volume of the pyramid by filling it with uncooked rice or sand. Ask students to pour the rice from the pyramid into the prism as many times as necessary to see how the volumes of the figures are related. Students will discover that it takes three batches of rice from the pyramid to fill the prism. That is, the volume of the pyramid is one-third the volume of the associated prism.

(B) The Great Pyramid in Giza, Egypt, is approximately a square pyramid with the dimensions shown. The pyramid is composed of stone blocks that are rectangular prisms. An average block has dimensions 1.3 m by 1.3 m by 0.7 m. Approximately how many stone blocks were used to build the pyramid? Round to the nearest hundred thousand.

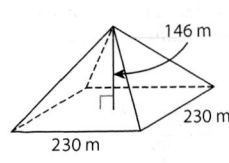

146 m

230 m

230 m

- Find the volume of the pyramid.

  The area of the base B is the area of the square with sides of length 230 m. So, $\underline{B = 52{,}900 \text{ m}^2}$.

  The volume V of the pyramid is $\frac{1}{3}Bh = \frac{1}{3} \cdot \underline{\ 52{,}900\ } \cdot \underline{\ 146\ }$.

  So $V \approx \underline{\ 2{,}574{,}466.7 \text{ m}^3\ }$.

- Find the volume of an average block.

  The volume of a rectangular prism is given by the formula $\underline{\ V = lwh\ }$. So the volume W of an average block is $\underline{\ 1.183 \text{ m}^3\ }$.

- Find the approximate number of stone blocks in the pyramid, divide $\underline{\ V\ }$ by $\underline{\ W\ }$. So the approximate number of blocks is $\underline{\ 2{,}200{,}000\ }$.

Reflect

2. What aspects of the model in Part B may lead to inaccuracies in your estimate?
   Possible answer: The given dimensions of the pyramid and the blocks are approximations,
   and the blocks do not form a true pyramid, and consist of layers or "steps".

3. Suppose you are told that the average height of a stone block 0.69 m rather than 0.7 m. Would the increase or decrease your estimate of the total number of blocks in the pyramid? Explain.
   Increase; this change would decrease W, so $\frac{V}{W}$ would increase. Since the size of each stone
   was slightly smaller, more would be needed to make a pyramid the same size.

Your Turn

4. A piece of pure silver in the shape of a rectangular pyramid with the dimensions shown has a mass of 19.7 grams. What is the density of silver? Round to the nearest tenth.
   $\left(\text{Hint: } density = \frac{mass}{volume}.\right)$

   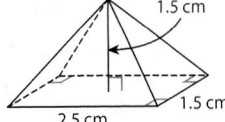

   1.5 cm

   1.5 cm

   2.5 cm

   - **Find the area of the base:** $B = (2.5)(1.5) = 3.75 \text{ cm}^2$
   - **Find the volume of the pyramid:** $V = \frac{1}{3}(3.75)(1.5) = 1.875$
   - **Find the density:** $D = \frac{19.7}{1.875} = 10.5$

DIFFERENTIATE INSTRUCTION

Modeling

To help students remember how to apply the formula for the volume of a pyramid, have students make a small poster showing examples of several types of regular pyramids, including ones with square, pentagonal, and hexagonal bases. Then have them use colored pencils to write the area of each base in one color, the heights in another color, and then list the formulas for the volumes in different colors. Have them label each figure with the formula and volume, and display the posters in the classroom. Invite students to share their posters with other students.

EXPLAIN 2

Finding the Volume of a Composite Figure

INTEGRATE MATHEMATICAL PRACTICES
Focus on Patterns

MP.8 Students should be able to recognize the solid figures that make up a composite figure. Ask them to make an organized list of all figures comprising the composite figures and then give the formulas for their volumes. Emphasize that the composite figure may include cylinders or prisms along with pyramids. After organizing how to find the volume of the composite figure, have students substitute for the variables in each formula, find the volume of each solid, then add or subtract the volumes to get the total.

QUESTIONING STRATEGIES

? How do you know whether to add or subtract the volumes of a composite figure? If the diagram indicates that one figure is cut out of or removed from another, subtract its volume from the volume of the larger figure. It the diagram indicates that two figures are connected to one another, add their volumes.

 Explain 2 **Finding the Volume of a Composite Figure**

You can add or subtract to find the volume of composite figures.

Example 2 Find the volume of the composite figure formed by a pyramid removed from a prism. Round to the nearest tenth.

Ⓐ

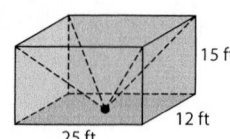

15 ft
12 ft
25 ft

- Find the volume of the prism.
  $V = lwh = (25)(12)(15) = 4500$ ft³

- Find the volume of pyramid.
  Area of base: $B = (25)(12) = 300$ ft²

  Volume of pyramid: $V = \frac{1}{3}(300)(15) = 1500$ ft³

- Subtract the volume of the pyramid from volume of the prism to find the volume of the composite figure.
  $4500 - 1500 = 3000$

So the volume of the composite figure is 3000 ft³.

Ⓑ

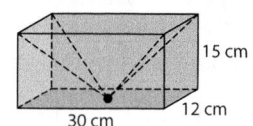

15 cm
12 cm
30 cm

- Find the volume of the prism.
  $V = lwh = (30)(\underline{12})(\underline{15}) = (\underline{5400})$ cm³

- Find the volume of the pyramid.
  Area of base: $B = \underline{(30)(12)} = 360$ cm²

  Volume of pyramid: $V = \frac{1}{3}(\underline{360})(\underline{15}) = (\underline{1800})$ cm³

- Subtract volume of pyramid from volume of prism to find volume of composite figure.
  $\underline{5400} - \underline{1800} = \underline{3600}$

So the volume of the composite figure is $\underline{3600}$ cm³.

© Houghton Mifflin Harcourt Publishing Company

LANGUAGE SUPPORT EL

Connect Vocabulary

To help them remember how the volume of a prism is connected to the volume of a pyramid, have students make a graphic organizer listing the volume formulas they know and adding the volume formulas from this module. Sample:

Volumes of 3-Dimensional Figures		
Formula	$V = Bh$	$V = \frac{1}{3}Bh$
Figure	prism	pyramid

Find the volume of the composite figure. Round to the nearest tenth.

5. The composite figure is formed from two pyramids. The base of each pyramid is a square with a side length of 6 inches and each pyramid has a height of 8 inches.

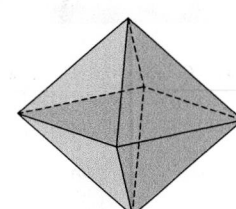

Area of base of each pyramid: $B = (6)(6) = 36 \text{ in}^2$

Volume of one pyramid: $V = \frac{1}{3}(36)(8) = 96 \text{ in}^2$

Volume of figure: $96 + 96 = 192 \text{ in}^3$

6. The composite figure is formed by a rectangular prism with two square pyramids on top of it.

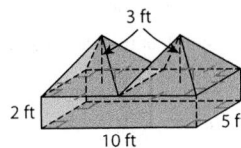

Volume of rectangular prism: $V_1 = (2)(10)(5) = 100 \text{ ft}^3$

Base of each pyramid: $(5)(5) = 25 \text{ ft}^2$

Volume of each pyramid: $V_2 = \frac{1}{3}(25)(3) = 25 \text{ ft}^2$

Volume of entire figure: $V_1 + 2V_2 = (100) + 2(25) = 150 \text{ ft}^2$

💬 Elaborate

7. Explain how the volume of a pyramid is related to the volume of a prism with the same base and height.

Three pyramids with equal volumes combine to form a prism. So a pyramid is $\frac{1}{3}$ the volume of the prism.

8. If the length and width of a rectangular pyramid are doubled and the height stays the same, how does the volume of the pyramid change? Explain.

The volume of the pyramid will be 4 times as great as the volume of the original pyramid.

If the original volume is Bh, and its length and width are doubled, then the area of the base is $(2\ell)(2w)$, or $4\ell w$, which makes the volume $V = 4 \times \frac{1}{3}Bh$.

9. Essential Question Check-In How do you calculate the volume of a pyramid?

The volume, V, of a pyramid with base area B and height h is given by $V = \frac{1}{3}Bh$.

ELABORATE

QUESTIONING STRATEGIES

? How is the volume of a pyramid related to the volume of a prism with the same base and height? The volume of the pyramid is one-third the volume of the prism.

SUMMARIZE THE LESSON

? How do you find the volume of a pyramid? The volume of the pyramid is one-third the area of the base of the pyramid times the height of the pyramid.

EVALUATE

ASSIGNMENT GUIDE

Concepts and Skills	Practice
Explore Developing a Volume Formula	Exercises 1–3
Example 1 Finding the Volume of a Pyramid	Exercises 4–7
Example 2 Finding the Volume of a Composite Figure	Exercises 8–9

INTEGRATE MATHEMATICAL PRACTICES

Focus on Reasoning

MP.2 When working with the volume of a pyramid formulas, remind students that pyramids have triangles for lateral sides. Each of these triangles has its own height, but these are not the height of the pyramid. (Instead, they are used to find the surface area of the pyramid.) The height of the pyramid is the perpendicular distance from the vertex to the base.

⭐ Evaluate: Homework and Practice

• Online Homework
• Hints and Help
• Extra Practice

1. Compare the volume of a square pyramid to the volume of a square prism with the same base and height as the pyramid.

Pyramid	Prism
$V = \frac{1}{3}Bh$	$V = Bh$
$= \frac{1}{3}\ell wh$	$= \ell wh$

The volume of the square pyramid is $\frac{1}{3}$ the volume of the square prism.

2. Which of the following equations could describe a square pyramid? Select all that apply.

A. $3Vh = B$

B. $V = \frac{1}{3}\ell wB$

C. $w = \frac{3V}{\ell h}$ ⃝

D. $\frac{V}{B} = \frac{h}{3}$ ⃝

E. $V = \frac{w^2h}{3}$ ⃝

F. $\frac{1}{3} = VBh$

C. $V = \frac{1}{3}Bh$
$3V = \ell wh$
$\frac{3V}{\ell h} = w$

E. $V = \frac{1}{3}Bh$
$= \frac{1}{3}w^2h$
$= \frac{w^2h}{3}$

D. $V = \frac{1}{3}Bh$
$\frac{V}{B} = \frac{1}{3}h$
$\frac{V}{B} = \frac{h}{3}$

3. **Justify Reasoning** As shown in the figure, polyhedron *ABCDEFGH* is a cube and *P* is any point on face *EFGH*. Compare the volume of the pyramid *PABCD* and the volume of the cube. Demonstrate how you came to your answer.

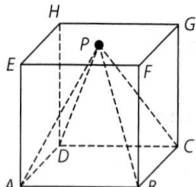

$V_{prism} = Bh$
$= \ell wh$
$= s \cdot s \cdot s$
$= s^3$

$V_{pyramid} = \frac{1}{3}Bh$
$= \frac{1}{3}\ell wh$
$= \frac{1}{3}s \cdot s \cdot s$
$= \frac{1}{3}s^3$

The volume of *PABCD* is $\frac{1}{3}$ the volume of the cube.

Find the volume of the pyramid. Round your answer to the nearest tenth.

4.

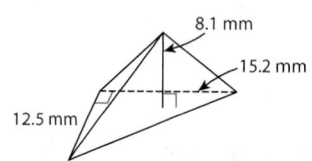

8.1 mm
15.2 mm
12.5 mm

$V = \frac{1}{3}Bh$
$= \frac{1}{3} \cdot \left(\frac{1}{2} \cdot 12.5 \cdot 15.2\right)(8.1)$
$= 256.5 \text{ mm}^3$

5.

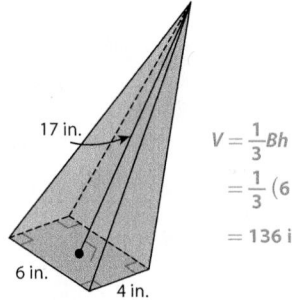

17 in.
6 in.
4 in.

$V = \frac{1}{3}Bh$
$= \frac{1}{3}(6 \cdot 4)(17)$
$= 136 \text{ in}^3$

© Houghton Mifflin Harcourt Publishing Company

Exercise	Depth of Knowledge (D.O.K.)	COMMON CORE Mathematical Practices
1	**2** Skills/Concepts	**MP.2** Reasoning
2	**2** Skills/Concepts	**MP.5** Using Tools
3	**2** Skills/Concepts	**MP.3** Logic
4–13	**1** Recall of Information	**MP.5** Using Tools
14–19	**2** Skills/Concepts	**MP.4** Modeling
20	**3** Strategic Thinking H.O.T.	**MP.3** Logic

6. Find the volume of a hexagonal pyramid with a base area of 25 ft² and a height of 9 ft.

$$V = \frac{1}{3}Bh$$
$$= \frac{1}{3} \cdot 25 \cdot 9$$
$$= 75 \text{ ft}^3$$

7. The area of the base of a hexagonal pyramid is $\frac{24}{\tan 30°}$ cm². Find its volume.

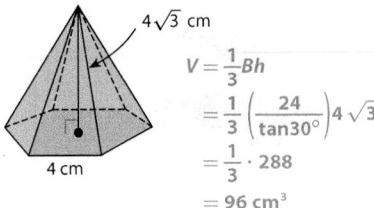

$$V = \frac{1}{3}Bh$$
$$= \frac{1}{3}\left(\frac{24}{\tan 30°}\right) 4\sqrt{3}$$
$$= \frac{1}{3} \cdot 288$$
$$= 96 \text{ cm}^3$$

Find the volume of the composite figure. Round to the nearest tenth.

8.

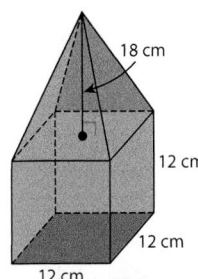

$$V_{prism} = Bh$$
$$= 12^3$$
$$= 1728 \text{ cm}^3$$
$$V_{pyramid} = \frac{1}{3}Bh$$
$$= \frac{1}{3}(12 \cdot 12)(18)$$
$$= 864 \text{ cm}^3$$
$$1728 + 864 = 2592$$
$$V_{total} = 2592.0 \text{ cm}^3$$

9.

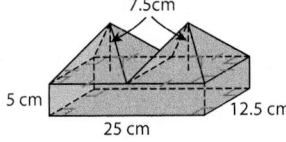

$$V_{prism} = Bh = (25 \cdot 12.5)(5) = 1562.5 \text{ cm}^3$$
$$V_{pyramid} = \frac{1}{3}Bh = \frac{1}{3}(12.5 \cdot 12.5)(7.5) = 390.625 \text{ cm}^3$$
$$1562.5 + 390.625 + 390.625 = 2343.75$$
$$V_{total} = 2343.8 \text{ cm}^3$$

10. Given a square pyramid with a height of 21 ft and a volume of 3969 cubic feet, find the length of one side of the square base. Round to the nearest tenth.

$$V = \frac{1}{3}Bh$$
$$V = \frac{1}{3}\ell wh$$
$$3969 = \frac{1}{3} \cdot x \cdot x \cdot 21$$
$$3969 = \frac{1}{3} \cdot x^2 \cdot 21$$

$$3969 = 7x^2$$
$$567 = x^2$$
$$\sqrt{567} = \sqrt{x^2}$$
$$23.8 \approx x$$
$$23.8 \text{ ft}$$

11. Consider a pyramid with height 10 feet and a square base with side length of 7 feet. How does the volume of the pyramid change if the base stays the same and the height is doubled?

The volume doubles.

Volume of pyramid with height 10

$$V = \frac{1}{3}Bh$$
$$= \frac{1}{3}\ell wh$$
$$= \frac{1}{3} \cdot 7 \cdot 7 \cdot 10$$
$$= 163.\overline{3} \text{ in}^3$$

Volume of pyramid with height doubled

$$V = \frac{1}{3}Bh$$
$$= \frac{1}{3}\ell wh$$
$$= \frac{1}{3} \cdot 7 \cdot 7 \cdot 20$$
$$= 326.\overline{6} \text{ in}^3$$

$326.\overline{6}$ is twice as great as $163.\overline{3}$.

Focus on Math Connections

MP.1 If the height of a pyramid stays the same and the side length of the base is doubled, then the volume of the pyramid is multiplied by the square of the dimension change, or 4. If all dimensions of the pyramid are doubled, however, then the volumes are in the ratio $1:2^3$, or 1:8.

Exercise	Depth of Knowledge (D.O.K.)	COMMON CORE Mathematical Practices
21	**3** Strategic Thinking H.O.T.	**MP.6** Precision
22	**3** Strategic Thinking H.O.T.	**MP.6** Precision

AVOID COMMON ERRORS

When finding the volume of composite figures, some students may think they need to always add the volumes of the figures that make up the composite figure. Caution students to study the composite figure carefully and then decide which volumes are added and which are subtracted.

12. Algebra Find the value of x if the volume of the pyramid shown is 200 cubic centimeters.

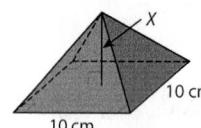

$$V = \frac{1}{3}Bh$$

$$V = \frac{1}{3}\ell wh$$

$$200 = \frac{1}{3} \cdot 10 \cdot 10 \cdot x$$

$$200 = \frac{100}{3} \cdot x$$

$$\frac{3}{100} \cdot 200 = \frac{100}{3}x \cdot \frac{3}{100}$$

$$6 = x$$

$$x = 6 \text{ cm}$$

13. Find the height of a rectangular pyramid with length 3 meters, width 8 meters, and volume 112 cubic meters.

$$V = \frac{1}{3}Bh$$

$$V = \frac{1}{3}\ell wh$$

$$112 = \frac{1}{3} \cdot 3 \cdot 8 \cdot h$$

$$112 = 8h$$

$$\frac{112}{8} = \frac{8h}{8}$$

$$14 = h$$

$$h = 14 \text{ m}$$

14. A storage container for grain is in the shape of a square pyramid with the dimensions shown.

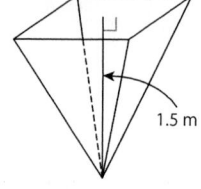

a. What is the volume of the container in cubic centimeters?

$$V = \frac{1}{3}Bh = \frac{1}{3}\ell wh = \frac{1}{3} \cdot 100 \cdot 100 \cdot 150 = 500,000 \text{ cm}^3$$

b. Grain leaks from the container at a rate of 4 cubic centimeters per second. Assuming the container starts completely full, about how many hours does it take until the container is empty?

$$\frac{500,000 \text{ cm}^3}{4 \text{ cm}^3 \text{ per sec}} = 125,000 \text{ sec}; \quad 125,000 \text{ sec} \cdot \frac{1 \text{ min}}{60 \text{ sec}} \cdot \frac{1 \text{ hour}}{60 \text{ min}} \approx 34.7 \text{ hours}$$

15. A piece of pure copper in the shape of a rectangular pyramid with the dimensions shown has a mass of 16.76 grams. What is the density of copper? Round to the nearest hundredth. $\left(\text{Hint: } density = \frac{mass}{volume}. \right)$

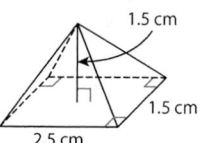

$$V = \frac{1}{3}Bh = \frac{1}{3}\ell wh = \frac{1}{3} \cdot 2.5 \cdot 1.5 \cdot 1.5 = 1.875 \text{ cm}^3 \qquad \frac{19.7 \text{ g}}{1.875 \text{ cm}^3} \approx 10.5 \frac{\text{g}}{\text{cm}^3}$$

16. Represent Real World Problems An art gallery is a 6 story square pyramid with base area $\frac{1}{2}$ acre (1 acre = 4840 yd², 1 story ≈ 10 ft). Estimate the volume in cubic yards and cubic feet.

$V = \frac{1}{3}Bh$

$= \frac{1}{3}\left(\frac{1}{2} \cdot 4840\right) \cdot 20$

$= 16,133.\overline{3}$

$\approx 16,100 \text{ yd}^3$

$V = \frac{1}{3}Bh$

$= \frac{1}{3}\left(\frac{1}{2} \cdot 4840 \cdot 3 \cdot 3\right) \cdot 60$

$= 435,600$

$\approx 436,000 \text{ ft}^3$

17. Analyze Relationships How would the volume of the pyramid shown change if each dimension were multiplied by 6? Explain how you found your answer.

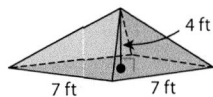

4 ft

7 ft   7 ft

Volume of original pyramid

$V = \frac{1}{3}Bh$

$= \frac{1}{3}(7 \cdot 7)(4)$

$= 65.\overline{3} \text{ ft}^3$

Volume of pyramid with dimensions multiplied by 6

$V = \frac{1}{3}Bh$

$= \frac{1}{3}(42 \cdot 42)(24)$

$= 14,112 \text{ ft}^3$

$\frac{14112}{65.\overline{3}} = 216$

The volume would be 216 times larger; dividing the volume of the enlarged pyramid by the volume of the original pyramid gives 216.

18. Geology A crystal is cut into a shape formed by two square pyramids joined at the base. Each pyramid has a base edge length of 5.7 mm and a height of 3 mm. What is the volume of the crystal to the nearest cubic millimeter?

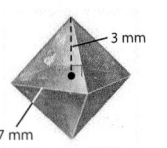

3 mm

5.7 mm

$V = \frac{1}{3}Bh$

$= \frac{1}{3}(5.7 \cdot 5.7)(3)$

$= \frac{1}{3} \cdot 97.47$

$= 32.49 \text{ mm}^3$

$2 \cdot 32.49 = 64.98$

$V \approx 65 \text{ mm}^3$

19. A roof that encloses an attic is a square pyramid with a base edge length of 45 feet and a height of 5 yards. What is the volume of the attic in cubic feet? In cubic yards?

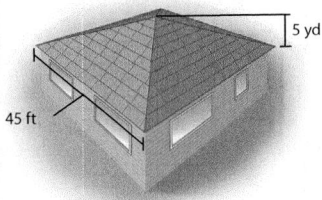

5 yd

45 ft

$V = \frac{1}{3}Bh = \frac{1}{3}(45 \cdot 45)(15) = 10,125 \text{ ft}^3$

$V = \frac{1}{3}Bh = \frac{1}{3}(15 \cdot 15)(5) = 375 \text{ ft}^3$

© Houghton Mifflin Harcourt Publishing Company

Have students work in pairs. Each student makes up two application problems, one involving the volume of a pyramid and one involving the volume of a composite figure. Then students exchange problems with their partners, and solve the problems that their partners have written.

JOURNAL

Have students describe how to use the general volume formula $V = Bh$ to write a formula for the volume of a square pyramid with base length ℓ and height h.

20. **Explain the Error** Describe and correct the error in finding the volume of the pyramid.

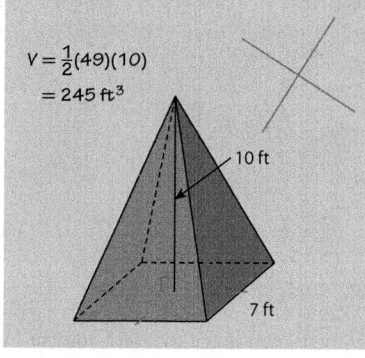

$V = \frac{1}{2}(49)(10)$

$= 245 \text{ ft}^3$

10 ft

7 ft

The formula for the volume of a pyramid is $V = \frac{1}{3}Bh$, not $V = \frac{1}{2}Bh$. The product of 49 and 10 should be multiplied by $\frac{1}{3}$, rather than $\frac{1}{2}$.

21. **Communicate Mathematical Ideas** A pyramid has a square base and a height of 5 ft. The volume of the pyramid is 60 ft³. Explain how to find the length of a side of the pyramid's base.

Let s be the length of a side of the pyramid's base. Then the area of the base is s^2, and $\frac{1}{3}s^2(5) = 60$. Solving shows that $s = 6$ ft.

$$\frac{1}{3}s^2(5) = 60$$

$$\frac{5}{3}s^2 = 60$$

$$\frac{3}{5} \cdot \frac{5}{3}s^2 = 60 \cdot \frac{3}{5}$$

$$s^2 = 36$$

$$\sqrt{s^2} = \sqrt{36}$$

$$s = 6$$

22. **Critical Thinking** A triangular pyramid has a length of 2, a width of x, and a height of $3x$. Its volume is 512 cm³. What is the area of the base?

$$V = \frac{1}{3}Bh$$

$$512 = \frac{1}{3}(2)(x)(3x)$$

$$512 = \frac{1}{3}(6x^2)$$

$$512 = 2x^2$$

$$x^2 = 256$$

$$x = 16 \quad or \quad x = -16$$

Since the width is not a negative number, $x = 16$. The area of the base is 2(16), which is 32 cm³.

Lesson Performance Task

Genna is making a puzzle using a wooden cube. She's going to cut the cube into three pieces. The figure below shows the lines along which she plans to cut away the first piece. The result will be a piece with four triangular sides and a square side (shaded).

1. Each cut Genna makes will begin at the upper left corner of the cube. Write a rule describing where she drew the lines for the first piece.

   Sample answer: Starting at the upper left corner, draw the diagonals of two adjacent sides of the cube. Then draw a diagonal through the cube from the upper left corner to the opposite corner.

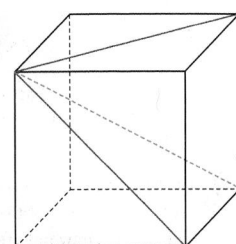

2. The figure below shows two of the lines along which Genna will cut the second piece. Draw a cube and on it, draw the two lines Genna drew. Then, using the same rule you used above, draw the third line and shade the square base of the second piece.

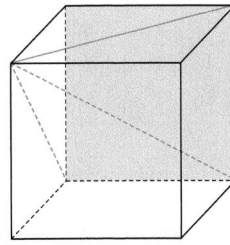

3. When Genna cut away the second piece of the puzzle, the third piece remained. Draw a new cube and then draw the lines that mark the edges of the third piece. Shade the square bottom of the third piece.

4. Compare the volumes of the three pieces. Explain your reasoning.

   Sample answer: The volumes of the three pieces are equal because the pieces are congruent to one another.

5. Explain how the model confirms the formula for the volume of a pyramid.

   Sample answer: Let B represent the area of the base of the cube, h represent the height of the cube, and s represent the length of the side of the cube. Then the volume of the cube is $V = s^3 = s^2 s = s^2 h = Bh$. Each pyramid has a volume equal to one-third the volume of the cube, so the volume of each pyramid is $V = \frac{1}{3} Bh$.

© Houghton Mifflin Harcourt Publishing Company

EXTENSION ACTIVITY

Countless *dissection puzzles* have been created over time, and new ones crop up every day. Students can research dissection puzzles on the Internet to find many such puzzles. Have students choose one or more puzzles that intrigue them, make copies, and challenge partners to solve them.

QUESTIONING STRATEGIES

The following questions lead students through a different derivation of the formula for the volume of a pyramid.

? Start with a cube with sides s units in length. What is its volume? $V = s^3$

? Connect the 8 corners of the cube with the cube's midpoint. Describe the shape and dimension of the figures formed. Six pyramids are formed. Each has a square base that is a face of the cube, so the base's area is s^2. Each pyramid has a height of $\frac{1}{2} s$.

? What is the volume of each pyramid? Explain. $V = \frac{1}{6} s^3$; 6 congruent pyramids make up s^3, the volume of the cube.

? Rewrite your expression for the volume of a pyramid using your expressions for the height of the pyramid, h, and the area of the base, B.

$$V = \frac{1}{6} s^3$$
$$= \frac{1}{3} \left(\frac{1}{2} s \right) s^2$$
$$= \frac{1}{3} hB$$

INTEGRATE MATHEMATICAL PRACTICES

Focus on Modeling

MP.4 Students can go online to find patterns for making three congruent paper pyramids that fit together to make a cube.

Volume of Cones

Common Core Math Standards

The student is expected to:

 G-GMD.A.1

Give an informal argument for the formulas for the circumference of a circle, area of a circle, volume of a cylinder, pyramid, and cone. Also G-GMD.A.3, G-MG.A.1

Mathematical Practices

 MP.4 Modeling

Language Objective

Explain to a partner how to apply the formulas for the volume of a cone.

ENGAGE

Essential Question: How do you calculate the volumes of composite figures that include cones?

Break the composite figure into familiar solids, such as cones, that you have a volume formula for. Then find the volume of each figure and add them.

PREVIEW: LESSON PERFORMANCE TASK

View the Engage section online. Discuss the photograph. Ask students to speculate on the connection between the photo and the topic of this lesson. Then preview the Lesson Performance Task.

Name _____ Class _____ Date _____

18.3 Volume of Cones

Essential Question: How do you calculate the volumes of composite figures that include cones?

⊘ Explore   Developing a Volume Formula

You can approximate the volume of a cone by finding the volumes of inscribed pyramids.

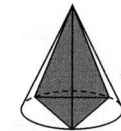 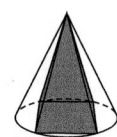 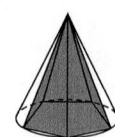

Base of inscribed pyramid has 3 sides

Base of inscribed pyramid has 4 sides

Base of inscribed pyramid has 5 sides

(A) The base of a pyramid is inscribed in the circular base of the cone and is a regular n-gon. Let O be the center of the cone's base, let r be the radius of the cone, and let h be the height of the cone. Draw radii from O to the vertices of the n-gon.

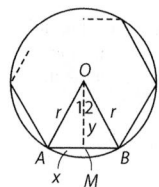

Construct segment $\overline{OM}$ from O to the midpoint M of $\overline{AB}$. How can you prove that $\triangle AOM \cong \triangle BOM$?

$\overline{OA} \cong \overline{OB}$ because they are both radii of the same circle. $\overline{AM} \cong \overline{BM}$ because M is defined

as the midpoint. Both triangles share the side $\overline{OM}$. So by the SSS Triangle Congruence

Theorem, the triangles are congruent.

(B) How is $\angle 1 \cong \angle 2$?

Since the triangles are congruent, and $\triangle AOM$ is a vertical reflection of $\triangle BOM$, then by

CPCTC, $\angle 1 \cong \angle 2$.

© Houghton Mifflin Harcourt Publishing Company

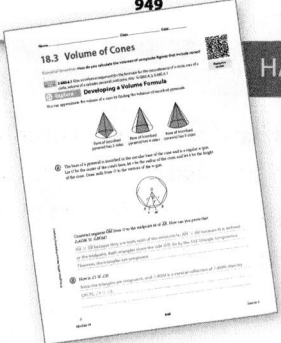

HARDCOVER PAGES 801–810

Turn to these pages to find this lesson in the hardcover student edition.

(C) How many triangles congruent to △AOB surround point O to make up the n-gon that is the base of the pyramid? How can this be used to find the angle measures of △AOM and △BOM?

There are n triangles congruent to △AOB in the n-gon, so the measure of $\angle AOB = \frac{360°}{n}$, and the measure of $\angle 1 = \frac{180°}{n}$. Since $\angle OMA \cong \angle OMB$ by CPCTC, and $\angle OMA$ and $\angle OMB$ form a linear pair, these angles are supplementary and must have measures of 90°. So, △AOM and △BOM are right triangles.

(D) In △AOM, $\sin \angle 1 = \frac{x}{r}$, so $x = r\sin \angle 1$. In △AOM, $\cos \angle 1 = \frac{y}{r}$, so $y = r\cos \angle 1$. Since $\angle 1$ has a known value, rewrite x and y using substitution.

Since $x = r\sin \angle 1$ and $y = r\cos \angle 1$, $x = r\sin \left(\frac{180°}{n}\right)$ and $y = r\cos \left(\frac{180°}{n}\right)$.

(E) To write an expression for the area of the base of the pyramid, first write an expression for the area of △AOB.

$$\text{Area of } \triangle AOB = \frac{1}{2} \cdot base \cdot height$$
$$= \frac{1}{2} \cdot 2x \cdot y$$
$$= xy$$

What is the area of △AOB, substituting the new values for x and y? What is the area of the n triangles that make up the base of the pyramid?

$$\text{Area}_{\triangle AOB} = xy$$
$$= r\sin \left(\frac{180°}{n}\right) r\cos \left(\frac{180°}{n}\right)$$

$$\text{Area}_{\text{base of pyramid}} = n\left[r\sin \left(\frac{180°}{n}\right) r\cos \left(\frac{180°}{n}\right)\right]$$
$$= nr^2\left[\sin \left(\frac{180°}{n}\right) \cos \left(\frac{180°}{n}\right)\right]$$

(F) Use the area of the base of the pyramid to find an equation for the volume of the pyramid.

$$\text{Volume}_{\text{pyramid}} = \frac{1}{3} Bh$$
$$= \left(\frac{1}{3}\right)\left[(nr^2) \sin \left(\frac{180°}{n}\right) \cos \left(\frac{180°}{n}\right)\right](h)$$

© Houghton Mifflin Harcourt Publishing Company

Developing a Volume Formula

INTEGRATE TECHNOLOGY

Students have the option of doing the Explore activity either in the book or online.

QUESTIONING STRATEGIES

? To develop a formula for the volume of a cone, why does it make sense to work with inscribed pyramids? We already have a formula for the volume of a pyramid.

? In general, what happens as the number of sides of the base of the inscribed pyramid gets larger? The volume of the pyramid gets closer to the volume of the cone.

PROFESSIONAL DEVELOPMENT

Math Background

The approach to finding a formula for the volume of a cone in this lesson is very similar to the approach to finding a formula for the circumference of a circle in Module 15-1, where students use inscribed regular polygons and an informal limit argument to show that the circumference, C, of a circle with radius r is given by $C = 2\pi r$. In this module, students inscribe a sequence of pyramids in a given cone and use similar reasoning to show that the volume, V, of the cone is given by $V = \frac{1}{3} Bh$, where B is the base area and h is the cone's height.

INTEGRATE MATHEMATICAL PRACTICES

Focus on Modeling

MP.4 When they look at models of cones, students sometimes think a cone has one-half the volume of a cylinder with the same height and base. Point out that a cone has a volume equal to $\frac{1}{3}$ the volume of the associated cylinder. Encourage students to use hollow models of cones and cylinders to verify this.

EXPLAIN 1

Finding the Volume of a Cone

QUESTIONING STRATEGIES

? How does the volume formula for a cone compare to the volume formula for a pyramid? The formulas are both $V = \frac{1}{3}Bh$, but B is the area of a circle, πr^2, for the cone, while B is the area of a polygon for the pyramid.

(G) Your expression for the pyramid's volume includes the expression $n \sin\left(\frac{180°}{n}\right) \cos\left(\frac{180°}{n}\right)$. Use a calculator, as follows, to discover what happens to this expression as n gets larger and larger.

- Enter the expression $n \sin\left(\frac{180°}{n}\right) \cos\left(\frac{180°}{n}\right)$ as Y_1, using x for n.
- Go to the Table Setup menu and enter the values shown.
- View a table for the function and scroll down.

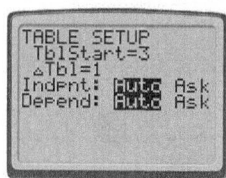 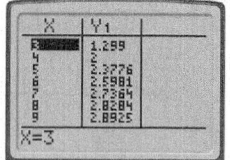

What happens to the expression as n gets very large?

The value gets closer and closer to π.

(H) If $n \sin\left(\frac{180°}{n}\right) \cos\left(\frac{180°}{n}\right)$ gets closer to π as n becomes greater, what happens to the entire expression for the volume of the inscribed pyramid? How is the area of the circle related to the expression for the base?

The expression gets closer to the formula for the pyramid, $\frac{1}{3}\pi r^2\, h$; πr^2 is the area of a circle.

Reflect

1. How is the formula for the volume of a cone related to the formula for the volume of a pyramid? Since πr^2 is the area of the base of the cone, the formula can be written as $A = \frac{1}{3}Bh$, which

is the same as the formula for the volume of a pyramid.

⊘ Explain 1 Finding the Volume of a Cone

The volume relationship for cones that you found in the Explore can be stated as the following formula.

Volume of a Cone
The volume of a cone with base radius r and base area $B = \pi r^2$ and height h is given by $V = \frac{1}{3}Bh$ or by $V = \frac{1}{3}\pi r^2 h$.

You can use a formula for the volume of a cone to solve problems involving volume and capacity.

COLLABORATIVE LEARNING

Small Group Activity

Have students each draw a cone and a cylinder, both with the same radius and height. Ask them to pass each drawing to another group member, who then measures and labels the radius and height of the cone. Have students pass the drawings again, to a group member who calculates the volume of the cone and cylinder. Have the group discuss the relationship between the volumes of the cone and the cylinder. If the volume of the cone is not exactly one-third the volume of the cylinder, have them explain why (for example, the measurements are not precise).

Example 1 The figure represents a conical paper cup. How many fluid ounces of liquid can the cup hold? Round to the nearest tenth. (*Hint*: 1 in³ ≈ 0.554 fl oz.)

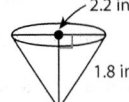

2.2 in.

1.8 in.

(A) Find the radius and height of the cone to the nearest hundredth.

The radius is half of the diameter, so $r = \frac{1}{2}(2.2 \text{ in.}) = 1.1$ in.

To find the height of the cone, use the Pythagorean Theorem:

$$r^2 + h^2 = (1.8)^2$$

$$(1.1)^2 + h^2 = (1.8)^2$$

$$1.21 + h^2 = 3.24$$

$$h^2 = 2.03, \text{ so } h \approx 1.42 \text{ in.}$$

(B) Find the volume of the cone in cubic inches.

$$V = \frac{1}{3}\pi r^2 h \approx \frac{1}{3}\pi \boxed{1.1}^2 \boxed{1.42} \approx \boxed{1.80} \text{ in}^3$$

(C) Find the capacity of the cone to the nearest tenth of a fluid ounce.

$$\boxed{1.80} \text{ in}^3 \approx \boxed{1.80} \text{ in}^3 \times \frac{0.554 \text{ fl oz}}{1 \text{ in}^3} \approx \boxed{1.00} \text{ fl oz}$$

Your Turn

Right after Cindy buys a frozen yogurt cone, her friend Maria calls her, and they talk for so long that the frozen yogurt melts before Cindy can eat it. The cone has a slant height of 3.9 in. and a diameter of 2.4 in. If the frozen yogurt has the same volume before and after melting, and when melted just fills the cone, how much frozen yogurt did Cindy have before she talked to Maria, to the nearest tenth of a fluid ounce?

2. Find the radius. Then use the Pythagorean Theorem to find the height of the cone.

$r = \frac{1}{2}(2.4 \text{ in.}) = 1.2 \text{ in.}$ $r^2 + h^2 = (3.9)^2$

$(1.2)^2 + h^2 = (3.9)^2$

$1.44 + h^2 = 15.21$

$h^2 = 13.77$

$h \approx 3.711 \text{ in.}$

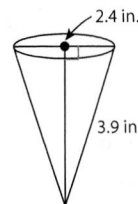

2.4 in.

3.9 in.

3. Find the volume of the cone in cubic inches.

$V = \frac{1}{3}\pi r^2 h \approx \frac{1}{3}\pi (1.2)^2 (3.711) \approx 5.596 \text{ in}^3$

4. Find the capacity of the cone to the nearest fluid ounce.

$5.60 \text{ in}^3 \approx 5.60 \text{ in}^3 \times \frac{0.554 \text{ fl oz}}{1 \text{ in}^3} \approx 3.1 \text{ fl oz}$

AVOID COMMON ERRORS

When calculating volumes of cones, some students may forget to multiply by $\frac{1}{3}$ (or divide by 3). Remind students that the volume of a cone needs the factor of $\frac{1}{3}$, but the volume of a cylinder does not. Watch for students who calculate the volume using the slant height of the cone instead of the height.

DIFFERENTIATE INSTRUCTION

Modeling

Have students make nets for a cone and a cylinder that has the same height as the cone. Then, have students cut out, fold, and tape the nets to form the three-dimensional figures. Students can model the volume of the cone by filling it with dry material. Ask students to pour the material from the cone into the cylinder as many times as necessary to see how the volumes of the figures are related. Students will discover that it takes three batches of material from the cone to fill the cylinder. That is, the volume of the cone is one-third the volume of the associated cylinder.

EXPLAIN 2

Finding the Volume of a Composite Figure

INTEGRATE MATHEMATICAL PRACTICES

Focus on Patterns

MP.8 Students should be able to recognize the solid figures that make up a composite figure, including cones, and whether the volumes of those figures are to be added or subtracted from the total volume. Ask students to make an organized list of all figures comprising the composite figures and then show the formulas for their volumes. After organizing how to find the volume of the composite figure, have students find the volume of each solid, then add or subtract the volumes, as needed, to get the total.

QUESTIONING STRATEGIES

? If a cone shares a base with a cylinder, and the volume of the cylinder is given, along with the heights of the cylinder and of the cone, how could you find the volume of the cone? Substitute the height of the cylinder and its volume into the formula for the volume of a cylinder and solve for r. Then use the value of r to find B, the area of the base of the cone. Substitute the values of B and the height into the formula for the area of a cone.

◉ Explain 2 **Finding the Volume of a Composite Figure**

You can find the volume of a composite figure using appropriate volume formulas for the different parts of the figure.

Example 2 Find the volume of the composite figure. Round to the nearest cubic millimeter.

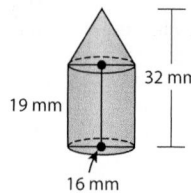

(A) Find the volume of the cylinder.

First, find the radius: $r = \frac{1}{2}(16 \text{ mm}) = 8$ mm

$V = \pi r^2 h = \pi(8)^2(19) = 3{,}820.176 \ldots$ mm³

(B) Find the volume of the cone.

The height of the cone is $h = \boxed{32}$ mm $- \boxed{19}$ mm $= \boxed{13}$ mm.

It has the same radius as the cylinder, $r = \boxed{8}$ mm.

$V = \frac{1}{3}\pi r^2 h = \frac{1}{3}\pi\left(\boxed{8}\right)^2\left(\boxed{13}\right) \approx \boxed{871.268}$ mm³

(C) Find the total volume.

Total volume = volume of cylinder + volume of cone

$= \boxed{3{,}820.177}$ mm³ $+ \boxed{871.268}$ mm³

$\approx \boxed{4{,}691}$ mm³

Reflect

5. **Discussion** A composite figure is formed from a cone and a cylinder with the same base radius, and its volume can be calculated by multiplying the volume of the cylinder by a rational number, $\frac{a}{b}$. What arrangements of the cylinder and cone could explain this?

The heights of the cylinder and the cone must be in an integer ratio. For instance, if they have the same height, and are joined base to base, the volume of the composite figure is

$V = \pi r^2 h + \frac{1}{3}\pi r^2 h = \frac{4}{3}\pi r^2 h$, or $\frac{4}{3}$ times the volume of the cylinder.

LANGUAGE SUPPORT **EL**

Connect Vocabulary

To help students remember how to apply the formula for the volume of a cone, have students make note cards showing examples of cones with different heights and bases. Then have them use colored pencils to write the area of each base in one color, the heights in another color, and then list the formulas for the volume in different colors. Have them label each figure with the formula and volume. Invite students to share their note cards with other students.

Making a cone-shaped hole in the top of a cylinder forms a composite figure, so that the apex of the cone is at the base of the cylinder. Find the volume of the figure, to the nearest tenth.

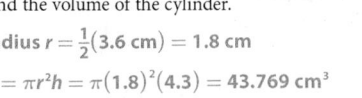

4.3 cm

3.6 cm

6. Find the volume of the cylinder.

 radius $r = \frac{1}{2}(3.6 \text{ cm}) = 1.8 \text{ cm}$

 $V = \pi r^2 h = \pi(1.8)^2(4.3) = 43.769 \text{ cm}^3$

7. Find the volume of the figure.

 Cone and cylinder have same height and radius, so volume of cone is $\frac{1}{3}$ times

 volume of cylinder.

 Therefore, volume of figure = volume cylinder − volume of cone

 $= \text{volume of cylinder} - \frac{1}{3} \text{(volume of cylinder)}$

 $= \frac{2}{3} \text{(volume of cylinder)}$

 $= \frac{2}{3}(43.769 \text{ cm}^3) \approx 29.2 \text{ cm}^3$

💬 Elaborate

8. Could you use a circumscribed regular n-gon as the base of a pyramid to derive the formula for the volume of a cone? Explain.

 Yes; the base area of the pyramid would be slightly larger than the base area of the cone,

 instead of slightly smaller, but you would still be using n congruent isosceles triangles

 with areas derived via $b = r \tan\left(\frac{180°}{n}\right)$ and $h = 2r$. Therefore the volume of the pyramid

 would have a factor of $n \tan\left(\frac{180°}{n}\right)$, and this would approach the value of π as n gets larger

 and larger.

9. **Essential Question Check-In** How do you calculate the volumes of composite figures that include cones?

 Sample answer: split the figure into simpler shapes, using the volume formula of each

 separate shape. The volume formula for a cone, $V = \frac{1}{3}\pi r^2 h$, is comparable to the volume

 formula for a pyramid, $V = \frac{1}{3}Bh$.

ELABORATE

QUESTIONING STRATEGIES

? How is the volume of a cone related to the volume of a cylinder with the same base and height? The volume of the cone is one-third the volume of the cylinder.

SUMMARIZE THE LESSON

? What are the main steps used to develop a formula for the volume of a cone? Sample answer: Inscribe a sequence of pyramids with ever-increasing sides in a given cone until the volume of the inscribed pyramid approaches the volume of the cone.

EVALUATE

Personal
Math
Trainer

ASSIGNMENT GUIDE

Concepts and Skills	Practice
Explore Developing a Volume Formula	Exercise 1
Example 1 Finding the Volume of a Cone	Exercises 2–6
Example 2 Finding the Volume of a Composite Figure	Exercises 7–10

INTEGRATE MATHEMATICAL PRACTICES
Focus on Communication

MP.3 Help students determine what information is required to use the volume formula for a cone. Sample questions: "What formula will you use?" $V = \frac{1}{3}\pi r^2 h$ "How can you find the radius?" Divide the diameter by 2. "How can you find the height?" Draw the right triangle formed by the radius, height, and slant height and then use the Pythagorean Theorem.

Personal
Math
Trainer

⭐ Evaluate: Homework and Practice

• Online Homework
• Hints and Help
• Extra Practice

1. **Interpret the Answer** Katherine is using a cone to fill a cylinder with sand. If the radii and height are equal on both objects, and Katherine fills the cone to the very top, how many cones will it take to fill the cylinder with sand? Explain your answer.

   It will take three cones to fill the cylinder with sand. Because the volume formula for a cylinder is $V = \pi r^2 h$, and the volume formula for a cone is $V = \frac{1}{3}\pi r^2 h$, the volume of a cone is $\frac{1}{3}$ the volume of the cylinder.

Find the volume of the cone. Round the answer to the nearest tenth.

2.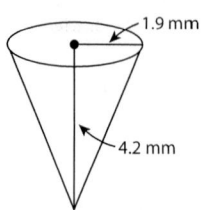
   1.9 mm
   4.2 mm

$$V = \frac{1}{3} Bh$$
$$= \frac{1}{3}\pi r^2 h$$
$$= \frac{1}{3}\pi(1.9)^2 \cdot 4.2$$
$$= \frac{1}{3}\pi(3.61) \cdot 4.2$$
$$\approx 15.9 \text{ mm}^3$$

3.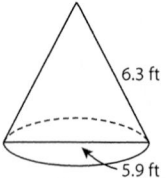
   6.3 ft
   5.9 ft

$$a^2 + b^2 = c^2$$
$$a^2 + 2.95^2 = 6.3^2$$
$$a^2 + 8.7025 = 39.69$$
$$a^2 = 30.9875$$
$$a \approx 5.6 \text{ ft}$$

$$V = \frac{1}{3} Bh$$
$$= \frac{1}{3}\pi r^2 h$$
$$\approx \frac{1}{3}\pi(2.95)^2 \cdot 5.6$$
$$\approx \frac{1}{3}\pi(8.7025) \cdot 5.6$$
$$\approx 51.0 \text{ ft}^3$$

4.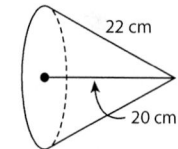
   22 cm
   20 cm

$$a^2 + b^2 = c^2 \qquad V = \frac{1}{3} Bh$$
$$a^2 + 20^2 = 22^2 \qquad V = \frac{1}{3}\pi r^2 h$$
$$a^2 + 400 = 484 \qquad = \frac{1}{3}\pi(84) \cdot 20$$
$$a^2 = 84 \text{ cm} \qquad \approx 1759.3 \text{ cm}^3$$

© Houghton Mifflin Harcourt Publishing Company

Module 18   **955**   Lesson 3

Exercise	Depth of Knowledge (D.O.K.)	COMMON CORE	Mathematical Practices
1	**3** Strategic Thinking		**MP.2** Reasoning
2–11	**1** Recall of Information		**MP.5** Using Tools
12–15	**2** Skills/Concepts		**MP.4** Modeling
16–19	**2** Skills/Concepts		**MP.5** Using Tools
20	**3** Strategic Thinking	H.O.T.	**MP.2** Reasoning
21	**3** Strategic Thinking	H.O.T.	**MP.3** Logic

Find the volume of the cone. Leave the answer in terms of π.

5.

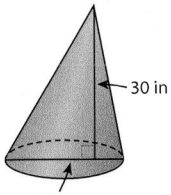

30 in

24 in.

$V = \frac{1}{3}Bh$

$= \frac{1}{3}\pi r^2 h$

$= \frac{1}{3}\pi(12)^2 \cdot 30$

$= \frac{1}{3}\pi(144) \cdot 30$

$= 1440\pi \text{ in}^3$

6.

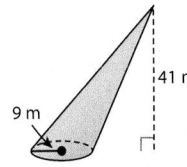

41 m

9 m

$V = \frac{1}{3}Bh$

$= \frac{1}{3}\pi r^2 h$

$= \frac{1}{3}\pi(9)^2 \cdot 41$

$= \frac{1}{3}\pi(81) \cdot 41$

$= 1107\pi \text{ m}^3$

Find the volume of the composite figures. Round the answer to the nearest tenth.

7.

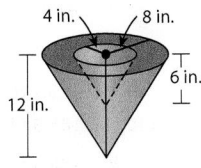

4 in.   8 in.

12 in.   6 in.

Volume of the large cone

$V = \frac{1}{3}Bh$

$= \frac{1}{3}\pi r^2 h$

$= \frac{1}{3}\pi(8)^2 \cdot 12$

$\approx 804.2 \text{ in}^3$

Volume of the small cone

$V = \frac{1}{3}Bh$

$= \frac{1}{3}\pi r^2 h$

$= \frac{1}{3}\pi(4)^2 \cdot 6$

$\approx 100.5 \text{ in}^3$

$804.2 - 100.5 = 703.7$

$V \approx 703.7 \text{ in}^3$

8.

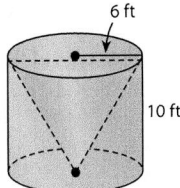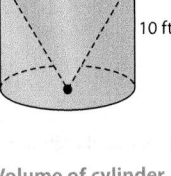

6 ft

10 ft

Volume of cylinder

$V = Bh$

$= \pi r^2 h$

$= \pi(6)^2 \cdot 10$

$\approx 1131.0 \text{ ft}^3$

Volume of cone

$V = \frac{1}{3}Bh$

$= \frac{1}{3}\pi r^2 h$

$= \frac{1}{3}\pi(6)^2 \cdot 10$

$\approx 377.0 \text{ ft}^3$

$1131.0 - 377.0 = 754.0$

$V \approx 754.0 \text{ ft}^3$

Exercise	Depth of Knowledge (D.O.K.)	COMMON CORE Mathematical Practices
22	**3** Strategic Thinking H.O.T.	**MP.2** Reasoning
23	**3** Strategic Thinking H.O.T.	**MP.3** Logic

AVOID COMMON ERRORS

When finding the volume of composite figures, some students may think they must always add the volumes of the figures that make up the composite figure. Caution students to study the composite figure carefully and then decide which volumes are added and which are subtracted. Watch for students who calculate the volume using the slant height of the cone instead of the height.

9.

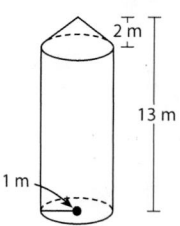

Volume of cone

$V = \frac{1}{3}Bh$

$= \frac{1}{3}\pi r^2 h$

$= \frac{1}{3}\pi(1)^2 \cdot 2$

$\approx 2.1 \text{ m}^3$

Volume of cylinder

$V = Bh$

$= \pi r^2 h$

$= \pi(1)^2 \cdot 13$

$\approx 40.8 \text{ m}^3$

$2.1 + 40.8 = 42.9$

$V \approx 42.9 \text{ m}^3$

10.

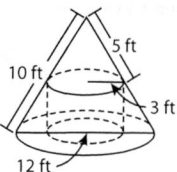

Height of cone

$a^2 + b^2 = c^2$

$h^2 + 6^2 = 10^2$

$h^2 = 64$

$h = 8 \text{ ft}$

Distance from top of cylinder to vertex of cone

$a^2 + b^2 = c^2$

$h^2 + 3^2 = 5^2$

$h^2 = 16$

$h = 4 \text{ ft}$

Height of cylinder

$8 - 4 = 4 \text{ ft}$

Volume of cone

$V = \frac{1}{3}Bh$

$= \frac{1}{3}\pi r^2 h$

$= \frac{1}{3}\pi(6)^2 \cdot 8$

$= 96\pi$

$\approx 301.6 \text{ ft}^3$

Volume of cylinder

$V = Bh$

$= \pi r^2 h$

$= \pi(3)^2 \cdot 4$

$\approx 113.1 \text{ ft}^3$

$301.6 - 113.1 = 188.5$

$V \approx 188.5 \text{ ft}^3$

11. Match the dimensions of a cone on the left with its volume on the right.

A. radius 3 units, height 7 units   <u>B</u> $\frac{25\pi}{6}$ units^3

B. diameter 5 units, height 2 units   <u>D</u> 240π units^3

C. radius 28 units, slant height 53 units   <u>C</u> $11,760\pi$ units^3

D. diameter 24 units, slant height 13 units.   <u>A</u> 21π units^3

Volume of cone A: $V = \frac{1}{3}Bh = \frac{1}{3}\pi(3)^2 \cdot 7 = 21\pi$ units^3

Volume of cone B: $V = \frac{1}{3}Bh = \frac{1}{3}\pi\left(\frac{5}{2}\right)^2 \cdot 2 = \frac{25}{6}\pi$ units^3

Height of cone C: $28^2 + h^2 = 53^2$, so $h^2 = 2025$ and $h = 45$

Volume of cone C: $V = \frac{1}{3}Bh = \frac{1}{3}\pi(28)^2 \cdot 45 = 11,760\pi$ units^3

Height of cone D: $12^2 + h^2 = 13^2$, so $h^2 = 25$ and $h = 5$

Volume of cone D: $V = \frac{1}{3}Bh = \frac{1}{3}\pi(12)^2 \cdot 5 = 240\pi$ units^3

12. The roof of a grain silo is in the shape of a cone. The inside radius is 20 feet, and the roof is 10 feet tall. Below the cone is a cylinder 30 feet tall, with the same radius.

a. What is the volume of the silo?

Volume of cone

$$V = \frac{1}{3}Bh$$
$$= \frac{1}{3}\pi(20)^2 \cdot 10$$
$$\approx 4188.8 \text{ ft}^3$$

Volume of the cylinder

$$V = Bh$$
$$= \pi r^2 h$$
$$= \pi(20)^2 \cdot 30$$
$$\approx 37,699.1 \text{ ft}^3$$

$4188.8 \text{ ft}^3 + 37,699.1 \text{ ft}^3 = 41,887.9 \text{ ft}^3$

$$V \approx 41,887.9 \text{ ft}^3$$

b. If one cubic foot of wheat is approximately 48 pounds, and the farmer's crop consists of approximately 2 million pounds of wheat, will all of the wheat fit in the silo?

$41,887.9 \text{ ft}^3 \cdot \dfrac{48 \text{ lb}}{1 \text{ ft}^3} = 2,010,619.2 \text{ lb}$

Yes, the crop will fit because the silo can hold over 2 million

pounds of wheat.

13. A cone has a volume of $18\pi \text{ in}^3$. Which are possible dimensions of the cone? Select all that apply.

A. diameter 1 in., height 18 in. $V = \frac{1}{3}Bh = \frac{1}{3}\pi(0.5)^2 \cdot 18 = 1.5\pi \text{ in}^3$

(B.) diameter 6 in., height 6 in. $V = \frac{1}{3}Bh = \frac{1}{3}\pi(3)^2 \cdot 6 = 18\pi \text{ in}^3$

C. diameter 3 in., height 6 in. $V = \frac{1}{3}Bh = \frac{1}{3}\pi(1.5)^2 \cdot 6 = 4.5\pi \text{ in}^3$

D. diameter 6 in., height 3 in. $V = \frac{1}{3}Bh = \frac{1}{3}\pi(3)^2 \cdot 3 = 9\pi \text{ in}^3$

(E.) diameter 4 in., height 13.5 in. $V = \frac{1}{3}Bh = \frac{1}{3}\pi(2)^2 \cdot 13.5 = 18\pi \text{ in}^3$

F. diameter 13.5 in., height 4 in. $V = \frac{1}{3}Bh = \frac{1}{3}\pi(6.75)^2 \cdot 4 = 60.75\pi \text{ in}^3$

CONNECT VOCABULARY [EL]

To remember how the volume of a cylinder is connected to the volume of a cone, have students make a graphic organizer listing the volume formulas they know and adding the volume formulas from this module.

Sample:

Volumes of 3-Dimensional Figures		
Formula	$V = Bh$	$V = \frac{1}{3}Bh$
Figure	prism	pyramid
Figure	cylinder	cone

14. The figure shows a water tank that consists of a cylinder and a cone. How many gallons of water does the tank hold? Round to the nearest gallon. (Hint: 1 ft³ = 7.48 gal)

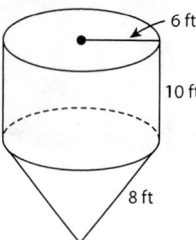

6 ft

10 ft

8 ft

Volume of cone

$$a^2 + b^2 = c^2$$

$$a^2 + 6^2 = 8^2$$

$$a^2 + 36 = 64$$

$$a^2 = 28$$

$$\sqrt{a^2} = \sqrt{28}$$

$$a \approx 5.3 \text{ cm}$$

$$V = \frac{1}{3}Bh$$

$$= \frac{1}{3}\pi(6)^2 \cdot 5.3$$

$$\approx 200 \text{ ft}^3$$

Volume of cylinder

$$V = Bh$$

$$= \pi(6)^2 \cdot 10$$

$$\approx 1131 \text{ ft}^3$$

$$200 + 1131 = 1331 \text{ ft}^3$$

$$1331 \text{ ft}^3 \cdot \frac{7.48 \text{ gal}}{1 \text{ ft}^3} \approx 9956 \text{ gal}$$

9956 gal

15. Roland is using a special machine to cut cones out of cylindrical pieces of wood. The machine is set to cut out two congruent cones from each piece of wood, leaving no gap in between the vertices of the cones. What is the volume of material left over after two cones are cut out?

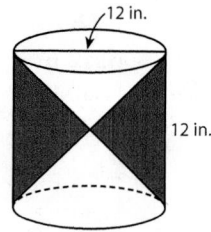

12 in.

12 in.

Volume of cylinder

$$V = Bh$$

$$= \pi(6)^2 \cdot 12$$

$$\approx 1357.2 \text{ in}^3$$

Volume of one cone

$$V = \frac{1}{3}Bh$$

$$= \frac{1}{3}\pi(6)^2 \cdot 6$$

$$\approx 226.2 \text{ in}^3$$

$$1357.2 - 226.2 - 226.2 = 904.8$$

904.8 in³

© Houghton Mifflin Harcourt Publishing Company

16. Algebra Develop an expression that could be used to solve for the volume of this solid for any value of x.

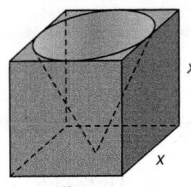

$$V = \left(s^3 - \frac{1}{3}Bh\right)$$

$$V = x^3 - \frac{1}{3}\pi r^2 h = x^3 - \frac{1}{3}\pi\left(\frac{x}{2}\right)^2 x = x^3 - \frac{1}{3}\pi\frac{x^2}{4}x$$

$$= x^3 - \frac{x^3\pi}{12}$$

$$= x^3\left(1 - \frac{\pi}{12}\right)$$

17. Persevere in Problem Solving A juice stand sells smoothies in cone-shaped cups that are 8 in. tall. The regular size has a 4 in. diameter. The jumbo size has an 8 in. diameter.

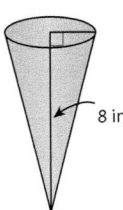

8 in.

a. Find the volume of the regular size to the nearest tenth.

$$V = \frac{1}{3}Bh$$

$$= \frac{1}{3}\pi(2)^2 \cdot 8$$

$$\approx 33.5 \text{ in}^3$$

b. Find the volume of the jumbo size to the nearest tenth.

$$V = \frac{1}{3}Bh$$

$$= \frac{1}{3}\pi(4)^2 \cdot 8$$

$$\approx 134.0 \text{ in}^3$$

c. The regular size costs $1.25. What would be a reasonable price for the jumbo size? Explain your reasoning.

$$\frac{134.0}{33.5} = 4$$

$$4 \cdot \$1.25 = \$5.00$$

$5; the large size holds 4 times as much.

18. Find the volume of a cone with base area 36π ft^2 and a height equal to twice the radius.

$$B = \pi r^2$$

$$36\pi = \pi r^2$$

$$36 = r^2$$

$$6 \text{ ft} = r$$

$$V = \frac{1}{3}Bh$$

$$= \frac{1}{3}(36\pi) \cdot 12$$

$$= 144\pi$$

$$V = 144\pi \text{ ft}^3$$

19. Find the base circumference of a cone with height 5 cm and volume 125π cm^3.

$$V = \frac{1}{3}Bh$$

$$125\pi = \frac{1}{3}\pi r^2(5)$$

$$\frac{3}{5} \cdot (125\pi) = \left(\frac{5}{3}\pi r^2\right) \cdot \frac{3}{5}$$

$$75 = r^2$$

$$5\sqrt{3} \text{ cm} = r$$

$$C = 2\pi r$$

$$= 2\pi\left(5\sqrt{3}\right)$$

$$= 10\pi\sqrt{3}$$

$$C = 10\pi\sqrt{3} \text{ cm}$$

Focus on Reasoning

MP.2 When working with the volume of a cone formula, remind students that cones have a slant height as well as a height. The slant height is used to find the surface area of the cone, while the height of the cone is the perpendicular distance from the vertex to the base.

JOURNAL

Have students describe how to use the general volume formula $V = Bh$ to write a formula for the volume of a cone with base radius r and height h. Use figures to illustrate the steps.

20. Analyze Relationships Popcorn is available in two cups: a square pyramid or a cone, as shown. The price of each cup of popcorn is the same. Which cup is the better deal? Explain.

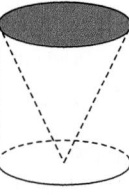

The pyramid is the better deal because you get a greater volume of popcorn (960 cm³ versus about 754 cm³) for the same price.

Volume of pyramid

$V = \frac{1}{3} Bh$

$= \frac{1}{3} (12^2) \cdot 20$

$= 960 \text{ cm}^3$

Volume of cone

$V = \frac{1}{3} Bh$

$= \frac{1}{3} \pi (6)^2 \cdot 20$

$\approx 754.0 \text{ cm}^3$

21. Make a Conjecture A cylinder has a radius of 5 in. and a height of 3 in. Without calculating the volumes, find the height of a cone with the same base and the same volume as the cylinder. Explain your reasoning.

$h = 9$ in.; the volume of a cone with the same base and height as the cylinder is $\frac{1}{3}$ the volume of the cylinder. For the cone to have the same volume as the cylinder, the height of the cone must be 3 times the height of the cylinder.

22. Analyze Relationships A sculptor removes a cone from a cylindrical block of wood so that the vertex of the cone is the center of the cylinder's base, as shown. Explain how the volume of the remaining solid compares with the volume of the original cylindrical block of wood.

The solid has $\frac{2}{3}$ the volume of the cylinder since the cone that is removed has $\frac{1}{3}$ the volume of the cylinder.

23. Explain the Error Which volume is incorrect? Explain the error.

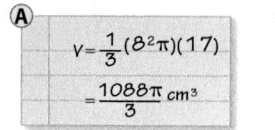
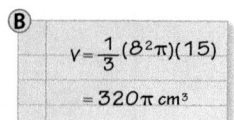
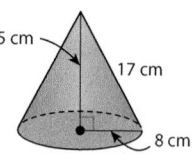

The calculation show in A is incorrect because it uses the slant height of the cone instead of the height.

Lesson Performance Task

You've just set up your tent on the first night of a camping trip that you've been looking forward to for a long time. Unfortunately, mosquitoes have been looking forward to your arrival even more than you have. When you turn on your flashlight you see swarms of them—an average of 800 mosquitoes per square meter, in fact.

Since you're always looking for a way to use geometry, you decide to solve a problem: How many mosquitoes are in the first three meters of the cone of your flashlight (Zone 1 in the diagram), and how many are in the second three meters (Zone 2)?

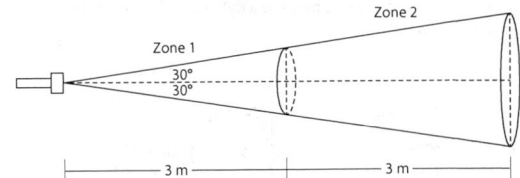

1. Explain how you can find the volume of the Zone 1 cone.
2. Find the volume of the Zone 1 cone. Write your answer in terms of π.
3. Explain how you can find the volume of the Zone 2 cone.
4. Find the volume of the Zone 2 cone. Write your answer in terms of π.
5. How many more mosquitoes are there in Zone 2 than there are in Zone 1? Use 3.14 for π.

1. **Sample answer: Find the radius of the circular base of the Zone 1 cone. Then use $A = \pi r^2$ to find B, the area of the base of the cone. Finally, use $V = \frac{1}{3} Bh$, with $h = 3$ meters, to find the volume of the cone.**

2. **The radius of the base of the Zone 1 cone is the length of the side opposite the 30° angle in a 30°-60°-90° triangle with a medium side measuring 3 m: $r = \frac{3}{\sqrt{3}} = \sqrt{3}$**

   $B = \pi r^2 = \pi \left(\sqrt{3}\right)^2 = 3\pi$

   $V = \frac{1}{3}(3\pi)\,3 = 3\pi$ **cubic meters**

3. **Sample answer: Find the volume of the combined Zone 1/Zone 2 cone, using the above method. Subtract from that volume the volume of the Zone 1 cone.**

4. **The radius of the base of the Zone 1/Zone 2 cone is the length of the side opposite the 30° angle in a 30°-60°-90° triangle with a medium side measuring 6 m: $r = \frac{6}{\sqrt{3}} = 2\sqrt{3}$**

   $B = \pi r^2 = \pi \left(2\sqrt{3}\right)^2 = 12\pi$

   $V = \frac{1}{3}(12\pi)\,6 = 24\pi$ **cubic meters**

   Volume of Zone 2 $= 24\pi - 3\pi = 21\pi$ cubic meters

5. **Number in Zone 1 $= 3\pi(800) = 2400(3.14) = 7536$**

   Number in Zone 2 $= 21\pi(800) = 16,800(3.14) = 52,752$

   There are 45,216 more mosquitos in Zone 2 than there are in Zone 1.

EXTENSION ACTIVITY

Ask students to complete the sentences below.

1. If you double the radius of the base of a cone, the volume of the cone is ____. **multiplied by 4**

2. If you double the height of a cone, the volume of the cone is ____. **multiplied by 2**

3. If you double both the height of a cone and the radius of its base, the volume of the cone is ____. **multiplied by 8**

INTEGRATE MATHEMATICAL PRACTICES
Focus on Math Connections

MP.1 Compare and contrast pyramids and cones. How are they alike? How are they different? Sample answer: Both are three-dimensional shapes that taper from a plane figure to a point. The plane figure is a polygon for a pyramid, a circle for a cone. A pyramid has triangles for lateral sides, a cone does not. The volume of both is found the same way: Find the product of $\frac{1}{3}$, the area of its base, and its height.

INTEGRATE MATHEMATICAL PRACTICES
Focus on Modeling

MP.4 A *surface of rotation* is generated by revolving a shape about a line called the *axis of rotation*. For example, if you rotate a half circle about a line that is a diameter of the full circle (the original circle), you generate a sphere. Describe how, using a shape and an axis of rotation, you could generate a cone. Sample answer: Use a right triangle as your shape. Use a line that contains one of the triangle's legs as the axis of rotation.

Scoring Rubric
2 points: Student correctly solves the problem and explains his/her reasoning.
1 point: Student shows good understanding of the problem but does not fully solve or explain his/her reasoning.
0 points: Student does not demonstrate understanding of the problem.

Volume of Spheres

Common Core Math Standards

The student is expected to:

COMMON CORE G-GMD.A.2(+)

Give an informal argument using Cavalieri's principle for the formulas for the volume of a sphere and other solid figures. Also G-GMD.A.3, G-MG.A.1, G-MG.A.2

Mathematical Practices

COMMON CORE MP.2 Reasoning

Language Objective

Explain to a partner how to apply the formula for the volume of a sphere.

ENGAGE

Essential Question: How can you use the formula for the volume of a sphere to calculate the volumes of composite figures?

Break the figures into familiar figures, including spheres and hemispheres, for which you know the volume formulas. Then find the individual volumes and add them.

PREVIEW: LESSON PERFORMANCE TASK

View the Engage section online. Discuss the photograph. Ask students to identify the subject of the photo and to judge whether or not it is built to scale. Then preview the Lesson Performance Task.

18.4 Volume of Spheres

Essential Question: How can you use the formula for the volume of a sphere to calculate the volumes of composite figures?

Resource Locker

⊘ Explore   Developing a Volume Formula

To find the volume of a sphere, compare one of its hemispheres to a cylinder of the same height and radius from which a cone has been removed.

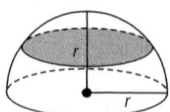 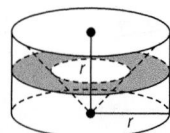

(A) The region of a plane that intersects a solid figure is called a **cross section**. To show that cross sections have the same area at every level, use the Pythagorean Theorem to find a relationship between r, x, and R.

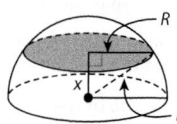

By the Pythagorean Theorem, $x^2 + R^2 = r^2$. Solving for R produces $R = \sqrt{r^2 - x^2}$.

To find the area of the disk that is a cross-section, use the area for a circle, $A = \pi R^2$, or $A = \pi\left(\sqrt{r^2 - x^2}\right)^2$. So $A_{disk} = \pi\left(r^2 - x^2\right)$.

(B) A cross section of the cylinder with the cone removed is a ring.

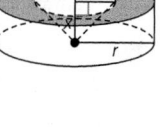

To find the area of the ring, find the area of the outer circle and of the inner circle. Then subtract the area of the inner circle from the outer circle.

The outer circle of the ring has a radius of r, so its area is $A_{outer} = \pi r^2$. The inner circle has radius of x, so its area is $A_{inner} = \pi x^2$.

The area of ring-shaped cross section is: $A_{ring} = A_{outer} - A_{inner}$

$$= \pi r^2 - \pi x^2$$

$$= \pi\left(r^2 - x^2\right)$$

The cross-sectional areas of the disk and the ring are equal.

© Houghton Mifflin Harcourt Publishing Company

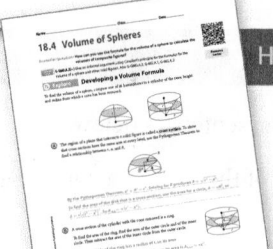

HARDCOVER PAGES 811–818

Turn to these pages to find this lesson in the hardcover student edition.

(C) Find an expression for the volume of the cylinder with the cone removed.

The volume of the cylinder is: $V_{cylinder} = \pi r^2 h$

$$= \pi r^2 r$$
$$= \pi r^3$$

The volume of the cone is: $V_{cone} = \frac{1}{3}\pi r^2 h$

$$= \frac{1}{3}\pi r^2 r$$
$$= \frac{1}{3}\pi r^3$$

The volume of cylinder with the cone removed is: $V_{cylinder} - V_{cone} = \frac{1}{3}\pi r^3 - \pi r^3$

$$= \frac{2}{3}\pi r^3$$

(D) Use Cavalieri's principle to deduce the volume of a sphere with radius r.

The sphere and cylinder with the cone removed have the same height and the same

cross-sectional area at every level x. By Cavalieri's principle, the two figures have the same

volume. Since the volume of the hemisphere is $\frac{2}{3}\pi r^3$, a sphere with radius r has twice this

volume, or $V_{sphere} = \frac{4}{3}\pi r^3$.

Reflect

1. How do you know that the height h of the cylinder with the cone removed is equal to the radius r?
   Possible answer: The height of the cylinder is the same as the height of the hemisphere, which must be r.

2. What happens to the cross-sectional areas when $x = 0$? when $x = r$?
   Possible answer: When $x = r$, the cross section of the hemisphere is a circle with
   the same radius r, and the ring-shaped cross section is also a circle with radius r
   (with a point of zero area removed), so both have area πr^2. When $x = 0$, the cross section
   of the hemisphere is a point with zero area, and the ring-shaped cross section is a ring
   with radius r but zero width, so also has zero area.

© Houghton Mifflin Harcourt Publishing Company

Developing a Volume Formula

INTEGRATE TECHNOLOGY

Students have the option of doing the Explore activity either in the book or online.

QUESTIONING STRATEGIES

? What do you need to show to use Cavalieri's Principle? The figures have the same cross-sectional area at every level.

? What does Cavalieri's Principle allow you to conclude? The two figures have the same volume.

INTEGRATE MATHEMATICAL PRACTICES
Focus on Communication

MP.3 Review the definition of *sphere* and discuss the related terms *hemisphere* and *great circle*. Explain to students that when a plane intersects a sphere, the cross-section that is formed is either a single point or a circle. If the plane passes through the center of the sphere, the cross section is a *great circle*.

PROFESSIONAL DEVELOPMENT

 Integrate Mathematical Practices

This lesson provides an opportunity to address Mathematical Practice **MP.2**, which calls for students to "reason abstractly and quantitatively." Students are already familiar with Cavalieri's Principle but, in this module, a surprising application of this principle is used. The argument is based on showing that a hemisphere and a cylinder from which a cone has been removed have the same cross-sectional area at every level and therefore must have the same volume. A bit of algebra shows that the volume of a sphere is equal to $\frac{4}{3}\pi r^3$.

EXPLAIN 1

Finding the Volume of a Sphere

QUESTIONING STRATEGIES

? What dimension or dimensions do you need to know to find the volume of a sphere? the radius

AVOID COMMON ERRORS

When calculating volumes of spheres, some students may forget to multiply by $\frac{4}{3}$ instead of $\frac{1}{3}$, as in the previous volume formulas. Remind students that the volume of a sphere needs the factor of $\frac{4}{3}$. Watch for students who calculate the volume using the second power of the radius instead of the third power.

Explain 1 **Finding the Volume of a Sphere**

The relationship you discovered in the Explore can be stated as a volume formula.

> **Volume of a Sphere**
>
> The volume of a sphere with radius r is given by $V = \frac{4}{3}\pi r^3$.

You can use a formula for the volume of a sphere to solve problems involving volume and capacity.

Example 1 The figure represents a spherical helium-filled balloon. This tourist attraction allows up to 28 passengers at a time to ride in a gondola suspended underneath the balloon, as it cruises at an altitude of 500 ft. How much helium, to the nearest hundred gallons, does the balloon hold? Round to the nearest tenth. (*Hint:* 1 gal ≈ 0.1337 ft³)

Step 1 Find the radius of the balloon.

The radius is half of the diameter, so $r = \frac{1}{2}(72 \text{ ft}) = 36$ ft.

Step 2 Find the volume of the balloon in cubic feet.

$$V = \frac{4}{3}\pi r^3$$

$$= \frac{4}{3}\pi \boxed{36}^3$$

$$\approx \boxed{195{,}432.196} \text{ ft}^3$$

Step 3 Find the capacity of the balloon to the nearest gallon.

$$\boxed{195{,}432.196} \text{ ft}^3 \approx \boxed{195{,}432.196} \text{ ft}^3 \times \frac{1 \text{ gal}}{0.1337 \text{ ft}^3} \approx \boxed{1{,}462{,}000} \text{ gal}$$

Your Turn

A spherical water tank has a diameter of 27 m. How much water can the tank hold, to the nearest liter? (*Hint:* 1,000 L = 1 m³)

3. Find the volume of the tank in cubic meters.

$$r = \frac{1}{2}(27 \text{ m}) = 13.5 \text{ m}$$

$$V = \frac{4}{3}\pi r^3 = \frac{4}{3}\pi(13.5 \text{ m})^3 = 10{,}305.9947\ldots \text{ m}^3$$

4. Find the capacity of the tank to the nearest liter.

$$10{,}305.9947\ldots \text{ m}^3 \approx 10{,}305.9947\ldots \text{ m}^3 \times \frac{1{,}000 \text{ L}}{1 \text{ m}^3} \approx 10{,}305{,}995 \text{ L}$$

COLLABORATIVE LEARNING

Whole Class Activity

Have students each draw a sphere and label the radius or the diameter. Then have each student pass the drawing to another class member who then calculates the volume of the sphere. Discuss with the class the relationship between the volumes of the spheres, given the diameter or the radius. Ask them how the volume would change if the radius is doubled or tripled. Also ask how they would find the volume of a hemisphere.

 **Explain 2** **Finding the Volume of a Composite Figure**

You can find the volume of a composite figure using appropriate volume formulas for the different parts of the figure.

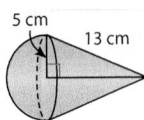

Example 2 Find the volume of the composite figure. Round to the nearest cubic centimeter.

Step 1 Find the volume of the hemisphere.

$$V = \frac{2}{3}\pi r^3 = \frac{2}{3}\pi(5)^3 \approx 261.799 \text{ cm}^3$$

Step 2 Find the height of the cone.

$$h^2 + \boxed{5}^2 = \boxed{13}^2$$
$$h^2 + \boxed{25} = \boxed{169}$$
$$h^2 = \boxed{144}$$
$$h = \boxed{12}$$

Step 3 Find the volume of the cone.

The cone has the same radius as the hemisphere, $r = \boxed{5}$ cm.

$$V = \frac{1}{3}\pi r^2 h$$
$$= \frac{1}{3}\pi \boxed{5}^2 \boxed{12}$$
$$= \boxed{314.159} \text{ cm}^3$$

Step 4 Find the total volume.

Total volume = volume of hemisphere + volume of cone

$$= \boxed{261.799} \text{ cm}^3 + \boxed{314.159} \text{ cm}^3$$
$$\approx \boxed{576} \text{ cm}^3$$

Reflect

5. Is it possible to create a figure by taking a cone and removing from it a hemisphere with the same radius?
No; possible answer: at the widest part of the hemisphere, its surface is almost vertical, so
part of it would have to lie outside the cone, even if the cone's height were much greater
than its radius.

Your Turn

6. A composite figure is a cylinder with a hemispherical hole in the top. The bottom of the hemisphere is tangent to the base of the cylinder. Find the volume of the figure, to the nearest tenth.

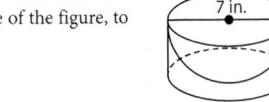

Volume of cylinder:
radius $r = \frac{1}{2}(7 \text{ in.}) = 3.5$ in; height $h = r = 3.5$ in.
$V = \pi r^2 h = \pi(3.5)^2(3.5) = 134.696 \text{ in}^3$
Volume of hemisphere: $V = \frac{2}{3}\pi r^3 = \frac{2}{3}\pi(3.5)^3 = 89.797 \text{ in}^3$
Volume of figure = volume of cylinder − volume of hemisphere
$= 134.696 \text{ in}^3 − 89.797 \text{ in}^3 \approx 44.9 \text{ in}^3$

DIFFERENTIATE INSTRUCTION

Kinesthetic Experience

Have groups of students brainstorm about how to find the radius of a real-world sphere (for example, use a measuring tape to find the circumference and then calculate the radius from the circumference formula). Then have them find the volumes of the types of spherical balls used in sports. Have them make a poster listing the sport, the size of the ball, and its volume. Invite students to share their posters with the class.

EXPLAIN 2

Finding the Volume of a Composite Figure

INTEGRATE MATHEMATICAL PRACTICES
Focus on Patterns

MP.8 Students should be able to recognize the solid figures that make up a composite figure, including spheres, and to know whether the volumes of those figures are to be added or subtracted from the total volume. Have students make an organized list of the volume formulas needed to find the volume of the composite figure. Then have them find the volume of each solid, and add or subtract the volumes, as needed, to get the total.

QUESTIONING STRATEGIES

? How do you calculate the volume of a composite figure that includes a sphere? Separate the figure into separate solids for which known volume formulas apply. Then add or subtract the volumes of each separate solid, depending on how the composite figure is formed.

AVOID COMMON ERRORS

Some students may have difficulty remembering to use the correct units of measure in their answers. Encourage students to list the measurements of spheres that are given in linear, square, and cubic units. Linear units are used for a radius, a diameter, or a circumference; square units are used for area or surface area (to be studied later); and cubic units are used for volume.

ELABORATE

QUESTIONING STRATEGIES

? How do you find the volume of a sphere given the diameter? The radius is one-half the diameter. The volume of the sphere is $\frac{4}{3}\pi$ times the cube of the radius.

SUMMARIZE THE LESSON

? Have students make a graphic organizer summarizing the volume formulas they have learned in this module. Sample:

Three-Dimensional Figure	Volume Formula
Prism	$V = Bh$
Cylinder	$V = Bh$
Pyramid	$V = \frac{1}{3}Bh$
Cone	$V = \frac{1}{3}Bh$
Sphere	$V = \frac{4}{3}\pi r^3$

💬 Elaborate

7. Discussion Could you use an inscribed prism to derive the volume of a hemisphere? Why or why not? Are there any other ways you could approximate a hemisphere, and what problems would you encounter in finding its volume?

Possible answer: no; no matter how many sides the base of the prism has, it will always be significantly smaller than the hemisphere; you could use discs (very thin cylinders) to approximate the hemisphere, but you would need some way to add up their volumes.

8. Essential Question Check-In A gumball is in the shape of a sphere, with a spherical hole in the center. How might you calculate the volume of the gumball? What measurements are needed?

I could subtract the volume of the spherical hole from the volume of the gumball. I would need to know the radius of both the gumball and the hole.

⭐ Evaluate: Homework and Practice

- Online Homework
- Hints and Help
- Extra Practice

1. Analyze Relationships Use the diagram of a sphere inscribed in a cylinder to describe the relationship between the volume of a sphere and the volume of a cylinder.

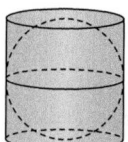

Pick an arbitrary radius common to the sphere and the cylinder.

Let $r = 1$ unit, which would make the height of the cylinder 2 units

$V_{cylinder} = Bh$

$\qquad = \pi(1^2)(2)$

$\qquad = 2\pi$

$V_{sphere} = \frac{4}{3}\pi r^3$

$\qquad = \frac{4}{3}\pi(1)^3$

$\qquad = \frac{4\pi}{3}$

$2\pi \div \frac{4\pi}{3} = 2\pi \cdot \frac{3}{4\pi} = \frac{3}{2} = 1.5$

The volume of the cylinder is 1.5 times the volume of the sphere.

© Houghton Mifflin Harcourt Publishing Company

LANGUAGE SUPPORT EL

Connect Vocabulary

To help students remember how to apply the formula for the volume of a sphere, have students make a small poster showing examples of spheres with different diameters or radii. Then have them use colored pencils to write the radius in one color and the formulas for the volume in a different color. Have them label each figure with its formula and volume. Invite students to share their posters with the class.

Find the volume of the sphere. Round the answer to the nearest tenth.

2.

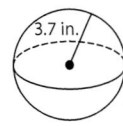
3.7 in.

$V = \frac{4}{3}\pi r^3$
$= \frac{4}{3}\pi (3.7)^3$
≈ 212.2
$V = 212.2 \text{ in}^3$

3.

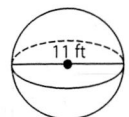
11 ft

$V = \frac{4}{3}\pi r^3$
$= \frac{4}{3}\pi (5.5)^3$
≈ 696.9
$V = 696.9 \text{ ft}^3$

4.

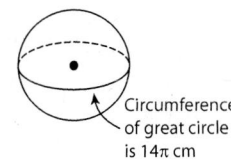
Circumference of great circle is 14π cm

$C = 2\pi r$
$14\pi = 2\pi r$
$7 \text{ cm} = r$
$V = \frac{4}{3}\pi r^3$
$= \frac{4}{3}\pi (7)^3$
≈ 1436.8
$V = 1436.8 \text{ cm}^3$

Find the volume of the sphere. Leave the answer in terms of π.

5.

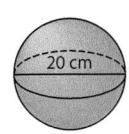
20 cm

$V = \frac{4}{3}\pi r^3$
$= \frac{4}{3}\pi (10)^3$
$= 1333.\overline{3}\pi$
$V = 1333.\overline{3}\pi \text{ cm}^3$

6.

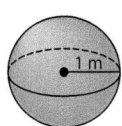
1 m

$V = \frac{4}{3}\pi r^3$
$= \frac{4}{3}\pi (1)^3$
$= \frac{4\pi}{3}$
$V = \frac{4\pi}{3} \text{ m}^3$

7.

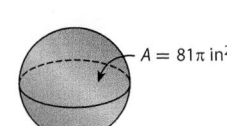
$A = 81\pi \text{ in}^2$

$A = \pi r^2$
$81\pi = \pi r^2$
$\frac{81\pi}{\pi} = \frac{\pi r^2}{\pi}$
$81 = r^2$
$9 \text{ in.} = r$
$V = \frac{4}{3}\pi r^3$
$= \frac{4}{3}\pi (9)^3$
$\approx 972\pi$
$V = 972\pi \text{ in}^3$

Personal Math Trainer

ASSIGNMENT GUIDE

Concepts and Skills	Practice
Explore Developing a Volume Formula	Exercise 1
Example 1 Finding the Volume of a Sphere	Exercises 2–7
Example 2 Finding the Volume of a Composite Figure	Exercises 8–14

INTEGRATE MATHEMATICAL PRACTICES
Focus on Communication

MP.3 Help students determine what information is required to use the volume formula for a sphere. Sample questions: "What formula will you use?" $V = \frac{4}{3}\pi r^3$. "How can you find the radius?" Divide the diameter by 2. "How can you find the volume of a hemisphere?" Find half the volume of the related sphere.

Exercise	Depth of Knowledge (D.O.K.)	COMMON CORE Mathematical Practices
1	**3** Strategic Thinking	**MP.6** Precision
2–11	**1** Recall of Information	**MP.5** Using Tools
12–16	**2** Skills/Concepts	**MP.4** Modeling
17–20	**2** Skills/Concepts	**MP.5** Using Tools
21	**3** Strategic Thinking H.O.T.	**MP.6** Precision
22	**3** Strategic Thinking H.O.T.	**MP.2** Reasoning
23	**3** Strategic Thinking H.O.T.	**MP.1** Problem Solving

Find the volume of the composite figure. Leave the answer in terms of π.

8.

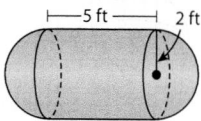

$V_{cylinder} = Bh$

$\qquad = \pi \cdot 2^2 \cdot 5$

$\qquad = 20\pi \text{ ft}^3$

$V_{sphere} = \frac{4}{3}\pi r^3$ (two hemispheres combine

to make a sphere)

$\qquad = \frac{4}{3}\pi(2)^3$

$\qquad = \frac{32\pi}{3} \text{ ft}^3$

$20\pi + \frac{32\pi}{3} = \frac{3}{3} \cdot 20\pi + \frac{32\pi}{3} = \frac{60\pi}{3} + \frac{32\pi}{3} = \frac{92\pi}{3}$

$V_{total} = \frac{92\pi}{3} \text{ ft}^3$

9.

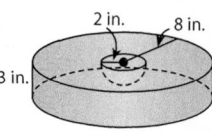

$V_{cylinder} = Bh$

$\qquad = \pi \cdot 8^2 \cdot 3$

$\qquad = 192\pi \text{ in}^3$

$V_{hemisphere} = \frac{1}{2}\left(\frac{4}{3}\pi r^3\right)$

$\qquad = \frac{2}{3}\pi(2^3)$

$\qquad = \frac{16\pi}{3} \text{ in}^3$

$192\pi - \frac{16\pi}{3} = \frac{3}{3} \cdot 192\pi - \frac{16\pi}{3}$

$\qquad = \frac{576\pi}{3} - \frac{16\pi}{3}$

$\qquad = \frac{560\pi}{3}$

$V_{total} = \frac{560\pi}{3} \text{ in}^3$

Find the volume of the composite figure. Round the answer to the nearest tenth.

10.

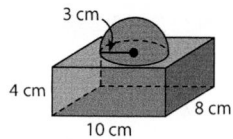

$V_{prism} = Bh$

$\qquad = 10 \cdot 8 \cdot 4$

$\qquad = 320 \text{ cm}^3$

$V_{hemisphere} = \frac{1}{2}\left(\frac{4}{3}\pi r^3\right)$

$\qquad = \frac{2}{3}\pi(3^3)$

$\qquad = 18\pi$

$\qquad \approx 56.5 \text{ cm}^3$

$320 + 56.5 = 376.5$

$V_{total} \approx 376.5 \text{ cm}^3$

11.

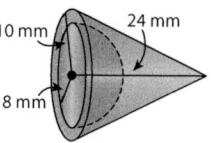

$V_{cone} = \frac{1}{3}Bh$

$\qquad = \frac{1}{3}\pi \cdot 10^2 \cdot 24$

$\qquad \approx 2513.3 \text{ mm}^3$

$V_{hemisphere} = \frac{1}{2}\left(\frac{4}{3}\pi r^3\right)$

$\qquad = \frac{2}{3}\pi(8^3)$

$\qquad \approx 1072.3 \text{ mm}^3$

$2513.3 - 1072.3 = 1441$

$V_{total} \approx 1441 \text{ mm}^3$

12. Analyze Relationships Approximately how many times as great is the volume of a grapefruit with diameter 10 cm as the volume of a lime with diameter 5 cm?

$$V_{grapefruit} = \frac{1}{2}\left(\frac{4}{3}\pi r^3\right)$$
$$= \frac{2}{3}\pi\left(5^3\right)$$
$$= \frac{250\pi}{3}$$

$$V_{lime} = \frac{1}{2}\left(\frac{4}{3}\pi r^3\right)$$
$$= \frac{2}{3}\pi\left(2.5^3\right)$$
$$= \frac{31.25\pi}{3}$$

$$\frac{\left(\frac{250\pi}{3}\right)}{\left(\frac{31.25\pi}{3}\right)} = \frac{250}{31.25} = 8$$

The volume of the grapefruit is about 8 times as great as the volume of the lime.

13. A bead is formed by drilling a cylindrical hole with a 2 mm diameter through a sphere with an 8 mm diameter. Estimate the volume of the bead to the nearest whole.

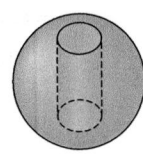

$$V_{sphere} = \frac{4}{3}\pi r^3$$
$$= \frac{4}{3}\pi\left(4^3\right)$$
$$\approx 268 \text{ mm}^3$$

$$V_{cylinder} = Bh$$
$$= \pi\left(1^2\right)(8)$$
$$= 8\pi$$
$$\approx 25 \text{ mm}^3$$

$$V_{bead} = V_{sphere} - V_{cylinder} \approx 268 - 25 = 243 \text{ mm}^3$$

14. Algebra Write an expression representing the volume of the composite figure formed by a hemisphere with radius r and a cube with side length $2r$.

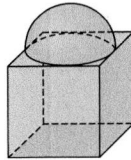

$$V = \frac{1}{2}\left(\frac{4}{3}\pi r^3\right) + Bh$$
$$= \left(\frac{2}{3}\pi r^3\right) + (2r)^3$$
$$= \frac{2}{3}\pi r^3 + 8r^3$$
$$= r^3\left(\frac{2}{3}\pi + 8\right)$$
$$r^3\left(\frac{2}{3}\pi + 8\right) \text{ or } \frac{2}{3}\pi r^3 + 8r^3$$

© Houghton Mifflin Harcourt Publishing Company • Image Credits: ©Jasmina81/iStockPhoto.com

PEER-TO-PEER DISCUSSION

Have students work in pairs. Each student should make up two problems, one involving the volume of a sphere and one involving the volume of a composite figure that includes a sphere. Then have students exchange problems with their partners, and each explain to the other how to solve the problem that the partner wrote.

15. One gallon of propane yields approximately 91,500 BTU. About how many BTUs does the spherical storage tank shown provide? Round to the nearest billion BTUs. (*Hint:* 1 ft³ ≈ 7.48 gal)

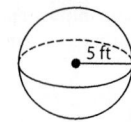
5 ft

$$V = \frac{4}{3}\pi r^3$$

$$= \frac{4}{3}\pi(5)^3$$

$$\approx 523.6 \text{ ft}^3$$

$$523.6 \text{ ft}^3 \cdot \frac{7.48 \text{ gal}}{1 \text{ ft}^3} \approx 3916.5 \text{ gal}$$

$$3916.5 \text{ gal} \cdot \frac{91,500 \text{ BTU}}{1 \text{ gal}} \approx 358,000,000 \text{ BTU}$$

16. The aquarium shown is a rectangular prism that is filled with water. You drop a spherical ball with a diameter of 6 inches into the aquarium. The ball sinks, causing the water to spill from the tank. How much water is left in the tank? Express your answer to the nearest tenth. (*Hint:* 1 in.³ ≈ 0.00433 gal)

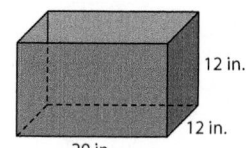
12 in.
12 in.
20 in.

$$V_{prism} = Bh$$

$$= (20 \cdot 12)(12)$$

$$= 2880 \text{ in}^3$$

$$V_{sphere} = \frac{4}{3}\pi r^3$$

$$= \frac{4}{3}\pi(3^3)$$

$$\approx 113.1 \text{ in}^3$$

$$V_{prism} - V_{sphere} = 2880 - 113.1 \approx 2766.9 \text{ in}^3$$

$$2766.9 \text{ in}^3 \cdot \frac{0.00433 \text{ gal}}{1 \text{ in}^3} \approx 12.0 \text{ gal}$$

The amount of water left is about 12.0 gallons.

17. A sphere with diameter 8 cm is inscribed in a cube. Find the ratio of the volume of the cube to the volume of the sphere.

Ⓐ. $\frac{6}{\pi}$

B. $\frac{2}{3\pi}$

C. $\frac{3\pi}{4}$

D. $\frac{3\pi}{2}$

$$V_{cube} = Bh$$

$$= 8^3$$

$$= 512 \text{ cm}^3$$

$$V_{sphere} = \frac{4}{3}\pi r^3$$

$$= \frac{4}{3}\pi(4^3)$$

$$= \frac{256}{3}\pi \text{ in}^3$$

$$\frac{512}{\left(\frac{256}{3}\pi\right)} = \frac{(3 \cdot 512)}{3 \cdot \left(\frac{256}{3}\pi\right)} = \frac{1536}{256\pi} = \frac{6}{\pi}$$

For Exercises 18–20, use the table. Round each volume to the nearest billion π.

Planet	Diameter (mi)
Mercury	3,032
Venus	7,521
Earth	7,926
Mars	4,222
Jupiter	88,846
Saturn	74,898
Uranus	31,763
Neptune	30,775

18. **Explain the Error** Margaret used the mathematics shown to find the volume of Saturn.

$$V = \frac{4}{3}\pi r^2 = \frac{4}{3}\pi(74,898)^2 \approx \frac{4}{3}\pi(6,000,000,000) \approx 8,000,000,000\pi$$

Explain the two errors Margaret made, then give the correct answer.
Margaret used the diameter rather than the radius, which she squared rather than cubed.

$$V = \frac{4}{3}\pi r^3 = \frac{4}{3}\pi(37,449)^3 \approx \frac{4}{3}\pi(52,520,000,000,000) \approx 70,027,000,000,000\pi$$

The correct answer is 70,027,000,000,000π.

19. The sum of the volumes of Venus and Mars is about equal to the volume of which planet?

Volume of Venus

$$V = \frac{4}{3}\pi(3760.5)^3$$

$$\approx 71,000,000,000\pi$$

Volume of Mars

$$V = \frac{4}{3}\pi(2111)^3$$

$$\approx 12,000,000,000\pi$$

$$71,000,000,000\pi + 12,000,000,000\pi = 83,000,000,000\pi$$

Volume of Earth

$$V = \frac{4}{3}\pi(3963)^3$$

$$\approx 83,000,000,000\pi \text{ Volume of Venus} + \text{Volume of Mars} = \text{Volume of Earth}$$

20. How many times as great as the volume of the smallest planet is the volume of the largest planet? Round to the nearest thousand.

Volume of Jupiter

$$V = \frac{4}{3}\pi(44,423)^3$$

$$\approx 116,885,000,000,000\pi$$

Volume of Mercury

$$V = \frac{4}{3}\pi(1516)^3$$

$$\approx 4,000,000,000\pi$$

$$\frac{116,885,000,000,000\pi}{4,000,000,000\pi} = \frac{116,885}{4}$$

$$\approx 29,200$$

About 29,000 times as great.

© Houghton Mifflin Harcourt Publishing Company

Focus on Math Connections

MP.1 Point out that if the radius of a sphere is doubled, then the volume of the sphere is multiplied by the cube of the dimension change, or 8. If the dimensions of the sphere change by a factor of k, then the volumes are in the ratio $1:k^3$.

JOURNAL

Have students describe how they would determine which solid has the greater volume: a cube with side length $2r$ or a sphere with diameter $2r$.

21. **Make a Conjecture** The *bathysphere* was an early version of a submarine, invented in the 1930s. The inside diameter of the bathysphere was 54 inches, and the steel used to make the sphere was 1.5 inches thick. It had three 8-inch diameter windows. Estimate the volume of steel used to make the bathysphere.

Possible solution:

$$V_{bathysphere} = \frac{4}{3}\pi r^3 \qquad\qquad V_{inside} = \frac{4}{3}\pi r^3 \qquad\qquad V_{window} = Bh$$

$$= \frac{4}{3}\pi(28.5)^3 \qquad\qquad = \frac{4}{3}\pi(27)^3 \qquad\qquad = \pi(4^2)(1.5)$$

$$\approx 96{,}967 \text{ in}^3 \qquad\qquad \approx 82{,}448 \text{ in}^3 \qquad\qquad \approx 75 \text{ in}^3$$

Amount of steel used: $96{,}967 - 82{,}448 - 3(75) = 96{,}967 - 82{,}448 - 225 = 14{,}294 \text{ in}^3$

22. **Explain the Error** A student solved the problem shown. Explain the student's error and give the correct answer to the problem.

A spherical gasoline tank has a radius of 0.5 ft. When filled, the tank provides 446,483 BTU. How many BTUs does one gallon of gasoline yield? Round to the nearest thousand BTUs and use the fact that 1 ft$^3 \approx$ 7.48 gal.

> The volume of the tank is $\frac{4}{3}\pi r^3 = \frac{4}{3}\pi(0.5)^3$ ft^3. Multiplying by 7.48 shows that this is approximately 3.92 gal. So the number of BTUs in one gallon of gasoline is approximately $446{,}483 \times 3.92 \approx 1{,}750{,}000$ BTU.

The student should have divided the total number of BTUs by 3.92 instead of multiplying; the correct answer is 114,000 BTU.

23. **Persevere in Problem Solving** The top of a gumball machine is an 18 in. sphere. The machine holds a maximum of 3300 gumballs, which leaves about 43% of the space in the machine empty. Estimate the diameter of each gumball.

$$V_{sphere} = \frac{4}{3}\pi r^3 = \frac{4}{3}\pi(9)^3 \approx 3054 \text{ in}^3$$

$$3054 \cdot (1 - 0.43) = 3054 \cdot 0.57 = 1740.78 \text{ in}^3$$

$$\frac{1740.78}{3300} \approx 0.5275$$

$$0.5275 = \frac{4}{3}\pi r^3$$

$$0.3956 \approx \pi r^3$$

$$0.1259 \approx r^3$$

$$\sqrt[3]{0.1259} \approx \sqrt[3]{r^3}$$

$$0.5 \text{ in.} \approx r$$

The diameter is twice the radius, so the diameter $= 2(0.5) = 1$.

The diameter of one gumball is approximately 1 in.

Lesson Performance Task

For his science project, Bizbo has decided to build a scale model of the solar system. He starts with a grapefruit with a radius of 2 inches to represent Earth. His "Earth" weighs 0.5 pounds.

Find each of the following for Bizbo's model. Use the rounded figures in the table. Round your answers to two significant figures. Use 3.14 for π.

1. the scale of Bizbo's model: 1 inch = _____ miles

2. Earth's distance from the Sun, in inches and in miles

3. Neptune's distance from the Sun, in inches and in miles

4. the Sun's volume, in cubic inches and cubic feet

5. the Sun's weight, in pounds and in tons (Note: the Sun's density is 0.26 times the Earth's density.)

Note: Answers may differ slightly due to rounding variations.

1. 2 inches = 4000 miles
   1 inch = 2000 miles

2. $\dfrac{9.3 \times 10^7 \text{ miles}}{\dfrac{2000 \text{ miles}}{\text{inch}}} = 46{,}500$ inches

   $46{,}500$ inches $\approx 47{,}000$ inches

   $\dfrac{46{,}500 \text{ inches}}{\dfrac{63{,}360 \text{ inches}}{1 \text{ mile}}} \approx 0.73$ miles

3. $\dfrac{2.8 \times 10^9 \text{ miles}}{\dfrac{2000 \text{ miles}}{\text{inch}}} = 1{,}400{,}000$ inches

   $\dfrac{1{,}400{,}000 \text{ inches}}{\dfrac{63{,}360 \text{ inches}}{1 \text{ mile}}} \approx 22$ miles

4. The radius of Bizbo's model sun is $\dfrac{4.3 \times 10^5 \text{ miles}}{\dfrac{2000 \text{ miles}}{\text{inch}}} = 215$ inches.

   The volume of Bizbo's model sun is $V = \dfrac{4}{3}\pi r^3 = \dfrac{4}{3}(3.14)(215)^3 \approx 4.2 \times 10^7$ cubic inches.

   $\dfrac{4.2 \times 10^7 \text{ cubic inches}}{\dfrac{1728 \text{ cubic inches}}{1 \text{ cubic foot}}} \approx 24{,}000$ cubic feet

5. First compute the volume of the model Earth: $V = \dfrac{4}{3}(3.14)(2)^3 \approx 33.5$ cubic inches

   Now find the density of the model Earth:

   $D = \dfrac{0.5 \text{ pounds}}{33.5 \text{ cubic inches}} \approx 0.0149$ pounds per cubic inch

   The sun's density is 0.26 times the density of the model Earth:

   $D = (0.26)(0.0149) \approx 0.003874$ pounds per cubic inch

   Multiply this by the Sun's volume to find its weight:

   $(0.003874 \text{ pounds per cubic inch})(4.2 \times 10^7 \text{ cubic inches}) \approx 160{,}000$ pounds

   $\dfrac{160{,}000 \text{ pounds}}{\dfrac{2000 \text{ pounds}}{1 \text{ ton}}} = 80$ tons

EXTENSION ACTIVITY

Give these directions:

1. Research the meaning and calculate the length of a light year. distance light travels in 1 year; about 6 trillion miles

2. Calculate the mileage to the nearest star and at least 5 other stars. nearest: Proxima Centauri; 4.2 LY ≈ 25.2 trillion miles

3. Compare the radius and volume of the red giant Antares with those of the Sun. If Antares were placed at the center of our solar system, its radius would reach to between Mars and Jupiter. Volume: many estimates given; 60 million times Sun

AVOID COMMON ERRORS

Unit conversions with huge numbers, such as are encountered in the Lesson Performance Task, can be simplified through the careful use of scientific notation and unit conversions:

$$\dfrac{9.3 \times 10^7 \text{ miles}}{\dfrac{2 \times 10^3 \text{ miles}}{\text{inch}}} =$$

$$\left(\dfrac{9.3}{2}\right) \times 10^{7-3}\left(\text{miles} \cdot \dfrac{\text{inch}}{\text{miles}}\right) = 4.65 \times 10^4 \text{ inches}$$

INTEGRATE MATHEMATICAL PRACTICES
Focus on Modeling

MP.4 The huge distances to the stars led to the creation of the light year, a unit that makes dealing with such distances far easier. There is no commonly used unit to measure the huge volumes of the stars, however, which are often given in cubic miles. Invent a unit that allows the volumes of stars to be expressed as manageable numbers, such as 10 or 100. Use your unit to express the volume of a star other than the Sun.

Sample answer: S, the volume of the Sun

The largest red supergiant star is VV Cephei. Its radius is close to 4 thousand times the radius of the sun, so its volume is close to 4000^3 times the volume of the Sun, or about $(6.4 \times 10^{10})S$.

Scoring Rubric

2 points: Student correctly solves the problem and explains his/her reasoning.

1 point: Student shows good understanding of the problem but does not fully solve or explain his/her reasoning.

0 points: Student does not demonstrate understanding of the problem.

Study Guide Review

ASSESSMENT AND INTERVENTION

Assign or customize module reviews.

MODULE PERFORMANCE TASK

COMMON CORE

Mathematical Practices: MP.1, MP.2, MP.3, MP.4, MP.6
G-GMD.A.3, G-MG.A.1

SUPPORTING STUDENT REASONING

Students should begin this problem by focusing on what information they will need. Here are some issues they might bring up.

- **The shape of the sinkhole:** Students can assume that the sinkhole is a cylinder. This shape should give a reasonable estimate of the volume of the hole.

- **The dimensions of the sinkhole:** Students can research this and use average numbers, or you can give them an estimate of 66 feet wide by 100 feet deep.

- **How to find the volume of the sinkhole:** Students can use the volume formula for a right cylinder, $V = \pi r^2 h$. The volume is $V = (\pi 33^2)(100) \approx 342{,}119$ cubic feet.

- **The cost of a cubic foot of concrete:** Students can research this or use \$4 per cubic foot.

- **Other costs for the repair:** Costs will include concrete, labor, and material transportation.

Essential Question: How can you use volume formulas to solve real-world problems?

© Houghton Mifflin Harcourt Publishing Company

KEY EXAMPLE　　　　　(Lesson 18.1)

Find the volume of a cylinder with a base radius of 3 centimeters and a height of 5 centimeters. Write an exact answer.

$V = \pi r^2 h$	Write the formula for the volume of a cylinder.
$= \pi(3)^2(5)$	Substitute.
$= 45\pi \text{ cm}^3$	Simplify.

KEY EXAMPLE　　　　　(Lesson 18.2)

Find the volume of a square pyramid with a base side length of 12 inches and a height of 7 inches.

$V = \frac{1}{3}Bh$	Write the formula for the volume of a pyramid.
$= \frac{1}{3}(12)^2(7)$	Substitute.
$= 336 \text{ in}^3$	Simplify.

KEY EXAMPLE　　　　　(Lesson 18.3)

Find the volume of a cone with a base diameter of 16 feet and a height of 18 feet. Write an exact answer.

$r = \frac{1}{2}(16 \text{ ft})$	Find the radius.
$= 8 \text{ ft}$	Simplify.
$V = \frac{1}{3}\pi r^2 h$	Write the formula for the volume of a cone.
$= \frac{1}{3}\pi(8)^2(18)$	Substitute.
$= 384\pi \text{ ft}^3$	Simplify.

KEY EXAMPLE　　　　　(Lesson 18.4)

Find the volume of a sphere with a radius of 30 miles. Write an exact answer.

$V = \frac{4}{3}\pi r^3$	Write the formula for the volume of a sphere.
$= \frac{4}{3}\pi(30)^3$	Substitute.
$= 36{,}000\pi \text{ mi}^3$	Simplify.

Key Vocabulary
right prism *(prisma recto)*
right cylinder *(cilindro recto)*
oblique prism *(prisma oblicuo)*
oblique cylinder *(cilindro oblicuo)*
cross section *(sección transversal)*

SCAFFOLDING SUPPORT

- The formula for the volume of a cylinder is $V = \pi r^2 h$, where r is the radius and h is the height.

- Encourage students to use unit analysis when they calculate the material cost to fill the sinkhole. The units of cubic feet should cancel, and \$ should remain in the numerator.

EXERCISES

Find the volume of each figure. Write an exact answer. *(Lessons 18.1–18.4)*

1. _____ 225

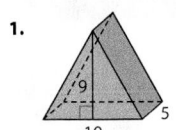
9
5
10

2. _____ 621.81

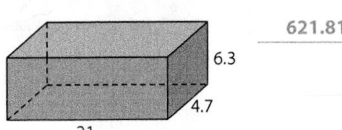
6.3
21
4.7

3. _____ 8448π cm³

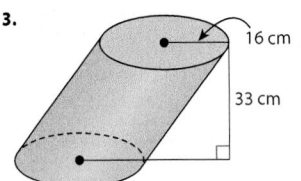
16 cm
33 cm

4. _____ 24 ft³

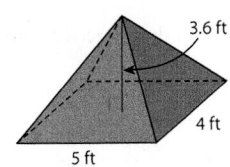
3.6 ft
4 ft
5 ft

5. _____ 24π m³

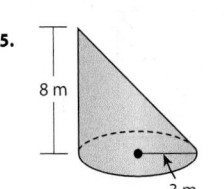
8 m
3 m

6. _____ 288π

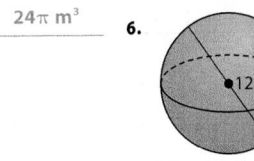
12

7. _____ 2997π yd³

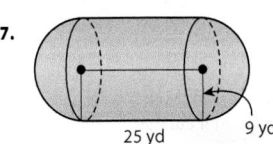
25 yd
9 yd

MODULE PERFORMANCE TASK
How Big Is That Sinkhole?

In 2010 an enormous sinkhole suddenly appeared in the middle of a Guatemalan neighborhood and swallowed a three-story building above it. The sinkhole has an estimated depth of about 100 feet.

How much material is needed to fill the sinkhole? Determine what information is needed to answer the question. Do you think your estimate is more likely to be too high or too low?

What are some material options for filling the sinkhole, and how much would they cost? Which material do you think would be the best choice?

© Houghton Mifflin Harcourt Publishing Company • Image Credits: ©Stringer/ Reuters/Corbis

---

DISCUSSION OPPORTUNITIES

- What other considerations may need to be made when planning to repair the sinkhole?

- How should the loss of a building also impact how this real-world problem is solved?

SAMPLE SOLUTION

Assumptions:

The sinkhole is in the shape of a right cylinder, with a diameter of 66 feet and a height of 100 feet.

The cost of concrete is $4 per cubic foot.

Method:

Find the volume of the sinkhole using $V = \pi r^2 h$, which is the volume of material needed to fill it. Then multiply the result by $4/ft³ to find the total cost.

Find the volume.

$$V = \pi r^2 h = \pi(33^2)(100) \approx 342{,}119 \text{ ft}^3$$

The estimate is likely to differ from the actual amount, but it is difficult to determine whether it is an overestimate or underestimate. The shape of the sinkhole will not be a perfect right cylinder, and the depth measurements will vary depending on where the measurement is taken.

Find the total cost.

$$(342{,}199 \text{ ft}^3)\frac{\$4}{1 \text{ ft}^3} \approx \$1{,}368{,}500$$

If concrete is used, it will cost well over a million dollars in materials alone to fill the sinkhole.

Assessment Rubric

2 points: Student correctly solves the problem and explains his/her reasoning.

1 point: Student shows good understanding of the problem but does not fully solve or explain.

0 points: Student does not demonstrate understanding of the problem.

Ready to Go On?

ASSESS MASTERY

Use the assessment on this page to determine if students have mastered the concepts and standards covered in this module.

ASSESSMENT AND INTERVENTION

Access Ready to Go On? assessment online, and receive instant scoring, feedback, and customized intervention or enrichment.

ADDITIONAL RESOURCES

Response to Intervention Resources

- Reteach Worksheets

Differentiated Instruction Resources

- Reading Strategies **EL**
- Success for English Learners **EL**
- Challenge Worksheets

Assessment Resources

- Leveled Module Quizzes

(Ready) to Go On?

18.1–18.4 Volume Formulas

Find the volume of the figure. *(Lessons 18.1–18.4)*

1. An oblique cylinder next to a cube.

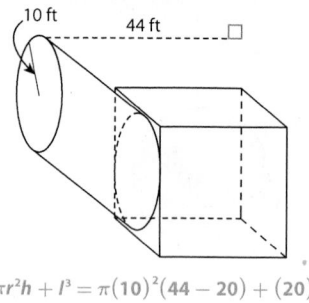

$$\pi r^2 h + l^3 = \pi(10)^2(44-20) + (20)^3$$
$$= 2400\pi + 8000$$

2. A prism of volume 3 with a pyramid of the same height cut out.

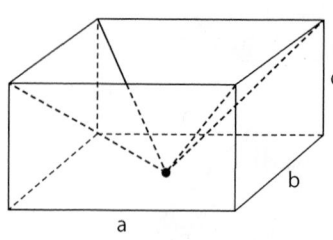

$$Bh - \frac{1}{3}Bh = \frac{2}{3}Bh = \frac{2}{3} \cdot 3 = 2$$

3. A cone with a square pyramid of the same height cut out. The pyramid has height l, and its square base has area l^2.

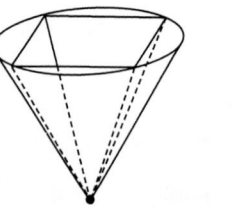 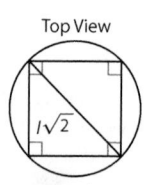

Top View

$l\sqrt{2}$

$$\frac{1}{3}\pi r^2 h - \frac{1}{3}l^2 h = \frac{1}{3}h(\pi r^2 - l^2) = \frac{1}{3}l\left[\pi\left(\frac{l\sqrt{2}}{2}\right)^2 - l^2\right]$$
$$= \frac{1}{3}l\left(\pi\frac{l^2}{2} - l^2\right) = \frac{l^3}{3}\left(\frac{\pi}{2} - 1\right)$$

4. A cube with sides of length s with the biggest sphere that fits in it cut out.

$$s^3 - \frac{4}{3}\pi\left(\frac{s}{2}\right)^3 = s^3 - \frac{4}{3}\pi\frac{s^3}{8} = s^3\left(1 - \frac{\pi}{6}\right)$$

ESSENTIAL QUESTION

5. How would you find the volume of an ice-cream cone with ice cream in it? What measurements would you need?

Answers may vary. Sample: An ice-cream cone is composed approximately of a semi-sphere and a cone. You need the radius of the cone and the height of the cone. Use the volume of a cone formula and add it to the volume of the sphere divided by 2: $\frac{1}{3}\pi r^2 h + \frac{1}{2}\left(\frac{4}{3}\pi r^3\right)$. You can then simplify.

Module 18   **977**   Study Guide Review

COMMON CORE **Common Core Standards**

Lesson	Items	Content Standards	Mathematical Practices
18.1	1	**G-GMD.A.3**	**MP.4**
18.1, 18.2	2	**G-GMD.A.3**	**MP.4**
18.2, 18.3	3	**G-GMD.A.3**	**MP.4**
18.1, 18.4	4	**G-GMD.A.3**	**MP.4**

Assessment Readiness

1. A simplified model of a particular monument is a rectangular pyramid placed on top of a rectangular prism, as shown. The volume of the monument is 66 cubic feet. Determine whether the given measurement could be the height of the monument.
   Select Yes or No for A–C.

   A. 10 feet   ○ Yes   ● No

   B. 13 feet   ● Yes   ○ No

   C. 15 feet   ○ Yes   ● No

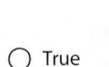

10 ft

2 ft

3 ft

2. A standard basketball has a radius of about 4.7 inches. Choose True or False for each statement.

   A. The diameter of the basketball is about 25 inches.   ○ True   ● False

   B. The volume of the basketball is approximately 277.6 in^3.   ○ True   ● False

   C. The volume of the basketball is approximately 434.9 in^3.   ● True   ○ False

3. A triangle has a side of length 8, a second side of length 17, and a third side of length x. Find the range of possible values for x.

   $9 < x < 25$

4. Find the approximate volume of the figure at right, composed of a cone, a cylinder, and a hemisphere. Explain how you found the values needed to compute the volume.

   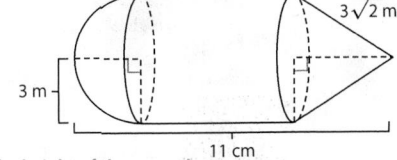

   3 m

   11 cm

   $3\sqrt{2}$ m

   Sample Answer: The volume of the figure is 226.2 m^3, or 72π m^3. The right triangle composed of the height of the cone, the radius of the cylinder, and the slant height of the cone is a special right triangle, so the height of the cone is 3 meters. The height of the cylinder is the length of the composite figure minus the radius of the hemisphere and the height of the cone, so it is $11 - 3 - 3 = 5$ meters.

MIXED REVIEW
Assessment Readiness

ASSESSMENT AND INTERVENTION

Assign ready-made or customized practice tests to prepare students for high-stakes tests.

ADDITIONAL RESOURCES

Assessment Resources

- Leveled Module Quizzes: Modified, B

AVOID COMMON ERRORS

Item 1   Some students will be confused that the question asks for the height when the height of the rectangular prism is given. Point out that the height of the monument includes both shapes in the composite figure, not just the prism.

Common Core Standards

Lesson	Items	Content Standards	Mathematical Practices
18.1, 18.2	1	G-GMD.A.3	MP.2
18.4	2	G-GMD.A.3	MP.1, MP.2
7.3	3*	G-MG.A.3	MP.6
18.1, 18.3, 13.3	4*	G-GMD.A.3	MP.2

* Item integrates mixed review concepts from previous modules or a previous course.

ESSENTIAL QUESTION:

Answer: For one example, visualizing a solid is useful for figuring out how much paint is needed to cover an object.

PROFESSIONAL DEVELOPMENT VIDEO

Professional Development Video

Author Juli Dixon models successful teaching practices in an actual high-school classroom.

Professional Development
my.hrw.com

MODULE **19**

Visualizing Solids

★

Essential Question: How can visualizing solids help you to solve real-world problems?

LESSON 19.1
Cross Sections and Solids of Rotation

LESSON 19.2
Surface Area of Prisms and Cylinders

LESSON 19.3
Surface Area of Pyramids and Cones

LESSON 19.4
Surface Area of Spheres

© Houghton Mifflin Harcourt Publishing Company • Image Credits: ©Stocktrek Images, Inc./Getty Images

REAL WORLD VIDEO
Check out how visualization of solids and surface area can be used to determine critical dimensions of the Space Shuttle and other spacecraft.

MODULE PERFORMANCE TASK PREVIEW

How Much Does the Paint on the Space Shuttle Weigh?

At some point, NASA stopped painting the fuel tanks for the Space Shuttle because of the extra weight it added. In this module, you will be challenged to use surface area to come up with an estimate for the weight of that paint. Let's start the countdown!

Module 19

979

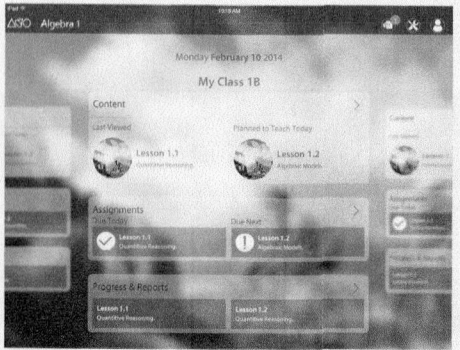

DIGITAL TEACHER EDITION

Access a full suite of teaching resources when and where you need them:

- Access content online or offline
- Customize lessons to share with your class
- Communicate with your students in real-time
- View student grades and data instantly to target your instruction where it is needed most

PERSONAL MATH TRAINER

Assessment and Intervention

Assign automatically graded homework, quizzes, tests, and intervention activities. Prepare your students with updated, Common Core-aligned practice tests.

Are YOU Ready?

Complete these exercises to review skills you will need for this module.

- Online Homework
- Hints and Help
- Extra Practice

Cross Sections

Example 1

What is the cross section of a plane that passes through (but not tangent to) a sphere?

No matter how or where the plane passes, the cross section will always be a circle with radius less than or equal to the radius of the sphere.

Find the cross section of the following.

1. A plane passing through a cylinder parallel to the bases.

    circle with radius equal to the radius of the bases

Volume

Example 2

Find the exact volume of a right cylinder with a radius 9 and height 5.

$V = Bh$	Volume of a cylinder
$B = \pi r^2$	Area of base equals the area of a circle.
$B = \pi(9)^2 = 81\pi$	Substitute and solve.
$V = (81\pi)(5) = 405\pi$	Substitute and solve to find the volume.

Find the volume of the following. Give exact values.

2. A sphere with radius 6

    288π

3. A pyramid whose base is a square with a base having sides of length 17 and whose height is 9

    867

Surface Area

Example 3

Given a cube with a side of length 5, find the surface area.

Since the surface area of a cube is 6 squares of equal area, find the area of one face of the cube and then multiply by 6.

$A = s^2$	Area of a square
$A = (5)^2 = 25$	Substitute and solve.
$SA = 25 \cdot 6 = 150$	Multiply by 6, the number of faces of a cube.

Find the surface area of a cube with the following side lengths.

4. 7

    294

5. 10

    600

© Houghton Mifflin Harcourt Publishing Company

Are You Ready?

ASSESS READINESS

Use the assessment on this page to determine if students need strategic or intensive intervention for the module's prerequisite skills.

ASSESSMENT AND INTERVENTION

TIER 1, TIER 2, TIER 3 SKILLS

Personal Math Trainer will automatically create a standards-based, personalized intervention assignment for your students, targeting each student's individual needs!

ADDITIONAL RESOURCES

See the table below for a full list of intervention resources available for this module.

Response to Intervention Resources also includes:

- Tier 2 Skill Pre-Tests for each Module
- Tier 2 Skill Post-Tests for each skill

Response to Intervention			*Differentiated Instruction*
Tier 1	**Tier 2**	**Tier 3**	
Lesson Intervention Worksheets	Strategic Intervention Skills Intervention Worksheets	Intensive Intervention Worksheets available online	
Reteach 19.1 Reteach 19.2 Reteach 19.3 Reteach 19.4	4 Area of a Circle 8 Cross Sections 24 Surface Area	Building Block Skills 9, 10, 11, 14, 31, 32, 38, 100, 101	Challenge worksheets Extend the Math Lesson Activities in TE

Cross Sections and Solids of Rotation

Common Core Math Standards

The student is expected to:

 G-GMD.B.4

Identify the shapes of two-dimensional cross-sections of three-dimensional objects, and identify three-dimensional objects generaterd by rotations of two-dimensional objects.

Mathematical Practices

MP.4 Modeling

Language Objective

Explain to a partner how to identify the three-dimensional objects generated by rotating two-dimensional shapes about a line.

ENGAGE

Essential Question: What tools can you use to visualize solid figures accurately?

A net allows you to visualize the whole surface of the figure; a cross-section allows you to think about the structure of the figure layer by layer; the relationship between a two-dimensional figure and the solid it generates by rotation tells you which figures can be generated in this way, and also tells you about their rotational structure.

PREVIEW: LESSON PERFORMANCE TASK

View the Engage section online. Discuss the photograph. Ask students to identify the subject of the photo and to speculate on the significance of the rings. Then preview the Lesson Performance Task.

Name_____ Class_____ Date_____

19.1 Cross Sections and Solids of Rotation

Essential Question: What tools can you use to visualize solid figures accurately?

Resource Locker

Explore Exploring Nets

A **net** is a diagram of the surfaces of a three-dimensional figure that can be folded to form the three-dimensional figure. To identify a three-dimensional figure from a net, look at the number of faces and the shape of each face.

(A) Complete each row of the table. Express the circumference of the cylinder as a multiple of π.

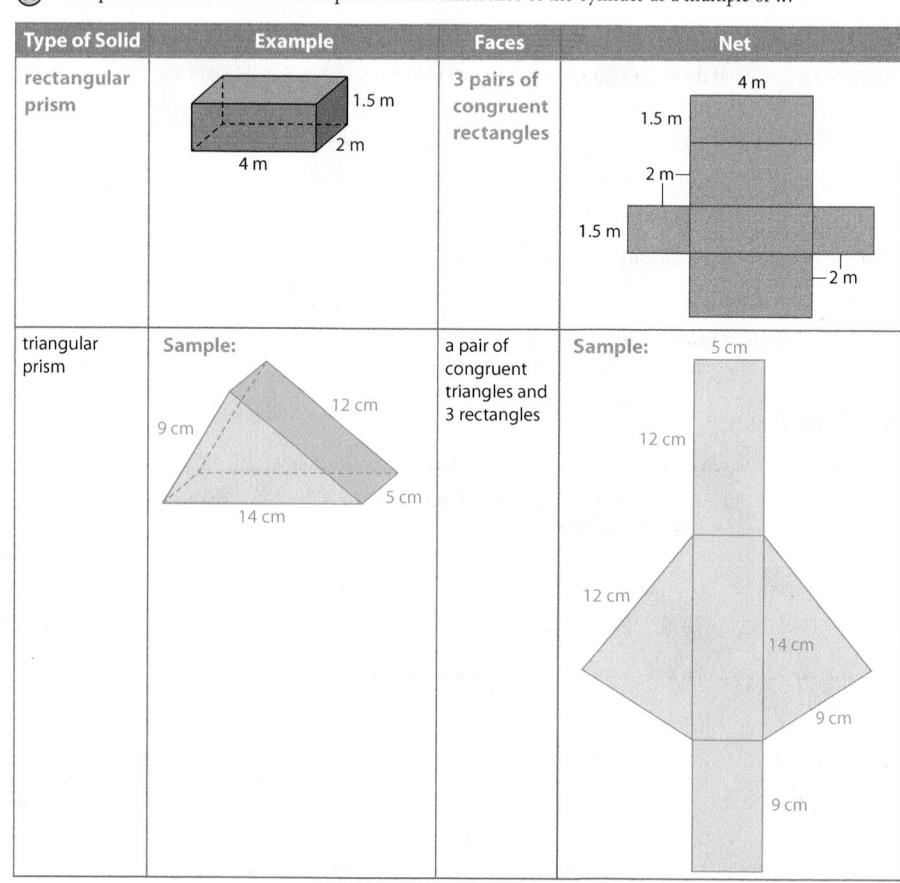

HARDCOVER PAGES 825–832

Turn to these pages to find this lesson in the hardcover student edition.

Type of Solid	Example	Faces	Net
rectangular pyramid	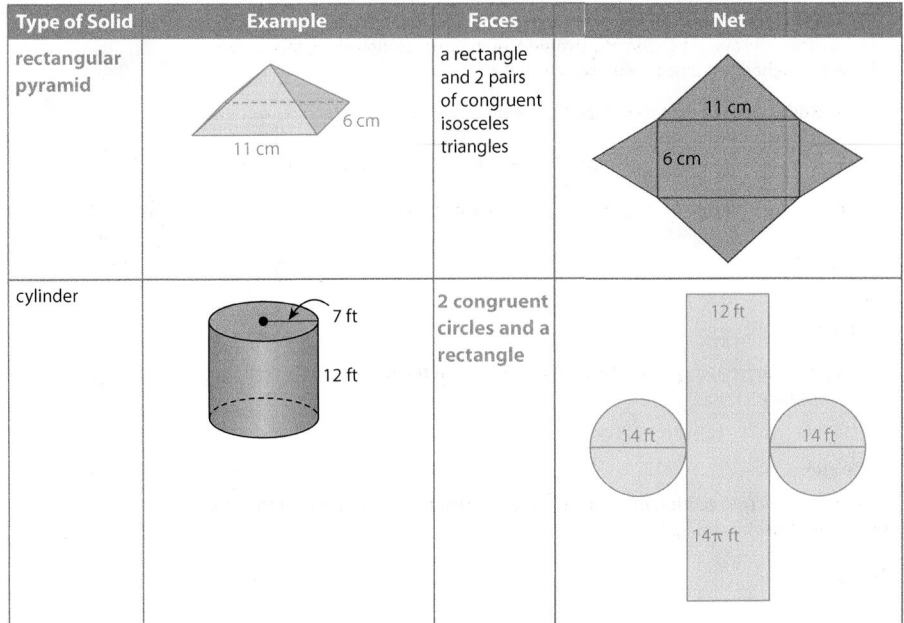6 cm 11 cm	a rectangle and 2 pairs of congruent isosceles triangles	11 cm 6 cm
cylinder	7 ft 12 ft	2 congruent circles and a rectangle	12 ft 14 ft 14 ft 14π ft

Reflect

1. **Discussion** Is there more than one way to draw a net for a solid? Are there rules for how the faces of a solid are joined to create a net for it?

   Yes; E.g., Any arrangement of the faces works as long as a) each face appears exactly once

   b) if two faces are joined at an edge in the net, they must be joined at this edge in the solid,

   and c) the faces form one non-overlapping surface.

Explain 1 Identifying Cross Sections

Recall that a *cross section* is a region of a plane that intersects a solid figure. Cross sections of three-dimensional figures sometimes turn out to be simple figures such as triangles, rectangles, or circles.

Example 1 Describe the cross section of each figure. Compare the dimensions of the cross section to those of the figure.

Ⓐ The bases of the cylinder are congruent circles.

The cross section is formed by a plane that is parallel to the bases of the cylinder. Any cross section of a cylinder made by a plane parallel to the bases will have the same shape as the bases.

Therefore, the cross section is a circle with the same radius or diameter as the bases.

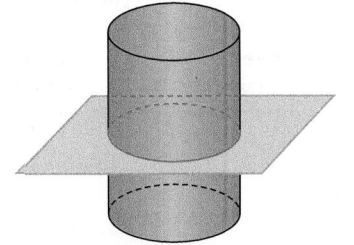

PROFESSIONAL DEVELOPMENT

 Learning Progressions

Previously, students learned about the properties of three-dimensional shapes and about rotational symmetry. The focus of this module is visualizing three-dimensional figures and generating solid figures by rotating two-dimensional figures. Students will identify cross-sections of the figures and review the terms related to three-dimensional figures, including *face, edge, vertex,* and *base.* As students progress through more advanced courses, they will see other three-dimensional figures and use cross-sections to generate *solids of rotation.*

EXPLORE

Exploring Nets

INTEGRATE TECHNOLOGY

Students have the option of doing the Explore activity either in the book or online.

QUESTIONING STRATEGIES

? How is a two-dimensional net related to a three-dimensional figure? If you fold the net, it forms a three-dimensional figure.

? Can a cube have more than one net? Explain. Yes; because all the edges have the same length, you can place the base squares in several different positions to form different nets.

EXPLAIN 1

Identifying Cross Sections

QUESTIONING STRATEGIES

? How many bases does a cylinder or prism have? What must be true about the bases? Two; the bases must be congruent.

? When is a cross-section of a prism congruent to its bases? when it is parallel to the bases

Focus on Reasoning

MP.2 Encourage students to use properties of three-dimensional figures to help them identify cross-sections. For example, knowing that the faces of a rectangular prism meet at right angles can help students identify the figure that is formed by a plane that intersects the prism.

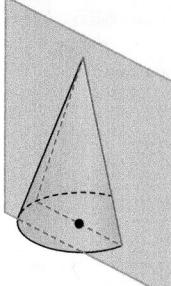

(B) The lateral surface of the cone curves in the horizontal direction, but not the vertical direction. Therefore the two sides of the cross section along this surface are straight line segments with equal lengths.

The third side is a diameter of the base of the cone. Therefore, the cross section

is a(n) [isosceles] triangle. Its base is the [diameter] of the cone

and its leg length is the [slant] height of the cone.

Reflect

2. A plane intersects a sphere. Make a conjecture about the resulting cross section.
It will be a circle.

Your Turn

Describe each cross section of each figure. Compare the dimensions of the cross section to those of the figure.

3.

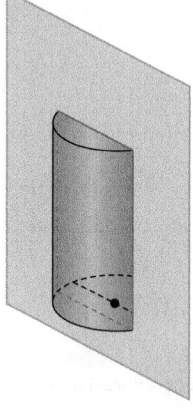

The bases of the cylinder are parallel, so the cross section is a quadrilateral with at least one pair of opposite sides parallel.

The bases of the cylinder meet the lateral (curved) surface at right angles, so the cross section must contain four right angles.

Therefore, the cross section is a rectangle. Its base is smaller than the diameter of the cylinder, because the plane does not pass through the widest part of the cylinder, and its height is the same as the cylinder's.

COLLABORATIVE LEARNING

Small Group Activity

Have students work in groups to generate prisms, cylinders, cones, and spheres by rotating two-dimensional figures about a vertical axis. Have students each choose a three-dimensional figure and conjecture which two-dimensional figure they will rotate to get the three-dimensional figure. Then have them create or draw a model to verify or disprove the conjecture. Have them present their results to the group.

⌾ Explain 2   Generating Three-Dimensional Figures

You can generate a three-dimensional figure by rotating a two-dimensional figure around an appropriate axis.

Example 2   Describe and then sketch the figure that is generated by each rotation in three-dimensional space.

(A)   A right triangle rotated around a line containing one of its legs

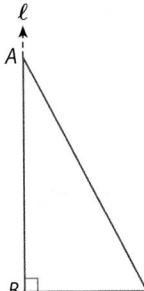

Leg $\overline{BC}$ is perpendicular to ℓ, so vertex C traces out a circle as it rotates about ℓ, and therefore $\overline{BC}$ traces out a circular base. The hypotenuse, $\overline{AC}$, traces out the curving surface of the cone whose base is formed by $\overline{BC}$. The figure formed by the rotation is a cone.

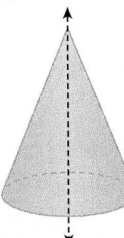

(B)   A rectangle rotated around a line containing one of its sides

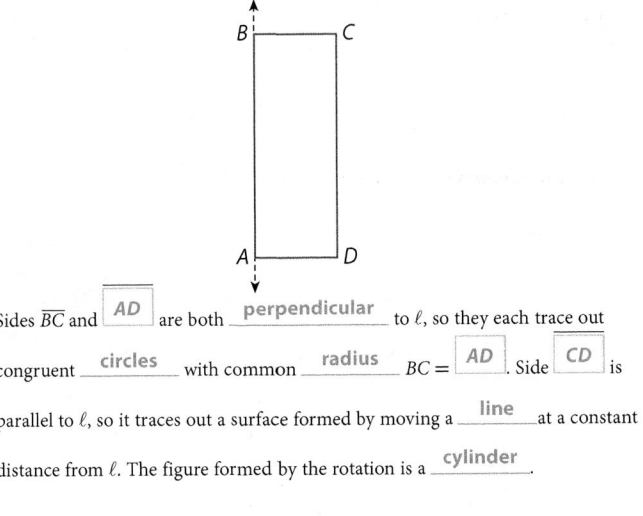

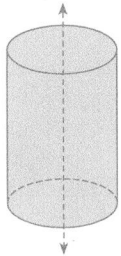

Sides $\overline{BC}$ and [AD] are both ___perpendicular___ to ℓ, so they each trace out

congruent ___circles___ with common ___radius___ $BC =$ [AD]. Side [CD] is

parallel to ℓ, so it traces out a surface formed by moving a ___line___ at a constant

distance from ℓ. The figure formed by the rotation is a ___cylinder___.

EXPLAIN 2

Generating Three-Dimensional Figures

INTEGRATE MATHEMATICAL PRACTICES
Focus on Critical Thinking

MP.3 Challenge students by asking them to describe the three-dimensional figures that are formed by rotating figures in a coordinate plane. For example, you might have students describe the figure formed by rotating the part of the line $y = -x + 2$ that lies in quadrant I around the x-axis. Students should find that the figure is a cone with radius 2 and height 2.

DIFFERENTIATE INSTRUCTION

Kinesthetic Experience

Some students may have difficulty visualizing the cross-sections in this lesson. Kinesthetic learners in particular might benefit from using clay to make small models of the relevant three-dimensional figures. Then, they can view cross-sections by making straight slices through the figures with a plastic knife or with a taut piece of string or dental floss.

QUESTIONING STRATEGIES

? How is a rotation around a line in space similar to a rotation around a point in a plane? In a rotation around a line in space, points move around the line in such a way that their distance from the line is unchanged, and points on the line of rotation are fixed. In a rotation around a point in a plane, points move in such a way that their distance from a point is unchanged, while the point itself remains fixed.

? How do you generate a cylinder from a rectangle? Rotate the rectangle along an axis that is one side of the rectangle.

AVOID COMMON ERRORS

Students may not be able to visualize the figure that results by rotating a figure along an axis in the plane. Encourage them to make a model by cutting out the figure and taping it to a pencil, then rotating the pencil while looking down on the pencil. Students should see the figure traced in the plane.

Reflect

4. **Discussion** What principles can you identify for generating a solid by rotation of a two-dimensional figure?

   E.g., Any vertex traces a circle, but only a side perpendicular to the axis of rotation (and with one endpoint on the axis) generates a circular surface. A side parallel to the axis generates a cylindrical surface. A side neither parallel nor perpendicular to the axis generates a conical surface (truncated if neither endpoint is on the axis).

Your Turn

Describe and then sketch the figure that is generated by each rotation in three-dimensional space.

5. A trapezoid with two adjacent acute angles rotated around a line containing the side adjacent to these angles

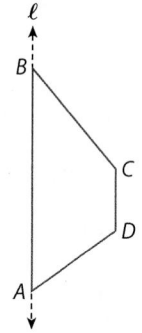

Sides $\overline{BC}$ and $\overline{AD}$ are neither perpendicular nor parallel to ℓ, so they form conical surfaces. Side $\overline{CD}$ is parallel to ℓ, so it forms a curved cylindrical surface. The figure formed by the rotation is a composite of two cones with a cylinder in between.

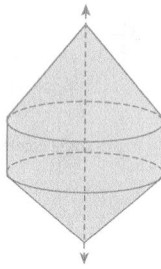

6. A semicircle rotated around a line containing its diameter

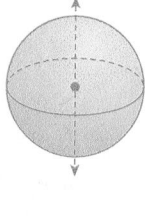

Each point on the semicircle traces out a circle. The figure formed by the rotation is a sphere.

LANGUAGE SUPPORT **EL**

Connect Vocabulary

To help students remember the vocabulary in the lesson, including *vertex, face, base, edge,* and *cross-section,* have students make a small poster showing labeled examples of several solid figures and their cross-sections. Have them use colored pencils to mark the bases of each in one color, the edges in another color, and so on. Have them label the figures with the vocabulary words, and highlight the cross-sections. Ask students to display the posters in the classroom and invite them to present their posters to the class.

💬 Elaborate

7. Discussion If a solid has been generated by rotating a plane figure around an axis, will the solid always have cross-sections that are circles? Will it always have cross sections that are not circles? Explain.

Yes. Every point on the figure rotated around the axis traces out a circle. So any slice through the solid that is perpendicular to the axis will either be a circle or a point. The solid will have cross sections that are not circles which can be created by taking a slice that is not perpendicular to the axis, unless the figure that has been rotated is a semicircle which results in a sphere.

8. Essential Question Check-In What tools can you use to visualize solid figures? Explain how each tool is helpful.

A net allows you to visualize the whole surface of the figure; a cross section allows you to think about the structure of the figure layer by layer; the relationship between a two-dimensional figure and the solid it generates by rotation tells you which figures can be generated in this way, and also about their rotational structure.

⭐ Evaluate: Homework and Practice

Personal Math Trainer
- Online Homework
- Hints and Help
- Extra Practice

1. Which of the figures is not a net for a cube? Explain.

a.
c.
b.
d.

Figure B; when the figure is folded, two of the faces will overlap.

Describe the three-dimensional figure that can be made from the given net.

2.

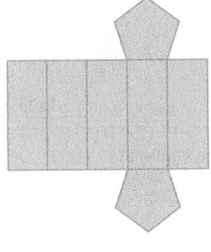

pentagonal prism

3.

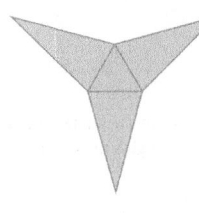

triangular pyramid

ELABORATE

QUESTIONING STRATEGIES

? How can you identify cross-sections of three-dimensional figures? Use visualization aids such as models and diagrams, and use known properties of three-dimensional figures to determine properties of the cross-section.

? How do you use rotations to generate three-dimensional figures? Rotate a two-dimensional figure about a line. The movement of its points in space traces a three-dimensional figure.

INTEGRATE MATHEMATICAL PRACTICES
Focus on Critical Thinking

MP.3 Challenge students to think about whether the three-dimensional figures they formed by rotating a two-dimensional figure about a line must themselves have rotational symmetry. Yes; the line must be an axis of symmetry for the figure, so the figure has rotational symmetry.

SUMMARIZE THE LESSON

? What is similar about nets and cross-sections, and what is different? Both nets and cross-sections are two-dimensional tools that can be used to help visualize three-dimensional figures. A net represents the surface of a three-dimensional figure, while a cross-section represents the intersection of a three-dimensional figure and a plane.

EVALUATE

ASSIGNMENT GUIDE

Concepts and Skills	Practice
Explore Exploring Nets	Exercises 1–3
Example 1 Identifying Cross Sections	Exercises 4–11
Example 2 Generating Three-Dimensional Figures	Exercises 12–15

INTEGRATE MATHEMATICAL PRACTICES

Focus on Modeling

MP.4 Some students may benefit from a hands-on approach for finding the cross-sections of solids. Have students draw simple figures like prisms and cylinders and then discuss in groups how they can add cross-sections to their drawings. Have them include a discussion of the properties of the solids and cross-sections that may help them add the two-dimensional figures to the drawing. Make sure they make some of the lines dashed to add perspective to the figures.

Describe the cross-section.

4.

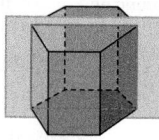

rectangle

5.

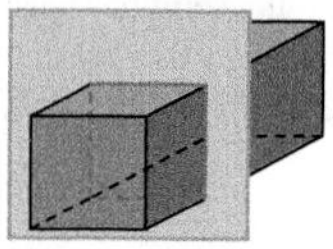

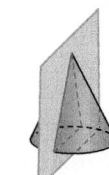

square

6.

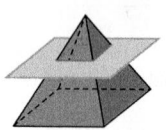

square

7.

(isosceles) triangle

8.

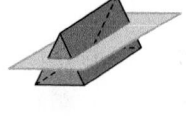

rectangle

9.

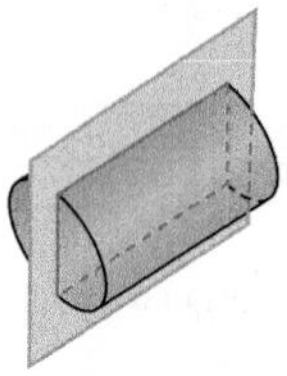

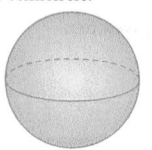

rectangle

10. Describe the cross section formed by the intersection of a cone and a plane parallel to the base of the cone.

circle

11. Describe the cross section formed by the intersection of a sphere and a plane that passes through the center of the sphere.

circle

Sketch and describe the figure that is generated by each rotation in three-dimensional space.

12. Rotate a semicircle around a line through the endpoints of the semicircle.

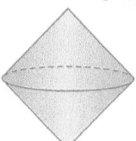

sphere

13. Rotate an isosceles triangle around the triangle's line of symmetry.

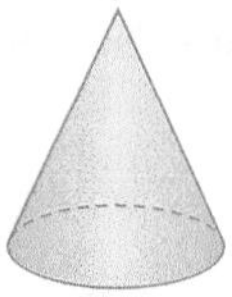

cone

14. Rotate an isosceles right triangle around a line that contains the triangle's hypotenuse

two cones that share a base

15. Rotate a line segment around a line that is perpendicular to the segment that passes through an endpoint to the segment.

disc (circle and its interior)

© Houghton Mifflin Harcourt Publishing Company

Exercise	Depth of Knowledge (D.O.K.)	COMMON CORE Mathematical Practices
1	**3** Strategic Thinking	**MP.6** Precision
2–15	**1** Recall of Information	**MP.2** Reasoning
16	**2** Skills/Concepts	**MP.6** Precision
17	**2** Skills/Concepts	**MP.2** Reasoning
18	**3** Strategic Thinking	**MP.6** Precision
19	**3** Strategic Thinking H.O.T.	**MP.4** Modeling

16. Multiple Response Which of the following shapes could be formed by the intersection of a plane and a cube? Select all that apply.

(A.) Equilateral Triangle

(B.) Scalene Triangle

(C.) Square

(D.) Rectangle

E. Circle

A plane through exactly three vertices of the cube forms an equilateral triangle, because the diagonal of every face of the cube is equal. A plane that intersects three edges at different distances from a vertex will form a scalene triangle

A plane parallel to any face of the cube forms a square. Every square is also a rectangle (it is also possible to form a rectangle that is not a square).

A cube has no curved sides, so a circular cross-section cannot be made.

17. A student claims that if you dilate the net for a cube using a scale factor of 2, the surface area of the resulting cube is multiplied by 4 and the volume is multiplied by 8. Does this claim make sense?

Yes. If the side length of a square in the original net is x, then a side length in the transformed net is $2x$. Original Surface Area $= 6x^2$; Transformed Surface Area $= 6(2x)^2 = 4(6x^2)$; Original Volume $= x^3$; Transformed Volume $= (2x)^3 = 8x^3$

18. Find the Error A regular hexagonal prism is intersected by a plane as shown. Which cross section is incorrect? Explain.

B; since the prism is regular, the bases are congruent, and the opposite sides of the cross section must be congruent.

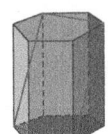 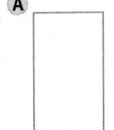 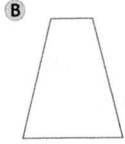

---

19. Architecture An architect is drawing plans for a building that is a hexagonal prism. Describe how the architect could draw a cutaway of the building that shows a cross section in the shape of a hexagon, and a cross section in the shape of a rectangle.

For a hexagon, cut parallel to the ground; for a rectangle, cut perpendicular to the ground.

20. Draw Conclusions Is it possible for a cross section of a cube to be an octagon? Explain.

No; the cube has 6 faces, so when a cross section is formed by the intersection of the cube and a plane, the resulting polygon can have at most 6 sides.

INTEGRATE MATHEMATICAL PRACTICES

Focus on Technology

MP.5 Some students may benefit from using geometry software to experiment with finding the cross-sections of solids. Have students draw simple figures like prisms and cylinders and then use technology to add cross-sections to their drawings. If possible, have them also use technology to draw solids by rotating two-dimensional figures about a line.

AVOID COMMON ERRORS

Students may be confused about how to find the height and radii of the solids they form by rotating a two-dimensional figure about a line. For the radius of a cylinder, have them measure the base of the rectangle that is perpendicular to the line. For the height of the cylinder, have them measure the side of the rectangle that is contained in the line. Have students think of strategies they can use to find the dimensions of other *solids of rotation*.

Exercise	Depth of Knowledge (D.O.K.)	COMMON CORE Mathematical Practices
20	**3** Strategic Thinking H.O.T.	**MP.6** Precision
21	**3** Strategic Thinking H.O.T.	**MP.6** Precision
22	**3** Strategic Thinking H.O.T.	**MP.6** Precision

INTEGRATE MATHEMATICAL PRACTICES

Focus on Reasoning

MP.2 There are many composite geometric solids that can be formed by rotating a two-dimensional shape about a line. Draw irregular two-dimensional figures and challenge students to predict the results of rotating the figures about a line.

JOURNAL

Have students illustrate and describe two different ways to use a rotation to generate a cylinder. Then, have students illustrate and describe two different cross-sections of a cylinder.

---

21. **Communicate Mathematical Ideas** A cube with sides of length s is intersected by a plane that passes through three of the cube's vertices, forming the cross section shown. What type of triangle is in the cross section? Explain.

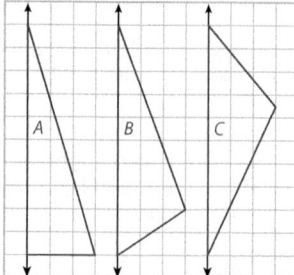

Equilateral triangle; by Pythagorean Theorem, each side of the triangle has length $s\sqrt{2}$.

$$a^2 + b^2 = c^2, \text{ so } 2s^2 = c^2 \text{ and } s\sqrt{2} = c.$$

22. The three triangles all have the same area because each base and each height are congruent. Make and test a conjecture about the volume of the solids generated by rotating these triangles around the base.

Conjecture: The volumes of the solids generated by triangles with congruent base and height will be equal. Calculating the volume of the solids generated by these three triangles suggests the conjecture is true.

Triangle A will generate a cone with height 9 and radius 3.

$$V = \frac{1}{3}\pi r^2 h = \frac{1}{3}\pi \cdot 3^2 \cdot 9 = 27\pi$$

Triangle B will generate two cones that share a base with radius 3. The top cone has height 6 and the bottom cone has height 3.

Volume of top cone $= \frac{1}{3}\pi r^2 h = \frac{1}{3}\pi \cdot 3^2 \cdot 6 = 18\pi$

Volume of bottom cone $= \frac{1}{3}\pi r^2 h = \frac{1}{3}\pi \cdot 3^2 \cdot 3 = 9\pi$

Total volume $= 18\pi + 9\pi = 27\pi$

Triangle C will generate two cones that share a base with radius 3. The top cone has a height of x and the bottom cone has a height of $9 - x$.

Volume of top cone $= \frac{1}{3}\pi r^2 h = \frac{1}{3}\pi \cdot 3^2 \cdot x = 3\pi(x)$

Volume of bottom cone $= \frac{1}{3}\pi r^2 h = \frac{1}{3}\pi \cdot 3^2 \cdot (9-x) = 3\pi(9-x) = 27\pi - 3\pi(x)$

Total volume $= 3\pi(x) + 27\pi - 3\pi(x) = 27\pi$

Lesson Performance Task

Each year of its life, a tree grows a new ring just under the outside bark. The new ring consists of two parts, light-colored *springwood*, when the tree grows the fastest, and a darker-colored *summerwood*, when growth slows. When conditions are good and there is lots of sun and rain, the new ring is thicker than the rings formed when there is drought or excessive cold. At the center of the tree is a dark circle called *pith* that is not connected to the age of the tree.

1. Describe the history of the tree in the diagram.

2. The redwood trees of coastal California are the tallest living things on earth. One redwood is 350 feet tall, 20 feet in diameter at its base, and around 2000 years old. Assume that the lower 50 feet of the tree form a cylinder 20 feet in diameter and that all of the rings grew at the same rate.

a. What is the total volume of wood in the 50-foot section? Use 3.14 for π.

b. How wide is each annual ring (springwood and summerwood combined)? Disregard the bark and pith in your calculations. Show your work. Write your answer in inches.

1. Sample answer: The tree appears to be seven years old. The first three years of its life there was ample sun and rain and the tree experienced excellent growth, especially in Year 3. After that conditions worsened and the tree grew less well, especially in the past two years. The pith is off center and the tree rings appear to be shifted to the left slightly. This could have happened because of high winds from the left side of the tree, causing the tree to grow less quickly on that side than on the right.

2. a.
   volume $= \pi r^2 h$
   $= 3.14(10)^2(50)$
   $= 15,700 \text{ ft}^3$

   b. radius $= 10$ ft $= 120$ in.
   number of rings $= 2000$
   width of each ring $= 120 \div 2000 = 0.06$ in.

© Houghton Mifflin Harcourt Publishing Company

INTEGRATE MATHEMATICAL PRACTICES
Focus on Math Connections

MP.1 A company sells redwood fence posts measuring 4 inches by 4 inches by 8 feet for $12. If all of the lumber in the 50-foot cylindrical section of the redwood tree described in the Lesson Performance Task were cut into fence posts, what would the total value be?

Volume of 1 post $= \frac{1}{3} \cdot \frac{1}{3} \cdot 8 = \frac{8}{9}$ ft^3;

Number of posts in the redwood

$= 15,700 \div \frac{8}{9} = 15,700 \cdot \frac{9}{8} = 17,662.5$;

Total value $= 17,662.5 \cdot \$12 = \$211,950$

INTEGRATE MATHEMATICAL PRACTICES
Focus on Reasoning

MP.2 If a lumberjack cuts a cylindrical tree parallel to the ground, the resulting cross-section will be a circle. Describe the cross-section formed if the cut is made at an angle to the ground, and the change in the cross-section if cuts are made at ever-increasing angles to the ground. As the angle of the cut increases, the circular cross-section will grow more and more elliptical, its width remaining the same but its length increasing continually.

EXTENSION ACTIVITY

Bristlecone pine trees of eastern Nevada and eastern California are identified as among the oldest living things on Earth. Have students research bristlecone pines and report on the ages, sizes, and typical ring widths of some of the oldest trees, and the environments where the trees are found, particularly as they relate to the bristlecone pines' remarkable longevity. Ages of several thousand years are common. Harsh conditions at the altitudes where the trees are found keep their sizes small and result in tiny tree-ring widths, as little as a fraction of a millimeter.

Scoring Rubric
2 points: Student correctly solves the problem and explains his/her reasoning.
1 point: Student shows good understanding of the problem but does not fully solve or explain his/her reasoning.
0 points: Student does not demonstrate understanding of the problem.

Cross Sections and Solids of Rotation   **990**

Surface Area of Prisms and Cylinders

Common Core Math Standards

The student is expected to:

 G-MG.A.1

Use geometric shapes, their measures, and their properties to describe objects (e.g., modeling a tree trunk or a human torso as a cylinder).

Mathematical Practices

 MP.2 Reasoning

Language Objective

Explain to a partner how to find the surface area of prisms and cylinders.

ENGAGE

Essential Question: How can you find the surface area of a prism or a cylinder?

You find the lateral area and then add twice the area of a base.

PREVIEW: LESSON PERFORMANCE TASK

View the Engage section online. Discuss the photograph. Ask students to identify the subject of the photo and to speculate on the significance of the surface area on determining how items are packaged. Then preview the Lesson Performance Task.

19.2 Surface Area of Prisms and Cylinders

Essential Question: How can you find the surface area of a prism or cylinder?

Resource Locker

⟳ Explore   Developing a Surface Area Formula

Surface area is the total area of all the faces and curved surfaces of a three-dimensional figure. The *lateral area* of a prism is the sum of the areas of the lateral faces.

Ⓐ Consider the right prism shown here and the net for the right prism. Complete the figure by labeling the dimensions of the net.

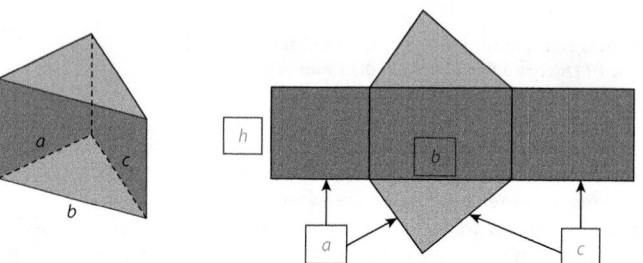

Ⓑ In the net, what type of figure is formed by the lateral faces of the prism?

rectangle

Ⓒ Write an expression for the length of the base of the rectangle.

$a + b + c$

Ⓓ How is the base of the rectangle related to the perimeter of the base of the prism?

They are equal.

Ⓔ The lateral area L of the prism is the area of the rectangle. Write a formula for L in terms of h, a, b, and c.

$L = h(a + b + c)$

Ⓕ Write the formula for L in terms of P, where P is the perimeter of the base of the prism.

$L = Ph$

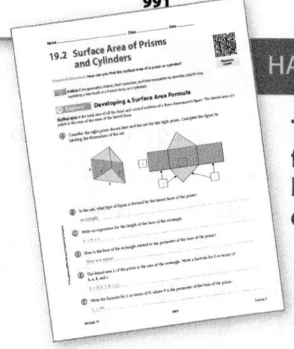

HARDCOVER PAGES 833–842

Turn to these pages to find this lesson in the hardcover student edition.

G) Let B be the area of the base of the prism. Write a formula for the surface area S of the prism in terms of B and L. Then write the formula in terms of B, P, and h.

$S = L + 2B; S = Ph + 2B$

Reflect

1. Explain why the net of the lateral surface of any right prism will always be a rectangle.
Sample answer: Each lateral face of any right prism is a rectangle. The net of the lateral

surface of any right prism is composed of rectangles joined end-to-end. Straight angles

are formed when the rectangles are joined in this manner resulting in one long

rectangular shape.

2. Suppose a rectangular prism has length ℓ, width w, and height h, as shown. Explain how you can write a formula for the surface area of the prism in terms of ℓ, w, and h.

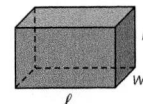

Sample answer: There are two faces with area ℓw, two faces with area wh, and two faces

with area ℓh, so the surface area can be written as $S = 2\ell w + 2wh + 2\ell h$.

Explain 1   Finding the Surface Area of a Prism

Lateral Area and Surface Area of Right Prisms

The lateral area of a right prism with height h and base perimeter P is $L = Ph$.

The surface area of a right prism with lateral area L and base area B is $S = L + 2B$, or $S = Ph + 2B$.

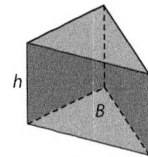

© Houghton Mifflin Harcourt Publishing Company

PROFESSIONAL DEVELOPMENT

 Integrate Mathematical Practices

This lesson provides an opportunity to address Mathematical Practice **MP.2**, which calls for students to "reason abstractly and quantitatively." In this lesson, students analyze three-dimensional figures to determine how they "decompose" into two-dimensional faces, each with its own area, and to find that the sum of the areas of the faces is equal to the surface area of the figure. Since the faces of the figures are polygons or circles, the combined areas generate the lateral area and surface area formulas students will use in this lesson.

EXPLORE

Developing a Surface Area Formula

INTEGRATE TECHNOLOGY

Students have the option of doing the Explore activity either in the book or online.

QUESTIONING STRATEGIES

(?) In a prism, how is the lateral area formula related to the surface area formula? The surface area formula consists of the lateral area plus the area of the bases.

INTEGRATE MATHEMATICAL PRACTICES
Focus on Reasoning

MP.2 Have students brainstorm how to determine what three-dimensional figure can be made from a given net and how the net can be used to find the surface area of the figure. Emphasize that prisms have parallelograms for sides, and cylinders have congruent circular bases.

EXPLAIN 1

Finding the Surface Area of a Prism

QUESTIONING STRATEGIES

(?) How can you use the formula for the area of a parallelogram to find the lateral area of a prism? Because the lateral faces of a prism are parallelograms, you can use the parallelogram formula to find the areas of the lateral faces and then add them together.

? When can the Pythagorean Theorem be used to find the area of the bases of a triangular prism? If the bases are right triangles, then the Pythagorean Theorem can be used to find the lengths of the legs of the triangles, which are necessary to find the area of the triangles.

Example 1 Each gift box is a right prism. Find the total amount of paper needed to wrap each box, not counting overlap.

(A) **Step 1** Find the lateral area.

Lateral area formula	$L = Ph$
$P = 2(8) + 2(6) = 28$ cm	$= 28(12)$
Multiply.	$= 336$ cm^2

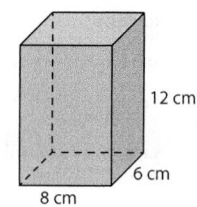

12 cm

6 cm

8 cm

Step 2 Find the surface area.

Surface area formula	$S = L + 2B$
Substitute the lateral area.	$= 336 + 2(6)(8)$
Simplify.	$= 432$ cm^2

(B) **Step 1** Find the length c of the hypotenuse of the base.

Pythagorean Theorem	$c^2 = a^2 + b^2$
Substitute.	$= \boxed{10}^2 + \boxed{24}^2$
Simplify.	$= \boxed{676}$
Take the square root of each side.	$c = \boxed{26}$

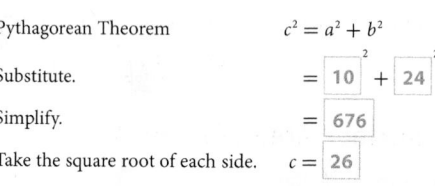

10 in   24 in

20 in

Step 2 Find the lateral area.

Lateral area formula	$L = Ph$
Substitute.	$= \boxed{60}\left(\boxed{20}\right)$
Multiply.	$= \boxed{1200}$ in^2

Step 3 Find the surface area.

Surface area formula	$S = L + 2B$
Substitute.	$= \boxed{1200} + 2 \cdot \frac{1}{2}\boxed{24} \cdot \boxed{10}$
Simplify.	$= \boxed{1440}$ in^2

Reflect

3. A gift box is a rectangular prism with length 9.8 cm, width 10.2 cm, and height 9.7 cm. Explain how to estimate the amount of paper needed to wrap the box, not counting overlap.
   Sample answer: Round each dimension to 10 cm. Then each face has an area of
   approximately $10^2 = 100$ cm^2, and the surface area is approximately $6(100) = 600$ cm^2.

COLLABORATIVE LEARNING

Small Group Activity

Have students work in groups to find the surface areas of various prisms and cylinders. Have students each choose a prism or a cylinder and conjecture how to find the surface area. Then have them draw and label a model or a net and describe how to find the surface area. Ask them to verify or disprove their conjectures, and present their results to the group.

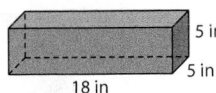

Each gift box is a right prism. Find the total amount of paper needed to wrap each box, not counting overlap.

4.

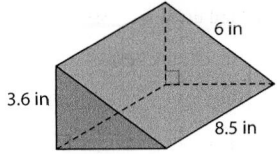

The lateral area is $L = Ph$.
$P = 2(18) + 2(5) = 46$ in.
So, $L = 46(5) = 230$ in².
The surface area is $S = L + 2B$.
$B = 18(5) = 90$ in²
So, $S = 230 + 2(90) = 410$ in².

5.

Let b be the unknown length of the leg of the base.
By the Pythagorean Theorem, $c^2 = a^2 + b^2$,
so $6^2 = 3.6^2 + b^2$, $36 = 12.96 + b^2$,
and $b^2 = 23.04$.
Taking the square root of each side shows that $b = 4.8$ in.
The lateral area is $L = Ph$.
$P = 3.6 + 4.8 + 6 = 14.4$ in.
So, $L = 14.4(8.5) = 122.4$ in².
The surface area is $S = L + 2B$.
$B = \frac{1}{2}(4.8)(3.6) = 8.64$
So, $S = 122.4 + 2(8.64) = 139.68$ in².

⊘ Explain 2   Finding the Surface Area of a Cylinder

Lateral Area and Surface Area of Right Cylinders

The *lateral area* of a cylinder is the area of the curved surface that connects the two bases.

The lateral area of a right cylinder with radius r and height h is $L = 2\pi rh$.

The surface area of a right cylinder with lateral area L and base area B is $S = L + 2B$, or $S = 2\pi rh + 2\pi r^2$.

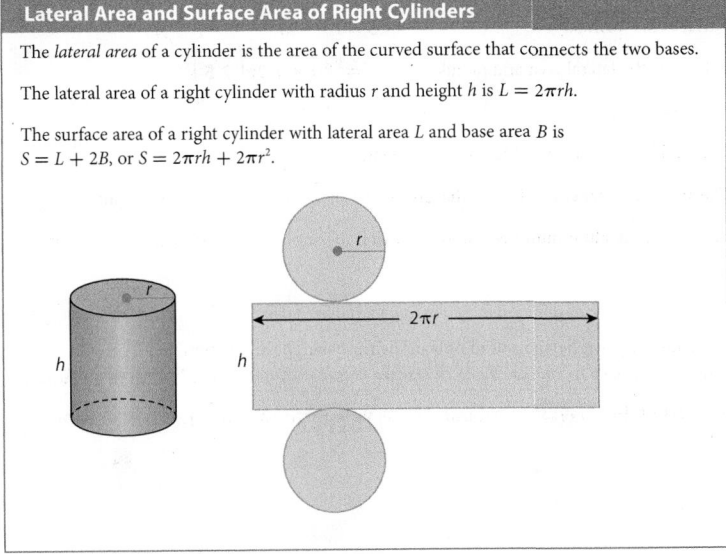

INTEGRATE MATHEMATICAL PRACTICES

Focus on Patterns

MP.8 Encourage students to make an organized list of the dimensions of the lateral sides and the bases of a prism as part of their plan for finding the surface area. Then have them substitute the appropriate values into the formulas for lateral area and surface area of a prism.

EXPLAIN 2

Finding the Surface Area of a Cylinder

QUESTIONING STRATEGIES

? How is the height of a right cylinder used to find its surface area? The height is used to find the lateral area. The lateral area is the circumference of the base times the height. Adding the lateral area to the area of the bases gives the surface area.

DIFFERENTIATE INSTRUCTION

Multiple Representations

Have students work in groups to cover boxes and cylinders with wrapping paper. Ask them to cut the wrap so that it does not overlap, and have them decompose the wraps into nets that they can use to find the surface area. Have groups discuss how the nets are related to the lateral area and the surface area formulas.

Common errors students make when applying the surface area formula include multiplying the height of the cylinder by the area of the base; using a diameter in the formula for cylinders instead of a radius; and forgetting to include the area of both bases. Caution students to look for these errors.

Example 2 Each aluminum can is a right cylinder. Find the amount of paper needed for the can's label and the total amount of aluminum needed to make the can. Round to the nearest tenth.

(A) **Step 1** Find the lateral area.

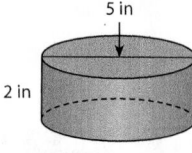
3 cm

9 cm

Lateral area formula	$L = 2\pi rh$
Substitute.	$L = 2\pi(3)(9)$
Multiply.	$= 54\pi \text{ cm}^2$

Step 2 Find the surface area.

Surface area formula	$S = L + 2\pi r^2$
Substitute the lateral area and radius.	$= 54\pi + 2\pi(3)^2$
Simplify.	$= 72\pi \text{ cm}^2$

Step 3 Use a calculator and round to the nearest tenth.

The amount of paper needed for the label is the lateral area, $54\pi \approx 169.6 \text{ cm}^2$.

The amount of aluminum needed for the can is the surface area, $72\pi \approx 226.2 \text{ cm}^2$.

(B) **Step 1** Find the lateral area.

5 in

2 in

Lateral area formula	$L = 2\pi rh$
Substitute; the radius is half the diameter.	$= 2\pi\left(\boxed{2.5}\right)\left(\boxed{2}\right)$
Multiply.	$= \boxed{10}\,\pi \text{ in}^2$

Step 2 Find the surface area.

Surface area formula	$S = L + 2\pi r^2$
Substitute the lateral area and radius.	$= \boxed{10}\,\pi + 2\pi\left(\boxed{2.5}\right)^2$
Simplify.	$= \boxed{22.5}\,\pi \text{ in}^2$

Step 3 Use a calculator and round to the nearest tenth.

The amount of paper needed for the label is the lateral area, $\boxed{10}\,\pi \approx \boxed{31.4} \text{ in}^2$.

The amount of aluminum needed for the can is the surface area, $\boxed{22.5}\,\pi \approx \boxed{70.7} \text{ in}^2$.

Reflect

6. In these problems, why is it best to round only in the final step of the solution?
   Sample answer: This results in a more accurate answer. If you round at an intermediate
   step, the inaccuracies may be compounded as you perform subsequent operations.

Each aluminum can is a right cylinder. Find the amount of paper needed for the can's label and the total amount of aluminum needed to make the can. Round to the nearest tenth.

7.

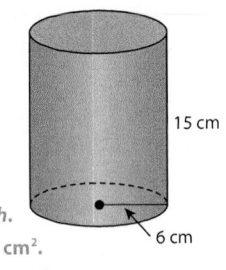

15 cm

6 cm

The lateral area is $L = 2\pi rh$.

So, $L = 2\pi(6)(15) = 180\pi$ cm^2.

The surface area is $S = L + 2\pi r^2$.

So, $S = 180\pi + 2\pi(6)^2 = 252\pi$ cm^2.

The amount of paper needed for the label is the lateral area, $180\pi \approx 565.5$ cm^2.

The amount of aluminum needed for the can is the surface area, $252\pi \approx 791.7$ cm^2.

8.

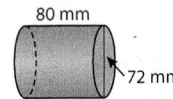

80 mm

72 mm

The radius of the cylinder is half the diameter, so $r = 36$ mm.

The lateral area is $L = 2\pi rh$.

So, $L = 2\pi(36)(80) = 5760\pi$ mm^2.

The surface area is $S = L + 2\pi r^2$.

So, $S = 5760\pi + 2\pi(36)^2 = 8352\pi$ mm^2.

The amount of paper needed for the label is the lateral area, $5760\pi \approx 18,095.6$ mm^2.

The amount of aluminum needed for the can is the surface area, $8352\pi \approx 26,238.6$ mm^2.

⊘ Explain 3   Finding the Surface Area of a Composite Figure

Example 3   Find the surface area of each composite figure. Round to the nearest tenth.

(A)   **Step 1**   Find the surface area of the right rectangular prism.

Surface area formula	$S = Ph + 2B$
Substitute.	$= 80(20) + 2(24)(16)$
Simplify.	$= 2368$ ft^2

4 ft

20 ft

16 ft

24 ft

Step 2   A cylinder is removed from the prism. Find the lateral area of the cylinder and the area of its bases.

Lateral area formula	$L = 2\pi rh$
Substitute.	$= 2\pi(4)(20)$
Simplify.	$= 160\pi$ ft^2
Base area formula	$B = \pi r^2$
Substitute.	$= \pi(4)^2$
Simplify.	$= 16\pi$ ft^2

Step 3   Find the surface area of the composite figure. The surface area is the sum of the areas of all surfaces on the exterior of the figure.

$S = $ (prism surface area) $+$ (cylinder lateral area) $-$ (cylinder base areas)

$= 2368 + 160\pi - 2(16\pi)$

$= 2368 + 128\pi \approx 2770.1$ ft^2

EXPLAIN 3

Finding the Surface Area of a Composite Figure

QUESTIONING STRATEGIES

?   Is the surface area of a composite figure always equal to the sum of the areas of the parts of the figure? Explain. No; you must subtract the areas of any parts of the surface that are overlapping.

Focus on Patterns

MP.8 Encourage students to carefully decompose a figure as part of their plan to find its surface area. Have them make an organized list of the dimensions of the lateral sides and of the bases for each figure, along with a list of those areas that are overlapping in the composite figure. Then have them write an equation for the total surface area of the parts, including subtractions for overlapping parts, and substitute the appropriate values into the formulas.

Ⓑ Step 1 Find the surface area of the right rectangular prism.

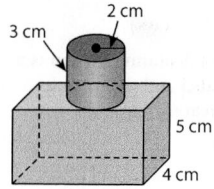
2 cm
3 cm
5 cm
4 cm
9 cm

Surface area formula $S = Ph + 2B$

Substitute. $= \boxed{26}\left(\boxed{5}\right) + 2\left(\boxed{9}\right)\left(\boxed{4}\right)$

Simplify. $= \boxed{202}$ cm²

Step 2 Find the surface area of the cylinder.

Lateral area formula $L = 2\pi rh$

Substitute. $= 2\pi\left(\boxed{2}\right)\left(\boxed{3}\right)$

Simplify. $= \boxed{12}\,\pi$ cm²

Surface area formula $S = L + 2\pi r^2$

Substitute. $= \boxed{12}\,\pi + 2\pi\left(\boxed{2}\right)^2$

Simplify. $= \boxed{20}\,\pi$ cm²

Step 3 Find the surface area of the composite figure. The surface area is the sum of the areas of all surfaces on the exterior of the figure.

$S = $ (prism surface area) $+$ (cylinder surface area) $- 2$(area of one cylinder base)

$= \boxed{202} + \boxed{20}\,\pi - 2\pi\left(\boxed{2}\right)^2$

$= \boxed{202} + \boxed{12}\,\pi \approx \boxed{239.7}$ cm²

Reflect

9. **Discussion** A student said the answer in Part A must be incorrect since a part of the rectangular prism is removed, yet the surface area of the composite figure is greater than the surface area of the rectangular prism. Do you agree with the student? Explain.

No; removing part of the rectangular prism produces a hole through the prism and this

creates additional exposed area on the interior surface of the hole.

Find the surface area of each composite figure. Round to the nearest tenth.

10.

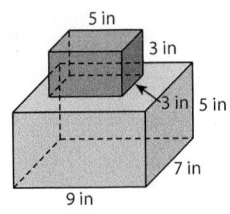

The surface area of the large prism is
$S_{large} = Ph + 2B$.
So, $S_{large} = (32)(5) + 2(9)(7) = 286$ in².
The surface area of the small prism is
$S_{small} = Ph + 2B$.
So, $S_{small} = (16)(3) + 2(5)(3) = 78$ in².
The surface area of the composite figure is
the surface area of the large prism plus the
surface area of the small prism minus 2 times
the area of the base of the small prism.
$S = 286 + 78 - 2(5)(3) = 344$ in²

11.

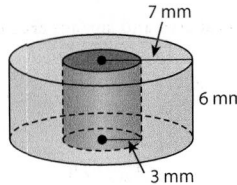

The surface area of the large cylinder is
$S_{large} = 2\pi rh + 2\pi r^2$.
So, $S_{large} = 2\pi(7)(6) + 2\pi(7)^2 = 182\pi$ mm².
The lateral area of the small prism is $L_{small} = 2\pi rh$.
So, $L_{small} = 2\pi(3)(6) = 36\pi$ mm².
The area of each base of the small cylinder
is $B = \pi r^2 = \pi 3^2 = 9\pi$ mm².
The surface area of the composite figure is the
surface area of the large cylinder plus the lateral
area of the small cylinder minus 2 times the area
of the base of the small cylinder.
$S = 182\pi + 36\pi - 2(9\pi) = 200\pi \approx 628.3$ mm²

💬 Elaborate

12. Can the surface area of a cylinder ever be less than the lateral area of the cylinder? Explain.
No. The surface area is the lateral area plus the area of the two bases. Since the area of the

two bases is greater than 0, the surface area must be greater than the lateral area.

13. Is it possible to find the surface area of a cylinder if you know the height and the circumference of the
base? Explain.
Yes. You can use the circumference of the base to find the radius of the base. Then you can

use the height, circumference, and radius in the surface area formula.

14. Essential Question Check-In How is finding the surface area of a right prism similar to finding the
surface area of a right cylinder?
In both cases, you can find the surface area by finding the lateral area and then adding

twice the area of a base.

ELABORATE

QUESTIONING STRATEGIES

❓ How do you find the surface area of a prism? You add the perimeter of the base times the height to twice the area of the base.

❓ How do you find the surface area of a cylinder? You add the circumference of the base times the height to twice the area of the base.

SUMMARIZE THE LESSON

❓ What is the same about finding the surface area of a prism and a cylinder? What is different? For both a prism and a cylinder, you find the surface area by finding the lateral area and then adding twice the area of the base; the bases of prisms and cylinders are different, so finding the lateral areas and base areas will require different processes.

LANGUAGE SUPPORT 🇪🇱

Connect Vocabulary

To help students remember the vocabulary in the lesson, including *lateral area* and *surface area,* have students make note cards of several different solid figures and their lateral and surface areas. Then have them use colored pencils to mark the dimensions of each in one color, and the formulas they will use in another color. Have them label the figures with the units and show the substitutions for the formulas. Ask them to share their note cards with other students

EVALUATE

Personal Math Trainer

ASSIGNMENT GUIDE

Concept and Skills	Practice
Explore Developing a Surface Area Formula	Exercise 11
Example 1 Finding the Surface Area of a Prism	Exercises 1–4
Example 2 Finding the Surface Area of a Cylinder	Exercises 5–6
Example 3 Finding the Surface Area of a Composite Figure	Exercises 7–10

INTEGRATE MATHEMATICAL PRACTICES

Focus on Modeling

MP.4 Some students may benefit from a hands-on approach for finding the surface area of solids. Have students draw simple figures like prisms and cylinders and then discuss in groups how they can find the lateral areas and the surface areas. Have them include a discussion of the properties of the faces of the figures that will help them find the lateral areas or the surface areas.

INTEGRATE MATHEMATICAL PRACTICES

Focus on Technology

MP.5 Some students may benefit from using the programming features of a graphing calculator to find the surface areas of right rectangular prisms and right cylinders. Have students enter the formulas for the surface areas of these simple solids as output from a program, with the dimensions of the solids as inputs.

- Online Homework
- Hints and Help
- Extra Practice

Find the lateral area and surface area of each prism.

1.

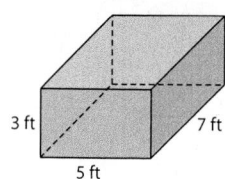

3 ft   7 ft   5 ft

$L = Ph$
$= (24)3$
$= 72 \text{ ft}^2$
$S = Ph + 2B$
$= 72 + 2(5)(7)$
$= 72 + 70$
$= 142 \text{ ft}^2$
$L = 72 \text{ ft}^2$
$S = 142 \text{ ft}^2$

2.

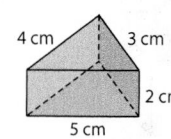

4 cm   3 cm   2 cm   5 cm

$L = Ph$
$= (12)2$
$= 24 \text{ cm}^2$

The base is a 3–4–5 right triangle, so in the area formula, $b = 3$ and $h = 4$.

$S = Ph + 2B$
$= 24 + 2\left(\frac{1}{2}(3)(4)\right)$
$= 24 + 12$
$= 36 \text{ cm}^2$
$L = 24 \text{ cm}^2$
$S = 36 \text{ cm}^2$

3.

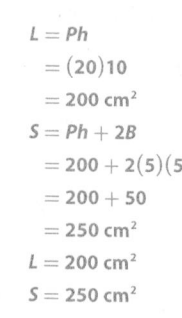

10 cm   5 cm   5 cm

$L = Ph$
$= (20)10$
$= 200 \text{ cm}^2$
$S = Ph + 2B$
$= 200 + 2(5)(5)$
$= 200 + 50$
$= 250 \text{ cm}^2$
$L = 200 \text{ cm}^2$
$S = 250 \text{ cm}^2$

4.

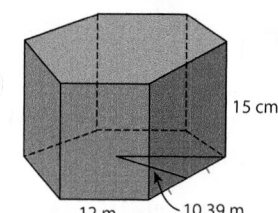

15 cm   12 m   10.39 m

$L = Ph$
$= (72)15 = 1080 \text{ m}^2$

The base can be divided into twelve right triangles, each triangle with a height of 10.39 m and a base of 6 m.

$B = \frac{1}{2}bh(12)$
$= \frac{1}{2}(6)(10.39)(12)$
$= 374.04 \text{ m}^2$
$S = L + 2B$
$= 1080 + 2(374.04)$
$\approx 1828.08 \text{ m}^2$
$L = 1080 \text{ m}^2$
$S = 1828.08 \text{ m}^2$

© Houghton Mifflin Harcourt Publishing Company

Exercise	Depth of Knowledge (D.O.K.)	COMMON CORE Mathematical Practices
1–10	**1** Recall of Information	**MP.5** Using Tools
11	**2** Skills/Concepts	**MP.4** Modeling
12–20	**2** Skills/Concepts	**MP.1** Problem Solving
21	**3** Strategic Thinking H.O.T.	**MP.4** Modeling
22	**3** Strategic Thinking H.O.T.	**MP.2** Reasoning

Find the lateral area and surface area of the cylinder. Leave your answer in terms of π.

5.

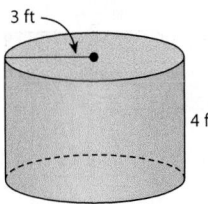

3 ft

4 ft

$L = 2\pi rh$

$= 2\pi(3)(4)$

$= 24\pi \text{ ft}^2$

$S = L + 2\pi r^2$

$= 24\pi + 2\pi(3)^2$

$= 24\pi + 18\pi$

$= 42\pi \text{ ft}^2$

$L = 24\pi \text{ ft}^2$

$S = 42\pi \text{ ft}^2$

6.

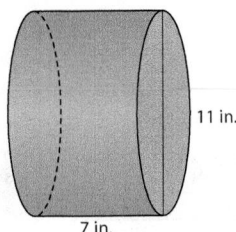

11 in.

7 in.

$L = 2\pi rh$

$= 2\pi(5.5)(7)$

$= 77\pi \text{ in}^2$

$S = L + 2\pi r^2$

$= 77\pi + 2\pi(5.5)^2$

$= 77\pi + 60.5\pi$

$= 137.5\pi \text{ in}^2$

$L = 77\pi \text{ in}^2$

$S = 137.5\pi \text{ in}^2$

Find the total surface area of the composite figure. Round to the nearest tenth.

7.

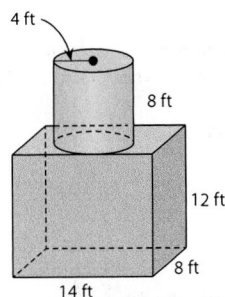

4 ft

8 ft

12 ft

8 ft

14 ft

Surface Area of Cylinder

$L = 2\pi rh$ $\qquad S = L + 2\pi r^2$

$= 2\pi(4)(8)$ $\qquad = 64\pi + 2\pi(4)^2$

$= 64\pi \text{ ft}^2$ $\qquad = 96\pi \text{ ft}^2$

Surface Area of Prism

$L = Ph$ $\qquad S = L + 2B$

$= (44)12$ $\qquad = 528 + 2(14)(8)$

$= 528 \text{ ft}^2$ $\qquad = 752 \text{ ft}^2$

$96\pi - \pi(4)^2 + 752 - \pi(4)^2 \approx 953.1 \text{ ft}^2$

$S \approx 953.1 \text{ ft}^2$

8.

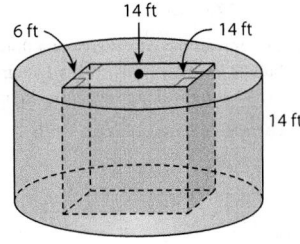

14 ft

6 ft

14 ft

14 ft

Surface Area of Cylinder

$L = 2\pi rh$ $\qquad S = L + 2\pi r^2$

$= 2\pi(14)(14)$ $\qquad = 392\pi + 2\pi 14^2$

$= 392\pi \text{ ft}^2$ $\qquad = 784\pi \text{ ft}^2$

Lateral Surface Area of Prism

$L = Ph$

$= (40)14$

$= 560 \text{ ft}^2$

$784\pi + 560 - 2(14 \cdot 6) \approx 2855.0 \text{ ft}^2$

$S \approx 2855.0 \text{ ft}^2$

AVOID COMMON ERRORS

As students find the surface area of cylinders, caution them to avoid the common errors of forgetting to include the areas of both bases, or using the diameter of the base instead of the radius in the formula.

INTEGRATE MATHEMATICAL PRACTICES

Focus on Critical Thinking

MP.3 Because a cylinder has circular bases, the circumference of the bases is the perimeter of the bases. Therefore, the lateral area of the right cylinder depends on the circumference of the base. If students think about the net for a cylinder, the net includes a rectangle and two circles. That means that the rectangle must have length equal to the circumference of the base.

Find the total surface area of the composite figure. Round to the nearest tenth.

9.

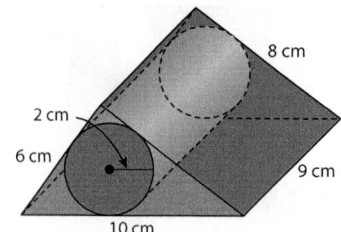

10.

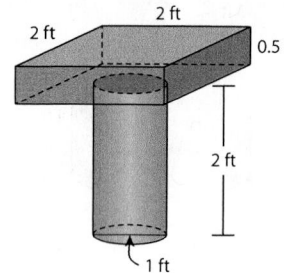

Surface Area of Prism

$L = Ph = (24)9 = 216$ cm²

The base is a 6–8–10, (3–4–5), right triangle, so in the area formula $b = 8$ and $h = 6$.

$S = L + 2B$

$= 216 + 2\left(\frac{1}{2}(8)(6)\right) = 264$ cm²

Lateral Surface Area of Cylinder

$L = 2\pi rh$

$= 2\pi(2)(9) = 36\pi$ cm²

$264 + 36\pi - 2\left(\pi 2^2\right) \approx 352.0$ cm²

$S \approx 352.0$ cm²

Surface Area of Prism

$L = Ph = (8)0.5 = 4$ ft²

$S = L + 2B$

$= 4 + 2(2)(2) = 12$ ft²

Total Area of Cylinder

$L = 2\pi rh$

$= 2\pi(0.5)(2) = 2\pi$ ft²

$S = L + 2\pi r^2$

$= 2\pi + 2\pi 0.5^2 = 2.5\pi$ ft²

$12 + 2.5\pi - 2\left(\pi 0.5^2\right) \approx 18.3$ ft²

$S \approx 18.3$ ft²

11. The greater the lateral area of a florescent light bulb, the more light the bulb produces. One cylindrical light bulb is 16 inches long with a 1-inch radius. Another cylindrical bulb is 23 inches long with a $\frac{3}{4}$-inch radius. Which bulb will produce more light?

Lateral Area of 16 inch bulb

$L = 2\pi rh$

$= 2\pi(1)(16)$

$= 32\pi$ in²

Lateral Area of 23 inch bulb

$L = 2\pi rh$

$= 2\pi(0.75)(23)$

$= 34.5\pi$ in²

The 23 inch bulb will produce more light.

12. Find the lateral and surface area of a cube with edge length 9 inches.

$L = Ph$

$= (36)9$

$= 324$ in²

$S = L + 2B$

$= 324 + 2(9)(9)$

$= 324 + 162$

$= 486$ in²

$L = 324$ in²

$S = 486$ in²

13. Find the lateral and surface area of a cylinder with base area 64π m² and a height 3 meters less than the radius.

Find the Radius

$A = \pi r^2$

$64\pi = \pi r^2$

$\dfrac{64\pi}{\pi} = \dfrac{\pi r^2}{\pi}$

$64 = r^2$

$8 = r$

$h = r - 3$

$h = 8 - 3$

$h = 5$

$L = 2\pi rh$

$= 2\pi(8)(5)$

$= 80\pi$ m²

$S = L + 2\pi r^2$

$= 80\pi + 2\pi(8)^2$

$= 208\pi$ m²

$L = 80\pi$ m²

$S = 208\pi$ m²

14. Biology Plant cells are shaped approximately like a right rectangular prism. Each cell absorbs oxygen and nutrients through its surface. Which cell can be expected to absorb at a greater rate? (*Hint:* 1 μm = 1 micrometer = 0.000001 meter)

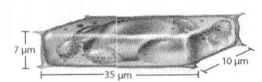 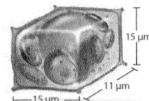

Surface Area of Cell 1

$L = Ph$ $S = L + 2B$
$= (90)7$ $= 630 + 2(35)(10)$
$= 630 \ \mu m^2$ $= 630 + 700$
                $= 1330 \ \mu m^2$

Surface Area of Cell 2

$L = Ph$ $S = L + 2B$
$= (52)15$ $= 780 + 2(15)(11)$
$= 780 \ \mu m^2$ $= 780 + 330$
                $= 1110 \ \mu m^2$

The cell that measures 35 μm by 7 μm by 10 μm will absorb at a greater rate.

15. Find the height of a right cylinder with surface area 160π ft^2 and radius 5 ft.

$S = 2\pi rh + 2\pi r^2$
$160\pi = 2\pi(5)h + 2\pi(5)^2$
$160\pi = 10\pi h + 50\pi$
$110\pi = 10\pi h$
$\dfrac{110\pi}{10\pi} = \dfrac{10\pi h}{10\pi}$
$11 = h$
$h = 11$ ft

16. Find the height of a right rectangular prism with surface area 286 m^2, length 10 m, and width 8 m.

$S = Ph + 2B$
$286 = 36h + 2(10)(8)$
$286 = 36h + 160$
$126 = 36h$
$3.5 = h$
$h = 3.5$ m

17. Represent Real-World Problems If one gallon of paint covers 250 square feet, how many gallons of paint will be needed to cover the shed, not including the roof? If a gallon of paint costs $25, about how much will it cost to paint the walls of the shed?

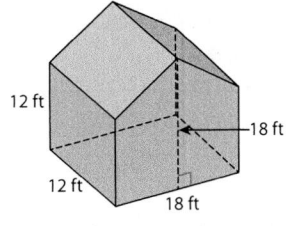

Front/Back Rectangles + Left/Right Rectangles +

Top Front/Back Triangles

$S = 2(18 \cdot 12) + 2(12 \cdot 12) + 2\left(\dfrac{1}{2} \cdot 18 \cdot 6\right) = 432 + 288 + 108 = 828$ ft^2

$828 \text{ ft}^2 \cdot \dfrac{1 \text{ gal}}{250 \text{ ft}^2} \approx 3.3$ gal

Since you can't get half a gallon, 4 total gallons will be needed.

$4 \cdot \$25 = 100$

4 gallons; $100

INTEGRATE MATHEMATICAL PRACTICES

Focus on Reasoning

MP.2 Have students brainstorm how they would find the surface area of a prism whose dimensions have all been doubled. Does the surface area double? no If not, what is the relationship? The area is 4 times as great. Have students also consider how the surface area changes if only the height of the prism changes. Ask students to use examples to justify their reasoning.

JOURNAL

Have students illustrate and describe how to use formula $S = L + 2B$ to find the surface area of a prism and of a right cylinder. Ask them to include all of the steps as well as the substitutions they will use in the formula.

18. Match the Surface Area with the appropriate coin in the table.

Coin	Diameter (mm)	Thickness (mm)	Surface Area (mm²)
Penny	19.05	1.55	C
Nickel	21.21	1.95	A
Dime	17.91	1.35	B
Quarter	24.26	1.75	D

A. 836.58

B. 579.82

C. 662.81

D. 1057.86

Penny $L = 2\pi rh = 2\pi(9.525)(1.55) = 29.5275\pi$ mm²
$\quad\quad S = L + 2\pi r^2 = 29.5275\pi + 2\pi 9.525^2 \approx 662.81$ mm²

Nickel $L = 2\pi rh = 2\pi(10.605)(1.95) = 41.3595\pi$ mm²
$\quad\quad S = L + 2\pi r^2 = 41.3595\pi + 2\pi 10.605^2 \approx 836.58$ mm²

Dime $L = 2\pi rh = 2\pi(8.955)(1.35) = 24.1785\pi$ mm²
$\quad\quad S = L + 2\pi r^2 = 24.1785\pi + 2\pi 8.955^2 \approx 579.82$ mm²

Quarter $L = 2\pi rh = 2\pi(12.13)(1.75) = 42.455\pi$ mm²
$\quad\quad S = L + 2\pi r^2 = 42.455\pi + 2\pi 12.13^2 \approx 1057.86$ mm²

19. **Algebra** The lateral area of a right rectangular prism is 144 cm². Its length is three times its width, and its height is twice its width. Find its surface area.

$\ell = 3w, h = 2w$
$L = Ph$
$144 = 2(w + \ell)h$
$144 = 2(w + 3w)2w$
$144 = 16w^2$
$\quad 3 = w$

$w = 3$ cm, $\ell = 9$ cm, $h = 6$ cm
$S = L + 2B$
$\quad = 144 + 2(9)(3)$
$\quad = 144 + 54$
$\quad = 198$
198 cm²

20. A cylinder has a radius of 8 cm and a height of 3 cm. Find the height of another cylinder that has a radius of 4 cm and the same surface area as the first cylinder.

$L = 2\pi rh$
$\quad = 2\pi(8)(3)$
$\quad = 48\pi$ cm²
$S = L + 2\pi r^2$
$\quad = 48\pi + 2\pi(8)^2$
$\quad = 48\pi + 128\pi$
$\quad = 176\pi$ cm²

$S = 2\pi rh + 2\pi r^2$
$176\pi = 2\pi(4)h + 2\pi(4)^2$
$176\pi = 8\pi h + 32\pi$
$144\pi = 8\pi h$
$\dfrac{144\pi}{8\pi} = \dfrac{8\pi h}{8\pi}$
$\quad 18 = h$

21. Analyze Relationships Ingrid is building a shelter to protect her plants from freezing. She is planning to stretch plastic sheeting over the top and the ends of the frame. Assume that the triangles in the frame on the left are equilateral. Which of the frames shown will require more plastic? Explain how finding the surface area of these figures is different from finding the lateral surface area of a figure.

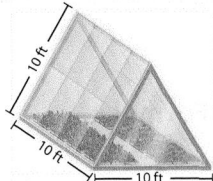 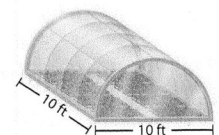

Surface Area of Triangular Prism (minus bottom side): $L = Ph = (30)10 = 300$ cm²;

$a^2 + b^2 = c^2$, so $5^2 + b^2 = 10^2$; $b = \sqrt{75}$; $S = Ph + 2B -$ Square $= 300 + 2\left(\frac{1}{2}(5)\left(\sqrt{75}\right)\right) -$

$10 \cdot 10 \approx 243.3$ ft²; Surface Area of Half Cylinder: $\frac{1}{2}L = \frac{1}{2}(2\pi rh) = \frac{1}{2}(2\pi(5)(10)) = 50\pi$ ft²;

$\frac{1}{2}S = \frac{1}{2}L + \frac{1}{2}2\pi r^2 = 50\pi + \frac{1}{2}(2\pi 5^2) \approx 235.6$ ft²

The triangular-prism-shaped frame will take more plastic; In lateral surface area, the area of the bases are not used. In this case, it is not the area of the bases that need to be removed.

22. Draw Conclusions Explain how the edge lengths of a rectangular prism can be changed so that the surface area is multiplied by 9.

Triple all the edge lengths.

Lesson Performance Task

A manufacturer of number cubes has the bright idea of packaging them individually in cylindrical boxes. Each number cube measures 2 inches on a side.

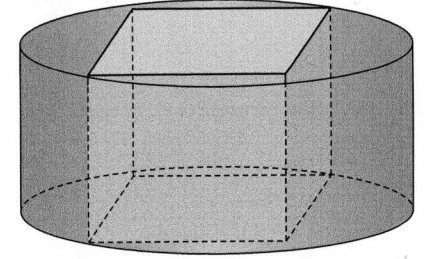

1. What is the surface area of each cube?

2. What is the surface area of the cylindrical box? Assume the cube fits snugly in the box and that the box includes a top. Use 3.14 for π.

1. The cube has 6 faces each with an area of $2 \times 2 = 4$ in². Total surface area of the cube: 6×4 in² $= 24$ in²

2. The top and bottom of the cylinder are circles, each with a diameter equal to a diagonal of one side of the cube, or $2\sqrt{2}$ inches. The radius of the top and bottom is half the diameter, or $\sqrt{2}$ inches.
Area of cylinder top $= \pi r^2 = 3.14\left(\sqrt{2}\right)^2 = 6.28$. Total area of top and bottom: $2 \times 6.28 = 12.56$ in² Lateral area of cylinder: $2\pi rh = 2(3.14)\sqrt{2}(2) = 12.56\sqrt{2}$ in².
Total surface area of cylindrical box: $\left(12.56 + 12.56\sqrt{2}\right)$ in².

© Houghton Mifflin Harcourt Publishing Company

EXTENSION ACTIVITY

A packaging engineer is designing a rectangular-prism-shaped container with a surface area of 64 square inches. Find the possible dimensions for at least three containers that have surface areas of 64 square inches.

Possible dimensions: $4 \times 4 \times 4$; $8 \times 2 \times 1.6$; $6 \times 2 \times 2.5$

Find the volumes of your containers. Then propose a hypothesis about the shape of a rectangular prism with the greatest volume for a given surface area.
Sample answer: The rectangular prism with the greatest volume for a given surface area is a cube.

AVOID COMMON ERRORS

To find the length of a diagonal of one side of the cube, students must use the Pythagorean Theorem to find h, the hypotenuse of a right triangle with 2-inch sides, and then must simplify the resulting square root. Here are the steps:

$$h^2 = 2^2 + 2^2$$
$$= 4 + 4$$
$$= 8$$
$$h = \sqrt{8}$$
$$= \sqrt{2^2 \cdot 2}$$
$$= \sqrt{2^2}\sqrt{2}$$
$$= 2\sqrt{2}$$

INTEGRATE MATHEMATICAL PRACTICES
Focus on Math Connections

MP.1 Describe how you could find the volume of an empty cylindrical number-cube container. Then find that volume. Use 3.14 for π. Subtract the volume of a number cube from the volume of a cylindrical container; about 4.56 cubic inches.

$V(\text{cylinder}) - V(\text{cube}) = \pi r^2 h - s^3$

$$\approx 3.14\left(\sqrt{2}\right)^2(2) - (2)^3$$
$$= 3.14(2)(2) - 8$$
$$= 4.56 \text{ in}^3$$

Scoring Rubric
2 points: Student correctly solves the problem and explains his/her reasoning.
1 point: Student shows good understanding of the problem but does not fully solve or explain his/her reasoning.
0 points: Student does not demonstrate understanding of the problem.

Surface Area of Prisms and Cylinders   **1004**

Surface Area of Pyramids and Cones

Common Core Math Standards

The student is expected to:

 G-MG.A.1

Use geometric shapes, their measures, and their properties to describe objects (e.g., modeling a tree trunk or a human torso as a cylinder).

Mathematical Practices

 MP.4 Modeling

Language Objective

Explain to a partner how to find the surface area of pyramids and cones.

ENGAGE

Essential Question: How is the formula for the lateral area of a regular pyramid similar to the formula for the lateral area of a right cone?

In both formulas, the lateral area is equal to half the perimeter of the base times the slant height.

PREVIEW: LESSON PERFORMANCE TASK

View the Engage section online. Discuss the photograph. Ask students to provide any information they may know about the pyramids of Egypt or the New World. Then preview the Lesson Performance Task.

Name_____ Class_____ Date_____

19.3 Surface Area of Pyramids and Cones

Resource Locker

Essential Question: How is the formula for the lateral area of a regular pyramid similar to the formula for the lateral area of a right cone?

⊘ Explore   Developing a Surface Area Formula

The base of a **regular pyramid** is a regular polygon, and the lateral faces are congruent isosceles triangles.

(A) The lateral faces of a regular pyramid can be arranged to cover half of a rectangle whose height is equal to the slant height of the pyramid. Complete the figure by labeling the missing dimensions.

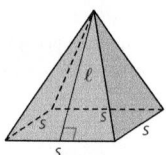 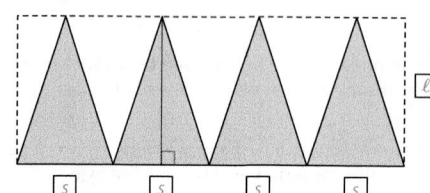

(B) Write an expression for the length of the rectangle in terms of s.

4s

(D) Write an expression for the area of the rectangle in terms of P and ℓ.

$P\ell$

(C) How does the length of the rectangle compare to P, the perimeter of the base of the pyramid?

They are the same.

(E) Write a formula for the lateral area L of the pyramid. (*Hint:* Use the fact that the lateral faces of the pyramid cover half of the rectangle.)

$L = \frac{1}{2} P\ell$

(F) Let B be the base area of the pyramid. Write a formula for the surface area S of the pyramid in terms of B and L. Then write the formula in terms of B, P, and ℓ.

$S = L + B;\ S = \frac{1}{2} P\ell + B$

Reflect

1. **Discussion** The pyramid in the above figure has a square base. Do your formulas only hold for square pyramids or do they hold for other pyramids as well? Explain.

The same reasoning may be used with any pyramid whose base is a regular polygon.

Therefore, the formulas hold for all regular pyramids.

© Houghton Mifflin Harcourt Publishing Company

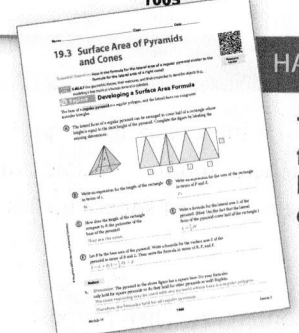

HARDCOVER PAGES 843–854

Turn to these pages to find this lesson in the hardcover student edition.

Finding the Surface Area of a Pyramid

Lateral Area and Surface Area of a Regular Pyramid

The lateral area of a regular pyramid with perimeter P and slant height

ℓ is $L = \frac{1}{2}P\ell$.

The surface area of a regular pyramid with lateral area L and base area

B is $S = L + B$, or $S = \frac{1}{2}P\ell + B$.

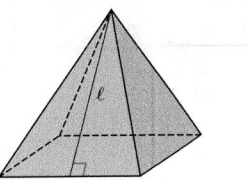

Example 1 Find the lateral area and surface area of each regular pyramid.

(A) **Step 1** Find the lateral area.

Lateral area formula $\quad L = \frac{1}{2}P\ell$

$P = 4(5) = 20$ in. $\quad = \frac{1}{2}(20)(9)$

Multiply. $\quad = 90$ in²

Step 2 Find the surface area.

Surface area formula $\quad S = L + B$

Substitute the lateral area;

$B = 5^2 = 25$ in. $\quad = 90 + 25$

Add. $\quad = 115$ in²

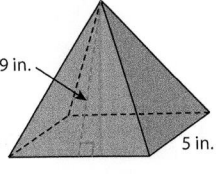

9 in.

5 in.

(B) **Step 1** Find the slant height ℓ. Use the right triangle shown in the figure.

The legs of the right triangle have lengths $\boxed{5}$ m and $\boxed{12}$ m.

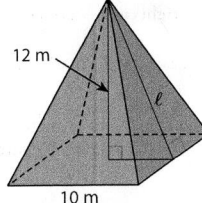

12 m

10 m

Pythagorean Theorem $\qquad \ell^2 = a^2 + b^2$

Substitute. $\qquad = \boxed{5}^2 + \boxed{12}^2$

Simplify. $\qquad = \boxed{169}$

Take the square root of each side. $\quad \ell = \boxed{13}$

Step 2 Find the lateral area.

Lateral area formula $\qquad L = \frac{1}{2}P\ell$

Substitute. $\qquad = \frac{1}{2}\left(\boxed{40}\right)\left(\boxed{13}\right)$

Multiply. $\qquad = \boxed{260}$ m²

Step 3 Find the surface area.

Surface area formula $\qquad S = L + B$

Substitute. $\qquad = \boxed{260} + \boxed{10}^2$

Simplify. $\qquad = \boxed{360}$ m²

Reflect

2. Can you use the formula $L = \frac{1}{2}P\ell$ to find the lateral area of a pyramid whose base is a scalene triangle? If so, describe the dimensions that you need to know. If not, explain why not.
No; the formula only holds for regular pyramids, so the base of the pyramid must be a

regular polygon. A scalene triangle cannot be a regular polygon.

PROFESSIONAL DEVELOPMENT

 Math Background

The surface area formulas of a regular pyramid and a right cone include the perimeter of the base and the slant height as variables. For a regular pyramid, the slant height is the height of one of the lateral triangles, and lateral area $= \frac{1}{2}$ (perimeter of base)(slant height). The surface area is the sum of the area of the base and the lateral area. The slant height of a right cone is the distance between the vertex and a point on the base edge, and lateral area $= \pi$(radius of base)(slant height). The surface area is the sum of the area of the circular base and the lateral area.

EXPLORE

Developing a Surface Area Formula

INTEGRATE TECHNOLOGY

Students have the option of doing the Explore activity either in the book or online.

QUESTIONING STRATEGIES

? How is the slant height different from the height of a pyramid? The slant height is the altitude of a lateral face, while the height of a pyramid is the distance between its vertex and its base.

INTEGRATE MATHEMATICAL PRACTICES
Focus on Reasoning

MP.2 Since the surface area formula for a pyramid includes the area of the base, emphasize that students will need to be able to find the area of any regular polygon. Encourage them to review the area formulas for regular figures from previous courses.

CONNECT VOCABULARY **EL**

Remind students of some of the vocabulary related to surface area, including *lateral area* and *slant height*. Have students make sketches that include the parts of the figures that make up the lateral area.

EXPLAIN 1

Finding the Surface Area of a Pyramid

QUESTIONING STRATEGIES

? Does the surface area formula for a pyramid apply to all pyramids? Explain. The surface area formula applies only to regular pyramids because each lateral side of a regular pyramid has the same slant height.

Surface Area of Pyramids and Cones   **1006**

Focus on Patterns

MP.8 Encourage students to distinguish a regular pyramid from other pyramids. A regular pyramid has a regular polygon for a base, and the slant height is the same for all lateral faces. Have students make an organized list of the dimensions of the pyramid as part of their plan for finding the surface area. Then have them substitute the appropriate values into the formulas for lateral area and surface area of a prism.

EXPLAIN 2

Developing Another Surface Area Formula

QUESTIONING STRATEGIES

? How is the slant height of a right cone used to find its lateral area? The cone is made up of a circular base and a sector of a circle with radius equal to the slant height ℓ. So, lateral area = the area of the sector = $\pi r \ell$, where r is the radius of the base.

Your Turn

Find the lateral area and surface area of each regular pyramid. Round to the nearest tenth, if necessary.

3.

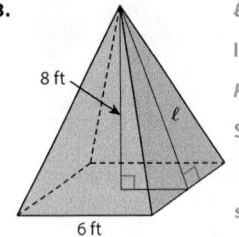

$\ell^2 = 3^2 + 8^2 = 73; \ell = \sqrt{73}$ ft

lateral area : $L = \frac{1}{2}P\ell$

$P = 4(6) = 24$ ft

So, $L = \frac{1}{2}(24)\sqrt{73} = 12\sqrt{73}$

≈ 102.5 ft².

surface area: $S = L + B$

$B = 6^2 = 36$ ft²

$S = 12\sqrt{73} + 36 \approx 138.5$ ft²

4.

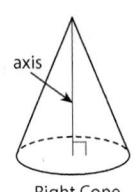

lateral area: $L = \frac{1}{2}P\ell$.

$P = 3(4) = 12$ cm

So, $L = \frac{1}{2}(12)(6) = 36$ cm².

surface area: $S = L + B$.

$B = \frac{s^2\sqrt{3}}{4} = \frac{4^2\sqrt{3}}{4} = 4\sqrt{3}$ cm²

$S = 36 + 4\sqrt{3} \approx 42.9$ cm²

🔎 Explain 2   Developing Another Surface Area Formula

The axis of a cone is a segment with endpoints at the vertex and the center of the base. A **right cone** is a cone whose axis is perpendicular to the base.

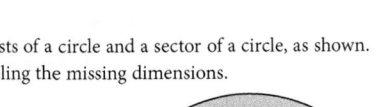

Example 2   Justify a formula for the surface area of a cone.

Ⓐ   A net for a right cone consists of a circle and a sector of a circle, as shown. Complete the figure by labeling the missing dimensions.

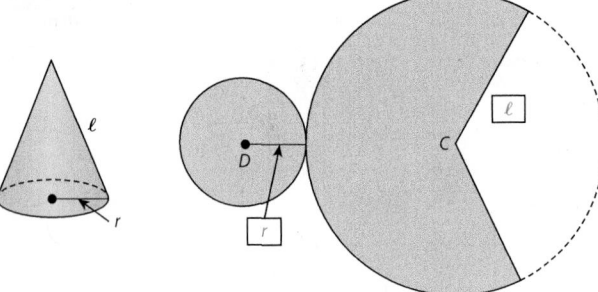

Ⓑ   Consider the shaded sector in the net. Complete the proportion.

$$\frac{\text{Area of sector}}{\text{Area of } \odot C} = \frac{\text{Arc length of sector}}{\boxed{\text{Circumference of } \odot C}}$$

Ⓒ   Multiply both sides of the proportion by the area of $\odot$ C. Complete the equation.

$$\text{Area of sector} = \frac{\text{Arc length of sector}}{\boxed{\text{Circumference of } \odot C}} \cdot \text{Area of } \odot C$$

COLLABORATIVE LEARNING

Small Group Activity

Have students work in groups to brainstorm how to relate the formula for the surface area of a right cone to the formula for the surface area of a square pyramid. (Start with the formula $S = B + \frac{1}{2}P\ell$ for the square pyramid and then substitute the corresponding parts for the cone to get $S = \pi r^2 + \pi r\ell$.) Ask them to draw diagrams to help them verify or disprove their results, and then present their results to the class.

(D) The arc length of the sector is equal to the circumference of ⊙ D. Therefore, the arc length of the sector equals $2\pi r$. Complete the equation by substituting this expression for the arc length of the sector and by writing the circumference and area of ⊙ C in terms of ℓ.

Area of sector = $\dfrac{2\pi r}{2\pi\ell} \cdot \boxed{\pi\ell^2}$

(E) Simplify the right side of the equation as much as possible.

Area of sector = $\boxed{\pi r\ell}$

(F) The area of the sector in Step E is the lateral area L of the cone. Complete the formula.

$L = \boxed{\pi r\ell}$

(G) Let B be the base area of the cone. Write a formula for the surface area S of the cone in terms of B and L. Then write the formula in terms of r and ℓ.

$S = L + B;\ S = \pi r\ell + \pi r^2$

Reflect

5. In Step D, why is the arc length of the sector equal to the circumference of ⊙ D?
When the net is folded to make the cone, the arc of the sector of ⊙ C will perfectly fit the
full circumference of ⊙ D to form the edge of the cone without gaps or overlap.

⦿ Explain 3 Finding the Surface Area of a Cone

Lateral Area and Surface Area of a Right Cone

The lateral area of a right cone with radius r and slant height ℓ is $L = \pi r\ell$.

The surface area of a right cone with lateral area L and base area B is
$S = L + B$, or $S = \pi r\ell + \pi r^2$.

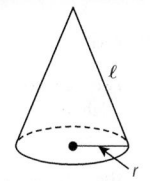

Example 3 A company packages popcorn in paper containers in the shape of a right cone. Each container also has a plastic circular lid. Find the amount of paper needed to make each container. Then find the total amount of paper and plastic needed for the container. Round to the nearest tenth.

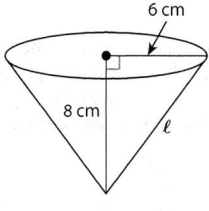

6 cm

8 cm

ℓ

(A) **Step 1** Find the slant height.

Pythagorean Theorem	$\ell^2 = 6^2 + 8^2$
Simplify.	$= 100$
Take the square root of each side.	$\ell = 10$

Step 2 Find the lateral area.

Lateral area formula	$L = \pi r\ell$
Substitute.	$= \pi(6)(10)$
Multiply.	$= 60\pi$ cm^2

Step 3 Find the surface area.

Surface area formula	$S = L + \pi r^2$
Substitute.	$= 60\pi + \pi(6)^2$
Simplify.	$= 96\pi$ cm^2

Common errors students make when finding the surface area of a cone include using the height of the cone instead of the slant height, using a diameter instead of a radius, and forgetting to include the area of the base. Caution students to look for these errors.

EXPLAIN 3

Finding the Surface Area of a Cone

QUESTIONING STRATEGIES

? How are the surface area formulas of a cone and pyramid similar and how are they different? The surface areas are similar because each is the sum of the lateral area and the area of the base. The shapes of the bases are different, so the actual surface area formulas are different.

DIFFERENTIATE INSTRUCTION

Modeling

Have students work in groups to make paper models of pyramids and cones. They should first create nets of the figures and then find the surface area of the nets. Have them compare their results to the surface areas they calculate using the dimensions of the completed figures. Have groups discuss how the nets are related to the lateral area and to the surface area formulas.

MP.1 Encourage students to distinguish a right cone from an oblique cone. The formulas in this lesson apply only to right cones, because oblique cones do not have a consistent slant height for the entire cone.

Step 4 Use a calculator and round to the nearest tenth.

The amount of paper needed for the container is the lateral area, $60\pi \approx 188.5$ cm². The amount of paper and plastic needed for the container is the surface area, $96\pi \approx 301.6$ cm².

Ⓑ **Step 1** Find the radius.

Pythagorean Theorem	$\boxed{25}^2 = r^2 + \boxed{24}^2$
Simplify.	$\boxed{625} = r^2 + \boxed{576}$
Subtract $\boxed{576}$ from each side.	$\boxed{49} = r^2$
Take the square root of each side.	$\boxed{7} = r$

24 cm, 25 cm

Step 2 Find the lateral area. $\qquad L = \pi r\ell$

Substitute and simplify. $\qquad = \pi\left(\boxed{7}\right)\left(\boxed{25}\right) = \boxed{175}\,\pi$ cm²

Step 3 Find the surface area. $\qquad S = L + \pi r^2$

Substitute and simplify. $\qquad = \boxed{175}\,\pi + \pi\left(\boxed{7}\right)^2 = \boxed{224}\,\pi$ cm²

Step 4 Use a calculator and round to the nearest tenth.

The amount of paper needed for the container is the lateral area, $\boxed{175}\,\pi \approx \boxed{549.8}$ cm².

The amount of paper and plastic needed for the container is $\boxed{224}\,\pi \approx \boxed{703.7}$ cm².

Reflect

6. Two right cones have the same radius. A student said that the cone with the greater slant height must have the greater lateral area. Do you agree? Explain.

Yes; $L = \pi r\ell$. Since π is a constant and the cones have the same radius, the slant height is the only variable in the expression So, increasing ℓ increases L.

Your Turn

A company makes candles in the shape of a right cone. The lateral surface of each candle is covered with paper for shipping and each candle also has a plastic circular base. Find the amount of paper needed to cover the lateral surface of each candle. Then find the total amount of paper and plastic needed. Round to the nearest tenth.

7.

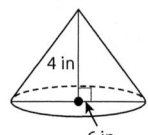

4 in, 6 in

$\ell^2 = 3^2 + 4^2,\ \ell^2 = 25$, so $\ell = 5$.
$L = \pi(3)(5) = 15\pi$ in².
$S = 15\pi + \pi(3)^2 = 24\pi$ in²
paper: $15\pi \approx 47.1$ in²
paper and plastic: $24\pi \approx 75.4$ in²

8.

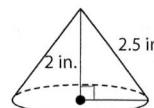

2.5 in., 2 in.

$2.5^2 = r^2 + 2^2,\ 2.25 = r^2$, so $r = 1.5$.
$L = \pi(1.5)(2.5) = 3.75\pi$ in²
$S = 3.75\pi + \pi(1.5)^2 = 6\pi$ in²
paper: $3.75\pi \approx 11.8$ in²
paper and plastic: $6\pi \approx 18.8$ in²

© Houghton Mifflin Harcourt Publishing Company

Explain 4 Finding the Surface Area of a Composite Figure

Example 4 **Find the surface area of each composite figure. Round to the nearest tenth.**

(A) **Step 1** Find the lateral area of the cone.

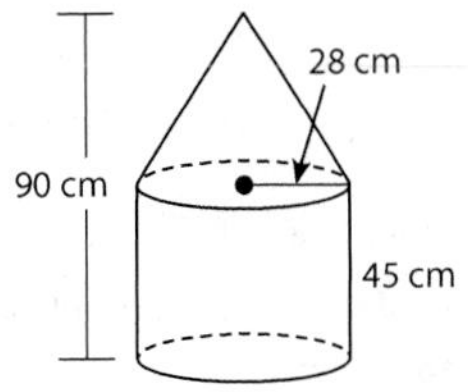

28 cm
90 cm
45 cm

The height of the cone is $90 - 45 = 45$ cm.

By the Pythagorean Theorem, $\ell = \sqrt{28^2 + 45^2} = 53$ cm.

Lateral area formula $L = \pi r \ell$

Substitute. $= \pi(28)(53)$

Simplify. $= 1484\pi \text{ cm}^2$

Step 2 Find the lateral area of the cylinder.

Lateral area $L = 2\pi rh$

Substitute. $= 2\pi(28)(45)$

Simplify. $= 2520\pi \text{ cm}^2$

Step 3 Find the area of the base of the cylinder.

Area of circle $B = \pi r^2$

Substitute. $= \pi(28)^2$

Simplify. $= 784\pi \text{ cm}^2$

Step 4 Find the surface area of the composite figure.

$S =$ (cone lateral area) + (cylinder lateral area) + (base area)

$= 1484\pi + 2520\pi + 784\pi$

$= 4788\pi \approx 15,041.9 \text{ cm}^2$

(B) **Step 1** Find the slant height of the pyramid.

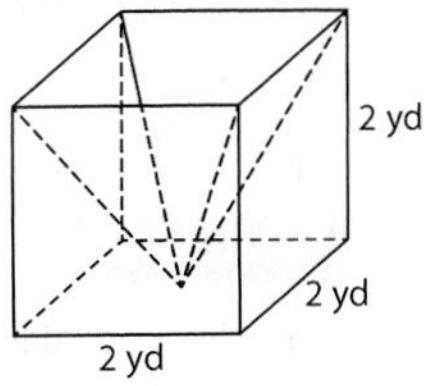

2 yd
2 yd
2 yd

By the Pythagorean Theorem, $\ell = \sqrt{1^2 + 2^2} = \sqrt{5}$ yd.

Step 2 Find the lateral area of the pyramid.

Lateral area formula $L = \frac{1}{2}P\ell$

Substitute. $= \frac{1}{2}(8)(\sqrt{5})$

Simplify. $= 4\sqrt{5} \text{ yd}^2$

Step 3 Find the lateral area of the rectangular prism.

Lateral area formula $L = Ph$

Substitute. $= (8)(2)$

Simplify. $= 16 \text{ yd}^2$

Step 4 Find the surface area of the composite figure.

$S =$ (pyramid lateral area) + (prism lateral area) + (base area)

$= 4\sqrt{5} + 16 + 4$

$= 20 + 4\sqrt{5} \approx 28.9 \text{ yd}^2$

EXPLAIN 4

Finding the Surface Area of a Composite Figure

QUESTIONING STRATEGIES

When is the surface area of a composite figure not equal to the sum of the areas of the parts of the figure? when the composite figure includes parts that overlap

Focus on Patterns

MP.8 Encourage students to make an organized list of the dimensions of each composite figure along with a list of the areas that overlap. Then have them write an equation for the total surface area of the parts, including subtractions for overlapping parts, and substitute the appropriate values into the formulas.

ELABORATE

QUESTIONING STRATEGIES

? How do you find the surface area of a pyramid? You add one-half the perimeter of the base times the slant height to the area of the base.

? How do you find the surface area of a cone? You add one-half the circumference of the base times the slant height to the area of the base.

Focus on Critical Thinking

MP.3 Challenge students to explain how the slant height is used to find the surface areas of a pyramid and of a cone.

SUMMARIZE THE LESSON

? What is difference between the formulas for the lateral area of a regular pyramid and the lateral area of a right cone? What accounts for this difference? The lateral area of a regular pyramid is half the perimeter of the base times the slant height, while the lateral area of a right cone is π times the radius of the base times the slant height. The formulas appear different because the base of a right cone is a circle, and π times the radius is half of its perimeter.

Reflect

9. How can you check that your answer in Part B is reasonable?
Sample answer: The surface area of the cube without the inverted pyramid is $6 \cdot 4 = 24$ yd^2.

The composite figure should have a surface area slightly greater than that of the rectangular prism, so the answer is reasonable.

Your Turn

Find the surface area of each composite figure. Round to the nearest tenth.

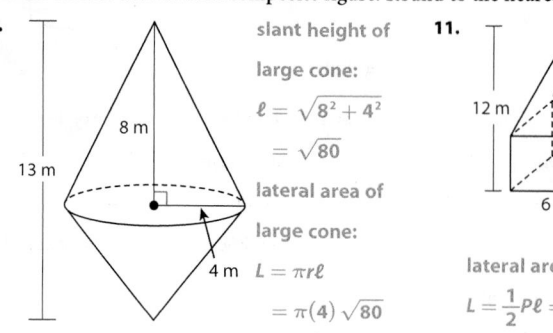

10. slant height of large cone:
$$\ell = \sqrt{8^2 + 4^2}$$
$$= \sqrt{80}$$
lateral area of large cone:
$$L = \pi r \ell$$
$$= \pi(4)\sqrt{80}$$
$$= 4\pi\sqrt{80} \text{ m}^2$$

height of small cone: $13 - 8 = 5$ m
$$\ell = \sqrt{5^2 + 4^2} = \sqrt{41}.$$
lateral area of small cone: $L = \pi r \ell$
$$= \pi(4)\sqrt{41} = 4\pi\sqrt{41} \text{ m}^2$$
$$S = 4\pi\sqrt{80} + 4\pi\sqrt{41} \approx 192.9 \text{ m}^2$$

11. height of pyramid:
$$12 - 4 = 8 \text{ cm}$$
slant height of pyramid: ℓ
$$= \sqrt{8^2 + 3^2}$$
$$= \sqrt{73}$$
lateral area of pyramid:
$$L = \frac{1}{2}P\ell = \frac{1}{2}(24)(\sqrt{73})$$
$$= 12\sqrt{73} \text{ m}^2$$
lateral area of prism:
$$L = Ph = (24)(4) = 96 \text{ m}^2$$
$$S = 12\sqrt{73} + 96 + 6^2$$
$$= 132 + 12\sqrt{73} \approx 234.5 \text{ m}^2$$

💬 Elaborate

12. A regular pyramid has a base that is an equilateral triangle with sides 16 inches long. Is it possible to determine the surface area of the pyramid? If not, what additional information do you need?
No; you also need to know the slant height of the pyramid.

13. Explain how to estimate the lateral area of a right cone with radius 5 cm and slant height 6 cm. Is your estimate an underestimate or overestimate? Explain.
The lateral area is $L = \pi r \ell$. Since $\pi \approx 3$, the lateral area is approximately $3(5)(6) = 90$ cm^2.

This is an underestimate, since the actual value of π is greater than 3.

14. **Essential Question Check-In** How is the formula for the lateral area of a regular pyramid similar to the formula for the lateral area of a right cone?
Sample answer: Both formulas involve the slant height, ℓ. Also, the formula for the lateral area of a regular pyramid is $L = \frac{1}{2}P\ell$, which is half the perimeter of the base times the slant height. The formula for the lateral area of a right cone is $L = \pi r \ell$, which is also half the perimeter (circumference) of the base times the slant height.

LANGUAGE SUPPORT **EL**

Connect Vocabulary

To help students remember the additional formulas in this lesson, have students work in groups to make a table of all surface area formulas they know, including the formulas for pyramids and cones. Have them discuss how to apply the formulas for the surface area of different pyramids and cones and then share their work with other groups.

Evaluate: Homework and Practice

• Online Homework
• Hints and Help
• Extra Practice

1. **Multiple Response** Which expression represents the surface area of the regular square pyramid shown? Select all that apply.

A. $\frac{t^2}{16} + \frac{ts}{2}$ B. $\frac{t^2}{16}$ C. $\frac{t^2}{4} + t\ell + \frac{t\ell}{2}$ D. $\frac{t}{2}\left(\frac{t}{8} + \ell\right)$ E. $\frac{t}{2}\left(\frac{t}{8} + s\right)$

$L = \frac{1}{2}P\ell = \frac{1}{2}t\ell = \frac{t\ell}{2}$

$S = L + B = \frac{t\ell}{2} + \left(\frac{1}{4}t\right)^2 = \frac{t\ell}{2} + \frac{t^2}{16} = \frac{t^2}{16} + \frac{t\ell}{2}$

$\frac{t^2}{16} + \frac{t\ell}{2} = \frac{t}{2}\left(\frac{t}{8}\right) + \frac{t}{2}(\ell) = \frac{t}{2}\left(\frac{t}{8} + \ell\right)$

2. **Justify Reasoning** A frustum of a pyramid is a part of the pyramid with two parallel bases. The lateral faces of the frustum are trapezoids. Use the area formula for a trapezoid to derive a formula for the lateral area of a frustum of a regular square pyramid with base edge lengths b_1 and b_2 and slant height ℓ. Show all of your steps.

Lateral Area = 4 trapezoids:

$A = \frac{(b_1 + b_2)h}{2} = \frac{(b_1 + b_2)\ell}{2}$

Because there are 4 trapezoids, multiply the area by 4.

$L = 4\frac{(b_1 + b_2)\ell}{2} \quad L = 2(b_1 + b_2)\ell$

$L = 2(b_1 + b_2)\ell$

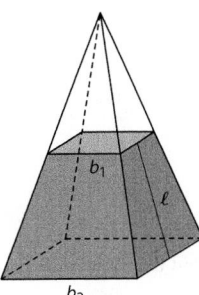

3. **Draw Conclusions** Explain why slant height is not defined for an oblique cone.

In an oblique cone, the distance from a point on the edge of the base to the vertex is not the same for each point on the base.

Find the lateral and surface area for each pyramid with a regular base. Where necessary, round to the nearest tenth.

4.
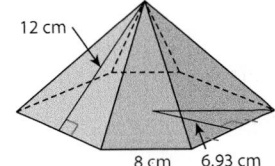
12 cm

8 cm   6.93 cm

$L = \frac{1}{2}P\ell = \frac{1}{2}(48)(12) = 288 \text{ cm}^2$

Twelve right triangles with $h \approx 6.93$ and $b = 4$ make up the base of the pyramid.

$B = \frac{1}{2}bh(12) = \frac{1}{2}(4)(6.93)(12) \approx 166.32 \text{ cm}^2$

$S = L + B \approx 288 + 166.32 \approx 454.3 \text{ cm}^2$

$L = 288 \text{ cm}^2; S \approx 454.3 \text{ cm}^2$

Exercise	Depth of Knowledge (D.O.K.)	COMMON CORE Mathematical Practices
1	**2** Skills/Concepts	**MP.2** Reasoning
2	**3** Strategic Thinking	**MP.6** Precision
3	**3** Strategic Thinking	**MP.2** Reasoning
4–17	**1** Recall of Information	**MP.5** Using Tools
18–19	**2** Skills/Concepts	**MP.4** Modeling
20	**2** Skills/Concepts	**MP.5** Using Tools

EVALUATE

ASSIGNMENT GUIDE

Concepts and Skills	Practice
Explore Developing a Surface Area Formula	Exercises 1–2
Example 1 Finding the Surface Area of a Pyramid	Exercises 4–7
Example 2 Developing Another Surface Area Formula	Exercise 3
Example 3 Finding the Surface Area of a Cone	Exercises 8–11
Example 4 Finding the Surface Area of a Composite Figure	Exercises 12–17

INTEGRATE MATHEMATICAL PRACTICES
Focus on Modeling

MP.4 Have students work in groups with models of pyramids and cones. Have them measure the models and find the surface area of a pyramid and a cone with the same slant height. Also have them find the surface area of a pyramid and a cone with the same radius and base length. Ask groups to discuss how the surface areas are related.

Surface Area of Pyramids and Cones   **1012**

AVOID COMMON ERRORS

Throughout the exercises, caution students to avoid the common error of using the height of the figure instead of the slant height in the surface area formula. Encourage students to think of mnemonic devices that will help them avoid this error.

5.

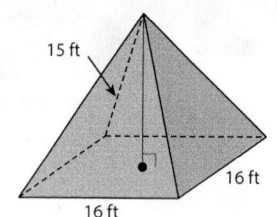

$c^2 = a^2 + b^2$

$c = \sqrt{a^2 + b^2}$

$\ell = \sqrt{a^2 + b^2}$

$\ell = \sqrt{15^2 + 8^2}$

$\ell = 17$ ft

$L = \frac{1}{2}P\ell = \frac{1}{2}(64)(17) = 544$ ft²

$S = L + B = 544 + (16)(16) = 800$ ft²

$L = 544$ ft²; $S = 800$ ft²

6.

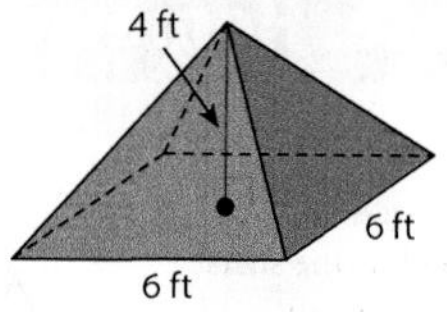

$c^2 = a^2 + b^2$

$c = \sqrt{a^2 + b^2}$

$\ell = \sqrt{a^2 + b^2}$

$\ell = \sqrt{3^2 + 4^2}$

$\ell = 5$ ft

$L = \frac{1}{2}P\ell = \frac{1}{2}(24)(5) = 60$ ft²

$S = L + B = 60 + (6)(6) = 96$ ft²

$L = 60$ ft²; $S = 96$ ft²

7.

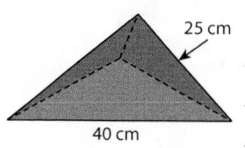

$b^2 = c^2 - a^2$

$b = \sqrt{c^2 - a^2}$

$\ell = \sqrt{c^2 - a^2}$

$\ell = \sqrt{25^2 - 20^2}$

$\ell = 15$ cm

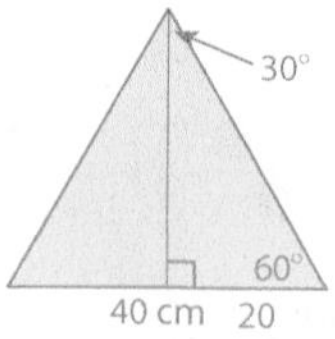

$L = \frac{1}{2}P\ell = \frac{1}{2}(120)(15)$

$L = 900$ cm²

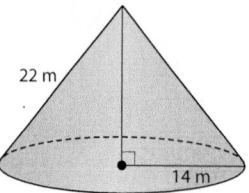

If the base is isolated

The height of the triangle, by the 30-60-90 Special Right Triangle Rules, is $20\sqrt{3}$.

$S = L + B = 900 + \frac{1}{2}(40)(20\sqrt{3})$

≈ 1592.8 cm²

$L = 900$ cm²; $S \approx 1592.8$ cm²

Find the lateral and total surface area for each cone. Leave the answer in terms of π.

8.

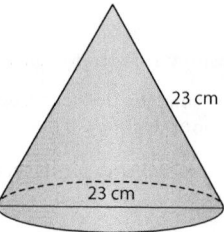

$L = \pi r \ell = \pi(14)(22) = 308\pi$ m²

$S = L + B$

$= 308\pi + \pi r^2$

$= 308\pi + \pi(14)^2$

$= 504\pi$ m²

$L = 308\pi$ m²; $S = 504\pi$ m²

9.

$L = \pi r \ell = \pi(11.5)(23) = 264.5\pi$ cm²

$S = L + B = 264.5\pi + \pi r^2$

$= 264.5\pi + \pi(11.5)^2$

$= 396.75\pi$ cm²

$L = 264.5\pi$ cm²; $S = 396.75\pi$ cm²

© Houghton Mifflin Harcourt Publishing Company

Module 19   **1013**   Lesson 3

Exercise	Depth of Knowledge (D.O.K.)	COMMON CORE Mathematical Practices
21–22	**2** Skills/Concepts	**MP.4** Modeling
23	**3** Strategic Thinking	**MP.1** Problem Solving
24	**3** Strategic Thinking H.O.T.	**MP.6** Precision
25	**3** Strategic Thinking H.O.T.	**MP.3** Logic

10.

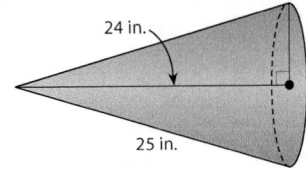

$b^2 = c^2 - a^2$

$b = \sqrt{c^2 - a^2}$

$r = \sqrt{c^2 - a^2}$

$r = \sqrt{25^2 - 24^2} = 7$ in.

$L = \pi r \ell = \pi(7)(25) = 175\pi$ in^2

$S = L + B = 175\pi + \pi r^2 = 175\pi + \pi(7)^2$

$\quad = 224\pi$ in^2

$L = 175\pi$ in^2; $S = 224\pi$ in^2

11.

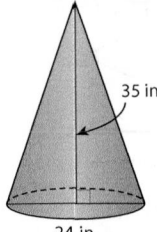

$c^2 = a^2 + b^2$

$c = \sqrt{a^2 + b^2}$

$\ell = \sqrt{a^2 + b^2}$

$\ell = \sqrt{35^2 + 12^2} = 37$ in.

$L = \pi r \ell = \pi(12)(37) = 444\pi$ in^2

$S = L + B = 444\pi + \pi r^2 = 444\pi + \pi(12)^2$

$\quad = 588\pi$ in^2

$L = 444\pi$ in^2; $S = 588\pi$ in^2

Find the surface area for the composite shape. Where appropriate, leave in terms of π. When necessary, round to nearest tenth.

12.

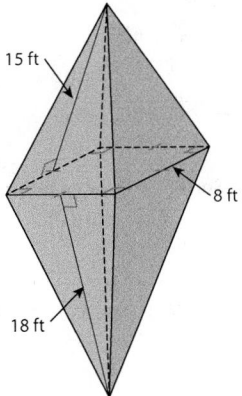

Lateral area of top pyramid

$L = \frac{1}{2}P\ell = \frac{1}{2}(32)(15) = 240$ ft^2

Lateral area of bottom pyramid

$L = \frac{1}{2}P\ell = \frac{1}{2}(32)(18) = 288$ ft^2

$240 + 288 = 528$

$S = 528$ ft^2

13.

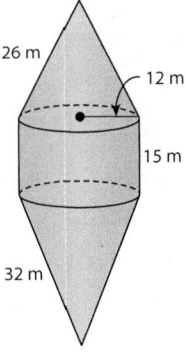

Lateral area of top cone

$L = \pi r \ell = \pi(12)(26) = 312\pi$ m^2

Lateral area of cylinder

$L = 2\pi r h = 2\pi(12)(15) = 360\pi$ m^2

Lateral area of bottom cone

$L = \pi r \ell = \pi(12)(32) = 384\pi$ m^2

$312\pi + 360\pi + 384\pi = 1056\pi$

$S = 1056\pi$ m^2

INTEGRATE MATHEMATICAL PRACTICES

Focus on Reasoning

MP.2 The surface area formulas of pyramids and cones are similar because they are derived from the basic formula $S = B + \frac{1}{2}P\ell$, where S is the surface area, B is the area of the base, P is the perimeter of the base, and ℓ is the slant height. Ask students to learn this formula and then make the appropriate substitutions for the area and perimeter of the base for either a pyramid or a cone.

Surface Area of Pyramids and Cones   **1014**

14.

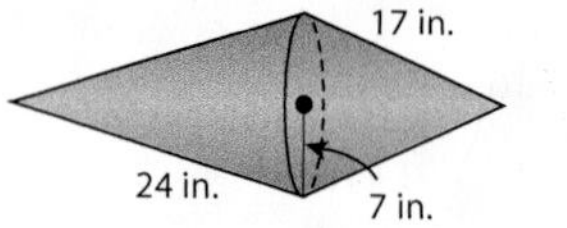

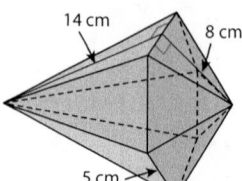

17 in.

24 in.

7 in.

Lateral area of left cone
$L = \pi r \ell = \pi(7)(24) = 168\pi \text{ in}^2$
Lateral area of right cone
$L = \pi r \ell = \pi(7)(17) = 119\pi \text{ in}^2$
$168\pi + 119\pi = 287\pi$
$S = 287\pi \text{ in}^2$

15.

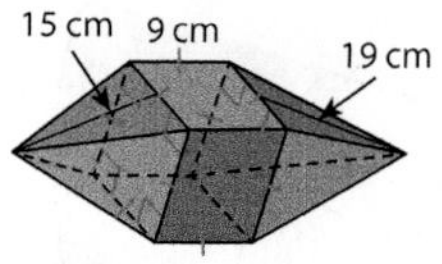

15 cm   9 cm   19 cm

Lateral area of left pyramid
$L = \frac{1}{2}P\ell = \frac{1}{2}(36)(15)$
$= 270 \text{ cm}^2$
Lateral area of cube
$L = Ph = (36)9 = 324 \text{ cm}^2$

Lateral area of right pyramid
$L = \frac{1}{2}P\ell = \frac{1}{2}(36)(19)$
$= 342 \text{ cm}^2$
$270 + 324 + 342 = 936$
$S = 936 \text{ cm}^2$

16.

14 cm

8 cm

5 cm

Lateral area of left pyramid
$L = \frac{1}{2}P\ell = \frac{1}{2}(30)(14) = 210 \text{ cm}^2$
Lateral area of right pyramid
$L = \frac{1}{2}P\ell = \frac{1}{2}(30)(8) = 120 \text{ cm}^2$
$210 + 120 = 330$
$S = 330 \text{ cm}^2$

17.

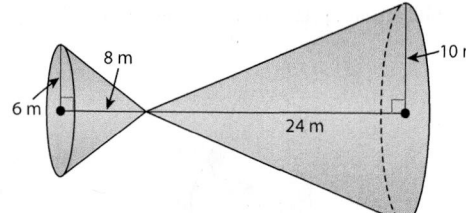

8 m

6 m

24 m

10 m

Slant height of left cone
$c^2 = a^2 + b^2$
$c = \sqrt{a^2 + b^2}$
$\ell = \sqrt{a^2 + b^2}$
$\ell = \sqrt{6^2 + 8^2} = 10 \text{ m}$

Surface area of left cone
$L = \pi r \ell = \pi(6)(10) = 60\pi \text{ m}^2$
$S = L + B = 60\pi + \pi r^2$
$S = 60\pi + \pi(6)^2$
$= 96\pi \text{ m}^2$

Slant height of right cone
$c^2 = a^2 + b^2$
$c = \sqrt{a^2 + b^2}$
$\ell = \sqrt{a^2 + b^2}$
$\ell = \sqrt{24^2 + 10^2} = 26 \text{ m}$

Surface area of right cone
$L = \pi r \ell = \pi(10)(26)$
$= 260\pi \text{ m}^2$
$S = L + B = 260\pi + \pi r^2$
$= 260\pi + \pi(10)^2 = 360\pi$
$96\pi + 360\pi = 456\pi$
$S = 456\pi \text{ m}^2$

18. Anna is making a birthday hat from a pattern that is $\frac{3}{4}$ of a circle of colored paper.
If Anna's head is 7 inches in diameter, will the hat fit her? Explain.

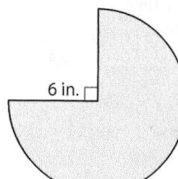

6 in.

Area of $\frac{3}{4}$ Circle/Lateral Area of Cone
$A = \frac{3}{4}\pi r^2 = \frac{3}{4}\pi(6)^2 = 27\pi \text{ in}^2$
$L = \pi r \ell$
$27\pi = \pi r(6)$
$\frac{27\pi}{6\pi} = \frac{6\pi r}{6\pi}$
$4.5 \text{ in.} = r$

No; the diameter is 9 in., so it is too large.

19. It is a tradition in England to celebrate May 1st by hanging cone-shaped baskets of flowers on neighbors' door handles. Addy is making a basket from a piece of paper that is a semicircle with diameter 12 in. What is the diameter of the basket?

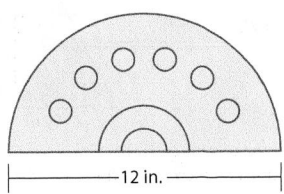

— 12 in. —

Area of $\frac{1}{2}$ Circle/Lateral Area of Cone

$A = \frac{1}{2}\pi r^2 = \frac{1}{2}\pi(6)^2 = 18\pi$ in^2

$L = \pi r \ell$

$18\pi = \pi r(6)$

$\frac{18\pi}{6\pi} = \frac{6\pi r}{6\pi}$

3 in. $= r$, so $d = 6$ in.

20. Match the figure with the correct surface area. Indicate a match by writing a letter for the correct surface area in the final column for each shape.

Shape	Base Area	Slant Height	Surface Area
Regular square pyramid	36 cm²	5 cm	C
Regular triangular pyramid	√3 cm²	√3 cm	B
Right cone	16π cm²	7 cm	D
Right cone	π cm²	2 cm	A

A. 9.4 cm²

B. 6.9 cm²

C. 96 cm²

D. 138.2 cm²

Regular square pyramid

$L = \frac{1}{2}P\ell$

$= \frac{1}{2}(24)(5)$

$= 60$ cm²

$S = L + B$

$= 60 + 36$

$= 96$ cm²

Regular triangular pyramid

$L = \frac{1}{2}P\ell$

$= \frac{1}{2}(6)(\sqrt{3})$

$= 3\sqrt{3}$ cm²

$S = L + B$

$= 3\sqrt{3} + \sqrt{3}$

$= 4\sqrt{3} \approx 6.9$ cm²

Right Cone 1

$L = \pi r \ell$

$= \pi(4)(7)$

$= 28\pi$ cm²

$S = L + B$

$= 28\pi + 16\pi$

$= 44\pi$

≈ 138.2 cm²

Right Cone 2

$L = \pi r \ell$

$= \pi(1)(2)$

$= 2\pi$ cm²

$S = L + B$

$= 2\pi + \pi$

$= 3\pi$

≈ 9.4 cm²

21. The Pyramid Arena in Memphis, Tennessee, is a square pyramid with base edge lengths of 200 yd and a height of 32 stories. Estimate the area of the glass on the sides of the pyramid. (*Hint:* 1 story ≈ 10 ft)

Lateral height of Pyramid

$c^2 = a^2 + b^2$

$c = \sqrt{a^2 + b^2}$

$\ell = \sqrt{a^2 + b^2}$

$\ell = \sqrt{300^2 + 320^2}$

$\ell = \sqrt{192,400}$

$\ell \approx 440$ ft

Lateral Area of Pyramid: $L = 1/2\,P\ell \approx \frac{1}{2}(2400)(440) \approx 528,000$ ft²

Possible Answer: 528,000 ft²

SMALL GROUP ACTIVITY

Have students work in groups. Each student should make up a surface area problem for a pyramid and for a cone. Have students pass the problems to another student, who solves the problems and then passes them to yet another student to be checked. Ask a fourth student to critique the problems to make sure the solutions are complete.

Surface Area of Pyramids and Cones   **1016**

Have students illustrate and describe how to use formula $S = B + \frac{1}{2}P\ell$ to find the surface area of a pyramid or cone. Ask them to include all of the steps as well as the substitutions they will use in the formula.

22. A juice container is a regular square pyramid with the dimensions shown.

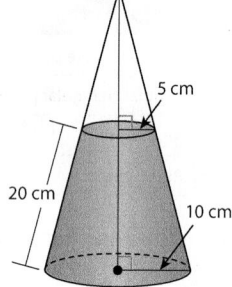

a. Find the surface area of the container to the nearest tenth.

$c^2 = a^2 + b^2$ ⠀⠀⠀$L = \frac{1}{2}P\ell = \frac{1}{2}(32)(\sqrt{116}) = 16\sqrt{116}$ cm²

$c = \sqrt{a^2 + b^2}$ ⠀⠀⠀$S = L + B = 16\sqrt{116} + 64 = 236.3$ cm²

$\ell = \sqrt{a^2 + b^2}$

$\ell = \sqrt{10^2 + 4^2} = \sqrt{116}$ cm

10 cm

8 cm

b. The manufacturer decides to make a container in the shape of a right cone that requires the same amount of material. The base diameter must be 9 cm. Find the slant height of the container to the nearest tenth.

$L = \pi r \ell$ ⠀⠀⠀⠀⠀$S = L + B$ ⠀⠀⠀⠀⠀$172.7 \approx 4.5\pi\ell$

⠀⠀$= 4.5\pi\ell$ cm² ⠀⠀⠀$236.3 = 4.5\pi\ell + 20.25\pi$ ⠀⠀So, $\ell \approx \dfrac{172.7}{4.5\pi} \approx 12.2$ cm

23. **Persevere in Problem Solving** A *frustum* of a cone is a part of the cone with two parallel bases. The height of the frustum of the cone that is shown is half the height of the original cone.

a. Find the surface area of the original cone.

$L = \pi r \ell = \pi(10)(40) = 400\pi$ cm²

$S = L + B = 400\pi + \pi r^2 = 400\pi + \pi(10)^2$

⠀⠀$= 400\pi + 100\pi = 500\pi$ cm²

5 cm

20 cm

10 cm

b. Find the lateral area of the top of the cone.

$L = \pi r \ell = \pi(5)(20) = 100\pi$ cm²

c. Find the area of the top base of the frustum.⠀⠀⠀d. Use your results from parts a, b, and c to find the surface area of the frustum of the cone.

$A = \pi r^2 = \pi(5)^2 = 25\pi$ cm²⠀⠀⠀⠀⠀$S = 500\pi - 100\pi + 25\pi = 425\pi$ cm²

H.O.T. Focus on Higher Order Thinking

24. **Communicate Mathematical Ideas** Explain how you would find the volume of a cone, given the radius and the surface area.

Possible answer: Substitute the given values for r and S into the surface area formula and solve for ℓ. Use the Pyth. Thm. and the values of r and ℓ to find h. Then substitute the values for r and h into the volume formula.

25. **Draw Conclusions** Explain why the slant height of a regular square pyramid must be greater than half the base edge length.

A triangle is formed with 2 vertices at the midpoints of opposite sides of the square base and the third vertex at the vertex of the pyramid. The side lengths of the triangle are ℓ, ℓ, and s, the edge length of the base. By the Triangle Inequality Theorem, $\ell + \ell > s$, so $2\ell > s$. Therefore $\ell > \frac{1}{2}s$.

Lesson Performance Task

The pyramid in the figure is built in two levels.

$AC = 200$ feet

You have a summer job as an intern archaeologist. The archaeologists you are working with need to apply a liquid microbial biofilm inhibitor to the pyramid to prevent bacterial degradation of the stones and have asked you to calculate the volume of inhibitor needed for the job. You find that you need 36,000 gallons of inhibitor for the top level. How many gallons will you need for the bottom level? (Keep in mind that you won't be treating the square bases of the levels.) Explain how you found the answer.

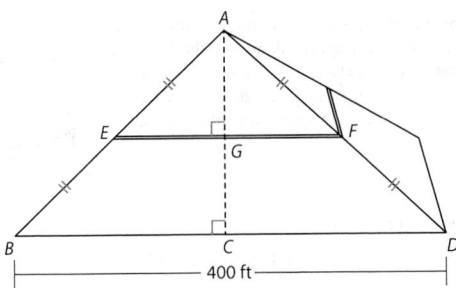

108,000 gallons of inhibitor will be needed.

According to the Triangle Midsegment Theorem, $EF = 200$ feet. Also, by the Triangle Proportionality Theorem, $AG = GC = \frac{1}{2} \cdot AC = 100$ feet.

perimeter of base of upper level: $4 \times 200 = 800$ ft

surface area of upper level (minus base): $\frac{1}{2}(800 \times 100) = 40,000$ ft^2

perimeter of base of complete pyramid: $4 \times 400 = 1600$ ft

surface area of complete pyramid (minus base): $\frac{1}{2}(1600 \times 200) = 160,000$ ft^2

surface area of lower level: $160,000$ ft$^2 - 40,000$ ft$^2 = 120,000$ ft^2

The surface area of the lower level is $\frac{120,000}{40,000} = 3$ times the surface area of the upper level and will require 3 times as much liquid as was used on the upper level. $3 \times 36,000 = 108,000$ gallons

© Houghton Mifflin Harcourt Publishing Company

LANGUAGE SUPPORT **EL**

A *biofilm* is a group of bacteria or other microbes that stick to a surface. A liquid microbial biofilm inhibitor is a liquid product that is applied to a surface to prevent a biofilm from forming.

INTEGRATE MATHEMATICAL PRACTICES
Focus on Reasoning

MP.2 Students may be intrigued to discover that after all their calculations, the surface area of the lower level of the pyramid turns out to be exactly 3 times that of the upper level. Challenge them to draw a diagram that uses congruent triangles to illustrate the relationship between the levels.

EXTENSION ACTIVITY

Ask students to research pyramids around the world, whether in the Middle East, the Americas, or Southeast Asia. Have them choose two pyramids, each from a different region, and use the dimensions they find to estimate their surface areas. Then have them compare the lateral areas of these pyramids in a presentation to the rest of the class.

Scoring Rubric

2 points: Student correctly solves the problem and explains his/her reasoning.

1 point: Student shows good understanding of the problem but does not fully solve or explain his/her reasoning.

0 points: Student does not demonstrate understanding of the problem.

Surface Area of Pyramids and Cones   **1018**

Surface Area of Spheres

Common Core Math Standards

The student is expected to:

 G-MG.A.1

Use geometric shapes, their measures, and their properties to describe objects (e.g., modeling a tree trunk or a human torso as a cylinder)

Mathematical Practices

 MP.4 Modeling

Language Objective

Explain to a partner how to find the surface area of a sphere.

ENGAGE

Essential Question: How can you use the formula for the surface area of a sphere to calculate the surface areas of composite figures?

Use the formula for the surface area of a sphere or hemisphere, together with area formulas for the other surfaces of the figure, being careful to exclude surfaces of those areas that are not part of the surface of the overall figure.

PREVIEW: LESSON PERFORMANCE TASK

View the Engage section online. Discuss the photograph. Ask students to explain what the equator is. Then preview the Lesson Performance Task.

19.4 Surface Area of Spheres

Essential Question: How can you use the formula for the surface area of a sphere to calculate the surface areas of composite figures?

Resource Locker

🧭 Explore   Developing a Surface Area Formula

You can derive the formula for the surface area of a sphere with radius r by imagining that it is filled with a large number of pyramids, whose apexes all meet at the center of the sphere and whose bases rest against the sphere's surface. It does not matter exactly what shape each base is, as long as all the bases have the same area, B, and they are not too far from regular polygons in shape. The figure shows a sphere with the first three pyramids inscribed.

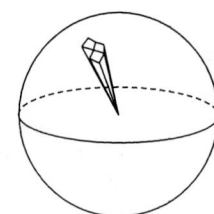

(A) What is the approximate volume of each pyramid?

Since each pyramid's base is small compared to the sphere, all points on the base are

approximately the same distance r from the center of the sphere; so for each pyramid,

$h \approx r$. Therefore each pyramid's volume is $\frac{1}{3}Bh \approx \frac{1}{3}Br$

(B) Express the approximate volume of the sphere in terms of the n pyramids.

Since the n pyramids almost completely fill the sphere, its volume $V \approx n\left(\frac{1}{3}\right)Br = \frac{1}{3}nBr$.

(C) Use the formula for the volume of a sphere to write an approximate equation that can be solved for B, and solve it.

$\frac{4}{3}\pi r^3 \approx \frac{1}{3}nBr$

$\frac{4\pi r^2}{n} \approx B$

(D) Write an approximate expression for the sphere's surface area S in terms of the pyramid bases.

Each base has almost the same area as the region of the sphere's surface immediately

above it. Therefore, since the bases almost completely fill the sphere, $S \approx nB$.

(E) Substitute your expression for the base area B of each pyramid from step C into your expression from step D. This gives you an approximate expression for the surface area S that does not involve the pyramids.

$S \approx nB \approx n\left(\frac{4\pi r^2}{n}\right) = 4\pi r^2$

© Houghton Mifflin Harcourt Publishing Company

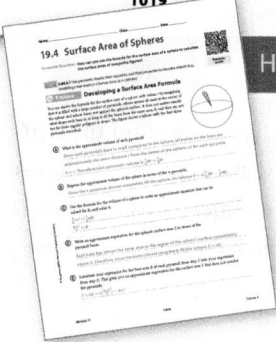

HARDCOVER PAGES 855–860

Turn to these pages to find this lesson in the hardcover student edition.

1. As *n* gets larger and larger, what do you think will happen to the closeness of the approximations in steps *A*, *B*, *C*, and *E*? Explain.

   E.g, All these approximations will get closer, because as the pyramid bases get smaller,

   the part of the surface of the sphere next to each base gets flatter and closer to the base.

2. As a conjecture, write the formula for the surface area *S* of a sphere with radius *r*.

   $S = 4\pi r^2$

🎯 Explain 1   Finding the Surface Area of a Sphere

Surface Area of a Sphere

The surface area of a sphere with radius *r* is given by $S = 4\pi r^2$.

You can use a formula for the surface area of a sphere to solve real-world problems.

Example 1 A spherical water tank is 21.5 ft in diameter. The corrosion-resistant alloy skin of the tank is $\frac{1}{8}$ in thick. How much alloy is used to make the tank, to the nearest cubic inch?

Ⓐ Find the radius of the tank in inches.

The radius of the tank is $\frac{1}{2}(21.5 \text{ ft}) = 10.75 \text{ ft} \times \frac{12 \text{ in.}}{1 \text{ ft}} = 129$ in.

Ⓑ Find the surface area of the tank.

$S = 4\pi r^2 = 4\pi \left(\boxed{129}\right)^2 = \boxed{209{,}116.973} \ldots \text{ in}^2$

Ⓒ Find the amount of alloy, to the nearest cubic inch.

Amount of alloy = surface area × thickness

$= \left(\boxed{209{,}116.973} \ldots \text{ in}^2\right) \times \left(\boxed{\tfrac{1}{8}} \text{ in.}\right) \approx \boxed{26{,}140} \text{ in}^3$

Your Turn

A basketball is a sphere 29.5 in. in circumference. A baseball is a sphere of circumference 9.0 in. How much material is needed to make each ball, and how does the ratio of these amounts compare to the ratio of the circumferences?

3. How much material is needed to make a basketball, to the nearest tenth of a square inch?

   radius of basketball $= \frac{29.5 \text{ in.}}{2\pi} = 4.695\ldots$ in.

   $S = 4\pi r^2 = 4\pi(4.695\ldots)^2 \approx 277.0 \text{ in}^2$

4. How much material is needed to make a baseball, to the nearest tenth?

   radius of basketball $= \frac{9.0 \text{ in}}{2\pi} = 1.432\ldots$ in.

   $S = 4\pi r^2 = 4\pi(1.432\ldots)^2 \approx 25.8 \text{ in}^2$

PROFESSIONAL DEVELOPMENT

 Math Background

The surface area *S* of a sphere is given by the formula $S = 4\pi r^2$, where *r* is the radius. This formula depends only on the radius of the sphere. If a plane passes through the center of the sphere, the circle (called a *great circle)* that is formed has the same radius and same center as the sphere. Great circles are the largest circles that lie on a sphere, and they have another important property: Given two points on a sphere, the shortest path on the sphere between the points lies along the great circle that passes through the points. For this reason, ships and airplanes generally follow routes that are arcs of great circles.

EXPLORE

Developing a Surface Area Formula

INTEGRATE TECHNOLOGY

Students have the option of doing the Explore activity either in the book or online.

QUESTIONING STRATEGIES

? How are pyramids used to approximate the surface area of a sphere? The volume of *n* pyramids with their bases on the surface of the sphere approaches the volume of a sphere as *n* increases. Since the volume formula of a pyramid includes the area of its base, setting the volume formula for a sphere equal to the volume formula for *n* pyramids, and then solving for the area, gives an expression for the area of the sphere.

EXPLAIN 1

Finding the Surface Area of a Sphere

QUESTIONING STRATEGIES

? How is the surface area of sphere related to its radius? The surface area is a function of the square of the radius, and it has a constant of variation equal to 4π.

INTEGRATE MATHEMATICAL PRACTICES
Focus on Math Connections

MP.1 Point out that all spheres are similar figures, so the formula for surface area, $S = 4\pi r^2$, where *S* is the area and *r* is the radius, depends only on the radius.

AVOID COMMON ERRORS

Students often confuse the surface area formula for a sphere with the volume formula for a sphere. Watch for students who do this and suggest that they think of mnemonics to help them distinguish the formulas.

EXPLAIN 2

Finding the Surface Area of a Composite Figure

QUESTIONING STRATEGIES

? When does the surface area of a composite figure include the area of a hemisphere? Sample answer: The area of a hemisphere is included if half of a sphere is part of the outer surface of the composite figure.

INTEGRATE MATHEMATICAL PRACTICES

Focus on Technology

MP.5 Have students use a spreadsheet or other technology to help them organize the calculations for composite figures. The spreadsheet should include cells for the dimensions of the figures, and the related surface area formulas. Then the **SUM** feature can be used to calculate the total surface area, including areas that are "negative" because they need to be subtracted.

---

5. Compare the ratio of the amounts of material to the ratio of the circumferences. What do you notice?
ratio of amounts of material $\approx \frac{277.0}{25.8} = 10.736\ldots$; ratio of circumferences $= \frac{29.5}{9.0} = 3.277\ldots$;
square of ratio of circumferences $= (3.277\ldots)^2 = 10.743\ldots \approx$ ratio of amounts of material

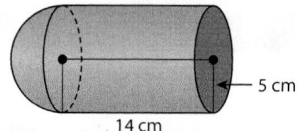 **Explain 2** **Finding the Surface Area of a Composite Figure**

You can find the surface area of a composite figure using appropriate formulas for the areas of the different surfaces of the figure.

Example 2 Find the surface area of the composite figure, in terms of π and to the nearest tenth.

5 cm
14 cm

(A) Find the area of the base of the cylinder.

$A_1 = \pi r^2 = \pi(5)^2 = 25\pi$ cm^2

(B) Find the area of the curved surface of the cylinder.

$A_2 = 2\pi rh = 2\pi\left(\boxed{5}\right)\left(\boxed{14}\right) = \boxed{140}\,\pi$ cm^2

(C) Find the surface area of the hemisphere.

$A_3 = \frac{1}{2}(4\pi r^2) = 2\pi\left(\boxed{5}\right)^2 = \boxed{50}\,\pi$ cm^2

(D) Find the surface area of the composite figure.

$S = A_1 + A_2 + A_3$

$= \boxed{25}\,\pi$ cm$^2 + \boxed{140}\,\pi$ cm$^2 + \boxed{50}\,\pi$ cm^2

$= \boxed{215}\,\pi$ cm$^2 \approx \boxed{675.4}$ cm^2

Reflect

6. **Discussion** Could you have used the formula for the surface area of a cylinder? Explain.
E.g., No, because only one base of the cylinder contributes to the surface area of the composite figure; or, Yes, but you would have to subtract the area of one of the bases

COLLABORATIVE LEARNING

Small Group Activity

Have students work in groups to brainstorm how to apply the formula for the surface area of a sphere when they need to find the area of a hemisphere or multiple spheres in the context of real-world problems. (Start with the formula $S = 4\pi r^2$ for the sphere and then find the fraction of the sphere that is needed for the application problem.) Ask them to draw diagrams to help them verify their conjectures, and then present their results to the class.

Find the surface area of the composite figure, in terms of π and to the nearest tenth.

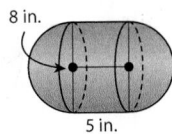

8 in.

5 in.

7. Find the lateral area of the cylinder.

$r = \frac{1}{2}(8 \text{ in.}) = 4 \text{ in.}$

$A_1 = 2\pi r h = 2\pi(4)(5) = 40\pi \text{ in}^2$

8. Find the surface area of each hemisphere.

$A_2 = A_3 = \frac{1}{2}(4\pi r^2) = 2\pi(4)^2 = 32\pi \text{ in}^2$

9. Find the surface area of the composite figure.

$S = A_1 + A_2 + A_3$

$= 40\pi \text{ in}^2 + 2(32\pi \text{ in}^2)$

$= 104\pi \text{ in}^2 \approx 326.7 \text{ in}^2$

💬 Elaborate

10. How does deriving the formula for the surface area of a sphere depend on knowing the formula for its volume?

The formula for the volume of a sphere is related to the sum of the volumes of *n* pyramids

that fill the sphere, with their apexes at the center of the sphere and their heights $h \approx r$

of the sphere. From that relationship, the sum of the areas of the bases of *n* pyramids will

equal the surface area of the sphere.

11. **Essential Question Check-In** How can you use the formula for the surface area of a sphere to calculate the surface areas of composite figures?

It is easier to form composite figures with a hemisphere, which has surface area

$S = \frac{1}{2}(4\pi r^2) = 2\pi r^2$. Use this formula together with area formulas for the other surfaces

of the figure, being careful not to include surfaces of parts of the figure that do not form

part of the surface of the overall figure.

ELABORATE

QUESTIONING STRATEGIES

? How could you use two-dimensional figures to represent the surface area of a given sphere? The surface area of a sphere with radius *r* is equal to four times the area of a circle with radius *r*. You could use four congruent circles, each with the same radius as the sphere, to represent the surface area of the sphere.

SUMMARIZE THE LESSON

? How do you find the surface area of a sphere? Determine the radius and use the formula $S = 4\pi r^2$.

DIFFERENTIATE INSTRUCTION

Critical Thinking

Have students work in groups to discuss how the surface area of a sphere changes if the radius is doubled, tripled, or halved. The group should be able to explain why the surface area changes more rapidly than the radius and show calculations to support their ideas (the radius is squared, so the surface area increases more rapidly). Have groups compare their results.

ASSIGNMENT GUIDE

Concepts and Skills	Practice
Explore Developing a Surface Area Formula	Exercise 1
Example 1 Finding the Surface Area of a Sphere	Exercises 2–5
Example 2 Finding the Surface Area of a Composite Figure	Exercises 6–9

⭐ Evaluate: Homework and Practice

• Online Homework
• Hints and Help
• Extra Practice

1. Using your knowledge of surface area and area, create a formula that will work to find the total surface area of the closed hemisphere for any value of r.

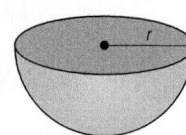

$$S = \frac{1}{2}\left(4\pi r^2\right) + \pi r^2$$
$$= 2\pi r^2 + \pi r^2$$
$$= 3\pi r^2$$
$$S = 3\pi r^2$$

Find the surface area of the sphere. Leave the answer in terms of π.

2.

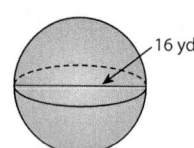

16 yd

$$S = 4\pi r^2$$
$$= 4\pi(8)^2$$
$$= 256\pi$$
$$S = 256\pi \text{ yd}^2$$

3.

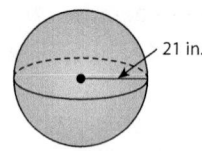

21 in.

$$S = 4\pi r^2$$
$$= 4\pi(21)^2$$
$$= 1764\pi$$
$$S = 1764\pi \text{ in}^2$$

4.

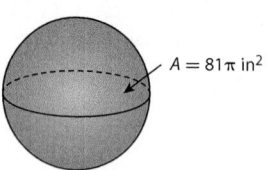

$A = 81\pi \text{ in}^2$

$$A = \pi r^2$$
$$81\pi = \pi r^2$$
$$\frac{81\pi}{\pi} = \frac{\pi r^2}{\pi}$$
$$81 = r^2$$
$$9 = r$$
$$S = 4\pi r^2$$
$$= 4\pi(9)^2$$
$$= 324\pi$$
$$S = 324\pi \text{ in}^2$$

5.

$A = 49\pi \text{ cm}^2$

$$A = \pi r^2$$
$$49\pi = \pi r^2$$
$$\frac{49\pi}{\pi} = \frac{\pi r^2}{\pi}$$
$$49 = r^2$$
$$7 = r$$
$$S = 4\pi r^2$$
$$= 4\pi(7)^2$$
$$= 196\pi$$
$$S = 196\pi \text{ cm}^2$$

Exercise	Depth of Knowledge (D.O.K.)	COMMON CORE Mathematical Practices
1	**2** Skills/Concepts	**MP.4** Modeling
2–11	**1** Recall of Information	**MP.5** Using Tools
12–13	**2** Skills/Concepts	**MP.4** Modeling
14–21	**2** Skills/Concepts	**MP.1** Problem Solving
22	**3** Strategic Thinking H.O.T.	**MP.2** Reasoning
23	**3** Strategic Thinking H.O.T.	**MP.2** Reasoning

Find the surface area of the composite figure. Leave the answer in terms of π.

6.

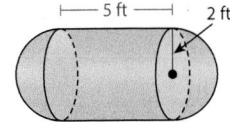

Surface area of one full sphere

$S = 4\pi r^2$

$\quad = 4\pi(2)^2$

$\quad = 16\pi$ ft^2

Lateral surface area of cylinder

$L = 2\pi rh$

$\quad = 2\pi(2)(5)$

$\quad = 20\pi$ ft^2

$16\pi + 20\pi = 36\pi$

$\quad\quad S = 36\pi$ ft^2

7.

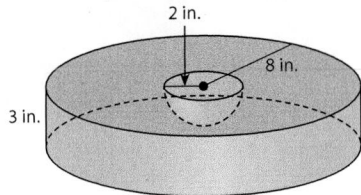

Surface area of cylinder

$L = 2\pi rh$

$\quad = 2\pi(8)(3)$

$\quad = 48\pi$ in^2

$S = L + 2\pi r^2$

$\quad = 48\pi + 2\pi(8)^2$

$\quad = 48\pi + 128\pi$

$\quad = 176\,\pi$ in^2

Surface area of hemisphere

$S = \frac{1}{2}(4\pi r^2)$

$\quad = 2\pi(2)^2$

$\quad = 8\pi$ in^2

Area of circle

$A = \pi r^2 = \pi(2)^2$

$\quad = 4\pi$ in^2

$176\pi + 8\pi - 4\pi = 180\pi$

$\quad\quad S = 180\pi$ in^2

8.

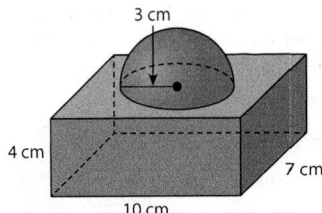

Surface area of hemisphere

$S = \frac{1}{2}(4\pi r^2)$

$\quad = 2\pi(3)^2$

$\quad = 18\pi$ cm^2

Area of circle

$A = \pi r^2$

$\quad = \pi(3)^2$

$\quad = 9\pi$ cm^2

$18\pi + 276 - 9\pi$

$S \approx 304.3$ cm^2

Surface area of prism

$L = Ph$

$\quad = (34)4$

$\quad = 136$ cm^2

$S = Ph + 2B$

$\quad = 136 + 2(10)(7)$

$\quad = 136 + 140$

$\quad = 276$ cm^2

9.

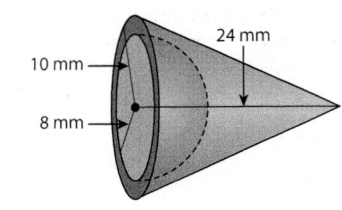

$c = \sqrt{a^2 + b^2}$

$\ell = \sqrt{10^2 + 24^2}$

$\ell = 26$ mm

Surface area of cone

$L = \pi r\ell = \pi(10)(26)$

$\quad = 260\pi$ mm^2

$S = L + B$

$\quad = 260\pi + \pi(10)^2$

$\quad = 360\pi$ mm^2

Surface area of hemisphere

$S = \frac{1}{2}(4\pi r^2)$

$\quad = 2\pi(8)^2$

$\quad = 128\pi$ mm^2

Area of circle

$A = \pi r^2$

$\quad = 64\pi$ mm^2

$360\pi +$

$128\pi - 64\pi$

$S \approx 1332.0$ mm^2

INTEGRATE MATHEMATICAL PRACTICES

Focus on Modeling

MP.4 Have students work in groups to find the surface areas of real-world spheres. Ask them to use a piece of string to find the circumference (and then the radius) of a great circle of the sphere. Then have them cut out four circles with the same radius and experiment with how to cover the sphere with the circles.

Exercise	Depth of Knowledge (D.O.K.)	COMMON CORE Mathematical Practices
24	**3** Strategic Thinking H.O.T.	**MP.6** Precision
25	**3** Strategic Thinking H.O.T.	**MP.2** Reasoning

Throughout the exercises, caution students to avoid the common error of using the volume formula instead of the surface area formula. Point out that one way to remember which to use is that area is in *square* units, and the radius is *squared* in the surface area formula.

10. Find the surface area of the closed hemisphere.

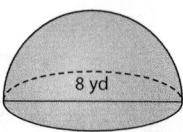

8 yd

$$S = \frac{1}{2}\left(4\pi r^2\right) + \pi r^2$$
$$= 2\pi(4)^2 + \pi(4)^2$$
$$= 48\pi \text{ yd}^2$$
$$\approx 150.8 \text{ yd}^2$$

$48\pi \text{ yd}^2$ or 150.8 yd^2

11. Find the circumference of the sphere with a surface area of 60π in². Leave the answer in terms of π.

$$S = 4\pi r^2$$
$$60\pi = 4\pi r^2$$
$$\frac{60\pi}{4\pi} = \frac{4\pi r^2}{4\pi}$$
$$15 = r^2$$
$$\sqrt{15} = r$$
$$C = 2\pi r$$
$$C = 2\pi\sqrt{15} \text{ in.}$$

12. **Geography** Earth's radius is approximately 4000 mi. About two-thirds of Earth's surface is covered by water. Estimate the land area on Earth.

$$S = \frac{1}{3}(4\pi r^2)$$
$$= \frac{4}{3}\pi(4000)^2$$
$$= 21,333,333.33\pi$$
$$\approx 67,000,000 \text{ mi}^2$$

13. A baseball has a radius of approximately 1.5 inches. Estimate the amount of leather used to cover the baseball. Leave the answer in terms of π.

$$S = 4\pi r^2$$
$$= 4\pi(1.5)^2$$
$$= 9\pi \text{ in}^2$$

14. Which of the following expressions represents the ratio of the surface area of a cylinder to the surface area of a sphere with the same radius, r?

A. $\frac{1}{2} + \frac{h}{r}$

B. $\frac{\pi + h}{r^2}$

C. $\frac{h}{4\pi}$

D. $\frac{r + h}{4r}$

E. $\frac{r + h}{2r}$

$$\frac{\text{cylinder}}{\text{sphere}} = \frac{2\pi r^2 + 2\pi rh}{4\pi r^2}$$

$$\frac{2\pi r^2 + 2\pi rh}{4\pi r^2} = \frac{2\pi r^2}{4\pi r^2} + \frac{2\pi rh}{4\pi r^2}$$
$$= \frac{1}{2} + \frac{h}{2r}$$
$$= \frac{1}{2} \cdot \frac{r}{r} + \frac{h}{2r}$$
$$= \frac{r + h}{2r}$$

15. **Explain the Error** Susana solved for the surface area of the sphere using the following method:

$$S = \frac{4}{3}\pi r^2$$
$$= \frac{4}{3}\pi(10)^2$$
$$= \frac{4}{3}\pi 100$$
$$= \frac{400}{3}\pi \text{ m}^2$$

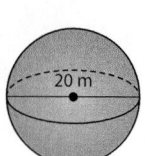

20 m

Find her error, and explain how to fix it.

Susana used $\frac{4}{3}$, which is part of the volume formula, not the surface area formula. The surface area formula is $4\pi r^2$.

16. Use the table to answer the question.

Planet	Diameter (mi)
Mercury	3,032
Venus	7,521
Earth	7,926
Mars	4,222
Jupiter	88,846
Saturn	74,898
Uranus	31,763
Neptune	30,775

a. Which is greater, the sum of the surface areas of Uranus and Neptune or the surface area of Saturn?

$S_{Uranus} = 4\pi r^2$

$\quad = 4\pi(15,881.5)^2$

$\quad = 1,008,888,169\pi$

$\quad \approx 3,000,000,000 \text{ mi}^2$

$S_{Neptune} = 4\pi r^2$

$\quad = 4\pi(15,387.5)^2$

$\quad = 947,100,625\pi$

$\quad \approx 3,000,000,000 \text{ mi}^2$

$2(3,000,000,000) = 6,000,000,000$

$S_{Saturn} = 4\pi r^2 = 4\pi(37,449)^2 = 5,609,710,404\pi \approx 17,000,000,000 \text{ mi}^2$

The surface area of Saturn is greater.

b. About how many times as great is the surface area of Earth as the surface area of Mars?

$S_{Earth} = 4\pi r^2$ $\qquad\qquad S_{Mars} = 4\pi r^2$

$\quad = 4\pi(3963)^2$ $\qquad\qquad\quad = 4\pi(2111)^2$

$\quad = 62,821,476\pi$ $\qquad\qquad = 17,825,284\pi$

$\quad \approx 200,000,000 \text{ mi}^2$ $\qquad \approx 60,000,000 \text{ mi}^2$

$\dfrac{200,000,000}{60,000,000} \approx 3.3$

About 3.3 times as great.

17. A globe has a volume of 288π in^3. What is the surface area of the globe? Give your answer in terms of π.

$V = \frac{4}{3}\pi r^3$ $\qquad \sqrt[3]{216} = \sqrt[3]{r^3}$

$288\pi = \frac{4}{3}\pi r^3$ $\qquad\quad 6 = r$

$\frac{3}{4} \cdot 288\pi = \frac{4}{3}\pi r^3 \cdot \frac{3}{4}$ $\qquad S = 4\pi r^2$

$216\pi = \pi r^3$ $\qquad\qquad = 4\pi(6)^2$

$\frac{216\pi}{\pi} = \frac{\pi r^3}{\pi}$ $\qquad\qquad = 144\pi \text{ in}^2$

$216 = r^3$ $\qquad\qquad S = 144\pi \text{ in}^2$

© Houghton Mifflin Harcourt Publishing Company

INTEGRATE MATHEMATICAL PRACTICES

Focus on Reasoning

MP.2 One half the surface area of a sphere is $2\pi r^2$. Emphasize that sometimes the area of the great circle must be added to find the total area of a real-world hemispherical object. For example, the surface area of half of an orange is $3\pi r^2$, where r is the radius of the orange.

Have students work in pairs. Each student should make up a surface area problem for a sphere, then pass the problem to the partner, who solves the problem. Have the pair then check each other's work to make sure the solutions are complete.

18. A bead is formed by drilling a cylindrical hole, with a 2 mm diameter, through a sphere with an 8 mm diameter. Estimate the surface area of the bead.

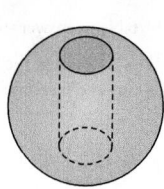

Surface area of sphere	Area of circle
$S = 4\pi r^2$	$A = \pi r^2$
$= 4\pi(4)^2$	$= \pi(1)^2$
$= 64\pi$ mm^2	$= \pi$ mm^2

Lateral area of cylinder $\quad 64\pi + 16\pi - 2(\pi) = 78\pi \approx 245$

$\qquad L = 2\pi rh \qquad\qquad\qquad S \approx 245$ mm^2

$\qquad = 2\pi(1)(8)$

$\qquad = 16\pi$ mm^2

19. The size of a cultured pearl is typically indicated by its diameter in mm. About how many times as great is the surface area of the 9 mm pearl as the surface area of the 6 mm pearl?

$S_{9\,mm} = 4\pi r^2 \qquad\qquad S_{6\,mm} = 4\pi r^2$

$\qquad = 4\pi(4.5)^2 \qquad\qquad = 4\pi(3)^2$

$\qquad = 81\pi$ mm^2 $\qquad\qquad\quad = 36\pi$ mm^2

About twice as great.

20. The diameter of an orange is 10 cm and the diameter of a lime is 5 cm. About how many times as great is the surface area of a half of the lime as the surface area of a half of the orange?

$S_{orange} = \dfrac{1}{2}\left(4\pi r^2\right) + \pi r^2 \qquad S_{lime} = \dfrac{1}{2}\left(4\pi r^2\right) + \pi r^2$

$\qquad\quad = 2\pi(5)^2 + \pi(5)^2 \qquad\qquad = 2\pi(2.5)^2 + \pi(2.5)^2$

$\qquad\quad = 50\pi + 25\pi \qquad\qquad\qquad = 12.5\pi + 6.25\pi$

$\qquad\quad = 75\pi$ cm^2 $\qquad\qquad\qquad\quad = 18.75\pi$ cm^2

$$\dfrac{75\pi}{18.75\pi} = 4$$

4 times as great.

21. A hemisphere has a surface area of 972π cm^2. If the radius is multiplied by $\frac{1}{3}$, what will be the surface area of the new hemisphere?

$$S = \frac{1}{2}\,4\pi r^2 \qquad S = \frac{1}{2}\,4\pi r^2$$

$$972\pi = 2\pi^2 \qquad = 2\pi\left(\frac{\sqrt{486}}{3}\right)^2$$

$$\frac{972\pi}{2\pi} = \frac{2\pi r^2}{2\pi} \qquad = 2\pi \cdot \frac{486}{9}$$

$$486 = r^2 \qquad = 108\pi \text{ cm}^2$$

$$\sqrt{486} = \sqrt{r^2} \qquad S = 108\pi \text{ cm}^2$$

$$\sqrt{486} = r$$

> **H.O.T. Focus on Higher Order Thinking**

22. Communicate Mathematical Ideas Describe the effect on the surface area if the dimension on the sphere is doubled.

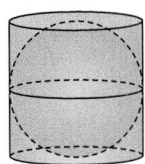

15 in.

Surface area of original sphere

$$S = 4\pi r^2$$

$$= 4\pi(15)^2$$

$$= 900\pi \text{ in}^2$$

Surface area of double the radius

$$S = 4\pi r^2$$

$$= 4\pi(30)^2$$

$$= 3600\pi \text{ in}^2$$

$$\frac{3600\pi}{900\pi} = 4$$

The surface area is multiplied by 4.

23. Analyze Relationships What is the relationship between the surface area of the sphere and the lateral area of the cylinder?

$$S = 4\pi r^2$$

$$L = 2\pi rh$$

$$= 2\pi r(2r)$$

$$= 4\pi r^2$$

The surface area of the sphere is equal to the lateral area of the cylinder.

INTEGRATE MATHEMATICAL PRACTICES

Focus on Math Connections

MP.1 Have students think of real-world examples of spheres and tell how to find their surface areas. Then have them tell how they would use that information for other real-world contexts. For example, the surface area of Earth is about $4\pi(3950)^2 \approx 196{,}000{,}000$ mi^2. Using the fact that 70% of Earth's surface is water, they could then find that about $137{,}000{,}000$ mi^2 of Earth's surface is water.

Surface Area of Spheres   **1028**

JOURNAL

Have students illustrate and describe how to find the surface area of a sphere. Ask them to include all of the steps as well as the substitutions they will use in the formula.

24. Persevere in Problem Solving A company sells orange juice in spherical containers that look like oranges. Each container has a surface area of approximately 50.3 in^2.

a. What is the volume of the container? Round to the nearest tenth.†

$$S = 4\pi r^2$$

$$50.3 = 4\pi r^2$$

$$\frac{50.3}{4\pi} = \frac{4\pi r^2}{4\pi}$$

$$4 \approx r^2$$

$$\sqrt{4} \approx \sqrt{r^2}$$

$$2 \approx r$$

$$V = \frac{4}{3}\pi r^3$$

$$= \frac{4}{3}\pi(2)^3$$

$$= \frac{4}{3}\pi(8)$$

$$\approx 33.5 \text{ in}^3$$

b. The company decides to increase the radius of the container by 10%. What is the surface area of the new container?

$$S = 4\pi r^2$$

$$= 4\pi(2.2)^2$$

$$= 4\pi(4.84)$$

$$= 19.36\pi$$

$$\approx 60.8 \text{ in}^2$$

25. Draw Conclusions Suppose a sphere and a cube have equal surface areas. Using r for the radius of the sphere and s for the side of a cube, write an equation to show the relationship between r and s.

$$S = 4\pi r^2$$

$$S = Ph + 2B$$

$$Ph + 2B = 4\pi r^2$$

$$4s \cdot s + 2s^2 = 4\pi r^2$$

$$4s^2 + 2s^2 = 4\pi r^2$$

$$6s^2 = 4\pi r^2$$

$$s^2 = \frac{4}{6}\pi r^2$$

$$\sqrt{s^2} = \sqrt{\frac{4}{6}\pi r^2}$$

$$s = 2r\sqrt{\frac{\pi}{6}}$$

$$s \approx 1.4r$$

$$s = 2r \cdot \sqrt{\frac{\pi}{6}}, \text{ or } s \approx 1.4r$$

Lesson Performance Task

Locations on Earth are measured in relation to longitude and latitude lines. Longitude lines run north and south through the North and South poles. The 0° longitude line is called the Prime Meridian and runs through Greenwich, England. Latitude lines circle the Earth parallel to the Equator, which is designated 0° latitude. Longitude and latitude lines intersect one another at right angles.

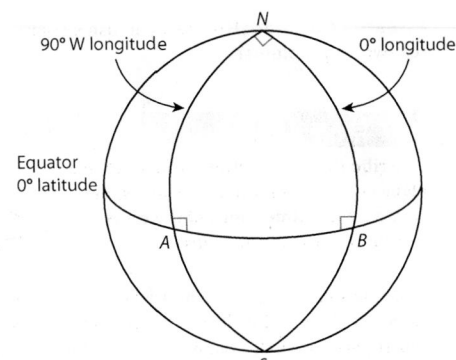

1. Triangle *ABN* is formed by the Equator and two lines of longitude. It is called a spherical triangle. Describe the ways that it is similar to a plane triangle and the ways that it differs.

2. Find the area of spherical triangle *ABN*. Explain how you found the area. Use 7912 miles as the diameter of the Earth. Use 3.14 for π.

1. **Sample answer:** Like a plane triangle, a spherical triangle has three sides and three angles. Unlike a plane triangle, its sides and its interior are curved, and the sum of the measures of its angles is not 180° (for triangle *ABN* it is 270°).

2. Because $\angle N$ measures 90°, there are three other triangles congruent to it in the Northern Hemisphere, with northern vertices at the North Pole, southern boundaries on the Equator, and sides of longitude 180° W, 270° W, and 0°. For similar reasons there are four more triangles congruent to it in the Southern Hemisphere. So, the area of triangle *ABN* is one-eighth of the surface area of the Earth.

   Earth radius $= 0.5 \times 7912 = 3956$ mi

   SA (Earth) $= 4\pi r^2 = 4(3.14)(3956)^2 = 196{,}563{,}196.2$ mi²

   SA (triangle *ABN*) $= 196{,}563{,}196.2 \div 8 \approx 24{,}570{,}400$ mi²

EXTENSION ACTIVITY

Pose this problem: Where on the Earth's surface can you walk one mile south, one mile east, and one mile north, and end up where you started? The easiest answer is the North Pole, but in fact there are an infinite number of places where it is possible. Have students try to find them on their own or, if necessary, by researching what is sometimes called "the Bear Problem" on the Internet. Surprisingly, a whole class of answers takes place near the *South* Pole. Start at any point on the circle that is $1 + \frac{1}{2\pi}$ miles north of the South Pole. Walk 1 mile south to the circle, 1 mile east (taking you around the circle), and 1 mile north to your starting point.

CONNECT VOCABULARY EL

The word *longitude* is derived from the Latin word for length. The word *latitude* is derived from the Latin word for breadth.

INTEGRATE MATHEMATICAL PRACTICES
Focus on Reasoning

MP.2 Quito, Ecuador is located approximately on the equator at 78.8° west longitude. Kampala, Uganda is located approximately on the equator at 32.6° east longitude. Find the distance between the cities. Explain your method. About 7701 mi; distance in degrees between the cities: 78.8° + 32.6° = 111.4°; fraction of equator represented by that distance $= \frac{111.4}{360} \approx 0.31$; circumference of equator ≈ diameter × 3.14 = 24,844 miles; Quito-Kampala distance ≈ 0.31 × 24,844 ≈ 7702 miles

Scoring Rubric

2 points: Student correctly solves the problem and explains his/her reasoning.

1 point: Student shows good understanding of the problem but does not fully solve or explain his/her reasoning.

0 points: Student does not demonstrate understanding of the problem.

Surface Area of Spheres   **1030**

Study Guide Review

ASSESSMENT AND INTERVENTION

Assign or customize module reviews.

MODULE PERFORMANCE TASK

COMMON CORE

Mathematical Practices: MP.1, MP.2, MP.4, MP.6
G-MG.A.1

SUPPORTING STUDENT REASONING

Students should begin this problem by focusing on what information they will need. Here are some issues they might bring up.

- **The shape and dimensions of the fuel tank:** Students can research this or you can tell them to assume the shape is a cylinder with a cone on the top, with the height of the cylinder 4 times the height of the cone.

- **The slant height of the cone:** Students can research this or use the Pythagorean Theorem.

- **How to find the surface area of the fuel tank:** Students can use a modified surface area formula for a right cylinder, $A = 2\pi rh + \pi r^2$ (only one end is closed), and for a right cone (the cone has no base), $A = \pi rl$, where l is the slant height.

- **The weight and coverage of a gallon of paint:** Students can research this or use the following: one gallon of paint may cover 300 square feet and weigh 10 pounds.

Essential Question: How can you use visualizing solids to solve real-world problems?

© Houghton Mifflin Harcourt Publishing Company

Key Vocabulary
net *(red)*
surface area *(área de la superficie)*
regular pyramid *(pirámide regular)*
right cone *(cono recto)*

KEY EXAMPLE   (Lesson 19.1)

Describe the cross section formed when a plane cuts through the center of a sphere. Compare the dimensions of the cross section to those of the figure.

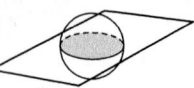

Since the sphere and the plane are both rotationally symmetric about the perpendicular axis, the cross section is also rotationally symmetric and is therefore a circle. Since it passes through the sphere's widest part, the circle's radius is equal to the radius of the sphere.

KEY EXAMPLE   (Lesson 19.2)

Find the surface area of a right prism with length of 10, width of 5, and height of 4.

$L = Ph$	Apply the lateral area formula.
$L = (2 \cdot 10 + 2 \cdot 5)4 = 120$	Substitute and solve.
$S = L + 2B$	Apply the surface area formula.
$S = 120 + 2 \cdot 10 \cdot 5 = 220$	Substitute and solve.

KEY EXAMPLE   (Lesson 19.3)

Find the surface area of a right cone with radius 12 and height 16.

$l^2 = 12^2 + 16^2$	Use the Pythagorean Theorem to find the slant height.
$l = 20$	Solve.
$L = \pi rl$	Find the lateral area.
$L = \pi(12)(20) = 240\pi$	Substitute and multiply.
$S = L + \pi r^2$	Find the surface area.
$S = 240\pi + \pi(12)^2 = 384\pi$	Substitute and solve.

KEY EXAMPLE   (Lesson 19.4)

Find the surface area of a sphere with radius 14.

$S = 4\pi r^2$	Use the formula for surface area of a sphere.
$S = 4\pi(14)^2 = 784\pi$	Substitute and solve.

SCAFFOLDING SUPPORT

- Encourage students to see the fuel tank as a composite three-dimensional shape.

- Students can use the figure to estimate the height of the cylindrical portion of the tank as a percentage of the total height, about 80%, and use this assumption to calculate the dimensions of the two shapes forming the tank.

- Remind students that if they use a cylinder and cone to model the tank, only one end of the cylinder will be covered in paint.

EXERCISES

Determine if it is possible to form the following shapes by rotating a two-dimensional shape around the *y*-axis. If so, state the shape needed to do so. *(Lesson 19.1)*

1. sphere   Yes, semicircle

2. right prism   No

3. cylinder   Yes, rectangle

Find the exact surface area of the following shapes. *(Lessons 19.2, 19.3, 19.4)*

4. right prism with length 3, width 4, and height 5   94

5. cylinder with radius 8 and height 3 176π

6. regular pyramid with side length 12 and height 8   384

7. right cone with diameter 8 and height 3 36π

8. sphere with radius 8 256π

9. hemisphere with radius 9 162π

MODULE PERFORMANCE TASK

How Much Does the Paint on a Space Shuttle Weigh?

NASA used to paint the fuel tanks for the Space Shuttle with white latex paint, but they decided to stop painting them because of the extra weight that the paint added. Just how much could that paint weigh?

The photo gives you a good sense of the shape of the fuel tank. According to NASA, the tank has a height of 153.8 feet and a diameter of 27.6 feet. Use one or more of the formulas you have learned to find the surface area of the tank. Then use your calculation to come up with your best estimate of the weight of the paint required to cover the fuel tank.

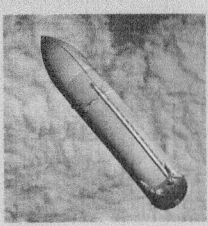

Start by listing in the space below any additional information you will need to solve the problem. Then use your own paper to complete the task. Be sure to write down all of your assumptions and data. Use tables, diagrams, words, or numbers to explain how you came to your conclusion.

DISCUSSION OPPORTUNITIES

- What other considerations may need to be made when finding the weight of the paint and how much paint was used?

- Why may there be more than one answer to this problem?

SAMPLE SOLUTION

Assumptions:

One gallon of paint weighs 10 pounds and will cover 300 square feet.

Only one coat of paint will be used.

The fuel tank can be modeled as a composite of two three-dimensional solids, a cylinder and a cone.

Cone height is 20% of tank height.

Method:

Find a general expression for the lateral surface area of the fuel tank.

A = curved side of cylinder

   + bottom of cylinder + lateral area of cone

   $= 2\pi rh + \pi r^2 + \pi rl$

Use the given values and assumptions to determine the dimensions of the tank. Height of the cylinder:

$0.8(153.8) \approx 123$ ft

Height of the cone:

$0.2(153.8) \approx 30.8$ ft

Slant height of the cone:

Use the Pythagorean Theorem with half the diameter of the cone, 13.8 ft, and the calculated height of 30.8 ft.

$x^2 = (13.8)^2 + (30.8)^2 \rightarrow x \approx 33.8$ ft

Calculate the surface area:

$A = 2\pi (13.8)(123) + \pi(13.8)^2$

$+ \pi(13.8)33.8 \approx 12{,}700$ ft^2

Use this value, the amount of surface area and weight per gallon of paint, to find the total weight of the paint.

$(12{,}700 \text{ ft}^2)\left(\dfrac{1 \text{ gallon}}{300 \text{ ft}^2}\right)\left(\dfrac{10 \text{ lbs}}{\text{gallon}}\right) \approx 420$ lbs

Assessment Rubric

2 points: Student correctly solves the problem and explains his/her reasoning.

1 point: Student shows good understanding of the problem but does not fully solve or explain.

0 points: Student does not demonstrate understanding of the problem.

Ready to Go On?

ASSESS MASTERY

Use the assessment on this page to determine if students have mastered the concepts and standards covered in this module.

ASSESSMENT AND INTERVENTION

Access Ready to Go On? assessment online, and receive instant scoring, feedback, and customized intervention or enrichment.

ADDITIONAL RESOURCES

Response to Intervention Resources

- Reteach Worksheets

Differentiated Instruction Resources

- Reading Strategies **EL**
- Success for English Learners **EL**
- Challenge Worksheets

Assessment Resources

- Leveled Module Quizzes

(Ready) to Go On?

• Online Homework
• Hints and Help
• Extra Practice

19.1–19.4 Visualizing Solids

State the figure obtained when rotating the figure about an axis along its largest side, and find the exact surface area of the resulting figure.

1. A rectangle with length 18 and width 14. *(Lesson 19.1)*

The widths of the rectangle are perpendicular to the axis, so they will trace out congruent circles around the axis. One length of the rectangle is on the axis, the other will connect the two circles together, forming a cylinder $S = L + 2\pi r^2$, where $L = 2\pi rh$. Substitute values to solve for L, $L = 2\pi (14)(18) = 504\pi$, and then substitute the values to find the surface area, $S = 504\pi + 2\pi(14)^2 = 896\pi$.

Find the exact surface area of the following. *(Lessons 19.2, 19.3, 19.4)*

2.

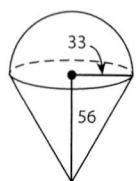

The composite figure is a cone and hemisphere. Start by finding the surface area of the hemisphere, $\frac{1}{2} S_1 = \frac{1}{2} 4\pi r^2$. Substitute the values in to find the hemisphere's surface area, $S_1 = \frac{1}{2} 4\pi(33)^2 = 2178\pi$. Next, find the lateral area of the cone. Find the slant height using the Pythagorean Theorem, $l^2 = (33)^2 + (56)^2$. Solving for l, $l = 65$. Now use the slant height to find the lateral area of the cone, $L = \pi(33)(65) = 2145\pi$. Finally, add the two surface areas together. $S = 2178\pi + 2145\pi = 4323\pi$.

ESSENTIAL QUESTION

3. When finding the surface area of a composite figure, why is it often necessary to subtract sides common to each individual shape?

Answers may vary. Sample: Identifiable shapes that are easy to find the surface area of in composite figures will often have portions that overlap with each other. This means that after adding the surface areas of the individual shapes, it is necessary to subtract sides common to both shapes to get the true surface area.

© Houghton Mifflin Harcourt Publishing Company

COMMON CORE **Common Core Standards**

Lesson	Items	Content Standards	Mathematical Practices
19.1	1	**G-MGD.B.4**	**MP.4**
19.3, 19.4	2	**G-MG.A.1**	**MP.7**

MODULE 19
MIXED REVIEW

Assessment Readiness

1. A rectangular prism has a surface area of 922 square units. Consider each set of dimensions. Could these be the dimensions of the right prism?
Select Yes or No for A–C.

   A. length = 23, width = 7, height = 10   ● Yes   ○ No
   B. length = 17, width = 8, height = 13   ● Yes   ○ No
   C. length = 10, width = 9, height = 12   ○ Yes   ● No

2. A sphere has a radius of 27. Choose True or False for each statement.
   A. The surface area of the sphere is
   729π square units.   ○ True   ● False
   B. The volume of the sphere is
   $26{,}244\pi$ cubic units.   ● True   ○ False
   C. The surface area of the sphere is
   2916π square units.   ● True   ○ False

3. $\triangle ABC$ maps to $\triangle DEF$ with the transformation $(x, y) \rightarrow \left(\frac{1}{4}x, \frac{1}{4}y\right)$. Choose True or False for each statement.
   A. If $BC = 8$, $EF = 2$.   ● True   ○ False
   B. If $BC = 4$, $EF = 16$.   ○ True   ● False
   C. If $BC = 20$, $EF = 5$.   ● True   ○ False

4. What solid is formed when rotating a square about a horizontal or vertical axis through the center of the square? Does this solid have a square for a base? Does this solid have a square for a cross-section?
   cylinder; no; yes

5. Draw the net of a right cylinder with a radius of 2 and a height of 6, and then explain if this answer is the only possible net for this cylinder.
   Sample Answer: No; any net that has a
   rectangle with length 6 and width 4π with two
   circles with radius 2 anywhere on either side
   will create a cylinder with similar dimensions.

   6 ft

   2 ft   2 ft

   4π ft

© Houghton Mifflin Harcourt Publishing Company

Assessment Readiness

ASSESSMENT AND INTERVENTION

Personal Math Trainer

Assign ready-made or customized practice tests to prepare students for high-stakes tests.

ADDITIONAL RESOURCES

Assessment Resources

• Leveled Module Quizzes: Modified, B

AVOID COMMON ERRORS

Item 5   Some students will reverse the length and width of the rectangle when labeling their nets. Remind students that the side of the rectangle touching the circles will always be equal to the circumference of the circles.

COMMON CORE   **Common Core Standards**

Lesson	Items	Content Standards	Mathematical Practices
19.2	1	**G-MG.A.1**	**MP.2**
19.4, 18.4	2*	**G-MG.A.1**	**MP.2**
11.3	3*	**G-SRT.A.1**	**MP.7**
19.1	4	**G-GMD.B.4**	**MP.2**
19.1	5	**G-GMD.B.4**	**MP.6**

* Item integrates mixed review concepts from previous modules or a previous course.

MODULE 20

Modeling and Problem Solving

ESSENTIAL QUESTION:

Answer: Modeling is useful for solving any real-world problem involving objects that are too large or unwieldy to manipulate or measure directly.

PROFESSIONAL DEVELOPMENT VIDEO

Professional Development Video

STEM Consultant Michael DiSpezio offers engaging suggestions and activities for integrating science, technology, and engineering into the math classroom.

Professional Development
my.hrw.com

MODULE 20

Modeling and Problem Solving

Essential Question: How can you use modeling to solve real-world problems?

LESSON 20.1
Scale Factor

LESSON 20.2
Modeling and Density

LESSON 20.3
Problem Solving with Constraints

© Houghton Mifflin Harcourt Publishing Company · Image Credits: ©Doug Berry/iStockPhoto.com

REAL WORLD VIDEO
Check out how GPS coordinates can be used to calculate the area of a region of the Earth's surface.

MODULE PERFORMANCE TASK PREVIEW

Population Density

It's easy to find the population density of a region once you know the population and the area. What's not always so easy is counting the population (New York City, 8,336,697 in 2012) and calculating the area (New York City, 302.64 square miles). Of course, there are some regions whose populations are much smaller than that of New York City and whose areas are easier to calculate. You'll find the population density of one of them after you complete this module.

Module 20   **1035**

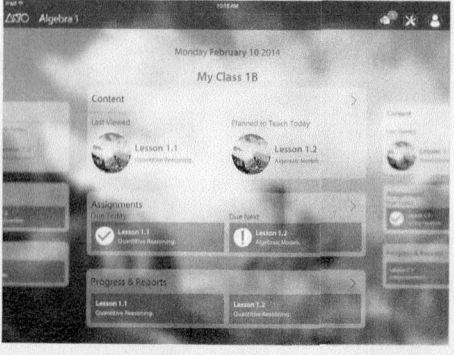

DIGITAL TEACHER EDITION

Access a full suite of teaching resources when and where you need them:

- Access content online or offline
- Customize lessons to share with your class
- Communicate with your students in real-time
- View student grades and data instantly to target your instruction where it is needed most

PERSONAL MATH TRAINER
Assessment and Intervention

Assign automatically graded homework, quizzes, tests, and intervention activities. Prepare your students with updated, Common Core-aligned practice tests.

Are (YOU) Ready?

Complete these exercises to review skills you will need for this module.

Scale Factor and Scale Drawings

- Online Homework
- Hints and Help
- Extra Practice

Example 1

The width on an architectural plan for a rectangular room is 8 cm. The actual room will be 12 ft wide and 18 ft long. How long is the length of the room on the plan?

$$\frac{\text{plan width}}{\text{actual width}} = \frac{\text{plan length}}{\text{actual length}} \rightarrow \frac{8}{12} = \frac{x}{18}$$

$$x = \frac{18 \cdot 8}{12} = 12 \quad \text{Multiply and simplify.}$$

The plan length is 12 cm.

Find the missing length for a rectangular room.

1. plan length: 4 in.
actual width: 28 ft
actual length: 32 ft
Find the plan width.

_3.5 in._

2. plan width: 6 in.
plan length: 8 in.
actual length: 24 yd
Find the actual width.

_18 yd_

3. plan width: 2.4 cm
plan length: 9 cm
actual width: 3.6 m
Find the actual length.

_13.5 m_

Volume

Example 2

The volume of a cylinder is 42 cm³. Its height is 3.5 cm. Find the diameter of the cylinder.

$$V = \pi r^2 h \quad \text{Write the formula.}$$

$$42 = \pi r^2 (3.5) \quad \text{Substitute.}$$

$$r^2 = \frac{42}{3.5\pi} = \frac{12}{\pi} \quad \text{Solve for } r^2.$$

$$r \approx 1.954 \quad \text{Solve for } r \text{ to the nearest thousandth.}$$

$$2r \approx 3.91 \quad \text{Find the diameter.}$$

The diameter of the cylinder is about 3.91 cm.

Find the missing measure of the cylinder to the nearest hundredth.

4. diameter: 7 ft
height: 2 ft
Find the volume.

76.97 ft³

5. radius: 10 in.
volume: 490 in³
Find the height.

_1.56 in._

6. diameter: 1.2 m
volume: 4.8 m³
Find the height.

_4.24 m_

Are You Ready?

ASSESS READINESS

Use the assessment on this page to determine if students need strategic or intensive intervention for the module's prerequisite skills.

ASSESSMENT AND INTERVENTION

TIER 1, TIER 2, TIER 3 SKILLS

Personal Math Trainer will automatically create a standards-based, personalized intervention assignment for your students, targeting each student's individual needs!

ADDITIONAL RESOURCES

See the table below for a full list of intervention resources available for this module.

Response to Intervention Resources also includes:

- Tier 2 Skill Pre-Tests for each Module
- Tier 2 Skill Post-Tests for each skill

Response to Intervention			*Differentiated Instruction*
Tier 1 Lesson Intervention Worksheets	**Tier 2** Strategic Intervention Skills Intervention Worksheets	**Tier 3** Intensive Intervention Worksheets available online	
Reteach 20.1 Reteach 20.2 Reteach 20.3	5 Area of Composite Figures 22 Scale Factor and Scale Drawings 27 Volume	Building Block Skills 9, 10, 11, 14, 30, 31, 35, 48, 50, 73, 77, 80, 83, 95, 106, 112	Challenge worksheets Extend the Math Lesson Activities in TE

Scale Factor

Common Core Math Standards

The student is expected to:

 G-GMD.A.3

Use volume formulas for cylinders, pyramids, cones, and spheres to solve problems. Also G-GPE.B.7

Mathematical Practices

 MP.2 Reasoning

To describe how changes in linear dimensions affect the area and

Language Objective

Explain to a partner the effect of a proportional dimension change on the area and perimeter of a geometric figure.

ENGAGE

Essential Question: How does multiplying one or more of the dimensions of a figure affect its attributes?

When you multiply one dimension of a figure by a scale factor, the area is also multiplied by that factor. You cannot predict how the perimeter changes. When you multiply both dimensions of a figure by the same scale factor, the perimeter is multiplied by that factor and the area is multiplied by the square of that factor.

PREVIEW: LESSON PERFORMANCE TASK

View the Engage section online. Discuss the photograph, and ask students to speculate on the purpose of the image. Then preview the Lesson Performance Task.

Name_____ Class_____ Date_____

20.1 Scale Factor

Essential Question: How does multiplying one or more of the dimensions of a figure affect its attributes?

Resource Locker

⊘ Explore Exploring Effects of Changing Dimensions on Perimeter and Area

Changes made to the dimensions of a figure can affect the perimeter and the area.

Use the figure to investigate how changing one or more dimensions of the figure affect its perimeter and area.

Ⓐ Apply the transformation $(x, y) \rightarrow (3x, y)$. Find the perimeter and the area.

Original Dimensions	Dimensions after $(x, y) \rightarrow (3x, y)$
$P = 6 + 4\sqrt{2}$	$P = 18 + 4\sqrt{10}$
$A = 6$	$A = 18$

Ⓑ Apply the transformation $(x, y) \rightarrow (x, 3y)$. Find the perimeter and the area.

Original Dimensions	Dimensions after $(x, y) \rightarrow (x, 3y)$
$P = 6 + 4\sqrt{2}$	$P = 6 + 4\sqrt{10}$
$A = 6$	$A = 18$

Ⓒ Apply the transformation $(x, y) \rightarrow (3x, 3y)$. Find the perimeter and the area.

Original Dimensions	Dimensions after $(x, y) \rightarrow (3x, 3y)$
$P = 6 + 4\sqrt{2}$	$P = 18 + 12\sqrt{2}$
$A = 6$	$A = 54$

© Houghton Mifflin Harcourt Publishing Company · Image Credits: ©Rex Features/AP Images

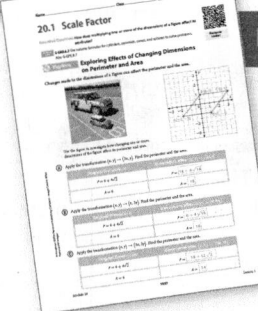

HARDCOVER PAGES 867–874

Turn to these pages to find this lesson in the hardcover student edition.

1. Describe the changes that occurred in Steps A and B. Did the perimeter or area change by a constant factor?
    Possible answer: When only one dimension was changed by a factor of 3, the area was

    changed by a factor of 3. There was no consistent rule for the change in perimeter.

2. Describe the changes that occurred in Step C. Did the perimeter or area change by a constant factor?
    Possible answer: When both dimensions were changed by a factor of 3, the perimeter

    changed by a factor of 3 and the area changed by a factor of 3^2 or 9.

⊘ Explain 1   Describe a Non-Proportional Dimension Change

In a non-proportional dimension change, you do not use the same factor to change each dimension of a figure.

Example 1   Find the area of the figure.

Ⓐ Find the area of the parallelogram. Then multiply the length by 2 and determine the new area. Describe the changes that took place.

Original Figure	Transformed Figure
$A = bh = 6 \cdot 5 = 30 \text{ ft}^2$	$A = bh = 12 \cdot 5 = 60 \text{ ft}^2$

When the length of the parallelogram changes by a factor of 2, the area changes by a factor of 2.

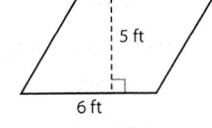

5 ft

6 ft

Ⓑ Find the area of the trapezoid. Then multiply the height by 0.5 and determine the new area. Describe the changes that took place.

Original Figure $A = \frac{1}{2}(b_1 + b_2)h = \boxed{\frac{1}{2}(3 + 12)8 = 60}$

Transformed Figure $A = \frac{1}{2}(b_1 + b_2)h = \boxed{\frac{1}{2}(3 + 12)4 = 30}$

When the height of the trapezoid changes by a factor of ____0.5____, the

area of the trapezoid changes by a factor of ____0.5____.

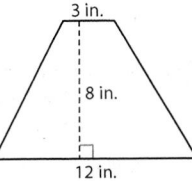

3 in.

8 in.

12 in.

3. **Discussion** When a non-proportional change is applied to the dimensions of a figure, does the perimeter change in a predictable way?
    Possible answer: No. Since the change to the dimensions is non-proportional, not all of the

    lengths are altered. Therefore, the perimeter will not change by the factor of the change.

4. Find the area of a triangle with vertices $(-5, -2)$, $(-5, 7)$, and $(3, 1)$. Then apply the transformation $(x, y) \rightarrow (x, 4y)$ and determine the new area. Describe the changes that took place.
    Possible answer: The original area is $A = \frac{1}{2}bh = \frac{1}{2}(9 \cdot 8) = 36$. After the transformation the

    area is $A = \frac{1}{2}bh = \frac{1}{2}(36 \cdot 8) = 144$. When the base length changes by a factor of 4, the area

    changes by a factor of 4.

Module 20   1038   Lesson 1

© Houghton Mifflin Harcourt Publishing Company

PROFESSIONAL DEVELOPMENT

Math Background

The use of scale factors and scale drawings is an important application of mathematics. If a figure in the plane is transformed proportionally with a nonzero scale factor of k, then the area of the transformed figure is k^2 times the area of the original figure, and the perimeter is k times the perimeter of the original figure. If only one dimension is changed by a factor of k, then the area is changed by a factor of k, and the change in the perimeter is not predictable.

EXPLORE

Exploring the Effects of Changing Dimensions on Perimeter and Area

INTEGRATE TECHNOLOGY

Students have the option of doing the Explore activity either in the book or online.

QUESTIONING STRATEGIES

? If all dimensions of a figure are changed by a factor of a, how does this change the area? the perimeter? The area changes by a factor of a^2; the perimeter changes by a factor of a.

INTEGRATE MATHEMATICAL PRACTICES
Focus on Reasoning

MP.2 If only one dimension of a geometric figure is changed by a factor of a, the effect on the perimeter is not as predictable as it is for area, which also changes by the same factor, a. This is because the perimeter total depends on which dimension is changed. For example, if a rectangle has dimensions of 2 in. and 3 in., doubling the 2 in. side makes the perimeter increase by 4 in. Doubling the 3 in. side, however, makes the perimeter increase by 6 in.

EXPLAIN 1

Describe a Non-Proportional Dimension Change

QUESTIONING STRATEGIES

? If one dimension of a non-circular figure is changed by a factor of a, how does this change the area? The area changes by a factor of a.

Some students may think that changing one dimension by a factor of a also changes the perimeter by a factor of a. Point out that the change in perimeter is not predictable when only one dimension is changed. Have students verify this with examples.

INTEGRATE MATHEMATICAL PRACTICES

Focus on Communication

MP.3 As you present each concept, ask students why they think each change in a dimension of a figure has a certain effect on its area. For instance, lead students to see that doubling the height of a rectangle doubles the rectangle's area because $b(2h) = 2(bh) = 2A$.

EXPLAIN 2

Describe a Proportional Dimension Change

INTEGRATE MATHEMATICAL PRACTICES

Focus on Reasoning

MP.2 Point out that if the radius of a circle or the side length of a square is changed, the size of the entire figure changes proportionally.

QUESTIONING STRATEGIES

? If the dimensions of a figure are changed proportionally, how does the area change? The area increases by the square of the dimension change.

---

5. Find the area of the figure. Then multiply the width by 5 and determine the new area. Describe the changes that took place.

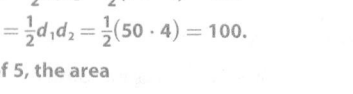

Possible answer: The original area is $A = \frac{1}{2}d_1d_2 = \frac{1}{2}(10 \cdot 4) = 20$.

After the transformation the area is $A = \frac{1}{2}d_1d_2 = \frac{1}{2}(50 \cdot 4) = 100$.

When the width changes by a factor of 5, the area changes by a factor of 5.

⊘ Explain 2 Describe a Proportional Dimension Change

In a proportional dimension change, you use the same factor to change each dimension of a figure.

Example 2 Find the area and perimeter of a circle.

Ⓐ Find the circumference and area of the circle. Then multiply the radius by 3 and find the new circumference and area. Describe the changes that took place.

Original Figure $C = 2\pi(4) = 8\pi$

$A = \pi(4)^2 = 16\pi$

Transformed Figure $C = 2\pi(12) = 24\pi$

$A = \pi(12)^2 = 144\pi$

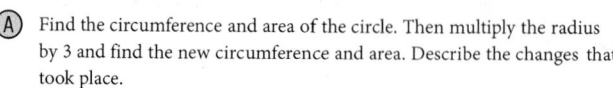

The circumference changes by a factor of 3, and the area changes by a factor of 9 or 3^2.

Ⓑ Find the perimeter and area of the figure. Then multiply the length and height by $\frac{1}{3}$ and find the new perimeter and area. Describe the changes that took place.

Original Figure

$P = 4(6\sqrt{2}) = 24\sqrt{2}$

$A = \frac{1}{2}d_1d_2 = \frac{1}{2}(12 \cdot 12) = 72$

Transformed Figure

$P = 4(2\sqrt{2}) = 8\sqrt{2}$

$A = \frac{1}{2}d_1d_2 = \frac{1}{2}(4 \cdot 4) = 8$

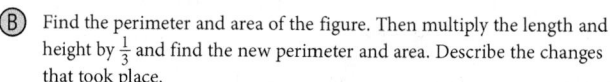

The perimeter changes by a factor of $\frac{1}{3}$, and the area changes by a factor of $\frac{1}{9}$ or $\frac{1}{3^2}$.

Reflect

6. Fill in the table to describe the effect on perimeter (or circumference) and area when the dimensions of a figure are changed proportionally.

Possible answer:

Effects of Changing Dimensions Proportionally		
Change in Dimensions	**Perimeter or Circumference**	**Area**
All dimensions multiplied by a	Changes by a factor of a	Changes by a factor of a^2

COLLABORATIVE LEARNING

Peer-to-Peer Activity

Have students work with partners to explore the effects of dimension changes. Have each student write two problems—one that shows a proportional dimension change to a triangle and another that shows a non-proportional dimension change to a parallelogram. Then have the partner find the area and perimeter of the new figure (if possible) and critique the solutions.

7. Find the circumference and area of the circle. Then multiply the radius by 0.25 and find the new circumference and area. Describe the changes that took place.

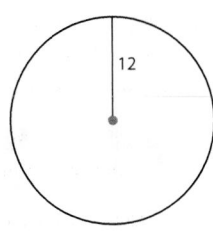

Possible answer: The original circumference is $C = 2\pi(12) = 24\pi$, and the original area is $A = \pi(12)^2 = 144\pi$. After the transformation, the circumference is $C = 2\pi(3) = 6\pi$, and the area is $A = \pi(3)^2 = 9\pi$. The circumference changes by a factor of 0.25, and the area changes by a factor of $(0.25)^2 = 0.0625$.

⚙ **Explain 3** **Describe a Proportional Dimension Change for a Solid**

In a proportional dimension change to a solid, you use the same factor to change each dimension of a figure.

Example 3 Find the volume of the composite solid.

(A) A company is planning to create a similar version of this storage tank, a cylinder with hemispherical caps at each end. Find the volume and surface area of the original tank. Then multiply all the dimensions by 2 and find the new volume and surface area. Describe the changes that took place.

The volume of the solid is $V = \pi r^2 h + \frac{4}{3}\pi r^3$, and the surface area is $S = 2\pi rh + 4\pi r^2$.

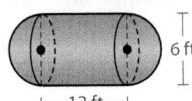

6 ft
⊢— 12 ft —⊣

Original Solid

$V = \pi(3)^2(12) + \frac{4}{3}\pi(3)^3 = 144\pi$ cu. ft.

$S = 2\pi(3 \cdot 12) + 4\pi(3)^2 = 108\pi$ sq. ft.

Transformed Solid

$V = \pi(6)^2(24) + \frac{4}{3}\pi(6)^3 = 1152\pi$ cu. ft.

$S = 2\pi(6 \cdot 24) + 4\pi(6)^2 = 432\pi$ sq. ft.

The volume changes by a factor of 8, and the surface area changes by a factor of 4.

(B) A children's toy is shaped like a hemisphere with a conical top. A company decides to create a smaller version of the toy. Find the volume and surface area of the original toy. Then multiply all dimensions by $\frac{2}{3}$ and find the new volume and surface area. Describe the changes that took place.

The volume of the solid is $V = \frac{1}{3}\pi r^2 h + \frac{2}{3}\pi r^3$,

and the surface area is $S = \pi r \sqrt{r^2 + h^2} + 2\pi r^2$.

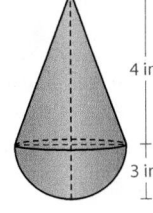

4 in.

3 in.

Original Solid

$V = \boxed{\frac{1}{3}\pi(3)^2 4 + \frac{2}{3}\pi(3)^3 = 30\pi}$ cu. in.

$S = \boxed{\pi(3)\sqrt{3^2 + 4^2} + 2\pi(3)^2 = 33\pi}$ sq. in.

Transformed Solid

$V = \boxed{\frac{1}{3}\pi(2)^2\left(\frac{8}{3}\right) + \frac{2}{3}\pi(2)^3 = \frac{80}{9}\pi}$ cu. in.

$S = \boxed{\pi(2)\sqrt{(2)^2 + \left(\frac{8}{3}\right)^2} + 2\pi(2)^2 = \frac{44}{3}\pi}$ sq. in.

The volume changes by a factor of $\frac{8}{27}$, and the surface area changes by a factor of $\frac{4}{9}$.

EXPLAIN 3

Describe a Proportional Dimension Change for a Solid

INTEGRATE MATHEMATICAL PRACTICES

Focus on Reasoning

MP.2 Point out that if a solid figure has a non-proportional dimension change, then the volume changes by the product of the factors of each dimension change. The surface area does not have a predictable change, just as perimeter does not have a predictable change for a two-dimensional figure.

QUESTIONING STRATEGIES

❓ If the dimensions of a solid figure are changed proportionally, how does the volume change? How does the surface area change? The volume increases by the cube of the dimension change; the surface area increases by the square of the dimension change.

DIFFERENTIATE INSTRUCTION

Modeling

Have students use blocks to study how the volume of three-dimensional figures changes if there is a change to the dimensions. Have student groups create a rectangular prism with blocks and give the volume, which equals the number of blocks. Then have them increase the dimensions of the prism proportionally and count the blocks (the volume increases by the third power of the dimension change). Ask them also to increase only one dimension of the original prism and explore how the volume changes.

ELABORATE

QUESTIONING STRATEGIES

? How does changing the dimensions of a figure proportionally by a factor of k affect the area?
The area is changed by a factor of k^2.

? What does a change to the area of a two-dimensional figure by a factor of k mean in terms of the perimeter? You cannot determine how it changes the perimeter.

SUMMARIZE THE LESSON

? What happens to a figure's area when a dimension of the figure is changed? What happens when two dimensions are changed? one dimension: area changes by the same factor as the dimension change and perimeter is not predictable; two dimensions: area changes by the square of the dimension change; perimeter changes by the same factor as the dimension change

---

Reflect

8. Fill in the table to describe the effect on surface area and volume when the dimensions of a figure are changed proportionally.

Possible answer:

Effects of Changing Dimensions Proportionally		
Change in Dimensions	**Surface Area**	**Volume**
All dimensions multiplied by a	Changes by a factor of a^2	Changes by a factor of a^3

Your Turn

9. A farmer has made a scale model of a new grain silo. Find the volume and surface area of the model. Use the scale ratio 1 : 36 to find the volume and surface area of the silo. Compare the volumes and surface areas relative to the scale ratio. Be consistent with units of measurement.

The volume of the solid is $V = \frac{1}{3}\pi r^2 h + \pi r^2 h$ (same height for cylinder

and cone), and the surface area is $S = \pi r \sqrt{r^2 + h^2} + 2\pi rh + \pi r^2$. For

the model, the volume is 64π cu. in., and the surface area is 60π sq. in.

For the silo, the volume is 2985984π cu. in. and the surface area is 77760π sq. in.

The volume changes by a factor of $46656 = 36^3$, and the surface area

changes by a factor of $1296 = 36^2$.

Elaborate

10. Two square pyramids are similar. If the ratio of a pair of corresponding edges is $a : b$, what is the ratio of their volumes? What is the ratio of their surface areas?
The ratio of their volumes is $a^3 : b^3$, and the ratio of their surface areas is $a^2 : b^2$.

11. **Essential Question Check-In** How is a non-proportional dimension change different from a proportional dimension change?
Possible answer: With non-proportional dimension changes, the effect on perimeter, area, and volume may not be clearly defined by a scale factor.

LANGAUGE SUPPORT **EL**

Connect Vocabulary

To help students understand what a *proportional dimension change* is, define *proportional* as *having the same ratio*, and a *dimension* as *a measurement of length in one direction*. So, a proportional dimension change is a change in each length measurement such that the lengths maintain the same ratio to each other.

Evaluate: Homework and Practice

A trapezoid has the vertices $(0, 0)$, $(4, 0)$, $(4, 4)$, and $(-3, 4)$.

1. Describe the effect on the area if only the x-coordinates of the vertices are multiplied by $\frac{1}{2}$.

Original Figure

$(0, 0)$, $(4, 0)$, $(4, 4)$, and $(-3, 4)$

Original Area

$A = \dfrac{(b_1 + b_2)h}{2} = \dfrac{(4 + 7)4}{2} = 22$

Transformed Figure

$(0, 0)$, $(2, 0)$, $(2, 4)$, and $(-1.5, 4)$

$A = \dfrac{(b_1 + b_2)h}{2} = \dfrac{(2 + 3.5)4}{2} = 11$

$\dfrac{11}{22} = \dfrac{1}{2}$

The area is multiplied by $\frac{1}{2}$.

2. Describe the effect on the area if only the y-coordinates of the vertices are multiplied by $\frac{1}{2}$.

Original Figure

$(0, 0)$, $(4, 0)$, $(4, 4)$, and $(-3, 4)$

Original Area

$A = \dfrac{(b_1 + b_2)h}{2} = \dfrac{(4 + 7)4}{2} = 22$

Transformed Figure

$(0, 0)$, $(4, 0)$, $(4, 2)$, and $(-3, 2)$

$A = \dfrac{(b_1 + b_2)h}{2} = \dfrac{(4 + 7)2}{2} = 11$

$\dfrac{11}{22} = \dfrac{1}{2}$

The area is multiplied by $\frac{1}{2}$.

3. Describe the effect on the area if both the x- and y-coordinates of the vertices are multiplied by $\frac{1}{2}$.

Original Figure

$(0, 0)$, $(4, 0)$, $(4, 4)$, and $(-3, 4)$

Original Area

$A = \dfrac{(b_1 + b_2)h}{2} = \dfrac{(4 + 7)4}{2} = 22$

Transformed Figure

$(0, 0)$, $(2, 0)$, $(2, 2)$, and $(-1.5, 2)$

$A = \dfrac{(b_1 + b_2)h}{2} = \dfrac{(2 + 3.5)2}{2} = 5.5$

$\dfrac{5.5}{22} = \dfrac{11}{44} = \dfrac{1}{4}$

The area is multiplied by $\frac{1}{4}$.

4. Describe the effect on the area if the x-coordinates are multiplied by 2 and y-coordinates are multiplied by $\frac{1}{2}$.

Original Figure

$(0, 0)$, $(4, 0)$, $(4, 4)$, and $(-3, 4)$

Original Area

$A = \dfrac{(b_1 + b_2)h}{2} = \dfrac{(4 + 7)4}{2} = 22$

Transformed Figure

$(0, 0)$, $(8, 0)$, $(8, 2)$, and $(-6, 2)$

$A = \dfrac{(b_1 + b_2)h}{2} = \dfrac{(8 + 14)2}{2} = 22$

$\dfrac{22}{22} = 1$

The area doesn't change. It would have been doubled by the change in the x-coordinates and halved by the change in the y-coordinates.

Exercise	Depth of Knowledge (D.O.K.)	COMMON CORE Mathematical Practices
1	**1** Recall of Information	**MP.5** Using Tools
2–4	**3** Strategic Thinking	**MP.2** Reasoning
5–12	**3** Strategic Thinking	**MP.5** Using Tools
13	**1** Recall of Information	**MP.2** Reasoning
14–16	**2** Skills/Concepts	**MP.4** Modeling
17–18	**1** Recall of Information	**MP.5** Using Tools
19–21	**3** Strategic Thinking	**MP.2** Reasoning

EVALUATE

ASSIGNMENT GUIDE

Concepts and Skills	Practice
Explore Exploring Effects of Changing Dimensions on Perimeter and Area	Exercises 1–4, 15
Example 1 Describe a Non-Proportional Dimension Change	Exercises 5–8, 13, 20–21
Example 2 Describe a Proportional Dimension Change	Exercises 9–10, 13–14, 16–18, 22–23
Example 3 Describe a Proportional Dimension Change for a Solid	Exercises 11–12, 19, 24

INTEGRATE MATHEMATICAL PRACTICES
Focus on Patterns

MP.8 Have students fill out a table like the one below to confirm that there is a pattern in the effects on a figure when one or more dimensions is changed.

Factor of k	Proportional Dimension Change	Non-Proportional Dimension Change
Area	Factor of k^2	Factor of k
Perimeter	Factor of k	Not predictable
Volume	Factor of k^3	Not predictable
Surface Area	Factor of k^2	Not predictable

INTEGRATE MATHEMATICAL PRACTICES

Focus on Reasoning

MP.2 Point out that there may be more than one way to produce a certain change in area. For example, suppose you want to double the area of a rectangle. You can do this by doubling the length, doubling the width, or by increasing the length and width proportionally by a factor of $\sqrt{2}$.

Describe the effect of the change on the area of the given figure.

5. The height of the triangle is doubled.

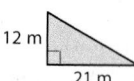

Original Figure

$A = \dfrac{bh}{2} = \dfrac{12 \cdot 21}{2} = 126 \text{ m}^2$

Transformed Figure

$A = \dfrac{bh}{2} = \dfrac{24 \cdot 21}{2} = 252 \text{ m}^2$

$\dfrac{252}{126} = 2$

The area is doubled.

6. The height of a trapezoid with base lengths 12 cm and 8 cm and height 5 cm is multiplied by $\frac{1}{3}$.

Original Figure

$A = \dfrac{(b_1 + b_2)h}{2} = \dfrac{(12 + 8)5}{2} = 50 \text{ cm}^2$

Transformed Figure

$A = \dfrac{(b_1 + b_2)h}{2} = \dfrac{(12 + 8)\frac{5}{3}}{2} = \dfrac{100}{6} = \dfrac{50}{3} \text{ cm}^2$

$\dfrac{50}{3} \div 50 = \dfrac{1}{3}$

The area is multiplied by $\frac{1}{3}$.

7. The base of the parallelogram is multiplied by $\frac{2}{3}$.

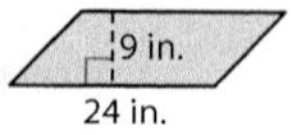

Original Figure

9 in.

24 in.

$A = bh = 24 \cdot 9 = 216 \text{ in}^2$

Transformed Figure

$A = bh = 16 \cdot 9 = 144 \text{ in}^2$

$\dfrac{144}{216} = \dfrac{2}{3}$

The area is multiplied by $\frac{2}{3}$.

8. Communicate Mathematical Ideas
A triangle has vertices $(1, 5)$, $(2, 3)$, and $(-1, -6)$. Find the effect that multiplying the height of the triangle by 4 has on the area of the triangle, without doing any calculations. Explain.

The area is mulitplied by 4. When only one dimension of a figure is multiplied by a factor, the area of the figure is multiplied by the same factor.

Describe the effect of each change on the perimeter or circumference and the area of the given figure.

9. The base and height of an isosceles triangle with base 12 in. and height 6 in. are both tripled.

Original Figure

$P = 8.5 + 8.5 + 12 = 29 \text{ in}$

$A = \dfrac{bh}{2} = \dfrac{12 \cdot 6}{2} = 36 \text{ in}^2$

Transformed Figure

$P = 25.5 + 25.5 + 36 = 87 \text{ in}$

$A = \dfrac{bh}{2} = \dfrac{36 \cdot 18}{2} = 324 \text{ in}^2$

Change in Perimeters $\dfrac{87}{29} = 3$

Change in Areas $\dfrac{324}{36} = 9$

The perimeter is tripled. The area is multiplied by 9.

10. The base and height of the rectangle are both multiplied by $\frac{1}{2}$.

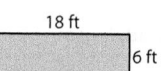

18 ft

6 ft

Original Figure

$P = 2(b + h) = 2(18 + 6) = 48 \text{ ft}$

$A = bh = 18 \cdot 6 = 108 \text{ ft}^2$

Transformed Figure

$P = 2(b + h) = 2(9 + 3) = 24 \text{ ft}$

$A = bh = 9 \cdot 3 = 27 \text{ ft}^2$

Change in Perimeters $\dfrac{24}{48} = \dfrac{1}{2}$

Change in Areas $\dfrac{27}{108} = \dfrac{1}{4}$

The perimeter is multiplied by $\frac{1}{2}$. The area is multiplied by $\frac{1}{4}$.

Exercise	Depth of Knowledge (D.O.K.)	COMMON CORE	Mathematical Practices
22	**2** Skills/Concepts H.O.T.		**MP.4** Modeling
23	**2** Skills/Concepts H.O.T.		**MP.4** Modeling
24	**3** Strategic Thinking H.O.T.		**MP.6** Precision

11. The dimensions are multiplied by 5.

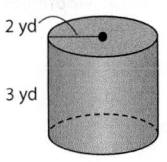

2 yd

3 yd

Original: $V = \pi r^2 h = 12\pi$ yd³;

Transformed: $V = \pi r^2 h = 1500\pi$ yd³;

change in volumes $\dfrac{1500\pi}{12\pi} = 125$;

volume is multiplied by 125.

12. The dimensions are multiplied by $\dfrac{3}{5}$.

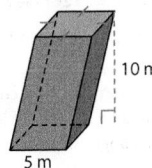

10 m

5 m

Original: $V = \ell wh = 250$ m³;

Transformed: $V = \ell wh = 54$ m³;

change in volumes $\dfrac{54}{250} = \dfrac{27}{125}$;

volume is multiplied by $\dfrac{27}{125}$.

13. For each change, check whether the change is non-proportional or proportional.

A. The height of a triangle is doubled. ○ proportional ● non-proportional

B. All sides of a square are quadrupled. ● proportional ○ non-proportional

C. The length of a rectangle is multiplied by $\dfrac{3}{4}$. ○ proportional ● non-proportional

D. The height of a triangular prism is tripled. ○ proportional ● non-proportional

E. The radius of a sphere is multiplied by $\sqrt{5}$. ● proportional ○ non-proportional

14. Tina and Kleu built rectangular play areas for their dogs. The play area for Tina's dog is 1.5 times as long and 1.5 times as wide as the play area for Kleu's dog. If the play area for Kleu's dog is 60 square feet, how big is the play area for Tina's dog?

Possible dimensions of play area: 10 feet by 6 feet; New Area: $A = \ell w = 135$ ft²

15. A map has the scale 1 inch = 10 miles. On the map, the area of Big Bend National Park in Texas is about 12.5 square inches. Estimate the actual area of the park in acres. (*Hint:* 1 square mile = 640 acres)

Possible map dimensions 2.5 in. by 5 in.; New Area: $A = \ell w = 1250$ mi²; $\approx$ 800,000 acres

16. A restaurant has a weekly ad in a local newspaper that is 2 inches wide and 4 inches high and costs $36.75 per week. The cost of each ad is based on its area. If the owner of the restaurant decided to double the width and height of the ad, how much will the new ad cost?

Original: $A = bh = 8$ in²; New: $A = bh = 32$ in²; $\dfrac{32}{8} = 4$; since the area is 4 times as large, it will cost $36.75 \times 4 = \$147.00$.

17. Suppose the dimensions of a triangle with a perimeter of 18 inches are doubled. Find the perimeter of the new triangle in inches.

Possible triangle dim. 6 in. by 6 in. by 6 in.; New Perimeter: $P = 3(12) = 36$ in.

A rectangular prism has vertices (0, 0, 0), (0, 3, 0), (7, 0, 0), (7, 3, 0), (0, 0, 6), (0, 3, 6), (7, 0, 6) and (7, 3, 6).

18. Suppose all the dimensions are tripled. Find the new vertices.

$(0, 0, 0)$, $(0, 9, 0)$, $(21, 0, 0)$, $(21, 9, 0)$, $(0, 0, 18)$, $(0, 9, 18)$, $(21, 0, 18)$, and $(21, 9, 18)$

19. Find the effect of the change on the volume of the prism.

Original: $V = \ell wh = 126$; New: $V = \ell wh = 3402$; $\dfrac{3402}{126} = 27$; the volume is multiplied by 27.

AVOID COMMON ERRORS

Students may make errors when finding the effects of proportional dimension changes on circles. Point out that because there is only one variable in the formula for a circle, changing the dimension is equivalent to doing a proportional dimension change. The area of the new circle increases by the square of the dimension change to the radius.

Divide students into groups. Have each group member find the effect of doubling all dimensions to the area and perimeter of a triangle, circle, parallelogram, and kite. Have them verify their results using algebra and share their results within the group.

JOURNAL

Have students describe the effects of a proportional dimension change on the area and perimeter of a two-dimensional figure, and on the volume and surface area of a three-dimensional figure. Ask them to include examples.

20. How would the effect of the change be different if only the height had been tripled?

Original: $V = \ell wh = 126$; New: $V = \ell wh = 378$; $\dfrac{378}{126} = 3$; the volume would have been multiplied by 3 instead of 27.

21. Analyze Relationships How could you change the dimensions of a parallelogram to increase the area by a factor of 5 if the parallelogram does not have to be similar to the original parallelogram? if the parallelogram does have to be similar to the original parallelogram?

Multiply the base or height by 5; Multiply the base and height by $\sqrt{5}$.

H.O.T. **Focus on Higher Order Thinking**

22. Algebra A square has a side length of $(2x + 5)$ cm.

a. If the side length is mulitplied by 5, what is the area of the new square?

$5(2x + 5) = 10x + 25$; $A = s^2 = (10x + 25)^2 = (100x^2 + 500x + 625)$cm^2

b. Use your answer to part (a) to find the area of the original square without using the area formula. Justify your answer.

$\dfrac{100x^2 + 500x + 625}{25} = 4x^2 + 20x + 25$; $(4x^2 + 20x + 25)$ cm^2; multiplying the side length of a square by 5 multiplies the area of the square by $5^2 = 25$, so dividing the area found in part (a) by 25 gives the original area.

23. Algebra A circle has a diameter of 6 in. If the circumference is multiplied by $(x + 3)$, what is the area of the new circle? Justify your answer.

If the circumference is multiplied by $(x + 3)$, then so is the radius. The original radius is 3 in. so the new radius is $3(x + 3) = (3x + 9)$ in. $A = \pi r^2 = \pi(3x + 9)^2$; The area of the new circle is $A = (9\pi x^2 + 54\pi x + 81\pi)$ in^2.

24. Communicate Mathematical Ideas The dimensions of a prism with volume V and surface area S are multiplied by a scale factor of k to form a similar prism. Make a conjecture about the ratio of the surface area of the new prism to its volume. Test your conjecture using a cube with an edge length of 1 and a scale factor of 2.

For a scale factor of k, the ratio of surface area to volume of the new prism is $\dfrac{1}{k}$ times the ratio of surface area to volume of the original prism. Original: $S = 1^2 \cdot 6 = 6$; $V = 1^3 = 1$; $\dfrac{S}{V} = \dfrac{6}{1}$; New: $S = 2^2 \cdot 6 = 24$; $V = 2^3 = 8$; $\dfrac{S}{V} = \dfrac{24}{8} = \dfrac{3}{1}$; $\dfrac{6}{1} \cdot \dfrac{1}{2} = \dfrac{3}{1}$

© Houghton Mifflin Harcourt Publishing Company

Lesson Performance Task

On a computer screen, lengths and widths are measured not in inches or millimeters but in **pixels**. A pixel is the smallest visual element that a computer is capable of processing. A common size for a large computer screen is 1024 × 768 pixels. (Widths rather than heights are conventionally listed first.) For the following, assume you're working on a 1024 × 768 screen.

1. You have a photo measuring 640 × 300 pixels and you want to enlarge it proportionally so that it is as wide as the computer screen. Find the measurements of the photo after it has been scaled up. Explain how you found the answer.

2. **a.** Explain why you can't enlarge the photo proportionally so that it is as tall as the computer screen.

   b. Why can't you correct the difficulty in (a) by scaling the width of the photo by a factor of 1024 ÷ 640 and the height by a factor of 768 ÷ 300?

3. You have some square photos and you would like to fill the screen with them, so there is no overlap and there are no gaps between photos. Find the dimensions of the largest such photos you can use (all of them the same size), and find the number of photos. Explain your reasoning.

1024 pixels

768 pixels

1. 1024 × 480; The photo must be scaled up in width by a factor of 1024 ÷ 640 = 1.6. So, apply the same factor to the height: 300 × 1.6 = 480.

2. a. You would have to scale the height of the photo up by a factor of 768 ÷ 300 = 2.56. Scaling the width by the same factor would create a photo that is 640 × 2.56 = 1638.4 pixels in width, which exceeds the width of the screen.

   b. You would increase the width by a factor of 1.6 and the height by a factor of 2.56, creating a distorted image.

3. 256 × 256. Sample answer: The height of the photos must be a factor of 768 pixels so that the photos fill the screen vertically. Two vertical squares would each have heights of 768 ÷ 2 = 384 pixels. But since 384 is not a factor of 1024, photos measuring 384 × 384 would not exactly fill the screen horizontally. Three vertical squares would each have heights of 768 ÷ 3 = 256 pixels. Since 256 is a factor of 1024, photos measuring 256 × 256 would fill the screen horizontally. The screen would have 3 rows of 4 photos each for a total of twelve 256 × 256 photos.

© Houghton Mifflin Harcourt Publishing Company

Module 20 **1046** Lesson 1

EXTENSION ACTIVITY

Computer screen resolutions are sometimes referred to by a set of acronyms, each with a corresponding size in pixels. Ask students to choose three of the following acronyms to research: VGA, SVGA, XGA, SXGA, and WUXGA. Have them find out the dimensions of each of their choices, then create a scale drawing on graph paper that relates the different sizes. Invite students to share their results with the class. VGA: 640 × 480; SVGA: 800 × 600; XGA: 1024 × 768; SXGA: 1280 × 1040; WUXGA: 1920 × 1200

INTEGRATE MATHEMATICAL PRACTICES
Focus on Patterns

MP.8 Question 3 in the Lesson Performance Task establishes that twelve 256 × 256 pixel photos can be placed on a 1024 × 768 pixel screen with no overlap and no gaps between photos. Find the sizes of other square photos larger than 50 × 50 pixels that can be placed on a 1024 × 768 pixel screen with no overlap and no gaps between photos. For each measurement that you find, give the number of rows, the number of squares in each row, and the total number of photos. Sample answers: 128 × 128 pixels: 6 rows of 8 photos each, 48 photos total; 64 × 64 pixels: 12 rows of 16 photos each, 192 photos total

INTEGRATE MATHEMATICAL PRACTICES
Focus on Math Connections

MP.1 A coordinate grid appears on a computer screen. A square on the grid has vertices at $(-4, 4)$, $(4, 4)$, $(4, -4)$, and $(-4, -4)$. A Web designer leaves the grid unchanged but scales up the square by a factor of 1.5 vertically and 0.8 horizontally.

a. What are the vertices of the new rectangle? $(-3.2, 6)$, $(3.2, 6)$, $(3.2, -6)$, and $(-3.2, -6)$

b. By what factor has the area of the rectangle been changed? 1.2

Scoring Rubric

2 points: Student correctly solves the problem and explains his/her reasoning.

1 point: Student shows good understanding of the problem but does not fully solve or explain his/her reasoning.

0 points: Student does not demonstrate understanding of the problem.

Scale Factor **1046**

Modeling and Density

Common Core Math Standards

The student is expected to:

COMMON CORE **G-MG.A.1**

Use geometric shapes, their measures, and their properties to describe objects (e.g., modeling a tree trunk or a human torso as a cylinder). Also G-MG.A.2

Mathematical Practices

COMMON CORE **MP.4 Modeling**

Language Objective

Explain to a partner how to model real-world situations involving density.

ENGAGE

Essential Question: How can you model real-world situations involving density?

Determine the area or volume involved. Then, divide the total number or quantity by the area or volume to calculate the density.

PREVIEW: LESSON PERFORMANCE TASK

View the Engage section online. Discuss the photo and how to calculate the density of gold. Then preview the Lesson Performance Task.

20.2 Modeling and Density

Essential Question: How can you model real-world situations involving density?

Resource Locker

⊘ Explore   Comparing Density

Density is the amount of matter that an object has in a given unit of volume. The density of an object is calculated by dividing its mass by its volume.

$$\text{density} = \frac{\text{mass}}{\text{volume}}$$

Density can be used to help distinguish between similar materials, like identifying different types of wood.

Data about two approximately cylindrical wood logs is shown in the table. Determine which wood is denser.

Type of wood	Diameter (cm)	Height (cm)	Mass (kg)
Douglas fir	6	17	254
American redwood	8	12	271

(A) Make a prediction, based on the data but without calculating, about which wood is denser. Describe your reasoning

Predictions will vary; reasoning might include a guess about which block is larger and

discussion of the mass of each log.

(B) Determine the volume of each log.
Douglas fir: $V = \pi(3\,\text{cm})^2(17\,\text{cm}) \approx 480\,\text{cm}^3$

American redwood: $V = \pi(4\,\text{cm})^2(12\,\text{cm}) \approx 603\,\text{cm}^3$

(C) Determine the density of each log. Identify the denser wood.

Douglas fir: density $= \frac{\text{mass}}{\text{volume}} = \frac{254\,\text{kg}}{480\,\text{cm}^3} \approx 0.529\,\text{kg/cm}^3$

American redwood: density $= \frac{\text{mass}}{\text{volume}} = \frac{271\,\text{kg}}{603\,\text{cm}^3} \approx 0.449\,\text{kg/cm}^3$

Based on this sample, Douglas fir is denser.

Reflect

1. What do your results tell you about the two types of wood?
Given pieces of wood with the same dimensions, the Douglas fir would be heavier than the

American redwood.

HARDCOVER PAGES 875–882

Turn to these pages to find this lesson in the hardcover student edition.

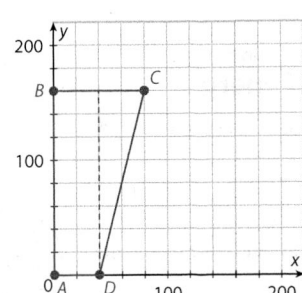

Explain 1 Calculating a Population Density

You can define density in other situations that involve area or volume besides mass per unit volume. For example, the population density of a region, or the population per unit area, can be found by using the density formula.

Example 1 Find the approximate population density.

(A) Burlington, Vermont has an area of about 160 km² and a population of 109,000 people. What is the approximate population density of Burlington?

$$\text{Population density} = \frac{\text{population}}{\text{area}} = \frac{109{,}000}{160} \approx 681 \text{ persons/km}^2$$

(B) The state of Vermont has a population of 626,000. Vermont's territory can be modeled as a trapezoid, as shown in the figure. Each unit on the coordinate grid represents one mile. Find the approximate population density of Vermont.

$$\text{Area} = \frac{1}{2}(b_1 + b_2)h = \frac{1}{2}\left(40 + \boxed{80}\right)\left(\boxed{160}\right) = \boxed{9600} \text{ mi}^2$$

$$\text{Population density} = \frac{\text{population}}{\text{area}} = \frac{626{,}000}{\boxed{9600}} \approx \boxed{65} \text{ persons/mi}^2$$

Reflect

2. **Discussion** The actual area of Vermont is 9,620 mi². Is your approximation an overestimate or underestimate? Explain.

    The approximation is a slight overestimate. The population is spread over a slightly larger area, and the exact population density is found by dividing by a greater value, so the population density is slightly less.

3. How would the population density of Vermont change if its given population doubled by 2100? Why?

    It would double. E.g., The population density is double the current population divided by the same area, which is double the current population density.

© Houghton Mifflin Harcourt Publishing Company • Image Credits: ©Albert Pego/Shutterstock

---

PROFESSIONAL DEVELOPMENT

 Integrate Mathematical Practices

This lesson provides an opportunity to address Mathematical Practice **MP.4**, which calls for students to "represent real-world problems with mathematical models." Students learn to find the density of real-life objects as the weight or mass per unit volume, and extend the idea of density to population density, or the population of a region per unit area of the region. Students learn some possible units of density and describe them mathematically.

EXPLORE

Comparing Density

INTEGRATE TECHNOLOGY

Students have the option of doing the Explore activity either in the book or online.

QUESTIONING STRATEGIES

? How do you calculate the density of an object? Divide the mass by the volume.

? What are some possible units of density? Possible answers: kg/m³, lb/ft³, g/cm³

EXPLAIN 1

Calculating a Population Density

QUESTIONING STRATEGIES

? What state would you expect to have a low population density? Why? Possible answer: Alaska, because the population of the state is relatively small while the area of the state is quite large. This makes for a low ratio of population to area.

? Suppose State A and State B have the same population, but State A has a greater area than State B. Which state has a greater population density? Why? State B; the same number of people are living in a smaller area, so the ratio of population to area is greater.

AVOID COMMON ERRORS

When calculating a population density, students may be confused about the order in which to form the ratio (that is, population divided by area, or area divided by population). Tell students that the units of population density provide a clue. Because population density is expressed as persons per square mile, the ratio should be formed by dividing the population by the area.

EXPLAIN 2

Calculating Measures of Energy

---

4. Critique Reasoning Marya claims that Burlington is about 10 times more densely populated than the state average. Is she correct? Explain your reasoning.

No; Marya seems to be comparing the numbers without paying attention to the units.

You cannot compare the numbers without converting to the same units. Converting the

population of Burlington to people per square mile, you get 1764 which is about 27 times

the average population density of the state.

Your Turn

5. Chicago has a population of about 2,715,000. Its territory can be modeled as a parallelogram, as shown in the figure. Each unit on the coordinate grid represents one mile. Find the approximate population density of Chicago.

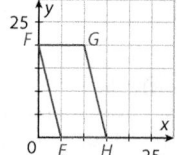

$$\text{Area} = bh = (10)(20) = 200 \text{ mi}^2$$

$$\text{Population density} = \frac{\text{population}}{\text{area}} = \frac{2{,}715{,}000}{200} \approx 13{,}600 \text{ persons/mi}^2$$

⚙ Explain 2 **Calculating Measures of Energy**

A British thermal unit (BTU), a unit of energy, is approximately the amount of energy needed to increase the temperature of one pound of water by one degree Fahrenheit. The energy content of a fuel may be measured in BTUs per unit of volume.

Example 2 A spherical tank is filled with a gas and it has the dimensions shown. Find the number of BTUs produced by one cubic foot of the gas. Round to the nearest BTU.

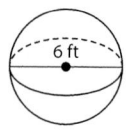

(A) When the tank is filled with natural gas, it provides 116,151 BTUs.

Find the volume of the spherical tank.

$$r = \frac{1}{2}(6 \text{ ft}) = 3 \text{ ft}$$

$$V = \frac{4}{3}\pi r^3 = \frac{4}{3}\pi(3)^3 = 36\pi \text{ ft}^3$$

Divide to find the number of BTUs in one cubic foot of natural gas.

$$\frac{\text{BTUs}}{1 \text{ ft}^3} = \frac{\text{BTUs in tank}}{\text{volume of tank}}$$

$$= \frac{116{,}151 \text{ BTUs}}{36\pi \text{ ft}^3}$$

$$\approx 1{,}027 \text{ BTUs}$$

COLLABORATIVE LEARNING

Peer-to-Peer Activity

To help students review how to find the number of BTUs per unit of volume, give each pair of students the radius of a sphere (in feet) and a sample BTU natural gas estimate for the sphere. Then have one student describe how to find the number of BTUs per cubic foot of the sphere and pass that information to the partner, who shows the work for finding the number of BTUs per cubic foot. Repeat the exercise with a different sample BTU natural gas estimate, but have the students switch roles.

Ⓑ When the tank is filled with kerosene, it provides about 114,206,000 BTUs.

The volume of the tank is $\underline{36\pi \text{ ft}^3}$.

$$\frac{\text{BTUs}}{1 \text{ ft}^3} = \frac{\text{BTUs in tank}}{\text{volume of tank}}$$

$$= \frac{\boxed{114,206,000} \text{ BTUs}}{\boxed{36\pi} \text{ ft}^3}$$

$$\approx \boxed{1,009,803} \text{ BTUs}$$

Reflect

6. Which fuel has a higher energy density?
   Kerosene has more BTUs per cubic foot, so it has a higher energy density.

7. One pint of water weighs approximately one pound. How many pints of water can be heated from 74°F to 75°F by one cubic foot of natural gas? How many pints of water can be heated from 75°F to 85°F by one cubic foot of natural gas?
   1,027 pints; each BTU of natural gas can increase the temperature of a pint of water by

   1°F; 102.7 pints; it takes 10 BTU to heat a pint of water by 10°F, so 1,027 BTUs can heat

   $\frac{1,027}{10} = 102.7$ **pints.**

Your Turn

8. A cylindrical tank has the dimensions shown. How many BTUs will the tank provide when filled with natural gas?

   Volume of tank $= \pi r^2 h = \pi(5)^2(14) = 350\pi \text{ ft}^3$

   From Example 2A, natural gas provides 1027 BTUs per cubic foot.

   BTUs in tank = volume of tank · BTUs in 1 ft³

   $$= 350\pi \cdot 1,027 \approx 1,129,245$$

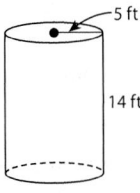
5 ft
14 ft

💬 Elaborate

9. Pressure is defined in terms of force per unit area. Is pressure an example of a density?
   Yes, because you divide the total amount of force by the area over which it is

   distributed so pressure is an example of density.

10. **Essential Question Check-In** Describe the general concept of *density* and give two real-world examples.
    Possible answer: Density is an average that describes the typical quantity of an item per

    unit area or volume. It is calculated by dividing the total number of items by the total

    area or volume. Two examples are density (mass ÷ volume) and population density (living

    things ÷ habitat area).

ELABORATE

QUESTIONING STRATEGIES

❓ Given a density, what additional information do you need to find the area or volume? To find the number or quantity? Given a density, you need to know the number or quantity to find the area or volume; to find the number or quantity, you need to know the area or volume.

SUMMARIZE THE LESSON

❓ How do you find density? For the density of an object, divide the object's mass by its volume. For population density, divide the population in a region by the area of the region.

DIFFERENTIATE INSTRUCTION

Kinesthetic Experience

Help students understand population density by providing them with a large grid and some kernels of popcorn. Ask them to spread the kernels randomly on the grid to simulate the population of a region. Have students brainstorm how they will find the population (of kernels) in one grid square and then describe the density of the population in that square in mathematical terms. Repeat the experiment with other sizes of squares, including 2 × 2 squares, until students find the density for the entire grid. Have them summarize by describing how to find the population density of a square region.

EVALUATE

ASSIGNMENT GUIDE

Concepts and Skills	Practice
Explore Comparing Density	Exercises 1–3
Example 1 Calculating a Population Density	Exercises 4–6
Example 2 Calculating Measures of Energy	Exercises 7–9

INTEGRATE MATHEMATICAL PROCESSES

Focus on Math Connections

MP.1 Remind students that they may need to review area and volume relationships to find density. Include how to find the area of irregular shapes and the volume of irregular solids, both of which may be needed for real-world applications of density.

⭐ Evaluate: Homework and Practice

• Online Homework
• Hints and Help
• Extra Practice

Determine which is denser.

1. Cylindrical logs of wood

Type of wood	Diameter (ft)	Height (ft)	Mass (lb)
Aspen	3.6	4.5	1,195
Juniper	3.0	6.0	1,487

Aspen $V = \pi(1.8)^2(4.5) = 14.58\pi$ ft³

Aspen Density $= \dfrac{1{,}195 \text{ lb}}{14.58\pi \text{ ft}^3} \approx 26$ lb/ft³

Juniper $V = \pi(1.5)^2(6.0) = 13.5\pi$ ft³

Juniper Density $= \dfrac{1{,}487 \text{ lb}}{13.5\pi \text{ ft}^3} \approx 35$ lb/ft³

Juniper is denser than Aspen.

2. Cylindrical bars of alloy

Alloy	Radius (cm)	Height (cm)	Mass (g)
Nichrome	3.9	27.2	10,800
Mild steel	4.6	18.8	9,840

Nichrome $V = \pi(3.9)^2(27.2) \approx 1{,}300$ cm³

Nichrome Density $\approx \dfrac{10{,}800 \text{ g}}{1{,}300 \text{ cm}^3} \approx 8.31$ g/cm³

Mild steel $V = \pi(4.6)^2(18.8) \approx 1{,}250$ cm³

Mild steel Density $\approx \dfrac{9{,}840 \text{ g}}{1{,}250 \text{ cm}^3} \approx 7.87$ g/cm³

Nichrome is denser than mild steel.

3. Spherical tanks of liquefied gases

Liquefied Gas	Radius (m)	Mass (kg)
Oxygen (O_2), at $-186°C$	0.8	2477
Hydrogen (H_2), at $-256°C$	1.2	514

Liquid oxygen

$V = \dfrac{4}{3}\pi r^3 = \dfrac{4}{3}\pi(0.8)^3 \approx 2.14$ m³

Liquid oxygen Density $\approx \dfrac{2{,}477 \text{ kg}}{2.14 \text{ m}^3} \approx 1{,}157$ kg/m³

Liquid hydrogen

$V = \dfrac{4}{3}\pi r^3 = \dfrac{4}{3}\pi(1.2)^3 \approx 7.24$ m³

Liquid hydrogen Density $\approx \dfrac{514 \text{ kg}}{7.24 \text{ m}^3} \approx 71$ kg/m³

Liquid oxygen is denser than liquid hydrogen.

LANGUAGE SUPPORT 🔲EL

Connect Vocabulary

Help students to understand how the term *density* is used. Explain that *density* means *the mass per unit volume* and is found by dividing the mass by the volume. Discuss that *population density* means *the population per unit area* and that it is found by dividing the population (of people, animals, and so on) of a region by the area of the region. Point out that both uses of *density* express a real-world quantity as a unit rate and have widespread applications in science, energy, and economics.

4. Colorado has a population of 5,268,367. Its territory can be modeled by a rectangle approximately 280 mi by 380 mi. Find the approximate population density of Colorado.

    Area $= bh = (280)(380) = 106,400$ mi^2

    Population density $= \dfrac{\text{population}}{\text{area}} = \dfrac{5,268,367}{106,400}$

    $\approx$ 50 persons/mi^2

5. Tennessee has a population of 6,495,978. Its territory can be modeled by a trapezoid, as shown in the figure. Each unit on the coordinate grid represents one mile. Find the approximate population density of Tennessee.

    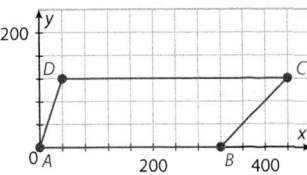

    Area $= \dfrac{1}{2}(b_1 + b_2)h = \dfrac{1}{2}(320 + 400)(120) = 43,200$ mi^2

    Population density $= \dfrac{\text{population}}{\text{area}} = \dfrac{6,495,978}{43,200} \approx$ 150 persons/mi^2

6. New Hampshire has a population of 1,323,459. Its territory can be modeled by a triangle, as shown in the figure. Each unit on the coordinate grid represents one mile. Find the approximate population density of New Hampshire.

    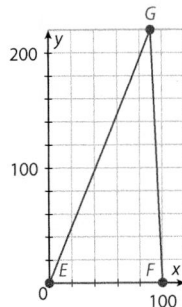

    Area $= \dfrac{1}{2}bh = \dfrac{1}{2}(100)(220) = 11,000$ mi^2

    Population density $= \dfrac{\text{population}}{\text{area}}$

    $= \dfrac{1,323,459}{11,000} \approx$ 120 persons/mi^2

7. A spherical gas tank has a 10 foot diameter. When filled with propane, it provides 358,000,000 BTUs. How many BTUs does 1 cubic foot of propane yield? Round to the nearest thousand.

    $r = \dfrac{1}{2}(10 \text{ ft}) = 5$ ft

    $V = \dfrac{4}{3}\pi r^3 = \dfrac{4}{3}\pi(5)^3 = \dfrac{500\pi}{3}$ ft^3

    $\dfrac{\text{BTUs}}{1 \text{ ft}^3} = \dfrac{\text{BTUs in tank}}{\text{volume of tank}}$

    $= \dfrac{358,000,000 \text{ BTUs}}{500\pi/3 \text{ ft}^3}$

    $\approx$ 684,000 BTUs

Exercise	Depth of Knowledge (D.O.K.)	COMMON CORE Mathematical Practices
1–10, 12	**1** Recall of information	**MP.6** Precision
11	**2** Skills/Concepts	**MP.2** Reasoning
13	**2** Skills/Concepts	**MP.6** Precision
14	**2** Skills/Concepts	**MP.2** Reasoning
15	**2** Skills/Concepts	**MP.6** Precision
16–17	**2** Skills/Concepts	**MP.1** Problem Solving

Students might make errors finding the population density of a region when they have difficulty finding the area of a region with an irregular shape. Remind students that breaking up the area into familiar shapes, such as triangles and rectangles, may be the most convenient way to find the area of an irregularly shaped region.

8. Ethan has collected information about the energy content of various fuels. Order the fuels by their energy density from greatest to least. (1 barrel = 42 gallons; 1 gallon = 8 pints)

Fuel	Heat Content
Jet fuel	5,670,000 BTUs/barrel
Gasoline	160,937 BTUs/gallon
Home fuel	138,690 BTUs/gallon
Propane	11,417 BTUs/pint

Convert jet fuel to BTUs/gal: 5,670,000/42 = 135,000 BTUs/gal.
Convert propane to BTUs/gal: 11,417 · 8 = 91,336 BTUs/gal.
From greatest to least energy density: gasoline, home fuel, jet fuel, propane.

9. A fuel tank has a volume of 32 gallons. When filled with biodiesel, it provides 4,000,000 BTUs. How many BTUs does 1 gallon of biodiesel yield?

$$\text{BTUs in 1 gallon} = \frac{\text{BTUs in tank}}{\text{volume of tank}}$$

$$= \frac{4,000,000 \text{ BTUs}}{32 \text{ gallons}}$$

$$= 125,000 \text{ BTUs/gallon}$$

10. A piece of marble has been machine-carved into the shape of a cone with the dimensions shown. It has a mass of 169 kg. What is the density of the marble, to the nearest kilogram per cubic meter?

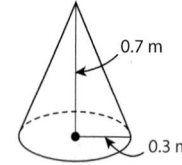

0.7 m

0.3 m

$$V = \frac{1}{3}\pi r^2 h = \frac{1}{3}\pi(0.3)^2(0.7) = 0.021\pi \text{ m}^3$$

$$\text{Density} = \frac{\text{mass}}{\text{volume}}$$

$$= \frac{169 \text{ kg}}{0.021\pi \text{ m}^3} \approx 2,562 \text{ kg/m}^3$$

11. **Metallurgy** The purity of gold is measured in carats. 24-carat gold is pure gold, and has a density of 19.3 g/cm³. 18-carat gold is often used for jewelry because it holds its shape better than pure gold. An 18-carat gold ring, which is 75% pure gold, has a mass of 18 g. What volume of pure gold was used to make the ring, to the nearest hundredth?

$$\text{Mass of pure gold used in ring} = (18 \text{ g}) \times 75\% = 13.5 \text{ g}$$

$$\text{volume of pure gold} = \frac{\text{mass of gold}}{\text{density of gold}}$$

$$= \frac{13.5 \text{ g}}{19.3 \text{ g/cm}^3} \approx 0.70 \text{ cm}^3$$

Exercise	Depth of Knowledge (D.O.K.)	COMMON CORE Mathematical Practices
18	**3** Strategic Thinking **H.O.T.**	**MP.7** Using Structure
19	**3** Strategic Thinking **H.O.T.**	**MP.2** Reasoning

12. Agriculture The maximum grain yield for corn is achieved by planting at a density of 38,000 plants per acre. A farmer wants to maximize the yield for the field represented on the coordinate grid. Each unit on the coordinate grid represents one foot. How many corn plants, to the nearest thousand, does the farmer need? (*Hint:* 1 acre = 43,560 ft^2)

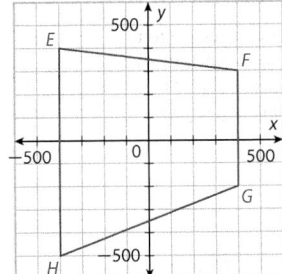

Area of $EFGH = \frac{1}{2}(b_1 + b_2)h = \frac{1}{2}(900 + 500)(800) = 560,000$ ft^2

plants per field $= \dfrac{\text{plants per acre}}{\text{area of 1 acre}} \times$ area of field

$= \dfrac{38,000}{43,560 \text{ ft}^2}(560,000 \text{ ft}^2) \approx 489,000$

13. The density of water at 4°C is 1000 kg/m^3. A cubic meter of water, when frozen to −20°C, has a volume of 1.0065 m^3. What is the density of ice at this temperature, to the nearest tenth?

One cubic meter of water has a mass of 1000 kg.

density of ice at $-20°C = \dfrac{\text{mass of ice}}{\text{volume of ice}}$

$= \dfrac{1000 \text{ kg}}{1.0065 \text{ m}^3} \approx 993.5$ kg/m^3

14. Space A launch vehicle is designed to carry up to 35 tons of payload into orbit. When fully fueled, it will contain 1,216,000 kg of liquid oxygen (LO$_2$) at a density of 1155 kg/m^3 and 102,000 kg of liquid hydrogen (LH$_2$) at a density of 71 kg/m^3. What is the total volume of liquefied gases carried by the launch vehicle, to the nearest tenth?

LO$_2$ volume $= \dfrac{\text{mass}}{\text{density}}$ LH$_2$ volume $= \dfrac{\text{mass}}{\text{density}}$

$= \dfrac{1,216,000 \text{ kg}}{1155 \text{ kg/m}^3} \approx 1052.8 \text{ m}^3$ $= \dfrac{102,000 \text{ kg}}{71 \text{ kg/m}^3} \approx 1436.6 \text{ m}^3$

Total volume $\approx 1052.8 \text{ m}^3 + 1436.6 \text{ m}^3 = 2489.4 \text{ m}^3$

© Houghton Mifflin Harcourt Publishing Company • Image Credits: ©Svetlana Foote/age fotostock

INTEGRATE MATHEMATICAL PRACTICES

Focus on Math Connections

MP.1 Encourage students to create a table of area and volume formulas they can use for reference as they work to find densities. Suggest that they include examples with units labeled.

Have students draw an irregular polygon in the coordinate plane and then describe how to find the population density for that region if 100 people live in it.

15. Manila, Philippines, has one of the highest population densities in the world with 111,002 people/mi². Manila's total population is 1,652,171. How large is Manilla, to the nearest tenth of a square mile?

$$\text{area} = \frac{\text{population}}{\text{population density}} = \frac{1{,}652{,}171 \text{ people}}{111{,}002 \text{ people/mi}^2} \approx 14.9 \text{ mi}^2$$

16. Multistep A building has apartments on 67 floors and each floor measures 110 feet by 85 feet. Currently, 2340 people live in the building. Find the population density of the building to the nearest person per square mile, in terms of the area occupied by the building at street level. Also find the population density of the building in terms of its total floor area. (*Hint*: 1 mi² = 27,878,400 ft²)

Area of each floor = (110 ft)(85 ft) = 9350 ft²

$$= \left(9350 \text{ ft}^2\right) \cdot \frac{1 \text{ mi}^2}{27{,}878{,}400 \text{ ft}^2} \approx 0.000335 \text{ mi}^2$$

$$\text{Population density (street level area)} \approx \frac{2340 \text{ people}}{0.000335 \text{ mi}^2} \approx 6{,}985{,}075 \text{ people/mi}^2$$

Total floor area $\approx 67 \times 0.000335 \text{ mi}^2 \approx 0.0224 \text{ mi}^2$

$$\text{Population density (total floor area)} \approx \frac{2340 \text{ people}}{0.0224 \text{ mi}^2} \approx 104{,}464 \text{ people/mi}^2$$

17. The caloric density of foods is a useful tool when comparing calorie counts. The table shows typical serving sizes for several foods and the number of calories per serving. Complete the fourth column. Then use the final column to number the foods from the lowest caloric density to the highest. Round to the nearest calorie per gram.

Food	Grams (g)	Calories (Cal)	Cal per 100 g	
1 cubic inch cheddar cheese	17	69	406	4
1 large hard boiled egg	50	78	156	2
1 medium apple	138	72	52	1
1.5 ounces raisins	43	129	300	3

H.O.T. Focus on Higher Order Thinking

18. Analyze Relationships The graph shows the relationship between mass and volume for pure silver. Use the graph to determine the density of pure silver to the nearest tenth and explain your method.

The density is equal to the slope of the graph.

$$\text{Density of silver} = \frac{105 \text{ g}}{10 \text{ cm}^3} \approx 10.5 \text{ g/cm}^3$$

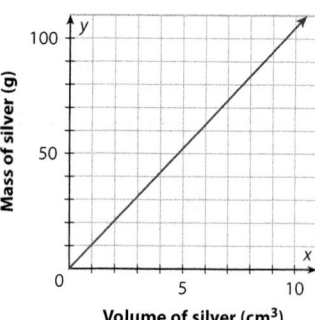

Volume of silver (cm³)

19. Communicate Mathematical Ideas According to Archimedes' Principle, an object placed in water will experience an upward force equal to the weight of water the object displaces. It is this upward force that causes objects less dense than water to float. For example, a cork floats when it is displacing a weight of water exactly equal to its own weight. When placed in water, what percent of a cork's volume will remain above the surface? Explain your answer.

	Density
Cork	0.24 g/cm³
Water	1.00 g/cm³

A sample of cork with a volume of 1 cm³ has a mass of 0.24 g, so it floats when displacing water with a weight of 0.24 g. This weight of water has a volume of 0.24 cm³, which is equal to the volume of cork beneath the surface. Therefore, 1 cm³ − 0.24 cm³ = 0.76 cm³, or 76% of the cork's volume, will remain above the surface.

Lesson Performance Task

A regular pyramid made of pure gold with the dimensions shown has a mass of 160.5 grams. Find the density of gold. Round to the nearest tenth. If the dimensions of the pyramid doubled, what would change about the mass and density?

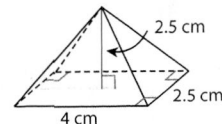

2.5 cm
2.5 cm
4 cm

$$V = \frac{1}{3}Bh = \frac{1}{3} \cdot 4 \cdot 2.5 \cdot 2.5 \approx 8.3 \text{ cm}^3$$

$$\frac{160.5 \text{ g}}{8.3 \text{ cm}^3} \approx 19.3 \frac{\text{g}}{\text{cm}^3}$$

Since the density of gold doesn't change, the mass would change when the dimensions are doubled.

$$V = \frac{1}{3}Bh = \frac{1}{3} \cdot 8 \cdot 5 \cdot 5 \approx 66.7 \text{ cm}^3$$

$$19.4 \frac{\text{g}}{\text{cm}^3} \cdot 66.7 \text{ cm}^3 = 1293.98 \text{ g}$$

© Houghton Mifflin Harcourt Publishing Company

EXTENSION ACTIVITY

A collector of rare artifacts wants to purchase a small regular pyramid which the seller claims is 80% pure gold and 20% silver. The collector carefully measures the dimensions of the pyramid, and finds the base is 1.7 cm by 2.1 cm, and the height is 2.2 cm. The density of silver is 10.5 g/cm³. What should be the mass of the pyramid if the seller is correct? volume: 2.618 cm³;

mass of gold: $(0.8)(2.618 \text{ cm}^3)(19.3 \text{ g/cm}^3) \approx 40.42$ g;

mass of silver: $(0.2)(2.618 \text{ g})(10.5 \text{ g/cm}^3) \approx 5.50$ g;

total mass: 40.42 g + 5.50 g = 45.92 g

MP.8 Have students describe how the volume of a regular pyramid changes as each dimension of the pyramid is multiplied by the same scale factor f. Students should see that the new volume is equal to the original volume multiplied by f^3.

INTEGRATE MATHEMATICAL PRACTICES
Focus on Math Connections

MP.1 In considering relationships among density, mass, and volume, students should recognize that because the density of a particular substance is constant, when the mass is increased, the volume increases by the same factor, and vice versa.

Scoring Rubric

2 points: Student correctly solves the problem and explains his/her reasoning.

1 point: Student shows good understanding of the problem but does not fully solve or explain his/her reasoning.

0 points: Student does not demonstrate understanding of the problem.

Modeling and Density   **1056**

Problem Solving with Constraints

Common Core Math Standards

The student is expected to:

 G-MG.A.1

Use geometric shapes, their measures, and their properties to describe objects (e.g., modeling a tree trunk or a human torso as a cylinder). Also G-MG.A.3

Mathematical Practices

 MP.4 Modeling

Language Objective

Explain to a partner how to model situations to meet real-world constraints.

ENGAGE

Essential Question: How can you model situations to meet real-world constraints?

Real-world situations often involve some sort of constraint, which means that the theoretical best solution might not be feasible. Volume formulas are often helpful in solving such problems.

PREVIEW: LESSON PERFORMANCE TASK

View the Engage section online. Discuss the photo and what shape of box is most efficient for packaging blocks. Then preview the Lesson Performance Task.

20.3 Problem Solving with Constraints

Essential Question: How can you model situations to meet real-world constraints?

Resource Locker

⊘ Explore   Maximizing Volume

Real-world problems often involve constraints. For example, for a given surface area, a sphere maximizes volume, but this is not usually the best shape for a package design.

Suppose you want to build a storage box from a rectangular piece of plywood that measures 4 ft by 8 ft. You must use six pieces, for the top, bottom, and sides of the box, and you can only make cuts perpendicular to the edges of the plywood. Given these constraints, what design appears to give the maximum possible volume for the box?

Ⓐ Consider the top, bottom, front, and back of the box. Which dimensions must these rectangular pieces have in common?

  All these pieces must have the same base length. The front and back must have the same

  height, as must the top and bottom.

Ⓑ Sketch two possible sets of cuts of the plywood. You do not have to use all the plywood in your design. Label your sketch with all the dimension information you have, using variable expressions if necessary.

  Possible answers are shown.

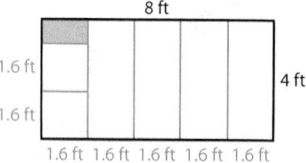

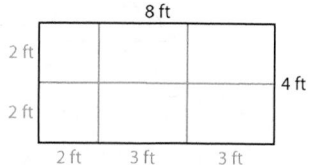

Ⓒ Calculate the volume of the resulting box for each of your designs.

  Possible answers.

  $V = \ell wh = (4\text{ ft})(1.6\text{ ft})(1.6\text{ ft}) = 10.24\text{ ft}^3$

  $V = \ell wh = (3\text{ ft})(2\text{ ft})(2\text{ ft}) = 12\text{ ft}^3$

Ⓓ Which design is better? Do you think one of your designs provides the greatest possible volume given the constraints of the problem?

  Check student answers. Answers might include "Yes; I used all of the wood and the square

  ends are most efficient." or "No; there should be a design that uses all of the wood."

HARDCOVER PAGES 883–892

Turn to these pages to find this lesson in the hardcover student edition.

1. How effective is this design in maximizing the volume? Explain.
   $4x = 4$ ft, so $x = 1$ ft; $8 - x = 7$ ft; $V = (7)(1)(1) = 7$ ft³.

   This design does not maximize the volume; the top,

   bottom, front, and back are long and thin, so the

   design uses a lot of plywood for its volume.

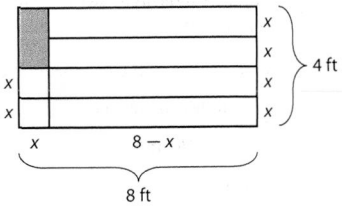

2. **Discussion** Compare results with others in your class. What seems to be a good strategy?
   Finding a layout that does not waste any plywood; finding a layout in which the

   rectangular pieces have similar base and height measurements.

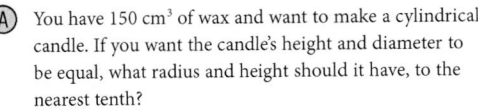 **Determining Dimensions Given a Volume**

Volume formulas are useful for solving problems where the constraint is to use a given volume of material for a given shape. For instance, suppose you want to make a cylindrical candle using a given amount of wax. You can use the formula for the volume of a cylinder to determine the candle's dimensions.

Example 1   Determine the necessary dimensions.

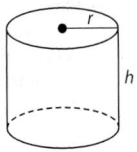 You have 150 cm³ of wax and want to make a cylindrical candle. If you want the candle's height and diameter to be equal, what radius and height should it have, to the nearest tenth?

The diameter of the candle is $2r$. The height is equal to the diameter, so $h = 2r$.

The candle's volume is:	$V = \pi r^2 h$
Substitute $2r$ for h:	$V = \pi r^2 (2r)$
Simplify:	$V = 2\pi r^3$
Substitute the given volume of wax:	$150 = 2\pi r^3$
Solve for r^3.	$r^3 = \frac{150}{2\pi} \approx 23.9$

Use a graphing calculator to graph each side of the equation as a separate function.

Graph $y = r^3$ and $y = 23.9$. The coordinates of the intersection are $(2.879..., 23.9)$.

The radius of the candle should be 2.9 cm. The height of the candle should be twice the radius or 5.8 cm.

PROFESSIONAL DEVELOPMENT

Math Background

Optimization problems are a common application in many calculus courses. For example, students may be asked to determine the cylinder with the maximum volume given a specific surface area. Students solve such problems in calculus by writing an equation for the quantity to be optimized and finding the derivative. This lesson gives students a preview of some of these ideas. Although no calculus is used, the lesson serves as an informal introduction to the types of design problems students will encounter in later courses.

EXPLORE

Maximizing Volume

INTEGRATE TECHNOLOGY

Students have the option of doing the Explore activity either in the book or online.

QUESTIONING STRATEGIES

? How would you describe the constraints for a given problem? Possible answer: The constraints are the conditions that minimize the costs or that determine how the final product or object should look.

INTEGRATE MATHEMATICAL PRACTICES
Focus on Math Connections

MP.1 Explain that a design problem is one in which you must design an object that satisfies the given conditions. You may want to give students a simple example, such as this: Design a rectangular picture frame that has the maximum possible area, given that the frame's perimeter is 24 inches. Ask students to suggest several combinations of length and width that give a perimeter of 24 inches, calculate the corresponding area, and then choose the dimensions with the largest area. Ask them to use their calculations to make a conjecture about the shape. For this example, the conjecture might be that the shape should be a square with side length 6 inches.

EXPLAIN 1

Determine Dimensions Given a Volume

QUESTIONING STRATEGIES

? How does a volume formula help you satisfy the constraints for a design problem? **Possible answer: If you are designing an object, the object has volume. So, since constraints are often related to size, finding the volume of the object is useful when comparing objects of different sizes.**

AVOID COMMON ERRORS

When solving a design problem, students may have difficulty getting started. Point out that students must not only identify important information, but decide which information to work with first. Ask students to work with a partner to explain how they prioritized the given information and decided which information to use in the first step of the solution process.

INTEGRATE MATHEMATICAL PRACTICES
Focus on Technology

MP.5 Point out that a graphing calculator can be used to help solve a design problem. Students can graph both sides of the equation for the problem and find the *x*-value of the intersection point of the two graphs.

 B You have 300 cm³ of wax and want to make a candle in the shape of a square prism. If you want the candle to be twice as tall as it is wide, what side lengths should it have, to the nearest tenth?

Let the length of the base be *b*. The height *h* is twice the base or _____2b_____.

The candle's volume is: $V = b^2 h$

Substitute 2b for h: $V = b^2(2b)$

Simplify: $V = 2b^3$

Substitute the given volume of wax: $300 = 2b^3$

Solve for b^3. $b^3 = 150$

Graph $y = b^3$ and $y = $ ___150___. The coordinates of the intersection are __(5.31, 150)__.

The side lengths of the square base of the candle should be ___5.3 cm___. The height of the candle should be twice the base or ___10.6 cm___.

Reflect

3. How can you check that your answer to Example 1B is reasonable?

Check that the volume of the candle is approximately 300 cm³.

$V = b^2 h = (5.3)^2(10.6) \approx 297.8$ cm³, so the answer is reasonable.

Your Turn

4. You want to make a conical candle using 15 in³ of wax. If the candle's height is twice its diameter, what radius and height should it have, to the nearest tenth?

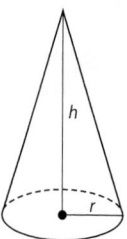

Height $h = 2(2r) = 4r$

$V = \frac{1}{3}\pi r^2(4r) = \frac{4}{3}\pi r^3$

$15 = \frac{4}{3}\pi r^3$

Graph $y = 15$ and $y = \frac{4}{3}\pi r^3$.

The intersection is at $(1.529..., 15)$.

Radius ≈ 1.5 in.

Height $= 4(1.5) = 6.0$ in.

5. You have an octagonal candle mold that has a base that is three inches across and has side length 1.2 inches. If you use this mold to make a candle using 50 in³ of wax, how tall will the candle be?

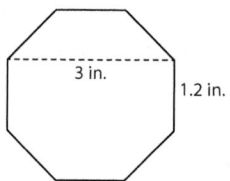

The base is made up of 8 congruent triangles each with height $= 1.5$ in. and base $= 1.2$ in.

Area of base $= 8 \cdot \frac{1}{2}(1.5)(1.2) = 7.2$ in²

$V = bh$

$50 = 7.2h$

$\frac{50}{7.2} = h$

$6.9 \approx h$

The candle will be almost 7 in. tall.

© Houghton Mifflin Harcourt Publishing Company

COLLABORATIVE LEARNING

Small Group Activity

To help students solve a design problem, have them work in groups of four. Ask one student to identify the important information in the problem and decide which information to work with first. Then have another student devise a plan and explain how to proceed in the solution process. Ask a third student to show the solution and a fourth student to check the work and make sure the solution fits the constraints in the problem. Then give the group another problem to solve and have them switch roles.

Modeling to Meet Constraints

A full-grown tree needs to have a minimum size canopy to photosynthesize enough sugar to feed the tree's bulk. This constraint can be modeled by relating the tree's canopy surface area to the volume of its trunk. By making some simplifying assumptions, you can explore this relationship.

Example 2   **What is the minimum radius for the described tree, to the nearest foot?**

Ⓐ Suppose a full-grown oak tree with trunk diameter 6 ft requires at least 8 ft² of exterior canopy area per cubic foot of trunk volume. Model the canopy with a hemisphere, and model the trunk with a cylinder whose height is three times its diameter.

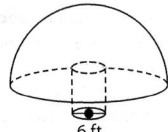
6 ft

Find the volume of the trunk.

Radius of trunk $= \frac{1}{2}(6 \text{ ft}) = 3$ ft   Height of trunk $= 3(6 \text{ ft}) = 18$ ft

Volume of trunk $= \pi r^2 h = \pi(3)^2(18) = 162\pi$ ft³

Find the minimum exterior canopy area for this size of trunk.

Minimum exterior canopy area $= \frac{8 \text{ ft}^2}{1 \text{ ft}^3} \times \left(162\pi \text{ ft}^3\right) = 1{,}296\pi$ ft²

Write an expression for the curved surface area of a hemisphere with radius r.

Surface area $= \frac{1}{2}\left(4\pi r^2\right) = 2\pi r^2$

Write an equation that shows the relation between the surface area and the canopy area.

Surface area $=$ Minimum canopy area

$2\pi r^2 = 1{,}296\pi$

$r^2 = \frac{1{,}296\pi}{2\pi} = 648$ $r = \sqrt{648} \approx 25$ ft

The minimum radius of canopy required for this oak tree is 25 feet.

Ⓑ Suppose a growing oak tree with trunk diameter 12 inches requires at least 12 ft² of exterior canopy area per cubic foot of trunk volume. Model the canopy with a hemisphere, and model the trunk with a cylinder whose height is 24 times its diameter.

radius of trunk $= \boxed{0.5}$ ft   height of trunk $= \boxed{24(1 \text{ ft}) = 24 \text{ ft}}$

Volume of trunk $= \pi r^2 h = \pi \left(\boxed{0.5}\right)^2 \left(\boxed{24}\right) = \boxed{6}\,\pi$ ft³

Curved surface area $=$ Minimum canopy area

$\frac{1}{2}(4\pi r^2) = \frac{\boxed{12} \text{ ft}^2}{1 \text{ ft}^3} \times \left(\boxed{6}\,\pi \text{ ft}^3\right)$

$2\pi r^2 = \boxed{72}\,\pi$ ft²

$r^2 = \frac{\boxed{72\pi \text{ ft}^2}}{\boxed{2\pi}} = \boxed{36}$ $r = \boxed{\sqrt{36}} = \boxed{6 \text{ ft}}$

The minimum radius of canopy required for this oak tree is 6 feet.

DIFFERENTIATE INSTRUCTION

Modeling

Help students understand how to create models that fit constraints by having them work in groups to create some of the simpler models in the problem set by using manipulatives. Ask the group members to reach a consensus about how to describe the models mathematically and how to determine whether the models fit the constraints of the problem they are solving. Have one group member describe the group's choice of models to the class.

EXPLAIN 2

Modeling to Meet Constraints

INTEGRATE MATHEMATICAL PRACTICES
Focus on Modeling

MP.4 Point out that more than one model may be appropriate to meet constraints, so students may need to experiment with different models before labeling one the best model.

QUESTIONING STRATEGIES

? How can you choose a model for a given problem situation? Possible answer: Determine which models fit a certain problem situation, and then choose the model that most closely meets the constraints of the problem.

AVOID COMMON ERRORS

Students may not be sure which model to choose for a given problem situation. Encourage them to determine the formulas that fit the model, as best they can (these may be volume formulas), and then use technology or other means to describe the model mathematically.

ELABORATE

QUESTIONING STRATEGIES

? How do you use geometry to solve design problems? Determine dimensions by using the given information and geometry formulas to write and solve an equation. You can also solve design problems by using the given information to draw and label one or more diagrams that meet the required conditions.

---

6. **Discussion** How could you use this model to make decisions about planting trees?
The model is accurate enough to compare the radius required for different trees, which could allow you to estimate whether you have room to plant a tree. For example, a 10 ft square area is probably not enough room for a full-grown oak tree, but a 50 ft square area should be enough space.

Your Turn

7. Assume a mature sequoia tree requires at least 0.6 m² of exterior canopy area per cubic meter of trunk volume. Also assume that the canopy can be modeled by a cone whose slant height is 4 times its radius, and that the trunk of the tree can be modeled by a cone whose height is 12 times its diameter. The formula for the lateral surface area of a cone is $A = \pi(\text{radius})(\text{slant height})$. What is the minimum base radius of canopy required for a sequoia with trunk diameter 5 m? Round your answer to the nearest tenth.

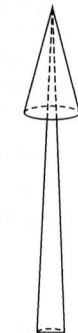

5 m

Radius of trunk $= \dfrac{1}{2}(5 \text{ m}) = 2.5 \text{ m}$ Height of trunk $= 12(5 \text{ m}) = 60 \text{ m}$

Volume of trunk $= \dfrac{1}{3}\pi r^2 h = \dfrac{1}{3}\pi(2.5)^2(60) = 125\pi \text{ m}^3$

Surface area $=$ Minimum canopy area

$$\pi(r)(4r) = \dfrac{0.6 \text{ m}^2}{1 \text{ m}^3} \times \left(125\pi \text{ m}^3\right)$$

$$4\pi r^2 = 75\pi \text{ m}^2$$

$$r^2 = \dfrac{75\pi \text{ m}^2}{4\pi} = 18.75$$

$$r \approx \sqrt{18.75} \approx 4.3 \text{ m}$$

💬 Elaborate

8. What is the role of a constraint in solving a real-world problem?
Possible answer: Often, a constraint gives you a value to be substituted into an equation relating a dimension to a volume or surface area, allowing the equation to be solved and the dimension found.

LANGUAGE SUPPORT **EL**

Connect Vocabulary

Help students to understand how the term *constraint* is used to describe a model that will fit a certain problem situation. Point out that the constraints, or conditions, for a problem may be related to size or volume. Thus, in a mathematical context, the constraints help define equations that can be used to solve the problem.

9. Essential Question Check-In How can you model situations to meet real-world constraints?
There are many methods, depending on the situation and the nature of the constraint. For example, in making a box out of a sheet of material, different designs must be considered to find the most efficient given the constraint of the sheet's dimensions. In other types of problem, such as making a candle in a certain shape out of a given volume of wax, a single design leads to an equation that can be solved when the constraint is substituted.

✪ Evaluate: Homework and Practice

- Online Homework
- Hints and Help
- Extra Practice

Find the volume of each design for a box built from a piece of plywood measuring 60 cm by 180 cm.

1.
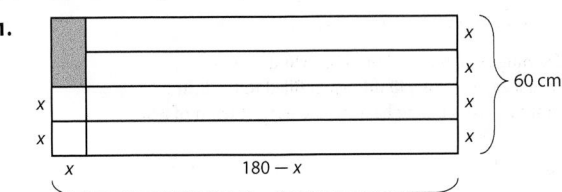

$4x = 60$ cm, so $x = 15$ cm

$180 - x = 165$ cm

$V = \ell wh$
$\quad = (165 \text{ cm})(15 \text{ cm})(15 \text{ cm});$
$\quad = 37{,}125 \text{ cm}^3$

2.

$2x = 60$ cm, so $x = 30$ cm

$V = \ell wh$
$\quad = (60 \text{ cm})(30 \text{ cm})(30 \text{ cm});$
$\quad = 54{,}000 \text{ cm}^3$

3.

$2x = 60$ cm, so $x = 30$ cm

$\dfrac{180 - x}{2} = \dfrac{180 - (30)}{2} = 75$ cm

$V = \ell wh$
$\quad = (75 \text{ cm})(30 \text{ cm})(30 \text{ cm});$
$\quad = 67{,}500 \text{ cm}^3$

4.

$x + 1.5x = 2.5x = 60$ cm,

so $x = 24$ cm and $1.5x = 36$ cm

$\dfrac{180 - 1.5x}{2} = \dfrac{180 - (36)}{2} = 72$ cm

$V = \ell wh$
$\quad = (72 \text{ cm})(36 \text{ cm})(24 \text{ cm});$
$\quad = 62{,}208 \text{ cm}^3$

© Houghton Mifflin Harcourt Publishing Company

SUMMARIZE THE LESSON

? What is a design problem? A design problem is one in which you are asked to find a model that will solve the problem within certain constraints.

EVALUATE

ASSIGNMENT GUIDE

Concepts and Skills	Practice
Explore Maximizing Volume	Exercises 1–4
Example 1 Determining Dimensions Given a Volume	Exercises 5–8
Example 2 Modeling to Meet Constraints	Exercises 9–12

INTEGRATE MATHEMATICAL PRACTICES

Focus on Math Connections

MP.1 Remind students that they may need to review area and volume relationships to find a model that will fit a problem situation. Review with them how to find the area of irregular shapes and the volume of irregular solids, as these may be needed for real-life modeling with constraints.

Exercise	Depth of Knowledge (D.O.K.)		COMMON CORE Mathematical Practices	
1–4	**1**	Recall of information	**MP.6**	Precision
5–20	**2**	Skills/Concepts	**MP.4**	Modeling
21	**3**	Strategic Thinking H.O.T.	**MP.7**	Using Structure
22	**3**	Strategic Thinking H.O.T.	**MP.4**	Modeling
23	**3**	Strategic Thinking H.O.T.	**MP.2**	Reasoning
24	**3**	Strategic Thinking H.O.T.	**MP.1**	Problem Solving

5. A cylindrical candle is to be made from 18 in³ of wax. If the candle's height is twice its diameter, what radius and height should it have, to the nearest tenth?

Height is twice the diameter, or 4 times the radius: $h = 4r$

$$V = \pi r^2 h = \pi r^2(4r) = 4\pi r^3$$

$$18 = 4\pi r^3$$

Using a graphing calculator, $r \approx 1.1$ in. and $h \approx 4.4$ in.

6. A conical candle is to be made from 240 cm³ of wax. If the candle's height is three times its diameter, what radius and height should it have, to the nearest tenth?

Height is 3 times the diameter, or 6 times the radius: $h = 6r$

$$V = \frac{1}{3}\pi r^2 h = \frac{1}{3}\pi r^2(6r) = 2\pi r^3$$

$$240 = 2\pi r^3$$

Using a graphing calculator, $r \approx 3.4$ cm and $h \approx 20.4$ cm.

7. The design specifications for a coffee mug state that it should be cylindrical, with height 1.5 times its diameter, and with a capacity of 450 mL when filled to the brim. What interior radius and height should the coffee mug have, to the nearest tenth of a centimeter? (*Hint:* 1 mL = 1 cm³)

Height is 1.5 times the diameter, or 3 times the radius: $h = 3r$

$$V = \pi r^2 h = \pi r^2(3r) = 3\pi r^3$$

$$450 = 3\pi r^3$$

Using a graphing calculator, $r \approx 3.6$ cm and $h \approx 10.8$ cm.

8. A bob for a pendulum clock will be a cone of equal height and diameter, made from 3 in³ of metal. What radius and height should the bob have, to the nearest tenth?

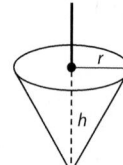

Height equals the diameter, so is twice the radius: $h = 2r$

$$V = \frac{1}{3}\pi r^2 h = \frac{1}{3}\pi r^2(2r) = \frac{2}{3}\pi r^3$$

$$3 = \frac{2}{3}\pi r^3$$

Using a graphing calculator, $r \approx 1.1$ in. and $h \approx 2.2$ in.

9. Assume a full-grown oak tree requires at least 8 ft² of exterior canopy area per cubic foot of trunk volume. Model the canopy with a hemisphere, and model the trunk using a cylinder whose height is three times its diameter. What is the minimum radius of canopy required for an oak with trunk diameter 9 ft? Round your answer to the nearest foot.

Trunk: $r = \frac{1}{2}(9 \text{ ft}) = 4.5 \text{ ft};$ $h = 3(9 \text{ ft}) = 27 \text{ ft};$ $V = \pi(4.5)^2(27) = 546.75\pi \text{ ft}^3$

Surface area = Minimum canopy area

$$\frac{1}{2}(4\pi r^2) = \frac{8 \text{ ft}^2}{1 \text{ ft}^3} \times 546.75\pi \text{ ft}^3$$

$$2\pi r^2 = 4,374\pi \text{ ft}^2$$

$$r^2 = \frac{4,374\pi \text{ ft}^2}{2\pi} = 2,187 \qquad r = \sqrt{2,187} \approx 46.8 \text{ ft}$$

10. A mature beech tree requires at least 20 m² of exterior canopy area per cubic meter of trunk volume. Model the canopy with a hemisphere, and model the trunk using a cylinder whose height is three times its diameter. What is the minimum radius of canopy required for a beech with trunk diameter 2 m? Round your answer to the nearest foot.

Trunk: $r = \frac{1}{2}(2\text{ m}) = 1\text{ m}$; $h = 3(2\text{ m}) = 6\text{ m}$; $V = \pi(1)^2(6) = 6\pi\text{ m}^3$

Surface area = Minimum canopy area

$$\frac{1}{2}(4\pi r^2) = \frac{20\text{ m}^2}{1\text{ m}^3} \times (6\pi\text{ m}^3)$$

$$2\pi r^2 = 120\pi\text{ m}^2$$

$$r^2 = \frac{120\pi\text{ m}^2}{2\pi} = 60 \qquad r \approx \sqrt{60} \approx 7.7\text{ m}$$

11. Assume a mature sequoia tree requires at least 0.6 m² of exterior canopy area per cubic meter of trunk volume. Model the canopy with a cone whose slant height is 4 times its radius. Model the trunk with a cone whose height is 12 times its diameter. What is the minimum base radius of canopy required for a sequoia with trunk diameter 8 m? Round your answer to the nearest tenth.

Trunk: $r = \frac{1}{2}(8\text{ m}) = 4\text{ m}$; $h = 12(8\text{ m}) = 96\text{ m}$; $V = \frac{1}{3}\pi(4)^2(96) = 512\pi\text{ m}^3$

Surface area = Minimum canopy area

$$\pi(r)(4r) = \frac{0.6\text{ m}^2}{1\text{ m}^3} \times (512\pi\text{ m}^3)$$

$$4\pi r^2 = 307.2\pi\text{ m}^2$$

$$r^2 = \frac{307.2\pi\text{ m}^2}{4\pi} \approx 76.8 \qquad r \approx \sqrt{76.8} \approx 8.8\text{ m}$$

12. Assume a mature Douglas fir requires at least 2 ft² of exterior canopy area per cubic foot of trunk volume. Model the canopy with a cone whose slant height is 4 times its diameter, and model the trunk with a cone whose height is 12 times its diameter. What is the minimum base radius of canopy required for a Douglas fir with trunk diameter 4 ft? Round your answer to the nearest tenth.

Trunk: $r = \frac{1}{2}(4\text{ ft}) = 2\text{ ft}$; $h = 12(4\text{ m}) = 48\text{ ft}$;

Volume of trunk $= \frac{1}{3}\pi r^2 h = \frac{1}{3}\pi(2)^2(48) = 64\pi\text{ ft}^3$

Surface area = Minimum canopy area

$$4\pi r^2 = \frac{2\text{ ft}^2}{1\text{ ft}^3} \times 64\pi\text{ ft}^3$$

$$4\pi r^2 = 128\pi\text{ ft}^2$$

$$r^2 = \frac{128\pi\text{ ft}^2}{4\pi} = 32$$

$$r = \sqrt{32} \approx 5.7\text{ ft}$$

Students may have difficulty choosing a model for a problem situation that has constraints. Point out that they may need some strategies to help them decide on a model; for example, determining the dimensions by using the given information and geometry formulas to write and solve an equation, or by using the given information to draw and label one or more diagrams that meet the required conditions.

13. None of the designs in Questions 1–4 actually maximize the volume of a box made from a 60 cm by 180 cm plywood sheet. Find a design that does maximize the volume. (*Hint:* Use two variables, x and y, for the dimensions of the two side pieces.)

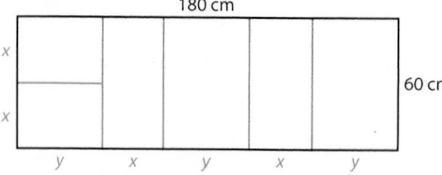

$2x = 60$, so $x = 30$ cm

$3y + 2x = 180$, so $3y = 120$, or $y = 40$ cm

$V = \ell wh = (60 \text{ cm})(40 \text{ cm})(30 \text{ cm}) = 72{,}000 \text{ cm}^3$

14. Jack is planning to build an aquarium in the shape of a rectangular prism. He wants the base to measure 90 cm by 40 cm. The maximum safe weight this type of aquarium can support is 150 kg. Given that the density of water is 0.001 kg/cm³ and that Jack estimates he will have 5 kg of rocks, sand, and fish to put in the aquarium, what is the aquarium's maximum height, to the nearest centimeter?

Tank dimensions: $\ell = 90$ cm, $w = 40$ cm, h to be determined.

Volume of tank: $V = \ell wh = (90)(40)h = 3{,}600h$

mass in tank = (volume of water) × (density of water) + 5

$\qquad 150 = 3{,}600h(0.001) + 5$

$\qquad 145 = 3.6h$

$\qquad h = \dfrac{145}{3.6} \approx 40$ cm

15. Rita is making a box from a 2 ft by 5 ft piece of plywood. The box does not need a top, so only five pieces are needed. Suggest two designs to maximize the volume of the box. Check your designs by calculating the volume.

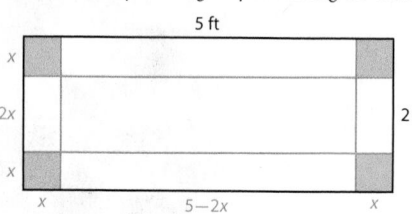 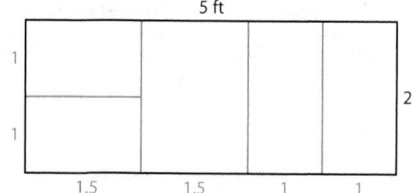

Sample answers are shown

$4x = 2$, so $x = 0.5$ ft and $2x = 2(0.5) = 1$ ft

$5 - 2x = 5 - 2(0.5) = 4$ ft

$V = \ell wh = (4 \text{ ft})(1 \text{ ft})(0.5 \text{ ft}) = 2 \text{ ft}^3 \qquad V = \ell wh = (2 \text{ ft})(1 \text{ ft})(1.5 \text{ ft}) = 3 \text{ ft}^3$

16. Multi-step A propane tank is designed in the shape of a cylinder with two hemispherical ends. The cylinder's height is twice its diameter, and the tank's capacity is 1,000 gal. What is the radius of the tank, to the nearest tenth of a foot? (*Hint:* 1 ft³ = 7.48 gal)

Height of cylinder is twice the diameter, or 4 times the radius: $h = 4r$

Volume of cylinder $= \pi r^2 h = \pi r^2(4r) = 4\pi r^3$

Volume of each hemispherical end $= \dfrac{1}{2}\left(\dfrac{4}{3}\pi r^3\right) = \dfrac{2}{3}\pi r^3$

Volume of tank $= 4\pi r^3 + 2\left(\dfrac{2}{3}\pi r^3\right) = \dfrac{16}{3}\pi r^3$

Capacity of tank in gallons $= 7.48\left(\dfrac{16}{3}\pi r^3\right) \approx 39.89\pi r^3$ gal

Therefore, $1{,}000 \approx 39.89\pi r^3$ gal.

Using a graphing calculator, $r \approx 2.0$ ft.

17. A cylindrical space station is 5 m in diameter and 12 m long, and it requires 0.2 m² of solar panels per cubic meter of volume to provide power. If it has two sets of rectangular solar panels, each 2 m wide, how long should each set of panels be? Round your answer to the nearest tenth.

Radius of space station $= \dfrac{1}{2}(5\text{ m}) = 2.5$ m

Volume of space station $= \pi r^2 h = \pi(2.5)^2(12) = 75\pi$ m³

Area of solar panels $= \dfrac{0.2\text{ m}^2}{1\text{ m}^3} \times (75\pi\text{ m}^3) = 15\pi$ m²

Area of each set of panels $= \dfrac{1}{2}(15\pi\text{ m}^2) = 7.5\pi$ m²

Length of each set of panels: $\ell w = 7.5\pi$

$\qquad\qquad\qquad\qquad\qquad 2\ell = 7.5\pi$

$\qquad\qquad\qquad\qquad\qquad \ell = 3.75\pi \approx 11.8$ m

18. Create a design to make a cylinder, including both circular ends, from a sheet of metal that measures 150 cm by 60 cm. Calculate the volume of your design, to the nearest thousand cubic centimeters.

Possible answer is shown.

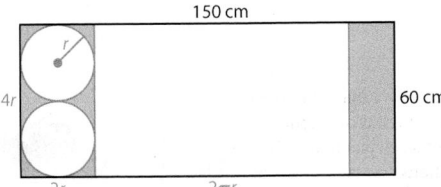

Radius of cylinder: $4r = 60$ cm, so $r = 15$ cm

Height of cylinder $= 60$ cm

Circumference of cylinder $= 2\pi r = 30\pi$ cm ≈ 94.25 cm

Check: $2r + 2\pi r \approx 30 + 94.25 = 124.25$ cm < 150 cm, so the design fits on the sheet.

Volume of cylinder: $V = \pi r^2 h = \pi(15)^2(60) = 13{,}500\pi$ cm³ $\approx 42{,}000$ cm³

MP.1 Encourage students to create a table of area and volume formulas they can use for reference as they work to find the models for problem situations. Suggest that they include examples with the units labeled.

19. A roll of aluminum foil is 15 in. wide. It has an interior diameter of 1.2 in. and an exterior diameter of 1.6 in. If the foil is 0.001 in. thick, what length of foil is rolled up, to the nearest foot? (*Hint:* Start by finding the volume of a 1-ft length of foil 15 in. wide.)

Volume of 1-ft length of foil 15 in. wide: $V = \ell wh = (15)(12)(0.001) = 0.18 \text{ in}^3$

Exterior radius $= \frac{1}{2}(1.6 \text{ in.}) = 0.8 \text{ in.}$

Volume of outer cylinder: $V = \pi r^2 h = \pi(0.8)^2(15) = 9.6\,\pi \text{ in}^3$

Interior radius $= \frac{1}{2}(1.2 \text{ in.}) = 0.6 \text{ in.}$

Volume of inner cylinder: $V = \pi r^2 h = \pi(0.6)^2(15) = 5.4\,\pi \text{ in}^3$

Volume of foil on roll: $9.6\,\pi \text{ in}^3 - 5.4\,\pi \text{ in}^3 = 4.2\,\pi \text{ in}^3$

Let the length of foil on the roll be x feet.

$0.18x = 4.2\pi$

$x = \frac{4.2\pi}{0.18} \approx 73 \text{ ft}$

20. Assume a full-grown oak tree requires at least 8 ft² of exterior canopy area per cubic foot of trunk volume. Model the canopy with a hemisphere. Model the trunk with a cylinder whose height is three times its diameter. Develop a formula for the minimum radius R of canopy required for an oak with trunk radius r, in feet.

Trunk: $h = 3(2r) = 6r;$ $V = \pi r^2 h = \pi r^2(6r) = 6\pi r^3$

Minimum exterior canopy area $= \dfrac{8 \text{ ft}^2}{1 \text{ ft}^3} \times (6\pi r^3) = 48\pi r^3$

In terms of canopy radius, canopy area $= \frac{1}{2}(4\pi R^2) = 2\pi R^2$

$2\pi R^2 = 48\pi r^3$

$R^2 = 24r^3$

$R = \sqrt{24r^3}$

H.O.T. Focus on Higher Order Thinking

21. What If? An animal's weight is proportional to its volume. The strength in its legs to support its weight is proportional to their cross-sectional area. Imagine magnifying a mouse to the size of an elephant. If its length is multiplied by 50, and its density and proportions stay the same, what are the multipliers for its weight and the cross-sectional areas for its legs? Would a mouse this size be able to support itself?

Weight multiplier $=$ volume multiplier $=$ (length multiplier)$^3 = (50)^3 = 125,000$

Cross-section multiplier $=$ (length multiplier)$^2 = (50)^2 = 2,500$

No, because the ratio of leg cross-section to weight has been reduced by a factor of $\frac{1}{50}$.

22. **Multi-step** A stopper will be the shape of the frustum of a cone. The height of the complete cone would be 8 times its base diameter, but the stopper's height is to be only twice the larger base diameter. The stopper is to be made from 10 cm³ of silicone. What should the stopper's base radius R, base radius r, and height be, to the nearest tenth?

Height of complete cone is 8 times the diameter,

or 16 times the radius: $H = 16R$

Smaller base radius: $r = \dfrac{8 - 2}{8}R = 0.75R$

Height of removed part of cone is 0.75 times

the height of the complete cone, or $h = 0.75(16R) = 12R$

Volume of entire cone:

$V = \dfrac{1}{3}\pi R^2 H$

$\quad = \dfrac{1}{3}\pi R^2(16R)$

$\quad = \dfrac{16}{3}\pi R^3 \approx 5.333\pi R^3$

Volume of removed part of cone:

$V = \dfrac{1}{3}\pi r^2 h$

$\quad = \dfrac{1}{3}\pi(0.75R)^2(12R)$

$\quad = 2.25\pi R^3$

Volume of frustum = Volume of entire cone − Volume of removed part

$V \approx 5.333\pi R^3 - 2.25\pi R^3$

$10 \approx 3.083\pi R^3$

Using a graphing calculator, $R \approx 1.010$ cm ≈ 1.0 cm.

$r \approx 0.75(1.010 \text{ cm}) \approx 0.8$ cm

$H - h = 16R - 12R = 4R$

$\quad \approx 4(1.010 \text{ cm}) \approx 4.0$ cm

23. **Look for a Pattern** An aluminum soda can holds 12 fl oz. Investigate the least amount of aluminum needed to make the can: Use the given volume to find a formula for the can's height h in terms of its radius r, substitute into a formula for the can's surface area, and use trial values to determine the values of r and h, to the nearest tenth of an inch, that minimize the can's surface area. (*Hint*: 1 fl oz = 1.73 in³)

$V = \pi r^2 h$

$12(1.73) = \pi r^2 h$

$\dfrac{20.76}{\pi r^2} = h$

$S = 2\pi rh + 2\pi r^2$

$\quad = 2\pi r\left(\dfrac{20.76}{\pi r^2}\right) + 2\pi r^2$

$\quad = \dfrac{41.52}{r} + 2\pi r^2$

By trial values, $r \approx 1.489$ in. ≈ 1.5 in. and $h \approx \dfrac{20.76}{\pi(1.489)^2} \approx 3.0$ in.

Have students explain what a design problem is and give an example of how they solved such a problem.

24. **Persevere in Problem Solving** People have a wide variety of body plans, from endomorphic (short and stocky) to ectormorphic (tall and slender). These body plans represent adaptations to cold or hot climates from earlier in human history. A higher surface area to volume ratio allows body heat to be shed more easily in a hot climate, while a lower ratio helps to retain body heat in very cold conditions. Complete the table. Find the ratio of surface area to volume for each body plan. How much greater is the ratio for the ectomorphic body plan than for the endomorphic one? (For each cylindrical form, count only one circular base in addition to the curved surface.)

Endomorphic body plan			
Part of Body	**Form and Dimensions**	**Volume**	**Exterior Surface Area**
Head	sphere, $d = 6$ in.	$\frac{4}{3}\pi(3)^3 = 36\pi$ in^3	$4\pi(3)^2 = 36\pi$ in^2
Torso	cylinder, $d = 15$ in., $h = 30$ in.	$\pi(7.5)^2(30) = 1{,}687.5\pi$ in^3	$2\pi(7.5)(30) + \pi(7.5)^2$ $= 506.25\pi$ in^2
Arms	cylinder, $d = 3$ in., $h = 24$ in.	$\pi(1.5)^2(24) = 54\pi$ in^3	$2\pi(1.5)(24) + \pi(1.5)^2$ $= 74.25\pi$ in^2
Legs	cylinder, $d = 6$ in., $h = 28$ in.	$\pi(3)^2(28) = 252\pi$ in^3	$2\pi(3)(28) + \pi(3)^2$ $= 177\pi$ in^2
Whole body		$36\pi + 1{,}687.5\pi + 2(54\pi)$ $+ 2(252\pi) = 2335.5\pi$	$36\pi + 506.25\pi + 2(74.25\pi)$ $+ 2(177\pi) = 1044.75\pi$
Ectomorphic body plan			
Part of Body	**Form and Dimensions**	**Volume**	**Exterior Surface Area**
Head	sphere, $d = 6$ in.	$\frac{4}{3}\pi(3)^3 = 36\pi$ in^3	$4\pi(3)^2 = 36\pi$ in^2
Torso	cylinder, $d = 10$ in., $h = 32$ in.	$\pi(5)^2(32) = 800\pi$ in^3	$2\pi(5)(32) + \pi(5)^2$ $= 345\pi$ in^2
Arms	cylinder, $d = 2$ in., $h = 34$ in.	$\pi(1)^2(34) = 34\pi$ in^3	$2\pi(1)(34) + \pi(1)^2$ $= 69\pi$ in^2
Legs	cylinder, $d = 4$ in., $h = 36$ in.	$\pi(2)^2(36) = 144\pi$ in^3	$2\pi(2)(36) + \pi(2)^2$ $= 148\pi$ in^2
Whole body		$36\pi + 800\pi + 2(34\pi)$ $+ 2(144\pi) = 1192\pi$	$36\pi + 345\pi + 2(69\pi)$ $+ 2(148\pi) = 815\pi$

Endomorph: $\dfrac{\text{surface area}}{\text{volume}} = \dfrac{1044.75\pi \text{ in}^2}{2335.5\pi \text{ in}^3} \approx 0.45 \text{ in}^{-1}$

Ectomorph: $\dfrac{\text{surface area}}{\text{volume}} = \dfrac{815\pi \text{ in}^2}{1192\pi \text{ in}^3} \approx 0.68 \text{ in}^{-1}$

The ectomorphic ratio is $\dfrac{0.68}{0.45} \approx 1.51$ times as great as the endomorphic ratio, or about 51% greater.

Lesson Performance Task

In trying to disguise a gift, Henry decides to put a box of blocks into a cylindrical box. The set of blocks is a cube that measures 4 inches on each side. About how much extra wrapping paper will Henry use as a result of this decision?

To wrap the 4 inch cube, Henry would need a sheet of paper that is long enough to cover 4 sides of the cube and wide enough to cover a little more than 2 sides of the cube.

length = 4(4 in.) + overlap = 16 + 2 = 18 in.

width = 2(4 in.) + overlap = 8 + 2 = 10 in.

So he would use about 180 in² of paper to wrap the cube.

To wrap the cylinder, Henry will need a sheet of paper that is as long as the perimeter of the cylinder and as wide as the height of the cylinder plus a little more than twice the radius of the base.

length = $2\pi r$ + overlap = $2(3.14)(2\sqrt{2})$ + 2 ≈ 19.76 in.

width = height + diameter + overlap = $4 + 4\sqrt{2} + 2$ ≈ 11.66 in.

So he will use about 230 in² of paper to wrap the cylinder.

Henry will use about an extra 50 in² of paper to wrap the cylinder.

© Houghton Mifflin Harcourt Publishing Company · Image Credits: ©LOOK Photography/Upper Cut Images/Alamy

EXTENSION ACTIVITY

Someone has a sphere and wants to package it in the cylindrical box used in the Lesson Performance Task. Assume the diameter of the sphere is equal to the diagonal of one side of the cube. What is the ratio of the surface area of the sphere to the surface area of the cylindrical box? Is packaging the sphere in the cylindrical box more or less efficient than packaging the cube in the same cylindrical box? Surface area of sphere: $4\pi r^2 = 4\pi\left(2\sqrt{2}\right)^2 = 32\pi$ ≈ 100.5, ratio: $\frac{100.5}{121.3}$, ≈ 0.83; Possible answer: Because the ratio is greater, packaging the sphere in the cylindrical box is more efficient.

AVOID COMMON ERRORS

When calculating the surface area of a cylinder, students will often forget to add the areas of the top and bottom. Remind students that the surface area is the lateral surface area plus twice the area of the top.

QUESTIONING STRATEGIES

? Which has a greater surface area, a cube with side length a or a sphere with diameter a? The surface area of the cube is $6a^2$ and the surface area of the sphere is $4\pi a^2$, so the sphere has the greater surface area.

Scoring Rubric

2 points: Student correctly solves the problem and explains his/her reasoning.

1 point: Student shows good understanding of the problem but does not fully solve or explain his/her reasoning.

0 points: Student does not demonstrate understanding of the problem.

Problem Solving with Constraints   **1070**

Study Guide Review

ASSESSMENT AND INTERVENTION

Assign or customize module reviews.

MODULE PERFORMANCE TASK

COMMON
CORE

Mathematical Practices: MP.1, MP.2, MP.4, MP.5, MP.6, MP.8
G-MG.A.1, G-MG.A.2

SUPPORTING STUDENT REASONING

To help students get started on this project, you may
wish to make these suggestions:

- **Draw an isosceles trapezoid shaped like
  Saskatchewan.** Label the map with the
  information you know about the province.

- **Use your drawing to estimate the area.** After
  you calculate the area exactly, you can use the
  estimate to check your work.

- **See if you can divide the trapezoid into smaller
  figures whose areas you can find.** If you can do
  this, the area of Saskatchewan will be the sum of
  the areas of the smaller figures.

Essential Question: How can you use modeling to solve
real-world problems?

© Houghton Mifflin Harcourt Publishing Company

Key Vocabulary
density *(densidad)*
scale factor *(factor de escala)*

KEY EXAMPLE   *(Lesson 20.1)*

Find the surface area and volume of a rectangular prism-shaped box measuring 6 inches by 8
inches by 12 inches. Then multiply the dimensions by 2 and find the new surface area and volume.
Describe the changes that took place.

$2(6 \times 8) + 2(6 \times 12) + 2(8 \times 12) = 96 + 144 + 192$	Find the original surface area.
$= 432 \text{ in}^2$	
$6 \times 8 \times 12 = 576 \text{ in}^3$	Find the original volume.
$2(12 \times 16) + 2(12 \times 24) + 2(16 \times 24) = 384 + 576 + 768$	Find the new surface area.
$= 1,728 \text{ in}^2$	
$12 \times 16 \times 24 = 4608 \text{ in}^3$	Find the new volume
$\frac{1728}{432} = 4$ Compare the surface areas. $\frac{4608}{576} = 8$	Compare the volumes.

The surface area is multiplied by 4. The volume is multiplied by 8.

KEY EXAMPLE   *(Lesson 20.2)*

Logan County, Kansas, has a population of 2,784. Its border can be modeled by a rectangle with
vertices $A(-18, 15)$, $B(18, 15)$, $C(18, -15)$, and $D(-18, -15)$, where each unit on the coordinate
plane represents 1 mile. Find the approximate population density of Logan County. Round to the
nearest tenth.

$18 - (-18) = 36 \text{ mi}$	The width of Logan County is the difference of the x-coordinates.
$15 - (-15) = 30 \text{ mi}$	The height of Logan County is the difference of the y-coordinates.
$36 \times 30 = 1080 \text{ mi}^2$	area = length × width
$\frac{2784}{1080} \approx 2.6$	Population density = $\frac{\text{population}}{\text{area}}$

The population density is about 2.6 persons per square mile.

KEY EXAMPLE   *(Lesson 20.3)*

The height of a filing cabinet is 1.5 times the width. The depth is twice the width. The volume of
the cabinet is 12,288 in³. What are the cabinet's dimensions?

Volume = $l \times w \times h$	Write the formula for the volume.
$12,288 = x \times 1.5x \times 2x$	Substitute for the volume, width, height, and depth.
$x = \sqrt[3]{4096}$	Simplify.
$x = 16$	Evaluate the cube root.

Width: 16 inches. Height: 1.5 × 16 = 24 inches. Depth: 2 × 16 = 32 inches.

SCAFFOLDING SUPPORT

- The formula for the area A of a trapezoid with
  bases a and b and height h is $A = \frac{1}{2}h(a + b)$.
  For this task, students are given a and b but
  cannot calculate the exact area until they find h.
  You may wish to provide this figure to give them
  some ideas about how to proceed.

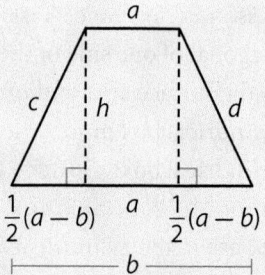

EXERCISES

1. One side of a rhombus measures 12 inches. Two angles measure 60°. Find the perimeter and area of the rhombus. Then multiply the side lengths by 3. Find the new perimeter and area. Describe the changes that took place. *(Lesson 20.1)*

    Original perimeter: 48 in.; original area: $72\sqrt{3}$ in² ; new perimeter: 144 in.; new area: $648\sqrt{3}$ in². The perimeter is multiplied by 3. The area is multiplied by 9.

2. A box of cereal measures 2.25 inches by 7.5 inches by 10 inches. The box contains 16 ounces of cereal. Find the cereal density, to the nearest thousandth. *(Lesson 20.2)*

    0.095 oz/in³

3. The height and diameter of a cylindrical water tank are equal. The tank has a volume of 1200 cubic feet. Find the height of the tank to the nearest tenth. *(Lesson 20.3)*

    11.5 ft

MODULE PERFORMANCE TASK

Population Density

Unlike most geographical regions, the Canadian province of Saskatchewan has a shape that is almost exactly a regular geometric figure. That figure is an isosceles trapezoid. Here are the lengths of the province's four borders:

North: 277 miles South: 390 miles East: 761 miles   West: 761 miles

- Saskatchewan's population in the 2011 census was 1,033,381. What was its population density?

- Saskatchewan is divided into 18 census divisions. Division 18, which makes up the northern half of the province (actually 49.3% of the area), has a population of 36,557. How does the population density of Division 18 compare with that of the southern half of the province?

Start by listing on your own paper the information you will need to solve the problem. Then complete the task. Use numbers, words, or algebra to explain how you reached your conclusion.

© Houghton Mifflin Harcourt Publishing Company

Module 20 — 1072 — Study Guide Review

SAMPLE SOLUTION

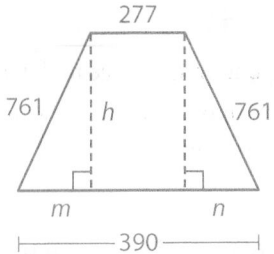

The two right triangles are congruent by the HL and AAS congruence theorems. So, $m = n$, and each equals $\frac{1}{2}(390 - 277) = 56.5$ miles. Applying the Pythagorean Theorem:

$$h^2 + 56.5^2 = 761^2$$

$$h^2 + 3192.25 = 579{,}121$$

$$h^2 = 575{,}928.75$$

$$h \approx 758.9 \text{ miles}$$

Trapezoid area $A = \frac{1}{2}h(a + b)$:

$$A = \frac{1}{2}(758.9)(277 + 390)$$

$$\approx 253{,}093 \text{ square miles}$$

$$\text{population density} \approx \frac{1{,}033{,}381}{253{,}093}$$

$$\approx 4.1 \text{ per square mile}$$

Division 18 population density:

$$\frac{36{,}557}{49.3\% \times 253{,}093} \approx 0.3 \text{ per square mile}$$

Southern half of province population density:

$$\frac{1{,}033{,}381 - 36{,}557}{50.7\% \times 253{,}093} \approx 7.8 \text{ per square mile}$$

The population density of the southern half of the province is more than 25 times as great as the population density of Division 18.

DISCUSSION OPPORTUNITIES

- On some maps, the northern and southern boundaries are slightly curved. Why? The Earth's surface is curved.

- Why might Division 18's population density be so much smaller than the other half of Saskatchewan? Sample answer: The climate is colder and the region less developed the rest of Saskatchewan, plus a large portion of the region is covered by lakes, which reduces the area that can be inhabited.

Assessment Rubric

2 points: Student correctly solves the problem and explains his/her reasoning.

1 point: Student shows good understanding of the problem but does not fully solve or explain.

0 points: Student does not demonstrate understanding of the problem.

Study Guide Review 1072

Ready to Go On?

ASSESS MASTERY

Use the assessment on this page to determine if students have mastered the concepts and standards covered in this module.

ASSESSMENT AND INTERVENTION

Access Ready to Go On? assessment online, and receive instant scoring, feedback, and customized intervention or enrichment.

ADDITIONAL RESOURCES

Response to Intervention Resources

- Reteach Worksheets

Differentiated Instruction Resources

- Reading Strategies **EL**
- Success for English Learners **EL**
- Challenge Worksheets

Assessment Resources

- Leveled Module Quizzes

(Ready) to Go On?

20.1–20.3 Modeling and Problem Solving

- Online Homework
- Hints and Help
- Extra Practice

Solve. Round answers to the nearest tenth. *(Lessons 20.1, 20.2, 20.3)*

1. A circle containing the point $(4, -2)$ has its center at $(1, 2)$. Describe the changes in the circumference and area of the circle if the radius is multiplied by 2.

  The radius of the original circle is 5 units. The circumference of 10π units is doubled to 20π units. The area of 25π square units is quadrupled to 100π square units.

2. Seven hundred people are gathered in a trapezoidal park with bases measuring 60 yards and 80 yards and a height of 50 yards.

  a. Find the population density of the park.

  b. Find the population density if the bases and height are halved.

  a. 0.2 person/yd^2

  b. 0.8 person/yd^2

3. An aquarium in the shape of a rectangular prism has a bottom, no top, two square sides, and two sides the same height as the square sides but twice their length. The total area of the five sides is 1800 in^2. Find the volume of the aquarium. Explain your reasoning.

  6750 in^2; Sample answer: Let x represent the length and height of the square sides. Then the longer sides and the bottom measure $2x$ by x. The total area of the five sides is $x^2 + x^2 + 2x^2 + 2x^2 + 2x^2 = 8x^2$. So, $8x^2 = 1800$. Solving, we get $x = 15$. The tank measures 15 in. $\times$ 15 in. $\times$ 30 in., giving a volume of 6750 in^2.

4. A triangle has base b and height h. The base is doubled. Describe how the height must change so that the area remains the same. Explain your reasoning.

  The height must be halved; sample answer: Area of original triangle $= \frac{1}{2}b_1 h_1$. Area of new triangle $= \frac{1}{2}(2b_1) h_2 = b_1 h_2$. This must equal the original area, $\frac{1}{2} b_1 h_1$: $b_1 h_2 = \frac{1}{2} b_1 h_1$. Diving both sides by b_1 gives $h_2 = \frac{1}{2} h_1$.

ESSENTIAL QUESTION

5. How can you use mathematics to model real-world situations?

  Sample answer: Use variables to represent what you want to know. Then write equations to represent the situations. Solve the equations, relating the solutions to the situations.

© Houghton Mifflin Harcourt Publishing Company

Common Core Standards

Lesson	Items	Content Standards	Mathematical Practices
20.1	1	G-GPE.A.1, G-GMD.A.1	MP.6
20.2	2	G-MG.A.1, G-MG.A.2	MP.4
20.3	3	G-MG.A.3	MP.6
20.3	4	G-MG.A.3	MP.6

Assessment Readiness

1. The dimensions of a cube are tripled. Choose True or False for each statement.

   A. The perimeter of each face is tripled. ⬤ True ◯ False

   B. The surface area of the cube is multiplied by 6. ◯ True ⬤ False

   C. The volume of the cube is multiplied by 27. ⬤ True ◯ False

2. A solid figure has a volume of 300 cubic centimeters. The radius and the height of the figure are equal. Select Yes or No for A–C.

   A. The figure could be a cylinder with a radius of $\sqrt{\frac{300}{\pi}}$. ◯ Yes ⬤ No

   B. The figure could be a cone with a radius of $\sqrt[3]{\frac{900}{\pi}}$. ⬤ Yes ◯ No

   C. The figure could be a cylinder with a height of $\sqrt[3]{\frac{300}{\pi}}$. ⬤ Yes ◯ No

3. A 4-square-mile community of prairie dogs in South Dakota has a total population of 12,000. Over a 3-year period, the total population increases at an average rate of 2% per year. Describe the change in the population density, assuming the total area of the community remains unchanged.

   The density increased by about 184 prairie dogs per square mile; sample answer: Population after 3 years $= 12{,}000(1.02)^3 \approx 12{,}734$. Original density $= \frac{12{,}000}{4} = 3000$ per square mile. Density after 3 years: $\frac{12{,}734}{4} \approx 3184$ per square mile. $3184 - 3000 = 184$ per square mile.

4. A city park in the shape of a right triangle has an area of $450\sqrt{3}$ square yards. One leg of the triangle measures half the length of the hypotenuse. What are the dimensions of the park? Explain your reasoning.

   30 yd by 30 $\sqrt{3}$ yd by 60 yd; sample answer: Let n represent the length of one leg of the triangle and let $2n$ represent the length of the hypotenuse. Then by the Pythagorean Theorem, the third leg measures $\sqrt{4n^2 - n^2} = n\sqrt{3}$. Area $= \frac{1}{2} \cdot n \cdot n\sqrt{3} = \frac{1}{2}n^2\sqrt{3}$. So, $\frac{1}{2}n^2\sqrt{3} = 450\sqrt{3}$. Solving for n gives $n = 30$ yd. The other sides measure 60 yd and 30 $\sqrt{3}$ yd.

MIXED REVIEW
Assessment Readiness

ASSESSMENT AND INTERVENTION

Assign ready-made or customized practice tests to prepare students for high-stakes tests.

ADDITIONAL RESOURCES

Assessment Resources

- Leveled Module Quizzes: Modified, B

AVOID COMMON ERRORS

Item 4 Some students will miss the indication that the triangle is a 30–60–90 right triangle. Encourage students to always consider the special triangle rules before attempting other methods of solving triangles. This will often save them time.

COMMON CORE   Common Core Standards

Lesson	Items	Content Standards	Mathematical Practices
20.1	1	**G-MG.A.1**	**MP.7**
20.3	2	**G-MG.A.3**	**MP.4**
20.2	3*	**G-MG.A.2**	**MP.4**
20.3	4*	**G-MG.A.3**	**MP.4**

* Item integrates mixed review concepts from previous modules or a previous course.

MIXED REVIEW

Assessment Readiness

ASSESSMENT AND INTERVENTION

Assign ready-made or customized practice tests to prepare students for high-stakes tests.

ADDITIONAL RESOURCES

Assessment Resources

- Leveled Unit Tests: Modified, A, B, C
- Performance Assessment

AVOID COMMON ERRORS

Item 2 Some students will forget the last step of finding the volume of a pyramid or cone, failing to multiply by $\frac{1}{3}$. Encourage students to double-check the formulas to ensure they have included every step.

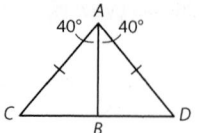
- Online Homework
- Hints and Help
- Extra Practice

1. Consider each congruence theorem below.
   Can you use the theorem to determine whether $\triangle ABC \cong \triangle ABD$?

   Select Yes or No for A–C.

   A. ASA Triangle Congruence Theorem   ○ Yes   ● No
   B. SAS Triangle Congruence Theorem   ● Yes   ○ No
   C. SSS Triangle Congruence Theorem   ○ Yes   ● No

2. For each pyramid, determine whether the statement regarding its volume is true.
   Select True or False for each statement.

   A. A rectangular pyramid with $\ell = 3$ m, $w = 4$ m, $h = 7$ m has volume 84 m³.   ○ True   ● False
   B. A triangular pyramid with base $B = 14$ ft² and $h = 5$ ft has volume 60 ft².   ○ True   ● False
   C. A pyramid with the same base and height of a prism has less volume.   ● True   ○ False

3. For each shape, determine whether the statement regarding its volume is true.
   Select True or False for each statement.

   A. A cone with base radius $r = 5$ in. and $h = 12$ in. has volume 100π in³.   ● True   ○ False
   B. A sphere with radius $r = \frac{6}{\pi}$ m has volume $\frac{8}{\pi^2}$ m³.   ○ True   ● False
   C. A sphere is composed of multiple cones with the same radius.   ○ True   ● False

4. DeMarcus draws $\triangle ABC$. Then he translates it along the vector $(-4, -3)$, rotates it 180°, and reflects it across the x-axis.
   Choose True or False for each statement.

   A. The final image of $\triangle ABC$ is in Quadrant IV.   ○ True   ● False
   B. The final image of $\triangle ABC$ is a right triangle.   ● True   ○ False
   C. DeMarcus will get the same result if he performs the reflection followed by the translation and rotation.   ○ True   ● False

---

COMMON CORE ## Common Core Standards

Items	Content Standards	Mathematical Practices
1	**G-SRT.B.5**	**MP.5**
2	**G-GMD.A.3**	**MP.5**
3	**G-GMD.A.3**	**MP.5**
4*	**G-CO.B.6**	**MP.1**
5	**G-GMD.A.1**	**MP.6**
6*	**G-CO.D.12**	**MP.5**

* Item integrates mixed review concepts from previous modules or a previous course.

5. Determine whether each statement regarding surface area is true.
   Select True or False for each statement.

   A. The surface area of a cone is the sum of the
      areas of a circle and sector of a circle.   ● True   ○ False

   B. The surface area of a sphere is greater
      than a cube's with $s = r$.   ● True   ○ False

   C. A composite figure's surface area is the sum
      of each individual figure's surface area.   ○ True   ● False

6. Can each of the shapes below be expressed as a composite figure of equilateral
   triangles? Select Yes or No for each shape.

   A. A pyramid   ○ Yes   ● No
   B. A hexagon   ● Yes   ○ No
   C. A pentagon   ○ Yes   ● No

7. The figure shows a composite figure formed by two right
   triangles, a square, and a circle. Determine whether the
   probability of throwing a dart into each shape is correct,
   assuming that the dart will always land in one of the shapes.
   Select True or False for each statement.

   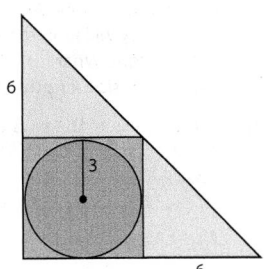

   A. The probability of
      landing in the circle is $\frac{\pi}{8}$.   ● True   ○ False

   B. The probability of landing
      in one of the triangles is $\frac{1}{4}$.   ○ True   ● False

   C. The probability of
      landing in the square is $\frac{1}{2}$.   ● True   ○ False

8. A cube is dilated by a factor of 4. By what factor does its volume increase? Explain
   your reasoning.

   The volume increases by a factor of 64. When the cube is dilated, each side
   length is increased by the dilation factor, so the volume is increased by the
   cube of the dilation factor.

9. The perimeter of $\triangle PQR$ is 44 cm, and $\triangle PQR \sim \triangle WXY$. If $PQ = 12$ and
   $XY + WY = 24$, what is the perimeter of WXY?

   Since the perimeter of $\triangle PQR = 44$, $QR + PR = 44 - PQ$, or 32 cm. This is
   proportional to the sum $XY + WY$, because the two triangles are similar so
   their corresponding sides are proportional. Their ratio is 24 : 32, or 3 : 4,
   which is the same ratio as their perimeters, $\frac{3}{4} = \frac{P}{44}$, so $P = 33$ cm.

PERFORMANCE TASKS

There are three different levels of performance tasks:

  * **Novice:** These are short word problems that
require students to apply the math they have learned
in straightforward, real-world situations.

  ** **Apprentice:** These are more involved problems
that guide students step-by-step through more
complex tasks. These exercises include more
complicated reasoning, writing, and open ended
elements.

  ***Expert:** These are open-ended, nonroutine
problems that, instead of stepping the students
through, ask them to choose their own methods for
solving and justify their answers and reasoning.

Common Core Standards

Items	Content Standards	Mathematical Practices
7	S-CP.A.1	MP.4
8	G-SRT.A.1	MP.3, MP.8
9	G-SRT.B.5	MP.6

* Item integrates mixed review concepts from previous modules or a previous course.

Item 10 (2 points)

Award the student 1 point for the correct scale factor, and 1 point for the correct volume.

Item 11 (6 points)

3 points for drawing of an orderly arrangement

3 points for correct volume

Item 12 (6 points)

A. 1 point for correct answer
   1 point for explanation

B. 2 points for correct ratio
   2 points for showing work

Performance Tasks

★**10.** A scientist wants to compare the densities of two cylinders, but one is twice as high and has a diameter two times as long as the other. How should the scientist compare the two densities of the cylinders if he doesn't know the volume of the larger cylinder? If the volume of the smaller cylinder is 30 cm³, what is the volume of the larger cylinder?

Use the scale factor 2 to find the volume of the larger cylinder. The larger cylinder's volume is equal to 8 times the volume of the smaller cylinder. The larger cylinder has a volume of 240 cm³.

★★**11.** You are trying to pack in preparation for a trip and need to fit a collection of children's toys in a box. Each individual toy is a composite figure of four cubes, and all of the toys are shown in the figure. Arrange the toys in an orderly fashion so that they will fit in the smallest box possible. Draw the arrangement. What is the volume of the box if each of the cubes have side lengths of 10 cm?

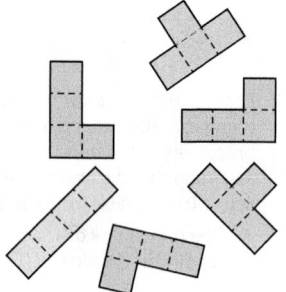

The lengths of the toys are 20 cm, 30 cm, or 40 cm (2 cube lengths, 3 cube lengths, or 4 cube lengths). So the smallest possible dimensions of the box are 20 by 30 by 40 cm, if the toys can be arranged to fit.

★★★**12.** A carpenter has a wooden cone with a slant height of 16 inches and a diameter of 12 inches. The vertex of the cone is directly above the center of its base. He measures halfway down the slant height and makes a cut parallel to the base. He now has a truncated cone and a cone half the height of the original.

A. He expected the two parts to weigh about the same, but they don't. Which is heavier? Why?

B. Find the ratio of the weight of the small cone to that of the truncated cone. Show your work.

A. The truncated cone is heavier because the bottom of the cone is wider than the top.

B. The vertical cross section of the full cone is an isosceles triangle, so the height of the cone is the third side of a right triangle with a hypotenuse of 16 in. and one leg, which is the radius, of 6 in. By the Pythagorean Theorem, the height is $\sqrt{220}$. The volume of the full cone is $\frac{1}{3}\pi \cdot 6^2 \cdot \sqrt{220} = 12\pi\sqrt{220}$. The radius of the small cone is 3 and its height is $\frac{\sqrt{220}}{2}$, so the volume of the small cone is $\frac{1}{3}\pi \cdot 3^2 \cdot \frac{\sqrt{220}}{2} = 1.5\pi\sqrt{220}$. The volume of the truncated cone is the volume of the full cone minus the volume of the small cone: $12\pi\sqrt{220} - 1.5\pi\sqrt{220} = 10.5\pi\sqrt{220}$. The ratio is $\frac{1.5\pi\sqrt{220}}{10.5\pi\sqrt{220}} = \frac{1}{7}$.

Model Maker A model maker wants to create a scale model of a sphere with a volume of 1000 m³. The model should have a volume of 1000 cm³. What scale factor should the model maker use? If a triangle drawn on the model has three right angles, what is its area?

The scale factor is $\frac{1}{100}$ because 1000 cm³ is one millionth of 1000 m³ and the scale factor is the cube root of the volume factors. The area is approximately 60.5 cm². Note that there is a lot of potential for rounding errors in this problem.

MATH IN CAREERS

Model Maker In this Unit Performance Task, students can see how a model maker uses mathematics on the job.

For more information about careers in mathematics as well as various mathematics appreciation topics, visit the American Mathematical Society http://www.ams.org

SCORING GUIDES

Task (6 points)

3 points for the correct scale factor

3 points for the correct area

UNIT 8

Probability

CONTENTS

Unit Pacing Guide

UNIT 8

45-Minute Classes

Module 21

DAY 1	DAY 2	DAY 3	DAY 4	DAY 5
Lesson 21.1	Lesson 21.2	Lesson 21.2	Lesson 21.3	Lesson 21.3

DAY 6	DAY 7	DAY 8		
Lesson 21.4	Lesson 21.4	Module Review and Assessment Readiness		

Module 22

DAY 1	DAY 2	DAY 3	DAY 4	DAY 5
Lesson 22.1	Lesson 22.2	Lesson 22.2	Lesson 22.3	Lesson 22.3

DAY 6				
Module Review and Assessment Readiness				

Module 23

DAY 1	DAY 2	DAY 3	DAY 4	DAY 5
Lesson 23.1	Lesson 23.1	Lesson 23.2	Lesson 23.2	Module Review and Assessment Readiness

DAY 6				
Unit Review and Assessment Readiness				

90-Minute Classes

Module 21

DAY 1	DAY 2	DAY 3	DAY 4
Lesson 21.1	Lesson 21.2	Lesson 21.3	Lesson 21.4
Lesson 21.2	Lesson 21.3	Lesson 21.4	Module Review and Assessment Readiness

Module 22

DAY 1	DAY 2	DAY 3
Lesson 22.1	Lesson 22.2	Lesson 22.3
Lesson 22.2	Lesson 22.3	Module Review and Assessment Readiness

Module 23

DAY 1	DAY 2	DAY 3
Lesson 23.1	Lesson 23.2	Module Review and Assessment Readiness
		Unit Review and Assessment Readiness

Unit 8 **1079B**

Program Resources

PLAN

HMH Teacher App

Access a full suite of teacher resources online and offline on a variety of devices. Plan present, and manage classes, assignments, and activities.

ePlanner
Easily plan your classes, create and view assignments, and access all program resources with your online, customizable planning tool.

Professional Development Videos

Authors Juli Dixon and Matt Larson model successful teaching practices and strategies in actual classroom settings.

QR Codes
Scan with your smart phone to jump directly from your print book to online videos and other resources.

Teacher's Edition

Support students with point-of-use Questioning Strategies, teaching tips, resources for differentiated instruction, additional activities, and more.

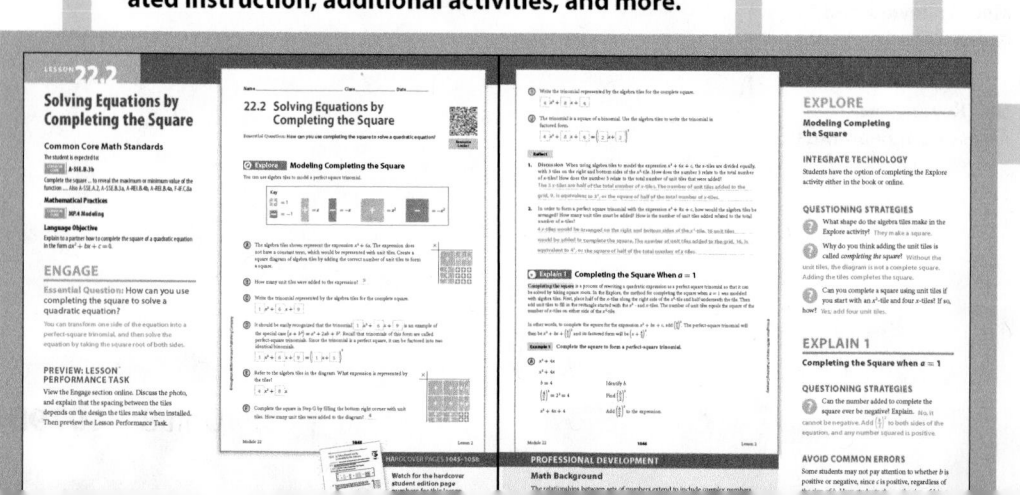

ENGAGE AND EXPLORE

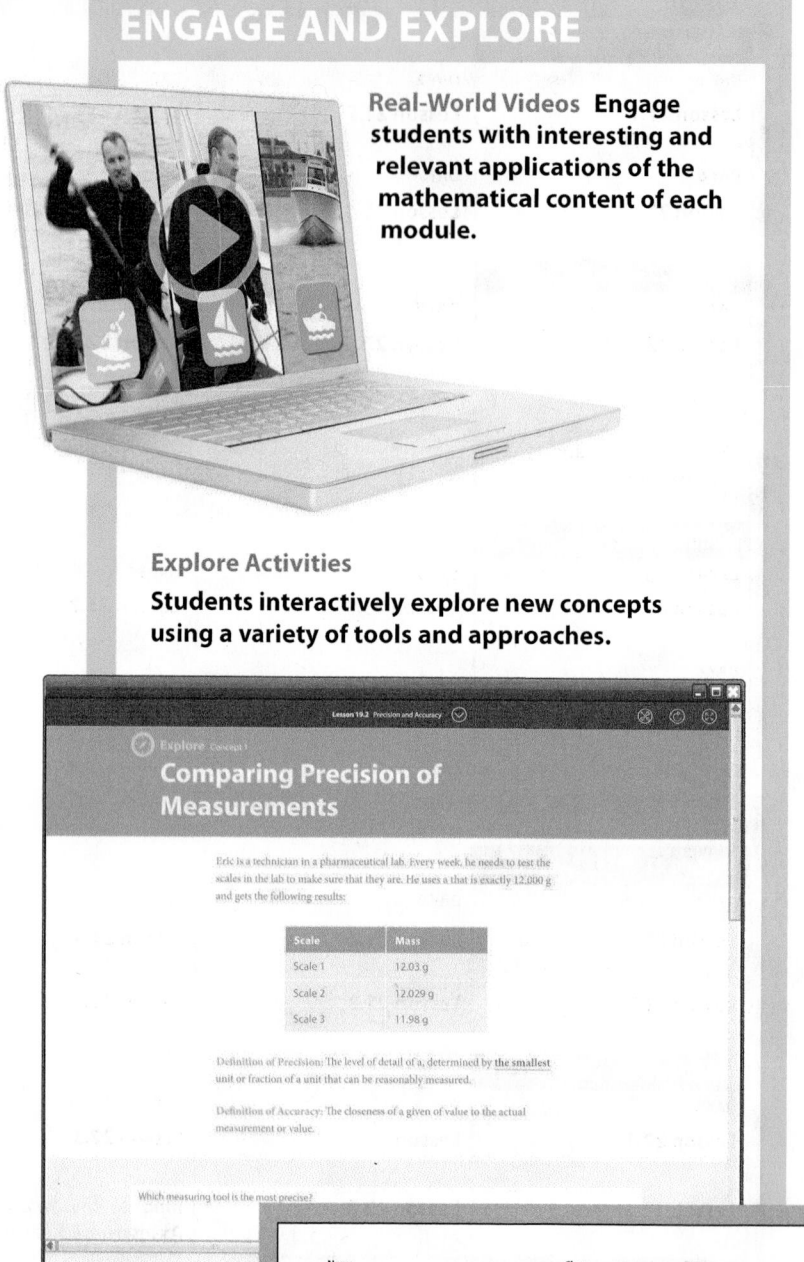

Real-World Videos
Engage students with interesting and relevant applications of the mathematical content of each module.

Explore Activities

Students interactively explore new concepts using a variety of tools and approaches.

Comparing Precision of Measurements

Eric is a technician in a pharmaceutical lab. Every week, he needs to test the scales in the lab to make sure that they are. He uses a that is exactly 12.000 g and gets the following results:

Scale	Mass
Scale 1	12.03 g
Scale 2	12.029 g
Scale 3	11.98 g

Definition of Precision: The level of detail of a, determined by the smallest unit or fraction of a unit that can be reasonably measured.

Definition of Accuracy: The closeness of a given of value to the actual measurement or value.

Which measuring tool is the most precise?

Name _____ Class _____ Date _____

22.2 Solving Equations by Completing the Square

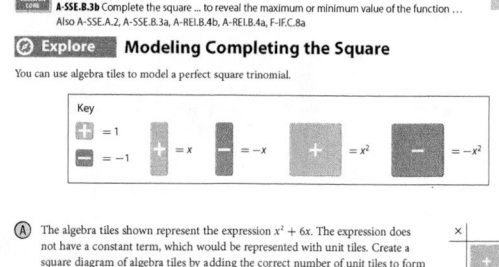

Essential Question: How can you use completing the square to solve a quadratic equation?

A-SSE.B.3b Complete the square ... to reveal the maximum or minimum value of the function ... Also A-SSE.A.2, A-SSE.B.3a, A-REI.B.4b, A-REI.B.4a, F-IFC.8a

Resource Locker

Explore   Modeling Completing the Square

You can use algebra tiles to model a perfect square trinomial.

(A) The algebra tiles shown represent the expression $x^2 + 6x$. The expression does not have a constant term, which would be represented with unit tiles. Create a square diagram of algebra tiles by adding the correct number of unit tiles to form a square.

(B) How many unit tiles were added to the expression? _____

(C) Write the trinomial represented by the algebra tiles for the complete square.

$$x^2 + \boxed{} x + \boxed{}$$

(D) It should be easily recognized that the trinomial $\boxed{} x^2 + \boxed{} x + \boxed{}$ is an example of

TEACH

Math On the Spot video tutorials, featuring program author Dr. Edward Burger, accompany every example in the textbook and give students step-by-step instructions and explanations of key math concepts.

Interactive Teacher Edition

Customize and present course materials with collaborative activities and integrated formative assessment.

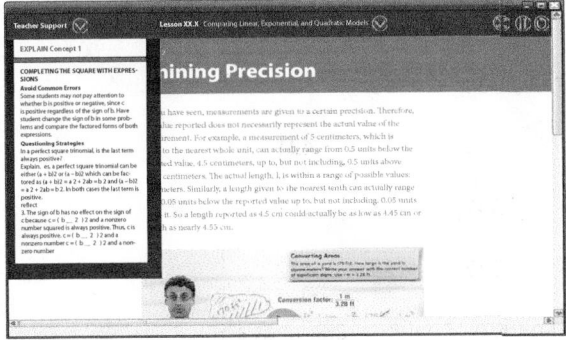

Differentiated Instruction Resources

Support all learners with Differentiated Instruction Resources, including

- **Leveled Practice and Problem Solving**
- **Reading Strategies**
- **Success for English Learners**
- **Challenge**

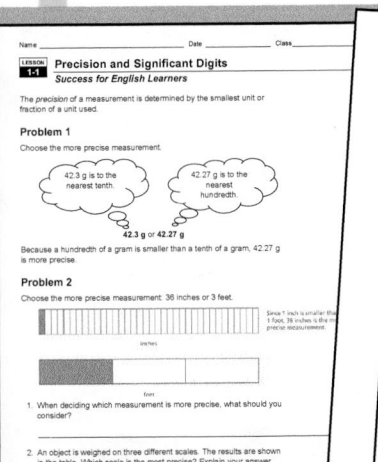
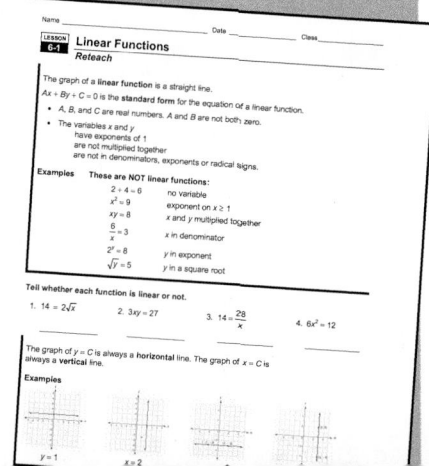

ASSESSMENT AND INTERVENTION

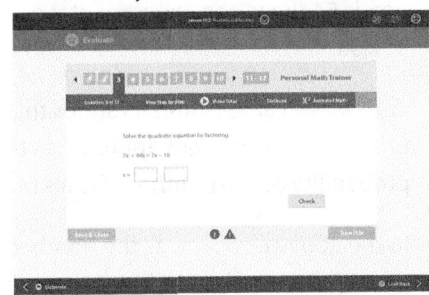

The **Personal Math Trainer** provides online practice, homework, assessments, and intervention. Monitor student progress through reports and alerts. **Create and customize assignments aligned to specific lessons or Common Core standards.**

- **Practice** – With dynamic items and assignments, students get unlimited practice on key concepts supported by guided examples, step-by-step solutions, and video tutorials.

- **Assessments** – Choose from course assignments or customize your own based on course content, Common Core standards, difficulty levels, and more.

- **Homework** – Students can complete online homework with a wide variety of problem types, including the ability to enter expressions, equations, and graphs. Let the system automatically grade homework, so you can focus where your students need help the most!

- **Intervention** – Let the Personal Math Trainer automatically prescribe a targeted, personalized intervention path for your students.

Focus on Higher Order Thinking

Raise the bar with homework and practice that incorporates higher-order thinking and mathematical practices in every lesson.

Assessment Readiness

Prepare students for success on high stakes tests for Geometry with practice at every module and unit

COMMON CORE

Assessment Resources

Tailor assessments and response to intervention to meet the needs of all your classes and students, including

- Leveled Module Quizzes
- Leveled Unit Tests
- Unit Performance Tasks
- Placement, Diagnostic, and Quarterly Benchmark Tests
- Tier 1, Tier 2, and Tier 3 Resources

Math Background

Probability  S-CP.A.1

LESSON 21.1

A *probability* is *a number between 0 and 1 inclusive that measures the likelihood of an event.* When an event consists of finitely many equally likely outcomes, the *theoretical probability* of the event is *the ratio of the number of outcomes in the event to the total number of possible outcomes.*

The probability of an impossible event is 0; the probability of a certain event is 1. When the set of all possible outcomes is finite, the converses of these statements are also true.

Probabilities may also be found by experimental means. The *experimental probability* of an event is *the ratio of the number of times the event occurs to the total number of trials.* For example, if you toss a coin 100 times and it comes up heads 54 times, the experimental probability of heads is $\frac{54}{100}$, or 0.54.

The Law of Large Numbers states that the experimental probability of an event approaches the theoretical probability as the number of trials becomes arbitrarily large.

In the above example, as the number of coin flips increases, the experimental probability of heads will approach the theoretical probability, 0.5.

Permutations and Combinations  S-CP.9

LESSONS 21.2 and 21.3

Combinatorics is *the branch of mathematics that deals with arranging and counting finite collections of items.*

One of the earliest known uses of combinatorial reasoning is in a medical text from India that dates from the 6th century B.C.E.

The author asserts that six basic tastes—salty, sour, bitter, sweet, hot, and astringent—may be combined to form 63 different taste combinations (6 individual tastes, 15 combinations of two tastes, 20 combinations of three tastes, 15 combinations of four tastes, 6 combinations of five tastes, and 1 combination using all six tastes). This is an example of a combination.

A *combination* is *a grouping of items in which the order does not matter.*

In a permutation, the order of the items does matter.

For a permutation of n items taken r items at a time $\left(_nP_r \right)$, there are

> n choices for the 1st item;
>
> $n - 1$ choices for the 2nd item;
>
> $n - 2$ choices for the 3rd item ; and
>
> $n - (r + 1)$ choices for the last item.

The total number of permutations is the product $n(n-1)(n-2)\ldots\left(n-(r+1)\right)$, or $\frac{n!}{(n-r)!}$.

Consider permutations of 4 numbers taken 3 at a time, shown in the array below. Each row shows six distinct permutations that are equivalent combinations.

123	132	213	231	312	321
124	142	214	241	412	421
134	143	314	341	413	431
234	243	324	342	423	432

In general, for a combination of n items taken r at a time $\left(_nC_r \right)$, each combination appears $r!$ times in the corresponding list of permutations. In other words,

$$\left(_nC_r \right) = \frac{_nP_r}{r!} = \frac{n!}{r!(n-r)!}.$$

Independent and Dependent Events

 **S-CP.A.2**

LESSONS 22.2 and 22.3

Two events are *independent* if *the occurrence of one does not affect the probability of the other.*

If A and B are independent, then $P(A$ and $B)$, also written $P(A \cap B)$, is $P(A) \cdot P(B)$.

More generally, events $A_1, A_2, \ldots, A_n$ are mutually independent if the occurrence of any one does not affect the probability of any other. Then,

$P(A_1 \cap A_2 \cap \ldots A_n) = P(A_1) \cdot P(A_2) \cdot \ldots \cdot P(A_n)$.

Mutually exclusive events cannot occur in the same trial.

For example, a coin cannot simultaneously show heads and tails.

If A and B are mutually exclusive, then $P(A$ or $B)$, also written $P(A \cup B)$, is $P(A) + P(B)$.

This addition rule is generally used when finding probability for a single trial, while the multiplication rule for independent events is usually applied to two or more separate trials, performed either simultaneously or in succession.

If all possible outcomes of an experiment can be expressed as numbers, then the *probability distribution* of the experiment is *a function that pairs each outcome with its probability*.

For example, the probability distribution for rolling a number cube is $P(X) = \frac{1}{6}$, where the input X may be the outcome 1, 2, 3, 4, 5, or 6.

Probability distributions obey all the rules of probability.

That is, for any X, $0 \leq P(X) \leq 1$ and the sum of all the probabilities $P(X)$ over all possible values of X is 1.

If X can take the values $x_1, x_2, \ldots, x_n$ and the corresponding probabilities are $p_1, p_2, \ldots, p_n$, then the expected value for the experiment is $x_1 p_1 + x_2 p_2 + \ldots + x_n p_n$.

The expected value for rolling a number cube is

$$1\left(\frac{1}{6}\right) + 2\left(\frac{1}{6}\right) + 3\left(\frac{1}{6}\right) + 4\left(\frac{1}{6}\right) + 5\left(\frac{1}{6}\right) + 6\left(\frac{1}{6}\right) = \frac{21}{6} = 3.5.$$

The expected value, 3.5, is the average outcome over a large number of trials.

In this sense, it is the "typical" value you expect to roll.

As this example shows, the expected value need not be one of the possible outcomes of the experiment.

Probability

MATH IN CAREERS
Unit Activity Preview

After completing this unit, students will complete a Math in Careers task by tracking the percentages of a population that are afflicted by infections. Critical skills include modeling real-world situations and applying knowledge of overlapping events.

For more information about careers in mathematics as well as various mathematics appreciation topics, visit The American Mathematical Society at http://www.ams.org.

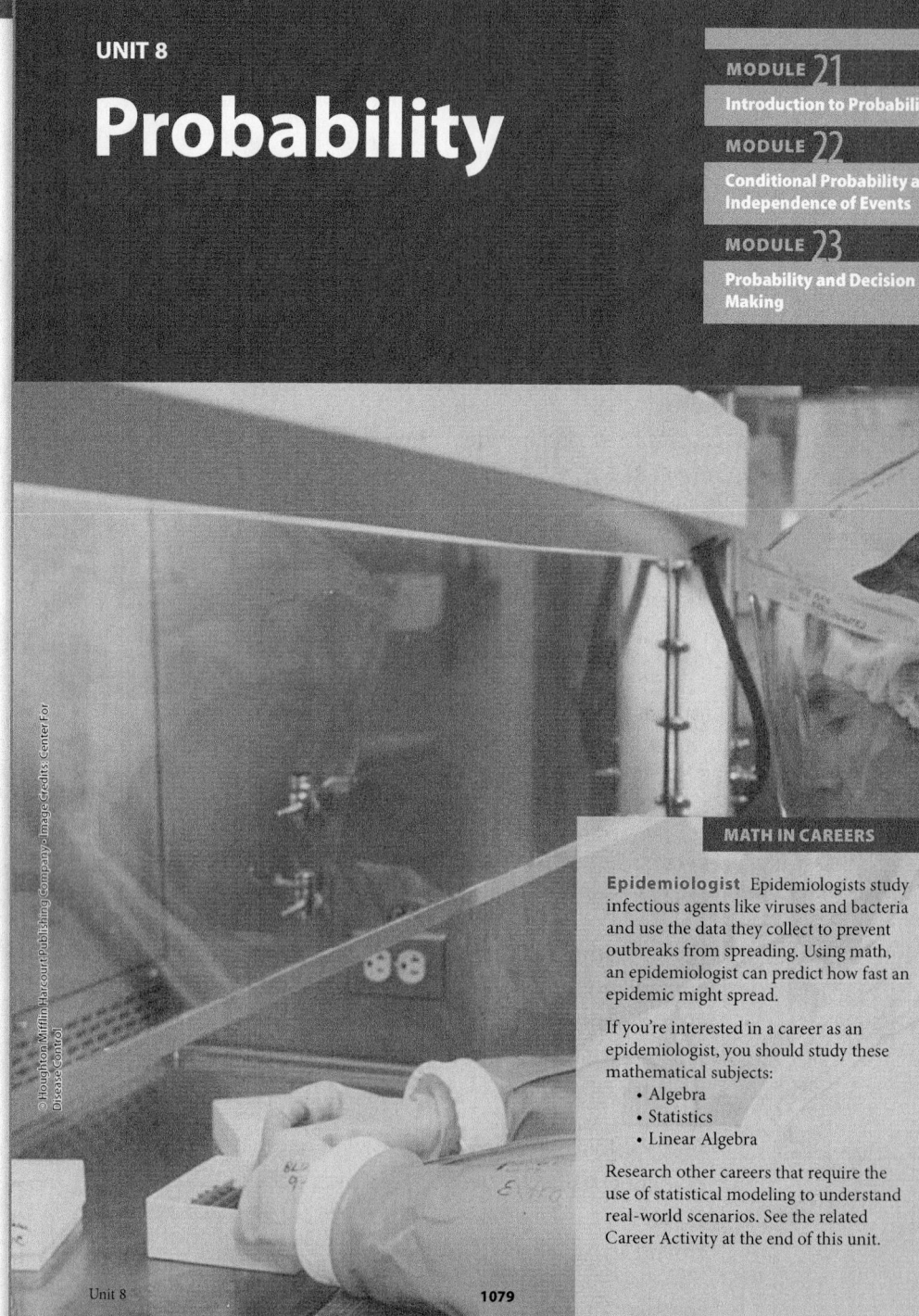

Probability

MODULE 21
Introduction to Probability

MODULE 22
Conditional Probability and Independence of Events

MODULE 23
Probability and Decision Making

© Houghton Mifflin Harcourt Publishing Company • Image Credits: Center For Disease Control

MATH IN CAREERS

Epidemiologist Epidemiologists study infectious agents like viruses and bacteria and use the data they collect to prevent outbreaks from spreading. Using math, an epidemiologist can predict how fast an epidemic might spread.

If you're interested in a career as an epidemiologist, you should study these mathematical subjects:
- Algebra
- Statistics
- Linear Algebra

Research other careers that require the use of statistical modeling to understand real-world scenarios. See the related Career Activity at the end of this unit.

Unit 8   1079

TRACKING YOUR LEARNING PROGRESSION

Before	In this Unit	After
Students understand: • finding the volume and surface area of a prism, cylinder, pyramid, cone, and sphere • cross sections and solids of rotation • scale factor • calculating densities • modeling to meet constraints	Students will learn about: • probability • set theory • permutations and combinations • conditional probability • independent and dependent events • using probability in making and analyzing decisions	Students will learn about: • analyzing functions, including end behavior • transforming function graphs and inverses of functions • graphing, writing, and solving functions including trigonometric functions

Reading Start-Up

Visualize Vocabulary

Match the review words to their descriptions to complete the chart.

Word	Description
probability	The measure of how likely an event is to occur
sample space	All possible outcomes of an experiment
event	Any set of outcomes
trial	A single repetition or observation of an experiment
outcome	A result of an experiment

Vocabulary

Review Words
- ✔ event (*evento*)
- ✔ outcome (*resultado*)
- ✔ probability (*probabilidad*)
- ✔ sample space (*muestra de espacio*)
- ✔ trial (*prueba*)

Preview Words
combination (*combinación*)
complement (*complementar*)
conditional probability (*probabilidad condicional*)
dependent events (*eventos dependientes*)
element (*elemento*)
empty set (*conjunto vacío*)
factorial (*factorial*)
independent events (*eventos independientes*)
intersection (*intersección*)
permutation (*permutación*)
set (*conjunto*)
subset (*subconjunto*)
union (*unión*)

Understand Vocabulary

Complete the sentences using the preview words.

1. The _empty set_ contains no elements.

2. If the occurrence of one event does not affect the occurrence of another event, then the events are called _independent events_.

3. A(n) _permutation_ is a group of objects in a particular order.

4. To find the _factorial_ of a positive integer, find the product of the number and all of the positive integers less than the number.

Active Reading

Key-Term Fold Create a Key-Term Fold with vocabulary words on the flaps and descriptions of the words behind them. Focus on how the vocabulary words for the unit relate. When speaking, describe the words when needed to make sure your ideas clear.

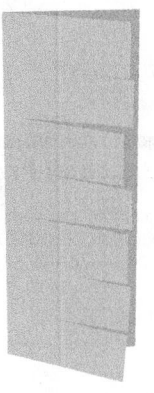

Reading Start Up

Have students complete the activities on this page by working alone or with others.

VISUALIZE VOCABULARY

The definition chart helps students review vocabulary associated with probability. If time allows, ask students to provide examples for each term.

UNDERSTAND VOCABULARY

Use the following explanations to help students learn the preview words.

A **set** is a collection of numbers or objects. Each member of the set is an **element**. The **empty set** contains no elements. A **subset** contains elements of a larger set. The **intersection** of two sets contains the elements common to both sets. The **union** of two sets contains all the elements of both sets. The **complement** of an event is all the outcomes in the sample space that are not in the event.

ACTIVE READING

Students can use these reading and note-taking strategies to help them organize and understand the new concepts and vocabulary. Encourage students to include examples to support the vocabulary on the key-term fold. Emphasize the importance to students of continuing to seek as much vocabulary clarification as needed throughout the unit to help them succeed in understanding problem contexts and applications.

ADDITIONAL RESOURCES

Differentiated Instruction

- Reading Strategies

Introduction to Probability

ESSENTIAL QUESTION:

Answer: Probability is useful for analyzing the likelihood that a particular event will happen; for example, that a die will show 6 on a throw, or that it will rain.

PROFESSIONAL DEVELOPMENT VIDEO

Professional Development Video

Author Juli Dixon models successful teaching practices in an actual high-school classroom.

Professional Development
my.hrw.com

MODULE 21

Introduction to Probability

Essential Question: How can you use probability to solve real-world problems?

REAL WORLD VIDEO
Check out how principles of statistics and probability are used to derive and interpret baseball players' statistics.

© Houghton Mifflin Harcourt Publishing Company • Image Credits: ©Tetra Images/Alamy

MODULE PERFORMANCE TASK PREVIEW

Baseball Probability

In this module, you will use concepts of probability to determine the chances of various outcomes for a baseball player at bat. To successfully complete this task, you'll need to calculate a theoretical probability for a real-world situation. Batter up!

Module 21   **1081**

DIGITAL TEACHER EDITION

Access a full suite of teaching resources when and where you need them:

- Access content online or offline
- Customize lessons to share with your class
- Communicate with your students in real-time
- View student grades and data instantly to target your instruction where it is needed most

PERSONAL MATH TRAINER

Assessment and Intervention

Assign automatically graded homework, quizzes, tests, and intervention activities. Prepare your students with updated, Common Core-aligned practice tests.

Are YOU Ready?

Complete these exercises to review skills you will need for this module.

Probability of Simple Events

Example 1 Find the probability of rolling a 4 when using a normal six-sided die with each side having equal probability.

• Online Homework
• Hints and Help
• Extra Practice

Each of the six faces has equal probability, so the probability of any face being rolled is $\frac{1}{6}$.

There is only one face with a four on it, so the probability of rolling a four is also $\frac{1}{6}$.

Find each probability.

1. The probability of flipping a coin and getting a heads, given that the probability of getting a tails is the same, and there is no chance that the coin lands on its side

   $\frac{1}{2}$

2. The probability of drawing a Jack of Hearts from a 52-card deck given the deck is properly shuffled

   $\frac{1}{52}$

3. The probability of any particular day being Sunday

   $\frac{1}{7}$

Probability of Compound Events

Example 2 Find the probability of drawing a red card or a black card when the probability of either is $\frac{1}{4}$ and you only draw one card.

Only one card is drawn and either card has a $\frac{1}{4}$ probability, so the probability of drawing one or the other is the sum of their probabilities.

Probability of drawing a red card or black card $\frac{1}{4} + \frac{1}{4} = \frac{1}{2}$.

Find each probability.

4. The probability of rolling a twelve-sided die and getting a 4 or a 6 given the probability of getting a 4 is $\frac{1}{12}$ and is equal to the probability of getting a 6

   $\frac{1}{6}$

5. The probability of pulling a red or a blue marble from a jar given the probability of drawing a red marble is $\frac{1}{4}$ and the probability of pulling a blue marble is $\frac{1}{2}$ and you only pull one marble

   $\frac{3}{4}$

Are You Ready?

ASSESS READINESS

Use the assessment on this page to determine if students need strategic or intensive intervention for the module's prerequisite skills.

ASSESSMENT AND INTERVENTION

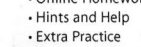

RtI Response to Intervention **TIER 1, TIER 2, TIER 3 SKILLS**

Personal Math Trainer will automatically create a standards-based, personalized intervention assignment for your students, targeting each student's individual needs!

ADDITIONAL RESOURCES

See the table below for a full list of intervention resources available for this module.

Response to Intervention Resources also includes:

• Tier 2 Skill Pre-Tests for each Module
• Tier 2 Skill Post-Tests for each skill

Response to Intervention			Differentiated Instruction
Tier 1 Lesson Intervention Worksheets	**Tier 2** Strategic Intervention Skills Intervention Worksheets	**Tier 3** Intensive Intervention Worksheets available online	
Reteach 21.1 Reteach 21.2 Reteach 21.3 Reteach 21.4	14 Probability of Compound Events 15 Probability of Simple Events	Building Block Skills 6, 12, 37, 39, 65, 72, 82, 86, 95, 112	Challenge worksheets Extend the Math Lesson Activities in TE

Probability and Set Theory

Common Core Math Standards

The student is expected to:

 **S-CP.A.1**

Describe events as subsets of a sample space (the set of outcomes) using characteristics ... of the outcomes, or as unions, intersections, or complements of other events ("or,""and,""not").

Mathematical Practices

 MP.6 Precision

Language Objective

Explain to a partner how to find the probability of rolling a certain number on a number cube and how to find its complement.

ENGAGE

Essential Question: How are sets and their relationships used to calculate probabilities?

To calculate the probability of an event, you need to know the number of items in the set of outcomes for that event, as well as the number of items in the set of all possible outcomes. The theoretical probability of the event is the ratio of the two numbers.

PREVIEW: LESSON PERFORMANCE TASK

View the Engage section online. Discuss the photograph. Ask students to describe math problems that could be illustrated by the two dogs. Then preview the Lesson Performance Task.

21.1 Probability and Set Theory

Essential Question: How are sets and their relationships used to calculate probabilities?

Resource Locker

⊘ Explore   Working with Sets

A **set** is a collection of distinct objects. Each object in a set is called an **element** of the set. A set is often denoted by writing the elements in braces.

The set with no elements is the **empty set**, denoted by ∅ or { }.

The set of all elements under consideration is the **universal set**, denoted by U.

Identifying the number of elements in a set is important for calculating probabilities.

(A) Use set notation to identify each set described in the table and identify the number of elements in each set.

Set	Set Notation	Number of Elements in the Set
Set A is the set of prime numbers less than 10.	$A = \left\{ 2, 3, \boxed{5}, 7 \right\}$	$n(A) = 4$
Set B is the set of even natural numbers less than 10.	$B = \left\{ \boxed{2}, \boxed{4}, 6, \boxed{8} \right\}$	$n(B) = \boxed{4}$
Set C is the set of natural numbers less than 10 that are multiples of 4.	$\boxed{C} = \left\{ 4, \boxed{8} \right\}$	$n(C) = \boxed{2}$
The universal set is all natural numbers less than 10.	$U = \left\{ 1, 2, 3, 4, 5, 6, 7, 8, 9 \right\}$	$n\left(\boxed{U} \right) = 9$

HARDCOVER PAGES 905–914

Turn to these pages to find this lesson in the hardcover student edition.

The following table identifies terms used to describe relationships among sets. Use sets *A*, *B*, *C*, and *U* from the previous table. You will supply the missing Venn diagrams in the Example column, including the referenced elements of the sets, as you complete steps B–I following.

Term	Notation	Venn Diagram	Example
Set *C* is a **subset** of set *B* if every element of *C* is also an element of *B*.	$C \subset B$		
The **intersection** of sets *A* and *B* is the set of all elements that are in both *A and B*.	$A \cap B$	 $A \cap B$ is the double-shaded region.	
The **union** of sets *A* and *B* is the set of all elements that are in *A or B*.	$A \cup B$	 $A \cup B$ is the entire shaded region.	
The **complement** of set *A* is the set of all elements in the universal set *U* that are *not* in *A*.	A^C or $\sim A$	 A^C is the shaded region.	

(B) Since *C* is a subset of *B*, every element of set *C*, which consists of the numbers __4__ and __8__, is located not only in oval *C*, but also within oval *B*. Set *B* includes the elements of *C* as well as the additional elements __2__ and __6__, which are located in oval *B* outside of oval *C*. The universal set includes the elements of sets *B* and *C* as well as the additional elements __1__, __3__, __5__, __7__, and __9__, which are located in region *U* outside of ovals *B* and *C*.

(C) In the first row of the table, draw the corresponding Venn diagram that includes the elements of *B*, *C*, and *U*. **See first row of table.**

(D) To determine the intersection of *A* and *B*, first define the elements of set *A* and set *B* separately, then identify all the elements found in both sets *A and B*.

$$A = \{\ 2\ ,\ 3\ ,\ 5\ ,\ 7\ \}$$

$$B = \{\ 2\ ,\ 4\ ,\ 6\ ,\ 8\ \}$$

$$A \cap B = \{\ 2\ \}$$

Module 21 1084 Lesson 1

© Houghton Mifflin Harcourt Publishing Company

PROFESSIONAL DEVELOPMENT

Math Background

A German mathematician, Georg Cantor (1845–1918), is considered to be the father of set theory. Cantor discovered that the rational numbers are countable but the real numbers are uncountable.

Two French mathematicians, Blaise Pascal (1623–1662) and Pierre de Fermat (1601–1665), are considered to be the founders of probability theory. The roots of probability theory lie in the letters they exchanged analyzing games of chance.

EXPLORE

Working with Sets

INTEGRATE TECHNOLOGY

Students have the option of doing the Explore activity either in the book or online.

INTEGRATE MATHEMATICAL PRACTICES

Focus on Modeling

MP.4 Discuss how the Venn diagrams provide pictures of set relationships to help students understand the terminology. Encourage students to practice drawing Venn diagrams to use when investigating set theory. For example, discuss how a Venn diagram can make it easier to identify the complement of an intersection.

AVOID COMMON ERRORS

Students may assume that a set that contains only 0 is the same as the empty set. Contrast the empty set, { }, with the set that contains only 0, {0}.

QUESTIONING STRATEGIES

? What word corresponds to the intersection of two sets? Is it *union*? Explain. *And* means the elements are in both sets, which corresponds to the intersection. *Or* means the elements can be in either set, which corresponds to the union.

? How is an intersection different from a subset? The intersection consists of the elements two sets have in common, while all of the elements of a subset lie within the set of which it is a subset.

? How do you know when sets overlap? Sets will overlap when they have some elements in common.

Probability and Set Theory **1084**

EXPLAIN 1

Calculating Theoretical Probabilities

INTEGRATE MATHEMATICAL PRACTICES
Focus on Math Connections

MP.1 Discuss the set notation used to define theoretical probability. Connect the notation to a word description of the probability ratio, such as, *the ratio of favorable outcomes in sample space to total number of outcomes in sample space.*

AVOID COMMON ERRORS

Students may have difficulty identifying an event based on a union or intersection. Suggest that students draw Venn diagrams to model the experiment. They can begin by defining each set and then create the Venn diagram to show where the sets overlap.

(E) In the second row of the table, draw the Venn diagram for $A \cap B$ that includes the elements of A, B, and U and the double-shaded intersection region. **See second row of table.**

(F) To determine the union of sets A and B, identify all the elements found in either set A or set B by combining all the elements of the two sets into the union set.

$$A \cup B = \left\{ 2, 3, 4, 5, 6, 7, 8 \right\}$$

(G) In the third row of the table, draw the Venn diagram for $A \cup B$ that includes the elements of A, B, and U and the shaded union region. **See third row of table.**

(H) To determine the complement of set A, first identify the elements of set A and universal set U separately, then identify all the elements in the universal set that are *not* in set A.

$$A = \left\{ 2, 3, 5, 7 \right\}$$

$$U = \left\{ 1, 2, 3, 4, 5, 6, 7, 8, 9 \right\}$$

$$A^C = \left\{ 1, 4, 6, 8, 9 \right\}$$

(I) In the fourth row of the table, draw the Venn diagram for A^c that includes the elements of A and U and the shaded region that represents the complement of A. **See fourth row of table.**

Reflect

1. **Draw Conclusions** Do sets always have an intersection that is not the empty set? Provide an example to support your conclusion.
   No. Using the example sets above, $A \cap C = \varnothing$ because they do not have any elements in common.

⚙ Explain 1   Calculating Theoretical Probabilities

A *probability experiment* is an activity involving chance. Each repetition of the experiment is called a *trial* and each possible result of the experiment is termed an *outcome*. A set of outcomes is known as an *event*, and the set of all possible outcomes is called the *sample space*.

Probability measures how likely an event is to occur. An event that is impossible has a probability of 0, while an event that is certain has a probability of 1. All other events have a probability between 0 and 1. When all the outcomes of a probability experiment are equally likely, the **theoretical probability** of an event A in the sample space S is given by

$$P(A) = \frac{\text{number of outcomes in the event}}{\text{number of outcomes in the sample space}} = \frac{n(A)}{n(S)}.$$

© Houghton Mifflin Harcourt Publishing Company

COLLABORATIVE LEARNING

Small Group Activity

Ask each group to draw a spinner with 6 or 8 equal parts. Then ask them to use letters, colors, or numbers to distinguish each section of the spinner. Have them define two events based on the spinners. For example, if letters are used, the set of vowels and the set of letters in the word *math*. Ask students to find the probability of each event, their complements, their union, and their intersection. Have students share their work. Review which events have a probability of 1, which have a probability of 0, and why.

Example 1 Calculate $P(A)$, $P(A \cup B)$, $P(A \cap B)$, and $P(A^C)$ for each situation.

(A) You roll a number cube. Event A is rolling a prime number. Event B is rolling an even number.

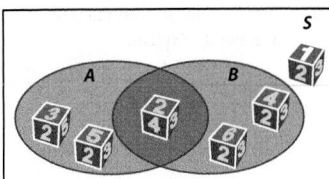

$S = \{1, 2, 3, 4, 5, 6\}$, so $n(S) = 6$. $A = \{2, 3, 5\}$, so $n(A) = 3$.

So, $P(A) = \dfrac{n(A)}{n(S)} = \dfrac{3}{6} = \dfrac{1}{2}$.

$A \cup B = \{2, 3, 4, 5, 6\}$, so $n(A \cup B) = 5$. So, $P(A \cup B) = \dfrac{n(A \cup B)}{n(S)} = \dfrac{5}{6}$.

$A \cap B = \{2\}$, so $n(A \cap B) = 1$. So, $P(A \cap B) = \dfrac{n(A \cap B)}{n(S)} = \dfrac{1}{6}$.

$A^C = \{1, 4, 6\}$, so $n(A^C) = 3$. So, $P(A^C) = \dfrac{n(A^C)}{n(S)} = \dfrac{3}{6} = \dfrac{1}{2}$.

(B) Your grocery basket contains one bag of each of the following items: oranges, green apples, green grapes, green broccoli, white cauliflower, orange carrots, and green spinach. You are getting ready to transfer your items from your cart to the conveyer belt for check-out. Event A is picking a bag containing a vegetable first. Event B is picking a bag containing a green food first. All bags have an equal chance of being picked first.

Order of objects in sets may vary.

$S = \{$orange, apple, grape, broccoli, cauliflower, carrot, spinach$\}$, so $n(S) = \boxed{7}$.

$A = \{$broccoli, cauliflower, $\underline{\text{carrot}}$, $\underline{\text{spinach}}\}$, so $n(A) = \boxed{4}$. So $P(A) = \dfrac{n\left(\boxed{A}\right)}{n\left(\boxed{S}\right)} = \dfrac{\boxed{4}}{\boxed{7}}$.

$A \cup B = \{$broccoli, $\underline{\text{cauliflower}}$, $\underline{\text{carrot}}$, $\underline{\text{spinach}}$, $\underline{\text{apple}}$, grape$\}$, so $n(A \cup B) = \boxed{6}$.

$P(A \cup B) = \dfrac{n\left(\boxed{A} \cup \boxed{B}\right)}{n\left(\boxed{S}\right)} = \dfrac{\boxed{6}}{\boxed{7}}$

$A \cap B = \{\underline{\text{broccoli}}, \underline{\text{spinach}}\}$, so $n(A \cap B) = \boxed{2}$.

$P(A \cap B) = \dfrac{n\left(\boxed{A} \cap \boxed{B}\right)}{n\left(\boxed{S}\right)} = \dfrac{\boxed{2}}{\boxed{7}}$

$P\left(\boxed{A^C}\right) = \dfrac{n\left(\boxed{A^C}\right)}{n\left(\boxed{S}\right)} = \dfrac{\boxed{3}}{\boxed{7}}$

? When you calculate the theoretical probabilities of events based on the same probability experiment, can the term in the denominator of the probability ratio change? Explain. No, the term in the denominator corresponds to the sample space, which does not change.

? If a set has no elements, what is the probability of the event represented by the set? Explain. 0, because there are no outcomes in the sample space that correspond to the event

? If the elements of a set are the same as the elements of the sample space, what is the probability of the event represented by the set? Explain. 1, because the number of elements in the set is the same as the number of elements in the sample space

DIFFERENTIATE INSTRUCTION

Manipulatives

Encourage students to design their own experiments to illustrate what they have learned about probability, such as calculating the complement of rolling a number with a number cube and then attempting to conform the calculation experimentally. Invite students to demonstrate their experiments before the class.

EXPLAIN 2

Using the Complement of an Event

AVOID COMMON ERRORS

Students may have difficulty understanding when to use the complement to find a probability. Point out that students may be able to find the probability directly but that the complement may provide a shortcut. Continue to remind students to create Venn diagrams to help them recognize relationships between sets.

QUESTIONING STRATEGIES

? Why are there different equations that relate the probability of an event and its complement? The three equations state the same relationship in different ways.

Reflect

2. **Discussion** In Example 1B, which is greater, $P(A \cup B)$ or $P(A \cap B)$? Do you think this result is true in general? Explain.

Since $P(A \cup B) = \frac{6}{7}$ is greater than $P(A \cap B) = \frac{2}{7}$, the union is more likely than the intersection. Yes, this is generally true since the union includes all the elements from both events, whereas the intersection contains only elements present in both sets. However, if $A = B$, then the probability of the union and intersection will be the same.

Your Turn

The numbers 1 through 30 are written on slips of paper that are then placed in a hat. Students draw a slip to determine the order in which they will give an oral report. Event A is being one of the first 10 students to give their report. Event B is picking a multiple of 6. If you pick first, calculate each of the indicated probabilities.

3. $P(A)$

$$P(A) = \frac{n(A)}{n(S)} = \frac{10}{30} = \frac{1}{3}$$

4. $P(A \cup B)$

$$A \cup B = \{1, 2, 3, 4, 5, 6, 7, 8, 9, 10, 12, 18, 24, 30\}; \quad P(A \cup B) = \frac{n(A \cup B)}{n(S)} = \frac{14}{30}$$

5. $P(A \cap B)$

$$A \cap B = \{6\}; \quad P(A \cap B) = \frac{n(A \cap B)}{n(S)} = \frac{1}{30}$$

6. $P(A^c)$

$$A^c = \{11, 12,..., 30\}; \quad P(A^c) = \frac{n(A^c)}{n(S)} = \frac{20}{30} = \frac{2}{3}$$

⊘ Explain 2 **Using the Complement of an Event**

You may have noticed in the previous examples that the probability of an event occurring and the probability of the event not occurring (i.e., the probability of the complement of the event) have a sum of 1. This relationship can be useful when it is more convenient to calculate the probability of the complement of an event than it is to calculate the probability of the event.

Probabilities of an Event and Its Complement	
$P(A) + P(A^c) = 1$	The sum of the probability of an event and the probability of its complement is 1.
$P(A) = 1 - P(A^c)$	The probability of an event is 1 minus the probability of its complement.
$P(A^c) = 1 - P(A)$	The probability of the complement of an event is 1 minus the probability of the event.

© Houghton Mifflin Harcourt Publishing Company

Module 21   **1087**   Lesson 1

LANGUAGE SUPPORT **EL**

Connect Vocabulary

Have students create a set of cards with diagrams to help them become familiar with the vocabulary introduced in this lesson. Help students connect the vocabulary to the notation used to represent a *set*, an *element*, the *universal set*, a *subset*, *union*, *intersection*, and *complement*. Have students use different colors to highlight and distinguish each relationship.

1087   Lesson 21.1

Use the complement to calculate the indicated probabilities.

(A) You roll a blue number cube and a white number cube at the same time. What is the probability that you do not roll doubles?

Blue Number Cube

White Number Cube	1	2	3	4	5	6
1	1, 1	1, 2	1, 3	1, 4	1, 5	1, 6
2	2, 1	2, 2	2, 3	2, 4	2, 5	2, 6
3	3, 1	3, 2	3, 3	3, 4	3, 5	3, 6
4	4, 1	4, 2	4, 3	4, 4	4, 5	4, 6
5	5, 1	5, 2	5, 3	5, 4	5, 5	5, 6
6	6, 1	6, 2	6, 3	6, 4	6, 5	6, 6

Step 1 Define the events. Let A be that you do not roll doubles and A^c that you do roll doubles.

Step 2 Make a diagram. A two-way table is one helpful way to identify all the possible outcomes in the sample space.

Step 3 Determine $P(A^c)$. Since there are fewer outcomes for rolling doubles, it is more convenient to determine the probability of rolling doubles, which is $P(A^c)$. To determine $n(A^c)$, draw a loop around the outcomes in the table that correspond to A^c and then calculate $P(A^c)$.

$$P(A^c) = \frac{n(A^c)}{n(S)} = \frac{6}{36} = \frac{1}{6}$$

Step 4 Determine $P(A)$. Use the relationship between the probability of an event and its complement to determine $P(A)$.

$$P(A) = 1 - P(A^c) = 1 - \frac{1}{6} = \frac{5}{6}$$

So, the probability of not rolling doubles is $\frac{5}{6}$.

(B) One pile of cards contains the numbers 2 through 6 in red hearts. A second pile of cards contains the numbers 4 through 8 in black spades. Each pile of cards has been randomly shuffled. If one card from each pile is chosen at the same time, what is the probability that the sum will be less than 12?

Step 1 Define the events. Let A be the event that the sum is less than 12 and A^c be the event that __the sum is not less than 12__ .

Step 2 Make a diagram. Complete the table to show all the outcomes in the sample space.

		Red Hearts ♥				
Black Spades ♠		2	3	4	5	6
	4	4+2	4+3	4+4	4+5	4+6
	5	5+2	5+3	5+4	5+5	5+6
	6	6+2	6+3	6+4	6+5	6+6
	7	7+2	7+3	7+4	7+5	7+6
	8	8+2	8+3	8+4	8+5	8+6

Step 3 Determine $P(A^c)$. Circle the outcomes in the table that correspond to A^c, then determine $P(A^c)$.

$$P(A^c) = \frac{n\left(A^c\right)}{n\left(S\right)} = \frac{6}{25}$$

ELABORATE

AVOID COMMON ERRORS

Students may have trouble identifying some outcomes associated with an event. Encourage students to carefully identify all outcomes by using tables, lists, or diagrams. They can circle the outcomes of interest (often called the favorable outcomes) in the sample space.

QUESTIONING STRATEGIES

? How does listing the elements in a set help you find the probability of an event associated with the set? The probability is based on the number of elements in the set, so you can just count the elements for the numerator of the probability ratio.

SUMMARIZE THE LESSON

? How can you use set theory to help you calculate theoretical probabilities? You can use the number of elements in a set to define theoretical probability: the theoretical probability that an event A will occur is given by $P(A) = \dfrac{n(A)}{n(S)}$, where S is the sample space.

Step 4 Determine $P(A)$. Use the relationship between the probability of an event and its complement to determine $P(A^c)$.

$$P(A) = \boxed{1} - P\left(\boxed{A^c}\right) = \boxed{1} - \dfrac{\boxed{6}}{\boxed{25}} = \dfrac{\boxed{19}}{\boxed{25}}$$

So, the probability that the sum of the two cards is <u>less than 12</u> is $\dfrac{\boxed{19}}{\boxed{25}}$.

Reflect

7. Describe a different way to calculate the probability that the sum of the two cards will be less than 12. **Use the table to count the number of outcomes in event A instead of A^c, which is 19, then divide that by the total number of outcomes to get $\frac{19}{25}$.**

Your Turn

One bag of marbles contains two red, one yellow, one green, and one blue marble. Another bag contains one marble of each of the same four colors. One marble from each bag is chosen at the same time. Use the complement to calculate the indicated probabilities.

8. Probability of selecting two different colors A^c is selecting the same color: $(R_1, R), (R_2, R), (Y, Y),$ $(G, G), (B, B); P(A^c) = \frac{5}{20} = \frac{1}{4}$, so $P(A) = 1 - \frac{1}{4} = \frac{3}{4}$.

9. Probability of not selecting a yellow marble A^c is selecting at least one yellow marble: $(Y, Y), (Y, Y),$ $(Y, G), (Y, B), (R_1, Y), (R_2, Y), (G, Y), (B, Y); P(A^c) = \frac{8}{20} = \frac{2}{5}$, so $P(A) = 1 - \frac{2}{5} = \frac{3}{5}$.

⊙ Elaborate

10. Can a subset of A contain elements of A^C? Why or why not? **No. The elements of a subset are contained completely within the parent set A, whereas none of the elements of the complement of a set A are in set A by definition, and thus they cannot be in a subset of A.**

11. For any set A, what does $A \cap \varnothing$ equal? What does $A \cup \varnothing$ equal? Explain. **The intersection of set A and the empty set is the empty set, $A \cap \varnothing = \varnothing$, since the two sets do not have any elements in common. The union of set A and the empty set is set A, $A \cup \varnothing = A$, since the elements of the union are the elements in set A or the empty set.**

12. **Essential Question Check-In** How do the terms *set*, *element*, and *universal set* correlate to the terms used to calculate theoretical probability? **Possible answer: To calculate probability, you need to know the number of possible outcomes in the sample space, which is the number of elements in the universal set. You also need to know the number of possible outcomes in the defined event, which is the number of elements in the defined set.**

⭐ Evaluate: Homework and Practice

- Online Homework
- Hints and Help
- Extra Practice

Set A is the set of factors of 12, set B is the set of even natural numbers less than 13, set C is the set of odd natural numbers less than 13, and set D is the set of even natural numbers less than 7. The universal set for these questions is the set of natural numbers less than 13.

So, $A = \{1, 2, 3, 4, 6, 12\}$, $B = \{2, 4, 6, 8, 10, 12\}$,
$C = \{1, 3, 5, 7, 9, 11\}$, $D = \{2, 4, 6\}$, and
$U = \{1, 2, 3, 4, 5, 6, 7, 8, 9, 10, 11, 12\}$. Answer each question.

1. Is $D \subset A$? Explain why or why not.
Yes, because every element of D is also an element of A.

2. Is $B \subset A$? Explain why or why not.
No, because there is at least one element of B that is not an element of A. For example, 8 is an element of B that is not an element of A.

3. What is $A \cap B$?
$\{2, 4, 6, 12\}$

4. What is $A \cap C$?
$\{1, 3\}$

5. What is $A \cup B$?
$\{1, 2, 3, 4, 6, 8, 10, 12\}$

6. What is $A \cup C$?
$\{1, 2, 3, 4, 5, 6, 7, 9, 11, 12\}$

7. What is A^C?
$\{5, 7, 9, 10, 11\}$

8. What is B^C?
$\{1, 3, 5, 7, 9, 11\}$

You have a set of 10 cards numbered 1 to 10. You choose a card at random. Event A is choosing a number less than 7. Event B is choosing an odd number. Calculate the probability.

9. $P(A)$
The sample space $S = \{1, 2, 3, 4, 5, 6, 7, 8, 9, 10\}$;
$A = \{1, 2, 3, 4, 5, 6\}$
$P(A) = \dfrac{n(A)}{n(S)} = \dfrac{6}{10} = \dfrac{3}{5}$

10. $P(B)$
The sample space $S = \{1, 2, 3, 4, 5, 6, 7, 8, 9, 10\}$;
$B = \{1, 3, 5, 7, 9\}$
$P(B) = \dfrac{n(B)}{n(S)} = \dfrac{5}{10} = \dfrac{1}{2}$

11. $P(A \cup B)$
The sample space $S = \{1, 2, 3, 4, 5, 6, 7, 8, 9, 10\}$;
$A \cup B = \{1, 2, 3, 4, 5, 6, 7, 9\}$
$P(A \cup B) = \dfrac{n(A \cup B)}{n(S)} = \dfrac{8}{10} = \dfrac{4}{5}$

12. $P(A \cap B)$
The sample space $S = \{1, 2, 3, 4, 5, 6, 7, 8, 9, 10\}$;
$A \cap B = \{1, 3, 5\}$
$P(A \cap B) = \dfrac{n(A \cap B)}{n(S)} = \dfrac{3}{10}$

13. $P(A^C)$
The sample space $S = \{1, 2, 3, 4, 5, 6, 7, 8, 9, 10\}$;
$A^C = \{7, 8, 9, 10\}$
$P(A^C) = \dfrac{n(A^C)}{n(S)} = \dfrac{4}{10} = \dfrac{2}{5}$

14. $P(B^C)$
The sample space $S = \{1, 2, 3, 4, 5, 6, 7, 8, 9, 10\}$;
$B^C = \{2, 4, 6, 8, 10\}$
$P(B^C) = \dfrac{n(B^C)}{n(S)} = \dfrac{5}{10} = \dfrac{1}{2}$

Module 21   **1090**   Lesson 1

EVALUATE

ASSIGNMENT GUIDE

Concepts and Skills	Practice
Explore Working with Sets	Exercises 1–8
Example 1 Calculating Theoretical Probabilities	Exercises 9–14, 22, 26, 29
Example 2 Using the Complement of an Event	Exercises 15–21, 23–25, 27–28

COMMUNICATING MATH

Discuss the importance of understanding the sample space. Encourage students to always list the members of the sample space before they find a probability. Discuss why this can help avoid errors, such as finding the probability of rolling a 2 with a number cube as $\frac{1}{5}$.

INTEGRATE MATHEMATICAL PRACTICES

Focus on Modeling

MP.4 Discuss when a Venn diagram might be useful in solving a probability problem, and when another method might be easier.

Exercise	Depth of Knowledge (D.O.K.)	COMMON CORE Mathematical Practices
1–8	**1** Recall	**MP.4** Modeling
9–14	**1** Recall	**MP.2** Reasoning
15–20	**2** Skills/Concepts	**MP.2** Reasoning
21	**3** Strategic Thinking	**MP.6** Precision
22	**3** Strategic Thinking	**MP.4** Modeling
23–26	**3** Strategic Thinking	**MP.3** Logic
27	**3** Strategic Thinking H.O.T.	**MP.3** Logic

INTEGRATE MATHEMATICAL PRACTICES

Focus on Math Connections

MP.1 Review the connection between likelihood and probability with students. Discuss how this can be useful when solving problems. When students calculate the probability of an event, be sure they understand what this means in the context of the original problem. For example, students should recognize that an event with a probability of 0.9 is very likely to occur, while an event with a probability of 0.1 is unlikely to occur.

AVOID COMMON ERRORS

Students may not consider the sample space when finding probabilities. Suggest that they summarize the probability ratio using words before they compute the probability.

Use the complement of the event to find the probability.

15. You roll a 6-sided number cube. What is the probability that you do not roll a 2?

The probability of rolling a 2, $P(2)$, is $\frac{1}{6}$.

The probability of not rolling a 2 is $1 - P(2) = 1 - \frac{1}{6} = \frac{5}{6}$.

16. You choose a card at random from a standard deck of cards. What is the probability that you do not choose a red king?

The probability of drawing a red king, $P(\text{red king})$, is $\frac{2}{52} = \frac{1}{26}$.

The probability of not drawing a red king is $1 - P(\text{red king}) = 1 - \frac{1}{26} = \frac{25}{26}$.

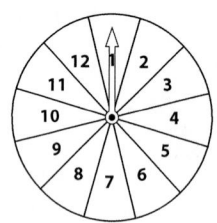

17. You spin the spinner shown. The spinner is divided into 12 equal sectors. What is the probability of not spinning a 2?

The probability of spinning a 2, $P(2)$, is $\frac{1}{12}$.

The probability of not spinning a 2 is $1 - P(2) = 1 - \frac{1}{12} = \frac{11}{12}$.

18. A bag contains 2 red, 5 blue, and 3 green balls. A ball is chosen at random. What is the probability of not choosing a red ball?

The probability of choosing a red ball, $P(\text{red ball})$, is $\frac{2}{10} = \frac{1}{5}$.

The probability of not choosing a red ball is $1 - P(\text{red ball}) = 1 - \frac{1}{5} = \frac{4}{5}$.

19. Cards numbered 1–12 are placed in a bag. A ball is chosen at random. What is the probability of not choosing a number less than 5?

The probability of choosing a number less than 5, $P(\text{less than 5})$, is $\frac{4}{12} = \frac{1}{3}$.

The probability of not choosing a number less than 5 is $1 - P(\text{less than 5}) = 1 - \frac{1}{3} = \frac{2}{3}$.

20. Slips of paper numbered 1–20 are folded and placed into a hat, and then a slip of paper is drawn at random. What is the probability the slip drawn has a number which is not a multiple of 4 or 5?

Multiples of 4 up to 20: 4, 8, 16, 20

Multiples of 5 up to 20: 5, 10, 15, 20

The set of multiples of 4 or 5 is $\{4, 5, 8, 10, 15, 16, 20\}$.
$P(\text{multiple of 4 or 5}) = \frac{7}{20}$

The probability of not selecting a card that is a multiple of 4 or 5 is $1 - P(\text{multiple of 4 or 5}) = 1 - \frac{7}{20} = \frac{13}{20}$.

© Houghton Mifflin Harcourt Publishing Company • Image Credits: ©Oleg Golovnev/Shutterstock

Exercise	Depth of Knowledge (D.O.K.)	COMMON CORE Mathematical Practices
28	**3** Strategic Thinking H.O.T.	**MP.3** Logic
29	**3** Strategic Thinking H.O.T.	**MP.3** Logic

21. You are going to roll two number cubes, a white number cube and a red number cube, and find the sum of the two numbers that come up.

a. What is the probability that the sum will be 6?

There are 36 possible outcomes. There are 5 ways to get a sum of 6, where the first addend is from the white cube and the second addend is from the red cube: $5 + 1, 4 + 2, 3 + 3, 2 + 4,$ and $1 + 5$. So the probability of getting a sum of 6, $P(6)$, is $\frac{5}{36}$.

b. What is the probability that the sum will not be 6?

The probability that the sum will not be 6 is $P(\text{not } 6) = 1 - P(6) = 1 - \frac{5}{36} = \frac{31}{36}$.

22. You have cards with the letters A, B, C, D, E, F, G, H, I, J, K, L, M, N, O, P. Event U is choosing the cards A, B, C or D. Event V is choosing a vowel. Event W is choosing a letter in the word "APPLE". Find $P(U \cap V \cap W)$.

$U \cap V \cap W = \left\{A\right\}$; $P(U \cap V \cap W) = \frac{1}{16}$

A standard deck of cards has 13 cards (2, 3, 4, 5, 6, 7, 8, 9, 10, jack, queen, king, ace) in each of 4 suits (hearts, clubs, diamonds, spades). The hearts and diamonds cards are red. The clubs and spades cards are black. Answer each question.

23. You choose a card from a standard deck of cards at random. What is the probability that you do not choose an ace? Explain.

$\frac{12}{13}$; there are 4 aces in the 52-card deck, so $P(\text{ace}) = \frac{4}{52} = \frac{1}{13}$. This means $P(\text{not ace}) = 1 - \frac{1}{13} = \frac{12}{13}$.

24. You choose a card from a standard deck of cards at random. What is the probability that you do not choose a club? Explain.

$\frac{3}{4}$; there are 13 clubs in the 52-card deck, so $P(\text{club}) = \frac{13}{52} = \frac{1}{4}$. This means $P(\text{not club}) = 1 - \frac{1}{4} = \frac{3}{4}$.

25. You choose a card from a standard deck of cards at random. Event A is choosing a red card. Event B is choosing an even number. Event C is choosing a black card. Find $P(A \cap B \cap C)$. Explain.

$A \cap B \cap C = \varnothing$ because you can never draw a card that is both red and black.

Therefore, $P(A \cap B \cap C) = 0$.

VISUAL CUES

When students create Venn diagrams to model a sample space and sets, caution them to be sure that an element is not used more than once on the diagram. For example, have students check that a number does not appear both in Set A and in its intersection with Set B.

Probability and Set Theory   **1092**

26. You are selecting a card at random from a standard deck of cards. Match each event with the correct probability. Indicate a match by writing the letter of the event on the line in front of the corresponding probability.

A. Picking a card that is both red and a heart.   ___B___ $\frac{1}{52}$

B. Picking a card that is both a heart and an ace.   ___A___ $\frac{1}{4}$

C. Picking a card that is not both a heart and an ace. ___C___ $\frac{51}{52}$

$P(\text{red} \cap \text{heart}) = \dfrac{n(\text{red} \cap \text{heart})}{n(\text{deck})} = \dfrac{13}{52} = \dfrac{1}{4}$

$P(\text{heart} \cap \text{ace}) = \dfrac{n(\text{heart} \cap \text{ace})}{n(\text{deck})} = \dfrac{1}{52}$

$P(\text{not }(\text{heart} \cap \text{ace})) = 1 - P(\text{heart} \cap \text{ace}) = 1 - \dfrac{1}{52} = \dfrac{51}{52}$; the only card that is both a heart and an ace is the ace of hearts, so there are 51 cards in the event not $(\text{heart} \cap \text{ace})$.

H.O.T. Focus on Higher Order Thinking

27. **Critique Reasoning** A bag contains white tiles, black tiles, and gray tiles. Someone is going to choose a tile at random. $P(W)$, the probability of choosing a white tile, is $\frac{1}{4}$. A student claims that the probability of choosing a black tile, $P(B)$, is $\frac{3}{4}$ since $P(B) = 1 - P(W) = 1 - \frac{1}{4} = \frac{3}{4}$. Do you agree? Explain.

    No; choosing a black tile is not the complement of choosing a white tile since the bag also contains gray tiles. It is not possible to calculate $P(B)$ from the given information.

28. **Communicate Mathematical Ideas** A bag contains 5 red marbles and 10 blue marbles. You are going to choose a marble at random. Event A is choosing a red marble. Event B is choosing a blue marble. What is $P(A \cap B)$? Explain.

    0; $A \cap B = \varnothing$ since a marble cannot be both red and blue. So $P(A \cap B) = 0$.

29. **Critical Thinking** Jeffery states that for a sample space S where all outcomes are equally likely, $0 \le P(A) \le 1$ for any subset A of S. Create an argument that will justify his statement or state a counterexample.

    Assume A is a subset of S. Then $0 \le n(A) \le n(S)$. For example, if S has 10 elements, the number of elements of A is greater than or equal to 0 and less than or equal to 10. No subset of S can have fewer than 0 elements or more than 10 elements. So $0 \le \dfrac{n(A)}{n(S)} \le 1$. When all the outcomes are equally likely, $P(A) = \dfrac{n(A)}{n(S)}$. Therefore $0 \le P(A) \le 1$.

Lesson Performance Task

For the sets you've worked with in this lesson, membership in a set is binary: Either something belongs to the set or it doesn't. For instance, 5 is an element of the set of odd numbers, but 6 isn't.

In 1965, Lofti Zadeh developed the idea of "fuzzy" sets to deal with sets for which membership is not binary. He defined a *degree* of membership that can vary from 0 to 1. For instance, a membership function $m_L(w)$ for the set L of large dogs where the degree of membership m is determined by the weight w of a dog might be defined as follows:

- A dog is a full member of the set L if it weighs 80 pounds or more. This can be written as $m_L(w) = 1$ for $w \geq 80$.
- A dog is not a member of the set L if it weighs 60 pounds or less. This can be written as $m_L(w) = 0$ for $w \leq 60$.
- A dog is a partial member of the set L if it weighs between 60 and 80 pounds. This can be written as $0 < m_L(w) < 1$ for $60 < w < 80$.

The "large dogs" portion of the graph shown displays the membership criteria listed above. Note that the graph shows only values of $m(w)$ that are positive.

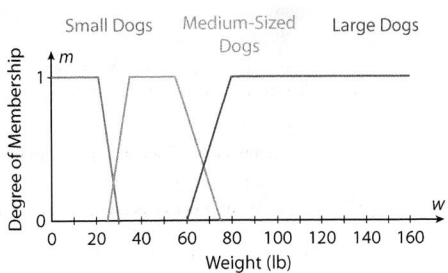

1. Using the graph, give the approximate weights for which a dog is considered a full member, a partial member, and not a member of the set S of small dogs.

   0 pounds to 20 pounds; between 20 pounds and 30 pounds; more than 30 pounds

2. The union of two "fuzzy" sets A and B is given by the membership rule $m_{A \cup B}(x) = \text{maximum}(m_A(x), m_B(x))$. So, for a dog of a given size, the degree of its membership in the set of small or medium-sized dogs $(S \cup M)$ is the greater of its degree of membership in the set of small dogs and its degree of membership in the set of medium-sized dogs.

   The intersection of A and B is given by the membership rule $m_{A \cap B}(x) = \text{minimum}(m_A(x), m_B(x))$. So, for a dog of a given size, the degree of its membership in the set of dogs that are both small and medium-sized $(S \cap M)$ is the lesser of its degree of membership in the set of small dogs and its degree of membership in the set of medium-sized dogs.

   Using the graph above and letting S be the set of small dogs, M be the set of medium-sized dogs, and L be the set of large dogs, draw the graph of each set.

   a. $S \cup M$

   Approximately size shown here

   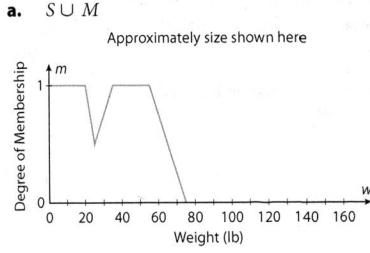

   b. $M \cap L$

   Approximately size shown here

   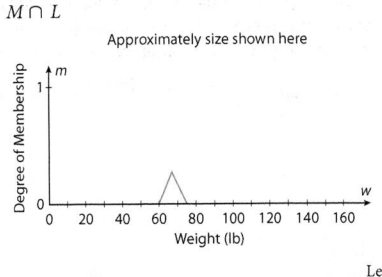

Module 21   1094   Lesson 1

INTEGRATE MATHEMATICAL PRACTICES
Focus on Reasoning

MP.2 Call attention to the point in the Lesson Performance Task graph where the green medium-sized dog line and the blue big-dog line intersect. Ask students to give as much information as they can about that point. Sample answer: The point represents a weight of around 100 pounds and a degree of membership of around 0.3. The point represents the highest degree of membership that a dog of around 100 pounds can obtain simultaneously in both the medium-sized and big-weight categories.

INTEGRATE MATHEMATICAL PRACTICES
Focus on Critical Thinking

MP.3 Arf has a small-dog degree of membership of x and a medium-sized dog degree of membership of y. Is $x > y$, $x < y$, or does the relationship between x and y depend on Arf's weight? Explain. The relationship depends on Arf's weight. The red and green graphs intersect at about 40 pounds. If Arf weighs less than 40 pounds, $x > y$. If Arf weighs more than 40 pounds, $x < y$. If Arf weighs 40 pounds, $x = y$.

EXTENSION ACTIVITY

Have students draw graphs showing fuzzy sets ranging from cold to hot. (Three sets could show *cold*, *warm*, and *hot*. Four sets could show *cold*, *cool*, *warm*, and *hot*. However, leave the choice of adjectives and the number of sets to students.) The vertical axis should record degrees of membership from 0 to 1. The horizontal axis should show either Fahrenheit or Celsius temperatures. Encourage students to be creative with their graphs, for example, by using colors to distinguish sets from one another. Students should write and answer at least three questions involving unions, intersections, and complements of the sets they have graphed.

Scoring Rubric
2 points: Student correctly solves the problem and explains his/her reasoning.
1 point: Student shows good understanding of the problem but does not fully solve or explain his/her reasoning.
0 points: Student does not demonstrate understanding of the problem.

Probability and Set Theory   **1094**

Permutations and Probability

Common Core Math Standards

The student is expected to:

 S-CP.B.9(+)

Use permutations and combinations to compute probabilities of compound events and solve problems.

Mathematical Practices

 MP.7 Using Structure

Language Objective

Give an example of a permutation to a partner and explain how you know it is a permutation.

ENGAGE

Essential Question: When are permutations useful in calculating probability?

Permutations are selections of groups of objects in which order is important. So, permutations are used to find the probability of a group of objects being selected in a particular order.

PREVIEW: LESSON PERFORMANCE TASK

View the Engage section online. Discuss the photograph, asking students what it might have to do with probability. Then preview the Lesson Performance Task.

Name _____ Class _____ Date _____

21.2 Permutations and Probability

Essential Question: When are permutations useful in calculating probability?

Resource Locker

⊘ Explore   Finding the Number of Permutations

A **permutation** is a selection of objects from a group in which order is important. For example, there are 6 permutations of the letters A, B, and C.

| ABC | ACB | BAC | BCA | CAB | CBA |

You can find the number of permutations with the **Fundamental Counting Principle**.

Fundamental Counting Principle

If there are n items and a_1 ways to choose the first item, a_2 ways to select the second item after the first item has been chosen, and so on, there are $a_1 \times a_2 \times \ldots \times a_n$ ways to choose n items.

There are 7 members in a club. Each year the club elects a president, a vice president, and a treasurer.

(A) What is the number of permutations of all 7 members of the club?

There are ___7___ different ways to make the first selection.

Once the first person has been chosen, there are ___6___ different ways to make the second selection.

Once the first two people have been chosen, there are ___5___ different ways to make the third selection.

Continuing this pattern, there are $7 \times 6 \times 5 \times 4 \times 3 \times 2 \times 1 = 5040$ permutations of all the members of the club.

(B) The club is holding elections for a president, a vice president, and a treasurer. How many different ways can these positions be filled?

There are ___7___ different ways the position of president can be filled.

Once the president has been chosen, there are ___6___ different ways the position of vice president can be filled. Once the president and vice president have been chosen, there are ___5___ different ways the position of treasurer can be filled.

So, there are $7 \times 6 \times 5 = 210$ different ways that the positions can be filled.

HARDCOVER PAGES 915–922

Turn to these pages to find this lesson in the hardcover student edition.

(C) What is the number of permutations of the members of the club who were not elected as officers?

After the officers have been elected, there are __4__ members remaining. So there are __4__ different ways to make the first selection.

Once the first person has been chosen, there are __3__ different ways to make the second selection.

Continuing this pattern, there are __$4 \times 3 \times 2 \times 1 = 24$__ permutations of the unelected members of the club.

(D) Divide the number of permutations of all the members by the number of permutations of the unelected members.

There are __5040__ permutations of all the members of the club.

There are __24__ permutations of the unelected members of the club.

The quotient of these two values is __$\frac{5040}{24} = 210$__.

Reflect

1. How does the answer to Step D compare to the answer to Step B?
   The values are the same.

2. **Discussion** Explain the effect of dividing the total number of permutations by the number of permutations of items not selected.
   This method can be used to calculate the number of permutations of a group of objects selected from a larger set.

✏ Explain 1 Finding a Probability Using Permutations

The results of the Explore can be generalized to give a formula for permutations. To do so, it is helpful to use *factorials*. For a positive integer n, **n factorial**, written $n!$, is defined as follows.

$$n! = n \times (n-1) \times (n-2) \times \ldots \times 3 \times 2 \times 1$$

That is, $n!$ is the product of n and all the positive integers less than n. Note that $0!$ is defined to be 1.

In the Explore, the number of permutations of the 7 objects taken 3 at a time is

$$7 \times 6 \times 5 = \frac{7 \times 6 \times 5 \times 4 \times 3 \times 2 \times 1}{4 \times 3 \times 2 \times 1} = \frac{7!}{4!} = \frac{7!}{(7-3)!}$$

This can be generalized as follows.

Permutations
The number of permutations of n objects taken r at a time is given by $_nP_r = \dfrac{n!}{(n-r)!}$.

© Houghton Mifflin Harcourt Publishing Company

PROFESSIONAL DEVELOPMENT

Learning Progressions

Combinatorics is the branch of mathematics that deals with arranging and counting finite collections of items. This lesson introduces students to permutations, which are groupings of items in which the order of the items matters. In the next lesson, students learn to count combinations, which are groupings of items in which the order does not matter. It is important for students to be able to distinguish between the two counting methods. Both provide useful formulas for counting large collections of items that can be applied to computing the probabilities of events with many equally likely outcomes.

EXPLORE

Finding the Number of Permutations

INTEGRATE TECHNOLOGY

Students have the option of doing the Explore activity either in the book or online.

INTEGRATE MATHEMATICAL PRACTICES
Focus on Reasoning

MP.2 Discuss why developing a counting rule for a group of objects is useful. Check that students recognize how quickly some visualizations become unwieldy, such as making a list or drawing a tree diagram, as the number of objects grows.

QUESTIONING STRATEGIES

? When finding probabilities of groups, what is the effect of specifying that order matters? Order distinguishes between groups with the same set of elements. For example, AB is not the same as BA if order matters, but it is the same if order does not matter. This affects numbers of outcomes, which affect probabilities of events.

EXPLAIN 1

Finding a Probability Using Permutations

AVOID COMMON ERRORS

Students may assume that the probability is the ratio of 1 to the permutation. Review the definition of the probability ratio and why a different permutation is needed to count the elements in the numerator and the elements in the denominator.

INTEGRATE TECHNOLOGY

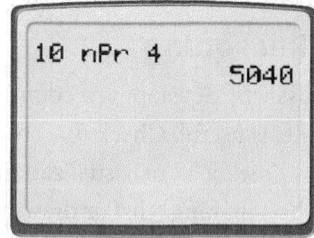

You may want to have students use their calculators to check their work. Graphing calculators have a built-in function that calculates permutations. For example, to find $_{10}P_4$, first enter 10. Then press **MATH** and use the arrow keys to choose the **PRB** menu. Select **2:nPr** and press **ENTER**. Now enter 4 and then press **ENTER** to see that $_{10}P_4 = 5040$.

```
10 nPr 4
              5040
```

QUESTIONING STRATEGIES

? The formula for a permutation is a ratio. Can a permutation ever be a fraction less than 1? Explain. No, although the formula is a ratio, it always simplifies to a whole number because it is a method for counting arrangements.

? Why is it important to be able to recognize a permutation to count an arrangement of objects? Why can't you just make a list or use a tree diagram? As the number of objects increases, the number of arrangements in a permutation gets large very quickly, and it becomes impractical and difficult to make a list or use a tree diagram.

© Houghton Mifflin Harcourt Publishing Company

Example 1 Use permutations to find the probabilities.

(A) A research laboratory requires a four-digit security code to gain access to the facility. A security code can contain any of the digits 0, 1, 2, 3, 4, 5, 6, 7, 8, and 9, but no digit is repeated. What is the probability that a scientist is randomly assigned a code with the digits 1, 2, 3, and 4 in any order?

The sample space S consists of permutations of 4 digits selected from 10 digits.

$$n(S) = {}_{10}P_4 = \frac{10!}{(10-4)!} = \frac{10!}{6!} = 5040$$

Event A consists of permutations of a security code with the digits 1, 2, 3, and 4.

$$n(A) = {}_4P_4 = \frac{4!}{(4-4)!} = \frac{4!}{0!} = 24$$

The probability of getting a security code with the digits 1, 2, 3, and 4 is

$$P(A) = \frac{n(A)}{n(S)} = \frac{24}{5040} = \frac{1}{210}.$$

(B) A certain motorcycle license plate consists of 5 digits that are randomly selected. No digit is repeated. What is the probability of getting a license plate consisting of all even digits?

The sample space S consists of permutations of $\underline{5\ \text{digits}}$ selected from $\underline{10\ \text{digits}}$.

$$n(S) = {}_{\boxed{10}}P_{\boxed{5}} = \frac{\boxed{10!}}{\boxed{5!}} = \boxed{30,240}$$

Event A consists of permutations of a license plate with $\underline{\text{all even digits}}$.

$$n(A) = {}_{\boxed{5}}P_{\boxed{5}} = \frac{\boxed{5!}}{\boxed{0!}} = \boxed{120}$$

The probability of getting a license plate with $\underline{\text{all even digits}}$ is

$$P(A) = \frac{n(A)}{n(S)} = \frac{\boxed{120}}{\boxed{30,240}} = \frac{\boxed{1}}{\boxed{252}}.$$

Your Turn

There are 8 finalists in the 100-meter dash at the Olympic Games. Suppose 3 of the finalists are from the United States, and that all finalists are equally likely to win.

3. What is the probability that the United States will win all 3 medals in this event?

$$n(S) = {}_8P_3 = \frac{8!}{5!} = 336; \quad n(A) = {}_3P_3 = \frac{3!}{0!} = 6$$

The probability of the United States winning all 3 medals is $P(A) = \frac{n(A)}{n(S)} = \frac{6}{336} = \frac{1}{56}$.

4. What is the probability that the United States will win no medals in this event?

$$n(S) = {}_8P_3 = \frac{8!}{5!} = 336; \quad n(A) = {}_5P_3 = \frac{5!}{2!} = 60$$

The probability of the United States winning no medals is $P(A) = \frac{n(A)}{n(S)} = \frac{60}{336} = \frac{5}{28}$.

Module 21   **1097**   Lesson 2

COLLABORATIVE LEARNING

Peer-to-Peer Activity

Have students work in pairs to confirm that the permutation formulas work. Suggest that they make a list of the number of ways the letters in the word CLUE can be arranged and then find the arrangements using the permutations formula. Next, have them examine what happens to the number of permutations as the number of letters in a word increases by starting a list for the word CLUES. Repeat for the words COOL and TOOT. Have students comment on the usefulness of the permutation formulas when counting items.

1097   Lesson 21.2

⊘ Explain 2 Finding the Number of Permutations with Repetition

Up to this point, the problems have focused on finding the permutations of distinct objects. If some of the objects are repeated, this will reduce the number of permutations that are distinguishable.

For example, here are the permutations of the letters A, B, and C.

| ABC | ACB | BAC | BCA | CAB | CBA |

Next, here are the permutations of the letters M, O, and M. Bold type is used to show the different positions of the repeated letter.

| **M**OM | MO**M** | **MM**O | **MM**O | O**MM** | O**MM** |

Shown without the bold type, here are the permutations of the letters M, O, and M.

| MOM | MOM | MMO | MMO | OMM | OMM |

Notice that since the letter M is repeated, there are only 3 distinguishable permutations of the letters. This can be generalized with a formula for permutations with repetition.

> ### Permutations with Repetition
>
> The number of different permutations of n objects where one object repeats a times, a second object repeats b times, and so on is
> $$\frac{n!}{a! \times b! \times \ldots}$$

Example 2 Find the number of permutations.

Ⓐ How many different permutations are there of the letters in the word ARKANSAS?

There are 8 letters in the word, and there are 3 A's and 2 S's, so the number of permutations of the letters in ARKANSAS is $\frac{8!}{3!2!} = 3360$.

Ⓑ One of the zip codes for Anchorage, Alaska, is 99522. How many permutations are there of the numbers in this zip code?

There are __5__ digits in the zip code, and there are __2 nines__, and __2 twos__ in the zip code, so the number of permutations of the zip code is

$$\boxed{\dfrac{5!}{2!2!}} = \boxed{30}\,.$$

Your Turn

5. How many different permutations can be formed using all the letters in MISSISSIPPI?
$$\frac{11!}{4!4!2!} = 34,650$$

6. One of the standard telephone numbers for directory assistance is 555-1212. How many different permutations of this telephone number are possible?
$$\frac{7!}{3!2!2!} = 210$$

© Houghton Mifflin Harcourt Publishing Company

Finding the Number of Permutations with Repetition

INTEGRATE MATHEMATICAL PRACTICES
Focus on Modeling

MP.4 Discuss the importance of identifying the permutation needed to count the sample space separately from the permutation needed to calculate the event when using permutations with probability.

QUESTIONING STRATEGIES

? How is the formula for the number of permutations where one object repeats different from the formula for the number of permutations with no repeats? How is it similar? In both formulas the numerator is $n!$ The denominator of the formula for no repeats is $(n - r)!$, while the denominator for repeats is $a! \cdot b!$ and so on to count the repeating objects.

DIFFERENTIATE INSTRUCTION

Multiple Representations

Have students calculate the number of permutations in various situations "by hand"; that is, by reasoning about the situation and using multiplication, by making a list, or by drawing tree diagrams. Then ask students what patterns they notice. A common element of every solution should be the product of a string of descending, consecutive integers, letters, or other items. Discuss how students can use this process to help them recall how to find the number of permutations.

EXPLAIN 3

Finding a Probability Using Permutations with Repetition

INTEGRATE MATHEMATICAL PRACTICES
Focus on Communication

MP.3 Discuss how students are able to identify n, r, a, b, and so on to use permutations with repetition to find probabilities.

QUESTIONING STRATEGIES

How can you use what you know about probability to check that the ratio makes sense when finding probability using permutations with or without repetition? The probability must be between 0 and 1.

Permutations with repetition can be used to find probablilities.

Example 3 The school jazz band has 4 boys and 4 girls, and they are randomly lined up for a yearbook photo.

(A) Find the probability of getting an alternating boy-girl arrangement.

The sample space S consists of permutations of 8 objects, with 4 boys and 4 girls.

$n(S) \frac{8!}{4!4!} = 70$

Event A consists of permutations that alternate boy-girl or girl-boy. The possible permutations are BGBGBGBG and GBGBGBGB.

$n(A) = 2$

The probability of getting an alternating boy-girl arrangement is $P(A) = \frac{n(A)}{n(S)} = \frac{2}{70} = \frac{1}{35}$.

(B) Find the probability of getting all of the boys grouped together.

The sample space S consists of permutations of $\underline{\text{8 students}}$, with $\underline{\text{4 boys and 4 girls}}$.

$n(S) = \boxed{\dfrac{8!}{4!4!}} = \boxed{70}$

Event A consists of permutations with $\underline{\text{all 4 boys in a row}}$. The possible permutations are BBBBGGGG, GBBBBGGG, $\underline{\text{GGBBBBGG, GGGBBBBG, and GGGGBBBB}}$.

$n(A) = \boxed{5}$

The probability of getting all the boys grouped together is $P(A) = \dfrac{n(A)}{n(S)} = \dfrac{\boxed{5}}{\boxed{70}} = \dfrac{\boxed{1}}{\boxed{14}}$.

Your Turn

7. There are 2 mystery books, 2 romance books, and 2 poetry books to be randomly placed on a shelf. What is the probability that the mystery books are next to each other, the romance books are next to each other, and the poetry books are next to each other?

$n(S) = \dfrac{6!}{2!2!2!} = 90$

Event A consists of permutations with books from each category next to each other.

The possible permutations are MMRRPP, MMPPRR, RRMMPP, RRPPMM, PPMMRR, and PPRRMM.

$n(A) = 6$

The probability of getting all the books from each category next to each other is $P(A) = \dfrac{n(A)}{n(S)} = \dfrac{6}{90} = \dfrac{1}{15}$.

LANGUAGE SUPPORT EL

Connect Vocabulary

Have students look up the meaning of the verb *permute* (it is *to change the order of*). Connect the definition to the mathematical definition of *permutation*, which is *an arrangement of objects in a definite order.*

8. What is the probability that a random arrangement of the letters in the word APPLE will have the two P's next to each other?

The sample space S consists of permutations of the letters in APPLE, and there are 2 P's, so $n(S) = \frac{5!}{2!} = 60$. Consider the two P's as a single block, so there are 4 positions for the letters to occupy.

$n(A) = 4! = 24$

The probability of getting the two P's next to each other is $P(A) = \frac{n(A)}{n(S)} = \frac{24}{60} = \frac{2}{5}$.

 Elaborate

9. If $_nP_a = {_nP_b}$, what is the relationship between a and b? Explain your answer.

The equation is true if $\frac{n!}{(n-a)!} = \frac{n!}{(n-b)!}$. This occurs only when $a = b$.

10. It was observed that there are 6 permutations of the letters A, B, and C. They are ABC, ACB, BAC, BCA, CAB, and CBA. If the conditions are changed so that the order of selection does not matter, what happens to these 6 different groups?

They would become a single group of the letters, ABC. The other five groups are duplicates of this result.

11. Essential Question Check-In How do you determine whether choosing a group of objects involves permutations?

Permutations are used when the order of selection matters.

☆ Evaluate: Homework and Practice

1. An MP3 player has a playlist with 12 songs. You select the shuffle option, which plays each song in a random order without repetition, for the playlist. In how many different orders can the songs be played?

$12! = 479{,}001{,}600$

The songs can be played in 479,001,600 different orders

2. There are 10 runners in a race. Medals are awarded for 1st, 2nd, and 3rd place. In how many different ways can the medals be awarded?

$10 \times 9 \times 8 = 720$

There are 720 possibilities for awarding medals.

3. There are 9 players on a baseball team. In how many different ways can the coach choose players for first base, second base, third base, and shortstop?

$9 \times 8 \times 7 \times 6 = 3024$

There are 3024 ways to arrange players.

Exercise	Depth of Knowledge (D.O.K.)	COMMON CORE Mathematical Practices	
1–11	**1** Recall of Information	**MP.2** Reasoning	
12–15	**1** Recall of Information	**MP.1** Problem Solving	
16–23	**2** Skills/Concepts	**MP.4** Modeling	
24	**3** Strategic Thinking H.O.T.	**MP.3** Logic	
25	**3** Strategic Thinking H.O.T.	**MP.2** Reasoning	
26	**3** Strategic Thinking H.O.T.	**MP.6** Precision	
27	**3** Strategic Thinking H.O.T.	**MP.3** Logic	

ELABORATE

AVOID COMMON ERRORS

Students may be able to identify the permutation needed for one part of the probability ratio but not the other. Remind students to first decide what the sample space is and then use a permutation to count the elements in the sample space. Next, they should use a permutation as needed to count the elements in the event. Review why $n(S)$ is always in the denominator.

SUMMARIZE THE LESSON

? What are permutations and how can you use them to calculate probabilities? A permutation is a group of objects in which order is important. You can use permutations to find the number of outcomes in a sample space or in an event.

EVALUATE

ASSIGNMENT GUIDE

Concepts and Skills	Practice
Explore Finding the Number of Permutations	Exercises 1–3
Example 1 Finding a Probability Using Permutations	Exercises 4–7, 18–19, 22–23, 26–27
Example 2 Finding the Number of Permutations With Repetition	Exercises 8–24
Example 3 Finding a Probability Using Permutations With Repetition	Exercises 12–17, 20–21, 25

4. A bag contains 9 tiles, each with a different number from 1 to 9. You choose a tile without looking, put it aside, choose a second tile without looking, put it aside, then choose a third tile without looking. What is the probability that you choose tiles with the numbers 1, 2, and 3 in that order?

   Let S be the sample space and let A be the event that you choose tiles with the numbers 1, 2, and 3 in that order.

   $$n(S) = {}_9P_3 = \frac{9!}{(9-3)!} = \frac{9!}{6!} = 504$$

   $$n(A) = 1$$

   $$P(A) = \frac{n(A)}{n(S)} = \frac{1}{504}$$

5. There are 11 students on a committee. To decide which 3 of these students will attend a conference, 3 names are chosen at random by pulling names one at a time from a hat. What is the probability that Sarah, Jamal, and Mai are chosen in any order?

   Let S be the sample space and let A be the event that Sarah, Jamal, and Mai are chosen in any order.

   $$n(S) = {}_{11}P_3 = \frac{11!}{(11-3)!} = \frac{11!}{8!} = 990$$

   $$n(A) = {}_3P_3 = \frac{3!}{(3-3)!} = \frac{3!}{0!} = 6$$

   $$P(A) = \frac{n(A)}{n(S)} = \frac{6}{990} = \frac{1}{165}$$

6. A clerk has 4 different letters that need to go in 4 different envelopes. The clerk places one letter in each envelope at random. What is the probability that all 4 letters are placed in the correct envelopes?

   Let S be the sample space and let A be the event that all 4 letters are placed in the correct envelopes.

   $$n(S) = {}_4P_4 = \frac{4!}{(4-4)!} = \frac{4!}{0!} = 24$$

   $$n(A) = 1$$

   $$P(A) = \frac{n(A)}{n(S)} = \frac{1}{24}$$

7. A swim coach randomly selects 3 swimmers from a team of 8 to swim in a heat. What is the probability that she will choose the three strongest swimmers?

   Let S be the sample space and let A be the event that the coach chooses the three strongest swimmers.

   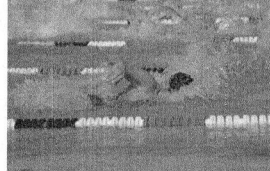

   $$n(S) = {}_8P_3 = \frac{8!}{(8-3)!} = \frac{8!}{5!} = 336$$

   $$n(A) = {}_3P_3 = \frac{3!}{(3-3)!} = \frac{3!}{0!} = 6$$

   $$P(A) = \frac{n(A)}{n(S)} = \frac{6}{336} = \frac{1}{56}$$

8. How many different sequences of letters can be formed using all the letters in ENVELOPE?

The three letter E's are not distinguishable.

$$\frac{_8P_8}{3!} = \frac{8!}{3!} = 6720$$

6720 sequences

9. Yolanda has 3 each of red, blue, and green marbles. How many possible ways can the 9 marbles be arranged in a row?

$$\frac{_9P_9}{3!3!3!} = \frac{9!}{3!3!3!} = 1680$$

1680 ways

10. Jane has 16 cards. Ten of the cards look exactly the same and have the number 1 on them. The other 6 cards look exactly the same and have the number 2 on them. Jane is going to make a row containing all 16 cards. How many different ways can she order the row?

$$\frac{_{16}P_{16}}{10!6!} = \frac{16!}{10!6!} = 8008$$

8008 row arrangements

11. Ramon has 10 cards, each with one number on it. The numbers are 1, 2, 3, 4, 4, 6, 6, 6, 6, 6. Ramon is going to make a row containing all 10 cards. How many different ways can he order the row?

$$\frac{_{10}P_{10}}{2!5!} = \frac{10!}{2!5!} = 15{,}120$$

15,120 row arrangements

12. A grocer has 5 apples and 5 oranges for a window display. The grocer makes a row of the 10 pieces of fruit by choosing one piece of fruit at random, making it the first piece in the row, choosing a second piece of fruit at random, making it the second piece in the row, and so on. What is the probability that the grocer arranges the fruits in alternating order? (Assume that the apples are not distinguishable and that the oranges are not distinguishable.)

Let S be the sample space and let A be the event that the grocer arranges the fruits in alternating order.

$$n(S) = \frac{_{10}P_{10}}{5!5!} = \frac{10!}{5!5!} = 252$$

$n(A) = 2$, AOAOAOAOAO or OAOAOAOAOA

$$P(A) = \frac{n(A)}{n(S)} = \frac{2}{252} = \frac{1}{126}$$

13. The letters G, E, O, M, E, T, R, Y are on 8 tiles in a bag, one letter on each tile. If you select tiles randomly from the bag and place them in a row from left to right, what is the probability the tiles will spell out GEOMETRY?

Let S be the sample space and let A be the event that the tiles spell out GEOMETRY again. The two letter E's are not distinguishable.

$$n(S) = \frac{_8P_8}{2!} = \frac{8!}{2!} = 20{,}160$$

$n(A) = 1$, GEOMETRY

$$P(A) = \frac{n(A)}{n(S)} = \frac{1}{20{,}160}$$

INTEGRATE MATHEMATICAL PRACTICES

Focus on Math Connections

MP.1 Discuss how to recognize when a probability evaluated using a permutation will be equal to the ratio $\frac{1}{n(S)}$.

AVOID COMMON ERRORS

Students may make errors when simplifying with factorials. Encourage students to write out the product a factorial represents, at least until they are sure which numbers to cancel.

PEER-TO-PEER

Have students work with a partner to write a probability problem about numbers, letters, or both in which a permutation is needed to count the objects. Have students solve their problems. Then ask them to exchange problems with another pair and solve those. Have the pairs review each other's solution methods.

VISUAL CUES

Discuss the locations of and relationship between n and r in the rule for permutations, and how they can be used to help students remember the formula for $_nP_r$. Make sure students do not confuse the P in the permutation formula for the P used to denote probability.

14. There are 11 boys and 10 girls in a classroom. A teacher chooses a student at random and puts that student at the head of a line, chooses a second student at random and makes that student second in the line, and so on, until all 21 students are in the line. What is the probability that the teacher puts them in a line alternating boys and girls, where no two of the same gender stand together?

$$n(S) = \frac{_{21}P_{21}}{11!10!} = \frac{21!}{11!10!} = 352{,}716$$

Because there are more boys than girls, there is only one way to alternate them: BGBGBGBGBGBGBGBGBGBGB. If a girl started first, the end would have too many boys. So $n(A) = 1$.

$$P(A) = \frac{n(A)}{n(S)} = \frac{1}{352{,}716}$$

15. There are 4 female and 4 male kittens are sleeping together in a row. Assuming that the arrangement is a random arrangement, what is the probability that all the female kittens are together, and all the male kittens are together?

$$n(S) = \frac{_8P_8}{4!4!} = \frac{8!}{4!4!} = 70, \; n(A) = 2, \text{ FFFFMMMM or MMMMFFFF}$$

$$P(A) = \frac{n(A)}{n(S)} = \frac{2}{70} = \frac{1}{35}$$

16. If a ski club with 12 members votes to choose 3 group leaders, what is the probability that Marsha, Kevin, and Nicola will be chosen in any order for President, Treasurer, and Secretary?

$$n(S) = _{12}P_3 = \frac{12!}{(12-3)!} = \frac{12!}{9!} = 1320, \; n(A) = _3P_3 = \frac{3!}{(3-3)!} = \frac{3!}{0!} = 6$$

$$P(A) = \frac{n(A)}{n(S)} = \frac{6}{1320} = \frac{1}{220}$$

17. There are 7 books numbered 1–7 on the summer reading list. Peter randomly chooses 2 books. What is the probability that Peter chooses books numbered 1 and 2, in either order?

$$n(S) = _7P_2 = \frac{7!}{(7-2)!} = \frac{7!}{5!} = 42, \; n(A) = _2P_2 = \frac{2!}{(2-2)!} = \frac{2!}{0!} = 2$$

$$P(A) = \frac{n(A)}{n(S)} = \frac{2}{42} = \frac{1}{21}$$

18. On an exam, students are asked to list 5 historical events in the order in which they occurred. A student randomly orders the events. What is the probability that the student chooses the correct order?

$$n(S) = _5P_5 = \frac{5!}{(5-5)!} = \frac{5!}{0!} = 120, \; n(A) = 1$$

$$P(A) = \frac{n(A)}{n(S)} = \frac{1}{120}$$

19. A fan makes 6 posters to hold up at a basketball game. Each poster has a letter of the word TIGERS. Six friends sit next to each other in a row. The posters are distributed at random. What is the probability that TIGERS is spelled correctly when the friends hold up the posters?

Let S be the sample space and let A be the event that that TIGERS is spelled correctly when the friends hold up the posters.

$$n(S) = {}_6P_6 = \frac{6!}{(6-6)!} = \frac{6!}{0!} = 720$$

$$n(A) = 1$$

$$P(A) = \frac{n(A)}{n(S)} = \frac{1}{720}$$

20. The 10 letter tiles S, A, C, D, E, E, M, I, I, and O are in a bag. What is the probability that the letters S-A-M-E will be drawn from the bag at random, in that order?

Let S be the sample space and let A be the event that the letters S-A-M-E will be drawn from the bag at random, in that order.

$$n(S) = \frac{{}_{10}P_4}{2!2!} = \frac{5040}{4} = 1260$$

$$n(A) = 1$$

$$P(A) = \frac{n(A)}{n(S)} = \frac{1}{1260}$$

21. If three cards are drawn at random from a standard deck of 52 cards, what is the probability that they will all be 7s? (There are four 7s in a standard deck of 52 cards.)

Let S be the sample space and let A be the event that all four cards are 7s.

$$n(S) = {}_{52}P_3 = \frac{52!}{(52-3)!} = \frac{52!}{49!} = 132{,}600$$

$$n(A) = {}_4P_3 = \frac{4!}{(4-3)!} = \frac{4!}{1!} = 24$$

$$P(A) = \frac{n(A)}{n(S)} = \frac{24}{132{,}600} = \frac{1}{5525}$$

22. A shop classroom has ten desks in a row. If there are 6 students in shop class and they choose their desks at random, what is the probability they will sit in the first six desks?

Let S be the sample space and let A be the event that the students sit in the first six desks.

$$n(S) = {}_{10}P_6 = \frac{10!}{(10-6)!} = \frac{10!}{4!} = 151{,}200$$

$$n(A) = {}_6P_6 = \frac{6!}{(6-6)!} = \frac{6!}{0!} = 720$$

$$P(A) = \frac{n(A)}{n(S)} = \frac{720}{151{,}200} = \frac{1}{210}$$

Have students cite real-world examples of permutations. Have them explain how they know the examples are permutations.

23. Match each event with its probability. All orders are chosen randomly.

A. There are 15 floats that will be in a town parade. Event A: The mascot float is chosen to be first and the football team float is chosen to be second.

B. Beth is one of 10 students performing in a school talent show. Event B: Beth is chosen to be the fifth performer and her best friend is chosen to be fourth.

C. Sylvester is in a music competition with 14 other musicians. Event C: Sylvester is chosen to be last, and his two best friends are chosen to be first and second.

$\dfrac{C}{A}\ \dfrac{1}{1092}$ $P(A) = \dfrac{n(\text{mascot 1st and football 2nd})}{n(\text{all floats in parade})} = \dfrac{_{13}P_{13}}{_{15}P_{15}} = \dfrac{1}{210}$

$\dfrac{A}{B}\ \dfrac{1}{210}$

$\dfrac{B}{}\ \dfrac{1}{90}$ $P(B) = \dfrac{n(\text{Beth 5th and friend 4th})}{n(\text{all contestants})} = \dfrac{_8P_8}{_{10}P_{10}} = \dfrac{1}{90}$

$P(C) = \dfrac{n(\text{Sylvester last, friends 1st and 2nd})}{n(\text{all musicians})} = \dfrac{2\cdot_{11}P_{11}}{_{14}P_{14}} = \dfrac{2}{2184} = \dfrac{1}{1092}$

H.O.T. Focus on Higher Order Thinking

24. **Explain the Error** Describe and correct the error in evaluating the expression.

$$_5P_3 = \frac{5!}{3!} = \frac{5 \times 4 \times \cancel{3!}}{\cancel{3!}} = 20$$

The denominator of the first fraction should be $(5-3)!$, not $3!$; $\dfrac{5!}{(5-3)!} = \dfrac{5!}{2!} = 60$.

25. **Make a Conjecture** If you are going to draw four cards from a deck of cards, does drawing four aces from the deck have the same probability as drawing four 3s? Explain.

Yes, they have the same probability. The probability of drawing 4 aces from a deck of cards would be $P(A) = \dfrac{n(A)}{n(S)} = \dfrac{_4P_4}{_{52}P_4}$ because the 4 aces could be drawn in any order, and there are 52 cards in the deck. There are also 4 3s in the deck that could be drawn in any order, so the probability would be the same.

26. **Communicate Mathematical Ideas** Nolan has Algebra, Biology, and World History homework. Assume that he chooses the order that he does his homework at random. Explain how to find the probability of his doing his Algebra homework first.

If he is doing his Algebra homework first, the only classes that can change homework order are Biology and World History, so $n(A) = {_2P_2}$. The sample space would have all three classes changing, so $n(S) = {_3P_3}$. Since $P(A) = \dfrac{n(A)}{n(S)} = \dfrac{_2P_2}{_3P_3} = \dfrac{2}{6} = \dfrac{1}{3}$, the probability of Nolan doing his Algebra homework first is $\dfrac{1}{3}$.

27. Explain the Error A student solved the problem shown. The student's work is also shown. Explain the error and provide the correct answer.

A bag contains 6 tiles with the letters A, B, C, D, E, and F, one letter on each tile. You choose 4 tiles one at a time without looking and line them up from left to right as you choose them. What is the probability that your tiles spell BEAD?

Let S be the sample space and let A be the event that the tiles spell BEAD.

$$n(S) = {}_6P_4 = \frac{6!}{(6-4)!} = \frac{6!}{2!} = 360$$

$$n(A) = {}_4P_4 = \frac{4!}{(4-4)!} = \frac{4!}{0!} = 24$$

$$P(A) = \frac{n(A)}{n(S)} = \frac{24}{360} = \frac{1}{5}$$

$n(A)$ should be 1 since the tiles must appear in the order B-E-A-D. The correct probability is $\frac{1}{360}$.

Lesson Performance Task

How many different ways can a blue card, a red card, and a green card be arranged? The diagram shows that the answer is six.

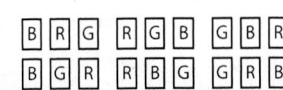

1. Now solve this problem: What is the least number of colors needed to color the pattern shown here, so that no two squares with a common boundary have the same color? Draw a sketch to show your answer.

   two

2. Now try this one. Again, find the least number of colors needed to color the pattern so that no two regions with a common boundary have the same color. Draw a sketch to show your answer.

   three

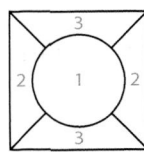

3. In 1974, Kenneth Appel and Wolfgang Haken solved a problem that had confounded mathematicians for more than a century. They proved that no matter how complex a map is, it can be colored in a maximum of four colors, so that no two regions with a common boundary have the same color. Sketch the figure shown here. Can you color it in four colors? Can you color it in three colors?

   Four colors are needed.

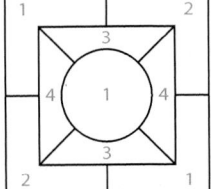

INTEGRATE MATHEMATICAL PRACTICES

Focus on Modeling

MP.4 Question 3 of the Lesson Performance Task shows a map containing nine regions that cannot be colored with three colors; four colors are required. Challenge students to draw a map containing fewer than nine regions that requires four colors. What is the fewest number of regions a map can contain that requires four colors? 5

AVOID COMMON ERRORS

Some students may draw a map with two regions that share a vertex point and must be the same color, and think they have disproved the theorem. Remind students that regions only require different colors if they share a boundary, not a corner.

EXTENSION ACTIVITY

Give each student several black-and-white copies of a map of a region containing a complex array of countries, and crayons or colored pencils in four colors. Challenge students to color the map in three colors, following the same restriction stated in the Lesson Performance Task: No two countries sharing a border can have the same color. Regardless of whether the map can be colored in three colors, have students show how it can be colored in four colors.

Scoring Rubric

2 points: Student correctly solves the problem and explains his/her reasoning.

1 point: Student shows good understanding of the problem but does not fully solve or explain his/her reasoning.

0 points: Student does not demonstrate understanding of the problem.

Permutations and Probability   **1106**

LESSON 21.3

Combinations and Probability

Common Core Math Standards

The student is expected to:

COMMON CORE S-CP.B.9(+)

Use permutations and combinations to compute probabilities of compound events and solve problems.

Mathematical Practices

COMMON CORE MP.7 Using Structure

Language Objective

Give an example of a combination to a partner and explain how you know it is a combination.

ENGAGE

Essential Question: What is the difference between a permutation and a combination?

You can choose a number of objects in such a way that the order matters, in which case you choose a permutation, or you can choose in such a way that order does not matter, in which case you choose a combination.

PREVIEW: LESSON PERFORMANCE TASK

View the Engage section online. Discuss the photograph. Ask students to guess the location where the photo was taken and describe what is happening there. Then preview the Lesson Performance Task.

21.3 Combinations and Probability

Essential Question: What is the difference between a permutaion and a combination?

⊘ Explore Finding the Number of Combinations

A **combination** is a selection of objects from a group in which order is unimportant. For example, if 3 letters are chosen from the group of letters A, B, C, and D, there are 4 different combinations.

ABC	ABD	ACD	BCD

A restaurant has 8 different appetizers on the menu, as shown in the table. They also offer an appetizer sampler, which contains any 3 of the appetizers served on a single plate. How many different appetizer samplers can be created? The order in which the appetizers are selected does not matter.

Appetizers	
Nachos	Chicken Wings
Chicken Quesadilla	Vegetarian Egg Rolls
Potato Skins	Soft Pretzels
Beef Chili	Guacamole Dip

Ⓐ Find the number appetizer samplers that are possible if the order of selection does matter. This is the number of permutations of 8 objects taken 3 at a time.

$$_8P_3 = \frac{8!}{\left(8 - 3\right)!} = \frac{8!}{5!} = 336$$

Ⓑ Find the number of different ways to select a particular group of appetizers. This is the number of permutations of 3 objects.

$$_3P_3 = \frac{3!}{\left(3 - 3\right)!} = \frac{3!}{0!} = 6$$

© Houghton Mifflin Harcourt Publishing Company · ©Tom Henderson/The Food Passionates/Corbis

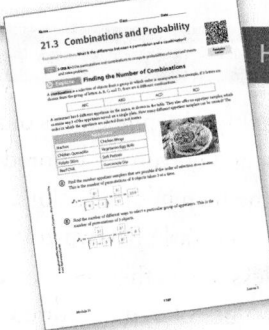

HARDCOVER PAGES 923–930

Turn to these pages to find this lesson in the hardcover student edition.

(C) To find the number of possible appetizer samplers if the order of selection does not matter, divide the answer to part A by the answer to part B.

So the number of appetizer samplers that can be created is $\dfrac{\boxed{336}}{\boxed{6}} = \boxed{56}$.

Reflect

1. Explain why the answer to Part A was divided by the answer to Part B.
   Since the order of selection does not matter, the answer to Part A contained duplications of each possible sampler. Dividing by the answer to Part B removed the duplicates of each sampler.

2. On Mondays and Tuesdays, the restaurant offers an appetizer sampler that contains any 4 of the appetizers listed. How many different appetizer samplers can be created?
   The number of appetizer samplers that can be created is $\dfrac{_8P_4}{_4P_4} = \dfrac{1680}{24} = 70.$

3. In general, are there more ways or fewer ways to select objects when the order does not matter? Why?
   There are fewer ways to select objects when the order does not matter. This is because multiple selections are counted as the same combination.

⊘ Explain 1   Finding a Probability Using Combinations

The results of the Explore can be generalized to give a formula for combinations. In the Explore, the number of combinations of the 8 objects taken 3 at a time is

$$_8P_3 \div {_3P_3} = \frac{8!}{(8-3)!} \div \frac{3!}{(3-3)!} = \frac{8!}{(8-3)!} \cdot \frac{0!}{3!} = \frac{8!}{(8-3)!} \cdot \frac{1!}{3!} = \frac{8!}{3!(8-3)!}$$

This can be generalized as follows.

Combinations
The number of combinations of n objects taken r at a time is given by $$_nC_r = \frac{n!}{r!(n-r)!}$$

Example 1   Find each probability.

(A) There are 4 boys and 8 girls on the debate team. The coach randomly chooses 3 of the students to participate in a competition. What is the probability that the coach chooses all girls?

The sample space S consists of combinations of 3 students taken from the group of 12 students.

$n(S) = {_{12}C_3} = \dfrac{12!}{3!9!} = 220$

Event A consists of combinations of 3 girls taken from the set of 8 girls.

$n(A) = {_8C_3} = \dfrac{8!}{3!5!} = 56$

The probability that the coach chooses all girls is $P(A) = \dfrac{n(A)}{n(S)} = \dfrac{56}{220} = \dfrac{14}{55}.$

PROFESSIONAL DEVELOPMENT

Math Background

In this lesson students are introduced to combinations. A combination of n objects taken r at a time is given by the rule $_nC_r = \dfrac{n!}{r!(n-r)!}$. Pascal's triangle is a number triangle with rows arranged according to the combination formula, starting with $n = 0$ and continuing indefinitely. Each successive row can be found by adding elements from the row above. It has many fascinating properties, and it can be used as a shortcut in algebra when factoring polynomials.

EXPLORE

Finding the Number of Combinations

INTEGRATE TECHNOLOGY

Students have the option of doing the Explore activity either in the book or online.

QUESTIONING STRATEGIES

❓ Why is it important to distinguish between a permutation and a combination when counting? They may have a different number of possible arrangements.

❓ How can you tell if an arrangement is a combination? An arrangement is a combination if the order of the items does not matter.

EXPLAIN 1

Finding a Probability Using Combinations

INTEGRATE TECHNOLOGY

Graphing calculators have a built-in function that calculates combinations. The $_nC_r$ function is available from the **MATH PRB** menu. Have students enter data in the same way they enter n and r when applying the permutation function. For example, to find $_6C_4$, first enter 6. Then press **MATH** and use the arrow keys to choose the **PRB** menu. Select **3:nCr** and press **ENTER**. Now enter 4 and press **ENTER** to see that $_6C_4 = 15$.

INTEGRATE MATHEMATICAL PRACTICES

Focus on Reasoning

MP.2 Check that students understand how the formula for the number of combinations of n objects taken r at a time is related to the formula for the number of permutations of n objects taken r at a time. The number of combinations is equal to the number of permutations divided by $r!$.

QUESTIONING STRATEGIES

? The formula for the number of combinations is a ratio. Can a combination ever be a fraction less than 1 ? Explain. No; as with the formula for permutations, although the formula is a ratio, it always simplifies to a whole number because it is a method for counting arrangements.

? Can the number of combinations ever be equal to the number of permutations? Explain. only when the combination is taken 1 at a time, when $r = 1$, which is the same as a permutation

---

(B) There are 52 cards in a standard deck, 13 in each of 4 suits: clubs, diamonds, hearts, and spades. Five cards are randomly drawn from the deck. What is the probability that all five cards are diamonds?

The sample space S consists of combinations of $\underline{5}$ cards drawn from 52 cards.

$$n(S) = {}_{52}C_5 = \frac{52!}{5!47!} = 2{,}598{,}960$$

Event A consists of combinations of 5 cards drawn from the $\underline{13}$ diamonds.

$$n(A) = {}_{13}C_5 = \frac{13!}{5!8!} = 1287$$

The probability of randomly selecting $\underline{5}$ cards that are diamonds is

$$P(A) = \frac{n(A)}{n(S)} = \frac{1287}{2{,}598{,}960} = \frac{33}{66{,}640}.$$

Your Turn

4. A coin is tossed 4 times. What is the probability of getting exactly 3 heads?

The number of outcomes in the sample space S is found by using the Fundamental Counting Principle since each flip can result in heads or tails.

$n(S) = 2 \cdot 2 \cdot 2 \cdot 2 = 2^4 = 16$

Event A consists of combinations of 3 heads taken from the set of 4 coin flips, so

$n(A) = {}_4C_3 = \frac{4!}{3!1!} = 4$

The probability of getting exactly 3 heads is

$P(A) = \frac{n(A)}{n(S)} = \frac{4}{16} = \frac{1}{4}$

5. A standard deck of cards is divided in half, with the red cards (diamonds and hearts) separated from the black cards (spades and clubs). Four cards are randomly drawn from the red half is the probability they are all diamonds?

The sample space S consists of combinations of 4 cards drawn from the 26 red cards, so

$n(S) = {}_{26}C_4 = \frac{26!}{4!22!} = 14{,}950.$

Event A consists of combinations of 4 cards drawn from the 13 diamonds, so

$n(A) = {}_{13}C_4 = \frac{13!}{4!9!} = 715.$

The probability of getting all diamonds is

$P(A) = \frac{n(A)}{n(S)} = \frac{715}{14{,}950} = \frac{11}{230}.$

© Houghton Mifflin Harcourt Publishing Company

COLLABORATIVE LEARNING

Small Group Activity

Have students create two situations in which 2 out of 16 objects are selected, with order important in one of the situations and not important in the other. Ask students to use the situations to compare and contrast permutations and combinations, explaining why the number of selections is greater in one than in the other, and describing the relationship between the two. Tell students it may be necessary to create several situations in which order is and is not important to be able to describe the relationship between permutations and combinations.

Explain 2 Finding a Probability Using Combinations and Addition

Sometimes, counting problems involve the phrases "at least" or "at most." For these problems, combinations must be added.

For example, suppose a coin is flipped 3 times. The coin could show heads 0, 1, 2, or 3 times. To find the number of combinations with at least 2 heads, add the number of combinations with 2 heads and the number of combinations with 3 heads $\left({}_3C_2 + {}_3C_3\right)$.

Example 2 Find each probability.

(A) A coin is flipped 5 times. What is the probability that the result is heads at least 4 of the 5 times?

The number of outcomes in the sample space S can be found by using the Fundamental Counting Principle since each flip can result in heads or tails.

$$n(S) = 2 \cdot 2 \cdot 2 \cdot 2 \cdot 2 = 2^5 = 32$$

Let A be the event that the coin shows heads at least 4 times. This is the sum of 2 events, the coin showing heads 4 times and the coin showing heads 5 times. Find the sum of the combinations with 4 heads from 5 coins and with 5 heads from 5 coins.

$$n(A) = {}_5C_4 + {}_5C_5 = \frac{5!}{4!1!} + \frac{5!}{5!0!} = 5 + 1 = 6$$

The probability that the coin shows at least 4 heads is $P(A) = \dfrac{n(A)}{n(S)} = \dfrac{6}{32} = \dfrac{3}{16}$.

(B) Three number cubes number cubes are rolled and the result is recorded. What is the probability that at least 2 of the number cubes show 6?

The number of outcomes in the sample space S can be found by using the Fundamental Counting Principle since each roll can result in 1, 2, 3, 4, 5, or 6.

$$n(S) = \boxed{6^3} = \boxed{216}$$

Let A be the event that at least 2 number cubes show 6. This is the sum of 2 events, <u>2 number cubes showing 6</u> or <u>3 number cubes showing 6</u>. The event of getting 6 on 2 number cubes occurs <u>5 times</u> since there are <u>5</u> possibilities for the other number cube.

$$n(A) = \boxed{5 \cdot {}_3C_2} + \boxed{{}_3C_3} = \boxed{5 \cdot \frac{3!}{2!1!}} + \boxed{\frac{3!}{3!0!}} = \boxed{15} + \boxed{1} = \boxed{16}$$

The probability of getting a 6 at least twice in 3 rolls is $P(A) = \dfrac{n(A)}{n(S)} = \dfrac{\boxed{16}}{\boxed{216}} = \dfrac{\boxed{2}}{\boxed{27}}$.

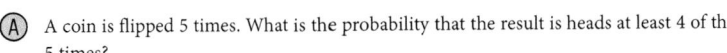
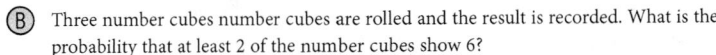

© Houghton Mifflin Harcourt Publishing Company · ©Eldad Carin/Shutterstock

---

AVOID COMMON ERRORS

Students may have difficulty using combinations to find probability. Have students break down the probability problem into parts. First find the size of the sample space. Then find the number of outcomes associated with the event. Finally, write the ratio.

EXPLAIN 2

Finding a Probability Using Combinations and Addition

INTEGRATE MATHEMATICAL PRACTICES
Focus on Communication

MP.3 Students may have difficulty recognizing how to use addition with combinations, and understanding why addition is used. Review how to find the probability of simple events that involve addition when rolling a number cube, such as rolling at least a 3 or at most a 4.

QUESTIONING STRATEGIES

? When you find a probability using combinations, will both parts of the probability ratio necessarily be combinations? Explain. No, the method used for counting each part of the ratio depends on the problem.

DIFFERENTIATE INSTRUCTION

Graphic Organizers

Have the class work together to create a graphic organizer that summarizes and demonstrates the rules for counting: the Fundamental Counting Principle, the permutation rule, and the combination rule. For each rule, have students include the formula and an example. Suggest that students highlight words in the examples that indicate why and how the rule is applied.

ELABORATE

AVOID COMMON ERRORS

Students sometimes compute a combination for $n(S)$ and then choose the numerator of the probability ratio carelessly. Emphasize the importance of accurately identifying both parts of the probability ratio.

SUMMARIZE THE LESSON

? What are combinations and how can you use them to calculate probabilities? A combination is a grouping of objects in which order does not matter. You can use combinations to find the number of outcomes in a sample space or in an event.

---

6. A math department has a large database of true-false questions, half of which are true and half of which are false, that are used to create future exams. A new test is created by randomly selecting 6 questions from the database. What is the probability the new test contains at most 2 questions where the correct answer is "true"?

The number of outcomes in the sample space S can be found by using the Fundamental Counting Principle since each question is either true or false.

$$n(S) = 2 \cdot 2 \cdot 2 \cdot 2 \cdot 2 \cdot 2 = 2^6 = 64$$

Let A be the event that at most 2 questions are true. This is the sum of 3 events: 2 true questions, 1 true question, or no true questions.

$$n(A) = {}_6C_2 + {}_6C_1 + {}_6C_0 = \frac{6!}{2!4!} + \frac{6!}{1!5!} + \frac{6!}{0!6!} = 15 + 6 + 1 = 22$$

Because the questions are equally likely to be true or false, the probability that the test contains at most 2 true questions is

$$P(A) = \frac{n(A)}{n(S)} = \frac{22}{64} = \frac{11}{32}$$

7. There are equally many boys and girls in the senior class. If 5 seniors are randomly selected to form the student council, what is the probability the council will contain at least 3 girls?

The number of outcomes in the sample space S can be found by using the Fundamental Counting Principle since each selection is either a boy or a girl.

$$n(S) = 2 \cdot 2 \cdot 2 \cdot 2 \cdot 2 = 2^5 = 32$$

Let A be the event that at least 3 girls are selected. This is the sum of 3 events: selecting 3 girls, 4 girls, or 5 girls.

$$n(A) = {}_5C_3 + {}_5C_4 + {}_5C_5 = \frac{5!}{3!2!} + \frac{5!}{4!1!} + \frac{5!}{5!0!} = 10 + 5 + 1 = 16$$

Because a senior is equally likely to be a boy or a girl, the probability that the council will contain at least 3 girls is

$$P(A) = \frac{n(A)}{n(S)} = \frac{16}{32} = \frac{1}{2}$$

💬 Elaborate

8. Discussion A coin is flipped 5 times, and the result of heads or tails is recorded. To find the probability of getting tails at least once, the events of 1, 2, 3, 4, or 5 tails can be added together. Is there a faster way to calculate this probability?

The sum of the probabilities of all possible outcomes is equal to 1. Determine the probability of getting no tails (or 5 heads) and subtract this value from 1.

9. If ${}_nC_a = {}_nC_b$, what is the relationship between a and b? Explain your answer.

The equation is true if $\frac{n!}{a!(n-a)!} = \frac{n!}{b!(n-b)!}$. This will occur when $a = b$ or $a + b = n$.

10. Essential Question Check-In How do you determine whether choosing a group of objects involves combinations?

Combinations are used when the order of selection does not matter.

© Houghton Mifflin Harcourt Publishing Company

Module 21   1111   Lesson 3

LANGUAGE SUPPORT EL

Connect Vocabulary

Have students make a chart to summarize what they know about combinations. Sample:

Combination	
Definition	A grouping of objects in which order does not matter
Formula	$${}_nC_r = \frac{n!}{r!(n-r)!}$$
Example	Combinations of 2 letters from A, B, and C: AB AC BC

• Online Homework
• Hints and Help
• Extra Practice

1. A cat has a litter of 6 kittens. You plan to adopt 2 of the kittens. In how many ways can you choose 2 of the kittens from the litter?

$$_6C_2 = \frac{6!}{2!(6-2)!} = \frac{6!}{2!4!} = \frac{720}{48} = 15 \text{ ways}$$

2. An amusement park has 11 roller coasters. In how many ways can you choose 4 of the roller coasters to ride during your visit to the park?

$$_{11}C_4 = \frac{11!}{4!(11-4)!} = \frac{11!}{4!7!} = \frac{39,916,800}{120,960} = 330 \text{ ways}$$

3. Four students from 30-member math club will be selected to organize a fundraiser. How many groups of 4 students are possible?

$$_{30}C_4 = \frac{30!}{4!(30-4)!} = \frac{30!}{4!26!} = 27,405 \text{ groups}$$

4. A school has 5 Spanish teachers and 4 French teachers. The school's principal randomly chooses 2 of the teachers to attend a conference. What is the probability that the principal chooses 2 Spanish teachers?

The sample space S consists of combinations of 2 teachers chosen from the 9 teachers, and event A consists of combinations of 2 teachers chosen from the 5 Spanish teachers.

$$n(S) = {_9}C_2 = \frac{9!}{2!(9-2)!} = \frac{9!}{2!7!} = \frac{362,880}{10,080} = 36$$

$$n(A) = {_5}C_2 = \frac{5!}{2!(5-2)!} = \frac{5!}{2!3!} = \frac{120}{12} = 10$$

$$P(A) = \frac{n(A)}{n(S)} = \frac{10}{36} = \frac{5}{18}$$

5. There are 6 fiction books and 8 nonfiction books on a reading list. Your teacher randomly assigns you 4 books to read over the summer. What is the probability that you are assigned all nonfiction books?

The sample space S consists of combinations of 4 books chosen from the 14 books, and event A consists of combinations of 4 books chosen from the 8 nonfiction books.

$$n(S) = {_{14}}C_4 = \frac{14!}{4!(14-4)!} = \frac{14!}{4!10!} = 1001$$

$$n(A) = {_8}C_4 = \frac{8!}{4!(8-4)!} = \frac{8!}{4!4!} = 70$$

$$P(A) = \frac{n(A)}{n(S)} = \frac{70}{1001} = \frac{10}{143}$$

EVALUATE

ASSIGNMENT GUIDE

Concepts and Skills	Practice
Explore Finding the Number of Combinations	Exercises 1–3, 22–23, 24–25
Example 1 Finding a Probability Using Combinations	Exercises 4–7, 12–21
Example 2 Finding a Probability Using Combinations and Addition	Exercises 8–11

COMMUNICATING MATH

After students have completed some of the exercises, ask them to discuss how they are able to distinguish combinations and permutations. Then have them explain how they were able to identify n and r in various examples. Ask them to tell whether they find one easier to work with than the other, and why.

Exercise	Depth of Knowledge (D.O.K.)	COMMON CORE Mathematical Practices	
1–12	**1** Recall of Information	**MP.2** Reasoning	
13–14	**2** Skills/Concepts	**MP.4** Modeling	
15–20	**2** Skills/Concepts	**MP.1** Problem Solving	
21	**2** Skills/Concepts	**MP.4** Modeling	
22	**2** Skills/Concepts	**MP.2** Reasoning	
23	**3** Strategic Thinking H.O.T.	**MP.3** Logic	

Focus on Communication

MP.3 Ask students to share their rationales for solving probability problems involving combinations. In particular, have them explain how they computed the values for $n(S)$ and $n(A)$ to find the probability.

AVOID COMMON ERRORS

Students often confuse permutations and combinations. They may not recognize which should be applied or they may apply the wrong formula. Have students begin by deciding whether the order is important or not. Then have them look up the formula. Note that this process may have to be repeated several times to solve a probability problem.

6. A bag contains 26 tiles, each with a different letter of the alphabet written on it. You choose 3 tiles from the bag without looking. What is the probability that you choose the tiles with the letters A, B, and C?

Let S be the sample space, which consists of combinations of 3 tiles chosen from 26 tiles, and let A be the event that you choose the tiles with the letters A, B, and C.

$$n(S) = {}_{26}C_3 = \frac{26!}{3!(26-3)!} = \frac{26!}{3!23!} = 2600$$

$$n(A) = {}_3C_3 = \frac{3!}{3!(3-3)!} = \frac{3!}{3!0!} = 1 \longrightarrow P(A) = \frac{n(A)}{n(S)} = \frac{1}{2600}$$

7. You are randomly assigned a password consisting of 6 different characters chosen from the digits 0 to 9 and the letters A to Z. As a percent, what is the probability that you are assigned a password consisting of only letters? Round you answer to the nearest tenth of a percent.

Let S be the sample space, which consists of combinations of 6 characters chosen from 36 characters, and let A be the event that you are assigned a password consisting of only letters.

$$n(S) = {}_{36}C_6 = \frac{36!}{6!(36-6)!} = \frac{36!}{6!30!} = 1{,}947{,}792$$

$$n(A) = {}_{26}C_6 = \frac{26!}{6!(26-6)!} = \frac{26!}{6!20!} = 230{,}230$$

$$P(A) = \frac{n(A)}{n(S)} = \frac{230{,}230}{1{,}947{,}792} \approx 11.8\%$$

8. A bouquet of 6 flowers is made up by randomly choosing between roses and carnations. What is the probability the bouquet will have at most 2 roses?

Let S be the sample space, which consists of combinations of 6 flowers (each of which is a rose or a carnation), and let A be the event that the bouquet will have at most 2 roses.

$$n(S) = 2 \cdot 2 \cdot 2 \cdot 2 \cdot 2 \cdot 2 = 2^6 = 64$$

$$n(A) = {}_6C_2 + {}_6C_1 + {}_6C_0 = 15 + 6 + 1 = 22$$

Because a flower is equally likely to be a rose or a carnation, $P(A) = \frac{n(A)}{n(S)} = \frac{22}{64} = \frac{11}{32}$.

9. A bag of fruit contains 10 pieces of fruit, chosen randomly from bins of apples and oranges. What is the probability the bag contains at least 6 oranges?

Let S be the sample space, which consists of combinations of 3 tiles chosen from 26 tiles, and let A be the event that the bag contains at least 6 oranges.

$$n(S) = 2 \cdot 2 \cdot 2 \cdot 2 \cdot 2 \cdot 2 \cdot 2 \cdot 2 \cdot 2 \cdot 2 = 2^{10} = 1024$$

$$n(A) = {}_{10}C_6 + {}_{10}C_7 + {}_{10}C_8 + {}_{10}C_9 + {}_{10}C_{10} = 210 + 120 + 45 + 10 + 1 = 386$$

Because a piece of fruit is equally likely to be an apple or an orange,

$$P(A) = \frac{n(A)}{n(S)} = \frac{386}{1024} = \frac{193}{512}.$$

© Houghton Mifflin Harcourt Publishing Company

Exercise	Depth of Knowledge (D.O.K.)	COMMON CORE Mathematical Practices
24	**3** Strategic Thinking H.O.T.	**MP.3** Logic
25	**3** Strategic Thinking H.O.T.	**MP.3** Logic

10. You flip a coin 10 times. What is the probability that you get at most 3 heads?

Let S be the sample space, which consists of the results of 10 coin flips (each of which is either heads or tails), and let A be the event that you get at most 3 heads.

$n(S) = 2 \cdot 2 \cdot 2 \cdot 2 \cdot 2 \cdot 2 \cdot 2 \cdot 2 \cdot 2 \cdot 2 = 2^{10} = 1024$

$n(A) = {}_{10}C_3 + {}_{10}C_2 + {}_{10}C_1 + {}_{10}C_0 = 120 + 45 + 10 + 1 = 176$

Because a flip is equally likely to result in heads or tails, $P(A) = \dfrac{n(A)}{n(S)} = \dfrac{176}{1024} = \dfrac{11}{64}$.

11. You flip a coin 8 times. What is the probability you will get at least 5 heads?

Let S be the sample space, which consists of the results of 8 coin flips (each of which is either heads or tails), and let A be the event that you get at least 5 heads.

$n(S) = 2 \cdot 2 \cdot 2 \cdot 2 \cdot 2 \cdot 2 \cdot 2 \cdot 2 = 2^8 = 256$

$n(A) = {}_8C_5 + {}_8C_6 + {}_8C_7 + {}_8C_8 = 56 + 28 + 8 + 1 = 93$

Because a flip is equally likely to result in heads or tails, $P(A) = \dfrac{n(A)}{n(S)} = \dfrac{93}{256}$.

12. You flip a coin 5 times. What is the probability that every result will be tails?

Let S be the sample space, which consists of the results of 5 coin flips (each of which is either heads or tails), and let A be the event that every result will be tails.

$n(S) = 2 \cdot 2 \cdot 2 \cdot 2 \cdot 2 = 2^5 = 32$

$n(A) = {}_5C_5 = 1$

Because a flip is equally likely to result in heads or tails, $P(A) = \dfrac{n(A)}{n(S)} = \dfrac{1}{32}$.

13. There are 12 balloons in a bag: 3 each of blue, green, red, and yellow. Three balloons are chosen at random. Find the probability that all 3 balloons are green.

Let S be the sample space, which consists of combinations of the 3 balloons chosen from the 12 balloons, and let A be the event that all 3 balloons are green.

$n(S) = {}_{12}C_3 = \dfrac{12!}{3!(12-3)!} = 220$

$n(A) = {}_3C_3 = 1$

$P(A) = \dfrac{n(A)}{n(S)} = \dfrac{1}{220}$

14. There are 6 female and 3 male kittens at an adoption center. Four kittens are chosen at random. What is the probability that all 4 kittens are female?

Let S be the sample space, which consists of the combinations of 4 kittens chosen from the 9 kittens, and let A be the event that all 4 kittens are female.

$n(S) = {}_9C_4 = \dfrac{9!}{4!(9-4)!} = \dfrac{9!}{4!5!} = 126$

$n(A) = {}_6C_4 = \dfrac{6!}{4!(6-4)!} = \dfrac{6!}{4!2!} = 15$

$P(A) = \dfrac{n(A)}{n(S)} = \dfrac{15}{126} = \dfrac{5}{42}$

PEER-TO-PEER

Have students work with a partner to write a probability problem about numbers, letters, or both in which a combination is needed to count the objects. Have students solve their problems. Then ask them to exchange problems with another pair to solve. Have the pairs review each other's solution methods.

AVOID COMMON ERRORS

Students sometimes attempt to simplify permutations or combinations by canceling factors. Remind students of the meaning of factorials, and suggest that they write out the multiplication to determine which factors actually cancel.

There are 21 students in your class. The teacher wants to send 4 students to the library each day. The teacher will choose the students to go to the library at random each day for the first four days from the list of students who have not already gone. Answer each question.

15. What is the probability you will be chosen to go on the first day?

Let S be the sample space, which consists of the combinations of 4 students chosen from the 21 students, and let A be the event that you will be chosen to go on the first day.

$$n(S) = {}_{21}C_4 = \frac{21!}{4!(21-4)!} = \frac{21!}{4!17!} = 5985$$

Since you are one group member, the rest of the group members can be made up of any of the 20 remaining students in your class.

$$n(A) = {}_{20}C_3 = \frac{20!}{3!(20-3)!} = \frac{20!}{3!17!} = 1140$$

$$P(A) = \frac{n(A)}{n(S)} = \frac{1140}{5985} = \frac{4}{21}$$

16. If you have not yet been chosen to go on days 1–3, what is the probability you will be chosen to go on the fourth day?

12 students have already gone, leaving 9 students to go to the library.

Let S be the sample space, which consists of the combinations of 4 students chosen from the 9 students, and let A be the event that you will be chosen to go on the fourth day.

$$n(S) = {}_9C_4 = \frac{9!}{4!(9-4)!} = \frac{9!}{4!5!} = 126$$

Since you are one group member, the rest of the group members can be made up of any of the 8 remaining who have not yet gone.

$$n(A) = {}_8C_3 = \frac{8!}{3!(8-3)!} = \frac{8!}{3!5!} = 56$$

$$P(A) = \frac{n(A)}{n(S)} = \frac{56}{126} = \frac{4}{9}$$

17. Your teacher chooses 2 students at random to represent your homeroom. The homeroom has a total of 30 students, including your best friend. What is the probability that you and your best friend are chosen?

Let S be the sample space, which consists of the combinations of 2 students chosen from the 30 students, and let A be the event that you and your best friend are chosen.

$$n(S) = {}_{30}C_2 = 435$$

$$n(A) = {}_2C_2 = 1$$

$$P(A) = \frac{n(A)}{n(S)} = \frac{1}{435}$$

© Houghton Mifflin Harcourt Publishing Company

There are 12 peaches and 8 bananas in a fruit basket. You get a snack for yourself and three of your friends by choosing four of the pieces of fruit at random. Answer each question.

18. What is the probability that all 4 are peaches?

The sample space S consists of the combinations of 4 pieces of fruit from the 20 pieces of fruit, and event A consists of combinations of 4 peaches.

$$n(S) = {}_{20}C_4 = \frac{20!}{4!(20-4)!} = \frac{20!}{4!16!} = 4845$$

$$n(A) = {}_{12}C_4 = \frac{12!}{4!(12-4)!} = \frac{12!}{4!8!} = 495$$

$$P(A) = \frac{n(A)}{n(S)} = \frac{495}{4845} = \frac{33}{323}$$

19. What is the probability that all 4 are bananas?

The sample space S consists of the combinations of 4 pieces of fruit from the 20 pieces of fruit, and event A consists of combinations of 4 bananas.

$$n(S) = {}_{20}C_4 = \frac{20!}{4!(20-4)!} = \frac{20!}{4!16!} = 4845$$

$$n(A) = {}_8C_4 = \frac{8!}{4!(8-4)!} = \frac{8!}{4!4!} = 70$$

$$P(A) = \frac{n(A)}{n(S)} = \frac{70}{4845} = \frac{14}{969}$$

20. There are 30 students in your class. Your science teacher will choose 5 students at random to create a group to do a project. Find the probability that you and your 2 best friends in the science class will be chosen to be in the group.

Since 3 of the group members are you and your friends, the additional 2 group members can come from any combination of the students left in class.

The sample space S consists of the combinations of 5 students from the 30 students, and event A consists of combinations of 2 students from the 27 who are left.

$$P(A) = \frac{n(A)}{n(S)} = \frac{{}_{27}C_2}{{}_{30}C_5} = \frac{351}{142,506} = \frac{1}{406}$$

21. On a television game show, 9 members of the studio audience are randomly selected to be eligible contestants.

a. Six of the 9 eligible contestants are randomly chosen to play a game on the stage. How many combinations of 6 players from the group of eligible contestants are possible?

$${}_9C_6 = \frac{9!}{6!(9-6)!} = \frac{9!}{6!3!} = 84$$

b. You and your two friends are part of the group of 9 eligible contestants. What is the probability that all three of you are chosen to play the game on stage? Explain how you found your answer.

The sample space S consists of the combinations of 6 contestants from the 9 who are eligible.

$$n(S) = {}_9C_6 = 84$$

After you and your friends are chosen, 3 other contestants from the remaining 6 can be chosen in any combination, so event A consists of combinations of 3 contestants from the 6 who are left.

$$n(A) = {}_6C_3 = 20, \quad P(A) = \frac{n(A)}{n(S)} = \frac{20}{84} = \frac{5}{21}$$

JOURNAL

Have students cite real-world examples of combinations. Have them explain how they know the examples are combinations.

---

22. Determine whether you should use permutations or combinations to find the number of possibilities in each of the following situations. Select the correct answer for each lettered part.

   a. Selecting a group of 5 people from a group of 8 people

   ○ permutation   ● combination

   b. Finding the number of combinations for a combination lock

   ● permutation   ○ combination

   c. Awarding first and second place ribbons in a contest

   ● permutation   ○ combination

   d. Choosing 3 books to read in any order from a list of 7 books

   ○ permutation   ● combination

   a. It doesn't matter in what order the people are selected.

   b. Order matters: numbers have to be in a specific order to open the lock.

   c. Order matters: awarding Sam first place and Elena second is different from awarding Elena first place and Sam second.

   d. It doesn't matter in what order the books are chosen.

H.O.T. Focus on Higher Order Thinking

23. **Communicate Mathematical Ideas** Using the letters A, B, and C, explain the difference between a permutation and a combination.

   In permutations, order matters. In combinations, order does not matter. In a permutation of A, B, and C, ABC is different from CBA, so they would be counted as two different permutations. In a combination, ABC is the same as CBA, and would not be counted again.

24. **Draw Conclusions** Calculate $_{10}C_6$ and $_{10}C_4$.

$$_{10}C_6 = \frac{10!}{6!(10-6)!} = \frac{10!}{6!4!} = \frac{3,628,800}{17,280} = 210$$

$$_{10}C_4 = \frac{10!}{4!(10-4)!} = \frac{10!}{4!6!} = \frac{3,628,800}{17,280} = 210$$

   a. What do you notice about these values? Explain why this makes sense.

   $_{10}C_6 = {_{10}C_4} = 210$; it makes sense that these values are equal because every combination of 6 objects that are selected has a corresponding combination of 4 objects that are not selected.

   b. Use your observations to help you state a generalization about combinations.

   In general, $_nC_r = {_nC_{n-r}}$.

© Houghton Mifflin Harcourt Publishing Company

25. Justify Reasoning Use the formula for combinations to make a generalization about $_nC_n$. Explain why this makes sense.

Using the formula for combinations and the fact that

$0! = 1,\ _nC_n = \dfrac{n!}{n!(n-n)!} = \dfrac{n!}{n!0!} = \dfrac{n!}{n!} = 1$; this makes sense because there is only 1 combination of n objects taken n at a time.

26. Explain the Error Describe and correct the error in evaluating $_9C_4$.

$_9C_4 = \dfrac{9!}{(9-4)!} = \dfrac{9!}{5!} = 3024$

The answer given was $_9P_4$, not $_9C_4$; $_9C_4 = \dfrac{9!}{4!(9-4)!} = \dfrac{9!}{4!5!} = 126$

Lesson Performance Task

1. In the 2012 elections, there were six candidates for the United States Senate in Vermont. In how many different orders, from first through sixth, could the candidates have finished?

2. The winner of the Vermont Senatorial election received 208,253 votes, 71.1% of the total votes cast. The candidate coming in second received 24.8% of the vote. How many votes did the second-place candidate receive? Round to the nearest ten.

3. Following the 2012 election there were 53 Democratic, 45 Republican, and 2 Independent senators in Congress.

   a. How many committees of 5 Democratic senators could be formed?

   b. How many committees of 48 Democratic senators could be formed?

   c. Explain how a clever person who knew nothing about combinations could guess the answer to (b) if the person knew the answer to (a).

4. Following the election, a newspaper printed a circle graph showing the make-up of the Senate. How many degrees were allotted to the sector representing Democrats, how many to Republicans, and how many to Independents?

1. $6! = 6 \cdot 5 \cdot 4 \cdot 3 \cdot 2 \cdot 1 = 720$

2. $\dfrac{208,253}{0.711} = 292,901.5471$ total votes

   $292,901.5471 \times 0.248 = 72,639.58 \approx 72,640$

3. a. $_{53}C_5 = \dfrac{53!}{5! \cdot (53-5)!} = \dfrac{344,362,200}{120} = 2,869,685$

   b. $_{53}C_{48} = \dfrac{53!}{48! \cdot (53-48)!} = \dfrac{344,362,200}{120} = 2,869,685$

   c. The person could reason that for each committee of 5 Democratic Senators in (a) there were 48 who were not on the committee. So, there is a one-to-one correspondence between the 2,869,685 committees of 5 and the 2,869,685 committees of 48.

4. Democrats $360° \cdot 0.53 = 190.8°$
   Republicans $360° \cdot 0.45 = 162°$
   Independents $360° \cdot 0.02 = 7.2°$

© Houghton Mifflin Harcourt Publishing Company

EXTENSION ACTIVITY

Each day, Senator Smith leaves his office and walks to the Committee Room along a grid of hallways that forms a 5 by 5 square. He moves only right (R) and down (D). The path shown can be written RRRDDDRDDR. The senator has developed a method to use combinations to find the number of different ways he can complete his walk. What is the method? How many ways can he do it? Find all possible combinations of five R's and five D's; $\dfrac{10!}{5!5!} = 252$ ways.

AVOID COMMON ERRORS

In Question 2, students may incorrectly conclude that the winning candidate received 71.1% of the total of 208,253 votes cast. The problem states, however, that 208,253 votes were 71% *of all the votes cast*. The part (208,253) and the percent (71.1) are given and the whole is asked for:

$\text{whole} = \dfrac{\text{part}}{\text{percent}} = \dfrac{208,253}{0.711} \approx 292,902$

INTEGRATE MATHEMATICAL PRACTICES

Focus on Patterns

MP.8 Shown below are the first 6 rows of an array called Pascal's Triangle. Each number in the array is found by adding together the two numbers above it.

Row 0						1						

Row 0   1
Row 1   1   1
Row 2   1   2   1
Row 3   1   3   3   1
Row 4   1   4   6   4   1
Row 5   1   5   10   10   5   1
Row 6   1   6   15   20   15   6   1

Find $_3C_2$, $_5C_3$, and $_6C_4$. Then propose a connection between the terms in the triangle and the quantity $_mC_n$. (You'll find the connection easiest to spot by numbering the first term in each row *Term 0*. So, Term 3 in Row 6 is 20.) $_mC_n$ equals Term n in Row m.

What is the 14th term in Row 17 of Pascal's Triangle? $_{17}C_{14} = 680$

Scoring Rubric
2 points: Student correctly solves the problem and explains his/her reasoning.
1 point: Student shows good understanding of the problem but does not fully solve or explain his/her reasoning.
0 points: Student does not demonstrate understanding of the problem.

Combinations and Probability **1118**

Mutually Exclusive and Overlapping Events

Common Core Math Standards

The student is expected to:

 S-CP.A.4

... Use the two-way table as a sample space to decide if events are independent and to approximate conditional probabilities. Also S-CP.B.7

Mathematical Practices

MP.6 Precision

Language Objective

Give a partner an example of a mutually exclusive event. Explain how you know the events are mutually exclusive. Repeat with an example of overlapping events.

ENGAGE

Essential Question: How are probabilities affected when events are mutually exclusive or overlapping?

The probability of mutually exclusive events is the sum of the individual probabilities, while the probability of overlapping events is the sum of the individual probabilities minus the probability that both events occur.

PREVIEW: LESSON PERFORMANCE TASK

View the Engage section online. Discuss the photograph. Ask students to estimate the probability that two people in the photo have the same birthday. Then preview the Lesson Performance Task.

Name_____ Class_____ Date_____

21.4 Mutually Exclusive and Overlapping Events

Essential Question: How are probabilities affected when events are mutually exclusive or overlapping?

◎ Explore 1 Finding the Probability of Mutually Exclusive Events

Two events are **mutually exclusive events** if they cannot both occur in the same trial of an experiment. For example, if you flip a coin it cannot land heads up and tails up in the same trial. Therefore, the events are mutually exclusive.

A number dodecahedron has 12 sides numbered 1 through 12. What is the probability that you roll the cube and the result is an even number or a 7?

(A) Let A be the event that you roll an even number. Let B be the event that you roll a 7. Let S be the sample space.

Complete the Venn diagram by writing all outcomes in the sample space in the appropriate region.

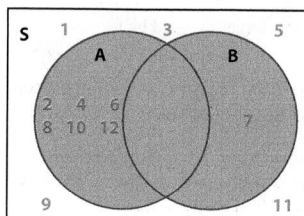

(B) Calculate $P(A)$.

$$P(A) = \frac{6}{12} = \frac{1}{2}$$

(C) Calculate $P(B)$.

$$P(B) = \frac{1}{12}$$

(D) Calculate $P(A \text{ or } B)$.

$$n(S) = 12$$

$$n(A \text{ or } B) = n(A) + n(B)$$

$$= 6 + 1 = 7$$

So, $P(A \text{ or } B) = \frac{n(A \text{ or } B)}{n(S)} = \frac{7}{12}$.

(E) Calculate $P(A) + P(B)$. Compare the answer to Step D.

$$P(A) + P(B) = \frac{1}{2} + \frac{1}{12} = \frac{7}{12}$$

$P(A) + P(B)$ __equals__ $P(A \text{ or } B)$.

© Houghton Mifflin Harcourt Publishing Company

Module 21   1119   Lesson 4

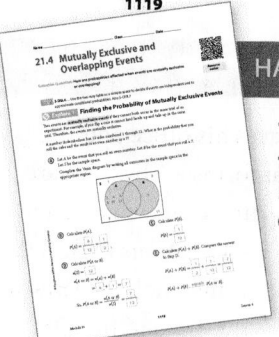

21.4 Mutually Exclusive and Overlapping Events

Turn to these pages to find this lesson in the hardcover student edition.

1. **Discussion** How would you describe mutually exclusive events to another student in your own words? How could you use a Venn diagram to assist in your explanation?
    Possible answer: Mutually exclusive events are events that have no common outcomes, meaning that any outcome that belongs to one of the events cannot also belong to the other event. The Venn diagram could assist in this explanation by visually showing that the events have no outcomes in common because their intersection would be empty.

2. Look back over the steps. What can you conjecture about the probability of the union of events that are mutually exclusive?
    The probability of the union of events that are mutually exclusive is equal to the sum of the probabilities of the events.

⊘ Explore 2 Finding the Probability of Overlapping Events

The process used in the previous Explore can be generalized to give the formula for the probability of mutually exclusive events.

Mutually Exclusive Events
If A and B are mutually exclusive events, then $P(A \text{ or } B) = P(A) + P(B)$.

Two events are **overlapping events** (or inclusive events) if they have one or more outcomes in common.

What is the probability that you roll a number dodecahedron and the result is an even number or a number greater than 7?

(A) Let A be the event that you roll an even number. Let B be the event that you roll a number greater than 7. Let S be the sample space.

Complete the Venn diagram by writing all outcomes in the sample space in the appropriate region.

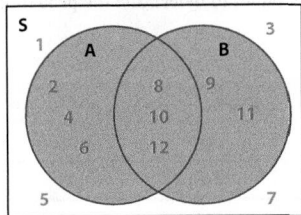

© Houghton Mifflin Harcourt Publishing Company

PROFESSIONAL DEVELOPMENT

🔷 Integrate Mathematical Practices

This lesson provides an opportunity to address Mathematical Practice **MP.6**, which calls for students to "communicate with precision." In this lesson, students must decide if events are mutually exclusive or overlapping in order to apply the correct version of the Addition Rule. They may examine a variety of representations, including set notation, Venn diagrams, language analysis, and two-way tables, to make and support their decisions.

EXPLORE 1

Finding the Probability of Mutually Exclusive Events

INTEGRATE TECHNOLOGY

Students have the option of doing the Explore activity either in the book or online.

INTEGRATE MATHEMATICAL PRACTICES
Focus on Communication

MP.3 Ask students to give examples of mutually exclusive events using outcomes from different probability experiments, such as a spinner, a number cube, or a deck of cards. Discuss with students how they can be sure the events they describe are mutually exclusive.

QUESTIONING STRATEGIES

? Explain why, in the case of mutually exclusive events, the probability of either event is equal to the sum of the probabilities of each event. The events have no outcomes in common so the probability will be the total of the individual probabilities.

? Why is a Venn diagram useful in finding the probability? The Venn diagram provides a picture of the sets and their outcomes that shows the sets do not overlap.

EXPLORE 2

Finding the Probability of Overlapping Events

INTEGRATE MATHEMATICAL PRACTICES
Focus on Communication

MP.3 Ask students to give examples of overlapping events using outcomes from different probability experiments, such as a spinner, a number cube, or a deck of cards. Discuss with students how they can be sure the events they describe are overlapping.

INTEGRATE MATHEMATICAL PRACTICES
Focus on Math Connections

MP.1 Review the set notation used for $P(A \text{ or } B)$ and $P(A \text{ and } B)$, as well as how they are represented on Venn diagrams for both mutually exclusive and overlapping events.

INTEGRATE MATHEMATICAL PRACTICES
Focus on Reasoning

MP.2 Discuss why $P(A) + P(B) - P(A \text{ and } B)$ can be used to find any probability $P(A \text{ or } B)$. For mutually exclusive events, $P(A \text{ and } B) = 0$.

QUESTIONING STRATEGIES

? How is $P(A \text{ or } B)$ different from $P(A \text{ and } B)$? *Or* refers to the union of the events; *and* refers to the intersection, or overlap, of the events.

? How can a Venn diagram help you remember the Addition Rule for overlapping events? A Venn diagram shows where the events overlap. This can help me remember to subtract the intersection so it is not counted twice.

(B) Calculate $P(A)$.

$$P(A) = \frac{6}{12} = \frac{1}{2}$$

(C) Calculate $P(B)$.

$$P(B) = \frac{5}{12}$$

(D) Calculate $P(A \text{ and } B)$.

$$P(A \text{ and } B) = \frac{3}{12} = \frac{1}{4}$$

(E) Use the Venn diagram to find $P(A \text{ or } B)$.

$$P(A \text{ or } B) = \frac{8}{12} = \frac{2}{3}$$

(F) Now, use $P(A)$, $P(B)$, and $P(A \text{ and } B)$ to calculate $P(A \text{ or } B)$.

$$P(A) = \frac{1}{2} \qquad P(B) = \frac{5}{12} \qquad P(A \text{ and } B) = \frac{1}{4}$$

$$P(A) + P(B) - P(A \text{ and } B) = \frac{1}{2} + \frac{5}{12} - \frac{1}{4} = \frac{2}{3}$$

Reflect

3. Why must you subtract $P(A \text{ and } B)$ from $P(A) + P(B)$ to determine $P(A \text{ or } B)$?

$P(A \text{ and } B)$ must be subtracted from $P(A) + P(B)$ to determine $P(A \text{ or } B)$ because the outcomes in the event A and B are counted twice. Therefore, the outcomes in the intersection must be subtracted from the total.

4. Look back over the steps. What can you conjecture about the probability of the union of two events that are overlapping?

The probability of the union of two events that are overlapping is equal to the sum of the probabilities of the two separate events minus the probability of both events.

🔎 Explain 1 Finding a Probability From a Two-Way Table of Data

The previous Explore leads to the following rule.

The Addition Rule
$P(A \text{ or } B) = P(A) + P(B) - P(A \text{ and } B)$

Example 1 Use the given two-way tables to determine the probabilities.

(A) $P(\text{senior or girl})$

	Freshman	Sophomore	Junior	Senior	TOTAL
Boy	98	104	100	94	396
Girl	102	106	96	108	412
Total	200	210	196	202	808

To determine $P(\text{senior or girl})$, first calculate $P(\text{senior})$, $P(\text{girl})$, and $P(\text{senior and girl})$.

© Houghton Mifflin Harcourt Publishing Company

COLLABORATIVE LEARNING

Peer-to-Peer Activity

Have students work with a partner to describe a situation in which the probability of two events is mutually exclusive. Have them formulate and answer a question about the probability. Repeat with inclusive events. Have students share their problems with the class.

$P(\text{senior}) = \frac{202}{808} = \frac{1}{4}$; $P(\text{girl}) = \frac{412}{808} = \frac{103}{202}$ $\qquad$ $P(\text{senior and girl}) = \frac{108}{808} = \frac{27}{202}$

Use the addition rule to determine $P(\text{senior or girl})$.

$P(\text{senior or girl}) = P(\text{senior}) + P(\text{girl}) - P(\text{senior and girl})$

$$= \frac{1}{4} + \frac{103}{202} - \frac{27}{202}$$

$$= \frac{253}{404}$$

Therefore, the probability that a student is a senior or a girl is $\frac{253}{404}$.

(B) $P\left((\text{domestic or late})^c\right)$

	Late	On Time	Total
Domestic Flights	12	108	120
International Flights	6	54	60
Total	18	162	180

To determine $P\left((\text{domestic or late})^c\right)$, first calculate $P(\text{domestic or late})$.

$P(\text{domestic}) = \dfrac{\boxed{120}}{\boxed{180}} = \dfrac{\boxed{2}}{\boxed{3}}$; $P(\text{late}) = \dfrac{\boxed{18}}{\boxed{180}} = \dfrac{\boxed{1}}{\boxed{10}}$; $P(\text{domestic and late}) = \dfrac{\boxed{12}}{\boxed{180}} = \dfrac{\boxed{1}}{\boxed{15}}$

Use the addition rule to determine $P(\text{domestic or late})$.

$P(\text{domestic or late}) = P(\text{domestic}) + P(\text{late}) - P(\text{domestic and late})$

$$= \frac{\boxed{2}}{\boxed{3}} + \frac{\boxed{1}}{\boxed{10}} - \frac{\boxed{1}}{\boxed{15}} = \frac{\boxed{7}}{\boxed{10}}$$

Therefore, $P\left((\text{domestic or late})^c\right) = 1 - P(\text{domestic or late})$

$$= 1 - \frac{\boxed{7}}{\boxed{10}}$$

$$= \frac{\boxed{3}}{\boxed{10}}$$

© Houghton Mifflin Harcourt Publishing Company · Image Credits: ©Elena Elisseeva/Cutcaster

EXPLAIN 1

Finding a Probability From a Two-Way Table of Data

AVOID COMMON ERRORS

Students may not use the correct total for the denominator of the probability ratio when they use a two-way table to find a probability. They may use a total from a row or column. As needed, have students extend the table to include a total that shows the sum of the columns is equal to the sum of the rows. This is the total needed for the denominator.

QUESTIONING STRATEGIES

? How do you know the events in the table are inclusive? **Possible answer: The overall total of the rows and columns is the same.**

? How do you identify the value that overlaps to apply the Addition Rule? **The overlap value is in the cell where the column and row intersect.**

DIFFERENTIATE INSTRUCTION

Multiple Representations

Discuss alternate ways to visualize the data in the problems presented. Have students make two-way tables, Venn diagrams, or tree diagrams as alternate ways to view the data and understand the relationships. Discuss the advantages of each representation.

ELABORATE

AVOID COMMON ERRORS

Students may forget to subtract the overlapping probability when finding the probability of overlapping events. Encourage students to draw Venn diagrams to help them remember how to apply the Addition Rule to solve probability problems.

SUMMARIZE THE LESSON

? How do you find the probability of mutually exclusive events and overlapping events? For mutually exclusive events A and B, $P(A \text{ or } B) = P(A) + P(B)$. For overlapping events A and B, $P(A \text{ or } B) = P(A) + P(B) - P(A \text{ and } B)$.

---

5. Use the table to determine $P(\text{headache or no medicine})$.

	Took Medicine	No Medicine	TOTAL
Headache	12	15	27
No Headache	48	25	73
TOTAL	60	40	100

$P(\text{headache}) = \frac{27}{100}$; $P(\text{no medicine}) = \frac{40}{100} = \frac{2}{5}$; $P(\text{headache and no medicine}) = \frac{15}{100} = \frac{3}{20}$; $P(\text{headache or no medicine}) = P(\text{headache}) + P(\text{no medicine}) - P(\text{headache and no medicine}) = \frac{27}{100} + \frac{2}{5} - \frac{3}{20} = \frac{13}{25}$ therefore, the probability that a person has a headache or takes no medicine is $\frac{13}{25}$.

💬 Elaborate

6. Give an example of mutually exclusive events and an example of overlapping events.
Possible answer: If you roll a number cube, the event of rolling a 3 and the event of rolling an even number are mutually exclusive because you cannot obtain both outcomes at the same time. If you pull a card from a deck, the event of pulling an ace and the event of pulling a spade are overlapping because you can obtain both outcomes by pulling the ace of spades.

7. **Essential Question Check-In** How do you determine the probability of mutually exclusive events and overlapping events?
To determine the probability of mutually exclusive events A and B, evaluate $P(A \text{ or } B) = P(A) + P(B)$. To determine the probability of overlapping events A and B, evaluate $P(A \text{ or } B) = P(A) + P(B) - P(A \text{ and } B)$.

⭐ Evaluate: Homework and Practice

• Online Homework
• Hints and Help
• Extra Practice

1. A bag contains 3 blue marbles, 5 red marbles, and 4 green marbles. You choose one without looking. What is the probability that it is red or green?
Let S be the sample space, A be the event that you choose a red marble, and B be the event that you choose a green marble. $n(S) = 12$, $n(A \text{ or } B) = n(A) + n(B) = 5 + 4 = 9$; $P(A \text{ or } B) = \frac{n(A \text{ or } B)}{n(S)} = \frac{9}{12} = \frac{3}{4}$; the probability that you choose a red marble or a green marble is $\frac{3}{4}$.

LANGUAGE SUPPORT 🇪🇱

Connect Vocabulary

For some students, the phrase *overlapping events* may be unclear. Separate the class into groups. Have students work together to create lists of overlapping events other than those in the examples from the lesson.

2. A number icosahedron has 20 sides numbered 1 through 20. What is the probability that the result of a roll is a number less than 4 or greater than 11?

Let S be the sample space, A be the event that you roll a number less than 4, and B be the event that you roll a number greater than 11.

$n(S) = 20$, $n(A \text{ or } B) = n(A) + n(B) = 3 + 9 = 12$

$P(A \text{ or } B) = \frac{n(A \text{ or } B)}{n(S)} = \frac{12}{20} = \frac{3}{5}$

The probability that the result is a number less than 4 or greater than 11 is $\frac{3}{5}$.

3. A bag contains 26 tiles, each with a different letter of the alphabet written on it. You choose a tile without looking. What is the probability that you choose a vowel (a, e, i, o, or u) or a letter in the word GEOMETRY?

Let S be the sample space, A be the event that you choose a vowel, and B be the event that you choose a letter in the word GEOMETRY.

$n(S) = 26$, $n(A \text{ or } B) = n(A) + n(B) - n(A \text{ and } B) = 5 + 7 - 2 = 10$

$P(A \text{ or } B) = \frac{n(A \text{ or } B)}{n(S)} = \frac{10}{26} = \frac{5}{13}$

The probability that you choose a vowel or a letter in the word GEOMETRY is $\frac{5}{13}$.

4. **Persevere in Problem Solving** You roll two number cubes at the same time. Each cube has sides numbered 1 through 6. What is the probability that the sum of the numbers rolled is even or greater than 9? (*Hint:* Create and fill out a probability chart.)

		Cube 1				
	1	**2**	**3**	**4**	**5**	**6**
1	1 + 1	1 + 2	1 + 3	1 + 4	1 + 5	1 + 6
2	2 + 1	2 + 2	2 + 3	2 + 4	2 + 5	2 + 6
3	3 + 1	3 + 2	3 + 3	3 + 4	3 + 5	3 + 6
4	4 + 1	4 + 2	4 + 3	4 + 4	4 + 5	4 + 6
5	5 + 1	5 + 2	5 + 3	5 + 4	5 + 5	5 + 6
6	6 + 1	6 + 2	6 + 3	6 + 4	6 + 5	6 + 6

(Cube 2 labels the rows)

Let S be the sample space, A be the event that the sum of the numbers is even, and B be the event that the sum of the numbers is greater than 9.

$n(S) = 36$, $n(A \text{ or } B) = n(A) + n(B) - n(A \text{ and } B) = 18 + 6 - 4 = 20$

$P(A \text{ or } B) = \frac{n(A \text{ or } B)}{n(S)} = \frac{20}{36} = \frac{5}{9}$

The probability that the sum of the numbers rolled is even or greater than 9 is $\frac{5}{9}$.

EVALUATE

Personal Math Trainer

ASSIGNMENT GUIDE

Concepts and Skills	Practice
Explore 1 Finding the Probability of Mutually Exclusive Events	Exercises 1–2, 22–23
Explore 2 Finding the Probability of Overlapping Events	Exercises 3–4
Example 1 Finding a Probability From a Two-Way Table of Data	Exercises 5–10, 11–21

COMMUNICATING MATH

Discuss the importance of filling in the total values for each row and column when the total values for a two-way table are not given.

Exercise	Depth of Knowledge (D.O.K.)	COMMON CORE Mathematical Practices
1–15	**2** Skills/Concepts	**MP.2** Reasoning
16	**2** Skills/Concepts	**MP.3** Logic
17–21	**2** Skills/Concepts	**MP.1** Problem Solving
22	**3** Strategic Thinking	**MP.3** Logic
23	**3** Strategic Thinking H.O.T.	**MP.3** Logic
24	**3** Strategic Thinking H.O.T.	**MP.4** Modeling
25	**3** Strategic Thinking H.O.T.	**MP.3** Logic

Mutually Exclusive and Overlapping Events   **1124**

Focus on Reasoning

MP.2 Discuss with students why it is easier not to simplify the fractions until after they have used the Addition Rule to calculate probabilities.

AVOID COMMON ERRORS

Students may not recognize overlapping events or may forget to subtract the overlap. Suggest that students first decide if the events can overlap. If so, students should identify the probability of this event first. Discuss how students can use *and* to help them recognize whether events overlap.

The table shows the data for car insurance quotes for 125 drivers made by an insurance company in one week.

	Teen	Adult (20 or over)	Total
0 accidents	15	53	68
1 accident	4	32	36
2+ accidents	9	12	21
Total	28	97	125

You randomly choose one of the drivers. Find the probability of each event.

5. The driver is an adult.

$$\frac{\text{Total Adults}}{\text{Total Drivers}} = \frac{97}{125}$$

6. The driver is a teen with 0 or 1 accident.

$$\frac{\text{Teen with 0 or 1 accident}}{\text{Total Drivers}} = \frac{19}{125}$$

7. The driver is a teen.

$$\frac{\text{Total Teens}}{\text{Total Drivers}} = \frac{28}{125}$$

8. The driver has 2+ accidents.

$$\frac{\text{Drivers with 2+ accidents}}{\text{Total Drivers}} = \frac{21}{125}$$

9. The driver is a teen and has 2+ accidents.

$$\frac{\text{Teens with 2+ accidents}}{\text{Total Drivers}} = \frac{9}{125}$$

10. The driver is a teen or a driver with 2+ accidents.

$$\frac{\text{Teen or Driver with 2+ accidents}}{\text{Total Drivers}} = \frac{28}{125} + \frac{21}{125} - \frac{9}{125} = \frac{40}{125} = \frac{8}{25}$$

Use the following information for Exercises 11–16. The table shown shows the results of a customer satisfaction survey for a cellular service provider, by location of the customer. In the survey, customers were asked whether they would recommend a plan with the provider to a friend.

	Arlington	Towson	Parkville	Total
Yes	40	35	41	116
No	18	10	6	34
Total	58	45	47	150

One of the customers that was surveyed was chosen at random.
Find the probability of each event.

11. The customer was from Towson and said No.

$$\frac{\text{Towson and said no}}{\text{Total}} = \frac{10}{150} = \frac{1}{15}$$

12. The customer was from Parkville.

$$\frac{\text{Parkville}}{\text{Total}} = \frac{47}{150}$$

13. The customer said Yes.

$$\frac{\text{Yes}}{\text{Total}} = \frac{116}{150} = \frac{58}{75}$$

14. The customer was from Parkville and said Yes.

$$\frac{\text{Parkville and said Yes}}{\text{Total}} = \frac{41}{150}$$

15. The customer was from Parkville or said Yes.

$$\frac{\text{Parkville or said Yes}}{\text{Total}} = \frac{47}{150} + \frac{116}{150} - \frac{41}{150} = \frac{122}{150} = \frac{61}{75}$$

16. Explain why you cannot use the rule $P(A \text{ or } B) = P(A) + P(B)$ in Exercise 15.

The events are not mutually exclusive because there are
41 customers who both live in Parkville and said yes, and they get
counted twice when adding $P(A)$ and $P(B)$, so you must use the more
general rule $P(A \text{ or } B) = P(A) + P(B) - P(A \text{ and } B)$.

Use the following information for Exercises 17–21. Roberto is the owner of a car
dealership. He is assessing the success rate of his top three salespeople in order
to offer one of them a promotion. Over two months, for each attempted sale, he
records whether the salesperson made a successful sale or not. The results are
shown in the chart.

	Successful	Unsuccessful	Total
Becky	6	6	12
Raul	4	5	9
Darrell	6	9	15
Total	16	20	36

Roberto randomly chooses one of the attempted sales.

17. Find the probability that the sale was one of Becky's or Raul's successful sales.

Let A be the set of Becky's successful sales attempts, let B be the set of Raul's
successful sales attempts, and let S be the set of all sales attempts.

$n(S) = 36$

$n(A \cup B) = n(A) + n(B) = 6 + 4 = 10$

$P(A \cup B) = \frac{n(A \cup B)}{n(S)} = \frac{10}{36} = \frac{5}{18}$

The probability that the sale was one of Becky's or Raul's successful sales is $\frac{5}{18}$.

© Houghton Mifflin Harcourt Publishing Company

Students might treat inclusive events as mutually
exclusive and double count a probability. A total
probability greater than 1 could indicate this error.
Remind students to consider whether the events can
occur simultaneously before they choose the form of
the addition rule to use.

Mutually Exclusive and Overlapping Events   **1126**

18. Find the probability that the sale was one of the unsuccessful sales or one of Raul's successful sales.

Let A be the set of all unsuccessful sales attempts, let B be the set of Raul's successful sales attempts, and let S be the set of all sales attempts.

$n(S) = 36$

$n(A \cup B) = n(A) + n(B) = 4 + 20 = 24$

$P(A \cup B) = \frac{n(A \cup B)}{n(S)} = \frac{24}{36} = \frac{2}{3}$

The probability that the sale was one of the unsuccessful sales or one of Raul's successful sales is $\frac{2}{3}$.

19. Find the probability that the sale was one of Darrell's unsuccessful sales or one of Raul's unsuccessful sales.

Let A be the set of Darrell's unsuccessful sales attempts, let B be the set of Raul's unsuccessful sales attempts, and let S be the set of all sales attempts.

$n(S) = 36$

$n(A \cup B) = n(A) + n(B) = 9 + 5 = 14$

$P(A \cup B) = \frac{n(A \cup B)}{n(S)} = \frac{14}{36} = \frac{7}{18}$

The probability that the sale was one of Darrell's unsuccessful sales or one of Raul's unsuccessful sales is $\frac{7}{18}$.

20. Find the probability that the sale was an unsuccessful sale or one of Becky's attempted sales.

Let A be the set of all unsuccessful sales attempts, let B be the set of Becky's sales attempts, and let S be the set of all sales attempts.

$n(S) = 36$

$n(A \cup B) = n(A) + n(B) - n(A \cap B) = 20 + 12 - 6 = 26$

$P(A \cup B) = \frac{n(A \cup B)}{n(S)} = \frac{26}{36} = \frac{13}{18}$

The probability that the sale was an unsuccessful sale or one of Becky's attempted sales is $\frac{13}{18}$.

21. Find the probability that the sale was a successful sale or one of Raul's attempted sales.

Let A be the set of all successful sales attempts, let B be the set of Raul's sales attempts, and let S be the set of all sales attempts.

$n(S) = 36$

$n(A \cup B) = n(A) + n(B) - n(A \cap B) = 16 + 9 - 4 = 21$

$P(A \cup B) = \frac{n(A \cup B)}{n(S)} = \frac{21}{36} = \frac{7}{12}$

The probability that the sale was a successful sale or one of Raul's attempted sales is $\frac{7}{12}$.

© Houghton Mifflin Harcourt Publishing Company

22. You are going to draw one card at random from a standard deck of cards. A standard deck of cards has 13 cards (2, 3, 4, 5, 6, 7, 8, 9, 10, jack, queen, king, ace) in each of 4 suits (hearts, clubs, diamonds, spades). The hearts and diamonds cards are red. The clubs and spades cards are black. Which of the following have a probability of less than $\frac{1}{4}$? Choose all that apply.

a. Drawing a card that is a spade and an ace

b. Drawing a card that is a club or an ace

c. Drawing a card that is a face card or a club

d. Drawing a card that is black and a heart

e. Drawing a red card and a number card from 2–9

a. $P\left(\text{spade} \cap \text{ace}\right) = \dfrac{n\left(\text{spade} \cap \text{ace}\right)}{n\left(\text{deck}\right)} = \dfrac{1}{52} < \dfrac{1}{4}$

b. $P\left(\text{club} \cup \text{ace}\right) = \dfrac{n\left(\text{club} \cup \text{ace}\right)}{n\left(\text{deck}\right)} = \dfrac{n\left(\text{club}\right) + n\left(\text{ace}\right) - n\left(\text{club} \cap \text{ace}\right)}{n\left(\text{deck}\right)} = \dfrac{13 + 4 - 1}{52} = \dfrac{16}{52} = \dfrac{4}{13} > \dfrac{1}{4}$

c. $P\left(\text{face} \cup \text{club}\right) = \dfrac{n\left(\text{face} \cup \text{club}\right)}{n\left(\text{deck}\right)} = \dfrac{n\left(\text{face}\right) + n\left(\text{club}\right) - n\left(\text{face} \cap \text{club}\right)}{n\left(\text{deck}\right)} = \dfrac{12 + 13 - 3}{52} = \dfrac{22}{52}$
$= \dfrac{11}{26} > \dfrac{1}{4}$

d. $P\left(\text{black} \cap \text{heart}\right) = \dfrac{n\left(\text{black} \cap \text{heart}\right)}{n\left(\text{deck}\right)} = \dfrac{0}{52} = 0 < \dfrac{1}{4}$

e. $P\left(\text{red} \cap 2 - 9\right) = \dfrac{n\left(\text{red} \cap 2 - 9\right)}{n\left(\text{deck}\right)} = \dfrac{16}{52} = \dfrac{4}{13} > \dfrac{1}{4}$

23. Draw Conclusions A survey of 1108 employees at a software company finds that 621 employees take a bus to work and 445 employees take a train to work. Some employees take both a bus and a train, and 321 employees take only a train. To the nearest percent, find the probability that a randomly chosen employee takes a bus or a train to work. Explain.

If 321 employees take only a train, and 445 total employees take a train, then

$445 - 321 = 124$ people take both a bus and a train to work.

$n\left(A \cup B\right) = n\left(\text{bus}\right) + n\left(\text{train}\right) - n\left(\text{bus and train}\right) = 621 + 445 - 124 = 942$

$n\left(S\right) = n\left(\text{total surveyed}\right) = 1108$

$P\left(A \cup B\right) = \dfrac{n\left(A \cup B\right)}{n\left(S\right)} = \dfrac{942}{1108} = \dfrac{471}{554} \approx 85\%$

The probability that a randomly chosen employee takes a bus or a train to work is 85%.

24. Communicate Mathematical Ideas Explain how to use a Venn diagram to find the probability of randomly choosing a multiple of 3 or a multiple of 4 from the set of numbers from 1 to 25. Then find the probability.

Let *A* be the set of multiples of 3 from 1 to 25 and *B* be the set of multiples of 4 from 1 to 25. Create a Venn diagram representing the sets *A* and *B*.

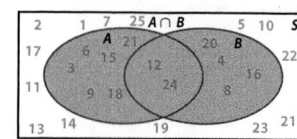

Add the numbers of elements in *A* and *B*, and then subtract the number of elements in the overlap to get the numerator of the probability. The denominator is 25.

$n(A \cup B) = 8 + 6 - 2 = 12$

$P(A \cup B) = \frac{12}{25}$

The probability of randomly choosing a multiple of 3 or a multiple of 4 from the set of numbers from 1 to 25 is $\frac{12}{25}$.

25. Explain the Error Sanderson attempted to find the probability of randomly choosing a 10 or a diamond from a standard deck of playing cards. He used the following logic:

Let *S* be the sample space, *A* be the event that the card is a 10, and *B* be the event that the card is a diamond.

There are 52 cards in the deck, so $n(S) = 52$.

There are four 10s in the deck, so $n(A) = 4$.

There are 13 diamonds in the deck, so $n(B) = 13$.

One 10 is a diamond, so $n(A \cap B) = 1$.

$$P(A \cup B) = \frac{n(A \cup B)}{n(S)} = \frac{n(A) \cdot n(B) - n(A \cap B)}{n(S)} = \frac{4 \cdot 13 - 1}{52} = \frac{51}{52}$$

Describe and correct Sanderson's mistake.

When finding $n(A \cup B)$, $n(A)$ should be added to $n(B)$, not multiplied.

$$P(A \cup B) = \frac{n(A) + n(B) - n(A \cap B)}{n(S)} = \frac{4 + 13 - 1}{52} = \frac{16}{52} = \frac{4}{13}$$

© Houghton Mifflin Harcourt Publishing Company

Lesson Performance Task

What is the smallest number of randomly chosen people that are needed in order for there to be a better than 50% probability that at least two of them will have the same birthday? The astonishing answer is 23. Follow these steps to find why.

1. Can a person have a birthday on two different days? Use the vocabulary of this lesson to explain your answer.

Looking for the probability that two or more people in a group of 23 have matching birthdays is a challenge. Maybe there is one match but maybe there are five matches or seven or fourteen. A much easier way is to look for the probability that there are *no* matches in a group of 23. In other words, all 23 have different birthdays. Then use that number to find the answer.

2. There are 365 days in a non-leap year.

   a. Write an expression for the number of ways can you assign different birthdays to 23 people. (Hint: Think of the people as standing in a line, and you are going to assign a different number from 1 to 365 to each person.)

   b. Write an expression for the number ways can you assign any birthday to 23 people. (Hint: Now think about assigning any number from 1 to 365 to each of 23 people.)

   c. How can you use your answers to (a) and (b) to find the probability that no people in a group of 23 have the same birthday? Use a calculator to find the probability to the nearest ten-thousandth.

   d. What is the probability that at least two people in a group of 23 have the same birthday? Explain your reasoning.

1. No; The set of days of the year when you have a birthday and the set of days of the year when you do not have a birthday are mutually exclusive, not overlapping.

2. a. Because assigned numbers must be different, find the number of permutations of 365 numbers taken 23 at a time: $_{365}P_{23}$

   b. Because assigned numbers can be the same, the number of choices for each person is 365, so form a product where 365 appears as a factor 23 times: 365^{23}

   c. Divide $_{365}P_{23}$ by 365^{23} and get 0.4927 to the nearest ten-thousandth.

   d. The complement of the event that at least two people in a group of 23 have the same birthday is the event that no people in a group of 23 have the same birthday, so P (at least two people in a group of 23 have the same birthday) $= 1 - P$(no people in a group of 23 have the same birthday) $\approx 1 - 0.4927 = 0.5073$ or 50.73%.

AVOID COMMON ERRORS

Students hearing the birthday paradox for the first time often misunderstand it as claiming that in a group of 23 randomly chosen people, the chances are better than 50–50 that one of them will have a specific given birthday, say July 23. Students are correct in thinking that that is highly unlikely. Stress that the paradox is that in a random group of 23, the chances are better than 50–50 that *two of them will have the same birthday*. The actual date of the birthday, however, is unstated.

INTEGRATE MATHEMATICAL PRACTICES
Focus on Critical Thinking

MP.3 Tammy's birthday is July 23. How large must a group of randomly chosen people be in order for there to be a better than 50% chance that one of them will have the same birthday she has?

$183; \dfrac{183}{365} \approx 50.1\%$

EXTENSION ACTIVITY

Present another surprising probability paradox: (1) Mister Jones has two children. The oldest is a girl. What is the probability that the other child is a girl? Explain your reasoning. $\frac{1}{2}$; 2 possible outcomes for second child: {B, G}; 1 favorable outcome: G (2) Mister Smith has two children. At least one of them is a girl. What is the probability that the other child is a girl? Explain your reasoning. $\frac{1}{3}$; 3 possible combinations: {GG, BG, GB}; 1 favorable outcome: GG It may seem counterintuitive that specifying "at least" changes the probability that the second child will be a girl. To test this, have students flip two coins (H = girl, T = boy). They should ignore TT (boy, boy). If one is a heads, they should count the number of times the other is also a heads.

Mutually Exclusive and Overlapping Events   **1130**

Study Guide Review

ASSESSMENT AND INTERVENTION

Personal Math Trainer

Assign or customize module reviews.

MODULE PERFORMANCE TASK

COMMON CORE

Mathematical Practices: MP.1, MP.2, MP.4, MP.7, MP.8
S-CP.A.1, S-CP.B.9

SUPPORTING STUDENT REASONING

Students should begin this problem by focusing on what information they will need. Here are some issues they might bring up.

- **How to find the probability of getting a hit at bat:** Students can make an organized list that shows the probability of getting a hit in the next turn and then in the next three turns at bat, the least number of turns at bat a player will get in today's game. The probability of getting a hit in three turns will be the sum of the probabilities associated with at least one hit at bat.

- **The probability of getting no hits at bat in one game:** Students can use the organized list to find this value for three turns at bat.

- **How to find the probability of getting exactly one hit at bat:** Students can use the organized list to find this value for three turns at bat. They should add the probabilities for all rows that show exactly one hit in three tries.

Essential Question: How can you use probability to solve real-world problems?

KEY EXAMPLE *(Lesson 21.1)*

When rolling two fair number cubes, what is the probability that the sum of the two cubes will not be even or prime?

The sum of two number cubes can be any integer from 2 through 12. Of these, the only possible sum that is not even or prime is 9. There are 36 possible outcomes for rolling two number cubes. Of these, the only ones that sum to 9 are (3, 6), (6, 3), (4, 5), and (5, 4). So, $P($sum is not even or prime$) = \frac{4}{36} = \frac{1}{9}$.

KEY EXAMPLE *(Lesson 21.2)*

Ten marbles are placed in a jar. Of the 10 marbles, 3 are blue, 2 are red, 3 are green, 1 is orange, and 1 is yellow. The 10 marbles are randomly placed in a line. What is the probability that all marbles of the same color are next to each other?

Marbles of the same color are indistinguishable objects. The sample space S consists of permutations of 10 objects, with 3 of one type, 3 of another type, and 2 of a third type.

$$n(S) = \frac{10!}{3!3!2!} = 50,400$$

Event A consists of permutations that have all marbles of the same color next to each other, so it is the number of ways of ordering the 5 colors.

$$n(A) = 5! = 120$$

The probability that all marbles of the same color are next to each other is

$$P(A) = \frac{n(A)}{n(S)} = \frac{120}{50,400} = \frac{1}{420}.$$

KEY EXAMPLE *(Lesson 21.3)*

A class of 15 boys and 15 girls is putting together a random group of 3 students to do classroom chores. What is the probability that at least 2 of the students are boys?

The sample space S consists of combinations of three student groups.

$$n(S) = \frac{30!}{3!27!} = 4060$$

Event A consists of combinations that have 2 boys or 3 boys in the group. The event of getting 2 boys in the group occurs 15 times, once for each individual girl in the class.

$$n(A) = 15 \cdot {}_{15}C_2 + {}_{15}C_3 = 15 \cdot \frac{15!}{2!13!} + \frac{15!}{3!12!} = 2030$$

The probability that there will be at least 2 boys in the group is $P(A) = \frac{n(A)}{n(S)} = \frac{2030}{4060} = \frac{1}{2}$.

Key Vocabulary

set *(conjunto, juego)*
element *(elemento)*
empty set *(conjunto vacío)*
universal set *(conjunto universal)*
subset *(subconjunto)*
intersection *(intersección)*
union *(unión)*
complement *(complemento)*
theoretical probability *(probabilidad teórica)*
permutation *(permutación)*
Fundamental Counting Principle *(principio fundamental de conteo)*
factorial *(factorial)*
combination *(combinación)*

SCAFFOLDING SUPPORT

- Students will first need to calculate the probability of getting a hit in any one turn at bat, using the information given. The probability is the ratio of the number of hits to the number of times at bat. The probability of not getting a hit in any one turn is 1 minus this value.

- To find the probability of any combination of hits and no hits, find the product of the probabilities for each individual event.

EXERCISES

Use the sets below to find the indicated set for problems 1–4. *(Lesson 21.1)*

$U = \{1, 2, 3, 4, 5, 6, 7, 8, 9\}$

$A = \{1, 3, 5, 7, 9\}$

$B = \{2, 4, 6, 8\}$

$C = \{1, 2, 4, 5, 7, 9\}$

1. $A \cup C$ ___{1, 2, 3, 4, 5, 7, 9}___

2. $B \cap C$ ___{2, 4,}___

3. A^C ___{2, 4, 6, 8}___

4. $A \cap B$ ___{∅}___

5. A computer password can use all digits (0–9) and all letters (*a–z*) that are case sensitive (upper and lower). How many different permutations of 5-figure passwords are there if there is no repeated input? *(Lesson 21.2)* **776,520,240**

6. Brandon is rolling a 10-sided number cube 5 times. What is the probability that he will roll at least two 7s? *(Lesson 21.3)* $\dfrac{26}{100000}$

Determine if the given events are mutually exclusive. If not, explain why. *(Lesson 21.4)*

7. Rolling a 3 or a 4 on a regular number cube **yes**

8. Drawing a queen or a red card from a standard deck of 52 cards
no; the card can be a red queen

9. Flipping a coin and having it land on heads or tails **yes**

10. Rolling an even number or a prime number on a number cube **no; 2 is both prime and even**

MODULE PERFORMANCE TASK
Baseball Probability

A baseball player will be batting three times during today's game. So far this season, the player has gotten an average of 1 hit in every 3 times at bat. Based on this data, what is the probability that the player will get exactly one hit in today's game? Is that outcome more or less likely than getting no hits?

Start by making notes in the space below about your plan for solving the problem. Then use your own paper to complete the task, using words, numbers, or diagrams to explain how your reached your conclusions.

DISCUSSION OPPORTUNITIES

- There are many baseball games in which a player gets more than three turns at bat. How does this change the probabilities shown in the organized list?

- Why is the probability of getting at least one hit in three turns at bat higher than the probability of getting exactly one hit in three turns at bat?

SAMPLE SOLUTION

Assumption:

The player will continue to bat the same percentage as batted in previous games of the season.

Method:

Make a model of the situation. Let a hit be represented by H and a miss be represented by M. The player will bat three times in today's game, so suppose there are three containers, each containing an H and two M's, and you draw a letter at random from each of the three containers to model the three at-bats.

For this model, the sample space **S** consists of the ways of drawing a letter from each container. So, by the Fundamental Counting Principle,

$n(S) = 3 \cdot 3 \cdot 3 = 27.$

Event **A** consists of combinations of the three letters chosen that have one H and two M's. If you draw the H from the first container, there are two ways to draw an M from the second and two ways to draw an M from the third. So there are $2 \cdot 2 = 4$ ways to draw an H from the first container.

If you draw the H from the second container, there are two ways to draw an M from the first and two ways to draw an M from the third. So there are $2 \cdot 2 = 4$ ways to draw an H from the second container.

Similarly, there are 4 ways to draw the H from the third container.

So, the probability that the player will have exactly one hit is:

$$P(A) = \frac{n(A)}{n(S)} = \frac{4 + 4 + 4}{3^3} = \frac{12}{27} = \frac{4}{9}$$

Assessment Rubric

2 points: Student correctly solves the problem and explains his/her reasoning.

1 point: Student shows good understanding of the problem but does not fully solve or explain.

0 points: Student does not demonstrate understanding of the problem.

Ready to Go On?

ASSESS MASTERY

Use the assessment on this page to determine if students have mastered the concepts and standards covered in this module.

ASSESSMENT AND INTERVENTION

Access Ready to Go On? assessment online, and receive instant scoring, feedback, and customized intervention or enrichment.

ADDITIONAL RESOURCES

Response to Intervention Resources

- Reteach Worksheets

Differentiated Instruction Resources

- Reading Strategies **EL**
- Success for English Learners **EL**
- Challenge Worksheets

Assessment Resources

- Leveled Module Quizzes

(Ready) to Go On?

21.1–21.4 Introduction to Probability

- Online Homework
- Hints and Help
- Extra Practice

Find the probabilities. *(Lessons 21.3, 21.4)*

1. Twenty-six tiles with the letters A through Z are placed face down on a table and mixed. (For the purpose of this exercise assume that the letter Y is a vowel.) Five tiles are drawn in order. Compute the probability that only consonants are selected.

The sample space S consists of combinations of 5 letters chosen from the 26 letters, and event A consists of combinations of 5 letters chosen from the 20 consonant letters.

$$n(S) = {}_{26}C_5 = \frac{26!}{5!21!} = 65780, \ n(A) = {}_{20}C_5 = \frac{20!}{5!15!} = 15504, \ P(A) = \frac{n(A)}{n(S)} = \frac{15504}{65780} = \frac{3876}{16445}$$

2. The two-way table shows the results of a poll in a certain country that asked voters, sorted by political party, whether they supported or opposed a proposed government initiative. Find the given probabilities.

	Party A	Party B	Other Party	No Party	Total
Support	97	68	8	19	192
Oppose	32	81	16	11	140
Undecided	9	23	10	26	68
Total	138	172	34	56	400

a. $P(\text{no party or undecided})$ $\quad \frac{56}{400} + \frac{68}{400} - \frac{26}{400} = \frac{98}{400} = \frac{49}{200}$

b. $P\left((\text{party A or support})^c\right)$ $\quad P\left((\text{party A or support})^c\right) = 1 - P(\text{party A or support}) = 1 - \frac{233}{400} = \frac{167}{400}$

ESSENTIAL QUESTION

3. A teacher is assigning 32 presentation topics to 9 students at random. Each student will get 3 topics, and no topic will be repeated. Somil is very interested in 5 topics. What is the probability that Somil will be assigned at least one of his preferred topics? Explain how you arrived at your answer.

Methods may vary. Somil being assigned at least one of his preferred topics is the complement of Somil being assigned none of his preferred topics. For the sample space S consists of combinations of 3 topics chosen from the 32 topics, $n(S) = {}_{32}C_3 = \frac{32!}{3!29!} = 4960$.

Event A consists of combinations of 3 topics in which Somil is not very interested:

$n(S) = {}_{27}C_3 = \frac{27!}{3!24!} = 2925$. The probability that Somil is not assigned any of his preferred topics is $P(A) = \frac{n(A)}{n(S)} = \frac{2925}{4960} = \frac{585}{992}$. Thus the probability that Somil is assigned at least one of his preferred topics is $P(A^c) = 1 - P(A) = 1 - \frac{585}{992} = \frac{407}{992}$.

© Houghton Mifflin Harcourt Publishing Company

COMMON CORE **Common Core Standards**

Lesson	Items	Content Standards	Mathematical Practices
21.3	1	**S-CP.B.9**	**MP.1**
21.4	2	**S-CP.A.4**	**MP.2**

MODULE 21
MIXED REVIEW

Assessment Readiness

1. Jonah is arranging books on a shelf. The order of the books matters to him. There are 336 ways he can arrange the books. Choose Yes or No for each statement.

   A. He might be arranging 3 books from a selection of 8 different books. ● Yes ○ No

   B. He might be arranging 4 books from a selection of 8 different books. ○ Yes ● No

   C. He might be arranging 5 books from a selection of 8 different books. ○ Yes ● No

2. Decide whether the probability of tossing the given sum with two dice is $\frac{5}{36}$. Select Yes or No for A–C.

   A. A sum of 6   ● Yes ○ No
   B. A sum of 7   ○ Yes ● No
   C. A sum of 8   ● Yes ○ No

3. Let H be the event that a coin flip lands with heads showing, and let T be the event that a flip lands with tails showing. (Note that $P(H) = P(T) = 0.5$.) What is the probability that you will get heads at least once if you flip the coin ten times? Explain your reasoning.

   About 0.999; Sample answer: Let A be the probability that heads appears at least once and B be the probability that it doesn't appear.

   $P(A) = 1 - P(B)$
   $\qquad = 1 - P(0.5^{10})$
   $\qquad \approx 1 - 0.001$
   $\qquad \approx 0.999$

4. There are 8 girls and 6 boys on the student council. How many committees of 3 girls and 2 boys can be formed? Show your work.

   840 committees; $_8C_3 \cdot {}_6C_2 = \dfrac{8 \cdot 7 \cdot 6 \cdot 5 \cdot 4 \cdot 3 \cdot 2 \cdot 1}{5 \cdot 4 \cdot 3 \cdot 2 \cdot 1 \cdot 3 \cdot 2 \cdot 1} \cdot \dfrac{6 \cdot 5 \cdot 4 \cdot 3 \cdot 2 \cdot 1}{4 \cdot 3 \cdot 2 \cdot 1 \cdot 2 \cdot 1}$

   $\qquad = 56 \cdot 15$

   $\qquad = 840$

MIXED REVIEW
Assessment Readiness

ASSESSMENT AND INTERVENTION

Assign ready-made or customized practice tests to prepare students for high-stakes tests.

ADDITIONAL RESOURCES

Assessment Resources

- Leveled Module Quizzes: Modified, B

AVOID COMMON ERRORS

Item 4 Some students have a hard time determining the difference between permutations and combinations. Remind students that with permutations, order matters, and with combinations, order does not matter.

COMMON CORE ## Common Core Standards

Lesson	Items	Content Standards	Mathematical Practices
21.2	1	S-CP.B.9	MP.2
21.1	2	S-CP.A.1	MP.2
21.1	3	S-CP.A.1	MP.4
21.3	4	S-CP.B.9	MP.2

* Item integrates mixed review concepts from previous modules or a previous course.

Conditional Probability and Independence of Events

ESSENTIAL QUESTION:

Answer: Conditional probability and independence of events are useful for analyzing how the occurrence of one event affects the probability of another.

PROFESSIONAL DEVELOPMENT VIDEO

Professional Development Video

Learn effective ways of integrating technology into your classroom to meet a variety of different needs.

Professional Development
my.hrw.com

MODULE **22**

Conditional Probability and Independence of Events

★

Essential Question: How can you use conditional probability and independence of events to solve real-world problems?

LESSON 22.1
Conditional Probability

LESSON 22.2
Independent Events

LESSON 22.3
Dependent Events

REAL WORLD VIDEO
Check out how principles of conditional probability are used to understand the chances of events in playing cards.

© Houghton Mifflin Harcourt Publishing Company • Image Credits: © Sergey Nivens/Shutterstock

MODULE PERFORMANCE TASK PREVIEW

Playing Cards

In this module, you will use concepts of conditional probability to determine the chance of drawing a hand of cards with a certain property. To successfully complete this task, you'll need to master these skills:

- Distinguish between independent and dependent events.
- Apply the conditional probability formula to a real-world situation.
- Use the Multiplication Rule appropriately.

Module 22   **1135**

DIGITAL TEACHER EDITION

Access a full suite of teaching resources when and where you need them:

- Access content online or offline
- Customize lessons to share with your class
- Communicate with your students in real-time
- View student grades and data instantly to target your instruction where it is needed most

PERSONAL MATH TRAINER

Assessment and Intervention

Assign automatically graded homework, quizzes, tests, and intervention activities. Prepare your students with updated, Common Core-aligned practice tests.

Are YOU Ready?

Complete these exercises to review skills you will need for this module.

Probability of Compound Events

- Online Homework
- Hints and Help
- Extra Practice

Example 1   Find the probability of rolling a pair of six-sided dice and the sum of their faces being even or equal to 3.

Three is not even, so the two probabilities are mutually exclusive. The probability is equal to the sums of the probabilities of rolling an even sum or rolling a sum of 3.

Probability of rolling an even sum $= \frac{18}{36}$ Count the number of outcomes for the first event.

Probability of rolling a sum of 3 $= \frac{2}{36}$ Count the number of outcomes for the second event.

Probability of rolling an even sum or a sum of 3 $= \frac{18}{36} + \frac{2}{36} = \frac{20}{36} = \frac{5}{9}$

Find each probability.

1. The probability of rolling two dice at the same time and getting a 4 with either die or the sum of the dice is 6. $\frac{7}{18}$

2. The probability of rolling two dice at the same time and getting a 4 with either die and the sum of the dice is 6. $\frac{1}{18}$

3. The probability of pulling red or blue marbles (or both) from a jar of only red and blue marbles when you pull out two marbles given that pulling red and pulling blue are equally likely events. 1

4. The probability of pulling a red marble and a blue marble from a jar of only red and blue marbles when you pull out two marbles given that pulling red and pulling blue are equally likely events. $\frac{1}{2}$

5. The probability of flipping a coin three times and getting exactly two heads or at least one tails given the probability of getting a heads is $\frac{1}{2}$ and the probability of getting a tails is $\frac{1}{2}$. $\frac{7}{8}$

6. The probability of flipping a coin three times and getting exactly two heads and at least one tails given the probability of getting a heads is $\frac{1}{2}$ and the probability of getting a tails is $\frac{1}{2}$. $\frac{3}{8}$

7. The probability of flipping a coin three times and getting at least two heads or at least one tails given the probability of getting a heads is $\frac{1}{2}$ and the probability of getting a tails is $\frac{1}{2}$. 1

Are You Ready?

ASSESS READINESS

Use the assessment on this page to determine if students need strategic or intensive intervention for the module's prerequisite skills.

ASSESSMENT AND INTERVENTION

RtI Response to Intervention **TIER 1, TIER 2, TIER 3 SKILLS**

Personal Math Trainer will automatically create a standards-based, personalized intervention assignment for your students, targeting each student's individual needs!

ADDITIONAL RESOURCES

See the table below for a full list of intervention resources available for this module.

Response to Intervention Resources also includes:

- Tier 2 Skill Pre-Tests for each Module
- Tier 2 Skill Post-Tests for each skill

Response to Intervention			Differentiated Instruction
Tier 1 Lesson Intervention Worksheets	**Tier 2** Strategic Intervention Skills Intervention Worksheets	**Tier 3** Intensive Intervention Worksheets available online	
Reteach 22.1 Reteach 22.2 Reteach 22.3	14 Probability of Compound Events 24 Surface Area	Building Block Skills 9, 10, 11, 14, 37, 39, 65, 72, 82, 86, 95, 101, 112	Challenge worksheets Extend the Math Lesson Activities in TE

Conditional Probability

Common Core Math Standards

The student is expected to:

 **S-CP.A.4**

... Use the two-way table ... to approximate conditional probabilities. Also S-CP.A.3, S-CP.A.5, S-CP.B.6

Mathematical Practices

 MP.4 Modeling

Language Objective

Explain to a partner how to find conditional probabilities.

ENGAGE

Essential Question: How do you calculate a conditional probability?

You can calculate the conditional probability $P(A \mid B)$ from a two-way frequency table using the formula $P(A \mid B) = \frac{n(A \cap B)}{n(B)}$. You can also calculate $P(A \mid B)$ using the formula $P(A \mid B) = \frac{P(A \cap B)}{P(B)}$.

PREVIEW: LESSON PERFORMANCE TASK

View the Engage section online. Discuss the photograph. Ask students to identify the celebrity and to describe the reasons for the celebrity's fame. Then preview the Lesson Performance Task.

Name_____ Class_____ Date_____

22.1 Conditional Probability

Resource Locker

Essential Question: How do you calculate a conditional probability?

⊘ Explore 1   Finding Conditional Probabilities from a Two-Way Frequency Table

The probability that event A occurs given that event B has already occurred is called the **conditional probability** of A given B and is written $P(A \mid B)$.

One hundred migraine headache sufferers participated in a study of a new medicine. Some were given the new medicine, and others were not. After one week, participants were asked if they had experienced a headache during the week. The two-way frequency table shows the results.

	Took medicine	No medicine	Total
Headache	11	13	24
No headache	54	22	76
Total	65	35	100

Let event A be the event that a participant did not get a headache. Let event B be the event that a participant took the medicine.

(A) To the nearest percent, what is the probability that a participant who took the medicine did not get a headache?

   __65__ participants took the medicine.   So, $P(A \mid B) = \dfrac{\boxed{54}}{\boxed{65}} \approx \boxed{83}$ %.

   Of these, __54__ did not get a headache.

(B) To the nearest percent, what is the probability that a participant who did not get a headache took the medicine?

   __76__ participants did not get a headache.   So, $P(B \mid A) = \dfrac{\boxed{54}}{\boxed{76}} \approx \boxed{71}$ %.

   Of these, __54__ took the medicine.

(C) Let $n(A)$ be the number of participants who did not get a headache, $n(B)$ be the number of participants who took the medicine, and $n(A \cap B)$ be the number of participants who took the medicine and did not get a headache.

   $n(A) = \boxed{76}$ $n(B) = \boxed{65}$ $n(A \cap B) = \boxed{76}$

Express $P(A \mid B)$ and $P(B \mid A)$ in terms of $n(A)$, $n(B)$, and $n(A \cap B)$.

$$P(A \mid B) = \frac{\boxed{n(A \cap B)}}{\boxed{n(B)}} \qquad P(B \mid A) = \frac{\boxed{n(A \cap B)}}{\boxed{n(A)}}$$

© Houghton Mifflin Harcourt Publishing Company

HARDCOVER PAGES 945–952

Turn to these pages to find this lesson in the hardcover student edition.

1. For the question "What is the probability that a participant who did not get a headache took the medicine?", what event is assumed to have already occurred?
   The event that a participant did not get a headache is assumed to have already occurred.

2. In general, does it appear that $P(A|B) = P(B|A)$? Why or why not?
   No, the calculations of $P(A|B)$ and $P(B|A)$ in Steps A and B show that these conditional
   probabilities are not equal, so in general $P(A|B) \neq P(B|A)$.

⊘ Explore 2 Finding Conditional Probabilities from a Two-Way Relative Frequency Table

You can develop a formula for $P(A|B)$ that uses relative frequencies (which are probabilities) rather than frequencies (which are counts).

	Took medicine	No medicine	Total
Headache	11	13	24
No headache	54	22	76
Total	65	35	100

(A) To obtain relative frequencies, divide every number in the table by 100, the total number of participants in the study.

	Took medicine	No medicine	Total
Headache	0.11	0.13	0.24
No headache	0.54	0.22	0.76
Total	0.65	0.35	1

(B) Recall that event A is the event that a participant did not get a headache and that event B is the event that a participant took the medicine. Use the relative frequency table from Step A to find $P(A)$, $P(B)$, and $P(A \cap B)$.
   $P(A) = 0.76$, $P(B) = 0.65$, and $P(A \cap B) = 0.54$.

(C) In the first Explore, you found the conditional probabilities $P(A|B) \approx 83\%$ and $P(B|A) \approx 71\%$ by using the frequencies in the two-way frequency table. Use the relative frequencies from the table in Step A to find the equivalent conditional probabilities.

$$P(A|B) = \frac{P(A \cap B)}{P(B)} = \frac{0.54}{0.65} \approx \boxed{83}\% \qquad P(B|A) = \frac{P(A \cap B)}{P(A)} = \frac{0.54}{0.76} \approx \boxed{71}\%$$

PROFESSIONAL DEVELOPMENT

Learning Progressions

This is the first of three related lessons that cover the concepts of conditional probability, independent events, and dependent events. Many texts begin by defining independent and dependent events. The approach in this module begins with a deeper treatment of conditional probability and then progresses to defining independent and dependent events. This approach gives students many opportunities to work with two-way tables, which they can use to make sense of a wide range of probability and statistics problems as they continue their study of mathematics.

EXPLORE 1

Finding Conditional Probabilities from a Two-Way Frequency Table

INTEGRATE TECHNOLOGY

Students have the option of doing the Explore activity either in the book or online.

QUESTIONING STRATEGIES

? As you read down the column of a two-way table, how do you find the probability that each event happened? Sample answer: Within the same column, you divide the number of outcomes for each event by the total number of outcomes in that column.

? What does the notation $P(A \mid B)$ represent? the conditional probability that event A will happen given that event B has already occurred

EXPLORE 2

Finding Conditional Probabilities from a Two-Way Relative Frequency Table

INTEGRATE MATHEMATICAL PRACTICES
Focus on Math Connections

MP.1 Two-way frequency tables are efficient ways to express quantitative data that can be categorized by two variables. Point out that there are two formulas for $P(A \mid B)$: $P(A \mid B) = \frac{n(A \cap B)}{n(B)}$ and $P(A \mid B) = \frac{P(A \cap B)}{P(B)}$. It is important for students to be able to identify each of the quantities in the two formulas, and for them to distinguish between $n(B)$, the number of outcomes for B, and $P(B)$, the probability of B.

EXPLAIN 1

Using the Conditional Probability Formula

AVOID COMMON ERRORS

Students may be confused about how to find the total number of outcomes in a two-way table. Tell them that the total number of outcomes (the number of outcomes in the sample space) should appear at the lower right corner. It equals the total of the bottom row of the table and the total of the right-most column of the table.

Ⓓ Generalize the results by using $n(S)$ as the number of elements in the sample space (in this case, the number of participants in the study). For instance, you can write $P(A) = \frac{n(A)}{n(S)}$. Write each of the following probabilities in a similar way.

$$P(B) = \boxed{\frac{n(B)}{n(S)}} \qquad P(A \cap B) = \boxed{\frac{n(A \cap B)}{n(S)}} \qquad P(A|B) = \frac{\boxed{\frac{n(A \cap B)}{n(S)}}}{\boxed{\frac{n(B)}{n(S)}}} = \boxed{\frac{P(A \cap B)}{P(B)}}$$

Reflect

3. Why are the two forms of $P(A \cap B)$, $\frac{n(A \cap B)}{n(B)}$ and $\frac{P(A \cap B)}{P(B)}$, equivalent?
   $\frac{n(A \cap B) \div n(S)}{n(B) \div n(S)} = P(A \cap B)$

4. What is a formula for $P(B|A)$ that involves probabilities rather than counts? How do you obtain this formula from the fact that $P(B|A) = \frac{n(A \cap B)}{n(A)}$?
   $P(B|A) = \frac{P(A \cap B)}{P(A)}$; you divide the numerator and denominator of $\frac{n(A \cap B)}{n(A)}$ by $n(S)$.

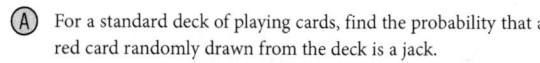 **Explain 1**   **Using the Conditional Probability Formula**

In the previous Explore, you discovered the following formula for conditional probability.

Conditional Probability

The conditional probability of A given B (that is, the probability that event A occurs given that event B occurs) is as follows:

$$P(A|B) = \frac{P(A \cap B)}{P(A)}$$

Example 1   Find the specified probability.

Ⓐ For a standard deck of playing cards, find the probability that a red card randomly drawn from the deck is a jack.

Step 1 Find $P(R)$, the probability that a red card is drawn from the deck.

There are 26 red cards in the deck of 52 cards, so $P(R) = \frac{26}{52}$.

Step 2 Find $P(J \cap R)$, the probability that a red jack is drawn from the deck.

There are 2 red jacks in the deck, so $P(J \cap R) = \frac{2}{52}$.

COLLABORATIVE LEARNING

Small Group Activity

Give groups of students sample two-way tables. Have one student verify all of the totals in the table and give the size of the sample. Ask a second student to explain how to find the conditional probabilities of one column of the table. Then have a third student explain how to find the conditional probabilities of the second column. Have a fourth student verify that the conditional probabilities for the table are consistent with the sample space and are correct. Then have students compare their results, and present them to the class.

Step 3 Substitute the probabilities from Steps 1 and 2 into the formula for conditional probability.

$$P(J|R) = \frac{P(J \cap R)}{P(R)} = \frac{\frac{2}{52}}{\frac{26}{52}}$$

Step 4 Simplify the result.

$$P(J|R) = \frac{\frac{2}{52} \cdot 52}{\frac{26}{52} \cdot 52} = \frac{2}{26} = \frac{1}{13}$$

Ⓑ For a standard deck of playing cards, find the probability that a jack randomly drawn from the deck is a red card.

Step 1 Find $P(J)$, the probability that a jack is drawn from the deck.

There are __4__ jacks in the deck of 52 cards, so $P(J) = \frac{\boxed{4}}{52}$.

Step 2 Find $P(J \cap R)$, the probability that a red jack is drawn from the deck.

There are __2__ red jacks in the deck, so $P(J \cap R) = \frac{\boxed{2}}{52}$.

Step 3 Substitute the probabilities from Steps 1 and 2 into the formula for conditional probability.

$$P(R|J) = \frac{P(J \cap R)}{P(R)} = \frac{\frac{\boxed{2}}{52}}{\frac{\boxed{4}}{52}}$$

Step 4 Simplify the result.

$$P(R|J) = \frac{\frac{2}{52} \cdot 52}{\frac{\boxed{4}}{52} \cdot 52} = \frac{2}{\boxed{4}} = \frac{1}{\boxed{2}}$$

Your Turn

5. For a standard deck of playing cards, find the probability that a face card randomly drawn from the deck is a king. (The ace is *not* a face card.)

Let F be the event of drawing a face card and K be the event of drawing a king. Then

$P(F) = \frac{12}{52}$ and $P(F \cap K) = \frac{4}{52}$, so $P(K|F) = \frac{P(F \cap K)}{P(F)} = \frac{\frac{4}{52}}{\frac{12}{52}} = \frac{4}{12} = \frac{1}{3}$.

6. For a standard deck of playing cards, find the probability that a queen randomly drawn from the deck is a diamond.

Let Q be the event of drawing a queen and D be the event of drawing a diamond. Then

$P(Q) = \frac{4}{52}$ and $P(Q \cap D) = \frac{1}{52}$, so $P(D|Q) = \frac{P(Q \cap D)}{P(Q)} = \frac{\frac{1}{52}}{\frac{4}{52}} = \frac{1}{4}$.

QUESTIONING STRATEGIES

❓ What is the conditional probability formula, and what does it represent?

$P(A \mid B) = \frac{P(A \cap B)}{P(B)}$; the probability that event A occurs given that event B has already occurred is represented by $P(A \mid B)$, and is equal to the probability that both A and B occur divided by the probability that event B occurs.

INTEGRATE MATHEMATICAL PRACTICES
Focus on Patterns

MP.8 Have students follow a pattern as they find the values to substitute into the conditional probability formula $P(A \mid B) = \frac{P(A \cap B)}{P(B)}$. First, identify which event has already occurred (B, in this case) and find the probability that B occurs (divide the number of B outcomes by the number in the sample space). Then find the number of events that are in the intersection of A and B and calculate the probability that both A and B occur (the sum of A and B divided by the number in the sample space). Finally, substitute the values and divide.

DIFFERENTIATE INSTRUCTION

Modeling

Some students may benefit from a hands-on approach for finding the conditional probabilities for a two-way table. Have groups of students complete a list of questions that they can ask about the table below, such as, "What is the probability that a household owns a dog given that the household owns a cat?" $15 \div 33 \approx 0.45$

		Owns a cat	
		Yes	No
Owns a dog	Yes	15	24
	No	18	43

Conditional Probability   **1140**

ELABORATE

QUESTIONING STRATEGIES

? How can you find conditional probabilities for the data in a two-way table? Label the events represented by the table as A and B and use the formula $P(A \mid B) = \frac{n(A \cap B)}{n(B)}$.

SUMMARIZE THE LESSON

? Given a two-way frequency table, how could you quickly verify that it has been filled out correctly? How could you do the same for a two-way relative frequency table? You could check that the sum of the frequencies in the bottom row and the sum of the frequencies in the right-most column are equal to each other and to the number of outcomes in the sample space; in a two-way relative frequency table, both sums should be equal to 1.

💬 Elaborate

7. When calculating a conditional probability from a two-way table, explain why it doesn't matter whether the table gives frequencies or relative frequencies.
A conditional probability is a ratio of two frequencies. If you divide those frequencies by the same number to convert them to relative frequencies, their ratio remains unchanged.

8. **Discussion** Is it possible to have $P(B \mid A) = P(A \mid B)$ for some events A and B? What conditions would need to exist?
Yes, it is possible for $P(B \mid A)$ to equal $P(A \mid B)$. This would happen if the probability of event A is equal to the probability of event B.

9. **Essential Question Check-In** In a two-way frequency table, suppose event A represents a row of the table and event B represents a column of the table. Describe how to find the conditional probability $P(A \mid B)$ using the frequencies in the table.
Divide the frequency that appears in the intersection of the row for A and the column for B by the total of all frequencies in the row for B.

☆ Evaluate: Homework and Practice

- Online Homework
- Hints and Help
- Extra Practice

In order to study the relationship between the amount of sleep a student gets and his or her school performance, a researcher collected data from 120 students. The two-way frequency table shows the number of students who passed and failed an exam and the number of students who got more or less than 6 hours of sleep the night before. Use the table to answer the questions in Exercises 1–3.

	Passed exam	Failed exam	Total
Less than 6 hours of sleep	12	10	22
More than 6 hours of sleep	90	8	98
Total	102	18	120

1. To the nearest percent, what is the probability that a student who failed the exam got less than 6 hours of sleep?

Let L be the event of getting less than 6 hours of sleep and F be the event of failing the exam. Then $P(L \mid F) = \frac{n(L \cap F)}{n(F)} = \frac{10}{18} = \frac{5}{9} \approx 56\%$.

2. To the nearest percent, what is the probability that a student who got less than 6 hours of sleep failed the exam?

Let L be the event of getting less than 6 hours of sleep and F be the event of failing the exam. Then $P(F \mid L) = \frac{n(L \cap F)}{n(L)} = \frac{10}{22} = \frac{5}{11} \approx 45\%$.

© Houghton Mifflin Harcourt Publishing Company

LANGUAGE SUPPORT **EL**

Connect Vocabulary

To help students describe the events represented in a two-way table and then determine the numbers used to find the conditional probabilities, have them first draw a line around the row or column of a two-way table representing the given information. Then ask them to circle the cell for the probability they are finding in another color. Then ask them to divide the number in that cell by the total in the respective row or column to find the conditional probability.

3. To the nearest percent, what is the probability that a student got less than 6 hours of sleep and failed the exam?

Let L be the event of getting less than 6 hours of sleep, F be the event of failing the exam, and S be the sample space. $P(L \cap F) = \dfrac{n(L \cap F)}{n(S)} = \dfrac{10}{120} \approx 8\%$.

4. You have a standard deck of playing cards from which you randomly select a card. Event D is getting a diamond, and event F is getting a face card (a jack, queen, or king).

Show that $P(D|F) = \dfrac{n(D \cap F)}{n(F)}$ and $P(D|F) = \dfrac{P(D \cap F)}{P(F)}$ are equal.

$P(D|F) = \dfrac{n(D \cap F)}{n(F)} = \dfrac{3}{12} = \dfrac{1}{4}$ $P(D|F) = \dfrac{P(D \cap F)}{P(F)} = \dfrac{\frac{3}{52}}{\frac{12}{52}} = \dfrac{\frac{3}{52} \cdot 52}{\frac{12}{52} \cdot 52} = \dfrac{3}{12} = \dfrac{1}{4}$

The table shows data in the previous table as relative frequencies (rounded to the nearest thousandth when necessary). Use the table for Exercises 5–7.

	Passed exam	Failed exam	Total
Less than 6 hours of sleep	0.100	0.083	0.183
More than 6 hours of sleep	0.750	0.067	0.817
Total	0.850	0.150	1.000

5. To the nearest percent, what is the probability that a student who passed the exam got more than 6 hours of sleep?

Let M be the event of getting more than 6 hours of sleep and Pa be the event of passing the exam. Then $P(M|Pa) = \dfrac{P(M \cap Pa)}{P(Pa)} = \dfrac{0.750}{0.850} \approx 0.882 \approx 88\%$.

6. To the nearest percent, what is the probability that a student who got more than 6 hours of sleep passed the exam?

Let M be the event of getting more than 6 hours of sleep and Pa be the event of passing the exam. Then $P(Pa|M) = \dfrac{n(M \cap Pa)}{n(M)} = \dfrac{0.750}{0.817} = 0.918 \approx 92\%$.

7. Which is greater, the probability that a student who got less than 6 hours of sleep passed the exam or the probability that a student who got more than 6 hours of sleep failed the exam? Explain.

Let L be the event of getting less than 6 hours of sleep, and let M be the event of getting more than 6 hours of sleep. Let Pa be the event of passing the exam, and let F be the event of failing the exam. Then $P(Pa|L) = \dfrac{P(L \cap Pa)}{P(L)} = \dfrac{0.100}{0.183} \approx 0.546 \approx 55\%$, and $P(F|M) = \dfrac{P(M \cap F)}{P(M)} = \dfrac{0.067}{0.817} \approx 0.082 \approx 8\%$, so the probability that a student who got less than 6 hours of sleep passed the exam is greater.

EVALUATE

Personal Math Trainer

ASSIGNMENT GUIDE

Concepts and Skills	Practice
Explore 1 Finding Conditional Probabilities from a Two-Way Frequency Table	Exercises 1–3, 14–15, 20, 22–23
Explore 2 Finding Conditional Probabilities from a Two-Way Relative Frequency Table	Exercises 4–7, 18–19
Example 1 Using the Conditional Probability Formula	Exercises 9–13, 16–17, 21

INTEGRATE MATHEMATICAL PRACTICES

Focus on Math Connections

MP.1 Two-way frequency tables express quantitative data that can be categorized by two variables. *Joint relative frequencies* are the values in each category divided by the total number of values, while *marginal relative frequencies* are found by adding the joint relative frequencies in each row or column. *A conditional relative frequency* is the quotient of a joint relative frequency and the marginal relative frequency. Conditional relative frequencies give an alternate way to find conditional probabilities.

Exercise	Depth of Knowledge (D.O.K.)	COMMON CORE Mathematical Practices
1–6	**1** Recall of Information	**MP.5** Using Tools
7	**2** Skills/Concepts	**MP.4** Modeling
8–13	**1** Recall of Information	**MP.5** Using Tools
14	**2** Skills/Concepts	**MP.4** Modeling
15	**2** Skills/Concepts	**MP.2** Reasoning
16–20	**2** Skills/Concepts	**MP.5** Using Tools
21	**3** Strategic Thinking H.O.T.	**MP.6** Precision
22	**3** Strategic Thinking H.O.T.	**MP.3** Logic
23	**3** Strategic Thinking H.O.T.	**MP.2** Reasoning

Students may assume that B always represents the event assumed to have taken place. Explain that A and B are simply variables and that the conditional probability formula holds true no matter which letters are used. For example, the formula can be used to find the probability of B given A:

$P(B \mid A) = \dfrac{P(A \cap B)}{P(A)}$. Emphasize that the letter *after* the vertical bar represents the event assumed to have taken place, and that its probability will always be in the denominator of the fraction.

You randomly draw a card from a standard deck of playing cards. Let A be the event that the card is an ace, let B be the event that the card is black, and let C be the event that the card is a club. Find the specified probability as a fraction.

8. $P(A \mid B)$ $P(A \mid B) =$

$\dfrac{P(A \cap B)}{P(B)} = \dfrac{1}{13}$

9. $P(B \mid A)$ $P(B \mid A) =$

$\dfrac{P(A \cap B)}{P(A)} = \dfrac{1}{2}$

10. $P(A \mid C)$ $P(A \mid C) =$

$\dfrac{P(A \cap C)}{P(C)} = \dfrac{1}{13}$

11. $P(C \mid A)$ $P(C \mid A) =$

$\dfrac{P(A \cap C)}{P(A)} = \dfrac{1}{4}$

12. $P(B \mid C)$ $P(B \mid C) =$

$\dfrac{P(B \cap C)}{P(C)} = 1$

13. $P(C \mid B)$ $P(C \mid B) =$

$\dfrac{P(B \cap C)}{P(B)} = \dfrac{1}{2}$

14. A botanist studied the effect of a new fertilizer by choosing 100 orchids and giving 70% of these plants the fertilizer. Of the plants that got the fertilizer, 40% produced flowers within a month. Of the plants that did not get the fertilizer, 10% produced flowers within a month.

a. Use the given information to complete the two-way frequency table.

	Received fertilizer	Did not receive fertilizer	Total
Did not flower in one month	$70 - 28 = 42$	$30 - 3 = 27$	$42 + 27 = 69$
Flowered in one month	$0.4 \cdot 70 = 28$	$0.1 \cdot 30 = 3$	$28 + 3 = 31$
Total	$0.7 \cdot 100 = 70$	$0.3 \cdot 100 = 30$	100

b. To the nearest percent, what is the probability that an orchid that produced flowers got fertilizer?

Let Fl be the event that an orchid produced flowers and Fe be the event that an orchid got fertilizer. Then $P(Fe \mid Fl) = \dfrac{n(Fe \cap Fl)}{n(Fl)} = \dfrac{28}{31} \approx 90\%$.

c. To the nearest percent, what is the probability that an orchid that got fertilizer produced flowers?

Then $P(Fl \mid Fe) = \dfrac{n(Fe \cap Fl)}{n(Fe)} = \dfrac{28}{70} = \dfrac{2}{5} = 40\%$.

15. At a school fair, a box contains 24 yellow balls and 76 red balls. One-fourth of the balls of each color are labeled "Win a prize." Match each description of a probability with its value as a percent.

A. The probability that a randomly selected ball labeled "Win a prize" is yellow   __B__ 76%

B. The probability that a randomly selected ball labeled "Win a prize" is red   __D__ 25%

C. The probability that a randomly selected ball is labeled "Win a prize" and is red   __A__ 24%

D. The probability that a randomly selected yellow ball is labeled "Win a prize"   __C__ 19%

	Winner	Not winner	Total
Red	$\frac{1}{4}(76) = 19$	$\frac{3}{4}(76) = 57$	76
Yellow	$\frac{1}{4}(24) = 6$	$\frac{3}{4}(24) = 18$	24
Total	25	75	100

Let R be the even that a ball is red, Y be the event that a ball is yellow, W be the event that a ball is labeled "Win a prize," and S is the sample space.

A. $P(Y|W) = \dfrac{n(Y \cap W)}{n(W)} = \dfrac{6}{25} = 24\%$ C. $P(W \cap R) = \dfrac{n(W \cap R)}{n(S)} = \dfrac{19}{100} = 19\%$

B. $P(R|W) = \dfrac{n(R \cap W)}{n(W)} = \dfrac{19}{25} = 76\%$ D. $P(W|Y) = \dfrac{n(Y \cap W)}{n(Y)} = \dfrac{6}{24} = 25\%$

16. A teacher gave her students two tests. If 45% of the students passed both tests and 60% passed the first test, what is the probability that a student who passed the first test also passed the second?

Let T_1 be the event that a student passed the first test and T_2 be the event that the student passed the second test.

$$P(T_2 | T_1) = \frac{P(T_1 \cap T_2)}{P(T_1)} = \frac{0.45}{0.60} = 0.75 = 75\%$$

17. You randomly select two marbles, one at a time, from a pouch containing blue and green marbles. The probability of selecting a blue marble on the first draw and a green marble on the second draw is 25%, and the probability of selecting a blue marble on the first draw is 56%. To the nearest percent, what is the probability of selecting a green marble on the second draw, given that the first marble was blue?

Let B be the event of selecting a blue marble on the first draw and G be the event of selecting a green marble on the second draw.

$$P(G|B) = \frac{P(B \cap G)}{P(B)} = \frac{0.25}{0.56} \approx 0.45 = 45\%$$

INTEGRATE MATHEMATICAL PRACTICES

Focus on Communication

MP.3 After making a two-way table, have students interpret the tables in terms of percentages. For example, if 10 students in the class own a cat, and 6 of those students also own a dog, have students verbalize that the conditional probability of owning a dog given that they own a cat is $\frac{6}{10} = 60\%$.

Conditional Probability   **1144**

You roll two number cubes, one red and one blue. The table shows the probabilities for events based on whether or not a 1 is rolled on each number cube. Use the table to find the specified conditional probability, expressed as a fraction. Then show that the conditional probability is correct by listing the possible outcomes as ordered pairs of the form (number on red cube, number on blue cube) and identifying the successful outcomes.

	Rolling a 1 on the red cube	Not rolling a 1 on the red cube	Total
Rolling a 1 on the blue cube	$\frac{1}{36}$	$\frac{5}{36}$	$\frac{1}{6}$
Not rolling a 1 on the blue cube	$\frac{5}{36}$	$\frac{25}{36}$	$\frac{5}{6}$
Total	$\frac{1}{6}$	$\frac{5}{6}$	1

18. P(not rolling a 1 on the blue cube | rolling a 1 on the red cube)

Let $N1B$ be the event that a 1 is not rolled on the blue cube and $1R$ be the event that a 1 is rolled on the red cube.

$$P\left(N1B\,|\,1R\right) = \frac{n(N1B \cap 1R)}{n(1R)} = \frac{\frac{5}{36}}{\frac{1}{6}} = \frac{\frac{5}{36} \cdot 36}{\frac{1}{6} \cdot 36} = \frac{5}{6}$$

Given that rolling a 1 on the red number cube has occurred, there are 6 possible outcomes (where the ordered pairs give the number on the red cube first): $(1, 1)$, $(1, 2)$, $(1, 3)$, $(1, 4)$, $(1, 5)$, and $(1, 6)$. Of these, the last 5 outcomes are successful because they involve a number that is not 1 on the blue cube. So, the probability of not rolling a 1 on the blue cube when a 1 is rolled on the red cube is $\frac{5}{6}$.

19. P(not rolling a 1 on the blue cube | not rolling a 1 on the red cube)

Let $N1B$ be the event that a 1 is not rolled on the blue cube and $N1R$ be the event that a 1 is not rolled on the red cube.

$$P\left(N1B\,|\,N1R\right) = \frac{n(N1B \cap N1R)}{n(N1R)} = \frac{\frac{25}{36}}{\frac{5}{6}} = \frac{\frac{25}{36} \cdot 36}{\frac{5}{6} \cdot 36} = \frac{25}{30} = \frac{5}{6}$$

Given that not rolling a 1 on the red number cube has occurred, there are 30 possible outcomes (where the ordered pairs give the number on the red cube first): $(2, 1)$, $(2, 2)$, $(2, 3)$, $(2, 4)$, $(2, 5)$, $(2, 6)$, $(3, 1)$, $(3, 2)$, $(3, 3)$, $(3, 4)$, $(3, 5)$, $(3, 6)$, $(4, 1)$, $(4, 2)$, $(4, 3)$, $(4, 4)$, $(4, 5)$, $(4, 6)$, $(5, 1)$, $(5, 2)$, $(5, 3)$, $(5, 4)$, $(5, 5)$, $(5, 6)$, $(6, 1)$, $(6, 2)$, $(6, 3)$, $(6, 4)$, $(6, 5)$, and $(6, 6)$. Of these, all but 5 outcomes—$(2, 1)$, $(3, 1)$, $(4, 1,)$ $(5, 1)$, and $(6, 1)$—are successful because they involve a number that is not 1 on the blue cube. So, the probability of not rolling a 1 on the blue cube when a 1 is not rolled on the red cube is $\frac{25}{36} = \frac{5}{6}$.

20. The table shows the results of a quality-control study at a computer factory.

	Shipped	Not shipped	Total
Defective	3	7	10
Not defective	89	1	90
Total	92	8	100

a. To the nearest tenth of a percent, what is the probability that a shipped computer is not defective?

b. To the nearest tenth of a percent, what is the probability that a defective computer is shipped?

Let *S* be the event that a computer is shipped, *D* be the event that a computer is defective, and *Nd* be the even that a computer is not defective.

a. $P(Nd \mid S) = \dfrac{n(Nd \cap S)}{n(S)} = \dfrac{89}{92} \approx 0.967 = 96.7\%$

b. $P(S \mid D) = \dfrac{n(D \cap S)}{n(D)} = \dfrac{3}{10} = 0.3 = 30\%$

H.O.T. Focus on Higher Order Thinking

21. Analyze Relationships In the Venn diagram, the circles representing events *A* and *B* divide the sample space *S* into four regions: the overlap of the circles, the part of *A* not in the overlap, the part of *B* not in the overlap, and the part of *S* not in *A* or *B*. Suppose that the area of each region is proportional to the number of outcomes that fall within the region. Which conditional probability is greater: $P(A \mid B)$ or $P(B \mid A)$? Explain.

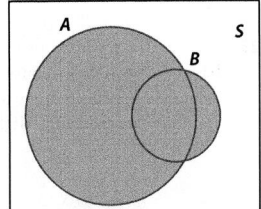

Since $P(A \mid B) = \dfrac{n(A \cap B)}{n(B)}$, you can think of $P(A \mid B)$ as the ratio of the area of the overlap of the circles to the area of the entire circle labeled B. Since more of circle B lies inside the overlap than outside the overlap, $P(A \mid B) > \dfrac{1}{2}$. On the other hand, since $P(B \mid A) = \dfrac{n(A \cap B)}{n(A)}$, you can think of $P(B \mid A)$ as the ratio of the area of the overlap of the circles to the area of the entire circle labeled A. Since less of circle A lies inside the overlap than outside the overlap, $P(B \mid A) < \dfrac{1}{2}$. So, $P(A \mid B) > \dfrac{1}{2} > P(B \mid A)$.

JOURNAL

Have students explain conditional probability in their own words. Also, ask students to give an example of how to use the formula for conditional probability.

22. **Explain the Error** A student was asked to use the table shown to find the probability, to nearest percent, that a participant in a study of a new medicine for migraine headaches did not take the medicine, given that the participant reported no headaches.

	Took medicine	No medicine	Total
Headache	11	13	24
No headache	54	22	76
Total	65	35	100

The student made the following calculation.

$P(\text{no medicine} \mid \text{no headache}) = \frac{22}{35} \approx 0.63 = 63\%$

Explain the student's error, and find the correct probability.

The student divided 22, the number of participants who did not take the medicine and did not report headaches, by 35, the number of participants who did not take the medicine. However, the student should have divided 22 by 76, the number of participants who reported no headaches. The correct calculation is

$P(\text{no medicine} \mid \text{no headache}) = \frac{22}{76} \approx 0.29 = 29\%$.

23. **Communicate Mathematical Ideas** Explain how a conditional probability based on a two-way frequency table effectively reduces it to a one-way table. In your explanation, refer to the two-way table shown, which lists frequencies for events A, B, and their complements. Highlight the part of the table that supports your explanation.

	A	Not A	Total
B	$n(A \cap B)$	$n(\text{not } A \cap B)$	$n(B)$
Not B	$n(A \cap \text{not } B)$	$n(\text{not } A \cap \text{not } B)$	$n(\text{not } B)$
Total	$n(A)$	$n(\text{not } A)$	$n(S)$

The conditional probability $P(A \mid B) = \dfrac{n(A \cap B)}{n(B)}$ restricts the discussion to event B because that event is assumed to have occurred. The numbers used to calculate $P(A \mid B)$ both come from the highlighted row in the table: $n(A \cap B)$ is the number of outcomes in event B that are also in event A, while $n(B)$ is the number of all outcomes in event B. The rest of the table is irrelevant.

© Houghton Mifflin Harcourt Publishing Company

Lesson Performance Task

The two-way frequency table gives the results of a survey that asked students this question:
Which of these would you most like to meet: a famous singer, a movie star, or a sports star?

	Famous singer	Movie star	Sports star	Total
Boys	20	15	55	90
Girls	40	50	20	110
Total	60	65	75	200

a. Complete the table by finding the row totals, column totals, and grand total.

b. To the nearest percent, what is the probability that a student who chose "movie star" is a girl?

c. To the nearest percent, what is the probability that a student who chose "famous singer" is a boy?

d. To the nearest percent, what is the probability that a boy chose "sports star"?

e. To the nearest percent, what is the probability that a girl chose "famous singer"?

f. To the nearest percent, what is the probability that a student who chose either "famous singer" or "movie star" is a boy?

g. To the nearest percent, what is the probability that a girl did not choose "sports star"?

For the following answers, let B be the event that a student is a boy, let G be the event that a student is a girl, let FS be the event that a student chose "famous singer," let MS be the event that a student chose "movie star," and let SS be the event that a student chose "sports star."

b. $P(G|MS) = \dfrac{n(G \cap MS)}{n(MS)} = \dfrac{50}{65} \approx 77\%$

c. $P(B|FS) = \dfrac{n(B \cap FS)}{n(FS)} = \dfrac{20}{60} \approx 33\%$

d. $P(SS|B) = \dfrac{n(B \cap SS)}{n(B)} = \dfrac{55}{90} \approx 61\%$

e. $P(FS|G) = \dfrac{n(G \cap FS)}{n(G)} = \dfrac{40}{110} \approx 36\%$

f. $P\big(B|(FS \cup MS)\big) = \dfrac{n\big(B \cap (FS \cup MS)\big)}{n(FS \cup MS)} = \dfrac{35}{125} \approx 28\%$

g. $P(\text{not } SS|G) = \dfrac{n(G \cap \text{not } SS)}{n(\text{not } SS)} = \dfrac{90}{125} \approx 72\%$

© Houghton Mifflin Harcourt Publishing Company

EXTENSION ACTIVITY

Have students fill out a table like the one in the Lesson Performance Task, using these facts: 300 students took part in the survey described in the Task; P(student who chose "Famous Singer" is a girl) $= \dfrac{7}{10}$; P(student who chose "Sports Star" is a boy) $= \dfrac{4}{5}$; of those who chose "Movie Star," 30% are boys; 80 students chose "Famous Singer"; 130 students chose "Sports Star."

	Famous Singer	Movie Star	Sports Star
Boys	24	27	104
Girls	56	63	26

INTEGRATE MATHEMATICAL PRACTICES
Focus on Patterns

MP.8 When dealing with tables like the ones in the Lesson Performance Task and the Extension Activity, students can check that the cell entries are consistent by (a) adding the row entries (for the Extension Activity, Boys + Girls = 155 + 145 = 300); (b) adding the column entries (Famous Singers + Movie Stars + Sports Star = 80 + 90 + 130 = 300); and (c) checking to see that the sums are equal (300 = 300).

INTEGRATE MATHEMATICAL PRACTICES
Focus on Communication

MP.3 Use the numbers in the "Movie Star" column of the Lesson Performance Task (15 and 50). Write at least four questions beginning with "Find the probability of___" that can be answered by writing a fraction that has either 15 or 50 in the numerator. For each question, give the fraction. Sample answers: Find the probability that a student who chose "Movie Star" is a boy $\left(\dfrac{15}{65}\right)$; find the probability that a student who chose "Movie Star" is a girl $\left(\dfrac{50}{65}\right)$; find the probability that a student who is a boy chose "Movie Star" $\left(\dfrac{15}{90}\right)$; find the probability that a student who is a girl chose "Movie Star" $\left(\dfrac{50}{110}\right)$.

Scoring Rubric

2 points: Student correctly solves the problem and explains his/her reasoning.

1 point: Student shows good understanding of the problem but does not fully solve or explain his/her reasoning.

0 points: Student does not demonstrate understanding of the problem.

Conditional Probability   **1148**

Independent Events

Common Core Math Standards

The student is expected to:

COMMON CORE S-CP.A.2

Understand that two events A and B are independent if the probability of A and B occurring together is the product of their probabilities, … . Also S-CP.A.3, S-CP.A.4, S-CP.A.5

Mathematical Practices

COMMON CORE MP.7 Using Structure

Language Objective

Work with a partner to brainstorm examples of independent events.

ENGAGE

Essential Question: What does it mean for two events to be independent?

Two events are independent provided the occurrence of one event has no effect on the occurrence of the other event. For independent events A and B, $P(A \mid B) = P(A)$; that is, the probability of event A does not change even when event B is assumed to have occurred.

PREVIEW: LESSON PERFORMANCE TASK

View the Engage section online. Discuss the photograph. Ask students to describe differences that they observe in the animals pictured. Then preview the Lesson Performance Task.

Name_____ Class_____ Date_____

22.2 Independent Events

Essential Question: What does it mean for two events to be independent?

Resource Locker

⊘ Explore   Understanding the Independence of Events

Suppose you flip a coin and roll a number cube. You would expect the probability of getting heads on the coin to be $\frac{1}{2}$ regardless of what number you get from rolling the number cube. Likewise, you would expect the probability of rolling a 3 on the number cube to be $\frac{1}{6}$ regardless of whether of the coin flip results in heads or tails.

When the occurrence of one event has no effect on the occurrence of another event, the two events are called **independent events**.

Ⓐ   A jar contains 15 red marbles and 17 yellow marbles. You randomly draw a marble from the jar. Let R be the event that you get a red marble, and let Y be the event that you get a yellow marble.

Since the jar has a total of __32__ marbles, $P(R) = \dfrac{15}{32}$ and $P(Y) = \dfrac{17}{32}$.

Ⓑ   Suppose the first marble you draw is a red marble, and you put that marble back in the jar before randomly drawing a second marble. Find $P(Y|R)$, the probability that you get a yellow marble on the second draw after getting a red marble on the first draw. Explain your reasoning.

Since the jar still has a total of __32__ marbles and __17__ of them are yellow, $P(Y|R) = \dfrac{17}{32}$.

Ⓒ   Suppose you *don't* put the red marble back in the jar before randomly drawing a second marble. Find $P(Y|R)$, the probability that you get a yellow marble on the second draw after getting a red marble on the first draw. Explain your reasoning.

Since the jar now has a total of __31__ marbles and __17__ of them are yellow, $P(Y|R) = \dfrac{17}{31}$.

Reflect

1. In one case you replaced the first marble before drawing the second, and in the other case you didn't. For which case was $P(Y|R)$ equal to $P(Y)$? Why?
   $P(Y|R) = P(Y)$ when the red marble was replaced because the total number of marbles in the jar, and therefore the proportion of marbles that are yellow, stayed the same.

2. In which of the two cases would you say the events of getting a red marble on the first draw and getting a yellow marble on the second draw are independent? What is true about $P(Y|R)$ and $P(Y)$ in this case?
   The events are independent when the red marble is returned to the jar. In this case, $P(Y|R) = P(Y)$.

HARDCOVER PAGES 953–962

Turn to these pages to find this lesson in the hardcover student edition.

To determine the independence of two events *A* and *B*, you can check to see whether $P(A|B) = P(A)$ since the occurrence of event *A* is unaffected by the occurrence of event *B* if and only if the events are independent.

Example 1   The two-way frequency table gives data about 180 randomly selected flights that arrive at an airport. Use the table to answer the question.

	Late Arrival	On Time	Total
Domestic Flights	12	108	120
International Flights	6	54	60
Total	18	162	180

Ⓐ Is the event that a flight is on time independent of the event that a flight is domestic?

Let *O* be the event that a flight is on time. Let *D* be the event that a flight is domestic. Find $P(O)$ and $P(O|D)$. To find $P(O)$, note that the total number of flights is 180, and of those flights, there are 162 on-time flights. So, $P(O) = \frac{162}{180} = 90\%$.

To find $P(O|D)$, note that there are 120 domestic flights, and of those flights, there are 108 on-time flights.

So, $P(O|D), = \frac{108}{120} = 90\%$.

Since $P(O|D) = P(O)$, the event that a flight is on time is independent of the event that a flight is domestic.

Ⓑ Is the event that a flight is international independent of the event that a flight arrives late?

Let *I* be the event that a flight is international. Let *L* be the event that a flight arrives late. Find $P(I)$ and $P(I|L)$. To find $P(I)$, note that the total number of flights is 180, and of those

flights, there are $\underline{60}$ international flights. So, $P(I) = \dfrac{\boxed{60}}{180} = \boxed{33\tfrac{1}{3}}\%$.

To find $P(I|L)$, note that there are $\underline{18}$ flights that arrive late, and of those flights, there are $\underline{6}$

international flights. So, $P(I|L) = \dfrac{\boxed{6}}{\boxed{18}} = \boxed{33\tfrac{1}{3}}\%$.

Since $P(I|L) \boxed{=} P(I)$, the event that a flight is international [is/is not] independent of the

event that a flight arrives late.

© Houghton Mifflin Harcourt Publishing Company • Image Credits: ©nmcandre/iStockPhoto.com

PROFESSIONAL DEVELOPMENT

Math Background

Two events are *independent* if the occurrence of one does not affect the probability of the other. In other words, for independent events *A* and *B*, $P(A) = P(A \mid B)$. Note that you can use this criterion to determine if *A* and *B* are independent. If *A* and *B* are independent, then $P(A \text{ and } B)$, also written $P(A \cap B)$, is $P(A) \cdot P(B)$. More generally, events *A*1, *A*2, …, *An* are *mutually independent* if the occurrence of any one does not affect the probability of any other. Then, $P(A1 \cap A2 \cap \ldots \cap An) = P(A1) \cdot P(A2) \cdot \ldots \cdot P(An)$.

EXPLORE

Understanding the Independence of Events

INTEGRATE TECHNOLOGY

Students have the option of doing the Explore activity either in the book or online.

QUESTIONING STRATEGIES

❓ How can you tell if two events *A* and *B* are independent? If $P(A) = P(A|B)$ or $P(B) = P(B|A)$, then *A* and *B* are independent events.

EXPLAIN 1

Determining if Events are Independent

QUESTIONING STRATEGIES

❓ How can a two-way frequency table help you determine whether two events are independent? A two-way frequency table makes it easy to find $n(A)$ and $n(A \mid B)$, which you can use to calculate $P(A)$ and $P(A \mid B)$. If the two probabilities are equal, the events are independent.

AVOID COMMON ERRORS

When given a two-way frequency table, some students may have trouble identifying which values to use to calculate *the probability of A given B*. Encourage them to circle the column that represents event *B*, and then put another circle around the cell within the column that represents event *A*. The number in the cell they have circled is $n(A \mid B)$.

EXPLAIN 2

Finding the Probability of Independent Events

INTEGRATE MATHEMATICAL PRACTICES
Focus on Math Connections

MP.1 Point out that independent events are not the same as mutually exclusive events, which are events that cannot occur in the same trial. For example, a coin cannot simultaneously show heads and tails. If A and B are mutually exclusive, then $P(A$ or $B)$, also written $P(A \cup B)$, is $P(A) + P(B)$. This addition rule is generally used when finding the probability for a single trial, while the multiplication rule for independent events is usually applied to two or more separate trials, performed either simultaneously or in succession.

QUESTIONING STRATEGIES

? Once you know that two events are independent, how can you find the probability that both events take place? Multiply the individual probabilities.

The two-way frequency table gives data about 200 randomly selected apartments in a city. Use the table to answer the question.

	1 Bedroom	2+ Bedrooms	Total
Single Occupant	64	12	76
Multiple Occupants	26	98	124
Total	90	110	200

3. Is the event that an apartment has a single occupant independent of the event that an apartment has 1 bedroom?
   Let SO be the event that an apartment has a single occupant, and let $1B$ be the event that an apartment has 1 bedroom. Then $P(SO) = \frac{76}{200} = 38\%$, and $P(SO|1B) = \frac{64}{90} \approx 71\%$.
   Since $P(SO|1B) \neq P(SO)$, the events are not independent.

4. Is the event that an apartment has 2 or more bedrooms independent of the event that an apartment has multiple occupants?
   Let $2B$ represent that an apartment has 2 or more bedrooms, and let MO be the event that an apartment has multiple occupants. Then $P(2B) = \frac{110}{200} = 55\%$, and
   $P(2B|MO) = \frac{98}{110} \approx 89\%$. Since $P(2B|MO) \neq P(2B)$, the events are not independent.

⊘ Explain 2 Finding the Probability of Independent Events

From the definition of conditional probability you know that $P(A|B) = \dfrac{P(A \cap B)}{P(B)}$ for any events A and B. If those events happen to be independent, you can replace $P(A|B)$ with $P(A)$ and get $P(A) = \dfrac{P(A \cap B)}{P(B)}$. Solving the last equation for $P(A \cap B)$ gives the following result.

Probability of Independent Events
Events A and B are independent if and only if $P(A \cap B) = P(A) \cdot P(B)$.

Example 2 Find the specified probability.

(A) Recall the jar with 15 red marbles and 17 yellow marbles from the Explore. Suppose you randomly draw one marble from the jar. After you put that marble back in the jar, you randomly draw a second marble. What is the probability that you draw a yellow marble first and a red marble second?

Let Y be the event of drawing a yellow marble first. Let R be the event of drawing a red marble second. Then $P(Y) = \frac{17}{32}$ and, because the first marble drawn is replaced before the second marble is drawn, $P(R|Y) = P(R) = \frac{15}{32}$. Since the events are independent, you can multiply their probabilities: $P(Y \cap R) = P(Y) \cdot P(R) = \frac{17}{32} \cdot \frac{15}{32} = \frac{255}{1024} \approx 25\%$.

© Houghton Mifflin Harcourt Publishing Company

COLLABORATIVE LEARNING

Small Group Activity

Have students work in groups to do a simple experiment like rolling a number cube twice. Have one student perform the experiment, while another student keeps track of the results both as a table and as a tree diagram. Have a third student determine the sample space for the experiment (for example, HH, HT, TH, TT), and a fourth student explain how to find the probability of the events in the sample space. Ask students to discuss their results, explain why the events are independent, and present their results to the class.

Ⓑ You spin the spinner shown two times. What is the probability that the spinner stops on an even number on the first spin, followed by an odd number on the second spin?

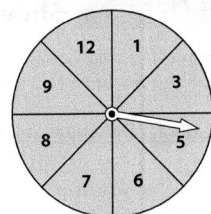

Let E be the event of getting an even number on the first spin. Let O be the event of getting an odd number on the second spin. Then $P(E) = \dfrac{\boxed{3}}{8}$ and, because the first spin has no effect on the second spin, $P(O|E) = P(O) = \dfrac{\boxed{5}}{8}$. Since the events are independent, you can multiply their probabilities:

$P(E \cap O) = P(E) \cdot P(O) = \dfrac{\boxed{3}}{8} \cdot \dfrac{\boxed{5}}{8} = \dfrac{\boxed{15}}{64} \approx \boxed{23}$ %.

Reflect

5. In Part B, what is the probability that the spinner stops on an odd number on the first spin, followed by an even number on the second spin? What do you observe? What does this tell you?

   The probability of getting an odd number on the first spin followed by an even number

   on the second spin is $\frac{5}{8} \cdot \frac{3}{8} = \frac{15}{64}$. This value is equal to the probability calculated in Part B.

   Because the spins are independent of each other, changing the order of the outcomes does

   not affect the overall probability.

Your Turn

6. You spin a spinner with 4 red sections, 3 blue sections, 2 green sections, and 1 yellow section. If all the sections are of equal size, what is the probability that the spinner stops on green first and blue second?

   Let G be the event of getting green with the first spin. Let B be the event of getting blue with the second spin. Then $P(G) = \frac{2}{10} = \frac{1}{5}$ and, because the first spin has no effect on the second spin, $P(B|G) = P(B) = \frac{3}{10}$. Since the events are independent, you can multiply their probabilities: $P(G \cap B) = P(G) \cdot P(B) = \frac{1}{5} \cdot \frac{3}{10} = \frac{3}{50} = 6\%$.

7. A number cube has the numbers 3, 5, 6, 8, 10, and 12 on its faces. You roll the number cube twice. What is the probability that you roll an odd number on both rolls?

   Let $O1$ be the event of getting an odd number on the first roll. Let $O2$ be the event of getting an odd number on the second roll. Then $P(O1) = \frac{2}{6} = \frac{1}{3}$ and, because the first roll has no effect on the second roll, $P(O2|O1) = P(O2) = \frac{1}{3}$. Since the events are independent, you can multiply their probabilities: $P(O1 \cap O2) = P(O1) \cdot P(O2) = \frac{1}{3} \cdot \frac{1}{3} = \frac{1}{9} \approx 11\%$.

DIFFERENTIATE INSTRUCTION

Critical Thinking

Distinguish between evaluating $P(A \mid B)$, when it is important to find the conditional probability that event A will occur given that event B has already occurred, and $P(A \text{ and } B)$, when it is important to consider whether events A and B are independent. The division rule $P(A \mid B) = \dfrac{P(A \cap B)}{P(B)}$ is used to find the conditional probability of A given B, while the multiplication rule $P(A \text{ and } B) = P(A) \cdot P(B)$ is used to find the probability that event A will occur in one trial and event B will occur in another trial, given that one trial does not affect the other.

EXPLAIN 3

Showing that Events are Independent

AVOID COMMON ERRORS

If students are confused about identifying independent events, have them try communicating their results from this lesson orally or in writing. Ask them to check that they are using terms correctly. In particular, be sure students understand that the word *independent* has a specific meaning in probability theory that may be different from its meaning in everyday conversation.

QUESTIONING STRATEGIES

? What are two ways of showing that two events are independent? Show or $P(A) = P(A \mid B)$ or $P(A \text{ and } B) = P(A) \cdot P(B)$.

INTEGRATE MATHEMATICAL PRACTICES
Focus on Patterns

MP.8 Have students follow a pattern to show that events are independent. Have them identify the total number in the sample space. Then ask them to find $P(A)$, $P(B)$, and $P(A \text{ and } B)$ and compare the values. $P(A \text{ and } B) = P(A) \cdot P(B)$ if and only if A and B are independent events.

⚙ Explain 3 **Showing That Events Are Independent**

So far, you have used the formula $P(A \cap B) = P(A) \cdot P(B)$ when you knew that events A and B are independent. You can also use the formula to determine whether two events are independent.

Example 3 Determine if the events are independent.

(A) The two-way frequency table shows data for 120 randomly selected patients who have the same doctor. Determine whether a patient who takes vitamins and a patient who exercises regularly are independent events.

	Takes Vitamins	No Vitamins	Total
Regular Exercise	48	28	76
No regular Exercise	12	32	44
Total	60	60	120

Let V be the event that a patient takes vitamins. Let E be the event that a patient exercises regularly.

Step 1 Find $P(V)$, $P(E)$, and $P(V \cap E)$. The total number of patients is 120.

There are 60 patients who take vitamins, so $P(V) = \frac{60}{120} = \frac{1}{2}$.

There are 76 patients who exercise regularly, so $P(B) = \frac{76}{120} = \frac{19}{30}$.

There are 48 patients who take vitamins and exercise regularly, so $P(V \cap E) = \frac{48}{120} = 40\%$.

Step 2 Compare $P(V \cap E)$ and $P(V) \cdot P(E)$.

$P(V) \cdot P(E) = \frac{1}{2} \cdot \frac{19}{30} = \frac{19}{60} \approx 32\%$

Because $P(V \cap E) \neq P(V) \cdot P(E)$, the events are not independent.

(B) The two-way frequency table shows data for 60 randomly selected children at an elementary school. Determine whether a child who knows how to ride a bike and a child who knows how to swim are independent events.

	Knows how to Ride a Bike	Doesn't Know how to Ride a Bike	Total
Knows how to Swim	30	10	40
Doesn't Know how to Swim	15	5	20
Total	45	15	60

Let B be the event a child knows how to ride a bike. Let S be the event that a child knows how to swim.

Step 1 Find $P(B)$, $P(S)$, and $P(B \cap S)$. The total number of children is 60.

There are __45__ children who know how to ride a bike, so $P(B) = \frac{45}{60} = \frac{3}{4}$.

There are __40__ children who know how to swim, so $P(S) = \frac{40}{60} = \frac{2}{3}$.

There are __30__ children who know how to ride a bike and swim, so $P(B \cap S) = \frac{30}{60} = \frac{1}{2}$.

LANGUAGE SUPPORT **EL**

Connect Vocabulary

Have students create notecards to help them understand the mathematical meaning of *independent*. Ask them to write, on the front of the card, an example of a time in their lives when they acted independently, and then write, on the back, an example of events that are mathematically independent. Connecting the idea to personal experience may help some students remember its meaning and use.

Step 2 Compare $P(B \cap S)$ and $P(B) \cdot P(S)$.

$$P(B) \cdot P(S) = \frac{\boxed{3}}{4} \cdot \frac{\boxed{2}}{3} = \frac{\boxed{1}}{2}$$

Because $P(B \cap S) \boxed{=} P(B) \cdot P(S)$, the events [are/are not] independent.

8. A farmer wants to know if an insecticide is effective in preventing small insects called aphids from damaging tomato plants. The farmer experiments with 80 plants and records the results in the two-way frequency table. Determine whether a plant that was sprayed with insecticide and a plant that has aphids are independent events.

	Has Aphids	No Aphids	Total
Sprayed with Insecticide	12	40	52
Not Sprayed with Insecticide	14	14	28
Total	26	54	80

Let S be the event that a tomato plant was sprayed with insecticide. Let A be the event that a tomato plant has aphids.

$P(S) = \frac{52}{80} = \frac{13}{20}$, $P(A) = \frac{26}{80} = \frac{13}{40}$, and $P(S) \cdot P(A) = \frac{13}{40} \cdot \frac{13}{20} = \frac{169}{800} \approx 21\%$.

Because $P(S \cap A) = \frac{12}{80} = \frac{3}{20} = 15\%$ and $P(S \cap A) \neq P(S) \cdot P(A)$, the events are not independent.

9. A student wants to know if right-handed people are more or less likely to play a musical instrument than left-handed people. The student collects data from 250 people, as shown in the two-way frequency table. Determine whether being right-handed and playing a musical instrument are independent events.

	Right-Handed	Left-Handed	Total
Plays a Musical Instrument	44	6	50
Does not Play a Musical Instrument	176	24	200
Total	220	30	250

Let R be the event that a person is right-handed. Let I be the event that a person plays a musical instrument.

$P(R) = \frac{220}{250} = \frac{22}{25}$, $P(I) = \frac{50}{250} = \frac{1}{5}$, and $P(R) \cdot P(I) = \frac{22}{25} \cdot \frac{1}{5} = \frac{22}{125}$.

Because $P(R \cap I) = \frac{44}{250} = \frac{22}{125}$ and $P(R \cap I) = P(R) \cdot P(I)$, the events are independent.

ELABORATE

QUESTIONING STRATEGIES

? How can you find the probability of independent events A and B? Use the multiplication rule $P(A \text{ and } B) = P(A) \cdot P(B)$.

SUMMARIZE THE LESSON

? Why is it important that the multiplication rule, $P(A \text{ and } B) = P(A) \cdot P(B)$, is true *if and only if* the events are independent? The fact that it is true if and only if the events are independent means that it can be used to determine whether events are independent, and vice versa.

EVALUATE

ASSIGNMENT GUIDE

Concepts and Skills	Practice
Explore Understanding the Independence of Events	Exercises 1–2
Example 1 Determining if Events are Independent	Exercises 3–4, 20
Example 2 Finding the Probability of Independent Events	Exercises 5–14
Example 3 Showing That Events Are Independent	Exercises 15–19, 21–22

💬 Elaborate

10. What are the ways that you can show that two events A and B are independent?
The ways that you can show that two events A and B are independent are by confirming that $P(A|B) = P(A)$ or that $P(A \text{ and } B) = P(A) \cdot P(B)$.

11. How can you find the probability that two independent events A and B both occur?
Multiply $P(A)$ and $P(B)$.

12. **Essential Question Check-In** Give an example of two independent events and explain why they are independent.
Sample answer: When flipping a coin twice, the events of getting heads on the first flip and on the second flip are independent. The occurrence of getting heads on the first flip does not affect the occurrence of getting heads on the second flip. The probability of getting heads on the second flip is $\frac{1}{2}$ regardless of what happens on the first flip.

⭐ Evaluate: Homework and Practice

- Online Homework
- Hints and Help
- Extra Practice

1. A bag contains 12 red and 8 blue chips. Two chips are separately drawn at random from the bag.

a. Suppose that a single chip is drawn at random from the bag. Find the probability that the chip is red and the probability that the chip is blue.
Let R be the event that the chip is red. Let B be the event that the chip is blue.
$P(R) = \frac{12}{20} = \frac{3}{5}$ and $P(B) = \frac{8}{20} = \frac{2}{5}$

b. Suppose that two chips are separately drawn at random from the bag and that the first chip is returned to the bag before the second chip is drawn. Find the probability that the second chip drawn is blue given the first chip drawn was red.
$P(B|R) = \frac{8}{20} = \frac{2}{5}$

c. Suppose that two chips are separately drawn at random from the bag and that the first chip is not returned to the bag before the second chip is drawn. Find the probability that the second chip drawn is blue given the first chip drawn was red.
$P(B|R) = \frac{8}{19}$

d. In which situation—the first chip is returned to the bag or not returned to the bag—are the events that the first chip is red and the second chip is blue independent? Explain.
Events R and B are independent when the first chip is returned to the bag because $P(B|R) = P(B)$ in that case.

© Houghton Mifflin Harcourt Publishing Company

Exercise	Depth of Knowledge (D.O.K.)	COMMON CORE Mathematical Practices
1–2	**1** Recall of Information	**MP.6** Precision
3–14	**2** Skills/Concepts	**MP.5** Using Tools
15–19	**2** Skills/Concepts	**MP.4** Modeling
20	**3** Strategic Thinking H.O.T.	**MP.2** Reasoning
21	**3** Strategic Thinking H.O.T.	**MP.3** Logic
22	**3** Strategic Thinking H.O.T.	**MP.4** Modeling

2. Identify whether the events are independent or not independent.

a. Flip a coin twice and get tails both times.

⬤ Independent   ◯ Not Independent

b. Roll a number cube and get 1 on the first roll and 6 on the second.

⬤ Independent   ◯ Not Independent

c. Draw an ace from a shuffled deck, put the card back and reshuffle the deck, and then draw an 8.

⬤ Independent   ◯ Not Independent

d. Rotate a bingo cage and draw the ball labeled B-4, set it aside, and then rotate the cage again and draw the ball labled N-38.

◯ Independent   ⬤ Not Independent

Answer the question using the fact that $P(A|B) = P(A)$ only when events A and B are independent.

3. The two-way frequency table shows data for 80 randomly selected people who live in a metropolitan area. Is the event that a person prefers public transportation independent of the event that a person lives in the city?

	Prefers to Drive	Prefers Public Transportation	Total
Lives in the City	12	24	36
Lives in the Suburbs	33	11	44
Total	45	35	80

Let T be the event that a person prefers public transportation. Let C be the event that a person lives in the city. Then $P(T) = \frac{35}{80} \approx 44\%$ and $P(T|C) = \frac{24}{36} \approx 67\%$. Since $P(T|C) \neq P(T)$, the events are not independent.

4. The two-way frequency table shows data for 120 randomly selected people who take vacations. Is the event that a person prefers vacationing out of state independent of the event that a person is a woman?

	Prefers Vacationing Out of State	Prefers Vacationing in State	Total
Men	48	32	80
Women	24	16	40
Total	72	48	120

Let O be the event that a person prefers vacationing out of state.

Let W be the event that a person is a woman. Then $P(O) = \frac{72}{120} = 60\%$ and $P(O|W) = \frac{24}{40} = 60\%$. Since $P(O|W) = P(O)$, the events are independent.

INTEGRATE MATHEMATICAL PRACTICES
Focus on Modeling

MP.4 To help students describe the independent events represented in a two-way table and then determine the numbers used to find the probabilities, have them also draw a probability tree representing the given information. Then ask them to show the probability for each branch and the calculations for each possible result in the experiment.

© Houghton Mifflin Harcourt Publishing Company

Independent Events   **1156**

AVOID COMMON ERRORS

When students start finding probabilities for successive events, it is easy to confuse the context. Have students read each exercise and highlight the key words and phrases.

INTEGRATE MATHEMATICAL PRACTICES
Focus on Communication

MP.3 Tree diagrams are useful for understanding the formula for the probability of independent events. Ask groups of students to practice constructing tree diagrams from two-way tables, and vice versa.

A jar contains marbles of various colors as listed in the table. Suppose you randomly draw one marble from the jar. After you put that marble back in the jar, you randomly draw a second marble. Use this information to answer the question, giving a probability as a percent and rounding to the nearest tenth of percent when necessary.

Color of Marble	Number of Marbles
Red	20
Yellow	18
Green	12
Blue	10

5. What is the probability that you draw a blue marble first and a red marble second?

   Let B be the event of drawing a blue marble first. Let R be the event of drawing a red marble second. Then $P(B) = \frac{10}{60} = \frac{1}{6}$ and, because the first marble drawn is replaced before the second marble is drawn, $P(R|B) = P(R) = \frac{20}{60} = \frac{1}{3}$. Since the events are independent, you can multiply their probabilities: $P(B \cap R) = P(B) \cdot P(R) = \frac{1}{6} \cdot \frac{1}{3} = \frac{1}{18} \approx 5.6\%$.

6. What is the probability that you draw a yellow marble first and a green marble second?

   Let Y be the event of drawing a yellow marble first. Let G be the event of drawing a green marble second. Then $P(Y) = \frac{18}{60} = \frac{3}{10}$ and, because the first marble drawn is replaced before the second marble is drawn, $P(G|Y) = P(G) = \frac{12}{60} = \frac{1}{5}$. Since the events are independent, you can multiply their probabilities: $P(Y \cap G) = P(Y) \cdot P(G) = \frac{3}{10} \cdot \frac{1}{5} = \frac{3}{50} = 6\%$.

7. What is the probability that you draw a yellow marble both times?

   Let $Y1$ be the event of drawing a yellow marble first. Let $Y2$ be the event of drawing a yellow marble second. Then $P(Y1) = \frac{18}{60} = \frac{3}{10}$ and, because the first marble drawn is replaced before the second marble is drawn, $P(Y2|Y1) = P(Y2) = \frac{18}{60} = \frac{3}{10}$. Since the events are independent, you can multiply their probabilities: $P(Y1 \cap Y2) = P(Y1) \cdot P(Y2) = \frac{3}{10} \cdot \frac{3}{10} = \frac{9}{100} = 9\%$.

8. What color marble for the first draw and what color marble for the second draw have the greatest probability of occurring together? What is that probability?

   The color marble with the greatest number in the jar has the highest probability of being drawn, so draw a red marble on each draw. Let $R1$ be the event of drawing a red marble first. Let $R2$ be the event of drawing a red marble second. Then $P(R1) = \frac{20}{60} = \frac{1}{3}$ and, because the first marble drawn is replaced before the second marble is drawn, $P(R2|R1) = P(R2) = \frac{20}{60} = \frac{1}{3}$. Since the events are independent, you can multiply their probabilities: $P(R1 \cap R2) = P(R1) \cdot P(R2) = \frac{1}{3} \cdot \frac{1}{3} = \frac{1}{9} \approx 11.1\%$.

You spin the spinner shown two times. Each section of the spinner is the same size. Use this information to answer the question, giving a probability as a percent and rounding to the nearest tenth of a percent when necessary.

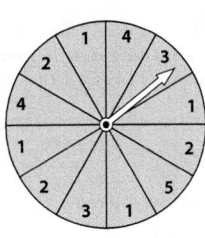

9. What is the probability that the spinner stops on 1 first and 2 second?

$P(1) = \frac{4}{12} = \frac{1}{3}$ and, because the first spin has no effect on the second spin, $P(2|1) = P(2) = \frac{3}{12} = \frac{1}{4}$. Since the events are independent, multiply their probabilities: $P(1 \cap 2) =$

$P(1) \cdot P(2) = \frac{1}{3} \cdot \frac{1}{4} = \frac{1}{12} \approx 8.3\%.$

10. What is the probability that the spinner stops on 4 first and 3 second?

$P(3) = \frac{2}{12} = \frac{1}{6}$ and, because the first spin has no effect on the second spin, $P(4|3) = P(4) = \frac{2}{12} = \frac{1}{6}$. Since the events are independent, multiply their probabilities: $P(4 \cap 3) = P(4) \cdot P(3) = \frac{1}{6} \cdot \frac{1}{6} = \frac{1}{36} \approx 2.8\%.$

11. What is the probability that the spinner stops on an odd number first and an even number second?

Let O be the event of getting an odd number on the first spin. Let E be the event of getting an even number on the second spin. Then

$P(O) = \frac{7}{12}$ and, because the first spin has no effect on the second spin,

$P(E|O) = P(E) = \frac{5}{12}$. Since the events are independent, multiply their

probabilities: $P(O \cap E) = P(O) \cdot P(E) = \frac{7}{12} \cdot \frac{5}{12} = \frac{35}{144} \approx 24.3\%.$

12. What first number and what second number have the least probability of occurring together? What is that probability?

The number that appears least often on the spinner has the

lowest probability of occurring, so you want to get 5 on each spin.

$P(5) = \frac{1}{12}$ and, because the first spin has no effect on the second spin,

$P(5|5) = P(5) = \frac{1}{12}$. Since the events are independent, you can multiply

their probabilities: $P(5 \cap 5) = P(5) \cdot P(5) = \frac{1}{12} \cdot \frac{1}{12} = \frac{1}{144} \approx 0.7\%.$

13. Find the probability of getting heads on every toss of a coin when the coin is tossed 3 times.

Let $H1$, $H2$, and $H3$ represent the events of getting heads on the first, second,

and third coin tosses, respectively. Because the events are independent,

$P(H1 \cap H2 \cap H3) = P(H1) \cdot P(H2) \cdot P(H3) = \frac{1}{2} \cdot \frac{1}{2} \cdot \frac{1}{2} = \frac{1}{8}.$

INTEGRATE MATHEMATICAL PRACTICES

Focus on Math Connections

MP.1 If A and B are independent events, the probability that both A and B occur is given by the multiplication rule $P(A \text{ and } B) = P(A) \cdot P(B)$. More generally, if n independent events occur, then the probability is the product of the n probabilities of the independent events.

Independent Events   **1158**

14. You are randomly choosing cards, one at a time and with replacement, from a standard deck of cards. Find the probability that you choose an ace, then a red card, and then a face card. (Remember that face cards are jacks, queens, and kings.)

Let A be the event of choosing an ace as the first card. Let R be the event of choosing a red card as the second card. Let F be the event of choosing a face card as the third card.

Because you replace each card you choose, the events are independent, and

$$P(A \cap R \cap F) = P(A) \cdot P(R) \cdot P(F) = \frac{4}{52} \cdot \frac{26}{52} \cdot \frac{12}{52} = \frac{1}{13} \cdot \frac{1}{2} \cdot \frac{3}{13} = \frac{3}{338} \approx 0.9\%.$$

Determine whether the given events are independent using the fact that $P(A \cap B) = P(A) \cdot P(B)$ only when events A and B are independent.

15. The manager of a produce stand wants to find out whether there is a connection between people who buy fresh vegetables and people who buy fresh fruit. The manager collects data on 200 randomly chosen shoppers, as shown in the two-way frequency table. Determine whether buying fresh vegetables and buying fresh fruit are independent events.

	Bought Vegetables	No Vegetables	Total
Bought Fruit	56	20	76
No Fruit	49	75	124
Total	105	95	200

Let V be the event that a shopper bought fresh vegetables. Let F be the event that a shopper bought fresh fruit.

$P(V) = \frac{105}{200} = \frac{21}{40}$, $P(F) = \frac{76}{200} = \frac{19}{50}$, and $P(V) \cdot P(F) = \frac{21}{40} \cdot \frac{19}{50} = \frac{399}{2000} \approx 20\%$.

Because $P(V \cap F) = \frac{56}{200} = 28\%$ and $P(V \cap F) \neq P(V) \cdot P(F)$, the events are not independent.

16. The owner of a bookstore collects data about the reading preferences of 60 randomly chosen customers, as shown in the two-way frequency table. Determine whether being a female and preferring fiction are independent events.

	Prefers Fiction	Prefers Nonfiction	Total
Female	15	10	25
Male	21	14	35
Total	36	24	60

Let Fe be the event that a reader is female. Let Fi be the event that a reader prefers fiction.

$P(Fe) = \frac{25}{60} = \frac{5}{12}$, $P(Fi) = \frac{36}{60} = \frac{3}{5}$, and $P(Fe) \cdot P(Fi) = \frac{5}{12} \cdot \frac{3}{5} = \frac{1}{4}$.

Because $P(Fe \cap Fi) = \frac{15}{60} = \frac{1}{4}$ and $P(Fe \cap Fi) = P(Fe) \cdot P(Fi)$, the events are independent.

17. The psychology department at a college collects data about whether there is a relationship between a student's intended career and the student's like or dislike for solving puzzles. The two-way frequency table shows the collected data for 80 randomly chosen students. Determine whether planning for a career in a field involving math or science and a like for solving puzzles are independent events.

	Plans a Career in a Math/Science Field	Plans a Career in a Non-Math/Science Field	Total
Likes Solving Puzzles	35	15	50
Dislikes Solving Puzzles	9	21	30
Total	44	36	80

Let MS be the event that a student plans a career in a math/science field. Let L be the event that a student likes solving puzzles.

$P(MS) = \frac{44}{80} = \frac{11}{20}$, $P(L) = \frac{50}{80} = \frac{5}{8}$, and $P(MS) \cdot P(L) = \frac{11}{20} \cdot \frac{5}{8} = \frac{11}{32} \approx 34\%$.

Because $P(MS \cap L) = \frac{35}{80} \approx 44\%$ and $P(MS \cap L) \neq P(MS) \cdot P(L)$, the events are not independent.

18. A local television station surveys some of its viewers to determine the primary reason they watch the station. The two-way frequency table gives the survey data. Determine whether a viewer is a man and a viewer primarily watches the station for entertainment are independent events.

	Primarily Watches for Information (News, Weather, Sports)	Primarily Watches for Entertainment (Comedies, Dramas)	Total
Men	28	12	40
Women	35	15	50
Total	63	27	90

Let M be the event that a viewer is a man. Let E be the event that a viewer primarily watches the station for entertainment.

$P(M) = \frac{40}{90} = \frac{4}{9}$, $P(E) = \frac{27}{90} = \frac{3}{10}$ and $P(M) \cdot P(E) = \frac{4}{9} \cdot \frac{3}{10} = \frac{2}{15}$.

Because $P(M \cap E) = \frac{12}{90} = \frac{2}{15}$ and $P(M \cap E) = P(M) \cdot P(E)$, the events are independent.

© Houghton Mifflin Harcourt Publishing Company

19. Using what you know about independent events, complete the two-way frequency table in such a way that any event from a column will be independent of any event from a row. Give an example using the table to demonstrate the independence of two events.

	Women	Men	Total
Prefers Writing with a Pen	40	60	100
Prefers Writing with a Pencil	20	30	50
Total	60	90	150

The ratio of women to men is 60:90, or 2:3. For independence of events, the 100 people who prefer writing with a pen must also be divided into a ratio of 2:3. Let m represent the common multiplier of 2 and 3, and solve $2m + 3m = 100$ to get $m = 20$. So, there must be $2(20) = 40$ women who prefer writing with a pen and $3(20) = 60$ men who prefer writing with a pen. To find the number of women who prefer writing with a pencil, subtract 40 from 60 to get 20. To find the number of men who prefer writing with a pencil subtract 60 from 90 to get 30.

Examples showing independence of events will vary. Sample answer:

Let W be the event that a person is a woman. Let Pe be the event that a person prefers writing with a pen. $P(W) = \frac{60}{150} = \frac{2}{5}$, $P(Pe) = \frac{100}{150} = \frac{2}{3}$, and $P(W) \cdot P(Pe) = \frac{2}{5} \cdot \frac{2}{3} = \frac{4}{15}$. Since $P(W \cap Pe) = \frac{40}{150} = \frac{4}{15}$ and $P(W \cap Pe) = P(W) \cdot P(Pe)$, the events are independent.

H.O.T.   Focus on Higher Order Thinking

20. Make a Prediction A box contains 100 balloons. The balloons come in two colors: 80 are yellow and 20 are green. The balloons are also either marked or unmarked: 50 are marked "Happy Birthday!" and 50 are not. A balloon is randomly chosen from the box. How many yellow "Happy Birthday!" balloons must be in the box if the event that a balloon is yellow and the event that a balloon is marked "Happy Birthday!" are independent? Explain.

Because half of the balloons are marked "Happy Birthday!", the probability of drawing a "Happy Birthday!" balloon is $\frac{1}{2}$. To be independent of the event that a balloon is yellow, the conditional probability of drawing a balloon marked "Happy Birthday!" given that the balloon is yellow also needs to have a probability of $\frac{1}{2}$. So, $\frac{1}{2}(80) = 40$ yellow "Happy Birthday!" balloons would need to be in the box.

21. Construct Arguments Given that events A and B are independent, prove that the complement of event A, A^c, is also independent of event B.

$$P(A^c \mid B) = 1 - P(A \mid B) \qquad \text{Definition of complementary events}$$

$$= 1 - P(A) \qquad \text{Definition of independent events}$$

$$= P(A^c) \qquad \text{Definition of complementary events}$$

So, events A^c and B are also independent.

22. Multi-Step The two-way frequency table shows two events, A and B, and their complements, A^c and B^c. Let $P(A) = a$ and $P(B) = b$. Using a, b, and the grand total T, form the products listed in the table to find the number of elements in $A \cap B$, $A \cap B^c$, $A^c \cap B$, and $A^c \cap B^c$.

	A	A^c	Total
B	abT	$(1-a)bT$	
B^c	$a(1-b)T$	$(1-a)(1-b)T$	
Total			T

a. Find the table's missing row and column totals in simplest form.

Row total for event B: $abT + (1-a)bT = [a + (1-a)]bT = bT$

Row total for event B^c: $a(1-b)T + (1-a)(1-b)T = [a + (1-a)](1-b)T = (1-b)T$

Column total for event A: $abT + a(1-b)T = a[b + (1-b)]T = aT$

Column total for event A^c: $(1-a)bT + (1-a)(1-b)T = (1-a)[b + (1-b)]T = (1-a)T$

b. Show that events A and B are independent using the fact that $P(A \mid B) = P(A)$ only when events A and B are independent.

$$P(A \mid B) = \frac{n(A \cap B)}{n(B)} = \frac{abT}{bT} = a = P(A)$$

c. Show that events A and B^c are independent.

$$P(A \mid B^c) = \frac{n(A \cap B^c)}{n(B^c)} = \frac{a(1-b)T}{(1-b)T} = a = P(A)$$

d. Show that events A^c and B are independent.

$$P(A^c \mid B) = \frac{n(A^c \cap B)}{n(B)} = \frac{(1-a)bT}{bT} = 1 - a = P(A^c)$$

e. Show that events A^c and B^c are independent.

$$P(A^c \mid B^c) = \frac{n(A^c \cap B^c)}{n(B^c)} = \frac{(1-a)(1-b)T}{(1-b)T} = 1 - a = P(A^c)$$

© Houghton Mifflin Harcourt Publishing Company

PEER-TO-PEER DISCUSSION

Have students discuss various pairs of independent events that they can create from the spinner below.

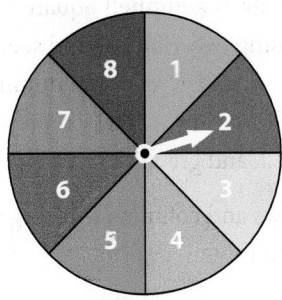

Have them describe in their own words the process they would use to find the probabilities for pairs of independent events.

JOURNAL

Have students explain what is meant by independent events and give an example of how to determine whether two events are independent.

Focus on Patterns

MP.8 Megan drew a Punnett Square to find the results of crossing two violet-round seed-yellow seed parents. Let V, R, and Y represent dominant violet, round, and yellow. Let v, r, and y represent recessive white, wrinkled, and green.

How many rows and columns will Megan's Punnett Square have? 8 rows, 8 columns

List the letter groups that will appear atop the columns and beside the rows in the square. *VRY, VRy, VrY, Vry, vRY, vRy, vrY, vry*

What is the probability that a second-generation flower will be white and wrinkled, and have green seeds? $\frac{1}{64}$

Lesson Performance Task

Before the mid-1800s, little was known about the way that plants pass along characteristics such as color and height to their offspring. From painstaking observations of garden peas, the Austrian monk Gregor Mendel discovered the basic laws of heredity. The table shows the results of three of Mendel's experiments. In each experiment, he looked at a particular characteristic of garden peas by planting seeds exclusively of one type.

Characteristic	Type Planted	Results in Second Generation
Flower color	100% violet	705 violet, 224 white
Seed texture	100% round	5474 round, 1850 wrinkled
Seed color	100% yellow	6022 yellow, 2011 green

1. Suppose you plant garden peas with violet flowers and round, yellow seeds. Estimate the probability of obtaining second-generation plants with violet flowers, the probability of obtaining second-generation plants with round seeds, and the probability of obtaining second-generation plants with yellow seeds. Explain how you made your estimates.

Mendel saw that certain traits, such as violet flowers and round seeds, seemed stronger than others, such white flowers and wrinkled seeds. He called the stronger traits "dominant" and the weaker traits "recessive." Both traits can be carried in the genes of a plant, because a gene consists of two *alleles*, one received from the mother and one from the father. (For plants, the "father" is the plant from which the pollen comes, and the "mother" is the plant whose pistil receives the pollen.) When at least one of the alleles has the dominant trait, the plant exhibits the dominant trait. Only when both alleles have the recessive trait does the plant exhibit the recessive trait.

You can use a 2 × 2 Punnett square, like the one shown, to see the results of crossing the genes of two parent plants. In this Punnett square, V represents the dominant flower color violet and v represents the recessive flower color white. If each parent's genes contain both V and v alleles, the offspring may receive, independently and with equal probability, either a V allele or a v allele from each parent.

© Houghton Mifflin Harcourt Publishing Company

	V	*v*
V	*VV*	*Vv*
v	*vV*	*vv*

2. After planting a first generation of plants exhibiting only dominant traits, Mendel observed that the second generation consisted of plants with a ratio of about 3:1 dominant-to-recessive traits. Does the Punnett square support or refute Mendel's observation? Explain.

3. Draw a 4 × 4 Punnett square for finding the results of crossing two violet-flower-and-round-seed parent plants. Let V and R represent the dominant traits violet flowers and round seeds, respectively. Let v and r represent the recessive traits white flowers and wrinkled seeds, respectively. Each column heading and row heading of your Punnett square should contain a two-letter combination of V or v and R or r. Each cell of your Punnett square will then contain four letters. Use the Punnett square to find the probability that a second-generation plant will have white flowers and round seeds. Explain your reasoning.

1. Estimate the probabilities using Mendel's data: If V represents violet flowers, then $P(V) = \frac{705}{705 + 224} = \frac{705}{929} \approx 76\%$. If R represents round seeds, then $P(R) = \frac{5474}{5474 + 1850} = \frac{5474}{7324} \approx 75\%$. If Y represents yellow seeds, then $P(Y) = \frac{6022}{6022 + 2011} = \frac{6022}{8033} \approx 75\%$.

2. The Punnett square supports Mendel's observation. The combination of alleles in each table cell occurs with a probability of $\frac{1}{2} \cdot \frac{1}{2} = \frac{1}{4}$. Since three of the four table cells contain a dominant V allele, you can expect three-fourths of the offspring to have violet flowers. Since one table cell contains two recessive v alleles, you can expect one-fourth of the offspring to have white flowers. So, the ratio of offspring with violet flowers to offspring with white flowers is $\frac{\frac{3}{4}}{\frac{1}{4}} = \frac{3}{1}$.

3.

	VR	Vr	vR	vr
VR	VVRR	VVRr	VvRR	VvRr
Vr	VVRr	VVrr	VvRr	Vvrr
vR	VvRR	VvRr	vvRR	vvRr
vr	VvRr	Vvrr	vvRr	vvrr

The combination of alleles in each table cell occurs with a probability of $\frac{1}{2} \cdot \frac{1}{2} \cdot \frac{1}{2} \cdot \frac{1}{2} = \frac{1}{16}$. For offspring to have white flowers, which is recessive, a table cell must contain two v alleles. For offspring to have round seeds, which is dominant, a cell must contain two R alleles or a combination of an R allele and an r allele. Three of 16 table cells satisfy those requirements ($vvRR$, $vvRr$, and $vvRr$), giving a probability of $\frac{3}{16}$.

INTEGRATE MATHEMATICAL PRACTICES

Focus on Critical Thinking

MP.3 A gardener claimed to have planted 10 violet-round seed-yellow garden pea seeds and to have obtained 10 white-wrinkled seed-green plants. Was the gardener telling the truth? Explain. Sample answer: The gardener's results were possible but highly unlikely. The probability that a single second-generation white-wrinkled seed-green plant will be produced is $\frac{1}{64}$. The probability that 10 will be produced is $\left(\frac{1}{64}\right)^{10}$, which is very small.

EXTENSION ACTIVITY

Have students work in pairs. Each pair should have two coins and a sheet of paper on which to record their results. Ask students to conduct 50 trials, each time flipping two coins and recording the results (2 heads, a heads and a tails, or 2 tails). Ask them to interpret their results in terms of the laws of heredity discovered by Mendel. Sample answer: We let H represent a dominant trait and T a recessive trait. We interpreted every HH, HT, and TH occurrence as an offspring displaying the dominant trait and every TT occurrence as an offspring displaying the recessive trait. About 75% of our trials resulted in HH, HT, or TH (offspring displaying the dominant trait), closely matching Mendel's results.

Scoring Rubric

2 points: Student correctly solves the problem and explains his/her reasoning.

1 point: Student shows good understanding of the problem but does not fully solve or explain his/her reasoning.

0 points: Student does not demonstrate understanding of the problem.

Independent Events   **1164**

Dependent Events

Common Core Math Standards

The student is expected to:

 S-CP.B.8

Apply the general Multiplication Rule in a uniform probability model, $P(A$ and $B) = P(A)P(B|A) = P(B)P(A|B)$, and interpret the answer in terms of the model. Also S-CP.A.3, S-CP.A.4, S-CP.A.5

Mathematical Practices

 MP.6 Precision

Language Objective

Work with a partner to brainstorm examples of dependent events.

ENGAGE

Essential Question: How do you find the probability of dependent events?

You can use the Multiplication Rule to find the probability of dependent events.

PREVIEW: LESSON PERFORMANCE TASK

View the Engage section online. Discuss the photograph. Ask students to describe the sport that is pictured. Then preview the Lesson Performance Task.

Name_____ Class_____ Date_____

22.3 Dependent Events

Essential Question: How do you find the probability of dependent events?

 Explore **Finding a Way to Calculate the Probability of Dependent Events**

You know two tests for the independence of events A and B:

1. If $P(A|B) = P(A)$, then A and B are independent.

2. If $P(A \cap B) = P(A) \cdot P(B)$, then A and B are independent.

Two events that fail either of these tests are **dependent events** because the occurrence of one event affects the occurrence of the other event.

Ⓐ The two-way frequency table shows the results of a survey of 100 people who regularly walk for exercise. Let O be the event that a person prefers walking outdoors. Let M be the event that a person is male. Find $P(O)$, $P(M)$, and $P(O \cap M)$ as fractions. Then determine whether events O and M are independent or dependent.

	Prefers walking outdoors	Prefers walking on a treadmill	Total
Male	40	10	50
Female	20	30	50
Total	60	40	100

$P(O) = \frac{60}{100} = \frac{3}{5}$, $P(M) = \frac{50}{100} = \frac{1}{2}$, and $P(O \cap M) = \frac{40}{100} = \frac{2}{5}$.

Since $P(O) \cdot P(M) = \frac{3}{5} \cdot \frac{1}{2} = \frac{3}{10} \neq P(O \cap M)$, events O and M are dependent.

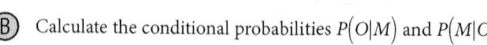

Ⓑ Calculate the conditional probabilities $P(O|M)$ and $P(M|O)$.

$$P(O|M) = \frac{n(O \cap M)}{n(M)} = \frac{40}{50} = \frac{4}{5}$$

$$P(M|O) = \frac{n(O \cap M)}{n(O)} = \frac{40}{60} = \frac{2}{3}$$

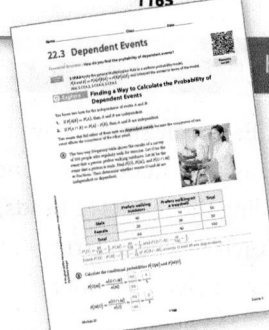

HARDCOVER PAGES 963–970

Turn to these pages to find this lesson in the hardcover student edition.

Ⓒ Complete the multiplication table using the fractions for $P(O)$ and $P(M)$ from Step A and the fractions for $P(O|M)$ and $P(M|O)$ from Step B.

×	$P(O)$	$P(M)$
$P(O|M)$	$\frac{3}{5} \cdot \frac{4}{5} = \frac{12}{25}$	$\frac{1}{2} \cdot \frac{4}{5} = \frac{2}{5}$
$P(M|O)$	$\frac{3}{5} \cdot \frac{2}{3} = \frac{2}{5}$	$\frac{1}{2} \cdot \frac{2}{5} = \frac{1}{5}$

Ⓓ Do any of the four products in Step C equal $P(O \cap M)$, calculated in Step A? If so, which of the four products?

Yes, the products $P(O) \cdot P(M|O)$ and $P(M) \cdot P(O|M)$ both equal $\frac{2}{5}$, the value of $P(O \cap M)$.

Reflect

1. In a previous lesson you learned the conditional probability formula $P(B|A) = \frac{P(A \cap B)}{P(A)}$. How does this formula explain the results you obtained in Step D?

   Multiplying both sides of $P(B|A) = \frac{P(A \cap B)}{P(A)}$ by $P(A)$ gives $P(A) \cdot P(B|A) = P(A \cap B)$.

   Letting $A = O$ and $B = M$ gives $P(O) \cdot P(M|O) = P(O \cap M)$, while letting $A = M$ and $B = O$

   gives $P(M) \cdot P(O|M) = P(M \cap O) = P(O \cap M)$,

2. Let F be the event that a person is female. Let T be the event that a person prefers walking on a treadmill. Write two formulas you can use to calculate $P(F \cap T)$. Use either one to find the value of $P(F \cap T)$, and then confirm the result by finding $P(F \cap T)$ directly from the two-way frequency table.

   $P(F \cap T) = P(F) \cdot P(T|F); P(F \cap T) = P(T \cap F) = P(T) \cdot P(F|T)$. Using the first of these

   formulas gives $P(F \cap T) = \frac{50}{100} \cdot \frac{30}{50} = \frac{1}{2} \cdot \frac{3}{5} = \frac{3}{10}$. Calculating $P(T \cap F)$ directly from the

   table gives $\frac{30}{100} = \frac{3}{10}$.

⚙ **Explain 1** **Finding the Probability of Two Dependent Events**

You can use the Multiplication Rule to find the probability of dependent events.

> **Multiplication Rule**
>
> $P(A \cap B) = P(A) \cdot P(B|A)$ where $P(B|A)$ is the conditional probability of event B, given that event A has occurred.

Example 1 There are 5 tiles with the letters A, B, C, D, and E in a bag. You choose a tile without looking, put it aside, and then choose another tile without looking. Use the Multiplication Rule to find the specified probability, writing it as a fraction.

© Houghton Mifflin Harcourt Publishing Company

PROFESSIONAL DEVELOPMENT

 Integrate Mathematical Practices

This lesson provides an opportunity to address Mathematical Practice **MP.6**, which calls for students to "communicate with precision." Students are already familiar with some aspects of probability but, in this lesson, they must analyze whether events are dependent or independent before they find the probabilities of the events. They use multiple representations, including formulas, two-way tables, and tree diagrams, to determine a probability. Students may also make an organized list of all outcomes.

EXPLORE

Finding a Way to Calculate the Probability of Dependent Events

INTEGRATE TECHNOLOGY

Students have the option of doing the Explore activity either in the book or online.

QUESTIONING STRATEGIES

❓ Suppose two events A and B are dependent. How are their probabilities related? If events A and B are dependent events, $P(A \text{ and } B) = P(A|B) \cdot P(B)$ or $P(A \text{ and } B) = P(B|A) \cdot P(A)$.

INTEGRATE MATHEMATICAL PRACTICES
Focus on Math Connections

MP.1 Point out that if two events occur with replacement, then the events may not be dependent. For example, if two marbles are drawn from a bag, the events of drawing a marble are dependent. But, if the first marble is replaced before the second one is drawn, then the events become independent, since the first event does not affect the second.

EXPLAIN 1

Finding the Probability of Two Dependent Events

QUESTIONING STRATEGIES

❓ Why is probability of dependent events different from the probability of independent events? The occurrence of one event affects the probability of the second event.

AVOID COMMON ERRORS

Help students who are confused about identifying dependent events by having them communicate their results from this lesson orally and in writing. Ask them to check that they are using terms correctly. In particular, be sure students understand that the word *dependent* has a specific meaning in probability theory that may be different from its meaning in everyday conversation.

INTEGRATE MATHEMATICAL PRACTICES

Focus on Math Connections

MP.1 Point out the two different ways to determine the probability of dependent events: (1) by using the formula for the multiplication rule, and (2) by making a tree diagram. You may also wish to tell students that they can determine the probability by thinking about permutations to find the number of outcomes in the sample space and the number of favorable outcomes.

(A) Find the probability that you choose a vowel followed by a consonant.

Let V be the event that the first tile is a vowel. Let C be the event that the second tile is a consonant. Of the 5 tiles, there are 2 vowels, so $P(V) = \frac{2}{5}$.

Of the 4 remaining tiles, there are 3 consonants, so $P(C|V) = \frac{3}{4}$.

By the Multiplication Rule, $P(V \cap C) = P(V) \cdot P(V|C) = \frac{2}{5} \cdot \frac{3}{4} = \frac{6}{20} = \frac{3}{10}$.

(B) Find the probability that you choose a vowel followed by another vowel.

Let $V1$ be the event that the first tile is a vowel. Let $V2$ be the event that the second tile is also a vowel. Of the 5 tiles, there are $\underline{2}$ vowels, so $P(V1) = \frac{\boxed{2}}{5}$.

Of the 4 remaining tiles, there is $\underline{1}$ vowel, so $P(V2|V1) = \frac{\boxed{1}}{4}$.

By the Multiplication Rule, $P(V1 \cap V2) = P(V1) \cdot P(V2|V1) = \frac{\boxed{2}}{5} \cdot \frac{\boxed{1}}{4} = \frac{\boxed{2}}{20} = \frac{\boxed{1}}{10}$.

Your Turn

A bag holds 4 white marbles and 2 blue marbles. You choose a marble without looking, put it aside, and choose another marble without looking. Use the Multiplication Rule to find the specified probability, writing it as a fraction.

3. Find the probability that you choose a white marble followed by a blue marble.

Let W be the event that the first marble is white. Let B be the event that the second marble is blue.

$P(W) = \frac{4}{6} = \frac{2}{3}$

$P(B|W) = \frac{2}{5}$

$P(W \cap B) = P(W) \cdot P(B|W) = \frac{2}{3} \cdot \frac{2}{5} = \frac{4}{15}$

4. Find the probability that you choose a white marble followed by another white marble.

Let $W1$ be the event that the first marble is a white marble. Let $W2$ be the event that the second marble is also a white marble.

$P(W1) = \frac{4}{6} = \frac{2}{3}$

$P(W2|W1) = \frac{3}{5}$

$P(W1 \cap W2) = P(W1) \cdot P(W2|W1) = \frac{2}{3} \cdot \frac{3}{5} = \frac{2}{5}$

© Houghton Mifflin Harcourt Publishing Company

COLLABORATIVE LEARNING

Peer-to-Peer Activity

Have students work in pairs. Give each pair a set of 5 to 10 playing cards or numbered index cards. Have students lay out the cards face up, write a list of possible independent and dependent events using the cards, and find the probabilities. Have one student identify the favorable outcomes and the other student identify the sample space for each event.

⊘ Explain 2 Finding the Probability of Three or More Dependent Events

You can extend the Multiplication Rule to three or more events. For instance, for three events A, B, and C, the rule becomes $P(A \cap B \cap C) = P(A) \cdot P(B|A) \cdot P(C|A \cap B)$.

Example 2 You have a key ring with 7 different keys. You're attempting to unlock a door in the dark, so you try keys one at a time and keep track of which ones you try.

(A) Find the probability that the third key you try is the right one.

Let $W1$ be the event that the first key you try is wrong. Let $W2$ be the event that the second key you try is also wrong. Let R be the event that the third key you try is right.

On the first try, there are 6 wrong keys among the 7 keys, so $P(W1) = \frac{6}{7}$.

On the second try, there are 5 wrong keys among the 6 remaining keys, so $P(W2|W1) = \frac{5}{6}$.

On the third try, there is 1 right key among the 5 remaining keys, so $P(R|W2 \cap W1) = \frac{1}{5}$.

By the Multiplication Rule, $P(W1 \cap W2 \cap R) = P(W1) \cdot P(W2|W1) \cdot P(R|W1 \cap W2) = \frac{6}{7} \cdot \frac{5}{6} \cdot \frac{1}{5} = \frac{1}{7}$.

(B) Find the probability that one of the first three keys you try is right.

There are two ways to approach this problem:

1. You can break the problem into three cases: (1) the first key you try is right; (2) the first key is wrong, but the second key is right; and (3) the first two keys are wrong, but the third key is right.

2. You can use the complement: The complement of the event that one of the first three keys is right is the event that *none* of the first three keys is right.

Use the second approach.

Let $W1$, $W2$, and $W3$ be the events that the first, second, and third keys, respectively, are wrong.

From Part A, you already know that $P(W1) = \dfrac{\boxed{6}}{7}$ and $P(W2|W1) = \dfrac{\boxed{5}}{6}$.

On the third try, there are 4 wrong keys among the 5 remaining keys, so $P(W3|W2 \cap W1) = \dfrac{\boxed{4}}{5}$.

By the Multiplication Rule,

$P(W1 \cap W2 \cap W3) = P(W1) \cdot P(W2|W1) \cdot P(W3|W1 \cap W2) = \dfrac{\boxed{6}}{7} \cdot \dfrac{\boxed{5}}{6} \cdot \dfrac{\boxed{4}}{5} = \dfrac{\boxed{4}}{7}$

The event $W1 \cap W2 \cap W3$ is the complement of the one you want. So, the probability that one of

the first three keys you try is right is $1 - P(W1 \cap W2 \cap W3) = 1 - \dfrac{\boxed{4}}{7} = \dfrac{\boxed{3}}{7}$.

EXPLAIN 2

Finding the Probability of Three or More Dependent Events

QUESTIONING STRATEGIES

? When does replacement affect independence? When there is replacement, the events are independent because the outcome of the first event does not affect the probability of the second event.

? Why can you use the multiplication rule $P(A \text{ and } B) = P(A) \cdot P(B|A)$ for both dependent and independent events? If the events are independent, $P(B|A)$ is equal to $P(B)$.

INTEGRATE MATHEMATICAL PRACTICES
Focus on Reasoning

MP.2 Ask students if they think that the multiplication rule for dependent events can be extended, as it was for independent events, and why. Yes; for example, a formula for three events is $P(A \text{ and } B \text{ and } C) = P(A) \cdot P(B \mid A) \cdot P(C \mid A \text{ and } B)$. Since each part of this formula can be found for dependent events, you can extend the rule.

DIFFERENTIATE INSTRUCTION

Modeling

Help students understand the difference between independent events and dependent events by discussing choosing two colored marbles from a bag: (1) with replacement and (2) without replacement. When you select a marble with replacement, you select the first marble, note its color, put the marble back in the bag, and then choose the second marble. In this case, the two selections are independent events. Without replacement, you select the first marble, put it aside, and then choose the second marble. In this case, the two selections are dependent events because the marble you chose first changed the sample space for your second selection.

5. In Part B, show that the first approach to solving the problem gives the same result. Let $W1$ and $W2$ be the events that the first and second keys, respectively, are wrong. Let R be the event that a key is right. Calculate three probabilities: $P(R)$, $P(W1 \cap R)$, and $P(W1 \cap W2 \cap R)$.

There is 1 right key among the 7 keys on the first try, so $P(R) = \frac{1}{7}$.

There are 6 wrong keys among the 7 keys on the first try and then 1 right key among the

6 remaining keys on the second try, so $P(W1 \cap R) = P(W1) \cdot P(R|W1) = \frac{6}{7} \cdot \frac{1}{6} = \frac{1}{7}$.

From Part A, you know that $P(W1 \cap W2 \cap R) = \frac{1}{7}$.

Because the three events R, $W1 \cap R$, and $W2 \cap W1 \cap R$ are mutually exclusive, the

probability that one of the first three keys is right is the sum of the probabilities of those

events: $P(R) + P(W1 \cap R) + P(W2 \cap W1 \cap R) = \frac{1}{7} + \frac{1}{7} + \frac{1}{7} = \frac{3}{7}$.

6. In Part A, suppose you don't keep track of the keys as you try them. How does the probability change? Explain.

If you don't keep track of the keys, the probability of trying a wrong key is always $\frac{6}{7}$, and

the probability of choosing the right key is always $\frac{1}{7}$. The events $W1$, $W2$, and R are now

independent, so you can multiply their probabilities without considering conditional

probabilities: $P(W1 \cap W2 \cap R) = P(W1) \cdot P(W2) \cdot P(R) = \frac{6}{7} \cdot \frac{6}{7} \cdot \frac{1}{7} = \frac{36}{343}$

Your Turn

Three people are standing in line at a car rental agency at an airport. Each person is willing to take whatever rental car is offered. The agency has 4 white cars and 2 silver ones available and offers them to customers on a random basis.

7. Find the probability that all three customers get white cars.

Let $W1$, $W2$, and $W3$ be the events that the first, second, and third customers, respectively,

get a white car.

$$P(W1 \cap W2 \cap W3) = P(W1) \cdot P(W2|W1) \cdot P(W3|W1 \cap W2)$$
$$= \frac{4}{6} \cdot \frac{3}{5} \cdot \frac{2}{4}$$
$$= \frac{2}{3} \cdot \frac{3}{5} \cdot \frac{1}{2}$$
$$= \frac{1}{5}$$

So, the probability that all three customers get a white car is $\frac{1}{5}$.

© Houghton Mifflin Harcourt Publishing Company

LANGUAGE SUPPORT EL

Vocabulary Development

Help students understand *dependent events* by having them create a poster with examples of dependent events that may be familiar, and that show simple calculations for the probability of the dependent events. You may want to prompt students to highlight the words that correspond to the event that is assumed to have already occurred and have them focus on the fact that this event affects the outcome of the other event.

8. Find the probability that two of the customers get the silver cars and one gets a white car.

Let $W1$ and $S1$ represent the events that the first customer gets a white or silver car, respectively. Let $W2$ and $S2$ represent the events that the second customer gets a white or silver car, respectively. Let $W3$ and $S3$ represent the events that the third customer gets a white or silver car, respectively. Calculate three probabilities: $P(W1 \cap S2 \cap S3)$, $P(S1 \cap W2 \cap S3)$, and $P(S1 \cap S2 \cap W3)$.

$P(W1 \cap S2 \cap S3) = P(W1) \cdot P(S2|W1) \cdot P(S3|W1 \cap S2) = \frac{4}{6} \cdot \frac{2}{5} \cdot \frac{1}{4} = \frac{1}{15}$

$P(S1 \cap W2 \cap S3) = P(S1) \cdot P(W2|S1) \cdot P(S3|S1 \cap W2) = \frac{2}{6} \cdot \frac{4}{5} \cdot \frac{1}{4} = \frac{1}{15}$

$P(S1 \cap S2 \cap W3) = P(S1) \cdot P(S2|S1) \cdot P(W3|S1 \cap S2) = \frac{2}{6} \cdot \frac{1}{5} \cdot \frac{4}{4} = \frac{1}{15}$

Because the events $W1 \cap S2 \cap S3$, $S1 \cap W2 \cap S3$, and $S1 \cap S2 \cap W3$ are mutually exclusive, you can add their probabilities:

$P(W1 \cap S2 \cap S3) + P(S1 \cap W2 \cap S3) + P(S1 \cap S2 \cap W3) = \frac{1}{15} + \frac{1}{15} + \frac{1}{15} = \frac{3}{15} = \frac{1}{5}$

So, the probability that two customers get the silver cars and one gets a white car is $\frac{1}{5}$.

💬 Elaborate

9. When are two events dependent?
Two events are dependent when the occurrence of one event affects the occurrence of the other.

10. Suppose you are given a bag with 3 blue marbles and 2 red marbles, and you are asked to find the probability of drawing 2 blue marbles by drawing one marble at a time and not replacing the first marble drawn. Why does not replacing the first marble make these events dependent? What would make these events independent? Explain.
The first marble you draw changes the sample space for your second draw. That is, the occurrence of the event that you get a blue marble on the first draw affects the occurrence of the event that you get a blue marble on the second draw. Replacing the first marble drawn returns the sample space to its original state so that the probability of getting a blue marble doesn't change from one draw to the next, which means that the events are independent.

11. **Essential Question Check-In** According to the Multiplication Rule, when finding $P(A \cap B)$ for dependent events A and B, you multiply $P(A)$ by what?
You multiply $P(A)$ by $P(B|A)$.

ELABORATE

QUESTIONING STRATEGIES

? How is the multiplication rule used to find the probability of dependent or independent events A and B? Sample answer: If A and B are dependent, then the rule is $P(A \text{ and } B) = P(A) \cdot P(B \mid A)$. If A and B are independent, then $P(B \mid A)$ can be replaced by $P(B)$ and the multiplication rule becomes $P(A \text{ and } B) = P(A) \cdot P(B)$.

SUMMARIZE THE LESSON

? State the multiplication rule, $P(A \text{ and } B) = P(A) \cdot P(B \mid A)$, in your own words. The probability that dependent events A and B take place is equal to the product of the probability that A takes place and the probability that B takes place given that A has already occurred.

EVALUATE

ASSIGNMENT GUIDE

Concepts and Skills	Practice
Explore Finding a Way to Calculate the Probability of Dependent Events	Exercise 1
Example 1 Determining the Probability of Two Dependent Events	Exercises 2–3
Example 2 Finding the Probability of Three or More Dependent Events	Exercises 4–14

INTEGRATE MATHEMATICAL PRACTICES

Focus on Communication

MP.3 Have students work in small groups to explain the difference between dependent and independent events. Then have them explain to each other how to find the probabilities associated with dependent and independent events. Ask them to use examples in their explanations.

1. Town officials are considering a property tax increase to finance the building of a new school. The two-way frequency table shows the results of a survey of 110 town residents.

	Supports a property tax increase	Does not support a property tax increase	Total
Lives in a household with children	50	20	70
Lives in a household without children	10	30	40
Total	60	50	110

a. Let C be the event that a person lives in a household with children. Let S be the event that a person supports a property tax increase. Are the events C and S independent or dependent? Explain.

$P(C) = \frac{70}{110} = \frac{7}{11}$, $P(S) = \frac{60}{110} = \frac{6}{11}$, and $P(C \cap S) = \frac{50}{110} = \frac{5}{11}$.

Since $P(S) \cdot P(C) = \frac{7}{11} \cdot \frac{6}{11} = \frac{42}{121}$ and $P(C \cap S) = \frac{5}{11} = \frac{55}{121}$,

$P(C) \cdot P(S) \neq P(C \cap S)$, so the events C and S are dependent.

b. Find $P(C|S)$ and $P(S|C)$. Which of these two conditional probabilities can you multiply with $P(C)$ to get $P(C \cap S)$? Which of the two can you multiply with $P(S)$ to get $P(C \cap S)$?

$P(C|S) = \frac{50}{60} = \frac{5}{6}$ and $P(S|C) = \frac{50}{70} = \frac{5}{7}$.

Multiplying $P(C)$ and $P(S|C)$ gives $\frac{7}{11} \cdot \frac{5}{7} = \frac{5}{11} = P(C \cap S)$.

Multiplying $P(S)$ and $P(C|S)$ gives $\frac{6}{11} \cdot \frac{5}{6} = \frac{5}{11} = P(C \cap S)$.

Exercise	Depth of Knowledge (D.O.K.)	COMMON CORE Mathematical Practices
1	**2** Skills/Concepts	**MP.4** Modeling
2–11	**2** Skills/Concepts	**MP.1** Problem Solving
12	**2** Skills/Concepts H.O.T.	**MP.4** Modeling
13	**3** Strategic Thinking H.O.T.	**MP.3** Logic
14	**3** Strategic Thinking H.O.T.	**MP.2** Reasoning

2. A mall surveyed 120 shoppers to find out whether they typically wait for a sale to get a better price or make purchases on the spur of the moment regardless of price. The two-way frequency table shows the results of the survey.

	Waits for a Sale	Buys on Impulse	Total
Woman	40	10	50
Man	50	20	70
Total	90	30	120

a. Let W be the event that a shopper is a woman. Let S be the event that a shopper typically waits for a sale. Are the events W and S independent or dependent? Explain.

$P(W) = \dfrac{50}{120} = \dfrac{5}{12}$, $P(S) = \dfrac{90}{120} = \dfrac{3}{4}$, and $P(W \cap S) = \dfrac{40}{120} = \dfrac{1}{3}$.

Since $P(W) \cdot P(S) = \dfrac{5}{12} \cdot \dfrac{3}{4} = \dfrac{5}{16} \neq \dfrac{1}{3} = P(W \cap S)$, the events W and S are dependent.

b. Find $P(W|S)$ and $P(S|W)$. Which of these two conditional probabilities can you multiply with $P(W)$ to get $P(W \cap S)$? Which of the two can you multiply with $P(S)$ to get $P(W \cap S)$?

$P(W|S) = \dfrac{40}{90} = \dfrac{4}{9}$ and $P(S|W) = \dfrac{40}{50} = \dfrac{4}{5}$. Multiplying $P(W)$ and $P(S|W)$ gives $\dfrac{5}{12} \cdot \dfrac{4}{5} = \dfrac{1}{3} = P(W \cap S)$. Multiplying $P(S)$ and $P(W|S)$ gives $\dfrac{3}{4} \cdot \dfrac{4}{9} = \dfrac{1}{3} = P(W \cap S)$.

There are 4 green, 10 red, and 6 yellow marbles in a bag. Each time you randomly choose a marble, you put it aside before choosing another marble at random. Use the Multiplication Rule to find the specified probability, writing it as a fraction.

3. Find the probability that you choose a red marble followed by a yellow marble.
Let R be the event that the first marble is red. Let Y be the event that the second marble is yellow. $P(R \cap Y) = P(R) \cdot P(Y|R) = \dfrac{10}{20} \cdot \dfrac{6}{19} = \dfrac{3}{19}$

4. Find the probabilty that you choose one yellow marble followed by another yellow marble.
Let $Y1$ be the event that the first marble is yellow. Let $Y2$ be the event that the second marble is yellow. $P(Y1 \cap Y2) = P(Y1) \cdot P(Y2|Y1) = \dfrac{6}{20} \cdot \dfrac{5}{19} = \dfrac{3}{38}$

5. Find the probability that you choose a red marble, followed by a yellow marble, followed by a green marble.
Let R be the event that the first marble is red. Let Y be the event that the second marble is yellow. Let G be the event that the third marble is green.
$P(R \cap Y \cap G) = P(R) \cdot P(Y|R) \cdot P(G|R \cap Y) = \dfrac{10}{20} \cdot \dfrac{6}{19} \cdot \dfrac{4}{18} = \dfrac{2}{57}$

6. Find the probability that you choose three red marbles.
Let $R1$, $R2$, and $R3$ be the events that the first, second, and third marbles, respectively, are red.
$P(R1 \cap R2 \cap R3) = P(R1) \cdot P(R2|R1) \cdot P(R3|R1 \cap R2) = \dfrac{10}{20} \cdot \dfrac{9}{19} \cdot \dfrac{8}{18} = \dfrac{2}{19}$

When students start finding probabilities for events A and B, it is easy to confuse the context. Have students read each exercise and highlight the key words and phrases. Suggest that they first decide whether the given events are dependent or independent. Then have them compute the probability and use it as a guide to determine whether the answer is reasonable.

INTEGRATE MATHEMATICAL PRACTICES
Focus on Modeling

MP.4 Tree diagrams are useful for understanding how to apply the formula for the probability of independent or dependent events. Ask groups of students to practice constructing tree diagrams for various given independent or dependent events A and B, and then use the multiplication rule to find the probabilities. Have them critique each other's work, switch roles, and repeat the exercise several times.

INTEGRATE MATHEMATICAL PRACTICES

Focus on Math Connections

MP.1 Using a smaller sample space may help students see the difference between independent and dependent events. Decrease the size of a sample space for an exercise and have students draw probability trees for two events. One should involve replacement and the other should not. Have students write the probability for each branch of the tree and use them to find the probability for each event.

AVOID COMMON ERRORS

Students should understand that $P(A \mid B)$ is not the same as $P(B \mid A)$, and they should not be confused in the formula $P(A \text{ and } B) = P(A) \cdot P(B \mid A)$. Emphasize that the order of the letters matters, and encourage students to articulate the expressions out loud to reinforce the difference.

© Houghton Mifflin Harcourt Publishing Company

The table shows the sums that are possible when you roll two number cubes and add the numbers. Use this information to answer the questions.

+	1	2	3	4	5	6
1	2	3	4	5	6	7
2	3	4	5	6	7	8
3	4	5	6	7	8	9
4	5	6	7	8	9	10
5	6	7	8	9	10	11
6	7	8	9	10	11	12

7. Let A be the event that you roll a 2 on the number cube represented by the row labeled 2. Let B be the event that the sum of the numbers on the cubes is 7.

a. Are these events independent or dependent? Explain.

Of the 36 outcomes in the entire table, a sum of 7 appears 6 times, so $P(B) = \frac{6}{36} = \frac{1}{6}$.

Of the 6 outcomes in the row labeled 2, a sum of 7 appears once, so $P(B|A) = \frac{1}{6}$.

Since $P(B|A) = P(B)$, events A and B are independent.

b. What is $P(A \cap B)$?

$P(A \cap B) = P(A) \cdot P(B) = \frac{1}{6} \cdot \frac{1}{6} = \frac{1}{36}$

8. Let A be the event that you roll a 3 on the number cube represented by the row labeled 3. Let B be the event that the sum of the numbers on the cubes is 5.

a. Are these events independent or dependent? Explain.

Of the 36 outcomes in the entire table, a sum of 5 appears 4 times, so $P(B) = \frac{4}{36} = \frac{1}{9}$.

Of the 6 outcomes in the row labeled 3, a sum of 5 appears once, so $P(B|A) = \frac{1}{6}$.

Since $P(B|A) \neq P(B)$, events A and B are dependent.

b. What is $P(A \cap B)$?

$P(A \cap B) = P(A) \cdot P(B|A) = \frac{1}{6} \cdot \frac{1}{6} = \frac{1}{36}$

9. A cooler contains 6 bottles of apple juice and 8 bottles of grape juice. You choose a bottle without looking, put it aside, and then choose another bottle without looking. Match each situation with its probability. More than one situation can have the same probability.

a. Choose apple juice and then grape juice. $\underline{\quad D \quad}$ $\frac{4}{13}$

b. Choose apple juice and then apple juice. $\underline{\quad A, C \quad}$ $\frac{24}{91}$

c. Choose grape juice and then apple juice. $\underline{\quad B \quad}$ $\frac{15}{91}$

d. Choose grape juice and then grape juice.

A1 = apple 1st, A2 = apple 2nd; G1 = grape 1st, G2 = grape 2nd

a. $P(A1) \cdot P(G2|A1) = \frac{6}{14} \cdot \frac{8}{13} = \frac{24}{91}$ c. $P(G1) \cdot P(A2|G1) = \frac{8}{14} \cdot \frac{6}{13} = \frac{24}{91}$

b. $P(A1) \cdot P(A2|A1) = \frac{6}{14} \cdot \frac{5}{13} = \frac{15}{91}$ d. $P(G1) \cdot P(G2|G1) = \frac{8}{14} \cdot \frac{7}{13} = \frac{4}{13}$

10. Jorge plays all tracks on a playlist with no repeats. The playlist he's listening to has 12 songs, 4 of which are his favorites.

a. What is the probability that the first song played is one of his favorites, but the next two songs are not?

Let $F1$ be the event that the first song played is a favorite. Let $NF2$ and $NF3$ be the events that the second and third songs, respectively, are not favorites. Then

$$P(F1 \cap NF2 \cap NF3) = P(F1) \cdot P(NF2|F1) \cdot P(NF3|F1 \cap NF2) = \frac{4}{12} \cdot \frac{8}{11} \cdot \frac{7}{10} = \frac{28}{165}.$$

b. What is the probability that the first three songs played are all his favorites?

Let $F1$, $F2$, and $F3$ be the events that the first, second, and third songs, respectively, are his favorites. Then $P(F1 \cap F2 \cap F3) = P(F1) \cdot P(F2|F1) \cdot P(F3|F1 \cap F2) = \frac{4}{12} \cdot \frac{3}{11} \cdot \frac{2}{10} = \frac{1}{55}.$

c. Jorge can also play the tracks on his playlist in a random order with repeats possible. If he does this, how does your answer to part b change? Explain why.

With repeats allowed, the probability that a favorite song is played is always $\frac{4}{12} = \frac{1}{3}$. The events $F1$, $F2$, and $F3$ are now independent, so you can multiply their probabilities without considering conditional probabilities:

$$P(F1 \cap F2 \cap F3) = P(F1) \cdot P(F2) \cdot P(F3) = \frac{1}{3} \cdot \frac{1}{3} \cdot \frac{1}{3} = \frac{1}{27}.$$

11. You are playing a game of bingo with friends. In this game, balls are labeled with one of the letters of the word BINGO and a number. Some of these letter-number combinations are written on a bingo card in a 5 × 5 array, and as balls are randomly drawn and announced, players mark their cards if the ball's letter-number combination appears on the cards. The first player to complete a row, column, or diagonal on a card says "Bingo!" and wins the game. In the game you're playing, there are 20 balls left. To complete a row on your card, you need N-32 called. To complete a column, you need G-51 called. To complete a diagonal, you need B-6 called.

a. What is the probability that the next two balls drawn do not have a letter-number combination you need, but the third ball does?

Let $NC1$ and $NC2$ be the events that the letter-number combination on the next ball and the ball after that, respectively, are not what you need. Let $C3$ be the event that the letter-number combination on the third ball is what you need. Then

$$P(NC1 \cap NC2 \cap C3) = P(NC1) \cdot P(NC2|NC1) \cdot P(C3|NC1 \cap NC2) = \frac{17}{20} \cdot \frac{16}{19} \cdot \frac{1}{3} = \frac{68}{285}.$$

b. What is the probability that none of the letter-number combinations you need is called from the next three balls?

Let $NC1$, $NC2$, and $NC3$ be the events that a letter-number combination you don't need is called from the next ball, the ball after that, or the ball after that, respectively. Then

$$P(NC1 \cap NC2 \cap NC3) = P(NC1) \cdot P(NC2|NC1) \cdot P(NC3|NC1 \cap NC2) = \frac{17}{20} \cdot \frac{16}{19} \cdot \frac{15}{18} = \frac{34}{57}.$$

JOURNAL

Have students use mathematical notation to define the probability of independent and dependent events. Then have students use their own words to explain what the notation means and how to use it.

12. You are talking with 3 friends, and the conversation turns to birthdays.

   a. What is the probability that no two people in your group were born in the same month?

   Use your birth month as a starting point. Let $NB1$ be the event that friend 1 has a different birth month than you. Let $NB2$ be the event that friend 2 has different birth month than you and friend 1. Let $NB3$ be the event that friend 3 has a different birth month than you, friend 1, and friend 2. Then
   $P(NB1 \cap NB2 \cap NB3) = P(NB1) \cdot P(NB2|NB1) \cdot P(NB3|NB1 \cap NB2) = \frac{11}{12} \cdot \frac{10}{12} \cdot \frac{9}{12} = \frac{55}{96}$.

   b. Is the probability that at least two people in your group were born in the same month greater or less than $\frac{1}{2}$? Explain.

   The event that at least two people in your group were born in the same month is the complement of the event in part a. So, the probability that at least two people in your group were born in the same month is $1 - \frac{55}{96} = \frac{41}{96}$, which is less than $\frac{1}{2}$.

   c. How many people in a group would it take for the probability that at least two people were born in the same month to be greater than $\frac{1}{2}$? Explain.

   Extend the results from part a:
   $P((NB1 \cap NB2 \cap NB3) \cap NB4) = P(NB1 \cap NB2 \cap NB3) \cdot P(NB4|NB1 \cap NB2 \cap NB3) = \frac{55}{96} \cdot \frac{8}{12} = \frac{55}{144}$
   The probability that at least two people in a group of 5 were born in the same month is $1 - \frac{55}{144} = \frac{89}{144}$, which is greater than $\frac{1}{2}$.

13. Construct Arguments Show how to extend the Multiplication Rule to three events A, B, and C.

   $P(A \cap B \cap C) = P((A \cap B) \cap C)$ Group events A and B as one event.

   $= P(A \cap B) \cdot P(C|A \cap B)$ Apply the Multiplication Rule to $A \cap B$ and C.

   $= P(A) \cdot P(B|A) \cdot P(C|A \cap B)$ Apply the Multiplication Rule to A and B.

14. Make a Prediction A bag contains the same number of red marbles and blue marbles. You choose a marble without looking, put it aside, and then choose another marble. Is there a greater-than-50% chance or a less-than-50% chance that you choose two marbles with different colors? Explain.

Let $R1$ and $R2$ be the events that a red marble is drawn on the first and second draws, respectively. Let $B1$ and $B2$ be the events that a blue marble is drawn on the first and second draws, respectively. Let n be the number of marbles of each color. Then $P(R1 \cap B2) = P(R1) \cdot P(B2|R1) = \frac{n}{2n} \cdot \frac{n}{2n-1} = \frac{n^2}{2n(2n-1)} = \frac{n}{2(2n-1)}$ and $P(B1 \cap R2) = P(B1) \cdot P(R2|B1) = \frac{n}{2n} \cdot \frac{n}{2n-1} = \frac{n^2}{2n(2n-1)} = \frac{n}{2(2n-1)}$. Since the events $R1 \cap B2$ and $B1 \cap R2$ are mutually exclusive, you can add their probabilities to get the probability of choosing two marbles with different colors:

$\frac{n}{2(2n-1)} + \frac{n}{2(2n-1)} = \frac{2n}{2(2n-1)} = \frac{n}{2n-1} = \frac{1}{2-\frac{1}{n}}$. Since the denominator of $\frac{1}{2-\frac{1}{n}}$ is always less than 2 for $n > 0$, the fraction is always greater than $\frac{1}{2}$. So, there is always a greater-than-50% chance that you choose two marbles with different colors.

Lesson Performance Task

To prepare for an accuracy landing competition, a team of skydivers has laid out targets in a large open field. During practice sessions, team members attempt to land inside a target.

Two rectangular targets are shown on each field. Assuming a skydiver lands at random in the field, find the probabilities that the skydiver lands inside the specified target(s).

1. Calculate the probabilities using the targets shown here.

 a. $P(A)$ a. 0.12

 b. $P(B)$ b. 0.2

       c. 0

 c. $P(A \cap B)$ d. 0.32

       e. 0

 d. $P(A \cup B)$ f. 0

 e. $P(A|B)$

 f. $P(B|A)$

2. Calculate the probabilities using the targets shown here.

 a. $P(A)$ a. 0.36

 b. $P(B)$ b. 0.14

       c. 0.04

 c. $P(A \cap B)$ d. 0.46

       e. $\frac{2}{7}$

 d. $P(A \cup B)$ f. $\frac{1}{9}$

 e. $P(A|B)$

 f. $P(B|A)$

3. Calculate the probabilities using the targets shown here.

 a. $P(A)$ a. 0.35

 b. $P(B)$ b. 0.01

       c. 0.01

       d. 0.35

 c. $P(A \cap B)$ e. 1

 d. $P(A \cup B)$ f. $\frac{1}{35}$

 e. $P(A|B)$

 f. $P(B|A)$

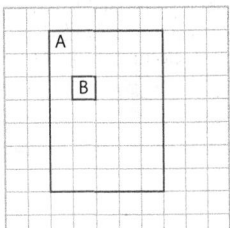

© Houghton Mifflin Harcourt Publishing Company

© Houghton Mifflin Harcourt Publishing Company

INTEGRATE MATHEMATICAL PRACTICES
Focus on Reasoning

MP.2 Two skydiver landing rectangles are outlined on a 10×10 grid. Describe the rectangles if the given probability is true.

- $P(A \text{ and } B) = 0$ The rectangles do not intersect.
- $P(A \text{ or } B) = 1$ the rectangles cover the entire grid.
- $P(A|B) = 1$ Rectangle B is contained in rectangle A.
- $P(B|A) = 0$ The rectangles do not intersect.

INTEGRATE MATHEMATICAL PRACTICES
Focus on Critical Thinking

MP.3 In the 10×10 grid for Question 2 of the Lesson Performance Task, rectangle A measures 6×6 units and rectangle B measures 7×2. Find the dimensions and amount of overlap of two rectangles different from rectangles A and B for which the answers to Questions 2c and 2d are unchanged.   Sample answer: rectangle A measures 6×5; rectangle B measures 10×2; amount of overlap: 4 squares.

EXTENSION ACTIVITY

Supply students with grid paper. Ask them to draw a 10×10 grid representing a skydiver landing area. Then have them draw two rectangles, A and B, so that $P(A \text{ and } B) = 0.06$ and $P(A \text{ or } B) = 0.58$. Ask them to find $P(A | B)$ and $P(B | A)$.   Many rectangles A and B are possible. All drawings must show two rectangles with an overlap of 6 squares. Additionally, Area rectangle A, in its entirety, plus Area rectangle B, in its entirety, must equal 64 square units. Sample: rectangle A measuring 6×4 units overlaps by 6 squares rectangle B measuring 8×5 units; $P(A|B) = \frac{3}{20}$ and $P(B|A) = \frac{1}{4}$.

Scoring Rubric

2 points: Student correctly solves the problem and explains his/her reasoning.

1 point: Student shows good understanding of the problem but does not fully solve or explain his/her reasoning.

0 points: Student does not demonstrate understanding of the problem.

Dependent Events   **1176**

Study Guide Review

ASSESSMENT AND INTERVENTION

Assign or customize module reviews.

MODULE PERFORMANCE TASK

Mathematical Practices: MP.1, MP.2, MP.4, MP.7, MP.8
S-CP.A.1, S-CP.B.6, S-CP.B.8

SUPPORTING STUDENT REASONING

Students should begin this problem by focusing on what information they will need. Here are some issues they might bring up.

- **How to find the probability of choosing one ace from a deck of 52 cards:** There are 4 aces in a deck of 52 cards, so the probability is $\frac{4}{52} = \frac{1}{13}$.

- **If choosing two aces or three aces in a row involves conditional probability:** Yes, because the second event of choosing a second ace in a row depends on a first ace having been chosen. Also, the third event of choosing a third ace in a row depends on the previous two choices being aces.

- **If choosing four cards in a row in which none are aces involves conditional probability:** Yes, because each successive event depends on the previous choice not being an ace.

Conditional Probability and Independence of Events

Essential Question: How can you use conditional probability and independence of events to solve real-world problems?

Key Vocabulary
conditional probability
  (probabilidad condicional)
independent events
  (eventos independientes)
dependent events
  (eventos dependientes)

KEY EXAMPLE (Lesson 22.1)

Find the probability that a black card drawn from the deck is a queen. (The deck is a standard one of 52 cards.)

The deck has 52 cards and 26 of them are black, so the probability of drawing a black card is $P(B) = \frac{26}{52}$.

There are 2 black queens in the deck, so the probability of drawing one of them from the deck is

$P(Q \cap B) = \frac{2}{52} = \frac{1}{26}$.

Using the formula for conditional probability, $P(Q \mid B) = \dfrac{P(Q \cap B)}{P(B)} = \dfrac{\frac{2}{52}}{\frac{26}{52}} = \dfrac{1}{13}$.

KEY EXAMPLE (Lesson 22.2)

Jim rolled a set of two number cubes. If these are standard 6-sided number cubes, what is the probability of obtaining 12? (That means the values of the top faces add up to 12.)

The only way to get 12 is for both of the top sides of the number cubes to be 6. The events of obtaining 6s are independent. Each of these events has the probability of $\frac{1}{6}$ (1 out of 6 options), so the probability of getting 12 is $\frac{1}{6} \cdot \frac{1}{6} = \frac{1}{36}$ by the multiplication rule.

KEY EXAMPLE (Lesson 22.3)

What is the probability of selecting 2 blue marbles out of a jar of 20, half of them blue? How did you obtain it?

Let event A be selecting a blue marble on the first pick. Let event B be selecting a blue marble on the second one. The first marble is not replaced, so these are dependent events. Of the 20 marbles, half of them are blue, so $P(A) = \frac{1}{2}$. Of the remaining 19 marbles, 9 of them are blue, so the probability of selecting one is $P(B) = \frac{9}{19}$. Thus, the probability of selecting 2 blue marbles is $P(A \text{ and } B) = \frac{1}{2} \cdot \frac{9}{19} = \frac{9}{38}$, using the multiplication rule.

SCAFFOLDING SUPPORT

- A common error in these types of problems is to forget to subtract one from the sample space after each choice. For example, for the first pick, the sample space is the entire deck of 52 cards. Each time one card is picked, the sample space decreases by 1.

- Students should realize that the probability of not picking an ace can be thought of as the probability of picking a card other than an ace. So for the first pick, there are $\frac{48}{52}$ ways for the first card to not be an ace.

Exercises

Determine the conditional probability. *(Lesson 22.1)*

1. What is the probability that a diamond that is drawn from the deck is a queen?

$$P(Q \mid D) = \frac{1}{13}$$

2. What is the probability that a queen drawn is a diamond?

$$P(D \mid Q) = \frac{1}{4}$$

Show that the following situation refers to independent events. *(Lesson 22.2)*

3. Isabelle believes that right- and left-footed soccer players are equally likely to score goals. She collected data from 260 players from a local soccer league. Using the following two-way frequency table, show that being right-footed and scoring goals are independent events.

	Right-Footed	Left-Footed	Total
Has scored a goal	39	13	52
Has not scored a goal	156	52	208
TOTAL	195	65	260

The events are independent because $P(A \text{ and } B) = P(A) \cdot P(B) = \frac{3}{20}$.

Identify whether a situation involves independent or dependent events. *(Lesson 22.3)*

4. Jim has 2 blue, 2 green, and 2 black socks in his drawer. He picks out 2 socks, one after the other. Determine the probability of him getting a matching pair of blue socks.

dependent

MODULE PERFORMANCE TASK

Drawing Aces

You have a standard deck of 52 playing cards. You pick three cards in a row without replacement. What is the probability that all three are aces?

Now you replace the three cards, shuffle, and pick four cards in a row without replacement. What is the probability that none are aces?

Begin by making notes in the space below about your plan for approaching this problem. Then complete the task on your own paper, using words, numbers, or diagrams to explain how you reached your conclusions.

© Houghton Mifflin Harcourt Publishing Company

SAMPLE SOLUTION

Let event A be the event that the first card is an ace, so $P(A) = \frac{4}{52} = \frac{1}{13}$ (4 out of 52 options). Let event B be the event that the second card is an ace as well, so $P(B|A) = \frac{3}{51} = \frac{1}{17}$. This is because out of the 51 remaining cards, 3 are aces. Use the multiplication rule.

$$P(A \text{ and } B) = P(A) \cdot P(B|A) = \frac{1}{13} \cdot \frac{1}{17} = \frac{1}{221}$$

Let event C be picking another ace out of the remaining 50 cards. There are 2 aces left, so

$$P(C|A \text{ and } B) = \frac{2}{50} = \frac{1}{25}.$$

By the multiplication rule:

$$P(A \text{ and } B \text{ and } C) = P(A \text{ and } B) \cdot P(C|A \text{ and } B)$$

$$= \frac{1}{221} \cdot \frac{1}{25} = \frac{1}{5525}$$

The probability of obtaining three aces in three picks is

$$P(A \text{ and } B \text{ and } C) = \frac{1}{5525} \approx 0.00018.$$

Now, find the probability that four out of four cards picked are not aces. 48 out of 52 cards are not aces in the first draw, then 47 out of 51, and so on.

$$P(A) = \frac{48}{52} \cdot \frac{47}{51} \cdot \frac{46}{50} \cdot \frac{45}{49} \approx 0.719$$

DISCUSSION OPPORTUNITIES

- Why is the probability of getting 4 aces in a game of cards so low?

- Why is the probability of getting 3 aces in a row without replacement lower than the probability of getting 3 aces in a row with replacement?

Assessment Rubric

2 points: Student correctly solves the problem and explains his/her reasoning.

1 point: Student shows good understanding of the problem but does not fully solve or explain.

0 points: Student does not demonstrate understanding of the problem.

Ready to Go On?

ASSESS MASTERY

Use the assessment on this page to determine if students have mastered the concepts and standards covered in this module.

ASSESSMENT AND INTERVENTION

Access Ready to Go On? assessment online, and receive instant scoring, feedback, and customized intervention or enrichment.

ADDITIONAL RESOURCES

Response to Intervention Resources

- Reteach Worksheets

Differentiated Instruction Resources

- Reading Strategies **EL**
- Success for English Learners **EL**
- Challenge Worksheets

Assessment Resources

- Leveled Module Quizzes

(Ready) to Go On?

22.1–22.3 Conditional Probability and Independence of Events

- Online Homework
- Hints and Help
- Extra Practice

Compute the requested probability and explain how you obtained it.

1. A farmer wants to know if a particular fertilizer can cause blackberry shrubs to produce fruit early. Using the following two-way table, compute the probability of a plant producing fruit early without receiving fertilizer. *(Lesson 22.1)*

	Early Fruit	No Fruit	Total
Received fertilizer	37	3	40
Did not receive fertilizer	19	21	40
TOTAL	56	24	80

In the study, 40 of the shrubs were not given fertilizer. Of these, 19 produced early fruit, so the desired probability is $P(\text{early}|\text{no fertilizer}) = \frac{19}{40} = 47.5\%$.

2. Lisa flipped the same coin twice. Determine the probability of the coin landing on tails on the second try. *(Lesson 22.2)*

The event of the coin landing on tails on the second try does not depend on the first try, and thus its probability is $\frac{1}{2}$.

3. Lisa flipped the same coin three times. What is the probability she obtained all tails? *(Lesson 22.2)*

The events of the coin landing on tails on different tries are independent, and thus the probability of flipping tails is $\frac{1}{2} \cdot \frac{1}{2} \cdot \frac{1}{2} = \frac{1}{8}$.

ESSENTIAL QUESTION

4. A jar contains 12 pennies, 5 nickels, and 18 quarters. You select 2 coins at random, one after the other. Does selecting a nickel affect the probability of selecting another nickel? Does not selecting a dime affect the probability of selecting a nickel? Describe how you would find the probability of selecting 2 nickels.

Answers may vary. Sample: A dime cannot be selected, so not picking one does not affect the second pick. These are independent events. Selecting two nickels in a row and not replacing the first means that there will be fewer coins to choose from on the second try. These are dependent events. Accordingly, the probability of selecting two nickels in a row is the product of selecting one and then selecting another given that a first one has been picked: $P(\text{two nickels}) = \frac{5}{35} \cdot \frac{4}{34} = \frac{1}{7} \cdot \frac{2}{17} = \frac{2}{119}$

© Houghton Mifflin Harcourt Publishing Company

COMMON CORE	**Common Core Standards**

Lesson	Items	Content Standards	Mathematical Practices
22.1	1	**S-CP.A.4**	**MP.6**
22.2	2	**S-CP.A.2**	**MP.6**
22.2	3	**S-CP.A.2**	**MP.2**

Assessment Readiness

1. Are the events independent? Choose Yes or No for each situation.

   A. Picking a penny and a marble out of a
   jar of pennies and marbles.   ● Yes   ○ No

   B. Drawing cards from a deck to form a
   4-card hand.   ○ Yes   ● No

   C. Rolling a 3 on a fair number cbe and
   flipping tails on a fair coin.   ● Yes   ○ No

2. Of the boys running for School President, 2 are juniors and 3 are seniors. Of the girls who are running, 4 are juniors and 1 is a senior. Decide whether the situation has a probability of $\frac{2}{5}$. Select Yes or No for A–C.

   A. A girl wins.   ○ Yes   ● No
   B. A candidate who is a boy is a junior. ● Yes   ○ No
   C. A candidate who is a junior is a boy. ○ Yes   ● No

3. You shuffle a standard deck of playing cards and deal one card. What is the probability that you deal an ace or a club? Explain your reasoning.

   $\frac{4}{13}$; sample answer: Four of the 52 cards in the deck are aces, so $P(ace) = \frac{4}{52}$. Thirteen of the cards are clubs, so $P(club) = \frac{13}{52}$. One of the cards, the ace of clubs, is both an ace and a club, so $P(ace \text{ or } clubs)$

   $= \frac{4}{52} + \frac{13}{52} - \frac{1}{52} = \frac{16}{52} = \frac{4}{13}$

4. Claude has 2 jars of marbles. Each jar has 10 blue marbles and 10 green marbles. He selects 2 marbles from each jar. What is the probability they are all blue? Explain your reasoning.

   About 0.056; sample answer: The probability of choosing 2 blue marbles from 1 jar is $\frac{1}{2} \cdot \frac{9}{19} = \frac{9}{38}$, a pair of dependent events. Picking from different jars is independent, so the probability is $\frac{9}{38} \cdot \frac{9}{38} = \frac{81}{1444} \approx 0.056$.

Assessment Readiness

ASSESSMENT AND INTERVENTION

Assign ready-made or customized practice tests to prepare students for high-stakes tests.

ADDITIONAL RESOURCES

Assessment Resources

- Leveled Module Quizzes: Modified, B

AVOID COMMON ERRORS

Item 4 Some students will recognize that there are two events but will not see that there are four—two marbles are picked from each of two jars. Remind students to read carefully and consider every event.

COMMON CORE Common Core Standards

Lesson	Items	Content Standards	Mathematical Practices
22.2	1	S-CP.A.2	MP.2
22.1, 21.1	2*	S-CP.A.1, S-CP.B.6	MP.4
21.4	3*	S-CP.B.7	MP.3
22.3	4	S-CP.A.5	MP.3

* Item integrates mixed review concepts from previous modules or a previous course.

Probability and Decision Making

ESSENTIAL QUESTION:

Answer: Understanding probability can help you solve real-world problems concerning long-term risk.

PROFESSIONAL DEVELOPMENT VIDEO

Professional Development Video

Author Juli Dixon models successful teaching practices in an actual high-school classroom.

Professional Development
my.hrw.com

MODULE **23**

Probability and Decision Making

Essential Question: How can you use probability to solve real-world problems?

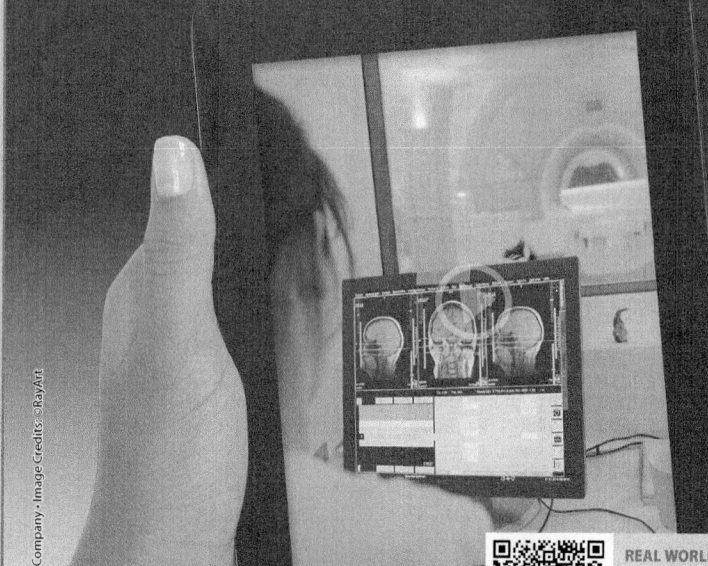

© Houghton Mifflin Harcourt Publishing Company • Image Credits: ··RayArt Graphics/Alamy

REAL WORLD VIDEO
Physicians today use many sophisticated tests and technologies to help diagnose illnesses, but they must still consider probability in their diagnoses and decisions about treatment.

MODULE PERFORMANCE TASK PREVIEW

What's the Diagnosis?

The science of medicine has come a long way since surgeries were performed by the neighborhood barber and leeches were used to treat just about every ailment. Nevertheless, modern medicine isn't perfect, and widely used tests for diagnosing illnesses aren't always 100 percent accurate. In this module, you'll learn how probability can be used to measure the reliability of tests and then use what you learned to evaluate decisions about a diagnosis.

Module 23   **1181**

DIGITAL TEACHER EDITION

Access a full suite of teaching resources when and where you need them:

- Access content online or offline
- Customize lessons to share with your class
- Communicate with your students in real-time
- View student grades and data instantly to target your instruction where it is needed most

PERSONAL MATH TRAINER

Assessment and Intervention

Assign automatically graded homework, quizzes, tests, and intervention activities. Prepare your students with updated, Common Core-aligned practice tests.

Are (YOU) Ready?

Complete these exercises to review skills you will need for this module.

Probability of Simple Events

- Online Homework
- Hints and Help
- Extra Practice

Example 1

Two 6-sided conventional number cubes are tossed. What is the probability that their sum is greater than 8?

+	1	2	3	4	5	6
1	2	3	4	5	6	7
2	3	4	5	6	7	8
3	4	5	6	7	8	9
4	5	6	7	8	9	10
5	6	7	8	9	10	11
6	7	8	9	10	11	12

There are 10 values greater than 8 and a total number of 36 values.

$$\frac{\text{number of favorable outcomes}}{\text{total number of outcomes}} = \frac{10}{36} = \frac{5}{18}$$

The probability that the sum of the two number cubes is greater than 8 is $\frac{5}{18}$.

Two number cubes are tossed. Find each probability.

1. The sum is prime.

$\frac{5}{12}$

2. The product is prime.

$\frac{1}{6}$

3. The product is a perfect square.

$\frac{2}{9}$

Making Predictions with Probability

Example 2

A fly lands on the target shown. What is the probability that the fly landed on red?

The area of the entire target is 6^2, or 36 units^2.

Red area is: $A = \pi r^2 = \pi(1)^2 = \pi$.

$$\frac{\text{number of favorable outcomes}}{\text{total number of outcomes}} = \frac{\pi}{36} \approx 8.7\%$$

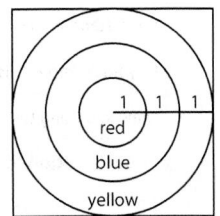

Use the target to find the percent probability, to the nearest tenth.

4. Blue

26.2%

5. Yellow or red

52.4%

6. Not within a circle

21.5%

Are You Ready?

ASSESS READINESS

Use the assessment on this page to determine if students need strategic or intensive intervention for the module's prerequisite skills.

ASSESSMENT AND INTERVENTION

🔺 **RtI** Response to Intervention **TIER 1, TIER 2, TIER 3 SKILLS**

Personal Math Trainer will automatically create a standards-based, personalized intervention assignment for your students, targeting each student's individual needs!

ADDITIONAL RESOURCES

See the table below for a full list of intervention resources available for this module.

Response to Intervention Resources also includes:

- Tier 2 Skill Pre-Tests for each Module
- Tier 2 Skill Post-Tests for each skill

Response to Intervention			Differentiated Instruction
Tier 1	**Tier 2**	**Tier 3**	
Lesson Intervention Worksheets	Strategic Intervention Skills Intervention Worksheets	Intensive Intervention Worksheets available online	
Reteach 23.1 Reteach 23.2	11 Making Predictions with Probability 15 Probability of Simple Events	Building Block Skills 6, 12, 39, 95	Challenge worksheets Extend the Math Lesson Activities in TE

Using Probability to Make Fair Decisions

Common Core Math Standards

The student is expected to:

COMMON CORE S-MD.B.6(+)

Use probabilities to make fair decisions (e.g., drawing by lots, using a random number generator).

Mathematical Practices

COMMON CORE MP.4 Modeling

Language Objective

Explain to a partner how to use a random number generator to simulate an experiment.

ENGAGE

Essential Question: How can you use probability to help you make fair decisions?

Probability offers a method for representing a population in an unbiased way so that decisions can be made fairly.

PREVIEW: LESSON PERFORMANCE TASK

View the Engage section online. Discuss the photograph. Ask students to describe the game that is pictured. Then preview the Lesson Performance Task.

23.1 Using Probability to Make Fair Decisions

Essential Question: How can you use probability to help you make fair decisions?

Resource Locker

🧭 Explore   Using Probabilities When Drawing at Random

You are sharing a veggie supreme pizza with friends. There is one slice left and you and a friend both want it. Both of you have already had two slices. What is a fair way to solve this problem?

(A) Suppose you both decide to have the same amount of pizza. This means that the last slice will be cut into two pieces. Describe a fair way to split this last piece.

Possible answer: One person gets to cut the pizza into two approximately equal pieces; the other person gets to choose which piece he or she wants.

(B) Suppose instead you decide that one of you will get the whole slice. Complete the table so that the result of each option gives a fair chance for each of you to get the last slice. Why do each of these possibilities give a fair chance?

Option	Result (you get last slice)	Result (friend gets last slice)
Flip a coin	Heads	Tails
Roll a standard die	2, 4, 6	1, 3, 5
Play Rock, Paper, Scissors	You win.	You lose.
Draw lots using two straws of different lengths	Long straw	Short straw

For each option, both results have a probability of $\frac{1}{2}$, so both people have the same chance of getting the last slice.

Reflect

1. Suppose, when down to the last piece, you tell your friend, "I will cut the last piece, and I will choose which piece you get." Why is this method unfair?
   Possible answer: I could cut the slice into two pieces with one much larger than the other and then choose the larger piece for myself.

Module 23   **1183**   Lesson 1

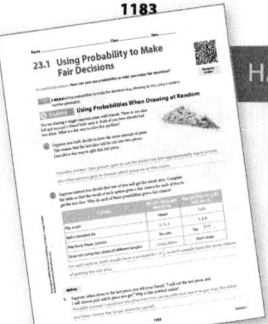

HARDCOVER PAGES 977–984

Turn to these pages to find this lesson in the hardcover student edition.

2. Your friend suggests that you shoot free throws to decide who gets the last piece. Use probability to explain why this might not be a fair way to decide.

Shooting free throws is not a random event. The player with more skill will have a greater

probability of winning.

🧭 Explain 1   Awarding a Prize to a Random Winner

Suppose you have to decide how to award a prize to a person at an event. You might want every person attending to have the same chance of winning, or you might want people to do something to improve their chance of winning. How can you award the prize fairly?

Example 1   Explain whether each method of awarding a prize is fair.

Ⓐ The sponsor of an event wants to award a door prize to one attendee. Each person in attendance is given a ticket with a unique number on it. All of the numbers are placed in a bowl, and one is drawn at random. The person with the matching number wins the prize.

The method of awarding a door prize is fair. Each number has the same chance of being chosen, so each attendee has an equal probability of winning the prize. If n attendees are at the event, then the probability of winning the prize is $\frac{1}{n}$ for each attendee.

Ⓑ A fundraiser includes a raffle in which half of the money collected goes to a charity, and the other half goes to one winner. Tickets are sold for $5 each. Copies of all the tickets are placed in a box, and one ticket is drawn at random. The person with the matching ticket wins the raffle.

The method of choosing a raffle winner is (fair)/not fair because

each _____ticket_____ has an equal probability of being drawn.

Reflect

3. In Example 1B, the probability may not be the same for each person to win the raffle. Explain why the method is still fair.

For each ticket, the probability of drawing the matching ticket is the same. A person who

buys more tickets should have a better chance of winning.

Your Turn

4. Each month, a company wants to award a special parking space to an employee at random. Describe a fair way to do this. Include a way to ensure that a person doesn't win a second time before each employee has won once.

Possible answer: Choose an employee's name at random from a list of all employees.

Each month, remove the previous winners from the list. Once every employee has won

once, begin again with the list of all employees.

PROFESSIONAL DEVELOPMENT

 Integrate Mathematical Practices

This lesson provides an opportunity to address Mathematical Practice **MP.4**, which calls for students to "represent real-world problems with mathematics." Students are already familiar with some aspects of probability; in this lesson, they will explore random sampling and the probabilities of events. Then they will use probabilities to help them explore the connections among random samples, convenience samples, and fair decision-making.

EXPLORE

Using Probabilities When Drawing at Random

INTEGRATE TECHNOLOGY

Students have the option of doing the Explore activity either in the book or online.

QUESTIONING STRATEGIES

❓ How can you find the probability that an event does not occur from the probability that an event does occur? If the events are independent, the probability that an event does not occur is the complement of the probability $P(E)$ that the event does occur, or $1 - P(E)$.

❓ How do you know if you have chosen a random sample? Possible answer: It is random when the probability of your selection has no predictability, and all choices are equally likely.

EXPLAIN 1

Awarding a Prize to a Random Winner

AVOID COMMON ERRORS

Students may assume that a certain method of awarding a prize is fair without finding the probabilities of the possible outcomes. Remind students that they can be sure a method is fair only if they can show, using probability, that each participant has an equal chance of winning.

QUESTIONING STRATEGIES

❓ How can you use probability to help make a game fair? You can use probability to help make sure every player has an equal chance of winning.

EXPLAIN 2

Solving Real-World Problems Fairly

INTEGRATE TECHNOLOGY

The random number generator of a calculator (**rand**) produces a random decimal number between 0 and 1. This should not be confused with the command to generate random integers, **randInt(1,n)**, which produces random integers from 1 to n. Point out that spreadsheets can also be used to generate random numbers. Students can use spreadsheets to add the number of trials for an experiment, as well.

QUESTIONING STRATEGIES

How could you use your calculator and the random number generator to generate random integers? Possible answer: Enter **randInt(1,n)** into the calculator and replace n with the highest integer you expect to generate.

Will every trial using the random number generator produce the same results? Explain. No; since the integers are generated randomly, each trial should produce a different sequence of random numbers.

Explain 2 **Solving Real-World Problems Fairly**

You can use a random number generator to choose a winner of a prize.

Example 2 Use a problem solving plan.

A class of 24 students sold 65 magazine subscriptions to raise money for a trip. As an incentive to participate, you will award a prize to one student in the class. Describe a method of awarding the prize fairly. Use probabilities to explain why your method is fair for the students listed.

Student	Subscriptions Sold
Miri	5
Liam	2
Madison	0

 Analyze Information

Identify the important information.
- There are __24__ students.
- They sold __65__ magazine subscriptions.
- There is one prize, so there will be one winner.

 Formulate a Plan

To be fair, students who sold more subscriptions should have a better chance of winning the prize than the students who sold fewer.
Find a method of assigning and choosing chances to win so that the chance of winning is proportional to the number of subscriptions sold.

Solve

The class sold 65 subscriptions, so assign the numbers 1–65 to the students. Each student gets as many numbers as the number of subscriptions he or she sold.

Student	Subscriptions Sold	Numbers Assigned	Probability of Winning
Miri	5	1–5	$\frac{5}{65} \approx$ 0.077
Liam	2	6, 7	$\frac{2}{65} \approx$ 0.031
Madison	0	none	$\frac{0}{65} =$ 0

Then use a calculator to find a random integer from 1 to 65. If the result is 7, then Liam wins the prize.

 Justify and Evaluate

This method seems (fair)/unfair because it gives everyone who sold subscriptions a chance of winning. You could award a prize to the student who sold the most subscriptions, but this might not be possible if multiple students all sold the same number, and it might not seem fair if some students have better access to buyers than others.

© Houghton Mifflin Harcourt Publishing Company

COLLABORATIVE LEARNING

Small Group Activity

Have groups of students brainstorm various examples of sampling methods that should produce random, unbiased samples. Have them compare these to methods that would be biased. For example, putting the names of all students into a hat and then drawing ten names should produce a random sample, while selecting student first names that begin with the letter S should produce a biased sample, because first names begin with some letters of the alphabet much more often than with other letters, such as X.

5. A student suggests that it would be better to assign the numbers to students randomly rather than in numerical order. Would doing this affect the probability of winning?

No, each number has the same probability of being chosen, so it does not matter which numbers are assigned to each student.

6. A charity is giving a movie ticket for every 10 coats donated. Jacob collected 8 coats, Ben collected 6, and Ryan and Zak each collected 3. They decide to donate the coats together so that they will get 2 movie tickets. Describe how to use a random number generator to decide which 2 boys get a ticket.

Possible answer: The boys collected a total of 20 coats. Assign Jacob numbers 1–8, Ben 9–14, Ryan 15–17, and Zak 18–20. Use the function randInt (1, 20) to generate 2 random numbers. If the second number is assigned to the boy who won the first ticket, generate another number until someone else wins the second ticket.

⚙ Explain 3 Solving the Problem of Points

The decision-making situation that you will apply in this example is based on the "Problem of Points" that was studied by the French mathematicians Blaise Pascal and Pierre de Fermat in the 17th century. Their work on the problem launched the branch of mathematics now known as probability.

Example 3 Two students, Lee and Rory, find a box containing 100 baseball cards. To determine who should get the cards, they decide to play a game with the rules shown.

Game Rules
• One of the students repeatedly tosses a coin.
• When the coin lands heads up, Lee gets a point.
• When the coin lands tails up, Rory gets a point.
• The first student to reach 20 points wins the game and gets the baseball cards.

As Lee and Rory are playing the game they are interrupted and are unable to continue. How should the 100 baseball cards be divided between the students given that the game was interrupted at the described moment?

Ⓐ When they are interrupted, Lee has 19 points and Rory has 17 points.

At most, 3 coin tosses would have been needed for someone to win the game.

Make a list of all possible results using H for heads and T for tails. Circle the outcomes in which Lee wins the game.

0T, 3H	1T, 2H	2T, 1H	3T, 0H
HHHH	THH	TTH	TTT
	HTH	THT	
	HHT	HTT	

© Houghton Mifflin Harcourt Publishing Company

AVOID COMMON ERRORS

Some students may not pay attention to the steps used for the problem-solving model. Point out the importance of each step in giving meaning to a problem rather than simply jumping to a solution attempt.

EXPLAIN 3

Solving the Problem of Points

INTEGRATE MATHEMATICAL PROCESSES
Focus on Math Connections

MP.1 Point out that making a list of all possible results for a game helps students see the sample space that is used for the game, which in turn is necessary to calculate the probability of winning the game.

QUESTIONING STRATEGIES

❓ How can you describe the sample space for the results of tossing a coin? Possible answer: Determine the number of times the coin is tossed and then represent the results of each toss of the coin with "H" for heads and "T" for tails.

❓ When does tossing a coin simulate the fair outcome of a game? Possible answer: When there are only two equally likely outcomes possible for a game, then the results of tossing a coin can simulate the two possible outcomes.

DIFFERENTIATE INSTRUCTION

Modeling

🖩 Some students may benefit from a hands-on approach for learning how to simulate a game with the random integer generator. For example, pairs of students can play a game to see which student gets the highest point total after 10 rolls of a die. Have them discuss the calculator command that is appropriate (**randInt(1,6)**), and how to proceed with the game. Then have students compare their results, declare a winner, play the game again, and compare the results of both games.

Students may not be sure which model to choose to represent the results of a game. Encourage them to determine the model that best simulates the expected results of the game, and then use technology or other means to describe the model mathematically.

There are 8 possible results. Lee wins in 7 of them and Rory wins in 1 of them.

The probability of Lee winning is $\frac{7}{8}$, so he should get $\frac{7}{8}$ of the cards which is 87.5 cards. The probability of Rory winning is $\frac{1}{8}$, so he should get $\frac{1}{8}$ of the cards which is 12.5 cards. Rather than split a card into two, they might decide to flip a coin for that card or to let Lee have it because he was more likely to win it.

(B) When they are interrupted, Lee has 18 points and Rory has 17 points.

At most, ____four____ more coin tosses would have been needed.

List all possible results. Circle the outcomes in which Lee wins.

0T, 4H	1T, 3H	2T, 2H	3T, 1H	4T, 0H
HHHH	THHH	TTHH	TTTH	TTTT
	HTHH	THTH	TTHT	
	HHTH	THHT	THTT	
	HHHT	HTTH	HTTT	
		HTHT		
		HHTT		

There are __16__ possible results. Lee wins in __11__ of them and Rory wins in __5__ of them.

The probability of Lee winning is $\frac{11}{16}$, so he should get __69__ cards.

The probability of Rory winning is $\frac{5}{16}$, so he should get __31__ cards.

Reflect

7. **Discussion** A student suggests that a better way to divide the cards in Example 3B would be to split the cards based on the number of points earned so far. Which method do you think is better?

   Possible answer: This suggestion would result in dividing the cards about evenly

   (51 for Lee; 49 for Rory). The solution in the example comes closer to the intended result

   that one student wins all of the cards.

Your Turn

8. Describe a situation where the game is interrupted, resulting in the cards needing to be divided evenly between the two players.

   Possible answer: If the game is interrupted when the players are tied, they each have a

   probability of winning equal to $\frac{1}{2}$.

LANGUAGE SUPPORT EL

Connect Vocabulary

Students may have difficulty understanding the word *random* as it relates to probability. When discussing randomness with students, you may want to conduct a short experiment with the names of 10 students who play basketball and of 10 students chosen by the last digits of their phone numbers. Ask students how they would design an experiment to find the average height of a high school student. Have them decide which group of students would be a representative sample of the heights of high school students and why.

9. Discussion In the situation described in the Explore, suppose you like the crust and your friend does not. Is there a fair way to cut the slice of pizza that might not result in two equal size pieces?

Possible answer: If you cut the slice so that one piece has all of the crust but less topping, then the crust piece might be larger, but your friend might find it more desirable.

10. How would the solution to Example 2 need to change if there were two prizes to award? Assume that you do not want one student to win both prizes.

You could award the first prize in the same way. Once the first prize is awarded, either all the numbers assigned to that winner have to be ignored when randomly generating a second winning number, or the winner's numbers have to be reassigned to people with the highest numbers. For example, if Liam won the first prize, then his numbers would be reassigned to the person who has the two highest numbers, 64 and 65. Then use randInt (1, 63) to award the second prize.

11. Essential Question Check-In Describe a way to use probability to make a fair choice of a raffle winner.

If people are buying raffle tickets, then each of the n tickets should have the same $\left(\frac{1}{n}\right)$ chance of winning. You can select a ticket randomly from a box, or use a random number generator to select the winning number.

☆ Evaluate: Homework and Practice

- Online Homework
- Hints and Help
- Extra Practice

1. You and a friend split the cost of a package of five passes to a climbing gym. Describe a way that you could fairly decide who gets to use the fifth pass.

Possible answer: You could split the cost of a sixth pass to the climbing gym so that you each get a third visit for half of the price of an additional pass. Or you could toss a coin and the winner gets the fifth pass. Tossing a coin gives each of you a 50% (or equal) chance of winning the last pass.

2. In addition to prizes for first, second, and third place, the organizers of a race have a prize that they want each participant to have an equal chance of winning. Describe a fair method of choosing a winner for this prize.

If the participants in the race each have a number, the organizers could select a number at random by using a random number generator or by putting slips of paper with each number into a box and randomly choosing one.

Exercise	Depth of Knowledge (D.O.K.)	COMMON CORE Mathematical Practices
1–3	**1** Recall of Information	**MP.2** Reasoning
4	**3** Strategic Thinking	**MP.1** Problem Solving
5–7	**1** Recall of Information	**MP.2** Reasoning
8	**3** Strategic Thinking	**MP.1** Problem Solving
9–11	**1** Recall of Information	**MP.2** Reasoning
12	**3** Strategic Thinking	**MP.1** Problem Solving

ELABORATE

QUESTIONING STRATEGIES

? How can you use probability in fair decision-making? Probability gives a quantitative way to choose a random, unbiased sample, which in turn can be used to represent a population so that fair decisions can be made.

SUMMARIZE THE LESSON

? How can a random number generator be used to simulate an experiment? Possible answer: Each possible result of an experiment can be assigned a number. When that number is produced by the random number generator, it simulates the corresponding experimental result.

EVALUATE

ASSIGNMENT GUIDE

Concepts and Skills	Practice
Explore Using Probabilities when Drawing at Random	Exercises 1–4
Example 1 Awarding a Prize to a Random Winner	Exercises 9–16
Example 2 Solving Real-World Problems Fairly	Exercises 5–8
Example 3 Solving the Problem of Points	Exercise 17

INTEGRATE MATHEMATICAL PRACTICES

Focus on Math Connections

MP.1 You may want to point out some different samples of a population to help students understand how random samples are different from non-random samples: A systematic sample uses a rule or pattern (like every third student) to select the members; a self-selected sample is one comprised of volunteers; and a convenience sample (like all students in first period lunch) chooses easy to reach members of the population.

Decide whether each method is a fair way to choose a winner if each person should have an equal chance of winning. Explain your answer by evaluating each probability.

3. Roll a standard die. Meri wins if the result is less than 3. Riley wins if the result is greater than 3.
   Not fair; $P(\text{Meri wins}) = \frac{2}{6} = \frac{1}{3}$; $P(\text{Riley wins}) = \frac{3}{6} = \frac{1}{2}$

4. Draw a card from a standard deck of cards. Meri wins if the card is red. Riley wins if the card is black.
   Fair; $P(\text{Meri wins}) = \frac{26}{52} = \frac{1}{2}$; $P(\text{Riley wins}) = \frac{26}{52} = \frac{1}{2}$

5. Flip a coin. Meri wins if it lands heads. Riley wins if it lands tails.
   Fair; $P(\text{Meri wins}) = \frac{1}{2}$; $P(\text{Riley wins}) = \frac{1}{2}$

6. Meri and Riley both jump as high as they can. Whoever jumps higher wins.
   Not fair; The person who is the better jumper is most likely to win

7. Roll a standard die. Meri wins if the result is even. Riley wins if the result is odd.
   Fair; $P(\text{Meri wins}) = \frac{3}{6} = \frac{1}{2}$; $P(\text{Riley wins}) = \frac{3}{6} = \frac{1}{2}$

8. Draw a stone from a box that contains 5 black stones and 4 white stones. Meri wins if the stone is black. Riley wins if the stone is white.
   Not fair; $P(\text{Meri wins}) = \frac{5}{9} \approx 0.56$; $P(\text{Riley wins}) = \frac{4}{9} \approx 0.44$

9. A chess club has received a chess set to give to one of its members. The club decides that everyone should have a chance of winning the set based on how many games they have won this season. Describe a fair method to decide who wins the set. Find the probability that each member will win it.

Member	Games Won	Probability of Winning	Member	Games Won	Probability of Winning
Kayla	30	0.30	Hailey	12	0.12
Noah	23	0.23	Gabe	12	0.12
Ava	18	0.18	Concour	5	0.05

Find the total number of games won: $30 + 23 + 18 + 12 + 12 + 5 = 100$. Assign numbers from 1–100 to the members so each has as many numbers assigned as the number of games won. Then use a random number generator to choose an integer from 1 to 100.

10. Owen, Diego, and Cody often play a game during lunch. When they can't finish, they calculate the probability that each will win given the current state of the game and assign partial wins. Today, when they had to stop, it would have taken at most 56 more moves for one of them to win. Owen would have won 23 of the moves, Diego would have won 18 of them, and Cody would have won 15. To 2 decimal places, how should they assign partial wins?
    Owen: $\frac{23}{56} \approx 0.41$ wins; Diego: $\frac{18}{56} \approx 0.32$ wins; Cody: $\frac{15}{56} \approx 0.27$ wins

© Houghton Mifflin Harcourt Publishing Company · Image Credits: ©T. Grimm/vario images GmbH & Co.KG/Alamy

Exercise	Depth of Knowledge (D.O.K.)	COMMON CORE Mathematical Practices	
13–18	**2** Skills/Concepts		**MP.2** Reasoning
19	**3** Strategic Thinking	H.O.T.	**MP.6** Precision
20	**3** Strategic Thinking	H.O.T.	**MP.4** Modeling

Represent Real-World Problems Twenty students, including Paige, volunteer to work at the school banquet. Each volunteer worked at least 1 hour. Paige worked 4 hours. The students worked a total of 45 hours. The organizers would like to award a prize to 1 of the volunteers.

10. Describe a process for awarding the prize so that each volunteer has an equal chance of winning. Find the probability of Paige winning.

Possible answer: Write the names on slips of paper, place them in a box, and draw a slip at random. The probability of Paige winning is 1 out of 20, or 0.05.

11. Describe a process for awarding the prize so that each volunteer's chance of winning is proportional to how many hours the volunteer worked. Find the probability of Paige winning.

Possible answer: Write the names on slips of paper, but for each hour that a student worked, write his or her name on an extra slip. Then draw a slip at random. The probability of Paige winning is 4 out of 45, or about 0.089.

There are 10,000 seats available in a sports stadium. Each seat has a package beneath it, and 20 of the seats have an additional prize winning package with a family pass for the entire season.

12. Is this method of choosing a winner for the family passes fair?

Yes. If the packages were attached randomly, then each seat has an equal chance of having the package containing the family pass.

13. What is the probability of winning a family pass if you attend the game?

$$P(\text{winning}) = \frac{20}{10,000} = \frac{1}{500}$$

14. What is the probability of not winning a family pass if you attend the game?

$$P(\text{not winning}) = 1 - \left(P(\text{winning})\right) = 1 - \frac{20}{10,000} = \frac{9980}{10,000} = \frac{499}{500}$$

A teacher tells students, "For each puzzle problem you complete, I will assign you a prize entry." In all, 10 students complete 53 puzzle problems. Leon completed 7. To award the prize, the teacher sets a calculator to generate a random integer from 1 to 53. Leon is assigned 18 to 24 as "winners".

15. What is the probability that a specific number is chosen?

$$P(\#) = \frac{\text{one number}}{\text{total numbers}} = \frac{1}{53} \approx 0.0189 \approx 1.89\%$$

16. What is the probability that one of Leon's numbers will be chosen?

$$P(\text{leon}) = \frac{\text{Leon's numbers}}{\text{total numbers}} = \frac{7}{53} \approx 0.1321 \approx 13.21\%$$

17. What is the probability that one of Leon's numbers will not be chosen?

$$P(\text{not leon's}) = 1 - \frac{\text{Leon's numbers}}{\text{total numbers}} = 1 - \frac{7}{53} \approx 0.8679 \approx 86.79\%$$

18. Is this fair to Leon according to the original instructions? Explain.

Yes. Leon did 7 of the total of 53 completed puzzle problems. He was assigned 7 of the 53 possible winning numbers, and each number has the same chance of being chosen.

Students might not understand the importance of an adequate sample size when trying to accurately represent a population for a survey. Point out the need to make the sample size large enough, as well as unbiased, when choosing a sample population.

INTEGRATE MATHEMATICAL PRACTICES
Focus on Math Connections

MP.1 A random sample of a larger population is sometimes called an *unbiased sample* if every other same-sized sample of the same population has an equal chance of being selected. Point out that random sampling is done when it is not convenient or feasible to survey the entire population.

Arrange students in small groups and have them discuss strategies for some of the exercises. Once they obtain their results, have them explain to one another how probability was used in the solutions.

AVOID COMMON ERRORS

Students may have difficulty understanding either how to generate unique random numbers or what the calculator's output represents. Encourage students to design alternative ways to generate random numbers, including using slips of paper in a bag.

MODELING

Give groups of students a hands-on activity to help them understand how the random-number generator is used to simulate the results of a survey. Have them compare their methods to the methods used in the Explore activity.

JOURNAL

Have students describe how probability can be used to help award a prize fairly.

---

19. **Make a Conjecture** Two teams are playing a game against one another in class to earn 10 extra points on an assignment. The teacher said that the points will be split fairly between the two teams, depending on the results of the game. If Team A earned 1300 points, and Team B earned 2200 points, describe one way the teacher could split up the 10 extra points. Explain.

Possible answer: Team A should receive $\frac{1300}{3500} = \frac{13}{35} \approx 37\%$ of the 10 extra points, or 3.7 points. Team B should receive $\frac{2200}{3500} = \frac{22}{35} \approx 63\%$, or 6.3 points.

20. **Persevere in Problem Solving** Alexa and Sofia are at a yard sale, and they find a box of 20 collectible toys that they both want. They can't agree about who saw it first, so they flip a coin until Alexa gets 10 heads or Sofia gets 10 tails. When Alexa has 3 heads and Sofia has 6 tails, they decide to divide the toys proportionally based on the probability each has of winning under the original rules. How should they divide the toys?

It would take at most 10 more flips for one of them to win $\big((10 - 3) + (10 - 6) - 1\big)$. The number of possible permutations of 10 Hs and Ts is 2^{10} or 1024, so there are 1024 possible results for those 10 flips. In the cases where 7 or more of the flips are heads, Alexa wins.

$7H/3T = \frac{10!}{7! \cdot 3!} = 120$; $8H/2T = \frac{10!}{8! \cdot 2!} = 45$; $9H/1T = \frac{10!}{9! \cdot 1!} = 10$; $10H = 1$

So Alexa wins in $120 + 45 + 10 + 1 = 176$ of the 1024 possible outcomes. The probability that she will win is $\frac{176}{1024} \approx 0.17$. So the probability that Sofia wins is $1 - 0.17 = 0.83$.

To divide the toys, 83% of 20 is 16.6, so Sofia should get 16 or 17 of the toys. Perhaps they could agree that she only gets 16, but gets first choice. Then they take turns choosing until Alexa has 4. Then Sofia gets the rest.

Lesson Performance Task

Three games are described below. For each game, tell whether it is fair (all players are equally likely to win) or unfair (one player has an advantage). Explain how you reached your decision, being sure to discuss how probability entered into your decision.

1. You and your friend each toss a quarter. If two heads turn up, you win. If a head and a tail turn up, your friend wins. If two tails turn up, you play again.

2. You and your friend each roll a die. If the sum of the numbers is odd, you get 1 point. If the sum is even, your friend gets 1 point.

3. You and your friend each roll a die. If the product of the numbers is odd, you get 1 point. If the product is even, your friend gets 1 point.

1. Unfair; The table shows that there is a probability of $\frac{1}{4}$ that two heads will turn up, giving you a win, and a probability of $\frac{2}{4} = \frac{1}{2}$ that a head and a tail will turn up, giving your friend a win. Your friend's probability of winning is twice as great as yours, so the game is unfair.

	H	H
H	HH	HT
T	TH	TT

2. Fair; The table shows all of the possible sums when two dice are tossed. Of 36 possible sums, 18 are even, so the probability of rolling even is $\frac{18}{36} = \frac{1}{2}$. Of 36 possible sums, 18 are odd, so the probability of rolling odd is $\frac{18}{36} = \frac{1}{2}$. Both players are equally likely to win, so the game is fair.

+	1	2	3	4	5	6
1	2	3	4	5	6	7
2	3	4	5	6	7	8
3	4	5	6	7	8	9
4	5	6	7	8	9	10
5	6	7	8	9	10	11
6	7	8	9	10	11	12

3. Unfair; The table shows all of the possible products when two dice are tossed. Of 36 possible products, 27 are even, so the probability of rolling even is $\frac{27}{36} = \frac{3}{4}$. Of 36 possible products, 9 are odd, so the probability of rolling odd is $\frac{9}{36} = \frac{1}{4}$. Your friend's probability of winning is three times as great as yours, so the game is unfair.

×	1	2	3	4	5	6
1	1	2	3	4	5	6
2	2	4	6	8	10	12
3	3	6	9	12	15	18
4	4	8	12	16	20	24
5	5	10	15	20	25	30
6	6	12	18	24	30	36

EXTENSION ACTIVITY

Divide students into pairs or teams. Give each pair game-playing materials such as dice, playing cards, blank cards to write on, counters, checkers, spinners, or paper they can use to play games like tic-tac-toe. Have pairs or teams then follow the directions below.

- Make up two games, one fair and one unfair, that utilize their materials.
- Write the rules of the games and the reasons they are fair and unfair.
- Calculate any probabilities associated with the games.
- Play the games and compare the outcomes with the predicted probabilities.

INTEGRATE MATHEMATICAL PRACTICES
Focus on Reasoning

MP.2 Explain how you could change the rules of Game 1 and Game 3 in the Lesson Performance Task to make the games fair. Possible answers: Game 1: If two heads turn up, you win. If a head and a tail turn up, you play again. If two tails turn up, your friend wins. Game 3: If the product of the numbers is odd, you get 3 points. If the product of the numbers is even, your friend gets 1 point.

INTEGRATE MATHEMATICAL PRACTICES
Focus on Communication

MP.3 Ask students to describe a simple game that appears to be fair but, due to a small alteration in the construction of the game—a change the player does not know about—is actually unfair. Possible answer: A spinner with six sections numbered 1 to 6. The player believes that all six sections have the same area, so that all the numbers have a $\frac{1}{6}$ chance of being spun. However, the section numbered 4 is slightly larger than the others, meaning that there is a slightly better chance that 4 will be spun.

Scoring Rubric

2 points: Student correctly solves the problem and explains his/her reasoning.

1 point: Student shows good understanding of the problem but does not fully solve or explain his/her reasoning.

0 points: Student does not demonstrate understanding of the problem.

Using Probability to Make Fair Decisions   **1192**

Analyzing Decisions

Common Core Math Standards

The student is expected to:

 S-CP.A.4

Construct and interpret two-way frequency tables of data when two categories are associated with each object being classified. Use the two-way table as a sample space to decide if events are independent and to approximate conditional probabilities. Also S-CP.A.5, S-MD.B.7(+)

Mathematical Practices

 MP.2 Reasoning

Language Objective

State Bayes's Theorem in your own words.

ENGAGE

Essential Question: How can conditional probability help you make real-world decisions?

You can use a two-way table and/or Bayes's Theorem to use given information to calculate a conditional probability. Then you can use the conditional probability to evaluate a decision that may have been made based on the given information.

PREVIEW: LESSON PERFORMANCE TASK

View the Engage section online. Discuss the photograph. Ask students to speculate upon the purpose of the three doors. Then preview the Lesson Performance Task.

Name_____ Class_____ Date_____

23.2 Analyzing Decisions

Essential Question: How can conditional probability help you make real-world decisions?

Resource Locker

⊘ Explore   Analyzing a Decision Using Probability

Suppose scientists have developed a test that can be used at birth to determine whether a baby is right-handed or left-handed. The test uses a drop of the baby's saliva and instantly gives the result. The test has been in development, long enough for the scientists to track the babies as they grow into toddlers and to see whether their test is accurate. About 10% of babies turn out to be left-handed.

The scientists have learned that when children are left-handed, the test correctly identifies them as left-handed 92% of the time. Also when children are right-handed, the test correctly identifies them as right-handed 95% of the time.

(A) In the first year on the market, the test is used on 1,000,000 babies. Complete the table starting with the Totals. Then use the given information to determine the expected number in each category.

	Tests Left-handed	Tests Right-handed	Total
Truly Left-handed	92,000	8,000	100,000
Truly Right-handed	45,000	855,000	900,000
Total	137,000	863,000	1,000,000

(B) What is the probability that a baby who tests left-handed actually is left-handed? $\frac{92{,}000}{137{,}000} \approx 67.2\%$

(C) What is the probability that a baby who tests right-handed actually is right-handed? $\frac{855{,}000}{863{,}000} \approx 99.1\%$

Reflect

1. Is the test a good test of right-handedness?
   Yes; 99.1% is a reliable indicator that the baby will be right-handed.

2. A baby is tested, and the test shows the baby will be left-handed. The parents decide to buy a left-handed baseball glove for the baby. Is this a reasonable decision?

   No; the test is correct only about $\frac{2}{3}$ of the time when the result is that the baby is left-handed.

© Houghton Mifflin Harcourt Publishing Company

HARDCOVER PAGES 985–994

Turn to these pages to find this lesson in the hardcover student edition.

3. Discussion Describe two ways in which the test can become a more reliable indicator of left-handedness.

The obvious way is to improve the test so that it is better than 92% for babies who are

really left-handed. But the better way is to improve how the test works on right-handed

babies so that there are fewer cases of right-handed babies who test left-handed.

⊘ Explore 2 Deriving Bayes' Theorem

You can generalize your results so that they are applicable to other situations in which you want to analyze decisions. Now, you will derive a formula known as Bayes' Theorem.

Ⓐ Complete the steps to derive Bayes' Theorem.

Write the formula for $P(B|A)$. $\qquad$ $P(B|A) = \dfrac{P(A \text{ and } B)}{P(A)}$

Solve for $P(A \text{ and } B)$. $\qquad$ $P(A \text{ and } B) = P(B|A) \cdot P(A)$

Write the formula for $P(A|B)$. $\qquad$ $P(A|B) = \dfrac{P(A \text{ and } B)}{P(B)}$

Substitute the expression for $P(A \text{ and } B)$. $\qquad$ $P(A|B) = \dfrac{P(B|A) \cdot P(A)}{P(B)}$

Ⓑ Explain how you can use a table giving the number of results for each case to find $P(B)$.

	B	B^c	Total
A	n	p	n + p
A^c	m	q	m + q
Total	n + m	p + q	n + m + p + q

Divide the total cases resulting in B by the total number of cases.

$P(B) = \dfrac{n+m}{n+m+p+q}$.

Ⓒ Explain how you can use the tree diagram to find $P(B)$.

Add $P(B|A) \cdot P(A)$ and $P(B|A^c) \cdot P(A^c)$.

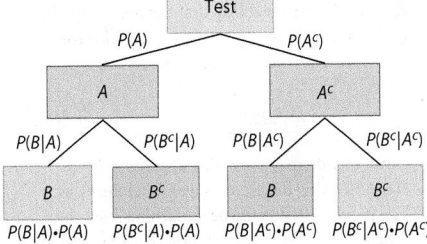

Ⓓ Use your result from Step C to rewrite your final expression from Step A to get another form of Bayes' Theorem.

$$P(A|B) = \dfrac{P(B|A) \cdot P(A)}{P(B)} = \dfrac{P(B|A) \cdot P(A)}{P(B|A) \cdot P(A) + P(B|A^c) \cdot P(A^c)}$$

PROFESSIONAL DEVELOPMENT

Math Background

At the heart of this lesson is Bayes's Theorem, a probability formula named after the English mathematician Thomas Bayes (1702–1761). The theorem is useful when you want to "reverse" a conditional probability. For example, you might know the probability that someone who has tuberculosis tests positive for the disease, but you want to know the probability that someone who tests positive actually has tuberculosis. Bayes's Theorem is generally the appropriate tool for calculating this probability. However, since constructing a two-way table seems more intuitive, it is the method used in the lesson.

EXPLORE 1

Analyzing a Decision Using Probability

INTEGRATE TECHNOLOGY

Students have the option of doing the Explore activity either in the book or online.

QUESTIONING STRATEGIES

? Does the size of a population always affect how you solve a problem? No. Sometimes any size of a population can be used because the size does not affect the relevant percents and probabilities.

? How can you tell if you have filled in all the relevant cells of a two-way table correctly? The totals across and down must be correct. The final total must be a sum of the totals in the bottom row.

EXPLORE 2

Deriving Bayes's Theorem

INTEGRATE MATHEMATICAL PRACTICES
Focus on Critical Thinking

MP.3 Point out that students should focus on interpreting the mathematical results in the context of the situation. When students use Bayes's Theorem to find a conditional probability, the specific value they find for the probability is less important than understanding what this value means. Interpreting the mathematical result is the essential step in determining whether a good decision was made.

? When does conditional probability apply to a problem situation? Possible answer: when the probability of one event is affected by the occurrence of a previous event

? How does a two-way table help you find conditional probabilities? A two-way table helps you organize information so that the probabilities can be calculated.

EXPLAIN 1

Using Bayes's Theorem

AVOID COMMON ERRORS

When using Bayes's Theorem, most errors arise from not being able to interpret and represent the conditional probabilities correctly. Suggest that students follow a pattern in identifying and describing each of the probabilities necessary to apply the theorem.

QUESTIONING STRATEGIES

? How does Bayes's Theorem help you analyze decisions? You can use the theorem and the given information to calculate a conditional probability. Then, you can use the conditional probability to evaluate a decision that was based on the given information.

Reflect

4. Explain in words what each expression means in the context of Explore 1.

$P(A)$ is the probability of actually being left-handed.

$P(B)$ is the probability of testing left-handed.

$P(A|B)$ is the probability of being left-handed if the baby tests left-handed

$P(B|A)$ is the probability of testing left-handed if the baby is left-handed

5. Use Bayes' Theorem to calculate the probability that a baby actually is left-handed, given that the baby tests left-handed. Explain what this probability means.

From the table, $P(B) = \dfrac{\text{Test left-handed}}{\text{Total tests}} = \dfrac{137,000}{1,000,000} = 0.137$

$P(A|B) = \dfrac{0.92 \cdot 0.10}{0.137} \approx 67.2\%$

About 67% of the time, a baby who tests as left-handed will be left-handed.

⚙ Explain 1   Using Bayes' Theorem

Bayes' Theorem is a useful tool when you need to analyze decisions.

> **Bayes' Theorem**
>
> Given two events A and B with $P(B) \neq 0$, $P(A|B) = \dfrac{P(B|A) \cdot P(A)}{P(B)}$.
>
> Another form is $P(A|B) = \dfrac{P(B|A) \cdot P(A)}{P(B|A) \cdot P(A) + P(B|A^c) \cdot P(A^c)}$.

Example 1   Suppose Walter operates an order-filling machine that has an error rate of 0.5%. He installs a new order-filling machine that has an error rate of only 0.1%. The new machine takes over 80% of the order-filling tasks.

(A) One day, Walter gets a call from a customer complaining that her order wasn't filled properly. Walter blames the problem on the old machine. Was he correct in doing so?

First, find the probability that the order was filled by the old machine given that there was an error in filling the order, $P(\text{old} \mid \text{error})$.

$P(\text{old}|\text{error}) = \dfrac{P(\text{error}|\text{old}) \cdot P(\text{old})}{P(\text{error})}$

$= \dfrac{0.005 \cdot (0.20)}{0.001 + 0.0008} = \dfrac{0.001}{0.0018} = \dfrac{5}{9} \approx 0.56$

Given that there is a mistake, the probability is about 56% that the old machine filled the order. The probability that the new machine filled the order is $1 - 0.56 = 0.44 = 44\%$. The old machine is only slightly more likely than the new machine to have filled the order. Walter shouldn't blame the old machine.

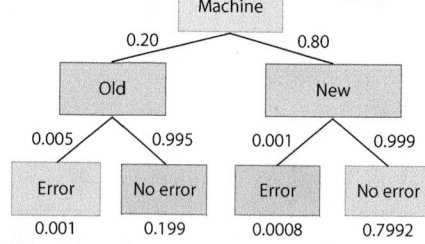

COLLABORATIVE LEARNING

Small Group Activity

Have groups of students discuss and analyze how the various branches of a tree diagram show the probabilities of the associated events. Have each student tell something about the diagram. For example, "the probabilities of complementary events add to 1." Then have them collate the information and make a conjecture about how to use a tree diagram to find the probability of an event. Invite students to share their information with the class.

(B) Walter needs to increase capacity for filling orders, so he increases the number of orders being filled by the old machine to 30% of the total orders. What percent of errors in filled orders are made by the old machine? Is Walter unreasonably increasing the risk of shipping incorrectly filled orders?

Find the probability that <u>the order was filled by the old machine</u>

given that <u>there is an error in filling the package</u>,

$P(\underline{\text{old}} \mid \underline{\text{error}})$.

Use Bayes' Theorem.

$$P(A|B) = \frac{P(B|A) \cdot P(A)}{P(B)} \quad \frac{0.005(0.30)}{0.0015 + 0.0007}$$

$$= \frac{0.0015}{0.0022} = \frac{15}{22} \approx 0.68$$

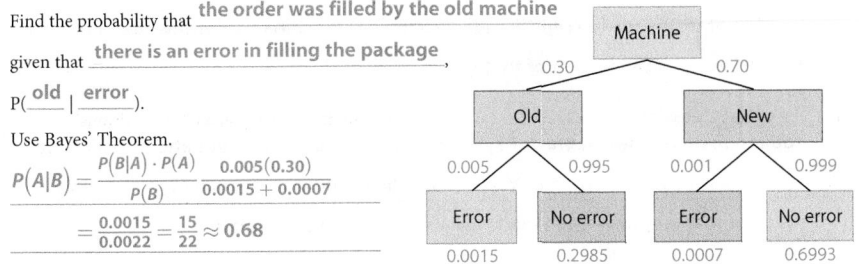

Describe the result of making this change.

Given that there is a mistake, the probability is about 68% that the old machine filled

the package. Making this change increases the number of errors by 4 orders for every

10,000 orders. This seems like a worthwhile risk.

Reflect

6. The old machine fills so few orders. How can it be responsible for more than half of the errors?
   The error rate of the old machine is five times the error rate of the new machine.

Your Turn

In the situation described in the Explore, suppose the scientists have changed the test so that now it correctly identifies left-handed children 100% of the time, and still correctly identifies right-handed children 95% of the time.

7. Complete the tree diagram.

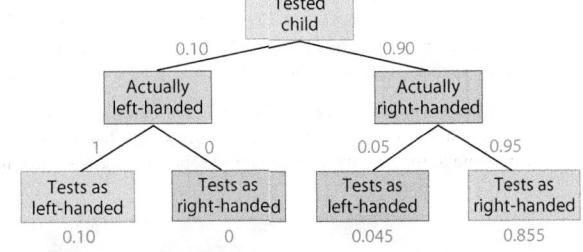

8. With the new test, what is the probability that a child who tests as left-handed will be left-handed? How does this compare to the original test?

$$P\left(\text{actual}_{\text{left}} \mid \text{test}_{\text{left}}\right) = \frac{1 \cdot 0.10}{0.1 + 0.045} = 69\%$$

The probability of the test being correct in this case increases about 2%.

9. With the new test, what is the probability that a child who tests as right-handed will be left-handed? How does this compare to the original test?

$$P\left(\text{actual}_{\text{right}} \mid \text{test}_{\text{left}}\right) = \frac{0.95 \cdot 0.05}{0.10 + 0.045} = 31\%$$

The probability of the test being correct in this case increases about 30%.

INTEGRATE MATHEMATICAL PRACTICES

Focus on Modeling

MP.4 Point out that a tree diagram or a two-way table helps to determine the individual probabilities that are used in Bayes's Theorem. Have students practice making tree diagrams or two-way tables, if necessary, to find each individual probability in the theorem.

DIFFERENTIATE INSTRUCTION

Auditory Cues

Help students understand Bayes's Theorem by having them restate the theorem in their own words and then verbalize how they will apply it. For example, "the probability that event *A* will happen given that event *B* happened is the product of the conditional probability that *B* happens given *A* with the probability of *A*, all divided by the probability of *B*." Stating the theorem in words may help students focus on the values they must find to apply the theorem.

ELABORATE

QUESTIONING STRATEGIES

? How would you say $P(A \mid B)$ in words? How is it different from $P(A)$? The probability of *A* given *B*; it is the probability that *A* occurs if it is given that *B* has already occurred, instead of simply the probability that *A* occurs.

SUMMARIZE THE LESSON

? What are some methods of using probability to analyze decisions? You can use two-way tables, tree diagrams, or Bayes's Theorem to calculate conditional probabilities, and then use those results to help you evaluate decisions made on the basis of the probabilities.

💬 Elaborate

10. **Discussion** Compare the probabilities you found in the Explore and Your Turn 8 and 9. Why did the percent of babies who test as right-handed and are actually left-handed increase?
    Possible answer: The increased accuracy of the test for left-handed reduced the overall

    number of tests showing right-handed, so the babies who test right-handed but are left-

    handed are a larger percent of that group.

11. **Essential Question Check-In** How can you use probability to help you analyze decisions?
    You can use a two-way table or Bayes' Theorem to use given information to calculate

    a conditional probability. Then you can use the conditional probability to evaluate a

    decision that may have been made based on the given information.

⭐ Evaluate: Homework and Practice

• Online Homework
• Hints and Help
• Extra Practice

1. A factory manager is assessing the work of two assembly-line workers. Helen has been on the job longer than Kyle. Their production rates for the last month are in the table. Based on comparing the number of defective products, the manager is considering putting Helen on probation. Is this a good decision? Why or why not?

	Helen	Kyle	Total
Defective	50	20	70
Not defective	965	350	1,315
Total	1,015	370	1,385

No; Of the 1,015 products that Helen completed, 50 were defective, which is about 4.9%. Of the 370 products that Kyle completed, 20 were defective, which is about 5.5%. Neither should be put on probation solely based on these data.

2. **Multiple Step** A reporter asked 150 voters if they plan to vote in favor of a new library and a new arena. The table shows the results. If you are given that a voter plans to vote *no* to the new arena, what is the probability that the voter also plans to vote no to the new library?

		Library		
		Yes	No	**Total**
Arena	Yes	21	30	51
	No	57	42	99
	Total	78	72	**150**

$P(\text{no library} \mid \text{no arena}) = \dfrac{42}{99}$, about 42%

Module 23   **1197**   Lesson 2

© Houghton Mifflin Harcourt Publishing Company

LANGUAGE SUPPORT 🇪🇱

Connect Vocabulary

If students comprehend some of the concepts in this lesson, provide them the opportunity to listen, share, and interact with other students in groups. Ask each group to make a poster representing a scenario in which one could use Bayes's Theorem to help make a decision, and then present the poster to the class.

3. You want to hand out coupons for a local restaurant to students who live off campus at a rural college with a population of 10,000 students. You know that 10% of the students live off campus and that 98% of those students ride a bike. Also, 62% of the students who live on campus do not have a bike. You decide to give a coupon to any student you see who is riding a bike. Complete the table. Then explain whether this a good decision.

	bike	no bike	Total
on campus	9,000(0.38) = 3,420	9,000(0.62) = 5,580	10,000(0.90) = 9,000
off campus	1,000(0.98) = 980	1,000(0.02) = 20	10,000(0.10) = 1,000
Total	4,400	5,600	10,000

Only 980 of the 4,400 bike-riding students live off campus, so only 22% of the coupons will go to the intended target of students living off campus. Therefore, this is not a good decision.

4. A test for a virus correctly identifies someone who has the virus (by returning a positive result) 99% of the time. The test correctly identifies someone who does not have the virus (by returning a negative result) 99% of the time. It is known that 0.5% of the population has the virus. A doctor decides to treat anyone who tests positive for the virus. Complete the two-way table assuming a total population of 1,000,000 people have been tested. Is this a good decision?

	Tests Positive	Tests Negative	Total
Virus	4,950	50	5,000
No virus	9,950	985,050	995,000
Total	14,900	985,100	1,000,000

Of the 14,900 people who tested positive, only 4,950 actually have the virus. The probability a person who tests positive for the virus actually has it is $\frac{4,950}{14,900}$, or about 33.2%. Most of the patients that the doctor treats for the virus do not need the treatment.

5. It is known that 2% of the population has a certain allergy. A test correctly identifies people who have the allergy 98% of the time. The test correctly identifies people who do not have the allergy 95% of the time. A website recommends that anyone who tests positive for the allergy should begin taking medication. Complete the two-way table. Do you think this is a good recommendation? Why or why not?

	Test Positive	Test Negative	Total
Allergy	196	4	200
No allergy	490	9,310	9,800
Total	686	9,314	10,000

No; Only 196 people out of the 686 who tested positive actually have the allergy. This is about 29% of those who test positive.

EVALUATE

Personal Math Trainer

ASSIGNMENT GUIDE

Concepts and Skills	Practice
Explore 1 Analyzing a Decisions Using Probability	Exercises 1–4
Explore 2 Deriving Bayes's Theorem	Exercise 5
Example 1 Using Bayes's Theorem	Exercises 6–9

INTEGRATE MATHEMATICAL PRACTICES
Focus on Communication

MP.3 Have students verbalize the solution process in finding conditional probabilities using a two-way table, tree diagram, and Bayes's Theorem. Then have them work in small groups. In each group, have one student pose a conditional probability situation from the real world, or use one of the exercises. The other students should check that conditional probability applies, and then solve the problem.

Exercise	Depth of Knowledge (D.O.K.)	COMMON CORE	Mathematical Practices
1–4	**3** Strategic Thinking	**MP.3**	Logic
5	**1** Recall of Information	**MP.5**	Using Tools
6–10	**1** Recall of Information	**MP.4**	Modeling
11	**1** Recall of Information	**MP.8**	Patterns
12	**1** Recall of Information	**MP.5**	Using Tools

Focus on Reasoning

MP.2 Using probabilities gives a way to quantitatively analyze decisions that need to be made based on the occurrence of past events. Ask students to think of situations that cause decisions to be made independently of the supporting probabilities. For example, a decision to close school for a "snow day" may be made based on factors other than the probability of snow.

6. Use the tree diagram shown.

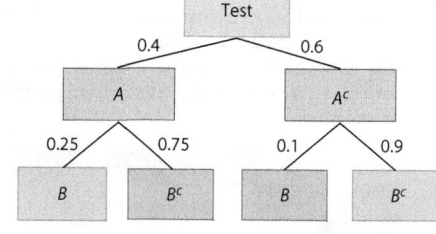

  a. Find $P(B|A^c) \cdot P(A^c)$.
  $$P(B \mid A^c) \cdot P(A^c) = 0.1 \cdot 0.6 = 0.06$$

  b. Find $P(B)$.
  $$P(B) = P(B \mid A^c) \cdot P(A^c) + P(B \mid A) \cdot P(A)$$
  $$= 0.06 + 0.25 \cdot 0.4$$
  $$= 0.06 + 0.1 = 0.16$$

  c. Use Bayes Theorem to find $P(A^c|B)$. $P(A^c \mid B) = \dfrac{P(B \mid A^c) \cdot P(A^c)}{P(B)} = \dfrac{0.06}{0.16} = 0.375$

7. The probabilities of drawing lemons and limes from a bag are shown in the tree diagram. Find the probability of drawing the two pieces of fruit randomly from the bag.

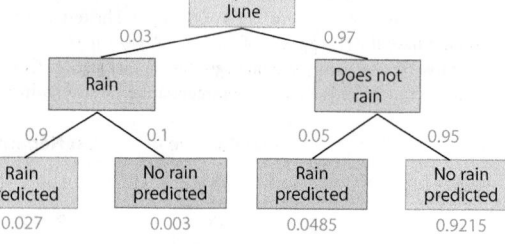

  a. two lemons
  $$\frac{2}{3} \cdot \frac{1}{2} = \frac{1}{3}$$

  b. two limes
  $$\frac{1}{3} \cdot 0 = 0$$

  c. lime, then lemon
  $$\frac{1}{3} \cdot 1 = \frac{1}{3}$$

  d. lemon, then lime
  $$\frac{2}{3} \cdot \frac{1}{2} + \frac{1}{3} \cdot 1 = \frac{1}{3} + \frac{1}{3} = \frac{2}{3}$$

8. **Multiple Step** A school principal plans a school picnic for June 2. A few days before the event, the weather forecast predicts rain for June 2, so the principal decides to cancel the picnic. Consider the following information.

  - In the school's town, the probability that it rains on any day in June is 3%.
  - When it rains, the forecast correctly predicts rain 90% of the time.
  - When it does not rain, the forecast incorrectly predicts rain 5% of the time.

  a. Find $P(\text{prediction of rain} \mid \text{rains})$ and $P(\text{rains})$.

  $P(\text{prediction of rain} \mid \text{rains}) = 0.9$ (given); $P(\text{rains}) = 0.3$ (given)

  b. Complete the tree diagram, and find $P(\text{Prediction of rain})$.

  P(Prediction of rain) = P(prediction of rain|rains) + P(prediction of rain|does not rain) = 0.027 + 0.0485 = 0.0755

  Days in June — 0.03 → Rain; 0.97 → Does not rain
  Rain: 0.9 → Rain predicted (0.027); 0.1 → No rain predicted (0.003)
  Does not rain: 0.05 → Rain predicted (0.0485); 0.95 → No rain predicted (0.9215)

  c. Find $P(\text{rains} \mid \text{prediction of rain})$.
  $$P(\text{rains} \mid \text{prediction of rain}) = \frac{0.9 \cdot 0.03}{0.0755} \approx 0.358 \approx 35.8\%$$

  d. Is the decision to cancel the picnic reasonable?
  No; there is only a 36% chance that it will rain.

Exercise	Depth of Knowledge (D.O.K.)	COMMON CORE Mathematical Practices
13–14	**1** Recall of Information	**MP.4** Modeling
15–16	**3** Strategic Thinking	**MP.3** Logic
17	**1** Recall of Information	**MP.5** Using Tools
18	**3** Strategic Thinking H.O.T.	**MP.3** Logic
19	**3** Strategic Thinking H.O.T.	**MP.3** Logic
20	**3** Strategic Thinking H.O.T.	**MP.3** Logic

9. Pamela has collected data on the number of students in the sophomore class who play a sport or play a musical instrument. She has learned the following.

• 42.5% of all students in her school play a musical instrument.

• 20% of those who play a musical instrument also play a sport.

• 40% of those who play no instrument also play no sport.

Complete the tree diagram. Would it be reasonable to conclude that a student who doesn't play a sport plays a musical instrument?

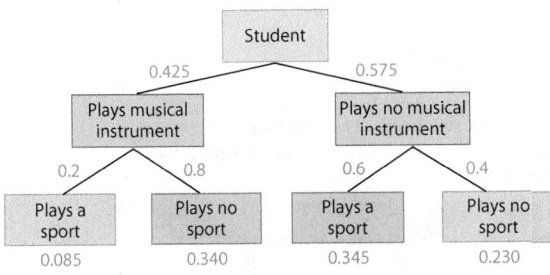

$$P(\text{music} \mid \text{no sport}) = \frac{P(\text{no sport} \mid \text{music}) \cdot P(\text{music})}{P(\text{no sport})} = \frac{0.8 \cdot 0.425}{0.34 + 0.23} \approx 0.60$$

The probability that a student plays a musical instrument given that he or she plays no sport is about 60%. So, it is somewhat likely that a student who doesn't play a sport does play an instrument, but it would not be reasonable to assume that this is true.

10. Interpret the Answer Company X supplies 35% of the phones to an electronics store and Company Y supplies the remainder. The manager of the store knows that 25% of the phones in the last shipment from Company X were defective, while only 5% of the phones from Company Y were defective. The manager chooses a phone at random and finds that it is defective. The manager decides that the phone must have come from Company X. Do you think this is a reasonable conclusion? Why or why not?

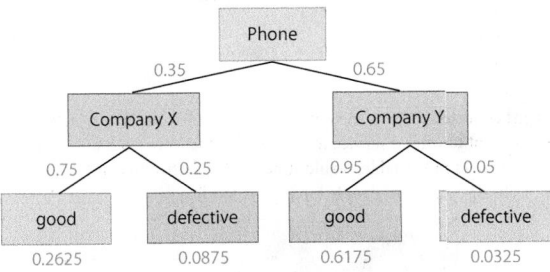

$$P\left(\text{Company X} \mid \text{defective}\right) = \frac{P\left(\text{defective} \mid \text{Company X}\right) \cdot P\left(\text{Company X}\right)}{P\left(\text{defective}\right)}$$

$$= \frac{0.0875}{0.0875 + 0.0325} \approx 0.73$$

This is a good decision because there is a 73% chance that a defective phone came from Company X.

Be sure students understand the difference between probabilities of independent events and of conditional probabilities. Emphasize that conditional probabilities are used for Bayes's Theorem.

11. Suppose that strep throat affects 2% of the population and a test to detect it produces an accurate result 99% of the time. Create a tree diagram and use Bayes, Theorem to find the probability that someone who tests positive actually has strep throat.

$$P(S|+) = \frac{P(+|S) \cdot P(S)}{P(+)} = \frac{0.99 \cdot 0.02}{0.99 \cdot 0.02 + 0.01 \cdot 0.98} \approx 0.67$$

About 67% of those tested positively for strep throat actually have strep throat.

12. A hand-made quilt is first prize in a fund-raiser raffle. The table shows information about all the ticket buyers. Given that the winner of the quilt is a man, what is the probability that he resides in Sharonville?

	Men	Women	Total
Forestview	35	45	80
Sharonville	15	25	40
Total	50	70	120

$\frac{15}{50} = 0.3 = 30\%$

13. Recall that the Multiplication Rule says the $P(A \cap B) = P(A) \cdot P(B \mid A)$. If you switch the order of events A and B, then the rule becomes $P(B \cap A) = P(B) \cdot P(A \mid B)$. Use the Multiplication Rule and the fact that $P(B \cap A) = P(A \cap B)$ to prove Bayes' Theorem. (*Hint*: Divide each side by $P(B)$.)

$$P(B) \cdot P(A \mid B) = P(A) \cdot P(B \mid A) \qquad \text{Substitution, because } P(B \cap A) = P(A \cap B)$$

$$\frac{P(B) \cdot P(A \mid B)}{P(B)} = \frac{P(A) \cdot P(B \mid A)}{P(B)} \qquad \text{Divide each side by } P(B).$$

$$P(A \mid B) = \frac{P(A) \cdot P(B \mid A)}{P(B)} \qquad \text{Bayes' Theorem}$$

14. **Sociology** A sociologist collected data on the types of pets in 100 randomly selected households. Suppose you want to offer a service to households that own both a cat and a dog. Based on the data in the table, would it be more effective to hand information to people walking dogs or to people buying cat food?

		Owns a Cat		
		Yes	No	Total
Owns a Dog	Yes	15	24	39
	No	18	43	61
	Total	33	67	100

$P(\text{cat} \mid \text{dog}) = \frac{15}{39} \approx 0.38$ and $P(\text{dog} \mid \text{cat}) = \frac{15}{33} \approx 0.45$, so it would be somewhat **more effective to approach people buying cat food.**

© Houghton Mifflin Harcourt Publishing Company

15. Interpret the Answer It is known that 1% of all mice in a laboratory have a genetic mutation. A test for the mutation correctly identifies mice that have the mutation 98% of the time. The test correctly identifies mice that do not have the mutation 96% of the time. A lab assistant tests a mouse and finds that the mouse tests positive for the mutation. The lab assistant decides that the mouse must have the mutation. Is this a good decision? Complete the tree diagram and explain your answer.

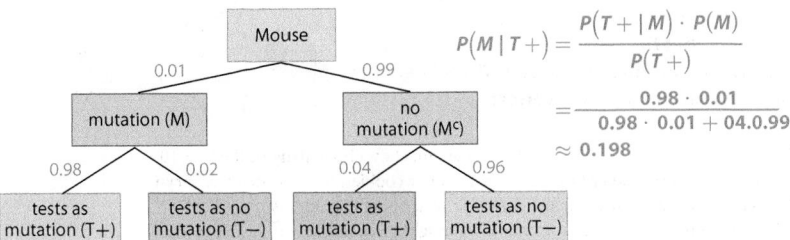

$$P(M \mid T+) = \frac{P(T+\mid M) \cdot P(M)}{P(T+)}$$

$$= \frac{0.98 \cdot 0.01}{0.98 \cdot 0.01 + 04.0.99}$$

$$\approx 0.198$$

It is not a good decision, because there is only a 19.8% probability that a mouse that tests positive for the mutation actually has the mutation.

16. Interpret the Answer It is known that 96% of all dogs do not get trained. One professional trainer claims that 54% of trained dogs will sit on one of the first four commands and that no other dogs will sit on command. A condominium community wants to impose a restriction on dogs that are not trained. They want each dog owner to show that his or her dog will sit on one of the first four commands. Assuming that the professional trainer's claim is correct, is this a fair way to identify dogs that have not been trained? Explain.

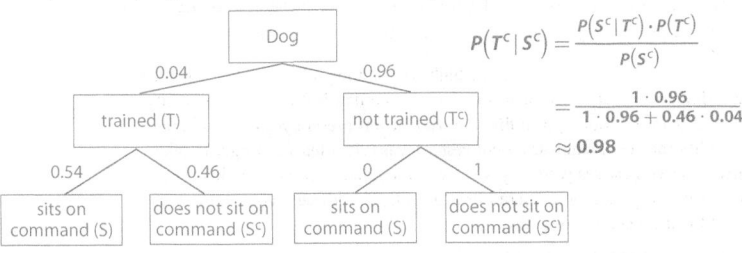

$$P(T^c \mid S^c) = \frac{P(S^c \mid T^c) \cdot P(T^c)}{P(S^c)}$$

$$= \frac{1 \cdot 0.96}{1 \cdot 0.96 + 0.46 \cdot 0.04}$$

$$\approx 0.98$$

It is fair, because there is a 98% probability that a dog that does not sit on one of the first four commands has not been trained.

17. Multiple Steps Tomas has a choice of three possible routes to work. On each day, he randomly selects a route and keeps track of whether he is late. Based on this 40-day trial, which route makes Tomas least likely to be late for work?

	Late	Not Late	Total
Route A	4	10	14
Route B	3	7	10
Route C	4	12	16

	Late	Not Late
Route A	IIII	HHT HHT
Route B	III	HHT II
Route C	IIII	HHT HHT II

$$P(Late \mid A) = \frac{4}{14} \approx 0.29; \quad P(Late \mid B) = \frac{3}{10} = 0.3; \quad P(Late \mid C) = \frac{4}{16} = 0.25$$

Based on the sample, Tomas is least likely to be late if he takes Route C.

Arrange students in small groups and have them discuss the different interpretations that may result from applying Bayes's Theorem. Ask them to brainstorm how the interpretations would change as more information is gathered from a probability experiment.

MODELING

Give groups of students a hands-on activity to help them understand how tree diagrams, two-way tables, and Bayes's Theorem are used to influence decision-making. Have them compare their results to the examples.

JOURNAL

Have students compare two methods of analyzing a decision: making a two-way table, and using Bayes's Theorem. Prompt students to describe the pros and cons of each method.

18. **Critique Reasoning** When Elisabeth saw this tree diagram, she said that the calculations must be incorrect. Do you agree? Justify your answer.

    Elisabeth is correct. The sum of the probabilities for the four outcomes is $0.44 + 0.2 + 0.3 + 0.16 = 1.1$, but the sum of the probabilities of all possible outcomes must be 1. Therefore, the calculations must be incorrect.

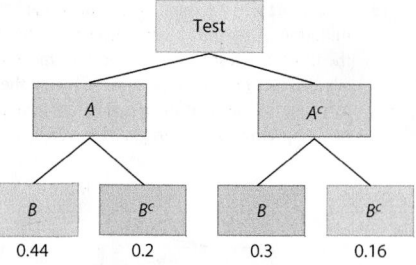

19. **Multiple Representations** The Venn diagram shows how many of the first 100 customers of a new bakery bought either bread or cookies, both, or neither. Taryn claims that the data indicate that a customer who bought cookies is more likely to have bought bread than a customer who bought bread is likely to have bought cookies. Is she correct?

		Bread		
		Yes	No	Total
Cookies	Yes	18	22	40
	No	54	6	60
	Total	72	28	100

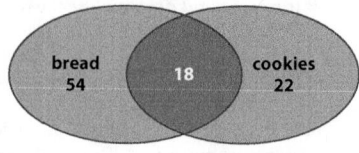

Yes, because $P(B \mid C) = \frac{18}{40} = 0.45$, while $P(C \mid B) = \frac{18}{72} = 0.25$. So, customers who bought cookies also bought bread almost half of the time, while customers who bought bread also bought cookies only a quarter of the time.

20. **Persevere in Problem Solving** At one high school, the probability that a student is absent today, given that the student was absent yesterday, is 0.12. The probability that a student is absent today, given that the student was present yesterday, is 0.05. The probability that a student was absent yesterday is 0.1. A teacher forgot to take attendance in several classes yesterday, so he assumed that attendance in his class today is the same as yesterday. If there were 40 students in these classes, how many errors would you expect by doing this?

    Students present yesterday = 90% of 40 = 36
    Students absent yesterday = 10% of 40 = 4

    $$P(PY \mid PT) = \frac{P(PT \mid PY) \cdot P(PY)}{P(PT)} = \frac{0.95 \cdot 0.9}{0.95 \cdot 0.9 + 0.88 \cdot 0.1} \approx 0.91; 91\% \text{ of } 36 = 33 \text{ students}$$

    $$P(AY \mid PT) = \frac{P(PT \mid AY) \cdot P(AY)}{P(PT)} = \frac{0.88 \cdot 0.1}{0.95 \cdot 0.9 + 0.88 \cdot 0.1} \approx 0.09; 9\% \text{ of } 36 = 3 \text{ students}$$

    $$P(PY \mid AT) = \frac{P(AT \mid PY) \cdot P(PY)}{P(AT)} = \frac{0.05 \cdot 0.9}{0.05 \cdot 0.9 + 0.12 \cdot 0.1} \approx 0.79; 79\% \text{ of } 4 = 3 \text{ students.}$$

    $$P(AY \mid AT) = \frac{P(AT \mid AY) \cdot P(AY)}{P(AT)} = \frac{0.12 \cdot 0.1}{0.05 \cdot 0.9 + 0.12 \cdot 0.1} \approx 0. \ 21\% \text{ of } 4 = 1 \text{ student}$$

    The cases where doing this would cause an error are $P(AY|PT)$ and $P(PY|AT)$. So based on the probabilities, he would have the attendance for yesterday wrong for about 6 students.

Lesson Performance Task

You're a contestant on a TV quiz show. Before you are three doors. Behind two of the doors, there's a goat. Behind one of the doors, there's a new car. You are asked to pick a door. After you make your choice, the quizmaster opens one of the doors you *didn't* choose, revealing a goat.

Door 1   Door 2   Door 3

Now there are only two doors. You can stick with your original choice or you can switch to the one remaining door. Should you switch?

Intuition tells most people that, with two doors left, there's a 50% probability that they're right and a 50% probability that they're wrong. They conclude that it doesn't matter whether they switch or not.

Does it? Using Bayes' Theorem, it can be shown mathematically that you're much better off switching! You can reach the same conclusion using logical thinking skills. Assume that the car is behind Door #1. (The same reasoning that follows can be applied if the car is behind one of the other doors.) You've decided to switch your choice after the first goat is revealed. There are three possibilities.

1. If I choose Door #1 first, my switch strategy dictates that I must switch my choice. If the quizmaster opens Door #2, I must switch my choice to Door #3. If the quizmaster opens Door #3, I must switch my choice to Door #2. Either way my strategy is unsuccessful and I lose.

2. a. If I choose Door #2 first, the quizmaster must open Door #3 because the car is behind Door #1.

   b. My switch strategy dictates that I must switch my choice, so I switch to Door #1. My strategy is successful and I win the car.

3. a. The quizmaster must open Door #2 because the car is behind Door #1.

   b. My switch strategy dictates that I must switch my choice, so I switch to Door #1. My strategy is successful and I win the car.

$\frac{2}{3}$; I win the car in two of the three case, the two where my first choice is wrong. I lose in only one of the three cases, the one where my first choice is correct.

EXTENSION ACTIVITY

Present the following to pairs of students: *There are three cards in a hat. One card is white on both sides. The second card is white on one side and red on the other. The third card is red on both sides. One card is removed and placed flat on the table. The side showing is red. What is the probability that the other side of the card is red?* Pairs should decide on an answer to the question and be prepared to give their reasoning. The answer seems paradoxical, so students may want to test it experimentally. $\frac{2}{3}$; the card cannot be white-white, so there are three possible cases. The other side may be (1) white, (2) side 1 of the red-red card, or (3) side 2 of the red-red card. Two of the three possibilities are favorable.

INTEGRATE MATHEMATICAL PRACTICES
Focus on Modeling

MP.4 Have students work in pairs to create and play games analogous to the game described in the Lesson Performance Task. Students should keep track of the results when they try various strategies for making the correct choice, and compare their results with the claim that switching is the best strategy.

AVOID COMMON ERRORS

Students may have difficulty understanding the logic behind the quizmaster's decision about which door to open after the initial choice has been made, and the reason why switching is a winning strategy in two out of three cases. Have students work in pairs to walk through the steps when the car is behind Door #1, as it is in the Lesson Performance Task; then when it is behind Door #2; and, finally, behind Door #3. Each time, students should begin by making an arbitrary choice of a door, then deciding how the quizmaster will react to the choice, and then seeing the result when they switch the initial choice.

Scoring Rubric

2 points: Student correctly solves the problem and explains his/her reasoning.

1 point: Student shows good understanding of the problem but does not fully solve or explain his/her reasoning.

0 points: Student does not demonstrate understanding of the problem.

Analyzing Decisions   **1204**

Study Guide Review

ASSESSMENT AND INTERVENTION

Assign or customize module reviews.

MODULE PERFORMANCE TASK

COMMON CORE

Mathematical Practices: MP.1, MP.2, MP.4, MP.5, MP.6, MP.7
S-CP.A.4, S-CP.A.5, S-MD.B.7

SUPPORTING STUDENT REASONING

Here are some questions students might have:

- **What is the "reliability rate" of a diagnostic test?** A test that is 100% reliable always correctly identifies a person who has the illness. A reliability of 85% means that 15% of the time the test fails to identify a patient who actually has the illness.

- **What is a "false-positive" rate?** A false positive result of a test is one that shows that a patient has the illness when in fact he or she does not. A false positive rate of 8% means that of every 100 people who do not have the illness and are tested, 8 will test positive for the illness.

Probability and Decision Making

Essential Question: How can you use probability to solve real-world problems?

Determine whether the method of awarding a prize is fair. Explain.

A festival has a baked goods fundraising raffle in which tickets are drawn for winners. The tickets are sold for $2 each, and the purchaser of the ticket places his or her name on the ticket before placing the ticket into a fishbowl on a table. There are 20 cakes for prizes. A ticket is drawn at random from the fishbowl for each cake.

The method of awarding the prize is fair. This is because each ticket has an equal probability of being drawn. For each of n tickets bought, that ticket has a $\frac{1}{n}$ chance of being drawn. The more tickets someone buys, the better chance they have of winning a cake.

Suppose Rhonda's Block Warehouse operates a block-making machine that has an error rate of 0.7%. Then Rhonda installs a new block-making machine that has an error rate of only 0.3%. The new machine takes over 75% of the block-making tasks. One day, Rhonda gets a call from a customer complaining that his block is not made properly. Rhonda blames the problem on the old machine. Was she correct in doing so?

Find Event A, Event B, $P(A|B)$, $P(B)$, and $P(A)$.

Event A is the error making the block, Event B is that the old machine made the block, $P(A|B)$ is the error rate of the old machine (0.007), $P(B)$ is the probability the old machine made the block (0.25), and $P(A)$ is $0.75 \cdot 0.003 + 0.25 \cdot 0.007 = 0.004$.

$$P(B|A) = \frac{P(A|B)P(B)}{P(A)} \qquad \text{Bayes' Theorem}$$

$$P(\text{old machine}|\text{bad block}) = \frac{0.007 \cdot 0.25}{0.004} \qquad \text{Substitute known probabilities}$$

$$P(\text{old machine}|\text{bad block}) = 0.4375 = 43.75\%$$

Given that the probability that a bad block is made by the old machine is less than 50%, Rhonda should not blame the old machine for the bad block.

SCAFFOLDING SUPPORT

- Students will find Bayes' Theorem useful in completing the Performance Task: $P(A \mid B) = \dfrac{P(B \mid A) \cdot P(A)}{P(B|A) \cdot P(A) + P(B|\sim A) \cdot P(\sim A)}$

- If students have trouble using Bayes' Theorem, suggest that they make a two-way table instead, divided into "Test Positive" and "Test Negative" on one side, and "Has Illness" and "Doesn't Have Illness" on the other. Suggest that they use a total of 100,000 patients and fill out the cells using the percentages given in the problem.

EXERCISES

Determine whether the method of awarding a prize is fair. Explain. If it is not fair, describe a way that would be fair. *(Lesson 23.1)*

1. A teacher gives a ticket to each student who earns a 90 or above on any homework assignment. At the end of each week, the teacher draws from the ticket jar and gives the winning student a free homework pass for the next week.

   Possible answer: This method of giving out tickets is not fair because it favors the students who make higher grades. A more fair way of distributing tickets would be giving a ticket to any student who turned in their homework, regardless of their grade on the assignment.

Suppose that a card dealing machine has a probability of 23% for pulling a face card. An older machine has a 14% chance of pulling a face card. Use Bayes' Theorem to find the probability. *(Lesson 23.2)*

2. If each machine is used 50% of the time, and a face card is the next card drawn, what is the probability the new machine drew the card?

   $$P\left(B|A\right) = \frac{0.23 \cdot 0.5}{0.185} \approx 0.622 = 62.2\%$$

MODULE PERFORMANCE TASK

What's the Diagnosis?

Lenny works in a factory that makes cleaning products. Lately he has been suffering from headaches. He asks his doctor if the chemicals used in the factory might be responsible for his headaches. The doctor performs a blood test that is routinely used to diagnose the kind of illness Lenny is concerned about.

Use the following facts to gauge the probability that Lenny has the illness if he tests positive:

1. The test has a reliability rate of 85 percent.

2. The test has a false positive rate of 8 percent.

3. The illness affects 3 percent of people who are Lenny's age and who work in conditions similar to those he works in.

Start by listing on your own paper the information you will need to solve the problem. Then complete the task. Use numbers, words, or algebra to explain how you reached your conclusion.

© Houghton Mifflin Harcourt Publishing Company

DISCUSSION OPPORTUNITIES

- Ask students to comment on the surprising fact that Lenny's chances of having the illness are only about 25%, even though the test has a seemingly high reliability rate of 85%. Sample answer: Along with the reliability rate, the false positive rate and the fact that only 3% of people who share Lenny's age and working conditions have the illness both have major effects on the probability that Lenny also has the illness.

SAMPLE SOLUTION

Apply Bayes' Theorem. Let $P(A)$ represent the probability that Lenny has the illness and let $P(B)$ represent the probability that the test was positive.

$$P\left(A \mid B\right) = \frac{P\left(B|A\right) \cdot P(A)}{P\left(B|A\right) \cdot P(A) + P\left(B|{\sim}A\right) \cdot P({\sim}A)}$$

$$= \frac{0.85 \times 0.03}{0.85 \times 0.03 + 0.08 \times 0.97}$$

$$= \frac{0.0255}{0.0255 + 0.0776}$$

$$= \frac{0.0255}{0.1031}$$

$$\approx 0.247$$

The probability that Lenny has the illness is about 24.7%.

Alternatively, fill out a table, using a total of 100,000 patients who have taken the test:

	Have Illness	Don't Have Illness	Total
Test Positive	2,550	7,760	10,310
Test Negative	450	89,240	89,690
Total	3,000	97,000	100,000

In this case, the answer 24.7% is found by dividing 2,550 (the number testing positive who have the illness) by 10,310 (the total number testing positive).

Assessment Rubric

2 points: Student correctly solves the problem and explains his/her reasoning.

1 point: Student shows good understanding of the problem but does not fully solve or explain his/her reasoning.

0 points: Student does not demonstrate understanding of the problem.

Ready to Go On?

ASSESS MASTERY

Use the assessment on this page to determine if students have mastered the concepts and standards covered in this module.

ASSESSMENT AND INTERVENTION

Access Ready to Go On? assessment online, and receive instant scoring, feedback, and customized intervention or enrichment.

ADDITIONAL RESOURCES

Response to Intervention Resources

- Reteach Worksheets

Differentiated Instruction Resources

- Reading Strategies **EL**
- Success for English Learners **EL**
- Challenge Worksheets

Assessment Resources

- Leveled Module Quizzes

(Ready) to Go On?

23.1–23.2 Probability and Decision Making

- Online Homework
- Hints and Help
- Extra Practice

Determine whether the method of awarding a prize is fair. Explain briefly. *(Lesson 23.1)*

1. Prize to every 500th customer

Not fair; not everyone can be 500th.

2. Ticket to every customer; drawing

Fair; every customer has a chance.

3. Choose number 1–10; draw number

Fair; each number has equal chance.

4. Ticket to all cars; two to red cars

Not fair; red cars have a higher chance.

Rodney's Repair Service has a lug nut tightening machine that works well 89% of the time. They got a new machine that works well 98% of the time. Each machine is used 50% of the time. Use Bayes' Theorem to find each probability. *(Lesson 23.2)*

5. new machine malfunctioned

$$P(B \mid A) = \frac{0.02 \cdot 0.5}{0.065} \approx 0.154 = 15.4\%$$

6. old machine malfunctioned

$$P(B \mid A) = \frac{0.11 \cdot 0.5}{0.065} \approx 0.846 = 84.6\%$$

7. old machine worked well

$$P(B \mid A) = \frac{0.89 \cdot 0.5}{0.935} \approx 0.476 = 47.6\%$$

8. new machine worked well

$$P(B \mid A) = \frac{0.98 \cdot 0.5}{0.935} \approx 0.524 = 52.4\%$$

ESSENTIAL QUESTION

9. How can probability and decision making help the organizer of a raffle?

Possible answer: The organizer of the raffle can make decisions about whether the raffle is fair or not fair. If it is not fair, they can find ways to make the raffle more fair, so more people will be willing to participate.

COMMON CORE   Common Core Standards

Lesson	Items	Content Standards	Mathematical Practices
23.1	1	**S-MD.B.6**	**MP.6**
23.1	2	**S-MD.B.6**	**MP.6**
23.1	3	**S-MD.B.6**	**MP.6**
23.1	4	**S-MD.B.6**	**MP.6**
23.2	5–8	**S-CP.A.5**	**MP.2**

MODULE 23
MIXED REVIEW

Assessment Readiness

1. Consider the situation. Is the method of awarding the prize fair?
   Select Yes or No for A–C.

   A. Ticket for every $10 spent   ● Yes   ○ No

   B. Coupon every 10 guests   ○ Yes   ● No

   C. Entry for every mile driven   ○ Yes   ● No

2. Consider the situation of having four tiles in a bag spelling M–A–T–H drawn randomly without replacement. Choose True or False for each statement.

   A. There is one way to draw all 4 tiles from the bag, if order doesn't matter.   ● True   ○ False

   B. There are six ways to draw 2 tiles from the bag, if order matters.   ○ True   ● False

   C. There are twenty four ways to draw 3 tiles from the bag if order matters.   ● True   ○ False

3. The band class has two trumpet players. Of the two, the first trumpet player plays a wrong note 4% of the time, and the second trumpet player plays a wrong note 9% of the time. If one song has the first trumpet player playing 75% of the song, and the second trumpet player playing the rest, use Bayes' Theorem to find the probability that a wrong note was played by the second trumpet. Explain whether your answer makes sense.

   $P(B \mid A) = \frac{0.09 \cdot 0.25}{0.0525} \approx 0.429 = 42.9\%$; Possible answer: It does make sense, because the trumpet player making the most mistakes pays much less of the time, so it would be less likely that the mistake would come from the second trumpet player.

4. Given a triangle with a side of length 11 and another side of length 6, find the range of possible values for x, the length of the third side. Explain your reasoning.

   $5 < x < 17$; Possible answer: By the Triangle Inequality Theorem, the sum of the lengths of any two sides of a triangle must be greater than the third side length. So $11 + 6 > x$, $x + 6 > 11$, and $x + 11 > 6$, which simplify to $x < 17$, $x > 5$, and $x > -5$. Ignore the third inequality and write a compound inequality to show the possible side lengths: $5 < x < 17$.

MIXED REVIEW

Assessment Readiness

ASSESSMENT AND INTERVENTION

Assign ready-made or customized practice tests to prepare students for high-stakes tests.

ADDITIONAL RESOURCES

Assessment Resources

- Leveled Module Quizzes: Modified, B

AVOID COMMON ERRORS

Item 1 Some students have a hard time considering the concept of fairness objectively and will only consider what they personally would consider fair. Remind students that they must use the mathematical definition of fairness to answer correctly.

COMMON CORE **Common Core Standards**

Lesson	Items	Content Standards	Mathematical Practices
23.1	1	**S-MD.B.6**	**MP.1**
21.2, 21.3	2*	**S-CP.B.9**	**MP.2**
23.2	3	**S-CP.A.5**	**MP.4**
7.3	4*	**G-MG.A.3**	**MP.6**

* Item integrates mixed review concepts from previous modules or a previous course.

MIXED REVIEW
Assessment Readiness

ASSESSMENT AND INTERVENTION

Assign ready-made or customized practice tests to prepare students for high-stakes tests.

ADDITIONAL RESOURCES

Assessment Resources

- Leveled Unit Tests: Modified, A, B, C
- Performance Assessment

AVOID COMMON ERRORS

Item 3 Some students will not recognize that drawing the cards are dependent events. Remind students to look for the words "with replacement" for independent events using cards. If the words are not present, it is likely the event is dependent.

UNIT 8 MIXED REVIEW
Assessment Readiness

- Online Homework
- Hints and Help
- Extra Practice

1. Figure *ABCDE* is similar to figure *LMNOP*. Select True or False for each mathematical statement.

   A. $\frac{BC}{AE} = \frac{MN}{OP}$ ○ True   ● False

   B. $\frac{AB}{DE} = \frac{LM}{OP}$ ● True   ○ False

   C. $\frac{BD}{AE} = \frac{MN}{LP}$ ○ True   ● False

2. The transformation $(x, y) \rightarrow (x - 2, y + 1)$ is applied to $\triangle XYZ$. Select True or False for each statement.

   A. The area of $\triangle X'Y'Z'$ is the same as the area of $\triangle XYZ$.   ● True   ○ False

   B. The distance from X to X' is equal to the distance from Z to Z'.   ● True   ○ False

   C. The transformation is a rotation.   ○ True   ● False

3. Does each scenario describe independent events? Select Yes or No for each situation.

   A. Drawing two cards from a standard deck of cards that are both aces   ○ Yes   ● No

   B. Rolling a fair number cube twice and getting 6 on both rolls   ● Yes   ○ No

   C. Rolling a 3 on a fair number cube and flipping tails on a fair coin   ● Yes   ○ No

4. Each student in a class has been assigned at random to draw a parallelogram, a rectangle, a rhombus, or a square. Select True or False for each statement about the likelihood that a student will draw a parallelogram.

   A. It is unlikely because the probability is less than 0.5.   ○ True   ● False

   B. It is likely because the probability is between 0.5 and 0.75.   ○ True   ● False

   C. It is impossible for it not to happen because the probability is 1.   ● True   ○ False

5. The events A and B are independent. Select True or False for each statement.

   A. $P(A \mid B) = P(B \mid A)$ ○ True   ● False

   B. $P(A \text{ and } B) = P(B)P(A)$ ● True   ○ False

   C. $P(A) = P(B)$ ○ True   ● False

© Houghton Mifflin Harcourt Publishing Company

Common Core Standards

Items	Content Standards	Mathematical Practices
1	**G-SRT.A.2**	**MP.5**
2	**G-SRT.A.2**	**MP.6**
3*	**S-CP.A.2**	**MP.3, MP.8**
4*	**S-CP.B.6**	**MP.3, MP.8**
5	**S-CP.A.3**	**MP.2, MP.7**

* Item integrates mixed review concepts from previous modules or a previous course.

6. Vera needs to place 15 student volunteers at a local fire station. Five students will wash fire trucks, 7 will be assigned to paint, and 3 will be assigned to wash windows. What is the number of possible job assignments expressed using factorials and as a simplified number?

$\frac{15!}{5! \cdot 7! \cdot 3!}$ or $\frac{15!}{10! \cdot 5!} \cdot \frac{10!}{3! \cdot 7!} \cdot \frac{3!}{0! \cdot 3!}$; **360 assignments**

7. The table below shows the number of days that a meteorologist predicted it would be sunny and the number of days it was sunny. Based on the data in the table, what is the conditional probability that it will be sunny on a day when the meteorologist predicts it will be sunny? Show your work.

	Sunny	Not Sunny	Total
Predicts Sunny	570	20	590
Does Not Predict Sunny	63	347	410
Total	633	367	1000

$\frac{570}{590} \approx 96.6$ or 97%

8. Complete the two-way table below. Then find the fraction of red cards in a standard 52-card deck that have a number on them and find the fraction of numbered cards that are red.

	Red	Black	Total
Number	18	18	36
No Number	8	8	16
Total	26	26	52

Red cards with numbers on them: $\frac{9}{13}$

Numbered cards that are red: $\frac{1}{2}$

Performance Tasks

★ **9.** Sixteen cards numbered 1 through 16 are placed face down, and Stephanie chooses one at random. What is the probability that the number on Stephanie's card is less than 5 or greater than 10? Show your work.

The cards that are less than 5: $\{1, 2, 3, 4\}$

The cards that are greater than 10: $\{11, 12, 13, 14, 15, 16\}$

Total number of cards that are either less than 5 or greater than 10: 10

$\frac{10}{16} = \frac{5}{8}$ or 62.5%

PERFORMANCE TASKS

There are three different levels of performance tasks:

*Novice: These are short word problems that require students to apply the math they have learned in straightforward, real-world situations.

**Apprentice: These are more involved problems that guide students step-by-step through more complex tasks. These exercises include more complicated reasoning, writing, and open ended elements.

***Expert: These are open-ended, nonroutine problems that, instead of stepping the students through, ask them to choose their own methods for solving and justify their answers and reasoning.

SCORING GUIDES

Item 9 (2 points) Award the student 1 point for the correct answer of $\frac{5}{8}$, and 1 point for showing work.

Common Core Standards

Items	Content Standards	Mathematical Practices
6	S-CP.B.9	MP.2, MP.7
7	S-CP.A.4	MP.2, MP.7
8	S-CP.A.4	MP.1

* Item integrates mixed review concepts from previous modules or a previous course.

2 points for correct probability for comedies given Class B

2 points for correct probability for Class B given comedies

1 point for explanation

1 point for showing work

Item 11 (6 points)

A. 1 point for correct answers
   1 point for explanation

B. 1 point for correct answer
   1 point for explanation

C. 1 point for correct answer
   1 point for explanation

★★**10.** Students in 4 different classes are surveyed about their favorite movie type. What is the probability that a randomly selected student in class B prefers comedies? What is the probability that a randomly selected student who prefers comedies is in class B? Explain why the two probabilities are not the same. Show your work.

	A	B	C	D
Action	12	9	8	11
Comedy	13	11	15	4
Drama	6	11	7	18

Total in class B $= 9 + 11 + 11 = 31$

$P(\text{comedies} \mid \text{class B}) = \frac{11}{31} \approx 0.355$

Total that prefer comedies $= 13 + 11 + 15 + 4 = 43$

$P(\text{class B} \mid \text{comedies}) = \frac{11}{43} \approx 0.256$

The conditional probabilities are different because the sample spaces are different, with 31 in class B and 43 that prefer comedies.

★★★**11.** A Chinese restaurant has a buffet that includes ice cream for dessert. The table shows the selections made last week.

	Chocolate	Vanilla	Strawberry
Cone	24	18	12
Dish	12	21	15

A. Which flavor is the most popular? Which serving method? Is the combination of the most popular flavor and serving method the most popular dessert choice overall? Explain.

B. Which of the following is more likely? Explain.
   • A customer chooses vanilla, given that the customer chose a cone.
   • A customer chooses a cone, given that the customer chose vanilla.

C. A class of 24 students gets the buffet for lunch. If all the students get ice cream, about how many will get a cone or vanilla? Explain.

A. The most popular are vanilla and cone because they have the largest marginal frequencies.

No; the most popular dessert choice is a chocolate cone and not a vanilla cone.

B. $P(\text{vanilla} \mid \text{cone}) = \frac{18}{24 + 18 + 12} \approx 33\%$

$P(\text{cone} \mid \text{vanilla}) = \frac{18}{18 + 21} \approx 46\%$

So a customer chooses a cone, given that the customer chose vanilla, is more likely because $46\% > 33\%$.

C. About 18 students because 75 of 102 is about 73.5% of 24 students

Epidemiologist An epidemiologist is aiding in the treatment of a community plagued by two different infectious agents, X and Z. Each infectious agent must be treated differently with a new treatment if the patient has been infected by both agents. The community has a total population of 15,000 people, where 5% are not affected by either agent and 60% are afflicted by the X infection. 39% of the population is afflicted by X but not by Z. Unfortunately, the treatment for the X infection fails 35% of the time. The same incident happened to 10 other communities with similar results as the first. What is the probability that people will be healthy? have the X affliction? have the Z affliction? have both afflictions?

Healthy people: 5%, X affliction: 60%, Z affliction: 56%, both: 21%

	Has X	Does not have X	Total
Has Z	$60 - 39 = 21\%$	$40 - 5 = 35\%$	$21 + 35 = 56\%$
Does not have Z	39%	5%	$100 - 56 = 44\%$
Total	60%	$100 - 60 = 40\%$	100%

$P(\text{Healthy}) = 0.05$

$P(\text{has X affliction}) = 0.6$

$P(\text{has Z affliction}) = 0.56$

$P(\text{has both X and Z}) = 0.21$

MATH IN CAREERS

Epidemiologist In this Unit Performance Task, students can see how an epidemiologist uses mathematics on the job.

For more information about careers in mathematics as well as various mathematics appreciation topics, visit the American Mathematical Society http://www.ams.org

SCORING GUIDES

Task (6 points)

2 points for correct probability of X affliction

2 points for correct probability of Z affliction

1 point for correct probability of health

1 point for correct probability of both afflictions

Glossary/Glosario

A

ENGLISH	SPANISH	EXAMPLES
acute angle An angle that measures greater than 0° and less than 90°.	**ángulo agudo** Ángulo que mide más de 0° y menos de 90°.	
acute triangle A triangle with three acute angles.	**triángulo acutángulo** Triángulo con tres ángulos agudos.	
adjacent angles Two angles in the same plane with a common vertex and a common side, but no common interior points.	**ángulos adyacentes** Dos ángulos en el mismo plano que tienen un vértice y un lado común pero no comparten puntos internos.	∠1 and ∠2 are adjacent angles.
adjacent arcs Two arcs of the same circle that intersect at exactly one point.	**arcos adyacentes** Dos arcos del mismo círculo que se cruzan en un punto exacto.	$\overset{\frown}{RS}$ and $\overset{\frown}{ST}$ are adjacent arcs.
alternate exterior angles For two lines intersected by a transversal, a pair of angles that lie on opposite sides of the transversal and outside the other two lines.	**ángulos alternos externos** Dadas dos líneas cortadas por una transversal, par de ángulos no adyacentes ubicados en los lados opuestos de la transversal y fuera de las otras dos líneas.	∠4 and ∠5 are alternate exterior angles.
alternate interior angles For two lines intersected by a transversal, a pair of nonadjacent angles that lie on opposite sides of the transversal and between the other two lines.	**ángulos alternos internos** Dadas dos líneas cortadas por una transversal, par de ángulos no adyacentes ubicados en los lados opuestos de la transversal y entre las otras dos líneas.	∠3 and ∠6 are alternate interior angles.
altitude of a cone A segment from the vertex to the plane of the base that is perpendicular to the plane of the base.	**altura de un cono** Segmento que se extiende desde el vértice hasta el plano de la base y es perpendicular al plano de la base.	h

altitude of a cylinder A segment with its endpoints on the planes of the bases that is perpendicular to the planes of the bases.

altura de un cilindro Segmento con sus extremos en los planos de las bases que es perpendicular a los planos de las bases.

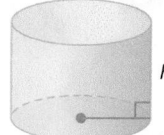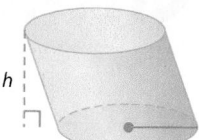

altitude of a prism A segment with its endpoints on the planes of the bases that is perpendicular to the planes of the bases.

altura de un prisma Segmento con sus extremos en los planos de las bases que es perpendicular a los planos de las bases.

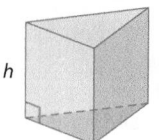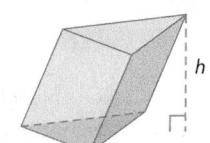

altitude of a pyramid A segment from the vertex to the plane of the base that is perpendicular to the plane of the base.

altura de una pirámide Segmento que se extiende desde el vértice hasta el plano de la base y es perpendicular al plano de la base.

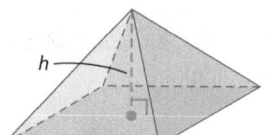

altitude of a triangle A perpendicular segment from a vertex to the line containing the opposite side.

altura de un triángulo Segmento perpendicular que se extiende desde un vértice hasta la línea que forma el lado opuesto.

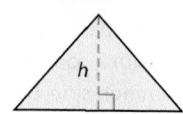

angle bisector A ray that divides an angle into two congruent angles.

bisectriz de un ángulo Rayo que divide un ángulo en dos ángulos congruentes.

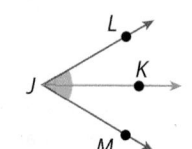

$\overrightarrow{JK}$ is an angle bisector of $\angle LJM$.

angle of rotation An angle formed by a rotating ray, called the terminal side, and a stationary reference ray, called the initial side.

ángulo de rotación Ángulo formado por un rayo rotativo, denominado lado terminal, y un rayo de referencia estático, denominado lado inicial.

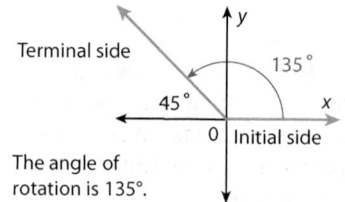

The angle of rotation is 135°.

angle of rotational symmetry The smallest angle through which a figure with rotational symmetry can be rotated to coincide with itself.

ángulo de simetría de rotación El ángulo más pequeño alrededor del cual se puede rotar una figura con simetría de rotación para que coincida consigo misma.

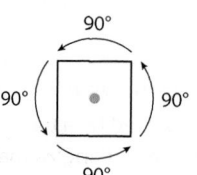

apothem The perpendicular distance from the center of a regular polygon to a side of the polygon.

apotema Distancia perpendicular desde el centro de un polígono regular hasta un lado del polígono.

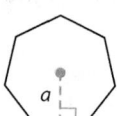

Glossary/Glosario

GL2

Glossary/Glosario

arc An unbroken part of a circle consisting of two points on the circle, called the endpoints, and all the points on the circle between them.

arco Parte continua de una circunferencia formada por dos puntos de la circunferencia denominados extremos y todos los puntos de la circunferencia comprendidos entre éstos.

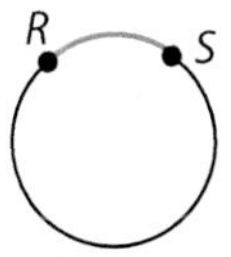

---

arc length The distance along an arc measured in linear units.

longitud de arco Distancia a lo largo de un arco medida en unidades lineales.

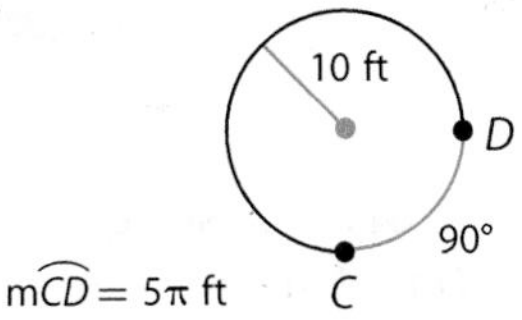

$m\widehat{CD} = 5\pi$ ft

---

arc marks Marks used on a figure to indicate congruent angles.

marcas de arco Marcas utilizadas en una figura para indicar ángulos congruentes.

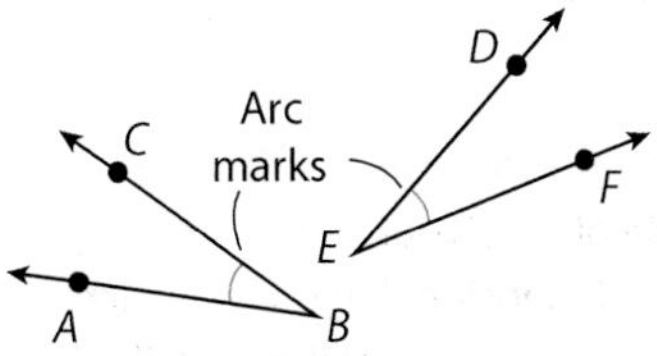

---

auxiliary line A line drawn in a figure to aid in a proof.

línea auxiliar Línea dibujada en una figura como ayuda en una demostración.

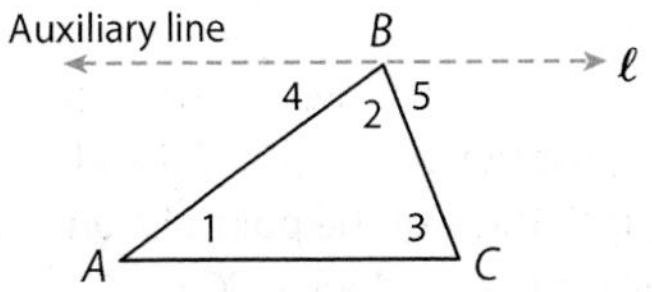

---

axiom *See* postulate.

axioma *Ver* postulado.

---

axis of a cone The segment with endpoints at the vertex and the center of the base.

eje de un cono Segmento cuyos extremos se encuentran en el vértice y en el centro de la base.

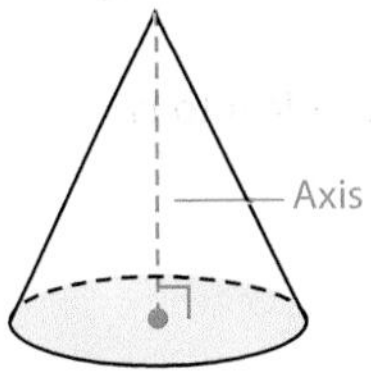

---

axis of a cylinder The segment with endpoints at the centers of the two bases.

eje de un cilindro Segmentos cuyos extremos se encuentran en los centros de las dos bases.

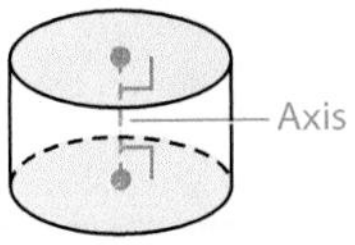

---

axis of symmetry A line that divides a plane figure or a graph into two congruent reflected halves.

eje de simetría Línea que divide una figura plana o una gráfica en dos mitades reflejadas congruentes.

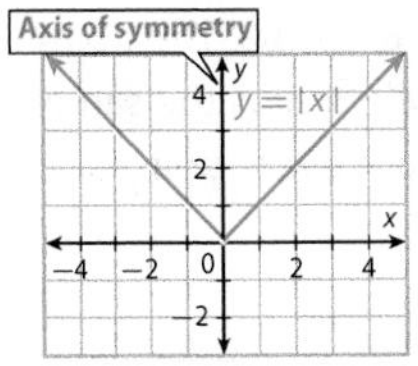

Glossary/Glosario

Glossary/Glosario

B

base angle of a trapezoid One of a pair of consecutive angles whose common side is a base of the trapezoid.

ángulo base de un trapecio Uno de los dos ángulos consecutivos cuyo lado en común es la base del trapecio.

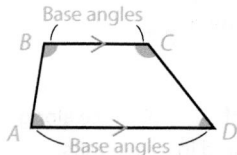

base angle of an isosceles triangle One of the two angles that have the base of the triangle as a side.

ángulo base de un triángulo isósceles Uno de los dos ángulos que tienen como lado la base del triángulo.

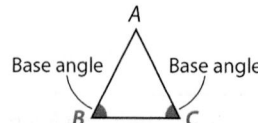

base of a geometric figure A side of a polygon; a face of a three-dimensional figure by which the figure is measured or classified.

base de una figura geométrica Lado de un polígono; cara de una figura tridimensional por la cual se mide o clasifica la figura.

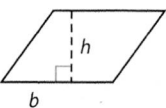 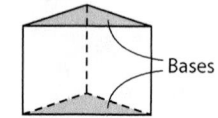

between Given three points A, B, and C, B is between A and C if and only if all three of the points lie on the same line, and $AB + BC = AC$.

entre Dados tres puntos A, B y C, B está entre A y C si y sólo si los tres puntos se encuentran en la misma línea y $AB + BC = AC$.

biconditional statement A statement that can be written in the form "p if and only if q."

enunciado bicondicional Enunciado que puede expresarse en la forma "p si y sólo si q".

A figure is a triangle if and only if it is a three-sided polygon.

bisect To divide into two congruent parts.

trazar una bisectriz Dividir en dos partes congruentes.

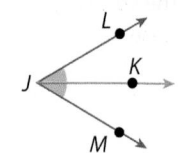

$\overrightarrow{JK}$ bisects $\angle LJM$.

C

center of a circle The point inside a circle that is the same distance from every point on the circle.

centro de un círculo Punto dentro de un círculo que se encuentra a la misma distancia de todos los puntos del círculo.

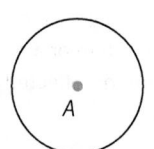

center of dilation The intersection of the lines that connect each point of the image with the corresponding point of the preimage.

centro de dilatación Intersección de las líneas que conectan cada punto de la imagen con el punto correspondiente de la imagen original.

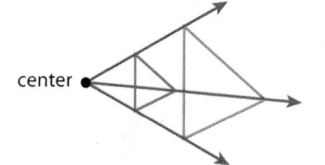

ENGLISH	SPANISH	EXAMPLES
center of rotation The point around which a figure is rotated.	**centro de rotación** Punto alrededor del cual rota una figura.	
central angle of a circle An angle whose vertex is the center of a circle.	**ángulo central de un círculo** Ángulo cuyo vértice es el centro de un círculo.	
centroid of a triangle The point of concurrency of the three medians of a triangle. Also known as the *center of gravity*.	**centroide de un triángulo** Punto donde se encuentran las tres medianas de un triángulo. También conocido como *centro de gravedad*.	The centroid is *P*.
chord A segment whose endpoints lie on a circle.	**cuerda** Segmento cuyos extremos se encuentran en un círculo.	
circle The set of points in a plane that are a fixed distance from a given point called the center of the circle.	**círculo** Conjunto de puntos en un plano que se encuentran a una distancia fija de un punto determinado denominado centro del círculo.	
circumcenter of a triangle The point of concurrency of the three perpendicular bisectors of a triangle.	**circuncentro de un triángulo** Punto donde se cortan las tres mediatrices de un triángulo.	The circumcenter is *P*.
circumcircle *See* circumscribed circle.	**circuncírculo** *Véase* círculo circunscrito.	
circumference The distance around the circle.	**circunferencia** Distancia alrededor del círculo.	Circumference
circumscribed angle An angle formed by two rays from a common endpoint that are tangent to a circle	**ángulo circunscrito** Ángulo formado por dos semirrectas tangentes a un círculo que parten desde un extremo común.	

ENGLISH	SPANISH	EXAMPLES
circumscribed circle Every vertex of the polygon lies on the circle.	**círculo circunscrito** Todos los vértices del polígono se encuentran sobre el círculo.	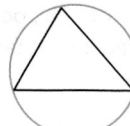
circumscribed polygon Each side of the polygon is tangent to the circle.	**polígono circunscrito** Todos los lados del polígono son tangentes al círculo.	
coincide To correspond exactly; to be identical.	**coincidir** Corresponder exactamente, ser idéntico.	
collinear Points that lie on the same line.	**colineal** Puntos que se encuentran sobre la misma línea.	 *K,L*, and *M* are collinear points.
combination A selection of a group of objects in which order is *not* important. The number of combinations of *r* objects chosen from a group of *n* objects is denoted $_nC_r$.	**combinación** Selección de un grupo de objetos en la cual el orden *no* es importante. El número de combinaciones de *r* objetos elegidos de un grupo de *n* objetos se expresa así: $_nC_r$.	For 4 objects *A, B, C,* and *D*, there are $_4C_2 = 6$ different combinations of 2 objects: *AB, AC, AD, BC, BD, CD*.
common tangent A line that is tangent to two circles.	**tangente común** Línea que es tangente a dos círculos.	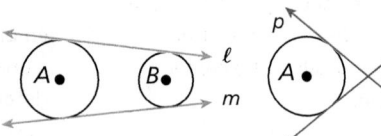
complement of an angle The sum of the measures of an angle and its complement is 90°.	**complemento de un ángulo** La suma de las medidas de un ángulo y su complemento es 90°.	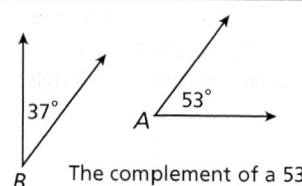 The complement of a 53° angle is a 37° angle.
complement of an event All outcomes in the sample space that are not in an event *E*, denoted $\bar{E}$.	**complemento de un suceso** Todos los resultados en el espacio muestral que no están en el suceso *E* y se expresan $\bar{E}$.	In the experiment of rolling a number cube, the complement of rolling a 3 is rolling a 1, 2, 4, 5, or 6.
complementary angles Two angles whose measures have a sum of 90°.	**ángulos complementarios** Dos ángulos cuyas medidas suman 90°.	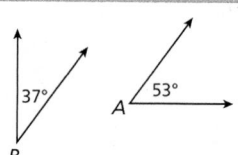

component form The form of
a vector that lists the vertical and
horizontal change from the initial
point to the terminal point.

forma de componente Forma
de un vector que muestra el cambio
horizontal y vertical desde el punto
inicial hasta el punto terminal.

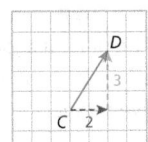

The component form of $\overrightarrow{CD}$ is $\langle 2, 3 \rangle$.

---

composite figure A plane figure
made up of triangles, rectangles,
trapezoids, circles, and other simple
shapes, or a three-dimensional
figure made up of prisms, cones,
pyramids, cylinders, and other
simple three-dimensional figures.

figura compuesta Figura
plana compuesta por triángulos,
rectángulos, trapecios, círculos
y otras figuras simples, o figura
tridimensional compuesta por
prismas, conos, pirámides, cilindros
y otras figuras tridimensionales
simples.

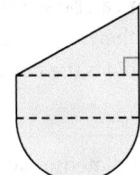

**composition of
transformations** One
transformation followed by another
transformation.

**composición de
transformaciones** Una
transformación seguida de otra
transformación.

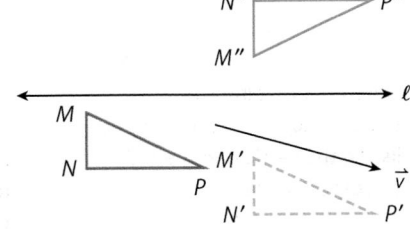

---

compound event An event made
up of two or more simple events.

suceso compuesto Suceso
formado por dos o más sucesos
simples.

In the experiment of tossing a coin and
rolling a number cube, the event of the coin
landing heads and the number cube
landing on 3.

---

concave polygon A polygon
in which a diagonal can be drawn
such that part of the diagonal
contains points in the exterior of the
polygon.

polígono cóncavo Polígono en
el cual se puede trazar una diagonal
tal que parte de la diagonal
contiene puntos ubicados fuera del
polígono.

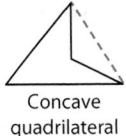

Concave
quadrilateral

---

conclusion The part of a
conditional statement following the
word *then*.

conclusión Parte de un
enunciado condicional que sigue a
la palabra *entonces*.

If $x + 1 = 5$, then $\underline{x = 4}$.
Conclusion

---

concurrent Three or more lines
that intersect at one point.

concurrente Tres o más líneas
que se cortan en un punto.

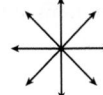

---

conditional probability The
probability of event *B*, given that
event *A* has already occurred
or is certain to occur, denoted
$P(B \mid A)$; used to find probability of
dependent events.

probabilidad condicional
Probabilidad del suceso *B*, dado
que el suceso *A* ya ha ocurrido o
es seguro que ocurrirá, expresada
como $P(B \mid A)$; se utiliza para
calcular la probabilidad de sucesos
dependientes.

Glossary/Glosario

conditional relative frequency The ratio of a joint relative frequency to a related marginal relative frequency in a two-way table.

frecuencia relativa condicional Razón de una frecuencia relativa conjunta a una frecuencia relativa marginal en una tabla de doble entrada.

---

conditional statement A statement that can be written in the form "if p, then q," where p is the hypothesis and q is the conclusion.

enunciado condicional Enunciado que se puede expresar como "si p, entonces q", donde p es la hipótesis y q es la conclusión.

If $\underline{x+1=5}$, then $\underline{x=4}$.
     Hypothesis   Conclusion

---

cone A three-dimensional figure with a circular base and a curved lateral surface that connects the base to a point called the vertex.

cono Figura tridimensional con una base circular y una superficie lateral curva que conecta la base con un punto denominado vértice.

---

congruence statement A statement that indicates that two polygons are congruent by listing the vertices in the order of correspondence.

enunciado de congruencia Enunciado que indica que dos polígonos son congruentes enumerando los vértices en orden de correspondencia.

$\triangle HKL \cong \triangle YWX$

---

congruence transformation *See* isometry.

transformación de congruencia *Ver* isometría.

---

congruent Having the same size and shape, denoted by $\cong$.

congruente Que tiene el mismo tamaño y la misma forma, expresado por $\cong$.

$\overline{PQ} \cong \overline{SR}$

---

congruent polygons Two polygons whose corresponding sides and angles are congruent.

polígonos congruentes Dos polígonos cuyos lados y ángulos correspondientes son congruentes.

---

conjecture A statement that is believed to be true.

conjetura Enunciado que se supone verdadero.

A sequence begins with the terms 2, 4, 6, 8, 10. A reasonable conjecture is that the next term in the sequence is 12.

---

consecutive interior angles *See* same-side interior angles.

ángulos internos consecutivos *Ver* ángulos internos del mismo lado.

---

contrapositive The statement formed by both exchanging and negating the hypothesis and conclusion of a conditional statement.

contrarrecíproco Enunciado que se forma al intercambiar y negar la hipótesis y la conclusión de un enunciado condicional.

Statement: If $n + 1 = 3$, then $n = 2$.
Contrapositive: If $n \neq 2$, then $n + 1 \neq 3$.

ENGLISH	SPANISH	EXAMPLES
converse The statement formed by exchanging the hypothesis and conclusion of a conditional statement.	**recíproco** Enunciado que se forma intercambiando la hipótesis y la conclusión de un enunciado condicional.	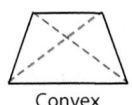 Statement: If $n + 1 = 3$, then $n = 2$. Converse: If $n = 2$, then $n + 1 = 3$.
convex polygon A polygon in which no diagonal contains points in the exterior of the polygon.	**polígono convexo** Polígono en el cual ninguna diagonal contiene puntos fuera del polígono.	 Convex quadrilateral
coordinate A number used to identify the location of a point. On a number line, one coordinate is used. On a coordinate plane, two coordinates are used, called the x-coordinate and the y-coordinate. In space, three coordinates are used, called the x-coordinate, the y-coordinate, and the z-coordinate.	**coordenada** Número utilizado para identificar la ubicación de un punto. En una recta numérica se utiliza una coordenada. En un plano cartesiano se utilizan dos coordenadas, denominadas coordenada x y coordenada y. En el espacio se utilizan tres coordenadas, denominadas coordenada x, coordenada y y coordenada z.	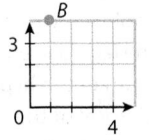 The coordinate of point A is 3. The coordinates of point B are (1, 4).
coordinate proof A style of proof that uses coordinate geometry and algebra.	**prueba de coordenadas** Tipo de demostración que utiliza geometría de coordenadas y álgebra.	
coplanar Points that lie in the same plane.	**coplanar** Puntos que se encuentran en el mismo plano.	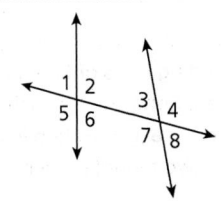
corollary A theorem whose proof follows directly from another theorem.	**corolario** Teorema cuya demostración proviene directamente de otro teorema.	
corresponding angles of lines intersected by a transversal For two lines intersected by a transversal, a pair of angles that lie on the same side of the transversal and on the same sides of the other two lines.	**ángulos correspondientes de líneas cortadas por una transversal** Dadas dos líneas cortadas por una transversal, el par de ángulos ubicados en el mismo lado de la transversal y en los mismos lados de las otras dos líneas.	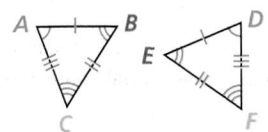 ∠1 and ∠3 are corresponding.
corresponding angles of polygons Angles in the same position in two different polygons that have the same number of angles.	**ángulos correspondientes de los polígonos** Ángulos que tienen la misma posición en dos polígonos diferentes que tienen el mismo número de ángulos.	∠A and ∠D are corresponding angles.

Glossary/Glosario

ENGLISH	SPANISH	EXAMPLES
corresponding sides of polygons Sides in the same position in two different polygons that have the same number of sides.	**lados correspondientes de los polígonos** Lados que tienen la misma posición en dos polígonos diferentes que tienen el mismo número de lados.	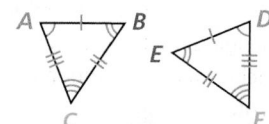 $\overline{AB}$ and $\overline{DE}$ are corresponding sides.
cosecant In a right triangle, the cosecant of angle A is the ratio of the length of the hypotenuse to the length of the side opposite A. It is the reciprocal of the sine function.	**cosecante** En un triángulo rectángulo, la cosecante del ángulo A es la razón entre la longitud de la hipotenusa y la longitud del cateto opuesto a A. Es la inversa de la función seno.	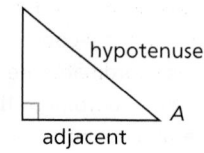 $\csc A = \dfrac{\text{hypotenuse}}{\text{opposite}} = \dfrac{1}{\sin A}$
cosine In a right triangle, the cosine of angle A is the ratio of the length of the leg adjacent to angle A to the length of the hypotenuse. It is the reciprocal of the secant function.	**coseno** En un triángulo rectángulo, el coseno del ángulo A es la razón entre la longitud del cateto adyacente al ángulo A y la longitud de la hipotenusa. Es la inversa de la función secante.	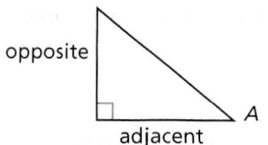 $\cos A = \dfrac{\text{adjacent}}{\text{hypotenuse}} = \dfrac{1}{\sec A}$
cotangent In a right triangle, the cotangent of angle A is the ratio of the length of the side adjacent to A to the length of the side opposite A. It is the reciprocal of the tangent function.	**cotangente** En un triángulo rectángulo, la cotangente del ángulo A es la razón entre la longitud del cateto adyacente a A y la longitud del cateto opuesto a A. Es la inversa de la función tangente.	$\cot A = \dfrac{\text{adjacent}}{\text{opposite}} = \dfrac{1}{\tan A}$
counterexample An example that proves that a conjecture or statement is false.	**contraejemplo** Ejemplo que demuestra que una conjetura o enunciado es falso.	
CPCTC An abbreviation for "Corresponding Parts of Congruent Triangles are Congruent," which can be used as a justification in a proof after two triangles are proven congruent.	**PCTCC** Abreviatura que significa "Las partes correspondientes de los triángulos congruentes son congruentes", que se puede utilizar para justificar una demostración después de demostrar que dos triángulos son congruentes (CPCTC, por sus siglas en inglés).	
cross section The intersection of a three-dimensional figure and a plane.	**sección transversal** Intersección de una figura tridimensional y un plano.	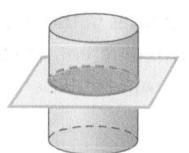

ENGLISH	SPANISH	EXAMPLES
cube A prism with six square faces.	**cubo** Prisma con seis caras cuadradas.	
cylinder A three-dimensional figure with two parallel congruent circular bases and a curved lateral surface that connects the bases.	**cilindro** Figura tridimensional con dos bases circulares congruentes y paralelas y una superficie lateral curva que conecta las bases.	

D

ENGLISH	SPANISH	EXAMPLES
decagon A ten-sided polygon.	**decágono** Polígono de diez lados.	
deductive reasoning The process of using logic to draw conclusions.	**razonamiento deductivo** Proceso en el que se utiliza la lógica para sacar conclusiones.	
definition A statement that describes a mathematical object and can be written as a true biconditional statement.	**definición** Enunciado que describe un objeto matemático y se puede expresar como un enunciado bicondicional verdadero.	
degree A unit of angle measure; one degree is $\frac{1}{360}$ of a circle.	**grado** Unidad de medida de los ángulos; un grado es $\frac{1}{360}$ de un círculo.	
density The amount of matter that an object has in a given unit of volume. The density of an object is calculated by dividing its mass by its volume.	**densidad** La cantidad de materia que tiene un objeto en una unidad de volumen determinada. La densidad de un objeto se calcula dividiendo su masa entre su volumen.	$\text{density} = \frac{\text{mass}}{\text{volume}}$
dependent events Events for which the occurrence or nonoccurrence of one event affects the probability of the other event.	**sucesos dependientes** Dos sucesos son dependientes si el hecho de que uno de ellos se cumpla o no afecta la probabilidad del otro.	From a bag containing 3 red marbles and 2 blue marbles, drawing a red marble, and then drawing a blue marble without replacing the first marble.
diagonal of a polygon A segment connecting two nonconsecutive vertices of a polygon.	**diagonal de un polígono** Segmento que conecta dos vértices no consecutivos de un polígono.	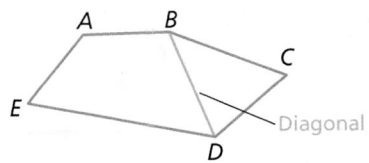
diameter A segment that has endpoints on the circle and that passes through the center of the circle; also the length of that segment.	**diámetro** Segmento que atraviesa el centro de un círculo y cuyos extremos están sobre la circunferencia; longitud de dicho segmento.	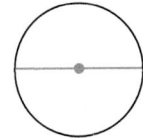

ENGLISH	SPANISH	EXAMPLES
dilation A transformation in which the lines connecting every point P with its preimage P' all intersect at a point C known as the center of dilation, and $\frac{CP'}{CP}$ is the same for every point P; a transformation that changes the size of a figure but not its shape.	**dilatación** Transformación en la cual las líneas que conectan cada punto P con su imagen original P' se cruzan en un punto C conocido como centro de dilatación, y $\frac{CP'}{CP}$ es igual para cada punto P; transformación que cambia el tamaño de una figura pero no su forma.	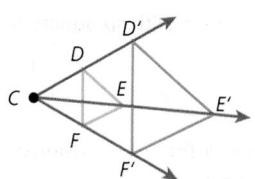
directed line segment A segment between two points A and B with a specified direction, from A to B or from B to A.	**segmento de una línea con dirección** Un segmento entro dos puntos con una dirección especificada.	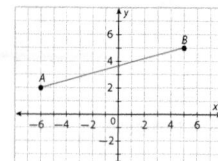
direction of a vector The orientation of a vector, which is determined by the angle the vector makes with a horizontal line.	**dirección de un vector** Orientación de un vector, determinada por el ángulo que forma el vector con una línea horizontal.	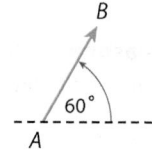
directrix A fixed line used to define a *parabola*. Every point on the parabola is equidistant from the directrix and a fixed point called the *focus*.	**directriz** Línea fija utilizada para definir una *parábola*. Cada punto de la parábola es equidistante de la directriz y de un punto fijo denominado *foco*.	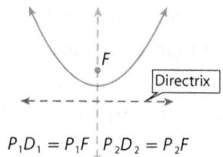 $P_1D_1 = P_1F \quad P_2D_2 = P_2F$
distance between two points The absolute value of the difference of the coordinates of the points.	**distancia entre dos puntos** Valor absoluto de la diferencia entre las coordenadas de los puntos.	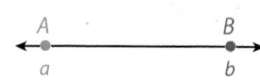 $AB = |a - b| = |b - a|$
distance from a point to a line The length of the perpendicular segment from the point to the line.	**distancia desde un punto hasta una línea** Longitud del segmento perpendicular desde el punto hasta la línea.	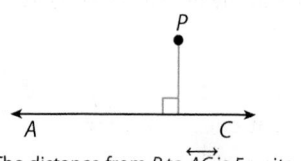 The distance from P to $\overleftrightarrow{AC}$ is 5 units.
dodecagon A 12-sided polygon.	**dodecágono** Polígono de 12 lados.	

E

element of a set An item in a set.	**elemento de un conjunto** Componente de un conjunto.	4 is an element of the set of even numbers. $4 \in \{\text{even numbers}\}$

ENGLISH	SPANISH	EXAMPLES
empty set A set with no elements.	**conjunto vacío** Conjunto sin elementos.	The solution set of $\lvert x \rvert < 0$ is the empty set, $\{\ \}$, or $\varnothing$.
endpoint A point at an end of a segment or the starting point of a ray.	**extremo** Punto en el final de un segmento o punto de inicio de un rayo.	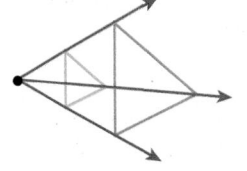
enlargement A dilation with a scale factor greater than 1. In an enlargement, the image is larger than the preimage.	**agrandamiento** Dilatación con un factor de escala mayor que 1. En un agrandamiento, la imagen es más grande que la imagen original.	
equally likely outcomes Outcomes are equally likely if they have the same probability of occurring. If an experiment has n equally likely outcomes, then the probability of each outcome is $\frac{1}{n}$.	**resultados igualmente probables** Los resultados son igualmente probables si tienen la misma probabilidad de ocurrir. Si un experimento tiene n resultados igualmente probables, entonces la probabilidad de cada resultado es $\frac{1}{n}$.	If a coin is tossed, and heads and tails are equally likely, then $P(\text{heads}) = P(\text{tails}) = \frac{1}{2}$.
equiangular polygon A polygon in which all angles are congruent.	**polígono equiangular** Polígono cuyos ángulos son todos congruentes.	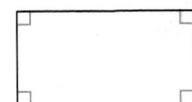
equiangular triangle A triangle with three congruent angles.	**triángulo equiangular** Triángulo con tres ángulos congruentes.	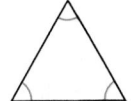
equidistant The same distance from two or more objects.	**equidistante** Igual distancia de dos o más objetos.	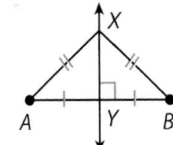 X is equidistant from A and B.
equilateral polygon A polygon in which all sides are congruent.	**polígono equilátero** Polígono cuyos lados son todos congruentes.	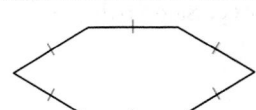
equilateral triangle A triangle with three congruent sides.	**triángulo equilátero** Triángulo con tres lados congruentes.	

Glossary/Glosario

Glossary/Glosario

ENGLISH	SPANISH	EXAMPLES
Euclidean geometry The system of geometry described by Euclid. In particular, the system of Euclidean geometry satisfies the Parallel Postulate, which states that there is exactly one line through a given point parallel to a given line.	**geometría euclidiana** Sistema geométrico desarrollado por Euclides. Específicamente, el sistema de la geometría euclidiana cumple con el postulado de las paralelas, que establece que por un punto dado se puede trazar una única línea paralela a una línea dada.	
event An outcome or set of outcomes in a probability experiment.	**suceso** Resultado o conjunto de resultados en un experimento de probabilidad.	In the experiement of rolling a number cube, the event "an odd number" consists of the outcomes 1, 3, 5.
experiment An operation, process, or activity in which outcomes can be used to estimate probability.	**experimento** Una operación, proceso o actividad en la que se usan los resultados para estimar una probabilidad.	Tossing a coin 10 times and noting the number of heads.
experimental probability The ratio of the number of times an event occurs to the number of trials, or times, that an activity is performed.	**probabilidad experimental** Razón entre la cantidad de veces que ocurre un suceso y la cantidad de pruebas, o veces, que se realiza una actividad.	Kendra made 6 of 10 free throws. The experimental probability that she will make her next free throw is $$P\left(\text{free throw}\right) = \frac{\text{number made}}{\text{number attempted}} = \frac{6}{10}.$$
exterior of a circle The set of all points outside a circle.	**exterior de un círculo** Conjunto de todos los puntos que se encuentran fuera de un círculo.	Exterior
exterior of an angle The set of all points outside an angle.	**exterior de un ángulo** Conjunto de todos los puntos que se encuentran fuera de un ángulo.	Exterior
exterior of a polygon The set of all points outside a polygon.	**exterior de un polígono** Conjunto de todos los puntos que se encuentran fuera de un polígono.	Exterior
exterior angle of a polygon An angle formed by one side of a polygon and the extension of an adjacent side.	**ángulo externo de un polígono** Ángulo formado por un lado de un polígono y la prolongación del lado adyacente.	$\angle 4$ is an exterior angle.

ENGLISH	SPANISH	EXAMPLES

external secant segment A segment of a secant that lies in the exterior of the circle with one endpoint on the circle.

segmento secante externo Segmento de una secante que se encuentra en el exterior del círculo y tiene un extremo sobre el círculo.

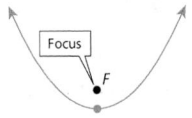

$\overline{NM}$ is an external secant segment.

F

factorial If n is a positive integer, then n factorial, written $n!$, is $n \cdot (n-1) \cdot (n-2) \cdot \ldots \cdot 2 \cdot 1$. The factorial of 0 is defined to be 1.

factorial Si n es un entero positivo, entonces el factorial de n, expresado como $n!$, es $n \cdot (n-1) \cdot (n-2) \cdot \ldots \cdot 2 \cdot 1$. Por definición, el factorial de 0 será 1.

$7! = 7 \cdot 6 \cdot 5 \cdot 4 \cdot 3 \cdot 2 \cdot 1 = 5040$
$0! = 1$

fair When all outcomes of an experiment are equally likely.

justo Cuando todos los resultados de un experimento son igualmente probables.

When tossing a fair coin, heads and tails are equally likely. Each has a probability of $\frac{1}{2}$.

favorable outcome The occurrence of one of several possible outcomes of a specified event or probability experiment.

resultado favorable Cuando se produce uno de varios resultados posibles de un suceso específico o experimento de probabilidad.

In the experiment of rolling an odd number on a number cube, the favorable outcomes are 1, 3, and 5.

focus (pl. foci) of a parabola A fixed point F used with a *directrix* to define a *parabola*.

foco de una parábola Punto fijo F utilizado con una *directriz* para definir una *parábola*.

Fundamental Counting Principle For n items, if there are m_1 ways to choose a first item, m_2 ways to choose a second item after the first item has been chosen, and so on, then there are $m_1 \cdot m_2 \cdot \ldots \cdot m_n$ ways to choose n items.

Principio fundamental deconteo Dados n elementos, si existen m_1 formas de elegir un primer elemento, m_2 formas de elegir un segundo elemento después de haber elegido el primero, y así sucesivamente, entonces existen $m_1 \cdot m_2 \cdot \ldots \cdot m_n$ formas de elegir n elementos.

If there are 4 colors of shirts, 3 colors of pants, and 2 colors of shoes, then there are $4 \cdot 3 \cdot 2 = 24$ possible outfits.

G

geometric mean For positive numbers a and b, the positive number x such that $\frac{a}{x} = \frac{x}{b}$. In a geometric sequence, a term that comes between two given nonconsecutive terms of the sequence.

media geométrica Dados los números positivos a y b, el número positivo x tal que $\frac{a}{x} = \frac{x}{b}$. En una sucesión geométrica, un término que está entre dos términos no consecutivos dados de la sucesión.

$\frac{a}{x} = \frac{x}{b}$
$x^2 = ab$
$x = \sqrt{ab}$

ENGLISH	SPANISH	EXAMPLES

geometric probability A form of theoretical probability determined by a ratio of geometric measures such as lengths, areas, or volumes.

probabilidad geométrica Una forma de la probabilidad teórica determinada por una razón de medidas geométricas, como longitud, área o volumen.

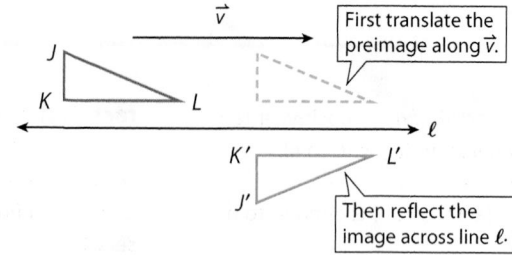

The probability of the pointer landing on 80° is $\frac{2}{9}$.

---

glide reflection A composition of a translation and a reflection across a line parallel to the translation vector.

deslizamiento con inversión Composición de una traslación y una reflexión sobre una línea paralela al vector de traslación.

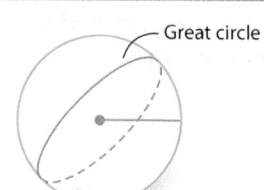

First translate the preimage along $\vec{v}$.

Then reflect the image across line ℓ.

---

great circle A circle on a sphere that divides the sphere into two hemispheres.

círculo máximo En una esfera, círculo que divide la esfera en dos hemisferios.

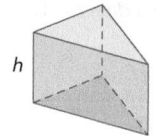

Great circle

H

---

height of a figure The length of an altitude of the figure.

altura de una figura Longitud de la altura de la figura.

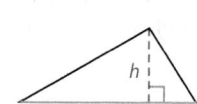

---

hemisphere Half of a sphere.

hemisferio Mitad de una esfera.

---

heptagon A seven-sided polygon.

heptágono Polígono de siete lados.

---

hexagon A six-sided polygon.

hexágono Polígono de seis lados.

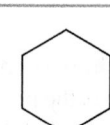

---

hypotenuse The side opposite the right angle in a right triangle.

hipotenusa Lado opuesto al ángulo recto de un triángulo rectángulo.

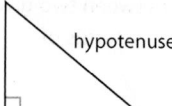

hypotenuse

---

hypothesis The part of a conditional statement following the word *if*.

hipótesis La parte de un enunciado condicional que sigue a la palabra *si*.

If $x + 1 = 5$, then $x = 4$.

  Hypothesis

I

---

identity An equation that is true for all values of the variables.

identidad Ecuación verdadera para todos los valores de las variables.

$3 = 3$
$2(x - 1) = 2x - 2$

---

image A shape that results from a transformation of a figure known as the preimage.

imagen Forma resultante de la transformación de una figura conocida como imagen original.

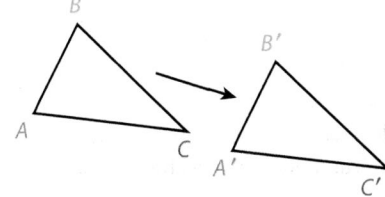

---

incenter of a triangle The point of concurrency of the three angle bisectors of a triangle.

incentro de un triángulo Punto donde se encuentran las tres bisectrices de los ángulos de un triángulo.

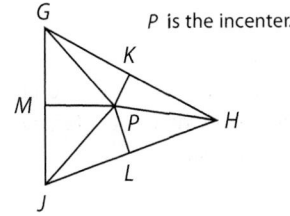

P is the incenter.

---

incircle *See* inscribed circle.

incírculo *Véase* círculo inscrito.

---

included angle The angle formed by two adjacent sides of a polygon.

ángulo incluido Ángulo formado por dos lados adyacentes de un polígono.

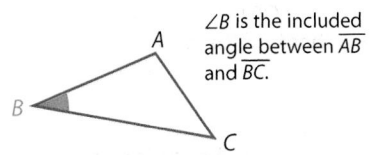

$\angle B$ is the included angle between $\overline{AB}$ and $\overline{BC}$.

---

included side The common side of two consecutive angles of a polygon.

lado incluido Lado común de dos ángulos consecutivos de un polígono.

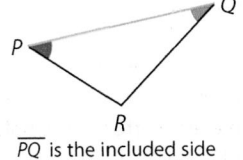

$\overline{PQ}$ is the included side between $\angle P$ and $\angle Q$.

---

independent events Events for which the occurrence or nonoccurrence of one event does not affect the probability of the other event.

sucesos independientes Dos sucesos son independientes si el hecho de que se produzca o no uno de ellos no afecta la probabilidad del otro suceso.

From a bag containing 3 red marbles and 2 blue marbles, drawing a red marble, replacing it, and then drawing a blue marble.

---

indirect measurement A method of measurement that uses formulas, similar figures, and/or proportions.

medición indirecta Método para medir objetos mediante fórmulas, figuras semejantes y/o proporciones.

Glossary/Glosario

ENGLISH	SPANISH	EXAMPLES
indirect proof A proof in which the statement to be proved is assumed to be false and a contradiction is shown.	**demostración indirecta** Prueba en la que se supone que el enunciado a demostrar es falso y se muestra una contradicción.	
indirect reasoning *See* indirect proof.	**razonamiento indirecto** *Ver* demostración indirecta.	
inductive reasoning The process of reasoning that a rule or statement is true because specific cases are true.	**razonamiento inductivo** Proceso de razonamiento por el que se determina que una regla o enunciado son verdaderos porque ciertos casos específicos son verdaderos.	
initial point of a vector The starting point of a vector.	**punto inicial de un vector** Punto donde comienza un vector.	
initial side The ray that lies on the positive *x*-axis when an angle is drawn in standard position.	**lado inicial** Rayo que se encuentra sobre el eje *x* positivo cuando se traza un ángulo en posición estándar.	
inscribed angle An angle whose vertex is on a circle and whose sides contain chords of the circle.	**ángulo inscrito** Ángulo cuyo vértice se encuentra sobre un círculo y cuyos lados contienen cuerdas del círculo.	
inscribed circle A circle in which each side of the polygon is tangent to the circle.	**círculo inscrito** Círculo en el que cada lado del polígono es tangente al círculo.	
inscribed polygon A polygon in which every vertex of the polygon lies on the circle.	**polígono inscrito** Polígono cuyos vértices se encuentran sobre el círculo.	
intercepted arc An arc that consists of endpoints that lie on the sides of an inscribed angle and all the points of the circle between the endpoints.	**arco abarcado** Arco cuyos extremos se encuentran en los lados de un ángulo inscrito y consta de todos los puntos del círculo ubicados entre dichos extremos.	$\widehat{DF}$ is the intercepted arc.

ENGLISH	SPANISH	EXAMPLES
interior angle An angle formed by two sides of a polygon with a common vertex.	**ángulo interno** Ángulo formado por dos lados de un polígono con un vértice común.	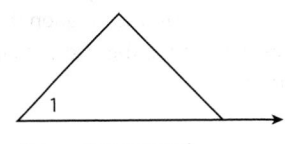 $\angle 1$ is an interior angle.
interior of a circle The set of all points inside a circle.	**interior de un círculo** Conjunto de todos los puntos que se encuentran dentro de un círculo.	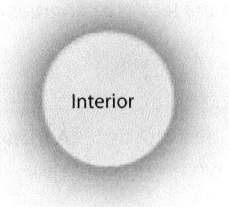
interior of an angle The set of all points between the sides of an angle.	**interior de un ángulo** Conjunto de todos los puntos entre los lados de un ángulo.	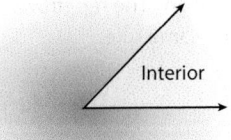
interior of a polygon The set of all points inside a polygon.	**interior de un polígono** Conjunto de todos los puntos que se encuentran dentro de un polígono.	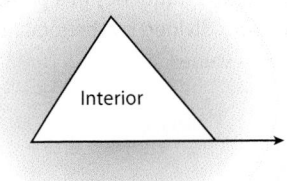
inverse The statement formed by negating the hypothesis and conclusion of a conditional statement.	**inverso** Enunciado formado al negar la hipótesis y la conclusión de un enunciado condicional.	Statement: If $n + 1 = 3$, then $n = 2$. Inverse: If $n + 1 \neq 3$, then $n \neq 2$.
inverse cosine The measure of an angle whose cosine ratio is known.	**coseno inverso** Medida de un ángulo cuya razón coseno es conocida.	If $\cos A = x$, then $\cos^{-1} x = m\angle A$.
inverse sine The measure of an angle whose sine ratio is known.	**seno inverso** Medida de un ángulo cuya razón seno es conocida.	If $\sin A = x$, then $\sin^{-1} x = m\angle A$.
inverse tangent The measure of an angle whose tangent ratio is known.	**tangente inversa** Medida de un ángulo cuya razón tangente es conocida.	If $\tan A = x$, then $\tan^{-1} x = m\angle A$.
irregular polygon A polygon that is not regular.	**polígono irregular** Polígono que no es regular.	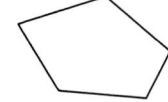

Glossary/Glosario

ENGLISH	SPANISH	EXAMPLES
isometry A transformation that does not change the size or shape of a figure.	**isometría** Transformación que no cambia el tamaño ni la forma de una figura.	Reflections, translations, and rotations are all examples of isometries.
isosceles trapezoid A trapezoid in which the legs are congruent but not parallel.	**trapecio isósceles** Trapecio cuyos lados no paralelos son congruentes.	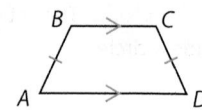
isosceles triangle A triangle with at least two congruent sides.	**triángulo isósceles** Triángulo que tiene al menos dos lados congruentes.	
iteration The repetitive application of the same rule.	**iteración** Aplicación repetitiva de la misma regla.v	

J

joint relative frequency The ratio of the frequency in a particular category divided by the total number of data values.	**frecuencia relativa conjunta** La razón de la frecuencia en una determinada categoría dividida entre el número total de valores.	

K

kite A quadrilateral with exactly two pairs of congruent consecutive sides.	**cometa o papalote** Cuadrilátero con exactamente dos pares de lados congruentes consecutivos.	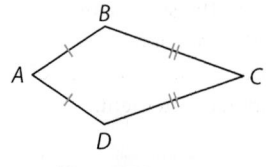Kite *ABCD*

L

lateral area The sum of the areas of the lateral faces of a prism or pyramid, or the area of the lateral surface of a cylinder or cone.	**área lateral** Suma de las áreas de las caras laterales de un prisma o pirámide, o área de la superficie lateral de un cilindro o cono.	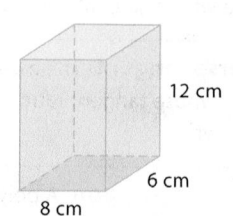Lateral area $= 4(6)(12) = 288$ cm²

Glossary/Glosario

ENGLISH	SPANISH	EXAMPLES
lateral edge An edge of a prism or pyramid that is not an edge of a base.	**arista lateral** Arista de un prisma o pirámide que no es la arista de una base.	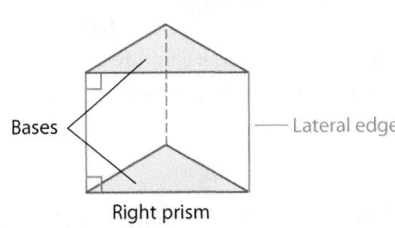 Bases — Lateral edge Right prism
lateral face A face of a prism or a pyramid that is not a base.	**cara lateral** Cara de un prisma o pirámide que no es la base.	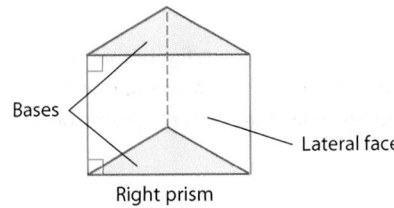 Bases — Lateral face Right prism
lateral surface The curved surface of a cylinder or cone.	**superficie lateral** Superficie curva de un cilindro o cono.	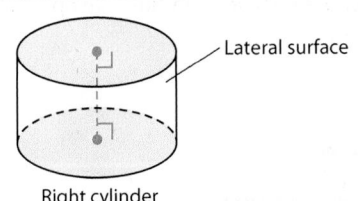 Lateral surface Right cylinder
leg of a right triangle One of the two sides of the right triangle that form the right angle.	**cateto de un triángulo rectángulo** Uno de los dos lados de un triángulo rectángulo que forman el ángulo recto.	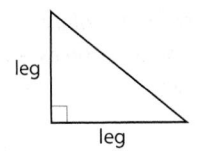 leg leg
leg of an isosceles triangle One of the two congruent sides of the isosceles triangle.	**cateto de un triángulo isósceles** Uno de los dos lados congruentes del triángulo isósceles.	 leg leg
legs of a trapezoid The sides of the trapezoid that are not the bases.	**catetos de un trapecio** Los lados del trapecio que no son las bases.	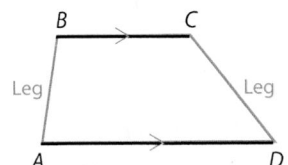 B C Leg Leg A D
length The distance between the two endpoints of a segment.	**longitud** Distancia entre los dos extremos de un segmento.	 A B a b $AB = \lvert a - b \rvert = \lvert b - a \rvert$
line An undefined term in geometry, a line is a straight path that has no thickness and extends forever.	**línea** Término indefinido en geometría; una línea es un trazo recto que no tiene grosor y se extiende infinitamente.	←——————→ ℓ

ENGLISH	SPANISH	EXAMPLES
line of symmetry A line that divides a plane figure into two congruent reflected halves.	**eje de simetría** Línea que divide una figura plana en dos mitades reflejas congruentes.	
line segment *See* segment of a line.	**segmento** *Véase* segmento de recta.	
line symmetry A figure that can be reflected across a line so that the image coincides with the preimage.	**simetría axial** Figura que puede reflejarse sobre una línea de forma tal que la imagen coincida con la imagen original.	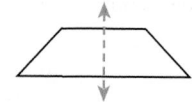
linear pair A pair of adjacent angles whose noncommon sides are opposite rays.	**par lineal** Par de ángulos adyacentes cuyos lados no comunes son rayos opuestos.	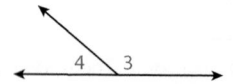 ∠3 and ∠4 form a linear pair.

M

ENGLISH	SPANISH	EXAMPLES
major arc An arc of a circle whose points are on or in the exterior of a central angle.	**arco mayor** Arco de un círculo cuyos puntos están sobre un ángulo central o en su exterior.	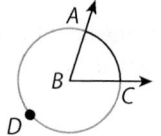 $\overset{\frown}{ADC}$ is a major arc of the circle.
mapping An operation that matches each element of a set with another element, its image, in the same set.	**correspondencia** Operación que establece una correlación entre cada elemento de un conjunto con otro elemento, su imagen, en el mismo conjunto.	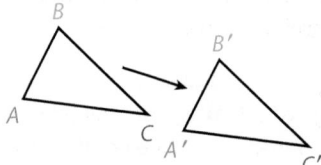
marginal relative frequency The sum of the joint relative frequencies in a row or column of a two-way table.	**frecuencia relativa marginal** La suma de las frecuencias relativas conjuntas en una fila o columna de una tabla de doble entrada.	
measure of an angle Angles are measured in degrees. A degree is $\frac{1}{360}$ of a complete circle.	**medida de un ángulo** Los ángulos se miden en grados. Un grado es $\frac{1}{360}$ de un círculo completo.	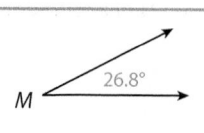 m∠M = 26.8°

ENGLISH	SPANISH	EXAMPLES
measure of a major arc The difference of 360° and the measure of the associated minor arc.	**medida de un arco mayor** Diferencia entre 360° y la medida del arco menor asociado.	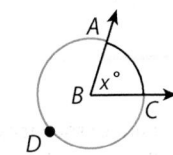 $m\widehat{ADC} = 360° - x°$
measure of a minor arc The measure of its central angle.	**medida de un arco menor** Medida de su ángulo central.	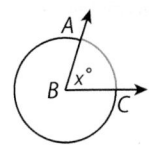 $m\widehat{AC} = x°$
median of a triangle A segment whose endpoints are a vertex of the triangle and the midpoint of the opposite side.	**mediana de un triángulo** Segmento cuyos extremos son un vértice del triángulo y el punto medio del lado opuesto.	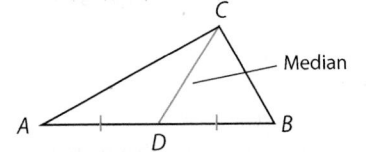
midpoint The point that divides a segment into two congruent segments.	**punto medio** Punto que divide un segmento en dos segmentos congruentes.	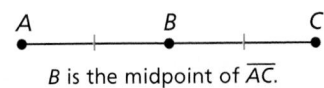 B is the midpoint of $\overline{AC}$.
midsegment of a trapezoid The segment whose endpoints are the midpoints of the legs of the trapezoid.	**segmento medio de un trapecio** Segmento cuyos extremos son los puntos medios de los catetos del trapecio.	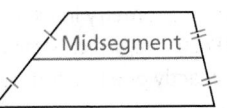
midsegment of a triangle A segment that joins the midpoints of two sides of the triangle.	**segmento medio de un triángulo** Segmento que une los puntos medios de dos lados del triángulo.	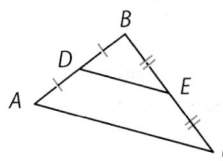
minor arc An arc of a circle whose points are on or in the interior of a central angle.	**arco menor** Arco de un círculo cuyos puntos están sobre un ángulo central o en su interior.	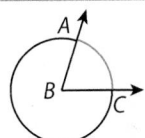 $\widehat{AC}$ is a minor arc of the circle.
mutually exclusive events Two events are mutually exclusive if they cannot both occur in the same trial of an experiment.	**sucesos mutuamente excluyentes** Dos sucesos son mutuamente excluyentes si ambos no pueden ocurrir en la misma prueba de un experimento.	In the experiment of rolling a number cube, rolling a 3 and rolling an even number are mutually exclusive events.

Glossary/Glosario

N

net A diagram of the faces of a three-dimensional figure arranged in such a way that the diagram can be folded to form the three-dimensional figure.

plantilla Diagrama de las caras de una figura tridimensional que se puede plegar para formar la figura tridimensional.

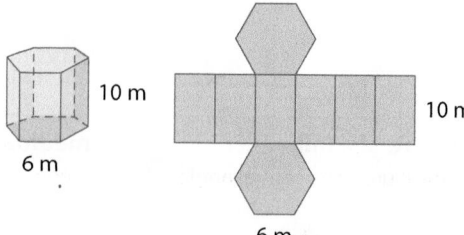

10 m

6 m

10 m

6 m

***n*-gon** An *n*-sided polygon.

***n*-ágono** Polígono de *n* lados.

---

nonagon A nine-sided polygon.

nonágono Polígono de nueve lados.

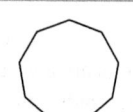

---

noncollinear Points that do not lie on the same line.

no colineal Puntos que no se encuentran sobre la misma línea.

Points *A*, *B*, and *D* are not collinear.

---

non-Euclidean geometry A system of geometry in which the Parallel Postulate, which states that there is exactly one line through a given point parallel to a given line, does not hold.

geometría no euclidiana Sistema de geometría en el cual no se cumple el postulado de las paralelas, que establece que por un punto dado se puede trazar una única línea paralela a una línea dada.

In spherical geometry, there are no parallel lines. The sum of the angles in a triangle is always greater than 180°.

---

noncoplanar Points that do not lie on the same plane.

no coplanar Puntos que no se encuentran en el mismo plano.

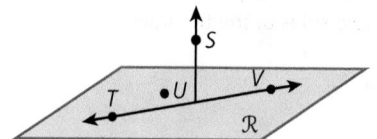

T, *U*, *V*, and *S* are not coplanar.

O

oblique cone A cone whose axis is not perpendicular to the base.

cono oblicuo Cono cuyo eje no es perpendicular a la base.

---

oblique cylinder A cylinder whose axis is not perpendicular to the bases.

cilindro oblicuo Cilindro cuyo eje no es perpendicular a las bases.

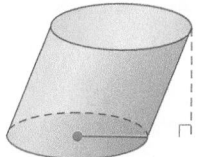

Glossary/Glosario

oblique prism A prism that has at least one nonrectangular lateral face.

prisma oblicuo Prisma que tiene por lo menos una cara lateral no rectangular.

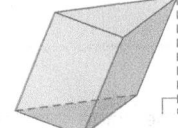

---

obtuse angle An angle that measures greater than 90° and less than 180°.

ángulo obtuso Ángulo que mide más de 90° y menos de 180°.

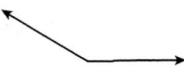

---

obtuse triangle A triangle with one obtuse angle.

triángulo obtusángulo Triángulo con un ángulo obtuso.

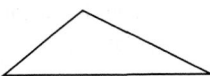

---

octagon An eight-sided polygon.

octágono Polígono de ocho lados.

---

opposite rays Two rays that have a common endpoint and form a line.

rayos opuestos Dos rayos que tienen un extremo común y forman una línea.

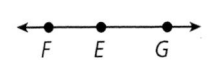

$\overrightarrow{EF}$ and $\overrightarrow{EG}$ are opposite rays.

---

order of rotational symmetry The number of times a figure with rotational symmetry coincides with itself as it rotates 360°.

orden de simetría de rotación Cantidad de veces que una figura con simetría de rotación coincide consigo misma cuando rota 360°.

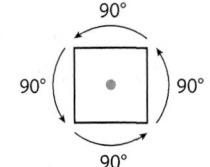

Order of rotational symmetry: 4

---

orthocenter of a triangle The point of concurrency of the three altitudes of a triangle.

ortocentro de un triángulo Punto de intersección de las tres alturas de un triángulo.

P is the orthocenter.

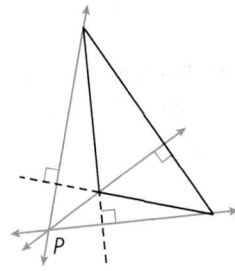

---

outcome A possible result of a probability experiment.

resultado Resultado posible de un experimento de probabilidad.

In the experiment of rolling a number cube, the possible outcomes are 1, 2, 3, 4, 5, and 6.

---

overlapping events Events that have one or more outcomes in common. Also called inclusive events.

sucesos superpuestos Sucesos que tienen uno o más resultados en común. También se denominan sucesos inclusivos.

Rolling an even number and rolling a prime number on a number cube are overlapping events because they both contain the outcome rolling a 2.

Glossary/Glosario

P

parabola The shape of the graph of a quadratic function. Also, the set of points equidistant from a point *F*, called the focus, and a line *d*, called the *directrix*.

parábola Forma de la gráfica de una función cuadrática. También, conjunto de puntos equidistantes de un punto *F*, denominado *foco*, y una línea *d*, denominada *directriz*.

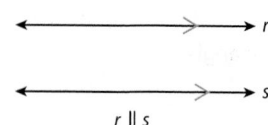

parallel lines Lines in the same plane that do not intersect.

líneas paralelas Líneas rectas en el mismo plano que no se cruzan.

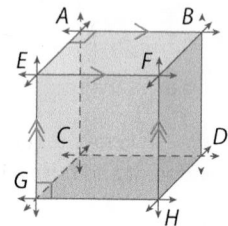

parallel planes Planes that do not intersect.

planos paralelos Planos que no se cruzan.

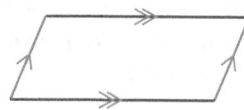

Plane *AEF* and plane *CGH* are parallel planes.

parallelogram A quadrilateral with two pairs of parallel sides.

paralelogramo Cuadrilátero con dos pares de lados paralelos.

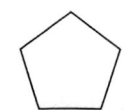

pentagon A five-sided polygon.

diagrama Polígono de cinco lados.

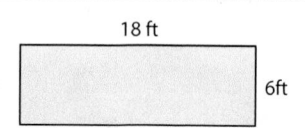

perimeter The sum of the side lengths of a closed plane figure.

perímetro Suma de las longitudes de los lados de una figura plana cerrada.

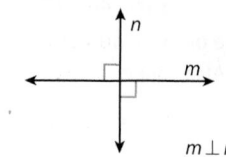

Perimeter = 18 + 6 + 18 + 6 = 48 ft

permutation An arrangement of a group of objects in which order is important. The number of permutations of *r* objects from a group of *n* objects is denoted $_nP_r$.

permutación Arreglo de un grupo de objetos en el cual el orden es importante. El número de permutaciones de *r* objetos de un grupo de *n* objetos se expresa $_nP_r$.

For 4 objects *A*, *B*, *C*, and *D*, there are $_4P_2 = 12$ different permutations of 2 objects: *AB*, *AC*, *AD*, *BC*, *BD*, *CD*, *BA*, *CA*, *DA*, *CB*, *DB*, and *DC*.

perpendicular Intersecting to form 90° angles, denoted by ⊥.

perpendicular Que se cruza para formar ángulos de 90°, expresado por ⊥.

$m \perp n$

perpendicular bisector of a segment A line perpendicular to a segment at the segment's midpoint.

mediatriz de un segmento Línea perpendicular a un segmento en el punto medio del segmento.

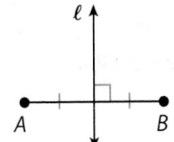

ℓ is the perpendicular bisector of $\overline{AB}$.

---

perpendicular lines Lines that intersect at 90° angles.

líneas perpendiculares Líneas que se cruzan en ángulos de 90°.

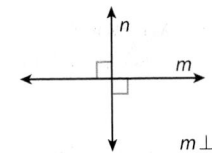

$m \perp n$

---

pi The ratio of the circumference of a circle to its diameter, denoted by the Greek letter π (pi). The value of π is irrational, often approximated by 3.14 or $\frac{22}{7}$.

pi Razón entre la circunferencia de un círculo y su diámetro, expresado por la letra griega π (pi). El valor de π es irracional y por lo general se aproxima a 3.14 ó $\frac{22}{7}$.

If a circle has a diameter of 5 inches and a circumference of C inches, then $\frac{C}{5} = \pi$, or $C = 5\pi$ inches, or about 15.7 inches.

---

plane An undefined term in geometry, it is a flat surface that has no thickness and extends forever.

plano Término indefinido en geometría; un plano es una superficie plana que no tiene grosor y se extiende infinitamente.

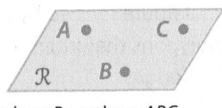

plane R or plane ABC

---

plane symmetry A three-dimensional figure that can be divided into two congruent reflected halves by a plane has plane symmetry.

simetría de plano Una figura tridimensional que se puede dividir en dos mitades congruentes reflejadas por un plano tiene simetría de plano.

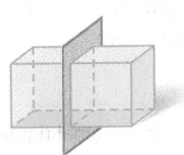

Plane symmetry

Platonic solid One of the five regular polyhedra: a tetrahedron, a cube, an octahedron, a dodecahedron, or an icosahedron.

sólido platónico Uno de los cinco poliedros regulares: tetraedro, cubo, octaedro, dodecaedro o icosaedro.

---

point An undefined term in geometry, it names a location and has no size.

punto Término indefinido de la geometría que denomina una ubicación y no tiene tamaño.

$P \bullet$

point *P*

---

point of concurrency A point where three or more lines coincide.

punto de concurrencia Punto donde se cruzan tres o más líneas.

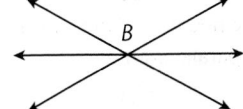

ENGLISH	SPANISH	EXAMPLES

point of tangency The point of intersection of a circle or sphere with a tangent line or plane.

punto de tangencia Punto de intersección de un círculo o esfera con una línea o plano tangente.

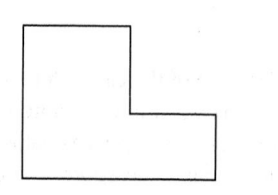

point-slope form
$y - y_1 = m(x - x_1)$, where m is the slope and (x_1, y_1) is a point on the line.

forma de punto y pendiente
$(y - y_1) = m(x - x_1)$, donde m es la pendiente y (x_1, y_1)es un punto en la línea.

polygon A closed plane figure formed by three or more segments such that each segment intersects exactly two other segments only at their endpoints and no two segments with a common endpoint are collinear.

polígono Figura plana cerrada formada por tres o más segmentos tal que cada segmento se cruza únicamente con otros dos segmentos sólo en sus extremos y ningún segmento con un extremo común a otro es colineal con éste.

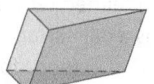

polyhedron A closed three-dimensional figure formed by four or more polygons that intersect only at their edges.

poliedro Figura tridimensional cerrada formada por cuatro o más polígonos que se cruzan sólo en sus aristas.

postulate A statement that is accepted as true without proof. Also called an *axiom*.

postulado Enunciado que se acepta como verdadero sin demostración. También denominado *axioma*.

preimage The original figure in a transformation.

imagen original Figura original en una transformación.

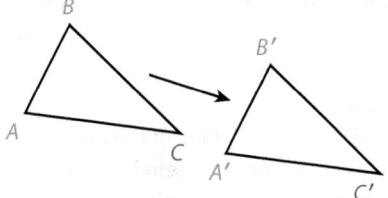

primes Symbols used to label the image in a transformation.

apóstrofos Símbolos utilizados para identificar la imagen en una transformación.

$A'B'C'$

prism A polyhedron formed by two parallel congruent polygonal bases connected by lateral faces that are parallelograms.

prisma Poliedro formado por dos bases poligonales congruentes y paralelas conectadas por caras laterales que son paralelogramos.

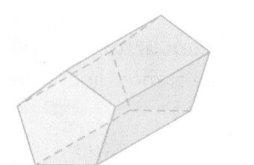

probability A number from 0 to 1 (or 0% to 100%) that is the measure of how likely an event is to occur.

probabilidad Número entre 0 y 1 (o entre 0% y 100%) que describe cuán probable es que ocurra un suceso.

A bag contains 3 red marbles and 4 blue marbles. The probability of randomly choosing a red marble is $\frac{3}{7}$.

Glossary/Glosario

ENGLISH	SPANISH	EXAMPLES
proof An argument that uses logic to show that a conclusion is true.	**demostración** Argumento que se vale de la lógica para probar que una conclusión es verdadera.	
proof by contradiction *See* indirect proof.	**demostración por contradicción** *Ver* demostración indirecta.	
pyramid A polyhedron formed by a polygonal base and triangular lateral faces that meet at a common vertex.	**pirámide** Poliedro formado por una base poligonal y caras laterales triangulares que se encuentran en un vértice común.	
Pythagorean triple A set of three nonzero whole numbers a, b, and c such that $a^2 + b^2 = c^2$.	**Tripleta de Pitágoras** Conjunto de tres números cabales distintos de cero a, b y c tal que $a^2 + b^2 = c^2$.	$\{3, 4, 5\}$ $3^2 + 4^2 = 5^2$

Q

quadrilateral A four-sided polygon.	**cuadrilátero** Polígono de cuatro lados.	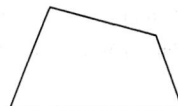

R

radial symmetry *See* rotational symmetry.	**simetría radial** *Ver* simetría de rotación.	
radian A unit of angle measure based on arc length. In a circle of radius r, if a central angle has a measure of 1 radian, then the length of the intercepted arc is r units. 2π radians $= 360°$ 1 radian $\approx 57°$	**radián** Unidad de medida de un ángulo basada en la longitud del arco. En un círculo de radio r, si un ángulo central mide 1 radián, entonces la longitud del arco abarcado es r unidades. 2π radians $= 360°$ 1 radian $\approx 57°$	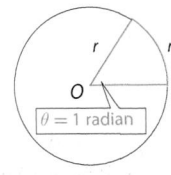
radius of a circle A segment whose endpoints are the center of a circle and a point on the circle; the distance from the center of a circle to any point on the circle.	**radio de un círculo** Segmento cuyos extremos son el centro y un punto de la circunferencia; distancia desde el centro de un círculo hasta cualquier punto de la circunferencia.	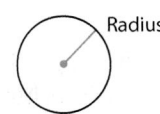
radius of a sphere A segment whose endpoints are the center of a sphere and any point on the sphere; the distance from the center of a sphere to any point on the sphere.	**radio de una esfera** Segmento cuyos extremos son el centro de una esfera y cualquier punto sobre la esfera; distancia desde el centro de una esfera hasta cualquier punto sobre la esfera.	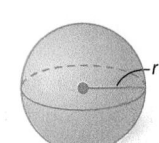

ENGLISH	SPANISH	EXAMPLES
ray A part of a line that starts at an endpoint and extends forever in one direction.	**rayo** Parte de una línea que comienza en un extremo y se extiende infinitamente en una dirección.	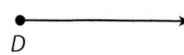
rectangle A quadrilateral with four right angles.	**rectángulo** Cuadrilátero con cuatro ángulos rectos.	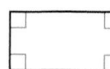
reduction A dilation with a scale factor greater than 0 but less than 1. In a reduction, the image is smaller than the preimage.	**reducción** Dilatación con un factor de escala mayor que 0 pero menor que 1. En una reducción, la imagen es más pequeña que la imagen original.	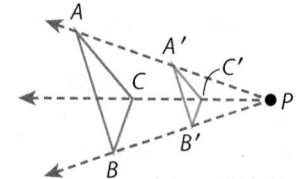
reflection A transformation across a line, called the line of reflection, such that the line of reflection is the perpendicular bisector of each segment joining each point and its image.	**reflexión** Transformación sobre una línea, denominada la línea de reflexión. La línea de reflexión es la mediatriz de cada segmento que une un punto con su imagen.	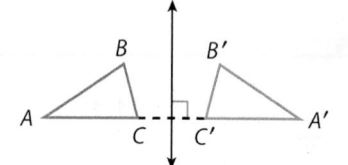
reflection symmetry *See* line symmetry.	**simetría de reflexión** *Ver* simetría axial.	
regular polygon A polygon that is both equilateral and equiangular.	**polígono regular** Polígono equilátero de ángulos iguales.	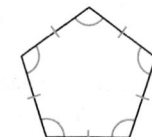
regular polyhedron A polyhedron in which all faces are congruent regular polygons and the same number of faces meet at each vertex. *See also* Platonic solid.	**poliedro regular** Poliedro cuyas caras son todas polígonos regulares congruentes y en el que el mismo número de caras se encuentran en cada vértice. *Ver también* sólido platónico.	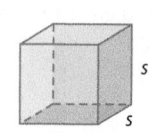
regular pyramid A pyramid whose base is a regular polygon and whose lateral faces are congruent isosceles triangles.	**pirámide regular** Pirámide cuya base es un polígono regular y cuyas caras laterales son triángulos isósceles congruentes.	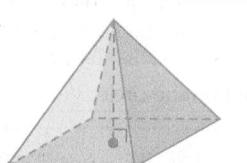
remote interior angle An interior angle of a polygon that is not adjacent to the exterior angle.	**ángulo interno remoto** Ángulo interno de un polígono que no es adyacente al ángulo externo.	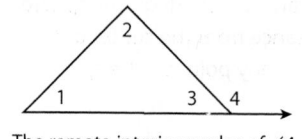 The remote interior angles of ∠4 are ∠1 and ∠2.

Glossary/Glosario

GL30

Glossary/Glosario

rhombus A quadrilateral with four congruent sides.

rombo Cuadrilátero con cuatro lados congruentes.

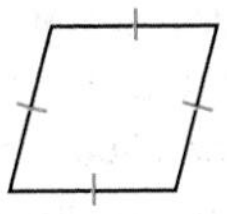

right angle An angle that measures 90°.

ángulo recto Ángulo que mide 90°.

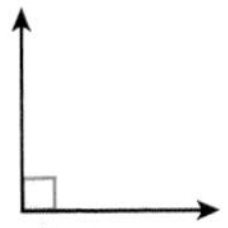

right cone A cone whose axis is perpendicular to its base.

cono recto Cono cuyo eje es perpendicular a su base.

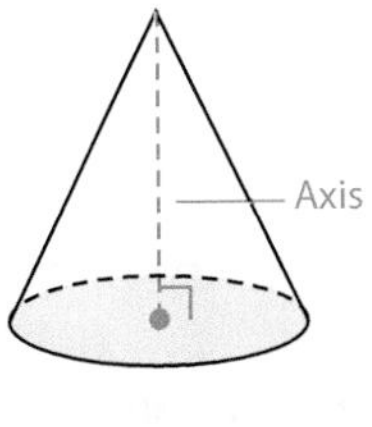

Axis

right cylinder A cylinder whose axis is perpendicular to its bases.

cilindro recto Cilindro cuyo eje es perpendicular a sus bases.

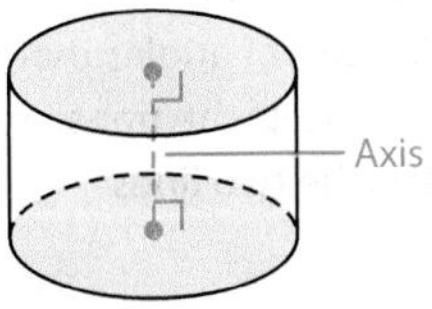

Axis

right prism A prism whose lateral faces are all rectangles.

prisma recto Prisma cuyas caras laterales son todas rectángulos.

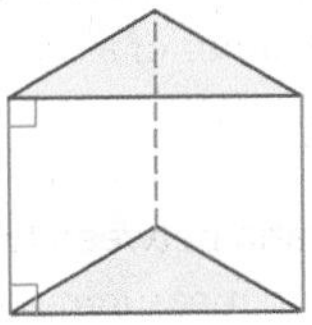

right triangle A triangle with one right angle.

triángulo rectángulo Triángulo con un ángulo recto.

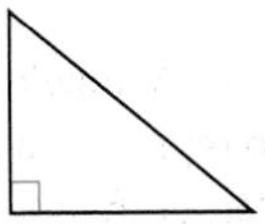

rigid motion *See* isometry.

movimiento rígido *Ver* isometría.

rigid transformation A transformation that does not change the size or shape of a figure.

transformación rígida Transformación que no cambia el tamaño o la forma de una figura.

rise The difference in the *y*-values of two points on a line.

distancia vertical Diferencia entre los valores de *y* de dos puntos de una línea.

For the points $(3, -1)$ and $(6, 5)$, the rise is $5 - (-1) = 6$.

rotation A transformation about a point *P*, also known as the center of rotation, such that each point and its image are the same distance from *P*. All of the angles with vertex *P* formed by a point and its image are congruent.

rotación Transformación sobre un punto *P*, también conocido como el centro de rotación, tal que cada punto y su imagen estén a la misma distancia de *P*. Todos los ángulos con vértice *P* formados por un punto y su imagen son congruentes.

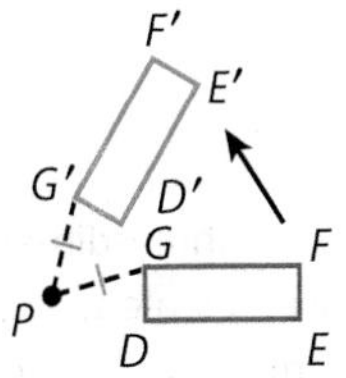

Glossary/Glosario

ENGLISH	SPANISH	EXAMPLES
rotational symmetry A figure that can be rotated about a point by an angle less than 360° so that the image coincides with the preimage has rotational symmetry.	**simetría de rotación** Una figura que puede rotarse alrededor de un punto en un ángulo menor de 360° de forma tal que la imagen coincide con la imagen original tiene simetría de rotación.	90° 90° 90° 90° Order of rotational symmetry: 4
run The difference in the *x*-values of two points on a line.	**distancia horizontal** Diferencia entre los valores de *x* de dos puntos de una línea.	For the points $(3, -1)$ and $(6, 5)$, the run is $6 - 3 = 3$.

S

ENGLISH	SPANISH	EXAMPLES
same-side interior angles For two lines intersected by a transversal, a pair of angles that lie on the same side of the transversal and between the two lines.	**ángulos internos del mismo lado** Dadas dos líneas cortadas por una transversal, el par de ángulos ubicados en el mismo lado de la transversal y entre las dos líneas.	1 2 5 6 3 4 7 8 $\angle 2$ and $\angle 3$ are same-side interior angles.
sample space The set of all possible outcomes of a probability experiment.	**espacio muestral** Conjunto de todos los resultados posibles de un experimento de probabilidad.	In the experiment of rolling a number cube, the sample space is $\{1, 2, 3, 4, 5, 6\}$.
scale The ratio between two corresponding measurements.	**escala** Razón entre dos medidas correspondientes.	1 cm : 5 mi
scale drawing A drawing that uses a scale to represent an object as smaller or larger than the actual object.	**dibujo a escala** Dibujo que utiliza una escala para representar un objeto como más pequeño o más grande que el objeto original.	E A F D B C H G A blueprint is an example of a scale drawing.
scale factor The multiplier used on each dimension to change one figure into a similar figure.	**factor de escala** El multiplicador utilizado en cada dimensión para transformar una figura en una figura semejante.	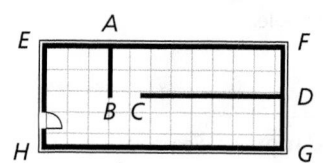 $A'(4, 6)$ $A(2, 3)$ $B'(0, 2)$ $B(0, 1)$ $C(3, 0)$ $C'(6, 0)$ Scale factor: 2
scale model A three-dimensional model that uses a scale to represent an object as smaller or larger than the actual object.	**modelo a escala** Modelo tridimensional que utiliza una escala para representar un objeto como más pequeño o más grande que el objeto real.	

Glossary/Glosario

scalene triangle A triangle with no congruent sides.

triángulo escaleno Triángulo sin lados congruentes.

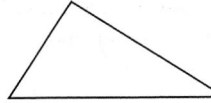

---

secant of a circle A line that intersects a circle at two points.

secante de un círculo Línea que corta un círculo en dos puntos.

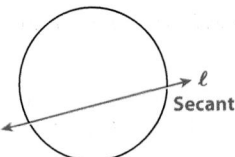

---

secant of an angle In a right triangle, the ratio of the length of the hypotenuse to the length of the side adjacent to angle A. It is the reciprocal of the cosine function.

secante de un ángulo En un triángulo rectángulo, la razón entre la longitud de la hipotenusa y la longitud del cateto adyacente al ángulo A. Es la inversa de la función coseno.

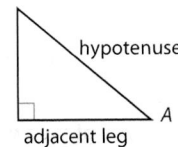

$$\sec A = \frac{\text{hypotenuse}}{\text{adjacent}} = \frac{1}{\cos A}$$

---

secant segment A segment of a secant with at least one endpoint on the circle.

segmento secante Segmento de una secante que tiene al menos un extremo sobre el círculo.

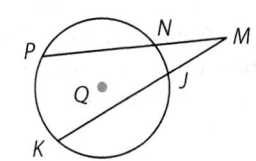

$\overline{NM}$ is an external secant segment.
$\overline{JK}$ is an internal secant segment.

---

sector of a circle A region inside a circle bounded by two radii of the circle and their intercepted arc.

sector de un círculo Región dentro de un círculo delimitado por dos radios del círculo y por su arco abarcado.

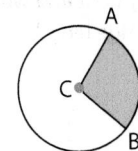

---

segment bisector A line, ray, or segment that divides a segment into two congruent segments.

bisectriz de un segmento Línea, rayo o segmento que divide un segmento en dos segmentos congruentes.

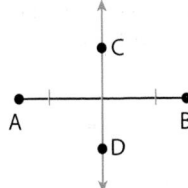

---

segment of a circle A region inside a circle bounded by a chord and an arc.

segmento de un círculo Región dentro de un círculo delimitada por una cuerda y un arco.

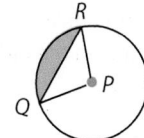

---

segment of a line A part of a line consisting of two endpoints and all points between them.

segmento de una línea Parte de una línea que consiste en dos extremos y todos los puntos entre éstos.

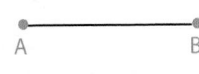

Glossary/Glosario

ENGLISH	SPANISH	EXAMPLES
semicircle An arc of a circle whose endpoints lie on a diameter.	**semicírculo** Arco de un círculo cuyos extremos se encuentran sobre un diámetro.	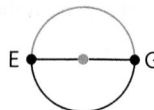
set A collection of items called elements.	**conjunto** Grupo de componentes denominados elementos.	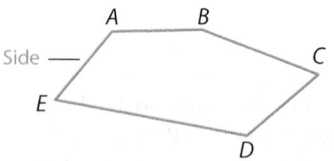
side of a polygon One of the segments that form a polygon.	**lado de un polígono** Uno de los segmentos que forman un polígono.	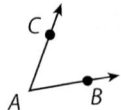
side of an angle One of the two rays that form an angle.	**lado de un ángulo** Uno de los dos rayos que forman un ángulo.	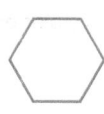 $\overrightarrow{AC}$ and $\overrightarrow{AB}$ are sides of $\angle CAB$.
similar Two figures are similar if they have the same shape but not necessarily the same size.	**semejantes** Dos figuras con la misma forma pero no necesariamente del mismo tamaño.	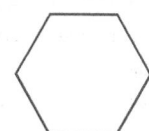
similar polygons Two polygons whose corresponding angles are congruent and whose corresponding side lengths are proportional.	**polígonos semejantes** Dos polígonos cuyos ángulos correspondientes son congruentes y cuyos lados correspondientes tienen longitudes proporcionales.	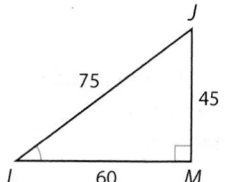 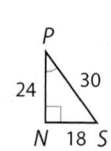
similarity ratio The ratio of two corresponding linear measurements in a pair of similar figures.	**razón de semejanza** Razón de dos medidas lineales correspondientes en un par de figuras semejantes.	Similarity ratio: $\frac{3.5}{2.1} = \frac{5}{3}$
similarity statement A statement that indicates that two polygons are similar by listing the vertices in the order of correspondence.	**enunciado de semejanza** Enunciado que indica que dos polígonos son semejantes enumerando los vértices en orden de correspondencia.	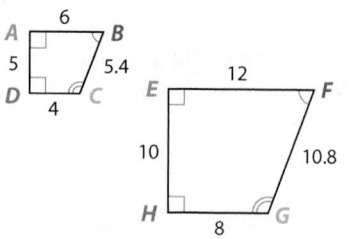 quadrilateral $ABCD \sim$ quadrilateral $EFGH$
similarity transformation A transformation that produces similar figures.	**transformación de semejanza** Una transformación que resulta en figuras semejantes.	Dilations are similarity transformations.

simple event An event consisting of only one outcome.	**suceso simple** Suceso que contiene sólo un resultado.	In the experiment of rolling a number cube, the event consisting of the outcome 3 is a simple event.
sine In a right triangle, the ratio of the length of the leg opposite $\angle A$ to the length of the hypotenuse.	**seno** En un triángulo rectángulo, razón entre la longitud del cateto opuesto a $\angle A$ y la longitud de la hipotenusa.	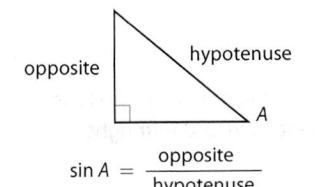 $\sin A = \dfrac{\text{opposite}}{\text{hypotenuse}}$
skew lines Lines that are not coplanar.	**líneas oblicuas** Líneas que no son coplanares.	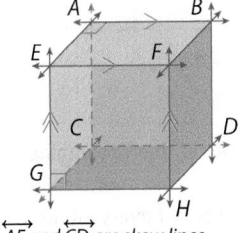 $\overleftrightarrow{AE}$ and $\overleftrightarrow{CD}$ are skew lines.
slide *See* translation.	**deslizamiento** *Ver* traslación.	
slope A measure of the steepness of a line. If (x_1, y_1) and (x_2, y_2) are any two points on the line, the slope of the line, known as m, is represented by the equation $m = \frac{y_2 - y_1}{x_2 - x_1}$.	**pendiente** Medida de la inclinación de una línea. Dados dos puntos (x_1, y_1) y (x_2, y_2) en una línea, la pendiente de la línea, denominada m, se representa con la ecuación $m = \frac{y_2 - y_1}{x_2 - x_1}$.	
slope-intercept form The slope-intercept form of a linear equation is $y = mx + b$, where m is the slope and b is the y-intercept.	**forma de pendiente-intersección** La forma de pendiente-intersección de una ecuación lineal es $y = mx + b$, donde m es la pendiente y b es la intersección con el eje y.	$y = -2x + 4$ The slope is -2. The y-intercept is 4.
solid A three-dimensional figure.	**cuerpo geométrico** Figura tridimensional.	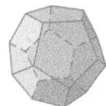
solving a triangle Using given measures to find unknown angle measures or side lengths of a triangle.	**resolución de un triángulo** Utilizar medidas dadas para hallar las medidas desconocidas de los ángulos o las longitudes de los lados de un triángulo.	
special right triangle A 45°—45°—90° triangle or a 30°—60°—90° triangle.	**triángulo rectángulo especial** Triángulo de 45°—45°—90° o triángulo de 30°—60°—90°.	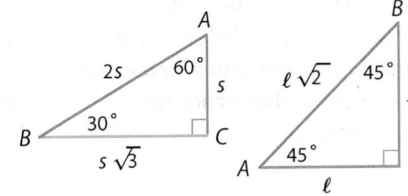

ENGLISH	SPANISH	EXAMPLES
sphere The set of points in space that are a fixed distance from a given point called the center of the sphere.	**esfera** Conjunto de puntos en el espacio que se encuentran a una distancia fija de un punto determinado denominado centro de la esfera.	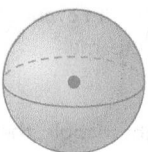
square A quadrilateral with four congruent sides and four right angles.	**cuadrado** Cuadrilátero con cuatro lados congruentes y cuatro ángulos rectos.	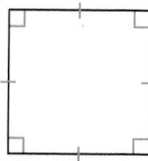
straight angle A 180° angle.	**ángulo llano** Ángulo que mide 180°.	
subset A set that is contained entirely within another set. Set B is a subset of set A if every element of B is contained in A, denoted $B \subset A$.	**subconjunto** Conjunto que se encuentra dentro de otro conjunto. El conjunto B es un subconjunto del conjunto A si todos los elementos de B son elementos de A; se expresa $B \subset A$.	The set of integers is a subset of the set of rational numbers.
supplementary angles Two angles whose measures have a sum of 180°.	**ángulos suplementarios** Dos ángulos cuyas medidas suman 180°.	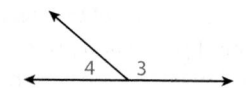 ∠3 and ∠4 are supplementary angles.
surface area The total area of all faces and curved surfaces of a three-dimensional figure.	**área total** Área total de todas las caras y superficies curvas de una figura tridimensional.	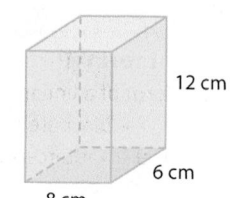 12 cm 6 cm 8 cm Surface area = 2(8)(12) + 2(8)(6) + 2(12)(6) = 432 cm²
symmetry In the transformation of a figure such that the image coincides with the preimage, the image and preimage have symmetry.	**simetría** En la transformación de una figura tal que la imagen coincide con la imagen original, la imagen y la imagen original tienen simetría.	
symmetry about an axis In the transformation of a figure such that there is a line about which a three-dimensional figure can be rotated by an angle greater than 0° and less than 360° so that the image coincides with the preimage, the image and preimage have symmetry about an axis.	**simetría axial** En la transformación de una figura tal que existe una línea sobre la cual se puede rotar una figura tridimensional a un ángulo mayor que 0° y menor que 360° de forma que la imagen coincida con la imagen original, la imagen y la imagen original tienen simetría axial.	

© Houghton Mifflin Harcourt Publishing Company

Glossary/Glosario

T

tangent circles Two coplanar circles that intersect at exactly one point. If one circle is contained inside the other, they are *internally tangent*. If not, they are *externally tangent*.

círculos tangentes Dos círculos coplanares que se cruzan únicamente en un punto. Si un círculo contiene a otro, son *tangentes internamente*. De lo contrario, son *tangentes externamente*.

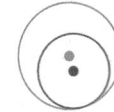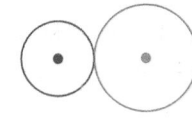

---

tangent of an angle In a right triangle, the ratio of the length of the leg opposite ∠A to the length of the leg adjacent to ∠A.

tangente de un ángulo En un triángulo rectángulo, razón entre la longitud del cateto opuesto a ∠A y la longitud del cateto adyacente a ∠A.

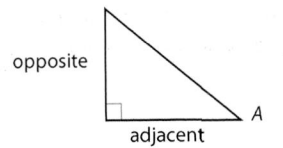

$$\tan A = \frac{\text{opposite}}{\text{adjacent}}$$

---

tangent segment A segment of a tangent with one endpoint on the circle.

segmento tangente Segmento de una tangente con un extremo en el círculo.

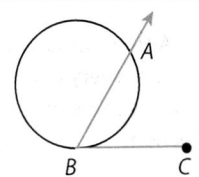

$\overline{BC}$ is a tangent segment.

---

tangent of a circle A line that is in the same plane as a circle and intersects the circle at exactly one point.

tangente de un círculo Línea que se encuentra en el mismo plano que un círculo y lo cruza únicamente en un punto.

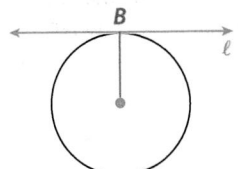

---

terminal point of a vector The endpoint of a vector.

punto terminal de un vector Extremo de un vector.

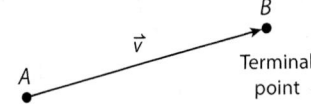

---

tetrahedron A polyhedron with four faces. A regular tetrahedron has equilateral triangles as faces, with three faces meeting at each vertex.

tetraedro Poliedro con cuatro caras. Las caras de un tetraedro regular son triángulos equiláteros y cada vértice es compartido por tres caras.

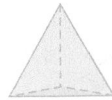

---

theorem A statement that has been proven.

teorema Enunciado que ha sido demostrado.

Glossary/Glosario

ENGLISH	SPANISH	EXAMPLES
theoretical probability The ratio of the number of equally likely outcomes in an event to the total number of possible outcomes.	**probabilidad teórica** Razón entre el número de resultados igualmente probables de un suceso y el número total de resultados posibles.	In the experiment of rolling a number cube, the theoretical probability of rolling an odd number is $\frac{3}{6} = \frac{1}{2}$.
tick marks Marks used on a figure to indicate congruent segments.	**marcas "|"** Marcas utilizadas en una figura para indicar segmentos congruentes.	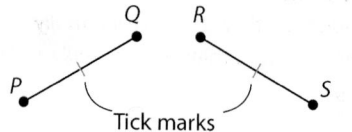
transformation A change in the position, size, or shape of a figure or graph.	**transformación** Cambio en la posición, tamaño o forma de una figura o gráfica.	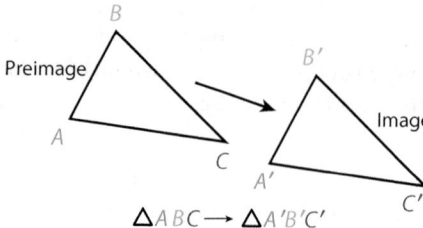
translation A transformation that shifts or slides every point of a figure or graph the same distance in the same direction.	**traslación** Transformación en la que todos los puntos de una figura o gráfica se mueven la misma distancia en la misma dirección.	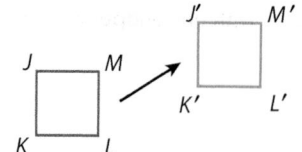
transversal A line that intersects two coplanar lines at two different points.	**transversal** Línea que corta dos líneas coplanares en dos puntos diferentes.	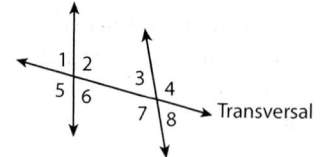
trapezoid A quadrilateral with at least one pair of parallel sides.	**trapecio** Cuadrilátero con al menos un par de lados paralelos.	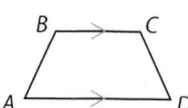
trial In probability, a single repetition or observation of an experiment.	**prueba** En probabilidad, una sola repetición u observación de un experimento.	In the experiment of rolling a number cube, each roll is one trial.
triangle A three-sided polygon.	**triángulo** Polígono de tres lados.	
triangle rigidity A property of triangles that states that if the side lengths of a triangle are fixed, the triangle can have only one shape.	**rigidez del triángulo** Propiedad de los triángulos que establece que, si las longitudes de los lados de un triángulo son fijas, el triángulo puede tener sólo una forma.	

ENGLISH	SPANISH	EXAMPLES
trigonometric ratio A ratio of two sides of a right triangle.	**razón trigonométrica** Razón entre dos lados de un triángulo rectángulo.	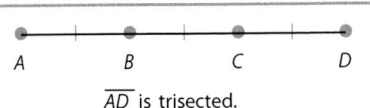 $\sin A = \dfrac{a}{c}; \cos A = \dfrac{b}{c}; \tan A = \dfrac{a}{b}$
trigonometry The study of the measurement of triangles and of trigonometric functions and their applications.	**trigonometría** Estudio de la medición de los triángulos y de las funciones trigonométricas y sus aplicaciones.	
trisect To divide into three equal parts.	**trisecar** Dividir en tres partes iguales.	A — B — C — D $\overline{AD}$ is trisected.
truth table A table that lists all possible combinations of truth values for a statement and its components.	**tabla de verdad** Tabla en la que se enumeran todas las combinaciones posibles de valores de verdad para un enunciado y sus componentes.	
truth value A statement can have a truth value of true (T) or false (F).	**valor de verdad** Un enunciado puede tener un valor de verdad verdadero (V) o falso (F).	

U

undefined term A basic figure that is not defined in terms of other figures. The undefined terms in geometry are point, line, and plane.	**término indefinido** Figura básica que no está definida en función de otras figuras. Los términos indefinidos en geometría son el punto, la línea y el plano.	
union The union of two sets is the set of all elements that are in either set, denoted by ∪.	**unión** La unión de dos conjuntos es el conjunto de todos los elementos que se encuentran en ambos conjuntos, expresado por ∪.	$A = \{1, 2, 3, 4\}$ $B = \{1, 3, 5, 7, 9\}$ $A \cup B = \{1, 2, 3, 4, 5, 7, 9\}$
universal set The set of all elements in a particular context.	**conjunto universal** Conjunto de todos los elementos de un contexto determinado.	

V

vector A quantity that has both magnitude and direction.

vector Cantidad que tiene magnitud y dirección.

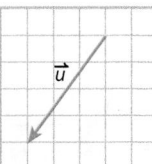

Venn diagram A diagram used to show relationships between sets.

diagrama de Venn Diagrama utilizado para mostrar la relación entre conjuntos.

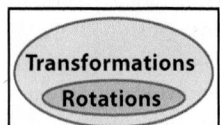

---

vertex angle of an isosceles triangle The angle formed by the legs of an isosceles triangle.

ángulo del vértice de un triángulo isósceles Ángulo formado por los catetos de un triángulo isósceles.

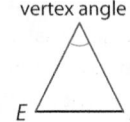

---

vertex of a cone The point opposite the base of the cone.

vértice de un cono Punto opuesto a la base del cono.

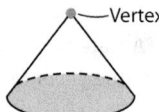

---

vertex of a parabola The highest or lowest point on the parabola.

vértice de una parábola Punto más alto o más bajo de una parábola.

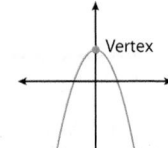

---

vertex of a polygon The intersection of two sides of the polygon.

vértice de un polígono La intersección de dos lados del polígono.

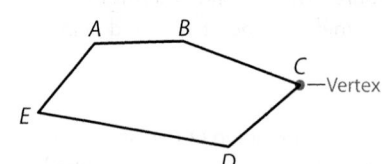

A, B, C, D, and *E* are vertices of the polygon.

---

vertex of a pyramid The point opposite the base of the pyramid.

vértice de una pirámide Punto opuesto a la base de la pirámide.

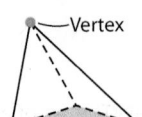

---

vertex of a three-dimensional figure The point that is the intersection of three or more faces of the figure.

vértice de una figura tridimensional Punto que representa la intersección de tres o más caras de la figura.

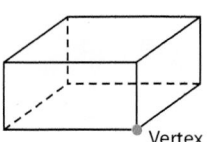

Glossary/Glosario

ENGLISH	SPANISH	EXAMPLES
vertex of a triangle The intersection of two sides of the triangle.	**vértice de un triángulo** Intersección de dos lados del triángulo.	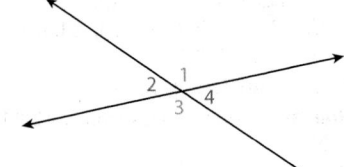 A, B, and C are vertices of △ABC.
vertex of an angle The common endpoint of the sides of the angle.	**vértice de un ángulo** Extremo común de los lados del ángulo.	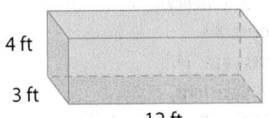 A is the vertex of ∠CAB.
vertical angles The nonadjacent angles formed by two intersecting lines.	**ángulos opuestos por el vértice** Ángulos no adyacentes formados por dos rectas que se cruzan.	∠1 and∠3 are vertical angles. ∠2 and∠4 are vertical angles.
volume The number of nonoverlapping unit cubes of a given size that will exactly fill the interior of a three-dimensional figure.	**volumen** Cantidad de cubos unitarios no superpuestos de un determinado tamaño que llenan exactamente el interior de una figura tridimensional.	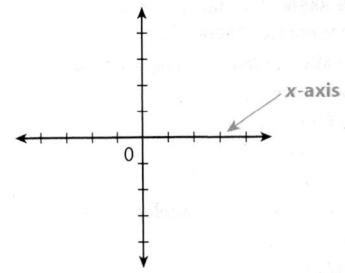 Volume $= (3)(4)(12) = 144$ ft^3

X

x-axis The horizontal axis in a coordinate plane.	**eje x** Eje horizontal en un plano cartesiano.	x-axis

Y

y-axis The vertical axis in a coordinate plane.	**eje y** Eje vertical en un plano cartesiano.	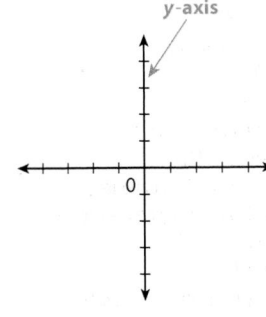 y-axis

Index

Index locator numbers are in Module. Lesson form. For example, 2.1 indicates Module 2, Lesson 1 as listed in the Table of Contents.

© Houghton Mifflin Harcourt Publishing Company

Index

© Houghton Mifflin Harcourt Publishing Company

Index

Table of Measures

LENGTH

1 inch = 2.54 centimeters

1 meter = 39.37 inches

1 mile = 5,280 feet

1 mile = 1760 yards

1 mile = 1.609 kilometers

1 kilometer = 0.62 mile

CAPACITY

1 cup = 8 fluid ounces

1 pint = 2 cups

1 quart = 2 pints

1 gallon = 4 quarts

1 gallon = 3.785 liters

1 liter = 0.264 gallons

1 liter = 1000 cubic centimeters

MASS/WEIGHT

1 pound = 16 ounces

1 pound = 0.454 kilograms

1 kilogram = 2.2 pounds

1 ton = 2000 pounds

Symbols

$\neq$	is not equal to	π	pi: (about 3.14)
$\approx$	is approximately equal to	$\perp$	is perpendicular to
10^2	ten squared; ten to the second power	$\parallel$	is parallel to
		$\overleftrightarrow{AB}$	line AB
$2.\overline{6}$	repeating decimal 2.66666...	$\overrightarrow{AB}$	ray AB
$\lvert -4 \rvert$	the absolute value of negative 4	$\overline{AB}$	line segment AB
$\sqrt{}$	square root	$m\angle A$	measure of $\angle A$

Formulas

Triangle	$A = \frac{1}{2}bh$	Pythagorean Theorem	$a^2 + b^2 = c^2$
Parallelogram	$A = bh$	Quadratic Formula	$x = \dfrac{-b \pm \sqrt{b^2 - 4ac}}{2a}$
Circle	$A = \pi r^2$	Arithmetic Sequence	$a_n = a_1 + (n-1)d$
Circle	$C = \pi d$ or $C = 2\pi r$	Geometric Sequence	$a_n = a_1 r^{n-1}$
General Prisms	$V = Bh$	Geometric Series	$S_n = \dfrac{a_1 - a_1 r^n}{1 - r}$ where $r \neq 1$
Cylinder	$V = \pi r^2 h$	Radians	$1 \ radian = \frac{180}{\pi} \ degrees$
Sphere	$V = \frac{4}{3}\pi r^3$	Degrees	$1 \ degree = \frac{\pi}{180} \ radians$
Cone	$V = \frac{1}{3}\pi r^2 h$	Exponential Growth/Decay	$A = A_0\, e^{k(t - t_0)} + B_0$
Pyramid	$V = \frac{1}{3}Bh$		